THE ENCYCLOPEDIA OF MIGRATION AND MINORITIES IN EUROPE
From the 17th Century to the Present

Although migration and integration have become important concepts today as a result of globalization, migration movements, integration, and multiculturalism have always been part of the history of Europe. Few people realize how many ethnic groups participated in migration within Europe or into Europe, and this ignorance has grave consequences for the social and political status of immigrants.

Newly available to an English-speaking audience, this *Encyclopedia* presents a systematic overview of the existing scholarship regarding migration within and into Europe. The first section contains survey studies of the various regions and countries in Europe covering the last centuries. The second section presents information on approximately 220 individual groups of migrants from the Sephardic Jews' emigration from Spain and Portugal in the 16th and 17th centuries to the present-day migration of old-age pensioners to the holiday villages in the sun. The first resource of its kind, *The Encyclopedia of Migration and Minorities in Europe* is a comprehensive and authoritative research tool.

Klaus J. Bade is Professor Emeritus of Modern History at the Institute for Migration Research and Intercultural Studies (IMIS), University of Osnabrück, Germany, and Chair of the Expert Council of German Foundations on Integration and Migration, Berlin, Germany.

Pieter C. Emmer is Professor Emeritus in the History of European Expansion at Leiden University in the Netherlands.

Leo Lucassen is Professor of Social History at Leiden University, where he also coordinates the profile area "Global Interactions: People, Culture and Power."

Jochen Oltmer is Associate Professor of Modern History at the IMIS, University of Osnabrück.

THE ENCYCLOPEDIA OF MIGRATION AND MINORITIES IN EUROPE

FROM THE 17TH CENTURY TO THE PRESENT

Edited by

Klaus J. Bade
University of Osnabrück, Emeritus

Pieter C. Emmer
Leiden University, Emeritus

Leo Lucassen
Leiden University

Jochen Oltmer
University of Osnabrück

Editorial Assistance
Corrie van Eijl, Marlou Schrover, Michael Schubert, and Jutta Tiemeyer

CAMBRIDGE
UNIVERSITY PRESS

CAMBRIDGE UNIVERSITY PRESS
Cambridge, New York, Melbourne, Madrid, Cape Town,
Singapore, São Paulo, Delhi, Tokyo, Mexico City

Cambridge University Press
32 Avenue of the Americas, New York, NY 10013-2473, USA

www.cambridge.org
Information on this title: www.cambridge.org/9780521895866

First published in German as *Enzyklopädie Migration in Europa:
Vom 17. Jahrhundert bis zur Gegenwart*
by Verlag Ferdinand Schöningh GmbH & Co. KG 2007

First English edition published by Cambridge University Press 2011

Printed in the United States of America

A catalog record for this publication is available from the British Library.

Library of Congress Cataloging in Publication data
Enzyklopädie Migration in Europa. English.
The encyclopedia of migration and minorities in Europe : from the
seventeenth century to the present / edited by Klaus J. Bade ... [et al.].
      p.   cm.
Includes bibliographical references and index.
ISBN 978-0-521-89586-6
1. Europe – Emigration and immigration – Encyclopedias.
2. Europe – Emigration and immigration – Economic aspects –
Encyclopedias.   3. Immigrants – Europe – History – Encyclopedias.
I. Bade, Klaus J.   II. Title.
JV7590.E4913 2011
304.8094′03–dc22   2010030605

ISBN 978-0-521-89586-6 Hardback

CONTENTS

Contents

Contents

PREFACE TO THE ENGLISH EDITION

After the publication of this *Encyclopedia* in German, Pieter C. Emmer and Leo Lucassen took on the task of overseeing the translation into English. Most contributions were translated by Thomas Dunlap in New York. All authors were given the opportunity to scrutinize the translation and to update the contents and the bibliography of their contributions. Special thanks are due to Jochen Oltmer and Jutta Tiemeyer at the University of Osnabrück for putting their experience in editing the German edition to good use a second time. We also would like to thank Annelieke Vries (Vienna) for preparing the figures and geographical maps in such an expert way and Steffen Pötzschke for proofreading. We are also extremely grateful to the Stichting Instituut Gak (Hilversum, the Netherlands) for providing us with an additional subsidy for the various translation and editing costs. And finally, we should mention the unstinting support of Wendy Bolton, Janis Bolster, Simina Calin, Patterson Lamb, Frank Smith, and Emily Spangler, all of Cambridge University Press, New York.

Leiden, the Netherlands
September 2009

Pieter C. Emmer and Leo Lucassen

PREFACE TO THE GERMAN EDITION

Migration and integration have become central topics of concern in contemporary Europe. Facing these challenges, many Europeans feel confronted with an exceptional historical situation. However, a look into the past shows that immigration, integration, and intercultural encounters have always been central elements of European cultural history. It also reveals that many "native" insiders who today feel anxious about the integration of immigrants are themselves the descendants of foreign outsiders. But apart from some well-known exceptions – for example, the Huguenots – little is known about the multitude and diversity of groups who have moved across political, cultural, and social borders in modern European history. Illuminating the rich multiplicity of these migratory events through selected examples is the purpose of this *Encyclopedia of European Migration*.

It all began at the Netherlands Institute for Advanced Study (NIAS) in Wassenaar. With the support of the German Research Council, which granted me a leave of absence from my chair at the University of Osnabrück, I spent the academic year 1996–7 at the research paradise in the dunes between Scheveningen and Noordwijk preparing my book *Europa in Bewegung*, first published in German in 2000, with editions in English, French, Italian, and Spanish appearing soon after.[1]

While I was still racking my brain at NIAS over the conception of such a synthesis of the history of European migration, I received an invitation from the Wissenschaftskolleg zu Berlin (Institute for Advanced Study at Berlin) to spend a research year there. For that purpose I was asked to sketch a research project.

As I worked on my book on the history of European migration, it had become increasingly clear to me how profoundly limited the scholarly groundwork was for such a historical synthesis. I learned how imbalanced and hard to compare the state of research was on the many migratory movements and migration regions of Europe, some of which overlapped in their historical importance against a historical background showing movements of people across borders as well as of borders across people.

Two things then, were missing: an additional effort to formulate a synthesis of the history of migration in Europe and an encyclopedic assembly of all available knowledge about these migratory movements and regions. It also became clear to me that in writing a synthesis I was trying to take the second step first, because an encyclopedic survey of what we knew about the history of European migration would have rendered such a synthesis much easier. However, this was a task I could take on only after I had finished my "NIAS book." Additionally, I realized that such an undertaking posed a conceptual challenge at least as great as that of my book project, for which I had already developed and abandoned a multitude of concepts at NIAS. I took comfort in the thought that the more complex and deeply layered reflections I had developed in conceiving this synthesis would ultimately benefit the conceptualization of the *Encyclopedia*.

From the outset, it was clear that in order to realize this plan of an *Encyclopedia of European Migration*, I would not only have to rely upon numerous specialists on individual migratory movements and regions but also utilize expertise in the field of Early Modern European history. To this end I asked my Dutch colleague Pieter C. Emmer, who had made a name for himself at Leiden University with studies on the migratory history of Early Modern Europe, if he would join me for a year at the Wissenschaftskolleg in Berlin in 2000–1 to serve as co-editor for the project. To my great delight he accepted the offer without hesitation.

I asked the rector of the NIAS, the historian Henk Wesseling, whether he could imagine hosting us for another year at the NIAS so we could continue to work on this large project after our stay at the Wissenschaftskolleg in Berlin. I was delighted when Henk gave his immediate approval. As a result, the idea for the first joint research project by the German Wissenschaftskolleg and the Netherlands Institute for Advanced Study was born.

Following the fall-summer orientation of the academic calendar of the NIAS, I initially suggested proceeding on a three-year schedule. The first year (2000–1) would consist of a conceptualization phase at the Wissenschaftskolleg in Berlin. The second year (2001–2) would be a writing phase, during which as many articles as possible would be written

---

[1] Klaus J. Bade, *Europa in Bewegung. Migration vom späten 18. Jahrhundert bis zur Gegenwart* (Munich, 2000). Translations: Italian (Rome, 2001); Spanish (Barcelona, 2003); French (Paris, 2002); English (*Migration in European History*, Oxford, 2003). See also Klaus J. Bade, ed., *Migration in der europäischen Geschichte seit dem späten Mittelalter: Vorträge auf dem Deutschen Historikertag in Halle a.d. Saale, 11.9.2002* (Osnabrück, 2002).

by their various authors. During the third year (2002–3), the project phase, clerical and editorial work would step into the foreground. Various workshops, editorial meetings, and the assembly of an interdisciplinary scientific advisory council as well as a group of specialists for countries and large regions, whom we referred to as "country coordinators," were planned to accompany all three phases of the project.

In reality it took us from the fall of 2000 until the spring of 2007 to prepare the print-ready version of the German edition of the *Encyclopedia*. While this was indeed longer than we expected, it was also quite a bit shorter than many had feared when they first heard about our ambitious plans.

From the very beginning and throughout the planning and project phases, we received substantial help from Jochen Oltmer, migration historian at the University of Osnabrück, and later co-editor. After the Wissenschaftskolleg in Berlin approved our research stay in 2000–1, Piet and I realized that our small German-Dutch editorial team was in urgent need of reinforcement. In order to fulfill this need, we invited Jochen Oltmer on the German side and Leo Lucassen (Leiden/Amsterdam) on the Dutch side to join the team as co-editors. To our delight, both readily agreed to do so.

During the academic year 2002–3, Piet Emmer and I met up at NIAS with Leo Lucassen, who was there as a result of his own application to prepare his book *The Immigrant Threat*,[2] as well as to collaborate as co-editor of the *Encyclopedia*. Jochen Oltmer, who in the meantime had defended his second PhD thesis (Habilitation) at the University of Osnabrück with a study on migration and migration policy in the Weimar Republic[3] and replaced me at my chair at the University of Osnabrück, worked as co-editor in close contact with the group at the NIAS. By then the approval of grants had secured the German-Dutch editorial assistance team, including the addition of cultural historian Michael Schubert (Osnabrück) on the German side and migration historians Marlou Schrover (Leiden) and Corrie van Eijl (Leiden) on the Dutch side, all of whom helped to oversee the various authors of the nearly 250 entries. At this point, members of the international scientific advisory council and the country coordinators were appointed to advise the editors. A total of 30 scientific experts from the most diverse fields of research (see appendix) also helped to select the migrant groups to be studied as well as to solicit the more than 200 authors who ultimately contributed to this project.

The rector of the Wissenschaftskolleg, sociologist Wolf Lepenies, had welcomed us to Berlin in the fall of 2000 with the well-intentioned warning that many perfect-seeming ideas had been discursively crushed in this place. If research Fellows left after a year with the result that everything had gone according to a preconceived plan, he told us, "the Wissenschaftskolleg has failed." It certainly did not fail in our case, and our concept underwent many changes as a result of

talks with other Fellows during and after the presentation of our ideas at the Wissenschaftskolleg.

Because of our different historiographical backgrounds, Piet Emmer and I also struggled at times to communicate with each other during our conceptual discussions in Berlin. Some of what seemed important to me epistemologically on the path from the conceptualization to the realization of the project struck Piet Emmer at times as somewhat "German," according to the spirit of the old Oxford joke: An English, a German, and a French student were told, "Write something on elephants!" The English student writes on "Elephants and Trade," the French student on "Les Éléphants et l'Amour," while their German counterpart begins a comprehensive work with volume one entitled "Prolegomena on Elephantology."

In the end we agreed on a pragmatic as well as user-friendly "middle ground." In the sense of a saying by my late friend Ernst Schubert (who was also involved in the *Encyclopedia*) that when building a house, it is not necessary to leave the scaffolding in place to avoid the impression that the house has risen from the ground on its own, we restricted our theoretical reflections for the authors (and later for the readers) to what was absolutely indispensable for understanding the overall concept. At its core, however, our approach retained the perspectives developed at the very beginning concerning what questions would be asked and how the project would be organized and put together. These conceptual ideas are outlined in the introductory articles.

The *Encyclopedia* was the first project undertaken jointly from the very beginning by two Institutes for Advanced Study, namely the NIAS in Wassenaar and the Wissenschaftskolleg in Berlin. Our thanks to NIAS and the Wissenschaftskolleg for hosting some of the editors of the *Encyclopedia* as Fellows in Wassenaar and Berlin and making the interdisciplinary workshops possible. We are grateful to the then-rectors, Henk Wesseling (NIAS) and Wolf Lepenies (Wissenschaftskolleg), and to the Fellows of both international research centers for their (at times) pleasantly trying suggestions.

I would like to thank the Fritz Thyssen Foundation (Cologne/Germany) and the Foundation Population – Migration – Environment (Stäfa/Switzerland) for their generous support of this project as a whole. Our thanks go also to the Otto and Martha Fischbeck Foundation in Berlin for funding a workshop at the Wissenschaftskolleg. I am grateful to the Deutsche Forschungsgemeinschaft/German Research Foundation for a grant of two research years to fund my replacement at the University of Osnabrück during my stays at the NIAS and at the Wissenschaftskolleg in Berlin. Jochen Oltmer expresses his gratitude to the Niedersächsischer Vorab of the Volkswagen Foundation for its support, which enabled him to work intensively on the *Encyclopedia* project in its last phase.

For their advice we thank the members of the interdisciplinary scientific advisory council and the country coordinators, among them especially Dirk Hoerder and Jan Lucassen. We thank the authors for their patience with demanding

---

[2] Leo Lucassen, *The Immigrant Threat: The Integration of Old and New Migrants in Western Europe since 1850* (Urbana, 2005).

[3] Jochen Oltmer, *Migration und Politik in der Weimarer Republik* (Göttingen, 2005).

editors and editorial assistants. We provided the authors with critical advice for the revision of their articles, although they were, of course, free to accept or reject our suggestions and are solely responsible for their entries.

We are especially indebted to Jochen Oltmer as co-editor for the thorough revision of the contributions for the German edition, which formed the basis for the English translation. Our thanks go also to the German-Dutch editorial assistance team of Michael Schubert, Marlou Schrover, and Corrie van Eijl for their work in cooperation with the editors and authors. We would also like to thank Jutta Tiemeyer from the editorial office of the Institute for Migration Research and Intercultural Studies (IMIS) at Osnabrück University. In cooperation with the editors and editorial assistants, she has conscientiously guided the German edition as well as the English edition on their way toward publication.

Berlin, July 2009   Klaus J. Bade

THE ENCYCLOPEDIA: IDEA, CONCEPT, REALIZATION

Klaus J. Bade, Leo Lucassen, Pieter C. Emmer, and Jochen Oltmer

Migration is as much part of the human condition as birth, procreation, sickness, and death, for Homo sapiens spread across the globe as "Homo migrans."[1] European social and cultural history, too, was decisively shaped by migration and integration. Throughout European history, insiders moving out and outsiders moving in, natives and foreigners of every stripe lived through, helped to shape, or suffered from all manifestations of border-crossing migratory activity. Their migratory experiences are to a certain extent historiographically comprehensible in contemporary internal ascriptions and external descriptions.

That is true for permanent emigrations and immigrations as well as for transit migrations and labor migrations that were either temporary or transitioned to permanent stays and definitive immigrations. And it is also true for refugee and coerced migrations, and of the processes – by no means fundamentally new from a historical perspective – that are today described with the umbrella term "transnationalism."

The encounter of foreigners and locals, of outsiders and insiders in European history, was not only shaped by the movement of people across borders, however. It was also determined by the movement of borders over people, which could turn minorities into majorities, majorities into minorities, and natives into strangers in their own land. Finally, it was often shaped by the exclusion (based on collective attributions in processes of alienation) of "strangers" or of groups and minorities declared as such within one's own "native" boundaries.

***

The period covered by the *Encyclopedia* stretches from the 17th century to today. Among the multitude of border-crossing migratory activities in Europe, special significance attaches to permanent immigrations within Europe and from outside regions into Europe. Of particular interest among these immigrations are the resulting intergenerational processes of integration lasting for at least two generations, including many forms of social and cultural composition and decomposition to the extent that they can be discerned in the sources. They range from the gradual disappearance and dissolution of group identities in assimilation processes to minority formations and diaspora situations.

Immigrations within and into Europe will be traced in the *Encyclopedia* only if (even without identifiable individuals) they formed more or less solid structural identities, that is, stable migratory patterns (e.g., migratory systems), and have left behind social constructions that are discernible in ascriptions and descriptions present in the contemporary imagination or deposited in the collective memory of the host population and/or the immigrant group. As to overseas emigrations, consideration is given only to their migratory structures (course and extent of the movements, origin and destination regions of the migrations), but not to the results of the migrations (e.g., diaspora or minority formation, integration/assimilation in the destination regions).

In line with the concepts of historical migration research as part of social and cultural historiography,[2] migration is understood here as a comprehensive social and cultural process within and between geographic and social spaces, encompassing three dimensions of time and space:

1. the mobilization in and dissolution from the regions of origin and their backgrounds;
2. the multifarious movements between regions of origin and of destination;
3. in the case of permanent immigration, the integration/assimilation in the destination regions, which sometimes spans generations.

At the forefront of the *Encyclopedia* is the question (number 3 above) about integration/assimilation in the destination regions. It could range from social accommodation/

---

[1] Klaus J. Bade, *Homo Migrans. Wanderungen aus und nach Deutschland. Erfahrungen und Fragen* (Essen, 1994).

[2] Concepts of historical migration research: Klaus J. Bade, "Migration History," in *International Encyclopedia of the Social and Behavioural Sciences*, ed. N. J. Smelser and Paul B. Baltes (Oxford, 2001), 9809–15; Klaus J. Bade, "Historische Migrationsforschung," in Klaus J. Bade, *Sozialhistorische Migrationsforschung. Gesammelte Beiträge*, ed. Michael Bommes and Jochen Oltmer (Göttingen, 2004), 27–48. Anthologies on methodological issues: Dirk Hoerder and Leslie Page Moch, eds., *European Migrants: Global and Local Perspectives* (Boston, 1996); Jan Lucassen and Leo Lucassen, eds., *Migration, Migration History, History: Old Paradigms and New Perspectives* (Bern, 1997). Surveys: Klaus J. Bade, *Migration in European History* (Oxford, 2003); Leslie Page Moch, *Moving Europeans: Migration in Western Europe since 1650* (Bloomington, 2003); Dirk Hoerder, *Cultures in Contact. European and World Migrations* (Durham, 2002); Patrick Manning, *Migration in World History* (New York and London, 2005); Jan Lucassen and Leo Lucassen, "The Mobility Transition Revisited, 1500–1900: What the Case of Europe Can Offer to Global History," *Journal of Global History* 4, 3 (2009): 347–78.

acculturation all the way to cultural and mental assimilation, though it could also lead to the formation of temporary or permanent minorities or diasporas.[3] However, mobilization in, dissolution, and finally departure from the regions of origin and the reasons behind them, as well as the movements between regions of origin and of destination, must remain discernible in the background because they are indispensable for a description of the migrant group in question. Equal attention is paid to temporary migrations without a permanent stay, provided these are migratory movements that, beyond personal or group identities, developed structural identities in the sense of enduring and stable spatial forms of movement or migration systems.

The *Encyclopedia* focuses exclusively on allochthonous groups that immigrated across borders or to the descendants of these immigrants. Thereby we not only deal with international migrations but also with groups that came from different cultural and social spaces. Their in-migration did not necessarily cross formal territorial boundaries, especially of states, but they certainly did cross informal boundaries, for example, ethnocultural or national-cultural, religious, or linguistic ones, which, too, could lead to the experience of the social construction of the "other" in ascriptions and descriptions.

A well-known example is the *Ruhrpolen* in 19th-century Germany, the majority of whom did not, contrary to conventional historical images, hail from across the eastern borders of Prussia, but from the Prussian east. They migrated in the late 19th and early 20th centuries into the likewise Prussian Ruhr region: as a result of the partition of Poland they were Prussian-German citizens, but of Polish nationality and mother tongue as well as Catholic in faith. In the Ruhr region they experienced a true immigration process, not in a legal but certainly in social, cultural, and mental senses, without having migrated across state borders.

Historiographically, migrant groups are usually defined or constructed through three kinds of ascriptions with fluid boundaries:

1. with reference to what were (or were believed to have been) the primary migration-shaping motives/intentions of the migrants behind their supposedly voluntary – in actual practice involuntary elements also played a role such as economic hardship – departure from the region of origin: for example, emigration, temporary labor migration, educational migration, or migration from economic-speculative or career motives, in the sense of what Charles Tilly called "subsistence migration," "betterment migration," or "career migration";[4]

2. in cases of refugee or forced migrations, with reference to their backgrounds: for example, religiously, politically, ethnically, and nationalistically motivated repression or expulsion;

3. with reference to ascriptions oriented toward the purpose of the stay, its duration, and technical-administrative status attributions in the destination region: for example, "immigrant," "seasonal workers," "contingent refugee," "asylum seekers."

The frequent result was the one-dimensional construction of group identities (e.g., "economic migrants," "religious refugees," "political refugees," or "ethnic minorities"). This was often done independently of the question as to whether – and if so, how long – such identities were preserved during the settlement and integration/assimilation process, and whether those identities actually reflected the way these groups viewed themselves. Moreover, they often were the product of ascriptions by host societies or technical classifications by authorities and bureaucrats. Such one-dimensional ascriptions cannot – or can only partially – capture the multiple identities of migrant groups, whose components change in the integration/assimilation process, overlap, or shift in priority.

As a result, they can lead to erroneous assessment. A migration that was triggered by religious-confessional oppression or ethnically motivated expulsion, for example, need not lead invariably – and especially not permanently – to a religiously or ethnically self-contained group. That is particularly unlikely if the religious-confessional or ethnic identity ascribed to the oppressed or expelled minority in the region of origin is identical to that of the majority society in the destination region: in that case, the exclusionary pressure that may have previously functioned as an identity-forming force loses its group-forming power. That was true, for example, in the early modern period of the "Salzburg Protestants" expelled from their bishopric: in the Protestant, Prussian east they were no longer considered "Protestants," but merely "Salzburgers." Today, much the same applies to ethnic Germans from the east (*Aussiedler*) oppressed in their regions of origin for more or less lengthy periods of time as a "German" ethnic or "national" minority – while in the ascriptions of their new host society, they are no longer regarded as "Germans" but, on the contrary, often are seen as "Russians."

Moreover, one-sided ascriptions of group identities based on presumed or actual migration motives or migration-shaping factors are misleading for the simple reason alone that during chain migrations or in more "mature" migration processes, the motivations of the pioneer migrants are not automatically "passed on" either in the immigration country or during the process of migration itself: the descendants of migrants persecuted in the region of origin for religious-confessional reasons, for example, do not remain "religious refugees" in the immigration lands. And migrations that may well have been originally triggered by specific motives

---

[3] Before settling on the final title of the *Encyclopedia* we had also contemplated, as the title for the project, "Migration – Integration – Diaspora." However, we abandoned placing the issue of diaspora in such a prominent position because it seemed to us more useful as an important subcategory of a broader integration approach than as an alternative to the concept of integration or even a replacement for it.

[4] Charles Tilly, "Migration in Modern European History," in *Human Migration: Patterns and Policies*, ed. William H. McNeill and Ruth S. Adams (Bloomington and London, 1978), 48–72.

and driving factors over time often develop a dynamic of their own, which can lead to even mere imitative action as a motive behind migration.

***

Against this complex and – because of the available sources – mostly only partially discernible background of multifarious and interdependent determining factors and developmental conditions, the *Encyclopedia* seeks to accomplish two things: (1) to document group-specific migrations on the latest state of research as exemplary cases and without claim to completeness, and (2) to render the long-term and multidimensional process of integration/assimilation proceeding over time at different rates and with different outcomes with the help of the available examples. At the same time, it is concerned with the question of how and under what conditions group identities developed in different ways in the tension between cohesion and diffusion in the settlement process, or became lost at different rates during the process of integration/assimilation.

Integration is here understood not as an intentional social or even political *concept*, but as a long-term intergenerational social and cultural *process* with fluid boundaries to assimilation, usually encompassing two and not infrequently three generations. This process begins with a phase of habituation to the new social context that can be understood as accommodation/acculturation or as social or partial integration. It ends – after various stages that look different from group to group – in the second or perhaps only a later generation, possibly in assimilation, which is here understood as "a process (neither one-sided nor linear or ineluctable) in which ethnic differences between immigrant groups and the local population fade away over time, in most cases after two to four generations, as a result of which ethnic characteristics lose weight and importance in a growing number of social contexts."[5]

Integration, in other more concrete words, can also be understood in this context as a social and cultural process that has two main dimensions: (1) structural, which focuses on the position of the migrants in the social structure of the receiving society (especially in the domains of work, education, and housing) and (2) identificational, which concentrates on the question of how migrants and their descendants identify with the receiving society (especially in the domains of friendships, marriages, organizations, and transnational and political activities). The outcome of these integration processes can differ considerably. Over generations some migrants become indistinguishable from the indigenous population. Others may be successful in the structural realm but hold on to contacts within their own ethnic groups (or vice versa). As Richard Alba and Victor

Nee have argued, integration (or assimilation) is often not a linear, but a "bumpy" process, depending on various factors.[6] Finally, integration is often highly influenced by institutional arrangements, which can lead to minority formation in the long run, as was the case for Jews and Gypsies, for example. After a phase of slowdown or stagnation, an integration process can resume again under changed circumstances. But integration processes can also be interrupted at various stages of development or undone by return or onward migration.[7]

In this broader context, there exists in the Atlantic realm a recent, international, and interdisciplinary scholarly discussion about the extent and limits of the assimilation model. For a long time, the dominance of the ideas of the Chicago School about the almost linear and more or less autodynamic integration of immigrants into a host society that was seen as virtually static and homogeneous influenced migration research (and not least also a part of the American self-understanding and of American immigration and integration policy). Once these guiding ideas ("one-sided" in the literal meaning of the word) had become obsolete in the scholarly and public discussion, the pendulum swung into the opposite direction.

Assimilation as a model and social goal, much like the guiding ideas and social concepts associated with it, now fell under what was virtually a blanket scholarly suspicion. For a long time, the mere mention of the pariah-term "assimilation" provoked collective reflexes of defensiveness and outrage in the scholarly community. In the process, the model of assimilation was completely denounced, with the lopsided exaggerations of the Chicago School as the target. The place of the assimilation model, now pronounced the original sin in the history of the discipline, was taken by endeavors that were sometimes no less "one-sided" in their focus – not only on ethnocultural heterogeneity as a program of research and social policies, but beyond that even on a seemingly permanent "migrant existence," on ethnocultural autonomy in permanent multicultural contexts, or on permanent transnational or transcultural identities of immigrants.

In all of this, many of the insights that the Chicago School already had arrived at were buried. That was true, for example, of the notion that migration has a process character, and especially of the view of integration as an intergenerational process with fluid boundaries to assimilation. This aspect is here expanded and differentiated through the question about the determinants of integration as an intergenerational cultural and social process. What we are dealing with is a dual-sided process in discernible (e.g. communal) social entities,

---

[5] Leo Lucassen, following Alba/Nee, in his "Assimilation in Westeuropa seit der Mitte des 19. Jahrhunderts: historische und historiographische Erfahrungen," in *Migrationsreport 2004: Fakten – Analysen – Perspektiven*, ed. Klaus J. Bade, Michael Bommes, and Rainer Münz (Frankfurt am Main, 2004), 43–66, here 44.

[6] Richard Alba and Victor Nee, *Remaking the American Mainstream: Assimilation and Contemporary Immigration* (Cambridge, MA, 2003). See also Leo Lucassen, *The Immigrant Threat: The Integration of Old and New Migrants in Western Europe since 1850* (Urbana and Chicago, 2005).

[7] Klaus J. Bade and Michael Bommes, "Einleitung: Integrationspotentiale in modernen europäischen Wohlfahrtsstaaten – der Fall Deutschland," in *Migrationsreport 2004: Fakten – Analysen – Perspektiven*, ed. Klaus J. Bade, Michael Bommes, and Rainer Münz (Frankfurt am Main, 2004), 11–42, here 34.

which changes not only the migrants and their descendants but also the receiving community, even if it does so with different intensity.[8] It involves various groups on both sides to differing degrees, actually or allegedly (ascriptions), and is accordingly reflected in different and not infrequently clashing ascriptions and descriptions.

Against this highly complex background of research questions the *Encyclopedia* combines historical-empirical, interdisciplinary, and largely cultural as well as social science–oriented approaches of international migration and integration research, along with the respective methodological reflections. They range, to give only four examples, from the double-sided research perspectives of Klaus J. Bade comparing the historical experiences past and present of immigrants in Germany with those of German emigrants abroad (1992) and from the likewise epoch-spanning research framework of Jan Lucassen and Rinus Penninx (1997), to Ewa Morawska's concept of "ethnicization" (1996), and to the comparison of old and new integration processes by Leo Lucassen (2005).[9]

It is not the purpose of the *Encyclopedia* to amass group descriptions for the purpose of further deepening the discussion on advantages and disadvantages of integration and/or assimilation concepts in migration research. Instead, the guiding notion is the concrete historical-empirical question as to why certain immigrant groups in certain reception contexts remained visible comparatively long in ascriptions and descriptions and in the collective memory on both sides, while other immigrations left only few, or historically "short" traces or no traces at all. Some of our early conceptual reflections on epistemology or research strategies have been incorporated into the following research overview by Dirk Hoerder, Jan Lucassen, and Leo Lucassen.

***

In implementing this approach in practice, we were from the beginning looking only at efforts to approximate our wide-ranging goals. That is true not only with respect to the often quite inadequate and usually highly disparate quality of the sources, which in many cases have only begun to be studied. Moreover, interdisciplinary historical research on migration, integration, and assimilation is only in its infancy in Europe. Finally, the study of groups, which arrived only in the second half of the 20th century and which are central to the current migration situation in Europe, can be only tentative for the simple reason that not enough time has passed to study their integration/assimilation from an intergenerational perspective.

To implement our conceptual aims, all contributors to this *Encyclopedia* have – where possible – used the same set of criteria (e.g., self-images or ascriptions of the migrant groups, stereotypes and images by the host society, social stratification, group-specific internal structures, language) by means of which groups and the changes over time can be described in a highly differentiated yet uniform way. When possible, they asked how these criteria as such and their significance or priority in the intergenerational process of integration/assimilation changed, until their distinctive function ceased possibly, but not invariably, in the assimilation process. For the criteria to identify groups, we in part relied on the (slightly revised) set of questions from the *Harvard Encyclopedia of American Ethnic Groups*.[10]

For example, in the case of a group that initially immigrated as a "confessional group" in their self-ascription or description by the host society, one may examine – given the sources to answer such complicated research questions – which or which additional criteria under the influence of which factors in the destination area kept the group together over a longer period of time. The chief reason was not necessarily the confessional identity and the communicative contexts it entailed. But the impact of the changes could also be such that only a small or core group that was receptive to the effectiveness of these criteria/factors remained together for a longer period, while the larger group dispersed. Even if impossible to do so in the individual entry the striving for a transparent structure based on the above-mentioned criteria had an important function for the cognitive strategy: it was to serve the authors as a guide or pattern, and thus contribute to give the essay a highly transparent parallel approach.

***

As mentioned earlier, the goal from the outset was not "completeness." Instead, in the face of the multitude of migratory movements, we set out to focus on exemplary case studies. However, an exemplary approach is possible only if an adequate overall view of the field in question exists – yet creating such an overall view is what the *Encyclopedia* set out to achieve in the first place. This raised a number of questions, which often had to be discussed in each individual case. From the wealth of groups we could only make a selection that was based on access to sources, the state of scholarship, and of course the availability of a suitable author.

Against this background we tried to focus on especially telling case studies. One example: beginning in the 1950s, many countries in central, western, and northern Europe were confronted with the phenomenon of what were called – following the German term – "guest worker migrations."

---

[8] For a good example, see Donna Gabaccia, *We Are What We Eat: Ethnic Food and the Making of Americans* (Cambridge, MA, 1998).

[9] Klaus J. Bade, ed., *Deutsche im Ausland – Fremde in Deutschland. Migration in Geschichte und Gegenwart* (Munich, 1992); Jan Lucassen and Rinus Penninx, *Newcomers: Immigrants and Their Descendants in the Netherlands 1550–1995* (Amsterdam, 1997); Ewa Morawska, *Insecure Prosperity. Small-Town Jews in Industrial America 1890–1940* (Princeton, 1996), and "Ethnizität als doppelte Struktur. Ein historisch-vergleichender Ansatz am Beispiel der US-amerikanischen Ethnohistorie," *Comparativ. Leipziger Beiträge zur Universalgeschichte und vergleichenden Gesellschaftsforschung* 8 (1998): 48–76; Paul van de Laar, Leo Lucassen, and Kees Mandemakers, eds., *Hier Rotterdam Stadsruimte. Stadsgeschiedenis en migratie* (Amsterdam, 2005).

[10] Stephen Thernstrom, Ann Orlov, and Oscar Handlin, eds., *Harvard Encyclopedia of American Ethnic Groups* (Cambridge, MA, 1980), viii.

Within these labor migrations, many of which ended in long-term settlement and family reunification, a number of groups – e.g., migrants from Portugal, Turkey, and Morocco – settled in several destination countries. A survey article on "Guest worker migrations in Europe" would not have offered adequate opportunities to look in depth at any particular group. A survey article on "Labor migrants from Portugal in central, western, and northern Europe," on the other hand, would have offered too little country-specific information. A collection from country-specific entries about "Labor migrations from Portugal to central, western, and northern Europe" would have led to numerous repetitions. In this instance, then, we decided instead to include an article titled "Portuguese Labor Migrants in Central, Western, and Northern Europe since the 1950s: The Examples of France and Germany"; its heading contains references to labor migrations from Portugal to other European countries while cross-references establish connections to information in other parts of the *Encyclopedia* that are relevant to this topic.

Extensive immigration areas, because of the desired analytical depth, require an exemplary focus on the destination area especially when relatively open groups (e.g., labor migrants) are being discussed. By contrast, migration and integration/assimilation processes can be meaningfully described also in broader and more differentiated immigration areas when we are dealing with groups that can be clearly demarcated in terms of their occupations, vocations, or region of origin (example: "Tyrolean Construction Workers in Central Europe from the 17th to the 19th Century"). In spite of such short, comparative surveys and cross-references, an alphabetical overview over various individual cases would be insufficient to give a thorough and systematic overview of migration and integration in Europe, especially since the changing migration structures in the origin and destination areas (e.g., changes in areas of emigration and immigration, different migratory regimes) were for their part highly important to the migratory activities. That is why we additionally included articles on countries or large areas that offer the overarching context. Finally, changes in the structures of migratory movements and migration policies (migration regimes) that applied to all of Europe are addressed in the following introductory, Europe-spanning section on terminologies and concepts of migration research.

***

The first part of the *Encyclopedia* offers 17 survey articles on large European regions and states. They trace the migratory history of these areas along with the social, economic, political, and cultural framework conditions of integration/assimilation. This first part sets the stage for the 219 entries on groups in the second part of the *Encyclopedia*. Footnotes in the larger survey articles point to the relevant entries. Cross-references establish connections between various entries. Finally, bibliographic references in both parts of the *Encyclopedia* offer guides to further reading.

In addition to this system of citation and cross-referencing, the articles in the *Encyclopedia* can be accessed in three other ways. The contents lists the individual entries in alphabetic order. The structure of the titles offers a uniform sequence of four items of information: (1) region(s) of origin (e.g., "Belgian"); (2) occupational group/migration or characteristics of the migration (e.g., "refugees"); (3) destination area of the migration (e.g., "western Europe"); (4) time period (e.g., "during the First World War") – in this case, then: "Belgian Refugees in Western Europe in the First World War."

Readers who are looking specifically for "French" or "Polish" groups, for example, will thus generally find the relevant entries already in the index. Two additional indices round out the *Encyclopedia*: first, the entries are systematized on the basis of the forms in which migration manifested itself; second, an additional register of countries, regions, and places allows readers to research the origin and destination regions of the groups discussed, as well as various other geographical or territorial, regional, or local connections.

***

Our hope is that with this *Encyclopedia* we have provided both a stimulus to scholarship and a platform for further research, a contribution to an emerging and ever-changing field of research, knowledge of which is of central importance to the question of European identity.

TERMINOLOGIES AND CONCEPTS
OF MIGRATION RESEARCH

Dirk Hoerder, Jan Lucassen, and Leo Lucassen

When asked about migration, people come up with a great variety of ideas, definitions, and concepts. Some may associate it with immigration from a neighboring country, others may reserve it for transatlantic moves, and many link it with the settlement process of migrants who are perceived as culturally different. What unites these reactions is the framework of the nation-state. Migrants are primarily people who move from one country to another and who draw the attention of the receiving society, as a consequence of the alleged difference in their social and cultural characteristics. This shared point of view is often closely linked to an explanatory model that considers migration simplistically as a one-way and one-time departure from unfavorable conditions ("push") in one state (emigration) and arrival in another one (immigration) with better conditions ("pull").

Since the 1980s, migration scholars have developed many new approaches and ideas that have produced a much more nuanced and multilayered perspective. The focus on the migrant, embedded in his or her networks, tries to understand geographical mobility, whatever form this may take. Moreover, the settlement process is also analyzed when people only stay temporarily and then move on or return to their place of origin. In this introduction we develop theoretical approaches and terminologies as they are currently used and will be used in this *Encyclopedia*. We will briefly refer to past concepts as well as to alternatives used in the current literature.

The traditional state-centered approach – as opposed to a human-agency or process-centered approach – to the complex phenomena of migration is still reflected in much of the terminology: an ethnic group is a cluster of immigrants from one nation-state in another; members of a diaspora are assumed to have continuous and lasting connections to their state of origin. Emphasis on human agency and social processes, however, reveals a large variety of decisions and patterns. On the whole, even if complicated, these new key concepts have enriched our understanding of migration.

Also new is the scope of the research: Europe's migration history is studied as a whole and placed in a global context, rather than separately as local, internal, international, or transatlantic. Such a comparative approach reveals the specificities of the European experience. From the late Middle Ages onward, populations had been settled for a long period, and no more large, thinly settled reservoirs of potentially usable agricultural land were available. In contrast, in sub-Saharan Africa the southward expansion of the Bantu-speaking people continued and in east Asia the densely settled Chinese Empire began a process of colonizing Manchuria and Mongolia. The Americas, after the postcontact population collapse, were being resettled. While societies on all continents were characterized by high internal population mobility, only Europeans moved in such large numbers – some 55 million from the early 19th century to the 1930s – to other continents, mainly to North and South America.

Far greater numbers still moved within Europe. After the Thirty Years' War (1618–48), which resulted in the death of one-third of central Europe's population, whole regions had to be resettled. At the same time, Sweden, the urban Netherlands, and central Spain required additional manpower, and three regional labor migration systems developed: the Baltic, North Sea, and French-Spanish systems. By the mid-17th century, agrarian populations in much of Europe had grown to a degree that land became insufficient for a farmer to feed all of the family. Thus, colonization movements of marginal lands began: wetlands were drained, steep hills tilled, mountainsides terraced. When the Habsburg as well as the Romanov empires pushed back the frontiers of the Ottoman Empire, lands vacated by refugees from war were resettled by the conquering Catholic or Orthodox Christian rulers with migrants from densely settled regions elsewhere.

Europe's towns had long attracted migrants, and by the 18th century numerous regional migration systems were centered on cities: the urban centers in the western part of the Netherlands, London, Paris, several cities of the Mediterranean littoral, and St. Petersburg and Moscow. Many of these migrants were unskilled laborers and domestics, but skilled artisans and technicians also circulated between cities over large distances, and for dairy and vegetable supplies each large city needed a belt of intensive agriculture that also required additional labor. Male and female migrants often stayed, married, and became part of the local population. In particular, when mercantilist rulers sought to expand port towns or capitals to establish new crafts or industries, they required mass in-migration.

Such migrations, driven by mercantilist economics and family dynamics, accounted for the majority of moves. However, European rulers had generated religious refugees by expelling those adhering to a different creed from that of the ruler. The 150,000 Huguenots forced to leave France are the most frequently cited example. Toward the end of the 17th century, flight for religious reasons abated, with the exception of special groups such as Mennonites and diverse groups of Old Believers, people unwilling to accept new rituals. While religious dissent, in general, no longer resulted in persecution, political dissent increasingly did and, in particular, since the age of revolution, political reformers and radicals sought refuge in distant, liberal cities, like London and Paris, but also in Switzerland.

In the 19th century, internal migrations intensified in much of Europe, as did transoceanic emigration and even seasonal migration. While the departure of whole peasant families from overpopulated regions to the Balkans, the south Russian Plains, North America, and also "white settler colonies" has captured the imagination, the vast majority of the moves were between rural and urban areas. Toward the end of the 19th century both a suburbanization movement and the fashion for wealthy middle-class families to own country houses also increased cultural exchange and city-outward mobility.

Transport, whether of migrants or of increasingly factory-produced goods required ever larger roads, and from the 1830s on, rail networks. These earthworks were readily carried out by men from rural regions and served as a mobilizing factor for further migrations. In a few decades, Europe's rail network expanded from 330 kilometers (1831) to 300,000 kilometers (1876), and labor for infrastructural improvements and huge transportation projects was even needed further afield: the Panama Canal and railroad building on other continents. In industry, from the 1880s on, skilled work was increasingly mechanized and divided into smaller tasks. As a result men, but in many industries also women, without artisanal or industrial training entered the factories. The concentration of new industries in England, France, Germany, Belgium, and the Netherlands, as well as in parts of Switzerland and Austria, drew millions of migrants from the periphery of Europe: Ireland; Scandinavia; east, middle, and southern Europe, especially Italy.

Toward the end of the 19th century, concepts of national identity had replaced local and regional belongings, and concepts of superior and inferior races had supplemented or replaced differentiation by culture. Societies that needed laborers began to exclude racially and nationally undesirable ones. While the political thought of the era of Enlightenment and of the French Revolution had postulated equality before the law, the nation-state, whether dynastic or democratic, restricted equality to nationals. Besides, economic nationalism replaced the liberal post-Napoleonic era. Thus, labor migrants faced ever more rigid passport controls at international borders, had to abide by special regulations, and could enter a state's labor markets only for a specified period of time. Internally, cultural groups other than those designated "national" became "minorities" and also suffered discrimination: Polish-speaking people in Germany, Yiddish-speaking

people in many societies, Basques or Bretons in France. Investments often bypassed "marginal" regions in which "minorities" lived, thus forcing them to migrate elsewhere for work – for example, Slovaks to Budapest, Vienna, or Pittsburgh.

The local wars of the Balkans and the First and Second World Wars emerged, rooted in, among other things, nationalism and racism, as well as in struggles of "minorities" for self-determination. For half a century, Europe became a refugee-generating continent. In the 1930s and 1940s, national-socialist German and Bolshevist Russian regimes established vast systems of forced labor and, by implication, of forced migration. Only with decolonization and the creation of nation-states in the former colonial areas, from the late 1940s on, did Africa and parts of Asia and Latin America replace Europe as a foremost refugee-generating cultural region.

In the second half of the 20th century, directions of internal migration changed and transatlantic migration came to an end. Instead, from the mid-1950s on, a south-north labor migration system from the Mediterranean countries – including Yugoslavia – emerged northward and, in a way, created a European (labor market) Union. While governments, as well as most of these labor migrants, intended such "guest worker" migrations to be temporary, many migrants settled for good. Moreover, after 1945 considerable numbers of immigrants from the colonies settled in western Europe, especially in France (Algeria and Vietnam), the UK (West Indies, India, Pakistan, and Bangladesh), Portugal (Mozambique and Angola), and the Netherlands (first Indonesia, later also Suriname). The demise of the East Bloc caused massive migration movement as well.

Toward the end of the 20th century, the south-north divide changed: asylum- and labor-seeking migrants increasingly came from south of the Mediterranean and from other countries in the southern hemisphere, where industrialization and incomes lagged behind, while demographic growth continued and political liberalization was wanting. Since Europe's states individually and, subsequently, collectively through the Schengen agreement, closed borders ("fortress Europe"), ever more men and women, without entry permits, came to increase their life-chances and work in the unofficial labor market. The newcomers, labeled with seemingly neutral terms as "undocumented" or *sans-papiers* are considered and treated as "illegals" by the state. Only now and then are regularization measures taken to redress their situation.

The majority of these European migrations were voluntary. Slave immigrations into Europe dwindled in the 16th century as did contract labor migration in the 18th. The return of forced migration under Hitler and Stalin does not change this overall conclusion. However, the term "free," as opposed to "forced," migration reflects only the decision making of families and individuals. It does not reflect the economic constraints that required that some members of a family or of a community seek labor and income elsewhere because they found neither land nor jobs at home. Given the number of children in most societies of Europe – France being the exception – more mouths had to be fed than families could provide for. Thus, the "free" decision merely concerned the question of who left. The same kinds of constraints in the lesser developed countries force families there to decide whom to send to Europe or other job-providing parts of the world.

The process of migration: forms and classifications, regimes and systems

For every migrant, the *process of migration* involves three phases: decision making in and departure from the society of origin; voyaging to the intended destination; and settling in the receiving society. With multiple migrations, these phases are repeated either as back-and-forth moves along the same geographical trajectory or to further new destinations.

The decision to migrate is made in a society of origin characterized by demographic specificities, the political system, social stratification, economic development (including the stage of industrialization and urbanization), ethnocultural and religious composition, and access to educational institutions, in particular, and societal resources, in general. Potential migrants, as well as their families, experience this frame in a particular regional setting and under the influence of regional migration traditions and resulting information flows, or the absence of them. If the frame is experienced as constraining, families or certain members look for life-course options elsewhere. Such constraints were formerly simplified to "push" factors, whereas "pull" factors can be defined as conditions elsewhere that are viewed as better in comparison with those at the place of origin.

The decisive step in a new understanding of the decision about whether or not to migrate occurred when scholars began to look at everyday lives in family and neighborhood groups. Before the mid-20th century, men and women made decisions individually and without family contexts only if they had broken local norms and were ostracized by their community: unruly young men and young women pregnant out of wedlock were the most common cases. The new paradigm involved a holistic view of human agency (micro-level) in cultural, societal, and economic regions (meso-level) encouraged or constrained by statewide codified laws, power hierarchies between sexes, age groups, generations, classes, and economic forces (macro-level). In the minds of migrants these levels are integrated, according to the information available and according to customary normative restrictions.

Decisions are made within a family economy, whether in traditional peasant, industrial wage, or 20th-century consumer societies. A family economy considers the income-generating capabilities of all family members according to their assigned gender and generational roles combined with the family's needs: reproductive; material as regards food, clothing, and housing; and emotional in terms of care, in particular, for children or elderly dependents. Thus, the pool of labor power is allocated according to societal norms in order to achieve the best possible results internally for all members

of the family and externally for their standing in the community. Allocation of resources and duties has to be negotiated in terms of benefits: maximization of income or of leisure, child care or waged work outside the home, education or labor for children, networking or individualist separation from the community. The process is neither equal nor democratic but depends on the respective stage of members in the family cycle as well as in individual life courses; it depends on traditional gender and intergenerational hierarchies.

The outcome of this process can very well be the departure of one of the members, but this is less common than older theories lead us to believe. Once it was decided whether the family would migrate as a whole – which necessitates adequate resources – or which particular member would be sent out or permitted to leave, information about potential destinations had to be compared. In some cases information was available for only one customary destination: a large city nearby or a labor market segment on a different continent. However, patterns of migration were usually complex and permitted selection among destinations.

In a late-19th-century north Italian village, girls and young women were sent to silk factories in neighboring towns, young men left for seasonal work in southern France, married men left for work in the Missouri iron mines and their wives tended the local agricultural plot. In the last case, women and children followed the male breadwinner once he could afford to pay their passage and support them in the new society. Through return migrants and emigrant letters, levels of information were high regarding one particular destination – e.g., a specific iron mine – but not other labor markets in North America.

Older interpretations assumed that emigrant letters would paint rosy pictures of achievements, but in sequential (or chain) migrations, in which friends and kin follow each other, the informant would in fact be expected to help the most recent newcomer to secure a job. Thus overly positive reports could be costly. If information was usually reliable, it was on occasion incomprehensible: late-19th-century agrarian villagers, who received descriptions of brilliantly lit train stations and huge factories, assumed the availability of accessible jobs and higher wage levels without taking into account the higher costs of living and slum living conditions. Migration research, if inspired by neoclassical economics, has pursued the reductionist approach of measuring wage differentials as sole or major "push and pull" factors while leaving all nonmeasurable cultural aspects of migration out of consideration.

In the actual geographical transition, migrants face obstacles and inducements. Obstacles might include political regulations limiting departure (of conscripts), poor relief systems, social norms (preventing women from traveling without male escorts), and economic systems, like proto-industry. The expected route could involve fear of little-known regions, an awareness of different languages, uneasiness about dangers on the road, or in transoceanic voyages fear of the deep blue sea. Travel time meant days or weeks without income from one's farm or from wages. Even cheap means of transport were costly in terms of unearned wages. Finally, immigration regulations could prevent entry or, alternatively, encourage people to come. Economists call these opportunity costs.

Given such costs, migration may take place in stages: to the next town to earn the fare for a further leg of the trip or to adjust to different lifestyles, later to a more distant and larger city, still later to a different country: from Anatolia via Istanbul to Munich or, in former times, from Lancashire via Liverpool to Boston. These kinds of migrations could be organized by labor recruiters, creating their own "spontaneous" chain migration patterns. In times of economic downswings on the receiving side or of good opportunities at the sending end such migratory connections may lie dormant until further socioeconomic changes increase the migratory potential again.

Inducements would include high levels of accurate information and supportive earlier migrants, kin or friends, at the destination. Of Europe's emigrants to North America around 1900, about 94% selected kin and acquaintances as a first port of call on their journey. Furthermore, migration may be stimulated with the help of migrant organizations (including churches), which were often supported and influenced by religious or state institutions in the sending country. Whether these various factors stimulate or hinder migration depends on the specific context. Thus, state policies, but also churches and unions, in receiving areas can be inclusive or exclusive, just like the networks of migrants themselves. Second-generation migrants in particular are not always keen on helping (or marrying) yet another cousin or relative and may also function as gatekeepers.

During their journey, most migrants cross some kind of border: between dialects and cultural regions; between farm and factory life; between communes, provinces, or states. Until the second half of the 19th century, international boundaries were not the most important ones. Passports for migration purposes, invented during the French Revolution, were predominantly used to check the identity of migrants in times of political unrest and not so much as a means of administrative control. Thus, a migrant moving within Belgium from the Flemish- to the French-speaking region had to overcome a cultural divide, while another moving within the French-language region from Belgium to France hardly noticed the change. Social spaces could be delineated more firmly than politically defined territories.

People on the frontier of new experiences might react intensely to border crossings: early modern pilgrims who left the social norms of their home community entered a state of liminality, of being temporarily outside of structured society. To help each other bridge cultural borders, 19th-century migrants bonded together during their travels and afterward. Modern international migrants traveling in planes have little time for savoring or fearing the route but at the point of arrival may face a formidable barrier of regulations and border bureaucrats. Thus, the border-crossing experience extends from one that is hardly noticed via cumbersome paperwork to an exhilarating experience (e.g., refugees escaping persecution) or a traumatizing and dangerous one (e.g., undocumented migrants).

Forms and classifications

Migration refers to geographic moves both over state borders and within the same political, social, or cultural space. It includes a change to a different location for a limited period of time with the intention to work and live there. As a form of human mobility it is distinguished from short-term mobility, such as daily or weekly commuting, tourism, or business travel, although such mobility may lead to migration: for example, German tourists deciding to migrate to Mallorca after retirement. Moreover, migration is distinguished from short-distance mobility, such as moving within the borders of a village or city. These moves are an interesting phenomenon of spatial history, but in general are not considered part of migration history.

When studying migration one may first distinguish between processes and their scientific analysis. With regard to manifestations, one can think of migratory labor systems, colonization, marriage migration, transhumance, and nomadism. Approaches are manifold and include disciplinary angles (economy, law, linguistics), thematic angles (family, generations, religion), and various aspects (discrimination, diaspora, integration, state control). In this introduction, however, we limit ourselves to "migration regimes" and "migration systems." In Table 1 we have listed the types of migration most commonly used.

Motives for migration are always related to degrees of constraint and therefore the distinction between free and unfree migration is blurred. Nevertheless, we may distinguish between situations in which migrants leave of their own free will because local economic opportunities are too limited – including sheer poverty – and situations in which they are compelled to leave. In the latter case a distinction has to be made between those who still have the freedom to choose their own destiny and those who do not. The Huguenots offer a good example of the first category: those who refused conversion (some 15%) to Catholicism had to leave France after 1685, but whether they would go to Geneva, England, Holland, or Prussia was of no consequence to the French authorities. Chattel slaves, i.e., forced migrants from west Africa to the Caribbean or from the Caucasus to Constantinople, had very little freedom, just like the forced migrants and deportees under Hitler and Stalin.

Migration may involve individuals – whose decision to depart usually occurs within family economies – families or segments of families, or whole or parts of groups defined by religion (Mennonites, for example), political persuasion, or ethnocultural patterns. Although families are thoroughly gendered arenas that determine, to a large extent, who leaves and who stays (depending on the prevailing family system), many migrants did not necessarily stay within the social and geographical reach of the family.

Table 1. Typology of migrations				
Motives	*Forced*	*Refugee*	*Economic*	*Cultural*
	By human or ecological force	Predominantly ideologically motivated	Also labeled as "betterment" migration	Such as grand tour, retirement
Distance	*Short*	*Medium*	*Long distance*	
	Local	Regional or national	Mostly international, including colonial and transoceanic	
Direction	*One-way*	*Circular*	*Multiple*	*Return*
Length of stay	*Seasonal*	*Multi-annual*	*Work-life*	*Lifetime*
Socioeconomic space	*Rural-to-rural*	*Rural-to-urban*	*Urban-to-urban*	*Colonial*
	E.g., the extension of agriculture after 1500, particularly in eastern Europe	Urbanization: the best-known type of migration in European history		Settlers, traders, soldiers, and sailors
Economic sector	*Agrarian*	*Industrial*	*Service-sector*	*Elite*
	Settler or farmer	Labor, including tramping by journeymen	Domestics, nurses, cleaning personnel, but also soldiers and sailors	Businesspeople, professionals

Moreover, there were other social entities – professional organizations such as the guilds, for example – that influenced these decisions deeply. The German *Wanderzwang* (forced itinerary) is a case in point: young men migrate on a regular basis because this is how the labor market in particular trades (bakers, for example) is organized. In this case the decision is significantly influenced by the preferences of employers, and the migrants themselves are not embedded in family or kin networks but in professional networks. For women a somewhat similar mechanism operates in the domain of domestic service. This in turn leads to quite different modes of accommodation, for when these migrants choose to stay in the place of destination their network is often much more fragmented than in the case of (mass) family migration.

Distance seems a logical criterion, as it can be measured simply by kilometers. However, as transport facilities change, kilometers measured in time and money change as well. However, this should not lead to the conclusion that distances were nearly insurmountable in the old days. Many Italian seasonal migrants at the end of the 19th century, for example, managed to work part of the year in North America, part of the year in South America, and part of the year in Italy. What is more, the distinction between internal (national) migration and international migration is quite different for inhabitants of Luxembourg than those of Russia. We have to be careful not to forget this when making international comparisons. The same goes for peculiar definitions of what is national. Algeria as a province of France for more than a century is a case in point.

It is important to distinguish between the intentions of migrants and the effects of migration as measured by migration historians. A substantial number of migrants die before they can fulfill their intentions, which, more often than not, is to return. The example of the millions of European sailors and soldiers who left for the colonies but who died of tropical

diseases before they could return is well known. The same applies, albeit in a less dramatic fashion, to most refugees, such as the inhabitants of Antwerp who, after 1585, fled to the north, expected the Spaniards to be defeated, and subsequently intended to return home. On the whole, migration historians have a tendency to overestimate permanent migration at the detriment of temporal migrations. This can be qualified for certain periods, destinations, and places of departure.

Nevertheless, migrants certainly can migrate with the intention to stay only seasonally, and they can succeed. They can also plan to go forever and never return, although many of them do return to their place of origin. It may be hard to establish such facts because this often requires nominal linking of data that not only costs considerable time but also may not be possible when only aggregate data are available, usually the case with most national and international statistics. Even if such nominal linking is possible the interpretation may not be easy. Age-, gender-, and class-specific life expectancy easily disturbs comparisons between different groups of migrants.

The distinction between rural and urban is not specific for migration. In fact, Europe in the period under scrutiny is characterized by rapid urbanization; for centuries this was due nearly exclusively to rural-urban migration but from the middle of the 19th century also because of autonomous natural growth. The intensity of urbanization has shifted along the so-called blue banana from northern Italy at the beginning of our period via the Low Countries and southern England in the 16th and 17th centuries to a more balanced growth in all parts of Europe, but mostly in the political and industrial centers. These shifts are clearly reflected in the migration history of this continent. Partially related to this is the maritime and colonial expansion of several parts of Europe, starting in the south with the maritime empires of several Italian cities in the eastern Mediterranean and the Portuguese expansion to Africa and then to Asia, followed by the Spanish adventures in the Americas. The emphasis then shifted to the Dutch Republic, which took the lead in the 17th century. The Dutch East India Company, for example, shipped more men to Asia than all other European colonial powers put together. Only at the very end of the 18th century did the French – for a very short period – and the English – for a much longer one – surpass the Dutch. In the 19th century a completely new pattern emerged, specifically related to the scramble for Africa.

Distinctions according to the economic sector where migrants work and want to work cannot be analyzed without taking into account the economic development of Europe. As a rule, major developments since the 16th century are described under the guise of proletarianization, i.e., the process in which people become wage earners. In the 17th and 18th centuries the so-called proto-industry was an important phenomenon. Not only in towns but especially in the countryside, many men and women who had previously been engaged in agricultural activities came to work on a loom or in another trade. Originally this might have been a disincentive to migrate, but with the unequal competition between rural industry and factories in the 19th century, many people left the countryside to go not only to the cities in Europe but also overseas. Second sources for proletarianization were the serfs in central and eastern Europe who were gradually liberated in the first half of the 19th century. These people also became available for the labor market. This process of proletarianization started in the Low Countries in the 14th century and shifted during the 19th and the greater part of the 20th century from roughly the northwest to the southeast of Europe. It determined what the poles of attraction for migrants were and which regions migrants left. The last major shift among economic sectors took place in the 20th century when in many countries the service sector took the lead from the industrial sector (which had previously surpassed the agricultural sector).

Migration regimes

Although geographical mobility is a structural element of human societies, the scope, direction, and form are partly influenced by the prevailing rules and regulations in the states that have made up Europe since the late 16th century. These formal *and* informal prescriptions for human behavior are not static. Feudal societies, for example, in principle curb migration because serfs are tied to the land, whereas liberal or capitalist societies often stimulate people to be mobile. Other political regimes, such as imperial China, find labor migration (labor to capital) problematic but stimulate settlement migration (labor to land). In this paragraph we distinguish several major societal types in Europe in the past four centuries, each producing different coherent sets of inducements and limitations with respect to migration. For these sets we use the term "regime." This does not imply that we assume legal and social rules to be always upheld. As we have argued before, to a certain extent migratory processes have a dynamic of their own, which becomes particularly visible at the micro and meso levels. The regime approach is chosen first of all to illustrate the scope of this autonomy and second to differentiate between specific forms of migration (and settlement) that various political systems have produced.

We discern several historical migration regimes according to the period under consideration and the political context. After a period of at least three centuries before 1800 in which migration regimes diverged rather widely inside Europe, the last two centuries show an increasing convergence.

Divergent migration regimes in the early modern period, 1500–1800

In the early modern period Europe is characterized by a number of competing regimes, which over the course of time became increasingly alike. We distinguish here among four major types: first, a liberal migration regime in a handful of small republics, in particular the Dutch and the Venetian republics; second, strong migration restrictions in most dynastic states; third, large territorial states inviting settlement migrations in specific parts of the country, like Russia and the Austro-Hungarian Empire; and last, the Ottoman Empire with a similar settlement policy, combined with a large internal mobility.

1. Liberal migration regimes in the Dutch and the Venetian republics

Rather exceptional, but very influential due to its overall successes in the 16th and 17th centuries, was the migration regime of small republics such as Venice and Holland. These European regions were characterized by high levels of urbanization and by low entrance levels for immigrants. The immigrants they attracted were not required to belong to the official religion of Venice (Catholicism) or of Holland (Protestantism). Even Jews and Armenians, and sometimes Muslims, were welcomed. The difference between the two republics lies in Venice's inability to rely solely on free immigrants. From the middle of the 16th century its navy employed slaves on the oars, and other slaves were also present in this major maritime port, something that was absent in Amsterdam, which heavily and exclusively depended on free immigration. The other early maritime power in Europe, Portugal, depended even more than Venice on the importation of slaves and might be seen as a subcategory.

2. Strong immigration regulations in most dynastic states

Starting in Spain and Portugal from the end of the 15th century and increasingly from the 17th century onward, dynastic states envisaged their inhabitants as useful beings who should share one religion and had to be prevented from leaving the empire. For those who did not want to adhere to the majority's religion, forced conversion or departure were the only options, as was the case in post-1492 Spain, in post–Henry VIII England, in Scandinavia, in post-1555 (Augsburg) Germany, and in all countries under the influence of the Counter-Reformation, such as post-1685 France. These dynastic states tended to depend on the estates and thus restricted migration and urbanization. On the other hand, immigration was not seen as important, with the exception of highly specialized craftsmen. Only certain groups were invited as protégés of the ruler. Such newcomers often negotiated a special status – for example, exemption from military service or from taxation during a period of initial establishment of an economic base, or the right to have separate cultural and, in particular, religious institutions (e.g., Huguenots). In a dynastic state the population shared only the status as subjects of a ruler; it did not necessarily share a culture or a language. The retention of the premigration culture at the new location was therefore possible as long as loyalty to the new ruler was explicitly declared.

3. Large territorial states inviting settlement migrations

Because of the domination of serfdom in East-Elbian Europe one easily assumes that there were few possibilities for migration. However, while serfdom, which lasted until 1800 in middle Europe and until 1861 in the Russian Empire, immobilized peasants, it did not prevent migration. Landlords rid themselves of serfs they no longer needed, or enticed serfs of other lords to work for them if they needed additional laborers. Estate owners could also allow serfs to perform wage labor under the terms of serfdom. In this case serfs were required to pay a recognition to their lord. Some serfs fled, such as the Cossacks who originated from runaway serfs and their descendants. Most important, however, the czars, in particular Catherine II (1762–3), invited immigrants to populate the newly conquered lands in the south. This attracted many free immigrants from German-language regions and other parts of central Europe.

4. The Ottoman Empire combining dedicated settlement policy and a large internal mobility

The Ottoman Empire's migration regime and patterns of cultural interaction constitute a special case. Its Eurasian territories – the Balkans, Hungary, the south Russian plains, Asia Minor, and the cultures of the eastern and southern Mediterranean – formed an integrated migration region. The top levels of the state were composed of voluntary and involuntary elite migrants: future administrators were recruited not only from the Muslim population but also from a forced levy of young Christian boys who were educated and raised Muslim, as well as of established ethnically Greek Phanariotes. The wives of the sultans and of ranking administrators came from slave catchment areas – Circassian or north African or other – and they too were highly educated. This bound service elite spoke a *lingua nullius*, the *Ottomanlica*, an artificial language created so as not to give advantage to any ethnic language, not even to Turkish.

Within the empire, migrations, both for economic and religious reasons, were manifold. If insufficient to fill a particular economic need the government used forced migration, *sürgün*, to establish urban or rural producers where needed. It provided them with a secure economic framework and thereby induced subsequent voluntary migration of co-ethnics of the involuntary *sürgün*-migrants. Religious groups (Jews, Christians) administered their own affairs and, except for a special tax, non-Islamic religions faced no discrimination. In the context of the Habsburg-Romanov-Ottoman rivalry, from the Balkans to the plains north of the Black Sea, Muslim peasant migrants settled in Bosnia. Later, Muslim settlers, nomads, and Central Asian peoples left with the retreating Ottoman forces, while settlers from Slavic-speaking cultures and southwestern German-language regions arrived.

From indirect to direct rule and the slow convergence of migration regimes, 1800–1900

In the course of the 19th century these divergent regimes slowly, and at differing paces, merged into either the empire (Habsburg, Ottoman, Romanov) or the nation-state regime. In western, southwestern, and northern Europe loyalty to a ruler or a dynasty was supplemented by a newly developed concept of nationhood. However, the model nation-states of Britain and France incorporated English, Scots, Welsh, Cornish, and Irish or French, Bretons, Basques, and Alsatians, while some French-speakers were Belgians or Swiss. In central, east-central, and eastern Europe the Hohenzollern, Habsburg, and Romanov empires, which collapsed during the First World War, remained states of many peoples throughout their existence, Russification and Germanization policies from the 1880s on notwithstanding. Throughout Europe, elites were mobile regardless of borders and states: the trans-European aristocracy intermarried and intellectuals used linguae francae – Latin, German, or French – to communicate. The time of substantial conversions had ceased, and tolerance, as in the Dutch Republic from the first half of the 17th century onward, now became the rule in postrevolutionary Europe. Maybe the most important exception at the very start of this period were the 30,000-odd political refugees from the Dutch Republic (1787) and a few years later an equal number of refugees who fled the revolutionary regime in France.

However, the lack of a political role for the citizenry in Europe's dynastic states led to increasing internal opposition. After the Age of Revolution, reactionary governments forced reformers and revolutionaries into exile, whereas after successful revolutions supporters of the old regimes fled in large numbers. Populations were no longer defined by faith and expelled for the "wrong" one (religious refugees), but were measured by political affiliation and confined or expelled for democratic or reactionary convictions (political convicts or refugees). However, religion continued to play a role in group construction. In the late 19th century the German state discriminated against Poles for being Catholic, whereas large segments of the Protestant English population stigmatized the Irish on the basis of their "popery" as the ultimate other, using discourse and stereotypes that resemble the anti-Muslim diatribes in western Europe from the 1990s onward.

In western Europe, the impact of the English urban bourgeoisie and of the French Revolution and its concept of equal citizens, and the Romantic concept of peoples' cultures, slowly welded the inhabitants into the nation-state ideology. This development, which also affected the Romanov Empire from the mid-19th century on and later also the Ottoman realm, had important ramifications for migrants but involved several internal contradictions. The territory of a state was usually not congruent with cultural regions. Britain, Belgium, and Switzerland contained several linguistically different groups; France, Spain, and Italy combined regions of culturally diverse inhabitants.

The imposition of the concept of nation onto culturally diverse peoples meant that some became "minorities," the Basques in Spain and France, for example. Others, such as German-origin people in Russia, became "co-nationals" outside of a nation's boundaries. The combination of the concept of the state with that of the nation led to a contradiction as every citizen was equal before a state's law but distinguished by a specific regional culture, not equal as regards cultural practice. "The nation" was elevated from one among several linguistic groups within a dynastic state. Usually the most numerous group became the hegemonic one with privileged access to state offices and, often, economic investments (e.g., of Magyar culture in many-cultured historic Hungary). This was paralleled by a cultural homogenization drive or by cultural and, often, economic oppression (e.g., of Slovaks). Postulated equality before the law went hand in glove with imposed inequality of cultures and unequal power relationships. It precluded negotiation of special cultural status. Nevertheless, the period 1850–1914 was characterized in Europe by far-ranging freedom to migrate over national boundaries.

The migration regime in liberal welfare states of the 20th century

For both the classical nation-state and the empires, the First World War marked the end of the long, laissez-faire, 19th century and the emergence of a new migration regime, which was first of all characterized by a much greater political as well as a socioeconomic role for the state. Differences in political and economic power between states, among other things, resulted in continent-wide warfare, beginning in the Balkans with wars between the competing Habsburg and Ottoman empires as well as with small wars of national liberation from imperial rule. From these decades through World Wars I and II the increasing number of new nation-states imposed new borders on long-settled people or shifted borders over them. Nation-states became institutions generating refugees by expelling "non-nationals" and by attempting to induce or force co-ethnics settling outside of the new nation's borders

to return "home." In the first half of the 20th century, imperial and nation-state Europe made the Continent the largest refugee-generating region in the world. From 1914 onward, the demand for laborers also led authoritarian regimes to force working men and women to change their location. Especially during the Second World War massive forced labor regimes were created, which in the case of Nazi Germany coexisted with the extinction of millions of people.

It would be one-sided, however, to paint the history of migration in the 20th century only in colors of war, expulsion, and mass murder. In terms of migration regimes, a more important and structural change influencing migration patterns was the large-scale intervention of the state in the socioeconomic domain. From 1914 onward, and in some states like Prussia a few decades earlier, the state assumed socioeconomic functions that had far-reaching consequences for the policy toward migrants. This was the side effect of the more general process of state building, which turned subjects into citizens with various kinds of rights and obligations: political (universal suffrage), but also socioeconomic (unemployment and sickness benefits, pensions, and the like). By laying the foundations of the later full-fledged welfare state, the state saw itself forced to demarcate much more clearly the difference between its own citizens and those belonging to another country.

This development had important consequences for the regulation of migration and the modes of integration. First, it was reflected in the legal restrictions on immigrants for entering the country or its labor market in the interwar period. Passports, abolished in most countries around 1860, were reintroduced and were used primarily for administrative purposes. States devised visa regulations to control entrance, especially to grant labor permits, admit refugees, and more generally to monitor aliens within its borders. Another sign of the changed state policy toward migrants were the active state recruitment policies, as followed by France in the 1920s. Furthermore, states became more restrictive with regard to the permanent stay of migrants and emerged as important actors in the discourse on the "assimilabilty" of immigrants. Fascism, National Socialism, and communism can be seen, in a way, as the apex of this ideology.

After the Second World War this new regime was further developed in the 1950s and 1960s. The only structural innovations were the implications of international agreements on refugees (Geneva Convention 1951) and the extension of the equality principle embedded in welfare state arrangements, leading up to what political scholars have labeled the "liberal paradox": growing legal differences between citizens and aliens and at the same time the building up of residence and social rights by immigrants due to the extension of their stay. Although noncitizens in a political (national) sense, their prolonged stay turned them into de facto citizens in a social and economic sense, whom the state could not easily deport and who even acquired the right to bring over family members. The best example of this development is the case of "guest workers." The whole of southern Europe from Portugal to Greece, as well as north Africa and Turkey, became a sending region. Migrants entered the social security systems of the receiving societies but, for decades in general, were not permitted to join the political system. They became denizens rather than citizens. At the same time, the eastern, socialist region of Europe was cordoned off with its own labor and rural-urban migration. (Former) Yugoslavia straddled the divide by combining a multiethnic socialist state with westward labor migration.

Whereas the migration of guest workers and to a lesser extent displaced persons can be regarded as the extension at a larger scale of the existing intra-European seasonal and labor migrations, the sometimes large-scale – partially – colored colonial immigration after World War Two (to Portugal, France, Belgium, Great Britain, and the Netherlands) was a new phenomenon. Interestingly, however, and notwithstanding the racial discourse and exclusionary acts, in the long run they were predominantly included in the nation, as (former) subjects of the colonial empire.

In addition, from the 1970s onward the origin of refugees shifted from (eastern) Europe to other parts of the world. First Latin America, then the Middle East, and subsequently parts of Asia and Africa, although Europe (as shown by the example of the Balkans in the 1990s) occasionally remained an important source. The upsurge in the numbers of refugees has different roots and analytically can be separated into factors of demand and supply. An important change in the demand side was the Geneva (Refugee) Convention (1951), which laid the legal basis for the right of refugees to seek asylum. During the first decades, however, the refugee definition was predominantly restricted to those fleeing eastern European communist regimes, like the Hungarians in 1956 and the Czechs in 1968, but from the 1970s it became clear that its reach was much more universal than originally intended. One of the reasons for the increase in the number of (non)European refugees was the restrictive immigration policy that emerged after the oil price crisis of 1973, which ended the relatively free entry of labor migrants, among whom were also migrants with political motives. With the restrictive regulations in place, the only way to enter western Europe for most migrants was either through family reunion, which multiplied the existing former guest worker population, or through the refugee/asylum channel. More important, however, the increase of refugees was caused by the growing economic inequality in the world and the military and political disruptions caused by the rivalry between superpowers (USA, USSR, and China) as well as the involvement of (former) colonial powers (Portugal, France, and Belgium, in particular). This caused grave military and political instability in Africa, the Near East, and Asia.

Most refugees, however, stayed within the region. To explain the often very selective refugee streams, the concept of "backward linkages" is useful. It points to the relation among political, economic, and military involvement of powerful states in other parts of the world, which then triggers migration. Examples are numerous: Vietnamese

(also to France) and people from Latin America to the USA, francophone Africans to France, Irish migrants and Tamils to England, and so on. Finally, more or less coincidental streams of migrants that lead to viable communities in specific countries often stimulate follow-up migration through chain migration and the dynamic of networks, thus linking macro-, meso-, and micro-levels. Notwithstanding the changes in the origin of the migrants after the Second World War, the political and economic causes are not new, and their insertion into western European societies is much more similar to that of earlier migrants than is often assumed.

A new regime emerging at the end of the 20th century?

Although it is clear that from the 1950s onward supranational arrangements and institutions have become important (EU, UN, etc.), this has not immediately weakened the nation-state, or the power of states to regulate immigration, nor has it diminished their claim to formulate and execute integration policies. This third regime changed somewhat in the 1980s and 1990s when the drive toward a common European immigration policy led to internal freedom of movement within the EU, the Schengen agreement, and the emergence of a fortress Europe. This complex of developments coincides with the disappearance of communism in eastern Europe in 1989 and the upsurge in asylum migration and may signal the transition to a new regime.

Migration systems

An empirically verifiable migration by many individuals from a particular geographic and economic region over a sizable period of time toward a common region of destination connected by information flows constitutes a migration system. This may be local (rural migration to the next city), regional (the North Sea system), continental, or transcontinental (migration in the Atlantic economies). The discourses about, norms, rules, regulations and laws, transport facilities, and patterns of mobility constitute a migration regime of a particular period and depend on both political organization and economic developments.

Migration systems consist of a long-standing mutual relationship between regions of departure and destination. They result from unequal economic or social development regionally, within a state, across Europe, or globally. In the 16th and early 17th centuries the three best-known migration systems were the Ottoman, the Venetian, and the Ibero-American ones. The Ottoman Empire (which reached its apex in Europe from 1526 to 1699) had an internal system. The Venetian one, partially in stiff competition with the Ottoman Empire, drew large numbers for its maritime and colonial needs from surrounding countries. The Spanish (and Portuguese) system was different because the 16th-century Iberian peninsula was outward-directed, mainly toward the Spanish and Portuguese crown colonies in the Americas and elsewhere. All three systems were untouched by the ravages of the Thirty

Years' War, 1618–48, which resulted in large intra-European repopulation migrations.

In the 17th century three new migration systems developed fully in western and northern Europe: a Franco-Spanish one, a North Sea–centered one, and a Baltic sea system. These three regional migration systems brought laborers and independent producers westward to the newly independent urban Netherlands, southward to Spain, and north- and eastward in particular to the Swedish Empire. Improved labor market opportunities for both men and women and migration of both sexes resulted in better marriage market conditions. The productive and reproductive spheres were closely linked. In the 1750s changes in economic and political predominance resulted in several new smaller systems centered on west and south European cities with the Dutch North Sea system remaining in force. In addition, two new settler migration systems linked regions with a rural population surplus to the Balkans and the south Russian plains, areas taken by Habsburg and Romanov armies from the Ottoman Empire.

In the wake of the Napoleonic Wars, 1789–1815 (involving an unprecedented mobility), and the reestablishment of several reactionary dynastic regimes at the Congress of Vienna (1814–15), migration systems changed again. Eastbound movements declined while transatlantic rural-to-rural and rural-urban migrations increased and, by the end of the 19th century, coalesced into one migration system in the Atlantic economies, the (mainly) proletarian mass migration along a northwestern Europe–to–North America axis and a smaller, peasant, middle-class, and worker southern Europe–to–South America axis. This system stagnated during the years 1914–45. This Atlantic system was replaced from the mid-1950s by the south-to-north intra-European labor migration system (guest workers) and joined by postcolonial migrants.

Adjustment to the receiving society

The past decade has witnessed increasing interest in the migrant settlement issue, with most studies focusing on the history of a single specific group of immigrants at the expense of the more general aspects of the settlement process of immigrants. Moreover, virtually all scholars deal with the first or, at best, the first and second generations, and focus particularly on the deviant characteristics of the group to which their study is devoted. They generally find minority formation to be a more interesting phenomenon than the way newcomers find their place in the new society. Thus, we know a lot about groups whose settlement process is characterized by a slackening or blocking of the assimilation process. Prominent examples include the many studies of Jewish migrants from the 16th century onward. In fact, the interest in the history of this religious minority is so keen as to eclipse the number of publications on other immigrant groups. Here too the emphasis lies predominantly on the special, "different" aspects of these (former) immigrants, muting their

similarities with the rest of the population. In the few cases in which this has been attempted, historical analyses show that the general idea of a separate position, apart from an *imposed* minority position, requires historical adjustment.

At this point we note that the *dominating interest* for ethnic differences and unique features is not a historical prerogative. Many social scientists direct their research efforts toward recent immigrants in line with their historian colleagues. Ethnicity, transnationalism, and diaspora have become buzzwords. While it cannot be denied that these concepts are important for a proper analysis of part of the "immigration reality," an inherent risk of a static and biased application is that insufficient attention is reserved for similarities with the receiving population and the, by nature, slowly evolving settlement process. Therefore, we need to pay more attention to the larger and more general socioeconomic, cultural, and political processes, of which immigration and settlement are a part.

The uneven emphasis on the first phase of the settlement process and on ethnicity is remarkable considering that in major parts of Europe assimilation has been the outcome in the long run. This means that structural integration has taken place, involving the removal of initial drawbacks in the labor markets, housing, and education. Consequently, the original convergence of a lower economic status and a primary identification with the original immigrant group has ceased after one or a few generations. Huguenots outside France, Germans in England or the Netherlands, Italians and Spaniards in France, to name a few examples, have ceased to form recognizable groups. And if it had not been for the Nazi terror, the assimilation process among Jews in western Europe, which started as early as the 18th century, would probably have been completed by now. A closer look at the 20th century reveals similar assimilation processes among the miners from Poland, Slovenia, and Italy in Germany, Belgium, and France. The postwar period poses a somewhat greater challenge in this respect because it is still unclear how the third and fourth generations will develop, but here an essentially similar process appears to be at work. Notwithstanding recent attention to their roots among the second and third generations, many descendants of colonial migrants who arrived in Europe in the 1940s and 1950s have become virtually invisible, with the notable exception of the Algerians in France and Pakistanis and Bangladeshis in Great Britain. Many children and grandchildren of former southern European guest workers (Italy, Portugal, Spain, Yugoslavia, and Greece) seem to follow a similar path, although some groups – Italians in Germany and Portuguese in France – show less progress when it comes to structural and identificational assimilation. Although these groups are less conspicuous, adhering to Christian religions and being Europeans, their slow assimilation process resembles that of labor migrants who dominate the current public debate about failing integration, and who often arrived more recently: Moroccans, Turks, recent *Aussiedler*, and other eastern European migrants and various groups of asylum seekers from outside Europe. The explanation for the slower, and sometimes (so far) failing, integration process, both in identificational and structural respects, is explained by a mixture of low human capital and different religions (Islam, Hinduism) on the part of the migrants and unfavorable economic structures and discrimination on the part of receiving societies.

If we are to understand the long-term and interactive assimilation process, it is necessary to avoid two obvious pitfalls: (1) the assumption of a linear and unconditional adaptation to a monolithic receiving society and (2) the one-sided approach, which emphasizes the (unique) cultural and ethnic characteristics of immigrant groups. The second approach emerged in response to the assimilation paradigm that had prevailed since the 1920s and had been developed and propagated by the Chicago School of Sociology headed by Robert Ezra Park. One of the basic premises of Park and his colleagues was that immigrants (most of whom originated from southern and eastern Europe) experienced a linear assimilation process in their country of settlement, gradually losing their own particular culture and habits as they stewed, so to speak, and eventually emerged from the "melting pot" of American society as genuine Americans. A second basic premise of this assimilation theory consisted of the characterization of immigrants and the receiving society as static entities. The homogeneity of society could only be achieved when immigrants succeeded in mastering its existing traditions, sentiments, and ideals. Park believed that most immigrants had come from a primitive rural society whose collectivist features formed an obstacle to the so celebrated American individualism. In his view, the assimilation process thus served to spark the immigrant's own initiative and "wipe out [his] memory of the past." With this, however, he merely referred to those elements that did not fit in the American democratic model, for he recognized that memories of the past could form a basis for building a new life and acknowledged that the original language and specific organizations of immigrants played a useful and valuable role, particularly where it concerned the first generation.

Nevertheless at the end of the 20th century the assimilation theory was updated and modernized, giving way to a version that is much more nuanced and differentiated and has a keen eye for the role of institutions. This new assimilation paradigm can be summarized as follows: most immigrants integrated structurally and did not simply adapt without further ado, but they made use (and took advantage) of a broad range of ethnic institutions and networks. Immigrants most definitely take an active stance in exerting influence on their own settlement process; they form their own image of the indigenous population and do not usually present themselves as mere victims overcome by a process of "displacement." Moreover, the overwhelming majority of migrants and their offspring combine multiple identities, which they profile depending on the situation. Although newcomers may have partly developed their own ethnic identity, such as that of "immigrant" or member of an ethnic minority, that certainly does not preclude them from also, or

additionally, experiencing a feeling of being connected with their indigenous counterparts in other respects (e.g., class, religion, political preference, gender). In this sense the new assimilation theory has much more in common than one would think at first glance with approaches that avoid the term "assimilation" and stress the de facto development of multiculturalism and diversity.

The distinction that can be made between *ethnicity* and *symbolic ethnicity* closely resembles this differentiated approach of the settlement process. "Ethnicity" points to a focus on the individuals' own group of immigrants sufficiently strong as to make its members see themselves primarily as members of that group: few marriages with outsiders, living spatially together, and the use of its own (ethnic) clubs and associations as well as economic circuits. This type of behavior may be observed among most first-generation and quite a few second-generation immigrants. "Symbolic ethnicity," on the other hand, points to a process of negotiating (respect for) diversity among subsequent generations that is essentially emphasized only in specific situations, whereas the actual social behavior, e.g., intermarriage, speaking to family members in the original language, or attending a place of worship, often shows signs of assimilation. Thus, ethnic identification is not per se connected to participation in ethnic practices, be they religion, language, or dress.

The new assimilation theory as well as approaches that favor the terms "accommodation" or "acculturation" also leave room for nonlinear developments, allowing for lapses and different outcomes. These may be caused by institutional factors, such as discrimination and stigmatization, but may also be the result of a deliberate choice to retain ethnicity, often for religious and cultural reasons. There are examples of groups of immigrants among whose offspring ethnicity has flared up and the feeling of belonging to a specific group has been (temporarily) emphasized in particular circumstances notwithstanding signs of assimilation. This is expressed not only in the form of symbolic ethnicity, but equally in actual social behavior. A worsening of the climate in the receiving society – in the form of a revival of discrimination to the point of actual persecution – is often to blame. Well-known examples are 19th-century anti-Semitism and the policy of extermination practiced by the Nazis, which encouraged a high degree of group formation among Jews (as expressed, among other things, in the Zionist movement). The nationalist influence of the country of origin may also have an impact on the assimilation process, as it did among Polish miners during the interwar period or among Moroccan and Turkish immigrants in the postwar period. Finally, the outcome of the settlement process also partly depends on the way receiving societies leave room for diversity and multiculturalism.

Assimilation or integration is therefore not the inevitable terminus of the settlement process. A well-known example is that of the Sinti and Roma (Gypsies), who have continued to exist as a segregated group for centuries, mainly due to stigmatizing government policies. Moreover, a structurally low position of immigrants in the labor market may contribute to sustained ethnicity. Finally, there are examples of self-imposed isolation, particularly in the case of immigrants who expect to stay only temporarily and who, for that reason, keep to themselves and continue to focus on their country or region of origin. This can be seen among trade minorities and independent professionals, such as Italian ice cream makers and Chinese restaurateurs. Once a situation of this specific type has continued to exist for a number of generations, it may give rise to what has been referred to as a "sojourn mentality," the idea of a kind of permanent temporary state of being.

The new assimilation paradigm also looks much more critically than the old Chicago School at the idea of the receiving society as a monolithic entity. A balanced analysis of the settlement process requires the deconstruction of the idea of a static receiving society, since the institutions of the state as well as those of the main social groupings and institutions (unions, churches, political parties) are far from uniform where their reactions to immigrants are concerned.

Notwithstanding the widespread, and largely justified, criticism of the old assimilation theory of the Chicago School, the emphasis by Park on assimilation as a *process* (instead of a *program*) continues to be relevant, particularly when the longer term (three to four generations) is the subject of study. Of particular use is the modified and modernized version for the USA as developed by Alba and Nee, who define assimilation as a two-sided sociological process in which immigrants adopt a number of major characteristics of the receiving society such as language and marriage outside their own group (*exogamy*), maintain external social contacts, and experience at least a modest upward social mobility. If these conditions are met, the offspring of immigrants will not *primarily* regard themselves as different, nor will they be regarded as such by the receiving society. The descendants may maintain specific cultural routines and foster a vague feeling of a shared ethnic background, but these cultural differences do not necessarily coincide with economic inferiority, as was the case with their parents and grandparents at the moment of their arrival. Moreover, the society where the immigrants take up residence also changes, albeit to a lesser extent, due to the dissimilarity in power and numbers. In most cases, this is a slow-moving process and many new elements are incorporated in such a way that the foreign origin is hidden for the majority of the public, thus leaving the myth of the uniformity of ethnic culture unaffected. This applies to linguistic influences as well as to a broad range of economic and cultural effects.

This approach is in line with Alba and Nee's distinction between *distal* and *proximate* causes. By "proximate" they mean causes that operate at the levels of individual and social networks, shaped by the social, cultural, and human capital of the individuals and groups involved. "Distal" refers to more structural causes such as institutional arrangements of the receiving society. This useful binary scheme is also recognizable in the "ethnicization" concept of Ewa Morawska, who distinguishes between group-specific social

and cultural patterns of immigrants and the traditions and ways of life of groups within the receiving society. These two dimensions constantly interact, but the final result of this process can vary enormously, depending on the opportunity structure of the environment where immigrants settle. Thus the settlement process of immigrants in small towns often differed from that in big cities, but it could also matter whether migrants settled in cities dominated by the service sector and light industry or in cities with mainly heavy industry. In all cases the influence of the "cultural tool kit" of immigrants is clear, but due to different economic, social, political, and cultural opportunity structures the character of the assimilation was quite distinct. The "ethnicization" model further distinguishes between different dimensions (economic, political, social, religious) in which assimilation takes place and shows that it is not a homogenous process, with different speeds per domain. Moreover, opportunity structures can differ not only at the local but also at the national level, as various comparisons between migration regimes or countries make clear.

Although the new assimilation theory is predominantly based on the American case, with its specific legacy of slavery, its conceptual tools and process approach have a broader reach and link up with European scholarship stressing diversity and multiculturalism as done by scholars such as Modood, Bauböck, and Favell. The revised assimilation model combines various terms that are also often used to describe specific parts or phases of the long-term process, such as adjustment, adaptation, accommodation, integration, insertion, and acculturation. Its heuristic value lies in the differentiation between generations, between domains, and between the economic, social, ideological, and cultural opportunity structure of the receiving society.

If we start with western Europe (lumping together dynastic states and republics) in early modern Europe religion, class, and gender were much more salient for one's social position than origin or nationality. Thus, the assimilation of co-religionists was accomplished much more quickly than in situations in which the religion of immigrants deviated, as in the case of Jews. Origin did matter, but only temporarily. Especially the admittance of immigrants to local institutions and the granting of rights mostly took time, but due to an implicit *ius soli* principle the second generation encountered the same chances and restrictions, depending on class and gender, as the rest of the indigenous population. In the non-Ottoman eastern part of Europe, developments were different. Here societies were much more segregated according to class (free versus unfree) or estate and ethnicity/language. Especially in the Habsburg Empire the difference between the German-speaking elite and the Slavonic Hungarian- and Romanian-speaking mass was considerable. This segregation also manifested itself spatially, with different living quarters in cities. Assimilation therefore had a different meaning, because as a consequence of this structural segregation there was no common culture to assimilate to. The Ottoman (*millet*) model was different again, in that society was split along religious lines, with each group having, to a certain extent, its own set of rules and institutional setting.

With the emergence of the nation-state in the 19th century and the shrinking of the Ottoman territory in southeastern Europe, the nation model gained ground and with it the greater stress on (alleged) origin. Also within the Habsburg Empire, the romantic idea of people with a common origin, language, and territory, often cast in racial terms, began to gain ground and became an important divisive element. Thus in this part of Europe the national idea could develop into ingrained ethnic and territorial conflicts, especially during the Balkan Wars of 1912–13, and lead to the dissolving of the Ottoman and Habsburg empires. In the case of the Ottoman Empire the genocide of the Armenians in 1915, planned by radical nationalist Turks, is a case in point.

At the end of the "long 19th century" in western Europe, the attitude toward immigrants from other states slowly but surely became embedded in the racial and national discourse. Due to the general aloofness of the state, however, immigrants from abroad – technically aliens – were, with few exceptions, fairly easily accepted and integrated. Citizenship did not yet entail much and the inclination to exclude people from other countries was quite weak. Parliamentary discussions about the guiding principles for nationality acts, centering around questions of *ius soli* or *ius sanguinis*, in France and Germany did attract much attention and stirred the emotions, but in practice these acts – for the time being – remained largely ideological constructions that only remotely interfered with the ordinary lives of immigrants.

As we explained earlier, this changed during and after the First World War when the line between citizens and immigrants was drawn much more firmly. Not only was migration more regulated and monitored, but states also became more interested in the assimilability of immigrants. This could be out of fear for national unity, as with the largely Catholic Polish-speaking population in the Ruhr area from the 1870s onward, or because the culture of some immigrants was deemed too strange and backward, or racially too deviant, for assimilation to be possible. Various groups, such as colonial migrants, Roma and Sinti, Chinese and Jewish immigrants, were considered, in many countries, as problematic cases.

Moreover, sending states also started to meddle with the affairs of "their" migrants abroad, mostly through migrant organizations. Well known are the attempts of the German state to stimulate the *Deutschtum im Ausland*, through German-language schools and (secret) subsidies to migrant organizations with a nationalistic program. This model was also followed in the interwar period by Poland and Italy, whose emigrants had settled in large numbers in France, Germany, and to a lesser extent in Belgium and the Netherlands. In this respect the more recent similar politics by countries like Turkey and Morocco are less new than one might think.

In Russia and eastern Europe the political opportunity structure was partly different. The dissolution of the empires

had brought about one new empire (Soviet Russia) and a number of newly created national states. In Russia with its many languages, ethnicities, and religions, the "nationality question" was not solved with the invention of the *homo sovieticus*. Instead, the national category was pivotal in the internal politics of the Bolsheviks, with Stalin as the most prominent and ruthless representative. Although the Soviet Union became officially a classless society, the parallel system of distinct ethnicities was inherited from the Czarist Empire and even refined and emphasized, officially in order to *protect* valuable cultural differences. Eventually, tens of millions of people were deported (and killed) within the vast Soviet territory, for reasons including the fact that their nationality was seen as a threat to the state. The centrality of "nationality" (including Jews as a nation) is illustrated by Russian passports until this very day, which not only list the adherence to the central state but also mention the bearer's nationality. In the rest of eastern Europe, nationality (inextricably mixed with racial and ethnic stereotypes) is also still very much alive, as the conflicts in the Balkans in the 1990s and the ongoing disputes about national minorities (e.g., Hungarians in Romania) underline.

Finally, we wish to briefly address the question of whether at the end of the second millennium a new migration regime is evolving, and with it new rules for the adjustment process. Many migration scholars argue that the nation-state is retreating and that as it does so immigrants have more room to create their own transnational or diasporic space, also over generations. Moreover, the possibilities to stay in contact with co-ethnics in other countries and in the sending community are greatly enhanced by transport and communication (satellite and Internet) revolutions that took place in the last decades of the 20th century. The consequence would be that the old, more or less linear assimilation model would not function anymore. Whether this is a likely scenario for the future, however, is still unclear. For the time being, among the second-generation immigrants in western Europe, integration in many domains is still very visible, notwithstanding the growing nativism in many countries.

SELECTED BIBLIOGRAPHIC REFERENCES

Alba, Richard, and Victor Nee. *Remaking the American Mainstream: Assimilation and Contemporary Immigration.* Cambridge, MA, 2003.

Bade, Klaus J. "Sozialhistorische Migrationsforschung." In *Bevölkerungsgeschichte im internationalen Vergleich: Studien zu den Niederlanden und Nordwestdeutschland*, edited by Ernst Hinrichs and Henk van Zon, 63–74. Aurich, 1988.

Bade, Klaus J. *Land oder Arbeit? Transnationale und interne Migration im deutschen Nordosten vor dem Ersten Weltkrieg*, www.imis.uni-osnabrueck.de/BadeHabil.pdf.

Bade, Klaus J. *Migration in European History.* Oxford, 2003.

Bauböck, Rainer, Agnes Heller, and Aristide Zolberg, eds. *The Challenge of Diversity: Integration and Pluralism in Societies of Immigration.* Aldershot, 1996.

Bauböck, Rainer, and John Rundell, eds. *Blurred Boundaries: Migration, Ethnicity, Citizenship*. Aldershot, 1998.

Brettell, Caroline B. *Men Who Migrate, Women Who Wait: Population and History in a Portuguese Parish*. Princeton, 1986.

Brettell, Caroline B., and James Hollifield, eds. *Migration Theory: Talking across Disciplines*. London and New York, 2000.

Brubaker, Rogers. *Citizenship and Nationhood in France and Germany*. Cambridge, MA, and London, 1992.

Burds, Jeffrey. *Peasant Dreams and Market Politics: Labor Migration and the Russian Village, 1861–1905*. Pittsburgh, 1998.

Crul, Maurice, and Hans Vermeulen. "The Second Generation in Europe." *International Migration Review* 37 (2003): 965–86.

Davids, Karel, and Jan Lucassen, eds. *A Miracle Mirrored: The Dutch Republic in European Perspective*. Cambridge, 1995.

Eltis, David, ed. *Coerced and Free Migration: Global Perspectives*. Stanford, 2002.

Fahrmeir, Andreas. *Citizenship: The Rise and Fall of a Modern Concept*. New Haven, 2007.

Favell, Adrian. *Philosophies of Integration: Immigration and the Idea of Citizenship in France and Britain*. Houndmills, 1998.

Foner, Nancy. *From Ellis Island to JFK: New York's Two Great Waves of Immigrants*. New Haven, 2000.

Gabaccia, Donna. *From the Other Side: Women, Gender, and Immigrant Life in the U.S., 1820–1990*. Bloomington and Indianapolis, 1994.

Gabaccia, Donna R. *Italy's Many Diasporas*. London, 2000.

Gans, Herbert J. "Symbolic Ethnicity: The Future of Ethnic Groups and Cultures in America." *Ethnic and Racial Studies* 2, 1 (January 1979): 1–20.

Hammar, Tomas. *Democracy and the Nation-State: Aliens, Denizens, and Citizens in a World of International Migration*. Aldershot, 1990.

Hammar, Tomas, Grete Brochmann, Kristof Tamas, and Thomas Faist, eds. *International Migration, Immobility and Development: Multidisciplinary Perspectives*. Oxford, 1997.

Harzig, Christiane, Danielle Juteau, and Irina Schmitt, eds. *The Social Construction of Diversity: Recasting the Master Narrative of Industrial Nations*. New York, 2003.

Hoerder, Dirk. "From Migrants to Ethnics: Acculturation in a Societal Framework." In *European Migrants: Global and Local Perspectives*, edited by Dirk Hoerder and Leslie P. Moch, 211–62. Boston, 1996.

Hoerder, Dirk. "Labor Markets – Community – Family: A Gendered Analysis of the Process of Insertion and Acculturation." In *Multiculturalism in North America and Europe: Comparative Perspectives on Interethnic Relations and Social Incorporation*, edited by Wsevolod Isajiw, 155–83. Toronto, 1997.

Hoerder, Dirk. *Cultures in Contact: World Migrations in the Second Millennium*. Durham and London, 2002.

Hoerder, Dirk, Christiane Harzig, and Adrian Shubert, eds. *The Historical Practice of Diversity: Transcultural Interactions from the Early Modern Mediterranean to the Postcolonial World*. New York and Oxford, 2003.

Hollifield, James. *Immigrants, Markets and States: The Political Economy of Postwar Europe*. Cambridge, MA, 1992.

Jackson, James H., Jr., and Leslie Page Moch. "Migration and the Social History of Modern Europe." *Historical Methods* 22 (1989): 27–36; repr. in Hoerder and Moch, *European Migrants*, 52–69.

Joppke, Christian. *Immigration and the Nation-State: The United States, Germany and Great Britain*. Oxford, 1999.

Lottum, Jelle van. *Across the North Sea: The Impact of the Dutch Republic on International Labour Migration, c. 1550–1850*. Amsterdam, 2007.

Lucassen, Jan. "Mobilization of Labor in Early Modern Europe." In *Early Modern Capitalism: Economic and Social Change in Europe, 1400–1800*, edited by Maarten Prak, 125–34. London, 2001.

Lucassen, Jan, and Leo Lucassen, eds. *Migrations, Migration History, History: Old Paradigms and New Perspectives*. Bern, 1997.

Lucassen, Jan, and Rinus Penninx. *Newcomers: Immigrants and Their Descendants in the Netherlands 1550–1995*. Amsterdam, 1997.

Lucassen, Leo. "The Great War and the Origins of Migration Control in Western Europe and the United States (1880–1920)." In *Regulation of Migration: International Experiences*, edited by Anita Böcker et al., 45–72. Amsterdam, 1998.

Lucassen, Leo. "A Many-Headed Monster: The Evolution of the Passport System in the Netherlands and Germany in the Long Nineteenth Century." In *Documenting Individual Identity: The Development of State Practices in the Modern World*, edited by Jane Caplan and John Torpey, 235–55. Princeton, 2001.

Lucassen, Leo. *The Immigrant Threat: Old and New Migrants in Western Europe, 1850–2002*. Urbana and Chicago, 2005.

Lucassen, Leo, David Feldman, and Jochen Oltmer, eds. *Paths of Integration: Migrants in Western Europe (1880–2004)*. Amsterdam, 2006.

Manning, Patrick. *Migration in World History*. New York and London, 2005.

McKeown, Adam. "Global Migration 1846–1940." *Journal of World History* 15, 2 (2004): 155–89.

Milward, Alan S. *The European Rescue of the Nation-State*. London, 1992.

Modood, Tariq. *Multicultural Politics: Racism, Ethnicity, and Muslims in Britain*. Minneapolis, 2005.

Morawska, Ewa. *Insecure Prosperity: Small-Town Jews in Industrial America, 1890–1940*. Princeton, 1996.

Noiriel, Gérard. *Le creuset Français. Histoire de l'immigration, XIXe-XXe siècles*. Paris, 1988.

Noiriel, Gérard. *La tyrannie du national. Le droit d'asile en Europe 1793–1993*. Paris, 1991.

Oltmer, Jochen. *Migration und Politik in der Weimarer Republik*. Göttingen, 2005.

Page Moch, Leslie. *Moving Europeans: Migration in Western Europe since 1650*. Bloomington, 2002.

Park, Robert Ezra, and Ernest W. Burgess. *Introduction to the Science of Sociology*. Chicago, 1924.

Polian, Pavel. *Against Their Will: The History and Geography of Forced Migrations in the USSR*. Budapest, 2004.

Portes, Alejandro. "Transnational Communities: Their Emergence and Significance in the Contemporary World-System." In *Latin America in the World Economy*, edited by Roberto P. Korzeniewica and William C. Smith. Westport, CT, 1996.

Schulze, Hagen. *Staat und Nation in der europäischen Geschichte*. München, 1999.

Sharpe, Pamela, ed. *Women, Gender and Labor Migration: Historical and Global Perspectives*. London, 2001.

Soysal, Yasemin Nuhoğlu. *Limits of Citizenship: Migrants and Postnational Membership in Europe*. Chicago, 1994.

Thomas, William I., Robert E. Park, and Herbert A. Miller, *Old World Traits Transplanted*. Montclair, 1971 (original 1921).

Thomas, William I., and Florian Znaniecki. *The Polish Peasant in Europe and America*. New York, 1918.

Tilly, Louise, and Joan Scott. *Women, Work and Family*. New York, 1978.

Torpey, John. *The Invention of the Passport: Surveillance, Citizenship and the State*. Cambridge, 2000.

Turner, Victor W. "Pilgrimages as Social Processes." In *Dramas, Fields, and Metaphors: Symbolic Action in Human Society*, edited by Victor Turner, 166–230. Ithaca, 1974.

Vermeulen, Hans, and Rinus Penninx, eds. *Immigrant Integration: The Dutch Case*. Amsterdam, 2000.

Zhou, Min. "Segmented Assimilation: Issues, Controversies, and Recent Research on the New Second Generation." *International Migration Review* (Winter 1997): 975–1008.

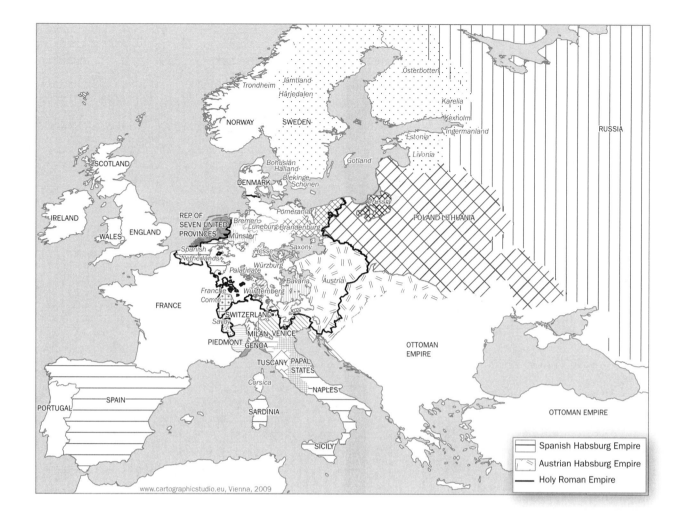

Europe 1648

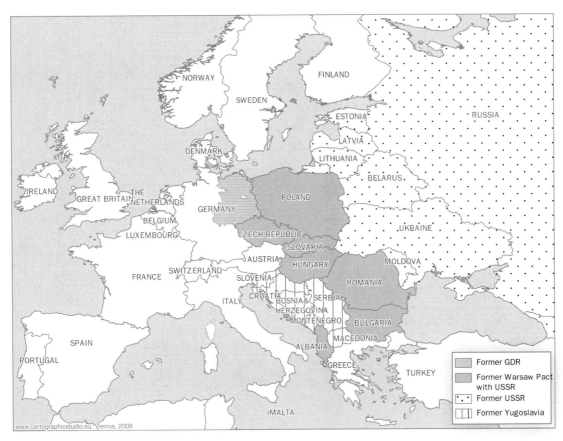

Europe 1999–2000

COUNTRIES

NORTHERN EUROPE

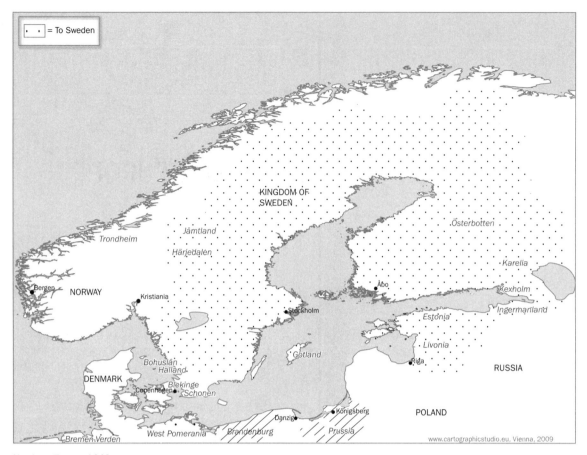

Northern Europe 1648

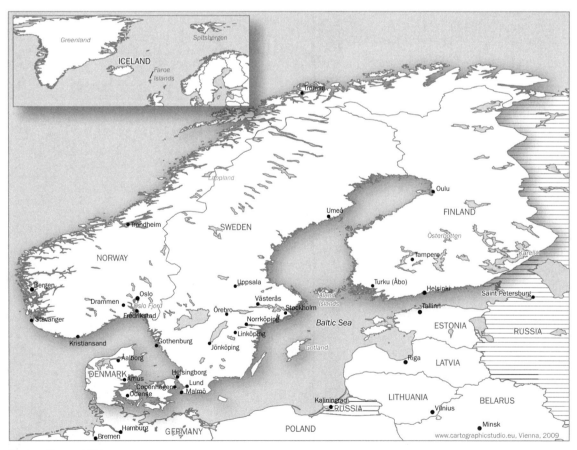

Northern Europe 2000

DENMARK, NORWAY, SWEDEN, FINLAND

Knut Kjeldstadli

The territory and its borders

Sweden, Denmark, and Norway were separate kingdoms in the early medieval period. Finland had been conquered and brought under the Swedish crown from the 12th to the 14th century. During the Kalmar union (1388–97 to 1523) all four countries were more or less united. The early modern history of Sweden is one of the rise and fall of a great power. Sweden split from the Kalmar union and started an expansion that led to the so-called great power period in Swedish history. The first wave of expansion crossed the Baltic Sea; between 1561 and 1620 Sweden swallowed the Kexholm province that is present-day North Estonia, Ingria, and Livonia. In the 17th century Riga was actually the largest Swedish town. The second wave of expansion was directed toward Denmark-Norway: in 1645 and 1658–60 Sweden conquered Gotland, Jämtland, and Härjedalen, then Scania, Halland, Blekinge, and Bohuslän. The third wave secured German territories, from Vorpommern to Bremen-Verden.[1]

This status as an important European power ended with the Great Nordic War 1700–21, when Sweden lost southern Karelia, most of its German, and all of its Baltic territories. During the War of Finland in 1808–9 Russia conquered the whole of Finland including the Åland Islands. This loss was somewhat compensated, as Norway was separated from Denmark after the Napoleonic wars and given to Sweden in 1814. Norway, however, was never integrated into the Swedish realm; two separate and internally sovereign states joined in a personal union under the Swedish king.

Among these border movements particularly the mid-17th century incorporation of Scania in present-day Southern Sweden took its time and was only accomplished in 1721. In the 18th and first half of the 19th century the Swedish state pursued a strict "Swedification" policy, particularly through the control of churches and schools, a policy that was in conflict with the peace treaties guaranteeing that Scania could keep her laws. The ban on books in Danish in Scania was only lifted in 1857. In the long run, the incorporation, at least from the state's perspective, was successful, as notions of a Danish Scania disappeared in the 19th century.

The Swedish conquest of Estonia in 1561, preceded by previous Swedish migration, left a legacy. Estonian Swedes

kept to themselves as a distinct minority for a long time. In the late 19th century they were roused into a kind of national awakening partly by Swedish cultural missionaries, partly by the czarist Russification project. Some hundred Estonian Swedes fled to Sweden in the 19th century to avoid being conscripted in the Russian army. In the 1920s some 8,000 people with Swedish roots still lived in Estonia; the majority migrated to Sweden during World War II.[2]

Orthodox Ingrians and a group called Votians inhabited Ingria, the territory in the vicinity of Petersburg. After the conquest of Ingria by Sweden in 1617, a conscious policy of immigration resulted in Lutheran Finns constituting three-quarters of the population in the late 17th century. The Russians recaptured the area in the early 18th century. In 1917, 140,000 speakers of Finnish still lived in Ingria; flight to Finland, forced collectivization, and relocations in the Stalin period decimated their numbers.

From a territorial point of view the history of modern Denmark is one of contraction. Territories were ceded to Sweden, as already mentioned, and there were conflicts over the status of Schleswig and Holstein. From 1773 until 1864, both were under Danish rule; until 1806 Holstein was part of the Holy Roman Empire of the German Nation, and between 1815 and 1864 it was part of the German Confederation. Schleswig, by contrast, remained until 1864 a Danish fief. After the German-Danish war of 1864 and the Prussian-Austrian war of 1866, both duchies were reunited as the Prussian province Schleswig Holstein.

After the end of the Danish-Norwegian personal union with the Peace of Kiel in 1814, Denmark kept its sovereignty over Iceland, the Faroe Islands, and Greenland. In 1944, Iceland broke away, in 1948 the Faroe Islands were granted autonomy, and in 1979 Greenland was granted home rule. As these islands have been fairly homogeneous in ethnic terms (Inuit and Danish in the Greenland case) and with little modern immigration until quite recently, they will not be treated any further in this overview.

After the Swedish-Norwegian personal union of 1814, the borders of Norway did not change. In 1905 the formal link to Sweden was loosened. In the northernmost parts of Norway, Sweden, and Finland there were no strict borders until the 19th century and in these frontier regions several groups

---

[1] Swedish Troops on the coasts of the North Sea and the Baltic Sea in the early modern period.

[2] Estonian and Latvian refugees in Sweden after World War II.

interacted and competed. From a historical point of view these areas may be viewed as Sami territories, where since the medieval period increasing numbers of migrants from Southern Scandinavia settled.[3] Finland emerged in 1809 as a separate unit, when Sweden ceded it to Czarist Russia. The former Swedish Finland, the county of Kexholm, and the county of Viborg (1812) merged into a separate grand duchy with far-reaching autonomy and the Russian emperor as duke.

Immigration in the era of mercantilism in the 17th and 18th centuries

Both Sweden and Denmark of the 17th and 18th centuries developed into multilingual, multireligious, and multiethnic empires. Underlying this policy was a mercantilist notion. Emigration was considered as a loss, even forbidden; immigration of people with capital or skills was encouraged. The authorities followed an active recruitment policy. To persuade people to move, migrants were rewarded fairly well and most career migrants entered society at the upper rungs of the social scale. This competition for skill took place among all European states, so that northern Europe not only gained specialists but also lost them – for example, in the case of Finland, which witnessed the departure of specialists to Russia. Furthermore, Norway experienced the emigration of male sailors and female domestics to the Dutch Republic, especially from the region of Bergen and Kristiansand. This labor migration reached its highest point in the third quarter of the 17th century. Norwegian sailors even continued to come to Amsterdam until the mid-19th century.[4]

The recruitment of skilled laborers helped Sweden to play an increasing important role in European politics. Sweden developed into a "heavy" centralized state, with a high degree of taxation and an efficient army. During Sweden's great power period, aristocrats from the new Baltic areas were included as functionaries in the administration and the army. Officers and mercenaries were recruited from several areas – in particular, these were Scots, Germans, and Baltic Germans. In the beginning of the 17th century, 45% of all high-ranking officers in the Swedish army were foreign born. Only a minority of them became permanent immigrants, although many were given land as part of their payment and several were elevated into the aristocracy. Because they owed their position primarily to the Swedish crown, foreigners were considered as particularly loyal and malleable. Apart from noblemen and mercenaries, other groups of immigrants were attracted as well in this mercantilist age, such as fortification engineers, artisans, merchants, bureaucrats, university professors, artists, and miners.

A similar import policy was pursued in Denmark. Initially there was a mercenary system and whole companies

were rented, but in the course of time soldiers were enrolled in the standing army and the Danish crown even lent them to other states as an auxiliary corps.[5] From the late 16th to the early 19th century Danish entrepreneurs, backed by purposeful state policies, also attracted foreign artisans and skilled workers into various manufactures, albeit not always with great economic success. There were also chances for career mobility in trade and industry for subjects from the more peripheral parts of the realm, as was the case with Norwegians in the capital of Denmark (Copenhagen) and Finns in Stockholm. Furthermore, Danish and German civil servants from Oldenburg (which became Danish in 1667) migrated to Norway, which was relatively underdeveloped.

Career migrants played an important role in the peripheral economy of Norway and helped to span the know-how gap to the more advanced regions in Sweden and Denmark. Several new economic branches rose to importance in the 17th and 18th centuries, such as export of planks and beams, shipping, mining, and glass works. Saxony, for instance, was the prime recruiting area for technical experts in mining.[6] Commercial expertise and knowledge of trade networks was also needed. The middlemen between Norway and Europe – originally Danes, Germans, Scots, or Dutch – often started as traders and in the end became the new Norwegian mercantilist bourgeoisie. The new upper classes had a foreign background and over time they became naturalized Norwegians.

In the 17th and 18th centuries geographic or ethnic origin did not play a decisive role in Scandinavia for a person's position in society. During the great power period in the 17th century, seventeen languages were spoken in the Swedish realm. At *Riddarhuset*, the assembly of aristocrats, German and Dutch were spoken along with Swedish. Language was primarily a practical means for communication, not an identity marker. German was the language of command in the Danish army until 1772–3. In the cosmopolitan upper class in both countries, Germans were the dominant element, whereas the most outstanding ministers in Denmark came from various German states. In reaction to this foreign competition the old Swedish nobility tried to monopolize the highest ranking commissions. In 1776 the so-called *infødsret* (the right of the inborn) was introduced in Denmark: only those who were born in the country could hold office in the upper ranks of the state administration. This decree, directed against the strong German influence, was exceptional in Europe but did not express any modern nationalism, since Norwegians and German-speaking subjects from the duchies were included as well.

In religious matters the Swedish power state followed the principle of *cuius regio, eius religio*. Catholicism, Calvinism, and Anabaptism were deemed unwanted, particularly from about 1650. These religions and Orthodox Christianity were outright forbidden by a church law in 1686. Orthodox

---

[3] Kvens and Torne-Finns in Norway and Sweden since the 18th century.
[4] German sailors in the Dutch merchant marine from the early 17th to the end of the 19th century.

[5] Scottish soldiers in Europe in the early modern period.
[6] Central and western European miners and smelters in Sweden and Denmark-Norway from the 16th to the 18th century.

Karelians under Swedish reign fled eastward by tens of thousands during the 17th century. The church and the "modernizing" secular elements in the state apparatus were at odds: this principle of religious uniformity could not be upheld in relation to foreigners, who were allowed to practice their religion in private, but not to congregate openly. Jews were to be evicted according to a law from 1658. This anti-Judaism did not imply any anti-Semitic biological notions; Jews could be baptized and were allowed into society. In 1775 Jews were accepted and allowed to practice their religion openly; the so-called Jew statute (1782) allotted them a fixed, but restricted, place in society. Between 1838 and 1870 almost all obstacles to equal citizenship were removed.

Initially Denmark-Norway was just as strict as Sweden, in tune with the Evangelical-Lutheran church ordinance of the reformation 1536–7, even more severely underlined in 1555. The state, however, in 1682 decided to follow the principle of free towns. Glückstadt outside Hamburg, Altona, Frederiksstad in southern Schleswig, Fredericia in Denmark and Frederikstad in Norway were open to people from all religions. Religious freedom was a way to entice people to come to these new towns. Jews, Catholics, Calvinists, Reformed, Mennonites, Socians, and Quakers found asylum.[7] A Moravian Brethren congregation was permitted to set up the small community of Christiansfeld, which has lasted until the present day.[8] An edict from 1685 opened Denmark to Reformed and Evangelicals and eased regulations on Catholics and Jews. In 1809, Jews were allowed in all parts of the country; in 1814, they obtained equal citizenship in Denmark. Oddly enough, the 1814 constitution of independent Norway, otherwise liberal and rather democratic, forbade Jews to enter the country, a ban that was only lifted in 1851.

Social class or status seems to have been an even more decisive factor than religion. Whereas Jews with capital were allowed, so-called beggar Jews were barred from entering Sweden in 1782. A similar distinction was drawn in Denmark where "Portuguese Jews" (Sephardim), often merchants, were allowed while "East Jews" (Ashkenazim) were suspected of barter trade and begging and therefore barred.[9] Another group suspected of being a burden were the Gypsies. A Swedish decree in 1637 prescribed that the men were to be killed without trial, the children and women immediately evicted. However, this harsh legislation was not enforced in an even manner. A third group that was sometimes marginalized was the "Forest Finns," slash-and-burn farmers from Savolax in Finland who settled in the forests of the southern border areas between Sweden and Norway, on the Swedish side from the late 16th and early 17th century; in Norway somewhat later.[10]

Two groups shed light on the preconditions preserving their ethnic identity: the Walloons in Sweden and the

Dutch at Amager outside Copenhagen. The Dutch were peasants, originally brought in 1521 to secure homeland food specialities to the Dutch-born queen. The community kept itself more than 300 years, with a measure of internal self-governance. In 1759 the first marriage outside the group took place; Dutch was used in sermons until 1811 and spoken well into the 19th century; customary practices and dress lasted even longer.

The Walloons were brought from the surroundings of Liège in present-day Belgium and Sedan in France in the first part of the 17th century. They were specialists in iron-work and charcoal production, lived in rather secluded communities, and were subject to a jurisdiction peculiar to the ironworks. They kept to their Calvinist pastors, passed on the trade from father to son, and were highly endogamous. Half a century later most had adopted Swedish as their primary language, but identification as Walloons – or better, as Walloon ironworkers – was still evident.

In their case, ethnicity and profession are hard to distinguish. One important point rises from the history of the Dutch and the Walloons: several characteristics that may be pinned on the group itself, such as trade, language, and customs, may help to explain their continued existence as a group. Still the relation to the surrounding society seems to have been most important and in both cases state policy mattered. Since the privileges bestowed on them by the state might be lost if their peculiarities disappeared, the state policy highly stimulated the drawing of ethnic borders.

Nation building the Nordic way

In northern Europe the Napoleonic wars dissolved two middle-sized European multinational empires, from which five nation-states emerged during the 19th century. Despite significant differences, the common traits were important enough to speak of a Nordic type of state. In all states there were dominant majority populations and Lutheran state churches that secured a link between religion and the concept of nationality. Besides, the peasants had been legally free in Norway, Sweden, and Finland since the Middle Ages, whereas in Denmark serfdom was abolished in 1788. The *folk*, the people, were regarded as the core of the nation, in particular the peasantry. Another common trait was early democratic features. In Sweden and Finland the peasants had been represented in the Diet since the 15th century, and their participation did not diminish after 1809, when new constitutions were introduced in both countries. Finland, as an independent grand duchy within the Russian Empire, got its own Diet and government. Also the new Norwegian constitution from 1814 secured broad political participation. In Denmark a modern national state came into being after 1849, with the establishment of a constitutional monarchy. The peasantry became a major political player especially after the defeat of Prussia and Austria in 1864.

What conditions for immigration did this Nordic, Lutheran, popular, democratic, and cultural nationalism

---

[7] Huguenots in Europe since the 16th century; Dutch Calvinist refugees in Europe since the early modern period.

[8] Moravian brethren in Europe since the early modern period.

[9] Sephardim in Europe in the early modern period.

[10] Forest Finns in Sweden and Norway since the late 16th century.

create? One might have expected skepticism of foreigners, but this is not reflected in the nature of citizenship. Although the concept of nation was related to history and language, both elements of "ethnic nationalism," Norwegian citizenship rested on the concept of *ius soli*, a territorial principle, from 1814 to 1888, when a new law underlined *ius sanguinis*, the principle of descent. The citizenship law of 1924 and its successors have upheld mixed principles. The other countries followed similar paths. At the same time there was an increasing expectation that newcomers should assimilate, "become Norwegian" or Danish, particularly in the second half of the 19th century.

In Denmark the 19th century was dominated by the German question. The population of Schleswig and Holstein was neither linguistically homogeneous nor neatly settled in clear-cut monolingual communities. Before the 19th century identities were fluid and malleable. Still, there was either a German or a Danish dominance in most areas, along with the minority along the west coast speaking the Frisian language. After the defeat in 1864 of the Prussion army, most Danes accepted a redefined version of the nation, more contracted and more inward looking. Denmark cultivated a self-image as a "small state." Still, within parts of the Danish-speaking population in Schleswig and in Danish nationalist circles, the idea of reclaiming the lost was kept alive after 1864. The northern part of Schleswig was rejoined with Denmark in 1920 after a referendum in which 91% of the voters participated. Some Danes suggested that southern Schleswig should be reincluded in Denmark after 1945, but the overwhelming majority refuted this "southern Schleswig-imperialism," both in 1920 and 1945.

Norway, ceded from Denmark to Sweden in 1814, joined a union under the Swedish king but was a separate and internally sovereign state; thus it is proper to speak of Swedish immigrants in Norway and vice versa in the 19th century. Norwegian nationalism was on the whole democratic, politically linked to liberal circles, the *Venstre* (national-democratic) party, which corresponded to a more egalitarian social structure in which the peasant movements were a major political actor. Claims have been made that this equality and relative homogeneity disposed Norwegians to be less open to cultural or ethnic differences. This, however, is not convincing since the labor movement that emerged in the 1880s was definitely more egalitarian and more internationalist than the other parties. A more plausible explanation is that the relatively short history as a reemerged independent nation created a more intense nationalism in Norway than in Sweden. Thus the policy of "Norwegianification" toward the Sami and the Kvæns – immigrants from Finland in northern Norway – was more aimed at forced assimilation than its Swedish equivalent.[11] Especially the peasantry supported the ideal of an ethnic homogeneous Norwegian population: when Parliament lifted the ban on the admission of Jews in 1851, peasant representatives were the most important opponents.

[11] Kvens and Torne-Finns in Norway and Sweden since the 18th century.

Finland-Swedes, Swedish-speaking Finns, descendants of immigrants who had settled before 1300, numbered 16% in 1750, 14% in 1865, and about 10% in 1930. They should, however, not be considered a national minority since they were not in any subaltern position in Finnish society. This duality is shown in present-day terminology: a Finlander is a citizen of Finland; a Finn is someone who uses Finnish as his mother tongue. Many Finland-Swedes lived as fishermen or peasants in northern Ostrobothnia, in the Åland archipelago and the southern coastal areas from Turku (Åbo) to Helsinki. In the capital Helsinki they formed a comparatively large part of the urban elite. Swedish was used as the official language. In the Finnish national movement, which grew stronger from the 1860s, both Finnish- and Swedish-speaking Finns participated. From 1863 Finnish was gradually introduced as an official language along with Swedish, to reach full equality in 1902; bilingualism was frequent and there was a high mobility between the language communities. In fact, some of the most ardent *Fennomanian* (Finnish nationalist) spokesmen were recruited from the Swedish-speaking educated class. The Swedish-speaking population of the Åland Islands strove for unification with Sweden, manifested in a self-staged referendum in 1917. But they received no support in the League of Nations and neither was Sweden willing to intervene. So they had to settle with a rather generous agreement of internal self-rule within the Finnish state in 1922, an autonomy that was expanded and confirmed in 1951 and 1992.

Since 1809 Finland was in practice a sovereign state with its own institutions and distinct nationality, able to resist the impact of the stern unification policy (in Finland seen as Russification) pursued from the 1890s. In 1917 Finland obtained external independence as one of the successor states to the Romanoff Empire. Some 33,500 Finns, Ingrians, and Karelians fled Russia, most of them in 1922. Karelia was included in Finland and nationalist academic and military circles dreamed of uniting Russian (or Eastern) Karelia with Finland as well. During the military advances in 1918–20 and once more in the middle years of World War II, it turned out that the Russian Karelians did not support this patriotism. As a result of the German-Finnish military defeat in 1944, 400,000 inhabitants of the Viborg county, about 10% of the population, moved to southern and central Finland. Statements on the remarkably low number of immigrants in contemporary Finland usually do not take into account this huge transfer and resettlement of migrants.

Labor migration and transatlantic emigration in the 19th and early 20th centuries

During the period of industrialization, skilled migrants were needed to introduce new technology and to train local workers. However, the typical migrant in this period was a labor migrant. Swedish industrial capitalism expanded spectacularly in the 20th century, but between 1860 and 1920 Swedish boys and girls from marginal agrarian areas migrated to farms, construction works, factories, and private households in the more rapidly growing economies of Denmark and Norway. Both were called "the poor man's America."

The real America loomed on the horizon. There had been international migration from the north earlier, such as the thousands of sailors and maids who went from Norway to the Netherlands (especially Amsterdam) in the early modern period. Still, this movement was dwarfed by the 2.5 millions emigrants who left the Nordic countries in the 19th and beginning of the 20th centuries. The Nordic countries contributed 5% of the total European emigration, while the population consisted of only 3% of the total European population. Among those who left before 1915 there were 1.1 million Swedes, 750,000 Norwegians, 300,000 Danes, and 300,000 Finns. The emigration rates of Sweden were above the European average, but were modest compared to Norwegian rates. From the 1850s to the 1890s the emigration intensity of Norway was second only to Ireland. From 1879 to 1893 as much as 77% of the natural increase of the population was absorbed by emigration. The Scandinavian countries belonged to the so-called old emigration countries; the most intense periods of emigration were 1866–73, 1879–93 (a peak in 1882), and to a lesser degree 1901–5. A majority settled in agrarian areas. In Finland, two-thirds of the emigration took place after the turn of the century, with a peak in 1902. Coming relatively late, the Finns entered wage labor in mining and forestry work. A new wave of emigrants left in the 1920s.

Swedes and Norwegians went mainly to the USA. Canada became an alternative from the turn of the century, particularly after the USA closed its gates in the 1920s. The USA was also the primary destination for Danes, but to Danes, Latin America, in particular Argentina, Australia, and Africa were important receiving areas as well.

These mass emigrations had effects on other forms of migration. First, the sheer magnitude tended to dwarf other forms of migration, both in the eyes of contemporary society and later historians. However, significant numbers actually moved into or within the Nordic or European countries. In the period 1868–1920, 60,000 to 80,000 Swedes went to Germany.[12] Emigrants from Norway between 1856 and 1900 numbered 528,000, including 20,000 Norwegians who went to Sweden. Immigration in the same period has been calculated at 130,000. Among the Nordic countries Norway received most of the immigrants, primarily Swedes and Finns. Besides, there were considerable internal population movements from countryside to towns, in Norway also from the inland to the coast and from the south to the north, which offered opportunities in fishery. "Northern Norway is our America," the saying went; similar utterances might have been made in Sweden. With a large emigration and immigration in the 19th century, Norway differed from France, for example, mainly a country of immigration, or from Ireland and Italy, which primarily exported their population.

Second, mass emigration could effect immigration – for instance through substitution of labor power. Thus in Scania there was both a high level of emigration and immigration. Such a theory, however, cannot be sustained generally because the most active emigration areas, both in Sweden and in Norway, were not areas of immigration. Neither were the immigration areas in Norway (Kvæns in the north, Swedes along the Oslofjord, and several nationalities in the capital) typical sending areas. However, there probably was an indirect link. The departure of half a million Norwegians before 1900, and 750,000 before 1915, did influence the labor market. Norway became a seller's market, thereby providing the structural precondition for the "liberating phase of capitalism" from the 1860s. Workers could shed social subordination by moving, and those who stayed could make a better bargain. Compared to working conditions in Sweden, wages in Norway were higher and labor conditions were deemed as more free, reasons mentioned for immigration by Swedish workers at the time.[13]

At the ideological level a somewhat peculiar notion developed around 1900. While emigration in the early decades was considered to relieve the country from a burden, rising labor costs also led to lamenting those who left the country. Commentators claimed that the most able, "the flower of the youth," went abroad; migration was portrayed as a loss of blood. The Swedes organized a huge official inquiry into emigration in 1911, Norway a more modest one in 1912. In all Nordic countries, societies were set up to reduce emigration or to maintain contacts with those who left: in Norway in 1907 and 1909, Sweden in 1907, Finland in 1911, and Denmark 1920. The paradoxical idea spread that while the best elements within the native population left, those who came from abroad belonged to the dregs of society. The Norwegian emigration inquiry put it succinctly: "Our nation cannot afford to be split by emigration and infected by immigration." Norwegian Americans who kept their mother tongue in the USA were praised, while Kvæns in Norway who kept their language were frowned upon as possible Trojan horses.

Emigration also resulted in return migration. In Europe as a whole an estimated 4 million returned between 1880 and 1931, 3 million between 1908 and 1923. The inclination to return varied: according to US statistics, Jews were least inclined to go back (5%), whereas as many as 89% of Bulgarians, Serbs, and Montenegrins returned. Among Scandinavians, 22% returned, on a par with other north and west European countries. Between 1875 and 1930, 178,000 Swedes (18%) came back from the USA; 155,000 Norwegians (19%) returned before 1940.[14] The majority of Swedes and Norwegians went back to rural areas and several of these invested in land. Return migrants brought back money, technical innovations, particular objects, and new habits

---

[12] Swedish labor migrants in Germany in the late 19th and early 20th centuries.

[13] Swedish labor migrants in Denmark and Norway in the 19th and early 20th centuries.

[14] Swedish return migrants from the USA, 1875–1930.

and ways of thinking. Migrant laborers in the southern and southwestern part of Norway imported US culture to such a degree that one may speak of Americanized areas.

Refugees and other immigrants from World War I until the 1950s

The 19th-century movements of labor migrants continued into the 20th century, to culminate before or during World War I. Immigrant Polish, Galician, and to a lesser extent Ukrainian women worked as seasonal beet pickers in south-eastern Scania and the southeastern parts of Denmark. Swedish workers, including navvies, still went to Norway and Denmark. To a large extent there was a south Scandinavian labor market and to some extent there was a parallel circumpolar market, consisting of Norwegians, Swedes, Finns, and to some extent Sami and Russians. The bulk of immigration to Norway was spontaneous, that is, not organized by companies or government agencies. Only east European agricultural workers were brought to Sweden and Denmark by recruiting agents who organized the tour and supervised the work. Private employment offices recruited Swedes to Denmark.

Denmark passed an immigration law in 1875, Norway in 1901. Both were primarily intended as a supplement to national poor laws, as instruments for evicting people who were considered a burden to the municipal budgets. Still, the Nordic states implemented fairly liberal immigration policies until World War I. A mixture of social unrest, political agitation, and espionage led the governments to introduce visas, registers, surveillance of foreigners, and central immigration authorities.

In all countries, but especially in Finland which gained its independence from Russia only on 6 December 1917, Russian refugees stayed on after 1918. In the years 1919 to 1923 tens of thousands of "Vienna children" were brought to the Scandinavian countries to keep or regain their health through nourishing summer stays in private homes, a humanitarian effort repeated at later occasions during World War II and its aftermath. The restrictive immigration regime and administration constructed during World War I were never fully dismantled, even though the visa restrictions were partly abolished. In fact, the core of the present legislation dates back to these years.

When new groups fled from Germany after 1933, there was an already developed system to handle the refugees. "Political" refugees were allowed more readily than Jews in all Nordic countries.[15] In 1940 there were 3,200 German-speaking Jewish refugees in Sweden, 2,300 in Denmark, and 840 in Norway after a peak of 1,000 in 1938. Relative to the population, the Danes admitted the greatest number. The Swedes were most restrictive in their immigration policies,

the Danes most lenient. During World War II, Sweden became a refuge for Finnish children, Finns, Norwegians, Estonians, Danes, Swedish-speaking Estonians, and Germans, to mention the larger groups, totaling some 180,000 in December 1944. One particular group became highly contentious after the war: 146 Estonians who had served with the Germans were extradited to the Soviet Union in 1945–6.[16]

During and after the war Swedish authorities pursued a conscious employment policy. Baltic and Polish refugees, several directly from the work and concentration camps were trained and hired as labor power, in forestry and agriculture and particularly in the commercial beet production in Scania where there was a lack of labor power. On a smaller scale this was also the case in Norway, which admitted a group of "displaced persons" (DPs), mostly Polish Jews.[17] Population movements created by the war included English women who married, for instance, Norwegian sailors or soldiers.[18] Cold war refugees in the Nordic countries were mainly Hungarians, Czechoslovakians, and Poles. In the anticommunist climate, the East Europeans were initially favored by their image as freedom seekers. Still, there were frictions and mundane problems similar to those experienced by other immigrant groups.

Labor migrations after the World War II

A common labor market in the Nordic countries was established in 1954. Citizens of the four states were free to enter the other countries without passports, free to take up residence and work, and to enjoy mutual rights to social benefits.

The Swedish economy was the most dynamic, as Sweden was now a leading industrial nation. There was an internal pool of labor power in the primary sector, created by structural rationalization in agriculture. Still there was a need for labor, so Sweden turned to Europe to look for workers to sustain its rapid economic growth and changed into a country of immigration. The most important countries supplying workers were Finland, Yugoslavia, and Greece. Finns came in numbers equal to the old transatlantic mass migration. Due to language differences and to lower standards of living in parts of Finland, Finnish-speaking Finns resembled other "foreign workers." In 1975, at the end of the period of labor migration, 45% of all foreign born were Finns, 10% were Yugoslavs, 8% Danes, 7% Norwegians, and well above 4% were Greeks and Germans.[19]

The Swedish policy was characterized by its conscious efforts to recruit, by an active state and by union participation, particularly from 1947 to 1972. Sweden had no colonial past it could rely on, like Great Britain or France, and developed a system similar to the German one. Immediately

---

[15] Political and intellectual refugees from Nazi Germany and from German-occupied Europe, 1933–1945; Jewish refugees from Nazi Germany and from German-occupied Europe since 1933.

[16] Estonian and Latvian refugees in Sweden after World War II.
[17] Displaced persons (DPs) in Europe since the end of World War II.
[18] British war brides in Norway since the end of World War II.
[19] Yugoslav labor migrants in western, central, and northern Europe since the end of World War II; Greek labor migrants in western, central, and northern Europe after 1950: the examples of Germany and the Netherlands.

after the war recruitment campaigns were launched in Western Germany, the Netherlands, Italy, Austria, Belgium, and Greece, both by industrial companies and the Swedish state. Formal state-to-state agreements were made with Italy, Austria, and Hungary. The state labor market board (*Arbetsmarknadsstyrelsen*) later set up agencies in Turin, Athens, Beograd, and Ankara. Vocational training was offered in the sending countries. Through this state participation, labor migrants secured some basic social rights. Sweden did not pursue a guest worker system and immigrants were not forced to leave after a period of work. On the other hand, from 1967 a non-Nordic immigrant was obliged to have a job, a work permit, and a residence permit before he or she could enter Sweden. This system lasted until 1972, when the demand for labor decreased and recruitment and labor immigration were formally brought to a halt. After the 1970s the population exchanges between the Nordic countries were fairly balanced, although with variations due to shifts in the economies.

In Denmark labor migration from Yugoslavia started in 1965, later from Turkey and Pakistan, with Turks as the largest group. In 1970 there was a temporary halt in labor immigration, which became permanent in 1973 with the oil price shock. Norway experienced a similar development, from 1967. The Pakistanis have been the dominant group since 1971, followed by Yugoslavs, Moroccans, and Turks.[20] The great majority of these were spontaneous migrants, not actively recruited. In 1975 Norway followed the other European countries, in the wake of the oil crisis, and introduced a halt in immigration. There was a double argument behind the law: immigration was restricted to prevent the emergence of a stable underclass, while those who had already arrived should have decent conditions. The unions supported this restrictive line, fearing that work and wage conditions might otherwise be undercut. However, as both reunification of families and marriages in the home country were allowed, the original labor migrant groups rapidly turned into stable minorities.

Finland has pursued the most restrictive immigration policy. After the dissolution of the Soviet Union more migrants have come, however. Among these were several ex-USSR Ingrians, mainly descendants of emigrants from the 17th century, allowed on the basis of *ius sanguinis* (nationality determined by ancestry) and linguistic closeness to the Finns. Still, while there were 12% foreign born in the Swedish labor force in 1993–4, 6% in Denmark and Norway, there were only 2% in Finland.

Refugee and labor migration, and integration policies since the 1970s

Like the labor migration, the new refugee movements from the 1970s also reached the Nordic countries. Apart from

Table 1. Percentage of the population with foreign citizenship, 1 January 2003				
	Denmark	Finland	Norway	Sweden
Nordic countries	0.61	0.17	1.22	1.83
Other EEAs*	0.79	0.18	0.67	0.68
Other Europe	1.55	1.01	0.72	0.88
Africa	0.46	0.16	0.38	0.26
Canada	0.02	0.01	0.03	0.02
United States	0.10	0.04	0.18	0.11
Other America	0.08	0.02	0.12	0.21
Asia	1.22	0.34	0.99	1.20
Oceania	0.03	0.01	0.02	0.05
Unknown	0.08	0.03	0.01	0.06
Total foreign	4.93	1.99	4.34	5.30

* European Economic Area (EEA): EU 15 + Norway, Iceland, and Liechtenstein.
Source: Nordic Statistical Yearbook (2003), 86–7.

the asylum seekers who fled the communist regimes in eastern Europe, before 1989 most refugees came from non-European countries.[21] To Sweden: Uganda-Asians, Chileans, Assyrians/Syrians, Palestinians, Kurds, Iranians, Vietnamese, Ethiopians, Eritreans, and Somalis. Denmark primarily received Chileans, Tamils from Sri Lanka, Iranians, Iraqis, and Somalis; to Norway came the same groups and many Vietnamese.[22] Since the fall of the iron curtain and the dissolution of the Soviet Union and Yugoslavia in the wake of 1989, Bulgarian Turks, Romanians, Bosnians, Macedonians, Kosovo-Albanians, and Croats have entered Sweden, whereas Bosnians and Kosovo-Albanians dominated in Norway.[23] In addition there have been new asylum seekers from the Middle East. In 2003 the majority of foreigners in northern Europe were from European countries (see Table 1). Around the turn of the millennium the percentage of foreign born in Sweden was around 11% of the total population.

From the 1970s onward Nordic states have followed an active integration policy, leaving room for the ethnocultural background of the immigrants. One example is the introduction of the municipal voting right, in Sweden in 1976, in Norway 1983, and in Denmark in 1991. In practice, however, assimilation is promoted: refugees are geographically dispersed to avoid ghettoes, foreigners are expected to change, and integration is not considered a two-way process. Furthermore, the policy aims at promoting equality between immigrants and native citizens but in order to secure welfare

---

[20] Turkish labor migrants in western, central, and northern Europe since the mid-1950s.

[21] Hungarian refugees in Europe since 1956; Czechoslovakian refugees in western, central, and northern Europe since 1968.

[22] Chilean refugees in Europe since 1973: the example of Switzerland; Vietnamese refugees in western, central, and northern Europe since the 1970s: the examples of France, Great Britain, and Germany; Iranian refugees in northern, western, and central Europe since 1980: the example of the Netherlands; Sri-Lankan Tamils in western and central Europe since the 1980s: the example of Switzerland; Kurdish refugees in western and central Europe since the late 20th century: the example of Germany.

[23] Refugees from former Yugoslavia in Europe since 1991.

for all, the numbers of refugees and asylum seekers are restricted.

Since the 1980s the general climate has changed from a rather liberal attitude to an emphasis on restriction. Denmark introduced one of the most liberal alien laws of Europe in 1983 and shifted toward control in 1986; lately, Danish insistence on control signals a general skepticism to foreigners. Norway has to some extent followed suit. In both countries strong right wing parties emerged. In the Danish elections of 2005 the Dansk Folkeparti (Danish People's Party) won 13% of the votes. In the same year the Norwegian Fremskrittpartiet (Progress Party) – established in 1973 by Anders Lange, who actively supported the South African Apartheid regime – won 22% of the votes.

A cluster of phenomena has been evoked to explain this change: rising numbers of immigrants from "foreign" cultures, for example, the different attitudes of Muslims toward the role of women and homosexuals. Furthermore, the policy to disperse immigrants led to the settlement of asylum seekers in regions with ample housing, but without sufficient jobs. Moreover, rising unemployment in general put the indigenous population in a position in which they had to compete with already established immigrants in the labor market. Finally, the fear of Muslims, who are seen as potential terrorists and extremists, has favored the anti-immigrant message of the populist parties. Sweden differs to some extent from its neighbors. Albeit violent right wing groups have been active, populist parties have remained weak and did not wreck the existing party system. Some have even pointed to Sweden as an example of a multicultural model.

Notwithstanding populist opposition, it is to be expected that immigration will rise in all Nordic countries. This increase is caused by the growing demand for labor of Nordic and European labor markets, ongoing family reunification, and international agreements to admit refugees from war-stricken areas. The current immigrant populations in northern Europe find themselves in a long-term process of social and economic integration. A longer period of residence leads unequivocally to greater participation in the education system and the labor market. At the same time, other newcomers keep coming. A reasonable suggestion is that cohabitation between the majority and the minorities will be decided by factors that in a sense are external to this relationship, such as the level of employment or the engagement of states in global conflicts.

REFERENCES

Blüdnikow, Bent, ed. *Fremmede I Danmark: 400 års fremmedpolitikk*. Odense, 1987.

Engman, Max. *Norden och flyttningerna under den nye tiden*. Copenhagen, 1997.

Finland, Folk. Nation. Stat. Historisk Tidskrift för Finland 3 (1987).

Kjeldstadli, Knut, ed. *Norsk innvandringshistorie*, 3 vols. Oslo, 2003.

Lottum, Jelle van. *Across the North Sea: The Impact of the Dutch Republic on International Labour Migration, c. 1550–1850*. Amsterdam, 2007.

Meyer, Frank. *"Dansken, svensken og nordmannen…": Skandinaviske habitusforskjeller sett i lys av kulturmøtet med tyske flyktninger: En komparativ studie*. Oslo, 2001.

Nyström, Keneth, ed. *Encounter with Strangers – the Nordic Experience*. Lund, 1994.

Olsson, Lars. *On the Threshold of the People's Home of Sweden: A Labour Perspective of Baltic Refugees and Relieved Polish Concentration Camp Prisoners in Sweden at the End of World War II*. New York, 1997.

Østergaard, Bent. *Invandrernes historie i Danmark*. Copenhagen, 1983.

Runblom, Harald. *Majoritet och minoritet i Östersjö-området: Ett historiskt perspektiv*. Stockholm, 1995.

Runblom, Harald, and Hans Norman, eds. *From Sweden to America: A History of the Migration*. Minneapolis and Uppsala, 1977.

Sane, Henrik Zip. *Billige og villige? Fremmedarbejdere i fædrelandet ca. 1800–1970*. Farum, 2000.

Sogner, Solvi. "Norwegian-Dutch Migrant Relations in the 17th Century." In *Dutch Light in the "Norwegian Night": Maritime Relations and Migration across the North Sea in Early Modern Times*, edited by Louis Sicking and Harry de Bles, 43–56. Hilversum, 2004.

Sørensen, Øystein, and Bo Stråth, eds. *The Cultural Construction of Norden*. Oslo, 1997.

Svalestuen, Andres A., Sune Åkerman, Reino Kero, Kristian Hvidt, and Bjarni Vilhjálmsson. *Migrationen fra Norden indtil 1: Verdenskrig. Rapporter til Det nordiske historikermøde i København 1971*. Copenhagen, 1971.

Svanberg, Ingvar, and Mattias Tydén. *Invandring: En svensk kulturhistoria*. Stockholm, 1992.

Tägil, Sven, ed. *Ethnicity and Nation Building in the Nordic World*. London, 1994.

WESTERN EUROPE

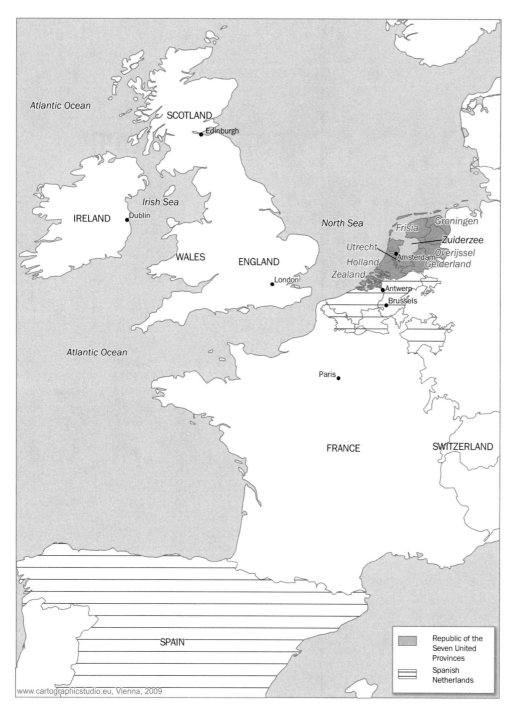

Atlantic Ocean

SCOTLAND
• Edinburgh

Irish Sea

IRELAND • Dublin

North Sea

Frisia Groningen

Utrecht Zuiderzee
Overijssel
Holland Gelderland
Zealand • Amsterdam

WALES ENGLAND

• London

Antwerp •
Brussels •

Atlantic Ocean

Paris •

FRANCE SWITZERLAND

SPAIN

Republic of the
Seven United
Provinces

Spanish
Netherlands

www.cartographicstudio.eu, Vienna, 2009

Western Europe 1648

Western Europe 2000

GREAT BRITAIN

Kenneth Lunn

Great Britain and its borders

The constitutional construction of the territory of Great Britain dates from 1707, with the consolidation of the kingdoms of England, Wales, and Scotland, although prior to this, there had been a single Scottish and English monarch from the beginning of the 17th century. Ireland was effectively a British colony, until in 1801 the Act of Union created the state known as the United Kingdom of Great Britain and Ireland. The division of Ireland in 1921 saw the emergence of the Irish Free State (later Eire), which left the United Kingdom of Great Britain and Northern Ireland. The devolution process in Great Britain implemented by the end of the 20th century has seen the creation of a Scottish Parliament and a Welsh Assembly, with some shifting of political authority from London.

Within the chronological and geographic framework of this overview, therefore, notions of "Britishness," particularly with regard to the Irish, are somewhat complex. Coupled with the existence of separate English, Welsh, and Scottish identities, with sets of cultural and social values, as well as the fluctuating importance of Welsh and Gaelic (Scots) languages, this can make for a complex framework of British history. Although the main emphasis in this encyclopedia is on immigration and migration beyond the boundaries of a state, some attention needs to be paid in particular to the movement of the Irish into mainland Britain, since this has had a dramatic impact upon British society and culture.

In addition, while recognizing the very long history of migration and settlement into Britain, and giving attention to earlier phases of this phenomenon, greater attention will be devoted to the processes of the 19th and 20th centuries, when numbers and impact become obviously more important. It is also the case that individuals have moved into and out of Britain over the centuries in a somewhat piecemeal fashion. Relative ease of access across the English Channel has seen much sporadic and temporary movement. While some reference will be made to these shifts, the essential focus will be on sustained migration of numbers significant enough for their experiences to be recorded and evaluated in terms of settlement and engagement with a receiving society. It is also worth pointing out the difficulties of assembling accurate statistical evidence for both migration and immigration. For the early period, accurate figures are virtually nonexistent and, even for the 20th century, are often estimates.

A key factor in much of the immigration into the British Isles was the development of imperialist and colonialist policies by the British state. It was also this phenomenon that encouraged large-scale migration from Britain to many territories elsewhere, such as the USA, Canada, Australia, New Zealand, and southern Africa in particular. Together with the patterns of world trade developed as part of these processes, this largely explains population movement and long-term settlement with regard to Britain. Since the end of World War II, decolonization and the breakup of the empire have added to these factors and have helped to shape the current population composition of Britain.

Early population movements in Britain during the 16th and 17th centuries

During the early modern period, there are many examples of migration from the Continent to Britain. In the 14th century, there was a significant flow of merchants from Lombardy into Britain. Individuals came and went according to the opportunities and, since the 17th century, the needs of trade, but there was always a presence during these early years. Merchants from the Hansa states, mostly German, also operated in a similar fashion, as did other economic migrants who had established clear patterns of movement by the 16th century. Records show the settlement of Flemish weavers in the southeast of England; Breton and Dutch miners in Cornwall, working the tin and copper resources; and French and Germans in the lead and iron mines of northern England.[1] There was also migration from the Netherlands from early in the century, where skills such as those displayed by Cornelius Vermuyden in the 1620s contributed to the drainage and development of agricultural land especially in eastern England. Artists, too, sought the patronage that was sometimes more readily available in Britain: Hans Holbein, who died in London in 1543, was one example of this movement.

Not all of these migrants journeyed or settled for purely economic reasons. Catholic persecution and pursuit of

---

[1] Netherlandish (Flemish) textile workers in 16th- and 17th-century England.

Protestants in Continental Europe meant the sporadic arrival of refugees from Germany, Switzerland, the Netherlands, and Spain.[2] The most significant contribution from the perspective of British immigration history came about as a consequence of the religious wars in France. From 1559, numbers of Protestant refugees (Huguenots) took up residence in Britain. The St. Bartholomew's Day massacre in Paris in August 1572 saw an upsurge in this migration, leading to the formation of Huguenot communities in London and the eastern counties of England.[3] In the capital, they settled in Spitalfields and developed the silk trade in particular but also contributed to several dimensions of new commercial ventures. In all, it has been estimated that Huguenot migration totaled around 50,000 arrivals in Britain. Their intellectual and cultural involvements have also made a significant impact on British life.

There is some evidence of hostility to these newcomers and challenges to their economic positions. The Hanseatic merchants gained significant political and financial privileges, which in turn sparked reactions from English merchants. In 1517, London apprentices attacked French and Flemish artisans, apparently because there were marriages between some incomers and local women. As part of a general xenophobia toward "foreigners" in the late 16th century, the Hanseatic merchants lost their special advantages. However, in the main, most of these minorities brought particular skills and met specific needs in the rapidly developing commercial sectors of British society and they were able to fit relatively easily into that culture.

The end of the 16th century also saw concern about the settlement of blacks in various British towns, including London.[4] There was considerable economic hardship at this time, with food shortages and moral panics about the movement of peoples with no obvious forms of support. It was in this context that, in 1601, a government proclamation ordering the expulsion of blacks from English towns was announced, although there is some doubt as to its efficacy. The origins of these black settlers – servants, slaves, entertainers, and seafarers – was varied but they became identified, at least in the eyes of Queen Elizabeth, as an "annoyance of her own liege people." There was also an Asian population in Britain from the early 16th century, as Indian servants, ayahs (nannies), and sailors settled in the country as links with the subcontinent through trade became more developed.

Another significant feature of the immigration into Britain in the 17th century was the formal return of Jews. Expelled from the country in 1290 by Edward I, the dictate was informally overturned in 1656 during the office of Oliver Cromwell. From the 16th century, individual Jews, Marranos from the Iberian Peninsula who had converted to Catholicism under duress during the Inquisition but maintained many of their original beliefs and practices, migrated to Britain.[5] The seizure of power by Cromwell had seen a revival of interest in the spirituality of Judaism and led to the arrangement that once more tolerated their presence in the country. At first, the arrival of Jews was barely detectable. By 1695, a figure of some 800 has been estimated. Most of these new immigrant Jews were Sephardim from Spain and Portugal, but others came from different European cities, such as Venice or Amsterdam, or from European colonies in the Caribbean, where there had been relative religious freedom. Others came from European states where forcible conversion to Christianity had been the only way to survive.

In the 17th century Britain was not merely a country that drew others to its shores. There were also many examples of Britons emigrating voluntarily and as a consequence of extreme "push" factors. Only a minority had economic motives, like Scottish traders, British merchants, and theater groups, who visited Continental Europe from time to time.[6] Many emigrants went to Ireland in the 17th century. After the victory in the Nine Years' War (1594–1603) the English crown sought to secure the northeast of Ireland by encouraging migration from England, Wales, and Scotland ("Ulster plantation").

The politically motivated settlement of over 300,000 migrants in Ireland added considerably to the country's population (1 million in 1600, 2 million in 1700), and the agricultural and commercial infrastructures saw considerable development.[7] Others found opportunities in continental Europe that were not available elsewhere. In particular, significant numbers of Scots offered themselves as mercenary soldiers in some of the European conflicts of the 16th and 17th centuries.[8] Small groups of Britons found religious and political refuge outside the country's shores: at various times, Royalists and Jacobins, Puritans, and Protestants sought greater freedoms within Continental Europe.[9]

However, during this early modern period, the most significant population movements out of the country were those that contributed to the growth of colonies in the Caribbean and in northern America. The settlement of Virginia began in 1607 and, with the intensification of tobacco cultivation in the 1620s, symbolized the beginning of the era of British colonial growth. Mainland North America and the West Indies were the destination for many hundreds of thousands of British people throughout the century. Exact figures are not available, but in the last four decades of the century, between 100,000 and 150,000 English people may have emigrated to the region, despite the limited demographic

---

[2] Waldensians in central Europe since the Early Modern Period; Dutch Calvinist refugees in Europe since the early modern period; Palatines in Europe since the 17th century.

[3] Huguenots in Europe since the 16th century.

[4] African slaves in Britain in the early modern period.

[5] Sephardim in Europe in the early modern period.

[6] Scottish traders and merchants in east-central Europe in the early modern period; British merchants in Portugal since 1640; English comedians in Europe in the early modern period: the example of the Netherlands.

[7] English and Scottish settlers in Ireland since the early modern period.

[8] Scottish soldiers in Europe in the early modern period.

[9] English Puritan refugees in the Netherlands in the 16th and 17th centuries; British Royalists in western, central, and southern Europe, 1640–60; Jacobites in Europe, 1688–1788.

growth in England during those years. Another estimate puts the number of Britons who moved to these colonies at near 400,000. The majority of those settlers were indentured laborers, young males who provided the labor that was later to be replaced by black slavery. They represented an aspect of labor mobility within Britain itself and colonial migration may well be viewed as an extension of that process. In addition, until 1776, there was a significant element of convict transportation. While the development of the colonies did allow greater opportunities for former servants to establish their own landholdings at the end of their indentured period, it also needs to be recognized that others sought to return to Britain and that there was a genuine movement both ways across the Atlantic in this period. In the 17th century, overall Britain experienced net emigration – pointing the way to later overseas development.

Empire building and migration effects in the 18th century

The large-scale introduction of black slavery into many of the Atlantic colonies significantly diminished the flow of British migrants. Nevertheless, these territories continued to attract those who saw opportunities for settlement in the New World. In particular, the second half of the century saw significant Scottish migration, mainly from the highlands. The nature of this movement was somewhat at odds with the bulk of 18th-century migration. The Scottish clan system helped to provide much closer kinship patterns of attraction and settlement and, especially in the 1770s, family group migration contrasted with the largely young single settlement from elsewhere in Britain.

Colonial and imperial linkages continued to contribute to the makeup of the population in Britain. As the 18th century progressed, imperial connections saw a significant increase in an Indian presence in Britain. One detailed study suggests a complex mix of settlers by this time, not simply servants and ayahs but also sailors (lascars) who were frequently left without return ships upon their arrival in Britain. The majority of these seafarers gathered in London and, in the 1780s, increasing attention was being given to the plight of these "black poor." In 1786, volunteer subscriptions were collected to provide support for distressed lascars and its remit was widened to become the Committee for the Relief of the Black Poor, including black seafarers as well as former African slaves now freed in Britain. By April 1786, the government had stepped in to provide relief for around 400 black and Asian needy and then supported the scheme to settle them in Sierra Leone. The plan was eventually implemented early in 1787, with 441 emigrants sailing to settle in Africa rather than face a life of continuing deprivation in Britain. This episode demonstrates the ways in which the presence of black and Asian people, brought to the country as a consequence of Britain's imperial adventures and unable to survive without support, became defined as a "problem." The moral and political debates about the issue shifted the focus of discussions about "solutions" from simple

philanthropic and voluntary gestures toward the need for state involvement.[10]

The 18th century also saw a continuing rise in the number of Jewish migrants to Britain, and by the middle of the century, the Jewish population was estimated to be 7,000 to 8,000. The majority of these newcomers, mainly still of Iberian origin, were now from the more impoverished communities in the Mediterranean region. However, what was more pronounced was a significant rise in the settlement of Ashkenazi Jews, from central Europe.[11] Estimates suggest some 6,000 in the first half of the century and 8,000 to 10,000 between 1750 and 1815. Faced by the restrictions placed upon Jews in many societies, they thus sought greater freedom and opportunity in Britain. In particular, small-scale trading was the pathway followed by those who remained in the country. However, in contrast to many of their Sephardic coreligionists, the Ashkenazim generally held to a more isolationist culture and thus limited the extent to which they were involved in any process of absorption and assimilation.

During this period, non-Jewish European immigrants also settled within Britain. By the end of the 18th century, it was possible to identify, in a meaningful way, a German community in London.[12] A number of merchants, manufacturers, and scientists were attracted to Britain by the perception of economic and intellectual opportunities. Britain's geographical position, as a stopping-off point in the Atlantic crossing, also ensured a random element of attraction, as some remained in what was initially meant as a transit break. While the majority remained in and around London, there are examples of settlement in other industrial and commercial centers in England and in Ireland. Other identifiable European groups included Greeks and Russians, as well as French – an exodus that was boosted by the French Revolution in 1789.[13]

The 19th century: the beginning of "mass migration"

From the end of the Napoleonic wars (1799–1815), Britain entered into a new phase of migration and immigration history. The upheavals of industrialization and urbanization created new "push" factors within Britain but also provided the attraction of new opportunities for those outside British shores. The story of the long 19th century reflects both these outgoings and incomings. The opening-up of Australia and New Zealand added to the older colonial outposts of northern America and the Caribbean, as did the later development of territories in southern Africa. New migrants into Britain also came from additional locations, particularly those of eastern Europe.

[10] African slaves in Britain in the early modern period.
[11] Ashkenazim in Europe since the early modern period.
[12] German industrial traders and spies in Great Britain in the 18th and 19th centuries.
[13] French Revolutionary refugees in Europe after 1789: the example of Germany.

One of the most significant migration stories of the 19th century in the British context concerns the exodus from Ireland. Essentially a phenomenon that impacted populations across the globe, it has been estimated that some 5 million Irish people left Ireland's shores in the first 70 years of the century. Between 1841 and 1901, the population of Ireland was halved – from over 8 million to around 4 million. While the United States took the largest share of these migrants, and other parts of the "old" empire such as Canada, Australia, and New Zealand provided settlement for many others, mainland Britain was also a significant locus for many Irish.[14]

Traditional explanations of this massive movement of Irish people to Britain have rested very heavily on notions of "push" and "pull" factors. Pressures in Ireland on the distribution of resources – land and food – were accentuated by particular crises such as the Famine of 1845–50. These prompted a continued, if somewhat uneven, exodus throughout the period. The pull factors were the relative ease of transport to Britain and the perceived economic opportunities offered by an industrializing country. The variety of occupations and trades was considerable. Work was often poorly paid but, nevertheless, the economic opportunities were often seen as preferable to the situation in Ireland.

Responses to this migration were also very complex. Reaction toward many of those migrants was often hostile, especially by those who perceived Irish workers as a threat against their own employment. There was also hostility from communities and from outside commentators who saw poor Irish migrants as lowering standards of living and respectable patterns of behavior. This was particularly the case in the new industrial settlements of England, Scotland, and Wales, where population increase generally was not matched by social improvements and the Irish were often scapegoats for these ills.

During the 19th century there was an influx of groups and individuals from Continental Europe. It is difficult to identify precise numbers and explanations for such movements without massive detail. A case study can illustrate the complex and often random nature of this process. Following the unsuccessful Warsaw rising of 1830–1 by Poles seeking to liberate themselves from Russian domination, there was an exodus to Prussia. One group of exiles was faced with the choice of being returned to Russian control or seeking a new life in the USA. Comprising 211 soldiers and one woman, they embarked on the *Marianne*. Bad weather forced them to shelter in Portsmouth, on England's south coast, and the Poles decided that they wished to remain there. Over the years, the Poles found permanent employment, learned English, changed their names to more Anglicized versions, and many married local women. In this way, they became part of a local community, and their presence is now marked only by a memorial in one of the city's cemeteries, where 80 of the original refugees were buried. This example represents the often complex combination of international, national, and local circumstances that determined the migration and settlement of European groups in Britain in these years.

Other European groups retained many more dimensions of their ethnic and cultural identities. The most-discussed dimension of Continental European migration to Britain at this time was the movement of Jews, largely from eastern Europe. Although there was a steady expansion of an established Jewish community in Britain throughout the 19th century, much of this population came from central and western Europe, Germany in the main. By the last quarter of the century, those who began to arrive in greater numbers in Britain were coreligionists from further east. The economic and political pressures in eastern Europe were such that Jewish citizens were compelled to look for new homelands. Britain was a relatively minor destination but had the advantages of an apparently stable Jewish community already in existence.[15] Many of those who settled in Britain during these years before World War I saw the United States as their final destination but ran out of funds or found opportunities for work and settlement in Great Britain.

Significant groupings of Jews became established in major towns in Britain during this period. London attracted considerable numbers but Leeds, Manchester, Liverpool, Glasgow, Hull, and Sheffield also had sizable communities. These new Jewish immigrants often found themselves on the receiving end of rising expressions of xenophobia and anti-Semitism. This found expression in forms of social and cultural hostility to the newly established communities, in trade union opposition to the alleged threat posed by these immigrants, and in a growing politicization of xenophobic and racist attitudes. The outcome was the Aliens Act of 1905, a hugely symbolic piece of legislation. Contemporary commentators and subsequent historians of immigration have noted its introduction of controls, which imposed limitations on the influx of poor migrants and were clearly aimed at the particular migration patterns of European Jews. It was this legislation that broke away from what has been seen as the relatively liberal 19th-century practice of free entry for immigrants into Britain and which established a framework that was to be redefined and focused during the 20th century. It should, however, be noted that reactions to these Jewish immigrants and the rise of a more articulated and insistent anti-Semitism was not a total experience. At work, Jewish employees could demonstrate their trade union credentials and political beliefs – numbers brought with them a strong left-wing perspective from eastern Europe and made considerable contributions to the emergence of socialist ideas within Britain.

One other group of eastern European immigrants who came to Britain in the late 19th century were those who were frequently described in the popular press as "Poles" but who, in fact, came from Lithuania. The reasons for moving were similar to those that prompted much of the Jewish migration

[14] Irish industrial workers in England, Scotland, and Wales since the 19th century.

[15] Eastern European Jews in London since the late 19th century.

of these years. However, this group of Lithuanians was of a different religion – Catholic – and was also seeking to move away from the Russification of their homeland, which involved the imposition of the Russian language and culture. There is some suggestion of a very quickly established chain migration process, with recruitment to work in the salt industry in Cheshire, England, and in the heavy industries in industrial Scotland, particularly in Ayrshire and Lanarkshire. Initial hostility, most obvious in Scotland, was aimed at their terms of employment, playing on the natives' fears about jobs and wages.

In time, there was a gradual acceptance of these workers, as they became members of the trade unions and the worries about their undermining conditions of employment were put into context. The support they gave to the national coal strike in 1912 provided much credence to their value within these working communities. There was ample evidence of a strong socialist element among the Lithuanians and the creation of a religious and social culture, including the establishment of a Lithuanian newspaper and various institutions. Their presence was eased by the existence of a strong Catholic tradition in the west of Scotland through Irish migration and settlement and, thus, despite the language and cultural differences, initial hostility was gradually overcome.

One significant contributor to both the short-term and long-term patterns of migration into Britain before the start of the 20th century was the merchant shipping industry. As already demonstrated, African and lascar seafarers had been employed by British shipping companies for some considerable time. Many would find themselves temporarily or permanently settled around the major ports, particularly London. Former seafarers would establish lodging houses and cafes to support these groups. In the 19th century, the diversity of employment patterns within the industry increased with the expansion of trade and the size of the fleet. During the second half of the century, there were numbers of Arabs and Somali seafarers, together with lascars, Chinese, West Indian, and West African crews.[16] Virtually all of the major shipping companies throughout the world sought to employ such workers to a greater or lesser extent and there was a complex pattern of employment history which, by the start of the 20th century, had begun to create immigrant communities in a number of British seaport towns. The range of different national and ethnic groups present in Britain by the early years of the 20th century is indicated in Table 1.

As with other earlier periods, British people also left their shores in considerable numbers. Indeed, throughout the 19th century, there was a net emigration count of some considerable size, over 1 million for most decades. The main period of migration to the USA and Canada were the decades between 1800 and 1860, when two-thirds of the immigrants in the United States came from Great Britain. Canada also attracted large numbers of British immigrants, drawn principally by the attractions of rural settlement and by the gold rushes.

Table 1. Main countries of origin of foreigners in England and Wales, 1871–1931				
	1871 (%)	1891 (%)	1911 (%)	1931 (%)
Europe	89	85	93	78
France	18	10	10	9
Germany	33	26	19	9
Italy	5	5	7	7
Poland	7	11	34	11
Russia*	2	12		12
Other European countries	24	21	23	27
USA	8	10	5	12
Asia	0	1	1	4
Other countries	3	5	2	6
Total foreigners (thousands)	100,600	198,100	284,800	307,600
% of total population	0.44	0.68	0.79	0.77

* In 1911: Russia (including Russian Poland).
Source: Censuses.

Australia began settlement in 1788 – convicts but also free labor – and throughout the 19th century, British immigration was a fundamental source of Australia's growing population. Scottish migrants began to be drawn more to Australia than the USA or Canada in the second half of the century, with the discovery of gold in 1851 and incentives for assisted passages encouraging this trend. The opening up of New Zealand by the middle decades of the century also attracted British migrants, as did southern African locations.

Many elements contributed to this massive population exodus from Britain. Some individuals perceived opportunities to practice their trades elsewhere. Coal and metal miners were in demand around the globe. Other skilled industrial workers found employment in Continental Europe, as other growing economies developed.[17] Economic pressures from the processes of industrialization, with people pushed off the land and the restructuring of skilled and unskilled work, undoubtedly drove many to look elsewhere. In the case of the Irish, and, to a lesser degree, Scottish migrants, disastrous crop failures in the 1840s meant there was little alternative to emigration. The attractions of the colonial territories and the apparent freedoms acted as powerful "pull" factors. Aided passages, funded first by Britain and then by colonial governments, speeded up and cheapened the processes while self-help groups and emigration societies worked to make passages available. The land clearances in Scotland, for instance, saw the establishment of the Highlands and Islands Emigration Society in 1852, which is estimated to have aided the move of some 5,000 to Australia in the space of a few years. The massive movement of British peoples remains a

---

[16] Kru seamen in Liverpool since the mid-19th century.

[17] English industrial workers (puddlers) in the Belgian iron industry in the early 19th century; British technical experts in France in the first half of the 19th century.

hugely significant population shift and contributed overwhelmingly to the establishment of new nations during this period.

Labor migrants and refugees in the 20th century

As in earlier times, economic changes in both Britain and those areas that contributed the bulk of immigrants were significant elements in population shifts. Other factors, such as major political upheavals, the impact of war, and the dismantling of empires, must also be taken into account. Alongside this rich and complex history of immigration must be set the story of migration from Britain during these years. While the older patterns of settlement in the United States became limited by that country's growing restrictions on such movement, the older imperial territories continued to attract British settlers. Indeed, for most of the century, there continued to be net emigration from the British Isles.

The early years saw the continuation of large-scale emigration. Between 1901 and 1910, nearly 2 million people left Great Britain and Ireland, half heading for the so-called Dominions of Australia, New Zealand, Canada, and South Africa. A similar number left in the period 1920–9, 65% for the Dominions. This movement slowed during the Depression years of 1930–9: fewer than 350,000 left and it was in this decade that immigration exceeded emigration for the first time in many years. In the post–World War II period, figures rose again and continued to be a significant aspect of population statistics until the last decades of the century.[18] Cooperation between the British government and governments of the receiving countries in implementing land settlement schemes and assisted passages facilitated this process. The 1922 Empire Settlement Act promoted these moves and it expired only in 1972, when the new territories themselves began to impose degrees of limitation on immigration. Table 2 indicates that only in the period 1931–51 did migration add to the mainland British population.

World War I and the subsequent population movements led to the intensification of legal restrictions. This period also witnessed an intensification of the debate about the integration of newcomers and the challenges to defined British culture. The basis for what may be seen as contemporary concerns and issues with regard to immigration became part of political discourse.

An example of the economic forces at work is the continuing expansion of the merchant navy and the ways in which this contributed to the growth of Britain's immigrant population. In the early decades of the 20th century, the increasing numbers employed in the merchant marine provoked both union opposition and clashes between the different elements in seaport communities. The so-called race riots of 1919 were, in fact, sparked by a complex web of economic grievances and also by cultural resentments of the different ethnic groups. During the interwar years, the union

Table 2. Net migration balance: England/Wales and Scotland, 1871/81–1981/91		
	England/Wales	**Scotland**
1871–1881	−164,000	−93,000
1881–1891	−601,000	−218,000
1891–1901	−69,000	−53,000
1901–1911	−501,000	−254,000
1911–1921	−620,000	−239.000
1921–1931	−170,000	−390,000
1931–1941	757,000	220,000
1951–1961	406,000	−282,000
1961–1971	−106,000	−327,000
1971–1981	−149,000	−151,000
1981–1991	385,000	−103,000

Source: Tranter, *British Population in the Twentieth Century.*

continued to pursue a campaign of hostility toward Chinese and Arab seafarers in particular. Moral crusades against race mixing and cultural difference were articulated in these decades and such attitudes continued into the postwar years. The state also sought to limit employment opportunities and contest citizenship status by introducing the 1925 Special Restrictions (Coloured Alien Seamen) Act, which sought to regulate more fiercely the work and presence in Britain of such "foreigners." In spite of all these hostile dimensions, however, there is ample evidence of community and work associations among the different ethnic groups.

The impact of World War I was not limited to recruitment in the merchant marine. Refugee groups, such as those from Belgium arrived on British shores,[19] as did considerable numbers of Empire citizens who contributed to the war effort. There was, however, a series of alarms about potential threats from population movement that led to the tightening of controls. In 1914, the Aliens Restriction Act empowered the government, for security reasons, to limit rights of entry into the country. At the end of the war, further legislation continued these limitations. The 1919 Aliens Restriction (Amendment) Act was superseded by the Aliens Order of the following year, by which immigration officials and other civil servants could limit entry, enforce registration, and deport "undesirables."

In the 1930s, there was an influx of mainly Jewish refugees from Germany and elsewhere in Continental Europe.[20] The rise of Nazism and of racial persecution prompted this exodus but it was not always viewed sympathetically in Britain. Professional groups, some trade unions, and government officials expressed fears about economic competition and of a perceived danger of increased anti-Semitism if more Jews were admitted to Britain. The government sought, therefore, to limit the number of refugees and voiced serious concerns

---

[18] British affluence migrants in the Costa del Sol in the late 20th century.

[19] Belgian refugees in western Europe during World War I.

[20] Jewish refugees from Nazi Germany and from German-occupied Europe since 1933; political and intellectual refugees from Nazi Germany and from German-occupied Europe, 1933–45.

about the potential disruption to society by their presence. As a result, although Britain did provide a haven for significant numbers of refugees – some 50,000 to 80,000 out of an estimated total of nearly 450,000 to 600,000 Jews who fled from the Greater Reich – this was a relatively small amount given the depths of persecution that the Holocaust was to display. It demonstrates the extent of hostility or perhaps simply the lack of concern within British society toward European Jews. Perhaps one exception to this was the acceptance of several thousand child refugees, those who came on the *Kindertransport*, and who did find a safe haven on British soil. Many of these refugees went on to make significant contributions to British cultural, political, and economic life.[21]

The war years, 1939 to 1945, saw the contribution of numerous imperial citizens, in both military and civilian capacities. Some remained after their war service; others returned home. A number of Britons returned from the conflict with "war brides" of different nationalities.[22] Other Europeans, fleeing from Nazi occupation, also found temporary location in Britain during those years,[23] and for some, like a large group of Poles, this became permanent residence in the postwar period.

The British government sought to restate its notions of empire citizenship in that period through the British Nationality Act of 1948, which confirmed the right of entry into Britain for all "subjects of the British crown," or citizens of the Commonwealth, as the old empire countries were now becoming known collectively. Indeed, it was this reaffirmation of the rights of entry into Britain of all "United Kingdom and Colonies" residents, which confirmed a common citizenship. It was not until the legislation of the 1960s and subsequent decades that this status became redefined and increasing limitations upon entry rights and citizenship were imposed.

One of the most daunting tasks facing British society at the end of World War II was the process of reconstruction and the social and economic changes championed by the newly elected Labor government in 1945. The establishment of a more effective social welfare program and the nationalization of several key industries were seen as fundamental to this process. In attempts to solve labor shortages in many sectors of the economy in the immediate postwar period, the British state looked outside its shores and also tried to redirect workers internally into those industries requiring labor.

One of the more traditional sources of labor, Ireland, was tapped to help in this process. In the period 1946–50, there was a net influx of between 100,000 and 150,000 Irish men and women. Specific recruitment schemes were introduced: the newly nationalized coal industry took over 2,000 Irish workers in 1946 alone. The following year, 29,000 men

and women were recruited for essential industries and services – agriculture, mining, and nursing being the main occupations.[24] However, as with previous periods of recruitment from Ireland, these schemes were not without their opponents. There was ample evidence of discrimination and prejudice within employment and some initial trade union resistance, expressing both the fear that British workers would be undermined and the possibilities of hostility within the workplace.

Other workers came from elsewhere in Europe. One group was those Poles who had come to Britain to fight on the Allied side during the war and who wished to remain in the country at the end of the hostilities. They became part of the Polish Resettlement Corps and were directed to fill specific labor shortages. Other Poles also arrived in England: those who had become refugees, been forced into slave labor or into the German army, and those who had escaped from camps and from the Soviet zones of occupation.[25] While some went back to the new Poland, a majority moved on to the USA and Canada, but some 140,000 settled in Britain.

The other major European group was made up of "displaced persons," mainly those from eastern Europe who found themselves unable to return home for a number of possible reasons. Many of them were housed in temporary camps and were recruited by Britain, among other European states, to fill temporary labor shortages. A number of schemes, attracting both men and women, operated under the general umbrella label of European Volunteer Workers (EVWs). Initially, these schemes, too, met with resistance. Trade unions, concerned with the possible threats to their members' pay and conditions, negotiated fiercely to ensure specific controls. Seventy percent of the men worked in agriculture and coal mining, at least for their initial contracts. Some went to work in the Cornish tin-mining industry, where the presence of Polish surnames even to this day records this involvement.

Ninety-five percent of the women were employed in textiles and domestic work. Most of the contracts, especially those involving members of the Polish Resettlement Corps who were seen as most likely to remain in Britain and to apply for British citizenship, stipulated that workers should be paid full union rates, be members of a union, and be employed only when all sides agreed there was an absence of suitable British labor. These agreements were negotiated nationally but there were often clashes on interpretation at a local level, which led to disputes and confrontation. Nevertheless, these were relatively minor occurrences and many of these foreign workers sought naturalization and went into very different forms of employment when circumstances allowed.

Other European groups were also recruited to participate in the rebuilding of Britain. Italian communities already existed in many parts of the country and there were regular patterns of migration to places such as the Welsh mining valleys and industrial Scotland. In the immediate postwar years,

[21] German and Austrian Jewish children transported to Great Britain since 1938–9.

[22] German war brides in western Europe since the end of World War II: the example of Great Britain.

[23] British war brides in Norway since the end of World War II.

[24] Irish nurses in England since World War II.

[25] Displaced persons (DPs) in Europe since the end of World War II.

economic conditions, particularly in the rural south of Italy, were often harsh. It was these circumstances, linked to the needs of British industries for labor, which saw the more regularized recruitment of Italian workers. In 1949, some 2,000 Italian women were brought to Britain to work in various industries and in domestic service in hospitals and private homes. The best-known example, however, of more systematic recruitment was the scheme established by the Marston Valley Brick Company of Bedfordshire. In 1951, the company was one of those granted permission by the Ministry of Labor to obtain workers from abroad on temporary contracts. The company set up a recruiting office in Naples and, from 1951 until the 1960s, engaged some 7,500 men for the industry. Other programs saw Italians being employed in the heavy metal industries and in coal mining through similar recruitment schemes in Italy. This form of controlled migration was operated in similar fashion to those schemes for EVWs and involved assisted passages, accommodation, and language and other classes to ease the difficulties of such a move. Fixed contracts and the agreement of trade unions to the conditions of employment generally meant that there was little overt hostility to the employment of these Italians in sectors of the economy where there were significant labor shortages.[26]

The other significant population movement into Britain in the immediate postwar period was from the Caribbean.[27] Although there was a wartime presence of both civilians and military personnel – men and women – most of them had returned home at the cessation of hostilities. Conditions were difficult in those initial years and the potential of other countries became an increasing attraction. The USA was the most powerful magnet but Britain was also a destination. The arrival in London of the *Empire Windrush* in June 1948 from Jamaica, with a passenger tally of 492, is symbolically taken as the start of large-scale migration into Britain. When the American government took steps in 1952 to limit immigration from the Caribbean, many who sought opportunities abroad turned to Britain. In contrast to the USA, entry rights for most West Indians had been protected by the 1948 British Nationality Act and so, by the early 1950s, a significant population movement was under way and around 1960 the numbers of West Indians in Britain had reached 200,000.

The arrival of the *Empire Windrush*, although receiving some publicity, was not perceived as a signal for the arrival of large numbers of West Indian immigrants. Initially, the right to settle in Britain was acknowledged and some provision was made for the new arrivals. Temporary accommodation was provided in London and the Ministry of Labor sought job opportunities for those who had no previously arranged work. There was concern about the concentration of these new settlers and a policy of dispersal throughout the

country was attempted. Essentially, what state officials feared was the rise of racism in response to these black immigrants. During the years of the Labor governments (1945–51), there were continual discussions with Caribbean authorities to try to limit migration and internal debates on the possibilities of introducing more restrictive legislation. Nevertheless, no formal steps were taken to change the status of those migrants; the expressed racial hostility in these years was relatively minor and many of the men and women who settled in Britain were able to find employment and were effective participants in the rebuilding of Britain.

Throughout the 1950s and 1960s, there were steady increases in the number of "New Commonwealth" immigrants – from the Indian subcontinent and the Caribbean – facilitated by the 1948 Nationality Act. There were also more direct moves to recruit workers for key areas that were understaffed. London Transport sought to recruit directly in 1956 from Barbados and in 1966 from Trinidad and Jamaica. The Ministry of Health advertised extensively in the Caribbean for hospital workers.

The decolonization of British India in 1947 and the partition in the republics of India and Pakistan added to the subcontinent's difficulties, and by the 1950s, economic pressure at home and the perceived benefits of opportunities in Britain saw the increase in migration from India, Pakistan, and Bangladesh, the last of which gained independence in 1971.[28] Workers, mostly young males at this stage, were drawn into skilled and unskilled work in the metal trades and many kinds of engineering and factory employment. By the 1960s, permanent settlement and the consolidation of family groups was a much more visible aspect of the Asian immigration process. Informal networks helped to provide information about employment possibilities and housing and cultural support. The initial intention was often to find employment and to remit money home, with no idea of permanent residence. Nevertheless, long-term immigration and settlement became a feature of this later postwar movement.

For many of those new arrivals from Southeast Asia and the Caribbean, London and some of the other major towns were key places of residence, but cities such as Bristol saw the growth of a significant black population, while other industrial areas in the Midlands received both Asian and black immigrants. The textile areas of Yorkshire and Lancashire were also boosted by this new element of the workforce and service industries across the country offered employment opportunities.[29]

While there can be little doubt that there was a need for these immigrants in the wider economic sense, by no means did they experience universal approval and acceptance. Both the state and the general population expressed concerns about the impact of these new arrivals. Fears about threats to white workers' jobs, concerns about pressure on housing

---

[26] Italian labor migrants in northern, central, and western Europe since the end of World War II.

[27] West Indians in Great Britain, France, and the Netherlands since the end of World War II.

[28] Indian, Pakistani, and Bangladeshi migrants in Great Britain since 1947; Pakistanis in Great Britain since the 1950s.

[29] African, Asian, and Latin American soccer players in western and southern Europe since the late 19th century.

Table 3. Main countries of origin of foreign born in Great Britain in 1971 and 2001				
	1971		**2001**	
	Numbers (000s)	**%**	**Numbers (000s)**	**%**
Europe	1,500	50.9	1,600	33.1
Ireland	*709*	*23.8*	*537*	*11.0*
Other Western Europe	*633*	*21.2*	*834*	*17.1*
Eastern Europe	*175*	*5.9*	*248*	*5.1*
North America, Oceania	253	8.5	397	8.1
South Asia	479	16.1	1,000	21.1
India	*322*	*10.8*	*467*	*9.6*
Pakistan	*140*	*4.7*	*321*	*6.6*
Bangladesh	*–*	*–*	*154*	*3.2*
Caribbean	237	7.9	255	5.2
Africa	210	7	834	17
Far East	109	3.7	398	8.1
Rest	178	6	359	7.3
Total foreign born	3,000	100.0	4,900	100.0
% of total population		5.8		8.3

Source: Rendall and Salt, "The Foreign-born Population," 133–4.

and social services, cultural clashes, and the strength of racist perspectives all contributed to tensions within British society.

Throughout the 1950s, there was ample evidence of discrimination against black and Asian immigrants in every area of life. The issues surrounding immigration also entered the political arena far more obviously than in earlier times. Members of Parliament for both the Conservative and Labor parties began to raise questions about the "problems" created by immigrants, as it was expressed, and to argue for the need to restrict immigration. The race riots of 1958 between white and black people, in Nottingham, in the Midlands, and in Notting Hill, in London, received considerable publicity and fueled the arguments for controls and restrictions. It was in this context that the Commonwealth Immigration Act was introduced in 1962, which, for the first time, specifically limited the rights of entry of black and Asian Commonwealth citizens into the United Kingdom. In 1964 further restrictions on Commonwealth immigrants followed, and race relations legislation was introduced that sought to engage with certain aspects of discrimination. Despite this, there were continuing pressures from the political right for further restrictions, and events such as the flight into Britain of Indians from Kenya in 1967 further heightened the tensions over race issues and led to the tightening of restrictions on rights of entry and settlement. The foundation of the National Front in 1967 from a number of anti-immigration and racist groups and Enoch Powell's famous "Rivers of Blood" speech in 1968 indicated the degree of support for such sentiments. In 1971, the Immigration Act ended the free right of entry

for all but those with parents or grandparents born in Britain.

During these years, other groups also contributed to the wider patterns of immigration and settlement, such as Maltese and Cypriot groups, and Moroccans and Turks.[30] In addition, the Chinese population of Britain increased, with Hong Kong, Malaysia, and Singapore being the main points of entry into Britain. The 1971 census suggested that almost 100,000 individuals of Chinese origin were present at that time and that there was a significant family presence rather than the previous pattern of single males. Again, there was evidence of dispersal away from London – Liverpool, Manchester, and Birmingham had sizable Chinese communities by the end of the 1960s. These smaller communities attracted both opposition and degrees of acceptance within wider British society. The diverse nature of the composition of British society by this time can be determined from the statistics in Table 3.

Considerable restrictions had been placed on many forms of immigration into Britain by the time that Margaret Thatcher and the Conservatives were elected in 1979. By that date, the opposition of elements of the political left and the encompassing of far-right ideas on immigration by the Conservatives had limited the appeal of the National Front. The economic and political changes ushered in by successive Conservative governments – the dismantling of traditional heavy industry and manufacturing, the privatization of many public services, changes in education and health care provision, and so on – exacerbated the inequalities in British society. It was hardly surprising that tensions were produced as a consequence of the long history of immigration and subsequent discrimination. In many inner-city areas with high proportions of ethnic minorities, disturbances in 1981 and 1985 prompted further debates about the consequences of immigration and the apparent lack of immigrants' integration into a wider "British" society. In addition to these concerns, which continue into the 21st century, there were now fears about new sources of so-called illegal immigrants, particularly from eastern Europe but also from Africa and Asia. The focus shifted away from Commonwealth citizens to those who were claimed to offer new forms of cultural, religious, and political threats to British society.[31]

The expansion of the European Union from 1 May 2004 has created considerable debate within Britain about the possible impact of migration from the new member states.

Various proposals for the registration and control of migrant workers have been debated in recent years and a "points" system for entry into the labor market will shortly

[30] Cypriots in Great Britain since 1945; Moroccan labor migrants in western, central, and northern Europe since the 1960s: the example of Great Britain; Turkish labor migrants in western, central, and northern Europe since the mid-1950s.

[31] Chinese migrants from Fujian Province in London at the end of the 20th century.

be introduced. The economic benefits of additional labor have been extolled, especially in sectors such as construction, catering, and hospitality, which have real shortages. Alongside the journalistic campaigns and some evidence of popular antagonisms toward asylum seekers and refugees, and the attempt by the British National Party to make political capital from issues of race and ethnicity, there has been a general sense of unease at the apparent challenges migration has provided to what have been identified as core British values.

The bombs that exploded in London in July 2005 have been seen by some as the British dimension of the Muslim challenge to Western culture and society. Concerns about these attacks, literal and metaphorical, on British values have come not simply from those on the political right but also from those who see themselves as operating within a broad liberal consensus. The concern is that those values and attitudes that acted as the essential social cement of a traditional British society have become eroded by concepts of plurality that fragment the population within the boundaries of the nation-state.

Other voices, however, have suggested that what migration has done is simply open up a discussion of what precisely constitutes British culture and whether such a homogeneous entity has ever existed. It has even been argued that the many different ethnic backgrounds of the majority white population have effectively demonstrated a commitment to what have been seen as the traditional strengths of a British culture. In education, while some young people of Caribbean origin have been defined as significant underachievers at school level, those of other ethnic groups have demonstrated strong commitment to educational achievement. In February 2004, the Department of Education and Skills announced that school students of Chinese origin were the best performing minority ethnic group at all subjects at all levels.

What this long history and current situation reflects, therefore, is the fluidity of what has been called postimperial Britain. The rich cultural mix of British society and the opening up of opportunities for some nonwhite individuals can be seen as a positive consequence of immigration into the country. On the other hand, the tensions and difficulties of such a history also complicate the changes taking place within that society and contribute to forms of hostility and fragmentation that could be said to characterize British society at the beginning of the 21st century.

REFERENCES

Bhachu, Parminder. *Twice Migrants: East African Sikh Settlers in Britain*. London, 1985.

Bridge, Carl, and Kent Fedorowich, eds. *The British World: Diaspora, Culture, and Identity*. London, 2003.

Colpi, Terri. *The Italian Factor: The Italian Community in Great Britain*. Edinburgh, 1991.

Constantine, Stephen, ed. *Emigrants and Empire: British Settlement in the Dominions between the Wars*. London, 1990.

Delaney, Enda. *Demography, State and Society: Irish Migration to Britain, 1921–1971*. Liverpool, 2000.

Endelman, Todd. *Radical Assimilation in English Jewish History, 1656–1945*. Bloomington, IN, 1990.

Endelman, Todd. *The Jews of Britain, 1656 to 2000*. Berkeley, 2002.

Frost, Diane. *Work and Community among West African Migrant Workers since the Nineteenth Century*. Liverpool, 1999.

Fryer, Peter. *Staying Power: The History of Black People in Britain*. London, 1984.

Gilroy, Paul. *There Ain't No Black in the Union Jack: The Cultural Politics of Race and Nation*. London, 1987.

Gray, Malcolm. *Scots on the Move: Scots Migrants 1750–1914*. Edinburgh, 1990.

Hammerton, E. James, and Alistair Thompson. *Ten Pound Poms: Australia's Invisible Immigrants*. Manchester, 2005.

Hansen, Randall, *Citizenship and Immigration in Post-War Britain*. Oxford, 2000.

Holmes, Colin. *John Bull's Island: Immigration and British Society, 1871–1971*. Basingstoke, 1988.

Kay, Diana, and Robert Miles. *European Volunteer Workers in Britain, 1946–1951*. London, 1992.

Kushner, Tony. *The Holocaust and the Liberal Imagination: A Social and Cultural History*. Oxford, 1994.

Lawless, Richard. *From Ta'izz to Tyneside: An Arab Community in the North-East of England during the Early Twentieth Century*. Exeter, 1995.

Layton-Henry, Zig. *The Politics of Immigration: Immigration, "Race" and Race Relations in Post-War Britain*. Oxford, 1992.

Lucassen, Leo. *The Immigrant Threat: The Integration of Old and New Migrants in Western Europe since 1850*. Urbana, IL, 2005.

Lunn, Kenneth, ed. *Race and Labour in Twentieth-Century Britain*. London, 1985.

Lunn, Kenneth. "'Race' and Immigration: Labour's Hidden History 1945–51." In *Labour's High Noon: The Government and the Economy 1945–51*, edited by Jim Fyrth, 227–42. London, 1993.

Lunn, Kenneth. "A Racialized Hierarchy of Labour? Race, Immigration and the British Labour Movement, 1880–1950." In *Racializing Class, Classifying Race: Labour and Difference in Britain, the USA and Africa*, edited by Peter Alexander and Rick Halpern, 104–21. Basingstoke, 2000.

MacRaild, Donald. *Irish Migrants in Modern Britain, 1750–1922*. Basingstoke, 1999.

Mason, David. *Race and Ethnicity in Modern Britain*. Oxford, 2000.

O'Leary, Paul, ed. *Irish Migrants in Modern Wales*. Liverpool, 2004.

Panayi, Panikos. *Immigration, Ethnicity and Racism in Britain, 1815–1945*. Manchester, 1994.

Panayi, Panikos. *German Immigrants in Britain during the Nineteenth Century, 1815–1914*. Oxford, 1995.

Paul, Kathleen. *Whitewashing Britain: Race and Citizenship in the Postwar Era*. Ithaca, NY, 1997.

Rendall, Michael, and John Salt. "The Foreign-born Population." *Focus on People and Migration* (2005): 133–4, http://

www.statistics.gov.uk/downloads/theme_compendia/fom2005/08_FOPM_ForeignBorn.pdf.

Solomos, John. *Race and Racism in Britain*. London, 2003.

Spencer, Ian R. G. *British Immigration Policy since 1939: The Making of Multi-Racial Britain*. London, 1997.

Sponza, Lucio. *Italian Immigrants in Nineteenth-Century Britain: Realities and Images*. Leicester, 1988.

Sword, Keith, Norman Davies, and Jan Ciechanowski. *The Formation of the Polish Community in Great Britain, 1939–1950*. London, 1989.

Tabili, Laura. *"We Ask for British Justice": Workers and Racial Difference in Late Imperial Britain*. Ithaca, NY, 1994.

Tranter, N. L. *British Population in the Twentieth Century*. Basingstoke, 1996.

Visram, Rozina. *Asians in Britain: 400 Years of History*. London, 2002.

Western, John. *A Passage to Britain: Barbadian Londoners Speak of Home*. London, 1992.

Whyte, Ian D. *Migration and Society in Britain 1550–1830*. Basingstoke, 2000.

Woodcock, Helen. *Rights of Passage: Emigration to Australia in the Nineteenth Century*. London, 1986.

IRELAND AND NORTHERN IRELAND

William J. Smyth

Located on the Atlantic fringes of western Europe, the island of Ireland for centuries has occupied a role of disproportionate significance in the history of European migration. At the beginning of the 21st century, the population of the island is about 5.5 million, yet it is frequently claimed that upward of 70 million people of Irish descent live elsewhere in the world, and there are reputed to be more churches named in honor of the Irish patron saint, St. Patrick, than for any other saint in Christendom. In 1901, 36% of all those born in Ireland were domiciled outside of their homeland. The equivalent figures for Scotland and England were 17% and 1%, respectively.

The country and its borders

During the Middle Ages, Ireland was the object of the Anglo-Norman conquerors, and from the time of the Norman invasion in 1167 through to the plantation of Ulster in 1609 the island gradually came into the possession of the English crown. In 1801 with the Act of Union Ireland was incorporated into the United Kingdom of Great-Britain and Ireland. In 1921, after many decades of political and even military strife, the British government granted 26 of the 32 counties in Ireland independence. In 1937 a new constitution established the Republic of Ireland. In 1973 Ireland joined the European Union. Until today, six counties in the northern province of Ulster remain part of the United Kingdom.

Long associated with prolonged and extensive out migration, Ireland has also been the recipient of distinctive and exceptionally large groups of migrants, and the present character of the country owes much to the contributions of these influxes. Throughout much of the 17th century, wars, rebellion, and forced dispossession of lands cleared the way for the plantation settlements of English and Scottish settlers who, by virtue of their Protestant religion and enduring links with their original homeland, radically transformed the politico-religious geography of the island. This British migration into Ireland was to be followed in the early 18th century by the emergence of net migration loss and by the 1760s the characteristics of mass emigration were discernible. With little respite, mass emigration from Ireland was to retain its potency over the next two and a half centuries with only a few interruptions. Not until the late 20th century did the number of emigrants become smaller than the number of immigrants. At present, the new immigrants, originating in central and eastern Europe, West Africa, Southeast Asia, and Latin America, are transforming a relatively homogeneous Irish population by their infusion of a very different and more complex mixture of race, religion, language, and color. In a strikingly obvious way, Ireland has now become a recipient demographic region in the new globalized economy and it has transcended its long-established image of an island of emigrants.

Irish emigrants were traditionally, but not exclusively, drawn from rural backgrounds. Until the 20th century, the Irish urban system was poorly developed. Rurality did, in itself, conceal significant variations in the motives of the emigrants. Arguably, many of the migrants of the first half of the 18th century were part of a self-regulating rural economy, wherein the emigration of some was designed to maintain a social and economic equilibrium among those remaining. This was in marked contrast to the increasing desperation evident among rural migrants in the 1840s, and especially during the years of the Famine, 1845–50. An increasingly dysfunctional rural Irish economy continued to export its sons and daughters in unprecedented numbers from that time until the mid-20th century. Migrants from urban areas became increasingly prevalent in the 20th century, and not all of them were lacking in education or skills.

The millions of Irish who emigrated over three centuries established themselves in economic and social niches that were a function of the time and place of settlement and reflected also the personal and economic environment out of which they moved. Diversity and adaptability were the chief characteristics of their new experiences. Over several generations and almost three centuries, there has been a remarkable persistence in the links between Ireland and specific destinations, much of it attributable to effective and resilient communications within the migration continuum. That explains why there was widespread knowledge in Ireland about the opportunities for migration, the migration process itself, and the various destinations. Ultimately, and in a circular logic, the best explanation of Irish migrant behavior is the existence of prior migration.

Demographic flux and the emergence of mass migration, 1600–1815

From the commencement of the 17th century Ireland was forcibly linked more closely with Britain and ultimately inserted into the wider world of British imperial expansion. That century began with the realization that the English settlements (plantations) created in Ireland in the previous century were largely in ruins and ongoing rebellion, assisted by Spanish military aid, and threatened to isolate England itself. Following the defeat of the Irish armies under the command of Aodh Mór Ó Néill, the second Earl of Tyrone during the Nine Years' War from 1594 to 1603, a new settlement scheme for Ulster (the Ulster Plantation) was designed to subdue the troublesome island. Lands were confiscated from the Irish chieftains, some of whom had sought refuge in Spain and Rome, and many of the Gaelic Irish who remained were pushed onto more marginal land.

Some 16,000 British migrants were settled in Ulster by 1622 – the majority of them Scots in contradistinction to earlier English-dominated plantations in Ireland. Since 1603, England and Scotland were united in a personal union and shared the same throne. The annual rate of inflow of the migrants, concentrated into a decade or so, was large by contemporary European standards.[1] The fragility of the Ulster Plantation was, however, demonstrated in the recurrence of warfare in the 1640s and again in the 1680s in the aftermath of which additional British settlers were allocated property in Ireland. Enforced settlement from Britain reduced the proportions of land owned by Catholics from 61% in 1641 to a mere 14% by 1704 and by the late 17th century, Protestants (largely, but not exclusively of immigrant stock) constituted almost 500,000 residents, or 25% of the total population of Ireland. Over the next several decades this Protestant population would be enlarged by small but distinctive European migrations of Huguenots and Palatines who settled primarily in urban centers.[2]

The immigrations of the 17th century were roughly balanced by an equivalent number of emigrants. Political and social dispossession of Catholics from 1600 generated an outflow to Continental Europe, the West Indies, and the eastern seaboard of the USA, and to those numbers there was later added a component of second-generation Protestant settlers seeking further adventure and opportunity in the New World to the west. Together these demographic movements created not only an environment in which population upheaval and migration were common but also engendered a tradition of linkages with other countries – linkages that would be vital for the 18th century.

Residual links with the European mainland influenced migration flows in the 18th century. A network of Irish colleges, stretching from Paris to Rome, provided university-level education for the sons of the better off – the majority of these students studied for the priesthood, and not all of them returned to Ireland. When Maynooth, Ireland's national seminary, was established in 1795, there were an estimated 400 Irish clerical students in the European colleges. These ecclesiastical connections were augmented by a tradition of military links with the armies of the European Catholic powers, for officer commissions, denied in the British Army on grounds of religion, met no such prohibition abroad. It has been estimated that more than 500 commissions were available to Irishmen in the armies of France, Spain, and Austria at any one time during the first half of the 18th century, and annual recruitment of officers may have been in the region of 100 per year – similar in scale to the ecclesiastical figure. To these figures there must be added the numbers of those serving abroad in the rank and file of the European armies and in the British army and navy. Estimates as high as 700 per annum have been suggested for this group.

Additionally, in the 18th century upward of 100 apprentices, clerks, and traders were attracted each year to Irish wineries and trading companies in coastal cities in France, Spain, and Portugal.[3] As with the military and ecclesiastical migrants, these Irish recruits were exclusively male and they did not give rise abroad to settlement groups of any significant size. However, all such groups did maintain, in their home regions, a conduit of information about foreign opportunities and thus qualified any description of isolated remoteness that might have been casually applied to contemporary Ireland.

The European focus of migrants naturally, and increasingly, included movement to Britain. From the 1730s onward there are increasing references to Irish beggars being accosted by parish officials in England, probably reflecting the emerging presence of Irish seasonal agricultural laborers. By the second half of the 18th century, annual migrations across the Irish Sea may have reached 400–500, but the numbers were slight compared with those who were to migrate in the following century. Overall, cumulative migration figures to Britain and Europe may have been on the order of 1,500 per year in the period 1700–75, and this from a total national population of about 2.2–2.6 million. As such, the scale of these migrations is comparable to the better-known movement to colonial America.

Transatlantic migrations during the early modern period

In both popular lore and professional histories, the distinctive role of Ulster-Scots from Ireland's most northerly province to colonial America is usually emphasized. It was no coincidence that Ulster, the part of Ireland colonized in the 17th century by Scottish and English settlers, should be the first region to prompt an out migration. By 1700, there remained little possibility of obtaining further land to colonize locally, and the population pressure naturally arising within the second and third generations of descendants of the colonizers was further extended by structural and regional changes within the maturing Ulster economy.

The first recorded migrations from Ulster to America in the 18th century occurred in 1717–18 when Presbyterian

---

[1] English and Scottish settlers in Ireland since the early modern period.
[2] Huguenots in Europe since the 16th century; Palatines in Europe since the 17th century.

[3] Irish brandy merchants in the Charentes in the 18th century.

clergymen organized a group migration of 3,000 individuals, but it was not until after 1720 that spontaneous large-scale migration began to emerge. It is generally agreed that in pre-revolutionary America, the Ulster-Scots were the largest single ethnic group in the nine colonies south of New England. The reliability of earlier figures has been called into question in recent years and there is now a tendency to revise downward the estimated number of migrants. It is now believed that about 108,000 Irish (two-thirds of them Ulster-Scots) migrated to colonial America between 1700 and 1785, but as such they still outnumbered arrivals from England and Scotland. Catholics may have constituted one-third of the migrants and, in exceptional years, southern regions rivaled the Ulster outflow. In 1753, for example, 4,000 departed from Dublin for America.

After 1780 there was a surge in the numbers of Irish migrants, with at least 100,000 leaving between then and 1815. In the years 1783–94, more than 5,500 Irish migrants arrived annually at Philadelphia, and many more arrived via other ports. As before, Ulster and southeast Ireland remained as the core source areas of the migrants, and the majority continued to be Presbyterian or Ulster-Scots, many of whom traveled in family groups. Once established in America, they displayed a strong tendency to locate in proximity to fellow Ulster people. Catholics, who predominated among the migrants from southeast Ireland and south Ulster, were much more likely to travel as single men, many of them earning their passage money by signing on as indentured servants for a fixed term. Lacking coreligionist spouses, this population appears to have disappeared into the cultural melting pot of the United States, although their distinctive family names have persisted.

Transoceanic migration was primarily focused on the USA, but it was not confined exclusively to it. Between the mid-17th and early 18th centuries, 40,000 Irish are estimated to have migrated to the West Indies – again, many of them traveled as indentured servants, although prisoners would have constituted a distinct minority. Catholic Irish overseers also were to be found in the French and Dutch, as well as British West Indian Islands, and as such they were the most widespread of all European settlers. Many of these Catholic Irish had arrived via France and were part of an earlier established Continental migration. Irish Protestants were located primarily on the British islands in the Caribbean.

Farther north, in the western Atlantic, another migration stream came into existence early in the 18th century. Seasonal migration to the Newfoundland fisheries commenced at the behest of English merchants, who called at Waterford and other ports of southeast Ireland to take on board provisions and men for the fishing fleets heading to the Grand Banks. The typical commitment was for two summers and a winter – with the fishermen over-wintering in Newfoundland, and returning home after a second summer of fishing. Upward of 5,000 young men traveled to the Newfoundland fisheries each year, but very few of them settled on the rocky island until the 1780s, when small communities began to develop.

Over the next 40 years, it is estimated that 25,000 to 30,000 may have decided to remain in the coves and fishing stations, where they have given rise to one of the most distinctive and regionally specific groups of Irish settlers anywhere in the Americas. From the closing decade of the 18th century, groups of Irish settlers in Newfoundland had migrated farther westward by sea and established niches of settlement in the Miramichi River valley of New Brunswick and also in the port city of Halifax, Nova Scotia.

The realization of mass migration, 1815–1920

In the 19th century the stream of migrants was to become a torrent. Oceanic migration rates of one per 1,000 had been common in the 18th century and those rates now rose to six per 1,000 in the 1840s, and were probably five times that during the Famine. Mass migration was now a reality, and by virtue of that process the relative balance of population size between Ireland and the remainder of the United Kingdom was fundamentally altered. In 1841 Ireland contained 33% of the total population of the United Kingdom; by 1911 that figure had dropped to 10%. Famine deaths and a relentless process of migration transformed the demographic landscape.

With the resumption of shipping after the end of the Napoleonic wars in 1815 and the expansion of trade in timber from the expansive forests of the Canadian colonies, a new momentum was generated. In an increasingly competitive environment the cost of passage dropped, and Liverpool, Glasgow, Belfast, and Derry enjoined in a lucrative trade in timber and people with Quebec, St. John, and a number of smaller New Brunswick out ports. To this new logistical development, and the pull of available land for agricultural settlement, was added an intensified push factor, emanating from an Irish countryside facing a developing rural crisis and rising population densities. Emigration was the inevitable solution: those with some capital and a familiarity with a regional tradition of migration were the first to move, but by midcentury virtually all regions and all social classes of Ireland were incorporated into the mass exodus.

Statistical information for the years 1815–25 is largely unreliable, but the general trend appears to show that the Canadian ports assumed precedence over the US ports, a pattern very evident by 1825 when more reliable data became available (see Table 1). In the 20-year period, 1825–45, approximately 1 million Irish arrived in North America, and about 60% of these landed in the Canadian colonies, having availed themselves of the cheapest transatlantic passage available. Of those who landed in New Brunswick, more than half may have gone immediately to the USA; among those who landed in Quebec, the attrition rate would have been much lower. Overall, North America was the destination, and specific locations within it were chosen on the basis of their economic possibilities or prior kinship links. An international border between Canada and the USA was not seen as a significant obstacle, although

Table 1. Overseas emigration from Ireland, 1825–1920					
Period	Total numbers (000s)	Destinations (%)			
		USA (%)	Canada (%)	Australasia (%)	Other (%)
1825–1830	129	39	61	N/A	N/A
1831–1840	438	39	60	1	N/A
1841–1850	1,299	70	28	2	0.3
1851–1860	1,216	81	10	8	0.6
1861–1870	818	84	5	10	0.6
1871–1880	542	83	5	11	1.0
1881–1890	734	85	6	8	1.0
1891–1900	461	93	2	2.5	2.5
1901–1910	485	86	8	3	3.0
1911–1920	229	75	14	7	4.0

N/A = not available.

Source: Akenson, *The Irish Diaspora*.

there is some evidence that the Protestant Irish from Ulster were more likely than their Catholic counterparts to remain in the Canadian colonies.

The scale of transoceanic migration from Ireland was unique in the experience of contemporary Europe, and no more so than during the period of the Famine, 1845–50. One million Irish died of starvation and disease at that time, and one and a quarter million fled to North America, with a further 300,000 settling in Britain. In 1847, the year of highest emigration, one quarter of a million persons departed for overseas destinations, the majority of them eventually choosing the USA in preference to Canada. As a result, Canada's Irish population is largely a pre-Famine creation, whereas that of the United States has much more immediate roots in the Famine and post-Famine experience.

In contradistinction to the Canadian experience, the post-Famine years witnessed significant growth in Irish migration to Australia and New Zealand. Australian migration had commenced with the transportation of convicts – 40,000 Irish prisoners had arrived in New South Wales before 1853. The discovery of gold, subsidized passage, and improved transportation combined to enhance the lure of the Antipodes. Between 1851 and 1920, one-third of a million Irish arrived in Australia and New Zealand, where they settled in almost equal numbers in rural areas and emerging urban centers. More than 80% of the Australian-Irish were Catholic, reflecting their regionally specific source areas in Munster and mid-Ulster. Protestants were more prominent in the New Zealand migration.

In an interesting offshoot to its Australian trade, Britain developed strong commercial links with Argentina, which provided supplies for ships sailing to the Antipodes. Out of those links emerged a fresh migration process. In the final third of the 19th century about 10,000 Irish migrated to Argentina. They were recruited mainly from two specific counties, Wexford and Westmeath.

No parish or region in Ireland was immune to the migration impulse by midcentury, and likewise all social classes were included. Chain migration and prepaid passages, especially to the USA, ensured participation of the poorest classes, who inevitably constituted the bulk of the migrants. However, even in the midst of the Famine, members of a wealthier and professional class continued to seek a new life in the colonies, and the numbers of teachers, religious leaders, surveyors, magistrates, and administrators reflected well the coexistence in Ireland of an emerging middle class and the most impoverished rural poor of western Europe. No social group was immune to the migration impulse although young unmarried adults, described as laborers or servants, constituted the bulk of the migrants. Neither was there any great distinction between the sexes; cohort analyses indicate that the gender balance of neither the residual population at home nor that of the new Irish communities abroad were seriously distorted by the mass migration.

Return migration was not a prominent feature. Returning migrants were very much the exception and in comparison with Italy, for example, the numbers were paltry. Indeed, in Irish life the "returned Yank" was traditionally seen as a figure of ridicule – an embodiment of personal failure abroad. Whatever their perception of exile, few Irish migrants found sufficient incentive or opportunity to resume life in Ireland. There were, however, always exceptions, and recent research has indicated that there may have been several thousand returned migrants to Ulster in the pre–World War I days, but the evidence remains somewhat inconclusive. For the majority who chose to migrate out of Ireland, the decision was irrevocable, and in many instances the migrants had more close relatives abroad than they had remaining in Ireland.[4]

---

[4] Irish return migrants from the USA in the 19th and early 20th centuries.

Mass migration to England, Scotland, and Wales during the 19th and early 20th centuries

The nature and scale of the transoceanic migration was further extended by mass migration to England, Scotland, and Wales.[5] In 1801 Ireland and Britain were politically united within the United Kingdom and, thereafter, little official attention was paid to collecting data for what was, in effect, now an internal migration. As a growing symbiotic relationship emerged between an increasingly overcrowded Irish rural economy and a rapidly growing British demand for labor, migration across the Irish Sea increased rapidly. In 1841, officials recorded the arrival of 57,000 seasonal Irish workers, 50,000 of whom were males, mostly between 16 and 32 years of age. Almost half came from a contiguous region in northwest Ireland. Most of these seasonal migrants stayed abroad for about six months, and during that period, they gained work in a multiplicity of niches. Their seasonal wages might well have stabilized the social structure at home, delaying, for a few decades, permanent mass migration, while simultaneously familiarizing their home regions with knowledge of the outside world. In the 1860s, Irish seasonal migration to Britain peaked at almost 100,000 per annum, and thereafter it declined rapidly, a decline that was accelerated by both the diminishing cohort from which the seasonal workers could be recruited, and also by the growing redundancy of manual labor in an increasingly mechanized farming economy.

The seasonal migrants were but a component of a much larger population of permanent Irish settlers in Britain. The 1841 census recorded 417,000 Irish born as permanent residents of Britain, but annual rates of arrivals are difficult to establish. In England and Wales, the percentage of Irish born peaked at 3% of the resident population in 1861, and from 1881 until 1921, it declined rapidly to less than 1% of the host population. Notwithstanding this dropoff in Irish migration, in the closing years of the 19th century, the Irish remained the largest immigrant minority in England and Wales, and especially so in Scotland.

The source areas of the Irish migrants to Britain are difficult to determine, but there is sufficient evidence to indicate that the Scottish migration was exceptionally specific in its regional origins. In the 1880s, more than 80% of the Irish in Glasgow and southwest Scotland had originated in Ulster, and in the years 1880–1910, Belfast and its adjoining county of Antrim supplied more than 30% of the Irish migrants to Scotland. In the mid-19th century, migrants bound for England were more likely to emerge from Dublin and the east coast, in the case of the Lancashire Irish, and from Munster and southeast Ireland, in the case of those going to London; but as the century progressed virtually the whole country was meshed into the flow. Most of the migrants were low-skilled laborers, and it has been argued by some historians that Britain received a greater proportion of the very poorest, compared with those who migrated to the British colonies. In the case of Scotland and some of the Lancashire textile towns, however, there is evidence that skilled textile operatives made their way from the Irish linen industry to employment in the British cotton industry.

Political independence and persisting migration, 1920–2000

In the 20th century, Britain emerged as the preferred destination of the majority of Irish migrants. This was especially true in the aftermath of World War II when tens of thousands of Irish laborers found employment in the reconstruction of British cities and, later, in the construction of a new motorway system. Britain was equally attractive to female migrants, many of whom worked on the assembly lines of factories. However, the female Irish migrants contained within their numbers a significant proportion of well-educated women who found employment as nurses and teachers.[6] They were socially distinct from the male Irish laborers, many of whom remained unmarried and increasingly impoverished as infirmity and old age took their toll.

The migration history of Ireland was comparatively unaffected by the political partition of the island in 1921 insofar as the demographic hemorrhage of the previous century continued unabated. Tens of thousands of Protestants may have migrated northward to Northern Ireland or to the rest of the United Kingdom in the immediate aftermath of the political upheavals. But overall the structural weaknesses in the rural economies of both parts of the island ensured a persistence of emigration. Ironically, Britain replaced the USA as the primary destination for the migrants from the newly independent state, as immigration restrictions created a relative downturn of interest in the latter country. In Northern Ireland, notwithstanding the stabilizing effect of the industrial economy of the Belfast region, migration continued, albeit at a pace lower than that of independent Ireland.

In the period 1921–51 a net migration loss of 650,000 was recorded for the whole island, but the rate per thousand in Northern Ireland was approximately half that of the Republic. A stagnating economy in the Republic pushed annual migration losses to a rate of 14 per thousand in the 1950s and the total population continued to fall until a slow revival occurred in the 1960s. In the 1970s a turnaround in the economy saw, for the first time, a net inflow of around 100,000. However, this was neutralized in the following decade when losses of 14 per thousand were once more recorded. Such extremes were not visible in Northern Ireland where a slow growth in total population was recorded in the 1950s and 1960s, but the rise of civil unrest in the 1970s saw a net out migration, including that of many Catholics who went south to the Republic.

Throughout the half century following Partition the United Kingdom continued to receive the majority of migrants from both jurisdictions, but in the 1980s a new trend emerged, with

---

[5] Irish industrial workers in England, Scotland, and Wales since the 19th century.

[6] Irish nurses in England since World War II.

Table 2. Ireland: Emigrants and immigrants, 1995–2000 (000s)						
	1995	**1996**	**1997**	**1998**	**1999**	**2000**
Total of Emigrants	33.1	31.2	29.0	21.2	29.0	22.3
United Kingdom	13.3	14.1	12.9	8.5	10.2	6.3
Rest of EU	5.1	5.1	4.1	4.3	4.5	4.3
United States	8.2	5.2	4.1	4.3	5.4	3.2
Total of Immigrants	31.2	39.2	44.0	44.0	47.5	42.3
United Kingdom	15.6	17.6	20.0	21.1	21.6	16.4
Rest of EU	6.3	7.2	8.1	8.7	10.0	9.8
United States	3.8	6.4	6.6	4.9	5.7	4.6

Source: *Ireland Census of Population* (2002).

Table 3. Principal countries of birth of Ireland's population, 2006 (000s)								
Ireland	**UK**	**Poland**	**Lithuania**	**Other EU**	**Africa**	**USA**	**Others**	**Total**
3,600	271	63	25	79	43	25	66	4,200

Source: Census of Ireland (2006).

some 50,000 undocumented Irish arriving in the USA. A further distinguishing feature of the migrations of that decade was the inclusion of a significant number of professionals and recent university graduates. Unlike earlier decades, the majority of migrants now came from urban areas.

In the early 1990s Ireland entered a phase of economic development that has proven to be unique in both scale and duration when compared with contemporary Organisation for Economic Co-Operation and Development (OECD) countries. This "Celtic Tiger" phase of national development has been underpinned by a doubling of the size of the national workforce – a transformation that has been made possible by increased female participation and by a period of sustained positive net migration. In the intercensal period 1991–6 a modest net migration balance of 2,000 per annum became discernible, but this expanded to annual figures of 26,000 and 48,000, respectively, in the years 1996–2002 and 2002–6. Indeed, net migration is now responsible for more than half of the annual rate of national population growth, exceeding the rate of natural increase by a significant margin. The net migration has been a function of both returning Irish nationals and foreign born. Table 2 indicates that in the 1990s the United Kingdom was the principal source of immigrants, followed by the rest of the European Union (EU) and the USA, but asylum seekers and economic migrants from Eastern and Central Europe, Africa, and Asia injected a more globalized dimension into the inflow. Northern Ireland attracted some of this diversified migration, but at a rate lower than that of the Irish Republic. Continuing emigration from Northern Ireland in the past decade and a half has included an increasingly visible subset of young, mainly Protestant, school-leavers going to universities in Britain. Many of these do not return to their home region after graduation.

The intercensal period 2002–6, a period that includes the recent expansion of the number of EU countries, reveals an ongoing dynamic of transformation of the national demography. During this four-year period the total population increased by 8.2% or 322,000 to 4.2 million. Of these, some 10% (419,733) were non-Irish nationals and 15% (612,629), including the children of previous Irish emigrants, had been born outside Ireland (see Table 3).

The number of Polish nationals resident in Ireland exceeded the number of Northern Ireland–born residents in the country and the plurality of the migration flow is very much dominated by the new accession countries of the EU. Almost two-thirds of immigrants arriving in Ireland in the 12 months before the 2006 census were young single people in their 20s and most found employment in the construction industry and in the service sector. The slowing down of the Irish economy in 2007–8 has led to an outflow of some recent migrants, and there is also evidence that not all of the social security registrations allocated to prospective immigrants have been actually activated. However, there is no doubt that the Irish national demographic has been altered fundamentally by the migration flows of the past decade and a half and the growth of the national economy has been very much dependent upon the scale of the net migration and the skill sets contained within it.

Conclusions

The population of Ireland has been subject to remarkable alteration through the forces of migration that have operated over more than four centuries. Since 1700 in particular, the small Atlantic island has manifested in a more extreme form than most European nations a level of demographic upheaval that has transformed the social, cultural, political, and economic life of the country in a prolonged and recurring manner. The insertion of Ireland into, initially, a British imperial world and, more recently, its immersion in a globalized economy has rendered it very susceptible to the push and pull forces of migration. Throughout three centuries those migration forces were expressed in the form of emigration – a process that tended to reinforce the intrinsic conservatism of Irish life – but the immigration of the past decade has opened Ireland to a period of unprecedented social and economic flux. A country that for a long time had exported its people has very few traditions or structures to resort to when faced with the rapid and large-scale arrival of culturally divergent groups. It is indeed fortunate that the present level of national prosperity can provide the resource potential necessary for the integration of the migrants. It will, however, require the will of government to translate that potential into constructive action.

REFERENCES

Adams, William Forbes. *Ireland and Irish Emigration to the New World: From 1815 to the Famine*. New York, 1932.

Akenson, Donald H. *The Irish Diaspora: A Primer*. Toronto, 1993.

Baines, Dudley. *Migration in a Mature Economy: Emigration and Internal Migration in England and Wales, 1861–1900*. Cambridge, 1985.

Barnard, Toby C. "New Opportunities for British Settlement: Ireland, 1650–1700." In *The Oxford History of the British Empire, Vol. I: The Origins of Empire: British Overseas Enterprise to the Close of the 17th Century*, edited by Nicholas Canny, 310–27. Oxford, 1998.

Bielenberg, Andy, ed. *The Irish Diaspora*. Essex, 2000.

Canny, Nicholas. *Making Ireland British*. Oxford, 2001.

Carrier, Norman Henry, and J. R. Jeffrey. *External Migration: A Study of Available Statistics, 1815–1950*. London, 1953.

Commission on Emigration and Other Population Problems, 1948–54 Reports. Dublin, 1954.

Cullen, Louis. "The Irish Diaspora of the 17th and Eighteenth Centuries." In *Europeans on the Move: Studies on European Migration, 1500–1800*, edited by Nicholas Canny, 113–49. Oxford, 1984.

Dickson, Robert J. *Ulster Emigration to Colonial America, 1718–1775*. London, 1966.

Doyle, David Noel. "The Irish in North America, 1776–1845." In *A New History of Ireland, Vol. V: Ireland under the Union 1801–70*, edited by William E. Vaughan, 682–725. Oxford, 1989.

Erickson, Charlotte, ed. *Emigration from Europe, 1815–1914. Selected Documents*. London, 1976.

Fitzpatrick, David. *Irish Emigration 1801–1921*. Dundalk, 1984.

Horn, James. "British Diaspora: Emigration from Britain, 1680–1815." In *The Oxford History of the British Empire, Vol. II: The Eighteenth Century*, edited by Peter J. Marshall, 28–52. Oxford, 1998.

Houston, Cecil J., and William J. Smyth. *Irish Emigration and Canadian Settlement*. Toronto, 1990.

Jones, Maldwyn. "The Scotch-Irish in British America." In *Strangers within the Realm: Cultural Margins of the First British Empire*, edited by Bernard Bailyn and Philip D. Morgan, 285–313. Chapel Hill, NC, 1991.

Kenny, Kevin. *Ireland and the British Empire*. Oxford, 2004.

MacDonagh, Oliver. "The Irish in Australia: A General View." In *Ireland and Irish Australia: Studies in Cultural and Political History*, edited by Oliver MacDonagh and William F. Mandle, 155–74. London, 1986.

Miller, Kirby. *Emigrants and Exile: Ireland and the Irish Exodus to North America*. Oxford, 1985.

O'Connor, Thomas. *The Irish in Europe, 1580–1815*. Dublin, 2001.

OECD. *Economic Survey, Ireland* 1997.

OECD. *Economic Survey, Ireland* 2001.

O'Farrell, Patrick J. "The Irish in Australia and New Zealand, 1791–1870." In *A New History of Ireland, Vol. V: Ireland under the Union 1801–70*, edited by William E. Vaughan, 662–81. Oxford, 1989.

O'Grada, Cormac. *Ireland: A New Economic History 1780–1939*. Oxford, 1994.

O'Sullivan, Patrick, ed. *The Irish World Wide: History, Heritage, Identity*. 6 vols. London, 1992/94.

Schrier, Arnold. *Ireland and the American Emigration, 1850–1900*. Minneapolis, 1958.

THE NETHERLANDS

Jan Lucassen and Leo Lucassen

With the exception of the period 1850–1914, immigration has always been an important feature of Dutch society. During the early modern period in particular, the western part of the Dutch Republic was dependent on immigrants, both as permanent settlers and as temporary workers in the agricultural sector and as sailors and soldiers in the merchant fleet. The share of foreign born of the total sedentary population in the 17th century was only slightly lower than in the last decades of the 20th century. The recent levels of immigration are therefore wrongly perceived as an unprecedented phenomenon (see Figure 1).

In this overview we will discuss the most important migrations to and from the Netherlands since the 16th century as well as the ensuing settlement process. Finally we will examine the similarities and differences between the migration and integration patterns in the past and in the present. We have chosen to use the present borders of the Netherlands. Although the national borders have changed somewhat in the period under observation, the present borders, decreed after the Dutch recognition of the new Belgian state in 1839, more or less overlap with those of the Dutch Republic after 1648.

Migration of labor migrants and religious refugees in the early modern period

In the 17th century the Dutch Republic was among the most highly developed and richest areas in Europe, if not in the world. In particular, during the 17th century the Dutch Republic created a global empire, based on the trade in spices and other colonial goods in the East (Indonesia) and in the West (Caribbean). In the case of the Caribbean, production depended almost exclusively on plantation slaves. A highly specialized agricultural and industrial base, especially in the western sea provinces, Zealand, Holland, and Frisia, backed up this commercial empire. This spectacular expansion was only possible due to a large inflow of migrants, especially following the one-sided secession of the northern Netherlands from the Spanish Empire in 1581. At least four categories can be distinguished.

First, large numbers of seasonal laborers came from abroad to help out in the peak periods. Each year tens of thousands of seasonal labor migrants left their homes in the western part of what is now Germany to work in the highly commercialized agricultural sector in the maritime provinces of the Dutch Republic, equaling about 5% of the population in the countryside. Second, there were transitory migrants who were recruited as soldiers (the Dutch Republic during its entire existence relied on mercenaries, half of whom were foreigners) as well as sailors to man the tens of thousands of ships, totaling more than half a million in the 17th and 18th centuries. Third, between 1600 and 1800, in total hundreds of thousands of domestic servants as well as journeymen, mainly from German lands, flocked to the cities to work as apprentices in urban trades, such as bakers, tailors, brewers, barrel makers, masons, and plasterers. Most of them stayed temporarily, from a few months to a few years, and only 10% to 15% became permanent immigrants. They joined the considerable number of migrants, predominantly from Scandinavia and the German states, who settled for good, again predominantly in the urban core of the Republic, and who constitute the fourth category of immigrants. Half of the migrants who settled in the urban area in the current provinces of South and North Holland, stretching from Dordrecht in the south to Hoorn and Enkhuizen in the north, were foreigners. This continuous immigration, an estimated 600,000 people in the period 1600–1800, resulted in high levels of foreign born in cities such as Amsterdam.

Although it is often assumed that the main reason for the huge immigration to the Dutch Republic in the early modern period was the absence of persecution and the climate of tolerance, recent research shows that economic motives prevailed. Only a quarter of those who settled can be categorized as political and religious refugees, such as the Iberian Jews, southern Dutch protestants, French Huguenots, and Jews from German and Polish lands.[1] And even for those refugees, economic opportunities clearly influenced their preference for the Netherlands. The remaining three-quarters were predominantly attracted by the booming economy, which was reflected in the spectacular process of urbanization and the Dutch primacy in foreign trade. Most of these migrants came

---

[1] Dutch Calvinist refugees in Europe since the early modern period; Sephardim in Europe in the early modern period; Huguenots in Europe since the 16th century; Ashkenazim in Europe since the early modern period; English Puritan refugees in the Netherlands in the 16th and 17th centuries; Waldensians in central Europe since the early modern period; Jacobites in Europe, 1688–1788; British Royalists in western, central, and southern Europe, 1640–1660.

Table 1. Percentage of foreign born in the 13 largest cities of South and North Holland, 1600–1800

	Total	From German lands	From the southern Netherlands and France	Total population
1600	33	*11*	17	250,000
1650	29	*13*	9	472,000
1700	16	*9*	3	545,000
1750	20	*13*	1	472,000
1800	16	*13*	1	466,000

Source: Jan Lucassen, *Immigranten in Holland*, 22.

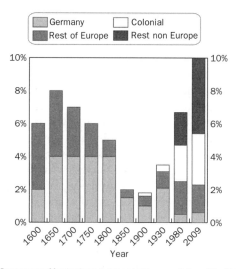

Figure 1. Percentage of foreign born in the sedentary population of the Netherlands, 1600–2009. *Key*: Colonial (mainly Indonesia and Suriname); rest non-European (mainly Turkey and Morocco). *Source*: Jan Lucassen and Rinus Penninx, *Newcomers. Immigrants and Their Descendants in the Netherlands 1550–1995* (Amsterdam, 1997); Jelle van Lottum, "Nieuwkomers in Nederland in de eerste helft van de negentiende eeuw," *Tijdschrift voor Sociale Geschiedenis* 29 (2003): 257–80; Leo Lucassen, "Herr Hagenbach en vele anderen. Migratie naar Holland na 1795," in *Geschiedenis van Holland 1795 tot 2000*, vol. IIIa, edited by Thimo de Nijs and Eelco Beukers (Hilversum, 2003), 299–344; Han Nicolaas and Arno Sprangers, "Buitenlandse migratie in Nederland 1795–2006: de invloed op de bevolkingssamenstelling," *Bevolkingstrends* (4e kwartaal 2007) (Rijswijk: CBS): 32–46; Central Bureau of Statistics.

during the "Golden" 17th century, but the level of immigration remained high until the Napoleonic period, as is shown in Table 1.

In some cities these percentages were much higher. A good example is Leiden, whose population multiplied sixfold between 1580 and 1672, due mainly to the immigrants from the textile area around Lille and Arras. All foreigners made up about 55% of the population around 1600. In the rest of the Dutch Republic immigration was considerably lower. Although coastal provinces, like Zealand, Frisia, and Groningen also attracted various sorts of migrants (harvest workers and sailors), the eastern and southern parts of the Netherlands were exporting rather than importing labor.

Emigration from the Netherlands was not a large-scale phenomenon in this period. During the second half of the 18th century only 15,000 went to the colonies in South America (Suriname), the West Indies (Dutch Antilles), and West Africa (smaller areas in Benin, Togo, Nigeria, Senegal, and Ghana). The number of emigrants to North America was even smaller and probably did not exceed 10,000, most of whom started their new life along the Hudson, where the Dutch West India Company (WIC) had established a trading post in 1625 (Manhattan). Not all of these emigrants were Dutch; also among them were a number of German and English dissenters, who often had adopted the Dutch language and customs before they started their voyage (for the – in theory – temporary emigration to Asia, see later in the chapter). A considerable, but very temporary, emigration took place at the end of the Ancien Régime when 40,000 Dutch fled to Belgium and France and often countries like Denmark, German States, and the Americas. These were the republican "patriots" who had been defeated by the royalist "orangists" in 1787 and who could return only in 1795. They were one of the earliest examples of political exile in Europe.[2] The number of emigrants between 1600 and 1800 was thus only a fraction of the number of immigrants who entered the country.

Who were these foreign migrants and to what extent did they settle and integrate in their Dutch surroundings? The demand for migratory seasonal workers started to grow in the second half of the 16th century, when the agricultural sector in the coastal provinces became more and more commercialized and labor intensive. Whereas many peasants lost their land and left for the city, increasing numbers of laborers were needed during the peak periods of the agricultural cycle from planting in early spring to grass mowing and harvesting in the summer and autumn. Furthermore many hands were needed to extract peat and for various infrastructural works, such as the construction of new polders in the province of Holland. The 20,000 men who migrated annually to do the bulk of this work came mainly from Westphalia, where most of them had their own small farms.[3] As their wives and children stayed behind to tend to their peasant holdings, the men profited from the much higher wages in the western part of the Dutch republic. This migration system, which is known as the North Sea System, would operate for more than two centuries and fade away only after the middle of the 19th century. As temporary wage labor in the Dutch Republic was part of their yearly work cycle, a way of complementing the meager and insufficient earnings from their own peasant holdings, these temporary migrants did not settle as a rule.

To a lesser degree this was also true for the second group of largely temporary, but not seasonally bound, labor migrants.

---

[2] Dutch political refugees from the Batavian Republic in France, 1787–1795.

[3] German seasonal agricultural laborers in the Netherlands from the 17th to the early 20th century; Lippe brickmakers in central, western, and northern Europe from the 17th to the early 20th century.

They were soldiers and sailors who worked on the large Dutch mercantile fleet.[4] During the early modern period, almost a million people traveled to the East Indies, half of whom were foreigners recruited by the Dutch, who served on the ships of the United East India Company (known as the VOC). About 70% never returned after one or more voyages. They either died from tropical diseases or stayed in the East Indies. Some 15% returned to their home country, so that another 15% settled in the Republic in the end, often in the cities where they had boarded their ships, like Amsterdam, Rotterdam, Delft, Hoorn, and Enkhuizen. Some started boardinghouses with the money they had earned and often attracted guests from their region of origin.

The thriving Dutch economy not only needed people for the agricultural sector but also for urban industries and the international trade networks. The first category comprised mainly journeymen, apprentices, and servants. Many men probably worked for German immigrants who had started small enterprises in Dutch cities, such as bakers, tailors, and hatmakers, and who preferred to employ German personnel.[5] Thus, annually thousands of German journeymen came to cities like Amsterdam, Haarlem, and Rotterdam to work for a couple of years and then move on again, often back to German lands. Less well documented is the influx of foreign female servants, from Germany and Scandinavia.

Apart from these largely temporary migrants there were some 600,000 foreigners who settled permanently and who changed the ethnic makeup of most cities in Holland. As previously mentioned, not the most numerous but the best-known immigrant group are the refugees. The largest group (about 100,000) were the southern Dutch, from both Antwerp and the region around Lille. Most of them had converted to Protestantism and fled from the Spanish Catholics, especially between 1580 and 1620. Economic motives also played an important role as their livelihood, generally textile production and trade, was jeopardized by the closing of the Scheldt River and by the devastation of the centers of textile (wool) production in what is now the border region between the southwest of Belgium and the northwest of France. These refugees were welcomed by Dutch cities, which justly considered them a source of economic prosperity. Cities such as Haarlem and Leiden even competed to attract these skilled migrants, offering them tax exemptions, full citizenship, and sometimes even guild membership.[6]

The Iberian Jews, of whom some 2,000 settled in Amsterdam in the 17th century, also played an important part in the ascendancy of the new Dutch Republic.[7] Although they were excluded from virtually all guilds, their capital and trade contacts in southern Europe and the Mediterranean assured them a good income and an influential economic position. Their coreligionists from Germany and some from eastern Europe, some 10,000 to 20,000 of whom settled in the Netherlands in the 17th and early 18th century, were less fortunate.[8] The last well-known refugee immigrant group were the 30,000 to 50,000 Huguenots who entered the country after the revocation of the Edict of Nantes in 1685.[9]

The large majority of the permanent immigrants, however, were not religious refugees but were mainly motivated by the high wages and abundant economic possibilities in the Dutch Republic. As their migration was spread out over a much longer period, they never attracted much attention. Most of them came from the western and northwestern part of what is now Germany and from Scandinavia, in particular southern Norway. The majority were Lutherans, who formed a minority church in the Calvinist-dominated Netherlands. In comparison to the Iberian Jews, southern Dutch, and Huguenots, hardly any of them were part of the commercial elite. Their socioeconomic position was rather modest and many of them would become part of the urban proletariat.

Most of these migrants who settled in the Netherlands integrated within two to three generations. Being a "foreigner" was a rather transitory phase, because the urban authorities made the admission to citizenship and guild membership relatively easy. Children of migrants automatically became part of the indigenous population. Many of them married Dutch partners and merged with the rest of the population. As a result most groups disappeared relatively quickly into the Dutch melting pot, which was easiest for immigrants with a Calvinist background. This was more difficult for Lutherans, Mennonites, Catholics, and Jews, who were all excluded from political functions in the Dutch Republic.[10] In some towns Catholics, and virtually everywhere Jews, were excluded from citizenship and membership of craft guilds. These degrees of legal discrimination lasted until the Emancipation Edict of the Batavian Republic in 1796 and it was not before the middle of the 19th century or even later that these minorities became integrated into Dutch society. This process involved much debate over the language to be used, especially on religious occasions (German or Danish/Norwegian among Lutherans, French among Huguenots, and Hebrew/Portuguese/Yiddish among Jews). Another group of immigrants, the Gypsies (or "Heathens"), was also discriminated against and were even more or less outlawed in the first half of the 18th century. As a result of "Gypsy hunts" a number of them were killed, whereas others fled and tried to become invisible to the authorities. During the early modern period local urban authorities, as well as intermediary institutions such as the guilds, played a crucial role in the integration process, because they – and the central state organs – determined who was entitled to full citizenship rights and thus admitted to the vital political and economic bodies.

---

[4] German sailors in the Dutch merchant marine from the early 17th to the end of the 19th century.

[5] German baker-journeymen in Amsterdam in the 17th century.

[6] Dutch Calvinist refugees in Europe since the early modern period.

[7] Sephardim in Europe in the early modern period.

[8] Ashkenazim in Europe since the early modern period.

[9] Huguenots in Europe since the 16th century.

[10] Mennonites in West Prussia since the 16th century.

Changing migration patterns in the 19th and early 20th centuries

From the end of the 18th century the magnet on the North Sea shore gradually lost its attraction and immigration levels reached rock bottom around 1900. The turning point was not so much the French occupation by Napoleon but the period after 1820 when the stagnating Dutch economy became increasingly unattractive to newcomers, especially from the German states. The economies of the eastern neighboring states started to grow and fewer emigrants departed for the Netherlands; as a consequence the foreign-born part of the Netherlands grew old and subsequently diminished in numbers. Thus, the old migration paths gradually waned, but did not disappear. The importance of seasonal migration decreased but remained considerable until the 1870s; the same pattern held true for sailors from northern Germany and Scandinavia – no large numbers anymore, but in the 1850s and 1860s the Amsterdam police still recorded hundreds of Norwegian and Danish sailors. Similar trends can be noticed among German apprentices who worked for Dutch (and German) bakers and tailors. German, Swiss, and other soldiers served in the Dutch army until the mid-19th century and in the colonial army until about 1900. Their numbers increased in the second half of the 19th century, due to the colonial expansion around 1830 and 1860 and the wars in Aceh and other parts of the Dutch East Indies from the 1880s onward. In total some 70,000 foreigners were recruited in the period 1815 to 1909.[11]

After 1850 the early modern migration system finally came to a creaking halt. This was reflected in the change of the occupational and geographical profile of the immigrants. The dominance of Scandinavian and German sailors and German craftsmen gave way to a much smaller stream of – again – German migrants, as well as newcomers from Belgium. The Germans who came to the Netherlands from the middle of the 19th century onward were predominantly to be found in new economic sectors, such as the transit trade, department stores, and the service sector in general.[12] The transit trade was closely linked to the spectacular development of the German Ruhr area. From 1850 onward the area around the small Ruhr River became the heartland of the heavy and chemical industry and the motor of the German economic success. The Netherlands functioned as an important transit country, especially the harbors of Rotterdam and – to a lesser extent – Amsterdam, where German trading companies and major industries set up their offices.

The second sector recruiting considerable numbers of German personnel was the retail trade, which has its roots in the early modern system of German peddlers. From the beginning of the 19th century onward a number of them changed from street trading to shopkeeping, some of which developed into successful department stores, specializing in textiles as well as a general assortment of goods.[13] Finally the flourishing entertainment sector (bars, restaurants, hotels, and brothels) attracted thousands of German men and women who worked as servants, waiters/waitresses, and prostitutes. Along with them other migrants settled, albeit in small numbers, often through highly specific chain migration patterns. Well-known groups are the Belgian straw hatmakers; Italian chimney sweeps and statue makers; Swiss, English, and French nannies; German wandering (Gypsy) musicians; Bosnian (Gypsy) bear leaders; and Hungarian (Gypsy) coppersmiths.[14]

In contrast to the early modern period, refugees did not constitute an important part of the total immigration. During the 19th century only small groups of political refugees (from Italy, German states, and Poland) entered the Netherlands.[15] A special group were several thousands of German Catholic priests and clergy who, due to Bismarck's anti-Catholic *Kulturkampf*, settled in the Dutch border province of Limburg and built monasteries there. Jewish refugees from Russia came to the Netherlands as well, particularly after 1880, but they preferred other destinations, such as France and England.

Compared to other European countries, with the notable exception of France, emigration in this period remained low. After the Napoleonic wars (during which an estimated number of over 20,000 was employed in military operations outside the Netherlands and never returned) emigration to the East Indies resumed. Between 1815 and 1910, some 89,000 Dutchmen left the Netherlands to serve in the Dutch East India Army, of whom a quarter died in the many colonial wars or during the voyage. Apart from the military, 41,000 civilian men and 17,000 women, most of them Dutch, migrated to the Dutch East Indies in this period. The "European" (i.e., including the descendants of mixed European-Asian marriages) civil population increased from 15,000 in 1815 to 70,000 around 1900. Because of a large demand for highly skilled labor in the first half of the 20th century, this number had almost quadrupled in 1930 to 240,000. This increase was not so much the result of massive immigration, as 87% was born in the Dutch East Indies. Behind these net numbers a vivid colonial circuit of in and out migration is hidden, numbering annually 2,000 to 4,000 emigrants before and 6,000 to 16,000 emigrants after the First World War.

Emigration to the Americas started in the mid-1840s and although the Netherlands was an unpromising source of emigrants compared to other European countries, still a

---

[11] Western and central European soldiers in the Dutch colonial army, 1815–1909.

[12] German traders and shopkeepers in the Netherlands, 1850–1900.

[13] German itinerant merchants from the Münsterland in northern, western, and central Europe in the 18th and 19th centuries

[14] Walloon straw hat makers in the Netherlands in the 19th century; Alpine chimney sweeps in western, central, and southern Europe from the 16th to the early 20th century; Bosnian bear leaders in western and central Europe, 1868–1940; Hungarian coppersmiths in western Europe from the 1860s to World War I.

[15] Polish political refugees in central and western Europe in the 19th century; Italian refugees of the *risorgimento* in central and western Europe in the 19th century.

quarter of a million left for the USA before the First World War. During the last decades of the 19th century, industrializing Germany, once the chief supplier of migrants to the Netherlands, became an attractive destination for Dutch workers. According to the German census of 1910 the number of Dutch born amounted to 145,000, a third of whom stayed for good.[16] With the outbreak of the Great War, emigration both to the Americas and to Germany came to a halt.

Migration in the interwar period, 1918–1940

After the First World War, the Dutch economy soon attracted new labor migrants and the share of foreign residents in the Netherlands increased from about 1.6% in 1918 to about 2.2% in 1930. In the big cities in the west (4%), as well as in the mining area of South Limburg concentrations were higher, with more than 20% in mining towns like Kerkrade and Heerlen. In the 1920s the bulk of the migrants came from Germany, but also from Belgium, Poland, Italy, and Slovenia. In the years following World War I the economy in the Netherlands and the Weimar Republic developed in opposite ways. Whereas the Dutch business cycle showed a clear upward trend until the beginning of the 1930s, Germany soon plunged into an unprecedented economic chaos, due to the internal political turmoil and the hyperinflation building up in the years 1918–23. The result of this divergent economic development was that many Germans tried to find employment in the Netherlands, whose strong currency and prosperity sharply contrasted with the situation at home. In the interwar period almost 200,000 German women found jobs as domestics in Dutch homes, especially in the western part of the country, and also in hotels and restaurants. Whereas women ended up in the lower segment of the labor market, German (and other foreign) men predominantly occupied skilled positions in industry.

The metal industry (mechanics, fitters), the building trade (masons, carpenters, and the like), the coal mines, and domestic services were short of workers and welcomed the immigration of Germans, who (men and women taken together) constituted almost 60% of all foreigners in the Netherlands in the 1920s and 1930s. German specialists were "hot" and employers went to great lengths to persuade Dutch immigration authorities to grant them work permits, which had become obligatory after 1918. Most migrants worked side-by-side with native workers, but the newcomers dominated a few niches. Well-known groups are the Italian ice cream vendors from the Belluno area in the northeast of Italy; and the *terrazzeri* from Friuli, also in the northeast.[17]

Domestic service, another sector occupied by a substantial number of foreigners, was dominated by German (and partly Austrian) women. They worked not only for the upper classes, but also in modest middle-class homes. Of the three big cities, the Hague, a typically service-dominated town and seat of government, attracted most servants. Nine out of 10 foreign women in this city worked as domestic servants around 1930, both in private homes and in the numerous hotels (especially in the adjoining sea resort of Scheveningen) and restaurants.[18]

With the world economic crisis, which affected the Dutch economy a few years later than the surrounding countries, but also lasted longer, immigration decreased, especially from 1933 onward. A group that was hit severely were former Chinese sailors from the Guangdong area; they had lost their jobs and lived mainly in Rotterdam and Amsterdam. Other Chinese migrants were traders from Zhejiang, who peddled in Chinese stoneware and textiles, in the Netherlands, Germany, Belgium, and France.[19] A few hundred were sent back to China, whereas many of those who stayed married Dutch women during the Second World War.

The first half of the 20th century produced many more refugees than the preceding 19th century and the Netherlands was not left untouched. Almost a million Belgian refugees crossed the southern border immediately after the outbreak of World War I and the siege of Antwerp. When it soon became clear that the German troops controlled large parts of Belgium and had reestablished order, the vast majority returned, but some 100,000, both soldiers and civilians, would stay until the end of the war.[20] Most of them were housed in large camps in the south of the country, whereas the more well-to-do rented housing themselves or were given shelter by Dutch people from the same social background.

Virtually all of these Belgians, except for some – Flemish nationalists – collaborators with the Germans, returned after the war. At the same time new refugees appealed for help. A group of German, Austrian, and Hungarian children (the majority being girls) were sent by the hundred thousands to Dutch families to recover. Although the stay of these "holiday children" was meant to be temporary (a few months at most), more than 10,000 stayed for good and were adopted.

The best-known group of refugees were those who fled the Nazi regime after 1933.[21] Whereas many German labor migrants returned to Germany, tens of thousands of mainly Jewish refugees as well as political refugees from Nazi Germany and Austria crossed the border seeking sanctuary. This was provided by coreligionists and by political sympathizers, not by the Dutch state, which, on the contrary, tried to hinder this kind of immigration as much as possible. Most

---

[16] Dutch labor migrants in Germany in the late 19th and early 20th centuries.

[17] Italian ice cream makers in Europe since the late 19th century.

[18] German maids in the Netherlands in the interwar period.

[19] Chinese restaurant owners in the Netherlands and Germany in the second half of the 20th century; Chinese itinerant merchants in Europe since the end of World War I.

[20] Belgian refugees in western Europe during World War I.

[21] Jewish refugees from Nazi Germany and from German-occupied Europe since 1933; political and intellectual refugees from Nazi Germany and from German-occupied Europe, 1933–45.

of these refugees remained for only a short while and left for other countries, in particular the USA. At the outset of World War II some 15,000 had settled in the Netherlands, most of them in Amsterdam. With the occupation by the Nazi army in 1940, the position of Jews soon became very difficult and from 1942 onward most of them, together with 100,000 Dutch citizens labeled as Jews by the Nazis, were taken to the death camps, from which only some 5,000 returned.

During the interwar period emigration from the Netherlands was insignificant. After the First World War most of the traditional destinations of Dutch emigrants had lost their attraction. The USA was closing its borders, and the German economy suffered from hyperinflation and mass unemployment. The colonies in the East remained, but the number of people who went there was low. Only the occupation of the Netherlands by German troops propelled larger numbers of people, both forced and voluntary, to leave for Germany. Apart from the 100,000 Jewish Dutchmen who were deported to the death camps, it concerned mainly male workers for the German (war) industry, prisoners of war, and some 22,000 volunteers for the SS wanting to fight the Soviet army.[22] With the exception of those killed by air raids or in combat, the bulk of these several hundred thousand temporary migrants returned after the war.

A new upsurge of immigration after the Second World War

In the postwar period the government stimulated citizens to emigrate to overseas destinations. The Netherlands, then with 10 million inhabitants, was considered overpopulated and in view of the large-scale destruction of its economy, unemployment was expected to remain high for decades. This propaganda fell on fertile ground. In 1948 one in three Dutchmen seriously considered leaving the country for good and between 1945 and 1960, half a million people (2%–3% of the population) emigrated to Canada, Australia, New Zealand, South Africa, and the USA, of whom 100,000 returned after a shorter or longer period.

The economic forecasts of the policy makers proved to be much too gloomy. From 1952 onward the first frictions in the labor market were noticed and soon a situation of full employment and even a scarcity of labor emerged. In particular, the metal industry, the coal mines, textiles, and domestic service had trouble recruiting enough workers. Although women's labor force participation was low in the Netherlands the promotion of female labor was not considered an option, since both the government and public opinion were against married women's work. When it soon became clear that internal migration would not solve the labor shortage, foreign migration under government supervision was considered. Special recruitment teams were sent to England to persuade former Polish soldiers to work as metalworkers or miners. In the course of 1947 the number of stateless displaced persons

and Poles increased, but in the end only some 12,000, mainly men, settled permanently.[23]

By and large, immigration in the postwar years was very limited. In 1947 the percentage of foreigners had been halved compared to 1930 and in 1960 their share had diminished even further. This could easily lead to the conclusion that in this period barely any immigration had taken place. In reality from 1946 onward one of the biggest immigration waves reached the Dutch shores. The main cause was the sudden decolonization of Indonesia and the colonial wars between the Netherlands and the nationalists in 1947 and 1948. In this tense atmosphere the situation for the Dutch expatriates and the much bigger group of Eurasians (most of them the offspring of Dutch fathers and Indonesian mothers), many of whom had occupied a privileged intermediary position in Indonesia, soon became difficult and many tried – with success – to travel to an unknown "fatherland." In total some 300,000 migrants, predominantly Eurasians, ended up in the Netherlands between 1946 and 1964, together with 12,500 Moluccans, who had been employed by the Dutch colonial army and arrived in 1951.[24]

Although the newcomers from the former East Indian colony were Dutch nationals, as explicitly underlined by the official inclusive term "repatriates," their settlement process had many elements in common with that of other immigrants. Moreover, their brownish skin color and peculiar Indonesian accent made them easily recognizable. Just like most of the other migrant groups, discrimination, mutual ignorance, and trouble between youngsters occurred in the first phase of their stay. On the other hand, three factors made their integration easier than that of other noncolonial migrants: they spoke Dutch, were reasonably well educated, and were categorized by the government as belonging to the Dutch nation, similar to the *Aussiedler* in Germany in the same period. Furthermore, they were lucky to arrive in one of the longest boom periods in western European economic history, so that their integration in the labor market and the educational system went relatively smoothly. Most of these "repatriates" settled in the major cities, especially in the Hague.

Even these huge numbers of colonial immigrants, most of whom found (predominantly clerical) jobs in the expanding Dutch economy, did not solve the labor shortage at the lower end of the labor market. When the displaced persons scheme offered no adequate solution, the Ministry of Social Affairs and employers decided in 1954 to systematically explore the possibilities of recruitment in Italy where unemployment was high. The big leap forward followed after 1960, when the business cycle reached its peak and the work permits for Mediterranean workers (from Italy, Spain, Portugal, Yugoslavia, Greece, and not long thereafter also Morocco and Turkey) increased within five years from

---

[22] Forced laborers in Germany and German-occupied Europe during World War II.

[23] Displaced persons (DPs) in Europe since the end of World War II.

[24] Dutch East Indian migrants in the Netherlands since the end of World War II; Moluccans in the Netherlands since 1951.

24,000 to 63,000 and reached a total of 100,000 around 1970. At first, most new labor migrants were concentrated in the south (mines) and the east (textile) of the Netherlands, but soon the center of gravity shifted to the western part of the country, where the metal and food processing industry, as well as labor-intensive sectors in agriculture attracted many guest workers.[25]

The oil price shock in 1973 and the ensuing recession did not stop immigration, on the contrary. Labor recruitment ended abruptly, but one of the unexpected and unintended consequences of the restrictive aliens policy was that many guest workers, especially those who came from countries where the economy was doing badly (Morocco and Turkey, but also Cape Verde), decided not to leave, because they would probably not be allowed to reenter the Netherlands. During their stay they had built up "embedded" rights, both by contributing to the welfare state and by the strong resident status caused by their prolonged stay and the role of activist lawyers, so it was difficult to expel them. Although until the 1990s many former guest workers held on to the myth of return, in reality their extended stay amounted to permanent settlement. Consequently they invited spouses and children and within a few years the Moroccan and Turkish part of the population that previously had been dominated by young and middle-aged men now consisted of complete families. In this way, and by way of subsequent immigration of marriage partners, substantial communities of first-, second-, and third-generation Turks (375,000 in 2009) and Moroccans (337,000 in 2009) emerged in many Dutch towns, but especially in the major cities, often concentrated in poor quarters. Given the fact that especially from 1980 onward unemployment increased, and remained high until the mid-1990s, the timing of this follow-up migration was unfortunate.

This was equally true for the immigration that directly preceded and followed the decolonization of Suriname in 1975, which had generated interethnic struggles in Suriname between the descendants of former African slaves (Creoles) and the group of former indentured laborers from India (Hindustanis). As a result of the atmosphere of ethnic tensions and uncertainty, after 1970 more than 190,000 Surinamese decided that they would have a better future in the colonial motherland. There had been small groups of Surinamese (mainly Creoles) in the Netherlands throughout the 20th century, mainly students, musicians, and nurses, but from 1970 onward the numbers rocketed from 27,000 to 336,000 in 2009 (including the descendants of the migrants). Just like the Antilleans, whose numbers increased in the

same period from 20,000 to 132,000, most of them preferred to settle in the major cities.[26]

If we set aside the colonial migrants from both the east and the west, who to a certain extent can be considered as refugees, the immigration of refugees after World War II remained low for a long time. As the government was preoccupied by the fear of overpopulation, the policy of accepting refugees was initially extremely restrictive. Even German Jews who had found refuge in the 1930s and had survived the death camps had great trouble being readmitted, whereas displaced persons were welcome only when they could contribute to the economy. Until the early 1970s only small groups of eastern Europeans (a few thousand Hungarians[27] in 1956 and some Czechs in 1968) were – reluctantly – given access, followed in the 1970s by groups of Chileans, Vietnamese, Kurds, and Iraqis.[28] After 1980 the annual number which until then had been in the hundreds changed to thousands (Iranians, Tamils, Ghanaians, Ethiopians, Pakistanis) and with the war in the Balkans to tens of thousands.[29]

The postwar immigration had important consequences for the composition of the population in the major Dutch cities and changed the outlook of many city quarters. Almost 60% of the Surinamese and half of the Moroccans live in one of the four major cities (Amsterdam, Rotterdam, the Hague, and Utrecht). The concentration of Turks in these cities is somewhat lower (37%), as many of them also live in substantial numbers in the eastern provinces Gelderland and Overijssel (the former textile area). Between the major groups there are important differences. Most Creole Surinamese live in Amsterdam, Hindustani Surinamese in the Hague, whereas Antilleans, Turks, and Cape Verdeans dominate in Rotterdam. Utrecht and Amsterdam have a substantial Moroccan community. Refugees and asylum seekers are more dispersed over the country, as a result of decentralized relief camps, but they also prefer the major cities, where various vibrant migrant communities, of both refugees and other migrants (like the Ghanaians in Amsterdam), have developed.

Around 2000 a public debate materialized on the integration of recent immigrants. Soon the idea became widespread that the integration (policy) had failed and that the much too tolerant multicultural policy of the successive Dutch governments since the 1970s was to blame. Dissatisfaction

---

[25] Spanish labor migrants in western, central, and northern Europe since the end of World War II; Greek labor migrants in western, central, and northern Europe after 1950: the examples of Germany and the Netherlands; Portuguese labor migrants in western and central Europe since the 1950s: the examples of France and Germany; Italian labor migrants in northern, central, and western Europe since the end of World War II; Turkish labor migrants in western, central, and northern Europe since the mid-1950s; Cape Verdeans in western and southern Europe since the 1950s: the example of the Netherlands.

[26] West Indians in Great Britain, France, and the Netherlands since the end of World War II.

[27] Hungarian refugees in Europe since 1956; Czechoslovakian refugees in western, central, and northern Europe since 1968.

[28] Chilean refugees in Europe since 1973: the example of Switzerland; Vietnamese refugees in western, central, and northern Europe since the 1970s: the examples of France, Great Britain, and Germany; Kurdish refugees in western and central Europe since the late 20th century: the example of Germany; Greek refugees in western, central, northern, and southern Europe during the military dictatorship, 1967–74.

[29] Sri-Lankan Tamils in western and central Europe since the 1980s: the example of Switzerland; Iranian refugees in northern, western, and central Europe since 1980: the example of the Netherlands; refugees from former Yugoslavia in Europe since 1991.

with the immigration and integration policies culminated in an unprecedented support for the populist party of Pim Fortuyn in the elections of May 2002. Although this party, whose leader was murdered shortly before the election, was dissolved in January 2008, the idea that integration had failed remained very strong, and since the elections in the fall of 2006, other populist anti-immigrant parties, such as the Party for Freedom (PVV) led by Geert Wilders, have filled the void.

There is no denying that since the 1990s severe problems have arisen with the (male) second generation of both former guest workers and Antillean migrants. Moroccan and Antillean boys in particular are overrepresented in mugging, street offenses, and drug-related criminality. Moreover, they perform poorly in school and in the labor market, with high percentages of dropouts and unemployed. Finally, many Dutch worry about the influence of Islam on the children of migrants, resulting in fierce discussion about headscarves and Islamic schools.

Nevertheless, it is not entirely clear whether there is a direct correlation between these problems and the (multicultural) integration policy in place since the 1980s. To a large extent the problems of these immigrant groups seem to be the product of the marginalized position of the first-generation guest workers, many of whom lost their jobs during the scaling down of the manufacturing industry at the end of the 1970s. This marginalization was greatly stimulated by the policy, endorsed by both employers and unions, of writing them off as disabled and granting them lifelong social security benefits. As a consequence, many badly educated men are no longer employed and have trouble in fulfilling their role as fathers in their families who joined them in the Netherlands in the 1970s and 1980s. Besides, their spouses are frequently not familiar enough with the Dutch language and customs to guide their children during their schooling and other activities outside the house. The situation is exacerbated by anti-foreigner feelings and Islamophobia, greatly enhanced abroad by the 11 September 2001 attacks in the USA, the terrorist attacks in Madrid and London, and at home by the murder of Theo van Gogh (2004); these feelings, sometimes strongly expressed by people like Ayaan Hirsi Ali and Geert Wilders (whose movie *Fitna* was released in March 2008), have led to reactions in the Muslim communities. Some believers retreat into strict orthodoxy, which in turn is grist for the mill of sympathizers of the PVV and similar movements. However, these pessimistic judgments on the integration policy ignore unmistakable progress in the key domains of integration, education, and work, whereas a moderate western European version of Islam is developing under the influence of young and better-educated members of the second-generation immigrants.

Looking back and ahead

When we compare the two peak periods of immigration in Dutch history, the early modern period and the second half of the 20th century, it is clear that the dynamics behind migration movements have changed. Before the 1970s it was largely the pull of the labor market that determined the rhythm of the migration from abroad. After World War II, however, this economic regime was partly replaced by a political, *statist*, regime, in which the mutually reinforcing effects of decolonization, a greater state control of immigration, "embedded liberal rights," and the welfare state partly disconnected migration from the demand for labor. The effects of this liberal democratic regime is best illustrated by the large-scale immigration in the 1970s and 1980s, which witnessed the family reunification among guest workers groups, immigration from Suriname, and high numbers of refugees, all three in a period in which the Dutch economy was not doing well and unemployment figures soared dramatically.

At the beginning of the 21st century, migration from the (former) colonies has largely subsided. Only immigration from the Antilles, still a part of the kingdom, continues. The ensuing migration from Turkey and Morocco is also decreasing. Many members of the second generation still overwhelmingly prefer marriage partners from these countries of origin, but since the turn of the century legislation is becoming more strict, which – together with increasing criticism on this preference within migrant associations – most probably will result in a gradual shift to Dutch-born partners from their own ethnic group. Only a small minority of the offspring of the guest workers from Turkey and Morocco marries native (and thereby non-Muslim) Dutch partners: around 2000 the rates for children of Turks and Moroccans were respectively 6% and 11%. Furthermore, the number of refugees and asylum seekers has decreased dramatically in recent years, as did the percentage of applications for asylum in the Netherlands compared to the European average, partly the result of a very restrictive Dutch policy.

To what extent the bad timing of the mass immigration in the 1980s and 1990s will change the integration patterns remains to be seen. At least two factors may have a slowing down effect on integration of offspring of the immigrants. One is the on-average low human capital (education and relevant work experience) of the former guest workers and of the more recent immigrants from the Antilles, which is partly reproduced among the second generation. Although it is remarkable how fast many children of these new migrants adapt to the new (cultural) environment and become more "Dutch" than their parents, a significant minority is not doing well. The prospect that part of the offspring of the migrants who settled in the 1970s and 1980s will develop into a persistent, ethnically tainted underclass is therefore not entirely illusory. Second, the Islamic background of most non-European former guest workers may also slow down intermarriage with non-Muslim partners, especially when the stigmatization of Muslims continues to be a major political factor.

Finally, we see a very recent immigration trend of eastern European workers from Poland, and to a lesser extent from Romania and Bulgaria, who work temporarily as seasonal workers in agriculture, but increasingly also in other sectors like building, cleaning, and other services. In 2008 it was estimated that some 120,000 of them (the bulk from Poland) work for longer or shorter periods in the Netherlands. While since the 1990s Poles, often illegally, already worked in the Netherlands, the numbers have increased considerably since the turn of the century. This pertains not only to temporary workers, but also to Poles who have taken up legal residence in Dutch municipalities (30,000 in 1999 versus almost 60,000 in 2008). This increase is explained by both demand and supply factors. On the one hand the booming Dutch economy and the high demand for labor in the sectors mentioned and on the other the freedom of movement for members of the new European Union states. Thus the entry of Poland (2004) and Romania and Bulgaria (2007) into the European Union has removed the barriers to enter and leave the country and pick up legal employment. In contrast to the guest workers, however, access to the welfare state is much more restricted, whereas those migrants who appeal to welfare run a great risk of being deported. These changes in the migration legislation have therefore to a large extent restored the primacy of the labor market, at least among the migrants from the European Union. This is well illustrated by the fact that many eastern Europeans left the Netherlands in the wake of the economic crisis that reached the Dutch shores in the first months of 2009.

REFERENCES

Bodian, Miriam. *Hebrews of the Portuguese Nation. Conversos and Community in Early Modern Amsterdam*. Bloomington, 1999.

Bosma, Ulbe. "Sailing through Suez from the South: The Emergence of a Dutch-Indies Migration Circuit 1815–1935." *International Migration Review* 41, 2 (2007): 511–36.

Bosma, Ulbe, and Remco Raben. *De oude Indische wereld 1500–1920*. Amsterdam, 2003.

Bossenbroek, Martin. *Volk voor Indië. De werving van Europese militairen voor de Nederlandse koloniale dienst 1814–1909*. Amsterdam, 1992.

Chotkowski, Margaret. *Vijftien ladders en een dambord. Contacten van Italiaanse migranten in Nederland 1860–1940*. Amsterdam, 2006.

Cottaar, Annemarie. *Ik had een neef in Den Haag. Nieuwkomers in de twintigste eeuw*. Zwolle, 1998.

Doesschate, Jan-Willem ten. *Asielbeleid en belangen: Het Nederlandse toelatingsbeleid ten aanzien van vluchtelingen in de jaren 1968–1982*. Hilversum, 1993.

Eijl, Corrie van. *Al te goed is buurmans gek. Het Nederlandse vreemdelingenbeleid 1840–1940*. Amsterdam, 2005.

Eijl, Corrie van, and Leo Lucassen. "Holland beyond the Borders: Emigration and the Dutch State, 1850–1940." In *Citizenship and Those Who Leave. The Politics of Emigration and Expatriation*, edited by Nancy L. Green and François Weil, 156–75. Urbana, 2007.

Gelderblom, Oscar C. "From Antwerp to Amsterdam: The Contribution of Merchants from the Southern Netherlands to the Commercial Expansion of Amsterdam (c. 1540–1609)." *Review* 26 (2003): 247–82.

Henkes, Barbara. *Heimat in Holland: Deutsche Dienstmädchen 1920–1950*. Straelen, 1998.

Hooghiemstra, Erna. *Trouwen over de grens. Achtergronden van partnerkeuze van Turken en Marokkanen in Nederland*. Den Haag, 2003.

Kuijpers, Erika. *Migrantenstad. Immigratie en sociale verhoudingen in 17e eeuws Amsterdam*. Hilversum, 2005.

Lesger, Clé. "Informatiestromen en de herkomstgebieden van migranten in de Nederlanden in de vroegmoderne tijd." *Tijdschrift voor Sociale en Economische Geschiedenis* 3 (2006): 3–23.

Lesger, Clé, Leo Lucassen, and Marlou Schrover. "Is There Life Outside the Migrant Network? German Immigrants in XIXth Century Netherlands and the Need for a More Balanced Migration Typology." *Annales de Démographie Historique* 2 (2002): 29–50.

Lottum, Jelle van. "Nieuwkomers in Nederland in de eerste helft van de negentiende eeuw." *Tijdschrift voor Sociale Geschiedenis* 29 (2003): 257–80.

Lottum, Jelle van. *Across the North Sea: The Impact of the Dutch Republic on International Labour Migration, c. 1550–1850*. Amsterdam, 2007.

Lucassen, Jan. *Migrant Labour in Europe 1600–1900: The Drift to the North Sea*. London, 1987.

Lucassen, Jan. "The Netherlands, the Dutch, and Long-Distance Migration in the Late 16th to Early 19th Centuries." In *Europeans on the Move. Studies on European Migration, 1500–1800*, edited by Nicholas Canny, 153–91. Oxford, 1994.

Lucassen, Jan. *Immigranten in Holland 1600–1800. Een kwantitatieve benadering*. Amsterdam, 2002.

Lucassen, Jan. "A Multinational and its Labor Force: The Dutch East India Company, 1595–1795." *International Labor and Working-Class History* 66 (Fall 2004): 12–39.

Lucassen, Jan, and Rinus Penninx. *Newcomers. Immigrants and Their Descendants in the Netherlands 1550–1995*. Amsterdam, 1997.

Lucassen, Leo. "En men noemde hen zigeuners." De geschiedenis van Kaldarasch, Ursari, Lowara en Sinti in Nederland: 1750–1944*. Amsterdam and Den Haag, 1990.

Lucassen, Leo. "Bringing Structure Back In: Economic and Political Determinants of Immigration in Dutch Cities (1920–1940)." *Social Science History* 26 (2002): 503–29.

Lucassen, Leo. "Herr Hagenbach en vele anderen. Migratie naar Holland na 1795." In *Geschiedenis van Holland 1795 tot 2000*, vol. IIIa, edited by Thimo de Nijs and Eelco Beukers, 299–344. Hilversum, 2003.

Lucassen, Leo, ed. *Amsterdammer worden. Migranten, hun organisaties en inburgering, 1600–2000*. Amsterdam, 2004.

Lucassen, Leo, David Feldman, and Jochen Oltmer, eds. *Paths of Integration. Migrants in Western Europe (1880–2004)*. Amsterdam, 2006.

Lucassen, Leo, and Boudien de Vries. "The Rise and Fall of a West European Textile-Worker Migration System: Leiden, 1586–1700." In *Les ouvriers qualifiés de l'industrie (XVIe–XXe siècle). Formation, emploi, migrations*, edited by Gérard Gayot and Philippe Minard, 23–42. Lille, 2001.

Lucassen, Leo, and Charlotte Laarman. "Immigration, Intermarriage and the Changing Face of Europe in the Post War Period." *History of the Family* 14 (2009) 1: 52–68.

Nicolaas, Han, and Arno Sprangers. "Buitenlandse migratie in Nederland 1795–2006: De invloed op de bevolkingssamenstelling." *Bevolkingstrends* (4e kwartaal 2007), Rijswijk: CBS: 32–46.

Roodt, Evelien de. *Oorlogsgasten: vluchtelingen en krijgsgevangenen in Nederland tijdens de Eerste Wereldoorlog*. Zaltbommel, 2000.

Rosendaal, Joost. *Bataven! Nederlandse vluchtelingen in Frankrijk 1787–1795*. Nijmegen, 2003.

Schrover, Marlou. *Een kolonie van Duitsers. Groepsvorming onder Duitse immigranten in Utrecht in de negentiende eeuw*. Amsterdam, 2002.

Smeets, Henk, and Fridus Steijlen. *In Nederland gebleven. De geschiedenis van Molukkers 1951–2006*. Amsterdam, 2006.

Vermeulen, Hans, and Rinus Penninx, eds. *Immigrant Integration: The Dutch Case*. Amsterdam, 2000.

Welten, Joost. *In dienst voor Napoleons Europese droom. De verstoring van de plattelandssamenleving in Weert*. Leuven, 2007.

Willems, Wim. *De uittocht uit Indië 1945–1995*. Amsterdam, 2001.

BELGIUM AND LUXEMBOURG

Frank Caestecker

For a long time the migration history of Belgium and the much smaller Luxembourg have run in parallel. The region experienced a period of affluence in the late Middle Ages, which led to an influx of immigrants. The 16th and 17th centuries were less prosperous in economic terms, which in turn changed the flow of migration. The region which today comprises Belgium and Luxembourg remained an area of emigration rather than immigration until the 20th century. This only changed when industrialization took hold in the 19th century and when, in the 20th century, heavy industry drew large numbers of migrant workers. Historical research focuses, for the most part, on migration in the last two centuries, while the migration streams in the early modern period remain underexposed.

The region and its borders

Until 1713 the region that today forms Belgium and Luxembourg fell under Spanish sovereignty followed by Austrian Habsburg rule. After a short French interlude (1795–1815) the area became a part of the Kingdom of the Netherlands under the Dutch king Willem I. In 1830 Luxembourg along with Belgium chose to secede from the Netherlands. An important part of the old Grand Duchy of Luxembourg became incorporated with Belgium while the remainder of Luxembourg, the part that held dynastic ties to the Netherlands, eventually became an autonomous state in 1839.

In the course of the 19th and in particular the 20th century Belgium grew into a bilingual country. In the 19th century state affairs were conducted in French, but by the end of this century the Dutch-speaking majority in the north and west of the country was demanding recognition for its language. In the course of the 20th century, this process would lead to the federalization of the country, and this wave of federalization would also see the small German-speaking community in the southeast of Belgium achieve recognition. Luxembourg, which during the 20th century also developed into a trilingual country, had long regarded French and German as official languages. Luxembourgish, which up to this point had been considered a dialect, was promoted to the third language of the country in 1984, as a result of influence from Luxembourg nationalism.

Aside from the linguistic divide, a second dividing line ran through Belgium: that between the Catholics and the liberals. While Luxembourg always remained a homogenous Catholic country, the position of the Catholic church in Belgium in the 19th and 20th centuries was a source of tension. The difficult relationship between the (Catholic) church and the (liberal) state provided for a unique institutional arrangement, whereby the church and state remained separated, but the state supported the religious structures. Not only churches and mosques but also private education establishments could enjoy such state support.

The consequences of denominational and political conflicts for migration relations in the early modern period

Flanders, in particular, experienced a strong period of prosperity in the late Middle Ages. Bruges and later Antwerp were important centers of international trade and were hubs in the international network of merchants. Flemish merchants established themselves in foreign trading centers, and foreign merchants came to Antwerp and Bruges.[1] In the middle of the 16th century Antwerp in particular attracted many immigrants, including painters and other artists.[2] In the course of the 16th century the economic downturn set in, and this along with powerful political upheaval led to an increase in the number of people who took up residence elsewhere. Between 1540 and 1590, approximately 175,000 people left the region, amounting to 15% to 20% of the population. Initially the destination was England or the German states, but after the campaign of the Spanish governor Alexander Farnese (1578–88) people left *en masse* for the Dutch provinces. The harbor city of Antwerp that surrendered itself to Farnese under relatively favorable terms – the emigrants were allowed to take their capital with them – saw half of her 80,000 inhabitants leave.[3]

The revival of Antwerp in the troubled 17th century meant that once again international trade made great strides and Flemish tradespeople ventured once more into the centers of world trade – for example in the Iberian Peninsula.[4]

---

[1] Spanish merchants in the Netherlands during the early modern period.

[2] Migrant artists in Antwerp in the early modern period.

[3] Netherlandish (Flemish) textile workers in 16th- and 17th-century England; Dutch Calvinist refugees in Europe since the early modern period.

[4] Flemish merchants in the Iberian Peninsula in the early modern period.

A number of small, but in economic terms important, migration streams of highly skilled workers were recorded. In the 17th century Italian and German glassworkers sowed the seeds of the Belgian glass industry, while a few thousand Wallonian metalworkers left for Sweden to instruct workers there in new techniques.[5] The prolonged economic recovery in the relatively calm 18th century stimulated the local merchants to truly integrate into the international trade networks.

In addition to the emigration of highly qualified workers and traders from Flanders, between 1724 and 1786, less skilled migrants from Luxembourg left for the Banat, a region annexed by Vienna. The colonization policy of the Austrian-Habsburg Empire was aimed at the creation of a Catholic and German-speaking population. The Luxembourgers satisfied these criteria and thousands of people left for the Banat in the hope of a better life. In Flanders and Liège on the other hand, the advancement of the proto-industry in the 17th and 18th centuries provided for sufficient means of subsistence and so there was less need for emigration. These relatively rich regions, where weaving and metalworking were practiced in cottage industries, were no part of the early modern North Sea seasonal migrant workers system.[6]

The Belgian-Luxembourg region functioned as a transit area for the seasonal migrant workers from the Rhineland that every year left for the North Sea area, which had a huge demand for seasonal labor. Furthermore, the traditionally highly mobile professional groups from various European regions were also drawn by the demand for various services in the coastal part of Belgium: boilermakers, knife grinders, and chimney sweeps from the Auvergne, as well as itinerant showmen with exotic animals from Parma and Naples. We see other, similarly specialized and strongly regional-centered groups also depart from this area, such as straw hatmakers from the Jeker valley (near Liège) who at the end of the 18th century and in the 19th century migrated to the Netherlands, as well as to France.[7]

Industrial labor migration in Belgium and Luxembourg during the 19th century

In Wallonia, in the 19th century, the proto-industry developed into a modern industry, and in particular, the area around the Sambre and the Meuse became the cradle of industrialization in Belgium. However, in the same period, the Flemish proto-industry was disappearing due to competition with mechanical production. The manufacturing town Ghent, which had modernized textile processing, was an island in a Flemish region in decline. From the middle of the 19th century there was a mass exodus from the Flemish proto-industry textile region. The exodus was

partly to the Wallonian industrial basin and the cities of Antwerp and Brussels.[8] France, however, formed the most important destination for migrants. In part they were seasonal migrants, but the majority settled permanently in the industrial area of northern France. Around 1815 the first Flemish migrant workers left for northern France to man the textile factories that had been set up by textile entrepreneurs from Ghent. After the political separation, Ghent's entrepreneurs wanted to keep providing for the French market with these French branches of their business. They attracted workers from the textile industry in Ghent that was in dire economic straits. In this way a close link between the northern French textile towns and Ghent was established, a link that would be sustained in the following century by the Flemish-French migration stream. The years of famine that began in 1840 caused this migration stream to explode. The appeal of France spread across the whole of Flanders. Toward the end of the 19th century half a million Belgians had established themselves in France, mostly in the industrial Département Nord.[9] Moreover, at least 50,000 Belgian seasonal workers worked annually in the French agricultural industry.

The emigration from agrarian Luxembourg was even more impressive; at the end of the century one-third of the population was domiciled outside of the borders. In 1891 30,000 Luxembourgers lived in France, mostly in Paris. With regard to transatlantic migration from Belgium and Luxembourg the USA was the preferred destination. Occasionally other American states successfully attracted transatlantic emigrants from the Belgian-Luxembourg region. Thus, the USA was less in demand in the 1880s when Argentina offered financial support for the transatlantic journey; from the 1890s Canada would also charm emigrants from Luxembourg and Belgium. For Luxembourg, the transatlantic migration rate was much more important than for Belgium: in 1900, 40,000 Luxembourgers were counted in the USA against 63,000 Belgians.

At the same time, Belgium and Luxembourg experienced immigration in the 19th century. The progressive liberalism of Belgium was appealing for persecuted political activists. Although these refugee streams, with Karl Marx as notorious representative, received much literary attention, these political activists formed only a small, albeit vocal, minority among immigrants in Belgium.

Belgium was the first industrialized country in Continental Europe and depended on highly skilled immigrants. The know-how of English technicians was after all crucial in the first phase of the industrialization. One of them, the mechanic William Cockerill, even became one of the most important entrepreneurs in 19th-century Belgium.[10] But also from other countries entrepreneurs and merchants came to

---

[5] Central and western European miners and smelters in Sweden and Denmark-Norway from the 16th to the 18th century.

[6] German seasonal agricultural laborers in the Netherlands from the 17th to the early 20th century.

[7] Walloon straw hat makers in the Netherlands in the 19th century.

[8] Flemish labor migrants in Wallonia since the 19th century.

[9] Flemish textile workers in western and central Europe since the 19th century: the example of France.

[10] English industrial workers (puddlers) in the Belgian iron industry in the early 19th century.

Belgium. Furthermore, Antwerp, as an important transit port city of great significance for German exports, attracted German traders and businessmen.[11]

When, half a century later, Luxembourg also industrialized, it leaned in particular on German capital and entrepreneurship, while German technicians also manned the command posts of this industry. The background of this strong German presence was the intensive political and economic German-Luxembourgian relations, resulting from the membership of Luxembourg in the German Confederation and the Customs Union (*Zollverein*). Unskilled workers for the Luxembourg industry in the region were scarce. Luxembourg's farmers chose overseas emigration over salaried work in industry in order to maintain their traditional lifestyles. If they chose to work in Luxembourg's industry, this work was merely an additional occupation, supplementary to their agricultural work. This local opposition to proletarianization meant that industry in Luxembourg mostly recruited its workforce from the French, Belgian, and German border regions. In 1913 half of all workers in Luxembourg's industry originated from these foreign border areas.

The industry in the Belgian cities of Liège and Verviers also attracted large numbers of short-distance migrants, sometimes from across the border. As industrialization continued, the need for workers significantly increased in the Wallonian area of the Sambre and the Meuse as well as in Luxembourg's industrial basin, while due to the agricultural crisis in the last quarter of the 19th century in Flanders a large labor pool existed. More and more people left Flanders for the industry in Wallonia and Luxembourg. The Belgian authorities, dominated by homogenous Catholic governments, realized that an economic shift from agriculture to industry was unavoidable. The population of the countryside got the chance, thanks to cheap railway subscriptions, to work in industry but still live in the countryside. The Catholic authorities hoped, in this way, to limit the social and political consequences of industrialization and to prevent a liberal and socialist advance in the Wallonian industrial basin. The number of rail subscriptions distributed to workers in Belgium grew from about 14,000 in 1870 to more than a million in 1890. These political interventions contributed significantly to the creation of a national labor market in Belgium. Improved transport infrastructure gradually transformed Flemish labor migration and seasonal work to northern France into a circular migration. In the 20th century the daily or weekly commute became the dominant form of migration in Belgium. At the end of the 1920s, 70,000 Belgian commuters left every day for northern France.

At the beginning of the 20th century emigration decreased and the Belgian-Luxembourg region became increasingly an area of immigration. Just before World War I, spontaneous immigration could no longer mitigate the need for workers, so recruitment took place on the periphery of Europe. In this way Italians arrived in the Luxembourg and Belgian industry. Alongside the labor migrants for unskilled work in heavy industry, there was also long-distance migration by an economic elite to these industrial economies. The significant economic intertwining of the German Empire with Luxembourg, but also with the port of Antwerp, meant that German entrepreneurs and employees settled in the region. In addition, immigration became more diverse as a result of the arrival, in the second half of the 19th century, of Jews from the German Empire and, from 1890, Jewish refugees from Czarist Russia. An important Jewish community was created in Antwerp and Brussels that specialized in semitraditional branches of industry, such as clothing, leather, and fur, enabling Jewish traders to bring these goods to the consumer. The Antwerp diamond sector was a branch of industry also heavily dominated by Jewish producers and traders. In the 1920s, the diamond sector became the most visible incentive for massive Jewish immigration, particularly from Poland. However, this new Jewish immigration established itself mostly in the semitraditional clothing, leather, and fur production and offered, thanks to vertical integration, an income source for considerable numbers of immigrants. This wave of immigration saw the small Jewish community from the 19th century grow to 50,000 members, who were highly visible due to their geographical and economic concentration.[12]

The migration to Belgium and Luxembourg in this period was barely influenced by political interventions. The ambitions of 19th-century Belgian and Luxembourg immigration policy were limited, as was apparent from the expulsion policy. Only criminal and subversive foreigners were expelled; all other foreigners were free to settle in Belgium and Luxembourg. Especially during the economic crisis of the 1880s, an economic decline that in Belgium coincided with a crisis of the political regime, the tolerance for immigrants decreased and more and more transient job seekers were expelled. By 1896 the regime crisis had been averted and the political will for a strict immigration policy was lost, but this by no means implied a return to the liberal policy from before 1880. Luxembourg also strengthened controls of foreigners toward the end of the 19th century. From 1893 foreign migrants had to register with local authorities, an obligation that had already existed in Belgium from the middle of the 19th century, for Belgians as well as foreigners. This Belgian call for registration was more the result of a liberal concern for a rational state that managed the country with business acumen than out of a need for control and repression of immigrants.

Although this obligation to register was the first step toward the protectionist immigration policy of the 20th century, the immigration policies of Luxembourg and Belgium remained generous. The increasingly relevant dividing line

---

[11] German traders in Antwerp in the 19th century.

[12] Ashkenazim in Europe since the early modern period.

between national citizen and foreigner became, as a result of a liberalization of the rules for obtaining citizenship, easier to bridge for established immigrants. The Luxembourg and Belgian nationality laws were based on the French Civil Code and the right to citizenship included, along with the naturalization of long-established immigrants, the right for children of immigrants who were born in the host country to claim Belgian or Luxembourg citizenship. The French liberalization of the nationality law in 1851 was copied, first in Luxembourg (1878) and later in Belgium (1909). Children born in the host country to immigrants who themselves were also born in the country of immigration automatically received citizenship.

Obtaining Belgian nationality did not require a complete integration into a Belgian cultural model. Long-term residence was by itself considered a sufficient guarantee. The fact that immigrants brought new religious movements into the country and even built up their own education networks was never problematized. The Belgian political regime that was supported by only a limited administrative apparatus considered this situation to be outside of its domain. Liberal anxiety over avoiding abuses of power led to a modest state, which respected the far-reaching autonomy of society. The liberal Belgian regime postulated the absolute neutrality of the state in religious affairs. At the same time, in order to give official support to the religious experience, the state was required to acknowledge the representatives of a religious cult. This paradox, an inheritance of the Roman Catholic tolerance of the Belgian liberal experiment of 1830, ensured that the Belgian state imposed the model of hierarchical and formal Catholicism on other religions. In analogy with the Catholic Council of Bishops, for example, Judaism – a more pluralistic religion – should also create a representative council. The Consistory, the mouthpiece of a liberal Jewish elite, assumed this role. The sustained Jewish immigration from east and central Europe meant that other religious movements within Judaism demanded recognition. The Consistory, to which liberal Judaism adhered, saw its hegemony endangered and was forced to acknowledge the diversity of the Jewish religion. In this way, Orthodox congregations established themselves and Zionist and Jewish education networks developed in Antwerp, all under the shield of the Belgian state.

The recruitment and establishment of an industrial workforce, 1918–1975

After World War I, Belgium and Luxembourg formed an economic union. The political and economic developments, and also the migration patterns, of both countries ran pretty parallel until the 1960s. In this period Belgium and Luxembourg were an immigration area. Emigration decreased significantly in the course of the 20th century, with two brief interruptions: the invasions of Belgium in 1914 and in 1940 were responsible for a massive exodus of refugees. In World War I this led to the long-term absence of roughly 10% of the population.[13] Moreover, in both wars Germany called on Belgian workers, albeit with or without force, to man the war industry.[14]

This emigration was of a temporary nature and that also applied to the migration stream to the Belgian Congo. After the Belgian authorities took over the Congo Free State in 1908 – until then the private domain of King Leopold II – this migration, mostly of the ruling elite, got under way. The emigration remained limited because the area was considered to be an exploitation colony, not a settlement colony. Nevertheless, the number of Belgians in the Belgian Congo rose from 6,000 in 1919 to 20,000 in 1940 and 90,000 on the eve of decolonization. The Belgian presence was scant in relation to the total population, which by Congo's independence (1960) was estimated to be 13 million. Both the Belgian authorities and large Belgian companies wanted a temporary presence of a white male elite, which had to be constantly renewed. The increase in the number of Belgians in the Belgian Congo was, particularly after World War II, accompanied by a more balanced distribution between men and women and also slightly more Belgian small businessmen and traders.

The invasion and occupation by the Germans in 1914–18 led after the war to a fracture of relations between the Belgian-Luxembourg region and Germany. Luxembourg traded-in Germany as an economic partner for Belgium, and the Belgian-Luxembourg region became an economic union. The war experience, the much weaker economic ties with Germany, and the return of many German migrants – often forced – to their home country led to a radical shake-up of the industrial labor market. Local workers became full-time industrial workers and for the remainder of the 20th century formed the core of the employees in Luxembourg's industry. Supported by their unions, they monopolized this labor market until the phasing out of industry in the 1970s. Foreign workers had only a supplementary role, most notably doing low-skilled jobs in the iron and metallurgical industries. It was Luxembourg's construction sector that became the main attraction for the foreign labor migrants.

Likewise, Belgium put out a call for foreign workers. Formal recruitment brought at least a quarter of a million foreign workers to Belgium in the period 1922–74. Eastern Europe, especially Poland, was an important source of workers, until the communist takeover in these countries. After that, only the Hungarian revolt in 1956 would draw another few thousand East Europeans to the heavy industry in Belgium. Half of the foreign labor force recruited for Belgian industry came from Italy. The dominance of Italian migrant workers was even stronger in Luxembourg (see Table 1). Toward the end of the 1950s Belgium also recruited in other Mediterranean countries, first in Spain and Greece and since

---

[13] Belgian refugees in western Europe during World War I.
[14] Polish and Belgian forced laborers in Germany during World War I; forced laborers in Germany and German-occupied Europe during World War II.

Table 1. Foreigners in Belgium and Luxembourg, 1875/1890–2001 (000s)

Belgium	1890	1900	1910	1920	1930	1947	1961	1970	1981	1991	2001
Neighboring countries (Luxembourg, Netherlands, Germany, France, Great Britain)	163	190	226	126	172	164	143	193	226	214	237
Italy	2	3	5	4	33	84	150	231	276	280	196
Turkey						0.6	0.3	20	64	85	56
Other European countries	4	11	21	17	104	100	88	139	116	116	153
Other continents	0.4	1.6	2	2	8	6	13	80	170	224	195
of which from Congo						0.01	3	5	9	12	11
of which from Morocco							0.5	39	105	142	107
Total number of foreigners	171	206	255	150	319	368	453	696	879	901	862
Share of population (%)		3	3.5	2	3.9	4.3	5	7.2	9	9	8.6

Luxembourg	1875	1900	1910	1922	1930	1945	1960	1970	1981	1991	2001
Neighboring countries (Belgium, Netherlands, France, Germany)	6	21	28	24	33	15	20	25	32	36	49
Italy	0.07	7	10	6	14	8	16	24	22	19	19
Portugal								6	29	39	58.7
Other European countries	0.07	0.7	2	2	7	3	2	4	9	14	28
Other continents	0.01	0.2	0.2	0.4	0.6	0.4	2	4	7	16	22.7
Total number of foreigners	5.9	29	39.7	33.4	55.8	29.1	41.5	62.5	95.8	114.2	162.3
Share of population (%)	2.9	12.3	12	12	18.6	7.5	13	18	26	29.7	36.9

Source: Censuses.

1964 also in Turkey and North Africa, while Luxembourg mainly attracted Portuguese migrant workers.[15]

The dynamics of migration and employment were strongly determined by economic conditions. A boom period attracted new migrants, while in times of economic decline the authorities tried to limit their number. In Luxembourg from 1929 and in Belgium from 1936 the government effectively controlled the labor market by making the employment of foreign workers dependent upon government permission. Thereafter, foreigners could only be appointed if there were no suitable Belgian/Luxembourgian workers. Citizenship became the key to the entry into the welfare community that was becoming ever more important with the extension of the welfare state.

[15] Greek labor migrants in western, central, and northern Europe after 1950: the examples of Germany and the Netherlands; Italian labor migrants in northern, central, and western Europe since the end of World War II; Portuguese labor migrants in western and central Europe since the 1950s: the examples of France and Germany; Spanish labor migrants in western, central, and northern Europe since the end of World War II; Turkish labor migrants in western, central, and northern Europe since the mid-1950s.

During the boom of the 1960s, when foreign investment in, among others, the car industry and petrochemistry, radically modernized Flemish economic life, the shortage of workers in the whole of Belgium and Luxembourg rose sharply. Hardly any use was made of long-winded and expensive recruitment methods in this period. As a result of the huge shortages in the labor market, the government lost its grip on labor migration. Migrant workers from Portugal, Turkey, and Morocco arrived spontaneously in Belgium and Luxembourg on tourist visas.

This spontaneous migration influenced the settlement process of the migrant workers. The formal recruitment of Spanish, Greek, and Italian migrant workers in the 1950s happened in discussion with the governments and in concurrence with the labor market politics in the country concerned and led to diversity in the area of origin of the migrant workers. The Turkish, Portuguese, and Moroccan labor migration was in contrast a much more spontaneous process that went hand in hand with chain migration and the phenomenon of transplanted villages.

In this period of mass labor migration, migrant workers were officially categorized as supplementary workers and were no longer considered to be (potential) citizens. The exclusion started after World War I as a nationalist reaction to the occupation, with a sharp mistrust of newcomers. Birth (and residence) was no longer sufficient for obtaining citizenship in the host country. From 1922 the conferring of citizenship to second- and third-generation newcomers in Belgium now depended on the political loyalty of candidate-Belgians. From the 1930s this widened to a call for assimilation of these foreigners in Belgian society. In Luxembourg this demand for cultural assimilation already became official on the eve of World War I, when the right to citizenship for foreigners who were born and raised in the country was radically scrapped. Long-term residence became insufficient for obtaining nationality; only integral assimilation could lead to citizenship.

Migrant communities that strengthened the cultural diversity within society encountered opposition from Flemish and Luxembourg nationalists, who favored an ethnically homogenous society. In Flanders, where after World War I the reduction of French speakers was high on the political agenda, the concomitant mass recruitment of foreign miners was accompanied by a plea for forced assimilation. In Wallonia, however, the elites strongly believed in the autonomous integration possibilities of the local society. For this reason people in Wallonia accepted the support of the country of origin for ethnic education for the children of migrants, while in Flanders this was radically rejected.

In Luxembourg too, until the 1960s, foreign workers, almost exclusively Italians, were considered supplementary labor. Family migration was not stimulated. Single men worked in Luxembourg in the prime of their lives after which they were replaced by new, fresh workers. In the Belgian mines, where there was a structural need for workers, settlement migration was viewed as a long-term solution for the labor shortages. Employers made family homes available or financed travel costs, while the Belgian government enabled the follow-up migration of family members. In the 1960s Luxembourg also subscribed to a similar diversified policy and encouraged Portuguese workers and their families to settle. This change of direction was a consequence of a widely, and now structurally, recognized labor shortage. At the same time the birth rate in both Belgium and Luxembourg declined to such a level that in both countries demographic concerns were voiced. The stimulation of family migration had to counter the drop in population.

Until well into the 20th century industry was the motor for immigration in the Belgian-Luxembourg region. The asylum channel was only a marginal gateway. Immediately after World War II Belgian heavy industry recruited displaced persons in the camps in occupied Germany. These refugee workers were considered first to be a solution to the labor shortage and not so much as persons in need of protection.[16] The protection rendered by the Belgian and Luxembourg authorities played a decisive role in the immigration of those who fled racial persecution in Nazi Germany. Belgium, both before and after World War II, had significantly more Jewish asylum seekers than Luxembourg. This can be explained because of the extensive Jewish community in Belgium that not only had religious but also familial or business ties with the persecuted Jews. To protect the border with Germany was not easy, and the unique refusal by the Belgian government to send Jewish refugees back to Germany once they were in Belgium, made Belgium in the 1930s and in the second half of the 1940s an important sanctuary. In Belgium these Jewish refugees were tolerated only until they found a definitive immigration country; many then departed for the USA or Israel.[17]

Migration and the postindustrial Belgian-Luxembourg region after 1975

In the course of the 20th century, Belgium and Luxembourg increasingly developed from countries of emigration to an area of immigration. At the end of the 20th century even the migration between France and Belgium changed direction. In 2000, every day 20,000 people left high-unemployment-afflicted northern France for Belgium. These commuters mostly did unskilled factory work in the economically strong performing Flemish region around Courtrai. Labor migration remained a gateway to Belgium and Luxembourg, despite the halt on immigration by both countries in 1974.

The economic crisis in the second half of the 1970s heralded the transition to a postindustrial economy. Belgium, and specifically Wallonia, had great difficulty with deindustrialization, while from the 1960s on Luxembourg switched from being an industrial country to a financial service center. In relation to the volume of managed capital, Luxembourg stands at first place in Europe (fourth worldwide) at the beginning of the 21st century, with more than 200 credit institutions. The service sector, the new work provider in Luxembourg, attracted an international elite migration. Many of these highly qualified labor migrants do not live in Luxembourg itself but in the neighboring countries. These commuters now account for more than a third of Luxembourg's workforce. In 2000, Luxembourg counted 430,000 inhabitants and 90,000 commuters. Belgium also has elite migrants, because of international or transnational companies that have had a significant presence in Belgium since the 1960s. This immigration of a few thousand highly qualified people every year, particularly from North America and Japan, relates mostly to internal company migration.

The immigration of skilled laborers grew with the establishment of supranational institutions in the city of Luxembourg

---

[16] Displaced persons (DPs) in Europe since the end of World War II.

[17] Jewish refugees from Nazi Germany and from German-occupied Europe since 1933; political and intellectual refugees from Nazi Germany and from German-occupied Europe, 1933–1945.

and in particular in Brussels while the latter developed into the European capital in the last quarter of the 20th century.[18] Finally, since the 1980s there has been an important immigration of wealthy and/or retired Dutch, and from the beginning of the 21st century, of French too, who mostly settle in the Belgian border area and Brussels for fiscal reasons.

The migration debate about highly qualified labor migration and free migration within the European Union has become overshadowed in the last two decades of the 20th century by the arrival of asylum seekers. This gateway for immigrants offered little prospect of permanent settlement: after the completion of the asylum process, roughly 10% of asylum seekers receive permanent residence status. This asylum channel has, however, led to a number of new migrant communities in Belgium and Luxembourg. In Belgium this has even brought a delayed legacy of the Belgian colonial past with a Congolese community of 30,000 people, two-thirds of whom have obtained Belgian nationality (see Table 1). In Brussels the community has even become identified with its own neighborhood: Matonge, named after the entertainment district in Kinshasa.[19]

The uninvited asylum migration provoked a strict immigration policy, mostly replicating the restrictive initiatives of the larger neighboring countries. Given their inability to come to terms with this asylum stream, Belgium (and Luxembourg) were strong advocates of "Europeanizing" the immigration policy. Today the influence of this Europeanization of the immigration policy, initiated by the Treaty of Amsterdam (1999), on the development of the Belgian and Luxembourg migration situation remains marginal.

In the wake of the labor migration, the immigration to Belgium from North Africa and Turkey persisted in the 1980s and 1990s in the form of family reunion and family formation. Initiatives to stop the flow of this migration stream had little success. Toward the end of the 20th century, the continued marriage migration – half of the second-generation Turks and Moroccans marries a partner from the country of their parents – keeps the close ties with the country of origin in place.

European integration in the 1980s and 1990s ensured free labor migration within the EU and an end to the discrimination of EU citizens in Belgium and Luxembourg. National egotism as expressed *par excellence* by immigration policy, became tempered from the 1960s in Belgium also by trade union pressure and demographic need. The rights within the social security system became less directly tied to citizenship. Also, immigrants from outside the EU became entitled to welfare benefits. The Belgian welfare state, which in the postindustrial transition was strongly engaged in the fight against poverty, functioned for the immigrants and their descendants in the last decades of the 20th century as a dam against impending poverty. Chances at the labor market

became restricted because the migrants remained focused on the industrial labor market, which was in serious crisis.

The Belgian discourse about immigrants and their offspring increasingly developed in the last decades of the 20th century along two lines. The Flemish fight to become "masters of their own destiny" and the desire for the boundaries of Flanders to correspond with the boundaries of the Flemish language produced an essentialist vision of ethnicity. This rather fundamentalist vision of "difference" of immigrant groups in Flanders strengthened in the last decades of the 20th century when social problems were increasingly emphasized in the electoral success of the Flemish Bloc (*Vlaams Blok*). The rise of this extreme-right xenophobic party in Flanders was a shock for the traditional parties and led to an institutional extension of the integration policies. This meant a break with the past, as immigrants became officially considered an integral part of Belgian society. There were differences, though, between both regions of Belgium. While in Flanders the traditional political elite cherished the cultural specificity of the migrant communities and developed a policy for ethnic minorities, French-speaking Belgium rejected a similar policy and advocated an ethnically neutral equal opportunities policy. A reconciliation between both points of view was realized at a national level with an integration policy that became institutionally supported by the Centre for Equal Opportunities and Opposition to Racism (Centrum voor Gelijkheid van Kansen en Racismebestrijding) established in 1993.

The Belgian integration policy concentrated on the fight against discrimination and making Belgian nationality available to immigrants. The 19th-century definition that long-term residence was a sufficient guarantee for obtaining Belgian nationality was once again adopted. Since 1991, third-generation foreigners – that is, children who are born in Belgium from parents of whom at least one was also born in Belgium – acquire Belgian nationality automatically, while children of immigrants born and raised in Belgium can claim Belgian citizenship again. In 2000 these rights to claim Belgian citizenship were radically extended to (nearly) everyone resident in Belgium for a minimum of seven years.

In Luxembourg, entry to the nation remained restricted to a select public: obtaining Luxembourg nationality was still considered to be the reward for a successful process of assimilation. With the promotion of Luxembourgish as the national language in 1984, this assimilation became a concrete and official objective: since 2001 an officially adjudicated basic knowledge of this language is required of candidate-Luxembourgers.

In Belgium the new integration policy led to a reluctant recognition of Islam, the second religion of the country. In 1974 Islam was recognized as a Belgian cult, but this acknowledgment came via an organization that worked under Saudi Arabian wings. This decision was more a diplomatic agreement – with oil as the lubricant – than an expression of the acceptance of Muslim immigration. The migrant communities, however, did not recognize themselves in this Saudi

---

[18] European and American civil servants of supranational organizations in Brussels since 1958.

[19] Congolese in Belgium since the 1960s.

version of Islam which, and together with the Islamophobia after the Iranian revolution of 1979, made the recognition of Islam virtually impossible. As a result, the financial advantages of recognition were not put into practice; the salaries of imams were not paid and the prayer rooms were not subsidized. With the extension of the integration policy in the 1990s, Islam could no longer be discriminated against. An internal solution, such as that for the Jews in the 19th century, turned out not to be possible for Islamic groups. In 1998 an election was held, under strict government control – "fundamentalists" should be excluded – to install an umbrella Muslim organization, and 70,000 people registered as Muslim on the electoral rolls. The chosen representatives had great difficulties in organizing a "Belgian Islam." Only in 2007 did scant public subsidies begin to be granted to Islam in Belgium.

Today one-third of the population of Luxembourg and at least one-ninth of Belgium's population have a migrant background. The migration to and from the Belgian-Luxembourg region was first and foremost a response to socioeconomic processes. The immigrants to this region have obtained a permanent place in these immigration societies. Since the last quarter of the 20th century immigrants from outside the European Union were increasingly considered undesirable, as it was found that they integrate only with great difficulty. The problematization of this immigration can be placed in a societal context of deindustrialization and rapid globalization – a globalization that expresses itself visually in new migrations. Regionalism as a reaction to strengthening globalization is expressed especially strongly in the Belgian-Luxembourg space with the development of a new national identity in Luxembourg and a decaying Belgian nation resurrecting itself in a Flemish and a Francophone, but not Wallonian, identity.

Migration is used by these 21st-century nationalists as a symbol for this budding nationalism. The state is being called on to defend its physical borders, and to curb the expressions of "being different" by "recent" immigrants and their offspring. This approach, which caricatures immigration, putting it face to face with national sovereignty, appears to be working and puts Flemish far-right extremism in a position to develop its extensive electoral following. As a result, the emotional rejection of immigrants and immigration is gaining a certain respectability. The management of migration, however, is not simply a question of political will and in any case the assimilation of the migrant cannot be forced. This impatience puts a heavy mortgage on the development of the Belgian-Luxembourg immigration society.

REFERENCES

Beyers, Leen. *Iedereen zwart? Het samenleven van nieuwkomers en gevestigden in de mijncité Zwartberg, 1930–1980.* Amsterdam, 2007.

Caestecker, Frank. *Vluchtelingenbeleid in de naoorlogse periode.* Brussels, 1992.

Caestecker, Frank. *Alien Policy in Belgium, 1840–1940: The Creation of Guest Workers, Refugees and Illegal Aliens.* Oxford, 2000.

Coudenys, Wim. *Leven voor de Tsaar. Russische bannelingen, samenzweerders en collaborateurs in België.* Leuven, 2004.

Gallo, Benito. *L'immigration italienne au Luxembourg.* Luxembourg, 1987.

Goddeeris, Idesbald. *Poolse migratie in België,* Amsterdam, 2005.

Lesthaeghe, Ron, ed. *Communities and Generations: Turkish and Moroccan Populations in Belgium.* Brussels, 2000.

Morelli, Anne. "L'appel à la main-d'œuvre italienne pour les charbonnages et sa prise en charge à son arrivée en Belgique dans l'immédiat après-guerre." *Belgisch Tijdschrift voor Nieuwste Geschiedenis* 19, 1–2 (1988): 83–130.

Morelli, Anne, ed. *Geschiedenis van het eigen volk. De vreemdeling in België van de prehistorie tot nu.* Leuven, 1993.

Morelli, Anne, ed. *Belgische Emigranten. Oorlogsvluchtelingen, economische migranten en politieke vluchtelingen uit onze streken van de 16de eeuw tot vandaag.* Berchem, 1999.

Pauly, Michel, ed. *Lëtzebuerg de Lëtzebuerger? Le Luxembourg face à l'immigration.* Luxembourg, 1984.

Rea, Andrea. "Immigration, Etat et citoyenneté. La formation de la politique d'intégration des immigrés de la Belgique." Unpublished PhD diss, Brussels University, 2000.

Reuter, Antoinette. "Luxembourg. Histoires croisées des migrations." *Migrance* 20 (2002): 4–9.

Schreiber, Jean Philippe. *Politique et religion: Le Consistoire central israélite de Belgique au XIXe siècle.* Brussels, 1995.

Schreiber, Jean Philippe. *L'immigration juive en Belgique du Moyen Age à la première guerre mondiale.* Brussels, 1996.

Scuto, Denis. "Qu'est-ce qu'un Luxembourgeois? Histoire de la nationalité Luxembourgeoise du Code Napoléon à nos jours." *Hémecht, Revue d'histoire Luxembourgeoise* 58, 2 (2006): 73–96.

Vranken, Jan, Chris Timmerman, and Katrien Van der Heyden, eds. *Komende generaties. Wat weten we (niet) over allochtonen in Vlaanderen.* Leuven, 2001.

Winter, Anne. "'Vagrancy'" as an Adaptive Strategy: The Duchy of Brabant, 1767–1776." *International Review of Social History* 49 (2004): 249–78.

FRANCE

Leslie Page Moch

Immigration to France has a long and fascinating history which has taken on considerable importance since the mid-19th century. Because France was the largest nation in western Europe in the early modern period, internal migration accounted for most human movement that supplied workers and artisans to needy fields, towns, and cities. Moreover, at this time, there was more emigration to France's colonies in the Americas than immigration from abroad. The Revolution of 1789 opened a period of political immigration to those attracted by French politics and émigré departures by those repelled by revolutionary politics. The postrevolutionary period signaled the beginning of France's declining birthrate, which was fundamental to the need for immigrant labor in the late 19th and 20th centuries. Three great waves of immigration (ca. 1900, 1920s, and 1960–75) brought unprecedented numbers of immigrants into France. The 20th century, marked by wars, economic crises, xenophobia, the collapse of the empire, and the globalization of migration patterns, created new and varied patterns of immigration and integration.

France and its borders

Compared with other European countries, France has current territorial borders that are are rather old. With the expansionist wars of Louis XIV in the second half of the 17th century as well as during the reign of his successor Louis XV, albeit more slowly, in the middle of the 18th century in the northwest, northeast, and southeast the current borders were set. The large-scale Napoleonic conquests in west, middle, and southern Europe were soon lost with the Congress of Vienna in 1814/15. Savoy and Nice were acquired in 1860 as a reward for the French support of the Italian unification movement. Alsace Lorraine, ceded by France after the war with Prussia in 1870, was recovered after World War I.

France was one of the most important European colonial powers. The extensive overseas possessions in the early modern period were largely lost, however, in the competition with the British Empire already in the 18th century. With the conquest of Algeria in 1830 and the expansion in Africa and Asia since the 1850s, a new vast colonial empire came about. The decolonization during the 1950s and 1960s was accompanied by numerous military conflicts and outright war, especially in Indochina and Algeria. The remains of the colonial empire are the overseas departments and territories in the Caribbean and the Pacific.

Internal migrations and emigration during the early modern period

Old regime France was alive with movement in countryside and city, most of which was internal migration. Harvest workers moved in a local or regional itinerary, and in the south they were aided by highland villagers. Regional towns and cities were, for the most part, fed by their geographically proximate demographic basin. Most fieldwork could be carried out by French labor – even in the vast fields of the Ile de France. By the end of the 18th century the coastal plain of southern France attracted Spanish and Italians to work the grape and grain harvests and to work in Marseilles.

Indeed, immigrants and visitors were crucial to old regime France. The city of Paris – largest city on the Continent from 1650 until after 1800 – attracted many foreigners. Perhaps best known are the artists and intellectuals who enriched the artistic community, court, and salons; these include the German composer C. W. Gluck, the philosopher Jean-Jacques Rousseau from Geneva, the German writer Melchior Grimm, and the US writer and politician Benjamin Franklin. Artisans and experts were not numerous but they were crucial to France's economic development in the 17th and 18th centuries. These include the Dutch engineers who managed the draining of the Marais neighborhood in Paris and large areas in southwestern France between the Loire and Gironde rivers; the Swedish tar experts who came to the aid of naval construction; the Dutch who instructed the French in fine textiles; and the English founders of the Creusot iron industry.

Foreign troops were an integral part of the old regime military landscape, and among these, Swiss served as the most stable recruits for the king.[1] Finally, the commercial elites of trade cities included international merchants. For example, Italians played a centuries-old role in Lyon; in Bordeaux, German, Anglo-Irish, and Dutch merchants were among the

---

[1] Swiss mercenaries in Europe from the 17th to the 19th century: the example of France.

elite, as were Jews of Iberian origin.[2] With the defeat of the Jacobites in England, some 12,000 officers, soldiers, women, and children escaped to France where smaller groups of their countrymen lived in Irish seminaries in Paris, Nantes, and Bordeaux.[3]

In the 17th and 18th centuries (especially ca. 1660–1730), emigration may have been more significant than immigration, particularly the loss of more than 150,000 Huguenots, most around the time of the Revocation of the Edict of Nantes in 1685; about a third departed for Britain, a third for the Netherlands, and a third for Switzerland, Germany, and North America.[4] No other emigration comes close; the founding emigrations to Canada called a total of perhaps 27,000, nearly half of whom were soldiers and most of the rest were single men, including temporary workers, priests, and missionaries, many of whom returned to France. Among the few women were the *filles du roi*, recruited from a Paris orphan hospice to marry settlers and who did stay on. French in the Caribbean colonies included about 28,000 on Saint Domingue and 25,000 on Martinique and Guadeloupe (in addition to 12,000 on the Pacific islands), where men outnumbered women more than in Canada.

Less exotic were the important colonies of French from the *massif central* who worked and traded in the cities and countrysides of Spain and which were estimated at 80,000 in 1789; like emigration to the Caribbean and Canada, this included both temporary and permanent departures and was almost exclusively male.[5] The Revolutionary upheavals and Napoleonic Empire to come would dramatically curtail emigrations to Spain and the Caribbean colonies.

Jews in France were welcomed in some areas and reviled in others, so the conditions of these so-called outsiders varied considerably. In the 1780s, communities of Jews included a total of 30,000 to 35,000, primarily in the southwest, northeast, Comtat Venaissin, and Paris. The Sephardic Jews from Iberia and Askenazis from German settlements entered France by distinct routes and histories. Askenazis faced the most hostility and violence in Alsace through the Revolutionary period, after which emancipation was almost completely realized under the Napoleonic Empire.[6]

The effects of the French Revolution

For the foreign-born as well as for Jews, old regime and Revolutionary France presented contradictions of welcome and expulsion. In the years of the 1789 Revolution and before, France attracted sympathetic political thinkers from abroad who were engaged in the struggles of the age against absolutism, including the likes of Thomas Jefferson and Thomas Paine. The waves of political refugees included those expelled from Fribourg in 1781, Geneva in 1782, the Dutch Republic in 1787, Belgium and Liège in 1790.[7] They came to a France that explicitly saw itself as a beacon of liberty. During the Terror, foreigners ceased to be welcome and came to be seen as part of a "foreign plot" until Thermidor, after which some of the friends of liberty, like Madame de Staël and Benjamin Constant, returned.

The Revolution was less attractive to conservatives like Edmund Burke, who preferred to make their commentaries from afar. Moreover, there was a mass departure of more than 150,000 anti-Revolutionary French and French whose lives and property were endangered by the Revolutionary government, particularly in 1793–4 under the Convention. These *émigrés*, some of whom were prepared to join forces invading France, came from all levels of society, but the one-fifth of them who were members of the royal family and wealthy nobles were influential in England, German territories, and in the friendly courts of the Continent. Over a quarter of the *émigrés* were women and most ultimately returned to France.[8]

The political practices of the Revolutionary period were on the whole inclusive of newcomers to France. Although at times neglected and ill-interpreted, between the laws of 1790 and the constitution of 1795, thousands of foreigners were naturalized by residing in France (for five years), marrying a French woman, or having a commercial enterprise in France; the majority of foreigners residing in France automatically were naturalized until 1795. Thereafter a declaration of intention was required and in 1799, ten years of residence – but throughout, the territorial principle of *ius soli* applied: one was French if one was born or resided in France. With the Civil Code in 1803, the principle of *ius sanguinis* triumphed: all those born of a French father were French.

Internal labor migrants and political refugees, 1815–1880

The end of the Napoleonic era left a million demobilized soldiers from the grand army – many were foreigners who only gradually returned home, leaving deserters and *trainards* behind who mixed with former subjects of the empire.[9] With the failed revolutions of 1820 came refugees from Spain, Italy, and Poland. Perhaps 20,000 refugees in all arrived between 1830 and 1850, half from Poland, but refugees were only a few of the foreigners in France.[10] For example, the 2,000 Italian

---

[2] German maritime traders in Cádiz and Bordeaux from the late 17th to the late 19th century; Irish brandy merchants in the Charentes in the 18th century; Sephardim in Europe in the early modern period.

[3] Jacobites in Europe, 1688–1788; British Royalists in western, central, and southern Europe, 1640–1660.

[4] Huguenots in Europe since the 16th century.

[5] Auvergnese in Spain in the early modern period.

[6] Sephardim in Europe in the early modern period; Ashkenazim in Europe since the early modern period.

[7] Dutch political refugees from the Batavian Republic in France, 1787–1795.

[8] French Revolutionary refugees in Europe after 1789: the example of Germany.

[9] European soldiers in the Napoleonic army.

[10] Polish political refugees in central and western Europe in the 19th century.

refugees who arrived in 1832 were a minority among 20,000 Italian compatriot seasonal and long-term immigrants.[11]

Although immigration would not become massive until after 1850, entrepreneurial families came early on whose enterprises would change working lives, internal migration, and immigration to France with the advent of factory industry. Commercial elites became important in banking and trade in Lyon, Marseilles, Bordeaux, and Paris. In a remarkable feat of national identity, German families such as the Krugs, Heidsiecks, and Pipers developed champagne into a quintessentially French product. More important to the labor force were the many foreign innovators who opened textile mills, such as the Englishman Rawle who employed 1,200 workers near Rouen at the beginning of the Restoration. Swedes, Swiss, Belgians, and especially English set up iron and steel mills in eastern France as well as machine shops in Paris, some during the Revolutionary and Imperial periods. In most cases, these entrepreneurs from neighboring nations integrated themselves with local elite families. Skilled laborers accompanied foreign enterprise – steelworkers and especially machinists.[12] Perhaps a peak of 60,000 skilled laborers gathered in the large cities, particularly in Paris and Marseilles, recruited by non-French employers. Thus among the 10,000 workers who built the Paris-Rouen railroad, half were British.

Germans in France had a different profile. Some had been coming to Paris as part of apprenticeships and *compagnonnages* since the 17th century, and many workers came to France after 1815, pushed out by agricultural crises and protectionist laws and by the conservative Carlsbad Decrees of 1819. Others simply traversed France as part of the wave of Germans en route to Le Havre and then the USA, but a great number remained in France and grew from about 30,000 in 1830 with about 7,000 in Paris to 170,000 at their peak with about 60,000 in Paris on the eve of 1848. Germans were well known among the tailors in Paris of the 1840s, where there were two Germans for every five male clothing workers, and one in three bootmakers; many were also cabinetmakers, typesetters, and blacksmiths.[13] This group included intellectuals and political activists as well as laborers, women as well as men. Germans would be expelled from France with the Franco-Prussian war of 1870–1, but would return to Paris after the war as shopkeepers, workers, and a majority of women who worked primarily as domestic servants – but also once again as political refugees, this time from Bismarck's antisocialist laws. The expulsions of World War I put an end to the German community in Paris.

Many Italians, Spanish, and above all, Poles, were also in France as political refugees. What was called the Great Emigration of Poles, 1830–1, included many intellectuals and artists like Frederic Chopin and many aristocrats;

Table 1. Principal nationalities in France, 1851–1946					
	1851 (%)	1881 (%)	1911 (%)	1931 (%)	1946 (%)
Belgians	42.4	50.4	28.6	11.9	11.1
Germans*	18.5	9.8	11.9	3.4	–
Spaniards	9.9	7.7	10.5	16.4	22.0
Italians	20.9	25.2	41.7	37.6	32.8
Swiss	8.3	6.9	7.3	–	–
Poles	–	–	–	23.6	30.8
Portuguese	–	–	–	2.3	1.6
Algerians	–	–	–	4.9	1.6
Total principal nationalities (000s)	302	957	1,005	2,148	1,373
Other nationalities (000s)	77	44	155	567	371
Total all foreigners (000s)	379	1,001	1,160	2,715	1,744

* Including Austria-Hungary until 1881.
Source: Calculated from Noiriel, *Population*.

nonetheless about 8,000 in total came to France.[14] At first welcomed by a France that wished to integrate and include asylum seekers, and urged them to join the French Foreign Legion which was established in 1831, France sought ways to reduce refugees by the mid-1830s by insisting that they join the Foreign Legion, turning them back at the border, or insisting that they abstain from political activity. Nonetheless, during the July Monarchy (1832–48), France took in many more refugees than any other country, and by 1846 an estimated 820,000 foreigners resided in France.[15]

With the crises and revolutions of 1848, France was briefly open to naturalizations in the spring of that year, but with more restrictive legislation, followed by the election of Louis Napoleon as president, France became more politically repressive and restrictive to outsiders. As a consequence the majority of the foreign born left France, so that by 1851 when the Second Empire was declared, and when foreigners were counted for the first time, the census enumerated only about 380,000 (see Table 1). These were primarily workers from neighboring countries who lived in the borderlands and Paris. One in three of these was a Belgian in the mines, factories, and fields of the north; one in six was an Italian, in the southeast and Paris; groups half that size came from Spain and Switzerland.[16]

---

[11] Italian refugees of the *risorgimento* in central and western Europe in the 19th century.

[12] British technical experts in France in the first half of the 19th century.

[13] German cabinetmakers in Paris in the 18th century.

[14] Polish political refugees in central and western Europe in the 19th century.

[15] Russian revolutionaries in western and central Europe in the 19th and early 20th centuries; German soldiers in the French Foreign Legion in the 19th and 20th centuries.

[16] Flemish textile workers in western and central Europe since the 19th century: the example of France; Italian industrial workers in western and central Europe in the late 19th and early 20th centuries; Italian workers in the construction industry in the Paris region since the 1870s.

Mass immigrations begin, 1880–1914

The second Industrial Revolution in France demanded more labor than its people could provide, particularly as the crises of the 1840s gave way to the prosperity of the Second Empire (1852–70). From the beginning, the recruitment of foreign workers was a managerial strategy to acquire an abundant, compliant, and inexpensive labor force. In the 1886–1911 period, the numbers of foreigners peaked for the first time at over a million. As ever, the history of each national group and French region is unique. The arrival of Belgians in the north was the strongest at first: the number almost quadrupled by 1886, when they reached their peak at some 486,000 and were nearly half the foreigners in France. They were, for example, 8,000 of the 14,000 miners at the Compagnie d'Anzin. Spanish doubled their numbers by 1876, and then tripled by 1911, working primarily in agriculture in the southwest. Swiss also doubled their numbers. Italians expanded the most: although relatively few arrived before the end of the Second Empire in 1871, they outnumbered Belgians and were nearly 40% of France's foreign born by 1911. Altogether, at the outbreak of the Great War, France's neighbors accounted for 89% of the foreign born (Italians, Belgians, Spanish, Swiss, and Germans), and a larger proportion than ever before were Italians.

Belgians performed primarily three kinds of work. In the Paris area, some 30,000 or more (in 1867) were industrial and construction workers whose numbers spread beyond eastern Paris out to the industrial suburbs. In the north, the labor of Belgian men and women was essential to the success of France's textile industry in and around Roubaix and Lille, where they provided weavers and less skilled millworkers. Finally, throughout the north and the Paris basin, Belgian seasonal laborers weeded and harvested as the sugar beet and potato became mass-produced crops. In 1906, Belgians were still a third of the foreigners in France and had in many cases settled, naturalized, and intermarried in the northern borderlands.[17]

Italian immigrants followed a long tradition, entering France to work as they had since the 16th century as artists, performers, and traveling workers: the bear trainers, musicians, and actors were accompanied by cobblers, knife-grinders, turners, glaziers, artisans who caned chairs, and street vendors of ices in the summer and chestnuts in the winter.[18] They were most numerous in the southeast (east of a line running from Nancy to Montpellier), especially in Savoy and Nice which had been part of Italy until 1860. When their numbers expanded from 1878 to 1882, Italians had begun to work as coachmen, tailors and other clothing workers, shoemakers, masons, carpenters, and stucco workers. They offered competition to the well-known masons and construction workers of central France who were particularly well known in Paris and Lyon. They were welcome as unskilled navvies in construction and infrastructure projects.[19]

Along the Mediterranean littoral, Italian men gathered salt and both men and women worked in the fields picking fruit, olives, and flowers. Women wound and spun silk in mills as far north as Lyon. Men worked in the quarries and mines of the east and even in Normandy. They specialized as metallurgists in naval yards and workers in the chemical factories of Marseille. Italians concentrated first in Nice, and in Marseilles, where they were a quarter of the population in 1911. Before World War I, there were important colonies of Italians in Lyon and Paris, and especially in the mines of Lorraine around Nancy and in Le Briey. Most traveled in male groups (especially seasonal workers), but Italians included family groups that would begin the integration into French society and men who would marry French women.

The massive immigrations of the end of the century – the first great wave – were not without problems. At the time of the end-of-century economic depressions, popular xenophobia brought out crowds that lashed out at foreigners. Belgians were attacked in the north; Italians were lynched in the south; and in 1893 there was a mass movement that ended in the murder of Italian salt workers in Aigues Mortes on the Mediterranean coast. A similar incident the following year in Lyon followed the assassination of French President Sadi Carnot by an Italian anarchist. At the same time, a more intellectual racism based on biological "science" was directed against the Jews of France, who were pictured as foreigners.[20] This anti-Semitism underlay the accusation of Captain Dreyfus of treason in 1898 and the long and divisive battle that subsequently divided the nation. The joint hostilities of xenophobia and racism in times of economic insecurity that marked the end of the 19th century would mark the 20th century as well.

Two groups of foreigners who did not hail from neighboring countries began coming to France before the Great War and would subsequently become very important. The first consisted of about 2,000 Polish miners who passed from Westphalia to the northern mines. The second were the Kabyles from the Algerian mountains, who came at about 5,000 per year after 1911; these men went primarily to the factories of Marseilles and the mines of the north. They were the first newcomers from the African and Asian colonies that France had taken since 1830, and as such, they were carefully supervised subjects, rather than citizens, of France. Cradle-loaders in the mines, cattle-drivers, dockworkers, and refinery workers, Algerian men held the least desirable jobs in France and in this period lived without families or sizable communities. The situation of the Kabyles of Algeria forecast immigration in a time of war, when the needs of war and

---

[17] Flemish textile workers in western and central Europe since the 19th century: the example of France.

[18] Italian street musicians in 19th-century Europe; Comici dell'arte in Europe in the early modern period.

[19] Italian industrial workers in western and central Europe in the late 19th and early 20th centuries; Italian workers in the construction industry in the Paris region since the 1870s.

[20] Eastern European Jews in Paris since the late 19th century.

the market for wartime products would dominate considerations of community, family, and integration.

It was in this period of peak immigration that the citizenship laws of France were articulated. Since 1848, foreigners had sought permanent residence in France rather than naturalization because it provided a less costly and restrictive avenue to living in France, particularly because it extended benefits to wives and children and obligated no one to military service. Moreover, the attitude of the French was assimilatory. Two kinds of considerations changed this situation – more internationalist trends embodied in the Anglo-French Cobden-Chevalier Treaty of 1860 and the formation of the German customs union pressured the French to be less restrictive to foreigners, and subsequently the residence requirement for naturalization was lowered from ten to three years in 1867 and the necessity for passports for entry (and internal travel) was ended by 1874. Second, France (and especially the northern provinces where the foreign population was most dense) was acutely aware that an increasing proportion of young men – immigrants and their sons – had no obligation to serve in the military. This was especially understood as a problem after France's defeat in the Franco-Prussian war of 1870–1. The numbers of children born to foreigners in northern France increased during the economic depression that began in 1873 – and they were more attractive to some employers than French young men precisely because they were not at risk of an absence for military service.

Debate in the senate began in 1882 around the question of citizenship by residence or bloodline. The resolution only came seven years later: the Citizenship Law of 1889 is considered to be an inclusive law of the "soil" because it granted citizenship to the children of foreigners born in France and encouraged assimilation – and so made them subject to army service as well. There are aspects of this legislation that made it a law of the "blood," since children born of French living abroad were also French citizens. The law was inclusive insofar as it welcomed the foreign born and included their children in the nation, thus providing a countercurrent to the popular xenophobia of the period. It was exclusive – and became more so – as it was amended in the 1890s to deny the foreign born medical benefits and to limit their numbers in construction and public work projects. Finally, citizenship law applied primarily to men alone, since a married woman was obliged to take her husband's nationality.

Although France employed many immigrant workers – men and women – and many foreigners settled in France, the international labor force of its mines, mills, and fields was not exceptional because workers of many nationalities also labored where industry, infrastructure construction, and farming were carried out on a large scale throughout western Europe and North America.

France was exceptional only in that the French did not participate in the mass emigrations to the Western Hemisphere that characterized most of Europe, 1845–1914. The primary explanation for limited emigration is the early decline of the birthrate in France, which enabled the French to stay home. Yet the state also discouraged emigration, and even despite this, over 816,000 French emigrated to North and South America before 1924.

The effects of the First World War

The Great War of 1914 signaled the 20th century's first abrupt change and crisis in international migration. Many immigrants were defined as the enemy and quickly left France. There were exceptions, however, as the army – the engine of integration *par excellence* – welcomed over 42,000 foreign born of 52 nationalities who volunteered to fight for France. Some were refugees or immigrants acting in opposition to their homeland or fighting out of gratitude to their adopted nation. Most were assigned to the Foreign Legion, designed as a military instrument to integrate foreigners. The largest group was over 7,000 Italians, who were able to form an autonomous regiment, the *Légion garibaldienne*, and joined with the Italian forces in 1915. Others, like the Jews among the 2,800 Russian volunteers, were treated less well and in some cases denied naturalization at the war's end.

During the war the French state took on essential functions in controlling migration that included building a systematic Parisian office to track immigrants under the auspices of the police. For wartime purposes, the state recruited labor migrants and soldiers abroad. Soldiers were predominantly enlisted in the colonies and partly deployed in Europe. For example, the state brought the *tirailleurs sénégalais* into the French army as part of the imperial fighting forces. Moreover, men were recruited to work in the war who had not before worked in France. They were recruited exclusively as wartime labor, and were expected to leave after the war. Integration, in other words, was hardly the concern of wartime recruitment.

Nearly 100,000 wartime workers were prisoners of war forced to join wartime construction and armaments efforts. Other labor recruitment began with neighbors – about 150,000, primarily from Spain; then a new recruiting service brought in over 80,000 Italians, Portuguese, Greeks, and Spaniards. About 86,000 Algerians were recruited to fight and 78,000 more – along with 55,000 Moroccans and Tunisians, 50,000 Vietnamese, and 37,000 Chinese – 220,000 colonial workers in all, who in many cases were not volunteers but more or less coerced workers. Of these, 100,000 worked in the armaments industries with French women, another new group of recruits. Most of the colonial workers were quickly sent home with the end of the war, in the first months of 1919.[21]

Not everyone could return. Some French, displaced by the German invasion, found their home area ruined and had to relocate. And newcomers quickly arrived; refugees and exiles from the war, the Russian Revolution, the Armenian

---

[21] Chinese student workers in France after World War I; Chinese contract workers in France during World War I.

genocide, and subsequent conflicts in central Europe and Russia sent 400,000 people to France before 1923.[22] Despite the official policy of welcome, each group – from Russians to Poles and Armenians – experienced the dislocations of moving into a new society in particularly stressful circumstances. In another result of the war, 50,000 French took up residence in Alsace-Lorraine in place of 150,000 Germans who fled to Germany after 1918, or were evicted by the French state.[23]

Immigration during the 1920s

The 1920s were an era of unprecedented immigration that built on the reputation of Paris as the capital of Europe for intellectuals, musicians, and other artists; it would also result in the settlement and integration of many Europeans in France.[24] In a sense, this is a decade that most deeply affected the French population to date with its infusion of newcomers who would stay on. On one hand, the groups from prewar times reasserted themselves and became more likely to become integrated into French society. On the other, some newer migration streams developed and the balance shifted among national groups. In any case, in the 1920s, immigration was so important that by 1931, the census reflected a record number of foreign born – over 2.8 million.

For the most part, this was labor migration, much encouraged by employers with the help of private recruiting agencies like the *Société générale d'immigration* (SGI), particularly for employers in mining, metallurgy, and agriculture. The state also negotiated accords with allies like Poland and Czechoslovakia. Mine companies arranged to bring in 7,000 Italians in January of 1919 and by the end of that year, the first train left Warsaw with 800 Polish miners on board. Lyonnais manufacturers sought out workers in Armenian communities. By 1924, mining, metallurgy, and agricultural employers joined forces to recruit foreign labor.

Italians doubled their 1911 numbers to 808,000 by 1931, probably a million including temporary and illegal migrants. A third were women. Although Italians remained the largest group of immigrants, the balance among foreigners was changing. Spaniards increased to 352,000. Neighbors – included Belgians, Germans, and Swiss – barely made up the majority of immigrants at 55%, and the rest were from groups that had been very small before the war. These included Poles, above all. While there were 46,000 in France in 1921, there were 508,000 a decade later, and Poles were second only to Italians among immigrants and nearly 20% of all foreigners in 1931. Many other people came out of Russia and Armenia (about 67,000 from each by 1931), Czechoslovakia, the Balkans, and eastern Europe. They were joined by about 300,000 North African citizens from the colonies, especially Algeria. The integration of each group followed a distinct trajectory.

Poles initially came to work as miners in the north, where many came by the trainload along with their families in the early 1920s. Among them were thousands who had worked for years or even decades in the German Ruhr area.[25] Wives and daughters found employment in the textile mills of the north, although in a foretaste of the late century, this sometimes demanded a long daily commute. As Poles moved to mining communities elsewhere in France and as new groups came into the mines, they entered other lines of work. In these years, Belgian immigration was on the wane and Italian immigration was becoming less important as Polish immigration was growing.

Many immigrant workers moved with the construction trades and seasonal work. Portuguese and Spanish cut slate in the Pyrenees; Italians worked the ovens in tile and brickworks, and split granite and quartz in quarries. Their glassmakers met competition from Bohemians. The building trades were hungry for masons, carpenters, and plasterers, particularly to rebuild in the war zones in the early 1920s. In Paris, immigrants worked to dismantle the old city walls and expand the metro. They built low-cost apartments and bourgeois villas and, in the end, the Maginot Line.

By the end of the 1920s, a third of coal miners were immigrants, 50% of cement workers, 50% to 70% of workers in the artificial silk mills, and 70% of men in the iron mines. Italians were the "men of iron" in the mines and mills of the east. Immigrants also took to the fields where Italians, for example, were recruited to southwestern France. Where there had been none in 1920, 100,000 became part of agricultural communities, primarily in the Haute-Garonne and the Gers.[26]

An international labor force manned the factories and fields, as it had at the turn of the century. For example, two-thirds of the labor force of the steelworks of Longwy were foreigners; already in 1920 these mills employed 1,700 French, 1,030 Italians, 497 Poles, 1,194 Belgians and Luxembourgers, 206 Czechs, Yugoslavs, and Russians, and 325 from a dozen other countries. French worked side by side with immigrants in the fields as well. For example, in the domain of Passy-en-Valois (Aisne), 50 French seasonal workers worked with 44 Poles, 16 Belgians, 8 Swiss, and 4 Czechs. France needed workers, and in the 1920s they came from abroad.

Acutely aware of its low birthrate and disastrous losses in the Great War, France welcomed immigrants and eased their integration. In 1927, the naturalization law was modified to facilitate assimilation and citizenship by reducing the 10 years of residency required before naturalization to three years. As at the turn of the century, immigration led in many

---

[22] Russian emigrants in Europe since 1917; Armenian refugees in France since World War I.

[23] German immigrants in Germany from territories ceded after World War I.

[24] American writers, visual artists, and musicians in interwar Paris; African students from the sub-Saharan Region in France since the late 19th century.

[25] Polish industrial workers in the Ruhr (*Ruhrpolen*) since the end of the 19th century.

[26] Italian agricultural workers in southwestern France since the 1920s; Italian industrial workers in western and central Europe in the late 19th and early 20th centuries; Italian workers in the construction industry in the Paris region since the 1870s.

cases to integration and upward social mobility, especially for Poles, Belgians, and Italians, but also history took a different course quite suddenly in the 1930s.

Migration and integration in times of depression, xenophobia, and war, 1931–1945

During the 1930s, France withdrew the welcome that was offered so extensively to newcomers in the 1920s: with the Great Depression, jobs disappeared and immigrants were sent packing; with rising anti-Semitism and xenophobia, many French demonstrated their objections to Jews and refugees from the Spanish Civil War; under the Vichy government, Jews and leftists were sent to their deaths. Thus, between 1931 and 1940, France was transformed from a welcoming and integrative liberal state into a suspicious and persecutory regime, a transformation set off by the great economic crisis of the 1930s and underwritten by popular anti-Semitism and xenophobia.

Mining and industries first sent foreigners home with the Great Depression. In the north, the number of foreign mine workers had declined by 24% by 1933, at which time the firings increased. Passage home was paid by the state or employer for many workers. By 1936, over 630,000 foreigners had left the country and the number of foreigners in Paris was reduced by a third. Generally, there was an effort to retain families, so bachelors were let go before families; one consequence of this was that the visibility of foreigners increased with the more important presence of children and women, which inflamed popular xenophobia.

Refugees became a focus of attention. France already served as a place of refuge for leftist Italians acting against Mussolini's 1927 ban on emigration, then the appointment of Hitler as chancellor of Germany in 1933 renewed the importance of refugees and refugee politics for France.[27] At first the church and public opinion were sympathetic, until it became apparent that many Jews were among the refugees. This time, crises of xenophobia came with a show of anti-Semitism, and it was not only workers who acted against outsiders. As Jews sought refuge in France and in many cases sent their children to professional schools, the liberal professions in France agitated against them. Demonstrations against Jewish medical and law students resulted in legislation restricting the ability of non-French to practice their profession in France; for example, the Armsbruster law of 1933 forbade medical licenses to non-French and imposed a 10-year residency before one could practice medicine. More generally, the laws of the 1890s that had eased naturalization and employment for foreigners were hardened by new legislation: a decree of 1935 limited the right to family reunification and to move within France; the right of free association was suspended for foreigners in

1939. The three-year residential period for naturalization was pushed back to 10 years under the Vichy government, and many who had gained citizenship under the 1927 law, "paper French" in the words of the right, were stripped of their citizenship. Such measures were designed precisely to lift the protection of citizenship from new arrivals such as Jews and also to prevent settlement and integration. The detailed records of the Parisian immigration service facilitated enforcement.

From 1936 to 1938, the Third Republic took on a policy of confinement to camps for certain groups; these camps would grow to house communists, Gypsies, Jews, and other foreigners during World War II. This was the apex of the murderous exclusion of foreigner and traveler wrought by the economic crises and triumph of fascism in the 1930s. There was more sympathy for Spanish refugees who came from the Basque region, Aragon, and Catalonia. In February 1939, a half million men, women, and children crossed the border from Spain. The wounded were sent to hospitals, others dispersed throughout France, and many returned to Spain. By July, 325,000 Spanish refugees remained.[28]

As during the Great War, questions of inclusion and integration of foreigners were obliterated during World War II. On the contrary, many newly arrived Jews and leftists were betrayed and deported rather than protected by the Vichy government: about 75,000 Jews were deported to the east, two-thirds of whom were foreign. And while France willingly shipped foreign and French-born Jews and leftists to Germany, the Vichy government also encouraged and coerced many other French to join the forced labor teams in Germany, so that by 1944, 1.25 million French were laboring in Nazi territory as forced laborers and prisoners of war.[29]

Immigration during the *trente glorieuses*, 1945–1975

With postwar recovery and growth, immigration from southern Europe, neighboring countries, the Mediterranean basin, and former colonies brought record numbers of newcomers to France. By 1971, their numbers passed the previous high of about 3 million in 1931 to reach 3.4 million in 1975. France was not exceptional in this period; rather, an infusion of immigrants was widespread throughout western Europe during this 30-year economic boom. It would bring a wide spectrum of newcomers into France. The degree to which newcomers settled and integrated depended upon national origins and the timing of arrival as one group gave way to another. Immediately after the war in 1946, Poles, Italians, Spaniards, and Belgians were the largest groups of resident foreigners, and these groups – especially Poles

---

[27] Political and intellectual refugees from Nazi Germany and from German-occupied Europe, 1933–1945; Jewish refugees from Nazi Germany and from German-occupied Europe since 1933.

[28] Spanish political refugees in Europe since the beginning of the civil war in 1936: the example of France.

[29] Forced laborers in Germany and German-occupied Europe during World War II.

Table 2. Principal immigrant groups in France, 1946–1999

	1946 (%)	1954 (%)	1962 (%)	1968 (%)	1975 (%)	1982 (%)	1990 (%)	1999 (%)
Spaniards	21.6	20.5	24.5	25.5	15.3	9.1	6.2	5.3
Italians	32.2	36.0	34.8	24.0	14.3	9.5	7.3	6.6
Poles	30.2	19.0	9.8	5.5	2.9	1.8	1.4	1.1
Portuguese	1.6	1.4	2.8	12.4	23.4	21.5	18.7	18.2
Algerians	1.6	15.0	19.3	19.9	21.9	22.5	17.6	15.6
Moroccans	1.1	0.8	1.8	3.5	8.0	12.3	16.5	16.6
Tunisians	0.1	0.4	1.5	2.6	4.3	5.3	5.9	5.1
Other Africans	0.9	0.1	1.0	1.4	2.5	4.4	6.9	9.3
Asians	5.0	2.9	2.0	1.9	3.2	8.1	12.2	13.5
Turks	0.6	0.4	*	0.3	1.6	3.4	5.7	6.8
Yugoslavs	1.5	1.2	1.2	2.0	2.2	1.7	1.5	1.6
Russians	3.6	2.4	1.4	0.8	0.4	0.2	0.1	0.4
Total principal nationalities (000s)	1,401	1,413	1,810	2,379	3,243	3,575	3,479	3,047

* Not available.

Source: Calculated from INSEE, censuses published in Blanc-Chaléard, *Les immigrés et la France*, 51.

and Italians who had arrived in considerable numbers in the interwar period – were quick to integrate, take better jobs, and move into growing areas of the labor force. For example, the sons of Polish laborers (1950–70) in the Cher were more likely to join the *cadres* and white-collar labor force than sons of French workers; sons of Italians were much more likely to be skilled workers or white-collar workers than the sons of French workers. Polish migration would decrease; Italian immigration, as massive as it was after the war, declined after the 1960s, and Italians became integrated into French society. These groups were the beneficiaries of the National Immigration Office (ONI, today the OMI, International Migration Office) that guaranteed foreign workers would receive benefits identical to those of the French, including family benefits and social security payments. These measures aided the integration of early arrivals. By 1975, 80% of Italians married someone outside the Italian community in France; others also married outside their communities – for Poles the figure was 65%, and for Spanish, 60%.

Immigration from southern Europe dominated until 1975, and Europeans remained well over half of the immigrants in France. Newcomers from Italy gave way to those from Spain, then Portugal.[30] By the late 1960s, there were nearly as many Spanish as Italians in France. Arrivals from Algeria increased dramatically after Algerian independence in 1962, so by 1968, Algerians were third after newcomers from Italy and Spain. Others from the Maghreb – Morocco and Tunisia – increased their numbers after 1968.[31] This was also the case for the growing stream of newcomers from former French

colonies in sub-Saharan Africa – particularly from Mali and Senegal (see Table 2).[32] In addition, many newcomers from the former colonies of the Caribbean traveled through the auspices of the Bureau pour les Migrations Intéressant les Départements d'Outre Mer (BUMIDOM) after 1962; this agency subsidized travel, provided job training, and encouraged family reunification in an era when immigration from overseas departments was considered more desirable than immigration from Africa. Many French Antilleans found work in the public sector working in the postal and health systems, and by 1975 over 100,000 Caribbean-born Antilleans lived in the metropole.[33] Portuguese suddenly began to come to France in great numbers in the late 1960s; by 1975, Portuguese outnumbered all other groups with over 750,000. Portuguese and Algerians would have distinct trajectories of integration in the years to come.

The years before 1975 were marked by a great deal of back-and-forth movement on the part of newcomers, many of whom were men who came to France to earn money, traveled without their families, and planned to return to their home area. As international as it had been in the 1920s, this labor force found Italians, Poles, and Spaniards working side-by-side in Paris construction, and Italians, Russians, and Poles in the steel mills of eastern France. This young and highly mobile labor force contributed more to unemployment, illness, and retirement funds than it drew because it included a smaller proportion of dependents than the French population. Questions of integration and second generation were of less importance than they would be in the future.

---

[30] Spanish labor migrants in western, central, and northern Europe since the end of World War II; Portuguese labor migrants in western and central Europe since the 1950s: the examples of France and Germany.

[31] Maghrebis in France after decolonization in the 1950s and 1960s.

[32] Vietnamese colonial and postcolonial immigrants in France since the World War I; Africans from the former colonies in France since the 1960s.

[33] West Indians in Great Britain, France, and the Netherlands since the end of World War II.

This changed with the oil price shock and economic downturn that began in 1974. Again, France was no exception; it closed borders to foreign workers in July of 1974, within months of Belgium and Germany. The policy was intended to stop newcomers from entering and to encourage returns home.

In fact, none of these was the result of border closures in and after 1974. Rather, the dynamic of immigrations changed in a way that neither reduced the numbers of foreign born nor encouraged returns home. Instead, immigrants chose to settle in France rather than return home, form or reunite families, and cross the borders illegally or overstay a tourist visa. As a consequence, the numbers of foreign born reached its final high point at about 3.5 million in 1982. Although newcomers wanted jobs, post-1975 immigration was not labor migration and was not negotiated and approved by the state as it had been until the 1970s.

During the 1970s and 1980s, Algerians and Portuguese outnumbered other immigrant groups. Although each group had its own trajectory and problems with integration in France, these two had particularly distinct profiles. The particular qualities of Algerian immigration warrant special attention. Immigration from Algeria is the numerically most important postcolonial movement to France and it has been marked by conflict and grave difficulties, despite the fact that Algerian immigration has been free since 1946 and Algerian Muslims became French citizens (rather than subjects) in 1947 – a legal change that applied to all members of the foreign empire (also important for Muslims from Mali and Senegal). Beginning in the 1960s, the long-standing immigration of workers from Algeria expanded at the end of the hard-fought war for independence, settled by the Evian Accords in 1962. This was the lion's share of a shift toward Maghreb immigration joined by Moroccans after 1968 so that by 1975, nearly 40% of immigrants in France came from the Maghreb.[34]

France encouraged the immigration of Algerians along with those of other workers from the Mediterranean basin after World War II. In this period, most Algerians came as workers without their families and planned to return home, so that questions of integration were not at issue. After 1960, as the war of independence against France became vicious and controversial, Algerians were repressed, hounded, and subject to murderous police actions that culminated on 17 October 1961 in Paris with the murder of at least 200 in response to a peaceful demonstration. Algerians were perceived to be the enemy of the French and subject to right-wing anti-immigrant politics that developed out of the Algerian war for independence. By the 1960s this had become primarily an immigration of Algerian Arabs, but it also included their former enemies, namely the *pieds-noirs* who had worked for the French government and who continued anti-Arab actions in France, and *Harkis*, Algerians who

had fought with the French army and who lived in camps apart from both French and Algerians.[35]

At the close of the war of independence, the French expected that Algerians would return home, but there was instead a surge in immigration, and immigration of a new kind that included wives, children, and other members of workers' families. Algerian newcomers were subject to racism and xenophobia from hostile segments of French society that culminated in a series of murders in the early 1970s which reflected a politics intolerant of integration that labeled Algerians as people who could not be assimilated into French society. This, in turn, led the Algerian government to forbid migration to France in 1973 out of concern for its people abroad. The following year, in response to the economic crisis brought on by the rise in oil prices, France suspended immigration. In 1975, the census counted over 700,000 Algerians in France.

Immigration and integration after 1975

Algerians were outnumbered by Portuguese who had come to France in the early 1970s, expanding from under 300,000 in 1968 to over 750,000 in 1975 and more than 780,000 in 1982. With the increased immigration of wives and children and formation of immigrant families in France, questions of integration also became questions about the second generation of all immigrants. In the case of the Portuguese, annual vacations (often the occasion for marriages and baptisms) maintained vital contacts with home, but also by the early 1990s, over half the sons of Portuguese parents born in France (59%) married a French women; for daughters the figure was nearly half (47%) and they registered to vote. This is also true of the sons and daughters of Spaniards in France. For both Portuguese and Spanish children, the younger the age at which they arrived in France, the greater their achievement in school.

Despite early difficulties, southern Europeans have for the most part assimilated into French society by intermarriage, electoral participation, and school achievement. The groups of longest standing – Italians and Spanish – have greater measures of achievement than the Portuguese, who are relatively recent arrivals. Indeed, one of the lessons of immigration history is that time is the greatest aid to integration.

Yet the situation for immigrants from the Maghreb is more complex because both Arab and Kabyle Algerians came to France and because Moroccans also had sent considerable numbers of immigrants to France since the interwar period. There are similar patterns of intermarriage in the case of Maghreb immigrants, but the difference between the experience of men and women is striking. As of 1992, over half the marriages of Algerian and Moroccan daughters were arranged by their families and this was the case for around 30% of the men. Moreover, half the sons of

---

[34] Maghrebis in France after decolonization in the 1950s and 1960s.

[35] Algerian "Harkis" in France since 1962; Algerian *pieds-noirs* in France since 1954.

Algerians born in France married French women; this was the case for only a quarter of Algerian daughters. As for schooling, Algerian men especially had high dropout rates (23%), but these were precisely the same as rates for young Portuguese men; the same is true for young Algerian and Portuguese women (16%). Finally, a significant minority of Algerian students (31% of men, 30% of women) completed the baccalaureate or went on to higher education. By 1999, this was true of even more Moroccan students (39% of men, 46% of women), although they too had high dropout rates (25%).

Such integration and achievement is particularly hard won given the material and political difficulties that came on the heels of the large-scale immigration of the postwar period. The Fifth Republic wrestled with issues of housing and integration, on one hand, and with growing anti-immigrant sentiment on the other. Housing presented the greatest impediment to humane conditions for immigrants beginning in the 1960s; shantytowns (*bidonvilles*) without running water, plumbing, or paved streets housed up to 15,000 migrant workers and their families in one location, steeped in mud and separated from housing for the French. In this case the location was Champigny, home to Portuguese southeast of Paris, in 1968, and others like Nanterre that housed about 10,000 in the same year, many of them Algerians. In 1964 the politics of eradicating these unsightly and unhealthy settlements produced *cités de transit* – temporary but walled dwellings with plumbing and windows, meant to house families for two years while permanent large apartment complexes were constructed. As two years stretched to up to 10 years and the politics of immigration became increasingly acrimonious, the construction of housing for newcomers was at the center of the social debate.

Just as the word "foreigner" became a code word for unwanted refugee and Jew in the 1930s, in the 1980s, the word "immigrant" no longer suggested an immigrant worker, but rather became a code word for Arab and an indicator of social problems. The word "immigrant" was applied not only to people born outside France but also to the children of recent arrivals. This was a denial of the processes of integration which were at work for groups as distinct as Italians in France since the late 1920s, and the children of immigrants from the Maghreb. It was inspired by the anti-Arab discrimination that blossomed during the Algerian war of independence and took root in French politics most famously with the encouragement of the Front National party under the leadership of Jean-Marie Le Pen. Such discrimination is apparently also at work for the educated second-generation North African and Turkish youth.

In the 1990s, new groups of immigrants increased their numbers, such as Turks who were already established elsewhere in western Europe.[36] Likewise, more Chinese, Vietnamese, and other Asians came to France.[37] Finally, with the collapse of communist governments in eastern Europe and Russia after 1989, more eastern Europeans and Russians came to France.[38] Some were part of the "globalization from below" of working people whose networks of contact reached western Europe, like the Chinese. Others came as part of long-standing colonial ties, such as the Vietnamese and Senegalese. Still others, like the Russians and Romanians, came because political shifts enhanced their chances for departure from their home countries. Finally, many entered as political refugees, especially from Cambodia, Vietnam, Zaire, and Turkey.[39]

Looking to the past and the future

France shares common patterns of immigration with other countries of western Europe. Like Germany, Switzerland, and England, France hosted an international labor force at the turn of the 20th century and again in the prolonged economic boom that followed World War II. Between the wars, however, France much more than other nations recruited workers from Poland, Czechoslovakia, and neighboring countries, many of whom stayed on and integrated into French life.

At the beginning of the 21st century, many immigrants and their children are also becoming part of France. One of the most telling signs is the willingness to become a French citizen. At the turn of the 21st century, well over 100,000 foreigners take on French citizenship every year, by marriage with a French citizen (over 26,000 in 2000), by taking citizenship at age 21 in the case of immigrants' children (about 43,000 in 2000), or applying for naturalization after five years of residence (over 50,000 people per year). Moreover, an important movement of *sans papiers* agitates for the regularization of their status. According to the 1999 census, 36% of France's immigrants have naturalized, many by marriage.

The integration process is clearly at work in the classrooms of public schools, the workplace, and the formation of new families. In the crucial matter of birthrates, there have been significant changes. The birthrates of Spanish, Italians, and Portuguese are now similar to those of the French; although those of Maghrebins and Turks are slightly more elevated, they have dropped significantly in the past 20 years.

In France, as elsewhere, two kinds of impediments are working against the integration of immigrants and their children. Economic restructuring and continued high unemployment mean that there is no economic boom at present like that of the *trente glorieuses* to provide immigrants and their children with the jobs that previous generations had been able to count on in their struggle to become established in France and to move from factory to shop or white-collar work.

---

[36] Turkish labor migrants in western, central, and northern Europe since the mid-1950s.

[37] Vietnamese colonial and postcolonial immigrants in France since World War I.

[38] Polish labor migrants in central and western Europe after 1989; eastern, east-central, and southeastern European prostitutes in western, central, northern, and southern Europe since the 1980s.

[39] Vietnamese refugees in western, central, and northern Europe since the 1970s: the examples of France, Great Britain, and Germany.

There are few new jobs for unskilled and semiskilled workers. For example, part of the reason the children of Algerian immigrants are less likely to marry than other groups is that Algerians in their 20s do not have the employment that can support the formation of an independent household. There is a demonstrable gap between the schooling and training systems, on one hand, and the job market, on the other.

In addition, growing identification of Muslim newcomers and anti-Islamic sentiments have grown from wider political tensions and the expansion of Muslim fundamentalist movements since Ayatollah Khomeini left France for Iran in 1979. This increased with the gulf wars, attacks on the New York World Trade Center in 2001, the war in Iraq since 2003, and actions against synagogues and Jewish cemeteries. The state response to anti-Islamic sentiment has been, in part, to focus on the public school as a shared secular space and thus to forbid the wearing of headscarves by Muslim schoolgirls, interpreting scarves as a religious symbol (along with large crosses, yarmulkes, and turbans). This has resulted in a law unique in Europe banning the wearing of headscarves in public schools, passed in the spring of 2003. French law intends to reinforce the national image of a secular state, welcoming to newcomers and promoting integration.

Unemployment and the alienation of an increasingly fundamentalist and politicized Muslim population are exacerbated by the housing segregation that locates many large groups of recent and second-generation immigrants outside major cities in the *banlieues*, where social tensions and unemployment are high. In November of 2005, riots around Paris and in *banlieues* across the country signaled a continuing gulf between the French and the portions of French society that are thought of as immigrant. Fulfilling the hope of integration and the promise of employment remain a challenge, and the response to the riots of 2005 and the French reaction to them locates the debate in issues of education and job training as engines of integration.

REFERENCES

Bade, Klaus J. *Migration in European History*. Oxford, 2003.

Blanc-Chaléard, Marie-Claude. *Les immigrés et la France, XIXe–XXe siècle*. Paris, 2003.

Bleich, Erik. *Race Politics in Britain and France: Ideas and Policymaking*. Cambridge, 2003.

Charbit, Yves, Marie-Antoinette Hily, and Michel Poinard. *Le va-et-vient identitaire. Migrants portugais et villages d'origine*. Paris, 1997.

Choquette, Leslie. *Frenchmen into Peasants: Modernity and Tradition in the Peopling of French Canada*. Cambridge, MA, 1997.

Favell, Adrian. *Philosophies of Integration: Immigration and the Idea of Citizenship in France and Britain*. New York, 2001.

Green, Nancy. *Ready-to-Wear and Ready-to-Work: A Century of Industry and Immigrants in Paris and New York*. Durham, NC, 1997.

Green, Nancy. *Repenser les migrations*. Paris, 2002.

Guy, Kolleen. *When Champagne Became French: Wine and the Making of a National Identity*. Baltimore, 2003.

König, Mareike, ed. *Deutsche Handwerker, Arbeiter und Dienstmädchen in Paris: Eine vergessene Migration im 19. Jahrhundert*. Munich, 2003.

Lequin, Yves. *La mosaïque France: Histoire des étrangers et de l'immigration*. Paris, 1988.

Lewis, Mary Dewhurst. *The Boundaries of the Republic: Migrant Rights and the Limits of Universalism in France, 1918–1940*. Stanford, CA, 2007.

Lucassen, Jan. *Migrant Labour in Europe, 1600–1900*. London, 1987.

Lucassen, Leo. *The Immigrant Threat: The Integration of Old and New Migrants in Western Europe since 1850*. Urbana, IL, 2005.

Mandel, Maud. *In the Aftermath of Genocide: Armenians and Jews in 20th Century France*. Durham, NC, 2003.

Noiriel, Gérard. *Longwy: Immigrés et prolétaires, 1880–1980*. Paris, 1984.

Noiriel, Gérard. *Le creuset français: Histoire de l'immigration (XIX–XXe siècle)*. Paris, 1988.

Noiriel, Gérard. *Population, immigration et identité nationale en France, XIX–XXe siècle*. Paris, 1992.

Poitrineau, Abel. *Remues d'hommes: Essai sur les migrations montagnardes en France, aux 17e–18e siècles*. Paris, 1983.

Ponty, Janine. *Polonais méconnus: Historie des travailleurs immigrés en France dans l'entre-deux-guerres*. Paris, 1988.

Poussou, Jean-Pierre. *Bordeaux et le sud-ouest au XVIIIe siècle*. Paris, 1983.

Rosenberg, Clifford. *Policing Paris: The Origins of Modern Immigration Control between the Wars*. Ithaca, NY, 2006.

Rygiel, Philippe. *Destins immigrés*. Besançon, 2001.

Simon, Patrick. "France and the Unknown Second Generation: Preliminary Results on Social Mobility." *International Migration Review* 37, 4 (2003): 1091–119.

Stora, Benjamin. *Ils venaient d'Algérie: L'immigration algérienne en France (1912–1992)*. Paris, 1992.

Stovall, Tyler. "Colour-Blind France? Colonial Workers during the First World War." *Race and Class* 35 (1993): 35–55.

Timera, Mahamet. *Les Soninké en France: D'une histoire à l'autre*. Paris, 1996.

Tribalat, Michèle. *Faire France: Une enquête sur les immigrés et leurs enfants*. Paris, 1995.

Tribalat, Michèle. *De l'immigration à l'assimilation: Enquête sur les populations d'origine étrangère en France*. Paris, 1996.

Weber, Eugene. *The Hollow Years: France in the 1930s*. New York, 1994.

Weil, François. "French Migration to the Americas in the 19th and 20th Centuries as a Historical Problem." *Studi Emigrazione/Etudes Migrations* 33 (1996): 443–60.

Weil, Patrick. *Qu'est-ce qu'un Français? Histoire de la nationalité française depuis la Révolution*. Paris, 2002.

Zehraoui, Ahsène. *Familles d'origine algérienne en France: Étude sociologique des processus d'intégration*. Paris, 1999.

CENTRAL EUROPE

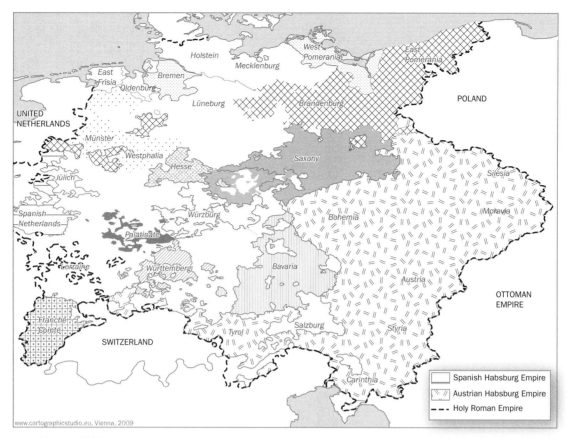

Central Europe 1648

Central Europe 2000

64

GERMANY

Klaus J. Bade and Jochen Oltmer

Migration in the German-speaking realm since the early modern period has encompassed not only peaceful cross-border movements and intercultural encounters. It has also included aggressive border crossings, flight across borders, and the exclusion of minorities within Germany and – after the violent expansion of Germany's borders in the Second World War – in other parts of Europe. Throughout German history, however, not only have people moved across borders, but borders have also moved over people – minorities became majorities, majorities were turned into minorities, and natives into strangers in their own land.

A survey of the main currents in the migratory activity to and from Germany from the early modern period to the early 21st century, leaving aside the multitude of everyday and ubiquitous small-scale migrations that are impossible to keep track of, reveals a number of striking focal points: they include above all the early modern immigration of religious refugees or those expelled for religious reasons, the tradition-rich settlement migrations to eastern, east-central, and southeastern Europe until the early 19th century, and the transatlantic mass exodus until the late 19th century. This was followed by a reversal – increasing over the long term – in the direction of the migratory movements, down to the varied immigration movements to Germany in the late 20th and early 21st centuries. Throughout its history, however, the German-speaking realm was rarely simply a land of either emigration or immigration; instead, it was usually both at the same time, though with enormous differences in the epochal importance of the two great directions of migration and the problems and perspectives on integration they entailed.

The region and its boundaries

During the period in question, Germany was a sphere with boundaries that were fluid over centuries – whether one looks at the development of the states of the Old Empire of the early modern era into the German nation-state of 1871 and its eventful – and in the 20th century also for other states and nations disastrous – history, or at the German-speaking realm, which became noticeably smaller, primarily as a result of the two world wars.

As supraordinated political entities, the Old Empire of 1806 and for the most part also the German Confederation (*Deutscher Bund*) from 1815 to 1866 were not states with fixed borders, comprising instead a multitude of more or less autonomous territories. To be sure, after the Thirty Years' War some of the territories within the Old Empire did develop – at very different rates and reach – into territorial states with firmly established institutions. However, even at this level there were rarely sharp boundaries. The backdrop was a multitude of overlapping jurisdictions, the result of still-potent feudal ties, complex dynastic relationships, and an orientation toward patronage relations. Likewise, it is not possible to identify a uniform realm of German language at the beginning of the period in question: first, because of numerous, very different German dialects, which made communication across regional boundaries difficult or even impossible; second, because of expansive border and mixed zones that extended far beyond the territory of the Old Empire, where variants of German and a great many other European languages interacted. The language of standard German developed only very slowly in the course of the early modern period.

Although the Congress of Vienna in 1814–15 led to more distinct territorial boundaries, given the specific structure of the German Confederation as a loose federation of states, central zones of territorial overlap continued to exist: parts of the state territory of Austria and Prussia were located outside of the Confederation, while European states such as Great Britain, the Netherlands, and Denmark were simultaneously linked to German territories in personal unions and were thus part of it. Only the establishment of the Empire in 1870–1 consolidated the borders of a central European nation–state. It stretched from Alsace-Lorraine in the southwest to the Baltic Memel region in the northeast, from southern Jutland in the north to the Alps in the south. However, it did not include broad German-speaking zones in Switzerland, Austria, and large minority regions in southeastern, east-central, and eastern Europe. The Empire encompassed strong cultural and linguistic minorities, especially Poles, Danes, and Alsatians/Lorrainians. Their number declined strongly after the territorial cessions at the end of World War I in the east (especially parts of Posen and West Prussia, eastern Upper Silesia, the Memel region), in the west (Alsace-Lorraine and Eupen-Malmedy), and in the north (Tonder). The end of World War II brought new territorial losses in the east: East Prussia, eastern Pomerania, eastern Brandenburg, Posen–West Prussia, and Silesia. What remained of Germany was encompassed by the two postwar German states after 1949, which were reunited in 1990.

Immigration and integration under the banner of the policy of demographic expansion in the 17th and 18th centuries

The immediate impact of war, and above all the side effects and consequences of the Thirty Years' War (1618–48), led to a massive demographic decline in the territory of the later German Empire, with a loss of about one-third of the prewar population of 15–17 million. By 1650, the population had only returned to the level of 1520 (10–12 million), though with considerable regional variations. On the whole, the rural population had been harder hit than the urban population by acts of war, epidemics caused by war (especially the plague), famines, flight, and expulsions, and the border regions had suffered more than the hinterland. Towns and settlements located on transit routes, on navigable rivers, and in strategically important regions had suffered losses of at times well over 50% of their prewar population. The corridor of devastation with the most heavily affected areas ran from northeast to southwest: from Pomerania and Mecklenburg to Brandenburg, Thuringia, Hesse, Franconia, the Palatinate, Württemberg, Swabia, and all the way to Alsace.

For about two generations, these ravaged areas became the primary regions of immigration in central Europe. With quite varying integration conditions, they were attractive economic destinations for settlement migrants from overpopulated regions spared by the wars. At the same time, territorialization in the wake of the Thirty Years' War led to the development of a mercantilist migration policy by territorial rulers, at the center of which was the desire for the greatest possible number of gainfully employed and tax-paying subjects. *Peuplierung* was therefore a central political concept of territorial governments in areas especially hard hit by the war. It involved the use of recruiters in the emigration regions and the granting of privileges and benefits to immigrants (tax exemption, free settlement land, favorable personal and property status, free lumber and firewood).

The confession was a central criterion of settlement and integration. That was true for religiously motivated flight as well as for immigration driven chiefly by economic considerations. Geographic mobility and social mobility worked hand in hand, because the settlement migrations of the postwar period were an essential catalyst of social advancement in the integration process for a majority of immigrants from overpopulated sending regions.

A survey of German regions ravaged by the Thirty Years' War – leaving aside the multitude and diversity of quantitatively dominant small-scale migrations – reveals the patterns of regional and interregional movements caused by the war: Alsace and Baden became the destinations for strong settlement migrations from Switzerland, and to a lesser extent also from Flanders and Wallonia. Swiss immigrants were also dominant in Württemberg, along with migrants from Vorarlberg, Bavaria, and Tyrol.[1] Religious refugees from the Austrian territories characterized the immigration to Franconia and Swabia. The same was true for Saxony and the Oberlausitz, which became the destination of several thousand Bohemian Protestant religious refugees seeking to escape the re-Catholicization in the Habsburg territories.[2] New arrivals from Bohemia, many of them cloth and linen weavers, also settled in the March Brandenburg. However, more important to that region was the influx of groups of Reformed Dutch, Swiss, and from the 1680s also Huguenot rural settlers, who were of particular interest to the ruling house of Brandenburg, which followed a related confession.[3]

Beyond Brandenburg, the Huguenots formed one of the largest and economically, culturally, and politically most important immigrant groups in early modern Germany. Of the 150,000 Huguenots who left France after the revocation of the Edict of Nantes (1598) in 1685, between 27,000 and 35,000 migrated to German territories, chiefly north of the Main. Brandenburg-Prussia was the most important destination, taking in about a third of the immigrants, followed far behind by Hesse-Kassel, the Guelph duchies, and the Hanseatic cities. Less than a quarter of the Huguenot migrants remained in southern Germany, here especially in the Palatinate, Württemberg, Ansbach, and Bayreuth. Only Germany saw the founding of self-contained Huguenot settlements that went back to initiatives by some princes: Kassel-Neustadt and Karlshafen (Hesse-Kassel), Friedrichsdorf (Hesse-Homburg), Christian-Erlang (Bayreuth). A central document for the link between the desire to admit and integrate confessionally related religious refugees and the interest in *Peuplierung* as an element of a mercantilist economic policy was – alongside a multitude of similar privileges – the Potsdam Edict issued by Prince-Elector Frederick William of Brandenburg in October 1685.

The most important receiving areas for Huguenots in Brandenburg-Prussia were regions that had been heavily depopulated by the war: the Ruppiner Land and the region around Potsdam, and here especially the Uckermark. The Ruppiner Land lost 60%–70% of its prewar population, the Uckermark no less than 90%. The primary urban migration destination was Berlin, where around 1700 one out of every five residents was of Huguenot background; many of them, because of their economic and cultural accomplishments, can be seen as an "imported *ersatz*-bourgeoisie" (in Stefi Jersch-Wenzel's phrase) that was of far-reaching importance to Berlin's emergence as a European metropolis. Still, the overall Huguenot contribution to Prussia's economic upswing since the late 17th century must not be exaggerated: although

---

[1] Swiss Protestant peasants in Alsace, southwestern Germany, and Brandenburg-Prussia since the mid-17th century.

[2] Bohemian exiles (*Exulanten*) in Saxony since the 17th century.

[3] Dutch Calvinist refugees in Europe since the early modern period; Swiss Protestant peasants in Alsace, southwestern Germany, and Brandenburg-Prussia since the mid-17th century; Huguenots in Europe since the 16th century; Waldensians in central Europe since the early modern period; Mennonites in West Prussia since the 16th century.

Huguenots may well have introduced new products and production methods, they were often among the producers of luxury goods and thus dependent on the demand from expanding court centers.

Only a small percentage of these immigrants was among the group of successful entrepreneurs and merchants, for among the Huguenots, as well, members of the middle and lower classes predominated. They, too, were sometimes in such high demand because of their special abilities and skills, for example, in manufacturing and agriculture, that one can speak in some areas of a veritable confession-driven technology transfer. In spite of many frictions with the natives in daily life because of special privileges and competition, the integration of the foreigners was greatly facilitated by the interest of the authorities in population growth, innovation, and an increase in their "industrial renown."

Brandenburg-Prussia remained one of the most important German immigration lands also in the 18th century. Central receiving areas were the March Brandenburg, East Prussia, and Silesia (after 1740). Between 1640 and 1786, Brandenburg-Prussia took in about half a million immigrants. In the process, there were two large-scale settlement schemes in war-devastated regions following the period of new settlements: the first came in East Prussia, heavily afflicted by the plague and other epidemics in the early 18th century; the second came during the reigns of kings Frederick William I (1713–40) and Frederick II (1740–86), in land newly opened up by large-scale reclamations in the lowlands of the Oder, the Neiße, and the Warthe. Into this context belongs also the settlement of Salzburg Protestants, who were expelled from their homeland in 1731–2 and formally invited to settle in East Prussia by Frederick Wilhelm I. The vast majority of the approximately 20,000 Salzburg emigrants were settled in East Prussia under favorable conditions. Smaller groups went to other Protestant territories in Germany, to the Netherlands, and to the English colony of Georgia in North America (settlement of Ebenezer/New Ebenezer).[4]

In addition to these long-distance movements for the purpose of settlements, the migratory activities in early modern Germany were characterized by a multitude of migrations within small areas. The vast majority of those functioned within the framework of the family economy and should be categorized especially as migrations specific to a particular phase of life, primarily as marriage migration and the movement of domestic personnel. Immigration into the cities, where mortality usually outpaced the birthrate, generally also came from nearby areas. Leaving aside the movement of pupils and students as specific types of educational migration, long-distance migrations from country to city and city to city were limited mostly to individuals who possessed particular qualifications. The armies of the German territories were recruited only in part from subjects of the respective princes: that was true, for example, of the Prussian army, which in the mid-18th century counted above all Hungarians,

Italians, Dutchmen, Swiss, and subjects from various other German princes among its many non-Prussian soldiers. In like manner, Germans served in the armies and navies of other states: the Dutch army, colonial forces, and navy had a high share of German mercenaries,[5] but German soldiers also fought under French,[6] Spanish,[7] and British command, as for example the approximately 30,000 mercenaries who were deployed by the British monarchy in the 1770s in its struggle against the North American colonies fighting for independence. More than half came from the Hessian territories of the Empire; the others were subjects from Braunschweig, Ansbach-Bayreuth, Anhalt-Zerbst, and Waldeck.

Equally strongly shaped by migrations were the labor markets of seamen in the merchant marine, of artists and artist craftsmen, of musicians, jugglers, and actors.[8] To a lesser extent that was also true for administrative officials, teachers, monks, secular priests, and pastors.[9] Added to this were the multifarious forms of specific vocational migrations. Here there was a strong overlap of regions of origin and specialization in crafts and trade, which developed via interregional migration networks and was linked with processes of acquiring qualifications through migration. The mark of this type of migration was the fact that the migratory professions were generally not or only rarely found in the small regions of origin, that migration and enhancement of skills were therefore closely linked. In German territories of the early modern period as either sending or destination regions, that was true, for example, of the brickmakers from Lippe[10] or of Italian chimney sweeps[11] and Italian pewterers.[12] This kind of job-specific migration can also be found in trade, for example, in the itinerant traders from the Münster region (referred to as *Tödden*) in northern, western, and central Europe in the 18th and 19th centuries.[13] Finally, there was diverse migration of journeymen – usually the result of "compulsory migration" enforced by the guilds – within the old crafts in the early modern period, the traces of which disappeared in the 19th century. Often the more or less stringent regulations of the guilds were concerned not only with the acquisition

---

[4] Salzburg Protestants in East Prussia since the 18th century.

[5] Western and central European soldiers in the Dutch colonial army, 1815–1909.

[6] European soldiers in the Napoleonic army.

[7] Spanish troops in the Netherlands in the 16th and 17th centuries: the example of Geldern.

[8] German sailors in the Dutch merchant marine from the early 17th to the end of the 19th century; musicians, showmen, jugglers, and acrobats in central Europe in the early modern period; comici dell'arte in Europe in the early modern period; English comedians in Europe in the early modern period: the example of the Netherlands; Italian and other "Alpine" (Grisons, Tecino, and Vorarlberg) architects and visual artists in Baroque Europe.

[9] Jesuits in Europe since the early modern period.

[10] Lippe brickmakers in central, western, and northern Europe from the 17th to the early 20th century.

[11] Alpine chimney sweeps in western, central, and southern Europe from the 16th to the early 20th century.

[12] Italian pewterers in Europe from the 16th to the 20th century.

[13] German itinerant merchants from the Münsterland in northern, western, and central Europe in the 18th and 19th centuries.

of artisanal and technical qualifications through regulated migration, but also with providing relief for local labor markets in the increasingly overcrowded crafts and trades.[14]

Continental and overseas emigration in the 18th and 19th centuries

Germany's population grew at an accelerated pace in the two centuries following the end of the Thirty Years' War. The enormous population losses from the war had been more or less made up within about two generations, by around 1700. The 18th century saw a substantial rise in the population of around 50%. For the territory of the later German Empire, a rise from 15 to 23 million between 1700 and 1800 is estimated. Comparable growth, though only in half the time, occurred between 1800 and 1850 (to 35 million) and between 1850 and 1900 (to 56 million).

Immigration contributed but little to this accelerated population expansion. On the contrary: after the century stretching from the end of the Thirty Years' War to the mid-18th century, which was characterized primarily by immigration in the context of official measures to increase the population, migratory movement was shaped increasingly by continental and overseas emigration. Continental emigration to eastern and southeastern Europe was dominant from the mid-18th century up to the 1830s, followed until the late 19th century by transatlantic emigration, chiefly to the USA.

Southeastern Europe and southern Russia offered important destinations for the settlement migration especially from southern German regions, where population growth had already picked up in the 17th and 18th centuries, and the territorial governments – in spite of a mercantilist tightening of prohibitions against emigration – were unable to stop the exodus. After the end of the Seven Years' War, the "Swabian treks" of 1763–70 and 1782–8 probably took around 70,000 German-speaking peasants and craftsmen from Franconia, Baden, Württemberg, Further Austria, Luxembourg, and Lorraine to the southeastern European Danube region, with settlement focal points in the Batschka, the Banat (Danube Swabians), and Transylvania.[15] Contemporaneous settlement migrations headed for the regions – just recently conquered by the Czarist Empire – along the lower Volga and in "New Russia" north of the Black Sea. As with the Swabian treks, along the Volga and in New Russia, as well, privileges and benefits were a central recruitment tool of the official population policy intended to develop and secure the settlement land.[16]

Confessional considerations, however, which had clearly structured the movements after the end of the Thirty Years' War, all but ceased to play a role any longer: the princes were willing to recruit and settle colonists of any confessional, regional, or social background for regions that were thinly populated or completely depopulated as a result of long wars. Highly desirable and courted especially were settlers from central Europe who were familiar with more advanced agricultural and artisanal skills. They could hope for especially enticing privileges, like the invitations issued by Russian Empress Catherine II in 1762–3, which promised free land, loans, favorable rights, exemption from taxes and dues for several years, and exemption from military service. Around 25,000 German settlers, most from the Palatinate, settled along the lower Volga within a few years after 1763. Other groups followed in subsequent decades, among them above all Mennonite settlers from West Prussia, who settled north of the Black Sea chiefly in the 1780s and 1790s; additional Mennonite groups and Pietists from southwestern Germany followed in the first two decades of the 19th century.[17]

All in all, the number of emigrants from the German-speaking realm to eastern, east-central, and southeastern Europe from the 1680s to 1800 can be estimated at around 740,000 people. By contrast, overseas migration to North America was a distant second during this period with around 170,000, whereby the origin regions of overseas emigrants were largely identical to those of the continental movement to eastern and southeastern Europe: Baden, Württemberg, the Palatinate, Alsace, and Lorraine.[18] The fact that nearly two-thirds of the emigrants from Württemberg were still heading for eastern and southeastern Europe at the end of the 18th and the early 19th centuries, while most of those from Baden were already going to the USA, had to do not only with the growing attractiveness of the New World across the ocean but also with migratory traditions shaped by the geography of transport communications: shipping along the Rhine offered emigrants from Baden a favorable link to the seaports in the north, while the Württembergers were still making greater use of shipping on the Danube for a continental west-east migration. Here the geography of communications was more important than confessional identity, which should have taken these two groups of emigrants into precisely the reverse direction: the Protestant Württembergers to North America, the Catholic Badeners to eastern and southeastern Europe.

Philadelphia was the chief port of destination of the German migration to North America until the 18th century. The initial focal point of settlement was Pennsylvania, though in the course of the 18th century it shifted increasingly to western Maryland, North Carolina, and Virginia. Years with a particularly strong overseas exodus were 1709, 1749–52, 1757, 1759, and 1782. Pennsylvania developed into the primary destination of religious dissidents (Quakers, Pietists,

---

[14] German baker-journeymen in Amsterdam in the 17th century; Saxon journeymen purse makers in Vienna in the 18th and 19th centuries; Tyrolean construction workers in central Europe from the 17th to the 19th centuries.

[15] German settlers (*Donauschwaben*) in southeastern Europe since the early modern period; Austrian Protestants (*Landler*) in Transylvania since the 18th century.

[16] German settlers in Russia since the 18th century; German merchants and industrial entrepreneurs in Russia since the 18th century.

[17] Mennonites in West Prussia since the 16th century.

[18] Palatinates in Europe since the 17th century.

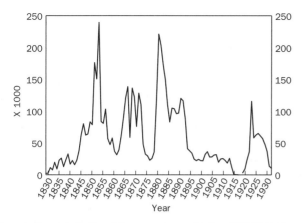

Figure 1. Phases in the flow of German overseas migration, 1830-1932. *Source:* Friedrich Burgdörfer, "Die Wanderungen über die deutschen Reichsgrenzen im letzten Jahrhundert," *Allgemeines Statistisches Archiv* 20 (1930): 161-96, 383-419, 537-51.

Mennonites, Dunkers, Schwenkfelders, and Moravian Brethren (*Herrnhuter*), whose migration was characterized by organized group movements and communal settlements. On the whole, however, group and family migrations driven by economic and social motives were already dominant in the 18th century. Estimates put the number of individuals of German origin in Britain's North American colonies at 225,000 in 1775, which amounted to 8.6% of the total population. One-third of the population of Pennsylvania was of German background; in Maryland it was 12%, New Jersey 9%, and New York 8%.

Beginning in the 1830s, the continental stream to the east and southeast receded decidedly behind the transatlantic migration, which quickly evolved into a mass movement after the mid-19th century. In the second half of the century, around 90% of that migrant flow led to the USA. The most important overseas destinations after that were Canada, Brazil, Argentina, and Australia. Between 1816 and 1914, about 5.5 million Germans emigrated to the USA, and since then another 2 million. Peaks of German emigration in the 19th century – with more than a million emigrants each – were the years 1846–57 and 1864–73; another 1.8 million emigrants followed in the last large phase of 1880–93 (see Figure 1). Between 1820 and 1860, the German-born population of the USA was the second-largest group behind the Irish at 30%, and from 1861 to 1890 it was even the largest.

One of the most important forces behind the transatlantic mass emigration of the 19th century in Germany was the imbalance between the growth in population and the availability of jobs during the crisis of transition from an agrarian to an industrial society. This imbalance took on very different forms in different regions and was soon joined by a tremendous internal migratory activity. It unfolded via transatlantic migration networks, through communication systems held together by relatives, acquaintances, and communities of shared origin, which connected European sending regions and overseas destinations, and especially by the "emigrant letters" that circulated within the circles of relatives and

friends back home. As chain emigration, the exodus began to follow its own tracks, as it were, and soon developed firmly entrenched overseas migratory traditions that connected certain regions and even certain communities with others in the New World – for example, Melle in the region of Osnabrück with New Melle on the Missouri river.

The various primary sending regions of the overseas migration entered the flow of transatlantic migration at different times, some earlier, some later: it began early in southwest Germany, whose agrarian structure was characterized by small and tiny holdings as agrarian land had to be divided equally among the heirs. Although the emigration from the southwest dominated until the mid-19th century, with a view to the overall German emigration, the share of western and northwestern regions, whose emigration was carried especially by members of strata below that of farmers, such as agricultural leaseholders (e.g., *Heuerlinge*, *Kötter* [cottagers]) and small craftsmen, grew larger. With continuing strong contributions from the southwest and northwest, German emigration in the late 19th century found its last focal point in the largely rural northeastern region of the Empire. The last great phase of emigration from 1880 to 1893 was dominated by the younger sons of farmers (*Anerbenrecht* meant that a farm was passed intact to the oldest son) and members of rural underclasses, chiefly day laborers and domestics. By this time, the structure of the emigration had also changed considerably in other respects: the rural settlement migration in family units had been replaced by migratory movements that were more strongly individualistic and ended by preference in the urban secondary and tertiary sectors.

Counter to the precipitous decline in German mass emigration, emigration to North America from eastern, east-central, southern, and southeastern Europe emerged as a mass movement in the early 1890s. In the United States it was referred to disparagingly as "New Immigration," in contrast to the "classic" immigration from western, central, and northern Europe. A large segment of the movement from eastern, east-central, and southeastern Europe used Germany as a transit country: the more German overseas emigration declined from the early 1890s, the more important this transit migration – the object of ruthless competition among international overseas shipping – became to the Hanseatic transatlantic lines. Between 1894 and 1910, only 11% (380,907) of overseas migrants departing from German ports were Germans, with foreigners making up 89% (2,752,256). From 1880 to World War I, more than 5 million emigrants from Russia (especially Russian Poland) and Austria-Hungary passed through the Empire on their way to the seaports. Only a few tens of thousands of these transit migrants remained in Germany, frequently only temporarily; this was the result also of the restrictive – by no means only health-related – "transit control" with which Prussia-Germany sought to prevent the immigration especially of Poles and Jews.[19]

[19] Eastern European Jews in Berlin from the late 19th century to the 1930s; Ashkenazim in Europe since the early modern period.

The employment of foreigners and the restrictive immigration policy from the late 19th century to the end of World War I

From the 1890s on, the growing German reservoir of workers was increasingly absorbed by the exploding job opportunities during the phase of high industrialization, as the period of economic growth that began in the 1890s continued – with two brief interruptions (1900/2, 1907/8) – until the eve of World War I. The attractiveness of the USA as the chief overseas destination receded behind the strong growth in opportunities in the domestic labor markets. Overseas emigration remained low from the early 1890s to World War I and flowed, as it were, into the stream of internal migration from rural into urban-industrial worlds of work and life. However, in Germany the central turning point in the enormous transition in transnational migratory movements around the turn of the century was the change from permanent transatlantic emigration to foreign continental immigration of limited duration. In terms of the primary thrust of migratory movements, this turned the Reich within a few years from a country of emigration into the second most important country of immigration in the world after the USA.

In this context, immigration into the industrial regions of the Ruhr and Emscher coal districts developed an almost magnetic attractiveness that drew in also internal long-distance migrations, in particular those of the "Ruhr Poles" and "Ruhr Mazovians."[20] After the end of the migratory "North Sea system," which, from the 17th to the early 19th century, had attracted thousands of German seasonal migrants to the coastal region of the Netherlands (*Hollandgänger*), the direction of migration all but reversed itself in some cases within the region of northwestern Europe: the place of the *Hollandgänger* from northwestern Germany was taken by Dutch migrants coming to Germany (*Preußengänger*), no small number of whom became immigrants. Before World War I, the Dutch constituted one of the strongest nationality groups – next to Poles and Italians – among the numerous foreign migrant workers in the Empire.[21]

From the early 1890s on, the employment of foreigners in Germany – especially in Prussia – grew into a mass movement. It reached its peak in 1914 with about 1.2 million foreign migrant workers. Most of them worked in Prussia: between three-quarters and four-fifths of all foreign migrants in the Empire went to Prussia. There the most important groups were Poles from Russian central Poland – and to a lesser extent those from Austro-Hungarian Galicia – who were employed in agriculture, along with Italians, who found work especially in brickyards and excavation, but also in mining and industrial production.

When it came to the "migrant worker issue," economic and political interests collided in Prussia: diametrically opposed to the economic interest in meeting the need for "cheap and willing" foreign manpower was the political interest in containing the predominantly Polish immigration into Prussia's eastern provinces. The Prussian anti-Polish policy was, leaving aside some ethnonational prejudices, determined largely by the Prussian government's anxieties about revolutionary dreams by Prussian, Russian, and Austro-Hungarian Poles about the resurrection of a Polish national state. This was also the policy motivation behind the mass expulsion in 1885 of foreign Poles who had been living, or at least working, in the Prussian border districts for years, in some cases decades, and the subsequent ban on immigration.

Since the end of the 1880s, the catastrophic "people shortage" (*Leutenot*) compelled a search for a solution that would satisfy the economic interests without endangering the strategy of the anti-Polish policy: the goal was to prevent the necessary influx of workers from the east from turning into immigration, keeping it instead on the tracks of temporary seasonal migration and in the process maintaining strict surveillance especially over the foreign Poles. The result was a system of restrictive control over foreigners that was developed in Prussia beginning in the 1890s and perfected in 1907, with *Legitimationszwang* (compulsory legitimizing papers) and *Rückkehrzwang* (compulsory return) during the *Karenzzeit* (waiting period) in the winter.

Legitimationszwang meant tighter control over foreigners with limited work and residence permits that had to be renewed annually. Foreign Polish migrant laborers who frequently arrived at the border or crossed it illegally (the recruitment of workers abroad was forbidden in Russian central Poland) were welcomed in the spring. It was repeatedly impressed upon the border authorities that they should not under any circumstances impede the influx of these workers, on which the agricultural labor market in eastern Prussia had become increasingly dependent, even if they had made their way to or even across the border illegally because of the impediments placed in their way by the Russian authorities. However, the foreign Polish workers should not turn into immigrants, but remain what they were – foreign migrant workers. As a result, they had to leave Prussian state territory before Christmas and return to their regions of origin, with failure to do so punishable by expulsion and deportation. No small number circumvented this compulsory return with the help of domestic employers and by crossing temporarily into neighboring German states which had not adopted the Prussian system of the anti-Polish security policy, in spite of Berlin's urging to do so.

Even in World War I, which cut off overseas emigration and continental immigration, foreign workers fulfilled a crucial replacement function in Germany: the lack of workers

---

[20] Polish industrial workers in the Ruhr (*Ruhrpolen*) since the end of the 19th century.

[21] German seasonal agricultural laborers in the Netherlands from the 17th to the early 20th century; German itinerant merchants from the Münsterland in northern, western, and central Europe in the 18th and 19th centuries; Polish agricultural workers in Prussia-Germany from the late 19th century to World War II; Italian industrial workers in western and central Europe in the late 19th and early 20th centuries; Dutch labor migrants in Germany in the late 19th and early 20th centuries; Swedish labor migrants in Germany in the late 19th and early 20th centuries.

was one of the fundamental problems of German wartime economic policy from 1914 to 1918. The demand for workers rose especially in three areas: the armament industry, mining, and agriculture. Measures to meet this need for labor were thwarted by the limited capacity of the domestic labor markets. As a result, the rapidly growing shortage of (skilled) workers during the war drove companies and relevant agencies to reach beyond the national labor pool and eventually pushed the forced recruitment of ever larger contingents of foreign workers.

Although there continued to be an appreciable number of foreign workers (men and women) who worked voluntarily in the German war economy, the employment of foreigners during the war was increasingly characterized by forced recruitment and forced labor. At the end of World War I the German labor force numbered at least 2.5 million, nearly one-tenth of the prewar level of those gainfully employed, and about one-seventh of all those in the workplace in the last year of the war. More than 1.5 million of them were prisoners of war.[22] Civilian foreign workers accounted for about 1 million of those employed in the German war economy. The German civil and military authorities did not treat them – unlike the prisoners of war – as a uniform category, even though most of them also belonged to the group of "enemy foreigners." That was especially true of the 500,000–600,000 foreign Polish workers at the end of the war in 1918. With the beginning of the war the policy toward the Poles from Russia, already restrictive, became even more so and was simultaneously reversed – from compulsory return to a ban on returning: as "hostile foreigners," the Poles from abroad were at the same time prohibited from leaving; in other words, they were not allowed to return home, something they had been compelled to do every year before the war. They were also prohibited from changing location and remained bound to their employer. Despite sharp protests from Vienna, the return of Poles and Ruthenians from Austro-Hungarian Galicia – i.e., a territory from an allied country – was initially made difficult to ease the transition from the peacetime to a wartime economy on the agricultural labor market.

The Poles had thus become de facto forced laborers who could not freely choose their place of residence or their employer. Beginning in 1915–16, the territories in Poland and Belgium occupied by German troops became the target of German labor policy. Poland remained primarily a recruiting ground for agricultural workers. By contrast, the workers recruited in Belgium were mostly for the armament industry. Because the number of "volunteers" overall was far below the level of what was desired or deemed necessary, the German authorities resorted increasingly to coercive measures.[23]

Given the massive military effort and the largely successful allied blockade of foreign trade, the employment of foreigners became a growing necessity for the German war economy during World War I. Without the rising internationalization of the labor markets, Germany would not have been able to wage the war for as long as it did. Moreover, in terms of the coerced mass movement of people, World War I was also beyond the military sphere a momentous "learning process" (Ulrich Herbert) with respect to the "use of foreigners" in the National Socialist war economy of Germany during World War II and in German-occupied Europe.

Flight and forced migrations in the interwar period and during World War II

With its extreme nationalism, World War I had given a strong boost to the exclusion of minorities and the spread of xenophobia. For the subsequent development of the employment of and the policy toward foreigners, World War I proved a pacesetter in that it substantially increased the state's capacity to intervene in the economy and society and thus also in migratory movements. The employment of foreigners during the Weimar Republic continued to be determined by the ethnonational anti-Polish policy that was carried over unchanged from imperial Germany. In admitting foreign Polish workers, German migration policy in the Weimar Republic continued to place economic considerations front and center, and preventing permanent settlement remained the primary goal of measures related to immigration policy. Despite the substantial decline in the size of the Polish minority in the Empire after World War I, the ethnonational bogeyman of a "Polonization" of eastern Prussia still formed the basis of the anti-Polish policy. The immigration of Polish workers continued to be seen as a threat to internal and external security, to the economy and the labor market, and to Germany's society and culture.

At the same time, labor market policy became increasingly important for the employment of foreigners. As a determining factor and dominant theme of the discussion in a Weimar Republic shaken by economic crisis, the slogan about the "protection of the national labor market" had replaced talk of a people shortage in industry and agriculture. In the Weimar Republic, the establishment of a nationwide labor bureaucracy, with the interlinking of labor market observation, job placement, and unemployment insurance, was the most important area of modernization in terms of labor market and social welfare policy. The far-reaching development of a modern labor administration created the preconditions for a foreigner policy oriented toward the labor market. Given the tense situation of the labor market in Germany, priority was given to German over foreign laborers who could take only replacement or additional jobs. This was also in line with demands by the German trade unions, which had already been articulated before the war and could be pushed through in the early years of the Weimar Republic in view of the new power of trade unions and labor parties: for example, to prevent wage dumping, foreigners could be employed only under the same working and wage conditions as nationals. After a transition phase of demobilization in 1919–20, these guidelines formed the foundation for increasingly

[22] Prisoners of war in Europe, 1914–1922.
[23] Polish and Belgian forced laborers in Germany during World War I.

sophisticated tools to regulate and guide the employment of foreigners.

Difficult economic conditions and a protectionist policy of immigration combined in bringing about a massive decline in the employment of foreigners in the Reich compared to the prewar period. In the 1920s, the number of foreign workers in Germany fluctuated between 200,000 and 300,000 and dropped to around 100,000 in the global economic crisis of the early 1930s. The growing pace of Germany's rearmament after the National Socialist takeover of power in 1933 made labor shortage once again a central theme of labor policy within a few short years. But even though the number of foreign workers in German industry and agriculture did rise, it reached only 436,000 by 1938–9. The chief reasons for this were economic and foreign currency policies and political-ideological factors, which caused the Nazi regime's immigration policy to remain restrictive even in the face of a growing labor shortage. For one, the employment of foreign workers was seen as problematic because the foreign currency situation in the Reich was exceedingly tight as a result of the rearmament efforts. For another, from the perspective of the radical ethnonationalistic and racist Nazi worldview, the employment of foreigners – especially with its traditionally large share of workers from eastern Europe – posed a threat of endangering the "blood purity" of the German population.

Germany remained a country of both emigration and immigration during the interwar period: compared to the prewar period, after the dismantling of the obstacles to emigration that had been thrown up by the war (a majority of the overseas destination countries, which had been allied against Germany in the war, initially did not accept any German immigrants), emigration rose sharply. The high point of emigration from the Weimar Republic was the crisis-ridden year 1923: 115,000 Germans left the country, a yearly figure that had not been reached since the last great exodus between 1880 and 1893. The rise in overseas emigration in the early years of the Weimar Republic was accompanied by a growth in continental emigration and labor migration; especially the Netherlands, which had been neutral during the war, became a central destination for tens of thousands of German immigrants, among them many young women who found employment in the service sector, primarily in private households.[24]

With the end of World War I and the processes of state formation in its wake, coercive migrations (flight, resettlement, expulsion) gained considerably in importance in the interwar period. The political changes as a result of the peace treaties caused about 10 million people in Europe to cross borders involuntarily. Germany, too, was massively affected by these movements. By the mid-1920s, about a million people had immigrated from the ceded territories. This was the largest immigration movement that the Weimar Republic had to deal with – and it had to do so between 1918 and 1923

within a few short postwar years that were marked by grave economic, social, and political crises.

From Alsace-Lorraine, alone, up to about 150,000 people came into what was left of the Reich, with another 16,000 immigrants from the former German colonies. Far more extensive still was the immigration from the eastern territories of the Reich ceded to Poland in the Treaty of Versailles. By mid-1925, the National Statistical Office had counted 850,000 German "border land expellees" from the western regions of Poland.[25] Added to these were the approximately 120,000 ethnic Germans who had come into the Reich from Czarist Russia during the war and postwar upheavals between 1917 and 1921–2, although around half continued overseas or migrated by the thousands back to Poland or the USSR.[26] The "ethnic Germans" are difficult to identify among the possibly one and a half million people who fled civil war and revolution in the former Czarist Empire. The Weimar Republic was initially one of the main destinations of this refugee movement: according to estimates (though they are probably too high), about 600,000 refugees from Russia were in Germany in 1922 and 1923, of whom around 360,000 supposedly found asylum in Berlin alone in 1923.[27]

Onward migrations quickly got under way. After 1923, the number of refugees from Russia in German exile continued to decline, down to 150,000 in 1925 and 100,000 in 1933. While "Russian Berlin" was initially the European center of exile with many important cultural and political functions, with the exodus of many refugees from Germany in the mid-1920s "Russian Paris" assumed that role and retained it until the invasion of German troops in 1940. One of the reasons France, and especially Paris and the adjoining *départements*, became the most important destination for Russian emigration is that the French government at times pursued an open immigration policy and the French economy was in search of workers. But the center of Russian emigration moved across the Atlantic further west: North America and especially "Russian New York" became with increasing frequency the final destination in the gradual geographic distancing from the Russian homeland. World War I shifted the center of Russian emigration to the USA for good, with the political and cultural focal point in New York. It was not only problems in the housing and labor markets that were behind the decline in the number of Russian refugees in Germany after 1923. There was also a restrictive German integration policy that showed little interest in having Russian refugees stay in Germany and therefore offered them neither legal nor economic support for integration.

Even more restrictive was the migration and integration policy of the Weimar Republic toward the immigration of eastern, east-central, and southeastern European Jews. Within the context of the formation of states in eastern, east-central,

---

[24] German maids in the Netherlands in the interwar period.

[25] German immigrants in Germany from territories ceded after World War I.

[26] Ethnic German "remigrants" from Russia in Germany, 1890s to 1930s.

[27] Russian emigrants in Europe since 1917.

and southeastern Europe, pogroms and other violent excesses against Jews had occurred against the backdrop of profound economic, social, and political crises. Many Jews sought, often illegally, to cross over the largely closed borders to the West. By 1921, probably around 70,000 asylum-seeking Jews from eastern Europe had come to Germany. In the beginning, those who had made it over the border barriers were granted asylum in Prussia. There, as well as in the rest of Germany, anti-Semitic excesses grew much worse between 1919 and 1923. There was open violence (street brawls, assaults, hostage-taking) against eastern European Jews, and the anti-Jewish policies were sharpened on the federal and state levels. In Bavaria, official anti-Semitism culminated in 1923 in a wave of internments and expulsions aimed at foreign Jews. But in Prussia, too, the granting of asylum that had still been generous in 1919 was soon increasingly restricted. Onward migration motivated by the anti-Semitic excesses, the increasingly restrictive asylum policy aimed at nonintegration, and the tense economic situation in the early years of the Weimar Republic caused the number of eastern, east-central, and southeastern European Jews, which had risen noticeably in World War I, to drop again rapidly.[28]

Processes of onward migration similar to those of refugees from Russia and eastern European Jews in the immediate postwar period can also be observed in the emigration from Nazi Germany after 1933, which comprised a total of about half a million individuals. It involved political opponents of the regime, those regarded as such by the regime, and especially all those who, as a result of the racist ideology of National Socialism, were humiliated as outcast aliens in Germany and increasingly persecuted. That was especially true of the Jews, 280,000 of whom fled the Reich. Around the world, more than 80 states took in refugees from Germany.[29]

World War II led to an unprecedented number of forced migrations, the result largely of the expansion and downfall of the National Socialist Third Reich. One can roughly identify four main types of forced migrations (with a good deal of overlap): (1) refugees from the immediate effects of military conflict, who fled or were evacuated from battle zones and advancing armies; (2) individuals who were deported during the war or forcibly detained: forced laborers, chiefly in the German war economy, prisoners of war, and civilian segments of the German or foreign populations who were resettled or deported; (3) the displaced persons (DPs) of the immediate postwar period; and (4) those expelled after the end of the war on 8 May 1945 from the former eastern territories of the German Reich and from the German settlement regions in eastern, east-central, and southeastern Europe.

During World War II, Germany was the engine and center of European forced mass migrations. It was able to wage war for nearly six years only because it had planned and pursued the conflict from the outset as a war of plunder and conquest. In this scheme, the states allied to Germany and the countries and territories acquired or conquered after 1938 were to serve the German war economy with their agricultural and industrial production, their raw materials, and their population. During the course of the war, the importance of the plundered goods and human resources to the German war economy grew immensely: in October 1944, nearly 8 million foreign workers were counted in Germany, among them nearly 6 million civilians and just under 2 million prisoners of war. Among the more than 20 countries of origin of the 8 million foreign workers registered in the fall of 1944, the Soviet Union dominated with a share of more than a third (2.8 million). It was followed by 1.7 million from Poland, 1.2 million from France, and several hundreds of thousands each from Italy, the Netherlands, Belgium, Czechoslovakia, and Yugoslavia.

A look at their share of the total employed population reveals the enormous economic importance of the foreign forced laborers to the German economy: all told, foreigners made up about a quarter of all workers in August 1944; they were found in all sectors of the economy, in enterprises of every size, and spread throughout the entire Reich. Their significance was especially high in specific sectors and enterprises. That was true for agriculture, where the percentage of foreign forced laborers was 46% in 1944, or in mining with 34%. Foreign forced laborers were also put to work in highly specialized areas and those important to national security and the war, for example, in the armament industry. In some industries with low qualification demands, four-fifths of all workers were foreigners. The average age of the foreign workers was 20 to 24 years, one-third were women of whom the majority were under the age of 20.

The German war economy during World War II, as a result of its very conception as a plunder economy, was from the beginning vitally dependent on foreign forced laborers: as early as in 1941, arms production would not have been able to fulfill its quotas any longer without foreigners, in agriculture that point was already reached in 1940. As a system of forced labor based to a large degree on foreign workers, the National Socialist "deployment of foreigners" remained historically without parallel.[30]

Throughout all of the newly conquered "living space" in the East, National Socialist policy sought to secure its rule permanently and to establish a German order that was focused strictly on racist criteria and set up a hierarchy of population groups and nationalities. Essential elements in the creation of this racist "world order" were the planning and extensive implementation of resettlements, expulsions, and deportations of entire populations in favor of the "Aryans," supposedly a "people without space." About 9 million people were affected by these actions. Between 1939 and 1944, 1 million

---

[28] Eastern European Jews in Berlin from the late 19th century to the 1930s.

[29] Political and intellectual refugees from Nazi Germany and from German-occupied Europe, 1933–1945; Jewish refugees from Nazi Germany and from German-occupied Europe since 1933; German and Austrian Jewish children transported to Great Britain after 1938–1939.

[30] Forced laborers in Germany and German-occupied Europe during World War II.

people of German background were lured and coerced back into the Reich from their settlement areas outside the boundaries of the Reich in southeastern, east-central, and eastern Europe in order to be settled in the conquered territories that had been directly annexed to the Reich.[31]

The precondition for the settlement of these ethnic Germans was always the deportation of the native Polish, Czech, and Jewish population, which was initiated on a large scale in 1939–40 and ended in genocide. In 1940–1, around 1.2 million Poles and Jews were expelled from the formerly Polish and now annexed *Reichsgaue* (Reich provinces) of Wartheland and Danzig–West Prussia to make room for the ethnic Germans to be newly settled. Frequently, expulsion and settlement occurred simultaneously, which meant that the treks of new settlers and deportees crossed paths. But that was only the beginning: according to the overall plan, of the more than 10 million people living in this region, only 1.7 million were considered capable of being "Germanized" (*eindeutschungsfähig*) – 7.8 million Poles and 700,000 Jews were to be driven out.

In the National Socialist hierarchy of races, Jews or those declared Jews were regarded as the population group with the lowest claim to so-called living space. They were hardest hit by the German policy of annihilation. When a ban on emigration was enacted in October 1941, 160,000 Jews were still living in the Reich, a time when the SS (Schutzstaffel) decisively began deportation into Poland, which was for most tantamount to a forced migration into death. In Poland itself, a total of nearly 3 million Jews were incorporated into the SS policy of "space planning" and annihilation. Of those, 2.7 million fell victim to murderous Nazi policies, which culminated in the industrial mass murder in extermination camps. The Jewish population of nearly all European countries suffered the same fate as the Polish and German Jews: 2.2 million from the Soviet Union, 550,000 from Hungary, 200,000 from Romania, 140,000 from Czechoslovakia, 100,000 from the Netherlands, 76,000 from France, 60,000 from Yugoslavia, 60,000 from Greece, and 28,000 from Belgium.

Flight and expulsion after World War II

After the end of the war, the surviving victims of the National Socialist labor, concentration, and extermination camps made up the majority of the 10–12 million displaced persons. They represented about 20 nationalities with more than 35 different languages. They stood under the direct authority of the four Allied occupying powers and of the international aid organizations authorized by them. Initially, the goal of the military authorities and aid organizations was to gather the DPs as quickly as possible and return them to their home countries. In the first four months after Germany's surrender in May 1945, alone, they were able to repatriate more than 5 million DPs. The majority voluntarily joined the countless

transports organized for them by the Allies. In accordance with an agreement between the western Allies and the USSR, DPs with Soviet citizenship were also forcibly repatriated. That was done even though officials of the western Allies knew that DPs, as alleged collaborators, faced internment, repression, and "reeducation measures," and officers frequently also the death penalty, which is why no small number of those affected chose suicide over deportation.[32]

Beginning in the fall of 1945, the numbers of those on the transports declined steadily. At the end of 1945 there were still around 1.7 million DPs in the three Western Occupation Zones. In 1946, the number of repatriations had dropped to only around 500,000. The emigration programs of the International Refugee Organization (IRO) that was set up in June of 1947 offered new prospects to a large number of DPs. Only a small portion remained in Germany. Those were mostly individuals who had not been considered for the emigration programs because of old age, illness, or disability to work. When the Western Allies handed responsibility for the DPs to the German government in 1950, around 150,000 were likely to still have been in West Germany, about a third of them still living in camps. With the Law on the Legal Status of Homeless Foreigners of 25 April 1951, Germany created a legal status for DPs that was generous compared to the international refugee law. Although it assimilated them in many areas to the legal position of West German citizens, it did not lead to complete equality with German refugees and expellees. The law did not regulate claims for compensation. Given the restrictive compensation practice of German administration and courts in the subsequent period, many "homeless foreigners" received no compensation for what they had suffered under the Nazi dictatorship.

In the immediate postwar period, the relationship of the German population to the DPs in the integration process was characterized by defensive attitudes, prejudices, contempt, but also envy: on the one hand, the discriminatory Nazi language about "subhumans" from the East was still reverberating. Added to this were generalized and fear-inspiring reports about violent outbursts and plundering by liberated forced laborers. On the other hand, DPs continued to be widely perceived as privileged persons under the care of the Allies, as they were removed from German police authority and also had opportunities for overseas emigration that were in the beginning closed to Germans, with few exceptions. German postwar society hardly regarded the DPs as anything more than an occupation problem – their fate as victims of Nazi rule was largely repressed and concealed.

Displaced persons were only one group among the millions of migrants in Germany in the immediate postwar period: in the territory that later formed the four occupation zones, around 10 million people had fled or were evacuated to rural regions in the face of the Allied carpet bombing of German cities. In many cases it was years before these evacuees could leave their makeshift quarters and return to their

---

[31] Ethnic Germans (*Volksdeutsche*) in the German Reich and in German-occupied territories in World War II.

[32] Displaced persons (DPs) in Europe since the end of World War II.

cities and towns; in 1947 there were still nearly 4 million evacuees in the four occupation zones. In the Federal Republic their return was then treated largely as a task of local communities and seen exclusively as a problem of the availability of housing in the cities. It was thus regarded as secondary to the reception and integration of refugees and expellees.

Of the approximately 18 million Reich Germans in the eastern provinces of the Reich and ethnic Germans in the German settlement areas in eastern, east-central, and south-eastern Europe, about 14 million had fled westward in the final phase of the war or had been expelled or deported after the end of the war. The census of 1950 reveals the result of the flight and expulsions of all these millions: nearly 12.5 million refugees and expellees from the former eastern territories of the German Reich, which had now passed into Polish and Soviet control, and from the settlement areas of the ethnic Germans had made their way into the Federal Republic and the GDR (German Democratic Republic); another 500,000 were living in Austria and in other countries, and perhaps around 300,000 had been deported to the USSR. Hundreds of thousands did not survive flight, expulsion, and deportation.

Of the 12.5 million refugees and expellees in the Federal Republic and the GDR in 1950, the largest group – just under 7 million – came from the formerly German territories east of the Oder and Neisse rivers. The second largest group were 3 million refugees and expellees from Czechoslovakia, joined by 1.4 million from Poland of prewar boundaries; 300,000 from the Free City of Danzig, until 1939 under the administration of the League of Nations; just under 300,000 from Yugoslavia; 200,000 from Hungary; and 130,000 from Romania.[33]

The refugees and expellees were not evenly distributed across the four occupation zones in Germany. Rural regions had to take in far more people than urban-industrial conurbations, many of which had been heavily damaged especially by the Allied bombing campaign; the housing situation and food supply seemed better in rural communities and small towns. All told, the eastern part of Germany was more heavily affected than the west, and within the three western occupation zones, the eastern regions were in turn more heavily burdened than the western regions. At the end of 1947, the share of refugees and expellees among the total population in the Soviet occupation zone stood at 24.3%. By contrast, the American occupation zone had 17.7% and the British 14.5%. In the French occupation zone the percentage was a mere 1%, a result of the refusal by French occupation authorities to take in refugees and expellees.

It seemed to many contemporaries that the problems of integrating these masses of immigrants could hardly be

solved by a smaller, overcrowded, and massively ruined postwar Germany. At the end of the war more than 4 million housing units were partially or completely destroyed, which was equal to more than one-fifth of the entire prewar housing stock. Added to this were the problems of supplying food and other goods. Only the sustained boom of the "economic miracle" that began in the early 1950s brought a fundamental improvement in the economic and social integration of the refugees and expellees, and of the at least 2.7 million immigrants from the GDR between 1949 and the building of the wall in 1961. Conversely, they altogether constituted a qualified labor force that played a major role in sustaining the economic miracle. However, in the process one could initially observe the stratification phenomenon usually associated with regular immigration: refugees and expellees at first took jobs mostly below their qualifications and thus also had a lower income. Opportunities for advancement existed for many of them primarily in the 1960s with the expansion of the job supply and the immigration of foreign workers, who in turn took the least desirable jobs.

The employment of foreigners and immigration into the Federal Republic of Germany

The enormous expansion of the West German labor market in the wake of a massive expansion of foreign trade, which was simultaneously the cause and consequence of the economic boom following the end of the immediate postwar period, formed the background to the recruitment of millions of migrant workers (guest workers), both men and women, from southern Europe. At first the strong influx from the GDR had additionally filled the growing need of the West German labor market. This influx ended abruptly in 1961.[34] Between the building of the Berlin Wall in 1961, which cut off the stream of workers from the GDR, and the outbreak of the economic crisis in 1973, which led to a halt in recruitment and saw the employment of foreigners pass its peak, the foreign labor force grew from around 550,000 to around 2.6 million. Between the end of the 1950s and the recruitment ban in 1973, around 14 million foreign workers came to Germany; around 11 million returned, the others remained and were joined by their families.

The initial recruitment treaties, signed with Italy in 1955 and Spain and Greece in 1960, were followed by agreements with Turkey (1961) and Morocco (1963), Portugal (1964) and Tunisia (1965), as well as Yugoslavia (1968). Of these agreements, only those with the two North African countries were largely ineffectual. Italians, Spaniards, and Greeks were most strongly represented in the beginning. Their share declined in the 1970s, while the number of Yugoslavs and Turks grew especially after the end of the 1960s. The share of foreigners among the West German residential population grew from 1.2% in 1960 to 4.9% in 1970 and

[33] German refugees and expellees from eastern, east-central, and southeastern Europe in Germany and Austria since the end of World War II; German deportees from east-central and southeastern Europe in the USSR after the end of World War II.

[34] German refugees and immigrants from East Germany in West Germany.

Table 1. Foreigners in the Federal Republic of Germany, 1961–2007 (rounded to hundreds, selected years).

	Number	In percentage of total population
1961	686,200	1.2
1967	1,806,700	3.1
1970	2,976,500	4.9
1974	4,127,400	6.7
1976	3,948,300	6.4
1979	4,143,800	6.7
1980	4,453,300	7.2
1982	4,666,900	7.6
1984	4,363,600	7.1
1988	4,489,100	7.3
1989	4,840,900	7.7
1990	5,342,500	8.4
1992	6,495,800	8.0
1995	7,173,900	8.8
1997	7,365,800	9.0
2001	7,318,700	8.9
2003	7,334,800	8.9
2005	6,755,800	8.2
2007	6,744,900	8.2

Source: Beauftragte der Bundesregierung für Ausländerfragen, ed., *Daten und Fakten zur Ausländersituation*, 18th ed. (Bonn, 1999), 19; Statistisches Bundesamt, Wiesbaden. The figures for 1992–2007 refer to reunited Germany.

7.2% in 1980, and then remained at nearly that level through the 1980s. In 1980, around 33% of foreigners were Turkish nationals, followed by Yugoslavs with 14% and Italians with 13.9%. The share of foreigners among the total number of wage and salary workers stood at nearly 10% in 1980; it subsequently declined slightly and stabilized at right around 8% (see Table 1).[35]

The term "guest worker," soon introduced in public discussion but not in official usage, implied an occupational-social classification with the emphasis on unskilled or semiskilled work, primarily in the central sectors of industrial production. In the 1970s, guest workers constituted around three-quarters of the foreign workforce (both men and women) in West Germany (1974 around 77%; 1979, 74%). Against the backdrop of sustained economic growth – interrupted only by the recession in 1966–7 – they formed a fluctuating pool of workers. It balanced out the tension between supply and demand in the labor market and pushed further economic

growth, first on the labor market, later also by increasing purchasing power.

Added to the development of a substratum below local labor was the economic buffer function of the employment of foreigners as periods of upswing and crisis alternated. This was revealed by the first recession in 1966–7 and during the oil price shock of 1973, which made evident the limits to growth and was the occasion for the recruitment ban that ended the guest worker period: as a result of the crisis of 1966–7, the employment of foreigners in West Germany declined by around 30% from 1.3 million to 0.9 million (January 1968). It then rose again, only to shrink once again by around 29% between around 1973 and 1977. This became especially apparent in areas strongly dependent on economic fluctuations, for example, the construction sector, in which the number of local workers dropped by around 15% between 1973 and 1976, while that of foreign workers declined by around 41%.

Although the recruitment ban in 1973 reduced the employment of foreigners, it also limited the transnational fluctuation of foreign workers, because after this time a voluntary, temporary return to the host countries could turn into a permanent, involuntary departure: foreign workers who left their jobs to return home generally had no chance to be readmitted as migrant workers. As a result, the number of new foreign workers who were less secure in terms of labor and social law declined, while the number of those who remained and had their families join them increased. Over time, however, their residence status solidified. Guest workers with permanent residence became immigrants. Although the number of gainfully employed foreigners dropped from 2.6 million in 1973 to around 1.8 million in 1977 and down to around 1.6 million by 1989, the foreign residential population stood at around 4 million in 1973 (3.97 million) and 1979 (4.14 million) and at just under 4.9 million (7.3%) by 1989.

Already in the late 1970s, a large number of the foreign families in Germany found themselves in a paradoxical social situation, living in an immigrant situation without an immigration country. This fact was suppressed in the political decision-making process and was taboo in administrative policies. However, the defensive self-description of West Germany as a non-immigration country became increasingly meaningless in the face of a pragmatic reorientation of administrative practice toward integration in every sense of the law. In cases of doubt, integration was assured by the judicial system: obligations toward foreigners with respect to residence, labor law, and social law were not to be suspended based on considerations of political opportunism. As the foreigners' duration of stay increased, so did their legal claims on the welfare state or its obligations to provide services to the immigrant foreign population. Still, the long-overdue comprehensive concepts regarding issues of immigration and integration were absent until the discussion emerged surrounding the report of the Independent Commission on Immigration in 2001 and the Immigration Law of 2002–3.

[35] Greek labor migrants in western, central and northern Europe after 1950: the examples of Germany and the Netherlands; Italian labor migrants in northern, central, and western Europe since the end of World War II; Portuguese labor migrants in western and central Europe since the 1950s: the examples of France and Germany; Spanish labor migrants in western, central, and northern Europe since the end of World War II; Turkish labor migrants in western, central, and northern Europe since the mid-1950s; Yugoslav labor migrants in western, central, and northern Europe since the end of World War II.

Table 2. Foreign contract workers in the GDR, 1966–1989 (selected years)	
1966	ca. 3,500
1967	14,000
1969	14,134
1971	14,800
1974	18,680
1979	20,567
1980	26,567
1984	29,000
1986	61,000
1988	87,793
1989	93,568

Source: Sandra Gruner-Domić, "Beschäftigung statt Ausbildung. Ausländische Arbeiter und Arbeiterinnen in der DDR (1961 bis 1989)," in *50 Jahre Bundesrepublik – 50 Jahre Einwanderung,* ed. Jan Motte, Rainer Ohliger, and Anne von Oswald (Frankfurt am Main and New York, 1999), 215–40, here 224.

The employment of foreign workers in the rotation system in the GDR

The GDR also gave employment to foreigners – on a smaller scale – on the basis of official state agreements. At the end, most foreign workers came from Vietnam and Mozambique. The employment of foreigners was officially hushed up in East Germany or trivialized as migration for the purpose of occupational training, which characterized only some of it in fact, especially in the beginning. Although the foreigners brought into the walled-in state with limited contracts had bureaucratic, authoritarian "supervision," they were often housed in separate communal dorms and thus also kept socially at a distance. Closer contacts required official permission and follow-up reporting.

Of the approximately 190,000 foreigners in the GDR in 1989, those employed in East German enterprises made up by far the largest group (93,600), among them on the eve of German reunification in 1989 around 59,000 workers from Vietnam and around 15,000 from Mozambique (see Table 2). Like the guest workers in West Germany, the foreigners in the GDR worked mostly in jobs that were least appreciated by local workers: in manufacturing and under the harshest conditions, for example, three-quarters in shift work.

Immigration problems in connection with the employment of foreigners emerged only in case of the – rare – marriages between foreign workers and citizens of the GDR, since the bilateral agreements stipulated that the arriving foreigners would have to return home once their contracts ended. Family reunification did not exist in this strict rotational system. The foreign workers in the GDR came as single migrant laborers of both sexes, with the agreements speaking above all of young, single workers. Some regulations were family-hostile: for example, in the case of pregnancy, the worker had the choice of abortion or deportation. This regulation was modified only shortly before the fall of the Berlin Wall. After that, Vietnamese women, for example, were allowed in exceptional cases to have their children in the GDR, provided their employer consented. Six weeks after the birth of the child they had to resume their job – the child was entitled to a place in day care – or leave the country.

The working and living conditions of the foreign workers were, for the duration of their stay, regulated in most areas through bilateral governmental agreements and special basic guidelines. There was virtually no sphere of life that was not in some way regulated or supervised. The East German Foreigners Act of 28 June 1979 and its attendant Foreigner Decree (*Ausländerverordnung*) regulated the fundamental questions of the foreign population's stay and legal status in the GDR. However, the legal framework articulated in these regulations remained very cursory: on the one hand, foreign workers living in the GDR were accorded the same rights as East German citizens, excluding those linked to citizenship, provided there were no separate agreements with the country of origin concerning the law on foreigners. On the other hand, it was stipulated that permission to reside in the GDR could, at any time and without any explanation, be restricted in duration and location, denied, withdrawn, or declared invalid.

In addition, measures were taken to immobilize and discipline the foreign workers: for example, as a rule they were tied to one employer for the duration of their stay, and their right to give notice was severely restricted. The threat to reduce or suspend payment of a compensation for separation from the family served to "strengthen work discipline." For Polish workers, for example, this "separation compensation" was paid after 1973 and calculated for every day of their stay. A single unexcused absence from work led to a 50% cut in this payment, a second unexcused absence resulted in its termination. The bilateral treaties also contained specific agreements about whether and how much of the gross income had to be directly transferred to the governments of the countries of origin, which portion of earnings would be paid directly to the workers, and which would be paid out only after their return.

Public discussion about foreigners living and working in the GDR were consistently suppressed by the government, and all official documents, treaties, and so forth were kept under lock until the fall of 1989. For that reason, foreigners living in East Germany had no lobby until then, with a few exceptions (e.g., the churches). Foreign workers had – leaving aside union activities in the workplace – neither a voice nor a right to participate in decisions relating to the policies dealing with foreigners. Separate lobbies for foreign workers did not exist. On the whole, there was state-mandated social segregation rather than social integration vis-à-vis the foreign workers in the GDR.[36]

Immigration and integration in unified Germany

The opening of the iron curtain, the change in the political systems in the states of the former Eastern Bloc, and the end

---

[36] Vietnamese, Mozambican, and Cuban labor migrants in East Germany since the 1970s.

of the GDR in 1989–90 transformed the patterns of migration in Europe and Germany. Unified Germany became once again the destination and hub of east-west migration. This was especially evident in the immigration of asylum seekers, ethnic Germans from the East (*Aussiedler*), and Jewish quota refugees.

The right of asylum enshrined in West Germany's Basic Law (*Grundgesetz*, GG) after World War II was intended to provide a secure stay to all those who felt entitled to that right until the decision on their application was made.[37] The growing number of refugees from all over the world who claimed that right led to an initial tendency to restrict it in practice, and eventually, following a surge in applications after the opening of the iron curtain, to restrict this basic right itself, a change that became reality in the Asylum Compromise of 1993. A right of asylum had also existed in the GDR, though not as a subjective right on the part of the applicant but as the right of state to grant asylum: compared to West Germany, the number of asylum seekers had been vastly smaller.

In West Germany, the trend line of asylum seekers crossed the 100,000 mark in 1988. During the year of European revolutions in 1989 it rose to about 120,000, reached around 190,000 in unified Germany, and surged to nearly 260,000 in 1991, and eventually almost 440,000 in 1992 (see Table 3).[38] The crises in eastern, east-central, and southeastern Europe, together with defensive measures against economic refugees from the third world, led to a complete reversal of the ratios: while 74.8% of asylum seekers were from the third world in 1986, by 1993, 72.1% came from eastern, east-central, and southeastern Europe.[39] This was the backdrop to the change in the basic right of asylum in 1993 (Article 16a of the Basic Law). Since that time, individuals have hardly any chance for asylum if they enter Germany via countries "free of persecution" or arrive from "safe third-countries," which now completely surround Germany. After the end of the wars and civil wars in southeastern Europe, the majority of asylum seekers came once again from the third world. Since the end of the 1990s, the number of yearly asylum applications has been on the whole in a down trend and consistently below the threshold of 100,000 that was crossed between 1988 and 1997.

However, the defensive measures did not only lead to a decline in the number of asylum seekers and an increase in the transit of asylum seekers through Germany to other European countries, but also to an increase in the number of illegal stays. The most important forms this has taken are not based on illegal border crossings put front and center in

Table 3. Asylum applications in the Federal Republic of Germany, 1972–2007 (selected years).	
1972	5,289
1976	11,123
1978	33,136
1980	107,818
1982	37,423
1984	35,278
1986	99,650
1987	57,379
1988	103,076
1989	121,318
1990	193,063
1991	256,112
1992	438,191
1993	322,599
1994	127,210
1997	104,353
1998	98,644
2000	78,564
2002	71,127
2003	50,563
2007	19,164

Source: Statistisches Bundesamt, ed., *Ausländische Bevölkerung in Deutschland* (Wiesbaden, 2001), 113; Bundesamt für Migration und Flüchtlinge.

sensational reports about organized human smuggling by the media. Rather, they derive from existing opportunities to enter the country legally, for example, as tourists, to visit friends or relatives, or as seasonal workers, business travelers, asylum seekers, or refugees. Illegality begins only when these individuals take jobs without a work permit, stay after their time of admission has expired (referred to as overstayers in the English-speaking and *sans-papiers* in the French-speaking world), or go underground after the request for asylum has been denied, when they are asked to leave, or the government announces it will take measures to terminate their stay (deportation). In addition, there is a great diversity of shifting migration patterns with fluid transitions.[40]

Less important, though much more spectacular, is clandestine immigration or crossing the borders with false papers, followed by an illegal stay in the country and illegal work, unregistered or registered on the basis of false papers. This is also the area in which smuggling organizations operate: for the most part internationally organized, sometimes linked by Mafia-like networks, they are the primary profiteers from Europe's closure to unwanted immigration. There are fluid boundaries to the illegal trade in contracts, to modern forms of debt bondage, and to human trafficking as internationally organized capital crimes – for example, trafficking in women.[41]

---

[37] Czechoslovakian refugees in western, central, and northern Europe since 1968; Hungarian refugees in Europe since 1956.

[38] Sri-Lankan Tamils in western and central Europe since the 1980s: the example of Switzerland; Chilean refugees in Europe since 1973: the example of Switzerland; Iranian refugees in northern, western, and central Europe since 1980: the example of the Netherlands; Kurdish refugees in western and central Europe since the late 20th century: the example of Germany; Vietnamese refugees in western, central, and northern Europe since the 1970s: the examples of France, Great Britain, and Germany.

[39] Refugees from former Yugoslavia in Europe since 1991.

[40] Polish undocumented immigrants in Berlin since the 1980s.

[41] Eastern, east-central, and southeastern European prostitutes in western, central, northern and southern Europe since the 1980s.

One characteristic of illegal migration is that – except for sometimes highly informative but unrepresentative participatory observations, interviews, social reportage, and local, limited case studies – it cannot be studied as such. For in its manifold and changing, partly mobile, partly also solidified structures, illegal migration is always merely a social or economic response to contextual conditions or changing structures of opportunity: it is a response to immigration restrictions against the backdrop of immigration pressure arising from conditions in the originating country and/or the attractiveness of the destination, to illegally available employment opportunities (at times created by the existence of a demand for illegal work, in the first place). And in its various forms of manifestation, it is also a mobile and flexible response to sanctions directed against it.

In addition to the influx of asylum seekers, the number of *Aussiedler* in the Federal Republic showed a particularly strong increase at the end of the 1980s and in the early 1990s. The immigration of *Aussiedler* is a kind of return migration across generations. Some of their ancestors had emigrated generations ago, some centuries ago, and some, as in the case of the Transylvanian Saxons, as far back as the late Middle Ages. Under the Laws on the Consequences of the Second World War (*Kriegsfolgenrecht*), recognized *Aussiedler* are entitled to German citizenship with all rights and obligations. Until the end of the 1980s, that is, until the end of the cold war, this involved a very generous practice of taking in *Aussiedler*. The 1953 Federal Law on Expellees and Refugees had created the legal basis and had charged the federal government with admitting individuals of German background from eastern, east-central, and southeastern Europe as *Aussiedler*, give them German citizenship, and promote their integration. Individuals of German background who had succeeded in penetrating the iron curtain were admitted into the Federal Republic and automatically assumed to have suffered persecution.[42]

The immigration of individuals of German descent from eastern, east-central, and southeastern Europe into the Federal Republic connected seamlessly to the history of organized expulsions and formed the third-largest migration movement after the arrival of refugees and expellees and the influx of migrant workers. In East Germany, the immigration of *Aussiedler*, here understood primarily as family reunification, was once again comparatively small.

Between 1950 and 2007, a total of around 4.5 million *Aussiedler* entered the Federal Republic and reunited Germany. The vast majority (around 3 million) came after 1987 in response to glasnost and perestroika in the USSR and the opening of the iron curtain. The influx of *Aussiedler* crossed the 200,000 mark in 1988 and reached nearly 400,000 by the end of 1990. In 1991, in spite of a large number of applications, it declined steeply to a little more than 200,000, and remained at this high level until 1995, after which

Table 4. Immigration of *Aussiedler*, 1986–2007	
1986	42,788
1987	78,523
1988	202,673
1989	377,055
1990	397,055
1991	221,995
1992	230,565
1993	218,888
1994	222,591
1995	217,898
1996	177,751
1997	134,419
1998	103,080
1999	103,599
2000	95,615
2001	98,484
2002	91,416
2003	72,885
2005	35,522
2006	7,747
2007	5,792

Source: Bundesministerium des Innern.

time it dropped precipitously (2003: 72,885; 2005: 35,522; 2007: 5,792) (see Table 4).

Between 1950 and 1987, Poland was the primary country of origin of *Aussiedler* in West Germany. Sixty-two percent of all *Aussiedler* (848,000) came from there, compared to only 8% (110,000) from the Soviet Union with its still restrictive emigration policy. In second place after Poland and well ahead of the USSR was Romania with 15% of the *Aussiedler* (206,000). After the opening of the iron curtain, mass immigration from the Soviet Union and its successor states quickly surpassed the influx from Poland and Romania. By 1990 its share rose to 37.3% and surged in 1991 to 66.4%. The immigration of *Aussiedler* from the Commonwealth of Independent States (CIS) reached more than 84.8% in 1992, 94.7% in 1993, and then 96.8% in 1996, when no fewer than 172,181 of the 177,751 *Aussiedler* admitted came from the former Soviet Union. The share of *Aussiedler* from Poland and Romania declined accordingly: only 2.6% and 2.4% of *Aussiedler* came from Romania in 1994 and 1996, while Poland's share dropped to 1.1% and 0.6%, respectively.

The shift in the regions of origin did not only result from the decline in the pool of emigrants in Romania and the surge in emigration from the vastly larger pool in the territory of the CIS. Beginning in 1990 it was also influenced by a change in the recognition procedures, which disadvantaged *Aussiedler* from Poland, Romania, and other regions vis-à-vis those from the CIS: since 1 January 1993, applicants must demonstrate in detail that they suffered from continuing "expulsion pressure" or discrimination because of their German ethnicity up to the time of application. By contrast, this is assumed unless otherwise demonstrated in the case of applicants from the CIS. All this is part of the

[42] *Aussiedler/Spätaussiedler* in Germany since 1950.

profound changes made to the basic regulations governing the immigration and integration of *Aussiedler* by the 1993 Law Dealing with Late Consequences of the Second World War (*Kriegsfolgenbereinigungsgesetz*), in conjunction with the asylum compromise, which was in reality a comprehensive compromise on migration. Since then, only *Spätaussiedler* born before 1993 are entitled to file an application. In addition, since the early 1990s there have been progressive cutbacks in integration measures, tending to bring the situation of the *Aussiedler/Spätaussiedler* closer to that of other migrant groups, even though they continued to be clearly privileged among all immigrant groups in Germany.

Fairly recent is the immigration of Jews from the successor states of the former Soviet Union. The prehistory of that migration began during the agony of the GDR between the fall of the East German Socialist Unity Party (SED) in early November 1989 and unification with West Germany on 3 October 1990. In this postrevolutionary interval, which also saw the introduction, for example, of the foreigner's right to vote in local elections in the GDR (repealed after unification), groupings in the East German parliament (*Volkskammer*) who had broken with the SED's anti-Zionist course declared their willingness, in a joint declaration in 1990, "to grant asylum to persecuted Jews in the GDR." This was also affirmed by the East German Council of Ministers in July 1990. In response, by mid-April 1991 nearly 5,000 Jews from the Soviet Union applied for admission to the state territory of the former GDR. The first 8,535 Jewish immigrants had been arriving since April 1990 in the then still existing GDR. Between the opening of the iron curtain to the end of 2005, more than 200,000 Jews migrated from the Soviet Union/CIS to Germany.[43]

Until the end of 2004, in the face of the everyday rather than state-sanctioned anti-Semitism in the CIS, they were treated analogously to "quota refugees" (*Kontingentflüchtlinge*), that is, they were given a collective status roughly corresponding with the one of those entitled to asylum. Following the passage of the Immigration Act of 1 January 2005, new regulations govern the admission of Jewish immigrants from the CIS. It is no longer sufficient to prove Jewish identity. Applicants must also demonstrate that they are able to support themselves after immigration into the Federal Republic. They must furnish proof of a basic knowledge of German, and Jewish authorities in Germany must also confirm the possibility of admitting the applicant into a Jewish community. Finally, since 2006 all this has made a positive integration prognosis a precondition for admission. The fact that in spite of these restrictions, Jews from the CIS are given preferential admission into the country responsible for the Holocaust is a response by the Germans to the darkest chapter in their history – a hesitant one, to be sure, following a protracted struggle over whether unified Germany would adopt this initiative from the GDR. Against this background, and notwithstanding all the efforts by the media to generate sympathy,

there are still some uncertainties in the encounter between Germans and Jewish immigrants from eastern Europe.

Added to this are identity problems among the immigrants themselves: they emigrated as Jews and were admitted into Germany as such. Around 80,000 – that is, far from all of them – joined Jewish communities (whose membership was back up to around 105,000 in 2005) who support them, even though a large number of them no longer had a Jewish identity in the religious and cultural sense back in their homelands, because many Jewish communities had been extinguished by the partly anti-Zionist, partly anti-Semitic pressure in the USSR. That feelings of guilt in the Federal Republic about mass crimes by the Nazis did not influence the treatment of all minorities affected is shown by the fate of the immigrant Roma. In this case the memory that, after the Jews, Sinti and Roma suffered most at the hands of the Nazis provided no bridge into Germany.

Official estimates put the number of Roma refugees in Germany from the beginning of 1990 to passage of the new asylum law on 1 July 1993 at around 250,000, mostly from Romania, but also from Yugoslavia and Bulgaria. Their treatment stands in stark contrast to that of the *Aussiedler* and Jews from eastern Europe. In the case of *Aussiedler* and Jews, we are dealing with state-overseen migration under the guiding perspectives of inclusion in the welfare state and integration into society. The opposite was true for the undesirable immigration of Gypsies from eastern Europe: exclusion and forced repatriation into countries where – as for example, in Romania – they are marginalized as least as much as the Jews are in the CIS.

At the center of the discussion over German migration and integration policy at the beginning of the 21st century stood the political and media debate about the report of the Independent Commission on Immigration set up by Interior Minister Otto Schily, and about the federal government's subsequently presented Law to Direct and Limit Immigration and to Regulate the Stay and Integration of EU Citizens and Foreigners (Immigration Law). It envisaged limited but controlled immigration, guided to the extent that was possible, based on a point system with criteria of admission derived from the Canadian model. It reduced the confusing multitude of residence permits to only two: a limited permit (*Aufenthaltserlaubnis*) and a permanent one (*Niederlassungserlaubnis*). And for the first time it elevated integration to a legal mandate, which also included obligatory courses for immigrants that promoted integration (e.g., language and orientation classes).

After protracted and difficult negotiations, a vote in the Federal Council (*Bundesrat*) that was declared invalid by the Federal Constitutional Court, an unchanged resubmission of the bill, another failure of the negotiations, and finally a successful round of talks in the chancellor's office, the Immigration Law was finally adopted in June 2004 and took effect on 1 January 2005. The price was high for an agreement between positions that were far apart, in a contested debate that was often less about the issue itself and more a

---

[43] East European Jews in Germany since 1990.

party-political proxy war: the point system as an instrument for guiding migration in the competition for the best talents fell victim to party quarreling. With a view to economic migration, the law eased immigration for highly qualified and self-employed migrants. With respect to the asylum law, the uncertain status of "toleration" was abolished, and with it the frequent de facto "chain-toleration"; moreover, in line with EU standards, gender guidelines for asylum determination were created.

All in all, the law, measured against the ideas of the Independent Commission on Immigration, but also against the government's original draft proposal, was a strongly curtailed step in the right direction. Its historical tardiness is reminiscent of the first German emigration law of 1897: the latter was created only when German mass emigration, which in the 19th century had brought 5.5 million emigrants to the United States alone, was already history. As a result, the protective measures of the law no longer reached the majority of German emigrants. The reason for the delay had been the political fear that an emigration law could further promote the troublesome emigration.

Much the same was repeated (in reverse direction) with the comprehensive immigration and integration law, the core of which migration researchers, commissioners for foreigners' issues, and those involved in practical migration and integration work had been calling for since the early 1980s. Because of political fears – also repeatedly invoked in populist discourse – that an immigration law could boost further immigration, relevant initiatives and the draft itself were blocked, delayed, and stripped of important guiding mechanisms. The law was not passed until 2005, when a quarter century of opportunities and maneuvering room in the area of integration policy had already been lost. It is striking that the very political forces that had blocked a comprehensive legislative response to migration and integration for decades, driven by a defensive refusal to acknowledge reality ("The Federal Republic is not an immigration country") in the end complained about failures in integration policy and about an "immigration into the social systems" which a timely law with clear perspectives and goals for guiding immigration and promoting integration could have substantially helped to contain.

The Immigration Law of 2005, about 20 years late compared to the social reality in the de facto immigration country, marked also the transition of the Federal Republic of Germany from an informal to a de jure formal modern immigration country with the requisite legal and administrative tools.

The term "informal immigration country" can be applied to a country in which immigration in the broadest sense consistently exceeds emigration. Such a county, in contrast to the classic overseas immigration countries, does not consider itself an immigration country, even though within its borders lives an immigrant population that can be described as such by all conventional criteria and regards itself as such. In spite of its self-description as a nonimmigration country, it might offer these immigrants fluid transitions, ranging from work migration, permanent stay, and formal immigration to the grant of citizenship. However, what is lacking is regular immigration legislation and an immigration policy, which are characteristic of a formal immigration country – independent of whether such a formal immigration country ever uses them to guide immigration (e.g., in accordance with certain criteria), increase it, or limit and possibly temporarily prevent free immigration. And in actual legal reality there are many transitional forms that lie somewhere in between.

The Federal Republic of Germany was an informal immigration country from the beginning of the 1980s, at the latest, in social and cultural terms, even if not yet in the legal sense. This gradually changed through the reform of the legislation on foreigners in 1990, which made nationalization easier, and especially through the reform of the Citizenship Law in 2000 with the limited introduction of the acquisition of citizenship through birth in the country and the temporary acceptance of dual citizenship, and, finally, in 2005 through the Immigration Law, which should be seen as historic even though it was historically late.

REFERENCES

Asche, Matthias. *Neusiedler im verheerten Land. Kriegsfolgen bewältigung, Migrationssteuerung und Konfessionspolitik im Zeichen des Landeswiederaufbaus: Die Mark Brandenburg nach den Kriegen des 17. Jahrhunderts.* Münster, 2006.

Bade, Klaus J., ed. *Auswanderer – Wanderarbeiter – Gastarbeiter. Bevölkerung, Arbeitsmarkt und Wanderung in Deutschland seit der Mitte des 19. Jahrhunderts.* 2nd ed. Ostfildern, 1985.

Bade, Klaus J., ed. *Deutsche im Ausland – Fremde in Deutschland: Migration in Geschichte und Gegenwart.* Munich, 1992.

Bade, Klaus J. *Europa in Bewegung: Migration vom späten 18. Jahrhundert bis zur Gegenwart.* Munich, 2000.

Bade, Klaus J., and Jochen Oltmer, eds. *Aussiedler: Deutsche Einwanderer aus Osteuropa.* Osnabrück, 1999.

Bade, Klaus J., and Jochen Oltmer. *Normalfall Migration: Deutschland im 20. und frühen 21. Jahrhundert.* Bonn, 2004.

Benz, Wolfgang, ed. *Die Vertreibung der Deutschen aus dem Osten. Ursachen, Ereignisse, Folgen.* Frankfurt am Main, 1995.

Bethlehem, Siegfried. *Heimatvertreibung, DDR-Flucht, Gastarbeiterzuwanderung. Wanderungsströme und Wanderungspolitik in der Bundesrepublik Deutschland.* Stuttgart, 1982.

Franzen, K. Erik. *Die Vertriebenen. Hitlers letzte Opfer.* Munich, 2002.

Friedmann, Alexander, et al. *Eine neue Heimat? Jüdische Emigrantinnen und Emigranten aus der Sowjetunion.* Vienna, 1993.

Gosewinkel, Dieter. *Einbürgern und Ausschließen. Die Nationalisierung der Staatsangehörigkeit vom Deutschen Bund bis zur Bundesrepublik Deutschland.* Göttingen, 2001.

Heckmann, Friedrich. *Die Bundesrepublik. Ein Einwanderungsland? Zur Soziologie der Gastarbeiterbevölkerung als Einwandererminorität.* Stuttgart, 1981.

Herbert, Ulrich. *Fremdarbeiter. Politik und Praxis des ›Ausländer-Einsatzes‹ in der Kriegswirtschaft des Dritten Reiches.* Berlin, 1985.

Herbert, Ulrich. *Geschichte der Ausländerpolitik in Deutschland. Saisonarbeiter, Zwangsarbeiter, Gastarbeiter, Flüchtlinge.* Munich, 2001.

Jacobmeyer, Wolfgang. *Vom Zwangsarbeiter zum heimatlosen Ausländer. Die Displaced Persons in Westdeutschland 1945–1951.* Göttingen, 1985.

Jasper, Dirk. "Ausländerbeschäftigung in der DDR." In *Anderssein gab es nicht. Ausländer und Minderheiten in der DDR*, edited by Marianne Krüger-Potratz, 151–89. Münster, 1991.

Jersch-Wenzel, Stefi, ed. *Von Zuwanderern zu Einheimischen. Hugenotten, Juden, Böhmen in Berlin.* Berlin, 1990.

Just, Michael. *Ost- und südosteuropäische Amerikaauswanderung 1881–1914. Transitprobleme in Deutschland und Aufnahme in den Vereinigten Staaten.* Stuttgart, 1988.

Lucassen, Jan. *Migrant Labour in Europe 1600–1900: The Drift to the North Sea.* London, 1987.

Marrus, Michael R. *The Unwanted: European Refugees in the 20th Century.* New York and Oxford, 1985.

Maurer, Trude. *Ostjuden in Deutschland 1918–1933.* Hamburg, 1986.

Motte, Jan, Rainer Ohliger, and Anne von Oswald, eds. *50 Jahre Bundesrepublik – 50 Jahre Einwanderung. Nachkriegsgeschichte als Migrationsgeschichte.* Frankfurt am Main and New York, 1999.

Oltmer, Jochen, ed. *Migration steuern und verwalten. Deutschland vom späten 19. Jahrhundert bis zur Gegenwart.* Göttingen, 2003.

Oltmer, Jochen. *Migration und Politik in der Weimarer Republik.* Göttingen, 2005.

Oltmer, Jochen, ed. *Kriegsgefangene im Europa des Ersten Weltkriegs.* Paderborn, 2006.

Oltmer, Jochen. *Migration im 19. und 20. Jahrhundert.* Munich, 2010.

Roeck, Bernd. *Außenseiter, Randgruppen, Minderheiten. Fremde im Deutschland der frühen Neuzeit.* Göttingen, 1993.

Schlögel, Karl, ed. *Russische Emigration in Deutschland 1918 bis 1941. Leben im europäischen Bürgerkrieg.* Berlin, 1995.

Schulze, Rainer, et al., eds. *Flüchtlinge und Vertriebene in der westdeutschen Nachkriegsgeschichte. Bilanzierung der Forschung und Perspektiven für die künftige Forschungsarbeit.* Hildesheim, 1987.

Spoerer, Mark. *Zwangsarbeit unter dem Hakenkreuz. Ausländische Zivilarbeiter, Kriegsgefangene und Häftlinge im Deutschen Reich und im besetzten Europa 1939–1945.* Stuttgart and Munich, 2001.

Stepién, Stanislaus. *Der alteingessene Fremde. Ehemalige Zwangsarbeiter in Westdeutschland.* Frankfurt am Main and New York, 1989.

AUSTRIA

Sylvia Hahn

Austria's geographic location in the heart of Europe, at the intersection of major east-west and north-south trade routes, has contributed to making the region one that has always been characterized by immigration, emigration, and transit migration. Neither the population growth nor the cultural diversity of the small and medium-size cities and of the former Habsburg capital and imperial residence of Vienna would be conceivable without immigration and the cultural baggage that the migrants brought with them over the centuries.

The region and its boundaries

Österreich, the German name for Austria, goes back to an Old German rendering of the Latin phrase *orientalia regna*, the "eastern land." It referred to the Danubian region east of the river Enns, which was the eastern boundary of the original Bavarian region. From about the middle of the 12th century, a Latin neologism *austria* was substituted for *ostarrîche*, using a Latinization of the German root "austar" (East). In the 14th and 15th centuries, the phrase "Dominion of Austria" (*dominium austrie*) was used: it encompassed the territories of modern-day Lower and Upper Austria, Styria, Carinthia, Carniola, the Windische Mark, Inner Istria, and Tyrol, along with the Habsburg ancestral lands around the upper Rhine in Swabia and Alsace. Triest, Freiburg im Breisgau, and some counties in what is now Vorarlberg were added a little later.

In the centuries that followed, the geographic parameters of the *dominium austrie* were altered repeatedly by wars, marriages, donations, and inheritances. In the wake of the internal creation of a state with the goal of forging the multitude of different lordships into a single state in the 18th century, this realm became the *Monarchia austriaca*, the Austrian monarchy – a dominion including a multitude of lands in central and southeastern Europe with a population of diverse ethnic and cultural backgrounds who spoke about a dozen different languages (including Yiddish).

By the middle of the 19th century, Österreich was used to refer to three different political-geographic levels:

1. the two Archduchies of "unter der Enns" (Lower Austria) and "ob der Enns" (Upper Austria)
2. the conglomeration of all the Habsburg crown lands except for Hungary and Lombardy-Veneto
3. the totality of the Habsburg monarchy, the Austrian Empire

The Austro-Hungarian Monarchy was created in 1867; it consisted of two imperial halves split along the line of the river Leitha that were sometimes called Cisleithania and Transleithania. Cisleitheinia was increasingly – and after 1915 also officially – called Österreich.

The end of World War I was a turning point as the once sprawling Habsburg monarchy was wiped from the map of Europe – leaving behind a rump Österreich, a small geographic area with just under 7 million inhabitants. On 12 November 1918 a Provisional National Assembly decided to set up a Republik Deutsch Österreich (Republic of German-Austria), which was intended to be a component of the German state. But the victorious powers prohibited the intended merger with Germany, and in the Peace Treaty of St. Germain they declared the official state name to be the Republic of Austria on 10 September 1919. Fifteen years later the corporatist dictatorship of the *Ständestaat* changed it to the Federal State of Austria. Following the annexation (*Anschluß*) by Nazi Germany in 1938, the name was completely eliminated and was replaced by the term Ostmark (Eastern March) until 1942, and then by the phrase Alpine and Danubian Reich Provinces (*Gaue*). After World War II, the Second Austrian Republic was set up covering the same territory as the First Republic.

Immigration to the cities and commercial regions from the 16th to the 18th century

Around 1525, the territory of modern-day Austria was home to about 1.5 million people (18 per square kilometer), and in 1754 there were 2.7 million (33 per square kilometer). The late Middle Ages and the early modern period were characterized by high population losses from epidemics (1348–9, 1410–11, 1436, 1521, 1630s, 1640s, and 1670s), wars (the Thirty Years' War 1618–48, the Turkish Wars 1526–52, 1566–8, 1593–1606, 1663–4, 1683–99, 1714–18, 1736–9, 1788–92), and expulsions of Jews and Protestants. Immigration had already helped make up for some of the population losses by the 16th and 17th centuries. Immigration was a demographic and economic necessity especially for cities devastated by wars, epidemics, and endemic high mortality.

Table 1. Population in Austrian cities, 1500–1900 (inhabitants in 000s)									
	1200	**1300**	**1400**	**1500**	**1600**	**1700**	**1750**	**1800**	**1850**	**1900**
Bad Ischl					1			5	6	
Dornbirn					1	2	4	5	6	
Eisenstadt							4	4	6	
Gmunden							2	3	5	
Graz		5		5	8	22	20	31	55	112
Innsbruck		1		4	6	7	10	12	13	41
Klagenfurt				1	4	5	7	10	12	
Krems					4		4	4	7	
Linz				3	3		10	17	27	58
Mattersburg								3	4	
Neunkirchen								2	5	
Salzburg				7	9	13	15	16	17	33
Schwaz				17	9	8	6	4	5	
Steyr				6	9	6	7	8	11	17
Wels					5	4	3	4	6	
Vienna	12	20	20	20	50	114	175	247	431	1,728
Wiener Neustadt			7		4	4	4	7	12	28

Source: Author's compilation based on Paul Bairoch, Jean Batou, and Pierre Chevre, *La population des villes européennes. Banque de données et analyse sommaire des resultants 800–1850* (Geneva, 1988); Knittler, *Die europäische Stadt.*

Between the 17th and the 19th centuries, many families in the remote mountain regions of Vorarlberg and Tyrol were economically dependent on the migration of their children for agricultural work in Upper Swabia in Württemberg, in Bavarian Swabia, and in Baden (*Hütekinder, Schwabenkinder*).[1] At the same time, however, a few early modern labor market areas in the rural-alpine region were characterized by immigration, the overall effect of which was a shift of population centers from east to west: while the centers were still in and around Vienna (modern-day Lower Austria) in the 14th and 15th centuries, new centers took shape in the alpine region through the mining of precious metals (the Inn valley around Schwaz, Kitzbühel, Gastein valley, Rauris, Schladming), salt (Hallein, Hall in Tyrol, Jallstadt), and iron mining and processing (Steyr, Eisenwurzen). The population of Tyrol, for example, rose from 45,000 in the 14th century to around 150,000 at the beginning of the 17th century, with a quarter of the residents employed in mining. The small village of Schwaz in Tyrol had a mere 200 inhabitants in 1312, but then grew into one of the most important mining centers in central Europe. At the beginning of the 16th century it had between 15,000 and 27,000 inhabitants (some estimates put the number as high as 40,000), which made it the largest settlement in Austria alongside Vienna (around 20,000). Thanks to the expansion of metal-processing industries in the 16th century, Steyr in Upper Austria also recorded a growth in population from 6,000 to 9,000 (see Table 1).

The various imperial residence cities were characterized by strong immigration, since the arrival of the ruling house and its court also brought a large number of merchants, artists, craftsmen, domestics, and small business owners in their wake. Take for example the city of Wiener Neustadt just south of Vienna. For a time in the 15th century it was the residence of Emperor Frederick III and experienced an economic upswing and a population growth to around 7,000. The departure of the ruling dynasty was followed by the decline of small businesses and trade and a sharp decline in the number of residents to about 4,000. The development of Prague when it was an imperial residence from 1583 to 1612 was similar: the number of newly enrolled citizens in Prague's new city rose by around 70% in the 1580s and 1590s, while it doubled in the old city (which amounted to around 60 new citizens a year). Following the return of the imperial residence to Vienna in 1612 the population of Prague dropped from 100,000 to 50,000 by 1700. Now it was Vienna's turn to profit from the role as an administrative-political center: only 29,000 inhabitants lived in the city around 1600, but by the 1670s their numbers had increased to 80,000. By around 1700 they were up to 114,000, and around 1800 to about 250,000. In the first half of the 17th century, alone, the city's gain from migration is estimated at around 25,000.

The migration of nobility in Austria played a role that was by no means unimportant in either economic or cultural terms. Moves by the court always entailed the (labor) migration of court staff and of the higher, middling, and low-level court employees, many of whom hailed from across almost the whole of Europe. When Emperor Ferdinand I moved to Vienna from Spain in the 1520s, about 4.7% of the 550 individuals of the court were Spaniards; under his son Maximilian II, their share stood at 7.4%. Hunting, raising animals, handling horses, and equestrian skills were particular

---

[1] Tyrolese and Vorarlberger children in Württemberg, Baden, and Bavaria from the early modern period to World War I.

domains of the Spaniards, and today's Spanish riding school in Vienna has its roots there.

Alongside the nobility, the most important migrant groups in Austria in the 16th and 17th centuries included scholars, artists, traders, and merchants from the northern and western parts of Germany, but also from southern, southeastern, east-central, and eastern Europe, as well as craftsmen and domestics. Because of its geographic location, Vienna also served as a way station and temporary stopping point for itinerant merchants, traders, or other traveling elites on their way to southern and eastern Europe. Moreover, Vienna had a constant presence of merchants from the Ottoman realm, especially Turks, Jews, Armenians, and Greeks, who specialized in importing textile raw materials, for example.[2]

Another important migrant group was construction workers, whose immigration and settlement was promoted and facilitated by a decree dating back to 1361. The masters of the "German nation" were followed by the travel-happy "Comoese" (*Comaskenvolk*), as the bricklayers and construction workers from the area of Lake Como and the environs of Milan were called. Furnished with patents, they had arrived as "troublemakers" (*Störer*), that is, as craftsmen working in small-scale trade outside the guilds; their work organization was largely based on familial and kinship networks. Most maintained ties with their regions of origin, with wives and children usually remaining behind in Italy. The intensive family networks that were based on a shared regional background formed the foundation for the creation of a de facto, generation-spanning monopoly in the construction industry in central Europe. These families were able to corner the labor market in the construction sector especially during the Baroque period in Vienna, Graz, Prague, as well as in smaller cities like Salzburg and Wiener Neustadt. There was often massive opposition to these immigrants and competitors by native craftsmen organized into guilds: accusations that they were not contributing to the defense of the city or assuming other duties were the order of the day.[3]

Many other craft trades also witnessed broad fluctuations of masters and journeymen through immigration and emigration.[4] Important regions of origin for craftsmen were Bavaria, Swabia, Württemberg, Baden, Rhineland-Palatinate, Switzerland, and the region of Bohemia-Moravia. As was the case with construction workers, merchants, and traders, among craftsmen, as well, one can identify regions of origin specific to certain trades: for example, chimney sweeps tended to come from certain valleys in the western Alps, most purse makers came from Saxon cities, while bakers were from Franconia and carpenters from Bavaria, Tyrol,

or Switzerland.[5] Among the *Störer* who were essential to the urban economy, about half were immigrants, among whom those from the region of Bohemia-Moravia and the German lands predominated – a similar proportion was found among master craftsmen. A very significant proportion of the immigrant *Störer* remained in the cities: for example, of the *Störer* present in Vienna between 1776 and 1781, about two-thirds had been living in the city for 10 years or more, and nearly all of these were married and had children.

The link between place of origin and work was even more evident among the many itinerant merchants who enlivened the city's alleys and squares with their wares and calls. They included the Silesian *Bandlkramer* (merchant-employers), the Tyrolean weavers (*Weyber*) and picture sellers (*Bildkrämer*), as well as the Savoyards who dealt in silk and woollens. Then there were the Italian lime merchants and cheese peddlers, or the tropical fruit dealers who came from Cilli (Celje) in southern Styria.[6]

Expulsions of Jews and Protestants up to the 18th century

These migrations into the cities and commercial regions were accompanied by waves of deportations and expulsions. One population group that was profoundly affected by this were the Jews. Though initially given letters of protection and privileges after being invited to immigrate, they were – beginning as early as the 14th century – repeatedly persecuted, expelled, or simply murdered. Expulsions of Jews from Styria, Carinthia (1496–7), and Salzburg (1498) were nearly contemporaneous with those in other German territories, Spain, and Portugal. At times the Jewish population itself was required to get rid of Jews who had become "unwelcome": in Vienna in 1582, the "freed Jews" who lived there had to help in the "deportation of the foreign Jews … from Venice, Poland, Bohemia, and Moravia." In 1670, Emperor Leopold I expelled the Jews once again from Vienna and Austria. The situation did not improve until the Edict of Toleration ended the expulsions in 1782, and even then the unrestricted right of settlement in regions that had already expelled Jews was only granted in the "basic law … pertaining to the general rights of citizens" that was promulgated in 1867.[7]

The expulsions of the Jews were followed by the persecution and expulsion of Protestants during the Counter-Reformation. About 40,000 religious refugees fled Austria for German Protestant states after the Thirty Years' War. These developments affected the miners and salt workers in the Alpine region (Tyrol, Salzburg, Carinthia, Upper Austria), and the population in cities like Vienna, where Protestants made up about two-thirds of the residents around 1620. One

---

[2] Greek traders and Phanariotes in southern and southeastern Europe from the early modern period to the 19th century.

[3] Italian and other "Alpine" (Grisons, Tecino, and Vorarlberg) architects and visual artists in Baroque Europe.

[4] Tyrolean construction workers in central Europe from the 7th to the 19th century.

[5] Alpine chimney sweeps in western, central, and southern Europe from the 16th to the early 20th century; Saxon journeymen purse makers in Vienna in the 18th and 19th centuries.

[6] Savoyard itinerant traders and merchants in central Europe in the early modern period.

[7] Ashkenazim in Europe since the early modern period; Galician Jews in Austria from the 18th to the early 20th century.

of the last large expulsions of Protestants occurred in 1731–2 when more than 20,000 were driven out of Salzburg. The majority migrated to Prussian Lithuania, but a few went as far as the British colony of Georgia on the east coast of North America.[8]

The recruitment of skilled workers in the age of mercantilism

These phases of expulsions up to the early 18th century were followed by the recruitment and immigration of skilled workers in the shift to mercantilist economic policies and the adoption of measures intended to boost the population. The Collegium Commerciorum (founded 1666), the first agency for trade and commerce in Austria, was responsible for initiating trade relationships, recruiting specialists, and granting privileges, for example to newly established companies and manufactures. The spectrum of immigrants deliberately brought in ranged from economic and financial advisors for the court, to artists, scientists, military and guard personnel, entrepreneurs and skilled craftsmen together with their helpers and families – all from the most varied regions of Europe. This recruitment reached a high point in the 18th century. For example, to set up silk factories, *Proponenten* and *Fundatores*, as the specialists and masters were called, were recruited from Italy, France, and the Netherlands. Alongside textile specialists, metalworkers and jewelers (*Galanteriearbeiter*) were brought in from England, watchmakers from Geneva, specialists in gilding and silvering copper from Würzburg, and comb makers from Italy. The English steelworkers recruited in 1765–8 included entrepreneurs like Rosthorn, Collins, Welsh, Lightowler, Winwood, and Robert and William Hikman who were crucial to the further development of Vienna's metalworking industry.

What all these immigrant specialists from diverse regions of Europe shared was that their arrival and settlement was supported and promoted by the authorities. The privileges granted to them ranged from buildings that were made available, customs relief or other financial support, and settlement permits for families and employees to exemption from military service and special permission to exercise their religion freely. In return, the immigrants obligated themselves to hire and train native workers, whose emigration the authorities in turn tried to prohibit by means of strict legal measures.

In spite of the pro-immigrant and foreigner-friendly stance during the period of mercantilism, one must not overlook the fact that these privileged specially recruited immigrants constituted only a small group of specialists who worked primarily in luxury trades and thus produced their goods more or less exclusively for the court and the nobility. Excluded from these privileges were the large numbers of immigrant workers in small-scale trades and those producing for the mass market, many of whom were also recruited on the trans-regional labor market – not to mention the numerous male and female domestics drawn from the environs of small, medium-sized, and large cities.

Natives and foreigners in the age of mass migration in the 19th century

While the second half of the 18th century was characterized by mercantilist economic and population-boosting policies, one pillar of which was the "increase in productive hands" whether from abroad or one's own lands, the 19th century developed into a century of intra-European and transatlantic mass migrations. Austrian industrialization (which arrived late by European standards) and the development of modern transportation technology led to a mass mobilization of workers across the monarchy.

In the 19th century the Austrian Alpine lands were clearly a region of in-migration. Thus, of the total population increase of 3.9 million between 1819 and 1913, about 1.3 million or 35% was accounted for by a positive net migration. The 730,104 female immigrants made up more than half of the immigration gain. The average annual net migration is estimated at around 14,680. The majority of immigrants were subjects of the monarchy who had left their hometowns and villages to seek employment in one of the industrial centers in Lower or Upper Austria, Styria, Vorarlberg, or in the imperial residence city of Vienna. The population of Vienna, for example, rose from about 250,000 around 1800 to about 1.7 million by 1900. In some regions and cities in the second half of the 19th century, immigrants made up between two-thirds and three-quarters of the local population. On the whole, two waves of immigration can be identified, one in the first third and another in the second third of the 19th century.

The geographic mobility of the population and the issues of poor relief, begging, and vagrancy this entailed were also reflected in legal measures. As early as the 16th century, care of the poor had been transferred to the communities; in the middle of the 18th century, *Zuständigkeitsrecht* and *Heimatrecht* (right of belonging and domicile) were created to regulate membership in Austrian communities. The law obligated the communities to care for the poor and aged and also governed the practice of deporting those in the population who were without subsistence and/or engaged in vagrancy. Closely linked to the *Heimatrecht* was citizenship. The first steps toward the establishment of citizenship in the German crown lands (without Hungary) were taken under Emperor Joseph II (1764–90) and the Civil Code (*Allgemeine Bürgerliche Gesetzbuch*, ABGb) of 1811 defined the term *Staatsbürger* for the first time, using it in the sense of "citizen of the state." Then 1849 saw the creation of a "general Austrian Reich citizen law (*Reichsbürgerrecht*) for all nations of the Austrian imperial state" (including Hungary) but the creation of the Dual Monarchy by the Austro-Hungarian Compromise of 1867 excluded the population of the "lands of the crown of St. Stephen" from Austrian citizenship. Immigrants from Transleithania were thus considered foreigners in the Austrian half of the Empire. The reciprocal

---

[8] Salzburg Protestants in East Prussia since the 18th century.

Table 2. Number and percentage of inhabitants with *Heimatrecht* and native inhabitants in selected cities of the Habsburg monarchy, 1890

	Total population (N)	Heimatrecht (N)	Native (N)	Heimatrecht (%)	Native (%)	Difference percentage points
Vienna	1,364,548	476,418	610,062	34.9	44.7	9.8
Prague	182,530	46,158	74,141	25.3	40.6	15.3
Triest	157,466	71,806	95,977	45.6	61.0	15.3
Lemberg	127,943	55,344	60,217	43.3	47.1	3.8
Graz	112,069	24,461	37,246	21.8	33.2	11.4
Brünn	94,462	29,665	35,896	31.4	38.0	6.6
Krakau	74,593	30,087	31,730	40.3	42.5	2.2
Czernowitz	54,171	26,726	30,702	49.3	56.7	7.3
Linz	47,685	12,774	15,271	26.8	32.0	5.2
Reichenberg	30,890	12,933	15,473	41.9	50.1	8.2
Laibach	30,505	7,390	10,408	24.2	34.1	9.9
Salzburg	27,244	8,164	7,647	30.0	28.1	-1.9
Wiener Neustadt	25,040	6,187	9,391	24.7	37.5	12.8
Iglau	23,716	8,418	11,289	35.5	47.6	12.1
Innsbruck	23,320	6,646	6,587	28.5	28.2	-0.3
Troppau	22,867	6,668	8,191	29.2	35.8	6.7
Görz	21,825	11,191	10,785	51.3	49.4	-1.9
Steyr	21,499	4,746	6,400	22.1	29.8	7.7
Trient	21,486	8,827	9,793	41.1	45.6	4.5
Marburg	19,898	2,836	9,870	14.3	49.6	35.4
Olmütz	19,761	3,967	10,918	20.1	55.3	35.2
Klagenfurt	19,756	5,624	9,472	28.5	47.9	19.5
Znaim	14,516	6,286	4,278	43.3	29.5	-13.8
Bielitz	14,573	4,608	6,166	31.6	42.3	10.7
Kremsier	12,480	4,921	6,152	39.4	49.3	9.9
Bozen	11,744	2,695	6,458	22.9	55.0	32.0
Rovigno	9,662	8,433	527	87.3	5.5	-81.8
Rovereto	9,030	4,852	5,070	53.7	56.1	2.4
Friedeck	7,374	2,498	3,464	33.9	47.0	13.1
Cilli	6,264	2,424	2,585	38.7	41.3	2.6
Ungarisch Hradisch	3,939	1,094	2,122	27.8	53.9	26.1
Pettau	3,924	867	2,011	22.1	51.2	29.2
Waidhofen/ Ybbs	3,665	1,175	1,375	32.1	37.5	5.5

Source: Author's compilation based on *Die Ergebnisse der Volkszählung vom 31. December 1890 in den im Reichsrathe vertretenen Königreichen und Ländern* (Vienna, 1895).

connection between *Heimatrecht* and citizenship remained intact until the early 20th century, citizenship could be attained only by individuals who had *Heimatrecht* in a community, and *Heimatrecht* was restricted to Austrian citizens.

The vast extent of migration within the monarchy and the political events of the *Vormärz* and the revolution of 1848–9 had already led to a noticeable tightening of laws on *Zuständigkeitsrecht* and *Heimatrecht* in the first half of the 19th century and after the passage of the revised law of 1863, only state officials and well-off individuals could obtain the *Heimatrecht* at their new place of residence. For hundreds of thousands of (labor) migrants and their wives and children this meant that they became legal foreigners in their own land. Beginning in the 1860s, the implementation of the restrictive legislation was reflected in the massive increase in the numbers of individuals who did not have the *Heimatrecht* in the places where they had been born. In nearly all of a selection of major

and minor cities in 1890 the percentage of the population with the *Heimatrecht* (i.e., those defined as legally native) was far lower than the percentage of those born there (see Table 2).

In Vienna, for example, 34% of the population had the *Heimatrecht*; but the percentage of those born in the city was far greater at nearly 45%, meaning that nearly a quarter of the native born were denied the benefits of the *Heimatrecht*. On the whole, one can make out two groups among the cities in this regard: cities that were located in the middle of the monarchy and were administrative, commercial, and/or industrial centers had greater percentage of native-born residents without the *Heimatrecht*; while cities that lay at the periphery of the monarchy, in the Alpine zone, in border regions, or in the poorer eastern section, had smaller discrepancies between the native born and residents with the *Heimatrecht*.

The number of foreigners in Austria rose from around 200,000 in the middle of the 19th century to a little more than half a million by the turn of the century. Given the natural growth of the population in those years, the share of foreigners continued to remain stable at around 2%. Numerically the largest numbers were Hungarians. As early as 1869 there were 90,000 immigrants from Hungary in the Cisleithanian half of the Empire; by the turn of the century, their number had tripled to about 300,000, and they now made up around half of the foreigners. Immigrants from German territories constituted the second-largest group, followed by Italian migrants and those from Russia. German immigrants made up around one-third of the foreigners in 1869, and one-fifth in 1910 (21%). Immigrants from Italy made up a steady 13%, those from Russia a total of 2% in 1869 and then 6% in 1910. Together, immigrants from Hungary, Germany, and Italy made up around 90% of all foreigners. The remaining 10% included immigrants from Great Britain (1869: 0.7% of all foreigners; 1910: 0.5%), France (1869: 1.1%; 1910: 0.5%), the USA (1869: 0.2%; 1910: 0.6%), and those from the rest of Europe (1869: 4.7%; 1910: 1.3%). The nationality of 1% of foreigners was unknown in 1869 and of 7.2% in 1910. Just under half of all foreigners lived in Lower Austria, including Vienna.

Short-distance migrations just across the borders predominated among the foreign migrants: for example, German immigrants lived chiefly in the territories near the German borders in Bohemia, Silesia, Upper Austria, Salzburg, and Vorarlberg; Hungarian immigrants, meanwhile, moved into the adjacent regions of Lower Austria, Styria, Krajina, and Moravia; Italian immigrants were dominant in Görz, Triest, Istria, Carinthia, and Tyrol – all of which were close to Italy;[9] and Russian migrants made up the largest share in Galicia near the Russian borders.

The way foreigners from the crown lands or abroad were treated varied a great deal and depended strongly on the social status and gender of the immigrants. As in the 18th century there were privileges, patronage, financial support, and exceptional permits for some, while the majority of immigrant faced harassment and humiliation through interrogations and the continuing risk of incarceration or deportation. The contradictory system of dealing with "own" and "foreign" foreigners was exacerbated by the restrictions in the granting of *Heimatrecht* that were implemented in the course of the 19th century. The granting or denial of the *Heimatrecht*, which was handled and regulated in a rather nebulous way over decades, drove a wedge into the local population and created an artificial foreignness that split the inhabitants into two legally and thus socially different groups: those who possessed *Heimatrecht* and participated in the social and political advantages that came with it, and those who did not possess it and were excluded from these benefits. The latter, defined as "unwelcome" natives (*Inländer*), could be deported to the communities responsible for them, while foreigners could be sent over the border. These inequalities stirred up resentments, hostilities, and a general sense of unease, which could erupt into violence. The confrontations were in part stoked by the rising nationalism and the (re)awakening racist and anti-Semitic currents.[10]

Overseas emigration and European internal out migration in the 19th century

Emigration to other European countries or overseas remained fairly insignificant in the 18th and at the beginning of the 19th century. Once the state began to pursue a policy of boosting population in the 18th century, it passed laws to prevent the population from emigrating across its borders. Already in the 18th century, unauthorized departures and any kind of aid to them were subject to harsh punishments; the year 1832 saw the introduction of the *Emigrationskonsense* (Emigration Permits), without which it was illegal to leave the country. The number of political refugees also remained small after the failed revolutions of 1848–9. A change came with the basic law (*Staatsgrundgesetz*) of 1867 that allowed every citizen to migrate across the borders (though men could do so only after having performed their military service). The only requirements were a valid passport and the means to cover travel costs. All in all, around 5 million people left Austria-Hungary in the 19th century, 70% of whom went overseas.

Between 1870 and 1910, about 1.8 million of the approximately 3.5 million overseas emigrants from Austria-Hungary hailed from Cisleithania; only Great Britain and Germany sent more people overseas during that same period. The majority went to the USA (see Figure 1), where they made up about one-quarter of the immigrants during these years. Only gradually did Canada and South America (especially Brazil and Argentina) become attractive as destinations.

Among the largest groups of migrants from Austria-Hungary to the USA at the turn of the century were Czechs and Slovaks (19.7%), Poles (18.9%), Serbo-Croatians and Slovenes (16.1%), Magyars (14.7%), Germans (11.8%), and Jews (7.1%). With the exception of the Germans and Jews who generally left in family units, most were single male emigrants of working age (14–40). Some went to America for only a few years or decades (e.g., Croats). The return rate at the turn of the century was high: of the approximately 1.2 million who went overseas from Austria-Hungary between 1903 and 1913, about 460,000 returned.

European countries remained the preferred destination for 30% of Austria-Hungary's emigrants. Around 1880, the German Empire alone was home to about 150,000 Austrians and they made up more than a third of all foreigners in that country. Their numbers rose rapidly in the following decades: by 1900 there were already 370,000 Austrian immigrants in Germany and around 622,000 in 1910. The majority

---

[9] Italian industrial workers in western and central Europe in the late 19th and early 20th centuries.

[10] Czech labor migrants in Austria in the 19th and early 20th centuries; Croatian and Slovenian labor migrants in Austria in the 19th and early 20th centuries.

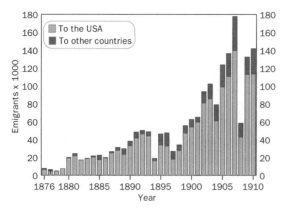

Figure 1. Overseas emigration from Austria, 1876–1910. *Source*: Based on the data in Heinz Faßmann, "Auswanderung aus der Österreichisch-ungarischen Monarchie," in *Auswanderungen aus Österreich. Von der Mitte des 19. Jahrhunderts bis zur Gegenwart*, ed. Traude Horvath and Gerda Neyer (Vienna, 1996), 33–55, here 35.

came from Austrian Silesia, Bohemia, and Moravia, and their preferred destination was the mining-industrial centers of the German Empire. The second-largest group were emigrants to Hungary and in the second half of the 19th century there were always more Austrians in Hungary than Hungarians in the Cisleithanian half of the monarchy: in 1880 their number was nearly 200,000, about 30,000 of whom lived in Budapest, alone. An eastward migration beyond Hungary was also considerable: about 85,000 Austrians were in Russia in the 1890s, while annexed Bosnia-Herzegovina was home to around 60,000 in 1910. Emigration to other European countries was always substantially lower. One important destination country was Switzerland with about 37,000 Austrian immigrants in 1910, followed by Great Britain and Ireland with just under 14,000, and Italy with nearly 11,000.

Labor migration, emigration, flight, and expulsion, 1918–1945

World War I profoundly transformed the working and living situation of people in the Habsburg Monarchy. Overseas migration was essentially blocked, and the massive internal labor migration was followed by waves of refugees. In the process, Vienna developed into a center for refugees from internal war zones. Refugees who had no financial or material resources could receive state support after registering with the police. At the end of 1915, the number of refugees in Vienna who were entitled to support stood at approximately 291,000; in March 1916 it had risen to 305,000; and in October 1916 it soared to half a million, 96,000 of whom were Jews. In 1917 the number of refugees declined to around 450,000, though it hit another high of 496,000 in March 1918. At the beginning of September, about 326,000 refugees were reportedly on the move in Austria-Hungary (110,559 Italians, 69,604 Slovenes, 68,289 Jews, 42,753 Ruthenians, and 23,802 Poles), around 100,000 of whom were on the territory of modern-day Austria. In December about 20,000 were receiving refugee support in Vienna, including 17,000

Jewish refugees from the east. By 1920, the number of Jewish refugees had risen to around 24,000.

The end of the war also meant the end of the multiethnic Habsburg state of Austria-Hungary. One of the successor states was the small Republic of Austria, which had been reduced to 13.2% of the former territory with 12.6% of the population (6.5 million). Austria also had about 32% of the factories of old Cisleithania and about 30% of the former national income; but cut off from their old suppliers and markets, years of economic depression followed with numerous factory closings and massive unemployment.

The shifting of borders and the creation of new states led to migrations and remigrations in every conceivable direction: after 1918 many Czechs living in Vienna and the southern industrial regions moved back into the territories of the newly created Czechoslovakia while a large number of former civil servants and military personnel from regions formerly belonging to the monarchy returned to Vienna or Austria and many German-speakers from the Czech Böhmerwald migrated into the central region of Upper Austria.

After the end of World War I the scale of both internal European migration and overseas emigration of Austrians declined precipitously. All told, between 1919 and 1937 only around 80,000 headed to non-European countries (USA: 34,000; Brazil: 15,400; Argentina: 11,300). Substantially fewer Austrians emigrated to Canada (5,400), the Soviet Union (3,200), and Palestine (1,900). Most emigrants hailed from the eastern states of Vienna, Lower Austria, Styria, and especially Burgenland, which had already had a pronounced tradition of overseas emigration before World War I. In the 1920s, Burgenland lost roughly 8% of its population to emigration; in some districts, such as Güssing in the south, 21% of the population left, chiefly for the USA. But industrial areas that had flourished in the late 19th century, especially those in metal- and ironworking and machine building like Steyr and Wiener Neustadt, experienced an economic crisis that especially prompted highly skilled workers to emigrate overseas along with their families. Some 8,000 Austrians were registered in European countries, with Germany still the most important destination. Around 10,000 Austrians went to France as migrant workers between 1925 and 1935, and about 4,000 headed to the Soviet Union between 1929 and 1935.

Following the dissolution and prohibition of the Social Democratic Workers' Party of Austria (*Sozialdemokratische Arbeiterpartei Österreichs* [SDAPö]) in 1934 by the Corporatist State (Austrofascism, 1933–8), around 3,000 Social Democrats fled to the Soviet Union while around 1,200 members of the Republican Guard (the SDAPö's paramilitary organization) given refuge by Czechoslovakia. After a failed putsch about 3,000 members of the Nazi Party escaped to Germany. From 1937 on there was a growing labor migration to Germany (around 20,000 individuals) in addition to about 60,000 Austrian Nazis who were in Germany for political reasons.

The expulsion of the Jews had already begun under the *Ständestaat* (Corporatist State), but it peaked after Austria's "annexation" by Nazi Germany when some 129,000 Jews were forced to emigrate between 1938 and 1941 and another 65,459 Austrian Jews were killed in the Holocaust by 1945.[11]

From a country of emigration to a country of immigration after World War II

At the end of World War II, around 1.6 million foreign forced laborers, prisoners of war, and former concentration camp inmates were in Austria. For the majority, Austria was a transit station on the way to the USA, Israel, or other destinations overseas. By around 1955, a million more refugees and expellees as well as displaced persons from eastern, east-central, and southeastern Europe had arrived in the country, though many of them also left as soon as they could arrange to move on. Among the largest and most durable immigrants were the *Volksdeutsche*, around half a million "ethnic Germans" from Czechoslovakia, Hungary, and Yugoslavia.[12]

For the most part, however, Austria developed into a country of emigration after World War II: the immediate postwar period was marked by a strong economic imbalance between the states in the east (Soviet Occupation Zone), with their armament and industrial sites that had been extensively damaged in and after the war, and the virtually intact Alpine west (American Occupation Zone). The massive economic disadvantages inflicted on the eastern states of Vienna, Lower Austria, and Burgenland (with wartime destruction compounded by the Soviet dismantling of industrial installations, the collapse of the transportation system, an energy shortage, and fewer funds from the European Recovery Program) led to a large-scale emigration – especially of younger workers, both male and female. The exodus was supported by state employment offices that recruited workers for foreign companies and organized a variety of courses (e.g., language, typing, and homemaking classes) for those willing to emigrate. This practice stood in opposition to the policy of the federal government, which wanted to prevent emigration as much as possible in order to shore up Austria's economic recovery, which was slowly gaining traction.

Still, the recruitment of migrants by Canada and Australia was permitted and to some extent even financially supported in Austria. The important destination countries also included countries in central and western Europe with a large demand for workers, including West Germany and Switzerland where about 50,000 Austrians migrated in the 1950s. The labor migration to those countries continued in the 1960s and 1970s. At the beginning of the 1970s, 177,000 Austrians were living in Germany; 101,000 of them were employees. All told, the migration of Austrians to Germany between 1961 and 1991 totaled about half a million – only a third of them were women, and 400,000 of them eventually returned to Austria. About 22,153 Austrians lived and worked in Switzerland in 1950; in 1970 there were 44,743. In the 1980s and 1990s, their number dropped to around 30,000. In contrast to Germany, in Switzerland the share of women was quite high: three-quarters of the migrants in the 1950s were female, 56% in 1960, and then a steady 40% to 45% since the 1970s. To this day, a not inconsiderable portion of these labor migrants are seasonal workers in the tourism sector and cross-border commuters (*Grenzgänger*) from Vorarlberg.

Next to these two German-speaking countries, relatively prosperous Sweden also exerted a particular attraction on migrant workers of both genders, especially in the 1960s and 1970s. The number of Austrians in Sweden quadrupled between the early 1950s and the mid-1960s and hit a high of around 5,500. By 1986 the number had dropped to around 2,800 and has been stable since then. The share of women among the emigrants to Sweden was and is to this day fairly low at one-third.

Small numbers of Austrians went to Great Britain, France, and Italy. Among non-European countries after 1945, the USA was initially the most important destination, followed by Brazil, Australia, and Canada. Since the 1960s, Brazil and South Africa have become the preferred destination countries for Austrian emigrants. By contrast, emigration to both the USA and Australia declined. All in all, about half a million Austrians were living abroad at the end of the 1990s, nearly three-quarters of those in another European country, chiefly Germany (188,000) and Switzerland (30,000).

Since the 1960s, Austria has clearly been transformed into a country of immigration. In 2001, Austria had 8.06 million inhabitants, which means that the population had grown by around 1.13 million since 1951. This growth was largely the result of strong immigration since the 1960s. In 1961, the foreign resident population of 100,200 made up merely 1.4% of Austria's population; by 1973–4, their share had increased to 4.1% (300,000).

Political refugees arrived in Austria in large numbers in 1956–7 from Hungary (more than 200,000), in 1968–9 from Czechoslovakia (around 162,000), and in 1981–2 from Poland (120,000–150,000).[13] Although nearly two-thirds of the refugees in each instance applied for asylum in Austria, only 5% to 10% actually stayed, as had been the case with the non-German refugees and expellees after World War II. Between 1973 and 1989 Austria also became a transit country for around 250,000 Jews from the Soviet Union, who emigrated via Austria to Israel, the USA, or other countries. Since 1990 Austria has lost this function as the hub for Russian-Jewish migrants, since they became able to migrate directly from Russia to their destination countries.

---

[11] Jewish refugees from Nazi Germany and from German-occupied Europe since 1933.

[12] Forced laborers in Germany and German-occupied Europe during World War II; displaced persons (DPs) in Europe since the end of World War II; German refugees and expellees from eastern, east-central, and southeastern Europe in Germany and Austria since the end of World War II.

[13] Hungarian refugees in Europe since 1956; Czechoslovakian refugees in western, central, and northern Europe since 1968.

With the opening of the iron curtain in 1989 and the outbreak of the Balkan wars in the 1990s Austria once again became a transit country as thousands of migrant workers from countries in east-central Europe, from the former Soviet Union, and from the Balkan states crossed Austria on their way to the West. There were also the military conflicts and the persecution and murder of ethnic minorities in Croatia (1991), Bosnia-Herzegovina (1992–3), and Kosovo (1999), which led to mass flights: all told, Austria took in 80,000–90,000 war refugees from Bosnia in the 1990s, which meant that Austria accepted more refugees than many other European countries. In 1991, around 13,000 war refugees from Croatia were given residence permits in Austria and official permission to work. Something similar happened with the refugees from Bosnia, who initially had temporary residence and employment rights until the National and State Act for Bosnian War Expellees expired in 1998. Two-thirds of the refugees remained in the country and received settlement permits; 11,000 refugees returned to their homeland, and about 12,000 moved on to other countries.[14]

The majority of foreign immigrants who came to and remained in Austria after the 1960s were deliberately recruited migrant workers of both genders, especially from Turkey (Recruitment Treaty 1964) and Yugoslavia (1966). In contrast to some other European countries, Austria confronted a labor shortage fairly late. As in Germany there was no interest in the integration or permanent settlement of these immigrant workers and here too they were referred to as "guest workers." In the beginning, the quotas agreed upon between Austria and the recruitment countries were barely met; only after 1969 did the number of guest workers start to rise rapidly, reaching a first peak of 226,800 in 1973. This was followed by an end to recruitment in 1974 and 10 years later the number of foreign workers had dropped by around 40% to 138,700.

At the same time, the end to recruitment caused some of the foreign workers to settle in Austria. This was then followed by family reunification and a follow-on migration of more distant relatives and friends – especially after the Balkan wars. Of the foreigners who came to Austria between 1989 and 1991, 56% joined relatives who had already been living there for a longer period and on whose support they could count. The demand for workers sparked by the rapidly growing economy after 1989 was filled with immigrants from the former Yugoslavia and Turkey. By contrast, migrant workers from Poland, Romania, Hungary, and Czechoslovakia (or its successor states) made up only around 3%.[15]

In the Second Republic, immigration and the labor market were guided by the cooperative interest politics of the state, unions, and employer organizations. This typical Austrian "Social Partnership" system of regulating immigration and the labor market was replaced in 1993 by a quota system that made new migration considerably more difficult. The respective quotas were assigned to the various federal states based on the state of the regional labor and housing markets as well as the capacities of the school and health systems. The introduction of this residence law marked a turning point in what had been until then a fairly open immigration policy. In 1997, Austria passed an integration package made up of an Aliens Act (*Fremdengesetz*) premised upon the slogan "integration before new immigration," along with amendments to the Alien Employment Act (*Ausländerbeschäftigungsgesetz*), the *Bundeshöchstzahlenüberziehungsverordnung* (a decree that had allowed the limit on foreign nationals to be exceeded), and the Unemployment Insurance Act. This legislation further restricted new immigration and introduced a system of graduated permits to stay in Austria. In the wake of Austria's accession to the European Union in 1995, the number of (legally employed) workers from non-EU countries has declined, while the number of workers from the EU area has increased (see Table 3).

After 1945, the integration of immigrants to Austria proved very difficult because of basic social and economic policies that promoted social and economic exclusion of immigrants. For example, the predominance of nationalized industrial enterprises and the extensive public sectors where the allocation of jobs and opportunities for advancement were strongly shaped by party-political and union interests, and where the employment of one's "own people" (i.e., party members) was given priority rendered the Austrian labor market much more impenetrable than the markets of other European countries. Something similar applied to the housing market where immigrants remained largely excluded from the publicly subsidized rental market. Moreover, the citizenship law based on the *ius sanguinis* made legal integration more difficult and restricted opportunities in professional and educational realms.

To this day, Austria has hardly experienced a global immigration: despite a steady rise since the 1960s, the share of immigrants from Asia (2001: 5.3%), Africa (2.1%), Oceania (0.2%), and the USA (0.9%) remains tiny at the beginning of the 21st century.

Even though integration has been made a priority in migration policy since the 1990s, many social and legal barriers to integration remain. Although immigrants in Vienna and other cities (like Salzburg, Linz, and Graz) do not live in large immigrant quarters cut off from the rest of the urban population, residential segregation is discernible by blocks and neighborhoods in the areas of inexpensive housing. In recreation and social life too, interaction and contact between immigrants and natives is often limited.

To be sure, since the 1960s a lively ethnic and/or religiously oriented organizational life has taken shape among the immigrants from Turkey and the former Yugoslavia: numerous organizations and clubs are aimed at different groups (e.g., small business owners, young people, women, or students) and in part also see themselves as representing their interests. The organizations established by the early Yugoslav immigrants in the 1960s and 1970s joined together into an

---

[14] Refugees from former Yugoslavia in Europe since 1991.
[15] Turkish labor migrants in western, central, and northern Europe since the mid-1950s; Yugoslav labor migrants in western, central, and northern Europe since the end of World War II.

Table 3. Residential population in Austria by selected nationality, 1961–2002

	1961 (N)	1971 (N)	1981 (N)	1991 (N)	2001 (N)	2001 (%)
Total population	7,073,814	7,491,526	7,555,338	7,795,786	8,064,500	
Native born	6,971,648	7,279,630	7,263,890	7,278,096	7,334,600	
Foreigners	102,166	211,896	291,448	517,690	730,000	100.0
From (selection)						
Germany	43,500	47,087	40,987	57,310	74,300	10.2
France	1,116	1,387	1,623	2,178	4,200	0.6
Great Britain	1,520	2,341	2,666	3,427	5,700	0.8
Italy	8,662	7,778	6,681	8,636	10,700	1.5
Netherlands	759	1,478	1,764	2,617	4,000	0.5
Yugoslavia and successor states	4,565	93,337	125,890	197,886	328,300	45.0
From						
Serbia, Montenegro					155,700	21.3
Kosovo						
Croatia					57,600	7.9
Bosnia-Herzegovina					96,200	13.2
Macedonia					12,400	1.7
Slovenia					6,400	0.9
Bulgaria	326	489	432	3,582	4,400	0.6
Poland	539	774	5,911	18,321	22,600	3.1
Romania	262	397	1,253	18,536	18,400	2.5
Czechoslovakia	741	2,991	2,032	11,318	13,800	1.9
Hungary	4,956	2,691	2,526	10,556	13,000	1.8
Turkey	217	16,423	59,900	118,579	130,100	17.8
Switzerland	3,307	3,860	3,569	4,901	6,300	0.9
Soviet Union, Russian Federation	226	192	495	2,112	3,700	0.5
Africa	626	1,279	3,127	8,515	15,200	2.1
Asia	1,630	4,254	12,304	25,677	38,400	5.3
North and South America	2,717	6,000	6,305	9,516	13,100	1.8

Source: Selected from Fassmann and Stacher, eds., *Österreichischer Migrations- und Integrationsbericht*, 42.

Umbrella Organization of Yugoslav Organizations in Vienna in 1976, but the disintegration of Yugoslavia led to a (national/ethnic) fragmentation of their organizational life in Austria. Fragmented or not, however, the organizational culture of the immigrants tends to be clearly separated from that of the natives. Nor has the recognition of the Islamic Community of Faith in Austria as an entity under public law in 1979 furthered the social acceptance of Muslims among the Austrian population. The lack of willingness on the part of most Austrians to engage more intensively with migrants, their living and working conditions, and their culture and religion has meant that while integration is demanded from the immigrants, the natives contribute little to it in everyday life.

REFERENCES

Bade, Klaus J. *Migration in European History*. Oxford, 2003.

Bauböck, Rainer. *"Nach Rasse und Sprache verschieden." Migrationspolitik in Österreich von der Monarchie bis heute.* Vienna, 1996.

Bauer, Ingrid, Josef Ehmer, and Sylvia Hahn, eds. *Walz, Migration, Besatzung. Historische Szenarien des Eigenen und des Fremden*. Klagenfurt and Celovec, 2002.

Brunold, Ursus, ed. *Gewerbliche Migration im Alpenraum*. Bolzano, 1994.

Chaloupek, Günther, Peter Eigner, and Michael Wagner. *Wien. Wirtschaftsgeschichte 1740–1938*. 2 vols. Vienna, 1991.

Chmelar, Hans. *Höhepunkte der Österreichischen Auswanderung. Die Auswanderung aus den im Reichsrat vertretenen Königreichen und Ländern 1905–1914*. Vienna, 1974.

Ehmer, Josef. *Soziale Traditionen in Zeiten des Wandels. Arbeiter und Handwerker im 19. Jahrhundert*. Frankfurt am Main and New York, 1994.

Fassmann, Heinz. *Emigration, Immigration und Binnenwanderung in der Österreichisch-ungarischen Monarchie*. Vienna, 1988.

Fassmann, Heinz, and Rainer Münz. *Einwanderungsland Österreich? Historische Migrationsmuster, aktuelle Trends und politische Maßnahmen*. Vienna, 1995.

Fassmann, Heinz, and Rainer Münz, eds. *Migration in Europa. Historische Entwicklung, aktuelle Trends, politische Reaktionen*. Frankfurt am Main and New York, 1996.

Fassmann, Heinz, and Irene Stacher, eds. *Österreichischer Migrations- und Integrationsbericht. Demographische Entwicklungen – sozioökonomische Strukturen – rechtliche Rahmenbedingungen*. Vienna, 2003.

Fassmann, Heinz, Helga Matuschek, and Elisabeth Menasse, eds. *Abgrenzen – ausgrenzen – aufnehmen. Empirische Befunde zur Fremdenfeindlichkeit und Integration.* Klagenfurt and Celovec, 1999.

Hahn, Sylvia. *Migration – Arbeit – Geschlecht. Mitteleuropa in vergleichender Perspektive, 17.-19. Jahrhundert.* Göttingen, 2007.

Hahn, Sylvia, and Karl Flanner, eds. *'Die Wienerische Neustadt.' Handwerk, Handel und Militär in der Steinfeldstadt.* Vienna, 1994.

Hahn, Sylvia, Andrea Komlosy, and Ilse Reiter, eds. *Ausweisung – Abschiebung – Vertreibung. Europa 16.-20. Jahrhundert.* Innsbruck, 2006.

Hanisch, Ernst. *Der lange Schatten des Staates. Österreichische Gesellschaftsgeschichte im 20. Jahrhundert.* Vienna, 1994.

Heindl, Waltraud, and Edith Saurer, eds. *Grenze und Staat. Paßwesen, Staatsbürgerschaft, Heimatrecht und Fremdengesetzgebung in der Österreichischen Monarchie (1750–1867).* Vienna, 2000.

Hoffmann-Holter, Beatrix. *"Abreisendmachung": Jüdische Kriegsflüchtlinge in Wien 1914 bis 1923.* Vienna, 1995.

Horvarh, Traude, and Gerda Neyer, eds. *Auswanderungen aus Österreich. Von der Mitte des 19. Jahrhunderts bis zur Gegenwart.* Vienna, 1996.

Jaritz, Gerhard, and Albert Müller, eds. *Migration in der Feudalgesellschaft.* Frankfurt am Main, 1988.

Johler, Reinhard. *Mir parlen Italiano und spreggen Dütsch piano. Italienische Arbeiter in Vorarlberg 1870–1914.* Feldkirch, 1987.

John, Michael. *Bevölkerung in der Stadt. 'Einheimische' und 'Fremde' in Linz (19. und 20. Jahrhundert).* Linz, 2000.

John, Michael, and Albert Lichtblau. *Schmelztiegel Wien – einst und jetzt. Geschichte und Gegenwart der Zuwanderung nach Wien.* Vienna, 1990.

Knittler, Herbert. *Die europäische Stadt in der frühen Neuzeit. Institutionen, Strukturen, Entwicklungen.* Vienna and Munich, 2000.

Komlosy, Andrea. *Grenze und ungleiche regionale Entwicklung. Binnenmarkt und Migration in der Habsburgermonarchie im 18. und 19. Jahrhundert.* Vienna, 2003.

Lohrmann, Klaus. *Die Österreichischen Juden zur Zeit Maria Theresias und Josephs II.* Eisenstadt, 1980.

Mathis, Franz. *Zur Bevölkerungsstruktur Österreichischer Städte im 17. Jahrhundert.* Vienna, 1977.

Parnreiter, Christof. *Migration und Arbeitsteilung. Ausländer-Innenbeschäftigung in der Weltwirtschaftskrise.* Vienna, 1994.

Pichler, Meinrad. *Auswanderer von Vorarlberg in die USA 1800–1938.* Bregenz, 1993.

Sandgruber, Roman. *Ökonomie und Politik. Österreichs Wirtschaftsgeschichte vom Mittelalter bis zur Gegenwart.* Vienna, 1995.

Sieder, Reinhard, Heinz Steinert, and Emmerich Tálos, eds. *Österreich 1945–1995. Gesellschaft, Politik, Kultur.* Vienna, 1995.

Stadler, Friedrich, ed. *Vertriebene Vernunft. Emigration und Exil Österreichischer Wissenschaftler 1930–1940.* 2 vols. Vienna and Munich, 1987/88.

Steidl, Annemarie. *Auf nach Wien! Die Mobilität des mitteleuropäischen Handwerks im 18. und 19. Jahrhundert am Beispiel der Haupt- und Residenzstadt.* Vienna and Munich, 2003.

Tálos, Emmerich, Ernst Hanisch, and Wolfgang Neugebauer, eds. *NS-Herrschaft in Österreich 1938–1945.* Vienna, 1988.

Walker, Mack. *The Salzburg Transaction. Expulsion and Redemption in Eighteenth-Century Germany.* Ithaca and London, 1992.

Weigl, Andreas. *Demographischer Wandel und Modernisierung in Wien.* Vienna, 2000.

Zatloukal-Reiter, Ilse. *Ausgewiesen, abgeschoben. Eine Geschichte des Ausweisungsrechts in Österreich vom ausgehenden 18. bis ins 20. Jahrhundert.* Frankfurt am Main, 2000.

SWITZERLAND

Marc Vuilleumier

The region and its boundaries

From the 17th century to the end of the Ancien Régime (1789), the Swiss Confederation remained territorially unchanged as a conglomerate of 13 sovereign cantons, subordinated lands (*Untertänen*), and associated towns and villages. In 1815, Switzerland became a confederation of 22 sovereign cantons with a nearly powerless central government. Since then, the territory of the Swiss state has changed only minimally. In small Switzerland, the border regions were far more extensive, relative to the overall territory, than in a large state. Two of the three largest cities, Geneva and Basel, are situated in a peripheral region that is nearly completely surrounded by the territories of other states. The languages of the surrounding states of Italy, France, Germany, and Austria are the same as the primary languages of Switzerland. Moreover, important south-north transit routes traverse the country. All this explains a migration that has been relatively strong for centuries, compared to larger countries in Europe.

Switzerland's political structure has changed considerably over the course of time: after the *Sonderbund* War in 1847, the new, federally oriented constitution of 1848 for the first time set up a central government, though its sphere of authority remained narrowly circumscribed. The powers of the government were gradually broadened in the 19th and 20th centuries and Switzerland was increasingly organized as a centralized state.

Still, the medieval institution of the *Bürgergemeinde* (civic community) with its political and economic privileges (autonomy or community of property) survived even after the 17th century. Membership was passed from the father to his children, as a way of limiting the number of privileged citizens and thus keeping the stake that each had in the common civic goods at the same level. Against this backdrop, members were constantly impeding the admission of new immigrants through prohibitive admission fees or negative replies. Since the community was obliged to support its poor members, few wealthy applicants were turned down and marriages among the citizens were controlled. Thus there arose, next to the full members of the community, the categories of *Einwohner*, *Beisässen*, or *Hintersässen* who were excluded from civic rights. Especially the cities, because of the monopoly on power by a small number of burgher families, moved increasingly toward being oligarchies.

In spite of the revolutionary upheavals at the end of the 18th century, the civic communities persisted into the next century. Parallel to it there developed the political community, which encompassed all residents. The tasks and resources were divided up between the two types of community. Occasionally there were mergers when the political community took over the privileges of the civic community. Civic communities still exist at the beginning of the 21st century, and the passport of each Swiss citizen does not record the place of birth, but the inherited place of citizenship (*Bürgerort*). Swiss citizenship depends on membership in a community and a canton, and the consent of a community is the precondition for the naturalization of a foreigner. Different from other countries, this is not merely an administrative act. Rather, it is an exclusively political decision that is made by the assembly of the citizens or their elected representatives (City Council or ad hoc commission).

Work and settlement migration in the 17th and 18th centuries

In the 17th and 18th centuries, Switzerland was not open to immigrants either politically or socially. The citizenry and the guilds increasingly closed themselves off socially. Immigrants, even if they had the right of residence, had to content themselves with less esteemed occupations and had virtually no opportunity for professional and social advancement. The wealthy rural regions generally rejected newcomers; only the less prosperous regions took in immigrants. The vast majority of immigrants came from neighboring countries, and their chances of integrating differed hardly from those of internal Swiss migrants. Because of the different growing periods in the various ecological niches, the migratory conditions were profoundly shaped by the seasonal labor migrations from the Alps into the valleys or the lowlands.

Scholarship has largely ignored the economically motivated migratory movements of the early modern period, focusing instead on the immigration of a large number of Protestant refugees into the Reformed territories between the 16th and the beginning of the 18th centuries. That wave of refugees from Italy, the southern Netherlands, southern Germany, and especially France crested with the exodus of the Huguenots after the revocation of the Edict of

Nantes in 1685.[1] For the vast majority of the nearly 140,000 religious refugees of this last wave until the beginning of the 18th century, Switzerland – with about 1.2 million inhabitants around 1700, among them 800,000 adherents to the Reformed faith – was merely a way station. The destinations were Prussia or other Protestant German states. By contrast, the majority of the Protestant refugees from France and Italy in the 16th century had settled permanently in Switzerland and integrated into the citizenry and urban patriciate within a few generations. At the end of the 17th century, however, against the backdrop of an economic situation that was more precarious than in the 16th century, the citizenry and the communities closed ranks more tightly: xenophobic reactions replaced religious solidarity and newcomers were turned away.[2]

The wealthiest and economically most adept among the Protestant refugees of the 16th and 17th centuries had been able to transfer part or all of their movable wealth – often in the form of letters of exchange – to the Frankfurt stock market. No small number of merchants and factory owners had been able to bring along their order books and the addresses of their customers; craftsmen, even if they came empty-handed, could fall back on their skills, which were at times far superior to those of their native counterparts. The capital, business connections, and skills brought by the immigrants boosted the economy in the cities and Reformed cantons of Switzerland and eventually led to lasting economic growth. Some refugee families spread out over several host countries, and their connections with one another were of great importance to the development of external trade and the banking system. Moreover, they contributed – especially in the 18th century – to the transfer of ideas and the rise of science.

However, Switzerland in the 18th century was not only a country of immigration, but also – and above all – a country of emigration. The interplay of growing population pressure and poor opportunities to make a living was exacerbated especially after famines or economic crises, and it intensified where grain cultivation was replaced by animal husbandry. By contrast, emigration remained on a lower level in proto-industrial regions. Many from the lower social strata left Switzerland as mercenaries, either as part of an individual contract with a private military entrepreneur or within the framework of a "capitulation," in which the canton or the patrician oligarchy regulated the merchandising of soldiers. During the Ancien Régime, this system formed a weighty economic factor, cemented the political cantonal structure, and ensured diplomatic influence abroad. It vanished with the French Revolution. While a few cantons reintroduced such regulations, liberal forces, however, which were gaining ground everywhere, regarded the support of absolutist

rulers (Naples, Papal States) by Swiss regiments as unwise. New capitulations were prohibited in 1848, still existing ones were abolished in 1859.[3]

In addition to the military exodus there was a civilian migration, which was rarely promoted by the authorities since they feared the loss of labor power and an impoverishment of the country. In Italy and other European countries, all the way to Russia, migrants from Ticino were working in the construction industry as bricklayers, plasterers, contractors, and architects, or in other skilled professions.[4] For example, numerous confectioners from the Grisons were found on the Italian peninsula since the early modern period and in Russia in the 19th century. Merchant entrepreneurs and watchmakers sent their workers to distant lands, often for longer periods. Of shorter duration were the foreign sojourns of industrialists, merchants, and bankers who went as part of their education and training. That was also true of young pastors, who began their careers by spending several years with a foreign congregation while they were waiting for a post to open up in Switzerland.

Extensive settlement migrations by Swiss men and women took place out of regions destroyed in the Thirty Years' War (1618–48): between 1660 and 1740, 15,000–20,000 Swiss left the French region of Franche-Comté for Alsace, the Palatinate, Baden, Württemberg, Bavaria, Brandenburg, and other German territories. These were frequently craftsmen from rural areas and small farmers with their families, who formed religious and geographic communities of common origin in their host countries.[5]

Until the beginning of the 19th century, the exodus was aimed almost exclusively at European countries. An exception were the Swiss regiments in the colonial forces of Great Britain, France, and the Netherlands. By comparison, emigration overseas remained small, even if 25,000 Swiss were already counted in the USA in 1790, most living in the cities.

Continental and overseas emigration from the 19th to the early 20th century

After 1815, overseas migration developed into a mass phenomenon, while continental migration simultaneously did not ease up. The backdrop to this development was the strong population growth that began in 1770 and was not accompanied by a corresponding expansion of work opportunities. In 1822, Czar Alexander I founded a colony in newly conquered Bessarabia and settled it with wine growers from the Waadtland. In 1940, most of their descendants fled the area – after 1918 in Romanian hands – before the advancing Red Army. Emigration to Russia, especially by

---

[1] Huguenots in Europe since the 16th century; Waldensians in central Europe since the early modern period; Dutch Calvinist refugees in Europe since the early modern period.

[2] Swiss Protestant peasants in Alsace, southwestern Germany, and Brandenburg-Prussia since the mid-17th century.

[3] Swiss mercenaries in Europe from the 17th to the 19th century: the example of France.

[4] Italian and other "Alpine" (Grisons, Tecino, and Vorarlberg) architects and visual artists in Baroque Europe.

[5] Swiss Protestant peasants in Alsace, southwestern Germany, and Brandenburg-Prussia since the mid-17th Century.

skilled workers, increased in the course of the 19th century and led to the establishment of a few successful companies. After the Russian revolution of 1917, more than 8,000 Swiss returned to their country of origin.

Until the 19th century, the emigrants were predominantly men, leaving aside the settlement migration in family units. But even among women there were individual migrants: they went from rural areas into nearby cities – also in neighboring countries – as domestics. The educational expansion in the 19th century promoted the specifically female emigration of cooks, governesses, and tutors. Russia, in particular, hired female French teachers and tutors. The destination regions of the Swiss changed in the 19th century: between 23% and 28% of all emigrants from Switzerland went to France; Germany in 1850 was home to about 11% of all Swiss abroad, their share dropped to 8.4% in 1880 and then rose again to 15% just before World War I. The fluctuations were less pronounced in the other countries, for example, in Russia, where the percentage hovered between 2.5 and 2.1. Italy was an exception: in 1850, 22.7% of all foreign-dwelling Swiss were living there, but after that the share declined rapidly, down to only 6.1% in 1870, and a mere 2.9% in 1913. This decline can be explained by the expulsion of the Ticinans from Lombardy-Veneto in 1853 (to which we shall return later), as well as the upheavals in the wake of the founding of the Italian nation-state in 1861 and the end of the migration of mercenaries.

The importance of the USA as a destination country for Swiss emigrants remained high throughout the 19th century and up to the US restrictions on emigration in the 1920s and the global economic crisis in the early 1930s. While 67.4% of Swiss living abroad were in Europe in 1850, that share dropped to 48.5% by 1870, and then rose again to settle around 51%. The corresponding share of Swiss living in the USA rose from 28.7% in 1850 to 36.5% in 1870, declined slightly thereafter, and eventually stabilized at around 34%. Overseas emigration as a whole fluctuated considerably and reached a first peak during the famine of 1816–17, when 0.47% of the total population of Switzerland left. That period saw the founding in 1819 of the settlement colony Nova Friburgo in Brazil, although its Swiss residents scattered throughout the country within a few years. Other settlement colonies in the USA, attested to this day by Swiss place names, survived longer and cultivated the traditions of their home country before they, too, eventually disbanded. The first high phase of overseas migration ended in 1820. With the economic crisis of the 1840s, the number of emigrants rose again rapidly. Even the renewed economic upswing around 1849–50 did not lead to a decline in overseas emigration, which reached a high point in 1854, when 0.7% of the Swiss population crossed the Atlantic. In addition to the economic problems of a growing population in the home country, the discovery of gold in California and Australia also played an important part in the decision to emigrate.

However, overseas migration was also pushed by political developments: seasonal movements from the valleys of Ticino to Italy already had a long tradition. Because of the precarious state of Ticinan agriculture, it became even more important in the middle of the 19th century: a series of failed harvests between 1848 and 1853, which drove up the price of grain by 50%, played a role in this. Following the failed revolution in February 1853 by the Italian democrat Guiseppe Mazzini in Milan, which was part of the Habsburg monarchy, Austria accused the canton of Ticino of being in league with the Italian national revolutionaries. By way of retaliation, Austria imposed a blockade of the borders, which lasted for more than two years. The seasonal workers who had returned for the winter could no longer go back to their jobs in the Po valley; in addition, 6,500 Ticinans were expelled from Lombardy-Veneto. Hundreds of male valley-dwellers who saw themselves deprived of their livelihood took passage to the USA and Australia. This simultaneously shifted the gender ratios in Ticino: for a long time, there was a pronounced surplus of women.

After the high point in the 1850s, overseas emigration declined rapidly in the years that followed. The phase of a global economic depression from the early 1870s to the early 1890s led to a renewed rise. In 1883, nearly 0.5% of the population of Switzerland crossed the ocean. Emigration to the USA declined again in importance in the final years of the 19th century.

Emigrants to America came mostly from rural regions, were small farmers and craftsmen, and left the country for the most part in family units. Emigration was supported by the communities, which rid themselves of their poor in this manner. Numerous communities paid some or all of the costs of passage if emigrants renounced their civic rights. In the 1880s, stagnating prices for agricultural commodities and the lack of a future for many small farms drove numerous farmers to sell their holdings to settle in the USA, Argentina, or Chile. This was no longer a flight from poverty, but a rational decision to improve their economic opportunities. At the same time, the urban population accounted for a growing share of the emigrants.

Immigrations in the 19th century

In the 19th century, Switzerland was not only a country of emigration but also a country of immigration. The political modernizations after 1830 and especially after 1848 facilitated the geographic mobility of the individual, as did the agreements about free settlement that were entered into with many European countries. Alongside a growing number of tourists, Switzerland also attracted migrant workers from neighboring countries. The border cantons had very high rates of foreign populations: Basel city, for example, had 23% foreigners around 1846, Geneva had 23.8% in 1850. At least half of the German immigrants were itinerant journeymen. They followed traditional routes, some of which led through Switzerland, moving from city to city in search of work as tailors, cobblers, locksmiths, or carpenters. In a few Swiss towns they accounted for a large portion or even the majority of craftsmen in these professions. They stayed in one place for several weeks or months, not infrequently crowded together in dilapidated accommodations. This group was very visible and soon associated with fixed attributes: they came without families; were young and outside of the traditional mechanisms of social control; lived an isolated, hand-to-mouth existence in a foreign land; spent much of their free time in taverns; were not infrequently addicted to alcohol; and were regularly involved in fights. Welfare organizations, initially often supported by the clergy or civic notables, tried to improve the living situation of German workers and journeymen. These organizations offered their members a place to talk, read the paper, prepare meals, and acquire a minimum of education through courses. This facilitated their integration into Switzerland and gave them a certain political awareness. That is why German republicans and democrats who had fled to Switzerland tried to gain access to these clubs to enlist the German craftsmen for their cause. For example, in the 1840s the social theories and political demands of the early German socialist Wilhelm Weitling were disseminated through these organizations.

Beginning in 1815, political refugees from the neighboring states began to pour into Switzerland in successive waves. Depending on the political orientation of their governments, the politically autonomous cantons were more or less receptive. In 1823 and once again in 1836, however, all cantons had to yield to the diplomatic pressure being exerted on the Confederation and expel the individuals who were classified as the most dangerous. With the exception of 1849, when about 12,000 refugees streamed into Switzerland following the failure of the European revolutions of 1848, political refugees accounted for only a very small portion of immigrants, presumably about 1% of all foreigners in Switzerland. Only a small number of the refugees of 1849 remained in Switzerland, since the Confederation promoted onward migration to England and America by issuing transit permits to the seaports.[6]

Around 2,000 Polish refugees came to Switzerland after the failed national uprising of 1863–4, and some settled there permanently. Together with their countrymen who had made a home there after the Polish November revolt of 1830–1, they formed small ethnic communities in which the memory of the lost Polish nation lived on. Until the reestablishment of the Polish state after World War I, the Polish National Museum in Rapperswil Castle was one of the cultural centers of the Polish diaspora.[7]

[6] Italian refugees of the *risorgimento* in central and western Europe in the 19th century.
[7] Polish political refugees in central and western Europe in the 19th century.

Table 1. Percentage of foreign nationals among the Swiss population, 1850–2000		
	Population	Foreign nationals in percentages
1850	2,392,740	2.9
1860	2,519,494	4.6
1870	2,655,001	5.7
1880	2,831,787	7.4
1888	2,917,754	7.8
1900	3,315,443	11.6
1910	3,753,293	14.7
1920	3,880,320	10.4
1930	4,066,400	8.7
1941	4,265,703	5.2
1950	4,714,992	6.1
1960	5,429,016	10.8
1970	6,269,783	17.2
1980	6,365,960	14.8
1990	6,873,687	18.1
2000	7,288,010	20.5

Source: Ritzmann-Blickenstorfer, *Historische Statistik der Schweiz; Statistisches Jahrbuch der Schweiz; Historisches Lexikon der Schweiz.*

Refugees, and foreigners in general, played an important role in the development of the Swiss education system. The majority of professors at the universities in Zurich and Bern that were set up in 1833 and 1834, respectively, were Germans. Numerous foreign teachers were also found in some cantonal schools and private educational institutions. In subsequent years, the proportion of Swiss teachers increased, especially at higher schools. On the whole, however, the share of foreign professors at Swiss universities has remained high into the 21st century (see Table 1).

In the second half of the 19th century, the economic upswing and the construction of the railroad attracted foreign workers and technical experts. At the same time, as we have seen, the overseas emigration and continental seasonal migration of Swiss nationals remained at a high level. Because of the many impediments to migration within Switzerland, many members of the rural lower classes preferred emigration to the USA to migration into the closest industrial city. The census of 1888 for the first time showed a positive migration balance, and it would remain that way in the future, with the exception of the war years 1914–45.

In the period of troubled growth in the global economy from 1873 to 1895, Swiss industry continued to expand at a moderate pace. This was followed until the beginning of World War I by a phase of explosive economic growth, as gross domestic product (GDP) rose by 35%–40%. Population meanwhile grew by 20%, two-fifths of which was the result of immigration and the high birthrate among foreigners in Switzerland. In 1910, foreigners made up nearly 15% of the total population. This meant that next to Luxembourg, Switzerland in 1914 had the highest share of foreigners among

Table 2. Foreigners in Switzerland, 1850–2000, by nationality (in percentages)											
	Countries of origin*								Continents		
Year	Germany	France	Italy	Austria	Spain	Portugal	Turkey	Yugoslavia	America	Africa	Asia
1850	39.6	41.8	8.6	4.4							
1860	41.6	40.8	12.0	3.2							
1870	37.9	41.2	12.0	3.9							
1880	42.6	28.3	19.7	6.0							
1890	48.9	26.3	18.2	6.0							
1900	41.0	18.2	30.5	6.4							
1910	36.7	14.7	36.7	7.1							
1920	37.2	14.2	33.5	5.8							
1930	38.0	10.5	35.8	6.2							
1941	26.0	10.9	43.0	9.7							
1950	19.6	9.6	49.0	8.3					1.4		
1960	16.0	5.4	59.2	6.8	2.3				1.9		
1970	11.0	5.2	54.0	4.3	11.2		1.1	2.3	1.7		
1980	9.3	5.4	44.3	3.6	11.3	2.0	4.1	6.5	2.2	1.2	2.3
1990	7.0	4.2	30.8	2.6	10.0	8.9	6.6	13.9	2.4	2.0	5.6
2000	7.7	4.3	22.5	2.0	5.9	9.5	5.6	24.2	3.5	2.6	5.1

* Only countries of origin are mentioned with more than 1% of the immigrants in Switzerland.

Source: Ritzmann-Blickenstorfer, *Historische Statistik*.

the population of any European country. That the size of the foreign population remained stable was due especially to naturalization law: since the status of a member of a community was inherited and no *ius soli* existed, many individuals with foreign nationality had been born in Switzerland. In 1910 that was true of more than one-third of these "foreigners," half of whom were under the age of fifteen. More than a quarter of those born abroad had already been living in Switzerland for more than 10 years.

One can therefore assume that more than half of all foreigners in Switzerland at the beginning of the 20th century were members of a stable ethnic community who had lived there for many years and had settled in for a permanent stay. For the most part they were workers and craftsmen, which explains their uneven geographic distribution: in 1910, about 80% of foreigners lived in the northern and eastern industrial regions and in the cities in 9 out of a total of 22 cantons. In the Canton Geneva, their share of the population reached 40%, in the Canton Basel city it was 38%, in Ticino, 28%, in the Canton Zurich, 20%. In some cities the percentage was even higher: 51% in Lugano, 34% in Zurich, 31% in St. Gallen, and 46% in the small industrial city of Arbon. Compared to the native population, foreigners were employed at higher rates in industry and the craft trades, and only rarely in agriculture. More than 95% came from neighboring countries, though the specific percentages varied: between 1888 and 1910, the share of immigrants from Austria-Hungary remained roughly the same, while the share of German and Frenchmen steadily declined and that of the Italians doubled (see Table 2). The number of Italians was regularly underestimated by a wide margin in the

statistics, since censuses took place in December and therefore failed to record the many seasonal migrants who had already returned home by then. That group was anywhere from 50,000 to 90,000 persons, depending on the state of the economy.

Ninety percent of French immigrants settled in the French-speaking western part of Switzerland. Their influx was part of a long tradition of migration, it rose at the slowest pace, and their share of the total population of Switzerland declined steadily. More than half of the French immigrants lived in the Canton Geneva, which geographically formed a Swiss enclave within France. Northern and eastern Switzerland were the destination of many workers, especially from poorly industrialized southern Germany. The higher wages in Switzerland also attracted many German skilled workers. About 20% of the Germans worked in trade, especially in French-speaking Switzerland, many had come for a few years to learn French. The emigration from Austria-Hungary was multiethnic; shortly before 1914 it also included several hundred Polish agricultural laborers from Galicia. On the whole it was almost exclusively workers who left the dual monarchy for Switzerland, with the proportion of unskilled workers higher than it was among the German immigrants.

Italian immigration grew the fastest after 1880; 87% of the immigrants came from the working class. Constantly improving and cheaper means of transportation made it possible for the poorest residents of the cities and especially of the rural regions in Italy to take jobs in industrial regions and on large construction sites in Switzerland. More than three-quarters of them came from northern Italy, nearly all others from central Italy as far south as Rome. The final phase of railroad construction in Switzerland, with the extremely labor-intensive building of tunnels, mountain lines, and cable railways, but also the rapid growth of the cities, led to a huge demand for workers. In 1910, about 81% of those employed in railroad construction were of Italian origins; 58% of the bricklayers came from abroad, chiefly from Italy. Since construction work, which employed 44% of all Italian laborers in Switzerland, was dormant in the winter, most were seasonal migrants. The families left behind in the country of origin often lived from a small farm or craft, earnings from which were so low that they depended on the additional income from abroad. It was not rare, however, for seasonal migrations to turn into longer stays.[8]

From 1900, the Italian immigration began to show increasing differentiation. Areas of employment like the textile, food, metal, and chemical industries gained in importance. More and more immigrants worked in factories. Employers in the textile industry in eastern Switzerland often turned to Italian women who were recruited directly in Italy. These young women frequently lived adjacent to the factories in dormitories run by nuns. They were joined by Italian women workers whose families or relatives were already living in Switzerland.

Female labor migration and the natural increase in the immigrant population led to a rise in the number of women among the foreign population at the beginning of the 20th century. The majority of new arrivals continued to come alone, independent of their marital status. The number of unmarried individuals was high in both genders. The Italian population, which lived geographically concentrated in certain neighborhoods or towns, was followed by other countrymen and women: merchants specializing in typical Italian products, tavern keepers, landlords renting out furnished rooms or running guest-houses – these, together with a certain number of industrial and commercial entrepreneurs who slowly managed to advance socially, formed transalpine colonies. Immigrants from the same regions of origin came together, established numerous organizations, and thus created elements of a separate social life.

The Italian-speaking Canton of Ticino was a special case, since it was home to 20% of all Italians living in Switzerland, who made up 27% of the inhabitants of the canton. They worked in particularly large numbers in the granite quarries of the Valle Leventina. Moreover, Ticino is the only canton in which Italians also settled as farmers, at times leasing or buying plots of land from emigrants leaving Ticino.

Many foreign students were educated at Swiss universities before World War I. Their number peaked in 1913–14 at 4,185, compared to 3,925 Swiss students. Between 1911 and 1915, they made up 20% of all students in Basel city and 80% of all students in Geneva. Since most Swiss universities admitted women quite early, from about 1870, many young women came to Switzerland to pursue a university education that was closed to them in their own countries. That was true, for example, of female students from Czarist Russia, some belonging to the Russian majority population but some also from ethnic or religious minorities (Armenians, Jews, Poles).[9] The influx of a large number of foreign students led to the emergence of a particularly international academic atmosphere, which has in part lived on into the 21st century. A special case is the inflow of patients – especially those suffering from tuberculosis – into the many Swiss health resorts, which sometimes led to very long sanitarium stays.

The response of the Swiss population to the immigration varied, depending on the period and the group in question. Immigration from France had a long tradition, and the social composition of the group was quite similar to that of the population in the western parts of Switzerland; the language of both groups was French, which meant that the immigrants were able to integrate fairly smoothly. Even in times of growing nationalist movements, the predominant Francophilia in western Switzerland facilitated the integration of French immigrants. German migrants, by contrast, were met there with a certain reserve, which ranged from suspicion to outright hostility. German-speaking Switzerland, on the other hand, sympathized with the German Empire. Within the bourgeoisie, the feeling of belonging to the realm of German culture eased the integration of Germans in this part of Switzerland. In the lower social strata, however, the inferiority that Swiss workers speaking their dialect felt toward the alleged "language fluency" of their German counterparts at times created tensions. Still, quite a number of immigrants integrated into their new environment so well that they were able to play an important role in the Swiss workers' movement. The organizations of the workers' movement formed for the immigrants, who joined them in large numbers, a network of protective institutions. This facilitated their integration into Swiss society.

Something similar applied later – though to a noticeably weaker degree – to the very rapidly growing population of Italian immigrations. Kept apart from the native population while working on large construction sites or concentrated in certain neighborhoods, the Italians for the most part lived isolated among themselves. If one takes the frequency of marriage between immigrants and natives as an indicator of integration, it was lowest among Italian immigrants. Conflicts between immigrants and natives were frequent both in the workplace and where they lived: Swiss workers saw their Italian colleagues as wage depressors and excessively obedient.

---

[8] Italian industrial workers in western and central Europe in the late 19th and early 20th centuries.

[9] Russian female students in Switzerland in the late 19th and early 20th centuries.

Resentment and contempt on the part of Swiss workers expressed itself also in other negative descriptions of the Italians: since they were eager to save as much money as possible, they were not participating in the activities of the workers, did not frequent taverns, and owned only ragged clothes – in other words, they lacked any feeling of self-esteem. Their low educational level – many were illiterate – was supposedly reflected in their overall behavior, but also in a lack of hygiene. Tensions mounted and escalated into xenophobic violence – for example, in Bern in 1893, when the local workers chased the Italians through the streets. The dilapidated housing of many Italians, and occasional homelessness, prompted talk of the "alien lifestyle habits and mores" of these immigrants. In July 1896, a trivial incident in Zurich triggered a three-day riot, during the course of which Italian cafés and restaurants were ransacked and a veritable manhunt was instigated. The Italians fled into the nearby forests. The police proved ineffective, and the intervention by the army was too late and inept. That abetted the actions of the agitators, among whom were also German immigrants.

World War I and its consequences for the conditions of migration

The mobilization of the European armies at the outbreak of World War I affected a large segment of the foreign population in Switzerland, which included many young adults. Some of the political refugees from Russia, who had been living in Germany or Austria-Hungary until then, moved on to Switzerland in August 1914.[10] Deserters on both sides crossed the borders into neutral Switzerland during the war; in 1918, their number reached 28,000. The attitude of the host country toward them fluctuated strongly, some were even sent back to their country of origin. Beginning in 1916, Switzerland, at its own request, took in injured and sick prisoners of war from both sides for treatment. They were housed in hotels – empty because of the war – in tourist-oriented towns and cities. Of the total of 68,000 prisoners of war, about 25,000 were still in the country when the armistice was signed in 1918.

An economic downturn and rising prices, the failure of wages to keep up with inflation, and the social inequalities that were becoming more apparent, had triggered a three-day general strike at the end of the war. The political elite, farmers, and many members of the urban population saw this event as a profound threat to the country's social and political order. Anger and hatred were directed not only against unionists and socialists, but also against foreigners, who were accused of having led Swiss workers astray. After that, broad segments of the Swiss public considered foreigners as a threat to the social order and the national values.

Another rupture had already occurred during the war. Until the outbreak of hostilities, Switzerland had no restrictions on immigration, except for the identity card requirement. But the national government now seized the authority to regulate the stay and supervision of foreign immigrants and linked the grant of an entry permit to the country's economic and political interests. In 1925, a new article in the constitution of the Confederation formally bestowed the authority to pass laws pertaining to the entry, exit, stay, and settlement of foreigners. During the course of the war, the number of foreigners living in Switzerland dropped by 150,000–200,000. It did not rise again significantly after the war, since economic growth remained weak during the interwar period and there was no strong need for labor; instead, emphasis was placed on rationalization and technological progress to boost labor productivity. In addition, Switzerland was especially hard hit by the economic crises of 1920–2 and the 1930s. To prevent a rise in unemployment, the cantons restricted or prevented foreign workers from settling in the country. Paradoxically, the decline in the number of foreigners saw a growth in the political and media debate about the supposed "foreignization" (Überfremdung) of Switzerland, which was driven by reactions to the general strike of 1918. But at the end of the 1920s, two-thirds of the foreigners in Switzerland had been living in the country for 20 years or more and were correspondingly well integrated.

World War II and the consequences for migration movements

The notion of a threat of foreignization shaped the restrictive orientation of Switzerland's refugee policy during the period of National Socialist rule in Germany and World War II. From 1945 down to this day, this policy has prompted passionate debates.

The Italian communities of origin in Switzerland slowly fell under the control of the Fascist regime in Italy. Beginning in 1933, the foreign organization of the German Nationalsozialistische Deutsche Arbeiterpartei (NSDAP) attained growing influence over the Germans living in Switzerland. Both developments harbored the potential for considerable diplomatic conflict. So as not to antagonize the regime in Rome, Swiss officials endeavored to keep out anti-Fascist refugees, who therefore headed elsewhere, especially to France. Until the outbreak of World War II, many Germans politically persecuted by the Nazi regime or considered "racially undesirable" also applied for entry into Switzerland.[11]

After 1933, Switzerland thought of itself as a transit country, but not an asylum country. In an effort to prevent

---

[10] Russian revolutionaries in western and central Europe in the 19th and early 20th centuries.

[11] Jewish refugees from Nazi Germany and from German-occupied Europe since 1933; political and intellectual refugees from Nazi Germany and from German-occupied Europe, 1933–1945.

refugees from staying, the government's refugee policy became increasingly restrictive: only those with a visa were permitted to enter, and immigrants were in principle forbidden from engaging in gainful employment. The outbreak of war in 1939, the closing of the border, and the occupation of France by German troops blocked all roads out of and into Switzerland. Although recognized political refugees and escaped prisoners of war who had secretly crossed the border were admitted, until the summer of 1944 that did not apply to Jewish refugees. The latter were expelled, in spite of the mortal danger posed by the Nazi policy of annihilation.

Estimates put the number of individuals expelled from Switzerland during World War II at around 20,000, mostly Jews. Admission was granted to about 51,000 civilian refugees. Added were about 2,000 individuals who were tolerated in the various cantons, and about 7,000–8,000 Jewish immigrants who were stuck in Switzerland when the war broke out: a total of around 61,000 refugees in a country with more than 4.2 million inhabitants. In addition, Switzerland admitted about 140,000 prisoners of war during the war. One French army corps, which had been interned in 1940, was sent back to France a year later on the basis of an agreement. Switzerland continued to regard itself as a transit country also after the war. High priority was therefore given to returning refugees to their home countries, or, since many no longer had a home, facilitating their departure for overseas destinations. Only after 1947 was there a growing willingness to grant permanent asylum; the last refugees of the interwar period and World War II who were still in Switzerland, just under 2,000, were now given permission to settle in the country.

Labor migration and asylum since World War II

With intact factories in the midst of a devastated Europe, Swiss industry experienced an unusually long phase of economic upswing after World War II. Leaving aside a few smaller economic downturns, it lasted until 1974 and brought profound changes in the country's social structure in its wake. Against the backdrop of a growing demand for labor, wages rose substantially. To slow this development and save costs, industrial employers began to recruit foreign workers already in the first phase of the upswing after the war (1945–8). The dire situation in neighboring countries and the relatively high and rising wage level in Switzerland prompted many Europeans to embark on labor migration to Switzerland. The Swiss authorities granted a large number of temporary residence permits that were valid for a season or a year. Initially, migrant workers came as part of private recruitment measures. Faced with about 2 million unemployed, the Italian government promoted the exodus to ease the social and political situation in the country. In 1948, it signed an agreement with Switzerland about social security and pension insurance

for the migrant workers. At that point, nearly all migrants from the southern neighbor came from northern and central Italy; in the years that followed the number of southern Italians increased.[12]

While the immigrants from Italy were chiefly men, between 1949 and 1959 Switzerland also saw the arrival of large groups of mostly young, single German and Austrian women. They found employment in the textile and food industry as well as in household-related services. As the rest of Europe began to recover economically from the beginning of 1950, Switzerland became less attractive. With the introduction of the freedom of movement for workers within the European Economic Union (EEC) in 1964, Germany became a serious competitor in the transalpine labor market; as a result, the number of Italians in Switzerland declined. Swiss recruitment measures were now aimed at more distant countries: initially Spain, with whom a recruitment agreement was signed in 1961 at the request of the Spanish government, then Portugal, Yugoslavia, Greece, and Turkey.[13]

Until around 1960, Swiss authorities pursued the strategy of using the employment of foreigners as an economic buffer. Several residence categories were developed to allow the government to reduce the numbers in a quick and uncomplicated way in case of an economic downturn: status A essentially limited the residence permit for seasonal workers to nine months per year, although it could be extended and de facto often led to substantially longer stays; status B was a permit for a full year; status C was an unlimited residence permit, which put foreigners on a par with Swiss citizens – except for political rights. The residence status was changed in the course of time and depending on the country of origin by varying, restrictive regulations. Immigrants with status A could not have their families join them, those with status B could do so only after they had been in the country for several years. In case of an economic downturn, the size of the foreign population could be quickly reduced by closing the doors to new immigrants and turning down applications for extensions. When these tools were put to use in 1974, the number of foreign workers dropped by around 300,000 within four years. The Swiss Confederation was thus able to export unemployment largely abroad. In addition, the geographic, social, and employment mobility of migrants was restricted by making residence permits valid for only a single canton.

---

[12] Italian labor migrants in northern, central, and western Europe since the end of World War II.

[13] Greek labor migrants in western, central and northern Europe after 1950: the examples of Germany and the Netherlands; Portuguese labor migrants in western and central Europe since the 1950s: the examples of France and Germany; Spanish labor migrants in western, central, and northern Europe since the end of World War II; Turkish labor migrants in western, central, and northern Europe since the mid-1950s; Yugoslav labor migrants in western, central, and northern Europe since the end of World War II.

Every change of location and job required a separate permit; self-employment was impossible. All these measures had the desired effect: at the beginning of 1960, the vast majority of foreigners in Switzerland had been living in the country for less than four years.

However, this policy also led to certain bottlenecks. Some countries of origin demanded an improvement in the status of their citizens. That was true of Italy, which signed a new agreement with Switzerland in 1964: it made the transition between the various residency categories easier, cut the waiting period for family reunification, and substantially loosened the mobility restrictions on immigrants. Three years later, these regulations were expanded to include immigrants from all other western and central European countries. At the same time, there was a growing recognition that the foreign workers were not temporary guests in Switzerland, but formed an indispensable and permanent element of the country's economy. In response, the rotation principle was gradually given up in favor of the integration principle. The goal now was to make a longer stay possible for the immigrants, to stabilize that stay, and to promote integration with the prospects of possible naturalization. It was now seen as disadvantageous that while the extensive importation of workers had allowed companies to grow, it had not raised labor productivity.

Beginning in 1963, the authorities enacted a variety of measures to limit new immigration. These measures did not have the desired effect, however, as the foreign population continued to grow, primarily through family reunification. This led to a change in the composition of the immigration with respect to geographic origins, employment structure – the percentage of those gainfully employed declined – and length of stay. Between 1969 and 1974 the number of C permits issued by the authorities doubled, a clear indication that permanence and integration were replacing uncertainty and rotation.

Immigrants took the least attractive, least desirable low-paying jobs. The rapidly shrinking group of Swiss who were part of the working class turned to the best-paying jobs and worked as foremen or shift leaders. Individual vocational-social advancement against the backdrop of a general rise in the level of prosperity (real wages had more than doubled between 1945 and 1975) led to a profound change in mentalities. Not everyone profited equally. Many who felt left out responded with bitterness and hatred toward the immigrants, who were seen as intruders and held responsible for the change in traditional roles and social relations within companies and businesses. The overburdening of the educational system and hospitals, the inadequacies of public facilities, and the housing shortage were also blamed on the "foreignization" by immigrants. Moreover, a multitude of everyday problems in the cohabitation of various cultures with different ways of life often led to tensions. Finally, a feeling of mistrust toward foreigners, whose settlement the Swiss government had looked at

askance for so long, also shaped the mentality of the native population.

Such feelings of xenophobia were picked up by some politicians and were reflected in the establishment of citizens' initiatives and voting lists against the alleged foreignization. The best-known of these actions, the Schwarzenbach Initiative, was aimed at limiting foreigners to 10% of the population. After an emotional campaign, it was rejected in 1970 by 54% of the voters. The large parties, businessmen, unions, and churches had opposed the initiative. Similar actions in subsequent years were less spectacular, especially since the number of foreigners was on the decline between 1975 and 1986. Still, the theme of foreignization keeps reappearing in the public discourse even at the beginning of the 21st century.

After 1985, the share of the foreign population in Switzerland started to rise again, in part because of extensive labor migrations, chiefly from Portugal and Yugoslavia. The peak phase occurred between 1989 and 1994. These were mostly semiskilled workers who replaced immigrants who had arrived years or decades earlier and had been able to move up in their working lives and advance socially in Switzerland. Although the economic downturn in the early 1990s triggered the departure of tens of thousands of foreign workers whose permits were not extended, it did not stop the immigration of nonworkers, which has continued to the beginning of the 21st century. Immigrants with an unlimited residence permit generally did not leave the country, even though they were often more strongly affected by unemployment than the native Swiss.

Added to this was the rising number of refugees. After 1945, unlike in the 19th century, the refugee issue was no longer of any consequence to Switzerland's foreign relations. The large majority of refugees came from socialist countries in eastern, east-central, and southeastern Europe. Their number fluctuated between 200 and 400 per year, with record peaks in 1956 during the uprising in Hungary (half of the 14,000 Hungarian refugees settled in Switzerland) and 1968 during the invasion of Czechoslovakia by Warsaw Pact forces (12,000–14,000).[14] Moreover, about 2,000 Tibetans came to Switzerland, initially under the protection of the United Nations High Commission for Refugees (UNHCR). The majority of European refugees had good vocational qualifications. Economic growth and an anticommunist climate facilitated their rapid integration. Until 1995, Switzerland always took in the refugee contingents organized by the UNHCR. Between 1978 and 1981, the largest group (8,500) came from Indochina.[15] Since then, most refugees have come from Latin America, Africa, and Asia, and

---

[14] Hungarian refugees in Europe since 1956; Czechoslovakian refugees in western, central, and northern Europe since 1968.

[15] Vietnamese refugees in western, central, and northern Europe since the 1970s: the examples of France, Great Britain, and Germany.

their integration has proved more difficult.[16] Moreover, the refugee status as defined in the United Nations (UN) convention of 1951 was starting to be dismantled: in the 1990s, the Swiss immigration authorities introduced several new residence categories, almost all of which offered refugees only a precarious status, enabling the authorities to turn away the majority of asylum seekers. The first Swiss Asylum Law of 1981 was repeatedly amended and tightened. The most recent, especially restrictive version was put to a referendum in September 2006: with a voter turnout of 48%, the law was approved by 68% of the votes.

While Italian immigrants had been the target of xenophobic projections and reactions in the 1970s, at the beginning of the 21st century these shifted to asylum seekers from the Balkans and Africa, whereas Italians, Spaniards, and Portuguese can be seen as largely accepted in Switzerland.

Although Switzerland is not part of the EU, it joined the EU member states in signing the bilateral treaties about individual freedom of movement, which took effect in 2002 and provided for a gradual implementation. Henceforth, applicants from non-EU countries will be selected on the basis of a point system that takes into account educational level, work experience, age, language skills, and vocational flexibility. This means, for example, that nationals from industrial countries (e.g., Japan and the USA), who are generally better qualified, can continue to enter Switzerland, while the majority of African, Asian, or Latin American migrants remain shut out. It also means, however, that companies that search around the globe for highly qualified personnel can siphon off pools of high-potential workers from the poorest countries.

Even though many of the difficulties of integration have evaporated for the "old" immigrant groups, they, too, continue to face problems. One of the most urgent is the granting of citizenship. All attempts to make it easier for foreigners born in Switzerland to become naturalized citizens have so far failed. Even the standardization of the naturalization taxes levied by the communities at a low level took a very long time. Since then, the number of naturalizations, which was very low until 1993, has risen strongly. In addition, a few of the cantons in the French-speaking part of Switzerland have granted foreigners living there for several years passive and active voting rights on the communal level.

Without question, Switzerland integrated a large part of its many immigrants in the decades of rapid economic and social change after World War II. However, especially economic crises and phases of accelerated social change have repeatedly revealed the distinct limits to the receptiveness of the Swiss population, and the penchant of the political system to respond to this chiefly with restrictive measures

intended to limit immigration and make the acquisition of permanent residence permits more difficult.

REFERENCES

Arlettaz, Gérald. *Emigration et colonies suisses en Amérique 1815–1918*. Bern, 1975.

Arlettaz, Gérald, and Silvia Arlettaz. *La Suisse et les étrangers. Immigration et formation nationale (1848–1933)*. Lausanne, 2004.

Boschetti, Pietro. *Les Suisses et les nazis. Le rapport Bergier pour tous*. Geneva, 2004.

Bühler, Roman, et al. *Schweizer im Zarenreich. Zur Geschichte der Auswanderung nach Rußland*. Zurich, 1985.

Ducommun, Marie-Jeanne, and Dominique Quadroni. *Le refuge protestant dans le Pays de Vaud. Aspects d'une migration*. Geneva and Lausanne, 1991.

Frei, Jürg. *Die schweizerische Flüchtlingspolitik nach den Revolutionen von 1848 und 1849*. Zurich, 1977.

Goehrke, Carsten, and Werner G. Zimmermann, eds. *"Zuflucht Schweiz." Der Umgang mit Asylproblemen im 19. und 20. Jahrhundert*. Zurich, 1994.

Halter, Ernst, ed. *Das Jahrhundert der Italiener in der Schweiz*. Zurich, 2003.

Historisches Lexikon der Schweiz, http://www.dhs.ch.

Hoffmann-Nowotny, Hans-Joachim. *Soziologie des Fremdarbeiterproblems. Eine theoretische und empirische Analyse am Beispiel der Schweiz*. Stuttgart, 1973.

Mahnig, Hans, ed. *Histoire de la politique de migration d'asile et d'intégration en Suisse depuis 1948*. Zurich, 1985.

Mesmer, Beatrix, ed. *Der Weg in die Ferne/Le chemin d'expatriation*. Bern, 1992.

Neumann, Daniela. *Studentinnen aus dem Russischen Reich in der Schweiz (1867–1914)*. Zurich, 1987.

Piguet, Etienne. *Einwanderungsland Schweiz: Fünf Jahrzehnte halbgeöffnete Grenzen*. Zurich, 2006.

Rauber, Urs. *Schweizer Industrie in Rußland. Ein Beitrag zur Geschichte des Kapitalexportes und des Handels der Schweiz mit dem Zarenreich (1760–1917)*. Zurich, 1985.

Ritzmann-Blickenstorfer, Heiner, ed. *Historische Statistik der Schweiz*. Zurich, 1996.

Ritzmann-Blickenstorfer, Heiner. *Alternative Neue Welt. Die Ursachen der schweizerischen Überseeauswanderung im 19. und frühen 20. Jahrhundert*. Zurich, 1997.

Schelbert, Leo, ed. *New Glarus 1845–1970. The Making of a Swiss-American Town*. Glarus, 1970.

Schelbert, Leo. *Einführung in die schweizerische Auswanderungsgeschichte der Neuzeit*. Zurich, 1976.

Schlaepfer, Rudolf. *Die Ausländerfrage in der Schweiz vor dem Ersten Weltkrieg*. Zurich, 1969.

Urner, Klaus. *Die Deutschen in der Schweiz. Von den Anfängen der Kolonienbildung bis zum Ausbruch des Ersten Weltkrieges*. Frauenfeld and Stuttgart, 1976.

Vuilleumier, Marc. *Flüchtlinge und Immigranten in der Schweiz. Ein historischer Überblick*. Zurich, 1992.

---

[16] Chilean refugees in Europe since 1973: the example of Switzerland; Sri-Lankan Tamils in western and central Europe since the 1980s: the example of Switzerland.

Vuilleumier, Marc. "Les ouvriers italiens en Suisse avant 1914: Les difficultés d'une intégration." In *L'intégration italienne en France,* edited by Antonio Bechelloni et al., 409–20. Brussels, 1995.

Wegmann, Susanna K. *Zur Migration der Schweizer nach Australien. Der Wandel schweizerischer Überseewanderung seit dem frühen 19. Jahrhundert.* Zurich, 1988.

Ziegler, Béatrice. *Schweizer statt Sklaven. Schweizerische Auswanderer in den Kaffeeplantagen von São Paulo 1852–1866.* Wiesbaden, 1985.

Zweiter Weltkrieg, vol. 17: *Die Schweiz und die Flüchtlinge zur Zeit des Nationalsozialismus,* edited by the Unabhängige Expertenkommission Schweiz. Zurich, 2001.

SOUTHERN EUROPE

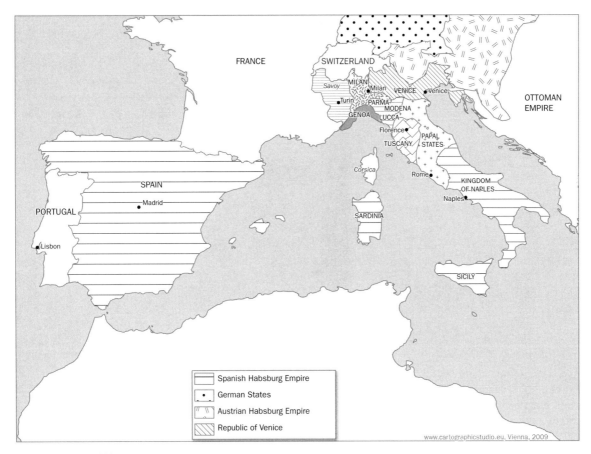

Southern Europe 1648

Southern Europe 2000

ITALY

Federica Bertagna and Marina Maccari-Clayton

Italy has been labeled the country of emigration par excellence. Not only did Italians migrate in larger numbers than any other European people but they did so for a longer period of time, and went to a greater variety of destinations. Economic factors were the principal stimulus to leave, but political and – to a lesser extent – religious factors also played an important role. The magnitude of Italian emigration between the last quarter of the 19th century and the First World War – when 14 million of the 50 million Europeans who went to the Americas were Italians – has tended to obscure the fact that significant population movements characterized the Italian peninsula from the late Middle Ages[1] and throughout the second half of the 20th century, when Italy completed its transition from that of a sending to receiving area.

Between the 16th century and the present time, three broad phases can be identified in Italian migration history. Up until the national unification in 1861, the Italian peninsula was both a sending and receiving area regarding international migration and experienced as well movements of population within the peninsula. The establishment of an independent state coincided with the beginning of Italian mass emigration, which was directed both to European and overseas destinations. Italy remained a country of out migration until 1973, when the Italian migration balance showed, for the first time, a positive sign. Since then, Italy has been a receiving country for immigrants from Africa, Asia, eastern Europe, and Latin America.

The territory and its borders

Throughout the early modern period, the Italian peninsula appeared as a patchwork of semi-independent states, mostly under the control of the major European powers (Austria, France, and Spain). Following the Treaty of Cateau-Cambrésis in 1559, the kingdoms of Sicily and Naples in the south and the Duchy of Milan in the north passed under the control of Spain, and France restored Piedmont and Savoy (in the northwest) to the Duke of Savoy. The Papal States extended throughout central Italy, while Genoa, Lucca, and Venice constituted independent republics. At the middle of the 18th century, Naples, Sicily, and the duchies of Parma and Piacenza passed to the Spanish Bourbons, and the duchies of

---

[1] Albanian settlers in Italy since the early modern period.

Milan, Mantua, Tuscany, and Modena to Austria. Remaining independent were the Papal States, the republics of Venice, Genoa, and Lucca, and the Kingdom of Sardinia, which had been created in 1720 by the union of Piedmont, Savoy, and Sardinia under the house of Savoy. Napoleon Bonaparte established the Kingdom of Italy in 1805, which included most of northern and central Italy. Savoy, Piedmont, Liguria, Tuscany, Parma, and the Papal States were annexed to the French Empire, while southern Italy became the Kingdom of Naples, with Joseph Bonaparte as king.

After Napoleon's defeat, Austrian influence became paramount in the Italian peninsula. The Congress of Vienna generally restored the pre-Napoleonic status quo and the old balance of power. The following changes in the political map of Italy took place: the former republic of Venice was united with Lombardy as the Lombardo-Venetian kingdom under Austrian control, and Liguria passed to the Kingdom of Sardinia, under the Savoy dynasty. Naples and Sicily were united as the Kingdom of the Two Sicilies. Italian unification was a result of the expansion of the Kingdom of Sardinia: Lombardy was annexed in 1859; Tuscany, Emilia, and southern Italy (including Sicily) in 1860. In 1861, the Kingdom of Italy was proclaimed, with Victor Emmanuel II of Savoy as its king. The Venetian territory was annexed in 1866, and Rome in 1870. Thus the Italian nation-state was established, which changed in some degree only in the north and northeast. The territorial gains were lost, however, after World War II, except for southern Tyrol and Triest.

Migration in the early modern period

The 17th century was a period of economic stagnation for Italy, as the center of economic life passed from the Mediterranean Sea to the Atlantic. Migration during this period was not the result of overpopulation nor of the pulling effect of the urban centers, as population growth was slow and the numbers residing in most great cities of Italy decreased in spite of the continuous arrival of vagrants and beggars from the countryside and – in the case of capitals such as Milan, Naples, Rome, and Venice – administrative and military personnel, merchants, and pilgrims from other European countries. The migrations of the early modern era continued traditions that had matured in the previous centuries. These included short-range movements from the Alpine and Apennine Mountains to the plains, medium-range movements among the various regional states, and further-reaching migrations that brought Italian vendors, artisans, bankers, and merchants to the major capitals of northern and central Europe.

In northern Italy, the villages and towns in the Alps of Piedmont, Lombardy, and Veneto represented an area of intense emigration toward the crop and rice cultivations in the Po valley, which attracted about 50,000 migrant workers each year. Other destinations were southern Italy (especially the city of Palermo in Sicily), and major cities of the Italian states and of the European countries (Milan, Turin, Lyon, Grenoble, Warsaw).[2] Emigration represented a regular occurrence in the economic life of the mountain people, an essential part of a well-established strategy to maintain the family income.

While agricultural activities in the plains attracted generic workers from the entire Alpine region, a significant number of emigrants were artisans whose movements were associated with specific migratory trades. Emigrants from the villages surrounding Lake Lugano and Lake Como – especially from the valleys of Intelvi and Valsolda – worked as masons and master masons in the towns of Piedmont and Lombardy, but also in Florence and Rome. Kiln men and master masons from the Belluno district and Carnia in the Udine province regularly left for the cities of the Habsburg Empire, Russia, and Poland. Carpenters from the Cadore region traveled to Venice and brought there the timber used in the Arsenale. Porters from the Bergamo area were present in all major Italian cities. Stonecutters, stone carvers, and plasterers from Valsesia and the Adorno valley exported their skills to the nearby Italian cities and into Switzerland, Prussia, and Alsace.

This migration was largely seasonal and temporary, but its regular occurrence led to the establishment of preferential links between specific areas of departure and arrival, and people moved along these familiar routes in ways similar to the well-known forms of chain migration of the 19th and 20th centuries.[3] Pioneering migrants promoted the diffusion of information and – in some instances – acted as recruiters of the new workforce. The migratory chains were reinforced at the point of arrival through the creation of village-based mutual aid associations and churches (emblematic is the case of the Intelvesi in Palermo), which also served the purpose of maintaining the connection between the immigrant and his place of origin. Since most emigrants were adult males, the absence of a large part of the male population for prolonged periods delayed the age of marriage and served as a natural form of birth control. During this period, overseas migration was still very limited, with the exception of the sailors and merchants from the coastal towns of Liguria who, by the late

18th century had already established a community in the Rio de la Plata region in South America.

In central Italy, population movements were linked to the specific landholding pattern of the area, where the sharecropping system (*mezzadria*) prevailed. Sharecroppers lived in complex family arrangements and owed half their crops to the landowner. When the family grew too large for the land assigned or the relations between estate managers and laborers became strained, the family – or part of it – moved. This migration was usually short in distance, was permanent, and involved entire families – men, women, and children. In a few instances, the state itself encouraged the relocation of families to colonize new land, as in the Tuscan Maremma, but such attempts met with little success. There were also noteworthy cases of seasonal migration from the Apennine Mountains to the plain, but unlike the Alpine model, the emigrants were largely unskilled workers. The harvesting of grain and other crops represented the main activity for about 100,000 emigrants reaching the central Italian coastal plain, and at the beginning of the 19th century the region represented the largest "pull area" of migrant workers in Europe.

Southern Italy was the land of latifundia and agricultural day laborers, and population movements were functional to that landholding system. Migration was most often the result of individual motivations and not of family and community strategy as in the north and center of Italy. The decision to migrate often meant a break with the place of origin and the move was in most cases a permanent one. There was also a seasonal migration in southern Italy, which was linked to the *transumanza* – the transfer of livestock from the mountain to the plain that took place every year – and it took shepherds from the Abruzzo region to Apulia, Lazio, and Tuscany. The shepherds involved in these transfers were also involved in a variety of other activities along the way.

The history of migration differed somewhat across the islands of Sicily, Sardinia, and Corsica. In the 17th century and up until the mass emigration to the USA at the beginning of the 20th century, Sicily was still a land of immigration, especially from the mountains of Calabria and Lombardy. Sicilian landlords promoted the settlement of Calabresi immigrants in the inland countryside, where they founded new rural villages, while the Lombardi moved more often to the cities. Sardinia remained largely untouched by the population movements of this period. Corsica, on the other hand, which was part of the Genoa Republic, was a major sending area. The emigrants from Corsica included soldiers, peasants who moved to the Tuscan Maremma, and wine sellers emigrating to Rome.

Since the Middle Ages, merchants from the Italian peninsula had been traveling in significant numbers to the major business centers in Europe and – in the case of Genoese and Venetian merchants – Asia, where they established "national" communities, which maintained strong links with the fatherland. In the early modern period, the declining importance of the Mediterranean economy and the Protestant reformation affected both the directions and magnitude of this

---

[2] Italian seasonal female workers in the Italian rice belt from the 16th to the mid-19th century.

[3] Italian and other "Alpine" (Grisons, Tecino, and Vorarlberg) architects and visual artists in Baroque Europe.

flow, which however remained relatively important. From the 16th century onward, Genoese merchants and bankers were active in Spain and the Kingdom of Naples, while merchants and bankers from the Tuscan cities of Lucca and Florence favored France.[4]

At the beginning of the early modern period, Italian cities entered an economic and demographic crisis. The capitals of the various regional states remained important receivers of immigrants from the countryside and from abroad,[5] but this immigration did not increase the number of inhabitants; it merely limited the demographic decline caused by high mortality rates. Only Naples and Turin experienced urban expansion resulting from immigration. The city of Livorno, in Tuscany, also represented a singular case: founded in 1577, it had an extremely liberal policy toward foreigners, which attracted Portuguese, Jewish, and Armenian merchants and transformed the city into a cosmopolitan center and one of the major ports in the Mediterranean.[6] Venice had been a receiver of Slavic and German immigrants since the Middle Ages, but also workers from closer inland associated with specific migratory trades, such as the already mentioned porters from Bergamo and carpenters from the Cadore area. Venice was also an important receiver of merchants from other European countries – especially the Netherlands – because of the city's prominence in the trades with the Levant. Rome remained an important center of immigration even after the Protestant Reformation. Apart from the pilgrims arriving every year, Rome received clergymen from all over Europe, who often traveled with their families and servants.[7]

International labor migrations from the Napoleonic period to Italian unification

Between the beginning of the 19th century and the unification in 1861, significant changes took place in the panorama of Italian migration. The Napoleonic campaigns brought most of Italy under the direct or indirect control of France. In the Cisalpine Republic – which included the former Duchy of Milan, Emilia Romagna, and part of the Adriatic side of central Italy – the new administration conducted the first population census in 1805, which revealed the magnitude of emigration from large areas of the territory. The introduction of mandatory drafts[8] induced young males to migrate in larger numbers, and the introduction of passports during this period can be linked to this phenomenon, as migration became increasingly a matter of police control.

The end of the Napoleonic wars and the settlements at the Congress of Vienna in 1814–15 inaugurated a period of peace in Europe, which, combined with the first phase of the Industrial Revolution in northern and central Europe, promoted the development of infrastructure and the initiation of large construction projects in many European countries. Italian emigrants from the northern regions, especially those associated with migratory trades related to the construction sector, provided an important part of the workforce employed in the completion of projects in France, Prussia, and the Habsburg Empire.[9] In the 19th century, emigration from the Italian peninsula increased both in magnitude and range. The surge involved primarily unskilled people of the lower classes, who could be found working as chimney sweeps, organ grinders, shoe polishers, and ice cream vendors in Paris, London, and Buenos Aires.[10]

The beginning of the 19th century also witnessed the development of a flow of political emigration associated with the struggle for Italian unification (*risorgimento*). Following the failure of revolts in the 1820s, 1830s, and 1848, Italian patriots escaped persecution by the Habsburgs in the Lombardo-Veneto, the Papal States in the center, and the Bourbons in the south and found refuge elsewhere in Europe (France and Switzerland, Belgium and Great Britain) and overseas (both in the USA and in South America), where many were involved in local political and military life. Giuseppe Mazzini, Giuseppe Garibaldi, Pietro Maroncelli, and Giovanni Battista Cuneo were some prominent figures of this flow.[11] The political exiles of the *risorgimento* opened the path to the political migration of Italian socialists and anarchists in the following decades. Yet, while the emigrants of the *risorgimento* constituted an "elite" migration, the socialist and anarchist émigrés came from all strata of the society, and once abroad they mixed with the traditional economic emigrants.

The age of transatlantic mass migration, 1876–1915

The 1870s marked the beginning of mass migration overseas from Italy. The intensification and spread of the Italian flow was a result of changes both at home and abroad. In Italy, the introduction of the military draft and the increased taxation that followed the country's unification in 1861 combined with the agricultural crisis of the early 1880s. While affecting all of Europe, the arrival of cheaper grains from the USA and Russia hit Italy especially hard, as it was still an overwhelmingly rural society and lagged well behind the other European nations on the path to industrialization. At the global level, the emancipation of African slaves in the Americas and the spread of the Industrial Revolution outside Europe created millions of jobs for Italian unskilled workers. The transportation revolution reduced the duration of the journey overseas

---

[4] Administrative elites in southern Italy and Sicily under Spanish rule in the early modern period.

[5] European students at Italian universities in the early modern period.

[6] Sephardim in Europe in the early modern period.

[7] European officeholders at the Roman Curia since the early modern period.

[8] European soldiers in the Napoleonic army.

[9] Italian workers in the construction industry in the Paris region since the 1870s.

[10] Alpine chimney sweeps in western, central, and southern Europe from the 16th to the early 20th century; Italian street musicians in 19th century Europe; Italian pewterers in Europe from the 16th to the 20th century; Italian ice cream makers in Europe since the late 19th century.

[11] Italian refugees of the *risorgimento* in central and western europe in the 19th century.

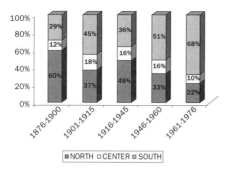

Figure 1. Italian gross emigration by main areas of origin. *Source*: Rosoli, ed., *Un Secolo di Emigrazione*.

from months to only a couple of weeks, and the cost of the passage also fell sharply in the 1860s.

Almost 14 million Italians left between 1876 – the first year for which official statistics are available – and the outbreak of the First World War. The emigration rate rose from less than 0.4% in 1876 to over 0.9% in the 1890s, and was well above 1% throughout the first 15 years of the 20th century. The peak years were 1906 and 1913, when the migration rate was 2.2% and 2.3%, respectively. From the 1890s onward Italy became the leader in both sheer numbers emigrating and in the rate of emigration. In the first phase (1876–1900), the majority of the emigrants came from northern Italy – where Genoa was the main port and South America was the main destination overseas. At the beginning of the 20th century emigration increased all over Italy, but the rise was more dramatic in the south and center, and the USA emerged as the principal recipient. Although Italian emigration in this period is commonly associated with the rise of overseas migration, European destinations remained very important.[12] (See Figure 1.)

In the last quarter of the 19th century, five countries each received about 15% of all Italian emigration: France, Brazil, Austria-Hungary, Argentina, and the USA. France and the lands of the Habsburg Empire had been a traditional destination for Italian immigrants for centuries. The former continued to be a major receiver of Italians until the mid-1960s, while the relative importance of the latter began to decline at the beginning of the 20th century, and the flow came to an end with the outbreak of World War I. Italian migration to Brazil was a circumscribed – albeit massive – event: almost 70% of the 1.2 million Italian immigrants between 1876 and 1914, arrived in the years 1888–1903. Following the abolition of slavery in 1888, the Brazilian government sponsored the arrival of Italian immigrants to work the coffee plantations by advancing the payment of their journey. The bad living conditions on the *fazendas* induced the Italian government to prohibit the system of prepaid tickets in 1902. Most Italians who went to Brazil were peasants from the Veneto region; they traveled in family groups and saw migration as a

permanent move. They settled mainly in the southern part of the country (Rio Grande do Sul and San Paolo) and signs of the Italian origin of large parts of the population in the area are still discernible today in the language and customs. The booming Italian migration to Argentina was associated with the economic growth and population policies of this Latin American country. The immigrants arriving at the end of the 19th century could count on an existing enclave of Italians – mainly from the Liguria region who had settled in the Rio de la Plata at the beginning of the century – who facilitated the integration of the new arrivals. The Italians who went to Argentina were generally young adult males with some professional skills and who were later joined by their families. In spite of the availability of agricultural land, most immigrants settled in Buenos Aires, where they were employed in the service and construction industries. By 1900, Italians constituted 12.5% of the Argentinean population, and they were present at every level of the society and in all socioprofessional groups. Migratory chains played a crucial role in the perpetuation of this flow until the first half of the 1950s.

Italian mass migration to South America represented an extremely profitable business for the shipping companies, which hired agents to recruit potential emigrants from the impoverished Italian mountains and countryside. At the beginning of the 20th century about 20,000 such agents were operating in Italy. Many of them were former emigrants, who returned to their places of origin to advertise the great opportunities available overseas, while neglecting to mention the harsh living and working conditions. In 1901 the Italian government established the Commissariato Generale dell'Emigrazione (CGE), to regulate migration and to protect the poorest strata of Italian society. The CGE was abolished by the fascist government in 1927.

The rise of emigration from the south of Italy coincided with the emergence of the USA as the major destination for Italians at the beginning of the 20th century. Almost 40% of all Italians who left between 1901 and 1914 went there. Central to the Italian flow to this country was the "*padroni*-system," which saw previously established Italians acting as intermediaries between American employers and the newly arrived immigrants. The immigrants were mainly peasants from Sicily and Campania, who settled in the big cities of the East Coast and became factory workers. The integration of Italian immigrants in the new country was difficult and they remained for a long time at the bottom of society. The American perception of the Italians also contributed to the difficult ascent of the immigrants. In the cities where they settled, Italians created ethnic neighborhoods where they imported the customs and traditions of their places of origin. (See Figure 2.)

An often neglected aspect of Italian emigration overseas during the age of mass migration was the extremely high rates of return that characterized those flows. About 50% of all emigrants who went to North and South America between 1905 (the first year for which statistics on return migration are available) and 1915 eventually returned to Italy. This fact

---

[12] Italian industrial workers in western and central Europe in the late 19th and early 20th centuries.

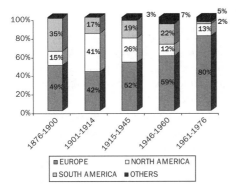

Figure 2. Italian gross emigration by main areas of destination. *Source*: ISTAT, *Sommario di Statistiche Storiche dell'Italia, 1861–1975* (Rome, 1976).

was well known to the contemporaries, who nicknamed the Italians *golondrinas* in Argentina and "birds of passage" in the USA. Most Italians who chose to emigrate saw their decision as a temporary one and many became seasonal workers across the ocean, completing the journey from Italy to the Americas many times during their lifetime. The magnitude and continuity of return migration preserved the links between the place of origin and the destinations, and was crucial to the creation of the Italian diasporas.

In Europe, France was the main destination of Italian immigrants throughout this period. Their numbers rose from over 300,000 at the beginning of the 20th century (38% of the foreign population) to over 400,000 on the eve of the First World War. The vast majority came from the northern and central regions (Piedmont, Tuscany, and Lombardy). In the last part of the 19th century, Italian emigrants went mainly to the southeast of France and to the cities of Marseille and Lyon. Their presence in Marseille increased from 11% of the population in 1866 to 25% in 1911. From the beginning of the 20th century onward, their numbers increased also in Paris and in Alsace and Lorraine, which at that time was still part of Germany. Italians in France were employed in a variety of sectors: textile, metal and construction, mining in the southeast, shipbuilding in the Provence, as well as agriculture in the southeast, and since the 1920s also in the southwest.[13] In 1900, Italians represented 10% of the unskilled workers in the building sector and 50% of all foreigners.[14] Most migration to France was seasonal and temporary, although a significant number of immigrants eventually settled there. The integration of the Italians into French society was difficult: episodes of intolerance and discrimination often resulted in the killing of the immigrants and the destruction of their properties, as happened in Aigues-Mortes in 1893 and Lyon in 1894.

The beginning of the 20th century also witnessed the emergence of Switzerland and Germany as important destinations for the Italian flow. The construction of the Brenner and St. Gothard railroads after 1860 opened the way to Germany for

Italian immigrants, whose numbers increased from almost 10,000 in 1876 to 50,000 in 1900. Besides building railroads, Italians in Germany worked in manufacturing (the third-largest immigrant group in 1906), mining (especially in the Ruhr, Lorraine, and Saar Basin), and construction (half of all foreign workers in 1906). Brassworkers, chair weavers, and other traveling vendors from northern Italy were also present in significant numbers in southern Germany.

The building of the St. Gothard tunnel played an important role also in Italian mass migration to Switzerland. There were about 42,000 Italians in Switzerland in 1880 and their numbers rose to almost 95,000 by the end of the century. In 1910, Italians represented 6% of the Swiss population, a figure that did not include the significant number of seasonal workers. The immigrants worked in the brick, silk, cotton, chocolate, footwear, and tobacco industries. As in France and Germany, a large number was employed in the construction sector, where they represented one-third of all workers in 1914.[15]

Changing migration patterns during the interwar period

The end of the age of mass migration is usually associated with the outbreak of the First World War. In the Italian case, however, a series of events at home and abroad in the decade after 1918 – rather than the conflict itself – marked the end of the great migration overseas. Between 1917 and 1924, the USA – still the major receiver of Italian immigration at the time – initiated a restrictive policy that reduced the admission of Italian immigrants to less than 5,000 a year. Almost concurrently, the fascist regime started to impose restrictions on emigration, in the belief that the power of a country resided in the size of its army and resident population.

There were two distinct kinds of emigration from Italy during the interwar years: the political exiles who opposed fascism and the movements associated with Italy's attempts at becoming a colonial power in eastern Africa. Following Benito Mussolini's rise to power, many opponents of the regime were forced to leave the country, and the expulsions were especially large between 1925 and 1930. The antifascist exiles were political opponents, intellectuals, trade union representatives, but also common citizens who resisted the fascist transformation of Italian society. As for the political migrations of the 19th century, most antifascists found refuge in Europe (Great Britain, Switzerland, and France), although some personalities such as Gaetano Salvemini, Carlo Sforza, and Alberto Tarchiani went to the USA.

The fascist government initiated a policy of land reclamation in Sardinia and in the Maremma and Agro-Pontino areas, which resulted in the foundation of about 100 new towns (among them Carbonia, Aprilia, and Sabaudia) and a fairly intense flow of internal migration, involving mostly peasants from the northeastern regions. Some of these resettlement

---

[13] Italian agricultural workers in southwestern France since the 1920s.

[14] Italian workers in the construction industry in the Paris region since the 1870s.

[15] Italian industrial workers in western and central Europe in the late 19th and early 20th centuries.

projects even recalled Italian emigrants from abroad, as in the case of some Venetians who returned from Bosnia, Romania, and Brazil. The restrictions imposed on Italian migration toward traditional overseas destinations were counterbalanced by an intensification of the flow directed to Africa. In Libya, which had been an Italian colony since 1912, the number of Italians increased from about 26,000 in the 1920s to 120,000 in 1940. In Ethiopia, which became an Italian colony in 1935, the fascist government declared a population of 300,000 Italians in 1940, but there is no other source available to verify this figure. The immigrants who went to Africa included a large number of military and bureaucratic personnel, but also engineers, construction workers, and drivers. Those who went to Libya came mainly from southern Italy, while Ethiopia received immigrants from all over Italy.

A special case in the panorama of Italian migration during this period was that of the Italians in Germany. In 1938, fascist Italy and Nazi Germany signed a migration agreement which brought about a half million Italians to work in German factories, mines, construction, and – to a lesser extent – agriculture. The flow to Germany was temporary and characterized by a large turnover. Mussolini's arrest and the signature of the armistice with the Allies in 1943 brought a dramatic deterioration to the living and working conditions of the more than 100,000 Italian workers in Germany, as they were now considered also citizens of an enemy state. During the German occupation of northern Italy, more Italian workers and soldiers were deported to Germany, where they were interned in the same labor camps as the Polish and other eastern Europeans.[16]

The post–World War II period

At the end of the Second World War, Italy received hundreds of thousands of refugees and displaced persons from eastern Europe, who were accommodated in camps that the International Refugee Organizations established throughout the peninsula.[17] Following the Peace Treaty, Italy was also required to surrender Istria and Dalmatia to Yugoslavia. As a result, about 300,000 Italian nationals residing in that area were forced to leave.[18] Only a small fraction of these refugees settled in Italy, while the majority went to Australia and the USA.

What characterized post–World War II Italian population movements until the mid-1960s in a significant way was a resumption of the migration flows directed abroad, both to other parts of Europe and overseas. Over 7 million Italians left between 1946 and the mid-1970s, but a high rate of return characterized the majority of these flows, and about half of the people who left eventually returned to Italy. Among the

emigrants who left in the years immediately following the end of the conflict were fascists who feared retaliation and imprisonment. In 1946, however, the newly created Italian republic granted a general amnesty and as a result the number of former functionaries of the Fascist Party among the emigrants declined.

At the end of the conflict the Italian government resorted to migration as part of its economic policy directed at lowering the unemployment rate – there were 2 million unemployed in Italy – and controlling social conflict. The international situation, however, had changed considerably and while pre–World War I migration had been largely free, the post–World War II flows were strictly regulated through bilateral agreements. In the first decade after the war, Italy signed migration agreements with France and Belgium in 1946, Argentina in 1947 and 1948, Czechoslovakia in 1947, Canada and Australia in 1951, and Germany in 1955. State intervention played a crucial role in the development of these migration flows: the potential emigrants were recruited through the Italian provincial labor offices and then sent to the departure points in Milan (for destinations elsewhere in Europe), Genoa, and Naples (those directed overseas), where they underwent a medical examination and – in some instances – an investigation of their political inclinations since the receiving countries did not want to import "troublemakers," especially if they were associated with the Italian Communist Party.

The country of immigration requested immigrants to be employed in specific sectors (miners in Belgium and the Netherlands, construction workers in Great Britain and Liechtenstein, farmers and domestic servants in Canada), and they usually signed a contract before leaving Italy. These flows were essentially demand-driven according to the needs of the receiving countries, and Italy tried incessantly to find new outlets for its surplus population. The USA maintained its quota law until the mid-1960s and only Argentina received a consistently high number of Italians after the Second World War. The resumption of population policies in Argentina and the industrialization programs initiated by the Peronist government coincided with the renaissance of the migration chains that had lain dormant throughout the interwar years. After an initial phase in the late 1940s and early 1950s, which saw an influx of new immigrants from Italy, most subsequent arrivals represented family reunions.

New destinations such as Australia, Canada, and Venezuela emerged, but the magnitude of Italian emigration remained well below what it had been before World War I and did not meet the expectations of the Italian government. Italian migration to Venezuela resulted after the discovery of vast oil fields in the South American country. The Venezuelan government initiated a major policy of industrialization and public works, which attracted Italian skilled workers, especially engineers, technicians, and entrepreneurs. In Canada there was already a small Italian community of about 140,000 people in 1946, and their numbers rose to over 270,000 by 1969. There was a considerable number of

---

[16] Forced laborers in Germany and German-occupied Europe during World War II.

[17] Displaced persons (DPs) in Europe since the end of World War II.

[18] Italian refugees in Italy from Adriatic territories that fell to Yugoslavia after 1945.

women, who were in demand as domestic servants, while the men, initially employed in agriculture, settled for the most part in Toronto and Montreal. Italian emigration to Australia had been limited in scope until World War II because of the distance and the cost of the journey, but more than 300,000 Italians arrived after 1945.

Overseas destinations entered a declining phase in the mid-1950s and Italian migration became more and more a European phenomenon. Switzerland was the country that received the largest number of Italians after World War II. Italians represented 50% of the foreign population in 1950 (3% of the total population), and 75% in 1975 (almost 9% of the total population). The immigrants worked mainly in the construction sector, in the metal and mechanical industries, and in the hotel sector. They were predominantly adult males, as Switzerland did not encourage the permanent settlement of these immigrants. Italian immigrants to Belgium were employed almost exclusively in the coal mines. The disaster of Marcinelle in 1956, in which 136 miners lost their lives, marked the end of this flow. France remained an important destination until the arrival of workers fleeing Algeria from 1962 saturated the French job market. The decline in the relative importance of France as a destination for Italian migration coincided with the emergence of Germany, which experienced an economic boom around the mid-1950s. Between 1957 and 1975, the Italians comprised 30% of the foreigners and in 1963, some 300,000 (38% of the immigrants) came from Italy.[19] Emigration also represented a major component of the attitude of the Italian government toward the unification of Europe, as Alcide De Gasperi – Italian prime minister and strong advocate of the European Economic Community (EEC) – made the free circulation of workers within the European Community a pillar of his European policy.

Not only did Italian emigration become more oriented toward Europe in the second half of the 20th century but the regional origins of the emigrants themselves changed as well, as the vast majority came from southern Italy. In the late 1950s and early 1960s, Italy entered an economic boom, which affected primarily the regions in the north and had its core in the industrial triangle formed by the cities of Genoa, Milan, and Turin. Northern emigration virtually stopped at this point, with the exception of the region of Veneto and the commuters crossing the border on a daily or weekly basis to work in Switzerland. Toward the end of the 1960s, the Veneto region also entered a phase of economic growth and Italian emigration remained a virtually exclusive southern phenomenon. The economic boom also prompted the beginning of a conspicuous movement of internal migration, with massive transfers from the rural regions in the south to the industrial centers in the north and Rome. This movement experienced its most intense phase in the 20 years between 1955 and 1975. It has been calculated that, by 1973, almost 4 million people transferred from southern Italy to the north and center and most of these movements became permanent.[20]

Italy as an immigrant country in the late 20th and early 21st centuries

The beginning of the 1970s marked the end of an era in the history of Italian emigration. In 1973 the Italian migration balance showed an immigration surplus for the first time since the beginning of official statistics. Italy was no longer a country of emigration and entered a phase of transition from sending to receiving country. Initially, this transformation was the result of an increase in return migration: more emigrants returned to Italy every year than left. The first wave of foreign immigrants consisted of women coming from the Philippines, Central America (especially El Salvador), Eritrea (a former colony), and Cape Verde, who found jobs as domestic workers in the big cities of northern and central Italy (Milan, Turin, Bologna, Rome); and by Tunisian men employed in the tomato harvest in southern Italy. The 1976 earthquake in Friuli attracted a flow of Yugoslavian immigrants in the reconstruction sector. By the end of the 1980s, Moroccans and Senegalese formed the two major immigrant groups in Italy. These arrivals were quantitatively insignificant, and the Italian government did not have any specific immigration policy. Most immigrants entered the country on a tourist visa and after finding an occupation remained without regularizing their position.

The collapse of the communist regimes in central and eastern Europe triggered the arrival of a substantial number of immigrants from those countries. Albanian immigrants constituted an especially significant flow, most of whom entered Italy illegally by crossing the Adriatic Sea. The image of boats arriving on the coasts of Apulia overflowing with distressed Albanians became emblematic of this phenomenon. In the following years, similar images became common in the press and on television with regard to the arrival on the Sicilian coasts of immigrants from northern and central Africa. While economic motivations remained the main reason for immigrating to Italy, many immigrants were escaping ethnic genocide and political persecution in their home countries.

The new waves of immigrants persuaded the Italian legislators of the necessity to regulate these movements. The Martelli bill in 1990 represented the first significant attempt at this – by increasing controls at the borders, requiring a visa for citizens of the principal sending countries, and enforcing expulsion for illegal immigrants. This bill was also the result of pressures from the other European countries that saw Italy as a bridgehead for immigrants trying to reach other European destinations, especially France, Germany, and Switzerland.

The Martelli bill, however, resulted in an increase in illegal immigration to Italy. Two negative features characterized all

---

[19] Italian labor migrants in northern, central, and western Europe since the end of World War II.

[20] Southern Italian workers in northern Italy, 1945–1975.

Table 1. Main foreign resident population in Italy

	October 2001 (%)	January 2005 (%)	Increase in absolute numbers
Albania	13.0	13.2	+146,000
Morocco	13.5	12.3	+115,000
Romania	5.6	10.4	+174,000
China	3.5	4.7	+65,000
Ukraine	0.6	3.9	+85,000
The Philippines	4.0	3.4	+29,000
Tunisia	3.6	3.3	+31,000
Senegal	2.3	2.2	+23,000
Other European countries	24.7	19.3	+134,000
Other countries	29.1	27.4	+270,000
Total foreign residents (abs.)	1,335,000	2,402,000	

Source: ISTAT, Censimento della popolazione straniera residente, Rome (2005).

subsequent legislation: the failure to regulate the incoming flows, which resulted in a strong presence of illegal immigrants; and the failure to assist the settlement and integration of the immigrant workforce. In the year 2000 there were over 1.3 million immigrants with regular permits in Italy. In 2005 the Bossi-Fini bill brought to light a population of almost 3 million immigrants in Italy, namely 5% of the Italian population and 10% of all foreigners in Europe. Most immigrants lived in the northern (64%) and central regions (24%), especially in the cities of Milan and Rome, which together had about 640,000 immigrants. Albanians, Moroccans, and Romanians represented the quantitatively largest national groups. Albanian immigrants were present throughout the Italian territory, both in the north and south. Almost half of the Moroccans, on the other hand, lived in two regions, Lombardy and Emilia, and the Romanians were concentrated into two other regions – Lazio and Piedmont.

Italian citizenship legislation is one of the most restrictive in Europe for foreigners – requiring 10 years of uninterrupted legal residence – but it is extremely liberal toward the descendants of Italian citizens, who can obtain it even after three or four generations have passed. That is one of the reasons for the recent "return" of the descendants of Italian emigrants from Argentina and Brazil – albeit limited in scope – following the economic crises in those two countries (see Table 1).

A large stratum of Italian society perceives immigration as a threat, giving proof of a short memory and applying to today's immigrants the stereotypes once attached to the Italians in other countries (criminal, thief, trickster, dirty, etc.). The emergence of political parties such as the xenophobic Northern League and numerous episodes of discrimination and open racism reported in the media have been symptomatic of this situation. On the eve of the second millennium, Italy provides the paradox of a country that needs the immigrants and yet is not entirely ready to accept them. The Italian economy needs immigrants in a variety of jobs that the Italian natives refuse because they are either dangerous or unappealing. In spite of significant unemployment (especially in the south), the demand for immigrants in some sectors of the economy is indeed strong. Eastern Europeans work in the construction sector, Chinese and Africans in the tanneries and textile factories, immigrant women in cleaning services and assistance to the elderly.[21] The immigrants are also reshaping the appearance of Italian society, and the fear of a loss of *italianitá* is widespread. Italian birthrates have been declining since the last quarter of the 20th century and the country's population is aging fast. In 2004, the children of immigrants represented almost 9% of all births in Italy, and over 4% of the student population.

At the beginning of 2005, foreign residents represented 4.1% of the total Italian population. In May 2006, a new government formed by a center-left coalition doubled the number of work permits for that year, bringing the number to 170,000. The total number of applications, however, was 540,000, of which 486,000 were eventually approved. While in the past the dramatic increase in the number of foreign residents was largely the result of governmental initiatives that encouraged irregular immigrants to legalize their position, in 2006 and 2007 the number of immigrants in Italy steadily increased as a result of larger annual quotas and family reunions. The majority of the immigrants going to Italy originated from other European countries: of every 10 foreign residents, 5 are Europeans, 4 are Asians or Africans, and 1 comes from the Americas.

At the end of 2007, immigrants represented 6.2% of the Italian population. After Spain, Italy is today the country with the largest annual increase in immigration as a percentage of the total population, a proportion even higher than that of the USA.

REFERENCES

Arru, Angiolina, and Franco Ramella, eds. *L'Italia delle migrazioni interne. Donne, uomini, mobilità in età moderna e contemporanea*. Rome, 2003.

Audenino, Patrizia. *Un mestiere per partire. Tradizione migratoria, lavoro e comunità in una vallata alpina*. Milan, 1990.

Bertagna, Federica. *La patria di riserva. L'emigrazione fascista in Argentina*. Rome, 2006.

Bevilacqua, Piero, Andreina De Clementi, and Emilio Franzina, eds. *Storia dell'emigrazione italiana, I: Partenze*. Rome, 2001.

Bevilacqua, Piero, Andreina De Clementi, and Emilio Franzina, eds. *Storia dell'emigrazione italiana, II: Arrivi*. Rome, 2002.

Bezza, Bruno, ed. *Gli italiani fuori d'Italia. Gli emigranti italiani nei movimenti operai dei paesi d'adozione 1880–1940*. Milan, 1983.

[21] Chinese migrants in the Italian fashion industry since the early 20th century; Peruvian female domestics in Italy since the end of the 20th century.

Bolaffi, Guido. *I confini del patto. Il governo dell'immigrazione in Italia*. Turin, 2001.

Boncompagni, Adriano. *The World Is Just Like a Village: Globalization and Transnationalism of Italian Migrants from Tuscany in Western Australia*. Fucecchio, 2001.

Choate, Mark I. *Emigrant Nation: The Making of Italy Abroad*. Cambridge, 2008.

Cinel, Dino. *The National Integration of Italian Return Migration, 1870–1929*. Cambridge, 1991.

Ciuffoletti, Zeffiro, and Maurizio Degl' Innocenti. *L'emigrazione nella storia d'Italia 1868–1975*. Florence, 1978.

Colombo, Asher, and Giuseppe Sciortino. *Gli immigrati in Italia. Assimilati o esclusi: Gli immigrati, gli italiani, le politiche*. Bologna, 2004.

Colucci, Michele. *Lavoro in movimento. L'emigrazione italiana in Europa, 1945–1957*. Rome, 2008.

Corti, Paola. *Paesi d'emigranti. Mestieri, itinerari, identità collettive*. Milan, 1990.

Devoto, Fernando. *Historia de los italianos en la Argentina*. Buenos Aires, 2006.

Franzina, Emilio. *Gli italiani al Nuovo Mondo. L'emigrazione italiana in America 1492–1942*. Milan, 1995.

Franzina, Emilio, and Matteo Sanfilippo. *Il fascismo e gli emigrati. La parabola dei Fasci italiani all'estero (1920–1943)*. Rome and Bari, 2003.

Gabaccia, Donna. *Italy's Many Diasporas*. Seattle, 2000.

Gabaccia, Donna, and Fraser Ottanelli, eds. *Italian Workers of the World: Labour Migration and the Formation of Multiethnic States*. Urbana, 2000.

Gabrielli, Patrizia. *Col freddo nel cuore. Uomini e donne nell'emigrazione antifascista*. Rome, 2005.

Iacovetta, Franca. *Such Hardworking People: Italian Immigrants in Postwar Toronto*. Montreal and Kingston, 1992.

Labanca, Nicola. *Posti al sole. Diari e memorie di vita e di lavoro delle colonie d'Africa*. Rovereto, 2001.

Lucassen, Jan. *Migrant Labour in Europe, 1800–1900: The Drift to the North Sea*. London, 1987.

Lucassen, Leo. *The Immigrant Threat: The Integration of Old and New Migrants in Western Europe since 1850*. Urbana, 2005.

Luzzi, Serena. *Stranieri in città. Presenza tedesca e società urbana a Trento (secoli XV–XVIII)*. Bologna, 2003.

Macioti, Maria Immacolata, and Enrico Pugliese. *L'esperienza migratoria. Immigrati e rifugiati in Italia*. Rome and Bari, 2003.

Mantelli, Brunello. *"Camerati del Lavoro." I lavoratori italiani emigrati nel Terzo Reich nel periodo dell'Asse, 1938–1943*. Florence, 1992.

Merzario, Raoul. *Il capitalismo nelle montagne. Strategie familiari nel primo periodo di industrializzazione nel comasco*. Bologna, 1989.

Milza, Pierre. *Les italiens en France*. Rome, 1986.

Pizzorusso, Giovanni, and Matteo Sanfilippo. "Rassegna storiografica sui fenomeni migratori a lungo raggio in Italia dal Basso Medioevo al secondo dopoguerra." *Bollettino di demografia storica*, 13 (1991). Special issue.

Porcella, Marco. *Con arte e con inganno. L'emigrazione nell'Appennino ligure-emiliano*. Genoa, 1998.

Pugliese, Enrico. *L'Italia tra migrazioni internazionali e migrazioni interne*. Bologna, 2002.

Pupo, Raoul. *Il lungo esodo. Istria: Le persecuzioni, le foibe, l'esilio*. Milan, 2005.

Rinauro, Sandro. "La disoccupazione di massa e il contrastato rimpatrio dei prigionieri di guerra." *Storia in Lombardia* 17, 2–3 (1998): 548–95.

Romero, Federico. *Emigrazione e integrazione europea 1945–1973*. Rome, 1991.

Rosoli, Gianfausto, ed. *Un secolo di emigrazione italiana 1876–1976*. Rome, 1978.

Sanfilippo, Matteo. *Problemi di storiografia dell'emigrazione italiana*. Viterbo, 2003.

Saskia, Sassen. *Guests and Aliens*. New York, 1999.

Sori, Ercole. *L'emigrazione italiana dall'Unità alla seconda guerra mondiale*. Bologna, 1979.

Sponza, Lucio. *Italian Immigrants in Nineteenth-Century Britain: Realities and Images*. Leicester, 1988.

Trento, Angelo. *La dov'è la raccolta del caffè. L'emigrazione italiana in Brasile, 1875–1940*. Padua, 1984.

SPAIN AND PORTUGAL

Horst Pietschmann

Because of its exposed geographical location between two large seas and as a bridge between Africa and Europe, the Iberian Peninsula has been a region of intense and wide-ranging migration movements since antiquity. Beginning in the Middle Ages, there were already numerous minorities on the Iberian Peninsula, who were given the opportunity – with sometimes more, sometime less, legal restriction – to preserve their linguistic, cultural, or religious identity. Thus the region was home to Jews, to Jews who had converted to Christianity either voluntarily or under coercion, to Moors, Moriscos (forcibly converted Muslims), but also to Christians under Muslim rule with no links to Rome. Added to these were colonies of foreign merchants (*nationes*), from the 15th century on increasingly individual migrant experts in various occupations (e.g., printers and artists), specialized artisans, merchants, or visitors to fairs in Medina del Campo. Moreover, a significant share of the population in Navarre and northern Catalonia came from France, and from the late Middle Ages the number of slaves of the most diverse backgrounds was on the rise.

The region and its boundaries

After 711, nearly the entire Iberian Peninsula was conquered by Muslim Arabs. The medieval Reconquest of the peninsula gave rise to the expansionary energy of the Christian Iberian kingdoms. Aragon began to expand into the western Mediterranean from the end of the 13th century, taking possession of Sicily and Naples and temporarily even of Greece. At the beginning of the 15th century, Portugal embarked on its expansion to North Africa and in the Atlantic, and around 1480 Castile, too, started to push outward. In a countermove, the Italian trading republics began their commercial penetration of the Iberian Peninsula and projected Mediterranean traditions into the Atlantic.

Portugal's Atlantic expansion led – initially with Italian and German participation – to the settlement of the Atlantic islands and the acquisition of bases on the coast of sub-Saharan Africa. This later gave rise to the discovery of the sea route to Asia and the conquest of the Americas. The beginning of the imperial age on the Iberian Peninsula in the late Middle Ages and at the beginning of the early modern period had far-reaching consequences for the political history of the region. It was only from the beginning of the 19th century that Spain and Portugal began to think of themselves as territorial states with European borders and clearly defined populations.

The problems of a history of Spanish and Portuguese migration

During the Middle Ages, the Christian realms of the Iberian Peninsula underwent a distinct internal development in many social areas, notwithstanding a multitude of political interactions among each other and with the rest of Europe (in 1426, the Portuguese infante Peter and 800 knights fought on the side of Emperor Sigismund against the Turks). They were separated from one another by mutual toll barriers. In each one of the Christian kingdoms – Navarre, Aragon, Castile, and Portugal – the population structure and distribution was as diverse as it was in Moorish Granada. With bases in North Africa, Madeira, the Azores, and along the coast of west Africa, Portugal at the end of the Middle Ages had possessions outside of the Iberian Peninsula, just as Castile did with the Canary Islands and Aragon with the kingdoms of Mallorca, Sicily, and Naples. Internal Iberian migration followed predominantly the north-south movement of the Reconquest; it rarely flowed in the opposite direction, and when it did it was limited to groups of elites in government service, and to occupational specialists such as clerics, soldiers, and merchants. The migration history of the two countries overlapped in part, especially during the time of the personal union of Portugal and Spain (1580–1640).

Attempts at replacing the traditional state of associated persons and at implementing the concept of a territorial state with a nation-state identity were not evident in Spain and Portugal until the 18th century. That signified the triumph of the principle of *ius soli* and thus the development of a modern concept of state citizenship. However, in the face of the outdated imperial, continent-spanning statehood, these developments also promoted disintegrative tendencies within the Spanish and Portuguese empires and the establishment of new independent states with pretensions as nation-states.

These historical processes in the late 18th and 19th centuries gave rise to problems defining the territory and the status of those born or living in it. In the wake of the independence movements in the 19th century, some Hispano-American states expelled all Spaniards who had been born in Europe but had settled in their territory, while, conversely, many royalist Spanish-Americans (Creoles) went to Spain voluntarily. At the same time, throughout the 19th century and down to the end of the 20th, many of the states that had once been part of the Spanish Empire made it very easy to acquire the citizenship of the other state. These regulations were in force for Hispano-Americans as late as the 1970s in Franco's Spain. Not only did they influence the migratory conditions of the most recent period and their statistical picture but they also resulted in the fact that those who were legally Spaniards could in fact be Hispano- or even Anglo-Americans.

Similar problems arose for Portugal, since the Portuguese Empire, with the exception of Brazil, formed a uniform legal territory down to the 1970s. Against this backdrop, migration in Spain and Portugal since the 19th century took on a character that was in many ways very specific to these two countries. Although it concerned primarily the two former colonial empires, it certainly could have repercussions also for the migratory situation within Europe and trigger a host of classification problems. For the imperial age and during the period in which the state was seen as a union of associates (*Personenverbandsstaat*), the territory understood as Spain and Portugal defined itself geographically through the royal courts and in their respective possessions by the presence of viceroyal courts.

Spain's colonial history in the Americas ended with the loss of the islands of Cuba, Puerto Rico, and the Philippines in 1898. To this day, the country has African possessions in the exclaves of Ceuta and Melilla, as well as overseas outposts in the Balearic Islands in the Mediterranean and the Canary Islands in the Atlantic. These outposts are uncontested parts of Spanish state territory and thus also of the European Union. Likewise, Portugal, irrespective of the end of its colonial past in the 1970s, has maritime outposts in the Atlantic islands that are politically part of Portugal and thus of the European Union, but which, like the Azores and the Spanish Canary Islands, do not belong to Europe geographically. Already at the beginning of their imperial history in the 16th century, both countries had granted their extra-Iberian territories an equal legal status as subrealms belonging to the crown of Portugal or Castile-Aragon.

The persistence of the political organization of the personal state in the medieval sense well into the 18th century makes it difficult to delineate phases in the migratory history of both Spain and Portugal. In the case of Portugal, it is possible to distinguish between Europe and non-Europe. That is not true for Spain, however: until the beginning of the 18th century, the Spanish crown possessed Sicily and Naples, at times also Sardinia and Corsica, Milan, the Spanish Netherlands, and Franche-Comté. The inhabitants of these European territories were all equally subjects of the Spanish king. According to the outdated legal and administrative structures in these various kingdoms and lordships, a person was a vassal of the Spanish crown only to the extent that he came from the Kingdom of Naples, the Duchy of Brabant, or some other lordship united to the Spanish crown, a situation

that was linked to a relative freedom of settlement. Within the area of the Spanish dominion, migration processes are difficult to distinguish from temporary population movements that had political, military, economic, or cultural causes: non-Europeans, too, made it to Portugal and Spain via these mechanisms, and through their service in the navy and army also to other regions of Europe.

The economic development in the Spanish and Portuguese overseas territories had a direct and indirect influence on the migration within Europe. That was true, for example, of the repercussions of the cyclical fluctuations in the production of precious metals in Spanish America, or of the Brazilian gold cycle of the 18th century. Already in the early modern period these first steps toward the development of an Atlantic economy caused Europe's focus to shift to the west or the Atlantic, a precursor, in a sense, of the great European migrations to America in the late 18th and 19th centuries.

In the course of the 18th century, and with the independence of Hispano-America in the 19th century, there developed increasing triangular European-Atlantic relationships, which were accompanied by migrations of certain social groups: these influenced economic relationships, political-ideological trends, and group formations, and they often operated in a border-crossing way. A few examples may illustrate this complex process. In the Peace of Utrecht (1713), the Asiento, the license for the importation of black African slaves to Hispano-America that was granted by the Spanish crown, was transferred from France to England. A short time later, this trade was controlled by the Irish Fitzgerald family in London, whose French branch had previously played that role in France.

Most of the Jesuits expelled from Portugal in 1757 and Spain in 1767, members of an order that was very international to begin with, settled in Italy. However, they maintained an extensive network of relationships within Europe, one that reached all the way to Russia under Empress Catherine the Great, who ensured the continuation of the order within her realm in spite of the Papal decision to dissolve it.[1] The writings of the expelled Jesuits about South America continued to circulate within Europe and were translated into all major languages. They played a role in the fact that initially Portugal and Spain, and in the 19th century also Ibero-America, became the destination of many travelers who published their accounts with a claim to scientific status.

After Spain and France had lost their navies in the battle of Trafalgar in 1805 and Napoleon had imposed the Continental blockade, the Spanish crown, which was dependent on the shipments of precious metals from its American colonies, was confronted with the problem of how to get its hands on the shipments that were ready to be dispatched in Mexico. This problem was solved in 1807 while units of the English navy where attacking Buenos Aires: the Irish trading house of Morfi (i.e., Murphy) based in Veracruz took over the shipments and sent the cargo to the English possession

---

[1] Jesuits in Europe since the early modern period.

117

of Jamaica, from where an English convoy of fleets brought it to London. There it was turned over to the trading house of Murphy & Gordon, which issued letters of exchange and sent them to the Spanish crown on the Continent, which cashed in the letters via its agents in Amsterdam and Hamburg, who had earlier supplied mercury for the Mexican mining operations. The cost for the entire operation was 20% of the total value.

More or less at the same time, Spanish political refugees in London were working with Spanish-Americans and transmitted liberal ideas to Spain. And Portuguese residing in London or Paris contributed to the emergence of two different liberal groups. Giuseppe Garibaldi, who had been socialized in the gaucho milieu of southern Brazil and Uruguay, was able to emerge as a leading figure of the Italian *risorgimento*, just as a century later Fidel Castro, who hailed from the Cantabrian region, became the *máximo líder* of Cuba and the political hero for an entire generation of young Europeans. At the end of the 19th century, Spanish and Italian seasonal workers in Argentina spread socialist ideas, organized themselves, and often joined forces upon returning to their respective home countries, with the result that an international anarchist movement was able to operate from Spain around 1880.

Many Spanish scientists and scholars in the most diverse fields, who had studied in Germany before, during, and after World War I, went to Mexico and other Latin American countries after the fall of the Spanish Republic in the civil war of the 1930s and set up scientific institutions and research fields. After World War II, they reestablished from there contacts to the German universities at which they had studied and in this way brought Germans back into international scientific and scholarly networks.

The examples of these kinds of multinational connections, influences, and triangular relationships created by this migration, onward migration, and return migration could be multiplied at will down to the present – one need only think of the new phenomenon of the widely promoted student migration, of the great number of binational marriages and relationships resulting from this, or of mass tourism, which often leads to permanent settlement.

It is a widely known phenomenon of Spanish migration history, already of the early modern period, that many migrations did not lead directly from one concrete starting point to a more or less distant destination; rather, they often represented migration-in-stages, interrupted by longer stays in other locations or even regions. Seville and Cádiz in western Andalusia and the Canary Islands are telling examples: like the Greater Antilles, they served during the colonial period as a launching pad for Spanish migrants to continental Hispano-America. Moreover, the economic, trading, and customs privileges that were always granted to the Portuguese and Spanish island groups in various forms promoted this role as outposts between the continents for shipping, trade, individuals from all over Europe, and for the acclimatization of plants and animals in both directions. In the 19th century,

then, they became important – because of their climate – to sick Europeans in search of healing, and as coal depots for the new steamships. In the 20th century they became strategically important as way stations for civilian and military air transportation and shipping, and after World War II they became destinations of mass tourism. Today, they are retirement homes for well-off European retirees and entry gates for African migrants to the European Union (EU).

The beginning of the 17th century does not constitute a turning point in the history of Spanish and Portuguese migrations. The periods in migration history coincide above all with turning points in political history. For example, from the perspective of migration history, the period between the beginning of Spain's imperial expansion in the age of the Catholic kings of Spain in the late 15th and early 16th centuries, and the decline of Spain's hegemony that became apparent in Portugal's independence in 1640, in the Peace of Westphalia in 1648, and in the Catalan uprisings and separatist tendencies in the middle of the 17th century should be seen as one coherent phase: there were major events beginning with the expulsion of the Jews, Spain's reach to Italy and into the Atlantic after 1492, and later with the beginning of Spain's decline, combined in 1609 with the expulsion of the Moriscos and the subsequent defeat in the Thirty Years' War. That same period saw numerically significant migrations of Spaniards – less so of Portuguese – to various European regions, and of European specialists to the Iberian Peninsula. These migrations were often temporary. As a result of the religious division of Europe, the stream of European pilgrims to Santiago de Compostela dried up at the same time.

From the perspective of structural history, the first manifestations of crisis became apparent in the age of Philip II in the second half of the 16th century, even though the king seemed to have attained the height of his power with the personal union of Spain and Portugal in 1580, while the failure of the Armada in 1588 also turned out to be a significant but not fatal setback. The effects of the price revolution, driven by the surge in the importation of precious metal from Latin America since the middle of the century and Philip II's borrowing following the first two bankruptcies of the state (part of the drastic measures of debt refinancing), manifested themselves after the 1570s in changed investment behavior (investments in durable consumer goods to safeguard one's assets). In a different way these phenomena also influenced the stream of European migration, since the European centers of finance shifted from Italy to the Netherlands, which changed the role of the Iberian Peninsula as the destination for specialized migrants. While the overseas colonies of both powers became increasingly attractive for immigrants, recruitment for military service in Spain and in the rest of Europe became more difficult. The Spanish *tercios* were increasingly filled with foreign units; later, forced recruitment and forced deployments in the European theaters of war became necessary also in Spain.

The first failed harvest at the beginning of the "Little Ice Age" after 1595 initiated Spain's long structural crisis in the

17th century. This crisis was partly responsible not only for Spain's political decline, but also for the shrinking population as a result of epidemics and famine. Added to this were manifestations of social dissolution, with repercussions for the history of migration. Spain experienced a phase of demographic decline that lasted beyond the middle of the 17th century. As a result, there was hardly any more emigration to other European countries. A slow phase of recovery commenced in the last two decades of the 17th century, still during the age of King Charles II (1665–1700) and the beginning of the end of Habsburg rule in Spain. It was promoted by initial reforms and a rise in profits from gold and silver mining in Latin America. This led to population growth and stronger overseas emigration in the 18th century. The provinces at the edges of the Levant and the Basque region benefited most from these trends. The economic upswing brought in its wake the emergence of relatively autonomous networks chiefly of Basques and Irish; the ways in which they functioned resembled the older networks of Sephardic Jews and transcended the territorial framework of the two empires.

The development of Portugal following independence in 1640 is comparable to that of Spain. Of course, the beginning of increasing emigration and immigration must be dated earlier in Portugal. Already the efforts of Henry the Navigator to advance along the coast of West Africa, following the Portuguese reach into North Africa in 1415, which had led to the (re)discovery and settlement of the Atlantic island groups, had given rise to a first Atlantic trading empire during his lifetime (1396–1460). It encompassed the coast of West Africa down to about Guinea and the maritime realm as far as the Azores, with rich fishing grounds, abundant sea mammals, and bases on the coast, from which trade – including already the slave trade – was conducted with the neighboring peoples. As early as the middle of the 15th century, this development attracted Italian as well as French, Flemish, and German economic interests and formed a magnet that drew specialists such as merchants, colonial and transportation entrepreneurs, and mercenaries from much of Europe to Lisbon.

From a German perspective, a prominent example of this development, given his renown as the creator of a famous globe, is Martin Behaim, a merchant from Nuremberg who lived in Lisbon and was married to the daughter of a Flemish governor of one of the islands of the Azores. But as early as the end of the 15th century, even ships from Danzig were not a rare sight in the port of Lisbon. Important parts of the sugar production of the Atlantic islands, which had started with crucial help from the Flemish, were sold to the North Sea and Baltic Sea regions by Hanseatic merchants. With the discovery of the sea passage to India by Vasco da Gama and the brief Portuguese monopoly in the pepper and spice trade that resulted from it, new streams of migration were set in motion both from Portugal overseas and from other European countries to Portugal and beyond. A mere five years after the beginning of the systematic colonization of Brazil (1537), a Rhenish entrepreneur operating out of

Antwerp took over the most productive sugar mill (*engenho*) near modern-day Rio de Janeiro.

These surges in Portugal's economy, which promoted migration, waned after King Sebastian's failed African enterprise around 1570. The crisis of succession triggered by his death helped those who advocated a personal union with Spain, from which they were hoping for new impulses for the domestic economy, to carry the day in 1580. As a result, Portugal entered a track of development that paralleled that of Spain in most economic, social, and political spheres until the 20th century, with the result that the history of migration in the two countries shows great similarities.

Henceforth, the Iberian migratory movements were powerfully shaped by the economic cycles in the two countries' overseas territories; the push factors at work in the two Iberian motherlands during the early phase of expansion were increasingly replaced by overseas pull factors. For example, the precious metals economy in Hispano-America in the late 17th century and the discovery of gold in Brazil (Minas Gerais and elsewhere) in the 18th century became determining forces for Spain and Portugal and influenced migratory conditions down to the first third of the 19th century. However, the strong familial and emotional ties to the communities of origin remained an important continuity in the history of Iberian migration. They found expression, for example, in aid shipments from successful migrants to family members who had remained behind, in gifts and religious endowments for the community of origin, in invitations to come overseas, and in the adoption of religious traditions from the home region.

The Iberian migratory movement overseas was followed in Spain by a stronger economic and trade penetration from France, which became noticeable even in Mexico around 1780. Portugal, meanwhile, had opened itself to English penetration since the Methuen Treaties of 1703, and so it comes as no surprise that in 1808 the English fleet brought the entire Portuguese court, some 15,000 persons, to Rio de Janeiro to protect it from Napoleon's troops.

At a time of population growth and overseas orientation by Spaniards and Portuguese, both countries became a magnet to the rest of Europe, a development that has not yet been comprehensively studied in terms of migration history. The political and administrative changes since the 18th century, along with the gradual improvement in sanitation, health, and social policies in their wake, put an end in the 19th century to the phase of the old demographic cycles (old type agrarian crises) characterized by weather conditions, periodic epidemics, and migration from the countryside to the cities. It gave rise to a phase of steadier population growth with a slow rise in life expectancy, though until the 20th century it lagged behind the rest of Europe.

This development was often interrupted by social and economic problems and by the internal and overseas migratory movements they triggered. Railroad construction, late industrialization, political liberalization and violent internal clashes, and deep-seated structural changes (such as the privatization of ecclesiastical and cooperative property and new colonial endeavors and entanglements) created incentives for migration in the 19th and 20th centuries: once again to South America, to North Africa, or to western and central Europe. Added to this, beginning in the 1960s, was the rapidly growing, temporary or permanent immigration into both countries, first from other European countries, then from Latin America, and most recently from Africa and southeastern Europe. Currently, the estimated 800,000 Romanians living in Spain legally and illegally are considered the largest immigrant group, followed by Ecuadorians and other groups of European and Latin American immigrants.[2]

Population and migration in the 16th and 17th centuries

At the beginning of the modern period, the Iberian Peninsula was a comparatively sparsely settled region. Around 1600, after a century of population growth, the approximately 580,000 square kilometers (of which Portugal had 90,000, Aragon 100,000, Navarre 12,000, and Castile 378,000) were home to about 11.4 million Iberians. Portugal had a population of around 1.5 million, Navarre nearly 185,000, Aragon about 1.4 million, and Castile more than 8.3 million. That yields a population density (inhabitants per square kilometer) of 13.6 for Aragon, 15.4 for Navarre, 16.7 for Portugal, and 22 for Castile, although these averages conceal an unequal population distribution. Just in the three mainland lands of the crown of Aragon, we find population densities of 8 in Aragon itself, 12 in Catalonia, and 30 in Valencia.

The imbalances were due in part to geographic conditions, in part to the degree of urbanization in the various regions, but in part also to their economic development. The numbers reflect demographic differences – some long term and occasionally persisting to this day – that were shaped, since the late 16th century, above all by the growth of urban metropolitan regions, such as Madrid, Barcelona, Valencia, Zaragoza, Bilbao, and Seville in Spain, and Oporto and Lisbon in Portugal.

Spain and Portugal had lost many economically active inhabitants through the expulsion of the Jews at the end of the 15th century. Estimates about the number of expellees have been recently corrected downward and now stand at around 100,000–150,000. Some migrated to North Africa and the eastern Mediterranean, to Thessaloniki, Constantinople, and Alexandria, but some also went to the North Sea region. Eager to preserve their Spanish language and cultural identity by establishing self-contained communities, these Sephardic Jews played an important role in the Atlantic region by establishing trading networks. They assumed special significance in Atlantic long-distance trade (especially sugar and tobacco), the import of other tropical and subtropical products, which were in growing demand in Europe, and in the Atlantic slave trade.[3]

In the course of the 16th century, the Jews who had remained in Spain and Portugal and had converted to Christianity (called *conversos*) were increasingly discriminated against by the old Christian population, less so by the nobility and the crown, and often denounced to the Inquisition, with the result that they came under growing pressure to emigrate. Attempts – apparent especially in Spain – to control overseas migration and to issue migration permits only to old Christian and "irreproachable" applicants seem to indicate that the *conversos*, in particular were eager to escape the pressure at home by emigrating. Since these regulatory efforts had little success, it can be assumed that there were many *conversos* among the large number of emigrants to Latin America.

Estimates about the number of Spanish overseas migrants in the 16th century, most of whom came from Castile, range from around 15,500 to 21,400 per year. As early as 1626, Pedro Fernández de Navarrete lamented, in his work *Conservación de Monarquias*, that the large number of *colonias* (here still in the sense of "nurseries") caused the departure of about 40,000 persons every year, who were suitable for all kinds of (productive) activity on land and sea. Global calculations put the number of Spaniards who had emigrated to Latin America by the end of the 16th century at around 200,000. They were predominantly men. Letters indicate that poverty and hardship were the primary motivations behind emigration. Men who had found a livelihood very often asked their wives, who had remained behind under the care of male relatives, to follow them to Latin America. At times the crown promoted the emigration and marriage of single women to limit the process of racial mixing (*mestizaje*) in Latin America, which was early on seen as an obstacle to the Hispanization of the colonies. It was only after the middle of the 16th century that the number of women among the emigrants to Latin America began to increase. There is very little coherent information about female migration to European theaters of Spanish politics. It is likely to have been fairly low and concentrated on the Netherlands and Italy, since migrants belonged overwhelmingly to the administration and the military and assumed that they would eventually return.[4]

Thinly settled to begin with, Spain lost around half a million people through expulsions and emigration in the 16th century, if we include the Moors who left for North Africa after the reconquest of Granada in 1492 and the soldiers deployed in Italy and the Mediterranean region, many of whom did not return home. Since Castile experienced a lengthy economic upswing in the 16th century and was spared larger epidemics, this loss was made up, at least in part, by high natural population growth. That trend reversed at the end of the 16th century: following the beginning of the "Little Ice Age" with its failed harvests, plague epidemics

---

[2] Latin American migrants in Spain since the end of the 1980s.
[3] Sephardim in Europe in the early modern period.

[4] Spanish troops in the Netherlands in the 16th and 17th centuries: the example of Geldern; administrative elites in southern Italy and Sicily under Spanish rule in the early modern period.

swept through the country between 1598 and 1602, bringing declining birthrates and high mortality in their wake.

By contrast, Catalonia, which was suffering through an economic crisis around the same time, experienced large migration gains from southern France and the Massif Central. Around a fifth of Catalonia's population in the 16th century is likely to have been born on the other side of the Pyrenees in France. With some fluctuation, this immigration to Catalonia persisted until around 1620. Thereafter, a thin but steady stream of French migration flowed from the Auvergne and Brittany into all regions of Spain.[5] In 1680, the French ambassador in Madrid estimated that about 70,000 of his countrymen were living in Spain. At the beginning of the 18th century, 25,000 French immigrants were counted in Andalusia, alone; most belonged to the underclass, and many probably continued onward to Latin America after a period of transition. French immigration can be explained, not least, by the fact that population-poor Spain paid higher wages than densely settled France. A powerful pull was exerted by the Spanish court, whose splendor continued to increase in spite of the economic and social problems and attracted individual migrants from all over Europe and South America, some of whom pursued their political or diplomatic affairs at the court for some period of time or remained there permanently. Many socially uprooted internal migrants and wounded mercenaries unfit for service also headed for the court and the capital of Madrid to support themselves with charitable meals for the poor, casual jobs, and criminal activities, or to try and collect outstanding payments or demand pensions and jobs in the administration, as illustrated in the literary genre of the Spanish picaresque novel.

In addition there was a numerically insignificant but economically important immigration of foreign merchants into the most important port cities. For example, the Germans who dominated southern German trading and economic interests in the 16th century were increasingly replaced by merchants from the Hanseatic cities and their hinterland. Because of their extensive network, they attained an economic importance that exceeded their numbers and were given a special diplomatic status as *nación hanseátic*. Thanks to its two merchant fleets that sailed every year between the mouth of the Guadalquivir and America, Cádiz became one of the great international ports of that time, functioning as a hub between the Mediterranean and the North Sea, on the one hand, and Latin America, on the other.[6]

The plague years 1598–1602 were followed in the course of the 17th century by further phases of devastating epidemics. Plague, smallpox, diphtheria, and other infectious diseases ravaged the Iberian Peninsula in fairly rapid succession, though their severity varied in different regions. Scholars have estimated that in their wake, the population declined by 7% to 10% around the middle of the 17th century. At the same time, there was a stronger internal migration into the cities. The many poor harvests and outright harvest failures caused by the weather went hand in hand with drastic price increases, which the hospitals in the cities sought to counteract with grain imports and other social measures; as a result, they continued to exert a strong attraction on the rural population. The state of research does not yet allow for a comprehensive overview of the extent and distribution of the population as a result of a heightened mortality caused by disease. Portugal was affected in much the same way. However, the densely settled northern part of the country, with its Atlantic climate and agriculture organized around small farms, was more heavily affected by these developments than the more thinly settled, Mediterranean south.

The loss of population in Spain from the expulsion of the Moriscos in the years after 1609 affected chiefly the crown of Aragon. In Castile, following the uprising of the Moriscos in the Alpujarras in the second half of the 1560s, which was put down with great effort, the self-contained settlements of this population group in Granada were dissolved through resettlement within Castile, and their members were dispersed within the central and southern regions of old Christian Castile. Census figures collected at the end of the 16th century showed 88,116 Moriscos in Castile, or 1.3% of the Castilian population. Aragon itself was home to 60,818 Moriscos (15.2% of the population), Valencia to 117,464 (26.1%), and Catalonia to only 3,716 (0.8%). The majority of the 272,140 expelled Moriscos were thus found in Valencia and Aragon. Although the realm of the crown of Aragon encompassed only 2.2% of the total Spanish population, it lost 12.6% of its inhabitants, and these losses could hardly be made up by gains from immigration. In conjunction with the pandemics of the first half of the century, they led to a noticeable decline in the population.

During the 16th century and down to about 1640, the Portuguese population doubled in size to around 2 million. At the same time, Portugal, like Spain, suffered high losses from migration: the number of Portuguese emigrants between 1500 and 1580 is estimated at around 280,000. Because Portuguese pursued trade colonization and not settlement colonization like Spain, its losses were smaller. Moreover, the country did not suffer as severely from the epidemics at the beginning of the 17th century. In addition, the importation of black African slaves since the later 15th century in part made up for the migration losses. The 60 years of personal union with Spain also witnessed strong emigration to Castile, though it is likely that Castile was merely a transit stop for onward migration to the economic centers of Hispano-America. After 1640, there were many Portuguese in these centers, some of which were expelled again. Although the average annual number of emigrants who went overseas rose to 8,000–10,000 individuals with the beginning of the Brazilian gold cycle in the 18th century, the population increased until the 1760s to about 2.6 million.

---

[5] Auvergnese in Spain in the early modern period.
[6] German maritime traders in Cádiz and Bordeaux from the late 17th to the late 19th century; British merchants in Portugal since 1640; Spanish merchants in the Netherlands in the early modern period.

During the Thirty Years' War (1618–48) and the successor wars that lasted into the 1660s (in part against "renegade" Portugal, in part against France and the rebellious Catalans allied with them), recruitment for the military in Spain was generally characterized more and more by forced conscription. Between 1635 and 1659, alone, between 8,000 and 12,000 recruits are said to have been levied each year; some were sent outside the country, some to other regions within the country. In total that comes to a figure of about 288,000 men. As a result of their departure from their home regions, 6% to 10% and more of the citizens were widows in many cities and towns at the time of the Peace of the Pyrenees. In contemporary sources we find reports from provincial and city authorities that outdid each other in the reported depopulation figures. Apparently very few of the conscripts ever returned to their hometowns. Only approximate information exists about the high numbers of those who deserted on the other side of the Atlantic from the ships of the fleets that traveled to South America every year. These desertions often turned into mass flights that led to delays in the return journey, since the crews had to be restocked with the help of impressments.

Slaves also arrived involuntarily on the Spanish Peninsula.[7] The importance of slave migrations is already evident from the existence of the mendicant order of the Mercedarians in Spain and Portugal. It saw its main mission in redeeming Christians who had fallen into North African slavery. The order decorated its churches – for example, in Toledo – symbolically with the chains of redeemed slaves. It is less well known that attacks and raids by the so-called Barbary pirates in the 17th century nearly depopulated entire coastal landscapes, beginning at the Cantabrian coast and along the Mediterranean shores as far as Barcelona. The Muslim pirates plundered towns and villages and enslaved their inhabitants, who fled into the hinterland. Conversely, Spaniards enslaved North Africans in the Mediterranean, though from the time of the Catholic kings they no longer did so with the native inhabitants of the Canary islands (prohibited in 1500). As a result of the Treaty of Tordesillas with Portugal (1494), Spain was blocked from access to the coasts of Africa, which meant that black African slaves could reach Spanish territories only through foreign intermediaries. The crown thus granted licenses (asientos) for the import of black African slaves, first to Portugal and then to other European powers, a trade in which German trading companies were also involved later on. However, the vast majority of black African slaves were shipped to South America to make up for the labor shortage brought about by the decline in the Amerindian population. It was only in roundabout ways that small numbers found their way to Spain, mostly to Andalusia. There, because of the relatively good conditions of integration, they gradually merged with the native population. By contrast, the number of black Africans was substantially higher in southern Portugal.

Population, migration, and integration in the age of territorialization in the 18th and early 19th centuries

The beginning of the 18th century marks a clear turning point in the history of Portugal and Spain. Following the stabilization of its dynasty and the recognition of its independence, Portugal bound itself closely to England in the Methuen Treaty. While this step is usually interpreted only in terms of politics and trade policy, it was evidently the result of fundamental reflections about the situation of the kingdom: years earlier, various high-ranking politicians had already recommended to the crown that it shift the center of the empire to Brazil. Since these ideas in the late 17th century came at a time when the Brazilian sugar economy was in decline as the dominant economic factor, these proposals were not acted upon, also for economic reasons. On the other hand, the advances of the *bandeirantes* into the interior of South America at that time opened up prospects that the long-sought deposits of precious metals would finally be found in Brazil. The Methuen Treaty thus fell into a period of uncertainty, which ended after around 1710 by significant discoveries of gold in Brazil, as a result of which the historiography in the 18th century speaks of an economic cycle of gold. Brazil therefore attracted immigrants not only from Portugal, but indirectly also from England, when substantial English merchant colonies established themselves in Portugal's most important port cities.[8] Despite its ties to Great Britain, the Portuguese crown in the 18th century tended more toward absolutist politics in the French tradition. This gave rise once more to parallels to the political development in Spain.

The beginning of the 18th century marked a more profound turning point in Spain, when the change in dynasty from the Habsburgs to the Bourbons led to a war of succession that dragged on until the Treaties of Utrecht and Rastatt in 1714, and in the course of which foreign armies for the first time operated in the country on a large scale. After the Bourbon pretender Philip of Anjou had been generally accepted in Spain as King Philip V, the realms of the crown of Aragon withdrew their allegiance again and joined the camp of the Habsburg pretender Charles, who was supported by England. At times two armies of the contending parties faced each other on Spanish soil, each with 20,000–25,000 men, with only about one-half of Philip's force consisting of Spaniards (mostly recruited from the northern part of the country), while 50% were French. The troops of the Habsburg pretender, by contrast, were mostly Englishmen and units recruited in the Empire. There is a good deal of speculation about the consequences of the war for Spain's demographic development, but little systematic research.

The wars constituted a dramatic rupture in the political history of Spain, which lost all its European territories in Italy and the Netherlands as well as Gibraltar and the Balearic Islands in the peace treaties of 1714. Spain kept

[7] African slaves on the Iberian Peninsula in the early modern period.

[8] British merchants in Portugal since 1640.

only its American territories relatively undiminished, even though it was forced to make concessions to England with respect to shipping and trade. These losses could be made up in part in the course of the 18th century in the Mediterranean region when the European powers consented to the establishment of a *secundogenitur* (home of the second son of the king) in Naples, Sicily, and Parma, and to the reconquest of the Balearic Islands. However, the political independence of these Italian territories closed a traditionally open door to extensive migration movements between the two peninsulas. With Gibraltar in English hands, Spain had to suffer a strategically important loss of territory that has rankled to this day and been the source of political problems.

Of course, elites in trade, the military, and the arts continued to migrate to the Iberian Peninsula also during the 18th century or left it to head for other European countries. Migration between the Netherlands and Spain, however, came to a halt after 1714, even if parts of the population from the former Spanish Netherlands settled permanently in Spain during the War of Succession; they were also joined by Catholic Irish from France. For some of these immigrants, the connection to Latin America may have been an important motivation to settle in Spain: in subsequent years, we find networks of family enterprises with familial branches in England, France, Spain, and North and South America.

The new dynasty was initially under the very direct influence of the French court, which abated only in the wake of Philip V's second marriage to Elisabeth Farnese. The new king took advantage of the rebellion of the Aragonese realms to abolish their special legal status after 1714 and subject them to Castilian law. As a result, only the Basque provinces and Navarre, which had supported Philip V, retained their old legal structure. Castilian became the official language, internal tariff barriers were dismantled, the assembly of estates was merged into a single body (though rarely summoned), and uniform succession regulations were introduced for all of Spain by solidifying the Salian inheritance law. The influence of the central councils from the time of Charles V was pushed back and they were restricted to the role as final courts of appeal. Their place was taken by state secretariats who ran the affairs of state with the king and quickly evolved into modern ministries. There followed the introduction of a new provincial administration under the leadership of intendants, who in their districts oversaw all administrative functions or performed them in person. At the same time, efforts were made to restrict the privileges of the Church.

These political and administrative measures initiated the transition from the traditional state of interpersonal relationships to a modern territorial state and thus a fundamental reinterpretation of state and society. It had consequences for the history of population and migration in that the standardization of legal conditions reduced the incentives for internal migration, while at the same time making it easier. Whereas under the Habsburgs, every vassal of the crown from this extensive conglomeration of realms could, in principle, approach the king directly with his concerns if he felt unfairly treated by the institutions, this was no longer possible. Henceforth, all petitions to the crown had to go through the intermediary levels, which then commented and passed them on. In order to make sure that justice would prevail after all, the intendants, as officials with executive function, were to form a new bureaucratic elite and be recruited from a professionally trained, educated officer corps that was committed to the common good of the state and to its highest interpreter, the king. However, the transition from crown vassal to subject that this entailed was only the beginning of a process that lasted into the 19th century.

The implementation of these measures against the entrenched opposition succeeded in Spain by the end of the reign of Philip V around the middle of the 18th century. That does not apply to Latin America, however, where the *Recopilación de las Leyes de Indias*, put in place in 1680 by Charles II, enshrined the old state of interpersonal relationships in the constitutional order. At the same time, the act guaranteed the overseas territories the status of separate kingdoms, which they had previously held only on a precarious legal basis. Moreover, politicians did not deem it wise to carry out these profound changes simultaneously in the mother country and the overseas territories. As a result, the motherland and its territories took increasingly divergent paths of political development. It was only on the basis of the concept of the territorial state, which made territory the crucial criterion for the definition of statehood, that one could conceive of a hierarchical order of the various territories in terms of their significance to "Spanish" statehood, and articulate the notion of mercantilism and the related idea of "colony" in the modern sense.

In 17th-century Spain, the term *colonia* was still used in the classic, ancient sense of "settlement." Now it was frequently defined as part of a state territory that was of lesser legal status, dependent on Spain, and tributary. Spaniards were now increasingly divided, according to birth, into those on either side of the Atlantic and gradually put at odds with each other, as Alexander von Humboldt described in his travel diary. Conflicts between European and American Spaniards had existed before, but they had always been the kinds of conflicts between individuals and groups that existed everywhere. Now, however, reinforced by relevant writings in Spain, they took on a fundamental meaning related to territory.

In the 18th and early 19th century, Latin America became the destination of many members of the Spanish lower classes, who in America, nevertheless, felt superior to their countrymen there. Conversely, the Hispano-Americans, "Creoles," developed an exaggerated sense of self-esteem that expressed itself in many ways. In the 16th and 17th centuries, Spaniards had emigrated to Europe and the Americas with the consciousness that as members of a superior power, they were fighting for the faith and for Spain and to achieve social recognition and social advancement. Now, however, 18th-century migrants were driven by doubts about Spain's role within Europe, for which they tried to overcompensate with a sense of superiority vis-à-vis the American-born population. Conversely, it would appear that the female population in Latin America preferred immigrant Spaniards, even of low social status, as marriage partners. It therefore comes as no surprise that as a result of these developments, Spanish migration to other countries in Europe no longer played a major role.

All this was reinforced further by a fundamental change in mentality. In Spain itself, in the wake of the development of tendencies toward individualization and in conjunction with the administrative and fiscal reforms, wealth was increasingly defined in different terms, namely, as the disposition over real estate, as revealed by the advance of physiocratic ideas since the middle of the 18th century. In thinly settled South America, the control of human labor remained the crucial criterion for wealth and the accumulation of land, often with the goal of preventing an excess of supply on a tight agricultural market.

The crown in the 18th century pursued mercantilist goals and promoted the growth of the population and the settlement of deserted tracts of land. It was eager, with the help of public investments and other supportive measures, to provide the poorer strata of the population with work and bread. In 1720, the crown established a *Junta de Sanidad*, which henceforth took on the problems of national health, battled epidemics and diseases, and supervised hospitals. From around the middle of the 18th century one can observe state action against existing monopolies and oligopolies and the promotion of the individual drive for profit, supplemented by far-reaching plans to reform the tax system, discussions regarding a land reform through the privatization of ecclesiastic and cooperative property, and the establishment of patriotic societies (*Sociedades Económicas de Amigos del País*) that were supposed to help propagate and implement the crown's policies. Since the expulsion of the Jesuits from all parts of the realm in 1767 for political reasons and the confiscation of the order's rich holdings, soon compensated for through the readmission of Jews to Spain, the political leadership began to propagate the concept of the "nation made up of individuals." This allowed the idea of nation to gain a wider foothold in Spain by the end of the 18th century. As a result, the first liberal constitution of Spain, adopted in 1812 in Cádiz after protracted negotiations, defined the land as a nation and laid down in detail who was to be considered a Spaniard and how foreigners were to be treated and, if circumstances called for it, naturalized.

It was only in 1812 that a long phase of legal uncertainty about the status of those who lived under the authority of the Spanish crown neared its end. This legal uncertainty resulted from the late medieval concept of the state, which assigned sovereignty to "king and kingdom, united in the Cortes." The "kingdom" was represented by deputies of the three estates of the clergy, the nobility, and the commoners, the latter represented by the cities. It was only in this constellation that *leges* – that is, laws carrying constitutional authority – could be passed. As there were no fundamental

legal regulations about the integration of foreigners before 1812, there were various possibilities for doing so: individuals and even groups could be integrated by being placed under the protection of great ecclesiastical or noble lords or acquiring "civic" rights, the status of a *vecino*, in a community. That status could usually be attained through marriage to a native woman and maintaining a household for 10 years in the city in question, or it was bestowed by the king through a privilege. However, the precondition was adherence to the Catholic faith.

The circumstances of the *reconquista* were such that larger groups of non-Christians – Jews and Moriscos – had to be integrated, which was done by placing them under the immediate protection of the king. They had to pay special taxes, in return for which they were given certain rights of self-governance. The crown always granted the latter with the caveat that these groups would be successfully assimilated also religiously. If that did not happen, and if the crown believed that these groups posed a political problem, royal protection could be withdrawn and expatriation ordered, as happened with the Jews and Moriscos and later with the Jesuits. A corresponding status as foreign *nationes*, which could likewise be revoked, for example, in times of war, was also granted to groups of foreign merchants.

The constitution of Cádiz for the first time clearly resolved this uncertain legal situation and transferred the right of naturalization to the central bureaucratic organs. The nation continued to define itself as Catholic, though it granted minority rights. Thus, after 1812 all those born on the soil of Spain and in the overseas territories were regarded as Spaniards including Indios, mestizos, and other groups, though not black Africans who hailed from non-Spanish and non-Christian territories. To be sure, the loss of the Spanish colonial territories in South America and the Caribbean at the beginning of the 19th century and in 1898 soon restricted the legal sphere within which this citizenship law applied; however, as part of the special relationship between Spain and the Hispano-American states that developed in the 19th century, it was undercut, at least in part, through all sorts of privileges that the states extended to each others' citizens when it came to naturalization.

In Portugal, a movement within the military likewise led to a constitutional assembly: in 1822, it adopted a constitution that drew heavily on the Cádiz constitution of 1812 and envisaged similar legal regulations concerning citizenship and national affiliation. However, since Portugal was able to hold on to its colonial empire largely undiminished until the 1970s (with the exception of Brazil), the legal definition of citizenship was only a partial clarification of the situation, especially since all kinds of special regulations were added in the 19th and 20th centuries.

The 18th century brought continuous population growth in Spain. The population initially grew slowly between 1717 and 1826, and thereafter at an accelerated pace from 8.8 to 14.2 million. Annual rates of growth rose from 0.31–0.32% to 0.64% toward the end of the century. In contrast to the development in the 16th century, it was now the peripheries that boasted considerably higher rates of growth. According to a census of 1787, Valencia, Galicia, Asturias, and the Basque provinces near the coast reached a population density of 30–60 inhabitants per square kilometer, Catalonia, Navarre, and Andalusia 11–29, while the once very densely settled central regions of Aragon, Old and New Castile, and Murcia had densities of only 0–10. Since the last were simultaneously the most strongly urbanized areas, the countryside in the center tended to depopulate, while the cities grew or at least kept their numbers stable.

The backdrop to the divergent distribution of population growth is to be found in structural conditions, changes in marriage behavior, and epidemiological factors. A smallpox epidemic at the end of the 18th century led after 1798 to state-mandated inoculation campaigns, which were also extended to the American colonies and in part explain the high growth rates after the end of the 18th century. At the same time, the northwestern regions with high population growth posted high rates of emigration. By contrast, the large Andalusian cities, as a result of the liberalization of trade and shipping with Spanish America and the economic growth it spurred, became very attractive to immigrants. Migrants, some of whom remained in Andalusia, some of whom left for America and once again boosted the number of immigrating Spaniards there, continued to impart great economic importance to the southwest of the country. That was also reflected in the tax revenues, the surplus of which was largely spent in the northern regions of the country.

The capital of Madrid and other cities with vigorous construction activity attracted many temporary migrant workers from the northwest, who returned to their hometowns and villages during the winter. With the rise of the textile industry in Catalonia and metal extraction in the Basque provinces, those regions also attracted internal migrants, who would evolve into a steady stream in the 19th and 20th centuries. Toward the end of the 18th century, in the wake of the commercial penetration of Spain by the French, the immigration of the French also increased, though they now tended to be members of the elite and no longer the poor in search of work and subsistence.

After 1808, Spain once again became the theater of military conflicts involving British, Dutch, Spanish, and French troops. Large segments of the civilian population, the Spanish army, and the provincial militias carried on a guerrilla war against the French invaders. Before that, regular Spanish troops had been embroiled in European conflicts alongside France and had been deployed as occupation troops. For example, Hamburg was occupied by a Spanish unit under the command of the Count of Romanones. This was the last military action of Spanish troops in Europe until the deployment of the "Blue Division" in World War II on the side of the Germans.

Although the Spanish model of the "national war" against Napoleon attracted a good deal of attention in Europe, we know very little about the consequences of these events for the demographic trend and the conditions of migration, since the latter were overlaid with the Hispano-American independence movements that occurred at the same time. While a large number of soldiers from western and central Europe who had become unemployed after 1814 were sent to South America with English help to support the rebels, King Ferdinand VII dispatched an army of around 16,000 soldiers to Venezuela and Colombia to fight the revolt. At the same time, the number of Spanish political refugees in France and England grew as a result of the repeal of the constitution of 1812 and the restoration policy initiated by Ferdinand VII.

Population and migration in the 19th and 20th centuries

The changes in Spanish and Portuguese colonial politics in the modern era revealed that both countries had, from a European perspective, at least temporarily lost their prominent position. Global political developments, however, brought both states back on the European stage from the middle of the 19th century onward. As a result, not only did the two states slowly regain their weight on the global diplomatic stage, but the importance of historical migratory traditions also increased again. This would change only when Portugal and Spain, after World War II, became part of a united Europe. This gave rise not only to new migratory developments and focal points but also to changed political and cultural orientations. Increasingly, immigration from Africa and Latin America to Europe favored the closer association of both countries with Europe and also turned them, from the last years of the 20th century, into the most vigorous proponents of a European-Mediterranean dialogue. This was also promoted by Basque terrorism, which at times found support in North Africa, and, finally, by the extensive illegal immigration from sub-Saharan Africa that flowed through these two countries into the EU via the North African enclaves of Ceuta and Melilla, the Straits of Gibraltar, and the Mediterranean and Atlantic islands.

Although the population grew in both countries from the beginning of the 19th century, life expectancy here long remained lower than in the rest of Europe. The fluctuating stream of migrants continued to flow primarily overseas. In the case of Spain, emigration into new colonial territories in North Africa also got under way toward the end of the 19th century.

The development of steamships made possible extensive overseas seasonal migration in the last third of the 19th century. Improved statistical recording of legal migratory movements began around the same time. While the surveys initially did not consistently reveal the destinations, European target countries appear increasingly at the beginning of the 20th century. These statistical overviews are not particularly revealing. They must be seen in connection with the conflict-ridden political and social developments of this period in both countries as well as in the destination countries: with the protracted dictatorships in Spain (1939–75) and Portugal (1933–74), and with the Spanish Civil War (1936–9), which deeply divided the population of the country down to individual families, and which attracted volunteers from all over the world on the side of the Republic, and military units from Italy and Germany on the side of the emerging dictatorship of General Franco. To this we must add as crucial factors since 1960 far-reaching structural changes in migration caused by the development of modern means of transportation, media, and communication technology, which gave rise to phenomena such as mass tourism and work and educational migration, and which triggered parallel migration processes in the opposite direction: labor migration from the Iberian Peninsula into the western and central European industrialized countries, and prosperity and educational migration in the opposite direction.

The first systematic census of Spain in 1857 counted a population of 15.5 million, a growth of 46.6% compared to the end of the 18th century. By 1900 the population had grown to 18.1 million; while this amounts to an increase of 76.4% from the late 18th century, it was still below comparable averages in the rest of Europe. Numerous epidemics, chiefly cholera, typhoid, diphtheria, and smallpox, along with endemic diseases like tuberculosis took countless lives, with the mortality seemingly higher among women than men. Other factors for a population growth that was slow compared to other European countries were the high rate of illiteracy (about 75%–80% around 1850), the low level of economic development, subsistence crises, the Carlist Wars, declining birthrates, and high mortality rates. Moreover, emigration to America increased once again as a result of growing political stability in most Hispano-American states after the middle of the century, with entrepreneurs from Spain helping to get industrialization processes (textile sector) started in Latin America. After 1860, the population grew more slowly. Average life expectancy even of wealthy burghers in the cities barely reached 40 around the middle of the century; for artisans it was around 25, for day laborers below 20. Life expectancy began to rise noticeably only with further advances in public health and sanitation after the late 19th century.

Here one must also bear in mind that the various surges of privatization of ecclesiastical, communal, and cooperative property up to 1860 had very different consequences from one region to the next. While the dissolution of monasteries and ecclesiastical institutions led to a drastic reduction in the size of the monastic population and the clergy in general, which meant that a higher number of men and women were integrated into the reproductive process, the loss of communal and cooperative property at the same time deprived especially the poorer strata of the population of their livelihood. The dissolution of ecclesiastical and cooperative property affected about 40%–60% of the arable land, which was now privatized. The intent was that this redistribution would benefit primarily small landless farmers and small leaseholders. Although middle-class urban dwellers also acquired land, in the end the redistribution boosted large-scale landholding. Since the population that was supposed to benefit had neither the necessary means of production nor access to credit, and since Church institutions lost their function as lenders, this measure favored land speculation, rural unrest, and migratory processes with demographic consequences.

With the military simultaneously keeping 100,000–110,000 men under arms continuously, who no longer tended to be housed close to home as had been the case in the Ancien Régime, there were far more extensive military migrations than in the 18th century. Alongside the higher military effort to secure Cuba and the Philippines, one must mention the Carlist uprising of 1846–9, the intervention in Portugal in 1847, the war against Morocco in 1859–60, the colonial expeditions in conjunction with France, such as the expedition to Cochinchina (1858–62), the intervention in Mexico (1861–2), the Spanish-Moroccan War (1859–60), the Pacific War (1865–71), the Second Carlist War (1872–6), and above all the wars in Cuba (1868–78 and 1898). Following the accelerating railroad construction after 1848, not only did the army become more mobile, but internal migration also increased into the expanding coal mining region of Asturias and the rapidly industrializing regions of the Basque provinces and Catalonia, which temporarily impeded the creation of families and split up existing ones.

The regionally very diverse rates of population growth in the last third of the 19th century (beginning of the Civil Registry 1882) and the first two decades of the 20th century reveal the influence of these factors. In the period between 1877 and 1920, population growth was less than 10% in some regions (Leon: 4.4%, Navarre: 8.5%), while in other areas it was between 10% and 30% (Old Castile: 12.27%, Galicia: 14.95%, Balearic Islands: 17.3%, Valencia: 27%, Andalusia: 28.6%, Asturias: 29%). Growth rates between 30% and 70% were found in Catalonia (33.8%), Aragon (33.8%), Murcia (38.7%), Extremadura (42.6%), New Castile (49.2%), on the Canary Islands (63.4%) – prompted in part by multistage migration with America as the final destination, and, finally, the Basque provinces (70.1%).

Growth was especially rapid in the two large cities of Madrid and Barcelona, whose population rose in the same period as a result of industrialization from 397,816 to 750,896 for Madrid, and from 248,943 to 710,335 for Barcelona. Traditional cities like Seville, Granada, Toledo, or Zaragoza had declining populations or only minor growth, whereas Valencia's population increased from 145,782 to 320,195. The two large metropolises, the Basque provinces, and the Canary Islands were the regions with the highest rates of growth. On the Continent the backdrop to this trend was industrialization and the internal migrations it triggered. The population of the Canary Islands grew because of the rising importance of shipping and trade (customs privileges), the boom in certain commodities (cochineal dye), and the increase in migration to Latin America.

With World War I, Spain began to fall increasingly in line with European demographic developments, with declining birth and death rates and higher growth rates; at the end of the 20th century, however, it slid into a process of demographic stagnation, much like Germany.

Extensive immigration from other European regions into the Iberian Peninsula is not discernible after the middle of the 19th century, but there was an influx of individual specialists. English and French investments in growing grapes for wine in the Guadalquivir region and in northern Portugal brought in specialists and merchants. The result was the general diffusion of the consumption of sherry and port in western and central Europe. In the wake of Romanticism, in which the literary and artistic interest in Spain played a large role, Spain as well as Portugal attracted a growing number of travelers and artists in the course of the 19th century. Their works boosted interest in these countries. At the end of the 19th century, then, with the "generation of 1898" and its demands for a modernization of Spain, more and more Spaniards went to other European countries to study. Parallel to this development we also find around the turn of the century several tens of thousands of immigrants from Portugal, France, Italy, Germany, and England in Spain, with specific regional distributions.

Earlier, the social problems had set in motion a Spanish labor migration – partly permanent, partly temporary – to southern France, and had caused a strong surge especially in the stream of emigrants to Latin America. Temporary labor migrations took Spanish rural laborers particularly into the South American agrarian states of Argentina and Brazil. The emigration of middle-class farmers headed chiefly to Cuba, Mexico, and other countries bordering the Caribbean. Most emigrants came from the regions with the highest demographic growth rates. Galicia, alone, provided about 38% of all Spanish migrants to Latin America in 1930. By contrast, the south and east of the country were affected by emigration to a much lower degree, as a result of which their share of the overall population increased considerably in the first third of the 20th century.

With the beginning of World War I, the emigrations overseas lost their importance. Instead, the strongly fluctuating migration of rural workers to France increased substantially, even from regions such as Catalonia, which in turn saw strong net gains from internal migration. Catalonia's gain totaled 340,800 between 1877 and 1920, which has given rise to the popular saying that the most ardent Catalans come from Andalusia. The provincial capitals in northern Spain generally benefited from immigration from their respective hinterland. At the same time, the south of the country attracted migrant workers from the Canary Islands. Cities also grew in the south, though more slowly. Whereas only 9% of all cities exceeded a population of 100,000 in 1900, by 1970, 36.7% were already in that category.

The civil war in the 1930s caused a deep rupture in the development of Spanish migration conditions. The number of casualties from the conflict is likely to have been 80,000. At the same time, there was a strong influx of foreign soldiers into Spain, alongside Germans, Italians on the side of General Franco, and volunteer fighters from Europe and overseas (Ernest Hemingway, for example). Around 300,000 Spaniards went into exile, both to European countries (France, Soviet Union) and to South America.[9] Many of these political refugees played an important role in the cultural and scientific life of their destination countries in Hispano-America. In European countries, opposition groups to the Franco dictatorship were formed. Many of the political refugees did not return home after the democratization of Spain.

After the end of World War II and the beginning of the strong and sustained economic growth in the countries of western, northern, and central Europe, the majority of the Spanish and Portuguese emigrants remained in Europe. By 1970, around 900,000 migrants had left Spain and Portugal with Latin America as their destination; during the same period (1945–70) around 400,000 returned from there to Europe. At the same time, however, France and Germany accepted more than 400,000 labor migrants from Spain up to about 1970, Switzerland more than 350,000. Adding the migrants to Great Britain, the Netherlands (more than 30,000), Belgium, and a few other countries, more than 1.4 million Spanish migrant laborers went to European countries. They were mostly men from rural areas, some of whom settled in their host country after getting married, while others returned to Spain after stays of varying durations and contributed to drawing Spain closer to Europe.[10]

Spain's economic upswing after it joined the European Community in 1986 led increasingly to a positive migration balance in that country. In part this was the result of returning migrants, but it was also due to European immigrants – some settling in the Iberian Peninsula in the wake of rapidly growing tourism since the 1960s or as prosperous immigrants with a second home, some arriving for economic reasons after Spain's accession to the EU and the Schengen Agreement that granted freedom of movement as they became active throughout Europe from there.[11]

In Portugal, the demographic development in the 19th century was different from that in Spain, the result of rapid population growth. In 1835 the country had 3 million inhabitants, by 1911 the number was already up to 5.5 million. Population density stood at around 40 per square kilometer in the middle of the 19th century; in 1900 it

---

[9] Spanish political refugees in Europe since the beginning of the civil war in 1936: the example of France.

[10] Spanish labor migrants in western, central, and northern Europe since the end of World War II; Portuguese labor migrants in western and central Europe since the 1950s: the examples of France and Germany.

[11] German affluence migrants in Spain since the late 20th century; British affluence migrants in the Costa del Sol in the late 20th century.

reached around 60 in the northern half of the country. Still, the country continued to have a largely agrarian imprint, for while the population of existing cities increased, new urban centers did not develop. As late as the turn of the 19th century, Portugal had merely around 100,000 industrial workers.

In the last third of the 19th century, the colonies once more took on greater political importance. That also led to a stronger exodus from the motherland to the colonies. In addition, social tensions beginning in the 1890s stimulated emigration to America. The primary destination countries were Brazil, the USA, and Venezuela. Portuguese authorities recorded a rise in migration across the border of more than 10,000 per year since the 1880s. In the mid-1890s, emigration at times even reached 50,000 per year, and between 1910 and 1920 it even exceeded this number. With the establishment of the dictatorship of António de Oliveira Salazar at the beginning of the 1930s, emigration returned to the level of the middle of the 19th century. After 1950 it rose rapidly and reached new heights in the 1960s and up to the Carnation Revolution of 1974.

Similar to Spain, the strong emigration since the 1950s was directed in part toward Latin America, but especially to western and central Europe. With the Carnation Revolution, Portugal became once again a land with a positive migration balance. The process of decolonization alone brought nearly a million people to the former motherland within a short period of time: Portuguese return migrants, descendants of Portuguese born in the colonies, but also black Africans who had closely collaborated with the Portuguese in the military and the administration. Although the majority possessed Portuguese citizenship or were able to obtain it immediately after their arrival, the integration of the postcolonial immigrants was a very slow process.[12]

Since the 1980s, a growing number of immigrants from other European states have flowed into the country. Among the 220,000 foreigners living in Portugal legally in 2001, about 30% came from European countries, 45% from Portuguese-speaking Africa, about 20% from North and South America, and around 3% from Asia. Since the turn of the 20th century, Portugal – like Spain – has seen a growing influx of migrants from eastern, east-central, and southeastern Europe. And the total number of immigrants, especially those from eastern, east-central, and southeastern Europe, is also likely to be substantially higher than the officially recorded number of immigrants. The first signs of economic crisis put the immediate future of this strong inflow from eastern, east-central, and southeastern Europe in question, while the influx from the southern states abutting the Mediterranean and from Africa is expected to grow (as in Spain). To what extent the number of prosperity migrants from western and central Europe will also

continue to grow is unclear at this time; on the whole, however, the number of residents with foreign citizenship in Spain and Portugal is likely to continue to increase in the years ahead.

REFERENCES

Altmann, Ida, *Transatlantic Ties in the Spanish Empire*. Stanford, 2000.

Alves Dias, João José, *Gentes e espaços. En torno da população portuguesa na primeirametade do século XVI*. Lisbon, 1996.

Angiolini, Franco, and Daniel Roche. *Cultures et formations négociantes dans l'Europe moderne*. Paris, 1995.

Arbell, Mordechai, ed. *Spanish and Portuguese Jews in the Caribbean and the Guianas: A Bibliography*. Providence and New York, 1999.

Bailyn, Bernard. *Atlantic History: Concept and Contours*. Cambridge, MA, and London, 2005.

Bernardini, Paolo, and Norman Fiering, eds. *The Jews and the Expansion of Europe to the West 1450–1800*. New York and Oxford, 2001.

Bernecker, Walther L. *Spanien-Handbuch. Geschichte und Gegenwart*. Tübingen, 2006.

Bernecker, Walther L., and Horst Pietschmann. *Geschichte Spaniens*. 4th ed. Stuttgart, 2005.

Bernecker, Walther L., and Horst Pietschmann. *Geschichte Portugals. Vom Spätmittelalter bis zur Gegenwart*. 2nd ed. Munich, 2008.

Bernecker, Walther L., Horst Pietschmann, and Rüdiger Zoller. *Eine kleine Geschichte Brasiliens*. Frankfurt am Main, 2000.

Boissellier, Stéphane. *Le peuplement médiévale dans le sud du Portugal: Constitution et fonctionnement d'un réseau d'habitats et de territoires, XIIe à XVe siècles*. Lisbon, 2003.

Brettell, Caroline B. *Men Who Migrate, Women Who Wait: Population and History in a Portuguese Parish*. Princeton, NJ, 1986.

Bustos Rodríguez, Manuel. *Cádiz en el sistema atlántico. La ciudad, sus comerciantes y la actividad mercantil (1650–1830)*. Madrid, 2005.

Canny, Nicholas, ed. *Europeans on the Move: Studies on European Migration 1500–1800*. Oxford, 1994.

Carmagnani, Marcello. *Emigración mediterránea y América*. Colombres, 1994.

Castillo, Alvaro. "Population et 'richesse' en Castille durant la seconde moitié du XVIe siècle." *Annales E.S.C.* 4 (1965): 719–33.

Correa Calderón, Evaristo. *Registro de Arbitristas, Economistas y Reformadores Españoles (1500–1936). Catálogo de Impresos y Manuscritos*. Madrid, 1981.

Covarrubias, José Enrique. *En busca del hombre útil. Un estudio comparativo del utilitarismo neomercantilista en México y Europa, 1748–1833*. Mexico, 2005.

Crosby, Alfred W., Jr. *The Columbian Exchange*. Westport, 1972.

---

[12] Angolan and Mozambican labor migrants in Portugal since the 1970s; Portugese *retornados* from the colonies in Portugal since the 1970s.

Driesch, Wilhelm von den. *Die ausländischen Kaufleute während des 18. Jahrhunderts in Spanien und ihre Beteiligung am Kolonialhandel.* Cologne and Vienna, 1972.

Elliott, John. *En búsqueda de la historia atlántica.* Las Palmas de Gran Canaria, 2001.

Emmer, Pieter C. "Barriers in the Atlantic. Success and Failure of the Minor European Nations." In *Latin America and the Atlantic World. El mundo atlántico y América Latina (1500–1850). Essays in Honor of Horst Pietschmann,* edited by Renate Pieper and Peer Schmidt, 263–77. Cologne, 2005.

Fernández Arrillaga, Inmaculada. *El destierro de los jesuitas castellanos (1767–1815).* Madrid, 2004.

Fuentes Quintana, Enrique. *Economía y economistas españoles.* 2 vols. Barcelona, 1999.

González Martínez, Rosa M. *La población española. Siglos XVI, XVII y XVIII.* Madrid, 2002.

González Portilla, Manuel, ed. *Demografía urbana, migraciones y envejecimiento. IV Congreso de la Asociación de Demografía Histórica.* vol. 1. Bilbao, 1999.

Gracia Rivas, Manuel. *Los Tercios de la Gran Armada (1587–1588).* Madrid, 1989.

Hellwege, Johann. *Die spanischen Provinzialmilizen im 18. Jahrhundert.* Boppard, 1969.

Herbers, Klaus. *Geschichte Spaniens im Mittelalter. Vom Westgotenreich bis zum Ende des 15. Jahrhunderts.* Stuttgart, 2006.

Herzog, Tamar. *Defining Nations. Immigrants and Citizens in Early Modern Spain and Spanish America.* New Haven and London, 2003.

Kamen, Henry. *The War of Succession in Spain 1700–1715.* London and Bloomington, 1969.

Kleinmann, Hans-Otto. "Der atlantische Raum als Problem des europäischen Staatensystems." *Jahrbuch für Geschichte Lateinamerikas* 38 (2001): 7–30.

Laferl, Christopher F. *Die Kultur der Spanier in Österreich unter Ferdinand I. 1522–1564.* Vienna, 1997.

Lida, Clara E., ed. *Una inmigración privilegiada. Comerciantes, empresarios y profesionales españoles en México en los siglos XIX y XX.* Madrid, 1994.

Lida, Clara E. *Inmigración y exilio. Reflexiones sobre el caso español.* Mexico City, 1997.

Lida, Clara E., José Antonio Matesanz, and Josefina Zoraida Vázquez. *La Casa de España y El Colegio de México. Memoria 1938–2000.* Mexico City, 2000.

Macías Hernández, Antonio M. *La migración canaria, 1500–1980.* Colombres, 1992.

Macías, Isabelo, and Francisco Morales Padrón. *Cartas desde América 1700–1800.* Seville, 1991.

Magalhães Godinho, Vitorino. "Portuguese Emigration from the Fifteenth to the Twentieth Century: Constants and Changes." In *European Expansion and Migration: Essays on the Intercontinental Migration from Africa, Asia, and Europe,* edited by Pieter C. Emmer and Magnus Mörner: 13–48. New York and Oxford, 1992.

Martínez, José Luis. *El mundo privado de los emigrantes a Indias.* Mexico City, 1992.

Martínez Shaw, Carlos, and José María Oliva Melgar, eds. *El sistema atlántico español (siglos XVII–XIX).* Madrid, 2005.

Morales Padrón, Francisco. *Atlas Histórico Cultural de América.* 2 vols. Las Palmas de Gran Canaria, 1988.

Mörner, Magnus. *Adventurers and Proletarians: The Story of Migrants in Latin America.* Pittsburgh and Paris, 1985.

Nadal, Jordi. *La población española (siglos XV a XX).* 4th ed. Barcelona, 1976.

Nunn, Charles F. *Foreign Immigrants in Early Bourbon Mexico, 1700–1760.* Cambridge, 1979.

O'Donnell y Duque de Estrada, Hugo José. *La fuerza de desembarco de la Gran Armada contra Inglaterra (1588). Su orígen, organización y vicisitudes.* Madrid, 1989.

Pardo, José Casas, ed. *Economic Effects of the European Expansion.* Stuttgart, 1992.

Pérez Mallaina, Pablo Emilio. *Spain's Men of the Sea: Daily Life on the Indies Fleets in the Sixteenth Century.* Baltimore, 1998.

Pieper, Renate. *Die Preisrevolution in Spanien (1500–1640). Neuere Forschungsergebnisse.* Wiesbaden, 1985.

Pietschmann, Horst. "Integration und Bürokratie in Lateinamerika aus historischer Sicht." In *Integration und Kooperation in Lateinamerika. Internationale Gegenwart,* vol. 1, edited by Manfred Mols, Dieter Nohlen, and Peter Waldmann, 53–99. Paderborn, Munich, Vienna, and Zurich, 1981. (Spanish edition in: Mols, Manfred, ed. *Integración y cooperación en América Latina,* 57–117. Mainz, 1981.)

Pietschmann, Horst. *Geschichte des atlantischen Systems, 1580–1830. Ein historischer Versuch zur Erklärung der "Globalisierung" jenseits nationalgeschichtlicher Perspektiven.* Göttingen, 1998.

Pike, Frederick B. *Hispanismo, 1898–1936. Spanish Conservatives and Liberals and Their Relations with Spanish America.* Notre Dame and London, 1971.

Pimentel, Manuel, ed. "Procesos migratorios, economía y personas." *Mediterráneo Económico* http://www.fundacioncajamar.es/mediterraneo/revista/migracion.pdf.

Portillo Valdés, José María. *Revolución de nación. Orígenes de la cultura constitucional en España, 1780–1812.* Madrid, 2000.

Quatrefages, René. *Los tercios españoles (1567–1577).* Madrid, 1983.

Romano, Ruggiero. *Conjonctures opposées. La ›crise‹ du XVIIe siècle: En Europe et en Amérique ibérique.* Geneva, 1992.

Russell-Wood, Anthony J. R. *The Portuguese Empire 1415–1808.* Baltimore and London, 1998.

Sánchez Albornoz, Nicolás, ed. *Población y mano de obra en América Latina.* Madrid, 1985.

Sánchez Rubio, Rocío, and Isabel Testón Núñez. *El hilo que une. Las relaciones epistolares en el Viejo y el Nuevo Mundo (Siglos XVI–XVIII).* Mérida, 1999.

Schaub, Jean-Frédéric. *Le Portugal au temps du Comte-Duc d'Olivares (1621–1640). Le conflit de juridictions comme exercice de la politique.* Madrid, 2001.

Schmidt, Peer. *Die Privatisierung des Besitzes der Toten Hand in Spanien. Die Säkularisation unter König Karl IV. in Andalusien (1798–1808).* Stuttgart, 1990.

Serrão, Joel. *A emigração portuguesa.* 2nd ed. Lisbon, 1974.

Sousa, Fernando de, and Jorge Fernandes Alves. *Alto Minho: População e economia nos finais do setecentos.* Lisbon, 1997.

Torales Pacheco, Josefina María Cristina. *Ilustrados en la Nueva España. Los socios de la Real Sociedad Bascongada de los Amigos del País.* Mexico City, 2001.

Vieira, Alberto. "The Fortune of the Fortunates: The Islands and the Atlantic System." In *Atlantic History. History of the Atlantic System 1580–1830,* edited by Horst Pietschmann, 199–248. Göttingen, 2002.

Vilar, Juan B., and María José Vilar. *La emigración española al Norte de Africa.* Madrid, 1999.

Weber, Klaus. *Deutsche Kaufleute im Atlantikhandel 1680–1830. Unternehmen und Familien in Hamburg, Cádiz und Bordeaux.* Munich, 2004.

Wohlfeil, Rainer. *Spanien und die deutsche Erhebung 1808–1814.* Wiesbaden, 1963.

Zylberberg, Michel. *Une si douce domination. Les milieux d'affaires français et l'Espagne vers 1780–1808.* Paris, 1993.

EAST-CENTRAL EUROPE

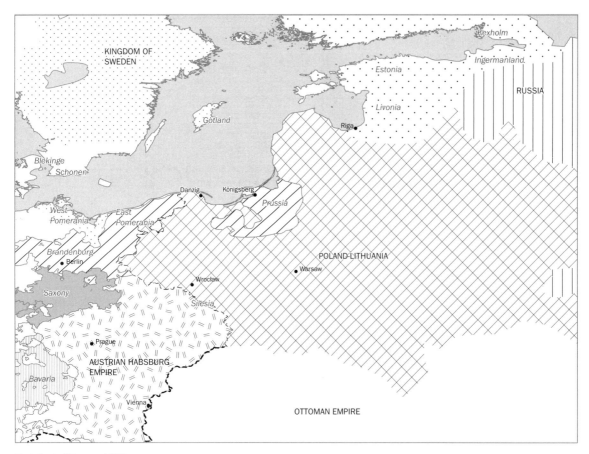

East-Central Europe 1648

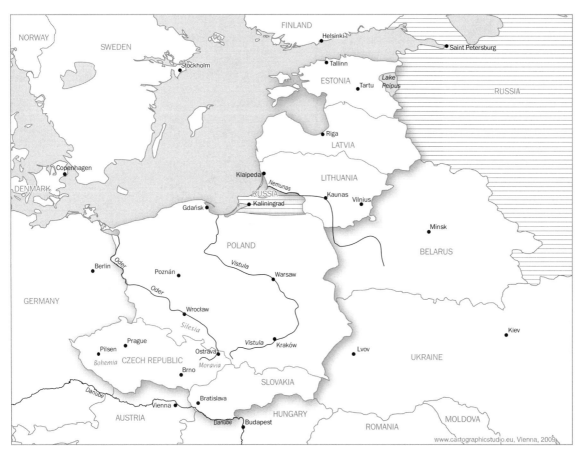

East-Central Europe 2000

THE BALTIC REGION: ESTONIA, LATVIA, LITHUANIA

Michael Garleff

Migrations occurred in the Baltic regions in various forms from the early modern period on, reaching their largest scale during and immediately after World War II. Germans immigrated on a regular basis beginning as early as the 16th/17th centuries. In the 19th century, the direction of the movement reversed: at first individuals of German extraction left, then larger and larger groups. Added to this were internal migrations by the native population triggered by industrialization, the first group emigrations to Russia, and overseas mass migration, especially from Lithuania to North America. Streams of refugees and deportations in the course of the revolutions and wars of the 20th century intensified these geographic population movements and led, along with the political upheavals, to a fundamental shift in the composition of the population. As shifts in regional and supraregional political power repeatedly redefined the role of majorities and minorities, the most diverse integrations had to be managed in the Baltic region.

The region and its boundaries

It is only in recent times that the Baltic area has been seen as a uniform entity, since Estonia, Latvia, and Lithuania embarked on a similar path of development after the end of World War I, at the earliest – both as independent states and during occupation by foreign powers. Following the union of 1569, Lithuania was increasingly drawn into Poland's sphere of influence. It was incorporated into the three partitions of Poland at the end of the 18th century (1771, 1793, 1795) and thus came under Russian rule. By contrast, Estonia and Livonia preserved their corporative privileges during the Great Nordic War (1700–21) with the Capitulation of 1710, reaffirmed in terms of international law in the Peace of Nystad in 1721. That was also true of the Duchy of Courland in 1795, which previously had been under Polish feudal suzerainty. The German-Baltic knightly estates, along with the groups of clergy and townsmen that were reinforced by continuous immigration from Germany, constituted the political, economic, social, and cultural elite, while the majority of the Estonian and Latvian peasants had no part in the political leadership of the state and fell into growing social and economic dependency. While a larger influx of German peasants did not take place, learned individuals had been joining the Baltic *Literatenstand* (estate

of men of letters) ever since the Enlightenment; the migration of czarist officials, meanwhile, remained limited.[1] On the other hand, many German Balts, especially in the 19th century, took advantage of the opportunities in the Czarist Empire to pursue careers as military officers, civil servants, or scholars.

During the process of state formation, borders shifted in 1917 when the former governments of Estonia and Livonia were turned into independent administrative units. This was the foundation for the states of Estonia and Latvia. They retained their borders after the wars of independence between 1918 and 1920, with Latvia acquiring with Lettgallen the former Polish Livonia, whose population differed from the Protestant Latvians and Estonians by their Catholic faith. Among the Catholic Lithuanians, the once close ties with Poland gave way after World War I to deep enmity, reinforced by Poland's annexation of the region around the historical capital of Vilnius (Vilna). The German Memel region (Klaipeda), meanwhile, was incorporated into Lithuania as an autonomous region.

The first phase of independence for the Baltic states ended when they were occupied by the Red Army and the German Wehrmacht in the wake of the Hitler-Stalin Pact in 1939. World War II and the Sovietization of the now Baltic Soviet Republics, with their streams of refugees and deportations, had grievous effects on the composition of the population in the Baltic region.

Only the second independence of the Baltic states, achieved during the "Singing Revolution" (1987–92) after of the collapse of the Soviet Union, offered the Baltic states the chance to rebuild free political and social structures, in part by returning deliberately to institutions of the interwar period. The altered composition of the population was a result of the resettlement of Germans and Swedes, the Holocaust, war casualties, deportations, and the emigration of Estonians, Latvians, and Lithuanians. Added to this was, finally, the accelerated influx of a Russian-speaking population, which threatened to turn Estonians and Latvians (but not Lithuanians) into minorities in their own countries during the Soviet period. The recovery of independence was followed, on the one hand, by a partial exodus of Russians, and on the other, by the return of some Balts from exile in the West.

[1] Russian elites in the Baltic states since the early modern period.

The alternating overlordship of foreign powers gave rise in the Baltic region to the special form of the settlement of military personnel. For example, the Swedish crown settled Finns in military colonies in several Livonian cities as early as 1625; like the Swedish farmers, they were free and thus different from the Estonian and Latvian peasants. However, the legal status of these immigrants deteriorated within a generation: in 1659 they became legally unfree as "hereditary colonists" (*Erbkolonisten*), and in 1668 their children were bound to the land. The sons gradually lost the original freedom of their fathers and sank into Livonian bondage by 1681. In the 19th century, the "cantonists" serving in the czarist armies formed in Estonia the core of Jewish communities that were able to establish themselves in this area outside of the Pale of Settlement. In the 20th century, finally, it was the members of the Red Army, together with Russian-speaking immigrants who had come through the state-sponsored labor migration to Estonia and Latvia, who exacerbated the integration problems in the restored states through their social separation.

Immigration and internal migration after the Northern War of 1721

Although the capitulations between the Estonian and Livonian estates and the Russian commanders had agreed on the return of all prisoners (both German nobles and commoners as well as Estonian and Latvian peasants), the disastrous destruction of the Northern War led to a strong decline in the population in Estonia and Livonia. Though Russian dignitaries received manors in the provinces, there was no larger Russian immigration; instead, measures were taken to curtail the infiltration of Russian rural dwellers from the bordering regions into Estonia.

The fate of Dorpat (Tartu) is an exemplary case for the decline and rebuilding of the Baltic cities. In 1708, Czar Peter I had the entire population taken into the Russian interior. Only in 1715 were the survivors of the 824 families, who had been deported as far as Vologda in northwestern Russia, allowed to return. With the help of immigrants, the rebuilding of the city was accomplished so swiftly that in 1785 it already had 2 preachers, 6 councilors, 35 burghers of the Great Guild and 57 of the Small Guild, who were joined by 22 nonguild Germans and several hundred Estonians. Between 1721 and 1761, more than 400 immigrants from Germany acquired civic rights in Dorpat. These academics and craftsmen no longer hailed from the once dominant sending regions of Lower Saxony, Westphalia, or Holstein, but from Mecklenburg, Pomerania, East Prussia, Thuringia, Saxony, and Silesia. Around 1790, Dorpat's population again numbered 3,600 (1,630 Germans, 1,625 Estonians, 337 Russians, 9 Swedes, 2 Poles).

The young academics who immigrated to Courland during this rebuilding phase especially from East Prussia formed the *Literatenstand*. Following their studies at European Protestant universities, young theologians, philologists, and jurists especially made their way to the Baltic region, where they were hired as *Hofmeister* (tutors) on manorial estates. With this kind of interim employment, Livonia became for many Germans once again a *Blivland* (a land in which to stay), as it had been during the Middle Ages. At the same time, some Germans also went from Russia's Baltic provinces to Germany: since the Reformation, the intellectual connections between the Baltic region and Germany had never been as strong as they were during the second half of the 18th century. Thus it was also primarily pastors who, after Pietism, spread Enlightenment to the Baltic region. Between 1711 and 1800, a total of 523 pastors were active in Livonia; of those, 270 had immigrated, mostly from Germany. In addition, Courland saw the emergence, as a result of strong immigration from East Prussia, of a rural German middling estate, which congregated around the manors, practiced crafts there, and comprised about 15,000 persons around 1800.

As part of her settlement policy, with the manifests issued between 1762 and 1764, Empress Catherine II had ordered the settlement of German colonists in the state domains (crown lands) of Hirschenhof and Helfreichshof in Livonia in 1766 and 1769. A total of 321 individuals were settled on 74 farmsteads; their path took them from the Palatinate via Jutland and Travemünde. As a legally self-contained settlement of dispersed individual farmsteads (*Einzelhofsiedlung*), the Hirschenhöfers grew into a solid farming entity that was distinct from the social structure that prevailed in the provinces. In spite of high initial child mortality, the population of the settlement grew to 4,444 by 1897 and stood at around 8,000 in 1914, but of those only about 2,000 were still living in the colony. The majority of the Hirschenhöfers migrated into Baltic rural communities and cities and to central Russia, though 60% headed for Riga, where they formed an essential part of the German commercial middle class and comprised about 5,000 persons in the 1930s. In contrast to the stagnant and then declining number of German Balts, the number of Hirschenhöfers increased substantially.[2]

Integration and emigration as a result of industrialization and Russification

Although the Baltic agrarian reforms at the beginning of the 19th century broke open the estate order of the Baltic Sea provinces economically, they cemented it politically. A core stock of productive Estonian and Latvian individual farms was able to develop, and their economic success resulted in a pronounced social differentiation: the landowning farmers were now joined also by tenant farmers and agricultural workers. On the whole, the intensification of agriculture along with industrialization and the urbanization it entailed offered opportunities also to Estonians and Latvians to advance into various professions. Several surges of modernization thus led to profound changes in the countryside and the cities: freedom of movement formed the precondition for new occupational branches, and urbanization transcended

---

[2] Palatines in Europe since the 17th century.

local limitations. The cities in the Estonian settlement area became more and more "Estonian," those in the Latvian area more and more "Latvian."

Urbanization led to a profound transformation in Estonia, Livonia, and Kurland, but not so in the Lithuanian governments with their stronger agrarian imprint. The background to this divergent development of Estonian and Livonian cities compared to Lithuanian cities was the effects of railroad construction, which took place at different times in the various regions. Following a direct link-up to the central grain-growing regions of southern Russia, Riga became exceedingly important as a seaport, and with the influx from the countryside, it increased its population fivefold within a mere generation and a half, from 103,000 in 1871 to more than 282,000 in 1897, and 520,000 in 1913. While Reval (Tallinn) developed into the second-largest import port of the Russian Empire, in the 1860–70s other cities in the Estonian settlement area also tripled their population within a generation. As a result, the Estonian and Latvian share of the population rose sharply in Reval and Riga, whereas in Lithuanian cities it was the share of Russians, Poles, and Jews that grew. Until the 20th century, the Lithuanians were a minority in Vilnius and Kaunas. In Riga in 1867, 43% of a population of about 103,000 were Germans and 23.5% Latvians: in 1913 the city's population was up to 514,500, of which just under 20% were still German, while 40% were already Latvians.

The transformation in agriculture in the wake of agrarian reforms also opened the way for the cultural emancipation of the Balts. Of crucial importance in this process of social and political differentiation was the degree of literacy. Whereas in 1897 only 30% of young people and adults in the interior Russian governments could read, the literacy rate was 95% in Estonia and over 92% in Livonia.

The emigration of German Balts to Germany began in 1860 with individual writers and scientists. The backdrop was Russification, which reached its high point in 1893 with the renaming of the university town of Dorpat to Yuryev, when several professors who were citizens of the German Reich also left the university because of the obligation to teach in Russian. The number of Russians studying here now surged quickly from 100 to 1,000, and more and more Estonians and Latvians advanced to higher positions via a Russian and instead of a German education.

In Lithuania, Russification took the added form of the settlement of Russian colonists, which was driven by strategic considerations. Along the most important railroad lines, Russians were settled in part on demesne land, in part on confiscated land – a corresponding process did not occur in the Baltic Sea provinces. One reaction to the rising pressure of Russian rule was the overseas emigration of Lithuanians (including Jews), which began at the end of the 1850s and increased strongly after 1864. At the beginning of the 1880s, the USA was already home to Lithuanian centers of settlement with several tens of thousands of immigrants, especially in and around Chicago. This movement continued, with the result that one-third of Lithuanians were already living overseas before World War I, primarily in the USA and Canada.

The emigration of Estonian individuals and groups to Russia had taken place quite early as a result of the upheavals of war. Thus, since the 16th century scattered settlements had emerged east of Lake Peipus. Even larger was the number of Estonians in St. Petersburg since the 18th century, where religious services in the Estonian language and separate church schools had existed since 1786. Estonians are said to have numbered 23,000 at the beginning of the 19th century, compared to only 7,000 Latvians. In the wake of failed harvests and peasant unrest, the middle of the 19th century witnessed an outflow of Estonian peasants to Samara and Saratov. Later, several hundred Estonians moved to the Caucasus and Crimea (Government of Tauria) as part of a religious-social movement. Emigration to Siberia began in 1878–80 and was followed a decade later by onward migration to the Far East. In both regions, released prisoners had previously already established Estonian settlement nuclei, which developed by 1897 into settlements with a total of 7,773 inhabitants. Beginning in the 1860s, the northwestern Russian trans-Peipus region became the primary destination of Estonian migration to Russia, with the city of Gdov as the center. In the environs of Gdov in 1917, Estonians numbered 45,000, no less than 23% of the population.

Flight and deportation from the Russian Revolution from 1905 to World War I

The revolutionary crisis of 1905–6 laid bare the political tensions between a German upper class, Russian state power, and an ethnic minority population in the Baltic Sea provinces. Revolutionary violence and punitive expeditions, in the course of which more than 4,500 suspects were banished to Siberia or stripped of their citizenship, permanently poisoned relations between the various population groups. Among the German Balts, the waning of the former solidarity with the rural population was apparent, not least, in the accelerated settlement of 15,000–20,000 German agrarian settlers from Volhynia in Courland and Livonia, where they were deployed as owners, tenants, or farmhands. The Estonian and Latvian revolutionary movement, with its fusion of national and social demands, was directed against the Russian aristocracy and the German-Baltic upper class. Lithuanian national groups allied themselves with the Catholic Church against Russian Orthodoxy, while the Estonian and Latvians opposed especially the Protestant territorial churches.

World War I had far-reaching consequences for the conditions of migration. In 1915, more than 750,000 Latvians from Courland and Livonia had fled or been evacuated to Russia with the retreating army. This was tantamount to three-fifths of the population in these regions or more than one-third of the entire Latvian population. In the destination areas, Latvian and Lithuanian refugees worked in the factories that had been moved to St. Petersburg, Charkiv, and Moscow and formed separate communities. Their Aid Committees developed into national gathering points with growing political importance, which Latvians and Estonians expressed with impressive mass demonstrations in the Russian capital. Moreover, the German occupation of Courland led to the creation of the first national Estonian military units within the czarist army; they eventually grew to a size of 130,000 men and took on an important function for the further development of Latvian national consciousness.

Germany's occupation policy in the Baltic region during World War I was determined, among other things, by claims to imperial power and by folkish-racial biological ideas; in the process, Germany consistently pursued annexationist goals. The agrarian nobility and propertied bourgeoisie of the German Balts were supposed to support a monarchist-conservative system of government. To "win the land for Germandom," plans called for a mass settlement of German farmers. The outcome of World War I had the opposite result, namely a mass flight of German Balts, many of whom – as had already been the case after the Revolution of 1905–6 – remained in Germany. In spite of the return of Baltic German refugees from Russia, the total number of Germans in Estonia and Latvia dropped by more than half between 1914 and 1934–5, from about 162,000 to 78,500.

Consolidation of the Baltic population in the interwar period

The establishment of independent Baltic states inaugurated a consolidation phase, at the beginning of which stood the return of many Balts and the emigration of more German Balts. Population losses were most severe in Latvia at 38.5%, and lowest, at 14.3%, in Estonia, which was directly affected by the events of the war fairly late. Of the 550,000 refugees from Lithuania in Russia at the beginning of 1918, nearly 350,000 had returned by 1924. Their varied social and ethnic structure strained the process of state formation, since the multiple identities could not be reconciled with the goal of a homogenous national state. As a result, the policy of repatriation became increasingly rigid to the middle of 1922. In fact, non-Lithuanian groups, especially the Jews, were even seen as a threat to the stability of the country. While all but 35,000 of the 250,000 ethnic Lithuanian refugees returned, only half of all Jewish refugees came back (80,000). In spite of the losses in World War I and the emigration of around 80,000 overseas by 1939, most of whom in the 1930s were Jews who went to Palestine, North America, and South Africa, Lithuania's population grew again rapidly.

The far-reaching agrarian reforms did have consequences for the national minorities: among other things, the German-Baltic large landowners were dispossessed. Still, the young Baltic republics offered the national minorities various rights of cultural autonomy and thus the possibility to integrate. This was most successful in Estonia (Cultural Autonomy Law of 1925) and, until the coup of 1934, also in Latvia (School Autonomy 1919), while Lithuania embarked upon the path to authoritarian forms of government as early as 1926. The

tensions, exacerbated by the growth of nationalist currents, had repercussions above all for the German and in part also for the Jewish minority, whose possibilities of living were increasingly restricted.

Resettlement, deportation, and flight during World War II

World War II constituted a profound disruption of the composition of the population, in three respects: through the resettlement of the Germans, the mass murder of the Jews, and the state-organized immigration of industrial workers after the end of the war.

Forced migrations began in the fall of 1939 in the wake of the Hitler-Stalin pact with the "dictated option" (*Loeber*) of the resettlement of the German Balts. In the German-Soviet Border and Friendship Treaty of 28 September 1939, the USSR, in a "Secret Protocol," had granted "Reich citizens and other persons of German extraction resident" in its sphere of interest the option of resettling to Germany. Most German Balts in Estonia and Latvia resettled: had they stayed, they would have been in danger of suffering the same fate that befell the middle-class Estonians and Latvians in the deportations that soon began. After the signing of resettlement treaties, the main resettlement action, which was completed by year's end, comprised around 14,000 from Estonia and around 52,000 from Latvia. A part of those who had remained behind then participated in the follow-up resettlement in the spring of 1940 and above all in the last resettlement following Soviet occupation in 1941. Among the 7,000 follow-up resettlers from Estonia and the 10,000 from Latvia in 1941 there were also about 3,500 Estonians and Latvians who escaped the threat of arrest this way. On the basis of agreements between the Swedish government and the occupying powers in 1940 and 1941, 7,000–8,000 Estonian Swedes living along the coast and on the islands were also resettled in Sweden.

Initially, the German population of Lithuania was not affected by this resettlement. It was only on the basis of a German-Soviet resettlement agreement on 10 January 1941 that the Lithuanian Germans were resettled to the Warthegau annexed by Germany, and all Lithuanians, Russians, and Belarusians from the Memelland and the Suvalki region to now Soviet-dominated Lithuania. In February–March 1941, 50,142 persons thus left Lithuania, among them nearly 20,000 Lithuanians who escaped Soviet occupation. From the German-controlled territory, 11,867 Lithuanians, 8,915 Russians, 57 Belarusians, and 50 persons of other nationalities were moved to Soviet Lithuania.[3]

The occupation of all of Lithuania by German troops was followed in 1942–3 by a return-settlement action that brought 20,000–30,000 of the resettled Lithuanian Germans back to their old homes. For the most part, the German authorities simultaneously expelled the Polish, Russian, and Lithuanian

---

[3] Ethnic Germans (*Volksdeutsche*) in the German Reich and in German-occupied territories in World War II.

population – a unique example for the forcible establishment of a German colony within a non-German majority population. The returning Germans set out for the West once again in the summer of 1944.[4]

Already in the wake of the first Soviet occupation, authorities began with the forced resettlement of "anti-Soviet elements" in November 1940, among them chiefly members of the former bourgeois and Social Democratic parties, officers, nobles, businesspeople, and landowners. As part of the mass deportations in June 1941, about 11,000 people from Estonia, 16,000 from Latvia, and 21,000 from Lithuania were deported into the interior of the Soviet Union.

German occupation in the summer of 1941 merely changed the forms of despotic power in the Baltic region, which was to be turned into a "German land" through the "Germanization" of the "racially positive elements," the colonization of "Germanic peoples," and the removal and liquidation of "undesirable national groups." The Jewish population was nearly completely exterminated through mass shootings. Approximately 1,000 Jews were killed in Estonia, 66,000 in Latvia, and 170,000 in Lithuania.

In 1944–5, tens of thousands fled the reach of the Soviet occupying power: 66,000 Lithuanians, 120,000 Latvians, and 80,000 Estonians, the majority civilians, but also several thousand who had served as soldiers under German command. Most came to Germany, where they were housed in camps for displaced persons (DPs). Many of them refused repatriation into their Soviet-occupied homelands out of fear of being punished as collaborators. The Soviet Union, however, regarded these Baltic refugees as its citizens and demanded their return. There were forced extraditions under tragic circumstances, and even mass suicides to avoid return. It was only through a decision by the United Nations (UN) General Assembly at the beginning of 1946 that the eastern European DPs were recognized as refugees and could no longer be repatriated against their will into the Soviet sphere of influence if they were afraid of being persecuted there.

In December 1946, the UNRRA (United Nations Relief and Rehabilitation Administration) was looking after 642,750 DPs worldwide. Of those, 558,850 were living in the western occupation zones of Germany; and of those, 27% were from the Baltic countries. Under the leadership of the IRO (International Refugee Organisation), founded in 1947 as the successor to the UNRRA, more than 27,000 Estonians and 100,000 Latvians were able to leave Germany by 1952. Estonians migrated chiefly to Sweden (20,000), Canada (19,000), the USA (16,000), and Australia (6,500). The majority of Latvians moved to the USA (45,000), Australia (21,000), Great Britain (18,000), and Canada (13,000).

A number of political exile organizations strove, with the help of numerous appeals to Western governments and at international forums, to sustain the legal continuity of the Baltic states in the awareness of the public and to remind the world of the occupation of their countries. A crucial role was also played by the cultural activities of the political refugees. Initial efforts in the DP camps gave rise to numerous national schools, scientific institutions, and even a "Baltic University" in Pinneberg. A major contribution to these endeavors to preserve the mother tongue and the cultural identity came from the Baltic writers who had gone to the West. At the beginning of the 21st century, more than 500,000 Lithuanians, more than 175,000 Latvians, and about 150,000 Estonians are living outside the Baltic states.[5]

The exceedingly multilayered, forced migration during World War II led to an enormous decline in the population. As a result, at the end of the war no other European country had suffered greater losses than the Baltic states: Lettland, 30%; Estonia, 25%; Lithuania, 15%. Between 1939 and 1945, 17% of Estonia's prewar population, 21% of Latvia's, and 6% of Lithuania's left because of resettlements, deportations, forced recruitment for "labor service" or military service, and flight from either the Soviet or the German occupation troops (see Table 1).[6]

The consequences of Sovietization for the Baltic Soviet Republics and for the conditions of migration

Following the retreat of the Germans, the measures of Sovietization started up again in 1944–5. They were aimed at giving the Baltic region economic and social structures identical to those in the Soviet Union. The deportation of the educated strata was now followed by the mass deportation of prosperous farmers.

The new rounds of deportations affected tens of thousands of Estonians, Latvians, and especially Lithuanians, mostly women and children. Parallel to the forced collectivization in agriculture after 1949, there was a forced industrialization, which led to fundamental structural changes. The middling farmers – the primary social class in the era of independence – were denounced as "kulaks" and forced into collective farms. In the spring of 1949 alone, a total of 90,000 Latvians, Lithuanians, and Estonians were affected by the deportations. The rising need for workers and the Sovietization of the administrative and party apparatuses triggered a steady immigration of Russians, but also of Estonians and Latvians from other parts of the Soviet Union, who often acted as pacesetters of Sovietization in positions of leadership. This resulted in a profound change in the ethnic composition of the overall population. The share of Latvians declined from about 76% in 1935 to 62% in 1959 and 52% in 1989, that of the Estonians dropped from 88% in 1934 to 74.6% in 1959 and 61.5% in 1989. During the same period, the Russian-speaking population (Russians, Belarusians, Ukrainians) rose in Latvia from 12.1% to 42.3%, and in

---

[4] German refugees and expellees from eastern, east-central, and south-eastern Europe in Germany and Austria since the end of World War II.

[5] Displaced persons (DPs) in Europe since the end of World War II.

[6] Estonian and Latvian refugees in Sweden after World War II; forced laborers in Germany and German-occupied Europe during World War II.

Table 1. Population development in the Baltic states (without new immigration) during and after World War II

	Estonia	Latvia	Lithuania
Population mid-October 1939 (Lithuania: with Vilna region, without Memel region)	1,130,000	2,000,000	2,950,000
Emigration November 1939 to May 1941 (incl. the German Balts)	–20,000	–70,000	–50,000
Soviet deportations and executions 1940–1	–15,000	–35,000	–35,000
Mobilization for the Soviet army 1941 and 1944–5	–35,000	–20,000	–60,000
Flight into the Soviet Union 1941	–30,000	–40,000	–20,000
Executions and deportations under German rule 1941–4 (among them ca. 250,000 Jews)	–10,000	–90,000	–200,000
Forced laborers brought to Germany 1941–4	–15,000	–35,000	–75,000
Killed as soldiers on the German side	–15,000	–40,000	–10,000
Soviet executions and deportations 1944–5	–30,000	–70,000	–50,000
Flight to the West 1942–5 (chiefly via Scandinavia)	–60,000	–100,000	–50,000
Return of forced laborers taken to Germany 1945	+5,000	+10,000	+20,000
Return from the Soviet Union and the Soviet army 1944–5	+20,000	+20,000	+20,000
Emigration to Poland	–	–	–150,000
Population development from territorial gains and losses 1940–5 (Estonia and Latvia: loss of strips of territory to the Russian Soviet Republic; Lithuania: gain of some White Russian territories and the Memel region)	–70,000	–50,000	+125,000
Other losses	–5,000	–80,000	–15,000
Population end of 1945	850,000	1,400,000	2,400,000
Soviet deportations 1946–53	–80,000	–100,000	–260,000
Victims of the partisan war	–15,000	–25,000	–50,000
Return from the Soviet Union or the Soviet army after 1945	+100,000	+100,000	+40,000
Immigration of Russian, Belarusians, and Ukrainians	+230,000	+535,000	+160,00
Excess of births over deaths	+70,000	+100,000	+350,000
Population beginning of 1955	1,155,000	2,010,000	2,640,000

Source: Helmut Meyer, "Geschichte der baltischen Länder," *Geschichte* 3 (1989): 37.

Table 2. National composition and languages of the population of Estonia

| | Number and percentage | | | | | | Language skills 1989 | | |
| | 1934 | | 1959 | | 1989 | | National | Second language | |
	Absolute	%	Absolute	%	Absolute	%	Language	Estonian	Russian
Total population	1,126,413		1,196,791		1,565,662		94.0	5.5	24.1
Estonians	993,496	88.2	892,653	74.6	963,269	61.5	98.9	0.6	33.6
Russians	92,656	8.2	240,227	20.1	474,815	30.3	98.6	13.7	1.1
Ukrainians	–	–	15,769	1.3	48,273	3.1	44.2	6.9	39.7
Belarusians	–	–	10,930	0.9	27,711	1.8	31.9	6.1	29.9
Finns	–	–	16,699	1.4	16,622	1.1	31.0	33.3	38.9
Jews	4,434	0.4	5,436	0.5	4,613	0.3	12.4	26.1	13.0
Tatars	–	–	1,535	–	4,058	0.3	55.4	6.3	51.2
Germans	16,345	1.5	–	–	3,466	0.2	36.0	14.7	35.5
Latvians	5,435	0.5	2,888	0.2	3,135	0.2	57.2	21.5	42.6
Poles	–	–	2,256	0.2	3,008	0.2	20.0	13.2	29.0
Lithuanians	–	–	1,616	0.1	2,568	0.2	62.7	12.6	56.3
Armenians	–	–	–	–	1,669	0.1	50.1	8.4	44.7
Azerbaijani	–	–	–	–	1,238	0.1	70.2	3.9	57.3
Moldavians	–	–	–	–	1,215	0.1	54.6	5.0	51.9
Chuvashi	–	–	–	–	1,163	0.1	47.5	5.3	45.0

Source: Census results in 1989, in *Baltisches Jahrbuch* 6 (1989): 266.

Table 3. National composition and languages of the population of Latvia

| | Number and percentage | | | | | | Language skills 1989 | | |
| | 1935 | | 1959 | | 1989 | | National | Second language | |
	Absolute	%	Absolute	%	Absolute	%	Language	Lithuanian	Russian
Total population	1,950,502		2,093,985		2,666,567		89.9	10.4	39.5
Lithuanians	1,427,612	75.7	1,297,881	62.0	1,387,646	52.0	97.4	1.3	65.7
Russians	206,499	10.6	556,448	26.6	905,515	34.0	98.8	21.1	1.1
Belarusians	26,867	1.4	61,587	2.9	119,702	4.5	32.2	15.5	29.7
Poles	48,949	2.5	59,774	2.9	60,388	2.3	27.1	22.8	33.8
Ukrainians	1,844	0.1	29,440	1.4	92,101	3.5	49.5	8.9	43.8
Lithuanians	22,913	1.2	32,383	1.5	34,630	1.3	63.9	40.3	36.0
Jews	93,479	4.8	36,592	1.8	22,897	0.9	22.5	27.0	17.5
Gypsies	–	–	4,301	0.2	7,044	0.3	84.7	52.3	28.6
Tatars	–	–	1,836	0.1	4,828	0.2	46.7	6.6	44.6
Germans	62,144	3.2	1,610	0.1	3,774	0.1	34.0	16.6	36.1
Estonians	7,014	0.4	4,610	0.2	3,312	0.1	50.3	28.7	40.1
Moldavians	–	–	230	–	3,223	0.1	69.0	7.7	60.6
Armenians	–	–	1,060	0.1	3,069	0.1	53.1	8.1	67.6
Azerbaijani	–	–	–	–	2,765	0.1	72.4	5.5	60.1
Chuvashi	–	–	–	–	1,491	0.1	47.9	6.8	44.8

Source: Census results in 1989, in *Baltisches Jahrbuch* 6 (1989): 264.

Table 4. National composition and languages of the population in Lithuania

| | Number and percentage | | | | | | Language skills 1989 | | |
| | 1923 | | 1959 | | 1989 | | National | Second language | |
	Absolute	%	Absolute	%	Absolute	%	Language	Lithuanian	Russian
Total population	2,158,159		2,711,445		3,673,362		99.6	0.2	37.4
Lithuanians	1,739,489	80.6	2,150,767	79.3	2,924,048	79.6	99.6	0.2	37.4
Russians	50,727	2.3	231,014	8.5	345,597	9.4	95.6	33.5	3.3
Poles	65,628	3.0	230,107	8.5	257,988	7.0	84.8	15.5	57.9
Belarusians	4,421	0.2	30,256	1.1	63,076	1.7	40.4	17.0	34.7
Ukrainians	–	–	17,692	0.7	44,397	1.2	50.9	16.9	41.9
Jews	154,321	7.2	24,672	0.9	12,312	0.3	35.7	38.0	22.2
Latvians	14,883	0.7	6,318	0.2	4,228	0.1	68.6	43.7	29.3
Tatars	–	–	3,023	0.1	5,107	0.1	32.0	14.3	43.5
Germans	88,568	4.1	11,166	0.4	2,058	0.1	42.1	35.7	26.1
Gypsies	–	–	1,238	–	2,718	0.1	81.8	45.2	26.5
Armenians	–	–	471	–	1,648	–	60.9	13.3	48.5
Usbeks	–	–	–	–	1,452	–	88.2	3.7	64.1
Moldavians	–	–	164	–	1,448	–	70.9	10.7	58.4

Source: Census results in 1989, in *Baltisches Jahrbuch* 6 (1989): 265.

Estonia from 8.2% to 35.2%. The changes in Lithuania were less profound: the share of Lithuanians remained nearly constant: from 80.6% in 1923 to 79.3% in 1959 to 79.6% in 1989. However, the share of Russian-speakers increased during that same period from 2.5% to 12.3% (see Tables 2, 3, and 4).

To be sure, the motto in cultural life and the educational system was "National in form, Socialist in content," and the national languages, literatures, or elements of folk culture were officially promoted. However, these measures served the "rapprochement of the national cultures," the goal being the creation of a "uniform, multinational Soviet culture." As a result, the Balts generally had to defend their ethnic autonomy against the ideal of the "Soviet man." Among the first actions by the new Soviet power was the transfer of the Transnarva regions and large sections of the Petschur district (Petseri) to the Russian Socialist Federated Soviet Republic (RSFSR), a total of 5% of the Estonian territory, with which Estonia also lost a large portion of its Russian and Setukesian inhabitants. After changes to the constitutions (1948 in Latvia, 1950 in Lithuania, 1953 in Estonia), the governmental structures of the Baltic republics were assimilated to the system of the USSR, which downgraded them to administrative units of a centrally governed state with, at best, cultural autonomy.

In a second land reform in 1944, the Soviet power had confiscated and distributed the land of the "emigrants, collaborators, and speculators." The struggle over collectivization intensified in 1947, and mass deportations after the Soviet model affected around 40,000 farmers in Estonia in 1949. The number of collectively managed farms rose from 530 to 3,017, and by 1959 there were no more private farms.

In Latvia, the Socialist transformation was completed by 1950. The Soviet rulers sought to resolve the conflict with the Latvian population's desire for autonomy by undermining the internal structures of the opposition. To that end, they employed, as they did in the Baltic sister republics, a diverse range of tools. The repression that began immediately was also here targeted against certain social groups. After the mass persecution of the old elites in 1940–1, the chief victims in 1944–5 were farmers. By 1951, 13%–17% of the Latvian population had fallen victim to this persecution. Measures of social disciplining created a strong sense of uncertainty, and the mutual distrust it fostered led to an "atomization" of society.

One element in the effort to secure Soviet rule was the encouragement of immigration by Russians. While the Russians believed they were helping the Balts establish Socialism after their "liberation," the latter saw them as unwelcome "colonialists." The state-promoted alienation between the two ethnic groups deepened the conflict between the Balts striving for emancipation and the Russians. However, the strong decline in the population ratio of Estonians and Latvians to Russians was the result not only of immigration, but also of war, flight, and repression. Thus, four decades after 1945, Latvians, Estonians, and Jews were the only European population groups whose disproportional decline during World War II had still not been made up.

Latvia and Estonia witnessed a state-sponsored transition to states with two large population groups, a process that was accelerated by a complex policy of the Russification of public life and a repression of the Latvian and Estonian languages. Bilinguality was a precondition for the emergence of a dual identity as a preliminary stage on the road to a uniform, Russian-speaking Soviet nation. The goal of this policy was thus the long-term assimilation of the non-Russians. A varied opposition to this development arose in all three Baltic states.

While Estonia and Latvia had lost smaller slices of territory during the transition to Soviet rule, Lithuania became significantly larger through the annexation of the Vilna region in 1939–40 and the Memel region in 1948. The Poles living in Lithuania were resettled in the People's Republic of Poland. This affected about 178,000 individuals; conversely,

an unknown number of Lithuanians came from the Suvalki region to Lithuania. Of the 134,000 inhabitants of the Memel region in 1941, about 86,000 made their way to West Germany by 1965 through flight and emigration; if we subtract the victims of war and deportations, only 10,000 of those inhabitants were left in the Memel region (Klaipeda).

After World War II, the Soviet Union defeated a partisan movement in all three Baltic states. The fighting in Lithuania lasted until 1953 and claimed more than 40,000 victims; Lithuanian sources put the number at nearly 60,000. About 350,000 farmers, intellectuals, and other political undesirables were deported. Alongside measures aimed at nationalization and collectivization that were comparable to those in Estonia and Latvia, the struggle in Lithuania was directed above all against the Catholic Church as the chief ideological enemy. As a result, a third of the clergy was also affected by the mass deportations.

Integration problems since independence in 1990

The transformation processes following the declarations of independence by the Baltic states in 1990 concerned especially the domestic political problem areas of minority law, citizenship law, and language. While problems of integration could be resolved relatively quickly in Lithuania, given the small size of the Russian-speaking population, the situation was substantially more conflict-laden in Estonia and Latvia.

Estonia and Latvia had never been uniform national states, but the ethnic composition of the population had now changed drastically through the high proportion of Russians. In Lithuania, meanwhile, old conflicts with the Polish minority continued to smolder, even if the issues were no longer the sorts of intense border conflicts that had occurred during the interwar period. In 1990, as already in 1918–20, the shaping of minority law brought together the goal of a cohesive national state with the granting of far-reaching rights of democratic participation. Among other things, this found expression in the special protection for the national language and in the granting of rights of cultural autonomy for ethnic minorities.

One central problem in all of this was in general the loyalty to the state on the part of all nationalities concerned. What is required is not only the unconditional recognition of the state's right to exist and exercise sovereignty (external loyalty) by the various groups, but also their willingness, as members of a minority, to participate actively in the tasks of the state and thus in all affairs of the political nation that is experienced as the binding community (internal loyalty).

As a result of mass migrations during and after the war, the Baltic titular nations were in danger of becoming a minority in their own countries. The directed immigration from the Soviet Union into the Baltic republic to secure Russian rule was intended to create a new Russian-speaking "Soviet people," with the goal of a long-term assimilation of the Estonian, Latvian, and Lithuanian nations. One serious consequence of this Soviet occupation policy was thus the existence of a large and initially integration-unwilling group of foreign immigrants. Of crucial significance for the nationalities policy of the Baltic states, which at the beginning of the 21st century is consciously connecting back to the minorities policy of the interwar period, is that it has become a function of European-Russian relations. That has given rise to the seeming paradox that a minority policy, however liberal it may be compared to other European states, will also be evaluated also as an element of foreign and security policy: especially the large, nonintegrated, Russian-speaking population group that immigrated after World War II and has not Estonian or Latvian citizenship is regarded by the European Union as a security risk along Europe's outer border.

After the Baltic states had become independent, this group initially did not receive a Latvian or Estonian equivalent of the lapsed Soviet passport, a situation that made many stateless. However, the political framework repeatedly compelled especially Estonia and Latvia to make compromises and come up with transitional regulations after 1990, especially on the issue of citizenship, whereby these states had to continuously mark out the boundary where they had to resist political blackmail by the Organization for Security and Co-operation in Europe (OSCE), the European Union (EU), and the North Atlantic Treaty Organization (NATO), on the one side, and Russia, on the other. At the beginning of the 21st century, nationalization was determined largely by language and civic tests which the Russian-speaking immigrants saw as discriminatory. Latvia was still home to more than 400,000 stateless individuals in 2005, Estonia to more than 130,000.

The policy regarding nationality as implemented by the Baltic parliaments and governments is based on the older understanding of a conservationist and protective minority policy. It confronts outside expectations about the creation of a new state identity, one that is based on a gradual assimilation of the minorities as part of a – in part overdue – modernization of the state and society. In the process, in everyday life ethnic factors generally seem to take a backseat to social and ethical concerns. For example, problems such as poverty, crime, or the environment now loom larger in the daily life of the people than ethnicity. Although the latter retains its importance in the cultural sphere, in other respects it is receding increasingly into the background.

The undoubted persistence of differences between the Baltic population and Russian-speaking immigrants should be continuously dismantled in the areas of citizenship and language laws, but that requires the understanding on the part of the Russian-speaking population that one should learn the language and culture of a country in which one wishes to live permanently.

One path toward integration could be a differentiated, multilingual school system, one that avoids and transcends the national lopsidedness of Russian-only (or Estonian-only or Latvian-only) schools. The contradictions between political intent and everyday practice that is occasionally still evident in the official school policy must be overcome, given the reciprocal interaction of assimilation, linguistic pluralism, and linguistic separation. The overarching long-term goal should be a democratically integrated and multiethnic democracy in which communication takes place in the respective national language. Other models posit the necessity of a dual integration process, one that achieves both the integration of the immigrants into the societies of Estonia, Latvia, and Lithuania, and the integration of the Baltic societies into Europe.

REFERENCES

Andræ, Carl Göran. *Sverige och den stora flykten från Estland 1943–1944*. Stockholm, 2004.

Angermann, Norbert, Michael Garleff, and Wilhelm Lenz, eds. *Ostseeprovinzen, Baltische Staaten und das Nationale. Festschrift für Gert von Pistohlkors zum 70. Geburtstag.* Münster, 2005.

Balkelis, Tomas. "Nation-Building and World War I Refugees in Lithuania, 1918–1924." *Journal of Baltic Studies* 34 (2003): 432–56.

Hehn, Jürgen von. *Die Umsiedlung der baltischen Deutschen – das letzte Kapitel baltischdeutscher Geschichte.* Marburg, 1982.

Hermann, Arthur. "Litauendeutsche zwischen Litauen und Deutschland 1939–1960." In *Jahrestagung 1989/90*, edited by Litauisches Kulturinstitut, 67–79. Lampertheim, 1991.

Hirschhausen, Ulrike von. "Die Wahrnehmung des Wandels: Migration, soziale Mobilität und Mentalitäten in Riga 1867–1914." *Zeitschrift für Ostforschung* 48 (1999): 475–523.

Jundzis, Tālavs, ed. *The Baltic States at Historical Crossroads: Political, Economic, and Legal Problems and Opportunities in the Context of International Co-operation at the Beginning of the 21st Century.* 2nd ed. Riga, 2001.

Kaubrys, Saulius. "Demographic Data on the Development of the German Community in Lithuania (1918–1939)." *Journal of Baltic Studies* 29 (1998): 253–60.

Kielyte, Julda, and d'Artis Kancs. "Migration in the Enlarged European Union: Empirical Evidence for Labour Mobility in the Baltic States." *Journal of Baltic Studies* 33 (2002): 259–79.

Loeber, Dietrich A. *Diktierte Option. Die Umsiedlung der Deutsch-Balten aus Estland und Lettland.* Neumünster, 1972.

Myllyniemi, Seppo. *Die Neuordnung der Baltischen Länder 1941–1944. Zum nationalsozialistischen Gehalt der deutschen Besatzungspolitik.* Helsinki, 1973.

Nollendorfs, Valters, and Erwin Oberländer, eds. *The Hidden and Forbidden History of Latvia under Soviet and Nazi Occupations 1940–1991.* Riga, 2005.

Pistohlkors, Gert von, Andrejs Plakans, and Paul Kaegbein, eds. *Bevölkerungsverschiebungen und sozialer Wandel in den baltischen Provinzen Rußlands 1850–1914.* Lüneburg, 1995.

Pistohlkors, Gert von, and Matthias Weber, eds. *Staatliche Einheit und nationale Vielfalt im Baltikum. Festschrift für Prof. Dr. Michael Garleff zum 65. Geburtstag.* Munich, 2005.

Raun, Toivo U. "Estonian Emigration within the Russian Empire, 1860–1917." *Journal of Baltic Studies* 17 (1986): 350–63.

Saar, Ellu, and Mikk Titma. *Migrationsströme im sowjetisierten Baltikum und ihre Nachwirkungen auf die baltischen Staaten nach Wiederherstellung der Selbständigkeit.* Cologne, 1992.

Schlau, Wilfried. "Zur demographischen Entwicklung in den baltischen Ländern seit der Mitte des 19. Jahrhunderts." *Zeitschrift für Ostforschung* 37 (1988): 581–96.

Schlau, Wilfried, ed. *Tausend Jahre Nachbarschaft. Die Völker des baltischen Raumes und die Deutschen.* Munich, 1995.

Schlau, Wilfried, ed. *Sozialgeschichte der baltischen Deutschen.* 2nd ed. Cologne, 2000.

Stossun, Harry. *Die Umsiedlungen der Deutschen aus Litauen während des Zweiten Weltkrieges.* Marburg, 1993.

Strods, Heinrihs, and Matthew Kott. "The File on Operation 'Priboi': A Re-Assessment of the Mass Deportation of 1949." *Journal of Baltic Studies* 23 (2002): 1–36.

Taagepera, Rein. "Litauen, Lettland, Estland 1940–1980. Gemeinsamkeiten und Unterschiede." In *Auch wir sind Europa. Zur jüngeren Geschichte und aktuellen Entwicklung des Baltikums*, edited by Ruth Kibelka, 21–35. Berlin, 1991.

Tegeler, Tillmann. "Esten, Letten und Litauer in der Britischen Besatzungszone Deutschlands. Aus Akten des Foreign Office." *Jahrbücher für Geschichte Osteuropas*, N.F. 53 (2005): 42–57.

Wittram, Heinrich, ed. *Der ethnische Wandel im Baltikum zwischen 1850–1950.* Lüneburg, 2005.

POLAND

Dorota Praszałowicz

During Poland's early modern history, far more people emigrated than immigrated. The country has experienced larger influxes only during a few phases of the early modern period and since the turn of the 20th century. Since the beginning of the 19th century, at least 7 million people have left Poland, whose population stood at more than 38 million in 2005. Mass emigrations commenced in the middle of the 19th century; they reached their height at the beginning of the 20th century and have continued, with a few interruptions, until the early 21st century.

Today, at least 15 million people of Polish extraction live outside Poland around the world. The Polish diaspora (Polonia) has become a central element in Polish collective memory. Among the most important target countries were the USA, Germany, and France, but also Brazil, Canada, Argentina, Great Britain, Australia, and Sweden. Moreover, because of the numerous shifts in the border between Poland and the Russian Empire and the USSR, many Poles and people of Polish origin continue to live in Russia and other successors states of the Soviet Union, especially in Belarus, Ukraine, Lithuania, and Kazakhstan. Alongside outflows that were economically motivated and some of which represented seasonal migrations, the Polish population experienced numerous refugee movements, forced resettlements, and deportations, especially in the 19th and 20th centuries.

The region and its boundaries

For a long time, ethnic diversity characterized the population of the Polish state. German, Ruthenian (Ukrainian), Lithuanian, and Jewish influences shaped the formation of its identity. The notion of belonging to a Polish nation developed within the Polish nobility between the end of the 16th and the middle of the 18th centuries. By the end of the 18th century, national ideas had spread also within the urban bourgeoisie. By contrast, within the quantitatively dominant rural population, the beginnings of the formation of a national identity are found only from the middle of the 19th century. Since a Polish state ceased to exist in the wake of the three partitions of the country in the late 18th century (1772, 1793, 1795), in the 19th century the Polish nation was understood exclusively as a cultural community based on the Polish language, the Catholic faith, and shared traditions.

The history of Poland can be roughly divided into the following phases: the Kingdom of Poland (966–1795) with the Piast (966–1370) and Jagiellon dynasties (1385–1572), the Noble Republic (1573–1795), the period of the partitions (1795–1918), the Second Republic (1918–39), the Communist People's Republic of Poland (1944–89), and the Third Republic (after 1989). In the 10th century, Wielkopolska (Greater Poland) with the cities of Gniezno and Poznán, and Małopolska (Little Poland) with Cracow formed the core territory of the state; later, Poland expanded to include Mazovia, Pomerania, and Silesia. At the end of the Piast Dynasty, the territory shifted eastward; Red Russia and Podolia were conquered, while Pomerania and Silesia in the west were lost. The beginning of the era of the Jagiellons was characterized by the union with Lithuania: during the "Golden Age," Poland-Lithuania comprised also modern-day Belarus and Ukraine and stretched to the Black Sea. During the period of the Noble Republic, the territory of the state shrank continuously down to the temporary end of Polish statehood in the partitions. The territory of the Second Republic (1918–39) was much smaller than that of the Noble Republic. Following World War II, the territory of the Polish state shifted westward by about 200 kilometers: about 180,000 square kilometers were lost in the east, 100,000 square kilometers were added in the west.

Religious minorities in the early modern period

The Polish kingdom was home to peoples of diverse languages and creeds. In spite of the successful implementation of the Counter-Reformation, the Confederation of Warsaw in 1573, as an edict of tolerance, offered protection to many religious refugees, for example, the Moravian Brethren.[1]

In the 16th century, Poland-Lithuania counted about 8 million inhabitants. Poles constituted the largest population group at 40%, but they inhabited only 20% of the territory of the state. Ruthenians (20% of the total population) and Lithuanians (15%) lived scattered over the expansive regions along the eastern border. Germans (10%) and Jews (5%) made up large segments of the urban population. Smaller shares of the population fell to the Armenians and Tatars, as well as to the 30,000–40,000 Scots who had immigrated to

---

[1] Moravian Brethren in Europe since the early modern period.

Poland at the beginning of the 17th century.[2] The minority population generally did not belong to the Roman Catholic Church. Ruthenians were Orthodox Christians or (after 1596) United Greek Catholics. Protestants were dominant among the Germans. Armenians, who lived predominantly in the eastern part of the kingdom, with their own Catholic Church, had erected a cathedral in Lemberg in the 15th century. The eastern region of Poland-Lithuania had more than 100 mosques of the Muslim Tatars in 1616.

Until World War II, Poland was home to the world's largest Jewish community. The first immigration of Jews occurred back in the 10th century. Privileges offered security: in 1264, the Treaty of Kalisz granted them what was presumably the first privilege. In the Middle Ages, several Jewish communities were founded in Silesia and Greater Poland. Jewish immigration rose strongly during the plague that devastated large parts of Europe between 1347 and 1350. The last king of the Piast Dynasty, Casimir II the Great (1333–70), granted Jewish refugees privileges that confirmed the rights already extended in 1264. Subsequently, too, the Jews stood under the protection of the kings and were able to preserve their faith and traditions.

The Jews earned their living primarily with trade and crafts. All Jewish communities in the Noble Republic were represented in the Council of the Four Lands that was created in 1590. Their numbers grew over the centuries from 200,000 in 1569 to more than 450,000 in 1648 and 800,000 by the end of the 19th century. In the wake of political unrest in Poland in the 17th century, Jews were frequent victims of violence, for example, during the Cossack revolt in 1648 under the hetman Bogdan Chmielnicki, when a number of Jewish communities were destroyed. This turbulent period saw the first wave of emigration by Jews from Poland, many of whom found refuge in the Netherlands. The Jews who remained in Poland rebuilt the community, which was focused on settlements (*shtetls*) in eastern Poland. As the power of kings disintegrated, the Jews increasingly lost their protection.[3]

Continental labor migration and overseas emigration in the 19th century

No Polish state existed between the Third Partition in 1795 and the end of World War I in 1918. The Polish national movement was suppressed, and Polish culture was prevented from expressing itself. The result was flights and expulsions. The collapse of the Polish state in 1795 triggered the first extensive wave of refugees.[4] The failed November Uprising against Russia in 1830–1 then led to the "Great Emigration," the largest exodus of Polish refugees. Its primary destination

was France, and it led to the formation of a strong Polish exile community in Paris. Important segments of the Polish intellectual elite congregated in the French capital, including influential poets of Romanticism, leaders of patriotic movements, and the most famous of all Polish composers, Fryderyk/Frédéric Chopin.

The uprising of January 1863 once more prompted a large flow of refugees, most of whom joined their countrymen abroad. All told, about 30,000 Poles left their homeland for political reasons between 1831 and 1870, with the majority going to France. Other important destination countries were Great Britain, the USA, Canada, and Switzerland. In Turkey, Polish refugees set up their own village near Istanbul. Still today, the name of the village, Polonezköy (formerly Adampol), points to its Polish founder. Many of the Polish refugees who had been taken in by the Netherlands decided to continue on to the Dutch colonies. A number of political prisoners escaped from Russia to Persia, others settled in Egypt and Algeria or moved to South Africa. But Poles were also living in the Philippines, India, and Japan. On the whole, though, only a small number of Poles reached the Far East or Africa, and they did not form self-contained communities of origin there.

The Russian authorities banished many of the Poles involved in the revolts to distant regions of Russia. In 1897, more than 11,000 Polish deportees were living in Kazakhstan, in 1911 at least 43,000 in Siberia. Following the failed Russian Revolution of 1905, another 8,000 Poles were banished to various parts of the Czarist Empire. Most of these were men.

However, Russia was also the destination of many Polish migrant workers; frequently these were well-trained specialists who worked as engineers or technicians, for example. A number of Poles served in the Russian army, others studied at Russian universities. These immigrants in search of work or education made up an estimated one-third of Polish migrants in eastern Europe. According to Russian statistics, on the eve of World War I, 426,000 Poles were living in Russia outside of the Polish provinces. The largest Polish communities were found in St. Petersburg (70,000), Kiev, and Odessa.

A relatively sizable Polish community of origin also developed in the Manchurian city of Harbin. It encompassed 7,000 Poles, whom the Russian authorities recruited between 1896 and 1903 for the construction of the east China railroad. This, the largest Polish community in Asia, maintained two elementary schools of its own, one high school, a library, a few Polish-language newspapers, and numerous clubs. It disintegrated after 1935 when the Soviet Union sold the east China railroad to Japan. Harbin's Polish population either returned to Poland or migrated overseas, to the USA, Brazil, or Australia.

A large number of the Polish migrant laborers came from the rural population. Russia was only one of their destinations, as many moved westward. The most important destination regions of the seasonal labor migration – often

---

[2] Scottish traders and merchants in east-central Europe in the early modern period.

[3] Ashkenazim in Europe since the early modern period.

[4] Polish political refugees in central and western Europe in the 19th century.

referred to as the "Saxon migration" (*Sachsengängerei*) – were the Prussian provinces of Saxony, Silesia, Pomerania, Brandenburg, and Hanover.[5]

Poles, Germans, and Jews from the Polish partition territory initially moved mostly to Berlin and the immediate environs of the metropolis, which offered many jobs to unskilled workers. In 1907, more than 856,000 inhabitants of Berlin and Brandenburg had been born in the part of Poland that had gone to Prussia. The stream of emigration from Prussian Poland shifted at the end of the 19th century and was now aimed increasingly at the new German industrial centers in the Ruhr region. In 1907, more than 512,000 of those living in the Prussian provinces of Rhineland and Westphalia had been born in Prussia's eastern provinces. They were Poles and Germans, rarely Jews. Poles were employed overwhelmingly in coal mining; they formed numerous local communities of origin in the Ruhr region and founded their own organizations, among them an influential union. However, they were not allowed to establish their own Polish-Catholic congregations.[6]

The strong exodus from Prussia's eastern provinces caused a steady rise there after the end of the 19th century in the number of Polish, Ruthenian, and Lithuanian rural workers of both genders from Austrian Galicia and Russian Poland.[7] In 1912, 300,000 foreign Polish seasonal workers were counted in Germany.[8]

At the turn of the 19th century, moreover, there were labor migrations from Poland to Denmark, Sweden, Bohemia, and Switzerland, as well as settlement migrations to Bukovina (modern-day Romania) and Bosnia and Herzegovina.[9] The USA was the most important destination of overseas migration from all three partition regions: its beginning dates to 1845, when a group of peasants left their Silesian village to settle in Texas. An estimated 1.4 million people left Prussian Poland between 1871 and 1914 with an overseas destination. Half were Poles, not much smaller than the group of Germans, while the number of Jewish emigrants was comparatively small. The high point of the overseas migration from Prussian Poland occurred in the 1880s; emigration began to decline strongly at the beginning of the 1890s, as it did in Germany as a whole.

Overseas emigration from Russian and Austrian Poland commenced two decades later. Between 1850 and 1914, more than a million people – mostly Poles and Ruthenians, but also Jews and Germans – left Galicia, Austria's share of partitioned Poland. The number of emigrants from Russian

Poland stood at more than 1.3 million between 1871 and 1914, among them Poles, Jews, Lithuanians, Ruthenians, and Germans. Because of inadequate statistical data, the composition of this migration movement can be determined only in vague outlines.

Jews were evidently the first emigrants who left Polish territories for good. The Jewish exodus from Posen began as early as the 1830s, initially to Berlin, but soon after to other German cities, to France, Great Britain, or North America. The Jewish population accounted for a relatively high percentage of the population in the Prussian province of Posen in the peak year 1846 (6.5%, about 80,000 individuals). By 1910, because of the strong continental and overseas emigration, their number had dropped to 26,500 (1.3%). Although Posen formed a settlement nucleus of the Jewish population in Prussia, the overwhelming majority of Jews lived further east in the Polish provinces of Russia and in the adjoining Baltic, Belarusian/White Russian, and Ukrainian territories. The migration pattern of the Jews from the province of Posen was followed, presumably since the middle of the 19th century, by Jews from Galicia and Russian Poland. About a third of all east-central and eastern European Jews went overseas.[10]

The main reason for the mass exodus from Poland was a disparity in the growth of the population and the available job opportunities, given the backward Polish agriculture. Serfdom was abolished in Prussian Poland in 1807, in Galicia in 1846, and in Russian Poland in 1864, but this did not improve the situation of the population engaged in small-scale farming. Poland was peripheral in a dual sense: large segments of east-central Europe lay at the margin of the Atlantic economic system, and the respective Polish partition territories formed the periphery of the territory of the partitioning powers. For example, in the second half of the 19th century, 80% of the population of the Prussian province of Posen was engaged in agriculture, and the ratios were no lower in the other partitioned territories. Everywhere there were many farms that were unable to support the family of the owner or leaseholder. "Galician misery" became proverbial. In addition, in Prussia's share of partitioned Poland, political motives also played a role in connection with the Germanization campaign supported by the government: the dividing up of landholdings belonging to the Polish nobility in eastern Prussia and their acquisition by German "colonists" was promoted by the state, while the sale of land to Poles was impeded.

In the USA, the first Polish communities of origin emerged in rural Texas, Wisconsin, and Minnesota. However, the majority of the new arrivals settled in cities and found employment as unskilled workers in construction, mining, and heavy industry. The US census of 1910 counted 1.7

---

[5] Polish agricultural workers in Prussia-Germany from the late 19th century to World War II.

[6] Polish industrial workers in the Ruhr (*Ruhrpolen*) since the end of the 19th century.

[7] Ukrainian labor migrants from Galicia in the Czarist Empire in the 19th and early 20th centuries.

[8] Polish agricultural workers in Prussia-Germany from the late 19th century to World War II.

[9] Polish settlers in Bosnia and Herzegovina since the end of the 19th century.

[10] Ashkenazim in Europe since the early modern period; eastern European Jews in Berlin from the late 19th century to the 1930s; eastern European Jews in London since the late 19th century; eastern European Jews in Paris since the late 19th century; Galician Jews in Austria from the 18th to the early 20th century.

million native speakers of Polish who had been born abroad or in the USA to parents born abroad. In 1920 the strongest concentrations of Polish immigrants were found in the states of Connecticut, New Jersey, Michigan, Illinois, and New York. The largest Polish American urban ethnic communities took shape in New York, Chicago, Detroit, Cleveland, Buffalo, and Milwaukee. Next to the USA, Canada, Brazil, and Australia were important destination countries.

Most Polish emigrants planned to leave their homeland only temporarily. That is why men were overrepresented among emigrants to the USA before World War I. The rate of return migration was an estimated 30%. Over the course of time, many decided to remain permanently and have their families join them; as a result, the proportion of women among Polish immigrants to the USA exceeded that of men in the period after World War I. In spite of the great distance, the Polish emigrants remained in contact with their relatives back home. Their letters provide insight into the functioning of chain migrations and the reestablishment of social bonds in the "New World."

Labor migration and forced migrations in the 20th century

Poland was a battlefield in World War I, and this had a multitude of consequences for the development of migration conditions. Traditional seasonal migrations, which secured the livelihood for many Polish families, were blocked. Flight and evacuations uprooted hundreds of thousands. Many Poles served as soldiers in the German, Russian, and Austrian armies and fought each other. In 1916, the number of Poles in the armies at war stood at 1.9 million.[11]

Poland recovered its sovereignty as a state after the end of the war, although the borders of the new state were not definitely fixed until 1921. Disagreements over where to draw the borders in the west, south, and east sparked bloody conflicts. According to the Polish census of 1931, which used native language as its criterion, around 70% of the population were Poles (22 million), 17% (5.6 million) Ukrainians and White Russians, 9% (2.7 million) Jews, and 2% (0.7 million) Germans. To this were added other minorities, for example, the Lithuanians at just under 3% (0.9 million). In the interwar period, Poland's political elite considered the high percentage of minorities within the population a problem. After 125 years of partitioning, many Poles desired a homogenous nation-state. The aggressively nationalistic party *Stronnictwo Narodowe* (National Party) emerged as a leading political force. Notwithstanding, many intellectuals of Jewish, German, and Ukrainian background continued to make important contributions to the development of Polish culture.

The reestablishment of the Polish state triggered a wave of return migration from the USA (1918–23: nearly 100,000), Brazil, Germany, and France. The flow of returnees from

the USA in the postwar period was aimed heavily at Galicia (48%) and the former Russian Poland (37%), while only a small minority headed back into the former Prussian territories. Apparently many descendants of the first Polish emigrants had already lost contact with their homeland.

The right of option laid down in the Treaty of Versailles compelled Poles who intended to remain in Germany to take German citizenship. In the first years of the Weimar Republic, about 100,000 Poles from the Ruhr region migrated into the coal mining regions of northern France and Belgium, which seemed to offer better economic opportunities.[12] Another 50,000 Poles went to other countries, and a larger number returned to Poland, not least from Berlin. Still, 216,000–270,000 Poles decided to remain in Germany. Meanwhile, the Polish authorities did not encourage return migration to Poland, and the political and economic chaos there discouraged many returnees so much that they turned their backs on Poland once again.

The economic misery within the context of the global economic crisis in the 1930s led to another peak in Polish labor migration. Because US immigration policy had become more restrictive, France became the most important destination country for Polish migrants. This migration had some tradition behind it: already at the end of the 19th century, many Poles – especially students, artists, and intellectuals – had journeyed to France. In the 1890s, Paris was home to more than 6,000 Poles. Between 1900 and 1914, about 25,000 to 35,000 Polish migrant workers arrived in France. Among them were Jewish artisans, Galician agricultural laborers in the environs of Dijon and Nancy, and the previously mentioned miners who had come from the Ruhr region. In 1939, the population of Polish background in France stood at more than 500,000, with settlements concentrated in the regions Pas-de-Calais, Nord, Alsace, and Lorraine, where they made up the second largest immigrant group after the Italians. Ninety percent of the Polish immigrants of the 1930s belonged to the working class and were thus noticeably different from the Polish migrants in Paris in the 19th century.

World War II led to new forced migrations of millions of Poles. Following the German occupation of the western portion of Poland, around 3 million Polish Jews, nearly the entire Jewish population of the country, fell victim to the Nazi genocide. At least another 3 million Poles were killed by Germans and Soviets during World War II. Approximately 3.5 million Poles fell into German hands as forced laborers, concentration camp inmates, or prisoners of war. About 920,000 Poles and Jews were expelled from the German-occupied territories of Wartheland and Danzig–West Prussia in favor of ethnic Germans, who were newly settled here from eastern, southeastern, and southern Europe as part of resettlement agreements.[13]

---

[11] Refugees in Russia during and after World War I; Polish and Belgian forced laborers in Germany during World War I.

[12] Polish industrial workers in the Ruhr (*Ruhrpolen*) since the end of the 19th century.

[13] Jewish refugees from Nazi Germany and from German-occupied Europe since 1933; forced laborers in Germany and German-occupied Europe during World War II; ethnic Germans (*Volksdeutsche*) in the German

Poles were also deported to the east, however. In 1939–40, the Soviet authorities deported about 1.5 million Poles from Ukraine and Belarus, and another half million from Lithuania in 1940–1. The destinations were mostly labor camps and special settlements in Siberia and Kazakhstan, where many of the deportees died.[14] The Polish army raised by the Soviets in 1941 from the ranks of the Polish prisoners of war, numbering 115,000 soldiers, was shipped to the west via Iran in 1942. The army stood under the command of the Polish exile government in London and joined the Western Allies in the fight against Nazi Germany. Another Polish army was set up in 1943 under Soviet control; in 1944, numbering about 90,000, it marched into Poland alongside the Red Army.

About 100,000 Poles managed to escape to France in 1939. Initially the Polish government in exile was headquartered in France, but it moved to London following the French defeat by Nazi Germany in the summer of 1940. The refugees from World War II were not the first immigrants from Poland in the British Isles: already in 1891, 5,000 Jews from Poland were living in Great Britain, 3,000 of them in London.[15] Most of the refugees who arrived after 1939 belonged to the political or military elite or were soldiers; the majority were men.

After the end of the war in 1945, many of the refugees decided not to return to Poland. That was also true of thousands of Poles who, as former forced laborers, concentration camp inmates, or prisoners of war, were now in West Germany under Allied care as displaced persons (DPs). They refused to recognize the communist regime imposed in Poland by the Soviets and thus became political refugees. More than 400,000 emigrated to the USA, about 55,000 went to Canada, and many remained in Great Britain and France or went to Australia. A very active Polish refugee community developed in Paris and revived the tradition of the "Great Emigration" of the 1830s. The monthly *Kultura*, the most important organ of Polish exile, also served as a bridge to the Polish intellectuals who continued to live in Poland. *Kultura* set high standards in political and philosophical discourse and supported, for example, a policy of reconciliation between Poland and its neighbors, especially Ukrainians, Belarusians, and Lithuanians.

In the immediate postwar period, the Roman Catholic Church, acting once again as an identity-creating force, stabilized the community of Polish political refugees around the world. This was a continuation of the tradition of national solidarity in times of oppression which had emerged in the 19th century. Already the mass emigrations of the 19th century and the concern that the Poles abroad might lose contact with the church, had led to the establishment of Polish Catholic missions abroad, which offered Polish-language masses (France: 1836, England: 1894, and Belgium: 1926).

Because the preservation of the Polish mother tongue was considered an important prerequisite for the preservation of the faith, many Polish priests, nuns, and monks traveled from place to place in distant lands to conduct masses and religious instruction in Polish. After World War II, Polish-Catholic congregations were also created in Germany, Denmark, the Netherlands, Switzerland, Spain, and Austria.

Following World War II, forced migrations continued to dominate the migratory activities in east-central Europe. As a result of Poland's westward shift, around 1.5 million Poles had been repatriated from Lithuania, Belarus, and Ukraine, after many had already left these regions in the wake of their occupation by the Soviet Union in 1939. About 3.5 million Germans were expelled from Poland.[16] More than 520,000 former Polish forced laborers returned from Germany, a smaller number from the Soviet Union.[17]

Governments saw the policy of "ethnic cleansing," including the expulsion of the Germans from eastern and southeastern Europe, as a preventive measure against future wars. Forcibly resettled in 1947 were also 140,000 Lemcos, Ruthenians in southeastern Poland, who were accused by the communist authorities of having supported anticommunist guerrillas. They were assigned new settlement areas in the former German territories in western Poland.

Polish Jews among the displaced persons encountered aggressive hostility after their return, since many Poles had taken over Jewish property, especially houses and apartments, after the deportation of the Jews. The most violent pogrom, in Kielce in 1946, left 46 dead and formed part of the backdrop to the emigration of more than 200,000 Polish Jews between 1945 and 1955.

The forcible migrations of the postwar period did not come to an end until the late 1950s. In Stalinist Poland, voluntary, border-crossing migrations and trips were initially prohibited; between 1949 and 1954, trips abroad were all but impossible. Thereafter the situation gradually improved: in 1954, only 4% of the 1,325 applications for passports were approved. In 1956, more than 30,000 could leave Poland temporarily or permanently, in 1957 as many as 148,000, and in 1958 around 141,000, mostly Jews and German who did not return.[18] In 1970, more than half of the 250,000 applications for a passport were turned down. However, Poland's passport policy changed at the end of the 1970s: in 1980, the regime approved 90% of the 800,000 applications. Between 1970 and 1980, 4.2 million Poles traveled abroad, four times as many as in the preceding decade. They were for the most part "tourists" who used their stay outside the country to earn money by working

---

Reich and in German-occupied territories in World War II; German settlers (*Donauschwaben*) in southeastern Europe since the early modern period.

[14] German deportees from east-central and southeastern Europe in the USSR after the end of World War II.

[15] Eastern European Jews in London since the late 19th century.

[16] German refugees and expellees from eastern, east-central, and southeastern Europe in Germany and Austria since the end of World War II; German deportees from east-central and southeastern Europe in the USSR after the end of World War II.

[17] Forced laborers in Germany and German-occupied Europe during World War II; displaced persons (DPs) in Europe since the end of World War II.

[18] *Aussiedler/Spätaussiedler* in Germany since 1950.

or selling Polish goods.[19] This income was utterly beyond compare with that in Poland, where the average monthly salary was about $US20 at the time.

According to official statistics, the number of emigrants from Poland in the 1970s and 1980s reached 20,000–30,000 annually; the real number was probably two or three times higher. Considerable attention in the West was given to the emigration of around 12,900 Polish Jews by 1971 in the wake of the anti-Semitic excesses in 1968. Much the same was true for the emigration of the activists of the Solidarity Union movement, who were expelled from the country by the authorities after the imposition of martial law in Poland in December 1981.

Emigration from communist Poland was certainly also prompted by economic motivations. Because the centralized planned economy gave citizens (leaving aside the functionaries in the state and the party) hardly any hope of social advancement, many left Poland in search of better prospects abroad. The economically motivated emigration reached a first high point in the 1970s, grew in importance in the 1980s, and remained at a high level also after 1989, because the transformation of the Polish economy after the end of the dictatorship, with its rigid free market reforms, led to a strong rise in competition for a shrinking number of jobs.

Beginning in the middle of the 1960s, Polish workers were employed abroad on the basis of bilateral treaties. They went for a few years to Czechoslovakia, the Soviet Union, Libya, and Iraq; other countries were added later, and the GDR eventually became the most important destination. In 1980 there were about 62,000 Polish contract workers abroad, most of them in the Eastern Bloc countries. About half worked in construction. After 1989, the bilateral treaties were adjusted to the new political realities. In 2003, more than 320,000 Polish migrant workers were employed abroad on this basis, 95% of them in Germany.[20]

In the 1990s, as in the two preceding decades, the number of registered emigrants averaged 20,000–30,000 a year. Germany, as the primary destination, accepted 75% of the Polish immigrants, 10% went to the USA. At the beginning of the 21st century, as well, Germany remained the chief destination of the Polish emigrants: in 2004, it counted more than 292,000 registered resident Poles. Poles of German extraction were given a privileged reception in Germany as *Aussiedler* (ethnic German emigrants) or *Spätaussiedler* (late ethnic German emigrants). Since 1950, about 1.4 million Poles of German background have emigrated to Germany.[21] Although the settlement and integration of the majority of *Aussiedler* and *Spätaussiedler* was successful, many are currently living in two worlds: since they hold both German and Polish citizenship, they can work in Germany and at the same time retain houses and land in Poland.

Since the beginning of the 1980s, Germany has seen a growing debate about illegal Polish migrant workers who enter with a tourist visa ("work tourists").[22] Most of the men are employed in construction, the women in household-related services. When it comes to agricultural work, the gender ratios are balanced. Polish immigrants are concentrated in cities that were already home to strong Polish communities before World War II. This is especially true for Berlin and the conurbations in the Ruhr region.

The change in the migration situation after the end of the Communist era

Alongside Germany, France and Great Britain also continue to be important destination countries for Poles at the beginning of the 21st century. Polish emigration especially to Great Britain has grown considerably since the late 1990s. Since the 1990s, new migration paths to Spain, Italy, and – not least – Ireland have emerged. For the inhabitants of some Polish communities with a long tradition of migration, Belgium has replaced the USA as the most important destination since the end of the 20th century. Women are overrepresented in several of the new migration movements out of Poland: in Italy and Belgium they are working in the large cities as nannies, geriatric nurses, and cleaning ladies. A Belgian newspaper estimated that around 50,000 Polish women were working illegally in Brussels in the 1990s. Cities like Liège, Charleroi, Antwerp, and Ostende have also become centers of Polish immigration. Spain in the 1990s was home to around 15,000 Polish immigrants, most of whom were working in Madrid and formed settlement centers in the cities of the Madrid metropolitan region: Alcalá de Henares, Torrejón de Ardoz, Fuenlabrada, and Móstoles. Much the same holds for Barcelona, Seville, and Valencia. In Ireland, students and university graduates from Poland are finding employment in qualified professions.

At the beginning of the 21st century, many of the Polish migrant workers are commuting daily or weekly between their jobs and where they live. The East-West salary gradient is an essential backdrop to the strong Polish emigration after the end of the Communist era. Especially regions with delayed economic development have very high rates of emigration: for example, many Polish immigrants in Brussels are from rural regions in northeastern Poland with particularly high unemployment. Among many Poles, the willingness to emigrate abroad is greater than the willingness to move into larger Polish cities. However, many migrant workers who had left Poland's rural areas to work abroad settled in the larger Polish cities upon their return. Years of work experience abroad improved their chances in the urban labor markets in Poland.

With the exception of the phases of urbanization and industrialization after World War II (1949–56), internal migrations were small in size during Poland's Communist

---

[19] Polish undocumented immigrants in Berlin since the 1980s.

[20] Polish labor migrants in central and western Europe after 1989.

[21] *Aussiedler/Spätaussiedler* in Germany since 1950.

[22] Polish undocumented immigrants in Berlin since the 1980s.

era. This has changed in the last years: between 2002 and 2004, about 4.2 million people changed their place of residence within Poland. More than 10% of the population was affected, whereby residents of the more weakly developed regions moved more rarely.

Contrary to what had been expected in Poland as well as in western and central Europe, Poland's accession to the EU in May 2004 did not lead to stronger border-crossing emigrations. To be sure, since then about 500,000 Poles have entered into regular employment in the EU states. However, these were by no means all emigrants from Poland; instead, many Poles who had already been working illegally in the EU states took advantage of the opportunity to legalize their status. In spite of the opening of a few national labor markets to the Poles (Great Britain, Ireland, the Netherlands, and Sweden), and in spite of rising emigration to Great Britain, Germany continued to be the chief destination.

Poles who work illegally in the western neighbor states face many dangers. Polish consulates and nongovernmental organizations (NGOs), as well as religious congregations, which are often attached to the Polish Catholic missions, offer aid in the destination countries. Polish-language masses can be found in Rome, Paris, Brussels, Amsterdam, London, Dublin, Madrid, Bochum, Chicago, New York, and in many other centers of Polish immigration. They offer Polish migrants an opportunity to exchange information with others and the chance to make connections for mutual aid – in looking for work, for example.

Beginning in the 1990s, Poland became a destination country for immigrants from the successor states of the Soviet Union and from Asia. Since 2003, all those wishing to enter from Ukraine, Belarus, and Russia are required to present a visa, but this has not affected the extent of the immigration from those countries. Men from the Commonwealth of Independent States (CIS) countries, among them mostly Ukrainians, found employment in Poland chiefly in construction, while women worked predominantly in household-related services. To a certain extent the immigrants from the East are taking the place of the Poles who migrated to the West – this seems to repeat a migration pattern from the late 19th and early 20th centuries. Polish statistics capture only a fraction of the immigrations: in 2002, the government counted nearly 50,000 foreigners and more than 500 stateless individuals who had been in Poland for more than a year, among them more than 9,000 Ukrainians, 4,000 Russians, 2,500 Belarusians, 2,000 Germans, nearly 2,000 Vietnamese, and more than 1,500 Armenians. In all probability, these figures are much too low.

The Aliens' Act of 2003 offered the possibility of legalizing the status of immigrants who had been living in Poland illegally for more than six years. By December 2003, more than 3,500 foreigners from 62 states (most from Armenia and Vietnam) had applied for a limited residence permit.

Dominant among the immigrants to Poland since the middle of the 1990s have been Ukrainian workers with good professional qualifications, though in Poland they often took on jobs that required low levels of qualifications. Because of the similarity of the two national languages, there are hardly any communication problems between Ukrainians and Poles. Still, many Ukrainian immigrants are learning Polish in order to integrate better.

Vietnamese immigrants had established connections to Poland already during the Communist era. Many young Vietnamese were studying in Poland in the 1970s. At the beginning of the 21st century, some used their old connections to find a niche in the Polish labor market. Many opened Asian or Chinese restaurants or sold textiles as itinerant traders at weekly markets. After a while relatives and acquaintances often came from Vietnam to join them.

Many eastern European border crossers engage in small-scale trade near the borders. In the 1990s their number was estimated at several million annually, though since the turn of the century it has been in strong decline. Unlike the number of migrant workers from eastern Europe, the number of asylum seekers in Poland has remained fairly small at the beginning of the 21st century. Nearly 7,000 asylum applicants were registered in 2003, mostly Chechens.

Poland's economic development since the middle of the 1990s led to a strong demand not only for unskilled workers but also for highly qualified experts. Tens of thousands of highly qualified individuals returned to Poland; some had lived for many years chiefly in Germany and the USA, and they included in the first decade of the 21st century also many *Aussiedler* and *Spätaussiedler* with dual citizenship. The returnees found work mostly in enterprises that have been set up in Poland by companies from western and central Europe. Among the returnees in the broadest sense were also Polish "repatriates," individuals of Polish descent who had migrated to the Czarist Empire generations earlier or had become Soviet citizens through the annexation of Polish territories by the USSR in the 1940s. Between 1998 and 2003, around 4,000 of them returned to Poland, mostly from Ukraine and Kazakhstan.

Beginning in the 1980s, Polish ethnic communities also emerged in states far from the original homeland, for example, in South Africa, where about 35,000 Poles live, most of them well educated. At the beginning of the 21st century, the largest number of people of Polish descent continue to be found in the USA (nearly 9 million), followed by Germany with 2 million, Brazil with 1.6 million, and France with 1 million.

The pronounced emigration tradition is a central element of the Polish culture of remembrance. During the time of the partitions in the "long" 19th century, the Polish exile formed a direct component of the nation. After World War II, the Polish diaspora supported the anticommunist movement; countless individuals and institutions abroad helped to carry the Solidarity movement of the 1980s.

At the beginning of the 21st century, the majority of Polish emigrants leave the country only for limited periods. They work abroad for a few months or years and then return to Poland. Most of the emigrants are young, between 18 and

35; many leave right after completing their education and training and seek employment abroad. The number of Polish students in the western neighbor countries is on the rise, and they are marrying non-Poles with growing frequency. In Poland, too, the number of mixed marriages is increasing; there were 4,000 in 2003 (2% of all marriages). More than half of the foreign husbands of Polish women come from EU member states, while 74% of the foreign wives of Polish men come from the successor states of the Soviet Union. Many of these couples have settled in Poland.

The experiences of eastern European immigrants in Poland resemble those of Poles in the West. Against the backdrop of rising unemployment, the rising immigration has triggered a controversial discussion. Given the developmental backwardness of the Polish economy, emigration is not likely to come to an end in the next 20 years. In the process, the share of qualified emigrants who will find jobs in line with their expertise in the western neighbor countries is likely to grow. At the same time, however, immigration to Poland will continue to increase strongly. More and more jobs are not or no longer attractive to unemployed Poles. Added to this is the low Polish birthrate, which, as in the western destination and neighbor countries, is likely to play an important role in the discussion over decisions related to immigration policy.

REFERENCES

Babiński, Grzegorz. *Pogranicze polsko-ukraińskie. Etniczność, zróżnicowanie religijne, tożsamość.* Cracow, 1997.

Baker, Thomas Lindsay. *The First Polish-Americans: Silesian Settlements in Texas.* College Station, 1996.

Bobińska, Celina, and Andrzej Brozek, eds. *Employment-Seeking Emigrations of the Poles World-Wide, XIX and XX Centuries.* Cracow, 1975.

Brozek, Andrzej. *Polish Americans 1854–1939.* Cracow, 1985.

Bukowczyk, John, ed. *Polish Americans and Their History: Community, Culture and Politics.* Pittsburgh, 1996.

Davies, Norman. *God's Playground: A History of Poland.* 2 vols. New York, 1982.

Davies, Norman. *Im Herzen Europas: Geschichte Polens.* 4th ed. Munich, 2006.

Diner, Hasia. *The Jews of the United States 1654 to 2000.* Berkeley, 2004.

Duda-Dziewierz, Krystyna. *Wieś małopolska a emigracja amerykańska. Studium wsi Babica powiatu rzeszowskiego.* Warsaw and Posen, 1938.

Florkowska-Francic, Halina, Mirosław Francic, and Hieronim Kubiak, eds. *Polonia wobec niepodległości Polski.* Breslau, 1978.

Greene, Victor. *For God and Country: The Rise of Polish and Lithuanian Ethnic Consciousness in America, 1860–1910.* Madison, 1975.

Greene, Victor. "Poles." In *Harvard Encyclopedia of American Ethnic Groups,* edited by Stephen Thernstrom, 787–803. Cambridge, MA, 1980.

Gross, Jan. *Fear. Anti-semitism in Poland after Auschwitz: An essay in Historical Interpretation.* New York, 2006.

Grzymała-Kazłowska, Aleksandra. "A Challenge of Transition: Polish Migrant Women in Brussels." *Ethnographica* 1 (2001): 46–55.

Jaworski, Rudolf. *Handel und Gewerbe im Nationalitätenkampf. Studien zur Wirtschaftsgesinnung der Polen in der Provinz Posen (1871–1914).* Göttingen, 1986.

Jaźwińska, Ewa, and Marek Okólski, eds. *Ludzie na huśtawce. Migracje między peryferiami Polski i Zachodu.* Warsaw, 2001.

Kemlein, Sophia. *Die Posener Juden 1815–1848. Entwicklungs prozesse einer polnischen Judenheit unter preußischer Herrschaft.* Hamburg, 1997.

Kępińska, Ewa. *Recent Trends in International Migration. The 2004 SOPEMI Report for Poland.* Warsaw, 2004.

Kleßmann, Christoph. *Polnische Bergarbeiter im Ruhrgebiet 1870–1945. Soziale Integration und nationale Subkultur einer Minderheit in der deutschen Industriegesellschaft.* Göttingen, 1978.

Kozłowski, Jerzy. *Rozwój organizacji społeczno-narodowych wychodźstwa polskiego w Niemczech w latach 1870–1914.* Breslau, 1987.

Kubiak, Hieronim. *The Polish National Catholic Church in the United States of America from 1897 to 1980: Its Social Conditioning and Social Functions.* Warsaw and Cracow, 1982.

Kubiak, Hieronim, Eugeniusz Kusielewicz, and Tadeusz Gro mada, eds. *Polonia amerykańska: Przeszłość i współczesność.* Breslau, 1988.

Kula, Marcin. *Polonia brazylijska.* Warsaw, 1981.

Kulczycki, John. *The Polish Coal Miners' Union and the German Labor Movement in the Ruhr, 1902–1934: National and Social Solidarity.* Oxford, 1997.

Makowski, Krzysztof. *Siła mitu. Żydzi w Poznańskiem w dobie zaborów w piśmiennictwie historycznym.* Posen, 2004.

Orłowski, Hubert, and Andrzej Sakson, eds. *Utracona ojczyzna. Przymusowe wysiedlenia, deportacje i przesiedlenia jako wspólne doświadczenie.* Posen, 1997.

Östreich, Cornelia. '*Des rauhen Winters ungeachtet.' Die Auswanderung Posener Juden nach Amerika im 19. Jahrhundert.* Hamburg, 1997.

Pacyga, Dominic. *Polish Immigrants and Industrial Chicago: Workers on the South Side, 1880–1922.* Columbus, 1991.

Pacyga, Dominic. "Polish Diaspora." In *Immigrant and Refugee Cultures around the World,* Vol. 2: *Diaspora Communities,* edited by Melvin Ember and Carol Ember, 254–63. New York, 2004.

Pilch, Andrzej. ed. *Emigracja z ziem polskich w czach nowożytnych i najnowszych (XVIII–XX w.).* Warsaw, 1984.

Praszałowicz, Dorota. "'Old Neighbors' in the New World: Jews, Germans, Poles and Ruthenians in Lower East Side." *Przegląd Polonijny* 31, 4 (2005): 77–93.

Rogmann, Heinz. *Die Bevölkerungsentwicklung im preußischen Osten in den letzten hundert Jahren.* Berlin, 1937.

Śladkowski, Wiesław. *Polacy we Francji.* Lublin, 1985.

Smout, T. Christopher, Ned C. Landsman, and Thomas Martin Devine. "Scottish Emigration in the Seventeenth and Eighteenth Centuries." In *Europeans on the Move. Studies on European Migration, 1500–1800*, edited by Nicholas Canny, 76–112. Oxford, 1994.

Stola, Dariusz. *Emigracja pomarcowa*. Warsaw, 2000.

Tazbir, Janusz. *A State Without Stakes: Polish Religious Toleration in the Sixteenth and Seventeenth Centuries*. New York, 1973.

Ther, Philipp. *Deutsche und polnische Vertriebene. Gesellschaft und Vertriebenenpolitik in der SBZ/DDR und in Polen 1945–1956*. Göttingen, 1998.

Thomas, William I., and Florian Znaniecki. *The Polish Peasant in Europe and America*. Boston, 1918.

Walaszek, Adam. "Return Migration from the United States to Poland." In *The Politics of Return: International Return Migration in Europe*, edited by Daniel Kubát, 213–19. Rome and New York, 1984.

Walaszek, Adam, ed. *Polska diaspora*. Cracow, 2001.

Zubrzycki, Jerzy. "Emigration from Poland in the Nineteenth and Twentieth Centuries." *Population Studies* 6, 3 (1953): 248–72.

Zubrzycki, Jerzy. *Polish Immigrants in Britain: A Study of Adjustment*. The Hague, 1956.

CZECHIA AND SLOVAKIA

Hermann Zeitlhofer

The territories of the Czech and Slovak Republics, sovereign since 1993, formed a joint state – Czechoslovakia – in 1918–39 and 1945–92. From 1939 to 1945, the Slovak Republic existed formally as an independent state, while the regions of the Bohemian lands that were not directly annexed to Nazi Germany were combined into the German-occupied "Protectorate Bohemia and Moravia." Before 1918, Czechia and Slovakia were parts of Austria-Hungary, though they belonged to different halves of the dual monarchy that existed after 1867. The Bohemian lands as part of the Austrian half of the state, and Slovakia as part of the Kingdom of Hungary, have had a separate history for most of the modern period. That applies also to the migration history of the two countries.

The following survey takes its cues from the dominant directions and forms of migration during the various periods. The section on preindustrial times therefore deals primarily with migrations caused by religious confessions. By contrast, during the "long" 19th century, the focus is on the economically motivated migration into the emerging industrial centers – as internal migration, but also overseas and to other European countries. During the first half of the 20th century, attention must be given especially to (forced) migrations brought on by ethnonational demarcations. A brief look at the situation after 1989 completes the survey.

The region and its boundaries

The border between the Bohemian lands and Slovak territory constituted simultaneously the border between the Austrian and the Hungarian halves of Austria-Hungary. Although it had been abolished in 1850 as a customs border, between 1867 to 1918 it was, in technical administrative terms, not considered an internal border but an external state border. The formation of borders in the Habsburg monarchy (and not only here) was a protracted and difficult process. For a long time, where a particular area belonged administratively and territorially was not precisely fixed and could overlap with another administration. For example, the Bohemian lands belonged not only to the Habsburg monarchy but were until 1806 simultaneously part of the Holy Roman Empire and in 1815–66 members of the German League (*Deutscher Bund*). At any rate, when it came to individual human migration, the internal borders between the various provinces (in part, even between communities) of the monarchy were more important before the middle of the 19th century than the external state borders. Thus, until 1857, passport controls were carried out – also during internal migrations – by all authorities along the way and at the destination point of a journey. After 1857, an attempt was made to guide and control internal migrations through a tougher variation of the *Heimatrecht* law, which linked support in old age and sickness to "membership" in a community.

The external borders of the Bohemian lands have remained essentially unchanged since 1742, when the better part of Silesia fell to Prussia and only a small part remained with the Habsburg monarchy as Austrian Silesia (later: Moravian Silesia). They were largely congruent with those of the modern Czech Republic. Minor gains in territory occurred vis-à-vis the German Reich and Austria when the state was founded in 1918–19, while a small region east of the Olsa river was ceded to Poland. By contrast, the modern-day Slovak Republic is substantially smaller in size than its historical counterpart, which was part of the Habsburg monarchy as Upper Hungary (*Oberungarn*). The Carpatho-Ukraine was part of the Czechoslavian state from 1918 to 1939 and went to the Soviet Union after 1945. Today it is part of Ukraine and home to about 1.3 million people.

From the beginning of the early modern period to the end of World War II, and with qualifications also in the period after 1945, the Bohemian lands and Slovakia can be characterized as multiethnic settlement areas. Strong ethnic, linguistic, cultural, and confessional minorities lived on the territory of the two states. Alongside the Czechs dominant in the Bohemian lands and the Slovaks dominant in Slovakia, one must point to the German-speaking settlement areas in the border regions between the Bohemian lands and Austria and the German Reich, as well as to the three German language islands in Slovakia – as well as to the Hungarian minority in Slovakia, which has remained strong to this day. In addition, there was a relevant Polish-speaking minority in Moravian Silesia, a strong Ruthenian (i.e., Ukrainian) minority in eastern Slovakia, and Croatian and Serbian settlements in western Slovakia (in the 17th and 18th centuries). A Roma minority lived dispersed across the region, but chiefly in Slovakia. Finally, one must add the Slovak minority in the Czech Republic and the Czech minority in Slovakia.

Until World War II, the Jewish population constituted a large religious minority. Confessionally, the Bohemian lands had been strongly imprinted by Catholicism since the Counter-Reformation; even after the right to the free exercise of religion was granted, Protestantism assumed some weight in the 19th century only in a few districts of eastern Moravia. Calvinists and remnants of the Hussite tradition formed merely a vanishingly small minority in the Bohemian lands. By contrast, in Slovakia, as in other parts of Hungary, the Counter-Reformation was less successful; as a result, the Protestants always formed a substantially larger share of the population here. The Ukrainian-speaking population of eastern Slovakia was of the Orthodox confession.

Migration and limits on migration under the banner of re-Catholicization and the expansion of manorialism in the 17th and 18th centuries

To this day, research on the migration history of the Bohemian lands and Slovakia in the 17th and 18th centuries has considerable shortcomings. The assumption has been that society was generally very stable and immobile during this period. Consequently, migration was studied only as an exceptional case. We know of both confessional migrations, which not infrequently took place under coercion and political pressure, and settlement migrations. However, a good deal of evidence suggests that less spectacular, quotidian forms of migration were also of great importance. However, to date there are no studies on the internal migration during this period.

During and after the Thirty Years' War, the Bohemian lands and Slovakia witnessed strong population movements, the result of profound confessional and political changes. Traditionally, the Thirty Years' War (1618–48) was accorded a very important role as a turning point in the history of the Bohemian lands. Although recent scholarship has, for good reason, strongly relativized this view, the war should be assigned a significant function as a catalyst for social change in at least two respects: the outcome of the war made possible the complete re-Catholicization of the population and the definitive establishment of the manorial system in the Bohemian lands. Both factors had a crucial influence on migratory events.

The Habsburg Counter-Reformation profoundly transformed Bohemia, which had had a Protestant majority before the Thirty Year's War. Especially in Bohemia, the Counter-Reformation was based on efforts to systematically record the non-Catholic population (1651). In the northern Bohemian border regions, the mass flight of Protestants across the nearby border was in part the result of the state's attempt at the systematic recording of the non-Catholic population. A large segment of the approximately 150,000 Bohemian religious refugees found a new home only a few kilometers on the other side of the border in Saxony and the region Oberlausitz.[1] The confessionally motivated exodus from Bohemia had finally lost its mass character with the dawn of the 18th century; only in the years 1741–2 did several thousand people leave eastern Bohemia for Prussia – often because of Prussian recruitment.

However, the confessional emigration from Bohemia had already begun during the Thirty Years' War: after the confessional minority of the pacifist Baptist and Hutterite communities, which probably comprised several tens of thousands of individuals and had grown out of the sociorevolutionary ideas of the German Peasants' War, had been expelled from Moravia in 1622. Most settled initially in what is today western Slovakia. In the 1670s and 1680s, they had to yield to the strong pressure of the Counter-Reformation. Many continued their migration to Transylvania. In the 18th century, the name "Habaner" became customary for the Slovak-speaking Baptists who had remained in Slovakia and converted to Catholicism. This population group, known especially for its pottery products, assimilated completely into the host society toward the end of the 18th century.

Between 1648 and 1658, as a result of the grievous anti-Jewish pogroms near Lviv (Lemberg) in the wake of the Cossack uprising under the hetman Bogdan Chemnicki, large groups of Polish, Lithuanian, and White Russian Jews came to Bohemia and Moravia. After 1670, the Jews expelled from Vienna settled in southern Moravia. This gave rise to the great importance of Jewish rural communities that was characteristic of the Bohemian lands in the modern period.[2]

Around 1690, western and southwestern Slovakia (around Bratislava and Komárno) witnessed a second wave of settlement by Serbs, after several thousand Croats, Serbs, and Slovenes had already immigrated in the 16th century. Thereafter, the city of Komárno formed for several decades the Serbian center in Hungary, before this population group was largely assimilated. After the number of Jewish families was legally limited in Moravia in 1726, many Jews migrated from Moravia to western Slovakia. Toward the end of the century, then, there were several migration movements from Galicia, since 1772 part of the Habsburg monarchy, to Slovakia. Jewish immigrants came above all to northern Slovakia, Poles to the region of Orava in the north, and Ruthenians to northeastern Slovakia.

The establishment of manorial structures in the Bohemian lands and Slovakian territories, which began in the 16th century and was fully completed after the Thirty Years' War, went hand in hand with restrictions on the subjects' freedom of movement. Leaving the manorial lord's realm of authority, which was often self-contained, required permission. Although this requirement existed undoubtedly everywhere, there were strong regional and temporal differences in the way it was handled and enforced. The Bohemian manorial lords controlled the geographic mobility of their subjects and sought to make it difficult, they were not able to nor did they intend to completely stop it, for the reason alone that they did

---

[1] Bohemian exiles (*Exulanten*) in Saxony since the 17th century.

[2] Ashkenazim in Europe since the early modern period.

not want to endanger the operation of their manors, which always depended to some degree on migratory wage labor.

The demographic consequences of the Thirty Years' War are difficult to measure precisely. The high population losses from the war – scholars often posit a decline of nearly 30% over the prewar level in Bohemia – cannot be adequately differentiated into direct or indirect consequences of the war, into demographic crises, and the results of migrations for confessional reasons; moreover, there were enormous regional differences. For example, while the central region of Bohemia was strongly affected, some of the mountainous border regions of Bohemia seem to have recovered quickly from the demographic crises – e.g., in the 1620s – and to have reached the prewar population levels immediately after 1648.

These regional differences had enormous influence on the policies of the manorial lords to control and guide the geographic mobility of their subjects. On some manors that were suffering from a considerable labor shortage in the immediate postwar years, during the first years and decades after 1648, entire population groups were moved to largely desolate and abandoned villages and settlements, and prohibitions against leaving were enforced with tough penalties. In the face of the economic recovery of Bohemia and the strong population growth in the second half of the 17th century, which continued throughout the 18th century at slower rates of growth, control over the mobility of subjects by the lords seems to have been handled in a less restrictive manner.

The numerous proto- and early industrial production sites (e.g., iron and glass manufactures, textile regions) and also the large estates in central Bohemia and the viticulture that was widespread in Moravia led to a strong demand for seasonal workers who were paid for piecework or received a daily wage. Well documented for the 18th century are the continuous migratory movements of harvest workers from the Giant Mountains, for example, to the Bohemian lowlands or the migration of domestics from the villages into the cities of other lordships. Many Bohemian lordships also experienced a border-crossing migration – authorized by the respective authorities – for marriage, work, or by journeymen into what are today Austrian or German territories between 1648 and about 1850. In many cases these permissions were granted on an individual basis, which makes it difficult to reconstruct the full extent of this migration; however, rare, complete registers of small Bohemian cities in the early 19th century indicate that a larger percentage of the population (at times more than 5%) requested an annual travel permit. From the second half of the 17th century, there are also reports about border-crossing seasonal labor migrations, for example, by inhabitants of the higher regions of the Bohemian Forest, who went to the Nuremberg area for the harvest.

In addition, one must bear in mind that in the 18th (and also in the 19th) century, the territorial rule of the Bohemian manorial lords did not extend de facto to all parts of their lands. That was even more true for the state. For example, the Bohemian Forest on the border with Germany and

Austria was an area that had been closed to effective control by the authorities. Marginal social groups and vagrants (*Vagierende*) – some of whom existed by cross-border smuggling – lived (and survived) in this remote area until the early 19th century.

Already during the early modern period, the exceedingly numerous traders, merchants, and craftsmen in the Bohemian lands were tied into diverse and extensive migration networks that regularly ranged across internal boundaries as well as external state borders.[3] The migrations of itinerant craftsmen from Bohemian lands to Vienna, for example, assumed the character of a mass migration as early as the first half of the 19th century. The northern districts of Bohemia, in turn, were closely linked to Saxony. This "Saxon migration," a seasonal migration that was long agricultural in nature and only toward the end of the 19th century industrial, had a tradition here that reached far back to the early modern period; it declined in importance around 1900, in contrast to the other seasonal migrations of east central European workers to the German Reich.

However, in the century following the Thirty Year's War, the Bohemian lands witnessed, alongside an emigration that was motivated chiefly by religious confession, also significant immigrations. Numerous Catholics came from Germany to Bohemia and settled in the mountainous border regions of the country. Much of this was a colonizing movement, which lasted into the 19th century and which led to the settling of the higher regions of the Bohemian Forest, for example. Glass production, which flourished in the early modern period, as well as the manifold forms of wood processing in the Bohemian Forest, repeatedly attracted workers from Bavaria and Austria. Other regions of Bohemia also saw notable German-speaking immigration, for example, by merchants from Tyrol to the city of Pilsen.

Migrations within the Habsburg monarchy during industrialization

Industrialization arrived early in the crown land of Bohemia. From the second half of the 19th century, the core industrial zones of the Habsburg monarchy lay in the north of the land. Both the quick transition from proto-industrial to industrial production in some regions of northern Bohemia, as well as another burst of strong industrial growth toward the end of the 19th century in several regions of northern Bohemia and northern Moravia and in the cities of Prague, Pilsen, and Ostrava, led to a rapid rise in the population, which was in part the result of strong immigration. These movements, however, were mostly internal migrations, hardly border-crossing ones. For example, the influx from the Czech-speaking interior into the predominantly German-speaking border regions carried the strong economic upswing in brown coal mining in northwestern Bohemia in the final decades of the 19th century. As a result, around 1900 it was by no means the

---

[3] Bohemian glass traders in Europe from the 17th to the 19th century.

most prosperous regions that had the highest percentage of persons born abroad (in Germany), but rather the northern and western Bohemian districts like Cheb (Eger), As (Asch), and Liberec (Reichenberg), which already had a tradition of receiving immigrants from the German Reich.

In spite of the massive industrial development, emigration was always dominant over border-crossing immigration in the Bohemian lands. From 1850 to 1914, around 1.6 million individuals emigrated from Bohemia and Moravia. Between 1900 and 1913 alone, the negative migration balance came to 400,000–500,000. About half of all those who left the Bohemian lands in the second half of the 19th century went to other parts of the Habsburg monarchy, mostly to its central region, to Vienna and Lower Austria. Inhabitants of the Bohemian lands formed the main contingent of immigrants to Vienna. Between 1857 and 1910, Bohemian-born individuals made up a steady 20% to 27% of Vienna's population. In 1910, around 470,000 residents of Vienna had been born in the Bohemian lands. Emigration to Vienna was significant in nearly all regions of Bohemia and Moravia in the second half of the 19th century. Although a clear majority of emigrants heading to Vienna came from southern Bohemian districts, measured against population size, the migration to Vienna was most important in Moravia, and here specially in the cities. This corresponded with the small-scale trade and artisanal structure that the immigration to Vienna retained in the phase of high industrialization.

The outmigration into the heartland of the monarchy around Vienna, but also to other parts of modern-day Austria (Lower and Upper Austria, Styria, and toward the end of the 19th century also Voralberg), was experienced in the judgment of most contemporaries as the crossing of a linguistic-cultural boundary, which the German-national propaganda regarded as a threat to Austria's German character. The pressure on the Czech-speaking immigrants to assimilate was correspondingly high.[4] However, the internal migration from Bohemia was by no means limited to the German-speaking realm of the monarchy: around 1870, for example, Bohemian and Moravian immigrants made up around half of all industrial workers in Budapest. In Cracow, too, which was growing rapidly, 5% of the residents around 1910 (about 7,000 people) had been born in Bohemian lands.

The agrarian regions of the southern half of Bohemia are regarded in the literature as the central source for the migration to Prague and other urban or industrial centers of Bohemia, to Austria's heartland, and overseas. These regions supposedly became the central emigration regions from about the middle of the 19th century. Scholars have advanced a variety of reasons for this: from the social hardships suffered by the population, poor soil conditions, and population growth, to the unequal distribution of land with very high ratios of landless, the loss of earning opportunities in the proto-industrial home industries, and the high costs

of buying one's way out of statute labor in the wake of the agrarian reform in 1848.

And yet, the dichotomous distinction – long dominant in the literature – between agrarian emigration regions, on the one hand, and industrial immigration regions, on the other hand, is false: around 1900, all agrarian districts of Bohemia also witnessed immigration. At least 10% of the population had been born outside of the districts.

Slovakia had a much stronger agrarian imprint than the Bohemian lands. A partly seasonal agricultural labor migration of Slovaks and Ruthenians from the territory of Slovakia to the Hungarian lowlands (*Tiefebene*) established itself at the end of the 17th century and remained highly important throughout the entire 19th century. This migration was increasingly focused on the industrial-urban zones. In 1910, about 300,000 Slovaks by birth lived outside the territory of modern-day Slovakia in the Kingdom of Hungary. This was an expression of the dominant north-south migration in the kingdom, which remained strongly oriented toward the Hungarian heartland around Budapest. For Slovaks, Budapest had about the same importance as Vienna had for the Czechs. In 1910, more than 93,000 Slovaks by birth were living in Budapest; about 80% had been born in western and central Slovakia. Eastern Slovak migrants, meanwhile, headed chiefly to other Hungarian industrial cities, for example, Mikolc. By contrast, immigration from the various parts of the Kingdom of Hungary into the territory of modern-day Slovakia was much smaller: according to the census of 1910, a total of just under 100,000 people living there had been born in other parts of the Kingdom of Hungary.

Vienna was also – if on a much smaller scale – an important destination region for Slovak emigrants. In 1910, about 55,000 immigrants from Slovakia were living in Vienna. Conversely, there were about 59,000 Austrians in Slovakia. Both in the Austrian part of the monarchy and in the Hungarian regions, the Slovaks were subject to strong pressure to assimilate, which grew even more intense after 1918 and between 1939 and 1945. In 1923, the Slovak minority in Austria was estimated at only 5,000; however, the seasonal agricultural labor migration from Slovakia had become very significant in eastern Austria in the interwar period. To this day, a small Slovak minority has persisted in Austria, especially in Vienna and in a few villages near the Slovak border. It was able to survive only because a constant stream of political refugees from Communist Czechoslovakia came to Austria.[5]

The migration movements between the Bohemian lands, on the one hand, and Slovakia, on the other, remained fairly unimportant on the whole during the time of the Habsburg monarchy: in 1910, only around 13,000 Slovaks by birth resided in Bohemia and Moravia. While the emigrants from the Bohemian lands largely integrated themselves into continental European migration networks and were part of the

---

[4] Czech labor migrants in Austria in the 19th and early 20th centuries.

[5] Czechoslovakian refugees in western, central, and northern Europe since 1968.

internal migrations within the Austrian state, Slovak migrants remained much more strongly tied into overseas and internal Hungarian migration systems.

Continental emigrations until 1914

In the modern period (especially the 19th century), the Bohemian lands witnessed a not insignificant emigration to eastern and southeastern Europe. Here one should mention especially the Czech-speaking settlements in the Ukraine (Volhynia) and in Romania (Banat). According to the 1897 census in the Russian Empire, more than 32,000 persons indicated Czech as their mother tongue in Ukraine alone; by comparison, only 6,450 did so in Russian Poland.[6] Bohemian emigration to the Banat began in the 1780s, peaked in the 1820s, and lasted until the 1850s. It followed the systematic settlement of the region with Catholic and largely German-speaking settlement groups that was fostered by the Habsburg administration.[7] From Bohemia came German- as well as Czech-speaking settlers. For the Bohemian Forest (*Böhmerwald*) one can note in the 1820s a short-lived, powerful surge of emigration to the Banat, which was driven especially by the landless and unpropertied population groups (*Hausgenossen*). Here a connection seems likely with the decline of the proto-industrial, manual yarn-spinning in the face of competition from the first machine-driven cotton-spinning factories – a development that robbed tens of thousands of individuals, almost overnight, of their additional income in many regions of Bohemian and Austria. In spite of several waves of return migration in the 20th century, villages with a Czech-speaking population survive in the Banat to this day.

From the end of the 19th century, immigrants from the Bohemian lands formed a significant part of the foreign workers in Imperial Germany. More than 33,000 foreign workers of Czech nationality were counted in Prussia in 1913. According to estimates by Austrian authorities, the number of Czech seasonal workers of both genders throughout the entire German Empire was as high as 50,000 in 1910. All these figures do not include German-speaking Bohemians, since they were generally not registered as a separate group among the German-speaking immigrants from the Habsburg monarchy by the statistic surveys focused on nationalities. However, as the small number of local studies available to date show, German-speaking Bohemians were strongly represented among the labor migrants to Germany. Important destination regions of the Bohemian migrant workers were above all Saxony, as well as Bavaria, the Rhineland, the Ruhr basin, and Bremen.

The seasonal labor migration to the German-speaking regions of modern-day Austria was, like the emigration into areas of the German Reich, an integral part of the way in which artisans and skilled workers, who were particularly numerous in Bohemia, advanced in their profession. Bohemian construction and brickworkers headed to the Vienna area and to Saxony, miners went in part to the Rhineland and the Ruhr basin, as well as Styria, while harvest workers made their way to Austria and Bavaria. Other occupational groups, such as musicians and peddlers, went to Hungary, Croatia, and France. The seasonal workers abroad exerted a fairly large influence on the emergence of the first workers' organizations in Bohemia in the second half of the 19th century.

Overseas migration since the middle of the 19th century

Overseas emigration from the Habsburg monarchy began around 1850 as a largely Czech immigration to the USA. Between 1850 and 1870, about 56,000 migrants from the Bohemian lands came to North America. About 55% of all emigrants from the Austrian part of the Habsburg monarchy between 1876 and 1885 came from the Bohemian lands. Since the annual number of emigrants from the Bohemian lands to the USA increased only slightly to 1914, Bohemia's share of overall emigration to America from the Austrian state declined to around 12% (1910) as a result of the Polish-Galician emigration that started up toward the end of the 19th century. Estimates put the total number of Czechs who had gone to the USA by 1914 at 350,000, at the least. The Czech emigration to the USA was largely a family migration. At the beginning it was driven by the desire for land in that country, and in the final years before 1914, as well, it tended to be dominated by skilled workers. Because of the relatively early onset of the emigration to the USA from Bohemian lands, the Czechs formed the only large, Slavic farming population there.

By contrast, Slovak emigration to the USA was – like the Galician movement – part of the "New Immigration" of largely unskilled workers into the industrial centers of the country, with their regions of origin largely in eastern, east-central, southeastern, and southern Europe. According to American statistics, about 620,000 Slovaks arrived in the country between 1880 and 1913. The high point occurred in the years 1905–7. The sending regions were largely in the northeast of the country. After the Galician Poles, the Slovaks formed the most important community of origin among the immigrants from the dual monarchy. In addition to economic reasons, Slovakian overseas migration was also driven by political and cultural factors. Many migrants were escaping the strong Magyarization pressure that began in their homeland after 1868. The 1870s witnessed the closing of all Slovak-speaking middle schools and the expulsion of the Slovak and German languages from elementary schools. As a result of the repressive measure against the use of the Slovak language, which grew in intensity until 1914, the USA eventually had more Slovak-language papers than Slovakia. In spite of a high rate of return migration among the Slovaks,

---

[6] Czech settlers in Volhynia from the 1860s to the 1940s.
[7] German settlers (*Donauschwaben*) in southeastern Europe since the early modern period.

nearly a quarter of all Slovaks were living in the USA before World War I. Shortly before World War I, Pittsburgh overtook Bratislava as the largest Slovak city in the world.

The transformation of migratory goals and form of migration after the establishment of Czechoslovakia, 1918–1938

Ethnically motivated resettlements, expulsions, and deportations of national minorities shaped the migratory conditions in east-central Europe in the first half of the 20th century. The nation-states newly created after 1918 defined themselves exclusively in ethnic terms. However, east-central Europe, in particular, with its great diversity – evolved over centuries – of different languages and cultures coexisting in small spaces, was anything but ethnically homogeneous. While attempts to bring the ethnic boundaries in line with the state borders were already made in the interwar period, they reached their high point only during and after World War II.

Concrete plans for the establishment of a joint nation-state of Czechs and Slovaks were drawn up during World War I especially by emigrants, for example, in the USA. The founding of Czechoslovakia in 1918–19 was followed by a first large, ethnically motivated wave of immigration: many nationally conscious Czechs and Slovaks returned to the newly created republic from many European states. The number of Czech returnees from Austria and Slovaks from Hungary was particularly high. The new Czechoslovakian state had propagated this return under the slogan of repatriation.

Conversely, thousands of Hungarians left Slovakia for Hungary. Still, after 1918 there was still a significant Hungarian minority in Slovakia, and there were about 400,000 Slovaks on Hungarian territory. Of no small importance to the creation of the Czechoslovakian state was also the Czechoslovakian Legion. After the end of the war, this military unit, made up of Czechs and Slovaks and deployed during World War I largely in Russia against the forces of the Habsburg monarchy, fought in the Russian Civil War on the side of the counter-revolutionary White Forces. At the beginning of 1919, it was about 60,000 strong. The legion returned to Czechoslovakia only in the course of 1920. Moreover, after 1918, Czechoslovakia was an important transit station for Jews fleeing pogroms in Poland, Ukraine, and Russia.

With the establishment of the new state, the previous internal migration from the Bohemian lands and Slovakia into the respective halves of the Habsburg monarchy came to a fairly abrupt end. Although this was no doubt the result largely of the new borders and of the nation-states closing themselves off against one another, that does not explain this development entirely. For example, a clear waning of Czech immigration into modern-day Austria (e.g., Vienna and Linz) is already evident in the decade prior to World War I.[8]

Only with the creation of the joint state did the mutual migration relationship between the Bohemian lands and Slovakia grow substantially stronger. And it has continued after the division into two separate sovereign states in 1993. Between 1918 and 1938, throughout the republic, many positions in the state administration, the military, or the schools were filled with Czechs. As early as 1921, 72,000 Czechs were living on Slovak territory. Even stronger, however, was the primarily economically motivated migration in the opposite direction.

A good many of the established, border-crossing migration paths of Czech and Slovak emigrants and immigrants remained intact after 1918. As a result, the migration balance of the newly created Czechoslovakian republic was negative. Between 1920 and 1937, about 180,000 migrants left the country. Initially, a majority of emigrants went to the USA; after that country had passed restrictive immigration laws, emigration to France and Germany increased. Czech labor migration into the German Empire attained a considerable size especially from the middle of the 1930s. Moreover, between 1922 and 1926, 13,000 citizens of Czechoslovakia emigrated to South America, with the vast majority going to Argentina. About 2,500 moved to the Soviet Union in the early 1920s, where they set up their own communes and cooperatives.[9] However, migration in the opposite direction, carried by political refugees after the Russian Revolution, was substantially larger at around 20,000.[10] Larger immigrations into Czechoslovakia also occurred in 1933–8 from the flight, from Germany and Austria, of tens of thousands who were politically and racially persecuted by the Nazi regime.[11]

Flight and forced migrations during and after World War II

The annexation of the Sudeten region by Nazi Germany in the spring of 1939 led to a first climax of ethnically motivated expulsions, which would subsequently assume unimagined dimensions during and after World War II. In this first phase, up to 400,000 Czechs from largely German-speaking border regions were resettled into the interior of the country. Moreover, most Czechs had to leave the now independent Slovak Republic, largely because they were no longer needed as civil servants and teachers.

Between 1939 and 1945, at least 140,000 Jews living in the territory of Czechoslovakia were deported and murdered. For the approximately 45,000 political refugees from Czechoslovakia, the Balkan route via Hungary and Yugoslavia was the most important escape route after the outbreak of the war. Among the destination countries for people fleeing the expansion of Nazi Germany, Great Britain played an especially important role.[12]

---

[8] Czech labor migrants in Austria in the 19th and early 20th centuries.

[9] European political emigrants in the USSR since 1917.

[10] Russian emigrants in Europe since 1917.

[11] Political and intellectual refugees from Nazi Germany and from German-occupied Europe, 1933–1945; Jewish refugees from Nazi Germany and from German-occupied Europe since 1933.

[12] German and Austrian Jewish children transported to Great Britain since 1938–1939; Jewish refugees from Nazi Germany and from German-occupied Europe since 1933.

After World War II, the German-speaking population was expelled from east-central Europe with the consent of the Allies. A great many of the approximately 150,000 German-speaking persons on the territory of Slovakia had already fled or been evacuated during the last year of the war. Although many of them tried to return to their hometowns and villages after the end of hostilities, they were expelled again in 1946. The vast majority of the German-speaking population in the Bohemian lands was expelled after the end of the war between 1945 and 1947. About 3 million people were affected by this on the territory of the Czechoslovakian republic. It led to the depopulation of entire regions – traditionally largely German-speaking – along the borders with Germany and Austria. Only about 180,000 German-speaking persons were allowed to remain in Czechoslovakia, for a variety of reasons.

Many German-speaking individuals had already been evacuated from their settlement areas before the end of the war as the front line drew closer. The first "wild" expulsions occurred during the Prague uprising at the beginning of 1945, which continued in many other locations during the first months after the end of the war. There were numerous deaths in the wake of acts of revenge against the German-speaking population (Brün Death March, 1945). To this day, the exact number of casualties is hotly debated; the number of deaths was probably 30,000. The great mass of the German-speaking population then had to leave the land as part of a "regulated" expulsion between January and December 1945. Although many came to Austria temporarily, most eventually found a permanent home in West Germany.[13]

After 1945, Czechoslovakia pursued a policy of "ethnic homogenization" through resettlement directed not only against the German-speaking population but also – to a lesser degree – against other nationalities. The measures were coordinated with other states in east-central and southeastern Europe: between 1945 and 1950, up to 200,000 Czechs and Slovaks returned to Czechoslovakia especially from Romania, Carpatho-Ukraine and Volhynia, Yugoslavia, France, and Bulgaria. They were joined by about 10,000 Czechs from Austria. About 70,000 Hungarians living in Slovakia were "exchanged" for Magyars who had been living in Slovakia until then. This reduced the share of the Hungarian-speaking population in Slovakia only insignificantly. The originally agreed-upon, far more extensive exchange never took place. After the annexation of Carpatho-Ukraine to the Soviet Union in 1945, about 8,000 Ukrainians left Slovakia, again as a part of a "population exchange" agreed upon in a treaty between the two states.

The repopulation of these nearly depopulated, formerly German-speaking territories was done largely with these returning migrants from east-central and southeastern Europe. Those settled in the border regions to Austria and Germany were mostly Slovaks from Romania – but also

sedentary and nomadic Roma from Slovakia and southeastern Europe. About 40,000 Slovakian Hungarians had been settled in these areas immediately after the end of the war, but following the repeal of the anti-Hungarian laws, more than half returned to Slovakia. The resettlement of these regions was not without problems and was only partially successful. Although the prospects of agricultural property seemed initially enticing to many, the general conditions were not especially favorable: interested individuals could not choose the land but had it allocated to them. Many returning migrants had no experience as independent farmers and quickly fell into debt. In many cases, the agricultural settlers therefore abandoned their farms again and headed for the industrial centers.[14]

Emigration during the Communist era, 1948–1989

The beginning of the Communist era in Czechoslovakia in 1948 brought with it, apart from many other profound changes, restrictions on border-crossing travel (*Reiseverkehr*) and emigration. The change in the political system was followed immediately by a first wave of emigration; the exodus was even more significant after the crushing of the "Prague Spring" in 1968.[15] A continuous emigration existed also after 1968, though on a smaller scale. After 1948, an estimated 60,000 left the country; after 1968, the number was probably 100,000–200,000. No exact figures on emigration in the Communist era exist, since the official statistics are highly unreliable in this regard. However, estimates put the negative migration balance in Czechoslovakia between 1948 and 1990 at 375,000–450,000. While the emigration after 1948 was directed largely at the USA, the exodus after 1968 went mostly to western and central Europe. It was only in the 1980s, as a result of a restrictive immigration policy by the European destination countries, that the USA and Australia became once again important host countries.

The emigrants during the Communist era had specific characteristics: most were young, male, had an above-average education, and came from the cities. In the 1980s, presumably one-fourth to one-third of all emigrants were from Prague. Beginning in the 1970s, economic motivations gained in importance alongside political reasons for emigration.

Although Czechoslovakia remained largely a country of emigration during the Communist era, there was immigration from other socialist states. Cheap workers were brought into the country from Cuba, as were immigrants from Vietnam, who continued to come in the postcommunist period. The Czech government also recruited tens of thousands of Polish migrant workers. The backdrop to this was a shortage of workers, which was quite pronounced at various times and was further exacerbated by the constant emigration losses.

---

[13] German refugees and expellees from eastern, east-central, and southeastern Europe in Germany and Austria since the end of World War II.

[14] Czech and Slovak settlers in the former Sudeten regions since the end of World War II; Magyar deportees from Slovakia in western Czechoslovakia since the end of World War II.

[15] Czechoslovakian refugees in western, central, and northern Europe since 1968.

During the entire communist period there was also a permanent Slovak immigration into the Czech industrial and urban centers which reached a first high point at the beginning of the 1950s and then surged again after 1989.

Change in the dominant migration direction after 1989

The upheavals of 1989 brought a turnaround in the migration pattern of Czechoslovakia. The Czech Republic that was established in 1993 became a transit and immigration country. At the end of the 1990s, more than half a million foreigners were living in the Czech Republic; the number of persons who did not reach the West or were sent back is estimated at more than 100,000. The majority of foreigners in the country most likely do not have residence status. Nearly a quarter of all foreigners living in Prague at the end of the 1990s without a residence permit were Americans. This group is characterized by a high level of education and in many cases stay only a short time. For the most part they are businesspeople and employees of multinational companies, as well as students who go to Prague for a semester or two.

After the division into two sovereign states on 1 January 1993, the Slovak citizens enjoyed a special status among the foreign workers in the Czech Republic: unlike others, they did not have to apply for a work permit but merely had to register. Still, the largest group of foreigners in the Czech Republic ahead of the Slovaks is the Ukrainians, just under 80,000 of whom had a residence permit in 2004. The foreign population in the Czech Republic after 1989 can be differentiated into three fairly distinct groups: (1) Immigrants from east and east-central European states, who – in a role comparable to that of the classic "guest workers" in western, central, and northern Europe – work in largely unskilled jobs (for example, as construction laborers). This category includes, apart from the Ukrainians, most of the Slovaks and Poles in the country. (2) The relatively high number of western and central Europeans as well as North Americans who should be seen as part of a migration of elites. At the end of the 1990s, two-thirds of these immigrants had a university degree; many were employed by multinational companies or worked as foreign language instructors or businessmen. (3) Asian immigrants, most of whom are from Vietnam and the People's Republic of China and are largely self-employed, especially in small-scale retail and street trades (textiles, electronics). This group grew – primarily in the 1990s – through immigration from the territory of the former GDR.[16]

A not unimportant segment of immigration after 1989 was made up by return migration of Czech refugees from the Communist era. It is likely that about 10% had returned to the Czech Republic by 2000; they came mostly from Germany and – in much smaller numbers – from the USA, Canada, Switzerland, and Austria. This return migration is

---

Table 1. The 15 most important origin countries of immigrants to the Czech Republic (including the share of Czech citizens) and emigration in the opposite direction, 2004

	Immigration from		Emigration to
	Number	% Czech nationals	Number
Ukraine	16,436	0.6	4,933
Slovakia	15,788	5.2	21,152
Vietnam	4,470	0.3	770
Russia	1,986	1.7	656
Poland	1,806	3.4	1,011
Germany	1,749	25.3	961
Moldavia	997	0.3	487
USA	874	24.5	601
Bulgaria	662	2.1	397
Great Britain	636	9.6	379
Belarus	587	0.7	248
Mongolia	558	0.0	255
China	516	0.0	135
Austria	476	14.3	330
France	413	7.7	323
Other	5,499		
Total	53,453		34,818

Source: Český statistický Úrad (2004), http://czso.cz.

---

continuing at the beginning of the 21st century, as evidenced by the strikingly high percentage of Czech citizens among the immigrants from certain western countries in 2004 (see Table 1). Since 2004, a change in the law has made it possible for foreign Czechs to recover the citizenship they lost when they fled the country.

Although the official statistics underestimate immigration as much as emigration, it seems notable that the most important destination countries of emigration from the Czech Republic were simultaneously the most important origin countries for immigrants to the Czech Republic. Hence, the current, border-crossing migration activities in the Czech Republic are shaped not so much by unilinear migration movements as by networks already created by migrants, which determine the direction of further migrations.

To this day, Slovakia has been shaped far more profoundly than the Czech Republic by the consequences of the historical migration movements. The share of minorities among the population is significantly higher here, and the problems of the integration and legal equality of these population groups are far more virulent. According to the census of 2001, about 10% of the population of the country should be assigned to the Hungarian nationality, which represents a very large share of the population in all border regions of Hungary. Especially weighty seems the question of social and economic equality for the minority of the Roma, estimated at several hundred thousand, most of whom live in the rural regions in the east of the country. The size of this population group, which suffers from extremely high unemployment and social discrimination, has been rising continuously since 1945, especially because of a relatively high birthrate.

---

[16] Vietnamese, Mozambican, and Cuban labor migrants in East Germany since the 1970s.

At the beginning of the 21st century, as well, the Slovak Republic is registering a fairly sizable emigration, especially among the better-educated population groups (brain drain). As the same time, the country is pursing a rigid immigration policy because of the implementation of the EU's Schengen laws: in 2004, only 15 immigrants were granted permanent residence status, while nearly 10,000 illegal border crossers were picked up by the authorities every year at the beginning of the 21st century.

All told, labor migration brings most of the foreigners to the Czech Republic. For asylum seekers, the country is often only a transit station, the real destination being the western states of the European Union. Special integration programs are targeted at the small minority of recognized refugees. Educational institutions are open to all legal immigrants free of charge, but the state medical insurance is not. For example, the self-employed and children of immigrants with a temporary residence permit must insure themselves privately. Nationalization is possible only after one has held an unlimited residence permit for five years. However, with the exception of cases of family unification, such permits are usually granted only after 10 years of legal residence. The waiting period for Czech citizenship is thus 15 years.

Ever since the Slovak and Czech republics sought accession to the EU, and even more so after they joined in 2005, the migratory challenges faced by these two countries have been closely linked to the goals of the EU's migration policies. As in many western European countries, a virulent tension remains between the attempt to close oneself off to new immigrants and the realization that one has become an immigration country that must make a greater effort to integrate the immigrants living in the country.

REFERENCES

Brandes, Detlef. *Der Weg zur Vertreibung 1938–1945. Pläne und Entscheidungen zum "Transfer" der Deutschen aus Polen und der Tschechoslowakei.* Munich, 2001.

Carter, Frank W. "Czechoslovakia in Transition: Migration before and after the 'Velvet Divorce.'" *IMIS-Beiträge* 6 (1997): 35–63.

Drbohlav, Dušan. "Die Tschechische Republik und die internationale Migration." In *Ost-West-Wanderung in Europa*, edited by Heinz Fassmann and Rainer Münz, 163–81. Vienna, 2000.

Ehmer, Josef, and Hermann Zeitlhofer. "Ländliche Migration in Böhmen vor dem Ersten Weltkrieg." *Zeitschrift für Agrargeschichte und Agrarsoziologie* 53, 1 (2005): 40–58.

Faßmann, Heinz. "Emigration, Immigration and Internal Migration in the Austro-Hungarian Monarchy 1910." In *Roots of the Transplanted. Late 19th Century East Central and Southeastern Europe*, edited by Dirk Hoerder, Horst Rössler, and Inge Blank, 253–308. New York, 1994.

Faßmann, Heinz. "Migration in Österreich 1850–1900. Migrationsströme innerhalb der Monarchie und Struktur der Zuwanderung nach Wien." *Demographische Informationen* (1986): 22–36.

Faßmann, Heinz, et al. "*Arbeitsmarkt Mitteleuropa.*" *Die Rückkehr historischer Migrationsmuster.* Vienna, 1999.

Fialová, Ludmila, et al., eds. *Dějiny obyvatelstva cěských zemí.* Prague, 1996.

Glettler, Monika. *Die Wiener Tschechen um 1900. Strukturanalyse einer nationalen Minderheit in der Großstadt.* Vienna and Munich, 1972.

Heumos, Peter. *Die Emigration aus der Tschechoslowakei nach Westeuropa und dem Nahen Osten 1938–1945.* Munich, 1989.

Hoensch, Jörg K. *Studia Slovaca. Studien zur Geschichte der Slowaken und der Slowakei.* Munich, 2000.

Kořalka, Jiří. "Some Remarks on the Future Model of Czech Emigration (1848–1914)." In *Overseas Migration from East-Central and Southeastern Europe 1880–1940*, edited by Julianna Puskás, 9–20. Budapest, 1990.

Kořalka, Jiří. *Tschechen im Habsburgerreich und in Europa 1815–1914. Sozialgeschichtliche Zusammenhänge der neuzeitlichen Nationsbildung und der Nationalitätenfrage in den böhmischen Ländern.* Vienna, 1991.

Kybal, Vlastimil. *Jiží Amerika a Československo.* Prague, 1928.

Laník, Jaroslav. "Urbanization and Industrialization in Bohemia before 1914." *Hospodářské dějiny/Economic History* 18 (1990): 317–33.

Maur, Eduard. *Gutsherrschaft und "zweite Leibeigenschaft" in Böhmen. Studien zur Wirtschafts-, Sozial- und Bevölkerungsgeschichte (14.–18. Jahrhundert).* Munich, 2001.

Nešpor, Zdeněk. "The Disappointed and Disgruntled: A Study of the Return in the 1990s of Czech Emigrants from the Communist Era." *Sociologický časopis/Czech Sociological Review* 38, 6 (2002): 789–808.

Puskás, Julianna. "Hungarian Migration Patterns 1880–1930. From Macroanalysis to Microanalysis." In *Migration across Time and Distance. Population Mobility in Historical Contexts*, edited by Ira A. Glazier and Luigi De Rosa, 231–54. New York and London, 1986.

Rubner, Heinrich. "En forêt de Bohême: Immigration et émigration, 1500–1960." *Annales de démographie historique* (1970): 135–42.

Tajtak, Ladislav. "Slovak Emigration: Its Causes and Consequences." In *Overseas Migration from East-Central and Southeastern Europe 1880–1940*, edited by Julianna Puskás, 74–88. Budapest, 1990.

Tajtak, Ladislav. "Slovak Emigration and Migration in the Years 1900–1914." *Studia historica slovaca* 10 (1978): 45–86.

Valeš, Vlasta, ed. *Doma v Cizině. Češi ve Vídni ve 20. století – Zu Hause in der Fremde. Tschechen in Wien im 20. Jahrhundert.* Prague, 2002.

SOUTHEASTERN EUROPE

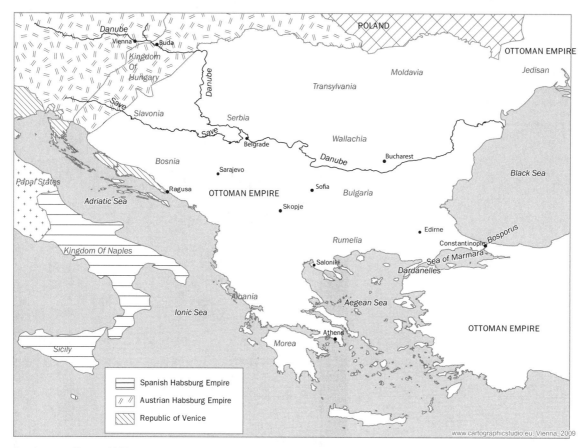

Southeastern Europe 1648

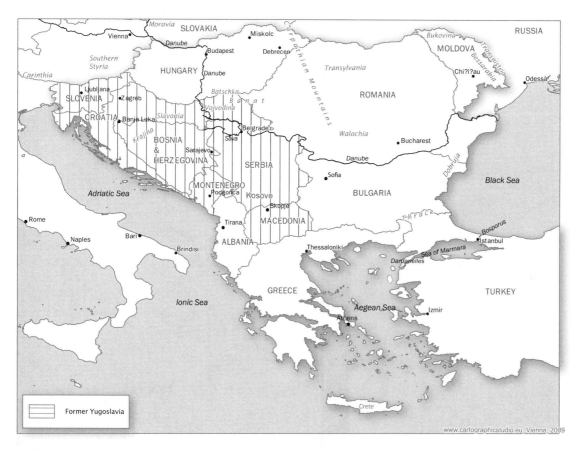

Southeastern Europe 2000

SOUTHEASTERN EUROPE

Holm Sundhaussen

For centuries, southeastern Europe was a region of movement. This was largely – but not entirely – a consequence of its geographic location. The southeastern European peninsula links central Europe with the Near East and the southern Russian steppe. In the east, south, and west it is bounded by five seas: the Black Sea, the Sea of Marmara, the Aegean, the Ionian Sea, and the Adriatic. The straits of the Bosporus and the Dardanelles have never formed a barrier to the route between Anatolia and Europe. The coastal regions, too, were relatively accessible from the sea. And the southern Russian steppe offered open access to the Romanian lowland and, following the Danube upstream, to the Great Hungarian Low Plain, or, along the Black Sea coast, in the direction of Constantinople (Istanbul). Even the mountains (especially the Carpathians and the Balkans) were not impassable, thanks to their passes. From the age of the great migrations during the transition from antiquity to the Middle Ages down to the eve of the modern period, nomadic horseman from the southern Russian steppe lands or Asia Minor, and in their wake also settled farmers (particularly Slavs), repeatedly pushed into southeastern Europe: e.g., Huns, Avars, proto-Bulgarians, Magyars, Petchenegs, Kumans, Mongols, and Turks.

The region and its boundaries

Although the lower reaches of the Danube also functioned as a border of empires and states at various times, it was never able to present a durable barrier to migration across it. Still, ever since the onset of Christianization, a religious-cultural differentiation emerged within southeastern Europe. The Roman Church with its Latin culture prevailed north of the lower reaches of the Sava and Danube and west of the Una, a tributary of the Sava, while the region south of the Sava and Danube was shaped by the Byzantine Empire with the Eastern Church and its Greek culture, and later – during Ottoman rule – given a partial Islamic overlay. As a result, on either side of the dividing line between the two subregions we find, in transitional zones, fluctuating state, religious, cultural, and ethnic boundaries.

Southeastern Europe thus divides into a northern and southern part. The northern part is formed by the territories of the former Kingdom of Hungary (especially modern-day Hungary, Slovakia, Croatia-Slavonia, Vojvodina, and the Romanian Banat and Transylvania). Since the 19th century, the southern part is usually referred to as the Balkans. The name is derived from the mountain range in central Bulgaria, which the Ottomans called "Balkan" (mountain forest). Among the determinative elements of this subregion south of the Sava and Danube (and east of the Una) is, alongside the Byzantine-Orthodox legacy, the approximately four centuries of Ottoman rule, which extended, depending on the specific area, from the middle or end of the 15th to the beginning of the 19th or 20th century. During this period there were no internal borders in the Balkan region, but there was a pronounced city-country dichotomy, as well as differences between the hard-to-reach mountain regions barely controlled by the Ottomans, on the one hand, and the more easily controlled lowlands, on the other. Of the utmost importance to migration history were the absence of internal borders and the differences in settlement history and geography.

The former Romanian Principalities of Wallachia and Moldava (including the modern-day Republic of Moldavia or Bessarabia, which was part of the Principality of Moldova until the beginning of the 19th century), are an exception: although they were likewise committed to the Byzantine-Orthodox legacy, they were never an integral component of the Ottoman Empire. As Ottoman vassal principalities, they had been able to preserve their political autonomy and separate social structure, with some restrictions during the reign of the Phanariotes (1711–1828). The Islamic overlay, which is characteristic for large swaths of the Balkan region, spared the Romanian Principalities (as it did northern southeastern Europe – Hungary with Croatia-Slavonia, which were only temporarily and partially incorporated into Ottoman rule). This situation also had repercussions for migration history. Finally, one must mention the Venetian colonial empire along the coasts of the Adriatic and the Ionian Sea, as well as in the Aegean and the eastern Mediterranean, which imparted a separate imprint to the western and southern periphery of the Balkan Peninsula.

Large sections of southeastern Europe stood under the overlordship of two multiethnic empires during the early modern period, the Islamic Ottoman Empire and the Catholic Habsburg monarchy, both of which contended for hegemony on the subcontinent, and a third powerful actor appeared in the course of the 18th century, i.e., the Czarist Empire: these circumstances shaped modern geographic population movements in decisive ways. The internal decay of Ottoman power since the second half of the 16th century, along with the subsequent changes in state borders or structures of rule and the cultural-civilizational regimes connected to them, was one of the primary factors behind the migration in the Balkans and the adjoining regions. The rising burden of dues within the Ottoman Empire, the purchase and sale of offices, corruption, and the despotism of local notables reinforced both internal migrations with the European provinces of the Empire, from the easily accessible lowlands to the difficult-to-reach mountain ridges, as well as transimperial migrations with entry or flight into the Habsburg realm, the Venetian Oltra mare, or the Czarist Empire.

Already in the second third of the 16th century, the Habsburgs had begun to establish the "Confinium militare" along their border with the Ottoman Empire, a military frontier that eventually stretched from Croatia-Slavonia, across the Banat, and all the way to Transylvania, and was subject to the direct authority of the war offices in Vienna. Only in 1851–81 was the special status of the military border gradually abolished and the approximately 20,000 square kilometer area returned to the kingdoms of Hungary and Croatia-Slavonia. The military farmers (border men) settled along the military border came overwhelmingly from the European provinces of the Ottoman Empire. At the end of the 17th century, the middle part of the Kingdom of Hungary, which the Ottomans had ruled for about a century and a half, was lost to the Habsburgs, as was Transylvania; southern Hungary followed in the first decades of the 18th century. At the end of the century, the Russians pushed to the north coast of the Black Sea and eliminated the Khanate of the Crimean Tatars, an Ottoman protectorate. In 1812 they also took control of Bessarabia. All changes to the borders were accompanied by intense waves of Muslim refugees on the one side, and the subsequent settlement of Christian colonists on the other.

The Balkan region south of the Sava and Danube (a total area of around 480,000 square kilometers) was still under the rule of the crescent at the beginning of the 19th century. The first two modern state entities arose in 1830–1 at the southern and northern peripheries of the Balkan region in the sovereign Kingdom of Greece and the autonomous Principality of Serbia. The birth of these two rump states did little to alter the accustomed picture: around 82% of the Balkan region between the straits in the east and the Bosnian-Croatian border in the west was still under the direct rule of the Sublime Porte. In the decades between the Congress of Berlin in 1878 and the beginning of the Balkan Wars of 1912–13, the Ottoman share of the Balkan area shrank to 44%, while the number of new states (with altered borders) rose to four: Greece, Serbia, Montenegro, and Bulgaria. To these must be added Bosnia-Herzegovina in 1908, which was administered by Austria-Hungary and had a special status within the dual monarchy.

The post-Ottoman creation of states came to an end in the second decade of the 20th century with the Balkan Wars, the establishment of Albania, and World War I. As a result, the Turkish share of the Balkan Peninsula dropped to 5% (Eastern Thrace). In other words, just under 460,000 square kilometers had changed their national identity in less than a century. While it was chiefly numerous Christians who fled from the crescent during the Ottoman period, the territorial losses of the Ottoman Empire and the establishment of post-Ottoman states triggered the flight of many Muslims from the cross. This flight was soon followed by the more or less successful expulsion of the remaining Muslims and the flight and expulsion of the Christians who did not belong to whatever nation a state was built upon.

World War I once again transformed the political map of southeastern Europe profoundly. The Austrian possessions along the Adriatic, in Carinthia, and in southern Styria, Bosnia-Herzegovina (jointly governed by Vienna and Budapest), and about two-thirds of the Kingdom of Hungary (Croatia-Slavonia, Slovakia, Carpatho-Ukraine, southern Hungary, and Transylvania) were absorbed by Italy, by the first Yugoslav state, by newly created Czechoslovakia, and by Greater Romania. The latter also incorporated Bessarabia. After the serious defeat by the Turks in 1922–3, the Greeks had to relinquish their claims to parts of Anatolia for good. The obligatory "population exchange" between Turkey and Greece buried the Greek "Megali idea." Although the order created by the Paris Treaties was subjected once again to drastic revisions before and during World War II, after 1945 the victorious powers reestablished the basic outlines of the status quo ante (with gains for Yugoslavia and losses for Romania).

The problems of a history of southeastern European migration

In view of the geographic and political framework outlined here – open peripheries and natural internal barriers, on the one side, and "Turkish wars" and fluctuating state borders, on the other – and of the resulting instability in settlement conditions, it is no surprise that a change of place of residence in its most varied forms was a familiar experience for large sections of the population in comparatively sparsely settled southeastern Europe. Although the study of the settlement and migration history has a great many gaps, the works from the school of the Serbian anthropogeographer Jovan Cvijić clearly show, for example, that the majority population of the post-Ottoman Principality and later Kingdom of Serbia was not old-established, but had immigrated only in the 18th and 19th centuries. In the basin of the Morava and in the districts of Valjevo and Podrinje, the old-established residents made up no more than 20%. And in extreme cases they accounted for only a fraction of the total population, as for example in the region of Takovo in Sumadija (major city: Gornij Milanovac), where they were less than 1%. A compilation of all available ethnographic data for 10 subregions of Serbia reveals that only 4.3% of the families studied were old-established; 34.2% had immigrated by the end of the 18th century, and 61.5% only in the course of the 19th.

So far, there has been no attempt to systematize the migration of southeastern Europe from the early modern period to the present beyond national-historiographic, national-linguistic, or microregional approaches. Not even the beginnings of a synthesis of the migratory events are on the horizon. This has to do, on the one hand, with the national focus of historical scholarship, and, on the other, with source problems and gaps in research. Many migrations left no or only fragmentary written traces. And the recollections passed down within families often turn out to be inaccurate. While archeology, ethnography, and linguistics can provide valuable clues about the origins, migration, and diffusion of certain population groups, these fields are – like historiography – often in the service of a "national cause." Much better documented and studied are the results of the migrations that have been included in research on minorities and diasporas. Nearly all studies about ethnic, religious, or linguistic minorities also contain more or less secure and detailed information or speculations about the origins of the group in question. It has become almost impossible to keep track of the wealth of such studies. Detailed studies exist especially on the history of the immigrants of German extraction in southeastern Europe. However, the central focus in works on minorities is usually not the migration itself but the life in the destination region, for which the sources are better.

The classification into ethnic or national minorities is a product of the creation of modern nations. The notion that modern-day minorities are the result of migrations is as widespread as it is false or misleading. The term "minority" is always used in reference to a "majority," and the latter is usually equated with the nation that forms the basis of the state. As a result of numerous changes in state borders, the relationship between majorities and minorities has repeatedly shifted. The movement of state borders often – but not always – followed the migration of people who had either become a minority and left (or were expelled), or who immigrated from a neighboring region since they saw themselves as part of the new majority nation. All international treaties creating new states in southeastern Europe in the 19th century contained an (individual) option right, which gave inhabitants affected by moving borders the choice to adopt the new citizenship and stay where they were, or migrate to the state of the nation to which they previously belonged. After the Balkan Wars of 1912–13, the individual option was replaced by the collective exchange of populations, initially optional, later (1923) compulsory. The second aspect of the process of ethnic segregation of heterogeneously settled regions was the immigration of co-nationals from the diaspora into the new national state. Especially the first two post-Ottoman states, Greece and Serbia, were immigration countries for several decades after 1830–1.

In and of itself, the modern-day allocation to a majority or minority thus tells us nothing about the preceding migrations. It can be the result of migrations in the area and of a change of cultures (e.g., a change of religion and language). Whether the Bosnian Muslims are Islamicized ("Turkified")

Serbs or Croats, or a separate ethnic group (with uniform or varied origins) cannot be unequivocally determined, especially since the terms "Serbs" and "Croats" are anything but clear-cut when projected back into the early modern period. And whether the Kosovo Albanians or a part of them are Islamicized and Albanianized Serbs (called Arnautasi in Serbian terminology) can be neither confirmed nor refuted. The same goes for a part of the Serbs, and – *mutatis mutandis* – for all majorities and minorities of the region. Some minorities have been living much longer in their settlement regions than the majority around them. And a majority can be made up of potential but not real minorities, which were able to avoid minority status as a result of their assimilation.

Finally, migrations in the distant past cannot always be clearly separated from later ones, either because the sources are fragmentary (for example with regard to the migrations of the "Gypsies"), or because the designations used in them resists clear ethnic interpretation (e.g., "Vlachs," "Greeks," "Saxons"), or because these were continuous movements or migrations that were temporarily interrupted and then resumed. A paradigmatic demonstration of this is the endless quarrel over the Albanian population in Kosovo, western Macedonia, and southern Serbia.

Well into the modern period, Vlachs, Greeks, or Saxons resist clear ethnic identification, which means that these designations tell us little about the (often controversial) regions of origin of these individuals. All three terms were used for occupational, religious, as well as ethnolinguistic groups. Not everyone who identified himself to travelers as a "Greek," because as an Orthodox Christian in the Ottoman Empire he was subject to the (Greek) Patriarchate in Constantinople or used Greek as the lingua franca, was ethnically Greek. "Vlachs" could be both ethnic Romanians as well as Romance-speaking population groups south of the Danube or Slavic-speaking members of the estate of shepherds, which was privileged during the Ottoman period. The term "Vlach" was used in early modern sources to describe a way of life and a legal status – not an ethnic group. The same is true for miners ("Saxons"), in Transylvania as well as in the Balkan region (e.g., the Serbian silver mines) or the territories of east-central Europe. Very few of the miners referred to as Saxons came from Saxony or modern-day Lower Saxony. A similar situation applies to the "Turks," though here it was not so much the vocation as the religious affiliation that formed the decisive criterion of identification. Still in the 19th century, it was customary to refer to all Muslims in the European provinces of the Ottoman Empire as Turks, irrespective of their background and language.

Another exacerbating factor is that many collective identities were (and in part still are) heavily contested, especially since members of these groups altered their ethnic or national identity depending on the situation, and some still do: for example, the Bosnian Muslims, who did this well beyond the end of the Second World War; or the Muslim, Bulgarian-speaking Pomaks in Bulgaria and western Thrace; the Muslim, Macedonian-speaking Torbeš in Macedonia; the

Orthodox, Greek-speaking Karakachans in Bulgaria; Muslim Roma in all countries of the region; or the Orthodox, Turkic-speaking Gagauzians in Moldavia, Romania, and northeastern Bulgaria.

A few designations appear sporadically, only to pass back into oblivion. Their substantive consistency is highly questionable. For example, since the beginning of the 1990s, the "Balkan Egyptians" have attracted the interest of minority scholarship. In the census in the Republic of Macedonia in 1991, more than 3,000 persons indicated that they were "Egyptians." By now, the Balkan Egyptians, who can be found under various designations in Macedonia, Albania, Kosovo, as well as in Greece and Bulgaria, have organized themselves across states as citizens of various countries "with origins in Egypt." While many outside observers define the Muslim "Balkan Egyptians" (with various mother tongues) as subgroups of the Roma, who themselves probably migrated to southeastern Europe at various times, the "Egyptians" regard themselves as a separate ethnic group whose ancestors immigrated from Egypt. It is completely unclear when the immigration is supposed to have occurred (already several centuries before Christ or only in Ottoman times). "But let us not forget one fact," proclaims a statement from the "Egyptians" organized in Germany: "From Alexander of Macedon in the fourth century before our reckoning, thanks to the Roman, Byzantine, and Ottoman Empires, the Balkan peninsula and the eastern Mediterranean, including Egypt, formed a state-administrate entity for 23 centuries, until the beginning of the 20th century. And within a state, internal migrations are perfectly normal."

Since many migrations cannot be directly reconstructed because of a lack of sources, and since the indirect method by way of minority and diaspora scholarship leaves many questions unanswered, the history of migration in southeastern Europe remains over long stretches a book with seven seals. Quantification, in particular, throws up a host of problems that are impossible or at best very difficult to resolve. That applies not only to the early modern period, but also to the 19th and 20th centuries. Immigration and emigration statistics are either not kept at all, or they are frequently inconsistent. Even the indirect method, that is, tracing the migration movements by way of population statistics, creates more questions than it answers. Especially Romanian and Greek statistics in the 19th and in part in the 20th century are highly deficient.

Working through the migrations is made even more difficult by the fact that some have become part of the national imagination and were removed from sober analysis. That applies, for example, to the "Great Exodus" of the Serbs from Kosovo to southern Hungary in 1690. The "memory" of this event entered Serbian national mythology in image and word and has weighed on Serbian-Albanian relations since the beginning of nationalism. Representative examples are the famous 1896 painting by the important Serbian history painter Paja Jovanovic, *Seobe Srba* ("Migrations of the Serbs"), the novel *Seobe* by Milos Crnjanski from the interwar period,

or the national agitation in the second half of the 1980s and in the 1990s. While the 19th- and 20th-century discourses about various population groups and especially those about autochthonousness/ancientness, as well as victimhood/expulsion have been well studied, hard facts often remain in the dark. Many aspects of migration history are in danger of dissolving into a history of discourse.

For the sake of clarity, the migration examples that follow, which make no claim to being complete, have been divided into three large, multilayered blocks. The first block is formed by the migrations in the age of the multiethnic empires (from the beginning of Ottoman expansion at the end of the 14th century to the collapse of the Ottoman Empire, the Habsburg monarchy, and the Czarist Empire at the end of World War I). Crucial characteristics of these migrations are, alongside economic and social motivations, religious factors and measures by the empires to secure their power militarily or economically (settlement/colonization). The second block is devoted to the migrations in the age of nationalism (since the second third of the 19th century). With the creation of national states and nations in southeastern Europe (patterned after the nation-state), a new motif for population shifts is added: the desire to create homogeneous ethnonational territories in a heterogeneous region and to expel "foreign" population groups (ethnic migrations).

There is overlap between the first two blocks during the "long" 19th century. Migrations that were caused essentially by the formation of national states are assigned to the second block, while migrations that lack this motif remain in the first block. Finally, the third block deals with the age of the East-West confrontation. During this period (from the end of World War II until 1989), political and ideological motifs assume preeminent importance for the migration activities in southeastern Europe. Here, too, as a result of the events in Russia since 1917, there is overlap with the second block during the interwar period. The "ethnic cleansing" in the former Yugoslavia during the 1990s can be seen as a continuation and radicalization of the ethnic population shifts examined in the second block. At all time, economic factors played an important role, for example, in the form of trade activities, poverty migration, and brain drain.

Migrations in the age of the empires

The expansion of the Ottomans in Europe and the integration of large parts of southeastern Europe into the Ottoman Empire (for periods of various lengths) was accompanied by intensive migrations (immigration, emigration, return migrations, internal migrations). The same was true for the long process of pushing the Ottomans out of the Danube-Balkan region and the territories north of the Black Sea. Many of these migrations were causally and reciprocally connected. The emigration or flight of Balkan Christians from the Ottoman Empire into Habsburg territory intensified the internal migration in the Ottoman territories. And the later return migrations of Muslims from territories captured by the Habsburgs or Russians triggered in their wake a colonization movement that was directed by the respective central authorities and landlords and included both internal and transimperial migrations.[1] The south-north migrations from the Balkan region onto Habsburg territory (emigration) were followed by the west-east migrations from central to southeastern Europe (immigration).

Among the early immigrations into the European provinces of the Sublime Porte was the forced settlement of Anatolian Turkic tribes (Yuruks) in the eastern Balkans (with a focal point in modern-day Bulgaria) and the admission of the Jews expelled from Spain and Portugal at the end of the 15th century (Sephardim), who quickly established flourishing communities above all in Constantinople (Istanbul) and Thessaloniki.[2] The meritocratic Ottoman system, which was based on pragmatism and religious toleration, offered those who belonged to the religions of the book many fields of economic activity and opportunities for advancement. In this respect, the Ottoman Empire was unique. Parallel to the immigration of new population groups, there was a migration of old-established inhabitants. The end of the 14th century already saw the beginning of the great migrations of southern Slavs, Albanians, and "Vlachs" within southeastern Europe and in adjoining territories. Specifically, one should mention the emigration of Albanians after Skanderbeg's death (1468) to Sicily and Calabria, where their descendants live to this day (Italo-Albanians or "Arbëresh"), the crossing over of Croat and Serbian refugees into Venetian and Habsburg territory ("Uskoks" since 1530), and the continuous stream of Orthodox (Slavic-speaking) "Vlachs" (who later usually defined themselves as Slavs) from the Ottoman Empire into the Habsburg military border on Croat-Slavonian soil.[3]

Particular importance would accrue to the northern migrations of the Serbs (1690 and 1739) from modern-day Kosovo and Serbia to southern Hungary (modern-day Vojvodina and beyond) as well as the expansion of the settlement area of the Albanians, among other things from the northern Albanian region to Kosovo and southern Serbia. The migrations of the Albanians were evidently a long-term process, which became more dynamic in the course of the 18th century, after the exodus of many Serbs. The occasion for the great northern migration of the Serbs was the conquest of Serbia by Habsburg troops, who had been joined by several thousand Serbian (and Albanian) volunteers. Following the successful Ottoman counteroffensive, segments of the population, fearful of retribution, fled into the Habsburg Empire under the leadership of the Serbian Patriarch Arsenije III. Emperor Leopold I guaranteed them freedom of religion and their own church organizations (Leopoldian Diploma of 21 August 1690). In 1716, the city of Karlowitz in Syrmia

(Sremski Karlovci) was chosen as the seat of the Serbian Metropolitan in the Habsburg monarchy.

However, the number and ethnicity of the migrants (from and to Kosovo) cannot be definitively determined. In a 1706 letter to the successor of Emperor Leopold, the Serbian Patriarch speaks of "40,000" souls who had left Kosovo under his leadership. By contrast, popular tradition speaks of up to 37,000 families (given an average family size of 5–6 persons, that would be over 200,000 migrants). It is highly likely that the majority of the refugees belonged to the Orthodox faith, even though some Catholic Christians are likely to have been among them. Whether they were ethnic Serbs remains an open question.

Much the same holds for the immigrants who moved into the abandoned regions. The fact that the vast majority of Kosovo Albanians today are Muslims, and that some of their ancestors immigrated only after 1690, does not mean that no Albanians existed in Kosovo before that, or that the immigrants at that time were Muslims, or that they were all ethnic Albanians. Similar uncertainties cloud the past of the Albanians (Arvanites) who have been living in Greece – mostly Attica – for centuries, and most of whom today define themselves as Greeks. Neither the date of their settlement nor their current number are free of controversy.

Just like the Serbs fled in 1690 and again in 1739 out of fear of retribution by the Ottomans, after the Russo-Turkish Wars of 1770–4 and 1787–91, many Greeks on the Peloponnese and the Aegean islands left their homes and settled in regions on the north coast of the Black Sea that had been conquered by the Russians (in Kerch on the Crimea, and above all in Odessa).[4] In addition to Greeks, members of other Balkan ethnic groups also came to "New Russia" in the wake of the colonization effort launched by Empress Catherine II. Before that, Greeks from various parts of their settlement territory had already fled to southern Italy, Venice, Transylvania, or the Czarist Empire. In the Ukrainian city of Nezin (northeast of Kiev), Greeks from Epirus and Macedonia set up a brotherhood in the 17th century that played a significant role in the trade between central Europe and the Ottoman Empire, but gradually lost its importance toward the end of the 18th century.

Several waves of refugees and settlement were also triggered by the repeated Veneto-Ottoman wars (e.g., over Crete and the Peloponnese) and by the Russo-Turkish wars of 1806–12 and 1828–9. The latter wars affected especially the Bulgarian population.[5] In the middle of the 19th century, more than half a million Bulgarians were living outside of the Bulgarian settlement area in the narrower sense: several hundreds of thousands in the Principality of Walachia (in Bukarest, alone, the Bulgarian community of merchants and craftsmen was more than 10,000 strong), 100,000 in

---

[1] Muslim brotherhoods in southeastern Europe since the early modern period.

[2] Sephardim in Europe in the early modern period.

[3] Albanian settlers in Italy since the early modern period; settlers on the Habsburg military border since the early modern period.

[4] Greek settlers from the Black Sea region in New Russia since the early modern period and Pontic Greeks in Greece since the end of World War II.

[5] Bulgarian and Gagauzian settlers in New Russia and Bessarabia since the 18th century.

Bessarabia and Ukraine, 50,000 in Istanbul, and about 25,000 in the Habsburg monarchy.

A special case was the rule of the Phanariotes in Walachia and Moldavia (1711–1828). In an effort to exert greater control over the vassal principalities and secure them against Russian and Austrian expansionary intentions, the Sublime Port installed wealthy Greeks from the Phanar quarter in Constantinople as princes. As a result of the rule of the Phanariotes, Greeks moved into the higher administrative positions in the principalities and displaced the native nobility (Boyars).[6] The process of Greekification proceeded especially quickly in Walachia; it was supported by Greek merchants, teachers, and monks, and led to a late flowering of Byzantine culture ("Byzance après Byzance"). At the same time, the dismal economic state in which the Romanian principalities found themselves after the Austro-Turkish war drove the Romanian peasants to emigrate en masse into the territories south of the Danube, with the result that the previous (ethnically diverse) population group of the Vlachs was strengthened in favor of the Romanian-Valachian ethnicity.

In a complementary movement to the Christian migrations from the Ottoman Empire into the Habsburg, Russian, and Venetian empires, or the Romanian principalities, Muslims left the territories lost by the Sublime Porte (e.g., Slavonia, central Hungary, Crimea) and moved into the Balkan area and Anatolia. Soon after the Russian annexation of Crimea in 1783, a large number of Crimean Tatars went into the Ottoman Empire. The remaining Tatars were resettled in the middle of the 19th century, during the Crimean War (1853–6). And when the Ottoman-Habsburg border at the turn of the 17th century shifted for two centuries into the lowlands of the Sava in the wake of the imperial conquests in Hungary and Slavonia, the entire Muslim population left the region north of the Sava. In western Slavonia, 180 years of Turkish rule led to considerable emigrations and resettlements. In the region of Ilova there is hardly a village that did not change its inhabitants once or even several times during this time. The same was true for the lowlands of the Drava and the Sava.

Slavonia's population presented a confessionally and ethnically mixed picture toward the end of Ottoman rule. Of the approximately 220,000 inhabitants, a solid one half were Muslims of varied ethnic backgrounds; they were joined by 72,000 Catholics, 33,000 Greek Orthodox ("Vlachs"), and 2,000 Hungarians. Together with the Sultan's troops, the entire Muslim population of the Slavonian interfluve withdrew to the Ottoman provinces south of the Sava, especially to Bosnia-Herzegovina. The sources provide no indication of any kind that even part of the Muslim population remained in Slavonia or central Hungary. Under classic Islamic law, if the territory in which a Muslim is living falls under non-Muslim rule and no change in that state of affairs can be expected, the Muslim has, strictly speaking, no choice but to emigrate

into the "realm of Islam." The movement of flight affected especially the urban settlements, which had been home to the majority of the Muslims.

After the Austro-Turkish Peace of Karlowitz in January 1699, the interfluve east of the Ilova was in a desolate state. Many of the once settled and cultivated regions were deserted. A majority of the inhabitants who had left the land temporarily or had withdrawn into the trackless forests and mountains of western Slavonia did not return to their old homesteads but took possession of the settlements abandoned by the Muslims if they offered more favorable living conditions. Once peace had stabilized, resettlement began in the regions of Hungary and Slavonia vacated by the Ottomans or Muslims, and it extended – with varying degrees of intensity – into the 20th century.

The carriers of this settlement movement in Slavonia were primarily Catholic and Orthodox Slavs, most of whom came from the adjoining provinces that had remained in Ottoman hands, from Bosnia, Herzegovina, and the *Pasaluk* (administrative seat of the Ottoman vizier) Belgrade, but also from the earlier Serbian refugee areas in central Hungary and Croatia proper. Three larger groups can be distinguished among the Slavic groups: Croats, Bunjevci (a group that came from the south and was closely related to the Croats), and Serbs, some of whom were referred to as "Vlachs" or even more frequently as "Raitzen." Immigrants of German background initially played only a minor role numerically. It was only relatively late, after the middle of the 19th century, that their importance in Slavonia gradually increased.

After the withdrawal of the Ottoman troops and the Muslims, Transdanubia and the land between the Danube and the Tisza initially witnessed a spontaneous return migration of Magyars, who were soon followed by members of other ethnic groups from the adjoining regions – Romanians, Slovaks, Ruthenians, and (Ashkenazi) Jews.[7] However, this did not remedy the low population density and the labor shortage in the eastern portion of the Habsburg monarchy, which is why the authorities in Vienna and the noble landowners started to recruit colonists from outside the Kingdom of Hungary. The first Habsburg settlement (*Impopulation*) edict was issued under Emperor Leopold I on 11 August 1689 and provided numerous privileges for colonists: lower land prices, heritable ownership of houses and land, tax exemption for three or five years, duty-free importation of construction material, the right to move away, and measures to promote trades, industry, and mining.

Settlement was pursued with particular resolve in the crown domains administered by the central imperial bureaucracy. The area of the military border was expanded along the Danube and extended all the way into Transylvania. Many ethnic groups were involved in the colonization of the territories conquered from the Ottomans: alongside the Magyars there were Czechs, Slovaks, Ruthenians,

---

[6] Greek traders and Phanariotes in southern and southeastern Europe from the early modern period to the 19th century.

[7] Ashkenazim in Europe since the early modern period.

Romanians, and southern Slavs. Beginning in the 18th century, German-speaking rural settlers also arrived in growing numbers; since the end of World War I, they have been referred to collectively as "Danube Swabians." Only a minority of those settlers was in fact of Swabian background; most came from modern-day Baden-Württemberg, Hesse, Bavaria, the Palatinate, and Austria. They were ethnically, dialectically, and confessionally heterogeneous and also diverse in their social stratification, whereby the percentage of tradesmen increased noticeably in the second half of the 18th century. As the preferred settlement areas of the "Danube Swabians" one must mention the Banat, the Batschka, Sathmar, southern Transdanubia ("Swabian Turkey"), Bakony north of Lake Balaton, and the mountainous region around Ofen (Buda). In the course of the 19th century, the Danube Swabians also set up branch settlements in the Slavonian interfluve and in Syrmia.[8] Multifarious migration movements took place between the older and younger German settlement areas (e.g., immigration of Germans from Zips and Bessarabia into the Banat, or emigration from Bessarabia and the Ukraine into the Dobrudscha).[9]

Parallel to the population movements caused by wars and their aftermath, there were population shifts and migrations that were linked to the re-Catholicization efforts in the Habsburg empire or were economically motivated. Examples are the Protestants (*Landler*) banned from Salzburg to multiconfessional Transylvania in the first half of the 18th century, the Tyrolean Baptists (Hutterites or Anabaptists), and the Lutherans forcibly resettled from Carinthia to Transylvania in 1734–56. In the language of the Austrian chancery in the 18th century, these subjects who were forcibly resettled from their home territories to other parts of the realm were referred to as "transmigrants."[10]

Far more numerous and more complex were the primarily economically motivated migration movements within the Ottoman Empire and beyond its borders. They can be roughly divided into two subgroups: the first group were merchants (and craftsmen), the second were peasants and herders. The backdrop to these migrations is easier to understand if one recalls that a kind of division of labor existed between the three large religious communities in the European provinces of the Ottoman Empire (Muslims, Orthodox Christians, and Jews). While the Muslims were active especially in the military, the administration, and the legal system as "servants" of the Sultan, Christians, Sephardic Jews, and immigrant Armenians played a leading role in commerce, the trades, and the "free professions"; peasants and herders, meanwhile, were responsible for food production. The movements of the "professional Ottomans" were guided chiefly by the needs as well as successes or failures of imperial policy. By contrast,

economic push and pull forces had the greatest importance for the economically active part of the Ottoman subjects. In both cases, religion played a role.

It is impossible, within the parameters of this essay, to lay out in detail all the migratory movements, settlements, and commercial networks associated with the group of merchants and craftsmen – from Sephardic Jews, "Greeks," Armenians, Aromuni, Ragusans – within the Balkan area, in broader southeastern Europe (Rumanian principalities, Transylvania, Hungary), and beyond (e.g., Venice, Marseille, Vienna, Leipzig).[11]

The borders between the Ottoman Empire and its northern and western neighbors were fairly porous in both directions in the early modern period. "Western" merchants were active in the territories of the Sultan and often entered into close ties with their local counterparts, while Ottoman subjects gradually expanded their radius and became active in the Habsburg monarchy and further west.

During the early modern period, Balkan merchants – Ottoman subjects of various ethnicities who were usually referred to as Greeks – were regular visitors at the fairs in Lemberg, Nezin, Leipzig, Pest, and Debrecen. Some joined into "Greek companies" that were furnished with special privileges (immunity, self-government, tax benefits) by the respective territorial lords. The first half of the 17th century saw the emergence of the first Greek companies in the Transylvanian cities of Kronstadt and Hermannstadt. After the Peace of Karlowitz (1699) and the annexation of the previous Ottoman vassal principality of Transylvania by the Habsburg Empire, Leopold I regulated the rights of the Balkan merchants in Transylvania. The Greek merchants in the Kingdom of Hungary also received a number of privileges in the course of the 18th century – often over the vehement opposition of the city magistrates. The Balkan merchants were especially active in the Hungarian export of wine and cattle (with companies in Tokaj, Eger, Miskolc, and other places).

Less well known than the Jewish and Greek traders with their numerous colonies is the role of the Armenians and Aromuni. In the 15th–16th centuries, the internal and external trade in the Rumanian principalities of Walachia and Moldavia was almost entirely in Armenian hands. In nearly all cities of southeastern Europe, Armenians were active in trade in disproportionate numbers (as tailors, lace makers, cobblers, silversmiths, or confectioners), later also as entrepreneurs or self-employed workers. The Aromuni – who were also called "Kutzo-Vlachs," "Megleno-Rumanians," or "Tsintsars," and who spoke a dialect closely related to Rumanian (with both Slavic and Greek and Albanian elements) – were initially present in the central Balkan region as nomadic herders or stock breeders engaged in transhumant, seasonal pasture

---

[8] German settlers (*Donauschwaben*) in southeastern Europe since the early modern period.

[9] German settlers in Russia since the 18th century.

[10] Austrian Protestants (*Landler*) in Transylvania since the 18th century.

[11] Greek traders and Phanariotes in southern and southeastern Europe from the early modern period to the 19th century; Sephardim in Europe in the early modern period.

farming. Their mobility predestined them for work as transportation entrepreneurs and traders. This then gave rise to a group of urban merchants who played a significant role in southeastern Europe's wholesale and long-distance trade in the early modern period. The larger Aromunian settlements in the area of northern Greece, Albania, and Macedonia represented important trading centers already in the 17th century. Aromunian merchants and the haulers associated with them handled trade not only within the Balkan Peninsula, but also to the Danubian principalities and central Europe. As early as 1658 they were enjoying privileges in the Habsburg monarchy.[12]

Moscopolis (Voskopojë along the modern-day Albanian-Greek border) was an important Aromunian entrepôt for trade with Venice, Brindisi, and Vienna. The legendary wealth of the city – which supposedly had 12,000 houses, 72 churches, an academy, and an extensive library – also led to a strong cultural flowering. In 1769 and 1788, however, the city was completely destroyed by Albanian mercenaries, because its inhabitants had supposedly supported the ill-fated expedition of the Russian fleet under General Grigorij Orlov into the southern Adriatic. This was followed by a strong wave of emigration, which headed, on the one hand, to central and northern Macedonia, and, on the other, to the Danubian principalities, to Hungary (e.g., the border town of Semlin/Zemun across from Belgrade), to Transylvania (where they became known as "Mocanii"), to Austria, Bohemia, and Moravia, and further onward to Silesia, Prussia, and Saxony, where the Aromunian immigrants often had trading partners or branches. In many parts of southeastern Europe, the (often assimilated) Aromunians were part of the core of the rising urban bourgeoisie. The Aromunians are an officially recognized minority in the modern-day Republic of Macedonia; in 1994, more than 8,600 self-identified with this group. The total number of Aromunians is estimated at more than 500,000; they are dispersed across a multitude of countries in the Balkan region (Romania, Greece [Sarakatchani], Albania, Bulgaria, and Macedonia), in central and western Europe, and in the USA.

A special group is constituted by the Catholics of European origins – the Levantines – in the eastern Mediterranean (Constantinople, Smyrna, and the Aegean). In part the members of this ethnoconfessional group are descendants of the medieval Genoese and Venetian settlers. Older sources refer to them as "Franks" or "'Latins," and they later stood under the special protection of the Sultan and the European powers (capitulations). In part they were reinforced by immigration from the "mother countries," especially from the mass immigration from western and central European countries after the Crimean War. While they played an important role in the business life of Constantinople and Smyrna, they were not able to present a consolidated collective identity during the process of

ethnicization in the final phase of the Ottoman Empire and either migrated back or assimilated.[13]

The collapse of Ottoman power and the "Oriental question" this entailed not only aroused the ambitions of the great European powers but also sparked lively debates within the states of the German League and later in the German Empire. Especially representatives of the liberal bourgeoisie and the *Augsburger Allgemeine Zeitung* demanded, beginning in the 1840s, that the German streams of emigrants be redirected from overseas to southeastern Europe, into the European provinces of "Turkey" in order to colonize and "civilize" the German hinterland along the lower Danube. In the view of Friedrich List, the lands of the lower Danube could "feed 10–20 million hard-working Germans, and become to our industry and trade what the American hinterlands are for the United States of America." And the future Prussian General Field Marshal Helmuth von Moltke proclaimed emphatically in 1842 in the *Augsburger Allgemeine Zeitung*: "The colonies of the German emigrants lie on the banks of the major German river, in the uncultivated, devastated, but rich and blessed lands along the lower Danube." In spite of active propaganda, the aimed-for emigration to southeastern Europe did not go beyond modest endeavors.

A very different kind of economically motivated migration during the period of the declining Ottoman Empire were the commuter movements by the Christian Balkan population into the European provinces. When the "pax ottomanica" – based on what was perceived as a balanced division of labor – began to weaken more and more after the middle of the 16th century, when dues and taxes rose rapidly, the despotic rule by local Ottoman dignitaries and troops could no longer be effectively contained by the Sublime Porte, and the illegal privatization of landholdings (formation of *tchiftliks*) took on ever larger dimensions, and robbery and social banditry (*hajduks, klephten*) spread. At the same time, parts of the agricultural population also moved into the cities (especially in the Bulgarian settlement region) or into the difficult-to-control mountain regions (Montenegro, Herzegovina, northern Albania), where they pursued transhumant cattle breeding. As soon as the natural food supply in the mountain ranges became constrained from population growth or ecological catastrophes or the situation in the lowlands improved, a partial return migration began, which was replaced, after a more or less lengthy period of time, by a renewed flight into the mountains. However, because of a lack of sources, the details and regionally varying intensity of these "metanastasic movements" (Jovan Cvijić) are difficult to reconstruct.

Until the 19th century, migratory cattle raising – often across large distances – formed a important livelihood for the population of the Balkans. The migratory herders were joined by the seasonal migratory craftsmen (*pečalbari*) and the itinerant traders in the 18th century. However, with the

---

[12] Greek traders and Phanariotes in southern and southeastern Europe from the early modern period to the 19th century.

[13] Levantines in the Ottoman Empire and in the eastern Mediterranean since the 19th century.

founding of the post-Ottoman states, many of the seasonal migration routes were transected by the new borders.

Migrations in the age of nationalism

The formation of nations and nation-states in the "long" 19th century initiated the collapse of the multiethnic empires. After some initial wavering, the concept of a national people (based on the *ius sanguinis* and the German model) prevailed across southeastern Europe. It led to the exclusion of those population groups who were actually or supposedly of different descent or were regarded as not part of the nation because of self-identification or external labels. Although the new states, in response to pressure by the great powers, had to adopt the *ius soli* into their regulations governing citizenship, and the protection of (religious) minorities in Romania, Serbia, Montenegro, Greece, and Bulgaria was for the first time enshrined in international law at the Berlin Congress in 1878, the practice relating to citizenship followed the principles of a nation of lineage.

Although all citizens had to be equal in formal law, in all Balkan states and in Romania there was an effort to limit citizenship as full members de facto to the members of one's own nation. The principle of equality was undercut by a flood of individual laws. The exclusionary regulations were aimed not only at unwanted immigrants but also – and especially – against old-established population groups that did not or did not wish to be part of the titular nation. They were thus not (only) aimed at foreigners or aliens but (also) against natives or groups that in many cases had been living for centuries on the territory in question. Those affected were chiefly Muslims (in the Balkan region), Jews (in Romania), and Gypsies.[14] Between 1851 and 1914, more than 80,000 Romanian Jews emigrated to the USA alone. After the beginning of the 20th century, members of Christian neighboring nations also became the target of the national homogenizers. All unwanted population groups were discriminated against in myriad ways, or – given an opportunity (usually during and after a war) – resettled or expelled. Spontaneous flight or expulsions during the war were followed by flight, pressure to emigrate, or resettlement after its end.

The "ethnic cleansing" reached its first climax during the Balkan War of 1912–13, when the remaining Ottoman territory in Europe was divided up between the rival Balkan states. The Bulgarian-Turkish peace treaty of Constantinople on 29 September 1913 for the first time provided for a mutual population exchange (on a formally voluntary basis), which extended to the inhabitants of entire towns and villages on both sides of the border. Population exchange was then made obligatory with the Greek-Turkish Convention of Lausanne

in 1923, a novelty in the history of international law. And for the first time it concerned individuals whose area of residence was not transferred from one state to another. Affected were Turkish citizens of the Greek Orthodox confession (almost exclusively ethnic Greeks) on the one side, and Greek citizens of the Islamic faith (with various ethnic identities) on the other side. Exempted were the Greeks in Istanbul and on the islands of Imbros and Tenedos, and the Muslims in western Thrace (Turks, Pomaks, Roma).

Because of the methodological problems mentioned at the outset, it is impossible to reliably quantify and summarize the extent of these ethnonational population shifts since the establishment of the nation-states. For example, there is no reliable ethnographic map of the Balkan region from the early 19th century that could be compared to a modern map. This deficiency is also – but not exclusively – attributable to statistical lacunae. The creation of an ethnographic map is the result of a process of classification. That requires specific and unequivocal distinguishing characteristics, without which any kind of classification is impossible. However, in many cases such characteristics did not exist until well into the 19th century. Either we have criteria that are insufficiently specific (e.g., Muslims, Orthodox, Catholics), or characteristics that cannot be clearly distinguished because of fluid boundaries (e.g., speakers of a southern Slavic idiom). In addition, the self-identification of many of the people in question was and is subject to repeated fluctuations.

Even for the 20th century, the extent of forcible population shifts can be reconstructed only in rough outlines. Although we have more statistical data and – as a result of the process of nation building – more classification criteria, in many cases this information is fragmentary or arbitrary. The streams of refugees have not been reliably recorded either in sending countries or the destination countries, not to mention the victims of mass murder. The calculation of overall demographic losses or gains also proves exceedingly difficult.

Analyzing the available demographic data, the American historian Marvin Jackson has tried to draw up at least an approximate balance sheet for the changes that affected the ethnic minorities in the four countries of Yugoslavia, Romania, Bulgaria, and Greece for the period 1912–70. According to his calculations, the migrations in and out of these states added up to 7.4 million individuals. That number includes some double counts, but those are of little consequence. Added to this is another million where it is impossible to determine whether the individuals in question assimilated (and thus lost their character as a minority) or emigrated. Only the officially registered national minorities were included in these calculations. If we add those persons who did not qualify in the analyzed censuses as a minority, but who nevertheless (in their quality as a temporary minority because of changes to the borders) became the victims of an ethnocide (e.g., Serbs and Bosnian Muslims in the Croatian Ustasa state during the Second World War), and if one considers the period from the founding of the respective

---

[14] Hungarian coppersmiths in western Europe from the 1860s to World War I; Bosnian bear leaders in western and central Europe, 1868–1940; Ashkenazim in Europe since the early modern period; eastern European Jews in Berlin from the late 19th century to the 1930s; eastern European Jews in London since the late 19th century; eastern European Jews in Paris since the late 19th century.

state to 1912, and from 1970 to the end of the 20th century, one would probably arrive easily at a total number of 12 million (with a high error rate either way).

This number must be set against the overall population: compared to western and central Europe, the four countries in question (Yugoslavia, Greece, Bulgaria, and Romania) were always more thinly populated, and around 1940, for example, they counted fewer than 50 million inhabitants. And to the extent that one replaces the total population of these states with those regions especially affected by the ethnic changes, the extent of the ethnic cleansing at times assumes an oppressive scale: during the course and as a result of these processes, the population in some regions was turned completely upside down.

All told, one can distinguish at least four large homogenization waves in the Balkan region (without northern southeastern Europe), which were generally triggered by wars. The first wave began in the 19th century after the founding of the respective state and affected especially the members of the previously politically dominant group (especially Turks and Muslims of non-Turkish background), but also the co-nationals of the Balkan peoples who were still living outside the boundaries of the young nation-state. It has been said that during the Balkan crisis of 1875–8, alone, about 1.5 million people (among them Turks, Albanians, Circassians) fled or were expelled. From Bulgaria alone, about 350,000 Turks had emigrated by 1912. The second large wave began with the Balkan Wars of 1912–13 and lasted to around the middle of the 1920s. This was the time of the first systematic national homogenizations (forced rebaptisms, name changes, expulsions, and massacres), which were for the first time documented – at least in fragmentary form – by an international observer commission from the Carnegie Foundation.

This period saw, on the one hand, bilateral resettlement treaties (e.g., the Bulgarian-Turkish treaty of 1913), and, on the other hand, the first agreement about a so-called population exchange that was internationally sanctioned (by the new League of Nations). The treaty concluded between Greece and Turkey in 1923 (Lausanne Convention) sanctioned ex post facto the flight and expulsions (at least in the case of the Greeks of Asia Minor) that had already occurred, that is to say, it concerned only individuals who were forcibly resettled after the signing of the treaty. About 1.2 million "Greeks," some of whom did not speak Greek, as well as nearly 400,000 Muslims (with various languages and ethnic affiliations) lost their traditional homeland and previous nationality. At the urging of Greece, the Greeks of Istanbul – the seat of the Ecumenical Patriarch – were exempted from the deportations. In return, the Muslims in the Greek part of Thrace were granted the right to stay.[15]

As a result of this and other population shifts, the ethnic landscape changed fundamentally in some regions of the Balkans. For example, the percentage of Greeks in Aegean

Macedonia rose from 43 to just under 90 between 1912 and 1926, while the share of Muslims among the population of Turkish Eastern Thrace increased from 39% to 95%. Invoking the Lausanne Convention, the Greek authorities also intended to resettle the more than 20,000 Muslim Albanians living in Chameria (southern Epirus), but these Muslims were spared deportation upon intervention by the League of Nations. Many of the Chamerians were later killed during gang wars and in the civil war during and after the Second World War, or they fled to Albania. The Lausanne Convention of 1923 served subsequent resettlements and expulsions as a model, one that was invoked by actors as different as Hitler (General Plan East, 1941–2) and Churchill (Potsdam Agreement, 1945). It was only in the 1995 Dayton Peace Agreements for Bosnia-Herzegovina that the international community made an about turn: instead of sanctioning the waves of flight and expulsions ex post facto, it codified the right of return.[16] All told, the number of victims of the second wave of flight and expulsions adds up to more than 3 million (especially Greeks, Turks, Bulgarians, and Macedonians).

The third large population shift encompasses the period from the beginning of the Second World War to about the end of the 1940s. It was characterized, among other things, by the Nazi resettlement and expulsion actions in the Yugoslav sphere (including Slovenes, Gottscheer Germans, Bosnian Germans), the ethnic cleansings in the Independent State of Croatia (especially against the Serbian population), by the persecution of minorities in the territories of Yugoslavia annexed by Hungary, Italy, and Bulgaria, the annihilation of Jews and Roma, and the flight or expulsion of the Yugoslav Germans.

In the territory of Yugoslavia, alone, which was turned into a motley quilt of occupied, annexed, and sham-sovereign entities after the German attack in April 1941, well over half a million people were affected by the forced resettlements before the end of the war: 260,000 Slovenes were deported to Croatia and Serbia; 160,000 were expelled from Croatia, and 35,000 from the Batschka region; 70,000 Croats had to leave "rump Serbia" and head toward Croatia. In addition, several tens of thousands of Jews and members of other population groups were deported and murdered in the Nazi concentration camps. About 122,000 Bulgarians settled in the Bulgarian occupation area of Macedonia, but they had to leave again after the end of the war. And the Germans living in Vojvodina until 1944–5 were replaced after the end of the war by nearly a quarter million Serbian and Montenegran colonists. The total number of victims of the third wave of expulsions in the Balkan region is likely to have been well over 2 million.[17]

---

[15] Greek Orthodox and Muslim refugees and deportees in Greece and Turkey since 1912.

[16] Refugees from former Yugoslavia in Europe since 1991.

[17] Ethnic Germans (*Volksdeutsche*) in the German Reich and in German-occupied territories in World War II; Jewish refugees from Nazi Germany and from German-occupied Europe since 1933; forced laborers in Germany and German-occupied Europe during World War II.

The fourth wave began with the outbreak of war in the former Yugoslavia in 1991 and lasted until the end of the 1990s. The world public was able to watch the flight, expulsions, and ethnocide on the television screen. The number of refugees, expellees, and dead (Bosnian Muslims or Bosniaks, Croats in the "Serbian Republic of Krajina" and in Bosnia, Krajina Serbs, Kosovo Albanians, and Kosovo Serbs) was substantially larger than in the third wave during the Second World War. Well over 4 million people were affected. It is likely that only about half of the refugees will return to their old homeland. The rest will fall victim to the homogenization of nation-states. Traumatic experiences, unresolved property issues, and the economic and social misery in the regions of origin are impeding the return guaranteed in the Dayton Agreements. By the end of May 2004, a total of just under a million refugees – less than half of those affected – had returned to their former homes in Bosnia-Herzegovina, among them 442,000 individuals into communities in which they do not represent the current majority ("minority returns"). All post-Yugoslav states (with the exception of Slovenia) find themselves confronted with enormous refugee problems.[18]

The period between these great currents of unmixing witnessed the comparatively unspectacular, but more or less continuous and daily departure of Turks/Muslims or Jews – emigrations that only occasionally intensified, as for example, in Bulgaria at the beginning of the 1950s and in the second half of the 1980s.

Northern southeastern Europe (including Romania and Moldavia) also saw the expulsion, flight, and forced assimilation of millions of people in the wake of the creation of new states, border shifts, and regime changes. After the First World War, Magyars, Croats, Slovenes, and Italians fled from neighboring countries into their respective nation-states or exercised their option right.[19] After the signing of the Treaty of Versailles, 350,000 Magyars streamed from the successor states of the Habsburg monarchy into Hungary, which had been substantially pruned territorially by the Peace Treaty of Trianon in 1920 (among them 197,000 Magyars from Romania and 47,000 from Yugoslavia). About 50,000 southern Slavs escaped from the south of what was left of the Hungarian state into Yugoslavia.

The Second World War saw a dramatic intensification of coercive measures, including the mass murder of undesirable minorities. This affected especially the Jews in Hungary, Bessarabia, and Transnistria, most of whom fell victim to the Holocaust. But these measures also targeted the Jews in Old Romania and Romanians in the Hungarian section of Transylvania; the Germans in Bessarabia, Bukovina, and Dobrudsch, who were resettled by the Nazis; the Germans expelled after 1945 from the northern sections of Yugoslavia

and Hungary; as well as those Magyars and Slovaks who had to leave their traditional homeland after 1945 because of a population exchange. About 320,000 Romanians fled from the part of Transylvania annexed by Hungary between 1941 and 1944, while 142,000 Magyars resettled there, though after the war they had to return to Hungary. Many of the Germans, Magyars, and Jews remaining in Romania left in the decades following the war or were bought off.

All told, the number of southeastern European Jews who fell victim to the Holocaust is estimated at more than 810,000: 476,000 from Hungary, at least 212,000 from Romania, including Bessarabia and Transnistria, 64,500 from Yugoslavia, and 58,000 from Greece. Among the victims were also a few tens of thousands who had fled from the Third Reich to southeastern Europe between 1933 and 1941. The number of Germans who were expelled from or left southeastern Europe added up to 763,500 by the fall of 1950: 297,000 from Yugoslavia, 253,000 from Romania, and 213,000 from Hungary.[20]

The second large current of migrations in the age of nationalism was tied to the modernization measures in the new states and their economic, social, and demographic consequences. In the second half of the 19th century, the societies of southeastern Europe reached the phase of demographic transition. Since urbanization and industrialization lagged behind population growth, a rapidly growing shortage of land made itself felt in the countryside toward the end of the 19th century. As emigration into the cities in many cases offered no way out, the modern labor migration overseas and into the European industrial countries began. Once again, the available numbers are fragmentary. Already before the First World War, around a million Balkan Slavs supposedly emigrated to North America. At the beginning of the 19th century, central Europe was home to about half a million industrial workers from the territory of the future Yugoslavia,[21] among them 17,000–45,000 Slovenes in the Ruhr basin. In the 1930s, an estimated 132,000 "Yugoslavs" emigrated to western and central Europe (mostly to Germany and France), with 41% coming from Slovenia and 24% from Croatia; 82,000 are said to have eventually returned.

At the beginning of the 1930s, the Greek authorities sought to ascertain the number of Greeks living abroad. They differentiated between Greek citizens and ethnic Greeks, that is to say, Greeks holding different citizenships but registered by foreign ethnic communities or the Greek Orthodox Church (see Table 1).

The palpable labor shortage in Germany after 1937, the result of the buildup of the armaments industry by the Nazis, triggered a wave of recruitment abroad, which was supplemented after the outbreak of the war by the use of prisoners

---

[18] Refugees from former Yugoslavia in Europe since 1991.

[19] Slovenian and Croatian emigrants in Yugoslavia from territories ceded to Italy after 1918; Italian refugees in Italy from Adriatic territories that fell to Yugoslavia after 1945.

[20] Jewish refugees from Nazi Germany and from German-occupied Europe since 1933; German refugees and expellees from eastern, east-central, and southeastern Europe in Germany and Austria since the end of World War II.

[21] Croatian and Slovenian labor migrants in Austria in the 19th and early 20th centuries.

Table 1. Greeks abroad at the beginning of the 1930s			
Region	Citizens	"Ethnic Greeks"	Total
Europe	146,024	441,787	587,811
Breakdown by country			
USSR	49,975	167,790	213,765
Turkey	26,431	140,000	166,431
Dodecanese	3,000	93,784	96,784
Albania	–	90,000	90,000
Cyprus	1,953	269,715	271,668
America	139,842	287,900	427,742
of those: USA	120,000	280,000	400,000
Other	100,167	34,703	231,654
Total	390,986	1,127,889	1,518,875

Source: Spiliotis, *Transterritorialität und Nationale Abgrenzung*, 28–9; not included in this table are individuals of Greek extraction living abroad who could not be identified either by the Greek authorities or on the basis of foreign statistics, or whose number was not revealed in deference to the sensitivities of the host countries.

Table 2. Southeastern European workers (civilian workers) in the Third Reich, 1943			
Country of origin	Men	Women	Total
Croatia	49,245	17,648	66,893
Serbia	34,395	12,035	46,430
Slovakia	29,010	16,384	45,368
Hungary	20,401	7,461	27,862
Bulgaria	19,753	1,415	21,168
Greece	9,285	1,892	11,177
Romania	6,641	2,075	8,716
Total	168,730	58,874	227,604

Source: Hans Zeck, "Erfahrungen mit dem Einsatz süodosteuropäischer Arbeiter, Mitte 1943," *Bundesarchiv R 63/629*, fol. 4ff.

Table 3. Yugoslav migrant laborers in Europe, 1971			
Country	Yugoslav census 1971	Estimate 1971	Estimate 1973
West Germany	411,503	594,300	700,000
Austria	82,957	90,000	197,000
France	36,982	60,000	75,000
Switzerland	21,201	25,000	28,000
Sweden	16,359	36,000	40,000
Other	27,867	13,000	35,000
Total	596,869	833,300	1,075,000

Source: Yugoslav Census 1971; Baučić, *Radnici u inozemstvu prema popisu stanovništva Jugoslavije*; Haberl, *Die Abwanderung von Arbeitskräften aus Jugoslawien*.

civilian population), who fled to Bulgaria and Yugoslavia in the 1920s, and the enemies of the communists who left their various "people's republics" after 1945. They were joined by refugees from the Greek civil war, who were dispersed to the socialist countries following the defeat of the communists in 1949, and the Hungarians who fled westward after the uprising in 1956.[23] The political refugees constituted a permanent irritant to the socialist governments, and they also kept the intelligence services busy. While the establishment of the socialist systems brought politically driven migrations in its wake, the collapse of these systems in 1989 triggered a stronger flow of migrations for economic reasons (both poverty migrations and brain drain).

As early as the 1950s, (illegal) labor migrants began to leave Yugoslavia – especially the karst regions in the Dalmatian-Bosnian border region – for Austria and West Germany. After the Yugoslav government (unlike other socialist regimes) legalized what was understood as temporary labor migration through bilateral treaties in the 1960s, the number of Yugoslav guest workers abroad surged. According to the Yugoslav census of 1971, just under 600,000 Yugoslav immigrants were in the various countries of western Europe, while estimates are substantially higher (see Table 3). Contrary to the official expectations in Yugoslavia and in the other recruiting countries, many of the guest workers never returned to their homeland.[24]

In nonsocialist Greece as well, emigration once again played an important role after the end of the Second World War. Between 1950 and 1975, just under 1.2 million individuals left, the vast majority in the 1960s. The majority had gone overseas in the 1950s; thereafter the ratio changed in favor of the European industrialized countries.[25]

of war and other forms of forced labor. In the spring of 1943, there were about 230,000 workers from southeastern Europe in the Greater German Reich (see Table 2).[22]

Migrations in the age of the East-West confrontation

After the October Revolution in Russia in 1917 and the victory of the Bolsheviks in the subsequent civil war, as well as in the wake of the establishment of socialist systems in Yugoslavia, Albania, Bulgaria, Romania, and Hungary after 1945, there began a stronger current of emigrations driven by political-ideological motivations. In addition, economically driven migrations took on new importance beginning in the 1950s. The first group included refugees from the Russian civil war (remnants of the "white" armies and segments of the

[22] Forced laborers in Germany and German-occupied Europe during World War II.

[23] Russian emigrants in Europe since 1917; Greek refugees in eastern and southeastern Europe after the civil war, 1946–1949; Hungarian refugees in Europe since 1956.

[24] Yugoslav labor migrants in western, central, and northern Europe since the end of World War II.

[25] Greek refugees in western, central, northern, and southern Europe during the military dictatorship, 1967–1974; Greek labor migrants in western, central, and northern Europe after 1950: the examples of Germany and the Netherlands.

Following the upheavals of 1989 and the beginning of the difficult process of transformation in the southeastern countries of the former Soviet Bloc, with its socioeconomic dislocations, there began a strong emigration to the West, which was reinforced further by streams of refugees and asylum seekers caused by the post-Yugoslav wars (1991–9).[26] In the wake of this development, the number of southeastern Europeans living in Germany, for example, also rose. Around 1.7 million foreigners of a southeastern European nationality were registered in that country in 1999: 737,204 from the Federal Republic of Yugoslavia (Serbia-Montenegro, including Kosovo); 364,354 Greeks; 213,945 Croats; 167,690 from Bosnia-Herzegovina; 87,504 Romanians; 53,152 Hungarians; and 49,420 from Macedonia. After subtracting those migrants who returned or continued on somewhere else, Germany had a positive migration balance with southeastern Europe (not counting Turkey) of just under 430,000 for the period 1991–2003.

Internal migration within southeastern Europe, which had played a key role both in the age of the empires and in the era of nationalism (including the events in the former Yugoslavia during the 1990s), has today receded entirely into the background. One exception is the immigration of Albanian workers into Greece. Estimates put the current number of migrant workers in Greece at 700,000–800,000 (most of them with unclear status). If a part of them stay on, Greek society will change. Officially, Greece has no minorities, with the exception of the Muslims of western Thrace listed in the Lausanne Convention of 1923. Many Greeks regard the Thracian Muslims as Islamicized (ethnic) Greeks, just as they see the Slavophone population in northern Greece as Slavicized (ethnic) Greeks. The fiction that there are no minorities in Greece cannot be maintained much longer in the face of the strong influx of Albanians.

Migrants and society of origin

The number of ethnic southeastern Europeans currently living abroad defies any reliable calculation. That holds true not only because the statistics are contradictory and full of gaps, but also because the problems of definition this creates remain impossible to resolve. Lists of immigrants, if they are maintained in the various countries, provide information only about the number of immigrants but tell us nothing about the subsequent generation or returning migrants. Taking our cues from the self-description of the individuals in question might be a solution, but it presupposes that corresponding information gathering is carried out in all countries, and that will simply not happen in the foreseeable future. The claims that more than 4 million Greeks (in the ethnic sense, that is, not only Greek citizens) are living abroad at this time (of those, 400,000 in Germany) is as unverifiable as the notion that more Albanians (not counting the Kosovo Albanians) are living abroad than in Albania itself.

Estimates like these always proceed from an essentialist premise, since they completely ignore the potential for change in collective identities and self-descriptions, and since they draw inferences from certain characteristics (such as language, religion, kinship) about the bearers of those characteristics. That is impermissible, for the genealogy of these characteristics is not identical with the genealogy of the people who have adopted (or cast off) these characteristics. Language and religion have a history of their own, which does not coincide with the history of the individuals who embody them. With some qualifications that apply also to kinship constructs, although they can remain fairly stable over long periods, they are also subject to change. For example, the agnatic (patriarchal) line of descent in the Balkan region has been replaced by cognatic (bilinear, referring to both parents) descent, while the once important elective affinity has receded entirely into the background. For the offspring of mixed ethnic marriages there is (in cognatic kinship systems) no clear ethnic classification, in any case. By contrast, those individuals who affirm their membership in a diaspora community or have joined one can be statistically captured, at least in theory. But while we have a multitude of scattered data in this respect, there is no overall number.

Diaspora research has been very active for several years and has produced a number of individual studies especially on relations between the foreign communities and the societies of origin, but this is not yet enough to create a complete picture. In international scholarship, questions of this kind are studied under the heading "transnationalism." At the center of this research are not only and primarily the financial relationships between society of origin and its foreign communities, but also, and above all, the cultural and political interdependencies and transfers: in other words, the question of how the society of origin influences the culture, identity management, and politics of the diaspora, and vice versa.

Both in the recent past and at present, diaspora communities have at times played and continue to play a decisive role in the processes of change in their societies of origin. This was especially evident during the processes of nation-building in southeastern Europe in the 19th century: the Greek or Bulgarian diaspora in the Romanian Principalities and in various parts of the Ottoman Empire, or the Serbian diaspora in the Habsburg monarchy exerted crucial influence on the "invention" of their nations. Something similar applies to the post-Yugoslav nation-building since the 1990s, particularly to the Croatian and Kosovo-Albanian diaspora. Because of their intercultural experience, diaspora communities can both take on a mediating role between various nations, and – by means of the transfer of ideas – function as pioneers in the struggle for their nation or, because of their foreign experience, as agents of national radicalization. The circumstances under which they assume one role or the other await study and clarification. In short: southeastern Europe's migration history remains an open history with many gaps, one that largely reduces the traditional national histories and their premises to absurdity.

---

[26] Refugees from former Yugoslavia in Europe since 1991.

REFERENCES

Adanir, Fikret. "Migration, Deportation, and Nation-Building: The Case of the Ottoman Empire, 1856–1923." In *Migrations et migrants dans une perspective historique. Permanence et innovations*, edited by René Leboutte, 273–92. Brussels, 2000.

Andrić, Ljubisav, ed. *Velika Seoba 1690–1990*. Belgrade, 1990.

Anselmi, Sergio, ed. *Italia felix. Migrazioni slavi e albanesi in Occidente. Romagna, Marche, Abruzzi secoli XIV–XVI*. Ancona, 1988.

Balogh, Sándor. "Die Aussiedlung der Bevölkerung deutscher Nationalität aus Ungarn nach dem 2. Weltkrieg." *Annales Universitatis Scientiarum Budapestinensis de Rolando Eötvös nominatae, Sectio historica* 22 (1982): 221–50.

Bandžović, Safet. "Iseljavanje muslimanskog stanovništva iz Srbije tokom XIX stoljćea." *Tutinski zbornik* 2 (2001): 79–128.

Batakliev, Ivan. "Bevölkerungsverschiebungen, Wirtschafts- und Siedlungspolitik Bulgariens, besonders nach dem Weltkriege." *Leipziger Vierteljahrsschrift für Südosteuropa* 3 (1939): 38–50.

Batakliev, Ivan. "Die Wanderung der Bulgaren in den letzten 30 Jahren." *Zeitschrift für Geopolitik* 18, 3 (1941): 155–63.

Baučić, Ivo. *Radnici u inozemstvu prema popisu stanovništva Jugoslavije*. Zagreb, 1973.

Baučić, Ivo. *Rückkehr und Reintegration jugoslawischer Arbeitnehmer aus der BRD, Deutsch-jugoslawische Untersuchung der Zukunftspläne jugoslawischer Arbeitsmigranten und ihre Realisierung nach der Rückkehr*. Bonn, 1987.

Beer, Mathias, ed. *Migration nach Ost- und Südosteuropa vom 18. bis zum Beginn des 19. Jahrhunderts. Ursachen – Formen – Verlauf – Ergebnis*. Stuttgart, 1999.

Benz, Wolfgang, ed. *Die Vertreibung der Deutschen aus dem Osten. Ursachen, Ereignisse, Folgen*. Frankfurt am Main, 1985.

Blanchard, Raul. "The Exchange of Populations Between Greece and Turkey." *Geographical Review* 15 (1925): 449–56.

Blank, Inge, "A Vast Migratory Experience: Eastern Europe in the Pre- and Post Emancipation Era (1780–1914)." In *Roots of the Transplanted, Vol. 1: Late 19th Century East Central and Southeastern Europe*, edited by Dirk Hoerder and Inge Blank, 201–51. New York, 1994.

Brandes, Detlef. *Von der Zarin adoptiert. Die deutschen Kolonisten und die Balkansiedler in Neurußland und Bessarabien 1751–1914*. Munich, 1993.

Brunner, Georg, ed. *Die Deutschen in Ungarn*. Munich, 1989.

Buchinger, Erich. *Die "Landler" in Siebenbürgen. Vorgeschichte, Durchführung und Ergebnis einer Zwangsumsiedlung im 18. Jahrhundert*. Munich, 1980.

Bur, Márta. "Das Raumgreifen balkanischer Kaufleute im Wirtschaftsleben der ostmitteleuropäischen Länder im 17. und 18. Jahrhundert." In *Bürgertum und bürgerliche Entwicklung in Mittel- und Osteuropa*, edited by Vera Bácskai, 17–88. Budapest, 1986.

Bur, Márta. "Handelsgesellschaften. Organisationen der Kaufleute der Balkanländer in Ungarn im 17.–18. Jahrhundert." *Balkan Studies* 25, 2 (1984): 267–307.

Carnegie Report: Report of the International Commission to Inquire into the Causes and Conduct of the Balkan Wars. Washington, DC, 1914.

Carter, Francis W. "Ethnicity as a Cause of Migration in Eastern Europe." *Geo-Journal* 30, 3 (1993): 241–48.

Chater, Melville. "History's Greatest Trek." *National Geographic Magazine* 48, 5 (1925): 533–90.

Čizmić, Ivan. "Emigration from Yugoslavia prior to World War II." In *Migration across Time and Nations: Population Mobility in Historical Contexts*, edited by Ira A. Glazier and Luigi De Rosa, 255–67. New York and London, 1986.

Čizmić, Ivan, et al., eds. *Iseljeništvo naroda i narodnosti Jugoslavije i njegove uzajamne veze s domovinom*. Zagreb, 1978.

Clogg, Richard, ed. *Balkan Society in the Age of Greek Independence*. Basingstoke, 1981.

Clogg, Richard. *The Greek Diaspora in the Twentieth Century*. Basingstoke, 1999.

Clogg, Richard. *The Greek Merchant Companies in Transylvania*. Cologne, 2000.

Constas, Dimitri, and Athanassios G. Platias. *Diasporas in World Politics: The Greeks in Comparative Perspective*. Basingstoke, 1993.

Cvijić, Jovan. *Metanastazićka kretanja. Njihovi uzroci i posledice*. Belgrade, 1922.

Devedji, Alexandre. *L'échange obligatoire des minorités grecques et turques en vertu de la Convention de Lausanne du 30 janvier 1923*. Paris, 1929.

Eberhardt, Piotr. *Ethnic Groups and Population Changes in Twentieth-Century Central Eastern Europe*. London, 2002.

Fassmann, Heinz, and Rainer Münz. "Geschichte und Gegenwart europäischer Ost-West Wanderung." *Österreichische Osthefte* 37 (1995): 747–78.

Fata, Márta. "Einwanderung und Ansiedlung der Deutschen (1686–1790)." In *Deutsche Geschichte im Osten Europas. Land an der Donau*, edited by Günter Schödl, 89–196. Berlin, 1995.

Ferenc, Tone. "Die Massenvertreibung der Bevölkerung Jugoslawiens während des Zweiten Weltkrieges und der mißglückte Plan einer Aussiedlung von Slowenen in Polen." *Studia historiae oeconomicae* 8 (1973): 51–76.

Frumkin, Gregory. *Population Changes in Europe since 1939: A Study of Population Changes in Europe during and since World War II as Shown by the Balance Sheets of Twenty-four European Countries*. New York, 1951.

Glamočak, Marina. "La genèse de l'émigration politique serbe et croate." *Balkanologie* 2, 1 (1998): 37–61.

Glatz, Ferenc, ed. *Études historiques hongroises*, Vol. 2: *Ethnicity and Society in Hungary*. Budapest, 1990.

Gondicas, Dimitri, and Charles Issawi, eds. *Ottoman Greeks in the Age of Nationalism*. Princeton, 1999.

Grečić, Vladimir, ed. *Seobe Srba nekad i sad*. Belgrade, 1990.

Grečić, Vladimir. *Migracije visokostručnih kadrova i naučnika iz SR Jugoslavije*. Belgrade, 1996.

Haberl, Othmar Nikola. *Die Abwanderung von Arbeitskräften aus Jugoslawien: Zur Problematik ihrer Auslandsbeschäftigung und Rückführung*. Munich, 1978.

Hecker, Hellmuth. *Die Umsiedlungsverträge des Deutschen Reiches während des Zweiten Weltkrieges.* Hamburg, 1971.

Heller, Wilfried. *Rumania: Migration, Socio-economic Transformation and Perspectives of Regional Development.* Munich, 1998.

Herbert, Ulrich, ed. *Europa und der "Reichseinsatz." Ausländische Zivilarbeiter, Kriegsgefangene und KZ-Häftlinge in Deutschland 1938–1945.* Essen, 1991.

Hirschon, Renée, ed. *Crossing the Aegean: An Appraisal of the 1923 Compulsory Population Exchange between Greece and Turkey.* Oxford, 2003.

Hockenos, Paul. *Homeland Calling: Exile Patriotism and the Balkan Wars.* Ithaca, 2003.

Höpken, Wolfgang. "Flucht vor dem Kreuz? Muslimische Emigration aus Südosteuropa nach dem Ende der osmanischen Herrschaft (19./20. Jh.)." *Comparativ* 6, 1 (1996): 1–24.

Jackson, Marvin R. "Comparing the Balkan Demographic Experience, 1860 to 1970." *Journal of European Economic History* 14 (1985): 223–72.

Janjetovic, Zoran. *Between Hitler and Tito. Disappearance of Ethnic Germans from Vojvodina.* Belgrade, 2000.

Kačavenda, Petar. *Nemci u Jugoslaviji 1918–1945.* Belgrade, 1991.

Kahl, Thede. *Ethnizität und räumliche Verbreitung der Aromunen in Südosteuropa.* Münster, 1999.

Kaser, Karl. *Freier Bauer und Soldat. Die Militarisierung der agrarischen Gesellschaft in der kroatisch-slawonischen Militärgrenze (1535–1881).* Graz, 1985.

King, Russell, Nicola Mai, and Stephanie Schwandner-Sievers, eds. *The New Albanian Migration.* Brighton, 2005.

Konstantinou, Evangelos, ed. *Griechische Migration in Europa. Geschichte und Gegenwart.* Frankfurt am Main, 2000.

Kyoseva [Kjoseva], Tsvetana. *Bulgaria and die Russian Emigration in Bulgaria: From the 1920s to the 1950s.* Sofia, 2002.

Levy, Avigdor. *The Sephardim in the Ottoman Empire.* Princeton, 1992.

Mackridge, Peter, and Eleni Yannakakis, eds. *The Development of a Greek Macedonian Cultural Identity since 1912.* Oxford and New York. 1997.

Mitrovicn, Andrej, ed. *Srbi i Albanci u XX veku.* Belgrade 1991.

Palairet, Michael. "The 'New' Immigration and the Newest. Slavic Migrations from the Balkans to America and Industrial Europe since the Late Nineteenth Century." In *The Search for Wealth and Stability*, edited by T. C. Smout, 43–65. London, 1979.

Pandevska, Maria. *Prisilni migracii vo Makedonija vo godinite na Golemata Istočna Kriza (1875–1881).* Skopje, 1993.

Pavlović, Radoslav Lj. "Seoba Srba i Arbanasa u ratovima 1876 i 1877–1878 godine." *Glasnik Etnografskog instituta* 4–6 (1955–7): 53–104.

Petrova, Darina. *Bulgarians from Istanbul.* Sofia, 2000.

Peyfuss, Max D. *Die aromunische Frage.* Vienna, 1974.

Popović, Dušan. *Velika seoba Srba 1690. Srbi seljani i plemići.* Belgrade, 1954.

Puskás, Julianna. "Hungarian Migration Patterns, 1880–1930: From Macroanalysis to Microanalysis." In *Migration across Time and Nations: Population Mobility in Historical Contexts*, edited by Ira A. Glazier and Luigi De Rosa, 231–54. New York and London, 1986.

Roman, Louis, ed. *Studii de demografie istorica românesca.* Bukarest, 2002.

Schieder, Theodor, ed. *Dokumentation der Vertreibung aus Ost-Mitteleuropa*, Vol. 2: *Das Schicksal der Deutschen in Ungarn;* Vol. 3: *Das Schicksal der Deutschen in Rumänien;* Vol. 5: *Das Schicksal der Deutschen in Jugoslawien.* Düsseldorf, 1956–61.

Schierup, Carl-Ulrik. *Migration, Socialism and the International Division of Labour: The Yugoslav Experience.* Aldershot, 1990.

Schmitt, Oliver J. *Levantiner. Lebenswelten und Identitäten einer ethnokonfessionellen Gruppe im Osmanischen Reich im "langen 19. Jahrhundert."* Munich, 2005.

Schödl, Günter, ed. *Geschichte der Deutschen im Osten Europas. Land an der Donau.* Berlin, 1995.

Schönfeld, Roland, ed. *Nationalitätenprobleme in Südosteuropa.* Munich, 1987.

Seewann, Gerhard, ed. *Minderheitenfragen in Südosteuropa.* Munich, 1992.

Seewann, Gerhard, ed. *Migrationen und ihre Auswirkungen. Das Beispiel Ungarn 1918–1995.* Munich, 1997.

Seewann, Gerhard. "Zwangsmigrationen von Minderheiten in Südosteuropa im 20. Jahrhundert." In *Südosteuropa im 20. Jahrhundert. Ethnostrukturen, Identitäten, Konflikte*, edited by Solomon Flavius, Alexander Rubel, and Alexandru Zub, 47–54. Konstanz, 2004.

Seewann, Gerhard, and Péter Dippold, eds. *Bibliographisches Handbuch der ethnischen Gruppen Südosteuropas.* 2 vols. Munich, 1997.

Siampos, George R. *The Greek Migration in the 20th Century.* New York, 1985.

Siupiur, Elena. *Bălgarskata emigranski inteligencija v Rumănija prez XIX vek.* Sofia, 1982.

Spiliotis, Susanne-Sophia. *Transterritorialität und nationale Abgrenzung. Konstitutionsprozesse der griechischen Gesellschaft und Ansätze ihrer faschistoiden Transformation, 1922/24–1941.* Munich, 1998.

Statelova, Elena, et al. *The Other Bulgarian: Documents about the Organizations of the Bulgarian Political Emigres 1944–1989.* Sofia, 2000.

Steiner, Stephan. *Reisen ohne Wiederkehr. Die Deportation der Protestanten aus Kärnten 1734–1736.* Munich, 2007.

Streit, Georg. *Der Lausanner Vertrag und der griechisch-türkische Bevölkerungsaustausch.* Berlin, 1929.

Subotić, Dragan, ed. *Neugasno srpstvo: srpska politićka emigracija o srpskom nacionalnom pitanju (1945–1990).* Belgrade, 1992.

Sundhaussen, Holm. "A délkelet-európai kisebbségek migrációs veszteségei a 20. Században." *Regio* 5, 4 (1994): 3–14.

Sundhaussen, Holm. "Bevölkerungsverschiebungen in Südosteuropa seit der Nationalstaatswerdung (19./20. Jh.)." *Comparativ* 6 (1996), no. 1: 25–40.

Švob, Melita. *Židovi u Hrvatskoj. Migracije i promjene u židovskoj populaciji. Jews in Croatia. Migrations and Changes in Jewish Population.* Zagreb, 1992.

Tasić, Nikola, ed. *Migrations in Balkan History.* Belgrade, 1989.

Todorova, Maria, and Nikolai Todorov. "The Historical Demography of the Ottoman Empire: Problems and Tasks." In *Scholar, Patriot, Mentor: Historical Essays in Honor of Dimitrije Djordjevic*, edited by Richard B. Spence, 151–72. New York, 1992.

Toumarkine, Alexandre. *Les migrations des musulmanes balkaniques en Anatolie (1876–1913).* Istanbul, 1995.

Tóth, Ágnes. *Migrationen in Ungarn 1945–1948. Vertreibung der Ungarndeutschen, Binnenwanderungen und slowakisch-ungarischer Bevölkerungsaustausch.* Munich, 2001.

Trajkov, Veselin N. *Bălgarskata emigracija v Rumănija XIV vek – 1878 godina I učastieto ih v stopanskija, obštestveno-političeskaja i kulturnija život na rumănskija narod.* Sofia, 1986.

Vickers, Miranda. "The Cham Issue: Albanian National and Property Claims in Greece." *Südosteuropa* 51 (2002): 228–49.

Weber, Georg. *Emigration der Siebenbürger Sachsen. Studien zu Ost-West-Wanderungen im 20. Jahrhundert.* Wiesbaden, 2003.

Winnifrith, Tom J. *The Vlachs: The History of a Balkan People.* London, 1987.

Zack, Krista, Flavius Solomon, and Cornelius R. Zach, eds. *Migration im südöstlichen Mitteleuropa. Auswanderung, Flucht, Deportation, Exil im 20. Jahrhundert.* Munich, 2005.

Zayas, Alfred-Maurice de. *A Terrible Revenge: The Ethnic Cleansing of the East European Germans, 1944–1950.* New York, 1994.

Živančević, Predrag. *Emigranti: Naseljavanje Kosovo i Metohije iz Albanije.* Belgrade, 1989.

EASTERN EUROPE

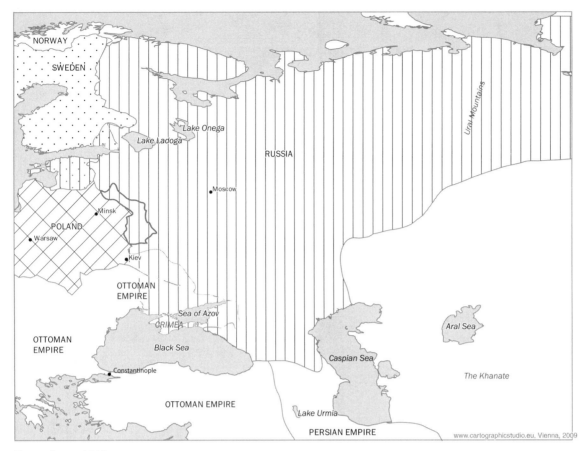

Eastern Europe 1648

Eastern Europe 2000

RUSSIA AND BELARUS

Richard Hellie

Since 1601 Russia has been the largest or one of the largest countries in the world. From 1601 to 1678, Russia annexed Ukraine and Belarus (White Russia). From 1678 to 1719, Russia annexed the Baltic region; from 1719 to 1795, Russia annexed much of Poland and Crimea; from 1795 to 1858, Russia annexed more of Poland, much of the Caucasus, and the Amur basin; from 1858 to 1897, Russia annexed the rest of the Caucasus and central Asia. The Russian Empire was at its peak in 1913 prior to World War I. Between 1913 and 1920, the Soviet Union lost Poland and the Baltic states, but in 1939 and 1940 the USSR re-annexed the Baltic States and much of Moldavia. In 1991 the USSR reached its maximum size, but after 1991 the USSR was reduced to the Russian Federation and lost the Baltic states, Moldova, Ukraine, most of the Caucasus, and central Asia.

The population-to-land ratio almost always and almost everywhere has been very low (see Table 1). Population has been concentrated in the European part of Russia, and only in a small fraction of that, primarily in the Volga-Oka mesopotamia – a triangle with Kazan as its eastern point, a line extending westward from Kazan along the northern part of the Volga to the Baltic or St. Petersburg/Leningrad, and the southern part of the triangle marked by the Oka river on a line extending to Smolensk and Russia's western frontier. To Russia's great historical misfortune, that area, the homeland of the Great Russians, has almost no natural resources, which are found outside the triangle. Gaining access to natural resources has been one of the motivating factors of Russian migration, both voluntary and compulsory. The area east of Kazan, the Urals and Siberia, primordially was inhabited by non-Slavs, and the East Slavic Russians and Belarusians generally have not desired to live there. Because of the resource value of those non-Russian areas of the Urals and Siberia, as well as for limited strategic concerns, the Russian government has always believed that some Eastern Slavs should be living in those areas, whether voluntarily or as the result of compulsion.

Inside the Volga-Oka mesopotamia there are almost no natural resources, a fact that travelers from western Europe commented on already in the 17th century. Not only is there no gold or silver but there is also no copper or coal, no petroleum or natural gas, not even any building stone much less any precious stones. Moreover, the surface natural endowment leaves much to be desired: primarily podzolic, acidic soil, about three inches thick, which gives very low grain yields in a climate with a short growing season and excessive precipitation. Until at least 1800, grain yields were "pre-Carolingian" (in Western terms); fewer than three grains were harvested for each one planted. After that, until at least the Khrushchev program of "chemicalization" in the early 1960s, yields rose only to 5:1. Before 1600, the forests may have provided wax and honey and fur-bearing animals, as well as meat to be hunted, but by that date most of that was gone and all that remained were the trees, birch and some pine. Also before 1600 the abundant rivers may have teemed with fish, but by 1600 much of the fish consumed had to be brought in from outside the area in question.

The Volga-Oka triangle could feed itself in normal times, but famines occurred there every six or seven years regardless of what the Great Russians did. The only way to increase yields was to migrate south of the Oka into the black soil (*chernozem*) region of Ukraine, which in 1600 was largely the "property" of the nomadic steppe peoples, the Crimean Tatars, the Nogais, and the Kalmyks. The Muscovites regarded the Oka as their southern frontier, and the middle service class provincial cavalry gathered there every year in anticipation of the annual raids from the steppes. The Crimean Tatars, who were primarily bent on slave-raiding, last crossed the Oka and reached Moscow in 1591.

Thus the Volga-Oka region was generally at best marginally hospitable to postneolithic man. This left the mesopotamian occupants with several options: (1) continue to live "at home" with a very low standard of living; (2) move elsewhere to better conditions permanently; (3) move outside the mesopotamia temporarily to gather desired items not available at home; (4) hire others to gather, produce, mine, or trap what was not available in the mesopotamia; (5) compel others to do this. All five of these options were utilized in varying proportions at different times.

Migration restrictions

Typically there has been a major obstacle in the exercise of these options since 1600 because Russia has rarely been a country in which its inhabitants could move freely for the last four centuries. At least from 1649 onward all peasants were permanently tied to the land that they cultivated. Since the early 1720s the peasant were no longer tied to the land, but to

Table 1. The Russian Empire/USSR/Russian Federation: Area, population, density/sq. km, 1601–2005

Year		Area/sq.km.	Population	Density/sq.km.	Sources used
1601		5,500,000	7,000,000	1.27	3, 7
1678			11,200,000		5, 6, 7
1719			15,000,000		3, 5, 6, 7, 11
1795			37,200,000		3, 7, 11
1858		19,600,000	74,000,000	3.78	3, 7, 11
1897		22,430,000	124,649,000	5.56	1, 7, 11
	Russia only	5,515,100	67,473,000	12.23	4, 11
1913			159,153,000		1, 7
	Russia only		89,902,000		4
1920			136,810,000		1
	Russia only		88,247,000		4
1926			147,027,900		1
	Russia only		92,735,000		4
1939			190,677,900		1, 3
	Russia only		108,377,200		3, 4
	Belarus only		8,912,200		3
1940			195,000,000		3
	Russia only		110,098,000		4
1959			208,826,700		1, 3
	Russia only		117,534,300		3, 4
	Belarus only		8,055,700		3
1979		22,402,200	262,436,200	11.71	1, 3
	Russian Feder.	17,075,400	137,551,000	8.06	4
	Belarus only	207,600	9,560,500	46.19	3
1991			278,100,000		2
	Belarus only		10,280,800	49.7	2
	Russia only		148,704,300		2, 4
2004			143,700,000		12

Sources: 1. TsSU SSSR. *Chislennost' i sostav naseleniia SSSR. Po dannym vsesoiuznoi perepisi naseleniia 1979 g*, Moscow (1984), 6. 2. Stat. komitet sodruzhestva nezavisimykh gosudarstv., *Strany-chleny SNG. Statiticheskii ezhegodnik*, Moscow (1992), 5, 168, 331. 3. *Demograficheskii entsiklopedichkii slovar'*, Moscow (1985), 271, 431, 561-2. 4. *Naselenie Rossii za 100 let (1897–1997). Statisticheskii sbornik*, Moscow (1998), 32-4. 5. Ia. E. Vodarskii, *Naselenie Rossii v kontse XVII-nachale XVIII veka*, Moscow (1977), 153, 192. 6. N. A. Gorskaia, *Istoricheskaia demografiia Rossii epokha feodalizma*, Moscow (1994), 96. 7. Ia. E. Vodarskii, *Naselenie Rossii za 400 let (XVI–nachalo XX vv)*, Moscow (1973), 151. 8. V. M. Kabuzan, *Izmeneniia i razmeshcheniia naseleniia Rossii v XVIII–pervoi polovine XIX v*, Moscow (1971). 9. V. M. Kabuzan, *Narodonaselenie Rossii v XVIII–pervoi poloviny XIX v. (Po materialam revizii)*, Moscow (1963). 10. A. G. Rashin, *Naselenie Rossii za sto let (1811–1913 gg.). Statisticheskie ocherki*, Moscow (1956). 11. *Rossiia. Entsiklopedicheskii slovar'*. Leningrad 1991 (reprint of *Entsiklopedicheskii slovar'*, published by Brokgauz-Efron, vol. 54, 1899), 12, 75, 115. 12. Johnson's Russia List, No. 8473.

the owner of the land, who could use the peasant as he or she saw fit. In 1861 this type of serfdom was abolished freeing the peasants from the control of their landlords. However, the peasants were still tied to the agricultural unit and had to pay redemption payments for the land that they cultivated. Migration to the cities was limited. Only after 1906–7 did this restriction disappear. Between 1861 and 1906–7 the number of migrants among the serfs had hardly been larger than before the abolition of serfdom. In spite of the freedom of movement granted to peasants in 1861 only a few peasants took the opportunity to move and to leave their former owners. The existing dependencies were simply too strong.

At the end of the 16th century, townsmen were not free to move anywhere, either. Landowners and landholders were expected to report for military duty whenever called up. This meant that only clergymen and freedmen were free to move whither their fancy drove them. In 1762 landowners in military service were freed from their service obligations, so that they were free to move as well. At some time before 1775, townsmen were permitted to come and go as they pleased.

But all of society was free to migrate wherever it wanted only between 1907 and the early Stalin period, the early 1930s, after which most farmers were bound to their collective and state farms and workers were bound to their places of employment. Moreover, major urban areas were decreed off-limits to most migrants throughout the Soviet period and beyond in an attempt to escape the ravages of modern rapid urbanization. N. S. Khrushchev, the secretary-general of the Communist Party in the Soviet Union and as such the political leader of the country between 1953 and 1964 tried to move the Soviet Union away from the horrors of Stalinism in 1957 and issued all peasants passports, which allowed them to move to any place that would accept them.

It should be stressed that the limitations represented a mesopotamian orientation that by no means all officials shared.

There always were figures in Moscow and St. Petersburg who welcomed the departure of Russians from the mesopotamia into the new territories. Moreover, Russian governors in the new territories always welcomed migrants and did almost everything in their power to avoid sending them back to the mesopotamia. Regardless of the prohibitions against migration, centrifugal movement (often illegal) persisted. This is evident in the census data of 1678 and 1719. In spite of the fact that the Law Code of 1649 bound most people to their place of residence, the traditional parts of Russia (the non-black-soil center, the northwest, and the north) increased in population 20% while the newly annexed areas (black-soil center, the east, southeast, northeast, and Siberia) increased 72%. The great discrepancy was due to migration, regardless of the law.

Migration within the Volga-Oka mesopotamia

The factors inducing inhabitants of the mesopotamia to move are probably beyond count, but certain of them must be singled out. Numerous peasants moved within the mesopotamia to escape rapacious, greedy, and cruel landlords. Victims of such landlords typically could move as little as one province away and normally escape detection by their lawful landlords. This changed only in the mid-17th century, when the government introduced *dragnets*, agents who interviewed everyone they could find to determine where they belonged. Runaways were returned to their lawful place of residence.

Serfdom's purpose was to curtail population mobility, and there can be no doubt that it did this. But regardless of that, seepage into the towns in the mesopotamia continued after 1649. The government was of two minds on this issue, for, while farming peasants supported the army both by the payment of taxes and especially by payments of rent, urban taxpayers amounting to only 2% of the population remitted a high proportion of the government's cash tax revenues and thus could not be overlooked. Towns did not grow very much in the second half of the 17th century, but every so often a town would petition the government to allow illegal migrants to remain in the town as they paid taxes. The government was often favorably disposed to such amnesties and in 1685 and 1686 blanket amnesties were decreed for all illegal migrants to towns. These people not only paid taxes but also engaged in handicrafts and trade, which contributed to the well-being of the Muscovite state. Urbanization has been a constant feature of Russian migration; in the census of 1897 this was expressed dramatically in the fact that 74% of the population of Moscow and 69% of the population of St. Petersburg had not been born there.

After the demographic explosion of the 1860s–1910s era, when the Russian population doubled, the Russian heartland for the first time in its history was overpopulated. As a result, increasing numbers of peasants seasonally migrated to urban areas, and they would return to the farms only perhaps for seeding time and always for the harvest. In later Soviet times, the seasonal migration was reversed as urban workers, students, and soldiers were sent out to the countryside to help bring in the harvest. In other places, such as Kalmykia, urbanites were sent to the countryside in February to help with the lambing season. Already in the 18th century serf-farmers from central Russia were forced to trek seasonally to the Urals, where they worked in the metallurgical industry in the off-agricultural season.[1]

During the Soviet period the most desirable destinations within the Volga-Oka region remained St. Petersburg/Leningrad and Moscow, which were classified by the Soviets as "deluxe towns" and provisioned accordingly. They were declared closed cities into which migration was illegal. Without official registration in legal housing (the notorious *propiska*), one could not legally get a job, and without a job, one could not get housing and registration. Centuries of practice provided Soviet citizens much experience in avoiding the *propiska* restrictions. Most enterprises ranging from factories to the Academy of Sciences were short of labor and thus were more than willing to hire qualified applicants. Housing still remained the dilemma. But many enterprises controlled and even owned and built their own housing. Such housing could be assigned to "absolutely essential" new employees. And presto, the *propiska* dilemma was solved.

An even more ingenious device was the following: maids, baby-sitters, and housekeepers were in very short supply in the USSR, an issue that became crucial especially when both spouses were employed and thus typically had surplus income. The famous "grandmother" was one solution, but an even cleverer one was to find a willing, rural teenage girl who desired to live in Moscow or Leningrad. Many girls and their parents desirous of escaping the intolerable boredom of rural life migrated to the big cities. When the girl turned 16, she was officially registered as a Muscovite. Another *propiska* had to be issued, for all living in Moscow on their 16th birthdays were given such documents. Such migrants benefited not only personally, but their families did as well. Living in Moscow, they could buy scarce commodities and mail them to their families and friends in the countryside. The mailing of goods out of Moscow was a project of enormous dimensions, so that Soviet post offices posted signs warning against mailing oranges in the winter because they would freeze in transit. Unquestionably ways could have been found to avoid giving a *propiska* to such migrants, but this would have cut off a source of labor deemed essential by the Soviet elite, and in the Soviet service state no leaders would have dared such a move. So the population of the desirable cities crept upward. The post-Soviet Supreme Court declared the *propiska* system illegal, but some Russian big cities have maintained it anyway in defiance of the law in an attempt to limit excessively rapid urbanization.

Migration usually moves where the wealth is, and in 2005 two of Russia's wealthiest regions were the ancient

---

[1] Russian peasant labor migrants in Russian factories from the end of the 19th century to the end of the 1920s; Russian labor migrants on large construction sites in the USSR since the 1920s; Soviet migrant construction workers (*shabashniki*) since the 1950s.

capital regions, Moscow and St. Petersburg. Inequality is ever increasing in Russia. The poorest regions in Russia are south of the Oka, the Briansk, Kursk, and Tula regions, as well as the north Caucasian regions of Karachaevo-Cherkessiia and Ingushetia, all of which are losing population. Historically, compensation in agriculture lags behind that in many urban occupations and partially accounts for rural-urban migration. At its end, however, in 1990, the Soviet Union largely overcame this gap so that wages in agriculture came close to 93% of average industrial wages. Since that time, however, agricultural wages had slipped to 35% of industrial wages by 2002. This has not resulted in a great leap in rural-urban migration because of lack of urban opportunities, but it has resulted in rural underemployment and the rise of underproductive small private farms.

Migration into the Volga-Oka mesopotamia from abroad

One might get the impression that the Russian heartland has done nothing but emit emigrants since the first Slavs completed their migration into and settlement of the region around 1300. But that is not completely true. Since at least 1470 the Russians have realized that they were technologically and especially militarily backward and that the only way to keep up to Western standards and to survive military pressures on their western frontier was to import Western specialists to assist with modernization. Since Grand Duke Ivan III invited Aristotel Fioravante to Moscow in 1470 to put a roof over the Kremlin's Assumption Cathedral and then introduce bronze casting of artillery, there has been a steady flow of specialists into Russia. Until around 1550 they mostly came from Italy, and after that from various areas of northern Europe. In the 17th century western European officers brought entire companies of soldiers to fight in the Smolensk War (1632–4) so that half of the Russian army at Smolensk consisted of foreigners. This was extraordinarily expensive, especially for a poor country such as was Muscovy, so that the recruiting of foreigners for the next major campaign, the Thirteen Years' War (1654–67) was more selective – only officers were hired, rather than entire companies of troops. The 17th century also witnessed the importation of all manner of other technologists, from metallurgists and prospectors to papermakers and druggists.

Between 1689 and 1725 Czar Peter the Great broadened this process. Military figures were his prime target, but one can safely say that he tried to recruit specialists in practically every area in which Russia was wanting. This ranged from canal builders and architects to shipwrights and city planners. His most enduring contribution was the creation of the Academy of Sciences in 1725, which was staffed entirely by foreign mathematicians and every manner of natural scientist and historian for its first decades because until 1755 Russia had no universities from which it might recruit scholars.

The recruitment of foreigners into Russia continued into the 19th century, when foreign engineers were hired to help build Russia's railways and foreign businessmen discovered that Russia needed entrepreneurs.[2] After the take-off of Russian industrialization was launched in the years 1892–1903, foreign entrepreneurs played a major role in the revitalization of Russian business in the years 1907–14, between the defeat in the war against Japan in 1904–5 and the revolution of 1905 and the outbreak of World War I.

The war, the Russian revolution of 1917, and the civil war greatly curtailed the inflow of foreigners into the Soviet Union and the vast majority of the foreign engineers fled during the civil war. Few returned during the 1920s and 1930s. That helps to explain why half of Stalin's university graduates were engineers, as the USSR needed them, didn't have any, and could no longer import them. Most of those who did migrate to the USSR were ideologues, enchanted by the notion that Stalin was practicing socialism, and people disenchanted by the failure of capitalism during the Great Depression.[3] Some of them were arrested and executed as "foreign spies" during the Great Purges (1936–8); those who were Germans and Austrians (including a number of Jews) were turned over to the authorities of national-socialist Germany after the signing of the Hitler-Stalin Pact on 23 August 1939.

After 1945 few foreigners were recruited to the USSR as the country embarked on a personnel-autarky policy. The mistaken idea was that the Soviet population was so well educated that any deficits could be covered by espionage and purchase of foreign prototypes for copying. Occasionally a foreign loser who had failed to sell his crackpot invention in the West or in Japan would turn up at a Soviet ministry, only to be laughed out of the door by Russians who understood full well what was coming their way.

The collapse of communism and the USSR in 1991 opened the floodgates to foreigners hoping to make a quick buck, whether it was those hoping to take advantage of the incredibly low wages paid to supposedly qualified Russian personnel or to sell products such as printing equipment that was so advanced that the backward Soviet economy could not absorb it. About the only foreigners who made money in the former USSR were those who were serving other foreigners hoping to make money in Russia. Few of them did, with the result that the West became disillusioned with the prospects of doing business in Russia. Postcommunist Russia remains as undeveloped as before and most decent consumer products are imported from abroad or sold by foreign companies. The country lacks a sufficient number of entrepreneurs, skilled managers, and capable workers. The situation is aggravated by the vast emigration of Jews abroad and the expropriation of some of the Jews who remained, caused by the various waves of anti-Semitism and anti-Zionism that have swept the country since the last years of Stalin. In order to remedy these shortcomings, the Russian

[2] German merchants and industrial entrepreneurs in Russia since the 18th century.

[3] European political emigrants in the USSR since 1917; German skilled workers and craftsmen in the USSR in the interwar period.

Table 2. Extent of Russian colonization of non-Russian areas of the USSR in 1970

Area/region/city	Ethnicity	Numbers	% of population
Russia proper			
Bashkiriia	Bashkirs	892,200	24
	Russians	1,546,300	41
Kareliia	Karelians	84,200	12
	Russians	486,200	68
Komi	Komi	276,200	29
	Russians	512,200	53
Tatariia	Tatars	1,536,400	49
	Russians	1,328,700	42
Caucasus			
Georgia	Georgians	3,130,700	67
	Russians	396,700	9
Azerbaijan	Azeris	3,776,800	74
	Russians	510,100	10
Armenia	Armenians	2,208,300	89
	Russians	66,100	3
Chechnya-Ingush	Chechens	508,900	48
	Ingush	113,700	11
	Russians	367,000	35
Baltics			
Estonia	Estonians	925,300	68
	Russians	334,600	25
Latvia	Latvians	1,341,800	57
	Russians	704,600	30
Riga	Latvians	299,100	41
	Russians	312,900	43
Kaliningrad	Germans	<1,000	0
	Russians	416,700	78
Siberia			
Buriatiia	Buriats	178,670	22
	Russians	597,000	74
Udmurtiia	Udmurts	484,200	34
	Russians	809,600	57
Iakutiia	Iakuts	285,700	43
	Russians	314,300	47
Altai Region	Altaitsy	51,100	2
	Russians	2,335,500	88
Central Asia			
Uzbekistan	Uzbeks	7,724,700	66
	Russians	1,473,500	13
Kazakhstan	Kazakhs	4,234,200	33
	Russians	5,521,900	42
Kyrgyzia	Kyrgyz	1,284,800	44
	Russians	855,900	29
Tajikistan	Tajiks	1,629,900	56
	Russians	344,100	12
Turkmenia	Turkmen	1,416,700	66
	Russians	313,100	15
Tashkent	Uzbeks	513,000	37
	Russians	564, 600	41
Alma-Ata	Kazakhs	88,200	12
	Russians	512,900	70
Semipalatinsk	Kazakhs	73,900	23
	Russians	188,200	59
Frunze	Kyrgyz	53,100	12
	Russians	284,700	66
Dushanbe	Tajiks	98,100	26
	Russians	157,100	42

Source: TsSU, *Itogi vsesoiuznoi perepisi naseleniia 1970 goda. Tom IV. Natsional'nyi sostav naseliia SSSR*, Moscow (1973).

government tried to recruit foreign executives and, comprehending the cost of the brain drain out of Russia, launched a campaign to encourage emigrants to return. In March 2006 the Russian Foreign Ministry announced that as many as 30 million Russians emigrants are residing outside their homeland and observed that Russians comprised more than 20% of the population of Kazakhstan, Ukraine, Estonia, and Latvia (see Table 2).

The alternative to importing skills has been to send Russians abroad to acquire them. Czar Boris Godunov in the 1590s was the first to attempt this, but none of the Russians returned. Czar Peter the Great had more success, and the dispatch of Russians to the West to gain skills has been a more or less regular practice ever since.[4] The major problem, of course, is the expense, which poor Russia has difficulty financing. The Soviets tried to lessen the expense by using student exchanges, so that the sole Soviet expense was to pay the foreigner's expenses in Russia while the receiving country had to pay for the Soviet's expenses plus all the transportation costs.

Migration south of the Oka

The first Slavic migrants south of the Oka were the Cossacks, beginning in the 15th century. They were freebooters who settled in river basins and lived by fishing, piracy, and as military mercenaries for whoever would hire them, or for themselves. They settled first along the Dnieper River, and then their settlements moved eastward as the Russian government tried to subject them to its power. From the Dnieper they moved to the Donets and Don River basins, and then to the Volga. Finally, they moved to the Iaik River, later renamed the Ural River. The Cossack communities removed much of the discontent from the Russian heartland because anyone who did not like being oppressed as a serf in Russia could flee to the borderlands and join the Cossacks. With the repression of the Cossacks, discontent sprang up increasingly in the Russian heartland.[5]

The black soil region south of the Oka was a continuous magnet for peasants from the gray earth (*podzol*) region. The attractiveness of the area south of the Oka induced peasant agriculturalists to keep moving ever southward until Catherine II annexed the Crimean peninsula in 1783. This southward Slavic migration also freed the Russians from the slave-raiding depredations of the Crimean Tatars. Big landlords moved into the area and forcibly moved their peasants with them into the more fertile land. No peasant seems to have protested against being forced to migrate from the mesopotamia into Left Bank Ukraine, which was completely unsettled.[6]

Migration to the Volga, Donets Basin, and northern Black Sea regions

The economic situation was comparable along both the eastern and western banks of the Volga, between Kazan and Astrakhan. Not only did this area have the Russian Empire's best farmland, but it also was the location of the Donets Basin, where vast quantities of coal are located. The Donets Coal Basin became the basic source of fuel for the central and southern regions of the European parts of the Russian Empire and the USSR. Discovered in the beginning of the 18th century, the Donets Coal Basin began to be exploited in a major way during the late 19th century thanks to the industrialization program of the Russian finance minister Count Sergei Witte; major waves of migrants were attracted to work in the mines and service enterprises around them. In the Soviet first five-year plan, the Donbas was a major industrial center. Much of its labor supply came from mesopotamian Russia, but a lot of it also was recruited Ukrainians and others on adjacent collective farms. The miners and other workers were almost exclusively male, whereas the laborers on the area's collective farms were almost exclusively female. On the other hand, other Donbas enterprises such as the stone and chalk quarries in Millerovo were manned by convict labor. Yet comparatively few of the Donbas workers were forced laborers, but that was not true in other Ukrainian mass projects. For example, nearly all the workers at the great Dneprostroi dam site (1927–32), were forced laborers.[7]

The northern Black Sea coast was a magnet for Russian settlers from the late 18th century down to 1991, as well as for other European migrants, who had been recruited in great numbers. Since the end of the 19th century much of that area, and especially the Crimea, has been developed as a resort territory. In 1944, Stalin expelled about 700,000 Crimean Tatars for being collaborators with the German occupiers during World War II, and Russians swarmed into the peninsula.[8] Khrushchev "awarded" it to Ukraine in 1954, and this turnover only became an issue after the collapse of the USSR in 1991. Just before that, in the late 1980s, the Crimeans were permitted to return to the peninsula, where about a quarter million of them have had to contest with the Russians and some Ukrainians, who had taken possession of the land.

Migration to and from Tatarstan and the Urals

When Kazan and the Volga were annexed in 1552, Russians flooded into the area. The Kama River Basin was soon inhabited by Russian migrants, opening the way to Siberia. There were so many Russians in Tatarstan, of which Kazan is the capital, that in 1991 the Kazan Tatars barely comprised a

---

[4] Russian students at German colleges and universities in the late 19th and early 20th centuries; Russian female students in Switzerland in the late 19th and early 20th centuries.

[5] Cossacks in Russia since the 17th century.

[6] Ukrainian and Russian settlers in New Russia since the 18th century.

[7] Russian peasant labor migrants in Russian factories from the end of the 19th century to the end of the 1920s; Russian labor migrants on large construction sites in the USSR since the 1920s; Soviet migrant construction workers (*shabashniki*) since the 1950s.

[8] Deportees in the Soviet Union during and after World War II.

Table 3. Causes of migration out of the territories of the Soviet Union in 1991 (percentages)

Country	Schooling	Job change	Ethnic strife	Unsettled life
Azerbaijan	5.1	7.7	47.9	3.0
Armenia	4.8	8.1	39.4	7.1
Belarus	11.5	15.5	1.4	8.9
Kazakhstan	11.1	14.1	10.9	8.5
Kyrgystan	8.0	12.8	32.7	6.5
Moldova	10.9	17.6	26.3	7.4
Russia	5.5	16.6	3.2	13.9
Tadzhikistan	5.5	9.1	40.6	4.4
Turkmenistan	13.1	13.9	15.4	5.7
Uzbekistan	8.3	10.0	27.3	6.2
Ukraine	11.3	18.8	3.2	10.2

Note: Omitted from the table have been the categories "Crime," "Family circumstances," and "Other." The data do not include the Baltic States.

Source: Statisticheskii Komitet Sodruzhestva Nezavisimykh Gosudarstv, *Strany-Chleny SNG. Statisticheskii ezhegodnik*, Moscow (1992), 7.

majority (see Table 2 for 1970 figures). Nevertheless, the Tatars were able to demand something approaching semiautonomy, a special tax system, and other privileges from the Russian Federation in the early 1990s. A significant number of Kazan Tatars have tried to make the ethnic Russians uncomfortable with the aim of forcing them out of the region. During the last years of the existence of the Soviet Union ethnic conflict constituted the main reason for the Russian emigration out of central Asia and the Caucasus. That was true, for instance, for Nagorno-Karabakh (in Azerbaijan and Armenia) and for the attempts to drive out Russians from Kyrgyzstan and Tadzhikistan (see Table 3).

Beyond Kazan lay the Ural mountains, which range from 300 to 1,200 meters above sea level. The Urals were covered with forests and underneath were many of the useful minerals desired by man. This was largely irrelevant to Russia until the Northern War (1700–21) cut Russia off from Swedish iron supplies. Russia required much iron for weapons, so Czar Peter the Great ordered the development of the Urals iron industry. Russia, which had relied on imports, had no iron industry, so had to develop one from scratch. Once prospectors had found the ore, the major problem was getting the labor to mine and refine it. There is no coking coal in the Urals, so men had to be found to fell the trees and turn them into charcoal to smelt the iron out of the ore. The solution was adopted of forcing serfs from European Russia to migrate to the Urals to work in the metallurgical industries. This was done in one of two ways: (1) private seigneurial serfs were forced to walk to and from the Urals enterprises in off-season, or (2) Urals entrepreneurs bought entire villages of serfs and transferred them en masse to their enterprises. This provided sufficient labor that Russia was able to become the largest manufacturer of iron in the world by 1800. The trouble was that by 1800 most of the forests had been logged

off; no coking coal had been found to substitute for the charcoal, so the metallurgical industries went into decline.

In 1929, Stalin in his striving for steel resolved to revitalize the metallurgical industry in the Urals on the basis of the Magnetic Mountain, which became the metallurgical city Magnitogorsk founded in 1931. It railroaded in its coking coal from the Kuznets Basin, the Kuzbas. Once again labor was the bottleneck, which Stalin solved by sending forced laborers to build and operate Magnitogorsk as well as the Kuzbas. The Magnetic Mountain was used up after Stalin died, and Magnitogorsk went into decline. In addition, the coal mines at Vorkuta, north of the Arctic Circle, also were of importance as its forced laborers provided 40% of Leningrad's coal. Since Khrushchev closed down the Stalinist system of forced labor and especially since 1991, the labor forces of those places have shrunk substantially as the freedmen migrated back to European Russia, or at least to more temperate climes, in spite of the fact that labor was now paid premiums of 100% and more over what could be earned in European Russia.

Migration and the exploitation of Siberia

Beyond the Urals lies Siberia, the Eurasian continent all the way to the Pacific. The first major Russian explorer was Yermak Timofeevič, who led a band of freebooter Cossacks to the Pacific to lay claim to Siberia for Russia in the late 16th century. Yermak was followed by adventurers interested in profiting from the furs in Siberia, which they purchased from the natives. They were followed by military governors with small garrisons who expressed Russian political hegemony in the region and collected taxes in furs from the natives. Those people rarely settled in the area. They did, however, manage to deplete the furs of Siberia by the end of the 18th century, with the result that the trappers crossed the Bering Strait in further search of furs. Once Alaska also had been "trapped out," the Russians sold it to the United States in 1867. Shortly after moving into Alaska, in 1816, Russians built Fort Elizabeth in Kauai (Hawaii), which they relatively soon evacuated. Other Russians went to California, but the initial adventurers were followed by insignificant migration.

That was different in Siberia. Between Czar Peter's time and 1991, Russians migrated to Siberia in sufficient numbers to become the majority ethnic group in the major river valleys and along much of the southern fringe of Siberia, the area bordering Kazakhstan, Mongolia, and China. Between 1851 and 1860 vast territories north of the Amur and Ussuri rivers, including Vladivostok, were seized from the Chinese Qing Empire. Some of the southern fringe is suitable for agriculture, and peasants who somehow were able to escape European Russia tended to set up farming there. This was greatly facilitated by the construction of the Trans-Siberian Railway at the turn of the 20th century, which transported "surplus population" from the Empire's mesopotamia to any point along the line. Between 1796 and 1916, 4.4 million migrated to Siberia and the Far East. In those years the population of Siberia rose from 1.2 million to 10.7 million, thanks largely to migration. One can see in Table 2 how the Russian migrants have tended to overwhelm the indigenous Siberian population, such as in Iakutiia, Udmurtiia, and the Altai.

Siberia contains all the 26 essential minerals, the only place on earth that does. Over the quarter millennium between the early 18th century and the mid-20th century, geologists located these minerals, which then were developed occasionally by the government, usually by private entrepreneurs, while during the Soviet period the state took over. Initially gold and diamonds were the prize, but by the 20th century everything else profitable was exploited as well. Manpower was extraordinarily scarce in many of those areas. Few of the natives were willing to work in the natural extractive industries, so entrepreneurs had to rely on Europeans. Before the building of the Trans-Siberian Railway, gangs of shackled exiles were formed and marched on foot to their destinations in Siberia. Laws of 1760 and 1765 permitted private serf owners to exile their obnoxious chattel to Siberia and have them counted as part of their quota of military recruits. This reveals that the settlement of Siberia was as important to the Russian state as manning the armed forces.

The involuntary migrants to Siberia were of two categories: exile (*ssylka*) and forced labor (*katorga*). For instance the Decembrists, many of those whom Czar Nicholas I did not execute for their failed coup/revolution in 1825, were exiled to Siberia. Some of them were followed by their wives. Those in exile were required to live in some remote Siberian location, in which they otherwise differed little from free men. Upon the expiration of their terms of exile (anything up to 25 years), the now free men often remained as residents in their place of exile. There were about 30 colonies of exiles in western Siberia in the 1880s. Each colony had between 4 and 60 people. The political exiles provided an extraordinary leavening to local life in the matter of museums, libraries, and other intellectual matters.

Forced laborers were marched on foot, and after the invention of the railroad, shipped in special *Stolypin* cars, which were subdivided into sections of iron cages in which the convicts were placed. The Soviets did not replace the *Stolypin* cars as they wore out, but instead stuffed the convicts into unheated boxcars. Much too frequently such transit was a death sentence, as the passengers froze to death or died of dehydration or starvation. The destinations of the forced laborers were often far from the railway station, and so the convicts had to walk the rest of the way, or were transported by ship. The forced labor camps are too many to list, but some of the most notorious were the Lena Gold Fields camp, a British concession in which the masters enjoyed rights of extraterritoriality, i.e., Russian law did not apply there. An uprising by the slave laborers in 1912 was brutally repressed, which led to a massive resumption of strikes throughout Russia that paralyzed the country from 1905 until the outbreak of World War I.

The Kolyma River contains numerous gold deposits, which the Soviets decided to exploit to the maximum by using hundreds of thousands of convict laborers, who had to labor in catastrophic working and living conditions. Much of eastern Siberia was put under the charge of the secret police and named *Dalstroi* (Far Eastern Construction). Moscow decided to build a new city, Magadan, to be the capital of Dalstroi, which has an area larger than France. Moscow had no idea what conditions were like on the Kolyma, with the result that the first boatload of guards, dogs, and convicts sent to initiate the construction of Magadan in 1932 all froze to death. Since 1991 the population of Magadan, as at all the other former Soviet slave labor projects, has declined markedly as the population capable of migrating – such as the employable, the young, and the better educated – have returned to European Russia. The Magadan airport, which used to have eight flights a week, in the early 21st century, had none.

Now fewer than 8 million Russians live in Siberia, while about 6 million of these live in the Far East. Because of the massive emigration, there is considerable apprehension among the population of Siberia that the East Slavs will be replaced by Chinese. In the mid-1990s the illegal Chinese population was reported to number 2 million, and at the beginning of the 21st century there is widespread recognition that Russians, who are demographically declining in numbers, do not want to live in Siberia. The fear is that Siberia's storehouse of minerals and petrochemicals will be transferred from Russian to Chinese possession. In recognition of this possibility, the Russian government developed programs to repopulate far eastern Siberia by attracting Russians from central Russia and the countries of the 14 non-Russian republics that became independent states when the USSR collapsed.

Migration and the conquest of central Asia

Fifteen hundred years ago the basic population of central Asia consisted of Indo-European Iranians, who were swamped by migrations from the east of Turkic and Mongol peoples. The Turks and Mongols tended to be rural pastoralists, whereas the Iranians were often urban dwellers. This distinction has persisted to the present day, although Soviet urbanization brought more Turkic peoples into the cities. Russians began to migrate in appreciable numbers into central Asia and especially into urban areas at the beginning in the mid-19th century, and by the end of the century they had annexed the entire area. By 1895 Russia reached the Pamirs.

Unlike Siberia, central Asia is not a storehouse of useful minerals, although some petrochemicals were discovered in the Caspian basin at the turn of the 20th century. During the second half of the 19th century, British adventurers entered central Asia; the Russians strove mightily to keep them out, and ultimately drove them out. The Russians wanted free access to India and the silks, spices, and other luxury goods of the Orient. In 1872 the British and the Russians signed a treaty on spheres of influence in middle and central Asia. Russia seized Khiva in 1873, Kokand in 1874, both on the Silk

Road, and Turkmenia in 1881–4. Other Anglo-Russian treaties over spheres of influence in central Asia were signed and as Russia's hold over the area became more secure, Russians migrated in a trickle into those areas.

Russians from Ivanovo, the textile center northeast of Moscow, in the 1870s discovered that cotton could be grown in what is now Uzbekistan by siphoning off waters from the Amu-Daria and Syr-Daria that flow into the Aral Sea. This became such a lucrative business that the Soviets turned the Aral Sea into a dead lake and salinated the soil and air of the region. The Ivanovo entrepreneurs who initiated the cotton enterprise including planting the cotton, harvesting, irrigating, ginning, and railroading it to the mills, did not survive the revolution, and the industry was largely turned over to the natives.

Russian migrants made up the majority of some major Soviet central Asian towns, such as Alma-Ata (which was founded by Russians in the 1860s), but by and large the Slavic migrants were political administrators sent by Moscow to control the region. Table 2 illustrates the numerical Russian presence in central Asia, especially the major urban areas, where Russians almost everywhere remained the population majority until the collapse of the USSR. Other colonists were engineers and factory directors who had skills the native working population did not. Since 1991 there has been a concerted effort by the natives to drive the colonists out of central Asia, and this has been quite successful in the more southerly parts of the region.

A major problem has been that until 2007 the post-Soviet authorities have not welcomed the return of the 23 million Russian "colonists" living in the former republics of the USSR, so that many of the returnees have been forced to live illegally on farms and on the outskirts of the cities in European Russia. In many respects, the lives of the returning colonists resemble those of the fugitive serfs and townsmen in centuries gone by: illegal in the eyes and the laws of the capital, but welcomed by the locals who need their labor.

Northern Kazakhstan has been a special case in central Asia. It has the same black soil that is found farther west in Ukraine, but it lacks Ukraine's precipitation. Nevertheless, this area proved very attractive to Russian farmers from the poorer soils of the gray earth (podzol) region. The political leader of the Soviet Union at the time, N. S. Khrushchev, launched the "virgin lands" program to plow up northern Kazakhstan in the late 1950s. This attracted an enormous stream of migrants, often enthusiasts of the Komosol, the youth organization of the Communist Party in the Soviet Union, who converted the region into an almost pure Russian colony. By 1964 the area was a dust bowl, but farming by the Russian colonists continues. The Kazakhs moved their capital in 1994 from Alma-Ata to Akmolina (formerly Tselinograd) out of fear that the majority Russian colonists in the area might insist that the region be annexed to the Russian Federation.

Transcaucasia as a destination of Russian migrants

Transcaucasia (Armenia, Georgia, and Azerbaijan) has been another destination of Russian migrants, but the numbers were different as very few Russians migrated to Armenia. Armenian merchants, however, have migrated to the Volga-Oka region since the late Middle Ages.[9] Azerbaijan is another story, especially because of its proximity to Persia as well as its location on the Caspian Sea and the Baku oil fields. Russians moved into the Baku region in large numbers after the discovery of oil at the turn of the 20th century. Georgia has attracted migrants from Russia especially since the end of the Caucasian Wars in the 1860s because of the pleasant climate in places such as Tbilisi (Tiflis) and Sukhumi on the Black Sea. Russians migrated to the North Caucasus to participate in the oil industry in Grozny, and to the administrative city of Vladikavkaz in North Ossetia.

In the years 1830–1900, many Russian religious dissidents such as Old Believers and others migrated to the North Caucasus to escape religious oppression in Russia itself. The migration flood into the North Caucasus was especially facilitated by the end of the Caucasian Wars, and between 1867 and 1897, 1.6 million people resettled into the region. The migration of those seeking religious freedom is similar to the Old Believers' migration to the Russian North (part of Karelia), north of the Volga, in the second half of the 17th century, and the flight of the strictly pacifist Dukhobors to Canada in the 19th century. Old Believers also migrated abroad to Canada, the USA, and Brazil to escape religious persecution.

Since 1991, or even shortly before, there has been perceptible reverse migration of Russians from the Transcaucasus back to Russia. The evidence of ethnic strife is shown in Table 3. During the attempted coup in Moscow in August 1991 against the then president of the Soviet Union, Mikhail Gorbachav, one of the groups voicing complaints were recent emigrants from Azerbaijan who alleged they had left the Caucasus because of harsh discrimination. At the time they were camped in temporary settlements outside Moscow. The sundry civil wars in Transcaucasia have prompted a number of Russian colonists to leave for Russia. The war over Nagorno-Karabakh (1992–4) provoked many population relocations, as have the wars over various parts of Georgia since the early 1990s. Perhaps worst of all have been the two Chechen wars (1994–6 and since 1999), which have left much of Chechnya a field of rubble and have forced much of the population to scatter, the Chechens to refugee camps, the Russians back to Russia.

Forced migration during World War II

The two Chechen wars remind people of Stalin's deportation to central Asia and Kazakhstan of hundreds of thousands of

[9] Armenian merchants in Russia since the late Middle Ages.

"punished peoples" because of their alleged collaboration with the German occupiers in World War II.[10] After Stalin's death most of the punished peoples were allowed to return to their homelands without any reparations, with the exception of the Crimean Tatars and the deportees of German origin, who were not allowed to return home until decades later.

Note that much of Siberia north of the Yalu River at one time was part of Greater Korea. Koreans continued to live there in Soviet times. As war with Japan appeared on the horizon in the late 1930s, Stalin ordered all the Koreans living in Siberia deported to Kazakhstan, where some of their heirs still live, because Korea had been annexed by Japan in 1905. Stalin and his minions feared that the Koreans living in Siberia would be loyal to Japan in case of war, so they were deported en masse. The 40,000 Germans, who had been imported into Russia by Catherine the Great and had migrated especially to the Volga region and New Russia in search of religious freedom, did not fare well during World War II.[11] Many of the descendants of the German immigrants were relocated or murdered by the Soviets. Some did survive the war and the Stalin era, and after 1950 the German government attempted to repatriate the surviving offspring of Germans in the USSR back to Germany.[12]

In this context, a few more words might be said about World War II. The war dislocated as many as 60 million people. In addition to the "punished peoples," other Soviet inhabitants moved because they were enslaved, forced to migrate, and sent to Germany as forced laborers by the German invaders.[13] Others were sent by the Soviet government to the "rear" (the Urals, central Asia) to man relocated industry or just to escape the Wehrmacht, were drafted and sent to the "front," were deported from areas annexed by the Soviets, and were moved for other reasons. After the war, millions returned to their old homes, but others did not – because they were dead, were forbidden to return home, voluntarily urbanized themselves, and so on.[14]

Migration and the Russian expansion westward

During the Thirteen Years' War (1654–67) Russian troops captured Riga, but then retreated. Czar Peter the Great annexed Courland, Livonia, and Estonia, areas in which the native Balts and Estonians were employed on the estates of the German nobility. The Germans were given very favorable terms by the Russians in what amounted to semiautonomy. The Germans proved very willing collaborators with the Russians up to World War I, and as a result very few

Russian colonists moved into those areas, either as settlers or as administrators.[15] After World War II, the victorious Soviets evicted all the Germans from the 700-year-old East Prussian city of Königsberg, renamed it Kaliningrad, and repopulated it with Russians (see Table 2; the 1970 census lists Germans as living elsewhere in the USSR, but not in Kaliningrad).

The reign of Catherine the Great witnessed the three partitions of Poland, dividing the country between the Austrian Habsburgs, the Prussians, and czarist Russia in 1772, 1793, and 1795. In 1815, the Congress of Vienna created the kingdom of Poland and linked it to Russia in a personal union. This made Warsaw part of the Russian Empire, and a handful of Russians moved into key centers to administer the region. Serfdom prevented Russian farmers from migrating westward into Poland-Lithuania, if any had wanted to do so.

More central for the history of migration, the annexation of Poland brought many Jews into the Russian Empire. According to laws of 1783, 1791, 1794, and 1835, Jews were not free to move anywhere they desired in the empire and were supposed to live in the Pale of Settlement, but by World War I many of them found their way to Russia's major cities. According to the census of 1897, there were about 5 million Jews living in the Pale and 320,000 outside of it. About 100,000 lived in Siberia, 80,000 in the Baltic provinces, 21,000 in St. Petersburg, and 20,000 in Moscow.[16] Numerically more important, between 1881 and 1914 about half of the 6 million Jews in the Russian Empire migrated abroad mainly to the USA.[17] The Jews who remained in the Russian Empire and the Soviet Union became russified, urbanized, and sovietized. The post-Stalin era found somewhere between 2 and 3 million Jews on the territory of the USSR. Leonid Brezhnev, who headed the Communist Party in the Soviet Union between 1964 and 1982, opened the floodgates when he allowed Jewish emigration, and by 1989 there were only 1.38 million Jews left in the USSR. Emigration continued to rise to massive proportions by 2000. At least a million Jews emigrated out of the USSR and the Russian Federation, with the result that in the early 21st century only between 200,000 to 400,000 Jews remained in the Russian Federation.[18] However, at least 57,000 Jews have returned from Israel to Russia and the other former Soviet republics.

The last remaining destination of Russian migration to discuss is the Baltic states, Estonia, Latvia, and Lithuania. Part of the region was "awarded" to the USSR in the Hitler-Stalin Pact of 1939. Soviet troops moved in, and the secret police immediately began to arrest those suspected of opposing

---

[10] Deportees in the Soviet Union during and after World War II; German deportees from east-central and southeastern Europe in the USSR after the end of World War II.

[11] German settlers in Russia since the 18th century; Ukrainian and Russian settlers in New Russia since the 18th century; Bulgarian and Gagauzian settlers in New Russia and Bessarabia since the 18th century.

[12] Aussiedler/Spätaussiedler in Germany since 1950.

[13] Forced laborers in Germany and German-occupied Europe during World War II.

[14] Displaced persons (DPs) in Europe since the end of World War II.

[15] Russian elites in the Baltic States since the early modern period.

[16] Jews from the Pale of Settlement in Odessa and in the cities of central Russia and Poland in the 19th century.

[17] Eastern European Jews in Berlin from the late 19th century to the 1930s; eastern European Jews in London since the late 19th century; eastern European Jews in Paris since the late 19th century.

[18] East European Jews in Germany since 1990.

the Soviet regime and to exile them to forced labor camps in the Soviet Union. After the German attack on the Soviet Union in 1941, the Wehrmacht forced the Soviets out of the Baltic region, but after the tide of war turned, Red Army troops marched through the area on their way to Berlin. The Baltic states were annexed to the USSR, and colonization of the Baltics by Russians and other Soviet citizens ensued. Russians especially admired Estonia and Latvia because of the higher standard of living, the urban culture, and the milder climate. Migration into Estonia was so intense that by 1991, Estonians were only a bare majority in their own country. Latvia, with its ancient and beautiful Germanic capital of Riga, also attracted numerous migrants from the USSR. Lithuania was far less attractive, so colonists comprised a far smaller portion of the population there than in the other Baltic republics when the Soviet Union broke up in 1991 (see Table 2 for 1970 figures).

Particularly offensive to many Baltic peoples was the outright, explicit refusal by many Russian colonists to learn their language. This was true, of course, not only in Estonia and Latvia, but also throughout the Russian Empire and the USSR. The Russians came as conquering rulers and dealt with the natives through those who could translate for them. Many Estonians and Latvians despised the Russians in their countries as "Asiatic barbarians" and hated them for having degraded their lands under the Soviet hammer and sickle. Having gained independence, they began to enact especially harsh linguistic laws whose intent was to tell the Russians to go home. The Russian colonists were forbidden to speak Russian, required to use Estonian and Latvian in official business, and given deadlines by which they had to learn these languages. Sensing that they were not wanted, thousands of Russians migrated eastward, when they could find some place to go. Russia imposed a three-year waiting period for a Russian passport. The major Russian cities were closed to them by the registration laws, and certainly Russians who had spent nearly half a century in Riga or Tallinn would have found it extremely distasteful to move to a labor-short Russian farm or village which would accept them. It is unknown how many Russian colonists in the Baltic states bit the bullet and returned to Russia even though Moscow put out the unwelcome mat for them.

Historical and contemporary migration patterns in Russia

In the past four centuries the part of the Eurasian landmass that has been occupied by Muscovy, the Russian Empire, the Soviet Union, and the Russian Federation and White Russia (Belarus) has witnessed a constant ebb and flow of population. Because of the low population densities and the intense shortage of and competition for labor, legal restrictions have frequently been placed on the mobility of most of the people living in that area. The extent to which these restrictions hampered economic development and the optimal allocation of labor has been much debated. It has always been obvious that regardless of the law, significant numbers of people moved of their own volition – and often with the connivance of officials and/or the local people in the places of the migrants' destinations. Frequently the involuntary relocation of people (serfs, convicts, military captives) has been resorted to by the state, serf owners, factory owners, and others to acquire scarce labor in places where free people are unwilling to live.

During the past four centuries there has been very little migration into Russia. The population is declining every year by 700,000 to 800,000, and predictions are that Russia with a population of about 142 million people in 2006 will have only 138 million inhabitants in 2012, 120 million in 2030, and 80 million in 2075. (See Table 1.) Always a "developing country," Russia has tried to make up for its skill deficiencies by importing (typically at great cost) foreigners, typically from the West. Jews have left Russia by the millions, but most migration has continued to be internal.

In the foreseeable future, one can only imagine similar patterns. The colonists in the former Soviet republics outside Russia will continue to attempt to return to Russia and may even be recruited and welcomed along with other émigrés. In 2007, Vladimir Putin, president of Russia at that time, attempted to curtail the collapsing population by extending the welcome mat for Russian colonists living in the non-Russian countries of the former USSR and even encouraged Russians living elsewhere "to return home" with their newly acquired skills. The Chinese, thousands of Vietnamese, and people from the Caucasus will continue to migrate into Russia, in spite of official attempts to stop them. In 2005, according to official estimates, about 70% of the undocumented, illegal immigrants from Asia and the former Soviet republics consign themselves to what amounts to voluntary slavery on construction sites, in the garment industry, in bakeries, and on farms. Other people from most of the rest of Europe, North America, and Australia and New Zealand will not attempt to migrate into Russia, for the climate and general conditions are too forbidding.

REFERENCES

Becker, Charles M., et al. "The Migration Response to Economic Shock: Lessons from Kazakhstan." *Journal of Comparative Economics* (2005): 107–32.

Bogdanovskii, Vladimir. "Agricultural Employment in Russia 1990–2003." *Comparative Economic Studies* 47, 2 (2005): 141–53.

Conquest, Robert. *The Nation Killers: The Soviet Deportation of Nationalities*. London, 1970.

Dallin, David J., and Boris I. Nicolaevsky. *Forced Labor in Soviet Russia*. New Haven, 1947.

Davies, Norman . *God's Playground: A History of Poland*. 2 vols. New York, 1982.

Gorskaia, Natalija A. *Istoričeskaia demografija Rossii épochi feodalizma*. Moscow, 1994.

Hellie, Richard. *Muscovite Society*. Chicago, 1967 and 1970.

Hellie, Richard. *Enserfment and Military Change in Muscovy.* Chicago, 1971.

Hellie, Richard. "The Stratification of Muscovite Society: The Townsmen." *Russian History* 6, 2 (1979): 119–75.

Hellie, Richard. *Slavery in Russia 1450–1725.* Chicago, 1982.

Hellie, Richard, ed. *The Muscovite Law Code (Ulozhenie) of 1649.* Irvine, 1988.

Hellie, Richard. "Migration in Early Modern Russia, 1480s–1780s." In *Coerced and Free Migration: Global Perspectives,* edited by David Eltis, 292–323. Stanford, 2002.

Hellie, Richard. "The Structure of Russian Imperial History." *History and Theory: Studies in the Philosophy of History* 44, 4 (2005): 88–112.

Hittle, J. Michael. *The Service City: State and Townsmen in Russia, 1600–1800.* Cambridge, 1979.

Iurkov, Iu. A., and V. L. Sokolin, eds. *Naselenie Rossii za 100 let (1897–1997). Statistićeskij sbornik.* Moscow, 1998.

Katorga i ssylka (Journal, 116 issues). Moscow, 1921–35.

Kazarian, Pavel Levonović. *Genezis politićeskoi ssylki v Rossii: konec XV–naćalo XIX v.* Vladivostok, 1999.

Kennan, George. *Siberia and the Exile System.* 2 vols. New York, 1891.

Kontorovich, Vladimir. "Can Russia Resettle the Far East?" *Post-Communist Economies* 12 (2000): 365–84.

Kuromiya, Hiroaki. "The Donbas between Ukraine and Russia." In *Dinamizm sotsial'nyckh protsessov v post-sovetskim obshchestve. Vyp. 2, ch. 2. Obshshestvennye nauki,* edited by L. A. Sinel'kova, I. F. Kompantseva, and G. A. Petrovskaia, 156–76. Luhansk, Zurich, and Geneva, 2001.

Leasure, J. William, and Robert A. Lewis. "Internal Migration in Russia in the Late Nineteenth Century." *Slavic Review* 27 (1968): 375–94.

Lewis, Robert A., and Richard H. Rowland. "East Is West and West Is East: Population Redistribution in the USSR and Its Impact on Society." *International Migration Review* 11 (1977): 3–29.

Moon, David. "Peasant Migration, the Abolition of Serfdom, and the Internal Passport System in the Russian Empire c. 1800–1914." In *Coerced and Free Migration: Global Perspectives,* edited by David Eltis, 324–57, 424–32. Stanford, 2002.

Nekrich, Aleksandr Moiseevich. *The Punished Peoples: The Deportation and Fate of Soviet Minorities at the End of the Second World War.* New York, 1978.

Rašin, Adolf G. *Naselenie Rossii za sto let (1811–1913 gg.) Statističeskie očerki.* Edited by S. G. Strumilin. Moscow, 1956.

Rośćevskaja, Larisa Pavlovna. *Revoljucionery-raznočintsy v zapadno-sibirskom izgnanii.* Leningrad, 1983.

Vodarskij, Jaroslav E. *Naselenie Rossii v kontse XVII-načale XVIII veka. (Čislennost', soslovno-klassovyj sostav, razmeščenie).* Moscow, 1977.

Wegren, Stephen, and A. Cooper Drury. "Patterns of Internal Migration during the Russian Transition." *Journal of Communist Studies and Transition Politics* 17, 4 (2001): 15–42.

Zimćenko, Iurij Borisović, et al., eds. *Deportacii narodov SSSR: 1930-e-1950-e gody.* 2 vols. Moscow, 1992.

UKRAINE

Frank Golczewski

Between the southern foothills of the Carpathians in the west and the now agriculturally used expanses of the steppe in the east, between the shores of the Black Sea and the Sea of Azov in the south, and Belarus (White Russia) and Russia's Muscovite heartland in the north lies a land – about 603,000 square kilometers in size and with a population of around 48 million at the beginning of the 21st century – that declared itself independent on 24 August 1991 under the name Ukraine. Traversed by several large rivers flowing north to south (Dniester, Southern Bug/Buh, Dnipro/Dnieper, Donez), it possesses an internal geographic structure only in the sense that forests and forest steppes predominate in the west and north, while the south – as far as the mountains of the Crimean peninsula that are close to the sea – and the east are covered by steppe regions, the "wild field."

The region and its boundaries

Lacking any natural barriers, Ukraine was a transition land for migrant groups moving between Asia and Europe. A non-nomadic settlement of the Dniester valley is presumed to have existed as early as the fourth century BCE in the Trypillya culture. But it was the nomadic horsemen (Cimmerians, Scythians, Sarmatians, Huns, later Avars, Hungarians, Chazars, Mongols/Tatars) from the east who, like the Greeks on the northern shore of the Black Sea and the eastward wandering Goths, at various times inhabited the territory of modern-day Ukraine. Between the fifth and eighth centuries CE, a Slavic population then began to trickle in from the northwest and settled initially above all in the river valleys.

Along the Dnieper trading route, which connected the Varangians of Scandinavia and the Greeks of Constantinople, a political center arose in Kiev, from which the state of the Ruś would develop in the ninth century with participation by Scandinavian warriors. This state, Christianized in the 10th century by Byzantium, to which both Russia and Ukraine trace back their own political traditions, extended in the west as far as Halyc (Galicia) and Volhynia, in the north to Ladoga and Novgorod; in the south, however, it only sporadically reached the Black Sea and lost itself in the steppe regions that remained the domain of the nomads.

When this realm disintegrated in the 12th–14th centuries from the violence of the Mongol and Tatar movements – but also because of internal clashes – and its tradition was transferred to the northwest (to Vladimir, later Moscow), the western principalities came under Hungarian and Polish rule, while the largest piece of the territory fell to the Grand Principality of Lithuania. This last pagan realm in Europe tolerated the Orthodox Christianity of its new subjects and used their East Slavic language in official business, a language that had developed away from the Muscovite (greater) Russian language on the basis of local dialects. The weak princely power in the distant south attracted people who preferred to avoid the growing legalization of the states in the region. In the steppe they formed unattached Cossack communities (from Turkic: *kozak* = free), which were given a semimilitaristic internal structure. At times they made themselves available as mercenaries to all the surrounding states, and they developed a social structure that has been romanticized as a kind of grassroots democracy, though in reality it very quickly led to feudal differentiation. Such aspects were reason enough to regard them as a social element specific to the region, and to declare the tradition of the Cossacks as one of the foundations of the modern Ukrainian state.

The successor states to the Mongol/Tatar "Golden Horde," which had kept Russia in a state of tribute-paying dependency, established themselves in the south of modern-day Ukraine. The Tatars dominated the southern steppes as far as the Dniester. The Khanate of the Crimea merged with the Ottomans, a move through which it gained control, alongside the other Tatar territories, also of the Greek and Genoese trading cities on the coast; however, after 1478 it had the status of an Ottoman vassal.

Between the 14th and 16th centuries, the Grand Duchy of Lithuania gradually united with the Polish crown; in the Union of Lublin in 1569, the Lithuanian territories of modern-day Ukraine were directly subjected to Polish rule, as previously the western sections of the land (Galicia-Volhynia) had already been. The nobles of the *Rzeczpospolita* ("Noble Republic," in actuality it was an elected monarchy) appropriated the new territories, extended the legal norms customary in Poland to the new lands and settled Jews, who were to take on intermediary and administrative functions. In the Ecclesiastical Union of Brest in 1596, the Orthodox of the Polish realm were, with partial success, placed under Roman Papal jurisdiction (Greek Catholic Church) while preserving the Byzantine rite.

After the term "Ukraina" (border land, mark) had been used in the Kievan state of the Ruś for several regions along the border, it consolidated itself in the 16th century for the Cossack territories at the edge of the Polish state, while the western Ukrainian provinces (voivodships), which had already been Polish for some time, continued to be referred to as Ruś. Conflicts between the Polish nobility, on the one hand, and the native peasants and Cossacks, on the other hand, culminated in 1648 in a large Cossack revolt under the hetman Bogdhan Chmelnicki; it brought in its wake traumatically remembered Jewish pogroms, during which the Jews were attacked as representatives of the often absentee Polish landowners. In a move that has sparked disagreement to this day, Chmelnicki in 1654 allied or subjected himself to the Moscow czars (Treaty of Perejaslav). In the Polish-Russian Peace of Andrusovo in 1667, the two partners divided up the non-Tatar part of modern-day Ukraine along the Dnieper. While Polish rule consolidated itself in the western/right-bank Ukraine, the eastern/left-bank territory fell into Russian hands, though Kiev went to Russia. After a period of autonomous development, this region was Russified in the wake of the absolutist standardization of the Russian Empire in the 18th century. The Cossack upper class was incorporated into the Russian noble registry.[1] In Russian parlance, this region was "Small Russia" (Malarossia), in contrast to the Greater Russian territories in the north.

The so-called Sloboda-Ukraine in the region of modern-day Charkiv had a special status. Moscow made this land, nearly unsettled until the middle of the 17th century, available to Cossacks who had fled from the areas of the revolt. The goal of the settlement was not least to protect the Russian core territory against incursions by the Crimean Tatars. The inhabitants were given Cossack (military) administrative units, but since these entailed no political rights, they were from the outset closely linked to the Russian state.

At the end of the 17th century, the territory of modern-day Ukraine was divided into the following regions: the modern-day trans-Carpathian Ukraine was part of the Kingdom of Hungary; the Podolian-Volynian-Galician voivodships had already been Polish for several centuries; to the east as far as the Dnieper mostly Polish landholding predominated, having been established here in the 16th century; the regions east of the Dnieper and the city of Kiev were parts of the Russian realm, with remnants of Cossack autonomy in some places; the south, inclusive of the Crimea, belonged to the territory of the Khanate of Crimea or the Ottoman Empire.

Population policy in the 18th century

In Ukraine on the right bank, the nobility sought to drive the Cossacks, who had risen up against Poland again in 1702, across the Dnieper. This failed, and under the hetman Ivan Mazepa, the Cossacks conquered parts of the right-bank Ukraine for Russia. Czar Peter I, however, aimed his reforms also against the Cossack privileges and deployed them as regular Russian troops. This prompted Mazepa, who was unhappy about this, to defect to the camp of the Swedish king Charles II in the decisive battle of the Great Northern War (1700–21) near Poltova in January 1709. Thereafter the Russians considered Mazepa a traitor, while the nationally conscious Ukrainians later saw him as a national hero. The Russian grip now tightened, and the administration of the region devolved onto the Russian state, apart from a brief interlude during the reign of Empress Elizabeth. Empress Catherine II abolished the autonomy of the hetmans in 1764.

Throughout nearly the entire 18th century, Ukraine was the battleground for Russian-Ottoman wars. Successful Russian offensives led to the conquest of the Black Sea coast and the Crimean peninsula by 1783, and thus also to the liquidation of the Khanate of Crimea. During the course of this war, the Cossack population was decimated. The Cossacks of the Zaparog Sic had granted refuge to the Russian peasant rebel Pugacev. That is the reason, once they seemed superfluous after the Russo-Ottoman Peace of Kücük Kainarci in 1774, that the last remnant of the earlier social system of the Cossacks was abolished: in June 1775, Russian troops destroyed the Sic – the upper class was taken captive and deported to Siberia, while many Cossacks fled to the Ottomans in the territory of the Danube estuary. The remaining Cossacks were resettled in 1784 to the newly conquered territories between the southern Bug and the Dniester, and in 1792, finally, to the Kuban region. A segment of the Cossacks who had fled to the Ottomans returned to Russia in 1828 and was also settled in the Kuban region. As a result, Ukrainian nationalists claim Kuban – which is today part of Russia – for Ukraine.

Russia recruited colonists in the west for the depopulated Ukrainian territory. The first, after 1752, were Orthodox Serbs, who escaped from the Habsburg Empire and were settled on the right bank of the Dnieper, on land that was now called "New Serbia" (Novaja Serbija). Like Austria, Russia initially practiced here the principle of the fortified border, meaning that it settled peasant-soldiers. The fortress of Saint Elisabeth erected in 1754 turned in 1775 into the city of Elisavetgrad (Kirovohrad). Around the same time, Austria also settled Ruthenians from the Hungarian trans-Carpathian Ukraine in Vojvodina to populate the border region.

Empress Catherine II opened the conquered land to general settlement with her manifest of 22 July 1763 and a second one in 1786. Russian noblemen were given land titles, but actually making the broad expanses arable required farmers, who were enticed into the steppe by the offer of better conditions than in Old Russia: corvée labor was lighter, and they were given tax exemption. In response, farmers immigrated from the north, but also from the still-Polish regions on the right bank of the Dnieper. Old Believers (opponents of the church reform carried out by Patriarch Nikon in the 17th century), who were persecuted or discriminated against in the rest of Russia, also followed the call of the south.[2]

---

[1] Cossacks in Russia since the 17th century.

[2] Ukrainian and Russian settlers in New Russia since the 18th century.

Since there were still insufficient settlers, however, and since the empress was also hoping for a modernization push from central European settlers, colonists were also brought from German territories to New Russia (Novorossija). They were given land, tax exemption, self-government, and the right to freely exercise their religion. They were even permitted to carry out missionary work among the Muslim Tatar population of the annexed territory. However, most German new settlers during Catherine's time moved to the Volga region. Those who remained along the Dnieper were above all Mennonites, near the island of Khortytsia, which had been a Cossack center for a while. Attractive to these new settlers was that Russia exempted them from military service. Larger immigrations of Germans occurred after another invitation from Alexander I in 1804. From the west German regions, settlers now came into the region between the estuary of the Danube and the Dnieper and into the land north of the Sea of Azov. The first reliable information about the size of this group of Black Sea Germans in the census of 1897 showed 283,000, a little less than 5% of the population. Until the German colonists were placed under the general administration in 1871, there was a special "welfare committee" (*popecitel'nyj komitet*), first in Katerynoslav (Russian: Yekaterinoslav, today: Dnipropetrovsk), then in Kishinev (Chişinău) and Odessa. In addition, the colonists enjoyed a high degree of self-governance.[3]

It was not only the Germans, however, who were much sought-after as colonists. Between 1778 and 1780, that is, still before the annexation of Crimea (1783), the new Russian administration organized the exodus of more than 30,000 Greeks and Armenians from Crimea to the steppe north of the Sea of Azov, centered in Mariupol.[4]

Podolia and parts of the voivodships of Kiev and Braclav on the right bank were under Ottoman rule in the second half of the 17th century. After Poland had signed an agreement with the Ottoman Empire in 1699 and the unrest waned, Poland also paid more attention to the Ukrainian regions beginning in 1714. Families of important magnates moved to Ukraine with the declared intent of bringing Polish culture to this "wild land." As this was done once again with Jewish administrators and craftsmen, about 250,000 Jews were living in Polish Ukraine in the 1760s.[5] Added to this was another internal migration: as settlers for the newly acquired lands, Polish landholders recruited Ukrainian and Polish farmers from the already Polonized voivodships of Galicia and Volynia (Ruś, Belz, Volyn) by offering them living and corvée conditions that were better than those in the western territories. While religious tolerance had prevailed under Ottoman rule in Podolia and the Russian new settlement regions (the immigrants from Germany were and remained Protestants,

Catholics, and Mennonites), the by now Catholicized Polish state sought to force Roman and Greek Catholicism over Orthodoxy, which led to tensions. The rebellious Cossacks had made the defense of Orthodoxy into one of the principles (if a secondary one) of their social order. In the 18th century, Poland was able to weaken Orthodoxy in eastern Poland and to incorporate the last remaining Orthodox bishoprics, as, for example, Lemberg, Przemysl, and Luck, into the Union of Brest.

Additional parts of the new southern coast of the Russian Empire were conquered in the subsequent wars. After Crimea had become Russian in 1783, the west coast of the Black Sea fell into Russian hands between 1787 and 1791, and in 1812, finally, Bessarabia as a whole. The Turkish fortress of Haci-Bey (Chadzibe) was expanded into a new, large Russian port after 1794. Empress Catherine was hoping to expand the economic contacts with the Mediterranean region. To that end, merchants were to be brought into the new city, among them especially Greeks, on whose account the city was given the name Odessa in 1795. Greeks, Jews (1859: 11% of the population, 57% of the merchants), Russian, and western and central Europeans made up a large share of the city's population.[6] Immigration also came from the surrounding Ukrainian land, and Cossacks were settled in a suburb.[7] Already in the first decades of its existence, Odessa's trade developed successfully, which led to an enormous expansion. Between the beginning of the 19th century and 1861, the population of the city grew tenfold. The high percentage of immigrants led to the emergence of a cultural identity separate from that of the surrounding Ukrainian lands.

The Polish-Russian integration of the Ukrainian territories did not proceed harmoniously for very long. The three partitions (1772, 1793, 1795) eliminated Poland from the map of Europe. The territories of Ukraine that had been Polish until then were divided up between Austria and Russia. In 1772, Austria appropriated Polish voivodships with Galicia and a part of Podolia, which, on the basis of a medieval legal title, were annexed to the Habsburg Empire as the crown land "Kingdom of Galicia and Lodomeria." In 1774, Austria acquired Bukovina (Buchenland), which had remained Ottoman until then, and created a separate crown land out of it. After the Austrian-Hungarian Settlement of 1867, the two crown lands remained part of the Austrian half of the Danubian monarchy, while the trans-Carpathian Ukraine continued to be part of Hungary. For the new East-Slavic subjects, referred to in Polish as *rusini*, the Habsburg monarchy used the word "Ruthenians," which established a reference to their emergence from the Kievan Ruś.

In the 1793 partition of Poland, Russia annexed eastern Volhynia, eastern Podolia, and the voivodships of Kiev and Braclaw. In 1795 there followed western Volhynia,

---

[3] German settlers in Russia since the 18th century.

[4] Greek settlers from the Black Sea region in New Russia since the early modern period and Pontic Greeks in Greece since the end of World War II.

[5] Ashkenazim in Europe since the early modern period.

[6] Greek settlers from the Black Sea region in New Russia since the early modern period and Pontic Greeks in Greece since the end of World War II.

[7] Ukrainian and Russian settlers in New Russia since the 18th century.

an annexation by which Russia reached the Bug border to Prussia, Austria, and (since 1815) the Kingdom of Poland allied to Russia.

Emigration and nationalization up to World War I

The annexations of the Polish (and thus also the Ukrainian) territories added considerably to Russia's and Austria's Jewish population. Russia, especially, had had relatively few Jews until 1772, most still in Ukraine on the left bank. Attempts by Catherine to grant the Jews the same rights as her other subjects were thwarted by opposition from the non-Jewish merchants and had to be rescinded. Instead, beginning in 1804 the so-called Pale of Settlement (*certa osedlosti*) was created, which remained in existence until World War I. Jews had the right of residence within the Pale, with only a few Jews able to settle outside of it. Ukraine, including the newly acquired, former Ottoman territories (with the exception of the governments of Charkiv and Sloboda-Ukraine), was part of the Pale of Settlement.[8]

While the status quo was initially preserved in the Russian partition territory following the annexations, Austria quickly launched efforts at bureaucratization and modernization in the newly acquired region. Under Polish rule, the United Christians had been neglected, the goal being to Latinize them. The Habsburg monarchy now made efforts to elevate the clergy of the Greek Catholic confession to the level of education of the Roman Catholic clergy. Theological training centers arose in Vienna and Lemberg, and the Vienna institutions, in particular, led the united clergy out of the provincial milieu.

As national ordering principles slowly began to replace religious ones in the 19th century, the United Christians could be identified in Austria as a Ukrainian (Ruthenian) population group. Their church became a Ukrainian-national agency (Agentur). In the Russian territories, the United Confession was prohibited after a grace period. Its congregations were incorporated into the Russian Orthodox church, with the result that the Ukrainians of the Austrian and the Russian territories were now confessionally different. While in Austria the Ruthenians were officially recognized as a population group of the monarchy, the Ukrainians in Russia were considered from the middle of the 19th century "Minor Russians," and thus a dialectic subgroup of the Russians. Political activity in favor of a separate Ukrainian nationality was persecuted in Russia, and administrative measures such as the prohibition against teaching (1862) and publishing (1876) in the Ukrainian language supplemented the efforts at Russification. These measures led to a first politically motivated emigration from Ukraine, which continued until World War I even though these restrictions were lifted after the Russian Revolution of 1905. However, this emigration involved only a small, nationally conscious

group of students and academics, most with connections to the Russian Left (Social Democrats and social revolutionaries), who dispersed across western and central Europe. Many of these refugees lived in the Austrian city of Lemberg, where the Kievan historian Michailo Hrushevskyi turned his chair in eastern European history into a center for Ukrainian studies. While this would have been an internal migration by today's borders, in actuality it was a flight into the bordering Habsburg monarchy, which was becoming increasingly hostile toward Russia.[9]

Austrian laws gave the Jews of the Polish partition regions that fell to the Habsburg monarchy an initially still restricted freedom of movement, which led to the migration of Galician Jews to other parts of the empire, such as Hungary and the formerly Ottoman Bukovina.[10] With the city of Czernowitz there arose in the Bukovina a metropolis that developed in the 19th century into an important and modern cultural center for Poles, Ukrainians, Romanians, and above all Yiddish- and German-speaking Jews. In the Russian part of Ukraine, massive efforts were made to bring the Jews from the countryside into the cities, which prompted many to emigrate to central and western Europe and overseas.[11]

Both Austria and Russia continued their efforts at populating these areas in the 19th century. German settlers moved to eastern Galicia, where they established a chain of German colonist villages in a strip between Zhovkva (Zolkiew) in the north and Stryj in the south. The territory that had become Russian attracted colonists especially to Volhynia. Here the first colonies were established at the beginning of the 19th century by Mennonites from the Netherlands and Prussia who were seeking to escape military service, though many of them subsequently continued on to southern Russia or Canada. Farmers from eastern Pomerania who did not adopt Russian citizenship after their arrival were often expelled from the country after 1871. Lutheran German colonists remained, however, and after 1861 there was a strong influx of Germans when the noble landowners lost their cheap labor with the liberation of the peasants and recruited replacements. While there were only about 13,000 Germans in Volhynia in 1861, by 1897 their number had risen to 170,000. Volhynia was also one of the settlement regions of the Czechs, who migrated from the Habsburg monarchy into the Czarist Empire, where some of them converted to Orthodoxy.[12]

A German emigration began in the second half of the 19th century: after the establishment of the German Reich in 1871, a Russification set in, which led to the abolition of the cultural privileges and special administration hitherto

---

[8] Jews from the Pale of Settlement in Odessa and in the cities of central Russia and Poland in the 19th century.

[9] Russian revolutionaries in western and central Europe in the 19th and early 20th centuries.

[10] Ashkenazim in Europe since the early modern period; Galician Jews in Austria from the 18th to the early 20th century.

[11] Jews from the Pale of Settlement in Odessa and in the cities of central Russia and Poland in the 19th century; eastern European Jews in Berlin from the late 19th century to the 1930s; eastern European Jews in London since the late 19th century; eastern European Jews in Paris since the late 19th century.

[12] Czech settlers in Volhynia from the 1860s to the 1940s.

granted to the Germans. In 1892, a law in Volhynia prohibited persons of foreign background, even if they held Russian citizenship, from settling outside the cities. This put a stop to the stream of colonists, and Germans now began to emigrate from Volhynia again. However, because of the high birthrate, the number of Germans continued to rise, to over 200,000 in 1911.[13]

The seasonal migration is difficult to gauge: before World War I, Ruthenian and Polish workers from Austrian Galicia worked on the estates in Prussia year after year.[14] At the end of the 19th century, the extremely nationalistic Pan-German League sought to recruit German settlers from Galicia for "internal colonization" in the eastern territories of Prussia.

Because of the introduction of the universal draft in 1874, many Mennonites who had come to Russia left to escape military service. However, the hope that they might improve their economic and social position also drove Lutherans and Catholics to continue their migration. Between 1870 and 1914, 116,000 Germans went from the Russian Empire (from the Volga region as well as from Ukraine) to the USA, where place names such as Odessa point to new German settlers from the Czarist Empire.

The Russian state remained officially neutral toward the Muslim Crimean Tatars in the territories acquired in 1783. In reality, though, there was tension between the Muslims and the Slavic immigrants or soldiers. While those who left the Crimean peninsula in 1783–4 were mostly Ottoman Turks from Caffa Feodosiya and individuals related to the Khan family, they were followed in 1789 by about 30,000 Tatars who had given up hope that the Ottomans might return.

Familial and cultural ties beyond the Black Sea continued to motivate new waves of emigration. After 1815 there was a continuous exodus, which the Russian state initially tried to prevent. That changed after the Crimean War (1853–6): on the basis of presumably false reports that the Crimean Tatars had supported the British and French expeditionary forces against Russia, emigration to the Ottoman Empire was eased and encouraged in 1859–60. It is likely that about 100,000 Tatars left at that time for the Ottoman Empire. The policy changed again in 1860: to prevent the land from becoming depopulated, the Tatars in the Czarist Empire were henceforth no longer to be marginalized. But already the Russian-Turkish War of 1877–8, which also led to nationalistic anti-Turkish eruptions, caused another surge in emigration, which continued at a low level until the beginning of the 20th century. The attempt by the czarist government, faced with a need for workers and settlers, to recall Tatars who had previously left met with very little success.

The move to bring Russian settlers to the Crimea also had little success. To be sure, the southern coast of the Crimea, because of its pleasant climate, developed into a

Table 1. Population groups in the Ukrainian regions of the Russian Empire, 1897	
	Number
Total	23,833,000
Ukrainians	17,040,000
Russians	2,970,000
Jews	2,030,000
Germans	502,000
Poles	406,000
Belarusians	222,000
Romanians	187,000
Crimean Tatars	220,000
Greeks	80,000
Bulgarians	68,000

Source: Russian Census, 1897.

popular recreation area for the Russians from the north, and Sebastopol became an important naval port. However, agricultural and urban settlers arrived in insufficient numbers, notwithstanding the grant of privileges and recruitment efforts abroad.

The census of 1897 revealed that the population of the Ukrainian regions of the Czarist Empire had grown from 13.4 million to 23.8 million (see Table 1). Jews made up 8% of the total population but 33% of the urban residents. In Ukraine on the right bank they even accounted for 80% of the population in the cities. In the governments of Tauria (Crimea and Vorland), Yekaterinoslav, and Cherson, the census showed about 280,000 German-speaking inhabitants, equivalent to about 5% of the population. In Bessarabia, whose northern (Chotin) and southern parts (Belgorod/Akkerman and Izmail) are today part of Ukraine, 60,000 German speakers were counted (about 3% of the population). The population of Galicia, Bukovina, and Transcarpathia came to about 5.9 million, about a third of whom were Ukrainians.

New immigrations into Ukraine were the result of the Russian liberation of the peasants in 1861 and of industrialization that began in the 1860s. This industrialization went beyond the light and agrarian industry (sugar refineries) that had been dominant until then: especially in the hinterland of the Donez (Juzovka/Donetsk; Luhansk) and the Ingulec/Inhulec (Kryvoy Rog/Kryvyi Rih) there arose coal mines, ironworks, and machine-building enterprises. This large coal district, financed with foreign money, developed into the most modern heavy industrial complex of the Russian Empire (by 1900 accounting for about 70% of the coal production and about 50% of the iron ore extraction) and had a large need for workers. Ukrainians were employed, though the entrepreneurs also recruited Russian peasants and, in order to quickly have skilled workers at their disposal, parts of the crews from Russia's older mining regions (Urals, Tula). The influx of Russians into the new industrial areas would continue in the 20th century as the Ukrainian industrial

[13] Ethnic German "remigrants" from Russia in Germany, 1890s to 1930s.

[14] Polish agricultural workers in Prussia-Germany from the late 19th century to World War II.

district was further expanded.[15] Not entirely reliable indications suggest that the share of Ukrainians among the population in the Dnieper-Donez region dropped from 84.5% in 1858 to 76.5% in 1897; presumably it declined even more than that. For the steppe areas in the south, the census of 1897 found a Ukrainian share of about one-third, and on the Crimea, 12%.

While the Czarist Empire sought to populate its newly acquired steppe regions further in the 19th century and made emigration more difficult, the situation in the smaller Ukrainian part of the Habsburg monarchy was soon characterized largely by emigration. High birthrates and the small plots of land because of the equal division among heirs caused the average size of agricultural enterprises to drop from 5 hectares in 1859 to 2.5 hectares in 1900. With this, the rural population, which accounted for the majority of the inhabitants, could no longer be sustained, and industrial jobs were available only in the small oil region of Boryslav. A large overseas emigration from the Danube monarchy began in the 1880s. According to estimates, 430,000 Ruthenians left Galicia and Bukovina between 1881 and 1912 and another 170,000 left the Carpatho-Ukraine; some US data even put the number at 700,000. According to official Austrian statistics, about 153,000 emigrated from the monarchy between 1902 and 1911.

It is difficult to say what share of the Polish and Jewish emigrants in the USA came from the territory of modern-day Ukraine, since they could also have come from what is today Polish western Galicia. According to Austrian emigration statistics, between 1881 and 1910 there were around 468,000 Polish emigrants from western Galicia as well as 137,000 Polish and 252,000 Ruthenian emigrants from eastern Galicia. Up until 1899, immigrants to the USA were registered by their nationality; after that there was a category called "Ruthenians," though it included only those who declared themselves as such. Given the nebulous options of national identification, that was by no means all of them, which means that the official declaration of about 255,000 Ruthenian immigrants to the USA between 1899 and 1914 is surely too low. The US emigration numbers for 1877 to 1887 (34,000) and 1888 to 1898 (74,000) are based on estimates.

The first wave of Galician Ukrainians found work after 1877 in the industrial regions in the eastern USA (Pennsylvania). Beginning in the 1890s, Ukrainians also went to Canada, where they were employed as railroad workers. To this day, they form relatively self-contained settlement areas in the western provinces (Alberta, Saskatchewan). Other destinations were Brazil and later also Argentina and Australia. Those who emigrated from the Russian part of Ukraine were mostly Jews. Legal restrictions, recurring pogroms (1871, 1881–2, 1891, 1903–6), and a precarious economic and social situation motivated their emigration to the USA, but also to Ottoman Palestine, where the initially philanthropic – later also politically motivated (Zionism) – settlement of Jews constituted a major factor.

Emigration had its counterpart in an internal migration in Russian Ukraine, in two directions. Although the agricultural production in Ukraine was enormously expanded in the course of the 19th century, the native population benefited little: the profits from the export of wheat went to the Russian entrepreneurs, merchants, and the state's treasury. The migration of the rural population aimed at the expansive, only recently opened territories of the Russian Empire. Ukrainians moved continuously into the area of the lower Volga and into the northern territories of the Caucasus, where there were about 1.7 million Ukrainians at the end of the 19th century. In the second half of the 19th century, about 100,000 Ukrainians moved from northern Ukraine to Siberia (Omsk region), Central Asia, and the land north of the Kazakh steppe. In these regions they were quickly subjected to a linguistic Russification. Other out-migration movements in the two decades before World War I were aimed at the far east of the Russian Empire: first by boat from Odessa to Vladivostok, later with the Trans-Siberian Railway, more than 200,000 Ukrainians came into the regions along the Amur and the coastal province (Primorsky Krai) on the Sea of Japan, in the so-called Green Wedge (Zeleny Klin), where they accounted for about 20% of the population.

The 19th century brought eastern Europe culturally defined ethnicity as a new categorization. That the Ukrainians belonged to a different ethnicity from Russians or Poles was controversial, and it was not rare for Polish/Ukrainian or Russian/Ukrainian self-descriptions to cut across families. To a high degree, membership in a modern Ukrainian nation was a result of subjective identity formation. While the debate of whether Ukrainians ("Minor Russians") and the "Great Russians" were part of a common ethnic group was dominated in the Russian Empire by the state, in the Habsburg Empire, competing self-descriptions were able to develop freely. The "Old Ruthenians" of Galicia saw themselves as an ethnic group belonging to Russiandom and presented themselves as pro-Russian (moskvofily). By contrast, the "Ukrainophile" Ruthenians emphasized a clear separation from the (Greater) Russians, though they saw themselves as part of the Ukrainians in the Russian Ukraine. The term sobornost was coined for this sense of togetherness. Most Poles, however, maintained that the Ruthenians did not possess the preconditions for a "historical nation," that they were an ethnographic mass that should be absorbed into "Polishness." In fact, an increasing Polanization is evident in Galicia before World War I; while the number of Polish-speaking inhabitants grew by 17.1% between 1900 and 1910, the number of Ukrainian speakers increased by only 4.3%, which was not the result of migratory differences or differences in the natural population growth.

---

[15] Russian peasant labor migrants in Russian factories from the end of the 19th century to the end of the 1920s.

Forced migrations in World War I

The unexpected advance of Russian troops in Galicia and Bukovina at the outbreak of the war in 1914 led to a large-scale movement of evacuation and flight into regions of Austria-Hungary not affected by the war. While precise statements about the extent of this movement are not possible, the War Surveillance Office (Kriegsüberwachungsamt) in Vienna posited a million people in May 1915. Among them were about 450,000 Jews who were fleeing from possible pogroms by Russian troops. After their flight they often made their way into the large cities, especially Vienna. No small number did not return to Galicia even after the Russians were pushed back in 1915. In addition, nationally minded Ukrainians and other Poles and Ruthenians also fled from the area of occupation.

Deportations occurred under Russian occupation. They affected the Jewish population, which was deported from the front line and border regions into the interior of Russia because of a general suspicion that they were spies. But these deportations also targeted Galicians with a national-Ukrainian attitude, among them also the Metropolitan of the United Church, Andrei Septicki. The coercive measures of the Russians compromised the pro-Moscow orientation of the Galician Ukrainians, which ceased to play a political role even after the reconquest of most areas of Galicia by the central powers.

Armed units composed of members of the various nationalities were set up on the Austro-Hungarian side in 1914, in Russia after the February revolution in 1917. Following the first Peace of Brest-Litovsk (9 February 1918) and the request by the Ukrainian People's Republic (UNR) to the central powers to take action against the Bolsheviks, the "Ukrainian Legion" of the Austro-Hungarian army was stationed near Aleksandrovsk (Zaporizhia) and Elizavetgrad (Kirovohrad), where it initiated Ukrainization. The UNR itself formed a unit of Ruthenian prisoners of war, which developed into one of its most important pillars. The German military authorities set up military units from Russian prisoners of war, which in 1918 were led back also to Ukraine, but were soon dissolved.

Following the Peace of Brest-Litovsk and the expulsion – with German help – of the Bolshevik troops from Ukraine, the latter – de facto since 29 April 1918 a German military protectorate under General Pavlo Skoropadski, who was declared hetman – was considered during the turbulent period of the beginning Russian Civil War a refuge for mostly Russian opponents of the Soviet Republic.[16] Together with failed national-Ukrainian politicians and intellectuals, they fled westward when – in the wake of Germany's capitulation in November 1918, Skoropadski's abdication in December 1918, and the defeat of the reestablished UNR in February 1919 – the Red Army pushed as far as Volhynia

and Podolia. The Ukrainian Galician Army (UHA), set up in the late fall of 1918 in eastern Galicia as the army of the West Ukrainian People's Republic, fought against Poland until July 1919; thereafter it crossed the Austro-Russian and – in the interwar period – Polish-Soviet border river of the Zbruc and fought for the UNR against the Bolsheviks. In August 1919 the UNR troops were able to advance as far as Kiev, but thereafter they were pushed back by the "white" forces of General Denikin, to whom the UHA deserted in November 1919; following Denikin's subsequent defeat in Odessa, they switched to the camp of the Bolsheviks. The remnants of the UNR army joined Poland in April 1920 and, together with the Polish army, occupied Ukraine once again as far as the Dnieper, only to be completely pushed out of Ukraine by the Red Army a few weeks later. Poland recognized Soviet Ukraine in the Peace of Riga in March 1921. In 1920, the Soviet troops also put the "whites" under General Vrangel to flight across the Crimea.

As a result, soldiers of the various Ukrainian and "white" Russian units as well as civilian refugees from Ukraine were dispersed among numerous European countries. Initially interned, the soldiers went on to develop exile communities with various political orientations in France, Germany, Poland, Czechoslovakia, Austria, and Yugoslavia. A segment of the refugees continued on to the USA. Many Jewish refugees from the region of the civil war, which had witnessed numerous pogroms between 1918 and 1920, went to Palestine (now under British rule), some went overseas, while others remained in central Europe, not least in Germany.[17]

Soviet nationalities policy and state-directed migrations during the interwar period

The territories east of the border agreed upon in the Polish-Soviet Peace of Riga in 1921 became one of the founding members of the USSR in 1922 as the Ukrainian Socialist Soviet Republic. The desire to establish Soviet power in the non-Russian regions led to the policy of *korenizacija* (rooting), in the course of which literacy education and a Ukrainization of cultural life came to the Ukrainian Soviet Socialist Republic. While the Ukrainian language had been outlawed in the Czarist Empire, the newly codified language now became the official state language in the Soviet Ukraine. In addition, national administrative units emerged in Ukraine on the communal and *rayon* level. In 1931, there were 254 German village soviets and even German-national *rayons*. In 1925, a Polish *rayon* was set up near Zitomir in Dovbys, renamed Marchlevsk. There were also nine Russian, three Jewish (Kalinindorf, Novozlatopol, Stalindorf), three Bulgarian, and three Greek *rayons*. Two additional Jewish *rayons* emerged on the Crimea (Freidorf, Larindorf). The result of this Ukrainizing and nationally tolerant policy was that a number of emigrants, among them also nationally

---

[16] Refugees in Russia during and after World War I; Russian emigrants in Europe since 1917.

[17] Eastern European Jews in Berlin from the late 19th century to the 1930s.

Table 2. Composition of the population of the Ukrainian SSR, 1926, 1959, and 1989

	1926		1959		1989	
	Number	%	Number	%	Number	%
Total	29,018,000	100	41,865,000	100	51,452,000	100
Ukrainians	23,219,000	80	32,158,000	76.8	37,419,000	72.7
Russians	2,677,000	9.2	7,091,000	16.9	11,355,000	22.1
Jews	1,577,000	5.4	840,000	2.0	486,000	0.9
Germans	394,000	1.4	23,000	0.1	–	–
Poles	476,000	1.6	363,000	0.9	219,000	0.4
Belarusians	76,000	0.3	291,000	0.7	440,000	0.8
Romanians	259,000	0.9	342,000	0.8	324,000	0.6
Greeks	108,000	0.4	104,000	0.2	–	–
Bulgarians	93,000	0.3	219,000	0.5	233,000	0.5
Tatars (Crimea)	179,000	0.5	61,000	0.1	–	–
Hungarians	–	–	149,000	0.4	163,000	0.3
Other	–	–	–	–	874,000	1.7

Source: Soviet censuses, 1926, 1959, and 1989.

conscious intellectuals like the president of the Central Rada, the parliament of the UNR, Michailo Hrushevski, returned to the Soviet Ukraine in a wave resembling the Russian national movement of the *Smenovechovstvo*. Since refugees with a socialist or sociorevolutionary motivation were more open to returning, the Ukrainian exile community experienced a pronounced political shift to the right. Poland, too, which had been awarded eastern Galicia for good in 1923 (Volhynia had also become Polish, Transcarpathia Czech, and the Bukovina Romanian), tolerated the return of nationalist Ukrainian emigrants after 1924.

Like the rest of the population, the colonists in southern Ukraine were affected by the civil war upheavals and the famine in 1921–2. That prompted many of them to leave the settlement areas temporarily or permanently. The closing of many churches that was decreed by the Soviets was also a motivation for emigration. In 1924, the authorities counted 360,000 Germans in the Ukrainian SSR, 56,000 of whom were Mennonites. The latter were the first to leave, with more than 8,000 leaving in 1924, mostly to Canada. The census of 1926 revealed that 20% of the 29 million inhabitants of the Ukrainian SSR were national minorities (see Table 2).

The expansion of the existing industries was intensified and pushed forward through the immigration of new workers, primarily from Russia. Other migrant laborers made their way to the Dnieper, where large-scale projects such as dams and power plants (Dneproges after 1927) created a need for workers that could not be met by the local population. The social and economic transformations following the consolidation of the Soviet state led to internal migrations within the Soviet Empire that paid no heed to administrative boundaries.[18] The urbanization of Ukraine also progressed during the Soviet period. World War I and the civil war still

had the opposite effect: since the provisioning of the cities was very poor, many city dwellers moved to the countryside, and the urban population dropped from 5.6 million in 1914 to 4.2 million in 1920. By 1928 the prewar conditions had been restored, and in 1939 nearly 40% (1914 about 20%) of the inhabitants of Ukraine were living in cities. The new immigrants in the industrial cities came in equal parts from Ukraine and other regions of the USSR. In this way the cities were, on the one hand, partially Ukrainianized (something they had not been before World War I), while, on the other hand, they retained a significant segment of a Russian-speaking population.

The dissolution of the Jewish Pale of Settlement in World War I caused especially younger Jews from the tight, small towns in western Ukraine to migrate into the industrial cities in eastern Ukraine and Russia. Compared to the census data of 1897 and 1926, the districts on the right bank of Ukraine lost 20% to 50% of their Jewish population, while their share in the Donets tripled. In Kiev, the number of Jews – who were not considered a religious community in the Soviet Union but a nationality and were statistically counted on that basis – rose fourfold. In Charkiv, which had not been within the Pale of Settlement, the number rose to seven times what it had been in 1897, while the increase in Odessa, already previously home to many Jews, was almost entirely the result of natural population growth.

In spite of the strong migration from the countryside to the city, the Soviet Union in 1922 launched a program for settling Jews in the country, the goal being the kind of occupational-social transformation that the Zionists also envisaged. Jewish settlement areas were set aside in southern Ukraine in the regions around Cherson, Kryvyj Rih, Zaporizhia, and on the Crimea peninsula. Between 1925 and 1927, about 80,000 Jews were settled here with help from the American Jewish Joint Distribution Committee (JDC). The chairman of the Settlement Organization for Working Jews (OZET),

---

[18] Russian labor migrants on large construction sites in the USSR since the 1920s.

Yuri Larin, planned to transplant up to 280,000 Jews to the Crimea, where a Jewish republic was to arise. Not least the opposition from the locals and anti-Semitic denunciations soon led to the abandonment of this project; subsequently, the streams of settlers were redirected into the region of Birobidzan in the Russian far east.

The moderate policy in the Soviet Ukraine did not last. At the end of the 1920s, the Soviet power under Stalin turned to industrialization and the forced collectivization of agriculture. In central and eastern Ukraine, as in other prosperous parts of the Soviet Union, this process was linked with the so-called de-kulakization campaign, which was supposedly expelling rich, supplies-hording farmers from their land and interning them under a coercive system in "special settlements" (*specposelenija*) in northern Russia and Siberia. The coercive measures and confiscations led to a famine in 1932–3 that cost the lives of millions of farmers. The year 1934 saw the beginning of a policy of Russification and the dismantling of the national administrative units that had just recently been created, a policy that came to a conclusion with the decree of the Central Committee of the Communist Party of the Ukraine on 1 April 1939 about the Liquidation and Transformation of the Artificially Created National Rayonsoi and Village Councils in the Ukraine. The advocates of this earlier policy were persecuted, banished, and murdered in 1937–8 in the wake of the great terror actions of the NKVD (Popular Commissariat of the Interior, home of the Secret Police). The Stalinist state's need for security led to the first national resettlements in 1935. Accused, among other things, of being part of the "active Fascists," about 13,000 German and additional Polish families from eastern Volhynia and the region of Odessa were deported between 1936 and 1938, chiefly to Kazakhstan.[19]

Migrations occurred also in the Polish part of Ukraine. The moderate forces in the Polish government held the upper hand only for a while. The cultural autonomy that Polish politicians had promised the Galician Ukrainians in 1923 was not granted. As a result, nationalist-Ukrainian veterans as well as secondary and university students were radicalized into the Ukrainian Military Organization and from 1929 in the Organization of Ukrainian Nationalists (OUN), which carried out terrorist campaigns against Poland and the alleged Ukrainian collaborators. The Polish side responded in 1930 with military "pacifications," in the course of which Ukrainian villages were burned down. In addition, Catholic Poles (among them demobilized soldiers) were settled in eastern Galicia, which Polish terminology of the interwar period referred to as Eastern Small Poland so as not to let the connection to Halyc and thus to Ruś be in the foreground. Both sides engaged in political and media skirmishes over the allocation of the inhabitants: for example, *Latynnyky*, Ukrainians who followed the Roman Catholic rite, were often counted among the Poles. In Volhynia there were efforts to foster a separate Ukrainian identity and prevent contacts with the Ukrainian nationalists in Galicia. That policy, however, had little success. Particular discontent was sparked by efforts to return churches that had become Orthodox in the 19th century to the Roman Catholic church (*rewindykacja*), and in the process as much as possible also win the faithful over to Roman Catholicism and thus to Polishness.

While emigration abroad was hardly possible for Ukrainians from the Soviet Ukraine, the situation was different in the Polish territories: according to the censuses, which here referred to religious affiliation, nearly 63,000 Greek-Catholic and 30,000 Orthodox emigrants left Poland between 1921 and 1929. As it is likely that half of the Orthodox were also Ukrainians, one can posit about 78,000 Ukrainian emigrants abroad. But a large part of the 125,000 Roman Catholic and nearly 200,000 Jewish emigrants from these years came from the territory of modern-day Ukraine. We can put the number of Ukrainians who left Poland between 1927 and 1938 at 134,000, with 45,000 returning migrants counted during the same period. The existing data do not allow us to determine how many of the 200,000 Jews and 398,000 Catholics who left Poland during this time were residents from East Galicia and Volhynia in what are today Ukrainian territories.

The dissolution of the Habsburg monarchy in the Peace of St. Germain in 1919 had assigned the Hungarian Transcarpathian region to Czechoslovakia. Alongside the 372,000 Ruthenians living there according to the census of 1921, there were 192,000 Hungarians, as well as Jews, Germans, Romanians, and Czechs. The autonomy promised to the region was granted only in part (cultural but not political autonomy). The interwar period also saw the immigration of Czechs and Slovaks (especially as civil servants).

From the estate of the former Danubian monarchy, Romania had been given Bukovina, home to a strongly mixed population. Ukrainians were found above all in the rural districts in the north, as well as in Bessarabia, which had also become Romanian. The resolutely pursued Romanization of the newly acquired territories led to cultural assimilation, but also to emigration.

When the easternmost region of Carpatho-Ukraine, as a result of the federalization of Czechoslovakia after the Munich Agreement in the fall of 1938, won autonomy and independence for two days in March 1939, many OUN followers crossed the border from Galicia in the hope of creating a Ukrainian national state with the help of the newly formed militia force Karpats'ka Sic. And this even though in the Carpatho-Ukraine, especially, the consciousness of belonging to a "Ukrainian nation" was only partially developed. A number of east Slavic inhabitants considered themselves (and in smaller groups still do at the beginning of the 21st century) members of a separate ethnicity of the Ruthenians (*Rusyny*), no small number also sympathized with a Magyarphile attitude. During the fall of Czechoslovakia in 1939, Hungary occupied the territory and murdered, deported, or imprisoned the nationalist Ukrainians who had not fled; in addition, a few Galicians were handed over to Poland.

---

[19] Deportees in the Soviet Union during and after World War II.

Forced migration in World War II

National Socialist Germany used the Ukrainian emigrants in Germany, Austria, and Czechoslovakia (as for example in the Polish campaign) as potential auxiliary troops.[20] In the occupied regions, the Germans protected the Ukrainians.

On the basis of the secret protocol to the German-Soviet nonaggression treaty of 23 August 1939, the Soviet Union occupied the previously Polish territories of East Galicia and Volhynia and proclaimed the liberation of the "West Ukraine." An "elected" Soviet popular representative body made the request to incorporate these territories into the Ukrainian SSR. Especially Ukrainian nationalists fled across the new demarcation line along the San to the German-occupied side, since the military and the politicians in the Nazi state sympathized with Ukrainian nationalism.

At the same time, Poles and Jews fled eastward from core Poland to escape the German troops – until 17 September 1939, within the legal Polish state, thereafter into the Soviet-administered region, into which the Germans deliberately expelled Jews from Upper Silesia and southern Poland. In the wake of the Sovietization of western Ukraine, a part of the refugees – inhabitants of the immediate border region and classified as "class enemies" – and often also Poles denounced to the Soviet authorities, Jews, and Ukrainians were deported from the new territories into the interior of the Soviet Union. The number of deportees for the Ukrainian and Belarusian territories should be put at about 320,000, among them around 200,000 Poles, 70,000 Jews, and 25,000 Ukrainians. Arrests, voluntary departures, and individuals joining the Red Army further reduced the size of the population.[21]

More migrations followed the resettlement agreement between Germany and the USSR: Ukrainians were supposed to resettle voluntarily from the German-occupied territory into Ukraine, while "ethnic Germans" (*Volksdeutsche*) from the new Soviet territories (East Galicia, Volhynia, in 1940 also from the northern Bukovina and Bessarabia) were to be brought "home to the Reich." Up to 1940, the authorities in charge registered around 130,000 ethnic Germans in Galicia and Volhynia, 97% of whom were resettled. The primary goal was the Warthegau, from where in 1939–40 a part of the Polish and Jewish population was deported to the so-called General Government. A segment of the resettled ethnic Germans came to the district Lublin in the General Government. But the resettlers also included some Ukrainian nationalists who took advantage of the opportunity to escape the Soviets.[22]

The annexation of the northern Bukovina by the Soviet Union made this area with the city of Czernowitz (Chernivtsi) for the first time part of Ukraine. When Romania, as Germany's ally, reoccupied the region, its policy was directed against the Jews as well as against the resident Ukrainians, many of whom fled across the border into the now German-occupied part of Ukraine.

These movements were already a result of a fundamental change in migratory conditions brought about by the German attack on the USSR in June 1941: once it was over its initial shock, the Soviet government tried to evacuate especially endangered groups. While nearly all the Jews further west fell into the hands of the Germans and their auxiliary forces, further to the east some of them could be taken to safety in areas east of the Volga. The higher-ranking administrative and party personnel were also evacuated. The plan, following the model of the deportation of the Volga Germans, also called for uprooting and removing the Ukrainian "ethnic Germans." However, because of the speed of the German advance, this succeeded only in part.[23] In the first month of the "Russian campaign," Ukrainian nationalists, who had been formed into smaller military units, led civil emigrants back into German-occupied territories.[24] The marching groups (*Pochidni hrupy*) of the OUN set up Ukrainian-national administrations, which the Germans tolerated. However, when the Ukrainians proclaimed a separate state in 1941, the Germans destroyed the higher Ukrainian administrative structures and arrested or murdered those responsible.

In the summer of 1941, the Germans divided the occupied territory. Under the designation of District Galicia, East Galicia, Austrian until 1918, was added to the General Government, which was otherwise made up of formerly Polish areas. The remaining areas formed the Reich Commissariat Ukraine (RCU) with the capital of Rivne (Rovno) in Volhynia, whose civil administration was given, as time went by, additional territories that had previously been under military governance. The Ukraine east of a line running about 100 kilometers east of the Dnieper remained under German military administration.

The Germans prohibited any further return migration of political refugees into Ukrainian territories, though this prohibition was repeatedly violated. Some of the Schutzmannschaften (a kind of auxiliary police force) made up of Ukrainians were deployed by the Germans in White Russia as security forces to prevent the paramilitaries from protecting friends and relatives. Later, the German occupiers brought especially Ukrainians from western Ukraine and the Cholm region to Travniki (in the district of Lublin) for military training, and used them as guard units in concentration camps, for example, in Auschwitz, Sachsenhausen (where Ukrainian nationalists were also interned), or Mauthausen. They also took part alongside the Germans in liquidating the ghettoes. The 14th Weapons Grenadier Division of the SS "Galicia," formed in 1943 with Ukrainian volunteers and ethnic Germans, was initially deployed in Galicia (Battle of Brody, July 1944) and largely wiped out; subsequently it was

---

[20] Russian emigrants in Europe since 1917.

[21] Deportees in the Soviet Union during and after World War II.

[22] Ethnic Germans (*Volksdeutsche*) in the German Reich and in German-occupied territories in World War II.

[23] Deportees in the Soviet Union during and after World War II.

[24] Russian emigrants in Europe since 1917.

replenished and led via Slovakia to Austria, where it was held in captivity by the Western Allies in Bellaria near Rimini. Cossack units and other auxiliary troops levied in Ukraine withdrew alongside the German Wehrmacht from Ukraine in 1944 and headed westward.

The murder of the Jews by Nazi Germany took place under the guise of a forced migration. Those Jews who were not immediately shot during the first days of the German occupation were briefly placed into ghettoes in the cities and were then murdered under the pretext of being resettled. In 1941, the German occupiers redirected transports of Jews from Hungary or the now-Hungarian Carpatho-Ukraine to Podolia and murdered most of them in the area around Kamieniec Podolski. Transports of Jews from western Ukraine headed mostly to the extermination camp of Belzec in the district of Lublin; in Volhynia and in eastern Ukraine, the shootings or killings in gas trucks took place in direct proximity to where the Jews were living.

In the summer of 1941, Germany ceded the southwestern part of Ukraine as far as the southern Bug to its ally Romania. This territory, referred to as Transnistria (region east of the Dniester) by Romania, was initially also included in the annihilation of the Jews, with many Romanians also involved in murdering Jews. Thus, a large segment of the Jewish population of Odessa fell victim to these pogroms. However, after the first wave of murders, the Romanians used Transnistria as a deportation region for the Jews of Old Romania. Although the living conditions were exceedingly bad and murders as well as deaths from exhaustion and epidemics were frequent, in the Romanian territory, in contrast to German-occupied Ukraine, Jews had a chance at survival, which also prompted a difficult-to-quantify flight from the German into the Romanian part of Ukraine.[25]

Additional forced migrations were due to the recruitment of workers for the Reich territory. Germany had an urgent need of workers in agriculture and (armament) industry to replace Germans drafted into military service. Until 1942, the Germans resorted to volunteers, which followed in the footsteps of the traditional movements of seasonal laborers. As word spread in Ukraine of how poor the living and working conditions were for eastern workers in Germany, the number of volunteers declined and eventually dried up completely. In response, the Germans resorted to coercive measures, and in 1942 they deported Ukrainian men and women for forced labor in the Reich, whereby Ukrainians from the district of Galicia in the General Government received somewhat better treatment (also compared to Poles drafted into forced labor) than the Ukrainians from the Reich Commissariat Ukraine and from the military administrative districts in eastern Ukraine.[26]

When it withdrew in 1943–4, the German occupying force led a majority of the ethnic Germans out of Ukraine. After an examination by the immigrant office of the SS, they could acquire German citizenship.[27] Also evacuated were Ukrainians and other population groups that had collaborated with the Germans and had reason to fear the reconquest by the Red Army. They included, among others, the representatives of the Ukrainian churches reauthorized by the Germans, members of paramilitary units, and administrative workers.

In the camps for displaced persons (DPs), set up in 1945 in Germany and Austria, they encountered former forced laborers of both genders, and Nazi victims (e.g., the Jews), in the deportation of whom some had participated. The number of Ukrainian DPs is difficult to gauge, and estimates that posit up to 3 million are surely exaggerated. It was only in 1946 that the Allied administrations of the DP camps accepted the nationality "Ukrainian," which meant that members of that group were until then registered in different categories. In this way about half of the members of the Armed SS Division Galicia escaped the forced repatriation agreed upon at the Yalta Conference in 1945: they declared themselves to be citizens of Poland, which was not the destination of any forced repatriation. By contrast, most of the DPs from the Soviet Union, the members of the Cossack troops and of the "Russian liberation army" under general Andrei Andreevic Vlasov, which fought against the Soviet Union and which had also been joined by a number of Soviet prisoners of war who hailed from Ukraine, were transported back to the USSR.[28]

Nation-state homogenization after the war and its consequences for the conditions of migration

After 1945, the re-Sovietized Ukraine had a different geographic shape than the Soviet Republic of the interwar period. In the west, the border followed the Bug then ran a few kilometers east of the German-Soviet demarcation line of 1939. In the summer of 1945, Carpatho-Ukraine, which had been part of Czechoslovakia until 1939 and of Hungary from 1939 to 1945, became Soviet and part of the Ukraine as the Transcarpathian Province. This gave the USSR a direct border with Czechoslovakia and Hungary. Moreover, the new Ukrainian SSR could advance a national claim: for the first time, all Ukrainian settled territories were united into the framework of a state.

Some of the people who had been evacuated when the Germans invaded returned to Ukraine with the Red Army. At the same time, however, people who had not previously lived in Ukraine were also settled there. That concerned not least the territories in the west of the land and along the new border with Poland, since the Ukrainians in the border region were seen as nationalistic and thus as a potential

[25] Jewish Refugees from Nazi Germany and from German-occupied Europe since 1933.

[26] Forced laborers in Germany and German-occupied Europe during World War II.

[27] Ethnic Germans (*Volksdeutsche*) in the German Reich and in German-occupied territories in World War II.

[28] Displaced persons (DPs) in Europe since the end of World War II.

threat. In the following years, the Soviet authorities subjected the Ukrainian population to an extensive review. Anyone who was compromised from having collaborated with the German occupation authorities, who had returned home from captivity as a prisoner of war, or was merely the victim of a denunciation was sentenced to lengthy banishment or internment in camps. Even those who survived the camps and were released and rehabilitated after Stalin's death in 1953 were in many cases not allowed to return to their original place of residence.

As in other parts of the USSR, after World War II, German prisoners of war as well as deportees from east-central and southeastern Europe had to rebuild in the Ukraine destroyed cities, among other things. Those who survived the exceedingly difficult conditions were generally able to leave the Soviet Union by the middle of the 1950s.[29] In western Ukraine, the Ukrainian Rebel Army (UPA), which had emerged in 1942, carried on a guerrilla war against Soviet rule until the early 1950s, in the course of which swaths of land were depopulated and resettlements occurred.

The new Soviet power brought about a change in the Ukrainian nationality structure, in two ways. The Crimean peninsula had been part of the Russian Socialist Federative Soviet Republic (RSFSR) ever since the founding of the latter in 1917. Until World War II, it had the status of an autonomous republic, primarily because of the strong Tatar population element. The German occupiers had murdered the Jews and Karaites on the Crimea. By contrast, the Crimean Tatars had been used to administer the peninsula and had been recruited for paramilitary units. On the charge of collaboration with the Germans, the entire Crimean Tatar population was deported to Soviet Central Asia in a forced action in May 1944. The ethnic Germans had left the peninsula along with the German troops, and the small groups of Greeks (15,000), Bulgarians (13,000), and Armenians (9,500) had likewise been resettled in 1944, so after this time the peninsula was inhabited almost entirely by Russians and Ukrainians. The geographic names were officially Russified in August 1944; Crimea lost its status as an autonomous republic and was henceforth a province of the RSFSR. In 1954, on the occasion of the 300th anniversary of the Agreement of Perejaslav, which was interpreted as the "reunification of Ukraine with Russia," it was handed over to the Ukrainian SSR.

Western Ukraine witnessed, on the basis of a Repatriation Agreement of 9 September 1944 between the USSR and the Soviet-installed communist government of Poland, a population exchange that was initially referred to as voluntary. Ukrainians living west of the new Polish-Soviet border, among them also the Lemkians of the northern foothills of the Carpathians, seen by some as a separate ethnic group, were supposed to resettle in Ukraine. In return, Poles and Jews who had held Polish citizenship before 17 September 1939 were supposed to come to the re-created Poland.

This resettlement was to be completed by 1 February 1945, although that date was repeatedly extended until June 1946.

According to official Soviet figures, about 790,000 people from western Ukraine resettled in Poland between 1944 and 1948, among them 4% to 5% Jews. However, Polish observers believed that outside of the registered repatriations in 1944 there was a "wild" movement of flight to Poland, estimated at around 100,000 and attributed chiefly to expulsion actions by the nationalistic Ukrainian underground. In a second phase of repatriation in 1956–7, a total of 256,000 people from the entire Soviet Union came to Poland, 76,000 of whom were from Ukraine, and of those about 72,000 from eastern Galicia. In the opposite direction, according to official figures, about 482,000 individuals were resettled from Poland in the Soviet Ukraine between 15 October 1944 and 2 August 1946.

At the same time, an attempt was made to tie the Ukrainians more closely to the Russians. Thus the United Church in the Soviet Ukraine was dissolved in 1946 and the faithful were received into the Russian Orthodox church. In Poland, the united priests and faithful were forced to join the Roman Catholic Church. In western Ukraine, the issue was the ethnic homogenization of various territories. The Soviet authorities were hoping that the resettlements would defuse interstate relations and local situations of conflict in Galicia, the Lublin region, and in Volhynia, which had seen tensions between nationalities before World War II. Already during World War II, Ukrainian nationalists had pursued a policy of homogenization to prepare Volhynia for an unchallenged integration into a Ukrainian nation-state after the war: in a coordinated campaign, with little interference from the Germans, the UPA called upon Polish farmers to leave, reinforcing their demands by burning down their villages and farms. This small-scale war between the UPA and Polish partisans, carried on with great cruelty, drove some Polish inhabitants to seek protection in fortified villages, and others to flee. Further to the west, actions by Polish forces of the right-wing underground were aimed, with a similar goal, against the old-established Ukrainians and Ukrainian settlers brought to the district of Lublin of the General Governmentby the Germans as part of the population shifts of the General Plan East.

On the Polish side of the border, as well, a three-sided civil war raged from 1944 to 1947 between communist Poles, the anti-Soviet Polish underground, and the UPA. Although it had been agreed that the resettlements would be voluntary, the Polish side expelled the Lemkians across the border and exerted pressure also on the other Ukrainians to leave their homeland and resettle in the Soviet Ukraine.

Given the still inadequately protected Polish-Soviet border and the difficult-to-control mountain region, this process was not entirely successful. When deported Lemkians began to wander back to Poland, the Polish authorities destroyed their abandoned villages to prevent them from resettling. Even though Poles were settled in parts of the former territory of the Lemkians, the region remained largely depopulated. Later it was transformed into a large nature preserve

---

[29] German deportees from east-central and southeastern Europe in the USSR after the end of World War II.

(*Bieszczady*), where still today one frequently encounters cemeteries and the chimneys of former villages.

Between 28 April and 28 July 1947, the Poles, in a measure referred to as Action Vistula (*Akcja Wisla*), deported a little more than 140,000 Ukrainians from the new southeast of Poland across the Vistula into the formerly German territories of Silesia, Pomerania, and East Prussia. The measure was justified with the argument that the Ukrainians still remaining on Polish territory after the expiration of the Polish-Soviet repatriation agreement posed a threat because of the proximity of the border and of the civil war that was raging on both sides. Although the intent was to assimilate the deportees into the Polish population, to which end no more than three Ukrainian families were to be placed into any one village, smaller Ukrainian settlement regions emerged, for example, in Liegnitz (Legnica). Beginning in the 1970s, there was no longer any major opposition to a return migration to southeastern Poland. It was officially permitted in 1991, and the cultural flourishing of the Ukrainians now encountered only local resistance.

Most of the Poles "repatriated" from Ukraine (more than 600,000) were used to populate Lower and Upper Silesia, from where the Germans had been expelled by 1947:[30] even if recent research has shown, for example, that only a small portion of the postwar population of Wrocław (Breslau) hails from Lemberg, this new Polish city took on the cultivation of the intellectual Polish traditions of Lemberg.

The further development of the industrial regions in the Soviet Union led to strong internal migrations that also affected Ukraine. On the one hand, Russians and members of other Soviet nationalities came to the industrial regions of Ukraine; on the other hand, Ukrainians had professional opportunities via the army or by means of a university degree in other areas of the large Soviet Empire. Although a phase of Ukrainization occurred under Petro Selest (1963–72), the party chief of the Communist Party of Ukraine, both before and after this time Ukraine stood under the banner of Russification ("rapprochement and melting"/*sblizenie I slijanie*). Russian was considered the language of interethnic communication within the Soviet Union, a clinging to Ukrainian was seen as "provincial" and "hostile to progress." The use of the Ukrainian language was denounced as almost reactionary, because it impeded the creation of a "Soviet people." The attitude of the national political exile community, which demanded the use of Ukrainian and whose most eloquent spokesmen had allied themselves with the USA, exacerbated the negative assessment of Ukrainian national culture in the Soviet Union under the banner of the cold war.

A specific form of internal migration began after the disaster at the Chernobyl nuclear power plant near Kiev on 26 April 1986. The Soviet authorities resettled the entire population from a radius of around 60 kilometers around the plant to other parts of the country. Pripiat became a ghost town,

Slavutic was created as a new urban settlement, and settlements sprang up on the outskirts of other cities. Evacuations also affected Belarus, where the radioactive fallout was more intense than in Ukraine. The catastrophe had a catalytic effect on the Ukrainian nationalist movement, which made the breakaway from Russia and thus the dissolution of the USSR the goal of its politics.

Migration after independence

Ukraine proclaimed its sovereignty in 1990 and its independence in August 1991, granting all its inhabitants the right to Ukrainian citizenship. Even though the first government of an independent Ukraine (1991–4) tried to carry out a massive Ukrainization, unlike in the other new states of Central Asia or the Baltic region, one cannot speak of an official or unofficial discrimination against minorities.

The hope of finding a better economic situation in Ukraine than in Russia, a perception that grew out of the nationalistic propaganda about the plunder of Ukraine by Russia, motivated Ukrainians from Russia to move to the new state, especially in 1991–2. But since the living standard in Russia remained higher after all, departures in the opposite direction subsequently predominated. The population of Ukraine declined. At the same time, there was a rise in the number of those who left Ukraine as migrant laborers in the direction of Poland, central, and western Europe, and especially overseas. The more active and younger Ukrainians, in particular, left the country. A special place belongs to the emigration of the Jews, large numbers of whom migrated to Israel, Germany, and overseas.[31]

However, immigration continued: while the Chechens, for example, who had likewise been deported in 1944, had been allowed back into the Caucasus decades earlier, it was only now that Ukraine lifted the prohibition on the return of the Crimean Tatars, who have never been officially rehabilitated. Return migrants were now allowed to settle on the Crimea and establish their own political assembly (*kurultaj*). In the quarrel between Ukraine and Russia about sovereignty over the peninsula and the Black Sea fleet stationed there, the Tatars usually took the Ukrainian side.

The first Ukrainian president, Leonid Kravchuk, also called upon the Russian Germans who had been deported to Siberia and Central Asia to come to the Ukraine. Since Russia continued to refuse their return to the Volga, some accepted this invitation and settled in the southern steppe regions, for example, in the region of Mykolaiv. However, since the material conditions were miserable, nearly all of them continued onward to Germany as soon as they had the opportunity.[32]

Statements about the number of ethnic Ukrainians and about the criteria by which the classification of ethnic identity should be made are controversial. Especially in Ukraine and in Russia, the question is whether individual self-definition,

---

[30] German refugees and expellees from eastern, east-central, and southeastern Europe in Germany and Austria since the end of World War II.

[31] East European Jews in Germany since 1990.

[32] *Aussiedler/Spätaussiedler* in Germany since 1950.

Table 3. Composition of the population of Ukraine, 2001		
	Number	**%**
Total	48,760,000	100.0
Ukrainians	37,541,000	77.8
Russians	8,334,000	17.3
Jews	103,000	0.2
Germans	33,000	0.1
Poles	144,000	0.3
Belarusians	275,000	0.6
Romanians	409,000	0.8
Greeks	91,000	0.2
Bulgarians	204,000	0.6
Tatars	311,000	0.7
Hungarians	156,000	0.3

Source: Ukrainian census, 2001.

the registration of nationality by the Soviet authorities, or the vernacular language is the relevant criterion. If the language were used, given the predominance of Russian in broad areas in southern and eastern Ukraine, the number of Ukrainians would be relatively small. The strong decline in the number of Russians in the census of 2001 compared to previous censuses was not due to emigration but to the growing profession of Ukrainian nationality. In absolute numbers, the ethnic Ukrainians have thus not become fewer, in spite of the strong decline in the population (see Table 3). According to the findings of Soviet researchers, in 1989 about 6.7 million Ukrainians lived outside Ukraine in the CIS, around 500,000 in the rest of Europe, about 1.4 million in America, and 25,000 in Australia.

Poland was the first state to recognize independent Ukraine. Fairly quickly, Poland and Ukraine, and later Hungary and Ukraine, entered into agreements about the cultural promotion of their respective minorities in the other country. On the local level, however, remnants of animosities persisted: in Przemysl, the local Catholics refused to return to the United Church, which had been revived in Poland and Ukraine, their former churches. In Lemberg, the controversy over the design of the restored memorial to the Polish defenders of the city against the Ukrainians in 1918 has not been settled even at the beginning of the 21st century. Ukraine has recognized the smaller communities as minorities, but not the Russians. With the presidency of Leonid Kuchma (1994–2005), who himself did not speak Ukrainian in the beginning, the program of Ukrainization was defused. The use of the Russian language was de facto tolerated in the east and south of the country (in the Autonomous Republic of Crimea, even officially). However, during the presidential elections in 2004, Minister President Victor Yanukovich was able to attract votes, especially in eastern Ukraine, with the promise to introduce Russian as the second official language and to separate the east and south of the country. The Ruthenians of Transcarpathia, who are struggling for recognition as a separate nationality, have had no success. The clash between

the "Blues" around Minister President Yanukovich and the "Orange Revolution" around State President Yushchenko is more about political than cultural or ethnic ties. Even if the "Blues" tend to favor cooperation with Russia, the question of the territorial integrity of Ukraine is not a contested issue at this time.

Outlook

The population numbers of Ukraine have been declining since the state's independence. This is the result of the negative growth rate (2000: –0.8%; birthrate: 9 per thousand; death rate: 16 per thousand) and emigration. Demographers expect a slowdown in the population decline, but not a reversal in the trend. A population of about 40 million is expected for 2040.

Until 2004, it was easy for Ukrainians to take illegal employment in Poland; since then, the introduction of the EU external border has made labor migration to the west a little more difficult. The heavy industry in eastern Ukraine, which has so far been hardly modernized, continues its production under catastrophic working conditions; over the long term, however, it is likely to survive only if substantial investments are made. Few indicators at this time show that Ukraine could prove to be an attractive country for the more flexible among its younger inhabitants. The question about the development of labor migration depends more strongly on opportunities in the target countries than the situation in Ukraine. Their fairly good training continues to allow Ukrainians to move to the Russian Federation, whose economic situation in some areas (surely not in all, and most of all not in the border regions to Ukraine) is substantially better than in the Ukraine.

Strong immigrations into the Ukraine from other CIS states can be expected only if successful investments – not least from abroad and here especially from the EU – can be implemented. However, establishing stronger ties between Ukraine and the EU could also contribute to a revival of emigration.

REFERENCES

Altshuler, Mordechai. *Soviet Jewry on the Eve of the Holocaust: A Social and Demographic Profile.* Jerusalem, 1998.

Ciesielski, Stanisław, ed. *Przesiedlenie ludności polskiej z kresów wschodnich do Polski 1944–1947.* Warsaw, 1999.

Dean, Martin. *Collaboration in the Holocaust.* Basingstoke, 2000.

Döring, Stephan. *Die Umsiedlung der Wolhyniendeutschen in den Jahren 1939 bis 1940.* Frankfurt am Main, 2001.

Džucha, Ivan. *Odisseja mariupol'skich grekov.* Vologda, 1993.

Golczewski, Frank, ed. *Geschichte der Ukraine.* Göttingen, 1993.

Govorskij, F. Ja, et al. *Evrei Ukrainy.* 2 vols. Kiev, 1992/1995.

Hryciuk, Grzegorz. "Zmiany liczby ludności Galicji Wschodniej w latach 1939–1946." In *Studia nad demografia historyczna i sytuacja religijna Ukrainy*, edited by Grzegorz Hryciuk and Jarosław Stoćkyj, 7–109. Lublin, 2000.

Jakovleva, Larysa V., et al. *Nimci v Ukraïni. 20–30-ti rr. XX st.* Kiev, 1994.

Kappeler, Andreas. *Kleine Geschichte der Ukraine.* 2nd ed. Munich, 2000.

Kostjuk, Mychajlo. *Nimec'ki kolonii na Volyni (XIX–počatok XX st.).* Ternopil', 2003.

Kuropas, Myron B. *The Ukrainian Americans: Roots and Aspirations, 1884–1954.* Toronto, 1991.

Magocsi, Paul Robert. *A History of Ukraine.* Toronto 1996.

Mark, Rudolf A. *Galizien unter Österreichischer Herrschaft. Verwaltung – Kirche – Bevölkerung.* Marburg, 1994.

Martynowych, Orest T. *Ukrainians in Canada: The Formative Phase, 1891–1924.* Edmonton, 1991.

Misylo, Jevhen. *Akcija "Visla." Dokumenty.* Lemberg and New York, 1997.

Naimark, Norman M. *Flammender Haß. Ethnische Säuberungen im 20. Jahrhundert.* Munich, 2004.

Neutatz, Dietmar. *Die "deutsche Frage" im Schwarzmeergebiet und in Wolhynien.* Stuttgart, 1993.

Pereselennja Poljakiv ta Ukraïnciv 1944–1946. Warsaw and Kiev, 2000.

Polishchuk, N. S., and A. P. Ponomarev, eds. *Ukraincy.* Moscow, 2000.

Slyvka, Jurij, ed. *Ukraïns'ka Emihracija.* Lemberg, 1992.

Stanko, V. N., ed. *Istorija Odesy.* Odessa, 2002.

Subtelny, Orest. *Ukraine: A History.* 2nd ed. Toronto, 1994.

Vjatkin, A. R., et al. *V dviženii dobrovol'nom i vynuždennom.* Moscow, 1999.

GROUPS

ADMINISTRATIVE ELITES IN SOUTHERN ITALY AND SICILY UNDER SPANISH RULE IN THE EARLY MODERN PERIOD

Martin Papenheim

Since antiquity, southern Italy and Sicily have been linked to the Mediterranean regions in various ways, and from the Middle Ages also with the political entities north of the Alps. Until the creation of the Italian nation-state in 1861, these regions were ruled by dynasties that were not from Italy. Between 1504 and 1713, they were vice-kingdoms under the suzerainty of Spain. The long period of "foreign rule" had a lasting impact on the political, social, economic, and cultural history of southern Italy.

The Kingdoms of Naples and Sicily played a preeminent role within the Spanish Empire: strategically in the fight against the Turks, economically and militarily as a resource in the defense of Habsburg positions in the contest between the European powers. At the same time, the two kingdoms were part of a dynamic economic, social, and cultural system that was connected to Spain, the Netherlands, Austria, and northern Italy and was based on the continuous exchange of ideas, goods, and people. The importance of this international sphere of communication for southern Italy and Sicily lay not least in the constant immigration of administrative and military personnel, bankers, merchants and seamen, as well as clergymen and artists from all over Europe, but chiefly from Spain.

Already in the 11th century, the Norman Roger I had filled important posts with his followers and with Frenchmen and Italians from other areas of the country. When the House of Anjou subsequently ruled Naples and Sicily (with interruptions from the 13th to the 15th century), it systematically recruited elites for the state administration. At the same time, foreign bankers functioned as creditors to the crown and as tax and customs farmers. The financial bureaucracy, in particular, was a central gateway for the upward mobility of immigrated elites down to the Spanish era. Thanks to their international connections and their presence in the important trading and financial centers of Europe, members of eminent banking families also attained top state offices outside of the financial world and high positions in the military. Their constant goal was to attain titles and fiefs and thereby gain a permanent foothold within the feudal system of southern Italy and Sicily. Until the 16th century, the intermixing of the private financial sector, private financing of the crown, and an official financial bureaucracy that was run by foreign banking families (and was characterized by the purchase and sale of offices) was typical for the administration of the southern Italian states.

During the Aragonese period, many Spaniards gained entry into the government and the administration from the time of King Martin I (1392–1409). Under King Alfonso V of Aragon, ruler of Sicily and Naples from 1442 to 1458, the Florentines installed by the Anjous were temporarily driven out. Still, they remained an important power factor within

the financial system, chief among them the Strozzi family, a branch of which occupied important offices in Sicily as late as the 17th century. But Aragonese and Catalans now began increasingly to occupy important positions in the public and private financial world in southern Italy, a process that reached its high point under King Ferrante I of Aragon (1458–94). Important families like the D'Avalos or the Guevara settled on the southern Italian mainland or in Sicily. Endowed with public offices, they obtained fiefs and integrated themselves into the nobility of southern Italy. The foreign administrative elite stood at the top of the social pyramid of the immigrants, led by the General Tax Collector and the General Treasurer and his staff – between 1432 and 1504 these were almost entirely Catalans. The base of the pyramid was made up of small Catalan tradesmen and merchants.

Another important segment of the immigrant elite was the Genoese, since the middle of the 14th century the leading merchants in the long-distance trade. For example, beginning in the 14th century under the Anjous, the Spinolas, one of the four leading patrician families of Genoa, were represented in Naples in the office of the Great Admiral of the Kingdom or in top posts of the financial administration. The Genoese attained preeminent influence under Emperor Charles I, because as the major financiers of the maritime republic they secured Habsburg-Spanish rule in Naples and Sicily. In the Kingdom of Naples, the Mari family, for example, was active as financiers of the state since the beginning of the 16th century by issuing *asientos* (short-term bills of exchange) or by farming revenues and taxes.

Beginning in the late 16th century, the Genoese, too, acquired a growing number of titles and fiefs and integrated themselves in this way into the southern Italian nobility. The purchase of high offices provided an important track of integration and at the same time a profitable investment opportunity. In the 17th century, we find Genoese families who had once come to Naples as bankers (e.g., as feudal lords in Calabria) in the highest offices as *governari*, *avvocati fiscali*, and *procuratori* of the land (Aurelio Musi) and as the holders of prerogatives from the Empire (Paolo Spinola).

During the Spanish period, Sicily was governed by vice-kings who came mostly from Spain or Sicily itself. In many cases these were high prelates who were both king and bishop on the island. A central administration based on immigrants never played the same role in Sicily that it did on the mainland. In Naples, meanwhile, the Spanish rulers, continuing an Aragonese practice, often placed Catalans at the top of the administration, both in the center and at the periphery of the land. After the Spanish rulers had fended off an impending pro-French conspiracy among the barons in 1527–8, they proceeded – as in other parts of the monarchy, to train an increasingly Spanish class of administrators in order to become independent from the ebb and flow of local politics. And beginning in the middle of the 16th century, the king alternated between loyal locals and foreigners also when filling the most important bishoprics. Royal appointments to top-level posts (which some individuals often held simultaneously in various parts of the Spanish monarchy), the purchase of offices, and financial business often went hand in hand. In the process, from the middle of the 16th century the tendency to pass on within the family offices in the leading state councils of Naples once they had been obtained was unmistakable.

While the kings of Naples came predominantly from the Castilian high nobility, in the wake of the Spanish administrative reform, the decree "De officorum provisione" in 1550 laid down rules about which offices were to be held by Spaniards or natives and which posts the king could hand out at his discretion. The king had the greatest decision-making freedom in awarding positions on the most important council, the Consiglio Collaterale. The three councilors who worked in Naples were appointed "at the king's pleasure." The councilor dispatched to the Council of Italy in Madrid was a Neapolitan. The seven highest honorary offices in the realm were divided between Neapolitans and Spaniards at a ratio of 4:3. The Consiglio di Stato that was in charge of military affairs was in the hands of the local feudal nobility. In all other state councils, the natives held at least half and mostly two-thirds of the seats. Two-thirds of the offices in the provinces and of the positions as tax collectors were staffed with Neapolitans. The chairmanship of the Gran Corte della Vicaria, the court of appeal for the provinces and the city court for Naples, rotated annually between a Neapolitan and a freely appointed official. Lower offices were left entirely to the natives. The specific formula of allocation, which was guided by a compromise between competing interests, resulted from the interaction of various factors: the desire to integrate the Neapolitan possessions into the Spanish realm, the relative independence of the king, consideration for local traditions, and the availability (or lack thereof) of native leadership personnel.

The tendency to integrate into the feudal structure and to position oneself in the highest offices of the state persisted in the Regno di Napoli. For example, Don Pietro di Toledo (actually Alvarez de Toledo) was appointed viceroy of Naples by Charles V, and had the longest reign of all (1532–53). He established a family dynasty which, among other things, was part of the patriciate of Naples until the end of the 19th century, held important fiefs, was related by marriage to many families of the kingdom, and provided further officials at the highest levels, among them several governors and another viceroy.

Büschges, Christian. "Konsens und Konflikt in der Spanischen Monarchie (1621–1635). Die vizeköniglichen Höfe in Valencia, Neapel und Mexiko und die Reformpolitik des Conde-Duque de Olivares." Habilitation, Cologne, 2002.

Intorcia, Gaetana. *Magistrature del Regno di Napoli. Analisi prosopografica. Secoli XVI–XVII*. Naples, 1987.

Musi, Aurelio. *Mezzogiorno spagnolo. La via napoletana allo Stato moderno*. Naples, 1999.

Musi, Aurelio. *L'Italia dei viceré. Integrazione e resistenza nel sistema imperiale spagnolo*. Cava de' Tirreni, 2000.

Papenheim, Martin. *Karrieren in der Kirche. Bischöfe in Nord- und Süditalien 1676–1903*. Stuttgart, 2001.

Cross-references: The Netherlands; Spain and Portugal; Italy

AFRICAN SLAVES IN BRITAIN IN THE EARLY MODERN PERIOD

David Killingray

There is evidence of people of African origin in the British Isles since Roman times. But the beginning of a small and steady immigration of black people into Britain began with the age of discovery in the 15th and 16th centuries. These men, and some women, mainly from the West African coast, came as slaves, visitors, or itinerant seamen. From the mid-17th century onward black people of African origin and descent were also coming into Britain from the American colonies, many brought as servants, others coming as "free" workers.

During the 17th century the transatlantic slave trade from Africa to the Americas grew rapidly. By the following century the slave trade was dominated by English/British shipping. This resulted in an increased number of black people, both free and in servile positions, coming to or being brought into Britain. Many came primarily as seamen but also as servants, few actually being referred to as "slaves." Servants and slaves were generally brought from the Caribbean and North American colonies by planters and those with commercial and professional interests there. Thus black workers were to be found in large houses in London and throughout the country. They included small children who were taken into wealthy households as lap-pets, as can be seen in numerous portraits and paintings of the period.

Little is known about the sex ratio or the geographical distribution of Britain's black population in the 18th century, although men outnumbered women. The majority of black people lived in the major Atlantic trading ports of London, Liverpool, and Bristol, with much smaller numbers in minor seaports such as Whitehaven, Lancaster, Preston, and Portsmouth. London had the largest black population, and the major concentrations were in Westminster and east of the City of London near the river Thames. However, it is clear from growing evidence that black people lived in towns and villages the length and breadth of the country. Contemporary estimates in the mid-18th century concluded that the total black population of Britain was about 20,000. This was surely an exaggeration. A recent estimate, based on research in parish registers and other records, suggests a total black population in Britain in 1770 of around 10,000, half living in London and the other half elsewhere in the country. Further research is required to answer crucial questions about the number, gender, geographical distribution, occupations, marital partners, and literacy of Britain's black population in the past.

Slave owners considered their slaves as movable property – chattels to be moved freely to and from Britain at will. In Britain black servants, and those who were slaves brought from the colonies, worked alongside whites and also fellow blacks, some of whom had formerly been slaves. Although slaves were few in number, their presence and status posed important moral and legal questions. Many Britons strongly opposed slavery when it involved the capture and enslavement of Europeans by the Muslim states of North Africa. Although black Africans were regarded as being part of humanity, whites in the 18th century generally considered them inferior, a view that some thought could be legitimized by the Bible. Eighteenth-century writers and philosophers began to systematize ideas of racial inferiority, but alongside their views were Enlightenment ideas that questioned the morality of slavery and the economy of using slave labor.

For blacks, the social and cultural environment in 18th-century Britain was vastly different from that of the American colonies, where slavery was firmly established and underwritten by law. English law (Scotland had a different legal system) had much to say on individual liberties but there was some ambiguity as to whether those rights also extended to black slaves. The difference between servile and free blacks was also, in some respects, unclear. Some black servants, even when dressed in finery for service in a grand house, might be forced to wear a collar as a symbol of their servile status. Blacks were occasionally listed in English wills as chattels to be passed on to heirs. However, very few blacks in Britain were called slaves. Labor law did not exist, and employees, whether white or black, were often bound to masters. Notices appeared in newspapers offering rewards for the return of runaway servants, both black and white, who had breached the terms of their unequal contract. Absconding servants who took clothes and possessions with them could be charged with theft.

Some black slaves believed that they would be free when they stepped on English soil, that the "air of England" would not tolerate slavery. Another idea that had popular currency was that baptism as a Christian confirmed a slave's freedom. The former slave Ottobah Cugoano wrote in his condemnation of the African slave trade in 1772: "I was advised by some good people to get myself baptized, that I might not be carried away and sold again." Legal opinion refuted both claims. The presence in Britain of black slaves from the colonies who believed they had certain rights in a free country was disturbing to some British masters and employers. As one man wrote of black slaves brought from the colonies, they "no sooner arrive here than they put themselves on a footing with other servants, become intoxicated with liberty, grow refractory, and either by persuasion of others or from their own inclinations, begin to expect wages according to their own opinions of their merits." Although little is known about the behavior of individual black servants or slaves, it can nevertheless be assumed that in Britain most did not run away, and

those that did often sought more favorable employment and "masters." Some must have been truculent and insubordinate. Others, perhaps the majority, were used well and were quiet about their lot, taking the rewards for their good behavior and trustworthiness. For example, Jack Beef, the slave of John Baker, a planter from the Leeward Islands, was highly trusted. He is often mentioned in Baker's diary as carrying out duties alongside white servants; Jack Beef was freed in 1771 but died before he could return to the West Indies.

A number of black servants who absconded sued their masters for wages. Some contacted their owners and negotiated terms for return to their employ. The terms they demanded might be concerned with new clothing, better conditions of service and personal treatment, and wages for labor, all indicating a desire to move from a servile to a more free status. Undoubtedly, fellow black and white servants encouraged slaves in these actions. Much more needs to be investigated about this important process of black people in Britain attempting to secure their own freedom by entering into contracts with their masters.

In the late 17th and 18th centuries English law was ambiguous and uncertain about whether black slavery was legitimate in England. A ruling of 1729 categorically stated "that a Slave by coming from the West-Indies to Great Britain, doth not become free," and it went on to say that a "Master may legally compel" a slave to return to the West Indies. Olaudah Equiano recounts how he was sold at Gravesend and forcibly shipped back to the West Indies in 1761. Such actions outraged the growing group of abolitionists, mainly Quakers and evangelical Christians. In 1765, Granville Sharp and his brother cared for a slave, Jonathan Strong, who had been harshly treated and then discarded by his master. When Strong had partly recovered, his master sued the Sharps for his return. The Sharp brothers contested the claim and secured Strong's liberty. The next important case also involved Granville Sharp and the slave James Somerset, who was in danger of being forcibly removed from Britain. Sharp secured a writ of habeas corpus on Somerset and as a result of the ensuing hearing Chief Justice Mansfield declared that a slave could not be forcibly removed from Britain.

Coming at a time when the campaign against the slave trade began to gain ground, this judgment was undoubtedly an important decision affecting the status and treatment of slaves living in England, as well as the antislavery movement. It did not, however, mean the end of black slavery in England. Black slavery remained technically legal in England until the Act of Emancipation in 1833, but slavery in England – and by extension the rest of Britain – was effectively dead by the 1790s. Slavery in Scotland had been ended by the case of *Knight v. Wedderburn* in 1778.

Following the independence of the United States, several hundred black loyalists, many being freed slaves resettled in Nova Scotia, came to Britain. Most were poor and while increasing the black population they also placed a burden on the parish poor assistance. Humanitarians, both white and black, helped to settle some poor blacks (both born in Africa and of African descent) at Freetown on the West African coast.

From 1787 onward the national campaign to end the slave trade created the largest extra-parliamentary lobby ever seen in Britain. It was the result of Enlightenment thinking and Christian, mainly evangelical, ideas. The leaders, both men and women, included prominent Christians such as Granville Sharp, Thomas Clarkson, Hannah More, and William Wilberforce, MP, but also a number of free black people, for example, Ottobah Cugoano and Olaudah Equiano. An act making the slave trade illegal for British subjects was passed in 1807. By then, probably few of the black people in Britain were slaves or were viewed as such by their masters. Following their success in ending British involvement in the slave trade, the abolitionists turned their attention to opposing its continuation by foreign powers, and also to the long campaign to end slavery in the British Empire and elsewhere. This was achieved in the years 1834–8.

Chater, Katherine. *Hidden Histories: Black People in England and Wales during the Period of the British Slave Trade c.1660–1807*. Manchester, 2009.

Drescher, Seymour. *Capitalism and Antislavery: British Mobilization in Comparative Perspective*. Basingstoke, 1986.

Fryer, Peter. *Staying Power: The History of Black People in Britain*. London, 1984.

Shyllon, Folarin O. *Black Slaves in Britain*. London, 1974.

Slavery and Abolition (journal).1980– (contains seminal articles and biographies).

Walvin, James. *England, Slaves and Freedom 1776–1838*. Basingstoke, 1986.

Cross-references: Great Britain

AFRICAN SLAVES ON THE IBERIAN PENINSULA IN THE EARLY MODERN PERIOD

William D. Phillips, Jr.

African slaves together with free people of color have formed a recognizable minority on the Iberian Peninsula from the late Middle Ages until the end of the 18th century. Their descendants partially account for the black minority in Portugal and Spain today. Already in classical times, small numbers of sub-Saharan Africans reached the peninsula, some traveling voluntarily as free individuals, others having been forced to make the trip as slaves. By the ninth century at the latest, Muslim caravan traders had brought blacks across the Sahara as slaves to Islamic Spain in small yet consistent numbers. As the Christian kingdoms of Iberia grew, they obtained black slaves through established channels of trade and the reconquest of Muslim-held territory. Nonetheless, the number of black slaves in Iberia remained small until the 15th century, when

the Portuguese developed direct trade with Atlantic Africa. Though their numbers were relatively small, they filled needs in the labor market in chronically underpopulated Portugal and in the Spanish kingdoms during the demographic trough following the Black Death of the mid-14th century.

Despite royal efforts to centralize the slave trade, the vessels that loaded slaves in West Africa did not always bring their cargo back to Lisbon, the main port of transit for slaves. Many ships stopped off in the Atlantic islands (Canaries, Azores, Madeira), where the Portuguese slave traders sold some slaves. Others unloaded their human cargo in Portuguese towns south of Lisbon, while still others sailed directly for Seville and other Andalusian ports. Recent estimates suggest that the number of sub-Saharan Africans transferred to the Atlantic islands and to Europe probably amounted to just over 200,000 between 1450 and 1600.

The major entry point for African slaves in Iberia was Lisbon, where officials of the House of Slaves met ships arriving from Africa, inspected their cargo and records, and assigned prices for the slaves. Not all slaves reached Lisbon in good enough physical condition to be sold immediately. Those who arrived ill were examined by the officials and treated. Many slaves remained in Lisbon while others were sold to other locations in Portugal, especially in the south, and abroad. Spain was the main importer. The eastern port cities on the Mediterranean and the towns and cities of Andalusia had the greatest number of slaves, but numbers were low everywhere. Seville in the 16th century probably had the greatest percentage of slaves at around 10% of the total population. No other city but Valencia approached that figure, and many parts of Spain had no slaves at all. Women accounted for more than half the slaves in Iberia.

Slave owners in Iberia came from many segments of the population. The higher ranks of society commonly made use of slaves as domestic servants, but in much smaller numbers than would later become common in the New World. Domestic service was the usual lot of slaves, who commonly were lodged in the households of their masters. Many female slaves also served their masters as concubines. The emergence of a large group of persons of mixed ethnicity (mulattos) testifies to a high degree of concubinage, common law unions, and – increasingly over time – intermarriage. Of those slaves who lived outside their masters' households, many in Seville lived in the city's poorer districts.

Slaves were also employed in income-producing ventures. They worked in soap factories and municipal granaries. They were porters and longshoremen, retail sellers in the streets and plazas, assistants for shopkeepers and merchants. Slaves even occasionally acted as agents for their merchant-owners. They were typically excluded from membership in the crafts guilds but guild masters could and did employ them as assistants. In Seville they worked in printing shops and municipal institutions, particularly as cleaners and launderers. Also at least two weapon makers employed black slaves. Owners of slaves either supervised their work directly or rented them out to craftsmen and tradesmen. It was common for slave women to be employed as washerwomen and garbage and refuse collectors. Slave men worked on the docks as stevedores and as laborers in the construction industry.

Slaves with greater skill worked in the craft guilds, although more prestigious guilds – of sword makers, goldsmiths, and lapidaries, for example – restricted slave access to the higher ranks of membership. Blacksmiths and shoemakers offered seemingly unrestricted advancement to slaves, but hosiers and pastry makers set limits on the rise of slaves. Sellers of water, vegetables, and processed food were often slaves whose activities were regulated by public health authorities. In Portugal, slaves were often employed as sailors and boatmen and ferrymen. There were also black seamen who worked as interpreters on trading vessels sailing to Africa. In Portugal, the ferries on the Douro and the Tagus were often worked by black slaves.

In contrast to the New World, where many slaves were used on plantations, a plantation economy hardly existed in the "motherlands" of Portugal and Spain, where slaves were used as agricultural labor, but in small numbers. This occurred more frequently in the south than in the north of Iberia. In Portugal, the Tagus River formed an important boundary: slave labor in agriculture was much more widespread south of the river than north of it. All slaves, regardless of their primary occupations in handwork or domestic service, could be assigned to work in agriculture seasonally during planting or harvesting periods. Slaves traditionally worked with horses and other domestic animals.

Attempts to flee were usually futile as only the African continent could be considered a relatively safe haven. Slaves could either be manumitted or could buy their freedom, with the total number of freed slaves reaching approximately 10% in Portugal in the 16th century. The treatment of slaves depended on the mood of their master, who enjoyed full authority over them. Black African slaves in Portugal and Spain were typically treated better than enslaved Muslims and Moriscos (Muslims who had converted to Christianity) who had become the property of their masters after being prisoners of war, victims of piracy, or captured during land raids in Morocco. Muslim slaves were considered enemies of Christianity or, in the case of Moriscos, unreliable Christians who continued to practice Islam in secret. In contrast, black Africans, who were typically animists, were seen as amenable to conversion. After forced baptism, many black Africans appeared to accept Christianity sincerely and joined religious communities. Some were even trained and ordained as priests, but were only allowed to practice in their lands of origin. Others joined Portuguese religious orders as laymen.

Slave owners and their relatives acted as godparents for the children of slaves, and black slaves were buried in Christian cemeteries and sometimes even in family vaults in churches. Slaves, especially those in the second generation

and after, were often sincerely pious and participated fully in religious life. In the parish of San Bernardo, where blacks and mulattos together made up a majority of the population, the Catholic Church set up the Hospital of Our Lady specially to serve the black population. A black brotherhood or confraternity emerged a few years later to run the hospital. By the late 16th century many other blacks lived in the parish of San Ildefonso, which also had a black religious brotherhood and even a Mulatto Street. Brotherhoods of slaves and free blacks were a common feature of community life in many other Iberian towns and cities. Blacks were, however, never completely accepted by lower-class whites, who viewed them as competition on the labor market.

As the population of the Iberian Peninsula grew, the resulting growth of the indigenous labor force reduced the need for slave labor. Starting in the early 17th century, slavery on the Iberian Peninsula continually lost importance and virtually disappeared by the start of the 18th century, but was not formally made illegal until the 19th century.

Earle, Thomas F., and Kate J. P. Lowe, eds. *Black Africans in Renaissance Europe*. Cambridge, 2005.

Martín Casares, Aurelia. *La esclavitud en la Granada del siglo XVI: Género, raza, y religion*. Granada, 2000.

Phillips, William D., Jr. *Slavery from Roman Times to the Early Transatlantic Trade*. Minneapolis, 1985.

Seabra Rodrigues, Ana María, et al. *Os negros em Portugal, sécs. XV a XIX*. Lisbon, 1999.

Saunders, A. C. de C. M. *A Social History of Black Slaves and Freedmen in Portugal, 1441–1555*. Cambridge, 1982.

Cross-references: Spain and Portugal

AFRICAN STUDENTS FROM THE SUB-SAHARAN REGION IN FRANCE SINCE THE LATE 19TH CENTURY

Sophie Dulucq

Beginning in the late 19th century, young people from the French colonies or the Francophone territories of sub-Saharan Africa that later gained independence came to France to pursue a university education. Until the 1930s, their numbers remained very small, and during the interwar period, as well, it rose to only about 100. The students went mostly to Paris. When more government scholarships were made available for study in France beginning in 1945, the number of sub-Saharan African students rose sharply: from about 2,000 (1949–50) to around 4,000 (1952–3) and approximately 8,000 10 years later (1959–60). All told, in the 1950s between 9% and 10% of male and female pupils from sub-Saharan French colonies went to France for higher education or university studies.

The number of African students in France rose even more after the French colonies in Africa gained independence.

It surged especially in the 1970s against the backdrop of the extensive expansion of the educational institutions in France. The influx remained strong also in the 1980s, in spite of a pullback because of an increasingly restrictive visa policy: in 2000–1, 30,000 students from sub-Saharan Africa were enrolled in French universities, which corresponded to about 20% of all foreign students. Former French colonial territories were dominant among the sending countries, among them Cameroon (3,600), Senegal (3,300), and Congo (2,300). Students continued to arrive also after decolonization, most of them young men: in 1959–60, the quotient of women was just under 17%, in 2000 around 35%.

Compared to the motherland, the educational system in the French colonies was poor. Until the 1950s there were hardly any *lycées* (high schools preparing students for university entry) and, with the exception of Senegal and Madagascar, no universities. Enrollment rates varied considerably in the various colonies: in French West Africa in 1949–50, for example, barely 4.2% of the children were in school, compared to 22% in Cameroon and 25% to 35% in Senegal and Ivory Coast. And there were also considerable differences within colonies: in general, a higher percentage of children were in school in the large conurbations compared to the rural regions, where the rates could be substantially lower. The first cohorts of students who came to France up to the 1930s were financially supported by missionary societies in the colonies or received government scholarships available since the 1920s. The majority of the students came from the group of the Westernized elites in Africa.

After the Second World War, France as the colonial power stepped up its efforts in the area of education. In the colonies it was especially the primary and secondary school systems that were expanded. The educational reforms in France and the greater availability of scholarships made it possible for the most successful students to study in France. The Office des Étudiants d'Outre-Mer (Office for Overseas Students) in Paris facilitated their stay in France. Even after decolonization, France did not want to lose its political influence in Francophone Africa and continued to promote the educational migration. A new scholarship program was developed jointly with the now-independent Francophone states, the financing of which was undertaken by France in cooperation with the new states.

At the beginning of the 21st century, the majority of the arrivals from sub-Saharan Africa continue to choose disciplines in the humanities and fields that open up professions in the service sector and rapid advancement in their countries of origin (e.g., law, business management, journalism). The minority continues to be students who opt for the natural sciences, medicine, or engineering.

For a long time, the majority of students returned to Africa after successfully completing their course of study: during the colonial period, a university education usually guaranteed a secure job back home in the colonial administration and in the French-dominated private economy (e.g., as teachers or employees in the administration or in the commercial sector). After independence, the young African states, faced with a shortage of experts, offered the returning university graduates from France at times very high positions in the public sector. Beginning in the 1970s, however, a return became increasingly unattractive: the African economies were stagnating, domestic political crises were coming to a head, structural adjustments in the 1980s and 1990s led to the elimination of jobs in the public sector, and many returnees were unemployed, often for years.

As a result, a growing number of sub-Saharan African students remained in France. One legal way to do so was marriage to a French citizen. The increase in exogamous marriages in France is known, even if the precise number cannot be determined. Beginning in the 1990s, highly qualified students moved on to other countries in the Western Hemisphere, especially to the USA, which became more open to PhDs from sub-Saharan Africa.

From the beginning, the students became culturally and politically engaged in the host society. Numerous organizations for that purpose were founded in the 1920s and 1930s: in 1933, for example, the Senegalese poet, philologist, and future president of Senegal, Léopold Sédar Senghor, set up a union of West African students in Paris; in 1934 he founded, together with Aimé Césaire from Martinique and Léon-Gontran Damas from Guyana, the journal *L'étudiant noir*, which would later be followed by a whole series of other journals. Many of the students from sub-Saharan Africa in Paris established contact with African American politicians or writers. Their worldview was shaped by Pan-Africanism. The black African concept of "négritude" was developed in the Latin quarter, and the Pavillon de la France d'Outre-Mer, erected in the Cité Internationale in the south of Paris, became one of the gathering places for the black intellectual community. Connections also existed between the students and politicians and union leaders in the colonies.

The years 1945–60 saw growth in the literary and political activities among the immigrants. By setting up publishing houses and journals that published works by African and African American artists, Paris asserted itself as the center of black African culture and of anticolonialism. The Féderation des Étudiants d'Afrique Noir en France (FEANF, Federation of Black African Students in France), founded in 1950, advocated the material interests of the students and created self-help organizations. At the same time, however, it was also the spearhead of the anticolonial struggle in Paris. The FEANF joined the communist International League of Students that had been set up in Prague in 1946. While the leaders of FEANF criticized black African politicians (parliamentarians of the Union Française, activists of the Rassemblement Démocratique Africain) as being too moderate, the journal *Les étudiants parlent*, first published in 1953 by the publishing house Présence Africaine, printed anticolonial polemics.

After the colonies gained independence, there was a decline in the degree of organized student activities, which now focused, among other things, on criticizing the political situation in the African states, some of which were autocratically governed, with some students conceiving of their activities as political resistance from French exile. At the beginning of the 21st century, the political discussions around migration, illegality, and integration, which were connected to the *sans-papiers* movement, also spread within the African student organizations.

Throughout the 20th century, the living conditions of students from sub-Saharan Africa in France remained precarious. That was especially true for those who were not the recipients of scholarships. Between 1945 and 1960, their number was twice as high as that of scholarship students. The housing shortage, high costs of living, and inflation hit the immigrants from the third world with full force. The devaluation of the franc of the states of the Communauté Financière Africaine (CFA, African Financial Community: Benin, Burkina Faso, Ivory Coast, Guinea-Bissau, Mali, Niger, Senegal, Togo) in 1994 drove up the impoverishment rates, even though there were repeated expressions of solidarity with black African students in France.

After decolonization in Africa, the group identity of black African students waned: crucial to this trend was the growing individualism within the group, the diversification of their geographic origins, their dispersal all over France, and the absence of a unifying ideology. At the beginning of the 21st century, this immigrant group no longer is a community sharing the same origin and is hardly visible within French society as a specific minority.

Dewitte, Philippe. *Les mouvements nègres en France (1919–1939)*. Paris, 1985.

Diané, Charles. *La FEANF et les grandes heures du mouvement syndical étudiant noir*. Paris, 1990.

Guimont, Fabienne. *Les étudiants africains en France (1950–1965)*. Paris, 1997.

Sot, Michel, ed. *Étudiants africains en France 1951–2001*. Paris, 2002.

Cross-references: France; American Writers, Visual Artists, and Musicians in Interwar Paris

AFRICAN, ASIAN, AND LATIN AMERICAN SOCCER PLAYERS IN WESTERN AND SOUTHERN EUROPE SINCE THE LATE 19TH CENTURY

Phil Vasili

The movement of African, Asian, and other players of color to professional soccer leagues in Europe in its pioneer era 1872–1919 was an unintended consequence of European colonial expansion. The majority of players of color were of African and African-Caribbean ethnicity.

Soccer increasingly gained importance in the local, indigenous cultures in colonial Africa and the Caribbean, while south and southeast Asians were stereotyped from the beginning as physically unsuited to the rigorous athletic demands of soccer. Their game par excellence was thought to be field hockey, because they supposedly possessed the necessary litheness and speed for that sport.

The majority of the professional soccer players of color who migrated to the metropolitan center of London came from well-to-do families and possessed an education that was above average. The grandmother of the world's first black professional soccer player, Arthur Wharton, was a Fante royal of the Stool family of Ekumfie in Ghana; the Scottish father of the world's first black international soccer player, Andrew Watson, was a successful merchant. Their social status contrasted sharply with that of the majority of British-born black soccer players, who were overwhelmingly of working-class origins. While their backgrounds may have been economically diverse, they shared a common identity as black players and thus represented a distinct social phenomenon.

Immigration into the professional soccer leagues of western and southern Europe after the Second World War and in the course of decolonization should not only be seen as an important feature of Europe's athletic and cultural development but also in the context of international economic developments: soccer in the developing countries of Africa and Asia, afflicted by the typical patterns of deskilling, underdevelopment, and poor organization, has been compelled to export "raw material" into the more advanced sectors of western Europe.

Players of color can be separated into four categories. The first consists of self-motivated individuals who themselves initiated contact with clubs. Their primary motivation tended to be the acquisition of economic and cultural capital. Nigerian international Elkanah Onyeali, for example, enrolled as a student in electrical engineering at Birkenhead Technical College in the autumn of 1960 before contacting and then signing a contract with the Tranmere Rovers.

A second group comprises indigenous players who were groomed to take on important positions both prior to and following independence of their respective countries. A representative of this group is the Nigerian Tesilimi Balogun, who came to Britain in 1949 as a member of the Nigeria Football Association touring team. Organized and led by expatriate civil servants and businessmen, the visiting Nigerian soccer players were showcased as models of the benefits of Empire. Balogun again visited Britain in 1955 and played for Peterborough United. After returning to Nigeria, he became a respected coach for the Western States Sports Council.

African or Asian players identified by European scouts as talented form the third category. The primary motivation of such players was the acquisition of economic capital and most returned to their homeland after finishing their contracts or career. An example is provided by Steve Mokone, the first black South African allowed to leave the apartheid state to play abroad, who joined Coventry City in 1956. In 1998, after his soccer career, time in prison, and a tenure as a professor, Mokone was named post-apartheid South Africa's Goodwill Ambassador for Tourism.

The fourth and by far largest category is made up by the offspring of locals and non-European immigrants, the vast majority of whom are of working-class origins. In cases of Anglo-African or Anglo-African-Caribbean heritage, the original migrant was most commonly the father. This was the case, for example, with Roy Brown, who played for Stoke City in the years 1938–53. His Nigerian father had studied in Great Britain and fought in the First World War. In cases of south Asian parentage, the parent of color was typically the mother, who had met her partner in her country of origin, in most cases India. An example here would be Norwich City's Kevin Keelan, born in Calcutta to an Indian mother and a British father.

The 1948 Nationality Act, which guaranteed colonial and Commonwealth citizens of British descent British passports and entry to the UK, allowed British clubs to recruit colonial players. Depending on their status, players recruited in this manner could also play for the national team, yet this only occurred in three cases in Britain until 1962: Watson for Scotland (1881, 1882), Eddie Parris for Wales (1931) and Hong Y "Frank" Soo for England (1940–5).

Until 1962, Africa provided the largest number of foreign-born black players, numbering at least 15. The passage of black soccer players to Britain, never very considerable to begin with, slowed appreciably with the introduction and gradual enforcement of the 1962, 1968, and 1971 immigration acts, which aimed to limit postcolonial immigration. It was not until 1978 that the Football Association relaxed the rules governing the signing of foreign-born players of non-Commonwealth status. Only in the 1990s did British clubs once again begin to recruit African players in any significant number, usually looking to other European – French in particular – rather than African clubs for talent. The most notable of these African imports are Ghanaian Tony Yeboah and South African Lucas Radebe. A survey from 1998 established the percentage of professional black soccer players at 15 with 33% of these playing in the Premiership.

Racism at matches was rather widespread but has decreased since the mid-1990s, largely due to the efforts of local, fan-based initiatives such as Football Unites–Racism Divides (Sheffield) and Show Racism the Red Card (Newcastle). The national organization Kick It Out, however, has been hindered by a lack of resources, bureaucratic interference, and ineffective leadership. Despite the relatively high proportion of professional players of color, the ethnic composition of spectators at professional games is still predominantly white. Inner-London Arsenal, where the ethnic minority population is 25%, is reckoned to have the largest proportion of supporters of color, at 5%.

Players of color, mainly from the colony of Algeria, have featured at the highest level of French soccer since the inception of the professional league in 1932. During the interwar period, clubs were allowed to field a maximum of five foreign-born players. Between 1945 and Algerian independence in 1962, a total of 117 players of color played professional soccer in France (76 Algerians, 34 Moroccans, 7 Tunisians), 12 of whom played for the national team. The situation of immigrant soccer players reflects the postcolonial situation in their countries of origin, as was the case with the Nigeria Football Association team that visited Britain in 1949. This also applies to France: eight Algerians left the French leagues in 1958 to fight for Algerian independence. All represent examples of the willing acceptance by the subjects of their symbolic cultural status and corresponding behavior. The more advantageous situation of French migrant soccer players in comparison with their British counterparts is the result of a better legal position and a higher rate of acceptance among their fellow players. In 1947 all Algerians automatically became French citizens while migrants from the British colonies never enjoyed a legal status equal to that of indigenous Brits, even though the majority held British passports.

The number of African players in the professional leagues of Portugal and Belgium also increased in the 1950s. As in France and Britain, the migratory routes followed colonial templates: Angolans and Mozambicans to Portugal, Congolese to Belgium. The legal status of migrants from African colonies to Portugal was similar to that in France as Angolans and Mozambicans could claim Portuguese citizenship. Like the French, the Portuguese integrated players of color into their national side. Angolan Miguel Arcanjo of Porto was one of the first black Portuguese internationals, closely followed by Mozambicans Lucas Figuerido "Matateu" of Belenenses and Hilario of Sporting Lisbon. However, the best-known Mozambicans were Eusebio, star and Golden Boot winner of the 1966 World Cup, and Mario Coluna, who captained that tournament's side. Eusebio and Coluna symbolized the cultural style of contemporary Portuguese soccer – a fusion of Iberian flair and cynicism with African spontaneity and athleticism – as vivacious, ingenious, and occasionally ruthless. In Belgium, by 1960, 30 indigenous players from the Belgian Congo played at professional clubs. This flow of talent ceased in 1962 when the newly independent Zaire, in an effort to stem the exodus of skilled and professional labor, made it virtually impossible for Zaireans to play abroad.

The presence of players of color in the national professional leagues of Britain, France, Portugal, and Belgium has reflected colonial ties and relations. British soccer, with its infamous insularity, had the least inclination to look to the nonwhite population of its colonies, though black players have had a continual presence there since the 1870s – before professionalization and the founding of the Football League. France, with its model of Greater France and rights of citizenship, had the largest proportion of players from former colonies and the greatest integration. Portugal and Belgium, too, gave greater legal and practical encouragement to their colonial subjects and citizens. Although France, Portugal, and Belgium had more players of color and enhanced integration, each country had restrictions on the number of foreign-born players clubs were allowed to field.

The presence of African professionals in the last decades has been most noticeable and controversial in Belgium. In 1985–95, a total of 126 Africans played in the first and second divisions of the Belgian professional league, 48 originating from Zaire. Nigeria, with 25, provided the second largest contingent. Belgium is a popular first point of arrival for young African talent. A number of factors explain this: the provision that foreigners who play soccer in Belgium before their 17th birthday are thereafter classified as Belgian players; the lack of indigenous talent; and the abundance of scouts and agents tracking African players. The Bosman ruling in 1995, and its subsequent deregulation of the transfer process, led to a further increase in migrant soccer players of color. By 1998 African professional soccer players were playing in 29 European countries.

In comparison with the total population of western and southern Europe, players of color are demographically overrepresented in professional soccer yet underrepresented at the coaching and administrative levels. The presence of players of color in the national leagues of European countries typically reflects the legacy of that country's colonial past and its particular legal relationship with formerly dependent states. The place of soccer within the national culture also influences a team's ethnic composition. For example, the relatively high proportion of black players in the French League is the result of the transformation of soccer's status in French society. Until the 1970s, rugby was considered the national sport and soccer a pastime favored by migrants. In Britain, the preeminent popularity of soccer ensures that the sport possesses an immense symbolic value, viewed as the embodiment of "typically British" athletic values, which also accounts for the reluctance of the Football Association until the 1970s to field players of color for the national team.

Darby, Paul. *Africa, Football and FIFA: Politics, Colonialism, and Resistance.* London, 2002.

Lanfranchi, Pierre, and Matthew Taylor. *Moving with the Ball: The Migration of Professional Footballers.* Oxford, 2001.

Vasili, Phil. *The First Black Footballer: Arthur Wharton 1865–1930: An Absence of Memory.* London, 1998.

Vasili, Phil. *Colouring over the White Line: The History of Black Footballers in Britain.* Edinburgh, 2000.

Cross-references: Belgium and Luxembourg; France; Great Britain; Spain and Portugal; Angolan and Mozambican Labor Migrants in Portugal since the 1970s; Congolese in Belgium since the 1960s; Maghrebis in France after Decolonization in the 1950s and 1960s

AFRICANS FROM THE FORMER COLONIES IN FRANCE SINCE THE 1960S

Ulrike Schuerkens

Several thousands of sub-Saharan Africans (SSA) emigrated to France in the 1960s, when French colonial rule was coming to an end. Apart from pupils and students, they were mostly composed of unskilled workers who were hired on merchant ships. They were living in French port cities like Marseille, Le Havre, Bordeaux, or Rouen. The origin regions of the immigrants of this first wave of migrants were the basins of the Senegal River (Mali, Mauritania, and Senegal) and the Casamance, the frontier between Senegal and Guinea Bissau. The second wave of sub-Saharan African immigration, up to the restrictions on entry in 1974, was also made up of unskilled, illiterate laborers from the river valley of the Senegal, whose inhabitants, because of continuing drought and crop failures, were dependent on the financial support of the emigrants.

In 1962, there were about 17,800 sub-Saharan Africans in France; by 1975, that number had already risen to 70,320. The immigrants relied on groups from the same home region who were already living in France as they sought to establish themselves in the country and receive initial help integrating them into the job market, especially in the region of greater Paris. At this point, the immigrants began concentrating on, among other things, trash collecting in Paris and public sanitation (cleaning of street and underground stations). Single male migrants lived in dormitories known as Foyers Sonacotra, today called ADOMA (from the latin *ad* meaning "to" and *domus*, which means "home") with a change in management for better living conditions. In these dormitories, rooms range from 7 to 18 m² where up to five or seven people can sleep. Until 1974, the group of sub-Saharan Africans in France was characterized by a strong fluctuation of its members, since emigration to their home countries often triggered the immigration of relatives and acquaintances to France. After 1974, restrictions on entry into France led to new forms of migration: it developed a permanent character not only structurally but also in terms of people. This third wave of migration comprised a noticeably larger number of individuals of diverse regional and social background and opened up new routes of access: first, laborers often immigrated illegally, as they had previously; second, wives and children followed the men as part of family reunification; third, there has been an increase of individual migrations of students and members of privileged professions, such as physicians and nurses at public hospitals or data processing professionals, engineers, etc.; fourth, asylum seekers formed another group of immigrants. The backdrop was formed above all by difficult economic situations, poverty, and in some cases political instabilities in many sub-Saharan African countries and the continuing, widespread idea of infinite wealth of the former colonial countries as privileged destinations. Given the numerous and difficult-to-fulfill entry requirements (e.g., visa, scholarships), families in the home countries invested in the migration of individuals who met the requirements. Following successful immigration, they expected financial transfers and presents in return.

In 1982, 127,332 immigrants from sub-Saharan Africa (not including naturalized immigrants) were living in France; by 1990, the number had already risen to 219,046, and in 1999, to 276,028. In the 1970s, it was initially the arrival of family members that led to the rapid increase. The most prominent indicator of that was the rise in the number of women: still rather few in number in 1975, in 1982, there were already 42,400. In 1990, their number grew to 72,970, which was equivalent to about 33% of the total number of sub-Saharan African immigrants; in 1999, the percentage of women born in sub-Saharan Africa and living in France stood at just under 47 (128,910). Between 1990 and 1999, 26% of all sub-Saharan African immigrants were under the age of 19, and many of them were women: among the 81,777 immigrants, there were 12,049 women aged 20–4. Of the 15,499 immigrants between 25 and 29 years old, 61% were female, as were 57% of the immigrants 30–4 years of age (a total of 14,138). Therefore, the rise in the number of sub-Saharan Africans resulted from the disproportionately strong immigration of women. After 1990, regular family reunifications were fairly rare at an average of 1,000 to 2,000 a year. Still, the majority of immigrants made up families, although their members in most cases immigrated individually. Since the 1980s, there have been immigrants from all sub-Saharan countries in France. A few regions of origin stand out: in 1982, 8,492 Congolese from the People's Republic of Congo were living in France; by 1999, the group had grown to 36,527. This puts it second behind the Senegalese with 39,014, followed by immigrants from Mali (35,015). There were 20,290 Cameroonians and 20,435 Ivorians. The two civil wars in Congo in 1993 and 1997 triggered a not insubstantial migration to France. Cameroon and Ivory Coast, in turn, are countries that have close ties with France and were economically fairly successful for a long time. The emigrants came mostly from the urban population, which was suffering from high unemployment rates since the 1990s as a result of the structural adjustment plans of the World Bank and the International Monetary Fund. In addition, the possibility of joining the already existing migration chains played a considerable role for the migration out of these countries of origin.

By contrast, poor countries like Chad, Burkina Faso, or Niger furnished only small immigrant groups to France (Chad 1,864, Burkina Faso 2,796, Niger 1,247). The reason behind this is the considerable prosperity gap between these countries and France. Potential emigrants are rarely able to raise the financial means for a migration with a decent prospect of success. At the turning point of the 21st century, the group of SSA immigrants in France is thus characterized

An African immigrant cleaning the streets of Paris, 1970 (*SV Bilderdienst*).

by a far greater heterogeneity than the group of unskilled laborers of the 1960s and 1970s, who came mainly from the rural Sahel region. Since the 1980s, the urban immigrants have altered the social composition of the sub-Saharan African population in France. In 1990, 34% of the gainfully employed of this immigrant population were engaged in unskilled work, 17% were skilled workers. Twenty-two percent worked as lower-level white-collar employees or as domestics in households, 10% held mid-level positions, 6% were academics, and 4% merchants, entrepreneurs, and craftsmen. In 1999, about 10% of those from the former French colonies who were in the labor market (20,480; not counting naturalized citizens) worked in the public sector; 19% worked in the field of education, health, and social services; 23% in private; and 20% in commercial services. By 1990, 22% of Africans from Francophone Africa had already become naturalized, though some had been French citizens already during the colonial period. That was true for 14% of the Togolese, 19% of the Ivorians, and 48% of the Congolese; by 1999, it applied to 26% of the Congolese, just under 34% of the Cameroonians, and about 35% of the Ivorians. In 1999, of the total of 72,991 naturalized Africans from former French administrative territories (and of the 114,142 who had kept their citizenship), 15.3% (9.4%) were employed in the public sector, and 13.4% (15.8%) were skilled workers of both genders; 5.7% (4.5%) held mid-level positions in commerce and 8.6% (3.7%) in the health sector, the education system, and the public sector; 3.5% (3.2%) worked as higher-level employees in commerce; academics made up just under 5% (3.8%); 3.8% (2.7%) worked at the corporate management level, 10.9% (15.8%) in private service industries. However, among the naturalized SSA there were also 11.3% unskilled workers and 3.8% unemployed persons who had never worked, whereas among nonnaturalized SSA, those percentages were 8.4 and 21.6, respectively.

Research on this immigrant group, which leaves much to be desired, applies the extensive social and economic discrimination against immigrants from rural regions in Mali and Senegal to all other groups of sub-Saharan origin.

However, the statistical data reveal that a remarkably large percentage of sub-Saharan Africans in France pursue skilled work and thus on the whole fulfill the conditions for integration into the labor market. But the same data confirm only to some extent that those with French citizenship represent a positive selection, since in many areas of the labor market the employment rates of immigrants with and without French citizenship are too close to support the thesis – still found in the literature at the beginning of the 21st century – of discrimination against nonnaturalized African immigrants. Instead, the data on the SSA immigrant population that is gainfully employed reveals a good deal more: 30% percent of the total of 175,807 persons are unemployed, divided equally between men and women. Among men, the age cohorts from 30 to 49 are especially hard hit, and among women those between 25 and 44, a fact probably related to their reproductive cycles.

Of significance with respect to the social integration of SSA in France is also the low naturalization rate among those who have lived the longest in France, the Malians and the Senegalese. Their migration projects involve remigration and a life in France without wives and children, whereby they continue to be responsible for the economic well-being of their families back at home through remittances. The integration of these rural migrants is also impeded by their low level of formal qualifications and sometimes minimal French language skills. The vast majority of the Francophone SSA immigrants is concentrated in the greater Paris region. Most of them live in the suburbs of Seine-Saint Denis. Among them, the rate of homeowners is very low, and at the same time the number of those living in shared accommodations very high at 2,769 (among them 10% students).

Thus, at the beginning of the 21st century, one can speak of a group of SSA immigrants that is heterogeneous with respect to social structure and regions of origin, and with chances of integration that vary depending on the time of arrival. It can be expected that the integration of the second generation born in France will depart from the patterns described here with respect to their course of education and training and their entry into the workforce. However, so far there are no recent research findings on this.

"Dossier: Africains, citoyens d'ici et de là-bas." *Hommes et Migrations* (2002) no. 1239.

"Dossier: Les Africains noirs en France. Aspects socio-économiques et conditions de vie." *Hommes et Migrations* (1990) no. 1131.

"La France et les migrants africains." *Politique africaine. Special issue* 67 (1997).

Schuerkens, Ulrike. "Migrants africains à Paris: L'intégration sociale en tant que problématique interculturelle." *Revue Internationale de Sociologie* 10 (2000) 3: 365–84.

Schuerkens, Ulrike. "African Women and Migration." *African Development Perspectives Yearbook* 8 (2001): 765–82.

Tardieu, Marc. *Les Africans en France. De 1914 à nos jours.* Monaco, 2006.

Cross-references: France; African Students from the Sub-Saharan Region in France since the Late 19th Century

ALBANIAN SETTLERS IN ITALY SINCE THE EARLY MODERN PERIOD

Peter Bartl

About 100 villages in Italy were newly established or refounded by Albanians in the late Middle Ages and early modern period. In 54 villages, Albanian is still spoken today in an ancient dialect (Arbëresh), though often only by members of the older generation. Currently the number of Arbëresh speakers is likely to be around 80,000. The other Albanian settlements have by now been completely Italianized, even if traditional Albanian dress and customs have been preserved among some parts of the population, along with a sense of their Albanian heritage. The centers of Albanian settlement were in southern Italy and on Sicily, in the modern provinces of Palermo, Cosenza, Catanzaro, Potenza, Foggia, Avellino, Campobasso, Taranto, and Pescara.

The Albanians came to Italy as mercenaries and refugees from Turkish rule. Most hailed from southern Albania and Greece. Immigration occurred in various stages and began already in the late Middle Ages. Even though Albanian refugees are mentioned in the area around Ancona in the 1430s and 1440s, the year 1448 can be seen as the beginning of Albanian colonization in Italy: Albanians followed the invitation by King Alfonso I of Naples to enter his service as mercenaries. They were commanded by Demetrio Reres and were given land to settle in the province of Catanzaro. At the same time, the sons of Reres, Giorgio and Basilio, established the military colonies Contessa Entellina, Palazzo Adriano, and Mezzojuso on Sicily.

The second wave of Albanian immigration also had a military background: in 1461, Albanian auxiliary troops under George Castriota Skanderbeg helped King Ferdinand I of Naples to quash a revolt of the nobility instigated by Anjou. While Skanderbeg returned to Albania as early as 1462, most of his people remained in Italy, settling in the modern provinces of Taranto, Campobasso, and Foggia.

The largest wave of Albanian immigration arrived when Albania was finally subjugated by the Turks following the death of Skanderbeg (1468). This time it was not mercenaries who came to Italy but refugees. We have no information about the size of this wave, but it must have been considerable: most Albanian colonies in the province of Cosenza that still have the strongest Italo-Albanian population component date from this time.

The immigration of Albanian refugees lasted into the first half of the 16th century. It was particularly strong in the wake of quashed uprisings against Ottoman rule in 1481, 1492, and 1506, and after the Ottoman reconquest of Corone in 1533. Corone and other coastal towns of the Peloponnesus had been taken by the Spaniards in 1532, with the native Christian population, the Albanians among them, supporting the Spanish conquest. When Corone returned to Turkish control, many Albanian families left Greece along with the Spaniards and settled in the Spanish Vice-Kingdom of Naples, preferring the towns of Barile, Maschito, and Brindisi di Montagna (province of Potenza), as well as San Demetrio Corone and San Benedetto Ullan (province of Cosenza). The refugees from Corone were given special help from the government: not only were they exempted from taxes but they also received financial support and had the right to bear arms, which was forbidden to other immigrants. Tracing one's ancestry back to these *nobili Coronei* was considered a special mark of distinction, and many Italo-Albanian families therefore tried to link themselves to them.

The *Coronei* brought an end to the time of the great Albanian migrations. Only smaller, scattered groups of Albanians settled in Italy in the 17th and 18th centuries: in the first half of the 17th century this occurred in Barile (Potenza) and in the area around Piacenza in northern Italy; in 1744, the residents of Piqeras in the Himara left their southern Albanian home and moved to Italy, where Charles III of Naples settled them in Villa Badessa (Pescara); in 1756, refugees from Skutari settled in Pianiano (Viterbo) in the Papal States; the last Albanian settlers came to Brindisi di Montagna (Potenza) in 1774, which already had an older Albanian colony.

In addition to the arrival of groups, there was also immigration by individuals. Beginning in the 16th century, a steady flow of Albanians came to Italy, where they sought to find work as mercenaries or sailors. Albanian cavalry regiments were found not only in Naples but also in Milan and in other Spanish possessions in Italy. For the most part they were Albanian immigrants who had already been living in Italy for some time, or Greeks offering to recruit soldiers on the Balkans for the Spanish crown. The best-known Albanian unit was the Regimento Real Macedone that existed in Naples until the beginning of the 19th century and was used in the end as a police force to combat crime and insurrections. The migration of individuals strengthened the already existing Albanian element in southern Italy. At the same time, it also ensured that the connection of the Italo-Albanians to the Balkan peninsula was not severed.

The residents of most Italo-Albanian communities do not have homogenous geographic origins. However, the majority surely hailed from the southern Albanian-Greek region. Evidence of that is not only the Toscan variety of their dialect, but also the Orthodox liturgy, which most Albanian communities in Italy once followed, still follow, or have returned to. The immigrants settled mostly in abandoned villages and initially lived completely isolated from the native population. Where contact did take place, the relationship was not without tensions: the newcomers wore foreign dress and had unfamiliar customs and habits. Religiously they were often regarded as heretics. The Italian clergy tried with some success to convert the immigrants to the Latin rite. Above all, however, the native population could not understand the Albanians, who clung tenaciously to their language. During the first two centuries, the immigrants married only within their own group. Mixed Albanian-Italian marriages occurred in the second generation exclusively in small Albanian communities that were isolated from other Albanian settlements. The Italo-Albanians displayed a typical minority behavior, which manifested itself among other things in a high opinion of themselves: they were proud of belonging to a dignified and noble people that had preserved its own culture in a foreign land. What set them apart from their Italian neighbors in their eyes was the *nostalgia alla patria lontana* (longing for the distant homeland), hospitality, a strong sense of honor, and faithfulness to one's word.

The Italo-Albanians made essential contributions to the development of the Albanian literary language. Since the 18th century there has also been an Italo-Albanian literature. The works of Giulio Variboba and Girolamo De Rada are part of Albanian literary history, even though today – because of their archaic language – they can be read in Albania only in versions that are adapted to standard Albanian. Last, in the 19th century the Italo-Albanians played a not insignificant role in the nationalist movement in their home country. In the revolutionary year 1848, Naples saw the publication of the very first Albanian newspaper, the *L'Albanese d'Italia*, with articles in Italian and Italo-Albanian, edited by De Rada. Between 1883 and 1887, De Rada published the monthly *Fiamuri Arbërit. La Bandiera dell'Albania*, which was also read in the mother country, in spite of Turkish and Greek censorship. Albanology congresses were organized in Italy (1895 in Corigliano Calabro, 1897 in Lungro) to call the public's attention to the Albanian question. At the same time, however, Italo-Albanians were also active in the Italian unification movement, the *risorgimento*.

As a result of the rural exodus, temporary labor migrations, and permanent emigration that are evident in southern Italy, as well as the influence of modern media, the survival of the language and culture of the Italo-Albanians is under threat. This is especially true of villages and towns that are distant from the Italo-Albanian heartland, the province of Cosenza. Still, there are efforts to retard this development. After World War II, it was above all the chairs in Albanian at the universities in Rome, Palermo, and Cosenza that made efforts to promote Italo-Albanian cultural life. Since 1919, the Italo-Albanian communities with the Byzantine rite in Calabria have had their own bishopric with the seat in Lungro; today it has 27 congregations. The bishopric of Piana degli Albanesi with 15 communities has existed on Sicily since 1937. Both bishoprics have close ties to the Abbey of Grottaferrata south of Rome, which also adheres to the Eastern Rite.

While the Italo-Albanians do not enjoy a national minority status, the preservation of their language and culture is promoted by the state in accordance with the autonomy statutes of Calabria, Molise, and Basilicata, and the 1980 regional law of Sicily. However, Italo-Albanian (Arbërisht) was not able to establish itself as a language of instruction in the state schools. The reasons were the insufficient number of speakers in many places, the lack of instructional material, and the lack of a standardized, uniform Italo-Albanian dialect. Only a few private elementary schools teach in Arbërisht. Modern Albanian is taught as a subject at the *gymnasium* in San Demetrio Corone.

Bartl, Peter. "Fasi e modi dell'immigrazione albanese in Italia." In *I rapporti demografici e popolativi. Atti del Congresso di Foggia e Gargano, 5–8 ottobre 1978*, 197–212. Rome, 1981.

Giordano, Emanuele. *Dizionario degli Albanesi d'Italia.* Bari, 1963.

Kellner, Heidrun. *Die albanische Minderheit in Sizilien. Eine ethnosoziologische Untersuchung der Siculo-Albaner, dargestellt anhand historischer und volkskundlicher Quellen sowie eigener Beobachtung in Piana degli Albanesi.* Wiesbaden, 1972.

Laviola, Giovanni. *Dizionario biobliografico degli Italo-albanesi.* Cosenza, 2006.

Petrotta, Salvatore. *Albanesi di Sicilia. Storia e cultura.* Palermo, 1966.

Rother, Klaus. "Die Albaner in Süditalien." *Mitteilungen der Österreichischen Geographischen Gesellschaft* 110, 2–3 (1968): 1–20.

Cross-references: Italy; Southeastern Europe

ALGERIAN "HARKIS" IN FRANCE SINCE 1962

Jean-Jacques Jordi

"Les Harkis" became a commonly used designation for tens of thousands of Muslim Frenchmen or Frenchmen of Muslim origin who immigrated to France as a result of the Algerian war (1954–62). The Algerian independence movement and the opponents of France's colonial policy regarded the "loyalists" and "legalists" who advocated the continuation of the French colonial empire as traitors and collaborators.

Algerian auxiliary troops had served the French from the beginning of French colonial rule in Algeria in 1830. They had been involved in most of the military clashes between the natives and the colonial power. In the Algerian war, as well, the French army drew on auxiliaries; the recruits were given a one month contract with a possibility of extension. As a rule, each unit (Harka) was made up of 25 men who were led by a French officer. Because of their local knowledge and language skills, the Harkis proved very effective in the conflict, and their number rose to 60,000 in the course of the war. Adding the Moghaznis (auxiliaries in the colonial administration), the Groupes mobiles de protection rurale (mobile rural protection units), the Groupes d'autodéfense des villages (village self-protection units), and a small number of professional soldiers, a total of about 200,000 Muslims fought on the French side in the Algerian war.

Arrival of "Harkis" in Marseilles (*Domenech, P.*).

After the victory of the Algerian independence movement FLN (Front de Libération Nationale), they were left behind in the country without protection, contrary to their expectations. Without prior announcement, the auxiliaries were disarmed shortly before the signing of the truce agreement of Évian in March 1962, and the French government prohibited them from resettling to France. The subsequent massacre among the "colonial collaborators" led to the death of about 35,000–40,000 individuals. France's political establishment kept silent about the events. In 1962 and the following years, thousands of Muslim families were able to flee to France. By 1968, the group had grown to nearly 140,000, of whom 88,000 had been born in Algeria. Officially they were considered repatriated Muslim Frenchmen. At the end of the 1980s, the number of Harkis in France was estimated at 350,000–400,000.

More than 40 years after the end of the Algerian war, the history of the Harkis continues to cloud relations between France and Algeria. Within France, large segments of the public view the Harkis with indifference or even rejection. The French governments responded with restrictive measures to the influx of Algerian refugees: between 1962 and 1966, about 55,000 Harkis, following their arrival, were housed in hastily erected camps (Larzac, Département Aveyron; Bourg-Lastic/Puy-de-Dôme; Rivesaltes/Pyrénées-Orientales; Bias/Lot-et-Garonne; Saint-Maurice l'Ardoise/Gard, La Rye/Vienne) and closed institutions for the purpose of integrating them into the job market. Only those who had advanced in the military hierarchy and the colonial administration, as well as members of the Algerian upper class and professional soldiers enjoyed freedom of movement.

The integration of the immigrants can be divided into three phases: 1962–75, 1975–91, and since 1991. The first phase (1962–75) was characterized by social exclusion. Camps and

View of the Larzac camp (*Domenech, P.*).

closed institutions were to ease the integration for the Harkis and their families. Here they received help in dealing with the authorities and other formalities, which included application for naturalization. Many within this group regarded it as humiliating that their French citizenship was not automatically recognized. The authoritarian camp regime prevented contacts with the natives.

The families were only gradually dispersed, in accordance with their professional qualifications and the possibilities of the housing market, to suburbs of Paris, northeastern France, the area between Lyon and Grenoble, and communities along the Mediterranean coast. Along the coast there were 75 smaller settlement reserved for the Harkis and 17 urban housing complexes. The isolation of the group in villages and suburbs impeded its integration. Two camps, in Bias and Saint-Maurice-l'Ardoise, remained open. Older immigrants continued to live there, along with large families, and individuals who were regarded as unplaceable in the job market. With the help of organizations, volunteers, and state agencies, about half of the immigrants were able to find a job by the mid-1970s; the other half remained dependent on government support.

At the beginning of the second phase of integration (1975–91), in the wake of numerous hunger strikes, there was an uprising throughout France on 7 May 1975 of Harkis in the camps and isolated settlements. The revolt was triggered largely by young people who had been born during the Algerian war. It was led by M'Hamed Laradji and his Confédération des Français Musulmans rapatriés d'Algérie et leurs amies (Association of French Muslims Repatriated from Algeria and their Friends). Camps were seized and hostages were taken. The Harkis were rebelling against their social exclusion and against the de facto denial of their existence in France since 1962. This was exemplified by their battle cry: "After the betrayal, abandoned; after the abandonment, exile; after exile, forgotten." Only now did all of France take notice of this group.

In response, the Council of Ministers had the camps of Bias and Saint-Maurice-l'Ardoise dissolved and torn down at the end of 1976. It promised an improvement in the housing situation, better opportunities for job training, more jobs, and compensation. However, the Harkis continued to live in

their settlements as a tightly knit community without substantial contact with the natives until the 1980s. The promises of the French government following the uprising in the mid-1970s could not be implemented politically or were not carried out for lack of funds.

This led to renewed unrest and the beginning of the third phase of integration: in the summer of 1991 the revolt was driven especially by young people born in France, most of whom knew nothing about the Algerian war of the land of the parents. The uprising began in the Cité des Oliviers, a suburb of Narbonne, and eventually spread across all of France. Particularly affected were cities and settlements with a high percentage of Muslim Frenchmen – for example, Saint-Laurent-des-Arbres in the Département Gard, Carcassonne, Jouques, Bias, Avignon, and Amiens. Once again the government promised the Harkis financial compensation. After modest compensation payments of 60,000 francs per person in 1987, a law in 1994 stipulated 110,000 francs for former auxiliary troops, combined with a housing allowance of between 15,000 and 80,000 francs.

Still, the years between 1997 and 2000 continued to be marked by numerous hunger strikes and other forms of protest. The immigrants continued to feel like second–class citizens and were usually not distinguished in the French public from Algerian migrant laborers. The Harkis demanded not only financial support and social recognition but also moral rehabilitation. French majority society increasingly supported these demands. At the end of the 20th century, 67% of the French believed that France had behaved wrongly toward the Harkis. The pressure on the French government grew. The political situation came to a head because of the intense discussion in the 1990s about the role of France in the Algerian war, and also because of the statements by the president of Algeria, Abd al-Aziz Bouteflika, about the "Harki collaborators" on the occasion of a state visit to France in June 2000. As a result, the history of the Harkis established itself within the cultural memory of France: September 25 was declared the national day of remembrance in honor of the Harkis and their descendants. Despite the recognition of the Harkis by the French state, a part of French majority society continues to see them as colonial collaborators or as part of the Algerian population in the French suburbs. At the same time, another part sees the acknowledgment of belonging to the group of the Harkis as a clear patriotic posture in favor of France.

Abrial, Stéphanie. *Les enfants de Harkis: de la révolte à l'intégration*. Paris, 2002.

Hamoumou, Mohand. *Et ils sont devenus harkis*. Paris, 1994.

Jordi, Jean-Jacques, and Mohand Hamoumou. *Les harkis, une mémoire enfouie*. 2nd ed. Paris, 2002.

Meliani, Abd-El-Aziz. *La France honteuse: le drame des harkis*. 2nd ed. Paris, 2002.

Cross-references: France; Algerian *Pieds-Noirs* in France since 1954; Maghrebis in France after Decolonization in the 1950s and 1960s

ALGERIAN *PIEDS-NOIRS* IN FRANCE SINCE 1954

Jean-Jacques Jordi

The postcolonial migrations that reached France in 1954–62 came in the wake of military clashes over the independence of French colonies: after the defeat of France in Indochina in 1954, the end of the protectorate over Morocco and Tunisia in 1956, the Suez crisis in 1956, the end of the fight over the military outpost of Bizerta in 1963, and the Algerian war from 1954 to 1962. During this period, the repatriation of parts of the population from the former colonies was always marked by flight from areas of war or civil war. No far-reaching concepts on how to integrate these immigrants existed in France.

From 1954 to 1964, France took in 1.8 million repatriates, 800,000 from Algeria, alone, in 1962 (all told, about 1 million came from Algeria). The French from Algeria, referred to as *pieds-noirs*, were largely of humble social origins and hailed from the large group of European settlers who had immigrated into northern Algeria after the French February revolution of 1848, chiefly from France, Spain, Italy, Malta, Switzerland, and Germany. Since 1848, the three *départements* of Alger, Constantine, and Oran were part of the territory of the French state. The *pieds-noirs* were French citizens. They also included Algerian Jews, who had been naturalized in 1870.

The intensification of the Algerian war in 1960–2, and especially the threat from the Algerian independence movement FLN (Front de Libération Nationale) that French citizens would have to leave the land of their birth after independence or expect being killed, led to the mass flight of *pieds-noirs*. The origin of the term "Black Feet" is unclear: according to one widespread interpretation, it is a pejorative reference to the fact that these people had supposedly settled in Africa only with "their feet" but without "their head," that is, with a European identity. At the same time, they were regarded as "violent colonizers." In the first years after their arrival in France, the *pieds-noirs* thus often encountered contempt, mistrust, and exclusion.

France tried to direct the immigration and to distribute the *pieds-noirs* evenly across the country. Still, three-quarters settled in the Mediterranean *départements* and in greater Paris. Between 1954 and 1968, the immigration of the repatriates accounted for more than half of the population increase in the southern French regions of Provence, Midi-Pyrénées, and Languedoc-Roussillon. In the Département Bouches-du-Rhône, in fact, more than 80% of the population growth was due to this influx. The immigration was even more important still for some communities in the Auvergne or in the region Poitou-Charentes, whose demography was characterized by aging because of low birthrates. Especially families and young people arrived: of those repatriated from Algeria in 1962, 31% were younger than 19 years of age, while only 28% of the natives fell into that cohort; conversely, only 16% of the repatriates were older than 65, while that

was true of 20% of the natives. The demographic structure of the immigrants affected the housing and labor markets and had a lasting influence on political decisions at the communal level.

The colonial myth disseminated the image of Algeria as the home of white agricultural settlers. In reality, though, more than 80% of the Algerian French were city dwellers already at the beginning of the 20th century. In France, as well, they settled mostly in medium-sized and large cities, with the exception of the Départements Gers, Dordogne, Lozère, and Corsica, where mostly rural immigrants were taken in. Two-thirds of the repatriates established their new residence in cities with a population of more than 100,000. That led initially to problems in the labor and housing markets, but also with schooling for the children of the immigrants, especially since the government efforts to direct the influx failed; in fact, in the mid-1970s there were signs of an onward movement from the north to the south by immigrants who wanted to live closer to the Mediterranean, but who had been sent to the Loire in 1962.

A special program or the construction of more than 35,000 housing units was hastily drawn up, 30% of which were intended for the repatriates. Neighborhoods with a high proportion of repatriates developed mostly along the outskirts of cities. Every large city in the south of France has a least one such neighborhood (e.g., Razimbaud in Narbonne). At the same time, entire settlements only for repatriates were laid out: Saint-Thys in Marseille, Le Morillon in Toulon, Corsy in Aix-en-Provence, Bagatelle and ZUP le Mirail in Toulouse (ZUP stands for Zone à urbaniser en priorité), areas that were given preference in urban development measures in the 1960s and 1970s. The influx of several hundred thousand families required a massive expansion of communal institutions. All large cities in the south, but also Lyon, Grenoble, Dijon, and the communities in greater Paris erected numerous schools using prefabricated construction methods. At the beginning of the school year 1962, the Département Bouches-du-Rhône counted 16,000 new students, 12,000 in Marseille, alone. The government's "Fourth Economic Plan" (1962–5; until 1993 there was a total of 10 Four- or Five-Year Plans) had to be hastily revised in order to accelerate the expansion of waste-water treatment and the new construction of schools and housing.

In 1962, the minister in charge of the repatriates, Alain Peyrefitte, had proclaimed that it would be easier to build housing where jobs were available than to create jobs where housing was available. Yet in spite of widespread fears of a sudden, sharp rise in unemployment and of wage declines because of the immigration, it proved possible to integrate the repatriates into the labor market fairly quickly and without any major problems. The backdrop was the long, sustained economic upswing of the years 1955–70 (the *quinze glorieuses*). In 1962, the government created a national labor office that found jobs for about 50,000 repatriates in 1963. That same year, 200,000 repatriates found work without government help. In 1964 there was hardly any more unemployment among the immigrants. Although the integration into the labor market was exceedingly rapid, the success must be qualified in so far as many *pieds-noirs* initially had to take low-status jobs.

The immigration had a stimulating economic effect, and this improved the image of the *pieds-noirs* in the host society. The end of the economic crisis in the Département Hérault, for example, was largely due to the repatriates. An economic report from the Département Bouches-du-Rhône therefore concluded in 1964 that the repatriates had been a "gain" and "a factor in the economic growth of the Département." Similar assessments were also found in economic reports from the Départements Gers, Dordogne, Haute-Garonne, Hérault, Lot-et-Garonne, Vaucluse, Gard, Isère, and the region Midi-Pyrénées.

The *pieds-noirs* contributed to the modernization of entire sectors of the economy, for example, fishing in the Mediterranean, which was done from Marseille, Sète, Toulon, Martigues, or Port-Vendres. That was also true of the agriculture of some regions, where they introduced new methods of intensive cultivation, such as the use of liquid manure, efficient machines, and the creation of cooperatives – for example, in the regions of Sud-Ouest, Midi provençal, and on Corsica. And the *pieds-noirs* were a factor of modernization also in other sectors, such as construction, transportation, the printing industry, the food industry, furniture making, advertising, and medical technology.

Some *pieds-noirs* advanced quickly in their careers as writers, actors, entrepreneurs, doctors, scientists, athletes, journalists, and politicians. Because of the pronounced occupational and social differentiation, the immigrant group cannot be seen as a homogeneous community, even if television and the movies in France were flooded with strongly folklorizing portrayals of a supposedly homogeneous culture of the *pieds-noirs*. In spite of the rapid social and economic integration of the *pieds-noirs*, many among them, especially the elderly, felt like foreigners in France, describing their presence as "exile" and continuing to refer to Algeria as their homeland.

Jordi, Jean-Jacques. *De l'Exode à l'Exil: Rapatriés et Pieds-Noirs en France, l'exemple marseillais 1954–1992.* Paris, 1993.

Jordi, Jean-Jacques. *1962: l'arrivée des Pieds-Noirs.* Paris, 1995.

Jordi, Jean-Jacques. *Les Pieds-Noirs (idées reçues).* Paris, 2009.

Leconte, Daniel. *Les Pieds-Noirs, histoire et portrait d'une communauté.* Paris, 1980.

Savarese, Eric. *L'invention des Pieds-Noirs.* Paris, 2002.

Verdes-Leroux, Jeanine. *Les Français d'Algérie de 1830 à aujourd-hui. Une page d'histoire déchirée.* Paris, 2001.

Cross-references: France; Algerian "Harkis" in France since 1962; Maghrebis in France after Decolonization in the 1950s and 1960s; Swiss Mercenaries in Europe from the 17th to the 19th Century: The Example of France; Vietnamese Colonial and Postcolonial Immigrants in France since World War I

ALLIED MILITARY PERSONNEL IN GERMANY SINCE THE END OF WORLD WAR II

Christian Th. Müller

The presence of foreign troops in Germany has been one aftereffect of World War II that has carried down to this day. From 1945 to 1994, between 300,000 and 500,000 Soviet (Russian) troops were permanently stationed on the territory of the SOZ/GDR (Soviet Occupation Zone/German Democratic Republic), while the Western zones and later the Federal Republic of Germany (FRG) were home to about 400,000 soldiers from the three Allied victorious powers as well as from Belgium, Canada, and the Netherlands. Until 1958 there was also a small contingent of Danish troops. In conjunction with the West German *Bundeswehr* and the East German National People's Army (*Nationale Volksarmee*), these military forces constituted the greatest concentration of troops and weapons of mass destruction in world history during peacetime and over the longest period. Along with the stationed troops, about half a million family members and foreign civilian employees of the military forces lived in the two Germanies. Table 1 gives an indication of the size of the national contingents and their composition.

The continuity of a massive presence of foreign troops on German soil contrasts with a change in their function and in how they were perceived and accepted by society. Initially, the primary purpose behind the stationing of troops was eradicating National Socialism and Germany's military potential, and, after the end of the war, guaranteeing reparations; however, with the emergence of the East-West conflict, securing western and central Europe – i.e., the Soviet Union's strategic glacis – over the long term became their most important task. It meant that the former allies of World War II confronted each other along the seam between NATO states and Warsaw Pact states as potential war enemies. The term "Allied troops" is therefore ambiguous. For one thing, between 1945 and 1990, the Western victorious powers France, Great Britain, and the USA exercised Allied rights – especially in Berlin – jointly with the Soviet Union, their ally in World War II and adversary in the East-West conflict. For another, as part of the stationing of troops within the NATO alliance, troops from additional states arrived as new allies of West Germany.

In addition, the presence of troops in conjunction with the gradual implantation of a bourgeois-parliamentarian democracy or a Stalinist regime after the Soviet model had domestic political tasks. While this process was completed fairly early in West Germany with the erection of a stable democracy, the Socialist Unity Party of Germany (Sozialistische Einheitspartei Deutschlands, SED), because of serious deficiencies in its legitimacy, remained dependent on the potential support of Soviet troops to maintain its power.

However, it was not only the respective domestic political role in the FRG and the GDR that showed clear differences. There was also no uniformity in living conditions, self-conception, and self-representation of the various national

Table 1. Foreign troops in the FRG, 1982, and GDR, 1990 (numbers rounded off)				
Country of origin	Military personnel	Family members	Foreign civilian employees	Total for country of origin
USA	233,000	161,000	16,800	410,800
Great Britain	65,000	90,900	2,400	158,300
France	50,000	32,000	9,000	91,000
Belgium	32,000	28,000	1,600	61,600
Netherlands	6,700	6,000	130	12,830
Canada	5,400	7,600	1,200	14,200
Total for FRG	392,100	325,500	31,130	748,730
Total for GDR: USSR	338,000	208,000		546,000

contingents, or in the way they were perceived by the Germans, depending on the Germans' political attitude, personal experience, place of residence, and the social strata and generation to which they belonged. In what follows, I will therefore take a closer look at the US troops in the FRG and the Soviet troops in the SOZ/GDR, which were simply the two largest groups.

Both the American and the Soviet troops came to Germany from western or eastern Europe during World War II in 1944–5 in the wake of military action. During that same time or shortly before, Soviet troops had entered Poland, Hungary, and Czechoslovakia, where they either stayed until their complete withdrawal in 1991 or to where they returned in 1956 and 1968, respectively, to put an end to undesirable political developments. The American troops had moved to Germany from Great Britain via France and Italy. With the exception of France, the USA has military bases in the countries mentioned to this day. While Belgium, France, Canada, the Netherlands, and the Soviet Union/Russia have withdrawn their forces from Germany, Great Britain and the USA, after a substantial troop withdrawal, still have 23,000 and 80,000 soldiers, respectively, on German territory at the beginning of the 21st century.

The ongoing presence of American forces and the long presence of Soviet troops in Germany as military organizations contrast with the individual stay of soldiers, their family members, and civilian employees, which was often limited to a few years and sometimes merely months. Transfers and discharges from military service constantly led to onward movements and returns. The duration of stay for US soldiers was for the most part between six months and two years. Sometimes, though, they stayed for much longer or – as could happen with binational marriages – permanently. By contrast, the tour of duty for Soviet soldiers in the GDR was much more uniform. Conscripts who did not first have to undergo specialized training in the USSR spent their entire military service of three – since 1968, two years –in the GDR, whereas unmarried professional soldiers remained three years, and married soldiers who brought their families with them, five years.

The answer to the question about the nature and degree of integration of foreign military personnel into German society is correspondingly contradictory. While the military

organizations had a network of institutional, economic, and social relationships that were official or at least semi-official in character and had long-term ties with the West German and East German state apparatus, there was virtually no social integration of military personnel. But because of their limited stay and a life that was largely shielded from the society of the host country, foreign military personnel rarely perceived themselves as a minority. In fact, given the almost completely separate existence of foreign troops in the FRG and the GDR, in each case with their own infrastructure, one can follow S. Seiler in asking whether the foreign soldiers, civilian employees, and their families lived in West or East German society at all.

Ghettoization in barracks, "military towns," and housing areas

Determinative for the daily existence of Soviet and the vast majority of American soldiers, civilian employees, and family members was life in barracks or special settlements (the housing areas or *Voennye Gorodki* [military towns]) that were separated from the German population. They had their own, group-specific infrastructure with commercial and service establishments, institutions of culture and leisure, and schools, all of which – in conjunction with a special legal status – endowed them with the character of a complete urban neighborhood. The construction of these "towns" began immediately after the end of the war; the occupying powers, moving beyond the continuing use of former barracks of the Wehrmacht and in order to house administrative offices and professional soldiers who increasingly came to Germany with their families after around 1947, sometimes confiscated streets and at times entire neighborhoods. The German population in these neighborhoods was resettled in the wake of the American occupying power's policy of nonfraternization, which was also pursued officially. Beginning in the 1950s, large-scale housing and infrastructure programs were carried out for the US forces, which led to the emergence of so-called Little Americas, which had the character of small American towns down to the four-digit house numbers so typical in the USA. While the American settlements were in principle freely accessible, entry into the Soviet military towns was restricted to members of the Soviet military forces, with the exception of tradesmen or official German visitors.

This more pronounced spatial separation found expression above all in the fence of wooden planks – mostly painted green – that was so typical of Soviet military settlements. In many Soviet garrisons, this spatial segregation corresponded also to a "side or regimental economy" that was unknown and unthinkable among the financially and materially much better off US forces: for example, Soviet soldiers ran chicken coops or pig breeding establishments or erected buildings on their own so as to overcome supply shortfalls on their own initiative.

Distinct differences were also evident in the housing for American and Soviet troops and their families. Whereas Soviet soldiers, even if they were in the GDR with their families, lived almost exclusively in barracks or military towns, a considerable portion of US soldiers lived in the midst of the German population outside the barracks and military settlements – as long as rents and the dollar exchange rate allowed them to, stretching the official policy of nonfraternalization. As far as the housing in military settlements was concerned, the respective national styles were carried on. For Soviet families this meant for the most part life in the *Kommunalka*, where several families shared an apartment and jointly used the kitchen and the bath. By contrast, the standard military housing of US forces – which was oriented toward the US standard of living – were noticeably more comfortable.

In both cases, however, a prosperity gap opened up sooner or later between the military and the society of the country in which the troops were stationed. For the GDR that was already evident from the mid-1950s. In West Germany, in the wake of the declining value of the US dollar since the end of 1960s, a clear impoverishment of the GIs – previously seen as the ambassadors of a desirable "American way of life" – compared to the West German population manifested itself. Especially enlisted men with families, who were not entitled to military housing, now found themselves, without rental subsidies and welfare benefits, increasingly unable to pay for private rental housing. In 1978, 16,000 GI families in the FRG were living below the poverty line, and in the same year, German CARE packages were for the first time handed out to US soldiers. Among Soviet conscripts, of whose tough and meager living conditions the East German population knew by way of rumors, poverty became obvious when they asked the German population for food and tobacco or tried to trade military equipment for money or alcohol.

The unsatisfactory or even impoverished living conditions of military personnel constituted one of the essential starting points for their black market activities, the abuse of alcohol and – among US soldiers – also drugs, as well as property crimes and crimes of violence. Because of the de facto extraterritorial status of barracks and military settlements, criminal behavior, in particular, was promoted to the extent that perpetrators were beyond the direct reach of the German police there. All this was exacerbated by conflicts within the forces. In the Soviet army, in addition to the different treatment of the various nationalities, there was the persistent problem of the *dedovscina*; this was the illegal and brutal treatment of the younger by the older soldiers, which characterized the daily life of Soviet conscripts to a large extent. By contrast, the internal conflicts of the US forces culminated in the first half of the 1970s, when protests against the Vietnam war coincided with tensions between black and white GIs and the relative impoverishment caused by the declining value of the dollar. This led to a dramatic erosion of discipline within and outside the barracks, one that was close to what Daniel J. Nelson has called a "regime of terror."

Both German societies were confronted in different ways and in different degrees of intensity with the problems and conflicts among the stationed troops. Characteristic are the differences in the way these problems were dealt with. While the negative manifestations linked to the presence of foreign troops were repeatedly and in part also very critically addressed in public by the West German media, in East Germany, given the propagandistically transfigured image of the Soviet Union and the Soviet army, such criticism was taboo. Criticism of the Soviet army and accompanying manifestations of their presence were expressed for the most part only behind closed doors, in part in the form of petitions and complaints, and very rarely in public protests such as leafleting actions and demonstrations.

On the whole, in spite of various forms of official and unofficial contacts with the native population, the stationed troops remained fairly isolated. Apart from the massive language barriers that existed for American and Soviet soldiers, in the case of the latter in the GDR one must mention above all the drastic curfews and the de facto prohibition against relations with East German citizens. Although American soldiers were not subject to these sorts of restrictions, most of them nevertheless spent most of their leisure time on the military bases and housing areas. The latter were well supplied with affordable eating establishments and recreational facilities, as a result of which the later decline in the value of the dollar led to a noticeable tendency toward self-isolation in the 'Little Americas.'

Occupiers, brothers-in-arms, and foreign friends

The spectrum of experiences, relationships, and conflicts produced perceptions of the foreign troops that differed according to generation, place of residence, and social status and were sometimes diametrically opposed. For example, even after occupying forces had turned into stationed troops, some of the Germans, in the wake of special incidents, crimes, and damage from maneuvers, claimed – especially with respect to the Soviet forces, but not infrequently also the US forces – that the military personnel had an occupation mentality, which was in stark contradiction to the propagated image of the great brother-in-arms. As a result, the way the forces described themselves or were officially depicted by their governments placed great emphasis on the legitimacy of their presence within the context of the East-West conflict.

Although the two leading powers always highlighted their differences, they spelled out the necessity of their presence with very comparable methods. In the second half of the 1940s, America Houses (*Amerikahäuser*) and Houses of German-Soviet Friendship (*Häuser der Deutsch-Sowjetischen Freundschaft*, DSF) were set up to spread the accomplishments of Western democracy and the "American Way of Life" or of the creation of socialism in the Soviet Union. There are also clear parallels in the institution of annual Months of DSF since 1949 and German-American Friendship Weeks since 1952, as well as in the periodic work deployment of American and Soviet soldiers in support of German municipalities and in the GDR also in industrial and agricultural enterprises. Such actions were intended to create acceptance for the presence of the troops, bind the German society to the respective leading power, and break down prejudices and fears of contact. In the process, the self-presentation of the US forces proved much more successful than the Soviet propaganda. Apart from the greater basic attractiveness of the American Way of Life among the German population and the considerable material and financial expenditures that the Americans invested in this publicity work, the primary reason for this divergence was the fact that the friendship propaganda in the SOZ/GDR from the very beginning bore highly ideological, doctrinaire, and strongly ritualized traits. All opposing opinions were branded as anti-Soviet or as simply hostile.

In both countries, however, the resonance among the population as well as the foreign troops to the organized expressions of friendship remained limited. For example, even the "Contact" program initiated in 1971 by the West German government and the US European Command with the goal of promoting contacts between German and American young people, reached only a tiny fraction of the German and American 18- to 25-year-olds living in the garrison towns and cities, since both groups generally preferred to stay among their own kind. As a result, as was the case in the relationship of the East German population to the Soviet forces, mutual feelings of otherness and resentment persisted also in West Germany, and they were continuously reproduced in connection with local conflicts with the troops.

By contrast, there were considerable differences in the way German officials worked with their American and Soviet counterparts to resolve problems. In East Germany, despite regular friendship meetings between the local and regional party and state officials and representatives of the Soviet army, it proved impossible right down to 1989 to set up a continuous collaboration of the relevant Soviet and German offices to contain damages from maneuvers or transgressions by Soviet soldiers. By contrast, the German-American Advisory Councils that were set up after 1952 at the state (Bundesland) and district levels were able to ensure ongoing institutional cooperation. As a result, problems and abuses in the garrisons could be responded to much more efficiently than was the case with Soviet installations in East Germany.

The spectrum of informal relations between the German population and foreign military personnel was nearly identical in both countries; these ranged from ad hoc contacts in taverns to economic relationships – including black marketeering and prostitution – all the way to friendships, intimate relationships, and binational marriages. However, the gradual articulation of the relationships was very different or even the complete opposite. For example, US soldiers constituted an important group of customers for the restaurants and red-light districts of their garrison towns and cities, while the mass of Soviet soldiers, because of their lack of money and the rigid restrictions on leaving their base, had no opportunity to take advantage of these "amenities." As a result, black market activities with clothing and equipment were all the more important in East Germany. In both countries only a small fraction of the military personnel entered into continuous business relationships, friendships, or intimate relationships with the German population. A lack of interest and distance predominated. For the mass of the German population, the foreign troops, civilian employees, and their family members thus remained "foreign friends."

All in all, in the case of foreign forces in West and East Germany, because of the constant personnel turnover and a de facto life in separated enclaves, there was no minority formation. To the extent that the troops were withdrawn from their German garrisons after the end of the cold war, their traces – except for contaminated sites and problems of how to convert their installations – practically vanished entirely. Alongside the above-mentioned differences in the presence of American and Soviet troops, the life in separate housing areas and barracks that were spatially clearly set apart from the society of the host country created a very similar potential for internal and external conflicts and comparable forms of friendship propaganda. There was a distinct difference, though, in the stance that the German authorities took vis-à-vis the troops stationed on their soil. While West German authorities were fairly consistent in insisting on adherence to agreements and law, and since the mid-1950s could generally count on a spirit of cooperation from the stationed forces, the position of the East German authorities and of the GDR as a state toward the "Group of Soviet Forces in Germany" was much weaker. As a virtual state within the state, these forces claimed special rights, some of which were not spelled out anywhere. Thus, every unusual incident involving members of the Soviet army in which bilateral agreements or East German laws were ignored contributed to the doubts regarding the sovereignty of the GDR and thus of the legitimacy of the SED regime.

Arlt, Kurt. "Sowjetische (russische) Truppen in Deutschland (1945–1994)." In *Im Dienste der Partei. Handbuch der bewaffneten Organe der DDR*, edited by Torsten Diedrich et al., 593–631. Berlin, 1998.

Arlt, Kurt. "'… stets wachsam zu sein im fremden Land!' Zum Selbstverständnis der sowjetischen Truppen in der DDR." In *Militär und Gesellschaft in der DDR. Forschungsfelder,*

Ergebnisse, Perspektiven, edited by Hans Ehlert and Matthias Rogg, 205–24. Berlin, 2004.

Höhn, Maria. *GIs and Fräuleins: The German-American Encounter in 1950s West Germany*. Chapel Hill, 2002.

Kowalczuk, Ilko-Sascha, and Stefan Wolle. *Roter Stern über Deutschland. Sowjetische Truppen in der DDR*. Berlin, 2001.

Leuerer, Thomas. *Die Stationierung amerikanischer Streitkräfte in Deutschland*. Würzburg, 1997.

Müller, Christian Th. "'O' Sowjetmensch!' Beziehungen von sowjetischen Streitkräften und DDR-Gesellschaft zwischen Ritual und Alltag." In *Ankunft – Alltag – Ausreise. Beiträge zur Geschichte von Migration und interkultureller Begegnung in der DDR-Gesellschaft*, edited by Christian Th. Müller and Patrice G. Poutrus, 17–134. Cologne, 2005.

Nelson, Daniel J. *A History of U.S. Military Forces in Germany*. Boulder and London, 1987.

Nelson, Daniel J. *Defenders or Intruders: The Dilemmas of US-Forces in Germany*. Boulder, 1987.

Seiler, Signe. *Die GIs. Amerikanische Soldaten in Deutschland*. Hamburg, 1985.

Cross-references: Belgium and Luxembourg; France; Germany; Great Britain; the Netherlands; Northern Europe; Russia and Belarus

ALPINE CHIMNEY SWEEPS IN WESTERN, CENTRAL, AND SOUTHERN EUROPE FROM THE 16TH TO THE EARLY 20TH CENTURY

Markus Walz

Migrant workers from the western Alps are considered innovators in chimney cleaning, because chimney construction in Europe spread from the south, and the last houses without chimneys in central Europe did not disappear until the 19th century. In fact, however, these workers hailed from regions where chimneys also arose late. They moved about not only without a fixed abode but beginning in the 16th century, they also took permanent residence in the destination regions. Some of them married into local families. Contemporaries regarded them as a homogenous group of origin: in 1547, Swiss-Germans called the segment of the valley between Domodòssola and Locarno the Kaemifägertal; in 1737, *Zedlers Universal Lexicon* listed the eastern half of the valley under the heading *Caminfeger-Thal* (chimney sweep valley).

The self-descriptions, however, changed with the language of the three concentrations of villages of origin in the upper or tributary valleys of the western Alps: the French Ramoneur and the Franco-Provençal Burna came from the Graian Alps (Val de Thônes, Maurienne, Tarentaise, Valle di Locana, tributary valleys of the upper Val d'Aoste), the Italian Spazzacamino from the Grisons (Misox/Val Mesolcina), or areas north of the Lago Maggiore (Val Vigezzo, Valle Cannobina in Milan/Piedmont, Centovalli, Valle Onsernone, Valle Lavizzara, Valle Mággia, Val Verzasca in the Tecino), sometimes called Rüsca in the Piedmontese dialect.

One peculiarity of the chimney sweeps from the western Alps was the male migrants between the ages of 7 and 14. The notion that all of them were apprentices is a misinterpretation, since child labor was cheap and efficient: a brushing of the chimney eliminated soot flakes but very little of the solid deposits (glaze) that posed a threat of fire; children fit into the inside of the chimney and worked there with wire brushes as they climbed up and down. Physical growth put a strict time limit on child labor. Had each child represented a chimney sweep in training, enormous numbers of journeymen without employment would have been the result. Underage workers therefore characterized the chimney sweep migration – as "non-domiciled" migrant workers in (accompanied) groups of young people and as labor migration. Only some went on to occupational migration as adolescents and adults.

The history of the chimney sweep profession is largely shrouded in darkness. The first references are found in Strasbourg (13th century), Augsburg (1432), and Bremen (1453), but up into the 18th century, this vocation was also pursued on the side by barber-surgeons, bricklayers, or roofers. Chimney sweeps from northern Italy appear in the sources in 1538 and 1547. The first documented instances concern men from Milan, while an accidental death (in Parma around 1630) and admissions into citizenship (in Swabia: Kaufbeuren 1679 and Mindelheim 1684; Mainz 1695) bring sweeps from the Tecino to light. The Valle di Locano as a place of origin does not show up until the 19th century. The final entries in the documentation were the last immigration into the Netherlands (1931) and the death of the last immigrant sweep in Vienna (1930).

Destination areas were the Italian peninsula and France, along with the Netherlands, western, central, and southern Germany, and the Danubian monarchy. At the beginning were the migrant workers who cleaned chimneys in large cities (Leipzig 1557) or in buildings of the territorial rulers (Duchy of Brunswick-Wolfenbüttel 1566, Principality Palatinate-Zweibrücken 1579, Bishopric Augsburg 1585, Bishopric Speyer 1606). Later, licensed migrant workers were active in the countryside – for example, one Italian in the District of Dülmen in the bishopric Münster (before 1754). Palatinate-Zweibrücken and the Electoral Palatinate auctioned off monopolies to the highest bidder, among them also Italians.

Immigration initially targeted the cities, where more chimneys were found: Leipzig 1577; Amsterdam 1604, 1617, 1670; Mainz 1623; Biberach an der Riss 1677; St. Goar/Rhine 1681; Rottenburg/Neckar 1687, 1690. Migrant work and immigration were not mutually exclusive: the Italian Baroggio, who was licensed in the Bishopric of Speyer in 1721–7 lived in Klingenmünster in the Electoral Palatinate.

What made this profession attractive was, first, the small operating capital it required (a few, easily transported implements, no real estate), and, second, the sale of secondary products: the tar-containing soot was used as a leather dye, as an auxiliary material in steel hardening, and as a fertilizer in agriculture and horticulture. Opportunities for profit were offered by an expansion of the business to the exacting field of stove building. Individual successes were demonstrated by a few chimney sweeps who reached the highest tax class in Vienna, but also one Piagetti in Augsburg, who had sold the business to his nephew for 2,000 gulden and was suing him in 1792–6 for a share of the profits.

Destination preferences by regions of origin are explained topographically (more westerly locations tended to be oriented toward France, more easterly ones toward the Habsburg lands) and accentuated a few local minorities. Much as in Nuremberg, the Vienna guild (which had about 18 businesses around the same time) was almost entirely in the hands of sweeps from the Grisons. This process was reinforced by occupational continuity across several generations in the same location (Vienna, Innsbruck, Prague, Bratislava).

Organizations of migrants appeared late and only in northern Italy. In 1925 in Milan, sweeps from Vigezzo and Cannobio sought to use their organization to control the quality of training and the work and secure their territory; a comparable organization in Turin was to standardize prices. In Rotterdam and the Hague, dense residential neighborhoods demarcated the chimney sweeps from the rest of the population. And the first Milanese in Amsterdam already lived in the Schoorsteenvegerssteeg (chimney sweep alley), an alley that bore this name since the 18th century. The languages and dialects of the origin regions no doubt had a cohesive effect.

A number of documented cases show that chimney sweeps divided the location of their business and the domicile of their family, thus combining weak social engagement with their destination with participation in their place of origin. From the 16th to the end of the 18th century, the Duchy of Württemberg always licensed chimney sweeps with the name Pironi, who presumably did not establish a permanent residence there. The imperial city of Kempten expelled the chimney sweep Johannes Cotta in 1742 after 24 years of citizenship rights because he had journeyed "to his fatherland" Savoy for more than three months without permission. Tombstones for native-born deceased bearing inscriptions in foreign languages – for example, in Cavergno (Valle Lavizzara) in Dutch, illustrate that migrants identified with their multiple localities.

Chimney work by children was still customary across Europe as late as the early 20th century. In Nuremberg in 1639 we find a reference to *Kehrrichtfegermägdlein* (chimney sweep maids), the only mention of female sweeps, and in 1695 the council of Kaiserslautern demanded from the chimney sweep "small boys for chimney crawling." In 1788, a commission of the English government reported about abuses in this form of child labor. Most of the chimney sweep boys from the western Alps were found in the 19th century, and – with declining numbers – until the 1930s. Their life stories depended on opportunity and happenstance. Joseph Laurent Fénix (1892–1958), the son of a small farmer from the area around Albertville (Département Savoie) began as a shepherd boy, at age 11 went to Dôle (Département Jura) as a chimney sweep because he could earn four times as much, and returned home at 14 to take up a carpenter apprenticeship. Johann Baptist Fernandis from Vigezzo took up his apprenticeship in Stuttgart in 1812 at the age of 18, and following his journeymen years, he took his master's exam in Augsburg in 1826. The journeymen chimney sweeps in that city complained in 1775 that Joseph Piagetti, in violation of guild rules, was employing "welsch" journeymen he had taken over from his brother in Eichstätt in central Franconia.

The working children and the chimney sweeps came from the same regions of origin. In the early 20th century, one chimney sweep from the Tecino working in Leeuwarden (province of Frisia, the Netherlands) annually brought in additional boys from his home village. But other specific, geographic dependencies are also noticeable: from the late 17th century, entrepreneurs from Maurienne (upper valley of the Arc) and Tarantaise (upper valley of the Isère) recruited the underage chimney sweeps along the lower reaches of the Arc; those in Rhêmes preferred the neighboring valley (Locana), and their counterparts in the Tecino turned to the Val Vigezzo in Piedmont. Something similar was probably also true of the Valle Cannobina, where around 1900 the adult chimney sweeps migrated for the summer half-year, and the chimney sweep boys for the winter half-year. The labor markets for the specific groups were characterized by different rates of pay. Around 1900, the usual seasonal wages for sweeps from Vigezzo were 50–60 lire, for those from Cannobio around 100 lire.

The underage chimney sweeps had few opportunities for participation and integration. The entrepreneurs employed few boys (probably four, at most); larger children's organizations are not known. The supposedly "secret language," a repertoire of terms coded in the language of origin and intended to prevent anyone from eavesdropping, had a separating and isolating effect. The chimney sweep boy Fénix listed words for master, house owner, mistress of the house, and foodstuffs.

In northern Italy in the 19th century, the chimney sweep boys aroused the public's sympathy; in 1880, women from Milan's upper class organized a festive Christmas meal for 144 chimney sweep boys. A number of charitable and church organizations appeared, such as a Catechesis for First Holy Communicants (Turin 1853), for which the bishop of Aoste provided French-language catechisms. In 1869, benefactors in Milan financed a Sunday school, in 1889 a rooming house and meals. An isolated case was the Societa di patrocinio dei piccoli spazzacamini (Turin 1873), which recruited boys between 6 and 14; guaranteed them clothes, housing, and meals; and offered homeowners chimney cleaning subscriptions.

The occupation structure of the chimney sweeps indicates that the chimney sweep boys did not necessarily take on an apprentice role. Fénix describes a group of three that worked on its own with an adult companion who offered chimney cleaning with a brush and negotiated prices; at age 13, Fénix took over that role himself. His employer ran a coal dealership and housed the group while it worked in the city or the suburbs in the summer; during the winter, it wandered widely from town to town.

Because of the income from the sale of glaze, autonomous groups of working children were already profitable if the seasonal wages for the children equaled the fees for the cleaning service. Depending on the season, around 1880 an entrepreneur from Verzasco was making 600–700 francs and paid the boys, depending on experience, 50–170 each. If the income was short, hungry children begged "successfully," and gifts in-kind from the population supplemented the clothing and food for the boys.

The acoustic signals announcing that the boys had arrived on the roof, and which were meaningful for coordinating the work, turned into the "chimney sweep song," and its performance became a begging custom – the widely accepted demand of a (monetary) gift for the singer. In France, listeners rewarded scurrilous songs based on vulgar secondary meanings of *ramoner* (instead of sweeping the chimney: vomiting or vaginal penetration).

The entrepreneurs who accompanied their underage workers in person had enough time to pursue an ambulatory trade (with rather weak sales): as peddlers with products from their hometown from the region around the Val d'Aoste or collectors of combed-out women's hair (to sell) from the Val de Rhêmes. The chimney sweeps from Vigezzo were quite successful with peddling crystal and iron goods in France (authorized by the French state in 1613, attested for the last time 1774), which de facto was their chief source of income. In the 18th century, several Paris jewelers hailed from the Val Vigezzo. In 1838, that valley counted 964 absent inhabitants – alongside 504 chimney sweeps and stove makers; also 81 craftsmen, 64 traders/peddlers, and 34 jewelers/goldsmiths.

The claim that the western Alps are the European cradle of the profession feeds the modern prominence of chimney sweeps from that region. A national chimney sweep organization headquartered in Santa Maria Maggiore (Val Vigezzo) seeks to promote research, culture, and tourism. The local chimney sweep museum and a chimney sweep statue indicate the identification with this profession. Since 1982, the Spazzacamini del 2000, an international special interest group with about 3,000 members, has been holding an annual festive procession in one town of the valley with about 800 participants.

The memory of the itinerant traders who simultaneously offered chimney work by children is the mental bridge for associating other kinds of migrants with the collective identification figure of the chimney sweep – for example, Givoanni Paolo de Feminis (d. 1736), a seller of miracle cures and inventor of *Kölnisch Wasser* (eau de Cologne). The underage chimney sweeps provided literary material. Several autobiographies have appeared, among them that by Fénix, which is already in its sixth printing. The well-known socialist, sociocritical authors of books for young adults, Lisa Tetzner and Kurt Held, used an accident in 1832 in their long-selling book *The Black Brothers* (1941), which was made into a TV

movie: a novel about the "living brooms" in Milan set within a framework of human trafficking, forced labor, and secret children's bands.

Bovenkerk, Frank, and Loes Ruland. "De schoorsteenvegers." *Intermediair* 20, 51 (1984): 23–39.

Bühler, Linus. "Die Bündner Schwabengänger und die Tessiner Kaminfegerkinder." *Schweizerisches Archiv für Volkskunde* 80 (1984): 165–82.

Fénix, Joseph Laurent. *Histoire passionnante de la vie d'un petit ramoneur savoyard, écrite par lui-même*. Lyon, 1994.

Mazzi, Benito. *Fam, füm, frecc – il grande romanzo degli spazzacamini*. Ivrea, 2000.

Mondada, Giuseppe. "Tra i nostri emigranti – gli spazzacamini." *Bolletino storico della Svizzera Italiana* 95 (1983): 9–21.

Cross-references: Austria; France; Germany; Italy; the Netherlands; Switzerland

AMERICAN WRITERS, VISUAL ARTISTS, AND MUSICIANS IN INTERWAR PARIS

Nancy L. Green

Since Thomas Jefferson and John Adams were sent to Paris to represent the young republic to the royal court, Americans have been visiting that city. In addition to statesmen and temporary travelers in Paris, it is estimated that between 1814 and 1848, some 500 to 1,000 Americans lived in the French capital on a more or less permanent basis. After the American Civil War and until the First World War, Americans continued to seek out European culture, going to France as part of an Americanized "Grand Tour" for the education of the well-to-do and sometimes staying on. Perhaps one of the best-known pre–World War I American writers in Paris was Edith Wharton. She settled there in 1907, became active in relief work during World War I, and was subsequently inducted into the French Legion of Honor. Henry James, who came often to visit her from England, where he lived, called Wharton the "pendulum woman" because of her regular trips back to the United States.

Indeed, many of the Americans in Paris throughout the 20th century have been "immigrants" of a particular sort: a better-heeled elite, very mobile in their transatlantic comings and goings. Wharton is one who chose life in the French metropolis (she is buried outside of Paris). The American "culture immigrants" as a whole, however long their stay in the City of Lights, represent a mixture of "Americanness," a critique of the same, and a cosmopolitan life of arts and letters.

The interwar period made famous by Gertrude Stein, Ernest Hemingway, F. Scott and Zelda Fitzgerald, Henry Miller, and so many others deserves special note because of the aura that has evolved around the expatriates who made

Paris their home during this period. Americans may not have been the most numerous nor were they the only cosmopolitan immigrant writers, artists, and musicians in the city. The British were more numerous, and other Americans were also present: "doughboys" (American soldiers) who remained after the war, businessmen setting up new ventures, and tourists. Living in Paris was cheap, and Prohibition was unthinkable in France. Yet the cultural immigrants of the Left Bank are those most remembered, and they have come to represent a particular comment on America itself. Wharton had already criticized "the long hypocrisy which Puritan England handed on to America." The "Lost Generation", as Gertrude Stein quipped, continued the search for a "new modernity" and engaged in an ongoing discussion about America itself.

Malcolm Cowley, both a participant in and biographer of this "literary odyssey," argued that the literary expatriates were indeed part of a "generation," but disagreed that they were "lost." Although they came from diverse backgrounds (albeit mostly middle class), they had started studying the "international republic of letters" even before their professors began preaching an abstract patriotism of world democracy as the United States prepared for entry into World War I. These sons and daughters of doctors, lawyers, and middling businessmen saw themselves as distinct from the elite of New England or the American South who had preceded them abroad. Many of them came to France after enrolling in the American ambulance corps, an experience that broadened the socially critical view of a generation of writers. What John Dos Passos, Ezra Pound, e. e. Cummings, Hart Crane, and others had in common was their engagement with the world of letters and a general sense of social change needed after the long, debilitating war.

The discussions started in New York's Greenwich Village; they continued in the cafés of Montparnasse: the Dôme, La Coupole, Le Sélect, and La Rotonde, where American writers and artists gathered with their French counterparts. Some, like the Fitzgeralds, alternated their stays in Paris with trips to the Côte d'Azur. Many of the American writers in Paris could be called "cultural workers" in that they paid their way as correspondents for newspapers such as the *Baltimore Sun*, the *New York Herald Tribune*, or the *Chicago Tribune*, sending home regular columns on literature, politics, society, or even horse racing news. (The last two newspapers also had their European editions: the Paris *Herald* and the Paris *Tribune*.) But even more important, the interwar cohort experimented in a host of new literary forms, publishing literary reviews that lasted several issues to several years if they were lucky: *Gargoyle, Broom, Secession, The Transatlantic Review, This Quarter, Tambour, The Little Review* (which had moved from Chicago to New York to Paris before folding), and *Exiles*. One of the longest lasting, *transition*, which sought "to present the quintessence of the modern spirit in evolution," published 27 issues from 1927 to 1939.

The American cultural immigrants were not all male or white or writers. Subsequent to Edith Wharton, an important generation of American women made their presence felt in Paris. They were booksellers and publishers such as Sylvia Beach, who founded the Shakespeare and Company bookstore and dared to publish James Joyce. They also established themselves as *salonières*, like Gertrude Stein with Alice B. Toklas, and Natalie Clifford Barney, and many were prolific writers in their own right: novelists, poets, journalists, critics, diarists: Stein, Djuna Barnes, Kay Boyle, Caresse Crosby, and Janet Flanner. Along with the Montparnasse cafés and Beach's lending-library, bookstore, and general gathering place at 12 rue de l'Odéon, the Stein and Toklas villa behind 27 rue de Fleurus, and Barney's apartment at 20 rue Jacob were important literary and artistic meeting places. An avid art collector since arriving in France in 1902 and friend of Picasso, Matisse, and others, Stein was also a novelist, poet, literary critic, and travel writer; her opera, *Four Saints in Three Acts*, was set to music by Virgil Thomson.

Indeed, key to the interwar culture was a mixing of literature and the arts, in the salons, the bookstores, and the literary reviews. It was also a mixing of French and Americans, interacting creatively. American composers such as Thomson, Herbert Elwell, Walter Piston, and Aaron Copland came to Paris to study with Nadia Boulanger. George Antheil's concerts were so avant-garde they sometimes ended in fistfights over their artistic merit. The French capital, home of the Ecole de Paris (itself a mixture of Russian Jews, Italians, and French artists), was also the place where American artists sought out the latest French trends, in inventive dialogue with the Cubists, the Surrealists, and others. Man Ray's first Paris exhibit was held in 1921, although the disappointing lack of interest in his paintings led him to become one of the most sought-after photographers in Paris. Gerald Murphy experimented with gadgets in his paintings, while Stuart Davis, who stayed but a year, captured Paris street scenes with his two-dimensional style. Alexander Calder's "mobiles" got their name from his French friend Marcel Duchamp.

The African Americans who came to Paris in the interwar years ranged from demobilized soldiers to writers, artists, and especially musicians. What Greenwich Village was to the white expatriates in Montparnasse, the African American art movement of the Harlem Renaissance was for the Left Bank black writers: a form of constant dialogue and argument with America. Langston Hughes, Claude McKay, and Gwendolyn Bennett did not come to Paris specifically to escape and criticize racism (as did African Americans in the 1950s), nor did they often end up staying beyond a year or several, but Paris made an impression on them. They wrote about "Paris noir" and inspired others to visit. Henry Ossawa Tanner, a well-known African American painter already in Paris before World War I, stayed on after the war and received the French Legion of Honor. The interwar black artists were influenced by their encounter with both French Cubism and African art. Some, such as Palmer Hayden and Archibald Motley, depicted the club life of Montmartre, while others were inspired by the African and Antilles worlds they met in the French capital. Hale Woodruff, Lois Mailou Jones, Nancy

Elizabeth Prophet, and Augusta Savage all made Paris home, and the French experience informed their art.

Montmartre developed as another center for Americans in Paris, particularly for the African American musicians. The numerous jazz clubs there provided jobs and were extremely popular with the French. Black musicians such as Opal Cooper and clarinetist Sidney Bechet came to play and stayed on. Eugene Bullard's nightclubs made him a central figure in the Montmartre African American community along with the singer Bricktop, who opened her own club. But it is Josephine Baker who came to epitomize the black American *artiste* in French eyes. Famous from her début in the "Revue nègre" in 1925 – immediately recognizable in her signature banana skirts – she later joined the Resistance and, after the Second World War, became a French star, always dressed in the latest Parisian fashion.

Black and white, male and female, wealthy and impecunious, in Montparnasse or on Montmartre, engaged in different forms of cultural activities, the American expatriates in interwar Paris were a diverse group. Several formed fast friendships and spent their Paris days together; many others participated only fleetingly in the American social life, or not at all. The expatriates were a separate group, and yet also integrated into Parisian life. American and French artists and writers crossed paths in Gertrude Stein's apartment; the Montmartre clubs drew the Fitzgeralds and other white Americans from the Left Bank along with enthusiastic French audiences. The Paris sojourn was also a productive encounter with French culture. Some of the literary reviews published half their articles in French. Others were vehicles for reading new French authors in translation; Beckett, for example, translated the Surrealists into English in *This Quarter*. The American writers were influenced by the French and other expatriates in Paris, from Proust and Valéry to the Dadaists and Surrealists to James Joyce. Perhaps the artists especially formed a truly cosmopolitan milieu, where language was not the necessary medium of exchange. Many came explicitly to study at the well-known French institutions such as the Académie Julien and the Ecole des Beaux Arts. Others were friends with and influenced by Jean Cocteau, Fernand Léger, Jean Miró, or Marcel Duchamp.

Ultimately, however, this crossroad of creativity came to an end. The Depression and the Second World War led to a two-stage exit of Americans from Paris. The stock market crash of 1929 and the subsequent economic crisis sent home those whose incomes depended on dollars. For those who remained into the 1930s, the outbreak of World War II sent most of them packing in haste. The myth would remain, however, and a next generation of Americans would come to Paris with Hemingway's *A Moveable Feast* in hand.

Allan, Tony. *Americans in Paris*. Chicago, 1977.

Benstock, Sheri. *Women of the Left Bank: Paris, 1900–1940*. Austin, 1986.

Cowley, Malcolm. *Exile's Return: A Literary Odyssey of the 1920s*. New York, 1934.

Fabre, Michel. *From Harlem to Paris*. Urbana, 1991.

Rotily, Jocelyne. *Artistes américains à Paris, 1914–1939*. Paris, 1998.

Stovall, Tyler. *Paris Noir: African Americans in the City of Light*. Boston, 1996.

Cross-references: France; European Elites on the Grand Tour in Early Modern Europe

ANGOLAN AND MOZAMBICAN LABOR MIGRANTS IN PORTUGAL SINCE THE 1970S

Cármen Maciel

In the last quarter of the 20th century, Portugal, traditionally a country with a high rate of emigration, became a significant destination for immigrants. These labor migrants came primarily from the former Portuguese colonies in Africa and today constitute the oldest immigrant communities in Portugal.

The Carnation Revolution in 1974 and the fall of the dictatorship in Portugal cleared the way for the decolonization of Angola, Mozambique, and other Portuguese colonies (in Africa: Cape Verde, Guinea-Bissau, São Tomé und Príncipe; in Asia: Portuguese India, Portuguese Timor). The sudden independence of the colonies in 1974–5, however, plunged the newly independent states, Angola in particular, into political chaos and extreme insecurity. Within several months, large numbers of people left the former colonies for the motherland.

Of those postcolonial migrants in Portugal characterized as *retornados* (returnees), only persons with Portuguese ancestry of the third degree or those born in the former colonies who had lived in Portugal for at least five years by April 1974 received Portuguese citizenship. The majority of black Africans did not meet these requirements. As a result of changes to Portuguese citizenship law in 1981, not even children born to African immigrants in Portugal were granted Portuguese citizenship.

Until the mid-1970s the number of immigrants from the colonies remained limited. The 1960 census registered 29,000 foreigners in Portugal, 22% of whom were from Brazil and 1.5% of whom were from Africa. Considerable migration from the Overseas Territories took place in the early 1970s: labor migrants from Cape Verde came to Portugal and replaced the growing number of Portuguese who emigrated to other European countries (mainly France and West Germany) to find work. Others, mainly from Angola and Mozambique, came to study at Portuguese universities. In 1980 almost half of the 58,000 foreigners in Portugal came from Africa, largely from Portuguese-speaking African countries (PSAC), with another 11% from South America (particularly Portuguese-speaking Brazil). Although the migration landscape in Portugal became more diverse from the late 1990s due to immigration from Asia, South America, and eastern Europe, the nearly 100,000 immigrants from the PSAC still represented 44% of the foreign population in 2001. Of these, Angolans made up the largest community (37,014) and Mozambicans the smallest (4,685). Portugal's foreign population increased to some 500,000 in 2004, with Cape Verdeans, Brazilians, and Angolans making up the main groups. The proportion of Mozambicans was by this point essentially negligible, likely because political and economic relations with South Africa intensified and Mozambique joined the British Commonwealth in 1995, leading to the establishment of other migration routes. These statistics, however, do not include illegal migrants, whose numbers increased when, from 1981 onward, the Portuguese government tried to restrict immigration by new entry and residence regulations as well as by the expulsion of foreigners.

In the 1990s amnesties were passed to provide legal status to immigrants who had entered or resided in the country illegally: this included almost 40,000 people in 1992 and another 35,000 in 1996. Since immigrants from the former colonies accounted for more than half of all legalized immigrants (72% in 1992 and 67% in 1996), the Portuguese government was accused of favoring these groups. Angolans were the largest group of legalized immigrants (21,783) and Mozambicans the smallest (1,173). Of African immigrants legalized in the 2001 amnesty, 46% were from Cape Verde and 36% from Angola.

Aside from the *retornados* in the second half of the 1970s, most migrants to Portugal from Angola came in the early 1980s and 1990s. These were mainly young men with average and below-average skills who wanted to escape the civil war in Angola and to find a job in Portugal. Approximately one-third of all Angolan immigrants between 1990 and 2002 came to Portugal because of family reunification.

The Memorandum of Understanding between the Angolan army and the military forces of the anti-Marxist UNITA in 2002 marked the end of 27 years of civil war in Angola. The Angolan government subsequently tried to stop emigration and adopted a framework program for repatriation. These measures had an effect, and the number of emigrants decreased, but the government's inability to stabilize economic and social conditions today still leads to the emigration of Angolans to Portugal, albeit in smaller numbers. Since 2002, the group has consisted equally of men and women of different ages, although the number of those of working age slightly predominates. The process of family reunification and the regularization of a sizable group of "illegal" children and youths in 1996, who then became included in official statistics, explain the extraordinary increase of the Angolan migrant population from less than 10,000 in 1991 to 37,000 in 2001.

Generally, Angolan immigrants came from the Angolan capital Luanda and other urban areas and speak only Portuguese. They live mainly in the Lisbon metropolitan area and, except for the small group of highly educated who arrived earlier, have semi- or unskilled jobs, whether in public works and building (men), manufacturing, or personal and domestic services (women). The great majority of the Angolans are Christian, particularly Catholic.

Although the flow of Mozambican immigrants lagged far behind that of Angolans, some similarities can be discerned. After the end of the *retornado* migration of the 1970s, several years passed until a continuous movement of families and individuals seeking employment in Portugal set in. Most of the migrants belonged to the Maconde ethnic group. Some were Indians (including those from the former Portuguese colony of Goa) and the confessional makeup of the group included Hindus, Muslims (including Ismailis), and Christians. Mozambican immigrants were generally better educated and more skilled than the Angolans, especially because a relatively high number of the Mozambican migrants of Indian descent were from either the middle or upper class. They work chiefly as professionals, traders, and civil servants or in services with ethnic characteristics, although there are also skilled workers, unskilled laborers, and independent business owners. Since a sizable part of this group is self-employed, Mozambicans are known as successful immigrants.

Migrants from Mozambique, as their Angolan counterparts, settled mainly in Lisbon, on the outskirts of the metropolitan area. Aside from African migrants of Indian descent, Mozambicans and Angolans are concentrated in run-down neighborhoods and social housing because of their scarce financial resources. Closed enclaves of African migrants have become common. African migrants of Indian descent, however, live dispersed throughout the city. The African migrants today have their own ethnic organizations and far-reaching social networks.

Only very few African immigrants marry in Portugal: the total number amounted to 137 Angolan and 58 Mozambican men and women (in equal proportions) in 2000. Although 90% of these couples included one Portuguese partner, the total number of exogamous marriages is far too small to be of any significance in assessing the social integration of the group.

African immigrants clearly benefit from their knowledge of the Portuguese language in the educational system. Their offspring currently represent 90% of all immigrant children in Portuguese schools. In elementary school, the performance of both African girls and boys is close to that of the natives, but in secondary school and university only Mozambicans (mainly men) approach the national average. Both Angolan and Mozambican children perform better than the children of migrants from other PSAC countries and have the lowest illiteracy rates.

African immigrants are generally associated with criminality and racism, but some studies indicate that public opinion is more favorable toward Angolans and Mozambicans than migrants from other PSACs. Angolans in particular, who are prominent in Portuguese society as a result of their associations and cultural activities, have encountered increasingly less racially motivated exclusion since the 1980s, which stands in contrast to the experience of Cape Verdeans, for instance. Angolan and Mozambican associations are mainly active at the local level, such as the Association of Angolan Residents of Odivelas or cultural and social organizations like the Portugal-Mozambique Association. There are some ethnic newspapers and magazines, mainly institutional ones like *Angola Informação*, published by the Angolan Embassy in Lisbon, and a number of restaurants concentrated in the metropolitan area of Lisbon. Angolans and Mozambicans occasionally organize cultural activities (meetings, expositions, or fairs), sometimes together with other groups from the PSAC.

Some circumstances complicate the integration process, especially for the second and third generations since children born to immigrants in Portugal do not possess Portuguese citizenship. This creates difficulties in terms of access to the labor market or in leisure, as sport teams, for instance, limit the number of foreign athletes who can play on a team.

While Mozambican immigration today has become rather insignificant, the number of Angolan immigrants in Portugal will likely continue to increase. The current stagnation of the Portuguese economy and growing unemployment, however, do not provide favorable conditions for the rapid integration of African migrants, who may face more and more problems in the future finding even unskilled positions.

Esteves, Maria, ed. *Portugal, país de imigração*. Lisbon, 1991.

Baganha, Maria, et al. *Is an Ethclass Emerging in Europe? The Portuguese Case*. Lisbon, 2000.

Pires, Rui. "A Imigração." In *História da Expansão Portuguesa*, vol. 5, edited by Francisco Bethencourt and Kirti Chaudhuri, 197–213. Lisbon, 1999.

Possidónio, Dora. "The Descendents of Angolans and Luso-Angolans in the Lisbon Metropolitan Area." *Finisterra. Revista Portuguesa de Geografia* (2004), no. 77: 39–58.

Cross-references: Spain and Portugal; Cape Verdeans in Western and Southern Europe since the 1950s: The Example of the Netherlands; Portuguese Labor Migrants in Western and Central Europe since the 1950s: The Examples of France and Germany; Portuguese *Retornados* from the Colonies in Portugal since the 1970s

ARMENIAN MERCHANTS IN RUSSIA SINCE THE LATE MIDDLE AGES

Tessa Hofmann

Permanent ethnic communities of Armenians, whose identity has been shaped since the fourth century by a separate Christian culture, a separate language and alphabet, and a distinctive literature and architecture, arose in the 11th century in Cilicia in southeastern Asia Minor as well as in the climatically favorable southern Crimea. The oldest Armenian inscriptions in Caffa (Feodosiya) date to 1027. The conquest of the Crimea in 1239 by the religiously tolerant Mongols promoted the influx of Armenians from the

expansive settlement areas in northern Asia Minor. In Caffa, the immigrant group possessed two Armenian-Apostolic churches and one Armenian-Catholic church as early as 1316. The Armenian-Catholic congregation was under the influence of the Genoese, to whom the Mongols had granted the trading monopoly for eastern and southern Crimea in 1267.

In close contact with the Armenian merchants on Crimea were the Armenian settlements along the lower reaches of the Volga, where the Mongols in 1235 and 1262 had settled numerous inhabitants of the northern Armenian trading and former capital city of Ani. Following negotiations with the Genoese consul in Crimea, they were permitted to move to the peninsula en masse in 1330. With an estimated half million inhabitants of Armenian origin, 46,000 of which were in Caffa alone, the Crimea was seen in some Western sources as Armenia maritima and the Sea of Azov as the Lacus armeniacus.

Especially from the settlement area of Crimea and from the Transcaucasus and Persia, Armenian merchants made their way via the Volga to the Khanate of Kazan and further, all the way to Moscow and Veliky Novgorod in northwestern Russia. So strong was their presence along this trade route that some chroniclers referred to it as an Armenian road. Kiev was home to Armenian merchants as early as the 10th century. Contacts between the Russian court and Armenian merchants intensified after Czar Ivan IV "the Terrible" conquered the Khanate of Astrakhan in 1556, thus initiating the southern orientation of the Muscovite state, and granted the Armenian community living there rights of free trade for the importation of "Armenian wares" – chiefly silk, precious stones, spices, incense, and other oriental goods.

At the beginning of the 17th century, Shah Abbas I established the Armenian trading company of Nor Jugha (Persian: Julfa), a suburb near his residence of Isfahan for up to 100,000 forcibly resettled Armenians from the territories of Nakhichevan, Van, and Yerevan; it became very important not only in the regional southern Russian region but also in the transit trade with silk between Persia, Russia, Sweden, and the Netherlands. Ten wholesale merchants of the company invested in the alliance with the Muscovite state in 1660 when, on the occasion of a visit to Moscow, they presented to Czar Alexey Michailovich, along with numerous other valuable gifts, a jewel-encrusted throne that can still be admired in the armory of the Kremlin in Moscow.

Beginning in the second half of the 17th century, merchants and manufacturers (together with Armenian church leaders and noblemen) from the trading colonies of Julfa, Astrakhan (e.g., the silk manufacturer Movses Sarafian), Moscow (e.g., the magnate Ivan Lazaryev), and Madras (Chennai; e.g., Iosif Emin and Shahamir Shahamirian) solicited political or even military support in Europe for the restoration of an Armenian state, or at the least Russian guarantees of protection. The latter did not succeed until October 1827, when Russian troops, with Armenian support, wrested from the Persians their previous Khanates of

Yerevan and Nakhichevan and incorporated them into the Russian Empire as an "Armenian government."

Under Empress Catherine II (1762–96), at the latest, who granted the Armenians from Astrakhan a special charter with the permission to establish the first Armenian-Apostolic bishopric in Russia, the Armenians were seen in Russia as capable merchants and entrepreneurs. In 1779, the empress, with the help of the newly appointed bishop of Astrakhan, Iosif Argutinskiy (Hovsep Arrutian), persuaded the Armenian population of Crimea to settle in her realm without restrictions. The prospect of extensive privileges, including the transit trade across Russian lands, was held out to the immigrants. The Armenians, who were initially slow to leave the Crimea, founded new cities and villages – which they called Nor (New) Nakhichevan – in the region around Rostov on the Don. Following the Russo-Turkish war and the conquest of Crimea in 1793, the special rights granted by Catherine II were transferred to the Armenians who had remained there or had returned.

By this time, an Armenian trading colony already existed in Moscow, where "a certain Armenian Avram" was first mentioned in writing in 1390 in the trading suburb of Kitaj-gorod (China city), which at that time already had an "Armenian section" and in the 16th century an "Armenian trading house." The first Armenian church in Moscow was erected in the 15th century between Ilyinka and Vavarka. In 1731, the East Georgian king Vakhtang IV, who was interested in an alliance with the Armenians, gave the Armenian community in Moscow land in the Georgian suburb for a new cathedral – the Uspenskiy Cathedral (Cathedral of the Assumption) still in use at the beginning of the 21st century – and a cemetery. Many Armenian merchants and manufacturers were economically successful as purveyors to the court and built their own houses, among them the Moscow silk manufacturer Zakhariaz Sheriman (Armenian: Sherimanian), who in the first half of the 18th century owned factories, houses, and land between Maroseyka and Myasnitskaya. The promotion of Armenian trading colonies in the Russian Empire in the 17th and 18th centuries, but especially the successful interlinking of Russia's mercantile interests with the political hopes of the Armenians, favored not only the economic development of the latter but also careers in the educational and cultural spheres and in service to the Russian state as interpreters, diplomats, and ministers (Interior Minister Count Mikhail Loris-Melikov [1880–1], Minister of Public Education Count Ivan Delyanov [1882–97]).

The first Armenian trading magnates elevated into the nobility in the middle of the 18th century came from the Lazaryev family (Armenian: Lazarian), which had migrated from Persia to Moscow; other ennobled Armenian families were the princes of Abamelek and Argutinskiy and the counts of Loris-Melikov. The Lazarevs owned numerous houses and factories in the center of Moscow as well as in Fryanovo in the Moscow area. The second half of the 19th century saw another wave of immigration by Armenian merchants, this time chiefly from the Caucasus and the Crimea. They opened shops and trading offices in the center of Moscow (Cherkaskiy pereulok and other streets of the Zaryadye neighborhood). Especially well known were the merchant families of Karamurzayev, Popov, Maslov, Boyajiyev (Armenian: Boyajian), the manufacturers Melikentsev, and the Lianosovs, who hailed from Astrakhan, had risen to become oil magnates in Baku, and had settled in Moscow and St. Petersburg.

With support from Armenian merchants and manufacturers, the Armenian trading colonies developed into centers of Armenian culture. The Lazaryevs, even more than the wholesale merchant family of the Djanumovs, made a name for themselves as patrons and benefactors. Their Moscow foundations included the church of Surb Khatch (1799) in an alley henceforth called Armyanskiy pereulok. Not far from the church, a higher language school donated by the Lazaryev family opened its doors in May 1815, initially as a three-grade *gymnasium*; its purpose was to train teachers and interpreters for government service, and alongside Armenian it taught Persian, Turkish, Arabic, and a number of European languages. From March 1928 it was called the Armenian Lazaryev Institute of Oriental Languages and it developed rapidly into one of the most important centers of Armenian education and Armenian studies in Russia. Attached to the institute were a boarding school and a printing shop, which between 1858 and 1864, in the new Armenian language and under the editorship of the philologist and orientalist Stepanos Nazarian, published the journal *Hyusisapayl* (Northern Lights), one of the most important periodicals of the Armenian enlightenment and "national awakening" or "rebirth" (*zartonk* or *veradznund*). The regular authors included the national-revolutionary democrat Mikayel Nalbandian. Among the prominent Armenian graduates of the Lazarev Institute were the poets Rafel Patkanian, Smbat Shahaziz, Gevork Dodokhian, Hovhannes Hovhannisian, and Vahan Tertsian (Ter-Grigorian), and the Armeniologists Mkrtitch Emin and Grigor Khalatian. Notable Russian graduates include the writers Ivan S. Turgenev, Yuri A. Veselovsky, and W. G. Lidin; the literary scholar D. D. Blagoy; and the stage director Constantin S. Stanislavskiy. The building of the Lazaryev Institute served as the House of the Culture of Soviet Armenia between 1921 and 1953, and since the dissolution of the Soviet Union in 1999 it has been the embassy of the second Republic of Armenia.

As in the Czarist Empire, during the Soviet period the Armenian communities in Russia, Georgia, and Azerbaijan were considered the "internal diaspora," with the difference that the tradition-steeped Armenian colonies of Soviet Russia were not permitted any official communal and cultural life. The many Armenian students in Moscow and St. Petersburg (Leningrad) were not even allowed to put on plays in Armenian. Armenian-Apostolic churches had to close because of the general repression of religion. The Armenian communities in Moscow and St. Petersburg, which had emerged out of the Armenian trading colonies, were revived only in the 1990s: the classicistic Armenian-Apostolic Church of St. Catherine (built 1771–9 by Yuri Velten) at Nevskiy Prospekt in St. Petersburg was returned to the community in 1992 and reconsecrated in 2000. By 1999, Moscow alone had about 15 Armenian organizations again; since 2000 they have been under the umbrella organization Union of Armenians in Russia. At the end of the 1980s, the majority of the just under 500,000 Armenians in Moscow, St. Petersburg, and other cities on Russian territory defined themselves as Russian citizens (*rossiyanye*) of Armenian descent. They regarded the refugees pouring into the communities from the war-torn and crisis regions of Azerbaijan, Georgia, and Central Asia as "un-Armenian," since they were strongly assimilated to their respective majority society. Following the collapse of the Soviet internationalism ideology and correspondent education, the attitude of the Russian society toward immigrant communities from former Soviet republics dramatically deteriorated in the 21st century: while Russian opinion polls revealed intolerance against immigrants from Caucasian and Central Asian countries, Armenians became targets of xenophobic and racist hate crimes in the megapolitan cities of Moscow and St. Petersburg.

At the beginning of the 21st century, the traditions of the Armenian trading colonies in Russia are probably most alive in the northern Siberian Republic of Yakutia. Although the ethnic Armenian community there is still small, because of the extraction of and trade in raw precious stones, it can be considered wealthy and also politically influential. Unlike the elite of the Armenian diaspora, which often has a critical attitude toward the political leadership of Armenia, the Armenian community of Yakutia sees itself as the medium for consolidating relations between Russia and Armenia, whose post-Soviet economy is based not least on the importation and processing of raw precious stones from Russian lands.

Arutyunyan, Yuri. "Armenians in Moscow." In *Immigration and Entrepreneurship: Culture, Capital, and Ethnic Networks*, edited by Ivan Light and Parminder Bhachu, 259–79. New edition, New York, 2004.

Galkina, Tamara A. "Contemporary Migration and Traditional Diasporas in Russia: The Case of the Armenians in Moscow." *Migracijske i etničeske teme* 22, 1–2 (2006): 181–94.

Petrosyan, Amalia, Albert Isoyan, and Kostandin Khudaverdyan, eds. *Hayern ashkharum*. Yerevan, 1995.

Suny, Ronald Grigor. "Eastern Armenians under Tsarist Rule." In *The Armenian People from Ancient to Modern Times*, vol. 2, edited by Richard G. Hovannisian, 109–37. New York, 2004.

Troebst, Stefan. "Die Kaspi-Volga-Ostsee-Route in der Handelskontrollpolitik Karls XI.: Die schwedischen Persien-Missionen von Ludwig Fabritius 1679–1700." *Forschungen zur osteuropäischen Geschichte* 54 (1998): 127–204.

Cross-references: Russia and Belarus; Southeastern Europe; Ukraine

ARMENIAN REFUGEES IN FRANCE SINCE WORLD WAR I

Tessa Hofmann

The genocide perpetrated by the regime of the nationalist Turkish party İttihat ve Terakki Cemiyeti (Young Turks) against the 2.5 million Armenians in the Ottoman Empire during and shortly after World War I claimed 1.5 million lives, according to contemporary estimates by the German embassy in Constantinople (Istanbul). Initially about 700,000 Armenians escaped the murder in 1915–17 by fleeing into neighboring Iran and the Russian Empire or by surviving death marches in the Middle East (northern Syria, northern Iraq, Lebanon). The invasion of the Turkish military into the eastern Transcaucasus in 1918 and 1920, which was accompanied by massacres, and the fighting of Turkish nationalists under Mustafa Kemal against Great Britain and France as the mandate powers of the Armenian settlement area of Cilicia in southeastern Asia Minor triggered further waves of refugees between 1919 and 1921. At the end of 1921, France, which had taken 105,000 survivors from Syria and Lebanon to Cilicia with the promise of making it a "secure homeland" for Armenians, evacuated 54,451 Christians from that area by train and boat, 40,000 of whom were Armenians of the Orthodox confession. Another 60,000 Christians fled by land.

The history of the intensive, but by no means conflict-free, relations between the Armenians and the French goes back to the Armenian principality and later small Kingdom of Cilicia (1080–1375), which prospered from transit trade under the protective umbrella of the neighboring crusader states; in 1342, Guy de Lusignan (Armenian: Lusinyan), a Frankish Catholic, acceded to the Armenian throne. Scattered Armenian immigrants are described in France since the 12th century. Permanent Armenian trading colonies arose from the end of the 17th century in Paris, Montpellier, and above all in Marseille, after the port city had developed into an international center of free trade. Between 1672 and 1683, the city was home to the print shop of the Armenian-Apostolic bishop Oskan Yerevantsi (Oskan of Yerevan), which played an important role in Armenian intellectual history. As early as 1666–8, the bishop printed the first Armenian Bible in Amsterdam and sent a copy to the French "Sun King" Louis XIV, who in response granted him a personal audience and gave him permission to move the print shop to Marseille. In 1810, a chair for Armenian studies was established as the École des Langues Orientales in Paris, and Armenian periodicals were published in France from the 1850s on. France was a magnet especially for intellectuals and exiles of the Armenian independence movement in the Ottoman Empire. In 1885, the educator, publisher, and founder of the first Armenian political party, Mkrtich Portugalian, launched from his exile in Marseille the party organ *Armenia* (until 1923), the purpose of which was to promote the "national awakening."

In spite of the cultural and political importance of France, especially for the Ottoman-ruled Armenians (Western

Armenians), their number in France remained small until 1914, at around 4,000. The stream of refugees, chiefly from the former mandate area of Cilicia, swelled that figure to 60,000 by 1926. The refugees were mostly laborers and artisans, to a lesser extent merchants and intellectuals. Marseille, the port of entry for many refugees, and Paris remained the centers of Armenian settlements, followed by Lyon and Nice.

The social status of the Armenian refugees, denaturalized in Turkey by law in 1923 and 1927 and stateless since that time, was initially precarious. Until the global economic crisis of 1929, 90% of Armenian refugees in France worked in industry. After that time, French Interior Minister Pierre Laval introduced the "primacy of nationals," which was supposed to drop the percentage of foreign workers to 10%. As a result, many Armenians tried to become self-employed craftsmen or shopkeepers, mostly in the suburbs of Paris with their more affordable rents. The commercial sectors preferred by the Armenians were – as they had been in their country of origin – manufacturing, processing, and trade in textiles (manufacture of clothes, hosiery goods, rope making) and the printing industry. Some Armenians were able to set themselves up as doctors. Self-contained Armenian villages arose in Alfortsville, Issy-les-Moulineaux, and Arnauville, which offered some protection in the 1930s against the xenophobia of extreme right-wing French nationalists.

During the German occupation of France between 1940 and 1944, the Armenians in France participated in the antifascist resistance through the Secret Armenian National Front. Of particular importance was the partisan group of the communist and workers' poet Misak Manouchian which operated in the Paris area. Manouchian had emigrated to France in 1925 as an orphan and a survivor of the genocide, and he saw Germany not only as the occupier of France but also as the co-perpetrator of the genocide as the former wartime ally of the Ottomans: "The politics of imperialist Germany in the past and of Hitler Germany today are the roots of the massacre of the Armenian people in 1914–1918 and today of the boundless misfortune of the peoples of Europe. When I throw my hand grenade, I ease my conscience."

The progressive assimilation since the end of World War I was and is seen by many Armenians in France as a threat to their ethnic identity. Eighty percent of the Armenian church weddings in Paris, Marseille, and Lyon are now mixed marriages, whereas before World War II, the Armenian community was characterized by endogamy. The speed with which the ethnic Armenian community is assimilating has been mitigated merely by the constant influx of Armenians from the Middle East following the civil war in Lebanon (1975–9), the ongoing crisis in Lebanon, the occupation of northern Cyprus by Turkey in 1974, and the Gulf Wars, 1980–8, 1990–1, and 2003. Added to this was the arrival of Armenians from the Republic of Armenia (*hayastantsiner*) since it became independent in 1991.

Since the 1970s, the self-confident third generation of refugees has become increasingly conscious of its roots. By contrast, the first and especially the already integration-willing

second generation were subject to strong pressure to assimilate. French officials and employers imposed French names. For example, Shahnour Aznavourian became the singer Charles Aznavour, the Russian Armenian Lev Tarasov (Armenian: Levon Torosian) became the writer and member of the Academy Henri Troyat, Garnik Zoulamian became the painter Carzou, and Achod Malakian the director Henri Verneuil. Shanour Kerestejian, who came to Paris from Istanbul in 1923 and wrote French poetry without any substantive reference to Armenia under the pseudonym Armen Lubin, published his major work *Nahanj arants yergi* (Retreat without Song) as Shahan Shahnour. Through the fate of Petros, who soon changed his name to Pierre, the novel recounts the alienation of the second immigrant generation after the genocide as the story of an unsatisfying, conflict-ridden relationship with the French woman Nanette, without sparing any details of the intimate life of the protagonists. With this provocation, misinterpreted as pornography within the conservative Armenian ethnic community, the author wanted to point to the double standard morality of the Franco-Armenians: clinging to patriotic phrases that have become hollow while at the same time assimilating as quickly as possible to French majority society and its values.

Many refugees were initially convinced that their stay in France would be temporary. As many as 10,000 Franco-Armenians followed the call of the Soviet Union in 1946–7 to "repatriate" into a Soviet Republic of which they knew nothing, and which became for most a shocking disappointment of their ideas of a strongly idealized "historical homeland." Most "remigrants" left Soviet Armenia in 1956 after France had negotiated permission for their return with the Soviet government.

Given the loyalty of the Armenians in two world wars, but also in consideration of the potential Armenian vote, French politicians of all parties at the municipal and later the national level have responded to the demands by Armenian and French organizations that the genocide in World War I, denied by Turkey since 1923, be acknowledged. In Marseille, a street was named after the victims of "24 April 1915" as early as 1973. The demands by the Armenian population, repeated over many years, also led to the erection of a monument to the victims of the genocide. This recognition policy reached its climax, in spite of vociferous protests by Turkey, when President Jacques Chirac signed a bill on 29 January 2001, which stated: "France publicly recognizes the Armenian genocide of 1915." On 12 October 2006, the French National Assembly passed a corresponding law that made denial of the genocide of the Armenians punishable. However, it takes effect only if it is also approved by the Senate and the president.

At the beginning of the 21st century, the naturalized Franco-Armenians define themselves overwhelmingly as French citizens of Armenian descent with an autonomous cultural identity, and they see it as their task, in spite of criticism of the political leadership in Armenia, to provide moral, political, and financial support to Armenia and Nagorno-Karabakh: "Origin and confession are important, but if you are Armenian then help Armenia, just as the Armenians in France and the US are doing!" (Charles Aznavour).

While language and the Armenian-Apostolic Church, which goes back to the year 301, have traditionally unified the Armenian diaspora, both have slowly lost their ability to create identity and provide national cohesion as a result of growing pressure to assimilate and increasing secularization. In the 20th century, their place was taken by the perception of the modern history of the nation as the community of fate of descendants of genocide victims.

Adalian, Rouben. "The Historical Evolution of the Armenian Diasporas." *Journal of Modern Hellenism* 6 (1989): 81–114.

Hofmann, Tessa. "Diaspora, Migration und Sprache: Am Beispiel der Armenier in Deutschland." In *Die armenische Sprache in der Diaspora*, edited by Jasmine Dum-Tragut, 37–57. Graz, 1997.

Hofmann, Tessa, and Gerayer Koutcharian. "Die Armenier in Frankreich." *Pogrom* 20 (1989), no. 146: 41–3.

Koutcharian, Gerayer. *Der Siedlungsraum der Armenier unter dem Einfluß der historisch-politischen Ereignisse seit dem Berliner Kongreß 1878: Eine politisch-geographische Analyse und Dokumentation.* Berlin, 1989.

Cross-references: France; Southeastern Europe; Russia and Belarus; Armenian Merchants in Russia since the Late Middle Ages

ASHKENAZIM IN EUROPE SINCE THE EARLY MODERN PERIOD

Stefi Jersch-Wenzel

At the dawn of the early modern period, both Sephardic (Sephardim) and Ashkenazi (Ashkenazim) Jews had been living in Europe for several centuries. While the Sephardim settled chiefly in Spain and Portugal and in the Mediterranean region (including North Africa), the East-Frankish German realm, "Ashkenaz" in Hebrew (derived from Genesis 10:3), that is, the region of France and Germany, formed the initial settlement area of the Ashkenazim. After the final expulsion of the Jews from France in 1349, whose existence there had been precarious for some time, Germany was more strongly equated with Ashkenaz in Jewish eyes. The term "Ashkenazim" now referred to all Jews who followed this branch of the religion from western Europe to Poland, from northern Italy to Hungary. The Ashkenazim differed from the Sephardim in the development of separate customs, the tight organizational structure of the community, and the heroic story of "kiddush hashem," the sanctification of the Holy Name through martyrdom during religious persecutions. The emphasis in their teaching and study was on Talmud and biblical exegesis, while the Sephardim devoted themselves also to secular sciences such as medicine, mathematics, astronomy, and languages.

Migration from the 15th to the 18th century

Although the German realm, unlike England, France, Spain, or Portugal, did not experience a general expulsion of the Jews in the Middle Ages, most likely because of its territorial fragmentation, numerous persecutions of the Jews led to early migration movements to east-central Europe. Beginning with the massacres of Jews during the crusades, Ashkenazim joined the eastward trek of German settlers to Poland as early as the 12th and 13th centuries. This exodus intensified in the wake of the bloody persecutions during the plague epidemic of 1348–9, which the Jews were accused of having caused by poisoning the wells. It reached its height during the 15th century, when nearly all larger cities and many of the largest territories expelled their Jews. Urban Jewish communities survived only in Frankfurt am Main, Worms, and Friedberg, though with restricted rights. The destination of the migration was initially northern Italy, but then increasingly and on a large scale Poland and Lithuania.

In the late 15th and well into the 16th centuries, Jewish expulsions occurred also in other European regions, for example, the Muscovite Empire, that is, Russia, the large cities in Switzerland, in parts of Hungary, and in some of the northern Italian cities. The Jews remaining in Germany changed from being largely urban to being rural and scattered. They settled in hundreds of villages in the territories of imperial counts and knights, often in groups of only a few persons, and they survived in part as cattle and grain dealers, in part as organizers of the trade between the city and the countryside. Exceptions were Jewish settlements in smaller towns, from where the temporary stay in a nearby, larger city for the purposes of trading was possible: for example, Fürth with access to Nuremberg, Deutz with access to Cologne, or Danish Altona with access to Hamburg. The rural settlement structure developed at this time also in Lower Austria and – with the exception of Prague – in Bohemia. It remained dominant until the middle of the 17th century. Very few Jewish religious communities were established, and the learning that was so highly esteemed from a religious perspective stagnated.

By contrast, new and favorable living conditions developed for Ashkenazi Jewry in Poland and Lithuania. As early as 1264, Prince Bolesław the Chaste had issued a privilege of admission for the Jews of Greater Poland, which King Kazimierz III the Great extended to Lesser Poland in 1334 and later to the entire realm. All subsequent Polish kings affirmed these privileges, which for four centuries formed the foundation for the general legal status of the Jews. The most important guarantees concerned the free exercise of religion, the self-governance of the communities, including Rabbinic jurisdiction, royal jurisdiction for their persons and property, and unrestricted economic activity.

The immigration from central and western Europe that followed, chiefly from Germany, grew in size throughout the late 15th century and continued throughout the entire 16th century. According to estimates for 1500, about 18,000 Jews lived in Poland and 6,000 in Lithuania; in the first half of the

17th century the total had already risen to nearly 500,000, which accounted for 5% of the total population. Initially they settled on royal lands (cities or leaseholds), but the weakening of the central power and the rise of the Polish nobility (*szlachta*) led to scattered settlement as early as the 16th century. Noble landholders increasingly founded their own cities in order to obtain, along with city rights, market rights and jurisdiction over their property, and they granted separate privileges to Jewish immigrants. The result was a multitude of different privileges, though their basis was always the original: personal protection for the Jews and respect for their communal autonomy.

Royal and seigneurial authorities desired the immigration of Ashkenazim into the overwhelmingly agrarian, underpopulated land largely for economic reasons. The Jews were initially active chiefly as money lenders to the king and the *szlachta*, but they soon shifted to trade in goods, specifically trade at fairs and in cattle and grain, and they supplied the population in the emerging small cities, market towns, and villages with nonagrarian products. In the cities they also formed a substantial share of craftsmen, unlike in Germany. Since they were not admitted into the Christian guilds they set up their own, which also took on social and religious functions. On the landed estates of the nobility, leases, which were increasingly left in their hands as time went by, constituted their most important livelihood. That holds for tax collecting, bridge tolls, mills, alcohol distilleries, and the taverns that went with them.

Since the largely poor rural population often fell behind in their payment of dues, the Jews, in their capacity as collectors, were often seen as exploiters, who allegedly impounded "the grain still green on the stalk" and who also enticed adolescents into consuming alcohol, thereby weakening their ability to earn a living. In the cities, too, where they filled important functions of an urban bourgeoisie between citizen-farmers (*Ackerbürger*) and the nobility or king, their position was nearly always contested. Fear of competition, economic behavior that was not guided chiefly by what Werner Sombart called the "idea of providing the necessities" (*Idee der Nahrung*), as well as religious and linguistic otherness created a latent antipathy toward them. Added to this were the protests of the Catholic Church, which was very strong in Poland, against tolerating believers of another faith.

Still, the time from the arrival of the Ashkenazim in Poland up to the middle of the 17th century is often referred to as the "Golden Age" of their history. Beginning in the 15th and 16th centuries, they developed a system of self-governance that was unparalleled in Europe. The basis was the community, the *kahal*. Its functions were comparable to those of a city magistracy, before which it represented the religious and economic interests of the community's members. The *kahal* was responsible for all internal and external affairs of its members and had to allocate the tax levied on the community to individual members and collect it. Superimposed on the communities on a regional level were the territorial councils, as

the umbrella organization for which the Council of the Four Lands – sometimes referred to as the "Jewish sejm" – was set up in 1582. The representatives of the four provinces of Greater Poland, Lesser Poland, Ruthania (Red-Ruthenia), and Volhynia (Lithuania established a separate territorial council in 1623) were chiefly charged with allocating the tax payment that the Jews as a whole had to pay. The council also dealt with economic, administrative, and religious issues, as well as educational guidelines and aspects of the well-developed system of social welfare. Until the 18th century, a flourishing learning that arose on this foundation and followed in the tradition of Talmudism remained the defining characteristic of Ashkenazi Jewry. In religious services and study, their language was Hebrew; in daily life, Yiddish, which was based on Middle High German and developed further through the incorporation of Hebrew and Slavic loan words.

The uprising of the Cossacks and Ukrainian peasants against the Polish magnates and the Jews as their alleged instruments, which began in 1648, triggered the downfall of the aristocratic republic as well as of the autonomous Polish Jewry. The massacres among the Polish and above all the Jewish population, which escalated into warlike clashes between Russia, Poland, and at times also Sweden, claimed the lives of at least 100,000–125,000 Jews. Although the loss of population could be made up in subsequent generations by a very high birthrate with a comparatively low infant mortality, many communities had been destroyed and the self-evidence of Jewish life had been permanently shattered by a 20-year threat to its existence. The *kahal* and the Council of the Four Lands also lost influence among the secular authorities as forms of protective self-governance and mouthpieces for the Jewish community.

The growing pauperization of the Jewish masses, the exploitation of community members by their leaders which had now begun, and the intellectual rigidity of the rabbis created fertile soil for messianic and mystical movements, which found numerous followers especially in the eastern parts of Poland-Lithuania. Positively fanatical were the followers of the Kabbalist Shabbetai Zevi, who declared in 1648 that he was the long-awaited Messiah, the messianic king by whom redemption would be proclaimed in 1666. The Shabbatian movement that arose spread rapidly, and even as far as Germany, and retained followers above all in Poland until the middle of the 18th century; here Jakob Frank declared himself the new Messiah and Shabbetai Zevi's successor in 1755 and also attracted numerous followers.

However, these movements could not match in sustainability and duration the mass movement of Hasidism, which originated around the middle of the 18th century, also in Poland, with the rabbi Baal Shem Tov and still exists today. In Hasidism, the place of learning and asceticism are taken by ecstatic prayer and life-affirming joy. It was a form of popular piety directed against the rabbinic oligarchy, though it can also be seen as a social movement of the poor and uneducated but pious mass of Jewry that spread from southern Poland to Ukraine, Belarus, Lithuania, and central Poland. It led to constant, intense conflicts with the rabbinic Orthodoxy and the governing representatives of the *kahal*. Hasidism found virtually no followers in western Poland and in Germany.

Already since the Cossack uprising and the subsequent wars, there was a remarkable remigration of Jewish refugees from Poland to central and western Europe. Although here, too, a messianic mass movement in the form of Shabbatianism had been emerging for a number of years, only a few small sects remained of it into the 18th century, while the majority of the Jews turned away from the mysticism of the Kabbalah. The Ashkenazim coming from eastern and east-central Europe, especially from Poland, did not arrive by any means in flourishing political entities, since large parts of Europe were suffering from the effects of the Thirty Years' War. Still, they encountered comparatively orderly – if strongly restricted – living conditions. In Germany, small and minuscule territories and smaller cities were still the predominant places of settlement, though with the rise of absolutist political structures, princely residences became places where the Jews' experience in financial dealings and the trade in goods proved useful. Although they were never incorporated into the policy of repopulating depopulated regions, Jews slowly regained access to the larger cities as tolerated individuals provided with letters of protection so they could provision the courts and generally invigorate trade. Although the prohibition against settlement remained in place in France, Alsace was part of France from the second half of the 17th century, and Ashkenazi Jews had been living there for centuries – though not unchallenged – chiefly in rural communities and had seen a steady growth through immigration in spite of restrictions on permits and very high levies by the state and the Church.

The northern provinces of the Netherlands, the union of the Estates-General, became home in the second half of the 16th century first to Maranos, that is, forcibly converted Sephardic Jews from Spain, who within a short period of time established several communities and built synagogues. Several decades later Ashkenazim from Germany also migrated to the Dutch Republic, followed within a few years by Polish Jews, who also established their own communities and erected synagogues, though they were combined into a single community in 1673. The chief settlement sites were initially Rotterdam, the Hague, and especially Amsterdam, where about 22,000 Ashkenazim lived in 1795, and later also smaller cities and villages. Here, too, there were restrictions on their economic activities, although the Sephardim were very successful especially in the first few decades in inland and overseas trade, while the Ashkenazim were initially active in retail trade and later in diamond cutting and the diamond trade. The traditional image is that of successful and respected Sephardim concerned with outward representation, contrasted against comparatively poor Ashkenazim who clung to their traditional Jewish way of life. Over time, however, this image did not comport with the social reality.

No Jews had been living in England since the expulsion in 1290, except for a few Jewish doctors invited into the country. As in the Netherlands, Sephardim were the first to settle there beginning in the late 16th century, and they responded in an almost hostile manner to the Ashkenazim who followed them and whom they regarded as a threat to their own position. Still, as early as the middle of the 17th century the Ashkenazim in London had a synagogue with rabbis of German background and other communal institutions. About the same time Ashkenazim also began to migrate again to Switzerland, coming from Alsace, the Palatinate, Boden, and in smaller numbers also from Poland.

At the end of the 17th century, central and western Europe were thus home again to a noteworthy Ashkenazi Jewry, though estimates of its size exist only toward the end of the 18th century. As already noted, settlement was almost everywhere diffuse and scattered. Yet Jewish life slowly developed, existing under special laws and aware of the latent anti-Jewish attitude of the Christian population. In the lands of the German Reich, Jewish life was aided by the emergence, over the course of the 17th century and after, of territorial Jewries (*Landjudenschaften*) in nearly all territories large and small. Although they were not autonomous institutions like the Council of the Four Lands in Poland or the organized Jewries in Bohemia, Moravia, and especially Prague, they did form supra-local bodies for both internal Jewish issues and for relations with the respective authorities. All in all, about 60 such territorial Jewries arose between 1662 and 1765; they were responsible for allocating and collecting the taxes imposed on the Jews, but they also settled all internal Jewish matters.

Alongside the emergence of these territorial Jewries, another development was taking shape: in the larger territories whose rulers were following the idea of the absolutist state, new Jewish communities were established or existing ones expanded beginning in the late 17th and especially in the 18th century. In the wake of the centralization of the state administration, protective privileges granted to individuals were now replaced with general privileges for all the Jews living in a dominion. They contained precise regulations about the permitted, restrictive living conditions for the Jews and interfered in communal autonomy. Exceptional regulations were found for the – sometimes highly privileged – court Jews, who in nearly all central European residential cities supplied the courts with money and luxury goods, provisioned the armies, and also leased state monopolies such as the minting of coins. In these always risky enterprises they benefited from their extensive business contacts – for the most part based on kinship connections – in various European countries.

The mass of the Jewish population, however, lived – in very restrictive legal conditions – from moneylending and pawnbrokering, from trade in goods permitted to them, and not least as peddlers and rag dealers. Religious practice was based on the traditional forms derived from the rules of *halachah*, which comprised the 613 commandments and prohibitions, and adherence to which determined all areas of life. Only slowly did Jewish scholars, especially rabbis, turn to secular sciences out of intellectual curiosity, especially to the natural sciences. They studied mathematical, medical, astronomical, and philosophical texts and for this purpose learned modern European languages. Unlike the situation among the Sephardim, who began to assimilate the culture of their environment through the acquisition of secular knowledge, the studies of the Ashkenazim initially had no effect on Jewish religion and philosophy and especially on Jewish life. That changed only with the emergence of the *Haskala*, the Jewish Enlightenment.

Against the ardent opposition of the traditional rabbinate, young Jewish intellectuals, most of them self-taught, began to turn to the educational ideal of the Prussian–northern German enlightenment. That included placing religion on the foundation of reason, which meant explaining Judaism as a religion of reason, not revelation. One of their important goals was to introduce High German as the language of daily life and culture, and to "purge" Hebrew as the language of religion from Yiddish, which was now seen as a kind of slang. The turn toward the sphere of German language and culture has often been referred to as the end of the "Jewish Middle Ages," and it constituted the beginning of the most profound transformation within Ashkenazi Jewry since its existence. The *Haskala* spread in a modified form via Austria also to Poland and Russia, where it led to controversies within the Jewish communities well into the 19th century, especially with the Hasidim. In variants that were specific to each country it also had a lasting effect in England, France, the Netherlands, Switzerland, and northern Italy.

Migration in the 19th and 20th centuries

As this intra-Jewish process of change was getting under way, the Polish Jews experienced the end of the state in which they lived when Poland was partitioned among Russia, Prussia, and Austria. Around the time of these annexations, the Jewish population in the partitioned territories was nearly a million, 200,000–250,000 of which fell under Austrian, around 160,000 under Prussian, and 500,000–550,000 under Russian rule. At this time Austria was already home to nearly 160,000 Jews, 150,000 of whom lived in the crown lands, in Bohemia, and in Moravia; Prussia had around 100,000 (with a further 70,000 in other German territories), while Russia, following several expulsions, had only scattered settlements of Jews. The final partitioning of the territory of the former Polish state that was agreed upon at the Congress of Vienna in 1815 lasted until the reestablishment of Poland after World War I. After that, Prussia had only the relatively small western portion of the land left (West Prussia and the area of the future Prussian province of Posen), with its 65,000 Jewish inhabitants; Austria retained Galicia (slightly enlarged in the north) with 250,000 Jews; Russia, meanwhile, annexed all the remaining territory of the former Polish state from Lithuania to Belarus, Ukraine, all the way to the Black Sea. The Kingdom of Poland, linked to the czars in personal union,

was established in a relatively small area around Warsaw. At this time, between 600,000 and 700,000 Jews lived in Russia's share of partitioned Poland.

The measures adopted in the various polities to incorporate the Jews legally and administratively were aimed at the abolition of Jewish communal autonomy (already weakened in some areas), the acquisition of secular education, the public use of a non-Jewish "high language" (in Prussia and Austria, German), the adoption of fixed family names, and a change in economic behavior. The Jewish *Patent* for Galicia in 1789, the *General-Juden-Reglement* for southern and New-East Prussia (Polish: *Prusy Nowowschodnie*) in 1797, and the Czarist Statute for the Jews in 1804 displayed various articulations of a comparable tendency. Freedom of movement was severly restricted for Jews; in the Russian partition territory it was even prohibited outside of the "settlement region." Although these regulations, if adhered to, did accord the Jews some civic rights, for the mass of the respective Jewish populations, and especially for the growing number of followers of Hasidism, they constituted a threat to their religiously determined world, whose strict rules they had been able to follow undisturbed for centuries.

Although the majority of Jews, who were able to settle again in central and western Europe only shortly before, continued to live as devout Jews, they were exposed to constant control by the authorities and intervention in the community's powers in most countries, although at times they themselves turned to the authorities if it appeared that conflicts within the community – say, over the election of elders or rabbis – could not be resolved. On this basis, constrained but not existentially threatened, they organized their life in partly externally imposed, partly self-chosen residential neighborhoods, set up the institutions necessary for the religious community, spoke their own idiom (West Yiddish), and maintained the necessary business contact with the Christian population. In this situation, representatives of the late Enlightenment, most of whom served in higher positions in government and whose arguments tended to be reality-based rather than philosophical, developed a different stance toward the Jews. It was consistent with their humanitarian goals grounded in natural law, combined with state law and etatistic considerations, to grant the Jews gradually the rights of citizenship – depending on the level of their "civic improvement," that is, assimilation – in order to integrate them into the existing social order. These considerations had their counterpart on the Jewish side in the ideas of the representatives of the *Haskala*, the Maskilim, who – with varying degrees of intensity – questioned the absolutely obligatory nature of Jewish ceremonial law and pushed emphatically for a broadly based secular education, and – as its prerequisite – the use of the respective national language.

This meeting of the minds between representatives of the late Enlightenment and of the *Haskala* in the last two decades of the 18th century began the process of Jewish emancipation, which extended in most European countries over nearly a century. On both the Christian and the Jewish sides it was accompanied by vociferous literary and scholarly disagreements, whereby the front lines of the debate tended to run within the two camps rather than against each other. While the non-Jewish side introduced traditional stereotypes, depending on the given political constellation, to prevent the Jews from being given civic equality at that time or at least not full equality, the central point of discussion on the Jewish side was the question of whether emancipation would lead to a loss of identity for the Jews. The result was the emergence of a reform Judaism in central Europe, with a radical wing, a moderately conservative to liberal Judaism, and – since the middle of the century – a neo-Orthodox current. All these factions of Ashkenazi Jewry eventually received civic equality: in France as early as 1791, in the French-dominated Batavian Republic in 1795–6 (fully realized in the Kingdom of Holland in 1806), in Germany and Austria between 1867 and 1871, in Great Britain in 1858, in Italy between 1861 and 1870, in Hungary in 1867, in Switzerland between 1866 and 1874, in the Kingdom of Poland in 1862, and in Russia not until February 1917, on the eve of the March Revolution.

During this process, which extended over decades, profound changes occurred within Ashkenazi Jewry: while the Jews in Galicia and in the Pale of Settlement remained largely committed to tradition and belonged to the poorer strata of the population, the Jews in central and western Europe began to develop into a permanent element of the urban bourgeoisie, thanks to the loosening and eventual abolition of restrictions on their economic activity. Since they had been living for centuries in a less secure state, it was easier for the Jews than for the old-established Christian bourgeoisie to adapt to the competitive capitalism that began with industrialization and to the flexibility and mobility it demanded. Initial attempts by governments to steer them more strongly toward crafts and agriculture had no lasting success. Instead, what transpired was a transformation from small and makeshift traders to middle-class merchants, from small moneylenders to bankers, or – in the textile sector, for example – from putting-out agents to early industrial entrepreneurs. This process was already in the first half of the 19th century accompanied by an increasing internal migration from small into medium-sized and large cities, where economic initiatives in the areas of trade, industry, and services were in demand. The acceptance of the Jewish fellow citizens by the Christian population was the greater, the less an urban structure was dominated by notables or a patriciate, and the more immigrants of diverse background were able to shape the changing urban landscape.

This change did not concern the Jews remaining in the countryside, in small villages, or in small towns. Among them, overseas migration emerged in the first half of the 19th century as an alternative to stagnating rural or small-town life under still constrained legal living conditions. In times of crisis – for example, the great crop failure in Germany in 1846 and the subsequent years of economic decline and stagnation until 1848 – about 26,000 of these Jews, chiefly from the Prussian eastern province of Posen and from Bavaria left in the wake of the first peak of a general German emigration. That was more than 6% of all the Jews who were living at this time in the German Confederation. Comparable waves of emigration occurred also in England, France, and northern Italy. They were repeated in the second half of the century, though without ever turning into a mass emigration. Rather, a majority of the Jews of central and western Europe were able, from the middle of the century, to advance socially into the economic and educational bourgeoisie, though service in government remained closed to them for a long time.

The development in east-central and eastern Europe was different. To be sure, under the influence of the industrialization that was taking place there also, a Jewish bourgeoisie and a secularly educated Jewish intelligentsia formed in parts of the Kingdom of Poland and in a few Russian provinces. However, expulsion orders and denials of residency permits, specifically in the central Russian governments, time and again impeded a continuous evolution. When all existing restrictions on settlement were abolished with the grant of near civic equality to the Jews in the Kingdom of Poland in 1862, there was a strong influx of Jews from the Russian Empire. The repeal of immigration restrictions into northern Italy, Bukovina, and Vienna, led to strong migratory movements also in the Habsburg realm after 1867. Jewish migrants from economically stagnant Galicia, from Bohemia, and from Moravia migrated into northern Hungary, Bukovina, and above all Vienna, whose Jewish population rose from 6,000 in 1857 to 175,000 in 1910. A mere 40,000 Jews from Poland, Russia, and Galicia came to Germany between 1870 and 1900. They settled above all in Prussia, Saxony, and Bavaria. During the same period nearly 300,000 made their way to Great Britain, though about 200,000 of those continued onward to North America with help from Jewish aid organizations. With the "Aliens Act" of 1905, the further immigration of east European Jews to England was reduced to a minimum.

This phase already saw the brutal pogroms in southern Russia (1881 and 1882), in the wake of which the largest wave of Jewish emigration from east-central and eastern Europe began. The trigger for the violence was, in addition to a deeply rooted, latent anti-Semitism, an economic crisis for which the Jews were blamed. During the even more brutal pogroms from 1903 to 1906, the Jews served as the object of aggression for both the growing revolutionary movement and for the government under pressure from it. By 1914, around 2.5 million of them had left, but so had a large part of the Galician Jews living in poverty.

The first destination for many was Germany, but because of its restrictive controls on transmigrants, it remained for the vast majority merely a transit country for emigration to the USA. Because German was virtually the lingua franca in many eastern and east-central European origin regions, the Jewish migrants expected an easy integration. There were also familial and economic ties to Germany, which gave them reason to hope that it would be easier to create a new life there. But the Jews who were already settled in Germany, faced with the mass of mostly impoverished fellow Jews who seemed to live up to the stereotype of the gibberish-talking Jews haggling for a living, were afraid that the limited integration they had won after a protracted struggle was in danger. This was all the more so because in the 1870s the hostility toward the Jews that had been grounded for centuries in religious and economic arguments receded into the background and a racially justified anti-Semitism was gaining ground. As a milestone, scholars usually point to the Berlin anti-Semitism controversy of 1879–80, which was triggered by Heinrich von Treitschke's essay "Unsere Aussichten" (Our Prospects, 1879) published in *Preußische Jahrbücher*, and led to a vast flood of writings. The anti-Semitic movement originating in Germany spread rapidly in Austria, Hungary, and France, and under different conditions also in Russia as well as in other eastern and southeastern European countries.

In the face of this threat as well as a feeling of otherness toward the immigrants, who were soon referred to as "Eastern Jews" and the majority of whom still lived firmly within the Jewish religious tradition, extensive and widely branching organizations and institutions were set up to look after the transmigrants and finance their passage, chiefly to North America, but also to Argentina and South Africa. The necessary funds came in part from Jewish welfare institutions, in part also from wealthy individuals. In Austria, Great Britain, and France as well, the existing organizations were concerned with providing aid for onward migration and not with measures to help the Jews integrate.

Parallel to the great wave of emigration, a national-Jewish movement, Zionism, arose, most concretely in Russia, but also in other European countries. Basic to the idea was the awareness of a separate "Jewish nationality," which was to find expression in national self-determination and at least cultural autonomy. The movement was initiated and carried by young Jewish intellectuals and a broadly organized Jewish working class that had emerged – unlike in central and western Europe – in the wake of industrialization. In spite of struggles within the movement over its direction, and opposition from Jews willing to assimilate, from Orthodoxy, and from the Hasidim, the ideas of Zionism spread rapidly, specifically among the younger generation in Europe. The official founding act of the Zionist movement is generally considered to be the First Zionist Congress in Basel in 1897 organized by Theodor Herzl, Oskar Marmorek, and Max Nordau, which, as a supraparliamentary institution, declared that its goal was a homeland for the Jews in Palestine that was protected by public law. The originally homogeneous Ashkenazi Jewry was fragmented into numerous currents, something Zionism did not cause but did accelerate; in part these currents existed side-by-side, in part they clashed vehemently.

Conversions to Christianity and withdrawals from Judaism also characterized Jewish life. The degree of acculturation in education and culture was at a comparably high level among the Orthodox, the moderate conservatives, the

liberal, the reform-oriented, and the radical reform current of Ashkenazi Jewry in central and western Europe, but also in Bohemia, Moravia, and Hungary. Differences were apparent especially in how closely everyday life followed the religious laws and what shape was given to the ritual of religious services. An added distinguishing characteristic in east-central and eastern Europe was the maintenance of Yiddish as the lingua franca, and from the end of the 19th century also as a modern literary language. The focal points of economic activity cannot be assigned to specific religious currents. Rather, in this regard the factor of geography was crucial. While a narrow Jewish upper class of wealthy Jews and a broad mass of petty merchants, artisans, and wage laborers existed in Poland, Russia, and Romania, a Jewish middle class remarkable in its size and economic importance had formed in neighboring countries to the west and southwest. Here, too, there existed a Jewish upper class and a Jewish petty bourgeoisie and the poor in need of support, established merchants, small-scale industrialists, representatives of the liberal professions, or the scientists and teachers who were slowly making their way into government service. They had a significant share in the general artistic and scientific production in Europe, whereby in Poland, in particular, Yiddish theater and literature also blossomed.

This Ashkenazi Jewry, richly diverse religiously and socially integrated in various ways, found itself confronted, in the first decades of the 20th century, by an anti-Semitism that was growing in most European countries, made its appearance in an aggressive and organized fashion, and was hardly combated by the respective governments. It was directed against a Jewish population that had grown by the 1920s to more than 9 million, for the most part because of a birth surplus. Since the emergence of smaller nation-states after World War I, that population was dispersed among approximately 20 countries. More than half lived in Poland (2.8 million), Russia (2.6 million), and Romania (1.1 million). Next came Germany (564,000), Hungary (473,000), Czechoslovakia (354,000), Great Britain (286,000), Austria (225,000), France (160,000), Lithuania (155,000), the Netherlands (115,000), Latvia (94,000), Yugoslavia (64,000), Belgium (50,000), Italy (45,000), Switzerland (21,000), and the Scandinavian countries (14,000). Virtually the only overseas migration in the period from 1915 to 1931 came from eastern and east-central Europe. However, its magnitude was now only a third of the wave between 1881 and 1914 (around 740,000), since the USA had radically reduced immigration quotas in 1924. In the quota system introduced that year, no more than 10,000 Jews from eastern and east-central Europe could immigrate, while the annual number in the years before World War I had been 100,000. In addition, the Soviet authorities were reluctant to grant exit permits. Other destinations outside of Europe were South America and, with 115,000 migrants, the British mandate of Palestine. Since England, as already mentioned, pursued a very restrictive immigration policy and Germany was almost exclusively a transit country, France, especially, became the destination of the intra-European immigration of Jews from eastern and east-central Europe. By 1939 their number was around 75,000, which accounted for 40% of all the Jews living in France. They settled almost exclusively in Paris.

Beginning in 1933, the Jews in Germany were stripped of their civic rights through the state-ordered anti-Semitism of the National Socialist regime. Their "civic death" was pushed through increasing restrictions and prohibitions on the exercise of certain professions, through a revocation of full citizenship by the Nuremberg Laws (1935) on largely racial grounds, and through countless special laws and decrees, with the goal of forcing the Jews into emigration. With the annexation of Austria in 1938 and the establishment of the Reich Protectorate of Bohemia and Moravia, this policy of exclusion was implemented there also. After the outbreak of World War II, it was then extended to all areas occupied by Germany, thus also to Poland with the largest Jewish population in Europe. The pogrom in November 1938 was followed by the large-scale material dispossession of the Jews through the "Aryanization" of their property, which was linked to the permission to emigrate, an emigration that was now nothing more than flight. Estimates put the number of emigrants from all of Europe at 500,000 between 1932 and 1945.

Those who stayed suffered an almost complete exclusion from all spheres of life. However, no large-scale exodus took place from Germany or the occupied territories. The reasons for this were, on the one hand, the subjective attachment, specifically on the part of the German Jews, to what they felt was their real and cultural homeland, and, on the other hand, the strict restrictions on admission in destination countries, especially the USA. Well known are the protracted and yet often futile attempts by Jews to procure at a relatively late date an immigration certificate for one of the few countries willing to take them in. Those unable to flee fell victim to the "Final Solution of the Jewish Question," i.e., they were murdered. After the death of 6 million Jews (the overwhelming majority of whom were Ashkenazim), traces of their centuries-long history in Europe are today found in only very few regions. In modified form that history lives on in Israel and the USA.

Battenberg, Friedrich. *Das europäische Zeitalter der Juden. Zur Entwicklung einer Minderheit in der nichtjüdischen Umwelt Europas.* Darmstadt, 1990.

Dubnow, Simon. *Weltgeschichte des jüdischen Volkes von seinen Uranfängen bis zur Gegenwart*, vols. 6–10. Berlin, 1927–1929.

Elbogen, Ismar. *Ein Jahrhundert jüdischen Lebens. Die Geschichte des neuzeitlichen Judentums.* Frankfurt am Main, 1967.

Haumann, Heiko. *Geschichte der Ostjuden.* Munich, 1990.

Hilberg, Raul. *The Destruction of the European Jews.* 3rd ed. New Haven, 2003.

Kotowski, Elke-Vera, Julius H. Schoeps, and Hiltrud Wallenborn, eds. *Handbuch zur Geschichte der Juden in Europa.* 2 vols. Darmstadt, 2001.

Cross-references: The Baltic Region; Czechia and Slovakia; France; Germany; Great Britain; Italy; Poland; Russia and Belarus; Southeastern Europe; Switzerland; Eastern European Jews in Berlin from the Late 19th Century to the 1930s; East European Jews in Germany since 1990; Eastern European Jews in London since the Late 19th Century; Eastern European Jews in Paris since the Late 19th Century; Forced Laborers in Germany and German-occupied Europe during World War II; Galician Jews in Austria from the 18th to the Early 20th Century; Jewish Refugees from Nazi Germany and from German-Occupied Europe since 1933

AUSSIEDLER/SPÄTAUSSIEDLER IN GERMANY SINCE 1950

Barbara Dietz

The term *Aussiedler* was coined in the early 1950s as the influx of German minorities from east-central and southeastern Europe and the Soviet Union continued after the flight and expulsion during the immediate postwar years had come to an end. The Constitution of the Federal Republic of Germany (Article 116, paragraph 1) guarantees the admission of these persons as German citizens: "Unless otherwise provided by a law, a German within the meaning of this Constitution is a person who possesses German citizenship or who has been admitted to the territory of the German Reich within the boundaries of December 31, 1937 as a refugee or expellee of German ethnic origin or as the spouse or descendant of such person."

Decisive for admission as *Aussiedler* are the "German ethnicity" of the immigrants and the "expulsion pressure" in their county of origin. These criteria were formulated shortly after World War II, when millions of Germans fled or were expelled from territories east of the Oder and Neiße rivers. The German Federal Law on Expellees (*Bundesvertriebenengesetz*, BVFG), passed in 1953, has regulated the conditions of admission for this group of immigrants. A major modification of the BVFG in connection with the 1993 Law on Dealing with the Consequences of the War (*Kriegsfolgenbereinigungsgesetz*) led to a change in terminology. Since that time, German immigrants from east-central and southeastern Europe and from the successor states of the Soviet Union have been called *Spätaussiedler* (late ethnic repatriates). The discussion that follows uses only the term *Aussiedler*, which here encompasses both groups.

The Federal Republic was pursuing primarily ethnic and political goals with the admission of *Aussiedler*. According to the view of the West German governments, the German minority in eastern Europe was threatened by an "expulsion pressure" after 1950, that is to say, by a state policy of ethnic discrimination. Against this background, *Aussiedler* were guaranteed admission to West Germany. However, the policy of taking in *Aussiedler* must also be seen within the context of the East-West conflict. The actual or potential immigration of *Aussiedler* from states east of the iron curtain could be understood during the cold war as a rejection of the Socialist social order and tallied up as a vote for the

Aussiedler on the platform of a West German border station, 1965 (*ullstein bild*).

liberal-democratic constitution of West Germany. This special background places the immigration of *Aussiedler* in line with the ethnically and politically motivated migrations by other minorities, for example, the migration of Jewish citizens from the USSR to Israel, or that of Black Sea Greeks from Ukraine, Russia, and Kazakhstan to Greece.

It is notable that the influx of *Aussiedler* affected almost exclusively West Germany, while the GDR attracted few migrants from the German minorities in east-central and southeastern Europe and the Soviet Union. The reason was not only that the GDR was comparatively less willing and would admit immigrants from German minorities in the Socialist "brother countries" only as apart of family reunification; the *Aussiedler* themselves preferred West Germany because of its democratic political system and economic stability.

While the migration of *Aussiedler* played no major role in the immigration that took place in Germany up to the end of the East-West conflict, a result of barriers to emigration in the countries of origin, this changed with the opening of the iron curtain. As *Aussiedler* began arriving in large numbers, they became a significant immigrant group in Germany in the 1990s. Unlike labor migration, which is initiated by economic motives, the immigration of *Aussiedler* was determined largely by ethnic and political factors, which have also significantly influenced the integration of this group.

The immigration of Aussiedler: *its background, motives, and development*

The historical background to the immigration of *Aussiedler* leads far back into the history of European migrations. Between the Middle Ages and the 19th century, several waves of settlement had taken migrants from the German-speaking lands to east-central and southeastern Europe as well as to Czarist Russia. The result were larger, German-speaking settlement areas in what are today Poland, Romania, and Hungary, and what were formerly Yugoslavia,

Czechoslovakia, and the Soviet Union. Toward the end of the 19th century, the essentially peaceful coexistence of the German minorities with the nation-states and with other ethnic groups in the host countries was made more difficult by national and nationalist ideologies that were becoming increasingly important in politics and daily life.

In the 20th century, political upheavals and two world wars initiated by Germany destroyed the basis of existence for the German minorities in eastern Europe. During and after World War II, Nazi Germany's policy of aggression and occupation caused large segments of the German minorities living in east-central and southeastern Europe and the Soviet Union to be stripped of their rights and expelled or forced to take flight. The ethnic Germans who remained had to suffer legal discrimination and social ostracism until the 1970s. However, the assimilation process that has prevailed since then has led to the extensive social integration of the group in east-central and southeastern Europe and the Soviet Union.

When the exodus of the *Aussiedler* got under way in the 1950s, the desire to live as "Germans among Germans" was front and center among the proclaimed motivations behind the migration. Responsible for this sentiment was the trauma of the deportation among the Germans in the Soviet Union, who in 1941 had been taken from the Volga Republic, southeastern Ukraine, and the Transcaucasus chiefly to Siberia and Kazakhstan, as well as the experience of ethnic discrimination in Poland and Romania. Moreover, many Germans were afraid of losing their mother tongue, their religious ties, and their cultural traditions and saw in emigration the only way to preserve their ethnic identity. In addition, the desire to reunite families played a major role, since the war and later the iron curtain had separated many of them. Although economic motives – that is to say, sharing in the West's higher standard of living – were mentioned in a number of cases, until the end of the 1980s they were of comparatively minor importance, since the *Aussiedler* were not doing badly at all, compared to the rest of the population, in the regions from which they departed.

The political upheaval in eastern Europe at the end of the 1980s led to a change in the motivation behind emigration, a change that resulted largely from the development of the exodus into a mass migration. It carried along a good many people who believed that Germany would offer a politically freer and economically better life. Family unification, however, continued to rank very high, and it reinforced chain migrations in the 1990s. Economic motives moved increasingly to the fore, the result of the crisis-riddled economic development in the countries of origin.

In the countries of origin, therefore, economic crises, processes of social disintegration, ethnic discrimination, and political instability promoted the exodus, while the guarantee of admission and Germany's economic and political security constituted a potent and growing attraction. A tendency to return to their original home was evident only among *Aussiedler* from Poland, who took advantage of the right

Aussiedler in the transit camp Friedland in Lower Saxony, 1988 (*ullstein bild*).

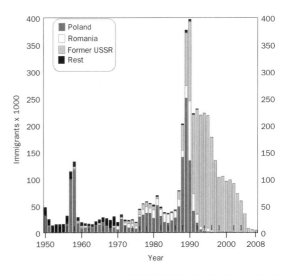

Figure 1. Immigration of *Aussiedler*, 1950–2006. *Source: Bundesverwaltungsamt.*

of *Aussiedler* to keep their previous citizenship, created the basis for a new life through work or professional qualifications in Germany, and for the most part lived as dual citizens in Poland after their return. Here one could discern, not least due to Poland's accession to the European Union, the first signs for the development of transnational networks, which manifested themselves, for example, in circular, short-term migration for gainful employment and in the emergence of dual residences in the country of origin and in the destination country.

Until the opening of the iron curtain, *Aussiedler* had to overcome large bureaucratic obstacles in their countries of origin before they were allowed to leave. As a result, the numbers of those who left the most important countries of origin – Poland, Romania, and the Soviet Union – were comparatively low: between 1950 and 1987, a total of 1.36 million *Aussiedler* came to Germany. This situation changed fundamentally with the collapse of the political systems in the states of east-central and southeastern Europe and the dissolution of the Soviet Union. The gradual lifting of restrictions on leaving opened the way for the *Aussiedler* to come to Germany.

All of a sudden, the Federal Republic of Germany, which for many years had demanded that the states of eastern Europe permit their citizens to leave, was confronted by a dramatic surge of *Aussiedler*: the number of immigrants rose from 78,000 *Aussiedler* in 1987 to 202,000 in 1988, and it reached its postwar peak in 1989 and 1990 with 377,000 and 397,000, respectively. Between 1988 and 2004, a total of 3 million *Aussiedler* came to Germany, of which 2.2 million hailed from the former USSR (see Figure 1).

The West German government responded to the dynamic development of the influx of *Aussiedler* primarily by trying to guide and limit it through changes in bureaucratic procedures, for example, the Law on the Admission of *Aussiedler* of 1 July 1990, and especially the Law on Dealing with the Consequences of the War (*Kriegsfolgenbereinigungsgesetz*, KfbG) of 1 January 1993. Until the passage of the KfbG, the general assumption was that all "ethnic Germans" in the named regions had suffered discrimination because of their ethnic identity. The KfbG retained this assumption only for applicants from successors states of the USSR, while all others had to offer individual proof that they had suffered discrimination. In addition, the KfbG set the annual quota for new arrivals at around 225,000 *Aussiedler*, a number that was revised downward on 1 January 2000 to 100,000 immigrants per year. Moreover, the law stipulated that only members of the German minorities in east-central and southeastern Europe and the former Soviet Union who had been born by 31 December 1993 could file an application for recognition as *Spätaussiedler*.

The establishment of a quota for immigrants caused the influx of *Aussiedler* to stabilize at a high level (about 220,000 annually) and led to a shift in the countries of origin to the successor states of the Soviet Union (95% of all *Spätaussiedler*, mostly from Russia and Kazakhstan). The years 1996 and 1997 posted the first, marked decline in the immigration of *Aussiedler* since the middle of the 1980s (see Figure 1). The primary reason for this was the introduction in the summer of 1996 of a test of an applicant's knowledge of the German language in the country of origin to prove his or her ethnic status (this did not apply to accompanying family members of non-German origin). Since the German minority in the former Soviet Union had little competency in the German language, the language test – which could not be retaken – constituted de facto a barrier to immigration. Recognition as *Spätaussiedler* is impossible for the approximately 50% of applicants who failed the language test.

247

The notice of admission to an applicant could also include spouses who did not belong to the German minority – provided the marriage had lasted at least three years at the time of the departure – and children from binational marriages. While in 1993 a comparatively high percentage (74%) of all *Aussiedler* were themselves applicants and thus of German origin, that number declined by 2004 to less than a fifth (19%). Since 1 January 2005, when the Immigration Law took effect, the non-German spouses and the children of applicants must also pass a language test, which has led to a further decline in the inflow of *Spätaussiedler*.

Aussiedler *in Germany: integration into the labor market and society*

Since the beginning of the immigration of *Aussiedler*, it was a political goal in Germany to ease and promote the integration of this group, something that had already been laid down programmatically in the immediate postwar period for refugees and expellees. Along with the granting of German citizenship to *Aussiedler*, this attitude led to the privileged admission of this group of immigrants.

As the number of *Aussiedler* rose in the 1990s, the policy of promoting the integration of *Aussiedler*, which had supported a relatively successful integration of this group up to the end of the 1980s, could no longer be financed on the scale that had been guaranteed until then. The federal government justified the substantial cuts it made to the subsidies for integration by pointing to the generally higher burdens and demands occurring in the economic and social spheres (among other things as a result of German reunification). In spite of this, special social support programs continued to characterize the integration of the *Aussiedler*. The government's aid package consisted of an integration subsidy of up to six months in cases of unemployment, an accelerated recognition of schooling and vocational training completed in the countries of origin, as well as social security payments in accordance with German social security law. Special subsidies were available for young *Aussiedler* to aid their integration into school, work, and society. For the reasons listed earlier, these integration subsidies were noticeably curtailed in the early 1990s; for example, language courses were cut back to six months.

However, it became clear in the 1990s that *Aussiedler* – just as labor migrants from the former "recruitment countries" – were no longer integrating into the labor market as easily and successfully as they had been, and that disintegrative tendencies were also becoming apparent in the social realm. In part, the explanation for this must be seen against the background of cuts in integration subsidies, but in part it was also the result of a change in the countries from which this immigrant group came and of the group's social and cultural characteristics in the early 1990s. Beginning at that time, the *Aussiedler* came overwhelmingly from the Soviet Union or its successor states that were wracked by economic and political crises. They had received their schooling and

occupational training in Russian, had been socialized in the (post) Soviet system, and had no links to German language and culture. Moreover, as mentioned earlier, there was a strong rise in the proportion of accompanying family members, most of whom came without any knowledge of German.

The economic integration of *Aussiedler* who arrived before German reunification in 1990 was comparatively successful. The situation in the labor market was favorable for this group of immigrants. Individual factors, like the lower average age compared to the age of the German population, and its occupational structure, which was characterized by a heavy emphasis on skilled trades and factory jobs, supported their occupational integration. Not least, the integration of the *Aussiedler* into the labor market was helped by the willingness of these immigrants to take jobs for which they were overqualified, and by the federal government's policy on vocational and professional qualifications.

Beginning in 1992, the labor market in Germany became less favorable, and this weakness persisted for a number of years. The reasons were economic, but also the result of an increase in immigration, not least by resettlers from the former GDR. This development was unfavorable to the occupational integration of the *Aussiedler*. In addition, the effort of these migrants to make a new beginning in the labor market was severely hampered by their lack of language competence, ignorance of the economic and social systems in the Federal Republic, and vocational and professional qualifications that did not meet the requirements in their new country. And the shortened language training, now only six months, was not sufficient to allow the new immigrants to establish themselves professionally in a way that reflected the qualifications with which they arrived. An added problem was that *Aussiedler* who had arrived since the 1990s were rarely able to work in their previous fields without additional training. Occupational reentry was especially difficult for those who had worked in the technical, information technology, or service fields. Here one could also feel the increasing competition in the German labor market, which affected especially *Aussiedler* and foreigners (particularly the second generation of the former guest workers).

Although there are no separate statistics about unemployment among the *Aussiedler* (because they are German citizens), a number of studies have shown that *Aussiedler* have a much higher risk of unemployment than the German population without a migration background. Female *Aussiedler* are especially hard hit. To a far higher percentage than men, they had worked in their countries of origin in professions (organizational and administrative jobs; social and educational jobs) they could no longer pursue without a good knowledge of German and additional qualifications. As a result of these difficulties in the labor market, *Aussiedler*, and especially the women among them, often had to change professions when trying to make a new beginning and/or accept jobs with lower levels of qualifications.

With respect to social integration, until the beginning of the 1990s it was assumed in Germany that *Aussiedler* would go through the process without major frictions – despite warnings from experts that *Aussiedler* of ethnic German origin, while Germans, were also at the same time immigrants. It was widely believed that a rapid integration into German society could be expected because the *Aussiedler* were German in origin and identity. While it is true that at that time there were few indications for a social segregation of *Aussiedler*, tendencies toward a social withdrawal were evident. For example, in many cases the contact that *Aussiedler* had to the native population was limited to the workplace, whereas in the private sphere they remained among themselves in their families or among their acquaintances from their countries of origin. Given their experiences with life in the formerly Socialist countries, family solidarity and reciprocal support within the circle of friends and acquaintances was far more important to *Aussiedler* than to the native population. *Aussiedler* often felt that social relationships in West Germany were individualistic and marked by strong competitive thinking.

One characteristic of the influx of *Aussiedler* is that this group of immigrants is clearly differentiated according to countries and regions of origin when it comes to German language skills, socialization, and confessional and cultural affiliation. *Aussiedler* from Poland, Romania, and the Soviet Union or its successor states developed noticeably distinct patterns of integration. For example, those from Romania already arrived with good German language skills, which considerably eased their economic and social integration. By contrast, among *Aussiedler* from the Soviet Union and its successor states, especially those who arrived after the beginning of the 1990s, tendencies of segregation were apparent, reflected in the use of Russian in everyday life and in exclusive contacts among one another.

From the late 1980s on, most *Aussiedler* who came to Germany already had relatives and acquaintances in that country who had left before. Hence there was among the new arrivals a widespread desire to move to the place or at least the state where relatives and acquaintances were living. As a result, strong concentrations of *Aussiedler* emerged in various states in certain communities or cities. The growth of these centers of settlement was promoted by the network of immigrants as well as developments in the housing market. As a frequently low-income group, especially after the sharp cut in integration subsidies, *Aussiedler* were largely locked out of the free housing market and were dependent on the allocation of subsidized or affordable housing. In the mid-1990s, one source of such housing, for example, was apartments and houses that became vacant with the departure of British, American, or Soviet troops. This led to the creation of self-contained settlements of *Aussiedler* from the Soviet Union or its successor states around former Allied bases. As a consequence, the spatial segregation among *Aussiedler* reached dimensions similar to what was found among other migrant groups in Germany. The mobility of *Aussiedler* out

of subsidized and into free-market housing, which was still evident at the beginning of the 1990s, largely ceased to exist after the mid-1990s.

Where *Aussiedler* from the Soviet Union or countries of the Commonwealth of Independent States lived in concentrated settlements, they created their own infrastructure. This is especially apparent in the use of the Russian vernacular, but also in forms of social behavior brought from the countries of origin. Interactions with the natives led not infrequently to reciprocal demarcation and exclusion, which increasingly separated the *Aussiedler* from the native population. Whereas *Aussiedler* in the previous decades had still voiced the desire to assimilate as rapidly and thoroughly as possible, that was no longer so consistently the case from the 1990s on. Conversely, the native population often denied that these immigrants were "German." Especially among *Aussiedler* from the Soviet Union or its successors states, natives noted with irritation that they frequently spoke Russian in everyday life and that they clung to consumer habits and behavior they had brought with them from their countries of origin.

The *Aussiedler* made up for the lack of integration into native neighborhoods, institutions, and circles of friends primarily by focusing on the network of familial relationships. Following the departure from their home countries, the family represented the most important emotional point of reference for *Aussiedler* in a foreign environment, and it was the group with whom they shared experiences of daily life in their countries of origin. That is also where intrafamilial structures had taken shape that often differed considerably from family structures in Germany. *Aussiedler* families saw themselves as a community whose generation-spanning cohesiveness was of existential importance to the individual family members. In intrafamily discourse, the authority of parents and grandparents was generally accepted, and the distribution of roles between men and women followed traditional patterns. *Aussiedler* families who came to Germany in the 1990s seemed self-contained and closed off to the outside, an impression that was further bolstered by the increasing use of Russian within the families. All indications suggest that young *Aussiedler* had a particularly difficult time getting accustomed to Germany from the 1990s on. Their German language competency was low and their schooling and vocational training were not accepted as equal in Germany. They often lived in isolated settlements among other *Aussiedler*, and their families were often in the low-income group. This marginal social position brought these young people into competition and conflict with young people in Germany who were in a comparably disadvantaged position, primarily young foreigners of the second and third generations.

In retrospect it can be noted that the immigration and reception of *Aussiedler* in Germany was heavily determined by (minority) politics. However, the influx of *Aussiedler* changed profoundly through the end of the East-West conflict and through the economic and political transformations in their countries of origin. From the beginning of the 1990s, at the latest, it became clear that *Aussiedler* constitute a special group within the spectrum of immigration in Germany, a group which – in spite of its privileged admission as German citizens – has had problems with integration that are comparable to those experienced by other immigrant groups.

Bade, Klaus J. *Ausländer–Aussiedler–Asyl: Eine Bestandsaufnahme.* Munich, 1994.

Bade, Klaus J., and Jochen Oltmer, eds. *Aussiedler: deutsche Einwanderer aus Osteuropa.* 2nd ed. Göttingen, 2003.

Brandes, Detlef. "Die Deutschen in Rußland und der Sowjetunion." In *Deutsche im Ausland – Fremde in Deutschland. Migration in Geschichte und Gegenwart,* edited by Klaus J. Bade, 85–130. Munich, 1992.

Dietz, Barbara. "Aussiedler in Germany: From Smooth Adaptation to Tough Integration." In *Paths of Integration: Migrants in Western Europe (1880–2004),* edited by Leo Lucassen, David Feldman, and Jochen Oltmer, 116–36. Amsterdam, 2006.

Dietz, Barbara, and Heike Roll. *Jugendliche Aussiedler – Portrait einer Zuwanderergeneration.* Frankfurt am Main, 1998.

Herwartz-Emden, Leonie, ed. *Einwandererfamilien: Geschl echterverhältnisse, Erziehung und Akkulturation.* 2nd ed. Göttingen, 2003.

Münz, Rainer, and Rainer Ohliger. "Long-Distance Citizens: Ethnic Germans and their Immigration to Germany." In *Paths to Inclusion: The Integration of Migrants in the United States and Germany,* edited by Peter Schuck and Rainer Münz, 155–202. New York, 1998.

Silbereisen, Rainer K., Ernst-Dieter Lantermann, and Eva Schmitt-Rodermund, eds. *Aussiedler in Deutschland. Akkulturation von Persönlichkeit und Verhalten.* Opladen, 1999.

Cross-references: Germany; Russia and Belarus; Allied Military Personnel in Germany since the End of World War II; German Refugees and Expellees from Eastern, East-Central, and Southeastern Europe in Germany and Austria since the End of World War II; German Settlers in Russia since the 18th Century; Greek Settlers from the Black Sea Region in New Russia since the Early Modern Period and Pontic Greeks in Greece since the End of World War II; Portuguese Labor Migrants in Northwestern Europe since the 1950s: The Examples of France and Germany; Spanish Labor Migrants in Western, Central, and Northern Europe since the End of the World War II; Turkish Labor Migrants in Western, Central, and Northern Europe since the Mid-1950s

AUSTRIAN PROTESTANTS (*LANDLER*) IN TRANSYLVANIA SINCE THE 18TH CENTURY

Mathias Beer

The collective term *Landler* has developed to describe the descendants of around 4,000 deported Austrian crypto-Protestants, a term used both by outsiders and these descendants themselves. These Protestants were "transmigrated" in the 18th century from core lands of the Habsburg monarchy to Transylvania, predominantly into the communities of Neppendorf, Großau, and Großpold north of Hermannstadt. The contemporary word "transmigrated" points to a special case of religiously motivated migration. It combines deportation (circumventing the freedom of faith and emigration laid down in the Peace of Westphalia) and colonization. The "transmigration system," instituted by the Catholic Viennese court under Emperor Charles VI and elaborated under Empress Maria Theresa, combined the cleansing of the Austrian heartlands of "Lutheran heretics" through forced resettlement with the grant of religious freedom and settlement that was driven by economic considerations. Despite their varied regional origins, the newcomers unexpectedly developed a group identity in the settlement regions. It found expression, among other things, in a shift in the meaning of *Landler*. As early as the 18th century it established itself as the term of origin for a segment of the deportees to Transylvania, and it slowly developed into a group name for all "transmigrants," irrespective of their regional origins.

The deportations, which initially targeted a limited number of "ringleaders" and their families, began in the Salzkammergut in the early summer of 1734. On short notice and without being told about their destination, the first transmigrants were put on ships in Linz. Sailing along the Danube under military escort, they reached the port of Titel on the Theiß River by way of Klosterneuburg and Ofen. From there they were taken to Temeswar and finally, by land, to Neppendorf via Deva and Mühlbach. Because the deterrent effect that the Viennese Court was hoping for failed to materialize, the deportations were subsequently expanded. In the first phase, 1734–7, 800 individuals were affected. The transmigrants hailed largely from the Salzkammergut (parishes of Goisern, Hallstatt, Ischl, and Gosau) and from Carinthia, and there especially from the lordship of Paternion. In contrast to the deportees from the Salzkammergut, among the Carinthians the families were separated and the children kept back. Moreover, their settlement sites in Transylvania were widely dispersed. Added to this was a mortality rate that was substantially higher than the already above-average death rate among transmigrants in the first period after settlement.

The second phase of the deportation began during the reign of Empress Maria Theresa. It affected more than 3,000 people and had decidedly repressive traits. The deportees came from the Upper Austrian Land ob der Enns and in smaller numbers from Styria and Carinthia. Except for a smaller number of Styrians who were settled in the Hungarian communities of Iklad and KeresztÚr, Transylvania was the destination of all transports. The chief settlement sites there were the communities of Großau and Großpold, the latter with a comparatively high proportion of Carinthians. The third and final phase of transmigration occurred in 1773–6. Around 200 Protestants were deported from Stadl in Styria. Shortly after the last transport had set out for Transylvania, Emperor Joseph II decreed an end to the deportations. Freedom of religion in the hereditary Austrian lands came with the Toleration Patent of 1781. However, the transmigrants were excluded from this patent. A return to their homelands, which many had aspired to and some had attempted, remained prohibited.

From the perspective of the Viennese Court there were several reasons for settling the transmigrants in Transylvania. In contrast to the Salzburg Protestants, who were expelled in 1731–3 and then settled in the Reich, the Netherlands, the British colony of Georgia, and above all in Prussian Lithuania, the freedom of religion demanded by the Protestants could be granted in Transylvania, within the boundaries of the monarchy but far enough away from the center. The Transylvanian Saxons, who had been living there since the medieval colonization of eastern Europe, as one of the recognized nations of the principality, had converted en bloc to Protestantism during the Reformation in the first half of the 16th century. In addition, the monarchy had economic interests. The influx of new workers and taxpayers was to help stabilize a Transylvania severely devastated by wars and uprisings. Given these preconditions, and because the Transylvanian Saxons and the transmigrants were "compatriots of the German nation and of their faith," Vienna was counting on the rapid assimilation of the newcomers. The specially created Inspectorate of Transmigrants, headquartered in Hermannstadt, was to help accelerate the settlement process and make the deportation irreversible.

But the measures to promote assimilation were overshadowed by the picture of heretics and troublemakers that the discrimination against the transmigrants on the part of the Viennese Court had created in the settlement region. It went hand in hand with the rejection of the newcomers by the population of the communities of Transylvanian Saxons. They saw the transmigrants, who were "incorporated as free people of the Saxon nation," that is, they were formally placed on an equal footing with the established population, as potential competitors, and not without reason. Frequent complaints by the transmigrants about the inadequate amount of building lumber allocated to them, about insufficient fields and meadows, and about discrimination in the craftsmen's guilds, as well as an anti-foreign "uprising" in Hermannstadt seem to indicate as much.

The number of marriages between Transylvanian Saxons and transmigrants grew only slowly, and newcomers moved into community offices at the same slow pace. These developments did not dismantle the differences between the two groups in the communities. On the contrary, differentiating factors like dialect, dress, and mentality were reinforced by the encounter with the old-established, Transylvanian-Saxon population. This resulted in conflicts that sometimes persisted into the 20th century, and it gradually led the transmigrants to develop their own group identities, which were initially determined by local conditions. This self-awareness as a group was determined by the conditions in the settlement site, the region of origin and thus the traditions of the transmigrants, the numerical ratio between the old-established and the immigrant population, and the specific age, wealth, and occupational structure. Beginning in the 19th century, there are clear indications that the *Landler* as a whole saw themselves as a group with characteristics unique to them, including their own history. They were perceived as such a distinct group also by the Transylvanian Saxons and the other ethnic groups of Transylvania – a culturally defined minority of around 7,000 persons within the Transylvanian Saxons, who themselves became a minority within Romania after World War I.

Along with the German minorities in Romania, the *Landler* shared the experience of the German groups of east-central Europe that were incorporated by the German Reich in the interwar period and especially during the Second World War: deportation to the Soviet Union and the discriminatory minority policy in Socialist Romania. By now, nearly all *Landler* have left, most going to the Federal Republic of Germany as *Aussiedler* (ethnic immigrants) and *Spätaussiedler* (late ethnic immigrants). The few who emigrated to Austria were classified in the 1990s as "Old Austrians" (*Altösterreicher*). The *Landler* as a group have been dissolving since the middle of the 20th century. It is foreseeable that they will soon exist only as a community of memory, as is attested, not least, by the *Landler* Museum in Goisern, Austria.

Beer, Mathias. "'Willkürliches Benehmen gegen den ererbten sächsischen Sitten und Bräuchen.' Aufnahme und Eingliederung der Transmigranten in Siebenbürgen" In *Migration nach Ost- und Südosteuropa vom 18. bis zum Beginn des 19. Jahrhunderts. Ursachen, Formen, Verlauf, Ergebnis*, edited by Mathias Beer and Dittmar Dahlmann, 317–35. Stuttgart, 1999.

Bottesch, Martin, Franz Grieshofer, and Wilfried Schabus, eds. *Die Siebenbürgischen Landler. Eine Spurensicherung*. Vienna, 2002.

Buchinger, Erich. *Die "Landler" in Siebenbürgen. Vorgeschichte, Durchführung und Ergebnis einer Zwangsumsiedlung im 18. Jahrhundert*. Munich, 1980.

Knall, Dieter. *Aus der Heimat gedrängt. Letzte Zwangsumsiedlungen steirischer Protestanten nach Siebenbürgen unter Maria Theresia*. Graz, 2002.

Sedler, Irmgard. *Die Landler in Siebenbürgen. Gruppenidentität im Spiegel der Kleidung von der Mitte des 18. bis zum Ende des 20. Jahrhunderts*. Marburg, 2004.

Steiner, Stephan. *Reisen ohne Wiederkehr. Die Deportation von Protestanten aus Kärnten 1734–1736*. Vienna and Munich, 2007.

Cross-references: Germany; Austria; Southeastern Europe; *Aussiedler/ Spätaussiedler* in Germany since 1950; German Deportees from East-Central and Southeastern Europe in the USSR after the End of World War II; German Refugees and Expellees from Eastern, East-Central, and Southeastern Europe in Germany and Austria since the End of World War II; Salzburg Protestants in East Prussia since the 18th Century

AUVERGNESE IN SPAIN IN THE EARLY MODERN PERIOD

Abel Poitrineau

Beginning in the Middle Ages, mountain dwellers from the Auvergne in central France migrated to Spain. A migration system developed that reached its high point in the 16th century and encompassed for the most part temporary labor migration. It weakened in the 19th century and eventually came to a complete end in the Second World War. The geographic movement of the Auvergnese became entrenched through oral traditions in the cultural memory on both sides of the Pyrenees.

In France, the migrants were called "Spaniards." Their region of origin extended over the arrondissements of Mauriac and Aurillac. By contrast, fewer people left from Châtaigneraie and from the basalt plateau of Planèze near Saint Flour. At the beginning of the 18th century, the centers of the migration lay in Ytrac and Crandelles in Aurillac. The Auvergnese initially went to Catalonia and to the kingdoms of Valencia and Murcia. However, because of the attraction of Madrid, Old and New Castile became over time the chief destination. Groups from the Auvergne also made their way to the region La Mancha and into the cities of Andalusia (Seville, Cádiz, Granada), though some of them are difficult to distinguish from the likewise numerous immigrants from the Limousin, which borders the Auvergne to the west.

Overpopulation, infertile soil, and the low level of development of the local economy prompted the mountain dwellers to leave the Auvergne in an effort to find, especially during the long winter months, an additional source of income in the south. The poor soil of the Auvergne allowed only extensive animal husbandry. Moreover, the Massif Central, located away from the great currents of goods and communication, and especially the high plain of the Auvergne lacked the nearby markets of large cities. The Auvergnese saw the Mediterranean region as a paradisiacal south of sunny coasts, luxuriant vineyards, and rich port cities.

Auvergne and Spain were politically and culturally linked. The kings of Aragon had inherited the lordship rights and title of a Vicomte of Carlat and Carladès in the Haute-Auvergne. The pilgrimage site Santiago de Compostela in Galicia also held property in the Massif Central, through which ran some of the longest routes of the pilgrims of St. Jacob (e.g., through the cities Le Puy and Aurillac). While the Massif Central never provided the population with sufficient opportunities for a livelihood in the late Middle Ages, the Christian Spanish kingdoms were suffering from a labor shortage. The backdrop was the reconquista, in which numerous feudal lords from Auvergne, the Limousin, and the Rouerge had also participated, and which had led to the exodus of the Muslim population as well as the expulsion of the Jews and Moriscos (converted Muslims) in the 15th century. Migration was facilitated by cultural and linguistic commonalities between Catalans, Castilians, and Aragonese, on the one side, and the inhabitants of Occitan France (Auvergne, Limousin, Gévaudan, Quercy, Rouerge), on the other. The religious wars that ravaged Occitan France in the 16th century eventually drove many Catholics to seek refuge south of the Pyrenees and to search for a livelihood there.

Gold and silver from the South American colonies made Spain rich and powerful in the 16th century. But the labor shortage continued, not least because many Castilians and Aragonese migrated overseas or entered the military or the church. As water carriers or as laborers in the cultivation of fields and in saw mills, the immigrants from the Auvergne were able to earn a comparatively high income until the 18th century. They were also welcome workers during the olive, grain, and grape harvest, and in forestry. The elites of Castile and Valencia also employed numerous Auvergnese as coachmen, kitchen helpers, or domestic servants.

Chain migrations developed. Relatives and friends provided help finding work and acted as interpreters; they also familiarized the newcomers with the mores of the host society. The often very young migrant workers traveled in groups as protection against highwaymen. They usually traveled on foot, sometimes by horse, and followed traditional routes: they stopped at specific taverns and inns, and crossed the Pyrenees at Somport, Roncevaux, through the Aran valley, or along the two foothills, via Bayonne or Perpignan.

Initially it was mostly seasonal work migration by men from the Auvergne to Spain. Only a few of the young migrants married Spanish women, established a family, and settled permanently in the destination country. The majority of the migrant workers were married or married in the Auvergne and returned regularly to their family, which continued to run the farm during the absence of the men.

The migration system changed in the 17th century. In the 16th century, so many Auvergnese were going to Spain that they made up 15% of the population in the Kingdom of Valencia, for example. Around 1550, nearly all water carriers in Toledo were Frenchmen. Thereafter, it was especially the influx of unskilled workers from the Massif Central that waned. A growing number of Auvergnese were now active in Spain as merchants and craftsmen: itinerant traders in the rural areas of Castile and Aragon, cobblers and coppersmiths who sold and repaired copper and tin ware, or cattle dealers specializing in the import of mules. From the end of the 17th century, members of these vocational groups returned more and more rarely to their country of origin, for the most part only every three or four years. Auvergnese continued to specialize, worked especially as bakers, dealt in fabrics and cloths, and organized bazaar-like markets. As a side business they lent money at interest, which earned the *gabachos*, as the Frenchmen were derogatorily called, the accusation of engaging in usury. Therein lay the core of the latent hostility toward the French, whom the Spanish writer Francisco de Quevedo in the 17th century alternately described as "lice who are sucking Spain dry," a "disgrace," "humiliation," and "abuse" for the land.

In many towns and villages, French merchants opened stores that were organized as family businesses. The most famous trading enterprises, Chinchón, Navalcarnero, and Segorbe, were named after the locations of their headquarters. They comprised several dozen partners bound by ties of kinship. The businesses earned considerable capital (real estate, merchandise, money). Selling or leasing shares in the business was subject to stringent rules; in principle, partners were forbidden to marry a Spanish woman, and if they did, they could face the loss of their rights. As a rule, the shares were passed down to sons or grandsons. Some more venturesome Auvergnese operated inns and taverns in Cádiz, Seville, Barcelona, and Madrid, taking in newly arriving countrymen. They also functioned as conduits for jobs and contacts to the native population.

Although the immigrants in Spain had adjusted fairly smoothly because of the linguistic and cultural kinship, the Auvergnese lived there in self-contained communities. In cities like Cordoba, Barcelona, or Saragossa, they congregated into self-contained residential neighborhoods. Some entered religious orders or joined the household troops of the Spanish king, the "Walloon Guard." Beginning in the 16th century, the Auvergnese, like all Frenchmen, were monitored and at times harassed by the Inquisition, which was afraid of an infiltration of Protestants.

Every political crisis between Spain and France led to repression by the state against the immigrants: on several occasions, the property of the Frenchmen was seized, confiscated, and sold for the benefit of the royal treasury. Information about the confiscated property points to the wealth especially of the trading companies. During the Spanish war of independence against Napoleonic rule (1808–13), the property of immigrants was expropriated again, as attested by reports from the French imperial compensation commission (Commission impériale des indemnités) set up in Bayonne and Toulouse in 1809 and 1810, respectively. The horse, mule, kettle, and blanket traders residing in the Kingdom of Valencia lamented losses that amounted in a few cases to more than 200,000 francs. The trading house of Chinchón, which employed about 80 Frenchmen in Spain in June of 1808, demanded compensation of no less than 1.5 million francs.

At the end of the stay in Spain, ranging from several months to several years, the migrant workers brought their often substantial savings back to Auvergne in the form of gold and silver coins or sent them ahead with traveling countrymen, in spite of Spanish decrees prohibiting the export of precious metals from Spain. The result was exaggerated tax increases in the communities of origin. The workers, merchants, and craftsmen who migrated to Spain played a major role in the fact that payment transactions in France were dominated by Spanish coins until the reign of King Louis XIV.

The men returning from Spain used the cash they had earned abroad above all to repay the debts their families had made to support themselves during their absence. Landlords and notables readily loaned money or crops to the wives or parents of "Spaniards," because repayment was assured. The income earned abroad also allowed the migrants to pursue specific marriage strategies: members of migrant families often married each other. Marriage contracts, for example, stipulated fixed agreements on the wife's education or payment of the dowry in installments, which was guaranteed by the regular return of the debtor. They also show that the migrant workers had much more cash than their nonmigrating neighbors of the same social status. Their prosperity affected land prices, which were unusually high in communities with strong migration earnings: the migrants, who often had sufficient financial means to buy fields, pastures, or forests year after year or establish a small agricultural or forestry enterprise, outbid each other upon their return. At times they even bought entire estates, mills, or feudal rights.

The migration also influenced the demographic development of the sending regions: although the birthrates rose after the periodic return of the "Spaniards," on the whole they were low compared to birthrates of other regions. Numerous migrants died in Spain. And in the Auvergne there was a strikingly large number of widows and women who had not found a spouse. Women whose husbands were missing were not allowed to remarry.

The migration system not only changed the demographic situation in the sending regions fundamentally and transformed the market for land. The "Spaniards" also brought new habits of dress and diet to the Auvergne and contributed to a change of the language by introducing many new words. In this way, the consequences in the Auvergne of the tradition-rich migration to Spain reverberated well beyond the decline of the migration system, which continued to lose importance during the 19th century.

Poitrineau, Abel. *Les Espagnols de l'Auvergne et du Limousin du XVIIIe au XIXe siècle.* Aurillac, 1985.

Cross-references: France; Spain and Portugal

BELGIAN REFUGEES IN WESTERN EUROPE DURING WORLD WAR I

Michaël Amara

The German invasion of Belgium in the First World War, stretching from August to October 1914 led to the flight of more than 1.5 million Belgian civilians. Several thousand settled in the Westhoek – the small part of Belgium that remained unoccupied – but the vast majority of men and women of every age and social background sought asylum abroad – in the Netherlands, France, or Great Britain. The choice of migration destination was usually determined by which border was closest: most of the inhabitants of the provinces of Hainaut and West Flanders tried to reach France, while thousands of people from Liège, Antwerp, and East Flanders traveled to the Netherlands or swelled the ranks of those hoping to flee the advancing German troops by crossing the English Channel.

The end of the German military advance in Belgium effectively brought the stream of refugees to an end. Only a few thousand Belgians continued to cross the Dutch border – mainly young men wishing to join the army or to find jobs abroad or wives of soldiers anxious to join their interned husbands. Although the electrical fence built on the Dutch-Belgian border by German occupation authorities curbed the flow of refugees, some Belgians continued to flee the country until the end of the war. For young men, the Netherlands was often a way station on the path to either France or England, but the families of internees who had managed to cross the border usually settled in the Netherlands and remained there until the end of the war. In May 1918, 6,640 such families lived in the Netherlands.

According to estimates, the number of Belgian refugees in the Netherlands reached 1 million in October 1914, but their number subsequently decreased rapidly, falling to about 100,000 by 1916. They were joined by some 30,000 Belgian soldiers, whom the Dutch authorities were compelled to intern in various camps scattered around the country. Another 200,000 Belgian refugees reached the coast of Britain in 1914, but their number gradually declined and remained stable at around 150,000. Due to the evacuation of Flemish civilians from the combat zone, the number of Belgians taking refuge in France increased throughout the conflict to reach 325,000 shortly before the armistice in November 1918. In total, more than 600,000 Belgians – some 10% of the Belgian population at the time – settled abroad during the First World War. For a large part of the Belgians who fled their country in 1914, the period of flight was an episode that lasted only weeks or months; most returned to their homeland long before the end of the war.

In each of the three countries involved, the arrival of Belgian refugees led to unprecedented humanitarian action. The immense scale of the relief efforts was prompted by the concern that the invasion of Belgium, in violation of international law, caused among the public of the affected nations. Britain and France justified their involvement in the war with Germany's violation of Belgian neutrality while the plight of the refugees gave a human face to the heroic struggle of "Poor Little Belgium."

Despite the massive flight caused by the war and the economic crisis within its own borders, France made no distinction during the conflict between French and Belgian citizens. Belgians received the same benefits from the state as the refugees from northeastern France. This financial help was maintained throughout the war and enabled the poorest refugees to avoid utter destitution. In Great Britain, the relief effort consisted almost solely, at first, of spontaneous acts of charity. Committees sprang up all around the country to help resettle refugee families, either with host families or in boardinghouses set up especially for that purpose. By the end of 1914, as people's generosity began to wane, the British government was forced to play a greater part in meeting the costs of helping the refugees.

In the Netherlands, in contrast, the scope of aid for the refugees remained significantly more limited. In order to maintain neutrality in the conflict, Dutch authorities were anxious for their actions not to be interpreted as a sign of support for the Allies. They imposed limitations on the personal freedom of the refugees and strongly encouraged them to return to Belgium. They were nevertheless forced to introduce new measures to cope with the massive influx of refugees. Makeshift camps were set up in the south of the country soon after the arrival of the first refugees. Many of these camps proved ill-suited to provide longer-term accommodation. The press and public opinion were quick to denounce the living conditions in the camps. The Dutch government, in order to appease critics, set up four large camps, euphemistically referred to as "havens" or "Belgian villages," in Nunspeet, Ede, Uden, and Gouda. The camps were designed to house up to 20,000 refugees and three of them remained in operation until the end of the war.

The scale of humanitarian aid for the refugees, particularly in Great Britain and the Netherlands, depended significantly on the social status of recipients. Those of higher social status were given preferential treatment from the British relief committees, including a more generous income and better housing. The Dutch government classified Belgian refugees in three distinct categories, largely according to social standing. Refugees were then sent to different camps based on which category they belonged to; upper-class refugees received a special allowance that enabled them to live outside the camps.

In France, Great Britain, and the Netherlands, the long months of war saw a gradual dwindling of the support offered to all refugees while access to financial aid from the state became increasingly restricted. Despite the considerable cost, each government continued to fulfill its humanitarian obligations throughout the course of the conflict and accepted the additional burden to their already strained state budgets. In Great Britain as in France, the sudden availability of Belgian refugees proved a particularly useful source of substitute manpower amid a severely depleted local workforce. In France, more than 22,000 refugees were put to work in a total of 1,600 companies, with a further 15,000 farmers sent to work on the land. In Britain, the government initially yielded to trade union pressure and discouraged the employment of refugees. As early as November 1914, however, Belgians began to play an increasingly important role in the British war industry. In 1918, with about 30,000 Belgians employed in ammunition factories, including more than 7,000 women, the refugees represented one of the largest foreign workforces in the country. This massive influx of foreign workers into the British labor market brought along its share of problems: with a poor command of English and little knowledge of British working traditions, the Belgians encountered enormous difficulties in their efforts of acculturation. British trade unions accused them of complying only half-heartedly with the main collective labor agreements, thus jeopardizing the social rights the trade unions had fought so hard to secure. To minimize these tensions, the refugees were often grouped together in Belgian-only teams and the authorities encouraged certain factories to employ only an exclusively Belgian workforce.

Unlike the situation in France and Great Britain, unemployment was very high among Belgian refugees in the Netherlands. Within the context of the economic crisis gripping the country, Dutch trade unions and many municipal authorities actively discouraged the hiring of Belgian refugees or endeavored to prevent them from competing with Dutch workers. Although some Belgians entered the Dutch labor market in the course of the war (for example, in 1918, 3,000 were employed in the mines of Limburg and 500 in the Philips factories in Eindhoven), the majority of qualified workers was drawn by the higher wages paid in war industries and chose to emigrate to Great Britain or France. In close collaboration with their Dutch counterparts, the British government earmarked considerable resources to bring skilled refugee workers from the Netherlands to Britain. At the beginning of 1916, the British Board of Trade supervised the transfer of 30,000 Belgian refugees across the English Channel.

In Great Britain and, to a lesser extent, France, the search for jobs prompted many refugees to settle in heavily populated working-class areas. In these communities, the refugees kept to themselves and felt a strong desire to maintain their traditional way of life, achieving only limited integration. Through the creation of dozens of choirs, theater groups, and various sports clubs, they used recreational activities to strengthen the bonds to their homeland. They set up a network of small shops in many city centers and the grocers and bakers offering Belgian specialties came to symbolize the Belgian presence abroad.

Anxious to prevent the refugee populations from permanently settling in their host countries, the Belgian government-in-exile attached great importance to preserving and promoting a strong sense of Belgian identity and national pride among the refugees. It urged those who found work abroad to continue sending remittances to their families back home so as to maintain the link between Belgian exiles and their relatives living in occupied Belgium. Throughout the entire war, ministers, members of parliament, and priests traveled the length and breadth of the host countries visiting Belgian communities to keep alive their hope for an imminent return. The swift assimilation of children into the host communities was a source of particular concern for the Belgian authorities. The creation of Belgian schools proved an extremely important weapon in the fight against the "denationalization" of the exile populations. A network of Belgian schools was set up in each host country. Thanks to the active support of the Dutch authorities, the network of schools in the Netherlands was particularly dense: in 1918 some 13,000 pupils were educated at more than 70 Belgian primary schools. The total number of refugee children being taught in such schools in the three host countries was estimated at 26,000 in 1917. This option, however, was not available to most Belgian refugee children since they lived dispersed across the host countries and thus had to attend local schools.

The proclamation of the armistice in November 1918 gave rise to great expectations among the refugees, the vast majority of whom were clearly impatient to return to their families and their property after years of absence. By July 1919, most of the Belgians who had taken refuge in the Netherlands had returned home; only very few decided to remain permanently. The British authorities, deeply concerned with the impending economic crisis threatening to engulf the country, immediately took measures for the repatriation of the refugees. By mid-1919, almost all Belgians who had resided in Britain had left the country. Although a small number requested to stay in Great Britain, the Home Secretary pressed for their departure.

In France, bled dry by four years of war, the repatriation of Belgian refugees was not as pressing an issue. A few thousand settled permanently in France, especially in Normandy, where many were granted fertile farmland. All in all, however, almost all of the hundreds of thousands of Belgian refugees during the First World War, returned to their homeland after the war – the unprecedented mass exile did not have the disastrous demographic consequences the Belgian authorities had feared.

Amara, Michaël. *Des Belges à l'épreuve de l'exil. Les réfugiés de la Première Guerre mondiale (France, Grande-Bretagne, Pays-Bas)*. Brussels, 2008.

Cahalan, Peter. *Belgian Refugees in England during the Great War*. New York and London, 1982.

Kushner, Tony. "Local Heroes: Belgian Refugees in Britain during the First World War." *Immigrants and Minorities* 18 (1999): 1–28.

Nivet, Philippe. *Les réfugiés français de la Grande Guerre – Les 'Boches du Nord'*. Paris, 2004.

de Roodt, Evelyn. *Oorlogsgasten. Vluchtelingen en krijgsgevangenen in Nederland tijdens de Eerste Wereldoorlog*. Zaltbommel, 2000.

Cross-references: Belgium and Luxembourg; France; Great Britain; The Netherlands

BOHEMIAN EXILES (*EXULANTEN*) IN SAXONY SINCE THE 17TH CENTURY

Alexander Schunka

In the discussion at the time, the label Bohemian Exiles (*Exulanten*) applied to groups which, in the wake of the Habsburg re-Catholicization efforts in the 17th century, left the lands of the Bohemian monarchy and went to various European states, among them Poland, England, the Netherlands, Brandenburg, and above all Saxony. In keeping with the confessional heterogeneity of Bohemia, they

255

Title page of the memorial book of Borek Materovský z Materova and his wife, Pirna, 1635 (*Herzog August Bibliothek Wolfenbüttel [Cod. Guelf. 1123 Novi. 8°, 4r]*).

were Lutherans, Utraquists (followers of the teachings of Jan Hus), Calvinists, or members of the Bohemian Brethren (*Brüderunität*) – all told, a large part of the non-Catholic population. The exodus involved Czech-speakers and German-speakers. In the older scholarship their number is given as 36,000 families, which would mean more than 100,000 individuals. However, this information owes more to Protestant mythologizing than solid statistical data. This has to do with the – already contemporary – stylization of the Bohemian Exiles into a unified group of religious refugees. In actuality, however, the process of migration cannot be reduced exclusively to religious motivations, nor can it be depicted as a straight-line migration from Bohemia to Saxony. The migratory activity persisted throughout nearly the entire 17th century and in some cases beyond. Especially neighboring Electoral Saxony was affected as a temporary or permanent immigration land. There, some of the immigrants were absorbed into the local population, some established their own settlements (e.g., Johanngeorgenstadt), or their own parishes (e.g., Zittau, Dresden), where religious services were at times held in Czech as late as the 19th century.

Beginning in the 1620s, Bohemia suffered a rapid population loss of about a million people, to which the effects of war, epidemics, and emigration motivated by religion and socio-economic interests contributed. After the suppression of the Bohemian uprising following the Battle of White Mountain (8 November 1620), there began a migration movement that initially encompassed political refugees but soon also included non-Catholic clergy and teachers who had been expelled by the Bohemian authorities. From the late 1620s on they were followed by citizens of royal cities, members of the nobility, and eventually also members of the rural population. The Habsburg re-Catholicization measures, carried out with help from the so-called Reformation Commissions

or the religious orders of the Counter-Reformation, were intended to persuade non-Catholic Bohemians to convert. However, in response to a subtle intensification of the confessional-political pressure, extending all the way to the confiscation of land, large segments of the population decided to leave. Because the concrete implementation of the policy of re-Catholicization varied in intensity in terms of timing and location, some areas in Bohemia continued to have some leeway with respect to religious orientation.

As a result of geographic proximity and confessional orientation, Calvinists and Bohemian Brethren headed primarily to Poland, Lutherans more to Saxony and to Saxon-administered Upper Lusatia (Oberlausitz). On a smaller scale there had actually been migrations out of Saxony to Bohemia or vice versa for confessional or professional reasons (pastors, merchants, craftsmen, intellectuals) long before 1620. In many cases, the choice of destinations by the immigrants during the re-Catholicization period was thus influenced by existing contacts or migration patterns.

Especially in the beginning, Electoral Saxony was torn between a pro-Habsburg policy and the reception of immigrants from Habsburg territories. Although the administrative capacities were increased, numerous lists of exiles were drawn up, and the obligatory registration of new arrivals was introduced, the officials in the end proved barely capable of dealing with the challenges posed by the immigration. Saxony neither pursued an organized settlement policy, nor was it possible to strictly maintain the idea of confessional unity. Depending on the course of the Thirty Years' War, there were also return migrations to Bohemia with subsequent conversions to Catholicism. In addition, exiled pastors or Bohemian merchants from Saxony ensured that the ties between the departure regions and the destination regions were cultivated. During and after the war they maintained the communication between Saxony and Bohemia, transported letters, or spread Protestant devotional literature to provide for the spiritual needs of those who had remained in Bohemia.

Electoral Saxony was not only an immigration land but also a point of contact for the emigrant politicians who worked for an organized return and a reinstatement of property. These efforts failed successively in the negotiations for the Peace of Prague (1635) and the Peace of Westphalia (1648). At the same time, Saxony was a transition station for many migrants heading for Protestant territories of the German Empire or other European countries.

From about the middle of the 1620s, the label Bohemian Exiles was used by the Saxon authorities or within Saxon society to describe the immigrants as a group. The Habsburg monarchy referred to the "emigrants" in part as "rebels," a view that was justified on the grounds of their resistance to the political-confessional measures or their abandonment of established relationships of dependency. The immigrants themselves valued their status as *Exulanten* which developed in the host country increasingly into a group-constituting, identity-creating characteristic.

The term *Exulanten* implied that individuals had abandoned their earthly possessions for religious reasons, that is, in favor of heavenly salvation. The status as an *Exulant* also connoted the aspect of a temporary migration, whose postulated limited temporal duration arose, on the one hand, from the hope of a return to the homeland, and, on the other, from religious expectations of redemption. And in many cases the return to the homeland should also be seen as a topos that took on a life of its own, since many exiles, especially pastors as the proponents of the idea of exile, were native and returned Saxons – for them, Saxon exile was thus de facto a remigration. The word *Exulant* changed in the course of the 17th century from a label for a religious refugee suffering a harsh personal fate to a marker of group membership in the destination lands. This had its counterpart in expectations of salvation and requests for help on the part of the immigrants, which were concretely expressed in applications for admission or in a separate status of *Exulanten* in the poor relief of Electoral Saxony.

Many of the Bohemian immigrants were temporarily or permanently dependent on the church's institutions of poor relief, a circumstance that reinforced an autonymous and exonymous characterization as a separate social group of poor (religious) refugees. They saw themselves as distinct from conventional beggars and vagrants by their religious flight and often knew how to use this fate to demand aid from the authorities. By contrast, geographic names of origin played a rather subordinate role as autonyms or exonyms; as a result, the term *Exulant* in Saxony soon ceased to refer only to immigrant Bohemians or Moravians and included also inhabitants of the Austrian crown lands, Silesians, or Hungarians.

Alongside an almost continuous rural short-distance migration in the border regions of the Bohemian-Saxon Erzgebirge (e.g., seasonal work, marriage ties), the destinations of the long-distance migrants were often larger cities, especially the residence city of Dresden, where the Prince Elector pursued a restrictive admission policy for a long time, or the mining towns in the Erzgebirge, which had become depopulated as a result of the decline of mining in that region and offered the immigrants good settlement opportunities. The situation was especially extreme in the 1620s and 1630s in the city of Pirna, whose geographic location had turned it into a center of immigration: at times the native population of about 4,000 confronted 2,000 immigrants. What is striking is that settlement habits from Bohemia were often adopted, especially in the first years of the exile, with individuals from the same sending place living close together also at the destination location. Cities like Pirna (until 1639), Zittau, or Dresden saw the emergence of Bohemian congregations that derived their cohesiveness above all from attendance at Czech services or from educational and various social institutions set up by the church. In the process, the cultivation of the Czech mother tongue served increasingly as a group-constituting factor, though hardly still as a necessary means of communication. In

contrast to some Huguenot settlements outside of Saxony, for example, no stable internal social structure was erected among the Bohemian Exiles.

Particularly after the end of the Thirty Years' War, some landowners in Upper Lusatia pursued a somewhat planned settlement policy on their devastated holdings. This led to the charge by Bohemian noblemen that many subjects were unlawfully walking away from their feudal ties to improve their economic situation in the neighboring land. There are only a few instances when Bohemian immigrants founded cities in Saxony: the most prominent example is the establishment – with the consent of the Prince Elector – of Johanngeorgenstadt in the Erzgebirge (1654) at the initiative of immigrants from the Bohemian mining town of Platten (Horní Blatná). We cannot speak in Saxony of a centrally organized policy of granting privileges or attracting settlers.

The Bohemian immigration to Electoral Saxony was a phenomenon that cut across social strata and status. Within the host society, however, the social bonds were at times questioned or abrogated. That applied, for example, to aristocratic immigrants, who for a long time faced the problem that as noblemen they could not swear the oath of citizenship, with the result that they had a difficult time acquiring property, lived as renters, and at times, even in periods of personal need, were not allowed to pursue regular employment. Exiled members of the aristocracy cultivated their consciousness of status among themselves, as is evident from the creation of family registers or the "Pirna Armorial."

Because of their writing activity, clergymen and teachers served primarily as the intellectual multipliers of exile. For some clergymen, the professional and social integration took place without any major problems. In the cities, immigrant craftsmen saw themselves for a long time confronted with the tenacious resistance of the guilds, who opposed the admission of outsiders largely for economic reasons. And yet, it was not rare for immigrants or their descendants to rise into city offices, especially after the Thirty Years' War.

Immigrants who settled on the landholdings of lords in Upper Lusatian territories often made a living as linen weavers, which, over the long term, provided the weaving business a developmental push toward the emergence of proto-industrial structure. This went hand in hand with a change in the settlement forms (from the peasant village to the weaver village), as well as with a transformation of gender roles and the division of labor in the countryside.

In many cases, the familiar situation had already changed profoundly through migration and exile. A large number of the single women who settled in Saxony were not widows but rather members of biconfessional families of which a part had remained behind in Bohemia, as well as domestics for whom migration opened up new employment relationships. In the case of Czech-speaking migrants, marriages among immigrants could come, as in Dresden, for example, through the infrastructure of the exile congregations, which served as the first point of contact also for non-Lutheran immigrants. German-speaking Bohemians were probably more rapidly absorbed into the host society than others: marriages or relations of godparenthood among immigrants and between immigrants and locals seem to have been about even.

Bohemian Exiles did not become a fixture in the collective memory beyond Saxony as was the case, for example, with the Huguenots of Brandenburg-Prussia. One important reason for this was probably that they sometimes quite rapidly merged with the host society. Still, they derived a sense of identification and uniqueness from their self-image as a religious persecuted group. Even though this migratory phenomenon cannot be reduced to an exact time period or precisely definable regions of origin and destination, to specific strata or to religious flight as the sole motive behind migration, or to followers of the Lutheran faith, some of them, especially in circles of the rather homogeneous Bohemian settlements or the urban exile's congregations, for a long time practiced their traditions as confessionally persecuted Protestants. And this image shaped the questions and results of the historical scholarship on the Bohemian Exiles in Saxony well into the 20th century.

Bobková, Lenka. "Böhmische Exulanten in Sachsen während des Dreißigjährigen Krieges am Beispiel der Stadt Pirna." *Frühneuzeit-Info* 10 (1999): 21–30.

Hrubá, Michaela, ed. *Víra nebo vlast? Exil českých dějinách raného novověku*. Ústí nad Labem, 2001.

Loesche, Georg. *Die böhmischen Exulanten in Sachsen. Ein Beitrag zur Geschichte des Dreißigjährigen Krieges und der Gegenreformation auf archivalischer Grundlage*. Vienna and Leipzig, 1923.

Schunka, Alexander. "Exulanten, Konvertiten, Arme und Fremde. Zuwanderer aus der Habsburgermonarchie in Kursachsen im 17. Jahrhundert." *Frühneuzeit-Info* 14 (2003): 66–78.

Schunka, Alexander. *Gäste, die bleiben. Zuwanderer in Kursachsen und der Oberlausitz im 17. und frühen 18. Jahrhundert*. Hamburg, 2006.

Wäntig, Wulf. *Grenzerfahrungen. Böhmische Exulanten im 17. Jahrhundert*. Konstanz, 2007.

Winter, Eduard. *Die tschechische und slowakische Emigration in Deutschland im 17. und 18. Jahrhundert*. Berlin, 1955.

Cross-references: Czechia and Slovakia; Germany; Huguenots in Europe since the 16th Century; Moravian Brethren in Europe since the Early Modern Period

BOHEMIAN GLASS TRADERS IN EUROPE FROM THE 17TH TO THE 19TH CENTURY

Klaus Weber

The production of high-quality glass doubtlessly numbers among the unique achievements of the West. One could even argue that the manufacture and use of such glass products made an essential contribution to the economic and cultural divergence that arose between the Orient and the Occident. There existed in early modern Europe, however, only two locations where the highest technological standards and production were developed and maintained: Venice and Bohemia. Although high-quality window and mirror glass was also produced in France and glass products of lesser quality in other countries, Venetian and Bohemian glass wares held a dominant position on the world market, even finding buyers in Africa and Asia.

Bohemia can look back on a long tradition of glassmaking; mass production, however, was first achieved in the late 17th century, when central European rural manufacturing had recovered from the depredations of the Thirty Years' War and began seeking new markets. In contrast to those in Venice, Bohemian glass manufacturers enjoyed the advantages of abundant raw material (firewood, potash, quartz sand) and the availability of cheap labor. Feudal lords encouraged new economic endeavors, created a suitable infrastructure, and even abolished socage to set free a workforce to a more liberal economy. One nobleman who in this respect particularly stood out was Count Josef Kinsky (1702–80), who in 1757 granted city and market privileges to the glass manufacturing village of Haida (today: Nový Bor) in the district of Leitmeritz (today: Litoměřice). Reliable figures for the 17th century are scarce, but estimates claim that by 1800 some 40,000 Bohemians made their living from the manufacture of an assortment of items, ranging from simple consumer articles to luxury items like goblets, mirrors, and chandeliers.

The 17th-century upsurge derived in part from new marketing strategies. The radius of the regional glass trade expanded considerably and traveling merchants increasingly replaced their traditional panniers with handcarts and sometimes even horse-driven carriages. A multitude of small "companies", whose members – all German-speaking Bohemians – were linked by familial ties and mutual involvement in production and commercial enterprises, lent the trade the character of the medium-size enterprises. These firms controlled the entire chain – from production and packaging to transport and sale. By 1700, sales expeditions had reached locales as remote as St. Petersburg and Moscow (1688) in the east and London and Cádiz (1691) in the west. In the following decades, Bohemians established permanent trading posts all over Europe: in Trieste, Ancona, Naples, Palermo, and Milan; in Amsterdam (before 1730), Rotterdam, the Hague, and Utrecht; in Porto (1730) and Lisbon; and in at least 17 locations in Spain, most notably in Cádiz (1720s), Bilbao (before 1733), and Madrid. Northern Europe was provided for by trading houses in Hamburg, Copenhagen, and Riga while trading posts in Istanbul and Smyrna supplied the Ottoman Empire. Despite Spanish regulations restricting foreign trade with its colonies, branches were even opened in Lima (1784) and Mexico City (1787). Bohemian traders used posts such as these as bases to launch trade expeditions to service even remote villages. Some 50 Bohemian merchants (not including clerks and apprentices) lived in Cádiz alone in the years 1720–1830. A number of the families that got their start in the 17th century – Kreybich, Preysler, Piltz, Palme, and Grosmann, to name only a few – remained active in glass commerce and trade well into the 19th century.

According to contemporary observers, Bohemian trading houses with their strict discipline and abstinence more closely resembled cloisters than commercial enterprises. A case study of the Spanish branches confirms that company contracts specifically forbade intermingling with the host society, marrying abroad, and even socializing with non-Bohemian merchants. Workdays began and ended with lengthy prayer recitations. Although their faith ought not to have been an obstacle to marriage between the thoroughly Catholic Bohemians and locals, the five Bohemian-Spanish marriages known to have taken place in Cádiz occurred only after 1800 – a stark contrast to the marrying behavior of other foreign traders in Spain. The main cause for this endogamous behavior lay in Bohemian feudal law, which until 1871 permitted marriage only with partners from the same lordly estate.

The traders thus chose wives from their native land and frequently traveled back and forth between Bohemia and the branches abroad. It was only while at home that they saw their families and settled accounts with their partners in glass production sites, in which they commonly held shares. Augustin Rautenstrauch, for example, after establishing a trading house in Cádiz, returned to Bohemia and directed the international enterprise from there. In the 1790s, his sons ran branches in Cádiz, Seville, and Lisbon, after one of them had previously been in Lima for a time. Although many Bohemian glass traders spent most of their lives abroad, they clearly valued the vertical integration of their businesses more than integration into the host societies. Furthermore, the prohibition of exogamy prevented the payment of dowries to partners from abroad and thereby minimized the outflow of money from what was a capital-poor region.

In light of the striking expansion of its commercial networks, covering key cities in Europe, the Americas, and the Ottoman world, the Bohemian family-based business model proved extremely successful. In spite of the general economic crises and political ruptures caused by the Napoleonic wars, Bohemian trading networks and branches abroad remained relatively stable into at least the 1830s. It was rather the transition to modes of modern industrial production and transport (replacement of firewood by coal, the emergence of railways) that undermined Bohemian preponderance in glassmaking and their migrant trader-based distribution networks.

Klíma, Arnost. "Glassmaking Industry and Trade in Bohemia in the 17th and 18th Centuries." *Journal of European Economic History* 13 (1984): 499–520.

Salz, Arthur. *Geschichte der Böhmischen Industrie in der Neuzeit.* Munich and Leipzig, 1913.

Schebek, Edmund. *Böhmens Glasindustrie und Glashandel. Quellen zu ihrer Geschichte.* Prague, 1878 (reprint Frankfurt am Main, 1969).

Weber, Klaus. *Deutsche Kaufleute im Atlantikhandel 1680–1830. Unternehmen und Familien in Hamburg, Cádiz und Bordeaux.* Munich, 2004.

Cross-references: The Baltic Region; Germany; Great Britain; Italy; The Netherlands; Russia and Belarus; Spain; Southeastern Europe; Czechia and Slovakia; German Maritime Traders in Cádiz and Bordeaux from the Late 17th to the Late 19th Century

BOSNIAN BEAR LEADERS IN WESTERN AND CENTRAL EUROPE, 1868–1940

Leo Lucassen

Bosnian bear leaders and their families started to migrate to western Europe in the late 1860s. Small groups were found in Germany (from 1867), the Netherlands (from 1868), and France (from 1872). These people were known as *Ursari*, derived from the Romanian (and Latin) word *urs* (bear). At the time, there were people of other nationalities traveling with dancing bears in western Europe, such as the French from the Ariège district in the Pyrenees, and Italians from Rome and Naples. However, they traveled alone, and so were not labeled Gypsies as the Bosnian families were.

It has been argued that the *Ursari* moved from Romanian and Bulgarian lands to Bosnia in the early modern period. The bulk of the Bosnian bear leaders who migrated to western Europe in the second half of the 19th century came from a fairly small area in the northwestern part of Bosnia around Banja Luka, and a few also came from Tuzla in eastern Bosnia. Both areas were part of the Ottoman Empire until 1878. Because they were stigmatized as Gypsies by the authorities in western Europe (as happened to the itinerant coppersmiths from Hungary in the same period), their movements and characteristics were well recorded, mostly by police officials. Thus we have quite a lot of information about the activities of bear leaders.

The chief source of income of bear leaders was the bears that they trained to dance and perform tricks in the streets or at fairs. Sometimes they were hired by schools to show children what real bears looked like. Whereas in the Balkans, many people believed that these bears also had magical powers, especially to cure the sick, in western Europe their function was primarily to entertain. Usually the bear leader would make his bear (or bears) dance to music played on the tambourine, the bagpipe, or a small barrel organ. Other animals, such as monkeys or camels, were sometimes also part of the show. It is known that in the last quarter of the 19th century the *Ursari* attracted a great deal of attention and many of them earned a modest living, some even reaching the middle class. Pero Geergovitch, for example, traveled through the Netherlands and Belgium in the 1880s with 2,000 francs in his possession, three times the average yearly wage of a day laborer at the time.

Bear leader with his family in Germany. Woodcut from a painting of Paul Meyerheim, around 1890 (*Kunstbibliothek, Staatliche Museen zu Berlin*).

However, traveling in wagons and living in tents was associated with idleness and begging, and so the *Ursari* were in permanent conflict with the police. In one example, Giovanni Vassilcovici and his family arrived by boat in Amsterdam in July 1869. They had four bears and a monkey and planned to take their animals through the streets dancing to the music of their bagpipes, but the chief of police stopped them from entering the city.

Although the bear leader was normally a man, women also led bears. In order to increase their income, they had to move around constantly. Performances in two or more different places in one day were not uncommon. Especially in the countryside, it was not profitable to stay in a small village longer than a day or so. One performance was enough to reach nearly all of the inhabitants of a small village. In more densely populated areas, bear leaders could make enough money in a fairly small area and stay for quite some time, as long as they were tolerated by local authorities.

It seems that most of these Bosnians did not intend to settle in western Europe. After 1890, traces of them largely disappear. From American sources, we know that many emigrated to North America, as did millions of other Europeans. They often took their bears with them and continued working as entertainers, although they now lived in either bought or rented houses. Not all left Europe: bear leaders worked in western Europe until the 1930s, including Great Britain. Only after bear leaders were banned by the new Nazi regime in 1933 did they disappear or change to other occupations. By then, most of them lived in caravans (mobile homes). Reliable data are lacking, but there were probably no more than a few thousands bear leaders active in western Europe by then.

As far as we know, these *Ursari* were Muslim (as are most Bosnians from rural areas). They neither spoke Romani, the language spoken by Gypsies, nor did they seem to mingle with other Gypsy groups. To what extent they integrated in the host societies is unknown. During the time they kept bears and performed, their movements and activities can be traced, but when they started to change occupations or gave up their itinerant life, they seemed to vanish from the field of observation by the police. With this, we lose their traces in available sources. It is certain, however, that unlike some other nomadic groups, these *Ursari* do not seem to have survived as an occupational or social group.

Lucassen, Leo. *En men noemde hen zigeuners. De geschiedenis van Kaldarasch, Ursari, Lowara en Sinti in Nederland (1750–1945).* Amsterdam and The Hague, 1990.

Lucassen, Leo, Wim Willems, and Annemarie Cottaar. *Gypsies and Other Itinerant Groups. A Socio-Historical Approach.* London and New York, 1998.

Vukanovic, T. P. "Gypsy Bear-Leaders in the Balkan Peninsula." *Journal of the Gypsy Lore Society* 38 (1959): 106–27.

Cross-references: France; Germany; The Netherlands; Southeastern Europe; Hungarian Coppersmiths in Western Europe from the 1860s to World War I

BRETON DOMESTICS IN PARIS SINCE THE LATE 19TH CENTURY

Didier Guyvarc'h

From the end of the 19th century until the 1950s, thousands of young girls left Brittany to work in Paris as domestics. This migration movement consolidated the image of the Breton woman as a "girl for every job" (*bonne à tout faire*), a frequently used designation for domestics. The stereotype found its embodiment in the comic strip *Aventures de Bécassine* (The Adventures of Bécassine) from 1905 and continued to be handed down. The author, Jacqueline Rivière, was inspired by her own role as the employer of a Breton domestic to create the figure of a young, naïve, ignorant, and clumsy Breton maid who was completely devoted to her mistress. The strip was continued until 1957 with great success. While "Bécassine" took her place within the French collective memory, her tale masked the real story of the migration of Breton girls to Paris.

The migration of domestics was part of a broader emigration from Brittany since the 1850s, which comprised more than a million people between 1861 and 1962. Until the First World War, the high birthrates made up for the loss of population from migration; after that, the population of Brittany went into decline. The background to the strong emigration was the decline of the traditional rural textile industry. Beginning in the mid-19th century, weavers and flax spinners in the Département Côtes du Nord (today Côtes d'Armor) increasingly lost their livelihoods in the structurally weak region and added to the growing army of beggars and needy, who made up more than 10% of the population of this *département*. The low agricultural yields of the small farmsteads and the high birthrate led to rural overpopulation: in 1882, one-seventh of all the maids in the 89 French *départements* were working on farms in the three Breton *départements*. The mechanization of agriculture slowly reduced the need for labor, while the region simultaneously remained barely industrialized and poorly urbanized. In 1914, only 14% of Bretons were living in cities, while 44% of the French population as a whole did so.

The cities evidently exerted a stronger attraction on young women than on young men. Many Breton girls from large families, most of whom lived in very small farmhouses that often had neither electricity nor running water until the 1950s, dreamed of a more comfortable life in the city. Through the railroad, which reached Brest in 1865, and in school they learned of other ways of living; an urban, modern life no longer seemed unattainable. The willingness of young Breton women to leave their agrarian region of origin encountered an urban supply of jobs. In the bourgeois society of France, hiring a domestic was a sign of social advancement. More than 900,000 domestics were counted in France at the end of the 19th century, 123,000 of them in Paris, alone; 83% were women, one-sixth of whom came from Brittany.

A variety of ways brought the young women to Paris: some joined up with tourists from Paris who promised to take them into their service. Others followed their girlfriends or relatives: a niece could replace her aunt, or sisters were successively employed in the same household. Religious organizations also placed domestics. Some women set out for Paris without having made any contacts, and some fell into the hands of shady characters upon their arrival at the Montparnasse train station. Between 1908 and 1911, alone, the organization L'Œuvre des Gares Parisiennes, set up in 1905, helped about 8,000 maids find a job when they had arrived with no employer and no place to live.

While the men who came from Brittany to Paris, most of whom worked as unskilled laborers, concentrated in certain quarters of the suburbs, like Saint-Denis, the young Breton women lived dispersed over the entire city. They often felt lonely, even though they formed the largest group of Breton immigrants in the capital up to the First World War. As the sole employee in service to a family, a domestic often worked more than 15 hours a day and had little opportunity to meet other Breton women. A 16- or 17-year-old girl had to make her way alone in a completely new social and cultural environment, had to dress differently, and was not allowed to speak her native language. The accustomed social norms of the rural community no longer applied, and at times the migrants had to break even with their religious convictions. Deracination was often the result, especially since the possibilities of home leave were severely restricted, since financial means were lacking and vacation was rarely granted until the social legislation of the French Popular Front in 1936.

The break with the cultural and moral world from which they came was also evident in sexual relations. In Paris in 1890, 50% of young, single mothers were domestics. They often lost their jobs, and some engaged in prostitution to survive: at the end of the 19th century, 40% of the illegal prostitutes were former domestics. But the integration process could also be very different: for one, at the end of the 19th century the economic situation of domestics was already better than that of female factory workers. Moreover, the attractiveness of new office jobs in the interwar period exacerbated the shortage of domestics and led to wage increases. For no small number of young women, life as a domestic was only a short phase of training and employment before marriage. Many returned to Brittany; others settled permanently in Paris.

For example, between 1890 and 1914, more than half of all Breton women in the 14th district of Paris married men not of Breton background; for male immigrants from Brittany, only 20% married a non-Breton. A comparison with the female Breton factory workers in Saint-Denis shows a broader social range among the husbands of Breton domestics; work as a maid could thus be a means of social advancement. After the Second World War, the integration of the domestics who had remained in Paris manifested itself, for example, in their activity in placing newly arrived Breton girls. Others, like Suzanne Ascoët, for instance, became advocates for the interests of the domestics. Born in Pont-l'Abbé in 1926 and employed as a domestic since age 17, Ascoët was active in the Jeunesse Ouvrière Chrétienne (Christian Working Youth), remained a domestic in Paris her entire life, and eventually became legal advisor to a union for domestics.

The ways in which domestics saw themselves and were perceived by others were very different in Brittany and Paris. Beginning at the end of the 19th century, the clergy and a number of Breton notables expressed grave concerns about the attraction of Paris and warned against leaving. For example, in 1913 the Union Régionaliste Bretonne published the poster "Les méfaits de l'émigration. Marie-Jeanne à Paris" (The ravages of emigration. Marie-Jeanne in Paris). In pictures, it told the fateful path of a young girl from her parents' farm to her deathbed in a Paris hospital. To prevent the deleterious effects of the exodus of domestics, Abbé Cadic founded the Breton Parish of Paris (La Paroisse Bretonne de Paris) in 1897. Through social and cultural activities, he sought to preserve the faith of Breton women and men living in Paris and their bonds to the homeland. This attempt to fight the deracination following emigration had some success until the First World War. Abbé Elie Gauthier revived this movement in 1947. The Breton initiatives to limit the exodus or mitigate integration problems point to the often negative assessment of the migration of domestics in their region of origin. In 1935, the church bulletin of Langonnet, a small community in the heart of Brittany, denounced the dangers of migration with the same words that had been used at the end of the 19th century: "If the parents knew, if the girls knew what awaited them in the city, they would not go away. They are exploited, badly housed, inadequately paid, exposed to the loss of their health, are lost and founder in the large city, without help, without support. Alas, how many of these young girls from our villages end up on the sidewalks of Paris!"

Around the same time, the picture of the Breton girl as a "maid for every job" spread in Paris at the end of the 19th century. Literature took hold of the stereotype. In 1900, Octave Mirabeau, in *Le journal d'une femme* (The Diary of a Woman), has the Breton Célestine say: "Being a domestic is something you have in your blood." The Breton maid, supposedly naïve and easy prey, formed a recurring theme in satirical publications. For many Bretons, however, Célestine and Bécassine symbolized the humiliation of an entire region, dominated and culturally overlaid by the French. The current of migration reversed direction at the end of the 1960s, not least as a result of growing tourism. Breton women increasingly found work in their homeland. In Paris, the jobs of Breton maids were taken over, first by Spanish and Portuguese women, and later by women migrants from Africa and Asia.

Corgniet, Viviane. *Les mouvements migratoires dans la commune de Langonnet de la fin du XIXe siècle à nos jours*. Brest, n.d.

Gautier, Élie. *L'émigration bretonne. Où vont les Bretons émigrants. Leurs conditions de vie*. Paris, 1953.

Guyvarc'h, Didier. "Le mépris et le chagrin, Un entre-deux." In *Femmes de Bretagne. Images et histoire*, edited by Alain Croix, 125–59. Rennes, 1998.

Martin-Fugier, Anne. *La place des bonnes. La domesticité féminine à Paris en 1900*. Paris, 1979.

Page Moch, Leslie. "Networks among Bretons? The Evidence for Paris, 1875–1925." *Continuity and Change* 18 (2003): 431–55.

Cross-references: France

BRITISH AFFLUENCE MIGRANTS IN THE COSTA DEL SOL IN THE LATE 20TH CENTURY

Karen O'Reilly

British people began migrating in increasing numbers to Spain's Costa del Sol during the last quarter of the 20th century. They were part of a trend that began with package tourism in the 1960s, second home ownership in the 1970s, and mass migration starting in the 1980s. Numbers are difficult to ascertain for various reasons – this is a largely undocumented and unregulated migratory flow – but commentators have noted that this migration has had significant local effects and has markedly changed the affected towns. It is important to distinguish between the migrants in terms of degree of permanence: there are those who migrate and live in their new destination, others who have seasonal visits, while others move back and forth between home and host countries. Spain has labeled the migrants "residential tourists." Of course, the British are not the only group to be part of this trend. There are now a number of retirees from northern European countries inhabiting areas of the Mediterranean coast, most notably from Germany, France, the Netherlands, Sweden, and Switzerland.

The British migrants to Spain are not integrated into Spanish society: they tend to be either retired, self-employed, or working in the informal economy; few speak Spanish; and they have constructed firm community boundaries which, while enabling them to settle more comfortably, also serve to marginalize them further. At the same time, however, they do not exhibit a strong longing for home nor the myth of return that is common among ethnic minorities. Indeed, they celebrate their new lives and new home and describe a desire to integrate that is continually frustrated when actually interacting with the local population. Younger migrants who grew up in Spain as well as those who settle inland are more likely than others to form bonds with Spanish people.

During the early 1960s, several factors contributed to the rapid growth of international tourism: the increase in real disposable incomes of northern Europeans, the increase in leisure time and paid holidays gained by workers across the social spectrum, and developments in transport that made long-distance travel cheaper and more comfortable. In the course of these developments, Spain became a preferred destination. The phenomenon of the all-inclusive package tour was crucial and created considerable business opportunities in the UK. Mass tourism as a form of mass consumption tends to be highly spatially concentrated. This applied particularly to the Mediterranean region, where new resorts like Fuengirola and Torremolinos in the Costa del Sol sprouted up almost overnight.

This period of large-scale vacationing by the British at Spanish resorts marked the beginning of what was later to become a mass migration trend. A few Britons settled in the resort areas more permanently in the 1960s but they were in the minority at least until the death of Franco in 1975. Then, through the 1970s, more and more Britons visited each year, some staying longer, returning, and eventually buying second homes. During the 1980s Spain's government became aware of the seasonal and regional nature of tourism, which brought a downward spiral in incomes each winter, and to compensate for this, it began actively to encourage foreign investment in Spain and foreign purchase of land and property. Developers capitalized on this new market, building cheap, often poorly constructed blocks of high-rise apartments in an unregulated fashion in many of the most popular resorts. As a result, *urbanisaciones* (new, densely concentrated developments of apartments and villas) sprang up in a spontaneous and often unplanned manner in and around these same resorts.

At this time, Britain was experiencing an economic boom, massive growth in the property market, and an increase in expendable wealth for many traditionally lower- and lower-middle class individuals. For the first time, many more people had money to spend on second homes, which, with the lengthening of holidays from work or while retired, they could visit for longer and longer periods. Others were able to sell properties in Britain, making huge profits with which to buy first homes in more affordable Spain, effectively securing a higher standard of living for themselves for their retirement.

Still others increased their income by establishing small businesses that served tourists and newly settled communities of expatriates in the resort areas. So began a migration trend with a snowball effect. During the mid-1980s the exchange rate fluctuated at around 200 pesetas to the pound sterling, reaching its high point of 220 pesetas to the pound in 1985. Tourists were now flocking to Spain in large numbers and, attracted by the low prices, favorable exchange rates, the sun and sea, and the welcoming infrastructure of the tourist areas, increasingly began to view Spain as a place to retire, but also to work. In Fuengirola and places like it, many Britons became aware of the business opportunities created by the presence of so many British tourists and started to offer various services: car hire, bars, restaurants, laundries, letting agents, and later, real estate agencies. Other individuals began to settle in search of work within these industries in resort areas with their beautiful surroundings and seemingly relaxed way of life.

During the 1990s, a recession in Britain together with the slump in the property market curbed the migration of Britons who had previously been able to sell their property at huge profits in Britain and buy real estate more cheaply in Spain. The peseta gained strength against the pound sterling for a time, and Spain was no longer as attractive and cheap for tourists and migrants. But in the 21st century, the flow has not been stemmed entirely: figures from real estate agents dealing in foreign properties estimated a 400% increase in purchases of Spanish property during 1999–2000.

Several authors have recognized the problems of obtaining hard data on this migration trend as little systematic research has been done and because official statistics do not reflect discrete migration trends within the main trend. Similarly, existing statistics are both difficult to obtain and rather unreliable because of the fluidity and unofficial nature of the migrant population. The best one can offer is a range of statistics from a variety of sources, with the caveat that the figures are not from comparable sources for comparable groups. For example, a Spanish study estimates the number of Britons living in 1990 in Mijas at 25,000 – this in a village whose total population at the time numbered only 36,000. This estimate is presumably far too high: only 6,500 British residents appeared in Mijas Council census figures in 1994. However, by 2001 the revision of the communal inhabitants registration counted 85,500 foreigners in the province of Málaga, 32,500 of whom were British (followed by Germans, French, and Danes as the main groups).

Figures for the whole of Spain vary widely. In June 1999 an English-language newspaper reported that 600,000 English-speaking foreigners were living in southern Spain. Another estimate set the number of British residents in Spain at almost 47,000 in 1986 and 73,000 by 1989. According to European Commission figures, 86,000 Britons lived in Spain in 1991 while other reports estimated that by 1994 there were between 100,000 and 300,000 of them. In 1993 the consulate in the Costa Blanca suggested a figure of 25,000 retired Britons living in the area alone. A 2006 academic study estimated that 750,000 Britons live in Spain. Among northern European migrants, the British are certainly the largest group overall in Spain, with the ratio of women to men remaining unclear.

In light of the transitory character of cross-border migration between Great Britain and Spain, a simple distinction between the phenomena of tourism and migration cannot be made. While some British migrants in Spain settle permanently, others move peripatetically back and forth during the year. Residence patterns are so fluid that the very concept of "permanent place of residence" is inadequate. However, the forms of movement can be loosely grouped into "ideal types" based on a combination of two factors: an individual's sense of belonging to one or another country and the time spent in one place of residence or another. In this manner, four main groups can be distinguished: full residents, returning residents, seasonal visitors, and peripatetic visitors.

Full residents are individuals who have moved to the area permanently. They generally identify as living in Spain and often state they have no intention of ever returning to live in their home country. Many own property or a business in Spain, while others rent their homes there. Many are retired but an equally large number works in Spain, most with an average age of 40 to 50.

Returning residents are resident in Spain in terms of home, orientation, and legal status. This group is made up mainly of retired or economically independent individuals who typically return to Britain each summer for anywhere from two to five months to escape the searing heat and overwhelming crowds of the Costa del Sol summer. Their temporary return home often provides the opportunity to spend time with their families. Many of these people own homes in Spain, but a significant number rent property in the form of apartments and small villas. A number of them own a second home or a "mobile" home in Britain, enabling their seasonal return, while others rely on friends and relatives to supply accommodation during their visits.

Seasonal visitors live in Britain but return to Spain each winter, attracted by, among other things, affordable prices for housing and leisure, the welcome of the established British community, and the health benefits of avoiding a harsh British winter. They are almost always retired individuals or couples who own property in Britain and who may also own property in Spain. Their winter stay can last anywhere from a couple of months to six months each year and is not always taken in one trip: many return to Britain for the Christmas period, for example. The qualitative difference between this group and the *residents* is their orientation, which is more strongly directed toward "home" than "host" country. However, they tend to have emotional ties and commitments in Spain and often spend enough time there for the visit to be much more than a simple diversion from their daily routine in Britain. Though their visit to Spain does not involve a clearly defined change of permanent residence, they are migrants rather than tourists. The average age of this group is about 60.

The fourth group, *peripatetic visitors*, usually own a second home in Fuengirola or the surrounding area and visit when they can. These visits typically have no pattern or routine and may be dictated by business or work in either Britain or Spain, by health, wealth, or family commitments. This group has a lower average age than the other groups, in the 30s to 50s. The orientation of peripatetic visitors is often divided between Britain and Spain and thus rather transnational, with either country alternately being considered "home." Commitments such as property, family, friends, and work in Spain mean their visits amount to more than leisure, travel, or tourism: peripatetic visitors identify themselves as migrants rather than tourists.

Figures for age, sex ratio, and household composition are not yet available for this still undocumented population. Couples and families, however, appear to predominate among the younger groups. The typical household unit for the *retired* British migrant is a married or cohabiting couple without dependent children who moved after retiring in early old age. Quantitative studies with a slightly higher proportion of male than female respondents report that approximately 70% of respondents live as part of a couple and a similar percentage lives in two-person households. Women predominate in single-person households, which make up approximately 25% of the samples.

British migrants in Spain have been characterized as retirement migrants and it is true to say that pensioners form a substantial part of the group. However, many of the migrants are much younger than retirement age and many move their entire families to Spain, where their children attend school or, if they are older, seek work. The seasonal visitor and returning resident groups discussed above are generally retired people, whereas full residents are often younger and include people in their 20s who migrate independently of their families. In fact, in June 1999, the English-language newspaper, the *Sur in English*, claimed that the age of its readership was decreasing as increasing numbers of working-age people were joining the community.

Labeling the British migrants in their totality as retirees is also problematic since many older migrants of retirement age in Spain are still working while some young migrants retired early as part of their migration. Older migrants insist that the experience of aging in this context is completely different from what it would be had they stayed in Britain and that they therefore cannot be understood through the general category of "the elderly." Older British people in Spain feel they have improved health and a better way of life than they would have in Britain.

It is the search for a new way of life that has prompted many of the migrants to leave Britain, be it permanently, seasonally, or peripatetically. Further reasons that people give for migrating to Spain can be separated into two distinct categories: negative views about life in Britain and positive views about life in Spain. Some of these negative factors, such as divorce, unemployment, and high crime rates, provided a specific trigger to the move, but a bundle of factors influencing the decision to "get out" can usually be identified.

At the same time, these push factors are often balanced by pull factors: the positive things about Spain that drew them to the country. These include, first, natural resources like the climate and the landscape; second, benefits offered by the settled British community such as social clubs, leisure opportunities, and a welcoming community; and, third, advantages offered by the Spanish community, such as respect for children and the elderly, friendliness, warmth, security, and a more leisurely pace of life.

A newfound anonymity also attracts some people: "the opportunity to start again in a new place, with a clean slate," as one respondent put it. Overwhelmingly, migrants who have settled permanently in Spain insist that they never want to return home. Indeed, a commitment to Spain is part of the community identity that distinguishes insiders from outsiders. Anyone who entertains the idea of returning home would admit so only privately and with regret.

Despite the fact that there is no myth of return and no romantic longing for home and even a strong identification with Spanish culture, Britons living in the Costa del Sol cannot be considered integrated within wider Spanish society, neither in terms of ethnic identity nor of social life. British bars are full of British customers and British clubs have almost exclusively British members. Britons spend their free time relaxing with other Britons in clubs and bars, on the beach, or making excursions to Gibraltar. There are British clubs for almost every interest and activity: bowling clubs, a cricket club, an arts center, a Scottish folk dancing club, bridge clubs, a theater group, Brownie Guides, walking clubs, social clubs, fund-raising groups, and many more. Clubs run by other nationalities – Spanish bars, the local pensioners club, and the Casa de la Cultura (Spanish arts center and local center for culture and adult education), for example – have very few British members, visitors, or customers. There are even an Anglican church and a British cemetery as well as a British bakery, English and Scottish butcher shops, an English grocery store, and several English bookshops. For many British, daily life involves talking to and spending time with other British people and very little interaction with the Spanish.

Some commentators have described affluence migration as a modern form of colonialism. However, the area of land to which these Britons have moved is governed neither by the country or state from which they emigrated nor by the migrants themselves; the migrants also are not subject to British jurisdiction. The situation also does not fit the model of more subtle economic domination or control commonly referred to as "neo-colonialism." In fact, the economic influence of many migrants is rather marginal, with most either living off their British pensions or working in the informal economy. Also not helpful is the categorization of these migrants as expatriates in the usual sense of the word, characterized by wealth, power, privilege, and status. The migrants are also not trying to reestablish "a little England in the sun."

These migrants also do not have much political or economic power. In fact, they are excluded from the main Spanish institutions. Britons in Spain have no power to vote in general elections and have only grudgingly been granted the right to vote in local elections. The absence of national voting rights for resident foreigners is in fact what differentiates them from Spanish citizens. Full rights of citizenship are further limited by the fact that European residents must prove they are financially independent or independent in terms of social security before being granted the right to remain in the host country. No matter how one is accepted in the new country, one remains in terms of citizenship a member of one's country of origin. At the same time, Britons in Spain have not sought to integrate more fully and seem content to live in a symbolic space between both countries, which allows them to take advantage of the benefits of each country as is necessary and possible.

Casado-Díaz, Maria. "Retiring to Spain: An Analysis of Difference among North European Nationals." *Journal of Ethnic and Migration Studies* 32, 8 (2006): 1321–39.

King, Russell, Anthony Warnes, and Allan M. Williams. *Sunset Lives: British Retirement Migration to the Mediterranean.* Oxford, 2000.

O'Reilly, Karen. *The British on the Costa del Sol: Transnational Identities and Local Communities.* London, 2000.

O'Reilly, Karen. "Intra-European Migration and the Mobility-Enclosure Dialectic." *Sociology* 41, 2 (2007): 277–93.

Rodríguez, Vincente, Maria A. Casado Díaz, and Andreas Huber, eds. *La Migración de Europeos Retirados en España.* Madrid, 2005.

Rodríguez, Vincente, Gloria Fernández-Mayoralas, and Fermina Rojo. "European Retirees on the Costa del Sol: A Cross-National Comparison." *International Journal of Population Geography* 4 (1998): 183–200.

Soysal, Yasemin. "Changing Citizenship in Europe: Remarks on Postnational Membership and the National State." In *Citizenship, Nationality and Migration in Europe*, edited by David Cesarini, 17–29. London, 1996.

Valenzuela, Manuel. "Spain: The Phenomenon of Mass Tourism." In *Tourism and Economic Development: Western European Experiences*, edited by Gareth Shaw and Allan M. Williams, 40–60. London, 1988.

Cross-references: Great Britain; Spain and Portugal; German Affluence Migrants in Spain since the Late 20th Century

BRITISH MERCHANTS IN PORTUGAL SINCE 1640

Cátia Antunes

In the second half of the 17th century, the British community in Portugal was mainly made up of English merchants and their families, joined by a small number of Irish and Scots.

The English presence in Portugal can be traced back to the 14th century, when, in 1359, the two main trading cities of the kingdom – Lisbon and Porto – obtained a safe-conduct, signed by King Edward III, to trade with England for the duration of 50 years. English merchants, like their German, Flemish, and Italian counterparts, became a common sight in Medieval and Renaissance Portuguese society.

When Portugal broke free of the Spanish Habsburg Empire in 1640, King John IV sought England's diplomatic and commercial support and England subsequently became one of Portugal's most significant political and commercial partners, alongside the United Provinces of the Netherlands and France. Even though England was in the middle of a civil war (1642–9), both royalists and parliamentarians declared their full support for the new Portuguese king. This amicable relationship with both the warring parties in the English civil war endangered the position of the British community in Portugal. Although the economic position of British merchants was never disrupted, religious and political disputes between Anglicans, Puritans, Presbyterians, and Catholics eroded social networks within the group. Portuguese authorities further fanned the conflict by at times favoring one or another group among the British merchants in accordance with their changing position toward the warring parties in England. This internal conflict among the British merchant community came to an end only when Portugal and England signed the commercial treaty of 1654. In 1703, the treaty of Methuen reinforced the treaty of 1654, seen by many as a sign that Portugal and England had become inseparable diplomatic and commercial partners.

In the second half of the 17th century, British merchants settled in Lisbon, Porto, Faro, and Madeira, all of which were centers with a long commercial tradition and which allowed British merchants to control the trade with English and continental European ports. The various communities of English merchants maintained close contacts with one another, but were not formally organized. It is impossible to establish the exact date when the British merchant community in Portugal was institutionalized as such, but the British in Lisbon, Porto, and Madeira were already organized into trading centers called factories by the mid-17th century. Access to membership in a factory depended principally on the volume of a merchant's trade. Residence in Portugal was advantageous but not absolutely necessary. Merchants, for example, could leave the country to operate from England or other British factories in Iberia, such as San Lucas de Barrameda in Spain.

The members of the factories acquired not only additional business opportunities but also social prestige as well as direct access to ports, products, and business partners in Portugal and its overseas possessions. At the same time, the social and economic authority of the factories guaranteed a secure environment for financial transactions among members, particularly for expensive investments and the granting of credit. The factories not only had merchants in their ranks but also a chaplain and a *conservador*. The factory often appointed the chaplain after he had been nominated by some of the notable members of the organization. The Treaty of 1654 institutionalized the position of the *conservador*, which was to be filled by a Portuguese and who was to be remunerated by the factory. As mediator between the British communities and the Portuguese authorities, the *conservador* dealt with questions covering trade rights, the exploitation of monopolies, the resolution of conflicts provoked by privateering or piracy, and the housing of merchants and their families. The *conservador* was also responsible for protecting the British merchants from the Inquisition.

The British factories of Lisbon, Porto, and Madeira existed for centuries. Families such as the Burrels, Maynards, or Coppendales formed merchant dynasties that decisively influenced trade throughout the entire early modern period. A prime example of the close cooperation between British and Portuguese merchants is provided by the letting of English ships to the Companhia Geral do Comércio do Brasil, which was founded in 1649. John Maynard used his extensive networks in Porto and Lisbon to obtain enough ships to cover the overseas trade of the Portuguese company. This trade agreement proved highly profitable not only for Maynard but also for his business associates and the Portuguese king. The Maynards were paid for their services in cash and sugar and were awarded indirect access to the Brazilian markets while Portuguese port cities were guaranteed significant economic support from the British merchant community.

British merchants in Portugal specialized in the re-export of colonial products, especially sugar and wood from Brazil, from Portugal to England, but they also took part in the trade within Europe. They made use of their extensive trade networks to import codfish, textiles, and books from England to Portugal. They also exported Portuguese wine, fruit, and salt to England and other European countries.

At the start of the 18th century the British community was mainly composed of merchants who came from British ports like London, Bristol, Plymouth, and Portsmouth, and from Dublin, and Cork. The immigrants were divided into two different groups. On the one hand, there were merchants who came to Portugal for a prolonged stay. Part of this group arrived at a young age; some men were newly married and came with their young families, and others were single and hoped to find a suitable wife within the British merchant community in Portugal. The other group was far more dynamic and stayed in Portugal for only short periods of time. This group included merchants who stayed temporarily to set up deals, solve conflicts, or solidify network relationships, but it also included diplomatic personnel and auxiliary troops who never became stable members of the British community in Portugal.

The relatively peaceful coexistence of the British merchants and the Portuguese authorities came to an end with the earthquake in Lisbon in 1755. The Marquis of Pombal, Sebastião José de Carvalho e Melo, minister of King José I, viewed the rebuilding of the capital as an opportunity to introduce fundamental economic, political, social, and cultural changes throughout the country. The policies of the marquis were disastrous for the British living in Portugal. His promotion of national production and the successful implementation of protective measures against imports created one of the most significant crises in Anglo-Portuguese commercial relations. The 1760s witnessed a massive decline in bilateral trade. Strict state control over the largest sources of national income – gold from Brazil and wine, especially port – worsened the situation. By restricting mass imports from Great Britain, the minister tried to block British access to Brazilian bullion and to bring the production and sale of port and other wines under Portuguese control. The British communities in Lisbon and Porto felt seriously threatened. They petitioned the royal minister and the king himself, calling attention to the millions of pounds invested by the community in Portugal, including support for the development of the textile industry. The conflict was resolved only when Pombal left his position and King José I died in 1777.

The British merchants were able to recover their previous position of dominance only in the 19th century, when they took over the production of port wine in the Douro valley (Porto region). The introduction of the British banking system and the import of textiles and other industrial products (e.g., railways, machinery) soon allowed British merchants to dominate the Portuguese market.

Fisher, Harold E. S. *The Portugal Trade: A Study of Anglo-Portuguese Commerce, 1700–1770*. London, 1971.

Gonçalves, Maria G. N. *A comunidade britânica no Porto. Inter-relações históricas, económicas, culturais e educativas*. Porto, 2003.

Magalhães, Joaquim R. "Os ingleses no Algarve nos séculos XVII e XVIII." *Anais do Município de Faro* 19 (1989): 31–40.

Sideri, Sandro. *Comércio e poder – colonialismo informal nas relações anglo-portuguesas*. Lisbon, 1978.

Shaw, L. M. E. *The Anglo-Portuguese Alliance and the English Merchants in Portugal, 1654–1810*. Aldershot, 1998.

Cross-references: Great Britain; Spain and Portugal

BRITISH ROYALISTS IN WESTERN, CENTRAL, AND SOUTHERN EUROPE, 1640-1660

Michael Schaich

In the 1640s, when the British monarchy was shaken by civil war and eventually overthrown by the revolutionary events at the end of 1648 and the beginning of 1649, a royalist movement arose on the European continent and, to a considerably lesser extent, also in North America, a movement whose sole raison d'être was the struggle against the rule of Parliament and the reinstatement of the house of Stuart. Over the course of the 1640s and the following decade, nobles loyal to the king, soldiers who had fought on the side of King Charles I in the civil wars, royal ministers and advisors, and members of the court left their homeland. The group of royalist exiles dissolved only with the return of King Charles II to the English throne in 1660.

The total number of refugees during this period of nearly 20 years, including women, children, and servants, is likely to have been at most a few thousand. The vast majority of royalists remained in the British Isles even after the final defeat of Charles I in 1648 and tried to endure the republic through accommodation, withdrawal into "internal emigration" ("cavalier winter"), or underground activity. Only a minority went into exile, and the motives that led to this decision were exceedingly diverse: they ranged from unshakable loyalty to the monarchy, which ruled out any form of coexistence with the new rulers, to pure love of adventure and fear of persecution, to rather pragmatic considerations resulting from the loss of all prospects of a career in the state, the church, or the university.

The composition of the royalist exile community was never stable: few refugees spent the entire time abroad until the restoration of the monarchy. Some returned from exile prematurely, and not only in the spring of 1652 when the Act of Oblivion passed by Parliament prompted many royalists to return. Some crossed back and forth over the English Channel, vacillating undecided between exile and longer stays at home, while others still returned repeatedly to British soil in secret to prepare and carry out uprisings and plots.

This instability of the refugee group notwithstanding, one can make some general statements about their migratory movements: the first royalists left the British Isles in 1640 after the forced summoning of the "Long Parliament," which for the first time took action against individual followers of Charles I. The royalists in exile received prominent reinforcement in 1644, when the king, in the midst of the first civil war, sent his wife, Henrietta Maria, and her court to France to remove her from the reach of Parliament. Two years later, following the defeat of the Cavaliers, the number of refugees experienced another surge. Among them was also the future Charles II, who fled with his advisors and courtiers via the Scilly Islands and Jersey to France, as well as a series of high-ranking royalists, chief among them Prince Ruprecht of the Palatinate. But the movement of refugees continued even during the 1650s: at the turn of 1656–7, for example, several hundred followers of the house of Stuart arrived on the Continent all at once when Spanish help seemed to make the raising of a potent invasion army an imminent possibility.

Most exiles sought refuge in the United Provinces of the Netherlands, in France, or in the Spanish Netherlands, though some also went to the Holy Roman Empire of the German Nation or southern Europe. In general, however, there was hardly a European country that did not host some royalists, however briefly. A few refugees even made it to Asia and Africa on their journeys. Less surprising is the existence of royalist exile communities in the British colonies in North America, especially in Virginia. The focal point of the exile was in western Europe, of course, which is explained not only by its geographic proximity to the British homeland but also by the close ties of the Stuarts to the ruling dynasties in these countries.

Both in Paris and the Hague, the refugee members of the British royal family found refuge with relatives in the 1640s. For example, Henrietta Maria, as the daughter of King Henry IV, was not only given an *apanage* by the French royal house but was also assigned as her residence a wing of the Louvre and after 1652 the Palais Royal, as well as outside of Paris the château of St. Germain-en-Laye. Until 1654, Charles II and the future king Jacob II, who fled London in 1648, also lived with their mother in Paris for long periods, though they also spent time in the Hague at the court of their sister Mary, the wife of King William II of Orange. It was only when the rapprochement between France and England since the early 1650s made the situation increasingly difficult for Charles II in Paris did he shift his residence, first to Cologne in 1654, and then, in the wake of financial and political help from the Spanish crown, to the Spanish Netherlands in 1656 (Bruges, Brussels), while the Queen Mother continued to live in France.

The courts of the various members of the royal house, as modest as they may have been at times given the chronic money shortage of the refugees, formed simultaneously the centers of the royalist exile. They offered the nobles a chance to earn their livelihood in a manner that was suitable to their social standing, and to define their social status through a position at court while abroad. First and foremost, however, the courts functioned as stages for the continued performance of monarchical ritual and political hubs, sites of tireless preparations for plots and uprisings against Parliament or even a fully fledged invasion of England. No less important than the plans to overthrow the Republic, which went hand in hand with diplomatic maneuvering to gain recognition throughout Europe for Charles II's claim to the throne, were the efforts to tap into ever new sources of financing to support the king who was suffering from a constant shortage of money. In the process, the ministers of Charles II not only sought support payments from friendly princes, loans from bankers, or aid payments from supporters abroad. They also went so far as to blackmail English merchant guilds on the Continent or resorted to the services of freebooters, who were given letters of marque in return for a share of the booty.

The courtiers spent a good deal of their time and energy, however, on power struggles between the various wings of the royalist camp. Condemned to political inaction over many years, they devoted themselves intently to carrying on internal rivalries that were triggered by different ideas about the best way to achieve the restoration of the monarchy and came to a head in countless intrigues and duels. For many observers, the internal factionalism at the courts of the exiled Stuarts became the true characteristic of the royalist exile.

However, away from the courts there also existed in various west European cities separate exile communities that helped new arrivals to find housing and local contacts or functioned as an information exchange. In Antwerp,

William and Margaret Cavendish, who had rented the house of Peter Paul Rubens from the artist's heirs, were active as patrons for artists and scholars, among them Constantijn Huygens and Nicholas Lanier. However, most of the refugees lived in meager material circumstances and just barely got by with occasional jobs or by taking out loans. By contrast, wealthier royalists often used their time on the Continent for educational trips. In fact, there was even a separate royalist travel guide for the most popular destination, Italy. In some cases it is difficult to decide where the Grand Tour began and the exile ended. Finally, many refugees, among them also the future king Jacob II, served as soldiers in the armies of European princes, with the result that refugee Englishmen repeatedly faced each other on opposite sides in the great battles in the middle of the century.

The British mercenaries were the only group that presumably integrated to any extent into their host countries. Most other royalists, leaving aside exceptions like William and Margaret Cavendish, probably remained outsiders in their new environment, as is revealed even by a look at the situation of the exiled courts. While Henrietta Maria, as "fille de France," had far-reaching access to court society in France, the courts of Charles and Jacob, especially after 1649, when the European powers did not wish to provoke the English Republic unnecessarily, remained largely isolated. Although Charles II himself and a few other high-ranking British nobles were a regular presence at the French court, especially in the 1640s, the exiled courts of the two Stuarts constituted separate enclaves during their time in Paris, barely noticed by the French nobility.

Conversely, the royalists rarely had to leave the circle of exiles to enjoy a minimum of sociability. For example, the Hague and Paris were home to English acting troops in the middle of the 1640s. Moreover, in the French capital, Anglican services were regularly held in the private chapel of the diplomatic representative of Charles II. The Paris exiles even had their own cemetery. In addition, the Continent already had older British exile communities, made up of Irish mercenaries or English Catholics, which could become destinations for the royalists. It would appear that the refugees often received support from the émigré Catholics, whether through refuge in monastic houses, the transmission of news and letters, or financial help. As a result, a stronger integration of the exiles into their host countries is not likely to have occurred. The relative brevity of the exile alone, as well as the already mentioned turnover within the refugee communities, rendered such a development unlikely.

While the royalists hardly left behind any traces on the Continent, the experience of exile did have some repercussions back in Great Britain. When the first returnees set out for home in March 1660, already two months before the official restoration of the monarchy, they carried in their luggage also new ideas and cultural influences. Scholars have seen ceremonial changes at the British court and the growing popularity of traveling on the Continent, as well as innovations in literature, architecture, and fashion, as consequences of a forced cultural transfer. At the same time, a transfigured memory of exile emerged in Great Britain after 1660. In memoirs, martyrologies, and – to some extent – in historical works such as Edward Hyde's influential *History of the Rebellion and Civil Wars in England* (first published Oxford 1702–4), the reader encounters a royalist refugee who, militarily defeated and living under strained material conditions, remained loyal to his king and worked indefatigably on the restoration of the divinely ordained monarchy. However, to what extent this view of the past took hold within the royalist movement beyond some individual groups must remain an open question, given the current state of scholarship. Moreover, after 1689 and the renewed expulsion of the Stuarts there arose in the myth of Jacobitism a competing memory which in the end displaced that of the refugees from the years 1640 to 1660.

Greenspan, Nicole. "Public Scandal, Political Controversy, and Familial Conflict in the Stuart Courts in Exile: The Struggle to Convert the Duke of Gloucester in 1654." *Albion* 35 (2003): 398–427.

Hutton, Ronald. *Charles II: King of England, Scotland, and Ireland*. Oxford, 1989.

Keay, Anna. *The Magnificent Monarch: Charles II and the Ceremonies of Power*. London, 2008.

Royalist Refugees: William and Margaret Cavendish in the Rubens House 1648–1660. Exhibition Catalogue. Antwerp, 2006.

Smith, Geoffrey. *The Cavaliers in Exile, 1640–1660*. Basingstoke, 2003.

Walker, Claire. "Prayer, Patronage, and Political Conspiracy: English Nuns and the Restoration." *Historical Journal* 43 (2000): 1–23.

Cross-references: France; Great Britain; The Netherlands; English Comedians in Europe in the Early Modern Period: The Example of the Netherlands; European Elites on the Grand Tour in Early Modern Europe; Jacobites in Europe, 1688–1788; Scottish Soldiers in Europe in the Early Modern Period

BRITISH TECHNICAL EXPERTS IN FRANCE IN THE FIRST HALF OF THE 19TH CENTURY

Michel Cotte

The migration of British technical experts to France in the first half of the 19th century was part of a long tradition of cultural and technological transfer via migration in Europe. The British experts were workers and engineers, occasionally also entrepreneurs. A clear label is often difficult, since the activities of the immigrants could change, depending on opportunities and personal skills. Social and geographic mobility was the rule. Because of the professional competence that was required, this phenomenon remained limited to a few thousand individuals; it may have reached 10,000 during the peak years in the second half of the 1820s.

The British experts came to France at the beginning of the first phase of that country's industrialization after 1815. Following the end of the Napoleonic wars, a kind of Anglomania developed among the French aristocracy, newly returned to power, and among entrepreneurs and engineers. Technical experts from the "motherland of industrialization" came into most European countries during the phase of industrial upswing. The immediate technological and economic consequences of this immigration can be hardly quantified, since a host of various factors contributed to industrial development. The migration to France and other European countries formed part of the expansion of the British manufacturing sector through the export of technical know-how and the presence of competent experts in the foreign markets.

Already in the second half of the 18th century, French authorities had put the technological development in Great Britain under close observation, though with middling success; the British spoke of "spying." After 1815 the French state pulled back as an actor in the economy, and within the framework of more liberal ideas, a comprehensive, privately organized French-British exchange of goods, money, and economically useful knowledge developed, which contributed to the spread of the Industrial Revolution in Europe.

The strong influx of British experts to France was limited to a brief period. It grew stronger after 1820, peaked during the social and economic crisis in 1830, dropped off rapidly thereafter, and was virtually over after 1850. Accordingly, the technical experts, who often traveled alone, stayed in France only temporarily, and usually returned to their home country. Only a few experts settled permanently in France as entrepreneurs. Some French companies recruited experts through Frenchmen living in Great Britain or through British intermediaries. Finally, French enterprises under British management – e.g., the Paris smelting works of Manby & Wilson, or several firms in Rouen – played a crucial role in the immigration of experts.

Only a few migrant workers, employed in large and well-organized enterprises like the iron works in Fourchambault in the Département Nièvre, for example, were accompanied by their families. As a rule, they, too, spent only a few years in France. For them, the migration constituted a phase in their professional life that was linked to the hope of earning as much money as possible. British technical experts, even the engineers among them, hardly spoke any French and very rarely tried to learn the language during their stay in France. As a result, the companies often had to fall back on translators. The temporary stays of the foreigners were not regulated by the French authorities. The arriving specialists remained embedded within the sociocultural system of their homeland and only in exceptional cases applied for French citizenship.

French companies wanted to close the gap with British industry through the influx of experts. Most of all, they were interested in modernizing conventional processes for carbonization and the production and processing of iron and steel, processes in the textile industry, and the use of steam engines. In 1820, British specialists were earning twice as much as Frenchmen with comparable qualifications, where they existed at all. After 1840, salaries converged, as there was a growing number of more highly qualified French technicians. The contract that British specialists signed with their employer often contained a clause about the training of local workers. The activities of the specialists ranged all the way to the erection of a turnkey factory – for example, the cotton mill of Ourscamp in the valley of Oise.

British experts did not go to all French regions in equal numbers. Initially they headed to Normandy, the area closest to their own regions of origin, especially to the area around Rouen. The influence of Great Britain on the industrial development and the introduction of new technological processes was more significant and lasting there than in other parts of France. A few enterprises in Normandy were run by the British, a situation that facilitated the immigration of their countrymen. Up to 5,000 British workers were involved in the construction of the railway line from Paris to Rouen. The next goal of the British migrants was Paris; many specialists also went to the large French ports of Bordeaux, Nantes, and Marseille, and from there on to other European port cities.

Far fewer British specialists made it into the interior. The French provinces were considered uncertain economic terrain, and migrations there took place only if they were preceded by clear agreements with a company. In technologically highly developed regions of France, like the area around Saint-Etienne and Lyon, the demand for British specialists was small or limited to a very brief period. Places of early industrialization, such as Mulhouse or Montbéliard in eastern France, did not resort to migrant workers at all.

The emigration of specialists quickly became a political issue in Great Britain. In the 1820s, the economic and political sectors sparked an intense debate over the "combination laws," which regulated the export of machine tools and prohibited the departure of experts in various professions. While entrepreneurs on the Continent emphasized the mechanism of a free labor market, the departing British experts were regarded by many British businessmen as "disloyal traitors." Others profited from the sale of machine tools on the Continent and from the export of know-how. To be sure, the migrants quickly brought new technological knowledge into the French enterprises and thus reduced the competitive advantage of British industry. At the same time, however, they proved to be competent conduits of commercial relationships with British companies and thus promoters of British export: the immigrant experts conceived new projects in France, ordered machines and equipment in Great Britain, and installed British machines. They familiarized native workers with the virtues of British industrial goods, which, in turn, could continue to promote the export of British machines to France even after the British experts had left.

Chassagne, Serge. *Le coton et ses patrons, France 1760–1840.* Paris, 1991.

Cotte, Michel. *De l'espionnage industriel à la veille technologique, la circulation des idées techniques durant la première industrialisation.* Besançon, 2005.

Harris, John. *Industrial Espionage and Technology Transfers, Britain and France in the 18th Century.* Aldershot, 1997.

Payen, Jacques. *La machine locomotive en France, des origines au milieu du XIXe siècle.* Lyon, 1988.

Raveux, Olivier. *Marseille, ville des métaux et de la vapeur au XIXe siècle.* Paris, 1998.

Cross-references: France; Great Britain; English Industrial Workers (Puddlers) in the Belgian Iron Industry in the Early 19th Century; German Industrial Traders and Spies in Great Britain in the 18th and 19th Centuries

BRITISH WAR BRIDES IN NORWAY SINCE THE END OF WORLD WAR II

Grete Brochmann

The Second World War and the German occupation of Norway caused many Norwegian young men to flee to Britain, both civilians and military personnel alike. During these years of exile, a number of these men married British women, with whom they traveled back to Norway to settle after the end of the war in 1945. British war brides differed from the major groups of migrants in that they did not emigrate for either political or economic reasons, but rather they simply fell in love with a foreign national. The phenomenon of marriage-related migration from Britain occurred relatively frequently during wartime, and in significant numbers: 45,000 British women married Canadian men, and more than a million European women (the majority British) married US citizens during the war and accompanied them home across the Atlantic. Compared to these figures, the number of war brides in Norway was very small; sources on the exact numbers are lacking.

How did these young women perceive their lives in the new home country? How quickly, if ever, did they find themselves at ease in their new surroundings, and on the other hand, how soon did the receiving society accept them as equals culturally and socially? There are more questions than answers in relation to this specific group of marriage migrants, because no comprehensive research has been undertaken. The only article available is based on a survey taken in 1982 among 38 women, almost 40 years after they moved to their husbands' home country. These women were all living in the Bergen area on the Norwegian west coast and described their experiences of integration in Norway.

Despite the relative proximity of Norway to Great Britain, "the North Sea can be a cultural barrier as real as the huge distances between Norway and more exotic places," reported one war bride. The emphasis on differences between Norway and Great Britain in the reports of war brides can be attributed to the general change in social status from a single woman to a married wife that they experienced, combined with the change involved in migration to a foreign country. However, even in the 1980s, these war brides still mentioned explicitly the considerable social, economic, and cultural adaptations that were necessary upon their arrival in Norway. The experience of war brides in Norway was similar to the much larger group of British war brides married to Americans or Canadians, who reported facing the same seemingly insurmountable hurdles, and who, despite a common language, complained about the process of integration.

Most of the women left England for Norway in their early 20s. They grew up in peacetime, reached adulthood during the war, and emigrated in a period when Europe was entering a process of comprehensive change. Norway was no exception, although the isolation the country had experienced during the war probably made the atmosphere even less familiar to newly arrived war brides. Norway was, apart from the specific conditions of the war, situated on the European geopolitical periphery. People were not particularly open to newcomers – even from a neighboring Allied country. According to the war brides, they were expected to slide inconspicuously into society – quickly and uncritically – with the least possible disturbance of the "Norwegian way of life."

These women perceived their lives in postwar Norway as an experience of difficult economic and social circumstances. The material standard, particularly housing, sanitary facilities, and access to consumer goods, was significantly worse than what they were used to in Britain. The German occupation had further decreased the Norwegian standard of living. Most couples began by living in a shared house – either with their in-laws or with strangers. Some of them lived in barracks without hot and cold water for as long as 14 years. Sharing a bathroom – if there was one – and a kitchen with other families was common. For most of the British women it took years to accomplish the same kind of life standard they were used to in Britain.

Furthermore, the women met with expectations of their social roles different from what they were accustomed to. In Great Britain most childless women over 17 had been mobilized to contribute to the war economy, in either the civil or the military sphere. This experience had increased their self-esteem and independence, and had contributed to an enhancement of their status in society. It was also through this public engagement that many of the women had met their future Norwegian spouses. Consequently, in contrast to many of the Norwegian women, who were excluded from paid work until after the war, most of the war brides had been engaged in paid work before marriage. The majority of them in fact had some kind of education – medicine, nursing, physiotherapy, teaching, banking, secretarial work, etc. – which they could not make use of in their new surroundings. From their youth in Britain, with the drama of war and accompanying new responsibilities, these women entered a new environment in Norway, where the woman's place was at home and where the rules of behavior for women were stricter than what they were used to. The women interviewed emphasized these differences strongly, even 40 years later.

Estrangement and alienation were familiar phenomena for most immigrants – at least in the beginning. The British women reported enduring homesickness, disorientation, and exhaustion in the first years in Norway. Inadequate knowledge of the "utterly unfamiliar" language and its subtle nuances, of customs and ways of life, and of Norwegian gestures and behavior frustrated the newcomers tremendously, leaving them with feelings of weakness, vulnerability, and inadequacy. With the husband's family as their only link to society, daily life seemed hard for the war brides. The relationship to the mother-in-law was the most vulnerable of all. It was often the task of the mother-in-law to teach the new member of the family correct rules and behavior for a Norwegian housewife. According to the contemporary norms for decent manners, daughters-in-law should not be independent, should not visit restaurants by themselves, should not talk politics with men, and remain quiet in public gatherings.

The feeling of being a second-class person as a woman was reported to be stronger in Norway than in Britain among the immigrants. Their main task was child care, but even this responsibility caused problems. Many of the British women wanted to raise their children in a firmer manner than was customary in Norway at the time, but had to give in to pressure to conform to their new surroundings.

Most of the women also reported that it was difficult to get acquainted with Norwegians. Norwegian women were cool to them and expressed shock about the war brides' ignorance of the local milieu. The social norms were perceived as "strange and unfamiliar"; Norwegians were described as "stiff," "inhibited," "insensitive" – and not least – "closed-mouthed." According to the British women, the expectation among Norwegians was that people should manage life and care for themselves without assistance from other people, or phrased differently, that one should respect the private life of others. Implicitly, when arriving in these communities from outside, one was expected to find one's way without being helped either socially or practically. Several war brides even reported that when their husbands died, their in-laws broke off contact, a fact that underlined their feeling of being accepted only as a function of their spouse.

In the late 1980s, when these British women had lived twice as long in Norway as they had in Britain, many of them still felt both Norwegian and British. The majority had managed to keep dual citizenship, due to a specific arrangement between Great Britain and Norway. Their Norwegian citizenship was valued for various purposes: it allowed them to vote, to travel easily in and out of the country, and also to have a feeling of belonging to Norwegian society. The British citizenship kept open the option of returning to England. They felt loyalty to both countries. Entering old age, a number of the women found themselves in a difficult dilemma: should

they remain in Norway where their children and grandchildren lived, or should they try to return to England?

How can we understand the adjustment process of these women as compared to other types of immigrants? The stories both compare and contrast the ones of other postwar immigrants to Norway. First, the war brides were not a visible minority. They were relatively few in number and were not concentrated in particular areas of the country. Consequently, they were not a part of an immigrant enclave and therefore did not enjoy the support mechanisms of such communities; conversely, they also did not have to endure the specific isolation that could accompany an ethnic community. They were mostly confined to the domestic sphere, in accordance with the social norms for women at the time, which also implied a different kind of isolation. As concerns assimilation, it seems that few of the British women subjectively assimilated. They remained loyal to their background and felt foreign throughout their lifetime. This alienation was admittedly not inherited by the next generation.

Hibbert, Joyce. *The War Brides*. Toronto, 1978.

Rokkan, Elizabeth. "Førti år i Norge: Livssituasjonen til britiske krigsbruder." In *Mellom to kulturer*, edited by Suzanne Stiver Lie. Oslo, 1986.

Shukert, Elfrieda, and Barbara Smith Scibette. *War Brides of World War II*. Novato, CA, 1988.

Virden, Jenel. *Good-bye Piccadilly: British War Brides in America*. Chicago, 1966.

Cross-references: Great Britain; Northern Europe; German War Brides in Western Europe since the End of World War II: The Example of Great Britain

BULGARIAN AND GAGAUZIAN SETTLERS IN NEW RUSSIA AND BESSARABIA SINCE THE 18TH CENTURY

Detlef Brandes

Bulgarian and Gagauzian villages still exist in Ukraine and Moldova at the beginning of the 21st century. The origins of the Turkic-speaking but Greek Orthodox Gagauzians is contested: Bulgarian scholars consider them Turkicized Bulgarians; Russian and Ukrainian researchers see them as remnants of Turkic-speaking nomadic people who migrated into northeastern Bulgaria from the Asian steppes at the turn of the first millennium. The largest settlement areas of the Bulgarians and Gagauzians are closely contiguous and in some parts merge into each other. In the Republic of Moldova, the Gagauzians, with about 153,000 members (1989 figure) outnumber the neighboring Bulgarians at 88,000 strong; by contrast, in Ukraine, the 233,800 Bulgarians outnumber the 32,000 Gagauzians in the regions of Odessa and Zaporizhia.

After her first Russo-Turkish war and the annexation of the Khanate of Crimea (1783), Empress Catherine II considered the territory north of the Black Sea as secure enough to settle foreigners there. This "New Russia," divided in 1802 into the *gubernii* of Cherson, Yekaterinoslav, and Tauria, was only thinly populated. The first Bulgarians and Greeks, who arrived between 1801 and 1810 on Russian ships in the ports of Odessa or Sebastopol, were driven to flee their homelands by fear of Turkish brigands who were infesting especially the area around Adrianople. They established six villages in the *gubernia* of Cherson and three on the Crimea and were therefore placed under the authority of the same special office that was responsible for German settlers. When the Russian army pushed across the Danube in the next Russo-Turkish War (1806–12), its task was to procure so-called Transdanubian settlers (*zadunajskie pereselency*) for New Russia, since the pioneer migrants had already shown themselves to be good sheep breeders, farmers, wine growers, and gardeners. The Russian troops reinforced Catherine II's "invitation" by burning down villages and deporting their inhabitants to the left bank of the Danube. In Bessarabia (annexed in 1812), the government granted the group of immigrants – which had grown to just under 6,000 families by 1819 – state land and the privileges of colonists, that is, financial help in establishing settlements, exemption from military service, and placement under a special agency.

Following the war that Czar Nicholas I waged against the Turks in 1829–30, more Transdanubian settler decided to migrate to Bessarabia. The already established settlers had to move together more closely and make do with an average of 50 instead of the previous 60 *desjatins* of land per family (1 *desjatin* = 1.09 hectares). However, nearly half of the new arrivals were prompted to return home by the Turkish government's offer of amnesty and the devastating failure of the harvest in 1833. In 1835, 57,000 Transdanubian settlers were living in Bessarabia, twice as many as had been there before the second wave of migration. After the Crimean War (1853–6), Russia had to give up a part of Bessarabia with 27 colonies to the Principality of Moldavia. When the new Romanian state in 1860 expanded compulsory military service and the payment of the customary taxes to the colonists, the Transdanubian settlers protested. Following clashes between demonstrators and Romanian troops, many of them hastily left their homeland and took refuge on Russian territory. Since it was not possible to accommodate all refugees in the Russian part of Bessarabia, 5,500 families were settled north of the Sea of Azov.

In keeping with the czarist laws pertaining to colonists, the Transdanubian settlers, like the German settlers, were entitled to 60 *desjatins* of land. However, the land remained in the possession of the community, which assigned each farmer a plot and divided the fields – depending on location and soil quality – into sections of which each farmer was given a strip. The pasture was used in common. After southern Bessarabia was ceded to the Principality of Moldavia, the land of the Transdanubian settlers was newly surveyed. Only now did the authorities discover that the settlers, in violation of the law, were not passing their claim to one son and have the remaining sons learn a trade. Instead, the settler redistributed the common farmland every three or four years and in the process allocated plots of equal size to each family, which meant that their shares became progressively smaller.

There are several reasons for this approximation to the practice in Russian redistribution communities: first, until the 1840s, the settlers engaged chiefly in animal husbandry, and the cattle was pastured on the commons. Second, the legally stipulated division into small families with and without land was foreign to the "house community" (*zadruga*), the large families of up to 100 members in which the Bulgarians and Gagauzians had lived at least before their resettlement to Bessarabia. Third, the settlers were not willing in 1830 to renounce part of their claim in favor of the new arrivals and deny it to their own sons. Only the two Bulgarian colonies on the Crimea used the land in keeping with the prescribed agricultural regulations, probably because horticulture and viticulture predominated here, and the intensive cultivation these required was not to be endangered by regularly handing it over to other families. The result was the emergence of a landless class that founded daughter colonies elsewhere. The Bulgarian and Gaugazians who resettled in the 1860s from Bessarabia to Tauria also introduced the use of farmsteads after the German model in most of their colonies.

The individual colonies in the *gubernii* of Cherson and Tauria set up "excellent agriculture," as the official in charge (*Hauptfürsorger*) reported in 1812. They supplied the nearby markets, but especially Odessa and the Crimean ports, with fruit and melons, wine and tobacco. Because the Transdanubian settlers of Bessarabia brought agricultural implements and animals (especially sheep) with them from their homeland, they required hardly any state aid. Officials were impressed by the "flourishing" and "admirably well-ordered" condition of their villages. The Bulgarians and Gaugazians cultivated summer grain on about 90% of their fields. Until 1840, they brought in better harvests than their neighbors who hailed from other regions.

Officials, their German neighbors, and travelers reported that the Transdanubian settlers were unusually hardworking and cultivated their fields more carefully than other farmers. From their homeland they brought the know-how to develop water resources, dig wells, and irrigate gardens. Because of their diligence, their moderate consumption of alcohol, and their thriftiness, which in the eyes of one controller bordered on miserliness, the Bulgarians and Gagauzians of Bessarabia were still better off than the Ukrainians and Romanians of this *gubernii* at the end of the 19th century. However, they did not reach the good economic situation of the German colonists. As late as the beginning of the 1860s, the Transdanubian settlers devoted themselves chiefly to animal husbandry, especially the mixed-wool tzigaga sheep. By the last years before World War I, sheep rearing had largely ceased to play a role in their colonies.

The Transdanubian settlers usually had two houses, a "kitchen" in which they did their daily living, and a living room that was used only to receive guests. Well-to-do farmers employed at least one laborer throughout the year. These laborers were mostly colonists who were saving their wages to buy draft animals. As late as the end of the 19th century, the Transdanubian settlers were not practicing regular crop rotation and no alternation of fallow and cultivated land; however, they had adopted improved agricultural implements from their German neighbors and had replaced their oxen with horses. A comparative ethnographic study at the beginning of the 20th century concluded that Bulgarian villages were better off: their yields of grain per *desjatin* and grape harvest per vine exceeded those achieved by the Gagauzians, and the houses and farm buildings of the Bulgarians were larger and more solidly built than those of their Gagauzian counterparts.

The colonies of Bulgarians and Gagauzians suffered from a shortage of smiths and coopers, especially in the first half of the 19th century. Only Bolgrad and Komrat developed into small towns in which tradesmen were in the majority or strongly represented. Their "factories" with an average of five to six employees included brickworks and potteries, fulleries and dyeworks, candle-making and soapworks. Both towns played a fairly important role in industrially underdeveloped Bessarabia.

In 1830, most villages of the Transdanubian settlers had one or two clergymen, though only two villages maintained a school. It was not long before schools were also found in Bolgrad and Komrat, where only male students learned to read and write Russian, to do basic arithmetic, and studied biblical history. Between 1833 and 1842, another 77 colonies opened schools in which boys outnumbered girls by 40 to 1. Still, in most communities of Transdanubian settlers, only the village clerks – who did not hail from the ranks of the settlers – were literate. As late as 1865, a controller noted that "because of the dismal state of school affairs," it was difficult to find teachers, clerks, and village mayors. He went on to say that this was why the Bulgarian population had made no progress of any kind either in public or private life since their settlement. They were lagging behind the German colonists by half a century.

When the *zemstva*, the organs of self-government in counties and *gubernii* set up in the wake of the great reforms by Czar Alexander II, took over the responsibility for schools, schooling also improved in the Bulgarian and Gagauzian colonies. In 1897, around 27% of Bulgarians in the three New Russian *gubernii* were able to read and write Russian, but only 0.1% could also read and write Bulgarian. Bulgarians sent about three times as many children to school as the Gagauzians, who had greater difficulty than the Bulgarians understanding the classes taught in Russian. However, since colonists had few opportunities to use their knowledge of Russian, most had forgotten it within a few years after leaving school.

In 1868, an upper-level, so-called central school opened in Komrat, where the teaching was supposed to be in Russian. However, representatives of the Bulgarians of Odessa and Izmail and the paper in Bolgrad demanded classes in Bulgarian, so that the school would do justice to its

importance for the "national development" of the Bulgarians not only in Bessarabia but also in the Ottoman Empire. When the governor-general of New Russia – noting the competition from the central school set up in 1859 under Romanian rule in Bolgrad (which had been ceded after the Crimean War) – lent his support to the demands of the Bulgarian settlers in 1870, Alexander II also agreed.

As directed by the Romanian government, the teaching at the central school in Bolgrad was in Bulgarian and Russian, at the elementary schools in Bulgarian. The central school was to train young people as teachers and clerks in a three-year course, and in a subsequent four-year course open the door to university for interested students. On the eve of the Bulgarian autonomy (1878), the school was granted the rights of a Romanian lyceum. Even after the re-incorporation of southern Bessarabia into Russia, the school was run by Bulgarian principals. Between 1865 and 1897, 350 students graduated from the lyceum, among them 261 Bulgarians. Most of them studied at European universities and played an important part in building the young Bulgarian state. In 1880, the school was forced to switch the teaching to Russian. Only religion and Bulgarian literature and history could be taught in Bulgarian in the afternoon. After that time, fewer and fewer Bulgarians sent their children to this school.

For the economic and social development of the Transdanubian settlements it was significant that sons were not drafted into service in the army or the navy and that families were not torn apart by military conscription. The government paid the immigrants a subsistence allowance until the first harvest and provided them with a minimum of draft animals, implements, and seed. However, since most settlements had adopted the essential elements of the Russian redistribution communities, they lacked the chief motivation for the acquisition of additional land, namely, the desire to provide for all sons. The adherence of the settlers to the traditional agrarian structures and their low educational level prevented a social differentiation into large farmers and farmhands and the emergence of a class of entrepreneurs and millers as well as priests and teachers, as was characteristic of the neighboring German colonies. Bulgarian and Gaugazian farmers occasionally sent their sons to the German colonies for an apprenticeship so they could learn modern agricultural techniques or be trained as smiths. Marriages, however, were out of the question because of the different confessions. Relationships between Bulgarians and Orthodox partners from other ethnic groups are reported in the sources only for the isolated, scattered colonies in New Russia, but not for the compact settlement area in Bessarabia. Even marriages between Gagauzians and Bulgarians were exceedingly rare.

Brandes, Detlef. *Von den Zaren adoptiert. Die deutschen Kolonisten und die Balkansiedler in Neurußland und Bessarabien 1751–1914.* Munich, 1993.

Deržavin, Nikolaj. *Bolgarskie kolonii v Rossii (Tavričeskaja, Chersonskaja i Bessarabskaja gubernija).* Sofia, 1914.

Djakovič, Vl. *Bŭlgarite v Bessarabija. Kratkij istoričeskij očerk s pet' priloženij.* Sofia, 1930.

Hadžinikolova, Elena B. *Bŭlgarskite preselnici v južnite oblasti na Rusija 1856–1877.* Sofia, 1987.

Cross-references: Russia and Belarus; Southeastern Europe; Ukraine; German Settlers in Russia since the 18th Century; Greek Settlers from the Black Sea Region in New Russia since the Early Modern Period and Pontic Greeks in Greece since the End of World War II; Ukrainian and Russian Settlers in New Russia since the 18th Century

CAPE VERDEANS IN WESTERN AND SOUTHERN EUROPE SINCE THE 1950S: THE EXAMPLE OF THE NETHERLANDS

Dóris Pires

Cape Verde, which literally means "the green cape," is a small archipelago 450 km off the west coast of Africa. The Cape Verdeans, descended from the first Portuguese colonizers in the 15th century and African slaves, migrated from their homeland because of poverty, drought, and repression during Portugal's colonial rule. Starting in the early 20th century, migration took on a mass character and became a central part of Cape Verdean life. At the end of the 20th century, ethnic Cape Verdeans living abroad (517,000) outnumbered inhabitants of the islands (430,000). There are significant groups of Cape Verdeans in the USA (400,000), Portugal (50,000), France (30,000), the Netherlands (19,000), and Italy (10,000). The sex ratio is more or less equal, except for Italy where women make up the vast majority due to gender-specific migration patterns. In most countries Cape Verdean men migrated first, while women and other family members followed after some time. In Italy, however, Cape Verdean women, working as servants in Italian households, arrived first and subsequently remained the majority.

In the late 1950s the first Cape Verdean men arrived in the Netherlands, working on European ships that passed through the port of Mindelo in Cape Verde. These pioneers, attracted to Rotterdam by the relatively high pay of sailors, set a pattern for the subsequent chain migration of friends and family members from Cape Verde as well as Cape Verdeans from France, Italy, Portugal, and Senegal. The newcomers easily found semi- and unskilled jobs in the cleaning and petrochemical industry. The first female migrants in the late 1960s were likewise employed in the cleaning industry or worked in factories on the west side of Rotterdam.

In the late 1970s, foreign sailors employed by Dutch companies were entitled to settle in the Netherlands and to acquire Dutch citizenship. Despite the economic recession of the 1970s and 1980s and subsequent immigration restrictions, the Cape Verdean community steadily increased, mainly due to family reunification and a birth surplus. Other Cape Verdeans overstayed their tourist visas and tried to work illegally in their traditional jobs. The only way to legalize their stay and eventually acquire Dutch citizenship was to marry a native or a Cape Verdean with a residence permit. According to estimates, there are between several hundred and 1,000 of such illegals.

In the 1990s, the growth of the Cape Verdean community in the Netherlands slowed. Family reunification was more or less complete and new regulations restricted the migration of marriage partners from Cape Verde. At the same time Cape Verdeans from third countries, mainly of the second generation from Portugal, came to the Netherlands to escape unemployment, lack of housing facilities, and racial discrimination in Portugal. These migrants were typically not affected by Dutch immigration barriers since they possessed the passport of another European state. Thanks to frequent contacts between the several diaspora communities, Cape Verdeans were well informed of the situation in other countries and were attracted to the more favorable economic and social conditions in the Netherlands. In contrast to the first group of predominantly unskilled workers, these Cape Verdeans usually had a higher level of education and were looking to improve their occupational standing. Another group of Cape Verdeans, composed of women who had previously worked in Italian households, settled in Rotterdam in the 1990s. They also hoped for better employment, income, and housing opportunities in the Netherlands

Three-quarters of Cape Verdeans in the Netherlands live in Rotterdam, where they make up an important minority group (about 15,000 in 2004), heavily concentrated in the municipality of Delfshaven. Within this community, 58% was born in Cape Verde, 40% in the Netherlands, and 2% in Portugal or elsewhere. The majority (58%) has Dutch citizenship while 29% has double citizenship (24% Cape Verdean–Dutch, 5% Portuguese-Dutch).

In the 1950s and 1960s, Cape Verdeans typically started their new lives in Rotterdam in one of the many cheap pensions in the city. Some opened their own boardinghouses, and in the 1970s there were five Cape Verdean boardinghouses in the west side of the city. The owners functioned as intermediaries for new immigrants and helped many men find a job in the shipping industry or elsewhere. The number of Cape Verdean migrants in Rotterdam continued to grow from 1975 as Cape Verdeans with a residency permit could then apply for housing. Older residents temporarily accommodated family and friends and helped them find a job and legalize their stay. The great majority of the first and second generation still lives in this initial settlement area, mostly in council housing (public housing), which reflects their low socioeconomic status.

Coming from a poor country with a low rate of literacy, Cape Verdean immigrants have been unable to move beyond the low-skilled jobs in shipping and the cleaning industry that they originally took. There is some social mobility, and members of the younger generation increasingly gain jobs that require vocational training, yet Cape Verdeans in occupational and university education remain an exception. Due to the relatively low rate of unemployment and unfamiliarity with the Dutch welfare system, Cape Verdeans make little use of social services offered by the Dutch state.

Despite their size and geographic concentration, Cape Verdeans have largely remained inconspicuous in Dutch society. They usually solve problems within the community, in which social control enjoys a high status. The first generation largely still has the feeling of being a guest in a foreign country. Cape Verdean children usually have a rather submissive attitude, which contrasts sharply with established patterns of social behavior in the majority society. The hierarchical family structure and strict discipline are also not typically found among the Dutch. As a result of such cultural differences as well as their low social position and a lack of knowledge about Dutch culture, Cape Verdean families do not easily integrate into Dutch society.

In segments of the Cape Verdean community, there are many households where single mothers live together with the grandparents of their children – a result of both irresponsible fathers and traditional family structures. In contrast to the situation on Cape Verde, these fatherless families cannot count on the community for help. Among the social consequences is teenage pregnancy, which is difficult to address because sexual education is taboo. Furthermore, there is a relatively high proportion of children who attend special education institutions or drop out of secondary schools.

Despite these differences with the locals, Cape Verdeans consider themselves to be rather "Western" due to their partial descent from Portuguese colonizers and their Catholicism. In comparison with other migrant groups, there is a somewhat higher tendency to marry a partner of a different background, especially Dutch. Some single men of the first generation married Dutch women, assimilated, and chose to educate their children in accordance with established Dutch models. Single women arriving from Cape Verde and Italy have also married Dutch men, but in smaller numbers.

Feelings of solidarity and the need to maintain contact among members of the community resulted in the creation of the Cape Verdean Association in 1967. This first initiative set an example: 67 Cape Verdean organizations were registered in the Netherlands in 2005. This proliferation of community organizations has been due to continual disagreements, poor organizational skills, and distrust of leaders. A remarkable feature is that most of these organizations are based on the regional background of the migrants. Traditionally, there has been little cooperation between the various Cape Verdean organizations. Since the 1990s, increasingly better organized associations have emerged, typically led by members of the second generation. These organizations aim their activities at integration and receive structural subsidies from municipal authorities. Other important elements that bind together Cape Verdeans are soccer and the Catholic Church. Soccer is very popular, and the 16 registered Cape Verdean clubs organize their own competition that involves Cape Verdean clubs from different countries. The Catholic Church has played a significant role in the development of the community. Church attendance has always been high and the Church has often functioned as a place to exchange experiences and to provide new immigrants with information.

All these organizations enable Cape Verdeans to maintain their culture and to find a place for themselves in their destination countries since they join emotional elements of their old homeland with material elements of their new homeland. Music has become the most visible expression of the community's identity. Younger generations have created a new style of music by fusing Western technology with Cape Verdean melodies and themes. Although outsiders are welcome at the associations' events, they are mostly attended by Cape Verdeans. Some members of the second generation consciously seek activities and friends outside the community. The younger generation usually communicates in Dutch while Creole remains the most important language of communication among older Cape Verdeans. This pattern is also visible in Cape Verdean communities in other countries, where the second and third generations speak the language of their parents increasingly less.

Although some segments of the new generation achieve upward mobility and the inconspicuousness of the Cape Verdean community as a whole seems to attest to a smooth process of integration, there is in fact a relatively low level of integration for the group in its entirety. The community is still inward-oriented and has been able to preserve its culture thanks to a well-organized system of community associations. Return migration is low, but Cape Verdeans remain closely connected to their homeland and to other Cape Verdean communities. In order to improve their social and economic position in the Netherlands, address community problems, and gain more support from state authorities, greater cooperation between the many Cape Verdean organizations is indispensable.

Carling, Jørgen. "Migration in the Age of Involuntary Immobility: Theoretical Reflections and Cape Verdean Experiences." *Journal of Ethnic and Migration Studies* 28 (2002): 5–42.

Carreira, Antonio. *Migrações nas Ilhas de Cabo Verde*. Lisbon, 1983.

Integratie en Inburgering in Rotterdam. Minderhedenmonitor 2003, edited by Instituut voor Sociologisch-Economisch Onderzoek. Rotterdam, 2003.

Pires, Dóris. *Immigratie en integratie op de arbeidsmarkt. Een vergelijkend onderzoek naar de arbeidsmarktpositie van Kaapverdianen in Lissabon en in Rotterdam*. Rotterdam, 1997.

Pires, Dóris. *Migratieonderzoek van de Kaapverdianen in Rotterdam, Conceptonderzoek naar de migratiegeschiedenis en de situatie van de Kaapverdianen in Nederland*. The Hague, 2005.

Cross-references: The Netherlands

CENTRAL AND WESTERN EUROPEAN MINERS AND SMELTERS IN SWEDEN AND DENMARK-NORWAY FROM THE 16TH TO THE 18TH CENTURY

Volker Seresse

The discovery of deposits of metal ores, technological innovations, and the availability of capital made possible the flowering of central European mining from the middle of the 15th century. Centers for mining precious metals were Tyrol, Salzburg, the Harz region (with Mansfeld), the Erzgebirge, and the northern Hungarian coalfield around Neusohl (in modern-day Slovakia); iron mining and smelting were found above all in the mountanous regions of central Europe. A period of stagnation and decline began in many places as early as the middle of the 16th century. Following the Thirty Years' War, further technological innovations and an increasingly scientific approach to mining facilitated the rebuilding of the mining industry, which was now for the most part administered and regulated by the territorial rulers.

Contemporary sources reveal that miners and smelters from central Europe developed, in both their own perception and that of outsiders, a professional identity that went beyond the norm. Emphasis was placed on the dangerous, partly underground work, the shift work by comparatively large groups of people, the separate mining jurisdiction, the specialized mining terminology, and the particular customs of miners.

Migration was virtually a constitutive element of the mining industry. That was true for the establishment of new mines, which was not thinkable without experts from already existing enterprises. But it was also true when unemployment and emigration became unavoidable because a deposit had been exhausted or became unprofitable. Economic crises, sometimes caused by regional factors and sometimes by economic fluctuations in supraregional metal markets, can be regarded as important driving factors behind mining migration. However, the onset of decline in a mine could also provide an incentive for highly qualified mining specialists from other coalfields to come in and introduce technological innovations. Likewise, the transfer of new smelting and forging techniques often came about through migration. The labor migration of miners and smelters thus repeatedly played a key role in the development of the various European mining districts.

The particular culture of the early modern glass industry was not as pronounced as that of mining. Instead, it resembled other specialized crafts for goods to satisfy sophisticated tastes, whose existence seemed desirable to early modern authorities from a mercantilist perspective. Compared to mining, a smaller number of skilled workers was required to secure a significant glass production.

However, the Scandinavian glass trade was even more strongly shaped by immigration from central and western Europe than was the case for mining: as far as we can tell, all efforts to build up a domestic glass production drew on foreign specialists, mostly from central Europe. For the glass foundries that were established around the same time (middle of the 16th century) in Denmark and Sweden, master glassmakers were recruited to produce goods in demand by the court and high nobility. The majority came from German regions; Italian masters were summoned more rarely.

Mining experts in Sweden and Denmark-Norway

The central importance of migration is revealed in exemplary fashion in the emergence of mining in Denmark-Norway and Sweden. The recruitment of experts from central and western Europe went back above all to the Vasa kings (1523–1654) and to the Danish-Norwegian monarchs Christian III (1534–59) and Christian IV (1596–1648). They were hoping that the targeted recruitment and privileging of mining experts and mining entrepreneurs would boost the crown's income and would help set up or expand a domestic metalware and weapons production.

The starting positions in the two Scandinavian kingdoms were quite different, since Norwegian mining on a meaningful scale did not begin until the 17th century, and, with the exception of silver mining, always lagged behind the Swedish mining industry that had existed since the High Middle Ages in importance. It is likely that from the beginning of silver, copper, and iron mining in Sweden, central European miners and metallurgical workers immigrated more or less continuously. In the 16th and 17th centuries, individual specialists or very small groups of miners came into the central Swedish mining regions of Bergslagen (parts of the provinces of Västmanland, Närke, Dalarna, Värmland, Gästrikland) and Uppland. Most were smiths and furnace masters, often from the northern German region (Lübeck, Danzig). Beginning in the time of King Gustavus Vasa, they were deliberately recruited for individual smelting works and hammer mills. Through the transfer of technological innovations, they made a major contribution to turning the mining sector into Sweden's most important export trade since the 16th century. Swedish copper (especially from Falun) and bar iron played an important role in the international market: around 1650, Sweden was producing about two-thirds of European copper, and from the middle of the 17th century to the middle of the 18th century, Sweden was Europe's most important iron exporter.

The migration of individuals and groups from Germany to Sweden is poorly documented and has been little studied. Better known is the immigration of 1,000 Walloons that was concentrated in the 1620s and 1630s, the importance of which is at times overestimated (including family members, it amounted to about 2,000 individuals). They came from the region between Liège, Chimay, and Sedan, one of the most important European iron districts in the 16th century, whose production was negatively affected after 1566 by the Dutch Revolt. Unemployment, low wages, and – in the Prince-Bishopric of Liège – pressure on the partly Calvinist

Illustration from the mining regulation (*Bergordnung*) for the Kingdom of Norway, printed in 1540 in Zwickau (*Thüringer Universitäts- und Landesbibliothek, Jena*).

population had increased the readiness to emigrate. The Walloon immigrants (the majority of whom were charcoal makers and forest workers) introduced a new type of charcoal kiln and built large furnaces; and the "Walloon forge" worked a little more productively than the "German forge." Larger groups of Walloons were active in the ironworks of Leufsta and Österby (North Uppland) as well as in Norrköping and neighboring Finspång. In smaller numbers they settled in about 50 other places.

A key role in the Walloon immigration was played by businessmen from the Low Countries, who first appeared in the Swedish mining industry as financiers and entrepreneurs at the end of the 16th century. The most important one among them was Louis de Geer, who had been born near Liège. He procured extensive privileges for the immigrants (e.g., exemption from military service, free exercise of their Calvinist faith, their own jurisdiction), organized the migrants, remained active on a large scale as financier and entrepreneur, and arranged the sale of the iron and steel products all over Europe. The mass production of cannons, muskets, harnesses, and pikes in his works in Finspång and Norrköping contributed to Sweden's successes in foreign policy during those decades.

Far less important than the iron industry was the Swedish manufacture of brass, which had been started in the 1570s by two entrepreneurs from Aachen. Until the 18th century, entrepreneurs and workers from the Aachen area migrated into various Swedish cities to produce brass goods.

Thanks to the German and Walloon immigration, Sweden developed in the 17th and 18th centuries into one of the leading European countries in the mining industry with respect to the scale of production and technology. The disappearance of Sweden's technology lag in the first half of the 17th

century reduced immigration from 1650–60 to the end of the 18th century to mostly individuals and the temporary stay of foreign mining experts in Sweden, which was customary throughout the mining industry in the 18th century as part of informational and educational trips.

The first attempt to operate mining on a larger scale in Norway was initiated by the Danish-Norwegian king Christian III around 1540. He had 300–400 mining experts recruited, mostly from the Erzgebirge, who were to engage in silver and copper mining in the southern Norwegian Telemark region. This endeavor was undone by plagues, a lack of infrastructure, and resistance from the local peasant population. Until the beginning of the 17th century, mining in Norway was thus merely sporadic and local and on a very small scale; a few immigrant English and German experts are recorded in the 16th century.

Only the discovery of silver in 1623 near soon-to-be-founded Kongsberg led to the recruitment of about 270 central European miners by 1632 and thus to the real beginning of Norwegian mining. As far as we can determine, the immigrants of this first wave and their successors until 1648 came chiefly from the Harz (including Mansfeld), where the Thirty Years' War had brought mining virtually to a halt. Another important region of origin was the Erzgebirge, where mining was already in a serious crisis before 1618. Some return migration apparently took place after the Peace of Westphalia in 1648.

Beginning in the middle of the 17th century, the onward migration of the experts recruited to Kongsberg or the first larger copper mine of Kvikne (in the northern Østerdal, founded in 1631) or their offspring was an essential characteristic of the mining migration. The only ones who now came directly from central Europe to Norway were a few individual, highly qualified experts and members of the mining administration – for example, until 1756, all Norwegian chief mining supervisors (*Oberberghauptleute*) were born in Germany. After the founding phase of Norwegian mining, the prevailing migration pattern thus resembled German immigration to Sweden.

Generally, the mining and foundry workers of German background were proportionately overrepresented in the more highly qualified occupational groups not only in the most important Norwegian copper mine of Røros but probably also in all Norwegian mines of the 17th century. All told, one can posit the immigration of about 500–550 German miners and foundry workers to Norway in the 17th century; in the 18th century, it was substantially smaller.

The sources provide hardly any information about the integration of the miners and foundry workers who immigrated to Scandinavia from the 16th to the 18th century. Two central aspects must be considered: for one, these immigrants were experts who knew that they were important or even indispensable at the periphery of Europe. They brought special skills with them and were therefore given privileges they were familiar with from back home; added to this were high wages. In every instance, they were socially distinct from their new environment – integration was not their concern, or at least not their very first concern. Conversely, in some places they had a decisive role in shaping a completely new segment of society and in turn influenced locals into new ways of working and living. The larger the number of immigrants and the higher the qualifications they brought with them, the more likely was this pattern to occur, which offered great opportunities for preserving a group identity. Second, the number of outsiders who immigrated at the same time and concentrated in a particular area was very small, with two exceptions (Walloons in Upland, Germans in Kongsberg), which means that the lasting formation of a group was severely circumscribed.

The Walloon immigration illustrates this: the settlement of the less-qualified charcoal makers and forest workers as individuals or very small groups was followed by their apparently swift integration. Integration was very different where the immigrants made up more or less the entire workforce of an ironworks and provided especially the respected hammer smiths and furnace masters, as was the case in the enterprises in Uppland, which formed closed settlement units. Especially in the large works of Leufsta and Österby, there developed separate economic-social and cultural milieus that did not exist in this form in the Walloon region of origin, where those working in the mining sector lived as part of agrarian society. The Walloon milieu in Uppland was dominated by families of smiths, who passed on their skills only within their own group and, if possible, also married within the group; marriages with Swedish women began only in the late 18th century. The closed nature of the Walloon settlements in Uppland was apparently broken open only during the 19th century, even though the linguistic assimilation – except for specialized terminology – had already begun at the end of the 17th century. Important steps toward integration were the repeal, in 1644, of the general exemption from being drafted into the Swedish army, and the incorporation of the largely Calvinist Walloons into Sweden's Lutheran Church from the end of the 17th century. The appointment of Calvinist pastors had repeatedly led to tensions with the native clergy since the middle of the century.

Most of the German immigrants in Norway were Lutherans. A German clergyman headed the parish in Kongsberg until 1770. The end to German-language services was the end point of an integration process that lasted nearly a century and a half. Unlike the Walloons in Uppland, the Germans in Kongsberg did not form a closed milieu, something that would have hardly been possible in any case under the conditions of what was by Norwegian standards a large city. As early as 1648, the German miners in the silver mine constituted a minority of 150 against 240 Norwegians. And since from that time only a few additional migrants arrived, while the workforce continued to grow substantially to about 700 around 1700, gradual integration was a given.

There are scant indications of tensions between immigrants and natives. Economic-social and cultural motivations can be hardly separated when, during Kongsberg's founding phase, for example, conflicts occurred between Germans and Norwegians, who performed less highly regarded jobs and were, accordingly, paid less. Much the same holds for the tensions that are occasionally attested in the sources between individual Germans in leading positions and the Swedish or Norwegian workers under them. By contrast, the uprising of the peasants of Telemark in 1540 against Christian III's mining endeavor was triggered largely by the heavy burdens that had been imposed on them to provide for the mine.

The immigration of western and central European miners lives on in the mining terminology of Norway and Sweden. They left hardly any traces in the collective memory, however. One exception is the Walloon immigration, which plays a certain role in the Swedish historical consciousness. It is remembered especially in the former Walloon settlements in Uppland. Since 1938, an organization that keeps the memory alive has existed in the Sällskapet Vallonättlingar (Society of the Descendants of the Walloons). This cultivation of the tradition began about the same time that the last Walloon enterprises were closed down around 1940. The migration of Walloon miners also found reflection since the 1920s in Swedish fiction, including youth books. In Norway, there are literary traces of the German immigration in the novels of Johan Falkberget (1879–1967), some of which are set in 17th- and 18th-century Røros.

Glassworks workers in Sweden and Denmark-Norway

The Danish glassworks in northern Jutland existed for only a few years. In operation the longest (1584–98) was an enterprise run by a master recruited from Hesse. Among other things, this glassworks supplied 20,000 glasses for the coronation festivities of Christian IV. At the beginning of the 17th century, the production in Jutland came to a complete halt primarily because of a shortage of wood, and two new projects around the middle and at the end of the century also failed. Lasting glass production began only after the establishment of the mercantilist-inspired Norske Kompani in 1739. It was aimed at autarchy for Denmark-Norway. It was largely Germans who migrated to the seven Norwegian glassworks that were set up by 1803, along with some Britons and a few Frenchmen. They received higher wages than in their regions of origin and brought their families with them. In the 1770s, separate schools were set up in the glassworks settlements. From the beginning, the immigrants had been granted their own jurisdiction. For Catholics and Calvinists, contact with clergy of their confession was facilitated. Because of these good conditions, the majority of immigrants remained in Norway. Apparently from the end of the 1770s, the immigrants instructed the natives systematically in the glassmaking art. Nevertheless, foreign masters were still running the Norwegian glassworks at the beginning of the 19th century, and two-thirds of the 160 workers were of foreign background. Immigration also continued: between 1855 and 1858, 75 glassblowers were recruited from Prussia,

Bohemia, Austria, and other central European glass regions for a new, large Norwegian glassworks.

The first Swedish glassworks developed from the middle of the 16th century in the Mälar See region near Stockholm, the most important market for glass products. Beginning in the 1620s, there were also glassworks in the forest of southern Småland. Most Swedish glassworks that were set up in the 16th and 17th centuries lasted only a few years, at best a few decades. Still, glass production never completely ceased. Time and again, individual master glassmakers or small groups immigrated from German territories and the Netherlands. In the Scanian glassworks of Henrikstorp, for example, all 14 glassmakers in the 1690s were probably of German background, possibly from Mecklenburg.

Around 1740 there began in Sweden a phase in which mostly noble entrepreneurs, with financial help from local merchants, set up new glassworks in various regions. To that end, they recruited foreign masters especially from Bohemia, Hesse, the Palatinate, Prussia, Saxony, Thuringia, and Württemberg. The Kosta glassworks in Småland, which still exists at the beginning of the 21st century, commenced operations in 1742 entirely with German glassmakers. It would appear that the number of migrants coming directly from central Europe declined during the remainder of the 18th century, as onward migration within Sweden became increasingly important. All told, around 130 glassworkers of German background can be attested in Swedish glassworks between 1736 and 1796. Some of these experts later migrated back, though most of their descendants remained in the country. Together with the locals who had learned the glassmaking craft, they formed a separate class of experts toward the end of the 18th century, as a result of which only few central European glassblowers went to Sweden in the 19th century.

When it comes to the integration of the master glassmakers who came to Scandinavia before 1740, all we can say is that either their very small numbers and the often brief existence of the various glassworks led to a rapid integration into the agricultural society, or that the individual experts continued onward or returned home. However, from the middle of the 18th century, the geographic isolation of the glassworks settlements contributed greatly to the fact that, in spite of small absolute numbers (usually no more than a dozen masters and workers with their families), there was no rapid integration. Rather, members of these families, who often had several masters or workers in their ranks, were active in glassmaking for several generations and preserved their occupational and cultural identity, which set them apart from their agrarian surroundings. In addition, there were close, border-crossing relationships between the northern European glassworks: 30 families were known in the 18th and 19th centuries in both Norway and Sweden.

The development of the two occupational groups examined here was shaped in a special way by migration not only for reasons specific to these sectors. The considerable technological gap that existed at times between Scandinavia and central or western Europe created the migration pattern. Added to this was the great interest by early modern authorities in mining and, to a lesser extent, in glass products. The integration patterns described here indicate that a special group identity was preserved longest where it was possible to maintain the separation from the native population through the special occupational status and self-contained places of working and living, with separate marriage markets, churches, and schools. This is exemplified in a special way by the Walloon-Upland ironworks and glassworks settlements of the 18th and 19th centuries.

Amdam, Rolv Petter. "Industrial Espionage and the Transfer of Technology to the Early Norwegian Glass Industry." In *Technology Transfer and Scandinavian Industrialization*, edited by Kristine Bruland, 73–93. New York and Oxford, 1991.

Berg, Bjørn Ivar. "Die frühen norwegischen Bergwerke. Zuwanderung, Technologie und Kultur aus Deutschland." In *Deutschland – Norwegen. Die lange Geschichte*, edited by Jarle Simensen, 34–49. Tano, 1999.

Florén, Anders, and Gunnar Ternhag, ed. *Valloner – järnets människor*. Uppsala, 2002.

Fogelberg, Torbjörn, and Friedrich Holl. *Wanderungen deutscher Glashüttenleute und Schwedens Glasindustrie in den letzten fünf Jahrhunderten*. Växjö, 1988.

Hillegeist, Hans-Heinrich. "Auswanderungen Oberharzer Bergleute nach Kongsberg/Norwegen im 17. und 18. Jahrhundert." In *Technologietransfer und Auswanderungen im Umfeld des Harzer Montanwesens*, edited by Hans-Heinrich Hillegeist and Wilfried Ließmann, 9–39. Berlin, 2001.

Nilles, Paul E. "The Walloon Immigration and the Swedish Steel Industry." In *Iron and Steel – Today, Yesterday and Tomorrow*, edited by Bertil Berg et al., vol. 3, 59–73. Stockholm, 1997.

Palmqvist, Arne. "Die Auswanderung Aachener Arbeiter und Unternehmer nach Schweden vom 16.–18. Jahrhundert und ihre Lage in Stockholm am Ende des 18. Jahrhunderts." *Zeitschrift des Aachener Geschichtsvereins* 66/67 (1954/55): 169–81.

Seresse, Volker. "Die Einwanderung deutscher Berg- und Hüttenleute nach Norwegen im 17. Jahrhundert und ihre Bedeutung am Beispiel des Kupferbergwerks Røros." In *Technologietransfer und Auswanderungen im Umfeld des Harzer Montanwesens*, edited by Hans-Heinrich Hillegeist and Wilfried Ließmann, 49–70. Berlin, 2001.

Cross-references: Belgium and Luxembourg; Germany; Northern Europe; Dutch Calvinist Refugees in Europe since the Early Modern Period

CHILEAN REFUGEES IN EUROPE SINCE 1973: THE EXAMPLE OF SWITZERLAND

Claudio Bolzman

Chilean political refugees came in ever-greater numbers to Europe after the military coup of September 1973 that overthrew the democratically elected socialist government of President Salvador Allende. The new regime was particularly repressive against militants and sympathizers from left-wing parties, trade unions, and grassroots associations. It is estimated that between 1973 and 1988, about 1 million people (almost 10% of the Chilean population) left the country for political reasons. This was an unprecedented situation in the history of the country, characterized until then by rather limited emigration movements. People of all social conditions and ages – including many families – fled. Around 100,000 Chilean refugees came to western Europe; Switzerland received around 4,500 exiles.

The first Chileans arrived in Switzerland in the fall and winter of 1973–4. They were part of a contingent of 255 refugees selected by a Swiss official from people who sought protection in different foreign embassies in the Chilean capital of Santiago. A further 450 Chileans arrived in Switzerland with the help of a solidarity movement called Free-Place Action, founded by Swiss humanitarian, religious, and left-wing groups with the aim of expediting the reception of refugees from Chile in Switzerland with financial and other assistance. Pressure from these movements and other initiatives on Swiss authorities, which repudiated the refugees across the board as "Chilean Communists," was ultimately so strong that most Chileans in the 1970s were given asylum. During the 1980s, however, the Swiss followed a more restrictive asylum policy toward Chileans.

Chilean refugees have gone through different phases of incorporation. During the first period, between 1973 and 1976–7, exiles organized themselves as a political community. Opposition to the military dictatorship and demonstration of solidarity with those who stayed in Chile was a part of everyday life in their new home. They founded political associations and met with other refugees as well as the Swiss who supported them in their work of solidarity.

Switzerland seemed a temporary place of residence for exiles. Problems that came with living in a foreign country were dismissed as relatively unimportant. Integration into the country that received them – for example, the search for a job and commensurate acquisition of skills – was considered by refugees to be illegitimate: political work took priority. In fact, exiles felt guilty for leaving their country and thereby giving up the direct fight against the dictatorship. Then every attempt to be more integrated in the new context was perceived as unfair; the duty was to work on solidarity and to prepare oneself for return. In this context, collective identity as political activists affected individual life plans, and the exile community exerted strong social control over its members. Thus, in this first stage, the issue of incorporation to the Swiss society did not really arise.

In the second half of the 1970s, the self-conception of the group slowly changed. As the military regime in Chile stabilized, the coherence grounded in common political ideals became less important. This situation made a return impossible, at least in the short term. Even if most refugees continued to think that they were not going stay forever in their host country, they realized that their sojourn might last many years. Facing this new perspective, they increasingly grappled with their situation in Switzerland and planned the future of their families there. This new definition of the situation had concrete implications: an increasing number of refugees began to define themselves not only with respect to political commitment but also to professional, family, and social resources. Private life and one's own progress were considered more and more important. Chileans organized themselves into friendly societies where they could organize their free time and at the same time work together on some issues (such as the education of children to preserve the Chilean identity over the generations, or gender-specific social problems), which were confined within the private sphere. Thus, at this stage refugees searched to combine, with more or less success, the need to solve problems that arose from everyday life with the need to keep a shared ideological community identity.

From the year 1983–4, Chilean domestic politics signaled slow change: the first steps toward political liberalization were initiated after the economic crisis of 1982 and important oppositional demonstrations. This situation had arbitrary consequences for exiles: some of them got permission to visit Chile, or even to return. For most, though, the country remained completely closed. Progressive liberalization was evaluated in very different ways: politically active refugees and those who maintained regular contact with the home country saw in these events the possibility of a quick return to Chile. Others, who had moved away from political activities and who did not maintain regular contact with Chile, had at this point largely given up a similar focus on return.

These differences of perception, along with important social strata differences between exiles, led to a great diversity of ways of life, of community organization, and of forms of incorporation into Swiss society. Besides the political groups, a large number of new, mostly local associations arose, emphasizing other social aspects instead of – or in addition to – only solidarity with Chile. Most were small groups; Chilean women, young people, inhabitants of the same suburbs, or people coming from the same region in Chile organized themselves in an autonomous way. Sports clubs, groups of artists, and ethnic businesses also developed. Most of the associations knew periods of effervescence and discouragement. Generally these periods where influenced by the Chilean political situation.

In March 1990, a democratic government was elected in Chile and a process of transition to democracy began. Chilean exiles were no longer compelled to live outside their homeland for political reasons. During this new period, many of the exiles who had structured their lives around the idea of return were now forced to make a decision and weigh their comparative future prospects in Switzerland and Chile. Ultimately, only around 20% of all Chilean refugees in Switzerland returned to Chile. This decision was much influenced by the sociopolitical context both in Chile and in Switzerland: on the one hand, exiles evaluated – perhaps for the first time – their chances of cultural and psychosocial adaptation to both countries and had also to take into account their political, social, economic, and legal situation. On the other hand, state-sponsored measures in Switzerland played a role: the number of exiles who decided to return to Chile during the early 1990s increased when the Swiss government promoted measures of assistance to refugees returning home.

In fact, it was at this stage that exiles, as an immigrant group, considered for the first time whether and to what extent they would constitute a community of origin with specific institutions and their own identity in Switzerland. This did not mean that most of them assimilated to the host country. The vast majority developed specific forms of cultural identities and kept various links with their home country. At the community level they created resident associations, representatives of all the Chileans living in the same canton. For the first time, these associations actively sought to promote citizen and social rights for Chileans living in Switzerland. For instance, in Geneva, the Chileans participated in a campaign to obtain the right to vote for foreigners at the local level. At the Swiss level, Chilean associations mobilized and negotiated with Chilean and Swiss authorities in support of a bilateral agreement on social security between both countries, the first signed by the Swiss state with a third world country. With the decision to stay in Switzerland came new social and political questions. Chilean immigrants realized that, for them, there was a gap between legal status and real status. They were citizens in a state where they were not residents and residents in a state where they were not citizens, effectively dispossessed of political rights in both states. The question of participation in social life at different levels became an important issue. They discovered themselves as an ethnic minority at the Swiss level, and as a diaspora at the international level.

Bolzman, Claudio. "Stages and Modes of Incorporation of Exiles in Switzerland: The Example of Chilean Refugees." *Innovation: The European Journal of Social Sciences* 7, 3 (1994): 321–33.

Bolzman, Claudio. *Sociologie de l'exil: une approche dynamique. L'exemple des réfugiés chiliens en Suisse.* Zurich, 1996.

Cross-references: Switzerland

CHINESE CONTRACT WORKERS IN FRANCE DURING WORLD WAR I

Nora Wang

In the course of World War I, British and French authorities experienced a severe labor shortage and, starting in the latter part of 1915, discussed various schemes for hiring European or "colonial" workers. The British seriously considered using Egyptian laborers in France (as they had in the Dardanelles in 1915) and the French planned to recruit some 200,000 laborers from their colonies in North Africa, Indochina, and Madagascar during the course of the war. However, since the demand for labor remained unfulfilled, some 140,000 Chinese contract laborers were recruited starting in 1916. They were to be employed in France both on the western front and behind the lines, while the British had ruled out employing colored workers in Britain itself.

The largest number was hired by the British, mainly to replace the British workers employed by the military command in France as well as to provide at least some relief for British soldiers. For this purpose the British Chinese Labor Corps was created. Other Chinese workers, contracted by the French army, were hired to compensate for the shortage of French longshoremen and factory workers and to do whatever handling work the war had rendered necessary. Identified in British contracts as "coolies" and in French contracts as *travailleurs chinois*, these men came to be known in China as *huagong* – actually an abridged name used for all Chinese migrant workers. They were recruited directly in China, by various British or French government agencies, and most were repatriated after the war, a process that lasted until 1922. These workers formed the first, albeit temporary, large-scale wave of Chinese migrants to France, preceding the mass arrivals after 1970.

Chinese contract workers had been hired under intergovernmental control prior to World War I, as early as the 1860s. After the outbreak of the war, the Allied Forces used this scheme as a way of gaining access to China's human resources without infringing upon the country's neutrality as China did not enter the war until August 1917, when it sided with the Allies. The first steps came from the French, who reached an agreement with the Huimin syndicate, purportedly a private Chinese agency, in January 1916. Recruiting offices were opened in various towns (Tianjin, Pukou, Qingdao, and incidentally Shanghai and Shamian, near Canton), leading to the departure of a first group of 5,000 men to Marseille in July 1916.

In May 1916, the British government set up its own agencies and staffed them with Chinese personnel. The first agency was opened in the leased territory of Weihaiwei, but Qingdao soon became the preferred site. The British were convinced that only people from north China could adjust to the French climate, and thus primarily hired workers from the Shandong province. After China entered the war, recruitment became easier and increased significantly. Until early 1918, large numbers of migrants were conveyed by sea, in groups ranging from a few hundred to a few thousand men. All in all, Great Britain employed some 100,000 men, France 40,000. Some 10,000 of these workers were leased to the American forces in autumn of 1917, to be returned upon the signing of an armistice.

British and French contracts differed in duration, level of pay, and punitive rules, though the provisions were in the main quite similar. The "British" workers were hired for a three-year term, were subordinate to army command, and were subject to military discipline, but they were not allowed to take part in military operations. They received an allowance upon enrollment and were paid one franc per 10-hour workday, while their relatives in China received a monthly allowance. No provisions were made in the case that they fell ill, but a thorough, one-time medical examination was performed. The "French" workers were enrolled for five years and were also subordinate to military command, but they were hired under civilian contracts and not allowed to take part in "national defense" operations. The average workday amounted to 10 hours and could not exceed 12 hours. Under pressure from French trade unions, it was agreed that the Chinese workers would be paid no less than French unskilled workers. The French "coolies" thus received five francs a day or three francs if they were fed and accommodated, which was usually the case. Their families would also receive compensation in the event of an accident or death. The French army directly employed some of the "French" workers, who were subject to military discipline; others were placed at the disposal of government departments, private firms, or harbor authorities and were subject to civilian jurisdiction. Both the British and the French allotted higher wages to skilled workers such as carpenters, fitters, and mechanics. Following the intervention of Chinese diplomats, the British and French granted Chinese contract workers one unpaid free day per week, while the French contracts also provided free days on French and Chinese holidays. Some 4,000 men, often students, were recruited to act as interpreters.

More than 90% of the contract laborers were from northern China. During the war, transportation of the migrant workers was difficult, as boats were in short supply and sea routes insecure. In August 1917, the French liner *Athos* was torpedoed in Mediterranean waters, killing more than 400 "coolies." Due to such risks, the ships usually preferred to sail around the Cape of Good Hope, which meant a three-month voyage to reach Le Havre.

Upon arrival, British "coolies" were sent to northern France and Flanders, to be employed in the *départements* of Pas-de-Calais, Somme, and Oise. The "French" contract workers were employed on the northern front as well, but also in large industrial centers or ports, such as Le Creusot, Brest, Marseille, or Bordeaux. Chinese laborers were generally praised, both by the French and the British. Their working and living conditions were, however, extremely difficult and did not correspond to their expectations. At the start of recruitment, the daily wage of the "British" workers was three times as high as that of unskilled workers in China, but the franc soon lost its value. The "coolies"– only known by their registration number, not their names – were housed in barracks or tents with poor sanitary conditions. Most were undernourished and had insufficient clothing. Despite provisions in their contracts banning employment in the military, quite a few workers were employed for "semi-military" tasks such as digging

trenches and recovering corpses and many were stationed directly in zones that were under fire. Some 3,000 men died in this manner, two-thirds of whom were British "coolies." The British set up a special Chinese hospital in Noyelles, although Chinese workers were admitted into other hospitals as well. A Chinese cemetery was later opened in the same place, a gesture the French government would never make for its own "coolies."

Chinese laborers also suffered from various epidemics, such as dysentery or influenza, and many were overworked, at times maltreated, or subjected to punishments they considered dishonorable. Others experienced racism, the British more so than the French "coolies." The payment of wages was often delayed or only paid in part. From 1916 to 1918 some strikes and a number of riots were recorded, which were heavily punished: workers were imprisoned or even executed, sometimes without trial. The *huagong* had little contact with Allied soldiers, other than the British or French officers who were in charge of their corps. Likewise, contacts remained scarce with the French people, who showed a whole range of attitudes toward the Chinese contract workers: fear, suspicion, curiosity, and sometimes sympathy. The unions in particular remained suspicious, especially after the Chinese laborers had been brought in to break the strike of Parisian gas workers in April 1920.

With the main aim of reducing fighting, gambling, and opium addiction among the Chinese contract workers, charitable organizations organized social and recreational activities and arranged Chinese classes for those who wanted to learn to read and write. The most notable and successful of such organizations was the YMCA. The workers themselves also set up organizations for improving their everyday life and managing their savings, recreation, and support. Some of these were continued after the war, mainly by workers who had not been repatriated.

Although most of the contract workers were repatriated after the war, some remained in France. After the armistice the British government was eager to repatriate the British "coolies" as the demand for labor had decreased and there were now plenty of ships available. From March 1919 until the end of that year, a monthly average of at least 5,600 "coolies" were sent back to China. The French government, unlike the British, allowed their contract laborers to stay in France on a voluntary basis. Roughly 3,000 men chose to do so. Some of them had married French women, although French authorities disallowed this in 1919 for fear of bigamy among the "coolies." Most of the men received civilian contracts and settled as industrial workers, mainly in central France and in the Parisian suburbs. It is difficult to assess the extent of their integration into French society. Until the 1940s the rate of women migrants in the Chinese colony never exceeded 8%. While Chinese men sometimes married French women, most remained single, especially as economic conditions deteriorated, but they often cohabitated with European women and their offspring. The Chinese colony in France stemmed mainly from this group.

As for the "French" migrants who returned to China, differing opinions exist about the impact and role of these returnees, a fact that probably reflects the variety of experiences. According to some accounts, the average savings collected by the "coolies" amounted to some 15 to 25 francs monthly, which was used for the payment of debts, the purchase of land, and for the establishment of small businesses in northern China. However, many returned penniless, some even as invalids. According to one source, the rate of illiteracy among these workers dropped from 80% upon enrollment to 62% at the time of their return. Some of the return migrants – in Shanghai, for instance – took part in the new labor movements and unions; many more returned to the rural provinces like Zhili or Shandong. Though short-lived, their experience proved an effective stimulus for other Chinese to migrate to France, particularly for the worker-students of the 1920s.

Chen, Sanjing. *Huagong yu Ouzhan*. Taipei, 1986.

Chen, Ta. *Chinese Migrations, with Special Reference to Labor Conditions*. Taipei, 1967.

Summerskill, Michael. *China on the Western Front: Britain's Chinese Work Force in the First World War*. London, 1982.

Cross-references: France; Great Britain; Chinese Student Workers in France after World War I

CHINESE ITINERANT MERCHANTS IN EUROPE SINCE THE END OF WORLD WAR I

Mette Thunø

In the late 19th century, the first Chinese small-traders started traveling from southern China to western Europe to sell carved jade-like soapstone and other Chinese curios. The majority of these small-traders originated from the mountainous towns and regions of Qingtian county in the province of Zhejiang in southeastern China. Situated in the mountains, Qingtian was historically an isolated and impoverished area with very few natural resources aside from the pale-green soapstone that for centuries had been carved into small figures, jewelry, and writing utensils.

Local anecdotes suggest that Qingtian artisans traversed Siberia to Europe to sell their handicrafts as early as the 17th century. More reliable historical sources document the presence of a handful of Qingtian traders in Moscow and St. Petersburg in the 1840s and in both England and France in the late 1870s. This suggests that although Qingtian soapstone had already for centuries enticed customers from all over China, Korea, and Japan, these carvings caught the interest of Europeans only in the late 19th and early 20th centuries, when they were displayed and earned prizes at various international exhibits, such as the World Exhibitions in Berlin (1896) and Paris (1899, 1900). These acclamations apparently convinced the Qingtian traders of the possibility of finding new markets in Europe. Migration from Qingtian to Europe in the early 20th century was the result.

Initially, some hundred Qingtian carvers and small-traders followed the pioneers to Europe. An upsurge in the number of Qingtian small-traders came with the numerous Chinese workers, contracted by the French and British army during the First World War. After the war, a large part of the Qingtian contingent of 2,000 young men remained in Europe. They found work in French factories, intermingled with the small number of Qingtian migrants already living in France, or traveled on to other European countries to sell Chinese handicrafts. This increase in numbers and the dispersal to other countries was followed by regular chain migration from Qingtian in the 1920s. The institutionalization of this migration – with black markets for passports, credits, and stowaway arrangements on ships from Shanghai to Naples and Marseille – attracted even Chinese peasants living in counties neighboring Qingtian (Wencheng, Ruian, Yongjia) to try their luck as small-traders in Europe.

Estimates indicate that some 25,000 Chinese small-traders in the mid-1920s and 10,000–18,000 in the mid-1930s resided in Europe. Chinese small-traders were primarily concentrated in France and the Netherlands, while their numbers were much smaller in Germany, Italy, Belgium, and Spain and insignificant in northern, eastern, east-central, and southeastern Europe and Britain. With Japan's occupation of China in 1937 and the ensuing civil war, Chinese migration to Europe gradually halted. The outbreak of the Second World War resulted in the return migration of some Qingtian traders while others settled in Europe on a permanent basis. In this way, the Qingtian small-traders came to constitute one of the primary groups of Chinese migrants in Europe during the second part of the 20th century.

The high rates of migration from the isolated Qingtian mountain villages and townships to western Europe reflect a close relationship between human mobility, sparse arable land, European predilections for Oriental handicrafts, European exploitation of cheap Chinese contract labor, and price level differences between China and Europe. European colonialism in Asia and the opening of the Suez Canal in 1869 resulted in direct maritime shipping connections between Shanghai, Hong Kong, and Mediterranean ports. Traveling over land also became easier with the Trans-Siberian Railway in 1904. Given these circumstances and the concurrent sealing off of Chinese immigration to the USA and Russia with the Chinese Exclusion Act of 1882 and the Russian Revolution in 1917, western, northern, central, and southern Europe now became the preferred destinations of Qingtian traders.

The majority of Qingtian migrants in the 1920s and 1930s were no longer professional stone carvers and traders but primarily peasants trying to earn a living in Europe. The initial trade in local Chinese stone carvings was gradually replaced by alternative commodities such as pearls, porcelain, neckties, carpets, paper flowers, glasses, tea, candy, wallets, and silk. Qingtian small-traders placed their orders with companies in major cities such as Paris or Berlin that were in contact with wholesale companies in Zhejiang and Shanghai. These wholesale companies shipped cheap Chinese goods all over Europe to local post offices where the Chinese traders paid for their orders. Frequently, these traders also fabricated goods from local material such as small wallets from leather purchased in Europe. In this manner Qingtian small-traders continued to engage in the practice of hawking and became known in many countries as "suitcase Chinese."

Traveling around with their bags filled with inexpensive handmade commodities to sell on the street and at local markets, Qingtian traders were in constant fear of being caught by the local police for hawking and lacking proper documents. They lived isolated from both the local population and other groups of Chinese migrants because they spoke a dialect among themselves and most were illiterate. In Marseille and Paris, the marginalization of Qingtian small-traders was illustrated by their secluded living quarters around, respectively, Saint-Charles railway station and Gare de Lyon. As a consequence, they supported each other, invited relatives and friends from China, and assisted them upon their arrival in Europe, sharing accommodation and provisions. They also set up associations to share information and extend mutual help to the needy such as the Amicale des Chinois de Zhejiang en France (Friendly Society of the Zhejiang Chinese in France), which was established in the early 1930s.

The Qingtian small-traders were all males, arriving without dependents and usually expecting to return home after achieving a certain level of wealth, but many remained in Europe. Some of them were able to establish themselves more permanently with residence and work permits. They shifted from hawking in Chinese curios to the sale of different services for the increasing number of Chinese immigrants (sailors, students, entertainers) in European ports. They set up hostels, restaurants, laundries, barbershops, import/export companies, and private banks for Chinese migrants as well as bean curd, leather, and furniture factories. Some were quite successful and achieved a high degree of economic as well as sociocultural integration. Quite a few of the more successful traders married European women while others did not possess adequate social, cultural, and financial resources to find a job or a local spouse in their European destination countries.

What was originally envisioned as a short-term stay became for some Qingtian traders a true process of immigration and settlement. Some Chinese remained in Europe despite the devastating effects of the depression of the 1930s and racial discrimination during the Second World War. After China's Communist Party took power in 1949, they started to apply for citizenship in the various European countries where they had settled. There they seized the opportunity to open Chinese restaurants as the local populations of Europe's larger cities started to show an interest in "exotic" and inexpensive Chinese cuisine. In the 1950s, countless Chinese restaurants and catering businesses flourished all over urban western Europe.

At this stage, competition from fellow Chinese was restricted to Chinese migrants from Taiwan, since emigration from China was prohibited after 1949. Between 1949 and 1965 only some 300 persons were permitted to leave Qingtian to be united with their families in Europe. Consequently, the former Chinese small-traders were finally able to achieve the level of wealth that they perhaps had anticipated when leaving Qingtian in the 1920s and 1930s. Only in the late 1970s, as China started liberalizing its emigration policy, Chinese migrants in Europe were able to reestablish their long dormant family ties to Qingtian. Since then, more than 200,000 Chinese men and women have migrated from the Qingtian area – primarily to Europe – to join the catering trade or to sell, more or less like their grandfathers, cheap Chinese commodities. Only this time, the markets for such Chinese goods have moved from western to central, east-central, and southeastern Europe.

Chen, Murong, ed. *Qingtian Xianzhi.* Hangzhou, 1990.

Pieke, Frank N., and Gregor Benton. *The Chinese in Europe.* London and New York, 1998.

Thunø, Mette. "Moving Stones from China to Europe." In *Internal and International Migration: Chinese Perspectives,* edited by Frank N. Pieke and Hein Mallee, 158–80. Richmond, 1999.

Understanding Migration between China and Europe. International Migration 41, 1 (2003) (special issue).

Wu, Chao. *Zhejiangji haiwai renshi yanjiu.* Shanghai, 2003.

Zhou, Wangsen, and Chao Wu. Sanbainian lishi, shibawan chizi – "Haiwai Qingtianren" sanlun (jiexuan). *Huaqiao huaren yanjiu luncong* (2001): 5, 16–44.

Cross-references: France; The Netherlands; Chinese Contract Workers in France during World War I; Chinese Restaurant Owners in the Netherlands and Germany in the Second Half of the 20th Century

CHINESE MIGRANTS FROM FUJIAN PROVINCE IN LONDON AT THE END OF THE 20TH CENTURY

Pál Nyíri

Great Britain has the longest history of a Chinese population in Europe, dating back to the mid-19th century. It has been dominated by Cantonese-speaking migrants from Hong Kong and Guangdong province. Between the Second World War and the late 1970s, direct migration between the People's Republic of China (PRC) and Britain came to a halt due to the closure of mainland China's borders for political reasons. In this time, Chinese came to Britain as colonial/postcolonial migrants from Hong Kong, Malaysia, and Singapore; as refugees from the Vietnam War; and as students and nurses from Taiwan, Malaysia, and Singapore. By the late 20th century, chain migration out of these areas as well as Guangdong had peaked and either stopped or shifted to the USA or Canada, which were considered more attractive destinations.

Starting in the 1970s, fresh migration chains began to emerge from other areas of the PRC, which once again became the chief source of Chinese migrants to Europe as it liberalized exit policies (although travel abroad remained accessible to only a privileged few). They went to Britain largely as students, but increasingly as irregular migrants as well. The latter group included those who overstayed business visitor visas – mainly from northeastern China – and those who entered the country illegally, overwhelmingly from the southeastern province of Fujian, particularly the regions around the provincial capital, Fuzhou.

In the course of economic reforms, the Fuzhou area experienced high economic growth, and urban wealth and consumption increased rapidly. Villages in the area, which despite the decades-long prohibition on leaving the country had retained a culture of migration and dependence on remittances, saw a resurgence of economic migration beginning in the late 1980s. Peasants in the Fuzhou area certainly did not belong to the most economically deprived population group in China, but their deprivation relative to the local context combined with the tradition of emigration provided a strong incentive to migrate. This ranged from the domestic migration of construction workers and watchmakers, through short-term legal labor migration to Singapore, to commercially brokered illegal migration to Taiwan, Japan, and the USA. Having lost most of their young male population to migration, primarily to the USA, many villages in the Fuzhou area became structurally dependent on overseas migrant remittances. But as illegal immigration from Fujian became a media topic in the traditional destination countries in the mid-1990s, entry and residence in these countries became increasingly difficult. The UK, promoted by migration brokers, emerged as a second-choice destination. Other new destinations included southern (Italy, Spain) and eastern (Hungary, Russia) European countries.

Most Fujianese in London in the 1990s came from the municipality of Fuqing, just south of Fuzhou, in particular from Jiangyin Township, as well as Jiangjing, Yuxi, Sanshan, and Gaoshan townships and the county seat, Fuqing. Migrants from Fuqing traditionally migrated to Japan and only began migrating to the West when access to the USA had already become difficult. A much smaller number came from the municipality of Changle, north of Fuzhou, where this wave of migration had begun earlier and targeted the USA. Most migrants to London were farmers and fishermen with little chance of social advancement in China. They were overwhelmingly young single men, with some single women and a few married women who followed their husbands. Given the lack of legal channels, children could not join their parents, and children born to Fujianese in London were sometimes sent back to China to be raised there by their grandparents .

The 1991 British census reported nearly 160,000 ethnic Chinese residents, almost 40% of whom lived in Greater London. Chinese organizations in Britain estimated a figure of 250,000 for the year 1997. The only way to estimate the number of Fujianese is to assume that all asylum applications by Chinese nationals were made by Fujianese. In the four years between 1996 and 2000, 11,916 such applications

were submitted. This number is commensurate with the estimates of Fujianese associations, which were in the tens of thousands. According to a London Chinatown real estate agent and restaurant owner, there were 300 to 400 Fujianese working in Chinatown restaurants in 1999, constituting half of the workforce in those restaurants. Chinatown, a compact business neighborhood of just one block in the central part of London officially known as the City of Westminster, became an information, employment, and housing exchange center and first destination for Fujianese immigrants, whose migration in the second half of the 1990s changed Chinatown's social and economic landscape. Previously controlled by businessmen from Hong Kong, the burgeoning Fujianese population, though largely undocumented and relegated to subordinate economic positions, increasingly challenged the economic and political power, sometimes achieved through criminal methods, of the Cantonese. Although Fujianese immigrants remained a small minority among Chinese in Britain at the end of the 1990s, London's Chinatown appeared to be locked in a struggle for dominance between them and the older Cantonese immigrants.

Although the chances to enter Britain legally or to regularize one's residence after entering illegally were lower than in many other European countries, throughout the late 20th century the UK retained a popular image in China as the most attractive destination in Europe. This was not due simply to economic reasons: Fujianese migrants to Britain faced income prospects comparable to some other countries in Europe, worse living conditions than in many other countries, and lower chances of legalizing their stay. In Italy, for example, several large-scale regularizations of "illegal" immigrants were conducted in the 1990s and 2000s. Here, most Fujianese work in garment and leather workshops operated by entrepreneurs from other Chinese provinces and some started their own businesses after acquiring legal documents. In Hungary, most Fujianese operated legally as traders just as other Chinese migrants did. The fact that Britain retained its attraction may have had to do with the image of Anglo-Saxon modernity that was familiar to the migrants through the media. This image, coupled with the greater freedom of movement and employment enjoyed by asylum applicants and other undocumented foreigners, translated into a perception of "better human rights." In any case, Great Britain was the most expensive destination offered by commercial migration brokers in China (*shetou*, or "snakeheads"). The discovery of the corpses of 58 Chinese in a refrigerator lorry in Dover in 2000 – by far the most lethal incident in the smuggling of migrants into Europe in recent memory – awakened the public's interest in this phenomenon.

Illegal Migration

The typical way for a Fujianese to enter the UK, highly publicized in both British and Chinese media, was to purchase the services of a broker for tens of thousands of pounds, collected by relatives or borrowed at high interest. Once

285

in Britain, most submitted asylum applications. Although these were almost always rejected, the appeals process (at least until 2001) lasted well over a year. During that period, the applicant had legal status, the right to housing from local authorities, and subsistence benefits and, until 2002, the right to work after an initial period of six months. After their applications were rejected, most Fujianese remained in the country because the British government was often both unable (since Fujianese migrants had no proof of their PRC citizenship, without which the Chinese government balked at accepting them) and reluctant (due to the absence of both political will and the resources to detain and deport all illegal migrants) to deport them to China. These rejected asylum seekers, if they had had the right to employment, retained it and attempted to obtain "exceptional leave to remain," a status usually granted after a number of years spent in Britain but attained by only very few Fujianese by 2001. The overwhelming majority remained in Britain either with temporary permits on the grounds that they could not be deported or without any residency permit.

Since the turn of the millennium, when the UK became the largest recipient of asylum applications in Europe (peaking at 110,700 in 2002), the subjects of illegal immigration, human smuggling, and bogus asylum seekers have become a major political issue. Although Chinese citizens were never at the top of UK asylum application statistics, the media treated them, after the incident at Dover in particular, as emblematic of the problem. They were well suited to embody the fear of mass immigration because of their cultural "otherness" in addition to the large population, increasing power, and "Communist dictatorship" of their country of provenance. Among Chinese migrants, Fujianese were most commonly associated with illegality, "snakeheads," and abuse of the asylum system. This perception was reinforced by several kidnappings of Fujianese by fellow migrants in the late 1990s.

For the migrants themselves, however, the various forms of legal and illegal migration constituted a continuum of alternatives in response to available opportunities. They saw illegal entry and asylum seeking, including the use of false claims in applications, as a response to the peculiarities of the British immigration regime rather than as a criminal activity. According to this understanding, "snakeheads" were service providers, whose main role was to supply information and to help, whether legally or illegally, in surmounting red tape and a multiplicity of restrictions on exit and entry. Rather than constituting an organized criminal network, most migration brokers were small-time peddlers of information and contacts who worked with others on a case-by-case basis to provide documents, transportation, and accommodation in the migration process.

The economic and social position of Fujianese in London

Most first-generation Chinese immigrants in Britain were engaged in the catering business. As that generation aged and the British-born second-generation Chinese were unwilling to continue in the same sector, choosing to go into the professions instead, Chinese restaurants experienced a labor shortage. As the market position of Chinese food was essentially based on low price, labor costs had to be kept close to the previous level, when most restaurants and take-out shops were family run. In the early 1990s, restaurant owners found their source of cheap labor in Malaysian Chinese students and "tourists." The former had the right to work, but the latter did not, which meant that the owners risked fines if they were discovered by the authorities. Thus, Cantonese restaurant owners welcomed Fujianese asylum seekers as a workforce that was, in many cases, legal, yet very vulnerable and docile.

Because these Fujianese spoke neither English nor – initially – Cantonese, the language of most Chinese customers, the Fujianese were confined to kitchen jobs, while Chinese students and Malaysian "tourists" were employed as waiters. Since most had no previous experience in such jobs, a typical Fujianese migrant started as a kitchen hand or dishwasher and hoped gradually to work his way up to assistant chef. But by 1999, the job market in London's Chinatown had become saturated. The wage of an experienced kitchen worker dropped from £300–400 (US$450–600) a week to £200. Those without any previous kitchen experience were paid £140–150 per week, and employers in Chinatown provided food but no accommodation. Yet, even these wages were attractive considering their value in China. The migrants remitted all the money they could to repay the debts they had incurred in order to travel to Britain as well as to support family members, themselves spending as little as £50 a week.

Job security was nonexistent; restaurant owners often asked workers to come to work only when business was good and sent them home when it was slack. There was constant pressure from newcomers who were willing to accept even lower wages. Most Fujianese worked less than a year in any given job. Many left Chinatown for jobs at Chinese restaurants across Britain and in Northern Ireland. But unemployment in Chinatown also increased, and scores of Fujianese hanging around in Gerrard Street waiting for jobs and exchanging advice became a daily sight, causing wariness among both Cantonese business owners and the police. Many others had only part-time jobs, working only on the two busiest days of the week.

Some Fujianese supplemented their income by hawking phone cards and smuggled cigarettes on the street. Although asylum seekers were entitled to housing and cash assistance from the local council, most Fujianese avoided using these facilities, fearing that if they did so they would be tracked down and eventually expelled from Britain. Flats rented from the council were often shared among several Fujianese.

The typical goal of Fujianese migrants was to start their own restaurant or take-out shop. But this path, which led to the mass takeover of cheaper Chinese catering by Fujianese in New York in the late 20th century, was seriously hindered in London by the inability of the Fujianese to gain legal residence, which made the large investment required extremely risky. By the early 2000s, there were only around 10 Fujianese-run take-out shops in London, limited to low-rent areas shunned by other Chinese caterers. More generally, the irregular status of the Fujianese and their resulting vulnerability impeded social stratification. Their socioeconomic status remained almost uniformly low. Apart from the few who had obtained legal residence and become business owners, most others shared the burden of heavy indebtedness, poor working and living conditions, unemployment, lack of local support networks, and little hope of reuniting with their children.

Fujianese in society in London

Two migrants from Fujian who had come to Britain on student visas in the late 1980s, gained legal residence rights, and started businesses in London, presented themselves to Chinese and British authorities as leaders of Fujianese associations. The first of these associations, the UK Futsing Association, was founded in 1996 by a Fuqing-born man. His rival, a migrant from Changle, split off to found his own group called the UK Fujian Association. The two "associations" performed no community functions and undertook no action on behalf of the Fujianese. Their leaders aimed primarily at personal recognition by the embassy of the People's Republic of China in London and by the Chinatown elite, which could bring useful business connections, and they also sought to tap the economic potential of the Fujianese. The Futsing Association operated on the premises of its president's Chinatown business, Futsing Finance, which became a meeting place and information exchange for Fujianese, also renting out Chinese DVDs. Futsing Finance attempted to organize association members into a savings association to help them lease restaurants and take-out stores, but neither the legality nor the success of the enterprise was clear at the turn of the millennium. The Futsing Association also joined the World Futsing Association, an international body strongly supportive of the communist government of China and headed by the Indonesian tycoon Liem Sioe Liong.

The Employees Gospel Evangelical Ministry, a mission run out of a London Methodist congregation with members mainly from Hong Kong, attempted to help Fujianese asylum seekers in translating documents and obtaining medical treatment or legal advice. It published a newsletter, *Fuxun*, specifically targeting Fujianese restaurant workers. But the church gained very few converts and the Cantonese congregation was wary of the newcomers. For most Fujianese, the streets of Chinatown remained the only support structure available to them. Their irregular legal status also isolated them to some extent from their "legal" and more mobile fellow provincials in southern and eastern Europe and limited their participation in transnational networks.

Illegal employment in the ethnic economy also isolated Fujianese migrants from British society. They shared crowded flats and rarely ventured outside Chinatown except to deal with their asylum claims or to visit friends working at other restaurants. Their incorporation into Chinatown society, too, was ridden with conflicts along lines determined by class and immigration history. While Cantonese restaurant owners benefited from Fujianese labor, they were wary of Fujianese as potential competitors for economic and social influence. They were opposed to and tried to prevent the opening of Fujianese businesses and associations in Chinatown. With the public justification that Fujianese were a threat to public safety and frightened away clients, business owners in Chinatown lodged repeated complaints against Fujianese hawkers and idlers, and even occasionally attacked them. The Chinatown elite stigmatized the Fujianese as criminal, uneducated, greedy, and uninterested in integration.

David Tan, head of the Westminster City Council's Chinese Community Liaison Office, led two delegations to the Home Office before the Dover incident, asking the government to get tough on illegal immigrants from Fujian. Soon afterward, however, the economic usefulness of the newcomers appeared to prevail over the fears of the establishment. In 2001, Tan made a statement supporting the granting of work permits. Yet the legal, social, and economic position of Fujianese in London remained extremely precarious because of the restrictive policy of the British government, while there was little hope for legalization. This, however, did not deter the Fujianese from entering the country illegally. Despite the fact that increasing numbers of illegal entrants were put in detention centers before they could apply for asylum, Chinese citizens filed 6,065 asylum applications in 2001–2.

Benton, Gregor, and Edmund Terence Gomez. *The Chinese in Britain, 1800–Present: Economy, Transnationalism, Identity.* Basingstoke, 1998.

Chin, Ko-lin. *Smuggled Chinese: Clandestine Immigration to the United States.* Philadelphia, 1999.

Friman, H. Richard. "Evading the Divine Wind through the Side Door: The Transformation of Chinese Migration to Japan." In *Globalising Chinese Migration*, edited by Pál Nyíri and Igor R. Saveliev, 9–34. Aldershot, 2002.

Giese, Karsten. *Irreguläre Migration vom chinesischen Festland nach Taiwan.* Berlin, 1999.

Li Minghuan, and Pál Nyíri. *The Chinese Community in Europe.* Amsterdam, 1999.

Pieke, Frank N. *Recent Trends in Chinese Migration to Europe: Fujianese Migration in Perspective.* Geneva, 2002.

Pieke, Frank N., et al. *Transnational Chinese: Fujianese Migrants in Europe.* Stanford, 2004.

Cross-references: Great Britain; Chinese Itinerant Merchants in Europe since the End of World War I; Chinese Migrants in the Italian Fashion Industry since the Early 20th Century; Chinese Restaurant Owners in the Netherlands and Germany in the Second Half of the 20th Century

CHINESE MIGRANTS IN THE ITALIAN FASHION INDUSTRY SINCE THE EARLY 20TH CENTURY

Antonella Ceccagno

Southern Zhejiang province is one of the few areas in China that since the early 20th century specialized in emigration to Europe. Migratory chains linked villages in this area with cities and industrial centers of Italy. Mass migration toward Europe and Italy first began in the mid-1980s. After the People's Republic of China initiated economic reforms and progressively opened China up to the world market, successive waves of Chinese migrants settled in Italy and a number of other European countries. They arrived as undocumented migrants and later were able to legalize their presence in the country. Italy was the first and most important destination in southern Europe for the Chinese because of frequent amnesties, legalization campaigns, and ample employment opportunities. In the mid-1980s, there were around 1,500 Chinese immigrants officially in Italy; by 1996, the number of adult Chinese with residency permits was around 29,000, and in 2003 it had grown to 100,109. In 2006 there were 128,000 Chinese adults with residence permits, but including those without papers, an estimated 168,750 Chinese were living in Italy.

Before 2005, when the Italian government recognized the growing importance of the People's Republic of China in the global marketplace and began to attract students from China, immigrants were largely unskilled workers. Initially, these unskilled Chinese were employed in the ethnic economy to perform contract work in the production of garments, leather goods, and later couches and furniture for Italian manufacturers.

In the 1980s, Chinese immigrants came almost exclusively from the province of Zhejiang, while newcomers from the province of Fujian arrived in the 1990s. Through the beginning of the 21st century, Zhejiang province was again the dominant area of origin for the Chinese in Italy. In southern Zhejiang and Fujian, migration was the traditional opportunity for advancement, and a specific culture of migration developed that stigmatized local alternatives to emigration as second rate or even as a sign of failure. Only at the turn of the 21st century has the recent wealth of opportunities for upward mobility in China changed this attitude toward migration.

Fujianese migrants originated from the central and western areas of the province and their destinations in Europe have mainly been Italy, Hungary, and England. Contrary to the Zhejianese, they had no history of migration to Europe and could not therefore rely on kinship chain migration structures, with the exception of a few pioneer immigrants. Once in Italy, most Fujianese entered the ethnic economy established by the Zhejianese and adopted existing working patterns.

Since the late 1990s, the most recent migrants from China have come from the northeastern Chinese provinces of Heilongjiang, Jilin, and Liaoning. They originated mainly in large urban centers and were primarily women who emigrated after losing their jobs during the restructuring of the Chinese economy. They could not generally count on previous contacts in Italy and therefore their condition in Italy has been far more precarious than that of the other groups from Zhejiang or Fujian. Some are employed in workshops owned by Zhejianese; some have found work as child care providers for other Chinese in Italy thanks to their better knowledge of standard Chinese. A growing number of them have become involved in the Chinese prostitution ring. Recently, as in other European countries, the proportion of women migrants has increased, as has the proportion of women who are the first in their family to migrate, or who migrated on their own.

From the beginning of the 20th century Chinese pioneers settled in the garment and leather goods industries in the cities of Milan, Bologna, and Florence/Prato, with some establishing themselves as entrepreneurs. These workshops were reclaimed and expanded by the large mass of new migrants in the late 1980s and early 1990s. At the turn of the century, new businesses in the garment industry with Chinese workers emerged, chiefly in Naples and Carpi, and later in other regions where enterprises were generally smaller. At the beginning of the 21st century, Chinese immigrant workers are employed chiefly in the production of garments and leather goods.

The garment industry is central to the Italian economy, and clothing from Italy enjoys a worldwide reputation. The participation of the Chinese is an important competitive edge for Italian garment producers, who regularly arrange to have work done by Chinese subcontractors for two reasons: production costs are lower because of the relatively low comparative wages for immigrants, and Chinese workshops can often procure material more economically from China. Resorting to Chinese subcontractors thus represents the main response of Italian manufacturers to increasing competition from countries with lower labor costs.

Since the 1980s, the number of independent businesses operated by Chinese citizens in Italy rose rapidly. In September 2005 there were 21,743 Chinese firms (sole proprietorships) in Italy, with a growth index of 21% over the last five years (average annual variation for 2000–5) and a 17.4% increase over 2006. These businesses are almost evenly distributed between trade/services and manufacturing.

The year 2004 represents a watershed as for the first time the number of Chinese businesses in trade and services overtook those in manufacturing (9,582 against 8,972). This trend continued in 2005 when out of a total of 21,743 Chinese migrants' businesses in Italy, 46.5% were in the commercial sectors while 44.4% were in the productive sectors. More recent data show that by December 2007 Chinese migrants' businesses in Italy have reached a total of 29,771; however, these data do not provide information on the percentage of commercial and productive activities.

Productive businesses employ on average 10 workers each while commercial and service businesses may employ only the owner and her or his family members. Therefore, the majority of Chinese are still employed in manufacturing.

Certainly, the data now available on working activities offer a new picture of Chinese immigrants: long associated with subcontracting in productive activities, they are repositioning themselves en masse outside manufacturing. This evolution is closely linked to the evolution of China, which in recent years has become an ever-stronger global exporter. Migrants have taken advantage of this evolution and have started to import goods from China themselves and, in a number of cases, they have set up their own production facilities in China with the aim of exporting part or all of their output.

The integration into mainstream culture of the offspring of Chinese pioneer migrants from Zhejiang was overshadowed in the 1990s by the problems in integrating the new Chinese migrants from Fujian and the northeastern provinces of China. The conditions of textile production in the ethnic economy do not favor integration. Workers often live inside the workshops and their children stay in China until their parents are able to open a business of their own. Only a tiny minority of Chinese adults speak Italian. Families are highly mobile as they try to establish themselves in Italy or elsewhere in Europe. Chinese migrants are accused of seeking only economic integration in Italy while avoiding cultural and social integration. The second generation of Chinese immigrants may in part be upwardly mobile, as is observed in Milan. But the example of Prato offers a very different picture: children of migrants must work in production as youngsters, and, as a consequence, they have an extremely high school dropout rate. Only a few students of Chinese origin complete school and go on to higher education. The young Chinese blame cultural barriers internal to Italian society for their integration problems. Even their Italian peers shut them out.

In contrast, Chinese importers and wholesalers, lead highly transnational lives. They spend much time in the motherland and are highly mobile in Europe. They perceive themselves as representative of a new, globalized, and economically strong China. Self-confident, they do not actively seek social or cultural integration in Italy.

Ceccagno, Antonella. *Giovani migranti cinesi*. Milan, 2004.

Ceccagno, Antonella, and Renzo Rastrelli. *Ombre cinesi? Dinamiche migratorie della diaspora cinese*. Rome, 2008.

Cologna, Daniele, and Lorenzo Breveglieri, eds. *I figli dell'immigrazione. Ricerca sull'integrazione dei giovani immigrati a Milano*. Milan, 2003.

Farina, Patrizia, et al. *Cina a Milano. Famiglie, ambienti e lavori della popolazione cinese a Milano*. Milan, 1997.

Pieke, Frank N., et al. *Transnational Chinese. Fujianese Migrants in Europe*. Stanford, 2004.

Cross-references: Italy; Chinese Itinerant Merchants in Europe since the End of World War I; Chinese Migrants from Fujian Province in London at the End of the 20th Century; Chinese Restaurant Owners in the Netherlands and Germany in the Second Half of the 20th Century

CHINESE RESTAURANT OWNERS IN THE NETHERLANDS AND GERMANY IN THE SECOND HALF OF THE 20TH CENTURY

Flemming Christiansen and Liang Xiujing

Since the Second World War, the Chinese restaurant sector in the Netherlands and Germany has been successful in achieving a reputation that contributed to the public stereotypes of Chinese as caterers and as a homogenous community. The rise of the Chinese restaurant sector after the Second World War, however, was based on heterogeneous groups of Chinese immigrants, who gradually developed it as a niche of entrepreneurship and employment in response to the limited opportunities for Chinese in the local labor market.

The Chinese in the Netherlands and Germany were, from 1945 until the 1990s, mainly chain migrants and refugees from the Pearl River Delta, Hong Kong's New Territories, southern Zhejiang, Suriname, the Dutch Indies and Indonesia, and Vietnam. Rough estimates indicate that there were over 100,000 Chinese in Germany in 2000 and 180,000 in the Netherlands. People in the Chinese restaurant sector in these two countries have different culinary and cultural origins and speak a variety of dialects and languages, including Cantonese, Hakka, various Zhejiangese versions of Shanghai dialect, Mandarin, Vietnamese, and Indonesian.

Due to the various migration patterns in the two nations after the Second World War, the restaurant sector in the Netherlands developed much faster than in Germany. Toward the end of the 20th century the relative density of Chinese restaurants in the Netherlands was five times greater than in Germany. In the Netherlands, most of the Chinese migrants in prewar Chinatowns left the country in the late 1930s. However, ex-colonial civil servants, army personnel, and other Dutch nationals were repatriated to the Netherlands at the time of Indonesia's independence, rising to a total of around 300,000 in 1966. As a response, the market for Chinese-Indonesian food increased, and the 10 Chinese restaurants in 1945 expanded to more than 60 by the early 1950s and 225 officially licensed in 1960 (and an estimated 400, if small outlets are counted). Their numbers further increased to 618 in 1970, 1,842 in 1987, and 2,250 licensed Chinese restaurants in 2003.

Their position in Germany was very different. Most Chinese who had remained in Germany during the war returned to China immediately after 1945. In Hamburg, for instance, there were only 30 Chinese residents after 1945 and only 5 Chinese restaurants in 1950. The number of restaurants in Germany grew, mainly due to secondary migration from the Netherlands and Britain, and increased to some 3,500 in 2000. When the Chinese restaurants in the Dutch Randstad (the conurbation stretching from Amsterdam to Rotterdam) and in London had reached a certain density in the 1960s, their activities not only shifted toward smaller cities in those countries but also in Germany. A Chinese shipping agent in Amsterdam helped people move to Germany. Restaurants in Rhineland-Westphalia first opened in the early 1960s and dozens of restaurant workers were employed in the first Chinese restaurant in Essen. Within a couple of years Chinese restaurants were established in many Rhineland cities, based on chain migration of people from the Pearl River Delta and Hong Kong's New Territories.

In the 1950s and 1960s, marriages between Chinese restaurant workers and German women were not uncommon; going back to Hong Kong to look for a spouse was expensive and difficult, and there were few women among the migrants. The employment of Hong Kong nurses in Cologne and other cities of the region during the mid-1960s enabled many of the men in the restaurant business to marry co-ethnics and settle down with families. This dramatically helped restaurant workers establishing new restaurants, as wives working alongside their husbands provided the necessary flexibility in the early stages of a new business.

Chinese employees, most migrating through Britain or the Netherlands, established themselves as restaurant owners in Germany once they had gained experience and earned sufficient capital, and subsequently they summoned more friends and relatives. In Hamburg, a Hong Kong entrepreneur who had worked in Britain, the Netherlands, and Belgium laid the foundation for several restaurants that recruited workers among Chinese in Britain, the Netherlands, and directly in Hong Kong. This pattern of recruitment changed in the 1990s when new Chinese Mainland migrants arrived through eastern Europe, and when former Vietnamese "boat people" and north Vietnamese workers originally recruited to work in the GDR began to enter the Chinese restaurant sector.

The Chinese restaurant sector, with its relatively low capitalization, low skills requirements, and limited interaction with mainstream labor recruitment proved highly efficient at absorbing migrant labor and responded rapidly and flexibly to changes in migration patterns. Key to the success of Chinese restaurants was the adaptation of food styles to the local markets and tastes. The Chinese cuisine in the Netherlands, accordingly, mainly consists of Chinese-Indonesian food, although the share of Cantonese-style restaurants gradually increased to almost one-fourth in 1994. In Germany, the main style is Cantonese food. In both countries this Cantonese cuisine is localized and adapted to European tastes.

The origin of the restaurant owners does not normally dictate the type of cuisine offered. Vietnamese immigrants in Germany, for example, have entered the Chinese restaurant sector, taking on Chinese menus, decorations, and so on. Similarly, Chinese entrepreneurs open Thai, Japanese, and other "oriental" restaurants according to demand, and in many cases abandon the ethnic label altogether, providing mainstream "European" foods or snacks.

After the German unification the demand for Chinese food in the new federal states of the former East Germany rapidly developed, giving cooks easy opportunities to start businesses of their own. This drained the established sector in the old federal states of the former West Germany of its prime staff, while at the same time strict German immigration rules made recruitment difficult. Some observers notice that this expansion caused a decline of quality in Chinese food, but "real" Chinese entrepreneurs blame the lower public image on the entry of the Vietnamese into their niche.

In the Netherlands, a surplus of Chinese restaurant workers with poor skills predominates, which then leads to chronic unemployment in this sector. Therefore labor and immigration authorities are hesitant to allow the recruitment of skilled cooks from abroad, requiring that the poorly skilled unemployed should be hired first. Government-sponsored vocational training measures seem, after initial success in the 1990s, no longer available.

In the Netherlands, the Chinese-Indonesian section of the federation of caterers organizes 40% of all Chinese restaurateurs; other organizations of Chinese caterers provide further structure to the sector. In Germany, no nationwide professional organization exists, although an attempt was made to found an organization after the "dog meat scandal" in 1995, when Chinese restaurants were unjustly accused of serving dog meat to their customers. Despite a nationwide hostility toward Chinese restaurant owners in the wake of the incident, it did not lead to the formation of an organization at the national level. Many regional associations, however, provide channels for communication among members and promote their interests generally.

The use of ethnic stereotypes has helped the sector to maintain its "exotic image." Variations in ethnic themes and emphasis on diverse cultural aspects allow for an enormous range of businesses, from luxury restaurants in prime locations to small suburban take-out shops, and a flexible response to the market. In this respect, the Chinese restaurant sector has a distinct advantage over other dominating restaurant chains with strong brand names and narrow business concepts. However, the ethnic branding of the Chinese restaurant sector also created a public image of the Chinese as a culturally homogeneous group. Thus the success of the ethnic brand in business and its positive symbolic function in ethnically diverse Dutch and German societies has helped to create and perpetuate stereotypes of ethnic difference in those societies.

Organizationally, the Dutch ethnic Chinese have been more able to assert their interests politically and in civil society than their German counterparts. This is partly due to different integration policies in the two countries. In the Netherlands, organized, culturally defined ethnic groups have more avenues for representation of their members, while in Germany, formal representation of non-European nationals is maintained by the German Federal Commissioners for Foreigners who deal with overlapping cultural and ethnic aspects of integration.

The children of the Chinese restaurant owners in both Germany and the Netherlands express a strong tendency to look for employment away from Chinese catering as a profession. The minimal opportunities for professional and social mobility within the ethnic economy have led members of the second and third generations to take a different professional direction. Catering families place great worth in the upbringing and education of their children to enable their entrance into prestigious professions, with less hard work and fewer inconvenient working hours.

While the social integration of Chinese restaurant owners and their employees is made difficult by the requirements of their work, the rise of an educated and articulate middle class of Chinese professionals and academics in the Netherlands and Germany, partly the result of the education migration to European universities, challenges the ethnic stereotypes of the Chinese communities in both countries. This, in turn, further contributes to the urge among ethnic Chinese to move away from the restaurant sector.

Christiansen, Flemming. *Chinatown, Europe: An Exploration of Overseas Chinese Identity in the 1990s*. London, 2003.

Ke, Peng (Pieke, Frank N.). *Helan Huaren de shehui diwei* (The Social Position of the Overseas Chinese in the Netherlands). Taipei, 1992.

Rijkschroeff, Boudewijn Roger. *Etnisch Ondernemerschap. De Chinese horecasector in Nederland en in de Verenigde Staten van Amerika*. Groningen, 1998.

Cross-references: The Netherlands; Dutch East Indian Migrants in the Netherlands since the End of World War II; Vietnamese, Mozambican, and Cuban Labor Migrants in East Germany since the 1970s; Vietnamese Refugees in Western, Central, and Northern Europe since the 1970s: The Examples of France, Great Britain, and Germany.

CHINESE STUDENT WORKERS IN FRANCE AFTER WORLD WAR I

Nora Wang

The Chinese worker-students who came to France around 1920 were largely young men with at least a minimal level of education. They came in search of learning, but at the same time they had to work for their living; to do so they relied on a small yet efficient network of Chinese migrants that had existed since the early years of the 20th century and had grown stronger after the arrival of Chinese contract workers during the First World War. Such worker-students were mainly of urban, lower-middle-class origins.

They formed a well-defined group of some 3,000 migrants, most of whom can be identified by name and who were representative of one distinctive generation. Despite the hardships stemming from the chaotic political and economic circumstances in China following the 1911 Republican Revolution, these migrants aspired to become a new, modern, and Western-minded but also strongly patriotic elite. More than a few of them would become political and administrative cadres as well as managerial leaders of the People's Republic of China (PRC) and would hold these positions well into the 1980s.

These young Chinese started carefully planning their journey as early as 1915 or 1916. The project became known as the Liufa Qingong jianxue yundong, or Movement for Diligent Work and Frugal Studies in France. Although a small number of the worker-students chose to go to Britain, Belgium, or Germany, most went for various reasons to France. On the one hand, they planned to teach the Chinese contract workers there, who were mainly illiterate peasants and who had stayed in France after the end of the war. They worked together with the interpreters (who also were often students) who had been hired by the British and French authorities. On the other hand, the Chinese expected that most European countries, particularly France, would experience a severe labor shortage after the war. The weakness of the franc also played a part in the decision, as did the (short-lived) Francophile trend among the educated Chinese youth, who identified the land of Victor Hugo with the esteemed values of science and democracy. Another reason to go was the network of Chinese migrants that existed in France and that had been created in the beginning of the 20th century by a few men, including the famous Li Yuying. Like many of the worker-students, Li had been inspired by anarchism, but also by the close ties with the French *libres-penseurs*, or freethinkers. A small but influential group had formed around him, including a number of radical politicians. Their goal was to train and select young Chinese in France, who would then go on to become important figures in their homeland while retaining their French ties. The group initially supported the worker-student movement, but turned away from it when the project escaped their control.

The journey to France required a great deal of preparation, including fund-raising and the establishment of preparatory schools in China to provide the worker-students with some training and a basic knowledge of French. Worker-students came from all over China, though the largest number originated from four provinces, two of which, Sichuan and Hunan, were located inland and did not have a pronounced migratory tradition. The movement, however, offered a unique opportunity for young people to go abroad. The other important provinces were Zhili, centered around Beijing, and Guangdong, which was the only province with a migratory tradition (apart from Fujian). All the students followed the same route: they traveled to Shanghai, boarded regular line ships and, once in Marseille, continued their journey by train to a site near Paris where they were received and could rely on assistance. The earliest groups left in the summer of 1919, the last near the end of 1920.

The organizers made great efforts to place the immigrant worker-students widely among the schools that had agreed to take them in. In most cases, these were high schools, as their level of training would not allow them to enroll in universities. At the same time, some were provided with employment in factories because their savings had been entirely used up. They had expected to stay in France for only a short time – an expectation that would keep them on the margins of French society. Circumstances, however, very soon altered their plans. In the early 1920s France suffered an economic disaster along with severe unemployment while nascent political disorder in China deprived the worker-students of financial support from home. Moreover, they soon discovered that it was hardly possible to combine their studies with factory work. By the end of 1920, the worker-students faced severe hardships. Most of them gave up their studies for lack of funds and slowly came to resemble other groups of migrant workers in that they spent most of their time looking for employment and congregated around those places where factory workers were wanted – mainly the Massif Central and the environs of Paris. They often found work with the help of "ethnic" networks. When the crisis began to abate, many were employed by a handful of firms, in particular the Schneider and Hutchinson plants in central France and Renault – the top automobile manufacturer in France at the time, employing many immigrant workers in a Parisian suburb. Although the worker-students did not integrate into French society to any significant degree, one might say that they adapted to the situation as other foreign workers did. Most of them were simply unskilled, low-paid workers, living in poor, overcrowded working-class lodgings close to the factory plants and alongside Italian, Polish, or North African workers. Unable and often unwilling to resume studying, they had little contact with the French, who in turn became aware of their existence only in a few, rare instances, when they staged protests, mainly against the representatives of the Chinese government on French soil. As a result of the public disturbances they caused – in February 1921 in Paris, in October 1921 in Lyon, and in the summer of 1925 in Paris again – some were arrested and deported.

The Chinese worker-student movement in France nourished political unrest among its members that was related to political events in their homeland. The group zealously cultivated its familial, political, and ideological ties to their homeland – a development that was enhanced by the isolation of the worker-students in French society. The focus on life and politics in China was expressed in gatherings as well as in the publication of mimeographed newspapers. The bulk of the worker-students, who initially had expressed a vague sympathy for anarchism, soon became attracted to socialism. Many of them adopted Marxist views and participated in the founding of the French branch of the Chinese Communist Party (CCP) in 1921. Although there were contacts between both groups, neither the French Communist Party nor the Comintern seems to have been the driving force behind the founding of the French CCP. The decisive factor was most likely the insulation of the worker-students from French society as well as their strong ties with the founders of the CCP. The French branch of the CCP produced several important activists for whom these years provided political schooling or greater ideological depth. Zhou Enlai, prime minister of the People's Republic of China until his death in 1975, provides a case in point; another prime example is Deng Xiaoping, who would lead the reform movement in the 1980s.

Most worker-students returned to China between 1922 and 1926. Some went home by sea, as they had come, while others, including political activists who were being deported, traveled through Belgium or Germany and then on to the USSR, where some stayed for various lengths of time. A few settled in France and participated in the activities of the Chinese migrant community there, which counted some 4,000 people in 1940. Apart from the worker-students, there were some 1,200 "regular" Chinese students in France in the 1920s and 1930s. In these years France counted the largest number of Chinese students in Europe. A few hundred of these received support from the Institut Franco-Chinois in Lyon, which itself grew out of the worker-student movement.

Levine, Marylin. *The Found Generation: Chinese Communists in Europe during the Twenties.* Seattle, 1989.

Wang, Nora. *Émigration et politique, les étudiants-ouvriers en France 1919–1925.* Paris, 2002.

Yunhou Zhang, et al. *Liufa qingong jianxue yundong.* Shanghai, 1982.

Cross-references: France; Chinese Contract Workers in France during World War I

COMICI DELL'ARTE IN EUROPE IN THE EARLY MODERN PERIOD

Otto G. Schindler

In the history of the theater, "Comici dell'arte" refers to Italian professional actors of the early modern period who organized themselves into larger acting troops of 10 persons, on average, and appeared on the scene starting in the middle of the 16th century. The term is modeled after the term "Commedia dell'arte," which has been used only since the 18th century for a form of theater originally called "Commedia improvvisa" or "Commedia mercenaria" in Italy. There were also women among the Comici dell'arte, something that was regarded as a revolutionary innovation. Their heyday is assumed to have been between 1580 and 1650.

Mobility being essential to their existence from the very beginning, the Comici dell'arte began early on to travel outside of Italy as well – preferably into areas and for occasions where the ground had been prepared through the humanistic influence of an "Italianità" and they could expect to find an audience that understood their language. The performances of Ariosto's *I Suppositi* or Bibbiena's *La Calandra* in 1548 at the wedding of Maximilian II of Austria to the Infanta Maria of Spain in Valladolid and at the entry of King Henry II of France and Catherine of Medici into Lyon might still have been staged by Italian members of the academy with a love for the theater. But the "Walhen" (Welsch) who that same year put on *ain Spil* (*a performance*) before Maximilian's sister in Innsbruck were already part of professional troupes of actors and acrobats, who, for example, also accompanied Emperor Charles V and his son Philipp II on their travels through Europe the following year. Most sources mention Venice as the hometown of these troupes. As early as 1532, the first professional Italian actor, Francesco de'Nobili (called Cherea) is said to have journeyed from Venice "to Hungary," which means he probably joined Charles V's campaign against the Turks.

Princely weddings, tournaments, and other courtly feasts, because of their growing theatricality and the rising demand for professional actors, provided more and more performance opportunities for Italian stage artists. The Prague wedding tournament of 1570, held for the marriage of Anna of Austria to Philipp II of Spain and staged by the Mannerist court painter Arcimboldo, for the first time brought together a larger number of Italian actors. Among them was the Venetian Giovanni Tabarino, who had already appeared in 1568 as a "Comediante" at an Austrian *Landtag*. He is considered the first Italian known by name who led a theater troupe across the Alps. Already at the beginning of 1568, a play by the troop of Alberto Naselli (called Ganassa) was arranged for Emperor Maximilian II by his court antiquarian, Jacopo Strada from Mantua. In subsequent years, Ganassa appeared at the imperial court with his wife, Flaminia.

A few Italian noblemen are also known to us as the organizers of courtly theater performances. In 1570, for example, Giovanni Alfonso Castaldo organized performances – in which Ganassa was also involved – before the emperor in Prague and Speyer. Together with Tabarino, Ganassa followed the wedding entourage of Elizabeth of Austria, the bride of King Charles IX, from Speyer to France. They were accompanied by the "imperial leaper" Arcangelo d'Abruzzo, who, as "Saltarin du roi," remained in French services until the end of the 16th century. After the death of Charles IX, Ganassa left Paris and headed for Spain, where he and his troupe remained for a full decade, not returning to Italy until 1584. Tabarino, who also maintained a company in Paris alongside Ganassa, achieved considerable renown at the court. The king and the highest-ranking court ladies were godparents to his son. Tabarino became so famous that even half a century later the legendary Parisian fair artist Tabarin named himself after him. Tabarino's engagements forced him to be remarkably mobile: during his tour in Paris in 1571, he traveled to Vienna to make himself available for yet another Habsburg wedding.

In subsequent years, the courts of the Austrian Habsburgs and the French royal court remained the most important destinations of the Comici dell'arte; dynastic links with princely houses in northern Italy facilitated the contacts. In most cases the trip came at the invitation or through a commission of the troupe's patron. Visits by foreigners to the centers of Italian theater, such as Venice, Florence, or Mantua, often resulted in invitations to the Comici dell'arte. For example, King Henry III of France, on his return from Poland in 1574, saw the famous Comici Gelosi in Venice. When he wanted to bring them to his court three years later, he had to await their return "de la Cour de l'Empereur." In 1614, a play by the Comici Accesi from Mantua was arranged for an Austrian *Landtag*. Subsequently, Emperor Matthias elevated their principal and first comedian Piermaria Cecchini to the nobility – an event that attracted considerable attention and improved the social standing of the Comici dell'arte. In 1627–8, Cecchini was again performing at the imperial court, this time as part of the Comici Fedeli, which the Duke of Mantua had sent to Prague for the coronation of his sister, Empress Eleonora I Gonzaga, and which was headed by Giovan Battista Andreini. Afterward the troupe performed in Vienna, where a new version of Andreini's successful play *La Maddalena* was also staged.

While further guest performances by the Comici dell'arte in Vienna are not attested until 1660 and after, tours by Italian companies to Paris occurred with much greater frequency. Here, too, the court of Mantua was the primary agent. As early as 1584–5, Tristano Martinelli, who was probably the first Arlecchino, journeyed to France with the Confidenti. Among the Comici dell'arte, Martinelli, a citizen of Mantua, was one of the most widely traveled: in 1576 and 1578 he could be found in Antwerp and London; after his stay in Paris he played in Madrid in 1588; between 1600 and 1601 he was back in France with the Accessi and dedicated his famous *Compositions rhetoriques* to King Henry IV and his wife Maria de' Medici. In 1613–14 and 1620–1 he was back in Paris. Even at the age of 70, the Duke of Mantua wanted to send him to the imperial court in Vienna, but illness prevented his trip. The Gelosi returned to France between 1603 and 1604 – this time with Francesco and Isabella Andreini, the most celebrated actors of their day. Beginning in 1606, the Fedeli of Mantua went on a major, sometimes multiyear tour to France every five years, on average. Many of the plays by their director, Giovan Battista Andreini, were printed in Paris.

In France, unlike in the countries of the Habsburgs, the Comici dell'arte from the outset played not only for the court but also in public theaters. The king or other patrons of the Italians sought to neutralize the opposition of officials, who objected to the competition the foreigner posed to native theater groups. From 1642 to 1647, a troupe invited by Cardinal Mazarin and led by Giuseppe Bianchi played in the hall of the Petit-Bourbon; it already included Tiberio Fiorillo, who later became famous as Scaramouche. In 1660, Mazarin decided to set up a permanent Comédie Italienne and to that end tried to engage the well-known Arlecchino Domenico Biancolelli. The latter was at that time at the court in Vienna, where his company, under the leadership of Andrea D'Orso, had a theater specially built by Burnacini at their disposal. However, opposition from the Viennese Jesuits prevented a continuation of this guest performance, whereupon Biancolelli accepted the invitation from Paris and became the most famous Arlequin at the Théâtre Italien. The group around Biancolelli became – next to Molière's troupe – the most popular in the French capital.

Like the native theater people, the Italians were fully integrated into the artistic and social life. As "Comédiens du roi" they enjoyed considerable prestige. They married into French families, the king was godfather to their children, they received precious gifts, and their stellar performances on stage were as much the talk of the day as their private affairs. At the same time, however, they also experienced the darker side of the Ancien Régime: when Louis XIV was informed of an alleged satire about Madame de Maintenon, he had the Théâtre Italien closed without further ado in 1697. A few of its members found a place at provincial French theaters, the rest – those who did not find employment at a German court, as for example Mezetin Constantini – had to return home. In 1716, Luigi Riccoboni was able to set up a new Comédie Italienne. Marivaux and others wrote French plays for this Nouveau Théâtre Italien. In 1762, this stage merged with the Opéra Comique, which had emerged out of the Théâtre de la Foire in 1714. The Italian company was disbanded for good at the end of 1779.

Members of the old Parisian Théâtre Italien also gave guest performances in London, for example, between 1673 and 1675 for a few months at a time under the direction of Tiberio Fiorillo. It was only in 1726–7 that a troupe from Italy returned to the English capital. Otherwise the plays of the Nouveau Théâtre Italien were usually put on in London during guest performances by French itinerant companies. During one such performance in 1749, there were tumultuous scenes involving Huguenots and other French immigrants. Xenophobic slogans were shouted from the galleries and gangs of thugs armed with clubs stormed the stage. Soldiers were used to protect the actors. The incident even became a campaign theme during the upcoming parliamentary elections.

Apart from these guest performances, the Parisian Comédie Italienne exerted considerable influence on European theater especially through printed collections of texts (by Évariste Gherardi and others). It was only in this way that the Commedia dell'arte made its way, for example, onto the playbill and into the acting method of the German-speaking theater, where it experienced a new heyday in the first half of the 18th century as German extempore comedy on the traveling stage and especially in the Viennese theater.

It would appear that in the German-speaking lands, the Italian theater troops – unlike the English actors – put on public performances alongside those at the courts only in the last decades of the 17th century. While the English had switched to the German language already at the beginning of the 17th century, few Italian companies performed their pieces also in German. One such piece was that of the Venetian Sebastiano di Scio, who traveled through almost all German-speaking lands between 1687 and 1711. Di Scio was an actor, puppeteer, wire-walker, and medicine salesman, which means he had strong ties to the theater of the fairgrounds, where there had always been a close symbiosis between actors, circus performers, and healers. But Di Scio also performed frequently in front of courtly audiences. He played Arlecchino at his very first performance in 1687 at the court of the Duke of Schleswig-Gottorf; soon after he appeared before King Charles XI in Stockholm, and on his return trip to Germany he performed for the Danish royal court in Copenhagen. In 1690 he was given a performance permit for Prussia, though for the time being he was employed in Celle with the Italian company of the Duke of Brunswick-Lüneburg.

Individual Italian actors also joined their German colleagues, as for example Giovanni Camillo Ganzachi from Bologna, who wrote several plays for them in Vienna. In the 1740s, Canzachi was active at the court of Electoral Saxony in Dresden and at the royal Polish court in Warsaw. Since 1697, the Italian Angelo Constantini, who had played the role of Mezetin in the Ancient Théâtre Italien, had been working in Warsaw as a theater agent; in 1699, he brought the troupe of Gennaro Sacco to Warsaw, and in 1715 that of Tommaso Ristori. The latter company also performed in Dresden starting in 1717. In 1719, this Saxon-Polish Comédie Italienne comprised 16 actors and actresses who were receiving 5,333 talers in fees.

After Italian actors from Poland had made their first appearance in Russia in 1731, Empress Anna Ivanova brought Italians back to St. Petersburg in 1733, presumably under the direction of Gaetano Sacco, who died in Moscow in 1734. Since Russian court society did not speak any Italian, plot summaries in Russian and German were handed out at the performances, numerous examples of which have survived.

The last-named Italian troupe was already made up in large parts from members of an Opera buffa ensemble. This development can also be observed in the rest of Europe: in the course of the 18th century, "operists" and other music and theater groups became the real domain of Italian itinerant and guest theater. It was also during this period that the companies supplemented themselves increasingly with actors from the host countries – in part through marriages with members of the company. Before that, marriages between Italian actors and their local colleagues were rare, at least in the German-speaking realm.

There does not seem to have been a pronounced discrimination against the Comici dell'arte abroad. In the destination countries, the Italians were generally the target of the typical contemporary expressions of hostility to the theater – e.g., on the part of the clergy – no more frequently than at home. They had more intense conflicts (especially in France in the beginning) with monopolies and other protective guild mechanisms of local theater organizations. In Vienna, too, one occasionally heard in declarations by the city government, alongside the usual moral concerns, that the Italians "are merely taking the cold cash out of the country." The harshest attacks against the Italians came from the theater reformers of the German Enlightenment: in Gottsched's eyes they represented, because of their "unnaturalness" and moral shortcomings, the very embodiment of what German theater had to be "cleansed" of. But only a few years later, Lessing splendidly rehabilitated the Comici dell'arte.

Artioli, Umberto, and Christina Grazioli, eds. *I Gonzaga e l'Impero. Itinerari dello spettacolo*. Florence, 2005.

Ferrone, Siro. *Attori mercanti corsari. La Commedia dell'Arte in Europa tra Cinque e Seicento*. Turin, 1993.

Mehnert, Henning. *Commedia dell'arte*. Stuttgart, 2003.

Schindler, Otto G. "'Mio compadre Imperatore.' Comici dell'arte an den Höfen der Habsburger." *Maske und Kothurn* 38 (1997): 2–4, 25–154.

Trautmann, Karl. "Italienische Schauspieler am bayrischen Hofe." *Jahrbuch für Münchener Geschichte* 1 (1887): 193–312.

Cross-references: Austria; France; Germany; Great Britain; Italy; Northern Europe; Poland; English Comedians in Europe in the Early Modern Period: The Example of the Netherlands; Huguenots in Europe since the 16th Century

CONGOLESE IN BELGIUM SINCE THE 1960S

Anne Morelli

In 2008, there were 971,448 foreigners living in Belgium. Among them, 20,980 were nationals of the Congo, who still represent the largest immigrant group from sub-Saharan Africa in Belgium. To this number must be added Belgian citizens of Congolese extraction and illegal immigrants from the Congo. In contrast to France, Canada, or the USA, which also have large groups of immigrants from the Congo, the presence of Congolese in Belgium is the result of postcolonial immigration since the independence of the Congo in 1960.

During the phase of the Congo's colonial dependence between 1885 and 1960 (until 1908 as the private colony of the Belgian king, Leopold II, thereafter as a colony of the Belgian state), there was, in contrast to other European colonial powers, hardly any colonial immigration to Belgium. Belgium did not import any colonial workers, since the colony was not densely populated and the existing labor pool was considered indispensable to the development of the colonial economy (plantation economy and later also raw material extraction). The colonizers feared that the employment of Congolese workers in Belgium could raise the wage costs in the colony. During the colonial period, the Congolese had no claim to Belgian citizenship and to the possibility of free entry into Belgium that would have come with it. The few Congolese who came to Belgium – for example, the workers who loaded and unloaded the ships that sailed between the Congo and Antwerp – were prohibited from entering the country. They had to live in special dormitories in the ports until their ships departed.

Before the 1950s there were, with the exception of the few transportation workers who had broken their work contract, had escaped from the dormitories, and were now engaged in low-wage jobs, only three Congolese groups that were in Belgium permanently or temporarily: domestics whose masters had returned from the colony, members of religious orders, and the "natives" put on display at "ethnological exhibitions." Beginning in the 1950s, Congolese also came to Belgium with growing frequency to study. Some of them developed into the elite of the Congolese ethnic community.

The first, exclusively male Congolese students regarded their migration to Belgian as a perfectly natural stage in their education and training. They received scholarships and were lodged in the African House (La maison africaine) established specifically for them in Brussels. Their number rose substantially after independence as the former colonial power saw in the training of Congolese leaders who remained intellectually and emotionally connected to Belgium an opportunity to continue to exert influence on the Congo.

The career of the scholarship students usually envisaged only a brief period of study, followed by a return to Africa. Many remained permanently, however, not least because they had often extended their studies due to their inadequate performance in an unfamiliar educational system and a foreign environment. Because the scholarships were not sufficient, some students took on additional jobs. As the period of study became extended, the wives of the students often followed, which created additional financial burdens. The student migration turned into an immigration. In response, Belgium in 1981 limited the student status for foreigners to the standard period of study. In 1988–9, 2,200 Congolese were registered as students in Belgium; in practice, however, they or their wives were active in the labor market. Although they usually had an advanced level of education, they took simple jobs as nurses or nursing home attendants, janitors, or baby-sitters. Even after completing their qualifying phase, Congolese doctors remained formally in training for many more years and took over the emergency services in most hospitals in Brussels.

The students were pioneering migrants, who were followed by a stream of immigrants who were relatives or acquaintances and whose social and residence status became more and more differentiated. Since the possibility of legal work by migrants to Belgium ended in 1974, the application for asylum was the only ticket to entry. Economic crises back home, the political upheavals following independence, the civil war, and authoritarian regimes led to a steadily rising stream of refugees. However, very few refugees made it to Belgium. Especially the dictatorship of Mobutu (1964–97) prompted some members of the political elite to go into exile in Belgium, from where they reorganized the political opposition. In their wake, many Zairean nationals (the Republic of the Congo was called Zaire between 1971 and 1997) tried to apply for asylum. In 1993, for example, their number stood at 4,122; less than 10% were successful, but nearly half of the rejected applicants remained in Belgium without a residence permit.

Even a completed course of training or study in Belgium rarely enabled the Congolese returnees to find work at home that matched their qualifications and was adequately compensated. This also contributed to diminishing the desire to return. Many first-generation immigrants were intent on providing their children, who were born and raised in Belgium, with a good education, which was still not possible in many areas of the Congo at the beginning of the 21st century. Thus there emerged in Belgium a large group of Congolese who were referred to back in the Congo good-naturedly as "les Belgicains" (half Belgian, half African).

The colonial past determined the outside image of the Congolese in Belgium. On the one hand, they are seen as mendacious, lazy, lacking in intellectual talent, and unreliable. On the other hand, they are said to possess a sense of family, respect for the elderly, musical rhythmicality, and a simple but deeply and outwardly displayed piety. To a certain degree, the Congolese living in Belgium at the beginning of the 21st century seemed to confirm the last set of stereotypes with their choice of jobs and professions: nursing, the performing arts, sports, and religion. Congolese singers (for example, Zap Mamas and Dieudonné Kabongo) have been as successful in Belgium as Congolese soccer players (for example, Ngalula Mbuyi, called "Junior"). In the religious spheres, many sects, but also Catholic parishes, owe their growth or mere survival to the commitment of Congolese priests.

More than half of all Congolese immigrants (7,178 in 2003) settled in a separate neighborhood in Brussels, the Matonge. This quarter, the scene of violent unrest in 2001 and since then socially restructured, is characterized by numerous Congolese stores and media. Congolese living in Brussels, who had come exclusively from cities in spite of the large agricultural population in the Congo, found there services and goods they knew from their homeland. The demand for imported foodstuffs, textiles, personal care products, communication, and money transfers gave rise to a group of Congolese merchants and entrepreneurs of both genders. Added to this were some illegal activities by the Congolese – for example, the trade in valuable raw materials from the Congo. The large number of multifarious business connections guarantee contact with the country of origin.

At the beginning of the 21st century, the Congolese immigrants in Belgium are socially very heterogeneous: while some have grown rich quickly, many are impoverished and forced to enter into precarious employment situations. Because of the breakup of many families or the lengthy period of study by the men, women must earn the livelihood for the family and look after their children's education. Not infrequently they are confronted with the academic failure or even criminal conduct of their disoriented children, who live in the most insecure and poorest neighborhoods of the city and attend the most poorly equipped schools. At the same time, however, women of Congolese background are experiencing a reversal of traditional gender relations and a secure social emancipation. They have control of their wages, can divorce an unfaithful or parasitical husband, and are often actively organized in churches and women's organizations.

Other Congolese immigrants have been able to hold respected positions within Belgian society. The acquisition of Belgian citizenship allowed them access to prestigious professions as doctors, lawyers, judges, teachers, or administrative officials. Increasingly, workers of Congolese background are also organized in socialist and Christian unions and are

participating in labor struggles. Candidates of Congolese background ran in the elections in 2003 but were not elected. Since 2004, a socialist councilor of Congolese background, Dorah Ilunga, has been serving in the community of St. Josse in Brussels.

How well integrated are Belgians of Congolese background at the beginning of the 21st century? There is no straightforward answer, even if social criteria – for example, the rise in the number of Congolese organizations and clubs (aid organizations, recreational clubs, religious groups) – can be measured with some precision. Mixed marriages have also become more commonplace, although they are often impossible to track statistically, since the children and grandchildren of the Congolese immigrants for the most part have Belgian citizenship. The nearly 50-year presence of Congolese immigrants in Belgium has produced new generations who have only symbolic ties to the Congo. The language of their ancestors – usually utterly foreign to them – is learned in language courses. The often still existing ties to the country of origin are familial in nature and tend to become looser and are limited to occasional visits and sporadic money transfers. Ethnic orientations are only of a symbolic character and are often limited to less conspicuous details of dress and eating habits. Progress in the social integration of the group will continue to depend crucially on the extent of its incorporation into the labor market.

Cornet, Anne. "Les Congolais en Belgique aux XIXe et XXe siècles." In *Histoire des étrangers et de l'immigration en Belgique de la préhistoire à nos jours*, edited by Anne Morelli, 361–87. Brussels, 2004.

Etambala, Aziza Zana. "Présences congolaises en Belgique (1885–1940): exhibition, education, emancipation, paternalisme." PhD diss., University of Louvain, 1989.

Lusdana, Ndamina. "Y-a-t-il des immigrés zaïrois en Belgique?" *Agenda intercultural* 112 (1993): 4–8.

Morelli, Anne. "Les Zaïrois en Belgique sont'ils des immigrés?" *Cahiers africains* (1994), no 10/11: 155.

Cross-references: Belgium and Luxembourg; Africans from the Former Colonies in France since the 1960s; African Students from the Sub-Saharan Region in France since the Late 19th Century; Portuguese *Retornados* from the Colonies in Portugal since the 1970s

COSSACKS IN RUSSIA SINCE THE 17TH CENTURY

Katrin Boeckh

The Cossacks are a phenomenon specific to eastern Europe, where they arose and spread because of the political, cultural, and geographic conditions in that region. The 17th century constitutes an important turning point when the polity of the Cossacks, established along the Dnieper by Bohdan Khmelnytsky (1595–1657), pledged loyalty to the Russian czar in the Treaty of Pereyaslav (1654).

The word "Cossack" comes from Turco-Tartar. Its literal meaning is something like "free warrior" and it originally referred to mercenaries in the service of the Mongols. The term passed to groups of soldier-peasants who settled in several border regions of the Russian Empire, along the Don, in the Ural Mountains, in the Caucasus, and along the Dnieper. The Polish kings and Russian czars took them into military service and gave them in return personal freedom and the right to landed property. It was only under Soviet rule in the 20th century that they lost their special status. Nevertheless, even in the postcommunist era there are many followers and descendants who are consciously reviving and carrying on Cossack traditions and ideals. As a result, the Cossacks developed a specific identity across centuries and in various centers of settlement. With a certain dynamism and by adjusting to political conditions they were able to preserve their self-identity to this day and embed it in their collective memory.

The genesis of the Cossacks goes back to migrations that led to land occupation and permanent settlement. But this migration was less an organized movement than a disorderly and spontaneous flight by which peasants since the 15th and 16th centuries sought to escape being tied to the soil and materially dependent on the lord of the manor. They joined nomadic Cossack units at the periphery of the Empire. Their fallback positions and emerging permanent settlements were located in regions that were far from the centers of power at the margins of the Russian Empire but militarily important and offering an adequate basis for a livelihood.

The settlement trek to the Cossack settlements (*stanicy*) rarely involved migration back home, since a return to the old homeland would have led to punishment. The emergence of Cossack settlements triggered further immigration, since Russian peasants, beginning in the 16th century, were subject to the growing pressure from landowners, whose estates they were eventually no longer allowed to leave. Although the lot of the rural population in the Russian Empire eased with the emancipation of the serfs in 1861, the influx into the Cossack settlements continued right up to the end of the 19th century. The number of Cossacks eventually rose to 4.4 million in 1916.

The target areas were characterized primarily by the fact that they were sparsely populated by nomadic, non-Slavic inhabitants and by other migratory bands – also referred to as Cossacks – who lived from attacks on Muscovite and Polish border fortifications, from hunting, fishing, extensive animal husbandry, and occasional mercenary service. The increased immigration led to a reorientation: the Cossacks established fixed domiciles and agriculture became the most important basis of their subsistence. For example, through the Don Cossacks it was possible to colonize the so-called Wild Field, the steppe north of the Black Sea through which horse-riding peoples had pushed westward for centuries. The 15th century saw the emergence of the Cossack settlement of Zaporozhian Sič along the rapids of the Dnieper in the south. Cossacks also clustered beyond the Ural Mountains

and played an important part in the conquest of Siberia. Likewise, "free warriors" congregated in the Caucasus and along the Terek. Although Cossacks were found in various regions of the Russian Empire, there were no close contacts among the individual Cossack settlements. Still, given the similarity of their way of life and their military employment, the Cossacks developed a community of shared values and culture that made all Cossacks visible to the outside world as a collective.

For all that, the majority of the Cossacks did not differ from the East Slavic population in their ethnic identity, even though their community also admitted indigenous peoples like the Tungusi, Tatars, Kalmucks, and other groups. Likewise, their Orthodox religious faith did not set them apart from their Slavic environment. While the Cossacks saw this faith as an important element of their culture, persecuted Old Believers were also taken in and even a Lamaist-Buddhist-dominated group of Kalmuck Cossacks existed along the Don. Rather, openness toward members of other ethnic and religious groupings and a willingness to integrate them – provided the newcomers submitted to the rules of their shared cohabitation – were a hallmark of the Cossack way of life. The tribal cohabitation encouraged the reception of new members into the respective communities.

The most important characteristics that distinguished the Cossacks from the rest of the rural population was the absence of the bondage of serfdom, the freedom of their way of life, and autonomy in judicial and administrative affairs. In addition to the peasant way of life, the military service they had to render shaped the identity of the Cossacks. Depending on their geographic distribution, Cossack units were used as "Registered Cossacks" by the Polish kings, to defend the Russian borders or expand them, to conquer new settlement territory, and to fight external enemies like the Golden Horde on the Crimea. Because of the military service of the men, the role and importance of Cossack women was also different from the rest of the female rural population. While women were initially not welcome in the Cossack bands, Cossack social behavior changed with the increased settlement activity, which also entailed the establishment of families and fixed clans. Cossack women, as peasants and guardians of home and hearth during the military absence of their husbands, and as auxiliary female soldiers, were granted near-equality with the men, even though they were given hardly any rights of public participation.

With the recognition of their demands by the czars, the Cossacks developed a specific order that also set them apart from the unfree rural population. Internally, the Cossacks organized themselves by means of a hierarchical structure of ranks modeled after the military, with certain predemocratic traits. At the head stood, as the executive, the *ataman* (among the Dnieper Cossacks: *hetman*), whom all Cossacks were obligated to obey in times of peace and to follow into the field. He was chosen by a council of elders (*staršyna*), which was made up of Cossack officers who met regularly. Among the peculiarities of the Cossack way of life was, in addition

"The Zaporozhian Cossacks draft a manifesto to Sultan Mehmed IV." Painting by Ilja Repin, 1891 (*akg-images*).

to the cohabitation of large clans under patriarchal leadership, that only a soldier was accepted as a full member of the community. A social differentiation emerged when individual Cossacks acquired more and more property, while others had to sell their land because they were unable to farm it due to their military obligations; the result was that a land-owning elite confronted the landless.

Although the Cossacks offered the socially discontented of various backgrounds the opportunity to join their circle, they themselves for a long time refused integration into the Russian state. Attempts by the czars to curtail the freedoms of the Cossacks led to rebellions. However, leaders like Ivan Bolotnikov (1606–7), Stepan Razin (1670–1), and Kondraty Bulavin (1707–8) gathered not only Cossacks around themselves, but they also incited malcontented peasants and sub-peasant groups to violent protest. The charismatic Don Cossack Emel'jan Pugačev, who led the last uprising of the Cossacks in 1773–5 in the Urals, was publicly executed in Moscow in 1775.

Catherine II abolished the office of *hetman* for good in 1764. In 1765, the so-called Slobodian Cossack regiments in eastern Ukraine were refashioned into regular hussar regiments. Slobodian Ukraine, the territory of the Cossacks, was placed under Russian administration. In 1775, the Zaporozhian Sič was destroyed. Even before that, the Zaporozhian Cossacks had come increasingly under the sway of the czarist authority as the Russian Empire expanded southward. At the end of the 19th century, the Cossacks were integrated into 11 armies as pure cavalry units. They were subject to the Ministry of War and initially had to serve 25 years, later 20, though they kept their personal freedom and the right to landed property and remained exempt from the capitation tax that nearly all male subjects had to pay.

In public they attracted attention because they were now used for a growing number of tasks related to internal security and to put down unrests. Special tasks were assigned to the Cossack Personal Standard of the czar. Infamous was the use of the Cossacks in the bloody suppression of a peaceful demonstration of workers before the Winter Palace in St. Petersburg on the "Bloody Sunday" of 9 January (22, new dating) 1905.

On the whole, the group identity of the Cossacks was hardly in danger of being eradicated under the czars, to whom they were militarily subject. After the end of the Cossack-led revolts in the 18th century, the czarist state no longer saw them as a potential source of unrest. Rather, through their military service the Cossacks now proved a military pillar of the state. To this was added their own ethos: they regarded themselves as the "better" Russians and for that reason alone did not seek assimilation to the rest of the population, and they were willing to defend their values, which lay in patriotism, protection of the needy, and their own freedom, as well as in their militarism.

A momentous rupture in Cossack unity occurred with the Bolshevik assumption of power in 1917. Henceforth, all previous qualities, activities, and political associations spoke against the continued existence of Cossacks in the new state. The creators of socialism saw in them representatives of the fallen aristocratic and autocratic regime and therefore regarded them as a threat to the new state, which tolerated neither a czar nor an Orthodox religion. Under Lenin they were therefore stripped of their special rights. But while other "enemies of the people" in the Soviet Union faced the threat of deportation or execution, like the so-called *kulaks* or the potential and real political opponents of the Communist Party, many Cossacks got off lightly. After the disbanding of their settlements, they came together again in new state-owned and cooperative enterprises. Despite the end to their privileged status, Cossacks, too, were willing to take up the Soviet cause. Red Cossacks fought on the side of the Bolsheviks both during the civil war and in World War II. Probably the most famous novel about the Cossacks, Michael Sholokhov's *The Quiet Don*, deals with the life of the Cossacks from World War I to the Russian civil war and describes the breakup of Cossack families in the face of the decision for or against Bolshevism.

Cossacks kept trying to achieve the legitimation of their own state through reference to their identity, which they tried to base on historical myths. Even so, it remains doubtful whether the elements of national statehood that are repeatedly attributed to the Cossack communities actually existed. While the notion of a Cossack nation corresponded to Cossack self-identity and the awareness of a special position in the Russian state, the Cossacks were not separated from their Russian environment by either language, religion, a self-contained settlement area that was administered completely autonomously, or any other element of nation creation. Although several attempts to proclaim a separate Cossack state were made in the 20th century by well-known *atamans* – during the civil war under Kaledin and Krasnov on the Don, under Dutov in Orenburg, and under *hetman* Skoropads'kyj in Ukraine – they were never able to last. Still, they attest to the popularity of these local Cossack leaders and to their power to assert themselves, even if only briefly.

That Cossacks at present are once again seen as models and idols worth imitating has to do with the fact that the values they propagated were not forgotten under Soviet rule and

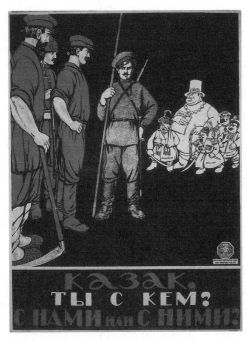

Placard of the Bolsheviks from the Russian civil war: "Cossack, on whose side are you?" Cossacks fought on both sides (*akg-images*).

were often uncritically transfigured and idealized. Moreover, many people in the countries of the former Soviet Union, because of the ideological emptiness and lack of models following the end of the socialist system, are now looking for new and positive political meaning – often in the prerevolutionary past. Especially in the former Cossack settlements in Russia and Ukraine, there is a belief that such meaning can be found among the Cossacks as the "better people." Today, several million people refer to themselves as Cossacks and see themselves in the Cossack tradition as "Russian, soldier, peasant, and believer." A pan-Russian Cossack League met for the first time in Moscow in 1990. In 1992, the Russian parliament, under the leadership of President Boris Yeltsin, passed a resolution that declared all measures since 1918 aimed against the Cossacks as illegal.

On the whole, the Cossacks have preserved a separate identity for centuries. Born under the conditions of Russian autocracy, they survived Soviet rule despite considerable interference and take their place as a new, conservative element in the contemporary transformation of Russian society.

Barrett, Thomas M. *At the Edge of Empire: The Terek Cossacks and the North Caucasus Frontier, 1700–1860.* Boulder, 1999.

Kumke, Carsten. *Führer und Geführte bei den Zaporoger Kosaken.* Wiesbaden, 1993.

O'Rourke, Shane. *Warriors and Peasants: The Don Cossacks in Late Imperial Russia.* Houndmills, 2000.

Stökl, Günther. *Die Entstehung des Kosakentums.* Munich, 1953.

Subtelny, Orest. *The Mazepists: Ukrainian Separatism in the Early 18th Century.* Boulder, 1981.

Cross-references: Russia and Belarus

CROATIAN AND SLOVENIAN LABOR MIGRANTS IN AUSTRIA IN THE 19TH AND EARLY 20TH CENTURIES

Sylvia Hahn

Three million Croats lived in the Habsburg monarchy on the eve of World War I. After the occupation of Bosnia in 1878, the Croatian areas outside of Italy had been consolidated in the monarchy and were divided between Hungarian Croatia-Slavonia (including the former military border district), Fiume (Rijeka), and a few western Hungarian *komitats*; the Austrian Crown Lands of Istria and Dalmatia; and Bosnia-Herzegovina (which was annexed in 1908 as an Imperial and Royal Province).

The vast majority of Croatian settlement areas remained basically agricultural into the 20th century. In the Austrian part of the Empire in 1910, 84% of the Croats and Serbs of Istria and Dalmatia depended on agriculture, as did 78% in Croatia-Slavonia and 86% in Bosnia-Herzegovina. Small farmers and small-scale tradesmen dominated. The emancipation of the serfs in 1848 led to fragmentation of landholdings, along with the breaking up of the large farms worked by extended families called *zadrugas* into small and very small holdings; this redistribution led to an increasing indebtedness and impoverishment of a large part of the rural-agrarian population. In the 1880s and 1890s, one-sixth of northern Croatian and other South Slav peasants were no longer able to feed their families.

By the late 19th century, the Croatian and South Slav populations could already look back on a long migratory tradition. Men's seasonal labor migration and itinerant trading in spices, or wooden goods (e.g., cooking spoons, sieves, bowls), or southern fruits, contributed to the family income from the 16th to the late 19th century. *Krawaten* peddlers followed the trade routes from south to north, via Styria and Lower Austria to Vienna and Prague. In the 19th century, Slovenian men of all ages left the Krajn district annually from the end of April to the end of September to work on building the Austrian railways.

The migration of Croats and South Slavs to other European countries played only a minor role between 1880 and 1914 (totaling only 10,000 individuals). Overseas migration was far more important on the other hand, and peaked between 1880 and 1914. The US government recorded 310,781 Croats as immigrants from the entire monarchy, but the real number was probably quite a bit higher as some Croatian immigrants were counted as Austrians rather than Croats because they had come from Austria. Between 10% and 20% of the emigrants eventually returned to Europe, generally after 10 or 20 years away.

In Vienna, the relatively few Croatians and other South Slavs in the city accounted for only around 1% of the entire immigrant population and their number remained quite moderate in the industrial areas of Lower Austria and in Styria as well. In contrast to other migrants like the Bohemians, Croatian and other South Slav labor migrants rarely set up or participated in clubs and organizations. At the end of the 19th and the beginning of the 20th centuries, the Slovenian writer Ivan Cankar made this loneliness of the migrants from the south the theme of several novels. There is, however, still a Croatian College in Vienna which dates back to the immigrant students and scholars of those years.

On the other hand, Croats from ethnic Croatian villages in the nearby Hungarian border region could be found in the numerous textile and paper factories of the Lower Austrian industrial region south of Vienna, as in Ebreichsdorf, Felixdorf, or Bruck an der Leitha. These were generally single young women and men, many of whom already had numerous acquaintances and relatives in these factory villages. They mostly lodged in the rooms for unmarried workers of the companies' own factory housing, and the proximity to their native villages made it possible for them to go home on weekends. Marriages within the factory worker milieu could lead to the creation of households by partners from different backgrounds. In many cases, additional moves from factory village to factory village took place, especially in times of economic downturns or unhappiness over wages, and these were often undertaken jointly by immigrants who had hailed from the same region. On the whole, strong bonds of kinship and friendship to the region of origin remained intact.

In the 19th century the chief destination in Austria-Hungary for migrant laborers from the Croatian and South Slav region was the port city of Trieste, which had been declared a free port by Empress Maria Theresa in 1766. That drew many immigrants into the city from the most diverse linguistic, ethnic, social, and regional backgrounds. Italian was the lingua franca in the 19th and 20th centuries. After the city's duty free status was rescinded in 1891, Trieste remained attractive to immigrants because it had evolved into a major industrial center.

After 1848, those who came to Trieste from rural Slovenian Krajina and the Gorizia region were mostly shepherds, day laborers, migrant laborers, domestics, and the younger members of peasant families. In the second half of the 19th century some of the villages in Trieste's hinterland ended up with large surpluses of men because most of their young women had gone to Trieste to work as domestics. Sometimes the short distance migration to Trieste was followed by a long distance migration across the Mediterranean. In 1900 about 3,500 people from Krajina, the coastal region, and Dalmatia lived in Egypt; about 2,000 in Constantinople; and about 1,300 in Turkey. In Egypt the majority of these Croatian and Slovene migrants were women: in Alexandria they made up 72% and in Cairo 61% of the migrants. Back home these female migrants to Egypt therefore were called *Alexandrinke*. These women generally worked as domestic servants, wet nurses, or maids, but some were high-status servants like governesses and English teachers. This migration stream of women from the Goriska region to Egypt started with the building of the Suez Canal in the 1860s and continued well into the 20th century – with some returning

only in the 1970s after staying and working in Egypt for 30 years. From interviews we know that most of these women provided important financial support to their families back home in Slovenia and that sometimes they were the main breadwinners.

Until around 1890 the migrants to Trieste from Gorizia-Gradisca (1890: 1,109; 1900: 1,040) and Krajina (1890: 583; 1900: 570) outnumbered those from further afield (1890: 937; 1900: 992). By 1910 there was a noticeable increase in immigrants from Istria (1900: 585; 1910: 884) and from abroad (1,170), while immigration declined slightly from Gorizia-Gradisca (967) and Krajina (498). Most immigrants from Krajina to Trieste worked at the port, transporting wood and coal. After 1895 other Krajinans worked in the blast furnaces of the Krajinan Industrial Society in the Servola district, taking poorly paid, dangerous, and unhealthy jobs that were avoided by native urban workers and were filled mainly by immigrants. Slovenian women rarely worked in the factories; instead they were mostly market vendors, washerwomen, bread bakers, or seamstresses, or in Italian households they were domestics who were under strong pressure to assimilate linguistically and culturally.

Until the turn of the century, Croatian and Slovenian immigrants put their clear stamp on various city neighborhoods; after that a new deliberate urban housing policy forced them to live more strongly intermixed with the Italian speaking population. The Slovenian immigrants had a vigorous associational life, both Catholic and liberal. In addition, Slovenian newspapers were established, as was a private system of Slovenian schools and kindergartens because teaching in the Slovenian language was prohibited in the public schools. The Slovenian immigrants were seen as assimilated; and it was only the growing Italian immigration after the turn of the century that led to a quickening of Slovenian and Croatian identity in a city that had become a target of Italian irredentists.

Barbič, Ana, and Inga Miklavčič-Brezigar. "Domestic Work Abroad: A Necessity and an Opportunity for Rural Women from Goriška Borderland Region of Slovenia." In *Gender, Migration and Domestic Service*, edited by Janet Henshall Momsen, 164–77. London and New York, 1999.

Božić, Saša. *Immigranten und Integration im Zusammenhang mehrschichtiger ethnischer Beziehungen. Am Fall der Kroaten in Wien.* Vienna, 1998.

Cattaruzza, Marina. "Slovenen und Italiener in Triest 1850–1914." In *Alpen-Adria-Städte im nationalen Differenzierungsprozeß*, edited by Andreas Moritsch, 199–255. Klagenfurt, 1997.

Grandits, Hannes. *Familie und sozialer Wandel im ländlichen Kroatien (18.–20. Jahrhundert).* Vienna, 2002.

Hahn, Sylvia. "Migranten als Fremde – fremd als Migranten. Zuwanderung in Wien und Niederösterreich im 18. und 19. Jahrhundert." In *Walz – Migration – Besatzung. Historische Szenarien des Eigenen und des Fremden*, edited by Ingrid Bauer, Josef Ehmer, and Sylvia Hahn, 77–119. Klagenfurt, 2002.

Hahn, Sylvia. *Migration – Arbeit – Geschlecht. Arbeitsmigration in Mitteleuropa vom 17. bis zum Beginn des 20. Jahrhunderts.* Göttingen, 2008.

Heuberger, Valeria. *Unter dem Doppeladler. Die Nationalitäten der Habsburger Monarchie 1848–1918.* Vienna and Munich, 1997.

Moritsch, Andreas. *Das nahe Triester Hinterland. Zur wirtschaftlichen und sozialen Entwicklung vom Beginn des 19. Jahrhunderts bis zur Gegenwart.* Vienna, Cologne, and Graz, 1969.

Cross-references: Austria; Southeastern Europe; Czech Labor Migrants in Austria in the Nineteenth and Early 20th Centuries; Settlers on the Habsburg Military Border since the Early Modern Period

CYPRIOTS IN GREAT BRITAIN SINCE 1945

Panikos Panayi

In the decades following the Second World War, Great Britain's borders were open to migrants from its former empire. While the vast majority of those who moved from the colonies originated in the West Indies and the Indian subcontinent, a significant number also came from some of the smaller British possessions, including Cyprus, an island with a population of 574,000 in the 1960s. Cypriots of both Greek and Turkish descent encountered a small group of their countrymen in Great Britain who had migrated there before the Second World War. The Greek Cypriot community in Great Britain is approximately four times as large as the Turkish Cypriot, which roughly corresponds to the proportion of Greek to Turkish Cypriots on Cyprus itself. The ethnic division of the population into Greek and Turkish Cypriots originated in 1571 with the Ottoman annexation of the island, which previously had belonged to the Venetian Empire.

Most of the migration from Cyprus to Britain occurred in the initial postwar decades so that between 1951 and 1971 the number of Cypriots in Britain increased from 10,343 to 72,665. A series of factors in Cyprus explains this growth, including a population surplus reaching maturity during the 1950s; a lack of economic opportunities in an overwhelmingly agrarian economy; and the emergence even at the local village level of the notion of England as a land of economic opportunity. This perception of England essentially developed through personal correspondence with relatives and led to the emergence of network migration. As a result, a significant percentage of the inhabitants of some villages, such as Lympia, moved to London while others, such as Mitseron, lost virtually none of their people. Another wave of Cypriot immigration took place in 1974 when Turkey occupied northern Cyprus, which led to the division of the island and the expulsion of the Greek population from the north of the island and the Turkish population from the south of the island. One result of this "ethnic cleansing" was the flight of as many as 10,000 persons to their relatives in Great Britain.

No significant migration from Cyprus to Great Britain has since taken place. Instead, the return migration of persons from the first and second generation has increased in importance. The only significant, usually temporary, migration has involved students who study at universities throughout the UK.

Of the approximately 100,000 Cypriots living in Britain in 1966, about three-quarters resided in London. According to the census of 2001, the number of Londoners born in Cyprus was 45,887, which meant that migrants of the second and third generations were not included in the total number. This concentration of Cypriots in London persists today. Although Greek Cypriots were initially concentrated in the inner London boroughs, forming ethnic neighborhoods in Camden Town, they subsequently moved farther north, first to Haringey and then on to the middle-class suburb of Palmers Green. Nevertheless, the main area of concentration of Greek and Turkish Cypriots remains the north of the capital. Aside from students, only those Cypriot migrants who run fish and chip and kebab shops throughout the country live outside of London.

The number of self-employed Cypriots in Great Britain is above average: as early as 1966 a total of 19.6% of Cypriots in London were self-employed when the national figure for the whole of the British population stood at 7.1%. Typical employment has included the ownership of grocery shops catering to members of the same ethnic group. The fish and chip shops, mentioned earlier, make up another conspicuous feature: in the town of Leicester as well as in the county of Leicestershire, for example, Greek Cypriots own virtually every fish and chip shop despite the fact only a few hundred live in the area. First-generation migrant women in London were usually employed as tailors by fellow Cypriots, either at home or in factories. The second generation has experienced much social mobility.

Language and religion have formed the basis of identification for Greek Cypriots in Britain. The first generation of Greeks spoke their own dialect, which they passed on to the second generation, while their grandchildren have increasing difficulty communicating in the language of their land of origin. The Greek Orthodox Church in Britain, which was founded in the late 19th century, continues to have great significance. In the early 1990s a total of 32 places of worship existed in London, together with dozens of others in the rest of Great Britain. Although mixed marriages with members of other ethnic groups have increased, Cypriots still possess strong ethnic ties and a distinct cultural identity at the start of the 21st century.

The few Greek Cypriots who moved to London before the Second World War had already established their own political and cultural organizations. By the 1960s, the community supported two newspapers: the Communist *Vema* and the nationalist *Helleniki*. Both had disappeared by the middle of the 1980s. In total there may have been up to 30 Greek Cypriot newspapers through the 1980s, with *Parikiaki* being the most important. By the 1990s numerous new organizations and clubs had developed among the Greek Cypriot community in London. These included community centers (which received some public funding), educational and youth associations, village societies, professional group-ings, women's associations, a Thalassemia Society devoted to fighting the genetic blood disease of the same name, at least one theater group – Theatron Technis – and, perhaps most important of all, London Greek Radio.

Cypriots in Britain have attracted relatively little hostile attention compared to the much larger African Caribbean and South Asian populations. Many racist groups see the Cypriots as white, although Cypriots are often dismissively viewed by native Britons as kebab shop owners. Although this stereotype, which has become increasingly prevalent since the 1980s, offers a very one-sided view of Cypriots in light of the variety of economic activities they are engaged in, the indigenous population has a generally positive estima-tion of Cypriots in Great Britain.

Anthias, Floya. *Ethnicity, Class, Gender and Migration: Greek Cypriots in Britain*. Aldershot, 1992.

Burrell, Kathy. *Moving Lives: Narratives of Nation and Migration among Europeans in Post-war Britain*. Aldershot, 2006.

Josephides, Sasha. "Associations Amongst the Greek Cypriot Population in Britain." In *Immigrant Associations in Europe*, edited by John Rex, Daniele Joly, and Czarina Wilpert, 42–61. Aldershot, 1987.

Pananyi, Panikos. *Spicing Up Britain: The Multicultural History of British Food*. London, 2008.

Visram, Rozina. "Turkish Cypriots." In *The Peopling of London: Fifteen Thousand Years of Settlement from Overseas*, edited by Nick Merriman, 106–10. London, 1993.

Cross-references: Great Britain; Southeastern Europe; Greek Labor Migrants in Western, Central and Northern Europe after 1950: The Examples of Germany and the Netherlands; Greek Refugees in Western, Central, Northern, and Southern Europe during the Military Dictatorship 1967-1974; Indian, Pakistani, and Bangladeshi Migrants in Great Britain since 1947; Turkish Labor Migrants in Western, Central, and Northern Europe since the Mid-1950s; West Indians in Great Britain, France and the Netherlands since the End of World War II

CZECH LABOR MIGRANTS IN AUSTRIA IN THE 19TH AND EARLY 20TH CENTURIES

Monika Glettler

Between 1860 and World War I, Czech labor migrants from the Bohemian crown lands went chiefly to Vienna and Lower Austria (until 1921 Vienna was part of Lower Austria), and to a much smaller extent to a few places in Upper Austria (primarily Linz) and Styria. The totality of the migrants and their pattern of integration were characterized by the high ratio of workers in industry and trades (85% vs. 46% among the native workforce), their well-developed system of clubs

and organizations, and their relatively narrow image of themselves.

The Czechs who settled in Vienna after the 1880s, because of the city's central function as the imperial capital and resi-dence and the industrial metropolis of the Habsburg multi-ethnic state, either stayed in Vienna temporarily to engage in seasonal work or slowly integrated, without forming closed ethnic communities of origin. In typological terms this was an interior migration from the rural/agrarian regions and small towns of southern Bohemia and Moravia that bordered on Upper and Lower Austria and usually had a population that was more than 90% Czech; the goal of the migrants was to find jobs and better life opportunities in the high-wage region of Vienna. These immigrants made up 44% of all migrants in the metropolis on the Danube. In the heyday of immigration around 1900, about 103,000 Czechs (referred to colloquially as Bohemian/Moravian/Slovakian) were officially counted in Vienna, among a total population of 1,675,000. Czech estimates even run as high as 300,000 to 600,000. As the new arrivals came and departing workers left in roughly the same numbers, the total population of Czechs in Vienna grew only slowly. Because of the large fluctuations, the membership in the Czech organizations could sometimes turn over completely within a year.

The factories in the Vienna Basin (textile, metal, electri-cal, and chemical industries), the large construction sites since 1860, and the brickworks in the southern environs formed the collection points especially for seasonal workers. In Upper Austria and Styria it was above all mining, metal- and ironworks, and railroad and shipbuilding that attracted immigrants. Czech labor migration to Linz began with the construction of the "salt line" from Linz to Budweis in 1825. Linz had about 2,000 Czechs in 1858, around 3,700 in 1890, and about 7,000 individuals of Czech descent in 1910. Comparable numbers do not exist for Styria (e.g., Graz, Donawitz, Voitsberg, Kapfenberg).

The Czech commercial workers and tradesmen were absorbed into the broad, traditionally rooted commercial sec-tor. At the forefront stood the clothing sector, especially since textiles made up the largest branch of industry in Bohemia/Moravia. In 1900, 28% of the Czechs in Vienna were working as tailors and shoemakers. They accounted for 44% of those gainfully employed in this sector; one-fifth were independent masters. In 1910, the Fortbildungsschule für Kleidermacher (School for Tailors) in Vienna had more than 67% Czechs. As early as 1869, 69% of all journeymen joiners came from Bohemia/Moravia. Over the course of three decades, the number of Czech locksmiths and tinsmiths in Vienna rose more than threefold. All in all, there was hardly a sector of the economy in Vienna in 1914 without Czechs.

The age cohort with the highest participation rate in the workforce among Czechs of Vienna was that between 11 and 30 (about 50% around 1900). While the men worked chiefly in the manufacturing sector, 75% of the women in the workforce were employed in the service sector, with only 21% in industry and trade. The preferred job was that of a domestic servant, since it solved the problem of food and housing for the time being and since single factory workers – especially those from the countryside – had a bad reputation, while employment as a nanny or parlormaid, cook, housekeeper, and wet nurse was seen as a transition to marriage. The large number of married Czech women between the ages of 20 and 30 indicates that many domestics married and it reflects the high numbers of female immigrants in the wealthy districts of central Vienna (districts I–IV).

While Czechs lived in all 21 districts of Vienna, their ratio among the respective populations varied. Self-contained ethnic communities of origin did not exist. Instead, the settlement patterns of the Czech immigrants were oriented primarily toward the predominant social and economic traits in the districts of Vienna. That the migrants accommodated themselves from the beginning to the functional differentiation of the city neighborhoods was especially evident in the workers' and industrial districts (X, XIV, XX). There the spatial concentration was limited to the level of blocks or houses (on average eight Czechs per house) or to self-contained, temporary housing in company-owned housing camps of the Wienerberger Tongruben- und Ziegelbrennereien in the suburb of Inzersdorf (for 3,000 Czech and Slovak workers). One in nine Czechs had no more than a place to sleep – known as a *Bettgeher* – with large working-class families, for a rent equal to half the monthly salary of a nursemaid.

The most important role for the self-constitution of the Czech migrants was played by the Czech system of clubs and organizations, which grew continuously from the 1860s; in Linz these were largely on a religious basis with Catholic masses held in the Czech language. To outside perception, these organizations were comparable, in terms of their function, "to what village, city and state mean to other people." Among many hundreds of organizations encompassing all spheres of life was the Česko-slovanský dělnický spolek (Czechoslovakian Worker's Organization) that was formed in Vienna in 1868 and which gave rise to the establishment of the Komenský League for the Establishment and Preservation of Bohemian Schools in Vienna (1872). Comenius, as the "founder of the modern school system," was chosen as the symbolic figure. The first private elementary school with a kindergarten was set up in 1883 with the goal of promoting the bilingual education of the children while preserving their Czech identity, especially since the proportion of Czech pupils was as high as 24% in some of the city's elementary schools. Around 1900, 47% of Czech households already had two or more children, who, through school attendance and street socialization, rapidly surpassed their parents in their knowledge of German and acted as translators in interactions with superintendents, employers, and officials. However, because of tight living quarters, very little time for a private life, and frequent moves, in addition to the fear of deportation as part of the *Heimatgesetz* (Homeland Law), the family was able to fulfill the function as the bearer of cultural identity only in part. As a result, the cultivation of the native culture and mother tongue for the most part remained on a low level, as well (*Böhmakeln* or *Kuchelböhmisch* as incorrect Czech/German).

There is no doubt that the structure of Czech organizations in Vienna – also because it endured for so long – solidified "the sense of belonging of the Bohemians in Lower Austria," even though the Imperial Court (Reichsgericht) clearly determined in 1910 that the Czech minority in Lower Austria had no "historical roots" and should therefore not be legally recognized as a "*Volksstamm* (ethnic group) of the country." The Czech private schools also strove in vain for recognition as public institutions.

The strong growth in immigration also gave rise to social and national discrimination against the Czechs through measures taken by the local bureaucracies. For example, Vienna's Municipal Council, in the words of the anti-Semitic politician and mayor of Vienna, Karl Lueger, was intent on "preserving the German character of the city of Vienna" and "eliminating these Slavic elements and replacing them with Germans." But in the perception of the Czechs themselves, Vienna became the "biggest Czech city," "in which the fate of the entire Czech nation will be decided." For Czechs with ambitions for social and economic advancement, integration was unavoidable: "He who wanted to be something had to speak German." The second generation usually remained in a more or less pronounced partial assimilation and decided to embrace a local identity: "I am not a German, I don't want to be a Czech, I am a Viennese."

The collapse of the Habsburg monarchy and the establishment of the first Republic of Czechoslovakia in 1918–19 triggered an enormous wave of remigration: against the backdrop of the Brünn Treaty of 1920 between Austria and Czechoslovakia, which provided the opportunity to choose, about 150,000 Viennese Czechs were repatriated whereas more than 81,000 remained in Austria. At the beginning of the 21st century, the remnants of the Czech organizations are united under the umbrella organization Minderheitsrat der Tschechen und Slowaken in Österreich (Minority Council of the Czechs and Slovaks in Austria). Only the school organization Komenský is deliberately leading a life of its own.

Glettler, Monika. *Die Wiener Tschechen um 1900. Strukturanalyse einer nationalen Minderheit in der Großstadt.* Munich and Vienna, 1972.

John, Michael, and Albert Lichtblau, eds. *Schmelztiegel Wien einst und jetzt. Zur Geschichte und Gegenwart von Zuwanderung und Minderheiten.* 2 vols. Vienna, 1990.

Rothmeier, Christa. *Die entzauberte Idylle. 160 Jahre Wien in der tschechischen Literatur.* Vienna, 2004.

Slapnicka, Harry. *Oberösterreich – unter Kaiser Franz Joseph (1861–1918).* Linz, 1982.

Soukup, František. *Česká menšina v Rakousku. Přehled vývoje české menšiny na Území dnešní republiky rakouské, zvláště ve Vídni,* Prague 1928.

Cross-references: Austria; Czechia and Slovakia

CZECH SETTLERS IN VOLHYNIA FROM THE 1860S TO THE 1940S

Jaroslav Vaculík

Czech migration to the Russian governorate of Volhynia began in the late 1860s and early 1870s and was the result of a migratory movement from the Czech (Bohemian) lands of the Habsburg monarchy to the region, which shared a border with Austrian Galicia as well as southern Ukraine and the Caucasus. The emigrants sought to improve their economic standing as the abolition of serfdom in czarist Russia in 1861 had made possible the acquisition of cheap land.

Recruitment on the part of the czarist government found great resonance in Bohemia, which is documented by peasant chronicles and letters from emigrants describing the favorable conditions of settlement in Volhynia. The czarist government recruited the Czechs to weaken the influence of the local, anti-Russian Polish nobility and to stimulate economic development in the governorate. Most of the migrants were young or middle-aged and traveled together with their families. The migrants comprised not only peasants and industrial workers, craftsmen, and merchants but also many rich farmers and members of the educated elite. After an often costly journey to their destination, the migrants bought land, livestock, and agricultural implements on site.

The emigrants came largely from the northern half of the Czech lands. According to contemporary accounts, "emigration fever" broke out in a number of Czech regions, while Habsburg authorities disapproved of the development. The embassy in St. Petersburg protested recruitment of the Czechs by the czarist authorities and invoked the Austro-Russian declaration of 5 June 1815 on the mutual extradition of deserters from military service. The Austrian authorities took action against the emigration by, among other acts, publishing unfavorable reports about settlement in Volhynia intercepted in the post. From 1868 onward Czech periodicals regularly printed accounts of the lives of Czech emigrants in Russia. While the liberal papers emphasized the advantages of emigration to slavic Russia over emigration to the USA, the conservative pro-Austrian press came out against emigration, publishing accounts of the difficult position of Czechs in Russia, the alleged perfidy of the Russian authorities, and the return migration of numerous individuals.

Despite the anti-emigration measures, some 15,000 Czechs left for Volhynia in the late 1860s and early 1870s. There was sufficient land for sale there and the journey was four times cheaper than traveling overseas. Linguistic affinities also played an important role in the decision of Czechs to emigrate. Various concessions provided to the immigrants by the imperial authorities also had a favorable effect. Some of the emigrants made the journey of several weeks by cart while others traveled by train to the last Austrian station of Brody in eastern Galicia, whence they continued by cart. The first Russian census in 1897 found 50,385 Czechs living in Russia, more than half of whom (27,670) lived in the Volhynia governorate.

With their knowledge of advanced agricultural methods the immigrants made a considerable contribution to the development of this area of Russia, which up to this point had been economically underdeveloped. The Czech immigrants also stimulated growth in industry and trade.

Most Czech migrants were engaged in agriculture and better educated than the local population: 59% were literate compared to only 9% among Ukrainians, who made up the largest indigenous population group. The Czechs formed a closed community. Even partners in mixed marriages, which were usually concluded between Ukrainian men and Czech women, typically oriented themselves toward Czech culture, which was also common among the few marriages of Czechs to German settlers.

At the beginning of the 20th century, the Czech press in Russia noted a reduction in cultural differences between the Volhynian Czechs and the local Ukrainian population: up to this point the economic and cultural influence exerted by the Czechs was manifested in farming methods, behavior, dress, and architecture. The clothing of the Volhynian Czechs, with a few exceptions, was also not influenced by their foreign environment. Their eating habits, however, were influenced by the adoption of a large number of Ukrainian dishes. The Czechs continued to observe the annual customs and feasts they had brought with them from the Czech lands.

Following the Revolution of 1905 and the granting of wide-ranging civil rights by the czar (the October Manifest), Czechs became politically engaged at the county, governorate, and state levels. Their political views, however, varied widely – some were supporters of constitutional democracy, others of social democracy; some were even supporters of great Russian policies while others took up the cause of Ukrainian national autonomy. Their involvement in various political currents increased following the fall of the czar in the Russian Revolution of 1917.

The outbreak of the First World War had a serious impact on the Czechs in Volhynia. Reservists were mobilized in addition to young men already performing basic military service. As many as 5,000 men from the ranks of the Volhynia Czechs alone fought in the Russian army. The war affected not only Czechs with Russian citizenship in Russia, but also thousands of Czechs with Austrian citizenship to whom the restrictive measures enforced against nationals of enemy states applied. The situation facing the local Czechs worsened considerably following the retreat of the Russian armies from Galicia to Volhynia in the spring of 1915, since their settlements were now on the front lines. Numerous Czech villages were evacuated several times by either Austrian or Russian forces and many were partially or fully destroyed.

During this war the Volhynia Czechs sided clearly from the very beginning with Russia against their old land, Austria. It was they who comprised the core of the Czech retinue, the nucleus of the Czechoslovak legions in Russia. From the very beginning of the war they favored the creation of an independent Czech state. The Bolshevik revolution in Russia led to a civil war, in which various political and military groupings (Ukrainian, White Russian, Bolshevik, and Polish) fought over Volhynia. The continual change of governing regimes led to a worsening of the general security situation, suffered most intensively by the civilian population. For this reason the occupation of western Volhynia by the Poles in the autumn of 1920 was welcomed by the local Czech population as a guarantee of stability and order.

Following the end of the Polish-Russian War with the Riga peace accord in March 1921 Volhynia was divided into a Polish and a Russian (Soviet) part. The majority of the Volhynia Czechs (around 80%) found themselves in the Polish part. In spite of the economic crisis at the turn of the 1920s and 1930s the interwar period in Polish Volhynia can be characterized as a period of new prosperity for the Czech minority, which was universally acknowledged by the Polish authorities and the population of all nationalities in Volhynia, in spite of the not altogether favorable development of Czechoslovak-Polish relations. The Czechs (25,000) were dispersed in 523 localities, in only 107 of which were there more than 50 Czechs. The majority were engaged in agriculture, although some were craftsmen, traders, owners of small companies in the food industry, or manufacturers of agricultural machinery. Of around 5,000 children of school age, 1,700 attended Czech schools while the remainder went to Polish schools.

The Czech School Foundation was responsible for private Czech education. In the prewar period, 25 Czech physical education units, 84 brass bands, 82 fire brigades, 47 amateur theater groups, and 27 libraries operated in Volhynia. The Polish census of 1921 showed the majority of the Volhynia Czechs belonging to the Orthodox Church. The mass conversion to Orthodoxy at the end of the 1880s was not inspired by the religious needs of the emigrants but was the result of political and economic pressure exerted by the Russian authorities of the day. Part of the Czech population also became engaged in Polish political life. In 1928 a Czech member of the governing Non-party Bloc from Volhynia was elected to the Polish assembly. The Czechs also published their own magazines – *Hlas Volyně* (1926–37), *Buditel* (1928–9), and *Krajanské listy* (1938–9), which brought together young poets and journalists.

The fate of the Czechs in eastern Volhynia (around 20% of the Volhynia Czechs), which became part of the Bolshevik Empire, was altogether different. After the initial generally liberal approach to national minorities and the new economic policy of the 1920s, the development of the USSR headed toward the forced mass collectivization of agriculture and political repression. This affected the Czech minority, particularly the intelligentsia and the peasantry. The All-Union census of 1926 showed more than 7,000 Czechs living in eastern Volhynia. Following the occupation of eastern Poland on 17 September 1939, totalitarianism, including deportation to Siberia, was also applied in western Volhynia.

Czech fire brigade in Polish Volhynia in the 1930s (*private ownership*).

The arrival of the Nazis in 1941 was initially seen as protection against further Soviet deportations. The situation in occupied Volhynia, however, came more and more to resemble a civil war, with Ukrainian nationalists, the Polish national resistance, and Soviet partisans all operating alongside one another. In this nationally and politically charged atmosphere the Czech minority, thanks to a number of members of the intelligentsia, united under the leadership of the illegal organization Blaník, which declared its support for the Czechoslovak foreign resistance. In 1944 this led to more than 10,000 of the Volhynia Czechs joining the 1st Czechoslovak Army Corps in the USSR.

The postwar fate of Volhynia lay in the hands of the Bolsheviks, who intended to complete what they had begun in 1939–41, most notably the forced socialization of agriculture (which was opposed by the Volhynia Czechs) and continued forced deportations. Efforts had already begun during the war to obtain the agreement of the Czechoslovak government to organized remigration to Czechoslovakia. This fitted in with the plans of the postwar Czechoslovak government, which called upon Czechs and Slovaks living abroad to return to their homeland. The Volhynia Czech soldiers were demobilized in the autumn of 1945 and the majority of them settled in Czechoslovakia. Negotiations on the organized return of the remaining Volhynia Czechs dragged on for a whole year until July 1946, in spite of the fact that the Soviets had given a binding promise in December 1945 to positive settlement of the Czechoslovak request for remigration. Even following the closure of a Czechoslovak-Soviet agreement, preparatory work by the joint Czechoslovak-Soviet committee continued until the beginning of 1947, when the first transport with returnees was allowed to leave. By May 1947 more than 33,000 people had been relocated from Volhynia to Czechoslovakia, which, along with the demobilized soldiers, amounted to around 40,000 persons.

The returnees differed from the rest of the Czechoslovak population in that they had had firsthand experiences of Soviet communism, and they did nothing to hide this fact in Czechoslovakia. The experiences of the Volhynia Czechs were, however, soon corroborated following the communist revolution in Czechoslovakia in February 1948, when the complete nationalization of the economy, the forced collectivization of agriculture, and the introduction of a one-party system and political trials were soon on the agenda. This affected the Volhynia Czechs more than other groups of the population, since they were all medium-sized private entrepreneurs in agriculture or crafts, whose property was confiscated. Many became victims of a number of large trials and many smaller trials, which ended in extraordinarily severe prison sentences in the 1950s.

Vaculík, Jaroslav. *Dějiny volyňských Čechů*. 3 vols. Prague, 1997–2001.

Cross-references: Czechia and Slovakia; Poland; Russia and Belarus; Ukraine

CZECH AND SLOVAK SETTLERS IN THE FORMER SUDETEN REGIONS SINCE THE END OF WORLD WAR II

Andreas Wiedemann

After the expulsion of the Germans from Czechoslovakia in the immediate postwar period, the former Sudeten regions were resettled from the summer of 1945 with Czech settlers from the interior of the Bohemian lands (more than 82% of the new settlers), with settlers from the Slovak part of the state (just under 9% of the new settlers), and with Czech and Slovak remigrants from abroad. The last made up about 7% of the new settlers and came from Hungary, the Soviet Union, France, Austria, Poland, Romania, Germany, Belgium, Bulgaria, and Yugoslavia. In addition, Magyars from southern Slovakia were compelled to settle as laborers in the border regions. The migration from the interior districts of the Bohemian lands to the former Sudeten regions was initially spontaneous in the summer of 1945, and then organized from the fall of 1945.

The special characteristic of the migration into the former Sudeten regions was that the new settlers as a whole did not form a minority there but the majority of the population. The resettlement of the Germans, largely carried out in 1946, opened up enormous tracts of land and both movable and fixed property. The chance to take possession of this property, and the opportunities for social advancement it offered, was a great incentive to the new interior settlers, most of whom came from the lower social strata. The chief interest was focused on settlement in areas with an intensive agricultural and a developed industrial production. The internal migration into the border regions was motivated chiefly by the poor economic and financial situation in the origin regions, the quest for a better job, the prospects of an apartment or house of one's own, the chance to own land with movable and fixed inventory, or the opportunity to run a commercial business and the potential to acquire it later on.

The agricultural settlers were recruited from rural workers, cottager families, and the landless. The majority of the Czech internal settlers, however, did not come from agriculture and was made up of operators of small-scale commercial enterprises, craftsmen, merchants, small entrepreneurs, and industrial workers. The Czech and Slovak remigrants from the eastern and east-central European countries saw in resettlement to Czechoslovakia, a country largely spared by the war, better prospects for the future than they did in their countries of origin, some of which had been severely ravaged by the war.

According to the census of 22 May 1947, the total number of new settlers in the border regions, including the children born there, stood at around 1.5 million. All told, 2,229,485 people were living at this time in the border regions of the Bohemian lands, 115,783 of whom (5.5%) had had their place of residence in Slovakia prior to 1 May 1945. About 180,000 Germans were still in the former Sudeten regions. Following the end of the mass settlement at the beginning of the 1950s, around 88% of the population in the former Sudeten regions were of Czech nationality, about 6% were of Slovak nationality, and only a bare 5% of German nationality. Since the number of those settled in the border regions was smaller than the number of Germans who were removed, the population in 1952 was only two-thirds of what it had been in 1930. At the same time, the population density dropped from 127 to 84 per square kilometer.

In 1950, about 155,000 Slovaks (including Slovak immigrants) were living in the border regions, most of whom had settled in northern and western Bohemia. However, this number also included the so-called re-Slovacized Magyars, a few thousand Roma, as well as Ukrainians from eastern Slovakia, who settled mostly in western Bohemia. The Roma were primarily from eastern Slovakia, settled in the cities of northwestern and western Bohemia (with half of the Roma from Slovakia settling in the cities of the interior), and worked mostly in industry, less so in agriculture. Most of the Slovak settlers were active in agriculture, construction, and the textile and metalworking industry.

According to information from the Ministry for Labor and Social Welfare, 202,526 remigrants had arrived by the end of 1949: 71,787 from Hungary, 38,859 from Volhynia, 21,001 from Romania, 12,915 from France, 11,117 from Austria, 10,341 from Poland, 5,197 from Yugoslavia, 4,059 from Germany, and the rest from other countries. About 120,000 returning migrants settled in the border regions, about half of whom worked in agriculture and forestry, and a third as wage laborers in industry, trade, and commerce. Most returning migrants were skilled and unskilled workers. By contrast, the Czechs from Volhynia, who constituted the largest returning group in the border regions with 40,000 settlers, came, to a large extent, from relatively high social positions as the owners of medium-sized farms. Many of them continued to run their own farms also after immigrating to the Bohemian lands.

An important general characteristic of the influx of new settlers was the low age and the high marriage and birthrates. In the spring of 1947, 35% of the population in the border areas were between 15 and 34 years of age. Although return migration exceeded immigration numerically after the end of the main wave of settlement (1947), the population in the border areas continued to grow. The natural rate of population growth in the border regions was 3.5%, higher than that in the interior (1950–2: 3.1%). That trend continued also in the following decades.

The pace and intensity of the formation of new social structures and the integration of the various settlement groups differed from region to region, and depended on a host of factors, for example, the number of new settlers, their rate of fluctuation, their origins, and the working and living conditions. The returning migrants sought to settle in groups wherever possible, something the authorities initially also promoted to make settlement easier for them. At first they retained the customs and traditions from their regions of origin, with substantial differences also found in this regard, depending on the size of the group, whether their settlement was concentrated, and how strong an imprint they had received from their country of origin. Communities with return migrants from various origin regions saw the emergence of heterogeneous cultural structures that differed from the local culture of the long-established population (dress, festivals, hair styles, diets). Some groups of new settlers worked harder than others at preserving their cultural identity.

None of the settlement groups living in the border areas after the Second World War had the status of a national minority. The Czech state reckoned with the gradual integration of the various population groups. Special lobbies for the new settlers did not exist. What did exist, however, especially on the regional level, were organizations of individual returning migrant groups, as for example the League of Czechs from Volhynia ("purged" after 1948 and dissolved in 1957), the Association of Foreign Czechs (returning migrants from Germany), the League of Exiles and Returnees from Poland, and the Association of Viennese Czechs. These organizations helped the respective remigrants with specific problems and, on the cultural level, connected with the customs of their clientele from the origin countries. In addition, the organizations served to maintain contact among settlers who sometimes lived dispersed. The Czechs of Volhynia founded the weekly paper *Věrná Stráž* (Faithful Watch). The League of Czechs from Volhynia also served the communist government, especially after the seizure of power in February 1948, also as an instrument to better control the Volhynia Czechs, who were considered unreliable by the government and hostile to communism. In the 1950s, many became victims of smaller and larger political trials.

In the first few postwar years, a few special characteristics of the remigrants, but also of the immigrants from Slovakia, formed barriers to contact among the groups. There were differences not only in way of life (dress, food), religious confession, language customs, and material situations but also in social status, literacy levels, and the degree of identification with the countries of origin. The remigrants did not always receive a friendly reception from the Czech majority society. The reasons for this were, on the one hand, the majority society's poor knowledge of the history of the Czechs and Slovaks and the causes and circumstances of their return, and on the other hand, the privileges granted to some remigrants (e.g., to the members of the Czech foreign army) and the competition with the internal settlers over acquisition of property in the border regions.

While the remigrants in the official language were described as Czechs or Slovaks, the majority society labeled them Romanians, Bulgarians, Magyars, and so on. The remigrants from Germany and Silesia had a particularly difficult time, since many of these settlers had only a poor command of the Czech language. The Slovak remigrants from Hungary, who frequently spoke Hungarian to each other in daily life, had a similar experience. As a result, various settlement groups at the margins of society entered into alliances for a variety of reasons: for example, in the glassblowing works in Karlovy Vary (Karlsbad) in western Bohemia, Germans who had not been removed and Slovaks from the Romanian Erzgebirge united in a common cause. In Cheb (Eger), also in western Bohemia, Czech remigrants from Romania received support from the local Germans, to which their shared Protestant confession likely contributed. When the Romanian Slovaks entered in the first exogamous marriages in the 1950s, their partners were more often Germans than Czechs.

After the Roma had settled in the border areas, the bureaucracy placed obstacles in their way when they were looking for jobs and housing. Their access to some border regions was blocked, and already settled Roma were expelled from others. There were also thoughts about separating the Roma from the rest of the population or strictly regulating their employment.

The work accomplishments of remigrants found special mention in reports about the fulfillment of the Two-Year Plan (1947–9) and the Five-Year Plan (1949–53). In the 1950s, the intensification of industrial production and the collectivization of agriculture had a considerable influence on the social structures in the border regions. Many settlers left the villages to look for work in the industrial sector in the cities. The stance of the remigrants toward collectivization varied. Especially the remigrant groups who belonged to the lower strata and had no traditional ties to the allocated land were hoping that the agricultural cooperatives would make their work easier and secure their circumstances. The Volhynia Czechs, on the other hand, rejected collectivization, since there were many farmers among them who had medium-sized farms and feared for their continued independence.

The linguistic and social process of integration was largely complete at the beginning of the 21st century. On the cultural level, however, it was still possible to make group-specific characteristics, whose intensity and manifestations were very different locally but no longer possessed divisive effect. Group identities remained intact among some remigrants, such as the Volhynia Czechs and the Viennese Czechs. After more than half a century of settlement, they were still holding commemorations, publishing their own journals, and cultivating their own historical culture.

Among the settler groups at the beginning of the 21st century, the Roma are considered the least integrated, though here, too, there are considerable local differences. The young generation is fully bilingual (Czech and Romani). With respect to culture and way of life, their employment structure and endogenous marriage circles, but also because of external descriptions from the majority society, the Roma remained a discernible minority in the border regions.

Heroldová, Iva. "Ethnische Prozesse in den böhmischen Grenzgebieten nach dem Zweiten Weltkrieg." In *Im geteilten Europa. Tschechen, Slowaken und Deutsche in ihren Staaten 1948–1989*, edited by Hans Lemberg, Jan Křen, and Dušan Kovač, 95–109. Essen, 1998.

Kastner, Quido. *Osidlování českého pohraničí od května 1945 (na příkladu vybraných obcí Litoměřicka*. Ústí nad Labem, 1999.

Nosková, Helena. *Návrat Čechů z Volyně. Naděje a skutečnost let 1945–1954*. Prague, 1999.

Radvanovský, Zdeněk. "Integrationsprobleme bei der Wiederbesiedlung der deutschen Siedlungsgebiete in den böhmischen Ländern nach 1945." In *Heimat und Exil. Emigration und Rückwanderung, Vertreibung und Integration in der Geschichte der Tschechoslowakei*, edited by Peter Heumos, 143–61. Munich, 2001.

Vaculík, Jaroslav. *Reemigrace zahraničních Čechů a Slováků v letech 1945–1950*. Brünn, 1993.

Wiedemann, Andreas. "Komm mit uns, das Grenzland aufbauen." *Ansiedlung und neue Strukturen in den ehemaligen Sudetengebieten 1945–1952*, Essen, 2007.

Cross-references: Czechia and Slovakia; German Refugees and Expellees from Eastern, East-Central, and Southeastern Europe in Germany and Austria since the End of World War II; Magyar Deportees from Slovakia in Western Czechoslovakia since the End of World War II

CZECHOSLOVAKIAN REFUGEES IN WESTERN, CENTRAL, AND NORTHERN EUROPE SINCE 1968

Dušan Šimko

The invasion of Czechoslovakia (CSSR) by the five "Brother Armies" of the Warsaw Pact on 21 August 1968 put a violent and final end to the "Prague Spring." The 450,000 soldiers of the invasion force brought the Czech utopia of a "Socialism with a human face" to a jarring halt. This dramatic event came as a shock to large segments of the Czech and Slovak population. After a few months of a relative social and political

End of the "Prague Spring": Czech refugees at the Austrian border, 1968 (*ullstein bild*).

opening, the citizens of the CSSR lost, at a single blow, all hope for a reform of the system. In the two decades that followed, thousands of Czechs and Slovaks tried to leave the country every year. For two decades, Czechoslovakia turned into a "spiritual/intellectual graveyard" (Heinrich Böll).

In 1974, the Czech exile writer Pavel Tigrid distinguished three main groups of Czechoslovakian refugees after 1968:

1. Individuals suffering political and social discrimination, such as former political prisoners of the Stalin period, former members of the penal units of the Czechoslovakian army, and former owners of shops or factories.
2. Well-qualified experts who no longer wished to pursue their careers under the dictates of the cadre politics of the Communist Party.
3. Active participants in the political and cultural renewal: reform functionaries of the Czech Communist Party, journalists, writers, and artists.

In the first years following the invasion, about 104,000 individuals left the CSSR. In the years 1969 to 1989, another 141,000 emigrated; the figures given by various authors vary. The official statistics are not reliable, since the issue was dealt with under the auspices of the Czechoslovak Ministry of the Interior. Three-quarters of the refugees were Czechs, one-quarter Slovaks.

Many of the refugees had left the country by the spring of 1969, when Gustáv Husák assumed the political leadership of the CSSR and initiated an era of "normalization" (1969–87), which was characterized by totalitarian control over all social, political, and cultural matters. By the spring of 1969, about 2,300 refugees had gone to Sweden, and about 1,750 to France. Because of traditionally close ties (German was still the first foreign language in Czech schools), good reachability, safety, and high living standard, the German-speaking countries – Austria (1968: 3,600 asylum applications),

Switzerland (1968: 4,200 asylum applications), and West Germany (1968: 4,000 asylum applications) – were among the most popular destination countries.

Vienna served as a gateway city into the West. Between 1968 and 1970, 162,000 Czechoslovaks made their way to Austria, the vast majority of whom (129,000) returned to the CSSR after a short stay. Next to the state-organized refugee aid, the 23 Czech or Czechoslovakian associations in Austria made a major contribution to securing the initial livelihood of the new immigrants. The better part of the refugees who remained behind in Austria later went to other countries or overseas (12,000), especially to Canada and the USA. Smaller contingents preferred Australia and New Zealand, two countries with tougher immigration laws. Given the unresolved legal situation in their homeland, the majority of refugees waited a few months before submitting an asylum application. Only after the border was hermetically sealed off did they decide to stay put. Only about 1% of the refugees took advantage of the amnesty decree issued by the Czechoslovakian President Ludvík Svoboda on 27 May 1969 to return to the CSSR.

More than 90% of the refugees had either a high school diploma or university degree. Many renowned scientists and professors left their universities at that time. University and secondary school students formed a large group. The refugees of the years 1968–9 as well as those of the "normalization period" thus belonged overwhelmingly to Czechoslovakia's educated elite. Thanks to the booming economy in western, central, and northern Europe, the refugees were often enthusiastically welcomed not only for political but also for economic reasons: politically as a kind of migratory vote against communism in Europe, economically on account of the labor shortage against a backdrop of continuing economic growth.

A special group were exiled writers and artists. Many well-known Czech writers and poets found asylum and new publication possibilities in the West: for example, Jiří Grusa, Rudolf Ströbinger, Karel Trinkewitz, and Ota Filip in Germany; Karel Michal in Basel; Jaroslav Strnad in Obstalden in the eastern Swiss canton of Glarus; Jaroslav Vejvoda in Zurich; Milan Kundera, Antonin J. Liehm, Jiří Kolář, Jan Vladislav, and Petr Král in Paris; and Pavel Kohout in Vienna. A central cultural-political role in the circumstances of the Czechoslovaks, who were regarded as exiles, was played by the newspaper Svědectví, published in Paris by Pavel Tigrid. At the same time, the Czechoslovak editorial teams of the radio stations Radio Free Europe, Deutschlandfunk, Deutsche Welle, and the British Broadcasting Corporation (BBC) received reinforcement in terms of personnel. An important political role in the destination countries was played by the Czechoslovak charitable foundations (e.g., the Swiss Masaryk Fund) and the editorial offices of exile journals. The latter pursued the dual strategy of informing the Western media and public and maintaining an uncensored flow of information into the CSSR. Through these organizations, contact between the dissidents at home and in exile was constantly maintained.

After 1970, the refugee groups in the European destination countries experienced a profound process of political and cultural differentiation: some Slovaks in the Czechoslovakian exile organizations now set up their own associations, the majority of which followed the national-separatist line of the "World Congress of Slovaks" (Svetový kongres Slovákov, SKS), whose umbrella organization had its seat in Toronto. The smaller part of the Slovaks, meanwhile, remained within the already existing or newly founded Czechoslovak organizations that argued in favor of the national integrity of Czechoslovakia. Because of the political and cultural differences, the dialogue between the two camps, which was pursued above all by the Czech or Czechoslovakian organizations, could not be continued in the 1980s.

A total of 27,622 Czechs and Slovaks sought asylum in West Germany between 1968 and 1990; of those, 22,654 were granted asylum. In the first two years after the crushing of the Prague Spring, on average 114 Czech citizens were given asylum in Germany every week. Doctors were fairly strongly represented among the refugees. The Czechoslovak immigrant group in West Germany had a very low percentage of workers (1.8%), but a high percentage of university graduates (30%). At the end of the 1980s, the average income of the Czechoslovaks in West Germany was nearly a quarter higher than the national average. It was primarily the large urban centers that attracted the immigrants because of the job opportunities they offered. Munich, Cologne, Bochum, and Frankfurt am Main developed into settlement centers of the Czechoslovak refugees. The conurbation of Munich is said to have been home to nearly 10,000 individuals of Czech or Slovak background at the beginning of the 21st century. The refugees of 1968 contributed significantly to the revitalization of old-established organizations – for example, the section of the Czechoslovak Society of Arts and Sciences, the Catholic organization Velehrad, and the sports club Sokol. The publishing house Index was founded in Frankfurt am Main. In Munich, the publisher Poezie mimo domov (PmD) published anthologies of the poetry of Czech and Slovak authors, and the Munich journal Obrys (1981–90) attained a high cultural-journalistic level. The Social-Democratic exile paper Právo lidu was published quarterly in Wuppertal (1978–90). All these journals and publishing houses shut down after the events of 1989.

In the first years following the occupation of the CSSR, Switzerland became the destination for about 8,000 Czech and 3,500 Slovak refugees. As early as February 1969, about 8,000 refugees were in the Swiss Confederation, and 4,200 individuals asked for asylum. Having pursued a restrictive refugee policy during the Second World War, Switzerland now sought to become demonstratively mindful of its humanitarian tradition. Already in 1956, following the crushing of the uprising in Hungary, the country had taken in 10,000 Hungarian refugees. Both the state bureaucracy and wide segments of the Swiss population extended a generous welcome to the Czechoslovak refugees. By 1989, about 14,500 citizens of Czechoslovakia had been granted asylum in Switzerland.

The first waves of refugees from the CSSR arrived by way of the assembly camps of the Red Cross in Buchs and St. Margarethen in the St. Gall Rheintal. The cantonal social welfare offices, the headquarters of aid for refugees, and the welfare sections of the federal Department of Justice and Police provided targeted financial help. In the years 1968–70, nearly all refugees were granted asylum in Switzerland. By the end of 1969, nearly 300 of the recognized asylum seekers had returned to the CSSR. In spite of the booming economy at the end of the 1960s and the beginning of the 1970s, it was fairly difficult to place the many lawyers, philologists, sociologists, and artists in the labor market. The many Czech and Slovak medical specialists among the refugees also posed a problem at that time, since Switzerland had a greater need for general physicians. The large number of doctors from the CSSR was the backdrop to the founding of the Czecho-Slovak-Swiss Medical Society in Zurich in the 1970s, which since 1990 has devoted itself primarily to working with doctors in the old homeland. In the first three years after 1968, cantonal offices as well as the private sector organized various language, retraining, and continuing education courses. For secondary school pupils and for students who had not yet studied three semesters in Czechoslovakia, courses leading to the acquisition of the matriculation diploma were set up at the University of Fribourg. Those admitted to study there received a monthly stipend of 500 francs.

The wave of refugees in 1968 gave rise in Switzerland to numerous new associations, joining a few that had already existed since the end of the 19th century, such as the Amitiés Helveto-Tchécoslovaques in Lausanne, and Masaryk in Solothurn; among them also were organizations that were active throughout Switzerland, such as the sports club Sokolská župa švýcarská and the already mentioned Czechoslovak Society of Arts and Sciences. After 1968, numerous periodicals were published in Czech and Slovak (*Zpravodaj, Bulletin, Slovenské zvesti, Horizont*), and a few publishing houses were set up (Poľana, Liber, Konfrontace).

Nearly half of the refugees from the CSSR had left their homeland together with their family members. At the time of flight, the majority were in the most productive age range of 18–40. This fact, combined with the high educational level (45% academics, 44% high school graduates), formed the basis for a successful integration into the Swiss labor market and society. Within half a year, 60% of all refugees found a job in line with their professional qualifications. Nearly 60% were able to communicate in German. Only a small part of the Czechoslovaks spoke French. To help explain the rapid integration into German Switzerland, by 1980, 73% of the former refugees understood Swiss German (*Schwyzerdütsch*) or even spoke it. The largest centers of Czechoslovak emigration were the urban agglomerations of Basel, Zurich, Lausanne, and Geneva. At no time did the refugees from the CSSR form ethnically defined quarters in the Swiss cities. Between 1980 and 1989, 10,355 Czechs and Slovaks were given Swiss citizenship. They formed a group of refugees which, from the perspective of both Swiss officials and the public, could be integrated without any problem. It would appear that the integration of the Czechs and Slovaks in all northern, western, and central destination countries seems to have in fact been completed with the second generation.

After the breakup of Czechoslovakia into the Czech and Slovak republics in 1992, many of the refuges were able to regain their respective citizenship. That circumstance, however, did not bring about a wave of remigration – the "homeland" passport was more of a symbolic bridge to the old home and at the same time it provided political and moral satisfaction.

At the turn to the 21st century, the many Czech, Czechoslovakian, and Slovak exile organizations were faced with an aging and declining membership. They tried to attract the second or third generation as new members. There is reason to believe that in spite of the completed integration in the second and third generation, the organizations will continue to play a cultural role.

Brouček, Stanislav, ed. *Czechs abroad/Češi v cizině*. Prague, 1996.
Formanová, Lucie, Jiří Gruntorád, and Michal Přibáň, eds. *Exilová periodika*. Prague, 1999.
Šimko, Dušan. *Exil in Basel*. Košice, 2003.
Špetko, Jozef. *Slovenská emigrácia v 20. storočí*. Bratislava, 1994.
Trapl, Miloš. "Tschechische politische Emigranten in den Jahren 1938, 1939, 1948 und 1968." In *Exile im 20. Jahrhundert*, edited by Claus-Dieter Krohn, 77–87. Munich, 2000.

Cross-references: Austria; Czechia and Slovakia; France; Germany; Northern Europe; Switzerland; Hungarian Refugees in Europe since 1956

DEPORTEES IN THE SOVIET UNION DURING AND AFTER WORLD WAR II

J. Otto Pohl

During the Second World War, the Stalin regime in several closely related actions forcibly deported a number of ethno-national minorities from their homelands to the interior of Soviet Asia. Decrees issued by the highest organs of the Soviet government ordered the deportation of the Russian-Germans in 1941; Karachais and Kalmyks in 1943; and Chechens, Ingush, Balkars, Crimean Tatars, and Meskhetian Turks in 1944 from their traditional areas of settlement to Kazakhstan, Central Asia, Siberia, and the Urals. In total, these deportations affected nearly 2 million people: some 850,000 Russian-Germans, 400,000 Chechens, 180,000 Crimean Tatars, 70,000 Karachais, 40,000 Balkars, and well over 90,000 Kalmyks, 90,000 Ingush, and 90,000 Meskhetian Turks. The Soviet regime in the final phase of the war and the immediate post-war period sent an additional 200,000 Russian-Germans from the formerly German-occupied territories in the Ukraine and Poland and from the Soviet-occupied parts of Germany to the eastern regions of the Soviet Union.

These decrees applied to the entirety of these ethnic groups and made no exceptions for individual political loyalty toward the Stalin regime. Communist Party members, Komsomolists (Communist Youth League), Red Army veterans, and even members of the NKVD (Peoples Commissariat of Internal Affairs, the Soviet security police) were almost without exception exiled to the interior of the USSR. Only women married to Russian men, a small minority of the targeted nationalities, received some exemptions from deportation.

The nationalities targeted by the Stalin regime for total exile from their traditional areas of settlement fell into two categories. The first category consisted of those nationalities with ethnic ties to foreign states. This included the numerous German communities throughout the European USSR and the Meskhetian Turks in Georgia. The Soviet government viewed these nationalities as a potential fifth column in any conflict between the Soviet Union and the states of their ancestral homelands. The Soviet government justified their forcible resettlement as a preventive security measure. Their deportation to confined areas deep in the interior of the USSR greatly reduced the possibility of foreign powers using them in intelligence, sabotage, and other military operations. This paranoid xenophobia, however, had deeper roots than worries about a fifth column. Its ultimate source was the inability of the Soviet government to completely Sovietize nationalities that still had cultural connections, however tenuous, to foreign countries.

The second category of deported nationalities consisted of those exiled on charges of collaboration with the Nazi occupation forces. This group included the Karachais, Kalmyks, Chechens, Ingush, Balkars, and Crimean Tatars. These native nationalities all shared a history of resistance to Russian and Soviet rule. This overt resistance to Sovietization marked them as "enemy nations" that could not be integrated into the USSR on an equal basis with other nationalities. Instead, the Stalin regime decided to dissolve them forcibly as distinct ethnic entities through a policy of dispersal and deculturation. The Second World War offered the opportunity to neutralize all sources of potential opposition from these nationalities. Despite the different official rationales for the deportation of these two categories, the Stalin regime subjected them both to forced exile and restrictions.

Deportation

The NKVD surrounded the villages of the condemned nationalities and informed them that they were to be resettled to distant regions of the USSR. Often roused from their homes in the middle of the night, many families had only a few minutes to pack necessities. They had to abandon most of their possessions. More important, they lost their ancestral homelands with their unique landscapes, monuments, historical buildings, houses of worship, and cemeteries. Women and children formed the majority of these deportees as most able-bodied men were at the front fighting in the Red Army. Subsequently, the Stalin regime discharged these soldiers and sent them into exile to those

regions their families had been deported. The deportation of these nationalities in their entirety was carried out with great speed.

The condemned nationalities made the long journey to Siberia, Kazakhstan, the Urals, and Central Asia in cattle cars. The NKVD packed an average of 40 to 50 deportees into each car. This number increased with each new deportation operation. The squalor and unhygienic conditions inside the unwashed cars likewise increased with each wave of human cargo. Only a hole in the bottom of each train car or a simple pail served as a latrine. The compact and unhygienic conditions of the sealed cattle cars led to the spread of contagious diseases such as typhus and tuberculosis. Every so often the trains would stop to remove the dead and seriously ill. During these stops, the NKVD shot those who strayed more than five meters from the rail lines. Despite instructions to provide food to the deportees, official Soviet records show that those conducting the deportations frequently ignored them. Often the food the deportees brought with them did not last the entire journey. The trip into exile generally lasted several weeks. During this time, tens of thousands died of dehydration, disease, and other causes. The surviving deportees arrived in the areas of exile weakened by hunger and with few possessions.

The "special settlement" regime

The Stalin regime placed the deported nationalities under the restrictions of the "special settlement" regime. The Soviet government confined the exiles to already existing villages and settlements. They even placed many of the deportees in houses already inhabited by Kazakhs and Russians under extremely cramped conditions. The deportations substantially changed the ethnic makeup of many villages and towns in Kazakhstan, Siberia and Central Asia. *Auls* (Kazakh encampments) formerly inhabited exclusively by Kazakhs became multiethnic villages with the arrival of resettled Russian-Germans, Karachais, Chechens, Ingush, Balkars, and Meskhetian Turks. Settlements in Siberia formerly inhabited exclusively by Russians likewise absorbed Russian-German and Kalmyk special settlers. Uzbekistan's industrial towns became even more multiethnic as Crimean Tatars joined Russians, Uzbeks, Koreans, and others.

Unlike the original inhabitants of these settlements, members of the deported nationalities could not leave their assigned settlements without permission from the special commandants of the NKVD. The Stalin regime denied them freedom of movement and free choice of employment. They had to register regularly with the office of the special commandant and fulfill their assigned work quotas. Failure to obey NKVD orders or attempts to leave their confined settlements carried severe penalties. The deportees lacked most of the rights accorded to other Soviet citizens and were subordinated to the authority of the NKVD special commandants.

Soviet nationality policy toward the deported groups resembled the creation of a racial caste system. The Stalin regime marked all members of the condemned nationalities as being inherent security risks by virtue of their ancestry. They had inherited the essential quality of being "anti-Soviet" upon birth. Indeed, children born in the special settlements automatically acquired the status of special settlers and had to be registered as such. The Stalin regime sought to confine the deportees to their special settlements permanently and prevent them from returning to their homelands. On 26 November 1948, this policy received legal codification from the Presidium of the Supreme Soviet when it made the exile of all national deportees and their descendants permanent. This permanent discrimination against groups defined by nationality has close parallels with other forms of racial discrimination elsewhere.

Living conditions in the areas of special settlement proved to be substandard. The local authorities did not have sufficient housing, food, or other resources to adequately accommodate the new arrivals and housed them in barracks, huts, club buildings, and structures in need of serious repair. Overcrowded and unsanitary housing conditions led to repeated outbreaks of typhus. Medical care to deal with such diseases remained inadequate. Food shortages remained critical among the deportees until 1949. These material deprivations led to an extremely high rate of mortality among the exiles. In total, the deported nationalities suffered over half a million deaths during the 1940s as a result of these miserable living conditions. Deaths significantly outnumbered births among the deportees until 1948–9. Even at the height of the Second World War, the total Soviet mortality rate did not exceed 2.4% per year, while some of the deported nationalities lost over 10% of their population in the first year of exile. This huge loss of life affected nearly every family among the deported nationalities.

In addition to these physical hardships, the deported nationalities also found their traditional cultures under assault. The Stalin regime sought to eradicate the previous cultural connections of the deportees and to absorb them into a greater Russian-speaking "Soviet people." The regime viewed cultural particularities as extremely deep-rooted. This view provided the background for the Soviet repression of the deported nationalities. In the absence of widespread intermarriage, total assimilation and the effacement of every trace of one's cultural heritage would require many generations. In the meantime the deportees remained suspect on the basis of their biological descent. For this reason, measures aimed at the destruction of their traditional culture were always accompanied by stigmatization as members of a group whose anti-Soviet orientation was supposedly inherent.

Pressure on the deportees to assimilate increased as a result of the widespread dispersal of the deportees among alien populations. The deportations meant the liquidation of all the cultural institutions of the deported nationalities and of all native language education. The Soviet regime decreed that their children had to attend Russian-language primary schools as Russian language education was regarded as one of the most important tools of "Sovietization." Initially, however, a very large number of deportees did not receive any education at all. In Kazakhstan and Central Asia, few Russian language schools existed in the areas of special settlement. Many of the deported children lacked proper clothing and shoes that would have allowed them to attend school during the first years of exile. Some families, Chechen ones in particular, refused to send their children, especially girls, to Russian schools. The education of the children in Russian thus proceeded slowly. As late as 1950, over a fifth of school-age children of the deportees in Kazakhstan still did not attend school. Only after 1950 did the Soviet efforts to provide universal Russian-language primary education to the children of the deportees make serious headway.

Release and partial rehabilitation

After Stalin's death, the new Soviet regime began to dismantle the special settlement regime. On 13 December 1955, the Presidium of the Supreme Soviet issued a decree freeing the Russian-Germans from the confines of their special settlement areas. This decree was followed by similar ones freeing the Kalmyks on 17 March 1956, the Crimean Tatars, Balkars, and Meskhetian Turks on 28 April 1956, and the Chechens, Ingush, and Karachais on 16 July 1956. These decrees freed the deportees from the restrictions of the special settlements and the surveillance of the MVD (Ministry of Internal Affairs, the successor of the NKVD), but they also expressly prohibited the newly freed deportees from returning to their former places of residence. They also barred the exiles from receiving compensation for property confiscated during the deportations.

The process of partially rehabilitating some of the nationalities deported by Stalin peaked during the late 1950s. At the XX Congress of the Communist Party of the Soviet Union on 25 February 1956, Nikita Khrushchev personally condemned the Stalinist deportation of the Karachais, Kalmyks, Chechens, Ingush, and Balkars. Deliberately excluded from his list of wrongfully deported nationalities were the Russian-Germans, Crimean Tatars, and Meskhetian Turks.

The members of these three groups had all proven to be a valuable and irreplaceable permanent workforce in Kazakhstan and Central Asia. The Soviet government's partial rehabilitation decrees of 1964 for the Russian-Germans, of 1967 for the Crimean Tatars, and of 1968 for the Meskhetian Turks all noted their important contributions to the economic development of the region. Unlike the largely peaceful Russian-Germans, Crimean Tatars, and Meskhetian Turks, the Chechens and other north Caucasians had been a source of constant unrest and the Soviet authorities experienced great difficulties integrating them into the local economies of Kazakhstan and Central Asia. By the late 1950s, this task appeared still to be more problematic than simply allowing them to return home.

The Soviet regime "rewarded" the hard work and loyalty of the Russian-Germans, Crimean Tatars, and Meskhetian Turks by continuing to prohibit these groups from returning to their areas of origin and denying them collective national rights. Decades of peaceful protests did nothing to redress this situation. Petitions, letters, and delegations could more easily be ignored than violent resistance.

In contrast, the nationalities named by Khrushchev in his speech received the right to return to their restored autonomous units. This right was expressed in a resolution passed by the highest organs of the ruling Communist Party on 24 November 1956, entitled "On restoring national autonomy to the Kalmyk, Karachai, Balkar, Chechen and Ingush peoples." During the next few years the vast majority of these exiles returned to their homelands.

The unrehabilitated nationalities

Despite their common plight, the Russian-Germans, the Crimean Tatars, and the Meskhetian Turks reacted very differently to their prolonged exile in Soviet Asia.

The Russian-Germans experienced a high degree of acculturation into the dominant Soviet Russian society of the USSR. The majority of Russian-Germans had Russian or Russified Ukrainian spouses and spoke fluent Russian and little or no German. During the mid-1960s, a small political movement sought to halt this acculturation. By 1968 this autonomy movement had largely collapsed because of its failure to achieve any results and its inability to mobilize popular support among the Russian-German population, and because of government persecution. In the 1970s, a more activist movement among the Russian-Germans aimed at securing the right to emigrate from the USSR to West Germany. The West German government exerted pressure on the USSR to allow the Russian-Germans to move to West Germany and presented that country as a welcoming homeland for the Russian-Germans. Ethnic Germans from communist countries, or *Aussiedler*, who came to West Germany received full citizenship and integration assistance automatically. This integration aid included assistance in finding housing and jobs, housing loans, language training, and vocational classes. After 1987, the Soviet government agreed to allow unrestricted emigration. The guarantee of German citizenship along with economic hardship and political instability in the former Soviet states made immigration to Germany an attractive option for the Russian-Germans. Over three-quarters of the ethnic German population of the former Soviet Union immigrated to Germany during the following decade.

In contrast, the Crimean Tatars retained a strong sense of national identity, reinforced by high rates of endogamy in exile. Crimean Tatar nationalism gathered strength in exile despite the loss of native language competency and other elements of their traditional culture. The strong emotional connection between the Crimean Tatar people and the land of the Crimean peninsula nourished a popular movement

for repatriation to their ancestral homeland and the restoration of the Crimean Autonomous Soviet Socialist Republic (CASSR). This movement had a strong grassroots base and could mobilize tens of thousands of people. In 1966, 130,000 people – virtually the entire adult Crimean Tatar population – signed a petition with demands addressed to the Soviet leadership. Throughout the 1960s, 1970s, and 1980s, the Crimean Tatars engaged in peaceful mass activities aimed at achieving their goals. The decades-long struggle by the Crimean Tatars to return to their homeland finally achieved partial success in the early 1990s: between 1989 and 1994, 260,000 people or more than half of the Crimean Tatar population of the former USSR returned to Crimea from Uzbekistan. After 1991, economic factors both in Uzbekistan and Crimea greatly slowed down this migration. The 1991 hyperinflation wiped out the savings accounts of most Crimean Tatars and made housing in Crimea inordinately expensive. At the same time, the collapse of real estate prices in Uzbekistan, largely as a result of sales by Crimean Tatars and others leaving the republic, meant that Crimean Tatars could no longer sell their houses in places like Tashkent and have enough money to move to Crimea and buy a house there. Today the Crimean Tatar struggle is focused on obtaining civil, cultural, and political rights for those who have returned to their historic homeland.

The Meskhetian Turks maintained their traditional language, religion, and other components of their culture in exile more thoroughly than did the two other groups. The experience of deportation and exile created a national consciousness among this group and galvanized them to defend their ethnic signifiers. As in the case of the Crimean Tatars, the Meskhetian Turks had a strong association with their historical homeland, and this spurred a political movement among them aimed at returning to Meskheti (in southern Georgia). However, both the Soviet and Georgian governments have adamantly prevented the Meskhetian Turks, except for a few thousand, from returning to Georgia permanently.

In the early 1970s, to the demands for repatriation to Meskheti the Meskhetian Turks added demands to immigrate to Turkey. The Soviet government also rebuffed these. In contrast to the position taken by the West German government toward the Russian-Germans, the Turkish Republic did not press for the immigration of Meskhetian Turks nor did they offer automatic citizenship or assistance to any of this group arriving on Turkish soil. The Turkish government has maintained this position up to the present day. Although the Turkish government does not deport these immigrants, it also does not grant them citizenship or most of the benefits associated with it. Since 1991, over 20,000 Meskhetian Turks have come to Turkey illegally. Most of them have taken menial jobs in the Bursa region. The Turkish government's unwelcoming posture, however, precludes immigration for most of the 365,000 Meskhetian Turks living dispersed across the former USSR.

Unlike the situation of the Russian-Germans or Crimean Tatars, the plight of the Meskhetian Turks worsened rather than improved as the Soviet Union entered its final years. A pogrom in the Fergana valley in Uzbekistan in 1989 led to another exodus of many Meskhetian Turks. In Krasnodar Krai, the local authorities dealt harshly with those who resettled there as a result of this incident; they were denied permanent residency permits and the right to own property, to work in most jobs, and to attend institutions of higher education. Local officials also turned a blind eye to violent attacks upon Meskhetian Turks by Cossack gangs. Since 2002 the US government has resettled most of the Meskhetian Turks from Krasnodar Krai as refugees in the USA. Neither return to Meskheti nor immigration to Turkey or the USA, however, are options for the vast majority of the Meskhetian Turks in the foreseeable future. They thus appear doomed to remain a vulnerable minority dispersed across the former Soviet states.

The deportation of entire nationalities during the Second World War remains a source of social problems in the former Soviet states. These problems are most evident in the cases of the Crimean Tatars and Meskhetian Turks. The failure of the post-Soviet states to adequately redress the collective criminal deportations of nationalities by the Stalin regime has greatly contributed to the continuation of ethnic conflicts in Eurasia.

Alieva, Svetlana, ed. *Tak eto bylo: Natsional'nye repressi v SSSR, 1919–1952 gody*. Moscow, 1993.

Bugai, Nikolai, ed. *Iosif Stalin-Lavrentiiu Berii:'Ikh nado deportirovat': dokumenty, fakty, kommentarii*. Moscow, 1992.

Pohl, J. Otto. *Ethnic Cleansing in the USSR: 1937–1949*. Westport, CT, 1999.

Polian, Pavel. *Ne po svoei vole: Istoriia i geografiia prinuditel'nykh migratsii v SSSR*. Moscow, 2001.

Weitz, Eric, D. *A Century of Genocide: Utopias of Race and Nation*. Princeton, NJ, 2003.

Cross-references: Russia and Belarus; *Aussiedler/Spätaussiedler* in Germany since 1950; Cossacks in Russia since the 17th Century; German Settlers in Russia since the 18th Century

DISPLACED PERSONS (DPS) IN EUROPE SINCE THE END OF WORLD WAR II

Frank Caestecker

American military authorities coined the concept of "displaced persons" (DPs) to include all non-German civilians, living outside their country of origin, who had been uprooted or deported during the course of the Second World War. Also, non-German civilians, who fled west in 1944–5 before the advancing Red Army were included in the DP category. In May 1945, at the moment of the German capitulation, about 10 million people in Europe qualified as displaced persons (*Personnes Déplacées*).

These DPs were to be brought back to their countries of origin. Prior to their repatriation, they were in the care of the Allied authorities. Camps were erected in occupied Germany, where the displaced persons had to wait until their return to their home country was organized. In keeping with the logic of the return project, the DPs were separated according to citizenship. Jews freed from the concentration camps and victims of the most brutal Nazi crimes, were therefore assimilated into the mass of persons displaced by the war. Repatriation to countries of origin was also planned for the Jews, who were likewise assigned to camps according to their national origin.

Repatriation

Repatriation proceeded at high speed. Many DPs returned on their own initiative, but in most cases highly organized schemes were set up to facilitate this process. In the aftermath of the war, transporting all these people back home presented an enormous logistical problem. Nevertheless, repatriation measures proceeded efficiently and under strict organization. In the first four months after the German capitulation alone, over 5 million DPs were successfully transported to their countries of origin. Of these DPs, the proportion of former forced laborers, prisoners of war, and concentration camp prisoners from western Europe was very high. The majority of DPs freely availed themselves of Allied-sponsored transportation. Under an agreement between the Western Allies and the USSR, repatriation of former prisoners of war and civilian workers with Soviet citizenship was given priority. If they refused, repatriation was forced, often against desperate individual resistance.

All Western Allies had agreed to the Soviet Union's demand for the speedy return of all its citizens, including those who had collaborated with the Germans. The term "collaborators" was defined broadly; 350,000 "traitors" were repatriated to the Soviet Union. Those who had joined the German armed forces, along with Soviet military officers who had surrendered and had been in German captivity were submitted to at least an undetermined period of forced labor upon return, which ended in amnesty only in 1955–6 following Stalin's death in 1953. Not even the Soviet citizens whom the Germans had forced to work in their war industry were allowed to merely return home upon liberation. Their stay abroad, albeit involuntary, placed them under suspicion. Slightly more than half a million were forced to join labor units upon their return. These units were allocated to work sites that were short of manpower due to extremely hard working conditions.

The Soviet authorities also demanded the repatriation of the former citizens of the Baltic states, eastern Poland, northern Bukovina, and all other territories which, due to border changes after 1945, were now Soviet possessions. The Soviet Union's Western Allies did not concede to the forced return of these people. The agreement with the Western Allies only sanctioned the forcible return of those citizens who had been residing within the borders of the Soviet Union on 3 September 1939. The new Soviet citizens were free to return, but no force was used by the Western Allies to make them do so.

Homeward movement fell off dramatically after autumn of 1945. At the end of that year, there were 1.7 million DPs still living in the three Western-occupied zones of Germany. In December 1946, about 700,000 DPs were still in the camps and another 200,000 living privately in Germany. Most of these DPs refused repatriation. Of the nearly 1 million DPs still in Germany about one-third were of Polish origin, one-fifth were of Baltic origin and another fifth – mainly in the US-occupied zone – were considered Jews. Only about 20,000 DPs who refused return had been Soviet citizens before the war started.

The refusal to return could be traced to the circumstances in which these DPs had left their homeland but also to the political changes that had occurred in their country of origin. Some had been deported by the Nazis from their homelands. The most striking among them were the Jews who had been deported to be exterminated. Others had been deported by the Nazis to work as forced laborers in the German war industry. Among the DPs, there was also a group who had been kept as prisoners of war by the Germans. Among the two latter categories, Soviet citizens were particularly reluctant to return as the information on the catastrophic economic situation in the Soviet Union slowly filtered through and because they were afraid – a fear partly justified – that they would be punished for their stay in the West. A last group among the DPs, were those who had fled westward as the Red Army advanced in 1944. A minority of them used their DP status to prevent possible persecution at home because of their wartime record. Numerous DPs were not eager to return home whether due to the shifting of borders in eastern and central Europe or to the change of political regimes in that region, all to the benefit of the Soviet Union. The citizens of the Baltic states and Ukraine, whose native lands had become part of the Soviet Union, as well as Poles loyal to the exiled anticommunist Polish government in London preferred to stay in Western-occupied Germany.

The persistence of the displaced persons issue beyond the immediate postwar years is to be attributed to international politics during the second half of the 1940s. The refusal of some Soviet citizens to be repatriated was viewed with apprehension among the Western Allies. In 1946, the United Nations with the creation of the International Refugee Organisation (IRO), successor to the UNRAA (United Nations Relief and Rehabilitation Administration), guaranteed displaced persons the individual right to refuse repatriation if they had well-founded fear of persecution due to race, religion, nationality, or political opinion. This IRO-definition meant the definite rupture between East and West in the management of international migration caused by the war. Soviet citizens were no longer obliged to return. The advent of the cold war stopped the collaboration between the Western powers and the Soviet Union and by the end of 1947 the Soviet repatriation missions could no longer count on any official cooperation from the West. DPs became pawns in the emerging anticommunist struggle.

Many Jewish survivors of the Holocaust made an effort to leave eastern, central, and southern Europe, particularly because anti-Semitism in these areas had grown stronger. In 1945, most Polish Jews had refused to return to the place from which they had been deported. From the summer of 1945 onward, the number of Jews among the displaced persons in occupied Austria and Germany swelled. Most of the 200,000 Polish Jews who had been in the Soviet Union during the war and who were authorized to return to Poland used their country of origin only as a place of transit on their way to the West. The pogrom in the provincial town of Kielce in July 1946 was a breaking point. Here, Holocaust survivors were accused of having committed a "ritual murder" and were attacked by their neighbors. More than 40 were killed and twice as many injured.

Hungarian Jews also showed with their feet that return to the prewar situation was not an option. Half of the approximately 50,000 Hungarian Jews who survived the Holocaust and who were repatriated in 1945 together with their gentile countrymen, were back in the DP camps by the spring of 1946. In 1947 the last group of Jewish emigrants, about 20,000 Romanian Jews, took their chances in occupied Germany. Although the Romanian dictator Antonescu had not gone along with German demands to send Romanian Jews to Poland to be killed, the Jewish population had suffered a barrage of anti-Jewish legislation after 1940, including the forcible seizure of Jewish property. After the war, the communist regime did not provide any facilities at all for the social and economic reintegration of Romanian Jews. The new regime took into account the virulent anti-Semitic feelings among the population, who had profited from the plundering of the Jews. By 1947, the Jews no longer hoped for a future in Romania and the famine that struck Romania in the winter of 1946–7 triggered a mass exodus. They were the last of the east European Jewry to be able to leave to the West. By the autumn of 1947 the borders of the Soviet Bloc were hermetically sealed.

These Jewish migrations from eastern-central and southern Europe further advanced the Zionist project for the foundation of a Jewish state. That the Zionists could, to a certain extent, manage this migration depended on the modus vivendi they found with the new regimes in eastern Europe. The Jewish migration was largely an organized movement, but at times – in particular the Romanian exodus – even the Zionists lost control. The Soviet Union and their eastern European allies played a seemingly passive role in this migration process by not obstructing emigration to the West. Absence of intervention was, however, a conscious political decision. By effectively forcing the Jewish migration to Palestine, Soviet interests aimed to weaken British influence in the Near East. In 1947, the emigration of Jews from what was becoming the Soviet Bloc was halted as the borders were closed definitively. The communist regimes, firmly in place by then, asserted their control over their territory.

The migration pattern of Jews from eastern Europe within occupied Germany and Austria was mainly determined by the American government's recognition of the specific fate of post-Holocaust Jewry. Immediately after the war, the survivors were not considered different from other DPs in any way. The fate of European Jews was linked to the general population displacements due to the war. But the Jewish displaced persons in occupied Germany, including the new arrivals, insisted on recognition as a separate group. Initially Jewish DPs were considered a distinct group only in the field of religion. German Jews, according to repatriation logic, were not displaced, and merely had to resettle in Germany. In the US zone of occupied Germany this undifferentiated policy toward DPs quickly gave way to special facilities for Jews. In the fall of 1945, Jews in the US zone, independent of their citizenship, were officially considered more in need of help than other DPs and subject to preferential treatment in the newly erected all-Jewish camps. This pro-Jewish American policy was largely instigated by the pressure in the USA of a well-organized Jewish lobby. The French and the British authorities were not prepared to privilege Jewish DPs over others. They adopted a common strategy to avoid the possible settlement of massive numbers of Jewish DPs in western Europe, namely that Holocaust survivors should return to their countries of origin and reconstruct their lives there, along with the rest of the population. French and British policy was motivated by fear of the increasing expenditure needed to provide for even more people in occupied Germany.

Palestine was the chief destination for the largest portion of Jewish DPs. Between the end of the war and the independence of Israel in May 1948, 6,500 survivors entered Palestine legally; another 69,000 Jews got in illegally. Few Jewish displaced persons were able to settle in western Europe. At the end of 1945, the British "Distressed Relatives Scheme" was designed for survivors in Europe, but only a few thousand survivors were allowed in. The Netherlands took in a few hundred survivors and Belgium gave temporary sanctuary to 10,000 Jewish DPs, nearly all of whom were forced to depart to a final destination.

The USA, with its more open attitude toward the Jewish plight, accepted a considerably greater number of survivors, albeit still a small number of those who were looking for a place to start a new life. In December 1945, President Truman announced a scheme of preferential treatment for displaced persons within the United States' immigration quota. In about two years, until 19 July 1948, only some 28,000 Jews entered the USA under these provisions. The independence of Israel in May 1948 brought to an end the difficulties Jewish DPs faced in finding a receptive home country. Two-thirds of all Jewish displaced persons who had been categorized as such in occupied Germany found a new home in Israel.

Resettlement

In the course of 1946, the perspective on the DPs slowly changed. Concern that the unrepatriated DPs would become an economic burden for the Allied authorities caused a policy review, resulting in a policy of controlled emigration, or

Departure of Jewish displaced persons to Israel, 20 August 1948 (*Haus der bayerischen Geschichte, Augsburg*).

resettlement. Early in 1946 the first openings for resettlement were offered by the UK, France, and Belgium, and later the Netherlands. All four countries experienced critical labor shortages in mining and identified DPs as a solution to this pressing need. France and Britain also needed agricultural workers; in Britain, the textile industry as well as domestic service were also short of workers.

These resettlement schemes were in fact labor recruitment schemes with selection based solely on labor capacity, combined with a number of control mechanisms to make sure this imported labor did not desert the undermanned industries for which they had been recruited. In terms of numbers of DPs recruited, Britain clearly outstripped the other western European countries. In the period 1946–50 about 100,000 displaced persons had been brought to Britain while France recruited about 35,000 DPs, Belgium 25,000, and the Netherlands a mere 5,000. Few dependents were brought in. In the case of the UK, spouses were allowed entrance as laborers in most cases and only a few thousand dependents could join the volunteers recruited for the understaffed industries. In Belgium, where only the mining industry had recourse to imported refugee labor, 15,000 dependents joined the recruited displaced persons.

In Britain and in Belgium no time limit was set over their occupational mobility. Due to international criticism and protest by the DPs themselves, British authorities in 1951 and Belgian authorities a year later decided that employment restrictions would be lifted after a three-year stay. The British authorities had more qualms about this crude manpower policy as it conflicted with another official goal of the government, i.e., to assimilate the DPs into British society, a preoccupation that was largely absent in Belgian policy making. The sensitivity of the British authorities to the human dimension of their recruitment operation can also be noticed in the decision not to use the label "displaced persons" for their refugee labor. The British considered this label to have a derogatory connotation and when the DPs entered Britain they were officially renamed "European volunteer workers." These qualms, however, brought little change in the conditions for settlement of refugee labor in Britain. Just as in Belgium, DPs were on a very long probationary period before they were finally accepted as permanent residents.

In 1947, the prospects of DPs altered fundamentally with the opening of the possibility of mass resettlement overseas. Relocation to the USA, Canada, and Australia increased in the course of 1948 and expanded rapidly in 1949. The decision to admit DPs was linked to foreign policy considerations. Relieving the war-shattered German economy from the burden of the DPs was considered necessary for the stability of the new democratic regime. At the same time, granting protection to those fleeing communist regimes was instrumental to the ideological struggle between East and West. The explicit goal of resettlement in the New World was permanent settlement, and a generous policy toward dependents was implemented. These new options were much more popular among DPs than the labor recruitment schemes of western European states. However, the New World countries' recruitment schemes were also guided to a certain extent by labor demands. Australia, for example, required newcomers to accept a two-year labor contract in industries with labor shortages. By 1951 about 700,000 DPs had been resettled overseas, mainly in North and South America, but also in Australia and New Zealand. Nearly 150,000 Jewish DPs found a new home in Israel and about 100,000 DPs had started a new life in the UK; France and Belgium each hosted about 40,000 DPs.

The resettlement schemes skimmed the cream of the population in the DP camps. Those who remained in the DP camps in Germany were deemed unattractive because they were too highly skilled, had too many dependents, or were in poor health because of forced labor and their long stay in the DP camps.

Immediately after the war, the standard of living for DPs in Germany was higher than that of the local population – for example, they received a larger food ration. This privileged treatment of DPs was heavily resented by the German population. DPs were disliked and looked upon as barbarians, in part reflecting the Nazi-promoted concept of *Untermenschen* from the east, an image strengthened by rumors of violent disturbances and looting by forced laborers after their liberation. As repatriation slowed and the economic burden of the occupation preoccupied the British authorities in particular, food rations were leveled downward and a compulsory work scheme was introduced to make the DPs self-sufficient. The number of DPs in camps in Germany dropped considerably at the end of the 1940s. While at the end of 1947 about half a million DPs were still living in camps in occupied Germany, two years later this number had been reduced by half. Emigration was the main cause of this decline, but a number of DPs remained in Germany, even though they had left the camps. In 1950, 150,000 DPs were still in Germany, a third of them still living in camps. In that year the DPs were handed over to the German authorities. The Law on the Legal Status of Homeless Foreigners, of 25 April 1951, created a special legal status for them. The Allied authorities had given the German

authorities strict instructions that the DPs could, under no conditions, be discriminated against. Notwithstanding their being equal to Germans before the law and thus having access to the German housing and labor market on the same terms as German citizens, most DPs, partly because of German xenophobia, remained unemployed in the camps. Those who lived outside the camps worked mostly for the occupation army. The denial that the *Heimatlose Ausländer* were, in the first instance, victims of the Nazi regime found expression in the restrictive German indemnification policy which largely excluded DPs from reparations. After 10 years of life in the camps, DPs in Germany were totally alienated from normal life. In the German state of Rhineland-Palatinate a group of former DPs left the DP camps to live in the woods and survived by robbery. Members of the group were rounded up in the 1960s. Some were given long prison sentences, while others were confined to psychiatric hospitals as incurable. One can only speak of integration of the *Heimatlose Ausländer* in the German economy from the 1960s onward. The large occupational opportunities in the wake of the German "economic miracle" enabled the DPs to leave their camps.

Integration into western European society

It is difficult to shed light on the integration of DPs in west European society, as displaced persons aroused hardly any sociological or social-historical interest in the decades after 1950. This gap in the research is in stark contrast to the research interest that DPs stirred up in the period immediately following the war. The abbreviation DP came into popular use in western Europe to self-identify or categorize others in the middle of the 1940s. Initially there was great interest in the Jewish displaced persons, who were called upon to regenerate the depleted Jewish communities in western Europe. They were the *She'erit Hapleita* (surviving remnants) and gave to many the expectation that the decimated Jewish communities of western Europe could be rejuvenated. The astonishingly high birthrate of the Jewish DPs in Germany in 1946–7, an expression of their determination to replace the dead, was seen as a sign of hope for the future of Jews in Europe. Still, the old conflict between Liberal and Orthodox Jews resumed and was more vehement than ever before. Some Jewish groups in western Europe viewed the Jewish displaced persons, because of their mostly Orthodox worldview, as a new avant-garde and called upon them to reinvigorate Orthodox Jewish life. The conflict between Liberalism and Orthodoxy was heated in the small Jewish communities in Germany. The few surviving German Jews who had been saved because of their mixed marriages were not ready to segregate themselves from the German community as the mostly Orthodox Jewish displaced persons required.

Hope was also bound up in the future of non-Jewish DPs, albeit of a different sort. The IRO, in its marketing campaigns directed to employers and officials in western Europe, depicted the DPs as people looking to seize whatever chance they could to start a new life. Employers and state officials looking for labor for industries short of manpower hoped that these refugees would not only be a hardworking labor force, but that they would also be resistant to communist ideology and be satisfied with the jobs that natives shunned.

The low social acceptance offered to DPs can be attributed to their refusal to remain in the employment sectors for which they had been recruited – frequently low-paying occupations with minimal social prestige. Along with this came suspicion and animosity based on their supposed political leanings. Above all, communists, a strong political force in Belgium and France, portrayed the DPs as "criminals" merely because of their refusal to be repatriated to their now communist-ruled home countries. That these DPs of a Slavic mother tongue had only German with which to communicate once they arrived in western Europe encouraged the idea of their political untrustworthiness. In some mines, the DPs had to undress on arrival to prove to the local miners that they had no SS-tattoos on their bodies.

Not only popular distrust but also official discrimination caused few DPs to feel at home in western Europe. The fact that they were tied to specific manual work for several years created considerable discontent among the DPs and they voiced harsh criticisms that they were, similar to their plight in Nazi Germany, again exploited as mere labor power. Discontent with their limited occupational choices exploded in Belgium in the summer of 1949 when most DPs had finished the two-year contract that they had signed upon arrival. They abandoned the jobs they were assigned to after their arrival in spite of the fact that the compulsory contracts they had been given were extended indefinitely. As a result, more than 1,000 DPs marched on Brussels, leading to a protracted and bitter battle for settlement rights. During this conflict the Belgian officials and the media portrayed the DPs as ungrateful guests. Only in the early 1950s did the DPs receive permanent residence permits in return for their years of hard labor. The long battle, which had proved necessary for the granting of settlement rights, left deep scars in the psyche of the DPs.

The integration of the DPs in west European societies was very difficult. DPs responded to the inhospitable climate and the poor job prospects by leaving western Europe en masse. Notwithstanding their dissatisfaction with living conditions in western Europe, only very few of the DPs returned to their native lands, and instead many departed for overseas destinations. The several thousand DPs that had been recruited for Dutch industry were nearly all gone in the 1950s. In the course of the 1950s at least half of the DPs recruited in DP camps for the Belgian mining industry had left the country, while in Britain, a quarter of the European volunteer workers had departed.

Along with access to fundamental social rights, any possible means for the development of their cultural needs likewise remained closed to DPs. Initially, the displaced persons wanted to retain their national identity, but they found hardly any support for this goal. Only in Germany did the DPs have the means for retaining and promoting their own culture through their own press and educational institutions. Elsewhere, no special facilities at all were provided for preserving the DPs' national culture or for supporting their integration into the host society. Although policy makers realized that the large number of DP laborers they took in would also become citizens in the end, the assumption was that their integration would simply proceed automatically. Civil society did not deem it necessary to make an effort. Employers did not see any use in attending to the special needs of their new workers. Trade unions were mostly not eager to set up branches organized on an ethnic basis, because it was regarded as being divisive. Only the freedom of religion of the DPs was, as a rule, supported.

By the end of the 1940s, the self-image of DPs had changed. With the cold war coming to its peak, their collective identification shifted toward that of refugees fleeing communism. The term "displaced persons" disappeared and was replaced by "refugee." After the 1950s, nobody claimed to be (or to have been) a displaced person anymore. The renewed attention for displaced persons in the 1980s was mostly linked to the search for war criminals, a connotation that the former DPs obviously wanted to avoid. At the turn of the 20th century due to the dissolution of the communist bloc and more importantly to the class actions of US lawyers against German companies, victims of Nazism – Jews and forced laborers alike – became the focus of public attention again. However, this public discussion did not cause a revival of the category DP, although the more than 1 million (former) DPs who were still alive at the start of the 21st century were the beneficiaries of the new German reparations policy that was more generous than before.

Caestecker, Frank. *Vluchtelingenbeleid in de naoorlogse periode*. Brussels, 1992.

Caestecker, Frank. "Holocaust Survivors in Belgium 1944–49: Belgian Refugee Policy and the Tragedy of the Endlösung." *Tel Aviver Jahrbuch für Deutsche Geschichte* 27 (1998): 353–81.

Cohen, Daniel G. "Naissance d'une nation: Les personnes déplacées de l'après-guerre, 1945–1951." *Genèse* 38 (2000): 56–76.

Dinnerstein, Leonard. *America and the Survivors of the Holocaust: The Evolution of the United States Displaced Persons Policy, 1945–1952*. New York, 1982.

Jacobmeyer, Wolfgang. *Vom Zwangsarbeiter zum heimatlosen Ausländer. Die Displaced Persons in Westdeutschland 1945–1951*. Göttingen, 1985.

Kay, Diana, and Robert Miles. *Refugees or Migrant Workers? European Volunteer Workers in Britain 1946–1951*. London, 1992.

Marrus, Michael R. *The Unwanted: European Refugees in the Twentieth Century*. New York, 1985.

Polian, Pavel. *Deportiert nach Hause. Sowjetische Kriegsgefangene im "Dritten Reich" und ihre Repatriierung*. Munich, 2000.

Proudfoot, M. J. *European Refugees: 1939–52: A Study in Forced Population Movement*. London, 1957.

Stepién, Stanislaus. *Der alteingesessene Fremde. Ehemalige Zwangsarbeiter in Westdeutschland*. Frankfurt am Main, 1989.

Zertal, Idith. *From Catastrophe to Power: Holocaust Survivors and the Emergence of Israel*. Berkeley, 1998.

Cross-references: The Baltic Region; Belgium and Luxembourg; France; Germany; Great Britain; The Netherlands; Poland; Russia and Belarus; Southeastern Europe; Ukraine; Forced Laborers in Germany and German-occupied Europe during World War II; German Refugees and Expellees from Eastern, East-Central, and Southeastern Europe in Germany and Austria since the End of World War II; Jewish Refugees from Nazi Germany and from German-occupied Europe since 1933; Political and Intellectual Refugees from Nazi Germany and from German-occupied Europe, 1933–1945

DUTCH CALVINIST REFUGEES IN EUROPE SINCE THE EARLY MODERN PERIOD

Dagmar Freist

The term "Dutch exiles" (German: *Exulanten*) has become established in recent historical scholarship to describe the Calvinist religious refugees from the Netherlands who were dispersed especially across northern, western, and central Europe in several waves of migration between 1525 and 1650. The word "Exulanten" goes back to the early modern description of a Protestant religious refugee as an "Exul" or "Exulant." Given the extant sources, scholars disagree on the number of migrants, with estimates ranging from 50,000 to 100,000 emigrants. The difficulty ascertaining reliable numbers has to do not least with the sometimes high degree of mobility among the refugees. Often refugees returned to their homeland after a brief period in exile or changed their place of refuge. The flight was motivated by confessional conflicts, that is, staunch Protestants were evading the inquisitorial measures of their territorial rulers, though economic and political reasons also played a role. Even if in most cases the interplay of various economic and social factors prompted flight, the Dutch exulants should be generally placed, alongside Jews and Huguenots, into the large group of early modern religious refugees ("confessional migration").

In the 16th century, the Netherlands, with 17 provinces and a total area of about 90,000 square kilometers, was part of the Habsburg Empire, under the rule of Emperor Charles V and after 1556 of his son King Philipp II until the Dutch Revolt. At the beginning of the early modern period, the urban landscape in the southern Netherlands was, next to northern Italy, among the economically and culturally most highly developed regions of Europe. The emphasis lay in the textile industry, though mining, canal construction, drainage technology, and shipbuilding were also prominent. Innovative economic sectors developed through the introduction of modern production methods outside of the guilds. While specialized knowledge and technical know-how made future migrants very attractive to their places of refuge, their exodus led to a tense economic situation in the sending regions and even to the decline of some economic sectors.

The repressive policy against non-Catholics, which had already begun under Charles V and had triggered a first wave of migration of Calvinists in the 1540s, was continued under Philipp II. This unpopular monarch, who spent very little time in the Netherlands, aroused the opposition of the Protestant nobility not only by retaining the heresy laws, documented in the "Segovia letter" of 1565, and implementing the Inquisition more vigorously, but also by carrying out a reorganization of the bishoprics that violated the traditional boundaries of the provinces. These measures threatened to increase the influence of the Catholic bishops, and the Protestant nobility saw its own benefices at risk. Criticism of Philipp II's confessional politics, combined with the nobility's desire to expand its own power, eventually led to the foundation of the Compromise League in 1565 under the leadership of William of Orange, a union of 2,000 members of the lower nobility. During a march on Brussels in 1566, the seat of the court of the governor-general, Margarete of Parma, was handed a petition with far-reaching demands in favor of the Protestants in the country. When Margarete suspended the Inquisition in response, there were outbreaks against Catholics combined with the public celebration of Reformed services. The return of émigré Protestants and the active and verbal support of the rebels by Calvinists in adjoining countries radicalized the protests. The result was the first "storm of the iconoclasts," which began in Steenvoorde at the beginning of summer 1566. The revolts were bloodily crushed in the spring of 1567 by the governor-general's troops, and numerous ringleaders were executed. The new governor-general, the Duke of Alva, cracked down on Protestants even more by setting up a Council of the Troubles, one of whose tasks was to punish the rebels. Thousands of people suspected of rebellion were condemned to death. The bloody suppression of the revolts of 1566–7 and the reign of Alva triggered a second wave of migration by Dutch Calvinists.

The revolt was rekindled in 1572, this time carried by the northern provinces of Holland, Zealand, and Frisia. The revolt was led by William of Orange, who demanded the withdrawal of all Spanish troops, freedom of religion, and a constitutional monarchy that brought in the Estates General and the provincial assemblies. His vision was a United Netherlands under the leadership of Brabant and the granting of religious freedom. This war, also known to history as the Dutch War of Liberation, ended on the one hand with the unification of the northern Netherlands into the Union of Utrecht in 1579, and, on the other hand, with a successful offensive by Spain between 1582 and 1585, which led to the reconquest of the southern Netherlands. That offensive concluded with the fall of Antwerp in 1585. Over the next four years, half of the population of this once flourishing trade city, about 38,000 individuals, migrated to the north.

The social composition of the emigration varied. In contrast to the time of the Duke of Alva, when above all craftsmen, textile workers, and wage laborers generally sought out places of refuge close to the border, in the 1580s many well-funded entrepreneurs and merchants operating on an international scale left the once flourishing trading, commercial, and financial centers in the southern Netherlands. Population loss, economic decline, and the shifting of traditional trade routes drove them to seek out new places from which to operate. Apart from a few quantitative approximations, scholarship to date has almost completely neglected gender-specific characteristics of migratory behavior, including the question about the possibilities of and motivations behind migration, the experience of migration, and the chances and willingness to integrate into the new societies. While women made up a rather high percentage of the internal migration, their numbers were much smaller in the long-distance migration.

Paths of migration

Initially, refugees from Flanders and Zealand found refuge in London, those from the northern provinces between 1544 and 1557 in Emden, and those from the southern Netherlands in various cities along the middle and lower Rhine (for example, 1544 in Aachen and Wesel). The first places of refuge had superb communication networks and trade connections with the country of origin, which allowed the emigrants to maintain close contact with their families and friends. In the 1560s, emigrants from Flanders and Maasland also went to the newly established exulant town of Frankenthal in the Palatinate. There were various reasons that the migrants often changed their place of residence: in part it had to do with the unstable political situation in their hometowns and cities, which not infrequently prompted them to return and then flee again; in part it had to do with changing conditions in their places of refuge, changes that usually concerned freedom of religion for the exulants and their economic opportunities or were the result of war and persecution. In addition, migrations were also triggered when the reception areas offered special privileges and when the trading markets shifted.

The persecution of Protestants in England during the reign of Queen Mary Tudor I led to the remigration of Dutch exulants to the Continent, though not back to their hometowns, but to the already proven refuge towns Emden and Wesel, as well as to Frankfurt am Main, Duisburg, and Strasbourg. The best-known refugee group was headed by the reformer Johannes a Lascos, which, after an unsuccessful request to Hamburg in 1553, eventually found a home in Emden. After Queen Elizabeth I assumed the throne in 1558, England became once again an important destination for Dutch exulants. Specialized craftsmen and traders settled in London at the invitation of Elizabeth I. The number of migrants grew so rapidly that the city government ordered a census in 1561, "commanding officials to search out & learne the hol number of Alyens & Straungers aswell Denizens as other dweiilinge and resiaunt at this point." Further censuses followed in 1568, 1593, and 1635. At the end of the 16th century, immigrants, most of whom came from the Spanish Netherlands, numbered 6,684 persons, about 6% of the total population of London.

Next to London, the textile and provincial city of Norwich was home to the largest colony of foreigners in England. The city council, with help from the Duke of Norfolk, had successfully petitioned Queen Elizabeth for permission to settle craftsmen from the southern Netherlands. The backdrop to this petition was a crisis in the textile industry. A patent of 5 November 1565 authorized the town fathers to admit "Therty Douchmen of the Lowe Countrys of Flaunders Alyens borne (not denizens) & being all householders or master workmen" along with their journeymen and families, a total of 300 individuals, a number that was soon exceeded. In the 1570s, the refugees numbered 4,000 and made up nearly a third of the total population of Norwich. In other English provincial towns, refugees were admitted and communities were established on orders from Queen Elizabeth. Among the most important were Sandwich (1561), Colchester (1565), and Maidstone (1567). These new foundations redirected the migration pressure on London into smaller towns and cities, which, in the face of population numbers that had been declining since the middle of the 16th century and economic stagnation, generally received the highly qualified migrants with open arms.

Until the remigration in the 1570s, the Dutch refugees in Wesel accounted for up to 40% of the total population; after that they were still 20%. Emden was home to around 5,000 Dutchmen between 1569 and 1573, at the time nearly half of the town's population. After 1573 a remigration to the northern provinces of the Netherlands set in, bringing down the number left in the town to about 1,000. Between 1581 and 1594, another 150 families whom the Spaniards had driven out of Groningen came to Emden. A tax register from 1562–3 for Emden attests to the wealth of the exulants. The upper class of the exulants consisted mostly of shipowners and very rich long-distance merchants; the middle and lower classes were made up of members of the textile trade. New immigrants were taxed at above average rates. Nearly all 175 immigrants who followed Johannes a Lasco came from the southern Netherlands and were relatively wealthy merchants with extensive trading networks. Their presence in Emden worked like a magnet for other refugees from the trading cities of Flanders and Brabant, some of whom brought immense economic resources and promoted the economic rise of Emden in the shadow of Hamburg and Amsterdam.

By contrast, Dutch refugees accounted for only 5% of the population of Aachen between 1544 and 1561. Following their expulsion from the city in 1559, the number of Dutch rose again at the beginning of the 1570s, and between the takeover of power in the city by the Protestants in 1581 and the Catholic reaction at the end of the 16th century, they made up as much as 15% to 20% of the local population. In addition to textile workers, after 1585 a growing number of members of the upper class arrived in the imperial city, among them bankers, large-scale merchants, and entrepreneurs from Antwerp. Dutch refugees who, after their expulsion from England, had made their way to Frankfurt am Main in 1554 via Wesel and Cologne under the leadership of Valérand Poullain, moved to the Palatinate in 1562 when the Frankfurt council restricted the religious liberties originally granted to the Dutch. The Reformed confession had been officially introduced in the Palatinate in 1559 under the Elector Frederick III. Following the departure of nearly all exulants from Frankfurt in 1562, a continuous influx began again at the end of the 1560s; around 1600, exulants made up nearly 20% of the population. A secondary migration between 1600 and 1620 brought additional Dutch families into the imperial city, especially rich merchants and entrepreneurs and wage workers in their employ.

In Cologne, immigration began in 1565. Following a first expulsion in 1570–1, the number of refugees started to rise again, initially slowly and after the fall of Antwerp in 1585 precipitously, eventually comprising around 5% of the total population. While craftsmen were numerically in the majority, the colony in Cologne also included many important merchants and entrepreneurs, mostly from the silk industry. Hamburg did not become a home to Dutch exulants until the end of the 1560s. Flight into the Hanseatic city took on larger dimensions after the fall of Antwerp. At the turn of the 16th century, the Dutch, most of whom came from Antwerp and were entrepreneurs and wholesale merchants, made up about 5% of the total population.

While the "miracle year" 1566, when the government of the southern Netherlands was compelled to tolerate Protestantism, prompted many migrants to return to their homeland, another exodus took place a year later, which either brought them back to their old places of refuge or gave rise to new centers of Dutch exulants. New Reformed communities formed in Goch, Emmerich, Rees, Cleves, and Siegen. A few entrepreneurs settled in the region of Thuringia–Upper Saxony in Gera (1572) and Meuselwitz (1578). The peace of Ghent in 1576 once again prompted a return home, first into the northern provinces of Holland and Zealand, after 1580 to the southern Netherlands, especially Antwerp, Bruges, Ghent, and Brussels. The fall of Antwerp in 1585 and the subsequent blockade by the northern Netherlands, along with the conquest of other large cities in the south as a result of the Spanish-Dutch war, triggered another large wave of migration into the northern Netherlands, to Haarlem, the Hague, Leiden, and Amsterdam, but also to England and Germany. In Leiden alone, around 55% of the population in 1600 consisted of foreigners, the overwhelming majority of whom were refugees from the southern Netherlands. Attractive destinations for Antwerp merchants were, in addition to the old places of refuge, the growing trading cities of Bremen and Hamburg as well as Stade and Emden. After Philipp II had lifted the embargo against Dutch ships and goods, and trade with the Iberian Peninsula was flourishing again, many exulants once again left their places of refuge in Germany and England and went to Holland and Zealand in the northern Netherlands.

A unique phenomenon were the so-called exulant cities, new foundations endowed with special privileges. Apart from confessional interests, the economic benefit that the various territorial rulers hoped to reap by attracting highly qualified workers was front and center when it came to establishing these planned settlements. The first new foundation came at the initiative of Frankfurt exulants in 1562 in the Palatinate. Not only were the exulants admitted into Heidelberg (at the time the residential city) but the territorial ruler also created four separate exulant settlements on the land of dissolved monasteries: 1562 in Schönau (east of Heidelberg) and Frankenthal (west of Mannheim), 1568 in Lambrecht (west of Neustadt), and 1579 in Otterberg (north of Kaiserslautern). Further exulant towns emerged around the turn of the century, for the most part through the onward migration from older settlements. Neu-Hanau was founded in 1597 on the territory of the Counts of Hanau who had embraced the Reformed confession, Joachimsthal in the March of Brandenburg in 1604, and, finally, Mannheim, the largest of all, in 1606. In Hesse the planned new foundation never got off the ground, which is why the Dutch settled in Kassel after 1604.

It was only in the 1620s that the fluctuations among the migrants in the various destination regions slowly declined, even if individual places of refuge, like Stade and Altona, recorded immigrants from cities in Holland and Zealand in the 17th century. Those willing to return had already left their places of refuge and the others had adapted more or less to a new life. In contrast to the immigrants of the 16th century, the refugees of the 17th century tended to settle in established urban communities.

The deliberate recruitment of skilled Dutch workers willing to migrate played a large role in the migratory events. In the 16th and early 17th centuries, individual Dutch entrepreneurs and merchants went to Sweden, among them Willem de Besche and Louis de Geer, who recruited workers from the Netherlands for their mining districts. For example, the Walloon immigrants were settled in the mining cities in Uppland (chiefly Löfsta and Österby) as well as in Finspang, later in Norrköping, where they received extensive privileges. Dutch merchants were recruited for the newly founded city of Gothenburg or its predecessor town of Nya Lödöse. The best-known European example is the population policy of the Elector Frederick William, who recruited specialists from Holland and Frisia for the stagnant agriculture in Brandenburg-Prussia, for canal building, and for architectural projects. While only scattered experts came at the beginning of the 17th century, a concerted effort was made to establish Dutch colonies after the Peace of Westphalia in 1648. The best known is the settlement created by the Electress Luise Henriette in 1651 in Bötzow, which was later named Oranienburg after her. Among the other settlements were those in Tangermünde, Cremmen, the districts of Chorin and Gramzow, and near Liebenwalde (Neuholland).

Criteria for the choice of destinations

Apart from the already mentioned proximity to the place of origin and existing networks and contacts, the conditions under which settlement occurred and migrants were granted the right of residency were crucial for the choice of destinations. An important practical role in selecting destinations was played by Reformed pastors and theologians (e.g., Johannes a Lasco, Valérand Poullain, and Petrus Dathenus), who had extensive networks in Europe and often acted as brokers between migrants and the authorities in the host towns and cities.

Among the material incentives were not least the privileges – enshrined in official letters of invitation – that were offered to those willing to migrate with the help of agents and often while they were still at home. Privileges stipulated the duration of the stay, taxes, the number of tolerated immigrants, property issues, requirements concerning economic activity, the precise settlement area, and, finally, regulations governing the exercise of religion.

The grant of religious freedom was handled differently in the various places of refuge and often depended on the confessional policy of the authorities. In London, until the reign of Mary Tudor, the Dutch exulants enjoyed extensive religious freedoms through the founding of the first "strangers church" in 1550 under Johannes a Lasco. However, the Walloon and Flemish strangers' churches established after Elizabeth I assumed the throne were no longer granted these extensive liberties. The bishop of London was placed at the head of these churches. The "Articles agreed upon at the Strangers fyrst coming hether" laid down the conditions of settlement in Norwich, including the founding of a separate congregation.

While the establishment of a strangers' church under the lax supervision of the State Church was permitted in London and Norwich, the city council of Wesel in the 1550 demanded that the strangers conform unconditionally to Lutheranism. This did not fail to produce conflicts, leading eventually to the formation of a voluntary church with a presbyterian constitution within the city church. After the Dutch group in the city had grown to nearly half of the local population as a result of further immigration, the Reformed doctrine spread within the local population through the influence of the strangers and their pastors. The Catholic council in Aachen tolerated only the private exercise of religion, though the clandestine establishment of a community was tolerated and the Reformed faith spread through the kinship ties between the exulants and some burgher families.

The settlement and external policy of Cologne, Hamburg, and Frankfurt was marked by conflicts of interest between economic policy and religious conviction. Tensions, expulsions, or voluntary departures were not infrequently the result of confessional politics. In Hamburg, the settlement of Calvinist Dutch led to constant clashes with the local Lutheran clergy, supported by large parts of the bourgeoisie and the guilds, who demanded conformity with Lutheranism, and the city council, which – for economic reasons – wanted to accord the exulants at least a minimum of religious freedom.

In the face of the prohibitions against establishing a Reformed community in Hamburg (which were on the books until the 18th century), the Dutch at first attended the Reformed service in Stade. In 1602, after having submitted a petition to the Counts of Holstein-Schaumburg, they were granted the right – much to the chagrin of the Hamburg clergy and the burghers – to build a Reformed church in nearby Altona and set up a consistory. By contrast, Emden, the erstwhile home of Johannes a Lasco, offered refuge to the exulant community expelled from London in 1553 from a sense of religious sympathy.

In spite of confessional reservations, many cities decided to admit the Dutch exulants for economic reasons and offered corresponding privileges. The Catholic council in Aachen recruited a group of 30 weaver families in Flanders and Artois and gave them "several hundred golden Brab. startup money"; in Aachen, the newcomers were helped by loans and by housing and commercial space that was made available to them. Cities that purposely recruited immigrants and in this process entered into direct negotiations with representatives of the migrants often promised, in public letters of invitation, religious freedom, exemption from taxes, and unrestricted economic activities. The 58 Dutch families that arrived in the exulant city of Frankenthal in June 1562 were presented with a capitulation that guaranteed them free entry, their own communal administration, and the exercise of their religion within the framework of the newly reformed ecclesiastical constitution of the Palatinate. English places of refuge also extended generous privileges to the exulants. For example, Colchester granted the Dutch the right to supervise the quality of their cloth and to set up a Reformed congregation, which existed there until the 18th century. In petitions for admission, the representatives of refugee groups also articulated the privileges they expected if they came to settle, assuring the authorities in return that they would see to the economic invigoration of their new place of refuge. For example, in his petition to the city council of Frankfurt in March 1554, Valérand Poullain not only praised the economic capacities of his refugee community and asked for houses and workshops but at the same time also underlined the necessity of founding a church in which the Reformed service could be celebrated in their own language without impediments.

It was not unusual for potential host cities to compete with one another. At the end of the 16th century, the northern Netherlands offered especially attractive places of refuge because of privileges and a vigorous economy. Many exulants returned and new ones were enticed from Brabant and Flanders. Haarlem, economically prostrate after the Spanish siege in 1573, used agents to recruit skilled workers in the southern Netherlands with the promise of large settlement bonuses and startup capital.

Cultural exchange and integration

The migrations had economic repercussions for their destination towns and cities as the new settlers implemented early modern economic forms and production methods, especially in the textile industry, influenced the local and regional confessionalization in many places, and led to a scientific, artistic, and cultural exchange across Europe.

The Dutch passed along skills and knowledge especially in the areas of textile manufacturing, copper working, silk making, goldsmithing, mining, and canal and shipbuilding. In addition, they provided important impulses to the stock and banking systems. Long term it was especially cities like Amsterdam, Hamburg, and Frankfurt am Main that benefited from the worldwide trading contacts that wealthy migrants from the southern Netherlands brought to their new homes. The surge in development that occurred in Brandenburg-Prussia in the second half of the 17th century was partly caused by the immigrant Dutch. Dutch craftsmen – mostly from the textile industry – and skilled workers often passed on their technical know-how when training local apprentices, an offer that Valérand Poullain, for example, made to the Frankfurt city council in his petition for admission of his group of exulants in 1554.

In some cities, however, local guilds, fearful of the competition, demanded that foreign weavers not pass on their skills and claimed a monopoly in training future journeymen and masters. Massive conflicts between the Dutch and the guilds occurred, among other places, in Frankfurt and Cologne, where the guilds, compared to those in cities like Emden or Wesel, were in a strong position. While the foreigners in Wesel were obligated to accept natives as apprentices and teach them new techniques, the Walloons in Sweden were accused of concealing their technical know-how in order to preserve their monopoly in mining. Dutch weavers in England faced similar accusations, while simultaneously obligated to accept only locals as apprentices.

Not all migrants were skilled and wealthy, however. In the 16th century, the foreign poor threatened to exacerbate the growing poverty problem. English cities made it a requirement that the foreign poor be supported by the exulant community, with the result that the Dutch had to fund both their own poor relief and the general poor relief in their host communities. Cities in the northern Netherlands demanded security deposits from migrants and required them to leave if they became impoverished. Still, all larger host towns and cities in England and Germany in the 1560s enjoyed – at least temporarily – a noticeably economic upswing in long-distance trade and in the textile industry from the economic activities of the exulants. The transfer of technology had a sustained effect: it put the domestic industry in a position to boost domestic production and win new markets as the workers learned new production methods and manufactured new goods. Not all social groups benefited equally from this development. Contemporary statements attest that people in the 16th century were aware of the economic benefit that came with the settlement of the Dutch.

Dutchmen worked at many European princely courts as painters, sculptors, artisans, and architects, even at the imperial courts in Vienna and Prague; traces of Dutch architecture have shaped the picture of many European cities to this day. Danzig, for example, where a Dutch Reformed community had established itself in 1585, was the city of Dutch architects, stonecutters, and sculptors, who were put to work chiefly on public buildings and occasionally also to decorate the façades of patrician houses. In conjunction with immigration, the development of autonomous art scenes in nearly all destination cities was important. In the late 1560s and early 1570s, Aachen and other exile towns along the Rhine were home to some prominent Dutch artists, among them the Antwerp architecture painter Hans Vredeman de Vries, his student Hendrick van Steenwyck the Elder, and the Malines (Mechelen) landscape painters Maarten and Lukas van Valckenborch. Most artists left their places of refuge at the end of the 16th century and resettled in Amsterdam, which replaced Antwerp as northern Europe's most important cultural metropolis.

Frankenthal assumed a special place because of the large number of artists there and the relatively long duration of their stay. By 1600, more than 20 Dutch painters had come to the exulant city, among them in the late 1580s the prominent Antwerp landscape painter Gillis van Coninxloo, the art dealer Cornelius Caimox, and the publisher Levinus Hulsius. Particularly attractive to Dutch artists was the Frankfurt fair, which accorded foreign artists the same rights as native artists. Cologne was for Dutch artists the city of printing and publishing. It became home to a scene to which many exulants sought contact. In Nuremberg and Frankfurt, Dutch emigrants were able to set up a publishing industry with a Europe-wide focus. In the 16th and as late as the early 17th century, Dutch artists followed the migration pattern typical of Dutch exulants and frequently changed their place of residence, which created a dense network of Dutch art in exile.

If there was already a close scholarly exchange in Europe during the time of Humanism, one in which Dutch scholars actively participated, this network was further intensified in the second half of the 16th century by the migratory movement from the Netherlands to Germany and England. For example, migrants enrolled in German universities, especially at the University of Heidelberg. A number of learned migrants occupied central positions at German courts and universities. One fixture of the exile communities was that they made scholarships available and founded schools which, because of their quality, were also attended by the children of the established city burgher class. At the same time, Dutch teachers worked at German schools.

The legal position of the foreigners was different from city to city and depended not least on who had the ultimate authority over a city's policy toward foreigners. In England, foreigners were generally excluded from the civic rights of the city, in accordance with a principle of 1521 which stated that only persons born in England could acquire citizenship. By means of a Letter of Denization, which could be obtained through petition and a payment of two pounds, foreigners were given the right to work as a master craftsman, to run a workshop, and to employ a limited number of foreign journeymen. Their children were allowed to complete the seven-year apprenticeship with a journeyman, a path by which the right of citizenship could be acquired. An Act of Naturalization accorded foreigners the same rights as the natives, though it was costly and had to be passed by Parliament. Between 1558 and 1603, 1,962 Letters of Denization were registered, but only 12 Acts of Naturalization.

Judging from the lists of foreigners and registry of citizens, Dutch exulants in Wesel and Emden were able to acquire full civic rights through payment of a fee. In Frankfurt am Main, as well, the exulants were admitted as new citizens in return for payment of a "burgher's fee." In Aachen, the Dutch were entitled to civic rights after the 1550s, and cloth weaving was exempted from the burgher's fee. In Cologne, the grant of civic rights was tied to the Catholic confession, in Hamburg to the Lutheran confession. At the turn of the 16th century, however, the policy on civic rights in Hamburg was revised: all Dutchmen were to be persuaded to obtain civic rights, though the Dutch often refused, out of concern for their religious independence or perhaps to evade the obligations that came with citizenship. A foreigner's contract in 1605 regulated fiscal, inheritance, and property issues. In return for a promise of protection by the council, the Dutch issued a statement of loyalty.

In some cities, the territorial ruler – at times also foreign powers, as in the case of Aachen – sought to influence the policy regarding foreigners as a way of curtailing urban autonomy or to prevent the settlement of Calvinists for reasons of confessional politics. Now and then the conflicts this gave rise to led to the expulsion of the foreigners. In Haarlem, Leiden, and other cities of the Dutch Republic, the acquisition of civic rights was also generally tied to the payment of a fee. However, even in the northern Netherlands, the prime example of religious tolerance, there were attempts, driven by confessional reasons, to deny civic rights and to exclude Catholics and other non-Calvinists from citizenship, as happened in Arnhem, Deventer, Utrecht, and Zwolle.

The process of integration in the destination towns of the immigrants took on very different forms and was shaped by the locals – as well as by the immigrants – through exclusion and xenophobia, but also through emulation and acculturation. A crucial characteristic of the Dutch religious refugees was initially their separateness, which manifested itself not only legally but also visibly in separate neighborhoods, schools, and churches and in their foreign language, customs, and clothes. Most exulants settled in certain neighborhoods of their host cities: the suburbs of Steinweg and Oberndorf in Wesel, the southwestern part of Haarlem, the eastern section of London, and in Norwich on both sides of the Wensum river. Wealthy refugees, however, settled deliberately in neighborhoods with a population of the same social background: in Norwich, for example, that meant West and Middle Wymer directly at important economic and political junctures of the town and close to the wealthy burgher class. While this social separation was in part the result of the conditions of settlement, some immigrant groups cultivated it intentionally, something that was observed especially by the native population in London and aroused resentment. After nearly 30 years of coexistence, Dutch exulants in London were still perceived as a group that did not wish to integrate itself into the host society. A complaint addressed to Queen Elizabeth I in 1571 spoke of "strangers though they be denized or borne here amongst us, yet they keepe themselves severed from us in church, in government, in trade, in language and marriage."

Dutch exulants in English cities learned the new language only with difficulty, sometimes not at all. In the United Netherlands, Flemings, Brabanters, and Walloons were criticized for speaking a "gibberish" of Dutch and French. By contrast, at the beginning of the 17th century, most of the exulants in cities in northwestern Germany were able to speak the German language. Because the wealthy foreigners brought along their own tailors, their style of clothing was also different from the clothes of their urban host societies. But here, especially, there was an imitation effect by the urban upper classes, which was commented upon very critically. In England it was especially French men's fashion that was branded as feminine, while French fashion for women fell into disrepute as being immodest.

In the United Netherlands in the early 17th century, the sumptuous dress and the foreign mores – seen as luxurious and disreputable – of the immigrants from Brabant repeatedly became the target of criticism in direct comparison to the native population. The women of Holland were accused of falling under the influence of fashionable women from Brabant and were now changing their clothes daily. While the women of Holland were described as dull and uncouth by the exulants, the women of Brabant had to face the accusation of being profligate and dissolute. In plays and satires, as well, most of the criticism was aimed at the exulants from Brabant, who were reproached for a luxurious lifestyle and accused of fraud, hypocrisy, and being close to the hated Spaniards. In the play *Spanish Brabanter* (1610) by the poet and playwright Gerbrand Bredero, we read the following: "This is how it is with the people of Brabant, men and women alike. They go about in the manner of the lord or lady of the world, but they have not a penny in their purse." In some German cities in immediate proximity to the Netherlands the degree of foreignness between migrants and the native urban population was apparently smaller. Here conflicts and xenophobia seem to have depended more on the power of the guilds, even though prejudices and urban unrest against migrants can be attested in nearly all refugee cities, simply because of the often far-reaching privileges that were granted to the foreigners.

While qualified foreigners were often welcomed by the authorities as an engine for the native industry and deliberately recruited with grants of numerous privileges, to the native population they always meant competition, which not infrequently led to conflicts. The population of early modern England, in particular, had the reputation of being xenophobic. In the 16th century we repeatedly find exclusionary statements directed at the Dutch exulants there, combined with the charge that "they take the bread out of our mouth." In 1586–7 and 1592–3, lampoons were circulating in London against the "beastly brutes, the Belgians, or rather drunken drones, and faint hearted Flemings." London apprentices threatened that "all the apprentices and journeymen will down with the Flemings and strangers." There was no violent assault, however. Often the strangers were blamed for all manner of deplorable conditions. The Dutch refugees in London, Norwich, or Colchester were accused, especially in times of economic or social crisis, of taking work away from the English, employing only their own countrymen, producing shoddy goods, engaging simultaneously in several trades, engaging in secret trade with each other, sending their profits back home, being responsible for the rise in food prices and rents, promoting the outbreak of the plague because of their tight and overcrowded living spaces, and conspiring against the state.

Even in the United Netherlands, the most popular destination of migrants from the southern Netherlands in the late 16th century, no less a man than the poet and dramatist Joost van den Vondel lamented the intolerance of his countrymen in the sonnet "Princely Presentation of the Animals" (1617): "Many nations are so uncivilized, dissolute, and uncouth that the poor foreigner does not wish to settle among them; all have won land for their own use, to others they would even begrudge the soil." In Haarlem and Leiden, tensions between the foreigners and the natives erupted from time to time, above all because of the completely overcrowded neighborhoods, economic competition, religious difference, and clear antipathy toward the southern Dutch; however, because of the broad network of political and social contacts at the level of city neighborhoods, there were no violent clashes. The complaint was heard that poor relief was being completely monopolized by the foreigners. Even in Emden, the guilds of the tailors, bakers, weavers, and barbers put pressure on the Dutch in 1567 and levied distraints upon all those active in their trades. In all cities, the city magistrates strove to protect the foreigners against assaults.

The Dutch exulants themselves did not necessarily feel like a cohesive group but saw themselves first and foremost as Walloons, Brabanters, Flemings, Hollanders, or Frisians. In Emden, for example, that was evident in their unwillingness to help one another in times of crisis: according to the deacons of the French Reformed community, aid should be rendered solely on the basis of need without distinction as to origins.

Depending on the duration of their stay, migrants of the first generation generally married within the refugee community, while in later generations up to 50% of spouses were not from the migrant community. With respect to the Dutch refugees in England, for example, this means that a fusion of migrants and the native population can be seen in the late 17th century. In Aachen, Wesel, and Emden the first marriages between exulants and families of the host society can be observed as early as the 16th century. To what extent this marriage behavior was gender or class specific has been hardly studied so far.

In many cases – for example, in Emden – the urban upper class sent its children to the French schools of the exulants. The United Netherlands witnessed a cultural fusion between the native upper classes and the bearers of culture from the more highly developed southern Netherlands, a development that should be seen as a process of social demarcation by the upper classes. As a result, the widespread criticism of the exulants and their luxurious lifestyle, articulated in sermons, plays, and pamphlets, was aimed simultaneously against the native upper class, which was in the process of copying this lifestyle. In the second and third generation, leading city offices, as well, were increasingly occupied by descendants of former immigrant families.

Archer, Ian W. "Responses to Alien Immigration in London, c. 1400–1650." In *Le Migrazioni in Europa Secc. XIII–XVIII*, edited by Simonetta Cavaciocchi, 755–74. Florence, 1994.

Eßer, Raingard. *Niederländische Exulanten im England des 16. und frühen 17. Jahrhunderts*. Berlin, 1996.

Frijhoff, Willem. "Migrations religieuses dans les Provinces-Unies avant le second Refuge." *Revue Du Nord* (1998), no. 2: 573–98.

Grell, Ole Peter. *Calvinist Exiles in Tudor and Stuart England*. Aldershot, 1996.

Israel, Jonathan. *The Dutch Republic: Its Rise, Greatness, and Fall 1477–1806*. 2nd ed. Oxford, 1998.

Lucassen, Leo, and Boudien de Vries. "The Rise and Fall of a Western European Textile-worker Migration System: Leiden, 1586–1700." *Revue du Nord* 15 (Hors serie, 2001): 23–42.

Papenbrock, Martin. "Bilder des Exils. Zur Kunst der niederländischen Glaubensflüchtlinge im 16. und 17. Jahrhundert." *Historisches Jahrbuch* 122 (2002): 111–40.

Po-Chia Hsia, Ronny, ed. *Calvinism and Religious Toleration in the Dutch Golden Age*. Cambridge, 2002.

Roosbroeck, Robert van. *Emigranten. Nederlandse vluchtelingen in Duitsland (1550–1600)*. Louvain, 1968.

Schilling, Heinz. *Niederländische Exulanten im 16. Jahrhundert. Ihre Stellung im Sozialgefüge und im religiösen Leben deutscher und englischer Städte*. Gütersloh, 1972.

Schilling, Heinz. "Die niederländischen Exulanten des 16. Jahrhunderts. Ein Beitrag zum Typus der frühneuzeitlichen Konfessionsmigration." *Geschichte in Wissenschaft und Unterricht* 43 (1992): 67–78.

Cross-references: Germany; Great Britain; The Netherlands; Spain and Portugal; Central and Western European Miners and Smelters in Sweden and Denmark-Norway from the 16th to the 18th Century; Huguenots in Europe since the Early Modern Period; Migrant Artists in Antwerp in the Early Modern Period; Netherlandish (Flemish) Textile Workers in 16th- and 17th-Century England

DUTCH CARAVAN DWELLERS IN THE NETHERLANDS SINCE 1870

Annemarie Cottaar

The first caravans (a type of mobile home) appeared in the Netherlands around 1870, after the completion of a road system that was crudely paved. Before that time itinerant salesmen and artisans spent the night in sheds in the countryside or in lodging houses in the cities. Tents were never widespread in the Netherlands. Living in caravans clearly deviated from the normal form of housing and the inhabitants were categorized as a distinct group within Dutch society. When Dutch, they were called "caravan dwellers," and when both itinerant and of foreign origin, they were called "Gypsies." The number of caravan dwellers in the Netherlands increased from some 2,000 in 1899 to 11,000 in 1930, 21,000 in 1960, and 23,000 at the end of the 20th century. In relation to the Dutch population the percentage of caravan dwellers has never exceeded 0.2% (the percentage reached in 1960).

The existing international literature makes only a vague distinction between foreign "Gypsies" and indigenous "travelers" (also called *Jenischen* or *Landfahrer*, tinkers, travelers, taters). At the same time, there are narratives about foreign origins of the "travelers." In the Netherlands, the dominant perception traces their roots back to western Germany (Westphalia), to drifters from the southern Netherlands, or to the Gypsy population. In addition, there is a notion that the itinerant way of life has been part of caravan dwellers' families for generations. Genealogical research on caravan dwellers who lived in the east of the Netherlands between 1920 and 1940, however, demonstrates that the majority of their ancestors were born either in this region or in nearby Germany and had generally lived and worked there for a long period of time. A sample of caravan dwellers in the city of the Hague from the same period, on the other hand, indicates that only the youngest generation was born there, while their parents came from the south or northeast of the Netherlands. Most likely, this was in the course of a general migratory movement from rural areas to major population centers after 1850. The mobile life of caravan dwellers in the Hague is representative of a relatively recent phenomenon. Only a small minority, such as knife grinders and chair caners, can be traced back to ancestors who practiced itinerant trades.

From the very beginning people in caravans were confronted with an existing negative image of itinerants in general. Living an itinerant life was believed to result from insufficient means of subsistence, which itself was seen to lead to begging and stealing. The process of social exclusion and the formation of caravan dwellers as a minority in the Netherlands is closely related to changes in the Poor Law. The new Dutch Poor Law of 1870 made municipalities responsible for relief, not only to the resident poor but also to all those who happened to stay there temporarily. Above all, smaller communities saw itinerants as a threat to their poor relief funds and tried to prevent their stay. This attitude was based on the long-standing popular notion that itinerant people were, by definition, poor. Municipal administrations were led more by their fears than by rational consideration: up to the Second World War, no municipal relief service provided any real volume of assistance to caravan dwellers. Only when the caravan dwellers were concentrated in special camps during the war did the relief develop into a burden on some municipalities. The Dutch government, however, paid for expenditures in these cases.

Although in the prewar period caravan dwellers could move about unhampered, they were not continuously on the road. During the winter months they usually remained in one place, mostly in a large town with many potential customers for their diverse economic activities. Many of their vocations, such as retail and street trade, were also practiced by "sedentary" people; sedentary traders were, however, limited to a small radius of activity. Caravan dwellers' products were either self-made or procured from a wholesaler. The self-made goods included slippers, artificial flowers, pegs, umbrellas, trivets, brushes, brooms, and baskets. The repair of used goods was also an important source of income. A man's earnings were regularly supplemented by those of his wife, and children after a certain age had to contribute to the family income as well. Peddling fancy goods was a woman's affair, but apart from selling things, women enquired after work for their husbands. Numerous artisans, such as knife grinders and basketmakers, lived in caravans as well. Caravan dwellers who worked as entertainers, showmen, and musicians covered an even larger area with their activities in order to attend the quick succession of festivals and yearly fairs held throughout the country.

After the Second World War it became more difficult for caravan dwellers to continue their trades. As a consequence of increasing prosperity, used utensils were no longer repaired but were replaced by new ones. Political decisions also hindered itinerancy in caravans. Their concentration in ever fewer large camps increased the competition between caravan dwellers, who more and more resorted to trade in secondhand cars and waste products. This in turn was curbed by state regulations. Although the possibility of remaining self-supporting diminished, the interest in wage labor did not increase. A central reason for this was that the entire group of caravan dwellers was declared as welfare recipients in the 1960s and 1970s. Although many remained active in trade, the official unemployment rate was 80% to 90%.

At the outset of the 20th century, caravan dwellers were hardly a homogeneous group. The process of minority formation in the next decades was mainly the result of government policies. The Caravan Act of 1918, intended to limit the number of caravans, was an important step. From then onward, municipalities were obliged to provide for a location where caravan dwellers could stay. These sites were usually located on the outskirts of the town, and the number of these sites, as well as the number of caravan dwellers allowed, remained limited. This was supposed to ward off bad living conditions in the camp sites. Still, up to the Second World War caravan

A Dutch knife grinder at work at a caravan camp in the Hague, 1921. To the left an umbrella peddler, in the background some musicians (*Spaarnestad Photo Sales*).

dwellers usually managed to escape from their spatial isolation and to keep in touch with the "sedentary" population. The first proposal, in 1938, to bring caravan dwellers together in large camps was not carried through. From 1943 onward, caravan dwellers were no longer allowed to circulate and had to move their caravans to large camps. Many caravan dwellers, however, abandoned their wagons and went "underground," in a house or an apartment, not infrequently in terrible condition. After the war their freedom of movement was restored and caravan dwellers resumed their old lives, if only for a short time.

The 1968 Caravan Act, aimed to adapt caravan dwellers to a sedentary way of life, provided for concentration in regional camps with their own schools, doctors, and social workers. The controversial ban on traveling limited the number of caravan dwellers by the stipulation that only their offspring had the right to live in a caravan. This hereditary right effectively strengthened their distinctiveness as a group. Although this policy aimed to improve the social position of caravan dwellers, it had more or less the opposite effect. It reinforced the segregation between the caravan dwellers and the rest of the Dutch population and, more crucially, it reduced the possibilities for caravan dwellers to earn their living.

The anxiety that itinerant people would burden the welfare system proved to be a self-fulfilling prophecy. In the 1970s and 1980s, the number of caravan dwellers dependent on welfare constantly increased. Due to their separation from the rest of society and their weak social position – in relation to employment, housing, and education – their situation has become more and more similar to that of ethnic minorities in the Netherlands. Consequently, they were included in the Dutch government's policies for ethnic minorities. Caravan dwellers mostly blame the government for the results of this policy of exclusion: their social isolation, the restriction of their right to freedom, and deprivation of the possibility to be self-supporting. This feeling of separation from the majority of society strengthens caravan dwellers' conviction that they are a distinct group with a special identity that is also entitled to a special legal status. As a result, some of the caravan sites

developed into extralegal areas, where, for example, cannabis was cultivated and tax authorities dared to enter only under police protection.

In 1999, the special legal treatment of caravan dwellers came to an end with the abolition of the Caravan Act. The right to live in a caravan was no longer hereditary but rather regarded as an adequate type of housing and therefore basically accessible for every Dutch citizen. Caravans became just like houseboats and houses, part of the regular housing policy of the municipalities.

Cottaar, Annemarie. *Kooplui, kermisklanten andere woonwagenbewoners. Groepsvorming en beleid 1870–1945*. Amsterdam, 1996.

Cottaar, Annemarie, Leo Lucassen, and Wim Willems. *Mensen van de Reis. Woonwagenbewoners en zigeuners in Nederland 1868–1995*. Zwolle, 1995.

Heymowski, Adam. *Swedish "Travellers" and Their Ancestry. A Social Isolate or an Ethnic Minority*. Uppsala, 1969.

Lucassen, Leo, Wim Willems, and Annemarie Cottaar. *Gypsies and Other Itinerant Groups: A Socio-Historical Approach*. London and New York, 1998.

Mayall, David. *Gypsy-Travellers in 19th-Century Society*. Cambridge, 1988.

Cross-references: Belgium and Luxembourg; The Netherlands

DUTCH EAST INDIAN MIGRANTS IN THE NETHERLANDS SINCE THE END OF WORLD WAR II

Wim Willems

Between 1945 and the late 1960s some 330,000 migrants from the former Dutch East Indies (Indonesia after achieving independence in 1949) settled in the Netherlands. The category was extremely heterogeneous: it included European-born migrants who had been in the Indies only temporarily, Indonesian-born Dutch, European nationals and their offspring who were often of mixed Indonesian-European descent, and indigenous persons with Dutch or other European passports. Then there were also 12,000 Moluccans – soldiers of the Royal Dutch East Indies Army – and their families as well as approximately 7,000 descendants of Chinese settlers to the Malayan Peninsula, the Peranakan, 3,000 Christian Malayans, Minahassers, and other small groups.

In the immediate postwar period, the acceptance and integration of migrants from Indonesia in the Dutch homeland were hampered by the destruction wrought by the war and German occupation, high unemployment, and an acute housing shortage. There was a large number of victims of the Japanese occupation among the more than 100,000 migrants in the first phase of migration (between 1945 and 1949) who expected, as did the Dutch government, to return to Indonesia, yet only one-third actually did. Many rejected, like the indigenous Dutch, Indonesian independence and the position of Sukarno, the first president of the new republic. After Indonesia was officially recognized as an independent state in 1949, however, many realized that their exile was likely to become permanent. A network of aid organizations that was established in the 1950s and that was active until the end of the 1960s took in the often penniless migrants and facilitated their integration.

The scope and timing of further migration was shaped by political developments in Indonesia. In the first seven years of Indonesian independence, some 150,000 persons with Dutch or European passports left the new republic to settle in the Netherlands. Since they were now increasingly viewed as foreigners in the former colony, their position in the job market, the housing market, and the educational system grew dramatically worse. Dutch who were born and raised in Indonesia were also affected. At least two-thirds of the migrants in this period were of mixed Indonesian-European descent, which also applied to the 65,000 persons who fled Indonesia between 1957 and 1963 after President Sukarno nationalized all Dutch possessions in response to the Dutch refusal to withdraw from New Guinea (West Papua). When the Dutch finally gave up their last colonial stronghold in the Pacific in 1963, another 13,000 persons with European citizenship, two-thirds of whom were born and raised in the East Indies, left for the Netherlands. The last category of persons to leave the former colony were those Europeans – mainly Dutch – who had taken on Indonesian citizenship. Many came to regret this decision in light of the economic boom in the Netherlands that began in the early 1950s. Of these 31,000 persons, some 23,000 eventually succeeded in reclaiming Dutch citizenship.

After the Second World War there was a political consensus in the Netherlands that the country was overpopulated. The large-scale immigration of former colonial subjects was therefore viewed as undesirable and for this reason successive Dutch governments in the 1950s and 1960s sought to prevent immigration from the former colony – no financial support was provided and immigrants who had taken Indonesian citizenship were treated as aliens. Many Dutch feared that the "Asian Dutch" could not be integrated into Dutch society and that they would become a pariah group and a financial burden on the state. It seemed instead to make more sense to provide financial support to the Dutch who were living in Indonesia. Only after much pressure from aid organizations like Pelita, NIBEG (an association to claim rights for former prisoners of war), and Nederland Helpt Indië (The Netherlands Helps the Indies) did support for a less restrictive admission policy grow.

This was the main reason that the term "repatriate" began to replace the term "migrant." A network of organizations was founded to help "repatriates" find housing, work, and education. All such initiatives – both from the church and private organizations – were coordinated by the Centraal Comité van Kerkelijk en Partikulier Initiatief voor sociale Zorg ten behoeve van gerepatrieerden, or CCKP, a committee that worked very closely with the government. Local branches throughout the country familiarized migrants with the demands of the new society. For nearly 20 years the CCKP worked together with the Ministry of Social Work to offer a broad range of services meant to facilitate the settlement and integration of the newcomers. This program included additional instruction for children and adults to eliminate gaps in their education and occupational training, two years of support in finding a job, special housing, state loans to purchase clothes and furniture, and various courses to familiarize especially women with the Dutch way of life.

Many "repatriates" nevertheless decided to leave the Netherlands and settle in the USA, Australia, or elsewhere. Approximately 30,000 received immigration permits for North America, some 9,000 for Australia. The heterogeneity of the migrants produced varying models of integration. The Indonesian-born migrants who had no familial ties in the Netherlands had an integration experience that differed significantly from that of migrants who had already lived in the Netherlands before settling in Indonesia. These "real" repatriates, some of whom had enjoyed a high social status in Indonesia, were frequently bitter toward restrictive Dutch admission policies and the unwelcoming attitude of Dutch society. They were the first to highlight the responsibility of the Dutch government for their loss of status. In contrast, the majority of migrants who had been born in Indonesia did not display a comparable bitterness, instead adapting to conditions in their new homeland and taking advantage of the available opportunities for social advancement.

As the process of decolonization seemed to be complete in 1968, the Dutch government ended its program of integration aid for migrants from Indonesia. Special state support appeared at this point as redundant, even if individual integration problems persisted and some migrants still felt alienated and had symptoms of trauma associated with the Japanese occupation or the war of independence. The 1950s nevertheless witnessed a far-reaching social integration of postcolonial migrants into Dutch society. Half of the newcomers, both men and women, married an indigenous Dutch and this percentage rapidly increased among successive generations. Young families with children in particular had little trouble in adapting and taught their offspring not to behave too "Indies." The result was successful integration – at least superficially – paired with the continued cultivation of some of their own cultural norms and values. In the 1980s and 1990s, this strategy of thorough outward adaptation met with criticism from some members of the second generation who emphatically called on their parents' generation to return to the history and cultural heritage of their ancestors.

At the beginning of the 21st century Dutch of partly Indonesian heritage, including both the first and second generations, comprised 582,000 persons. Approximately 458,000 live in the Netherlands, making up more than 3% of the population, and 124,000 in other countries. The sociodemographic profile of this group since its arrival in the Netherlands is not well defined. Its members have never been recognized as a minority and have therefore not benefited from a minorities policy and have seldom been the subject of sociological research. Almost half of the group lives in the conurbation the Randstad in the western Dutch provinces of north and south Holland. This reflects the situation in the 1950s, as most newcomers, notwithstanding the state policy to encourage settlement throughout the country, tended to settle in the Randstad. In this respect they resemble other migrants, who are also heavily concentrated in the urbanized core of the Netherlands.

Beets, Gijs, et al. *De demografische geschiedenis van de Indische Nederlanders.* The Hague, 2002.

Bosma, Ulbe, Remco Raben, and Wim Willems. *De geschiedenis van Indische Nederlanders.* Amsterdam, 2006.

Willems, Wim. *De Uittocht uit Indië, 1945–1995.* Amsterdam, 2001.

Willems, Wim. "No Sheltering Sky: Migrant Identities of Dutch Nationals from Indonesia." In *Europe's Invisible Migrants,* edited by Andrea L. Smith, 33–59. Amsterdam, 2003.

Willems, Wim, et al. *Uit Indië geboren. Vier eeuwen familiegeschiedenis.* Zwolle, 1997.

Cross-references: The Netherlands; Moluccans in the Netherlands since 1951

DUTCH LABOR MIGRANTS IN GERMANY IN THE LATE 19TH AND EARLY 20TH CENTURIES

Corrie van Eijl

Labor migration between Germany and the Netherlands has a long tradition. The large-scale migration of German workers to the North Sea region of the Netherlands started in the late 16th century. Labor migration between the two countries then changed direction with Germany's enormous economic growth from the 1860s on. An increasing number of Dutch headed for Germany and sought employment in industrial production, construction, or agriculture. At the start of the 1870s, Germany replaced Belgium as the main destination for Dutch labor migrants and remained so until the start of the First World War.

Most Dutch labor migrants returned to the Netherlands after a stay of a few months, sometimes years, in Germany, yet some also remained for a longer period of time or settled permanently. Research has hardly investigated the patterns and experiences of Dutch labor migrants and their families in Germany, focusing instead on emigration to the USA.

Although precise numbers are lacking, all estimates indicate a strong increase in the number of Dutch migrants toward the end of the 19th century, reaching a peak in the years before the outbreak of the First World War. According to census data from the German Kaiserreich, the number of Dutch migrants increased between 1871 and 1914 from approximately 22,000 to nearly 145,000. Since the total number of foreigners in Germany grew simultaneously, Dutch made up 11% of all migrants in both 1871 and 1914. During the First World War and the subsequent crisis years during the Weimar Republic, migration from the Netherlands to Germany flagged considerably: the total number of Dutch in 1925 was only 85,000, approximately half of whom were women.

How the employment of foreigners in the German Kaiserreich developed over time can be determined with the aid of the *Nachweisungen* (documentation) of Prussian *Landräte* (regional councils) on *Zugang, Abgang und Bestand der ausländischen Arbeiter im preußischen Staate* (arrival, departure, and number of foreign laborers in Prussia), especially considering that the overwhelming majority of Dutch labor migrants in Germany went to Prussia. According to the *Nachweisungen*, Dutch made up 116,000 of the total 916,000 labor migrants in Prussia in 1913, or the fourth largest group. The proportion of women was relatively low at 13%.

Industrialization in the Netherlands in the late 19th century did not keep up with the relatively high level of population growth. Meanwhile, the western provinces of Prussia, where labor shortages were widespread, were nearby and easy to reach by train and the wage gap between the two areas was growing: a blacksmith in Germany around 1900, for instance, earned 1.80 gulden per day while his Dutch counterpart earned only 80 cents. The salary of a Dutch factory worker averaged 50 cents per day while it could go as high as 1.80 gulden per day in Germany.

Entry restrictions for Dutch workers were minimal before 1914. According to the Dutch-German immigration treaty of 1904, a Dutch certificate of nationality, which would allow someone to return to the Netherlands at any time, was generally sufficient to enter the country. In the interwar period, however, the introduction of stricter labor market regulations as well as the *Inländer Vorrang* (priority for natives) limited labor migration from the Netherlands. In the second half of the 1920s, the number of Dutch workers in Germany fluctuated between 19,400 (1926) and 21,800 (1929), most of whom were longtime workers and had a permanent residence status.

In contrast, the number of seasonal laborers and those who crossed the border daily or weekly to work in Germany was much higher in the Kaiserreich period. Four thousand textile workers from Enschede and its environs regularly crossed the border to work at the textile factories in Gronau and Nordhorn in 1910.

The overwhelming majority of Dutch immigrants traveled to areas of Prussia that bordered on the Netherlands, mainly in Rhineland-Westphalia. In Duisburg, for instance, nearly 90% of all foreign workers in 1890 were of Dutch origin. Initially, Dutch workers were mainly from the eastern border provinces, like Limburg and Gelderland, but from 1906 onward, when unemployment in the Netherlands was rising, migrants also came from the western, urbanized part of the country.

The Dutch who went to work in Germany were mainly young adult men who commonly traveled with others from the same town to perform seasonal labor. Many informed themselves about working conditions in Germany and entered into a contract before departing, although this was not very common among Dutch migrants from the border provinces. For instance, in 1908 almost half of the migrants from Drenthe, a border province, left for Germany without any preparations whatsoever, while more than 90% of those from the western province of South Holland had already secured employment before departing. The Dutch Employment Exchange, founded in 1908 by the Dutch government, in the next 25 years aided some 11,000 Dutch job seekers find employment in the industrial centers of Germany, particularly on the Rhein and Ruhr.

In the beginning of the 20th century nearly 25% of Dutch male migrants in Prussia worked in agriculture, the remaining 75% in industry or trade. The situation in the 19th century was similar: in 1867 some two-thirds of all Dutch migrants, both men and women, lived in villages or small towns, which suggests that they were mainly agricultural workers. In 1913 the majority of Dutch female migrants still worked as agricultural workers, yet little is known about their living and working conditions

Male Dutch migrant workers, mainly unskilled or semi-skilled, worked in the brickyards in Rhineland and Westphalia; in canal and railroad construction; in the textile industry in Aachen, Münsterland, and Nordhorn; in heavy industry in Hanover and Oberhausen; in the tile and food industry. The Dutch who were active in the agricultural sector were employed as milkers in Niederrhein, in peat cutting in Hanover province, and in related activities.

The living and working conditions of Dutch migrants employed as canal workers are relatively well documented. More than half of the workforce in the northern section of the Dortmund-Ems canal, constructed between 1892 and 1900, was Dutch, who were mainly employed as unskilled construction workers. The high number of Dutch workers resulted partly from the shortage of labor for this kind of work but also from the employers' preference for Dutch migrants, who were willing to accept lower wages than their German counterparts and were considered more amenable to that type of labor. The majority of these workers originated from cities near the German border like Coevorden and Emmen. Most were employed for only a few months and less than 10% stayed for more than six months. They were often housed in barracks, sometimes termed "Dutch barracks" because they were inhabited exclusively by Dutch. A few years later, during the construction of the Nord-Ostsee canal, more Dutch men were employed in semiskilled jobs, which led to complaints from German machinists and heaters about Dutch workers, who were willing to work longer hours and whose presence brought wages down.

The fact that the Dutch appear to have made little, if any, cultural impact and that no separate Dutch communities emerged may indicate that Dutch migrant laborers integrated quickly and without difficulty into their German host society. Little is known, however, about the course the integration may have taken and about temporal, geographic, social, and gender peculiarities. Studies on Duisburg shed some light on the experiences of the Dutch community in this city, where the number of Dutch immigrants increased from around 130 in 1867 to 5,400 in 1900 and 12,000 in 1910. Of all foreign immigrants in Duisburg, 64% were Dutch-born in 1867 and 85% in 1900. In 1922 their numbers had been halved, and they decreased further to approximately 5,000 in 1925 and remained fairly constant until 1936.

Because there was such a large Dutch community in Duisburg, ecclesiastical authorities in Holland sent a Dutch missionary there in 1873. Concern about the large number of foreigners in the city was probably the cause for the institution of a special alphabetical residency register for Dutch immigrants.

In the mid-19th century, Neuenkamp, located in the low-lying grassy fields bordering on the Rhine and Ruhr rivers to the north of the city's inner core, became home to Duisburg's greatest concentration of Dutch immigrants. However, statistics show that migration patterns changed between 1867 and 1905. The proportion of male migrants – and also of Dutch male lodgers – diminished while the proportion of Dutch women and children increased, indicating a growth in the number of families. As was presumably the case in other German cities as well, seasonal labor migration developed into longer-term settlement.

Dutch primary schools were founded in many cities with a high proportion of Dutch, such as Gronau, Elten, Kleve, Goch, Gladbach, and Aachen. These schools employed 11 Dutch teachers in 1914; the number of pupils fluctuated widely and amounted to nearly 300 in 1917. Religious communities in the Netherlands maintained contact with Dutch citizens in Germany. In the decade before the First World War both Catholic and Protestant charitable organizations were founded to promote the spiritual welfare of Dutch migrants in Germany. The Catholic organization published its own magazine for Dutch migrants in Germany.

Those Dutch who remained in Germany after the First World War were often bound to the country through marriage, friendship, or longtime residence. During the economic depression in the immediate postwar years, these Dutch migrants were affected particularly hard by the growing unemployment in Germany. Duisburg, for instance, had some 1,800 Dutch citizens out of work in 1920, which was 18% of the city's total unemployed. This resulted in the foundation of the Dutch League in Germany (De Nederlandsche Bond in Duitschland) in 1921. This organization attempted to make the Dutch press and the parliament in the Hague aware of the deteriorating living conditions in Germany and it sought help from the Dutch government. To improve the condition of Dutch migrants and to prevent their expulsion from Germany, poor relief from the Dutch government for Dutch citizens in Germany drastically increased after 1922. This relief was cut back only when economic conditions improved in the 1930s as a result of the rearmament poli- cies of the National Socialists. The recovery of the economy again attracted new migrants from the Netherlands, but their numbers fell far short of those from before the First World War: from 1936 to 1938 the number of Dutch laborers in Germany increased from approximately 22,000 to 31,000. Only toward the end of the 20th century would Germany again become the main destination country for Dutch emigrants.

Bade, Klaus J. "'Preußengänger' und 'Abwehrpolitik'. Ausländerbeschäftigung, Ausländerpolitik und Ausländer- kontrolle auf dem Arbeitsmarkt in Preußen vor dem Ersten Weltkrieg." *Archiv für Sozialgeschichte* 24 (1984): 91–162.

Eijl, Corrie van, and Leo Lucassen. "Holland beyond the Borders: Emigration and the Dutch State, 1850–1940." In *Citizenship and Those Who Leave*, edited by Nancy L. Green and François Weil, 156–75. Urbana, IL 2007.

Eiynck, Andreas, et al. *Wanderarbeit jenseits der Grenze. 350 Jahre auf der Suche nach Arbeit in der Fremde.* Assen, 1993.

Gargas, Sigismund. "Die niederländische Auswanderung." *Economisch-Historisch Jaarboek* 14 (1928): 179–81.

Jackson, James H. *Migration and Urbanisation in the Ruhr Valley 1821–1914.* Atlantic Highlands, NJ, 1997.

Kösters-Kraft, Michael. *Großbaustelle und Arbeitswanderung. Niederländer beim Bau des Dortmund-Ems-Kanals 1892– 1900.* Osnabrück, 2000.

Oltmer, Jochen. *Migration und Politik in der Weimar Republik.* Göttingen, 2005.

Cross-references: Germany; The Netherlands; German Itinerant Merchants from the Münsterland in Northern, Western, and Central Europe in the 18th and 19th Centuries; German Seasonal Agricultural Laborers in the Netherlands from the 17th to the Early 20th Century; German Traders and Shopkeepers in the Netherlands, 1850–1900

DUTCH POLITICAL REFUGEES FROM THE BATAVIAN REPUBLIC IN FRANCE, 1787–1795

Joost Rosendaal

In the 17th century, thanks to its solid political, religious, and commercial infrastructure, the Dutch Republic enjoyed a golden age in which culture, art, and science flourished. Economic development, however, stagnated in the following century. Instead of continuing to invest in new businesses, the ruling financial elite lived off their previous economic successes. Power was monopolized by an aristocracy under the patronage of William V, Prince of Orange. The Provincial Estates, which officially governed the country, had appointed the prince *stadtholder*. However, William possessed consider- able unofficial authority of his own. The well-to-do burghers, who were effectively excluded from government, became increasingly dissatisfied with the prevailing corruption, nep- otism, and abuse of power. Influenced by the ideas of the

Enlightenment, which in the Dutch Republic had acquired a markedly Christian slant, they called for democratic reforms and started a revolution. The country's decentralized struc- ture meant that the revolution developed in each respective local context and spread from city to city. Not content with removing the aristocracy from power, the revolutionaries – who first called themselves Patriots and later Batavians – focused their attacks on the *stadtholder*. In 1786 the conflict escalated into civil war.

The *stadtholder* was able to secure his position only when a Prussian army of 30,000 men entered the Netherlands in September 1787 and, together with supporters of the House of Orange, mainly Orthodox Protestant farmers and rural and urban lower-class workers, suppressed the Patriot move- ment. This counter-revolution was accompanied by extensive violence and looting, and many Patriots were put on trial. In Holland, the most powerful and pro-Patriot of the seven prov- inces, persons loyal to the Prince of Orange replaced almost half of the city councilors. The terror of the Orangist move- ment drove the Patriots into exile. In the first few months after September 1787 large numbers of people – an esti- mated 5% of the population – fled from the cities where the counter-revolution raged to nearby towns or villages, or even abroad. More than 40,000 Patriots took refuge in Denmark; the German territories of Bentheim, Burgsteinfurt, and Altona; the USA; and above all, the Austrian Netherlands (later Belgium) and France.

At first, most of the refugees remained in the Austrian Netherlands. Emperor Josef II hoped that the Patriot leaders' wealth and economic initiative would benefit the country, but his hopes were to be dashed. His enlightened reforms led to an uprising and finally a full-blown revolution (1789–90) among conservatives, who joined with Orangists from the north to take action against the Patriots. By a process of con- tinual intimidation they forced most of the Patriots to leave the country so that by mid-1790 only a few were left in the Austrian Netherlands.

France now became their main place of refuge. Like Josef II, the French king Louis XVI hoped his country would ben- efit from the wealth the Dutch brought with them. Moreover, he was under a moral obligation to give them shelter. As part of his continuing struggle with the British and the Prussians, Louis had supported the Patriots in their conflict with the Anglophile Orangists and had promised to come to their aid if ever they were threatened or attacked. In the event, how- ever, he was unable to keep his promise. His Royal Council was divided on the matter, and two ministers resigned. France simply could not afford to finance a war.

In the opening months of 1788 France began making arrangements for the reception of the Patriot refugees. More than a thousand of them were granted a weekly allowance by the king and they were housed, together with their families, in unoccupied barracks around Saint-Omer and Gravelines in northern France where much of the population still spoke Dutch. Most of the refugees were young, middle- and upper-class men aged 20 to 30 and mainly from towns and provinces where the conflict between Patriots and Orangists had been fiercest. They felt that even their activities as volunteers in Patriot paramilitary organizations gave them sufficient reason to flee. Regular army officers who supported the Patriots were incorporated into a special regiment (the *Royal-Liégeois*) or were granted pensions as French officers. About 25 leaders and publicists received special treatment and were paid out of a secret foreign ministry fund.

Half of the 5,000 refugees, some 1,500 men and their families (600 women and 900 children), still lived in France after one year. For most, their stay in France would last altogether seven years. Although the majority stayed in the allotted barracks for seven years, some moved into private apartments in nearby cities or the surrounding countryside. In order to make a living, several resumed their original trade, which in some cases was met by opposition from local guilds, which feared the competition. However, over time the local population accepted the refugees and several young Dutchmen married French women. The differences in language and religion – about half of the Patriots were Protestant – made it necessary to create their own clubs and churches. The Catholics, however, joined existing parish communities. Those who spoke French, most of them affluent and well-educated, were accepted in established circles, political clubs, and *loges*.

There was a vigorous debate among the refugees as to whether they should accept France's proposal to settle there permanently or wait for a change in the political situation in the Netherlands and remind the French of their promise of military support. A committee was set up to find a suitable place for a permanent settlement. Its report was met with mixed feelings. Under the influence of opponents of a permanent settlement who were in close touch with French opposition circles (the Duke of Orléans, Lafayette, and Mirabeau), the plan was rejected. The majority of the refugees remained in northern France while some of their leaders went to Paris to lobby the French government and remind it of its obligation to liberate the Netherlands from the rule of the House of Orange.

Although some Patriot noblemen frequented the court of Louis XVI and Queen Marie-Antoinette, the king and his government were not at all eager to accede to the lobbyists' requests. Their minds were focused on their own political problems. France was on the brink of revolution. The radical democrats among the refugees were active members of the revolutionary clubs in Paris, and some of them took part in the storming of the Bastille on 14 July 1789. Although the refugees had their own publishers, newspapers, and revolutionary clubs in northern France as well as Paris, the liberation of the Netherlands would not make headway by the time of the fall of the Ancien Régime in August 1792.

The Patriot refugees saw themselves as the true heirs of the Batavians, the freedom-loving native population of the Netherlands who had once fought against the Roman occupiers. The new French government granted the refugees' request to form a military unit called the Batavian Legion.

In October 1792 a Batavian Revolutionary Committee made up of democratic publicists, lawyers, and senior officials from small towns was recognized as a provisional government. Its efforts were finally rewarded when the French National Assembly declared war on the *stadtholder* and the British king on 1 February 1793. The Batavians and the French invaded the south of the Dutch Republic and, after free elections in one of the main towns and the surrounding villages, a democratic administration was installed. However, the French army suffered a crushing defeat in the Austrian Netherlands, forcing the Batavians to retreat and ending the revolution after just two months.

The defeat of the French army also led to the fall of the Girondins, the French revolutionary faction in favor of exporting the revolution. During Robespierre's Reign of Terror, the Batavians had to abandon their hopes of liberating their country. One of the leaders of the Batavian Revolutionary Committee, Joannes Conradus de Kock, was beheaded, while others were incarcerated and were saved from the guillotine only by the fall of Robespierre's party in the summer of 1794.

The French now resumed the fight against their foreign foes and the Batavian Legion was incorporated into the regular French army, where some of its officers were given the rank of general. In the winter of 1794 this army launched a second assault on the Dutch Republic. The new attack, which was accompanied by internal upheaval, proved successful and in January 1795 the Batavian Revolution drove the *stadtholder* and his party from power. Practically all refugees returned to the Netherlands and helped bring the Batavian Republic into being. Their reintegration was very successful: most ended up in important government, judicial, and military posts. Even after the restoration of 1813, King William I, son of the former *stadtholder*, was to be greatly indebted to these Batavians.

Rosendaal, Joost. *Bataven! Nederlandse vluchtelingen in Frankrijk, 1787–1795*. Nijmegen, 2003.

Cross-references: Belgium and Luxembourg; France; Germany; The Netherlands; Northern Europe

EASTERN EUROPEAN JEWS IN BERLIN FROM THE LATE 19TH CENTURY TO THE 1930S

Trude Maurer

Jews from central Europe had been migrating to the east since the 13th century, but already after the massacres and devastation of the Chmelnicki uprising in Ukraine (1648), a movement in the opposite direction set in, even if it was for a long time on a small scale. This changed considerably with the famine and cholera epidemic in the Russian Empire in 1869, and then the pogroms of 1881 and the discriminatory laws in their wake. Together with the economic misery that had been affecting them for some time (including also Austrian Galicia), this acute deterioration of the situation drove millions of Jews into emigration, the chief destination of which was the USA.

On the way to America, the majority passed through Germany (transit migration) because the overseas emigration route went primarily through German seaports (Hamburg, Bremerhaven). However, a small segment of the migrants remained in the Empire temporarily, while others eventually settled permanently. In response to a quota for Jews at Russian higher secondary schools and universities that was introduced in 1887, another group came to Germany to study. Finally, there were merchants who took advantage of the growing economic intertwinement of Germany, Russia, and Austria-Hungary to set up or expand border-crossing trading enterprises.

They thought of themselves simply as Jews and were "eastern Jews" only to the Germans, including also the modern, assimilated German Jews. The generalizing term "eastern Jew" (*Ostjude*), which encompassed groups previously referred to mostly by their region of origin as Polish, Russian, or Galician Jews, established itself only in World War I, when the occupation and hoped-for annexation of Russian Poland by German and Austro-Hungarian troops sparked fears of a massive immigration of Jews.

The major waves of emigration from the Russian Empire occurred in the 1880s and in the period of the Russo-Japanese War (1904–5) and the first Russian revolution (1905). In 1880 there were about 16,000 Jews from eastern and east-central Europe in the German Reich; in 1910 that number was already 70,234. But while the immigrants in France, Great Britain, and the USA were concentrated in each country's largest city, in Germany only one-fifth lived in Berlin. Still, Berlin was typical of the settlement pattern of Jewish migrants as a whole, in that 78% of them lived in (a total of 48) large cities (in contrast to 50% of the German Jews and 21% of the overall population). The Scheunenviertel in Berlin, which was considered the embodiment of the eastern Jewish settlement in Germany, offered them above all an initial destination: before World War I, it was home to no more than one-quarter of the Jews living in the capital.

While Russian subjects made up two-thirds of all eastern and east-central European Jews in Berlin in 1880 (2,048 compared to 957 from Austria), by 1910 that ratio had been inverted in the capital (3,606 Russian against 6,098 Austrian Jews) and in the Reich as a whole. This large number of Jews from the Habsburg Empire also set the eastern Jewish population of Germany and Berlin apart from its counterpart in Western countries. It was the result of a Prussian policy that was unable to effectively control and prevent the immigration, but which reduced the migrant population through expulsions. This was aimed especially against Russian subjects, not only because they were assumed to be subversive but also because the Russian officials did not protect them as much against such measures as the Austrians did. This policy reached its high point in 1885–7, when around 10,000 Jews (and 20,000 Poles) were expelled from Prussia. From the perspective of the Prussian government, naturalization was to be granted to eastern Jews only in exceptional cases, when it was in Germany's interest; in Berlin, only 11% of immigrant Jews were naturalized citizens in 1910.

The high percentage of merchants also set apart the eastern Jewish migrants in Berlin (1910: 43%) from those in Paris, London, and New York, who were concentrated in trades and industry (Berlin: 48%). At the same time, this occupational structure provided the basis for stereotypical perceptions: many non-Jews regarded Jewish trade as unproductive, indeed as mere hucksterism.

During World War I, about 30,000 Jewish laborers were recruited from occupied Russian Poland or brought to Germany under coercion. In 1918, however, a closing of the border especially against eastern Jews was imposed. Although eastern European Jews in Germany were initially spared "repatriation" in the immediate postwar period because of attacks and pogroms in east-central and eastern Europe, German officials were eager to stop further immigration by keeping the border closed. Still, between the end of the war and the spring of 1920, another 20,000 or so Jews came to Berlin. In the first two years after the war, officials launched large-scale raids against these illegal immigrants and alleged "profiteers." Special deportation camps existed between 1921 and 1923. Although the Social Democratic-led Prussian government advocated the principle of equal treatment with other foreigners, the bureaucracy and the police certainly did not implement this policy consistently.

Anti-Semitism, which had already increased during the war, now expressed itself in violent actions, the worst of which occurred during the general unrest over rising prices in 1923: in the Scheunenviertel in Berlin, they turned into pogrom-like excesses. Inflation, economic crisis, and this violence also led to an onward migration to the West and (on a small scale) a return migration home. According to official statistics, 40,406 eastern and east-central European Jews were living in Berlin in 1925. Their share of the Jewish migrant population in the Empire had doubled (40%). That is also reflected in the continuing rise in the degree of urbanization: 89% of the eastern Jews in Prussia were now living in large cities. Likewise, the percentage of those employed in industry and the trades was higher than in the prewar period. Thousands more already left during the global economic crisis of the early 1930s and then during the first months of National Socialist rule. Finally, in October 1938 the German Reich undertook the partially successful attempt at a mass deportation to Poland.

In Berlin, the eastern and east-central European Jews constituted a considerable segment of foreigners living in the city (in the Empire about a third). And since many Jewish transit migrants were also passing through the city (around 5,000 per month at the end of 1921), they shaped the image of the foreigners well beyond their numerical strength. Anti-Semites, taking the Scheunenviertel as representative, stylized them deliberately into the embodiment of the "foreignness" of all the Jews.

At the beginning of the 1920s, the population density in the Scheunenviertel was, compared to the average for Berlin (296 inhabitants per hectare), exorbitant at 1,477 persons per hectare. The streetscape was shaped by the Orthodox with beard and kaftan; the infrastructure reflected the needs of a population whose vernacular language was Yiddish and which adhered to the religious laws much more strictly than the majority of German Jews: numerous bookstores for Hebrew and Yiddish writings were found there, along with shops for kosher foods and ritual objects, as well as prayer rooms (which were often maintained by Jews from the same place or region – even though they were all, by law, also members of the Jewish community of Berlin).

Among the eastern Jews themselves, the insecurity and uncertainty of their life promoted a penchant for behavior that attracted the least possible attention. Thus, in the German Empire, unlike in other countries, they set up hardly any organizations for mutual aid, especially no political bodies, cultural institutions, or press organs of their own. Since they regarded German culture as superior, they soon adapted to German ways of life or the ways of the German Jews: they quickly learned German and sent their children to the best possible schools. The second generation, at the latest, became largely integrated into German Jewry and thus into the German bourgeoisie, with differences generally persisting only in religious practice. Thus, even though the group as such met with skepticism or even contempt, the individual could certainly be integrated, provided he became sufficiently bourgeois. However, that process is less well documented than the policy of the state or the conflicts between eastern Jews and German Jews in some Jewish communities.

The aid for the refugees who arrived after World War I was borne largely by the organizations of German Jewry – but dispensed in collaboration with the League of Eastern Jews. Their goals were to support onward migration to other countries or return to their homeland, as well as the integration into the German economy. The Jewish communities, too, made efforts toward integration – among other things through Jewish schools set up for that purpose in the 1920s.

During the Weimar period, in contrast to the Empire, the eastern Jews developed a rich organizational life. The traditional synagogue communities and a few charitable organizations founded in the last years before the war (e.g., in Berlin in 1905), whose number now continued to rise, were joined by youth clubs, workers' cultural organizations, and regional organizations, though they also devoted themselves chiefly to charitable work and at the same time provided places of sociability. In addition, however, the Jews from eastern and east-central Europe also organized themselves on a supraregional level. Since they did not form a culturally homogeneous group either socially or culturally, they created two organizations for themselves, the Association of Eastern Jews, whose members were overwhelmingly of Polish background, and the much smaller Association of Russian Jews, which was made up largely of intellectuals, the self-employed, and a small number of merchants. They were largely Russian acculturated and had fled after the October Revolution. This organization was about effective but discreet self-help for circles that had once been well-off. In Berlin, the Association of Russian Jews even maintained its own club. Still, in spite of the social and cultural differences, it cooperated with the Association of Eastern Jews, which was set up in 1919 with help from – and perhaps even at the initiative of – the German Zionist Federation (which was interested in recruiting new members for its movement). Initially it was based on individual membership (500 members in Berlin in 1919), but from 1924 on it sought to bring together the existing organizations as an umbrella organization. In Berlin a total of 34 organizations were affiliated with it in 1931, in the Reich as a whole around 100.

In the beginning, the association worked chiefly toward providing aid to newly arriving refugees; later the work for the resident eastern Jews moved to the fore, especially activities on behalf of the middle class. From the end of the 1920s, the association devoted itself increasingly to cultivating the eastern Jewish identity within the framework of a Jewish-national orientation and to representing the eastern Jews within the Jewish communities. This created tensions with the Zionists, who demanded unquestioned loyalty, while the association demanded to be an equal, independent partner.

This self-confidence also allowed the association to appreciate specific creations of Germany Jewry and to seek to connect to Western Jewish life without becoming completely absorbed by it. It sought a synthesis between the old Jewish life, the spirit of the new milieu, and the exigencies of economic and cultural life. The fact that the association had several thousand members who were German citizens points not only to long-term settlement but also to assimilation in language and culture (which was the precondition for naturalization). Even the association's weekly – and later monthly – paper was published in German. At the same time, however, the self-description as eastern Jews speaks to its self-assertiveness vis-à-vis German Jews and non-Jews.

Aschheim, Steven E. *Brothers and Strangers: The East European Jew in German and German Jewish Consciousness, 1800–1923.* Madison, WI, 1982.

Geisel, Eike. *Das Scheunenviertel. Bilder, Texte und Dokumente.* Berlin, 1981.

Maurer, Trude. *Ostjuden in Deutschland 1918–1933.* Hamburg, 1986.

Weiss, Yfaat. *Deutsche und polnische Juden vor dem Holocaust. Jüdische Identität zwischen Staatsbürgerschaft und Ethnizität 1933–1940.* Munich, 2000.

Wertheimer, Jack. *Unwelcome Strangers. East European Jews in Imperial Germany.* New York and Oxford, 1987.

Cross-references: Austria; Germany; Poland; Russia and Belarus; Ashkenazim in Europe since the Early Modern Period; Eastern European Jews in London since the Late 19th Century; Eastern European Jews in Paris since the Late 19th Century; Jews from the Pale of Settlement in Odessa and in the Cities of Central Russia and Poland in the 19th Century

EASTERN EUROPEAN JEWS IN GERMANY SINCE 1990

Paul A. Harris

Since the fall of the Berlin Wall in November 1989, over 200,000 Jews from the former Soviet Union have immigrated to Germany, making it the fastest growing Jewish community in the world and the third largest Jewish community in Europe after France and the UK. So great is the influx of Russian-speaking Jews that in 2003, 2004, and 2005, Germany resettled more Jews than did the state of Israel. In one of this century's most unlikely waves of emigration, tens of thousands of Russian-speaking Jews voluntarily chose to live in a country that nearly annihilated them over a half century ago.

Before the collapse of the Berlin Wall, Russian-speaking Jews immigrated primarily to Israel and the USA. Between 1968 and 1988, roughly 170,000 Russian Jews migrated to Israel and an estimated 300,000 to other Western countries, mainly the USA. During that time, Russian Jews who wished to resettle in the USA were accorded automatic refugee status under US immigration law. Conversely, those Jews who wished to settle in Israel were permitted to do so under Israel's Law of Return that gives every Jew the right to settle in Israel. With the collapse of communism in the late 1980s, a major wave of Jewish emigration from the former Soviet Union ensued. In the 15 years that followed (1990–2005), an estimated 1.1 million Jews left the former USSR: approximately 800,000 migrated to Israel, 300,000 migrated to the USA and over 200,000 to Germany.

Out of this large number of Russian-speaking Jewish immigrants who are living in Germany, only an estimated 80,000 are officially registered with Germany's 84 Jewish communities. The total number of Jews officially belonging to Germany's Jewish community is estimated at 105,000, thereby giving Russian-speaking Jews an overwhelming majority. That less than half of all estimated Russian-speaking émigrés participate officially in Germany's established Jewish communal structures can be attributed to the political environment of the former Soviet Union, where religion and religious practice were forbidden under the communist system. As a result, Jewish communal existence in the former Soviet Union was virtually obliterated and Russian-speaking Jewish migrants in Germany bring with them little to no understanding of Jewish religious practice and communal life.

In the late 1980s, the Jewish community in Germany was slowly dying out. Numbering roughly 30,000, in 1990 the small Jewish community in Germany was predominantly elderly and their children were inclined to go abroad. In fact, the situation was so grave that Jewish leaders concluded that for all practical purposes the community would cease to exist in about 2007. Revolutionary changes on the international and German domestic scene in the late 1980s set the stage to reverse this decline.

The fall of the Berlin Wall in November 1989 coincided with the decision of the US government to rescind the automatic refugee status of Russian-speaking Jews, thereby restricting their entry. Although Israel and the United States were the preferred destination countries, several thousands sought refuge on German soil fueled in part by the US government's new immigration restrictions and the German decision to open its borders for Russian-speaking Jews. The collapse of the Berlin Wall and the subsequent social, political, and economic upheaval that immediately followed provided the soil for several grassroots citizens' initiatives (*Bürgerinitiativen*) in East Berlin that sought to advance the cause of Jewish immigration and resettlement to East Berlin. These initiatives slowly spread to West Germany culminating in a series of parliamentary debates in the fall of 1990.

The parliamentary debates surrounding Jewish immigration placed a newly unified Germany in an awkward situation. Still haunted by its National Socialist past, it wanted to tighten immigration controls but did not want to be perceived as anti-Semitic. The issue of Russian-speaking Jewish immigration was finally formalized in the accord in 1991 that permitted Jewish persons living in the territory of the former Soviet Union to enter legally and resettle in Germany. This decision, based upon humanitarian grounds, came as a result of the increasing pressure on Germany to legalize 8,513 Russian-speaking Jews who had arrived since spring 1990 and to accommodate the rising number of Jewish émigrés seeking haven in Germany. This new policy remained the legal basis for the continued migration and permanent resettlement of Russian Jews to Germany.

Unlike the USA, where migrants resettle in established migrant communities, German refugee law allows a proportional resettlement whereby each state and locale are required to take in a certain number of Russian-speaking Jews so as to equalize the financial burden on each of Germany's 16 states. As a result of this apportionment scheme, many Russian Jews are resettled in small villages with no established Jewish community and far removed from the larger cities. As long as the émigrés receive social assistance, they are required to live in the towns and cities where they were placed. Because of the high unemployment rate of this cohort (roughly 40%) the majority of émigrés do not resettle to other German towns. In cities and villages with a local Jewish community in place, the Jewish community plays an exceedingly important social welfare and integrative role. Although the law guarantees a wide range of social benefits such as language instruction, job retraining, and unemployment and housing assistance, migrants are faced nevertheless with an alien environment and foreign society. The established Jewish communal structures provide integration assistance in the form of language training, support groups, explanations of general principles of civil society, and religious socialization or Jewish acculturation, to name a few.

The organization officially charged with providing integration assistance to Russian-speaking Jewish migrants is the Central Welfare Board of Jews, funded by federal and state governments and governed by the Central Council of Jews, the official representative of Germany's Jewish community.

In early 2003, the German government signed the first-ever agreement with the Central Council of Jews granting Judaism the same legal status in Germany as the Roman Catholic and Lutheran churches. Because of its official recognition, it is eligible to receive public funds for its operations. Yet, because funding is tied to matching contributions from the federal church tax, the Central Welfare Board is chronically underfunded due to the Jewish community's small size (105,000 registered members) and considerable mandate in having to serve such a large and recently resettled immigrant community.

One of the key challenges facing Germany's Jewish community is to promote Jewish communal living and religiosity among the newly arriving émigrés. These new immigrants coming into Germany since 1990 spent most of their life under a communist regime in which opportunities to practice their faith were strictly limited. Another hardship faced by newly arriving migrants is finding employment. Russian Jews are overrepresented in professions such as engineering, medicine, and the natural sciences; finding suitable employment in an already strained German labor market is difficult at best. This failure to find a secure position has led many of the "first generation" migrants to essentially resign and stop the job search, creating a sense of loss and low self-esteem among large numbers of middle-aged and elderly émigrés. A recent survey found that 60% of Russian-speaking Jewish émigrés reported feeling "not at all" integrated into German society and an additional 29% felt only "a little" integrated into German society. The challenges to societal integration among this cohort have been highlighted in the German government's decision in late 2004 to restrict the number of Russian-speaking Jewish migrants, allowing Jews from the former Soviet Union to immigrate to Germany only if they speak German, can show an invitation from a German Jewish community, and can prove that they will not receive social welfare. These controversial changes in the law are designed to improve the integration of the immigrants. Impressionistic evidence shows that the children of these migrants are beginning to enter the German middle class after becoming fluent in German and taking advantage of educational opportunities, thereby leaving a hopeful sign for future generations.

Many Russian-speaking Jewish migrants have created their own cultural niches by forming cultural and social clubs. Russian-speaking Jews in Germany have demonstrated a strong willingness to retain their Russian cultural heritage and pass these same cultural traits along to their children. When asked which culture – Russian or German – was most important to be part of, an overwhelming majority (80%) responded that both were important identity goals. Although there are no current data on intermarriage, roughly 60% of respondents preferred their children to marry a Russian-speaking Jew. Since German society is still "foreign" to them, many Russian-speaking Jewish immigrants resort to their own cultural group. They wish to preserve Russian culture and language not only at home and among friends, but also in public. They are eager to meet fellow Russian speakers in Russian cultural centers or clubs and even to socialize with Russian-speaking German repatriates (*Spätaussiedler*) from the former Soviet Union. As such, Russian Jews have established Russian-language newspapers, radio programs, and television stations that offer special programs for Russian speakers in Russia, the United States, Israel, and Germany. Unfortunately, this has led many in the German-speaking Jewish community to assert that "the Russians" are more concerned with being Russian than with integrating into the German-Jewish community.

As incredible as it may seem, barely half a century after Germany tried to exterminate European Jewry, Germany now has the world's largest growing Jewish population. Although the number of Jews in Germany is only a little more than one-third of their prewar population, the immigrants have begun to rejuvenate and reestablish what was once a dying community. Jewish cultural centers, schools, restaurants, and synagogues have opened in Berlin, Frankfurt am Main, Munich, and elsewhere. Even in provincial towns such as Augsburg, Potsdam, and Fulda, Jewish life is enjoying an improbable renaissance and rebirth. Yet, major challenges still remain since many migrants have been unable to successfully integrate into the German labor market. Successful integration into German society is the single most important indicator of their willingness to make Germany their permanent home.

Ben-Rafael, Eliezer, et al. *Building a Diaspora: Russian Jews in Israel, Germany and the United States.* Leiden, 2006.

Harris, Paul A. "The Politics of Reparation and Return: Soviet Jewish and Ethnic German Migration to the New Germany." PhD diss, Auburn University, AL, 1997.

Kessler, Judith. "Jüdische Immigration seit 1990. Eine Studie über jüdische Migranten in Berlin." *Migration und Soziale Arbeit* 1 (1997): 40–7.

Pinto, Diana. "Towards a European Jewish Identity." *Golem. Europäisch-jüdisches Magazin 2000,* http://www.hagalil.com/bet-debora/golem/europa.htm.

Schoeps, Julius H., Willi Jasper, and Bernhard Vogt. *Russische Juden in Deutschland. Integration und Selbstbehauptung in einem fremden Land.* Berlin, 1996.

Tress, Madeleine. "Soviet Jews in the Federal Republic of Germany: The Rebuilding of a Community." *Jewish Journal of Sociology* 37 (1995): 39–54.

Cross-references: Germany; Russia and Belarus; *Aussiedler/Spätaussiedler* in Germany since 1950

EASTERN EUROPEAN JEWS IN LONDON SINCE THE LATE 19TH CENTURY

David Feldman

East European Jews who came to England in the late 19th and early 20th centuries formed one offshoot of a far larger movement of Jews, most of whom were destined for the USA. The vast majority of these migrants had been born in Russia or in those parts of the former Kingdom of Poland under Russian jurisdiction, but some too came from German Poland (Posen), Austrian Poland (Galicia), and Romania. Between 1880 and 1914, 120,000 to 150,000 east European Jews settled in England, but at any single moment their number was inflated by thousands of transmigrants – perhaps 15% of the 2 million headed for the USA – who broke their journey in England.

The great majority of the east European Jews in England lived in London. In 1911 the census found 61% of all Russians and Russian Poles in England and Wales (almost all of whom were Jews) living in the capital. Women comprised a large and growing minority among these immigrants. In 1881, they comprised just 42% of Russian and Russian Poles in London but by 1911 they made up 48% of the total. By 1871, the concentration of east European Jews in the districts just to the east of the city of London was well established. Higher rates of immigration only served to make this concentration more intense, though the area of concentrated settlement also grew. In 1911, 83% of London's Russian and Russian Polish population lived in the East End, a working-class and immigrant quarter.

The rising and consistent flow of Jewish emigration was a response to economic hardship underpinned by population growth, rural stagnation, and government-imposed restrictions on where Jews could settle and which occupations they could practice. Despite large-scale emigration, the Jewish population in the Russian Empire grew from 1–1.5 million at the beginning of the 19th century to more than 5 million at the century's end. The agrarian economy developed too sluggishly to support the growing number of Jews dependent on petty commerce in the countryside. Government interventions, which from 1882 aimed at evacuating Jews from rural areas, amplified these trends. Emigration was not the only response to these developments. Overcrowding in rural trading also led to a shift toward urbanization and to manufacturing occupations, particularly in Lithuania and White Russia. At the same time that 2 million Jews left the Russian Empire, there was a huge internal migration movement of Jews from Lithuania and White Russia to Poland and "New Russia" north of the Black Sea.

The pogroms of 1881–2 did accelerate the emigration movement but were not the starting point of Jewish emigration, which had been growing slowly for over a decade. Except over short periods, the rhythm of emigration did not coincide with anti-Jewish violence or new government restrictions. Nevertheless, the memory of flight from violence or religious persecution informed the self-perception of Jewish immigrants who settled in London. Their understanding of their own experience was underpinned by a well-founded appreciation of the legal disabilities suffered by Jews in eastern Europe whereas in Britain they enjoyed full equality before the law. However, the idea that the Jewish immigrants were fleeing violence or religious persecution was a half-truth propounded by Jews (though not exclusively by them) in order to promote integration. It was an image calculated to appeal to the native population, who would be encouraged to welcome the immigrants as refugees and victims of religious persecution rather than as fierce economic competitors who would usurp the jobs and homes of Englishmen. As for the immigrants, it was likely to make them think well of their new home despite their many hardships.

When Jewish immigrants began to arrive in London in the 1870s and 1880s, the British government did not possess a mechanism for counting accurately the number of immigrants entering the country, nor was there a law to prevent or regulate their entry. Both these absences were filled in 1905 when the Conservative government introduced the Aliens Act. Henceforth immigrants were required to demonstrate to an official that they were able to keep themselves and their families "decently" and without being a burden on the state. They would otherwise be prevented from entering the country. The Aliens Act generated a fear among immigrants that further laws discriminating against immigrants already in the country would follow. These fears may have inhibited integration among some immigrants but, at another level, the act may have improved conditions for the immigrants by alleviating the intensity of competition at the bottom end of the housing and labor markets.

Before 1905, therefore, the state had no role in the processes of settling and integrating Jewish immigrants in London or elsewhere in the UK. In an arrangement that was characteristic of Victorian Britain, these functions were the remit of voluntary assistance organizations, of which the most important for Jewish immigrants was the Jewish Board of Guardians. However, Anglo-Jewish charities did more than relieve applicants and strive to improve the immigrants' social situation and their cultural integration; they also returned thousands to eastern Europe. Between 1882 and 1906, when the Aliens Act came into force, the board and its associated agency, the Russo-Jewish Committee, returned 31,000 Jewish immigrants to eastern Europe. These were immigrants who had applied to the board for help but were designated as "hopeless cases" and were offered no assistance other than their passage home. We can gauge the significance of repatriation if we keep in mind that the figure of 31,000 returnees is equivalent to 56% of the increase of Russians and Russian Poles in London between 1881 and 1911. The board in this way promoted the economic and social integration of those who remained at the expense of the thousands it expelled.

For most east European Jews the process of migration to London was also a process of proletarianization. The Russian census of 1897 found just 41% of Jews engaged in mechanical and manufacturing trades and in transportation. By contrast, at the end of the 19th century just over 80% of east European Jews in London were engaged in what the census classified as manufacturing, mechanical, and laboring trades. We can estimate that at the end of the century roughly 70% of Jewish immigrants were wage laborers. Tailoring accounted for the occupation of the largest number of Jewish immigrants – 42% of men and 59% of women. In many spheres of production, particularly in tailoring and boot/shoemaking, Jewish immigrants competed with English journeymen. There was also competition in the housing market. As a result of immigration, there were ever fewer apartments available. The inevitable outcome was upward pressure on rents. Economic competition generated friction between locals and immigrants.

There was no single image ascribed to Jewish immigrants by the British population. Some people sympathized with them as victims of pogroms and czarist oppression, but others regarded them as marked indelibly by Russian origins, signs of which were to be found in their uncouth "ghetto" religiosity and their alleged low standard of living. It was widely accepted, both by their supporters and detractors, that the immigrants' identity as Jews was not only a mark of religious difference but was also something that had cultural and social significance. Controversy lay in the different ways these qualities were valued. The immigrants' supporters saw them as hardworking individualists who aspired to improve themselves and rise out of the ranks of the laboring classes. By contrast, their opponents considered them unscrupulous competitors who undercut native laborers and employers alike.

The growth of the Jewish immigrant working class from the 1880s on was the context for the emergence of a labor movement in this milieu. In 1889 and 1890, there were large and successful strikes pursued by immigrant tailors and boot and shoe workers, supported vigorously by the English trade unions and by Jewish revolutionaries. However, the Jewish labor movement in London was unable to create a sustained and cohesive organization. Employers withdrew their concessions in a counterattack in 1891–2. In defeat, relations between immigrants and English trade unions became embittered. In each year from 1892 to 1894, the Trades Union Congress passed a resolution calling on the government to enact legislation to restrict immigration.

It was not trade unions but small synagogues and, above all, benefit societies that were the most commonplace and durable associations in the Jewish East End. Many benefit societies were attached to a synagogue but a growing number were independent. A survey in 1898 of some streets in the heart of the Jewish East End found that between one-half and two-thirds of adult men were members of at least one society. Most of these societies offered benefits in the event of sickness and a lump sum payment to relatives upon death. Some were *landsmanshaftn* – nominally, at least, combinations of men from particular towns or regions – but others imitated

English Masonic orders or named themselves after British royalty or Anglo-Jewish notables. Thus some societies identified with eastern Europe while others connected themselves with England and English Jews. Along with the small synagogues of the Jewish East End, these institutions provided male immigrants with a civil society and public life.

The relationship of the immigrants to English-born Jews was very important in shaping the economical, social, political, and cultural integration of Jewish immigrants. In part, this was a matter of the relationship between the immigrants and the institutions created by Anglo-Jewry, whose leaders worked to integrate the immigrants into the existing communal framework. They did so because they feared independent immigrant organizations would undermine the terms of Jewish emancipation. It was very important, for example, that the chief rabbi should remain unchallenged as a religious authority, not least so that Jewish law would be interpreted in ways that also conformed to the laws of Parliament. Similarly, the Board of Deputies of British Jews jealously guarded its position as the body that represented Jewish interests to the British government. However, at the same time as the Anglo-Jewish elites asserted their leadership, they also established institutions, such as the Federation of Synagogues (1887), that helped to integrate Jewish immigrants within the Anglo-Jewish community and, thereby, within British society more widely.

The Jewish community had to take account of the growing influence of the state, which increasingly involved itself in regulating social relations and providing social services. The question of how the state should relate to non-Anglican and non-Christian religious communities was raised in new ways. For example, the state contributed to the financial costs of schools administered by the Jewish community, as it did for Anglican and Roman Catholic schools. The 1870 Education Act created a new sort of school – board schools – funded by local taxation, administered by local school boards and answerable to central government. Jewish parents were allowed by law to remove their children from these schools during Christian religious instruction. But in the East End of London, special attention to Jewish needs went a step further: in 1902, as many as 16 board schools were run on what were called "Jewish lines." This meant that the schools observed Jewish holidays and Jewish men and women served on their boards of management; in some cases the schools employed a Jewish head teacher and in all cases at least one teacher was Jewish. As a result, the daily attendance of Jewish children at these schools was notably high, which had also an important influence on their integration.

In the early 20th century, in some respects, the actions of the state became more hostile to immigrants. Above all this was signaled by the passage of the Aliens Act of 1905 and the restrictions introduced on the outbreak of the war. The war itself produced contradictory effects. Thousands of men from the Jewish East End served in the armed forces, but some Russian Jews declared themselves reluctant to fight on the same side as the czarist regime from which they fled. Following the revolution of February 1917, 3,000 men chose to return to Russia with the stated intention of serving in the armed forces. More friction arose in the 1920s as the Home Office appeared to discriminate against Jewish immigrants who applied for naturalization and when Jews became targets for the "red scare" that followed the Russian revolution.

At the start of the 20th century some 120,000 Jews lived in the East End. Just one-half of these Jews were immigrants. The East End was populated by successive waves of immigrants. Some came as children and were educated in London schools. Others, who were older but married and had children in the 1880s and 1890s, produced a generation of English-born Jews that reached adulthood in the decade before and the decade after the First World War. This English-born population played an important part in the integration process. After 1918, a new English-speaking leadership came to prominence in the Jewish East End, not least in the trade unions. In politics, Jewish support in the East End was divided between the Liberal and Labor parties but it was the latter that became the stronger force.

Demographic and social change helped to shape the path of integration. One way in which we can observe the integration of Jewish immigrants is through their process of family formation. When the immigrants arrived in London they came from societies in which the birthrate was higher and the age of marriage lower than in England. In England and Wales at the beginning of the 20th century the average age of marriage for men was 26.9 and for women it was 25.4. Among the Jewish population (a population that included both immigrants and established Jews) the figures were 25.1 and 22.9 years of age, respectively. However, by 1934, the figures for Jewish immigrants and the general population in England and Wales were identical for brides, at 25.6 for women, and almost identical for men – whereas Jewish immigrant bridegrooms married for the first time on average at age 28.0, the figure in the general population was 27.5. It is also possible for us to trace, in broad terms, the social and economic integration of the Jewish immigrants and their children. In the period before 1914, there was a movement out of the East End to Soho, the West End, and Hackney. In the interwar period this movement both accelerated and struck out in new directions. The Jewish population became more widely distributed and lived in newly emerging quarters that were easier to reach because of the expansion of the public transit system. In the same period, occupations among the Jewish population became increasingly diverse, even in the East End of London. By the end of the 1920s, just 29% of Jewish men were involved in textile production and trade. Among women, though, at 50%, the concentration was higher. There was also a reduction in the involvement of Jews in furniture making. In these years, Jewish men and women were moving instead into the service sector: into office work and into jobs as salesmen, either traveling, in the street markets, or in shops. The

Jewish working class continued to dwindle in the following decades. Occupational mobility and integration led to Jews having a higher occupational-social status on average than the rest of the population in London. A 1971 survey of Jews in the poor inner London borough of Hackney found that whereas only 7% of occupied men in the borough were self-employed, among Jews the figure was 21%.

Black, Eugene C. *The Social Politics of Anglo-Jewry, 1880–1920*. Oxford, 1988.

Cesarani, David, ed. *The Making of Modern Anglo-Jewry*. Oxford, 1990.

Feldman, David. *Englishmen and Jews: Social Relations and Political Culture, 1840–1914*. London, 1994.

Gartner, Lloyd P. *The Jewish Immigrant in England, 1870–1914*. 3rd ed. London, 2001.

Godley, Andrew. *Jewish Immigrant Entrepreneurship in New York and London, 1880–1914*. Basingstoke, 2001.

Kosmin, Barry A. "Nuptiality and Fertility Patterns of British Jewry 1850–1980." In *Demography of Immigrant and Minority Groups in the United Kingdom*, edited by David A. Coleman, 245–61. London, 1982.

Pollins, Harold. *Economic History of the Jews in England*. London, 1982.

Cross-references: Great Britain; Poland; Russia and Belarus; Ashkenazim in Europe since the Early Modern Period; Eastern European Jews in Berlin from the Late 19th Century to the 1930s; Eastern European Jews in Paris since the Late 19th Century; Jews from the Pale of Settlement in Odessa and in the Cities of Central Russia and Poland in the 19th Century; Russian Revolutionaries in Western and Central Europe in the 19th and Early 20th Centuries

EASTERN EUROPEAN JEWS IN PARIS SINCE THE LATE 19TH CENTURY

Nancy L. Green

The assassination of Czar Alexander II in 1881 and the pogroms that ensued marked the beginning of a mass emigration of Jews from the Russian Empire. Emigration had begun before that date and subsequent departures were linked as much to famine and the increasingly restrictive economic and geographic restrictive legislation as to periodic violent outbreaks against the Jews. Between 1881 and 1925, approximately 3.5 million Jews left east and central Europe (including Romania and the Austro-Hungarian Empire); 2.65 million headed to the USA, 210,000 went to England, 150,000 left for Argentina, and approximately 100,000 went to France. It is estimated that by 1939 approximately 130,000 eastern European Jews were living in Paris alone, including some 28,500 who had been naturalized.

France was a destination of transit as well as of choice. For some, it was seen as a way station even if they ended up staying. After the USA imposed nationality quotas on immigration in the 1920s, France (even more than England, which had imposed its own restrictive Alien Law in 1905) provided an important alternative. But France was also a chosen location for those imbued with the image of the French Revolution and its early emancipation of the Jews in 1791. For Russian Jewish revolutionaries as for many tailors, bakers, and artists, France represented a land of political, economic, or cultural opportunity, different from the pulls of the New World.

Not surprisingly, the eastern European Jews in France congregated mostly in Paris. Although families also settled in the major provincial cities (Nancy, Metz, or Strasbourg), which had sizable Jewish populations as well, the oft-noted French centralization led to a concentration of Jews, like many other immigrants, in the capital city. A large French Jewish community was already established there. Its philanthropic organizations, an immigrant safety net, were known in the east, even if relations between the wealthier French Jews and their poor immigrant coreligionists would at times be fraught with tension. News of the Paris job market spread through migrant information networks. A Yiddish almanac of 1910 advised newcomers that they should head to the Rue des Rosiers, the heart of the Pletzl, the Jewish quarter of Paris. There, the eastern European Jews found apartments, shops, and synagogues in the neighborhood where Alsatian Jews had settled after the Franco-Prussian War. Kosher restaurants, bakeries, and cafés all functioned as meeting places and labor exchanges. After World War I, the Yiddish-speaking areas of interwar Paris expanded to other working-class districts of Belleville and the Place de la République. The eastern European Jews were never the sole inhabitants of those areas; they lived alongside similarly modest French artisans and workers.

The Russian-Polish Jews played a considerable role in the growth of the ready-made garment industry in the city. In 1910, according to one estimate, approximately 11,410 Jewish immigrants (one-third of the entire community) worked in the Paris garment trade: 3,500 in men's wear, 2,800 in women's wear, and 1,400 in the fur trade. Another 1,400 were capmakers, a specialty of the eastern European Jews in Paris. The immigrants were also woodworkers, leatherworkers, shoemakers, bakers, butchers, and waiters, and some joined the French unions. An *Intersektsionen byuro* (Yiddish language sections bureau) representing all of the Jewish crafts within the Confédération générale du travail (main French labor federation) was created in 1910. A revamped *Intersindikale komisie* (Yiddish language sections commission) served the same function as of 1923. Mutual aid societies, oratories (immigrant synagogues, set up because the French Jewish synagogues seemed too foreign), burial societies, social balls, and reading rooms enriched community life. Internal differentiation meant that political groups multiplied. Lively disputes among socialists (Bundists), communists, and Zionists also marked the interwar period on the

"Jewish street." Some 200 Jewish *landsmanshaftn* (hometown clubs) existed in Paris before the Second World War, and 127 Yiddish newspapers or journals were founded in the interwar period. Twenty immigrant societies joined to create an umbrella organization called the Fédération des sociétés juives de Paris (Federation of Jewish societies in Paris) in 1913; some 190 Jewish immigrant organizations united to form its successor the Fédération des sociétés juives de France (Federation of Jewish societies in France) in 1926.

If the story of eastern European Jewry in Paris were written ending in 1930, the tale of integration would be a classic one describing a vibrant first- and second-generation community living *heureux comme Dieu en France* – happy as God in France – as the old (German/Yiddish) adage went. The sights, sounds, and odors of the immigrant neighborhood did not mean isolation nor prevent a whole range of adaptations to *la vie parisienne*, from modes of eating and living to ways of praying (here, becoming less demonstrative). As one old Russian woman in an early immigrant novel decried Jewish assumption of French customs: "Why the Jews even eat frogs' legs there!" But the integration process was not only a matter of a slow shift of culinary habits for some, from Jewish laws of kosher to strange French delicacies, anathema to Orthodox Judaism. The immigrant Jews showed their patriotism to the land that had given them refuge and work by volunteering alongside the French in the First World War. Although many had left the Russian Empire to avoid military service and some remained pacifists, approximately 8,500 foreign-born Jews signed up to fight. Some 3,400 were enrolled, many of whom never returned from the battlefield. During the 1920s, France's borders, unlike those of the USA, were open to foreigners. Polish Jews continued to immigrate and to organize their social life, burials, and after-school Jewish classes in the style to which they were accustomed. Ladino-speaking Jews from the former Ottoman Empire and Jews fleeing Germany after 1933 also came to France in this period.

The vast majority of Jewish immigrants sent their children to French public schools. For some, integration also occurred thanks to the efforts of the French Jewish community's philanthropic organizations (notably the Comité de Bienfaisance [Welfare Committee]). Concerned lest their foreign coreligionists' modes of dress, speech, and poverty prompt renewed anti-Semitism, French Jews sought to "Frenchify" the newcomers through their aid. The latter also created their own self-help institutions (e.g., a shelter called the Société philanthropique de l'Asile israélite de Paris). Politics – particularly in the French labor movement – was another vector of integration for some immigrants. Charles Rappoport, for example, an active socialist before World War I, helped found the French Communist Party in 1921 before breaking with it in 1938. Last but not least, Russian Jewish artists such as Marc Chagall, Ossip Zadkine, and Chaim Soutine helped give the Ecole de Paris its reputation, if not its name.

Things began to change in the 1930s, and not only for eastern European Jews. Xenophobic attitudes and policies began affecting the daily life and opportunities for all immigrants in France. A law of 10 August 1932, restricting access to wage labor in order "to protect national labor," affected Poles and Italians; their contracts were terminated, and they were sent home. Jews too were affected by the 10% quota placed on the hiring of foreigners in certain industries. One solution was to become self-employed. But as anti-immigrant sentiment grew along with economic depression, subsequent restrictive laws in 1935 aimed at foreign artisans and peddlers had an even greater impact on the large number of Jewish immigrants who had concentrated in the small workshops of the garment industry. At the same time, the medical and legal professions excluded foreigners and the newly naturalized from their ranks. Growing anti-Semitism was countered, among other ways, by the creation of a Union des sociétés juives (Union of Jewish societies) in 1938, organized by politically left immigrants who felt that the Fédération des sociétés juives was too tepid in its response to the situation.

The worst, however, was yet to come. During the Second World War, in France, as elsewhere in Europe, Jews were singled out for discrimination, deportation, and death. While some immigrants were able to continue sewing piece-work while in hiding and others engaged in sabotage while working in firms producing for the German army (making sweater neck holes too small, foreshortening glove fingers, etc.), for many, the war meant deportation. Jewish firms and businesses big and small were "Aryanized." In occupied France 1,233 garment firms had been closed as of December 1943 and some 4,000 sewing machines were confiscated. It was subsequently estimated that the industry's labor force declined by 45% during the war. Naturalization proved to be no barrier as foreign Jews were denaturalized, and two Jewish Statutes (3 October 1940, and 2 June 1941) legalized anti-Semitism. Ultimately, one-quarter of French Jewry was deported, representing 10% of French Jews and 40% of foreign-born Jews.

After the war, some returned; other survivors of the Holocaust emigrated elsewhere, especially to Israel, the USA, and Australia. The Jewish community in France began a slow but determined process of reconstruction. The eastern European presence persisted, and by 1968 there were still 10 Yiddish periodicals being published in Paris, while simultaneously a new wave of Polish Jews fleeing renewed anti-Semitism at home came to the city. In the meantime, the French Jewish community was profoundly rejuvenated and transformed by the arrival of yet another wave of Jewish immigrants: North African Jews coming to France in the wake of decolonization, some of whom would settle in the same neighborhoods as their predecessors. By the end of the 20th century, the old eastern European delicacies in the Yiddish neighborhoods of the Pletzl and Belleville had serious competition from Jewish North African treats.

In 1996, *Unzer vort*, the last Yiddish periodical in France, closed, the symbol of a dying immigrant generation. Yet two important spaces on the Parisian scene continued to mark, for the time being, the transformation of the eastern European Jewish generation into a place of memory: the Pletzl and the Bibliothèque Medem. The Pletzl preserved, through its remaining bookstore and east European delicatessen, the signs of the heyday of Yiddish Paris, even as falafel shops and fancy clothing boutiques came to proliferate. The Bibliothèque Medem, founded in 1929 and the largest Yiddish library still existing in late 20th-century Europe, moved in 2002 to a newly renovated "Maison de la culture yiddish" (Yiddish cultural center) and continued to expand.

Adler, Jacques. *The Jews of Paris and the Final Solution: Communal Response and Internal Conflicts, 1940–44*. New York, 1987.

Caron, Vicki. *Uneasy Asylum: France and the Jewish Refugee Crisis, 1933–1942*. Stanford, 1999.

Green, Nancy L. *The Pletzl of Paris: Jewish Immigrant Workers in the Belle Epoque*. New York, 1986.

Green, Nancy L. *Ready-to-Wear and Ready-to-Work: A Century of Industry and Immigrants in Paris and New York*. Durham, 1997.

Hyman, Paula. *From Dreyfus to Vichy: The Remaking of French Jewry*. New York, 1979.

Weinberg, David A. *Community on Trial: The Jews of Paris in the 1930s*. Chicago, 1977.

Cross-references: France; Poland; Russia and Belarus; Eastern European Jews in Berlin from the Late 19th Century to the 1930s; Eastern European Jews in London since the Late 19th Century; Forced Laborers in Germany and German-occupied Europe during World War II; Jewish Refugees from Nazi Germany and from German-occupied Europe since 1933; Jews from the Pale of Settlement in Odessa and in the Cities of Central Russia and Poland in the 19th Century; Maghrebis in France after Decolonization in the 1950s and 1960s; Russian Revolutionaries in Western and Central Europe in the 19th and Early 20th Centuries

EASTERN, EAST-CENTRAL, AND SOUTHEASTERN EUROPEAN PROSTITUTES IN WESTERN, CENTRAL, NORTHERN, AND SOUTHERN EUROPE SINCE THE 1980S

Rutvica Andrijasevic

The political changes that followed the fall of the iron curtain in 1989 were decisive for a large increase in the number of women from central, eastern, and southeastern Europe in the western European sex industry. In the late 1970s and the early 1980s, Latin American women were the predominant migrant group in the sex industry. The number of women from Africa increased throughout the 1980s and in the second half of the 1980s considerable numbers of migrants from Thailand and the French Overseas Territories came to work in the western European sex industry. In 2000, migrant prostitutes were estimated to make up 70% of the total population of sex workers in western Europe, some 30% to 40% of whom were women from central, eastern, and southeastern Europe.

Although the phenomenon is relatively widespread, qualitative and quantitative data on the migration and integration of prostitutes from central, eastern, and southeastern Europe is extremely scarce. For the most part, their presence in the sex industry is researched within the framework of trafficking in women and the debate on forced versus voluntary prostitution.

The economic transformation of eastern European countries after 1989 was accompanied by increasing unemployment. The reduction of jobs in low-income light industries and education affected women in particular. As a result, women often had to move into "informal" sectors of the economy or emigrate in search of alternative employment opportunities. At the same time, the demand for low-wage women's labor in the service industry, including the sex industry, grew in western Europe in combination with a significant wage gap between west and east. The desire to improve one's economic situation was the main cause of sex worker migration from eastern to western Europe while the possibility of escaping patriarchal social relations and creating new life opportunities provided a secondary motivation.

The European Union (EU) enlargement process, especially changes in border regimes and immigration policies, affected the geographical distribution of sex-work migration, even raising the possibility that current countries of origin for prostitution migration might soon become countries of destination. As part of the integration process, internal borders between EU member states were abolished while the external border regime was strengthened. Candidate states for EU membership were required to implement the border and visa regulations of the Schengen Agreement and to harmonize their immigration and asylum legislation according to EU guidelines. These changes created a system of differing regulations governing freedom of movement between the EU-15, the central and eastern European countries (CEECs) that joined the EU in May 2004–January 2007, and noncandidate states. This system permits labor migration for citizens of the EU-15, but it defers the right of citizens of the CEECs to reside and work freely in the EU-15 until 2011 and heavily restricts labor migration from the non-EU member states through visa regulations.

Available data for 2000–2 point to the importance of geographic proximity in determining the country of destination for migrants in the sex industry: women from Ukraine, Moldova, Russia, and Belarus work in the sex industry in Poland, Hungary, Romania, and Bulgaria. Romanian and Bulgarian prostitutes also work for shorter periods of time (between one and three months) in Poland and Hungary. A similar pattern exists in relation to the western European countries on the border to eastern Europe. In the Scandinavian countries, women from the Baltic states and Russia make up the majority of migrant prostitutes. In Germany and Austria, most women in the sex industry come from central Europe and the Balkans.

Aside from geographical proximity, preexisting migrant communities and the intensity of economic ties between the countries of origin and destination play an important role in shaping the composition of the migrant sex worker population. In Italy, for example, most migrant sex workers come from Bulgaria, Romania, Moldova, and Ukraine while migrant prostitutes in Greece are mainly from Russia, Ukraine, Albania, and Bulgaria. In Spain the majority of sex workers come from Latin America rather than eastern Europe, but in Portugal large numbers of eastern European women work in the Algarve, where, as part of informal recruitment schemes, male members of a family are channeled into the construction sector and female members into the sex industry.

In contrast to those women who arrived shortly after 1989, when the immigration laws of EU member states were less restrictive, women who have migrated since the late 1990s seldom have the means and resources to organize and finance their visa, travel, and residency and to work independently. Most women rely on the services of individuals or agencies to supply the papers required for immigration and to find work. Such arrangements are often characterized by a certain degree of deception concerning the type of work to be performed as well as labor and living conditions. Women commonly contract financial debts toward the third parties who organize their journey and/or the owners of the clubs in which they work. As a result, some migrant sex workers work under a high level of control and exploitative labor conditions.

Women who arrived in the early and mid-1990s were usually between 20 and 30 years old and had previously been employed as factory workers, high school teachers, nurses, secretaries, sex workers, students, or waitresses or were self-employed. Their level of education was rather high and they commonly had completed professional training or had begun university education. However, in the late 1990s some significant changes occurred: women tended to be younger, with a lower level of education and with little or no work experience.

Migrant women often combine prostitution with other activities such as petty trade during shuttle migration between their country of origin and destination. They also alternate prostitution in western Europe with short-term agricultural or other types of seasonal labor. A few sources indicate that the length of time women work in prostitution varies according to the type of work available and the residency and labor regulations of their host country. For example, Ukrainian women in street prostitution in Italy commonly work on a three-month basis while Moldavian women in nightclubs in northern Cyprus have six-month contracts.

What migrant sex workers across Europe have in common is a high level of mobility and turnover due to restrictive immigration policies as well as the pursuit of economic gain and the control exercised over them by third parties. The geographic origin of migrant sex workers has also changed. For example, while Albanian women were present only in Italy and Greece until the mid-1990s, today they are also part of the sex industry in Belgium, France, and Germany. The high level of mobility today resembles the situation in 19th-century Europe, when prostitutes generally stayed in one location only for a short period of time and traveled back and forth between major cities in the Netherlands, Germany, France, and Belgium. This frequent turnover in the sex industry is driven today as in the past by customer demand for "new" women as well as by the efforts of women to avoid residency restrictions and stigmatization.

In the majority of EU countries, sex work is not covered by labor legislation, and where it is, as in Germany and the Netherlands, different regulations apply to EU and non-EU citizens. Rather than improving the condition of all sex workers, the legalization of prostitution widened the gap between EU and non-EU prostitutes. As a result of restrictive residency and labor regulations as well as frequent police prosecution, many undocumented prostitutes went underground. This resulted in enhanced dependency on third parties for the provision of work and accommodation, greater vulnerability to exploitation, enforced mobility, and heightened social isolation.

Sex workers from the countries that joined the EU in 2004 are in a better legal situation than those from non-EU countries since they enjoy the right to a visa-free stay of three months as well as the right to self-employment. As a result, some countries have witnessed a significant increase in the migration of prostitutes from central and eastern Europe, such as the Netherlands, which is also an attractive destination since several sex worker interest groups exist there, like the association of room-owners that aids prostitutes in the regulation of their residency status.

The practical implementation of EU residency law on the national level has proven difficult time and time again. In the case of six window prostitutes from Poland and the Czech Republic (the so-called Jany case) – who, according to EU law that had already come into effect in 1999 through the association of their countries of origin with the EU, should have been able to work independently – the Dutch Ministry of Justice refused them residency permits. While this decision was later overruled by the European Court of Justice, the Dutch state initially argued that the women were not independent workers since it was impossible to establish whether they were in fact working of their own free will.

The perception of eastern European women in the sex industry as victims rather than workers is based on the prominence of "trafficking" rhetoric throughout Europe and the USA starting in the 1990s. This rhetoric favors the idea of a simple distinction between victims and criminals and depicts mafia-like organizations as enslaving women in prostitution by coercive means or debt bondage. The opinion of scholars, however, is divided on whether criminal organizations or the restrictive immigration and labor regulations bear the main responsibility for the vulnerability to abuse and labor exploitation of migrant sex workers.

The trafficking discourse prompted the development of measures aimed at combating organized crime and aiding trafficking victims. In this respect, the Netherlands and Italy offer contrasting examples. While the policies of the Dutch state are geared toward prosecuting the offenders, preventing irregular migration, and repatriating the women, the Italian state has developed policies aimed at the reintegration of trafficking victims. The Italian Immigration Law of 1998 grants renewable six-month residence and work permits to victims on the condition that they give up prostitution and participate in a program of social reintegration. The Italian integration model, however, has one significant drawback: it is built on a concept of victimhood, and it does not acknowledge women's agency. It also establishes a normative concept of victimhood (i.e., forced migration, coercion into prostitution, and economic exploitation) that denies social and legal protection to women who do not exactly correspond to the established model.

Due to the stigmatization of prostitution, the police, customers, and local men often harass women in ways that vary from verbal and physical abuse to detention and deportation. The so-called Natasha discourse – predominant in England, Turkey, Israel, and the USA – labels all migrant women from the former Soviet Union as prostitutes whether they are sex workers or not. By identifying themselves as victims of deception or poverty, some women from central, eastern, and southeastern Europe in the sex industry try to avoid the "whore" stigma and achieve social acceptance. Women also pursue social and legal inclusion by not telling their family in their country of origin about their activity as prostitutes, allowing them to establish a relationship or marriage with local men.

The limited period of residency, the stigmatization among the women themselves, and the discrimination by some European sex workers toward migrant women have hindered the active participation of migrant women in the existing interest groups for the protection of the rights of sex workers. Collective political self-organizing of sex workers from central, eastern, and southeastern Europe is still to take place.

Anderson, Bridget, and Julia O'Connell Davidson. *Is Trafficking in Humans Being Demand Driven: A Multi-Country Pilot Study*. IOM, Geneva, 2003.

Andrijasevic, Rutvica. "Problematizing Trafficking for the Sex Sector: A Case of Eastern European Women in the EU." In *Women and Immigration Law: New Variations on Classical Feminist Themes*, edited by Sarah van Walsum and Thomas Spijkerboer, 86–103. London, 2007.

Augustín, Laura. "Migrants in Mistress's House: Other Voices in the 'Trafficking' Debate." *Social Politics* 12 (2005): 96–117.

Gülçür, Leyla, and Pinar İlkkaracan. "The 'Natasha Experience':
Migrant Sex-Workers from Former Soviet Union and Eastern
Europe in Turkey." *Women's Studies International Forum* 25
(2002): 411–21.

*Research Based on Case Studies of Victims of Trafficking in
Human Beings in 3 EU Member States, i.e., Belgium, Italy
and The Netherlands*, edited by Payoke, On the Road, and De
Rode Draad (Commission of the European Communities,
DG Justice & Home Affairs, Hippokrates JAI/2001/HIP/023),
2003, www.prostitutie.nl/studie/documenten/mensenhandel/
researchcasestraffick.pdf.

Tampep 5 Final Report: 2000–2002, edited by TAMPEP, 2002,
http://www.tampep.com.

Cross-references: Austria; The Baltic Region; Belgium and Luxembourg; Czechia and Slovakia; France; Germany; Great Britain; Italy; The Netherlands; Poland; Russia and Belarus; Southeastern Europe; Spain and Portugal; Ukraine; Latin American Prostitutes in the Netherlands since the 1970s

EGYPTIAN UNDOCUMENTED IMMIGRANTS (*SANS-PAPIERS*) IN PARIS SINCE THE 1980S

Detlef Müller-Mahn

Beginning in the 1980s, the number of Egyptian immigrants in Paris rose sharply, a development that was triggered by changes in the system of temporary labor migration in the Middle East and was carried by new transnational migrant networks. Although the Egyptian immigrants initially came to France illegally (*sans-papiers*), at the beginning of the 21st century many of them did have a secure legal status and were able to establish themselves successfully in economic niches, such as the vegetable trade, weekend markets, or segments of the construction industry.

A group of 300–400 persons from the village of Sibrbay in the central Nile delta, most of whom worked in Paris as painters, can be seen as a prime example of the internal social structure and the economic activities of the Egyptian immigrants: their migrations were determined by the transnational social relationships among the migrants. The labor organization of the group was hierarchical, and their economic success was based on the specific course of their integration and the legalization of their presence in France.

Immigration from Egypt to Paris increased when temporary labor migration to the Arab oil-producing states declined as a result of certain economic and political developments in the Middle East. However, Europe as the new migration destination confronted the immigrants with entirely different challenges from those of the Arabian peninsula: migration to Arab destination countries was legal, often organized by intermediaries, in principle affordable for everyone, and within the sphere of Arab-Islamic language and culture. By contrast, access to Europe involved far greater economic and social exertions and cultural accommodations. The response

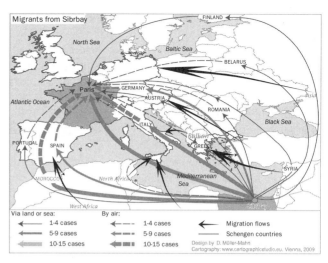

Paths of migrants from Sibrbay to Paris.

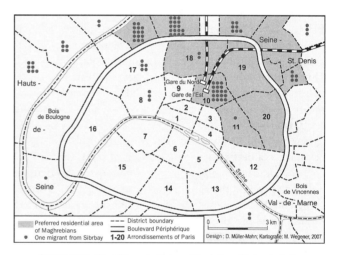

Spatial distribution of houses of labor migrants from Sibrbay in Paris.

to the changed circumstances was the emergence of migratory patterns that were substantially based on networks with fairly exclusive access.

The pioneer in the long chain of migrants from Sibrbay was a man who had worked as a cook for a French family in Egypt and had accompanied his employers on their return to Paris as early as the 1950s. In spite of marriage and naturalization in France, he did not break off contacts with his relatives in Sibrbay. At the end of the 1970s, he was the point of contact for a first group of Egyptians, who subsequently set up small businesses and brought more countrymen to Paris as workers.

Most migrants had to rely on their families to pay for the journey. They sold land or cattle or borrowed the necessary sum from relatives, if possible. The second option was the preferred one, with migrants who had already been living in France for some time acting increasingly as funders. Because of the large initial investment required, the migrants were under intense pressure to succeed, since they could not possibly repay their debts by pursuing wage labor in Egypt.

Thus, those who failed on their way to Europe had all the more reason to try again.

At the beginning of the 21st century, the trips to France were organized by "travel agents" in Egypt, most of whom had migration experience themselves. Working with contacts in Europe, they arranged to get the travelers safely to France in small groups. In 1998, such a journey "with a guarantee of success" cost the equivalent of 3,000–4,000 euros; by 2004 the price had already risen to 7,000 euros. A trip organized by the migrants themselves was substantially cheaper at 1,000–1,500 euros, but it also involved considerably higher risks. It is difficult to estimate the ratio of failed attempts to enter the country or deportations relative to all immigrations. It would appear that entry into Europe had become fairly predictable for migrants from Sibrbay in the second half of the 1990s: with the expansion of network relationships and the establishment of the first group in Paris, there was now sufficient social and economic capital to find fairly safe paths for newly arriving men – and recently also some women – from Sibrbay.

Few migrants returned to Sibrbay voluntarily and for good, even though most had originally come to Paris to earn money to establish a family, acquire property, and build a house in their native village. This apparent contradiction between intent and reality can be explained by the integration patterns in the destination country.

The integration of the immigrants in France generally occurred in three phases, which went hand in hand with a gradual change and loosening of ties to the native village. The ways in which the immigrants managed their adjustment to the new spatial and social environment in France could be quite varied. But in the process many Egyptians found themselves in personal conflict over their goals. At the beginning of the 21st century, about two-thirds of the men were between 30 and 40 years old and had already been living in France for more than five years. Although they worked for years toward a successful return to Egypt, regularly sent money home, and were able to fulfill at least some of their material wishes, they kept postponing their original goal.

The first phase following the entry into France was the most difficult one for the migrants. They had to survive the first year or two in Paris to be able to pay off their debts. As illegal aliens with no familiarity with the city and no language skills, they faced a heightened risk of being picked up by the police and deported to Egypt. A massive sense of cultural insecurity and the separation from their families in Egypt made their lives even more difficult. A large number of migrants spent their time withdrawn into Egyptian housing communities; their social contacts focused on visits with countrymen in Paris, where they cooked together and watched Egyptian videos. There were also phone calls with relatives and friends back in Egypt. In this way a piece of Sibrbay was reproduced in their daily life. Nearly all immigrants from Sibrbay lived in northeastern Paris, in neighborhoods with the highest proportion of immigrants from the Maghreb.

Many newcomers reacted to the encounter with a foreign world with a deepened religiosity. The large mosque of La Chapelle became the most important meeting place outside their homes. This is also where the first contacts beyond the original group were established. Moreover, the mosque was an authoritative institution for the Egyptians, who as *sans-papiers* were not able to take advantage of government services. In this context, an imam from Sibrbay played a central role for the migrants from his village because he was the only authority recognized by all. He acted as mediator in conflicts, most of which revolved around wage and money issues. He also organized medical care for the sick and collected contributions to help in emergencies.

In the second integration phase, the primary goal of the *sans-papiers* living in permanent insecurity, once they had repaid their debts, was to legalize their presence as the basis for securing a livelihood for the long term. The prerequisite for that was integration into the host society, although that integration did not take place as an incorporation into French society as a whole, but as integration into the North African–Muslim immigrant society in the *banlieues* of the French capital. Some immigrants were able to legalize their stay after only a few years; others were still living without papers after 20 years. There were essentially two options for acquiring a residence permit. The first was to take advantage of one of the campaigns for the legalization of illegal immigrants (regularization) that were carried out repeatedly in France and some neighboring countries. During the most recent legalization campaign in Italy, many *sans-papiers* crossed the border from France to have themselves officially registered in Italy with forged certificates of employment. The Italian residence permits, valid for 10 years, allowed their holders also to engage in legal employment in France. Although a host of men from Sibrbay were victims of con men in Italy, for others the cost of 1,500–2,000 euros for the trip and the forged certificate of employment turned out to be a useful investment.

The second option for acquiring a residence permit was marriage to a woman with French citizenship. The partners were frequently divorcées of Arab background, mostly from Morocco or Algeria, often with children. Contacts were established through the mosque or through acquaintances. Egyptian men for the most part regarded these matrimonial ties with a North African woman as a "temporary marriage" – especially if they also had a wife and children in Egypt. Through marriage the men acquired not only the right to a 10-year residence permit but also a household of their own. Most of the women, especially those with children, lived in public-assistance housing, which was more affordable and comfortable than the often dark and cramped housing of the *sans-papiers*.

The course of integration was influenced in crucial ways by the circumstances of work. About 90% of the men from Sibrbay worked in Paris as painters or owners of painting businesses. Their success was based on a work organization that was hierarchical and flexible in its adjustment to the market. At the top of the hierarchy stood a few men who had already immigrated at the beginning of the 1980s, had French citizenship, and were active as self-employed small businessmen (patrons). The services they offered had no competition in terms of price, as they were able to keep wage costs low by employing illegal workers.

A key role in the organization of work was played by informal middlemen, subcontractors (*muqawillîn*), who at the behest of their patrons looked for workers among the *sans-papiers*; because of their personal contacts, they gave preference to countrymen from Sibrbay. Most middlemen had a residence and work permit; a few even had French citizenship at the beginning of the 21st century. Via cell phones they kept in constant contact with the patrons and the *sans-papiers*, who were employed only on a day-by-day basis. Their circuits led them through the city to the shifting work sites to check on the execution of the jobs and, if necessary, provide additional men and materials. The jobs were contracted by both private individuals and state-owned institutions.

The trust between the patrons, middlemen, and hired painters, the result of their common background, formed the basis of the work organization, since the relationship between employers and employees could not be contractually regulated. The low wages, high flexibility, and relatively low-risk combination of legal economic activity by the patrons and the profitable shadow-economy of the *muqawillîn* and *sans-papiers* allowed the immigrants from Sibrbay after the 1980s to establish themselves in a service sector that had previously been in the hands largely of other immigrants from North Africa.

The third phase of integration began after the legalization of residence status. Advancement within the work hierarchy to a position of *muqawillîn* or patron was now possible. The integration process led to a growing distancing of the group from its country of origin, a result of a diversification of social contacts. At the same time, however, the connection to Egypt could not break off, since it was the reservoir of labor. With the rise in the work hierarchy and a higher income and living standard, the original intention of a permanent return to Egypt slowly receded into the background for many. Those who could afford to do so commuted seasonally between their home region and the destination country.

Müller-Mahn, Detlef. "Ein ägyptisches Dorf in Paris. Eine empirische Studie zur Süd-Nord-Migration am Beispiel ägyptischer 'Sans-papiers' in Frankreich." *IMIS-Beiträge* (2000), no 15: 79–110.

Müller-Mahn, Detlef. *Fellachendörfer. Sozialgeographischer Wandel im ländlichen Ägypten.* Stuttgart, 2001.

Cross-references: France; Maghrebis in France after Decolonization in the 1950s and 1960s

ENGLISH COMEDIANS IN EUROPE IN THE EARLY MODERN PERIOD: THE EXAMPLE OF THE NETHERLANDS

Ton Hoenselaars

During the late 16th century, English actors and musicians – also known as comedians, strolling players, or *Wandertruppen* – began to perform in various places on the European continent. The earliest known group arrived in the autumn of 1585, following their patron Robert Dudley, Earl of Leicester, to the Low Countries. On 23 April 1586, Lord Leicester's men performed the semidramatic, semi-acrobatic show, *The Forces of Hercules*, in the garrison town of Utrecht.

In the following years there was a stream of comedians who sought their fortune in the Low Countries, often on their way to Germany, Denmark, Sweden, and Austria. They performed both in marketplaces and at the royal courts. In 1590, Robert Browne's company played at Leiden and the next year the States General were asked to grant permission for performances of Lord Howard's men in the Dutch provinces of Zealand, Holland, and Frisia. In 1597 new English comedians were seen in Utrecht. Between 1604 and 1607 English actors performed every year at Leiden or at the fair in the Hague. Strolling players from England visited the Continent until well into the 17th century, despite the fact that the Thirty Years' War (1618–48) hampered their movements.

Occasionally the comedians belonged to the retinue of a nobleman like the Earl of Leicester who used them for the purpose of public relations and prestige. Another reason that comedians traveled in England or on the Continent and performed at markets, fairs, or inn yards could be the closure of residential theaters in England due to plague, which forced the players to seek their fortune elsewhere. Furthermore, competition among the glut of entertainment companies in late 16th- and early 17th-century England might have driven the comedians across the English Channel. These well-known reasons for the high mobility of actors, however, fail to account fully for the choice of their destinations. An often-ignored reason that actors crossed the channel was the refusal by the authorities to allow them to travel to England's overseas colonies. The more puritanical investors and settlers had ideological reasons for excluding "Papists and Players," but they also refused them because their colonial expectations were founded on trade and labor, not on idleness, the "sin" for which the English theatrical tradition had been attacked since the mid-16th century. Moreover, they feared that the players might be unpleasantly critical of the colonial enterprise. For these reasons, Puritan preacher and writer William Crashaw stated in his 1609 sermon addressed to the Lord Governor and Captain General of Virginia: "we send all trades to Virginia, but will send no players."

The English comedians performed a specific type of drama: with stage images and movement it appealed to the eye, and the ear was graced with music. In this way they avoided the language barrier and often left a deep impression on their audience. Thus, it was reported that during a performance in Amsterdam a woman in the audience witnessed a murder played out on stage and was so deeply moved that she confessed a murder that she herself had committed 12 years before.

Such spectacular performances, as well as the commercial success of the English comedians, attracted the attention of the ancient Chambers of Rhetoric in the Low Countries, where gifted amateurs from the upper middle classes gathered to write and recite poetry in private, while only rarely performing plays in public. It was not without envy that the rhetoricians from The Eglantine and The White Lavender chambers looked down on these professional and commercial players who, rather than observe the elevated, classical ideals of the *ars retorica*, kept the audience riveted with conjuring tricks, pantomime, song, and dance. However, the chambers were forced to take the English players seriously, as they managed after all to be successful both with the man in the street and with royalty across Europe. In 1610, the chambers offered the public an opportunity to attend their own indoor events, including plays that were presented on a repertory basis.

While taking the cue from the traveling comedians by starting a commercial repertory theater system in the Low Countries, the representatives of the Amsterdam Chambers remained ambivalent toward the English actors. In a speech to his fellow members at The Eglantine chamber, the local playwright G. A. Bredero argued that there might be one or two fairly good players among the English comedians, but added that most of them were "wooden actors," "riffraff," and without any proper sense of morality. In his comedy entitled *Moortje*, Bredero let his characters articulate both the aversion to and the admiration for the strolling players from across the channel.

English comedians gave rise to a number of changes elsewhere in the Low Countries. In Leiden, for example, a Dutch traveling company named Bataviersche Comedianten was founded in 1617 following the English model. These Dutch performers traveled to the local fairs and across the national borders to Germany and Denmark, taking over many of the English routines and tricks, while enjoying the advantage of being able to communicate with the Dutch audience in their own language. Nevertheless, the Dutch and English troupes were not rivals, and collaboration was common practice, especially after the outbreak of the Thirty Years' War in 1618. Travel in Europe was a hazardous matter, and so the English and Dutch companies in the Low Countries tended to work more closely together, even if each sometimes put its own interests first. This collaboration provides the best explanation for the occurrence of similar characters in different European stage traditions. The character of Pickelherring, for example, which resembles various types of the commedia dell'arte, also occurs in slightly modified form as Hans Stockfish, Hans Supp, Jean Potage, Hans Leberwurst, and John Sausage.

International collaboration also accounts for the emergence of London stage plays on the Continental stages. By way of the English strolling players, the Utrecht rhetorician Adriaan van den Bergh probably became acquainted with Shakespeare's *Titus Andronicus*, and with Thomas Kyd's *The Spanish Tragedy*, of which Van den Bergh made an adaptation, entitled *Don Jeronimo*, that he performed at his Utrecht chamber in 1626. He also founded a traveling theater company. His fame, however, also rests on his daughter Adriana, who, given the absence of rules against female participation in the theater, joined her father's traveling company at an early age. With the experience thus gained, Adriana van den Bergh became the first professional Dutch "actress." In 1654 she made her first appearance on the stage of the Municipal Theater of Amsterdam, acting the part of Katherina in a Dutch translation of *The Taming of the Shrew*. This play, the first Shakespeare comedy performed in the Low Countries, reached the official stage through the international strolling player circuit to which the Van den Berghs had belonged for decades.

The Amsterdam rhetoricians' highbrow aversion to the English comedians has long determined our perception of the early modern theater companies that toured the European continent. Only in recent years have theater historians been able to fit the English comedians into a nomadic reading of culture. They have come to recognize the traveling circuit as a site for the training of female actors and to appreciate it as a place for unique theatrical enterprises that were professional in commercial terms, as well as multidisciplinary and international.

Albach, Ben. *Langs kermissen en hoven. Ontstaan en kroniek van een Nederlands toneelgezelschap in de 17de eeuw.* Zutphen, 1977.

Bachrach, Alfred Gustave Herbert. "Bredero en de Engelse Toneelspelers." In *Rondom Bredero. Een viertal verkenningen*, edited by A. G. H. Bachrach et al., 71–89. Culemborg, 1970.

Cohn, Albert. *Shakespeare in Germany in the Sixteenth and Seventeenth Century: An Account of English Actors in Germany and the Netherlands and of the Plays Performed by Them during the Same Period.* London, 1865.

Hoenselaars, Ton. "The Pollicie of Playes Is Very Necessary: *The Tempest* and the Idle Players in the New World." In *L'Oisiveté au temps de la Renaissance*, edited by Marie-Thérèse Jones-Davies, 181–208. Paris, 2002.

Hoenselaars, Ton, and Jan Frans van Dijkhuizen. "Abraham Sybant Tames The Taming of the Shrew for the Amsterdam Stage (1654)." *Ilha do desterro: A Journal of English Language, Literatures in English, and Cultural Studies* 36 (1999): 53–70.

Limon, Jerzy. *Gentlemen of a Company: English Players in Central and Eastern Europe, 1590–1660.* Cambridge, 1985.

Riewald, J. G. "New Light on the English Actors in the Netherlands." *English Studies* 41 (1960): 65–92.

Schrickx, Willem. "Pickelherring and the English Actors in Germany." *Shakespeare Survey* 36 (1983): 135–47.

Cross-references: Great Britain; The Netherlands; Comici dell'arte in Europe in the Early Modern Period

ENGLISH INDUSTRIAL WORKERS (PUDDLERS) IN THE BELGIAN IRON INDUSTRY IN THE EARLY 19TH CENTURY

Wim Lefebvre, Sofie De Caigny, and Erik Buyst

When France conquered the "Belgian" provinces in 1793, they introduced the ideals and principles of the French Revolution that would later shape the Belgian nation. The abolition of the guilds, the access to the French market, and the continental blockade against British products stimulated industrial development in Belgium. Foreign, mostly British, engineers and workers played an important role in setting up new industries since the export of new technologies from Britain was prohibited. The immigration of British puddlers in Belgium, which lasted about 30 years (around 1820–50), is a typical example of this type of labor migration. As the Walloon part of Belgium had a geophysical structure almost identical to that of the British Midlands, these workers found coal and iron ore deposits there very similar to those at home.

Puddling is a manual way of refining pig iron into wrought iron. Since it was an extremely difficult and heavy job and a crucial process in iron production of the 19th century, the puddler was one of the most important industrial workers at that time. English workers were active in Belgium in an early stage, since it was the first country on the Continent to adopt the new British method of iron production.

Puddlers often emigrated in groups to Belgium, France, and Germany, but they were forced to split up once they arrived on the Continent, having to work in different regions. They nonetheless kept in close contact with each other. Most of them were paid laborers, who spent part of their life working in Belgian, French, or German iron factories and later returning to their native countries. They were recruited by friends or relatives already employed in a continental iron factory. Others simply tried their luck, moving frequently from one place to another in search of the highest wages. Unfortunately, the number of these industrial workers migrating into continental Europe is unknown, nor is it certain how many brought their families with them.

Impoverished English puddlers were attracted by the higher wages on the Continent, even before the abolition in 1824 of an act prohibiting the emigration of skilled workers from Britain. Both push and pull factors determined the immigration of English puddlers in Belgium. Many puddlers were working at low wages in Lancashire iron industries. Around 1830, English puddlers earned 50% more in Belgium than in their homeland. On the other hand, Belgian entrepreneurs needed skilled workers to introduce the puddling process to their factories. Importing machines, blueprints, and books was not adequate to pass on the technology, since the technical terminology of puddling was vague. The craft was passed on to others mostly by practical experience. Moreover, the transfer of British technologies to the Continent was prohibited until 1843. Foreign puddlers were therefore needed to instruct local workers.

Both their superior technological knowledge, compared to indigenous laborers, and their higher wages gave the English puddlers a high sense of self-esteem. Puddlers were at the top of the wage hierarchy in the Belgian iron industry, initially earning seven to eight times the average wage of local workmen. During the first half of the 19th century, however, this wage divergence gradually diminished. Their high wages and self-esteem, combined with their short stay in Belgian host communities, stood in the way of a smooth integration. Most important, they were unwilling to learn the language of the country where they worked and lived. The local population often saw this high conception of personal worth as arrogance. Contrary to this negative image in the local community was a high appreciation by the national government for these industrial immigrants. Their contributions to industrial development were seen as an essential stimulus factor, accelerating the pace of the national economy.

Because of their relatively short stay and limited integration, English industrial workers left hardly a trace in Belgium, neither in daily life nor in the archives. A few of them, however, managed to become important industrialists in Belgium and never went back to their native country. Best known, even today, is William Cockerill, an impoverished Lancashire laborer who had wandered through Sweden and Russia but ultimately landed in the textile factory of Simonis-Biolley in Verviers in 1798. William and, more important, his son John managed to build an industrial empire; they started with the production of machines for textile production but soon expanded their activity to other industries. In 1817, John Cockerill opened in Seraing the first vertically integrated iron factory on the Continent, with its own mines, coke ovens, and machine construction sites. Twenty years later it had become the world's largest iron plant, employing over 2,000 laborers. Other examples of successful English industrialists are Thomas Bonehill and James Hodson. They rapidly grew rich and soon even were influential in Belgian politics. These entrepreneurs not only kept in close contact with the industrialists in Britain but also with each other, creating strong networks. An example of this is the marriage of two sons of William Cockerill with the daughters of Pastor, an English engineer. Before that, Cockerill's daughter Nancy had already married James Hodson.

As a rule, however, English craftsmen did not stay permanently in Belgium. Puddlers played a significant role in the Belgian iron production, but only for a relatively short period. They helped start up new plants but moved on once they had trained a sufficient number of indigenous puddlers and became superfluous. Around the middle of the 19th century, most of these engineers and workers had returned to Britain.

Chlepner, Ben Serge. "L'étranger dans l'histoire économique de la Belgique." *ULB. Revue de l'Institut de Sociologie* 11 (1931): 695–734.

Fremdling, Rainer. "The Puddler: A Craftsman's Skills and the Spread of a New Technology in Belgium, France and

Germany." *Journal of European Economic History* 20 (1991): 529–67.

Lemoine, Robert J. "Les étrangers et la formation du capitalisme en Belgique." *Revue d'histoire économique et sociale* 20 (1932): 252–336.

Cross-references: Belgium and Luxembourg; Great Britain

ENGLISH PURITAN REFUGEES IN THE NETHERLANDS IN THE 16TH AND 17TH CENTURIES

Ronald G. Asch

"Puritans" refers to those English Protestants of the late 16th and 17th centuries who opposed the official Church of England with various degrees of intensity, because they believed that the Reformation was incomplete even after the "Elizabethan settlement" in 1558–9. While a few radical splinter groups (Separatists) formally broke away from the Church of England, most remained within the state church until the Civil War of 1642–9, though they found themselves repeatedly confronted by church and state measures that sought to coerce them into religious conformity. A considerable number of Puritans, both clergy and laity, escaped these measures – especially from the 1580s on – by seeking refuge abroad, primarily in the northern Netherlands and later also in North America.

As a result of close trading relationships with England that existed already before the outbreak of the Dutch revolt at the end of the 1560s, numerous settlements of English merchants existed in the northern Netherlands and, until the reconquest of these regions by Spanish troops in the 1580s, also in the south, especially in Antwerp. Moreover, in 1585, Queen Elizabeth had placed several regiments – initially about 6,000 soldiers – at the disposal of the Dutch Republic, and they remained stationed in the Netherlands after the Dutch-Spanish truce of 1609. In return, England had been given control (until 1616) of the cities of Vlissingen and Brielle/Den Briel, which were home to a few sizable English congregations that included civilians alongside soldiers. Beginning in 1603, the date of the personal union of England and Scotland, Scotsmen also served in the treaty regiments, which had an authorized strength of 13,000 soldiers. In addition, several thousand British soldiers and officers served as mercenaries in the regular army of the Republic. Last, Dutch universities, especially Leiden and later also Utrecht, were a strong magnet for British students.

Thus, even before the beginning of a religiously motivated emigration, many Britishers lived in the Netherlands at least temporarily, and in the 17th century, the flight from religious persecution was often all but impossible to distinguish from emigration that was driven largely by economic motives. That is the reason the scale of the Puritan emigration cannot be quantified, especially since in the Netherlands, English Puritans (those who were not Separatists) and Scottish Presbyterians – who prior to 1660 rarely had any reason to

The harbor district of Rotterdam with the stock exchange in the middle. Numerous Scots traded here (*Gemeentearchief Rotterdam*).

leave their country for religious reasons – often belonged to the same congregations.

We do know, however, that the official English Reformed Church in Amsterdam had a total of 450 members in 1623. In addition to this community, to whom the city had given a church of its own in 1607 in the old courtyard of the Beguines, there were five other English churches in Amsterdam. Leiden in 1609 had a total of 200 British families, who petitioned for a church of their own; Vlissingen had 128 in 1619, Utrecht somewhat fewer with 120 in 1622, and Delft around 70 in 1636. Other English settlements are found at this time above all in Middelburg, Utrecht, the Hague, Rotterdam (around 1640, the English church here numbered about 1,000), Dordrecht, and Brielle/Den Briel. All told, there must have been several tens of thousands of individuals of British origin in the Dutch Republic, though by no means did all of them belong to a separate English or British church, nor had they all come to the Netherlands for religious reasons. Moreover, many thought of their sojourn in the republic as merely temporary.

For those who did in fact feel persecuted in their homeland as Puritans, the Netherlands must have been attractive not only for its geographic proximity. The Dutch provinces and cities pursued a relatively tolerant policy toward most religious minorities; moreover, de facto the creed and, at least formally, the church constitution of the official Calvinist Church of the republic accorded with the ideals of most English Puritans. In addition, before the beginning of the exodus there were already a few Puritan-minded clergy in the Netherlands, who were either employed by the trading company of the Merchant Adventurers (as for example the well-known theologian Thomas Cartwright, who was chaplain to the Adventurers in Antwerp and Middelburg from 1580 to 1585) or served as army chaplains in the English regiments. As a rule, the emigrants came from the urban milieu; they were artisans, small tradesman, and merchants, more rarely peasants and farmers, who could hardly hope to acquire land favorably in the Netherlands and later tended to emigrate to America instead. Still, there is likely to have been some emigration from the social strata below the peasants.

While most English Puritans tended to leave alone or accompanied only by their family, the so-called Separatists – radical Protestants who rejected any state or national church and formed communities composed only of the "elect" – often left their homeland in larger groups. The first Separatists to settle in the Netherlands in 1582 were about 100 Puritans from Norwich, who initially formed a congregation in Middelburg. Their leaders were Robert Browne (whence "Brownists" or Dutch *bruynisten*) and Robert Harrison. However, the Separatists, whose presence was frowned upon by the town authorities, soon moved to Amsterdam, where a Separatist congregation would endure until the end of the 17th century, in spite of internal divisions, schisms, and intense hostility from Presbyterian and English clergy. Some also turned to the Baptists and a part of them joined the Dutch Mennonites. Another group of Separatists, also around 100 individuals, had settled in Leiden in 1609 under the leadership of pastor John Robinson.

When the Church of England returned more strongly to pre-Reformation traditions in the 1620s – and especially the 1630s – during the reign of King Charles I (1625–9), the pressure on the Puritan wing of the church increased. Emigration to the Netherlands thus intensified especially after 1629. London and the east of England (a stronghold of Puritanism) seem to have been particularly important as areas from which the emigrants originated. Prominent Puritan clergy, though they were now more likely Congregationalists than Puritans, sought refuge in the Netherlands, and some members of their congregations followed them. Bishop Wren of Norwich alone supposedly expelled 3,000 Puritan-minded believers – several hundred, for sure – from his diocese during his tenure (1635–8), though in this case, as well, it is difficult to distinguish confessional from economic motivations for the exodus. Most found refuge in the Netherlands, some in other European countries, and no small number made it to America.

Beginning in the 1640s, when the rule of Charles I collapsed, many clergy and laity made their way back to England from the Netherlands, while emigration to the Netherlands largely came to a halt. After 1660, however, a new crop of pastors arrived in the Dutch Republic from the circles of the Dissenters, the successors to the Puritans. Many had lost their parishes in England following the Restoration. The religious refugees were joined – especially in the 1680s – by prominent political opponents to Stuart rule, like the Earl of Shaftesbury; however, this was by no means a mass exodus, especially since the military conflicts between England and the Netherlands after 1660 made migration more difficult. A stronger outflow now began from Scotland, where the radical Presbyterians, the so-called Covenanters, suffered persecution at the hands of the Episcopal Church. Especially Rotterdam, long a center of Scottish immigrants to the Netherlands, admitted many Covenanters, who around 1690 had their own church with

This map by Joan Blaeu from 1649 gives an impression of Rotterdam from the south, with the Scottish colony at the left bottom (*Gemeentearchief Rotterdam*).

about 1,000 congregants. Next to Rotterdam, Leeuwarden as well as Amsterdam and Utrecht had larger congregations of Scottish immigrants in the later 17th century, though no small number of their members returned to Scotland after the Glorious Revolution of 1688.

Puritan immigrants were generally given a friendly reception in the Netherlands. Theologically close to the Dutch Calvinist Church, some of the English-speaking congregations – for example, the Reformed Congregation of Amsterdam – early on directly joined the Dutch church and its local "classes" (unions of several local congregations below the level of the provincial synod which jointly assumed the tasks of church governance). Other congregations – the majority – temporarily united into a separate English Synod between 1621 and 1633, which was recognized by the Estates-General as part of the Calvinist church. After the dissolution of the Synod, most congregations were directly joined to the official Dutch church, even if the English and Scottish congregations in Rotterdam, for example, retained a relatively high degree of independence.

Less clear was the position of the Separatists and other sects, especially the Quakers, who were initially even sporadically persecuted by the Dutch authorities on account of their radicalism. At any rate, the sects generally could not count on support from the Dutch state. For the most part, however, the less radical English and Scottish congregations chose to subordinate themselves at least formally to the public church in the Netherlands as a way of avoiding the threat of supervision by the local authorities. Incidentally, the Puritan clergy active in the Netherlands in turn exerted a considerable influence on the development of the church in England, because they were able to have works printed in the Dutch Republic that would have fallen victim to censorship in England. Before 1640 and again after 1660, cities like Amsterdam and Rotterdam were centers of an extensive Puritan network that reached all the way to America.

The first generation of immigrants – that was especially true of the clergy, much less so of the merchants among the congregants – generally had no or only an inadequate command of Dutch. From the second half of the 17th century, however, some clergy had already grown up in the Netherlands and had studied there, and a few English theologians even held lectureships at Dutch universities. Finally, after 1660–70, the church records of the English congregation in Amsterdam, for example, show that even its office-holders had adopted Dutch phrases and forms of expression and had in part forgotten their own language. Marriages between Englishmen and Dutch women – the reverse seems to have been rarer or is less frequently documented – were numerous from the beginning. In those instances, however, the wives often remained official members of their original congregation, a situation that led to complications in marital disputes, since, for example, the presbyteries and consistories of the English congregations punished violence by a husband against his wife much more leniently or not at all, in contrast to the Dutch religious authorities. Conversely, initially the English congregations often insisted on a strict observance of Sunday and also applied other principles of church discipline against sin with special rigor. As the decades went by, however, they usually adapted themselves to the prevailing Dutch practice.

As the numerically significant migration from England into the Netherlands came to an end around the middle of the 17th century, most English congregations went into decline. After 1660, especially in the smaller communities, English-speaking Dutchmen were a significant portion of the congregants. Most congregations lost their earlier importance completely after 1690, when emigration from Scotland also dried up. Around 1700, only 12 of what had originally been around 30 English or British congregations in the Netherlands still existed, and two of those have survived to this day, the English Reformed Church in Amsterdam and the Scots Church in Rotterdam. In the 18th century, however, the clergy of the English-speaking congregations in the Netherlands were all Scottish Presbyterians, since it was no longer possible to recruit any new blood in England.

Catterall, Douglas. *Community without Borders: Scots Migrants and the Changing Face of Power in the Dutch Republic, c. 1600–1700.* Leiden, 2002.

Clare Carter, Alice. *The English Reformed Church in Amsterdam in the Seventeenth Century.* Amsterdam, 1964.

Coggins, James Robert. *John Smyth's Congregation: English Separatism, Mennonite Influence and the Elect Nation.* Waterloo, Ontario, 1991.

Collinson, Patrick. *The Elizabethan Puritan Movement.* Oxford, 1967.

Sprunger, Keith L. *Dutch Puritanism: A History of English and Scottish Churches in the Netherlands in the Sixteenth and Seventeenth Centuries.* Leiden, 1982.

Watts, Michael. *The Dissenters: From the Reformation to the French Revolution.* Oxford, 1978.

Cross-references: Great Britain; The Netherlands; Scottish Soldiers in Europe in the Early Modern Period

ENGLISH AND SCOTTISH SETTLERS IN IRELAND SINCE THE EARLY MODERN PERIOD

Nicholas Canny

Ireland had been subject to the authority of the English crown since the 12th century, and this subjugation brought with it a significant migration of people of Anglo-Norman origin. The descendants of the Anglo-Norman invaders were to dominate political life in the eastern parts of the country until the 16th century; in addition, many farmers, traders, and artisans, also Anglo-Norman descendants, settled in these areas with their families. These people constituted the largest element in the population of Irish towns until the 17th century and, in the 21st century, still form a substantial element of the farming population in the more fertile low-lying areas of the eastern part of the country.

Throughout the medieval centuries, political and cultural connections were maintained between the Gaelic lordships in Ulster (Ireland's northern province) and the Gaelic regions in the highlands and islands of Scotland. This connection also led to significant population movement from Scotland to Ireland, especially by fighting men who put themselves at the service of Gaelic Irish lords either for money or the assignment of land within the various Gaelic lordships. One Scottish Gaelic family, the McDonalds, ultimately established themselves as the dominant ruling family of the northeast coast of Ulster. Their right to rule there was formally recognized by the English crown after 1603 when their Scottish overlord, King James VI of Scotland, become King James I of England.

The descendants of these Anglo-Norman immigrants continued to be recognizable as a group. The first generation of Anglo-Normans had justified their 12th-century incursion into Ireland on religious and moral grounds, and their descendants continued, even into the 16th century, to identify themselves as the upholders of the interests of the English crown in Ireland. Furthermore, they adhered to the theory, at least until English rulers assumed the title of kings (or queens), as opposed to lords, of Ireland in 1541, that their purpose in Ireland was to assist the English crown with the completion of the conquest of Ireland that had been started by King Henry II in 1172. Their claim to distinctiveness and elevated position was rendered credible by their use of English as their preferred language and by their adherence to the principles of English common law and to English administrative procedures. Their noble leaders took part in England's strife over succession to the throne, even while they simultaneously competed with lords of Gaelic ancestry and against dynastic rivals within the anglicized community in Ireland. These immigrants were also a recognizable group because of their Anglo-Norman surnames (e.g., Fitzgerald,

Butler, Burke, Power, etc.) and because they referred to themselves as the "English in Ireland" or the "English-Irish."

They also remained a visible migrant group in the eyes of others. Gaelic leaders continued to regard the Anglo-Normans as intruders upon their ancestral lands. Gaelic lords might, when it suited their purposes, intermarry with Anglo-Norman families, but they generally identified with the political principle that they were obliged to resist and to reverse the Anglo-Norman partial conquest, as their ancestors had resisted the Norse Viking invaders.

Such tendencies toward separation and resistance in the Gaelic population did not hold true for Scots-Gaelic settlers in Ireland. By contrast, they were in Ireland at the invitation of Gaelic lords, and they belonged to the same cultural and linguistic group. Scots of Gaelic ancestry introduced a new range of surnames to Ireland (McDonnell, Sweeney, Sheehy, and Fleming, e.g.), and until 1603, they were persistently regarded by both the English crown and the anglicized population of Ireland as a foreign presence that had no entitlement to be involved in Irish politics and warfare, much less to settle there permanently.

The composition of the population of Ireland became more and more diverse during the early modern period. The English government strove to advance its authority at the expense of local potentates in complete disregard of the cultural background of the population. Lords of Anglo-Norman descent, conscious of their political independence, tended to resist the English policy of centralization until it was decided in London to administer the country through loyal English-born officials and soldiers. Another critical factor that contributed to crown preference for "New English" over the "English-Irish" (who at this point came to be known as the "Old English") was that the Old English remained adamantly attached to Catholicism rather than conforming to the Protestant church favored by the English state. The crown always rejected the Old English contention that their confessional preference in no way compromised their political loyalty. This argument was further exposed as threadbare when a series of provincial lords, initially of Anglo-Norman extraction but ultimately also of Gaelic ancestry, invoked the 1570 Papal bull of excommunication of Queen Elizabeth to justify the withdrawal of their allegiance to the English crown and their entry into political alliance with England's continental enemies (above all, France and Spain). This development, added to a series of rebellions, explains why successive English governments over the period 1580–1690, undertook a policy of establishing English settlers after the suppression of these rebellions to pacify Ireland.

Plantation migrations

The series of military campaigns and ensuing settlement resulted in the transfer of at least 80% of the land from Catholic to Protestant ownership and a corresponding shift of political power into Protestant hands. In an effort to increase the Protestant presence – and this proved especially successful in towns – substantial numbers were induced to move to Ireland from England and the Scottish lowlands. According to the best estimates, the total migration from England and the Protestant areas of lowland Scotland into Ireland over this interlude reached a possible maximum of 310,000 people, and this was composed of possibly 180,000 English (including Welsh) migrants, and 130,000 Protestant migrants from lowland Scotland. In both instances the larger portion of the migration happened after 1650, and the largest population flow from Scotland was a phenomenon of the 1690s. The scale and impact of the migration that occurred becomes evident when it is placed against the total population of Ireland – it grew from around 1 million in 1600 to 2 million in 1700.

English, Welsh, and lowland Scottish immigrants were found at all levels of society. They occupied positions as administrators and in the military (which was retained to uphold English authority in Ireland), worked as traders and artisans, and farmed as tenants on the estates that fell into Protestant possession. The most prominent immigrants were those who became members of the new elite as landowners, army officers, and officials in state or church. Besides being socially prominent, these leaders were also the instigators of a larger scale migration, since proprietors of plantations had a contractual obligation to populate their estates with settlers. The essential requirement of the government was that these settlers be "British Protestants" who would also be capable of improving the economy of the country because of their mastery of agricultural or manufacturing skills. Proprietors were also obliged to found villages and market towns on their properties, and to settle traders and artisans. The planters were not indifferent to the confessional requirement, but their principal concern was to recruit people who could be relied upon both to pay rent for their farms and to improve their holdings. The astute landlords quickly learned that their interests were best served if they concentrated on the recruitment of artisans and professionals who would both pay rents for the properties they leased in the plantation towns and would simultaneously lease and improve farms in the vicinity of these towns.

Despite their control of the land, Protestants were, for the most part, town dwellers. They were present in large numbers in Dublin, which was both the administrative capital and the chief port of Ireland, but also in the few port towns of the south and of Ulster, and in the multitude of garrison and administrative towns that came to dot the countryside.

The Protestant ascendancy

These migrants formed the core of the Protestant community that was to dominate Ireland for the 18th and much of the 19th century, and whose members aspired to govern the Northern Ireland state to the close of the 20th century. Their belief that Protestantism was the only "true religion" justified, in their view, their dominance over their "eternally damned" Irish Catholic neighbors, who outnumbered them by at least three to one in the 18th century. The fact that they, over the course of a short period of time, monopolized political power and enjoyed a privileged position in the economy seemed to provide tangible proof of this proposition. Intermarriage with Catholics was always discouraged by Protestant divines.

The clergy were diverse. There were zealous English Protestants, either immigrants or the children of settlers, who as a rule graduated from Trinity College, Dublin, which early on established a reputation for being a dogmatic Protestant institution. In the case of Ulster, Presbyterian ministers, usually graduates of the Scottish universities, served the spiritual needs of many of the Ulster population of Scottish ancestry, despite the existence in every parish of Protestant clergy from the official Church of Ireland. The presence of Presbyterian ministers makes it clear that despite a shared opposition to, and dread of, Catholicism, the Protestant community in Ireland was a fractured body. Besides the sizable Presbyterian element of Scottish descent in Ulster, there was a significant number of Protestant dissenters in the country at large. In the 17th century, these minority groups were made up principally of Quakers and Baptists, most of whom arrived with the conquest pursued by Oliver Cromwell in 1649. The Irish Protestant community of the 18th century also incorporated continental refugees, both Huguenots and inhabitants of the Palatinate, who were perceived by English and Irish Protestants alike as innocent victims of the tyranny of Louis XIV of France.

Each of the elements within this Protestant community retained its distinctive identity for a considerable time. Huguenots, for example, were permitted to have their own French-language Calvinist services conducted by their own ministers so long as these took place within Church of Ireland buildings. Language, together with memories of a common fate, set the Huguenots apart as a closely knit immigrant community for much of the 18th century, but they were gradually assimilated into the Church of Ireland community principally through intermarriage. They remained visible as a distinctive group only in those few communities, notably Portarlington in the Queen's County, which were pure Huguenot settlements. The inhabitants of the Palatinate, primarily those settled in County Limerick, also retained their linguistic and confessional distinctiveness until well into the 18th century, when they turned more toward Methodism and away from the Church of Ireland. Quakers differed in their dress code, rigid discipline, and consciousness of belonging to a wider commercial network that spanned the Atlantic. These connections were sustained both by networks of correspondence and by visits from male and female itinerant preachers. Some of the more financially successful Quakers entertained advantageous marriages outside their congregation, usually to members of the Church of Ireland, and suffered ostracization for doing so.

By contrast, the identity of members of the Church of Ireland was the least threatened because theirs was the legally defined established church, which was present in every area. Moreover, their clergy and church organizations (including Trinity College, Dublin) were maintained both by landed estates and by tithes collected from the entire farming population of the country regardless of their own confessional preference. The most privileged of the community (besides the clergy) were Church of Ireland Protestants who commanded wealth, whether urban or rural. They alone enjoyed full membership of town corporations and full participation in elections to the Irish Parliament of the 18th century. Political control also meant access to privilege and position in Great Britain and its expanding empire. As a result, the poor in the Church of Ireland community enjoyed a more advantageous position than their equivalents in the other Protestant confessions.

The one group from within the Irish Protestant community who aspired to challenge the dominance of the Church of Ireland were the Presbyterians of Scottish ancestry, who became more numerous after the final great influx of the 1690s. Their ethnic distinctiveness was heightened by the continued use of Scottish dialect and of Scottish attire mainly by the less elevated among their ranks, while the purity of their Presbyterianism was sustained by prolonged spiritual contacts with Scotland and its universities. Since the mid-17th century, the Presbyterians aspired to have their religion on an equal footing with Church of Ireland Protestantism. However, all they attained was a semi-official status conceded by King Charles II (1660–85), whereby they received some monetary support from the crown for the payment of ministers and the maintenance of their churches. They were, however, still obliged to pay the tithe to the Church of Ireland and to have their marriages registered by the clergy of that church. They had good reason to expect an improvement on this position after the victory of William of Orange's forces over those of the Catholic King James II in 1690; the incoming monarchs were known to be sympathetic to Calvinism, Ulster Protestants had been steadfast in their support for William against James, and Protestants were now more numerous than ever before, particularly in the province of Ulster. The disappointment of these aspirations for equality created considerable disenchantment among Presbyterians, which was principally expressed by resistance to tithe payment, particularly during years of bad harvest.

While fractures within the Irish Protestant community persisted for a considerable time, fission was avoided, at least until the close of the 18th century. All elements recognized that, as Protestants, they had more in common with each other than with Irish Catholics. In addition it was accepted among Protestants that historical experience had demonstrated that they had been forced to endure a Catholic uprising every half century. Moreover, Catholics were seen to derive moral sustenance from their kinsfolk living in exile in Catholic Europe, and the hope that, in the event of Britain's forces being defeated in the wars on the Continent, these exiles would return in arms to release the Catholic Irish from Protestant overlordship. The Catholic army of France maintained an Irish regiment that was replenished through recruitment from Ireland. The Catholic Church, and many Catholics in Ireland, continued to recognize the exiled Stuarts as their legitimate monarchs until well into the 18th century. The Protestant admission that Catholics were not reconciled to their loss of power and status, and that Gaelic authors as well as Catholic priests cultivated a memory of their past independence and political strength, reminded Protestants of their vulnerability. However, because Protestants held all positions of power, it seemed that they would be exposed to overthrow only if they became divided among themselves. Protestants were therefore regularly reminded by the state and church of the proven animosity that Catholics in Ireland felt toward Protestants and Protestantism. Protestant cohesion was also fostered by the cultivation of the memory of King William, whose timely intervention in Ireland had supposedly saved Irish Protestants from yet another bloody massacre.

A historical irony lay in this cultivation of the memory of King William, because Irish Protestants who had lived through the 1690s in fact felt embittered by their treatment at the hands of King William and his associates. This, they contended, had placed the Irish Protestant interest in jeopardy, first by conceding excessively generous terms to their Jacobite opponents when the Williamites had achieved total victory, and second by granting much of the property of the defeated supporters of King James to favorites of King William, including the royal mistress, rather than to Irish Protestants who had most endured the heat of battle. It was this sense of betrayal that persuaded Irish Protestants that they must look primarily to their own resources to prevent the "further growth of Popery."

The leaders of this Protestant community in Ireland therefore pressed for legislation to curb the political influence of Catholicism. The ensuing enactments came to be known as "Popery laws" or "Penal laws" and were designed to uphold the Protestant interest in perpetuity. Those who supported this legislation, partly gained in defiance of the British administration, had taken the first step on the road to becoming "patriots," a stance much admired by Irish Protestants. Among the factors that gave rise to such "patriotism" were resentment over English curtailments on the independence and integrity of Irish institutions and concern over the appointment of English government favorites to hold senior positions in the administration of the Irish church and state. The challenge of the patriots led to acrimonious debates, but this, in turn, fostered unity among Protestants of different confessions while it also enhanced the reputation of those who were willing to stand against English "interference" as well as against Irish Papists.

19th-century challenges

The fight against influence from London and against Irish Catholics held the Irish Protestant community together until the close of the 18th century. Thereafter a significant rift occurred, leading to the 1798 insurrection, when radicals from within the Church of Ireland allied with alienated Ulster Presbyterians and many disenchanted Catholics to lay claim to political equality such as had been enunciated by the French Revolution. The crushing of that revolt and the subsequent passage of the Act of Union cementing Britain with Ireland into a single UK, seemed to have salvaged the dominant position of Irish Protestants and underlined the need for unity. Despite that, some Irish Protestant radicals continued to make common cause with Catholics during the course of the 19th century, as Catholics advanced successive bids first for political emancipation from the Penal Laws, then for an improvement of the legal position of tenant farmers relative to their landlords, and finally for a greater degree of autonomy for Ireland within the Union.

However, the number of Protestants who identified with such issues dwindled over the course of time, more particularly as the expanding franchise of the later 19th century added a new political significance to the numerical minority of Protestants in Ireland. Therefore Catholic demands for an improvement in their position provoked a mobilization of Protestants to defend their own interests. The most significant of such mobilizations was the resistance to the passing of a Home Rule Bill for Ireland. But despite appeals for unity, many pragmatic Protestants recognized that they could not resist indefinitely. They settled for an arrangement whereby six of Ulster's counties – in which there was a clear Protestant majority – would be under Protestant self-administration. The price of this security was the independence, after 1922, of the remaining 26 counties of Ireland, and with it the abandonment of the Protestant minority in that jurisdiction to the Catholic majority who held sway in the new state.

20th-century realities

The initial enthusiasm for the creation of "a Protestant parliament for a Protestant people" was so great that the social cleavages and the confessional differences that existed within the ranks of Northern Ireland Protestantism could safely be ignored. Under those circumstances politicized Protestantism in Northern Ireland assumed a patrician aspect up to the 1960s enabled by favorable economic conditions, bolstered largely by shipbuilding and aircraft construction, both of which enjoyed a boom during the Second World War and the postwar reconstruction of Europe. A common front and common identity was also facilitated by Protestant organizations such as the "Orange Order," which were open to Protestant men of all social categories, and which evoked unity through the commemoration of past victories and the anticipation of others to come.

However, once the boom was over and recession set in, leading to the collapse of the industrial sector of Northern Ireland, the days of Protestant power were numbered. Its authority eroded as the legitimacy of the polity of Northern Ireland was challenged from two sides: by Catholics who contended they had been denied their civil rights, and by self-styled Republicans determined to destroy it by force. Under these circumstances the united front, which Protestantism in Ireland had always previously presented whenever its authority was challenged, became fragmented. Thereafter, all that united the Protestant community in Northern Ireland was a detestation of Catholicism and a pride in their earlier political, economic, and social importance for Ireland. Moreover, as Protestants in Northern Ireland assumed ever more dogmatic positions, they increased the distance between themselves and their co-religionists in Independent Ireland. The latter group had suffered an initial decrease in their numbers after the independence of the Irish Free State as many, especially in the public service, withdrew to Britain or to Northern Ireland. Their numbers, especially in rural areas, were further depleted through intermarriage with Catholic partners, whose children were more likely to be raised as Catholics than as Protestants. Those who endured as Protestants in Independent Ireland tended to be the more affluent and the city dwellers who, in the second half of the 20th century made the accommodation necessary to survive in a Catholic, and ultimately in a more pluralist society. For these and for many middle-class Protestants in Northern Ireland, it was difficult to identify themselves with the militant Protestant anti-Catholicism of previous decades. Such militant organizations remained, into the 21st century, a bulwark for those Protestants in Northern Ireland who saw themselves threatened by globalization and the increasing local pluralistic political options and lifestyles being forced upon them by external and internal pressures. Even these, however, have recently abandoned their intransigence and have entered into power sharing relationships with their former Catholic and Republican enemies.

Barnard, Toby. *A New Anatomy of Ireland: The Irish Protestants, 1649–1770*. New Haven and London, 2003.

Canny, Nicholas. *Making Ireland British, 1580–1650*. Oxford, 2001.

Canny, Nicholas, ed. *Europeans on the Move: Studies on European Migration, 1500–1800*. Oxford, 1994.

Connolly, Sean J. *Religion, Law and Power: The Making of Protestant Ireland, 1660–1760*. Oxford, 1992.

Jackson, Alvin. *Home Rule: An Irish History, 1800–2000*. London, 2003.

McBride, Ian. *Scripture Politics: Ulster Presbyterians and Irish Radicalism in the Late Eighteenth Century*. Oxford, 1998.

Tyler Blethen, H., and Curtis W. Wood, Jr., eds. *Ulster and North America: Transatlantic Perspectives on the Scotch-Irish*. Tuscaloosa, AL, 1997.

Cross-references: Great Britain; Ireland and Northern Ireland; Huguenots in Europe since the 16th Century; Jacobites in Europe, 1688–1788; Palatines in Europe since the 17th Century

ESTONIAN AND LATVIAN REFUGEES IN SWEDEN AFTER WORLD WAR II

Matthew Kott und Harald Runblom

Sweden has long-standing historical and cultural ties to Estonia and Latvia. As a result, Sweden has periodically attracted refugees from war and civil war, labor migrants, and political dissidents from the Baltic countries throughout the 20th century. World War II led to the flight, deportation, and displacement of around 400,000 civilians from the Baltic states. Only a minority were successful in reaching neutral Sweden.

The largest single group of these refugees was comprised of about 25,000 ethnic Estonians. The number of Latvian refugees at its immediate postwar peak was around 5,000. Another noteworthy group was the *estlandsvenskar*, or Estonian Swedes. Some Baltic German, Russian, and Jewish refugees also fled to Sweden from Estonia and Latvia. This article concentrates on the Estonian and Latvian refugees.

Most Baltic refugees came to Sweden in the autumn and winter of 1944–5 by making the dangerous sea crossing from the Estonian islands and western coast of Latvia in fishing boats. In addition, some 2,000 ethnic Estonians were able to "repatriate" to Sweden in 1944 under the auspices of a Swedish–German agreement to evacuate the indigenous Swedish community from Estonia.

Flight itself often occurred by individual initiative, particularly in Estonia. Here, the availability of boats was a significant factor, with many refugees being coastal dwellers. Estonian and Latvian resistance groups also organized limited boatlift operations. In return for providing intelligence to Sweden and the Western Allies, these resistance groups received financial and technical aid to rescue key figures who were required for political activity in exile.

Adverse weather conditions, as well as hostile German and Soviet naval patrols, made the crossing a hazardous undertaking. An estimated 2,000 Estonians perished at sea. Infants and the elderly were particularly vulnerable. Balts who survived the crossing usually made landfall on Gotland or in the Stockholm archipelago. The Swedish civilian and military authorities, with the help of the local population, did their utmost to attend to the hungry, freezing survivors. In all, 271 camps for Baltic refugees were set up in Sweden.

The demographics of the Baltic refugee groups reflected the circumstances of their flight: there were very few elderly, and most refugees were in their 20s and 30s. Men were overrepresented, likely due to the danger of conscription into either the German or Soviet army. More Estonian than Latvian families came to Sweden. Over a fifth of the Estonian refugees (22%) were housewives, compared to only 15% of Latvians, while the proportion of Estonian children was also slightly higher. Among the Latvian refugees were many white-collar workers and intellectuals (almost a quarter). Clergymen, medical professionals, and academics were generally well represented among all Baltic refugees.

The attitude of the Swedes toward the Baltic refugees was influenced by a major trauma in recent history, which is deeply rooted in the cultural memory of the Baltic states and Sweden alike: the "extradition of the Balts" (*baltutlämningen*). Three thousand interned soldiers who had fought in German uniform were extradited to the USSR. Despite protests, the Swedish government handed over hundreds of Germans and

146 Balts to the Soviets in January 1946. Many of those extradited ended up in the Gulag. The extradition inspired a novel (*Legionärerna*, 1968) by Per Olov Enquist and a motion picture (*A Baltic Tragedy*, 1970). A museum exhibition in 2004 on the extradition provoked heated media debates, proving that this event still retains a strong emotive resonance.

Radical elements on the Swedish Left viewed interned Baltic soldiers as quislings and war criminals. Besides, trade union leaders played upon fears that an influx of foreigners would have negative consequences for the Swedish labor market. In September 1945, a union in Norrköping urged the government to extradite all Balts from Sweden. The booming Swedish economy attracted a few Balts to Sweden from the displaced persons (DP) camps in Germany in the late 1940s; but the hostile rhetoric of the Swedish Left before the extradition, coupled with rumors that Sweden would soon forcibly repatriate civilian refugees as well, instead incited thousands of Balts to emigrate to other countries. Negative perceptions of the entire Baltic community persisted in some leftist circles, which coined the slur "Baltic fascists" (*baltfascister*) for the Baltic refugees. In general, however, there was broad public sympathy for the Baltic internees, due to the growing fear of Soviet aggression against Sweden.

Following their release from the refugee camps in 1945–6, Balts and other refugees were not allowed to settle in Stockholm and Gothenburg. This situation began to change in the 1960s when many of them obtained Swedish citizenship. In the meantime, Baltic communities had developed in many smaller towns, as well as in suburban municipalities like Solna, which borders the city of Stockholm.

Life in Sweden involved a social downgrading for many Baltic refugees. Almost all Baltic refugees were directed into industrial jobs – on the railways or in factories – even though only 40% of the Estonians were of working-class background. Some Balts started to work as agricultural laborers but switched to industrial jobs later on. The lucky exceptions were employed under the "archive workers" (*arkivarbetare*) scheme, developed in the 1930s to provide clerical jobs for unemployed university graduates, and which in 1945 created jobs for 2,000 refugee intellectuals from the Baltic states and elsewhere.

In 1960, 65% of Estonians held working-class jobs. Despite a strong trend in upward social mobility from that time on, the proportion of the Estonia-born cohort employed in industry remained somewhat higher than the Swedish average into the 1980s. The refugees' children often went on to higher education, thereby regaining the social status that many of their parents' generation had lost. Some even rose to national prominence in the Swedish elite, such as foreign minister Laila Freivalds, who served from 2003 to 2006.

The Balts created a vibrant network of organizations to maintain their cultural identity in Sweden. They founded choirs, amateur theaters, academic societies, professional associations, newspapers, publishing houses, religious congregations, veterans' organizations, and scout troops. Saturday classes in the various centers of Baltic settlement taught the language and culture. The Estonian community in Stockholm was large enough to support a private day school. Both Estonian and Latvian communities formed umbrella organizations, whose elected representatives served as the officially recognized representatives in relation to the Swedish government and as channels for state support of their communities' cultural activities. In addition, these representative bodies maintained ties with organizations of their fellow Baltic exiles at home and abroad.

Because of their social mobility and organizations, Estonians and Latvians were often portrayed as model immigrants and as an example for later immigrants, despite the fact that acculturation in Sweden was undeniably easier for the northern European, predominantly Lutheran, Balts. Successful acculturation did not necessarily mean rapid assimilation. Among the Balts, there was a strong impetus to maintain group cohesion through an ideology of exile. This exile identity was not only propagated through the aforementioned cultural activities but also reinforced by the political climate of the cold war. Those who were deemed by the promoters of the "Baltic cause" as insufficiently supportive were often socially marginalized. Disillusionment with the community leadership often led excluded dissenters to break ties with their ethnic community and culture and to assimilate into the Swedish majority.

Even though the initial surplus of men restricted the possibility of finding a partner within their own group, marrying outside the refugee community was discouraged. For the second generation, intermarriage became more common in the 1960s and 1970s, often as a rebellion against the conservative ideology of exile.

In the late 1980s, the Balts in Sweden actively helped their homelands regain independence from the USSR. Yet, despite decades of exile ideology, only a few Balts decided to repatriate after 1991, most notably Estonia's president Toomas Hendrik Ilves. The majority of Estonians and Latvians felt fully integrated in Sweden and chose to remain there. At the beginning of the 21st century, Sweden's Baltic ethnic communities have been reinvigorated by new immigrants from their now independent homelands.

Andræ, Carl Göran. *Sverige och den stora flykten från Estland 1943–1944*. Uppsala, 2004.

Byström, Mikael. *En broder, gäst och parasit: Uppfattningar och föreställningar om utlänningar, flyktingar och flyktingpolitik i svensk offentlig debatt 1942–1947*. Stockholm, 2006.

Eriksson, Lars-Gunnar, ed. *De första båtflyktingarna: En antologi om balterna i Sverige*. Norrköping, 1986.

Holmert, Bengt Göran. *Gotland under beredskapsåren 1939–1945*, vol. 1: *Flyktingströmmarna från Baltikum i andra världskrigets slutskede*. Västervik, 1999.

Olsson, Lars. *On the Threshold of the People's Home of Sweden: A Labor Perspective of Baltic Refugees and Relieved Polish Concentration Camp Prisoners in Sweden at the End of World War II*. New York, 1997.

Raag, Raimo, and Harald Runblom, eds. *Estländare i Sverige: Historia, språk, kultur*. Uppsala, 1988.

Cross-references: The Baltic Region; Northern Europe; Displaced Persons (DPs) in Europe since the End of World War II; Ethnic Germans (*Volksdeutsche*) in the German Reich and in German-Occupied Territories in World War II

ETHNIC GERMAN "REMIGRANTS" FROM RUSSIA IN GERMANY, 1890S TO 1930S

Jochen Oltmer

Beginning in the 1870s, many of the German colonists who had settled in czarist Russia in the late 18th and early 19th centuries moved on to the USA, South America, Canada, and Australia. In the 1860s, the Russian government had step by step rescinded important privileges, a policy of Russification had increased the assimilation pressure, and a shortage of arable land hampered the economic development of the German settlements. Between 1870 and 1914, 116,000 Russian Germans emigrated to the USA alone, out of a total German-speaking population of 1.8 million (according to the 1897 census). Beginning in the 1890s, Germany was also one of the destination countries: by the early 1930s, around 200,000 Russian Germans had arrived in the country.

German recruitment policy formed the background to the onset of an intensified emigration into the German Reich: in 1886, the Prussian government had passed a highly funded settlement law to purchase Polish landholdings in the Prussian provinces of Posen and West Prussia for the purpose of settling German farmers. Because the number of domestic applicants for settlement was in steady decline, the authorities switched to recruiting colonists in eastern, east-central, and southeastern Europe, chiefly in czarist Russia. Of the 21,683 families that were settled between 1888 and 1914 – a result that was far below expectations – about a quarter, 5,480 families (around 25,000–30,000 persons) came from abroad. Dominant among them were ethnic German families from Russia (4,900), the majority of which came from Russian Poland (3,540) and the rest chiefly from Volhynia in northwestern Ukraine. The percentage of ethnic German settlers recruited from abroad rose especially after the turn of the century. The peak year was 1905 with 41.9%.

Similar in size was the recruitment of Russian-German agricultural workers (men and women) for the estates in the Prussian east. Here, too, the intent was to displace Poles, though in this case not Prussian citizens of Polish nationality but the hundreds of thousands of Polish agricultural labor migrants who annually poured into Prussian agriculture from Russian central Poland and Austro-Hungarian Galicia. In the final six years before World War I, the Relief Association for German Remigrants (Fürsorgeverein für deutsche Rückwanderer) created in Berlin in 1909 with massive support from Prussian official agencies, recruited around 26,000 Russian-German agricultural workers.

During World War I, the Relief Association for German Remigrants brought about 60,000 Russian Germans into

Russian Germans arriving at the harbor of Swinemünde in Pomerania, 1929 (*SV Bilderdienst*).

the German Reich. The primary goal was the recruitment of (agricultural) workers to ease the labor shortage in Germany brought on by the war. The center of emigration was the settlement area of the Volhynia Germans, which had been hard hit by the immediate effects of the war and a Russian policy of deportation. It had been occupied in 1915–16 by German and Austro-Hungarian troops.

"Remigration" also became an essential topic of the German policy of annexation during World War I. The plan was to annex a broad swath of Russian territory along the Prussian border in the east. It seemed that this kind of occupation would be able to fulfill Germany's economic and military-strategic hopes only in conjunction with a settlement policy: following an extensive "resettlement" of the native population, the "border strip" (*Grenzstreifen*) was to be "Germanified" through ethnic German colonists from Russia. Germany's defeat in 1918 made the implementation of this plan impossible.

In the Weimar Republic, the discussion surrounding the Russian-German remigrants receded entirely behind the economic and social problems of postwar society. Remigrants were no longer considered an economic or – in view of the desired settlement in the Prussian eastern territories marked by emigration – ethnonational gain, but were seen as a burden on the economy, the society, the labor market, and diplomatic relations with the countries of origin. An active "remigration" policy was no longer pursued. Ethnic German minorities in eastern, east-central, and southeastern Europe seemed useful to German foreign and minority policy only as long as they did not leave their settlement areas. To be sure, in the chaotic years of German Occupation, Russian revolution, and Russian civil war (1917 to 1921–2), about 120,000 Russian Germans were able to leave their settlement areas and head for Germany. However, the vast majority arrived already during the war or in the wake of the retreat of the German troops from the territories of the former Russian Empire.

Even life-threatening economic, social, and political crises for the Russian Germans such as the famine of 1921–4 and the collectivization of agriculture from the end of the 1920s, did not lead to a more open reception policy in the Weimar Republic. The grave famine in 1921–2, a result of the Russian civil war and the first Soviet measures to restructure the economy, also hit the settlement areas of Russian Germans along the Volga and north of the Black Sea. Tens of thousands fled the hunger by leaving their villages for regions that seemed to offer a better food supply: Siberia, Central Asia, the Caucasus, Ukraine, and central Russia. Several thousands among them also managed to make their way to central Europe, and possibly 2,000–3,000 Volga-German famine refugees arrived in Germany, even though the German government quickly sealed off the border to this group. The waning of the famine in 1922 meant at the same time the end of large-scale migrations from Russia. With the victory of the Red Army in the Russian civil war, the Soviet Union became the first state in the world that systematically and efficiently controlled external and internal migration in order to implement its large-scale program of industrialization.

The Soviet goal of preventing emigration was very much in the interest of the German policy of restricting immigration. That was evident in late 1929 when, in the wake of forced collectivization, 13,000–14,000 Russian-German farmers descended on Moscow in the hope of receiving help from the German embassy to emigrate: against the backdrop of the beginning global economic crisis, it was only after very protracted negotiations that the German government declared itself willing to receive the farmers provisionally. About 5,700 Russian-German colonists were transported to Germany. The German condition for taking them in was that the costs of transporting and housing them be borne by the interest organizations of the Russian Germans. Moreover, the German government obligated them to make sure that the colonists continued their migration to countries overseas. The Russian-German colonists who arrived in Germany at the end of 1929 were initially put up in camps from where they continued their migration to Canada, Brazil, Paraguay, and Argentina in 1930–1. In February 1930, the German government decreed an immigration stop for Russian-German colonists. This was motivated by the expectation that the exodus from the Soviet Union would swell in the wake of further collectivization in agriculture. Germany maintained, however, that it was in no position to receive additional immigrants because of the economic crisis, and that relations with the USSR should not be burdened any further.

The integration of Russian Germans into imperial Germany and the Weimar Republic is still an unexplored topic. It is likely that well over half of the approximately 200,000 ethnic German remigrants who reached Germany between the 1890s and the global economic crisis at the beginning of the 1930s either returned to eastern Europe or continued on to countries overseas. That was true for nearly all of the Russian Germans recruited as agricultural laborers (of both genders) before 1914 and also for a large portion of the remigrants who arrived as workers or refugees during

and at the end of World War I. They returned to their regions of origin in Russia – especially after the waning of the famine there – or were found among the large number of overseas emigrants from Germany at the beginning of the 1920s. According to the pressure groups of the Russian Germans in the Weimar Republic, the strong tendency toward remigration and onward migration overseas resulted chiefly from the shortcomings of the German integration policy that had been criticized from the outset: Germany, they claimed, had showed no interest in providing farm holdings for the immigrants with their mostly agricultural background. The publications by the pressure groups of ethnic Germans from Russia were dominated by the picture of disappointment over the conditions of reception: the Russian Germans had always been seen just as unwelcome foreign immigrants, as competitors in the labor market, but only rarely as members of the same nation that deserved privileges.

One method of preventing the immigration and permanent settlement of ethnic German foreigners in the Weimar Republic lay in a relatively restrictive application of the Reich and Citizenship Law of 1913. This stands in distinct contrast to the practice, closely intertwined with the Law Pertaining to the Consequences of War, of recognizing and admitting *Aussiedler* (ethnic Germans from the east) and *Spätaussiedler* (late resettlers) into the Federal Republic of Germany after World War II. The legal equality of "ethnic Germans of foreign citizenship in the Reich" (*Volksdeutsche*) with citizens of the Reich was rejected by the Weimar Republic, as was a rapid nationalization of the ethnic Germans. The prevailing thrust in the political and public discussion was that putting "ethnic Germans of foreign citizenship" and members of the Reich on an equal legal footing would have two consequences: first, it would alienate the ethnic Germans from their homeland and thereby weaken the ethnic German minorities abroad, especially since it would make the Reich even more attractive to these immigrants and thereby further reinforce the dissolution of the minority groups; second, a generous granting of Reich citizenship would threaten the interests of the Reich in economic and labor market policies. The goal of Weimar politics vis-à-vis the ethnic German remigrants was thus preventing immigration into the Reich by preserving the settlement centers in eastern, east-central, and southeastern Europe out of considerations relating to domestic, foreign, and economic policies, and if need be also against humanitarian interests.

Oltmer, Jochen. *Migration und Politik in der Weimarer Republik.* Göttingen, 2005.

Cross-references: Germany; Russia and Belarus; Ukraine; *Aussiedler/Spätaussiedler* in Germany since 1950; Ethnic Germans (*Volksdeutsche*) in the German Reich and in German-Occupied Territories in World War II; German Refugees and Expellees from Eastern, East-Central, and Southeastern Europe in Germany and Austria since the End of World War II; German Settlers in Russia since the 18th Century; Polish Agricultural Workers in Prussia-Germany from the Late 19th Century to World War II

ETHNIC GERMANS (*VOLKSDEUTSCHE*) IN THE GERMAN REICH AND IN GERMAN-OCCUPIED TERRITORIES IN WORLD WAR II

Isabel Heinemann

Under National Socialism, the term *Volksdeutsche* (ethnic Germans) described German minorities outside Germany (by virtue of descent, language, or affirmation of "German culture") who did not have German, Austrian, or Swiss nationality. They were distinguished from *Reichsdeutsche* (Reich Germans) and *Auslandsdeutsche* (German nationals living outside of the borders of the Reich). Most ethnic Germans lived as national minorities in the countries of eastern, east-central, and southeastern Europe. During World War II they became the target of Nazi ethnic policy: as part of the conceptions of a racist order, these "settlers tested in the ethnic struggle" were to help "Germanicize" the territories that were annexed or occupied by Germany. This ended the policy of supporting minorities of German origin that was still practiced in the Weimar Republic – for example, in the Association for Germans Abroad (Verein für das Deutschtum im Ausland, VDA). Under the slogan "Home to the Reich!" a population transfer organized by Heinrich Himmler began in 1939. During World War II, more than a million "ethnic Germans" were resettled to the Altreich (Germany before the annexation of the Sudeten region and Austria) and to German-occupied regions (chiefly Danzig–West Prussia and the Warthegau) and were given German "Reich citizenship."

This resettlement began after the defeat of Poland as a population exchange between the German Reich and the Soviet Union. While the ethnic Germans left east Poland and the Baltic area and went westward, Balts, Belarusians, and Ukrainians were to be resettled to the east from territories annexed by Germany. Several resettlement agreements with the Soviet Union and the Baltic states in the fall of 1939 regulated the procedure.

The westward migration of the ethnic Germans cannot be fundamentally seen as "forced resettlement." The majority left their homeland voluntarily, spurred on by Nazi propaganda and by the hope that they would be better off in material terms. Many wished to escape communism or their oppressive minority status. The resettlement of the ethnic Germans was closely interlinked with the expulsion of the non-German local civilian population in the "settlement areas" and especially with the murder of the Jews: for every "ethnic German new farmer," at least five Polish farmers lost their farms. The new settlers were given furnishings and clothing that had once belonged to murdered Jews. However, because it was not possible throughout the duration of the war to provide enough settlement locations – that is, farms, trade businesses, houses, and apartments – the journey ended for the majority of ethnic Germans in special reception camps.

Phases in the resettlement of the "ethnic Germans"

Shortly after the outbreak of the war, Hitler gave SS Reich Leader Heinrich Himmler the order to "bring home" the "ethnic Germans" and to "Germanify" the annexed Polish territories. Himmler chose for himself the title of Reich Commissioner for the Strengthening of Germandom (Reichskommissar für die Festigung deutschen Volkstums, RKF) and set up a separate SS administration RKF to plan and implement the resettlements. In addition, he used the Ethnic German Assistance Center (Volksdeutsche Mittelstelle, Vomi) to care for the migrants. This organization had been established in 1935 as the Nationalsozialistische Deutsche Arbeiterpartei (NSDAP) office to provide financial support to the ethnic Germans, indoctrinate them ideologically, and align their political orientation with the "people's community" (*Volksgemeinschaft*). In 1941, Vomi was elevated into an SS chief office.

While the ethnic Germans were still in their homeland, their property was registered by resettlement trust organizations so as to make later compensation possible. The best known among these was the SS enterprise German Resettlement Trust Office, Ltd. (Deutsche Umsiedlungstreuhandstelle m.b.H., DUT). Under the supervision of Vomi, the ethnic Germans were subsequently registered, gathered together, and transported on foot, by train, or by boat to the occupied regions of western Poland. There they had to first pass a political and racial-anthropological test in the reception camps, the result of which decided their subsequent fate: in a process that was referred to as "sluicing," they passed through the so-called Immigrant Central Office (Einwandererzentralstelle, EWZ) of the SS in Łódź/Litzmannstadt or one of its branch offices, or they were dealt with by one of the mobile EWZ commissions. This "sluicing" involved the participation of the Reich Health Leader, the Reich Interior Ministry, the Reich Labor Office, the Order and Security Police, the Security Service Reich Leader SS (SD), and the Race and Settlement Office of the SS. The vote of the representatives of the last two offices carried special weight. Only "racially pure" individuals should, as settlers, build the new Europe under German hegemony. There was no room for the "racially unsuitable" – even if they spoke German or could point to German ancestors.

The decision of the EWZ divided the ethnic Germans into three groups: "E(ast) Cases" to be used as settlers in the occupied territories, "A(ltreich) Cases" for "labor deployment" in Germany, and "S(pecial treatment) Cases" to be sent back since they were unsuited for "eastern settlement." Only the first two groups were granted the Reich citizenship certificate. The original plan to send back the "S Cases" proved impossible to carry out during the war, and these individuals were instead placed into camps for observation. As it was, life in camps was the dominant characteristic of the resettlement of the ethnic Germans; in peak times the Vomi maintained between 1,500 and 1,800 camps in the Reich and the occupied territories.

"Autochthonous and resettled farmers in the East and in the West": The resettlement of "ethnic Germans," 1 January 1942 (*from Konrad Meyer,* Landvolk im Werden [*Berlin, 1941*]).

The first large-scale project of the Nazis to resettle ethnic Germans was the elaborately conceived plan in the Fall of 1939 to "bring home" the approximately 200,000 German-speaking south Tyroleans of Italian nationality. Although 80% of those concerned had come out in favor of a resettlement, by the middle of 1940, in actuality only around 82,700 south Tyroleans emigrated to the German Reich and the Ostmark.

The subsequent development of the ethnic German question reads like the history of National Socialist expansion. Austria, the Sudeten region, Bohemia, Moravia, and the Lithuanian Memelland became part of the German Reich in 1939. The Carpathian Germans of Slovakia remained a national minority in one of Germany's vassal states. The war saw the resettlement of ethnic Germans from eastern, central-eastern, and southeastern Europe. It occurred in waves, with a peak in 1939–41. First came the ethnic Germans from the Baltic region, initially from Estonia and Latvia (together just under 62,000 in the fall of 1939, another 17,000 during the "follow-up resettlement" in the spring of 1941), a little later from Lithuania (around 48,000 at the beginning of 1941). The next large group were the resettlers from eastern Poland, more specifically, from the Soviet-annexed regions of Galicia (between Bug and San, which belonged to the General Government from 1941), Narew (region around Białystok, attached to East Prussia in 1941), and Volhynia (between Bug and Dnieper). Between the end of December 1939 and the beginning of February 1940, about 128,000 individuals were transported from eastern Poland to the Warthegau by train.

The ethnic Germans from the territories around Chełm and Lublin in the General Government formed the third large wave. Between September and December 1940, about 30,000 persons came to western Poland. They were followed by Germans from Romania (from southern Bukovina, northern Dobrudscha, and Old Romania, a total of just under 77,000 persons between the middle of October and the middle of December 1940) and from the territories of northern Bukovina and Bessarabia that belonged to the Soviet Union (end of 1940, 137,000). In 1941 and 1942 came the resettlement of the ethnic Germans from Croatia (18,000), Serbia (around 2,000), Slovenia with the German-language enclave of Gottschee and the territory around Ljubljana/Laibach (around 14,600, who were settled in Lower Styria and Carinthia). A small number of ethnic Germans came from Greece (144) and Bulgaria (2,500). Over 17,000 from occupied France settled in Germany or in annexed Alsace-Lorraine, a few were used as "east settlers."

All told, just under half a million ethnic Germans migrated from abroad to the annexed territories between October 1939 and the end of 1940, and another 500,000 between 1941 and 1944. To settle them in the annexed western Polish territories, the SS drove around 800,000 Poles from their homes and farms during the war: they were threatened and harassed, dispossessed without compensation, forcibly resettled into the General Government, or locally "displaced." No small number of them paid with their lives for the National Socialist visions of a "German East." Tens of thousands lost their homes and farms also in the other occupied regions of eastern and east-central Europe: they, too, were to make room for the settlement of the ethnic Germans. Hardest hit by the German settlement utopias were the European Jews: the murder of the entire Jewish population of east-central Europe formed the basis of all resettlement plans. The murder of the Jews, the expulsion of, among others, Poles, Czechs, Ukrainians, and Lithuanians, and the settlement of ethnic Germans went hand in hand.

From the middle of 1942 to the end of 1943, the National Socialist settlement policy entered a new phase. Within the framework of the colonial settlement ideas of the General Plan East and of the General Settlement Plan, which envisaged the permanent stabilization of Nazi rule in eastern and east-central Europe through settlement, members of the German minorities were consolidated into certain "settlement cores." While a broad "Germanification" of the occupied western Polish territories through the resettlement of ethnic Germans was the order of the day between 1939 and 1941, the settlement plans changed with the expansion of the war after the attack on the Soviet Union. Because of the size of the territories that were now occupied, the plans for the rest of the east called for a partial Germanification by means of "German settlement pearls." These plans were implemented in two cases: in the district of Lublin, the SS pulled together 10,000 ethnic Germans at the end of 1942 in the district of Zamość; at least 50,000 Poles lost their farms and homes because of it. In 1942–3 in the Ukraine, around

30,000 ethnic Germans from the General Commisariat of Shitomir were concentrated into two settlements at the explicit wish of Himmler, at the expense especially of the Ukrainian population; the Jewish population of the territory had already been deported or killed in the fall/winter of 1941. These settlements of ethnic Germans in the occupied Ukraine would not last long: already at the end of 1943, the settlers fled in treks from the Red Army. Their resettlement ended in the Vomi reception camps in the occupied Polish territories.

At the same time, also following the premises of eastern colonization, ethnic Germans from Lithuania migrated back to their settlement regions. The resettlement to the west in 1941 was reversed a little over a year later at the express order of Himmler: with help from German settlement experts, the ethnic Germans were to return to their homeland from which they had previously been brought "back home into the Reich." A total of 26,000 of the formerly 48,000 ethnic German Lithuanian resettlers returned to Lithuania in 1942. Of those, 19,000 were settled once again on farmsteads from which 22,000 Lithuanians, Poles, and Russians had been expelled. The officially organized return of the Lithuanian Germans arose from the impossibility of settling them on new farms in the occupied territories of western Poland – the majority was still housed in Vomi camps in the spring of 1942. Beyond that, however, the Nazi settlement experts were also hoping that the resettlement would consolidate German rule over Lithuania, which had by now also been conquered.

Resettlement as a punitive measure was suffered especially by ethnic Germans from western Europe: several thousand Germans from Alsace-Lorraine and Luxembourg were taken against their will to resettlement camps in the Altreich for purposes of "re-education." This affected individuals who had been guilty of anti-German statements and activities and families of conscientious objectors. It is only in these cases, rather insignificant in quantitative terms, that one can speak of a "forced resettlement" of ethnic Germans.

The "ethnic Germans" in the Nazi state: loyalty, coercive measures, and integration into the "people's community" (Volksgemeinschaft)

The ethnic Germans were not only a favorite target group of Nazi propaganda; in many instances they also placed themselves willingly in service of the Nazi state. Although the SS, which was responsible for settlement policy, repeatedly emphasized the importance of the ethnic German settlers for a "German East" and their racial superiority over the populations of their countries of origin, most ethnic Germans at the same time liked to claim a privileged place in the Nazi's hierarchy of peoples in Europe by highlighting their "Germanness." There is no other way to explain the enthusiasm with which the ethnic German minorities of the Baltic region, eastern Poland, and later southeastern Europe took up the Nazis' offers of resettlement. They

were willing to leave their homeland for the realization of an ideology, even if many also associated that with concrete material hopes. Among the 140,000 ethnic German recruits who joined the SS Armed Forces (Waffen-SS) by the end of 1943, which means before the beginning of the most intense forced recruitment, there were many resettlers who were not yielding merely to the pressure put on them by SS recruiters in the camps. Resettlers participated readily in Nazi institutions, but especially in the SS – for example, as interpreters for Vomi, as settlement officials of the RKF, and also as guards in concentration camps.

The intense loyalty and willingness to cooperate to the point of committing crimes contrasts with the rising discontent that many ethnic Germans felt in the wake of their resettlement. To the extent that the settlement experts of the SS were unable to settle them – as hoped – on new farms and in new businesses, the resettlers began to complain about the continuing life in the camps or fell into a state of apathy. In many camps the sanitary conditions and the provisioning were so poor that children and old people, in particular, were dying. Moreover, the "racial" classification of people was felt to be degrading. Those who, for lack of "racial suitability" were classified not for "eastern settlement" but for assigned work in the Altreich or placement into observation camps (A and S Cases) felt especially discriminated against and cheated out of their hopes.

In keeping with the Nazi state's ideas of racial order, the treatment of the ethnic Germans turned coercive precisely when they did not match the biological ideals of the National Socialists or resisted the SS settlement policy. For example, "hereditarily ill ethnic Germans" became victims of forced sterilization, and seriously ill and mentally ill individuals were murdered as part of the euthanasia actions. Ethnic Germans who showed themselves unhappy in the camps or resisted the settlement orders were threatened by the SS with internment in concentration camps.

While the Nazi state postulated the complete merger of the ethnic Germans into the "people's community," until 1945 one could speak of an integration of this group only in very qualified terms. A few managed to create a (temporary) new existence as settlers under German occupation or as members of German institutions, but the majority of the ethnic German resettlers were stuck in camps until 1945 (and in many cases even longer). Instead of managing their own farm in Danzig–West Prussia or in the Warthegau, many ethnic Germans were working as agricultural laborers on the farms of others or as workers in the (armaments) industry of the Altreich. Even though the Nazi state claimed that it made no differentiation between Reich citizens once "racial suitability" had been demonstrated, reality was different, especially for the ethnic Germans: integration was most successful for immigrants from Estonia and Latvia, since they formed the first large resettler group and at the same time possessed a relatively high level of skills and education and/or had left behind substantial property for which they were suitably compensated. The other immigrants, especially from eastern Poland, the Soviet Union, and Romania, had a much more difficult time of it in the Reich and the occupied territories: they arrived when hardly any settlement places were left for allocation and were often poor and badly educated. In addition, many had problems with the German language and the National Socialist "guiding culture." That made them immediately identifiable as members of a minority and caused the locals to look upon them disparagingly as "Poles," "Russians," or "Romanians." Complaints about ethnic Germans who were "racially unsuitable" and acting in an "un-German" manner pervade also the reports of the SS's resettlement agencies.

The National Socialists viewed the resettlement of the ethnic Germans as permanent and as the foundation stone for an ethnic reordering of Europe under German hegemony. Still, during the war many had to endure several resettlements across the occupied territories, as was the case, for example, with the Lithuanian Germans who were resettled in 1941 and returned in 1942. Those families who had been settled as part of the "policy of Germanification" in the annexed western Polish territories, in the General Government, in Lithuania, or even in Ukraine had to flee their farms again before the advancing Red Army in 1943–5. No small number had already lost their lives to partisan attacks, to which the settlements of the ethnic Germans in the occupied territories were constantly exposed.

The ethnic Germans who initially remained in their homelands at the end of the war were affected in varying degrees by expulsion and state punitive measures: in the Potsdam Agreement in August 1945, the victorious Allies agreed on the "resettlement" of the German minorities – both Reich Germans and ethnic Germans – from the People's Republic of Poland, Czechoslovakia, and Hungary. However, contrary to the stipulations of the Potsdam Agreement, violent attacks on the ethnic Germans occurred especially in Poland and Czechoslovakia, where people took revenge for the cruel ethnic policies of the Nazi State. The Romanian ethnic Germans, meanwhile, were dispossessed but not expelled, even though the Soviet Union had 60,000–65,000 of them deported. While the ethnic Germans of South Tyrol were not affected by expulsion, camp internment or deportation into the Soviet Union awaited many of the ethnic Germans remaining in Yugoslavia. The background to this was the bloody partisan war that the Germans had waged against the local civilian population – especially by the Waffen-SS division Prince Eugen that was composed largely of ethnic Germans.

The many ethnic German resettlers who were still living in reception camps in the Reich at the end of the war blended with the "Reich Germans" fleeing and expelled since the end of 1944 from the People's Republic of Poland and Czechoslovakia into the large group of refugees and expellees. In the Federal Expellee and Refugee Act of 1953, this group was placed in West Germany legally on a par with the Reich Germans and with respect to state aid. After the war, the ethnic Germans considered themselves mostly as victims of the war, of National Socialist policies, or "forced resettlement" – of their "Germanness" as such. However, one would fail to do justice to the fate of the ethnic German minorities in eastern and southeastern Europe during World War II if one did not also take into account their enthusiasm for the Nazi regime, their anti-Semitism, their willingness to collaborate, and their participation in the murder of the Jews and the policy of annihilation.

Aly, Götz. *"Endlösung." Völkerverschiebung und der Mord an den europäischen Juden*. Frankfurt am Main, 1995.

Dieckmann, Christoph. "Plan und Praxis. Deutsche Siedlungspolitik im besetzten Litauen 1941–1944." In *Wissenschaft, Planung, Vertreibung. Neuordnungskonzepte und Umsiedlungspolitik im 20. Jahrhundert*, edited by Isabel Heinemann and Patrick Wagner, 93–118. Stuttgart, 2006.

Heinemann, Isabel. *"Rasse, Siedlung, deutsches Blut." Das Rasse- und Siedlungshauptamt der SS und die rassenpolitische Neuordnung Europas*. Göttingen, 2003.

Kochanowski, Jerzy, and Maike Sach, eds. *Die "Volksdeutschen" in Polen, Frankreich, Ungarn und der Tschechoslowakei. Mythos und Realität*. Osnabrück, 2006.

Lumans, Valdis O. *Himmler's Auxiliaries. The Volksdeutsche Mittelstelle and the German National Minorities of Europe, 1933–1945*. Chapel Hill and London, 1993.

Cross-references: Austria; The Baltic Region; Czechia and Slovakia; France; Germany; Poland; Russia and Belarus; Southeastern Europe; Ukraine; *Aussiedler/Spätaussiedler* in Germany since 1950; Ethnic German "Remigrants" from Russia in Germany, 1890s to 1930s; Forced Laborers in Germany and German-Occupied Europe during World War II; German Refugees and Expellees from Eastern, East-Central, and Southeastern Europe in Germany and Austria since the End of World War II; German Settlers (*Donauschwaben*) in Southeastern Europe since the Early Modern Period; Jewish Refugees from Nazi Germany and from German-Occupied Europe since 1933

EUROPEAN AND AMERICAN CIVIL SERVANTS OF SUPRANATIONAL ORGANIZATIONS IN BRUSSELS SINCE 1958

Christian Kesteloot

As the political decision-making center of the European Union, Brussels is better known in the world than Belgium. This started with the provisional housing of the administration of the European Commission and EURATOM (European Atomic Alliance) in the city in 1958. Gradually, Brussels became the most prominent location of European institutions and the symbolic seat of the European Union. Although the European Parliament Committees initially met in Brussels, the plenary monthly sessions were held in Strasbourg, while the Parliament's Secretariat was located in Luxembourg. At the instigation of the members of Parliament, who wanted to avoid the tiresome journeys between the three cities, it was finally decided to concentrate the activities in Brussels and to use the newly built International Conference Centre. Since 1992, Brussels has officially housed the European Commission, the European Council, the Social and Economic Committee, and the Committee of the Regions and the Parliament (except for the secretariat and the ordinary plenary sessions).

Brussels furthermore houses most of the NATO institutions since the withdrawal of France from NATO in 1966. For security reasons the SHAPE (Supreme Headquarters of the Allied Powers Europe) was located in Casteau, near Mons. The Atlantic Council, the Military Committee, and the 15 NATO delegations have their seat in Evere, near the Brussels airport. A few other less important international public institutions are present in Brussels as well.

The European Union and NATO attract numerous diplomatic delegations, while many regions and cities have their own representation in the city. All of these institutions and their numerous employees from various nations have led to an even greater foreign presence in Brussels, ranging from international schools, media, hotels, restaurants, lobbyists, lawyers, and financial services. These organizations, in turn, recruit a portion of their personnel from abroad, or bring in employees from overseas to Brussels.

NATO employs about 1,500 civilians and an undisclosed number of military staff, which is by nature much more mobile. The number of EU civil servants working in Brussels increased from 3,200 in 1965 to 7,122 in 1974, 21,189 in 2000, and about 35,000 in 2008, of whom between 70% and 80% are not Belgian citizens. Most of them live in Brussels with their families. Together they represented about 36,900 persons in 2000 and 42,000 in 2005, which is about 2.5% of the metropolitan area population (64 municipalities). Although nearly half of the civil servants are female, women are underrepresented in managerial functions. The total number of foreigners related to the EU or other organizations is difficult to assess, but there are probably over 100,000 foreigners, of whom about two-thirds live within the Brussels Capital Region (BCR, 19 central municipalities).

Originally, the civil servants of the European institutions were recruited in the first six member states (Belgium, Luxembourg, the Netherlands, France, and the Federal Republic of Germany). Each time the European Community and the European Union (after 1992) were enlarged, the number of civil servants increased as well, especially because the growing number of official languages called for new armies of translators and interpreters. In 1973, the UK, Ireland, and Denmark joined the Community, followed by Greece in 1981, Portugal and Spain in 1983, and Austria, Finland, and Sweden in 1992. Nationals of each new member country have the right to apply for a job at the European Community and European Union institutions. Enlargement is now an ongoing strategy of the European Union. Ten southern and eastern European countries (Estonia, Latvia, Lithuania, Poland, the Czech Republic, Slovakia, Hungary, Slovenia, Malta, and Cyprus) joined in May 2004. Romania

and Bulgaria followed in 2007. A share of the human resources of the Union's institutions is assigned for each new member state. For the last enlargement, nearly 5,800 new posts were foreseen by 2009, of which about 5,000 will be located in Brussels.

Initially, the Brussels urban community was proud of the European Community presence. There was the feeling of living in a metropolis with a high international importance. However, support for the European Community did not necessarily foster the integration of the foreign civil servants in the city. In the 1970s, the positive feelings in Brussels turned into mutual indifference, if not antipathy, between the Brussels community and the "eurocrats," as the civil servants of the European Community were mockingly called. Both the commission and the Brussels cultural world felt the need to build bridges between the European Community/Union civil servants and Brussels. The former opened an Information Office for Belgium and the latter created Europalia in 1969, a biennial festival presenting the history, traditions, and culture of a European country.

The civil servants remained, however, encapsulated in their own networks, while the Brussels inhabitants blamed them for increasing housing prices and the privileges of the eurocrats such as high wages and low taxation. The EU/EC officials earn on average twice as much as national civil servants and they pay around 15% in taxes (against up to 50% for Belgians). Since they pay these taxes to the European Union itself, and no land tax is paid for the offices occupied by the European institutions, they do not bear the costs they generate in the municipalities in which they live and work, unlike the other residents. As a result, both the Brussels politicians and the inhabitants have a rather equivocal attitude toward the institutions and their civil servants, which does not encourage their integration in the urban community.

There are further reasons for this negative attitude. The expansion of the EU offices encroaches on the surrounding residential area, for example. The building of the European Parliament in the late 1990s resulted in the eviction of some 2,500 inhabitants from their much-loved neighborhood. The European institutions' insistence on ample parking facilities for their offices has thwarted local policies for public transportation: eurocrats, easily identifiable by the EUR number plates on their cars, are seen as main contributors to the daily traffic jams.

Additionally, the EU/EC foreigners have voting rights at the municipal level and the Flemish fear they will reinforce the strength of francophone political parties both in the BCR and the suburbs. There is a delicate balance between the protection of the francophone minority at the federal level and in the suburbs of Brussels within the Flemish Region on the one hand, and of the Flemish minority in the BCR on the other hand. However, less than 10% of the Europeans take up their right to vote, and so they are not an important factor in communal politics. This is in part due to the cumbersome voting registration procedure and also to a lack of interest in the complex, conflict-ridden francophone-Flemish politics.

The integration of the EU/EC civil servants was further hindered by their residential distribution. They reside in the upper-class neighborhoods of the city, especially in the southern and eastern suburbs surrounding the Zoniën Forest. On the one hand, their housing conditions in the country of origin and their high wages drive them into these areas, but on the other the housing market has adapted to their presence, increasing the tendency toward creation of "golden ghettoes." Mutual help between EU/EC staff members and the development of specialized real estate companies tend to direct the newcomers to the same neighborhoods, while housing costs adjust to the purchase power of the newcomers and exclude citizens of other social levels from the areas. Finally, schools – including three European schools – as well as clubs and shops adapt to their new patrons, making their concentration in these areas even more obvious. For reasons of administrative efficiency the offices of the international civil servants are concentrated in the European Quarter, preventing natural contacts with other employees in the city.

International civil servants also have little contact with the lower strata of their own national community in the city, such as the immigrant workers who were already present in Brussels of Italian, Spanish, Greek, and Portuguese origin. Likewise, future eastern European civil servants will not use the networks set up by their legal and illegal poorer co-nationals. This does not preclude the development of expatriate communities, as long as members are of similar social strata: EU officials, as well as temporary or permanent employees of private concerns from the same nation, and independent or other highly qualified labor migrants who take advantage of the easy mobility within the EU all visit the same locales, particularly the Irish pubs of the inner city. They also read the English-language weekly *Bulletin*, use communal online networks (e.g., chat rooms), and invite one another to house parties.

Regardless of the antipathy toward them from the people of Brussels, EU officials are increasingly happy with their city. Although a survey among 5,000 commission employees in 1981 showed that 60% were unhappy with their location and wanted to leave Brussels, today most EU foreigners appear to be very positive about the city and the quality of life it offers. In 1998, 53% had a house of their own (compared to 41% of all households of the BCR in 2001) and only half of them want to leave Brussels after retirement. Surveys also disclose a movement to the inner city: the share of Germans living in the suburbs (outside the BCR) dropped from 47% in 1981 to 38% in 2003; similar changes apply to the British, Danes, Irish, Swedes, and Austrians. Many civil servants enjoy the quality of life in the inner city, including a large spectrum of cultural events and the closeness to the European institutions where they work.

Since the 1990s, Europe and Brussels have been much more involved in the integration of the European institutions and its employees in Brussels. Brussels is increasingly considered an embodiment of European identity. Brussels rightly considers EC/EU institutions and their employees

one of its main economic assets. In the early 1990s, the new Brussels Capital Region opened a Brussels-Europe Liaison Office that promotes the image of Brussels as the capital of Europe and increases its citizens' awareness of the Region's importance for Europe. Within the francophone Belgian population, however, there is still a strong reluctance to accept the multicultural character of the city and many would like to see these residents adopt the dominant culture of the francophone elite. But the bicultural character of the BCR institutions, equally divided between Flemish and Walloons, prevents such monolithic integration.

Brussels is also a dual city in terms of social and spatial structure, with a deep segregation between the deprived neighborhoods in the western part of the inner city, mainly inhabited by low-skilled immigrants from various nations, and the southeastern suburbs. Many EU officials and their families have tried to overcome the social consequences of these divisions. A group of EU parents, for example, is engaged in attempts to locate a fourth European school in the northwestern part of the Brussels region in order to breach this barrier. At the same time, the hybrid character of the cultural and social institutions in Brussels opens many possibilities to integrate in an international city, without giving up one's own identity. The ability to live with diversity thus becomes a challenge for both the immigrants and the native population.

Bureau de Liaison Bruxelles-Europe. Bruxelles – Europe en chiffres. http://www.blbe.be/files/EU%20-%20Bruxelles%20en%20 chiffres%20octobre%202008%20FR.pdf (accessed 10 March 2009).

Cailliez, Julie. *Schuman City: Des fonctionnaires britanniques à Bruxelles.* Louvain-la-Neuve, 2004.

Christiaens, Etienne. "Rich Europe in Poor Brussels: The Impact of the European Institutions in the Brussels Capital Region." *City* 7 (2003): 183–98.

Communication from the Commission to the Council and the European Parliament: Activities and Human Resources of the Commission in the Enlarged European Union. Edited by the Commission of the European Communities. Brussels, 2002.

Demoulin, Michel, ed. *Bruxelles, l'européenne. Regards croisés sur une région capitale. Brussel, hart van Europa. Een verkennende blik op een kapitale regio.* Brussels, 2001.

Elmhorn, Camilla. *Brussels, a Reflexive World City.* Stockholm, 2001.

Favell, Adrian. *Free Movers in Brussels: A Report on the Participation and Integration of European Professionals in the City.* Brussels, 2001.

Grimmeau, Jean-Pierre, and Anne David-Valcke. "Les cadres étrangers à Bruxelles." *Revue Belge de Géographie* 102 (1978): 33–42.

Cross-references: Austria; The Baltic Region; Belgium and Luxembourg; Czechia and Slovakia; France; Germany; Great Britain; Ireland and Northern Ireland; Italy; The Netherlands; Northern Europe; Poland; Spain and Portugal; Southeastern Europe

EUROPEAN ELITES ON THE GRAND TOUR IN EARLY MODERN EUROPE

Mathis Leibetseder

The term "Grand Tour," which is used internationally, goes back to the linguistic usage of the 17th century, when the "grand tour de France" referred to a tour of the most important provinces and royal residences in France. At the end of the 17th century, British writers detached the term from its original geographic reference and established it as a description for the tour through Europe. In what follows, Grand Tour will be used as a collective term for specific study and educational trips by early modern elites, especially from western and central Europe, other terms for which were *peregrinatio academica, Kavalierstour, Prinzenreise*, or *Bildungsreise*.

The historical roots of the Grand Tour reach back to the Middle Ages, when knights traveled to visit courts, to fight heathens, or to make pilgrimages to holy sites. However, in its specific form, the Grand Tour appears first in the study and educational trips of the 16th century, and over the next two centuries, as well, it was subject to a constant change in function and form. Generally, the young men who made the tour had already undertaken initial studies in pertinent educational institutions at home prior to their departure. Inspired by travel literature, they would then venture abroad between the ages of 15 and 25. They were accompanied by study companions or friends recruited through family and kinship networks; if they hailed from the nobility or the patrician class, they would also travel with private tutors and servants. The trip usually lasted between two and four years, though it could also be substantially longer. While travelers for the most part spent only a few days at each stop, they often lingered for months in cities with educational institutions or courts. Since a return was fully intended, an integration into the society of the countries visited was sought only to a certain degree. Only in exceptional cases did the travelers remain in a destination country.

While the *peregrinatio academica*, with its strong burgher imprint, was strongly focused on visits to learned institutions such as universities and academies, to collections, or outstanding monuments, the nobility also had access to the knight academies as exclusive training establishments. Moreover, the sons of noble families on their tours were eager visitors to the courts and attended theaters, salons, and other meeting places of high society. Along with the acquisition of theoretical knowledge and practical skills (foreign languages), practicing norms of behavior specific to one's social estate was also at the forefront of the Grand Tour until the early 18th century.

Destinations were chiefly in Italy and France, more rarely in the Netherlands, England, the Holy Roman Empire, and Scandinavia. The Iberian Peninsula and the states of eastern Europe were at the margins of the routes. And while the routes did change over time, on the whole they tended to become standardized, since visits to certain sites were absolutely required. Thus France in the age of Louis XIV became increasingly the real goal of young travelers and Paris their capital, while Italy's great era did not begin until the second half of the 18th century. During this period the outdated trip to polish one's upbringing was slowly replaced by the *Bildungsreise*, where travelers no longer learned the values and behavioral norms of their class but, in keeping with bourgeois educational ideals, were supposed to develop their individual talents.

The *Bildungsreise* probably found its high point in the mania for Italy during the age of Goethe. In reality, though, the practice of travel was already at that time undergoing yet another change in form and function. It was increasingly rare for travelers to leave their home for several years, and it was increasingly uncommon for them to journey through several countries. Even if the traditions of the Grand Tour began to lose their power to shape culture from the beginning of the 19th century, the destination countries and the catalog of sites to be visited have influenced travel behavior down to the present.

The itinerant sons of the nobility went to considerable expense to adapt to the customs of the upper classes of the countries they visited. They acquired a knowledge of the languages of learning and the court, namely Latin, French, and Italian, and strove also to express abroad the rank and status they enjoyed at home through the choice of appropriate symbolic means. For example, even before they could be seen in society, they had to furnish themselves with a wardrobe that identified them as the son of a duke, baron, or knight according to the rules of the host society. They also needed means of transport appropriate to their social rank, which usually meant sedan chairs or carriages. Moreover, anyone who wished to participate in the social intercourse of the upper classes required lodging with rooms in which to receive guests. Then it was important to familiarize oneself with the local etiquette and to look up individuals who could provide contacts to high society. Alongside academics and scholars, that role was played above all by the envoys who had been present at the European courts in ever-growing numbers since the 17th century. These individual efforts did not clash with the formation of a group feeling among the young travelers, for they strove to help one another by making connections with new acquaintances and to multiply the possibilities of social contact.

The adoption of the customs of the local societies, however, was always a temporary one with clear boundaries that were set by both the society from which the travelers came and the society they visited. One of the boundaries that was drawn by the society of origin concerned the religious integrity of the travelers: since Europe had been divided into different confessional camps since the 16th century, the young men could hardly avoid contact with adherents of other confessions. The territorial rulers of Bavaria therefore sought, around 1600, to make the Grand Tours of their subjects contingent on their permission and – wherever possible – regular attendance at Catholic mass. In a Protestant country like England, as well, there were concerns that the traveling sons of the nobility could secretly convert to Catholicism in Italy. In addition to the question of confession, the loyalty of the noblemen to their respective territorial lord was always an issue. For example, the trips abroad by young noblemen in 18th-century Prussia were subject to strict regulations. However, such trips were by no means unwelcome to the territorial rulers. Rather, the princes were certainly interested in officeholders who were widely traveled and multilingual.

In addition to attempts by the state to direct these trips, the traveling young men were also controlled by their guardians, who laid down their principles of upbringing in "instructions." One point of these instructions concerned adherence to the confessional principles of the parents (which could, of course, be opposed to those of the countries visited); another was contact with women. Initial contacts in the destination country were to be established mostly with elderly women, specifically noblewomen and princely ladies of the home country who were married to prominent locals, while the acquaintance with unmarried noblewomen was undesirable as it posed a threat to the family's marriage strategies. Sexual contacts with the other gender were publicly described as a perilous risk to health (venereal diseases); to what extent they were nevertheless tolerated by the guardians cannot be ascertained from the sources.

The official and familial prescriptions and prohibitions raise questions about possible ways of supervising and sanctioning behavior. Princes and families relied in equal measure on the close-knit communication networks of the upper classes in early modern Europe. News about unauthorized travel activities or misbehavior abroad could reach guardians and the authorities through diplomatic networks or other travelers. As punishment, the princes threatened to impose monetary penalties and potentially refuse to later accept into their services travelers who had left the land without official permission. Parents, who additionally were kept informed about the progress of the journey through letters from the tutors and their charges, could at any time refuse to continue financing the trip, forcing their sons to return home.

The host societies, too, knew how to prevent the multiyear travels from turning into an immigration. They drew boundaries on the efforts of the young travelers to fit in, boundaries they were not allowed to cross. A symbolic expression of these boundaries could be seen during court visits to Versailles, where travelers beginning in the late 17th century were assigned a place beside envoys. But the relationships to the local nobility also proved quite short-lived in most cases. Acquaintances that were cultivated after travelers had left – through correspondence, for example – are documented as rarely as marriages to women that the travelers met abroad.

Although the return was usually planned ahead of time, there were also cases in which the Grand Tour did in fact turn into immigration. In Europe that was especially true in the 16th and early 17th century, less so in later periods. However, the specific political constellation of the Holy Roman Empire offered the social elite plenty of opportunity

to emigrate to another territory also in the 17th and 18th centuries. Moreover, the personal unions between the European states offered room for the immigration of members of leading bourgeois and noble strata.

An integration of noble travelers into the host societies generally took place via an appointment to service at the court, in the administration, or in the military. Conditions were particularly favorable in the environs of courts where there were military units of the traveler's home country, where military alliances existed, or where countrymen had already gained a foothold as officeholders. Still, even in such cases the wives, at least in the first generation, generally continued to come from the traditional marriage circles of the family.

Two test cases show that the conditions for the reception and integration of travelers were quite diverse: Kaspar von Schönberg, from the Meissen nobility, traveled to France to study in the late 16th century and settled there permanently. In this instance military skill, conversion, and marriage into the French high nobility smoothed his way into French society. The most important channel of social advancement was a German cavalry corps, in which Schönberg rose to the rank of captain. Having achieved military fame, Schönberg was eventually naturalized, and King Henry IV of France appointed him councilor in the financial administration. As Gaspard de Schomberg he was the father of a dynasty that produced several influential men and was linked with the first families of the French nobility through numerous marriages.

The second example reveals how the social elite in the host societies reacted to foreign officeholders: in 1732, the tour of the Imperial Count Henry VI Reuß eventuated in service in Denmark. However, the precondition for this development was not the contacts the young nobleman himself had established during the trip but the familial network of the Reuß family and the personal union between Denmark and the duchies of Schleswig-Holstein. But the native courtiers were by no means enamored of the new officeholder. We are told that on the occasion of his appointment, there was "real grumbling among the courtiers, whereby the poor new chamberlain had no lack of envious faces, in that the jealousy and displeasure can be read from the face of most of them, and that all the more so since the chamberlains here have such a high rank and esteem, and there are in fact not many of them, and many who have sought it have been turned down by the king." The appointment of the foreign nobleman had been made possible in the first place only by the intercession of other German office- and title holders at the court in Copenhagen. In the rare cases in which the Grand Tour resulted in immigration, the travelers were thus generally integrated in terms of their social estate and at the same time highly visible owing to their elevated social position.

However, the Grand Tour had immigration potential not only for the young noblemen themselves but also for those traveling in their entourage, e.g., servants, doctors, or tutors. Of course, only the latter have left traces, while the fate of other servants is lost among the masses. Johann Friedrich Reifenstein, for example, who looked after a nobleman's son on his tour through Italy, left his master in Florence to live in Rome. It was not an official post that cushioned his arrival but the milieu of German scholars and artists who resided in the Eternal City. Although he was active as a painter himself, he presumably earned his living primarily as a tour guide for noble travelers.

Babel, Rainer, and Werner Paravicini, eds. *Grand Tour – Adeliges Reisen und europäische Kultur vom 14. bis zum 18. Jahrhundert*. Sigmaringen, 2004.

Black, Jeremy. *The British Abroad: The Grand Tour in the Eighteenth Century*. New York, 1992.

Frank-van Westrienen, Anne. *De Groote Tour. Tekening van de educatiereis der Nederlanders in de zeventiende eeuw*. Amsterdam, 1983.

Helk, Velo. *Dansk-norske studierejser*, 2 vols. Odense, 1987.

Leibetseder, Mathis. *Die Kavalierstour. Adlige Erziehungsreisen im 17. und 18. Jahrhundert*. Cologne, 2004.

Cross-references: France; Germany; Great Britain; Italy; Northern Europe

EUROPEAN OFFICEHOLDERS AT THE ROMAN CURIA SINCE THE EARLY MODERN PERIOD

Birgit Emich

"Curia romana" (Roman Curia) is the term commonly used since the 11th century to describe the ensemble of institutions and individuals that assisted the pope in the fulfillment of his duties. That these duties could be both spiritual and secular was one of the specific peculiarities of the papacy until the dissolution of the Papal States in 1870: the supreme pontiff was not only the spiritual head of the world church but also the territorial ruler of a state. Alongside the departments for the governance of the church, to which the label Curia exclusively refers today, until 1870 there were also bodies charged with the governance of the state and foreign policy. As early as the 12th century, the Latin "curia romana" was translated as "la corte di Roma" or "la corte pontificia": the Curia was a court, the center of monarchical power. At the beginning of the early modern period, the term "Roman court" was used as self-evidently in France and elsewhere as at the Curia itself.

As the center of a world church with universal pretensions, the Curia should have been staffed with members from a great many states. However, with the Curia representing the court and seat of government of a territorial ruler with political goals in the competition of powers, there were limits to such an "internationalization" in the sense of a representation spanning the "nations." In fact, the 16th century saw an Italianization of the Curia, which determined its geographic composition into the 20th century. Still, Rome remained an international center with great attractive force: the Catholic powers of Europe sought to exert influence on the policies of the popes by sending ambassadors to the Curia and pushing for the elevation of their own countrymen to the office of cardinal; bishops from around the world regularly appeared at the Curia, and pilgrims were drawn to Rome alongside students, tradesmen, and artists. While the Curia is therefore not a prime example of a system characterized by mobility for spiritual reasons, it is the embodiment of a world church that must also be seen as a political system and which functioned, until 1870, simultaneously as the court of a territorial ruler and was shaped until the end of that symbiosis by the tensions between mobility and Italianization.

The term *natures*, which refers more to language groups than to political boundaries, played an important role in the history of group formation and the self-perception and outside perception at the Roman Curia. In the 15th century, five great nations (*nazioni*) were differentiated at the Curia: France, England, Spain, Italy, and Germany. However, smaller communities, too, could be conceptualized as nations. That applied not only to the Castilians, Aragonese, Lorrainers, and Bretons, but also to the regions of Italy.

The geographic composition of the Roman Curia

From the death of the Dutchman Hadrian VI in 1523 to the election of John Paul II in 1978, all the popes came from Italy. In terms of social background, the pontiffs of the modern era were recruited from the urban patriciate; geographically the cities of northern and central Italy dominated.

Parallel to the papacy, the college of cardinals also experienced an Italianization in the 16th century. After a phase of French dominance in the 14th century, the explanation for which is the sojourn of the Curia in Avignon and which corresponded with the election of almost exclusively French candidates to the papacy, the college had initially internationalized itself following the upheaval of the schism between a French and an Italian faction. For example, while Pope Eugene IV (1431–47) bestowed the red cardinal's hat on 13 Italians, 4 Frenchmen, and 3 Spaniards, which gave the Mediterranean group a three-quarter majority, he also appointed one cardinal each from Portugal, Hungary, England, and Poland, two cardinals from Germany and Greece, and one humanist from the region of what is today Turkey; as a result, the college was more international than ever before. But the quota of non-Italians declined again rapidly: in 1455, they still commanded a two-thirds majority plus one that was crucial for the election of the pope, but by 1484 their share was already below the blocking minority of one-third. Pope Sixtus V violated his own decree of 1586, which stipulated that the cardinals should be recruited from all parts of the Christian world, and in the subsequent centuries, as well, it was not honored.

Until the 20th century, the non-Italian minority was dominated by Frenchmen and Spaniards. Portuguese candidates were able to catch up in the 18th century, while representatives from Protestant countries like England or the territories of the Holy Roman Empire remained rare. Among the Italians, the largest group came from the Papal States, and of those the largest group in turn was from Rome itself. The numbers in detail: 1566–1605: 72% Italians (36% from the Papal States), 12% Frenchmen, 9% Spaniards; 1605–55: 82% Italians (51% from the Papal States), 7% each Frenchmen and Spaniards; 1655–1799: 80% Italians (43% from the Papal States), 7% Frenchmen, 5% Spaniards, 2% Portuguese; 1800–46: 78% Italians (60% from the Papal States), 8% Frenchmen, 4% Spaniards. The number of cardinals grew in tandem with the internationalization of the college. Alongside shared regional identity, kinship (nepotism) intensified the regional focal points.

Italianization is evident in the early 16th century also among the lower ranks of the curial hierarchy. According to the *ruoli* of the popes, in which they listed the members of the pontifical household as well as officeholders down to the simple servant, the percentage of Italians rose from 41% under Leo X (1513–21) to 65% at the court of Paul III (1534–49). Here, too, Spaniards and Frenchmen dominated the dwindling group of non-Italians, and here, too, the Italians came with increasing frequency from Rome and the Papal States as time went by. This trend intensified in the following decades. For example, of the candidates who sought a prelature in the first decades of the 18th century, 27% came from the Papal States outside of Rome and an additional 12% were Romans. There were no non-Italians among those interested in the career of a prelate, which required noble birth, judicial experience, and a minimum level of wealth, but not specific geographical origin. Here, too, shared regional identity played a central role alongside kinship, as shown by the affinity of various regional groups for specific offices: the chances were greatest when countrymen were already in office and could work in a supportive fashion. Conversely, the prospects for a post declined if the number of countrymen who were potential patrons in high positions declined. Thus the Italianization of the lower ranks resulted also from the declining presence of non-Italian cardinals.

Shared regional identity played a central role also in the way in which Italian members of the Curia saw themselves and were perceived by outsiders. Whether in self-descriptions or official lists of officeholders, whether in the reports of the Roman Avvisi writers or in private correspondence: detailed information about the curiales usually begins with a reference to their regional background. Finally, regional identity was an important factor not only for individual careers but also for the formation of factions within the college of cardinals and thus for what was of paramount interest to most observers: the power relationship among the individual client groups that gathered around the still-living nephews (*nepote*) of the previous popes or other leadership figures from their entourage. They formed the so-called nephew factions and decided the outcome of the next papal election with their alliances and enmities.

Regional identity referred here to *patria* or *nazione*, to small spaces, an identity that was defined chiefly but not exclusively by political boundaries. For example, when it came to the label Genoese, Florentine, or Venetian, it was of no consequence whether the member of the Curia came from the eponymous city itself or from the hinterland of the respective state. But even within a political entity, several regional groups could be differentiated and likewise described as different *nazioni*; in the Papal States there were the Bolognese, Ferrarans, or Perugians, for example. A special role was attached to the city of Rome: because it was the goal of families who rose into the Curia to gain a foothold within the high nobility of the city, *romanitas* as such was socially attractive. That was evident, for example, in the marriage market or the collecting of Roman antiquities, a way in which especially successful social climbers demonstrated their attachment to Rome. And it was evident in the self-Romanization of popes like Paul V Borghese, who, though hailing from a Sienese family, presented himself on the façade of St. Peter's in gigantic letters as "Paulus V. Burghesius Romanus."

Still, this kind of assimilation at the highest level did not prevent individuals from favoring their own countrymen. Members of a regional nation different from one's own were always considered *stranieri* or *forestieri*, foreigners. While the particular attributions that were made could vary, depending on the traditional relationships between the groups, a few common stereotypes can be identified and sometimes linked to the relationship between the *nazione* in question and the Curia. For example, the proverbial avarice of the Genoese probably had something to do with their involvement in the financial system of the papacy. And since a career in the financial sector represented an early form of advancement by merit and thus created fewer obligations toward a patron, the often-invoked unreliability of the Genoese in terms of patronage could also have had a basis in real life.

The international presence at the Curia

If the Italianization of the Curia reflected the political interests of the popes, it raises the question of why *any* non-Italians were given the red cardinal's hat. The answer lies in the pressure of the European powers. While the popes were able to rebuff the demand – as expressed during the reform councils in the 15th century – to fill the college of cardinals on a proportional basis and to turn it into a kind of representative body of the world church, they always yielded to the steady pressure of the Catholic monarchs to elevate their countrymen. After all, the appointment of cardinals, just like canonization, offered popes the opportunity to fulfill the requests of royal petitioners and to call on a return favor when the time was ready.

One expression of this political horse-trading, which favored the most important Catholic monarchies and thus explains the preponderance of the Spanish and French cardinals in the college, is the institution of the "crown cardinals" that arose in the 15th century and lasted into the 20th: these were cardinals who were appointed at the specific recommendation of a secular sovereign. The unofficial privilege of nominating a candidate initially belonged only to the emperor, but in the 16th century it was also granted to the kings of France and Spain and in 1729 finally also to the Kingdom of Sardinia. There were two large groups of crown cardinals who did not reside in Rome: politicians like Richelieu, who needed the red hat for reasons of prestige and for their own political purposes, and relatives of the royal houses, who were likewise concerned about prestige and a source of income from the church.

Alongside the crown cardinals there was another group who contributed to the decline of the number of cardinals residing in Rome: the "national cardinals." They owed the red hat to their appointment to an office in their own country that came with the cardinal's honor. In this case, the monarchs, who were unable to prevent the Italianization of the Curia but at the same time ensured the "nationalization" of their national churches and guaranteed themselves the right to fill the lucrative posts in their own territory, pushed hard for linking certain bishoprics with a cardinalate.

In general, the commentators in the *Relazioni della Corte di Roma* could say nothing about the crown and national cardinals, who were never or only very briefly at the Curia, or only what they had been able to glean from their countrymen in Rome. However, given that these cardinals would most likely be absent at the next conclave, that is all one needed to know about them. By contrast, when it came to the non-Italian cardinals residing by the Tiber, analysts were usually content with a reference to their nationality, from which contemporaries believed their political affiliation could be readily inferred. In the process, the political relationships between states could lead to the formation of a supranational block, which was also perceived as such by the college, as can be seen in cardinals from the Holy Roman Empire: as long as both Spain and the imperial court were ruled by the Habsburgs, German cardinals were assigned without further ado to the Spanish national party. The only exception was the small minority of non-Italians who owed their red hat not to the recommendation of their king but to a career in a monastic order or to other church activities. Since these cardinals could definitely feel greater loyalty to the pope who appointed them than to their territorial sovereign, they were at times associated with one of the nephew factions.

The mechanisms by which the European powers sought to exert their influence were also reflected in the way Roman observers perceived the Italian cardinals. In the portraits of the cardinals, the reference to their geographic origins and other information that determined their membership in one of the nephew factions was therefore always followed by an assessment of their position between the poles of Spain and France, and – de facto closely tied to this – by information about pensions and other perquisites from one of the Catholic powers.

To be sure, the self-perception and self-presentation of the Italian cardinals did not revolve solely around their outside connections and relationships. For them, the client ties to the Italian faction chiefs were front and center; after all, they had a far stronger impact on daily life at the Curia than a pension in France or Spain. This is evident, for example, in their self-description as a "creature and faithful servant of the pope," who had bestowed the red hat on them. But it also becomes clear in the custom, following the appointment to the cardinalate, to integrate the pope's family crest into one's own cardinal crest and thus express the status as client in heraldic terms. Still, the Italian cardinals contributed indirectly to the presence of the European powers in Rome, because they were always perceived also as partisans of either Spain or France, and because they presented themselves as such, for example, during events held by the respective regional associations (national brotherhoods).

Among non-Italian cardinals, the way they were perceived from the outside was largely congruent with the way they perceived themselves. That they saw and wished to show themselves as members of their nation is illustrated by their involvement in the national brotherhoods. That they understood themselves as servants of their monarchs is made clear, apart from their function as national protectors or interim ambassadors, by their behavior in conclaves. In general, the non-Italian cardinals followed the instructions they received from Vienna, Paris, and Madrid for the papal elections. The leader of the respective national party in the college also uttered, at the behest of his territorial sovereign, the right of exclusion against certain candidates and thus prevented their election. The cardinals worked closely with the ambassador of their country not only, but especially, in these important situations.

As early as the 16th century, ambassadors from Italian states and representatives from the Catholic monarchies of Europe were accredited at the Curia. The highest status was enjoyed by the representatives of the Emperor, France, and Spain, and by the Venetian envoy as the highest ranking Italian diplomat. They were followed by the ambassadors of Savoy and Tuscany, then the representatives of other Italian princes or republics, next the representatives of the Order of the Knights of Malta and the envoys of Bologna and Ferrara, the two last cities within the Papal States who had been able to secure the privilege of permanent representation at the Curia. Far below in rank, though ever present in the daily life of the Curia, was the army of agents who offered their services to smaller political entities as well as to church institutions and private individuals, and who at times represented the interests of their sometimes numerous employers only in a specific case.

The Curia, its many observers, and the actors themselves kept careful watch over the status that was assigned to the ambassadors in ceremonies and to the way diplomats perceived themselves and were perceived by others: they were the representatives of their country, whose position at the Curia was reflected in their treatment. Conversely, the ceremonial integration of the ambassadors, who had their fixed place in processions, for example, and were virtually paraded before the public, also reveals that the Curia used the international presence for its own self-representation: Rome was *il teatro del mondo*, the world's stage – namely, less in the ecclesiastical than in the political sense.

At times the international presence at the Curia was boosted by bishops paying their *ad limina* ("to the threshold") visit. Depending on the geographic distance of their bishopric from Rome, since 1585 bishops had been obligated to appear in Rome every 3, 4, 5, or 10 years (since 1909 uniformly every 5 years) and give an account to the pope of the state of their dioceses.

General councils in Rome would have provided another reason for the bishops of the world church to journey to the Tiber. However, not a single general council was held in Rome between the Fifth Lateran Council of 1512–17 and the First Vatican Council in 1869–70. Moreover, the First Vatican Council showed that even assemblies such as these did not have to represent the world church exactly: of the approximately 700 participating bishops, 35% came from Italy and 17% from France, which guaranteed the traditional dominance of Romance countries. The approximately 200 bishops from dioceses outside of Europe were exclusively white and the majority was of European background.

The nazioni of the city of Rome

The migratory movements triggered by the Curia were by no means limited to the non-Italian cardinals, ambassadors, and bishops. For one, both cardinals and ambassadors had households with numerous members who, by the rules of the time, were often from the native country and thus contributed to the internationalization if not of the Curia, then certainly of the city of Rome. For another, since its return from Avignon, the Curia had contributed substantially to Rome's rise in the 15th century as the most cosmopolitan city of its day and to its perception in the 16th century by both Romans and foreign visitors as the "capital of the world." After all, the Roman court not only offered clerics a chance to make a living and pursue a career but it also handed out commissions and contracts to artisans, artists, and merchants. A contemporary topos said that even the most obscure person from far away could attain the highest honors in Rome. And in fact, according to a rare source, the percentage of non-Italians among the Roman population may have been nearly 20% in 1527 (a different calculation puts it at only 7.5%). Another 64% had immigrated from Italian regions outside of Rome, and only 16% of the 50,000 inhabitants were native to the city. However, in the course of the 16th century the percentage of Romans born in the city continued to grow.

The weights shifted in the 16th century also within Rome's non-Italian population. While the German nation had initially been dominant, the Reformation as well as bad memories of the plundering of the city in the *Sacco di Roma* in 1527, attributed largely to German mercenaries, led to a collapse of the German presence in Rome. Henceforth, the Spanish nation constituted the largest group among the non-Italians at the Tiber. This points once again to

the central role that the Curia played in the migration to Rome: the initial sparks for the influx from Iberia came from the pontificates of the two Spanish Borgia popes Calixtus III (1455–8) and Alexander VI (1492–1503), who gave preferential treatment to their countrymen. In addition, the growing presence of Spaniards in Rome was in line with Spain's growing influence on the popes. The great period of Spanish presence in Rome came to an end when the Bourbons ascended the Spanish throne in 1700. Just as the balance of power had shifted in Europe, the situation at the Curia and between the *nazioni* now also shifted in Rome in favor of the French side.

That the non-Italians remained present in Rome and identifiable as *nazioni* in spite of their declining share of the total population had to do chiefly with the so-called national brotherhoods. The latter formed the organizational core of the *nazioni*: among their members were also the ambassador, crown cardinals, and other officeholders at the Curia from the respective country, and they helped their nation to attain a visibility in Rome that the political representation by the ambassador could have never achieved on its own. Initially established to look after pilgrims from their home country, and thus usually in possession of a pilgrim hostel and a national church with a cemetery, the brotherhoods always devoted themselves to religious and charitable tasks.

At all times it was the regional identity that provided the internal bond and external boundary of the non-Italian national brotherhoods and of the respective organizations of the Italian *nazioni*. The national language always played a large role among non-Italian groups; for example, it was the language of preaching at the national churches. However, that did not prevent the division of language communities into various brotherhoods nor their fusion into larger entities. On the one hand, one can therefore observe a fragmentation of the large nations: first to split off from the German brotherhood (founded in the 14th century by a soldier from Dordrecht) centered around the national church of Santa Maria dell'Anima were the Flemings, followed in the 17th century by the Swiss. Moreover, members of the same nation could organize themselves into various brotherhoods, which became more differentiated especially in the 15th century through new foundations and revealed a certain social affiliation: curial officials from the German language region preferred to join the brotherhood centered around the Anima, while German craftsmen gathered in the brotherhood around Campo Santo Teutonico, the German cemetery, or set up separate occupational groups (brotherhoods of shoemakers and bakers). The Florentines, for example, also organized themselves into two socially different brotherhoods. Occasional dual memberships as well as lively social and professional contacts between the members of the various brotherhoods of a nation indicate that these brotherhoods did not necessarily compete with one another and that the shared geographical background remained a unifying element.

On the other hand, several brotherhoods could give rise to a single one in the sense of forming a mental nation. That process could be initiated by political interests and be financially supported by a government, as in the case of the fusion of the Castilian, Aragonese, and Portuguese brotherhoods into the Iberian Brotherhood in 1579: "Because they enhance our reputation and authority at the papal court," so King Philipp II, the ambassador was to bring together and promote all subjects of the Spanish crown in Rome. This points to the functions of the national brotherhoods in the political context: for their members they formed a social network that offered patronage relationships alongside charitable services and economic connections, and which was able to provide, for example, career-advancing contacts to the Curia.

With respect to their home country, the brotherhoods took on the task of demonstrating the strength of their nation in Rome. A central tool to that end was the organization of religious ceremonies that took place on national feast days, in honor of national patron saints or on the occasion of the country's political and military triumphs, and which always referred symbolically to one's homeland, for example, through relevant coats of arms on the religious paraphernalia. Then there were charitable events that were also publicly staged and identified as national. Finally, the *nazioni* made their appearance on social occasions, for example when their members accompanied a newly arrived ambassador on his first visit to the Curia, thus increasing the number of coaches in the diplomat's entourage, something that was attentively noted by observers. But there is another factor, in particular, which demonstrates that this participation in the city's religious and social life was simultaneously intended and perceived as a political demonstration: the Italian supporters of a particular country within the college of cardinals often participated in the activities of the national brotherhoods as a way of declaring their loyalty to the national party and in the process also strengthening it symbolically.

The political function of the national brotherhoods was additionally expressed in the efforts by popes and monarchs to shape the legal status of the organizations in their own interests: in 1604, the popes pushed through a provision that brotherhoods could be founded only with their approval. The European monarchs, meanwhile, sought to gain control of their respective national brotherhoods along with their property. Since most states were able to do just that with the help of their ambassadors, numerous brotherhoods were placed under the direct administration of the permanent embassies in the 17th and 18th centuries. Occasionally the Holy See was able to prevent this: for example, when Italy entered the war in 1915, it took over the administration of the Anima to protect the holdings of the German national church from being confiscated by the Italian state. As a result of these actions by the church and the state, the only brotherhoods in the traditional sense that still exist today are the foundations of the Italian and the Campo Santo Teutonico.

Within the brotherhoods, which were not structured along the lines of professional estates, the social spectrum of members ranged from the crown cardinals, ambassadors, and auditors of the Rota (tribunal of the Curia), to wealthy merchants and prosperous artisans, all the way down to servants of noble households. Although the lower social strata were not able to occupy the offices of the organizations, they did play a large role: they were the recipients of the charity with which the brotherhoods not only demonstrated solidarity with their countrymen, but also – and above all – staged their piety to maximum public effect. Support (dowries) was also given to some of the women who joined the brotherhoods as "sisters" but could not expect to hold any position of leadership.

At first glance, the non-Italians in Rome were hardly identifiable as members of their nations. To be sure, dress made it possible to distinguish clerics and laypersons and in both groups the various estates or hierarchical ranks or orders. And since observers at festive occasions occasionally detected ornamentations *alla spagnuola* on the livery of the participants, ceremonial garb may well have been identifiable in terms of nation. Among the mass of the population, however, nationalities are not likely to have expressed themselves in dress. That is also true for the settlement structure, which was oriented more toward occupation than geographic origin. That some *nazioni* were overrepresented in certain professions and thus also in the respective neighborhoods can be seen, for example, from the Florentine banking quarter in Rione Ponte. In general, however, place of residence does not permit any inference about nationality.

Nationality can be very easily recognized and demonstrated only through participation in the national brotherhood and the use of the national language, which was prescribed in the statutes at least of the German brotherhoods and was presumably widespread especially among their members. Churches and cemeteries often carried the nation in their names (e.g., San Luigi dei Francesi, Campo Santo Teutonico), and their architectural design often resembled an affirmation of their homeland, up to a certain point (the Italian Renaissance was the measure of all things).

Even if the number of members of a nation who never joined the respective brotherhood is impossible to determine, it is likely that it accounted for the majority in all nations. Just how far the lack of interest in one's own geographic identity could go is revealed by the number – by no means small – of Italianized foreign names.

Given the stereotypes that were common and cultivated in Rome, one can assume that this kind of assimilation was a helpful career move. Non-Italians were perceived in Rome not only as foreigners, like the immigrant Italians; someone who came from beyond the Alps was considered "ultramontane," a term that would become synonymous with "heretic" in the 18th and 19th centuries. The image of the Germans was particularly negative and from an especially early date. Already in the 15th and 16th centuries, both popular and learned literature disseminated the stereotype of the boorish, perennially drunk German, whose language was considered the embodiment of the incomprehensible. The image grew even more negative through the *Sacco di Roma*, and the Reformation added another aspect: Luther's countrymen became the incarnation of the anti-Roman heretics.

Skepticism toward foreigners in general and Germans in particular was widespread also at the Curia, as attested by its intensive efforts in the 17th century to establish better oversight of foreign visitors in Rome. Their salvation was deemed to be especially imperiled in the environment around the Anima: by the scandalous life that German bakers, the strongest occupational group among the Germans in Rome, in particular were accused of leading, and from the heretical teachings that seemed to have a stubborn hold in this nation.

To what extent such perceptions impaired the everyday life of non-Italians in Rome is difficult to say. On the flip-side, there is no small number of indications that point to social integration. For example, a German-Italian brotherhood of weavers existed from the early 15th century, which points to the unifying force of the shared occupation, which was also important to the settlement structure. And in the Spanish national brotherhood, 14% of the young women in the organization who received a dowry between 1578 and 1628 had one Roman parent. Evidently, the marriage circles were limited far less to one's own nation than the national stereotypes would suggest. While membership in a national brotherhood might therefore point to a certain identification with one's own nation, it did not invariably make integration into the Roman population more difficult.

The dual role of the pope as head of the church and territorial ruler placed limits on the mobility at the Roman Curia. The dissolution of the Papal States in 1870 made possible the very internationalization at the Curia and the college of cardinals that had been thwarted for centuries by the worldly political interests of the papacy. This development found its most striking expression in 1978: when the Pole Karol Wojtyla was elected pope, it was the first time in more than 450 years that a non-Italian had ascended to the papal throne. However, this was preceded by a process that was manifested in the legal realm much earlier: for example, the right of exclusion was prohibited in 1904, and the 1917 version of canon law declared that cardinals were to be recruited from all parts of the world. Neither stipulation was new, but both were now implemented for the first time.

With respect to the background of the cardinals, following tentative steps under Pope Pius IX (1846–78), a genuine internationalization began with Pius XII (1939–58). Although John XXIII (1958–63) once again appointed Italians with greater frequency, he also appointed the first African cardinal. Paul VI (1963–78) and John Paul II (1978–2005) vigorously pushed this development forward. And so while Italy in absolute numbers still furnishes more cardinals than any other country in the world (end of 1994: 20), the percentage of Italians dropped from 35% in 1963 to 24% in 1978 to 17% in 1994. Western Europe's share (without Italy) also declined from 29% (1963) to 20% in 1978 and 19% in 1994. The winners of this restructuring were Latin America (increase from 3% to 16%) and Asia (1939: 1.6%; 1958: 7.3%) under Pope Pius XII, Africa under Paul VI (1963: 1%; 1978: 10.5%), and Africa (1994: 12.5%) and eastern Europe (1978: 6%; 1994: 10%) under John Paul II.

Pope Paul VI gave clear proof for the changed perception of the international character of the college of cardinals. While non-Italian cardinals were still seen by the popes as a threat to their political freedom in the 19th century, Paul VI addressed the newly elevated cardinals in 1973 as representatives not only of their dioceses, but also of their nations. And in 1976 he declared that the goal of the most recent elevations was to make the college a mirror of the world church with members from all nations.

Ago, Renata. *Carriere e clientele nella Roma barocca*. Rome, 1990.

Broderick, John F. "The Sacred College of Cardinals: Size and Geographical Composition (1099–1986)." *Archivum Historiae Pontificiae* 25 (1987): 7–71.

Dandelet, Thomas James. *Spanish Rome 1500–1700*. New Haven, 2001.

Fosi, Irene. "Roma e gli 'ultramontani.' Conversioni, viaggi, identità." *Quellen und Forschungen aus Italienischen Archiven und Bibliotheken* 81 (2001): 351–96.

Füssel, Stephan, and Klaus A. Vogel, eds. *Deutsche Handwerker, Künstler und Gelehrte im Rom der Renaissance*. Wiesbaden, 2001.

Hurtubise, Pierre. "La présence des 'étrangers' à la cour de Rome dans la première moitié du XVIe siècle." In *Forestieri e stranieri nelle Città basso-medievali*, 57–80. Florence, 1988.

Levillain, Philippe, ed. *Dictionnaire historique de la Papauté*. Paris, 1994.

Reese, Thomas J. *Im Innern des Vatikan. Politik und Organisation der katholischen Kirche*. Frankfurt am Main, 1998.

Reinhard, Wolfgang. "Herkunft und Karriere der Päpste 1417–1963. Beiträge zu einer historischen Soziologie der römischen Kurie." *Mededelingen van het Nederlands Historisch Instituut te Rome* 38 (1976): 87–108.

Schulz, Knut, and Christiane Schuchard. *Handwerker deutscher Herkunft und ihre Bruderschaften im Rom der Renaissance. Darstellung und ausgewählte Quellen*. Rome, 2005.

Signorotto, Gianvittorio, and Maria Antonietta Visceglia, eds. *La Corte di Roma tra Cinque e Seicento. "Teatro" della politica europea*. Rome, 1998.

Cross-references: France; Germany; Italy; Spain and Portugal

EUROPEAN POLITICAL EMIGRANTS IN THE USSR SINCE 1917

Hannes Leidinger and Verena Moritz

With a decree in March 1918, the Russian Socialist Federal Soviet Republic (RSFSR) granted "all foreigners who are being persecuted for political or religious crimes the right of asylum." The decree was incorporated into the first version of the constitution of the RSFSR in July 1918. With the creation of the USSR, the reference to persecution on religious grounds disappeared. In the constitution of the Soviet Union of 1936, admission was to be granted to "citizens of foreign states" who were being persecuted "for defending the interests of workers or for scientific work or for a national liberation struggle."

Reality, however, was very different from these pronouncements, for the right of asylum was applied in an extremely restrictive fashion. Bodies that dealt with political emigration to the USSR – the commission of the All-Russian Central Executive Committee, the Communist International (Comintern) and its national branches, and later especially the Central Legitimation Committee of the International Red Aid (IRA) – came from a position of class warfare and emphasized that "the political emigrants" should "be preserved for the fighting proletariat." Therefore, the IRA communists had to choose either illegality in their own country or resettlement in a capitalist country with a liberal asylum practice. The USSR could grant asylum only if there was a "threat of the death penalty or long prison term," and even then only with the approval of the applicant's own and the Soviet Communist Party. Those who were in the end admitted were among the Communist Party cadres or at least among those who sympathized with the Soviet power and the "Socialist experiment."

In addition to "political emigrants," many who were politically interested in the "Soviet experiment" spent some time in the USSR: between April 1925 and October 1926, for example, 19 delegations of foreign workers and unions, some of them with several hundred participants, visited the country. From 1929 to 1933 there were nearly 2,000 delegates from 33 countries. Moreover, many "comrades" dispatched from their countries of origin attended the cadre or party schools in the USSR: in 1926–7, for instance, around 170 foreign communists were studying at the International Lenin School in Moscow.

Moscow did not develop into a center of exile for European Social Democrats. At the beginning of World War II they fled to France and Czechoslovakia, and after 1939 from there directly or indirectly to the USA, Switzerland, the UK, and Sweden. The same is true of many communists. Until the 1930s, they escaped the persecutions in Italy, southeastern Europe, and east-central Europe by going chiefly to Vienna and Paris.

Between 1923 and 1932, more than 10,000 individuals found refuge in the USSR, mostly from Poland, Bulgaria, Latvia, Germany, and Romania. The number of German-speaking refugees to the Soviet Union increased once more following the Nazi takeover of power in Germany. In 1936, this group alone is said to have comprised 4,000–5,000 persons, about 30%–40% of whom were women. However, neither the highest circles of the Communist Party nor the Comintern had precise numbers. The control commission or cadre section of the Comintern estimated that the number of political emigrants for the period between 1920 and

1936 was at least 35,000–37,000, although the reports on which this estimate was based were incomplete. Thirteen "sister parties," among them the Romanian and Bulgarian parties, which were so important for questions dealing with emigrants, furnished no information at all.

The integration of the political emigrants proved difficult. For one, civil war, ethnic conflicts, and Allied intervention had created a kind of siege mentality in the Kremlin leadership, which led to the surveillance of the foreigners. Surrounded by "class enemies," the leadership mistrusted even its own Soviet diplomats or, for example, prisoners of war from the ranks of the czar's army who had come into contact with "foreign capitalist countries" between 1914 and 1918. For another, the emigrants were not interested in staying long in the Socialist fatherland. Many were awaiting a favorable moment to return to their home countries, regardless of whether they were put to work in the central apparatus of the Communist International or – as for instance the members of the German, Latvian, and Polish sections of the Comintern as well as the approximately 750 Austrian emigrants of the Military Organization (Schutzbund) of the Austrian Social Democratic Workers' Party – they had been brought together in their own housing, national clubs, and cultural institutions.

Still, there were some efforts by the Communist Party of Russia (CPR) to create ties that bound the foreign communists to the USSR. In 1923, the Comintern decided to dissolve foreign communist associations in the USSR and to demand admission into the CPR as the condition for "political emigration." Until 1934, the decision to adopt Soviet citizenship was voluntary; thereafter, that step also became a requirement for recognition as a political emigrant.

The climate toward all foreigners deteriorated from the 1930s on: the abolition of the special "provision for foreigners," which until 1935–6 involved access to a better range of available goods in separate stores and the possibility of paying with foreign currency, also affected the political emigrants. Remigrations were the result. Those who opted to extend their stay in the Soviet Union and in many cases brought their families to join them, not least for economic reasons, witnessed the Stalinist cadre investigations that culminated in the Great Purge (1936–8), with a relatively high number of victims among the foreigners and ethnic minorities of the Soviet Union. Those affected included nationalities that were associated with potentially hostile states, such as National Socialist Germany.

Communists and socialists who were forced into illegality in their own countries and were thus without diplomatic protection were especially helpless in the face of the persecutions by the NKVD (Soviet Ministry of Internal Affairs, which ran the Secret Service). A number of emigrant groups lost a large number of their members. Some sections of the Comintern, including the Polish one, ceased to exist entirely in the wake of the repressions. Even though the reported numbers may not be quite accurate, one can assume that 315 of the 875 Belarusian and 140 of the 200–300 Yugoslav political emigrants were persecuted. The German representation on the Executive Committee of the Comintern reported on 29 April 1938 that more than 70% of the members of the Communist Party had been arrested. We know the precise number of Bulgarian emigrants to the Soviet Union between 1917 and 1944: 3,000. Of those, 1,200 were persecuted and either shot or – with a survival rate of 10% – sentenced to prison and forced labor. Members of foreign communist parties who were spared continued to work for the party. Among other things, they were put to work during World War II on the "ideological schooling" of captured soldiers of the German Wehrmacht and its allied armies.

After the advance of Soviet troops at the end of the war, the leadership cadres returned to their own countries. Some subsequently occupied high state and party offices in the communist-dominated satellite states of the USSR. A few remigrants took over functions in the Soviet Occupation Zones in Germany and Austria. And finally, those who had been in prison or were still in camps also managed to leave the Soviet Union. The "land of the October Revolution" had largely lost its fascination.

Chase, William J. *Enemies within the Gates? The Comintern and the Stalinist Repression, 1934–1939*. New Haven and London, 2001.

Leidinger, Hannes, and Verena Moritz. *Gefangenschaft, Revolution, Heimkehr. Die Bedeutung der Kriegsgefangenenproblematik für die Geschichte des Kommunismus in Mittel- und Osteuropa 1917–1920*. Vienna, 2003.

McLoughlin, Barry, Hans Schafranek, and Walter Szevera. *Aufbruch – Hoffnung – Endstation. Österreicherinnen und Österreicher in der Sowjetunion 1925–1945*. Vienna, 1996.

Müller, Reinhard. *Menschenfalle Moskau. Exil und stalinistische Verfolgung*. Hamburg, 2001.

Tischler, Carola. *Flucht in die Verfolgung. Deutsche Emigranten im sowjetischen Exil 1933 bis 1945*. Münster, 1996.

Weber, Hermann, and Dietrich Staritz, eds. *Kommunisten verfolgen Kommunisten. Stalinistischer Terror und ›Säuberungen‹ in den kommunistischen Parteien Europas seit den dreißiger Jahren*. Berlin, 1993.

Cross-references: Austria; The Baltic Region; Czechia and Slovakia; Germany; Poland; Russia and Belarus; Southeastern Europe; Ukraine; Deportees in the Soviet Union during and after World War II; Political and Intellectual Refugees from Nazi Germany and from German-Occupied Europe, 1933–1945; Prisoners of War in Europe, 1914–1922

EUROPEAN SOLDIERS IN THE NAPOLEONIC ARMY

Erich Pelzer

The European war that the nation in arms (*nation armée*) launched in 1792 under the banner of liberty, equality, and the right of self-determination of nations, and which Napoleon Bonaparte carried on in altered constellation until 1815, demanded a heavy blood sacrifice from France. Between 1792 and 1815, the wars of revolution and empire cost around 1.4 million lives, out of a French population of 25 million (5.8% of the total population). In three important respects the Napoleonic army followed the tradition of the French Revolution: it adopted the same recruitment methods, it supported the motivation of each participant in the wars through a system of promotion, and it embraced the policy of expansion through conquest and subjugation.

However, the numerous wars between 1796 and 1815 were not waged solely and exclusively by French troops. From the beginning, and after 1805 on a larger scale, foreign troops were incorporated into the French army. In 1812, at the latest, the Napoleonic army was a European one. Of the Grande Armée that crossed the Memel on 12 June 1812 to bring down czarist Russia, less than half were Frenchmen. There is hardly a European nation that was not involved in the Napoleonic wars. Even Danish and Swiss auxiliary troops fought for France. About 720,000 foreign soldiers served in the Grande Armée between 1805 and 1813.

The particular ratio, however, including casualties, varied considerably from one country to the next. For example, Italians fought in the Lecchi Division in the Veneto in 1805 and in Naples in 1806. Until January 1804, 7,900 Italians were stationed in the camp of Boulogne; deployed to Prussia in 1807, they assisted the French in the siege of Kolberg and Stralsund. After their return to Milan they were used in the Spanish campaign in 1808. Between 1808 and 1813, 30,183 Italians served on the Iberian Peninsula, and only 8,958 returned home. Under the command of Eugène de Beauharnais, the viceroy of Italy installed by Napoleon, they participated in the campaigns in Russia and Germany. Of the 10,300 Italians who crossed the Memel in June 1812, merely 500 survived the Russian campaign. A total of 121,000 Italians served in the French army from 1806 to 1814. Their losses amounted to 50%. The contingent from the Kingdom of Naples was smaller and was deployed chiefly in Catalonia (9,000 men). As late as 1813, 13,000 Neapolitans were still fighting in Germany; of those, 1,454 were killed and 400 taken prisoner.

The largest contingents among the foreign Napoleonic troops were made up of Germans (chiefly from the Kingdoms of Saxony, Bavaria, Württemberg, and Westphalia, and from the Grand Duchies of Baden, Cleves-Berg, Hesse-Darmstadt, Nassau, and Frankfurt) and Poles (from the Grand Duchy of Warsaw). A summary overview reveals the various troop levels and casualties for the period 1805–13: Bavaria (110,000; casualties: 36,500); Saxony (66,000; 30,000); Württemberg (48,000; 19,000); Baden (24,500; 12,000); smaller states of the Rhenish Confederation (60,500; 26,500); Cleves-Berg (13,000; 8,500); Westphalia (52,000; 36,000, most through desertion); Warsaw (85,000; 40,500). The Austrian auxiliary corps in 1812 comprised 30,000 men, of whom 6,000 were killed and wounded and 4,000 died from disease. The smallest contingent of all was the Prussian auxiliary corps of 1812, which had only a single division, served in the 10th Army

Corps under Marshal Jacques MacDonald, and was stationed in Riga and St. Petersburg. Because it was not involved in actual warfare, its losses remained comparatively small (500 men).

The age of the mass armies since the French Revolution had rendered the mercenary armies obsolete. Their place was taken by drafted subjects who were sworn to a new kind of obligatory military service. The military recruitment was unpopular in France because the system of levying soldiers was made dependent on demand and social criteria. Wealthy families could buy out their sons with an official certificate by providing a replacement. Between 1801 and 1805, one out of every four Frenchmen avoided the draft; between 1805 and 1810 it was one out of five. Next to buying an exemption, the only way to escape military service was desertion, which Napoleon fought implacably as an act of treason.

Most Frenchmen, convinced of their own political and cultural superiority, saw the Spaniards, Germans, Dutchmen, Austrians, and Russians as backward subjects imperturbably loyal to king and priest. What the populations in the occupied and annexed territories experienced as harassment and oppression were above all the heavy war contributions, the disregard of their religion, and the plundering of churches and museums. This created a climate of popular hostility toward France, which erupted in Germany, for example, in the War of Liberation of 1813. National hatred, effectively stoked by poets and writers (e.g., Ernst Moritz Arndt, Heinrich von Kleist), had primarily economic, social, and cultural motives. All told, opposition to French occupation erupted three times in popular revolts: 1806 in Calabria, 1808 in Spain, and 1809 in Tyrol.

Rates of desertion and flight from conscription were correspondingly high. Between 1805 and 1809, more than 42% of the conscripts in Belgium deserted, as did one-third of those called up in Rome in 1810. More than 18,000 soldiers deserted in the Kingdom of Italy in 1809. Tens of thousands of deserters lived as bandits and vagrants and terrorized the rural population. Although many efforts were made to maintain order, even in France some regions were not free of vagabond deserters.

The Napoleonic age generated hundreds of thousands of prisoners of war on all sides. The European sovereigns showed little interest in them. After the end of the war in 1815, tens of thousands of prisoners were still interned in camps. In France alone, 130,000 were yearning for the day of their liberation, among them no fewer than 16,000 English soldiers and 1,000 English civilians. They were housed in the fortresses of Verdun, Sedan, Bitche, Longwy, and Valenciennes in northern France. During the campaign of 1805, 70,000 Austrians fell into French hands, and nearly as many Prussians did in the campaigns of 1806–7. The Austrians were released from French captivity in March 1806, the Prussians in December 1808. During their captivity, the Prussian prisoners of war worked on canal construction (Burgundy, Saint-Quentin, the Ourcy Canal, and in the port of Rochefort) and drained swamps in the Rhone delta and in

Charente. After the campaign of 1809, 20,000 Austrians were taken to France as prisoners.

At times, captivity gave rise to permanent settlement, which could then also lead to family reunification. The largest such group were captive soldiers in czarist Russia: the majority of the Grande Armée was taken prisoner by the Russians in 1812. According to Russian sources, they numbered 150,000 men, not counting about 50,000 to 60,000 injured and sick. According to French sources, a mere 60,000 to 72,000 men who had survived the Russian winter returned to France. The czar sought to prevail upon the prisoners remaining in Russia to stay: in July 1813 a letter from the Russian Minister of Police was circulated throughout Russia, followed by an identical *ukase* from the czar in November 1813, which offered the prisoners settlement as foreign settlers and naturalization. The czar guaranteed them freedom of religion, exemption from military service, a tax exemption for five or ten years, and a plot of land in Ukraine or Siberia. The decree initially envisaged a provisional citizenship for two to three years, which could then be converted into a permanent one. By August 1814, two years after the Russian campaign, one-quarter of the former soldiers of the Grande Armée had taken advantage of this offer. About 15,000 to 20,000 of them became subjects of the czar.

Bernard, Léonce. *Les prisonniers de guerre du Premier Empire.* Paris, 2002.

Elting, John R. *Swords around a Throne: Napoleon's Grande Armée.* New York, 1988.

Lucas-Dubreton, Jean. *Les soldats de Napoléon.* Paris, 1977.

Rothenburg, Gunther. *The Napoleonic Wars.* London, 1999.

Smith, Digby. *The Greenhill Napoleonic Wars Data Book: Actions and Losses in Personnel, Colours, Standards and Artillery, 1792–1815.* London, 1998.

Sokolov, Oleg. *L'armée de Napoléon.* Saint-Germain-en-Laye, 2003.

Tulard, Jean, ed. *Dictionnaire Napoléon*, 2 vols. Paris, 1999.

Cross-references: Austria; Belgium and Luxembourg; France; Germany; Great Britain; Italy; The Netherlands; Northern Europe; Poland; Russia and Belarus; Spain and Portugal; Switzerland

EUROPEAN STUDENTS AT ITALIAN UNIVERSITIES IN THE EARLY MODERN PERIOD

Gian Paolo Brizzi

From the establishment of the first European universities in Bologna and Padua in the 11th century, geographic mobility was part and parcel of student life: in the early modern period, students often changed their place of study several times. In 16th-century Ferrara and Pisa, for example, 55% to 82% of all students had been at least at one other university. And the founding of numerous Italian universities in the early modern period did not reduce the rates of student mobility, even if some older and more famous universities were frequented more than some new ones.

Geographic mobility of students in Italy, the *iter italicum*, developed at the turn from the Middle Ages to the early modern age into the prime example of student migration in Europe. There was the migration of the *citramontani*, who migrated regionally but certainly did cross the borders of Italian states. This must be distinguished from the migration of the *ultramontani*, who came from countries beyond the Alps and some of whom visited several Italian universities in succession. Although *ultramontani* were in the minority, their influx is a sign of pronounced academic motivation, which prompted young students to embark upon the sometimes adventurous and financially costly journeys and put up with a separation from home and family that often lasted for years. The more *ultramontani* were studying at a university, the higher its reputation and that of its teachers.

From the beginning of the 16th to the middle of the 17th century, Italian universities attracted the most foreign students, compared to their European counterparts. Signs of the presence of foreign students in Italian university towns that are still visible today are family coats of arms, which can be found, for example, on the walls of university buildings (Archiginnasio in Bologna, Bò in Padua). Other reminders of the influx of students are names of streets in some university towns that refer to the geographic origins of the students, or the adoption of patron saints that were unknown to the local tradition.

The students enrolled not only at the university, but overwhelmingly also in their respective *nationes*. These institutions can be seen as communities of origin or common language. Many Italian universities in the early modern period, however, distinguished only between *natio citramontana* and *natio ultramontana*. But we are told that there were 14 *nationes* in Bologna as early as the 13th century: they included the "Polish nation" (*natio polonica*) and the "German nation" (*natio germanica*).

The Italian universities of historical renown especially attracted *ultramontani*: Bologna, Padua, Pavia, followed by the universities of Siena, Rome, Perugia, and Ferrara. The enrollment registers attest that many of the newly established universities of the 16th and 17th centuries, by contrast, had a marked regional character: Macerata (1549) and Fermo (1558), for example, only sporadically attracted students from outside the region, especially since the overall student turnover at these universities was less pronounced. Even the most heavily attended university in Italy, that in Naples founded in 1224, seems to have drawn mostly from the surrounding regions, against a backdrop of low student turnover: only 0.4% of the graduates between 1584 and 1648 were not local.

In many cases, family traditions determined the choice of a place of study. Beyond that, the influx of students into early modern Italy was driven by a variety of motivations. Italy exerted a particular attraction as the cradle of Humanism. The

iter italicum had already been trod by important scholars – for example, the astronomer Nikolaus Kopernikus, the theologian John Colet, the philologist and philosopher Erasmus of Rotterdam, and the philologist Antonio de Nebrija. The mobility of the professors, some of whom changed university every semester, also furthered the migration, especially among those students who were willing to follow their teachers: Galileo Galilei, for example, was accompanied by students to Pisa, Padua, and Florence. They came from many European countries and often lived with their teacher in the same house.

The student migration, frequently referred to also as an academic pilgrimage (*peregrinatio academica*), had developed especially because of the rising demand for well-educated administrative elites in the territorial states. University degrees were generally recognized throughout Europe. Since the late 15th century, a course of study at a faculty of law had offered students of burgher background good prospects of professional and social advancement. Students who had studied Roman law in Bologna, for example, could enter the service of their territorial lord in the Holy Roman Empire of the German Nation as councilors and syndics. As doctors of law, they pushed into positions that had hitherto been reserved for the nobility, or they became city officeholders. According to the law of the Empire, doctors were on a par with the lower nobility. Unlike members of the nobility, who often had to show only a brief course of study, they were dependent on a degree to assume offices in the state, the cities, or the church. Against this backdrop, the number of students of burgher background at Italian universities rose from the end of the 15th century. Only in the 17th century was the proportion of noblemen and commoners among the students in balance again, not least because it was becoming increasingly important also for the nobility to hold a degree to have a successful career in state service.

Since the 17th century, the educational goals developed in pedagogical theses emphasized the formation of the perfect gentleman. As a result, music schools as well as weapons and riding academies were increasingly established in university towns. The new educational goals turned the traditional *peregrinatio academica* into a Grand Tour, within the framework of which the universities were seen as merely one educational institution among many; for the nobility, there were, for example, the Colleges of the Nobility in Parma, Bologna, Siena, Naples, Rome, and Palermo, as well as the Collegio Nazareno and the Collegio Clementino in Rome.

For the 16th century, 1,217 French students (from France, Franche-Comté, and French Savoy) were recorded in Italy: of those, 481 were enrolled in Padua, 305 in Pavia, 220 in Ferrara, and 123 in Bologna; to a lesser extent they also studied in Pisa, Turin, Siena, Perugia, and Rome. Political events and treaty alliances determined their migration: the French occupation of the Duchy of Milan (1515–25), for example, led to a growth of the francophone student group in Pavia, which was part of Milan. Following the French defeat in the Battle of Pavia in 1525 against the Habsburgs, the francophone students tended to migrate in the direction of Padua, which was under Venetian rule. Ferrara was a preferred destination of the French, above all during the rule of Duke Ercole II (1528–59) and his wife Renata, the daughter of Louis XII of France. The city showed itself very hospitable not only to Frenchmen, but also to John Calvin and other reformers.

The universities in northern Italy were a destination also for Dutch students: between 1500 and 1575, 107 were recorded in Bologna, 108 in Padua, and 32 in Ferrara. The development of their migration suggests an increase in the following decades. While fewer and fewer students from the British Isles came to Italy during the 16th century, because universities of European-wide renown (Oxford, Cambridge) were emerging in their own country, the number of Poles seems to have remained stable in Padua and especially Bologna, where 679 Polish students were enrolled between 1500 and 1650.

On a much larger scale was the influx of students from the Holy Roman Empire of the German nation. Between 1500 and 1650, Bologna, Siena, Padua, and Perugia together recorded about 40,000 enrolled students from the Empire. Since some of the students attended several universities, their total number may have been around 25,000. Padua attracted about 44% of German students, Siena around 28%, Bologna 22%, and Perugia right around 6%.

Geographic proximity did not determine the choice of a place of study: of German graduates in the fields of medicine and philosophy in Padua, only 34% came from a region in the Alps or immediately adjoining territories (Austria, Tyrol, Styria, Carinthia, Bohemia, or Swabia), while the remaining 66% hailed from regions farther north (Silesia, Saxony, Westphalia). In Bologna, Siena, Padua, and Perugia combined, an average of 19 young men from the southern regions of the Reich were enrolled each year, compared with 12 from Silesia, alone. The link between the Italian universities and certain German cities remained stable throughout the entire period (1500–1650), as attested by the migration from Strasbourg, Augsburg, Cologne, Freiburg im Breisgau, Halle, Würzburg, Leipzig, Lüneburg, Munich, Münster, Nuremberg, Innsbruck, Salzburg, Graz, and Ulm.

The influx from other European cities (Antwerp, Brussels, Alcañiz, Barcelona, Mallorca) to Italy also continued. Spanish students went almost exclusively to the university in Bologna, where 11% of graduates in the law faculty came from Spain, and in smaller numbers to the University of Pisa, where Spaniards accounted for 7% of the doctoral candidates in the 16th century, though only 2.6% in the 17th. Spanish students avoided Padua because of the conflicts between Venice and Habsburg, and they preferred Bologna because the Spanish king Philipp II (1556–98) authorized only Bologna and Rome as destinations for Spanish students in an effort to promote the establishment of universities in his own country.

Of the 616 students from the German nation who completed their studies in Padua between 1616 and 1673, 36% spent less than six months in the city, and 58% between six months and three years. The majority of students who came to Padua for only a few months had already studied in another city. The purpose of the stay in Padua was to acquire an academic degree from a renowned university. By contrast, those who stayed longer completed studies they had pursued mostly in Padua. In the 16th and 17th centuries, Padua had gained an excellent reputation in medicine, natural sciences, mathematics, and philosophy, while Bologna was especially famous for its legal faculty: 25.6% of the graduates of the law school in Bologna between 1500 and 1650 were *ultramontani*, the majority from the Holy Roman Empire and Spain.

Confessionalization had a decisive influence on the choice of places of study as early as the second half of the 16th century: after 1564, students were compelled to make a profession of their faith. Since that time, the doctoral colleges could grant a title only to Catholic students. Still, in the enrollment lists of the *natio germanica* in Bologna we can find some non-Catholics, who may have concealed their true confession (as did, for example, Duke Frederick I of Württemberg, Georg Erasmus von Tschernembl, Karl von Zierotin, and Prince Johan Georg I of Saxony).

Venice remained neutral in the confessional conflicts because it wanted to underscore its independence vis-à-vis the pope, and because as a trading city, it did not wish to strain its relationships with the Protestant German states. In 1616, the Serenissima established its own doctoral college. In this way, it circumvented the obligation to demand a profession of faith from the students. Subsequently, between 1616 and 1673, around 89% of the members of the German nation at the University of Padua completed their studies at the college in Venice.

Padua remained the exception. More common was the Counter-Reformation solution of recruiting Catholic students by setting up scholarship or educational colleges and keeping students increasingly at a single university for the duration of their studies. Their education and training at Italian universities was to turn them into champions of Catholicism in their countries of origin. Colleges were set up especially for students from countries in which reform efforts were strong or the Orthodox faith seemed to be spreading. A Hungarian-Illyrian college was set up in 1533 in Bologna.

Rome, however, became even more of a center of colleges: while the German College had been established as early as 1552, followed by the Hungarian, English, and Greek-Maronite colleges between 1577 and 1584, the year 1622 saw the founding of the College "de Propaganda Fide," which was intended to train the missionary clergy. Students from southeastern Europe had the College Paleocapa (1633) and the Seminar Cottunio (1653) in Padua, the Illyrian College in Loreto (1581), and the Illyrian-Albanian College near Fermo (1663).

The *nationes* were centers of student life at the universities and were self-administered. They represented the student body to the academic and city administrations and to other nations. Students from the Empire, for example, participated for at least one semester in the self-governance of the German nation in Bologna as procurators, consiliari, and librarians and in this way exerted influence on the university. The German *nationes* in Padua and Bologna enjoyed city privileges thanks to their many and highly esteemed members: they had their own jurisdiction and were exempt from certain taxes. At events put on by the city, a front-row seat among the city's burghers was reserved for the Consiliar as the representative of the German nation. His privileges included the right to carry arms in public. Not all students enrolled in the *nationes* did in fact pursue university studies: the advantage of an enrollment lay in the protection that the nation offered as legal counsel, for example, against actions taken by the Inquisition, which happened from time to time.

The students were completely integrated into the nations. The nations had their own residential houses, estates, economic enterprises, facilities for tests and academic festivities, as well as cemeteries and churches in which they held their own masses. Noble students, more than non-nobles, were far more strongly integrated into the society of the host country: as members of an early modern noble society that transcended countries, they attended balls and princely audiences or spent time at the courts. After completing their studies, the vast majority of the students – now with expertise, well read, with a knowledge of languages and travel experience – returned to their regions of origin to assume positions in the state, the cities, and the church.

Brizzi, Gian Paolo. "La pratica del viaggio d'istruzione in Italia nel Sei-Settecento." *Annali dell'Istituto storico italo-germanico in Trento* 2 (1976): 203–91.

Dotzauer, Winfried. "Deutsches Studium und deutsche Studenten an europäischen Hochschulen (Frankreich, Italien) und die nachfolgende Tätigkeit in Stadt, Kirche und Territorium in Deutschland." In *Stadt und Universität im Mittelalter und in der frühen Neuzeit*, edited by Erich Maschke and Jürgen Sydow, 112–41. Sigmaringen, 1977.

Ridder-Symoens, Hilde de. "Mobility." In *A History of the University in Europe*, vol. 2: *Universities in Early Modern Europe (1500–1800)*, edited by Hilde de Ridder-Symoens, 416–48. Cambridge, 1996.

Tervoort, Ad. *The Iter Italicum and the Northern Netherlands. Dutch Students at Italian Universities and Their Role in the Netherlands' Society (1426– 1575)*. Leiden, 2005.

Verger, Jacques. "Peregrinatio academica." In *Le università dell'Europa. Gli uomini e i luoghi, secoli XII–XVIII*, edited by Gian Paolo Brizzi and Jacques Verger, 107–35. Milan, 1993.

Zonta, Claudia A. *Schlesische Studenten an italienischen Universitäten. Eine prosopographische Studie zur frühneuzeitlichen Bildungsgeschichte*. Cologne, 2004.

Cross-references: Germany; France; Italy; The Netherlands; Poland; Spain and Portugal; Southeastern Europe; European Elites on the Grand Tour in Early Modern Europe

FILIPINO MAIL-ORDER BRIDES IN WESTERN, CENTRAL, AND NORTHERN EUROPE SINCE THE 1980S

Virginia O. del Rosario

The term "mail-order bride" was first coined in the popular press in the 1980s and used to label Filipino and other Asian women introduced to foreign men through the mediation of commercial institutions (for example, marriage bureaus, friendship clubs, and so on) with the goal of marriage. The system of this marriage market, as in the use of the phrase, manifests ethnic and social inequalities between women of the third world and men from industrialized nations of the West. Once an introduction had been made, the man and the woman involved underwent a period of correspondence prior to an actual meeting that could eventually lead to marriage. The migration of the woman either as fiancée or wife to the man's country of domicile usually resulted – hence, the term "mail-order brides."

The view of this marriage market is frequently laden with biases, which have led to narrow perceptions about the role played by women involved and their personal options: the marriages of mail-order brides were purely commercial contracts and were doomed to failure. This argument justified institutional measures, such as the tightening of immigration policies by the state in the brides' destination countries, aiming at the control of the women involved. This explanation assumed that the flight of female "economic refugees" from the third world to the West was disguised as marriage. The escape from poverty was seen to be the sole motive for women portrayed as immoral.

The background for female marriage migration, important since the 1980s, is much more complex. Mail-order bride migration represents an important migratory stream of women from the Philippines since the 1980s and, equally, has had an impact on destination countries. In the country of origin, deeply embedded conceptions of family, work, and female migration were reformed by the possibilities and limitations of global migration. The migration of Filipino women as mail-order brides is the result of the interaction of domestic and global forces that operated in the 1970s and 1980s. In the Philippines, the following forces were in operation: (1) the continued use of migration as a strategy for the social mobility if not the survival of individuals and families in the framework of reciprocal obligations among Filipino family members; (2) narrowing employment options abroad for Filipino women; (3) the strong cultural pressure on women to get married, related to the deeply seated perceptions of women's role, marriage, and the value of having one's own family; and (4) the social acceptability of marriage as a woman's reason for migration.

In industrialized countries, the sociopolitical, economic, and ideological processes during the same period contributed to the major shifts in the understanding of the traditional roles of men and women, and an identity crisis for men was not an uncommon consequence. A certain portion of the male population wished for a more traditional division of roles in marriage. A male demand arose for particular types of potential marriage partners associated with such roles and values, and this demand was in turn exploited by mail-order bride agencies. Filipino migrants came from various regions: the biggest group originated from the Visayas island group, followed by those from the island of Mindanao. A considerable number also comes from the Southern Tagalog region, Bicol province on Luzon island, the central Philippines, and the northern Philippines. In relative terms, only a few come from the national capital region (Metro Manila), suggesting that the recruitment operation of mail-order bride agencies tended to concentrate more in the provinces than in big cities.

Among the most commonly documented European destinations of Filipino mail-order brides are Belgium, the Netherlands, Germany, Switzerland, Sweden, Norway, Denmark, and the UK. Filipino mail-order bride migrants have also been documented in Australia, New Zealand, the USA, Canada, Japan, and more recently, Taiwan. Regardless of their nationality – whether in Europe or elsewhere – the majority of the foreign husbands of Filipino mail-order brides are not urban dwellers, a characteristic shared with their Filipino wives. Swiss, Australian, and Japanese husbands come mostly from agricultural and farming communities. Many Australian husbands married to Filipino mail-order brides live in the remote Outback.

Accurate statistics on the number of mail-order brides migrating to each destination are extremely difficult to find. Foreign embassies in the Philippines keep a record of the number of Filipinos given entry visas to their country. However, the statistics are not always disaggregated according to sex; when disaggregated, these are restricted to the number of fiancée or spouse visas granted to Filipino women with no indication of their method of introduction. Government institutions in the mail-order bride's country of migration, such as the Netherlands' Central Bureau of Statistics, might keep statistics on Filipino-Dutch couples married in the Netherlands, but not elsewhere. The difficulty of ascertaining the method of introduction of couples is further aggravated by the denial by Filipino mail-order brides of being mail-order brides themselves, because of the pejorative attitudes toward the concept.

In general, women migrating as wives in order to join their foreign spouses in their countries of domicile tend to settle and establish their own family in such countries. After migration, most mail-order brides become full-time housewives, a condition that leads to minimal social contact and further adds to their feelings of isolation abroad. Only in a few cases does marriage not last due to unsuccessful adjustment between the partners. Some Filipino mail-order brides separated from their foreign husbands migrate back to the Philippines and rejoin their families. Others, however, remain in their former husband's country of domicile mainly because they feel shame to return to the Philippines because of their failed marriage. The latter option is available only to those who have achieved an independent resident status in their country of migration. Marriage migration for fiancées is not always successful. Mail-order brides who did not ultimately marry either engage in correspondence with another prospective foreign husband or might be introduced through the informal Filipino network to another prospective husband. Successive migration and return can be the result.

The links with her Filipino family are sustained after the Filipino mail-order bride's migration in a number of ways: regular communication; remittances in money or in goods from the woman to her family in the Philippines; visits to the Philippines by the Filipino woman, her foreign husband, and their children; or visits by the Filipino family to their daughter in her country of domicile. Other couples set up a business partnership with the bride's relatives in the Philippines, thereby also ensuring constant communication between them. However, while the mail-order brides might have settled and built their own families in their foreign husbands' country of domicile, many express a desire to return to the Philippines in their old age. In yet other cases, some mail-order bride couples decide to relocate to the Philippines to settle in the brides' home country.

The Filipino mail-order bride's integration in her new country of domicile is determined by a number of factors, among which are the quality of the ensuing marriage and how the mail-order bride is seen in the wider society. The responses of individuals and organized groups in Europe and other destination countries have been fundamentally shaped by the dominant discourse on the mail-order bride phenomenon that focuses on the women far more than on the introduction agencies or the men involved. The resulting moral isolation was further exacerbated by possible xenophobic attacks on the women. In addition, a discourse emphasizing the woman as a victim, encouraged by assistance organizations intensified this distance. Not only the direct reproach of women as "immoral" or "economic opportunists" but also the image of these women as "sex-slaves," "prostitutes," and "poor innocent victims" can legitimize migration control, limitations, and prohibitions. Feminist groups in countries of destination shared these attitudes about the migration of women from the third world. In 1985, West German feminists were reported to demand that the entry of Asian brides into the country be strictly regulated or banned completely. The women were seen as exploited by the mail-order bride system.

In contrast, nongovernmental and church-based third-world organizations also engaged in lobbying activities aimed at providing support to women who did not have successful marriages (regardless of the method of introduction) or those who had been brought into the country illegally (regardless of the channel). In the former Federal Republic of Germany, one women's organizations, AGISRA (Arbeitsgemeinschaft gegen internationale sexuelle und rassistische Ausbeutung, or Consortium against international sexual and racist exploitation) lobbied to repeal immigration laws detrimental to the foreign wives of German men.

The majority of mail-order brides belong to the Roman Catholic Church. The fatalist attitude often accompanying her religious faith can, on the one hand, give a Filipino mail-order bride the strength to endure problematic situations in the marriage or in an unfamiliar environment but can also, on the other hand, force her to sustain the marriage at all costs. Because of their strong religious faith, these brides usually turn first to the church in search of stable human contact and relationships in their new environment. The church provides a place for meeting compatriots and represents a ready refuge where the clergy and other church representatives are seen as providers of support to women in trouble. But among Roman Catholic communities, the issue of mail-order brides in the Philippines or in destination countries reflect the church's controversial position: it is caught between a sustained support of women amid physical or emotional suffering and the fight against the further outgrowth of a quickly growing international marriage market.

During mail-order brides' early residence in Europe, they were frequently discriminated against by virtue of their being "foreign" or "colored." Interestingly, women were more likely than men, in the woman's new country of residence, to display indifference or prejudice toward them. The brides attributed this to Western women's jealousy that their male compatriots had married foreigners. In the Dutch context, the discriminatory behavior of the nationals toward the Filipino bride seemed to dissipate with her being able to speak the Dutch language and relate better with the indigenous community. In Britain as well, closer social contact led to more relaxed intercultural relations.

Filipino women also became targets of covert as well as overt discrimination and harassment from the wider community in their new countries of domicile by virtue of their established or suspected identity as mail-order brides. European women, even when their marriage was completed through the brokering of marriage agents, evaded such discrimination. In Germany, where commercial matchmaking has been a tradition for some time, it is not uncommon for German people to frown upon the German man and his Asian wife who have used the services of commercial matchmakers. A similar situation exists in Japan.

Fellow Filipinos in their new countries are often indifferent to mail-order brides. The Filipino community abroad is divided concerning this issue: goodwill and support stand alongside distanced sympathy and clear rejection. These indifferent attitudes account for the isolation of many Filipino mail-order brides in their new countries of domicile. Women develop more or less successful integrative strategies. They establish and maintain an informal network of support and solidarity with other Filipino mail-order brides in similar circumstances, where information is exchanged about prospective paid employment, experiences of their own marriages are shared, and common problems and their solutions

are identified. They also work tenaciously to learn the indigenous language in their foreign husbands' countries to enable them to interact with the wider community. Some engage in remunerative activities within or outside the home to reduce boredom, isolation, and feelings of financial dependence on their husbands, as well as to enable them to send money to their families in the Philippines. Others continue to count on their Filipino families for constant emotional support despite their physical separation from them. Often, they develop a form of self-denial in the face of the images ascribed to them as mail-order brides.

Del Rosario, Virginia O. *Lifting the Smoke Screen: Dynamics of Mail-Order Bride Migration from the Philippines*. The Hague, 1994.

Hollnsteiner, Mary R. "Reciprocity in the Lowland Philippines." In *Four Readings on Philippine Values*, edited by Frank Lynch and Alfonso de Guzman, 69–91. Quezon City, 1973.

Thadani, Veena N., and Michael P. Todaro. *Female Migration in Developing Countries: A Framework for Analysis*. New York, 1979.

Truong, T. D., and Virginia O. Del Rosario. "Captive Outsiders: The Sex Traffick and Mail-Order Brides in the European Union." In *Insiders and Outsiders*, edited by J. Wiersma. Kampen, 1995.

Cross-references: Germany; Great Britain; The Netherlands

FLEMISH LABOR MIGRANTS IN WALLONIA SINCE THE 19TH CENTURY

Frank Caestecker

Migration from Flanders, the northern, Dutch-speaking region of Belgium, took place continuously throughout the 19th century. While Flemish preindustrial society was relatively prosperous with its proto-industrial linen industry, industrialization caused severe economic decline. Overseas destinations were hardly popular among Flemish emigrants as they had alternatives in neighboring areas. Both the textile industry in northern France and the Walloon heavy industry in the southern part of Belgium were in need of manpower. Distance from their home region and occupational opportunities shaped the direction of Flemish emigration. Certainly from the mid-19th century onward, East Flanders and Limburg, Flemish provinces bordering Wallonia, provided surplus labor for the Walloon industrial basin, while Flemish provinces bordering France sent their surplus labor en masse to France.

In the 1880s Flemish emigration to Wallonia saw a strong upsurge. The language census of 1890 indicates that the purely Flemish speakers and the bilingual Flemish in the two Walloon provinces where heavy industry was located had increased from 80,000 in 1890 to 110,000 in 1890. The language censuses are, however, of limited use. Mainly because of the strong Walloon pressure to assimilate in a French-speaking community, the censuses provide quantitative information only for the first generation of immigrants.

This rise in Flemish immigration runs parallel to the increasing demand for workers in Walloon heavy industry, the expansion of which was threatened by the constantly declining growth rate of the Walloon population, itself linked to the demographic transition of industrialization. New employment opportunities arose in a time when the traditional agrarian economic livelihood in all Flemish provinces was threatened. From then onward, Walloon heavy industry recruited nationally. At that time, because of the expanded railway network and the cheap transportation for workers introduced by the Catholic government to protect the rural population against the subversive influence of the city, long-term displacement was no longer necessary for earning a livelihood in faraway industries. Weekly movement between workplace and home became possible for Flemish labor migrants. After the First World War, with the introduction of the eight-hour day, even daily commuting from rural Flanders to industrial Wallonia was feasible. Although no research has been done on the size of this migration movement, it seems that from the end of the 19th century onward, only a minority of the Flemish labor migrants actually settled in the Walloon industrial basin and the number of transients increased in the first decades of the 20th century. To estimate the number of these transients we have at our disposal only a snapshot picture from the winter of 1928 when 12,000 Flemish workers commuted by train to the mines in Wallonia, and 10,000 of them returned home daily. This stream of migration dried up after the Second World War, when the center of the Belgian economy shifted toward Flanders. Migration between Flanders and Wallonia resumed in only small numbers in the 1990s, but this time in the opposite direction, toward Flanders, due to the economic decline of Wallonia.

For those Flemish labor migrants who settled in industrial Wallonia, integration into the local society was a great opportunity. It implied integration not only into an industrial world which promised a steady income, but also in a French community, which thereby offered a higher status, as French was the preferred national language.

At the end of the 19th century when industrial workers in Wallonia started to organize in a socialist counter-society this reorganization of the Walloon social space did not give way to a greater tolerance toward Flemish particularism. An industrial worker of Flemish origin in Wallonia had to be assimilated to be considered a full-fledged member of this organized working class.

At the end of the 19th century, the Belgian Catholic Church considered the Flemish a bulwark against progressive secularization, especially socialism, which was considered highly dangerous. The church therefore attempted to counter this assimilation process, promoting Flemish facilities in Wallonia and sending Flemish-speaking priests to congregations. Later, in the interwar period, these Catholic initiatives expanded to include the founding of friendly associations and trade unions. Only when this Catholic workers' movement had gained popularity among the Flemish labor migrants in Wallonia in the 1930s did the Walloon socialist community offer specific services for Flemish workers, but only half-heartedly. These services were aimed at the daily Flemish commuters only; all the others were expected to assimilate. With the integration of the Flemish into the socialist workers' movement, Catholic initiatives to preserve the Flemishness of the immigrants in Wallonia proved ultimately unsuccessful.

The integration of the Flemish immigrants in Wallonia even became a symbol in the political fight against the Flemish movement. The Walloon society, without providing any facilities for Flemish-speakers, assimilated them easily, and this was seen as a sign of its generosity and superiority.

At the beginning of the 21st century, the only remaining traces of the immigration of the Flemish migrant workers are Dutch surnames. The spatial distribution of these names is an indicator of the degree of assimilation of subsequent generations of immigrants: when the Walloon population increasingly left industrial areas for the rural hinterland, some carried Dutch-Flemish surnames. Another sign of the far-reaching integration of the offspring of Flemish immigrants is their relatively frequent ascendance into the local political elite. Their Flemish origins, visible in their surname, played no role at all. Inhabitants of Wallonia of Flemish origin do not see any reason to claim this heritage; it is considered merely a footnote in their biography.

Caestecker, Frank. "Vakbonden en etnische minderheden, een ambigue verhouding. Immigratie in de Belgische mijnbekkens, 1900–1940." *Brood en Rozen* 1 (1997): 51–63.

Poulain, Michel, et al. "Flemish Immigration in Wallonia and in France, Patronyms as Data." *History of the Family* 5, 2 (2000): 227–42.

Quairiaux, Yves. "Les 'Flamands' avant 1914 en Wallonie. Du dénigrement à l'assimilation." In *L'image de l'autre dans l'Europe du nord-ouest à travers l'histoire. Actes du colloque*, edited by Jean-Pierre Jessenne, 237–52. Villeneuve d'Ascq, 1996.

Cross-references: The Baltic Region; Belgium and Luxembourg; France; Germany; Great Britain; The Netherlands; Poland; Russia and Belarus; Southeastern Europe; Ukraine; Forced Laborers in Germany and German-Occupied Europe during World War II; German Refugees and Expellees from Eastern, East-Central, and Southeastern Europe in Germany and Austria since the End of World War II; Jewish Refugees from Nazi Germany and from German-Occupied Europe since 1933

FLEMISH MERCHANTS IN THE IBERIAN PENINSULA IN THE EARLY MODERN PERIOD

Eddy Stols

On the Iberian Peninsula, Flemish merchants – who came from the modern-day states of Belgium, the Netherlands, and Luxembourg, as well as the neighboring areas of northern France, the Duchy of Cleves, and the Rhineland – had been called *flamengos* (Portuguese) or *flamencos* (Spanish) since the late Middle Ages. A distinction between the *holandeses* and the *flamencos* loyal to Spain was made, at the earliest, after the uprising of the northern Netherlands against Spanish rule in 1568. With their independence following the Peace of Westphalia in 1648, the Republic of the United Netherlands established consular legations on the Iberian Peninsula, which now existed alongside the *naciones flamencas*, the privileged communities of the Flemish. The southern Netherlands remained under Spanish rule until 1713, and even thereafter, the *naciones flamencas* often invoked their loyalty to Spain and the privileges they had been granted by the Spanish crown. In Portugal, the separation of Dutchmen and Flemings occurred only when that country became independent from Spain in 1668 following the Peace of Lisbon. After its separation from the United Kingdom of the Netherlands in 1830, Belgium laid claim to the patrimony of the Flemish nations in Spain.

The flow out of the Low Countries to the south increased beginning in the early 15th century. Most young migrants also went to the Iberian Peninsula in addition to Italy and France. From the middle of the 16th century, the annual number of migrants was over 100. At first they came mostly from Bruges and other Flemish cities, later also from Antwerp and regions farther north. The departure had economic reasons: the flourishing crafts trades in the growing cities of the Low Countries produced a surplus of young journeymen who were hoping to find work in the south. The trade links between Bruges – later also Antwerp – and southern Europe led to the immigration of many Italians, Portuguese, and Spaniards into the Low Countries, which in turn made it easier for Flemish craftsmen and artists to make their way south. The marriages of the male representatives of the reigning dynasties in the Low Countries (Duke Philip the Good of Burgundy and the Habsburgs Philip I, Charles V, Philip II, Alexander Farnese, and Archduke Albert) to Portuguese and Spanish princesses stimulated the emigration of Dutch courtiers, servants all the way down to kitchen personnel, painters, printers, tapestry layers, musicians, and gardeners to Lisbon and Madrid, and to the royal residences in Aranjuez and El Escorial. At the same time, the Iberian expansion overseas attracted not only sailors and cannoneers but also transoceanic merchants, who came increasingly from the Low Countries.

The first Flemish brotherhoods and nations were established by merchants on the Iberian Peninsula in Lisbon in 1414 and after 1500 in Cádiz, Seville, and Málaga. Most of these institutions were headquartered in a monastery chapel. In Lisbon, next to the Confraria de Santo André in the monastery of São Domingo, a second, mixed German-Flemish brotherhood of São Bartolomeu was set up in the church of São Gião. Within the brotherhoods and nations was the office of the almoner: originally in charge of supporting the needy, this priest was now supposed to guarantee the orthodoxy of the members of the group. Some brotherhoods and nations set up a hospice to take in needy countrymen, the best example being San Andrés de los Flamencos in Madrid in 1594. There were fewer Flemish merchants in the Basque and Cantabrian ports and therefore no brotherhoods and nations, since the wool and iron trade that was the mainstay here remained more strongly in the hands of the local merchants. Outside of the Iberian Peninsula, these Flemish institutions were not able to establish themselves, with a few exceptions in Rome and Paris.

The Flemish nation on the Iberian Peninsula followed the example of the Iberian nations in Bruges and Antwerp, even if they differed in various respects: the Flemish on the Iberian Peninsula received more extensive personal privileges than the Spaniards did in the Low Countries. The Flemish did not have to pay dues; they were allowed to engage in retail trade, ride on mules, wear silk garments, and carry weapons. The Flemish nation never attained the strict organization with staple right and separate business offices as did, for example, the nation of Vizcaya (Biskaia) in Bruges. They operated with loose connections to countrymen in Venice, Livorno, North Africa, the Middle East, and even Goa in India. Moreover, the nations facilitated onward migration to the Atlantic islands, into the Vice-Kingdom of New Spain, and to South America. Flemish communities emerged on Tenerife and La Palma, in Funchal, Ponta Delgada, Mexico, Lima, Potosi, Salvador da Bahia, and Recife. They were active in the sugar plantations or in mining and trade, even though they did not have their own organization. Through royal permits (*licencias*) or on the basis of letters of naturalization (*cartas de naturaleza*), Flemish merchants from Seville and later Cádiz were allowed to load goods onto the ships of the Spanish flotilla headed to America; under certain circumstances, they could sail along themselves. In addition, the illegal trade with the colonies was flourishing.

It was especially the transoceanic trade that allowed the group of Flemings to grow by around 1600 to about 100 in Lisbon and 300 in Seville. We know of approximately 660 names of *flamencos* and *holandeses* in Cádiz during the 18th century; in 1791, that city had still about 20 Flemish trading houses. They traded not only with their own wares but also brokered trading contacts in French, Hanseatic, or Italian ports. During the Eighty Years' War (1568–1648) between the Dutch rebels and the Spanish crown, they were suspected of being agents for the outlawed trade with the enemy, or even of preparing a Dutch invasion.

Xenophobic reactions grew louder after the beginning of the 16th century because of the alleged "greed" of the Flemish councilors to the Spanish kings Philip I and Charles V, the "quick enrichment" of many merchants, and the "drunkenness" of the sailors and craftsmen. Especially in the second half of the 16th century, religious dissenters among the immigrants were persecuted by the Inquisition, which had about 250 Flemings arrested in Spain, Mexico, and Peru, and about 100 in Portugal, Brazil, and Goa. A few were even burned at the stake. After 1600, however, Protestants were for the most part tolerated, provided they did not live their faith in an overly conspicuous and public manner.

To secure recognition and renew their privileges, the Flemish nations showed deference toward the Spanish as well as to the Portuguese kings. For example, they participated in major festivities like the marriage of the hereditary prince John in Lisbon in 1552, or the visit of the Spanish king Philip IV (1621–65) to Seville. In Lisbon, the Flemings set up their own triumphal arches for Philip II's assumption to the throne in 1581, for the visit of Philip III in 1619, and for the wedding of the Portuguese king Peter II in 1687. This ensured a measure of influence, which went so far that the consuls of the Flemish nations were able to prevent the arrest of Flemish merchants for smuggling and the embargo against ships from the northern Netherlands, if it was in the interest of their economic success. Another move that proved economically beneficial was the establishment of the Almirantazgo by leading Flemish and German merchants in Seville in 1625, an escort company with 24 warships that was supposed to secure the ships sailing north against attempts by captains from the rebellious Dutch ports to seize them.

The majority of the *flamencos* returned to the southern Netherlands with their accumulated wealth. In Antwerp they were mocked as Spanish Brabantines, who supposedly continued to cultivate the noble ways of life they had brought back from Spain. A few families remained on the Iberian Peninsula for several generations and passed the business from father to son or nephew. Other Flemish families settled permanently on the Iberian Peninsula, with family members often migrating onward to the colonies of Portugal and Spain in the New World. Endogamy and exogamy were balanced. Even if the Flemings visited their own taverns and Cádiz had a calle de Flamencos (Street of the Flemings), no concentrated settlement by the immigrants was found in any city. For the most part, their integration took place within two generations, at the most: the Flemings quickly learned the native language, had African slaves as servants, purchased country houses and estates, held posts within the city administration or with the Inquisition, acquired titles of nobility, were admitted into the large knightly orders – for example, those of Santiago or the Ordem do Cristo – or joined monasteries and religious foundations. The Hospital de Venerables Sacerdotes in Seville was even founded by a *flamenco*, Justino de Neve. In Lisbon the Convento das Flamengas was founded in 1582 with fugitive nuns from the Low Countries and started to receive the daughters of Flemish families.

In general, Portuguese and Spanish society received the several hundred *flamencos* kindly because many Spaniards and Portuguese had often personal experiences or connections in Flanders and appreciated Flemish textiles, jewels, clocks, knives and scissors, paintings, engravings, and sculptures, as registered in their saying: "*No hay más Flandes*," "There is no other Flanders." On their side the emigrants benefited on their return in the southern Netherlands from the experiences in transoceanic trade.

Bustos Rodríguez, Manuel. *Burguesia de negocios y capitalismo en Cádiz: Los Colarte (1650–1750)*. Cádiz, 1991.

Crespo Solana, Ana. *Entre Cádiz y los Países Bajos. Una comunidad mercantil en la ciudad de la ilustración*. Cádiz, 2001.

Fagel, Raymond. *De Hispano-Vlaamse wereld. De contacten tussen de Spanjaarden en Nederlanders*. Brussels and Nijmegen, 1996.

Joukes, Veronika. *Os Flamengos no Noroeste de Portugal (1620–1670)*. Porto, 1999.

Stols, Eddy. *De Spaanse Brabanders of de handelsbetrekkingen van de Zuidelijke Nederlanden met de Iberische Wereld, 1598–1648*. 2 vols. Brussels, 1971.

Stols, Eddy. "No hay más Flandes en o tempo dos flamengos in koloniaal Amerika." In *De Lage Landen en de Nieuwe Wereld, De zeventiende eeuw* 21, 1 (2005): 3–28.

Thomas, Werner, and Eddy Stols. "La integración de Flandes en la Monarquía Hispánica." In *Encuentros en Flandes*, edited by Werner Thomas and Robert Verdonck, 1–73. Louvain, 2000.

Thomas, Werner. *Los protestantes y la Inquisición en España en tiempos de Reforma y Contrarreforma*. Louvain, 2001.

Cross-references: Belgium and Luxembourg; The Netherlands; Spain and Portugal; African Slaves on the Iberian Peninsula in the Early Modern Period; German Maritime Traders in Cádiz and Bordeaux from the Late 17th to the Late 19th Century; Spanish Merchants in the Netherlands in the Early Modern Period

FLEMISH TEXTILE WORKERS IN WESTERN AND CENTRAL EUROPE SINCE THE 19TH CENTURY: THE EXAMPLE OF FRANCE

Carl Strikwerda

Flemish textile workers emigrated in the 19th century principally to France, but in smaller numbers also to England, the Netherlands, and Germany. The language spoken in Flanders, the northern part of modern-day Belgium, is Dutch, although the Flemish dialects can vary significantly from the language spoken just to the north in the Netherlands. Consequently, observers, especially in the 19th century, often referred to the spoken language as "Flemish." Into the 20th century, Dutch or Flemish was the language of farmers, workers, and the middle class in Flanders. Business, administrative, and government elites as well as the Catholic Church used French. Since the Counter-Reformation of the 16th century, Flanders has been an almost completely Catholic region.

Flanders has a long history of textile production, especially of linen. After flourishing in the Middle Ages, Flanders and its textile production fell into economic decline. Intensive agriculture in Flanders, however, meant that the region remained one of the most densely populated areas in Europe. In the 18th century, Flanders developed a large rural textile industry. Poorly paid spinners and weavers produced linen cloth for export from locally grown flax. Many depended on part-time agricultural work to survive. Mechanized cotton production and steam engines were introduced in 1801 into Flanders, presumably the first location outside of England. Factory production of both cotton and linen soon became centralized in Ghent, which experienced a population explosion leading up to the 1840s. The impoverished rural industry sector continued to decline slowly for decades.

The uneven business cycles of mechanized production in Ghent and the continued decline of textile production in the countryside periodically drove Flemish workers and their families to emigrate. More than 90% of the emigrants went to France, the northern part of which could be reached within a few days on foot. Canals and, in the 19th century, railroads connected the two regions. Despite the differences in language and political boundaries, there were close historical ties between Flanders and northern France. Much of northern France had been part of medieval and early modern Flanders, until Louis XIV conquered it. So-called French Flanders, the area around Lille and Dunkerque, was roughly equivalent to the departments of Nord and Pas-de-Calais, where Dutch was spoken in some areas. The Nord, like Belgian Flanders, was devoutly Catholic and a strong center of textile production, both with rural industry in the 18th and factory production in the 19th century. Northern French textile production was in cotton and wool, the latter especially in Roubaix. Flemish Belgium produced cotton and linen goods. Nonetheless, much similar work was done in the two regions. Most Flemish workers from Ghent and even some from the villages knew enough French to understand how to operate the machines and how to change money.

The immigration of Flemish workers was essential to the success of the northern French textile industry throughout the entire 19th century. The potato famine of the "hungry forties," which hit Flanders harder than any other European region aside from Ireland, drove thousands of rural spinners and weavers to France. Ghent's factories were starved in the "cotton famine" of the American Civil War in the early 1860s, when the federal government blockade of southern ports prevented cotton from reaching Europe. Even skilled cotton weavers and spinners from Belgian factories migrated to Lille and Roubaix to seek work.

Roubaix's population grew from 8,000 in 1800 to 124,000 in 1896. In 1872, 55% of Roubaix's population was Belgian, many of them born in France to Belgian parents. The Nord-Pas-de-Calais region had about 250,000 Belgians, almost all of them Flemish – equal to approximately 5% of Belgium's total population. The initial wave of migration in the 1840s had mainly been male. By the 1860s, more families and women began to migrate. Belgians made up the largest migrant group in France throughout the 19th century. Sixty percent of the Belgians in France lived in the Nord. It was only in 1910 that Italians replaced Belgians as the largest migrant group in France.

Isolated numbers of Flemish textile workers migrated to other cities, such as Paris, Rouen, and Arras, where several thousand found work. Some also sought work in the English Midlands and textile centers in the Netherlands and Germany such as Münchengladbach, but these were small migratory movements that left few records. Only 15,000 Belgians, for example, lived in the Netherlands at the end of the 19th century, most of whom were day laborers or tradesmen. Textile workers employed in the Midlands kept their Flemish colleagues informed about newly developed textile machinery and unionism in England. Labor unions in both Ghent and the Nord in textiles, transportation, and metallurgy all had contact with British unions.

After the 1880s, the migration of Flemish textile workers gradually declined. Flanders had always competed with England by focusing on cheaper cloth, working longer hours, and relying more on female and child labor. Ghent's industry diversified with the expansion of its port and metallurgy, while the textile industry became more efficient with the adoption of more modern technology. Textile factories also spread from Ghent to smaller cities in Flanders, providing an alternative to migration for rural workers. Textile production meanwhile stagnated in northern France as the coal and iron industries grew.

While immigration to France declined, Flemish workers still came to the Nord, but they did so on a daily or weekly basis. These commuters were known as *frontaliers*, or cross-border workers. Instead of settling long term in Lille or Roubaix, Belgians moved to towns near the French border and commuted into France each day to work. Others commuted by tram or railroad each week from the countryside or small Flemish towns. About a third of these cross-border workers were women, virtually all unmarried. Wages were higher in France while the cost of living was lower in Belgium, partly due to lower taxes. The Belgian government encouraged commuting by building tramlines or light railways and providing cheap workmen's tickets on the national railroads, partly to slow urbanization and to check the growth of the Socialist Party in Belgium. While in much of Belgium this policy was designed to slow the growth of large cities, it increased the number of *frontaliers* in the region near the Nord. By 1908, an estimated 40,000 Belgians crossed the border to France every day or every week. In the interwar period, the number reached its highest point – 100,000 – before gradually declining after the Second World War.

In comparison with Italians and Germans in other parts of France, the Flemish in the north had few difficulties integrating into French society. Between 1870 and 1890, Belgians made up almost half the foreign workers in France but had only 11 incidents of violence against them. Italians had 67 while Germans, only one-fifth as numerous as the Belgians, were targets in seven incidents. Despite differences of language and citizenship, the French and Flemish had a shared history of trade, textile work, ardent Catholicism, and certain customs, such as local sports, carnivals, and beer drinking (as opposed to wine drinking, as occurred in much of the rest of France). Although there were riots between French and Belgian workers in the north in 1819 and again in 1849, relations between the two groups were otherwise generally good. In 1867, the French observer Louis Reybaud reported that friendships between French and Belgian workers in Roubaix were uncommon, but there were no instances of open hostility, although the French mocked the Flemish for their incomprehensible language and what was perceived as clannishness.

A simple classification of Flemish migrants as rural and French as urban is inaccurate. The migration of Belgians and the migration of native French to cities in the north had similar features. Many of the Flemish migrants came from Ghent and other cities, while a large number of migrants went to cities in the Nord from the French countryside. Belgians, many of whom were skilled and experienced textile workers, were compensated almost as well as their French counterparts. Belgians also often distinguished themselves by introducing new ideas and methods of organization into the north. Of the 26 founders of La Paix (Peace), the most important consumer cooperative in Roubaix, 19 were born in Belgium, 13 in Ghent. The Belgians, according to historian Michelle Perrot, were "the teachers of Socialism in northern France." Catholic labor organizing in the region, too, was heavily inspired by Belgian examples.

The Belgian community in the north gradually assimilated as immigration decreased. The use of Dutch declined in the second and third generations of migrants and intermarriage increased. In Lille in 1853, about a quarter of the Belgians married a French partner; by 1869, about one-third did, with the majority being Belgian men who married French women. In Roubaix and other cities where the Belgians amounted to over half the population – in contrast to Lille, where they formed about a quarter of the population – the process of assimilation occurred only later, in the 1880s. In 1889 French law made it easier to become a citizen, leading to the naturalization of an increasing number of Belgians. In 1886 in Halluin, located very close to the Belgian border, 77% of the population possessed Belgian citizenship; by 1900, the number was only 32% due to the large increase in naturalizations.

More serious problems, however, existed between Flemish *frontaliers* and workers in France, both native French and Belgians or their offspring. The *frontaliers* came only to work; they failed to join unions or neighborhood associations and very few learned French. A major textile strike in 1903–4 failed in part because Belgian *frontaliers* continued to work while French unions went on strike. In contrast, a strike in 1910 in Halluin succeeded because French socialist and Catholic unions and Belgian Catholic and socialist unions in Meenen, a town just over the border, formed a close alliance. Yet in the interwar period there were also cases when Belgian Catholic and socialist unions of *frontaliers* went back to work while French socialist and communist unions stayed on strike.

Precisely the hostility that sometimes arose between the French and the Belgian *frontaliers* furthered the assimilation of Flemish immigrants living in France. Both French and Belgians in the north saw the *frontaliers* as more conservative and rural. The target of French labor hostility was

the *frontaliers*, not the Belgian Flemish who lived in France. In contrast to the Belgian *frontaliers* commuting across the border, Flemish immigrants living in France more closely resembled the French because they were more proficient in the language and joined French labor organizations.

Balthazar, Herman, and Nicole de Rykere. "Betrekkingen tussen het socialisme in Vlaanderen en Noord-Frankrijk (1870–1914)." *De Franse Nederlanden. Jaarboek Stichting Ons Erfdeel (Les Pays-Bas Français)* 4 (1979): 11–29.

Couton, Phillipe. "Ethnic Institutions Reconsidered: The Case of Flemish Workers in 19th Century France." *Journal of Historical Sociology* 16 (2003): 80–110.

Lentacker, Firmin. *La Frontière Franco-Belge: Etude géographique des effets d'une frontière internationale sur la vie de relations.* Lille, 1974.

Schepens, Luc. *Van vlaskutser tot Franschman: bijdrage tot de geschiedenis van de Westvlaamse plattelandsbevolkings in de negentiende eeuw.* Brugge, 1973.

Stengers, Jean. "Les mouvements migratoires en Belgique aux XIXe et XXe siecles." In *Les migrations internationales de la fin du XVIIIe siècle à nos jours*, 283–317. Paris, 1980.

Strikwerda, Carl. "France and the Belgian Immigration of the Nineteenth Century." In *The Politics of Immigrant Workers: Labor Activism and Migration in the World Economy since 1830*, edited by Camille Guerin-Gonzales and Carl Strikwerda, 3–52. 2nd ed. New York, 1998.

Cross-references: Belgium and Luxembourg; France; Italian Industrial Workers in Western and Central Europe in the Late 19th and Early 20th Centuries

FORCED LABORERS IN GERMANY AND GERMAN-OCCUPIED EUROPE DURING WORLD WAR II

Ulrich Herbert

The use of millions of workers in forced labor during the Second World War was one of the salient features of National Socialist labor policy – in Germany itself as well as all over German-occupied Europe. To be sure, the term "forced laborer" encompasses a multitude of groups with at times very different working conditions. We can distinguish four large groups that were very distinct in terms of their status, the nature of their recruitment, their social status, the legal status of their deployment, and the duration and circumstances of their working condition:

1. Foreign civilian workers who were brought to Germany between 1939 and 1945 for "work deployment" (*Arbeitseinsatz*) and referred to in popular parlance as "foreign workers" (*Fremdarbeiter*); they formed by far the largest of these four groups.
2. Foreign prisoners of war, chiefly from Poland, the Soviet Union, and France, who were used as workers in Germany. However, a considerable portion of the Polish

prisoners were transferred to the status of civilian workers. This group included also the approximately 600,000 military internees – Italian soldiers who were interned by the Wehrmacht after Italy left the Axis and came to Germany as forced laborers.

3. Inmates of SS concentration camps on Reich territory.
4. European Jews who were forced to perform forced labor for shorter or longer periods in their homelands (first in Poland) and then especially after their deportation – in ghettoes, forced labor camps, or in concentration camps, satellite camps, and after 1944 also on a larger scale on Reich territory.

Finally, one must also take into account those inhabitants of states occupied by the Wehrmacht who were compelled to perform forced labor at home or were taken to third countries. However, to this day quite different definitions of forced labor have been used in the various countries, ranging from compulsory work in concentration camp–like facilities to the obligation to work imposed by native labor administrations on the recipients of state aid.

"Foreign workers" and prisoners of war

The National Socialist "deployment of foreigners" between 1939 and 1945 constitutes the largest instance of the large-scale, coerced use of foreign workers in history since the end of slavery in the 19th century. In the late summer of 1944, 7.6 million foreign civilian workers and prisoners of war were officially registered as working on the territory of the Greater German Reich, the majority of whom had been brought into the Reich by force for work deployment. At that time they made up about one-quarter of all registered workers in the entire economy of the German Reich.

Immediately after the outbreak of the war in September 1939, about 300,000 Polish prisoners of war who had fallen into German hands were very quickly put to work, especially on agricultural enterprises. At the same time a campaign began to recruit Polish workers: initially it followed in the footsteps of the long tradition of Polish agricultural workers in Germany, but it very soon shifted toward increasingly harsh recruitment measures, and from the spring of 1940 it turned into veritable manhunts in the General Government section of occupied Poland. Here the workers were captured through the imposition of obligatory service on entire age cohorts, collective oppression, raids, and by rounding up those attending movie theaters, schools, or churches. By May 1940, more than a million Polish workers had been brought into the Reich in this way.

Still, the leadership of the regime continued to see the "deployment of Poles" as a violation of the "racial" principles of National Socialism. In February 1940, SS Reich Leader Heinrich Himmler argued that the "*volks*-political dangers" arising from it had to be counteracted with appropriately harsh measures. Subsequently, an extensive system of repressive measures aimed at the Poles was developed: they had

to live in barracks camps (though this soon proved impossible to implement in the countryside), received lower wages, were not allowed to use public facilities (from express trains to swimming pools), were forbidden from attending German religious services, had to work longer than the Germans, and were required to wear a badge – the "Polish P" – on their clothing. Contacts with Germans outside of work were prohibited, sexual relations with German women were punished with the public execution of the offending Pole. Moreover, "to protect German blood," it was decreed that at least half of the recruited Polish civilian workers had to be women.

Overall, German authorities could rate the test case of the "Polish deployment" a success: it was possible to bring a large number of Polish workers to Germany against their will within a short time, and to establish within the German Reich a two-class society based on "racial" criteria.

As early as May 1940, however, it was impossible for the Germans not to admit that the recruitment of Poles was unable to meet the German economy's demand for workers. As a result, during and soon after the campaign against France, a little over a million French prisoners of war were brought into the Reich as workers. In addition, stepped-up recruitment of workers took place in the Allied countries and occupied territories in the west and north. These groups, too, had special stipulations regarding their treatment, wages, housing, and so forth, though these were far more favorable than those for the Poles. The result was a multitiered system of national hierarchies, a stepladder with the "guest workers" from Allied Italy and the workers from northern and western Europe at the top, and the Poles at the bottom. Until 1941–2, the proportion of "voluntary" workers was relatively high in northern and western Europe; thereafter, in the face of declining supply, various systems of forced recruitment for work deployment to Germany were instituted there also.

The vast majority of foreign civilian workers and prisoners of war during the Blitzkrieg phase until the summer of 1941 were put to work in agriculture. At this time, foreigners played no important role in industrial enterprises; instead, industry's strategy was to recover its workers from the military soon after the end of the Blitzkrieg. At the same time, the ideological reservations about expanding the "deployment of foreigners" were so strong within the party and the bureaucracy that the decision was made to freeze the number of foreigners where it stood in the spring of 1941, at just under 3 million. This approach worked as long as the strategy of short, sweeping campaigns did not require a transition to a long war of attrition.

The situation changed profoundly following the first military setbacks for the Wehrmacht in the Soviet Union in the fall of 1941. A Blitzkrieg was now out of the question. Instead, the German armaments industry had to adjust to a lengthy war of attrition and substantially increase its capacities. Moreover, industry could no longer count on returning soldiers as workers; quite the contrary: a massive wave of conscription now took hold of the workforce of the previously protected armaments industry. The intensive efforts that now began to draw workers from the western European countries were no longer sufficient by themselves to close these gaps. Only the deployment of workers from the Soviet Union would have been able to provide additional, effective relief.

Before the beginning of the war, however, the Nazi regime had explicitly ruled out the work deployment of Soviet prisoners of war or civilian workers in the Reich. The opposition to any employment of Soviet citizens in Germany by the party leadership, the Main Reich Security Office, and the SS was driven not only by "racial" reasons and national security considerations. Rather, the departments of the regime and the sectors of the economy involved in war preparations were so confident of victory that such a deployment was simply seen as unnecessary. Thus, since there seemed to be no need, in terms of the war economy, for their use within the Reich, the millions of Soviet prisoners of war were abandoned to their fate in the mass camps in the hinterland of the German eastern front – very much in keeping with the principles of the Russian campaign, agreed upon by the regime as early as the spring of 1941, that the majority of the "superfluous" Soviet population would not be fed and would be left to starve. More than half the 5.7 million Soviet prisoners of war who had fallen into German hands by the end of the war starved, froze to death, died of exhaustion or diseases, or were killed, a substantial portion during the first 10 months of the war.

But when Germany's military situation – and thus also the state of its war economy – changed rapidly in the fall of 1941, the result was massive economic pressure for the deployment of Soviet prisoners, which found expression in relevant orders in November. This time the initiative came from industry, especially mining, where the lack of labor had already reached an ominous stage. The majority of Soviet prisoners, however, was no longer available for work deployment. Of the more than 3 million prisoners by that time, a mere 160,000 had come into the Reich for work deployment by March 1942. For that reason the authorities and the economy now switched on a large scale to the recruitment of Soviet civilian workers. The procurement of as many workers as possible as quickly as possible became the most urgent matter and primary task of Fritz Sauckel, newly appointed as the Plenipotentiary for Labor Deployment in March. Under his direction, the special operations staffs of the Wehrmacht and the German labor offices deported nearly 2.5 million civilians from the Soviet Union to the Reich as forced laborers – 20,000 per week.

Parallel to the development of the "Polish deployment," a system of comprehensive repression and discrimination characterized the use of Soviet forced laborers in the Reich. That system, however, was far more radical even than the regulations governing the Poles. The Soviet civilian workers, now officially called "East workers," were externally marked with a badge (Ost), had to live in guarded camps surrounded by barbed wire, and were to a special degree exposed to the whims of the Gestapo and the factory protection units.

Within the Reich, a virtual universe of camps had by now emerged; camps of foreigners were found everywhere in the large cities as well as the countryside. In the city of Berlin, alone, there were several hundred of them. All told there may have been more than 30,000 in the Reich, and about 400,000–500,000 Germans were directly involved in the organization of the "deployment of foreigners" in various functions, from camp director to administrator of foreigners in a factory.

The living conditions of the various groups of foreigners were differentiated by a national hierarchy that was strictly regimented down to the smallest detail. Workers from the occupied western lands and so-called friendly nations did have to live for the most part in camps, but they received roughly the same wages and food rations as Germans in comparable jobs, and they were also subject to the same working conditions. By contrast, workers from the east, especially Soviet citizens, were in a much worse position. The rations for the "East workers" were often so skimpy that within a few weeks after their arrival (and especially in the years 1942–3), the workers became completely undernourished and unfit for work. As early as the early summer of 1942, numerous companies were reporting that the "Russian deployment" was totally unprofitable, since effective employment would presuppose not only better food and adequate breaks, but also training measures for the forced laborers that were in line with the work process. Among French prisoners, measures like these had achieved an output level close to that of German workers, while the situation of Soviet forced laborers was different from one business to the next, from one camp to the next. Workers were generally much better off in agriculture than in industry, but even there, the differences in treatment and diet, especially after the end of 1942, can be described as extreme. That, however, points to the great differences in individual companies' leeway for action and discretion. It would be simply wrong to blame the living conditions of the workers from the east entirely on the compulsory regulations of the bureaucracy.

When it came to wages, there was – roughly speaking – a four-tiered system. The civilian workers from all countries, except for the formerly Polish and Soviet regions, received the same wages as the German workers (men and women) in comparable jobs – at least nominally. Polish workers, too, were supposed to receive the same wages, nominally, but they had to pay a special tax of 15%, the "Polish tax" – which was introduced by the German labor authorities with the remarkable justification that this was compensation for the Poles not being conscripted for military service, like the Germans. By contrast, the Soviet workers of both genders received special, fixed wages, which were substantially lower than those for Germans and the other foreign workers – nominally by about 40%, in reality in most cases probably much lower still. Moreover, the labor authorities complained that many enterprises paid no wages at all to the Soviet civilian workers, considering them "civilian prisoners" and treating them accordingly.

In September 1944 there were 7.6 million foreign workers in jobs in the Empire: 5.7 million civilian male and female workers and just under 2 million prisoners of war. Of those, 2.8 million were from the Soviet Union, 1.7 million from Poland, and 1.3 million from France; all told, individuals from about 20 countries were put to work in the Reich. More than half of the Polish and Soviet civilian workers were women, on average less than 20 years of age – the average forced laborer in Germany in 1943 was an 18-year-old female student from Kiev. In September 1944, about 23% of all those employed in the Reich were foreign civilian workers of both genders or prisoners of war. We know from studies of forced labor in individual companies – for example, Daimler-Benz or Volkswagen – that the proportion in the armament-intensive sectors was more than 40% and 50%; in many manufacturing sectors it stood at 70% and 80%, which meant that German employees – apart from the administration – worked mostly as trainers and supervisors. Especially high ratios of foreign forced laborers were reached – in addition to direct military production – in the construction sector and in agriculture.

The employment of foreign forced workers was by no means limited to large enterprises, however, but extended to the entire economy (except for the administration) – from small farms, to a locksmith shop with six employees, to the Reich railroad, to local communities, and to the large armament enterprises.

Concentration camp inmates

From the beginning of 1944, however, it became clear that even these large numbers were no longer adequate for the labor requirements, especially of the Reich's large armament projects. Labor recruitment declined as a result of the military development particularly in the Soviet Union, which meant that the ever larger gaps in labor resulting from stepped-up conscription could no longer be filled. In response, interest turned increasingly to the only organization that still controlled a considerable pool of laborers: the SS and the concentration camps under its control.

During the first years of the war, the work deployment of concentration camp inmates had had no importance to the war economy. To be sure, as early as 1938 the SS ran its own economic enterprises (especially quarries, brickworks, and repair workshops), and nearly all inmates were put to some kind of forced labor. However, the character of work as "punishment," "education," or "revenge" was retained also here, and toward the groups that were especially low in the political and "racial" hierarchy of the Nazis, it took the form of annihilation before 1939 and increasingly thereafter. The establishment of SS-run enterprises like the Deutsche Ausrüstungswerke (German Equipment Works) and the Deutsche Erd- und Steinwerke (German Earthworks and Quarries) did show that the SS was seeking to utilize the concentration camps increasingly as economic factors. Still, in practice, the economic function of the forced labor of the inmates remained subordinate to the political goals of camps well into the war.

Following the military setbacks along the eastern front in the fall of 1941, and subsequent refocusing of the German armament industry toward the necessities of a long war of attrition, the Reich Leader SS now also undertook organizational reorganizations to make production for armament – and not only, as previously, for construction, the production of building materials, and military equipment – the primary task in the concentration camps. In fact, however, the concentration camps were not set up for such a rapid conversion, nor was there sufficient economic expertise in the Economic and Administrative Main Office (Wirtschafts- und Verwaltungs-Hauptamt, WVHA) of the SS, newly established as the organizational central office of the concentration camps, to create large-scale armament production out of nothing. In addition, it was difficult to switch the concentration camp guards themselves, accustomed by long practice to regard human life in the concentration camp as worthless, to making work deployment their primary concern. In April 1942, the WVHA made the labor deployment of concentration camp inmates the chief task of all camp commanders: in actuality, though, of the 95,000 inmates registered in the second half of 1942, 57,503 died, that is, more than 60%. It was only in the spring of 1942 that the SS began to employ camp inmates on a larger scale for armament purposes, especially in the construction of the IG Farben plant near Auschwitz. However, the inmates were here initially used only for construction work, with their use in armament production beginning only a year later. In the clashes among the various interest groups within the SS, the idea of punishment and annihilation continued to override the idea of labor and productivity – above all, because the mass deportations of Soviet workers to Germany, which began at this time, did not yet create any need to deploy camp inmates.

Not until September 1942 did Adolf Hitler decide, on the recommendation of Minister of Armaments Albert Speer, that the SS should henceforth make its concentration camp inmates available to industry on loan and that industry in turn should integrate the inmates into the existing production processes. In this way the principle of lending camp inmates to private industry, which would henceforth dominate the work deployment of camp inmates, was firmly established. Thereafter, their use within existing industrial enterprises was stepped up. For that purpose, private companies would register their labor needs with the WVHA, which then reviewed the accommodations and security arrangements and issued the authorization. Once that was done, company representatives in the camps were usually able to personally select the inmates who seemed suitable. After that, the inmates were moved into a "satellite camp" of the concentration camp, generally located in direct proximity to the work site. The fees that the companies had to pay to the SS for the inmates were 6 Reichsmark per day for skilled workers and 4 Reichsmark for unskilled laborers and women. At the same time, the SS-run economic enterprises in the Reich also began to switch increasingly to armament production; from the end of 1942, the German Equipment Works (DAW) was already engaged largely in armament and war-essential activities, especially maintenance and repair work.

To enhance the armament deployment, the chief interest of the WVHA was now to vigorously boost the number of inmates in the shortest possible time. Within seven months, the occupancy rate for all concentration camps rose from 110,000 (September 1942) to 203,000 (April 1943). By August 1944, the number of inmates had already risen to 524,268, and it reached more than 700,000 at the beginning of 1945. However, the monthly mortality rates for inmates remained extraordinarily high and began to decline only in the spring of 1943: from 10% in December 1942 to 2.8% in April 1943. This shows that the rising demand on the part of private and SS-run industry led to higher rates of incarceration in concentration camps, not to a change in the working and living conditions for inmates in the camps.

The average period during which inmates were fit to work – and thus their life expectancy – was between one and two years in 1943–4, though there could be significant differences depending on where inmates were deployed and to which group they belonged. Real improvement in the working and living conditions of concentration camp inmates occurred only when the labor of an individual was difficult or impossible to replace because he or she possessed certain skills or had been trained for a skilled job.

In the summer of 1943, of the 160,000 registered prisoners in the WVHA camps, about 15% were employed in running the camps, and 22% were categorized as unfit to work. The remaining 63%, that is, about 100,000, were distributed among the SS's construction projects and economic enterprises, as well as private companies. At the end of 1942 there were 82 satellite camps on the territory of the Reich; a year later there were 186. In the summer of 1944 that number rose to 341; by January 1945 it had grown to 662. However, since the numbers of the SS and the Speer ministry sometimes diverge strongly, it is difficult to make a precise statement.

Forced labor of the Jews

With respect to the Jews, the transition to the systematic forced labor can be dated to the beginning of 1939. From that time on, Jews in Germany who applied for unemployment benefits were deployed, following a relevant decree of the German labor administration, as unskilled laborers in "closed labor deployment" (*geschlossener Arbeitseinsatz*). By the summer of 1939, the number of these Jewish forced laborers, mostly men, had grown to about 20,000; they were put to work on road construction, land improvement, canal and dam projects, and on garbage dumps, and after the beginning of the war also on short-term snow removal and harvesting actions. In 1940, the obligation for compulsory labor was extended to all able-bodied German Jews (both men and women), regardless of whether they were receiving unemployment benefits. Henceforth, employment was mainly in industry.

However, from the spring of 1941, at the latest, efforts to put the German Jews to forced labor in armament enterprises in the Reich territory clashed with the goal of the German regime to deport the Jews from Germany. Even for the Jewish forced laborers deployed in armament industries (about 50,000 in the summer of 1941), the jobs, many of which had been rated "important to armament," offered no secure protection against deportation, but merely a delay staggered according to the importance of their activity. Remarkable in this context is that the deportations also of Jews employed in war-essential enterprises were justified with the argument that there were, after all, plenty of Poles and Ukrainians available as a replacement – and this was, in the end, the decisive factor in the decision to eventually deport the previously spared *Rüstungsjuden* (armament Jews) in Berlin. In the summer of 1943, there were – with few exceptions – no more Jews within Germany, and thus also no more Jewish forced laborers.

The forced labor of Jews in German-occupied countries, especially in east-central and eastern Europe, showed a similar development, though with a different timing. In the General Government of Poland, compulsory labor for Jews was enacted as early as October 1939. All male Jews between 14 and 60 years of age had to perform labor in forced labor camps to be established for that purpose. It was the task of the Jewish Councils (Judenräte) to register and classify the workers accordingly. A few weeks later, compulsory labor was also extended to Jewish women between 14 and 60.

Originally, however, the SS had intended to put all Jews in the General Government to work in large forced labor camps. However, so many Jews were de facto employed in free work relationships that a sudden incarceration in camps was hardly possible just on organizational grounds. However, the Jewish work deployment was to be increasingly concentrated in ghettoes, the establishment of which had not progressed very far by this time.

The work administration in the General Government had decreed as early as the summer of 1940 that Jewish workers freely employed were to receive wages that were at most 80% of what was usual for Poles in comparable jobs. Many German businesses or organizations subsequently dismissed their Jewish workers, whom they had previously paid lower wages or none at all. That changed, however, with the beginning of the systematic "Final Solution." The flight into jobs in the ghettoes – called "shops" – and the terrible situation of Jewish workers, who had to fear being deported or murdered if their work performance was deemed inadequate, resulted in Jewish workers becoming increasingly cheaper and thus more attractive to entrepreneurs. The division into war-important and less important production sites meant for the Jewish forced laborers of both sexes to an increasing degree a decision of life and death.

The contradictions grew more intense with the switch to the primacy of work deployment after the beginning of

1942: in March of that year, the authorities in the General Government began to dissolve the ghettoes and to deport the Polish Jews to the annihilation camps. However, some of them were taken into special work camps under the supervision of SS and police, where they were put to work on construction projects and armament production. To that end, the SS set up its own economic enterprises in these camps, in part using the relocated factory equipment of former Jewish businesses. These measures created considerable conflicts especially with the Wehrmacht interested in preserving "its" Jewish laborers in the ghetto workshops. The SS, however, was willing to leave the Jewish workers to the armaments enterprises for the time being only if the Jews were given over to the enterprises for work deployment as concentration camp inmates under the oversight of the SS.

On 19 July 1942, Himmler ordered all Polish Jews to be murdered by the end of 1942. Only those Jews who were engaged in forced labor important to the armament industry would be left alive for the time being. However, the relevant production sites were to be gradually transferred to SS oversight and be brought together into forced labor camps. In response, ghetto after ghetto was now liquidated and the production facilities with tens of thousands of Jewish workers were shut down; the forced workers were deported into the annihilation camps and were murdered. The situation was no different in the occupied territories of the Soviet Union. After the first phase of mass shootings in the summer of 1941, the Jews had been deployed in work gangs and workshops here as well. But even after the retooling of the war economy from the beginning of 1942, the practice of liquidation was continued with no concern for economic considerations.

A change occurred only after the beginning of 1944, in the final phase of the war, when the main political goal of the Nazis toward the Jews had been achieved and the labor shortage had grown dramatically worse: Jewish prisoners were deployed also on Reich territory as workers in SS-run enterprises, on the relocation of factories underground, and in private businesses, especially in major industrial enterprises. As early as August 1943, the top leaders of the Nazi regime decided to produce the A 4 rocket, one of the so-called V-weapons, with the help of concentration camp inmates in underground facilities. As 1943 turned to 1944, the Germans began to move war-important production throughout the country into underground facilities, mostly caves or mine shafts, where they were protected from bombing raids. These projects, driven forward under enormous time pressure, had horrifying consequences for the camp inmates who were put to work on them. Especially in the start-up phase in the fall and winter of 1943–4, the death rates were immensely high. The easy replaceability of the inmates on work that was technically simple but physically arduous, enormous time pressure, poor nutrition, and dismal living conditions were the reasons for the high death rates, which began to drop only when the housing camps had been completed and production began. Until then, however, the inmates were "worked out" (*abgearbeitet*) within a few weeks after their arrival.

These kinds of projects, which required tens, even hundreds, of thousands of workers in three-day shifts, could be carried out only with concentration camp inmates, because only the SS still had labor pools on that scale. But when even those were soon inadequate to complete the intended tasks, the work deployment of Jews was discussed in the spring of 1944. Until then, the employment of Jews within the Reich was explicitly forbidden; after all, it was considered a success of the Reich Security Main Office of the SS to have made the Reich *judenfrei* (free of Jews). That changed now. Of the approximately 485,000 Hungarian Jews deported to Auschwitz in the spring of 1944, about 350,000 were immediately gassed, while about 100,000 who seemed especially able-bodied were selected out for work deployment in the Reich. As the influx of "foreign workers" had almost completely dried up by then, more and more enterprises in the Reich had requested inmates from the labor offices and sometimes directly from the concentration camps, and they were now also willing to employ Jewish forced laborers of both genders from the "Hungarian action." These inmates coming from Auschwitz, among them a large number of women, were now formally placed under the concentration camps in the Reich and distributed among the enterprises that had requested camp workers.

The number of work details (*Arbeitskommandos*) attached to the main concentration camps grew rapidly from the spring of 1944; by the end of the war there were about 660 satellite camps on Reich territory. The list of German companies that established such satellite camps and used concentration camp inmates grew ever longer and comprised hundreds of well-known companies. The working and living conditions of the inmates were very different in the various companies. On the whole, though, one can say, with a great deal of caution, that the inmates used in the production of the armament industries themselves had a much greater chance of survival than those who were deployed on the large construction sites, especially for the expansion of underground production facilities, and in the production in the caves and mine shafts after the enterprises had been moved there.

Forced labor: an overview

In a final attempt to determine the overall numbers of humans put to forced labor in Nazi Germany by the authorities and enterprises, precise figures that are based on the statistics of the labor administration can be given only for the work deployment of foreign civilian workers and prisoners of war: the highest number of the simultaneously deployed "foreign workers" was reached in the summer of 1944 at 7.6 million. However, given the considerable fluctuations, it is more realistic to posit a total of about 9.5–10 million foreign civilian workers and prisoners of war who were used as forced laborers in Germany for a shorter or longer period of time. A credible estimate of the number of concentration camp inmates who had been used for forced labor in main or satellite camps is hardly possible. All told, between 1939 and 1945 about 2.5 million inmates were taken to concentration camps of the future WHVA of the SS, among them about 15% Germans and 85% foreigners. A credible estimate puts the number of those who died in the camps during these years at 836,000–995,000 (this does not include the camps of Majdanek and Auschwitz, where a total of about 1.1 million died, the vast majority of whom were Jews).

It can be assumed that virtually every concentration camp inmate was used for forced labor for a shorter or longer stretch during his or her period of incarceration, though in very different and changing ways. Of the approximately 200,000 inmates in April 1943, fewer than half are likely to have been deployed in the armaments sector. At the end of 1944, the total number of inmates stood at about 600,000, of whom 480,000 were in fact registered as fit to work. According to estimates by the WVHA of the SS, about 240,000 were used on the underground relocations and on the construction projects of the Organization Todt, and about 230,000 in private industry.

The number of Jews who were used for forced labor before or after their deportation cannot be given with sufficient accuracy, especially since it varied widely in the individual European countries. In the summer of 1942, the number of Polish Jews crammed into the ghettoes and forced labor camps was around 1.5 million; it seems reasonable to assume that at least half of them were used for forced labor for shorter or longer periods. Substantially smaller was the number of those who, after their deportation from various European countries into the camps of the East, were selected out as fit to work. Likewise, for the territory of the Soviet Union we have no numbers that would allow us even an approximate estimate.

In 1944, foreign forced laborers – civilian workers, prisoners of war, concentration camp inmates, and Jewish workers – made up about a fourth of all those employed in the economy within the Reich. After 1942–3 that also included camp inmates and Jews. In the final phase of the war, the expansion of underground production sites, especially for airplane production, rested mainly on the use of forced labor.

So far it has not been possible to find even a single larger enterprise in the manufacturing sector that did not employ foreign forced laborers during the war. That applies especially to civilian workers and prisoners of war, while concentration camp inmates and Jewish forced laborers were requested chiefly by the larger enterprises. The initiative for the use of forced laborers came consistently from the enterprises themselves; if they did not request any forced laborers, they did not receive any. Arguments that the economic enterprises were compelled by the regime to employ forced laborers have no foundation in fact and misrepresent the nature of the cooperative structures in the German labor administration during the war.

All in all, this brief overview makes clear that the German economy was dependent on the employment of foreign forced laborers with no other alternative at the latest from the time when the fortunes of war suffered a reversal in the winter of 1941–2. Without them it would have been impossible to maintain the armament production, and thus continue the war, or to feed the German population at what was until 1944 a relatively high level. Forced labor in the German war economy was thus not a regime-induced peripheral phenomenon but was one of the essential preconditions for a war waged by Germany for nearly six years.

Chiari, Bernhard, and Jörg Echternkamp, eds. *Ausbeutung, Deutungen, Ausgrenzung (Das Deutsche Reich und der Zweite Weltkrieg*, vol. 9/2). Stuttgart, 2005.

Darstellungen und Quellen zur Geschichte von Auschwitz, edited by the Institut für Zeitgeschichte, 4 vols. Munich, 2000.

Echternkamp, Jörg, and Ralf Blank, eds. *Politisierung, Vernichtung, Überleben (Das Deutsche Reich und der Zweite Weltkrieg*, vol. 9/1). Stuttgart, 2005.

Gruner, Wolf. *Der geschlossene Arbeitseinsatz deutscher Juden. Zur Zwangsarbeit als Element der Verfolgung 1938–1943.* Berlin, 1997.

Hammermann, Gabriele. *Zwangsarbeit für den "Verbündeten." die Arbeits- und Lebensbedingungen der italienischen Militärinternierten in Deutschland 1943–1945.* Tübingen, 2002.

Herbert, Ulrich. *Fremdarbeiter. Politik und Praxis des "Ausländer-Einsatzes" in der Kriegswirtschaft des Dritten Reiches.* 3rd ed. Bonn, 1999.

Herbert, Ulrich, Karin Orth, and Christoph Dieckmann, eds. *Die nationalsozialistischen Konzentrationslager. Entwicklung und Struktur*, 2 vols. Göttingen, 1998.

Mommsen, Hans, and Manfred Grieger. *Das Volkswagenwerk und seine Arbeiter im Dritten Reich.* Düsseldorf. 1995.

Naasner, Walter. *Neue Machtzentren in der deutschen Kriegswirtschaft 1942–1945. Die Wirtschaftsorganisation der SS, das Amt des Generalbevollmächtigten für den Arbeitseinsatz und das Reichsministerium für Bewaffnung und Munition/ Reichsministerium für Rüstung und Kriegsproduktion im nationalsozialistischen Herrschaftssystem.* Boppard, 1994.

Spoerer, Mark. *Zwangsarbeit unter dem Hakenkreuz.* Stuttgart, 2001.

Wagner, Jens-Christian. *Produktion des Todes. Das KZ Mittelbau-Dora.* Göttingen, 2001.

Cross-references: France; Germany; Italy; The Netherlands; Northern Europe; Poland; Russia and Belarus; Southeastern Europe; Ukraine; Jewish Refugees from Nazi Germany and from German-Occupied Europe since 1933

FOREST FINNS IN SWEDEN AND NORWAY SINCE THE LATE 16TH CENTURY

Einar Niemi

The Forest Finns (*skogfinner*) in Sweden and Norway have their historical roots in migration from Finland between the end of the 16th and the early 18th century. Their main areas of settlement were the vast forests of Värmland in Sweden and the neighboring forest regions in Norway, with a core area in Finnskogene (the Finn Forests) in the county of Hedmark. In Sweden their settlement areas were named Finn Forests as well, but here the term has also been applied to the individual settlements. From the very start of the Forest Finns' settlement, the most characteristic feature of their culture was the swidden agricultrue (slash and burn) techniques they used for clearing the forests and tilling the soil. The name Rye Finns (*rugfinner*) has also been used: a reference to their most characteristic agricultural product. The Forest Finns of Norway enjoy the status of a "national minority" as a result of Norway's ratification in 1999 of the Council of Europe's Framework Convention for the Protection of National Minorities of 1995, whereas Sweden did not include its Forest Finns among its minorities when ratifying the same convention.

The migration of the Finns was a combination of both pull and push factors. The most important pull factor was the labor market for artisans, miners, mariners, servants, farmhands, and peasants in a period marking the early stages of Sweden's development as a Baltic empire and the country's "grand era." Royal recruitment to certain trades and enterprises added to the pull factors. Among the decisive push factors were population growth, warfare, crop failure, and hunger. The first known settlement of Forest Finns in Sweden took place around 1580. During this first phase of Finnish migration, until circa 1630, southern Värmland was the main destination. In the next phase, from 1630 until the end of the 17th century, the Finns settled in some 60 of Värmland's 90 parishes, and in 200 parishes in the whole of central Sweden. The Forest Finn population of Värmland increased from an estimated 8,000–9,000 at the end of the 17th century to 25,000 (7% of Värmland's population) by the early 19th century.

The first Forest Finns in Norway settled in Hedmark around 1620 and were connected with the Finn Forests of Värmland across a region that was not divided by an official state border until 1751. The expansion proceeded in stages, often based on chain migration mechanisms – neighbors and relatives followed in the wake of pioneers. Over a time span of 80 years most parts of the Finn Forests of Värmland and Hedmark were colonized, although sparsely, and during the 18th century the gaps in these core areas of colonization were filled. At the same time, the Finns moved farther west and north in Norway, until about 40 parishes hosted Forest Finns.

The special Finn census in Norway in 1686 registered about 1,200 Finns. Although women and children were counted as well, the census has severe lacunae and accounts for only a minimum number of Finns in Norway. This source indicates not only that many people had been born in Sweden but also that integration into society at large had begun: in the case of 160 individuals, one of their parents was either Swedish or Norwegian, the remainder were "pure" Finns.

The 1845 census, the next registration of Finns in Norway, only counted Finns when their ethnicity was clearly proven through descent or regional provenance. Finns were registered in only two parishes in Hedmark –and the total number of Finns was set at 1,740, about the same number that was registered in the 1855 census, in addition to some 500 persons from mixed marriages. By the turn of the century approximately 500 Finns were counted in the same parishes in the old core area of the Norwegian Finn Forests.

Although the Finns were welcomed by the central state authorities, they were opposed from the very start by established local farmers who had not cultivated the deep forests, but used parts of them for hunting, shooting, fishing, and producing hay in outlying fields. Their main complaint against the Finns was that their agricultural methods destroyed the forests for future agricultural and forestry use and diminished the value of game and fishing. Sometimes local ironmill owners had reservations about the Finns as well, although the Finns produced charcoal for the mills. This conflict was possibly one of the reasons the Finns ventured ever deeper into the forests or participated in the establishment of the first Swedish colony in North America, New Sweden in Delaware, in 1638.

The tradition of swidden agriculture remained a constant source of conflict until it was totally banned in the 19th century and the Forest Finns had to switch to other methods of agriculture. During the 18th century the inland forests increased in market value due to the expansion of forestry and the export of timber and planks to the European continent, which led to an increasingly critical view of the Finns' traditional form of agriculture. In the second part of the 17th century and throughout the 18th century, large stretches of crown land were sold to merchant entrepreneurs and mill owners and turned into estates, with forestry as their economic backbone. As a result, many Finns became dependent on the new owners and most had to accept the status of tenant farmer or crofter.

Around 1820 the Forest Finns of Värmland and Hedmark tried to improve their economic conditions and to protect their culture. The catalyst for this movement was Carl Axel Gottlund, a young Uppsala student with family roots in the eastern Finnish region Savolax who began his studies and "missionary" activities in the Finn Forests in 1817. Under his guidance, the Finns asserted the right to establish a large, cross-border parish of their own as well as their own chapels and churches; sought to select Finnish-speaking parsons, teachers, and judges; and attempted to improve their economic situation. In 1823, Gottlund led a march of 12 Finn leaders, 6 from either side of the border, to Stockholm, the capital of the Swedish-Norwegian Union, to present a petition of 500 folio pages signed by 600 Finns to the National Assembly and the king. Their claims were rejected due to fears of the establishment of a "miniature state" on the border. Gottlund (the apostle of the Forests Finns) was expelled from Sweden and ended up as scholar at the University of Helsinki. Although the protest failed, economic conditions among the

Finns improved in the 1820s when one of the great estates of the region went bankrupt, its land was divided up, and the parcels were sold at auction; many Finns bought farms and became peasant proprietors.

The suppression of Forest Finn mobilization undoubtedly paved the way for increased efforts at assimilation. Nevertheless, at the end of the 19th century there were still signs of the persistence of Finnish language and culture such as the archaic smoke sauna or steam bath, the smoke ovens in farmhouses and *ria*, the characteristic sheds for drying and threshing of the Finns. It was not until well after the Second World War that the last Forest Finns who spoke Finnish as their mother tongue died out.

In the last few decades there has been a strong renewed interest in the Forest Finns' culture and history. Scholars have taken particular interest in topics such as the swidden agricultural methods, secular architecture, and family names and place names; more than 1,500 Finnish toponyms, for example, are registered only in the Norwegian Finn Forest area and some 7,000 in the Swedish *Finnmarker*. There is widespread ethnosymbolic cooperation across the Swedish-Norwegian border between museums, cultural heritage bodies, and local and regional history associations. Summer festivals have become popular, not least the "Finn Forest Days" in the heart of the Norwegian Finn Forest in July every year. The recognition of the Norwegian Forest Finns as a national minority has encouraged new initiatives to revitalize their culture and ethnicity.

Bladh, Gabriel. *Finnskogens landskap och människor under fyra sekler: En studie av samhälle och natur i förändring*. Karlstad, 1995.

Kjeldstadli, Knut, ed. *Norsk innvandringshistorie*, vols. 1–3. Oslo, 2003.

Østberg, Kristian. *Finnskogene i Norge*. Grue, 1978.

Tarkiainen, Kari. *Finnarnas historia i Sverige*, vols. 1–2. Helsinki, 1990–1993.

Wedin, Maud, et al., eds. *Det skogsfinska kulturarvet*. Falun, 2001.

Wedin, Maud. *Den skogsfinska kolonisationen i Norrland*. Falun, 2007.

Cross-references: Northern Europe; Central and Western European Miners and Smelters in Sweden and Denmark-Norway from the 16th to the 18th Century; Kvens and Torne-Finns in Norway and Sweden since the 18th Century

FRENCH MARITIME MERCHANTS IN HAMBURG SINCE 1680

Klaus Weber

In the 18th century, Hamburg was home to a significant group of French maritime traders who made a considerable contribution to the city's economic strength. Some French had long been present in Hamburg, particularly since the

religious conflicts of the 16th and 17th centuries had driven many Huguenots from their homeland. Although Hamburg also attracted Catholics, the majority of the French merchants were Calvinists, particularly after the revocation of the Edict of Nantes in 1685, when the French community rapidly became the largest group of foreign merchants in the Hanseatic city.

The Senate of the free city of Hamburg traditionally welcomed foreign entrepreneurs, even those belonging to non-Lutheran minorities, but the burghers, guilds, and a part of the Lutheran clergy were rather hostile toward them. Non-Lutheran foreigners – both Catholics and Calvinists – were not allowed to become burghers, were subject to higher levies, and were not permitted to maintain their own places of worship or cemeteries until 1785. Well into the 1720s, religious minorities suffered public attacks. Only the intervention of the Dutch government as protector of the Calvinist diaspora checked threats of violence and derogatory pamphlets. The prevailing image of the Huguenot migration is one of a persecuted religious minority that found refuge in tolerant Protestant states, where they achieved considerable economic success. Although this picture is certainly true for the majority of Huguenots, the case of Hamburg illustrates that Huguenots sometimes settled in places where favorable religious and political conditions were clearly lacking. Only the extremely profitable economic conditions offset restrictions that nearly equaled those in their country of origin.

The 1680s and 1690s, decades that witnessed significant Huguenot migration to Hamburg, coincided with French colonial expansion in the Caribbean. Saint-Domingue and a number of smaller islands became the principal producers of commodities like sugar, coffee, and indigo. French Atlantic seaports, traditionally strongholds of French Protestants, increasingly provided colonial goods for central European and Baltic markets, with Huguenots as major agents in the trade. Their relatives and co-religionists in Hamburg soon transformed the city into one of the principal markets for such goods in northern Europe, surpassing even Amsterdam – far more hospitable toward Huguenots – by the 1730s.

By transferring energy-intensive sugar refineries from French Atlantic seaports to the estuary of the Elbe River, Huguenot immigrants were able to take advantage of lower costs for labor and fuel. In French port cities, chambers of commerce and royal officials frequently complained about Hamburg's low wages and cheap coal in the 18th century. Hamburg also benefited from its proximity to central and eastern Europe, the Continent's primary markets for sugar. The Huguenots thus dominated the most expansive and most lucrative sector of Hamburg's economy: the import and processing of colonial goods such as sugar, cotton, and tropical dyes like indigo, which was used for textiles. At the same time, German trade recovered following the Thirty Years' War and increasing amounts of its products, textiles in particular, were exported into the Atlantic basin. Huguenots also conducted much of this export trade, which likewise profited from the comparatively low costs of labor and became highly competitive in western Europe, Africa, and the New World. Aside from wanting to escape the religious oppression they experienced at home, French migrants were mainly drawn to German territories by economic prospects. It must be mentioned, however, that those who went to Hamburg were part of the economic elite; Huguenots who settled in the German hinterland typically were of more modest social origins.

Compared with the total number of Huguenots throughout Europe, the Hamburg community was small: out of the more than 150,000 Huguenot refugees no more than 1,500 settled in the Hanseatic cities of Bremen, Lübeck, and Hamburg. The majority went to Hamburg and the neighboring Danish city of Altona (today a part of Hamburg), where the Danish government allowed the community to maintain its own chapels. While Altona offered religious tolerance and free trade, Hamburg's assets were its political neutrality and its favorable position as a major transit point for colonial goods, financial services, and commercial information. The French who resided in Hamburg attended church services in Altona, while the French in Altona also traded at the influential Hamburg Stock Exchange. In the 1770s, when Hamburg's population had exceeded 100,000, its Huguenot community comprised some 200 persons, that of Altona about 300. Considering the overlap between both groups, the total number of Huguenots at the time likely lay below 500 persons. Though very small in number, the community was very powerful in terms of commerce and trade. The Boué (from Bordeaux) and His (from Rouen) families were its most prominent representatives.

Among the far smaller group of French Catholic merchants in Hamburg, those belonging to the trading house Michel & Grou from Nantes, which established a branch in Hamburg in the first half of the 18th century, stood out. The company also maintained branches in Paris, Saint-Domingue, London, Amsterdam, and Bilbao. The company was heavily involved in the Atlantic slave trade as well as in the Compagnie des Indes (the French East Indian Company) and maintained excellent contacts with the nobility of the French court. Between 1749 and 1755 alone the company's various branches sold more than 10,000 slaves in the New World. Michel & Grou left the city before 1750 due to a dispute with the Senate over the amount of port duties to be paid.

The sugar trade best illustrates French economic domination in Hamburg. In the 1750s, five of Hamburg's seven major importers were Huguenots and together these five controlled almost 40% of the sugar imports registered by the customs authorities, although it should be emphasized that the imports of Lutheran burghers were largely exempt from import duties. Nevertheless, the total of Hamburg's annual imports from France in the period is estimated at some 14 million marks, with sugar likely accounting for half, and the total of Hamburg's maritime imports at 77 million marks, with France being the city's largest trading partner. Seen in this light, the imports of Pierre His registered by customs authorities in 1755 – exceeding 1.8 million marks, including wine, brandy, coffee, dyes, and sugar worth more than

1 million marks alone – accounted for a significant share of Hamburg's total trade.

French merchants were also major exporters of central European manufactures and acted as agents in the German linen market. Émigré Huguenot textile experts who had relatives in French Atlantic port cities used these excellent commercial relations to their own benefit. Thanks to such contacts Pierre Boué & fils was commissioned by the Real Compañía de Caracas to send entire shiploads of linen from Hamburg to Spain. For the same company, Boué also sent vessels loaded with hemp, tar, and timber from the Baltic Sea area to Spanish shipyards. Other Huguenots were likewise involved in this trade, including Bernard Texier, Pierre His, Jean Boyer, and Alexandre Bruguier. The Boué brothers also founded a shipyard in Altona and constructed warships and commercial vessels there for the Compagnie des Indes. In 1723 the Senate succeeded in attracting this business to Hamburg, where it became the city's major shipyard for the entire century. By 1732 the Boué shipyard had delivered at least 23 ships to France, including battleships of up to 500 tons. In this sector too, French investors benefited from the lower cost of labor and raw materials.

French efforts to integrate into Hamburg's bourgeois community met with less success. Franz Peter His and Peter Boué (Hamburg-born sons of the aforementioned His and Boué) were involved in the creation of a Patriotic Association (Patriotische Gesellschaft, 1765) and the experiment to create a German National Theater (Deutsches Nationaltheater, 1767). Jean Pierre Vidal, Guilleaumont His, Pierre Texier, and Guilleaume Courtier became important figures in the early history of freemasonry in Hamburg and were active participants in the cultural exchange that took place among the various ethnic and religious groups within the city's economic elite. Despite such initiatives, Hamburg's Lutheran oligarchy remained closed to the immigrants. The oligarchs had already created a Patriotic Association in 1724, whose 1726 manifesto stipulated the hegemony of only a single faith within the city. The association of 1765, in which the Huguenots were active, did not make this tradition its own. Its focus was on charitable works and the formation of an enlightened world that their predecessor organization had viewed as God-given and immutable.

The marriage patterns of the Boué family clearly reveal the exclusionary behavior of local residents. Three-quarters of the 36 Boué marriages in the 18th century (including both male and female family members) were concluded with partners of French origin, most of whom were from Hamburg or Altona, some from France. Only after 1790, when the economic significance of familial bonds to French seaports began to recede as French trading predominance in Hamburg weakened, did the rate of exogamous marriages grow – yet these partners were of British rather than German origin.

Following the French Revolution and the Napoleonic wars, the French community shrank considerably, both in number and in economic performance. The Huguenots soon became a tiny minority among Hamburg Calvinists, who counted some 8,000 members. Surprisingly, the community's most severe crisis came from within. Although the emergence of 19th-century liberalism had attenuated previously existing socioreligious conflicts between locals and outsiders, the Franco-German war of 1870–1 provoked a grave identity crisis within the community as the Hanseatic City and other German states sided with Prussia against France. Numerous members of the community called on their pastors to take a more pronounced German-national stand or converted themselves to Lutheranism, which was viewed as genuinely Prussian and legitimized the aggressive Prussian path toward a German nation-state. Conversion to German Calvinism, in contrast, represented a less radical alternative.

Members of the most eminent Huguenot families in particular converted, thus depriving the community – already shrinking – of its social and economic grounding, and putting an end to the ambiguous cosmopolitan identity of Hamburg's French community. Once a generous donor to poorer communities in Prussia, the French Reformed Church in Hamburg had itself become a supplicant for financial support by the 1880s. At the end of the 19th century the community barely counted 40 adult members in a Lutheran city of almost 1 million inhabitants. Only after the Second World War did the parish recover in any substantial way, again numbering several hundred members by the 1970s.

Kopitzsch, Franklin. "Franzosen in den Hansestädten und in Altona zwischen 1685 und 1789." In *Deutsche in Frankreich, Franzosen in Deutschland 1715–1789*, edited by Jean Mondot, Jean-Marie Valentin, and Jürgen Voss, 283–95. Sigmaringen, 1992.

Schrader, Fred E. "Handel und Aufklärungssoziabilität in Hamburg und Bordeaux, 1750–1820." In *Lumières et commerce*, edited by Jean Mondot and Catherine Larrère, 67–87. Frankfurt am Main, 2000.

Weber, Klaus. *Deutsche Kaufleute im Atlantikhandel 1680–1830. Unternehmen und Familien in Hamburg, Cádiz und Bordeaux.* Munich, 2004.

Weber, Klaus. "French Migrants into Loyal Germans. Huguenots in Hamburg (1685–1985)." In *Enlarging European Memory. Migration Movements in Historical Perspective*, edited by Mareike König and Rainer Ohliger, 59–70. Ostfildern, 2006.

Whaley, Joachim. *Religious Toleration and Social Change in Hamburg 1529–1811*. Cambridge, 1985.

Cross-references: France; Germany; Huguenots in Europe since the 16th Century

FRENCH REVOLUTIONARY REFUGEES IN EUROPE AFTER 1789: THE EXAMPLE OF GERMANY

Daniel Schönpflug

The importance of migration in the age of the French Revolution is revealed by the fact that the term "émigré"

appeared in everyday French only in the last decade of the 18th century. More than 150,000 French men and women left their country between 1789 and 1794. Generally speaking, this migration was caused by the revolutionary upheaval, although this statement must not blind us to the fact that the motivations of the migrants were as diverse as their social and regional origins and destinations. After an initial phase during which émigrés headed above all to the cities close to the border (Turin, Worms, Koblenz, Brussels), France's military expansion forced the refugees to move on. Thereafter, London was home to the largest emigrant colony, but no European country was without revolutionary refugees. For the majority of the emigrants, blocked from returning by French laws that were gradually tightened between 1792 and 1794, exile ended with the Napoleonic amnesty of 1801–2. To do justice to the complexity of the phenomenon, the discussion that follows will focus on the emigrant colony that emerged in Koblenz in 1791, composed mostly of counter-revolutionary nobles who were hoping for military intervention in France, which will be compared to other places and manifestations of exile.

Scholarship distinguishes two main phases of emigration prompted by the revolution: in the first phase, which lasted from 1789 to the August unrest of 1792 and the proclamation of the Republic, it was mostly members of the nobility – and to a lesser extent also clerics and members of the bourgeoisie – who left the country. Emigration in this phase was based on a free decision and was in most cases determined by political opposition, a desire to resist, or a feeling of danger. In the second phase from September 1792, when the stream of emigrants grew significantly, the social profile and the motives of the refugees changed. A substantially higher proportion now came from the Third Estate. It also included former supporters of the revolution who had run into conflict with the radicalizing leadership in Paris or were suffering political persecution.

New factors behind the rise in emigration were the growing economic problems, war, and civil war, which drove above all petty bourgeoisie and farmers from the French periphery into exile, increasingly vehement attacks on the church and the clergy, and the terror from the fall of 1793 to the summer of the following year. According to official data, the emigrants came from all social strata: 25% were clerics, 17% from the nobility, 11% from the grand bourgeoisie, 6% from the petty bourgeoisie, 14% were workers, and 19% farmers; for 7% the social origins cannot be identified. They came chiefly from regions of the French periphery. The department with the largest number of emigrants was Bas-Rhin.

The formation of a French colony in Koblenz was a phenomenon of the first phase of emigration after the summer of 1789. The key figure was the Comte d'Artois, a brother of the king, who had been one of the first French noblemen to leave the country. Following expulsion from his first place of exile in Brussels, he briefly set himself up in Turin. The move to Koblenz took place in July 1791, simultaneously with King Louis XVI's attempt to flee, which came to an inglorious end at Varennes. In Koblenz, the count was festively received by his uncle, the Elector Clemens Wenceslaus, and put up in castle Schönbornlust outside the gates of the city. Artois was completely open about his counter-revolutionary intentions, and his appeals for emigration that were circulated in France bore some fruit. The stream of emigrants to Koblenz grew; nearly 80% of them were officers from the royal army (more than 7,500 persons). At times, the city was overwhelmed by the influx, as housing, means of transportation, and food-stuffs were in short supply.

The emigrants in Koblenz tried to preserve the Ancien Régime that was in full decline. A court modeled after Versailles arose around the Comte d'Artois and the Comte de Provence. Both appointed a *Maison* in keeping with their rank. The repertoire of dignitaries, officials, household and ceremonial guards, and servants known from Versailles was revived; even officer ranks, which had been abolished before the revolution to save money, were handed out again. Offices were awarded largely on the basis of a person's noble status and favor; however, since the offices were highly sought-after and the funds scarce, the buying of offices played a significant role. Contemporary estimates put the size of the Bourbon court in Koblenz at around 800 persons. In feasts, receptions, balls, and musical and theatrical performances, the court sought to revive the splendor of the old days. Social hierarchies and the elaborate and strict ceremonial activities followed old patterns; the informal structures of the old court life also reappeared: the struggle for favor, intrigues, and reign of mistresses.

The political center of the Koblenz court was the Conseil des Princes in which the princes and their ministers deliberated the measures to be taken. Their main goal was to enter into alliances with European monarchs. Likewise, emissaries and letters made it possible to establish contact with confidants in France, who in turn were to call for emigration and resistance to the revolution. To that end, the French royalist press was asked to print brochures and articles. There was also a finance minister, the former Controlleur des Finances Charles Alexandre de Calonne, who – since the support payments from the Elector of Trier were by no means sufficient – had to continuously collect donations and ask for loans to finance the sumptuous life and the army.

The Conseil was above all the center of the military opposition to the revolution and the place where plans for an invasion were hatched and the recruitment of an army of emigrants was coordinated. It was also the command headquarters of the Armée des Princes, though it did not see action before the Prussian-Austrian campaign in the late summer of 1792. The places where the troops were stationed were dispersed over the entire Electorate. For that reason, individual units, often located far apart, became very independent. On the whole, the troops, because of a lack of equipment, poor training, and scanty pay, had little military effectiveness. One structural problem was also the fact that the noblemen, in keeping with their social status, were for the most part placed into the rank of officers, which meant

that there were virtually no common soldiers. The few commoners in the Armée des Princes were grouped into separate units. It is impossible to determine the total strength of the emigrant army; contemporary estimates put it at 13,000 to 14,000 men.

While the court and the army were the organizational centers of the emigrants in and around Koblenz, these were by no means the only forms of sociability. According to estimates at the time, 2,000 to 4,000 emigrants over and beyond the courtiers were in Koblenz. Depending on their financial resources, they lived in the various inns and hotels of the city. In addition, parks and squares, restaurants, the theater, and the churches offered opportunities for social interactions. Although the colony in Koblenz had a disproportionately large number of males, the result of Artois's military projects, there were also a few salons run by Parisian ladies. Thus the emigrants in Koblenz lived for the most part within a closed social sphere. Given their project of creating a counterweight to the new order in France by reestablishing the world of the Ancien Régime, and because of the possibility of supporting oneself temporarily with funds brought into exile or borrowed, it did not seem necessary to them to seek a place within the foreign society. To be sure, they were dependent on the services of native hotelkeepers and merchants, of lenders and local servants, but differences in social status, language problems, fundamentally different ways of life, and the unwillingness of the emigrants to engage a culture they regarded as inferior created a deep gulf between the colony and the residents of the city.

The self-perception of the emigrants was based on a deeply rooted sense of superiority, which derived its legitimacy from the "radiance" of French court culture. The courts and cities on the fragmented map of the Old Empire struck them accordingly as incomplete copies of Versailles and Paris. "Provincial," "backward," "gothic," and "baroque" are labels that frequently recur in the emigrants' description of Germany. The German clinging to tradition was rarely commented upon positively, in spite of the exiles' hatred of innovation in France. As a result, the emigrants in Koblenz struck a self-confident pose. They showed themselves in public in uniform, in arms, and with white cockades. Marches and parades in military formation and with music in the middle of the city were no rarity.

The reaction of the Koblenzers to the flood of immigrants varied: the hospitality and generosity of Elector Clemens Wenceslaus, who not only financed the court of the emigrants but also accorded it sovereign rights (such as a separate jurisdiction and police forces), was confronted by the concerns and mistrust of the territorial estates. They repeatedly pointed to the danger that Electoral Trier was running by taking the side of the enemies of the revolution. It was only pressure from the Empire that led to a first emigrant ordinance that demanded – without any effect – the disbanding of the troops. The response by the population at large was no more positive. The heightened demand for housing and consumer goods invigorated the city's economy, though it also meant a higher cost of living for the locals. The debts that the emigrants owed to citizens of Koblenz became a growing problem. They were no doubt the background for the increasing complaints about the excessive and immoral life of the emigrants. Reports like the autobiography of Friedrich Christian Laukhard suggest that the cohabitation was marked increasingly by accusations and conflicts. The French were labeled "impudent," "puffed up," and "proud"; their "corrupted morals" were supposedly the reason there were "no more virgins" in Koblenz.

The end of the emigrant colony came with the outbreak of the first Coalition War. The Armée des Princes joined the advance of the Prussian forces and was defeated along with them at Valmy (20 September 1792). Clemens Wenceslaus thereupon changed his attitude and prevented the emigrant court from returning to his land.

Koblenz can be considered the best-organized colony, which acted as a shining symbol of the counter-revolution. However, the situation there was not very representative for the emigration as a whole. Only in Electoral Trier did a prince become a magnanimous host for a large group of emigrants; in many places in Europe, the emigrants were merely tolerated or even systematically expelled. Only in Koblenz did the political will of an elite driven away by the revolution present itself so clearly. Elsewhere, the emigration was socially and politically more heterogeneous, it organized itself into small groups, with life characterized by more modest circumstances and the need to earn money. In London, where about 25,000 Frenchmen and women, chiefly nobility and common people, sought refuge, the emigrants at least enjoyed a reliable right of residence. In certain areas of London – for example, Soho and Marlyebone, where the wealthy emigrants lived – an active social life took shape; but in other neighborhoods there was also dire poverty, although it was relieved by charitable organizations and a government support fund.

Worse still were the conditions of admission for French emigrants in Prussia. The law permitted foreigners to stay on Prussian territory only in exceptional cases; since 1792, political refugees had been granted a special legal status, which was largely identical to the status of vagabonds. Even those among the approximately 5,000 emigrants who became Prussian subjects were not equal in legal terms to those born in the country. With few exceptions, the emigrants did not receive state support. By far the most common way for the noble refugees to secure a livelihood was the search for employment as a private language tutor or instructor in courtly arts such as fencing, dancing, or riding. Emigrants were prohibited from enrolling in a university, and only in rare cases were they admitted into the Prussian army. The situation was easier for members of the Third Estate. French domestics could find employment also with Prussian families, while those who possessed modern specialized knowledge, like the refugee workers from the French textile industry, were actually in demand in the labor market. Due to these conditions, emigrants in Prussia were much less

able than their counterparts in Koblenz to cut themselves off from their host society. Accommodation proved a necessity of survival in an environment whose dealings with foreigners were determined chiefly by utilitarian motives. Yet in spite of a certain number of marriages between migrants and the host population, there is nothing to suggest a further-reaching integration of the group.

The short duration of their exile also argues for the weak integration of the French emigrants. Through the Concordat of 1801, Napoleon created the possibility for exiled clerics to return without punishment. The senatorial decree of 26 April 1802, which amounted to an amnesty for all emigrants, triggered a great wave of remigration. However, the confiscated property of the emigrants could be returned only if it had not been sold again. The restoration period opened the path for the *milliard des émigrés*, an agreement about reparation payments for dispossessed emigrants.

Carpenter, Kirsty. *Refugees of the French Revolution: Emigrés in London 1789–1802*. London, 1999.

Henke, Christian. *Coblentz: Symbol für die Gegenrevolution. Die französische Emigration nach Koblenz und Kurtrier 1789–1792 und die politische Diskussion des revolutionären Frankreichs 1791–1794*. Stuttgart, 2000.

Höpel, Thomas. *Emigranten der Französischen Revolution in Preußen 1789–1806. Eine Studie in vergleichender Perspektive*. Leipzig, 2000.

Rance, Karine. "Mémoires des nobles français émigrés en Allemagne pendant la Révolution française: La vision rétrospective d´une expérience." *Revue d'histoire moderne et contemporaine* 46 (1999): 245–62.

Schönpflug, Daniel, ed. *Révolutionnaires et émigrés. Transfer und Migration zwischen Frankreich und Deutschland 1789–1806*. Stuttgart, 2002.

Cross-references: Belgium and Luxembourg; France; Germany; Great Britain; Italy

FRENCH, BELGIAN, BRITISH, AND US OCCUPATION TROOPS IN WESTERN AND SOUTHWESTERN GERMANY, 1918–1930

Michael Schubert

After the end of World War I, the victorious powers occupied territories in western and southwestern Germany: Belgian troops were stationed in the northern Rhineland along the Dutch and Belgian borders; British troops in the area around Cologne and Solingen; French troops in the area east and west of Bonn up to the Belgian border and in the Bavarian Palatinate, in Hesse around Wiesbaden, and in the Rhine bridgehead of Kehl. American forces occupied the Prussian Rhine province in the north along a line between Honnef and Koblenz, westward as far as Trier, and up to the border with Luxembourg. The occupied territory was expanded with the addition of the city of Frankfurt and its environs in April 1920, and of several territories on the right bank of the Rhine in March 1921. Beginning in January 1923, French and Belgian troops occupied the Ruhr region as a punitive measure because German reparation payments were in arrears. The USA rejected this measure and withdrew its troops from Germany; the territory formerly occupied by the USA was taken over by the French army. The Young Plan of 1929–30, which restructured the reparation payments, ended the occupation of all territories of the Rhineland on 30 June 1930, with the Belgians already having vacated their occupied territory in 1926.

The total size of the occupying forces was in constant flux and can no longer be determined precisely. Estimates put the number of troops at well over 100,000 after the Treaty of Versailles took effect at the beginning of 1920. The French provided the vast majority of the occupation forces in the Rhineland, with 200,000 soldiers in the winter of 1919 and still around 85,000 in 1920. In 1921, the British forces in Cologne numbered around 11,000 to 12,000. They increased their troop strength in 1923 in the wake of the occupation of the Ruhr region.

The experience of the German civilian population with occupation varied considerably. The backdrop was differences in the intensity of contacts with soldiers and the occupation policy in the different occupation zones, which showed strong regional and local variations. Additionally, some hostile and nationalistic mayors and members of local governments tried to influence the behavior of the civilians and incite them against the occupation forces. The occupation of the Rhineland lodged in Germany's collective memory under the slogans "Rhenish separatism," "Ruhr struggle," and "black disgrace." All three aspects concern the French occupation, which was painted in starkly propagandistic colors at the time and seen as occupation by a hostile power, the history of which largely blocks out the daily experience of social contact between the natives and the occupiers.

Very little scholarly research has been done on the Belgian and US occupation, and few studies include the daily experience of occupation. Against the background of the shortages after the war, including the housing market, the poor state of the finances of the Empire and local communities, and the hyperinflation of 1923, occupation constituted an added burden in daily life. In the first months of occupation, mail traffic between occupied and nonoccupied territories was interrupted in many places, the use of telephone and telegraph was prohibited, the water supply was blocked, and the operation of the administration was impeded, with the result, for example, that payments of pensions and wages were not made and the transport of goods by railroad was strongly curtailed, if not entirely stopped. Crossing the boundary between occupied and nonoccupied territory was possible only with an additional passport that had to be applied for.

The initial attitude of the natives to the troops was one of distance, contempt, or even enmity: while the streets in Koblenz were largely deserted when the US troops entered,

the population in Cologne watched the arrival of British troops for the most part with sullen silence or indifference. During the first few months of its existence, the Office of Occupation Issues set up by mayor Konrad Adenauer was deluged with complaints about soldiers who were driving over sidewalks in their vehicles or about the Royal Air Force, which was holding maneuvers above cemeteries. It aroused the anger of the people of Cologne that violations of the new regulations were handled in summary proceedings and harshly punished: failure to salute an officer could be punishable by a fine of 7,000 marks or six months in jail. Some municipal politicians decried a brutal "occupation mentality" on the part of the French soldiers, who supposedly drove civilians from the sidewalks with blows from their rifle butts. Only in rare instances did locals greet the arrival of the soldiers with admiration, whose discipline and good provisioning attracted attention. By contrast, a daily occurrence was the provocations of soldiers by the civilian population through disparaging looks, gestures, and jeers.

The noncommissioned officers and enlisted men of the occupying forces lived in closed-off areas, often in barracks vacated by German troops. Officers were housed in private lodgings: in confiscated houses and apartments, with German families, or, as soon as family members had joined them, increasingly in their own housing. Hotels and other private buildings were often confiscated for the military administration. In Cologne, for example, the British army in 1919 occupied not only all hotels and 300 private houses, but also 96 schools as temporary accommodations, with the result that the German city administration could blame the British for problems in providing schooling for the locals.

Especially the arrival of families in 1919 caused considerable friction in the British case. The arriving wives, influenced by the war propaganda at home, struck the native women as pushy and aggressive in the peremptory manner in which they confiscated housing. In Wiesbaden, where seven schools and many private dwellings were confiscated by French troops, the housing shortage grew much worse. Koblenz had to bear the heaviest burden; in 1923, following the takeover of the city by the French, there were 1,881 confiscated housing units for 59,000 residents. By contrast, in Cologne, with a population of 670,000, only 590 units had been seized.

Despite the multitudinous conflicts, indications of a gradual normalization are evident in the daily encounters between natives and occupiers, which manifested itself in friendly interactions all the way to intimate relationships. In the British military papers *Cologne Post* and *Bystander*, the "Rhinelander" appeared less as an enemy than a figure of ridicule. Eventually he was occasionally even described as a friend in whom a little "French blood" flowed. Many encounters between quartered soldiers and local families were characterized in the British case by mutual generosity and friendliness as early as 1918. Soldiers were given Christmas presents and were looked after by their "guest family" if they fell ill.

Although fraternization was prohibited, neither the British nor the Germans did anything to stop it. British soldiers met German *Mädels* in the cafés, and some British women – who were employed in the occupied zone as secretaries, nurses, or mess-hall workers – looked at these developing romantic relationships with mistrust and even jealousy. Even though the *Cologne Post* railed against mixed marriages, by September 1921, 157 marriages had already been concluded between British soldiers – including seven officers – and German women. By 1925 the number of mixed marriages had risen to 700. After marriage, the women were formally part of the occupying army. Prostitution was decried by the British, but especially against the backdrop of the inflation, it developed into a profitable business.

In the course of the 1920s, the British and French garrison towns and cities saw the appearance of stores selling everyday provisions and clothing from back home, bookstores, or bakeries offering white bread. Already in 1920 there were enough British entrepreneurs in Cologne to sustain three British banks and a chamber of commerce. In 1922, the chamber registered 47 British enterprises and 2,500 British businessmen. Organizations (e.g., women's clubs and scout troops) and establishments of public life – such as movie houses, theaters, and opera houses – emerged in the British and French occupation zones. The Rhine Army Dramatic Company in Cologne put on plays by British playwrights. In 1919 the French opened a public reading room in Kaiserslautern that was stocked with French literature, newspapers, and magazines.

French cultural offerings were increasingly seen as a deliberate cultural policy within the context of the French *pénétration pacifique*. As early as 1918, a German separatist movement had appeared in the French-occupied Rhineland, whose goal it was to turn the Rhineland into an independent state affiliated with France. The French cultural policy that was launched in 1920 and did not end until 1923–4 was intended, among other things, to promote the Frenchification of the only "superficially German" Rhinelanders through French language courses and lectures about French history, geography, and culture. In publications spawned by French cultural policy, for example the *Revue Rhènane* that appeared in Mainz from 1920 to 1930, the Rhinelander was seen as close to French culture because he was, like the French, of "Celto-Romanic" background, and had also been shaped for centuries by French influences, most especially by the 20 years after 1792 when his homeland was part of France.

The occupation of the Ruhr region led to an escalation of the occupation situation. The Reich government under Wilhelm Cuno called for passive resistance, and former members of the Free Corps, as well as communists, committed acts of sabotage and attacks on the occupying troops. Many Germans were stripped of their offices, driven from their homes, arrested, or deported to the nonoccupied zone along with their entire families. That was the case, for example, with railroad workers who refused to work for the occupying power, but also with leading officials and simple state and Reich employees. In Koblenz, alone, about 1,500 persons had to leave the city in 1923, at least temporarily. The "Ruhr struggle" had a lasting negative impact on the relations between the occupiers and the natives.

However, the most profound reverberations from the occupation of the Rhineland were generated by the nationalistic and racist agitation against the "black disgrace": while Great Britain did not deploy any colonial troops in the Rhineland, and only a few non-European soldiers served in the Belgian and American units, France had stationed around 30,000 to 40,000 soldiers of north and west African background and a few hundred Indonesian soldiers in the Rhineland in 1920–1. In the city of Wiesbaden, for example, of a total of 3,635 French occupation troops, 855 were of Algerian, 600 of Tunisian, and 25 of Indochinese background. In the small town of Erbenheim (population 2,700) near Wiesbaden, 55 Moroccans and west Africans served among the total of 125 soldiers stationed there.

With the use of colonial troops in World War I already having led to a larger international debate, the deployment of French colonial troops and the crimes imputed to them – especially rapes – triggered a flood of German publications. They argued on racist grounds and emphasized that members of "lesser races" should never be allowed to rule over Europeans, let alone Germans. For example, Heinrich Schnee, the former governor of German East Africa and Reichstag deputy of the German People's Party, wrote in 1924 that "rapes of German women and the forced establishment of brothels with white women for the black troops" entailed "the gravest dangers for the future of the white race." The Reich government supported the demand for the withdrawal of non-European soldiers with diplomatic initiatives. As early as 1923, Reich president Friedrich Ebert had attacked the "use of colored troops of the lowest culture as overseers of a population of such high intellectual and economic importance as the Rhinelanders" as a "violation of the laws of European civilization."

Sexual relationships between German women and soldiers were repeatedly portrayed in the political and public discussion in Germany as a violation of "moral and social honor (*Standes-Ehre*)," which had been brought about only by the material desires of the women in difficult economic situations. And sexual relationships between German women and non-European soldiers were regarded by nationalistic agitation as "racial defilement" (*Rassenschande*) already in the 1920s. In Cologne, alone, according to a report by Adenauer, about 600 illegitimate children of occupation soldiers had been born by 1920. A statistical survey of 1934 speaks of a total of 385 children from sexual relationships between German women and soldiers of non-European backgrounds. In 1937, these "Rhineland bastards" were subjected to forced sterilization for reasons of "racial hygiene."

After the withdrawal of the troops and the end of the occupation of the Rhineland, British and French social, cultural, and economic life largely collapsed. Only a few foreign soldiers, most of them married to German women, remained in the Rhineland after leaving military service.

Koller, Christian. *"Von Wilden aller Rassen niedergemetzelt." Die Diskussion um die Verwendung von Kolonialtruppen in Europa zwischen Rassismus, Kolonial- und Militärpolitik (1914–1930).* Stuttgart, 2001.

Koops, Tilmann, and Martin Voigt, eds. *Das Rheinland in zwei Nachkriegszeiten. 1919–1930 und 1945–1949.* Koblenz, 1995.

Kreutz, Wilhelm, and Karl Scherer, eds. *Die Pfalz unter französischer Besetzung (1918/19–1930).* Kaiserslautern, 1999.

Pommerin, Reiner. *Sterilisierung der Rheinlandbastarde. Das Schicksal einer farbigen deutschen Minderheit 1918–1937.* Düsseldorf, 1979.

Williamson, David G. *The British in Germany 1918–1930: The Reluctant Occupiers.* New York and Oxford, 1991.

Cross-references: Belgium and Luxembourg; France; Germany; Great Britain

GALICIAN JEWS IN AUSTRIA FROM THE 18TH TO THE EARLY 20TH CENTURY

Michael John

Galicia was annexed to the Habsburg monarchy in 1772 as consequence of the partition of Poland. From 1867 to 1918 it belonged to the Austrian half of the Austro-Hungarian dual monarchy. Thereafter it became part of the Republic of Poland. The crown land of Galicia was always home to the largest number of Jews in the Habsburg monarchy: in 1775 there were 250,000, and by 1880 already 450,000 (8.5% of the population of the crown land). Around 1900 the number of Jews stood around 770,000, and in 1910 at around 900,000 (12%). The Jews of Galicia formed a rapidly growing population with a very high birth surplus. By Jewish standards, an unusually large number worked in agriculture (about 20% around 1900). In addition, many Jews lived as small independent merchants and tradesmen, whose trade also included peddling.

A statistical report in 1903 described one-quarter of the Galician Jews as "utterly propertyless and unemployed." The mortality rate was high, with hunger or typhus a frequent cause of death. The widespread existence of begging and prostitution testifies to the dire living conditions of part of the Jewish lower classes in Galicia. Originally the Galician Jews spoke mostly Yiddish, but until the 1860s the educated classes used exclusively German as the hegemonial language. Into the 1890s, assimilated Galician Jews had a pronounced affinity for German culture; alongside Vienna and Berlin, other German cities were often also the desired destination for one's path through life and were seen as the embodiment of civilization. By contrast, nonassimilated Jews remained more strongly attached to religion and a traditional way of life.

The orientation toward German culture came to an end in 1867, when various reforms establishing Galicia's new autonomous status within the Habsburg monarchy took effect. Henceforth, Poles, in particular, took over the key positions in the regional administration. The educational and judicial systems were given a stronger Polish imprint. Although the idea of German as the language of culture remained as a mythic notion, a growing majority of Galician Jews indicated Polish as their vernacular during censuses. *Shtetl*, traditional dress, Hasidism, and religious Orthodoxy characterized a substantial portion of the Galician Jews as further cultural elements and identified them as a specific group. The migration of these Jews to the crown lands of Inner Austria, but especially to Vienna and Lower Austria, developed into a chain migration that grew substantially even during unfavorable economic times. A focal point were labor migrations with a perspective of long-term settlement. At the lower end of the social scale one can speak of poverty migrations (beggars, peddlers). For the Jewish middle and upper classes of Galicia one can also identify a good deal of career migration. Migration by individuals was common; family migrations remained more rare during the entire 19th century.

If we look back in time, as early as 1812, the representatives of the Jews in Vienna – only accepted at that time because they paid a toleration tax – issued a "call … to initiate suitable measures to remove as best as possible the foreign, Israelite beggars (from Galicia) that are found here." Until 1848 it was illegal for propertyless Galician migrants to come to Vienna, and their influx was very limited. By contrast, Jews of greater means and income were allowed to move to Vienna. About 15,000 Jews lived in Vienna around 1850. Outside the city there were virtually no immigrant Jews. Like Styria, Tyrol, and Carinthia, Upper Austria (including Salzburg) was among the lands from which Jews were nearly completely excluded after the great expulsion in 1669. Although Jewish merchants were allowed to visit the large markets, until the first half of the 19th century they were not allowed to settle and as a rule had to leave the land again within three days. A liberalization of the law began in the revolutionary year 1848, and the last regulations restricting the choice of a profession and the geographical mobility of Jews were rescinded in 1867.

The reforms set in motion a sustained Jewish immigration into the western portions of the monarchy, with the migration from Galicia to Vienna and lower Austria initially no stronger than the migration from other parts of the realm. Galician immigrants accounted for around 10% of the Jews in Vienna in 1857, and by 1880 their share had risen to only 10.7%. The absolute numbers, however, rose from 1,511 to 7,801. At first the exodus occurred chiefly from the larger centers of Galicia. Beginning in the 1880s, it shifted strongly to the eastern part of the region: for one, railway connections to smaller towns and villages had improved with the expansion of local lines; for another, the pogroms in Russia (1881), especially in regions close to the border, uprooted hundreds of thousands of Galician Jews. In response, more than 200,000 emigrated, mostly to the USA. However, beginning in the 1880s thousands also went to Vienna and lower Austria year after year. By the eve of World War I, the share of Galicians among Vienna's Jewish population had risen to around 20%. In 1910, 42,695 persons among Vienna's resident population had been born in Galicia. And here the dominant regions of origin were the districts of Lemberg (City) and eastern parts of the country like Brody, Tarnopol, and Stanislau, and in the west Cracow and Tarnow. Vienna and a few of its suburbs formed the center of immigration from Galicia. The only other place to which the large eastern crown lands sent out an appreciable number of migrants was Graz in Styria.

The immigration of Galician Jews to Vienna increased once more from the late 1890s. These immigrants now included more low-income, tradition-bound Jews in need of social charity. Within the social spectrum, the majority of Galician Jews were now found in the lower segments of the middling strata and in the lower classes, and especially because of the older generation of immigrants they formed an "anti-modern element." Because the Galician Jews for the most part also used Yiddish (sometimes also Polish), they contrasted culturally with the assimilated majority of Jews already living in Vienna. Moreover, the Galician immigrants were often deeply religious and committed to Hasidism.

Unlike other Viennese Jews, the tradition-bound Galician immigrants often lived in the districts of Leopoldstadt (2nd district) and Brigittenau (20th district). For example, 57% of all Jews from Galicia who married between 1870 and 1910 lived in one of these two districts, compared to 35% of all Jews born in Vienna and 30% of all Jews born in Bohemia. Upon closer inspection the difference is particularly striking in Brigittenau, which stood at the lower end of the Viennese districts in the social hierarchy: 10% of Galician Jews lived there, compared to 1% of Jews from Hungary, 1% of those from Bohemia, and 3% of Vienna-born Jews – they were beggars and peddlers, furniture movers, laborers, and skilled workers.

By contrast, Galician Jews were rarely found in the middle class or among major entrepreneurs. Among the rare exceptions was Sigmund Reitzes (1835–1906) from Lemberg, who had settled in Vienna as a banker and major stockholder and lived there to the end of his life. Reitzes can be seen as the prototype of a successful stock market player who took advantage of the economic crisis of 1873 for profitable stock speculations. Among other things he owned a large number of shares in various railway companies and had decisive influence on Vienna's Pferde-Tramway-Gesellschaft. In 1889, Viktor Adler's Social Democratic journal *Gleichheit* (Equality) pilloried the particularly harsh working conditions of tramway employees and portrayed Reitzes as the capitalist exploiter par excellence.

Although the differences between the Galician Jews and the other Jews living in Vienna should not be exaggerated, it is possible to point to the formation of a specific minority, which manifested itself in cultural orientation, marriage behavior, diet, dress, religious and linguistic peculiarities,

Most Jewish immigrants in Austria at the end of the 19th century came from Bohemia, Moravia, Galicia, and Bukovina. Photo: Emil Mayer, around 1910 (*ullstein bild*).

and a specific settlement pattern. The social and cultural integration of the Galician Jews into Vienna's Jewish society progressed rather slowly. Already the growth of Jewish *Gymnasium* students who had been born in Galicia was no more than modest, and in some districts of Vienna the number of Galician students at higher secondary schools actually declined between 1890 and 1910. Jews who had already resided in Vienna for some time consistently displayed prejudices against the newcomers. Theodor Herzl (1860–1904) developed his Zionist idea in Vienna, and it reflected many facets of assimilated Viennese Jewish culture. Herzl's attack on Yiddish as the language of the ghetto was symptomatic of the exclusion practiced by Jews who were already assimilated or came from regions where Yiddish was not spoken. This rejection was summarized in the term *Ostjuden* (Eastern Jews); German culture was seen by many Viennese Jews as valuable and superior to any "Eastern" culture. Part of the liberal-patriotic majority of Viennese Jews was Rabbi David, who, on the occasion of the trial of a "Galician swindler" in 1906, criticized in synagogue the behavior of the "Eastern Jews." At the same time, Zionist as well as national-Jewish magazines launched vehement polemics against the Galician women for allegedly assimilating to Austrian custom in terms of fashion (e.g., the wearing of *Dirndl* dresses).

The establishment of sports clubs, like the *Hakoah* (Hebr.: "strength") founded in Vienna in 1909, can be seen as a renewed attempt by the Galician Jews to preserve their Jewish identity while at the same time emancipating themselves from the Galician "culture of avoiding violence" that was taken to the point of "submissiveness" during anti-Semitic attacks. The *Hakoah* had many Galician Jews of the first and second generation among its members and achieved its greatest success in the interwar period when its soccer team became the first Austrian professional champion. The athletic ambitions of the *Hakoah* revealed a "masculine," "militant" side of Judaism that played an important role in strengthening Jewish self-confidence. Along the same lines were also the dueling student fraternities like *Kadimah* (Hebr.: "forward"), which was set up primarily by Jews from Galicia. Out of the intellectual environment of the *Kadimah* came Joseph Samuel Bloch (1850–1923), who had been born in Dukla, Galicia. He was a rabbi in a suburb of Vienna and for many years a delegate to the Reichsrat from a Galician electoral district. As early as 1884, Bloch founded the journal *Oesterreichische Wochenschrift*, which served as an important weapon in the battle against anti-Semitism as well as against assimilationist currents. In 1886 came the Österreichisch-Israelitische Union (Austrian-Israelite Union), a kind of civil rights organization whose primary mission was to combat the surging anti-Semitism.

In fact, it was largely due to this anti-Semitism that the Galician Jews were not integrated into society either around 1880 or around 1914. The parties of the Christian-social and German-national spectrum that were dominant in many Austrian cities disseminated a massive anti-Semitism, an important element of which was the image of the "caftan-Jew." This stereotype was fomented with lasting impact in the so-called province, the largely German-speaking crown lands west of Vienna: "The street life of Linz," we read for example in the *Linzer Morgenpost* in June 1897, "was enriched in the last few days in an unpleasant way by the sight of unadulterated, original Polish Jews. The strange pair wandered through the streets in dirty caftans and nicely curled sidelocks – a living call for anti-Semitism." Because no Galician Jews lived in Linz, the attacks against Jews were aimed at visitors passing through. The virulent anti-Semitism also affected Adolf Hitler, who grew up in Upper Austria and was eight years old at this time. For example, Hitler devoted a lot of space in his book *Mein Kampf* to the actions of the leading anti-Semites Schönerer and Lueger and developed his hostile image of "the Jew" chiefly from the outward appearance of the Galician immigrants in Vienna: "Once, as I was strolling through the inner city, I suddenly encountered an apparition in black caftan and black locks…. This racial conglomeration disgusted me."

Following the outbreak of World War I, the advance of Russian troops triggered the flight of entire Jewish families from Galicia and Bukovina. They sought safety in the interior and thus for the first time also made their way to other regions of Austria in larger numbers. "Refugees crowd into Vienna," was a headline in the *New York Times* in October 1914: "Capital unable to accommodate Jews from Galicia…. The stream has now been diverted to various places in Moravia, Upper Austria and Salzburg." The future film director Samuel "Billy" Wilder, eight years old at the time, was among the refugees coming to Vienna. In 1914 he moved with his parents to the Austrian capital, where he later passed his *Abitur* and began to study at the university. By May 1917, according to official figures, 40,637 indigent Jewish refugees were already in Vienna. The anti-Semites engaged in a verbal persecution

of the *Ostjuden*. As anti-Jewish pogroms occurred immediately after the end of the war in the Galician homeland of the Jews, which was now part of the Polish state, most of those who had fled to Vienna did not want to return. The Galician Jews turned into "Polish Jews." In the interwar period, as well, they served as the negative image of "the Jew" in the new Austrian republic. After the somewhat more tolerant 1920s, anti-Semitism reemerged in harsher forms in the wake of the global economic crisis. In Vienna that affected especially the *Ostjuden*, who ended up in even greater social isolation. After the annexation of Austria by the German Reich in 1938, the number of Jews who left the country to save their lives grew rapidly. The National Socialist genocide of the Jews utterly destroyed Jewish-Galician culture in Austria.

Binder, Harald. *Galizien in Wien. Parteien, Wahlen, Fraktionen und Abgeordnete im Übergang zur Massenpolitik*. Vienna, 2005.

Botz, Gerhard, Ivar Oxaal, Michael Pollak, and Nina Scholz, eds. *Eine zerstörte Kultur. Jüdisches Leben, Antisemitismus in Wien seit dem 19. Jahrhundert*. 2nd ed. Vienna, 2002.

Hödl, Klaus. *Als Bettler in die Leopoldstadt. Galizische Juden auf dem Weg nach Wien*. Vienna, 1994.

John, Michael, and Albert Lichtblau. "Jewries in Galicia and Bukovina, in Lemberg and Czernovitz: Two Divergent Examples of Jewish Communities in the Far East of the Austro-Hungarian Monarchy." In *Jewries at the Frontiers*, edited by Sander Gilman and Milton Shain, 29–66. Urbana and Chicago, 1999.

Klanska, Maria. *Aus dem Schtetel in die Welt 1772 bis 1938. Ostjüdische Autobiographien in deutscher Sprache*. Vienna, 1994.

Kohlbauer-Fritz, Gabriele, ed. *Zwischen Ost und West. Galizische Juden in Wien*. Vienna, 2000.

Lichtblau, Albert. "Juden in Österreich – Integration, Vernichtungsversuch und Neubeginn. Österreichisch-jüdische Geschichte 1848 bis zur Gegenwart." In *Geschichte der Juden in Österreich*, edited by Evelyn Brugger et al., 447–556. Vienna, 2006.

Cross-references: Austria; Poland; Eastern European Jews in Berlin from the Late 19th Century to the 1930s; Eastern European Jews in Paris since the Late 19th Century; Eastern European Jews in London since the Late 19th Century; Jewish Refugees from Nazi Germany and from German-Occupied Europe since 1933

GERMAN AFFLUENCE MIGRANTS IN SPAIN SINCE THE LATE 20TH CENTURY

Klaus Schriewer

As Europe began to recover economically after World War II, it saw the gradual beginning of mass tourism from the northern countries into the Mediterranean region. This tourism was slowly followed by a kind of affluence mobility that brought elderly individuals from northern and central Europe to the Mediterranean at the end of their working lives. Initially, France and Italy were the preferred destination countries. After the 1960s, Spain developed into the most popular and important destination. This form of migration is described as old-age migration or retirement migration and recently as affluence mobility.

Although there are numerous statistical sources on internal European migrations, the number of old-age migrants cannot be precisely determined. One reason is that the data collected by governmental and public institutions provide only limited information about retirement migrants. For example, since 1990 it is no longer possible to identify departures from Germany in terms of age cohorts. It is also clear that only a portion of the emigrants are recorded by the official statistics. Many seniors do not migrate officially, remain formally registered in their home country, and do not apply for a residency permit in their destination country, largely because registration has negative consequences for them. For example, German insurance companies only pay Germans registered as residents in Spain for health care expenses according to Spanish standards. As a result, it can be assumed that merely half of the European seniors in Spain are registered by the authorities.

The data provided by statistical offices (e.g., Eurostat, the German Federal Office of Statistics, the Instituto Nacional de Estadistica) can thus be used only to describe a trend. It indicates that the number of retirement migrants in Spain has steadily grown since the 1960s. The official German statistic for departures to Spain records only 34 persons in 1962, but 158 persons in 1986. Clearer still is the statistic of the Instituto Nacional de Estadistica (INE; National Statistical Institute), which shows that the number of German seniors living in Spain increased in the period from 1996 to 2008 from 13,302 to 61,164 persons.

Detailed information about the social breakdown of old-age migration does not exist. However, it is evident that well into the 1980s, migration to Spain was a phenomenon that was limited to the upper middle class. According to estimates by the German honorary consul in Alicante, that changed in the 1990s, with the majority of retirement migrants who have gone to Spain since that period coming from the lower middle class.

The motives behind affluence mobility are often easy to explain. The reason given by seniors is that they wish to enjoy and be active in the phase following their working life in a place with a friendly climate. Affluence mobility is thus also one of the phenomena that must be seen in connection with the process of individualization in central, western, and northern European societies. Closely linked to the search for sunny climes is the second motive given by retirees for their decision to migrate: health. The mild Mediterranean climate enjoys the reputation – also among doctors – of easing rheumatoid and respiratory ailments.

The settlement of European seniors in Spain is limited to a few chosen regions that are of interest also to tourism: the Canaries, the Balearic Islands (and here chiefly Mallorca), and Spain's Mediterranean coast. Along the coast the settlement stretches from the Costa Brava to the Costa del Sol, with heavy concentrations around Alicante and Malaga. Here the majority of European seniors have acquired a house or an apartment. This property is often located in settlements that were built specifically for vacationers and foreign seniors. Such artificial residential facilities are erected mostly "in the open field" close to Spanish villages and towns and are referred to as *urbanizaciones* in Spanish. Some of the *urbanizaciones* on the Mediterranean are inhabited mostly by Spaniards and only the occasional foreigner, while others are home almost exclusively to Europeans from northern regions. Simply because of the way these developments have been marketed, often focused on a single country, those who settled there were initially of the same nationality. For example, the *urbanización* Ciudad Quesada near Alicante is considered a Swiss village. This characteristic of the settlement changes when the houses are sold. In many settlements this turnover gradually creates a mix of individuals from different countries.

The interest that German retirees take in their host country of Spain and their contacts with Spaniards vary considerably. A small segment, most of them from the upper middle class, try to learn Spanish, travel throughout the country, and often have close contacts with the locals. However, the majority of seniors quickly give up initial attempts to learn the native language. They are content with a rudimentary knowledge and move largely in areas where seniors have settled. There, shops, banks, official agencies, and doctors frequently offer services in English and German. Whereas European seniors as late as the 1980s still had to conduct the essential business of everyday life in Spanish, at the beginning of the 21st century that is no longer necessary. Seniors can find out what is going on in Spain and their respective region through the German-language weeklies that are published in the various coastal regions.

Interviews with old-age migrants clearly reveal that the change in the infrastructure of daily life has led to closer ties with Germany, and that an intensive engagement with the country and people of Spain is no longer necessary. Essential milestones of this change were the expansion of the telephone network, the spread of satellite dishes for television reception, and the regular supply of German newspapers and magazines. For example, until the 1990s, many seniors phoned family members and friends only occasionally, because using public phones was considered cumbersome. Today, a phone in one's home is standard, and phone calls to Germany several times a week are the norm. The close ties of seniors to their home country are also evident from the trips that many retirement migrants make to Germany several times a year. Important reasons for these trips are contact with family and friends as well as visits to doctors. An indicator of life in two worlds is that some of the seniors have made only a partial migration and spend several months a year in Germany. So one could say that affluence mobility is a typical example of so-called transnational migration.

In Spain, the response to European seniors is mixed. Economically it has become an important factor, and those who benefit from it regard it on the whole as positive. Others speak of Spain on sale – *España en venta*. On the one hand they point to the changes in the landscape, arguing that the consequences of these changes are more serious than those from mass tourism. On the other hand, they warn against a profound transformation in the structure of Spanish society and in the culture of the Spaniards.

So far, old-age migration has not been studied in depth from the perspective of the emergence of an international environment in which people from different European countries live in direct proximity and encounter each other in daily life. The senior areas are one of the few examples in Europe in which the issue of a European culture and a European consciousness manifests itself in practice. What makes this "laboratory" especially important is that the individuals here are not primarily social elites, as is the case in the administrative metropolis of Brussels or in cities like Frankfurt am Main, where business and economic leaders congregate.

Findings reveal, however, that national identification is very important and that the use of national stereotypes is widespread. For example, Germans and Spaniards claim that the English refuse to learn Spanish. German seniors encounter Spaniards with a broad repertoire of ideas, like the notion that punctuality holds a different value for them. How strongly value judgments can diverge is especially evident in questions of environmental protection and care for the landscape, areas in which German seniors maintain that Spaniards lag behind. Language competence is very important in building a sustained network of social contacts (circles of acquaintances and friends), which is very important after immigration and demands a high degree of social flexibility from the retirees. Since only a minority of migrants have an adequate command of Spanish and English, social contacts take shape primarily within the same language communities. Germans, for example, are frequently in contact with Swiss nationals, and there are many organizations of German speakers of various nationalities.

If one can speak of the beginnings of a European consciousness, the reason lies in the importance that the old-age migrants themselves accord to the sporadic contacts with people of different nationalities. Any interpretation of this positive assessment must be colored by the realization that these German migrants came from a generation that grew up with strong national resentments, lived through World War II, and belong to the nation that was responsible and is blamed for the Holocaust. First, German seniors in Spain like to see sporadic contact especially with English and Dutch nationals as a step toward the reconciliation of a European community of nations torn apart by the war. Second, the beginnings of a European consciousness are evident when seniors compare the different social realities in Germany and Spain on the basis of a more or less thorough knowledge. These comparisons of nations and societies in everyday life are the expression of a Europeanism that transcends the nation as the frame of reference. A third indicator of a Europeanization is the growing geographic mobility itself. In the case of the old-age migrants, life between and in two societies and among different nationalities promotes their self-conception as Europeans. This becomes clear – the fourth factor – as the European seniors carry on a specific political discourse about the European Union. It deals with the discrepancy between economic and social integration and of the concrete problems posed by life in Spain, for example, in connection with health care. That Europe forms a frame of reference for the European seniors finds symbolic expression among some – especially the Germans – in the flying of the flag of the European Union in front of their house.

Garcá Jiménez, Modesto, and Klaus Schriewer. *Ni turistas ni migrantes. Movilidades residenciales europeas en España*. Murcia, 2008.

Jurdao Arrones, Francisco. *España en Venta: Compra de Suelos por Extranjeros y Colonización de Campesinos en la Costa del Sol*. Madrid, 1990.

O'Reilly, Karen. *The British on the Costa del Sol: Transnational Identities and Local Communities*. London, 2000.

Rodríguez, Vicente, Maria A. Casado, and Andreas Huber. *La migración de jubilados europeos en España* (CSIC, Colección Politeia, no. 23). Madrid, 2005.

Schriewer, Klaus, and Irene Encinas. "Being Misleading about Where One Resides. European Affluence Mobility and Registration Patterns." *Ethnologia Europaea* 37, 1–2 (2007): 98–106.

Seiler, Diana. *Sozialpolitische Aspekte der internationalen Mobilität von Rentnern – insbesondere von deutschen Rentnern in Spanien*. Frankfurt am Main, 1994.

Williams, A. M., and C. M. Hall. *Tourism and Migration: New Relationships between Production and Consumption*. London, 2002.

Cross-references: Germany; Spain and Portugal; British Affluence Migrants in the Costa del Sol in the Late 20th Century; European and American Civil Servants of Supranational Organizations in Brussels since 1958

GERMAN AND AUSTRIAN JEWISH CHILDREN TRANSPORTED TO GREAT BRITAIN AFTER 1938–1939

Claudia Curio

Between December 1938 and the outbreak of World War II in September 1939, 9,354 unaccompanied children of both genders and up to the age of 17 found refuge from Nazi persecution in Great Britain. About 80% belonged to Jewish religious communities; the rest were of Jewish origins. The rescue action, which became known under the name *Kindertransporte* (children's transports), was made possible by the decision of the British government, in response to the pogrom in Nazi Germany in November 1938, to

Jewish refugee children after their arrival in England in 1938-9. Most of the children came from Vienna and were first interned before being placed with families (*ullstein bild*).

ease immigration restrictions for children and teenagers. Alongside the escape of many children and teenagers to the safety of Palestine (Youth *Aliyah*), the children's transports were the most extensive rescue action for unaccompanied, persecuted children. British aid organizations and private persons assumed responsibility for their financial expenses and care, chief among them the Movement for the Care of Children from Germany/Refugee Children's Movement (RCM). Assembling and carrying out the transports of several dozen to several hundred children was done in Germany by the division Children's Emigration of the Reich Representation of Jews in Germany, and in Austria by the division Youth Care of the Jewish Community in Vienna (for Jewish children) and a few Christian organizations (for children of Jewish background).

About two-thirds of the children came from the Altreich (Germany before the annexation of Austria); of those 30% were from Berlin, and about a third came from annexed Austria (nearly all from Vienna). Smaller groups came from Czechoslovakia (669), though among them were many originally from Germany, and the Free City of Danzig (124). An unknown number of children and teenagers came from the Polish border town of Zbąszyń. They had just reached this town as part of the "Polish action," during which about 17,000 Jews of Polish citizenship were expelled from Germany in October 1938.

Initially, the British government and aid organizations saw the children as transit migrants or temporary immigrants. The goal was reunification with their own families abroad or after a return to their homeland, or onward travel to Palestine, as in the case of several hundred candidates for the Youth *Aliyah* who had come to Great Britain to foreign *hachsharah* centers (which provided preparatory training and education for emigration to Palestine). However, in the 1940s, in the face of the Holocaust, it became clear that a majority of the children would settle permanently in the country.

Immediately after the outbreak of the war, all refugee children under the age of 15, together with British children of the same age, were evacuated from large cities and metropolitan areas and sent to the countryside. The war also led to the expulsion of "enemy aliens" from the southern and eastern coastal regions and from important military areas (restricted areas), which also affected these children. About 1,000 children over the age of 16 were temporarily interned in 1940 on the Isle of Man and at other remote sites on the British Isles. A few hundred children were deported to Canada and Australia, where some settled permanently.

By 1944, 1,600 to 1,700 children had moved on to be reunified with family members in the USA or other countries abroad. After the war, another large wave of children – most of whom had lost their parents in the Holocaust – left Great Britain, heading especially for the USA and Palestine/Israel. Even where parents had survived, reunification sometimes failed because children and parents had grown apart, which could sometimes result merely from the lack of a common language. Only in exceptional cases did the young refugees return to their countries of origin. The majority remained in Great Britain and took advantage of the simplified naturalization procedure that the government offered to war orphans.

According to a sample study carried out by the Board of Deputies of British Jews, in 1950 15% of the children had moved on to the USA, 7% to Palestine/Israel, and 4% each to Australia and other countries. Sixty percent continued to live in Great Britain. More recent data about the distribution of the young refugees to the various countries do not exist.

To a much greater extent than was the case with adult refugees, the conditions of integration for children in Great Britain were shaped by the ideas of the aid organizations, especially the RCM, which in turn were influenced by the expectations of the British majority society about a complete assimilation of the children and related conceptions of integration held by the Anglo-Jewish community. In the 1930s and 1940s, Jewish refugees in Great Britain had to expect anti-Semitic, anti-German, and general xenophobic reactions. That is why the Anglo-Jewish aid for new immigrants to Great Britain, for example, was strongly characterized by the desire to render the new arrivals "invisible" and anglicize them as quickly as possible. The areas in which the RCM brought its influence to bear in this direction were the housing and distribution of the children, schooling and vocational training, and religion. A possible return to their families and societies of origin (e.g., through education in their mother tongue) was not promoted.

The strategies promoting assimilation of the refugees had an especially strong impact on the integration path of small children. As a result of attendance in British schools until age 14, life in British families (placement in foster families was favored by the RCM because it allowed for an even distribution of the children across the country), the rapid language acquisition common at this age, and an identity of origin that was not strongly fixed, younger children were very rapidly anglicized. Many children placed with Christian families were baptized.

Refugees who came to Great Britain as adolescents were subject to conditions different from those facing smaller children. These young adults often lived with others in hostels that were usually located close to Jewish communities, which allowed them to have ties with the religious milieu. Those who looked after them were often refugees from Germany themselves. Because they were older, language acquisition proved more difficult, and their identity of origin was more solidified. The integration of these young adults was accelerated neither by placement in families nor by attendance at British schools – higher education and academic ambitions were usually not promoted; for a long time, they moved exclusively within refugee circles. Participation in World War II in the British military – which often entailed the adoption of an English name – was for many young refugees of both genders (the Auxiliary Territorial Service was open to young women) an important step toward integration. This was the first time they did not feel they were being looked upon as "refugees."

In looking at the ways in which the former child refugees were integrated after the end of the war, one must bear in mind that the segment for which we have information – thanks to autobiographies, interviews, and other biographical documents – constitutes a nonrepresentative minority for the simple reason that it has an awareness of and interest in its own identity of origin. Nothing is known about the vast majority of the refugees after they reached the age of adulthood and thus left the aid organizations' sphere of responsibility. In many cases, especially among the younger age cohorts, one must reckon with the complete loss of their identity of origin. However, since 1989, about 1,000 of the former child refugees, as the result of a first meeting, have been in regular contact and have formed an international community of remembrance of the *Kinder*, who have organized local groups and a communication network in the USA, Great Britain, and Israel.

The refugees' assessment of their own social integration varies depending on the country that took them in: those who moved on to the traditional immigrant country of the USA generally feel better integrated into the majority society than those who remained in Great Britain. Nearly all express the sense of being outsiders – against a backdrop of what is usually a successful integration outwardly through careers, material well-being, and marriage to British and American citizens. Many regret the loss of educational opportunities in their childhood and youth, though an astonishingly large number made up later in life for the opportunities lost to persecution and life under conditions of exile and they have had great professional success. The most problematic result of persecution and exile, however, is the loss of the family of origin, a loss that still weighs on most of the former child refugees at the beginning of the 21st century.

Benz, Wolfgang, Claudia Curio, and Andrea Hammel, eds. *Die Kindertransporte 1938/39. Rettung und Integration*. Frankfurt am Main, 2003.

Curio, Claudia. *Verfolgung, Flucht, Rettung. Die Kindertransporte 1938/39 nach Großbritannien*. Berlin, 2006.

Göpfert, Rebekka. *Der jüdische Kindertransport von Deutschland nach England 1938/39. Geschichte und Erinnerung*. Frankfurt am Main, 1999.

Leverton, Bertha, and Shmuel Lowensohn, eds. *I Came Alone: The Stories of the Kindertransports*. Sussex, 1990.

Cross-references: Germany; Great Britain; Jewish Refugees from Nazi Germany and from German-Occupied Europe since 1933

GERMAN BAKER-JOURNEYMEN IN AMSTERDAM IN THE 17TH CENTURY

Erika Kuijpers

Throughout the 17th century, baking bread was a typical migrant profession in Amsterdam. Of all the bread bakers who registered their first marriage at the town hall between 1600 and 1700 (2,768 in all), 91.2% were born outside of Amsterdam. Instead of a replacement by second and third generations, the share of first-generation immigrants from beyond Amsterdam and the coastal provinces of the Republic even increased in the 17th century. Most of these immigrants originated from the eastern provinces of the Dutch Republic and the neighboring German areas of Lower Saxony and Westphalia. In the first half of the 17th century, they came especially from villages and towns of East Frisia, Oldenburg, and Bremen. Later, the recruitment area also began to include the Northern Rhineland and Westphalia.

Half of all bakers who married in Amsterdam came from Germany; 95% of the bakers were still working as journeymen upon marriage, at least in the years between 1641 and 1650. Among the master bakers, who generally owned their own shops, the number of immigrants was much lower. Exact numbers are not available, but at least half of the master bakers were natives of Amsterdam. Generally speaking, bread consumed in Amsterdam was produced by "foreign" journeymen, while the bakery shops were predominantly owned by burghers originating from Amsterdam and other Holland towns, and only a small number of shops were the property of successful immigrants from the east of the Dutch Republic, Lower Saxony, and Westphalia.

In the course of the century, the number of bakery shops increased from about 169 in 1611 to between 275 and 330 in 1688, while the population of Amsterdam grew from about 70,000 to 200,000 in the same period. It can be assumed that the average size of individual bakeries and therefore the number of journeymen per shop also increased. There are no figures concerning apprentices and journeymen. In 17th-century London, the average number was three to four journeymen for each bakery as well as an apprentice. If the same ratios applied in Amsterdam, it is clear that the majority of these journeymen would have had no hope of ever reaching the master status. Some of them may have returned to their homes with their savings; perhaps they managed to settle as a master upon their return.

One could become a master baker in Amsterdam only after working for at least two years for an established Amsterdam master and passing the exams of the guild. Second, one had to become a burgher of Amsterdam. Citizenship was automatically bestowed on those born into a citizen family and could be acquired by marrying the daughter or widow of a citizen, or by paying a fee to the city that by 1650 was 50 guilders. To put this fee into perspective, we have to keep in mind that a baker-journeyman earned between 1.20 and 2.45 guilders a week (on top of room and board), so 50 guilders equaled four to five months' wages. In addition, a contribution of 10 guilders had to be paid to the guild.

Still these administrative costs were small compared to the capital required to start a business. Bakery shops that were usually built as such, with fixed ovens and chimneys, were sold for 1,000 to 3,000 guilders in the late 17th century, not including the inventory of necessary utensils. This explains why bakery shops remained in the same families and on the same location over many generations. For a foreign journeyman with no substantial capital of his own, it was almost impossible to reach the rank of master unless he was lucky enough to marry a baker's widow. The same situation applied in the journeyman's hometown. Unless he were to inherit a bakery or marry a baker's widow the capital investment was as high as it was in Amsterdam and presented an insurmountable hurdle. Many of the conditions for becoming a master and settling down in a German town were even more difficult to meet. Those immigrants who managed to set up their own business in Amsterdam were assured of a regular income. With few exceptions, the bakers of Amsterdam belonged to the middle class. Many bakers possessed both their home and bakery, and some owned a second house or a plot of land.

Amsterdam was a possible destination for the obligatory journeyman travel (*Gesellenwanderung*) of various northwestern German bakers' guilds. The 1630 ordinance of the small East Frisian town of Aurich stated that every baker-journeyman who finished his apprenticeship there should go to serve in a bakery shop in Holland for an additional two years. Indeed, many baker-journeymen must have returned home, or possibly traveled farther afield: of the 19 immigrants from Aurich who became Lutheran church members in and just after 1626, only 10 married in Amsterdam. Only two out of five of the men registering as bakers could be traced in the marriage banns. The remaining three either never married or went elsewhere. Nonetheless, a remarkable 23% of all male immigrants from Aurich marrying in Amsterdam during the 17th century were bakers. The fact that they married makes a possible return to Germany unlikely, because in many German guilds, only single men were admitted to the master's exam. German scholars also agree that, generally, the number of artisans who were trained within the guilds was greater than the number of

vacant places or opportunities for masters to start a business. Although training and experience may have been the reason for the migrations of journeymen, the lack of opportunities in the local labor market could have been the root cause. Apprentices went from the countryside to small cities like Aurich, and from Aurich they then traveled on to a metropolis like Amsterdam. The big city was at the end of the line. Information spread through familial or acquaintance networks, leading ultimately to chain migration, and it may have become common knowledge that one might as well go directly from one's village to Amsterdam. Many of the journeymen whose status and reputation still depended on their corporate identity in their hometowns became modern wage earners in Amsterdam with very little hope of further social mobility.

Very little is known about the living conditions and social position of journeymen bakers in Amsterdam. In the more specialist trades, one had to pay for an apprenticeship, but bakery boys were lodged and boarded in the baker's household without payment for their training, making bakery work an attractive option for migrant workers. The recruitment of journeymen probably took place through social networks and in the bakers' inns, where free journeymen used to gather. They did not have organizations of their own and the guild did not regulate the rights or duties of journeymen. They were mentioned in the guild records for the first time only at the end of the 17th century. Journeymen wages were very low. Even common sailors had a higher daily wage, and the prospects of social mobility were more limited for bakery journeymen than for sailors. Much of the work in a bakery shop, such as cleaning or carrying flour, water, and wood was unskilled and merely required physical strength. In his voluminous work on the bakers of Paris, Steven Kaplan described the work as very unhealthy. It was the combination of low status, harsh conditions, little skill, and the informal mechanisms of selecting compatriots as apprentices and journeymen that made work in bakeries typical work for migrants. Those who lacked the social and financial capital necessary to start their own business in Amsterdam or back home were condemned to a life of wage dependency, or even forced to leave the trade.

Kaplan, Steven L. *The Bakers of Paris and the Bread Question: 1700–1775*. Durham, 1996.

Knotter, Ad, and Jan Luiten van Zanden. "Immigratie en arbeidsmarkt te Amsterdam in de 17e eeuw." *Tijdschrift voor Sociale Geschiedenis* 13 (1987): 403–31.

Kuijpers, Erika. *Migrantenstad. Immigratie en sociale verhoudingen in 17e-eeuws Amsterdam*. Hilversum, 2005.

Lourens, Piet, and Jan Lucassen. "Gilden und Wanderung: Die Niederlande." In *Handwerk in Europa. Vom Spätmittelalter bis zur Frühen Neuzeit*, edited by Knut Schulz, 65–79. Munich, 1999.

Cross-references: Germany; The Netherlands

GERMAN CABINETMAKERS IN PARIS IN THE 18TH CENTURY

Hans-Ulrich Thamer

In 1779, King Louis XVI listed in his private expense account payments of 2,400 and 12,000 livres to *les Allemands* for a dresser and a secretary desk. In the linguistic usage of the 18th and 19th centuries, names of geographic origin were often linked with certain occupational groups who had carved out a more or less permanent place in the Paris labor market as migrant workers or journeymen: bricklayers came from the Limousin, coal heavers from the Auvergne, and street sweepers from southwest German Nassau. In like manner, no small number of cabinet and furniture makers from Germany made a name for themselves in Paris in the 18th century. Many of them were considered highly skilled specialists, who possessed knowledge and skills that were rarely in demand in the modest circumstances in their home villages but for which a market existed in France, also because few local craftsmen there had comparable specialized skills.

With the differentiation of their work and the refinement of their products since the 17th century, the Paris carpenters had split into various guilds. The *menuisiers*, who made large cabinets from ebony or who "ebonized" lesser-quality woods through blackening, called themselves *menuisiers-ébénistes* from the beginning of the 18th century, and soon merely *ébénistes*. Eventually, the label was applied only to those who used the economical technique of veneering. This provided an opportunity for German specialists, who were particularly skilled in this technique.

One center of the domestic and foreign cabinet and furniture makers was the Faubourg Saint-Antoine. The suburb, which bordered the Bastille in the east of the city, was among the *lieux privilégiés* and was, through special laws, exempted from many of the restrictions of the guild economy. As a result, in a confrontation with the strict regime in the city, it had developed into what Michael Stürmer called "a free market island." Although the tough quality standards of the guild applied here also, operating costs were lower since the free worker in the Faubourg paid nothing into the guild treasury, no master's qualification (*maîtrise*) had to be purchased, and no brotherhood had to be supported. On the other hand, there was no corporative protection, no standing of a sworn master, and no guarantee of the free pursuit of his business in and around the city. The only thing that mattered were the individual's performance and inventiveness. Moreover, the free labor market of the Faubourg offered the liberty to divide the work up individually and to produce precious furniture in small series. This made it more flexible and cost effective. As a result, many merchants had their goods made in the small workshops of this suburb. Many Parisian guild masters had begun their artisanal careers in the *lieux privilégiés* of Saint-Antoine or the Enclos du Temple and had family ties to the suburb, which explains why the tendency to boycott the nonguild furniture makers and their products was weaker here than in other Paris guilds. This was therefore an open and partially tolerated system of cooperation with merchants and guild masters, which served as a social safety valve and model of advancement into the time of the French Revolution, when the Faubourg Saint-Antoine would become the center of the revolutionary popular movement.

About 50% of the German immigrants living in the suburb in the second half of the 18th century were *ébénistes*, which was about 1% of the total population of the Faubourg. For the 18th century we can trace a total of 89 German cabinet and furniture makers through their products, the vast majority of whom worked in Paris as *ébénistes*. Beginning in the middle of the 17th century, more and more German craftsmen from Rhenish regions and southern Germany had come to Paris to find work there in the wake of the devastation of the Thirty Years' War. Those workers were especially welcome who, as a directive of the city of Lyon put it, "brought with them the secret of a few new textiles." Since the reign of Louis XIV, under the auspices of a mercantilist industrial policy as conceived by the French finance minister Jean-Baptiste Colbert, foreign skilled workers had been recruited to France, provided they were considered experts. The successors of the Sun King carried on this policy. These workers were enticed with an exemption from the waiting years usually necessary for the acquisition of a master's diploma; with a temporary exemption from the burdens of citizenship, such as taxes and quartering; and with the guarantee of confessional tolerance and easy naturalization.

The German territories, meanwhile, imposed a complete prohibition on migration for various trades and renewed it time and again; the authorities were afraid of losing subjects and know-how. Other trade codes, however, envisioned temporary migration, also and precisely to other countries, because there "every trade could be brought to a perfection that brought it close to the free arts." The temporary migration of craftsmen was to remain a phase of professional training and ideally end with the tradesman settling down in his native land as a master. Of course, whether French crafts were in fact superior in every area remained debated in the 18th century, and often the presumed gradient between Germany and "developed" France with respect to the level of technical know-how and possibilities of production was much vaguer and less clear. The German *ébénistes* in Paris were evidence of that.

As trades became increasingly overcrowded, the migration of journeymen also provided temporary relief for the local labor markets. However, such regulatory concepts existed above all on paper: the practice of the Ancien Régime was characterized by exceptions and the inability to exert effective control.

At the beginning of the 18th century, and especially after the death of Louis XIV in 1715, the influx of German craftsmen increased markedly. Especially highly skilled craftsmen from Alsace and Germany were in demand as a result of a change in taste in French society. Those craftsmen included cabinet and furniture makers, who were welcome in addition to the veneer workers as experts for inlay work (*marqueteurs*) and lacquer works (*liqueurs*), as well as wallpaperers and bronze workers.

The Lutheran parishes were the first point of contact for those craftsmen who were Protestants. There they found information about the city and their first work contracts. The majority of the newcomers recorded in the parish registers after 1763 came from the western territories of the Reich. They were employed by countrymen who already had their own workshops or by French masters. At times difficulties arose from the strict regulations of the Paris guilds. The admission and working conditions were more favorable in the *lieux privilégiés*, which attracted carpenters as well as furniture and cabinetmakers.

German was spoken in the Lutheran communities. But even in the suburbs with their many foreigners and their own social and neighborhood systems, German immigrants were not necessarily forced to learn French. In the restless Faubourgs, social conflicts and violence were daily occurrences, and this could make the integration of the foreign workers very difficult. In many cases the protest actions were directed against foreign journeymen and apprentices, who were to be excluded as unwelcome competitors. Especially difficult and prolonged was the integration of the newcomers if they belonged to the group of the first immigrants and exercised less-specialized professions and crude trades. In the case of a blacksmith who arrived in Paris in 1759, it took nine years before he could call himself a *forgeron au Faubourg*, another four years before he became a master, and another eight before he married and settled in the city as *maître et bourgeois de Paris*.

The integration of highly skilled craftsmen was much faster. As early as 1740, the number of masters with German names slowly began to increase among the *ébénistes*. Johann Jakob Stadler, who had immigrated in 1772 from Silesia, was listed a short time later in the register of the Lutheran-Danish community as *ébéniste Faubourg Saint-Antoine, rue de Charenton, chez M. Wolf*; three years later he was *menuisier, rue de Colombier, chez Hermès, facteur de clavecins*, in 1778 he was a piano builder himself, and in 1786 he married a French woman with a *brevet de permission*. A few *ébénistes* in Paris managed to become court artisans as *ébéniste privilégié du Roi*, or as *ébéniste du comte d'Artois*. That meant the highest recognition in the market and a partial exemption from the excessively constraining requirements of the guild regulations, but by no means did it secure financial success, since many of the high-ranking customers were very bad at paying and not a few of the trade masters were fairly inept in business matters.

Among the 89 German cabinet and furniture makers who can be identified by their products were *ébénistes* like F. Bayer, J.-G. Beneman, J. G. Frost, Johann Franz Oeben, Jean-Henri Riesener, and Adam Weisweiler. Johann Franz Oeben, who is attested as living in Paris in 1749, had also begun his career in the Faubourg Saint-Antoine. From November 1751 to October 1754, he rented his own rooms in the workshops of the Louvre as a *compagnon Ébéniste et Menuisier du Roy*,

that is, as a court artisan. With his appointment as *Ébéniste du Roy* in November 1754, he was given an apartment and a workshop in the Gobelins and in 1756 he moved to the Arsenal, where, as an *Ébéniste mécanique du Roy* he enjoyed a lifetime right of residence after 1760. In 1761 he was then admitted into the Paris guild. After many commissions for the court, he began at the Arsenal with his most famous piece, a roll-top desk for Louis XV, which was finished after his death by his successor Jean-Henri Riesener, who also married his widowed wife. In 1782, Riesener finally acquired the title of a "royal cabinetmaker" himself.

Important to the self-assertion in a foreign environment and characteristic of the old trade were also the kinship and neighborhood networks of artisans. Oeben's brother Jean Simon was also drawn to Paris, where he, too, became an *ébéniste*. His younger brother Girard chose the same path. We know that he, too, married a French woman, whose sister in turn was married to the *ébéniste* Martin Carlin from Freiburg im Breisgau and also a resident in Paris. Jean Francois Oeben himself married the sister of the important Flemish *ébéniste* Roger Vandercruse, who owned a house in the Faubourg Saint-Antoine.

Other furniture makers from the Reich were not nearly as successful and also stayed in Paris only temporarily. Very little of any certainty can be said about the return migration of German journeymen and masters, apart from some fragmentary bits of information. The products of the majority of the German cabinetmakers working as journeymen or master have not survived; we know their names at most from business accounts or the parish registers of the Lutheran communities, who, with special toleration by the French crown and protection from Protestant princes and envoys in Paris, were able to celebrate their services. On the lists of those who partook of the Eucharist in the Lutheran communities, we find a total of 151 *ébénistes* from 1744 to 1784, of whom 44 had acquired the master's diploma by 1784.

Among the *ébénistes* who were in Paris only temporarily was also one David Roentgen from Neuwied. To be sure, his world of work and sales had European dimensions, and his much-admired products brought him a top position within the European world of commercial art. In 1779, since the economy of the princely manufacturing city of Neuwied remained too constricted, and the reach of his sale of luxurious furniture equipped with perfect mechanics remained limited to the Old Reich, he had successfully sought out the privilege of an *artiste ébéniste et machiniste du Prince* in Brussels, and that same year in Paris he was given the title of an *ébéniste mécanicien du Roi et de la Reine* at the initiative of the Count d'Angiviller. Of course, he could sell in the city only after he had been formally accepted into the guild of the *menuisiers-ébénistes*. For a foreigner like him that cost an admission fee of 1,000 livres, which remained unaffordable for most of his countrymen. It is not clear whether even his monumental pieces, like the secretary desk for Louis XVI, were made in Paris or instead in his workshop in Neuwied and only assembled in Paris. In any case, as the Paris luxury trade slid into a general depression after 1784, Roentgen withdrew increasingly from the Paris market. At the end of 1785, the word was that he intended to let his workshop and establishment in Paris "close down."

Even if the revolution temporarily interrupted the manufacturing of luxury goods, Paris remained also in the 19th century a magnet for German specialists in fine crafts, but even more so for masses of poor journeymen from all sectors. Their number would soon rise to several tens of thousands.

Kaplan, Steven L. *La fin des corporations*. Paris, 2001.

König, Mareike, ed. *Deutsche Handwerker, Arbeiter und Dienstmädchen in Paris. Eine vergessene Migration im 19. Jahrhundert*. Munich, 2003.

Malettke, Klaus. "Deutsche protestantische Handwerker in Paris und die französische absolute Monarchie im 17. und 18. Jahrhundert." In *Ein gefüllter Willkomm. Festschrift für Knut Schulz zum 65. Geburtstag*, edited by Franz J. Felten et al., 617–27. Aix-la-Chapelle, 2002.

Pallach, Ulrich-Christian. "Fonctions de la mobilité artisanale et ouvrière-compagnons, ouvriers et manufacturiers en France et aux Allemagnes (17e–19e siècles)." *Francia* 11 (1983): 365–406.

Pallach, Ulrich-Christian. "Deutsche Handwerker im Frankreich des 18. Jahrhunderts." In *Deutsche in Frankreich – Franzosen in Deutschland 1715–1789. Institutionelle Verbindungen, soziale Gruppen, Stätten des Austausches*, edited by Jean Mondot, Jean-Marie Valentin, and Jürgen Voss, 89–102. Sigmaringen, 1992.

Stürmer, Michael. *Handwerk und höfische Kultur. Europäische Möbelkunst im 18. Jahrhundert*. Munich, 1982.

Cross-references: France; Germany

GERMAN DEPORTEES FROM EAST-CENTRAL AND SOUTHEASTERN EUROPE IN THE USSR AFTER THE END OF WORLD WAR II

Mathias Beer

During the final six months of World War II, hundreds of thousands of citizens of the German Reich (*Reichsdeutsche*) and especially members of ethnic German minorities in east-central and southeastern Europe (*Volksdeutsche*) were deported to the Soviet Union for forced labor. These deportations, which lasted until 1949, affected civilians from the areas east of the Oder and Neiße, the Baltic states, Romania, Hungary, Yugoslavia, Czechoslovakia, and Bulgaria. By virtue of their ethnicity alone, they were held collectively responsible for the devastation caused by German troops in their war of aggression against the USSR.

The displaced did not form a homogeneous group. The deportations occurred at various times and affected individuals from different regions of origin. The destinations and duration of the deportations differed regionally and individually. What all deportees shared was merely the terms used to describe them ("mobilizees and internees" in Russian, "displaced persons," "deportees," and "forced laborers" in German), the goal of the action (a temporary exploitation of their labor to rebuild the Soviet Union as part of the reparations it demanded), and a work and camp experience for women and men that was characterized by coercion, humiliation, disease, and death. They referred to themselves as "Russia abductees" (*Rußlandverschleppte*) and more recently also as "deportees" (*Deportierte*). Because of the difficult state of the sources and the differing criteria used in categorizing the displaced persons, the numbers – corrected downward since the postwar years – show a broad range: from 270,000 to well over 360,000 deportees, with an average mortality rate of around 20%.

Reparations figured prominently in Soviet postwar planning. The Soviets saw them as compensation for the material losses inflicted on them by the German Reich. Reparations were intended to aid in the rebuilding of the USSR and at the same time weaken Germany and its former allies. Alongside the confiscation of German assets, the dismantling of German industrial installations, and shipments from ongoing industrial production, these goals were to be achieved through the deportation of German workers into the Soviet Union. Plans to that effect go back to the period following the German defeat at Stalingrad in 1943, when it became apparent that fortunes had turned on the Eastern Front.

Special weight was given to the ideas of Ivan Michajlovič Majskij, who was the Soviet ambassador in London, Deputy Foreign Minister, and chairman of the Commission to Study the Reparations Question. On 5 January 1943, he wrote in his diary: "We must also demand another form of reparations – German laborers." He assumed that the work of German civilians in the rebuilding of an economy destroyed by German troops was permissible, just, and also desirable. The Soviet Union did not fail to point to the millions of civilian workers deported to Germany during the war. Although the Soviet Union was not given concrete commitments for its plans in this regard during the major Allied war conferences, the "use of German labor" as laid down in the protocol of the Yalta Conference in February 1945 was not a controversial topic in the negotiations. Accordingly, Foreign Minister Vyacheslav Mikhailovich Molotov informed his deputy at the end of November 1944 that there would be no complications with the Western Allies on the question of the use of German labor. By this time, preparations were already under way for the centrally directed, large-scale, and systematic deportation.

Soviet military authorities first took an inventory of the groups of individuals of German nationality in the territories of east-central and southeastern Europe occupied by the Red Army. Of the 551,000 identified individuals, more than 97,000 men between the ages of 17 and 45 were considered fit for work. Initially only they were to be deployed in rebuilding the coal industry in the Donets Basin and the metallurgy industry in the south of the Soviet Union. Directive No. 7161,

No.	Region (Oblast') and Union Republics	Number of labor battalions	Interned		% of male workers
			Persons	% of total	
1.	Stalino	63	49,452	37.4	55.8
2.	Vorošilovgrad	30	26,015	19.7	64.6
3.	Dnepropetrovsk	27	18,556	14.0	61.2
4.	Čeljabinsk	6	5,185	3.9	42.8
5.	Rostow	5	4,314	3.3	50.9
6.	Swerdlovsk	6	3,470	2.6	45.9
7.	Georgian SSR	4	2,972	2.2	88.8
8.	Čkalow	3	2,780	2.1	95.0
9.	Charkiv	4	2,409	1.8	69.6
10.	Molotow	3	1,946	1.5	41.7
11.	Zaporizhia	2	1,608	1.2	77.1
12.	Minsk	3	1,526	1.2	100.0
13.	Komi ASSR	2	1,357	1.0	22.3
14.	Tschuwakaja ASSR	2	966	0.7	7.9
15.	Grozny	2	927	0.7	35.0
16.	Moscow	3	877	0.7	100.0
17.	Kurgan		788	0,6	7.7
18.	North Ossetian ASSR	2	762	0.6	63.1
19.	Others	14	6,243	4.8	
	Total	183	132,133	100.0	58.7

Source: Polian, *Against Their Will*, 278.

signed by Stalin on 16 December 1944, expanded the circle of persons to be deported, laid down the lines of responsibility and the organizational process, and specified the areas in the Soviet Union where the deportees would be put to work. The decree stated the following: "All Germans fit to work between the ages of 17 and 45 (men) and 18 and 30 (women) who are in the territories of Romania, Yugoslavia, Hungary, Bulgaria, and Czechoslovakia liberated by the Red Army shall be mobilized and interned in order to deport them with the goal of labor deployment in the USSR." Oversight of the mobilization was put in the hands of the Soviet secret service NKVD. The deportations were to be carried out in December 1944 and January 1945 and be completed by 15 February. The "Plan of the primary measures to prepare the implementation of the operation to intern and deport the Germans to the USSR," issued on 26 December 1944, summed up the previous ideas and thinking. It laid down the timetable for carrying out the deportations in the various countries.

Internment began earliest in Hungary (November 1944), followed by Yugoslavia. The affected individuals were ordered to report within a specified period of time at fixed collecting places with no more than 20 kilograms of clothes and articles of daily use. On the way to these sites, the deportees were policed by NKVD troops and Soviet army units. The roundup of the deportees in Romania, the main theater for the mobilization and internment of the German population in southeastern Europe that was fit to work, took place in two stages, 11–26 January and 27 January–2 February 1945. The Romanian police and constabulary participated in these actions. The deportations from southeastern Europe also affected German nationals whom Soviet troops encountered and interned there.

The mobilization of civilian workers for the Soviet Union in the eastern territories of the German Reich was somewhat different from the way it was done among the German minorities in east-central and southeastern Europe. At the beginning of 1945, the NKVD was initially charged with taking "measures to cleanse the areas behind the front of the fighting Red Army from hostile elements." These measures were the responsibility of the respective Soviet army groups. At the beginning of February, when the deportations from southeastern Europe had been largely completed, internment and deportation began in the eastern territories of the Reich. They peaked in March 1945, waned in April, and ceased on 8 May 1945, following the unconditional surrender of the German Reich. Of the more than 215,000 "mobilizees," of whom more than 148,000 were deported to the Soviet Union, more than 138,000 were Germans. The other displaced persons were Poles, citizens of the USSR (mostly members of non-Russian nationalities), Hungarians, Slovaks, and Italians. The interned and mobilized Germans from the eastern territories of the Reich were later joined by another 70,000 civilians from the Soviet Occupation Zone, who filled the labor battalions of the Soviet labor camps.

The roundups, the marches on foot to the collection sites, and the transport of the deportees to the target regions in poorly heated freight cars with inadequate provisions and medical care took two to six weeks. Thirty to forty-five people were tightly packed into each freight car. This stage of the deportations already saw deaths on the trains that were

Table 2. Release and repatriation of the internees, 1945–1949						
Country	**Released and repatriated individuals**					
	1945	**1946**	**1947**	**1948**	**1949**	**Total**
Germany	32,867	10,526	11,051	11,802	11,446	77,692
Romania	9,064	10,639	9,126	11,439	20,804	61,072
Hungary	3,991	4,860	12,082	3,999	4,169	29,101
Yugoslavia	1,001	1,857	2,506	1,062	2,608	9,034
Japan	–	740	2,210	347	1,715	5,012
Czechoslovakia	876	666	372	248	216	2,378
Austria	13	42	69	27	48	199
Bulgaria and other countries	161	472	182	112	–	927
Total	63,463	35,834	42,572	29,803	41,746	213,418

Source: Polian, *Against Their Will*, 294.

carrying up to 2,500 passengers. The chief destination areas – alongside many other regions – were above all Ukraine and southern Russia, and there primarily the Donets Basin and the centers of heavy industry. Among the most important beneficiaries of forced labor were the People's Commissariats for coal mining, the construction industry, and the iron industry. However, German forced laborers of both genders were also found on the collective farms of socialist agriculture. German civilians participated as forced laborers on all large construction and industrial projects in the immediate postwar years in the Soviet Union. As such they represented – at least in terms of the specifications of the plans – a not inconsiderable production factor in fulfilling the first Five-Year Plan.

The deportees were housed, separated by gender, in the barracks camps of the GUPVI, the Main Administration for Prisoners of War and Internees. Forced laborers were clearly worse off than prisoners of war. The various economic sectors in which they were deployed regarded them as workers that were replaceable at will. The labor battalions, made up of 1,000 and more deportees, formed an administrative unit in the area of the People's Commissariat to which they were assigned. The battalions had a strict military structure. Guarding the battalions, ensuring their orderliness, and political work were the responsibility of the Ministry of the Interior in Moscow (NKVD/MVD).

Shift work and meeting work quotas under conditions of poor housing (somewhat better conditions as early as 1948, two square meters per person), extreme weather, poor hygienic conditions, and inadequate food and medical care characterized daily life in the developed camp societies. The surviving memoirs and sparse artifacts open only a crack onto the world of this camp system, which damaged the deportees for life. During the first two years, which show the highest mortality rate, the daily confrontation with death dominated the struggle for survival. The death rates among the deportees from the eastern territories of the German Reich were noticeably higher than among the deported ethnic Germans from east-central and southeastern European countries. Moreover, substantially more men than women died. Under

these conditions, the goals of the plans – generally much too ambitious – were not always attained. In some battalions, the income that was generated did not cover the costs for the scanty rations of food, clothing, and shoes, and the expenses for the organization and personnel of the camps.

Considerations of economic efficiency were the essential reason the first sick deportees and those unfit to work were released as early as 1945. In the beginning, those released were largely *Reichsdeutsche*. On 27 July 1946, the Council of Ministers of the USSR decided to release all German forced laborers, irrespective of their citizenship. In 1947 the majority of those released were Hungarian Germans; in the final phase they were Romanian Germans. The return took place separated by citizenship by way of several transit camps. *Reichsdeutsche* were released through Frankfurt an der Oder; citizens of Hungary, Austria, and Czechoslovakia through Marmaros Sziget; citizens of Romania, Yugoslavia, and Bulgaria through Focşani. The planning often did not match reality. For example, a quarter of the Transylvanian Saxons were not released directly to Romania, but to Germany. Efforts to return to their regions of origin often took years or were unsuccessful.

The following entry in the release pass of a woman born in 1925 and deported from Banat in Yugoslavia is symptomatic for the history of German civilians deported into the Soviet Union for forced labor at the end of World War II: on 19 November 1949, the 24-year-old woman "was released and is on her way back to homelessness." The survivors are homeless to this day. Those who were able to return found behind the iron curtain a different, fundamentally changed world. Often stateless, they came home to a foreign land, where they gradually had to make their way without being allowed to speak publicly about their experiences. The vast majority of the deportees came to the Federal Republic of Germany in the second half of the 20th century as *Aussiedler* and *Spätaussiedler* (ethnic German immigrants). Their lobbying organization is seeking compensation from the Federal Republic. So far, the deportees have been excluded from the Russian rehabilitation of political victims in the Soviet Union. The legal aspects of these forced migrations in Europe have not been considered. Essential impulses for its study have come from those who lived through it.

Baier, Hannelore, ed. *Deportarea etnicilor germani din România în Uniunea Sovietică. Culegere de documente de arhivă.* Sibiu, 1994.

Karner, Stefan. *Im Archipel GUPVI. Kriegsgefangenschaft und Internierung in der Sowjetunion 1941–1956.* Vienna and Munich, 1995.

Klier, Freya. *Verschleppt ans Ende der Welt. Schicksale deutscher Frauen in sowjetischen Arbeitslagern.* Berlin, 1996.

Mitzka, Herbert. *Zur Geschichte der Massendeportation von Ostdeutschen in die Sowjetunion im Jahre 1945. Ein historisch-politischer Beitrag.* 2nd ed. Einhausen, 1987.

Polian, Pavel. *Against Their Will: The History and Geography of Forced Migrations in the USSR.* Budapest and New York, 2004.

Schieder, Theodor, et al., eds. *Dokumentation der Vertreibung der Deutschen aus Ost-Mitteleuropa.* Published by the Bundesministerium für Vertriebene, Flüchtlinge und Kriegsgeschädigte. 5 vols., 3 supplements, index of places. Bonn, 1953–62.

Weber, Georg, et al. *Die Deportation der Siebenbürger Sachsen in die Sowjetunion 1945–1949.* 3 vols. Cologne and Weimar, 1996.

Wolf, Josef. *Deutsche Zwangsarbeiter aus Ostmittel- und Südosteuropa in der Sowjetunion 1945–1949.* Munich, 2005.

Cross-references: The Baltic Region; Czechia and Slovakia; Germany; Poland; Russia and Belarus; Southeastern Europe; *Aussiedler/ Spätaussiedler* in Germany after 1950; Forced Laborers in Germany and German-occupied Europe during World War II; German Refugees and Expellees from Eastern, East-Central, and Southeastern Europe in Germany and Austria since the End of World War II; German Settlers (*Donauschwaben*) in Southeastern Europe since the Early Modern Period

GERMAN IMMIGRANTS IN GERMANY FROM TERRITORIES CEDED AFTER WORLD WAR I

Jochen Oltmer

The political and territorial changes in the wake of World War I probably caused 5 million people in Europe to cross borders. Many of these migrations resulted from the loss of territories by the defeated countries. The successor states of the central and southeastern European losers of the war (Germany, Austria, Hungary, Bulgaria) were compelled, in the immediate postwar period, to take in a total of at least 2 million people from the lost territories. This influx of former citizens achieved especially large dimensions in a few successor states of the destroyed Habsburg Empire. Of the people who were living in Austria at the end of the 1920s, nearly 800,000 – more than 10% of the total population – had been born outside of the new borders in one of the territories of

the other successor states. Something similar was true for Hungary, which took in 500,000 people who had arrived after the war from Czechoslovakia, Romania, and Yugoslavia.

In the German Reich, the number of immigrants who were German nationals from territories ceded after World War I to Poland (large parts of Posen and Western Prussia, as well as Eastern Upper Silesia), France (Alsace-Lorraine), Belgium (Eupen-Malmedy), Denmark (Tondern), and Czechoslovakia (Hultschiner Ländchen) was much smaller than in Austria and Hungary. Still, this immigration of around 1 million people was the largest of all the immigration movements that the Weimar Republic had to deal with, most of them in the postwar years of 1918–23, which were characterized by grave economic, social, and political crises. From Alsace-Lorraine, 150,000 settled in what was left of the Reich; another 16,000 arrived from the former German colonies. Far greater still was the influx from the eastern territories of the Reich ceded to Poland after the Treaty of Versailles. By the middle of 1925, the Reich Statistical Office had counted 850,000 German arrivals from the new Polish western territories. In this entry the focus will be on the Weimar Republic's immigration and integration policy as it related to this group because this is what research to date has concentrated on. Further central aspects of the integration of this immigrant group that go beyond these aspects have so far remained unexamined; the same is true for the way this movement was perceived by the receiving society. Unlike the millions of German refugees and expellees from east-central, southeastern, and eastern Europe after World War II, the migration of Germans from the ceded territories after World War I is today no longer present in the collective memory of the Germans.

Among the politically motivated migrations of the immediate postwar period, the integration of immigrants from Alsace-Lorraine was considered fairly unproblematic in the political and administrative discourse as well as in public perception. The overwhelming portion of the immigrants from the former Reichsland, about four-fifths, arrived within a year after the armistice of 11 November 1918.

That the economic and social integration was relatively free of tension can be attributed to various factors: most Germans from Alsace-Lorraine arrived so early after the end of the war that they were not confronted with the increasingly deteriorating housing market in the same way as immigrant groups that arrived later. The fairly rapid job placement was facilitated by the above-average number of civil servants (from administration, the postal service, and the railroad, along with judges, teachers, priests) among them, who were taken over into the public sector of the Rest-Reich. Contemporary estimates at the beginning of the 1920s concluded that more than 40% of the emigrants, many of whom were accompanied by their family members, were civil servants or railroad workers working for the Reich. Among the emigrants who were not from the public sector, an above-average number came from jobs in the mining industry. Most of them soon found employment in the mines along the Ruhr and the Emscher, which suffered from a shortage of labor in the immediate postwar period.

About a quarter of all immigrants from Alsace-Lorraine settled in Rhineland-Westphalia. Dominant among the other destinations were areas bordering Alsace-Lorraine: Baden (18%), Hesse-Nassau (8%), Württemberg (7%), and the Palatinate (6%). The integration of the Alsace-Lorrainians was also facilitated by the fact that instrumentalizing the ethnic minority in Alsace-Lorraine for revisionist purposes was not paramount for the political and public discussion in Germany in the immediate postwar period. While Alsace-Lorraine was among the territories that were supposed to revert to Germany through a revision of the Treaty of Versailles, given France's position of power, such a revision did not seem likely, even in the medium term.

By comparison, the reception of German nationals from the former territories of eastern Prussia that were ceded to Poland proved far more conflictual. This resulted primarily from the image of the German minority in territories handed over to Poland that was very different from that of the immigrants from Alsace-Lorraine. It was accorded a far more important role in the revisionist policy of the Weimar Republic. German foreign politics considered Poland, precisely because of its strong minority population, as a weak *Saisonstaat* (seasonal state) with considerable economic and social problems and dependent on massive support from France. A revision of the territorial changes in the former eastern territories of the Reich brought about by the Treaty of Versailles seemed achievable in the foreseeable future. As part of this plan, preserving the German minority in the ceded territories was highly important to German foreign policy. Departures were therefore not in the interest of the Reich, even if the "border region expellees" (*Grenzlandvertriebene*), the official designation of this immigrant group in Germany, were supported out of considerations related to the laws pertaining to the consequences of the war, domestic politics, and humanitarian concerns.

Moreover, the number of immigrants was far greater than in the case of the migrants from Alsace-Lorraine. The majority of them came later into the shrunken territory of the Reich and encountered a far less favorable situation on the housing market. While the short-term provisioning for housing had been sufficient for the immigrants from Alsace-Lorraine in 1918/19, this was no longer the case with immigrants from the ceded territories in the east who came after 1921 and especially after 1922.

Moreover, the immigrants from the territories ceded to Poland fitted much less well in the labor market: about half of all immigrants from the east probably came from agriculture and forestry, with the majority most likely independent farmers and their family members. Because of the limited possibilities for farmers in the Reich, and because cash from compensation payments or a possible sale of property rapidly lost value in the massive postwar inflation in Germany, the chance to acquire new agricultural property was slim. A survey in 20 transit camps on a given day in February 1923 revealed that of the 1,736 families from the rural population

Distribution of food by the Red Cross in the refugee camp Schneidemühl in Posen-West Prussia to Germans from territories ceded to Poland, 1925 (*ullstein bild*).

that were polled, 1,244 had previously been independent owners of farmland. This points to the overrepresentation of agrarians in this group. Of the 1,450 families with agricultural property surveyed in 20 camps in April of the same year, more than a third (579) had no assets and only 16 had assets of more than a million marks – which by that point was equivalent to around $50.

Few additional statements are possible about the social structure of the immigrants from territories ceded to Poland: initially and most strongly dominant during the exodus in 1918 and 1919 was the urban population with a considerable number of those working in public service or as employees in the private sector, tradesmen, merchants, and industrial workers. Much like those from Alsace-Lorraine, these urban emigrants – who often had good to excellent qualifications – still had relatively favorable opportunities in the labor market in the Reich. As described, that was no longer the case for the agrarian emigrants who followed later in larger numbers. On the whole, the number of women and children was disproportionately high among this later group. This was a result of the high number of casualties among men during the war, but also because many male heads of households had initially resettled into the Reich in search of housing and work and had their families join them later, or had sent their families ahead while they remained behind to make final arrangements (e.g., settling property questions).

According to data from the German Red Cross for the years 1918 through 1922, this development led to a clear shift in the way the emigrants from the ceded territories in the east were received: while the vast majority of emigrants in 1918 and 1919 had arrived in the Reich without support from the Red Cross and the government, by 1920 that ratio was reversed. In 1918–19, around 70% of immigrants came without support; in 1920 and 1921 that number was down to only 40%. In 1922 it dropped further still to a mere 30%.

As a consequence of the growing economic and social problems of integration, and seeking to better control the emigration and direct the immigration, the government set up large "returnee camps" (*Heimkehrlager*) that were organized along military lines. This, in turn, led to other problems, especially since the states and municipalities, in the face of the deteriorating conditions in the housing and labor market, became increasingly resistant to the allocation of immigrants from the ceded territories. Between 1920 and 1925, Germany set up 26 such transition camps, which reached their highest occupancy in late 1922 and in early 1923 with around 40,000 persons. Thereafter the influx from the ceded territories declined rapidly, and the number of camp residents also dropped considerably in 1923–4.

The largest share of emigrants from the east was registered in the Prussian administrative districts and provinces at the eastern border: of those who left Posen and western Prussia, 18% lived in Berlin in 1925, 15% in Brandenburg (here especially in the most easterly district Frankfurt/Oder), 12% in Lower Silesia, 11% in Pomerania, and 8% in east Prussia. Among those who left eastern Upper Silesia, the geographical concentration in the neighboring provinces was even more pronounced: 57% were counted in Upper Silesia in 1925 and 19% in Lower Silesia.

All told, the reception of Germans from the ceded territories put the Weimar Republic under considerable legitimation pressure. First, because of laws pertaining to the consequences of the war and citizenship, it was compelled to organize the reception of the emigrants. Second, this reception seemed a considerable burden for the economy, the labor market, and the social security system in Germany in the immediate postwar period. Third, remaining in the ceded territories was considered an option for the Germans there: strong German minorities in the lost territories seemed to substantially boost the chances of a successful revision of the European postwar order. Still, Weimar's migration policy was unable to prevent the massive exodus of German citizens from the ceded territories. Even the attempts to direct and guide this movement failed in the end, with the result that the number of Germans in the new western regions of Poland declined considerably.

This dilemma of Weimar policy vis-à-vis the immigrants from the ceded territories, caught up in the thicket of foreign political interests in revision, concerns over economic and sociopolitical burdens, and obligations arising from laws pertaining to the consequences of the war and citizenship, all of which were dressed up with humanitarian gestures, gave rise to a contradictory policy of reception and integration. It was never proactive, but reacted by setting up structures for receiving the immigrants only when tens of thousands of immigrants from the ceded territories were already in Germany. The Weimar Republic set up a layered, militarily organized system for transporting the immigrants and passing them on to reception centers and transitional "returnee camps." However, this infrastructure for taking in the immigrants from the ceded territories was not backed up by an adequate infrastructure of economic and social integration.

Essentially, the immigrants were left to themselves to find jobs and housing. The integration institutions set up by the state were never able to accomplish their mission. The only option for immigrants who were considered unplaceable in the labor market was to remain in the camps, in some cases for years.

Oltmer, Jochen. *Migration und Politik in der Weimarer Republik.* Göttingen, 2005.

Cross-references: Austria; Czechia and Slovakia; France; Germany; Poland; Southeastern Europe; German Refugees and Expellees from Eastern, East-Central, and Southeastern Europe in Germany and Austria since the End of World War II

GERMAN INDUSTRIAL TRADERS AND SPIES IN GREAT BRITAIN IN THE 18TH AND 19TH CENTURIES

Stefan Manz

From the middle of the 18th century, a growing number of German entrepreneurs, engineers, and state officials traveled to the motherland of industrialization for the specific purpose of procuring information. The growing technology and productivity gap between Great Britain and other parts of Europe had also driven home to the Germans the need to catch up. In the early industrial phase up to around the middle of the 19th century, journeys by specialists played a far more important role than in later phases, since technological and entrepreneurial knowledge often did not exist in the form of descriptions or blueprints but was accessible only as experiential knowledge gained through direct observation. Added to this were British prohibitions on the export of smelting and textile machinery put in place in 1750, which could be circumvented only by industrial espionage and were not lifted until 1825 and 1842, respectively. Advanced knowledge thus had to be acquired on location, whether by legal or illegal means.

Although Great Britain was the most important destination country of German entrepreneurs, it was not the only one. Travelers also headed to France and Belgium, and beyond Europe to the USA. Conversely, the stream of visitors to Great Britain drew from all western, central, and northern European countries. For example, in the second third of the 19th century, nearly all Norwegian industrialists spent some time in Great Britain. Entrepreneurial trips from Germany to Great Britain should thus be seen as a case study for a form of migration that was common throughout Europe during the early industrial period.

While the social background of travelers was relatively homogenous, they can be roughly classified, with respect to their occupational status, into independent entrepreneurs, employed engineers (occasionally also craftsmen), and state officials. Whereas representatives of the first two categories could not leave their factories for more than a few weeks to travel, officials often remained in Great Britain for as long as a year. Occasionally there were also state-sponsored informational trips by farmers. In 1764, for example, King Frederick II of Prussia sent six sons of tenants from Pomerania, the Old Prussian territories, and Silesia to England for one year. In all cases these were merely short, purely professional cultural contacts, which generally did not involve social integration or settlement, especially since even longer stays were characterized by active travel within Great Britain. This form of mobility thus has long-term repercussions less for the destination country than for the country of origin. The returning travelers acted as bearers and multipliers of advanced know-how that substantially advanced the course of German industrialization.

Because of the ephemeral nature of this pattern of geographic mobility, the size of the groups cannot be precisely determined. Snapshots merely convey an impression. In Rhineland and Westphalia, for example, a stay in England has been confirmed for nearly every important industrialist of the early 19th century. As early as the 1770s, the Birmingham machine factory of Matthew Boulton, the partner of James Watts, was a popular destination frequented almost daily by foreign visitors. The same was true of Josiah Wedgwood's enterprise in Derby, the leading European pottery factory. Other important destinations were the industrial regions around London, Manchester, Sheffield, and Glasgow. German territorial rulers were also interested in questions relating to infrastructure and dispatched state officials to inspect canals and railroads.

In the early phase, the British hosts and officials took a benevolent view of the travelers. They demonstrated to the foreigners their own advances with an air of satisfaction, and their long-term hope – in spite of the ban on exports – was to find markets for their machine-building industry. But when the first foreign imitations pointed to an emerging competition, the perception turned negative. The Germans were now perceived as parasitical beneficiaries of the British spirit of innovation, and in travel accounts the visitors described "the scant openness … and the mistrust that they have toward foreigners in this regard." For example, beginning in 1786, Boulton and Wedgwood imposed a strict ban on visitors in their factories. Important industrial cities followed suit. The prohibitions on the export of machines and tools of smelting and textile manufacture were tightened in the 1780s.

Given the unrelenting pressure to come up with innovations, German entrepreneurs were now left with only the path of industrial espionage. To gain insight into the production factories, they held out the prospects of promising business relationships, bribed factory workers, obtained stellar letters of recommendation, or falsified their identities. Alfred Krupp, for example, had himself introduced into the English business world in 1838–9 under the name A. Schroop and presented himself as an interested but not very knowledgeable private person. In Prussia, this kind of information procurement received state support, in that outstanding graduates of the Berlin Industrial Institute received

travel grants. The influential founder of the Institute, Peter Christian Beutch, coordinated the trips and reserved for himself the right to decide, upon the return of these travelers, "how they could become most useful to their fatherland by applying their knowledge."

The London World's Fair in 1851 was simultaneously the high point and turning point in the travels of German entrepreneurs to Britain, in that it symbolized for the last time Great Britain's market-dominating position and attracted numerous businessmen and decision makers. A total of 11,292 persons traveled to London from the German states. During the fair, 2,499 persons reported just to the Prussian legation in London, among them 13 princes, 1 count, 1 minister, 1,128 merchants and factory owners, 298 civil servants, 86 military men, 111 mechanics, 310 farmers and landowners, and 298 craftsmen and small-scale tradesmen. The visits were often financially supported as a form of industrial training. The Prussian state railroads, for instance, offered reduced fares, and the Stettin merchants sent a commission of tradesmen to London for a four-week stay. Especially also the southern German states of Baden, Württemberg, and Bavaria used the World's Fair quite deliberately to promote their domestic industry.

As a result of changes in the structural background conditions, informational trips to Great Britain by established German entrepreneurs occurred rarely in the second half of the 19th century. Germany for its part was now developing into a center of innovation that attracted specialists from abroad. However, Great Britain remained an attractive destination for young entrepreneurs and engineers – some still in the process of training – who could profit from global trade connections and technological innovations. For example, Hermann Blohm and Ernst Voß worked in that country around 1870 independent of each other as shipbuilding engineers before founding the Hamburg shipyard of Blohm & Voß.

Kroker, Werner. *Wege zur Verbreitung technologischer Kenntnisse zwischen England und Deutschland in der zweiten Hälfte des 18. Jahrhunderts.* Berlin, 1971.

Manz, Stefan. *Migranten und Internierte. Deutsche in Glasgow, 1864–1918.* Stuttgart, 2003.

Muhs, Rudolf. "Englische Einflüsse auf die Frühphase der Industrialisierung in Deutschland." In *Wettlauf in die Moderne. England und Deutschland seit der industriellen Revolution,* edited by Adolf M. Birke and Lothar Kettenacker, 31–50. Munich, 1988.

Schumacher, Martin. *Auslandsreisen deutscher Unternehmer 1750–1851 unter besonderer Berücksichtigung von Rheinland und Westfalen.* Cologne, 1968.

Weber, Wolfhard. "Industriespionage als technologischer Transfer in der Frühindustrialisierung." *Technikgeschichte* 42 (1975): 287–305.

Cross-references: Germany; Great Britain; Swedish Return Migrants from the United States, 1875–1930

GERMAN ITINERANT MERCHANTS FROM THE MÜNSTERLAND IN NORTHERN, WESTERN, AND CENTRAL EUROPE IN THE 18TH AND 19TH CENTURIES

Hannelore Oberpenning

In early modern Europe, itinerant trade developed – with regional differences in extent and importance – into a constitutive element of traditional agrarian societies. Whole armies of traveling merchants were on the road in the 18th and 19th centuries and brought to the consumers nearly everything that could be transported in knapsacks or portable chests and baskets. Whether in Germany as *Hausierer*, in the Netherlands as *marskramers*, in France as *colporteurs*, or in Italy as *venditori ambulanti* – there was hardly a region between Scandinavia in the north and Italy in the south in which traveling merchants were not part of the everyday picture in villages and cities, on farms, and on the small and tiny plots of cottagers or hired hands.

Among the many groups of traveling merchants who sold goods in short- and long-distance trade – especially after the 17th century – to rural consumers were the *Tödden* from the northern Münsterland. From there, their trading organization encompassed, with a far-reaching trading network, a large part of western, central, and east-central Europe; while its core regions were part of the "North Sea system" of the *Hollandgänger* (migrant workers who went to Holland), its scope was much greater. The border-crossing long-distance trade took the *Tödden* from northern France in the west to the Baltic region in the east. In the process there was a merger of peddling and eventually also retail trade of an initially subpeasant class that sought to escape the threat of pauperization or to boost the meager income from their small agricultural plots. The regions of origin of the exclusively Catholic *Tödden* were the county of Lingen and the parish of Hopsten in the Prince-bishopric of Münster – that is, the area between Lingen in the north and Tecklenburg in the south, in what is today the western border region between the states of North-Rhine Westphalia and Lower Saxony. Around the middle of the 18th century, 40% to 50% of the male working population (more than 1,000 registered traveling merchants) was living here from the trans-regional sale of goods.

The term *Tödden* is an orally transmitted word, which in the argot of the peddling traders was used as an autonym. The word is not found in contemporary sources. In German administrative documents, the *Tödden* were referred to as *Hopster* or *Höpster*, as *lingensche Packenträger* or *Messerträger*, in Dutch sources as *bontdrager* or *bonddrager* or also as *pakkedrager*. *Pakken* was used to describe knapsacks, the preferred means for transporting goods among textile traders. Along with textiles goods such as fabric (e.g., linen and wools) and small finished textile goods (e.g., caps, socks, gloves, cloths), the specialized assortment of trading wares of the *Tödden* included metal goods, especially small iron wares (e.g., scissors, knives, buckles, sewing needles).

The emergence and spread of itinerant trade represented an answer to the growing disparity between population growth and employment opportunities, which in many parts of Old Europe forced a large part of the rural population to search for additional sources of income. In the wake of the strong population growth, especially from the middle of the 18th century, the mass of land-poor and subpeasant classes often engaged in traveling trade as a necessary side or even a primary job because they lacked other options. The geographic origins of this trade lay in economically disadvantaged marginal zones, especially mountain regions, and in other areas that were not very productive agriculturally. Spatially, the larger groups of wandering merchants in 18th-century Europe were shaped largely by regional concentrations in several neighboring villages of traveling merchants, and thus by the formation of distinct communities of traveling merchants with a high proportion of *colporteurs*.

Every group of traveling merchants specialized in certain types of wares. Trade was done with goods procured from wholesalers or manufacturers, often with the products of domestic industrial trade. The so-called self-peddlers who produced their own goods belonged more to an earlier developmental phase. In addition, the structure of some highly developed movements of itinerant trade was shaped by certain commercial or entrepreneurial forms of organization or cooperation. Those ranged from formal mergers into trade associations called "companies," often on the basis of kinship ties, to informal agreements on the basis of separate secret languages, which were always suspect to the respective authorities. Also characteristic were the organization of trade on the basis of a division of labor, the maintenance of storehouses in the trading area, and the dividing up of the trading districts among the traveling merchants.

In most European countries, the estate-based, corporative notions of order were difficult to reconcile with the practice of itinerant trading, with the result that such trading was made very difficult if not impossible. The rigid defensive battles waged by representatives of urban trades and commerce against traveling merchants grew out of the intensifying economic competition to which urban craftsmen, merchants, and shopkeepers found themselves exposed in the face of overcrowded small trades, the expansion of the putting-out system, and the increase in manufactures or rural domestic industries after the 18th century. If the peddlers did not wish to settle in the host country and pay regular dues tied to the acquisition of citizenship rights, they were to remain excluded from economic activity. However, acquiring citizenship of a city was usually quite elaborate, tied among other things to proof of the requisite wealth, and it involved costs that were not inconsiderable.

The tool kit of Cameralistic economic policies based on large-scale government intervention did encourage a system of ordinances with numerous mechanisms of restriction, prohibitions, and control, but those often existed merely on paper and were unable to prevent the spread of global trade. The Prussian state, for example, actually granted the

Tödden a de facto monopoly for the sale of the "Bielefeld linen" produced in the country of Ravensberg in the Prussian provinces east of the Weser river. Around the middle of the 18th century, the Prussian king placed the traders under contractual obligation to take fixed quotas of domestic manufactured goods, in return for which they received permission to engage in largely unrestricted itinerant trade with them. The *Tödden* were thus to take over the sale of the goods produced by the proto-factories of the textile and metal goods industries, which were substantially promoted by the Prussian state.

During their more than 150-year-long history, the migratory activities in the itinerant trade of the *Tödden* were characterized by multifarious forms and stages of immigration and integration in the destination region, as well as emigration and separation in the region of origin – forms that varied from one destination region to the next and could range, in fluid and sometimes overlapping manifestations, from itinerant trade to partial integration, the founding of businesses, and family reunification. In the process, there were forms that were typical for one destination region but never developed in another one. As a rule, the *Tödden* spent the better part of the year – mostly nine months and more – in their accustomed sales regions and returned to their home villages only once or twice a year to buy merchandise and visit their families. The traders usually returned on Christian feast days in the summer and winter, St. Jacob and Christmas, after which they would spend the following summer or winter months (often only a few weeks) at home. To sell their goods, the *Tödden* thus used above all the time of year most favorable for itinerant trade, that is, the spring and fall. When their customers were busy with the harvest in the summer, the *Tödden* returned to their home villages to provision themselves with new goods and take care of business and personal affairs. The extent to which they were still bound to the context of agrarian production and acquisition in the villages varied, but in general it was no longer extensive. The ties that the traders still had to their home were maintained mostly for psychological and hardly at all for economic reasons. Stays of several months in the sales regions usually required the full-time commitment of individual traders and were not compatible with earning a primary livelihood on the family's farm. In addition, the dates of fairs, at which trading goods were purchased, also influenced the cycles of migration. The forms and duration of migration were thus oriented primarily toward the internal structures and necessities of the migratory business.

For all the existing exclusivity of the group that was in part closed off to the outside, the itinerant trade provided comparatively intensive integration into the economic and social structures of the destination regions. Whether in the Netherlands, Prussia, Mecklenburg, or Pomerania, the *Tödden* usually lived the better part of the year as independent entrepreneurs or employees of companies, as inhabitants or residents, in the cities or the countryside. A rented room served as housing and storehouse. After the trading

regulations were tightened in the Netherlands, the *Tödden* proceeded, toward the end of the 18th century, to establish tax-liable households in the destination areas. The traveling business was made considerably easier through the more or less thorough penetration of the trading areas. That required a certain measure of infrastructure and logistics: the traders had to set up or expand stable and yet flexible systems and networks for trouble-free transportation, for the storing and sale of goods, and for places to stay and spend the night. In addition, they needed a solid knowledge of the local languages and the regional and local mentalities and buying habits, and the establishment of a permanent stable of customers. Integration into the life of the church community went without saying, provided there was a Catholic parish. In the process, *Tödden* not infrequently exerted considerable influence on the establishment and development of church communities; two examples are Brandenburg and Pomerania.

The political and economic transformations, and above all the economic reform legislation in the early 19th century, meant for the *Tödden* and many other groups of traveling merchants an end to trade in its traditional forms. While itinerant trade in the area of origin dried up almost completely by the middle of the century, the commercial sector in the destination areas transitioned for many to stationary trade through the founding of urban textile businesses. However, this path into the life of an urban entrepreneur could be taken only by those whose itinerant trade had earned them enough to spend the considerable finances it took to create a new livelihood. The slow, lengthy process by which the *Tödden* established new businesses and settled down in the destination regions stretched into the late 19th century. The businesses were set up in the central towns of their former customer areas, and some of them now developed into centers of stationary trade by families from northern Westphalia. In the Dutch coastal province of Frisia, for example, the concentration was so high in the 19th century that a not insignificant share of the textile trade carried on there is traced back to *Tödden* businesses. They included the textile enterprise founded in 1841 in the Frisian town of Sneek by Clemens and August Brenninkmeyer, which was given the name C & A Brenninkmeyer. The remarkable thing is that we find here the roots of well-known textile companies today, among them, for example, C & A, Hettlage, Boecker, Lampe, or Voss.

In spite of the establishment of businesses in the destination area, many merchants and their families for a long time kept their original domicile and center of their lives in their regions of origin. Even now, they clung to the traditional migratory activity, to the regular commuting migrations between the origin and destination regions between the district of Tecklenburg in the northern Münsterland and the neighboring Kingdom of Hanover or Brandenburg, Pomerania, Holstein, and the Netherlands. The traveling business continued to be pursued for a long time in addition to the stationary trade. It was only at the end of the 19th century that the great majority had brought their families into the immigration regions and settled down there with a permanent domicile. But the social bonds to the places of origin remained even then. Many returned to their communities of origin after withdrawing from an active life of business, to live out their lives and be buried there, while the next generation carried on the business in the former destination region of the traveling merchants.

Characteristic of the itinerant trade of the *Tödden* was thus commuting in groups, a pattern that was maintained across centuries, and the bilocal living and working situation of the traveling merchants, which turned them into locals and outsiders in several places at the same time. This gave rise to a migratory behavior that was handed down within local contexts and within group and family structures and was maintained until the period when businesses were set up and developed in the 19th century. The migratory traditions of the merchants took on an almost ritual stability, which remained even when the traveling trade itself came to an end with the transition to an industrial society, and the regular return into the regions of origin was also no longer necessary in economic terms.

Fontaine, Laurence. *Histoire du colportage en Europe (XVe–XIXe siècle)*. Paris, 1993.

Lucassen, Jan. *Migrant Labour in Europe 1600–1900: The Drift to the North Sea*. London. 1987.

Oberpenning, Hannelore. *Migration und Fernhandel im "Tödden-System." Wanderhändler aus dem nördlichen Münsterland im mittleren und nördlichen Europa des 18. und 19. Jahrhunderts*. Osnabrück, 1996.

Page Moch, Leslie. *Moving Europeans: Migration in Western Europe since 1650*. Bloomington, 1992.

Reininghaus, Wilfried, ed. *Wanderhandel in Europa*. Dortmund, 1993.

Cross-references: The Baltic Region; France; Germany; The Netherlands; German Seasonal Agricultural Laborers in the Netherlands from the 17th to the Early 20th Century; German Traders and Shopkeepers in the Netherlands, 1850-1900

GERMAN MAIDS IN THE NETHERLANDS IN THE INTERWAR PERIOD

Barbara Henkes

For centuries German women had traveled to the Netherlands to look for work. However, their number increased dramatically after the First World War. During the interwar years tens of thousands of young German women left their country to try their luck in the neighboring country that had remained neutral during the Great War. The need to earn a living led many young women especially from the northwest, to the enticing "Guilder Paradise" (*Guldenparadis*). Those who arrived first helped their sisters, girls next door, or friends to

obtain positions with their mistresses' relatives, neighbors, and acquaintances. Initially they were received with open arms, since the demand for domestics in the growing middle class was rising while Dutch working-class girls were able to find work outside the domestic sphere, in factories, sweatshops, and department stores. The shortage of cheap domestic labor could be alleviated by the arrival of German girls.

In 1920, only 9,100 female foreign workers were registered in the Netherlands, most of them German. Three years later their number had increased fivefold. The foreigners' registers indicate that the number of German maids in 1923 must have been about 40,000. After the economic situation in the Weimar Republic stabilized in November 1923, many of them returned home, though not for long. As soon as the global economic crisis in 1929 hit Germany fast and hard, the presence of German domestics in the Netherlands increased in the early 1930s again to about 40,000 in 1934. After that, their number decreased rapidly: by the time German troops invaded the Netherlands in May 1940, there were only about 3,500 German maids left. These figures do not take into account the many German women who had acquired Dutch citizenship, usually through marriage to a Dutchman, and were therefore no longer counted as Germans in the Dutch statistics. How many of them married Dutchmen can no longer be determined with precision, but it must have been several tens of thousands.

For many young women, this labor migration was limited in duration. On average, they spent two years as domestics in the Netherlands before they returned to Germany, changed position, or settled permanently in the Netherlands after marriage. It is estimated that at least 175,000 German maidservants worked and lived in Dutch households during the 1920s and 1930s. Just like their Dutch colleagues they had to cope with the precarious relationships within the private households, though they found themselves more frequently in difficult situations because of unfamiliarity with the Dutch language and habits. Moreover, if they did not live up to the expectations and were dismissed, they faced not only the loss of their job and place to stay, but also the possibility of being forced to leave the country. Because of their vulnerable legal and social status as foreign workers, many of them were prepared to do more work for less money than their native counterparts.

Women's organizations for the protection of girls in Germany as well as in the Netherlands were actively involved as consultants and employment agencies in the migration of single women across the national borders. Since the end of the 19th century, young women's wanderlust was accompanied by warnings against the increased moral and physical dangers that the girls' stay away from home entailed. The ignorant young women were said to be in imminent danger of falling into the wrong hands through unverifiable newspaper advertisements or shady intermediaries. During the journey, they ran the risk of encountering ruthless white slave–traders. Once they had arrived at the place of destination, misfortunes like pregnancy out of wedlock and prostitution still lay in

A staff member of the Railway Mission meets a young traveler at a railway station in Germany, around 1930 (*Archiv des Diakonischen Werks der EKD, Berlin*).

wait. In particular, girls outside the realm of parental surveillance were supposed to be subjected to temptations that not only brought danger to them personally but also constituted a threat to public morality, in general, and the reputation of German women abroad, in particular. Morality and patriotism became irrevocably intertwined in the discourse about the international migration of unmarried women.

When the labor migration of maidservants had turned into a mass movement, the Dutch and German organizations for the protection of girls jointly focused on supervising the female migrants at the railway stations and after they had reached their destinations. In the process they cooperated with German organizations in the Netherlands like the Deutsche Evangelische Gemeinden (German Protestants Congregations), the Vereine für Deutschsprechende Katholiken (Associations for German-speaking Catholics) and the evangelical Jugendbünde für Entschiedenes Christentum (German Youth Leagues of the Christian Endeavour Society). Together they tried to offer young German women a safe home base (*ein Stück Heimat*) in the unfamiliar Dutch surroundings, where they could meet and exchange experiences once or twice a week under the leadership of a German or German-speaking sister or a laywoman (*Fürsorgerin*).

In doing so, the German *Mädchenvereine* (organizations for German girls) played an important role in the care for and thus integration of the newcomers in their Dutch surroundings. At the same time, however, they could hamper this process as they organized the young women on the basis of their Germanness. Their identification with the home country was promoted even more after 1933, when German organizations abroad increasingly fell under the spell of National Socialist Germany. However, most German domestics joined these German gatherings only for a short time or not at all. The numbers of participants varied from 200 in the big cities to 10 or 15 girls in the smaller towns. Otherwise they went out to meet with others in the park, at dancehalls, or at the movies where they often got acquainted with Dutch youngsters. As the maid period was experienced

as a transitional phase between school and marriage, the decision to settle down in the Netherlands or return to Germany was often determined by the encounter of a future spouse. And at the same time the orientation toward the "old" or the "new" homeland influenced the choice of a partner. Marriage to a Dutchman brought the young women not only a certain independence in their own household but also Dutch citizenship.

The Netherlands did not escape the global economic crisis of the 1930s. As unemployment grew, employers were urged by the government to replace their foreign servants by Dutch maids. While legal measures were taken in the Netherlands to prevent German maids from staying or entering the country, the German authorities took action to stop the women from migrating and to make them return home. Moreover, improved prospects on the German labor market prompted many to return voluntarily. Those who remained in the Netherlands often had good employers, had serious suitors, or had become anchored in Dutch society in some other way. If they had not exchanged their German nationality for a Dutch one by marrying a Dutchman, they were confronted in December 1938 with a summons by the German authorities to return to Germany. The Action for the Collective Return of German Maids, or the *Hausmädchenheimschaffungsaktion*, as it was called in German official jargon, aimed at recruiting more women to alleviate the shortage on the German labor market.

But there were other motives as well. The warnings that had been voiced all along about the alleged moral dangers that migration posed to single women were now increasingly combined with nationalistic and anti-Semitic tones: the Netherlands, it was said, were "anti-German" and "Jewified." German women were told to stop being "a servant people for other states" (*ein Dienstbotenvolk für andere Staaten*), and thereby evade their true destiny in their own country. For it was only in the latter that they could fulfill their task as future mothers for the German people (*das deutsche Volkstum*). The large number of written requests from German maids and Dutch mistresses for dispensation indicate that there was not much enthusiasm among the remaining German maids to return. The action did, however, mark the end of the intensive migration of young, unmarried women from Germany to the Netherlands during the interbellum.

Women of German descent who were living in the Netherlands in May 1940 had found a way to reconcile the ties to their homelands with their position in Dutch society. However, the German invasion revealed how vulnerable this position was. Under the conditions of war, their national origins took on central importance: one was either on the German side, or on the Dutch side; in-between positions were not accepted. The tormented feeling that went along with this was aptly expressed in the anxious question of whether a girl's own brother would have to fight against her. The few remaining German domestics and the many German-Dutch housewives were too often classified as "Nazi-Germans." While the Nazi authorities urged them to join the German side, the Dutch looked at them with suspicion.

The German occupation and the sharp dividing line between Dutch and German in terms of "friend" and "foe" continued to reverberate long after the liberation in 1945. For decades to come, the war experience shaped a negative image of Germany and Germans in the Netherlands. The result was that many former German domestics, in spite of Dutch citizenship, Dutch family names, and command of the Dutch language, were tainted by their background. Their attempts to hide their German accent, the embarrassing confrontations when German family members came to visit, and the experience of having to justify oneself because of one's German background reveal that what was initially a smooth process of integration and acceptance of German women into Dutch society could turn into the opposite.

Henkes, Barbara. "Changing Images of German Maids during the Inter-war Period in the Netherlands: From Trusted Help to Traitor in the Nest." In *The Myths We Live By*, edited by Paul Thompson and Raphael Samuel, 225–39. London, 1990.

Henkes, Barbara. "German Maidservants in the Prosperous Guilderland and the Land of Moral Threats: Nation-Images and National Identity during the Interwar Period." In *Images of the Nation: Different Meanings of Dutchness, 1870–1940*, edited by Annemieke Galema, Barbara Henkes, and Henk te Velde, 133–59. Amsterdam, 1993.

Henkes, Barbara. *Heimat in Holland. Deutsche Dienstmädchen 1920–1950*. Straelen, 1998.

Henkes, Barbara. "Maids on the Move: Images of Femininity and European Women's Labour Migration during the Interwar Years." In *Women, Gender and Labour Migration. Historical and Global Perspectives*, edited by Pamela Sharpe, 224–43. London and New York, 2001.

Lucassen, Leo. "Bringing Structure Back In: Economic and Political Determinants of Immigration in Dutch Cities (1920–1940)." *Social Science History* 26 (2002): 503–29.

Cross-references: Germany; The Netherlands

GERMAN MARITIME TRADERS IN CÁDIZ AND BORDEAUX FROM THE LATE 17TH TO THE LATE 19TH CENTURY

Klaus Weber

The existence of large communities of foreign merchants was a typical characteristic of European port cities in the early modern era. This was possible due in large part to the trade monopolies maintained by mercantilist west European colonial powers. Only a country's own subjects were to benefit from its colonial trade – the involvement of foreigners was allowed in only certain ports in the mother country, not in the colonies, and it was precisely these places that attracted many merchants from abroad.

Until approximately 1830, thousands of German-speaking traders are assumed to have established settlements in British, Dutch, French, Portuguese, and Spanish ports. Since they lacked their own colonies, the economic success of German-speaking merchants dealing in export-oriented trades from the 17th to the 19th century was largely dependent on commerce with their western neighbors. In value, German ports conducted more trade with Bordeaux, Europe's largest port for the re-export of colonial wares, than with all British ports combined while Cádiz served as one of the main transit points for German export wares. This essay deals with these two port cities. Recent studies have established the number of German merchants living in Cádiz and Bordeaux at approximately 240 and 230, respectively, for the time period 1680–1830. These figures refer only to shareholding partners and their male offspring who also became shareholders. The number would be at least 50% higher if bookkeepers, family members, apprentices, and members of related professions were included.

The two port cities attracted specific groups of merchants who fit the respective economic profile of each city. Starting in the late 17th century, Bordeaux gradually became the principal transit port for products from the recently acquired French Caribbean islands. In the 1780s, more than 50% of French colonial exports to other European markets – which did not include the significant trade in wine – passed through Bordeaux. For nearly the entire 18th century, Cádiz was the only Spanish port fully authorized to trade with the Spanish colonies in the Americas, receiving at least 80% of American goods designated for Spain. Although a more productive plantation system developed in the French colonies, the Spanish colonies with their far greater acreage and larger population formed a more important market for European manufactures, most of which were paid for not by trade in colonial goods but rather with Mexican and Peruvian silver, which was in fact the top export commodity of the Spanish colonies in the Americas.

The Spanish Atlantic commerce attracted an immense number of French, Dutch, Italian, British, German, and other traders. The largest group was the French, who were favored by the Bourbon dynasty ruling in Madrid. The relatively small number of German merchants in Cádiz nevertheless competed rather successfully. Surprisingly, the vast majority of the German merchants came not from the Hanseatic seaports but rather from relatively small locales in the remote German hinterland. Of the 237 Germans whose origins are documented, only 88 came from Hamburg, 6 from Bremen, and 3 from Lübeck. More than half of the German merchants in Cádiz came from Germany's proto-industrial regions such as the Westphalian and Silesian linen weaving areas and the iron manufacturing region of the Rhineland. Linen and metalware, luxury goods less so, constituted the bulk of German export articles to Spain (and France). Among individual regions, the area providing the single greatest number of German merchants in Cádiz was northern Bohemia, with at least 47 traders from the glass manufacturing city of Haida (Nový Bor). A number of the Bohemians and Westphalians had begun their careers as merchants as humble peddlers in their home region. Eighteen of the traders in Cádiz came from the Bavarian Ammer Valley and the Tyrolian Valley of Gardena, which were renowned for their production of carved wooden religious icons, an ideal item for export to Catholic countries.

The production of all German trade articles was highly labor intensive, which was decisive for their success in the western markets. Silver production in Mexico and Peru was one of the main causes of a long-lasting period of inflation and led to the emergence of a wage and price gradient that stretched from the Americas across the Atlantic and deep into central and eastern Europe. This early modern price revolution and considerable demographic growth in 18th-century Europe favored the development of central European proto-industries, whose products were made very competitive in western Europe, Africa, and the Americas thanks to low labor costs. Manufacturers reduced transaction costs and increased profits by establishing familial networks that stretched into western markets. The Westphalian Ellermann family managed to establish branches in Hamburg, Amsterdam, Cádiz, and temporarily (presumably illegally) in the New World. Its Cádiz branch existed over the course of four generations – from the early 1720s into the 1840s. Bohemians established permanent branches over the entire Iberian Peninsula and serviced even remote rural areas by peddling.

Very different economic conditions shaped the German trading colony in Bordeaux. The French Caribbean, colonized by France in the late 17th century, thereafter rapidly became a highly productive plantation empire, providing for three-quarters of the sugar consumption in the 18th-century western world. At the same time, French manufacturing was far more competitive and better protected by custom duties than Spanish manufacturing, which made German imports into France less lucrative – a fact that was reflected in the origins of the Germans in Bordeaux. They mainly came from Hanseatic ports, financial centers (e.g., Frankfurt) and centers of trade (e.g., Magdeburg), purchasing, for instance, French sugar, coffee, indigo, wine, and brandy for Germany, where these products had already found a mass market. Although French ports received large quantities of German textiles, these were designated for re-export into Hispanic and African markets. On the basis of its plantation economy, France had become the leading nation in the slave trade. With textiles being the most important article of exchange, some German merchants – in particular Friedrich Romberg and his sons, who hailed from the iron and textile manufacturing town of Iserlohn (Mark) – were able to establish veritable Atlantic trading empires, which consisted in complementary enterprises, such as textile manufactures in the Rhineland and Flanders; shipping and maritime insurance companies in Bordeaux, Bruges, and Ostend; slaving companies; indigo and cotton plantations in the Caribbean; and wine estates in the Bordeaux region.

Many German migrants in Cádiz and Bordeaux married the daughters of French or Spanish merchants, less so of the resident British, Irish, and Dutch. It already became difficult to identify the national identity of such families with the second generation, particularly among the most successful. They all lived in the respective harbor district of each city, where numerous commercial and kinship links between the respective minorities combined to create one single cosmopolitan group.

Yet in this respect as well there existed differences among Germans in the two cities. In contrast to thoroughly Catholic Cádiz, there had always been Calvinist and Sephardic minorities in Bordeaux, which aided the mainly Protestant Germans in establishing familial ties with important trading and shipping dynasties there. From 1769, non-French Protestants had their own cemetery and from 1776 were allowed to attend Calvinist religious services. In Spain, in contrast, Protestants were prohibited from maintaining their own churches well into the 19th century and had to bury their dead outside city walls.

Starting in the 1740s, French law increasingly opened the possibility of direct trade with the Caribbean to foreigners. A number of Germans subsequently became involved in transatlantic shipping and even ran their own Caribbean plantations. Marriage to a French woman facilitated gaining such privileges and enhanced acculturation. For this reason as well, German merchants and their offspring were considerably better integrated in Bordeaux than in Cádiz. Of the Germans who either immigrated to or grew up in Bordeaux in the 18th century, 49 are known to have married; 32 chose a French and only 11 a German partner. Among Germans in Cádiz in the 18th century, there are 48 documented marriages, 18 involving a Spanish woman and at least 20 a German woman. Integration through conversion to Catholicism and subsequent marriage seems to have been more frequent in Cádiz in the late 17th than in the 18th century. Women were not only marriage partners but also took an active part in the family business as they, for example, ably filled in for their husbands while the men were traveling. A number of widows continued to run the family business successfully when there were no male heirs, they were too young, or they seemed unfit. Sons or nephews, however, were typically the ones who took over the business.

However, the local Catholics were not the single factor to explain the less successful integration of foreign merchants in Cádiz. The significant group of nearly 50 German-speaking Bohemians was Catholic without exception, but Bohemian feudal law allowed them to marry only women from the lordly estate to which they themselves belonged, which meant that partnerships with Spanish merchants were extremely rare. It was only in the 1780s, in the course of founding settlements in Mexico City and Lima, that Bohemian merchants cooperated with Spanish partners, who then acted as front men – a common practice aimed at getting around the trade monopoly.

The importance of such cosmopolitan familial networks, however, began to dwindle as soon as France had lost part of its Caribbean empire and Spain its colonies on the American mainland. The independent republics of the New World preferred direct trade routes that did not rely on intermediary trading posts in Cádiz or Bordeaux. The impact of the Atlantic revolutions on the early modern trading networks clearly demonstrates that such networks could exist and thrive only under the Old Regime. German migration to Bordeaux virtually stopped in 1789. Only the firms of those German families who had invested early enough in the lucrative wine trade survived the French Revolution and the Napoleonic Empire. This group later provided a number of important notables in Bordeaux in the 19th century who still maintained close social and cultural contacts with Germany. Their business contacts with Germany, the Baltic, and eastern Europe secured their dominance in these wine markets. This cultural ambivalence was challenged only in 1870, with the outbreak of the Franco-Prussian War. Modern nationalism compelled the Germans in Bordeaux to take on French citizenship, which put an end to their simultaneous German and cosmopolitan identity in Bordeaux that dated back to the Old Regime.

The decline of the German trading post in Cádiz set in later, around 1810, after Spain's colonies in the Americas had gained independence. In the face of poor social integration and limited opportunities for investment outside of maritime trade, the fate of the colony was sealed. A small number of Westphalian and Bohemian families were, however, able to maintain their Spanish businesses into the 19th century while others moved to Mexico, Chile, or Peru. Only a branch of the Böhl family, hailing from Hamburg and active in the wine trade since approximately 1815, succeeded, as several German trading and wine growing dynasties had in Bordeaux, in taking advantage of the changes; it still exists today as a successful retailer of spirits and foodstuffs.

Henninger, Wolfgang. *Johann Jakob von Bethmann, 1717–1792. Kaufmann, Reeder und kaiserlicher Konsul in Bordeaux.* 2 vols. Bochum, 1993.

Jeannin, Pierre. "La clientèle étrangère de la maison Schröder et Schyler, de la Guerre de Sept ans à la Guerre d'Indépendance." *Bulletin du Centre d'Histoire des Espaces Atlantiques*, nouvelle série 3 (1987): 21–83.

Ruiz, Alain, ed. *Présence de l'Allemagne à Bordeaux du siècle de Montaigne à la veille de la Seconde Guerre mondiale.* Bordeaux, 1997.

Schebek, Edmund. *Böhmens Glasindustrie und Glashandel. Quellen zu ihrer Geschichte.* Prague, 1878 (reprint Frankfurt am Main, 1969).

Weber, Klaus. *Deutsche Kaufleute im Atlantikhandel 1680–1830. Unternehmen und Familien in Hamburg, Cádiz und Bordeaux.* Munich, 2004.

Cross-references: France; Germany; Spain and Portugal; Bohemian Glass Traders in Europe from the 17th to the 19th Century; Irish Brandy Merchants in the Charentes in the 18th Century

GERMAN MERCHANTS AND INDUSTRIAL ENTREPRENEURS IN RUSSIA SINCE THE 18TH CENTURY

Dittmar Dahlmann

Though German entrepreneurs were found in many Russian cities and in nearly all sectors of industry, in trade, and in banking, the primary centers were St. Petersburg, Moscow, Lodz, and Warsaw. There were also larger groups in the Baltic cities of Riga and Reval, along the Volga River in the area stretching from Samara to Saratov and all the way to Tsaritsyn, and in Odessa and a few other larger cities of the Black Sea region. The immigration occurred over a long period of time, and special conditions can be observed for each region. For example, German industrial entrepreneurs in the Volga and Black Sea region were recruited mostly from the ranks of the German colonists who had arrived in the 18th and the beginning of the 19th century, whereas in most other areas they had already arrived as craftsmen, merchants, or entrepreneurs. In the Baltic cities, the German class of industrial entrepreneurs came from the circles of craftsmen and merchants, many of whom had been living there since the late Middle Ages and the early modern period. A collective term "German entrepreneurs" or "German merchants" did not exist in the Russian Empire at the time, either as self-description or an outside label. And there were no ethnically based organizations of German merchants and entrepreneurs on the local, regional, or countrywide level.

Into the 19th century, the immigration of German-speaking merchants and entrepreneurs to Russia was a typical case of the migration of individuals or families. Individual merchants made their way to Russia even before the reign of Mikhail Feodorovich Romanov (1613–45), primarily to Moscow and the port city of Arkhangelsk. A stronger flow of immigration began in the 1630s. Since the cohabitation of Russians and foreigners was not tolerated by the czars and the church for political, religious, and cultural reasons, especially in Moscow, the foreigners lived in the "foreign or German suburb" (*nemeckaja sloboda*). It is not clear whether a foreigners' suburb existed in Arkhangelsk. The suburb in Moscow had about 100 families at the turn of the 17th century; about a third were merchants.

Vigorous immigration began with Russia's opening to the West under Peter I (1682–1725) and especially after 1712 with the move of the capital from Moscow to the newly founded St. Petersburg. Many immigrants hailed from northern Germany, especially the two large Hanseatic cities of Lübeck and Hamburg, but also from the ranks of the Baltic-Germans in Estonia and Livonia. In addition, there was a numerically significant immigration of Dutchmen and Englishmen, which continued into the 19th century.

Foreign merchants and entrepreneurs encountered exceedingly favorable conditions in the Russian Empire from the time of Czar Peter I. Russian merchants had too little capital and knowledge to engage in long-distance trade with Europe and Asia and set up manufactures, and a Russian merchant fleet was virtually nonexistent. In part because of their highly favorable commercial treaties, which largely excluded any competition, English merchants, active in the Muscovite Empire since the mid-16th century, dominated the Russian market until the end of the 18th century. During the Napoleonic period, but especially after the Congress of Vienna, the German merchants developed into the dominant trading group as the interests of the English shifted to the British colonies.

Many of the German entrepreneurs who arrived in growing numbers in the 19th century initially arrived as individual migrants. Often they had few assets and in some cases they came as employees or on behalf of a company. Family members – especially brothers, uncles, or nephews – for the most part followed only after receiving a positive assessment of the market opportunities or in the wake of the first commercial successes. With support from his family, an entrepreneur began to build a company that would remain in family hands for decades. Family members received shares or stocks with or without voting rights. In some cases, an entrepreneur's rise was also supported by a family that resided in German lands or in other parts of Europe.

The German entrepreneurial class that emerged from the ranks of the colonists in the compact German settlement regions along the middle Volga and on the Black Sea for the most part processed agricultural products of the region or supplied the agricultural sector with technical equipment: along the Volga there arose a mill industry and a textile manufacture that specialized in *sarpinka*, a blend of linen and cotton. The Black Sea region saw the development especially of an agricultural machine industry.

It is hardly possible to provide reliable figures on the size of the group of German entrepreneurs or merchants in Russia. Data on the urban population, for the most part collected only from the middle of the 19th century onward, are too vague in their categories to furnish clear information. For example, Russian statistics recorded only social estates and lumped together all foreign citizens in the category "nationality." In the larger cities of the Russian Empire, the share of German entrepreneurs at the turn of the 19th century can be estimated at about 10%–12% of the entire German population. In St. Petersburg and Moscow, that amounted to substantially less than 1% of the entire urban population – in St. Petersburg, the German-speaking population made up 2.6% of the total population (41,280), in Moscow 2% (20,000).

In the two urban centers of the Empire, the immigrant German entrepreneurs formed part of a German group that was already broadly differentiated in social terms. They largely retained their language and religion. The overwhelming majority (80%–90%) was Protestant. The most important focal points of German life were the parishes, which maintained their own schools and charitable organizations and developed an active social life. From the middle of the 19th century, German entrepreneurs supplanted the previously dominant, German-speaking nobility in the major offices, on the committees of the community, in schools, and in charitable institutions (for example, municipal and school councils, presbyteries, advisory boards).

Within the larger Russian cities in the 19th century, the Germans thus formed a largely self-contained community, whose institutions were crucially dependent on financial support from the entrepreneurial class. Alongside the already mentioned ecclesiastical institutions, there were German-language publishers who published newspapers, magazines, and books; there were also associations, clubs, restaurants, and numerous shops run by Germans. Integration was not a compelling necessity either for daily or commercial life. Until the end of the 19th century, the Russian state, too, did not in principle expect any moves toward integration. The foreigners living in the country were not even consistently encouraged to become Russian citizens. Consequently, as documented by the history of the German family business Wogau (established in the 1840s), several generations remained German citizens until the outbreak of World War I. And this family was not an isolated case: it was only in the decades before the outbreak of World War I, which were characterized by a heightened nationalism, that the German immigrants in Russia were linked to the idea of a "German threat."

In nearly all German families of entrepreneurs, marriages were concluded only within the German group until the third – and sometimes even the fourth – generation. Alongside economic and class interests, this endogamous behavior resulted from the strong integration of these families into the German communities and especially the confessional differences: in principle, children who resulted from a marriage to an Orthodox partner could only be baptized as Orthodox.

A cultural process of integration often began with the language, which was frequently laced with Russianisms. The use of diminutives as the first name, as is customary in Russia, as well as the custom of addressing someone by the person's first and father's name point to this development. This process carried over into the decoration of domestic space: the "nice corner" of the living room was at times even adorned with an icon. The Germans often began to celebrate church feast days, especially Easter, according to Russian customs. Above all, however, the entire family along with some of their servants and household goods moved to the dacha for the summer months.

German entrepreneurs participated actively in the self-governing bodies of the entrepreneurial class in the Czarist Empire and were often elected to leading positions. For example, numerous German entrepreneurs held the important post of alderman of the stock exchange in Moscow. They were also deeply involved in the establishment of associations of the entrepreneurial class of the Russian Empire, which began especially after the revolution of 1905–6, though at no time did they form a separate association with an ethnonational basis.

The tremendous economic success of German entrepreneurs in Russia in the 19th and early 20th centuries is documented in St. Petersburg by Alexander Baron Stieglitz, who made his mark primarily as a banker; Leopold König, who

The Moscovite textile entrepreneur Ludwig Baron Knoop and his wife, Luise, in the 1880s (*private ownership*).

The villa of the König family in St. Petersburg at the end of the 19th century (*private ownership*).

became known as the "sugar king"; and the merchant houses of Spies, Amburger, and Mollwo. Moscow witnessed the unparalleled rise of the textile company of Ludwig Knoop, on whom Czar Alexander II conferred the hereditary title of baron, and whose company operated around the world. The entrepreneurial elite of the city included also the families of Wogau, Marc, Bansa, Zenker, Spieß, Heuss, and List. In Odessa the families Mahs, Schulz, Fenderich, Kommerell, and Höhn made a name for themselves; in Lodz it was the entrepreneurs Scheibler, Heinzel, Grohmann, Meyer, Herbst, Geyer, and Kunischer. In the Volga region the companies Borell, Reinecke, Schmidt, and Bender became especially prominent; in the Black Sea region were found the enterprises Lepp & Wallmann and Neufeld. In spite of its marginal location, the merchant house of Kunst & Albers, with headquarters in Vladivostok, was known throughout Russia.

The nationalization policy of the Bolsheviks who emerged victorious from the October Revolution of 1917 put an end to the successful activities of the German entrepreneurs. A great many families left Soviet Russia and moved their activities to Germany or other countries. However, in many cases their factories and company headquarters still existed at the beginning of the 21st century, though under different names.

Amburger, Erik. *Fremde und Einheimische im Wirtschafts- und Kulturleben des neuzeitlichen Rußland. Ausgewählte Aufsätze.* Wiesbaden, 1982.

Amburger, Erik. *Deutsche in Staat, Wirtschaft und Gesellschaft Rußlands. Die Familie Amburger in St. Petersburg 1770–1920.* Wiesbaden, 1986.

Dahlmann, Dittmar. "Lebenswelt und Lebensweise deutscher Unternehmer in Moskau vom Beginn des 19. Jahrhunderts bis zum Ausbruch des Ersten Weltkrieges." *Nordost-Archiv,* N.F. 3 (1994): 133–63.

Dahlmann, Dittmar. "Unternehmer als Migranten im Russischen Reich." In *Migration nach Ost- und Südosteuropa vom 18. bis zum Beginn des 19. Jahrhunderts. Ursachen – Formen – Verlauf – Ergebnis,* edited by Mathias Beer and Dittmar Dahlmann, 235–44. Stuttgart, 1999.

Dahlmann Dittmar, and Carmen Scheide, eds. "*... das einzige Land in Europa, das eine große Zukunft vor sich hat.*" *Deutsche Unternehmen und Unternehmer im Russischen Reich im 19. und frühen 20. Jahrhundert.* Essen, 1998.

Cross-references: The Baltic Region; Germany; Poland; Russia; German Settlers in Russia since the 18th Century

GERMAN REFUGEES AND EXPELLEES FROM EASTERN, EAST-CENTRAL, AND SOUTHEASTERN EUROPE IN GERMANY AND AUSTRIA SINCE THE END OF WORLD WAR II

Arnd Bauerkämper

The place that German refugees and expellees held in the "collective memory" in West and East Germany as well as Austria after World War II was shaped not only by the respective interests of the actors but also by how they saw themselves and how others saw them. The relationship between the new arrivals and the old-established population was always an asymmetrical interaction in which diverse ascriptions and projections overlapped and intermixed. At the same time, there was a discrepancy between the official culture of remembrance and personal memory, especially in the Soviet Occupation Zone (SOZ) and the GDR. Remembering and forgetting were not only individual processes; they were also socially negotiated and simultaneously interrelated in complex ways. Flight and expulsions as "places of remembrance" can therefore be grasped analytically as social constructs that were subject to the specific political conditions prevailing in Germany and Austria after World War II and the social change that took place.

What follows, after a brief explanation of the terms, is an account of the various migratory movements and the basic outlines of the integration of the refugees and expellees. Since the integration of refugees and expellees in Austria has been studied far less intensively than in the occupation zones in Germany and in the Federal Republic of Germany (FRG) and the German Democratic Republic (GDR), the essay will concentrate chiefly on the two German states.

German forced migrants: terms and categories

In common parlance, "refugees" in Germany and Austria were persons who had left their homes under circumstances that were at least in part of their own choosing, for example, with respect to the timing of the forced migration. By contrast, "expellees" (*Vertriebene*) described persons who had no or very few options during the forced migration. In all German occupation zones and in Austria, the terms "refugee" and "expellee" were largely used as synonymous in everyday life. This linguistic usage was as widespread among the old-established population as it was among the forced migrants.

In the official language, however, differing political goals and structures emerged early on in the SOZ and the GDR, on the one hand, and in the Western occupation zones and the FRG, on the other. In Sepember 1945, the Soviet occupying power pushed through the term "resettler" (*Umsiedler*). This linguistic policy reflected above all the goals of the leadership of the German Communist Party (KPD) and of the relevant Soviet and German authorities to integrate the forced migrants rapidly into their "new homeland" and to stop a debate about a revision of the postwar borders. The subsequently established term "former resettler" was intended to signal that the immigrants held the status of "resettlers" only during a transition phase. This focus on the future was even more obvious with the use of "new citizen" (*Neubürger*) by the Soviet occupational administration and the party leadership of the Socialist Unity Party of Germany (SED). By 1948–9, the integration of the refugees was seen as largely completed. As a corollary, the new rulers forbade discussion of the specific identities and problems of the forced migrants in the GDR. After the SED leadership recognized the Oder and western Neiße as Poland's western borders in the Treaty of Görlitz on 6 July 1950, the pressure to suppress all these issues became overwhelming. As a result, even the term "new citizen" disappeared in the GDR in the 1950s. Expulsion and expellees remained important themes only in literary works, at least until 1955 and then again during the final 15 years of the SED regime.

In West Germany, uniform legal terms were established only in the Federal Expellee Law of 19 May 1953. According to this law, "expellees" (*Vertriebene*) were Germans of the Reich (*Reichsdeutsche*) and "ethnic Germans" (*Volksdeutsche*) who had been expelled from their homelands. The term "homeland expellees" (*Heimatvertriebene*) applied to those individuals in this group who had already lived in the "expulsion area" (*Vertreibungsgebiet*) on or before 31 December 1937. Administrative practice distinguished from this group the "newcomers" (*Zugewanderte*), those who had lived on the territory of the SOZ/GDR or in greater Berlin on 1 September 1939 and were not refugees. However, in the self-description of the forced migrants, these terms overlapped as frequently as they did in the constructions of the "other" by the native population.

Basic outlines of the migratory movement

The flight set in when the Soviety army units reached the German settlement areas in eastern, east-central, and southeastern Europe in the fall of 1944. The majority of the forced migrants fled into the territory of what was to become occupied Germany later on. Others were overrun by the Red Army, since German officials and the Wehrmacht had given the order to evacuate the threatened areas too late. Numerous refugees who were overtaken by the Soviet troops subsequently returned to their native towns and villages. After the end of World War II, Germans were systematically expelled, especially in Poland, Czechoslovakia, and Romania. Once Soviet officers and Polish officials had closed the crossing points on the Oder and Neiße in July 1945, the refugees and expellees were no longer able to return to their homeland east of these rivers. In addition, the Soviet Union prohibited the "unorganized" expulsions to stop the chaos of an uncontrolled influx of refugees and expellees. But the prohibition was also due to the imminent Potsdam Conference, where the victorious allies demarcated Poland's western border at the Oder and the western Neiße and agreed on the "transfer" of the Germans from Poland, Hungary, and Czechoslovakia "in an orderly and humane fashion." Although the spontaneous expulsions were not completely stopped, the focus was increasingly on transports following bilateral agreements. After the Allied Control Council presented its "transfer plan" in November 1945, 1.38 million German citizens were moved in 1946 alone from the new western Polish territories into the British Occupation Zone (Operation Swallow).

Although migration movements in the opposite direction were recorded until the summer of 1945, the westward flight dominated the migratory processes, which had been triggered not least by the Nazi regime with its brutal policy of moving and annihilating populations in east-central Europe. By the end of October 1946, around 10 million German refugees and expellees had reached the four occupation zones; 1.7 million had been victims of forced migration. In December 1947, 4.4 million refugees lived in the SOZ, where they made up 24.3% of the population; 3 million had settled in the American zone (17.7%), 3.3 million in the British zone (14.5%), and 60,000 in the French zone (1%). By 1950, the Federal Republic had taken in 7.9 million refugees and expellees, the GDR 4.1 million, and Austria 370,000. In the territory of the FRG, the share of these forced migrants of the overall population rose between 1950 and 1956 from 16.5% to 17.5%. By contrast, refugees (including displaced persons and former prisoners

Expellees arrive at the Berlin railway station Lichterfelde-South in June 1945 (*Deutsches Historisches Museum, Berlin*).

of war) in Austria made up only around 6% of the population in 1953. The largest group of expellees to reach Austria were the 170,000 Danube-Swabians, although nearly as many Germans from Czechoslovakia (151,000) had arrived in Austria. All told, between 1945 and the end of 1958, around 481,000 German refugees and expellees came to the Alpine Republic; of those, 47% acquired Austrian citizenship.

In West and East Germany, as in Austria, the refugees and expellees were initially steered to the countryside, where they found shelter and could be provisioned with food. As late as September 1950, 47.2% of forced migrants in the FRG were still living in communities with fewer than 3,000 residents, where only 32.8% of the old-established population lived. The agrarian regions of the SOZ/GDR recorded an even higher concentration of the refugee population in the countryside. Of the total of 12.5 million German refugees and expellees registered in the two German states in 1950, 56.1% came from the former German territories in the east, 24.5% from Czechoslovakia, and 11.3% from territories that had already been part of the Polish state before World War II.

The 1950s saw the beginnings of an internal migration in both German states; it was smaller in Austria, but in all three states it was inadequately recorded statistically. In the SOZ the "resettlers" were the most important target group of the "labor force guidance" (*Arbeitskräftelenkung*) that began in 1946 and was intended to provide workers and employees especially to the new industrial enterprises and the growing public administration. In the FRG the state-guided resettlement began in 1949: between 1950 and 1960, four large-scale resettlement actions brought a total of 957,462 forced migrants from Schleswig-Holstein, Lower Saxony, and Bavaria into other federal states. Even more important in both German states, however, was the voluntary onward migration of refugees and expellees. For example, in the 1950s in the FRG, 1.7 million moved to a different state. Overall, with the rebuilding of the cities and the industrial enterprises in the two German states and in Austria, the forced migrants generally moved from the countryside to the growing urban centers and from the primary sector into the commercial economy. In addition, between 1950 and 1961, the FRG registered 3.6 million individuals who had arrived from the GDR. Of those, around one-quarter were refugees and expellees. However, 487,000 West Germans also resettled in the GDR in the 1950s. Internal migration and the migration processes between and within the two German states intermixed the population and corrected the initial misdirection of workers.

Thousands of forced migrants moved on to other countries. Especially "ethnic German" refugees and expellees, many of whom the Allied government evidently categorized as displaced persons, left East and West Germany for France and Great Britain, later also for Canada and the USA.

Formation of minorities and patterns of integration

In the initial postwar years, German refugees and expellees in Germany and Austria were clearly identifiable minorities, whose marginal social status was consolidated and prolonged in equal measure by external ascriptions and self-images. To begin with, the minority status arose chiefly from the gross material discrimination against forced migrants. As late as the 1950s, refugees and expellees who had to apply for aid were still provided with much less living space and far fewer essential consumer goods than the old-established population. In Austria, for example, 45,000 to 50,000 German newcomers were still living in camps in the early 1950s. Unemployment was also above average among the forced migrants. Refugees and expellees who had been able to find work were often hired below their qualifications.

The arrival of the forced migrants led to a far-reaching occupational and social process of descent into lower social classes. The newcomers suffered much more strongly from inter- and intragenerational social decline than the old-established population. Until the 1960s, refugees and expellees in the Federal Republic and Austria were overrepresented among dependent employees, while they remained underrepresented among the self-employed. In the GDR, even though the policy of nationalization and collectivization that began in the late 1940s in industry and agriculture had an equalizing effect, it did not immediately remedy the material disadvantage of the forced migrants. The loss of status was especially pronounced for the farmers among the refugees and expellees. The occupational integration of the forced migrants into the agrarian economy was on the whole too weak in both German states to make a significant contribution to the social integration of this population group. In Austria, as well, around a third of the German refugees and expellees worked in agriculture in 1950. However, contrary to the hopes of the political elites, the deployment of the new arrivals did not boost the efficiency of agricultural production, just as it failed to increase productivity in industry, where another third of the forced migrants worked as skilled laborers in 1950.

Beginning in the late 1940s, newly arrived Germans also began to take jobs at an increasing rate in industrial and

Emergency accommodation for refugees and expellees, around 1946 (*Deutsches Historisches Museum, Berlin*).

commercial enterprises, often following a change in their place of residence. In the SOZ, it was especially state-supported "resettler cooperatives" that aided integration into the commercial economy, in which private property had already been largely eliminated in the 1950s. Here officials also helped refugees and expellees to find jobs in the service sector. However, in both German states currency reform and currency conversion in 1948 delayed the occupational integration, which made significant progress only with the economic upswing in the 1950s. In Austria, the signing of the State Treaty in 1955 formed an important foundation for the integration of the expellees alongside economic growth, not least in that the agreement established the framework for the government's refugee policy. Thanks to their pronounced desire to rise up the social ladder, their resultant willingness to work hard, and their high mobility, the refugees and expellees slowly overcame their minority status in the three countries in question.

However, this did not mean that the social integration of the forced migrants had been achieved because the marginalization of this group resulted not only from material inequality but also from specific sociocultural factors. When it became clear that an immediate return of the newly arrived refugees and expellees to their homeland was out of the question, conflicts between the newcomers and the natives over how to divide up the economic resources generally surged in the two German states and in Austria. Bitter conflicts broke out in many communities over the allocation and use of housing, especially in the countryside. The distribution of other goods, such as furniture, was also intensely controversial.

Cultural differences between the forced migrants and the established population exacerbated the conflicts. In the villages, where the majority of refugees and expellees initially settled, rural dwellers encountered city dwellers, Protestants encountered Catholics, and refugee farmers encountered farmers whose property had come through the war unscathed. The social envy of the newcomers, but also defensive reflexes by the native population, triggered social conflicts that were

difficult to resolve. In the eyes of many natives the newcomers were unwelcome foreigners onto whom were projected the traditional prejudices against "the East" and "the Slavs," as is clearly revealed by the name "Polacks" that was given to them. Only slowly and reluctantly were the forced migrants accepted into local organizations, at first always into sports clubs. The combination of material inequality and different customs, habits, and way of life created a minority status that the refugees and expellees were unable to overcome even with growing intermarriage.

Religious difference also contributed to the marginalization of the forced migrants, especially that between Roman Catholics and Protestants. Although in many places even Protestant-Lutheran and Protestant-Reformed congregations drew lines of separation between one another, the social circles of refugees and natives slowly intersected more and more, especially among the young generation. In West Germany, 53.9% of the newcomers were already marrying natives between 1946 and 1950, and in 1961–70 the figure was up to 68%. However, one must take into account the unequal size of the two population groups. Moreover, marriages between expellees and natives often created serious intrafamilial tensions and conflicts. On the whole, the integration of the forced migrants had made progress in the 1950s, but it was by no means complete. Social integration was completed only by the change in generations, as especially the sociologist Paul Lüttinger has demonstrated in the case of the FRG.

Government subsidies mitigated the privation of the refugees and expellees but were unable to prevent their marginalization. In 1945 and 1946 all zones of occupation saw the establishment of special agencies that were to ensure a rapid integration of the forced migrants. However, the measures ordered by the bureaucracy in charge of the refugees were contradictory, for while they improved the material situation of the newcomers, they simultaneously solidified their minority status. For example, redistribution and collections in favor of the refugees and expellees reinforced the envy of the natives. State laws also heightened the aversion to the unloved newcomers, though the latter were slowly able to shake the stigma of welfare recipients with the help of government aid. For example, the Law to Remedy Urgent Social Distress (Immediate Aid Law) took effect on 8 August 1949 in the Bizone; it provided monthly assistance with a base amount of 70 Deutschmarks (DM). This was the first time the refugees and expellees were given a legal claim to state allocations. Finally, on 16 May 1952, the German parliament approved the law about burden sharing, which granted German newcomers compensation for property losses. The payment modalities favored those who had suffered minor losses, as they were able to reclaim a larger share of their lost property than victims who had suffered substantial losses. By 1979, a total of around 150 billion DM had been distributed to refugees and expellees in the Federal Republic to promote integration and provide compensation.

In the SOZ, by contrast, the SED leadership blocked a prepared law on burden sharing in October 1948. Under the Law on the Further Improvement of the Situation of Former Resettlers (Resettler Law) that was eventually passed on 8 September 1950, refugees and expellees could apply for an interest-free loan of 1,000 marks per household for furniture and household goods. However, German migrants who had a high income were excluded from receiving aid, and the repayment requirements scared off especially pensioners and welfare recipients. In the GDR, all laws dealing specifically with the group of forced migrants expired in 1952–3. The agencies charged with looking after and integrating the forced migrants, which had been set up immediately after the war, had already been dissolved in 1948. The emergence of state socialism went hand in hand with a policy of coerced social homogenization. However, the temporary special administration that had been set up for the forced migrants had to suspend its operation also in West Germany in the late 1940s, as it encountered resistance from the regular municipal authorities and the native population.

In Austria, the first equalization laws were not passed until 1952. Legally, too, the German refugees and expellees remained noticeably disadvantaged compared to the native Austrians in the 1950s. In expectation of a final regulation in the announced state treaty with the Allied Powers, the Austrian government refused in principle to recognize an obligation to integrate German refugees and expellees. The integration of this group was closely linked with the policy toward former forced laborers and prisoners of war who had been taken to Austria during World War II. Even though the government increasingly accepted integration as a political goal, it still had no coherent concept in the late 1950s. Since fear of a rise in unemployment was widespread also within the native population, the state did not provide much financial support. The expenditure on refugees, which had reached 3.4% of the bugdet and 0.5% of GDP in 1948, had dropped to 1.1% and 0.2%, respectively, by 1951. However, important impulses toward an integration of refugees and expellees had already come in the postwar period from churches and voluntary aid organizations, who got involved in housing construction and setting up new businesses. And from the end of 1951, a representative of the United Nations' High Commission for Refugees in Vienna also offered support intended to promote the integration of refugees into postwar Austrian society.

Immediately after the end of the war, the Allied Powers had suppressed the establishment of refugee and expellee organizations in all zones in Germany and Austria in order to prevent political protests. The refugee committees that had already been set up in 1945–6 were tightly controlled by the military governments and the German authorities. Beyond these committees, the authorities only occasionally permitted autonomous local organization that were largely nonpolitical. After interest communities of refugees and expellees had been organized as early as 1947, in part in close imitation of occupational organizations, the

"prohibition on association" (Koalitionsverbot) was finally lifted in West Germany in the summer of 1948. However, this had a quite ambivalent effect on the integration of the newcomers: on the one hand, it allowed them to articulate their identity as refugees or expellees; on the other hand, in many cases it reinforced their marginalization in that they themselves construed their "otherness" and thereby unwittingly confirmed the ascriptions of outsiders. Still, even membership in the League of Expellees and Those Deprived of their Rights (Bund der Heimatvertriebenen und Entrechteten, BHE), founded in 1950–1 as the political lobby of the expellees in Schleswig-Holstein, delayed the integration process only insignificantly. The BHE, which prefixed the phrase All-German Bloc (Gesamtdeutscher Block, GB) to its name in 1952, encompassed at most one-fifth of the refugees and expellees. Although the GB/BHE, whose goals were supported by only 5% of the longtime residents, was represented in a few state parliaments and from 1953 to 1957 also in the Bundestag, the party folded in 1961.

By contrast, in the SOZ/GDR the formation of separate refugee organizations was ruthlessly suppressed. The Soviet military administration, in close collaboration with leading functionaries of the KPD, pushed through a policy of controlled integration. For example, the newly established Central Administration for German Resettlers ordered as early as September 1945 the formation in communities and districts of Resettler Committees that were to be made up of representatives of the native population and of the newcomers and promote the interests of the "resettlers" in the local and regional bureaucracies. However, in 1947 the SED leadership rejected the formation of a Central Resettler Committee as originally planned in order to contain the danger that the refugees and expellees might organize themselves. And in November of 1948, the Central Secretariat of the SED even decided to dissolve all "resettler committees." Subsequently, the party leadership and agencies reduced the policy of integration even further to its material and economic dimension, and they suppressed the cultural identity of the refugees and expellees. For example, in 1950 the East German Ministry of the Interior prohibited public statements that made reference to the homeland of migrants. However, that did not rule out private meetings or the formation of informal groups. Even though the refugees and expellees – now labeled at best "new citizens" – were spied on and monitored, the early 1950s did see secret meetings that were broken up by the police.

The "expellees" retained a much longer and more intense presence in the collective memory of the West Germans. Anticommunism and revisionist demands, which were in principle supported by the federal government under Konrad Adenauer, sustained the memory of flight and expulsion, as did the obsolete notion of the "German homeland in the East." In the final analysis, however, the experiences and history of the forced migrants were not incorporated into the historical awareness of the West Germans. Flight and expulsion did not find a central place of commemoration in the Federal Republic; rather, they were politically instrumentalized. For example, 400–500 monuments that were set up in the 1950s were intended to document the migrants' right of return. In addition, numerous films and literary works supported the tendency to morally equate crimes *against* Germans with crimes committed *by* Germans during World War II.

In this discourse of remembrance, the expellees appeared once again as victims, but not as subjects acting autonomously and with their specific emotional ties to their homeland. The result was a tendency in the Federal Republic to privatize and marginalize individual experiences and the status of these people as refugees and expellees. Finally, in the 1960s and 1970s, the forced migrants and their experiences of flight and expulsion were pushed as thoroughly to the margins of political discussion as was their memory of their homeland. In Austria it was – until the 1980s – seemingly above all the official self-conception of the Republic as an object or even victim of the Nazi policy of expansion that deflected attention away from the refugees. However, in the two German states and in Austria there were also many German forced migrants who – determined to climb back up the social ladder – suppressed their own experiences of flight and expulsion as well as the memory of their homeland. In so doing they not only adopted outside categorizations without reflecting on them, but they also unwittingly delayed or blocked an open debate about the forced migration of Germans from eastern, central-eastern, and southeastern Europe.

Only the change of generations and the unification of Germany have cast a clearer light on the successes and limitations of refugee integration in the GDR, the FRG, and in Austria. On the whole, the extent of the integration defies a monocausal explanation. Rather, integration was shaped by numerous factors – such as life experiences before 1945, the routes of flight, the reactions of the native populations after the arrival of the refugees in the new settlement regions, and the intensity of the desire to return. In addition, one must take into account generation- and gender-specific differences as well as differences between various occupational groups. But integration was not unidirectional either in the two German states or in Austria: although the refugees and expellees were for a long time pushed into a marginal social position, they rattled entrenched milieus – especially in the countryside – and altered outmoded ways of life in the societies that took them in. However, the cultural and mental pressure toward integration was generally so strong in the countries in question that conformity and the striving for professional, economic, and social advancement were rewarded in the host societies. While this did not by any means break the identities of the refugees and expellees as minorities, the individual memory of the homeland in the official culture of remembrance was largely tailored to the needs of the old-established elites. Though largely displaced from the collective memory of the German and Austrian postwar societies, the minorities of the forced migrants after 1945 have certainly left distinct traces in Germany and (less noticeably) in Austria.

Bade, Klaus J., ed. *Neue Heimat im Westen. Vertriebene, Flüchtlinge, Aussiedler*. Münster, 1990.

Bauerkämper, Arnd. "Assimilationspolitik und Integrationsdynamik. Vertriebene in der Sowjetischen Besatzungszone/DDR in vergleichender Perspektive." In *Integrationen. Vertriebene in den deutschen Ländern nach 1945*, edited by Marita Krauss, 22–47. Göttingen, 2008.

Benz, Wolfgang. *Die Vertreibung der Deutschen aus dem Osten. Ursachen, Ereignisse, Folgen*. Frankfurt am Main, 1985.

Bingen, Dieter, Włodimierz Borodziej, and Stefan Troebst, eds. *Vertreibungen europäisch erinnern? Historische Erfahrungen – Vergangenheitspolitik – Zukunftskonzeptionen*. Wiesbaden, 2003.

Faulenbach, Bernd. "Die Vertreibung der Deutschen aus den Gebieten jenseits von Oder und Neiße. Zur wissenschaftlichen und öffentlichen Diskussion in Deutschland." *Aus Politik und Zeitgeschichte* B 51–52 (2002): 44–54.

Frantzioch, Marion. *Die Vertriebenen. Hemmnisse, Antriebskräfte und Wege ihrer Integration in der Bundesrepublik Deutschland*. Berlin, 1987.

Franzen, K. Erik. *Die Vertriebenen. Hitlers letzte Opfer*. Munich, 2001.

Hahn, Eva, and Hans Henning Hahn. "Flucht und Vertreibung." In *Deutsche Erinnerungsorte*, edited by Etienne François and Hagen Schulze, vol. 1, 335–51, 695–7. Munich, 2001.

Hoffmann, Dierk, Marita Krauss, and Michael Schwartz, eds. *Vertriebene in Deutschland. Interdisziplinäre Ergebnisse und Forschungsperspektiven*. Munich, 2000.

Lotz, Christian. *Die Bedeutung des Verlusts. Erinnerungspolitische Kontroversen im geteilten Deutschland um Flucht, Vertreibung und die Ostgebiete (1948–1972)*. Cologne, 2007.

Lüttinger, Paul. *Integration der Vertriebenen. Eine empirische Analyse*. Frankfurt am Main, 1989.

Schwartz, Michael. *Vertriebene und "Umsiedlerpolitik." Integrationskonflikte in den deutschen Nachkriegs-Gesellschaften und die Assimilationsstrategien in der SBZ/DDR 1945 bis 1961*. Munich, 2004.

Stanek, Eduard. *Verfolgt – verjagt – vertrieben. Flüchtlinge in Österreich*. Vienna, 1985.

Cross-references: Austria; The Baltic Region; Czechia and Slovakia; Germany; Poland; Russia and Belarus; Southeastern Europe; *Aussiedler/Spätaussiedler* in Germany since 1950; Austrian Protestants (*Landler*) in Transylvania since the 18th Century; Displaced Persons (DPs) in Europe since the End of World War II; Ethnic Germans (*Volksdeutsche*) in the German Reich and in German-Occupied Territories in World War II; German Deportees from East-Central and Southeastern Europe in the USSR after the End of World War II; German Refugees and Immigrants from East Germany in West Germany; German Settlers in Russia since the 18th Century; German Settlers (*Donauschwaben*) in Southeastern Europe since the Early Modern Period; Salzburg Protestants in East Prussia since the 18th Century

GERMAN REFUGEES AND IMMIGRANTS FROM EAST GERMANY IN WEST GERMANY

Helge Heidemeyer

The category of refugees and immigrants from the Soviet Occupation Zone (SOZ) and the GDR to West Germany applies to those who left the territory of the future GDR after the Soviet Red Army crossed the borders of the Reich and came to West Germany. No general term for this group has been established. This was the result of the legal differentiation within this group in West Germany (to be discussed below), the use of a similar label for expellees, and the different label given to this group of individuals in West and East Germany. Here the totality of these migrants is subsumed under the phrase "emigrants from the SOZ/GDR."

The decision to leave the SOZ/GDR was made on an individual basis, though it was always shaped by the occupation of the Soviet army and the establishment and expansion of a socialist system, even if at times the influence was only indirect. Thus, this migration had a political dimension even if the concrete background to the exodus was at first glance nonpolitical but economic in nature. Still, legally the immigration could be described as flight only if the person was escaping "danger to life and limb" (federal Emergency Admission Law of 22 August 1950). This applied to a great many migrants, but not to all of them.

Culturally and socially the migration from East to West Germany can be seen as internal migration because it took place within the same linguistic region, there were few cultural inhibitions to overcome, and the problems of integration therefore remained fairly minor.

The immigration from the SOZ/GDR occurred continuously through the entire period; the only aspect that varied was its extent. Table 1 provides an overview of the immigration, supplemented by the migration from West Germany to the GDR. Since the absolute numbers are not reliable, the figures from the migration statistics are juxtaposed to the statistics of emergency admissions. At the very least, the numbers offer an indication of certain magnitudes and trends.

The two turning points of 1961 and 1989 are immediately apparent: they were the result of the construction of the Berlin Wall and the opening of the border. All other fluctuations can be attributed to the policy of the GDR. It created the atmosphere that favored the decision to leave East Germany: the motivations ranged from vague discontent about economic conditions to an acute threat to a person's safety and life. Some of the reasons directly mirror the politics and the situation in the SOZ/GDR, such as the flight of Nazi officials from the advancing Soviet army, the departure of farmers during the phases of planned collectivization, or the wave of refugees in the years of increasing political and economic pressure in 1952–3 and after June 17, 1953. The strong immigration in 1984, when the number of applications in the emergency admission procedure surged from 10,700 to 38,700, on the one hand shows the influence of the billion-marks loan arranged by Bavarian Minister-President Franz Josef Strauß, and on the other documents the decision by the GDR government to "release" 32,000 individuals willing to abandon their GDR citizenship in an effort to improve the country's international image and calm the political situation at home.

These events reveal that the migration was largely determined by the push from the political, economic, and social situation in the GDR, but that to a certain extent the political and economic conditions in West Germany also exerted an attraction throughout the period. East Germans were well aware of conditions in the West thanks to West German media and a multitude of private contacts between the two Germanies.

On the whole, the migration was a mass phenomenon up to the building of the wall, after which time the final closing of the border substantially limited the possibilities of leaving. Only a small number of the immigrants after 1961 were – to use East German terminology – *Sperrbrecher* (blockade runners), whose often spectacular flight attracted attention in the West. Most immigrants left the GDR legally. Most of those were individuals who were not gainfully employed: of the immigrants registered in 1970, 85% fell into this category; 74% were pensioners who arrived largely as part of family reunification. In other words, East Germany gave permission to leave chiefly to those who were not only no longer economically productive, but were drawing social benefits.

For the most part the immigrants found a new home in the West. There was no significant onward migration to other countries. However, in the early years of the young West German republic such a migration was certainly discussed as a possible option, as long as the economic and social problems were still severe. These debates did not result in anything, but they do show that the immigrants from the SOZ/GDR were perceived as a burden. In the late 1940s and early 1950s they further exacerbated an economic and social situation already made difficult by the arrival of millions of expellees. At the same time, however, the Federal Republic could not and would not prevent these Germans from entering – all the more once the competition between the political systems was in full swing during the cold war. In that tense situation, the West German government made every effort to underscore the political nature of the immigration. It introduced the systematic vetting of the immigrants in the so-called emergency admission procedure. Those who could present credible political reasons for leaving were given preference and received government benefits, including especially quick access to housing and jobs. Those who did not meet these standards were left to their own devices, though they were allowed to remain in West Germany. By excluding a part of the immigrants from benefits, the federal government at the same time increased the acceptance by the population of those given preferential admission as political refugees.

Table 1. Immigration from the SOZ/GDR and the new federal states, 1944–1965 and 1986–1990, to West Germany (in thousands)				
	Census 1961	Migration statistics		Emergency admission statistics
	Citizens of the FRG with residence in 1939 in the future GDR, by year of arrival	Immigration from the GDR including East Berlin to the FRG without West Berlin	Emigration from the FRG without West Berlin to the GDR including East Berlin	Applicants
1944/45	290.3	–	–	–
1946	169.9	–	–	–
1947	133.0	–	–	–
1948	138.9	–	–	–
1949	144.1	–	–	59.2
1950	–	337.3	56.7	197.8
1951	–	287.8	45.3	165.6
1952	–	232.1	30.9	182.4
1953	–	408.1	28.1	331.4
1954	–	295.4	49.0	184.2
1955	–	381.8	48.7	252.9
1956	–	396.3	46.7	279.2
1957	–	384.7	52.6	261.6
1958	–	226.3	38.7	204.1
1959	–	173.8	38.7	143.9
1960	–	225.4	28.5	199.2
1961		233.5	23.1	207.0
1962		15.3	6.9	21.4
1963		35.0	4.1	42.7
1964		29.5	4.4	41.9
1965		29.5	5.6	29.6
1986		29.5	2.6	26.2
1987		22.8	2.4	19.0
1988		43.3	2.5	39.9
1989		388.4	5.1	343.9
1990		395.3	36.2	238.4
Total		4,571.1	556.8	3,471.5

Source: *Statistisches Jahrbuch* and author's calculations.

The government benefits extended to those immigrants classified as "genuine" refugees included their distribution among the federal states on the basis of quotas negotiated by the states. The channeling of the immigrants from the GDR was guided by the situation of the labor market in the various states. The primary destination state was therefore North Rhine–Westphalia, which at times had to take in two-thirds of those recognized as refugees. Finding housing for all of them subsequently proved to be the biggest problem. After North Rhine–Westphalia, during the height of the immigration in 1952–3, threatened to refuse admission to any more refugees, the federal government began to provide funds for housing construction starting in 1953.

With the economy moving into high gear during the time of the "economic miracle" and the demand for labor surging, the immigrants from East Germany were seen less and less as a burden: given the social structure of the immigrants, among whom single, young, skilled men predominated until 1961 (a year that marked a turning point

also in this regard), they made up the reservoir of workers that the West German labor market so urgently needed. That these workers came in a steady stream and could be integrated without social disruptions added to their value. As for the immigrants, it was very important that they were immediately entitled to social services in West Germany, if necessary. Assistance for special groups, such as political prisoners from the GDR, rounded out the support system (Prisoner Assistance Act of 6 August 1955). Still, a generous expansion of benefits – among them, for example, the complete inclusion in the equalization of war-related burdens – occurred only after 1961, when the influx had all but dried up and the improved benefits could no longer represent an incentive to leave the GDR. The assistance for refugees was first consolidated in 1953 in the Federal Expellee and Refugee Act (Bundesvertriebenen- und –flüchtlingsgesetz, BVFG). However, the legislature redefined the circle of those entitled ("Soviet zone refugees") more narrowly than the Emergency Admission Act had; the confusion of labels increased. In 1965, the "Soviet zone refugees" were given equal status to the expellees in terms of legal benefits in their own Refugee Assistance Act.

What characterized the groups of immigrants from the SOZ/GDR was their heterogeneity. The reasons that had prompted them to leave East Germany were very diverse. A small part of the immigrants were accused of having dishonest motives, such as spying for the GDR – not without reason, as we now know from documents from the East German State Security and as was demonstrated by the case of Günter Guillaume, after whose unmasking Chancellor Willy Brandt resigned office in 1974. Because the migrants left the GDR at different times, they had been shaped politically in very different ways. Not infrequently the immigrants of the first decade saw themselves as – sometimes – militant anticommunists who were strongly supportive of West Germany's "inner ties to the West." Later generations of immigrants had been socialized in the GDR, had internalized ideological elements of the political system even as they had reservations about it, and were often distanced and critical toward the system in West Germany. For example, some of the leading figures of the student movement in 1968 had immigrated from the GDR, the most prominent among them being Rudi Dutschke.

The way immigrants were treated in West Germany deepened their original heterogeneity as a group. The separation into Soviet zone refugees and nonrecognized refugees prevented the emergence of a group consciousness. Given the rapid integration into the labor market, in a society, furthermore, that seemed largely familiar, no collective consciousness of being different developed. It also helped that they were not as profoundly rejected as was initially the case with many expellees. To be sure, resentment existed in West German society also toward the immigrants from the GDR, especially in the early 1950s. On the whole, however, the relationship was much more relaxed, given the smaller (and also annual) extent of the influx, the more favorable economic preconditions for their admission, the politically desired acceptance of the immigrants as escapees from political despotism, and the emergence of an underclass of non-German "guest workers."

One mirror of this is the development of the associational life of the immigrants: it remained fractured into different territorial, occupational, and political organizations and showed a low level of organization. Only in the fall of 1969 was an umbrella organization for all immigrants from the SOZ/GDR founded with the League of Central Germans (Bund der Mitteldeutschen). The driving force behind this was the fundamental reorientation of the Germany policy since the middle of the 1960s, which culminated in the *Ostpolitik* of the Brandt government. The foundation of this organization at precisely this time was in line with the policy of the existing associations, which never conceived of themselves as purely interest organizations, but as the "conscience of the nation," as the Minister for Pan-German Affairs Jakob Kaiser (CDU) emphasized in 1953. They wanted to keep alive the issue of reunification and articulate the interests of the Germans in the GDR.

The tendency toward group cohesiveness remained weak among the immigrants. The only uniting characteristic, flight from the SOZ/GDR, was an individual act, and life in the Federal Republic also remained a personal experience for the immigrants. They were never present in the societal awareness of the receiving country as a social group. At the same time, leaving aside some initial signs during the distribution battles in the early years of the Federal Republic, they were not excluded or discriminated against. The precondition for integration without any larger social distortions was, first of all, their good potential for occupational integration, but also their basic mentality, which was positive toward West Germany. As a result, the immigrants from the SOZ/GDR retained an individualistic orientation and placed little stock in strong associational representation. With regard to the time of migration, geographic settlement, reception by West German society, self-conception, and interest representation, they formed a group that must be clearly distinguished from the German expellees from east-central, southeastern, and eastern Europe.

Ackermann, Volker. *Der »echte« Flüchtling. Deutsche Vertriebene und Flüchtlinge aus der DDR 1945–1961*. Osnabrück, 1995.

BMD-Handbuch, edited by the Bund der Mitteldeutschen. Part 2. Bonn, 1987.

Effner, Bettina, and Helge Heidemeyer, eds. *Flucht im geteilten Deutschland. Erinnerungsstätte Notaufnahmelager Marienfelde*. Berlin, 2005.

Heidemeyer, Helge. *Flucht und Zuwanderung aus der SBZ/DDR 1945/1949–1961. Die Flüchtlingspolitik der Bundesrepublik Deutschland bis zum Bau der Berliner Mauer*. Düsseldorf, 1994.

Kaase, Max. "Bewußtseinslagen und Leitbilder in der Bundesrepublik Deutschland." In *Deutschland-Handbuch. Eine doppelte Bilanz*, edited by Werner Weidenfeld and Hartmut Zimmermann, 203–20. Bonn, 1989.

Cross-references: Germany; *Aussiedler/Spätaussiedler* in Germany since 1950; German Refugees and Expellees from Eastern, East-Central, and Southeastern Europe in Germany and Austria since the End of World War I; Turkish Labor Migrants in Western, Central, and Northern Europe since the Mid-1950s

GERMAN SAILORS IN THE DUTCH MERCHANT MARINE FROM THE EARLY 17TH TO THE END OF THE 19TH CENTURY

Karel Davids

From the 17th century until well into the 19th century, German maritime labor migrants made up the most stable group of foreign sailors in the Netherlands, even though they were not the largest contingent of foreigners on all routes and in all branches of the Dutch merchant marine. Travel accounts and records of the personnel department of the Dutch East India Company (Verenigde Oostindische Compagnie, or VOC) show that Germans were already sailing on Dutch East-India ships in the first half of the 17th century. Their share among crews in the Dutch merchant marine probably was greatest between 1700 and 1870. In the 18th century, about one in two of all foreign seamen sailing on ships of the VOC hailed from Germany. The share of Germans among all seafarers employed on Dutch East India ships rose from about 10% in 1700 to more than 20% in the period between 1740 and 1790. In other branches of the Dutch mercantile marine, the percentage of Germans among foreign sailors increased from about 34% in 1700–10 to 52% in 1774–5 and finally to 73% in 1814–26. Their share of the total crew on Dutch merchant ships rose from an estimated 8% in 1700–10 to more than 30% in 1774–5, before dropping to around 17% in 1814–26. Although the presence of Germans on Dutch merchant ships in the later 19th century declined both in relative and absolute terms, they still formed in 1877 53% and in 1920 26% of all foreign seamen. In this period, they composed 8% and 2%, respectively, of the total crew of Dutch sailing vessels and steamships hired in Dutch ports.

The number of Germans who served on Dutch merchant ships is based on the estimated number of newly recruited personnel per year in all branches of merchant shipping. In the early 1700s, the inflow of German sailors in the East India Company may have been around 350, and in the rest of mercantile marine approximately 750 per year, given an annual total of 1,100 men (apart from a few women dressed as men, sailors were indeed all male). By the 1770s, these figures had probably risen to 1,000 and 6,300, respectively, resulting in an annual total of 7,300. In the mid-1820s, the number of Germans signing on for service on Dutch merchant ships had probably declined to no more than about 2,900 per year, sinking still lower, to around 750, by the early 1900s. Given the fact that total employment in the Dutch mercantile marine in the mid-19th century was much higher than in the 1820s (30,000 as opposed to 17,000 men), and assuming that the share of Germans had decreased to some 12% of the total crew, the annual inflow in the 1860s may have amounted to about 3,600 men.

German sailors had not always seen the sea before signing on. Many of them were in fact not trained sailors at all, particularly those thousands of Germans sailing on ships of the Dutch East India Company after 1750. Most of the German seamen on VOC ships in the early 18th century came from the Wadden Islands, Schleswig-Holstein, East-Frisia, and other areas bordering the North Sea or the Baltic Sea. In the final decades before the VOC dissolved in 1799, close to half of the German sailors originated from Saxony, Thuringia, Swabia, Westphalia, Hessen-Kassel, and other German-speaking regions in the interior of the Holy Roman Empire. These areas largely lay outside the "North Sea System" of seasonal labor migration, which brought thousands of peat cutters and reapers primarily from northwest Germany to the agricultural areas of the Netherlands. German sailors in

other branches of the merchant marine about 1700 also came almost exclusively from the coastal areas along the North Sea and the Baltic Sea. Whether the geographical distribution of these seamen later in the 18th century changed in the same way as in the case of East India Company remains unclear.

There are hardly any indications of systematic campaigns to recruit Germans for service in the Dutch merchant marine. Even the East India Company never staged a full-blown recruiting drive in Germany to fill its ships. Germans traveled of their own accord, individually or in small groups, to Amsterdam, Hoorn, Enkhuizen, or other seaports in the western Netherlands before engaging on a merchant ship or entering the service of the VOC. If these migrants fell into the hands of impressment agents, which was not uncommon, it was only after their arrival in a port town in Holland.

Germans enlisted on Dutch merchants with varied motives. Some of the new recruits of the VOC were primarily driven by curiosity to see the world – according to travel accounts by Germans who sailed on East Indiamen. Others joined the company to escape creditors at home or to evade the reach of the law. But the vast majority of the Germans who decided to sign on with the VOC did so for economic reasons. Although the pay of seamen on VOC ships was low compared to the wage level in other jobs in the Dutch economy, migrants from Germany nevertheless earned more in the company's service than in most forms of employment in their own region. Given the lower standard of living in his home country, a German sailor's VOC salary of seven to twelve guilders a month was essentially a higher real income than it was for a native Dutchman. Signing on with the VOC thus could serve as a way to escape misery at home, and the possibility to save up some money for a better start in life once he had returned. Other branches of the Dutch merchant navy, which generally paid higher wages than the East India Company, must in this respect have exerted an even more powerful attraction.

The prospects for career mobility for Germans in the Dutch mercantile marine were on the whole rather bleak, however. Although 13% of all the shipmasters who married in Amsterdam in the period between 1651 and 1665 originated from Germany, the chances for an ordinary German sailor to reach the highest ranks aboard a Dutch merchant ship were in fact slim. These German shipmasters most likely had made a career on German ships, or had started their career in the Dutch merchant navy in the rank of mate or even higher. Research on career patterns in the Dutch merchant navy (excepting the VOC) around 1700 has shown that foreigners who had first signed on as a sailor or a petty officer, in contrast with native Dutchmen, seldom managed to reach the position of mate, let alone to receive the command of a ship. Prospects for promotion appear to have been marginally better in the East India Company. German seamen with much experience and a long record of service in the VOC could attain the rank of captain, especially if they hailed from a region that boasted a lengthy tradition of seafaring, such as the Wadden Islands. In comparison to Dutch sailors, German sailors achieved promotion through the ranks much less often. Sailors from Germany normally just remained sailors.

The barriers that hampered the upward mobility of German sailors cannot be found primarily in the spheres of language or religion. Dutch had been a sort of lingua franca for a long time among seafarers on the Baltic and North Seas. Up to the middle of the 19th century, it was not unusual for Germans from the coastal areas of the North Sea and the Baltic to have at least a smattering of Dutch. The fact that most German seamen were Lutherans became in course of time a less important factor in integration. Although formal rules still existed in the 18th century within the VOC that discriminated against people of other denominations than the Dutch Reformed Church, they were increasingly less significant in practice. The relatively lower career prospects for German seamen in the Dutch merchant marine were also not based on ethnic prejudice but had to do with requirements of literacy, sufficient experience at sea, and good connections with shipmasters and other high-placed persons in the shipping industry. Literacy rates among foreign seamen were in the 17th and 18th centuries lower than among seafarers from Holland, Zealand, or Frisia. Sailors from the interior of Germany were naturally less familiar with the sea than crew members recruited from seafaring communities in the Netherlands. Being outsiders in the Dutch merchant marine, German sailors also possessed less social capital that could help to further their career than seamen from the Netherlands who had been embedded in the relevant social networks all their life. If seamen from Germany were sometimes the victims of prejudice on the part of Dutchmen, as in the notorious outburst by surgeon Nicolaas de Graaff (1701) against *moffen, poepen, knoeten, hannekemaijers*, and other green *kassoepen* with "grass still sticking between their teeth" flocking to ships of the VOC, they suffered abuse for their lack of sea legs rather than for their German birth.

Seamen who entered the service of the VOC signed on for three to five years. But many of them in fact never saw their homeport again. "Geht nach Ostindien; und von dort, Ihr wißt, kehrt von drei Männern einer nur zurück" (Go to the East Indies, and you know that only one in three men will return): Heinrich von Kleist made one of the protagonists exclaim this in his play *Der zerbrochne Krug* (1806). Although the rates of return of VOC personnel varied in the course of time and by employment category, this statement is indeed a fairly accurate description of the actual statistics for German sailors: two out of three perished at sea, died in a port en route, or settled somewhere in Asia. Sailors who enlisted in other branches of the Dutch merchant navy normally only signed on for the duration of a voyage. Accidents, sickness, or desertion (in the 19th century, sailors often jumped ship in an American port) led to a low rate of return in the rest of the Dutch merchant navy, though still much higher than in the East India Company.

Once a foreign sailor had been paid and had no further contract, he could choose to settle down in the Netherlands.

A number of German seamen no doubt preferred to head home; most German accounts of voyages to Asia were, significantly, not completed in Holland, but after the author's safe return in Germany. If a sailor was young and single, however, it was not unusual to find him staying in the country where he had found employment in the mercantile marine and marrying a local or immigrant woman. During the 17th century, more than 5,700 seamen from Germany married in Amsterdam. The actual process of integration of German sailors in Dutch society between 1700 and 1900 is still in need of further study, however.

The absolute and relative decline of the flow of migrant maritime labor from the German hinterland to the Netherlands in the later 19th century was partly related to economic growth in Germany itself, which made employment in the Dutch merchant marine relatively less attractive than before. Apart from this, the portion of "cheaper" sailors, recruited mostly from China or the Dutch East Indies, grew steadily.

Bruijn, Jaap, Femme Gaastra, and Ivo Schöffer, eds. *Dutch-Asiatic Shipping in the 17th and 18th Centuries*, vol. I. The Hague, 1987.

Davids, Karel. "Maritime Labour in the Netherlands, 1570–1870." In *"Those Emblems of Hell": European Sailors and the Maritime Labour Market 1570–1870*, edited by Paul C. van Royen, Jaap R. Bruijn, and Jan Lucassen, 41–71. St. John's, 1997.

Gelder, Roelof van. *Het Oost-Indisch avontuur. Duitsers in dienst van de VOC*. Nijmegen, 1997.

Lottum, Jelle van. *Across the North Sea: The Impact of the Dutch Republic on International Labour Migration, c. 1550–1850*. Amsterdam, 2007.

Royen, Paul van. "Manning the Merchant Marine: The Dutch Maritime Labour Market about 1700." *International Journal of Maritime History* 1 (1989): 1–28.

Schuman, Peter. *Tussen vlag en voorschip. Een eeuw wettelijke en maatschappelijke emancipatie van zeevarenden ter Nederlandse koopvaardij 1838–1940*. Amsterdam, 1995.

Cross-references: Germany; The Netherlands; German Seasonal Agricultural Laborers in the Netherlands from the 17th to the Early 20th Century; Western and Central European Soldiers in the Dutch Colonial Army, 1815–1909

GERMAN SEASONAL AGRICULTURAL LABORERS IN THE NETHERLANDS FROM THE 17TH TO THE EARLY 20TH CENTURY

Jan Lucassen

Hollandgänger in its broadest sense is used in reference to all migrants originating from German-speaking lands who left for the Netherlands between 1600 and 1900, in particular to the province of Holland, but also to other maritime provinces like Frisia (*Frieslandgänger*). This broad definition refers to over 1 million proto-industrial and industrial migrant laborers of both sexes who either resided temporarily or settled permanently in the Netherlands; hundreds of thousands of soldiers, sailors, and servants; and finally tens of thousands of seasonal agricultural laborers. The term *Hollandgänger* in its narrower and more precise sense, however, refers to the last group of seasonal migrants mentioned above who traveled every year from northwestern Germany to the maritime Dutch provinces to work as mowers and haymakers or in peat cutting and other jobs. This entry deals with the *Hollandgänger* of the second, more restricted sense of the term.

The economic and social roots of seasonal migration

Starting in the beginning of the 17th century, the booming Dutch economy exhibited a quickly rising demand for labor, including a need for workers in agriculture and rural industries. Dairy farming became dominant in central and northern Holland and Frisia, while, aside from wheat, peat became especially important in southern Holland, Zealand, and Groningen as the urban population and industry in particular depended on peat for ovens, kilns, and water pans in sugar and salt refineries, among others.

The increased need for seasonal laborers in these areas could not be fulfilled by the diminishing number of peasant farmers in the Netherlands. The loss of population in north Holland and population stagnation in south Holland were due to the lack of year-round employment opportunities. Peasants could no longer make a living through the traditional combination of different sources of income as the stagnation of dike building and polder construction starting in the 1640s, the depression in deep-sea fishing, and the fall in agricultural prices after 1650 reduced the demand for labor. There were far fewer jobs available throughout the rural areas of north Holland after 1640–50 and, to a lesser extent, of south Holland after 1680 in farm work (yearlong), groundwork (spring), herring fishing (June to December), hunting and inland fishing (summer and autumn), and cleaning ditches and domestic industry (winter).

Animal husbandry in north Holland, however, remained important and, as a result, the demand was high for workers in mowing and haymaking in June and July. Since these tasks required intensive work in an extremely short time span, acute labor shortages existed during the seasonal peak period. Increasing demand created a similar situation in the cutting of peat. Since the rural population of north Holland diminished and that of south Holland stagnated, opportunities were created for peasants from areas farther away, e.g., the sandy regions in the east and the south of the Netherlands and even more so peasant labor migrants from bordering German-speaking areas like Westphalia.

In these areas, the population grew rapidly following the Thirty Years' War (1618–48). In Westphalia this resulted in a marked increase of landless peasants who were unable to subsist on their earnings from small leased farms. These farmers were known as *Heuerlinge* in many parts of northwestern Germany. As a rule, dividing large farms among different heirs was not permitted (e.g., in Osnabrück since 1618), so the number of such farms remained more or less constant. *Heuerlinge* became dependent on additional employment opportunities, which middle- and large-sized farms in Westphalia could not offer, particularly during the period of sinking grain prices (c. 1650–1750). One solution for these workers was to supplement their work on small farms with domestic textile production and migratory labor within a single work cycle.

Consequently, the demand for seasonal labor in the Netherlands met an increased supply of potential labor migrants from northwestern Germany whose willingness to migrate was likely further stimulated by the inclination of large Westphalian farmers to keep wages low. The highly divergent economic development within the Dutch Republic – especially the gap between the maritime provinces and the hinterland, which in turn prompted differences in the standard of living and wages – also incited many Dutch workers to leave their homes in search of work farther west. Wages in the province of Holland for agricultural work during the summer, for example, were twice as high as in Twente and the Achterhoek (border regions in the east) and even three times as high as in Tecklenburg in Westphalia.

Around 1800, Westphalian migrant laborers were in a position to earn a third of their annual household income by working only a quarter of the year in Holland. This was also possible because seasonal migrants took with them as much nonperishable food as possible, like salted meat, flour, groats (if possible homegrown), to avoid the high prices for such goods along the coast of the North Sea. Consequently, this extensive temporary migration hardly resulted in permanent settlement in the Dutch maritime provinces. The economic rationale behind *Hollandgängerei* lay in the combination of several sources of income: the peasant farm at home, some cottage industry, and, most important, migrant labor in Holland – while avoiding or reducing the effects of the high prices that prevailed there.

Not every combination of small farming and domestic industry, however, led to seasonal migration. The eastern part of Tecklenburg illustrates that peasant families whose land yielded more than subsistence harvests and who continued domestic weaving throughout the year, required all members of their households to remain at home.

Changing migration patterns

Holland- and *Frieslandgängerei* for the first decades of the 17th century were reported in various parts of Westphalia, including Lippe (1604), Münster (ca. 1605 and 1608–9), and Osnabrück (1608). It is, however, not fully clear whether these workers were involved in permanent, temporary, or seasonal migration. One of the few exceptions is provided by reports in Münster (1608–9) and Hadeln (1632–3) that mention grass cutting and seasonal migration in Holland and Frisia. In the latter case, the misery of the Thirty Years' War seems to have been a decisive reason for the migration.

For the period after 1650, indications of westward seasonal migration are much more numerous. On the German side, a list of 3,000 *Heuerleute*, including 925 *Hollandgänger*, has been preserved. On the Dutch side, there are clear records from Frisia (1666) and from Groningen of the transport of *Hollandgänger* to Amsterdam in 1679. The number of seasonal migrants on ferries across the Zuiderzee between Overijssel and Amsterdam increased in the first half of the 17th century, followed by a second, more rapid increase in the second half of the century. Throughout the 18th century, the figures stagnated until they finally decreased in the first decade of the 19th century. This development is consistent with data available for some regions within Westphalia.

Available data from the beginning of the 19th century are more precise, which is mainly due to the French occupation of western Germany. In 1811 about 30,000 workers traveled between various jobs in the coastal strip from Calais to Bremen, which was never more than 50 km wide. Over 20,000 of these spoke (Low) German and thus can be considered typical *Hollandgänger*. The yearly average of *Hollandgänger* in the 18th century was possibly some 30,000 persons. As a proportion of the total population, the figures were highest for the Département de l'Ems Supérieur (2.89%), the Principality Lippe-Detmold (1.70%), the Département de la Lippe (0.88%), and the Département des Bouches du Weser (0.61% to 0.64%). On the local level, these figures could amount to one-quarter of the total male working population. Most *Hollandgänger* thus came from the countryside of the following areas: Osnabrück, the Niederstift Münster, and further east, Lippe and Paderborn. Adjacent regions to the south and the north of these lands supplied fewer seasonal migrants and the intermediate Prussian lands with their strong textile industries, such as around Bielefeld, saw even less emigration. The predominant position of the prince-bishopric of Osnabrück is confirmed by fragmentary figures: 925 *Hollandgänger* in 1656, 6,000 around 1780, and some 4,700 in 1811.

The declining importance of this traditional migration pattern proceeded unevenly over the 19th century. After decreasing in the period of French occupation, the level of *Hollandgängerei* remained at a rather stable, if low, level for some time and then rapidly dwindled to insignificance after 1870. In the Landdrostei Osnabrück there were about 8,000 *Hollandgänger* in 1811, at least 3,500 in 1871, and only a few hundred around the turn of the century. This was not so much the result of diminishing demand in the traditional pull areas along the North Sea coast but rather of the emergence of successfully competing pull areas in northwestern Germany. It started with the economic development of Hamburg and Bremen after the Napoleonic period, but it was mainly the rise of the Ruhr area in the second half of the 19th century that tolled the death knell of the North Sea system of migratory labor. Not only did this new pull area offer attractively higher wages but its drawing power was enhanced above all by the variety of jobs it could provide: both seasonal work in summer (especially in construction) and winter as well as year-round employment. Push areas that had previously supplied labor to the North Sea coast were now drawn into the sphere of the Ruhr system, including seasonal and other workers from the eastern provinces of the Netherlands. Some former *Hollandgänger* may also have joined the mass migrations from Westphalia to the USA, which increased in the 1840s. At the end of the 19th century only a few areas still witnessed the annual departure of *Hollandgänger*, areas such as Weener/Aschendorf and, to a lesser extent, Diepholz, Lippe, and Bentheim. The First World War put an end to even this small trickle.

Work and earnings

Considering that *Hollandgängerei* continued over so many generations and that it only lost its attraction because of external causes like the successful competition of the Ruhr area, it must have been profitable for those who engaged in it. Without doubt, the work was hard, strenuous, and even dangerous. To earn their wages, which could be considerable, *Hollandgänger* had to be in good health. If a migrant worker fell ill, which was not unlikely since malaria was endemic in the coastal marshes, or lost his job for some other reason, the costs of medical care or lost wages could exceed the salary for an entire season.

The overwhelming majority of the *Hollandgänger* were married men, who often brought along their sons and the sons of relatives and neighbors. There were only small numbers of females among *Hollandgänger* in 1811, typically employed as weavers, haymakers, weeders, bleachers, and peddlers. Around 1811 *Hollandgänger* from Westphalia brought home on average 40 Reichsthaler or 160 French francs. The rest of the household income (90 Reichsthaler) was derived from the small cottage farm, from cottage industry activities, and from wage labor on the large properties in the workers' home village. All family members were involved in these tasks, although the wife bore sole responsibility during the absence of her husband.

The Dutch labor market offered many opportunities for migrants, but some of the more seasonally bound jobs developed into occupational specialties for *Hollandgänger*. The 1811 statistics illustrate that two types of work were most important: at least an estimated 12,000 workers came to the North Sea coast to mow grass and prepare hay on dairy farms and approximately 9,000 migrants worked in the peat bogs. To a considerable extent these activities were complementary: many migrant laborers left the peat fields by the end of May or the beginning of June so as to reach the dairy farms for the next job by the start of the hay harvest. Gardening for well-to-do Dutch also became a specialty of *Hollandgänger*. Since Holland imported most of its bread grain, the demand for grain harvesters was not as important. This work, as well as the digging of madder, attracted more seasonal laborers from Belgium than from Germany.

Next to agriculture and peat digging, construction in general and brickmaking in particular were important trades. Well-known examples of *Hollandgänger* are the plasterers from Oldenburg and the brickmakers from Lippe. Marsh reclamation, dike building, and the dredging and digging of canals and harbors were activities that took place especially in spring and early summer and that could be combined with harvesting later in the year. Finally, bleaching, rafting, and peddling (by the *Tödden* among others) were important occupations in the 1811 statistics. The bleacheries in the dunes to the west of Haarlem were one of the few sectors that attracted more women than men, in this case from Lingen. Timber-raft shipping on the river Rhine was a specialty of men living north of Bingen and Koblenz. In early spring these raftsmen lashed together the smaller rafts that had been assembled on the tributaries of the Rhine in order to float them down to the Dutch sawmills and shipyards.

Two important sectors are missing in the 1811 data: seasonal herring fishing and whaling. Due to Napoleon's blockade of England, these trades were insignificant in 1811 but before and, to a certain degree, also later on they were certainly considered part and parcel of *Hollandgängerei*. Over one thousand whalers (*Grönlandfahrer*) came from the north Frisian Islands, but they also hailed from places farther south, e.g., hundreds from the prince-bishopric of Osnabrück. Herring fishing was a specialty of people from Schaumburg-Lippe.

Starting in the 17th century, most farmers in the low-lying meadowlands of the provinces of Holland and Frisia engaged exclusively in raising livestock, particularly dairy cattle. Practically all milk was processed into cheese or butter on the farms. The cattle grazed in the grasslands in summer but had to be fed with hay in stables during the winter. Grass mowing began in early June in Frisia, two weeks later in Holland, and all the grass had to be mowed and brought in within six weeks. This work was performed by migrant workers who were recruited in two ways. Most typically, a single farmer developed a working relationship over several years with a number of workers whose work he could rely on. Other workers traveled to the meadowlands without prior arrangements, going door to door selling their labor, but they also offered their services at the markets of regional centers, like the Frisian towns of Sneek, Leeuwarden, or Joure, or Purmerend in north Holland.

Mowers were typically hired as a pair and slept among the hay in barns. They rose as early as possible in the morning, at about 3:00 A.M., and were brought coffee with buttermilk from the farm in the fields at about 8:00 A.M. They rested for a while in the mid-afternoon, usually in the fields, shielded by a crude tent, and in the early evening, at about eight o'clock, they received a bowl of porridge at the main farmhouse. On such a day, working in teams of two, each mower cleared with his scythe more than half a hectare of grass, weighing nearly 3,000 kg. After a week or two the farmer summoned a pair of haymakers, sometimes also including women, who usually came from a lesser distance than the mowers. Their work consisted in turning and finally gathering the grass that the mowers had laid in the swaths. Four weeks after the start of the hay harvest, all grass was cut and, within another two weeks, if not too much rain had fallen, the hay was safely stored. Once the mowing was finished, wages were paid in cash according to piece rates, based on the surface mowed by the team or processed into hay, and payment was typically accompanied by a modest celebration. The relationship between mowers and their employer was a rather personal one as grass mowers and haymakers commonly worked for the same employer year in, year out.

Major industrial consumers of peat were distilleries and refineries, soap and salt production factories, breweries, bleach works, and brick ovens. Along the North Sea coast there were two kinds of peat-yielding territories: *hoogvenen* (high peat bogs) in the northeast of the Netherlands stretching into adjacent Germany and *laagvenen* (low peat bogs), mainly between Amsterdam, Utrecht, and Rotterdam. The distinction between the two types of bogs is based on the water table, which determines the growing conditions of the peat. High peat bogs, which lie above the water table, can be drained by excavating canals. The exposed peat can then be cut in sods with a shovel. In such bogs, an estimated 3,000 migrants found employment in 1811. Digging waterways could not drain low peat bogs and here the peat usually had to be scooped out in muddy clumps. In 1811, approximately 6,000 migrants were employed digging peat under such conditions, most of them in the low peat bogs of Holland-Utrecht.

Standard procedures were developed and implemented in the extraction of peat from high bogs. First, a stretch of drainage ditches was dug to bring down the water level. Next, canals were excavated for the transport of the cut peat. At times canal diggers worked together in large crews of as many as 80–90 persons. But smaller groups of five to ten canal diggers are also cited, which was also common for the ensuing task of cutting the peat itself. A worker who was part of a team could cut about 2,000 sods of high peat (measuring $40 \times 15 \times 15$ cm on removal) daily. Cutting peat and, initially, the excavation of canals were limited to three months of the year, roughly from March to June. Earlier in the year the bog was either frozen or it was too wet and the cutting process had to stop in the early summer because peat requires a drying time of many weeks or even months. Peat had to be dry by the end of the summer because it disintegrates when exposed to below-freezing temperatures.

The social organization of *Hollandgänger* who dug high peat was in many respects reminiscent of that of the grass cutters. Wages, based on piece rates, were paid to the group that had offered itself as a team to the contractor. For this purpose they chose a leader who was responsible for negotiating wages with their employer and for divvying up wages. For the duration of the job, members of the team worked and lived together and a number of unwritten rules existed to keep disturbances to a minimum. Each man's place in bed and at the dinner table was determined by specific regulations and even the baking of pancakes was governed by rules.

The organization for mining low peat was rather different. Low peat was dredged up from under the water with a scoop. A dredger usually emptied the net of his scoop into a small boat while he either stood in the boat or balanced on a plank linking the boat to dry land. Part of the marshy polder that was not yet dredged was earmarked as a drying field for the extracted peat. The dredger worked with a partner who spread out the low peat and stamped on it while wearing wooden shoes with boards fastened to their bottom. Only when the muddy peat had dried sufficiently could it be cut into neat sods, followed by a further drying period of some months. Mining low peat was thus bound to roughly the same seasonal rhythm as the mining of high peat. Foreign migrant laborers performed the dredging, spreading, and stamping of the peat while local workers performed the remaining tasks throughout the rest of the year. Pairs of migrant workers lived in sheds that housed some 20 workers. These sheds stood on edges of the bog in remote areas that were not yet being exploited.

There was a clear sense of solidarity among the peat cutters. At the beginning and end of the season, groups of peat cutters discussed wage rates and labor conditions. The employers tried to adhere to a common policy on these issues, which prompted the teams of cutters, even if employed by different men, to act in league with each other. The isolated living in remote sheds presumably also reinforced the workers' solidarity in their dealings with employers and outsiders. Strikes broke out particularly at the outset of the peat-cutting season when – with an eye on the market situation – the piecework rate was set and diggers tried to extract better remuneration for the whole season.

Relations between employer and employee – with the exception of the grass mowers – were largely impersonal. Workers hardly met their employer and typically settled their business with a supervisor or (sub-)contractor, who was responsible for the organization of payment and work. Migrant laborers, who usually worked in narrowly demarcated sectors and performed specific seasonal bound tasks, only sporadically came into contact with local workers. The obvious exceptions to the rule are the peddlers who depended on the rural population of the maritime provinces as the buyers of their goods. In spite of this isolation, *Hollandgänger*, and especially *hannekemaaiers* (the Dutch expression for the grass mowers from the east), became central characters in Dutch theater. From the late 17th until well into the 19th century farces that portrayed the "stupid German grass mower" were immensely popular. It is difficult to determine to what extent this display of Dutch feelings of superiority had negative consequences for the everyday life of the *Hollandgänger*.

Bölsker-Schlicht, Franz. *Die Hollandgängerei im Osnabrücker Land und im Emsland. Ein Beitrag zur Geschichte der Arbeiterwanderung vom 17. bis zum 19. Jahrhundert.* Sögel, 1987.

Eiynck, Andreas, ed. *Wanderarbeit jenseits der Grenze. 350 Jahre auf der Suche nach Arbeit in der Fremde.* Assen, 1993.

Gladen, Albin, et al., eds. *Hollandgang im Spiegel der Reiseberichte evangelischer Geistlicher. Quellen zur saisonalen Arbeitswanderung in der zweiten Hälfte des 19. Jahrhunderts*, 2 vols. Münster, 2006.

Küpker, Markus. *Weber, Hausierer, Hollandgänger. Demografischer und wirtschaftlicher Wandel im ländlichen Raum: Das Tecklenburger Land 1750–1870.* Vienna, 2009.

Lucassen, Jan. *Naar de kusten van de Noordzee. Trekarbeid in Europees perspektief, 1600–1900.* Gouda, 1984; English translation: *Migrant Labour in Europe 1600–1900: The Drift to the North Sea.* London, 1987.

Lucassen, Jan. "Hannekemaaiersbrieven 1860–1889. Een bijdrage tot de geschiedenis van de arbeidsverhoudingen in de Friese hooibouw." *It Beaken* 19 (1987): 200–29.

Nolte-Schuster, Birgit, Jaap Vogel, and Winfried Woesler. *Zur Arbeit nach Holland. Arbeitswanderung aus der Region Osnabrück zwischen 1750 und 1850.* Osnabrück, 2001.

Oberpenning, Hannelore. *Migration und Fernhandel im "Tödden-System." Wanderhändler aus dem nördlichen Münsterland im mittleren und nördlichen Europa des 18. und 19. Jahrhunderts.* Osnabrück, 1996.

Riet, Arte Johannes Jan van 't. "Meeten, boren en besien." *Turfwinning in de buitenrijnse ambachten van het Hoogheemraadschap van Rijnland 1680–1800.* Hilversum, 2005.

Rößler, Horst. *Hollandgänger, Sträflinge und Migranten: Bremen und Bremerhaven als Wanderungsraum.* Bremen, 2000.

Cross-references: Germany; The Netherlands; German Baker-Journeymen in Amsterdam in the 17th Century; German Itinerant Merchants from the Münsterland in Northern, Western, and Central Europe in the 18th and 19th Centuries; German Sailors in the Dutch Merchant Marine from the Early 17th to the End of the 19th Century; Lippe Brickmakers in Central, Western, and Northern Europe from the 17th to the Early 20th Century; Western and Central European Soldiers in the Dutch Colonial Army, 1815–1909

GERMAN SETTLERS IN RUSSIA SINCE THE 18TH CENTURY

Detlef Brandes

At the time of the first Russian census in 1897, the Russian Empire was home to 1,790,489 persons who listed German as their mother language. More than three-quarters of them lived in the countryside, and more than two-thirds were Lutherans. If we subtract the German inhabitants of Russian Poland, Lithuania, and the Baltic provinces, who are not counted among the "Russian Germans" in the narrower sense, the number of German settlers in Russia drops to 1,168,515. To be sure, travelers in all *gubernii* (provinces) of the Empire could encounter Germans who often made a living as doctors, apothecaries, foresters, gardeners, and tutors, and who in many cases had assimilated in language and religion to the Russian Orthodox majority population already in the second generation. However, the large German groups in St. Petersburg and Moscow, like the Germans in the countryside, largely clung to their language, customs, and confession. All told, only 0.75% of the Germans in Russia had converted to Orthodoxy. Among the German settlers, the two largest groups in 1897 were the Volga Germans at 402,565 and the Black Sea Germans at 377,798. Of the 209,072 Germans in Ukraine west of the Dnieper, 171,300 were living in the *gubernia* of Volhynia, alone. Northern Russia outside of the city boundaries of St. Petersburg had 25,652 German-speaking residents, and 16,669 were living in the Transcaucasus. By 1897, 40,060 Germans had settled in the northern Caucasus, and 14,298 in the Asian part of the Empire.

The first large influx of immigrants was triggered by Empress Catherine II (1762–96) with a manifesto of 1763, in which she promised "foreign settlers" land, travel costs, settlement loans, religious freedom, and exemption from recruitment into military service. With these privileges, the empress, like Emperor Joseph II in Austria and King Frederick II in Prussia, took advantage of the opportunity to lure individuals who had been uprooted and impoverished by the Seven Years' War into thinly settled areas. By 1774, 30,623 individuals had taken up Catherine's invitation, four-fifths of them in the years 1763–6. A large number of the immigrants came from Hesse, where their plots were small but the encumbrances on them were large. Although small villages were also established near St. Petersburg, in Livonia, and in Ukraine west of the Dnieper, the majority of the settlers were sent to Saratov at the middle Volga, where they settled in 104 villages with 25,781 persons on both banks of the river. The prospects of being able to do missionary work among the Kazakhs and the Kalmyks prompted the headquarters of the Moravian Brethren in Herrnhut to set up a small – and later famous – community of Sarepta near Tsaritsyn (Volgograd).

Following the First Turkish War (1768–74) and Russia's annexation of the Khanate of the Crimea (1783), the new province of "New Russia" on the northern coast of the Black Sea was opened to immigrants. The first German migrant settlers left Danzig in 1786–7 and the Werder River and headed for New Russia. Most of them were Mennonites, whom the Prussian state had prohibited from buying more land because they refused to perform military service and on whom it had imposed compensation payments to the cadet corps in Kulm. They created the district of Chortica: a few villages, so-called colonies, along the Dnieper south of Yekaterinoslav (Dnepropetrovsk). By contrast, the large groups of Mennonite immigrants between 1804 and 1806 and the smaller ones of the following decades were steered into the *gubernia* of Tauria. They set up their villages east of the Molochna River, which flows into the Sea of Azov. In 1803–4 and 1808–9, large groups of Lutherans, Reformed, and Catholics from southwestern and western Germany and Alsace (and Switzerland, as well) followed the invitation of Czar Alexander I. Revolutionary and coalition armies had

devastated their homeland and the rulers had raised taxes drastically to finance the rebuilding. Their villages were distributed along the western bank of the Molochna, the hinterland of Odessa, the lower Dnieper, and the Crimea. Impoverished German settlers whom Alexander I encountered in the Duchy of Warsaw were given permission to migrate onward to Bessarabia, which had been conquered in 1812. Devastating harvest failures and chiliastic hopes prompted a large number of Württembergers to set out for Mount Ararat in 1816–18. Some of these emigrant groups insisted on their original destination and established colonies beyond the Caucasus, while others accepted the offer of the czarist government and remained in New Russia and Bessarabia. Between 1823 and 1842, Lutheran and Catholic settlers from West Prussia, Baden, and Hesse were given land north of Mariupol on the Sea of Azov.

While the recruitment until then had been undertaken by the state, behind the immigration of German settlers to Volhynia stood Polish estate owners, though by 1860 they had prevailed on only 11,400 Germans to settle as tenants on their holdings. When many estate owners in Russia were forced to lease or sell their land after the abolition of serfdom in 1861, when the Polish January uprising in 1863–4 had triggered fears about the future among the German farmers loyal to the czar, and roadways and railway lines had been built between Warsaw and Kiev, many Germans streamed from their now overcrowded villages in Russian Poland to Volhynia.

Special privileges and economic success

Already Catherine II had set the "foreign settlers" apart from the rest of the peasant population as "colonists." They were placed under a Guardianship Chancellery in St. Petersburg with "offices" in the main settlement areas. The government repaid the immigrants the costs for the trip and gave them loans to build houses and buy a minimum stock of animals and agricultural implements. She had so much land allocated to the colonies that every German farmer in the Volga region was able to work 30 *desjatins* – a *desjatin* is about one-tenth larger than a hectare. In the Black Sea region, Lutherans and Catholics received 60 *desjatins*, Mennonites even 65 *desjatins*. Colonists were supposed to pass on their share of the common fields undivided to their youngest son – they could neither sell nor lease their land. The Volga Germans were granted tax exemption for 30 years, the Black Sea Germans for only 10 years. Meanwhile, most of the Germans of Volhynia were given a lease with only a few years free of taxes.

The Germans on both sides of the Volga deviated from the legally prescribed agrarian order as early as 1785 and adopted the system of their Russian neighbors, who regularly, at intervals of a few years, redistributed all fields to the families or their male members ("redistribution"). Every Volga German now had a claim to a share of the land, and no father was forced to make provision for the acquisition of land for his usually numerous offspring. In addition, some of the settlers were able to lease land from fellow villagers who devoted themselves entirely to a trade. By contrast, until the reform of 1871, the settlers in New Russia clung to the practice of leaving their entire landholding to a single son. The others sons had to acquire or lease land or learn a trade. However, with support from the government, the growing number of landless sons laid claim to help in purchasing land. Unlike the Volga colonists and the Russian state peasants, the Black Sea Germans had large sources of communal funds available to acquire land, funds that came from income from the leasing of land belonging to orphans until they came of majority and the land of former district sheep farms. The communities deployed this "orphan" and "sheep farm capital" to buy land, on which daughter colonies were set up for the landless.

When official auditors examined the situation of the German colonies in 1890, the colonists had established 198 villages on the Volga and 225 in New Russia on state land. But while the number of New Russian settlements had more than quadrupled through the establishment of daughter colonies on purchased and leased land, no new settlements had taken place in the Volga colonies during the preceding two decades. The government had given the Volga Germans nearly 1.4 million *desjatins*, more than twice as much state land as the settlers in New Russia. Whereas the land of the Volga colonies increased by only 12% up to 1890, the landholdings of the New Russian colonies doubled. In addition, individual colonists in New Russia together had acquired more than a million *desjatins* – four times more than individual Volga Germans. The entire landholdings of the Black Sea Germans had thus nearly quadrupled since the last allocation, while those of the Volga Germans grew by only 30%.

However, the distribution of land in New Russia remained very unequal: the *gubernii* of Yekaterinoslav and Tauria had 455 Germans with private landholdings of more than 100 *desjatins*. Of those, 156 owned more than 10,000 *desjatins*, and 26 more than 5,000 *desjatins*. Within the mother colonies still established on state land, as well, the "full farmers" with their original share of 60 to 65 *desjatins* existed alongside "half" and "quarter" farmers, a class of smallholders and a class of landless without a farm of their own. Although their number had decreased through the extensive purchases of land during the previous 25 years, as well as the emigration of Mennonites to North America, it still amounted to 16% in the *gubernii* of Bessarabia and Tauria, 25% in the *gubernia* of Yekaterinoslav, and no less than 67% in the *gubernia* of Cherson. A major difference for the German farmers continued to be whether they worked state land, their own land, or leased land. To sell or pawn state land, they first had to redeem their share with a payment of 20 times the land tax. Leaseholders could lose their land to financially more solvent farmers or buyers.

In the 1890s, the growth in German landholdings in New Russia began to slow, since the colonists began to purchase cheaper land in North America as well as in other provinces of the Empire. Black Sea Germans, and in smaller numbers also Germans from the Volga and Volhynia, moved into the

land of the Don army, the northern Caucasus, and the Ural region, and from the turn of the 20th century they joined the eastward migration of Russian and Ukrainian farmers into the Asiatic part of the Empire, where the state was once more offering free land to the settlers.

The Lutheran and Catholic colonists were slow in getting used to living conditions in the steppe. About half of them had belonged to the urban or rural lower class back at home and had possessed little or no wealth at all. The others had used up their savings during the journey to Russia. Lack of food and clean water, inadequate housing, and along the Volga also attacks by nomads cost many colonists their health or even lives in the first two decades. Only the second generation was able to make the farms of their parents flourish. Quicker progress was made by the Mennonites, who had experience in agriculture as independent farmers. As "model settlers" they were to set up "model farms" and were given greater start-up capital. With their horses, with implements and handcarts they had brought from home or soon produced themselves, they were able to work more efficiently than their neighbors using oxen and Russian tools. Moreover, economic progress was ensured by an agricultural association that obligated all Mennonites to a four-field system with crop rotation and fallows, and which promoted sheep raising by distributing Merino sheep.

The Mennonites also used plows with three or more blades and later sewing, harvesting, and threshing machines earlier than other farmers in New Russia. In addition, they enjoyed the privilege of having their taxes frozen at 15 kopeks per *desjatin*. As a result, between 1812 and 1840, Mennonite taxpayers paid only a third – and from 1841 to 1869 as little as one-eleventh – of the taxes owed by Lutheran and Catholic colonists or even Russian state farmers. This made it possible for more capital to flow into private or communal economic enterprises in the Mennonite colonies. The Volga Germans grew grain and tobacco. Wholesalers transported the commodities on the Volga to the customers. The Black Sea Germans reduced their sheep herds once Russian grain had found a stable market in central and western Europe.

The German farmers in New Russia were able to use their workers, draft animals, tools, and machines more efficiently on their holdings of 60–65 *desjatins* than could the Volga Germans, whose area under cultivation became smaller and smaller because of the redistribution among the ever-growing number of families. Moreover, one *desjatin* in the hands of a large-scale farmer yielded more than one in the hands of a small farmer. Since the number of families with a claim to land remained constant in the Black Sea colonies, the common fields did not have to be divided up into as many strips as in the Volga colonies, with their larger population and redistribution system: in the Volga colony of Galka, for example, nearly 50,000 strips were measured out and distributed to the families according to the number of their male "souls." Thirty kilometers lay between the most distantly separated fields of every farmer. It was only in the 1880s that the first Volga German colonies adopted the multifield system with regular crop rotation and a one-year fallow period – two to three decades later than the Lutheran and Catholic colonies of New Russia.

Beginning in the 1870s, German colonists set up steam-powered mills in their villages, the capitals of the *gubernii*, and the chief cities of the districts. In Saratov, Yekaterinoslav, and Aleksandrovsk (today Zaporizhia), they owned more than half of the mills. German village craftsmen took advantage of the rising demand for robust handcarts and agricultural implements and sold them far across the boundaries of the colonies from the 1850s on. When the government imposed higher tariffs on the importation of iron goods, the domestic production of agricultural machines increased. New Russia took over the leadership from the western and Baltic provinces and raised its share of the manufacture of agricultural implements and machines to nearly 50% by 1911. The workshop of the former smith Höhn in Odessa, with its 1,200 workers, developed into the largest plow maker of the Empire.

The colonists on the western bank of the Volga, like their Russian neighbors, earned part of their livelihood as home workers, especially weavers. They processed above all *sarpinka*, a blend of cotton and linen. The Moravian Brethren from Sarepta had disseminated the art of weaving *sarpinka* to the Volga colonies. In the early stages of production, this blue cloth was still sold in the immediate surroundings. As production increased, the entrepreneur opened up more distant markets. Some invested their capital in the Volga region in the lucrative grain trade with the centers of Seelmann and Katharinenstadt. While these colonies flourished through trade along the Volga, a few of the formerly exclusively agricultural colonies of New Russia, like Chortica, Einlage, Halbstadt, Neuhalbstadt, and Hoffental, developed into prosperous industrial villages, with settlements for workers and several factories for agricultural implements and machines.

The organization of church and schools

The colonial administration obliged the clergy and magistrates (*Schulzen*) to admonish the colonists "to piety, church attendance on Sundays and feast days, prayer, and the taking of the Eucharist." The district and village magistrates were to see to it that the colonists led "a sober, quiet, and industrious life, as was appropriate to their status." In Lutheran villages, the pastors had great influence, and together with the wealthy farmers they guided the life of the parish. On the whole, however, the pastoral care of the German parishes was barely adequate. Most German villages were visited only a few times a year by their pastor, who usually had to look after several, often widely dispersed villages. Many Protestant parishes saw the emergence of Pietist parishes. The Catholic colonies were cared for overwhelmingly by Polish and Lithuanian clergy sent out by the archbishopric of Mohylev, whose seat was later transferred to St. Petersburg. Poor language skills limited their influence on the parishes.

It was only in 1857 that a seminary was founded in Saratov to train German priests for the colonies. The Mennonites chose their spiritual "teachers" and "elders" on their own. Mutual care and the threat of exclusion from the parish through the "ban" ensured a pronounced social control.

In the German parishes, the village teachers simultaneously held the office of sexton and cantor. When the clergy was absent, they read from the sermon books and took their place at funerals and weddings. The teaching in the village school prepared young people primarily for confirmation. When these youngsters left the school, they were at least literate and numerate. In the Mennonite communities, by contrast, better-educated teachers, smaller classes, and teacher conferences ensured a higher educational level.

Beginning in 1834, at the initiative of the government, "central schools" were set up to train the colonists' children as teachers and community clerks and spread knowledge of the Russian language. In the 1860s, many teachers initially demanded a division of the large classes and an improvement in the teaching of Russian, precisely also because many Germans were forced to work outside the colonies. The interest of the colonists in educating their children at state-recognized higher schools grew after the introduction of compulsory military service (1874), since the period of military service was reduced for graduates from these institutions. The central schools were Russified in the 1880s, the church schools at the beginning of the 1890s. Henceforth, only German and religion were to be taught in the mother language. After the revolution of 1905, the *gubernii* allowed children to be once again instructed in the mother language in all subjects during the first two years, while a few subjects had to be taught in Russian from the third grade on.

Social and political integration

External and internal descriptions characterize the colonist as a person who found fulfillment exclusively in the small world of his village and perceived life outside of the community as alien. Church, school, and community were supposedly the entire content of his intellectual and social life. The German settlers were said to desire self-government and to be left alone by the authorities. That is why, according to the colonial authorities, they fulfilled their duties with "admirable alacrity." The colonists maintained close ties among themselves but kept aloof from the rest of the population. They were eager for good relations with the inhabitants and supported them especially after failed harvests with seed, foodstuffs, and money. However, they accepted only Germans of their own confession as tenants, heirs, and spouses. The colonists jealously guarded their "nationality" and prohibited especially their daughters from marrying Russians. However, the reforms of Alexander II, the abolition of the special administration of the colonies in 1871, and the introduction of compulsory military service in 1874 forced the colonists – now officially referred to as "settler-owners" – increasingly to leave their villages, at least temporarily. The contacts of the Germans to the outside world intensified. What contributed to this was the growth in the exchange of goods, the expansion of transportation networks, and the urbanization and social differentiation that went hand in hand with economic modernization; also, the administrative districts were now no longer organized according to ethnic criteria, and military service required that young men learn the Russian language.

The essentially positive outside image of the colonists changed with the gradual deterioration of the political relationship between Germany and Russia from the end of the 1870s on. Russian nationalists saw the German immigration into the southwestern *gubernii* as well as in the land purchases of the colonists as a "peaceful conquest of Russia by the Germans." In the face of the seemingly unstoppable increase in German landownership, such warnings found a ready audience among Russian and Ukrainian farmers unable to compete with the more solvent German colonists when it came to leasing and buying land. At the same time, the Orthodox Church was irate at the missionary successes of Pietists and Mennonites among its flock. Controllers were therefore charged with overseeing the main settlement areas of the Germans. They reported about Ukrainian settlers who perceived their German neighbors as a "higher estate" – both estates, they said, were alienated from each other, though only one controller reported envy and hatred toward the Germans. The Germans, in turn, felt threatened. After an anti-Jewish pogrom in Aleksandrovsk in 1881, they claimed that they had heard cries like "Now against the Jews, but later against the Germans." This controller also related that despite their dislike of the Germans, the Ukrainians and Russians took the Germans as their model: they built their houses and worked their fields on the German pattern, used horses instead of oxen, raised the so-called German or red cow, and purchased increasingly more efficient agricultural machines. Beginning in the early 1890s, German settlers were prohibited from leasing or buying land in Volhynia. When land prices had risen sharply in the old settlement areas, a part of the Russian-German farmers sold their landholdings and emigrated to North America and Brazil, but also to the northern Caucasus, Siberia, and Courland, where Baltic estate owners offered them land beginning in 1905.

After the creation of organs of self-governance (*zemstva*) in 1864 on the level of the districts and *gubernii*, the German colonists participated in the political life of the Czarist Empire: they were delegated to service in the *zemstva* of the *gubernii* and the *zemstvo* administrations. At the first elections to the Duma (the pan-Russian parliament) in 1905, the Germans on the Black Sea and in the two capitals supported the liberal-conservative Union of October 17, while the Volga Germans voted for the left-liberal Constitutional Democrats. With the help of the Octobrists, the German delegates were able, between 1910 and 1912, to block attempts by the government to constrain the economic activities of former colonists.

During the First World War, doubts about the loyalty of the German settlers grew. The German soldiers of the Russian army were moved to the Caucasus front. The government decided to "liquidate" the landholdings not only of Germans of the Reich but also of Germans of Russian citizenship. The use of the German language in school and in public was forbidden.

The February Revolution of 1917 led to the abolition of these "liquidation laws." Soviet nationalities' policy rested on the assumption that territorial units in which the population was governed and educated in the schools in its own language would solve the state's "nationalities problem." The new government combined the German rural settlement areas into 550 national village soviets and 15 national *rayons* (counties). Added to this was the establishment of the Volga German Autonomous Soviet Socialist Republic. For the Germans, the period up to the Second World War – with the exception of the years 1925–8 – was marked by catastrophes: during the civil war, which followed the October Revolution of 1917, and during the famine of 1921–4, they lost many members and a large portion of their property. During the phase of collectivization, the Soviet regime degraded the majority of the peasants into *kolchosniks*, that is, into landless cottagers, deported the minority of the *kulaks* (a category of relatively affluent peasants with relatively large endowments) as right-less "special settlers" to inhospitable regions in the high north, closed the churches, arrested the clergy, and outlawed religious ceremonies. At the beginning of the 1930s, many German Russians once again starved to death. Following the National Socialist seizure of power in Germany, the situation of the German Russians deteriorated. They were persecuted even more than the other nationalities in the Soviet Union – offers of help from Germany after the failed harvests of 1933 and 1934 further increased the suspicion of the authorities against the German Russians. The State Police, GPU, and the People's Commissariat of Internal Affairs (NKVD) combed the German villages for potential "fascists," with the result that numerous German families lost their able-bodied male members. In 1938 their schools were Russified and the national village soviets and *rayons* were dissolved.

After the German attack on the Soviet Union in 1941, Stalin had the Germans deported into the Asiatic part of the Soviet Union. A few days after the deportation decree, the Volga Republic disappeared from the map: a decree of 7 September 1941, integrated its *rayons* into the territories of Saratov and Stalingrad. Under the impact of the radical German policy of occupation and the anti-German propaganda, the German Russians continued to be treated in a hostile fashion as "fascists" by their new neighbors. It was only under the pressure in the camps, in the "labor army," and in exile that a part of the Germans assimilated to the Russian-speaking majority. Young people now grew up without religious education. To some extent the government itself countered this forced assimilation by insisting that this group's passports were stamped "German." In their applications for resettlement to Germany, German Russians still invoke this stamp at the beginning of the 21st century.

Brandes, Detlef. *Von den Zaren adoptiert. Die deutschen Kolonisten und die Balkansiedler in Neurußland und Bessarabien 1751–1914.* Munich, 1993.

Dahlmann, Dittmar, and Ralph Tuchtenhagen, eds. *Zwischen Reform und Revolution. Die Deutschen an der Wolga 1860–1917.* Essen, 1994.

Dönninghaus, Victor. *Revolution, Reform und Krieg. Die Deutschen an der Wolga im ausgehenden Zarenreich.* Essen, 2002.

Dönninghaus, Victor. *Minderheiten in Bedrängnis. Sowjetische Politik gegenüber Deutschen, Polen und anderen Diaspora-Nationalitäten 1917–1938.* Munich, 2009.

Long, James. *From Privileged to Dispossessed: The Volga Germans, 1860–1917.* Lincoln and London, 1988.

Neutatz, Dietmar. *Die "deutsche Frage" im Schwarzmeergebiet und in Wolhynien. Politik, Wirtschaft, Mentalitäten und Alltag im Spannungsfeld von Nationalismus und Modernisierung (1856–1914).* Stuttgart, 1993.

Stricker, Gerd, ed. *Deutsche Geschichte im Osten Europas: Rußland.* Berlin, 1997.

Cross-references: The Baltic Region; Germany; Poland; Russia and Belarus; Ukraine; *Aussiedler/Spätaussiedler* in Germany since 1950; Bulgarian and Gagauzian Settlers in New Russia and Bessarabia since the 18th Century; Ethnic German "Remigrants" from Russia in Germany, 1890s to 1930s; German Merchants and Industrial Entrepreneurs in Russia since the 18th Century; Moravian Brethren in Europe since the Early Modern Period; Ukrainian and Russian Settlers in New Russia since the 18th Century

GERMAN SETTLERS (*DONAUSCHWABEN*) IN SOUTHEASTERN EUROPE SINCE THE EARLY MODERN PERIOD

Márta Fata

Historical Hungary (the modern-day countries of Hungary, Slovakia, Croatia, the regions of Transylvania, Banat in Romania, and Batschka in Serbia) was an immigration country for nearly a thousand years. As had happened after the end of Mongol expansion in east-central and southeastern Europe in the 13th century, following the reconquest of Hungary by the Ottomans around the turn of the 17th century, immigrants from diverse European regions participated in the reconstruction of the country, with the majority of the settlers coming from the German-speaking realm. For one reason, the population in central Europe was significantly larger than in Hungary. For another, the emperors from the house of Habsburg had been simultaneously the kings of Hungary since 1526, a circumstance that promoted immigration from the German territorial states to Hungary. Not least, the recruiting of German settlers was justified on the grounds that "they come with good determination and their

own means, and they behave exceedingly well." Compared to the old-established population, the immigrant Germans generally possessed something that was much desired by Hungarian landowners: knowledge of modern agriculture and trade. Consequently the pars-pro-toto term "Swabian" (ung. *sváb*, rom. *şvab*, kroat. *švaba*, serb. шваба) that was initially used for the Germans – most of whom immigrated from the Imperial Circle of Swabia – reflected high esteem. It was only in the wake of Magyarization that began in the last third of the 19th century that the word took on a negative connotation in the Hungarian language.

The self-descriptions of the descendants of the settlers reflected the process of differentiation within "Swabian society" that began in the 19th century. The rural population continued to use the term "Swabian." By contrast, the Swabian bourgeoisie that had arisen from the peasant class adopted the term "German-Hungarians" – known since 1641 as the self-description of the Saxon burghers in the region of Zips in Upper Hungary – and in so doing emphasized their close intertwinement with the Hungarian majority. When the German settlement areas were divided up among the successor states to the throne of St. Stephen as a result of the peace treaties following World War I, the Swabians proved themselves loyal to their new states, which was expressed – among other ways – by the self-descriptions as "Hungarian-Germans," "Yugoslav-Germans," and "Romanian-Germans." By contrast, the outside description "Swabian" took on the character of a term of abuse in Hungary (where the national minorities were blamed for the breakup of historical Hungary) and in Yugoslavia (as a result of the German occupation of the country in World War II).

The term "Danube Swabian" was introduced by German southeastern European studies in 1922 to emphasize the historical and cultural unity of the Swabian settlement areas also after the division of Hungary. The term took on a new meaning after World War II when several hundreds of thousands of Germans were expelled from Hungary, Yugoslavia, and Romania and found a new home in Germany as "Danube-Swabians." An identity tied to their countries of origin (Hungary, Romania, or Yugoslavia) still dominated their collective memory at the beginning of the 21st century.

Background and goals of migration

Lack of immigration statistics makes it impossible to determine precisely the volume of German immigration in the 18th century. For the first half of the 18th century, scholars have estimated the number of Germans in Hungary at around 350,000–400,000. In 1773, the number was put at around 637,000, in 1840 it was already up to 1,038,000, and in 1880 to nearly 2 million, including those in Zips and the Transylvanian Saxons who had settled in the Middle Ages and the urban immigrants from the Austrian half of the Austrian-Hungarian dual monarchy.

The recruitment of settlers for the territories under the direct administration of Vienna, which began in 1689 with an imperial Population Patent (*Impopulationspatent*), was aimed at increasing the population as an element of mercantilist economic policy. In 1722–3, the Hungarian landowners also recognized how important the settlement of qualified workers was to their lordships in a law concerning the settlement of the land with colonists. The rights guaranteed by Vienna and the Hungarian parliament (freedom of movement, temporary exemption from taxes, etc.) were very attractive to people in the German territorial states, who were often plagued by wars and famines and who wished to free themselves from oppressive legal burdens (law of real division, marriage restrictions, etc.) and the economic hardships so closely linked to them.

The regions from which the settlement movement to Hungary originated were chiefly the lands of the Habsburgs themselves or their close allies, especially Hesse and the southern and southwestern regions (Baden, Bavaria, Alsace, Lorraine, Swabia, the Palatinate, Upper Austria). The Germans settled in the region around Ofen (Ofener Bergland), in the Hungarian Highlands, in southern Hungary ("Swabian Turkey"), in the region around Sathmar, in the Batschka area, and in the Banat, later via satellite villages in Slavonia, with the immigration directed more toward villages than market towns or cities. As a result, the term "Swabian" was simultaneously associated with the German-speaking peasantry.

Nowhere did the newcomers form larger, ethnically self-contained areas. They were settled alongside Hungarians, Romanians, Slovaks, and southern Slavs, which from the outset required that the immigrants communicate with their ethnically different neighbors. However, in the villages of the Banat and along the military border the government enforced a more or less consistent separation of German-speakers from other groups, often in the form of dual settlements. Other settlement areas witnessed frequent segregation, which resulted largely from the different ways in which the ethnic groups engaged in economic activities.

The Swabian settlements were linguistically and confessionally diverse. For example, in the Ofener Bergland residents spoke dialects with Bavarian and Rhenish-Franconian elements, in the south largely with Franconian, Palatine, and Swabian elements. While in the Banat and especially along the military border, where Emperor Charles VI and his successor, Maria Theresa, pursued simultaneously military and political goals with their settlement policy, it was mostly Catholics who were given a new home as the "bulwark (*Vormauer*) of Christendom." What mattered most to Emperor Joseph II and the secular landowners was not confessional identity but solely the qualifications of the settlers. As a result, Lutherans were also settled in larger numbers in the Batschka and the Komitat Tolna. Catholic and Protestant Germans did not form their own ecclesiastical organizations but were incorporated into the Hungarian churches, which promoted their integration. At the time of the growth of the Hungarian national state in the 19th century, the Catholic Church became – alongside the state – the promoter of the assimilation of minorities, including the Germans. This was especially successful in the case of the "Sathmar Swabians."

What became the driving force behind the geographic and social mobility of the settled Swabians was *Anerbenrecht*, the right of an heir to inherit an undivided farm estate, which diverged from Hungarian custom and became the uniform practice only after settlement. Sons excluded from the inheritance learned a trade, sought to establish their own farmstead by buying land within or outside the boundaries of their village, or pursued higher qualifications by attending secondary schools or even university. The dissolution of the Croatian military border in 1858 and its settlement and the industrialization of Hungary in the second half of the 19th century brought in their wake an intensive domestic migration from the Swabian villages to the southern Slavic and Hungarian settlement areas.

While farmers and artisans preserved their culture also in their new surroundings, for the university-educated sons of farming families social advancement meant simultaneously the path of voluntary assimilation. The reason was that the fundamental economic and political reforms of the 19th century did not originate from the weak, mostly German-speaking bourgeoisie but from the Hungarian nobility. As a result of the Magyarization of the bourgeoisie, the Swabians – unlike the Zipser and Transylvanian Germans in the countryside – lost their leadership stratum.

Integration between "fatherland" and "motherland"

The German settlers were economically successful in Hungary. For one, they had brought with them more efficient farming and commercial methods than were generally practiced in Hungary. For another, Hungarian landowners had granted the settlers a less severe system of dues and boon work – unpaid work required by the landowner, which took the tenant away from his own farm – which made it easier for the settlers to produce for the market and engage in rational farming. *Anerbenrecht* imparted to their way of life another special characteristic, one that from the outset promoted the dynamic participation of the settlers in the money economy. That in turn allowed for the adoption of bourgeois norms, among them a greater willingness to work hard and save (no strict division of work according to gender, fewer holidays, simpler festive meals, less expensive clothing, etc.), which became the most important identity-creating values and at the same time the fundamental characteristics that outsiders ascribed to the Swabians. A saying that became widespread in southern Hungary especially in the 20th century vividly encapsulates this outsider perception: "If you throw a Swabian over a fence naked, he'll land on the other side clothed."

Differences in the forms and conditions of state-sponsored and private settlement influenced the social status of the settlers. Those settled on state-owned land, as in the Banat and along the military border, were placed into villages laid out by engineers, where the government built houses, schools, and churches for them and helped them create a new life by providing equipment, draft animals, seed, and loans. Here the farmers generally had large agricultural acreage and switched to the more profitable cultivation of grain. Under Habsburg administration there arose a legally free and self-confident peasant class, which was able to preserve its elevated status also after the return of the Banat (1779) and the Banat military border (1873) to Hungary.

By contrast, private settlement on the noble *komitats* (county) was often less capitalized, and the development of the estates from the second half of the 18th century led to the gradual dismantling of the special legal status of the Swabian farmers. The villages within Hungary, generally with smaller boundaries and soil that was sometimes of lesser quality, were dominated by extremely small farms, which were able to expand their sources of income by switching to specialized crops (tobacco, wine, and fruit), animal husbandry, and small-scale trades.

A social divide thus ran along the Danube: the number of large and medium-size farms held by Swabian farmers was twice as high in the Banat and the Batschka as in Transdanubia. However, those areas also had a significantly higher number of day laborers with little chance for social advancement, especially after the middle of the 19th century. It is therefore not surprising that around 1900, when Hungary's economic modernization stalled and the excess Swabian population failed to find work in industry, these regions, in particular, witnessed – alongside a small-scale labor migration to Germany – mass emigration to the USA. But while the Hungarian and Slovakian emigrants to the USA left Hungary for good, the majority of the Swabians returned within a few years to buy land with their savings.

The economic and social differences that already existed between the German settlement areas at the time they were established remained in place and played a role in the fact that the Swabians did not form a political community when the modern Hungarian nation-state was created, but merely an ethnic group without corporate rights or their own ecclesiastical organization. The reality was that until the second half of the 19th century the Swabians had no need to express specific group interests, since the forces behind the settlement were not pushing for their sociocultural integration. The Swabians were able to preserve their language, way of life, and customs for a long time undisturbed while at the same time absorbing elements from the culture of their host region. For example, in the religious sphere the immigrants introduced the worship of the saints Rochus, Valentine, and Urban, previously unknown in Hungary, while conversely adopting the saints from the medieval Hungarian royal house, especially the founder of the crown, Saint Stephen. In other spheres of life, as well, there was more or less necessary accommodation, for example, in terms of food culture. The cultivation of certain types of grain, vegetables, and fruit, determined by the climate and soil of the Pannonian region, became the basis of a specifically Swabian cuisine: the descendants of the settlers supplemented their most important foods from their old homeland, such as potatoes and cabbage, with Hungarian vegetables like paprika, onions, and garlic.

Acculturation was most pronounced among the Swabian landowners in the Banat, which led to the adoption of the values and way of life of the Hungarian gentry and eventually promoted assimilation. The Swabian educated middle class (writers, university professor, deputies of regional parliaments), which had taken on Swabian interests at the end of the 19th century, was able to draw support from the owners of large and medium-size farms in the Banat. The latter were most threatened with respect to their livelihood: the backdrop was an agrarian crisis triggered by the importation of cheap American grain and the infestation of the vineyards with the vine pest, but also the increasing fragmentation of land as a result of the gradual suppression of *Anerbenrecht* in favor of an equal division among the heirs. Initially they tried to represent their interests in economic organizations and eventually in the Hungarian German People's Party (Ungarländische Deutsche Volkspartei), which was founded in 1906. But the political rallying cry "Jolt yourself! Extend yourself, Swabian farmer!" remained limited to the Banat and the dissolved military border. The German farmers in the Batschak and especially in the interior could hardly be mobilized for these kinds of economic and political goals because as small and very small-scale farmers they were less exposed to the fluctuations of the market than the large farmers of the Banat engaged in monoculture. In addition, they felt that the Hungarian Nationalities Law of 1868, which provided extensive guarantees for the public use of traditional languages, was adequate, even after it was trimmed back at the beginning of the 20th century.

After 1918, the Swabians were divided up among various states. However, in the trenches of World War I they had experienced a national sense of German unity beyond their settlement areas and state borders and they now wished to have a political organization. The minority protection treaties that were signed by the successor states to the Hungarian monarchy and guaranteed by the League of Nations awarded the minorities personal and collective rights. Yet the granting of these rights depended on the goals the new nation-states were pursuing in foreign policy. In practice this meant that the German minorities had various degrees of freedom of movement. The Hungarian government, which was seeking a territorial revision, pushed the linguistic assimilation of the minorities and tried to prevent any cultural and political organization of the Germans. In Yugoslavia, the Germans were economically weakened by the agrarian reforms that were carried out also to their disadvantage, but with an eye toward Hungarian revisionism, they – as well as the Germans in Romania – were permitted (at least for a time) to freely organize themselves politically, economically, and culturally. The new states wooed their loyalty in an effort to stabilize the new state borders in Yugoslavia and Romania, which were not coterminous with the ethnic boundaries.

Village judge and jurymen of the German-Hungarian municipality Cseledoboka, 1934 (*Institut für donauschwäbische Geschichte und Landeskunde, Tübingen, Collection Rudolf Hartmann*).

After 1933, the politics of the German minority groups in all three successor states to the Danubian monarchy, which had been traditionally focused on patriotism toward the respective state and constitution and, above all, their own culture, found itself in a dead end. In its pursuit of great power status, Hitler's Germany was demanding political loyalty from the Germans of southeastern Europe, and this aroused the suspicion of the national governments. In this situation of conflict between the "fatherland" and the "motherland," the "policy of protection" offered by the German Reich seemed to the young representatives of the German "renewal movement" the only way to preserve a minority status they regarded as under threat (Hungary, Romania) and to find a solution to pressing social problems (Yugoslavia). Since the mostly national-liberal or conservative representatives of the older generation tended to be skeptical toward these aspirations, strong tensions emerged within the German minority groups. The fears of the elders were realized: the price for Germany's advocacy of the goals of the German minorities to the governments of the successor states was their instrumentalization for the foreign policy interests of the Third Reich and the *Gleichschaltung* of the German "ethnic groups." The organs of the German minorities supported this as compliant instruments of the Nazis' hegemonic policy. After 1938, at the latest, the German minority groups found themselves in a tight spot, however, since Hungary, Romania, and Yugoslavia supported Germany's hegemonic policy, if for different reasons and to varying degrees of intensity. That is why critical voices among the Swabians in Hungary and the opposition in the German-Catholic camp in Romania went unheard.

After the end of World War II, the Germans in southeastern Europe were collectively punished through mass killings (Yuogoslavia), expulsion (Hungary), deportation within their homelands and to the Soviet Union (Yugoslavia, Hungary, Romania), and by being stripped of their rights, dispossessed, and stigmatized as "Hitler's fifth column."

The Swabians in Yugoslavia tried to escape these revenge measures by fleeing and later emigrating legally to the Federal Republic, especially as part of the family reunification program. In Hungary they chose to migrate to the cities, Magyarize their names, and give up the use of their language and traditional dress. The Swabians, the majority of whom had been active in the agrarian sector until 1945, found new employment as industrial workers in the socialist industry. To compensate for the economic and social decline they suffered as a result, the second generation after 1945 was often eager to pursue an academic profession. More strongly than in the 19th century, this social advancement entailed assimilation. Modern, urban forms of a Hungarian-German culture were not able to arise. The self-description of the Germans continues to point to traditional values like work ethic and religiosity. A Swabian folklore, meanwhile, was preserved.

In Romania, by contrast, the German bourgeoisie in its settlement area in the Banat soon found itself in the minority vis-à-vis the immigrant Romanians, and even though the Germans were in demand as skilled workers, they remained excluded from management positions. As a result of the 1977 German-Romanian treaty about the resettlement of the Germans, the majority of Romanian-Germans found a new home in the Federal Republic. Although an urban German culture had been able to establish itself in Romania after 1918 in the form of secondary schools, papers, theaters, and the production of literature and books, mass emigration beginning in the 1970s reduced it to the point where only rudiments are left.

With the demise of communist rule in eastern Europe at the end of the 1980s, minority protection laws leading in the direction of administrative and cultural autonomy were passed in Romania and especially in Hungary. However, these laws did not stop the ongoing process of assimilation. The cultural identity of the Swabians in Hungary is disappearing, since the number of those speaking the Swabian mother tongue has dropped precipitously and continues to decline.

Aschauer, Wolfgang. *Zur Produktion und Reproduktion einer Nationalität. Die Ungarndeutschen*. Stuttgart, 1992.

Fata, Márta. *Die Donauschwaben. Deutsche Siedlung in Südosteuropa. Exhibition catalogue*, edited by Immo Eberl. Sigmaringen, 1987.

Fata, Márta. *Die Schwäbische Türkei. Lebensformen der Ethnien in Südwestungarn*. Sigmaringen, 1997.

Schödl, Günter. *Land an der Donau*. Berlin, 1995.

Senz, Ingomar. *Die Donauschwaben*. Munich, 1994.

Cross-references: Germany; Austria, Southeastern Europe; *Aussiedler/ Spätaussiedler* in Germany since 1950; German Deportees from East-Central and Southeastern Europe in the USSR after the End of World War II; German Refugees and Expellees from Eastern, East-Central, and Southeastern Europe in Germany and Austria since the End of World War II; Settlers on the Habsburg Military Border since the Early Modern Period

GERMAN SKILLED WORKERS AND CRAFTSMEN IN THE USSR IN THE INTERWAR PERIOD

Sergei Zhuravlev

Large-scale migration from Germany to the Soviet Union took place between 1928 and 1931, as the Soviet government sought German workers to aid in the industrialization of the country. Although they formed part of a larger group of foreign workers in the USSR, Germans outnumbered Americans, Austrians, Czechs, and others. In 1931 alone – according to various estimates – 6,000 to 8,000 skilled workers and craftsmen from highly developed branches in the German industry, accompanied by approximately the same number of family members, found employment in key Soviet enterprises in Moscow, Leningrad, the Volga regions, Ukraine, the Urals, and western Siberia. Most German workers returned to their homeland by 1936.

This migration movement was closely tied to the cultural and political developments in the USSR. The idealism associated with the Soviet experiment of reshaping economic, social, cultural, and political life found sympathizers throughout the West. Economic developments, however, played an important role as well: the Soviet Union had a shortage of qualified industrial workers, which was only intensified after 1927 with the introduction of the first Five-Year Plan and the massive import of modern technology from the West, particularly from Germany. Finally, the depression of the early 1930s, which did not affect the Soviet Union, also made the USSR an attractive destination for specialists who either had lost their jobs or faced the threat of unemployment.

Soviet migration policy in the 1920s and 1930s did not follow a consistent pattern. In the initial period between 1920 and 1927, economic migration was strictly limited, but after the introduction of the first Five-Year Plan in 1927 the "best representatives of the foreign proletariat" were welcomed. In connection with the large-scale import of modern German technology in 1928–31, the USSR sought to hire German workers in particular. These experts, so they hoped, would help Russian workers handle the complicated equipment and familiarize them with modern industrial production.

In 1927–9 several thousand Germans, mainly unemployed miners from the Ruhr area, were contracted to work in the Donbass coal basin in Ukraine. Enthusiastic workers from Essen traveled by train to help in building socialism. Due to poor organization, however, many workers did not find jobs that matched their qualifications and appropriate equipment and tools were often not available. The Germans suffered because of the low payment, the lack of food and medicine, and the harsh working and living conditions of the rural Soviet Union. This frequently resulted in public outcries, complaints, refusal to work, and contract violation through large-scale return migration as well as general disillusionment.

In order to improve the situation, Soviet authorities in 1930 reformulated their recruitment of, hiring of, and employment practices with foreign workers. Professional skills no longer represented the decisive criterion for recruitment. The selection of "loyal" and "conscientious" workers with the support of communist party cells in Germany and measures preparing candidates for temporary shortages in Russia were intended to prevent further disappointments. New arrivals were no longer settled in small towns or the countryside, but only in industrial centers, where living and working conditions were more acceptable to foreign workers. Finally, they also received privileges in the rationing system and special efforts were made to integrate the foreigners into Soviet society.

The large-scale recruitment of foreign workers stopped in 1932 and the living and working conditions for foreign workers in the Soviet Union steadily worsened. Germans no longer received privileged contracts and could not extend existing ones. A guaranteed wage and partial payment in marks – the most important stipulations of the contracts signed with skilled German metalworkers in 1929–30 – were soon abolished. The Soviet authorities, knowing that they could easily recruit skilled machinists from among the ranks of the numerous unemployed in Germany, lowered the guaranteed monthly wage from 250 to 150 rubles between December 1930 and October 1931. The Germans had either to accept the same conditions as Soviet workers or return to Germany. Many skilled German workers who had originally intended to remain in the Soviet Union now considered themselves temporary labor migrants and waited for the German labor market to improve.

Germans were mainly recruited on an individual basis by the Soviet government or the key ministries (*Narkomaty*) through their representatives in the Soviet Trade Mission (Torgovoe Predstavitel'stvo) in Berlin at the request of Soviet enterprises in search of skilled workers. In some cases candidates were asked to demonstrate their skills before a contract was signed. Workers were in great demand, especially in the metal industry and at power stations, and not only those who were highly skilled but also those who were less skilled, such as turners, fitters, toolmakers, and welders. Preference was given to comparatively young (27–35 years), qualified male workers with at least 10 years of experience in firms like Siemens, Krupp, or AEG. Contracts were set for a year and could be extended. Soviet authorities covered the costs of travel and baggage transportation to and from the USSR for the workers themselves and their families and also provided living accommodations.

The migrants often came in groups of people who had earlier worked together in a German enterprise or had been active in the same cell of the KPD (Communist Party of Germany). For example, many German workers in the Moscow electricity combine (Elektrozavod, which had a monopoly position in the field) had been employed by either the lightbulb manufacturer Osram or the electrical equipment company AEG. A further example is provided by skilled workers from Thüringer Wald who were employed in various Soviet regions (automobile production and the Stanko machine construction factory in Moscow, radio production in Alexandrov, machine tool construction in Kunzewo, milling machine production in Gorki, or factories in Uljanowsk and Penza). Dozens or sometimes even hundreds of German skilled workers and their families formed "German colonies" connected to factories all over the USSR.

The majority of German migrants to the Soviet Union were KPD members or sympathizers. The proportion of communists increased to 50% after 1930, when the KPD assisted Soviet authorities in the selection process. Many migrant workers planned to settle long term or permanently in the USSR and sold their property in Germany. Few, however, renewed their contracts beyond the original one-year term or remained longer than three to four years in the Soviet Union.

About a quarter of all German workers were unmarried. Some married workers were compelled to arrange for their families to move to the USSR due to the cancellation of the foreign currency clause in their contracts, which left them unable to provide for their families in Germany. While the presence of one's family may have served as a stabilizing factor in a difficult period of acclimatization, it also frequently created problems in terms of accommodation, food, and medical care. The high cost of living in the USSR in the early 1930s forced many German spouses to take up paid work.

The high fluctuation among German migrants began to ebb only in 1932, when the Soviet government initiated a policy meant to recruit foreign labor in a more cost-effective manner. The USSR increasingly delegated German political refugees with industrial work experience to the plants (2,000 to 3,000 persons) or hired Germans who were already in Russia (tourists, members of the workers' families) without privileged individual contracts. Further, German workers provided factory officials with the names of colleagues or relatives in Germany who were then recruited. Sometimes entire families were put under contract, a policy that became rather popular, not least for propaganda reasons. For example, three generations of the Huth and Zint families (grandfather, father, and children) worked in the Moscow electricity combine in 1931. The German "colony" in the plant comprising about 300 employees and family members – was the largest one in Moscow. Other large "colonies" could be found at the Stanko factory in Moscow, the automobile factories in Gorki and Moscow, the tractor factories in Stalingrad and Kharkov, and the plant in Kuznetsk.

The Germans did not speak Russian and initially had to get their bearings on their own. In enterprises with a sufficient number of German workers, German labor brigades were formed. Although the practice complied with their wishes and put their skills to use most effectively, it also isolated them even more from their Russian workmates. Russian apprentices later joined such teams. Germans who demonstrated organizational talents and who managed to learn Russian quickly were employed as foremen, instructors, shop managers, or even constructors and engineers.

Housing and living conditions were poor. In the best case, the Germans were accommodated in communal apartments (*kommunalka*), in which two to three families (or unmarried men) each had their own (single) room and shared the kitchen, bathroom, and toilet. Many found that the *kommunalka* solution undermined their privacy and family life. During periods of strict rationing and general shortages all employees took their midday meal in the factory canteen (*stolovaia*), but the simple fare often drew critical comments from the Germans, who particularly missed their beloved beer. The abolition of the rationing system in 1935 increased the supply of food but also led to a sharp increase in the prices of basic foodstuffs, including bread. A modest improvement in real wages took place in 1936–7, at a time of continuing inflation, but the standard of living for most workers still lagged behind that of 1928, when the program of massive industrialization had begun.

From a cultural, psychological, and economic point of view, adopting the USSR as a new "motherland" was not an easy task, even for German communists. While the Soviet authorities highlighted their wish to integrate German skilled workers into the Soviet society, the migrants were essentially left to their own devices in a foreign country with an unfamiliar culture and language. In 1930, however, a special order was issued to local party organizations in industrial enterprises, requiring them to take personal care of each foreigner. They were supposed to acquaint them with social life and activities in the plant, help them learn Russian, and familiarize them with the political situation in the country. The new law granted foreign workers the right to vote and to stand for election. Dozens of Germans were elected to district Soviets and even the Moscow Soviet in the 1930s.

In 1929 and 1930 plants employing a sufficiently large number of foreigners received funds to build apartment buildings specially designed to accommodate foreign workers in more comfortable housing. This corresponded to the wishes of German workers to live together, where they could help one another when faced with acclimation and integration problems, but it also increased their isolation from Soviet society.

A network of "foreigners' offices" (*inobiuro*), each of which was responsible for a specific nationality and which extended from the local unions to the Central Soviet of Trade Unions in Moscow, were meant to aid migrant workers in their everyday lives. These offices helped to resolve visa issues, settled disputes, and pursued complaints, but they also were responsible for political control. In addition to the well-known *Deutsche Zentral Zeitung* (*DZZ*), published by the German section of the Communist International (Comintern), the number of local German newspapers increased, such as *Echo* in Stalingrad, and even factory newspapers. German workers were invited to describe their impressions of life in the USSR or to publish suggestions for increasing productivity. A foreign workers' club with a large German section was established in Moscow at the end of 1929 and organized cultural and political events for Germans. Since the club typically had a German-speaking audience, however, it also failed to promote integration into Russian society.

The children of German workers did not encounter language problems as they learned Russian at school or at summer pioneer camps and had Russian playmates. The workers themselves only learned as much Russian as they needed to communicate in the workplace or to secure a better position. German housewives, who had to bear the main burden in an economy characterized by shortages, mainly kept to themselves, did not learn Russian, and longed for their homeland.

Starting in 1933, the Soviet regime employed compulsory measures intended to better integrate Germans into Soviet society and to prevent return migration. A campaign was started to prompt Germans to renounce their German citizenship and become Soviet citizens. It was "strongly recommended" that they end all relations with the National Socialist German state: visits to Germany or German diplomatic posts in the USSR as well as correspondence with friends and relatives in Germany were to cease. Workers who ignored these appeals and bought tickets for a vacation or a return journey to Germany were expelled from the Communist Party. The result was the mass flight of German skilled workers out of the USSR. In many cases party discipline was the only means of stopping return migration – by 1936 at least 2,600 German migrants had been transferred from the KPD to the Soviet Communist Party.

Many Germans turned their backs on the Soviet Union because they were simply unable to adjust to the living conditions there: the precarious supply situation, high prices for basic foodstuffs, a low family income, and the intolerable life in the *kommunalka* were the most important reasons. The decision to return to National Socialist Germany clearly illustrates the depth of the disillusionment that had set in since their arrival in the USSR. Many who had come to the USSR as dedicated communists returned to Germany as sympathizers of the Nazis' "new order," which promised work for all. Their fellow countrymen who remained in the Soviet Union dubbed them "deserters from the front of Socialist construction." The phenomenon of return migration to National Socialist Germany after 1933 contributed to the emergence of increasingly xenophobic Soviet propaganda, which contrasted sharply with the much-publicized communist internationalism.

The majority of German workers left the country in several waves of return migration during the years 1934 through 1936, before the onset of mass political repression. Those who remained in the USSR after 1936 – craftsmen who had married Soviet women or had become Soviet citizens – fell victim to the *massoperatsii* of the Soviet secret police (NKVD) during the Great Terror (1936–8) particularly following enactment of the NKVD's "German Order no. 00439" on 25 July 1937. Almost all of these workers were arrested or killed during the Stalin terror. Families were torn apart; male breadwinners were executed or sent to camps. A small number of

German workers survived in the Gulag and returned to East Germany in the late 1950s.

Dehl, Oleg. *Verratene Ideale. Zur Geschichte deutscher Emigranten in der Sowjetunion in den 30er Jahren*. Berlin, 2000.

Jarmatz, Klaus, Simone Barg, and Peter Diezel. *Exil in der UdSSR*. Leipzig, 1979.

Kaiser, Gerd. *Russlandfahrer. Aus dem Wald in die Welt. Facharbeiter aus dem Thüringer Wald in der UdSSR, 1930–1965*. Tessin, 2000.

Schafranek, Hans. *Zwischen NKWD und Gestapo: Die Auslieferung deutscher und Österreichischer Antifaschisten aus der Sowjetunion von Nazideutschland, 1939–1941*. Frankfurt am Main, 1990.

Tischler, Carola. *Flucht in die Verfolgung: Deutsche Emigranten im sowjetischen Exil 1933 bis 1945*. Münster, 1996.

Zhuravljev, Sergei. *Ich bitte um Arbeit in der Sowjetunion. Das Schicksal deutscher Facharbeiter im Moskau der 30er Jahre*. Berlin, 2003.

Cross-references: Czechia and Slovakia; Germany; Poland; Russia and Belarus; Ukraine; Deportees in the Soviet Union during and after World War II; European Political Emigrants in the USSR since 1917; Russian Labor Migrants on Large Construction Sites in the USSR since the 1920s

GERMAN SOLDIERS IN THE FRENCH FOREIGN LEGION IN THE 19TH AND 20TH CENTURIES

Eckard Michels

The French Foreign Legion, an elite unit for colonial wars, was originally founded in 1831 merely as a temporary institution to accommodate political refugees of the revolutionary events across Europe in 1830–1, and it recruited foreign volunteers for a minimum of five years. The unit, at all times commanded by French officers, always accepted Germans along with other European nationalities (non-Europeans were not tolerated until the mid-1960s) in the ranks of its soldiers and noncommissioned officer ranks. Especially in the first 60 years of the 20th century, the Germans constituted an indispensable reservoir for the mercenary force. This was especially true in the 1920s during the war in French Morocco against the Rif rebellions and during the French decolonization wars after 1945, which ended with Algeria's independence. During the entire 170-year history of the force, the Germans were by far the strongest nationality, even if the trend has been in strong decline since the Algerian war.

Women were still not being recruited at the beginning of the 21st century; for a few years there have merely been a few French female medical officers and female noncommissioned officers in the administration, who had been posted temporarily to the Legion from the regular army. An estimated 550,000–600,000 men served in the Legion between

1831 and the end of the 20th century. Of those, about 220,000 are likely to have been Germans, followed by about 100,000 Frenchmen who usually joined the Legion under a false nationality, and around 70,000 Italians. In three phases of the Legion's history, the Germans constituted about a third to a half of all legionnaires: between 1871 and 1900, from the beginning of the 1920s to 1933, and from 1946 to 1962. The highest absolute number of Germans in the Foreign Legion was reached around 1953–4, when about 20,000 were serving as legionnaires, which amounted to about 55%. If one considers that for every volunteer actually accepted into the Legion, three to five candidates were usually turned away for lack of physical fitness, a past history of serious crimes, presumed political unreliability, or for racist reasons (Jewish candidates were often refused), the existence of the Foreign Legion brought about no small labor migration in the 19th and 20th centuries between Germany (to a lesser extent also Italy, Spain, and Switzerland) and France or its colonies in North Africa and Indochina.

The number of volunteers crowding into the Legion's recruitment offices was always a barometer for political upheavals and for social and economic crises in Europe in the 19th and 20th centuries, and for the migratory movements to France they triggered. For example, in the 1870s and 1880s, men from Alsace-Lorraine furnished more than half of the recruits, since they were not willing to serve in the hated army of the German emperor. In the 1890s, this stream dried up when the new generations made their peace with life in Imperial Germany. The 1920s saw a wave of anti-Bolshevist emigrants from Russia who sought refuge in the Legion, and after the end of the Spanish Civil War in 1939, Spaniards who were loyal to the Republic briefly made up the largest contingent among new recruits.

Finally, the upheavals in eastern, east-central, and southeastern Europe since 1989–90 led to a surge in the percentage of legionnaires from the formerly communist states. At the beginning of the 21st century, they accounted for around 55% of all newly inducted legionnaires, while the percentage of German volunteers among the recruits dropped to below 2%. As a result of the ups and downs in French interests overseas, the size of the Legion and thus the need for recruits also fluctuated considerably: the strength of the mercenary force oscillated between a minimum of about 3,000 in the 1870s and a maximum of nearly 50,000 mercenaries in 1939–40, and still 36,000 at the height of the war in Indochina in 1953–4. At the beginning of the 21st century, the Legion had about 7,900 officers, noncommissioned officers, and soldiers from 130 nations, though Europeans continued to furnish about 90% of the personnel.

The motives for joining the Legion were always varied, though in most cases material need, often triggered by political persecution at home and a life in exile, family uprooting, or a lack of occupational opportunities were crucial factors that led men to seek out the recruitment office. By contrast, a love of adventure, fascination with the military life, the desire to acquire further professional training, political convictions, or fear of criminal prosecution at home were more rarely motives behind the decision to join the Legion. The bundle of economic and social motives played a decisive role especially among German legionnaires; also, Germany was France's neighbor with the largest population. A persistent and – compared to the period before 1914 – high rate of unemployment in the 1920s and early 1930s led, for example, to a strong influx of German volunteers, whose decision to join was also influenced by the presence of nearby recruiting offices: the Foreign Legion maintained recruitment offices in the occupied Rhineland until 1930. In 1945–6, thousands of German prisoners of war held by the French were recruited. Beginning in 1947 there was a wave of mostly young Germans, who flocked to the recruitment offices of the Legion in the French occupation zone in southwestern Germany (which did not close until 1955). They often came from the group of German refugees and expellees from the east, who had been uprooted by the war and therefore had problems integrating into the labor market in the Western zones. After World War II, as well, there were – at times coincidentally – particularly good recruitment circumstances for the Legion in Germany, at a time when protracted military engagements in the colonies were creating a heavy demand for recruits. Finally, the option of serving in German military units to escape unemployment was initially nonexistent after 1945.

The fact that Germans went to France to serve in the Foreign Legion led Germany – from the end of the 19th century until the 1960s – repeatedly to press campaigns that denounced this alleged scandal. In most cases domestic and foreign political motives were in the background, less so a concern for the fate of the legionnaires. The phenomenon of German-speaking foreign legionnaires was widely known in Germany at the time, and it has survived as a linguistic relic in the sense that the press occasionally refers to German soccer players who change to foreign clubs as "legionnaires." However, in Germany the quantitative dimension of this work migration was usually significantly overestimated or deliberately exaggerated. In France, little attention was paid to German legionnaires – after all, the French motherland, especially Strasbourg and then Marseille, were at most brief transit stations on the way to the colonies in North Africa and Indochina.

Most candidates wanted to enlist for a single tour to escape a momentary emergency at home or in the asylum country of France, especially since the Legion hardly offered foreigners any career prospects and also paid poorly until the 1960s. However, the Legion always had a high rate of reenlistment after the end of the first tour, as a result of which about one-third to half of all legionnaires remained in the Legion for 10 or more years, for the most part because reintegration into civilian life in their homeland had failed. The possibilities of establishing a life outside of the military community of the mercenary force – for example, in France or its colonies – were extremely limited. Because the Legion

Germans in the Foreign Legion captured in 1954 in Indochina during the battle of Dien Bien Phu. They were released that same fall; North Vietnamese propaganda photo (*ullstein bild*).

held a special position within the French army, there were no contacts with regular French units. Moreover, the units were usually stationed in remote garrisons in Indochina and North Africa, which meant that in a geographical sense they were separated from the French population even in the colonies.

During the five-year tour of duty, the basic legionnaire ranks had neither home leave nor leave to go to France; vacation days had to be spent in the Legions' holiday homes in the colonies. Added to this were language problems, since the Legion, until the end of the Algerian war, placed no stock in having its members acquire a thorough knowledge of French. Moreover, a legionnaire could hardly acquire vocational qualifications for a civil job after the end of his enlistment: until the end of the Algerian war, the Legion was a force with an infantry focus and required hardly any technical knowledge from the simple soldier. Finally, the legionnaires encountered an overwhelmingly negative attitude from the French public, which on the whole had an ambivalent view of the Legion. As an institution it was cheered, most strikingly during the parade on 14 July on the Champs-Elysées. If nothing else, it did embody France's claim to be the second home for Europe's castaways, who in return were willing, out of gratitude, to risk their lives for the "Grande Nation" and the universal values it stood for.

The individual legionnaire, however, was met with distrust; after all, he carried the reputation of being a failure in life. In the case of the German legionnaires, this attitude was reinforced by traditional anti-German prejudices. Thus, after the two world wars, the public responded at times with alarm to learning that the Germans constituted by far the largest contingent among the legionnaires. The legionnaires' reputation

of being particularly good soldiers, which preceded them and was always confirmed by the Legion's officers, was behind the fear that the Legion could escape the control of the French officers and mutate into a kind of German "fifth column." The German legionnaires (and probably also ex-mercenaries of other nationalities) for their part often retained a certain respect for – indeed, an attachment to – the Legion after the end of their service, though it was frequently combined with an anti-French attitude. For them, if anything was a second home it was the Legion rather than France.

Comor, André-Paul. *La Légion Etrangère*. Paris, 1992.
Hallo, Jean-Pierre. *Monsieur Légionnaire. L'homme et ses traditions*. Paris, 1994.
Michels, Eckard. *Deutsche in der Fremdenlegion 1870–1965. Mythen und Realitäten*. 5th ed. Paderborn, 2006.
Porch, Douglas. *La Légion Etrangère 1831–1962*. Paris, 1994.

Cross-references: France; Germany; German Refugees and Expellees from Eastern, East-Central, and Southeastern Europe in Germany and Austria since the End of World War II; Russian Emigrants in Europe since 1917; Spanish Political Refugees in Europe since the Beginning of the Civil War in 1936: The Example of France

GERMAN TRADERS IN ANTWERP IN THE 19TH CENTURY

Greta Devos and Hilde Greefs

The reopening of the river Scheldt to international maritime traffic in 1796 – after being closed off for more than two centuries – turned Antwerp into an attractive commercial metropolis. Immigrants from surrounding regions and abroad contributed to the explosive population growth that accompanied the economic expansion: the city grew from 60,000 inhabitants in 1812 to 112,000 in 1860 and 224,000 in 1890. Trade and maritime activities attracted immigrants from the Netherlands – even after the separation and the declaration of Belgian independence in 1830 – and from Great Britain, France, the USA, and Germany. Throughout the whole 19th century Dutch immigration strongly prevailed, while the Germans formed the second largest immigrant group. In 1846, some 1,650 Germans lived in the province of Antwerp (compared to 9,932 migrants from the Netherlands). The number of German immigrants increased to 8,660 in 1910, but declined after the First World War to 1,716 in 1920.

Unlike their countrymen in Brussels and Liège, a substantial portion of the Germans in Antwerp seem to have been traders. Exact numbers are not available, but some surveys indicate that around the middle of the century some 30% to 40% of the German immigrants were engaged in trade. As a young, cheap, and modernizing port, well situated for transit trade to Germany (especially the Rhineland), Antwerp strongly appealed to newcomers.

In general, two groups can be distinguished among the German traders. The first group consisted of elderly businessmen who had received their training in other ports or commercial centers outside of Belgium. If they did not already belong to the upper middle class, they were able to climb up the social ladder rather swiftly. The establishment of branches from existing firms as well as the delegation of representatives, often family members, indicate that their settlement in Antwerp was often part of a deliberate strategy to reinforce economic activities and to extend international trading networks. The second group consisted of youngsters who often made their entrée in Antwerp through apprenticeship, frequently working in the firms of other, often newly established, entrepreneurs. Apprenticeship not only offered technical skills, experience, and status but was also a good starting point for the construction of one's own commercial networks. Some of these apprentices left Antwerp after a few years, while others stayed and made a career in a local firm or started up their own business.

The most important German merchants were active in the international maritime trade or in related sectors such as shipping or maritime insurance. German merchant houses dominated important niches, such as the early stages of trade in hides and wool, all the more as Antwerp developed into one of the main hide markets in Europe.

The main part of the German immigrants originated from northern Rhineland and Westphalia, especially from Aachen and Cologne near the Belgian border. Although not all German immigrants grew up in an urban environment, stepwise migration via cities – often even port cities – defined their migration patterns. Forms of cooperation between immigrated businessmen with identical geographical or community origins or family background, reveal that migration was rarely an individual matter. Clearly, the presence of family members, relatives, or friends in Antwerp resulted in forms of chain migration. Not only business partners but also wives, children, and German-speaking domestics followed the immigrant traders to Antwerp. During the first decades of the 19th century they often temporarily returned to their hometown to marry a fellow countrywoman. The children of these first-generation migrants were preferably married off to successful businesspeople, often also from Germany. Later on their sons and daughters intermingled with Antwerp entrepreneurial or other well-to-do families, a practice that could expand their own business prospects.

The German traders sustained contact with their place of origin after moving to Antwerp. Reliable partners abroad were important not only for trade but also for the exchange of information about products, prices, suppliers, and buyers as well as about the local political and economic situation. As information exchange between relatives was considered more reliable than news from other sources, these contacts contributed to the expansion of the traders' international commercial activities.

The number of German traders was not exceptionally high; the craftsmen, domestic servants, shopkeepers, and catering personnel who followed in their wake were more numerous. Despite their small number, German businessmen were influential, since many of them had belonged to the elite in Antwerp since the early 19th century. When the Chamber of Commerce was founded in 1802, three of the five foreign merchants were Germans and their presence in the Chamber as members and presidents was striking during the 19th century. Since the Chamber was responsible for many economic issues, their influence on economic policy was considerable. Rich Germans also quickly joined the existing literary or music societies of the local French-speaking upper class and in due course set up their own German societies. Their interests varied from music (small ensembles, symphonic music, choral singing) and literature (reading circles) to gymnastics and sport activities. By the end of the century most of the German clubs and societies were coordinated by the Centralausschuß der deutschen Vereine. As promotors of various arts, they supported young artists, built up rich collections of old paintings, organized concerts, and invited celebrated musicians. Together with the local elite they organized events and festivities although not all of the French-speaking elite appreciated their presence.

German traders also attended to charity and mutual aid societies. Mutual aid societies became better organized toward the end of the 19th century, with German services for health care, cheap housing, employment, and assistance to female immigrants and seamen. Rich traders organized funds for needy Germans and locals or participated in other charity works. The Deutsche Schule, founded in 1873, assumed a special prominence. The good reputation of the school drew children from well-off families, though only half of the pupils were German subjects. German newspapers, bakeries, butchers, and public houses completed the image of a strong German presence in prewar Antwerp. There was no segregation as such and the spread of Germans over the town was determined by profession and status. Just like the local upper classes, German traders acquired large properties outside town and contributed to the establishment of residential areas in the suburbs.

Some of the German traders were naturalized as Belgian citizens and fully integrated into Belgian society. Others maintained their German nationality and remained loyal to national traditions, such as the yearly celebration of the Kaiser's birthday after 1871. A few members of the colony meddled with local political life, nourishing the distrust of the Flemish Catholic voters, while others propagated pan-German ideas that were rejected by the francophone upper class. These internal tensions took on new meaning at the outbreak of the First World War. A portion of the immigrants returned to their native country to fulfill their military service while some stayed and collaborated with the German occupiers and met with the hostility of the Belgian population after the war. Another group abstained from political interference and sided with the local population. After the war, German trade in Belgium took a nasty blow while German firms and the belongings of German subjects were confiscated. The number of German nationals in Antwerp decreased significantly. From the mid-1920s onward, German shipping lines and their agents could regain a foothold, but the heyday of the German traders – also as a consequence of new commercial structures after the war – in Antwerp was over.

Devos, Greta. "De Duitse kooplui en het Antwerps cultuurleven." In *De Nottebohmzaal. Boek en Mecenaat*, edited by Roger Rennenberg, 147–54. Antwerpen, 1993.

Devos, Greta. "Inwijking en integratie van Duitse kooplieden te Antwerpen in de 19de eeuw." In *Minorities in Western European Cities (16th-20th Centuries)*, edited by Hugo Soly and Alfons K. L. Thijs, 135–56. Brussels and Rome, 1995.

Devos, Greta, and Hilde Greefs. "The German Presence in Antwerp in the 19th Century." *IMIS-Beiträge* (2000), 14: 105–28.

Cross-references: Belgium and Luxembourg; Germany; The Netherlands

GERMAN TRADERS AND SHOPKEEPERS IN THE NETHERLANDS, 1850–1900

Leo Lucassen

In the 19th century German traders and shopkeepers in the Netherlands formed a highly visible subgroup within the total German migrant population. Some of them established well-known chain department stores while others played an important role as commercial agents, street traders, or peddlers, both in cities and in the countryside. They were part of a much larger wave of immigration from German-speaking lands that began in the early modern period and started to subside slowly after 1800, by which point the heyday of economic growth in the coastal regions of the Netherlands was over, while from the 1850s onward the German economy experienced a long period of unprecedented industrial growth. Instead of Germans traveling to the Netherlands for work, in the second half of the 19th century, Dutch workers started to come to the Ruhr area, the heartland of German industrialization. These macro-economic changes are clearly reflected in the development of German migration to the Netherlands. Whereas around 1800 some 4% of the Dutch population was born in German lands, this share steadily declined, amounting to only 1% at the end of the 19th century (see Table 1).

German migrants were not evenly distributed across the Netherlands. As in the early modern period, many settled in the urban centers of the coastal region, especially in cities like Amsterdam, Rotterdam, and the Hague, but also in smaller towns like Haarlem, Utrecht, Dordrecht, Gouda, and Delft. The number of Germans in the Dutch-German border area increased markedly in the 19th century, especially in the south of Limburg, where almost 5% of the inhabitants were of German origin in 1879.

Most migrants came from the northwestern part of Germany, today encompassing the states of North-Rhine Westphalia and Lower Saxony, and from the Rhine Valley

Table 1. Germans in the Netherlands, 1849–1909				
	Male	**Female**	**Total**	**% of the total population**
Born in Germany				
1849	25,000	16,000	41,000	1.4
1859	21,500	15,500	37,000	1.1
1869	18,700	15,000	34,000	0.9
1879	21,500	20,500	42,000	1.0
German citizenship				
1889	14,462	14,805	29,267	0.7
1899	16,661	15,204	31,865	0.6
1909	18,613	18,921	37,534	0.6

Source: Dutch Censuses 1849-1909. Starting in 1889, Dutch censuses no longer registered place of birth, but rather citizenship, which means that the figures for 1849-79 cannot be directly compared with those for 1889-1909 as the number of persons born in Germany was larger than those with German citizenship. Likely because of the relatively high rate of naturalization, the total number of foreigners in the Netherlands in 1889-1909 was only around 65%-70% of those born outside the Netherlands.

stretching south to Hesse. A small minority came from eastern and southern Germany. Cities like Rotterdam in particular, which functioned as an important transit port for the Ruhr area, drew many migrants from the Rhine Valley, especially the area between Mainz and Düsseldorf. Traditional emigration areas in the northwest, like East-Frisia, Oldenburg, and Münsterland, in contrast, were predominant in the migration to Amsterdam and Utrecht.

The occupations of German immigrants in the Netherlands were extremely varied. The previously large share of journeymen and artisans decreased slowly in the course of the 19th century, in smaller places like Utrecht already from 1820 onward, whereas in Amsterdam the decline in the number of bakers, tailors, and brewers started only in the 1860s. Their place was to a large extent taken by migrants working in the service sector (musicians, prostitutes, domestics, waiters) and the transportation sector (sailors, bargemen), but most importantly by traders. In the urban centers in the west of the Netherlands some 35% to 40% of all Germans worked in the trade sector,

One of the best-researched groups is the German (Catholic) peddlers from small villages like Hopsten, Recke, Mettingen, and Ibbenbüren in the northern part of Münsterland, west of Osnabrück and close to the Dutch border. Peddlers with textiles and other products, known as *Tödden*, already were coming to the Netherlands in the 18th century to sell from door to door, especially in the countryside in the northern and western parts of the country. Some opened shops at the beginning of the 19th century that would eventually become very successful, such as C&A (established by August and Clemens Brenninkmeijer), Peek & Cloppenburg, and V&D (Vroom and Dreesmann). In the shadow of these tycoons, numerous German shopkeepers settled in Dutch towns and soon became an integral part of the booming retail sector. In contrast to their Dutch colleagues, many German shopkeepers ran large and modern enterprises, with new sales techniques and fixed low prices, instead of negotiating each individual transaction separately, which was common at the time. Furthermore, they advertised in local newspapers and were often part of larger chains of shops with the same name.

Most entrepreneurs recruited their personnel, both men and women, from their (largely Catholic) home region, stretching from Oldenburg in the north to Münster in the south. In Utrecht, but also in other cities, they usually lived behind or above the store and sometimes in special boardinghouses nearby. The turnover was considerable and many shop assistants moved from city to city from one German store to the next. A good illustration of this highly mobile migration pattern is the impressive Sinkel store in Utrecht, well known at the time, where between 1860 and 1879 some 238 different Germans of both sexes were employed for a shorter or longer period of time. Only a few of them succeeded in setting up their own shops. At the end of the 19th century, the link with the Münsterland slackened and the use of German personnel gradually diminished.

Whereas the German shopkeepers from the Münsterland can be considered an example of (successful) niche formation, where migrants from a certain area specialized in a given type of economic activity, this was not the case for the growing German business houses and commercial establishments that were concentrated in port cities like Rotterdam and, to a lesser extent, Amsterdam. With the tempestuous growth of the German industrial economy, the port city Rotterdam became a vital transit point that attracted a substantial number of German commercial clerks and other administrative personnel. In their wake numerous other Germans flocked to Rotterdam. In contrast to Utrecht, where the majority were chain migrants from specific small German regions, in Rotterdam the majority of the migrants came from all over the Rhine valley, which stretched from the Dutch border to Switzerland.

Apparently, through the continuous exchange of goods and information in the entire Rhine region, it became generally known that Rotterdam offered ample opportunities for work: for traders and shopkeepers, but also for musicians, prostitutes, servants, and domestics. Different migration patterns resulted in different residential patterns: whereas in Utrecht most Germans lived alongside fellow countrymen and were concentrated in certain parts of the city, in Rotterdam the majority of German migrants lived in housing rented from Dutch landlords and were dispersed throughout the entire city.

Another important group of German migrants (of both sexes) in the trading sector were peddlers in stoneware from the Westerwald in Nassau (north of Koblenz). They formed a close-knit migrant network and were active in many Dutch cities, like Utrecht, Amsterdam, Delft, Gouda, and Rotterdam. Their main product was stoneware pots (*Kannenbäckerware*) used to store oil, wine, beer, or other liquids as well as to preserve sour and salty vegetables, meat or fish, and butter. Most of these pots were produced in the Westerwald and bought by traders who transported them by water to the Netherlands. The pots were sold by peddlers to Dutch customers in urban and rural areas, at markets or from door to door. Some of these peddlers became wholesale traders, employing people from their home region to do the actual selling. The first peddlers had already arrived at the end of the 18th century and their activities increased and spread in the course of the 19th century. Initially, they worked only between March and November, returning home in winter, but gradually they settled in small but permanent concentrations in Dutch cities.

Most German labor migrants stayed for only a short while in the Netherlands. Those with the highest rate of mobility were men and women working as prostitutes, sailors, peddlers, and musicians, followed by skilled industrial workers and tradesmen. Only a small percentage settled permanently and integrated into Dutch society.

In general, the number of Germans was too small for them to leave their stamp on Dutch cities. In most towns they lived dispersed among different neighborhoods. However, in Amsterdam around 1850 the proportion of German-born residents exceeded 10% in certain areas while the city average was 3%. Other cities had concentrations of German migrants on certain streets. Shopkeepers, for example, mainly settled downtown close to shopping streets. The street traders from the Westerwald were also commonly concentrated on specific streets, partly because of commercial and logistic reasons (close to waterways), but also because they preferred to live close to one another.

Marriage patterns among these groups were extremely varied. The peddlers from Nassau were rather endogamous and they rarely married outside their own regional group. Only at the end of the 19th century, when their trading monopoly dwindled, did exogamous marriages increase. Shopkeepers from Münsterland also typically chose partners from their home region. They kept in contact with those who stayed behind and some even had considerable property in their villages of origin. Others, however, married Dutch women and saw their contacts with Germany quickly disintegrate. The highest rates of exogamy were found among commercial agents, which is reflected by the differences in marriage patterns between German immigrants in Utrecht (mostly shopkeepers and peddlers) and Rotterdam (many commercial agents and shopkeepers). Between 1860 and 1880, 50% of all Germans in Utrecht married other Germans while in Rotterdam this proportion was only 25%. In both cases men were more exogamous than women. Religious endogamy in both cities was much higher than ethnic endogamy. Most Germans married co-religionists, be they of German or Dutch descent.

The social status and social mobility of the German immigrants in the trading business varied. In Rotterdam and probably also in Utrecht, their social position was above average. Some belonged to the elite and some to the working class, but many were relatively well-to-do shopkeepers or tradesmen. Social advancement within a single generation was also possible. For example, Friedrich Oehlschläger, born in Drohne (Prussia), arrived in Rotterdam in 1872 as a waiter and within 13 years was the owner of a large hotel. For most other Germans, social mobility was not as spectacular, but many managed to improve their position, for example, by advancing from shop assistant to shop owner. The peddlers, such as the stoneware traders from the Westerwald, probably did less well as they lived in the poorer parts of town. Some families, however, succeeded in entering the middle class.

At the beginning of the 20th century, the importance of the trading sector for German migrants decreased. Especially in the interwar period, when emigration from Germany soared, we see a shift to industrial occupations (men) and domestic service (women).

Delger, Henk. "Chancen in Rotterdam. Eine Untersuchung der sozialen Mobilität zweier deutscher Migrantengruppen (1870–1879 und 1920–1929)." In *"Wir sind auch da!" Über das Leben von und mit Migranten in europäischen Großstädten*, edited by Angelika Eder, 47–72. Hamburg, 2003.

Lesger, Clé, Leo Lucassen, and Marlou Schrover. "Is There Life Outside the Migrant Network? German Immigrants in XIXth Century Netherlands and the Need for a More Balanced Migration Typology." *Annales de Démographie Historique* 4, 2 (2002): 29–50.

Lucassen, Leo. "De selectiviteit van blijvers: een reconstructie van de sociale positie van Duitse migranten in Rotterdam (1870–1885)." *Tijdschrift voor Sociale en Economische Geschiedenis* 1 (2004): 92–115.

Lucassen, Leo. "Huwelijken van Duitse migranten in Nederland (1860–1940): De rol van herkomst, religie, beroep en sekse." *Tijdschrift voor Sociale en Economische Geschiedenis* 2 (2005): 54–80.

Oberpenning, Hannelore. *Migration und Fernhandel im "Tödden-System": Wanderhändler aus dem nördlichen Münsterland im mittleren und nördlichen Europa des 18. und 19. Jahrhunderts*. Osnabrück, 1996.

Schrover, Marlou. *Een kolonie van Duitsers. Groepsvorming onder Duitse immigranten in Utrecht in de negentiende eeuw*. Amsterdam, 2002.

Cross-references: Germany; The Netherlands; German Baker-Journeymen in Amsterdam in the 17th Century; German Itinerant Merchants from the Münsterland in Northern, Western, and Central Europe in the 18th and 19th Centuries; German Maids in the Netherlands in the Interwar Period; German Seasonal Agricultural Laborers in the Netherlands from the 17th to the Early 20th Century

GERMAN WAR BRIDES IN WESTERN EUROPE SINCE THE END OF WORLD WAR II: THE EXAMPLE OF GREAT BRITAIN

Raingard Eßer

"War brides" are among the mythically overrated set pieces of the time of war and occupation in western Europe and the Far East during and after World War II. The intimate relationships between German *Frauleins* and especially American GIs, but also English and to a lesser extent French occupation soldiers, continue to loom large in the collective West German memory. The phrase "war brides," however, is inaccurate: strictly speaking, the German women who married the members of an occupation army or administration after World War II were not war brides but postwar or occupation brides. Still, the phrase was already used in the contemporary press and has established itself in historical scholarship.

Most women emigrated to the USA as the brides of American soldiers. In the period from 1945 to 1949, for which statistics are available, 15,028 women left Germany for the United States as the fiancées of American military personnel, among them also those who used marriage in an attempt to circumvent the prohibition against emigrating from Germany and immigrating to the USA. Less precise numbers are available for the emigration of the fiancées of British occupation troops. Estimates put the figure at around 10,000 women. The relationships of German women with French occupation soldiers have so far not been studied. The comparatively tiny number of German men who married female occupation personnel has been hardly looked at, except for emigration to the USA (323 husbands between 1945 and 1949). Here the phenomenon of the "war groom" becomes entangled with the former German prisoners of war who remained abroad after their release, which has also been little studied.

War brides were generally young (between 16 and early 30s) and traveled alone. As such, they reflect the overall profile of overseas emigration after World War II: 60%–70% female, mostly between the ages of 20 and 29, and more than 50% unmarried. Initially, children from previous relationships could not be brought along or only with difficulty, while there were no problems for entering the destination country for children from the relationship with the future husband.

Both the American and the British occupation authorities had issued a strict prohibition against fraternization with the German population, but it could not be upheld in any of the Western zones. In the American zone, regulations allowing marriage between Americans and Germans (though involving a cumbersome bureaucratic procedure) were passed as early as December 1945. The British occupation authorities did not sanction marriages between British citizens and Germans until August 1946.

The American and British occupying powers used similar control procedures in authorizing marriage between a member of the armed forces and a German. The issuing of a permit was preceded by a detailed moral, physical, and political examination of the woman. In addition, she had to furnish character references from the mayor and priest of her community. If there were no concerns, the local military commanders could grant a marriage permit. However, for German-British couples, the permit contained the stipulation of a six-month waiting period, during which the man had to return to Britain for at least three weeks to discuss his wedding plans with his family. If the wedding plans went forward, the bride had to apply for emigration and immigration permits, which were individually reviewed by the British Home Office. If the future husband was by then stationed back in Great Britain, he had to promise in writing that he would marry the woman and to declare that there were no legal obstacles to performing the marriage at the earliest possible date. As a rule, the woman would then be given a temporary residence permit for Great Britain, which expired once the wedding took place. Upon marriage, the woman lost her German citizenship in accordance with German law. Until 31 December 1948, she was automatically given a British passport; because of a revision of the British Nationality Act, women who married their British spouse after that date had to submit an application to the Home Office.

The majority of women left Germany in the first two years after the Allied marriage regulations of 1945–6 took effect. The precarious economic conditions in Germany played a decisive role in the decision to emigrate. Other important aspects were the imbalance in the gender ratio in Germany and ideas about the new homeland conveyed in the press. The number of war brides rose steadily until the founding of the Federal Republic of Germany in 1949. Thereafter, the rate of marriages between Germans and members of the occupying powers declined. Even though the Occupation Statute was not repealed until 1955, war brides were no longer a topic of public discussion.

There are hardly any documents about the stay of women in Great Britain. Information about separations, divorces, and remigration is nonexistent. There are no records about the regional distribution of the women within the country, and to date no social profile of the women emigrants has been drawn up. However, using interviews of contemporary witnesses, an oral history project by German and English scholars was able to collect information about this group of female migrants. It is revealing, first of all, that the German women did not organize themselves into clubs, as was customary among other foreign war brides. Rather, the women tried to conceal their identity as Germans in public by pretending that they were Swiss, Dutch, or Austrian, for example. In retrospect, many war brides described their marriage as an unhappy one, which was often attributed to disillusionment over their social status and the economic situation of the husband after his release from the military.

Still, the women tried to assimilate in the new society. The overall picture reveals a pronounced mentality of social advancement. Many tried and also succeeded in rising into the British middle class. Their children were given English names. On the whole, however, the British host society was perceived as foreign and unfriendly. The women experienced xenophobia until the 1970s, which was lessened only by the massive influx from the former British colonies and the Commonwealth countries, as new images of the foreigner and the enemy established themselves. Most women maintained

contact with their former homeland, and it was repeatedly invigorated especially in old age. Privately, cuckoo clocks and beer steins constituted set pieces of German cultural identity, though as a construct they had very little connection any longer to daily life in the Federal Republic. Integration into British society had succeeded for many externally but not mentally. That is also true from an intergenerational perspective: many children from international marriages left Great Britain and sought to make a life for themselves in their mother's native country.

Eßer, Raingard. "'Language No Obstacle' – War Brides in the German Press, 1945–1949." *Women's History Review* 12, 4 (2003): 577–603.

Höhn, Maria. "Frau im Haus und Girl im Spiegel: Discourse on Women in the Interregnum Period of 1945–1949 and the Question of German Identity." *Cultural European History* 26 (1993): 57–90.

Shukert, Elfrieda Berthiaume, and Barbara Smith Scibetta. *War Brides of World War II.* Novato, CA, 1988.

Steinert, Johannes-Dieter, and Inge Weber-Newth. *Labour & Love. Deutsche in Großbritannien nach dem Zweiten Weltkrieg.* Osnabrück, 2000.

Cross-references: Germany; Great Britain; British War Brides in Norway since the End of World War II

GREEK LABOR MIGRANTS IN WESTERN, CENTRAL, AND NORTHERN EUROPE AFTER 1950: THE EXAMPLES OF GERMANY AND THE NETHERLANDS

Hans Vermeulen

Greek migration to "Europe" – as the Greeks tend to say – began a few years after the end of the Greek Civil War (1946–9). Transatlantic migration initially far outweighed migration to Europe, but this situation changed rapidly starting in 1960, when 57% of Greek migrants – twice as many as in the previous year – left for destinations in northern, central, and western Europe. The main phases of migration took place 1960–5 and 1969–70. After 1988, when Greeks could move freely within the European Community, migration to Europe increased again, but this new immigration falls outside the scope of this essay.

In the period from 1955 until 1977 some 760,000 persons left Greece for European destinations. West Germany attracted by far the largest share of these Greek "guest workers" (84%). The other main destinations were Belgium (4%), Switzerland (2%), Sweden (1%), and the Netherlands (1%) while 8% went to other European countries. To judge the total volume of emigration one must take into account that in the same period almost 440,000 Greeks (of a total population of less than 8.5 million in 1961) left for transatlantic destinations. While Greek communities currently exist in Austria, France, Italy, and the UK, these groups are not comprised

Table 1. Greek nationals in countries of the European Union, 2000

Country	Number of Greeks
Germany	363,202
UK	21,000
Belgium	19,216
Italy	11,388
France	6,091
The Netherlands	5,265
Sweden	4,413
Luxembourg	1,250
Austria	990
Denmark	653
Spain	652
Finland	287
Portugal	96
Ireland	no data
Total	434,503

Source: Eurostat 2000, European Social Statistics.

of "guest workers" but mainly of students, artists, intellectuals, political refugees, and entrepreneurs. Many of the labor migrants returned to Greece after a few years, although still half a million Greek nationals lived in other European countries in 2000.

Greek labor migrants started working in Belgian coal mines in 1953. After the influx of Italian workers decreased following a number of severe accidents in the mines, the Belgian government concluded a recruitment agreement with Greece in 1957. Working conditions, however, remained so poor that some Greek workers found employment in Germany or the Netherlands and broke their contracts with the Belgian government. Soon thereafter, Greece concluded recruitment agreements with Germany (1960) and the Netherlands (1966). However, many Greek workers – in Germany about one-third for example – were not recruited but came on their own initiative.

Exact data on the development of the number of Greek labor migrants in the individual destination countries are lacking. The data in Table 1, which are drawn from an EU survey, represent citizens of Greece, which means they include those who did not come to northern, central, and western Europe as guest workers and do not include those who became citizens in their respective destination countries. Switzerland, which is not included in the table, had 8,500 residents with Greek citizenship in 1990.

The economic crisis of the mid-1960s led to a dramatic drop in Greek labor migration, which, however, increased again starting in 1968. Important for this development were the wage gap that still existed between Greece and Germany, the political repressions during the Regime of the Colonels (1967–74), continuing underemployment in the countryside, and the increasing significance of migration networks. A third of those who entered Germany during the second immigration period of 1968–73 had already been there before.

The often small Greek migrant communities aroused little political and public – and therefore little scholarly – interest in their destination countries. Interest in the group almost completely disappeared in the 1980s, particularly because the community did not create any serious problems. Interest on the Greek side was more extensive and enduring, but this research focused mainly on return migration and remittances. This lack of research hinders a systematic comparison of the integration of Greek guest workers and their descendants in the different destination countries.

Most Greek labor migrants in Europe hailed from regions in northern Greece (Macedonia, Thrace) that had suffered heavily from a decade of war, civil war, and the following political repression. Initially workers formed the majority of migrants; after 1964 it was peasants. The level of education was low among both groups, and in the early 1980s still 6% of male and 21% of the female migrants in Germany were illiterate.

Greek labor migration was originally an overwhelmingly male phenomenon. In contrast to Turkish and Moroccan migrants, however, Greeks began to resettle members of their families in their respective destination countries within a few years after their arrival. In the Netherlands, for example, women joined their husbands as early as 1965 and family reunification peaked between 1968 and 1972. The children, however, often remained in Greece in the care of grandparents to allow women to earn money outside the home so that the couple could return more quickly to Greece.

Integration of first- and second-generation immigrants

During the 1960s and early 1970s the overwhelming majority of Greek male immigrants worked in industrial enterprises (e.g., metal industry, car factories). The majority of Greek women also participated in the labor market. In the Netherlands, for example, 55% worked outside the home in the early 1980s, while 21% of these women were unemployed and 6% disabled. Only 18% never participated in the labor market. Greek women worked in industry (e.g., assembling electrical equipment), but were more commonly employed in the service sector. The oil crisis of 1973 resulted in large-scale unemployment and economic restructuring. One consequence was that both women and men increasingly moved from industry to the service sector. Greeks commonly worked for cleaning agencies, particularly in Sweden.

In the 1970s, partly as a reaction to the economic crisis, more and more Greeks opened small businesses, often a Greek restaurant but sometimes a grocery store, building company, or tourist agency. In the Netherlands, this development began in the mid-1970s. By the early 1980s, 12% to 15% of the Greeks – a high percentage compared to other immigrant groups – was self-employed. In Germany the proportion of self-employed rose from 3% in 1976 to 10% in 1982.

The integration of the Greek population in Germany has differed remarkably from that of Italians, Spaniards, and immigrants from the former Yugoslavia. The Greek integration pattern has been characterized by both a high degree of ethnic cohesion and a relatively high degree of structural integration. Second-generation Greeks perform well at school, although below the level of Spanish immigrants. In 1997, 21% of Greek pupils attended schools that belonged to the highest level of secondary education, as compared to 28% of the Spanish, 15% of the former Yugoslavs, and only 12% of the Italians. University attendance of second-generation Greeks is also below that of the Spanish but higher than that of the other immigrant groups.

In the labor market in Germany, Greeks perform less well, which is reflected particularly in unemployment figures – 18% in 1998, compared to 18% among Italians, 12% among Spaniards, and 11% among former Yugoslavs, but 24% among Turks. The strong ethnic cohesion of the Greek immigrant communities may restrict their access to the German labor market. This high degree of ethnic cohesion manifests itself in several ways. First, Greeks are more endogamous than other groups: less than a quarter of children of Greek origin stemmed from mixed marriages in 1997, compared to 81% of Spanish origin and 42% of Italian origin. Greeks are also known to hold on to their native language. In Germany this has been reflected in the fierce struggles of Greeks for national schools – Greek secondary schools in particular. Furthermore, Greeks possess a high degree of internal organization. Greek voluntary associations are often directed at issues of (Greek) education and Greek culture and many have strong relations with Greece and their respective regions of origin. Particularly important are the so-called *kinotites*, the Greek communities to which virtually every Greek belongs. The limited and often outdated information available on Greeks in Belgium, the Netherlands, Sweden, and Switzerland suggests that the character of the integration process of Greeks in these countries has been similar to that in Germany. Here also the high rate of return migration can be seen as the result of strong internal organization and orientation toward the region and country of origin.

Return migration and the integration of returnees

The mid-1960s witnessed the emergence of a certain concern in Greece about the effects of large-scale emigration. Employers complained about the lack of skilled labor, and Xenophon Zolotas, the director of the Bank of Greece, urged the government to promote return migration. Shortages became more common in the late 1960s and contributed to an increase in immigration to Greece: by 1972 there were already 15,000 to 20,000 foreign workers in Greece.

The first large-scale wave of return migration in 1966–7, documented in Figure 1, was, however, not caused by labor shortages in Greece but rather by a temporary recession and the pressure exerted by the German government on unemployed foreign workers to return to their country of origin.

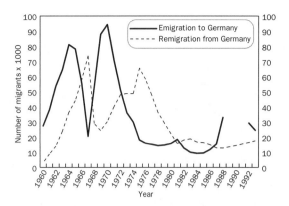

Figure 1. Greek migration to Germany and Greek return migration. *Source*: Nickolas P. Glytsos and Louka T. Katseli, *Greek Migration: The Two Faces of Janus* (Athens, 2000). The figure is based on data from the *Statistisches Bundesamt* and the National Statistical Service of Greece.

When the recession was over, emigration to European destinations once again increased. The second wave of return migration was again the result of economic crisis – the oil crisis of 1973 – but this time positive factors in Greece also played a role in bringing migrant laborers back to their homeland: the economic situation in Greece improved toward the end of the Regime of the Colonels and the regime finally fell in 1974. The large-scale return migration reduced the Greek population in Germany from about 400,000 in 1973 to about 300,000 in 1978. It is estimated that in the entire period from 1950 to 1978 about 1 million Greeks migrated to Germany while 800,000 returned to Greece. After 1978 the rate of fluctuation decreased markedly, but the general pattern of emigration and return migration persisted. Migration then slowly lost its guest worker character, particularly after 1988 when Greeks could move freely within the EC.

Toward the end of the 1970s interest in the returnees on the part of the Greek government as well as the church, social scientists, and intellectuals began to grow. In cooperation with the German Evangelical Church, the Greek Orthodox Church opened a center for the reintegration of returnees in Athens in 1978 and in Thessaloniki in 1980. The Greek employment office (OAED) opened new branches in Athens and Thessaloniki to help returning migrants find work. At the same time, special reception classes for the children of returnees were introduced. Notwithstanding these and other measures by the Greek government, children of return migrants typically do poorer in school than the children of nonmigrants, especially if they returned to Greece after the age of nine or ten.

The majority of the return migrants did not go back to their native villages but rather to urban centers, where most found work within half a year. Approximately one-third was self-employed. Return migrants brought on average savings of 64,000 Deutschmarks (DM). Part of this money was spent during the first period of unemployment; the rest was used for housing and to invest in small businesses. Many return migrants viewed conditions in Greece more critically than those who had never left the country, particularly in relation to labor relations, social services, the bureaucracy, and widespread corruption. Women were even more critical than men since they felt the loss of freedom they had gained in Germany or in other destination countries. Many migrants regretted returning to Greece – 53% according to one study – and emigrated again, often after having spent the savings they had earned abroad. Many former guest workers, however, still live in Greece, particularly in the north.

The Greek diaspora in Europe and the role of the Greek state

During and after the Cyprus crisis of 1974 the Greek lobby in the United States made it clear to the Greek government that Greeks living abroad were not just a source of remittances but could also serve the nation as a political and cultural force. Ever since, the Greek government has much more actively promoted Greek language, culture, and political interests abroad, making use of the large Greek diaspora – an estimated 5 million persons, or half the population of Greece itself. To this end, the position of deputy minister for Greeks abroad was created in the Ministry of Foreign Affairs in 1983. In the early 1990s a number of Greek cultural institutes were founded in London, Berlin, and other cities, which were joined in 1995 by the World Council of Hellenes Abroad. This semi-independent institution appears to cooperate more fruitfully with institutions of the church than with those of the state. It remains to be seen to what extent these initiatives will contribute to the strengthening of Greek identity among persons of Greek descent abroad, but they will in any case promote the creation of a large transnational network of people interested in "the Greek cause."

Bruneau, Michel. "Politiques de l'état-nation grec vis-à-vis de la diaspora." Revue européenne des migrations internationales 17, 3 (2001): 9–22.

Glytsos, Nickolas P., and Louka T. Katseli. Greek Migration: The Two Faces of Janus. Athens, 2000.

Hopf, Diether. Herkunft und Schulbesuch ausländischer Kinder: Eine Untersuchung am Beispiel griechischer Schüler. Stuttgart, 1987.

Lauth, Jutta. Fremder Frauen Wege: Eine ethnologische Fallstudie mit griechischen Migrantinnen. Zurich, 1994.

Thränhardt, Dietrich. "Einwandererkulturen und soziales Kapital: Eine komparative Analyse." In Einwanderer-Netzwerke und ihre Integrationsqualität in Deutschland und Israel, edited by Dietrich Thränhardt and Uwe Hunger, 15–51. Münster, 2000.

Unger, Klaus. Die Rückkehr der Arbeitsemigranten. Eine Studie zur Remigration nach Griechenland. Saarbrücken, 1983.

Venturas, Lina. "The Beginning of Greek Post-war Emigration to Belgium: Networks and Strategies." In Griechische Migration in Europa. Geschichte und Gegenwart, edited by Evangelos Konstantinou, 217–26. Frankfurt am Main, 2000.

Vermeulen, Hans, et al. Migranten in de Nederlandse samenleving: De Grieken. Muiderberg, 1990.

Vermeulen, Hans. "The Greek Labour Diaspora in Western Europe, Its Integration in the Receiving Societies, Especially Germany, and Its Relation with the Home Country." In Ethnicity and Migration: A Greek Story. Migrance 30 (2008), Special Issue, edited by Martin Baldwin-Edwards, 18–36.

Zolotas, Xenophon. International Labor Migration and Economic Development. Athens, 1966.

Cross-references: Belgium and Luxembourg; Germany; The Netherlands; Switzerland; Greek Refugees in Western, Central, Northern, and Southern Europe during the Military Dictatorship, 1967–1974; Greek Settlers from the Black Sea Region in New Russia since the Early Modern Period and Pontic Greeks in Greece since the End of World War II; Italian Labor Migrants in Northern, Central, and Western Europe since the End of World War II; Spanish Labor Migrants in Western, Central, and Northern Europe since the End of World War II; Turkish Labor Migrants in Western, Central, and Northern Europe since the Mid-1950s; Yugoslav Labor Migrants in Western, Central, and Northern Europe since the End of World War II

GREEK ORTHODOX AND MUSLIM REFUGEES AND DEPORTEES IN GREECE AND TURKEY SINCE 1912

Erik-Jan Zürcher

As a result of its shocking defeat at the hands of a coalition of small Balkan states in the Balkan War of 1912–13, the Ottoman Empire lost 80% of its European territories, along with 4.2 million inhabitants (about 16% of the total population of the Empire). The Balkan War uprooted approximately 800,000 persons. Around half were Muslim civilians who fled for fear of attacks by Greek, Serbian, or Bulgarian soldiers and followed the retreating Ottoman army. A large number of the refugees died of cholera, which had been introduced to the area by Ottoman troops stationed in Syria while those who remained gravitated toward Constantinople or were transferred to Asia Minor.

The new border demarcation following the war left Thrace west of the Maritza River, which had a large Muslim majority, in Greek hands and Eastern Thrace, which was two-thirds Greek and Bulgarian, in Ottoman hands. During the war, about 50,000 Bulgarians from Eastern Thrace had fled to Bulgaria and roughly an equal number of Turks had gone in the opposite direction. In the hope of relieving tension on the border, Bulgaria and Turkey attached a supplementary protocol on population exchange to the peace agreement concluded in Constantinople on 29 September 1913. Under the protocol, a mixed commission was to be formed, which was to act as an impartial arbiter and was to assess and liquidate the property left behind by the emigrants. Although the agreement was never actually implemented due to the outbreak of World War I less than a year later, it served as a model for later agreements on population exchange in the Balkans and the Near East. It should be noted, however, that the population exchange envisaged in 1913 was to take place on a strictly voluntary basis.

The loss of the Balkan provinces had a devastating effect not only because of the symbolic and economic importance of the provinces for the Ottoman Empire but also because a disproportionate part of the administrative and political elite of the Empire hailed from the Balkan provinces. Yet, the Ottoman irredentist movement was of a limited scope. Instead, the political leadership of the Empire after 1913 focused on the development of Asia Minor, or Anatolia, as the Turkish heartland. The leadership consciously adopted the area as their new homeland to compensate for the loss of the Balkan provinces.

The first effects of this policy could already be seen in the early months of 1914. Mahmut Celâl, general secretary of the Smyrna branch of the ruling Young Turk movement, which had established a one-party dictatorship after a coup d'état in January 1913, was instructed to Turkify the western seaboard of Asia Minor. Through threats and intimidation, the militias under his command succeeded in forcing up to 200,000 Greek Orthodox to flee from the coastal provinces to the Greek islands in the Aegean sea directly opposite the mainland. Greek businessmen and commercial farmers bore the brunt of these expulsions as the drive behind the campaign was economic as much as it was political: the Ottoman government aimed to replace the non-Muslim bourgeoisie, which completely dominated the modern industrial, financial, and commercial sectors of the economy, with a "national," that is, Muslim bourgeoisie of their own.

In May 1914, the Ottoman government sought to make the changes permanent by concluding an agreement on population exchange with the Greek government. Greek prime minister Eleftherios Venizelos accepted the plan in principle but on the condition that it would be voluntary. A mixed commission patterned on the model established by the Turkish-Bulgarian agreement of 1913 was to guarantee the equitable disposal of property, but nothing ever came of the initiative. The plan was suspended indefinitely in August 1914 due to the outbreak of the war in Europe. During the war, the Ottoman Greeks were not persecuted in the same way as Armenians and Syrian Christians, and no large-scale massacres took place; but once Greece joined the war on the side of Great Britain, France, and Russia in 1917, many Greek families were moved inland for fear they would support the landing of Entente troops.

After the war ended with the armistice of Moudros on 31 October 1918, it was apparent that any future peace agreement would entail far-reaching territorial losses for the Ottoman Empire. Greece advanced claims to Smyrna and its hinterland and to Eastern Thrace. In May 1919, the Greek army occupied Smyrna and the surrounding area. Almost as soon as the Greek army had arrived, large numbers of Greeks, who had had to leave the Ottoman Empire in 1914, began to return and to reclaim their former houses and businesses. When a peace treaty was concluded between the victorious Entente and the Ottoman Empire at Sèvres in July 1920, the Greek claims were acknowledged. The Ottoman state was reduced to central and northern Asia Minor and

Constantinople, but by this time a strong nationalist resistance movement had emerged in Anatolia that refused to recognize the Sèvres treaty. Great Britain and France were in the process of demobilizing their troops and therefore not in a position to enforce the treaty. The Greek government of Venizelos saw in this an opportunity to unite all Greek Orthodox living around the Aegean and the Sea of Marmara in a single Hellenic state. The Greek army moved inland but was halted by the Turkish army before Ankara in September 1921 and then routed in August 1922. The Turkish army took Smyrna on 9 September 1922.

When the Greek army collapsed and its remnants retreated toward the sea, the vast majority of the Greek population, fearing Turkish reprisals, also fled. The exact number involved is not entirely clear, but realistic estimates run between 400,000 and 500,000. These people as a rule left in great haste with only the things they could carry. They were transferred to Greece by a host of larger and smaller vessels of all descriptions and flags. In the following months, mass emigration continued. When the Turkish nationalists demanded the surrender of Eastern Thrace, the Greeks living there, some 250,000, as well as some 50,000 Armenians, left for Greece, but as British forces still occupied the Bosphorus and the Dardanelles, the Turks had no means of transferring troops there. As a result, the refugees from Eastern Thrace could prepare their departure much more carefully and take many more of their belongings with them. After the Turkish victory, only two groups of Greek Orthodox were left in Asia: the communities in central Anatolia, which were partly Turkish-speaking (the so-called Karamanlis) and those living on the eastern Black Sea coast, the Pontian Greeks. Each group numbered about 200,000 persons. In addition there were several hundred thousand Greek Orthodox in the Constantinople area, partly residents of long standing, partly refugees.

The population exchange

The idea of exchanging the Greeks of Asia Minor for Muslims living in Greece was first broached by the Norwegian Fritjof Nansen (1861–1930), who had been the League of Nations' High Commissioner for Refugees since 1919. It was quickly taken up by the Greek government. The inflow of three-quarters of a million refugees posed almost insurmountable housing problems in Greece and the removal of the 600,000 Muslims in Greece would go some way toward alleviating the problem, as the vacated homes of the Muslims could be used to house the immigrants. Greece already had some experience with population exchanges. A clause allowing the exchange (on a voluntary basis) of 92,000 Bulgarians for 46,000 Greeks was contained in the peace agreement of Neuilly with Bulgaria, concluded in August 1920.

Nansen was given the green light by the League of Nations to explore the plausibility of an exchange on 14 November 1922, one week before the start of the peace negotiations in Lausanne between Great Britain, France, Italy, and Greece on the one hand and Turkey on the other. Turkey agreed in principle, on the condition that the Turkish-Muslim population of Western Thrace (for which the Turkish delegation in Lausanne demanded a plebiscite on their inclusion in Turkey or Greece) would be exempt. In return, the Greeks then demanded an exemption for the Greek Orthodox inhabitants of Constantinople. A convention was concluded between the two countries on 30 January 1923. It covered those "Turkish nationals of Greek Orthodox religion and Greek nationals of the Moslem religion" who had emigrated voluntarily or had been forced to emigrate since 18 October 1912 (the date of Greece's declaration of war at the start of the Balkan War). This, of course, included those groups who had remained in their place of residence but would now be forced to emigrate. The convention came into force when it was included in the peace treaty of Lausanne, which was concluded on 24 July 1923.

Three things are remarkable about the convention. First, the only criterion was one's religious affiliation. There was no reference to linguistic or ethnic categories. The majority of the Muslims from Macedonia were Greek speaking and a considerable proportion of the Greek Orthodox of central Anatolia spoke Turkish. Nevertheless, these groups were also resettled based on their religious affiliation. Second, the convention was retroactive: it was not limited to the migrations that had started in 1922 but legitimized all of the – largely forced – migrations in the course of the wars that had taken place since 1912. A third important feature was the compulsory character of the resettlement. This was the first time that deportations had been legalized under international law.

As almost all Greeks from western Asia Minor had already left the country; the population exchange mainly involved the transfer of the central Anatolian Greek Orthodox (Greek- and Turkish-speaking) and the Pontic Greeks. Of the latter community, it was primarily the inhabitants of the towns on the Black Sea littoral who were resettled, as most of the Greeks of the mountainous inland areas, some 80,000 persons in all, had already fled into Georgia and Russia after their defeat at the hands of the Turkish nationalists.

Resettlement and integration

The resettlement of the refugees posed tremendous problems in Greece. The country, which had a population of only 5.5 million inhabitants, was faced with an influx of approximately 1.2 million persons, according to estimates. The immigrants were settled first in camps, then in settlements on the outskirts of towns and cities, especially the two major cities Athens and Salonika. These cities, each of which had fewer than 200,000 inhabitants before the exchange, now doubled in size and huge new tracts of land were developed on their outskirts. The properties of Muslims in the countryside of Macedonia and Crete now became available, but as those communities had only had approximately 400,000 inhabitants, there was not enough land to house the immigrants and

provide them sustenance. State and church lands were therefore also made available for settlement purposes.

As a rule, the Greek immigrants from Turkey moved and resettled as communities. The names of their new settlements often recalled the places they came from, e.g., "New Smyrna." They brought their own clubs and organizations with them and founded numerous migrant organizations. The social and cultural traditions of the immigrants were different in many ways from those of the native inhabitants of Greece, but also from those of one another: Pontic Greeks, Greeks from Thrace, central Anatolian Greek Orthodox, and former inhabitants of the west coast and Smyrna could not be regarded as a single community. The integration and economic survival of the migrants were aided by the fact that there was a relatively high proportion of skilled professionals among them, from shippers and bankers and hazelnut, tobacco, and raisin traders to railway engineers and hotel and restaurant owners. This allowed them to become a dynamic element in the economy. Many migrants, however, saw better prospects outside of Greece and reemigrated to France, Britain, or the USA.

The pattern of resettlement of Macedonian Muslims in Turkey was quite different. The migrants from Macedonia formed a much smaller group than the Greek Orthodox who had left Turkey. They also overwhelmingly came from rural areas, so it was logical that they should be assigned farmland. The Turkish authorities dealt with individual families rather than with whole communities and in assigning land they classified the immigrants according to agricultural specialization: tobacco growers, olive growers, or grape growers. They were resettled in areas suitable for their respective type of agriculture. For example, tobacco growers who had produced the famous Macedonian tobacco that went into Egyptian cigarettes were resettled in the Samsun area on the Black Sea coast, where they grew tobacco for the state monopoly.

In Turkish society, the immigrants, like those who had come to the country in earlier waves of immigration (1878, 1913), remained recognizably different and were collectively known as *muhacirs*. They lived in separate villages or neighborhoods and largely maintained their social and cultural traditions. The use of minority languages was actively discouraged by the government of the republic, but the first- and second-generation migrants still often spoke Greek or Albanian among themselves. Like the immigrants from the Balkans and the Caucasus before the First World War, they built up strong networks of immigrant associations, which remain active to this day.

A common characteristic shared by the Greek and the Muslim migrants is that they had to rebuild their lives from scratch. The Lausanne convention included a stipulation for the establishment of a mixed commission on the pattern of the earlier agreements with Bulgaria, but the task of assessing the value of property left behind and disposing of it in an equitable manner proved simply too complicated. The mixed commission continued its work until October 1934, but the bulk of the migrants never received any compensation for their lost property.

The Muslims of Western Thrace and the Greek Orthodox of Constantinople were, as mentioned above, exempt from the exchange. The former comprised approximately 200,000 persons and the Turkish authorities did their utmost to reduce the number of the latter group to a similar figure by demanding proof from each individual that he or she had actually been resident within the municipality of Constantinople in October 1912. The main task of the mixed commission was assessing the status of these so-called *établis*. The fate of the two communities in the following years and decades followed very different patterns. The Muslims of Western Thrace were mistrusted by the Greek state. Expressions of their Turkish (as opposed to Muslim) identity were strictly forbidden and there has been constant pressure on the community to hellenize. Nevertheless, it has survived more or less intact as a separate community living in a clearly circumscribed area with a strong sense of separate identity. The same cannot be said for the Greek Orthodox of Constantinople, or – as it has been known since 1923 – Istanbul. In the interwar period, the community diminished in size but held onto its socioeconomic position in spite of the nationalist economic policies of the state, which still pursued the goal of creating a native Turkish bourgeoisie at the expense of non-Muslims. The skills possessed by the community were simply indispensable.

The trust of the Greek community in the impartiality and secular character of the Turkish state was fatally weakened, however, by two events: first, the imposition of a hugely discriminatory wealth tax in 1942 that ruined many Greek businesses and then large-scale, politically inspired riots in September 1955. That stimulated the vast majority of Istanbul Greeks to emigrate to Greece or the USA. At the end of the 20th century, the Greek Orthodox community in Istanbul had shrunk to about 2,000 persons, about 1% of its former size.

The perceptions of the population exchange have differed widely on both sides. The Greek mainland had had no previous experience with large-scale immigration and found itself in 1922–4 suddenly faced with a mass influx of migrants amounting to over 20% of its autochthonous population. In addition, this wave of immigration coincided with a grave political and military crisis. The Greek army had been handed a humiliating defeat and the entire political system had been discredited. Against this backdrop, the exchange has been perceived as the gravest national catastrophe. As time has passed, attributions of guilt have been directed less and less toward the mistakes of the Greek government and its occupation of Asia Minor and more and more toward the purported injustice and barbarism of the Turks. In addition, a strong sense of nostalgia for the lost world of Anatolian Hellenism has emerged that has been particularly fostered by the countless immigrant organizations. The magnitude of the problem and the size of the migrant population have

meant that Greek society as a whole has come to identify strongly with the fate of the migrants. This is reflected in the number of archives, research institutes, and publications devoted to the Greek communities of Asia Minor and the population exchange. As early as 1930 a large-scale survey of the social and cultural heritage of the Anatolian Greeks was initiated.

The Turkish situation has been very different. In Turkish eyes, those who came in 1924–5 constituted only one among many groups of Muslim refugees that had to be resettled after the 1820s. In line with the tradition of their predecessors, the Young Turk movement, the political elite of the Turkish republic, viewed the homogenization of Anatolia as a positive development: the area, which had been 80% Muslim in 1912, had become 98% Muslim. The population exchange was therefore seen as an integral part of the nation-building process. The loss of a modern industrial middle class was considered the necessary price for the achievement of full independence. This interpretation still prevails today, in Turkey itself as in European and American historiography.

The population exchange has aroused neither significant scholarly nor public interest, because the Macedonians represented only one among many migrant groups and made up only 3% of the population in a relatively thinly populated country. Whereas in Greece an entire library offers publications and rich sources for further study, in Turkey only a single, rather slim monograph has been published on the topic. Only recently have social historians begun to take an interest in the human aspect of the population exchange. Several television documentaries and planned oral history projects illustrate the new interest in this long-forgotten topic.

Andreades, Andreas. *Les effets économiques et sociaux de la guerre en Grèce*. Paris, 1929.

Ari, Kemal. *Büyük mübadele. Türkiye'ye zorunlu göç 1923–1925*. Istanbul, 1995.

Kitromilidis, Paschalis. "The Greek-Turkish Population Exchange." In *Philologiae et Historiae Turcicae Fundamenta V. History of Turkey in the Twentieth Century*, edited by Erik-Jan Zürcher, 255–70. Berlin, 2008.

Ladas, Stephen. *The Exchange of Minorities: Bulgaria, Greece and Turkey*. New York, 1932.

McCarthy, Justin. *Muslims and Minorities: The Population of Ottoman Anatolia and the End of Empire*. New York, 1983.

McCarthy, Justin. *Death and Exile: The Ethnic Cleansing of Ottoman Muslims 1821–1922*. Princeton, 1995.

Pekin, Müfide. *Yeniden kurulan yaşamlar. 80. Yýlýnda Türk-Yunan Nüfus Mübadelesi* [Rebuilt lives. The Turkish-Greek Population Exchange in its 80th Year]. Istanbul, 2005.

Cross-references: Southeastern Europe; Armenian Refugees in France since World War I; Greek Settlers from the Black Sea Region in New Russia since the Early Modern Period and Pontic Greeks in Greece since the End of World War II

GREEK REFUGEES IN EASTERN AND SOUTHEASTERN EUROPE AFTER THE CIVIL WAR, 1946–1949

Theodoros Lagaris

The Greek Civil War (1946–9) between leftist partisan groups under the leadership of the Communist Party of Greece (CPG) and units of the conservative Greek government cost the lives of tens of thousands. In their struggle against the antisocialist politics of the conservatives, the partisans wanted free parliamentary elections and the withdrawal of the foreign troops stationed in Greece since the end of World War II. Great Britain supported the Greek government militarily until 1947, thereafter the USA offered money and arms and sent military advisors.

With the victory of the Greek army and the end of the civil war in 1949, about 56,000 men and women as well as 28,000 children fled into the neighboring "People's democracies" of Albania and Bulgaria. Among the refugees were not only partisans who had taken up arms voluntarily but also forced recruits who had been coerced into joining the ranks of the partisans as fighters or auxiliary personnel. The volunteers were made up of very diverse groups: there were members of the CPG alongside former resistance fighters against the German occupation, who were persecuted in Greece by right-wing extremist groups and the Greek police. A third group were Slavo-Macedonians fighting for their autonomy with support from the CPG. Moreover, some of the Slavo-Macedonian refugees were among the forced recruits; others were forced to flee because of their ethnic background as a part of a "national cleansing" by advancing Greek troops. Many of the refugees who were initially taken in by Albania and Bulgaria were subsequently distributed to other countries in eastern and southeastern Europe (see Table 1). The majority of partisans capable of working went to the Soviet Union to close gaps in that country's production.

Even at the beginning of the 21st century, the *Paidomazoma* (abduction of the children) continues to be vigorously debated in Greece. The government accused the partisans of abducting all children between the ages of 3 and 14 from territories they controlled during the civil war and taking them to eastern and southeastern European countries. According to the government, the intention of the partisans was to raise the children as communists, to let them grow up as "Slavs" and thus contribute to the "destruction of the Greek race." By contrast, the partisans depicted the sending of children to eastern and southeastern European countries as an act of humanity: the children were supposedly removed from the areas of conflict with the consent of their parents to protect them from the brutality of the approaching army, the bombardments, and being dragged off to the children's villages set up by the royal family itself.

The children, distributed among various eastern and southeastern European countries, lived in homes and were raised as Greeks. While many children were taken away by partisans and Slavo-Macedonians at the request of their

Country	Adults	Children	Members of the CPG among the refugees
Romania	9,100	3,801/5,132	1,279
Czechoslovakia	11,941	2,235/4,148	1,707
Poland	11,458	3,000/3,590	3,132
Hungary	7,253	3,000/2,589	1,017
Bulgaria	3,021	2,660/672	1,140
GDR	1,128	-/1,128	
Soviet Union	11,980		8,173
Albania		2,000/-	
Yugoslavia		11,600/-	
Total	55,881	28,296/17,259	16,448

Table 1. Distribution of Greek refugees in eastern and southeastern Europe, 1949–50

Source: Stelios Giatroudakis, *Taskendi: 30 chronia prosfygia* (Athens, n.d.); the first number under the Children column is based on data by the Greek Red Cross in 1950. Information about this from Bærentzen, "Paidomazoma."

parents, other parents felt coerced, out of fear of reprisals, to consent to the separation from their children. Shortly after the end of the war, those parents, with the help of the Red Cross, demanded the return of their children to Greece; according to data from the Red Cross, 12,127 requests had been submitted by 1950. All told about 5,000 children who had furnished proof of Greek nationality as demanded by the Greek state were sent back.

During the civil war, the conservative political elite rejected a peaceful solution to the conflict. Decades after the civil war, it was still refusing any reconciliation with the communists. In their view, a "conspiracy of Communist Pan-Slavism" against the territorial integrity of the country formed the backdrop to the civil war. The partisans had acted "anti-national" and had been in service to a hostile nation. This version of history shaped the refugee policy of the Greek governments. As early as December 1947, parliament passed a decree that made it possible to strip citizenship from "Greek nationals who are residing temporarily or permanently abroad and can be shown to be behaving anti-national in the current rebellion or in any way support the war of the bandits directed against the state." In this way, a total of 22,266 refugees who were living in eastern and southeastern European countries lost their citizenship between 1948 and 1963.

This punitive measure was followed, in a decree of 21 January 1948, by the confiscation of the property of the denaturalized refugees. It was even possible to seize the property of spouses. The confiscated wealth, chiefly landholdings, was divided up among the members of groups with close ties to the conservative governments. Not only did this eradicate the memory of the refugees in their native towns and villages, but the refugees were simultaneously deprived of a material basis for a potential return.

A first wave of returnees reached Greece in the second half of the 1950s. For the most part they were former forced recruits. An application for return had to be submitted in person to the closest Greek embassy. Applicants had to prove both Greek nationality and their status as prisoners of war or hostages, i.e., the fact that they had been coerced into leaving. Returning refugees founded the Association of Repatriates from the States behind the Iron Curtain, which also published a number of autobiographies of former refugees. They recounted dismal working conditions in the factories, at construction sites, and in the fields; minimal pay; food shortages; wretched housing; and the splendor with which the party cadres surrounded themselves. The association put the number of returnees at the beginning of the 1960s at 15,000. They were able to reintegrate themselves into Greek society through the same mechanism used for the "national suspects" who had been captured by government troops during the civil war and interned in reeducation camps: a declaration of remorse in which they distanced themselves from the "anti-national" goals of the CPG and condemned them. A large number of disillusioned refugees suffering discrimination used this path, which was not discouraged either by the CPG or the Soviet government.

The larger part of the partisans transported to the Soviet Union came to Tashkent (Uzbekistan) to work in the (heavy) industry that had been set up there during World War II. In Tashkent, the refugees lived surrounded by fences in former prisoner of war camps with communal accommodations that also provided space for meetings and cultural events. In other places of refuge, as well, the refugees initially had to content themselves with communal accommodations until the local authorities – for example, in Sofia (Bulgaria) – erected new buildings for them. A few escaped life in the camps by marrying natives.

The eastern and southeastern European host countries refused to recognize the Greek immigrants as "political refugees" in keeping with the international agreements they had signed. As a result, their support took on the character of charity, not of the fulfillment of international treaties. The refugees had no rights of any kind in the host countries. Neither the host countries nor the leaders of the CPG were willing to tolerate oversight by the United Nations (UN). As stateless persons, the refugees were initially given the "yellow identification card," which, among other things, restricted their freedom of movement to their place of residence – similar documents were issued to, for example, individuals politically persecuted at home and those with a criminal record. In the mid-1960, the refugees were granted the status of "political immigrants," which was de facto hardly any different from their previous one.

The refugees were distributed among the various countries in self-contained units of the partisan army. During the first two years they lived in accordance with military rules (early morning exercise, military ranks, military drills), since in the eyes of the CPG leadership the civil war was not over yet and the slogan therefore was "ready for battle." It often took years before the members of one family who had been spread out to different locations were reunited. One goal in

making family reunification difficult was the intent of the leadership of the CPG to impose upon the refugees the idea that the party was the most important source of identity. Accordingly, the oath of party members went as follows: "I swear: from this moment on I no longer belong to myself. I belong completely to my party and its great cause. First the party and then I. First the party and then my mother."

For most refugees, who hailed from agrarian regions and were barely literate in their own language, learning the local language was a difficult task. At the same time, the refugees were faced with a shortage of goods, corruption, and black marketeering, which was a profound disillusionment to many. The children were integrated into the local educational systems and in addition attended special courses set up by the CPG to learn the Greek language and culture.

In the eastern and southeastern European host countries, the refugees became increasingly subject to the control of the CPG leadership. The communist governments of the destination countries accorded the Greek "sister party" the right to make decisions about the future of the refugees. In the process, the Soviet-installed CPG leadership could resort to the apparatus of repression in the host countries. For example, the leadership alone decided about access to educational institutions and the allocation of jobs and housing. Opportunities for education and vocational training were considered rewards for loyalty toward the party. The CPG leadership encouraged younger functionaries among the refugees to learn technical-scientific professions. To that end, it provided a certain number of university places without admission tests. However, those who kept their distance from the party, as for example, the recruits, had to perform simple and physically hard work in factories and on construction sites.

In addition, the CPG leadership had an information monopoly: information about the events in Greece and in the various host countries was passed on by the CPG's radio station Phoni tis alitheias (Voice of Truth), by the newspaper published in each country by the local party organization (in Hungary, for example, it was called *Laikos agonas*, Popular Struggle), or the monthly CPG magazine *Neos Kosmos* (New Order). The party's Office of Enlightenment was tasked with controlling the flow of information; listening to western European radio stations, for example, the BBC, was prohibited. The CPG's printing house published Marxist-Leninist writings and "analyses" of the respective dominant party factions. Literature was first examined for its loyalty to the party line.

Intraparty conflicts and the struggle between various party factions shaped the history of the Greek refugees in eastern and southeastern Europe. Discussions about the backgrounds of the civil war and the defeat of the partisans were to be avoided. Criticism was punished – with expulsion from the party and the demeaning defamation as "agent of the class enemy and of imperialism," or even as "rapist"; with the loss of a privileged job, exclusion from the educational system, and the loss of housing. Many former functionaries ended up as brickmakers or metalworkers after having been kicked out of office. Members and functionaries who were classified as "dangerous" to the "intraparty discipline" were arrested, interrogated, and tortured. The CPG set up a *kolkhoz* camp in Poland where inmates were forced to perform grueling work under the supervision of CPG guards.

Immediately after his flight, Kostas Karagiorgas, for example, a well-known partisan and high-level functionary of the CPG, had called for an extensive debate about the events of the 1940s and had criticized the political course and the authoritarian style of the leadership group. On orders from the CPG leaders, he was arrested in 1950 in Bucharest by the Romanian police, interrogated, and tortured in an effort to extract from him a confession about his alleged activity as an "agent" and "traitor." He died from the effects of the torture. The faction of the CPG around General Secretary Nikolaos Zachariadis, which had been dominant since 1945, lost its power in 1956 in the wake of de-Stalinization. It fell victim to the practices of the intraparty struggle against "deviants" which it itself had institutionalized: the former general secretary, now considered "suspect," was demoted to the status of an industrial laborer. When he began to make efforts to return to Greece, the Soviet authorities deported him to Siberia, where he committed suicide in 1973. His closest collaborators and dozens of his supporters suffered the fate of deportation to Siberia, the Hungarian Puszta, or northern Kazakhstan.

Even after the collapse of the military dictatorship in 1974, the conservative governments that followed (1974–81) refused to put a quick end to the odyssey of the political refugees by rescinding existing laws. They insisted on individual applications, but they no longer required declarations of remorse. Between 1974 and 1981, 21,650 refugees made their way back to Greece. In many cases, restrictive Greek regulations in the economic and social spheres continue to prevent a return: many refugees were unable to find a job in Greece, their old property remained confiscated, and those not recognized in Greece as former political refugees did not receive an integration subsidy from the state. And the governments of the eastern and southeastern European host countries initially also refused to pay back social security contributions and to remit pensions to Greece.

It was only the governments led by Panellinio Sosialistiko Kinima (PASOK; Pan-Hellenic Socialist Movement) that facilitated remigration in the 1980s. Greek refugees were allowed to return without conditions, confiscated property was returned, academic degrees were recognized. In response, about 45,000 individuals returned to Greece. The high number of returnees more than 30 years after the end of the Greek Civil War leads to the conclusion that the refugees had been barely integrated into the eastern and southeastern European host countries, had preserved their Greek identity in relatively tight and cohesive ethnic communities, and had lived with the dream of returning. Excluded from a privileged return in the 1980s was the group of refugees from the Slavo-Macedonian minority: "descent from the Greek national group" remained the precondition for a return.

Bærentzen, Lars. "The 'Paidomazoma' and the Queen's Camps." In *Studies in the History of Greek Civil War 1945–1949*, edited by Lars Bærentzen, John O. Iatrides, and Ole L. Smith, 127–57. Copenhagen, 1987.

Baev, Iordan. "Ellines politikoi prosfyges stin Voulgaria." In *Ptyches toz emfyliou polemou 1946–1949*, edited by Kleomenis Koutsoukis and Ioannis Sakkas, 207–15. Athens, 2000.

Dritsios, Thomas. *Giati me skotoneis syntrofe*. Athens, 1983.

Lambatos, Gavrilis. *Ellines politikoi prosfyges stin Taskendi (1949–1957)*. Athens, 2001.

Ravanis-Rentis, Dimitrios. *To imerologio tis prosfygias enos andarti*. Athens, 1991.

Cross-references: Czechia and Slovakia; Germany; Poland; Russia and Belarus; Southeastern Europe

GREEK REFUGEES IN WESTERN, CENTRAL, NORTHERN, AND SOUTHERN EUROPE DURING THE MILITARY DICTATORSHIP, 1967–1974

Theodoros Lagaris

After the takeover of power by the military in Greece following the putsch in April 1967, a great many politically engaged Greeks were confronted with repressive measures by the new rulers. Conservative and liberal politicians, as well as intellectuals, were now also among the circle of those who were suspected of acting in a "subversive," "anti-Greek," and "anti-national" manner. Until then, this accusation had been leveled only against supporters of the Communist Party of Greece (CPG), especially the partisans and refugees of the Greek Civil War (1946–9). Even royalist civilians and army officers fled, for example, after the failed counterputsch by the king in December 1968 and after the revolt of royalist navy officers in May 1973. As long as the military was in power, a steady stream of refugees left Greece and sought admission to countries in western, central, northern, and southern Europe. We have no statistical data about the magnitude of this stream of refugees. Immediately after the overthrow of the dictatorship, virtually all refugees returned home. Only a very small minority had shifted the center of their lives permanently abroad, had found work, or had established a family.

In the immediate aftermath of the putsch, the new rulers had nearly the entire political elite arrested in 1967. The detainees were imprisoned or placed into collection camps on islands or in the interior of the country, for example, the notorious camp of Oropos near Athens. Conservative politicians, among them the former prime minister Panagiotis Kanellopoulos, were placed under house arrest. In response, many who feared they might be swept up by other waves of arrest fled the country. They went to the UK, France, Italy, West Germany, Switzerland, the Netherlands, and Scandinavia and applied for political asylum. The refugees included many members of resistance organizations, for example, the Pan-Hellenic Liberation Movement (PAK). One of them was the future prime minister Konstantinos Simitis, a member of PAK, who managed to escape to Germany in 1969 shortly before he was to be arrested.

Greeks who were under military surveillance or wanted by the military could be smuggled out of the country to western, central, northern, and southern Europe with the help of countrymen who already resided or had recently arrived there. These first groups of refugees, which included also the later founder of the Pan-Hellenic Socialist Movement (PASOK), Andreas Papandreou, were followed later by those released from prison and the camps, among them the politician and composer Mikis Theodorakis. The releases were a response to international protests. The military regime referred to them as "deportations" abroad and justified them as a measure to reduce the potential influence that individuals considered "anti-Greek" would be able to exert on the population.

Even in the 1970s, the regime still felt compelled – because of international pressure – to expel members of resistance groups who had been arrested or already sentenced by military courts. That was true, for example, of Amalia Fleming, a socialist politician and wife of the Scottish bacteriologist Alexander Fleming, and of the lawyer and socialist politician Georgios Mangakis. Some managed to flee the country in spite of strict surveillance and internment: examples are the publisher of the conservative papers *Kathimerini* and *Mesimvrini*, Helen Vlachos, who had been under house arrest, and the liberal politician Georgios Mylonas. In 1968 another case caused a stir: the regime had sent two individuals – under secret surveillance – to Strasbourg to testify against the exclusion of Greece from the Council of Europe by affirming that there was no violation of human rights in Greece. After requesting asylum from the Norwegian delegation, they acted as witnesses for the prosecution.

During the last two years of the dictatorship, the refugees were above all students seeking to escape imminent arrest and torture or avoid military conscription. In response to growing protests at the universities, the regime had the leaders arrested, and in 1973 it suspended the long-standing practice of deferring military service while students were enrolled at university for all those under political suspicion.

The Greeks who fled to various western, central, northern, and southern European countries were not immediately recognized by the authorities as political refugees; instead, the crossing of the border was generally followed by a lengthy and complicated asylum process. Only the Scandinavian countries and the Netherlands pursued a generous policy of recognition. Within the context of the cold war, the late 1960s and early 1970s were characterized in the West by fear of "communist revolutionaries." For example, the Office for the Protection of the Constitution in West Germany classified nearly all Greek resistance organizations as "extremist."

Many European politicians and intellectuals, and not only conservative ones, believed that the military in Greece was the only alternative to a socialist or communist dictatorship.

As a result, even Swiss authorities initiated protracted investigative procedures against well-known refugees, for example, Georgios Mylonas. Immigrants whose passports were not renewed or even canceled by Greek consulates got into trouble with the alien laws in the host countries and lived in constant fear of being deported. Some refugees became stateless when their citizenship was revoked. A prominent example was the actor and future Greek minister of culture (1981–9), Melina Mercouri, who had been living abroad already before the putsch and who was punished for her political activism against the military regime by having her citizenship revoked and her property confiscated. However, these kinds of sanctions against Greeks who allegedly acted in an "anti-national" manner abroad were already part of a law passed by the conservative government in 1962.

Other Greek migrant workers, intellectuals, or students who had already been living in the destination countries before the military putsch also became politically engaged members of the opposition: for example, the journalist Pavlos Tzermias, who was working for the *Neue Zürcher Zeitung*, emphasized that his decision to work against the regime cast him into the status of refugee. Every Greek consulate had surveillance officers – among them the infamous "Work Commissions" in West Germany – who took note of all public actions by Greek citizens and reported them back to Athens.

The situation was particularly difficult for Greek students who participated in actions against the dictatorship at European universities. Not only did the regime revoke their passports but it also forbade their families in Greece from sending money abroad. Especially in Italy, where a very politicized Greek student body was active, the number of the "paperless" grew continuously. Among them was Kostas Georgakis, who, in an act of protest against the regime, set himself ablaze in Genoa in 1970.

The struggle against the military government shaped the daily life of the refugees. For many, work and family were only secondary. Information about the situation in Greece was collected and disseminated; acts of solidarity, rallies, and demonstrations were planned. Many hours a day were spent participating in meetings of various committees, organizations, and local branches of resistance organizations, to which nearly every refugee belonged.

In the European metropolises that were home to prominent and less prominent refugees, the political camps that had been at loggerheads since the Greek Civil War (1946–9) entered into a political dialog: the conservative faction around Konstantinos Karamanlis ceased to stigmatize the socialist and communist opponents as "anti-national" and "anti-Greek," since the military had now seized this discourse and was aiming it also against those who had invented it, the conservative government in power between the civil war and the military coup.

In bulletins, journals, and other publications, the committees of the Greek refugees informed the Western public about the repressive measures of the military regime – like the decrees abolishing freedom of the press, expatriations, arrests, military courts, internment in camps, and torture – and about its anti-European nationalism, anticommunism, and anti-Semitism. At the center stood the weekly information bulletin *Athènes-Presse Libre* that was edited by refugees in Paris. Further publications of this kind were the London *Hellenic Review* and *Griechische Dokumente und Informationen*, the latter published by the Action Democratic Greece in Cologne. Other organizations aimed exclusively at the active – and also armed – struggle against the dictatorship, as for example, the Demokratiki Amyna (Democratic Defense). That was especially true for some radical organizations like the Movement 20 October that was founded by students in Paris in 1969 and was influenced by terrorist actions (e.g., of the Basque ETA) in Europe and by guerrilla fighting in Latin America.

However, the majority of refugees joined resistance organizations that had been set up by political parties already active in Greece before the dictatorship. Chief among them were the Panellino Apeleftherotiko Kinima (PAK, Pan-Hellenic Liberation Movement) founded in Stockholm in 1968 by Andreas Papandreou, the leading functionary of the Center Union, and by the Patriotiko Antidiktatoriko Metopo (PAM, Patriotic Anti-Dictatorial Front) led by the Communist Party. In the final analysis, their politics were also aimed at setting themselves clearly apart from one another in the struggle for influence among the Greek refugees in western, central, northern, and southern Europe, and to present themselves as the only true representative of the fight against dictatorship.

Papagiannopoulos, Giorgos. *I skoteini plevra tou iliou*. Athens, 1989.

Vlachos, Helen, ed. *Dokumentation einer Diktatur: Griechenland*. Munich, 1972.

Cross-references: France; Germany; Great Britain; Italy; The Netherlands; Northern Europe; Southeastern Europe; Switzerland; Greek Labor Migrants in Western, Central, and Northern Europe after 1950: The Examples of Germany and the Netherlands; Greek Refugees in Eastern and Southeastern Europe after the Civil War, 1946–1949

GREEK SETTLERS FROM THE BLACK SEA REGION IN NEW RUSSIA SINCE THE EARLY MODERN PERIOD AND PONTIC GREEKS IN GREECE SINCE THE END OF WORLD WAR II

Ioannis Zelepos

Greeks settled in the Black Sea region were uniformly referred to as "Pontians" or "Pontic Greeks," labels derived from the Greek name for this sea (*Pontos Euxeinos*). The area of settlement was the Pontus region in northeastern Asia Minor. It comprised the coastal strip with the ports of Sinope, Samsun, and Trabzon, along with its mountainous interior, where the

cities of Amasia, Tokat, Sivas, Gümüshane, and Erzerum are located. Until 1923, this core region was home to compact Greek settlements from which, at various times, extensive migrations took place to territories north of the Black Sea, to the Caucasus region, and finally, to Greece. The Orthodox Greeks, who made up about 93% of the total population in the 16th century (an estimated 200,000 out of 215,000), still accounted for just under 30% (about 380,000 of 1.3 million) on the eve of the Balkan wars at the beginning of the 20th century. In addition to emigration, this decline was also due to conversion to Islam, though its rate can no longer be determined.

The area of Greek settlements on the Crimea had a center in the south of the peninsula around the cities of Sebastopol, Simferopol, and Yalta, and in the east in Kertch. As a result of the colonization efforts of New Russia since the 1770s at the initiative of Empress Catherine II and her successors, Greek settlements arose on the northern coast of the Sea of Azov and the mouth of the Don, with focal points in Mariupol, Taganrog, and Rostov, and northeast of the Black Sea with focal points in Novorossiysk, Yekaterinodar, and Sukhumi. In this context belongs also the founding of Russian trading ports that attracted numerous Greek traders from the Ottoman Empire – for example, Odessa (created in 1794 as a free port), where a flourishing Greek community grew up.

Since the end of the 18th century, settlements of Pontic Greeks were also established in the Caucasus region, primarily in Tchalka near Tiflis, but also in Baku, Erivan, and Dagestan, and later in Kars and Batum. Toward the end of the First World War, about 165,000 Pontians were living in the Caucasus, and about 335,000 in Ukraine (including the Crimea). The majority of the Russian Black Sea Greeks were deported in 1941 as part of Stalin's minority policy and forcibly resettled in Central Asia, namely Kazakhstan and Uzbekistan. A part of them returned to their previous settlement areas on the Black Sea after Stalin's death in 1953, another part left for Greece. Today, about 500,000 Greeks still live in the successor states of the Soviet Union. The last great migration push died down following the breakup of the Soviet Union after the middle of the 1990s, and these settlements once again form vigorous communities in the CIS.

Migration waves and their reasons

Beginning in the 18th century, the migration of Greeks in the Black Sea region was directed primarily to Russia. It took place almost entirely in family units. An essential driver for the migrations was initially the settlement policy of the czars, which was motivated by the desire to settle and economically develop the territories of New Russia acquired since the end of the 18th century. Settlers from many parts of Europe were recruited with the help of targeted propaganda and the grant of numerous privileges, such as exemption from taxes and military service and allocations of land, animals, equipment, houses, and even cash. To this were added the guaranteed exercise of the settlers' religion, local self-government, and schools of their own. Apart from geographic proximity, there were two primary reasons that recruiting Pontic Greeks from the Ottoman Empire made sense: first, among them were productive and in part specialized workers; second, as Orthodox Christians they were brothers in faith and thus seemed better suited than the local population groups of the Muslim faith for securing the governance of the newly acquired territories.

The second reason became especially important in the Caucasus region, where the Russian state had been undertaking targeted efforts at confessional homogenization since the second third of the 19th century. It promoted the immigration of Christians from the neighboring Ottoman regions, primarily Armenians and after them Greeks, while it suppressed the Muslim population (Cerkessians, Abkhazians, Kurds) and in part also forced them to emigrate in the opposite direction. Tens of thousands were affected, which means that the beginnings of a regular population exchange are evident.

But even independent of the deliberate measures of settlement policy by the state, there were many economic reasons for the Pontic Greeks to migrate. Apart from the Russian trading ports in the Black Sea, where merchants could find lucrative areas of activity especially in the increasingly important grain trade, the Russian mining regions also developed into magnets for specialized craftsmen and miners. Initially the latter came mostly as seasonal workers, though after some time they began to have their families join them. Independent migrations into rural regions – for example, the Caucasus regions of Kars and Tchalka – could also be observed. These were driven by economic motives but also by the increasingly precarious safety situation in the Ottoman border provinces: one important, repeated cause of the migration of Greeks from the Ottoman Empire to Russia were the military clashes between the two states. For example, the Russo-Ottoman wars of 1768–74 and 1828–9 had already led to massive refugee movements. The same was true of the Crimean War of 1853–6, the Russo-Ottoman War of 1877–8, and the First World War; during the latter conflict alone, around 130,000 Pontians left their homeland and headed north.

At the beginning of the 20th century, Greece replaced Russia as the most important destination area of Pontic migration. The period between 1895 and 1907 was the first time that a small number of families, as part of a state settlement project, moved out of the Caucasus region to what was then the northern border of Greece. However, no permanent settlement came about. In fact, it would appear that the majority of those immigrants returned to their homes in the Caucasus within a short period. Already during the First World War, refugee movements from the Black Sea region reached Greece, initially from the Ottoman Empire

(especially following Greece's entry into the war in 1917 on the side of the Entente), then from Russia as a consequence of Greek participation in the Allied expedition to Ukraine in 1918–19. The high point was the population exchange between Turkey and Greece that was carried out in 1923 in line with the Treaty of Lausanne, and which put a radical end to the long history of Greek settlement in Asia Minor within a short time.

The last great migration push of Pontic Greeks to Greece followed after 1987 and the subsequent collapse of the Soviet Union, after there had been two smaller peaks in emigration in 1937–9 and 1965–7. The emigration after 1987 was driven primarily by economic motives, though to some extent it was also in response to the rise of the new nationalism in the successor states to the Soviet Union. Starting with 527 officially registered persons in 1987, the immigration to Greece reached its high point between 1990 (13,853) and 1993 (10,926); thereafter, it declined noticeably (1994: 5,793; 1996: 5,578). Estimates put the total number of immigrants from the former Soviet Union to Greece today at slightly more than 70,000.

Integration and segregation

An overall heterogeneous picture of the Greeks in the Black Sea region as a group emerges, on the one hand, from the various historical phases and causes behind its formation as a minority, and, on the other hand, from the divergent sociocultural profile of its various parts. For example, the Pontic Greeks of the core region in Asia Minor were an old-established population with developed cultural traditions and separate statehood in the Middle Ages. Here was the location of the Empire of Trapezunt between 1204 and its conquest by the Ottomans in 1461; to this day, its history is instrumentalized as a historical mythos to emphasize Pontic identity. Already the short-lived "Pontic Republic," which declared its independence in 1918 in the upheavals at the end of the First World War, chose as its national coat of arms the eagle of the emperor of Trapezunt, which also today serves as the symbol of numerous Pontic organizations within and outside of Greece.

The overwhelming majority of the Russian Greeks, recruited largely from the core region of Asia Minor, were farmers (at the beginning of the 1920s, at least 80%) who gradually lost their numerous privileges after the second half of the 19th century in connection with the policy of Russification. A much smaller segment of the population was free wage workers (for example, miners) and craftsmen. Finally, there was the group of merchants: though numerically the smallest, it had important social functions for the formation of identity. As a rule they formed the core of the numerous communities that were established in most Russian cities and functioned as receptors and multipliers of a discourse that was becoming increasingly focused, after the independence of Greece, on the national state. That debate also led to the establishment and financing of schools whose curricula followed those of the Greek "motherland," and it made a major contribution to the development of a specific diaspora mentality.

In the first half of the 19th century, however, this development was only in its infancy. Alongside these new trends, older orientations continued to affect the self-perception of the Greeks: next to Russia as the "new" homeland stood the Pontus region as an "old" homeland, to which multifarious connections were maintained. For example, new settlements were often given the names of places of origin, which contributed across generations to an internal differentiation according to communities of origin and the maintenance of kinship relationships between regions of origin and the destination regions. One important aspect of the mental anchoring of the Greek settlers in Russia was not least the traditional religious centers of the Pontus region (e.g., the Soumela monastery).

The orientation to the Greek nation-state, to which initially only the weakest geographical, historical, or cultural ties existed, eventually took on extraordinary significance in the 20th century, especially after the loss of the "old homeland" on the Black Sea. This development had already manifested itself on the eve of World War I in the large-scale grant of Greek citizenship to Pontic Greeks.

The formation of the Black Sea Greeks as a minority was characterized by segregative elements that clearly outweighed integrative factors. The basic social conditions in Russia and in the Ottoman Empire favored the formation and preservation of separate group identities, from the religious community to the village community and down to the family. In part this was also due to the long absence of state initiatives to integrate the various segments of the population. A state that was in this sense "weak" remained characteristic of the Czarist Empire until the second half of the 19th century, and its conquests in southern Russia and the Caucasus could not, initially, be regarded as consolidated in any way. For that reason, the Pontic Greeks who had been recruited to secure Russian rule lived for a long time in closed village communities with a high degree of local autonomy, in areas whose ethnic structure was largely heterogeneous because of the colonists from the most varied parts of Europe. This fragmentation extended equally to the rural and the urban areas and led to the near-complete absence of a "majority people" or a "majority culture" as a point of reference for integration.

In Orthodox Russia, just as in the Ottoman Empire, though in slightly different ways, confession retained its identity-creating power for the Black Sea Greeks, in the sense that their privileges included, alongside local self-government, also the free exercise of religion. Thus the community preserved Greek as the liturgical language in religious services until the beginning of Russification in 1860.

This points to language as a second important criterion of identification: use of the Pontic dialect – which fulfilled the function of an everyday language – undoubtedly had a strong, group-binding effect. In addition, standard modern Greek was also taught in the schools, which were operated and financed in part by the churches, and in part by the Greek communities in Russia. One example is the Greek Trading School of Odessa (founded in 1817), where in 1872 a higher Greek school was set up, the future, highly renowned Rodokanakeion Parthenagogeion. On a lesser scale, this language and cultural policy was also supported by the Greek state after the end of the 19th century. However, its effect must not be exaggerated, given the absence of compulsory school attendance. Moreover, the use of the Pontic dialect declined from the second half of the 19th century, which had to do in part with the systematic Russification but in part also with Greek-Russian mixed marriages that were not impeded by any confessional barriers.

The assimilation process seems to have been most pronounced in the environs of Mariupol'. Most of the Greeks of Tchalka and Kars in the Caucasus were already Turkish speaking when they settled, while instruction in the Greek schools in this area was exclusively in Russian. On the whole, Greek language proved relatively resilient, though that likely applies more to the Pontic dialect than to the standard language, which was probably as an everyday language in use only among the Greeks in the Odessa area. According to official statistics in 1926, 72.7% of individuals identifying themselves as Greeks in the Soviet Union indicated Greek as their mother tongue; by 1959 there were still 41.5%, and by 1970 the number had dropped to 39.3%.

As part of Lenin's minority policy, Greek was strongly promoted and in 1928 codified as an official minority language with a greatly simplified orthography. The generally favorable conditions in the early Soviet Union led to a veritable flowering of Greek cultural life, but it came to an abrupt end in 1937 with the restrictive minority policy of Stalin and his head of the secret police, Lavrenti Beria. The cultural flowering showed itself, among other things, in the establishment of a Greek state theater in Sukhumi (from 1928 to 1936), and, after 1930, in the emergence of Greek-language papers in Rostov on the Don (*Komunistis*, successor to *Spartakos*, which had already been published before 1920), in Mariupol' (*Kolechtivistis*), and in Sukhumi (*Kokinos Kapnas* – "Red Tobacco Planter"), but also in a remarkable production of Greek-language literature. About 39% of these publications appeared in the Pontic dialect, which was also codified for the first time with Kostis Topcharas' *Grammar of the Pontic Language*, published in 1932 in Rostov on the Don. This was connected with a plan, discussed at this time, to make Pontic the official language of the Greek minority. In the end, modern standard Greek was retained, a decision that was motivated by the hope of carrying the communist revolution also to Greece at a later time. In that process, the Soviet Greeks were to play a multiplier role, which would have been hampered by their linguistic separation. Still, it must be noted that the years between 1926 and 1937 in the Soviet Union saw far-reaching efforts to strengthen a genuine Pontic Greek identity, even though in a strictly socialist context.

Title page of the Greek newspaper *Red Tobacco Planter*, published in Sukhumi until 1937, issue of 21 January 1934 (*Chatziiossif, Christos, ed. Istoria tis Elladas tou 20ou aiona, vol. II/1. Athens, 2001, p. 385*).

By contrast, in their "national homeland" of Greece, the Pontic Greeks long remained marginalized as refugees. However, to the extent that their integration into the supraordinated group of the Greek nation succeeded, the only room that was left for a Pontic cultural identity in the end was in the form of ethnic folklore. The first signs of such an integration process became visible in Greece in the 1930s, a process that was based on the gradual overcoming of the initial, dire social situation of the refugees. War and the occupation period of the 1940s accelerated this process, even if all of this did not lead to the complete integration of the Pontic Greeks. One indication of this is the fact that they made up a disproportionately large share of the Greek labor migrants who left the country in large numbers beginning in 1950, first to Australia and the USA, and after 1960 also increasingly to West Germany.

In the 1980s, the overwhelming majority of the Pontic Greeks in the USSR held Greek passports, which is what made their "remigration" to Greece after the end of the century possible in the first place. However, this has had and continues to have little effect on the problem of integrating Russian Pontic Greeks into Greek society. Upon their arrival in Greece, most immigrants after World War II spoke only Russian or the Pontic dialect, which in actual practice, compared to modern standard Greek, posed as many barriers to communication as a foreign language. The problems arising from this massive communication barrier in school or on the job market played a crucial role in the social marginalization and isolation of the immigrants. But the immigrants also encountered strong resentments within Greek society. In contrast to the Pontic refugees of 1923, whose labor power was welcome in the agriculture of Greece's northern regions, the Pontic Greeks after the Second World War settled in the urban centers – mostly in the environs of Athens, to a lesser extent also in Thessaloniki – in the hope of better earnings opportunities. Within the framework of chain migrations,

this soon led to the emergence of rapidly growing settlement concentrations in the suburbs of these cities, which led some to speak of "ghettoes." The Greek state ignored this problem for a long time.

In the anticommunist climate of the cold war, the Pontic Greeks, though themselves often victims of Stalinism, were at times suspected of engaging in "subversive activities" simply because they had come from the Soviet Union. For example, during the military dictatorship (1967–74), they were for that reason prohibited from setting up organizations. Only with the sustained democratization of Greece, and when the problem seemed to take on unsettling dimensions for Greek society with the mass arrival of more Pontic Greeks, did the state take the first initiatives to integrate this group, for which the name *Rossopontioi* (Russian Pontians, not Russian Greeks) had become established in common parlance. Important state measures were, for example, the establishment of language courses (after 1987) with special textbooks, the creation of reception centers, the allocation of housing, and the granting of start-up loans. This went hand in hand with a gradual revaluation of Russian-Pontic identity in social awareness, an identity that is present in the cultural life of the country also at the beginning of the 21st century and is seen as an enrichment. The beginnings of an integration of the *Rossopontioi* who have immigrated since the late 1980s are thus apparent.

Bornträger, Ekkehard W. "Les Grecs de Russie. Une histoire mouvementée et un avenir incertain." *Europa Ethnica* 50 (1993): 200–8.

Fotiadis, Kostas. *O Ellinismos tis Krimaias. Marioupoli, dikaioma sti mnimi*. Athens, 1990.

Henrich, Günter S. "Die Griechen der Gemeinschaft Unabhängiger Staaten." *Folia Neohellenica* 9 (1999): 76–113.

Kappeler, Andreas. "Die griechische Diaspora im Zarenreich." In *Griechische Kultur in Südosteuropa in der Neuzeit. Beiträge zum Symposium in memoriam Gunnar Hering (Wien, 16.–18.12.2004)*. In *Byzantina et Neograeca Vindobonensia*, vol. XXVI, edited by Maria A. Stassinopoulou and Ioannis Zelepos, 351–62. Vienna, 2008.

Karidis, Vyron. "The Mariupol Greeks: Tsarist Treatment of an Ethnic Minority ca. 1778–1859." *Journal of Modern Hellenism* 3 (1986): 57–74.

Karpozilos, Apostolos. "Pontic Culture in the USSR between the Wars." *Journal of Refugee Studies* 4 (1991): 364–71.

Cross-references: Russia and Belarus; Southeastern Europe; Bulgarian and Gagauzian Settlers in New Russia and Bessarabia since the 18th Century; German Settlers in Russia since the 18th Century; Greek Labor Migrants in Western, Central, and Northern Europe after 1950: The Examples of Germany and the Netherlands; Greek Orthodox and Muslim Refugees and Deportees in Greece and Turkey since 1912; Ukrainian and Russian Settlers in New Russia since the 18th Century

GREEK TRADERS AND PHANARIOTES IN SOUTHERN AND SOUTHEASTERN EUROPE FROM THE EARLY MODERN PERIOD TO THE 19TH CENTURY

Ioannis Zelepos

The general political instability of southeastern Europe since the late Middle Ages initially prevented trade in this area from undergoing a development similar to that in western, central, and southern Europe. While the continental trading links ceased entirely in some areas as a result of the numerous military conflicts, the maritime trade in the eastern Mediterranean was largely in the hands of the Italian maritime republics of Venice, Genoa, and Pisa. This situation changed around the middle of the 16th century with the establishment of the Ottoman Empire as the most important force of political order in southeastern Europe, and with the substantial waning of its urge toward military expansion westward.

Within the context of a general economic upswing in the region, for which the revival of the urban centers on the Balkan Peninsula were both cause and indicator, there arose new possibilities of development for trade. In the process, native population groups profited substantially from the closure of the Black Sea to non-Ottoman ships, and from the displacement of the Italian trading powers from the eastern Mediterranean.

The chief beneficiaries of this development were initially Armenians and Sephardic Jews who had immigrated in large numbers from Spain since 1492, and only secondarily Orthodox Christians, namely Greeks, who were living in Constantinople and some of whom were descendants of Byzantine noble families. They were called "Phanariotes" after the neighborhood in which they lived, Phanar (Fener), which has also been the seat of the Ecumenical Patriarchate since 1453. Their spheres of activity were largely in the Black Sea region, where they played a role, among other things, in the import of Russian furs, and on the eastern Balkan peninsula, which was critically important to the capital's grain supply, and an important part of whose trade they already controlled around 1600.

When we speak of Phanariotes, we must bear in mind that in the 18th century they included many families who were originally not from Constantinople but had settled there as social parvenus only after having established themselves successfully as traders in southeastern Europe. For the sake of simplicity, they can be divided into two categories: one category was made up Greeks from Epirus (e.g., Ioannina) and Macedonia (e.g., Kastoria), who, in addition to Macedonian Slavs, Aromuni, and Serbs, were able to use the continental trading routes largely without competition, thanks to their knowledge of the area and their language skills. Those routes ran from the southern Balkans via Belgrade and Hungary to central Europe, specifically to Vienna or Leipzig, where important Greek trading colonies arose. After the 18th century, these locations frequently became way stations also in a circular trading route that included Russia.

The other category consisted of Greeks from the Aegean region who were active in maritime trade. Many came originally from the island of Chios and had settled in nearby Smyrna (Izmir). During the Cretan War of 1645–69, Smyrna had replaced Thessaloniki as the second-most important trading metropolis of the Ottoman Empire (after Constantinople), and since that time it had also attracted merchants from there. Greek trading houses in Smyrna soon established numerous branches in Italy, namely, in Livorno, Genoa, and Trieste, which acquired growing importance vis-à-vis Venice, where a large Greek community had already formed after the end of the Byzantine Empire. Branches were also established in France, the Netherlands (primarily in Amsterdam), as well as in the English ports of London, Manchester, and Liverpool. Since the 18th century, the hitherto unimportant Aegean islands of Hydra, Spetses, Psara, and Kasos were also able to gain a foothold in Mediterranean trade on a smaller scale.

Some of the Phanariotes accumulated enormous cash wealth with trade and tax farming (the practice of assigning the responsibility for tax revenue collection to private citizens or groups) and were soon active as bankers, too. Since about the middle of the 17th century, the Phanariotes had been able to play a dominant role in trade in the Ottoman Empire, namely, to the same degree that the Jews and Armenians lost their positions in this area. This went hand in hand with their political rise, which peaked in the 18th century and then came to an abrupt end with the Greek War of Independence in 1821.

Within the context of Ottoman society, "Greek traders" must be seen primarily as a socioprofessional group, whereas an ethnic interpretation is potentially misleading and of limited evidentiary value. Into the 19th century, Greek fulfilled the function of a lingua franca in the domestic trade in southeastern Europe and was used as such by most groups that participated in this trade. In addition to Slavs and Aromuni, that affected also Albanians, who formed the population of the trading islands of Hydra and Spetses and thus provide a good example of the ex post facto revaluation of socioprofessional affiliation into national identity. External perception, too, largely lacked ethnic criteria until the establishment of nation-states, since in central Europe all traders of the Orthodox faith who came from the Ottoman Empire were called "Greeks." The chief characteristic of this group was its geographic and social mobility. In the Ottoman Empire it succeeded very quickly in translating economic success into political influence, eventually also forming a culturally specific stratum as a "moneyed nobility." Thus the courts of the Phanariotes in the Danubian hegemonies, as centers of literary production in the 18th century, among other things played an important role in the reception of the European Enlightenment and indirectly also of the ideas of the French Revolution in southeastern Europe, which was an important precondition for the emergence of national movements in this region.

It is therefore no coincidence that the 1821 Greek War of Independence also began in the Danube hegemonies and not in the region that would later form independent Greece. In these semiautonomous principalities, members of this group functioned as an "embryonic bourgeoisie," while the formation of nation-states in southeastern Europe simultaneously marked the beginning of the end of the Phanariotes as a phenomenon closely tied to the prenational context of Ottoman society.

In central and western Europe, by contrast, the social advancement of Greek traders was often accompanied by assimilation into the local civic elites, whereby the change of confessions from Orthodoxy to Catholicism or Protestantism was usually decisive. In addition to offering broader possibilities of lucrative marriages, assimilation also opened access to previously closed professions within the state apparatuses, for example, in administration, politics, or science, while at the same time promoting the dissolution of older relationship networks, for which the loss of language (in a context that had until then been fundamentally characterized by multilinguality) is the chief indicator. Apart from a few exceptions (e.g., the Leipzig fur traders from Kastoria, whose last descendants resettled to Frankfurt am Main after the founding of the GDR in 1949), they thus ceased to exist as a group at the end of the 19th century. Their visible traces can at times still be found in names for streets and squares, on buildings, and in family names.

Faroqhi, Suraiya, ed. *The Cambridge History of Turkey: The Later Ottoman Empire, 1603–1839*. Cambridge, 2006.

Held, Hans W. *Die Phanarioten, ihre allmähliche Entwicklung zur fürstlichen Aristokratie bis zu deren Untergang*. Elberfeld, 1920.

Inalcic, Halil, and Donald Quataert. *An Economic and Social History of the Ottoman Empire 1300–1914*. Cambridge, 1994.

Pippidi, Andrei. "Phanar, Phanariotes, Phanariotisme." In *Hommes et idées du Sud-Est européen à l'aube de l'âge moderne*, edited by Andrei Pippidi, 341–50. Paris, 1980.

Stoianovich, Traian. "The Conquering Balkan Orthodox Merchant." *Journal of Economic History* 20 (1960): 234–313.

Cross-references: France; Great Britain; Italy; The Netherlands; Southeastern Europe

HABSBURG OFFICIALS IN THE AUSTRIAN NETHERLANDS IN THE 18TH CENTURY

Renate Zedinger

The Peace Treaties of Utrecht, Rastatt, and Baden (1713–14) described as "Austrian Netherlands" the southern Dutch provinces that Habsburg Emperor Charles VI was to receive from the rich Spanish inheritance. It is roughly comparable to the area of modern-day Belgium and Luxembourg, excluding the Prince-Bishopric of Liège: specifically, the duchies of Brabant, Geldern, Limburg, and Luxembourg, the counties of Flanders, Hainaut, and Namur, as well as the lordships of

Mechlin, Tournay, and Tournay-Tournaisis. Each of these territories had its own privileges, institutions, and laws.

A separate administrative apparatus had to be set up in Vienna for these territories, previously governed from Madrid. In Brussels, the structures still in place from the Spanish days were carried on: here governors, *Obersthofmeister* (lord stewards), and plenipotentiary ministers represented the legitimate territorial prince. In a nod to the former status of these territories, they were initially administered, beginning in 1714, by the "Spanish Council" in Vienna; however, as early as 1717 a separate chancery that reflected the specific needs of this region, the "Highest Council of the Netherlands," was created.

With all the advantages and disadvantages of an institution in which regional interests collided with the interests of the larger state, the Highest Council of the Netherlands functioned until the middle of the 18th century. Wenzel Anton Graf von Kaunitz-Rietberg, from 1753 court and state chancellor under Empress Maria Theresa, wanted to adjust the Dutch business of state to the guidelines of his overall administrative concept and forced its incorporation into the state chancellery's sphere of competence. However, Kaunitz respected the special status of the Austrian Netherlands, unlike Emperor Joseph II, whose radical reforms triggered the first unrest in the southern Netherlands (1787), which in the end, intensified by the repercussions of the French Revolution, led to the split-off of the Austrian Netherlands (1794).

A significant contribution to keeping these diverse areas together came from the Habsburg officials, both in Vienna and in Brussels. While in the first years Belgian jurists were called to Vienna to participate in setting up the administration, the migration movement reversed in the second half of the 18th century. The Peace of Aachen (1748) had created stable conditions after the War of the Austrian Succession, and the Austrian Netherlands would now enjoy decades of prosperity. The land owed this not least to the wise policy of Prince Charles Alexander of Lorraine, who succeeded in keeping the Belgian provinces out of all European conflicts and to provide effective economic impulses. When the governor died in 1780, the population was estimated at 2 million, and at 75 inhabitants per square kilometer, the population density was considerable by European standards.

A not inconsiderable contribution to the land's economic upswing came from the many immigrants from the Austrian crown lands, Bohemia, Moravia, and Hungary – migrants who arrived to make a life for themselves in the Austrian Netherlands. Posts in the local administrative apparatus also seemed very attractive, especially in Brussels. This went hand in hand with a development that had already begun in this area decades before: it proved to be increasingly important to place the business of government and financial affairs into the hands of trained experts. Different from the central government in Vienna, this substantially reduced the proportion of the nobility in the mid-level hierarchy of officials in the Austrian Netherlands;

Prince Charles Alexander of Lorraine, Governor of the Austrian Netherlands, 1744–80. Painting by Martin van Meytens (*Kunsthistorisches Museum, Vienna*).

to a growing extent, only the high political and representative positions, high church posts, and military offices were reserved for them. However, the rulers now took advantage of the possibility of ennobling deserving officials, which proved a lucrative business for the state's finances and conveyed recognition, renown, and success. This ennoblement had social repercussions, though the difference between the old and new nobility was preserved. One example is August Gottlob Lederer, who was born in 1723 in the area of Lower Saxony: after studying in Louvain, he was hired by the administration in Brussels, transferred to Vienna, was ennobled in September 1763, and was eventually appointed to the highest post in the state chancellery (today's equivalent of the chief of the cabinet) at the side of Kaunitz. Lederer exemplifies a multitude of officials whose descendants also had careers in the administration and shaped the forms of bourgeois life in the 19th century.

The practical needs of the state were the ideal and yardstick for the education of the officials. The career in public service began after the study of the law at a university, often in Vienna or Louvain. Those who could afford it studied in Leiden or Paris and thus gained a certain career advantage by doing so. But indispensable for advancement in Habsburg services were extensive language skills – French, German, Latin – and for appointment to the administration in the Austrian Netherlands, also Flemish. The career path and the social ambience developed largely along the same lines in Brussels and Vienna: from university study to the proper marriage, the life path of Habsburg officials corresponded in both cities to the traditional patterns of behavior.

The sons of successful fathers at the imperial court in Vienna, such families as the Bartensteins, Lederers, or Van Swietens, had no problems getting along in the administration

in Brussels or in the social environment, which, much as in Vienna, was oriented toward the classic norms of the developed educated bourgeoisie. While the officials, regardless of their qualifications and the position they held, received no meaningful salary during their initial career phase, lucrative prospects were opened up to them. Those included a well-endowed marriage, which made it possible to keep up one's standard of living, solidified social integration, and provided additional insurance for social recognition. Only after years of service did the officials receive quarterly salaries, which could be supplemented by gifts for special services. However, these special payments depended on the state's financial situation and can therefore hardly be considered a predictable source of income. Still, one must not overlook that those employed in the administration could exercise several functions simultaneously; this quite common and deliberately accepted practice saved the state considerable sums of money while allowing officials to boost their meager income without suffering any damage to their status within Habsburg services.

Recognition by the ruler and with it recognition within the social hierarchy brought – alongside the already mentioned ennoblement – advancement into higher estates: the title *Staatsrat* (State Councilor) was considered the crowning conclusion to a career in Habsburg services. That was true even though appointment to the State Council of the Austrian Netherlands was merely an honor, since this body no longer possessed any political weight in the second half of the 18th century. State chancellor Kaunitz was well aware of this: in his presentation to Maria Theresa on 10 January 1768, he recommended that this practice be maintained by pointing out that it could be used to achieve the same effects as special payments, which would merely burden the state treasury unnecessarily. For many officials, a career in Brussels was more desirable than one in Vienna, as it offered far better career opportunities once you got your foot in the door: in the administrative apparatus of the Austrian Netherlands, the imperial acts of grace were bestowed according to performance and not according to birth.

In the second half of the 18th century, the Habsburg officials formed a largely homogeneous group within the Belgian regional administration. Their number is not recorded. One indication, a biased one, though, comes from the petitions for pensions and employment that officials sent to the Court Chamber after their flight in 1794: of the approximately 500 petitions that have been examined, about half of the officials themselves or their fathers had migrated from Vienna to Brussels. State Chancellor Kaunitz, who was in charge of the administration of the Austrian Netherlands after 1757 and who sought to centralize the various lands, preferred to staff the top posts with lawyers who did not hail from the Belgian provinces so as to prevent the formation of a specific patriotic outlook in the administration.

The Habsburg officials were socially recognized and professionally and financially secure. Regardless of their background and in spite of certain differences in the career paths, they played an important role – in both the Austrian Netherlands and the capital and residence city of Vienna – in the development of an early educated burgher class: the officials represented an impulse-giving and dynamic element on the road to the Belgian bourgeoisie of the 19th century.

Galand, Michèle. "Gages, honneurs, mérites: les hauts fonctionnaires dans les Pays-Bas autrichiens." In *Le travail: Reconnaissance et représentations*, edited by Michèle Galand, 557–80. Brussels, 2001.

Galand, Michèle. "Les Lorrains à la Cour de Bruxelles durant la seconde moitié du XVIIIè siècle: Entre exil et integration." In *Franz Stephan von Lothringen und sein Kreis. Tagungsband (Jahrbuch der Österreichischen Gesellschaft zur Erforschung des 18. Jahrhunderts, 23)*, edited by Renate Zedinger. Bochum, 2009.

Heindl, Waltraud. *Gehorsame Rebellen. Bürokratie und Beamte in Österreich 1780 bis 1848.* Vienna, 1991.

Zedinger, Renate. "Un fonds à découvrir pour l'histoire des Pays-Bas autrichiens: Les requêtes des fonctionnaires émigrés conservées au 'Finanz- und Hofkammerarchiv Wien.'" *Bulletin de la Commission royale d'Histoire de Belgique* 164 (1998): 173–256.

Zedinger, Renate. *Die Verwaltung der Österreichischen Niederlande in Wien.* Vienna, 2000.

Zedinger, Renate. *Migration und Karriere. Habsburgische Beamte in Brüssel und Wien im 18. Jahrhundert.* Vienna, 2004.

Cross-references: Austria; Belgium and Luxembourg; The Netherlands

HUGUENOTS IN EUROPE SINCE THE 16TH CENTURY

Matthias Asche

Modern scholarship no longer traces the name Huguenots to a contemporary corruption of the German word *Eidgenossen* but locates the etymological roots in the diminutive of the French name *Hug* or *Hugues* (*Huguenin, Hugnot, Huguenot*). It probably was a name of abuse used by outsiders and may refer to the legendary Le Roy Huguet, after whom a city gate in Tours is named and where the first local Protestants are supposed to have secretly gathered at night. The negative connotation of the term Huguenot is also indicated by its use as a popular designation for a French coin of low value.

The word Huguenots was common throughout France as early as 1560, and after 1561 it appeared in official designations – without distinction – for followers of Calvin and Luther. The name was given a greater specificity (or broadened) during the French religious wars in the second half of the 16th century. In the Peace of Alès (1629) which ended the 10th religious war, on the one hand, the term described followers of the French Reformed Church (*huguenots de religion*) and, on the other hand, supporters of the political party (*huguenots d'etat*) which fought for recognition as a religious community

Frederick William, the Great Elector of Brandenburg (1620–88) receives a delegation of Huguenots. Lithograph after a painting of Carl Röchling (*akg-images*).

and for political participation. Presumably because of this dual meaning and the negative connotation of the expression, the Huguenots called themselves almost exclusively *François réformés*. After 1629, when the Huguenots had been eliminated as a political force, the word referred in France only to this special denominational group.

Beginning in the 1660s, the Huguenots came under massive pressure in France. The high point was the revocation of the Edict of Nantes (1598) by Louis XIV's Edict of Fontainebleau (1685), which outlawed the practice of the Protestant religion and initiated the systematic destruction of French Reformed churches and parishes in France. The Edict only permitted conversion to Catholicism, not emigration. More than 150,000 Huguenots fled across the borders after 1685. In the countries that took them in they were referred to as *réfugies* or, more simply, as "Frenchmen."

The majority of the approximately 700,000 Huguenots who remained in France had to convert to Catholicism under pressure from the French authorities. The number of sham converts who continued to adhere to the underground Protestant Church in France (*Église du desert*) was presumably high. After the proclamation of the general freedom of religion and conscience in the French Revolution (1789) and the concession of complete freedom of worship in the first French Constitution (1791), French Protestants and the returning descendants of the *réfugiés* quickly reestablished parishes. Under Napoleon I for the first time the French Reformed Church was officially recognized in the Organic Articles of 1802.

In the narrower sense, the word Huguenot refers to all members of the French Reformed Church in France, along with all reformed, French-speaking religious refugees between approximately 1550 and 1789 who in their host countries professed membership in the French Reformed Church (officially established in 1559); their creedal foundation was Jean Calvin's *Confession de Foi* (*Confessio Gallicana*), which was partly modified during the period of exile. The constitution of the church came from the pen of Calvin, too (*Discipline ecclésiastique des églises réformées de France*). Originally the French Reformed Church was not organized along episcopal-hierarchical but synodal-presbyterial lines with elected bodies (*consistoire, ministres, diacres, anciens*). The Huguenots also include the *Orangeois*, Protestants from the southern French Principality of Orange, part of the Duchy of Nassau-Orange, who were expelled in 1703 after the principality had been ceded to France and most of whom settled in the cities of Brandenburg-Prussia.

The great flows of European Huguenots included – during different phases – various groups of Protestants who are counted among the Huguenots in the broader sense. Among them there were the Reformed Walloons and Flemings from the Spanish Netherlands, who were expelled by the Spaniards during – but also before – the Dutch Revolt, and who settled, for the most part permanently, in the Republic of the United Netherlands and in German territories and cities along the Rhine. Their descendants had intermixed with descendants of Reformed Swiss and Germans as well as Waldensians, who in their settlement areas in the Electoral Palatinate were impelled to emigrate by re-Catholicization measures during the late 17th century and the poor economic situation in the 18th century. The emigrants left Electoral Palatinate in several large waves; in their new host countries they were referred to as *Pfälzer* (Palatines), inhabitants of the Palatinate.

The wider circle of Huguenots also included the French and Savoyan Waldensians, who had left their homeland because of the growing oppression that began in the middle of the 1650s, and most of them – especially the French Waldensians – found a new home in the Protestant territories of the Empire. In addition, the streams of Huguenots were joined by numerous Reformed French-speaking (*Welsch*) Swiss from the Waadtland and the Geneva region, from the Principality of Neuchâtel, and from lordships of the Prince Bishopric of Basel in the Bern Jura, by Graubünden Rhaeto-Romanians from the Pays de Grisons, and by Mompelgarders from the Württemberg Duchy of Montbéliard.

Beyond that, the Huguenots frequently included French, Dutch, and Swiss Catholics, too, who passed themselves off as religious refugees to take advantage of the economic and social privileges in the host countries. However, some of them remained Catholics in their new countries and offered their services in the establishment of manufacturing enterprises or at court.

Migration, settlement, and settlement policy

It is impossible to give precise figures for the number of Huguenots who left France in several waves, beginning as early as the middle of the 16th century. The emigration of individuals and groups, which was part of the larger context of religious persecution in the Confessional Age, took the Huguenots – until the Edict of Revocation (1685) – above all to the Netherlands, Switzerland, England, and the Protestant territories of the Holy Roman Empire (especially Electoral Palatinate) bordering France; some settled permanently and some stayed only temporarily. Realistic estimates for the great exodus of Huguenots can merely be found for the period after 1685. Around 1670 there were about 900,000 Huguenots in France. By 1700, of that number, some 150,000 had fled to other European countries, and in a second step many went on to overseas colonies for economic reasons. Additional, though substantially smaller, waves of refugees left France until well into the 18th century.

Because of double counting during onward migration and uncertainties in determining who should be considered a Huguenot, the following numbers also are presumably too high: the majority of the Huguenots were admitted into England (50,000, including Ireland and the English colonies in North America), the Netherlands (35,000–50,000, including the Cape colony), and Germany (27,100–34,350, especially Brandenburg-Prussia, the Rhine-Main area, Franconia, and the large trading cities). Smaller contingents went to Switzerland (10,000), Denmark (2,000), and Russia (600).

Since most Huguenots were forced to flee their homeland in haste and without organization, many host places, especially in Switzerland, were merely way stations, which usually had older refugee communities but rarely a church infrastructure. The onward migration of refugees went to countries with which their admission had been negotiated, often by delegates of the refugees. Upon their arrival, the local authorities assigned them a final place of residence.

Some of the refugees were received into towns as a minority (e.g., in 1554 in Frankfurt am Main; in 1689 in Dresden), in villages occasionally even as a new majority (e.g., in the Uckermark in Brandenburg), with more or less extensive privileges. Others were prompted to establish new towns, town districts, or villages, where they were allowed the free exercise of their religion (e.g., in 1699 in Karlshafen an der Weser, in 1597 in Neu-Hanau, after 1662 in the new cities founded by the prince elector in Berlin, in 1686 in Erlangen-Neustadt, Huguenot- and *Pfälzer*-villages in the Uckermark, Waldensian villages in Hesse and Württemberg). Because of legal impediments, problems with church organization, or economic difficulties, many new settlers – as individuals, in groups, or as an entire colony – moved on to other towns and territories (e.g., the partial exodus of the Walloon emigrants from Heidelberg to Frankenthal in 1577, or the total exodus of the Walloons from Mannheim to Magdeburg in 1689).

Every single refugee group had a different sense of self-identity. For example, the Huguenots from France and the Waldensians lived for a long time with the hope of returning to their homeland. However, only the Savoyan Waldensians (1690) were able to do so, while the others were forced – because of the prohibition against returning that was reissued by Louis XIV in the Peace of Rijswijk (1697) – to settle permanently in their new homes. That is why some of them moved from German territories adjoining France into the interior of the Holy Roman Empire. In fact, the situation was different with the *Pfälzer*, most of whom had left their homeland voluntarily.

When a comparative survey is made of the conditions of admission and settlement, of the legal background conditions, and of the ways in which Huguenots assimilated in the various European countries, there must also be a comparison of the different privileges granted to them (*Freiheiten, Kapitulation, Begnadigung, Edikt, Patent, Concessions, Franchises, Déclaration en faveur*). These privileges contained specific rights, special provisions, and concessions for all *réfugiés* (general privileges), for special groups of Huguenots, or for individuals (special privileges for those operating manufacturing businesses, for artisans or farmers), some of which deviated strongly from the customary law of the land. The numerous privileges given the Huguenots were often the result of tenacious negotiations in the circles of the territorial ruler. Sometimes these negotiations involved direct participation and lobbying by princely councils, the local clergy, the territorial estates, deputies of the refugees, or the Protestant "protective powers" (Switzerland, the Netherlands, England).

While a range of very different motives played a role in the granting of Huguenot privileges, one can usually identify three main reasons behind the admission of religious refugees: first, helping brethren of a related faith who were in dire straits; second, boosting the number of one's subjects; and third, developing new or restoring war-ravaged land (colonization), with recruitment aimed preferentially at the operators of specialized manufacturing or artisans (mercantilist promotion of the economy to establish new commercial sectors and production techniques). There could be a definite shift in focus when privileges were renewed or modified, and when specific implementing regulations were passed. Huguenot privileges were legal instruments in the hands of the territorial rulers that made it possible for them to quickly and flexibly intervene in social and economic life. As means of imposing the absolutism of the territorial ruler, the Huguenot privileges stood against the existing church constitution, the "old estate-society," and the guild-organization of trades in the host countries.

The privileges contained concessions and special rights in the areas of church organization, civil and criminal law, and the economy: for example, the granting of a community status on a corporatist basis (colonies) and separate parishes with self-elected pastors, participation in or the complete exemption from the usual legal system, exemption from taxes and dues for a specific period (exempt years), as well as personal freedom for the new subjects. Special privileges could grant full civic rights and start-up loans for tradesmen and exempt workers dependent on them from military service and the billeting of soldiers. However, only a small minority of the refugee Huguenots were part of the highly specialized commercial or artisanal upper class; most came to the host countries as simple merchants, tradesmen, or farmers.

The legal and administrative organization of the emigration of minority groups that were confessionally, and for the most part also linguistically and culturally, foreign was accomplished in the European host countries in various ways. The behavior of the authorities toward the Huguenots depended on the respective level of economic and social development, the internal and external political conditions, and the political, administrative, and ecclesiastical constitution of the host country. Especially the degree of ecclesiastical freedom granted to the *réfugiés* depended on the relationship between state and church in the host countries.

In England, where numerous west European refugee communities of the most diverse Protestant creeds had already existed since the reign of Queen Elizabeth I, King Charles II, in the face of the worsening persecution of Protestants in France (*dragonades*), issued as early as 1681 privileged and free permanent residency permits to religious refugees willing to settle: the "Letters of Denization" allowed them the free exercise of their religion and the right to freely engage in their professions and trades, and also gave them free access to all educational institutions. Additionally, the Huguenots were given equal status with the natives in regard to taxes and dues. Following the ouster of the Catholic king Jacob II, William III and Mary II continued the policy of rapid integration of the Huguenots in England by issuing the "Declaration for the encouraging of French protestants to transport themselves into this kingdom." In 1689, however, as in 1681, the refugees were not granted status as a separate church.

Like England and Switzerland, the Netherlands largely experienced an influx of refugees of higher social status. At the end of the 17th century, the Netherlands could already look back on a long tradition of Protestant refugee communities. Because of the intense competition among Dutch mercantile communities to recruit tradesmen and specialized artisans, the privileges had included special economic concessions since the 1680s: for example, the acquisition of citizenship at no cost, exemption from dues, free entry into the guild, favorable loans to craftsmen without financial means, or legal equality with the local residents; however, in good mercantilist fashion, these concessions were also offered to other foreigners willing to settle. In essence, the settlement policy of the Dutch communities moved between two models: either the granting of full citizenship with free entry into the guilds, or – with a corresponding special legal status – the exemption of Huguenots from compulsory guild membership and a temporary exemption from taxes and dues.

In comparison to other European countries, the German territories went the furthest in granting special rights to the Huguenots – in both church organization and economy. Numerous privileges were granted by German princes – usually at the expense of the native subjects: extensive tax exemptions, free building sites and building material, and an exemption from the billeting of soldiers. At times, for example in the two Reformed territories of Electoral Brandenburg and Hesse-Kassel, the package included the settlers' own community administration with a more or less pronounced separate jurisdiction. In the County of Solms-Greifenstein, an entire village (Daubhausen) was forced to evacuate to make room for the immigrants. The reasons for the granting of such extensive special rights are found in the considerable devastation and depopulation of entire areas by the continuous wars in the 17th century, as a result of which territorial rulers were in dire need of new settlers. Moreover, representatives of the refugees had a much more active role in the drafting of many German privileges than was the case elsewhere in Europe. The far-reaching demands of the refugees, who not only came as petitioners but also offered a boost to the population and economic innovation, could thus be forced through much more effectively, in part by playing against each other the various princes willing to take them in.

During the great Huguenot exodus at the end of the 17th century, a division of tasks emerged among the European Protestant powers: because of its geographic location, Switzerland often became the first country of refuge, but because of its limited capacity, it was forced to divert the streams of refugees – at great logistical effort and financial expense – to Germany, where the German territorial lords admitted the Huguenots as new settlers for confessional, population-policy, and economic reasons. Like Switzerland and England, the economically advanced Netherlands, with its high population density, provided financial support for the transport of refugees and for the construction of settlements and churches by the immigrants in Germany. As powers that provided protection and security to the refugees, these states exploited the exodus propagandistically against French hegemonic policies under Louis XIV. The close collaboration of the Protestant states on refugee policy at the end of the 17th century is apparent at several levels: the dynastically interrelated Protestant ruling houses organized a network of legal and administrative communication by taking over the privileges and settlement conditions of other refugee countries, and by negotiating, through diplomatic channels, the settlement of the refugees depending on the capacities of the host territories.

Pathways and forms of integration

The special role of the Huguenots within their host societies, which has often persisted for a long time, resulted primarily from their French Reformed creed and their language. The privileged status was above all manifested in their own administration with separate jurisdiction, their own churches and schools (e.g., the founding of the French *Gymnasium* in Berlin in 1689), and in certain tax concessions.

Additional to the legal provisions for the settlement of the Huguenots, which reflected the personal, religious, or economic interests of the territorial rulers in the new subjects, acceptance by the host society determined the course of the integration process. None of the early modern states pursued an active policy of integration. On the contrary, by retaining the policy of privileges, they further reinforced the special status of the Huguenots. The new subjects and their

descendants also rejected integration into the host societies until the early 19th century and clung to their socially exclusive special status. On the whole, it should be emphasized that the great Huguenot exodus occurred at a time of French cultural hegemony in Europe. That is why contemporaries gratefully received the influence of the refugees – of course, only of a small upper class – in art, science, education, military, and the economy: French private tutors, language teachers, officers, and manufacturers disseminated French culture in many princely capitals, trading cities, and military strongholds.

One important precondition for the integration of the Huguenots was the acquisition of full civic rights. By avoiding special legal, economic, and ecclesiastical privileges already during the process of immigration, England from the outset placed the Huguenots on an equal footing to the natives – with the result that as early as the beginning of the 18th century nothing stood in the way of their rapid naturalization as full citizens (native subjects). In the English colonies in North America, corresponding regulations were in some cases enacted even earlier (e.g., 1666 in Massachusetts and Maryland, 1671 in Virginia, 1703 in New York). In the Netherlands and Switzerland, the first restrictions to curtail the special status of the Huguenots were enacted in the 1690s. At the beginning of the 18th century they initiated a trend toward the complete naturalization of the refugees. In 1715 the Huguenots were fully naturalized in the Netherlands, though initially without access to political offices ("small naturalization"). That restriction was abolished in the 1730s ("large naturalization").

The Huguenots placed great stock in getting their own French Reformed church organization – and ideally in getting a completely autonomous ecclesiastical system. In the Netherlands, in England, and in the colonies they therefore sought to link up with the churches that had a synodal-presbyterial constitution or with the Dutch Reformed churches, where at least in the beginning separate French-speaking pastors were appointed for the newcomers. However, French as the language of sermons and schooling had noticeably declined in the Dutch Reformed churches from the middle of the 18th century (e.g., prohibition against the French language in the Dutch Cape colony in 1739). In England and the Netherlands, half of the French Reformed churches had been closed by the end of the 18th century. The remaining parishes were able to continue only because of financial support from the congregants.

Because of their comparatively pronounced and persistent special status in terms of the economy, the law, and church organization, the Huguenot colonies in the German territories developed in a fundamentally different way from that in the west European countries. Of course, it is important to bear in mind that the specific conditions varied from one territory to the next, which means that the integration of the Huguenots also took different courses. The essentially benevolent policy of privileges pursued by the territorial rulers at times encountered vigorous opposition from the native population. The generous privileges and the policy of preferential treatment for the refugees – for example, by prohibiting German settlers from moving into French neighborhoods and colonies or outlawing marriages between Huguenots and Germans – as well as the patronage and clientelism at court generally did not lead to a rapid integration of the new subjects.

Impediments to integration were the prosperity of the Huguenots that emerged rapidly in many places and the standing they enjoyed at court, which created feelings of jealousy. The extensive economic privileges led especially to lasting competition with the guilds, who showed no willingness to admit the refugees. In some cases the highly specialized artisans among the Huguenots responded by creating their own guild-like organizations (e.g., button makers in Berlin, glove makers in Halle). The everyday conflicts between natives and foreigners were numerous and concerned, for example, the joint use of fields, churches, and cemeteries as well as jurisdictional quarrels between native courts and the courts of the French settlements.

Fundamental to Huguenot self-identity was, alongside the French Reformed creed, the French language, which was generally still retained in the liturgy, in church music, and in the schools after it had ceased to be the vernacular of the congregants. With the Protestant church unions in some German states at the beginning of the 19th century, French, after a phase when French and German coexisted as the language of the sermon, gradually disappeared completely from the liturgy. In the Kingdom of Denmark, where conditions were comparable to those in Germany in many respects and where there were two Huguenot colonies – in Copenhagen and Fredericia – French as the language of the sermon was given up in favor of German in 1814. In a deviation from the strict Lutheran orientation of the Danish state church, a separate Huguenot-French consciousness persisted in Denmark until the end of the 19th century.

In addition to the conflicts between the old-established and the newly settled population, there were many instances of intense quarrels and mutual intolerance among the various immigrant groups, especially over the use of church buildings and the extent of the special rights that had been granted. The sometimes strict division into separate Walloon Reformed, Dutch Reformed, and French Reformed parishes and the specific self-identity and endogamous behavior of the various immigrant groups show how important it is to clearly distinguish among the various Protestant refugee communities. There were language barriers not only with Flemish-speaking, Walloon-speaking, and French-speaking refugees but also – and especially – with the Waldensians who spoke alpine Provençal (Occitan dialect), and among whom a separate religious consciousness, endogamy, and cultural practices usually persisted longer than among other immigrant groups.

Although the use of the French language was not generally prohibited by the authorities, a process that led to the increasing adoption of the German vernacular and to the end of the ability to write and speak French had begun early on. For example, the Prussian school code of 1763 explicitly permitted – on a voluntary basis – German-language instruction for children from Huguenot families because of their poor knowledge of French. By contrast, however, some Huguenot women, especially in the countryside, did not understand or speak German until well into the 19th century.

The purely Huguenot marriage circles maintained in the countryside at least at the start began to loosen in the 18th century; at first German Reformed, later Lutheran, spouses, too, were chosen. At the urging of their German spouses and because of a poor knowledge of French, a growing number of Huguenots turned to the German Reformed Church, and some also converted to the Lutheran denomination. The traditional baptismal names of the Huguenots, drawn by preference from the Old Testament, have become increasingly less common since the middle of the 18th century. A process of assimilation also occurred with family names, whereby various developments – corruption, German pronunciation, external or internal Germanization – can be observed.

Among the territories of the Holy German Empire, the development of the identity of the Huguenots and their descendants has been best studied to date in Brandenburg-Prussia, especially since this was a very successful story of integration. However, one must bear in mind that the intellectual engagement with questions of Huguenot identity was largely carried on within circles of the educated upper class. After their admission, the Huguenots, who came from two politically, culturally, and socioeconomically very different regions of France (*pays de droit* in the south, *pays de coutoume* in the north), grew into a single group only slowly and with difficulty. Alongside the consciousness of belonging to a European-wide, mutually supportive, religious community of fate, a specific form of Borussophilia and patriotism arose within the Huguenot economic and intellectual elite as early as the 18th century. The respect for the crown and the state of Brandenburg-Prussia was rooted in older traditions from their French homeland, where the Huguenots had always seen themselves as loyal subjects. For a long time, the independent political-social administrative structures of the French colony and the autonomy of the French Reformed Church were not touched. The sustained preservation of special Huguenot privileges gave rise to an endogenous, exclusive group identity among the Huguenot descendants, which was grounded in the shared religious creed, a shared French language of ritual and vernacular, and the memory of a shared fate as refugees.

In 1772 the introduction of the right of elective citizenship (*Wahlbürgerrecht*) in Brandenburg-Prussia as part of King Frederick II's large-scale policy of boosting the population (*Peuplierung*) for the first time rattled the group consciousness of the descendants of the *réfugiés*. The option for all newly recruited colonists of placing themselves either under the general Prussian jurisdiction or that of the French colony broke up the unity of the French colony (as a community of privileges and law) and the French Reformed denomination (as a religious community). Since the legal community of the French colony thus turned into a colony of foreigners and new citizens of any background, the tradition-minded descendants of the Huguenots withdrew into their parishes, which alone could still offer them a separate group identity. At the same time, the occasion of the 100th anniversary of the Potsdam Edict in 1785 saw a rise in public manifestations of loyalty to the crown and the state of Brandenburg-Prussia, the goal of which was to set oneself apart from the non-French fellow citizens within the French colony.

The rehabilitation laws of the French Revolution (1787 Edict of Toleration by King Louis XVI, 1789 Declaration of the Rights of Man and of the Citizen, 1790–1 Restitution laws about the return of Huguenot property seized after 1685 and the offer of French citizenship) triggered discussions about a return within the host countries of the refugees. The new legal state of affairs in France, which no longer had any restrictions on the exercise of religion, and the enticement of restitution meant that those descendants of the Huguenots who did not return to the land of their ancestors could no longer legitimately think of themselves as Frenchmen in their host countries. This was seen as a problem, since the much-invoked refugee identity always implied at least the potential return from exile.

The pressure was so intense that it put a final ending to a separate Huguenot identity. For those who did not migrate back to France – the vast majority of the Huguenot descendants – the decision to stay was the last step toward a complete assimilation within the host society. Added to this, the privileges of the French colony in Prussia were abolished in 1809 and the French sections within the Prussian ministries (upper level state and ecclesiastical offices, colony courts) were closed. As it was, the French language had been in a pronounced retreat in the religious and everyday realms since the end of the 18th century. And the church unions at the beginning of the 19th century also in many places put an end to the separate French Reformed church organization. As a result, the Huguenots who had remained in their host countries largely kept their distance from refugees of the French Revolution and from the Napoleonic occupation troops.

While the term Huguenots was hardly used any more in France as early as the Napoleonic period, it experienced a veritable renaissance in the former host countries in the 19th century, whereby the Huguenot descendants always placed great stock in being seen as loyal patriots and a social elite. The lavish commemoration in 1885 of the 200th anniversary of the Huguenot exodus led in many German states to a sustained rediscovery of the historical legacy by families of pastors, officials, and officers with Huguenot roots, as well as among holders of hereditary farms and those in hereditary occupations, even if it did not involve the requisite church ties and any special cultivation of the French language. Historical and genealogical research – reflected also in the establishment of organizations (e.g., in 1883 the Huguenot Society of

America in New York, in 1885 the Huguenot Society of Great Britain and Ireland in London, and in 1890 the Deutscher Hugenotten-Verein in Friedrichsdorf in the Taunus), separate journals and publication series, and since the end of the 20th century touristic exploration trips by Huguenot descendants to the homeland of the *réfugiés* – ensure also at the beginning of the 21st century an undiminished interest in the origins, legacy, and fate of the Huguenots.

Bischoff, Johannes E. *Lexikon deutscher Hugenotten-Orte*. Bad Karlshafen, 1994.

Cottret, Bernard. *Terre d'exil. L'Angleterre et ses réfugiés français et wallons, de la Reforme à la Révocation de l'Edit de Nantes, 1550–1700*. Paris, 1985.

Dölemeyer, Barbara. *Die Hugenotten*. Stuttgart, 2006.

Duchhardt, Heinz, ed. *Der Exodus der Hugenotten. Die Aufhebung des Edikts von Nantes 1685 als europäisches Ereignis*. Cologne and Vienna, 1985.

Gresch, Eberhard. *Die Hugenotten. Geschichte, Glauben und Wirkung*. 2nd ed. Leipzig, 2005.

Hartweg, Frédéric, and Stefi Jersch-Wenzel, eds. *Die Hugenotten und das Refuge. Deutschland und Europa*. Berlin, 1990.

Höpel, Thomas, and Katharina Middell, eds. *Réfugiés und Emigrés. Migration zwischen Frankreich und Deutschland im 18. Jahrhundert*. Leipzig, 1997.

Magdelaine, Michelle, and Rudolf von Thadden, eds. *Le réfuge huguenot*. Paris, 1985.

Reaman, George Elmore. *The Trail of the Huguenots in Europe, the United States, South Africa and Canada*. London, 1963.

Yardeni, Myriam. *Le réfuge protestant*. Paris, 1985.

Cross-references: France; Germany; Great Britain; The Netherlands; Northern Europe; Switzerland; Dutch Calvinist Refugees in Europe since the Early Modern Period; French Maritime Merchants in Hamburg since 1680; French Revolutionary Refugees in Europe after 1789: The Example of Germany; Palatines in Europe since the 17th Century; Swiss Protestant Peasants in Alsace, Southwestern Germany, and Brandenburg-Prussia since the Mid-17th Century; Waldensians in Central Europe since the Early Modern Period

HUNGARIAN COPPERSMITHS IN WESTERN EUROPE FROM THE 1860S TO WORLD WAR I

Leo Lucassen

From the end of the 1850s onward small groups of coppersmiths from Hungary, but also from Bohemia, migrated to European countries, like France, Belgium, the Netherlands, Great Britain, Spain, Italy, Poland, Russia, Scandinavia, and German states. In the literature on "Gypsies" these coppersmiths are often subsumed under the heading *Kalderaš* (or *căldăraşi*, literally "boiler-makers"), a term that is still used for certain Gypsies in present-day Hungary and Romania with a background in metalwork.

Although according to their passports most of these migrants were born in Hungary, there is ample evidence that suggests their forefathers originated from Romanian lands, especially the principalities of Wallachia and Moldavia, where until the mid-19th century Gypsies were enslaved. Various contemporaries have mentioned and described the *Kalderaš* in the first half of the 19th century. Moreover, the language of the Hungarian-born coppersmiths contained many Romanian words, and it has been recorded that from the end of the 18th century onward Gypsies from these principalities fled to Transylvania and Hungary. It is therefore not very plausible, as many have argued, that there is a direct link between the history of coppersmiths and the emancipation of the Gypsy slaves in Moldavia and Wallachia in 1856. The overwhelming majority of those coppersmiths who were registered in western Europe in the 1860s and 1870s were born in Hungary and had probably settled there at least one generation earlier.

These coppersmiths traveled in relatively large family groups (normally 20–60 people, sometimes as many as 150), consisting of men, women, and children. In itself this was not unusual because most emigrants from eastern Europe migrated with their families. The *Kalderaš* combined this with an itinerant way of living. Instead of staying in hotels or boardinghouses during their travel, they set up small camps with large tents, which they transported on open four-wheel carts, drawn by horses. In addition, they made a living in ambulant occupations – in their case the mending of copper and iron pots, pans, and utensils. Due to this combination of characteristics, together with their Hungarian (or at least eastern European) origin, locals soon associated the *Kalderaš* with the category "Gypsy." The stereotypes attached to this label were largely negative. Gypsies were assumed to cheat, steal, and use their occupations as a cover for begging. Although these coppersmiths (whose total number in the period 1860–80 probably did not exceed a few thousand) behaved in an orderly way and earned enough money to make a living, police and border authorities in western Europe were very suspicious. The extremely negative official reaction to coppersmiths effectively constituted them into a unified group: they were considered the ultimate unwanted aliens, and much energy was devoted to deporting them or even preventing them from entering the country. Most of these coppersmiths did not aim to stay in western Europe and only few settled there. Just like millions of other eastern Europeans, they wanted to emigrate across the Atlantic and only used their stay in western Europe to make money for the journey and for a new start in the Americas.

In order to overcome the suspicion they met, many combined coppersmithing craftsmanship with a folkloristic show. On occasion they opened their encampment to the public for money; some even advertised their activities ahead of their arrival in local newspapers. For the Netherlands and France we know that thousands of people took the opportunity to visit these camps, where the coppersmiths gave

Hungarian coppersmiths at work. On the right a fortune-teller. Lithograph, around 1850 (*ullstein bild*).

demonstrations of their craftsmanship but also performed music and dance in Hungarian costumes. The most successful groups were quite rich and put golden and silver objects, like staffs and drinking goblets, on display.

Apart from these public gatherings, the men (women were not involved in the trade) were busy obtaining commissions to repair copper objects of all sorts. Notwithstanding the initial suspicion of the public and the competition of sedentary coppersmiths, many seem to have been rather successful in earning money in this way, while traveling from place to place. Their business success was probably due to a combination of low prices and good craftsmanship.

Groups of coppersmiths functioned as one company, with an appointed leader who planned the itinerary and negotiated with the authorities about their stay. They not only worked for individuals, but – especially after 1900 – also for factories and small businesses, especially bakers, dairy factories, and laundries, who asked them to do repair work. Women and children remained in the encampment but occasionally begged in the streets and (the women) told fortunes. Begging was often not a sign of poverty but was considered a normal way of adding to the family income.

Most coppersmith groups traveled through western Europe in the 1870s and 1890s and then emigrated to South and North America. The migration from eastern to western Europe did not stop entirely, however. In the period up to the First World War, especially between 1905 and 1913, small groups made their appearance in western Europe. In 1911, one of these groups arrived in England, where they drew the attention of local authorities, journalists, and scholars. The regions of origin of this second wave seem to have become more diverse – including Russia, Greece, Romania, and Silesia – reflecting their migrations after their departure from Romania and Hungary in the first half of the 19th century. Although by then many (but not all) had changed from tents to caravans (a type of mobile home), their conduct had not changed. Customers praised them for their skill, and authorities labeled them as Gypsies, trying hard to evict them from their territories. A small minority did stay in countries like Germany, the Netherlands, Great Britain, and France, but little is known about their integration process in the long run. For those who stayed in caravan camps, together with other groups who were labeled Gypsies, their descendants are still confronted with social marginalization. Those who went their own way have vanished into mainstream society in the lands where they immigrated.

Achim, Viorel. *The Roma in Romanian History*. Budapest, 2004.

Fraser, Angus. *The Gypsies*. Oxford, 1992.

Lucassen, Leo. *En men noemde hen zigeuners. De geschiedenis van Kaldarasch, Ursari, Lowara en Sinti in Nederland (1750–1944)*. Amsterdam and The Hague, 1990.

Lucassen, Leo. "The Clink of their Hammer was Heard from Daybreak till Dawn: Gypsy Occupations in Western Europe." In *Gypsies and Other Itinerant Groups: A Socio-Historical Approach*, edited by Leo Lucassen, Wim Willems, and Annemarie Cottaar, 153–73. London and New York, 1998.

Cross-references: France; Maghrebis in France after Decolonization in the 1950s and 1960s

HUNGARIAN REFUGEES IN EUROPE SINCE 1956

Jan Willem ten Doesschate

After the death of Stalin in 1953, the communist regime in Hungary, lead by Imre Nagy, tried to follow a more liberal course. The new Russian leader Nikita Khrushchev was afraid that this would have far-reaching consequences for the security of Russian dominance in eastern Europe. When rioting broke out in the streets of Budapest in 1956, and with the declaration of Hungarian neutrality and withdrawal from the Warsaw Pact, the communist regime was seriously threatened. Khrushchev thereupon sent Russian troops to occupy the country, crushed the revolution, and replaced Nagy, who was soon thereafter executed by President János Kadár.

As a result, some 225,000 Hungarian refugees left the country and crossed the border into Austria and, to a lesser extent, into Yugoslavia. From there they went to some 35 countries, mostly to the USA and Canada, but a significant number chose destinations in northern, central, and western Europe (see Table 1).

There are surprisingly few studies on the migration and integration processes of Hungarian refugees in western Europe. The occasional research is concentrated on the arrival and reception of the refugees. Most of them were young and male and originated from Budapest and the western part of Hungary. In contrast to the media images, many of them had not taken part in the uprising against the Russian occupation; they used the opportunity to leave the country in the hope of a better future in the West. The cold

Table 1. Countries of destination of Hungarian refugees after 1956	
Destination	**Numbers of refugees**
United Kingdom	22,000
Austria	18,000
Germany	16,000
France	13,000
Sweden	7,000
Switzerland	7,000
Belgium	6,000
Netherlands	3,300
Norway	1,500
Europe	*93,800*
United States of America	80,000
Canada	37,000
Australia	14,000
New Zealand	1,000
Outside Europe	*132,000*
Total	**225,800**

Source: See references.

Hungarian refugees reach Austria at the end of October/early November 1956 (*ullstein bild*).

war image of Hungarian refugees as "freedom fighters" therefore applies to only a small minority. Many wanted to escape the difficult economic situation in their country and applied for visas at the American consulates in Vienna and Salzburg. Others kept the option open for return, for when the situation in Hungary had normalized, and chose to stay in nearby Austria, Germany, or Switzerland. The overwhelming majority was housed in refugee camps in Austria, helped by the International Red Cross and private relief organizations.

The policy to grant refugee status to everyone who left the Eastern Bloc during the cold war did not imply that all European countries opened their borders to Hungarian refugees in 1956. There was official and popular sympathy for these "freedom fighters," but many policy makers had their reservations about admitting large groups of refugees because of housing shortages, insecure economic prospects, and concerns about overpopulation.

The Dutch government, for instance, allowed only a limited number of refugees and tried to select those who could fill vacancies in the labor market, for example, in the coal mines. Other countries sent teams to Austria to select the most useful refugees for their labor markets. The immigration of Hungarian laborers sometimes led to friction in destination countries. In the UK, British miners were afraid that the Hungarians would work too hard and thus weaken the bargaining power of their labor unions. As in the Netherlands, however, the British unions supported the decision to welcome Hungarian refugees who could help fill the vacancies in the labor market. Apart from industrial workers in the mining and metal sectors, quite a few refugees with good language skills found jobs in skilled professions in Britain, especially in hospitals as doctors and psychologists. Finally, several countries selected a large number of students for entry into European universities, supported by a special fellowship program of the Rockefeller Foundation.

In general the prospects for a rather smooth and fast integration were good, both in the Netherlands and in other countries. Most Hungarians were skilled, and the receiving societies regarded them as "useful" immigrants. Besides, from an economic perspective the timing of the immigration was very fortunate, as they arrived at the beginning of a long period of unprecedented high economic growth of the world economy. The limited research suggests that most Hungarians did indeed have little trouble finding jobs that fit their qualifications. This was facilitated by intense language courses, which the Netherlands and many other countries offered immediately after the immigrants' arrival.

The integration process in the USA has been studied in greater detail; until further research is available, we may assume that it resembles to a large extent the experience in western European countries. The general conclusion of American studies is that the insertion of the Hungarian refugees into society was rather successful. At the end of 1957 most had found stable jobs, which can be attributed to both the characteristics of the migrants and the structure of the receiving society. The migrants were young, predominantly male, well educated, and highly motivated to stay and build their new lives in the USA. More than half the refugees of working age had college degrees or were skilled or semiskilled laborers; many others were university students. The exodus cost Hungary tens of thousands of its most highly educated and best-skilled citizens. Moreover, it is clear that rather than being politically motivated, most just wanted a better future. This explains why there was not a strong exile mentality or strong transnational ties. With regard to the structure of the receiving society, it is important that – as in western Europe – public opinion was very favorable, which made identification with the country of settlement relatively easy.

In conclusion, it seems that integration of the Hungarian refugees in western Europe and in overseas countries shared a number of similar features, although future research will undoubtedly uncover national differences as well. In general, the integration process went smoothly because the migrants were relatively highly skilled, wanted to stay permanently, and were met by a relatively open and welcoming society and a favorable economic situation.

Doesschate, Jan-Willem ten. "Het Nederlandse toelatingsbeleid ten aanzien van Hongaarse vluchtelingen." MA thesis. Nijmegen, 1985.

John, Michael, and Albert Lichtblau. *Schmelztiegel Wien, einst und jetzt: Zur Geschichte und Gegenwart von Zuwanderung und Minderheiten.* Vienna, 1993.

Joly, Danièle, and Robin Cohen, eds. *Reluctant Hosts: Europe and Its Refugees.* Aldershot, 1989.

Kuyer, H. J. M. *Twee jaar na de vlucht. Een onderzoek naar aanpassing en persoonlijkheid van Hongaarse vluchtelingen.* Nijmegen, 1963.

Marrus, Michael R. *The Unwanted: European Refugees in the Twentieth Century.* New York and Oxford, 1985.

Puskás, Julianna. *Ties That Bind, Ties That Divide: One Hundred Years of Hungarian Experience in the United States.* New York, 2000.

Zierer, Brigitta. "Willkommene Ungarnflüchtlinge 1956." In *Asylland wider Willen. Flüchtlinge in Österreich im europäischen Kontext seit 1914,* edited by Gernot Heiss and Oliver Rathkolb, 157–71. Vienna, 1995.

Cross-references: Austria; Belgium and Luxembourg; France; Germany; Great Britain; The Netherlands; Northern Europe; Southeastern Europe; Switzerland

INDIAN, PAKISTANI, AND BANGLADESHI MIGRANTS IN GREAT BRITAIN SINCE 1947

Roger Ballard

Britain's south Asian population currently includes about 2.2 million people, of whom more than half were born in the UK. Virtually all the remainder were born in the British Commonwealth and are consequently de facto UK citizens. Their presence in Britain is relatively recent: prior to the outbreak of the Second World War it included no more than a few thousand souls. While this rapid increase in population was largely precipitated by a large inflow of labor migrants from the former Crown Colony of India during the three decades of industrial boom that followed the end of hostilities, its members' roots can in large part be traced back to the identity of the early prewar pioneers. Since the mid-1960s onward, vigorous efforts have been made to control the arrival of further adult males, but the inflow nevertheless continued as wives and children came to join men who had already established themselves in Britain.

The exponential growth of the south Asian presence was not so much the result of further immigration but the

Table 1. South Asian presence in the United Kingdom, 1961–2001					
Ethnic group/National origin	1961	1971	1981	1991	2001
Indian	81,400	240,700	673,700	823,800	1,028,500
Pakistani	24,900	127,600	295,500	449,600	706,800
Bangladeshi			64,600	157,900	275,200
East African *	–	44,900	181,300	–	–
Other Asian	–	–	–	–	214,400
Total South Asian population	106,300	413,200	1,215,100	1,431,300	2,224,900
% of South Asians in UK population	0.2	0.9	2.5	3.0	4.4

* An ethnic question was introduced in 1991, but it did not include the category "East African Asian," which primarily applies to commercial and migrant workers who emigrated from the Indian subcontinent during the period of European expansion in east Africa.

Source: UK decennial censuses.

result of the inevitable expansion of a group that was heavily skewed toward the youthful end of the age spectrum, further reinforced by its members' – and most especially its Muslim members' – relatively high fertility rates. Hence there are good reasons to expect that numbers will double their current level within the next two decades.

Diversity

Over 90% of migrants trace their ancestry to just three tightly restricted areas of the Indian subcontinent. Around 60% originate from a small number of submontane districts in northern Punjab, which now fall on both sides of the border between India and Pakistan. This demarcation was a result of the division of the subcontinent in 1947 into Hindu (India), Muslim (Pakistan), and Buddhist (Sikkim, until 1950) states; wars between India and Pakistan, refugee movements, deportation, and displacement followed. A further 20% of south Asian migrants came from the coastal districts of the Indian province of Gujarat, and around 10% trace their origins to Sylhet District, in the northeastern corner of Bangladesh, a country that came into existence only when it seceded from Pakistan in 1971. The migrant population includes a much smaller number of Tamils, mainly from Sri Lanka, as well as the families of professional migrants who arrived from towns and cities scattered the length and breadth of the subcontinent. While most made their way directly to Britain, a significant minority spent an intermediate period of residence in one of the British Commonwealth nations or in nations that remained colonies into the 1980s.

All Britons of south Asian origin display a number of cultural commonalities, primarily in similar family structure and cuisine, as well as a passionate interest in Mumbai's "Bollywood" films. Nevertheless they exhibit a wide range of internal variations in national origin (Indian, Pakistani, Bangladeshi, Mauritian, Sri Lankan), religion (Hindu, Sikh, Muslim, Christian), and language (including Punjabi, Urdu, Hindi, Hindko, Gujarati, and Bengali). In addition, active local communities, each of which is strongly endogamous,

have crystallized around commonalities of caste (*zat, jati*), further divided internally into yet more tightly focused descent groups (*biraderi*), which still have adherents in the UK at the beginning of the 21st century. The significance of these levels of differentiation is largely contingent on the specific context. *Biraderi*-based reciprocities are overwhelmingly significant in domestic contexts, but in more public arenas, factors of caste, religion, and regional origin become increasingly salient. By contrast, purely national loyalties (as among Indians, Pakistanis, and Bangladeshis) now mean relatively little – except when cricket matches are being played.

Census data between 1961 and 2001 indicate that while the British Indian population showed clear signs of leveling off by 2001, both the Pakistani- and Bangladeshi-origin populations were still expanding rapidly (see Table 1). The principal causes of such differences are different fertility rates and the scale of further immigration, which are still substantially greater among both these groups than among the Indian group – whose restricted growth is also partly accounted for by onward migration to the USA and Canada. Although people of Indian origin still formed a clear majority of British south Asians in 2001, they will soon be outnumbered by those of Pakistani origin.

Pakistani and Bangladeshi immigrants display a high level of religious homogeneity: more than 98% identified themselves as Muslims in the 2001 census. Hindus made up just under half of Britain's Indian population and Punjabi Sikhs contributed a further third, with Muslims (most of whom are from Gujarat) making up most of the remainder. There is also a significant Christian presence among the Indian and the Pakistani groups. Among the former, the Christians are mostly Goan, and among the latter, mostly Punjabi (see Table 2).

Creation of communities of origin and upward social mobility

Prior to 1947, the great majority of south Asians in Britain were sojourners rather than settlers. Their numbers were so limited and their backgrounds so diverse that there was

Table 2. The religious adherence of Britain's south Asian population, 2001								
	Indian		Pakistani		Bangladeshi		Other Asian	
	Persons	%	Persons	%	Persons	%	Persons	%
Muslim	131,700	13.8	657,700	98.6	259,700	98.7	90,000	42.0
Hindu	466,600	49.0	500	0.1	1,700	0.6	64,600	30.1
Sikh	301,300	31.6	300	0.1	100	0.0	15,000	7.0
Buddhist	1,900	0.2	200	0.0	200	0.1	11,700	5.5
Christian	50,700	5.3	7,800	1.2	1400	0.5	32,400	15.1

Source: England and Wales Census, 2001.

little prospect for the emergence of a coherent community. Rather, those with similar occupations – such as trainee doctors in Edinburgh, trainee barristers in London, Sylheti former seamen in London's dockland, and the Punjabi peddlers working out of Glasgow, Liverpool, Bristol, and Southampton – formed small-scale local networks. Each such band had a highly parochial character. Sojourners of differing class and regional origins had no significant contact with one another.

As prosperity grew from 1950 onward, indigenous workers took the opportunity to move upward through the labor market, generating acute labor shortages throughout Britain's heavy industries and in poorly paid jobs in the service sector. Established reservoirs of additional labor in Ireland and eastern Europe (Poland, Lithuania) had by then either become exhausted or inaccessible because of the cold war, and south Asian migrants proved to be an excellent alternative. Pioneers who had established themselves in Britain smoothed the way for immigrants who followed. They notified their friends and kinsfolk about the advantageous situation in the labor market and helped with initial contact with the authorities and with the search for apartments and jobs. Because of high demand, it was easy enough to find employment by presenting oneself at factory gates, and once hired, to enthusiastically recommend one's relatives as employees – leading to an ever-escalating process of chain migration from specific rural locations in the subcontinent to equally specific destinations in urban industrial centers of Britain. Employers gained access to a self-recruiting workforce prepared to work long hours in unpleasant jobs for relatively low wages.

Despite their status as British subjects, the only forms of employment readily accessible to the newcomers – who were also readily identifiable as people of color – were those which the indigenous population preferred to avoid. Neither familiarity with English linguistic and cultural conventions nor the acquisition of educational and professional qualifications greatly reduced the impact of such handicaps. Moreover, when settlers (and even more so their British-born offspring) subsequently sought to gain entry into more senior positions in the employment market, the forces of exclusionism became progressively greater. Yet despite all the exclusionary obstacles they encountered, members of Britain's south Asian

population have managed to achieve a substantial degree of upward socioeconomic mobility.

The secret of their success is not difficult to locate. In addition to hard work, settlers and their offspring have made extensive use of the cultural capital embedded within their kinship networks. At every step – from facilitating migration to Britain, finding employment, generating the capital required to start business enterprises, and facilitating the passage of their offspring through the higher education system and into professional employment – kinship reciprocities have played a central role. Moreover a dual adaptive strategy – the acquisition of the linguistic and cultural skills required to ease active participation in the English social order and the exploitation of the resources of their ancestral heritage – has enabled them to make the best of both worlds. But although broadly similar strategies have been deployed within every component of this population, outcomes have been far from uniform, largely as a result of differences in the character and quality of the social, familial, cultural, educational, and professional resources available within each specific network.

British Pakistanis and Bangladeshis originating from poor rural areas where educational facilities were virtually nonexistent have so far made limited upward progress. Groups who fall into this category include Hindko-speaking Pathans from Attock District, Potohari-speaking Kashmiris from Mirpur District (both located in Pakistan), and Sylhetis from northeast Bangladesh. Paradoxically, all three areas have a long history of engagement with the transnational labor market and were the British merchant navy's principal recruiting grounds for engine-room stokers from the 1880s onward. Former seamen from all three areas were among the earliest pioneer migrants in Britain, where they subsequently carved out a niche for themselves in the textile mills of the Pennine region of northern England. Nevertheless, they chose to give much greater priority to facilitating the passage of their kinfolk to Britain than to maximizing their own upward socioeconomic mobility in the UK. While their numbers increased rapidly after 1947, relatively few of the migrants from Mirpur and Attock have moved beyond the inner-city areas where they initially settled. Many stepped sideways into self-employment – particularly as taxi-drivers and operators of take-out restaurants – following the collapse of the textile industry. By contrast, the vast majority of Sylhetis, whose rural backgrounds were otherwise very similar, have created a niche of their own: a network of "Indian" restaurants that now extends across the length and breadth of Britain.

By contrast, the Indian migrants from areas with substantially higher levels of agricultural prosperity – such as Jat Sikhs from the Jullundur Doab in Indian Punjab, Muslim Arains from Pakistani Punjab, and Pattidar Patels from Gujarat – have achieved considerably faster upward socioeconomic mobility. Taking advantage of their higher levels of education and craft skills, they moved much more rapidly into semiskilled industrial work than their Mirpuri and Sylheti counterparts. When further upward progress was blocked by systematic discrimination, they also moved into self-employment and set up businesses that soon began to operate on a much more substantial scale. Some of their enterprises have been so successful that they are now listed on the stock exchange. Although the first generation of migrants had enjoyed relatively limited educational opportunities, their greater familiarity with the strategies and processes of education meant that they tended to have much more ambitious plans for their children than their largely illiterate Mirpuri and Sylheti counterparts. As a result, the British-born children of Hindu Pattidars, Jat Sikhs, and Muslim Arains have by now moved en masse into professional occupations.

Differences in gender rules have been a further determinant of upward mobility. Virtually all Muslim groups arrived with a stronger commitment to female seclusion than did their Hindu and Sikh counterparts. This has had far-reaching consequences. Most Muslims waited much longer before reuniting their families in Britain. While Hindu and Sikh women took waged employment almost immediately after their arrival, most overseas-born Muslim women have remained extremely reluctant to take employment which would cause them to break *purdah*, rules governing relations between the sexes and wearing the veil, leading many to take on low-paid work as seamstresses at home. Female employment among Muslim women has become the norm only with the emergence of a British-born generation.

The different origins of migrant populations have had an important effect on their settlement structures. The income-earning opportunities available to Muslim families were significantly limited compared with their Sikh and Hindu counterparts, making it largely impossible to move to suburbs or more upmarket neighborhoods. In addition, the rules of *purdah* made continued residence in spatially close-knit ethnic colonies more attractive: in such circumstances it was much easier for women to slip inconspicuously between each other's houses. Yet this has also led many young Muslim women to decide that the best way to overcome these limitations was to make the most of the educational opportunities open to them. Besides enabling them to delay the prospect of an early arranged marriage, it also enhances their prospects of gaining well-paid employment. British-born Muslim women are now substantially outperforming their male peers, especially in higher educational contexts, and have become active

participants in the employment market, very often in professional occupations.

The top-most section of the socioeconomic spectrum of south Asian–origin Britons is currently occupied by the offspring of settlers who made their way to Britain by way of east Africa. Although their ancestral origins also lay in Gujarat and Punjab, the "east Africans" arrived with significant additional resources. Their parents had been drawn overseas either as craftsmen to build and run the east African railways, or to open the small businesses through which British trading networks were extended into the interior. Those who worked on the railway were for the most part Ramgarhia Sikhs from the Punjab and Prajapati Mistris from Gujarat, whose traditional occupation had been as blacksmiths and carpenters. Most of those drawn into the commercial sector belonged to one of Gujarat's many trading castes, such as the Lohanas, the Khojas, and the Bohras; they were also accompanied by a smaller number of Punjabi Khatris and Brahmins. Sandwiched as they were between first the German (in mainland Tanzania until 1918) and then the English colonial elite and the subordinated African multitudes, the settlers engaged actively in the economic development and the administration of the colony. Besides enhancing their own professional abilities, they also ensured that their locally born children gained first-class educational and professional qualifications.

When the British lost control of east Africa during the 1960s, it was not just European settlers but also those from south Asia, who found themselves required to leave. As subjects of the British crown, most were entitled to settle in the UK, and after much deliberation the British authorities eventually allowed most of them to do so. Having arrived in Britain, east African Asians of both sexes soon gained a legendary reputation for entrepreneurial success. Although most families had been forced to abandon most of their financial assets in Africa, they used the same entrepreneurial strategies as those deployed by their direct-migrant counterparts, albeit with a number of highly effective supplemental resources. These included greater levels of fluency in English, better educational and professional qualifications, and above all the reinforced levels of personal and collective self-confidence that they had developed during their previous experience of colony construction. Hence, while the east Africans appeared much more "Westernized" than their direct migrant counterparts, they remained acutely aware of the value of ethnic consolidation, and hence just as strongly committed to maintenance of their religious and cultural traditions.

Social inclusion and exclusion

Despite substantial variations in the socioeconomic achievement among Britain's many south Asian communities, all have sustained a high level of coherence among themselves – with the result, for example, that levels of endogamy within each community remain extremely high. Large sections of the local British population look with mistrust at the socioeconomic upward mobility that immigrants achieve, especially those of Indian origin, and separate themselves in part according to racist descriptions of themselves and others. Immigrants' commitment to "alien" faiths such as Hinduism, Sikhism, and Islam, is routinely treated as an indicator of nonbelongingness. Nevertheless, at the beginning of the 21st century, the great majority of settlers – and even more so their locally born offspring – are wholly conversant with indigenous linguistic, social, and cultural conventions. Hence they have no difficulty in acting like "real" English when it is strategically advantageous to do so. But however great the efforts they may make to "fit in," such strategies do not end exclusion and marginalization: nominal acceptance displays a remarkable tendency to evaporate when there is active competition for scarce resources.

Such experiences have an adverse mental effect on immigrants, who only seldom answer back, because any attempt to do so invariably triggers explosive reactions among the host English community. Many immigrants of south Asian origin instead attempt to be inconspicuous and hope to avoid discrimination through large-scale assimilation. They maintain strict boundaries in the private sphere: here, the community of origin provides a distinct ethnic and religious identity. The second generation holds onto this identity, because it can offer a positive feeling of self-esteem.

Only a small portion of south Asian immigrants and their offspring leave behind completely the connections to their community of origin. One example is seen in the predominantly male members of the second generation, whose upbringing and education have completely collapsed and who, as a result, fall from the social network of their community of origin directly onto "the street." For other immigrants, an exogamous marriage means abandonment of the ethnic community. However, the frequency of boundary-crossing in the reverse direction – such that persons of alien origin are incorporated within the network – is much lower and invariably involves women who marry immigrant men. Their success is normally dependent on the comprehensive adoption of all the social and cultural behavioral attributes of *biraderi* (Pakistani clan systems) by these women. In diverse social arenas, immigrants are nevertheless totally integrated, such that British south Asians routinely participate in the social milieus of the majority *ghore* (whites), while very few members of the indigenous English majority have yet gained the cultural and linguistic competence that would permit them to participate in a similar fashion in the world of the *apne* (British south Asians).

Given both their unwillingness and inability to cross these boundaries, the vast majority of indigenous Britons know very little about the lives of south Asians and look with fear and alarm on the ethnoreligious pluralism of British society. Calls for greater "community cohesion" (assimilation) have become increasingly strident, and have been further reinforced since the suicide bombings on London's underground railway system in July 2005.

Akhtar, Shabbir. *Be Careful with Muhammad! The Salman Rushdie Affair*. London, 1989.

Ballard, Roger. *Desh Pardesh: The South Asian Presence in Britain*. London, 1994.

Banks, Marcus. *Organising Jainism in India and England*. Oxford, 1992.

Burghart, Richard. *Hinduism: The Perpetuation of Religion in an Alien Cultural Milieu*. London, 1987.

Desai, Rashmi. *Indian Immigrants in Britain*. London, 1963.

Helweg, Arthur. *Sikhs in England*. New Delhi, 1986.

Hinnells, John, ed. *Religious Reconstruction in the South Asian Diasporas: From One Generation to Another*. London, 2007.

Modood, Tariq, ed. *Ethnic Minorities in Britain: Diversity and Disadvantage*. London, 1997.

Mukta, Parita. *Shards of Memory: Woven Lives in Four Generations*. London, 2002.

Tambs-Lyche, Harald. *London Patidars: A Case Study in Urban Ethnicity*. London, 1980.

Visram, Rozina. *Ayahs, Lascars and Princes: The Story of Indians in Britain 1700–1947*. London, 1986.

Cross-references: Great Britain; Pakistanis in Great Britain since the 1950s

IRANIAN REFUGEES IN NORTHERN, WESTERN, AND CENTRAL EUROPE SINCE 1980: THE EXAMPLE OF THE NETHERLANDS

Halleh Ghorashi

Since the mid-20th century, there have been two major waves of emigration of Iranians. The first wave, between 1950 and 1981, consisted mainly of students and political or religious opponents to the Pahlavi regime (1926–79). Some loyalists who were associated with the regime anticipated the upcoming political unrest that culminated in the Iranian Revolution of 1979 and started leaving Iran. The majority of these early emigrants, who were largely able to preserve their assets, went to the USA, especially to southern California.

The second wave of emigration was far more extensive and started about 1981. Many of these Iranians had to leave the country because of their political convictions or religious backgrounds. In addition, many young men left Iran during the Iran-Iraq War (1981–8) to escape being sent to the front. Estimates of the number of Iranian emigrants in the 1980s and 1990s vary from 1 million to 4 million. English-speaking countries such as the USA and parts of Canada were the most popular destinations, since English had been taught as the second language in Iranian schools since World War II. Besides, Iranians could get a residence permit in European countries only if they applied for political asylum. Policy was less restricted in the USA, where many Iranian exiles applied for other types of residence permits. The USA now hosts the second largest Iranian community in the world. However, possibilities for migration to the USA and Canada gradually became more limited.

In Europe, France was a popular country of destination because of cultural and political interactions with Iran, and England and Germany because of the student exchange. In Europe, Germany probably hosts the largest group of Iranians: the estimated number is around 120,000. Sweden also witnessed a steep increase in the number of Iranians between the end of the 1980s and the beginning of the 1990s. It had received some 55,000 Iranians by the beginning of the 21st century – now the largest non-Western immigrant group in Sweden.

Initially, Iranians were not interested in migrating to the Netherlands, due both to the language barrier and the lack of historical relations. However, in the 1990s, the Netherlands became popular because of its rather liberal policies for granting asylum. Asylum requests by Iranians in the Netherlands increased in 1992–3 and reached a record level of 6,000 in 1994. This number decreased drastically because of more restricted asylum policies introduced in the mid-1990s.

In January 2000, 24,642 Iranians were officially registered in the Netherlands. This number, however, excludes the Iranians in the refugee centers waiting for recognition of their status (some 4,000) and those whose applications for asylum were rejected and who became illegal. Thus, the estimated number of Iranians living in the Netherlands is up to 30,000, of whom fewer than half are women.

Up to 1987, refugees were free to settle in the city of their own choice and most Iranians preferred to live in larger cities such as Amsterdam, Rotterdam, and the Hague. The official number of Iranians in 2003 in these cities was around 3,000, 2,400, and 1,800, respectively, although the actual number is probably higher. In 1987, a restricted housing policy was introduced. Refugees were accommodated in special centers until they were granted asylum, after which they were distributed throughout the country.

An important characteristic of Iranians in the Netherlands is that they are generally highly educated. Iranians are present in Dutch higher education institutions in different fields and have been able to secure various positions in politics, science, arts, and the media. Some examples of active Iranian participants in the public arena are Farah Karimi, ex-member of the Dutch parliament and general director of Oxfam-Novib; Kader Abdolah, writer and columnist; Soheila Najand, artist; and Afshin Ellian, scholar and publicist.

Women seem to have been more successful than men in exploring possibilities and achieving new goals in their adopted countries. This new space for women has of course affected their family structure. Many who entered the countries as couples have divorced. There have also been tensions and violence within Iranian families since the traditional privileges of men have been threatened or limited. As the result, almost one out of five Iranian families in the Netherlands is a single-parent family. These cultural conflicts could also be one of the possible reasons for an increase in marriages to partners of other nationalities. Although official figures on intermarriage are lacking, observations in the

community illustrate that many Iranians, especially women, choose non-Iranian partners.

Iranians in the Netherlands do not live in a closed community. The few gatherings they organize are mainly related to Iranian national festivities or political events. The only festivity that is celebrated every year in almost every large city is the Iranian New Year on 21 March. This individualistic orientation of Iranians in the Netherlands has to do with a combination of factors. The group who entered the Netherlands in the 1980s could stay in the country only if they applied for political asylum, and being granted a residence permit depended on the applicant's political story. Most of these Iranians were very politically oriented and many applicants saw the Iranian embassy in the Hague as "the enemy." They could face danger because of the nature of the stories they told to Dutch officials to gain asylum, and the presence of the embassy led many to feel threatened. Their fear proved justified during the 1980s when several prominent members of the Iranian regime's opposition were assassinated in Europe. Among the Iranian migrants these events served to undermine trust in their own security in Europe.

Although Iranians have shown an increasing interest in cultural, social, and democratic activities since the mid-1990s, leading to the foundation of new organizations, these activities have not yet resulted in the formation of a real Iranian community in the Netherlands. Different political orientations, political reticence in the public sphere, and mutual suspicion among Iranian immigrants in the Netherlands were, however, not the only reasons for this lack of community development. The influence of the Dutch context has to be taken into consideration as well.

Immigrants with Islamic backgrounds in the Netherlands are associated with the history of the postwar "guest workers." These immigrants came from traditional areas of their countries, with little education, and they provided cheap labor for the reconstruction of Europe. The Dutch considered their stay temporary, which affected the policies of the time: group formation and the maintenance of the migrants' own culture were encouraged, while integration into Dutch society was not. However, in the 1980s, the realization came that this migration was not temporary, which led to replacing the term "guest worker" with "migrant." Policies also changed, this time toward stimulation of integration into Dutch society. From the mid-1990s, rightist political discourse gained more popularity in the country by claiming that the cultural backgrounds of Islamic migrants were the main reason for their isolation and that they presented a major social problem in Europe. Thus, Turkish and Moroccan migrants who were encouraged to keep their culture before the 1980s were, in the 1990s, blamed for having done so. The attacks in New York and Washington on 11 September 2001 gave these rightist discourses even more legitimacy in viewing migrants from Islamic countries as the scapegoat of the nation.

Due to this history of recent migration and changes in integration policy, group formation of migrants is no longer encouraged and is considered undesirable. Among Iranian refugees, this context has contributed to an emphasis on their individuality and a lack of a sense of community. Their political past has been essential in the construction of their self-image, as they consider themselves part of the intellectual elite of Iran. It is because of this background that Iranians want to differentiate themselves from other migrants in the Netherlands and go along with the dominant discourse that is against the group formation of migrants and in favor of individual integration.

In comparison, the formation of an Iranian community has progressed further in some other European countries. In Germany, several cultural, social, and women's organizations have been founded, but a strong nationwide organization is lacking. The Iranian presence in Sweden is as recent as in the Netherlands, and yet this group has been able to establish one of the strongest Iranian communities in all of Europe.

The self-image of Iranians as intellectual elites of their society often does not coincide with the dominant perception held by the host country. In many European countries including the Netherlands, since the end of the 1990s rightist discourse is becoming dominant; in these views, the migrants of Islamic background are understood as problems or, even worse, as (potential) enemies. They are often regarded as uneducated, traditional, and violent, in the case of men, and victimized, in the case of women. These images seem to have become so strong that there is little room left for differentiation. Iranians, who consider themselves "enlightened intellectuals," are often perceived as simply "Islamic" or "Islamist." Most Iranians resent the use of these stereotypes and emphasize that they are not traditional believers in Islam, all the more because they are refugees from an Islamic country. Some even go so far as to position themselves either as atheists or anti-Islamic.

Iranians in the Netherlands work hard to become part of the new society and do their best to present themselves in the role of "intellectual immigrants" by their contributions to art, politics, public debates, and science. Nevertheless, they are often seen and treated as "others," and this can ultimately hinder their complete integration into the new society. Studies in Germany, Sweden, and the Netherlands show that this feeling of being treated as a foreigner or an "unwanted other" results in the Iranians' searching for a sense of belonging by formation of a group or an orientation directed toward the past. Tension between their self-image and the image of them in the host society may urge Iranians to build their own community in order to gain a sense of belonging in the new country. The history of Iranians in Europe is too short to come to any conclusions, but the interaction between the self-image and the image of the host society will play a decisive role in the development of Iranians within European countries.

Agh, Tahereh. *Lebensentwürfe im Exil: Biographische Verarbeitung der Fluchtmigration iranischer Frauen in Deutschland*. Frankfurt am Main, 1997.

Darvishpour, Mehrdad. *Invandrarkvinnor som bryter mönstret: Hur maktförskjutningen inom iranska familjer i Sverige paverkar relationen*. Stockholm, 2003.

Fathi, Asghar, ed. *Iranian Refugees and Exiles since Khomeini*. Costa Mesa, 1991.

Ghorashi, Halleh. *Ways to Survive, Battles to Win: Iranian Women Exiles in the Netherlands and the United States*. New York, 2003.

Hessels, Thomas. "Iraniërs in Nederland." *Bevolkingstrends* 52 (2004): 54–8. Centraal Bureau voor de Statistiek.

Kamalkhani, Zahra. *Iranian Immigrants and Refugees in Norway*. Bergen, 1988.

Spellman, Kathryn. *Religion and Nation: Iranian Local and Transnational Networks in Britain*. New York, 2004.

Cross-references: France; Germany; Great Britain; The Netherlands; Northern Europe; Moroccan Labor Migrants in Western, Central, and Northern Europe since the 1960s: The Example of Great Britain; Turkish Labor Migrants in Western, Central, and Northern Europe since the Mid-1950s

IRISH BRANDY MERCHANTS IN THE CHARENTES IN THE 18TH CENTURY

Louis M. Cullen

The migration of Irish merchants in wine and spirits to Spain, France, and the Austrian Lowlands (later Belgium) was a feature of the 17th and 18th centuries. In these areas, the Irish, along with migrants of other nationalities, effectively replaced the Dutch who had all but disappeared from the trade by 1750. At the peak of wine and spirits trading, several dozen Irish trading houses each operated in Cádiz, Nantes, and Bordeaux, where ethnic communities in excess of 100 people also existed. Along with these communities were others, who operated with smaller numbers and for shorter intervals in lesser ports. While Irish immigrants in most port cities were generally Catholic, among the Irish in Bordeaux there were Protestant as well as Catholic merchants. The hope for economic success was the chief impetus to migrate in a period of soaring trade, but in a context where personal contacts among the merchants offered both information and security.

From the late 17th century, demand expanded for the great clarets and burgundies, for gin and factory beer, and for cognac. In the long war years of 1689–1713, Irish merchants replaced the English on the Canary Islands and in the ports of Spain itself. They also emerged as the dominant force in the trade between France and the British Isles. Irish merchants, together with German ones, were the strongest foreign buying force in Bordeaux. Their business in Bordeaux and in other French ports was a well-balanced activity of matching imports and exports. Today, the names of surviving houses or "chateaux" include Barton, Johnston, Lynch, MacCarthy, Kirwan, Boyd, and Lawton, the most famous brokers in the history of Bordeaux wines.

The cognac trade was only a small one compared with the large and dynamic wine trade. Trading houses in the Charentes date from a period when the market for brandy – different from that for wine, which was in constant demand – changed drastically. The market for spirits was characterized by intense competition with other spirits and by fluctuating grain prices. Another crucial factor was a variable demand in Paris for brandy: demand for cognac grew ever stronger to replace brandy produced along the Loire valley, which declined in importance due to its greater vulnerability to weather and frost. While some houses had appeared in the 1730s, notably those founded by the Londoner John Baker and the Irishman Walter Geoghegan, most of the houses were established in years of speculative upturn in trade after 1750. Anthony Galwey appeared in 1755, James Delamain in 1760, Saule & Jennings in 1763, and Richard Hennessy and Luke Bellew in 1765.

Thus, the Irish houses in the Charentes appeared predominantly during the Seven Years War (1756–3), or in the few years of postwar boom when retarded recovery in the rum trade and poor grain harvests in Ireland made brandy wildly lucrative. Four of the young Irish traders in the Charentes died in short succession, but two of the houses successfully survived the main travails of the late 1760s. Further Irish brandy trading houses were founded in Bordeaux, in the belief that periodic upswings in brandy demand in the huge port were a prelude to a stable custom. However, the Irish houses there fared badly, with the exception of the Dubliner Andoe who settled there in 1773 to leave only in the revolution in 1793. Richard Hennessy moved to Bordeaux in 1776, leaving the cognac house to a nephew of Laurence Saule, but returned once more to Cognac in utter failure in 1788. The surviving houses in 1789 were a mere two: Ranson & Delamain whose business from 1760, directed by James Delamain, had been a stable one, and Hennessy, who took over the business of John Saule who died in 1788.

Many Irish houses of the 1760s exported most of their goods to Ireland. Due to especially volatile demand in Ireland, their dependence on the Irish market posed a decisive risk. The two surviving houses could compete because they had other and more stable outlets for their goods. Circumstances had given Richard Hennessy a small stake in the London market, and comparatively little in the Irish trade. Ranson & Delamain benefited from being the only house in Cognac and Jarnac that had a stable Paris business.

Successful marriages between the members of different trading houses secured the success of the business. In this regard, the brandy trade followed the typical pattern of commodity trades of the time. Marriages to local women played a part in the success of the businesses of Anthony Galwey, John Saule, and Samuel Turner. The houses of Hennessy and Martell benefited from matrimonial alliances in 1795 and 1816. Two local marriages were decisive in the survival of the business of Jean Martell, who arrived in France in 1718, and whose business suffered initially in the post-boom crisis.

Cullen, Louis M. "The Irish Merchant Communities of Bordeaux, La Rochelle and Cognac in the Eighteenth Century." In *Négoce et industrie en France et Irlande au XVIIIe et XIXe siècles*, edited by Paul Butel and Louis M. Cullen, 51–64. Paris, 1980.

Cullen, Louis M. *The Brandy Trade under the Ancien Regime: Regional Specialisation in the Charente.* Cambridge, 1998.

Cullen, Louis M. *The Irish Brandy Houses of Eighteenth-Century France.* Dublin, 2000.

Guimerà Ravina, Agustin. *Burgesia extranjera y comercio atlantico: La empresa comercial en Canarias (1703–1771).* Santa Cruz de Tenerife, 1985.

Cross-references: France; Ireland and Northern Ireland; German Maritime Traders in Cádiz and Bordeaux from the Late 17th to the Late 19th Century

IRISH INDUSTRIAL WORKERS IN ENGLAND, SCOTLAND, AND WALES SINCE THE 19TH CENTURY

Donald M. MacRaild

Significant numbers of Irish workers have been present in the British economy since the 18th century. The number of Irish-born workers in England and Wales reached a high point in 1861, when the combination of famine, privation, and diminishing opportunities at home and employment prospects in Britain prompted more and more Irish to seek to improve their economic and social situation by emigrating. The proportion of Irish-born workers in the Scottish population peaked 10 years earlier than in England and Wales, although the highest total figure there was not achieved until 1881 and was always higher than in England and Wales. In the latter two areas, the figure never exceeded 3%; in Scotland, the figure was regularly two or three times the rate for England and Wales.

These rates of migration are explained partly as a function of distance (only 13 miles separated Northern Ireland and Scotland at the closest point); but population flow was also encouraged by the concentration of mining and heavy industry in the parts of western Scotland closest to Irish ports. Moreover, heavy overseas out migration from Scotland created further opportunities for Irish labor. Irish immigration to the UK also remained high after the Second World

Table 1. Irish-born population of England, Wales, and Scotland, 1841–1951

	England & Wales	%	Scotland	%
1841	289,404	1.8	126,321	4.8
1851	519,959	2.9	207,367	7.2
1861	601,634	3.0	204,083	6.7
1871	566,540	2.5	207,770	6.2
1881	562,374	2.2	218,745	5.9
1891	458,315	1.6	194,807	4.8
1901	426,565	1.3	205,064	4.6
1911	375,325	1.0	174,715	3.7
1921	364,747	1.0	159,296	3.3
1931	381,089	0.9	124,296	2.6
1951	627,021	1.4	89,007	1.7

Source: Census of England and Wales, 1851–1951; Census of Scotland, 1851–1951.

Table 2. Irish-born settlers in the four major British centers, 1841–1871								
	1841		1851		1861		1871	
	Numbers	%	Numbers	%	Numbers	%	Numbers	%
London	75,000	18.0	108,548	14.9	106,879	13.3	91,171	11.8
Liverpool	49,639	11.9	83,813	11.5	83,949	10.4	76,761	9.9
Manchester	33,490	8.1	52,504	7.2	52,076	6.5	34,066	4.4
Glasgow	44,345	10.7	59,801	8.2	62,082	7.7	683,308	8.8
Total	202,474	48.7	304,666	41.8	304,986	37.9	270,328	34.9

% = proportion of entire Irish-born population of England, Wales, and Scotland found in these cities.

War: in the mid-20th century, the absolute number of Irish in England and Wales became larger than it had been for a century (see Table 1).

Irish migrants in the 19th century were perceived as marginal and poor. Socially critical writers such as Thomas Carlyle and Friedrich Engels portrayed the Irish as a hard-pressed population of unskilled workers, undercutting wages, negatively affecting indigenous morality, and languishing as an urban subproletariat. A similar image was portrayed by the *Morning Chronicle* surveys of the provinces (1849–50). In contrast to such stereotypical contemporary descriptions, however, the Irish were a variegated and diverse migrant population. They came to occupy jobs in well-paid occupations and were not merely restricted to the worst sorts of labor on docks, in tanneries, chemical works, or construction – although such outlets were important for the unskilled element that was most numerous among them.

Irish migration was fundamentally a reflection of the wage gap between Ireland and Britain. It has been argued that Britain was simply the outlet for the poorest migrants, those who could not afford to go to the USA. The Irish tended to prefer the US option and the American flow outstripped that to Britain from the 1850s until the 1920s. But many of those who settled in Britain improved their prospects by staying there. Some of the Irish also consciously treated Britain as a stopping point on the way to other destinations. The flow of Irish labor migrants was overwhelmingly in the direction of commercial and industrial zones; Irish movement to Britain, however, did not necessarily follow the rhythms of the business cycle. Quantities of Irish went to Britain regardless of the economic climate they found there. The Famine generation provides a case in point for they arrived en masse at a time of depression in Britain.

By the mid-19th century, the Irish population was spread across Britain, although clustered in centers of industrial development and urban growth. Consequently, there were relatively few Irish in the rural shires but significant numbers across central and western Scotland, in the northeast of England and west Cumberland, in urban Lancashire and Yorkshire, in the Midlands, and in London. Pockets of settlement appeared elsewhere, in ports such as Bristol, and in dockyard, navy, and maritime towns, such as Plymouth, Portsmouth, Southampton, and around the Thames. They

were also found in the administrative centers and commercial capitals of otherwise rural regions, for example, in York, Lancaster, and Carlisle (the latter two having textile mills that sustained more diverse Irish communities). The great concentration of Irish was to be found in the major cities: Liverpool, Glasgow, Manchester, and London, which in 1841 were home to more than half of the Irish population in England, Scotland, and Wales, as Table 2 illustrates.

One of the most enduring images of the Irish is of a disorganized community that lacked the institutions of social cohesion or the necessary guile to take advantage of opportunities for social advancement and which relied upon laws protecting the poor. However, one of the most remarkable features of Irish settlement was the parallel and simultaneous development of a series of religious and social affinities that became a whole way of life at the level of neighborhood and parish.

The pre-Famine generation

At the turn of the 19th century, long-established migration patterns between Irish and British ports were beginning to solidify as growing industrial towns attracted increasing waves of Irish. One of the earliest permanent industrial settlements began to emerge in this period in western and central Scotland within the growing textile industries. Most of these early settlers were Protestant weavers from Ulster.

In other industries, such as coal and iron, an Irish presence was also building up, though there is some debate, and little clarity, about the position that the Irish achieved in the labor hierarchy of the collieries. The coal industry, despite its inherent characteristics of hard and dangerous toil, did not offer a universal or regular labor experience for incoming migrants. In the northeast of England, where arcane employer-worker relations prevailed until the mid-19th century and workers struggled to control access to mine work, Irish labor tried hard to achieve a foothold in the better-paid underground work in the mines. There also seems to have been an initial restriction of the Irish to pit laboring in Welsh collieries. In Scotland, where labor experiences were harsher and social relations more primitive than in England, there is much less evidence of the Irish being excluded in this way. Just how far Irish workers were restricted to pithead laboring because of a failure to break the native stranglehold on hewing (cutting coal) is not known.

From the 1780s, textile workers, miners, and general laborers from Ireland were becoming increasingly important to the burgeoning Scottish economy, one of the most advanced in the world. By the 1830s, the Irish in the big cities had become synonymous with the social problems associated with industrial growth and urbanization. Irish settlements in the big towns and cities and related social problems did indeed grow quickly. By 1831, the Irish-born populations of Glasgow, Liverpool, and Manchester were becoming focal points for the settlement of Irish workers in a great variety of unskilled laboring occupations. The metropolis of London provided all manner of work for the Irish who had been settled there since the Elizabethan period (1533–1601). By the 19th century, they were to be found in the poorest parts of the most overcrowded parts of the city.

Along the Thames, as on the Mersey or the Clyde, the Irish worked as laborers, porters, and carters; they also achieved higher status work as lightermen and stevedores. The work they did in these places was hard, unremitting, and often prone to the contractions of trade. Alehouses, lodging houses, and brothels attracted the Irish, both as customers and providers, owners and servants. The streets of London were traversed by Irish lawyers and doctors as well as the laboring men. The waterfront environment of the world's busiest port also created opportunities for white-collar workers, such as clerks, as well as for the working class. Irish navvies were also numerous among those who built the major railway arteries during the "railway mania" of the 1840s.

There were far more skilled workers among the pre-Famine Irish than has been acknowledged in a historiography overwhelmingly skewed toward emphasizing the poverty and wretchedness of the Irish. According to Samuel Holme, a prominent local builder in Liverpool, one-fifth of the Irish labored in the poorest trades, while one-tenth of them were mechanics, a craft occupation noted for high skill and wages and strong worker organization. Even in Liverpool – home of the archetypal Irish slums – the ethnic workforce was variegated. Irish labor in Manchester dominated the poorer aspects of the building trades, though migrants were also well represented as bricklayers and masons, as was common elsewhere. Once the Irish were established in these trades, moreover, they, like Durham miners or Clydeside shipwrights, fought to exclude all but their own kind from entry. While employers viewed Irish labor favorably, they also noted the propensity of the Irish to strike in order to gain redress.

While the Irish shared experiences with their non-Irish counterparts, class allegiances could be restricted by ethnic friction. Such occurrences led to what employers perceived as difficulties. Mill owner Joseph Bell, who employed more than 100 Irish hand-loom wool weavers, felt compelled to keep them apart from the English because it was "unpleasant to have both together." Similar tensions also emerged in Wales, where immigrants posed a threat to native workers that, though more apparent than real, led to widespread enmity and violence. As in other parts of Britain, Welsh anti-Irish hostility was particularly intense from the 1830s to the 1860s, but continued until the 1880s. At that point, Wales was a major producer of iron and coal, but the Irish seem not to have achieved a proportionate share of skilled work: in iron foundries, for example, they tended to be laborers rather than puddlers. Despite an apparently ethnically stratified workforce, tensions were commonplace and violence sometimes occurred. Religion provided one reason for this reception, but cultural factors also played a role.

The Famine and 1848

The Great Famine (1845–50) turned Ireland into the embodiment of poverty and distress. However, by the time the blight struck the Irish potato crop in 1845, several generations of Irish men and women were established in the urban hierarchy of British towns. Those who had attained better sorts of work in mines or factories, as mechanics or smiths, were eclipsed by the waves of poor Irish who swept into British ports in these years looking for refuge or onward passage to the New World. The degree of misery and privation panicked onlookers, not least the taxpayers of Liverpool, where local taxes increased dramatically to pay for the paupers. The Famine thus brought dramatic consequences for Irish labor migration. First, the proportions of destitute Irish greatly increased, initially in the coastal towns of western Britain and south Wales: from Cardiff and Swansea, round to Liverpool, the northwest coast, and Clydeside. The spread of the pauper Irish soon affected inland parishes, including small rural villages with very little previous experience with the problem of itinerant Irish poverty. The poor Irish became the focus of attention among newspaper journalists and social critics who lamented the Famine and stressed the destabilizing effect of the high numbers of new poor immigrants.

The increased migration caused by the Famine also had an effect on the many stable, established Irish communities in Britain. Hostility toward the Irish, who were already tainted by their association with poverty, increased in the context of political conflicts around the issue of equal rights for Catholics in Great Britain. The situation only worsened in the 1850s and 1860s with competition for jobs and the growth of anti-Catholic and anti-Irish sentiments in response to the movement for Irish independence. Wales, the northwest, and central Scotland were particularly affected.

Any assessment of whether the Irish inhabited what we might call ghettoes depends partly upon the definition of the term itself. For instance, residential inequality, or spatial segregation does not itself necessarily create a ghetto. In Liverpool, occupational and social status limited the Irish community's choice of dwellings, while segregation was defined by poor quality housing and in the multiple occupancy of low-quality housing. Slum conditions were not limited to the big cities: Caribee Island in Wolverhampton and the alleys of York also housed compressed communities of, at times, outcast Irish. In London, networks of Irish businesses, homes, and services were not sufficiently compact to constitute separate geographic neighborhoods.

Beyond the Famine

Family settlements were important to the early establishment of Irish communities in Britain; as single migrants became more prominent they still tended to migrate in clear patterns. Indeed, associations between certain Irish and British regions became important, and strong kinship bonds were a central feature of Irish migrant life. Letters and word-of-mouth ensured that friends, family, and acquaintances received the sorts of social knowledge that facilitated not only migration but also choice of work and lodgings. This helped to foster a strong sense of ethnic solidarity and bonds of togetherness, and the migrants were also able to utilize such ties to gain a foothold in the new communities. Detailed information on the number of return migrants is lacking. Those who crossed the Irish Sea to Britain, however, were far more likely to return to Ireland than those who migrated to the USA. By 1900, there was a flow of holidaying migrants who returned home to visit relatives.

Irish settlement ensured that by the mid-Victorian period Roman Catholicism in Britain had the highest rate of growth of all confessions and that the Irish were not merely passive recipients of Catholic culture. A prodigious church-building program was based in part upon the contributions of the low-income Irish. English and Scots Catholics came to be massively outnumbered by their working-class Irish counterparts. The Irish patron saint St. Patrick and the pope represented the central symbols of an increasing unification between Irish nationality and Irish Catholicism. On top of the spiritual dimension, the provision of social functions became a key marker of Catholic success among the impoverished urban Irish in Britain. The Catholic Church came to view the erection of schools and the training of teachers as vitally important. By the mid-Victorian period, an elaborate and broad-based church had come into being, including social work, welfare, leisure pursuits, and schooling, which strengthened the faith and provided the young with an upbringing based on Irish cultural traditions.

A generation of violence was also part of a wider hardening of ethnic divisions, and these worked their way into community life in palpable ways. Levels of intermarriage, for example, declined with the Famine generation. In some ways, the much larger Irish community of the 1850s provided more opportunities for Irish to marry Irish, and of course the Famine influx included far higher, but still unexamined, proportions of family migration, which precluded the need for intermarriage. In both London and York intermarriage rates halved during the Famine years and shortly after. Recent research on the Irish in the northeast shipbuilding town of Wallsend-upon-Tyne has revealed that endogamy rates were around 60% in 1851, climbing steadily to nearly 75% in 1871. Religious influences may also have facilitated the preservation of Irish-Irish marital patterns, for the post-

Famine Irish were also more devout, with the growing network of churches, schools, priests, and nuns putting pressure upon the Irish to marry within the community. It was only with the children and grandchildren of the Famine generation that the rate of mixed marriages gradually increased. By 1891, in Wallsend, the proportion of Irish-only marriages had dropped over 50%, and this proportion only grew smaller with time. Although the Vatican issued the *Ne Temere* decree in 1907 forbidding marriage between Catholics and non-Catholics, the impact was weakened by growing secularization among the Irish in the 20th century.

As in Ireland itself, there were also conflicts between Catholics and Protestants among Irish migrants in Britain, which included a Protestant minority. The militant Protestant Orange Order, the majority of whose members were Irish migrants from Ulster, provided a counterpoint to the majority Catholic element of the Irish community between the 1820s and 1880s. The order organized numerous activities that went far beyond the ritual celebration of the "Glorious Twelfth" of July. In some places, attempts were made to provide modest social welfare, for example, sickness and death benefits. The Orange Order represented the collective consciousness of one rarely studied ethnic group – Irish Protestants – and the foundation, meaning, and the forms of their social and cultural worlds. Orangeism was also used in some places as a lever to control access to the job market. The order ensured an intra-Irish sectarian dimension to community life and was also part of a continuing pattern of violence. Such violence faded slowly starting in the later 1860s, especially after the Fenian episodes of 1867 and 1868, when a panic about armed insurrection and raids spread across Britain.

By the 1870s, most British workers had the daily experience of living side-by-side with Irish workers. Though the classic perception of the Irish as laborers in the poorest grades of work is borne out by the realities of many lives in this period, there are many indications that a significant proportion of these arrivals found better sorts of work. By the end of the mid-Victorian period, up to half of Irish workers were in skilled work. Even in York, where work was often of menial character, there was a substantial skilled element averaging around 25% among the Irish-born male workforce. In the iron-ore centers of Cumberland, semiskilled or skilled work was engaged in by about 90% of Irish-born males. In shipbuilding towns, the Irish found skilled and semiskilled work, as blacksmiths, fitters, turners, riveters, and drillers. The Irish remained at the forefront of the waterside trades into the 20th century and were an important element in the dock strike in London in 1889 and in the syndicalist struggles of 1910 and 1914.

Social and occupational advancement among Irish migrants in Britain made slow progress. While the poorest of the Famine Irish undoubtedly saw their offspring improve their lot, the industrial workers who represented a more normal experience in the later period were clearly held up in certain trades by the privileges of craft and tradition. The Irish in the 1880s were still underrepresented as coal miners; both the Irish-born and their sons failed to attain their share of face work. Most remained surface laborers. In shipbuilding, complex ethnic demarcations were in place until well into the 20th century as native and Protestant workers crowded the apprenticed trades and Catholics were held in the unskilled and ancillary work, which was subordinate to that of the highly paid craftsmen.

The 20th century

The Irish continued to migrate to Britain after the Victorian heyday. The movement took on a more settled aspect than was previously the case, though the Irish remained preponderant in the sorts of work that native workers did not want. The 1911 census figures for Scotland show that 28% of the almost 90,000 Irish were employed in the manufacture of iron and metals, while 13% were employed in mining. The patterns that had emerged in the 1870s, when the Irish became established across the urban-industrial hierarchy, clearly became entrenched in the early 20th century.

The interwar years saw the continuing improvement of the socioeconomic status of now well-established Irish communities. The restrictive immigration policy of the USA resulted in the renewal of large-scale migration to Britain, but this migrant community was much less visible than its 19th-century counterpart. The second-generation Irish remained strongly unionized and, by the 1920s, were also filling the ranks of the growing Labor Party. This association between the Irish and labor organization began in the 1820s in the early unions, has parallels in other countries, and continued until after the Second World War. The Irish continued to work in construction, railways, factories, metal manufacture, and chemicals. They provided important labor during wartime, too, though traveling back and forth to Ireland became more problematic and the state's attempt to control labor supply and placement and the threat of military conscription made things more difficult.

By 1951, Irish workers were widely dispersed in England, Wales, and Scotland. Low skill levels and metal industries, building, and laboring were still predominant, but engineers, doctors, and other white-collar graduates also appeared as a force among the ranks of the Irish. Nearly one-quarter of the Irish were professionals. With the advent in 1948 of the National Health Service, which dramatically increased the need for personnel to fill nursing and related positions, this group came to include many Irish nurses and midwives. Irish men and women also occupied the lower grades of work in the NHS, though these positions increasingly went to newer immigrants, for example, from the West Indies. The Irish cornered the labor market on major arterial construction projects, such as tunneling for water, power, and transport systems.

As the economy changed in the interwar period and particularly after the Second World War and old industries died out, the geographical distribution of the Irish in Britain also began to change. Northern industrial towns became less appealing while southern towns, such as Luton and Bedford with their car plants and brickworks, attracted more new Irish settlers than Liverpool or Manchester. London continued to attract many Irish, with centers such as Kilburn associated with a vigorous expatriate culture. Existing migration links and movements between shipyard towns continued to be significant until the 1980s, thus denoting a continuity of industrial labor migration that had first taken shape in the mid-Victorian years.

Delaney, Enda. *Demography, State and Society: Irish Migration to Britain, 1921–1971.* Liverpool, 2000.

Delaney, Enda. *The Irish in Postwar Britain.* Oxford, 2007.

Fielding, Steven J. *Class and Ethnicity: Irish Catholics in England, 1880–1939.* Buckingham, 1992.

Finnegan, Frances. *Poverty and Prejudice: A Study of Irish Immigrants in York 1840–1875.* Cork, 1982.

Handley, James E. *The Irish in Modern Scotland.* Cork, 1947.

Hollen Lees, Lyn. *Exiles of Erin: The Irish in Victorian London.* Manchester, 1979.

MacRaild, Donald M. *Irish Migrants in Modern Britain, 1750–1922.* Basingstoke, 1999.

MacRaild, Donald M. *Faith, Fraternity and Fight: Irish Migrants and the Orange Order in Northern England, c.1850–1920.* Liverpool, 2005.

Mitchell, Martin J. *Irish in the West of Scotland, 1797–1848: Trade Unions, Strikes and Political Movement.* Edinburgh, 1998.

Mitchell, Martin J., ed. *New Perspectives on the Irish in Scotland.* Edinburgh, 2008.

O'Leary, Paul. *Immigration and Integration: The Irish in Wales, 1798–1922.* Cardiff, 2002.

Swift, Roger, and Sheridan Gilley, eds. *The Irish in Britain, 1815–1939.* London, 1989.

Swift, Roger, and Sheridan Gilley, eds. *The Irish in Victorian Britain: The Local Dimension.* Dublin 1999.

Cross-references: Great Britain; Ireland and Northern Ireland; Irish Nurses in England since World War II; West Indians in Great Britain, France, and the Netherlands since the End of World War II

IRISH NURSES IN ENGLAND SINCE WORLD WAR II

Margaret Ó hÓgartaigh

There was a long tradition of Irish women migrating to England to pursue professional careers since the mid-19th century. This was due to the lack of employment opportunities for women, especially in rural Ireland. After the Second World War Irish women profited from shortages of staff in English hospitals. They were consciously recruited because many nurses were needed, and English women were reluctant to opt for a nursing career. Given the limited opportunities for single women in Ireland and the fact that the British state was introducing a national health service, there were both push and pull factors operating for Irish women who sought careers and social advancement in England.

These Irish women were primarily economic migrants who could profit from free access to the British labor market. Unlike citizens from other parts of the former British Empire, the Irish were not subjected to discriminatory immigration policies. The majority of the Irish immigrant women did not opt for a nursing career. In 1946, some 20% of the Irish women who traveled to England were trained nurses, while more than 60% worked in domestic service. However, it was possible to begin training as a nurse after a period of domestic service.

Nursing gave women from working and lower middle-class backgrounds an opportunity to pursue a professional career. Irish women in England were overrepresented in low-paid employment but, due to their strong presence in nursing, they were also overrepresented in professional occupations. One-third of all Irish-born women in England worked as a professional, as opposed to only one-quarter of English-born women.

Clearly, there was a large market for Irish women who wished to become a nurse in England. In January 1945 the *Irish Nursing World* included 64 advertisements for positions in various English hospitals. Both trainees and qualified nurses were sought. Most hospitals sought women who were educated at second level ("well-educated girls") and were at least 17 years old. The Ministry of Labour calculated in 1946 that 34,000 nurses were needed for the postwar National Health Service. In 1950 the need for nurses in British hospitals was still very great and posters were also used to attract Irish women.

As early as 1946 12% of the nursing staff in Britain were born in independent Ireland. One-quarter of all Irish-born women in paid work in Britain were nurses. According to the *Irish Democrat* in 1948 some 40% of nurses in London were Irish. This proportion declined in later years to approximately 10% to 15%, due, in part, to the influx of emigrants from the New Commonwealth. By the early 1960s, 11% of all the nursing recruits were Irish born; almost half were born outside the UK. By the 1971 census, nurses born in the Republic of Ireland and Northern Ireland constituted 12% of the total nursing population. Women from Northern Ireland were less strongly represented in nursing (9%) than women from the Republic (12%). More revealingly, in Ireland in 1971 there were 19,000 nurses as opposed to 12,000 Irish-born nurses in Britain.

The arduous working conditions in hospitals hindered the recruitment of English girls and women, who were not inclined to choose a nursing career. Irish women were willing to accept these conditions and were seen as particularly suited to nursing given their willingness to work long hours. The high status of nursing in Ireland had attracted them to the nursing profession, but there were few openings for either trainee or registered nurses in their home country. In the mid-1950s, the Commission on Emigration and Other Population Problems found that many women in the nursing profession left Ireland because the remuneration, facilities for training, pension schemes, and hours of work were considered unattractive. Furthermore, in Ireland women had to pay for nurse training, while in Britain the training was paid for. According to advertisements in 1946, trainees even received a small salary, between £45 and £60 per annum, and were provided with a uniform as well as a holiday and sick allowance. Hence, for many Irish women a nursing career in England was an attractive option. Given the security of having accommodation provided and the likelihood that there would be other Irish in the vicinity, it is not surprising that young Irish women were allowed to emigrate by their families.

Working conditions varied from institution to institution. State Registered Nurses received £110 to £150 as well as a yearly £5 allowance for past service. Student nurses were usually provided with residence, laundry, and uniforms. However, the majority of nurses in London seem to have been dissatisfied with their hospital accommodation. Many nurses worked more than 50 hours a week with, typically, 28 days of paid leave a year. Elizabeth O'Sullivan, trained in the 1950s in London, remembered working for seven hours six days a week and ten hours one day a week. However, in many other countries in Europe these hours were not unusual in the nursing profession. In keeping with the authoritarianism prevalent in nursing generally, nurses remembered that wards were run like "battleships" and that cleanliness was more highly valued than care.

Irish immigrant women did not see themselves as exiles. Migrant networks and pathways facilitated the emigration of friends and siblings and were fully utilized to encourage others to join the profession. By the mid-1960s 11% of senior nursing staff in England and Wales was Irish born. Irish women were also far more likely to be promoted than their African-Caribbean colleagues, due to discrimination. In general, Irish-born members of the medical profession in Britain were highly integrated and there were 4,000 Irish-born dentists and doctors in Britain compared to 3,500 in Ireland by the early 1970s. Assimilation was furthered by the intermarriage of Irish women and English men. Nearly half of all Irish women in Britain did not marry Irish men.

A specific study of Wirral Midwives near Liverpool, a magnet for Irish emigrants, paints a very positive picture of the experiences of Irish women. Respondents had siblings already nursing in England and one interviewee suggested that "England was just an extension of Ireland." Moreover, these women enjoyed the "intense loyalty" and "comradeship" of other Irish women. At the same time, discrimination was rare as there were many Irish women in senior positions. All of these women had enjoyed professional advancement and their offspring were far more likely to be educated at third level than their English counterparts.

Irish nurses maintained regular contact with their relatives in Ireland. The National Health Service subsidized trips to Ireland and nurses were allowed to accrue holiday entitlements so as to enjoy extended holidays at home. Hence, they maintained their sense of Irishness, though they were perceived as industrious professionals in England. For Irish nurses in England, emigration was more opportunity than exile.

There are no figures available for the return migration of Irish women, but given the oversupply of nurses in Ireland until the 1990s, it is unlikely that many returned to Ireland. Moreover, by the 1970s women constituted 75% of emigrant outflow from Ireland and only 39% of return movement.

Barrington, Clare. *Irish Women in England: An Annotated Bibliography*. Dublin, 1997.

Daniels, Mary. *Exile or Opportunity? Irish Nurses and Midwives in Britain*. Liverpool, 1993.

Delaney, Enda. *Demography, State and Society: Irish Migration to Britain, 1921–1971*. Liverpool, 2000.

Delaney, Enda. *Irish Emigration since 1921*. Dundalk, 2002.

Walter, Bronwen. *Outsiders Inside, Whiteness, Place and Irish Women*. London and New York, 2001.

Cross-references: Great Britain; Ireland and Northern Ireland; Irish Industrial Workers in England, Scotland, and Wales since the 19th Century

IRISH RETURN MIGRANTS FROM THE UNITED STATES IN THE 19TH AND EARLY 20TH CENTURIES

Patrick Fitzgerald

Emigration to colonial America had been significant in the 18th century. The century after 1815, however, witnessed an exodus that could only be described as massive and predominantly made up of Catholics. Of the 8 million migrants who departed between 1815 and 1914, around two-thirds ended up in the USA. The decade of the Great Potato Famine (1845–55) saw approximately 2.5 million emigrants depart. Throughout the latter 19th century, Ireland consistently topped the European table for overseas emigration (proportionate to population), usually sustaining a rate that was often double, sometimes triple, that of the European average. Although part of these emigrants returned to Ireland after their stay in the USA, Irish return migration rates seem to have been exceptionally low.

A good deal of evidence suggests that return migration rates to Europe from the USA in the later 19th and early 20th centuries were higher among males than females. Many men came back in search of a marriage partner or to invest savings earned overseas in a farm or house. Emigrants to America from continental Europe tended to be predominantly male. In the later 19th century, however, Ireland was unusual among European countries in that the gender balance among emigrants remained remarkably even. The even gender balance of Irish transatlantic emigrant flow from Ireland and the relatively modest rate of return to Ireland from the USA are closely connected. In short, Ireland sent to the USA a higher proportion of those who were less predisposed to return. Many of the young single women who left Ireland for the USA gained employment as domestic servants, which

brought them into regular and direct contact with generally well-to-do American families and may well have accelerated their integration into the new country. While the evidence drawn from rural folklore suggested the pattern of the single female migrant returning to Ireland, having saved up a dowry to lure a farming husband, other sources do not corroborate this. Analysis of passenger lists containing details of those who returned to Ireland from the USA between 1856 and 1867 demonstrates that two-thirds of these were male and that half of the females were already married. Evidence relating to the age of those returning in the 1850s and 1860s suggests an average age of 29.8 years for men and 26.5 for women. Comparison with the average age of those departing suggests that many returned after around five years in America.

In terms of their occupational profile and skills level, the returnees appear to have been drawn from the average, middle range of emigrants. Most had improved their skills somewhat through migration and only a minority of those coming back to Ireland fitted the contemporary popular stereotypes of spectacular success or failure in the New World. Undoubtedly a proportion of those returning had set out with the intention of social and economic advancement, achieved through savings earned in the course of labor migration, following a pattern more common in southern and eastern Europe. This also reflected, to some degree, an extension of patterns of temporary migration to Britain. Family commitments such as the care of aged parents or inheritance after death drew others home. Ill health, sometimes the consequence of harsh employment conditions particularly during the middle decades of the century, brought migrants back across the ocean, while others had found difficulties adjusting to an unfamiliar cultural environment. For most Irish emigrants movement to the USA meant a fairly sharp and rapid transition from a rural, agricultural world to an urban, industrial world. For many who had moved directly from the rural west of Ireland, the world of New York, Boston, or Philadelphia was profoundly foreign and for some unbearably discomforting.

Statistics compiled in the USA between 1908 and 1923 suggest a European average return rate of 35% compared to a much lower rate of 11% for the Irish. Of 26 ethnic or national groups across the continent of Europe, only the Jews (5%) recorded a lower return rate. This minimal importance of return migration in the broader context of Irish overseas migration is confirmed by other research, which indicates a return rate at the beginning of the 20th century of approximately 10% or an even lower rate of 6.25%, just prior to the outbreak of World War I.

Research also indicates fluctuations in Irish return migration. First, particular peaks in return correlated with downturns in the US economy. Even prior to the influx of Irish immigration during the Famine decade, there is evidence to suggest that the financial panics of 1819 and 1837 and subsequent recessions reduced the flow from Ireland and increased the flow of returnees. Similarly, recessions in 1858, 1873, and most notably in the mid-1890s spurred Irish immigrants to make their way back across the Atlantic. It is as yet unclear if the relative economic buoyancy of the period 1876–8 in Ireland, which checked emigration, had any similar effect. Second, while return migration was far from unknown during the "age of sail," it has been suggested that the widespread introduction of Atlantic steam passages during the 1860s helped to encourage a gradual increase in return traffic, even if all of those who came back did not necessarily do so permanently. By the close of the 19th century instances of both permanent and temporary return had increased from that which had prevailed a generation before. The transition in transport technology had made both the "returned Yank" and the "American tourist" more commonplace figures in the Irish countryside.

Undoubtedly, there is no simple or singular explanation for the exceptionally low rate of return to Ireland from the USA. Clearly, in rational, economic terms, there was little in Ireland to draw migrants home. However, one could point to similar circumstances in other parts of Europe, which conversely experienced heavy rates of return, such as southern Italy (60%). The fact that Ireland experienced such consistently heavy emigration in the seven decades after 1840 meant in a real sense that there were fewer people – family, friends, neighbors, and relatives – to induce migrants to come back to their place of nativity or earlier settlement in Ireland. The relatively modest rates of return were also connected with the even gender balance of the transatlantic emigrant flow from Ireland. Women were less predisposed to return, and the even gender balance reduced the imperative for young adults wishing to marry within the ethnic group to recross the ocean to find a suitable partner. The extent to which emigration became such an ingrained aspect of life in post-Famine Ireland, an anticipated stage in the life cycle, should not be forgotten. As primogeniture and the consolidation of farms replaced partible inheritance and the subdivision of holdings during the 19th century, siblings who came back had no obvious niche at home and could return to quite a precarious situation. The particular custom often enacted in rural Ireland on the eve of departure – the "American wake" or "living wake" – reinforced the idea of the permanence of the departure. The wake was an Irish funeral custom and this consciously emotionally charged ritual equated emigration with death. It served to remind emigrants to remember the home farm in their letters and remittances rather than necessarily turning up again on the doorstep to stay permanently.

Ultimately, the answer to this question of low return migration may lie more in the USA than Ireland. Certainly from the 1880s on, as the volume of emigration from southern and eastern Europe began to overtake that from northern and western Europe, there are solid grounds for regarding Irish immigrants as enjoying certain distinct advantages in the New World. The very fact that they had a well-established and influential Irish American ethnic network to offer support was one factor. More significant

still was the fact that the majority of those Irish migrants passing through Ellis Island to the USA were white and literate in English. Comparative analysis of the relative ease or difficulty of integration among ethnic immigrant groups, including those coming to the USA from across the Pacific as well as the Atlantic, shows that immigrants from Ireland, whether Protestant or Catholic, enjoyed a relatively privileged position by this stage.

Finally, let us look at the experience of return migrants once they had disembarked in Ireland. Although returnees had generally acquired or enhanced skills in the USA, the extent to which this contributed to innovation or modernization in Ireland was blunted by the fact that most returned to an agricultural, rural environment in Ireland from a predominantly urban, industrial USA. Readjustment to "Irish ways" was undoubtedly taxing for many, and the estimation that a similar proportion (10%) of those who came back to Ireland returned again to the USA may be indicative of such difficulties. Many went back into a rural world, with more apparently drawn toward north Leinster and the northwest of Ireland, where access to land was more open than would have been the case in the south and west. Those not taking up farms could invest New World savings in a shop, pub, or spirit-grocery. Many returnees in early 20th-century Ireland became pub owners, and some also combined this with the role of emigrant agent. Thus they could profit in Ireland from their experience overseas and play their part in encouraging other Irish emigrants.

There was inevitably enormous variation in the experience of individual returnees but one should be cautious of underestimating the difficulty of reintegration even after a relatively short sojourn in the USA. Irish rural society had become conditioned to accepting the gaps in their ranks left by the departed and had very little experience of other immigrant arrivals. Even the familiar face of someone who had done well or was thought to have done well overseas could find many detractors who resented that success and were not slow to give voice to their feelings. Those who returned not having "made it" in the "land of opportunity" would equally expect to encounter many ready to deride their failure. Many of the patterns relating to reintegration persisted into the 20th century. With the relatively rapid expansion of the economy in the Republic of Ireland in the 1990s and the more positive representation of the Irish diaspora in the USA, those who have returned perhaps found the process less problematic than it once was.

Eccles Wight, J. "'It Is a Lonesome Thing to Be Away from Ireland Always': Returned Emigrants." *Irish Roots* 25 (1998): 12–13.

Fitzgerald, Patrick. "'Come Back Paddy Reilly': Aspects of Irish Return Migration 1600–1850." In *Emigrant Homecomings: The Return Movement of Emigrants 1600–2000*, edited by Marjory Harper, 32–54. Manchester, 2005.

Fitzpatrick, David. "Emigration, 1801–70." In *A New History of Ireland: Ireland under the Union 1801–70*, vol. V, edited by William E. Vaughan, 562–616. Oxford, 1989.

Fitzpatrick, David. "Emigration, 1871–1921." In *A New History of Ireland: Ireland under the Union 1801–70*, Vol. VI, edited by William E. Vaughan, 606–52. Oxford, 1996.

Gould, John D. "European Inter-Continental Emigration: The Road Home: Return Migration from the U.S.A." *Journal of European Economic History* 9 (1980): 41–111.

Gmelch, George. "Return Migration." *Annual Review of Anthropology* 9 (1980): 135–59.

Schrier, Arnold. *Ireland and the American Migration, 1850–1900.* Minneapolis, 1958.

't Hart, Marjolein. "Irish Return Migration in the 19th Century." *Tijdschrift voor Economische en Sociale Geografie* 76 (1985): 223–31.

Wyman, Mark, *Round-Trip to America: The Immigrants Return to Europe, 1880–1930.* Ithaca, 1993.

Cross-references: Ireland and Northern Ireland; Swedish Return Migrants from the United States, 1875–1930

ITALIAN AGRICULTURAL WORKERS IN SOUTHWESTERN FRANCE SINCE THE 1920S

Laure Teulières

Between 1923 and 1926, approximately 40,000 Italian agricultural workers migrated to southwest France, into what is today the Midi-Pyrénées and Aquitaine regions, and remained there long term. Nearly all the migrants came from the northern part of Italy, principally the provinces of Venetia, Friuli, and Piedmont, also Lombardy and, more marginally, Emiglia and Tuscany. They left their country due to overpopulation and economic hardship. Moreover, a minority left to flee political persecution from the fascists, who had seized power in 1922.

The migration movement began quite abruptly. Until the 1920s, there were only a few Italians in the region – stallholders, small craftsmen, builders, or woodcutters – whereas Spanish immigrants were traditionally well represented. After an initial boom – some commentators spoke of "a rush to Gascony" – the rate of immigration decreased. The fascist government increasingly monitored those seeking to emigrate and limited the number of departures with the help of numerous regulations and bureaucratic obstacles. However, Italians continued to migrate to southwest France, either by leaving Italy without valid papers or by coming legally via other French regions. Some Italian ironworkers or miners, for instance, abandoned their difficult jobs in Lorraine to find employment in agriculture. At that time it was quite easy, even for undocumented migrants, to change jobs due to existing labor shortages in France.

According to the 1936 census, more than 80,000 Italians were settled in the southwest of France. Although the statistics on return migration are not very precise, it was a rare phenomenon, particularly at the end of the 1930s when

Mussolini tried to convince emigrants to move back to their "motherland." Involved in agricultural work and connected with the rural world, the emigrants had already become firmly rooted. After the Second World War, chain migration continued into the 1950s: as a result of family ties and preexisting migratory networks, immigration from Italy to France did not slacken. The main occupational goal remained agricultural work.

Several circumstances contributed to the integration process of the Italian migrants. The favorable sociodemographic framework of southwestern France was the decisive factor in the initial migration movement: due to a constant decrease in the birthrate since the early 19th century, the population was continually declining. The large number of casualties of the First World War accelerated the demographic trend: from 1911 to 1921, southwest France lost about 235,000 inhabitants. The Garonne Valley was particularly hard hit as the region had also experienced emigration away from the countryside. Male agricultural workers were lacking everywhere and Italian rural migration filled this gap. The migration concentrated on the core agricultural areas of the *départements* of Haute-Garonne, Gers, Tarn-et-Garonne, and Lot-et-Garonne as well as the neighboring areas of Lauragais (to the east), Quercy and Rouergue (to the north), Gironde and Périgord (to the west) and Pyrenees piedmont (to the south).

Sociocultural features also played an important role in the successful integration process. From its beginning this immigration was a familial one: men typically went first and sought an appropriate location and then sent for their women and children and sometimes other relatives like parents, siblings, or cousins. Also, the intention of many migrants to settle permanently contributed to a favorable reception in the host society. Their willingness to work eased social accommodation while their strong Catholicism commonly favored a willingness to adapt. They were said to be discreet, adaptable, capable, and hardworking.

Another key factor was that French farmers and landowners, urgently in need of laborers, initially actively promoted the recruitment of Italian migrants. After many unsuccessful attempts to gain local agricultural workers, agricultural associations, local notables, and government authorities encouraged migration from Italy. The Italian peasants were welcomed as a remedy for depopulation and the crisis in agriculture. The majority started as sharecroppers, paying rent in proportion to the harvest, partially or even entirely in kind, which increased the income from previously unprofitable agricultural enterprises – to the great satisfaction of the French owners. A considerable minority of the newcomers settled as landowners from the outset, contributing to a positive image of the entire Italian community. Settlement in this thinly populated area with scattered, isolated farms precluded the concentration of immigrants in closed ethnic communities. Furthermore, shared rural values as well as comparable ways of life and occupational experiences likely had a positive effect on day-to-day interaction with the locals.

However, integration into French society did not always proceed without difficulty, and the Italian state appears to have been the main obstacle to assimilation. Mussolini's policies aimed to preserve "Italianness" and strong patriotism among Italians abroad by means of various social and political organizations run by the Italian consulates. At that time, however, French society viewed suspiciously every manifestation of nationalist attachment to one's home country among foreigners. Therefore, every diplomatic disagreement between France and Italy caused tensions between natives and immigrants. This was the case in 1926 and particularly in the late 1930s, when Rome made claims on French territories, encouraged emigrants to return to their homeland, and finally entered into an alliance with Nazi Germany.

The Second World War worsened the situation. Mobilization in September 1939 caused tremendous resentment in the region: French citizens were drafted whereas their Italian neighbors could remain at their places of employment. When Italy entered the war on the side of Germany against France in May 1940, the French accused the Italians of having "stabbed them in the back" in the middle of a military catastrophe. Italians in France were henceforth considered traitors and enemies – a situation that the signing of an armistice a few weeks later between France and Germany and Italy could do little to change. During the Vichy regime, rumors spread that Italian immigrants were collaborating with the Germans and taking advantage of their privileged position to enrich themselves on the black market. The hatred culminated in the spring of 1943 when young Frenchmen were obliged to go work in Germany while the Italians were again exempt. The events of these years would have a lasting effect. Despite having taken part in the resistance and the struggle for liberation, the Italian community had been discredited. The French never forgave the Italians for the political stance of their home country. In everyday life, a distinct Italophobia prevailed in French public opinion.

Nevertheless, progress in the integration process was also made. The primary school system played an important role, socializing and acculturating children, although Italians did not gain higher or even secondary education until the third generation. Long-term socioeconomic development in France also eased the integration process. The "Thirty Glorious Years" (1944–74) were marked by unparalleled prosperity and profound modernization, especially in rural areas, and the Italian community in southern France profited from these developments. The agrarian reform of 1946 improved the position of sharecroppers, some of whom took out loans and, over the course of several years, acquired their own agricultural enterprises. Moreover, the second generation of migrants entered the labor market when the economy was booming. Many young men who desired a better life entered the construction industry, for which no special training was required, and to this day there are many entrepreneurs of Italian origin in construction. The large and closely knit families also contributed to social advancement, and some successful businessmen improved the image of the entire community of Italian migrants. Naturalizations began in 1930 and remained steady until the Second World War, when all proceedings were stopped. In 1954, the southwest region (i.e., Midi-Pyrénées and Aquitaine) counted almost 80,000 naturalized citizens of Italian descent, one-third of whom were born in Italy. A large survey by the French National Institute of Demographic Studies in 1951 revealed that the population of Italian descent was largely integrated, preserving in the private sphere just a few cultural features brought with them from their home country – particularly eating habits and recipes.

Since the 1950s Italian immigrants in France thus seem to have become gradually invisible as a discrete group. Nowadays, however, there appears to be a trend for a return to an Italian identity, even if, according to the 1999 census, only a small group of approximately 7,000 persons in Midi-Pyrénées still possess Italian citizenship. In general, the interest of subsequent generations in their ancestors' past depends on how well their parents fared in French society. Some look for their roots in an attempt to revive their "Italianness." Although the migrants and their offspring possess only a residual identity, Italian associations have succeeded in preserving and passing on their beloved symbolic patrimony. The public events, meetings, commemorations, and language courses for teenagers and adults they offer meet with great popularity. The phenomenon of city partnerships between municipalities in Italy and southwest France is also particularly revealing. Their number has increased steadily from the late 1980s thanks to initiatives from migrant associations. In most cases, the partnerships are oriented around a cross-border migratory network between the departure sites in Italy and the destination sites in France and thus contribute to the preservation of historic ties between two European regions.

Guillaume, Pierre, ed. L'immigration italienne en Aquitaine. Talence, 1988.

Rouch, Monique, ed. "Comprar un prà." Des paysans italiens disent l'émigration (1920–1960). Talence, 1989.

Rouch, Monique, and Carmela Maltone, eds. Sur les pas des Italiens en Aquitaine au vingtième siècle. Talence, 1998.

Saint-Jean, Dominique. "L'intégration des Italiens dans le Sud-Ouest." Hommes et migrations (1994), no. 1134: 22–8.

Teulières, Laure. Immigrés d'Italie et paysans de France (1920–1944). Toulouse, 2002.

Teulières, Laure. "Rural Dimensions at Stake: The Case of Italian Immigrants in Southwestern France." In Paths of Integration: Migrants in Western Europe (1880–2004), edited by Leo Lucassen, David Feldman, and Jochen Oltmer, 63–77. Amsterdam, 2006.

Cross-references: France; Italy; Italian Industrial Workers in Western and Central Europe in the Late 19th and Early 20th Centuries

ITALIAN ICE CREAM MAKERS IN EUROPE SINCE THE LATE 19TH CENTURY

Frank Bovenkerk and Loes Ruland

The seasonal migration of Italian ice cream makers from the 37 villages of the parallel valleys of Zoldo and Cadore in the northern Italian Dolomites (as well as the cross valley with the village of Cibiana connecting the two) into what are today all countries of Europe established itself in the second half of the 19th century. Austria, Germany, and the Netherlands were among the initial destination countries. Even at the beginning of the 21st century, a majority of Italian ice cream makers and their families continue to return every year in October to their home villages in (often very expensive) cars bearing foreign license plates.

The international trade show for ice cream making (Mostra internazionale del Gelato), established in 1960 and held in the first week of December in Longarone (between the valleys of origin along the main artery from Venice to the north), is still today completely dominated by ice cream makers from the region. Here the entrepreneurs gather to share their experiences and compare the economic opportunities in the various target countries.

Already at the end of the Middle Ages, the region from which the seasonal migrants originated had been economically exploited to its ecological limits. The monetary economy that penetrated this part of the Dolomites as early as the 11th century under the influence of Venice led in the valleys to economic structures that went beyond agricultural self-sufficiency. In all valleys, hemp and flax as well as rye and barley were cultivated for the market. The Cadorini family was active especially in forestry, until a flooding of the Piave in 1882 washed away most of the sawmills. Between the 13th and the 17th centuries, the Zoldani mined iron ore and subsequently developed a metal industry – which flourished until 1900 – by processing scrap iron brought in by mules. They also manufactured barrel staves and oars and engaged in charcoal making. Cottage industry during the winter months took on a special importance in the valleys: some villages specialized in the production of glasswares and glasses, in tinkering, and in other repair work. Beginning in the Middle Ages, the Cadorini additionally established themselves in the transport business along the trade route between Venice and southern Germany across the Brenner Pass.

Flexibility and early, small-scale migrations (e.g., trading migrations to sell products manufactured by the cottage industry) characterized the economy of the valley dwellers. The direct precursors to the ice cream makers went into the large cities of northern Italy in the winter to sell pears and chestnuts, the latter kept warm in small copper kettles that sat atop a small, smoldering charcoal fire which they carried with them with a strap around their shoulders and on a pillow to protect their stomachs.

The technique for producing ice cream is said to have been developed in China thousands of years ago. The first reliable European sources reveal that the sweet was consumed in the 17th century at the courts in Italy and France. A mixture of frozen water and salt made it possible to cool the mostly white, milk-based ice cream. The cultural innovation that the *Gelatieri* brought to their target countries lay in the production of water ice enriched with fruit extracts. The production took its cues from the fruit that was available in the target countries at any given time. The strictly secret recipes became part of a family's culture and ice making was styled into an art form and a calling.

Ice cream makers took pains to work in a sanitary manner. The squeaky clean ice palaces of marble and steel that have been erected since the 1980s reflect these efforts. After World War II, ice cream makers increasingly adjusted to youth culture and the purchasing power of their young customers. Beginning in the 1960s, ice cream makers followed the herds of tourists to the beaches of the Mediterranean in Spain and Italy. Especially the ice cream parlors in Germany developed in the 1960s into an integral part of leisure culture at a time when the first "vacation wave" had taken the West Germans to Italy.

The ice cream industry that emerged in the 20th century put the *gelatieri* on the defensive. Ice cream makers tried to secure their market position by placing special emphasis on hygiene, introducing ever new varieties, and cultivating family recipes in an almost cult-like fashion. The individualistically minded entrepreneurs even started to organize. In Germany at the beginning of the 21st century, around 1,500 ice cream makers with 2,200 ice cream parlors are organized in UNITEIS (Union der italienischen Speiseeishersteller, Union of Italian Ice Cream Makers), which was founded in 1969, and about half of the 150 Italian ice cream makers in the Netherlands are members of ITAL (Vereniging van Italiaanse ijsbereiders in Nederland, Association of Italian Ice Cream Makers in the Netherlands).

Migration began in the 19th century as a seasonal migration of men to secure a livelihood and developed into the seasonal commuting of entire families who spent the winter in their home communities. The fact that *gelatieri* rent out their stores during the winter (for example, to a complementary fur business) and return to Italy is no longer an economic necessity at the beginning of the 21st century, but a luxury they can afford thanks to their extraordinarily good income during the summer. According to estimates, 80% of ice cream makers from the Val di Zoldo still return to their native villages in the winter.

The pioneers of the migration are still held in high esteem by ice cream makers from the province of Belluno at the beginning of the 21st century. Silvio Molin Pradel was one of the first *gelatieri* in Austria (Vienna) in 1886, and Guido De Lorenzo opened his business in the Netherlands (Utrecht) in 1928. Once the business had been established – a mobile trade often turned into an ice cream parlor – the men, in the next phase of migration, brought along their families and sometimes also neighbors or acquaintances, who after some years as employees opened their own stores in other towns.

Later, the seasonal migration was so common among the residents of the immediate regions of origin that the owners of ice cream parlors were forced to recruit employees from a larger region and to fall back on the province of Treviso to the south.

The chain migration led to typical settlement patterns. Germany, for example, was home largely to Zoldani, while those who had settled in the Netherlands were chiefly Cadorini. Such structures can reach down to the village level: the residents of Fornesighe migrated to Hungary, while the Vodesi headed for the Netherlands.

Vienna was the first center of ice cream making, and it flourished here until the outbreak of World War I in 1914. No fewer than 22 families with an estimated size of several hundred individuals dominated the Viennese market for ice cream. In Vienna, the handcarts developed into the first ice cream parlors: in 1894, the Viennese authorities denied the Italian seasonal migrants a license in order to protect the domestic street vendors. In response, the Italians set up their first parlors. After the war, many of them returned to the city while others tried to set up their businesses farther north, in Germany and the Netherlands. World War II brought another temporary interruption in the spread of ice cream makers from the province of Belluno across all of Europe. At the beginning of the 21st century, Vienna has 115 ice cream parlors, 49 of which are Italian. Of those, 20 are being run by families from the Val di Zoldo in the third or fourth generation. The rest belong to other northern Italian families, chiefly from the province of Treviso, whose members had initially migrated as employees of the Zoldani.

While approximately 10–15 ice cream–making families had opened a store temporarily in Triest and along the Dalmatian coast between the late 19th century and the end of World War I, some ice cream makers migrated from Vienna to Hungary as early as the 1880s. In 1885 they made it to Budapest and from there to other cities in Hungary. Their immigration peaked in that country around 1900. After World War I they resumed their seasonal migration, and in 1930 there were 20 families from the Val di Zoldo in Budapest.

Before World War I, the *gelatieri* had 20 ice cream parlors in Prague, and from there they went to other cities in Bohemia and Moravia. Breslau and the industrial cities in Upper Silesia were the first destinations in northern east-central Europe. The heyday of the Italian ice cream business in Poland was in the 1930s, when that country must have had hundreds of ice cream parlors. Before World War I, the ice cream makers had even penetrated as far as Tallin, Riga, and Kaunas. Today, Stockholm still has the ice cream parlor of Zoldano Pietro Ciprian. He arrived in 1905, married a Swedish woman, and had some economic success in the 1920s.

However, the business of his successor cannot match the ice palaces in Germany, which can accommodate 70–80 guests on average. Both in number and in terms of economic success, the Italian ice cream makers in Germany rank at the top in Europe. Of all Italians who have organized in UNITEIS, 29% are Zoldani and 16% are Cadorini. Twelve

Italian ice vendors in Utrecht (The Netherlands) on the verge of the Second World War (*De Lorenzo*).

percent originate from other towns and villages in the province of Belluno. They are spread evenly across the country and are no longer found only in larger cities. Their rule of thumb is that it is possible to set up an ice cream parlor in every town of more than 3,000 inhabitants. Those from the Val di Zoldo are for the most part of the second, third, or even fourth generation. A mere 17% of the Zoldani say that they are newcomers. Among the Cadorini, a majority is likewise from at least the second generation; 38% are newcomers. By contrast, among the ice cream makers from the province of Treviso, 88% are the first generation in Germany.

The willingness of the *gelatieri* and their families to commute between Italy and Germany is on the decline. Some now select Germany as the center of their life and are sending their children – who previously had spent part of the season with the grandparents in the region of origin – to German schools. Bilingual education is very important to the families: the "Italian identity" must not be lost.

Ampezzan, Don Ernesto. *Storia Zoldana*. Belluno, 1985.

Bovenkerk, Frank, Anna Eijken, and Loes Ruland. *Ijscomannen en schoorsteenvegers*. Amsterdam, 2004.

Catomeris, Christian. *Gipskattor och Positiv, Italienare i Stockholm 1896–1910*. Stockholm, 1988.

Fini, Franco. *Cadore e Ampezzano*. Bologna, 1981.

Panciera, Donato, Paolo Lazzarin, and Tarcisio Caltran. *Wie das Eis entstand. La storia del gelato*. Verona, 1999.

Cross-references: Austria; Germany; Italy; The Netherlands; Northern Europe; Southeastern Europe; Spain and Portugal

ITALIAN INDUSTRIAL WORKERS IN WESTERN AND CENTRAL EUROPE IN THE LATE 19TH AND EARLY 20TH CENTURIES

René Del Fabbro

"The Chinese of Europe" – that is what contemporary observers called the hundreds of thousands of Italian migrant workers who sought work and bread on the other side of the Alps in the decades before World War I. On the one hand, attributes like hardworking, thrifty, and quiet were thus attached to the Italians, while on the other hand, they were given – primarily from the ranks of the workers' movement – labels such as "wage depressors," "dirty competitors," or even "strikebreakers." Especially the labor markets of France, Switzerland, Austria, Germany, Luxembourg, and Belgium experienced – at different times – a strong influx of Italian workers, an influx that surged explosively shortly before the turn of the century. The term *Transalpini*, which is now commonly used for Germany, can be taken as a collective term for the entire migratory movement across the Alps, since its social structures were decidedly homogeneous.

The Italian migration to Europe was initially a periodic (seasonal) or temporary (multiyear) labor migration of persons eager to earn a living for a limited period of time. Accordingly, the group was referred to in contemporary terminology as *ausländische Wanderarbeiter* in Germany (foreign migrant workers) or *Saisoniers* in Switzerland (seasonals). However, already before World War I there were signs that the immigrant group was assimilating culturally to the native population. World War I constituted a turning point for the integration of the Italians into their European host countries: especially the highly mobile segment among the immigrants returned home after the outbreak or the end of the war; the segment that had already established closer ties in the host country remained there. The migrations northward in the decades before World War I should not be seen in isolation from the geographic population movements later on, as they formed a kind of bridgehead for all subsequent transalpine proletarian migration streams of the 20th century, which were closely interconnected with the older immigrations.

Between high mobility and stabilization: patterns of movement

Of the total volume of 14.5 million, officially registered Italian emigrants between 1876 and 1915, 7.6 million were part of the "wet," transatlantic migration to the USA, and 6.1 million belonged to the "dry" migration within Europe. The Italian migration statistics, whose numbers tend to be too low especially for the continental migration, recorded during this period 1.7 million emigrants to France, more than 1.4 million to Austria, more than 1.3 million to Switzerland, and more than 1.2 million to Germany. Along the way, the focal points shifted, as France increasingly lost its dominant position as the primary destination country of the Italians. The Habsburg monarchy also lost its attraction and recorded the fastest decline in the immigration of Italian workers. By contrast, Switzerland and Germany saw a rising influx of immigrants: before 1890, the two countries received only around 10% of the migrant laborers, but after the turn of the century they regularly received about 30% and 25%, respectively.

In 1910–11, the statistics of the host countries that were collected in the winter showed a total of 420,000 Italians in France, just under 200,000 in Switzerland, 104,000 in Germany, and around 80,000 in Austria. The figures were much higher still during the height of the season in the summer. The ratio of Italians within the total population was by far the highest in Switzerland at 5.4%. France, with a stagnant demographic trend, recorded more than 1% Italians, while the share was less than 1% in Germany and Austria.

The end of the 19th century witnessed an almost explosive surge in the number of migrants and a geographic expansion in both the regions from which migrants left and where they went. In Germany, 23,000 Italians were in the country in the winter of 1895, and by the same time five years later the number had soared to 70,000. Switzerland recorded a growth from 42,000 in 1888 to 117,000 by the turn of the century. In France and Austria, by contrast, the rise – from an already high level – was only moderate. What explains the rapid rise in the readiness to leave one's home, which spread almost like a "wandering fever" from the north of Italy to the south, was – apart from demographic, economic, and domestic political problems – the breathtakingly fast expansion of the European railroad network also in the Alpine region. That expansion made possible the large-scale, fast, and cost-effective transport of workers – on tracks, through tunnels, and over bridges that had for the most part been laid and built with the migrants' own hands.

In France, the transalpine migrants ended up chiefly along the Mediterranean coast (Départements Alpes Maritimes, Bouches de Rhône, and Var), in the northeast (Département Meurthe-et-Moselle), and in the southeast of Paris. The port city of Marseille, alone, was home to about a third of all migrants to France. In northern Switzerland, the target destinations of the immigrants were – apart from the large cities of Zurich, Bern, Lucerne, and Basel – primarily the Cantons of Basel-Land, Thurgau, Wallis, Waadtland, Neuchâtel, Geneva, Graubünden, and St. Gallen. In southern Germany, the states of Bavaria, Baden, and Württemberg were focal points of the immigration; in Austria they were the Cisleithanian regions of the Empire. Numerically smaller branches of the migration movement reached nearly all European states. In turn, regional and local focal points of immigration emerged in the various countries, with the border region of Germany, France, Luxembourg, and Belgium becoming the center and hub of the Italian migration. The geographic origins of the Italians within the host countries was clearly marked by the geographic proximity to the destination countries. However, after the turn of the century many Italians from the Romagna and Abruzzi were also found in France, Germany, and Switzerland.

Despite the clustering of the *Transalpini* in several – mostly industrial – locations, the Italian labor migrants were generally distributed across the immigration regions in groups ranging in size from small to very small. The penchant for forming colonies was weak. This settlement pattern was also a result of the fact that the diverse groups of brickmakers and quarry and construction workers labored either widely dispersed in largely rural areas or followed construction sites that moved across the landscape (railroads, tunnels, canals, defensive fortifications).

As one would expect for labor migrants, four characteristics applied to the *Transalpini* with respect to gender, age, family status, and occupational status: they were male, young, single, and active. However, in the period between the turn of the century and World War I, the ratio of women to men increased as a result of the migration of working women and nonworking wives and the birth of female children. Conversely, the ratio of unmarried to married workers and the ratio of those gainfully employed to unemployed declined, while the rise in the number of children led to a drop in the average age.

Developments that were roughly comparable across Europe also occurred with respect to the occupational structure. It is striking that with the exception of southeastern France, the agricultural sector was almost entirely avoided. The numbers are most striking for Germany. In 1907, there was a grand total of 864 agricultural laborers alongside 121,000 industrial workers. The lion's share of Italian workers were employed in the construction sector and its affiliated occupations (bricklayers, stonecutters, excavators, brickmakers, tunnel builders, plasterers, terrazzo layers, and asphalters). In Switzerland around 1910, 90% of the workers in railroad, tunnel, and cable car construction were foreigners and thus in this case nearly entirely Italians. In addition, a growing number of these southern Europeans worked in the mining and smelting industries, which were not seasonal and therefore promised steady employment. Tens of thousands of very young Italian women worked in the textile industry with its traditionally low wages.

Although a considerable percentage of the migrants were skilled workers with an artisanal tradition, the rise in the number of *Transalpini* after the turn of the century also entailed a decline in professional qualifications. Odd-job men and unskilled laborers, especially hosts of excavators and transportation workers, increasingly dominated the stream of migrants numerically. This gave rise to a pronounced occupational proletarization or even subproletarization.

Nowhere, with the exception of the special case of Marseille, did the *Transalpini* form larger and stable, genuine immigrant colonies. What the relevant sources refer to as colonies were entities characterized by strong fluctuations, transitory "cultural sluice gates" (Klaus J. Bade) that were grouped around small, fixed cores. The typical length of stay by an Italian at a place of employment was between several weeks and a few months. In addition, however, there were a few smaller, stable settlement colonies especially of miners, for example, along the Ruhr or in northern France, some of whom were deliberately immobilized by entrepreneurs because they represented a valuable workforce.

When it comes to the formation of neighborhoods, one must therefore distinguish very precisely between genuine colonies of stationary immigrants and transitory structures that were characterized by a strong flux of migrant workers. In Switzerland, for example, the Italians lived in veritable slums that were called "Italian quarters" or *quartiers italiens* and degenerated into no-go-areas for the native Swiss. In spite of the virtual absence of colony formation in all European host countries, all destination regions showed a clear trend – already before World War I – toward a stabilization of migration processes and the progressive integration of Italians.

In legal terms, the Italians had free access to all labor markets. During the "Golden Age" of unimpeded labor migration, the *Transalpini* did not even need passports to cross the borders heading north. It was only in reaction to the Milan uprising of 1898 that Italy itself introduced a passport requirement for Switzerland in 1901. And characteristically enough, the era of the national states also did not know any measures to regulate the labor market – leaving aside the measures against Polish migrant workers in Prussia, which were largely based on political premises and constituted a special case in Europe. In this regard, the host societies were thus open to the Italians without putting major legal obstacles in their way.

On the whole, the *Transalpini*, in spite of certain tendencies toward stabilization, remained highly mobile until World War I and the vast majority were oriented toward their regions of origin, a posture that encompassed money transfers and regular return trips to Italy as well as the acquisition of land and real estate in their hometowns and villages. However, a small number of migrant workers already embarked on the path of integration and permanent settlement in the destination regions.

"Self-chosen" exclusion and the beginnings of integration

The native populations gave the Italians all kinds of collective names, most of which had to do with their eating habits. *Bolänteschlugger*, *Maisdiiger*, and *Spaghettifrässer* were some of the words that emerged in Switzerland because the immigrants ate polenta or pasta. However, the most common term for the Italians in Switzerland was the peculiar word *Tschingge*. It is derived from the cry of *cinque* or *cinq* in the northern Italian dialect, which the Italians used to conclude the popular outdoor game of Morra. *Eckensteher* (loafers), *Macaroni*, *Les Crispi* (after the Italian prime minister), *Chinesen Europas* (Chinese of Europe), *Chinoise de l'Occident*, or *Polen der Schweiz* (Poles of Switzerland) were other terms and phrases used in Europe to describe the Italian workers.

When local elites – businessmen, diplomats, labor inspectors, scholars – characterized the *Transalpini*, they used stereotypical adjectives like sober, hardworking, intelligent, industrious, docile, and thrifty. This positive view by far outweighed the occasional criticism of the conduct of the migrant workers and did in fact apply to the hardworking and thrifty groups of Italians who often lived in isolation. A deviation from these patterns of behavior and assimilation to the standards of the host country quickly diminished the value of the *Transalpini* to employers. As a result, it could happen that the Italian workers, in the wake of the formation of a new underclass, were replaced by east Europeans who were even less demanding.

In many cases, however, the native proletariat perceived the immigration of Italian workers as the displacement of domestic workers from traditional labor markets. In Upper Bavaria, for example, the labor press in 1876 described the immigration as the "onrushing deluge of Italian labor competition." It went on to say that the Italians had subjected themselves to a "truly beastly way of life," one to which German workers were not accustomed. Thus the migrant workers found themselves in serious conflicts with the strong and tightly organized free unions, especially in Germany. In the heated debates, the migrant workers were given the pejorative labels "scabs," "wage depressors," and "dirty competitors." In all destination countries, the conflicts – in spite of a variety of causes – had their roots in the final analysis in the clash between the interests of migrant workers and those of the natives, or a clash between preindustrial and industrial mind-sets. The migrant workers sought to accomplish their earning goals in the destination countries, ambitious goals and usually limited to a few months of the season, while the workers' movement saw the achievements as a threat to the relationship between employers and workers, the fruit of decades of struggle.

For example, the term *Furlan* was virtually synonymous for "strikebreaker" among German bricklayers around 1900. In many cases, the southern workers were enticed to places where strikes were going on by employers or their agents and were sometimes shielded from local workers by the police; as a result they were to some extent ignorant about their unsupportive behavior. However, at least the *capi-crumiri*, the leaders of the strikebreakers who cooperated with employers, were fully aware of what they were doing.

The behavior of the Italians in their host countries can be explained in part by a mentality that was rooted in the world of small landholding in the mountainous regions from which they hailed: at times this mentality expressed itself in defensively oriented thriftiness but also in a desire for social advancement. Thus many migrant workers arrived at a simple conclusion about unions: "I don't need a workers' organization; I need money and nothing else." Not least, the life in two worlds, characterized by seasonal migration, gave rise to split identities, as exemplified by young workers from the province of Udine, who acted as strikebreakers in Germany and then turned around and presented themselves as "socialists" in their hometowns and villages. Different from these workers were the unskilled agricultural laborers from the Po valley, which was characterized by large-scale landholding, and the mountainous regions of central Italy with their archaic structures: these laborers were considered troublemakers. The penchant for rebelliousness expressed itself by these workers in spontaneous actions, primarily walking off the job, occasionally accompanied by threats of violence against employers.

German workers' organizations sought to defend their achievements through educational work by means of leaflets, meetings, informational trips to the places the migrant workers came from, and the Italian-language newspaper *L'Operaio Italiano*, first published in 1898. These efforts had some – if modest – success. Following serious clashes around the turn of the century, one unionist noted in 1912 the almost complete disappearance of strikebreaking. The pressure on wages exerted by the migrant workers and the excessively long working hours remained in place. However, that was only true of jobs where the immigrants were directly competing with native workers, but not of those that were avoided by Germans because they were dirty, strenuous, and unhealthy. Moreover, the number of Italians who were organized into the free unions remained low – in Germany in 1912 it was a little over 7,000. On the whole, the assimilation of the Italians to the working conditions of the destination country progressed only slowly.

French, Swiss, and Austrian unions had to wrestle with problems similar to those confronting their German counterparts. With the influx of socialist and anarchist circles, and thus of an intellectual elite, the political organization of the Italians in Switzerland was more highly developed than in any other destination country. There was even a Socialist Party (Partito Socialista Italiano in Svizzera) with the relevant suborganizations. Conflicts between immigrants and natives could be channeled somewhat better within the institutional framework.

Internal class opposition between native and foreign proletariats usually formed the starting point for acts of violent xenophobia, which struck the *Transalpini* with varying degrees of brutality in the various host countries. Virtual anti-Italian pogroms with numerous fatalities and dozens of injured occurred in France in Marseille (1881), in Lyon (1894), and especially in Aigues Mortes (1893). Countless numbers were injured during the "Italian riots" in the large cities of Switzerland, during which the population's "Tschingen hatred" exploded: Bern 1893, Zurich 1896, and Basel 1900 and 1904. By contrast, violent attacks remained a marginal phenomenon in Germany.

In all destination regions there are indications of a clearly felt gulf between northern and southern Italians. For example, in 1906 the office of trade inspection in Lorraine described it as a "worrisome accompanying manifestation" of the Italian migration that it included a steadily rising number of "weak and degenerate south Italians, who are poisoning the native population with their dirty and corrupt mores." Analogously, in France the northern Italians were regarded as easy to assimilate, while south Italians were considered incapable of integration. This north-south contrast found its expression, for example, in the pronounced differentiation by the French police between *Piémontais* and *Napolitains*. German employers preferred northern Italians as workers, especially those from the Veneto; the Romagni were less popular, while the Abruzzi were seen as very lazy. Job ads in the Italian emigrant paper *La Patria* were occasionally looking explicitly for *Furlani* or "northern Italians." The sociocultural ascriptions that went along with this were articulated not only by the native population. The dividing line – analogous to the internal Italian centrifugal forces that were part of the *Mezziogiorno* problem – was certainly brought up by the Italians themselves. A contemporary *Furlan* witness emphasized the north-south contrast by praising the *Furlani* as the best brickyard workers, in contrast to the "Neopolitans," who "never feel like working."

The forces of group cohesiveness within the *Transalpini* were weak, with the exception of the factors of place of origin and kinship ties. They liked to portray Italy as an allegorical stepmother who denied her sons a living in their own land, or they went so far as to revile her as *porca Italia* – the "Italian swine." Group cohesion thus hardly operated through cohesive forces with a national or merely regional motivation; instead, it manifested itself primarily in a way of thinking the Italians call *campanilismo* (from *campanile*, church tower), which did not look beyond the boundaries of one's own place of origin or kinship bonds. This attitude was abetted by the fact that the Italians in most cases did not leave their homes as individual migrants but in larger groups of sometimes as many as two or three dozen interrelated individuals of the same local origin. Under the leadership of a subcontractor, called *capo* or *Akkordant*, they lived during their months abroad in direct proximity to their workplace in some kind of "voluntary prison." Because they spoke different dialects (the Ladini language of the *Furlani* is even a separate language), the various regional groups could hardly communicate with one another. No small number of Italians were illiterate.

The proportion of self-employed among the *Transalpini* remained relatively low in all host countries, also in comparison to other immigrant nationalities (for example, 1.4% in Germany in 1907, 6% in Switzerland in 1905). Still, the sources do contain numerous clues pointing to the initiatives of Italian entrepreneurs, primarily in the construction industry and its supply sectors. In many cases the founding of a business was done with the simplest means. "A canvas was being laid on top of a trestle above some blocks of stone and the 'new granite works' are opened," wrote one author about Italians in Baden. But there were also larger Italian companies, for example, in specialized trades like the making of terrazzo floors. For the most part, though, they were small family businesses that employed almost exclusively relatives of the owner. There were very few workers' pubs and guesthouses or grocery stores that had been set up by Italians.

Before World War I, the *Transalpini* developed in all destination regions only the weakest rudiments of clubs and associations. Alongside a few organizations of the bourgeoisie, chiefly welfare and aid associations, we find only sporadic indications of proletarian initiatives, most of which involved music, theater, or sports. Cologne, for example, had a Società Operaia Italiana, and Stuttgart had a Sezione Edile Italia, both of which created theater groups. Ückingen in Lorraine was home to a few short-lived bike racing clubs. The Union musicale italienne founded in Lyon in 1885 had a grand total of 32 active members, while 23 individuals belonged to the Armonia Italia, which was set up in the same year.

The exceedingly weak development of a separate system of clubs and associations should be seen, on the one hand, as the result of the very high horizontal mobility among the migrant workers within the destination regions and the anemic formation of entrenched colonies, but on the other hand also a sign of a willingness to assimilate. Thus among *Transalpini* who were immigrants already before World War I one can note a tendency to become very active in local clubs and organizations. Another reason was undoubtedly also the dispersed pattern of migration, because in many cases there were simply not enough Italians in one place to set up associations.

Geographically, the *Transalpini* moved overwhelmingly within Catholic regions. France and Austria were considered Catholic powers plain and simple. In the German Empire, the chief areas into which Italians migrated were precisely coterminous with the region referred to as "Catholic Germany." The biggest friction between Italians and Swiss, the "Italian riots," occurred in cities with a Protestant imprint: Zurich, Bern, and Basel. Here there were repeated clashes with members of the Protestant petty bourgeoisie, to whom the Italians, *ultramontan* in the literal sense of the word, were suspect because of their "different" way of life. For the Italians, the transnational Catholicism could constitute a bridge, so to speak, from the region they left to the host society. Generally, however, the specific circumstances of life in migration had a secularizing effect on the highly mobile segment of migrants who were disconnected from their home communities.

Public perception in the destination countries was that the rates of crime were far higher among Italian migrant workers than among the local population. Especially the gravitational center of Italian migration in Europe, the prospering industrial region in the border area of Belgium, Germany, France, and Luxembourg, won a sad notoriety in the eyes of contemporaries. This is already attested by labels such as "Transvaal," "Klondyke," and "Tour de Babel" for the Arrondissement Briey in the year 1909. Rumor had it that the largely unmarried Italian workers had indulged in veritable "saturnalia" in their taverns run by fellow Italians. In Villerupt, for example, there were around 100 canteens and cafés in 1912, and there were 1,300 applications for permits for dances. The local papers did their part with reports about "bloody murders" by Italians – the picture of the knife- or gun-wielding Italian had wide currency.

A superficial look at crime statistics could confirm the suspicion that Italians were more criminal than members of other nations or the natives. However, the demographic makeup of the immigration was very different from that of the local population in terms of age, gender, and social status. As in every population, the majority of crimes were committed by a group that was strongly overrepresented among migrant workers: young men from the lower classes. The criminality of the Italians took place for the most part within their ethnic subgroup. The habit of some Italians – especially those from central Italy – to carry weapons like knives or even guns, which were used with an astonishingly low threshold of inhibition, led to the often very bloody outcome of fights. Especially the acts committed by the Abruzzi point to divergent notions of honor and law, not only between the immigrants and the local population but also between Italians from the north and those from the south. As the adjusted statistics make clear, only a small minority of Italians were prone to acts of violence. To a certain extent, however, the deviant behavior of these few shaped the image of the entire group, which was eyed by the public with suspicion.

In general it can be stated that while many marriages were concluded between Italians and native women before World War I, marriage behavior was largely endogamous all the way into the second generation. In fact, in the final years before the war, marriages between Italian partners increased because more Italian women spent time abroad. What is true of men did not apply in the same degree to women. In a sample of 1,000 Italians in Lyon at the turn of the century, 189 heads-of-household could be identified, of whom no fewer than 40 had married a French woman. At the same time, of the 385 Italian women of the sample, only 10 lived with a French partner. Among the 105 married Italians who became naturalized citizens between 1899 and 1914, 61 had married a French woman.

The transalpine mobility of work largely ground to a halt with the outbreak of World War I and the waves of return migration it triggered. Between 1 August and 15 September 1914, nearly 620,000 returnees from Germany, France, and Austria were counted in Italy. France, in particular, because of the political constellation (Italy was a member of the Triple Alliance), saw the outbreak once again of an open and in part violent hostility toward the Italians. The immigrants were all but forced by French workers to return home. While the border regions between Germany, France, and Belgium – which now constituted military battle or security zones – were completely depopulated of Italians, by no means all of the *Transalpini* returned to their homeland. In neutral Switzerland, many Italians returned to their jobs shortly after the outbreak of the war. About 25,000 Italians remained in Rhineland and Westphalia. In most cases these were workers who had family members in the country or German wives. Following Italy's entry into the war against Germany in August 1916, the Italians were declared to be hostile foreigners who were required to register with the police. Still, the interest in the urgently needed workers always trumped that interest in political reprisals. It was only the shortage of jobs after the end of the war that prompted most Italians to leave Germany, or they were asked by the authorities to do so.

From migrant workers to immigrants

Italian migration into Germany and into Austria, which was also struggling with economic problems, no longer played a meaningful role in the 1920s. The continuity of migration on the scale of the prewar period ruptured. In 1922, the principle of primacy for natives was legally enshrined for the German labor market: it stipulated that an employer could hire a foreigner only if he had demonstrated that no German was available to fill the job. By 1925, the number of Italians in Germany who were in an immigration situation was down to a mere 24,000. It was only from the end of the 1930s that several hundreds of thousands of Italian workers returned into what was now Nazi Germany. By contrast, after World War I, labor migration into Switzerland and France resumed on a vigorous scale. The influx from Friuli to France, before the war relatively unimportant at 8% of the total volume, now developed an enormous vigor and was overrepresented in formerly German Lorraine. In a sample of 840 individuals, nearly 40% hailed from Friuli. France thus became for the *Transalpini* in the 1920s and early 1930s a replacement option for the lost labor markets in Germany and Austria. The number of Italians in France rose from 420,000 in 1921 to over 760,000 in 1926 and 808,000 in 1931. The southeastern part of Paris experienced a massive influx of Italian migrant workers in the interwar period. Lyon had a total of 28,500 Italians in 1926, well over twice as many as in 1911. Longwy was home to 18,500 Italians in 1931. Because of their *proximité culturelle*, their use in the French economy, which was plagued by a labor shortage, was in fact welcome.

The interwar period saw the emergence of an epochal change in the transalpine migration processes, a change that had merely been hinted at before 1914: highly mobile migrant workers turned into immigrants. Because of the large number of Italians who were present, the intergenerational integration of the *Transalpini* can be studied especially well in France. To a certain extent the stabilization of immigration into France and Switzerland was also helped by political disagreement with Mussolini's fascist regime, which additionally put a damper on the inclination of the Italians to return home. In the second generation, integration made noticeable progress on the most diverse levels, especially in France – measurable by social assimilation with respect to language (literacy), fashion, food, the system of clubs and associations, religion, political participation, profession, marriage behavior, child rearing, and women in the workplace. The rates of naturalization increased and the French picture of the Italians underwent a change. For example, in northeastern France the skilled Italian miners of the second generation were now considered the spearhead of the workers' movement. The intergenerational social integration was promoted by Italian parents, who encouraged their children to socialize with their French schoolmates.

While southeast Paris, for example, witnessed very high mobility still in the 1920s among the Italians, whose preferred work continued to be in construction, a sustained trend toward permanent settlement began in the 1930s, especially among those born between 1895 and 1905. The field of work changed only for the age cohort born between 1920 and 1930, from construction worker to more "modern" occupations such as electrician, car mechanic, or factory worker. Only the third generation of *Transalpini* assimilated also in their marriage behavior. Just under 200,000 Italians became naturalized in France in the period from 1900 to 1940 in accordance with the relevant laws of 1899 and 1927. There is reason to believe that the integration process was a little faster still in Germany and Austria because of the small numbers of Italians and in view of the fact that of the once dispersed immigration, only a few families were still left. The "Chinese of Europe" became French, Swiss, German, and Austrian. Nevertheless, a pronounced, almost "atavistic" propensity toward individualism but also toward transnational thinking is still mentioned as a characteristic of the descendants of Italians.

Bechelloni, Antonio, Michel Dreyfus, and Pierre Milza, eds. *L'intégration italienne en France. Une siècle de présence italienne dans trois régions françaises (1880–1980)*. Brussels, 1995.

Blanc-Chaléard, Marie-Claude. *Les Italiens dans l'est parisien: Une histoire d'intégration (1880–1960)*. Rome, 2000.

Del Fabbro, René. *Transalpini. Italienische Arbeitswanderung nach Süddeutschland im Kaiserreich 1870–1918*. Osnabrück, 1996.

Foerster, Robert F. *The Italian Migration of Our Times*. Cambridge, 1919.

Gabaccia, Donna R. *Italy's Many Diasporas*. Seattle, 2000.

L'immigration italienne en France dans les années 20. Published by the Centre d'études et de documentation sur l'immigration italienne. Paris, 1988.

Manz, Peter. *Emigrazione italiana a Basilea e nei suoi sobborghi 1890–1914. Momenti di contatto tra operai immigrati e società locale*. Comano, 1988.

Noiriel, Gérard. *Longwy. Immigrés et prolétaires 1880–1980*. Paris, 1984.

Wennemann, Adolf. *Arbeit im Norden. Italiener im Rheinland und Westfalen des späten 19. und frühen 20. Jahrhunderts*. Osnabrück, 1997.

Cross-references: Austria; Belgium and Luxembourg; France; Germany; Italy; Switzerland; Italian Labor Migrants in Northern, Central, and Western Europe since the End of World War II; Polish Agricultural Workers in Prussia-Germany from the Late 19th Century to World War II; Southern Italian Workers in Northern Italy, 1945–1975

ITALIAN LABOR MIGRANTS IN NORTHERN, CENTRAL, AND WESTERN EUROPE SINCE THE END OF WORLD WAR II

Yvonne Rieker

The topos *emigrazione* is a permanent part of Italy's historical iconography. That is evident from numerous publications, exhibits, and conferences about *gli italiani all'estero* – the "Italians abroad." The phrase *pezzo di pane*, the "piece of bread" for which one had to take on the burden of migration, has taken on symbolic meaning in Italy.

Italian postwar government saw in the traditional overseas emigration to North and South America or Australia, as well as in the equally traditional intra-European labor migration, a means of supplementing the internal structural reforms, which were slow to get off the ground, and of containing unemployment, underdevelopment, and social protest. Especially the Mezzogiorno south of Rome was suffering from high structural unemployment, poverty, and underdevelopment. Temporary labor migration for the provisional export of unemployment was to be accelerated through treaties with France, Belgium, Switzerland, West Germany, and, quantitatively less important, Great Britain, Sweden, Luxembourg, the Netherlands, Czechoslovakia, and Hungary, as well as by regulations governing freedom of movement on a European level.

The quantitative trend of Italian labor migration is difficult to determine. Still, basic trends can be identified. Switzerland had 140,280 Italian residents in 1950; by 1960 the number had already risen to 346,223. After hitting a peak of 583,850 (1970), their number declined to 418,989 (1980) and 322,203 (2000). In West Germany, the number of Italians rose from 25,802 (1955), to 196,672 (1961), 573,648 (1970), and 617,895 (1980), declining thereafter to 552,440 (1990). By 2001, the number of Italians living in Germany was up again to 601,258. Belgium in 1947 counted 84,134 Italians; in 1961 their number was 200,086, in 1970 it stood at 249,490, in 1981 at 279,700, in 1991 at 241,175, and in 2001 at 195,586. All we have for France are data about the immigration within a specific period of time, but it provides no information about the number of Italians who were in the country at any particular moment: 175,000 (1946–50), 491,000 (1951–60), 898,000 (1961–70), 492,000 (1971–80), 20,000 (1981–5). There were several reasons for the decline – from 1980, at the latest – in the number of Italian residents or immigrants in the four main immigration countries of Switzerland, Germany, Belgium, and France: regulations that made naturalization easier (Belgium), an expansion of recruitment to additional sending countries (Switzerland), and increased return migration as a result of economic crises and structural weakness in the industrial sectors in which Italians were chiefly employed.

Migration substantially altered Italy's socioeconomic condition in the postwar years. Between 1955 and 1971, emigration from rural regions into the industrial areas of northern and central Italy and into the industrial centers of western, central, and northern Europe comprised a total of 9.14 million persons. In the process, a particular effort at adjustment was demanded from the numerically largest group of southern Italian migrants: they had to find their way not only in a world of industrial labor with a comparatively rigid discipline, but also in sociocultural conditions that were completely new for them. What most migrants from southern Italy saw as particularly positive were the regular wage in industry, the resulting ability to plan for the future, increased opportunities for consumption, and regular working hours – the region they came from was dominated by day labor and tenant farming.

Immigration conditions in the destination areas

Immediately after 1945 the migration of Italian workers to France began, some of which was seasonal. It was based on a long tradition that was at times marked by intense conflicts between French and Italian workers. The new migrant workers encountered the 450,800 Italians who were already living in France in 1946. The French government emphatically supported the immigration for reasons of labor market policy. It regarded the integration (culminating in naturalization) of Italian workers and their families as desirable. The government noted a "cultural closeness" between the French and the Italians that eased assimilation. To promote migration, a bilateral agreement was signed in February 1946, which stipulated the immigration of 20,000 workers in 1947. In actuality, the number of immigrants substantially exceeded the parameters set by the government. But Italian workers who had immigrated illegally could legalize their stay without any difficulties. Beginning in 1951, they were immediately granted a residence permit valid for three years, and after five years they received complete freedom of movement.

The Italians in France in the 1940s and 1950s came chiefly from the following areas: the regions of Piedmont and Liguria, in the north Friaul, the Trentino, the Veneto, and the Mezziogiorno (about 58%). Immigration was concentrated in the French mining regions in the northeast; in Paris, where Italians had already been working for some time as small-scale entrepreneurs or in the automobile industry; and in the south. The ratio of Italians among the population was especially high in Nice, Grenoble, Toulon, Marseille, Lyon, and Strasbourg. Until the 1960s, the Italian migration was extremely important to the migratory activities in France: between 1950 and 1955, a total of 76% of permanently employed foreign workers came from the southern neighbor. In 1961, the number of Italians in France stabilized at just under 700,000. The main thrust of the Italian migration had by then shifted toward Switzerland and Germany.

In 1946, Belgium and Italy also signed a treaty for the recruitment of workers who were to be employed in mining. Temporary work contracts were issued, although they could be extended, if necessary, without any bureaucratic hassle. The Italians soon developed into the largest group of foreign workers in Belgium. They hailed primarily from southern Italy, and most went to the heavy industrial zones of Wallonia and to Brussels.

After World War II, Switzerland developed alongside West Germany into the most important destination country for Italian migrant workers. As early as 1945, the Swiss Federal Office for Industry, Trade, and Labor had approached the Italian embassy in Bern to indicate a need for workers. A recruitment treaty was signed in 1948. To keep the permanent immigration of Italians low, the Swiss granted residence permits only after 10 years; unskilled workers were permitted to bring their families into the country only after three years. However, the idea of a rotation of workers that the Swiss government was pursuing could not be implemented for economic reasons. As it was, the turnover rate of Italian workers was nearly 70% in the 1950s.

As early as 1948, Switzerland no longer required a visa for Italians. An employment contract was not necessary for entry into the country. This promoted immigration that was not controlled by the state. Between 1958 and 1960, the proportion of immigrants who entered as "tourists" was 37.5%; by 1962 it had already risen to 54%. Until the end of the 1950s, the Italian migrant workers came mostly from Lombardy, the Piedmont, and the Veneto. Only after northern Italy experienced an economic upswing in the early 1960s did the majority of immigrants to Switzerland come from the Mezziogiorno. While the Swiss government tried to exclude workers from southern Italy from recruitment, the Italian government prevented it from doing so. Moreover, pressure from Italy was able to improve the conditions of immigration in 1964: henceforth, Italian workers would be given preferential treatment after five years when it came to extending their stay, and families could join them after 18 months.

In the recruitment treaty that the German government agreed upon with Italy in 1955, an important role on the German side was played – alongside the rising need for workers reported by employers and caused by the liberal economic policy – by the desire for state regulation and control of the migration. Initially this had consequences for the social and collective wage policy, as the Italian employees were placed on an equal footing with German workers in the social system, something that was in the interest especially of the German unions. Strict border control and targeted recruitment via the "German commission" in Verona were supposed to put a stop to the uncontrolled immigration. However, since the economic conditions favored unimpeded immigration, both German employers and Italian workers were able to successfully circumvent the bureaucratic burdens of state recruitment.

As it was, after the end of 1961 the state's efforts at exerting control were rendered moot by the European Economic Union's (EEC) new regulations on freedom of movement. Hereafter, a valid personal identification card was sufficient to cross the border. While 58.9% of Italian labor migrants in 1959, and no less than 64.6% in 1961, had entered the country through the German Commission, that percentage dropped to 46.5% in 1962 and to 23.6% a year later. The number of Italian workers in West Germany stood at 14,894 in 1957, at 162,250 by 1962, reached a high of 204,288 in 1965, and hovered around 168,300 in 1970. The Italians were not only the first group of foreign labor migrants in Germany; until 1970 they were also the largest. The vast majority came from the Mezzogiorno. Relative to the resident population, emigration to Germany was especially pronounced in Agrigento, Foggia, and Enna; in absolute numbers it was prominent once again in Agrigento and Foggia as well as in Bari. Chain migration played a considerable role, but with varying consequences.

Within the West German government there was a variety of opinions about the permanent settlement of foreign workers. The concept of temporary employment was undercut by the fact that the recruitment treaty of 1955 already allowed family reunification. After 1973, the number of Italians living in West Germany stabilized at around 600,000, with the economic crises at the end of the 1960s and the beginning of the 1970s leading to an extensive return migration as well as accelerated family reunification. Still, West Germany clung to the credo that it was "not an immigration country."

Economic, social, and cultural integration

In the 1960s and early 1970s, the Italians in Germany worked chiefly in the construction sector, in the iron- and metalworking industry, and in other manufacturing sectors. At that time agriculture had only marginal importance for them, even though the state-regulated recruitment of Italian workers was initially intended precisely for this sector. At the beginning of the 21st century, as well, Italian workers were employed far more frequently than their German counterparts in unskilled and semiskilled jobs, while they were far more rarely found in white-collar professions. Public sector jobs were almost completely closed to them. Italian men were found in disproportionately high numbers in jobs involving heavy physical labor, high noise levels, and strong emissions, and Italian women in poorly paid service professions. The proportion of self-employed was higher than the average for other groups of foreigners and was second to the Greeks. This points to the importance of Italian ice cream parlors, restaurants, and retail shops. A majority of these businesses have a high proportion of working family members. Compared to Germans and to the average of foreign groups in the workforce in Germany, the Italians come off badly with respect to both net income and professional advancement within and between generations. In 1989, the percentage of young Italians employed as unskilled and semiskilled workers was about the same it had been in their parents' generation. In addition, unemployment is very high among Italians in West Germany.

In Switzerland, too, the majority of Italians fall into the lowest occupational categories and the lower income groups. Moreover, the 1960s saw a decline in the level of qualifications among the immigrants, most of whom now came from the Mezzogiorno. The percentage of Italians employed in trades and industry (not counting the construction sector) rose from 28.8% in February 1951 to 60.3% in February 1964; the strongest increase was recorded in the metalworking and machine-building industries. By contrast, the number of Italians employed in households and in the hospitality industry shrank. In the face of the labor shortage in Switzerland, it was fairly easy for Italian workers to improve their situation, in part by acquiring skills, in part by becoming self-employed. Some Italians established small family businesses also in this country. A similar constellation prevailed in Belgium, although the structural changes in the economy had a very negative impact on the old industrial regions in Wallonia, the most important immigration

region of the Italians. Measured against the average in the host countries, the social situation of the Italians who had migrated abroad was, on the whole, not favorable. Opportunities for economic advancement were offered especially by the founding of family restaurants and in the food retail sector.

Only France offered a different picture. The social differentiation among the Italian immigrants in that country had to do not least with the strong Italian influx that dated to the decades before 1945. At that early time, already, self-employment had increased among the Italians: native networks were reproduced in France and extended not only to food retail and eating establishments but also to the construction sector and small landholdings. Also unusual was the number of Italian women in the workforce, which was high already in the mid-1970s. All this made the patterns of integration for Italians in France significantly different from those in West Germany, Switzerland, or Belgium. For example, in 1976 the monthly income of Italians in France was above the average for other immigrant groups. Geographically they were not very mobile, and this, in turn, stood in contrast to the other immigration countries, where the turnover and mobility of Italian workers were noticeably higher, and where commuting migration also played a larger role.

The occupational integration of Italian workers in France was also aided by the unions in that country; although they achieved a lesser degree of organization than in West Germany, for example, they had been able to gain experience with immigration from the southern neighbor during the interwar period. The German unions, for their part, were at first slow to take on the concerns of the foreign workers, but then did so vigorously, whereas the Swiss workers' organization did not do so consistently until the 1970s.

The scholastic integration and the prospects of success for young Italians in vocational and professional training were most favorable in France, by far. The assimilation-oriented educational system in France presumably contributed as much to this circumstance as the specific characteristics of the Italian immigration, which are evident in its long tradition and a region of origination that lay primarily in northern Italy. Notwithstanding the pitfalls that bedevil any comparison of different school systems, clear parallels in the alarmingly poor schooling of Italian children can be noted in Switzerland, Belgium, and Germany. In Switzerland, the difficulties that Italian children were experiencing in school did not lessen even as the duration of their stay grew longer, as documented by the consistently high numbers of Italian children in special education schools. In Belgium, the poor scholastic success of young Italians was equal only to that of young Turks. Italians frequently had to repeat a grade and ended up in the lowest types of schools in disproportionately large numbers. The few Italians who had achieved a university degree were compelled – much more frequently than Belgian graduates – to take jobs below their level of qualification.

An analogous educational underperformance by Italian immigrants was evident in West Germany. In the school year 1996–7, the ratio of *Gymnasium* students to special education students was 5:1 among German – and, incidentally, Croatian – children, and 4:1 among Spaniards. By contrast, more Italian children and youngsters were attending a special education school than a *Gymnasium*. The data on vocational and professional training yields a similar picture. It is revealing that Italian girls were achieving noticeably better school diplomas than Italian boys. They were taking advantage of opportunities that were broader here than in the southern Italian society from which they came. But it is equally revealing that in spite of their better education, Italian girls and women had little success in the labor market.

While the indicators of schooling, training, and occupation point to considerable disadvantages and shortcomings among the Italians, surveys speak of a successful social integration when it comes to spheres of life outside of school and work. Representative polls in West Germany in 1985 and 1995 arrived at the unanimous conclusion that Italian men were more likely than immigrants from the other, former recruitment countries to marry a German woman. Findings in France were similar. In 1976, among marriages involving an Italian, 20.6%, were Italian-French marriages compared to 9.6% with spouses of other nationalities. The results were similar when it came to friendships and the sphere of leisure activities. Italians were widely seen as open and communicative. In Germany, in particular, these attributed qualities derived in part from the ubiquity of Italian restaurants, the German fondness for Italy, and tourism to Italy.

Unlike other groups, the Italians who settled in Switzerland, Germany, France, or Belgium did not really establish distinct, separate ethnic communities. However, they frequently lived in close kinship networks and communication circles that facilitated their entry into a foreign environment, and in part these still exist at the beginning of the 21st century. The dissolution of large family units into nuclear families, typical of industrial nations, was slower among southern Italians than among some other immigrant groups. Given this dominance of social relationships based on kinship, the low value placed on more impersonal institutions such as unions, party, or immigrant clubs is hardly surprising.

The high degree of social acceptance of Italians in the destination countries did not go hand in hand with a broad cultural assimilation. That is evident from the persistence of Italian cuisine everywhere. In Belgium, southern Italians often followed traditions from the Mezzogiorno in the design of their homes and gardens, and in their marriage and funeral customs. These Italians were drawn to the Partito Communista Italiano, while the Belgian Communist Party remained without influence. In West Germany, young Italians were found to be much more religious than their German counterparts.

All told, in all four primary destination countries the Italian immigration is very frequently held up as the example of a successful integration and contrasted positively with immigrants of the Muslim faith and with asylum seekers. However, along with the integration shortcomings in school and workplace that are dramatically apparent in Switzerland,

Belgium, and West Germany, the way Italians see themselves also indicates that the picture of the smoothly integrated Italians is too simplistic. The perception in the host societies is an affirmative, at time socioromantic image of Italy, one that hardly coincides with the socioeconomic and cultural situation of the immigrants. Although Italians represent in the eyes of the host societies the "other," they are not the problematic "foreign." Yet the fact that the problems of social and economic advancement, education, and training among Italian immigrants are rarely noticed helps to perpetuate them.

Nationalization rates are low among Italians in Germany. In part that has to do with the long prohibition against dual citizenship, which was lifted for Italians only in 2002 in an agreement between Germany and Italy. Especially in the second and third generation, there is still a desire, even at the beginning of the 21st century, to retain a visible symbol of being part of Italy. Many Italians felt that the need to give up their Italian citizenship when they became German citizens curtailed their possibilities of participating in the democratic process in their country of origin and was an expression of a lack of tolerance.

Switzerland, which – like Germany – was long unwilling to regard itself as an immigration country and where xenophobic tendencies were explicitly directed against Italians at the beginning of the 1960s, allowed dual citizenship in the 1990s. Especially young Italians were vocal about the significance of this option, which granted them the right to vote in elections to the Swiss National Council without having to deny their "roots." In response to this change in Swiss law, the rate of nationalization rose markedly among Italians.

The situation in France was entirely different: between 1946 and 1990, 425,190 Italians became French citizens. Moreover, a child born in France is automatically considered French if one parent is a French citizen. If that is not the case, the child is given citizenship once it reaches the age of majority and if it has lived in France for at least five years. Precisely for that reason, statistics in France recorded only 252,759 Italian nationals in 1990. At the same time, many Franco-Italians emphasized their background through the Italian spelling of their names. In Belgium, the rate of nationalization appears to be not much lower than in France. In addition, the third generation of Italians is automatically granted citizenship if both parents were born in Belgium. However, in this country, as well, young Italians continue to see themselves as part of the Italian nation.

Characteristic of the Italian labor migration to other European countries was a strong fluctuation and a high rate of remigration. For example, about 3.07 million Italians went to West Germany between 1964 (exact figures are available since that year) and 1996, and 2,892,000 left again. What remains unclear is how many migrants went back and forth repeatedly between Italy, Germany, and other countries, since the statistics on arrivals and departures record only raw numbers, not personal data. Remigration can be attributed in part to the employment of many Italians in the low-wage sector of the respective host country, which made a financially secure life in old age difficult there, and in part to the creation of a specific welfare economy in southern Italy. A number of returnees were able to use their savings in their hometowns and villages to purchase a house with a plot of land for a subsistence livelihood, and this, along with benefits from the Italian state, allowed them a modest but secure living.

The undecidedness of many Italians regarding their permanent place of residence influenced the life plans of even the second and third generations. A representative survey in West Germany showed that as late as 1989, only one in three of 15- to 25-year-old Italians indicated the intention of remaining permanently in Germany; 61% of those polled spoke of an uncertain sense of their future or none at all. In a similar study in Switzerland in 1988, half of the Italian young people surveyed reported that they might return to Italy, but they did not articulate any concrete ideas, let alone plans. Even in France, only 54% of the Italian nationals living there had definitively decided in favor of their host country by the mid-1970s.

The roots of this Italian "myth of return" lie in an identity construct that was guided by the desire – now obsolete but still resonating – to return home from abroad as an acknowledged success. Against this backdrop, avoidance of a definitive decision and a view of migration as not final characterize especially the actions of migrants from the Mezzogiorno. The fairly short distances between the homeland and the destination countries, and the freedom of movement that has prevailed within the EEC since 1961, made it possible for the Italians, without many complications, to leave their jobs if they were unhappy with them and perhaps try again later.

Blanc-Chaléard, Marie-Claude, ed. *Les Italiens en France depuis 1945*. Rennes, 2003.

Ginsborg, Paul. *A History of Contemporary Italy. Society and Politics 1943–1988*. London, 1990.

Halter, Ernst, ed. *Das Jahrhundert der Italiener in der Schweiz*. Zurich, 2003.

Perrin, Nicolas, and Michel Poulain. *Italiens de Belgique. Analyses socio-démographiques et analyse des appartenances*. Louvain-la-Neuve, 2002.

Rieker, Yvonne. *"Ein Stück Heimat findet man ja immer." Die italienische Einwanderung in die Bundesrepublik*. Essen, 2003.

Studi Emigrazione. Rivista trimestrale del Centro Studi Emigrazione 42 (2005): *La collettività di origine italiana in Europa occidentale dagli anni 1970 ai giorni nostri*.

Cross-references: Belgium and Luxembourg; France; Germany; Italy; Switzerland; Greek Labor Migrants in Western, Central, and Northern Europe after 1950: The Examples of Germany and the Netherlands; Italian Industrial Workers in Western and Central Europe in the Late 19th and Early 20th Centuries; Portuguese Labor Migrants in Northwestern Europe since the 1950s: The Examples of France and Germany; Spanish Labor Migrants in Western, Central, and Northern Europe since the End of World War II; Southern Italian Workers in Northern Italy, 1945–1975; Turkish Labor Migrants in Western, Central, and Northern Europe since the Mid-1950s

ITALIAN AND OTHER "ALPINE" (GRISONS, TECINO, AND VORARLBERG) ARCHITECTS AND VISUAL ARTISTS IN BAROQUE EUROPE

Michael C. Maurer and Anton Schindling

The history of European art of the Baroque is inconceivable without the contribution of artists from Italy and the Alpine regions. Numerous ecclesiastical residences in the Holy Roman Empire, such as Salzburg (Solari), Würzburg (Petrini, Tiepolo, Bossi), Eichstätt (Gabrieli, Pedetti), and Passau (Carlone), secular courts like Dresden (Chiaveri, Canaletto) and Ludwigsburg (Retti, Frisoni), and monasteries in the Habsburg patrimonial lands, in southern Germany, Switzerland, and outside the Empire in St. Petersburg (Trezzini, Chiaveri, Rastrelli) received the imprint they carry to this day from these itinerant artists.

The international movement of architects and visual artists in the Baroque period includes a range of migratory events, from seasonal migrations lasting several months to labor migrations with multiyear contracts, all the way to permanent settlement and integration in the destination region. One remarkable phenomenon, unique in the history of contacts and encounters between European regions, are the "Maestri Comacini" (i.e., the masters from Lakes Como and Lugano), men from the Grisons (Misoxans), the Tecino, and not least the Vorarlberg Baroque architects from the Bregenzerwald: architects, painters, and frescoists, plasterers, and sculptors from small, dynamic regions along the old south-north link from northern Italy via the Grisons or Tecino to southern Germany.

The external conditions under which this migration occurred were structurally nearly identical for the departure areas located north and south of the main ridge of the Alps. They arose chiefly from the geographical and demographic conditions of the valley communities in the Alps and the alpine foothills: with these communities having reached the limits of their economic possibilities and suffering subsistence crises, migration – temporary, if nothing else – in various sectors of trade and commerce had to have a balancing effect. Great importance was attached to the monopolization of and specialization in certain crafts by families, villages, or valley communities, which is often attested very early. Around 1500, Misox (Mesolcina) saw the beginning of the emigration not only of builders, but parallel to them also of mercenaries, chimney sweeps, and itinerant traders. In the Bregenzerwald it was initially the shoemakers who, after the Thirty Years' War, sought a living north of the Alps, followed only later by architects, plasterers, and bricklayers. Such occupational traditions and traditional migratory systems, in which the sons at an early age were taken on the road in family and kinship units, often replaced individual migratory decisions. On the one hand, the preconditions for a commercial migration were thus already in place, namely, knowledge about possible employment far from home and the ability to tap into it. On the other hand, the growing demand for skilled workers in the construction and furnishings industries, especially in the period after the end of the Thirty Years' War that was characterized by the desire of the nobility and the clergy for outward representation, led to a growth in employment opportunities and thus also to labor migration. In the territories of the Holy Roman Empire, in particular, the Maestri Comacini and craftsmen from Misox, the Tecino, and Vorarlberg were able to satisfy the sophisticated tastes of clients who took their cues from Italy. In return, the migrant workers could hope for opportunities for economic and social advancement. A corresponding migration of architects and artists from French-speaking regions did not exist (with a few exceptions) even when French art and culture became increasingly a point of reference in the 18th century.

In service to courts and monasteries

The Val d'Intelvi between Lake Lugano and Lake Como, as home to a whole series of artist families connected by kinship ties, is an outstanding example of the places from which the Maestri Comacini originated. By the 17th century, the architects and visual artists of the valley had already been working north of the Alps for generations. Embedded in the artisanal family traditions (Carlone, de Allio, Frisoni, Retti, Lurago), the Comoese, who worked mostly in groups, profited from their kinship connections by recommending one another to important clients. Especially in the art of plastering, the Comoese together with the neighboring Ticinians had a monopoly-like hold in the later 17th and early 18th centuries. Like the Italian painters (Pellegrini from Venice), sculptors (Benedetti from Castione), and theater architects and set builders (Bibiena from Bologna) who journeyed through half of Europe, they transported the current formal language, their artistic self-confidence, and the tight organizational principle of their workshops to the north. In their area of work they would continue to be exemplars and pioneers for local artists. The Comoese crossed territorial and confessional boundaries and could be found at many courts not only seasonally but usually for several years or even permanently.

The men from the Grisons, mostly from the two towns of Roveredo and San Vittore in Misox, were active north of the Alps for more than 200 years. Architects and visual artists from other valley communities in the Grisons never attained the mastery and the renown of those from Misox. Initially, the men from Misox worked primarily as hands-on construction craftsmen with Comoese and Ticinians, who had a much longer tradition as migrants and builders. It therefore comes as no surprise that the Italian-speaking Misoxans and Ticinians were lumped together with the Comoese and referred to as "Italian" artists by foreign contemporaries and for a long time also in art history scholarship. Only at the beginning of the 18th century was a corporative organization established in Misox, of the kind that was found earlier

among the Comoese and in a highly developed form among the baroque architects of Vorarlberg. While the construction crews from the Misox generally returned home in the winter, that is, they worked abroad only seasonally, the architects and artists from the valley remained abroad longer, with some settling permanently within the court environments (Zuccalli, Viscardi, Gabrieli).

It was above all Catholic courts in the Holy Roman Empire – led by the imperial court in Vienna and the court of the Prince-Archbishop of Salzburg (the latter because of his city's geographic location, lively trade, and particularly active artistic contacts) – that held a preeminent place as the conduits and hubs of Italian influence. In Salzburg, which was spared the horrors of war, the early baroque heyday began still during the Thirty Years' War, and it is closely associated with the name of the Comoese Santino Solari (1576–1646), who influenced the construction activity in the archbishopric from 1612 until his death, first as court and later also as fortification architect. The rebuilding of the cathedral signaled the beginning of the Baroque north of the Alps and reflected the influence of Italians in Salzburg, which dominated nearly all spheres of courtly life at that time and was pushed back only toward the end of the 17th century. The churches of Giovanni Gaspare Zuccalli (1667–1717) – Erhard Church, Kajetaner Church – marked the end of the long creative period of the Comoese in the archbishopric. Their place was taken by native artists like Johann Bernhard Fischer von Erlach (1656–1723).

In Eichstätt, residence of the prince-bishop, Misoxans worked for nearly two centuries uninterrupted as court architects and bricklayers. Before the Thirty Years' War, and on an even larger scale during the rebuilding following the destruction of 1634, well-known builders were working in Eichstätt, men like Giovanni Albertalli (around 1575–1657), Giovanni Giacomo Angelini (1632–1714), and Gabriele di Gabrieli (1671–1747), who came from Roveredo but died in Eichstätt and was buried there, whose churches and secular buildings have shaped the appearance of the city to this day. In addition, a large group of master bricklayers and stonemasons whose identity is no longer known worked in the city along the Altmühl River; in 1661, more than half of all construction workers employed there came from Misox. After Gabrieli, the Comoese Maurizio Pedetti (1719–99) continued the Italian building tradition in Eichstätt.

Another important destination of the Misoxans was the Electorate of Bavaria, where the most important representative of the well-known architect family of the Zuccalli from Roveredo, Enrico Zuccalli (1642–1724), had worked as court architect in Munich since 1672. His buildings (Theatiner Church, Schloß Schleißheim, Ettal Monastery), and those of the younger Giovanni Antonio Viscardi (1645–1713), a native of San Vittore (Cistercian Abbey of Fürstenfeld, Trinity Church in Munich) mark the High Baroque in Bavaria. Both masters remained in Bavarian service to the end of their lives. While Zuccalli surrounded himself mostly

F. A. Kannegießer: The *Hofbauschreiberei* in the "Italian village" in Dresden, 1827 (*Sächsische Landesbibliothek – Staats- und Universitätsbibliothek Dresden/ Deutsche Fotothek*).

with countrymen and spoke hardly any German, the younger Viscardi drew increasingly on native workers in carrying out his commissions.

The activities of Italian-speaking builders and artists were not limited to Catholic courts and territories, as is evident from several examples in the Empire (Dresden, Ansbach and Bayreuth, Ludwigsburg) and other European countries (Sweden, Russia). At the Württemberg court in Ludwigsburg, a larger group of Italian immigrants formed around the Comoese artists Donato Giuseppe Frisoni (1683–1735) and Paolo Retti (1691–1748) during the time of the Protestant Duke Eberhard Ludwig (1693–1733). Around 1720, this group comprised several hundred individuals, who remained there also beyond the Baroque heyday of the court in the time of the Catholic dukes. The integration of the immigrants was quick and unproblematic in a Catholic territory. In a Protestant territory under a Catholic dynasty, there were at least initial steps toward integration within the environment of the court: in Dresden, a Catholic family had been ruling a Protestant territory since the conversion of the Elector August the Strong in 1697. The building of the Catholic court church by Gaetano Chiaveri (1689–1770), along with the separation of the Italian builders in an "Italian village," can be seen as an indication that the integration of the Catholic migrant laborers was not desired and intended, or was at least looked at askance in the Protestant residency city. Still, cases like that of the painter Guercino (1591–1666), who turned down a lucrative commission in England on the grounds that he did not wish to live with "heretics," was the exception in the Baroque period.

Russia's integration into the history of European art and architecture began with the founding and construction of St. Petersburg in 1703, a task for which Czar Peter the Great recruited hundreds of skilled workers from Germany, France, and Italy. One man who had a particularly large impact in the first few decades was Domenico

Trezzini from Lugano (1670–1734), who had previously been active in Copenhagen and who lived and worked in the Russian capital from his arrival in 1703 until his death. As architect and especially as the educator of the first generations of native builders, Trezzini shaped Russian architecture for decades to come. The czar rewarded him with numerous privileges and was godfather at his first son's baptism (Trezzini had brought his wife from his homeland in 1709). The Comoese who had come with Trezzini, most of whom worked as plasterers, likewise initiated a thoroughgoing orientation to Italian models when it came to the interior furnishings of churches and castles. This was carried on by the later builders in service to the czars, men like Gaetano Chiaveri and Niccolò Michetti (1672–81 to 1759). Bartolomeo Francesco Rastrelli (1700–71), the leading architect of the 1740s and 1750s, who had already come to St. Petersburg as a young man with his father in 1716 and was intimately familiar with the Russian language and customs, nevertheless returned to his home in northern Italy after decades of work in Russia. It would appear that a return migration to Italy in old age was always a serious option, even for those with a privileged status and in spite of apparent integration.

The life of Carlo Innocenzo Carlone (1686–1775), a native of Scaria in the Val d'Intelvi, can be seen as exemplary for the course of an artist's career between northern Italy and the Baroque Empire. Early on he accompanied his father, Giovanni Battista (died 1707), across the Alps to acquire a knowledge of German and to learn the family's traditional plasterer's craft in his father's workshop, which was then located in Passau. However, he decided on a career as a painter and apprenticed himself to his countryman, the frescoist Giulio Quaglio (1668–1751), among other places in Laibach. His subsequent training in Venice and Vienna predestined him for a career north of the Alps. Following his first independent work in Passau, where the family's renown paved the way, he moved his workshop to Vienna. The following decades were characterized by important commissions in the environment of the imperial court (Upper Belvedere of Prince Eugen) as well as in Ludwigsburg and Ansbach, where important posts were already occupied by artists from the Val d'Intelvi, namely Paolo and Leopoldo Retti (1705–51) and Frisoni. These years of work by Carlone (which took him also to Breslau, Prague, and Weingarten, for example), were interrupted by frequent trips home, where he married Caterina Corbellini from another family of artists.

At the end of the 1730s, Carlone returned to the Val d'Intelvi for good, acquired – as a wealthy returnee – houses in Scaria and Como, donated liturgical vessels, and participated in founding a brotherhood. To what extent Carlone's waning popularity north of the Alps contributed to his return must remain an open question. He worked one more time at the request of the elector of Cologne in Augustusburg castle near Brühl; otherwise the years until his death were characterized by projects in northern Italy, above all the native church in Scaria, which he and his brother Diego Francesco Carlone (1674–1750) turned into a masterpiece of the Comoese Roccoco. This example illustrates that the native art in northern Italy received a number of stimuli through the returning migrants. Migrants who had grown rich abroad sometimes helped the community to build or restore churches and donated numerous sacral objects.

There is no other group of architects and artisans who over generations retained the same sort of cohesion as did the families Beer, Thumb, and Moosbrugger from the Bregenzerwald. The basis for this kind of cohesiveness had been provided by the organization in the Aue Guild since the middle of the 17th century, which was both an occupational association and a religious brotherhood, and the tight network of family and kin, within which training, occupation, and commissions, but also enduring contacts with specific clients, were handed down. Because of it, the masters from Vorarlberg repeatedly recruited their countrymen for building projects, even when – as was rarely the case – they had settled permanently abroad and maintained less intense contacts with the homeland. Unusual also is the number of architects who hailed from Vorarlberg, especially from the Bregenzerwald around Au-Schoppernau: nearly 1,000 building craftsmen and artists are attested from the late 16th into the 19th century. In Au-Schoppenau itself, more than 90% of the male population was active in the building trade between 1670 and 1700. The best-known masters were Michael Beer, the founder of the Aue Guild (1605–66; Abbey Church in Kempten, Abbey of Rottenmünster), Michael (around 1640–90; Obermarchtal), and Peter Thumb (1681–1766; St. Gallen, Birnau), Fr. Caspar Moosbrugger (1656–1723; Einsiedeln), as well as Franz (1660–1726; Salem, Weingarten) and Johann Michael Beer von Blaichten (1700–67; St. Blasien).

While the men from Vorarlberg had initially competed with the master builders from Misox in the southwest of the Empire and in Switzerland, in the last third of the 17th century they were able to gain an almost monopolistic position in this area when it came to the construction of churches and monasteries. The commissions came from the reciprocal relationships, contacts, and recommendations between monasteries and religious orders (especially Benedictines, Cistercians, Premonstratensians, Jesuits). The activities of the men from Vorarlberg in at least 400 locations – centered most heavily between the Alsace and the Allgäu, Switzerland, and the Black Forest, especially among the imperial prelates and in Further Austria, but extending as far as Bohemia – could not have been accomplished without the qualities of "hard work," "thrift," and "a sense of family and community" already attested by contemporaries, and without a smooth organization. The master builders and construction foremen (*paliere*) began to assemble the individual construction crews during the winter, and the upcoming seasonal migration was jointly planned before the exodus began in the spring. The size of the construction crews always varied, though they probably rarely exceeded in number the 200 men that Peter Thumb took to the Alsace in 1729.

When families of architects settled in places where they were active, their generation-spanning integration became visible as social advancement. One exemplary case is the history of the Bagnato family of architects, which was active for the Commandery of the Teutonic Order in Alsace-Lorraine in the 18th century and whose roots lay in the Val di Peccia in the Tecino. In the late 17th century, the bricklayer Paul Bagnato found employment with one of the many construction crews working on the French fortresses in Freiburg and Landau. His son Johann Caspar (1696–1757; Altshausen, Mainau) succeeded in specializing and advancing to become an independent master builder in service to the Teutonic Order. He settled in the seat of the provincial Commandery of the Order in Altshausen and successfully applied for citizenship in the imperial city of Ravensburg, in which the confessions were evenly split. His children, among them his successor as architect for the Teutonic Order, Franz Anton (1731–1810), consolidated and accelerated the family's social and economic rise by marrying into leading patrician families of the Swabian, Catholic imperial cities. In the following generations, the family became civil servants, first of the Teutonic Order and then of the new Kingdom of Württemberg, and it was ennobled in the 18th century.

Surviving traces of the migration

The traces of the architects and interior artists from Italy, the Grisons, the Tecino, and Vorarlberg are still visible today in their works, although German historiography – especially under the influence of *völkisch* ideas in the first half of the 20th century – certainly did try to minimize or even erase their presence. The Bagnato family is a good example of the changing historical scholarship, characterized by the artists' names that sometimes appear in Italian, sometimes in German as Giovane Gaspare/Johann Caspar and Francesco Antonio/Franz Anton. In the same vein, the architects were sometimes considered Italians and sometimes native Germans. In the process, the Italian version of the names often went hand in hand with a view that tended to be derogatory: it was argued that the Italian builders merely transposed the art form of their homeland, which had a chance in the German territories only because of the generally dire state of affairs in the wake of the Thirty Years' War and the resulting lack of native talent.

Well into the 20th century, historical scholarship was pervaded by a dictum by Hans Jacob Wagner von Wagenfels that the work of Fischer von Erlach had been the glorious victory of "German art and skill over the veneration of the foreigners." The result was an antithetical juxtaposition of the work of the "foreign," meaning Italian, artists, who had "foreignized the soil," with the preceding artistic era of the German Renaissance, on the one hand, and that of the late Baroque and Roccoco, on the other. The German students and successors of the Italian builders had supposedly developed their own, native conception of art that was superior to the Italian High Baroque (Fischer von Erlach, Lukas von Hildebrandt, Dominikus Zimmermann, the Asam brothers, the Dientzenhofer family, Balthasar Neumann). The work of the men from Vorarlberg was also given a *völkisch* connotation in that they were depicted as "genuine Germanic builders" who were "averse to the clever Italian art" and had functioned as a connecting link to the "perfected southern German Roccoco."

The artistic migrations of the Italians ended in the Habsburg lands and in southern Germany with the success of native architects, some of whom had learned their craft from the Italians. The men from Vorarlberg were displaced above all by the spread of French taste and the early Classicism that went along with it after the middle of the 18th century. The migration in the field of architecture and the visual arts would remain a phenomenon especially of the Baroque, even though work migration from the valleys of the Alps has remained alive in other sectors down to the present.

Della Torre, Stefano, et al., eds. *Magistri d'Europa. Eventi, relazioni, strutture della migrazione di artisti e costruttori dai laghi lombardi.* Milan, 1996.

Kühlenthal, Michael, ed. *Graubündner Baumeister und Stukkateure. Beiträge zur Erforschung ihrer Tätigkeit im mitteleuropäischen Raum.* Locarno, 1997.

Lieb, Norbert. *Die Vorarlberger Barockbaumeister.* 3rd ed. Munich, 1976.

Natter, Tobias G., and Ute Pfanner, eds. *Architectura Practica – Barockbaumeister und moderne Bauschule aus Vorarlberg.* Exhibition catalogue. Bregenz, 2006.

Pfister, Max. *Baumeister aus Graubünden – Wegbereiter des Barock. Die auswärtige Tätigkeit der Bündner Baumeister und Stukkateure in Süddeutschland, Österreich und Polen vom 16. bis zum 18. Jahrhundert.* Munich, 1993.

Pfister, Ulrich, ed. *Regional Development and Commercial Infrastructure in the Alps.* Basel, 2002.

Schindling, Anton. "Bei Hofe und als Pomeranzenhändler: Italiener im Deutschland der Frühen Neuzeit." In *Deutsche im Ausland – Fremde in Deutschland. Migration in Geschichte und Gegenwart,* edited by Klaus J. Bade, 287–94. 3rd ed. Munich, 1993.

Cross-references: Austria; Germany; Italy; Switzerland; Northern Europe; Russia and Belarus; Alpine Chimney Sweeps in Western, Central, and Southern Europe from the 16th to the Early 20th Century; Italian Pewterers in Europe from the 16th to the 20th Century

ITALIAN PEWTERERS IN EUROPE FROM THE 16TH TO THE 20TH CENTURY

Markus Walz

Beginning in the 17th century, "Italian pewterers" became a negative label, used by German authorities for unqualified, fraudulent migrant craftsmen, by German pewterers for (supposedly nonresident) Italian competitors (as in 1715 in Minden/Westphalia), and by naturalized pewterers of Italian extraction for their unwelcome countrymen (as in 1809 in Plattling/Lower Bavaria).

Pewterers of Italian extraction offer a vivid example of migrants in a profession that was common because of the production of tableware, but one that had few practitioners. In central Europe, the itinerant profession was almost entirely in the hands of Italians either as pewterers with a mobile workshop (repair craftsmen, spoon makers) or as traders. However, pewterers are also found as immigrants with a settled local business and/or itinerant marketing.

The total volume of this itinerant group cannot be determined with precision, though it exceeded the 132 pewterers of Italian extraction listed by Georg Wacha for central Europe many times; in 19th-century Rhineland-Westphalia, alone, Italians accounted for 28 of 180 (1822) or 26 of 136 (1862), or about one-fifth, of all pewterers. Since they were more productive thanks to their higher numbers of helpers, they contributed significantly to this craft.

Italian pewterers are said to have lived in Prague (14th century) around the same time that specialized pewter workers first emerged (first corporation in Nuremberg around 1285). Further documented instances range from 1553 (Ödenburg/Sopron, Hungary) into the 1930s. The quantitative high point probably occurred in the first half of the 19th century. The gradual disappearance of this trade also brought the wanderings to an end – the 20th century preferred more stable (enamel, steel), lower-maintenance (nickel silver), or more colorful materials (porcelain), and some pewter goods went out of fashion entirely (funeral plaques, tin soldiers, tankard lids for warm beer).

The region of origin of these migrants encompassed Alpine valleys west of the Lago Maggiore in a radius of around fifty kilometers belonging to the Duchy of Milan and since 1748 to Savoy/Piedmont-Sardinia. In addition, there were Italian-speaking pewterers of migratory movements that differed in origin and destinations (Venetians in Bohemia, men from Valais and the Tecino in France, men from Trent from the Val di Non in German Tyrol).

The destinations of the migrations lay between southern France (1603 Nîmes), Palatinate (1589 Speyer), and Bohemia (1590 Jungbunzlau/Mladá Boleslav); around 1800 between the Netherlands (before 1785 Luxembourg), Hamburg (1805), Ermland (before 1718 Mehlsack/Pieniezno), Silesia (1707 Reichenstein/Zloty Stok), Transylvania (before 1715 Hermannstadt/Sibiu), and Tyrol (1744 Kufstein). Pewterers of Italian origin also appeared in Denmark, but they never reached the British Isles, Scandinavia, and the Baltic region. Although pewter wares played a (secondary) role in all classical cultures of the Mediterranean region, so far we have no knowledge of postclassical pewter objects from the Iberian Peninsula or southeastern Europe.

Pewter foundries were completely absent in the Italian region of origin, which meant that no masters could emigrate from there. The patterns of movement of the Italian group resembled those of the majority of central European pewterers, who crossed medium and long distances and de facto emigrated (apprenticeship mostly not in the parents' home, journeymen migration, independence, shift of location). Pewterers of Italian extraction differed from the other groups through their adaptable combinations of business, which disregarded the traditional boundaries between craft and trade, and the gradient in prestige between stationary business and itinerant trade – for central Europe a structural novelty in the economy. They opened up locations with weak sales by separating the residence of their family from the location of their business, sometimes running several locations that were staffed only some of the time and in this way reduced risks. Cologne ceased being a "second residence" only for the fifth Sesiani (from 1822); in the process, the pewter foundry expanded into a metal dealership and metal goods factory.

Pewterers of Italian extraction were not able to satisfy their need for assistants with their own sons. They took in almost exclusively apprentices and journeymen from their own regions of origin, where young men were looking for opportunities. Independent of a prohibition against the employment of *welsch* (Romance) assistants in several guilds (e.g., in Alsace) and of the general exclusion of *welsch* migrant journeymen from the allowances in those guilds where this was customary, a parallel craft structure emerged in this way. In cases of economic success it grew through its own internal dynamic when those willing to be trained followed and went out on their own after completing their training. If demand declined, it shrank on its own through the elimination of trainee positions.

The region of origin participated in the development of the trade through a pan-European social network with numerous participants (in various professions) and direct communication through migrant workers and the (minority) of return migrants. Cultivating contacts was facilitated by the destination preferences of individual villages or several neighboring villages of the region of origin.

A self-definition and an organization as pewterers of Italian extraction were lacking. The authorities of the destination areas often urged the migrants to acquire local citizenship rights. After 1820, Prussia limited engagement in an itinerant trade almost exclusively to its own subjects, but it carried out naturalizations with very few problems. With this, every less than flattering name for the group disappeared – beyond the label "Italian pewterers."

We know of only one group of pewterers in St. Wendel (today Saarland) who lived a separated life in the second half of the 19th century: however, their daily life with few local contacts, their large numbers, and their limited stays (at times there were up to 13 itinerant pewterers without families) were atypical. The Italians often lived locally as the only pewterer, and we have no evidence for housing in close proximity to Italians of other professions. Opportunities to represent themselves as a separate group among the groups of migrants or the Catholic pastoral care for migrants emerged only around 1900.

A characteristically fluid change of trade in the late 19th century. The flourishing pewter foundry developed by Joseph Giacometti (naturalized in 1865) was developed by his widow into a diversified metal and housewares business. Advertisement in the *Wohnungs- und Geschäfts-Anzeiger für den Stadtbezirk Recklinghausen*, Recklinghausen, 1899 (*Stadt- und Vestisches Archiv Recklinghausen*).

The membership of pewterers of Italian extraction in small-town collective guilds, as well as products that are indistinguishable from "local" goods in form and quality point to the acceptance of the group among the population of the destination region. A few Italian pewterers cultivated close business ties in the destination region: they cast wares from the stocks of scrap metal dealers, peddled products of the pewter foundries in Frankfurt am Main that were expanding in the 18th century, and worked as specialized suppliers for large businesses in the 19th century.

Pewterers of Italian extraction were informed and skilled in their dealings with the authorities: in the 18th century they avoided territories with restrictions on immigrants; after 1818 they avoided locations in the Prussian border control district, where the authorities were on the lookout for smuggling; they applied – successfully even when their residence was elsewhere – for the monopolistic territorial concessions for itinerant pewterers that were customary into the 19th century. Their dealings with the authorities were made easier by their level of literacy that was equal to that in central Europe and an apparently adequate command of the German language.

Broad social contacts are indicated by sources from Rhineland-Westphalia, which say that the population unrelated by marriage acted as godparents to more than 60% of the children of Italian pewterers and that the problematic choice of female partners was rare. We don't know about the stay and activities of the wives of migrant workers or pewterers who hailed from the regions of origin, and whose husbands had separated their place of domicile and their occupational location. The majority in Rhineland-Westphalia appear to be wives from the destination town or its environs, nearly always from the lower-middle and upper-lower class. The daughters of craftsmen were well represented, but we have no instance where existing workshops were acquired by marriage (daughters who stood to inherit them, widows of masters).

The majority of children of pewterers of Italian extraction who grew up in Rhineland-Westphalia also married into local, comparable circumstances. Compared to craftsmen overall, the 19th century was positive for sons: only 15% of them declined socially into the lower class.

It stands to reason that the migrant workers among the Italian pewterers were not keen to integrate. However, the category "migrant labor" is not a good description of their multivarious ways of life. The immigrants among them could integrate to the point of "invisibility": they became specialized craftsmen with little local competition, had an economic livelihood, and had favorable connubial contacts at the destination location. The authorities of less important locations promoted them in order to boost the local availability of wares; in these cases, the potential of conflict with "local" craftsmen disappeared almost entirely.

The contemporary focus was entirely on "Italian pewterers," regardless of whether they were "nondomiciled" itinerants or immigrants with a fixed abode. The history of craftsmanship at the end of the 20th century also describes migrant workers, though it tends to look more at the products of immigrants who left lasting traces with the handiwork they left behind them.

Bella forma. Zinn und Edelstahl aus Piemont. Peltro e acciaio del Piemento. Exhibition, Westfälisches Freilichtmuseum Hagen, 3.5.–3.8.1997. Hagen, 1997.

Egg, Erich. *Das Handwerk der Tiroler Zinngießer*. Innsbruck, 1998.

Wacha, Georg. "Übersicht über italienische Zinngießer nördlich der Alpen." *Adler* 12 (1980–2): 73–7, 169–72, 207–10, 341–3, 442–7.

Walz, Markus. *Zinngießerfamilien aus Italien in Westfalen und im Rheinland*. Münster, 1998.

Walz, Markus. *Region – Profession – Migration. Italienische Zinngießer in Rheinland-Westfalen 1700–1900*. Osnabrück, 2002.

Wiswe, Mechthild. "Italienische Zinngießer im südlichen Niedersachsen." In *Beiträge zur niedersächsischen Landesgeschichte. Zum 65. Geburtstag von Hans Patze*, edited by Dieter Brosius et al., 285–306. Hildesheim, 1984.

Cross-references: Austria; Czechia and Slovakia; France; Germany; Italy; Northern Europe; Switzerland

ITALIAN REFUGEES IN ITALY FROM ADRIATIC TERRITORIES THAT FELL TO YUGOSLAVIA AFTER 1945

Rolf Wörsdörfer

The departure of Italians from Adriatic territories after the Second World War is usually described with the term "exodus" (*esodo*). The word appeared for the first time in March 1944 in a letter by a high functionary of the northern Italian Repubblica Sociale Italiana (RSI, Republic of Salò); he was warning against the emigration of Italian civil servants from Italy's eastern border regions. And in the years that followed, about 250,000 Italians did leave the Adriatic territories; a smaller number of anticommunist Slovenes and Croats also went to the West. Most protagonists of the exodus saw themselves as *esuli* (exiles), *profughi* (refugees), or *optanti* who had opted for Italian nationality. The mass emigration lasted until 1955; thereafter, only smaller groups left the formerly Italian territories of Yugoslavia.

In the weeks following Italy's surrender on 8 September 1943, the Slovenian and Croatian partisans had formulated territorial claims of the new Yugoslav state to the northeastern coastal regions and had passed annexation decrees that were retroactively legitimized by AVNOJ (Anti-Fascist Liberation Council of the People of Yugoslavia), the political leadership body of the resistance. In addition to decrees against the presence of the Italian state and its representatives in the northeastern Adriatic that were sanctioned by meetings of the delegates, September 1943 and May 1945 witnessed attacks by the partisans or their security forces against parts of the civilian population. These acts of violence, known as *foibe* and *deportazioni* (murders, kidnappings), were one reason the relationship between the largely Slavic partisans and the Italian coastal residents remained tense. Only in the strongholds of the Italian communists was there cooperation, until 1948 under the banner of the "brotherhood and unity" propagated by Tito.

The emigration of the Italians extended over 12 years because the border issue was far from decided immediately after the end of the war. As a result, the exodus fragmented into at least five submovements:

1. The "black exodus." The protagonists were largely civil servants from Italy's old provinces, who, out of fear of reprisals by the partisans, had already left the border region months before the end of the war. They were then followed, shortly after hostilities had ceased, by the Fascist Party and militia leaders or notables (hence the name *esodo nero*).

2. The evacuation of Zara (Croatian: Zadar). The residents of this enclave in Dalmatia, the majority of its 21,000 inhabitants being Italians, were prompted to leave the city primarily by Allied bombing raids in 1943–4. Many Zarans crossed the Adriatic to settle in the region of Ancona; others made their way northward to Istria.

3. The exodus from Fiume and Istria. After the end of the war and during the peace negotiations, there was no longer any debate that the city of Fiume (Croatian: Rijeka) would belong to Yugoslavia. The excesses by the Yugoslav secret police, the "war-communist" measures of the People's Committee that had been set up during the partisan war, the closing of many enterprises, and the growing unemployment spurred the departure of the Italians from the city in the first years after the war (20,000 by January 1946 alone). Around the same time Italians were leaving those parts of Istria whose return to Italian administration had already become unlikely. The triggers were, among other things, the occupiers' dismantling policy; the introduction of a new currency (Jugolira) pegged to the dinar; the repressive policy toward the Catholic Church, which was accompanied by murders and kidnappings; a general legal uncertainty; and finally, the growing signs that the peninsula would remain under Yugoslav rule.

4. The exodus from Pola. The fate of the Istrian port city of Pola, initially occupied by partisans in May 1945 but then handed over to the Western Allies 40 days later, remained contested until the signing of the peace treaty in February 1947. When the treaty stipulated the handover of Pola to Yugoslavia, nearly all Italian residents of the city left by sea (28,058 optanti by July 1946).

5. The exodus from Zone B of the Free Territory of Trieste. Not until 1954–5 did the majority of the Italian population leave the Yugoslav-administered part of the Free Territory of Trieste (FTT), the so-called Zone B. Many residents of Zone B, which consisted of the Slovenian district Koper (Italian: Capodistria) and the Croatian district of Buje (Italian: Buie), had hoped to the very end for the survival of the FTT or a return of the zone to Italy. When the unfavorable decision was made, they moved to the West.

The question of how the protagonists of the exodus from the formerly Italian territories were received in Italy itself and in Trieste (Zone A), which was administered by the Western Allies until 1954, cannot be answered without reference to the fractured political culture of the land. Thus, until the outbreak of the Comintern conflict in 1948, the communists displayed an indifferent, if not hostile, attitude toward the refugees. In a few cases, the workers of leftist strongholds blocked convoys of refugees from passing through their cities. In the eyes of the communist rank and file, anyone who fled from Tito's socialist Yugoslavia could only be a "reactionary" or "fascist." The PCI leadership was more cautious and described the mass of emigrants as "misled people." The communists accused their Christian Democratic coalition partners of having provoked the exodus by making material promises to the refugees (money, jobs).

The political parties of the center, especially the Christian Democrats who regularly had a governing majority after 1947, had not directly triggered the exodus. But they did woo the refugees once they had arrived in Italy or Trieste.

The Italian state-owned television regularly broadcast a show about the Adriatic regions. And the center parties held positions of leadership in the aid organizations that helped the Istrians in finding work and building houses. The role of the clergy in the distribution of state and private aid money to the refugees secured the Catholic Church considerable influence on an originally national-liberal and secular-urban population like the one in Trieste. All told, Trieste took in just under a third of all emigrants from the ceded Istrian territories.

The settlement of the Istrians, Fiumans, and Dalmatians in Trieste and in other cities of the border regions benefited the center parties, in that the overwhelmingly anticommunist new arrivals immediately had Italian citizenship and the right to vote. A small but influential segment supported the parties of the extreme right. In the end, the official policy oscillated between the goal of integration into Italian society and the desire to keep territorial or financial claims against Yugoslavia alive, which could undermine the efforts toward integration.

The Istrians in Trieste were not really strangers; already before the exodus they were known in the port city as commuters or migrant workers. Jokes made the round among the native population about the Istrian peasants and their proverbial frugalness. Moreover, the old-established population of Trieste was jealous of the refugees' seemingly easy access to state aid funds and programs, an attitude that helped at least in part to solidify the well-worn stereotypes. Among the refugees from Zone B was an especially large number of bi- or trilingual farmers whose national identity had not been fixed before this time. It was only in exile that they then embraced an Italian identity all the more emphatically.

More important was the clash of interests that developed between the refugees and the members of the Slovene minority in the city and in Zone A. In part this stemmed from the general political polarization and a hostility toward the Slavs that was deeply rooted in Trieste to begin with, a hostility that was intensified by the experiences of wartime and the postwar years. The housing construction policy of the Roman ministries, communal offices, aid organizations, and private entrepreneurs was aimed at settling the Istrians in the Slovenian neighborhoods of Trieste and in the minority-inhabited Kars and coastal villages. When the Allies withdrew from Trieste and the city returned to Italian suzerainty, the refugees, some of whom had spent years in camps, were housed in compact apartment blocks (borghi) with their own infrastructure (e.g., shops, meeting rooms), all of which were put up near Slovenian settlement areas.

The residents were to cultivate their traditions and dialects in the borghi, which were often named after local Istrian saints. Sometimes the arable land was expropriated by circumventing the communal administrations dominated by Slovenian parties; in the costal town of Duino (Slovenian: Devin) west of Trieste, the Italian authorities turned the original Slovenian majority population into a minority by settling Istrians. The settlement form of the *borghi* was initially aimed at leaving the new arrivals intact as a self-contained community. However, the maneuvering room of the Slovenian minority was constrained with the help of the refugees, and this also helped to facilitate the integration of the latter into the Italian-dominated society.

The refugee organizations ensured that their issues and concerns became part of a "borderland discourse" that was also engaged in by the majority of the autochthonous population. That discourse picked up many motifs of the traditional Adriatic irredentism and included demarcation against the Yugoslav neighbor as well as the preservation of certain material demands (border revision, compensation for confiscated property). A temporary and partial understanding between the center parties and the political representatives of the Trieste Slovenes was possible only at the time of the center-left coalitions in the 1960s. The Triestans – both natives and refugees from Istria and Dalmatia – reacted to the Italian-Yugoslav Treaty of Osimo (1975) by returning to the mobilization of local patriotism and anti-Slavism (*Lista per Trieste*).

The crisis of the Italian party system in the first half of the 1990s and the breakup of Yugoslavia put the status of the refugees and the situation of the Italian minority in Slovenia and Croatia once again on the political agenda. When newer anthropological studies report about the Adriatic irredentism of the *esuli* organizations, the focus is no longer on the majority of the Istrians who fled and emigrated in the 1940s and 1950s, but only on their politically active and organized segment, which has kept the memory of the exodus alive at the turn from the 20th to the 21st century. The situation of the Istrians in Trieste is comparable to that of the Cubans in Miami, especially in regard to what Ballinger has called the "absurd closeness" of the lost homeland.

Ballinger, Pamela. *History in Exile: Memory and Identity at the Borders of the Balkans*. Princeton, 2003.

Cattaruzza, Marina. "Der "Istrische Exodus": Fragen der Interpretation." In *Erzwungene Trennung. Vertreibungen und Aussiedlungen in und aus der Tschechoslowakei 1938–1947 im Vergleich mit Polen, Ungarn und Jugoslawien*, edited by Detlef Brandes, Edita Ivaničková, and Jiri Pešek, 295–322. Essen, 1999.

Colummi, Cristiana, et al. *Storia di un esodo. Istria 1945–1956*. Trieste, 1980.

Gombač, Jure. *Esuli ali optanti. Zgodovinski primer v Luči sobodne teorije*. Ljubljana, 2005 .

Volk, Sandi. *Esuli a Trieste. Bonifica nazionale e rafforzamento dell'italianità sul confine orientale*. Udine, 2004.

Wörsdörfer, Rolf. *Krisenherd Adria 1915–1955. Konstruktion und Artikulation des Nationalen im italienisch-jugoslawischen Grenzraum*. Paderborn, 2004.

Cross-references: Italy; Southeastern Europe; Slovenian and Croatian Emigrants in Yugoslavia from Territories Ceded to Italy after 1918

ITALIAN REFUGEES OF THE *RISORGIMENTO* IN CENTRAL AND WESTERN EUROPE IN THE 19TH CENTURY

Marc Vuilleumier

The term *risorgimento* arose in Italy shortly after 1750 and referred initially to the striving for the "rebirth" of a uniform Italian culture. Later, the meaning of the word shifted: it now referred to the goal of the Italian national movement to create a modern, unified Italian state. Already during the French Revolution, and then increasingly so in the phase between the restoration of the small and medium-sized Italian states at the Congress of Vienna in 1815 and the emergence of the Italian nation-state (1861–70), many of its champions, from the *moderati* (moderate Liberals) to the *democratici* (Democrats), were forced to go into exile in other European countries.

The restoration reestablished the pre-Napoleonic order in Italy and reinstalled the various dynasties: the Spanish Bourbons ruled in Naples-Sicily (Kingdom of the Two Sicilies), the Habsburgs and their collateral branches governed four Italian states in central and northern Italy (Kingdom of Lombardy-Veneto, Grand Duchy of Tuscany, duchies of Parma and Modena), the house of Savoy ruled the Kingdom of Sardinia-Piedmont, the Bourbon ducal house of Parma held the Principality of Lucca (after 1847 part of the Grand Duchy of Tuscany), and the pope presided over the Papal State.

Political repression, and especially the failure of the revolutionary uprising in the Kingdom of the Two Sicilies and in Sardinia-Piedmont in 1820–1, in the Papal State and in central Italy in 1831, as well as the revolution of 1848–9, drove large numbers of the liberal opposition out of Italy. The chief destination countries were Switzerland, France, Great Britain, and Belgium. A smaller number of refugees went to South and North America or settled in Greek or African port cities on the Mediterranean, as well as in Malta, in order to remain in the closest possible contact with their homeland.

The size of the group cannot be accurately determined, especially since it fluctuated wildly, as amnesties or pardons frequently allowed a return to Italy. Onward migrations within Europe were the rule, voluntary or forced, if the host country wanted to rid itself of guests who had overstayed their welcome. For example, Geneva, like other Swiss cantons that yielded to the pressure from foreign powers, revoked the residence permits of the many refugees it had admitted in 1821. It did the same after the attempt to invade Savoy from Geneva under the leadership of the democratic Giuseppe Mazzini in 1834 and after the revolution of 1848–9, when the neighboring states demanded that the Swiss Confederation expel the refugees. By this time France had already stopped accepting refugees, who were only allowed to transit the country on their way to Great Britain or the USA.

The Kingdom of Savoy-Piedmont, by contrast, which was led by a liberal government, took in many refugees from the rest of Italy. Many of them became naturalized. However, the kingdom was not so willing to open its doors to refugees who were democratic or republican in their political orientation. The arriving intellectual elite provided the kingdom with many high-level personnel for the administration, the military, and the educational system. The immigrants helped in allowing the kingdom to take a leading role in the unification of Italy.

The social composition of the refugee groups changed between 1815 and 1849. National ideas had undergone a crucial development especially within the Napoleonic army, which brought together soldiers from all over Italy. From 1820–1 to the end of the 1830s, it was chiefly former officers and noncommissioned officers of the Napoleonic army who participated in the conspiracies and revolutionary uprising in Italy and made up the majority of the refugees.

Since many members of the opposition saw the Spanish Revolution of 1820 as an example to be imitated, some of the refugees went to the Iberian Peninsula after the failed uprisings in Italy in 1821. When France intervened in Spain in 1823 in the name of the restorationist "Holy Alliance" (Russia, Great Britain, Austria, Prussia, and France) to overthrow the liberal government, about 1,200 Italian refugees fought in the army of the Spanish constitutionalists. Italian refugees were also involved in the struggles for Greek independence against Ottoman rule (1821–9). Among them was Santorre di Santarosa: the subprefect of La Spezia during Napoleon's rule, he joined the Piedmontese guard as a captain in 1815 and was killed in Greece in 1825.

Some of the refugees after 1821 were of bourgeois background; many belonged to the high nobility. The proportion of bourgeois refugees grew considerably after 1831. In 1848–9, the urban population as a whole took an active part in the revolution and consequently made up a large share of the refugees (small and middling merchants, craftsmen, and workers).

The refugees were eager to recruit to the national movement the many migrant workers from all regions and states of Italy who were in other European countries. However, because of the great social difference between the political refugees and the migrant workers, that effort had only meager success, even if the political exiles did in fact develop a social movement after the 1830s. Giuseppe Mazzini, for example, founded the Unione degli operai italini (Union of Italian Workers) in London in 1840, which also operated a free evening school for the children of Italian migrant workers. In addition to the basic skills in reading, writing, and arithmetic, the children were taught Italian and history.

There was no uniform organization of the Italian refugees. The political convictions were too diverse, and mutual blame for the defeats of the national movement split the group into a multitude of political camps. The refugees composed, often in French, numerous historical treatises that were intended to legitimate their struggle for the "rebirth" of an Italian national state. They also penned programmatic political tracts and articles, most of which appeared in French and English magazines. All over Europe, the refugees fanned a discussion about the situation in Italy and its political future. Printing and publishing houses were set up in the Italian-speaking Swiss canton Ticino, one example being the famous Tipografia Elvetica de Capolago, which was run in 1849 by the liberal politician and philosopher Carlo Cattaneo.

In the early 19th century, trips to Italy remained fashionable among the European nobility and bourgeoisie. Political, social, and cultural trends in Italy were attentively watched and discussed. For that reason, the refugees from Italy encountered goodwill in the other European states. Added to this was their high social status, especially in the 1820s and 1830s, which made their reception easier. For example, the poet Ugo Foscolo, who had left Italy voluntarily, immediately found supporters and friends among his admirers in Zurich in 1816 and later in London. The Piedmontese and Neapolitan noblemen and -women were received with open arms in the salons in Paris and London. As soon as they had set themselves up, they put on their own social events: the famous gatherings of Princess Cristina Belgiojoso in Paris and of Marquis Guiseppe Arconati-Visconti at castle Gaesbeek near Brussels became meeting places for the refugees and facilitated contact with members of the native elite.

Individual personalities aided in the reception and integration of the refugees. Among them was the Swiss economist and historian Jean-Charles-Léonard Simonde de Sismondi in Geneva in the 1820s. In Paris, the philosopher Victor Cousin acted as a conduit between the refugees and French defenders of constitutional monarchy. Cousin, who had become a kind of philosophical mouthpiece of the July Monarchy established in 1830, exerted great influence on the moderate Italian liberals. A number of refugees had academic careers in the destination countries, taught Italian literature and history, and in this way played an important role in disseminating national ideas.

The refugees sympathized with specific political currents in the host countries. In France, they supported the liberals of the July Monarchy, in spite of their disappointment that the liberals had refused to become involved in the Italian uprisings of 1831. In Belgium, the majority joined the side of the liberal and national opposition: after the Brussels uprising of 1830, no small number of Italians participated in the fight against the Netherlands. In Switzerland, left-liberal politicians supported the Italian refugees by offering them the possibility of acquiring citizenship in the cities and cantons in which they governed. For example, the majority of the citizens of the Swiss community of Grenchen demanded the naturalization of Mazzini and the Ruffini brothers who were part of his movement to protect them against the threat of expulsion. The semi-canton of Basel-Landschaft granted citizenship to Michael Napoleon Allemandi, whose family had initially fled to Geneva in 1821 and then went to Spain and France, and in 1847 appointed him a colonel in the confederate army. In 1848 he hurried to Italy, where he was appointed general of the Italian volunteer armies. After their defeat he left Italy for good and returned to Switzerland, where he died in 1858. Like so many other refugees, he did not live to see the successful creation of the Italian nation-state in the 1860s.

In 1831, Guiseppe Mazzini founded the movement Giovane Italia (Young Italy) in Marseille. Thus began the 40-year career of the democrat from Genoa as leader of the democratic, republican, and patriotic movement among the Italian refugees. With the intent of using the national currents in other European countries for Italy's patriotic struggle, he founded in succession the movements Young Poland, Young Germany, and Young Switzerland, which merged to form Young Europe in 1834 in Bern. While this ambitious movement was short-lived, it created lasting contacts among similarly oriented groups that were fighting for their goals in the most varied European states. Still, Mazzini's influence declined. The failure of his mostly improvised endeavors and the entanglement of some of his supporters in the attempts on the life of Emperor Napoleon III cost him part of his followers, who reinforced the camp of the *Moderati* and thus assured their triumph in the founding of the Italian national state between 1859 and 1861.

Battistini, Mario. *Esuli italiani in Belgio (1815–1861)*. Brussels, 1968.

Furiozi, Gian Biagio. *L'emigrazione politica in Piemonte nel decennio preunitario*. Florence, 1979.

Galante Garrone, Alessandro. *Filippo Buonarroti e i rivoluzionari dell'ottocento (1828–1837)*. Turin, 1972.

Martinola, Giuseppe. *Gli esuli italiani nel Ticino 1791–1870*. Lugano, 1980–94.

Mastellone, Salvo. "La composition sociale de l'émigration italienne en France (1816–1847)." *Rassegna storica toscana* 8 (1962): 223–38.

Cross-references: Belgium and Luxembourg; France; Italy; Switzerland; European Elites on the Grand Tour in Early Modern Europe; European Soldiers in the Napoleonic Army; Italian Industrial Workers in Western and Central Europe in the Late 19th and Early 20th Centuries

ITALIAN SEASONAL FEMALE WORKERS IN THE ITALIAN RICE BELT FROM THE 16TH TO THE MID-19TH CENTURY

Elda Gentili Zappi

Rice cultivation was introduced into Italy in the second half of the 15th century and gradually became the most advanced example of capitalist agriculture in what was to become a united Italy in 1861. Ideal conditions for growing rice existed in the Po Valley between Piedmont (Vercelli and Novara) and Lombardy (Lomellina). The success of this agrarian enterprise led to the formation of a powerful class of rice growers who employed both local and migratory wage earners to weed, harvest, and thresh the rice. Seasonal weeders worked in the rice fields during the flooding period, when the rice plants were two months old, for about 40 days, from the end of May to the beginning of July. The weeding (*monda* or *mondatura*)

required more extensive and more labor-intensive work at a greater expense than the other operations.

Rice growers hired weeders from the local workforce in public squares, but this was not sufficient for a thorough weeding. By the 16th century, growers began to rely on agents or middlemen (*capi*, *caporali*, or *capisquadre*) to recruit labor squads from distant locations. The *capi*, who accompanied the weeders to the labor sites and also acted as overseers, were notorious for the verbal and physical abuses they inflicted on the migrants, and edicts of local administrators repeatedly called for the elimination of the *capi*. However, the system, once in place, was self-perpetuating for four centuries.

From the 17th century on, the rice weeders were mostly women (*mondariso*, *mondine*, or *mondatrici*), joined by a small percentage of men and children. In wintertime *capi* hired squads of about 50 women for the weeding; there were young and old, single and married women, including mothers sometimes accompanied by their children, who were hired at half the stipulated wage. The recruiting sites were both nearby and distant. In the east, workers were sought from locations 100 kilometers away, such as Piacenza, in Emilia, and Lodi, in Lombardy. They were also hired from as far as Reggio Emilia and Modena, in Emilia – over 200 kilometers away. But the majority of the migratory weeders came from communities in the Alps and the Apennine mountains: the Novarese Highlands, the Biellese, Ivrea, Valsesia, Pallanza, Ossola, Voghera, Bobbio, Monferrato, and Tortonese, all of which were less than 100 kilometers away.

In the mountain communities of the Alps and the Apennines, whence the largest number of seasonal weeders came, the land was distributed among subsistence farmers living off small holdings. The poor yield of their crops, even when supplemented by resources available in adjacent common lands, was still not sufficient to cover the needs of a family. Many skilled and unskilled workers from the mountains migrated seasonally to urban or rural sites to perform various jobs and earn money to supplement their family income. Their interest was to preserve, or even better, their economic status.

Beginning in the 1850s the squads could travel by train from some regions at discounted fares. Previously, they had come on carts or simply walked. Once in the fields, they performed the same exhausting work as the local women, but for a longer period of time. Their bodies bent over, they had to spend long hours wading in the water up to their knees, carefully extricating the weeds that were stifling the growth of the rice plants. The migrants' meals, provided by the *caporali*, were prepared with cheap and often rotten foods cooked in polluted water. All migratory workers slept in the open air or in stables. These conditions caused ailments such as bronchial infections, intestinal disorders, typhoid and rheumatic fevers, and ulcers of the legs. Without proper protection during the night, migrants could contract malaria from the bite of the anopheles mosquito, which proliferated in the stagnant waters covering the fields.

Rice growers recognized the advantages of female labor, such as the presumed greater docility and dexterity and, most important, the lower wages women could be paid. By the late 1860s the area of rice cultivation had grown to encompass 140,000 hectares, annually requiring more than 75,000 workers, almost half of them migrants. The rice belt ranked third in attracting seasonal immigrants in Italy from May to July, surpassed only by Capitanata in northern Apulia and Rome. Starting in the 16th century, these circular flows formed three discrete medium-distance migration systems within Italy that together employed 1 million migratory workers in the 1880s. Seasonal workers, a fifth of them women, crossed not only country, regional, provincial, district, and communal administrative borders, but cultural and dialectal boundaries as well.

Many factors discouraged the integration of the migrant weeders into the host society. In particular, members of the middle and upper classes in the rice-belt communities felt burdened and threatened by the thousands of strangers whom they perceived to be part of a dangerous class. From the perspective of the locals, women outside the oversight of their male relatives did not fit into any of the traditional gender roles for females: daughter, mother, wife, or nun. They were also viewed as licentious since workers of both sexes mingled during the weeding season and since the young women were subject to the *capi*'s sexual abuses. If a migrant woman succeeded in escaping the *capi*'s control and ventured into the streets of the rice-belt cities seeking other jobs, such as domestic service, they ran the risk, as nonresidents, of being stopped by the police. The police stereotyped these women, who clearly belonged to the lower class, as prostitutes. As such, they faced prosecution under the prostitution laws, including forced repatriation.

Migrants and local weeders rarely socialized. The rice growers sometimes provoked antagonism between the two groups by hiring the migrants and leaving the local weeders unemployed as reprisal for requesting higher wages. Some confrontations took place in the 1880s and 1890s, when the local unemployed *mondine* pressured the migrants to stop their weeding; but this and other forms of protest remained limited and usually ineffective.

Family structure and socioeconomic conditions, such as the availability of land and the structure of land tenure systems, varied in the migrants' places of origin. These differences, however, do not appear to have influenced the intention of most migrant workers to be away from their home communities for only as long as the seasonal work required. A woman's meager earnings had to support her family, often compensating for the inadequate income of other family members. For this reason, weeding, as a source of ready income, was an eagerly sought after form of employment but at the same time was only one among several paid and unpaid jobs performed year-round, such as tending the domestic animals or an orchard. Many families went into debt during the winter, so at that time women felt forced to join a weeding squad. In return, they would sometimes receive a sack of grain or money as an interest-bearing advance from the *capi*. In an Emilia weeders' song entitled "The Mondine's Bitterness," the returning migrants bear the brunt of the responsibility for paying family debts:

When we arrive at Reggio Emilia
The creditors will come to us:
"Mondariso, out with the money purse,
We want to be paid."

In Reggio Emilia, as in many places east of the rice belt, capitalist investments in land gave rise to a class of landless workers whose subsistence depended on wages earned by both the young and old. In this recruiting area, the *capi* found many weeders. In the 1880s these workers fought within the newly organized, militant farmworkers' leagues to improve local working conditions and to secure better wages. The rice-belt workers, too, began to establish leagues at the turn of the 20th century. These leagues organized protests and solidarity actions between local and migratory *mondine*, endeavoring to counteract the rice growers' control of the labor market.

These militant weeders usually staged seasonal work stoppages throughout the rice belt to compel their employers to negotiate with the leagues. One exceptional event took place during the fascist era when, in 1931, the *mondine* faced the threat of wage reductions. The 1926 fascist laws had prohibited independent labor actions, but 200,000 weeders organized a fierce and finally successful strike in defiance of these laws. Their militancy carried on into the mid-1950s, by which time the introduction of chemical herbicides made weeding by hand dispensable and thus eliminated the need for *mondine* – and the centuries-old seasonal migration of women to the rice belt then came to an end.

La Marchesa Colombi (Torriani Torelli-Viollier, Maria Antonietta). *In risaia. Racconto di Natale.* Milan, 1890.

Faccini, Luigi, ed. *Uomini e lavoro in risaia. Il dibattito sulla risicoltura nel '700 e nell '800.* Milan, 1976.

Pugliese, Salvatore. *Due secoli di vita agricola. Produzione e valori dei terreni, contratti agrari, salari e prezzi nel Vercellese nei secoli XVIII e XIX.* Milan, 1908.

Ramella, Franco. "Emigration from an Area of Intense Industrial Development: The Case of Northwestern Italy." In *A Century of European Migrations, 1830–1930*, edited by Rudolph J. Vecoli, 261–74. Urbana, 1991.

Zappi, Elda Gentili. *If Eight Hours Seem Too Few. Mobilization of Women Workers in the Italian Rice Fields.* Albany, 1991.

Cross-references: Italy

ITALIAN STREET MUSICIANS IN 19TH-CENTURY EUROPE

John Zucchi

Italian street musicians started traveling to other parts of Europe in the late 18th century and particularly after the end of the Napoleonic wars. This migration was caused by the agricultural crisis, population pressure, and land parcelization. Their numbers sharply increased in the 1860s and 1870s and then dropped toward the end of the 19th century. The musicians were part of a broader migration stream that included peddlers, tinkers, and traders from various Italian states. Like all these migrants, the musicians were petty entrepreneurs from Italian towns and villages in search of economic opportunity in European cities. By the mid-19th century, however, Italian street musicians alone formed a discrete migration stream, comprising one part of that flow of entertainers that was so visible on the streets of Europe's cities.

The Italian street musicians did not constitute a homogeneous migratory group but were composed of various subsegments, originating from different regions with their own respective traditions. The first significant migrant musicians originated from the Val di Taro, in the Duchy of Parma. These street organists, incorrectly known as "hurdy-gurdy men," came from towns and villages in the region stretching from Bardi to Borgotaro, such as Berceto, Compiano, and Bedonia, as well as from towns south of Genoa along the Ligurian coast and their hinterlands, primarily Santo Stefano d'Aveto, Borzonasca, Mezzanego, Varese Ligure, Zoagli, and Chiavari. Migration was a familiar phenomenon in this region. In the early 19th century hundreds of ink vendors, animal exhibitors, lace makers, hatters, cooks, saddlers, and wax figurine makers, both male and female, migrated from the Val di Taro to Paris and London, but also to smaller French and British cities, as well as to Bremen, Lübeck, Vienna, Istanbul, Smyrna, Thessaloniki, Moscow, and the Americas.

The early wandering musicians can be understood as part of the migratory movement of beggars who practiced quasi-legitimate "trades." Indeed, in early 19th-century Paris and in mid-19th-century London, street musicians shared boardinghouses with fellow townspeople who practiced various street trades. The street music trade might be seen as a short-term solution to cash shortages in periods of crisis. In the late 1850s many, and perhaps the majority, of the migrants from the Duchy of Parma were street musicians. In Barcelona as well as St. Petersburg, more than half of the migrants originating from this region were hurdy-gurdy men or street organists. Another 31 were to be found in Moscow.

These street organists from the Val di Taro were followed by violinists and harpists from a number of agricultural towns in the southern Lucania region, in hilltop settlements south of the city of Potenza, and especially the towns of Viggiano and Laurenzana, Corleto Perticara and Calvello, Marsiconuovo, Marsicovetere, and Brienza. Here too the population crisis, lack of cash, and shortage of arable lands prompted tradesmen, agricultural laborers, and small landholders to export their trades or develop new ones. Among these were shoemakers and jewelers from Laurenzana and coppersmiths from Lagonegro who plied their trades and peddled their wares in Marseille, Barcelona, Madrid, or Paris, and eventually made their way to South America in some cases.

In the 18th century these towns also witnessed the migration of pipers, or *zampognari*, to the Neapolitan coast, traditionally during the Christmas season. By the early 19th century, harpists began to undertake more extensive peregrinations from Viggiano, along with clarinetists and

A young musician on his first trip (*Title page of the book* The Blackgown Paper *by Luigi Mariotti, London, 1846*).

violinists. The idea of playing the harp as a migratory musician emerged from the harpmaking tradition of the town itself. Harpmakers in Viggiano made smaller, 37-string harps that could easily be transported. The town's most famous harpmaker, Vincenzo Bellizia, was said to have made 145 harps for his town's migrants in the 1840s and early 1850s while local musicians had to look elsewhere for their instruments. Historical records, folk poetry, and folklore indicate that by mid-century the *viggianesi* had traveled to numerous towns and cities in Russia, Spain, France, Britain, and the Americas. Children and adults apparently received some basic instruction, whereby some became accomplished harpists.

By the late 19th century, fifers and pipers typically came from the lower Apennines in the Ciociaria area, from towns such as Picinisco, Roccasecca, or Sora. Each of these three districts had its own respective migration tradition, at first in agricultural labor and later in urban trades. Peasant families from the Ciociaria region attained a sort of prominence in France, where their children and young women were prized as artists' models. The fifers and pipers thus fit into the broader pattern of urban migrants from agricultural towns in the Apennines or coastal Ligurian towns. Like other migrants, they tended to be small landholders or tenants who initially sought to supplement their family incomes through yearly migration.

It is difficult to establish the number of Italian street musicians in this period with any exactitude. In the late 1860s and early 1870s – the high point of the street music trade – there were probably between 3,000 and 6,000 child musicians and no more than 10,000 musicians total throughout Europe and the Americas. For the mid-1890s there are estimates of 2,500 Italian musicians on Britain's streets, with 1,000 in London alone. Street musicians were to be found in many towns and cities in Europe, but the most important centers were the Left Bank and Place Maubert in Paris, Saffron Hill in London, and Five Points in New York. These neighborhoods were not only centers for street musicians but were also home to a number of Italian immigrants engaged in various trades and commercial activities. In these areas, southern Italian musicians eventually came to replace the hurdy-gurdy men and barrel-organists from Liguria and Parma.

In the course of the 19th century, Italian street musicians became an increasingly visible minority on the streets of Europe's cities – a development that was both reflected and reinforced by their continuous appearance in contemporary literature. The works of Fyodor Dostoyevsky, Thomas Carlyle, Charles Dickens, George Eliot, and American writers such as Edgar Allan Poe, Louisa May Alcott, and Nathaniel Hawthorne all contain significant allusions to the musicians. Numerous poems and short stories were also written about them, even including one of Horatio Alger's children's novels, *Phil the Fiddler*, which was based on a young Italian violinist.

Something that brought the street musicians a degree of notoriety, particularly from the mid-1860s on, was the high proportion of children involved in the trade. By the 1860s, Italian consuls in Barcelona, Paris, Madrid, Rio de Janeiro, Paramaribo, Havana, and New York regularly issued complaints about the presence of extremely young harpists and fiddlers. The migration of children in mid-19th century Italy was not a rare occurrence as children made up a considerable segment of the migrants from Liguria, Parma, and southern Italy. Like other young migrants in their regions, child musicians – both boys and girls – practiced their craft in the framework of an apprenticeship system. Contracts typically lasted for three years and outlined the obligations that both child and master were expected to fulfill. The masters were known as *padroni*, a term that was used at the time to denote a labor agent and would later be used in reference to Greek, Italian, and Japanese labor agents.

In the late 19th century, state and municipal authorities undertook action – at times rather aggressively – against the street musicians. The initiatives mainly targeted child labor in the trade, but adults were affected as well. Paris, for example, occasionally rid the city of the immigrant musicians, arresting over 2,500 of them between 1867 and 1869. Following these actions, the young fifers from Sora became a major nuisance for the Parisian police. In the Netherlands, Italian street musicians were regularly expelled in the 1860s and 1870s for their mendicant status. In London, a long campaign to control noise in the metropolis complicated the situation of street organists. After the 1889 Act for the Prevention of Cruelty to Children, Italian child musicians became less numerous and less visible on the streets of Britain. Street musicians had virtually disappeared from Austria-Hungary by the turn of the century, although they were able to continue their activities in Sweden and Norway in large numbers. Their numbers dropped in North America, even if barrel-organists were to be found in most cities until the First World War and even beyond. The 1874 Padrone Act, meant to protect

foreign children against involuntary service, proved a formidable tool against child street musicians in the USA. This law was reinforced by an Italian law of 1873 to protect Italian children from being sent abroad with masters in mendicant trades. The law effectively rendered contracts between these children and their masters null and void, which permitted US authorities to press charges against the *padroni*.

The accumulation of cash by street musicians, and particularly by *padroni*, provided capital for new entrepreneurial activities. It is not clear whether this shift to other forms of enterprise was inspired by government legislation and the negative images propagated by the press in the 1870s or rather by the end of the recession of that decade. However, it is evident that by the 1880s many of the traditional areas of origin produced far fewer migrants involved in the street music trade. Italian child musicians from Caserta, for example, entered French industry – the glassworks in Lyon, for example – while adults from the region continued their activities as street musicians in European cities. By 1870 immigrants from the Val di Taro gained prominence in the ice cream business in London, while migrants from Laurenzana became involved in the boot shine trade in New York and later continued their musical careers in Toronto, but no longer on the streets.

Italian musicians did not completely disappear from the streets; they remained relatively prominent even into the 1930s, but by this time they originated from other Italian towns. There is no exact data on return migration, but one might speculate that a great many of the emigrant musicians to North America remained there while the itinerant musicians in Europe more frequently returned to Italy.

Angelini, Massimo. "Mestieri girovaghi e moralismo storiografico: Studi sulla 'Tratta dei fanciulli' nell'appennino settentrionale (sec XIX)." *Il risorgimento* 3 (1996): 425–37.

Carpaneto, Oreste, and Marco Porcella. *Popolare i monti. Storia demografica della comunità di Tribogna*. Genoa, 1990.

Porcella, Marco. *La fatica e la Merica*. Genoa, 1986.

Sponza, Lucio. *Italian Immigrants in Nineteenth-Century Britain: Realities and Images*. Leicester, 1988.

Zucchi, John. *The Little Slaves of the Harp: Italian Child Street Musicians in Nineteenth Century Paris, London, and New York*. Liverpool, 1999.

Cross-references: Austria; France; Germany; Great Britain; Italy; The Netherlands; Russia and Belarus; Spain and Portugal; Southeastern Europe; Italian Ice Cream Makers in Europe since the Late 19th Century

ITALIAN WORKERS IN THE CONSTRUCTION INDUSTRY IN THE PARIS REGION SINCE THE 1870S

Marie-Claude Blanc-Chaléard

From the end of the 19th century, the Italian construction worker was considered the prime example of the border-crossing labor migrant in Europe. The construction of extensive rail networks, including the necessary tunnels, accelerated the industrialization of Europe. Central and western Europe were now easier to reach for seasonal workers from northern Italy. Piedmontese and Lombards went to Switzerland and France, while migrants from Friuli and the Veneto moved to Germany and into the Habsburg Empire or to the Balkans; later, they even pushed into the Czarist Empire via the trans-Siberian railroad. Cities were growing, and the capitals, in particular, were to be made resplendent with representative architecture.

The construction industry developed a huge need for tough and nondemanding proletarians. With exceptions like stonecutters and mosaic craftsmen (terrazzo), the northern Italians in the construction industry were rarely skilled workers. Their strength lay above all in their willingness to work extremely hard for relatively poor pay under harsh conditions, and in the well-established traditions of migration. Those traditions were based on village and family networks that became a central element of the specific pattern of work organization. This had already been behind the success of the bricklayers from the Limousin who migrated annually to the Paris construction sites in the 18th century. In the 19th century, northern Italian construction workers were soon found throughout Europe.

In France, with its low population growth and the reluctance of the rural population to leave their farms for industrial employment, construction was one of the most attractive sectors to foreign workers. In 1900, the northern Italians, collectively referred to as *Piedmontese*, already held 10% of all jobs in the French construction sector. In southeastern France, they far exceeded that number: in 1913, 40% of the bricklayers employed in Marseille came from Italy. All told, more than a quarter of all Italians in France worked in the construction industry, ranging from bricklayer assistants to decorators, tilelayers, painters, or heating engineers. After 1900, the social advancement of an Italian from worker to entrepreneur was no longer a rarity. Already before 1914, many Italian brick workers, coal miners, and metalworkers in the German Ruhr area and Alsace-Lorraine had left for France where they found work in the construction sector and the possibility of establishing their own businesses.

The *Piedmontese*, who for a long time worked chiefly in southeastern France, came into the northern half of France in larger numbers after the Franco-Prussian War of 1870–1. In Paris, the measures of large-scale urban renewal initiated by Haussmann in his function as prefect of Paris were yet to be completed – although Haussmann had to step down from his post as prefect because of the harsh criticism of his plans in the Third Republic. Moreover, structures destroyed in the war – for example, the viaduct of Nogent-sur-Marne located a few kilometers from Paris – had to be rebuilt. Subsequently, one of the most important immigrant communities in the Paris region developed here: in 1896, Nogent was the Paris suburb with the highest percentage of Italians (7%).

According to the census of 1872, 117 Italians were living in Nogent (before the war there had been only 3), mostly young men (only 4 adult women), nearly all of whom were bricklayers or bricklayer assistants and hailed from the Val Ceno (province of Parma) and the Val Nure (province of Piacenza): no less than 40% came from a single community, Ferriere in the upper Val Nure. A pronounced migration tradition developed between Nogent and Val Nure, which led to formation of a tight-knit and permanent community of origin. The small farmers from Ferriere who had previously worked as pit sawyers during their seasonal winter migration worked in Nogent as bricklayers, without being able to show any qualifications other than the ability to work hard and to quickly organize communal life outside of their native village. Beginning in 1872, two of their Italian wives rented out rooms, and the immigrant group grew rapidly. Women found jobs locally as washerwomen or they made feather ornaments (*plumassières*). According to the census of 1891, there were already more than 100 couples or families among the 480 immigrants. At the last census before the outbreak of World War I, the gender ratios among the 800 immigrants were nearly equal.

The construction sector in Nogent employed 70% of the Italian men, and beginning in 1900 there were already several Italian entrepreneurs in the community. The first buildings that these new entrepreneurs built was housing for the men they employed, countrymen from the same region of origin as their own. The Italian colony in Nogent developed into a kind of outpost of Ferriere: a hotel was built, stores sold Italian products. Mobility within the community was extremely high: very few families appeared in the same place in two successive censuses (1891 and 1901: only 25%), and the children were usually sent to Italy until they were old enough to work.

The living and working conditions of the construction workers fused the colony together and set it apart from the native population: in Nogent itself, less than 10% of the local workers were employed in the construction sector. The community itself was made up largely of the petty bourgeoisie: pensioners, employees of the railroad company Chemins de Fer de l'Est, and notables for whom the town was attractive because of its proximity to the Bois de Vincennes. The Italian bricklayers lived in comparatively poor circumstances in the narrow, dirty alleys in the center of town. The natives despised the Italians, and this xenophobia could turn violent – for example, after the Italian anarchist Sante Jeronimo Caserio assassinated the French president, Marie-François Sadi Carnot, in Lyon in 1894. During these times of aggressive xenophobia, the Italians in Nogent never left their homes alone.

Although the immigrants lived isolated from the host society and focused on their homeland, after 1900 there were signs that an integration process was beginning. The entrepreneurs were respected as experts by both their clients and by builders, who accepted them as members of their sociétés de secours mutuel (societies for mutual economic asistance). Some Italian families decided to send their children to local schools, and the mobility of the families declined: 32% of families appeared in both the 1901 and the 1911 census. Twelve percent of marriages in the second generation of immigrants were exogamous. The second generation also tried to escape the bricklaying profession: in 1911, only 45% of Italian workers born in France were still bricklayers. Some Italians showed their ties to France by founding the organization Lyre Garibaldienne Nogentaise, invoking Guiseppe Garibaldi, who was considered in equal measure the champion of the Italian *risorgimento* and a French national hero, who had defended the Third Republic with his army of volunteers in the Franco-Prussian War. However, the organization found little resonance among its own ranks. The First World War intensified the rapprochement between immigrants and natives. Sons of Italians died at the front fighting for France; in 1920, the mayor of Nogent honored them. Thereafter, the Lyre Garibaldienne, by now more successful in attracting members, participated in the local parades celebrating 14 July.

After the First World War, France developed into the chief destination for European migration. The Italians – whether antifascist émigrés or simple workers – formed the main immigrant group, helping to satisfy the enormous demand for workers: in 1931, they accounted for one-third of all immigrants to France, numbering about 1 million. They were present above all in the construction sector, which in the Département Seine in 1931, for example, employed about 41% of the Italian workers. Italian construction businesses flourished during this period. The establishment of additional Italian businesses took place not only on the Seine: at the end of 1920, there were 7,000 throughout the country.

The Italian colony in Nogent also flourished. In 1931 it had more than 1,500 persons, while the region of origin was shifting: the percentage of immigrants from Ferriere and the Val Nure dropped to 30%, since the Italian entrepreneurs in Nogent were now offering jobs to many individual immigrants from Italy, who increasingly settled throughout the environs of Paris. At the same time, however, Italian life became more visible: in Nogent, famous for its *guinguettes* (open air cafés for dancing) along the banks of the Marne where Parisian workers went to dance, talented accordion players born in the "Italian" city center were most welcome. Families tended to band together in the uncertain times of fascism; many decided to stay permanently. The colony was made up mostly of immigrants from traditionally strongly Catholic regions, anti-fascist in the minority though active fascists were equally rare. The identity of the group was in fact oriented less toward national models, cultivating instead the village bonds.

The integration process in the 1930s unfolded full of contradictions. A new wave of xenophobia accompanied the economic crisis and rising international tensions. The Italians in France were confronted with harsh criticism by the French of Italy's policy of expansion after Mussolini had attacked Ethiopia. Many who lost their jobs and were excluded from the communal unemployment benefits left Nogent after 1932. At the same time, in the wake of the liberal citizenship law of 1927, any Italians in the city, especially those from the

Val Nure, some of whom were already living in France in the third generation, took French citizenship. As early as 1926, 23% of persons of Italian background born in France had already done so. The integration of the group was promoted by attendance at school, membership in Catholic youth groups, and shared sports activities. The number of mixed couples was more than 25% in 1936. It was especially painful for these young French people to be accused of treason when Italy entered the war in June 1940. By this time, a little over one-third of those in the colony in Nogent, whether born in France or not, had returned to Italy.

Similar contradictions appeared at the end of World War II after the liberation of France. While the public discussion in France was often shaped by hostility toward the Italians, there was a rapprochement on the private level: young people of the most diverse backgrounds danced in the excursion restaurants and celebrated the *Libération*. The percentage of mixed marriages reached 50. Through postwar reconstruction the building industry experienced a boom that was even more spectacular than the one after the First World War. New construction businesses were set up. In the Paris region, businesses headed by Italians accounted for 20% of all enterprises active in the construction sector, and one-third of all bricklaying shops. In 1962, there were 15 construction businesses run by individuals of Italian background from Nogent. Many had passed from father to son. Others survived only for a brief period. That was the case, for example, for the business Nogentaise run by Jean Maloberti, which was organized as a cooperative by a group of friends who had known each other since their youth and shared a past as ardent Christians in the Catholic Youth Relief Work and as prisoners of war. By contrast, other businesses that had been established by third-generation immigrants were in existence much longer.

In the 1960s, the Italian construction workers were gradually replaced by the Portuguese and the Algerians. A last stream of Italians from the Val Nure reached the colony in the 1950s, which after 1954 counted more Frenchmen of Italian background than Italians. Among a total of 1,260 persons in 1962 there were 804 French citizens, just under 20% of whom worked in the construction sector. Many were factory workers, more than 20% were white-collar workers. By contrast, more than 60% of the Italian workers from the last wave of immigrants was working in construction.

As the occupational profile of the children of Italians in Nogent approached that of the children of the French, the colony, which had existed for a century, was eventually barely visible any longer, because its members had dispersed across the entire Paris region. Legal equality through nationalization and especially through birth in France had formed the first stage on the road to integration. Even if the construction industry was for many entrepreneurial families a path of social advancement, for others integration only came with the disappearance of the stigma of being an "Italian bricklayer." Cultural integration accelerated after the Second World War when the immigrants were increasingly considered French and the hostility of the French aroused by the war waned. Entry into the age of consumption since the 1950s has further promoted integration.

The immigrants had early adopted the prevailing customs in Nogent and saw themselves as part of the community. In spite of the segregation in the 1930s, in the postwar period the colony merged completely with the suburban community. The war caused the colony to shrink. Among those who eventually settled in Nogent and had offspring, many preserved a kind of Italian "reserve identity." The ties to Italy remained intact and were strengthened by a city partnership between Nogent and the Val Nure. It is said that in Ferriere, everyone speaks French in August. An organization to solidify the relationship between the Val Nure and the suburb east of Paris was founded in 1978 (ASPAPI: Association de Parme et Plaisance en France). A revival of Italian culture in Nogent was promoted by the growing trend after the end of the 20th century of becoming aware of one's roots. The Italian state also took a growing interest in the Italian diaspora and, for example, offered Italian citizenship to all residents of Nogent who had Italian parents.

The occupational specialization in the construction industry undoubtedly shaped the identity of the Italian immigrants and kept the group together. Chain migrations and the establishment of businesses reinforced the ties to the place of origin while at the same time reproducing the occupational specialization. As a result, it was precisely the Italian construction workers and entrepreneurs in Nogent who remained connected to their Italian origins, more strongly than other Italian migrant laborers in neighboring communities and in Paris itself. The Italians had succeeded in finding a specialization in an occupation that held little prestige and to turn it into a positive, identity-creating characteristic.

Blanc-Chaléard, Marie-Claude. *Les Italiens dans l'Est parisien. Une histoire d'intégration (années 1880–1960)*. Rome, 2000.

Blanc-Chaléard, Marie-Claude. "La petite entreprise italienne du bâtiment en banlieue parisienne: Passage vers la société industrielle." *Actes de l'Histoire de l'immigration* 1 (2001), http://barthes.ens.fr/clio/revues/AHI/articles/volumes/chalea.html.

Blanc-Chaléard, Marie-Claude, ed. *Les petites Italies dans le monde*. Rennes, 2007.

Colin, Mariella, ed. *L'émigration-immigration italienne et les métiers du bâtiment en France et en Normandie*. Caen, 2001.

Milza, Pierre. *Voyage en Ritalie*. Paris, 1995.

Milza, Pierre, and Marie-Claude Blanc-Chaléard. *Le Nogent des Italiens*. Paris, 1995.

Rainhorn J., ed. *Les petites Italies dans l'Europe du Nord-Ouest. Recherches valenciennoises*. Valenciennes, 2005.

Cross-references: France; Italy; Italian Industrial Workers in Western and Central Europe in the Late 19th and Early 20th Centuries; Italian Labor Migrants in Northern, Central, and Western Europe since the End of World War II; Maghrebis in France after Decolonization in the 1950s and 1960s; Portuguese Labor Migrants in Northwestern Europe since the 1950s: The Examples of France and Germany

ITALIANS IN SOUTHERN TYROL SINCE THE END OF WORLD WAR I

Günther Pallaver

A stable Italian language group in southern Tyrol emerged essentially in the first half of the 20th century. State-guided settlement was joined by economically motivated immigration. Using historical turning points, one can also reconstruct how the Italian language group underwent a change in its self-understanding during the last third of the 20th century. Whereas that group saw itself as part of the Italian nation until the 1970s and thus as the dominant majority population, today the Italian language group regards itself as an ethnic minority. Finally, for a number of years now one has been able to trace the process of an emerging "South Tyrolean nation" among the Italian-speaking southern Tyrolese. All three language groups (Germans, Italians, Ladin speakers) are embarked on the difficult path to a common regional identity.

Southern Tyrol has always been a trilingual land. In the Duchy of Tyrol, until 1918 a crown land (province) of the Habsburg monarchy, Italians lived in Welsch Tyrol or in the Trentino, Ladin speakers round the Sellastock/Passo Sella, and German-speaking Tyroleans and Vorarlbergers in the remaining parts. According to the last official census by the monarchy (1910), modern-day southern Tyrol had about 7,000 Italians among a total population of 251,500 (3%). There may have been substantially more. Most settled in the southern Tyrolean Unterland/Bassa Atesina, a valley bordering the Trentino. The immigration from the Trentino was a consequence of the economic gap between north and south in Tyrol. The Trentino migrants found employment above all in agriculture, in timber rafting on the Etsch/Adige River, and then in the construction of the railway lines. Many of these Austrian citizens with Italian as their native language had assimilated over the decades.

The end of World War I and the occupation (1918) and annexation of southern Tyrol by Italy (1920) led to a first wave of Italian immigration. The emigrants were first representatives of the state apparatus, especially military men and high-ranking civil servants. After fascism came to power in October 1922, the Italian immigration was deliberately directed. To Italianize the German-speaking population, the regime employed repressive measures in the administration of the area, the schools, and the culture. Within a few years, personnel from other Italian regions had replaced the majority of South Tyrolese teachers and civil servants. In 1926, Bolzano/Bozen was made the capital of the newly created province of Bolzano, which led to the establishment of a series of new agencies as well as military and civilian installations in which Italians were employed.

Beginning in the 1930s, the politics of cultural repression was supplemented by the policy of demographic majorization. Since the German-speaking population of southern Tyrol would not let itself be forcibly assimilated, the fascist government was intent, using a targeted economic policy, on pushing Italian immigration to make the German-speaking population a numerical minority in their own land. A key element was creation of the industrial zone in Bolzano/Bozen, though it was also driven by the state's overall employment policy. Beginning in 1935, the industrial settlement was realized with the participation of the most important representatives of industrial enterprises in Lombardy (Falck, Feltrinelli, Viberti, Lancia, Montecatini). The settlement of thousands of workers in a separate neighborhood (the *semirurali*) that this entailed drastically altered the ethnic composition of Bolzano/Bozen. Of about 80,800 Italians living in the province of Bolzano/Bozen in 1939, about half (36,000) resided in Bolzano. While the civil servants came from all parts of Italy, the industrial workers were chiefly from the Veneto and Lombardy, the areas from which the industrial enterprises drew their skilled workers. The composition of the language groups was affected especially by the 1939 Option Agreement between Italy and the German Reich, on the basis of which just under 80,000 German-speaking southern Tyrolese emigrated to the German Reich by 1943. Conversely, during the German occupation of southern Tyrol between 1943 and 1945, there was a small exodus of Italians.

In 1910, about 7,000 (3%) Italians had officially lived in South Tyrol, mostly from the Trentino. According to the first census after World War I (1921), their numbers had risen to about 20,000 (8%). By 1939, South Tyrol was home to 81,000 Italians (24%) and by 1943, this number was 95,000 – an increase between 1921 and 1943 of 75,000.

Immigration was largely restricted to the cities. The only larger, more or less stable Italian population group active in agriculture came after the regulation of the Etsch/Adige River in 1926–8. This river had routinely flooded, making the surrounding land unusable for agriculture. When the river's course was stabilized, more reliably arable land was created, and migrant farmers were invited to cultivate this property. Approximately 140 families from the Veneto came and settled in the "Borgo Vittoria" of Sinigo/Sinich near Meran/Merano. As agricultural sharecroppers they constituted, together with several hundred immigrants who were working in the new Sinich chemical factory of the Montecatini, a self-contained and outwardly closed-off Italian island in a purely German environment. That remained so also after 1945.

As early as 1945, a series of negative factors confronted the Italian immigrants. In sociodemographic terms there was an abundance of Italians in the bureaucracy, in industry, and in trade, while they were virtually nonexistent in agriculture. By 1945, immigrants were coming to South Tyrol from many different regions, and because of their varied origins, the resulting group had little social and cultural cohesion. Only three territories, the Veneto, the Trentino, and Lombardy, were sending immigrants at above-average rates. From the late 1940s, another numerically strong group was made up of Italians from Istria and the adjoining Adriatic coastal region; they had been expelled from Yugoslavia and had migrated to South Tyrol. The Italians of South Tyrol thus remained socially splintered with respect to their regions of origin. In 1951, of the 115,000 Italians in South Tyrol, 91,400 had been born outside the province of Bolzano/Bozen.

The conditions for peaceful cohabitation of the language groups were not favorable after 1945. Fascism and National Socialism had left behind deep wounds on both sides. Opposition to the dictatorships in Italy and Germany had not generated any shared experiences among the Italians and Germans of South Tyrol. While the Italian resistance had been focused chiefly on the preservation of the Brennero/Brenner border, the German resistance had pursued the return of South Tyrol to Austria. The ethnically competing resistance, the failed de-Nazification and de-fascization, as well as the lack of democratic traditions in both camps, led to a resurgence of nationalism and to "ethnic blockbuilding," understood as the consolidation of ethnic segregation within the population and the political system.

One of the few elements of cohesion among the Italians in South Tyrol was based on their awareness of confronting another group on foreign territory. They did not have strong territorial ties to the land where they were, and the substitute for this lack was their shared national membership in and identification with the Italian state, which was seen as a kind of national and social patron. Many Italians saw themselves as the outpost and defenders of *Italianità* in a border region whose national ownership was still contested and which had to be defended against possible German annexation ambitions. That, not least, is the reason the neo-fascist Movimento Sociale Italiano (MSI), which was stoking nationalism, was always more successful in South Tyrol than in the rest of Italy.

While many Italians thus saw themselves as a group charged with a "national mission," they were often perceived and labeled by the German-speaking population as "nationalists" and "fascists." The reasons for this were the charged nationalistic climate in the land, the slow implementation of South Tyrol's autonomy after 1948, a creeping "re-fascization" (e.g., harassment by the Italian bureaucracy, violation of basic rights), and a lack of employment opportunities in the region: the modernization process in agriculture released a large number of German-speaking workers, who found few job opportunities in Italian industry and administration and therefore often were compelled to emigrate. One result of this political and social development was South Tyrolean terrorism in the 1960s. These attacks were carried out by German-speaking inhabitants of South Tyrol who demanded autonomy for South Tyrol and who accused the Italian state of marginalizing the German-speaking inhabitants.

Judging from Table 1, the development of the Italian language group after 1945 can be divided into two phases: until the 1960s, one can speak of a second immigration to South Tyrol, though it was smaller compared to the period until 1945. After passage of the second Autonomy Statute of 1972, the size of the Italian population group declined.

The primary characteristics of the migratory movements within Italy in the first years after World War II were a

Table 1. Population trends in South Tyrol, 1900–2001,* according to language groups, in percentages

Year	Italians	Germans	Ladin speakers
1900	4.0	88.8	4.0
1910	2.9	89.0	3.8
1921	10.6	75.9	3.9
1961	34.3	62.2	3.4
1971	33.3	62.9	3.7
1981	28.7	64.9	4.1
1991	27.6	67.9	4.2
2001	26.4	69.1	4.3

* Next census: 2011.
Source: Italian Census.

pronounced flight from the rural land and a resulting concentration in the cities. During that time, several thousand additional Italians settled in the cities of South Tyrol, especially in Bolzano/Bozen. Apart from industry, public service continued to motivate immigration into the provincial capital. This trend deepened the already existing social and economic structural differences between the language groups. The economically motivated immigration of the Italian population was politically supported by the government in Rome, for example through a generous housing construction program.

Between 1946 and 1952, around 25,000 Italians, mostly from the region of northern Italy, moved to South Tyrol. Just under 40% of the immigrants came from the Trentino and the Veneto each; the immigration from the regions of central Italy was a little below 10% and that from southern Italy around 5%; the rest came from other regions of northern Italy and Istria, whose Italian population had fled to Italy from Yugoslavia.

Passage of the second Autonomy Statute in 1972 constituted an important turning point for the psychological condition of the Italians in South Tyrol. This statute provided for protection of minorities, which improved the condition of the German-speaking and Ladin-speaking South Tyroleans, and the territorial self-administration of all three language groups – and thus also of the Italians. With this statute, the Italian language group lost a series of privileges, while the formerly dominated German-speaking minority became the dominant language group in the land. The repercussions of the new autonomy of 1972 – which was based on recognition of the numbers of the respective language groups and on ethnic separation – became evident at the end of the 1970s. The Italian South Tyroleans, who were caught off guard by the autonomy statute of 1972, were most strongly affected by the new rules of territorial self-government, since the ethnic proportionality that was now introduced – i.e., the allocation of public sector jobs based on the relative strength of the language groups and the requirement that applicants be bilingual – blocked their privileged access to these jobs.

Added to this was the onset of a crisis in industry, which likewise affected primarily those segments of the labor market

that were occupied chiefly by Italians. The ethnic division of labor was now exacting its revenge. Suddenly the Italians of South Tyrol felt like a minority in their own state, which no longer held out its protective hand over them. Many decried the state's withdrawal in South Tyrol and the capitulation of the nation before the German minority, which evoked a powerful sense of impotence. The new situation not only reinforced the already existing nationalistic attitude of some of the Italians but also bitterly disappointed those who had fought for the new autonomy statute of 1972.

This discontent was further strengthened by the census of 1981, when it became statistically evident that in the preceding 10 years the Italian language group had declined from 33.3% to 28.7% of the population. The reasons were a stronger emigration – triggered by the crisis in industry and the removal of unlimited access to public sector jobs – and a birthrate that was lower that that of the largely rural German-speaking population. Discontent gave rise to political protest, which in turn led to the rise of nationalism, occasional terrorist acts at the beginning of the 1980s, a loss of votes for Italian parties that were pro-autonomy, and – conversely – growing support for the neo-fascist MSI, after 1995 the Alleanza Nazionale (AN). Frustration mounted when the Italians' massive backing for the MSI/AN in the various provincial elections did not lead to the hoped-for change in the political course in Bolzano/Bozen and Rome. Although the AN formed the strongest Italian group in the South Tyrolean provincial council (since 2008 with Forza Italia as Popolo della libertà), it was always excluded from participation in the government because of its politics and its past. The realization among many Italians that they achieved nothing with their protest votes has caused voter turnout in elections, and thus the political participation among the Italians of South Tyrol, to decline by several percentage points compared to that of the German-speaking population.

The attempt by the Italians to overcome this discontent expressed itself in two different directions. A smaller group is striving for stronger integration and closer contacts with members of the other language groups. This endeavor is running into institutional barriers, especially since the Second Autonomy Statute is based on the ethnic separation of the language groups. Institutional separation (schools, clubs, media, church) and the concentration of the Italians in monolingual conurbations impede this cultural exchange. By contrast, a larger share of the Italians is concerned about its own identity, leading to a greater emphasis on Italienità, an attitude that repeatedly slips into a nationalistic tenor.

As of the census of 2001, the Italian language group seems to have stabilized at 26.4% of the population, even if the internal turnover (immigration from and emigration to other regions) remains relatively high. Alongside the 113,494 Italians there are 296,461 German-speaking South Tyrolese, who make up 69.1% of the population. There are also 18,736 Ladin speakers (4.3%); 3.3% of the population are not EU citizens (2008: 6.7% foreign residents – 33% EU citizens and 67% non-EU citizens). Even more than before 1945,

South Tyrol's Italians live in the cities and a few villages of the South Tyrolean Unterland/Bassa Atesina. They constitute the majority in only five of 116 communities in South Tyrol, with the two neighboring cities of Bolzano/Bozen (73%) and Laives/Leifers (70%) heading the list. These two cities are also home to just under 70% of the Italians in South Tyrol. In six communities they reach a proportion of more than 30%, in five more than 20%, and in ten more than 10%. In the remaining communities (with a few exceptions) they make up less than 5%.

Gatterer, Claus. *Im Kampf gegen Rom. Bürger, Minderheiten und Autonomien in Italien*. Vienna, 1968.

Pallaver, Günther. "South Tyrol's Consociational Democracy: Between Political Claim and Social Reality." In *Tolerance through Law: Self Governance and Group Rights in South Tyrol (European Academy Bozen/Bolzano)*, edited by Jens Woelk, Francesco Palermo, and Joseph Marko, 303–27. Leiden and Boston, 2008.

Statistisches Jahrbuch für Südtirol 2008, edited by ASTAT. Bolzano/Bozen, 2009.

Südtiroler Sprachbarometer/Barometro linguistic dell'Alto Adige 2004, edited by ASTAT. Bolzano/Bozen, 2006.

Wanderungen und demographische Entwicklung in Südtirol. Jüngste Entwicklungen und aktuelle Tendenzen 1960–1997, edited by ASTAT. Bolzano/Bozen, 2000.

Cross-references: Austria; Germany; Italy; Italian Refugees in Italy from Adriatic Territories That Fell to Yugoslavia after 1945

JACOBITES IN EUROPE, 1688–1788

Christoph von Ehrenstein

The term "Jacobite" is derived from the Latin name of the English Stuart monarch James II, who was deposed in the wake of the "Glorious Revolution" (1688–9) of William of Orange (from 1689 King William III of England, Scotland, and Ireland). Accordingly, from the early 1690s, Jacobites were all those who strove for a restoration of the Stuart dynasty that was in exile in France. For three generations after 1688, the Stuarts maintained their claim to the British throne. The constellation of European powers in the 18th century allowed them to undertake numerous attempts at invading the island with the help of continental allies. Supporters of the dynasty tried to bring it back in two larger uprisings in Great Britain (1715, 1745). Only after 1750 was it perfectly clear that there would be no second restoration of the Stuarts.

One upshot of the smoldering "British war of succession" after 1688 was the emergence of a widely dispersed, socially and religiously heterogeneous Jacobite diaspora in Europe. In five waves of migration, a total of 30,000–40,000 Stuart supporters left the British Isles after their political or military defeats of 1689, 1691, 1716, 1719, and 1746. Only a minority of a few thousand returned over the course of the 18th century. Until the uprising in Scotland and parts of northern England in 1715, the almost exclusively Catholic Irish Jacobites made up the majority of the exiles (at least 60%); however, even before 1715, Stuart supporters were also recruited among the Protestant communities in England (about 30%) and Scotland (around 6%). Jacobites hailed from nearly all regions of Great Britain, and their confessional and geographic composition changed over the course of time. In spite of the very diverse experiences of exile, which depended strongly on the exiles' region of origin, their confessional background, and the time of their departure, something they had in common was that many were received into already established communities of British natives. The Stuarts' supporters, often of noble lineage, integrated quickly into the elites of their respective host country. For that reason the Jacobite identity of most immigrants had long since faded when the last pretender to the throne, Charles Edward Stuart, died in 1788.

The two waves of refugees following the change of ruler in England and the military defeats of the Jacobites in Scotland (1689) and Ireland (1691) were by far the largest. In the winter of 1688–9, a first group around the court of James II, his wife, Maria of Modena, and their son, the future James III, left the island. From 1689 to 1713, the royal family, along with its ministers, advisors, and staff, found refuge at Saint-Germain-en-Laye, the former chief residence of Louis XIV. Financed by the French king, a representative Jacobite court-in-exile comprising around 300 people established itself there within a few short months. In the 1690s as many as 1,000 additional families arrived in the city, and their strong aristocratic background (about 40%) substantially shaped the exile community. Alongside the immediate royal household, military and court personnel, the staff of the many noble families, Catholic clergy, and tradesmen formed the largest occupational groups among the exiles.

Almost all the soldiers were part of the second wave of migration during these years. After the defeat of a counter-revolution in Ireland in the fall of 1691, initiated by James II, a total of 15,000 Irish soldiers and officers with about 4,000 wives and children followed their king to France. Since the 18th century, often referred to as the climax of the "flight of the wild geese," the subsequent service of these regiments under French and later Austrian, Spanish, or Russian command was part of the tradition of Irish mercenary service on the Continent. At the same time, however, multifarious contacts with the court in exile were maintained, and until the 1730s the British public looked askance at these "Irish regiments" as a potential army of the Stuarts – and not entirely without reason. In many cases, for example, the Irish exiles worked hand in hand with freebooters to whom James II had granted letters of marque in return for a share of the booty. At the exiled court itself, however, the Irish played no important role, in spite of their large numbers. They occupied only about 7% of all posts at court, while Englishmen and Scotsmen held the most important positions in roughly equal parts.

Next to Saint-Germain-en-Laye, Paris became the most important place of exile. Here, more than 1,000 Jacobites settled in sections of the city that had been traditionally marked by a strong British presence. In addition to the university neighborhood, where the various monasteries and seminaries of the British Catholics were located, they lived in Saint-Sulpice and Saint-German-des-Prés, where they rubbed elbows with the British who were passing through on their "Grand Tour." Some 300–400 exiled clergy functioned alongside the resident British priests as legal advisors, translators, messengers, and agents in financial matters. Their services were used especially by the Jacobite soldiers in the French army. Social conflicts were not absent in these centers of Jacobite exile. For example, in the 1690s bands of Irish highwaymen haunted the road between Saint-Germain-en-Laye and Paris, and the tense relationship between Jacobites and French citizens erupted on the local level in several violent clashes.

The smoother integration in the coastal cities of France and in the Netherlands was aided by the close contacts the Jacobites had to established communities of British immigrants. Traditional trade relationships between southern Ireland and the coastal regions of western Europe made it easier for many Irish exiles to survive. In French port cities like Nantes, Saint Malo, or Bordeaux, soldiers and sailors as well as numerous tradesmen joined the communities of ethnic Irish, which maintained long-established connections with their region of origin and were characterized by the comings and goings – as well as the remigration, though small – of Irish Jacobites. Much the same holds true for the English and Scottish Jacobites, who were often taken in by the already existing ethnic communities in the Netherlands and northern France.

Many of the exiles who arrived en masse lived in poverty or were able to survive only with the help of occasional donations from better-off members of the group. Some of the wealthier Jacobites brought substantial assets with them from home; for years some even derived income from their British estates, which were mostly run in their absence by family members, often by wives who had remained behind. Given such frequently close familial ties, the Jacobite elite tended to remigrate to their country of origin when the political climate improved.

The Jacobite exile, concentrated in this first phase in France and the Netherlands, is usually described as a phenomenon motivated purely by politics. It is true that loyalty to the exiled dynasty, often coupled with practical hopes of new career opportunities after a restoration, played a central role. However, added to this were confessional reasons, since the Stuarts had lost the English throne not least because of their Catholicism. Especially among the Irish Jacobites, who were almost exclusively Catholic, the longing for a return to their homeland was combined with the hope of religious equality and with Counter-Reformation ideas.

The regional and confessional background played a crucial role also in the way the Jacobites perceived themselves and were perceived by outsiders. For example, the French population often did not see the Jacobites as political refugees at all, since they became part of the ethnic Irish-Catholic communities that had existed for generations. Moreover, the marriage patterns of the exiles and the choice of godparents in communities in France show that the orientation toward the countries of origin and the confessional identities were still dominant in the second generation. The local social models of the regions of origin lived on in the destination countries; patronage relationships were maintained. At the exiled court, the various "national" and confessional groups among the Jacobites were engaged in grim struggles over the political and religious path to a restoration of the Stuarts. Although these conflicts rendered an effective policy more difficult, until the end of the reign of Queen Anne (1702–14; after 1707 Queen of Great Britain), all groups shared the belief that they would triumph in the end. Since exile was seen as a temporary experience, few made efforts to become citizens of the countries in which they took refuge.

The exiled court of the Stuarts, the Catholic seminaries and monasteries on the Continent, and the Irish and Scottish regiments in service to the great European powers were the nodal points of the continental network of Stuart supporters. These institutions also made possible the existence of a Jacobite diaspora following the defeat of the uprising in 1715, which had sought to place a Stuart on the throne. The central point of reference, despite its waning cultural importance, remained the court of the Stuarts, which, after stops in Bar-le-Duc, Avignon, and Urbino, resided in Rome after 1719. In the Palazzo del Re north of the capitol, the Scottish nobility now dominated the conspiratorial endeavors to restore Stuart rule in Great Britain. Since the military stage of Jacobite uprisings had shifted to Scotland and northern England, the regional and confessional composition of the Jacobite exile also changed. Although it has so far not been possible to come up with precise numbers, we must assume that the movements of refugees to the Continent were noticeably smaller during this phase. After the rebellion of 1715, between 400 and 2,000 Scottish and English Jacobites reached French exile directly or via Scandinavia. Even smaller was the number of refugees following the equally unsuccessful Scottish uprising of 1719. The Jacobite diaspora experienced a brief revitalization after the military defeat of Culloden in 1746, when several hundred Stuart loyalists fled Scotland. The percentage of noble Jacobites among the new exiles was as high as it had been as late as the 1690s. In all, well over half of the refugees probably came from noble families or the gentry. Already before 1715, their aristocratic status had eased the integration of many Catholic exiles in their host countries. Once again, positions in (financial) administration, the military, or the diplomatic corps were the usual career stations. Especially the noble Stuart supporters of the second generation, because of their language skills and experiences, provided diplomats to Austria, Spain, and France. In Spain, moreover, the Jacobites already enjoyed equal rights under the law thanks to relevant decrees (1680, 1701, and

1718). On 30 November 1715, France also carried out a general nationalization of all foreigners who had been in French service for more than 10 years.

The new stream of Protestant Jacobites from Scotland, however, had few opportunities to pursue work appropriate to their status in the Catholic monarchies. Moreover, Protestant services were either officially prohibited, as in France, or only tolerated unofficially, as in Rome. Unless they converted, Protestants were generally barred from service in the French military or administration. Numerous petitions to the exiled court provide insight into the life of the Scots in the French provinces, and it was characterized by poverty, loneliness, and alcoholism. Quite a few managed, through legal loopholes and family connections, to have their forfeited estates in their home countries run by family members, and eventually some were able to return home after several years of dismal experiences in exile. For the others, thanks to the by now established patronage network of the Stuarts, positions in Prussia, Scandinavia, or Russia opened up over time. James Keith of Inverguie, the son of a Scottish earl from Aberdeenshire who had a stellar military career in Russia and Prussia as Field Marshal Keith, is merely the most prominent example. Dozens of Jacobites were also among the foreign experts on administration and the economy that Czar Peter the Great brought to St. Petersburg.

The integration of the elites into their various destination countries did not necessarily mean that the refugees lost their political identity as Jacobites. However, after 1715, loyalty to the Stuarts was gradually joined by a second political identity as subjects of the respective host countries. It was precisely the Jacobite network, which was especially strong between the 1720s and the 1740s and promoted integration in the destination countries, that could lead to conflicts of loyalty, which were – in cases of doubt – resolved in favor of the new employers. In the end it was not only another defeat of a Scottish uprising in 1745–6, but also the physical and intellectual decline of the Jacobite crown prince Charles Edward Stuart in the 1750s that reduced the number of politically committed exiled Jacobites to a hard core around the exiled court in Rome.

Important throughout the period in question was the transfer of knowledge and culture between England and the Continent. In Gothenburg, for example, the Swedish East Asia Company was founded after the British model. The machines and workers that the Jacobite John Holker brought to Rouen in 1749 made a crucial contribution to the development of the French textile industry. However, a uniform artistic taste, shaped by the respective host country, did not develop in the Jacobite diaspora. The preference of the Jacobite elite for Italian painting and music led to a clear cultural profile from the very beginning only in the case of the exiled court. What was disseminated in Europe was John Locke's political philosophy as well as Catholic mysticism. It is occasionally argued that the Jacobite presence in fact had a crucial role in shaping the early European Enlightenment, but that remains a questionable proposition

considering that the Jacobite diaspora was culturally very heterogeneous.

The prominent role of individual Jacobites and the Europe-wide patronage network gave rise to contemporary conspiracy theories, which have lived on into the historiography of the 21st century. For example, the exiled Stuart dynasty was assigned the leading role within European Freemasonry. This rumor was fed by the knowledge that Jacobite elites had a crucial hand in setting up the first lodges in Paris, Rome, Madrid, Russia, and Switzerland. However, the establishment of Freemason lodges points not so much to secret plans to control European politics as to a characteristic feature of the Jacobite diaspora: it is best understood as an exiled military and administrative elite which, in the first half of the 18th century, participated actively throughout all of Europe in the processes of political, social, economic, and cultural change from absolutism to the Enlightenment.

Chaussinand-Nogaret, Guy. "Une élite insulaire au service de l´Europe: Les Jacobites au XVIIIe siècle." *Annales* 28 (1973): 1097–122.

Corp, Edward. *A Court in Exile. The Stuarts in France, 1689–1718.* Cambridge, 2004.

Cruickshanks, Eveline, and Edward Corp, eds. *The Stuart Court in Exile and the Jacobites.* London, 1995.

Genet-Rouffiac, Nathalie. "La Première Génération de l´exil jacobite à Paris et Saint-Germain-en-Laye (1688–1715)." Thèse de Doctorat, Ecole Pratique Des Hautes Etudes. Paris, 1995.

Szechi, Daniel. *The Jacobites. Britain and Europe 1699–1788.* Manchester, 1994.

Szechi, Daniel. " 'Cam Ye O´er Frae France': Exile and the Mind of Scottish Jacobitism, 1716–1727." *Journal of British Studies* 37 (1998): 357–90.

Wills, Rebecca. *The Jacobites and Russia 1715–1750.* East Linton, 2002.

Cross-references: France; Germany; Great Britain; Italy; The Netherlands; Russia and Belarus; Spain and Portugal; British Royalists in Western, Central, and Southern Europe, 1640–1660; English Puritan Refugees in the Netherlands in the 16th and 17th Centuries; European Elites on the Grand Tour in the Early Modern Period; Scottish Soldiers in Europe in the Early Modern Period

JESUITS IN EUROPE SINCE THE EARLY MODERN PERIOD

Birgit Emich

"Jesuits" is the name – originally used as a derisive nickname – for members of the Society of Jesus (Lat. *Societas Jesu*), an order of Catholic clerks regular that is active around the world. Though the term was never officially recognized, it was used by members of the order themselves as early as the 16th century. The word referred to the Jesuits' perception of themselves as serving the Church militant as successors to Jesus, though its semantic connotations (false, sanctimonious, hypocritical) also reflect the polemic that has accompanied the order since its canonical establishment by the pope in 1540.

The Jesuit Order is a prime example of the mobility that is structurally inherent in the Catholic Church by virtue of its missionary impulse: the group around Ignatius of Loyola, the founder of the order, placed themselves at the pope's disposal in 1540 that he might send them "where the need is the greatest." Initially the goal was to spread the faith, and after 1550 also to defend it. Alongside missionary work among the pagans, Jesuits thus became active in fighting against the Reformation and consolidating the Catholic faith in Europe.

In pursuing its efforts, the order became known for its pastoral work (reforms of individual pastoral care) as well as its educational offerings, which ranged from schools for Jesuits-in-training (1749: 61 around the world), to seminaries (176), colleges for the laity (669), and universities (24). In view of the missionary ideology, the traditional monastic way of life – including fidelity to place, divine offices, and the monastic habit – was given up and the dispersal of the members all over the world was laid down in the order's constitution. The coexistence of strict centralized leadership (superior general at the top, absolute obedience to the pope) and heightened demands on the training of the members of the order (membership in four graduated levels from novice to full member) reflected the order's view of itself as a spiritual-intellectual elite, but also its perception by outsiders as the spearhead of the pope and of the Counter-Reformation completely obedient to Rome, as well as the image of the Jesuits as Europe's schoolmasters.

The patterns of the Jesuits' movements – members of the order were active on all continents (India, Japan, Congo, Brazil) as early as 1550 – break down into two phases within Europe. The period of the quantitative and geographic expansion began with the systematic dispersal of the group around Ignatius during his lifetime. When Ignatius died in 1556, the order had around 1,000 members. That number rose to 5,000 by 1580 and 14,000 by 1620. The order attained its maximum size of 22,600 members around 1750. While about one-seventh of the entire order was at that time active in missionary work outside Europe, the great majority of Jesuits were dispersed among the countries of Europe. Organized into provinces, the Jesuits were represented in all Catholic countries of Europe as early as the beginning of the 17th century, with focal points in Flanders and along the Lower Rhine, in northern Italy, and in central and southeastern Spain. Since the settlement of Jesuits had to be approved not only by the leadership of the order but also by the respective secular authorities, the order was not able to gain an official foothold in Protestant countries. However, the Society of Jesus was present even there through its participation in missionary work (in England since 1580).

In the first decades after its founding, the society spread chiefly through the migration of Italian Jesuits, who, after a brief phase of Spanish predominance, dominated the order

Expulsion of the Jesuits by the Bohemian Protestants at the beginning of the Thirty Years' War (1618/19). Contemporary satirical engraving (*Germanisches Nationalmuseum, Nuremberg*).

from the late 16th century. However, the recruitment of new members was soon undertaken in the host societies. In France, for example, only Frenchmen could be active as Jesuits after 1604. Still, migration movements occurred: within a province through reassignments, necessitated for instance by the foundation of new colleges, and across country borders, primarily for training and teaching at the national colleges in Rome (e.g., Collegium Germanicum for German priests). As a rule, Jesuits from non-Catholic countries had to undergo their training and education abroad, for example, English Jesuits at the English College in Rome or at the colleges in Flanders founded by and for Englishmen.

The second phase in the history of the order's migration commenced with the expulsion of the Jesuits from several Catholic countries and their colonies beginning in 1759, the prohibition of the society in France in 1764, and the official dissolution of the order in 1773. For some members this meant a time of forced migration: while the Jesuits from Portugal (1,100 of 1,700), Spain (5,100), Naples (1,400), and Parma (170) were taken in by the Papal State, the former members in France (3,500) and in most territories of the Empire were able to stay where they were and continue to work as priests or teachers. That was also true in Russia and Prussia, whose monarchs appreciated the Jesuits as teachers in their Catholic provinces and did not enforce the dissolution, or only did so years later.

With the reestablishment of the order in 1814 and its reauthorization in most countries, some Jesuits returned to their former lands. Jesuits were expelled from many countries up until the 20th century: Belgium 1816, Russia 1820, Portugal and Spain 1834–5, Austria and Galicia 1848–52, Switzerland 1847–1973, Germany 1873–1917, France 1880, and Spain 1932. All told, more than 1,000 Jesuits died in the persecutions since 1540. The number of members rose only slowly after 1814, to 4,600 in 1850. In 1880 it stood at 10,500, in 1900 the order had 15,000 members worldwide, and by 1930 it had 22,000. A new high point was reached in 1965 with 36,000 members, and the numbers have been declining since then. In 1999, membership was 21,700, the level of 1750. Today, more than half of new members come from traditionally non-Christian countries.

Antipathy toward the Jesuits was often linked with their self-image as a spiritual-intellectual elite and the way in which that expressed itself ("Jesuit pride"). Anti-Jesuit polemics existed at all times and even in Catholic countries. From the *Monita secreta* (a forgery, but widely accepted; published in 1614 by a former Polish Jesuit and allegedly representing the secret directives of the superior general of the order) to Blaise Pascal's *Léttres écrites à un provincial* (1657), which also met with wide resonance, the following attributions were part of the fixed stock of the negative image that outsiders had of the order: the "striving for power," as evidenced by the large number of Jesuit confessors at the Catholic courts in Europe; the "enrichment of the order and its members," a charge whose substantive core is found in the dependence of the society, committed to poverty, on donations and foundations; and "loose morals," a charge that was theologically grounded in the rejection of Jesuit teachings (free will, doctrine of probability).

Within Catholicism, the image of the worldly, scheming Jesuit to whom every means was acceptable was also disseminated by representatives of the old and new monastic orders who felt threatened (above all the Capuchins) by the more mobile and thus often more successful Jesuit competition, and by members of the church hierarchy: cathedral chapters and bishops saw the Jesuits, as the standard bearers of the Tridentine Reform, as a challenge to their customary ways, their status, and their resources – whom one could dismiss, in the words of one canon from Münster in the 17th century, as "beardless Roman playactors," but not ignore.

When it comes to the attributions that characterized the Jesuits as outsiders within their host societies, one must distinguish between images of the confessional age up to around 1700, and ideologically driven perceptions since the Enlightenment. In the first phase, the Jesuits, independent of the confession of the majority society, were seen as tools of the papacy and its allies, chiefly Spain. The fact that members were actually recruited from the host society was irrelevant. Italy as the order's place of origin and the center of its training played a role in the perception of the Jesuits especially in the phase of immigration: the priests of the first decades were readily recognizable as southern Europeans and as such met with rejection north of the Alps. Later, the labeling of locally recruited Jesuits as "Roman" was used to denounce the order that was loyal to the pope and to rebuff its claims within the church. In Protestant England, but also in Catholic France, the dominant label that was attached to the Jesuits was that of being "Spanish," partisans of Spain and thus in the final analysis enemies of the state. This referred to Spain's dominance in the order's hierarchy, which was factually no longer true after around 1600, and was, in the end, the product of the constellation of foreign politics.

Political-ideological attributions gained weight with Spain's and Rome's loss of power, but especially with the decline in the importance of the confessional conflict. After 1814, the Jesuits, who had also been put intellectually on the defensive by the Enlightenment, represented the Counter-Revolution (Jules Michelet 1845) and the Restoration, which supposedly aided them in reestablishing the order. During the time of the *Kulturkampf*, the Jesuits saw themselves as champions of Ultramontanism both within (Vatican I) and outside the Church. Their enemies in the emerging nation-states, meanwhile, saw the members of the international order sworn to loyalty to the pope as "fellows without a fatherland." At the same time, one can observe a racial charging of the image of the enemy: Houston Stewart Chamberlain declared Ignatius an "anti-Aryan" (*Die Grundlagen des neunzehnten Jahrhunderts* [The Foundations of the 19th Century] 1899), while Wilhelm Busch's anti-Jesuit allegorical poem "Pater Filucius" of 1872 or Erich Ludendorff's polemical tract *Das Geheimnis der Jesuitenmacht und ihr Ende* (The Secret of Jesuit Power and Its End) in 1929 presented the Jesuits in their illustrations in a way that was reminiscent of the depiction of the Jews in Nazi propaganda a little later.

The order lost its conservative image in the second half of the 20th century: since the Second Vatican Council (1962–5) and the opening of the Society of Jesus to questions of social justice, the Jesuits have been seen as modernizers, at least within the Church. The status of the Jesuits in the host countries depended chiefly on the confession of the respective authorities. In Protestant regions there was a threat – if not of persecution – of legal and tax-related discrimination. But even in Catholic regions, the order was not always given the necessary permission to set itself up, or, as the expulsions show, that permission was revoked. Alongside the granting of legal status, attention must also be paid to the financial and political support of the order from Catholic princes and governments, support that declined as conditions for the order in Protestant countries improved.

If one looks at the outside perception of the order, the basic fact to consider is the relationship of tension between the willingness of the Jesuits – grounded in their pastoral concerns – to accommodate themselves to the local conditions, and the desire to preserve, along with the order's unity, its visible identity as a group. A complete integration into a host society could therefore never be the goal of the Jesuits. Examples are the question of customs and mores in general, and the issue of dress, in particular. On the one hand, the constitution of the order instructs its priests "to adopt the general and recognized custom of honorable priests on matters concerning diet, clothing, and other matters in life." On the other hand, the bylaws, in order to strengthen the unity within the society, call for a certain uniformity not only in doctrine, but also "externally in dress."

This tension between unity and accommodation is also evident in practice. The first Jesuits who came from Italy into the German-speaking regions wore their accustomed Roman priestly dress, including the three-cornered biretta, which caused offense and impeded their pastoral work. In response, many Jesuits wanted to dress like German secular clergy. However, Superior General F. Borgia, who was concerned for the unity of the expanding order, allowed only a middle path: Jesuits working in the Empire had to wear the typical Roman biretta with its three corners (instead of the four typical in the German territories) as well as a wide-brimmed hat. Caricatures from the 16th century to Wilhelm Busch attest that the biretta and the hat became the external identifying signs of the Jesuits in the German lands.

That the Jesuits were and wished to be visible is evident from their symbol "IHS" (*Iesus hominum salvator*, Jesus savior of man) on churches and buildings and by their settlement structure. The branches were concentrated in cities, where, following the Roman model, they occupied central spaces. The majority of Jesuits lived in colleges, that is to say, in communities that were simultaneously educational institutions for the next generation of Jesuits as well as for young men from outside the order. Jesuits were thus chiefly active as teachers: as late as 1961, more than a third of the members of the society worked in school service, the same proportion as in 1556.

The relationship of the Jesuits to their host societies was characterized, chiefly in the Catholic regions, by the efforts of the order to participate in and shape the religious-confessional and thus also the social life of their environment. Through their more narrowly pastoral work (preaching, hearing confession, teaching catechism, popular missionary work, prison ministry), as well as – and probably primarily – through their educational institutions, Jesuits came into contact with a relatively broad segment of the population. Before the official dissolution of the order in 1773, which was reinstated in 1814, as many as 200,000 students yearly probably attended these institutions worldwide. In 1961 that number stood at around 1 million, whereby the focal point had shifted from Europe to the United States and above all to the countries of missionary work. Especially in the early modern period, the success of the Jesuit colleges is largely because the order's educational offerings were free and open also to the lower social strata through scholarships and boarding schools.

In spite of the humanistic orientation of the educational program, the students' mother tongue played a large role in the teaching provided by the order, which accepted the local language as the precondition for and medium of its work. That is also confirmed by the Jesuit theater, which supported the pastoral-pedagogical work and allowed the order to shape its own self-image: for didactic purposes, passages in Latin were translated. The performances of the Jesuit dramas became mass events in the public sphere. During their heyday in the 17th century they reached a broad public, but from the middle of the 18th century they were seen as increasingly out of step with the times and were mocked by the enemies of the order.

The goal of the Jesuits – to influence religious life and through it also society as a whole – was served not only by school and theater but also by the Marian Congregations, pious confraternities that were open to all male Catholics after 1586 and were intended to mold their members religiously and morally in all areas of life. The strong demand for such congregations under Jesuit leadership led to the founding of about 2,500 of these sodalities (as they came to be called) throughout the Catholic world between 1563 and 1773. In their heyday, the congregations had nearly 100,000 members in the northern German province of the order alone.

The value system of the Jesuits held some attraction also for women, as suggested by their interest in the Marian Congregations. Although separate sodalities for women were authorized only in 1751, women from higher social strata were at times admitted into the male congregations, and purely female circles had formed long before the papal authorization – the circle in Ingolstadt, for example, had more than 700 members in 1656. The strong female interest in the congregations may have had something to do with the Jesuit preaching of a family life that departed from the traditional, hierarchical models and placed men and women on equal footing within marriage. But the order, which always rejected a female branch, attracted the interest of women also beyond its ideas of marriage. The 16th and 17th centuries, in particular, witnessed the foundation of numerous semireligious women's communities, which took the Society of Jesus as their model (e.g., Mary Ward Sisters, Ursulines).

On the whole, the Marian Congregations with their numbers and the composition of their members attest what other indicators for the social acceptance of the order – such as attendance at its schools, the choice of Jesuit confessors, entry into the order itself, and above all donations and legacies to the Society of Jesus – also demonstrate: the rupture in the history of the order in 1773 can also be felt in the status of the Jesuits within society. While they had a polarizing effect before the dissolution of the order, though it was precisely this that made them visible and attractive to Catholics loyal to Rome, they were not able to win back their former importance in Europe after the refounding in 1814. After 1773, the order had to dispense with the support of Catholic princes who, during the age of confessionalization, had been hoping to derive political advantages from the work of the Jesuits. And for the upper social circles, as well, who had been clearly overrepresented among the supporters of the Society of Jesus before 1773, the Jesuits, as the embodiment of Catholic militancy, seem to have lost their attractiveness with the waning of confessional tensions.

However, at no time can one speak of a complete integration of the Jesuit order into the host society. The idea of calling and migration was part of the Jesuits' self-conception. Like the Church as a whole and every other religious community, the order never pursued an assimilation that would have led to the loss of identity. As a result, the Society of Jesus preserved its specific profile in accommodation.

Châtellier, Louis. *The Europe of the Devout: The Catholic Reformation and the Formation of a New Society*. Cambridge, 1989.

Decot, Rolf, ed. *Konfessionskonflikt, Kirchenstruktur, Kulturwandel: Die Jesuiten im Reich nach 1556*. Mainz, 2007.

Falkner, Andreas. "Jesuiten." In *Kulturgeschichte der christlichen Orden in Einzeldarstellungen*, edited by Peter Dinzelbacher and James Lester Hogg, 204–41. Stuttgart, 1997.

Haub, Rita. *Die Geschichte der Jesuiten*. Darmstadt, 2007.

Koch, Ludwig. *Jesuiten-Lexikon. Die Gesellschaft Jesu einst und jetzt*. Paderborn, 1934.

Niemetz, Michael. *Antijesuitische Bildpublizistik in der frühen Neuzeit: Geschichte, Ikonographie und Ikonologie*. Regensburg, 2008.

O'Malley, John W., and Gauvin Alexander Bailey, eds. *The Jesuits and the Arts 1540–1773*. Philadelphia, 2005.

Pavone, Sabina. *Le astuzie dei Gesuiti. Le false istruzioni segrete della Compagnia di Gesù e la polemica antigesuita nei secoli XVII e XVIII*. Rome, 2000.

Vogel, Christine. *Der Untergang der Gesellschaft Jesu als europäisches Medienereignis (1758–1773): Publizistische Debatten im Spannungsfeld von Aufklärung und Gegenaufklärung*. Mainz, 2006.

Wild, Joachim, Andrea Schwarz, and Julius Oswald, eds. *Die Jesuiten in Bayern 1549–1773*. Munich, 1991.

Worcester, Thomas, ed. *The Cambridge Companion to the Jesuits*. Cambridge, 2008.

Cross-references: France; Germany; Great Britain; Italy; Spain and Portugal; European Officeholders at the Roman Curia since the Early Modern Period

JEWISH REFUGEES FROM NAZI GERMANY AND FROM GERMAN-OCCUPIED EUROPE SINCE 1933

Wolfgang Benz

In response to anti-Semitic propaganda, discrimination against the Jews in law, politics, and administration, as well as the open terror following the takeover of power by the National Socialists, about 38,000 Jews left Germany in 1933. They were followed in 1934 – the year the consolidation of Nazi rule was completed – by just under 23,000. About 20,000 emigrated in 1935; the most significant event of that year, the "Nuremberg Laws," which stripped the Jews of their civic rights, showed up in the statistics for 1936, which saw the departure of 25,000 refugees. The apparent easing of the situation in 1936, the year of the Berlin Olympics, when the regime's anti-Semitic actions seemed to wind down, was reflected in a smaller number of only 23,000 emigrants in 1937. The intensification of the regime's anti-Jewish policy, its switch from discrimination and persecution through legislative and administrative acts to naked violence, demonstrated by the expulsion of Polish Jews in October and especially the pogroms of "Reich Crystal Night" (*Reichskristallnacht*) in November 1938, led to the largest waves of emigration: a total of 33,000–40,000 emigrants left in 1938, and about 75,000–80,000 in 1939. This was the time of the greatest emigration pressure.

Following the *Anschluß* (annexation) of Austria in the spring of 1938, that country became a testing ground for the

German-Jewish refugee children in a Parisian kindergarten in the late 1930s (*ullstein bild*).

bureaucratically accelerated emigration of the Jewish minority. According to the census of March 1934, Austria was home to 191,481 persons "of the Israelite confession" (according to the definition used by the Nuremberg Laws, there were a few thousand additional Jews; their total number was estimated at 206,000). The census of 17 May 1939 still showed 94,601 Jews as defined by Nazi racial ideology and 84,214 *Glaubensjuden* (religious Jews). Around 130,000 Austrian Jews had thus emigrated between the *Anschluß* and the outbreak of World War II. In part this exodus was the result of private initiatives, in part a response to the pressure exercised since August 1938 by the Central Office for Jewish Emigration (Zentralstelle für jüdische Auswanderung) in Vienna, which had been set up by Adolf Eichmann on orders from the Reich Main Security Administration (Reichssicherheitshauptamt) and the Reich Commissioner for the Reunification of Austria with the German Reich, Josef Bürckel. The Central Office issued passports in exchange for a fee of 5% of personal assets and organized the departure while stripping the emigrants of more of their property. However, as an agency whose sole mission was to push the Jews out, the Central Office did not organize visas and passages or other prerequisites for entry into a destination country. The basic idea was to finance the emigration with Jewish money and to organize the departure also of poor Jews with the help of these forced levies.

About two-thirds of the Jewish population had left Austria by the time World War II broke out. According to a census by the Central Office for Jewish Emigration in Vienna, 66,260 "religious Jews" were still in Austria on 15 September 1939, added to whom were 8,359 Jews as defined by the National Socialist race laws.

The outbreak of World War II meant the end to most possibilities of emigration, as diplomatic offices were closed down and travel and transport opportunities disappeared. Only 15,000 Jews were able to leave Germany in 1940; another 8,000 departed in 1941. In spite of the prohibition against emigration that was issued on 23 October 1941, six weeks after the police ordinance requiring Jews to wear the

Jewish Star, about 8,500 Jews managed to get out between 1942 and 1945. According to reports regarding the activities of the emigrant aid organization Central Committee for Aid and Rehabilitation (Zentralausschuß für Hilfe und Aufbau) and the Reich Representation of German Jews (Reichsvertretung der deutschen Juden), between 257,000 and 273,000 Jews left Germany from 1933 to 1941. The total number of Jewish emigrants from Germany is estimated at 278,500. Under the best of circumstances, the initial destination countries in Europe – France, Czechoslovakia, Belgium, Luxembourg, and the Netherlands – were a stopover for the emigrants before they moved on. For many, these host countries turned into a trap after German occupation, a trap from which the path led to the Holocaust. Outside of Europe, the most important destination regions became Australia, South America, and the USA. Within Europe, Great Britain was the most important country for German-Jewish emigration. Of course, many were tolerated only because they had transit visas, but after the outbreak of the war they were unable to continue on.

Since World War I, British immigration and asylum policy had been essentially restrictive, to which was added the population's economic fears about immigrants. When war broke out, about 40,000 Jewish refugees from Germany, Austria, and Czechoslovakia had entered the country; the total number of exiles is estimated at 50,000 to 80,000. Beginning in the fall of 1939, some of the refugees from the areas under Hitler's rule were interned in camps as "enemy aliens." Internment was expanded in May of 1940, and the government decided to deport all internees to Canada and Australia. Following the sinking of one ship by German torpedoes, the restrictions were relaxed, and by August 1941 more than half of the approximately 30,000 internees had been released again.

The Children's Transports, by which nearly 10,000 Jewish children from Germany and Austria escaped Nazi persecution to Great Britain between December 1938 and August 1939, constitute a high point of organized aid and solidarity in the history of efforts to save Jews from the Holocaust. At the same time, the Children's Transports were a tragedy of unimaginable personal suffering, which the toddlers, children, and teenagers experienced as the trauma of separation from their families and home, and their farewell to their parents who faced an uncertain future and for many, their own doom.

Immigration requirements were difficult to meet, the altruism of British foster parents had clear limits, and bureaucratic rigidity refused the saving entry into Britain to those who stood out by their behavior, those not in perfect health, or those conspicuous through their "Jewish appearance" and external disabilities (for example, surgery scars in the face). The demands that the host society placed on Jewish children from Germany with respect to their attractiveness, good behavior, and ability to integrate was a death sentence for many, since they were given no opportunity to leave in spite of all the efforts and pleas by aid organizations on the Continent. Most sought-after were infants, who could

A Jewish refugee child arriving in the British port of Harwich in 1938. The girl from Berlin is welcomed by a nurse and an immigration official (*SV Bilderdienst*).

fulfill the desire for adoption; the least popular was the most endangered group – adolescent boys.

The problems of reception and socialization included the way in which the young emigrants were housed: camplike in hostels or individually in foster families. Alongside the organizational, financial, and administrative difficulties that British politics and private charity found themselves confronted with, there were differences within the Jewish community about the treatment of the newcomers and expectations about the departure of the refugees after a temporary stay, though during their presence they certainly had claims to support, education, and religious identity that had to be met. Moreover, the young immigrants triggered a variety of fears, with the old-established Jews afraid, for example, of anti-Semitism as a reaction by the majority society.

The Children's Transports should be seen as the collective fate of persecuted young people who not only had to make their way in a foreign world unprepared but also had to constantly prove to their environment through good behavior, assimilation, and gratitude that they were worthy objects of an often rigid system of care. Personal fates reflect the individual tragedies that in fact make up the reality of the redemptive story of the Children's Transports. The majority of the children and teenagers were integrated into British society while preserving their Jewish identity. After the war, Great Britain took in another 7,000–8,000 orphans who had lost their parents in the Holocaust.

Most Jewish immigrants stayed in Great Britain for good. Their integration into society was often accompanied by the need to develop their own identity, which, for all its adaptability, emphasized different regional and cultural origins (continental Britons). For that reason, and because the reaction of British-Jewish communities and institutions tended to be cool, separate communities and organizations emerged, like the Leo Baeck Loge or the Association of Jewish Refugees from Germany and Austria (AJR), and later the Association of the Children of Jewish Refugees.

Palestine was originally the destination of only a minority of Jews, the Zionists. The idea of Eretz Israel – Theodor Herzl's vision of a homeland of the Jews on biblical soil – was attractive to Polish and eastern European Jews. Even the takeover of power by the National Socialists had little impact on the reservations German Jews felt about Zionism. Only slowly, after the Nuremberg Laws of 1935 and the prohibitions against exercising one's profession in the Nazi state, and then in the fall of 1938 following the November pogroms, did Palestine become a desired emigration destination.

Of course, emigration to Palestine posed special obstacles. For one, there were the physical and practical demands placed on the settlers. Academic and commercial skills and knowledge were not in demand in Palestine, but agricultural and related handicraft skills certainly were, as the goal was to make inhospitable land fertile. The young Zionists, organized into *Hechalutz* (Pioneers), prepared as *Chaluzim* for life in the new homeland; they acquired the necessary skills in workshops and practicums, they attended *Hachsharah* (Preparation), and they trained on training farms for the future in Eretz Israel. The acquisition of Hebrew language skills was also a precondition for Zionist settler life in Palestine.

Organizing the Jewish immigration, the *Aliyah* (Going Up), was the task of the Jewish Agency for Palestine in Tel Aviv. It maintained the "Palestine Office" with branches throughout the German Reich, responsible for selecting and counseling immigrants, transferring funds, and procuring visas, certificates, and means of transportation. The crucial hurdle for entry into Palestine was the Immigration Certificate, which the British Mandate Government issued only within very limited quotas. There were various categories: A Certificates for those with capital, the self-employed, tradesmen, and others whose income was assured; B Certificates for members of religious professions, pupils, and students; C Certificates for laborers (with handicraft or agricultural training); D Certificates for persons whose family members were already living in Palestine. The problem of the transfer of assets was regulated in the Haavara Agreement. An agreement between the Reich Economic Ministry and a company in Palestine, it functioned between 1933 and 1939 on the principle of "goods for people." Capital was paid into trustee accounts in Germany; the funds were used to purchase German goods and ship them to Palestine, where Jewish immigrants from Germany were given the equivalent value in the form of real estate. In this way about 140 million Reichsmarks were transferred between 1933 and 1942, which ensured the livelihood of about one-fifth of the emigrants from Germany.

Around 60,000 Jews emigrated legally to Palestine between the spring of 1933 and the fall of 1941, when the Nazi state formally prohibited emigration. *Aliyah Beth*, illegal emigration to Israel, was the last hope of many desperate individuals fleeing persecution and destruction at the hands of the National Socialists. Organized by Zionist organizations like the Mossad le Aliyah Beth and supported by the Jewish underground organization Haganah in Palestine, the illegals came into the land in various ways, with false or illegally used papers, after concluding sham marriages, as tourists, overland through eastern Europe, but above all by sea, mostly in decrepit, overloaded, and barely seaworthy ships. The journey across the sea was often preceded by a trip – during World War II often no less hazardous and difficult – from Vienna down the Danube and through the Black Sea.

After the shock of the Reich Crystal Night in November 1938 and the subsequent incarceration of about 30,000 Jews in concentration camps to pressure them into emigrating, the British government's White Book in May 1939 was another signal for the difficult situation faced by Jews willing to leave. Great Britain was planning to limit Jewish immigration to Palestine to a total of 75,000 by 1944, with an annual quota of 10,000 and the possibility for another 25,000 refugees, provided the country's economic situation allowed this, in the estimation of the High Commissioner. After that, no immigration at all was to occur without the consent of the Arab population. The proportion of Jews in the total population of Palestine was not to exceed one-third. In addition to drawing protests from the Zionists, the British plans led to a surge in *Aliyah Beth*. In the first half of 1939, 10,000 illegal immigrants reached Palestine alongside 8,000 legal ones. As punishment, no immigrants were admitted between October 1939 and April 1940. "Special *hachsharah*" (given the disguising abbreviation S.H.) was the name for the seven illegal passages that were financed with the help of the American Joint Distribution Committee. Few refugees of the S.H. reached their goal, some only after years of British internment. The boats sank, ran aground, were intercepted by the British navy, or fell victim to the Germans in Serbia, like the Kladovo Group (so named after the place where the transport was captured).

The end of Nazi rule liberated Jews from concentration and forced labor camps. Most of the Jews from east-central Europe, who had become displaced persons, as well as other survivors had the desire for a new homeland. Palestine was a sought-after destination after the Holocaust. But that meant continued illegal immigration with the help of the legendary organization Bricha (Escape), which scouted transit routes from eastern and east-central Europe via Germany and Austria and organized transports overland and then by boat, with which the "rest of the saved" were to make their way to Palestine.

Until the establishment of the state of Israel, at least 65 illegal boat transports tried to bring the survivors of the Holocaust into the land of their hopes, against the restrictions of the British, which remained in force until 1948. At least the escape routes in Europe had become more passable after the spring of 1945. The *Exodus* became the symbol of the Jewish determination to immigrate and British attempts to keep the Jews out. The ship set sail for Eretz Israel on 10 July 1947 with 4,515 passengers. It had been purchased by the Haganah in the United States. The vessel carried the name *Exodus* for only a few days on its voyage to Israel, which was shadowed by British agents and the British navy. Late in the evening of 17 July 1947, British warships intercepted the *Exodus* on the high seas, shortly before it reached its destination, Tel Aviv.

The heavily damaged *Exodus* was towed to Haifa. With a considerable use of force, the passengers were transferred to three British troop transporters, which set out the next day. Since the internment camps on Cyprus were already overcrowded, they were supposed to take the Jewish refugees to France. However, the Jews refused to disembark in that country. After three weeks, the boats then set course for Hamburg. The disembarkation on 8 September, following many protest demonstrations in displaced person camps on German soil, became a moral defeat for the British, since public opinion had finally become aware of the fate of the Jews and turned against Britain. The fate of the illegal Jewish immigrants in Palestine touched public opinion. The literary and film treatments of the voyage of the *Exodus* created a monument to the *Aliyah Beth*, of course in heroicizing and trivializing forms that were at best approximations of reality. Ideological bonds and a Zionist attitude were at least tacit prerequisites for immigration to Palestine. Of course, even in dire straits the majority of German Jews were no Zionists. That found expression in this well-known saying among immigrants in Israel: "Are you here from conviction or from Germany?" but it also became part of the social situation of the *Jeckes* (a nickname for German Jews in Israel). Still, the trauma suffered by the circumstances of the illegal acquisition of a homeland was offset by the gain to Jewish identity from *Aliyah*, the "going up" to Israel, though initially it meant under the best scenario simple physical survival.

The reserved attitude of the Jews from the German-speaking region of central Europe toward Zionism paralleled the difficulties they experienced in their acculturation to Palestine and after 1948 to the state of Israel. Resentment among those who had immigrated before 1933, mostly from eastern and east-central Europe; language problems (German was seen by some as an element of cultural identity, by others simply as the language of Hitler); and the clash between the dominant milieu, shaped largely by Jews from eastern and east-central Europe on the one side and the German *Jeckes* on the other side made integration more difficult. For most German Jews, the new life meant social decline and economic hardship. Unemployment, high rents, homesickness for Germany, the external problems of the Jewish-Arab conflict, and the lack of infrastructure complicated life in Israel. German-language papers and the cultivation of traditions from back home in clubs were also signs of the difficult process of acculturation. The immigrants from central Europe

influenced the development of urban life in business methods (department stores), architecture, and infrastructure. They shaped culture and science and scholarship, especially in the fields of law, medicine, music, and higher education. In politics, however, the Jews from Germany remained under-represented. The shared experience of arrival was for most German Jews the feeling of having suffered a step back in civilization.

Among non-European destination countries, Australia played only a very minor role in the hopes of German Jews during the Nazi period; and in the catalog of potential or even desirable countries for central European Jews during Nazi rule, it was not exactly at the top of the list. Larger numbers of the first survivors from the Holocaust and Jews from central Europe who had sought refuge in Shanghai headed for the fifth continent after World War II. Jewish communities were established especially in Melbourne and Sydney, and through the influx of displaced persons freed from Hitler's camps, they grew to a considerable size. After the war, more than 20,000 survivors of the Holocaust found a new home in Australia. Relative to the size of its population, Australia thus accepted more victims of the Nazi regime as immigrants than all other countries, with the exception of Israel.

By contrast, before 1939 Jewish immigration to Australia had been fairly limited: all told, a little over 7,000 Jews from German-speaking lands (just under 5,000 from Germany, 2,000 from Austria, others from Bohemia and Moravia; most came after the November pogrom of 1938). The year 1939 was an exception, with 5,098 Jewish refugees among the 21,100 immigrants who arrived in Australia that year.

The USA became the most sought-after destination country for Jews fleeing Hitler. Since World War I, immigration to the USA had been regulated by quotas, and entry required the affidavit of a US citizen. For immigrants from Germany, the quota had been set at 51,227 in 1921 (of a total of 164,667 per year); under the impact of the global economic crisis, it was reduced to 25,957 in 1929. However, until the annexation of Austria and the November pogroms of 1938, these quotas did not even come close to being filled. The high point of the demand occurred in 1939; however, because of transit problems following the outbreak of the war, the closing of consulates, and the prohibition against emigration (1941), the possibilities could be taken advantage of only to a very limited extent. On average, only 36% of the German quota was used.

Among the reasons for the failure to take full advantage of the quota, the belated realization of the danger was not the most important. The crucial role was played by bureaucratic obstacles that were thrown up by the USA as a result of isolationist xenophobia, racism, and anti-Semitism. Unions, veterans (the American Legion), nationalistic and fundamentalist organizations (American First), and others agitated successfully for a restrictive refugee policy by the USA, which manifested itself in the lack of success at the League of Nations conference on refugee questions in 1936 and the Evian Conference in 1938 and also influenced the stance of other nations. Exemplary of the American attitude was the fate of the more than 900 Jewish refugees who were on their way from Hamburg to Cuba on the *St. Louis*. Because of invalid visas, they were refused admission in Cuba and sent back to Europe. In spite of the intervention of the American Jewish Joint Distribution Committee, they were not given asylum in the USA, and the Coast Guard secured the country's territorial waters against attempts by the ship to land illegally.

American immigration policy remained ambivalent also after the outbreak of World War II. Humanitarian appeals and activities by politicians, organizations, and private persons confronted the unchanged xenophobic attitude of the administration and public opinion. The initiative by a senator, who sought the admission of 20,000 Jewish children on a special quota after the November pogroms, had already failed in its initial stages: Undersecretary Long, who had run the visa department in the State Department since the beginning of 1940, instructed the consulates to erect every possible obstacle against the immigration of undesirable Jewish and political refugees from Europe and thus limited the success of an Emergency Visitor's Visa Program, for which aid organizations had nominated 3,000 persons facing grave danger. Only a third were given a visa, and only a part of those were able to actually enter the USA. On the other hand, numerous aid organizations worked on behalf of the refugees by providing material support and help in social integration; chief among them the American Jewish Joint Distribution Committee, the Hebrew Sheltering and Immigrant Aid Society (HIAS), the Jewish Labor Committee, and the Emergency Rescue Committee (ERC), which was represented in Marseille by Varian Fry and helped especially prominent refugees to gain life-saving entry into the USA.

Beginning in 1936, and peaking after the outbreak of the war, Latin America also developed into a destination of Jewish emigrants. In the period 1939 to 1945, up to 35,000 Jews from central Europe lived in Argentina, about 17,000 in Brazil, 13,000 in Chile, 7,000 in Uruguay, more than 5,000 in Bolivia, with smaller numbers of Jews finding refuge in Colombia, Ecuador, Peru, Paraguay, Mexico, and other countries. The refugees in Cuba (around 8,000) and in the Dominican Republic (2,000) remained there only out of necessity, the goal being the USA, which they tried to reach as quickly as possible. The entire Latin American exile is characterized by migratory tendencies: after the war, streams moved to the USA, Palestine/Israel, and from the poorer countries like Bolivia, Paraguay, and Chile to Argentina (Buenos Aires) and Brazil (Sao Paulo).

Jewish refugees from Nazi Germany were not welcome anywhere in Europe. A few countries that were the first destinations of emigration – such as Austria, Czechoslovakia, France, and the Benelux states – sooner or later fell within the sphere of Nazi power, with disastrous consequences for the Jews who had found asylum there. One can single out Czechoslovakia and Luxembourg for their generous refugee policy, which was ended, of course, when the Nazis invaded,

and acknowledge Great Britain – which until World War II saw itself at best as a way station for onward migration overseas – for the eventual integration of Jews from the German sphere of power. By contrast, the role of Switzerland remains problematic. Although the Swiss policy of turning away refugees, practiced in part in cooperation with German authorities, was no doubt grounded in the country's geopolitical situation, it was nevertheless unique in its harshness. The reserved stance of European nations toward Jewish refugees from Germany, for which the Swiss attitude is exemplary, constituted a major reason that the destination countries of Jewish emigrants were mostly outside of Europe. Another, probably equally important, motive was the desire of the Jews to find a new homeland outside the European continent, either under the banner of Zionism (but also from sheer necessity) in Palestine, or in the hope of finding security and prosperity in the USA.

Armbrüster, Georg, ed. *Exil Shanghai: 1938–1947. Jüdisches Leben in der Emigration.* Teetz, 2000.

Benz, Wolfgang, ed. *Das Exil der kleinen Leute. Alltagserfahrung deutscher Juden in der Emigration.* Munich, 1991.

Benz, Wolfgang. *Flucht aus Deutschland. Zum Exil im 20. Jahrhundert.* Munich, 2001.

Benz, Wolfgang, and Marion Neiss, eds. *Deutsch-jüdisches Exil. Das Ende der Assimilation? Identitätsprobleme deutscher Juden in der Emigration.* Berlin, 1994.

Berghahn, Marion. *Continental Britons: German-Jewish Refugees from Nazi Germany.* Oxford, 1988.

Curio, Claudia. *Verfolgung, Flucht, Rettung. Die Kindertransporte 1938/39 nach Großbritannien.* Berlin, 2006.

Franke, Julia. *Paris – eine neue Heimat? Jüdische Emigranten aus Deutschland 1933–1939.* Berlin, 2000.

Heumos, Peter. *Die Emigration aus der Tschechoslowakei nach Westeuropa und dem Nahen Osten 1938–1945.* Munich, 1989.

Picard, Jacques. *Die Schweiz und die Juden 1933–1945. Schweizerischer Antisemitismus, jüdische Abwehr und internationale Migrations- und Flüchtlingspolitik.* Zurich, 1994.

Röder, Werner, and Herbert A. Strauss, eds. *Biographisches Handbuch der deutschsprachigen Emigration nach 1933.* Munich, 1980.

Saint Sauveur-Henn, Anne. *Zweimal verjagt. Die deutschsprachige Emigration und der Fluchtweg Frankreich-Lateinamerika 1933–1945.* Berlin, 1998.

Saint Sauveur-Henn, Anne. *Fluchtziel Paris. Die deutschsprachige Emigration 1933–1940.* Berlin, 2002.

Wyman, David S. *The Abandonment of the Jews: America and the Holocaust 1941–45.* New York, 1984.

Cross-reference: Belgium and Luxembourg; Czechia and Slovakia; France; Germany; Great Britain; The Netherlands; Poland; Switzerland; Displaced Persons (DPs) in Europe since the End of World War II; German and Austrian Jewish Children Transported to Great Britain after 1938-1939; Political and Intellectual Refugees from Nazi Germany and from German-Occupied Europe, 1933-1945

JEWS FROM THE PALE OF SETTLEMENT IN ODESSA AND IN THE CITIES OF CENTRAL RUSSIA AND POLAND IN THE 19TH CENTURY

Yvonne Kleinmann

The Jewish Pale of Settlement – in official parlance the "Pale of Permanent Jewish Settlement" – was born from the Belarussian, Lithuanian, and Ukrainian territories that had been annexed by Russia during the three partitions of Poland (1772, 1793, and 1795). Ashkenazi Jews had been settling here in large numbers since the 15th century. In Poland-Lithuania they had enjoyed extensive cultural and administrative autonomy, embodied at the local level in the *kahal* (communal administration) and on the transregional level between 1580 and 1764 in the Council of Four Lands (Hebr.: Va'ad arba aratzot). A lack of accurate statistics makes it impossible to determine precisely the number of Jewish subjects who came under Russian rule in the wake of Poland's partitions. Estimates posit 30,000–35,000 Jews for the Belarussian territories annexed in 1712, and about 400,000 in the territories annexed in 1793 and 1795. Given these magnitudes, the expulsion of the Jews as the traditional instrument of czarist policy was neither practicable nor in the state's fiscal interest.

In a supplement to the urban reform of 1775, which was aimed at promoting the cities and their economy, Empress Catherine II in 1783 classified the entire Jewish population of Belarus, even though the majority lived in village settlements, as city dwellers – depending on the tax payment as either guild merchants or members of the *meshchanstvo*, the heterogeneous conglomerate of all other urban residents. This gave Jewish merchants the same privileges as their Christian counterparts, especially the right to leave the province in which they were registered. Moreover, the guild tax removed them from the collective tax liability of the Jewish community, which thus lost the most effective instrument of social control over its wealthiest members.

The status of Jewish merchants is of particular importance in view of the long-term development of migration, especially the migration of Jewish subjects to St. Petersburg and Moscow after the 1850s. The geographic range of their trading activities must have expanded rapidly: as early as 1788, old-established Muscovite merchants protested that Jews were joining the guilds in the capital. That prompted Catherine II in December 1791 to issue a decree (*ukase*) which for the first time tied Jewish merchants to a specific territory, namely, their traditional settlement region in Belarus. Jewish subjects were expressly banned from joining the merchant guilds of central Russian cities and ports. This *ukase* is seen in Jewish historiography as the origin of the Pale of Settlement, but the fact is that restrictions on mobility existed for all other social groups with the exception of the nobility, which had the right to move freely.

Reflecting economic pragmatism, the *ukase* took the additional step of expanding the area of permanent settlement "for the Hebrews beyond the Belarussian province to the provinces of Yekaterinoslav and Tauria." Those regions were thinly populated and were supposed to be colonized. Within the defined territory, which was subsequently expanded especially through the territories annexed during the second and third partitions of Poland, the mobility of the Jewish population remained unrestricted; the only requirement was registration in an urban magistracy and in a *kahal*. The czarist Jewish Decree of 1835 for the first time listed all 15 provinces open to permanent settlement by Jewish subjects: Vitebsk, Kovno, Vilna, Grodno, Minsk, Mogilev, Volhynia, Kiev, Chernigov, Poltava, Podolia, Kherson, Yekaterinoslav, Bessarabia, and Tauria. This formally established the Pale of Settlement. Although the Pale continued to exist in its described form until World War I, as the decades went by it formed less and less a defined territory, let alone a self-contained legal sphere.

A controversial question within the czarist government concerned the settlement of Jews in rural areas. With the exception of agricultural colonies, the government of Alexander I had prohibited such settlement in his Enactment concerning the Jews in 1804, a prohibition that was repeatedly reinforced by expulsion. This was based on the regulation that the Jews as a whole were to be classified among the urban population. After 1827, Jews were once again tolerated in villages, and the Decree of 1835 explicitly authorized their settlement in the countryside, with the exception of the governments of Mogilev and Vitebsk. Settlement restrictions were tightened again by the "May Laws" in 1882, which banned Jews in principle from establishing new settlements in the countryside and stripped those who had been traditionally living there of the right to own real estate and land. As a result of the changes in economic structure that went along with this, the Pale of Settlement represented for its Jewish population in the last decades of the 19th century less and less an encompassing settlement area and increasingly a geographic framework for a network of scattered urban settlements. These profound changes notwithstanding, czarist officials and Jewish subjects continued to speak of the Pale of Settlement as a uniform entity.

Russian-Jewish historiography as well as Western travelers in the late 19th century in retrospect often pointed to the geographic limitation on the Jews in the Pale of Settlement and coined the phrase, the "large ghetto." Nevertheless any comparison with the early modern archetype of the Venetian ghetto is inappropriate. The Pale of Settlement was neither an exclusively Jewish area of residence – it was home to a multiethnic population, the majority of whom were Lithuanians, Belarussians, Ruthenians/Ukrainians, along with their historical elites (Swedish, Polish, and German nobility) – nor was its Jewish population locked up. Rather, before the abolition of serfdom in the Czarist Empire in 1861, Jews lived within the large territory of the Pale of Settlement with far fewer constraints on their mobility than the peasant majority and the Christian members of the *meshchanstvo*, a pejorative term used by the Russian intelligentsia to label the

541

Russian peasant masses, whom they saw as stupid, ugly, and primitive. Apart from this they had a number of options for leaving the Pale, at least temporarily. Until the 1860s, Jewish subjects and czarist officials perceived the Pale of Settlement, whose provinces were by and by incorporated into the economic system of the rest of the Empire, primarily as an economic and not as a geographic restriction: beginning in the 1840s, Jewish merchants sought repeatedly to obtain permission from the government to expand their trading networks to the entire realm.

The exodus of Jews from the Pale of Settlement in the course of the 19th century can be seen as a continuation of the strong, unrestricted internal migration within the Pale, which had already begun in the last years of the 18th century and grew continuously until the late 19th century. The areas of departure were primarily the infertile and industrially barely developed Lithuanian and Belarussian provinces, with the chief destinations the new ports and industrial cities of Ukraine and "New Russia," especially Odessa, Kherson, Yekaterinoslav, and Poltava.

Between 1859 and 1878, the czarist government, driven by economic considerations and in response to numerous interventions by the Jewish mercantile elite, granted the privilege of settling throughout the empire to wholesalers, university graduates, members of medical professions, military veterans, and artisans, thereby also opening up to them the central Russian provinces from which they had been expelled for centuries. Since neither legal security nor civic rights existed under czarist rule, the liberalization of the settlement laws cannot be seen as a limited civic emancipation of the Jewish population by western and central European standards, but merely as a personal privilege. Jewish newcomers to St. Petersburg and Moscow set themselves apart from the Jews in the Pale of Settlement by a high degree of mobility and their striving for secular education. Still, they by no means disappeared within the big city anonymity of the Russian metropolis. The religious identity recorded in all official documents and the unchangeable personal and paternal name were sufficient to identify them as Jews and to subject them to official and subtle daily forms of discrimination. Little changed in this regard until the end of czarist Russia, notwithstanding the religious freedom declared in 1905.

Simultaneously with the development of Jewish overseas emigration out of the Pale of Settlement into a mass phenomenon since the 1880s, the migration into the neighboring Polish regions gained importance: in 1862, the essential restrictions on economic life, settlement, and the acquisition of land had disappeared for Jews in the Kingdom of Poland; in 1864, the Russian occupiers put a violent end to the autonomy of the Polish state by putting down the January uprising. Unimpeded by legal regulation, in particular Jewish merchants from the Pale settled in the Polish industrial centers, first of all Warsaw and Łódź, to integrate Polish production into the Empire's market. For Russian-speaking Jews, the introduction of Russian as the official language in annexed Poland opened up new opportunities. The existing sources, however, do not allow us to determine the extent and duration of this immigration. A contemporary estimate exists only for the years 1893–1913, which were characterized by a strong rise in migrations as a result of the expulsion of Jews from Kiev and Moscow. This estimate puts the number at about 250,000. In general, however, the long-asserted connection between anti-Jewish violence and emigration can be clearly refuted in the case of migration within the Russian Empire as well as emigration overseas, since the exodus from the northwest of the Pale of Settlement into the south continued after the Odessa pogrom in 1871 and even increased after the Ukrainian pogroms in 1881–2.

The Jewish population in the three New Russian provinces of Kherson, Yekaterinoslav, and Tauria grew from around 46,000 in 1844 to half a million in 1897, the result of intensive immigration from the northwestern provinces, and to a lesser extent of the generally above-average natural rate of growth among the Jews. Growth in the Lithuanian and Belarussian emigration regions was relatively anemic: in 1847 around 947,000 Jewish subjects were already living there; in 1881 there were 2,291,000, and by 1897 the number had risen to only 2,622,000.

A striking example for the extensive migration into the young cities of "New Russia" and Ukraine is offered by the Jewish population of Odessa, whose history provides insight into the connections between socioeconomic constraints, migration, and cultural transformation. Already in 1794, the year the city was founded, Jews made up about one-tenth of the ethnically homogeneous population. The new port, which was rapidly integrated into the flourishing Black Sea trade as an important base, the free trade promoted by liberal governors and city chiefs, and tax privileges for colonists of any religion and confession always attracted more immigrants. Odessa's population grew from 2,350 in 1794 to about 400,000 within a century. By 1843 the number of Jewish residents had risen to around 12,000, by 1873 to 51,400, and by 1897 to 138,900. Their share of the overall population in those years stood at 15%, 27%, and 34%, respectively, which meant that in quantitative terms the Jews could be seen less and less as a minority.

In the first years of the 19th century, Odessa attracted those who sought to multiply their wealth in the young port city but also those who felt their livelihood was threatened elsewhere. The latter included many Jewish tradesmen, small-scale merchants, and tavern keepers from Lithuanian and Belarussian territories, who in the wake of the prohibition against rural settlements and the operation of taverns in 1804 first set out to the agrarian colonies of "New Russia," and after their failure sought a new livelihood in Odessa. Here they made a living until the 1850s, largely as tradesmen, small-scale merchants, money changers, and modest brokers in the grain trade. Starting from a better position were about 300 Jewish merchants from Habsburg Galicia, especially from Brody, who settled with their families in Odessa after 1814 to position themselves more favorably on the trading route that ran from Leipzig via Breslau, Brody, and Odessa all the way to Persia. Within a few decades, many of them advanced to become the city's most successful large-scale merchants, bankers, and stockbrokers, and after the 1850s they displaced their Greek competitors in the lucrative grain export trade thanks to optimal links with Jewish dealers in the hinterland.

The immigration paved the way not only for economic success but also for cultural and religious innovations. Typical of the new Jewish communities in the southern Pale of Settlement, and thus also in Odessa, was the absence of generally recognized religious authorities. This went hand in hand with a rather casual attitude toward religious law, which manifested itself in an acculturation to the ways of the big city. As early as 1810, a considerable number of Odessa Jews set aside the traditional rites and replaced their traditional dress with contemporary urban fashion. To be sure, between 1795 and 1800, prayer houses and charitable institutions were founded on the model of traditional Jewish communities, and a *kahal* as the organ of Jewish self-government, but its religious authority was very limited in the face of the cultural heterogeneity of the immigrants.

Until the 1820s there was no such thing as a strictly organized Jewish community. It was only at that time that the minority of the Maskilim, the followers of the Jewish Enlightenment that had made its way to Odessa via Brody, with support from the city commander, prevailed against the Orthodox groups of the Hasidim and the Mitnagdim and occupied the influential positions in the *kahal*. Subsequently, 1826 saw the establishment of the first Jewish reform school in the Czarist Empire, whose curriculum fused the traditional study of religion with secular subjects. In 1841, the first Choral Synagogue opened its doors. The Orthodox population boycotted it because of its far-reaching innovations in interior architecture and ritual, and as late as the 1870s the majority of Odessa's Jews gathered in four other synagogues, more than 30 houses of prayer, and countless prayer rooms. Migration did not invariably go hand in hand with religious reform, but Jewish Orthodoxy in Odessa approached the ways of the life of the Maskilim in a way that would have been unthinkable in Vilna, for example.

The social system that established itself in Odessa in the early 19th century was segmented with respect to social status and – with the exception of the nobility – ethnicity. Until the 1850s, Russian, Greek, Jewish, and other immigrants socialized in their private lives largely within their own ethnic communities and maintained their own schools, press organs, clubs, charitable institutions, churches, and synagogues. Still, there were public tasks that were regarded as a common matter, especially the urban self-government, in which Jews had been actively involved since the first years of the city's founding. Only the reactionary city code of 1893 limited the number of Jewish officeholders to 10%. Other important arenas of contact between different immigrant groups were state-run and private schools and after 1865 the New Russian University. Many Jews studied there, especially in the medical and law schools, after the 1880s also in

technical fields, and contributed to the steady growth of the academic elite.

Tensions between the various ethnic groups had religious but especially economic roots. As early as 1821, 1848, and 1859, the Greek residents had launched violent assaults against the Jewish population – quickly stopped by the city's police – during the Easter holidays. Hostility toward the Jews reached a new dimension in Odessa during the pogrom of 1871. For the first time, numerous Russians participated in the acts of violence and plundering alongside the Greek instigators. The result of the unrest, which lasted several days, was eight dead, many gravely wounded, thousands left homeless, and property damage in the millions. Even though more than 1,000 aggressors were arrested and some of them were punished, this could not hide the fact that the Jewish population was without police protection for several days. Representatives of the czarist government and the Russian press accused the Jews across the board of "exploitation."

The Odessa pogrom in May 1881 was only one of many organized pogroms in the urban centers of Ukraine that were directed chiefly against the property of Jews. In this instance, as well, police and army units intervened only after three days. Although contemporaries overestimated the government's responsibility for the pogrom, there is no denying the psychological consequences among the Jewish population of the repeated experience of violence and the lack of protection by the state. In the 1870s and 1880s, Odessa developed into the center of Palestinophilia, Jewish-national and proto-Zionist ideas, and a debate over emigration, while Russophile convictions receded into the background and press organs of the Haskala (Jewish Enlightenment) moved their editorial offices to St. Petersburg or closed down their activities entirely.

The settlement of Jews from the Pale in the central Russian provinces was fundamentally different from the extensive and unimpeded migration to Odessa. Until 1859, the presence of Jewish subjects there was merely temporary, illegal, or – in the case of Jewish recruits in the army – involuntary. But even in the reform era of Czar Alexander II (1855–81), who granted Jewish subjects individually the right to settle throughout the realm, czarist officials clung to the notion that they had to "protect" ethnic Russian territory from the Jewish population collectively. Until World War I, resident permits for Jewish subjects beyond the Pale of Settlement were tightly controlled. This had grave consequences for the Jewish minority in central Russia, which will be examined here by way of the quantitatively and politically important colony in St. Petersburg.

According to the statistics of the czarist censuses, the Jewish population in the capital had grown to around 6,700 by 1869 and to 16,800 by 1881; in 1890, only 15,300 Jewish residents were recorded. Their number increased again to 16,400 by 1897 and hit around 19,300 in 1900. St. Petersburg's Jews achieved their highest percentage of the population overall in 1881, when they accounted for just over 2%; in the subsequent decades, it was no more than 1.5%. This decline was a result of the city's strong population growth from 667,000 in 1869 to 1.25 million by 1900, driven by an immigration that was mostly rural in character. While men initially predominated among Jewish immigrants, in the following decades the gender ratio nearly evened out, so that – unlike in the case of the male-dominated rural immigration – we can assume that the migration was largely in the form of family units. The Jewish immigrants came from all provinces of the Pale and settled in all central quarters of the capital, without forming a distinctive Jewish neighborhood. The censuses of the Central Statistical Committee essentially captured only those Jews (men and women) who were living legally in the capital. Surveys by the city's police often came up with a substantially higher number of Jewish subjects in St. Petersburg – for example, about 27,000 in 1897. Jewish journalists assumed that the Jewish population in the capital was generally about twice what the official census reported.

Leaving aside the academic elite and the military veterans, the right of residence in St. Petersburg was tied to a stable membership of the guilds or to the exercise of a declared trade – for women and children it was tied to the status of the head of the household. This meant that the right to reside in St. Petersburg could be lost at any time. Social mobility in the capital was possible only within those occupational categories whose members had the right to settle throughout the realm. As a result, a Jewish proletariat on the scale that had developed in Odessa by the late 19th century could not emerge in St. Petersburg. The Jewish minority in the capital established itself largely in the middle and upper class, without leaving its traditional domain in trade and commerce. The percentage of the Jewish population in the academic professions rose to about 14% by the turn of the century. In spite of this above-average prosperity and level of education, Jews did not play nearly as important a role in the public life in St. Petersburg as they did in Odessa. Before 1892, Jewish officeholders were rare in the city's government. The reason was largely the relative insignificance of the local authorities in a city that housed the czarist government. Influential Jews like the Gincburgs and Poljakovs took their concerns directly to the various ministries and government representatives.

The most important structural difference between the Jews of St. Petersburg and all other Jewish minorities in central Russia on the one hand and the Jewish communities in the Pale of Settlement on the other was that the former had no corporative character. A great many of the tradesmen remained within the collective tax and recruitment bodies of their respective Jewish communities of origin and in terms of taxation did not exist in St. Petersburg. The other Jewish immigrants in central Russia were, from the perspective of the Ministry of the Interior, members of a specific estate (for example, merchants of the *meshchanstvo*) or of an occupational group, while their Jewish identity was regarded exclusively as a religious one and assigned to the sphere of private life. The establishment of a Jewish community as the representative of the entire Jewish population of St. Petersburg was therefore forbidden by the autocratic authorities from the outset. In St. Petersburg, the legally guaranteed religious tolerance concerned each individual Jewish subject and his concrete prayer community, but certainly not a centralized community and the public celebration of Jewish rituals.

Nevertheless, the secularized Jewish elite around the banker Goracij Gincburg, made up of large-scale merchants and a few academics, sought to set up in the capital an oligarchically governed community, one that was not only to encompass the entire Jewish population but also establish itself as a new center of Jewish politics in the Czarist Empire. Although the new elite always invoked the ideals of the Haskala, set up a reform school for boys and girls, and financed a splendid choral synagogue, it remained committed to the power structures of the premodern, autonomous Jewish communities. This manifested itself, for example, in the self-evident way in which it clung for a decade to the traditional taxation of kosher meat in the capital to finance its institutions. In fact, over the long term it was able to establish in St. Petersburg all the elements of a traditional Jewish community, filled with new content. Still, it did not attain secular authority and an official status.

Even though the Jews of St. Petersburg enjoyed the reputation – mediated by the memoirs of contemporaries – of a secular orientation, a reputation that persisted down to the recent scholarly literature, the majority observed the religious laws. However, there was no such thing as a uniform Jewish ritual life. In addition to the traditional distinctions between the Hasidim, the Mitnagdim, and the Maskilim, within the individual currents, depending on the geographic origins of the immigrants, there were also divergent notions on what constituted a proper religious service, reflected in the large number of places of prayer. With the exception of the elite, the Jews of St. Petersburg were well served by the government's insistence on decentralized structures in Jewish ritual life. Completely outside the world of the various prayer houses were the many students and academics, who had given up all religious rituals after migrating into the Russian capital.

Contacts with members of other religious communities beyond business dealings were as rare in St. Petersburg as they were in Odessa. Beginning in the 1860s, there arose a small number of settings – scientific organizations, circles of students and artists – in which religious and national identity was deliberately subordinated to a liberal ideal of society. Parallel to this, in the 1870s there were already Jewish student groups that were organized around regional origins; they met for discussions and readings with Jewish poets and advocated proto-Zionist ideas. No forums for transconfessional encounters beyond the world of work are known from the environment of the multiethnic body of tradesmen and merchants. Customary were ties to the prayer houses of the respective minority and to the school and charitable organizations it maintained. Since all ethnic-religious communities were in a minority position vis-à-vis the dominant Russian-Orthodox population, violent clashes between the various minorities did not take place. But that in no way means that religious and national antagonism were irrelevant in the capital. Still, pogroms did not happen in St. Petersburg, primarily because the police and the military maintained strict control over public order in the capital.

Largely unexplored is the immigration of Jews from the Pale of Settlement into the neighboring Polish territories that had been integrated since 1864 into the administrative system of the Czarist Empire. The Jewish population grew from about 212,000 in 1816 to 1.32 million in 1897 and 1.53 million in 1905. The degree to which this substantial increase was due to natural growth or immigration has not been determined. Jewish immigrants from the Pale of Settlement who attracted the attention of the Polish public after the 1860s were given the exonym *Litwak*. Originally this was the value-neutral word for a person of Lithuanian background. Orthodox Polish Jews, however, applied it in a pejorative sense to all foreign Jews who ignored the religious law. Polish-patriotic journalists and Polish acculturated Jews in turn distinguished between *Litwaks* of the older generation, who stood for Russification and economic exploitation, and those of the younger generation, who were considered followers of either socialism or Jewish nationalism. Jewish immigrants, who did *not* come only from Lithuania but from the entire Pale of Settlement and after 1891 also from Moscow, became the projection screen for the fears of traditional Jewish society that felt its integrity was being threatened, as well as for the trauma that Poles and Polish acculturated Jews associated with foreign political rule, cultural subjugation, and subordination to the economic interests of the Russian partition power.

A number of these fears had a basis in reality: Jewish immigrants from the Pale of Settlement who had learned Russian communicated much more easily than the elite of Polish Jews with the new czarist administrative institutions and occupied positions within government service. Moreover, Jewish entrepreneurs who had migrated to Moscow after 1891 soon competed with the long-established Jewish, Polish, and German industrialists in Łódź. In Warsaw, merchants from Moscow quickly monopolized the sale of Polish shoes in the large market of the Russian Empire and posed a threat to manual production by setting up mechanized workshops. The given examples refer exclusively to the small elite of the immigrants. Further research is needed, however, to determine whether the *Litwaks* formed a self-contained and dynamic immigrant group or whether they were instead a myth propagated by Polish-patriotic forces who feared for the integrity of an imagined Polish nation vis-à-vis the Russian authorities.

Anderson, Barbara A. *Internal Migration during Modernization in Late Nineteenth-Century Russia.* Princeton, 1980.

Guesnet, François. *Polnische Juden im 19. Jahrhundert. Lebensbedingungen, Rechtsnormen und Organisation im Wandel.* Cologne, 1998.

Kleinmann, Yvonne. *Neue Orte – neue Menschen? Jüdische Lebensformen in St. Petersburg und Moskau im 19. Jahrhundert.* Göttingen, 2006.

Nathans, Benjamin I. *Beyond the Pale: The Jewish Encounter with Late Imperial Russia.* Berkeley, 2002.

Rowland, Richard H. "Geographical Patterns of the Jewish Population in the Pale of Settlement of Late Nineteenth Century Russia." *Jewish Social Studies* 48 (1986): 206–34.

Stampfer, Shaul. "Patterns of Internal Jewish Migration in the Russian Empire." In *Jews and Jewish Life in Russia and the Soviet Union*, edited by Yaakov Ro'i, 28–47. London, 1995.

Zipperstein, Steven J. *The Jews of Odessa: A Cultural History, 1794–1881.* Stanford, 1985.

Cross-references: The Baltic Region; Poland; Russia and Belarus; Ukraine; Ashkenazim in Europe since the Early Modern Period; Greek Settlers from the Black Sea Region in New Russia since the Early Modern Period and Pontic Greeks in Greece since the End of World War II

KRU SEAMEN IN LIVERPOOL SINCE THE MID-19TH CENTURY

Diane Frost and Melvin Walker

The term "Kru" refers to the West African ethnic group that originated in eastern Liberia and migrated and settled along various points of the west African coast (notably Freetown, Sierra Leone, but also the Ivorian and Nigerian coasts). They settled further afield as well, in the British port cities of Liverpool, London, and Cardiff. Kru people established distinct ethnic communities in those places where they settled, though research is yet to be done on Kru communities outside of Freetown and Liverpool.

Kru people were employed on board both British Royal Navy and merchant marine ships during their long association with Britain. Initially they were used as interpreters and navigators on merchant vessels that traded on the treacherous Liberian coast, where they learned to be highly skilled in negotiating the surf. Such skills paved the way for their employment aboard British ships. This took two forms. First, Kru sailors were employed on ships that sailed along the coast. These were merchant ships that utilized Kru stevedores to load and discharge cargoes around the west African coast. Second, Kru were used on deep-sea voyages. There is evidence that these sailors were used on European slave ships bound for the Americas. They also worked as sailors on the Royal Navy Anti-Slave Trade Squadron that operated from Freetown and whose job was to suppress the slave trade by apprehending and prosecuting slave ships off the west African coast.

Many factors operated in the decision to employ Kru people as sailors on British ships. Initially they were used to fill labor shortages left by white crews who had died or fallen sick on the malaria-infested west African coast. Second, they were used as laborers or stevedores on the coast to save white labor from the arduous task of loading and discharging cargoes in the steamy climate of tropical west Africa. Kru labor was also cheaper to employ and organized less often into trade unions.

It was their work on board British merchant ships that brought Kru people to ports in the UK and in particular to Liverpool. Because many Kru people were transient (due to the nature of seafaring) before they permanently settled, the community was predominantly male with much smaller numbers of Kru women. As a result, those Kru men who did eventually settle more often than not formed relationships with local white women (though some married local black women). The marriage of Kru men to British women meant that Kru cultural expressions from west Africa were not on the whole perpetuated through the second generation. Such children tended to be "black British of African descent" or, as many would today term themselves, "Liverpool-born black people."

A purely assimilationist concept of migration, wherein each immigrant group ultimately gives up its ethnic identity through the process of absorbing the norms and values of the host society is problematic with reference to groups whose ancestry lies outside of Europe, including the Kru. Because of the visibility of different ethnic groups, often accentuated by racism, a dark-skinned immigrant group in Great Britain – despite many commonalities with the white majority, such as Christianity or the English language – could never "disappear" or be "absorbed," as was essentially the case for Irish or Jewish immigrants. "Race" or skin color became the main signifier of difference and was used to marginalize and discriminate against all such groups.

Kru people could be found in Liverpool from at least the latter half of the 19th century, when they were employed in increasing numbers on Liverpool merchant ships that traded with west Africa. Black sailors from west Africa and the Caribbean had been part of English society much earlier, from the 18th century, and had been conspicuous in English ports since the 17th century if not before. While it is difficult to find conclusive and hard evidence that Kru people formed part of this early black presence, it seems highly likely they would have, given their contacts with British merchants and their work aboard British ships at this time.

Kru people settled in the south docklands areas of Liverpool during the late 19th and throughout the 20th century. Because of the transient nature of their work, precise estimates of their numbers are difficult to ascertain. But records for membership of a Kru social club in the 1940s and 1950s indicate those registered as numbering several hundred. The true numbers of Kru in Liverpool were likely to be higher than this. The establishment of black seamen's boardinghouses and the close proximity of the docks encouraged the Kru to settle initially in the southern docklands, alongside other black immigrants and sailors from the four corners of the world. Because the Kru community was predominantly male, marriage or unions to local white women saw such families clustering in a mixed community that was predominantly white but which had a concentration of black or mixed-race families.

This initial settlement pattern was strengthened over the next 100 years by three processes. First was the discrimination of the local authority in neglecting to provide public housing outside the docklands. Second came the refusal of banks and building societies to give loans or mortgages to allow these groups to purchase houses elsewhere. And third, black families faced hostility and racism if they went outside this area and attempted to settle in all-white areas. Consequently, the black community in Liverpool, of which Kru people formed an important component, was confined and some would say "ghettoized" in a particular part of the south end of Liverpool. The location of this community has gradually moved away from the docks because of slum clearance programs, though the concentration of black people has remained intact and in the south end of the city. Those white women who married or had black partners became "assimilated" into the black community since they were often ostracized by their own families but accepted by the wider black community.

Kru men in Liverpool continued to work on board British ships throughout the first half of the 20th century, except when they were between ships or unemployed in the 1920s and 1930s due to a slump in world shipping. Many Kru sailors were often able to retain a strong link with their homeland in west Africa because of the frequent sailings there, though this began to decline gradually during the 1950s, 1960s, and 1970s. By the 1980s, there were very few ships sailing to Liverpool with Kru crews.

Ethnic identity as Kru people was thus reinforced through a number of contributory processes. First, the consistent contact Kru men maintained with their homeland, family, and wider community, even though they were permanently settled in Britain upheld this identity. They were in a unique position as migrants to maintain such close and regular links with their home. Second, because Kru identity was something that was constructed out of the particular work that these people became famous for, namely, seafaring, their continued work on board British ships perpetuated and reinforced this label. "Kru" was an ethnic-cum-occupational identity that became synonymous with seafaring. Third, Kru ethnic identity was maintained in the context of Liverpool through the regular contact with transient Kru seamen who came from Freetown in west Africa in the course of their work. Finally, Kru ethnic identity in common with other migrant groups was maintained and modified in the context of Liverpool because of their experience of racism and hostility. Thus Kru identity was not an attempt to hang on to archaic and "traditional" forms of life just for the sake of it. Nor was it because they did not want to "fit in." Rather, the maintenance of ethnicity was a reaction to the way they were received by the majority white population. This was true of other migrant groups as well.

Ethnic identity among Kru migrants in Liverpool was characterized by a great fluidity. Kru adopted various and simultaneous ethnic and national identities. They identified themselves as Kru, as Sierra Leonean/Liberian, west African and black, as well as being officially British citizens (as British subjects of Sierra Leone, which was or had been a British colony). These multiethnic labels were the product of both external labeling and the need to identify with wider groups.

Through the maintenance of ethnic identity, the Kru people were active agents in the creation of their history, consciousness, and allegiances. This fluid identity represented practical attempts to come to terms with their predicament as migrant workers.

During the 1950s, there were more voluntary associations among Liverpool's black communities than in most other black communities in Great Britain. Perhaps this was because west Africans formed a large part of Liverpool's black population and such organizations were an established part of their culture in Africa. The Kru people of Freetown, as both immigrants and workers, had established numerous organizations that helped them adapt to a new urban setting and gave them a degree of protection in the event of sickness, unemployment, and death. It is hardly surprising, then, that such organizational structures were transported, albeit in a modified form, to the Liverpool context where similar needs and situations arose.

The Liverpool Kru community throughout the 20th century was never larger than several hundred at any one time, and this meant that they did not organize independent associations to the same extent as they had in Freetown. In Liverpool in 1948, the "United Kroo National Society" was established and registered under the "Companies Act." Its membership totaled around 250 in 1948. The organization began as a burial club where money was collected from individual Kru. This was a tradition that had been carried from Freetown, where the absence of a welfare state made such provision essential. As membership expanded, so too did the functions of the club. The stated objectives of the society were to safeguard the interests of the "Kroo Tribe and the various clans." As well as a burial function, society funds provided for a host of discretionary needs, including legal assistance and repatriation. Recreational facilities were also provided in the club building. Subscriptions were levied according to whether members were employed or unemployed. Almost all its membership was male, though there is little doubt that Kru men's families also used the club building for recreational functions.

The Kru people also became involved in all kinds of organizations not only among their own ethnic group but also with other national groups who originated from the same country or countries in west Africa (such as the Nigerian Club, the Sierra Leonean Club, and the Liberian People's Welfare Organisation). Moreover, Kru people in common with others from Africa and the Caribbean and black British developed cultural institutions that catered to the needs of black workers and their families more generally. In 1943, Stanley House was set up as a community center for the black population of Liverpool in an effort to foster better interracial relations between local blacks and whites. In the late 1940s, the Colonial People's Defence Association was set up in the aftermath of racial disturbances in Liverpool in 1948. In this umbrella organization, different sections of the black community came together to organize their own defense against these xenophobic attacks and to provide support to those charged with disorderly behavior. The organization sought to promote the interests of all black people through the formation of ties with local trade unions, political parties, and other bodies.

Black people who shared a sense of exclusion and racism used the notion of a "black community" to describe their own affiliation. It gave them a strong sense of identity and belonging especially when faced with attacks (such as those in 1919 and 1948). It did not work against smaller, more individual ethnic identities, which could coexist alongside this broader one. The notion of "black communities" in Britain (including Liverpool) became prominent again in the 1980s and 1990s.

The majority of first-generation Kru people experienced much hostility and at times violence and racial discrimination in all aspects of their lives. As the second and third generation came through, hope grew in the community that they would be accepted and assimilated into British society like other immigrant groups before them. However, this was not the case. Continuing discrimination and racism encouraged first-generation Kru to assert their Kru ethnic identity, while second and subsequent generations described themselves not as Kru but along more overtly political lines as African, as African Caribbean, as black, as black British, or as Liverpool-born Black. This they share in common with other second-generation black people. These self-descriptions are indicative of their need to retain distinct ethnic and racial identities in the face of racial discrimination, economic marginalization, and political exclusion. For many, such labels are a source of group support and an assertion of their distinct identity within British society, of which they are an integral part.

The sea and port life dominated the lives of all Liverpool-born people up until the introduction of container ships and the decreasing need for sailors and dockworkers, beginning in the 1970s. Before then, most working-class families in Liverpool had someone whose job was connected with the sea. This was no different for the male children of Kru sailors. Hereafter, the male offspring of Kru were no more likely to go to sea than any other Liverpool-born male. Today, there are few Liverpudlian people engaged in seafaring, including second-generation Kru. This can be explained by global structural changes in the shipping industry rather than with a change in the Kru community, whose members were so long active in one particular branch of employment.

Dahya, Badr. "Pakistanis in Britain: Transients or Settlers?" *Race* 14 (1973): 241–77.

Frost, Diane. *Work and Community among West African Migrants Workers*. Liverpool, 1999.

Hall, Stuart, et al. *Policing the Crisis: Mugging, the State and Law and Order*. London, 1978.

Khan, Verity. "The Pakistanis: Mirpuri Villagers at Home in Bradford." In *Between Two Cultures: Migrants and Minorities in Britain*, edited by James Lee Watson, 57–89. Oxford, 1977.

Pryce, Ken. *Endless Pressure*. Harmondsworth, 1979.

Cross-references: Great Britain

KURDISH REFUGEES IN WESTERN AND CENTRAL EUROPE SINCE THE LATE 20TH CENTURY: THE EXAMPLE OF GERMANY

Birgit Ammann

Kurdistan is a cohesive cross-border area that includes eastern Turkey, northern Iraq, parts of western Iran, and northern Syria. Moderate estimates put its population at some 28 million: 16 million in Turkey, 4 million in Iraq, 5 million in Iran, and 1.5 million in Syria. Even though the absence of a Kurdish nation-state and Kurdish citizenship complicates the definition of Kurds, they represent an identifiable group with a common language, other ethnic attributes, and a distinct sense of community. Kurds have migrated to neighboring countries but also to North America, Australia, and Europe, especially Germany. About three-quarters of the official Turkish and Iraqi asylum seekers who have entered Germany since the 1970s are Kurds, and more or less unnoticed by the public, they have developed into the largest group of refugees and one of the largest groups of migrants in Germany.

Well over 1 million Kurds lived in western Europe at the turn of the 20th century, including 700,000 to 800,000 in Germany, some 100,000 in France, and 60,000 in the Netherlands. Among Kurds in Germany there are approximately 100,000 official asylum seekers with varying residency status from both Iraq and Turkey and a few thousand from both Syria and Iran. While Kurds who did not migrate as refugees can often be defined only on the basis of their ethnic self-ascription, refugee status is typically linked directly with the acknowledgment of Kurdish ethnicity.

Before the number of Kurdish migrants began to increase rapidly in the 1980s, a few academics from different Kurdish regions lived in Europe for political, economic, and other reasons: diplomats, supporters of the Kurdish national movement, scholars, and university students from privileged families. From the late 1950s until the beginning of the 1970s, the recruitment of laborers from Turkey as well as subsequent family reunification led to the immigration of all ethnic groups from Turkey to western and central Europe.

At that time Turkey's extremely restrictive politics regarding its ethnic minorities resulted in the repression of their cultural expressions. This applied especially to the central and western parts of Turkey and its cities, where many migrants from Kurdish families had settled before they migrated to Europe. In their countries of destination Kurdish migrants were usually not recognized as such due to this background and their adaptation to the majority culture of Turkish society.

In the 1980s the number of involuntary Kurdish migrants increased, and the 1990s witnessed waves of refugees from both Turkey and Iraq to nearly all western and central European countries. To a large extent these Kurds originated from rural areas in the far east of Turkey where assimilation to the majority culture of the Turkish society had hardly taken place, or from neighboring Iraq where a clear ethnic identity traditionally prevailed. These waves were now

Kurdish students hand out flyers at the Berlin Kurfürstendamm in the 1970s (*Muhamed, Alaaddin, Archiv Europäisches Zentrum für Kurdische Studien – Berliner Gesellschaft zur Förderung der Kurdologie e.V.*).

perceived as Kurdish in the countries of destination. Besides, the large numbers of political refugees changed the composition of the Kurdish diaspora from more or less apolitical labor migrants to homeland-oriented political activists.

The motives for migration overlap: on the one hand, Kurdish migration to Germany to a large extent was politically motivated and partly imposed by the deliberate destruction of resources such as housing, water, and food supplies, and by ecological damage; there was also systematic ethnic discrimination in all four countries of origin. On the other hand, labor migration and the pursuit of economic improvement also played a role. To some extent, the movement can be labeled chain migration since, for many refugees, the presence of relatives was the only criterion in their choice of the country of destination. Apart from asylum seekers, Kurds also entered Germany as marriage migrants, which represented the only possibility for migration after labor recruitment was halted in 1973. At the end of the 20th century Kurdish migration from both Turkey and Iraq, as well as from Syria and Iran, comprised all age groups, single men and women, unaccompanied minors, and nuclear or extended families.

Except for forced remigration, Kurdish return migration has been insignificant. None of the refugees from Iraq have been expelled from Germany. Kurdish migration to western Europe not only resulted in permanent settlement but also in the formation of a diaspora with all of its typical characteristics. In contrast to most other refugee populations, Kurds often commute between their country of origin and the new country of settlement. In the case of the Kurdish refugees from Turkey, this trait was the result of strong ties to co-ethnic labor migrants and their offspring, who freely travel back and forth. In the case of the Iraqi Kurds it is the unique situation of the formerly protected no-fly zone and now largely self-controlled region in northern Iraq that allows back and forth movement. Many Kurdish refugees from Iraq and Turkey as well as from Syria and Iran have acquired German citizenship because it allows them to visit their countries of origin safely.

Although the geographic distribution of newly migrated refugees in the federal states (*Bundesländer*) and municipalities in Germany is subject to state control in order to ensure regional proportionality, Kurds mainly choose to live in cities in former West Germany as soon as they are able to do so because they have strong ethnic and familial networks in these areas. Many live in neighborhoods with high proportions of immigrants, but specific Kurdish neighborhoods do not exist. Because of increased contact among Kurdish refugees within the European diaspora, politically active Kurds placed great hopes in the common ethnic interests of Kurds from all parts of Kurdistan in Europe for an independent Kurdish nation or at least some form of autonomy or cultural rights; this has resulted in a historical reunion of central elements of the Kurdish populace for the first time since the widespread persecution of Kurds before and after the fall of the Ottoman Empire. The divergent influence of varying regimes and states, however, quickly dashed such hopes. Social relations tend to be regionally oriented and intermarriage between the different Kurdish groups is rare. Nevertheless, the Kurds view themselves as belonging to a common group. Kurdish political parties and media reinforce sentiments of belonging to a transnational community and promote commitment to the larger Kurdish cause.

Religious affiliations such as Sunni Muslim or Yezidi, a religion found only among Kurds, do not play a major role in the diaspora. Religion is viewed as a private matter and very few Iraqi, Syrian, and Iranian Kurds attend mosque. However, a growing solidarity between Kurds and Turkish Islamists can be observed since the Turkish state is fiercely fighting the beliefs of both groups. In their daily lives, many migrants still define their moral concepts of honor and shame in religious terms and therefore argue on religious grounds when expressing their opposition to "Western behavior" and their aversion toward marriage with Germans.

Although Iraqi Kurds have faced repression and persecution, they have maintained a clear ethnic identity and keep Kurdish as a first language. Turkish Kurds, who to a large degree lost their language due to its decades-long prohibition, often lack this cornerstone of their ethnic identity. The fact that command of the Kurdish language in Turkey is often associated with a rural background and a low level of education further adds to the problem.

The psychological disposition and social ties of Kurdish migrants, particularly among the refugees, are strongly oriented toward the homeland. This applies both to Iraqi Kurds, whose migration only began in the 1980s, and Turkish Kurds, who first came to Germany in the 1960s. This tendency is encouraged by social discrimination, high unemployment rates, and educational deficits. The vast majority of Kurdish refugees, however, clearly perceive these problems as marginal compared to the conditions in their respective countries of origin.

The sense of belonging and notions of ethnic distinctness among the Kurds have largely been neglected by German authorities, even though recognition of Kurdish asylum seekers emphasizes exactly this ethnic criterion. In contrast to some European countries like Sweden or France, there has never been significant public funding for Kurdish activities in Germany – be it in the arts, research, social affairs, education, media, and cultural activities or human rights actions. When the privately financed ethnopolitical activities of the communist-oriented Kurdistan Workers' Party (PKK) in the 1990s achieved a scale of violence previously unknown among migrants in Germany, it created a vicious circle, where it was sometimes no longer clear whether the target of the movement was Turkish government policy or the German state and German society.

Although Turkey, seeking to join the European Union, is in the middle of an extensive transformation process, every expression of ethnic difference is still considered a threat to the unity of the country and remains forbidden in large parts of the society. Although the German attitude only slightly reflects and parallels this situation it severely hinders societal integration, especially of the Turkish Kurds. Furthermore, the portrayal of Kurdish violence in the media has resulted in an enduring, very one-sided and negative public opinion of the Kurds. At the same time, the temporary increase in the strength of the former PKK, dissolved in 2002, can be interpreted as an indication of the group's defective integration into German society. Yet, support for the successor organizations of the PKK has clearly declined since the imprisonment of its head, Abdullah Öcalan, in 1999.

As the Kurdish refugees lack a realistic perspective of returning to their homeland, they are eager to integrate into their new surroundings. Especially among Iraqi Kurds – most of whom are professionals – there are high aspirations for the education of their children. Historical familiarity with cultural and linguistic diversity appears as a favorable precondition for multicultural sensitivity and successful integration. But, because Kurds in all their states of origin have had to struggle to define themselves in opposition to the dominant national group, they are not likely to give up their notions of ethnicity easily. Developments among the second and even the third generation highlight this point.

One of the obstacles to the integration of Kurds in Germany, especially those from Turkey, is that they are perceived as Turks in Germany, while ethnic Turks, following official Turkish policy, tend to exclude them. The situation for Iraqi Kurds in Germany is different: they are perceived as Iraqi Kurds, not as Iraqis, let alone as Arabs. They also have their own political representatives who are not only accepted within Germany but who have been partially integrated into the administrative system.

The Kurds are a very heterogeneous group. Little systematic research has been done on their integration into German society even though their cultural identity and ethnicity arouse great interest. Policy aimed at strengthening their ethnic identity does not necessarily lead to a refusal to integrate into the host society, as shown by Kurdish migrants in other countries, where their cultural heritage is fundamentally respected and efforts to develop it are taken seriously and often subsidized by the state. Particularly in Sweden, but also in Norway, France, and Belgium, Kurdish immigrants have a more open and positive attitude toward the government and the majority population of their host country than those living in Germany. Diasporic, transnational consciousness does not necessarily conflict with integration into mainstream society. It is precisely the political elite of Kurds in Europe that is highly integrated.

Ammann, Birgit. *Kurden in Europa. Ethnizität und Diaspora.* Münster, 2001.

Bruinessen, Martin van. "Shifting National and Ethnic Identities: The Kurds in Turkey and the European Diaspora." *Journal of Muslim Minority Affairs* 18 (1998): 39–52.

Eccarius-Kelly, Vera. "Political Movements and Leverage Points: Kurdish Activism in the European Diaspora." *Journal of Muslim Minority Affairs* 22 (2002): 91–118.

Østergaard-Nielsen, Eva. *Transnational Politics: The Case of Turks and Kurds in Germany.* London, 2002.

Wahlbeck, Östen. *Kurdish Diasporas.* London, 1999.

Cross-references: Germany; Northern Europe; Southeastern Europe; Turkish Labor Migrants in Western, Central, and Northern Europe since the Mid-1950s

KVENS AND TORNE-FINNS IN NORWAY AND SWEDEN SINCE THE 18TH CENTURY

Einar Niemi

The Kvens and the Torne-Finns are related groups of people, both categorized linguistically as Finno-Ugric. In older Scandinavian historical sources Kvenland was the name of their common area of origin, situated around the inner parts of the Gulf of Bothnia, with the region at the mouth of the Torne River Valley as their core area. Kvenland and the people living there, the Kvens, are mentioned as early as the end of the ninth century. The Kvens' specific form of social organization was based on agriculture, animal husbandry, and trade. The Finns started to colonize the Torne River Valley in the 16th century, then spread out further north and west, and have since been dominant culturally and ethnically in large parts of the river valley area, which encompasses parts of both Sweden and Finland today.

The presence of the Torne-Finns as a separate group in Sweden was a consequence of the border demarcation between Sweden and Russia following the Finnish War of 1808–9, which led to the creation of the Russian Grand Duchy of Finland. The eastern border of Sweden, running through the Torne Valley, split the Finnish population in the valley and turned the Finns on the Swedish side of the valley into an ethnic minority group. In 1860 approximately 14,000 Finns lived on the Swedish side of the border, equivalent to 20% of the population in Norrbotten, Sweden's northernmost county. The population in some of the municipalities on the border was almost entirely Finnish speaking. The 1930 census was the last one in Sweden to attempt to register the Finns on a systematic basis. In the whole of Norrbotten, approximately 30,000 persons used or understood Finnish, while 4,000 spoke Finnish exclusively.

The migration of Kvens to northern Norway took place in two main waves. The first extended from the early 18th century until the early 19th century, producing agricultural settlements in valleys and inner fjords in the northern parts of northern Norway. This first wave was primarily an expansion of the Finnish agricultural colonization of Lapland, but it was also precipitated by the Russian campaign in the Gulf of Bothnia region during the Great Northern War (1700–21). During this period the Kvens of Norway were already viewed as a separate "nation," with characteristics that differentiated them from their neighbors, such as their language, material culture, and traditions. State borders did not present a serious obstacle for the Kvens since clear boundaries between Norway and Sweden and Norway and Russia were only established in 1751 and 1826, respectively.

The second wave of Kven immigration to northern Norway began around 1830 and extended until the end of the 19th century, with the peak years in the late 1860s and early 1870s. During this period, the migration turned into a mass phenomenon, pushed by demographic factors and structural changes in the economy in the migrants' areas of origin and pulled by the labor market of northern Norway, which was rapidly expanding in mining, fisheries, whaling, and sealing. Many Finns were also attracted to northern Norway by the prospect of moving on to the USA via the Arctic harbors and only stayed temporarily in Norway.

Kvens of the second wave of migration settled mainly in the fjords and on the coast, with the eastern parts of the Norwegian province Finnmark now forming the main destination region. According to the 1875 census, the Kvens mainly lived in two thinly populated counties: 5,800 in Finnmark (25% of the population) and 5,500 in Troms (8% of the population). As was the case in Sweden, the 1930 census in Norway was the last one to register the Kvens but was hindered by problems of "mixed" ethnicity and unclear criteria concerning ethnic identity. Altogether, approximately 6,000 individuals in Norway were defined as Kvens, the great majority of whom still lived in Troms and Finnmark.

The Kven settlements established by the first generation of immigrants were, as a rule, separated from the neighboring settlements of Sami and Norwegians. In some towns, ghetto-like Kven neighborhoods were built, the best known being the two "Kven towns" of Vadsø on the northern shore of the Varanger Fjord, which received the names Eastern and Western Kven Town (in Finnish Ulkopää and Sisäpää). Vadsø hosted the largest concentration of Kvens in Norway; in 1870 more than half of the town's population of approximately 2,000 people was made up of Kvens. For this reason, the town came to be known as the "Kven capital of Norway." Kven villages in the countryside differed from both Norwegian fishing villages and the traditional single farm system through the collective organization of seasonal work, expansive agriculture, and intensive animal husbandry as well as their building tradition. This ethnic spatial pattern was maintained until well after the Second World War, and clearly visible features still remain. Cultural elements such as the Kven language, which is mainly spoken by the elderly, have also been preserved.

A state minority policy that aggressively sought the assimilation of the Kvens first developed in Norway with the advent of modern nationalism. Nation building in the northern area bordering Russia and Finland was regarded as a national task of the utmost importance. The goal of creating a homogenous Norwegian state was pursued until the Second World War. This policy included the mandatory usage of Norwegian in schools, churches, and administration; Norwegian agricultural colonization and the establishment of industrial enterprises and military establishments in areas of Finnish settlement; prohibitions on Finns taking certain jobs; and surveillance and control measures.

Kven attempts at ethnopolitical organization in defense of their culture were swiftly opposed by the authorities. The Læstadian denomination, a Puritan-pietistic evangelistic Lutheran movement started by the Swedish Lapland pastor Lars Levi Læstadius in the 1840s, represented a haven for the Kvens as well as for the Sami. In Læstadian congregations preaching was delivered in the mother tongue, turning it into a kind of *lingua sacra*.

Nineteenth-century Swedish minority policy toward the Torne-Finns followed more or less the same pattern as Norwegian policy toward the Kvens, also spurred by the notion of the "Russian menace." During the interwar period, the policy of Swedification took a more lenient direction. There was permission, for example, to introduce the Finnish language as a voluntary subject in some schools in the Torne Valley. In Norway, such initiatives were rejected.

Although the assimilation policy was no longer systematically pursued during the postwar period, it was implemented in practice in many schools in both the Torne Valley and in northern Norway. The last formal school guidelines concerning Norwegianization and Swedification were not abolished until about 1960. The 1970s marked a political watershed for minorities in the Torne Valley. The Torne-Finns started to organize along ethnopolitical lines with considerable success. During the 1970s and 1980s, Finnish language teaching in schools was widely introduced and efforts for the preservation and revitalization of Finnish language and culture found broad support in the movement *meän kieli* (our language). The leading organization of the Torne-Finns, Svenska Tornedalingars Riksförbund (in Finnish Tornionlaksolaiset), founded in 1981, was at the center of the movement.

The ethnopolitical mobilization of Kvens since the 1970s was without doubt inspired by the *meän kieli* movement as well as by the political achievements of Sami. Their national association, Norske kveners forbund (in Finnish Ruijan kveeniliitto), was founded in 1987, followed by the newspaper *Kaiku* (Echo). Starting in the 1970s a weekly radio program

in Finnish has been produced and Finnish has been taught as a voluntary "foreign language" subject in both primary and secondary schools in Troms and Finnmark as well as in some high schools. Finnish language instruction has been extended since 1990. Starting from the time they became politically active, the Kvens claimed the status of a national minority, but this encountered considerable reservations on the part of state authorities, which actually still categorized the Kvens as immigrants. It was not until Norway and Sweden ratified the Council of Europe's Framework Convention for the Protection of National Minorities of 1995 that both the Kvens in Norway and the Torne-Finns in Sweden were recognized as national minorities. And it was not until 2005 that the Kven language was defined as a language in its own right, rather than a dialect, a status also granted in recent years to the language of the Torne-Finns.

The out migration of young Torne-Finns and Kvens has resulted in a comparative increase in elderly people in the original areas of settlement in Norway and Sweden. At the start of the 21st century, the Torne-Finns and Kvens still occupy specific niches of the labor market in agriculture, cattle breeding, forestry, and crafts. Within both groups there are debates about ethnic identity, including discussions on the "correct" designation. But on the whole, both they themselves and the larger society regard them as ethnic groups in their own right.

Elenius, Lars. *Både finsk og svensk: Modernisering, nationalism och språkförendring i Tornedalen 1850–1939*. Umeå, 2001.

Eriksen, Knut Einar, and Einar Niemi. *Den finske fare: Sikkerhetsproblemer og minoritetspolitikk i nord 1860–1940*. Oslo, 1981.

Huss, Leena. *Reversing Language Shift in the Far North: Linguistic Revitalization in Northern Scandinavia and Finland*. Uppsala, 1999.

Kjeldstadli, Knut, ed. *Norsk innvandringshistorie*, vols. 1–3. Oslo, 2003.

Niemi, Einar. "Norway – National Minorities and Minority Policy in Norway." In *International Obligations and National Debates: Minorities around the Baltic*, edited by Sia Spiliopoulou Åkermark et al., 397–451. Mariehamn, 2006.

Ryymin, Teemu. *"De nordligste finner": Framstillingen av kvenene I den finske litterære offentligheten 1800–1939*. Tromsø, 2004.

Cross-references: Northern Europe; Russia and Belarus; Forest Finns in Sweden and Norway since the Late 16th Century

LATIN AMERICAN MIGRANTS IN SPAIN SINCE THE END OF THE 1980S

Rosa Aparicio Gómez

In the late 1980s, Spain began to change from a country of emigration to immigration. In this period, the number of migrants from Latin America grew steadily but reached a high level only in the second half of the 1990s. In 2005 the official number of Latin Americans in Spain was 676,000, but, given the large number of irregular residents, the total number was likely well over a million. By 2008, the number had risen to 1,269,053 which represented almost one-third of the total number of foreign migrants in Spain without counting another probable half million irregular migrants. Moreover, the statistics do not take into account the more than 100,000 Latin Americans who have been naturalized since 1992.

The immigrants have come from all 19 countries in Latin America and have settled in each of the 17 Spanish autonomous regions with only a single exception: no Nicaraguans are registered in La Rioja. Five countries account for almost 80% of the total number of Latin American immigrants in Spain: Ecuador (33%), Colombia (21%), Peru (10%), Argentina (8%), and the Dominican Republic (6%). Ecuador is the only country where more than 1% of the population has emigrated to Spain; in all other countries the proportion has been much smaller. Many irregular immigrants come from Bolivia, Brazil, and Paraguay. During the regularization process in Spain in the first half of 2005, when illegal immigrants could apply for residency permits, Bolivians made up the largest group of applicants alongside Ecuadorians and Colombians: almost 50,000 Bolivians applied for a residency permit while only 7,000 Bolivians were legal residents at the time.

Latin American migrants in Spain display a clear preference for settlement in the urban areas of Madrid and Catalonia, where nearly 60% of the Latin American population lives. The enormous appeal of large urban centers is attributable not only to the widespread availability of employment opportunities in such areas. Irregular immigrants also prefer large cities because they are more likely to go unnoticed there as a result of less social control. The high proportion of women among Latin American immigrants also contributes to the preference for large cities as they offer an abundance of jobs in professions in which women are typically active, such as domestic and personal services.

Beyond this general tendency, the respective national groups tend to live concentrated in certain areas. Ecuadorians typically settle in agricultural regions, which accounts for their strong presence, for example, in Murcia. Dominican migrants, with a high proportion of women and typically possessing a lower level of occupational training, have settled in larger cities because of the high demand for domestic services there. Nearly 70% live either in Madrid or Barcelona. In contrast, Peruvians and Colombians, who also initially settled in cities due to the easier access for women to the labor market there, appear to have succeeded in advancing socially. Colombians of both sexes, for example, have spread in larger numbers than other Latin American migrants to middle-sized towns throughout Spain, such as Las Palmas, Valencia, or Bilbao. While most Peruvians (77%) have remained in Madrid and Barcelona, they have commonly been able to move on to better jobs.

In light of the favorable employment opportunities for female labor migrants, women have been predominant among Latin American migrants to Spain since migration began. As a result of family reunification and a shift in countries of origin, however, this trend has recently declined. In March 2005, some 55% of Latin American migrants to Spain were women while the number among African migrants was just 35% and among Asian migrants was 42%. For certain groups of Latin American migrants, the proportion of women is even higher: well over 70% of Brazilian and Guatemalan migrants in Spain are women while the number among at least eight other national groups exceeds 60%. The proportion of women among migrants from the Dominican Republic, for example, was 63% in 2005 and at 67% was even higher in 2004. The differences in gender composition among the various Latin American migrant populations in Spain reflect different patterns of migration. In most cases, women have tended to migrate first due to the better employment opportunities for women available in Spain while men have come later, mostly in the course of family reunification.

The migrants do not identify themselves as part of a comprehensive group of Latin Americans, but rather as Ecuadorians, Colombians, and so on. In Spain, however, they are considered "Latin Americans" and they accept this designation. The Spanish population usually only distinguishes between five broad groups of migrants – Moroccans, Latin Americans, sub-Saharan Africans, Chinese, and eastern Europeans – although they know that these groups can be divided into many smaller ones. "Latin American" has a positive connotation among Spaniards partly due to earlier Spanish settlement of large swaths of Latin America, the existence of a common language, and the widespread notion that Latin Americans and Spaniards possess a shared cultural heritage (*Hispanidad*), which facilitates positive relations between the two groups. Prejudices about Latin America, however, are also rather widespread. Latin Americans, for example, are said to act in a sycophantic manner toward Spaniards in order to get preferential treatment when seeking employment, particularly in the service sector. The undifferentiated characterization of "Latin Americans" is also the result of the preferential legal treatment, ostensibly justified by their shared history, accorded to Latin American migrants: while other immigrants must reside in the country for 10 years, Latin American migrants can be naturalized after just two years of uninterrupted legal residence. This regulation also applies to citizens of Spanish Guinea and the Philippines, both of which are former Spanish possessions. Finally, the marked presence in the media of a purportedly coherent "Latin world" folklore, which spread from the USA to Spain, also contributes to a unified view of Latin Americans in Spain.

Preferential treatment in naturalization is not the only privilege Latin American migrants in Spain have enjoyed. For many years, they could enter Spain without a visa and remain in the country for up to three months. This was especially valuable when the USA and Canada – previously among the preferred countries of destination – started to tighten their entry regulations during the late 1980s. Such Spanish entry privileges, however, have been successively curtailed for citizens from the Latin American countries with the highest rate of migration to Spain. Thus in the early 1990s a visa was required of Peruvians, in 2002 of Colombians, and in 2003 of Ecuadorians. While these measures have considerably reduced immigration from those countries, the number of migrants from countries whose citizens can still enter Spain without a visa has increased. Peruvians and Ecuadorians, however, continue to enjoy some privileges on the labor market as they, in contrast to other migrants, are exempt from the regulation requiring that Spanish citizens be given priority in employment.

Migration to Spain is commonly explained as an answer to economic problems, criminality, and political violence in many Latin American countries; the common language is often cited as a central reason for selecting Spain as country of destination. These reasons alone, however, are insufficient. In the first place, this migration, in contrast to how it is often depicted in the media, is not motivated by existential want. On the contrary, the immigrants are predominantly from the lower middle classes, seeking to enhance their quality of life. If poverty were the main reason for migration, the number of migrants from the respective countries should correspond to the level of income per capita, but this is not the case: Ecuador, Colombia, Peru, and the Dominican Republic send many more migrants to Spain than other countries with similar levels of income per capita and many more than countries with a lower per capita income. Furthermore, while Spain was earlier a land of refuge for many who sought to escape dictatorial regimes or political violence in the 1970s – Argentineans and, to a lesser degree, Peruvians – this no longer holds true. The example of Colombian migration to Spain at the end of the 1990s suggests rather that the respective political situation does not decisively influence the decision to migrate as the proportion of those coming from regions most affected by violence did not exceed that of those coming from more peaceful areas.

Migration networks established through chain migration are significantly more important than poverty or political instability for the decision to migrate, as recent studies on Ecuador, Colombia, and Peru illustrate. For example, some 43% of all Colombian migrants to Spain had contact with relatives before they left and 35% had contact with Colombian friends or acquaintances in Spain. Sixty percent of Ecuadorian migrants of both sexes in Murcia had previous contact with either relatives or fellow countrymen in the area.

Limited employment opportunities and poor housing conditions hamper the integration of Latin American migrants in Spain. Apart from Ecuadorians, who have a disproportionately high representation in agriculture and construction, most migrants work in the service sector in unstable, low-paying jobs with little prestige. Recent data suggest that Latin Americans working in this sector continually move from one job to another and thereby steadily increase their earnings, yet their salaries usually remain below their level of qualification.

Upon arrival, migrants usually have provisional lodging, provided by relatives or acquaintances, or live in cheap boardinghouses. Afterward, they typically move on to a rented room in an apartment shared with other migrants. Within approximately a year of arriving, most are able to rent their own apartment together with their family or close friends. After six or eight years they can usually afford to buy a home, which conforms to common practice in Spain.

Although data on contact between Latin American migrants and native Spaniards are scarce, some studies point to significant differences based on land of origin. Peruvians and Colombians seem more frequently to have private relationships with Spaniards and intermarriage between the groups is not infrequent. Ecuadorians, in contrast, tend to form close-knit networks with fellow nationals. Dominicans in turn are more open toward the recipient society, illustrated by their willingness to rely on state social services and private aid organizations supported by the state, not just on the aid of their own community.

Latin American migrants in Spain do not stand out in terms of their outward physical appearance. The Spanish public classifies them as "Latin Americans" based on the "accent" with which they speak Spanish, but they typically cannot differentiate between them based on country of origin. Such differences, however, are already less pronounced in the second generation, meaning that in this respect many members of the Latin American minority in Spanish society are now hardly recognizable as non-Spanish.

Aparicio, Rosa, and Carlos Giménez. *La Migración Colombiana en España*. Ginebra, 2003.

Gómez, José, Andrés Tornos, and Colectivo IOE. *Ecuatorianos en España. Una aproximación sociológica*. Madrid, 2007.

Gregorio, Gil C. *Migración femenina, su impacto en las relaciones de género*. Madrid, 1998.

Izquierdo, Antonio, Diego López de Lera, and Raquel Martínez. "Los preferidos del siglo XXI: La inmigración latinoamericana en España." In *III Congreso de la Inmigración en España*, vol. II, edited by Francisco Javier Garcia Castaño and Carolina Muriel López, 237–49. Granada, 2002.

Martínez Buján, Raquel. *La Reciente Inmigración Latinoamericana a España*. Santiago de Chile, 2003.

Pedone, Claudia. "Diversificación de las cadenas migratorias ecuatorianas hacia el mercado de trabajo agrícola en Murcia." In *La condicióninmigrante: exploración e investigaciones desde la Región de Murcia*, coordinated by Andrés Pedreño Cánovas, 255–72. Murcia, 2005.

Tornos, Andrés, et al. *Los Peruanos que Vienen*. Madrid, 1997.

Tornos, Andrés, and Rosa Aparicio. *Las Redes Sociales de los Inmigrantes Extranjeros en España. Un estudio sobre el Terreno*. Madrid, 2005.

Cross-references: Spain and Portugal; Moroccan Undocumented Immigrants in Spain since the End of the 20th Century

LATIN AMERICAN PROSTITUTES IN THE NETHERLANDS SINCE THE 1970S

Marie-Louise Janssen

Since the 19th century, foreign women have worked in Dutch prostitution. In the beginning, the majority of these women hailed from surrounding countries, such as Germany and France. However, since the 1970s, an increasing number of female migrants coming from different parts of the world have entered the world of prostitution in the Netherlands. Women from east Asia, Latin America, west Africa, and central and eastern Europe began to migrate to the Netherlands, ending up as workers in the sex industry. As in many other European countries, the migrant prostitutes employed in the Dutch sex industry outnumbered local sex workers at the end of the 20th century.

During the last three decades of the 20th century, the most conspicuous group among all migrant sex workers has come from Latin America and the Caribbean. Since the mid-1970s the number of Latin American women has risen noticeably. In the Netherlands, where an estimated 25,000 to 30,000 women and men are working in prostitution, the number of all Latin American sex workers is estimated between 5,000 and 7,000. The first Latin American women occupying seats behind the windows in the famous red light district of Amsterdam were from Suriname, a former Dutch colony. Some years later, at the beginning of the 1980s, women mainly from the Dominican Republic and Colombia, and to a lesser degree from Brazil, Chile, Peru, and Argentina started to arrive and spread out all over the country.

Due to the stigma attached to prostitution, and the discrimination that often accompanies it, many prostitutes do not openly admit to the exact nature of their work. In addition, many Latin American sex workers are illegal residents, without resident status or work permits. This particular group mostly operates in an illegal circuit, beyond the reach of official data gathering. The high mobility that characterizes this migrant group constitutes another major obstacle to any attempts at civil registration. Most of these women tend to travel a lot, inside both the Netherlands and Europe, constantly, sometimes daily, changing their workplace. Sometimes they even alter their window or brothel on a daily basis. They also constantly commute between Europe and their home country.

Several factors can explain the intensive migratory movement of women from Latin America to the European continent. The vast majority of the women are labor migrants who have left their country because of persistent economic or political crises and rising unemployment. They migrate to Europe seeking a source of income and a better future for their children. Most of them are young women aged between 18 and 30 years, single mothers who carry the main financial responsibility for their family. Once the women have arrived in the Netherlands, their options in the labor market are limited. In general, the women come from the lower economic classes, having received little more education than a few years

of primary school. In some cases they are illiterate. A certain segment of these women have previous experience working as prostitutes either in their own country or elsewhere in Latin America. For these women, who often speak only Spanish, prostitution is, apart from domestic work and housecleaning, one of the few possible ways to survive in Europe.

Further reasons for the increasing number of Latin American sex workers in the Netherlands are developments on the Dutch labor market. Since the 1970s, there has been a growing demand in the Netherlands for cheap, female workers in the informal service sector, including domestic work in private households, cleaning services, and child care, as well as in the sex industry. This demand is often accompanied by ethnic, and sometimes racist, stereotypes. Frequently women from the so-called third-world countries are preferred by employers in these sectors, due to their vulnerable status as undocumented immigrants; they are considered to be cheaper than Western women, as well as less astute and demanding. Many clients of prostitutes also express their preference in terms of nationality, grounding their choice in specific ethnic stereotypes that are associated with particular nationalities or cultures. Since the 1970s, an increasing demand for black and colored "exotic" women can be observed among many clients and sex tourists. Often this demand is based on stereotypical ideas of ethnic femininity and sexuality that presumably enhance the popularity of these women. Latin American women, for instance, are appreciated for a supposedly "natural appetite for sex" and being "passionate lovers," while European women, on the other hand, are considered to be "cool" and "commercial."

In addition to economic factors, there are also social reasons that may play a part in the decision to migrate to Europe, such as the desire to escape from the restrictions of an oppressing traditional gender role and a longing for more personal freedom. This particular aspect manifests itself especially in the case of transgender sex workers, who are strongly represented among the Latin American migrants. This applies to men who dress up like women when engaged in sex work, or transsexuals, who regard themselves as female both in their work in prostitution as well as in daily life, and who satisfy mainly the lusts of male clients. Many have experienced violence and discrimination in their native countries, where they are marginalized as homosexuals or transgenders. The climate of relative tolerance prevailing in the Netherlands with respect to homosexuality and transsexuality encourages many to migrate.

The women use different strategies to migrate to Europe. Social networks, for instance, play a vital role, triggering a chain of migration. Many women are recommended by relatives, such as a sister or cousin, or friends who assist them in finding their way to Europe or who lend them money to make the crossing. In due course, an increasing number of women have been leaving on their own initiative and migrate independently to Europe, thus giving rise to an autonomous migration process. They enter the Netherlands with a tourist visa that is valid for three months. Once their visa is expired, the women disappear in the illegal circuit or look for an appropriate European husband. On the basis of a marriage with a European they can obtain a legal status as well as a work permit, which gives them the opportunity to work and travel freely throughout Europe.

Especially during the 1980s, an important migration route to Europe was established via the Dutch Antilles in the Caribbean. A considerable number of Dominican and Colombian women had been working in the famous brothel Campo Alegre (Happy Camp) on the Dutch-Antillean island Curaçao before they migrated to the Netherlands. This notorious brothel was founded and legalized in 1949 by Dutch authorities to satisfy the sexual demands of European and North American marines and businessmen who were temporarily quartered on Curaçao. Dutch prostitution policies prevailed, which brought forth toleration and regularization of brothels by the state. Most of these Colombian and Dominican women were recruited in their native countries by *buscones*, a common term in the Caribbean for people who recruit women for prostitution and mediate between the women and the brothel owners. Since the 1980s, this practice has become more widespread in the Caribbean, giving rise to a flourishing sex industry in the region based on an organized network.

At first the women were set to work in prostitution for a period of time in one of the Antillean islands; subsequently they were trafficked to Europe. In this manner hundreds of Latin American women came to the Netherlands every year as victims of human trafficking. In general, it is estimated that about 3,500 women are trafficked each year and forced into Dutch prostitution by third parties, either by deception, violence, or the threat of violence. Internationally organized networks of traffickers recruit the women in Latin America, lending them the money to undertake the voyage, facilitating their stay in several European countries, and rapidly incorporating them into the international sex industry. The women are lured with false promises and misled about the true nature of the work they will have to perform, as well as the terms of employment and working conditions.

The women have to pay thousands of dollars in advance for their airline tickets and the procurement of documents. Many women have signed contracts and taken out a mortgage on a house of a relative. Prior to traveling to Europe, they find themselves heavily indebted to the traffickers, which leads to a situation of dependency, also known as debt bondage. Added to this is the situation of lawlessness in which they live and work, and both make the women extremely vulnerable. Even the new prostitution policy that legalized prostitution in the Netherlands in 2000, by granting the prostitutes the same rights and duties enjoyed by any other professional group, has further aggravated this situation because this alteration of the law does not apply to persons from outside the European Union. After decades of tolerance, non-European migrants are currently being excluded from working in the Dutch sex industry. To detect illegal prostitutes, increased police control of brothels and areas of street prostitution has been stepped up in all Dutch cities. After being picked up by the vice squad, illegal prostitutes are taken to the police

station and handed over to the immigration police, which then immediately start deportation procedures.

Latin American women work in various forms of prostitution, such as clubs, private houses, window prostitution, streetwalking, and escort services. Especially in certain quarters in Arnhem, the Hague, and Amsterdam, cities where window prostitution is a common practice, their presence is strongly felt and determines the street image and atmosphere of the neighborhood. Walking past the open windows and doors, one is surrounded by the sounds of Spanish-language and Caribbean dance music, such as *merengue* and *bachata*, as well as the smell of traditional dishes, such as *arroz con habichuela y chicharrón* (rice with beans and beef).

Frequently these Latin American women live their lives in complete isolation from Dutch society. Working generally six or seven days per week, apart from their contacts with clients and brothel keepers, they hardly associate with the "natives." Many of them live in the same place where they work and rarely leave their neighborhood. For many, their stay in the Netherlands is mostly restricted to their workplace, which, in the case of window prostitution, for example, consists of a tiny rented room of two by three meters. They usually order take-out meals that are delivered by an errand boy and cooked by a compatriot who makes a living of selling traditional dishes to prostitutes. Other factors contributing to the isolation of these women are the language barrier as well as their dynamic migration patterns, preventing them from staying at the same spot for long periods.

Usually the women maintain contacts with some Latin American colleagues or other compatriots. They look for each other's company to exchange experiences and information grounded in their common culture, language, and religious tradition. Most women are Catholic and visit, if possible, churches with a Spanish-language mass that are found in some of the big cities. Also, there are specific religious meetings, especially for the Dominicans, like the celebration of the Virgin of Alta Gracia, the nation's patron saint.

The Latin American women maintain strong ties with their family in the country of origin. They call their families weekly, regularly send money, and frequently visit their home and family. Mostly they work between 8 and 10 months and then return home, usually around Christmastime. During these visits, the nature of their work in Europe is not revealed. Because of the moral condemnation of prostitution, they anxiously keep their work secret from their children, family, and friends. This is also one of the reasons the women in general do not want to invite their children to visit or to live with them in Europe. Their life takes place in two separate worlds: one in Europe working as a prostitute and sometimes living with a European husband, and one in their home country with their children.

In general, Latin American prostitutes do not identify themselves professionally with other prostitutes. For this reason the women are not very interested in organizing themselves within the national organization the Red Thread (an interest group for prostitutes in the Netherlands founded in 1985). Before leaving their countries, the Latin American women believe in the existing myth that the life of a prostitute in foreign countries is considered *una vida fácil*, an easy life, that will enable them to get rich quickly, but many times this does not correspond with reality.

Most women perceive their migration to Europe as a temporary or seasonal migration. They migrate to Europe with the idea that they will return after having earned a sufficient amount of money to raise their social status in the country of origin and to finance a good upbringing for their children. A plot of land and their own house made of stone are important status symbols that confirm their migration success.

As a consequence of their financial contributions to the family, these women obtain a respected position within the family and the community and experience upward social mobility. Their acceptance or rejection by their families depends on the financial success they have achieved. As the women succeed in sending money home or bringing it with them when they return, they are indeed considered successful and are admired, although their families know or suspect that they have worked in prostitution. In this case, the women serve as an example to other women in the country who also want to migrate. But when their return is unexpected as the result of deportation or escape from a situation of deceit and violence, the migrants are considered to have failed.

Brussa, Licia. "The TAMPEP Project in Western Europe." In *Global Sex Workers: Rights, Resistance, and Redefinition*, edited by Kamala Kempadoo and Jo Doezema, 57–82. New York and London, 1998.

Kempadoo, Kamala. *Exotic Colonies: Caribbean Women in the Dutch Sex Trade*. Denver, 1994.

Kempadoo, Kamala, ed. *Sun, Sex, and Gold. Tourism and Sex Work in the Caribbean*. Lanham, 1999.

Rode Draad, ed. [The national organization that defends the rights of sexworkers in the Netherlands] *Opheffing Bordeelverbod. Een onderneming voor prostitutie*. Amsterdam, 2000.

Stichting Tegen Vrouwenhandel, ed. [The Dutch Foundation against Trafficking] *Registratiegegevens inzake aanmeldingen van (mogelijke) slachtoffers van vrouwenhandel over de periode 1992–2000*. Utrecht, 2000.

Cross-references: The Netherlands; Eastern, East-Central and South-Eastern European Prostitutes in Western, Central, Northern, and Southern Europe since the 1980s; Peruvian Female Domestics in Italy since the End of the 20th Century

LEVANTINES IN THE OTTOMAN EMPIRE AND IN THE EASTERN MEDITERRANEAN SINCE THE 19TH CENTURY

Oliver Jens Schmitt

"Levantines" was the term given to Catholics of the Roman rite living in the Ottoman Empire and in the Islamic states of the eastern Mediterranean, most of whom had immigrated from Europe since the high Middle Ages. Levantine, an exonym coined by Europeans, acquired its pejorative connotation with respect to the group defined only in the 19th century. Before about 1800, the term usually referred to all non-Muslim residents of port cities in the eastern Mediterranean. Members of that group used it to describe themselves only after 1900, and even then only in exceptional cases. Levantines themselves preferred primarily the prestigious term "Europeans." Their Greek-speaking neighbors referred to the Levantines as "Franks" or "Francolevantines"; their Turkish-speaking Muslim neighbors called them "Freshwater Franks" (*tatlý su frengi*).

The oldest centers of settlement for the Levantines were Constantinople (Istanbul; since the 10th and 11th centuries), Aleppo (since the late Middle Ages), Smyrna (Izmir; heavily since the beginning of the 17th century), and in the 19th century Alexandria, Thessaloniki, and to a lesser extent ports like Beirut, Athens, and the Black Sea ports of Varna, Odessa, and Trebizond. As late as the 19th century, the core element was formed by the descendants of Venetian and Genoese families, most of whom had settled in the Aegean after the Fourth Crusade (1204). Beginning in the 16th century, the Ottoman Empire signed treaties (capitulations) with various European states (France, Venice, England, the Netherlands) in which the privileges of the Europeans were spelled out in detail (e.g., exemption from dues, consular jurisdiction, protection of the domicile).

These capitulations had fundamental importance for the Levantines and their identity formation, for until the 19th century, Catholics of the Roman rite had no representation of their own set up and recognized by the Ottoman state, but fell into the legal categories of *dhimmis*, so-called *protégés* (protected individuals), and subjects of European states. Especially at the end of the 18th and in the first decades of the 19th century, European embassies and consulates were generous in handing out letters of protection (*Berate* or *Firmane*). Beneficiaries were especially the already resident Roman-Catholic *dhimmis* of various ethnic backgrounds, but also Arab-speaking Aleppians, mostly Turkish-speaking Armenians from Nachitchewan (the "Persians" in Smyrna), Greek-speaking island Catholics from the Aegean, Greek-speaking Catholics from the Ionian Islands, and Maltese, large numbers of whom migrated into the "Frankish quarters" of Galata-Pera and to Smyrna between 1700 and 1850.

The immigration was driven by various motives: the "Persians," fleeing war and persecution, came to Smyrna in three larger waves. The Greek-speaking island Catholics escaped the double pressure from the Ottoman administration and the growing hostility of the surrounding Orthodox world, especially after the Greek revolt of 1821. Economic reasons and the prospects of enjoying the privileges laid down in the treaties explain the immigration of a maritime proletariat (seamen, petty merchants, criminals) from Malta, Dalmatia, and the Ionian Islands. In the first half of the 19th century, these immigrants encountered solidified social structures among the local Levantines of Galata-Pera and Smyrna. Alongside ethnic Italian Catholics, in the 17th and 18th centuries it was especially French merchants who migrated to the trading cities of Galata, Smyrna, and Aleppo. Until around 1800 they formed a largely self-contained unit among the Levantines.

Since the Levantines, because of their varying legal status within the Ottoman Empire, never made up a constitutional entity, group cohesion was assured through a shared religious confession, confessional institutions, close family bonds, and common economic interests. Next to the dragomans, who had been settled in Galata since the 15th century and who de facto played a part in shaping the eastern policy of the European powers around 1800 as interpreters at embassies and consulates, the great merchants of the European trading houses formed the second element of the elite. A small group of middling merchants and craftsmen formed the middle class, below which was a numerically large underclass of day laborers, seamen, economic failures, and "adventurers." While the ethnic Italian and ethnic French families began to intermix around 1800, the rate of endogamy remained high into the second half of the 19th century among island Catholics, Ionians, Dalmatians, and Maltese. The group of the dragomans was absent in Smyrna as a power factor. Dominant here were the merchant families from Italy, France, Great Britain, and the Netherlands which had been immigrating since the 17th century; after 1800 they made marriage alliances across confessional boundaries, and from about 1840 on they increasingly integrated also "Persian" and "island Catholic" families.

In the second half of the 19th century (especially during and after the Crimean War 1853–5), the reforms of the *Tanzimat* (reorganization), the opening of the Ottoman Empire to free trade (Treaty of Balta Liman 1838), the greatly increased influence of the European powers, and the great demand for European capital, technology, and goods brought several tens of thousands of European immigrants into the Ottoman eastern Mediterranean region, to Constantinople, in particular. The upswing of trade in the eastern Mediterranean, the rapid rise especially of Alexandria, the growing importance of Odessa to the European grain trade, and the barely diminished economic position of Smyrna also led to an expansion of the settlement areas of the Catholics, who now settled also outside the existing "Frankish quarters" and set up bases in smaller ports and in the inland areas of the Balkans and Asia Minor that were close to the coast. The already existing communities, especially in Galata-Pera, underwent a profound change. The old dragoman dynasties were replaced by a new elite of immigrant technocrats (bankers, engineers, merchants, craftsmen, and independent professionals like lawyers, doctors, and journalists), who satisfied the demand of a segment of Ottoman society for a European lifestyle.

The new immigrants deliberately set themselves apart from the already established urban residents with European roots by distinguishing between themselves as "Europeans" with a correspondingly high social prestige and the orientalized and

therefore "lower-ranking" Levantines. As a result, the term "Levantine" with its modern negative connotation emerged after 1850. It should be understood as the product of a fierce competitive struggle over who could lay claim to the economically very lucrative European identity in a Westernizing society. Still, the largely male immigrants quickly mixed with native women. Especially the newly arriving members of the lower and middle classes soon adopted the Greek vernacular that was widely spoken among the Levantines and assimilated quickly. It was also this rapid process of assimilation that made it possible for the majority of these new immigrants to be called Levantines after only a few decades.

That same period also saw the breakup – through mixed marriages – of the isolated milieu of the island Catholics, Dalmatians, and Maltese. The strong rise in the number of exogenous marriages within the Catholic milieu, the rapid increase also in mixed confessional marriages, especially with Orthodox women, gave rise toward the end of the 19th century of a group in Galata-Pera that could no longer be traced back to a particular milieu of origin. It defined itself solely through its Catholic confession, which established the link to the prestigious self-description and external description as Europeans. A dual identity of the Levantines took shape. For one, there was an "inner identity" that was shaped entirely by confession and family bonds. For another, on the outside – that is, vis-à-vis the European diplomatic representations and Ottoman officials – the Levantines presented themselves as citizens or protected individuals of European states. The social capital of European descent and the legal privileges from passes and letters of protection established the unique position of the Levantines within Ottoman society. Toward the end of the 19th century, about 40,000 Catholics of the Roman rite lived in Constantinople and its environs; in Smyrna this group counted between 15,000 and 20,000 before World War I.

In contrast to most other non-Muslim communities in the Ottoman Empire, with their highly developed self-governance (*millets*) in the 19th century, the Levantines never constituted a legal or political entity. Since the Levantines thought of themselves as citizens of European states, they hardly developed any interest in helping to shape the political system of the Ottoman Empire, which was in the process of reforming itself. With two exceptions, political expressions on the part of the Levantines did not occur: the "indigenous" opposition of the Catholics of Pera, during the revolutionary period after 1792, to the protective power France, which had become anticlerical, and the vague project of a city-state of Smyrna under Levantine leadership around 1862. In fact, many Levantines left officials deliberately in the dark about their ethnic identity. The switch from one protective status to another, depending on personal advantage, was a common phenomenon. It was only a tightening of European passport laws in the 1860s and the introduction of Ottoman citizenship in 1869 that forced the Levantines to make a decision. However, final adoption of a European citizenship was only a formal step. For in spite of the absence of a political organization of the Levantines as a group, there were strong bonds among them. A particularly important role was played by church organizations, which flourished in the 19th century. New forms of sociability (casinos, clubs, theater, European-style cafés) became a bonding agent of the group. The numerous exogamous marriages gave rise to a special, confessionally defined, and nonnational group, whose Catholic and European identity seemed exclusive toward the other ethno-confessional communities.

Between about 1850 and 1923, the social differentiation of the Levantines was heightened by new immigration from Europe. Old-established families of the elite moved into the second tier, and European technocrats into the top tier of the social hierarchy. Characteristic of this development was the decline of the great Levantine banking houses Alléon (bankers to the Sultan) and Glavany, which were displaced by large European banks. In Smyrna, the Levantines were able to hold their own until after World War I especially in trade. Because of the cohesiveness and self-confidence of the Levantine community (about 10% of the city's population), Smyrna can be considered the center of the Levantines in the eastern Mediterranean. Smyrna, in particular, saw the creation of Greek-language texts in Latin script (*Frankochiotika*), which should be seen as a genuine Levantine cultural form.

The decline of the Levantines was closely connected with the modernization, nationalization, and secularization of Ottoman society. As a purely confessional group without a uniform legal status and political organization or goals, without prominent leaders, and without a class of intellectuals, the Levantines were passive in the face of these changes. They gave in to the pressure to declare their allegiance that was asserted by the protective powers, which after 1855 deliberately reshaped the old "colonies" into nationally conscious bridgeheads of imperialist interests in the Ottoman Empire. Since the passport from a European state made possible the privileged position of the Levantines in the Ottoman state in the first place, they were unable to resist the pressure to give in. The considerable leeway that existed until around 1870 for an individual social articulation of their identity as Catholic inhabitants of the Ottoman Empire and as persons under the protection of European powers was increasingly curtailed. The nationalistic policy of the Young Turks after 1908 put further pressure on the Levantines. The Italo-Turkish War (1911) and World War I forced large numbers of Levantines with Italian, French, and British passports to leave their homeland. Their dilemma became evident upon their arrival in the countries of origin. In Naples, the Levantine war refugees were greeted with the call "The Turks are coming."

After World War I, as well, and especially in the wake of the xenophobic legislation of the Turkish Republic after 1923 (prohibition against practicing one's profession, restrictions on property rights), most Levantines left their homeland and migrated to Europe or countries overseas. Today, Izmir and Istanbul, which are now largely homogeneous ethnically, have small, aging communities of around 2,000 or a few hundred individuals, respectively.

Dalleggio, Eugène. "Bibliographie analytique d´ouvrages religieux en Grec imprimés avec des caractères latins." *Mikrasiatika Chronika* 9 (1961): 385–499.

Gautier, Antoine, and Marie de Testa. *Drogmans et diplomats européens auprès de la Porte ottomane.* Istanbul, 2003.

Hitzel, Frédéric, ed. *Istanbul et les langues orientales.* Paris, 1997.

Schmitt, Oliver Jens. *Levantiner. Lebenswelten und Identitäten einer ethnokonfessionellen Gruppe im Osmanischen Reich im langen 19. Jahrhundert.* Munich, 2005. (French translation Istanbul, 2007)

Smyrnelis, Marie-Carmen. *Une société hors de soi. Identités et relations sociales à Smyrne aux XVIIIème et XIXème siècles.* Paris, 2005.

Cross-references: France; Great Britain; Italy; The Netherlands; Southeastern Europe

LIPPE BRICKMAKERS IN CENTRAL, WESTERN, AND NORTHERN EUROPE FROM THE 17TH TO THE EARLY 20TH CENTURY

Piet Lourens and Jan Lucassen

The Duchy (since 1789 Principality) of Lippe-Detmold was one of the core regions of what was referred to as *Hollandgängerei* (migration to Holland). Some regulations by the authorities in the first half of the 17th century sought to prevent the migration from Lippe-Detmold. At that time a few men from Lippe appeared in Amsterdam, chiefly as bakers and sugar makers. A strong exodus from Lippe-Detmold began only a century later. Evidently emigration and seasonal migration were already so extensive toward the end of the 17th century that the ducal government outlawed them. The considerable rise in the volume of migrants resulted probably from a strong increase in the large number of grass mowers and peat cutters who were working until around 1900 in the western and northern provinces of the Netherlands and in neighboring East-Frisia.

Presumably some of these peat cutters in East-Frisia or possibly also in Groningen became acquainted with brickmaking. This trade had a long tradition there and was rapidly expanding in the 17th century. In Lippe, by contrast, where the customary building style was half-timbered houses with mud walls, brickmaking was scarce. The earliest mention of brickmakers from Lippe dates to 1657 from Weener (East-Frisia). The year 1682 saw the first ordinance that explicitly referred to brickmaking as the vocation of migrant workers. Beginning around that time, one Johann Jost Eckensträter from Lippe became active as a "messenger" (job broker) for his countrymen. In 1714, at his request, the government of Lippe granted his son a monopoly as "messenger" for East-Frisia and Groningen. In 1737–8, the brickworks at the estuary of the Ems counted 27 molders and 206 workers from Lippe.

The number of brickmakers from Lippe rose from 288 men in 1790, to 1,060 migrant laborers in 1820, up to 7,786 migrants in 1860. At the same time, the traditional destination regions increasingly declined in importance: the percentage of those who migrated to Groningen and East-Frisia declined from nearly 100% around 1800 to 50% in 1820, down to less than 20% in 1860. The number of Lippe brickmakers continued to grow also after 1860, though at a slower rate: there were 12,000 brickmakers from Lippe in the 1880s and 1890s, and the high point was reached around 1900 with about 14,000. After World War I the number of migrant workers dropped dramatically and stood after 1923 continuously at a little over 5,000.

As the number of brickmakers from Lippe rose almost without interruption until World War I, so did the ratio of migrant workers to the overall population in their homeland: from 1.7% in 1811, to more than 7.6% 50 years later, and a high of 10% on the eve of World War I. At that time, about a quarter of the grown men in Lippe were migrant workers.

Throughout the entire 18th century, East-Frisia remained the most important destination area of the brickmakers from Lippe. Beginning in about 1780, Oldenburg also offered work alongside Groningen. From about 1820 on, more and more men from Lippe went to the brickworks along the banks of the Elbe and Oste in the Hanoverian rural bailiwick of Stade. From there, the brick region extended especially northward and in the late 1840s reached as far as Denmark. In addition, the entire Kingdom of Hanover also developed into a brick region. In the last quarter of the 19th century, migrations were increasingly concentrated within the borders of the German Empire, with the focal point in Rhineland and Westphalia. This new pattern of migration southward persisted until the first decades of the 20th century. Occasional brickmakers from Lippe have also been documented in southern Norway and in Sweden, in the Baltic region, in Russia, and in Austria-Hungary. However, they constituted fully formed monopolies in this segment of the labor market only along the Dutch and German North Sea coast as well as in large enterprises in Schleswig-Holstein and Jütland. In the factories of all other brick regions, the men from Lippe always worked in competition with other migrant laborers, for example, the Walloons in the Rhineland.

From the 17th until well into the 19th century, the brickmakers from Lippe usually worked in brickworks whose production capacity was large enough to employ a Lippe brickmaker group for the entire season. During such a season, a group was responsible for the entire production process, from mixing the clay to firing the bricks and preparing them for shipment.

Throughout the season, which lasted from April to November, the Lippeans worked from early in the morning to late at night. The first step in brickmaking was grinding the clay. The carter brought the prepared clay to the *Aufstecher*, who in turn brought it to the molder. The molder passed his product on to the carrier (*Abträger*), who stored the molded bricks in the drying shed. Once a stock of about 100,000 bricks had been dried, they were fired in the kiln under the direction of the kiln master (*Brandmeister*). The entire cycle – from preparing the clay to firing the bricks – could be accomplished five times in a season.

Far-reaching changes took place after 1880: with the help of the extrusion press, every worker was able to produce far more moldings than before. Stocks could be laid in, and Hoffmann's circular kiln (*Ringofen*), patented in 1858, allowed firing during nearly the entire winter. Since brickmaking thereby increasingly lost its seasonal character, in the end the seasonal labor migration of the brickmakers also vanished.

Crucial to the productivity of a group of brickmakers was the quality of the cooperation of all its members. The better they worked together, the higher the output of the entire group and thus also of each individual brickmaker. Oversight was in the hands of the kiln master, who in the small brickworks was also the molder. The brickmaking group was often composed of neighbors or even family members. Brickmakers generally worked in a group for many years. During the winter, the workers were recruited, the tasks assigned, and the wages negotiated. In the brickworks, the workers shared a common room and slept two to a bed. Meals were also taken together in the same room.

The piece wages were calculated for nearly all workers at the end of the season. The factory owner counted all the well-fired bricks and reckoned the final compensation for the group. From that he subtracted the costs authorized by the kiln master for the shared lunch and coffee – the "communal account" (hence the reference to the group as the "Lippe commune") – as well as any advances. After that, the kiln master distributed the money to the members of the group according to their jobs.

The Lippeans, especially as represented by the kiln master, stood in contact with the employer and with the brick messenger privileged by the government. The brick region of the Lippeans was divided into four districts in 1802, 1842, and 1867: (1) Groningen and East-Frisia; (2) Oldenburg and Hanover; (3) Saxony, Schleswig-Holstein, and Scandinavia; (4) Brandenburg and all other regions. The brick messengers and the various factory owners in the districts worked out the number of laborers needed in the next season and the wage per 1,000 fired bricks. The messenger recruited the necessary groups, often by first recruiting the kiln masters, who then in turn put together their groups. In the summer, the messenger (or his underling) came to the workplace of the brickmaker groups and brought letters and parcels. In the middle of the 19th century, the brick messengers took on additional important functions, like oversight of the burial and sick fund and the courts of mediation. The introduction of freedom of trade in the North German League in 1869 put an end to the state-licensed messenger system in Lippe, though unofficially it continued to exist for decades.

With the growing mechanization and the resulting decline in the seasonality of brick production, the relationship between the kiln master and the other workers slowly changed. It was the beginning of the end of the cooperative brickmaking commune. The kiln masters evolved increasingly into *Annehmer* and intermediate masters paid by the piece, the other brickmakers into unionized, dependent workers paid by the hour. Only a very small group of Lippeans settled permanently in the immigration regions during this period. It was most likely to happen in the industrialized, new brick regions like the Ruhr area.

Fleege-Althoff, Fritz. *Die lippischen Wanderarbeiter*. Detmold, 1928.

Gladen, Albin, et al., eds. *Hollandgang im Spiegel der Reiseberichte evangelischer Geistlicher. Quellen zur saisonalen Arbeitswanderung in der zweiten Hälfte des 19. Jahrhunderts*. 2 vols. Münster, 2007.

Linderkamp, Heike. *"Auf Ziegelei" an der Niederelbe. Zur saisonalen Wanderarbeit lippischer Ziegler im 19. und 20. Jahrhundert*. Stade, 1992.

Lourens, Piet, and Jan Lucassen, *Arbeitswanderung und berufliche Spezialisierung. Die lippischen Ziegler im 18. und 19. Jahrhundert*. Osnabrück, 1999.

Lourens, Piet, and Jan Lucassen. "Karrieren lippischer Ziegler: Das Beispiel Delfzijl 1855." In *Lippische Mitteilungen aus Geschichte und Landeskunde* 76 (2007): 63–80.

Wessels, Paul. *Ziegeleien an der Ems. Ein Beitrag zur Wirtschaftsgeschichte Ostfrieslands*. Aurich, 2004.

Cross-references: Germany; The Netherlands; Northern Europe; German Baker-Journeymen in Amsterdam in the 17th Century; German Seasonal Agricultural Laborers in the Netherlands from the 17th to the Early 20th Century

MAGHREBIS IN FRANCE AFTER DECOLONIZATION IN THE 1950S AND 1960S

Ulrich Mehlem

The word Maghrebis, which is used to refer to people from the North African states of Morocco, Algeria, Tunisia, and Libya, is derived from Arabic *Al-maghrib* (west). In France, the word has gained currency since the 1980s along with the terms *Nord-Africains* and *Arabes*.

Table 1 shows that France is the dominant immigration country for Maghrebis. In most countries, these numbers, which are derived from the statistics for foreigners, represent merely a lower limit, since individuals from the Maghreb are no longer counted once they have acquired citizenship in the immigration country. That is especially true for France.

Even after the independence of the Maghreb states, immigration to France continues to stand in the shadow of colonial history, which links especially Algeria to the former colonial master even at the beginning of the 21st century. French rule lasted 132 years there (1830–1962), the Algerian *départements* were a direct part of the motherland after 1848, and

after 1947 the Muslim inhabitants of Algeria were French citizens. By contrast, Morocco and Tunisia were considered protectorates (1912–56 and 1881–1956, respectively), a model of governance that combined the traditional political and social institutions of those countries with institutions introduced from France.

In France, colonial and postcolonial migration and migration of recruited "guest workers" flowed together seamlessly. At the beginning of the Algerian war of independence in 1954, 212,000 Algerians were already living in France, compared to only 34,000 Tunisians and 49,600 Moroccans by the time the war ended in 1962. It was only during the subsequent years, down to the ban on recruitment of foreign workers in 1974, that immigration from the two other Maghreb states rose noticeably: in that year, France was home to 884,000 Algerians, 270,000 Moroccans, and 140,000 Tunisians. What began as labor migration of single men with high rates of turnover led, via permanent stays, to a real immigration situation in the course of the 1960s and early 1970s.

Beginning in the 1980s, the integration of immigrants from the Maghreb became in France not only a central theme of social and domestic politics but also a basic component of the French Republic's political and cultural self-conception. For a long time, the focus was on aspects of socioeconomic exclusion: the especially high unemployment among the immigrants, their concentration in government housing on the outskirts of the conurbations (the *banlieues*), and the poor performance of these young people in the school system, all of which became strikingly apparent from the youth unrest in Lyon and Paris in 1981 and 1991, and in Paris and other large cities in 2005. Later, the discussion was overlaid with cultural and religious questions, which revolved chiefly around the compatibility between secularized west European societies and Islam. The rise of the New Right and of the antiracist movement, as well as the various patterns of self-organization among the Maghrebis, are directly related to these developments. The sense of group belonging is slowly losing importance for some of the immigrants, while the majority still emphasizes it by setting itself apart from the native French.

History and pattern of immigration from the Maghreb

The central importance of France as the reception country for Maghrebis has above all historical reasons. Until the independence of Algeria, the open border between France and that country facilitated population movement between them across the Mediterranean. However, this freedom of movement, still enshrined in the Treaty of Evian (1962), came under growing pressure from an uncontrollable immigration to France and was increasingly constrained by quotas set by the two countries. The recruitment ban of 1974 put an almost complete stop to legal immigration for work. Family reunification had begun among the Algerians as early as the end of the 1960s. To counter a permanent settlement of Algerians, France, at the beginning of the 1970s,

Table 1. Maghrebis in Europe by nationality, 1997

Destination countries in the EU	Countries of origin in the Maghreb			Maghreb as a whole
	Morocco	Algeria	Tunisia	
Belgium	145,363	10,177	6,048	161,588
Germany	82,803	23,082	28,060	133,945
Spain	61,303	3,259	378	64,940
France	572,652	614,207	206,336	1,393,195
Italy	77,189	3,177	35,318	115,684
Netherlands	164,567	905	2,415	167,887
Sweden	1,533	599	1,152	3,284
Great Britain	3,000	2,000	2,000	7,000
Total	1,108,410	657,406	281,707	2,047,523

Source: Eurostat 1997.

increasingly recruited migrant workers from Morocco, though after the ban on recruitment, these also began to bring over their families.

French citizenship law in principle created good conditions for the equality of the Maghrebis as citizens, though it simultaneously made it difficult to regulate their immigration. All children born in France to foreigners with legal residence status can acquire French citizenship when they reach the age of majority. This regulation in the sense of the *ius soli*, replaced in 1986–8 by the principle of descent, still forms, at the beginning of the 21st century, the precondition for the acquisition of French citizenship by the majority of the second generation of North Africans. And since Algerians were French citizens until 1 January 1963, their children born in France could be seen as doubly French: they were entitled to nationalization not only because of their birth on French soil but also because of their descent from parents who themselves had been born on French territory. Until the 1980s, the Algerian state, which was concerned about its influence over its own citizens, sought to counteract the easier access of the second generation to French society. Thereafter, opposition to the automatic granting of citizenship grew even in France. In 1989, the number of Maghrebine youth with a claim to nationalization in France was estimated at 700,000.

Over time there was a shift in the regions of origin from which immigrants came. In Algeria, Berber-speaking Greater Kabylia was initially a preferred region of departure – on the one hand because of France's vigorous assimilation policy, on the other hand because of the traditionally scanty employment opportunities in this region. In Morocco, too, rural regions – Souss, the Middle and High Atlas – were in the beginning the point of departure for labor migration to France. As time went by, however, regional background became differentiated, as large cities in the Maghreb increasingly became stopovers or even the primary areas of origin of the immigrants.

The immigrants' level of education has risen since the migration began. According to a study by the French National Office of Statistics, in 1992 a total of 47% of Moroccan women and 44% of Algerian women in France had no education of any kind; the same was true of 31% of Moroccan men and 41% of Algerian men. Since the mid-1970s, only men with a school diploma have been coming into the country; moreover, because of improvements in the school system in the countries of origin, the study also found that language skills in French were improving.

Although some of the Maghrebis migrated back home, by and large the immigrants gradually shifted the focus of their lives to France. Ideas about return to the homeland were usually given up for good with family reunification and the birth of children in the host country.

Aspects and forms of integration

The Maghrebis constituted themselves into a community of origin through a reciprocal process of external and internal ascription. In the process, affiliation with Islam has been gaining importance since the 1980s, whereas colonial ideas of cultural difference had still predominated in the 1960s and 1970s. Certain dress codes have helped to make Muslims highly visible also in public. However, more important than such outward signs is the inner attitude of many Muslims in a secularized world, which requires special efforts to maintain ritual obligations and certain moral values and lead to the preservation of specific group identities. By contrast, other factors of "visibility," such as skin color, play only a minor role because the differences are so minor. Language is also inconsequential when it comes to the perception of differences, since French is used in all countries of the Maghreb as a second, unofficial lingua franca and is taught, at least in spoken form. The tendency to stop using the native language even within the family and to switch to the exclusive use of French is more pronounced among Maghrebi immigrants of the second and third generation than it is among other immigrant groups.

On the other hand, one important factor in their self-identification is the orientation toward a language of origin (regional variations of Arabic and Berber). However, this point of reference was initially for the most part regional, limited to the common region of origin with a very specific dialect in each instance. It was only the immigrants of the 1980s who saw spoken Arabic as a language of national prevalence that was no longer tied to regions – though it did not have the status of a national language. For the Kabyles, the use of the Berber language is developing increasingly into a political factor. The controversies over the Algerian government's language policy, which culminated in the "Berber Spring" of 1980, reverberated also among the immigrants in France, where the greater political freedoms were used for intensive cultural and educational work.

At the beginning of the 21st century, the primary function that is left for Modern Standard Arabic – whose role as an element of identification in the 1960s and 1970s was also supported by a secular, pan-Arabic ideology – is a religious one. Within the French population, it is equated to a large degree with Islam and Islamism, which has contributed to a strong devaluation of this language, though it can still be selected as a second or third foreign language at some French upper secondary schools.

The national self-description of the Maghrebis is marked by strong ambivalences. That holds true not only for the relatively large group of dissidents and oppositionists, who tended to belong more likely than not to left-wing groups, especially in the 1960s and 1970s, but who have also been found in the Islamist camp since the outbreak of the Algerian civil war in 1992. The idea of an imagined homeland, which is cultivated in the context of real problems with integration in the destination country, often contradicted the reality of everyday life in the Maghreb that was experienced during the frequent visits to relatives: hassles with the bureaucracy, a lack of interest on the part of the states in the concerns of the emigrants, and difficulties of remigrants in their efforts to reintegrate. In no small number of cases, such experiences made the picture of one's own country an increasingly negative one.

These markers of identity were joined by new elements in the second generation: emblematic in France was the term *beur* (a corruption of *arabe* in the French vernacular), which was initially used pejoratively for the second generation of Maghrebis but was then adopted by them as symbol of their own identity. Moreover, the spread of the term *Maghrébin* shows that importance attached no longer to a concrete state but increasingly to a large region with many sociocultural commonalities. At the turn of the 21st century, French youth culture was pervaded by many Maghrebine elements.

The essential inconspicuousness of the Maghrebis in terms of external physical characteristics, language, and citizenship stands in contrast with a discrimination conceded not only by themselves but also by members of the majority society; as late as the 1990s, that discrimination was still so strong that immigration and Maghrebine origin were largely equated in France. One source of these attitudes is France's colonial history and a racism that was widespread especially among the Algerian French, which initially saw the Maghrebis as members of a defeated ethnic group, but at the same time also as the enemy who had proved himself superior in the war of independence. The trauma of the lost colonial empire also nourished notions of a cultural racism, which is closely linked to the rise of the New Right and – through an engagement with the discourse on multiculturalism – no longer uses "racial" membership to exclude others but cultural characteristics like Islam. The topos of the "dangerous classes," which has a long tradition going back to revolutionary France of the late 18th and the first half of the 19th centuries, the Paris Commune of 1870–1, and the Popular Front of the 1930s, has taken on an increasingly

ethnocultural meaning with the youth unrest of 1981, 1991, and 2005. It seemed that the integrity of French society was under threat from the suburbs.

The state itself laid down certain criteria that ascribed status. The French citizenship of the immigrants, in conjunction with their social position as blue-collar workers, determined residency and work permits, the allocation of housing (at first largely in workers' hostels), and the entitlement to social services, which were administered by an institution set up for this specific purpose in 1958, the FAS (Fonds d'action sociale pour les travailleurs immigrés et leurs familles). As part of measures to prevent violence, affirmative action programs for young Frenchmen of Maghrebine origin also moved to the fore. As a result of the formal equality of a growing number of Maghrebis as French, there was a growing effort to avoid the ascription of a special status in official discourse. Symptomatic of that trend was also the renaming of the FAS into the FASILD (Fonds d'action et de soutien pour l'intégration et la lutte contre les discriminations). Conversely, however, the immigrants of various national origins, their specific attitudes and behaviors, became increasingly a topic of the social sciences, after this kind of research was rejected by many still in the 1990s for being itself an act of discrimination and overemphasis on differences.

In the 1950s, the available housing failed to keep up with the massive and only partly government-directed Maghrebine immigration. In all large cities, but especially in the conurbations of Paris, Lyon, and Marseille, there arose *bidonvilles*, slums, where the foreign population, especially of Algerian origin, was concentrated in houses or shelters that were partly dilapidated and repaired or patched-up by the residents themselves.

A first governmental measure to remedy this situation was the establishment in 1956 of the housing construction company SONACOTRA (Société nationale pour la construction de logements pour les travailleurs), whose work was initially limited to French Muslims of Algerian background who were living in France as migrant workers, and their families. The elimination of the *bidonvilles* was also intended to deprive the Algerian FLN (Front de Libération Nationale) of its recruiting grounds. Only after the end of the Algerian war did the mandate of the housing company expand to include all immigrants as well as French workers. The latter, however, were rarely dependent on the housing that was made available.

Family reunification in the late 1960s and early 1970s led initially to a concentration of Maghrebi immigrants in the traditional working-class neighborhoods of the large cities. In the wake of urban renewal efforts, many families moved to the social housing complexes that were erected at the periphery of large cities and conurbations in the 1960s and whose number doubled between 1970 and 1973. At the same time, a large number of French renters moved into better apartments as the economy experienced an upswing.

Since the unrest in Lyon in 1981, the *banlieues* have become synonymous with "ghetto," with the social exclusion and separation of the Maghrebis. These clichés, cultivated by the media of the French Right and Left and which are also found in the discourse of Maghrebine organizations and young people, mask the fact that the move from the *bidonvilles* and the workers' hostels into new apartments with central heating, interior toilets, and laundry rooms was initially a social advance and an improvement in the living situation.

In the 1960s, however, the shortcomings of the large housing complexes became apparent: a lack of infrastructure, anonymity, little sense of responsibility on the part of the tenants and local officials, as well as weak social control promoted the rapid decay of the housing stock, dilapidation, criminality, and drug use. The state authorities responded with repression and stepped-up police presence.

After the youth unrest in 1981 and the coming to power of the socialists, the first steps were taken to redevelop the housing complexes. However, those measures were not able to prevent the outbreak of new unrest in 1991 in Vaulx-en-Velin, a satellite town of Lyon. The unrest in 2005, the largest to date and affecting nearly all large French cities, put the focus of political attention once again on the problem of a failed urban policy.

In the 1980s, Islam developed into a relevant factor in the suburban settlements. Residents demanded that prayer rooms be set up in the apartment complexes, which would also be used for children's supervised homework or Arabic lessons as well as for other activities. These facilities, established by younger fathers of the second generation, were mostly run by parents' associations who financed their work through membership dues but also received some support from the municipalities. Somewhat problematic was support for the parents' associations by the immigrants' countries of origin, who thereby gained some influence over these facilities. The integration of the children and young people into French society is something the organizations promoted only to a very limited extent.

In socioeconomic terms, a growing differentiation within the Maghrebine population in France has taken place. Of the adult Algerians who had immigrated before 1974, 83% were still largely unskilled laborers in 1992, while this was true of only 67% of young people who had arrived in the same period. That figure dropped to 56% among those born in France. The percentage of unskilled laborers was somewhat lower among Moroccans: in the first generation it stood at 75%, among young immigrants at 51%, and among youths who came after 1974 it was only 39%. Conversely, the percentage of mid-level and higher occupational groups rose from 2% (3% for Moroccans) in the first generation, to over 10% (25% for Moroccans) among young immigrants, to 13% for Algerians born in France and no less than 33% among young Moroccans who arrived after 1974.

In France there is a tendency toward social advancement in the second and third immigrant generation, although this must be qualified by noting the high unemployment among the immigrants. Of the sons of workers of Algerian background who were between the ages of 20 and 29 in 1992, only 38% remained simple laborers, something that was the case in France as a whole for 55% of working-class sons. Conversely, 19% of sons of Algerian workers became skilled workers (countrywide 14%), 6% tradesmen and entrepreneurs (countrywide 1%), and 6% mid- and upper-level white-collar workers in private industry (countrywide 1%).

The proportion of women of Moroccan and Algerian background who were in the workforce was initially far below the French average. Women generally followed their husbands only as part of family reunification and worked as housewives. However, this model, which was the predominant one in the 1970s, always had exceptions: migrant female workers who created a livelihood for themselves in the host country and sometimes married there.

In 1992, the employment rate of Algerian women stood at 50% in the first generation, but at 80% in the second. The younger women thus reached a percentage that was in line with the national average. A tendency for social advancement is evident also among the daughters of Algerian workers: about half had white-collar jobs (48%, equal to the national average), but 13% were in mid- and upper-level professions in private industry (countrywide 11%). About 20% had remained in the industrial sector as skilled or unskilled workers. The ethnic economy is less important among the Maghrebis in France than it is among other immigrant groups. There was, however, a particularly strong increase in the proportion of self-employed Maghrebis in the trades. The establishment of businesses was increasingly supported by organizations whose primary goal was procuring the necessary loans. They include organizations founded by French of Maghrebine origin like 3 CI (Cohabitation des Communautés et Coopération Internationale) in Marseille, or Entreprendre en France, which was founded by a former president of the FAS, Pierre Patrick Kaltenbach.

The domains of social advancement for young Maghrebis in France include also political and union organizations. However, the majority of these activists from an educated Maghrebine elite were able to fill only lower to mid-level positions in the federations and parties since the 1970s; many became social workers and coordinators of state programs in social trouble spots, or they assumed leadership positions in immigrant organizations and educational institutions. Few rose to the national leadership levels of these organizations and into corresponding positions in government service. In the 1980s, the focal points of the activities shifted to organizations that were more religious in nature. Increasingly, young Maghrebis combined their political and social engagement with their own working life, though limited to the specific interests of their own community.

Only a fairly small group of immigrants – mostly of Algerian background (Kabylis, "Harkis"), with especially high educational degrees and defining themselves primarily as Frenchmen – succeeded in advancing into national, nonethnic organizations. They rose into leadership positions not only in government service but also in the private sector and in independent professions. Within the established political parties, they developed into a new political class as city, regional, or general councilors. They were also represented in the national leadership of organizations like SOS Racisme and France Plus.

However, the social advancement of some of the *beurs* and the assimilation this entailed was hardly registered by the French public. One of the reasons is that successful integration takes place precisely when it remains unnoticed. Moreover, the move into neighborhoods with a low concentration of Maghrebi residents, which often accompanied social advancement, meant that the better-integrated individuals disappeared from the radar screen of the media. In addition, immigrant organizations themselves engaged in a discourse of pauperization to legitimize the need for state support and their own role as mediators.

In spite of the clear trends toward social advancement, the unemployment following the economic crisis after 1973 hit the Maghrebi immigrants disproportionately hard because they tended to have low professional qualifications, and the jobs eliminated in the wake of automatization were predominantly those for unskilled workers. However, unemployment has been even harder on members of the second generation and those who immigrated after 1974. Women, too, are at a disadvantage compared to men: in 1992, for example, 55% of Algerian women of the first generation were unemployed, 10% were employed through a job-creation scheme, and 16% had only a temporary employment contract. A mere 7% received assistance from the labor office. By contrast, only 16% of Algerian men between 40 and 49 years of age were unemployed (nationwide: 4%). Of those in the 50 to 59 age group, 23% had no work (nationwide: 10%). However, while the number of indigenous unemployed rose by 52% between 1984 and 1988, it rose by only 18% among Maghrebi immigrants in the same period. Even in 1984, Maghrebis still formed by far the largest group of unemployed immigrants (just under 80,000).

In the second generation, the disparity between the sexes shrank, especially at the expense of young males, whose unemployment rate stood at 39% (Algerians) and 37% (Moroccans) – compared to 33% for young Algerian women and 31% for young Moroccan women. Poor educational achievement is not adequate to explain the low employment level among young Maghrebi men. For those with a school diploma below the *baccalauréat*, 36% of Algerian women and 39% of Algerian men were unemployed (nationwide: 10% of men and 20% of women). The lower unemployment rate of young Algerian women even bucked the national trend. More than half of young Algerian men of the second generation remained unemployed for more than a year after completing their education (nationwide: 29%). There are various reasons that the school achievement of children of Maghrebine background in France is below average for the country: it could be explained more by social than cultural factors, and was comparable to that of indigenous, educationally and socially disadvantaged children. The lower level of education of the parents and their limited ability to support their children played a role in this. However, compared to comparable French social milieus, the interest of the parents in a good education for their children was relatively high.

Another explanation for the high unemployment rate among male youth of Maghrebine background is ethnic discrimination. In 1992, 80% of the children of Algerian immigrants, and on average no fewer than two-thirds in the country as a whole, believed that "Arabs" (North Africans, Maghrebis) were the group most strongly discriminated against, followed by black Africans. Skin color and religion played no prominent role as factors for this discrimination.

The self-organization of the Maghrebine immigrants is weak and characterized by a strong dependence on the country of origin, a dependence that has been overcome only in part even at the beginning of the 21st century. The Algerian and Moroccan friendship clubs, the *amicales*, were controlled by the embassies of the home countries and were infested with informants. In the 1970s, organizations of the radical Left also played a certain role, like the Movement of Arab Workers (MTA: Mouvement des Travailleurs Arabes), which were also involved in the strikes at Renault in 1975 and in the SONACOTRA residences in 1975–8. In the beginning these activists were characterized by Marxist ideologies and *Tiersmondisme*, which sees political conflicts above all through the lens of a global clash between North and South. They formed the core of the great political mobilization of the *beurs* in the 1980s, appropriated concepts of multiculturalism during this time, and remained largely secular also in subsequent years.

In the 1980s, antiracism formed a crystallization point for the mobilization of the nationwide movement of Maghrebi youth. Their rallies in 1983 and 1984 resonated among Maghrebis and made possible a broad alliance with other organizations of the Left, church groups, critical unions, and the Jewish educational elite. However, in organizations like SOS Racisme, it became apparent very early that young Maghrebis were inadequately represented – relative to the number of activists – in the leadership bodies on the national level. A variety of factors account for the breakup of the movement toward the end of the 1990s, not least the growing importance of Islamism and anti-Islam.

Although the history of Islam in France dates back to the 19th century, and the Grand Mosque of Paris – after initial efforts at the end of the 19th century – was erected as early as 1926, Islam did not emerge as the second-largest religion until the 1970s and especially the 1980s. Its history in France is closely connected with Maghrebi immigration.

Alongside traditional forms of organization like brotherhoods and mystical orders, there also increasingly emerged – as in other parts of the Islamic world – reformist groups who saw in the diaspora a particularly fertile field for their missionary work. They included especially the Associations of Islamic Awakening (Gamaat at-tabligh), whose program was developed by Mohamed Ilyas in India. Within the framework of its identity model, the overcoming of social ills (petty criminality, drug abuse), this Islam acquired growing attraction also for the youths of the *banlieues* through common experiences, meditation (*dhikr*) and mission, and the shared stepping out (*khuruj*) from the accustomed milieu to work for the faith. But the Islam of the Gamaat at-tabligh was not a political movement, nor did it instruct its followers in the personal study of the religious sources. For many new converts it was therefore merely a transit station to more radical groups, like the Islamic organizations brought together in 1983 under the umbrella organization UOIF (Union des Organisations Islamiques de France). In addition, the FFM (Fédération française des musulmans), which is shaped by Algerian reform Islam that is closely aligned with the state, and the FNMF (Fédération nationale des musulmans de France), which is under Moroccan influence, continue to play an important role.

The fusion of social protest with religious forms of expression gave rise to a new generation of "communitarians," who no longer advocate individual assimilation or the right to equality in diversity but a participation of cultural communities as such in public life. Although these groups propagate Islam in the sense of a personal confession and oppose secularism, most of them distance themselves from militant groups.

The headscarf controversy in 1989 represented a turning point in a number of ways. The very heated debate over whether religious symbols like the headscarves of Muslim girls (generally prohibited among teachers) were permissible in secular schools split not only SOS Racisme but also the socialist camp and the *beur* movement itself. It revealed the potency of the discourse of the New Right, which was able to draw strength from the widespread uncertainties within French society about its encounter with Islam, and also the growing self-confidence of French Muslims.

At the same time, there were efforts to use the special living conditions of Muslims and the various compromises they had to make with secular society to shape a genuinely European Islam. Although Prime Minister Lionel Jospin had already made efforts in that direction, it was not until 2002 that Interior Minister Nicolas Sarkozy was able to bring about an agreement among the three most important Islamic umbrella organizations that regulated the procedure for electing a Conseil Français du Culte Musulman (CFCM). The first elections for this representative body were held in French mosques in the spring of 2003.

The contrast between the cultures from which the Maghrebis originated and the culture of the host society is most obvious in family structures and in the Islamic prescriptions about marriage and the relations between men and women. The large number of marriages within a person's own community or at least within the group of Muslims shows that the absorption of the Maghrebine groups into French society is not yet in sight, or is possible only for a small group of assimilated Maghrebis.

The irreconcilability of family structures is particularly evident in the first generation. Here family unification in migration led to the dissolution of the large family and, because of the disappearance of the control of the in-laws over the daughter-in-law, also to a new definition of relations between spouses. Initially thrown back into their own homes and cut off from outside relationships, many women soon gained greater freedoms than they had experienced in the country from which they came: they established contacts with women in the neighborhood, acquired the right to go to the market by themselves and make purchases, and were forced to look after the concerns of their children in contact with the school and other institutions of the host society. While the status of the husband thus grew weaker, wives and mothers had to take on a host of new tasks, though they were often not able to handle them (as demonstrated, for example, in Mehdi Charef's film *Tea in the Harem of Archimedes*).

Through the school attendance of the children and because of their close contact with French institutions, the conflict between the traditions of Maghrebine and French society moved into the family: the children experienced their parents as backward, the parents in turn saw them as "children of sin," who had deviated from the proper path.

Young men and women devised different strategies for dealing with these problems. Girls often chose a more cautious, slower path of emancipation, along which they usually proceeded through success in school. To be sure, they were frequently unable to freely choose their spouse and rarely entered into a mixed marriage with a non-Muslim without breaking with the family, since Islamic law forbids a woman from marrying a non-Muslim (although a Muslim man may marry a non-Muslim woman). Still, many women were able to negotiate acceptable solutions with their parents. According to a poll in 1992, the vast majority of Algerian women born in France married either immigrants or their descendants (54% and 31%, respectively), while those figures were only 17% and 33% among Algerian men. However, at the beginning of the 21st century, a stronger political movement developed among young women of Maghrebine background, which called itself programmatically *ni putes, ni soumises* (Neither whores nor submissives).

The path of compromise was also taken by some of the young males, who are called *Bu* (from the colloquial word for head, *bugne*), an allusion to their willingness to work hard in school. By contrast, the *Sonac* – so named after the workers' housing of the SONACOTRA – remains tied to his ethnic community: although he takes advantage of some freedoms of French society, he follows the marriage wishes of his parents. The *Lascar*, finally, remains torn between these two camps: he is neither able to integrate through success in school, nor is he able to find his place within the ethnic community. His world is the youth gang of the neighborhood, which becomes highly visible during youth unrest. The experience of social decline concerns above all young males: simple physical labor, where it still exists, ranks at the very bottom of the scale of the social hierarchy; social advancement succeeds only through education and thus through stronger integration; at the same time, men of Maghrebine origin, in particular, are the target of ethnic prejudices, while their traditional authority is being questioned. This explains part of their special difficulties integrating.

Jelen, Christian. *Ils feront de bons Français. Enquête sur l'assimilation des Maghrébins*. Paris, 1991.

Kepel, Gilles. *Les banlieues de l'Islam. Naissance d'une réligion en France*. Paris, 1987.

Khellil, Mohand. *L'intégration des maghrébins en France*. Paris, 1992.

Lamchichi, Abderrahim, and Dominique Baillet, eds. *Maghrébins de France, Regards sur les dynamiques de l'intégration*. Paris, 2001.

Tribalat, Michèle. *Faire France. Une grande enquête sur les immigrés et leurs enfants*. Paris, 1995.

Cross-references: France; Moroccan Labor Migrants in Western, Central, and Northern Europe since the 1960s: The Example of Great Britain; Algerian "Harkis" in France since 1962; Moroccan Undocumented Immigrants in Spain since the End of the 20th Century; Algerian *Pieds-Noirs* in France since 1954

MAGYAR DEPORTEES FROM SLOVAKIA IN WESTERN CZECHOSLOVAKIA SINCE THE END OF WORLD WAR II

Adrian von Arburg

Between 1945 and 1947, at least 55,000 Magyars from southern Slovakia came to the Bohemian lands (Bohemia, Moravia, Bohemian Silesia). They were deported by the Czech authorities in two main waves within the boundaries of the state. After World War II, the Magyar ethnic group, with more than 550,000 members, continued to account for around 15% of the total population of Slovakia. They were settled fairly compactly in the southern and southeastern districts along the Danube (Žitný ostrov/Rye Island), the Matra Mountains, and farther to the east in the direction of Košice. This area, settled by Hungarian-speaking peoples since the Hungarian occupation of the land in the basin of the Danube in the ninth century, had been incorporated after World War I into the newly established state of Czechoslovakia in the Treaty of Trianon with Hungary (1920). Those deported in the winter of 1946–7 came almost exclusively from the smaller rural settlements in a total of 17 Slovakian districts, the vast majority from the fertile Rye Island directly southeast of Bratislava (Preßburg), in the heartland of the Magyar minority in Slovakia (for example, the districts of Šamorín, Galanta, Dunajská Streda, Nové Zámky, Komárno, Parkan/

Štúrovo, and Želiezovce). The proportion of deportees was noticeably smaller in the eastern districts (for example, Tornaľa, Rožňava, Krupina, and Moldava). The deportations, which began in the west and proceeded rapidly eastward, were suspended at the end of February 1947 shortly before reaching Košice, primarily in response to Western protests and diplomatic negotiations between Czechoslovakia and Hungary.

As it became increasingly apparent in 1945–6 that the Allies of World War II would not acquiesce to the forced transfer of the Magyar minority to Hungary, the government in Prague began to focus increasingly on a solution to the "Hungarian question" within the territory of the state. Two paths to a complete "Slovakization" of the Slovakian part of Czechoslovakia (resurrected in 1945) were taken: first, after 1946 those Magyars who in 1945 had been stripped of their citizenship in the First Republic of Czechoslovakia (1918–38) but were able to prove their Slovak origins were allowed to "re-Slovakize" themselves. Second, depending on the diplomatic situation, there was a concurrent deportation of a large part of the Hungarian-speaking population. The motivation for "Slovakizing" Slovakia was joined by the goal of alleviating the labor shortage in the Bohemian lands. Workers were in short supply primarily because of the expulsion of the Sudeten Germans. Moreover, the government wanted to put pressure on Hungary with the deportation of the Magyars as a way of achieving its primary goal, the complete forcible resettlement of the ethnic Hungarian minority to Hungary.

As part of the first deportation action in the fall of 1945, at least 9,247 individuals, at first only men but then entire families, were forcibly removed as agricultural workers to the Czech part of the republic; half of them had previously been independent farmers. The second deportation, which lasted from November 1946 to February 1947, comprised – according to official statistics – 43,900 Magyars (11,642 families) from 393 communities, who were transported, along with their movable property, in 219 railroad transports (passenger and freight cars). Again, half of the deportees were farming families with landholdings of less than five cadastral acres (2.9 hectares), the others were agricultural laborers. The deportees had owned 6,596 houses and 14,149 cadastral acres (8,143 hectares). Even though the action was presented to those affected and to the public as a temporary "work deployment," it was the intention of the Czechoslovakian government, according to archival documents, that the deported families would remain permanently and assimilate in the Bohemian lands.

Contrary to a notion that was long handed down and is still widespread in the oral tradition as well as in scholarly literature, the majority of the deported were not settled in the border regions of the Bohemian lands (Sudetenland), but transported to their interior districts. The reason was concerns about settling a population group officially regarded as "untrustworthy" in a border region that was considered especially important militarily. Less than one-fifth of the

Magyars deported westward were settled in the region that had previously been inhabited chiefly by German-speaking populations, and even here they were – with only a few exceptions for state-owned forest and pasture lands – placed into regions that were not close to the border and adjoined the traditionally Czech-speaking districts. One exception was the hops-growing area of Žatec (Saaz), which was relatively close to the border.

In the second wave of deportations, according to official statistics, 37,639 Magyars came to Bohemia and 6,261 to Moravia and Silesia, most as agricultural laborers on the holdings of Czech farmers who had to pay the authorities a "transportation fee" for each laborer and could pick the workers at will at the arrival train station. Most Magyars were transported into Labor Office Districts with especially intensive agriculture: Žatec (4,690), Mladá Boleslav (3,868), Kolín (3,611), Kladno (2,952), Prague (2,832), and Pardubice (2,146). In Moravia, the focal point of the settlement lay in the fertile plain of Haná south of Olomouc (Olmütz) and in the northern environs of Znojmo (Znaim).

The remigration of the deported began immediately after arrival at their destinations, and over time it intensified. By June 1947, 1,000 deported Magyars had already fled either back to their origin regions in southern Slovakia or into Hungary. By March 1948, 4,973 Magyars had done the same in Bohemia alone, and by the beginning of June the number for all settlement areas had already reached 12,014. A "re-escorting" ordered by Prague was an initial failure, in most cases thwarted by a lack of interest on the part of the local Slovak authorities (by June 1948 only 800, according to other sources 1,180 were redeported). After a rapid improvement in relations between Prague and Budapest, following the successful establishment of the communist monopoly on power, it quickly became evident that Czechoslovakia could no longer afford to deport members of a "brother nation," confiscate their property, and strip them of citizenship. This change in the political and diplomatic situation encouraged thousands of additional deportees to make the illegal return to their homelands between March and December 1948. In June 1948, 32,201 Magyars were said to still be in the Bohemian lands, in October around 27,000, in December only 24,000. Between January and mid-April 1949, the authorities transported another 19,000 back to their regions of origin. According to official data, this left about 5,000 in the western sections of Czechoslovakia. When the Czech government, in the spring of 1948, announced that Magyars could have their Czech citizenship restored after staying in the deportation regions for at least three years, only a minority took the offer (3,627 persons).

In March 1950, 13,201 Hungarians were counted in the Bohemian lands. The majority is likely to have been voluntary – and often merely temporary – migrant laborers, members of the "intelligentsia," Roma, and ethnic-Slovak remigrants from Hungary. According to a survey in 1992, only 10% of Hungarians living in the Czech Republic had arrived between 1940 and 1950, the vast majority arriving only after the 1950s as part of labor migrations not directed by any state. Only 1.5% of those polled indicated that they themselves had been affected by the deportations or had family members who had suffered that fate.

The sojourn of the greater part of the deportees in the western regions of Czechoslovakia was thus of short duration. As early as April 1949, about 90% were back in southern Slovakia, though not necessarily at their original place of residence. The Czech population referred to the deportees – officially given the euphemistic label of "recruits" – simply as "Magyars." While Czechoslovakian historiography until 1989 for the most part used the contemporary term *nábor* (recruitment) to describe the forcible resettlement, the term "deportation" has established itself in the scholarly literature and publications since the 1990s. The shared fate of the loss of the homeland and forced labor on foreign soil promoted the emergence of a group identity that is still evident at the beginning of the 21st century – in the organization of the deportees in the Association of the Deported Citizens of the Slovak Republic, in compensation demands that are made as a group, and in a centralized documentation and literary processing of the experience of deportation. This self-identity of the group, based on a shared history, does not clash with their identity as a Hungarian-speaking, autochthonous population of Slovakia.

In most instances, there was not even the beginning of an integration into the new Czech surroundings. Although integration was desired by the state, those affected, who regarded their deportation as an injustice, did not seek it. Given the possibility of escape and later also of an official return to their origins, there was no real incentive for integration, especially since the deportees faced an exceedingly difficult social situation and were, as people de facto without any rights, among the poorest strata of the population. As it was, the majority of the deportees thought of their stay as merely temporary to begin with, since they evidently believed for a long time in the official pronouncements about a "labor deployment." Moreover, nearly every forcible resettled family had relatives or acquaintances back home who informed them that most of those who escaped back to their homelands had not been returned and had found at least makeshift housing and work.

The Czech employers were rarely satisfied with the performance of their Magyar laborers. Social contacts to the employer's family and to the Czech population have so far not been studied in detail; in memoirs they appear partly as "hate-filled" and "deeply broken," but partly also as "correct" or even "cordial." Since the residence permit of the deportees was restricted to the area of the "labor deployment" and there was little time or money for leisure activities, social contacts were largely limited to the local level. For the most part a community would have only a few scattered families of deportees, which usually came from the same or neighboring villages. Still, communication across entire regions was very dense. Visits by Hungarian-speaking priests, not welcomed by the authorities but tolerated by the Czech clergy, led to veritable pilgrimages by the largely Roman Catholic deportees. Resistance manifested itself in the form of strikes and numerous, vigorously pursued complaints to the Czech authorities. In addition, many deportees made contact with the Hungarian or Western missions in Prague. Complaints often concerned the failure by the employer to observe the state-guaranteed working conditions, poor living conditions, inadequate provisioning with shoes and clothing, the lack of any minority rights and thus also of Hungarian-language schools, religious services, and sources of information (the government did not begin publishing a Hungarian information paper, *Jó Barát*, until June 1948), the corrupt and arbitrary selection of deportees, the impossibility of freely engaging in an occupation (just under half had previously not been involved in agricultural work), the absence of opportunities for continuing education, and inadequate care and infrastructure for older or ailing family members and children. Above all, the deportees emphatically demanded the right to return to their homelands or at least depart for Hungary.

What traces the presence of a few tens of thousands of Slovak Magyars – which lasted on average less than two years – left in the target regions has so far not been studied. Returning deportees brought back to their home regions at least a rudimentary knowledge of Czech and knowledge of more progressive methods in planting, harvesting, and stabling. It is also impossible to make adequate statements about the continuity of social contacts (often also with other agricultural laborers, for example, Germans, Romanians, Bulgarians, and Slovaks).

Arburg, Adrian von. "Zwangsumsiedlung als Patentrezept. Tschechoslowakische Bevölkerungspolitik im mitteleuropäischen Vergleich 1945–1954." In *Vertreibung und Minderheitenschutz in Europa*, edited by Matthias Niedobitek and Frank-Lothar Kroll, 43–113. Berlin, 2005.

Arburg, Adrian von. "Abschied und Neubeginn. Der Bevölkerungswechsel in den Sudetengebieten nach 1945." In *Als die Deutschen weg waren. Was nach der Vertreibung geschah: Ostpreußen, Schlesien, Sudetenland. Das Buch zur WDR-Fernsehserie*, 185–217. 2nd ed. Berlin, 2006.

Janics, Kálmán. *A hontalanság évei. A szlovákiai magyar kisebbség a 2. világháború után 1945–1948*. Budapest, 1989.

Šutaj, Štefan. *Maďarská menšina na Slovensku v rokoch 1945–1948 (Východiská a prax politiky k maďarskej menšine na Slovensku)*. Bratislava, 1993.

Vadkerty, Katalin. *A kitelepítéstöl a reszlovakizációg. Trilógia a csehszlovákiai magyarság 1945–1948 közötti történetéröl*. Bratislava, 2001.

Cross references: Czechia and Slovakia; Southeastern Europe; Czech and Slovak Settlers in the Former Sudeten Regions since the End of World War II; German Refugees and Expellees from Eastern, East-Central, and Southeastern Europe in Germany and Austria since the End of World War II

MENNONITES IN WEST PRUSSIA SINCE THE 16TH CENTURY

Stefi Jersch-Wenzel

Among the religiously driven migration movements of the early modern period, those of the Anabaptists, to which the Mennonites belong, are comparable in size only to those of the French Protestants, the Huguenots, and of the Protestant Salzburgers, though these movements began a century or two later. After the radical beginnings of this Protestant current, which spread rapidly in central Europe after around 1525, a group of Anabaptists emerged in the Netherlands, along the lower Rhine, and in the rest of lower Germany around the eponymous leader Menno Simons (1496–1561). Simons, a Roman Catholic priest from Witmarsum in Frisia, had joined the Anabaptists in 1536, and in the following decades he became, with his teachings focused on nonviolence, the dominant figure of this initially small but continuously growing group.

This group differed in its orientation from the other Protestant denominations that were taking shape, especially from the followers of Luther and Calvin. Its doctrine included adult baptism in place of infant baptism, the strict separation of church and state, the refusal to swear any oath to secular authority, and the postulate of nonviolence, which included a fundamental rejection of military service. This placed them in opposition not only to the Catholics but also to the Lutherans and Calvinists, and they were subjected to many restriction and also to persecution from both the secular and ecclesiastical authorities. As "sectarians," the Mennonites were therefore explicitly excluded from the Peace of Augsburg in 1555.

Under the pressure of persecution, the Mennonites began to emigrate as early as the first half of the 16th century to Alsace, the Palatinate, West Prussia, and later also to North America. Alsace and Switzerland proved way stations for many, since they were not safe from persecution there. The accelerated immigration of Mennonites into West Prussia that subsequently extended over the following decades led toward the end of the 17th century to a shortage of land that had originally been set aside for new settlers. For a new wave of Mennonite refugees, the Polish king as well as ecclesiastical and noble landholders expanded the potential settlement area by adding more underpopulated, uncultivated land. This was the swampy floodplain between the cities of Danzig, Marienburg, and Elbing with the broad Weichsel delta, the Large and Small Marienburger Werder, the Danziger Werder, and the Elbinger Werder.

West Prussia, formerly part of the territory of the Teutonic Order, was under the suzerainty of the Polish crown since 1466. The polyethnic and multiconfessional Polish "aristocratic republic" developed a tradition of tolerance that was unique in Europe in the early modern period. Although the king and the majority of the population professed Catholicism, segments of the nobility had turned to the

Reformed confession, while the largely German population of Danzig, Elbing, and Thorn, as well as the populations in the Weichsel region gradually embraced Lutheranism. Added to the mix was Ashkenazi Jewry, the largest Jewish group in Europe. Alongside smaller Protestant sects, the Mennonites, too, were able to freely practice their religion here.

Thanks to the close trading links between the Netherlands and the cities in northeastern Europe, the Dutch, and thus also the Anabaptists or *Taufgesinnte* (baptism-inclined), as the Mennonites were frequently referred to, knew that broad swaths of land in the former territory of the Teutonic Order were uninhabited. Villages had been abandoned and the irrigation system, including dams, was no longer maintained, with the result that marshy, depopulated areas were lying fallow. Royal administrators (*Starosten*) took advantage of the experience that the Dutch immigrants had with dyking and cultivating marshy soil and settled them on such holdings; the revenues from cultivation were used to defray the expenses for the princely court. In addition, a considerable rental income could be expected, since the Mennonites were initially prohibited from acquiring land and received it only for a longer period in tenancy (*Emphyteuse*).

Only a small number of Mennonites sought to settle in West Prussian cities, and those who did were often thwarted in their efforts to create a livelihood by opposition from the local notables organized into guilds. The majority formed so-called Dutch settlements (*Hauländereien*) in the countryside, in which the community of settlers (all equal in status) faced the landlord. An annually elected mayor was merely charged with supervising the performance of the lease obligations. If a village was home to both Mennonites and other believers – usually Lutherans – a mayor was elected for each group.

Although the Mennonites were included in the Warsaw Confederation of 1585, which the estates of West Prussia joined, and therefore enjoyed the freedom to practice their religion, their status was not entirely secure. In some cases they could avert threats of expulsion from the Catholic Church only with substantial payments. In addition, like the Lutherans they were subject to the Catholic *Pfarrzwang* (obligation to obtain all sacraments from the Catholic priest), which meant that they had to help defray the church expenses of the Catholics through dues in kind. The Lutherans, too, managed to compel the Mennonites to help defray their ecclesiastical costs, on the grounds that they were employing Protestant domestics who were using the services of Lutheran preachers and teachers.

Other dues were the result of their religious principles. Since they rejected any form of military service, they had to pay for the exemption from military service and billeting, as well as for release from compulsory labor for state institutions, and from the obligation to take on administrative offices.

When it came to the legal constitution of their religious communities, the Mennonites were subject to restrictions.

Because of the dominant position of the Catholic Church in Poland, based as it was on state law, neither Lutherans nor Mennonites were able to establish religious communities under public law. They were merely allowed to gather for the private practice of their religion and thus unite into a "personal community," but all this within the existing Catholic parish, because the Catholic *Pfarrzwang* remained in force. They were private associations formed through the voluntary agreement of the interested parties, "quasi-parishes" (Hermann Nottarp) without supervisory authorities, who appointed their preachers, organists, and schoolmasters and built churches and schools.

The extent of the Mennonite migration is difficult to estimate for the period of Polish rule, since it occurred in bursts and fluctuated a good deal. One indication of the growth of the Mennonite settlements may come from the increase in royal lease income in the period between 1590 and 1649: the rent that non-Mennonite inhabitants had to pay had risen by 12%, but that of the Mennonites had shot up by 170%. This was due in part to higher interest rates that were repeatedly raised, in part also to additional immigration and thus to a constant enlargement of the farmland.

Precise numbers exist only for the period after the First Partition of Poland (1772) and the annexation of West Prussia by Prussia. The *Special-Consignation aller in Westpreußen befindlichen Mennoniten im Jahre 1776* (Special Census of all Mennonites present in West Prussia in 1776) counted 12,032 individuals, who made up 3% of the population in the province but 10% and more in their primary settlement area. Smaller groups of Mennonites had already attempted to settle in East Prussia in the first half of the 18th century, specifically Königsberg and the Memel lowland, which meant that the local authorities were not unfamiliar with the religious principles of this immigrant group. Their strict refusal of military service led to repeated expulsions there or at least to threats of expulsion by King Frederick William I. However, only a few hundred persons came to East Prussia in response to King Frederick II's permission to settle there.

For the Mennonites in West Prussia a positive development seemed in the offing with the change on the throne: in 1774 they were granted an exemption from military service in return for an annual payment of 5,000 talers to the cadet school in Kulm, and in 1775 they were released from payments to the Catholic clergy, a move that was in line with Prussian ecclesiastical policy. A privilege (*Gnadenprivileg*) granted to them by Frederick II in 1780 secured their legal status. At the level of the provincial administration, however, these years saw the beginning of harsh restrictions of Mennonite rights, which were enshrined in an edict in 1789. They concerned above all an exclusion of the Mennonites from the right to acquire real estate, and a confirmation of the dues to the Lutheran Church, which had risen precipitously since the beginning of Prussian rule. The chief point of attack was the Mennonites' exemption from military service. However, their economic success also factored into the restrictions, since it put them into a position of buying landholding on a larger scale, also from impoverished Lutherans.

Since the numerous complaints and petitions submitted by the Mennonites against these regulations were unsuccessful, and since it was no longer possible in the now Prussian province, as it had been during Polish times, to move to the lands of other landholders, poorer families, in particular, decided to emigrate. At the behest of the empress, Russian recruiters offered potential colonists land and payment of travel costs. Since the West Prussian authorities – ignoring warnings from Berlin about harm to the province – did little against this inclination to emigrate, about 4,000 Mennonites left West Prussia between 1786 and 1806 and migrated to Russia. Thereafter, the remaining Mennonite population in West Prussia still amounted to between 12,000 and 13,000, thanks to a high birthrate.

Although the living conditions were less favorable under Prussian rule than they had been under Polish rule, the beginnings of a Prussian patriotism developed among those who had remained in West Prussia during the Napoleonic period and in the wars of liberation. To be sure, the communities, with their members who had been living for 250 years a moral life of pronounced simplicity, continued to represent the only acceptable organizational form for the Mennonites and the basis for their self-identity. However, they discharged their contribution to the defense of the country not only through substantial monetary payments and supplies in kind for the army; they also volunteered for alternative civilian service, for example, in caring for the injured or serving in the fire brigade. Individual young Mennonites also joined the volunteer troops in the wars of liberation.

This set off an intra-Mennonite conflict between the strictly Orthodox Flemings and the liberal Frisians, on the one hand, and between the generations in both camps, on the other, a conflict that dragged on for several decades. While in the area of language, Low German was predominant without controversy in daily life as early as the end of the 18th century and High German for dealings with the authorities, marriages to non-Mennonites, which, in accordance with the Mennonites' religious maxims, had to lead to exclusion from the community, and the continued adherence to the refusal of military service remained points of contention. While the problem of mixed marriages persisted into the 20th century, the Mennonites were made subject to military service by the constitution of the North German Confederation in 1867. The only concession they obtained by a Cabinet Order in 1868 was the permission to perform that service as nurses, to train as soldiers to provide logistical support, or to serve as military artisans.

When the law of 1874 "concerning the conditions of the Mennonites" made them equal under civic and ecclesiastical law, all special state regulations for the exercise of their religion, on which they had insisted much longer than other minorities, came to an end. As their stagnating numbers indicate – between 1815 and 1910 it hovered between 10,000

and 13,000 – many Orthodox believers left the West Prussian settlement areas and migrated to North America. This high rate of emigration could also be observed in other European regions.

Attempts to strengthen the group consciousness and establish a uniform representation internally and externally – for example, through the periodical *Mennonitische Blätter* (since 1854) and their merger into the Vereinigung der Mennonitengemeinden im Deutschen Reich (Association of Mennonite Communities in the German Reich) since 1884 – are comparable to initiatives by other minorities. Still, it is unmistakable that the Mennonite religion transformed itself in West Prussia, as in central Europe in general, from a comprehensive way of life into a confession. As a result of the participation of the Mennonites in World War I, also as soldiers, the partition of their settlement areas into German and Polish sovereign territories after the war, and flight and expulsion after World War II, the traces of the Mennonites disappeared in West Prussia.

Beheim-Schwarzbach, Max. *Hohenzollernsche Colonisationen. Ein Beitrag zu der Geschichte des preußischen Staates und der Colonisation des östlichen Deutschlands.* Leipzig, 1874.

Goertz, Hans-Jürgen, ed. *Die Mennoniten.* Stuttgart, 1971.

Goertz, Hans-Jürgen. *Religiöse Bewegungen in der Frühen Neuzeit.* Munich, 1993.

Nottarp, Hermann. *Die Mennoniten in den Marienburger Werdern. Eine kirchenrechtliche Untersuchung.* Halle a.d. Saale, 1929.

Penner, Horst. *Die ost- und westpreußischen Mennoniten in ihrem religiösen und sozialen Leben, in ihren kulturellen und wirtschaftlichen Leistungen. Teil I: 1526 bis 1772.* Weierhof, 1978; *Teil II: Von 1772 bis zur Gegenwart.* Kirchheimbolanden, 1987.

Cross-references: Germany; The Netherlands; Poland; Russia and Belarus; Switzerland; Ashkenazim in Europe since the Early Modern Period; German Refugees and Expellees from Eastern, East-Central, and Southeastern Europe in Germany and Austria since the End of World War II; German Settlers in Russia since the 18th Century; Huguenots in Europe since the 16th Century; Salzburg Protestants in East Prussia since the 18th Century

MIGRANT ARTISTS IN ANTWERP IN THE EARLY MODERN PERIOD

Natasja Peeters

When Antwerp supplanted Bruges as western Europe's main commercial metropolis in the 1480s, its population was estimated at approximately 30,000. Eighty years later, it had some 100,000 inhabitants. As a center of production, consumption, and trade, Antwerp attracted migrants of the most varied regional and social backgrounds. Its cosmopolitan atmosphere and the presence of foreign communities and various humanist groups augmented Antwerp's attraction. The town held a virtual monopoly in the production of luxury goods: diamond cutting, stained glass, books, prints, tapestries, paintings, musical instruments, sculpture, and many other goods. To stay productive, the town required a large yearly influx of migrants. A nearly complete series of *Poorterboeken* (inscription lists of people applying for citizenship in Antwerp) from 1533 to 1795 provide evidence of the great attraction Antwerp possessed. Between the years 1533 and 1584, 300 new citizens on average were granted citizenship every year. This number decreased to approximately 86 in the last decade of the 16th century, 45 by the late 17th century, and 30 around 1720.

However, the *Poorterboeken* account for only a small number of actual migrants to Antwerp: those who gained legal residence and could afford the fee for citizenship. Many temporary migrants thus remained overlooked. Migrants who married a woman from Antwerp and consequently became citizens were also not registered in the inscription lists. It is therefore impossible to give an estimate of the total number of migrants or total number of migrant artists for any given period. Artists who migrated to Antwerp were men as the artists' trade was predominantly male. Sources do not say whether they migrated with their families or alone.

Although specific reasons for migration to Antwerp certainly varied, one factor outweighed all others: the availability of work. Antwerp's promise of prosperity was a magnet for artists. Economic motives could be combined with occupational motives (e.g., desire to work in a creative atmosphere, the prospect of artistic training in one of Antwerp's many studios) or specific problems in one's country of origin (e.g., political problems in France, religious oppression). The influx of artists remained strong until the third quarter of the 16th century. The guild of Saint Luke thrived under these favorable economic circumstances: between 1500 and 1570 some 78% of the studio's masters, 70% of its painters, and 79% of its sculptors were migrants. In the early decades most migrants were skilled, but as Antwerp grew in importance it also attracted many young apprentices. In the 1550s the workshops in Antwerp became a training ground for journeymen painters from all over Europe.

Due to increasing signs of unrest (such as the iconoclasm of 1566) and the economic downturn of the city, many artists began to leave Antwerp after 1565. After the Spanish recaptured the town in 1585, the authorities stipulated that only Catholics were allowed to remain in Antwerp after a four-year period in which it was possible for residents to convert to Catholicism. This resulted in a large-scale exodus (including artists) that led to a severe demographic crisis; in 1589 Antwerp's population shrank to approximately 42,000, only to return to 68,000 in the course of the 17th century.

Those migrants of the 16th century, who were accounted for in available sources, came mostly from around Antwerp and other provinces of the Low Countries: an estimated 54% from within the boundaries of present-day Belgium and another 24% from the (current) Dutch provinces. Twelve percent came from Germany, 8% from France, and 2% from more distant European countries. The situation remained largely the same in the early 17th century, but from 1625 onward some 70% of the migrants came from within the boundaries of present-day Belgium, an indication that Antwerp's influence had decreased substantially.

A good and well-studied example, which also confirms the general picture, is provided by the case of migrant painters. Most migrant painters came from the villages and small towns around Antwerp or from Brabant, Herentals (the Francken family), and Mechelen, for instance. Another sizable group of artists came from towns in the other Flemish provinces: Courtrai, Ghent (Lucas de Heere), Alost (Pieter Coecke van Aalst), Bruges (Gerard David), Brussels (Goswin van der Weyden), and Louvain (Quentin Metsys), and from Wallonia (Joachim Patinir) as well. This geographical background also applies to other artists: sculptor Jan Ghenoots came from Mechelen and there was a considerable influx of tapestry makers and paper makers from Alost, Oudenaarde, Brussels (Peter van Uden), and Mechelen starting in 1540. The city also tried to attract specific professional groups and actively encouraged the establishment of lucrative trades. In 1559, for example, the Antwerp town board offered free citizenship to tapestry makers from Brussels if they were willing to settle in Antwerp.

Many artists came from the Northern Provinces: 208 of them are mentioned in documents between 1500 and 1569. To name a few: from Leyden (Otto Vaenius), Nijmegen (Gerard de Jode), Amsterdam (Pieter Aertsen), Haarlem (Philip Galle), Utrecht (Antonio Moro), Breda, and Frisia.

Although only 8% of the migrants came from France and less than 1% from Italy, some branches of the trade in luxury goods virtually owed their existence exclusively to Italian or French migrants. Indeed, a steady trickle of migrants from France to Antwerp never let up. The painter and art dealer Bartholomeus de Momper, for example, came from Lyon and the sculptor Robert Moreau came from Paris. Most famous were the French goldsmiths, five of whom worked in Antwerp in 1550. Venice supplied mirror makers like Giovanni Cornachini while many potters, majolica makers, and crystal glass blowers came from Brescia – Jan Fransisco, for instance. Antwerp even allowed an Italian monopoly in glass production in order to strengthen its position on the international glass market. The printing business was another trade where many migrants were employed: Christopher Plantin and Martin Lempereur came from France, but other nationalities were also active, such as the Spaniard Francisco de Enzimas and the German Arnold Mylius. Artists from Cologne were active in the music industry, e.g., Tielman Susato in music printing and Joost Carreest as an instrument maker.

As an estimated 78% of the artists in the guild of Saint Luke in the 16th century were migrants, they decisively shaped the artistic identity of Antwerp, which was then further disseminated by migrant artists. Antwerp painting, for instance, had no "local" style or artistic identity before 1500.

The arrival of migrant painters in the first decades of the 16th century, however, resulted in the creation of a multifaceted Antwerp style: different German, Italian, and French elements of composition and style, Renaissance and late Gothic motifs, fell on fertile ground and were reinvented and diffused among the city's painters. Dürers' brief stay in Antwerp in 1520–1, when he sold his prints and made many contacts with the local artistic community, resulted in the so called woodcut convention, eagerly adopted by painters in the city. Early 16th-century Antwerp painting stood for a sophisticated, elegant style, characterized by serpentine, undulating figures and voluminous bodies, a background painted with attention to color, and a manner of portrayal that provided noise and drama. This distinctive style is called "Antwerp mannerism" and it shows vividness – but also capriciousness and a certain theatricality – that was lacking elsewhere.

One of its key themes was the Adoration of the Christ Child by the Magi. Its countless depictions, specifically those between 1510 and 1560, feature the Magi as foreign traders bearing exotic gifts for Jesus. These paintings were popular with international merchants who could identify with the Magi and were attracted to the exoticism, the symbols of trade, and the spirit of travel that they conveyed.

The town also stood at the vanguard of new genres, enthusiastically introduced or eagerly embraced by the newcomers: landscapes or peasant pieces (Pieter Bruegel), grotesques (Cornelis Bos), and kitchen pieces (Pieter Aertsen). Thus, the artistic prosperity of Antwerp was largely created by its immigrants.

Although Antwerp continued to welcome foreign artists, the situation in the 17th century has been less thoroughly studied and the 18th century remains totally uncharted. In the early 17th century the fine arts continued to prosper; Antwerp remained an important site for employing and training painters, engravers, and others. The painter Abraham van Diepenbeek from 's-Hertoghenbosch, for example, migrated to Antwerp because it was home to the workshop of Peter Paul Rubens. Apprentices and journeymen continued to trickle into the workshops of Anton Van Dijck, Jacob Jordaens, and others. Other trades that continued to attract skilled artisans in the 17th century were the printing industry and sculpture, which enjoyed considerable popularity as propagators of the Catholic faith during the Counter-Reformation. They helped propagate the renewed vigor of the Catholic Church in paintings, engravings, books, and sculptures, giving the baroque style an international and sophisticated allure. By 1650, however, Antwerp's international artistic, economic, and demographic golden age had passed.

Guicciardini, Ludovico. *Beschrijvinghe van alle de Nederlanden, anderssins ghenoemt Neder-Duytschlandt.* Amsterdam, 1612 (1567).

Mander, Karel van. *The Lives of the Illustrious Netherlandish and German Painters: Preceded by the Lineage, Circumstances and Place of Birth, Life and Works of Karel van Mander, Painter and Poet and Likewise His Death and Burial,* vol. 1, edited by Hessel Miedema. Doornspijk, 1994 (1604).

Thijs, Alfons K. L. "Antwerp's Luxury Industries: The Pursuit of Profit and Artistic Sensitivity." In *Antwerp, Story of a Metropolis, 16th–17th Century,* edited by Jan van der Stock, 105–13. Antwerp, 1993.

Thijs, Alfons K. L. "Minderheden te Antwerpen (16de/20ste eeuw)." In *Minorities in Western European Cities (16th–20th Centuries),* edited by Hugo Soly and Alfons K. L. Thijs, 17–42. Brussels, 1995.

Verbeemen, Jozef. "Immigratie te Antwerpen." In *Mededelingen van de Geschieden Oudheikundige Kring voor Leuven en omgeving (›de Brabantse stad‹)* 5 (1965): 81–100.

Cross-references: Belgium and Luxembourg; Germany; France; Italy; The Netherlands; Spain and Portugal

MOLUCCANS IN THE NETHERLANDS SINCE 1951

Henk Smeets

Between 21 March and 21 June 1951, some 12,500 Moluccans arrived in the Netherlands from Indonesia. The group consisted of some 3,500 soldiers of the former Royal Dutch Colonial Army (Koninklijk Nederlands-Indisch Leger, KNIL) and their wives and children. The majority of these soldiers originated from Ambon, the center of the Moluccas, and the adjacent islands. Most were Protestants, but there were also some Muslims and Catholics among them. Until the 1970s, they were referred to as "Ambonese"; afterward this term was replaced with the more correct "Moluccan."

After the Netherlands had granted independence to the Indonesian archipelago in December 1949, the indigenous soldiers of the KNIL were given the choice of either joining the new Indonesian army or demobilizing and settling somewhere in Indonesia. Many soldiers transferred to the new army, but some 4,000 – mostly Moluccan – soldiers objected to serving the former enemy or feared persecution as former "colonial collaborators." Therefore, they opted for demobilization and settlement on the Moluccas. However, the Indonesian government forbade former KNIL soldiers to settle there since they believed they would reinforce the rebels who had proclaimed the Republic of the South Moluccas (Republik Maluku Selatan, RMS) in April 1950.

As a result, the Moluccan soldiers mainly were moved to the island of Java and protected there by Dutch troops. The presence of a colonial army in an independent Indonesia, however, met with increasing criticism. Following a case that reached the Dutch Supreme Court, it was ruled that the Moluccan soldiers could not be held in Indonesia against their will. The Dutch government then decided to transport the soldiers and their families temporarily to the Netherlands. Facing discharge from military service, the soldiers now had to decide between joining the Indonesian army, settlement on Java as civilians, or a temporary exile in the Netherlands. Since the first two possibilities were not acceptable alternatives for many Moluccans, they had no choice but to leave for the Netherlands. Several hundred soldiers initially refused to board the ships but then made the journey to Europe when threatened again with discharge from the army.

While the soldiers were still en route, the Dutch government decided to discharge them upon arrival in the Netherlands. The Moluccans had become Indonesian citizens when the country gained independence and the Netherlands did not want non-Dutch soldiers in the ranks of its armed forces. The Netherlands had also promised the Indonesian government not to keep these soldiers on active duty. The Moluccan soldiers resisted the discharge and went to court, which ruled in their favor, but this judgment was overturned by a higher court. The discharge from military service, the ensuing period of high unemployment and the Moluccans' total dependence on the Dutch government had a traumatic effect, at least on the first and second generation of the Moluccan community in the Netherlands. Several decades later, the Dutch government acknowledged that this discharge had caused an unfortunate "false start."

Since their stay in the Netherlands was supposed to be only temporary, integration was considered undesirable and government policy was aimed at keeping the Moluccans isolated from Dutch society. Upon arrival, the Moluccans were housed in empty buildings, including former labor and concentration camps. Responsibility for housing and provisions was given to the Agency for Ambonese Care (Commissariaat van Ambonezenzorg, CAZ), a highly centralized government agency set up in 1952. The goals of the CAZ were oriented toward prompting the Moluccans to return to Indonesia, but as the duration of their stay in the Netherlands grew longer, pressure to change this policy increased. After only a short while, Moluccan children were allowed to attend schools in the regular Dutch educational system. Meanwhile education for adults still focused on the return to Indonesia, and aid for integration in the labor market was also lacking. At the same time a significant number of Dutch – mainly conservatives and Protestants – supported the Moluccan struggle for an independent state but never attained much influence in Dutch politics.

In the camps, the former soldiers were housed, fed, and received pocket money from the state, but persistent unemployment undermined morale and caused disturbances. For this reason, the Dutch government required the Moluccans to care for their own livelihood, which led to massive protests among the Moluccans, who accused the government of shirking its responsibilities for the consequences of the discharges from military service. The protests gradually abated as the Moluccans lacked political influence, but Dutch government policy remained a bitter disappointment for the Moluccans. Since the first generation of Moluccan men possessed only military training, they, along with their wives who in most cases were also unskilled, mainly found employment as unskilled laborers.

A Moluccan family in front of their barrack in camp Ybenheer near Oosterwolde, province of Frisia, in the northern part of the Netherlands, early 1950s (*Moluks Historisch Museum, Utrecht, The Netherlands, Collection Oosterbaan*).

In 1959 the government decided to disband the camps and to establish small living quarters, consisting of some 50 Moluccan families, in areas with sufficient employment opportunities. This measure also met with some resistance. The camps still bore a resemblance to military barracks and the transfer to regular houses was perceived by the Moluccans as a further attack on their rights as former KNIL soldiers. Due to this resistance as well as to the limited willingness of the designated cities to participate, the original plan was only partially implemented. As a result, Moluccan living quarters emerged that were much larger than those originally planned, yet without consideration of whether employment opportunities were available. Some of the camps had to be evacuated by force and some 30 years elapsed until the last camp had been finally liquidated. In 1980 these closed Moluccan living quarters housed 60%, in 2000 some 40% of the Moluccan population in the Netherlands.

Participation in the educational system and labor market and the improvement of living conditions were important steps toward the integration of the Moluccan population. The effect, however, remained limited until the 1970s. This was the result of, among other things, an inconsistent government policy, aimed at integration but at the same time highly oriented toward the perspective of return. The CAZ, which existed until 1970 and blocked the involvement of other government agencies, obstructed the integration process still further. The Moluccans, for their part, did not desire integration, but focused on the past and on the injustices they had experienced.

In the later 1960s second-generation Moluccans became increasingly visible in Dutch society. Young men became involved in the Dutch party scene and were viewed by their indigenous peers as fierce competition for the favor of young women. Contact with Dutch society soon assumed a confrontational character with frequent fights, vandalism, and more serious forms of criminal behavior such as thefts and robberies. Dutch society soon became aware of the presence of this second-generation minority group that was shaped by both Moluccan and Dutch culture. These were the times of student protests, Black Power, and resistance against the war in Vietnam. A large number of young Dutch sympathized with these goals, and the use of violence was not always rejected outright. Many Moluccan youths concluded that the peaceful protests of their parents on behalf of an independent Moluccan state had not yielded any results. Although only a few eventually crossed the border toward violence, many felt that changes had to be made and action had to be taken.

This development was reinforced in 1966 when Indonesia executed the second president of the RMS, Chris Soumokil, at the behest of General Suharto. When Suharto, now president, was planning a state visit to the Netherlands in 1970, the situation escalated. Moluccan youths stormed the residence of the Indonesian ambassador and took several hostages. In subsequent years, the number of violent acts increased. In 1975 plans were made to take Queen Juliana hostage. Some months later, Moluccans hijacked a train in Wijster in the northern Netherlands and occupied the Indonesian Consulate in Amsterdam. In 1977 near De Punt, another train was hijacked and pupils and teachers of a primary school in Bovensmilde were taken hostage. The next year Moluccans occupied the building of the provincial administration in Assen. They wanted to gain international attention for the cause of an independent Moluccan state and demanded the release of those involved in earlier actions. Their goal was not only to influence Indonesia but also the Dutch government, which, in the eyes of Moluccan activists, could have done much more to strengthen the position of the RMS. The actions in 1977 were also aimed at the Moluccan government-in-exile and its leader Johannes Alvarez Manusama, who was considered to be too weak. In the course of these actions, five Dutch nationals and one Indonesian were killed. The violent conclusion of the 1977 hijacking took the lives of another two Dutch nationals and six Moluccans.

The actions of the Moluccans in the 1970s resulted in worldwide public interest in their situation and the RMS, but they did not bring about an independent Moluccan state nor lead to the fulfillment of other demands. Relations between the Moluccans and a large part of the Dutch population deteriorated over the course of several years. A favorable, yet unintended, result of the violent actions was an acceleration of the integration process of the Moluccans as the Dutch government now gave high priority to their integration into Dutch society. The socioeconomic position of young Moluccans proved much worse than had been assumed: almost 90% of Moluccans between 15 and 30 years old left school at the lowest level of secondary education. New measures, implemented between 1980 and 1990, aimed to deal with these arrears in education and to provide more job opportunities.

At the same time, Moluccan society itself changed: Moluccan parents of the second generation realized that the future of their children was in the Netherlands. Government actions meant to improve their position now found more acceptance, even among RMS supporters who until then had considered such actions a tactic to distract them from political struggle. Thus, in 1990 the government and Dutch and Moluccan organizations began to cooperate closely in order to find steady employment for long-term unemployed Moluccan youths. Thanks to this project, 1,200 steady jobs were created and nearly every second-generation Moluccan became integrated into the labor market.

The attitude of the Moluccans toward the RMS also changed. Without renouncing the fundamental right to establish an independent state, many Moluccans realized they would not return even if a Republic of the South Moluccas would materialize. Time spent in the motherland during holidays demonstrated clearly that returning to a "third world" country was no longer a realistic possibility; they had become too accustomed to life in the Dutch consumer society.

The bond with the Moluccas, however, did not disappear. When a civil war broke out in Ambon in 1999, Dutch Moluccans were very concerned about the fate of family members and fellow villagers. They initiated numerous relief actions with the remarkable involvement of third-generation boys and girls, including children of mixed marriages (some 35%) who only knew the Moluccas from stories or holidays.

On the surface level, these young Moluccans seem to be well integrated in Dutch society. Recent research nevertheless shows that their position in education and employment is weak: 70% still do not advance beyond the lowest level of vocational training. The integration process is clearly not yet complete.

Bartels, Dieter. *Moluccans in Exile: A Struggle for Ethnic Survival*. Leiden and Utrecht, 1998.

Chauvel, Richard. *Nationalists, Soldiers and Separatists: The Ambonese Islands from Colonialism to Revolt 1880–1950*. Leiden, 1990.

Manuhutu, Wim, and Henk Smeets, eds. *Tijdelijk Verblijf. De opvang van Molukkers in Nederland 1951*. Amsterdam, 1991.

Smeets, Henk, and Fridus Steijlen. *In Nederland gebleven. De geschiedenis van Molukkers 1951–2006*. Amsterdam and Utrecht, 2006.

Smeets, Henk, and Justus Veenman. "More and More at Home: Three Generations of Moluccans in the Netherlands." In *Immigrant Integration. The Dutch Case*, edited by Hans Vermeulen and Rinus Penninx, 36–63. Amsterdam, 2000.

Steijlen, Fridus. *RMS, van ideaal tot symbool. Moluks nationalisme in Nederland 1951–1994*. Amsterdam, 1996.

Cross-references: The Netherlands

MORAVIAN BRETHREN IN EUROPE SINCE THE EARLY MODERN PERIOD

Dietrich Meyer

The Church of the Moravian Brethren is a free Protestant church that was formed after 1722 under the protection and spiritual leadership of Count Nikolaus Ludwig von

Count Nicholas Ludwig von Zinzendorf (1700–60), theologian and founder of the community of the Moravian Brethren, portrayed and cut by Hugo Bürkner (*ullstein bild*).

Zinzendorf from Moravian and Bohemian *Exulanten* (religious exiles) and soon also from numerous additional immigrants from Germany. In the Anglo-American world, the renewed Unitas Fratrum – the Latin name of the church of the Bohemian Brethren (Jednota bratrská) that emerged in 1457 out of the Hussite Reformation – is referred to as the Moravian Church, since Moravians were dominant among the faithful who, starting in Herrnhut, spread the religious beliefs of the community in the first years of its existence. Among the Bohemian *Exulanten*, who settled in large numbers in Saxony and Silesia in the 17th and 18th centuries, those who went to Herrnhut constituted a special group because of their particular religious conviction, which had a Pietistic imprint.

With respect to the content of their faith, they were of a mind with Zinzendorf, who followed the missionary and reform plans of August Hermann Francke. By adopting the statutes that Zinzendorf drew up in 1727, the Moravian Brethren constituted themselves as a transconfessional, philadelphian community (following Philipp Jakob Spener's idea of an *ecclesiola in ecclesia*) within the Lutheran state church of Saxony. Following Zinzendorf's expulsion from Saxony in 1736, the Brethren spread in Germany, the Netherlands, Great Britain, Switzerland, the Scandinavian countries, the Baltic region, and North America (Pennsylvania: e.g., Bethlehem, Nazareth, Lititz) and became a magnet for religiously awakened individuals. Since the Moravian Brethren settled in separate communities or formed self-contained settlement nuclei in cities, their community has survived to this day not only as an independent free church but also as a special form of settlement and social organization.

The region of origin of the Moravian, German-speaking emigrants was especially the Kuhländchen around Neutitschein (Nový Jičin) with Zauchtental (Suchdol n.O.), Sehlen (Žilina), Kunewalde (Kunin), Schönau (Šenov), Senftleben (Ženklava), and Seitendorf (Hladke Zivotice). After 1548 and even more after 1620, members of the Unitas Fratrum – under pressure from the Habsburg Counter-Reformation – took refuge in Poland, especially in the area around Lissa (Leszno), where they established an important school and where their descendants lived into the 20th century. Poland was also the true destination of the Moravians, who made contact with Zinzendorf through the initiative of the carpenter Christian David.

In 1727, about 150 of the 300 residents at Herrnhut were from Moravia. By 1731, according to an imperial list, 263 persons had emigrated from the Kuhländchen to Herrnhut, where they made up the majority of the nearly 500 inhabitants. By contrast, the number of German-speaking and Czech-speaking Bohemians who joined the Brethren was smaller.

In response to an imperial complaint in 1731, migration from Bohemia and Moravia to Herrnhut was largely blocked by decrees of the Saxon state as early as 1732–3.

Crucial to the development of the community was that the immigrants for the most part embraced Zinzendorf's missionary ideas. As they saw it, their task in life was not so much to integrate successfully into their new homeland, as to spread the "good news of the Gospel" among the "slaves of Central and South America," the "poor Eskimos in Greenland and Labrador," the "oppressed and exploited Indians of North America," and the "despised indigenous tribes of South Africa and Australia."

The attraction of the Brethren increased especially after their settlement in the Wetterau after 1738 (communities in Herrnhaag and Marienborn) and had purely religious reasons: discontent among believers with the overly rigid and regulated piety of the territorial churches, enthusiasm for the missionary idea and the modern Christian educational institutions, and the "relaxed joyfulness" of Moravian piety. In England, the Moravians were closely connected with the beginnings of Methodism around the Anglican clerics John and Charles Wesley, until the two movements split in 1741. In the Netherlands they met with fierce opposition from the Reformed Church, but with sympathy among the Mennonites, who were inclined toward Pietism. As a result, from around 1738, the Brethren attracted members of the Anglican Church in England, followers of the Mennonites in the Netherlands, Calvinists from the Netherlands and Switzerland, and Lutheran Christians from the Baltic region.

The influx of new immigrants also altered the social stratification in the various settlements of the Brethren. Whereas most of the initial settlers were simple farmers or craftsmen, after 1740 there was a rise in the number of nobles, especially from the Oberlausitz and Silesia, but also from the Baltic region, Switzerland, and the Netherlands. The Dutch were often merchants who invested their money in enterprises of the Brethren. The integration of the immigrants of diverse backgrounds and their identification with their chosen community of Moravian Brethren happened fairly quickly: they all saw themselves as a spiritual elite that was leaving behind the confessional Christianity of the 18th century and giving an ecumenical interpretation to Moravian, Lutheran, and Reformed confessional writings.

At the same time, the Brethren, for a variety of reasons, maintained their own identity separate from other churches and communities in the receiving countries: first, since they were recognized as a church by Prussia in 1742 and England in 1749, they were able to hold their own alongside the territorial and state churches as a separate free church with important elements of the Moravian church constitution (transferral of the office of bishop by the senior of the Polish Moravian Church, Daniel Ernst Jablonski, to David Nitschmann in 1735 and Zinzendorf in 1738; adoption of the office of acolyte and of the ecclesiastical ordination of deacon, presbyter, and bishop from the Unitas Fratrum; elements of church discipline). Second, with the Herrnhuter Statutes of 1727 and the election of Jesus Christ as the Senior Elder of all communities in 1741, Zinzendorf gave the settlements of the Brethren a theocratic constitution in which the secular organization of social and economic life and the spiritual order of religious service and pastoral care formed a specific unity. Critics spoke of a "state within the state." This constitution had to be given up in the various German states with changing legislation after 1848 and the growing separation of state and church.

Third, the settlements of the Brethren were laid out everywhere along a largely identical scheme and their church halls were erected in accordance with a uniform building program, which points to centralized leadership by Zinzendorf and his co-workers (such as Siegmund August von Gersdorf) and the directorate of the church. Fourth, the structuring of the communities into different "choirs" depending on age and gender (e.g., unmarried brothers, unmarried sisters, married persons, widows, widowers) led to the building of choir houses in which the various choirs lived separated from one another, celebrated daily liturgical assemblies, and organized their own forms of work. Fifth, until 1945, the administration of the European communities of Brethren – with the exception of those in Great Britain – was overseen in centralized fashion from Herrnhut. This led to a strong dominance of Germans, with the result that in Zeist in Holland, for example, German was spoken as late as the first third of the 20th century.

The migration of church members is not determined by outward reasons but by the engagement for specific tasks of the church, particularly mission work and fellowship formation. This meant that members of the community were constantly journeying to their missionary regions or on home leave. Since a large number of Brethren was born in the overseas missionary fields, they formed a group of "cosmopolitans" unusual for the 18th and 19th centuries. The Moravians did not pursue any missionary goals within Europe to avoid conflict with the confessional churches. Instead, they worked with the territorial churches and offered forms of intensive fellowship as assemblies, missionary hours, and home visits to all those receptive to them, especially in areas underserved by the churches. This "diaspora work" was done, where possible, by co-workers of the local communities of the Brethren, and where no communities existed the Brethren set up "societies" with their own meeting rooms or halls. The picture of wandering Moravian Brethren on their way to community meetings and individual pastoral care was shaped by the lay Christians of the diaspora work, who usually traveled by foot for lack of money and could not expect large audiences.

The Brethren in Great Britain did not engage in diaspora work, following instead the model of evangelization of an independent denomination that maintained preaching locations for evangelical events in various locales. Today's small communities in England and Ireland form a separate province and have experienced an influx from the missionary regions in the second half of the 20th century, especially from the West Indies. That is even more true for the Netherlands, with the Dutch communities shaped by a strong inflow from Suriname, where a larger, independent missionary church of the Brethren has emerged. The Brethren communities in Czechia do not go back to the 18th century but arose from the "Bohemian-Moravian work," which was created for evangelical work after the publication of the Religious Patent of 1861. In 1931 the movement became independent and today it forms its own province.

Buijtenen, Mari P. van, Cornelis Dekker, and Huib Leeuwenberg, eds. *Unitas Fratrum. Herrnhuter Studien – Moravian Studies.* Utrecht, 1975.

Crews, C. Daniel. *Faith, Love, Hope: A History of the Unitas Fratrum.* Winston-Salem, 2008.

Hahn, Hans Christoph, and Hellmut Reichel. *Zinzendorf und die Herrnhuter Brüder. Quellen zur Geschichte der Brüder-Unität von 1722 bis 1760.* Hamburg, 1977.

Hamilton, J. Taylor, and Kenneth G. Hamilton. *History of the Moravian Church: The Renewed Unitas Fratrum.* Bethlehem, 1967.

Mason, J. C. S. *The Moravian Church and the Missionary Awakening in England 1760–1800. (Royal Historical Society Studies in History).* Chippenham, 2001.

Moeschler, Felix. *Alte Herrnhuter Familien. Die mährischen, böhmischen und Österreichisch-schlesischen Exulanten.* 2 vols. Herrnhut, 1922/1924.

Podmore, Colin. *The Moravian Church in England 1728–1760.* Oxford, 1998.

Uttendörfer, Otto. *Alt-Herrnhut. Wirtschaftsgeschichte und Religionssoziologie Herrnhuts während seiner ersten zwanzig Jahre (1722–1742),* part 1. Herrnhut, 1925.

Uttendörfer, Otto. *Wirtschaftsgeist und Wirtschaftsorganisation Herrnhuts und der Brüdergemeine von 1743 bis zum Ende des Jahrhundert,* part 2. Herrnhut, 1926.

Cross-references: Czechia and Slovakia; The Baltic Region; France; Germany; Great Britain; The Netherlands; Northern Europe; Poland; Russia and Belarus; Switzerland; Bohemian Exiles (*Exulanten*) in Saxony since the 17th Century; Mennonites in West Prussia since the 16th Century; West Indians in Great Britain, France, and the Netherlands since the End of World War II

MOROCCAN LABOR MIGRANTS IN WESTERN, CENTRAL, AND NORTHERN EUROPE SINCE THE 1960S: THE CASE OF GREAT BRITAIN

Myriam Cherti

After the Second World War, France was the most important European destination for Moroccan migration to western Europe. Moroccan migration then expanded to other European nations with recruitment agreements with West Germany, Belgium, and the Netherlands. The Moroccan population in Europe increased from 400,000 in 1975 to 2.8 million by 2008. Most of the European Moroccans are concentrated in France (39.86%), Spain (19.28%), and Italy (13.36%) with smaller groups in the Netherlands, Belgium, Germany, and the UK. Although there is a relatively greater amount of information about immigration to France and the Netherlands, much less is known about the situation of Moroccans in the UK, even though the main migration movement to these three countries started roughly in the same period during the early 1960s and into the 1970s.

An accurate estimate of the size of the Moroccan community currently living in the UK is not available, mainly because British government statistics do not register nationality but place of birth. Second- and third-generation migrants are thus grouped together with everyone else born in the UK. However, unofficial estimates indicate the number of Moroccans in the UK to be over 50,000 with at least 30,000 in London alone.

In contrast to other European countries, no bilateral labor agreement exists between Great Britain and Morocco; migration was therefore shaped mainly by social networks of friends and relatives. Moroccan migration to Britain can be divided into four phases. The first started in the 1960s and consisted of unskilled workers, mostly from northern Morocco, with a smaller community from Meknes and Oujda. The second phase – family reunification – followed from the early 1970s onward. The third phase started in the mid-1980s, and was made up of a sizable number of young semiskilled professionals and entrepreneurs, mostly from Casablanca and other larger cities. The fourth and most recent migration wave started in the early 1990s with the emigration of highly skilled Moroccan professionals, both from Morocco itself and from France. This short essay concentrates on some of the social-economic and cultural characteristics of these labor migrants, the most quantitatively significant group of the 1960s and 1970s.

Moroccan migration to the UK in the 1960s and early 1970s was characterized as labor migration and influenced by the traditional push and pull factors. Economic reasons and the attraction of a Britain imagined as "Eldorado" were the main motivations for Moroccan labor migrants. Since this migration was not regulated by any government schemes, anyone who wanted to emigrate had only to write to a recruiting agency and pay for a work permit to be sent a conditional contract to work in the UK.

Most Moroccans who came to England in the 1960s were hired to work in the service industries, such as hotels and small businesses that started to prosper in the climate of economic growth during this period. The majority of these immigrants were unskilled workers from the northern part of Morocco, more specifically the Jbala region (Khmiss Sahel, Beni Gharfet, Beni Arouss), Larache, Tetouan, Tangiers, and the surrounding areas, and with smaller communities from Meknes and Oujda. The majority settled in large cities such as London and Edinburgh with smaller concentrations in towns like Slough, Crawley, and Trowbridge.

One of the key specificities of Moroccan migration to England lay in the large number of women who arrived as independent migrants in the early 1970s. They were single, widowed, divorced, or single female heads of households, who supported their families with their earnings. This indicates an earlier feminization of migration, as opposed to frequent descriptions of migrant labor, where female migrants first come into view in connection with family reunification. In the UK, however, many wives came first with work permits and were joined later by their spouses and children. The absence of bilateral agreements indirectly enabled this process of early female migration. The recruitment of potential Moroccan migrants was subject to few restrictions without any interference from the state. The minimal state interest in steering this migration also meant that migrations hardly left a trace in migration statistics.

The increasingly restrictive immigration rules set in motion in the late 1960s and early 1970s encouraged many immigrants to bring their families over from Morocco. This transformed what was originally a temporary migration in search of a livelihood into longer-term settlement, leading to the beginning of family reunification in the 1970s. However, unlike other European nations, in England, Moroccan women have played a key role in the economic life of the family: in an estimated 80% of households, both partners have integrated into the job market simultaneously at some point in their lives.

Moroccan settlement was concentrated mainly in large cities such as London. The great majority of those who originated from the north of Morocco ended up living in an equally specific part of London, in close proximity to each other. Their presence is visible through Moroccan mosques, grocery stores, cafes, restaurants, voluntary organizations, and supplementary schools. In fact, the area in and around Golborne Road in North Kensington, where there is a high concentration of people of Moroccan origin, is commonly known as "little Morocco." Cheap rents as well as the local council's policy in housing allocation played a key role in influencing the geographical distribution of Moroccans.

Most Moroccans were recruited to fill job vacancies in the English labor market, mainly in the hotel and catering businesses, and in the National Health Service. Because of their limited skills and poor knowledge of English, they almost inevitably took the lowest paid jobs that provided little opportunity for career mobility. This picture is still prevalent in the job market, as according to the 2001 census data, Moroccan-born migrants in London are most likely to be working in hotels and restaurants (23.7%), wholesale and retail trades (14.6%), and real estate (13.9%). Spanish-speaking immigrants, especially those who originated from the north of Morocco, purposefully chose Spanish employers to overcome their English language barrier. The same networks of friends and relatives that frequently encouraged migrants to come to the UK also assisted with their job search once there. The increasing labor shortage in the UK has encouraged employers in some cases to give incentives to their employees in recruiting more workers, particularly in the hotel and catering industries.

Many Moroccans in the UK have ultimately maintained social contact with the members of their own group in order to support one another. The relatively low educational and skill levels of the first generation have served to relegate Moroccans to the margins of British mainstream society, allowing only minimal opportunities for upward mobility. This applies particularly to immigrants from the 1960s. Over years of intensive work, they established their own religious and social facilities, mosques, and Koran and Arabic classes for members of the younger generation. In London alone there are more than 20 Moroccan voluntary organizations catering to the needs of their local communities by providing advice and support in accessing services. These organizations are especially important in the case of the first generation, which still remains relatively isolated because of the language barrier and lack of knowledge of the British social system.

The younger generation of Moroccans is most likely to attend schools with a majority of other ethnic minority students, as the choice of school is mostly determined by the area of residence. Although it is difficult to make general statements, since school statistics are not arranged by ethnicity, a discrepancy is often seen between second-generation Moroccans born in England and the generation born in Morocco who arrived in England at a young age. While the second generation have evident difficulties in school, partly because of the lack of parental support and partly because of a lower level of ambition, the young migrants of the first generation in general display a strong eagerness to learn as well as high career aspirations.

The average educational achievement of the generation who migrated as children is somewhat higher than second-generation Moroccans, but it is still lower than that of their English and other ethnic minority peers. According to the North Westminster Community School Report on examination results in 1997, Moroccan boys underachieved as compared to Moroccan girls and other Arab groups. Peer group pressure is perceived as one of the factors contributing to this discrepancy in school achievement. There is evidence that Moroccan students pose problems to schools in adopting an antisocial style as a means of demarcating their identity, thereby also challenging the school's authority. This often leads to their expulsion from school, making it more difficult for expelled children – more often boys than girls – to rejoin mainstream schools, joining instead special learning units.

Among Moroccans students at the beginning of the 21st century, an increasing differentiation in educational careers is taking place. A small group achieves the marks needed for higher professional and university education, while there is another group that reaches only the level of secondary education or of lower vocational education. Between these two extremes is a large group of youth who graduate from the highest level of vocational education and college education. Whereas the first group can secure elevated professional positions within different sectors of the economy, the second and third groups face difficulties accessing the job market and often experience significant levels of unemployment.

The young generation of Moroccans living in the UK is very heterogeneous. While some of its members gain access to the middle class, the majority still experience exclusion. Some of them identify themselves as "Moroccan Muslims born in Britain," others as "British Moroccans" or "British Muslims." Very few see themselves as "English" or "Moroccan Arab," or choose another hyphenated identity if they are children of "mixed marriage." There is, however, one shared experience: a feeling of detachment. Many young Moroccans feel that they do not belong either to the host country or to their country of origin.

The process of settlement of this group represents, in a sense, "a minority within a minority," making it increasingly more difficult to define, count, or even give a name to this population, which occupies divergent positions in the social structure. Depending on their age group, their family background, and the neighborhoods in which they grew up, second-generation Moroccans in the UK experience an ongoing process of identity construction where Islam plays an increasingly significant role. However, their interpretation of Islam differs from that of their parents: it is individualistic and pluralistic, allowing room for a personal and selective experience of their faith, for internal debate, and for tolerance toward other ways of thinking. This Muslim identity grants second-generation Moroccans a stronger and wider sense of belonging that transcends their local neighborhoods or communities and connects them to the larger Muslim community in Britain and Europe. In other words, the Muslim identity of young Moroccans in the UK and in Europe in general can be considered as part of an ongoing process for integration and recognition of their rights.

Migrant communities often pass through a number of development stages in order to reach full emancipation and a sizable representation at the social, economic, and political levels of the host country. Moroccans in the UK are part of a community that, in social terms, is still very young. Among the main strengths of the community are its self-containment, its mutual support networks, and its inherently strong transnational identity. While the first generation, to a large extent, is still perceived as withdrawn and disengaged from mainstream society, the second generation appears relatively more integrated and civically engaged.

Borkwood, Jerome. *From Kensal Village to Golborne Road, Tales of the Inner City*. London, 2002.

Cherti, Myriam. "Reconstructing the History of Moroccan Migration to the UK: An Oral History Approach." In *Enlarging European Memory: Migration Movement in Historical Perspectives*, edited by Mareike König and Rainer Ohliger, 169–78. Munich, 2006.

Cherti, Myriam. *Paradoxes of Social Capital: A Multi-Generational Study of Moroccans in London*. Amsterdam, 2008.

Cherti, Myriam. *British Moroccans: Citizenship in Action*. Runnymede Trust, London, 2009.

Raising Educational Achievement amongst Arabic-Speaking Children: A Report by Al Hasaniya Moroccan Women's Centre. London, 1999.

Westminster Ethnic Minority Needs Audit (WEMNA) 2007. Making People's Voices Heard, Imperial College, 2007.

Cross-references: France; Great Britain; The Netherlands; Maghrebis in France after Decolonization during the 1950s and 1960s

MOROCCAN UNDOCUMENTED IMMIGRANTS IN SPAIN SINCE THE END OF THE 20TH CENTURY

Mohand Tilmatine

The immigration of Moroccans to Europe began when northern, western, and central European countries needed additional workers beginning in the 1950s as a result of their economic development and recruited "guest workers." At that time, the situation in Morocco was characterized by a structural imbalance between a rapidly growing population and the labor market's poor ability to absorb it. Treaties with states of the European Union (West Germany 1961, France 1963, Belgium 1964, and the Netherlands 1969) regulated the recruitment of the Moroccan migrant workers. After a period of growth (1969–74), the size of the group largely stagnated following a recruitment stop in the destination countries at the beginning of the 1970s. Moroccan immigration only picked up again at the end of the 1980s. However, the Moroccans who now arrived increasingly as part of family reunification encountered a satiated labor market in the destination countries in the 1960s and 1970s. The quest for legal – and increasingly also illegal – employment opportunities led the migrants to change their focus, and Spain, in particular, became the new primary destination.

The developmental potential of the southern part of Morocco (the Rif region), still fundamentally weak at the beginning of the 21st century, the almost persistent dryness, and the high demographic pressure are factors that favor exodus and emigration from this area. At the same time, pictures from Europe that are carried into North African households via satellite, reveal the different living standards between Morocco and Europe. These impressions are often reinforced by the "wealth"-promising appearance and behavior (cars, money, clothes) of those who have successfully made the leap across the Mediterranean.

It was especially Spain's admission as a new member of the European Union (1986) that piqued the interest of Moroccan migrants. As a direct result of accession to the EU, Spain in 1991 introduced a restrictive visa policy following the provisions of the Schengen Agreement. However, as Spain at that time did not consider itself an immigration country, it did not see the necessity of simultaneously opening up legal channels of immigration. Thus, while Spain turned into a southern outpost of "Fortress Europe," it also remained an important transit country for all those illegal migrants who wished to make their way into the traditional destination countries overland. In addition, beginning in the mid-1990s, Spain itself was becoming increasingly an immigration country. Thus the visa requirement after 1991 and also the Spanish Foreigners' Law of 1985 did not prevent Moroccan immigration but merely drove it into illegality.

For Morocco, illegal immigration is undoubtedly of great economic importance, both with respect to financial support for the families back at home and for the economy as a whole. Emigrations are individual or collective, but mostly they are familial projects and are generally carried out as such. Migration as part of one's life's path is so deeply rooted within the population in Morocco that no end to the exodus is to be expected, nor are remigration programs likely to be successful, especially if one considers that in Morocco, returning is interpreted as a failure and a disgrace for the individual and the family.

Only a rough estimate is possible of the percentage of Moroccans among the total illegal immigrants in Spain. A clue comes from the number of applicants during the legalization campaigns, which illegals very frequently take advantage of. In total, nearly 700,000 applications for legalization were received by the Spanish authorities as part of the campaign carried out between February and May 2005. In contrast to previous programs, this measure was aimed primarily at the status of migrants in the labor market. The largest percentage of applicants came from Madrid, Catalonia, the autonomous region of Valencia, and from Andalusia. Twelve and a half percent of the applicants were Moroccans (86,000).

Criminal organizations, most of which were involved in the drug trade, quickly adapted to the "new market" of illegal immigration. The business with the *Harragas*, as the illegals are called in North Africa, offered new opportunities and was linked with a broad spectrum of "services": from simply putting the migrants on ships to the complete transport to the destination, including procurement of a job and the necessary papers. The gangs of smugglers encompass, at the most varied levels, middlemen, subcontractors, and agents, who recruit possible clients, as well as owners of means of transportation and specialists (*Mdebber*) who take care of papers and money exchange and establish contacts. The price for a "trip" ranges from 5,000 to 50,000 dirhams (500–5,000 Euros), depending on the services offered and requested.

A large portion of the illegal immigrants who make their way to Spain from North Africa, cross the narrow (14 km-wide) strait between Morocco and Spain in *pateras*, small wooden boots that can sometimes hold up to 60 persons. In an effort the elude the border patrol, the landing sites alternate between Gibraltar, the Canary Islands, the coast of Cádiz, and the area around Motril near Granada and Malaga. The most important launching site on the Moroccan side, the "great gate" to Europe, is without a doubt Tangiers. But the expansion of surveillance installations and above all the heavy demand for smuggling trips prompted a search for alternatives. They were found farther south, in the area of Tetuán, Larache, Sidi Ifni, Tarfaya, or Dakhla, El Aaiún (western Sahara) along the Atlantic coast with the Canary Islands as the goal. A migration using trucks, buses, and ferries – though much smaller in size – heads for Spain also from the two Spanish enclaves on Moroccan soil, Melilla and Ceuta, which are secured by strong border fortifications.

In spite of the high price and the risks, illegal immigration to Spain on the whole is increasing. In 2003, 942 *pateras* were counted (up 28% from 2002), and at the same time the number of victims grew. This trend is confirmed by data from the Spanish Red Cross, which registered 15,819 humanitarian responses by its organization (2001: 10,457) on Fuerteventura and Lanzarote, as well as in Tarifa, Algeciras, Barbate, and Motril. When a *patera* with 50 migrants on board sank on 25 October 2003, and 37 bodies washed up on the beaches of Cádiz, there were numerous reports in the media. The obviously worsening situation prompted the king of Morocco to suggest a Spanish-Moroccan cooperation to fight illegal immigration to Spain: as part of that effort, 2,500 policemen have been deployed since January 2004 to control the sea and land borders.

The motives of legal and illegal immigrants are essentially the same. The most important factor leading to the decision to emigrate without a legal permit seems to be the intention of finding work in Spain, even if it is illegal. Jobs that require no special skills were taken over by the Moroccan illegals while skilled and/or more prestigious work is hardly accessible to Moroccans with legal papers, let alone to illegals. According to the data of the Spanish legalization campaign in 2005, 31.7% of applicants were employed in private households, 20.8% in construction, 14.6% in agriculture, and 10.4% in the hotel and restaurant industry. Women especially can be found in private households and increasingly in prostitution. The social profile of the illegals is therefore not substantially different from that of the legal immigrants. Moroccans as a group can be seen as typical for illegal immigrants in their gender and age structure: 87% of Moroccans are male, and 50% are under the age of 30.

For some years, Morocco has experienced a new phenomenon: the illegal migration of underage children to France, Italy, Belgium, and especially Spain. Various agencies and aid organizations in Spain have been trying since 1995–6 to call attention to this continuously growing problem. In the destination countries, the children of poor families, mostly from villages and cities near Tangier but also from places like Agadir, Fez, or Salé, generally end up on the street or in reception centers for underage foreigners. Many of these children and teenagers are victims of human traffickers and are sexually exploited and abused. Members of the Spanish police and special units for fighting illegal immigration were able to break up numerous trafficking networks that specialized in young migrants. Because of its explosive nature, the issue also became the topic of a resolution addressing "Unaccompanied minor citizens from third countries," passed by the European Union on 26 June 1997.

Word that underage migrants were not being sent back quickly spread in Morocco, with the result that this form of immigrant rose sharply. In the first half of 2005, 871 new arrivals were registered at the reception centers in Andalusia. However, with the information that these children were not returned to Morocco immediately, the number of underage migrants taken in by the centers rose to 1,357 just for the period between 1 January and 30 June 2005. This amounted to an increase of 123% over the comparable period in 2004.

The Spanish legalization campaigns eased the precarious social situation of the illegals. However, the Spanish government announced in June 2005 that there would be no further legalizations under Minister President Zapatero. Instead, the plan was to carry out tougher workplace controls and make possible faster deportations.

Berriane, Mohamed, and Bernabé López García, coord. *Atlas de la inmigración marroquí en España*. Madrid, 2004.

Erfand, Rob van der, and Liebeth Heering. *Moroccan Migration Dynamics: Prospects for the Future*. Geneva, 2002.

García Castaño, F. Javier, and Carolina Muriel López, eds. *La inmigración en España. Contextos y alternativas*. Seville, 2002.

Inmigración extranjera en Andalucía. II Seminario sobre la investigación de la inmigration extranjera en Andalucía. Junta de Andalucía: Dirección general de políticas migratorias. Seville, 2002.

López García, Bernabé, ed. *Atlas de la inmigración magrebí en España*. Madrid, 1996.

Cross-references: Spain and Portugal; Moroccan Labor Migrants in Western, Central, and Northern Europe since the 1960s: The Example of Great Britain

MUSICIANS, SHOWMEN, JUGGLERS, AND ACROBATS IN CENTRAL EUROPE IN THE EARLY MODERN PERIOD

Ernst Schubert

The early modern history of players (*Spielleute*) and jugglers (*Gaukler*) in the Holy Roman Empire was not a linear continuation of medieval traditions. Too deep were the ruptures that affected the life of these traveling folk. While in the Middle Ages the term *ioculator* could still encompass all entertainers, from musicians to rope-walkers, the etymology of the German word *Gaukler*, for example, already reveals a specialization. Likewise, the German term *Spielmann*, used in the high Middle Ages in the comprehensive sense of the Latin *ioculator*, had given way to a more specific meaning: musician.

There are two reasons that the terms *Spielmann* and *Gaukler* in the early modern period had taken on a meaning that was clearer than in the Middle Ages and came close to our modern understanding. For one, there was the specific early modern pressure toward professionalization, which drove journeymen – for example, many of whom had still possessed qualifications in several crafts in the late Middle Ages – to concentrate on a single trade. The *Spielmann* now became the person who performed songs and instrumental music. Henceforth he was distinct from the *Gaukler*, the entertainer who made a living by performing stunts of the most varied kind. For another, the terminological clarification has to do with the fact that the vague charge of dishonesty that often excluded the medieval *ioculator* from the Eucharist was defined more precisely in the early modern period, when dishonor became a problem of the law pertaining to the craft trades. Anyone who wanted to exclude from the guilds the members of certain professions and their sons had to define these groups with greater precision.

In the early modern period, the mobility of simple folk stood under the general social suspicion – developed in the 16th century – of the now impermissible idleness. That was especially true of the itinerant musicians and jugglers. Astonishingly enough, the medieval suspicions lived on in circles of the Protestant clergy: even a man like August Hermann Francke believed that it was necessary to demand the exclusion of musicians from the Eucharist. Secular authority struggled to reconcile the suspicion – pronounced in countless decrees – that itinerant entertainers were idlers and people without masters who were not welcome in the land, with the need of the common man for some diversion in his dreary everyday life. As a result, permits were granted to musicians, who were allowed to perform in the region but had to make an effort to behave morally. These permits applied only to musicians – more precisely, musicians for village dances – but not to jugglers and acrobats, who could never make a living in a circumscribed regional area, and also not to itinerant music troupes, who did not shy away from covering long distances.

Official decrees constitute the most important source for the history and diversity of the early modern jugglers and acrobats. For example, a territorial decree from Bavaria in 1553 declared that "women shall henceforth be prohibited from jumping." The medieval *saltatrix* who could perform acrobatic leaps thus still existed: in a world in which sports were still foreign, a back handspring was probably enough to elicit gaping amazement.

It was not so much zealous clerics or the reputation of dishonor of the crafts that placed the itinerant musicians and entertainers under the shadow of social suspicion. For that, the primary reason were the decrees by the authorities.

Musicians in the 16th century. Copper engraving by Lorenz Strauch (*Germanisches Nationalmuseum, Nuremberg*).

The power of these insistently repeated decrees to shape the mentality of the people was considerable (the German saying "Idleness is the beginning of all vice" can be traced back to them), although their practical reach was minor. For example, Bishop Franz Ludwig von Erthal complained in 1792 that a troupe of Savoyard musicians had disturbed him for an entire afternoon by playing outside of his residence. Groups of musicians continued to travel the land even without special official permits and were greeted as a welcome addition to village feasts and fairs.

Groups of wandering musicians were sometimes found in the 15th century in the environs of large cities; and what is new in the early modern period is that these troupes of musicians were bound together by a common origin, often from a single village – for example, Hundeshagen in Eichsfeld. That also meant, however, that they had a home to which they repeatedly returned. In essence we are dealing with the descendants not of medieval minstrels but of medieval migrant workers. These itinerant groups were closer to the migrant hawkers – for example, the Westphalian *Tödden* – than to their sedentary colleagues in cities, at church, and at courts. Their musical style, too, had picked up the trend toward artful music only in rudimentary forms at best. Their audience was at village fairs and festivals. German musician groups went as far as Russia in search of a living, and Savoyards performed for the common people in northern German lands.

A special group among wandering performers were the Jewish musicians. The term *Klezmer*, for a long time common only in eastern European Jewry, came into use as a general term for Jewish music only after 1975; in the West, the term was *Lezim*. Originally limited to the feasts within their religious community, Jewish musicians acquired in the early modern period a reputation that made them known beyond the circle of Jewish communities. Their paths of migration were very extensive.

The extraordinary, country-spanning mobility of the musicians in early modern culture was the continuation of a tradition dating back to the late Middle Ages, when, for example, German violinists were highly esteemed in Italy as itinerant musicians. Cultural changes had a direct effect on the range of earning opportunities for traveling folk. The printing of what scholarship has labeled "historical folk songs" in broadsheets diminished the standing and impact of the medieval wandering reciter, who had been so important to the diffusion of views and ideas. His successor, the *Zeitungssinger* (newspaper reciter) scratched out a living at fairs with few earnings opportunities. The last traces of his existence vanished in the early 18th century. Political news was now spread entirely via newspapers and the oral circulation of the information they contained. The knowledge of the "newspaper reciter" became obsolete too rapidly to sustain his time-consuming wanderings. He overcame the problem of his dated information by reciting ballads of murders from distant lands because unimagined cruelties are always topical. The newspaper reciter transmuted into the balladeer (*Bänkelsänger*). In response to attempts to romanticize and elevate ballad singing, the following should be noted: the ballads were not an emanation of any kind of folk tradition – in the case of the murder ballads, they were based on printed, official *Urgichten* (confessions of the accused), which were versified with more or less skill. And above all, ballad singing was completely nonpolitical, very much in contrast to the importance, responsibility, and impact of the medieval reciter.

But the traveling entertainers could also take advantage of new cultural developments. Flexibility and the ability to adjust, in particular, are among the most important characteristics of the early modern world of traveling folk. People in this world reacted quickly to cultural changes, while traditional elements were not forgotten. The traveling entertainer with rare, exotic animals, the rope-walker, the *Seilriese*, and the acrobat encountered each other in the Middle Ages. If we add to them also the wandering puppeteer, we can see them as the descendants of the medieval *Himmelreicher*, who performed biblical stories as puppet plays to an urban audience. A new phenomenon, created by cultural developments, were the "peepshow box" people, who presented at fairs precursors of slide shows by using the technical capabilities of the *laterna magica*.

As during the Middle Ages, a wide variety of wandering entertainers could earn a living as fairground attractions – from rope-walkers to "strongmen" to escape artists. One special category in the early modern period, whose audience was initially found only in the noble-courtly sphere, were trick riders. They often appeared in larger troupes and formed a *circus equestre*. Trick riding was not one of the fairground attractions. It seems to have spread only in the

18th century out of England, as a specialized art form of interest not only to cavalrymen. However, the sort of circus rings for artistic horsemanship that were built as permanent installations in Paris in 1767 and in London in 1770 did not exist in German lands. The special case of the trick riders reveals one fundamental factor of the early modern culture of traveling folk: cross-border exchange as the result of European mobility. For example, "Jumpers" were differentiated according to the technique named after their region of origin, thus performing either the "Brabantine" or the "Lorrainese" jump.

As they had already done in the Middle Ages, early modern traveling folk traveled the land with rare animals. In the Middle Ages there had been bear tamers or jongleurs who traveled with monkeys (one man had even wandered down the Rhine with an elephant in the hope of finding passage to England); in the early modern period, especially after the 17th century, wandering troupes appeared who went on extensive travels with several animals, not just one. These mobile menageries were the beginnings of the zoo.

The female dancers still common in the Middle Ages, a description that often meant acrobats, disappeared in the early modern period. This vocation had an exceedingly bad reputation of immorality, which caused it to die out in the 16th century, when the culture of medieval brothels also vanished. In keeping with the general trend of suppressing independent women's work, entertainment became in the early modern period a domain of men, notwithstanding the occasional female instrumental virtuoso and female singers. With respect to the women's parts in the traveling theater that arose in the late 16th century, these theaters, to avoid suspicions of immorality, initially had men play the female parts. In general, German actresses, who existed since the end of the 17th century, had a much harder time than their counterparts from Italy, Spain, France, and England. They enjoyed no protection from the high nobility and the courts, quite apart from the fact that courts preferred foreign performers, prior to the development of permanent theaters. At the end of the 18th century, a permanent theater culture emerged in many residential cities, which over the long term transformed the traveling troupes into a manifestation of lower popular culture. Around the same time there arose in some large cities – though with less impact over the long term than the theater – a stationary form of entertainment that was no longer dependent on mobility. We encounter it for the first time in 1766 at the Prater in Vienna, but this kind of precursor to the circus had also taken shape outside the Millerntor in Hamburg. To fully appreciate the opening of the Prater in Vienna in 1766 as a cultural turning point, one must recall the thundering suspicions against useless pleasure in shows and entertainments that are so abundant in the territorial decrees after the 16th century. To be sure, the players who worked at the Prater had to obtain permits in the traditional ways in line with the requirements set by the authorities. The goal – which was also in line with traditional patterns – was to transform a wandering profession into a stationary one. However, the actions by the authorities were merely a response to the assertiveness of the entertainers who had been looked down upon for a long time. What the authorities had denounced for two and a half centuries as idleness was now taken seriously as having positive repercussions for the better society. In Book Two of *Wilhelm Meisters Lehrjahre*, Goethe describes the performance of rope-walkers and jumpers, and what has fascinated people at fairs since time immemorial, namely, the potential of the human body, which was never realized under the constraints of everyday life. And Goethe already had an inkling that the tricks of the acrobats had set in motion a development that would lead to modern gymnastics.

The admittedly somewhat daring suggestion that modern gymnastics derived from the artistry of early modern acrobatics gains credibility from a contemporaneous development. Classical music from at least the 1700s had drawn on "folkloristic" motifs. However, these so-called folk songs were often based not on something created by the "common people" but were the inventions of traveling musicians.

The range of performances included the flexible exploitation of new opportunities. The discovery of the New World and the intensifying commercial contacts with Africa revealed a previously unknown richness of the animal world. Beginning in the 17th century, performers took advantage of this by buying exotic animals, especially in Amsterdam and Genoa. They traveled the lands with these creatures, not shying away from the long trek all the way to Russia. All indications are that these animals were well treated, though not in a species-appropriate way; after all, they were the very livelihood of the traveling entertainers. Old animals were frequently sold at considerable profit. If zoos and circuses owe their beginnings to princely menageries, they also were influenced by the traveling exhibitors of exotic animals.

The traveling entertainers of the early modern period were always alert to new possibilities for earning a living. When "taking the waters" became increasingly popular with the better society in the 18th century, groups of traveling musicians responded and "spa music" (*Kurmusiken*) and "well music" (*Brunnenmusiken*) were born. Because of the difference in external description, these were not like the separate spa orchestras that would emerge in the 19th century; the wandering troupes of musicians who played before better society were considered traveling folk.

One can imagine that many musicians, players, jugglers, and acrobats, seeking protection from the dangers of the open road, would travel in the company of other groups of itinerant folk, such as peddlers and hawkers. And the musicians from Savoy, on their long journeys through southern Germany, would probably have sought the company of "Welsh chimney sweeps," of lemon and sour orange merchants, or of Swiss "marmot fat-makers" (*Murmeltier-Schmalzler*, marmots were in fact a source of food). The situation was different with those singers, actors, and acrobats who depended on the protection of and proximity to better society. They

had to be concerned about an "honorable" appearance, which included good clothes, respectable accommodations, and, not least, refined manners.

Erchenbrecher, Boris. "Zum Wandel des komischen Gaukler, Sänger, Komödianten in der Frühen Neuzeit, untersucht an ausgewählten regionalen Beispielen." *Hannoversche Geschichtsblätter* N.F. 50 (1996): 31–51.

Irsigler, Franz, and Arnold Lassotta. *Bettler und Gaukler, Dirnen und Henker. Außenseiter in einer mittelalterlichen Stadt; Köln 1300–1600*. 10th ed. Munich, 2004.

Roeck, Bernd. *Außenseiter, Randgruppen, Minderheiten. Fremde im Deutschland der frühen Neuzeit*. Göttingen, 1993.

Schubert, Ernst. *Alltag im Mittelalter. Natürliches Lebensumfeld und menschliches Miteinander*. Darmstadt, 2002.

Schubert, Ernst. "Latente Mobilität und bedingte Seßhaftigkeit im Spätmittelalter." *IMIS-Beiträge* (2002), no 20: 45–67.

Cross-references: Germany; Alpine Chimney Sweeps in Western, Central, and Southern Europe from the 16th to the Early 20th Century; Comici dell'arte in Europe in the Early Modern Period; English Comedians in Europe in the Early Modern Period: The Example of the Netherlands; German Itinerant Merchants from the Münsterland in Northern, Western, and Central Europe in the 18th and 19th Centuries

MUSLIM BROTHERHOODS IN SOUTHEASTERN EUROPE SINCE THE EARLY MODERN PERIOD

Valeria Heuberger

Through the expansion of the Ottomans into southeastern Europe from the end of the 14th century, members of Dervish orders, as representatives of Sufism, a mystical strain of Islam, wandered into the Balkan region. Here they played an important role in the Islamization of the various population groups of the region. These orders had their origin mostly in modern-day Iran, Afghanistan, and central Asia. They showed great diversity in their structures, doctrines, and rituals, in many cases while incorporating elements of pre-Islamic, shamanistic, Hindu, or Christian faith and practice. Almost all of them were hierarchically structured communities gathered around a master; some, for example, the Baktashiye order under the Albanians, were rooted above all in the countryside. Others, like the Qadiriya and the Mevleviye orders, tended to be found in the urban area, in the upper class, or among tradesmen. With the spread of the various orders in the Balkan region, not only did their faith become rooted in the local population but their leadership stratum was also made up increasingly of autochthonous Slavs or Albanians.

The various Dervish orders had very diverse religious-spiritual orientations. Alongside hierarchically structured communities with convents and attached religious schools and guest houses, which were also open to non-Muslims, there were also Dervishes who were not organized into brotherhoods and who wandered about as mystics, ascetics, and miracle healers. Characteristic for some orders, for example, the Bektashiye, was a strong orientation toward Shi'ite Islam or its elements. This led repeatedly to the persecution and suppression of these brotherhoods by representatives of official Sunni Islam, which was the state religion in the Ottoman Empire. Added to this was an occasional socio-revolutionary attitude that regarded the Ottoman rulers and their state as corrupt, or currents that drifted into sectlike offshoots. One example of this is a branch of the Malamatiya order, which established itself in the 16th century in Bosnia. One of the spiritual leaders, Hamza Bali, who was himself from Bosnia, was executed in Istanbul.

Dervishes had frequently come into the Balkan areas as "warriors of the faith" in Ottoman military units. Both during their lifetimes and after their deaths, they were venerated by the local population, among them also non-Muslims, since miraculous powers and deeds were often attributed to them. Their tombs became pilgrimage sites for non-Muslims, too, since the cult surrounding these warriors of the faith and saints was often linked to already existing Christian – and even pre-Christian – cult sites. This syncretism is characteristic of popular religion in southeastern Europe. Some of the brotherhoods had strong ties to institutions of the Ottoman Empire; that was true, for example, of the Bektashiye order and the elite units of the Janissaries. In addition, there was a close relationship between certain orders and trade guilds, evident in the guild rules or the use of certain Suras of the Koran in certain work processes.

The centuries-long rule of the Ottomans in the Balkan region had a formative influence on the shape of the urban space. Buildings benefiting the general public – such as bridges, fountains, and soup kitchens – were financed through pious foundations, and the type of the "Turkish city on the Balkans" emerged. Brotherhoods also played a role in this, since convents of Dervishes and associated buildings additionally enriched the cityscape with its Ottoman-oriental influence. For example, the Ottoman governor in Bosnia, Isa-Beg Isakovic, erected a meetinghouse (*tekke*) of the Mevleviye order in Sarajevo in 1462. Other orders represented in Bosnia as well as in the entire Balkan region under Ottoman rule, some existing to this day, were the Qadiriya, with its main centers in the 16th and 17th centuries in Sarajevo, Travnik, Jajce, and Zvornik, and the Rifa'iya, Halvetiye, and Naqshbandiya orders.

The influence of the brotherhoods in the Ottoman Empire gradually declined in the 19th century, even though the Bektashiye order played an important role in the emerging national movement of the Albanians. The communist takeover in most states of southeastern Europe after 1945 brought prohibitions and restrictions for all religious communities. For example, the Dervish orders were officially outlawed in Yugoslavia in 1952, though they continued to exist underground. A renaissance of Islam and the brotherhoods began in 1970, and 1974 saw the founding of an Alliance of Islamic Dervish Orders in Yugoslavia (SIDRA,

Savez Islamskih Derviskih Redova Alijje u SFRJ), which changed its name to ZIDRA (Zajednica Islamskih Derviskih Redova Alijje) in 1979. However, the orders continued to be regarded with suspicion by Belgrade, since in the case of the Bektashiye among the Albanians they were associated with demands for more autonomy for Kosovo; the official Islamic institutions, in Bosnia-Herzegovina as well as Macedonia, also regarded the brotherhoods as not always in compliance with the norms of Islam. However, this dichotomy between "Orthodox Islam" and "popular Islam" had already been around since the founding of the brotherhoods in the Middle Ages and was not a 20th-century phenomenon. In the middle of the 1980s, estimates put the number of followers of Dervish orders in Yugoslavia at around 50,000, among whom the Kosovo-Albanians of the Bektashiye order were dominant. Of the 70 Dervish meetinghouses in Yugoslavia in the 1980s, fully 58 were in Kosovo, 10 in Macedonia, and 7 in Bosnia-Herzegovina.

The conflicts and wars that erupted in the 1990s in Bosnia-Herzegovina, Kosovo, and Macedonia led in general to a stronger interest in Islam among Balkan Muslims, and, connected with it, in the brotherhoods, which for centuries have represented a specific current among the multitudinous forms of Islam in southeastern Europe.

Balić, Smail. *Das unbekannte Bosnien. Europas Brücke zur islamischen Welt.* Cologne, 1992.

Duijzings, Ger. *Religion and the Politics of Identity in Kosovo.* London, 2000.

Frembgen, Jürgen Wasim. *Reise zu Gott. Sufis und Derwische im Islam.* Munich, 2000.

Thirlwall Norris, Harry. *Islam in the Balkans. Religion and Society between Europe and the Arab World.* London, 1993.

Cross-reference: Southeastern Europe

NETHERLANDISH (FLEMISH) TEXTILE WORKERS IN 16TH AND 17TH-CENTURY ENGLAND

Raingard Eßer

The great confessional struggles of the 16th and 17th centuries brought far-reaching social and political upheavals to Europe. They led not only to the creation of new states – for example, the United Provinces of the Netherlands – but also profoundly altered the living conditions of burghers, peasants, artisans, and merchants. Next to the flight of French Huguenots following the revocation in 1685 of the Edict of Nantes (1598), the movement of Netherlandish exiles into the neighboring countries of England and Germany between 1550 and the beginning of the 17th century was the most important migration event in the period of confessionalization. While the French refugees of the late 17th century already found relatively established political, social, and religious structures, the Netherlanders encountered a situation of transition from late medieval to early modern economic forms and social structures, especially with respect to the system of guilds.

In this phase of transformation the exiles were able to influence many situations, though this often led to tensions within the host society. The exiles, collectively referred to in England as "strangers," came primarily from the organized and economically highly developed textile regions of the Spanish Netherlands (Flanders and Brabant). At home and abroad, they were considered pioneers in the introduction of new, attractive product palettes, such as the so-called "New Draperies," and luxury goods such as trims and socks. Another feature that characterized them was the development of "modern" production methods. They used these skills, which were attractive to the economic elite of the host society, to bargain for favorable settlement conditions. Until the 1970s, scholarship emphasized the particular importance of this immigration for the modernization of the English textile industry. That view has been revised in the last few years. Scholars now highlight the innovative impulses in English industry and have questioned what was previously assumed to be the early capitalist character of the Dutch economy.

The extent of the migration out of the Spanish Netherlands can be only estimated. Contemporaries, like the historian Emmanuel von Meteren, for example, spoke of about 100,000 families who fled in the second half of the 16th century. However, an average family size of five persons would yield the improbable number of 500,000 refugees. Modern research has put the number of those who left their homeland between 1525 and 1650 at 30,000 to 50,000.

Little of any certainty can be said about the relative weight of religious, political, and economic motives behind the exodus. An important backdrop to the migration was undoubtedly the coercive measures against followers of the Calvinist movement, which was gaining ground in the textile centers of Flanders especially in the 1560s. Added to this was the brutal suppression of political opposition to the centralizing policy of Philip II by the royal governors (especially the Duke of Alva). However, of particular importance to the exodus was surely also the economic weakness in the textile sector from the 1560s to the 1580s, which was caused by political unrest and difficulties finding markets for its products. The trade embargo between the Netherlands and England in 1563–4 and a food crisis caused by an interruption in grain shipments from the Baltic region, the result of the Danish-Swedish conflict over who would rule the Baltic Sea region, led to a strong flow of migration in the second half of the 1560s.

The provinces of the Netherlands and the centralized Spanish power had been locked in war since the 1570s, and the economic damage from this conflict was felt heavily in an economy dependent on export. Additional factors in the emigration were the overpopulation of the Netherlands and fluctuating inflation rates in the 16th century. The precarious political and economic situation of the Netherlands hit the workers in the textile sector especially hard, and they formed the largest group among those who left. However, after the capture of Antwerp in 1585, there was a growing number of merchants and entrepreneurs among the emigrants. Not infrequently they were able to transfer their capital to the host country and invest it profitably. In many cases, business connections with the homeland could be maintained.

There is very little solid information about how long the immigrants stayed. The sources do not reveal whether the refugees left their homeland for good, returned to Flanders and Brabant at a later time, or migrated to the economically more successful northern Netherlands after the consolidation of the United Provinces. The study of the movement of émigrés between the various Netherlandish communities in England or Germany is also in its infancy, apart from a few exceptions limited to high-profile members of the refugee group such as preachers or intellectuals.

The initial place of refuge for the émigrés was London, where a first officially recognized and legally secured community of foreigners appeared as early as 1550. However, it came to a forced end only a few years later with the death of the Protestant king Edward VI and the subsequent accession to the throne of the Catholic Mary I Tudor. The émigrés were expelled from the country because of their Protestant leanings. It was only after Mary's death in 1558 that Netherlandish refugees arrived again in England. Popular destinations were London, which continued to receive the largest share of the refugees, and the southern English cities of Dover, Yarmouth, Southampton, Canterbury, Colchester, and Sandwich. The most important Netherlandish community in England after London was founded in Norwich in 1565. There was no settlement in rural regions.

The most significant social, political, and religious institutions of the émigrés were the Calvinist congregations, whose establishment was in many cases the required precondition for the admission of Netherlanders into a city. For example, the official letter of invitation from the community of Sandwich to the Netherlanders demanded membership in the foreign church. Similar stipulations were made by the councilors in other émigré cities. The organization of congregations created an instrument of control for both the immigrants and the local population.

Jurisdiction over their countrymen as well as supervision of the ecclesiastical and thus the social discipline of their fellow brothers and sisters was left in the hands of the consistories of the foreign churches. Poor relief, the care of orphans, and education likewise remained internal matters for the émigré community. As for the city governments, in the preachers and elders of the congregation they had someone to go to for all matters concerning the foreigners. However, scholars have discovered that a segment of the Netherlanders did not join the foreign congregations. Especially in London, many immigrants lived outside the Netherlandish network of churches. In conflicts with city governments over economic issues, the leading members of the foreign communities served as spokesmen for the émigrés. Various bodies were established to supervise training in the Netherlandish textile trade. These organizations mediated legal quarrels over the training of apprentices and the size of businesses and represented their countrymen before the English authorities in conflicts between the English and the Netherlanders.

Concerning the economic expectations of the English host society regarding the settlement of the Netherlanders, the picture for the second half of the 16th century is quite mixed. Native textile workers not infrequently complained about a lack of cooperation of the newcomers: the foreigners were not willing to pass their knowledge and skills on to the English, but recruited their apprentices from their own ranks, contrary to the official agreements. On the other hand, the supply industry of the textile sector benefited from their presence. On the whole, the urban economic elite showed itself rather generous toward enterprises that departed from the traditional guild system. They pointed to the general economic upswing that had supposedly been achieved through the Netherlanders, even if it occasionally came at the expense of domestic competition. The regulation limiting the Netherlanders to economic sectors not already occupied by the English had to be abandoned fairly soon. The Netherlanders developed their own economic infrastructure and, in violation of prohibitions to the contrary, they supplied their own communities with food and other articles of daily life. In a number of cities this situation led to sporadic attacks on the foreigners, but the city governments were generally quick to suppress them.

When it comes to the self-image of the exiles, two forms can be identified. On the one hand, many Netherlanders maintained contact with their land of origin. Studies of wills and letters have shown a strong loyalty to friends and family members in the old homeland that extended into the second generation. On the other hand, in the second generation, in particular, contact with the native population increased considerably. The number of English men and women who became spouses, godparents, and business partners of the émigrés grew especially at the turn of the 16th to the 17th century. The émigré church lost its importance as a center of Netherlandish identity after the 1620s and 1630s. Dutchmen of the second generation were no longer willing to support the financing of a separate church in addition to the taxes and dues they had to pay the cities. However, in spite of attacks by the conservative Anglican archbishop William Laud in the 1630s, the institution of the foreign church remained intact – with declining membership – in many cases until the 19th century, in London even to this day. In spite of occasional xenophobic attacks, one can speak of a successful integration of the Netherlandish immigrants in England. The Netherlanders were allowed to cultivate their identity of origin and often set the pace of their integration.

Backhouse, Marcel. *The Flemish and Walloon Communities at Sandwich during the Reign of Elizabeth I (1561–1603).* Brussels, 1995.

Eßer, Raingard. *Niederländische Exulanten im England des späten 16. und frühen 17. Jahrhunderts.* Berlin, 1996.

Goose, Nigel, and Lien Bich Luu, eds. *Immigrants in Tudor and Early Stuart England.* Brighton, 2005.

Grell, Ole Peter. *Dutch Calvinism in Early Stuart London: The Dutch Church in Austin Friars 1603–1642.* Leiden, 1989.

Luu, Lien Bich. *Immigrants and the Industries in London 1500–1700.* Aldershot, 2005.

Pettegree, Andrew. *Foreign Protestant Communities in Sixteenth Century London.* Oxford, 1986.

Spicer, Andrew. *The French-speaking Reformed Community and Their Church in Southampton, 1567–c.1620.* Stroud, 1997.

Cross-references: Great Britain; The Netherlands; Dutch Calvinist Refugees in Europe since the Early Modern Period; Huguenots in Europe since the Early Modern Period

ORTHODOX MONKS ON MOUNT ATHOS SINCE THE EARLY MODERN PERIOD

Wolfgang Nikolaus Rappert

About 80 kilometers east-southeast of the Greek city of Thessaloniki, the Athos peninsula extends into the Aegean Sea, 50 kilometers long and 10 kilometers at its widest point. The highest elevation, from which the peninsula derives its name, is Mount Athos at 2,033 meters. At the beginning of the 21st century, the peninsula, home to monks since the ninth century, has 20 large, fortress-like monasteries. Outside their walls are affiliated settlements: 12 village-like *sketes* and several so-called *kalyves* (houses for several monks), *kellia* (cells, somehow similar to farmhouses and with small chapels), *kathismata* (small houses for single monks), and *hesychasteria* (hermitages). Today, all monasteries prescribe a regulated daily schedule for their monks; private property is not permitted. Only in a few outlying locations are monks able to control their time and property.

From the time of the Byzantine Empire through Turkish rule to today, Athos has always been politically and religiously self-governing. Since the Treaty of Lausanne in 1923, Athos has been under the suzerainty of Greece, is protected by the Greek constitution, and is administered jointly by all monasteries on the basis of a separate charter: a four-member Holy Administration (Iera Epistasia) exercises executive power, while legislate power rests with a 20-member Holy Community (Iera Koinotita) on which every monastery is represented and which meets three times a week. In addition, twice a year the 20-member assembly of the abbots (Synaxis) meets as the highest legislative and judicial body. Spiritual oversight is in the hands of the Ecumenical Patriarch of Constantinople; secular oversight rests with a governor who reports to the Greek Foreign Ministry. The administrative seat is in the centrally located town of Karyes. Women are not allowed to enter Athos. This prohibition on entry (*abaton*), which probably existed from the very beginning, was first confirmed by an imperial decree in 833 and was subsequently renewed by additional imperial decrees, ordinances (*firmane*) of the Sultans, and by the Greek Constitution.

Economically, the monasteries were initially supported by the Byzantine emperors and by the Bulgarian and Serbian czars. After the Turks had conquered these states, the principalities of Moldova and Wallachia guaranteed the economical survival of Athos in the 15th, 16th, and 17th centuries. In return, Athos enriched the lands from which the monks came spiritually and culturally. Today, Athos is economically self-sufficient through agriculture and forestry, fishing and viticulture. The production of incense, wood carving, and icon painting brings in additional revenues.

From the outset, the monks were recruited not only from Greek but also Russian, Georgian, Serbian, Bulgarian, and Romanian regions with a Byzantine ecclesiastical tradition. In the early period there was also a Benedictine monastery of the Roman-Latin tradition with monks from Sicily, but it soon died out as a result of the increasing ecclesiastical tensions between Rome and Byzantium. During Ottoman rule over Athos (1430–1912), the monks were considered citizens of the Ottoman Empire. Most of the regions from which the monks originated (Greece, Serbia, Bulgaria, and Romania) were under Turkish rule, which meant that migration to the monasteries from those areas was not impeded by political conditions. Movement from territories outside the Ottoman Empire was more difficult: the number of Georgians in Athos had already declined precipitously in the 14th century when the Mongols swept over Georgia.

The influx of Russians to the Russian monastery of Panteleimon, which was still flourishing in the early modern period, was severely impeded from the 17th to the early 19th century by the Russo-Turkish wars. As a result, monks from Greek parts of the Ottoman Empire as from the vassal principalities of Moldova and Wallachia dominated Athos during this time. The northern areas' initially unsuccessful Greek uprising against the Turks in 1821, in which some Athonites also took part, led to the exodus of many monks from Athos and an economic crisis for those remaining. In that situation, the Greeks who were at the time predominant at the Panteleimon monastery once again tried to attract Russian novices, who could contribute to the economic revival. The Russian presence on Athos was therefore strong once again after 1839 (soon, in the eyes of some Greeks, too strong). In 1912, Athos was occupied by the Greeks. Responding to Russian demands, the Russian monks were placed under the authority of the Russian ambassador in Constantinople in civil matters and under that of the Russian Synod in spiritual ones. After the October Revolution in 1917, there was hardly any influx of Russian monks for many decades.

Since 1923, monks who are not from Greece must renounce their citizenship and apply for a residence permit from both the Greek government and the Ecumenical Patriarchate, to whose jurisdiction they are subject. If their application is accepted, they are given Greek citizenship without any further formalities – something that could impair their ties to their countries of origin; especially in the decades of the cold war, visa regulations made trips back home difficult. As a result, the number of non-Greeks on Athos declined. For example, between 1920 and 1940, the number of Russian monks in the Panteleimon monastery dropped from 800 to 215, in the Russian Andreas *skyte* from 150 to 45, in the Russian Elias hermitage from 160 to 52, and in the Russian *kellia* from around 1,000 to about 200. By December 1965, the number of monks on Athos as a whole had dropped to a mere 1,491: 1,290 Greeks, 62 Russians, 17 Bulgarians, 28 Serbs, and 94 Romanians. Since then, however there has been a substantial increase: until the opening of the iron curtain mostly through the influx of Greek monks; thereafter also through the renewed migration of non-Greeks.

Looked at from the outside, Athos seems like a single entity – which is why one can refer to the inhabitants uniformly as Athonites or Hagiorites, that is, individuals who have chosen to live on the Holy Mountain for religious reasons. Internally, the above-described settlement structure gave rise to a more differentiated picture, which is reflected in different customs at the various monasteries (e.g., the language of liturgy and everyday life; icons in the style of different schools of painting), depending on the national origins of the monks.

A diachronous continuity of the various monastic communities was created by the presence of several generations of monks, through which the liturgical, spiritual, and cultural customs of the individual monasteries were passed down between the generations and new members were integrated into the community. An essential factor of integration is the daily routine, which strictly regulates the times of personal and communal prayer, work, meals, and periods of rest. During the first few months, a new arrival – in most cases not yet a monk but a layman – practices the rhythm of monastic life. By assuming the monastic habit, he is eventually accepted into the novitiate, a trial period lasting two to three years during which he is assigned the most humble jobs and is barred from corresponding with the outside world. Monastic ordination makes him a full member of the community, in which he can now develop his spiritual, artisanal, and intellectual abilities. However, the most important tasks of the monk are constant prayer and meditation. After a longer period of time in the community of the larger monastery, the monk is free to remain within the community or move into a *skyte* or hermitage affiliated with his monastery. At the beginning of the 21st century, the average age of Athonite monks was around 45 to 50. Twenty percent of the monks had a university degree (about half of those in theology). Less than 2% had failed to complete their primary education.

The Athonite monks leave their mark on the Orthodox world by the model they provide in their lived imitation of Christ, as well as in their encounters with the thousands of pilgrims who visit them each year on Athos, or on their own travels. They offer advice in confessional conversations, but influence is also exerted by the published writings of the monks. With the icons they create, they reach people all over the world.

Billetta, Rudolf. *Der Heilige Berg Athos in Zeugnissen aus sieben Jahrhunderten.* 5 vols. Vienna, 1992–4.

Lemerle, Paul, ed. *Archives de l'Athos, fondées par Gabriel Millet.* 20 vols. Paris, 1937–8.

Cross-references: Russia and Belarus; Southeastern Europe

PAKISTANIS IN GREAT BRITAIN SINCE THE 1950S

Alison Shaw

The immigration and integration of Pakistanis in Great Britain can be divided into three partially overlapping phases: male labor migration during the 1950s and 1960s; family reunification from the mid-1960s through the 1980s; and transnational marriage from the 1980s to the present day. Britain's Pakistani population increased from about 10,000 in 1951 to about 747,000 in 2001, according to the census from that year. Pakistanis now comprise over 1.2% of the total British population of 60 million and 43% of Britain's 1.6 million Muslims. Over the past 50 years, British life has been influenced by various aspects of south Asian culture – in cuisine, music, and popular comedy, for example – while its south Asian minorities have achieved varying levels of socioeconomic and cultural integration within British society. Pakistanis, along with Bangladeshis, remain the most economically and socially marginalized of Britain's south Asian minorities, reflecting, among other factors, their low socioeconomic starting point in the UK, low levels of female employment, and their continuing socioeconomic commitments in Pakistan.

South Asians have traveled between Britain and the Indian subcontinent since the early days of British colonialism. The first Pakistanis to enter Britain in substantial numbers were men who came as economic migrants in the 1950s and 1960s from what was West Pakistan (since 1947) and, in 1971, became Pakistan after civil war with East Pakistan (which became Bangladesh). In the 1950s, the British government actively encouraged migration from its former colonies in south Asia and the Caribbean to meet labor shortages in the industrial cities of London and the Midlands and in the textile towns of Yorkshire and Lancashire after the Second World War. As British subjects under the 1948 British Nationality Act, Commonwealth immigrants at that time had unrestricted right of entry.

Many of the Pakistani migrants had had some previous contact with Britain through army and navy service. Attracted by the laborer's wage in Britain – over 30 times higher than the wage for similar work in Pakistan – they came mainly from districts in the northern Punjab, such as Jhelum, Gujrat, Gujranwala, Rawalpindi, Attock, and Mirpur in Pakistan-held Kashmir, as well as from districts in central Punjab, such as Faisalabad, Sahiwal, and Sargodha. All these areas were bound by a common history of migration that was the result of British colonialism. Viewing their stay in Great Britain as temporary, the Pakistani migrants were essentially sojourners or international commuters who usually lived in shared rented accommodation provided by Pakistani landlords and remitted money to support relatives in Pakistan or to sponsor another kinsman's migration. Migrants also made periodic return visits home, sometimes risking their jobs in Britain. The resulting pattern of chain migration accounts for the district- and sometimes village-specific characteristics of most Pakistani settlements in Britain, which persists to this day.

Pakistani emigration to Britain significantly increased with the prospect of stricter immigration controls in the 18 months before the introduction of the 1962 Commonwealth Immigrants Act. It was also accelerated, in Mirpur, by the construction of the Mangla Dam, which displaced more than 110,000 people, many of whom joined relatives in Britain. The 1962 Act restricted Commonwealth immigration but permitted wives and dependent children (if under 18 and accompanied by their mothers) to join husbands or fathers already in Britain. They also received the right to apply for British citizenship. Many Pakistani men made use of this opportunity and brought their wives and children to Britain. More Pakistani children were subsequently born in Britain and family size was generally larger than the UK average.

The second phase of immigration continued throughout the 1970s and 1980s, eventually transforming the transitory all-male settlements into family-based communities. Reflecting earlier migration patterns, the largest Pakistani populations, according to the 2001 census, are found in Birmingham (100,000) in the West Midlands and Bradford (70,000) in the north. Although precise figures are unavailable, people from Mirpur district in Pakistan-held Kashmir probably comprise about half of the British Pakistani population. With family reunification and new childbirth, the Pakistani population increased from 25,000 in 1961 to 119,000 in 1971, more than doubling again in the following decade. This did not, however, necessarily signal a commitment to adopt the lifestyle of the local population; on the contrary, the arrival of wives and children helped reestablish some significant features of Pakistani family life and culture in the new environment.

In keeping with family understandings of *purdah* (female modesty) and because of their poor knowledge of English and preoccupation with the care of preschool children, many Pakistani wives did not seek paid work outside the home. They were able to overcome their initial isolation, however, by quickly establishing social contact with other Pakistani women, by drawing on preexisting ties of kin and village, and making contact with new Pakistani neighbors. Women's networks provided mutual support and opportunities for shared religious activities including Qur'an readings at home and celebrations of Islamic festivals, such as *Id ul fitr* and *Id ul Zoha*.

The presence of wives and children also brought into sharp focus migrants' concerns about the potentially corrupting influences of Western social and sexual mores on

British-raised Pakistani children. One response was the establishment of Qur'an classes for children at local mosques through family- and community-based initiatives. By the 1980s, mosques had been established in most towns where Pakistanis had settled. All major Pakistani religious movements and organizations are represented in Britain today. Special state provisions for Muslim pupils (providing *halaal* meat in school meals, exempting students from sex education, etc.) and the issue of separate Muslim schools have been increasingly debated in the public domain. By 2002, there were about 50 mostly private Muslim schools in Britain. Pakistanis participate in local British politics: Bradford, in 2004, had 13 Muslim councilors and has had two Muslim Lord Mayors. Bradford also houses offices of all of Pakistan's major political parties.

In the 1980s and early 1990s, as the older children of pioneer-generation migrants reached marriageable age, their marriages to men and women from Pakistan marked the beginning of a significant new phase of migration that has continued to the present day. In 2000, over 10,000 Pakistani nationals gained entry clearance to join partners with British citizenship. This type of spousal immigration is a south Asian and particularly Pakistani phenomenon, with Pakistan sending more migrants than India and Bangladesh combined. Whereas wives of pioneer-generation migrants had initially expected to remain in Pakistan, today's spouses from the subcontinent usually expect to join their partners in Britain once they have obtained entry clearance. The number of interethnic marriages between Pakistanis of both sexes and persons of British descent is negligible.

Transnational Pakistani marriages are often consanguineous, reflecting the preference for marriage within the kin group in Pakistan (as well as in the Middle East, North Africa, and elsewhere in south Asia, where first cousin marriage is a significant minority marriage pattern). Recent surveys suggest there are more first cousin marriages among second- and third-generation British Pakistanis than among the pioneer generation. This reflects the continuing strength of emotional and socioeconomic ties between siblings living continents apart, ties that migrants seek to cement through their children's marriages. Younger British Pakistanis stress the value of marrying someone who is known and who understands the culture and religion of their homeland. For some incoming grooms, migration also offers opportunities to provide economic support to kin in Pakistan. In the UK, arranged transnational marriage has generated controversy on grounds of human rights following cases of forced marriage. Marriage to a first cousin has also been criticized on grounds of elevated risk of genetic problems in children. Negative British stereotypes of Pakistanis also include the perception that they "keep to themselves," fraudulently use state benefits, or are Islamic fundamentalists.

Most British Pakistanis retain links in Pakistan, often making periodic visits "back home." Retired pioneer-generation men commonly travel between Britain and Pakistan, living in houses financed by remittances, and expect to be buried in Pakistan. The bodies of the deceased are still routinely returned to Pakistan for burial, although women may expect to be buried in Britain, where their children live and where deceased infants and children are usually buried in the Muslim sections of local British cemeteries. Transnational connections are also maintained by younger UK-raised Pakistanis, especially those with spouses from Pakistan. Some of these couples live and raise families in Pakistan, making periodic visits to the UK. These continuing transnational links are likely to help maintain connections to Pakistan in generations to come.

There are approximately 1 million Indians (Hindus and Sikhs) and approximately 1 million south Asian Muslims (750,000 Pakistanis and 250,000 Bangladeshis) in Britain. Yet national surveys and census data indicate that there are far fewer (by almost 50%) Pakistanis and Bangladeshis than Indians in the UK labor force. The south Asian Muslim population has a younger age structure than other south Asian groups because family reunification occurred later. The proportion of highly qualified Pakistani professionals in the labor force is also low, as is the participation of Muslim women, although the number of young employed Muslim women is increasing. These factors affect the relative wealth of the Pakistani population as a whole.

Comparisons across ethnic groups reveal the relative economic disadvantage of British Pakistanis but conceal socioeconomic differences within the Pakistani population that reflect differences in social background and regional variations in the British economic climate and corresponding economic opportunities. The most disadvantaged Pakistani groups tend to be of rural Punjabi or Pakistan-held Kashmiri origins who in the first generation had poor social class resources and who comprise perhaps half of the Pakistani population. This is reflected in comparatively low, though improving, levels of education among Pakistani children, despite significant gender and regional differences and the fact that Pakistanis are well represented among university entrants. Families living in the north were also affected by the economic decline and rising unemployment of some inner-city areas. When combined with relatively limited opportunities for educational and social mobility, this situation prompted some families to move to the south. These factors have impeded the social mobility of the younger generation, contributing to the alienation of young British Pakistanis noted in Home Office reports on the riots in Oldham in May 2001, which spread to Burnley, Leeds, and Bradford. Involving clashes between Asian Muslim youth and the police, these were reportedly the most violent instances of civil unrest to have occurred in Britain for 20 years.

Pakistani migration has always included some people from the educated middle classes. In Manchester, a sizable Pakistani middle class, which includes expatriate representatives of Pakistani commercial interests, has influenced social dynamics in the city. Successful British entrepreneurs represent a range of backgrounds, including the Arain, traditionally a caste of vegetable growers from Faisalabad district that

Students from Nigeria, Pakistan, England, and Scotland at the faculty of neuropsychology, University of Edinburgh (*ullstein bild*).

lived in Indian Punjab before the waves of flight and expulsion that occurred in the course of Indian and Pakistani independence in 1947. In such industrial towns and cities as Glasgow, Manchester, Birmingham, Newcastle, and Oxford, favorable opportunities for business enterprise, often facilitated by redundancy pay from factory closures and interest-free loans from fellow migrants, enabled ventures into the *halaal* meat trade, ethnic food stores, and fabric and clothing trades. Manchester, Preston, and Rochdale have become important centers of Pakistani-run wholesaling and manufacturing.

Pakistanis have established a niche as landlords in the housing rental market, especially in university cities with student populations, and they dominate the taxi businesses of many British cities. This sometimes dangerous but lucrative work offers flexible working hours compatible with domestic and family commitments. Many Pakistanis have also invested in new properties and sometimes in business ventures in Pakistan, often in cities near their villages of origin rather than in the villages themselves. Their continuing commitments in Pakistan, including support of relatives, are important in understanding the relative wealth of the Pakistani population in Britain. In 2003–4, remittances from the UK to Pakistan conducted through banks amounted to approximately $334 million. By contrast, south Asians who have emigrated from east Africa to the UK and who have fewer direct links with Pakistan have invested all their savings in the UK.

As members of the Muslim community (*umma*), British Pakistanis have a transnational religious identity oriented toward both Pakistan and the Middle East. Today, modern transport facilitates the pilgrimage to Mecca (*haj*) and other visits to Islam's holy sites. Since the 1980s, issues associated with British Pakistanis' religious and cultural identity have received increased public attention. The Rushdie affair of 1989, including the anti-Rushdie demonstration in London and television broadcasts showing Bradford Muslims burning Rushdie's book *The Satanic Verses* brought the previously low public profile of Pakistanis and Muslims into the political spotlight. These events generated considerable anti-Muslim

sentiment and gave Pakistanis a sharper sense of their religious distinctiveness.

Pakistanis have since contended with several other international crises involving Muslims. They joined other British protestors against the first Gulf War (1990–1) and against the wars in Afghanistan (2002) and in Iraq (2003). Attacks on British Muslims increased dramatically after 11 September 2001 and again following the London bombings on 7 July 2005. The increasing perception of Islam in the UK as a political problem is reflected in the rise of Islamophobia and in the inclusion in the 2001 census, for the first time since 1871, of a question on religious affiliation.

Ballard, Roger, ed. *Desh Pardesh: The South Asian Presence in Britain*. London 1994.

Choudhury, Tufyal, ed. *Muslims in the UK: Policies for Engaged Citizens*. Budapest and New York, 2004.

Lewis, Philip. *Islamic Britain: Religion, Politics and Identity among British Muslims*. London, 1994.

Modood, Tariq, et al. *Ethnic Minorities in Britain: Diversity and Disadvantage*. London, 1997.

Shaw, Alison. *Kinship and Continuity: Pakistani Families in Britain*. London, 2000.

Werbner, Pnina. *The Migration Process: Capital, Gifts and Offerings among British Pakistanis*. Oxford, 1990.

Cross-references: Great Britain; Indian, Pakistani and Bangladeshi Migrants in Great Britain since 1947

PALATINES IN EUROPE SINCE THE 17TH CENTURY

Mark Häberlein

Between the late 17th century and the late 19th century, southwestern Germany was among the central European regions with the highest migratory activity. Until 1806, southwestern Germany was characterized by a multitude of small and tiny lordships – noble and knightly territories, territories of imperial cities, and monasteries under the direct suzerainty of the Holy Roman Empire. Larger, geographically more or less cohesive territorial units were formed by the Electoral Palatinate, the Duchy of Palatinate-Zweibrücken, the Prince-Bishopric of Speyer, the Duchy of Württemberg, the Margravates of Baden, and Habsburg Outer Austria. During the Napoleonic age, the many ecclesiastical and secular lordships were secularized or mediatized and were absorbed into larger territorial states: into the Grand Duchies of Baden and Hesse-Darmstadt, the Kingdoms of Württemberg and Bavaria, and Prussia's Rhine province. Between the 17th and the 19th centuries, hundreds of thousands left this region, which was politically fractured, confessionally fragmented, and had an economy structured around agriculture and small-scale trade and commerce. In many destination areas they became known as Palatines (*Pfälzer*), despite their quite varied regional origins.

The destination of the migration were the English colonies in North America, later the USA, as well as Great Britain and Ireland, but also Hungary (settlement in the Banat and Batschka) and Galicia, which belonged to the Habsburgs following the first division of Poland in 1772. Beginning in the early 1740s, King Frederick II of Prussia (1740–86) recruited settlers in southwestern Germany to colonize the Oderbruch and the lowlands of the Warthe and Netze. Numerous emigrants from the Electoral Palatinate, the Duchy of Zweibrücken, and neighboring territories settled in Pomerania, the Mark of Brandenburg, and in the Neumark in newly founded or already existing villages. Frederick's Prussia also pursued colonization projects along the lower Rhine: beginning in 1741 the settlement Pfalzdorf arose in the Duchy of Cleves; additional settlement in Cleves and the Kurmark followed in the 1760s. As late as the beginning of the 19th century, several thousand southwest Germans migrated to the provinces of South Prussia and New East Prussia, which had become Prussian after the second and third division of Poland (1793, 1795).

Russia, too, intensively recruited German colonists under Empress Catherine II (1762–96). By 1768, between 25,000 and 30,000 colonists, the majority from the Palatine region and Hessian territories, were settled in 104 confessionally largely homogeneous villages in the Volga region. A side current of this migratory movement was the reception of about 70 Palatine families on crown lands in Livonia (1766). Czar Alexander I (1801–25) continued this population policy: between 1804 and 1842, more than 11,000 families were brought to the Black Sea region and the southern Caucasus, after 1814 also to Bessarabia. Among them were more than 5,000 families from Württemberg and more than 2,000 from Baden and the Palatinate.

Denmark settled southwestern Germans in Jütland and Schleswig between 1759 and 1762. The officer Johann Kaspar von Thürriegel recruited several thousand Palatines for a colony in the Sierra Morena in Spain from 1767 to 1769. The Palatine settlement of Veltenhof was created in the Duchy of Brunswick in 1750. After the unification of the Palatinate and Bavaria (1777), several dozen Palatine families moved to the Bavarian Donaumoos. Failed settlement projects and the problems many migrants encountered in eastern, east-central, and southeastern Europe led to return migrations and in part to onward migrations, for example, from Ireland to North America or from Prussia to Russia.

On the whole, the character of the migrations changed from being predominantly an internal European migration before 1815 to a largely transatlantic emigration after 1830. In the 18th century, and still in the 19th, it was chiefly families and groups from rural or small-town regions that left. For the Palatine region, the first out migrations of groups are documented as early as the 1670s and 1680s. The beginning of the mass exodus of the 18th century was marked by the departure of 13,000 to 15,000 southwest Germans who set out for England after the extremely harsh winter of 1708–9, leaving behind a homeland that had already suffered from

LONDON: Printed for J. Baker, at the Black-Boy in Pater-Noster-Row. 1710.

Tent camp of the Palatinates (*Pfälzer*) in London, 1709/10 (*The State of the Palatines for Fifty Years Past to His Present Time [London, 1710]; anonymous leaflet, private ownership*).

the War of the Spanish Succession (1701–14). Their goal was the North American colonies, which were touted in writings like those of the Palatine minister Josua Harrsch (known as Kocherthal). Toward the end of the 19th century, the overseas migration of southwest Germans receded again in favor of internal migrations to the industrial centers of the German Reich. These migrants were for the most part single young men, whose share among the emigrants grew steadily.

In the discussion of what prompted the emigration in the 18th century, the following factors head the list: destruction from war, the burden of seigneurial forced labor and dues, a growing disparity between population growth and the possibilities of creating a livelihood, a shortage of agrarian resources, frequent crop failures, damage from game animals, and despotic behavior by the lord or ruler. For the 19th century as well, scholars point mostly to the symptoms of economic and social crisis in southwestern Germany: the progressive fragmentation of landholdings, pauperization, crises caused by inflationary prices, and a lack of economic alternatives. By contrast, religious and political motivations were the predominant driving force only among a minority of southwest German emigrants: the Palatine Mennonites who migrated to Pennsylvania and Galicia in the 18th century, the Württemberg Separatists who moved to the USA and Russia in the early 19th century, and the political activists who emigrated after the failed revolutions of 1848–9.

The migration policy of the authorities in the southwest varied in the 18th century. Those in Outer Austria and the territorial lords who were part of the Habsburg clientele in the Empire generally did not put any obstacles in the way of emigration to southeastern Europe, or even promoted it. Larger lordships, like the Margravates of Baden, Württemberg, and Palatinate-Zweibrücken, tried to keep wealthy subjects in the land. In addition, they siphoned off a considerable portion of the possessions of those departing – generally at least 20% to 25% – through manumission and departure taxes, as well as chancery, clerical, and other seigneurial fees, and in most cases those released from subject status were refused permission to return. With the adoption of the cameralist maxim that the wealth of a state depends on the number of its subjects and the rise in emigration, some territorial rulers took harsh measures against foreign recruitment after 1750 and prohibited emigration. In 1768, the states in the southwest even obtained an imperial edict that generally prohibited emigration to territories that were not part of the Empire. In general, however, such prohibitions had little effect: illegal departures presented a problem that most authorities were unable to control. In the early 19th century, the southwestern states initially continued the cameralist principles and responded to the waves of emigration with further bans. Beginning in the 1830s, under the influence of political and public discussions surrounding emigration and pauperism, the notion of protection moved to the fore. The state was now intent on enforcing a paternalistic obligation of caring for those who were leaving. At the height of the pauperism crisis between 1849 and 1855, Baden and Württemberg supported the departure of the poverty-stricken with state funds; many communities also financed the exodus of the "local poor" so they would no longer be the responsibility of the community's treasury.

In the English-speaking world, the German migrants were often referred to as Palatines across the board since the mass exodus of 1709, even though many migrants came from other territories. The court preacher of Prince George of Denmark, in a sermon delivered in London in 1710, spoke of the "so-called Palatines" who "wish to move to the so-called New World from all ends of Germany, but especially from the Palatinate." In addition to the actual importance of the Palatinate as a sending region, what gave rise to this external label were also the close political ties between the ruling house of the Palatinate and the English government, as well as the pioneering role played by the group around Kochertahl, which had emigrated to America via England as early as 1708. The frequently used formula of the "poor distressed Palatines," which seems to go back to Kocherthal, emphasized the misery of the migrants and their need for aid. The discussion about the Palatines in Parliament in London, in pamphlets, and in the press disseminated the term in the English-speaking world.

The English authorities were not prepared for the influx following the extremely cold winter of 1708–9 and housed most southwest German immigrants temporarily in tent cities near London. Around 3,000 Palatines were shipped off to New York in 1710, about 600 to the Carolinas. Another 3,000 were transported by the authorities to Ireland, and several hundred were settled in England or recruited for the army. About 4,000 returned to Germany, predominantly Catholics.

The label Palatines for the German immigrants and their descendants has survived until recent times especially in Ireland, even though the number of Palatines who settled in Ireland permanently was relatively small. In spite of support from the government, the majority soon left the island again: at the end of 1711, only 312 of the originally 821 families were still in the country. The largest group among those who stayed settled as tenants on the holdings of Protestant landlords in County Limerick, where they engaged in diversified

agriculture and processed hemp and flax. Since no pastors had accompanied the emigrants to Ireland, most joined the Anglican Church or, from the middle of the 18th century, the Methodist movement. Because of the confessional difference with the Catholic population and the loyalty of the Palatines toward the Anglo-Irish upper class, there was hardly any intermarriage or intensive social contact with members of the Gaelic majority. In spite of high rates of emigration and a gradual sociocultural integration, the Palatines were still perceived as a separate group by travelers and novelists as late as the middle of the 19th century, as exemplified, for example, in Gerald Griffin's 1842 novel *Suil Dhuv the Coiner*.

By contrast, in eastern, east-central, and southeastern Europe, the southwest German immigrants were often referred to as "Swabians." The Palatine origin of the population was indicated at most by settlement names such as Neu-Mannheim and Pfalzheim in Prussia, or Kandel, Landau, and Heidelberg in southern Russia, though they were generally the product of nomenclature chosen by the authorities. In Prussia, "Palatine colonies" were perceived as a special form for an extended period only on the local level. Theodor Fontane, in the second volume of his *Wanderings through the Mark of Brandenburg*, noted that there were still differences "in the appearance and character of the inhabitants" between the settlements of the Palatines in the Oderbruch and those in neighboring villages settled by Poles or Bohemians. However, he was unable to decide whether the appearance of a settlement was shaped more by the regional origins of its inhabitants or by local conditions.

In a few larger settlements that were entirely or mostly inhabited by Palatines, such as Neu-Ansbach near Driesen (Neumark) and in Pfalzdorf on the lower Rhine, a dialect related to the Palatine vernacular was still spoken in the early 20th century. In Jütland in the 1830s, the Danish pastor Frederik Carl Carsten noted a distanced relationship between the descendants of the remaining German colonists, whose origins were at that time supposedly still apparent from their dialect and dress, and their Danish neighbors. By contrast, the larger German settlement enclaves in Russia and southeastern Europe were generally made up of colonists from various territories, which prevented the formation of an identity oriented toward specific regional origins.

In German literature, the picture of the Palatinate as the classic emigration region solidified after the Enlightenment. In 1776, the Göttingen historian and journalist August Ludwig von Schlözer even went so far as to assert that "from no country in the world have more people emigrated, proportionately, than from Germany's paradise of the Palatinate." In 1857, the conservative cultural historian Wilhelm Heinrich Riehl described the "modern Palatine's appetite for emigration" as "an Alamannic-Suebian legacy." The "true emigration fever" was for Riehl "Swabian-Alamannic and Palatine." The assumption of the existence of such a quasi-natural wanderlust among the Palatines influenced the scholarship on migration, which was focused on local history and ethnography, until well into the 20th century.

Fenske, Hans. "Die deutsche Auswanderung." *Mitteilungen des Historischen Vereins der Pfalz* 76 (1978): 183–220.

Heinz, Joachim. *"Bleibe im Lande und nähre dich redlich!" Zur Geschichte der pfälzischen Auswanderung vom Ende des 17. bis zum Ende des 19. Jahrhunderts.* Kaiserslautern, 1989.

Hippel, Wolfgang von. *Auswanderung aus Südwestdeutschland. Studien zur württembergischen Auswanderung und Auswanderungspolitik im 18. und 19. Jahrhundert.* Stuttgart, 1984.

Paul, Roland. "Auswanderungen aus der Pfalz vom 18. Jahrhundert bis zur Mitte des 20. Jahrhunderts." In *Pfälzische Landeskunde. Beiträge zu Geographie, Biologie, Volkskunde und Geschichte*, vol. 3, edited by Michael Geiger et al., 221–43. Landau, 1981.

Renzing, Rüdiger. *Pfälzer in Irland. Studien zur Geschichte deutscher Auswandererkolonien des frühen 18. Jahrhunderts.* Kaiserslautern, 1989.

Schulte Beerbühl, Margrit. "Frühneuzeitliche Flüchtlingshilfe in Großbritannien und das Schicksal der Pfälzer Auswanderer von 1709." In *Über die trockene Grenze und über das offene Meer. Binneneuropäische und transatlantische Migrationen im 18. und 19. Jahrhundert*, edited by Mathias Beer and Dittmar Dahlmann, 303–28. Essen, 2004.

Cross-references: Germany; Great Britain; Ireland and Northern Ireland; Russia and Belarus; Southeastern Europe; *Aussiedler/Spätaussiedler* in Germany since 1950; German Refugees and Expellees from Eastern, East-Central, and Southeastern Europe in Germany and Austria since the End of World War II; German Settlers in Russia since the 18th Century; German Settlers (*Donauschwaben*) in Southeastern Europe since the Early Modern Period; Mennonites in West Prussia since the 16th Century

PERUVIAN FEMALE DOMESTICS IN ITALY SINCE THE END OF THE 20TH CENTURY

Felicitas Hillmann

Since the beginning of the 1980s, Italy has developed from a classic emigration country into an immigration country. Earlier than in the other southern European countries, certain patterns of immigration emerged in Italy that solidified in the late 1990s: a large segment of the immigration was now characterized by a high degree of informality and in part illegality. In addition, for some of the groups of immigrants whose development was particularly dynamic, a feminization of migration could be observed. The example of female Peruvian domestics in Italy shows how closely more recent patterns of migration are linked, on the one hand, with processes of transnationalization, that is, with the emergence of border-transcending social structures, and, on the other hand, with a change in gender relations in the destination country.

Peruvian men and women constitute a relatively young and steadily growing immigrant group in Italy. In December 2000, around 32,000 Peruvian nationals were registered in

Italy. That was 18% more than the year before; compared to the preceding decade, their number had grown 10-fold. Women accounted consistently for 65% (about 22,000 persons).

The immigration of Peruvian women to Italy had started at the beginning of the 1980s, after the military junta that had ruled Peru from 1968 to 1980 had been overthrown, and the conflict between the new government and the socialist guerilla organization Sendero Luminoso (Shining Path) was pushing the country increasingly into political and economic uncertainty. In the early 1990s, the migration targeted a few cities – above all Milan, Rome, and Naples. Until March 1993, many female migrants were able to enter the country with a tourist visa and then remain as "overstayers." Since then, most Peruvian women have come with the help of travel agencies, though these often operate with exaggerated promises and false contact addresses. A trip from Lima to Italy cost between US\$1,800 and US\$4,000. Two basic travel routes had been established in the 1990s. One route to Europe ran through Czechia, Slovakia, and Hungary, countries that were undergoing a transformation at the time. The migrant women arrived by plane with a transit visa valid for several days. That gave them enough time to organize their onward journey. *Pasadores* (smugglers), often of Italian or South American origin, contacted the "tourists" at stopovers at airports and train stations and offered to help them continue their journey and cross the border into Italy. The risk of a *foglio di via*, of being turned back at the Italian border, was accepted by the migrants. A second route led through Germany by means of a transit visa and from there, mostly on foot, to Italy across the Swiss or Austrian Alps.

Many Peruvian women made their way to Italy via chain migration. Initially these were apparently migration chains organized by relatives; as the 1990s went on, they took on a distinct work-focused orientation. For example, several graduates of a nursing class departed in succession and helped each other in doing so. This kind of training as nurses is often found among Peruvian women – occasionally while they were waiting for a place at a university. Other large segments of the group were formed by teachers or those employed in the social services sector. Financial support for the migrants from family members or colleagues in other countries made the trip possible.

Nearly all female immigrants came from urban areas in Peru. Although the motivations for the migration remained diverse, with few exceptions the primary driver was the desire to improve one's standard of living. Two groups can be distinguished here: one group wished to secure the survival of their own family back home by migrating. These migrants depended on finding employment quickly in the informal sector so they could immediately send money back home. If these women had any children, they placed them in care in their home country. Women who did not have to care for children usually had several younger brothers and sisters and were unmarried. Many of these migrants also mentioned problems with violence as a motivation behind emigration alongside poverty. In many cases the women had tried for a long time to improve their family's living standards at home.

A short-term securing of the survival of the family at home was not always the motivation. A second group of migrants worked toward securing a long-term livelihood and future after their own plans for a vocation at home had been endangered or thwarted by political and economic turmoil. In contrast to the first group, these migrants can be described as privileged, since they possessed sufficient capital to leave and were often already tied into transnational households that were able to pass along migration experience and provide financial backing.

An example of the second group is the transnational Bordega household from Lima (see Figure 1). The parents lived in Lima with a daughter and a grandson. After the first family members – two nieces and a nephew – had emigrated to the USA in the late 1980s, Latin American countries formed the destination countries, for example, for a niece who is a doctor. At the beginning of the 1990s, two daughters, because of immigration restrictions in North America and the worsening political situation in some parts of South America, went to Italy – one had worked in a bank, the other as a police officer. Money to pay for their emigration came from family living in the USA and Latin America. The existence and persistence of such transnational households, along with the deregulation of financial markets and easier international money transfers (including remittances from Italy) have favored intercontinental migrations since the 1990s, migrations that were usually characterized by illegal border crossings and irregular stays. These kinds of transnational networks also came into play with the first group of migrant women: they accepted becoming indebted to members of their own family, countrymen, or intermediaries.

In the 1990s, Italy offered Peruvian women without a residence permit a wide variety of job opportunities in the informal economy. Most of the women worked as household help: cleaners, nannies, caretakers for the elderly and the sick. Traditionally, this work had been done by native workers from poorer rural regions. Since the 1990s, however, these jobs have been dominated by immigrant women: in 2002, 60% of all the household help was of foreign origin, 87% of them women. Compared to native workers, the female migrants were younger, better educated, and usually worked more hours per week. Household workers who have by now become regularized – that is, are officially registered – are working chiefly in northern Italy (Lombardy) and Latium (with the capital of Rome), as well as in Naples; in southern Italy and on Sardinia and Sicily, only about one-sixth of all household workers are registered and thus have legal residency status.

Two reasons, in particular, have led to the growing employment of domestic help since the 1980s: first, the increasing entry of Italian women into the labor market especially in the first three regions mentioned above. It became increasingly normal for young native women who had vocational

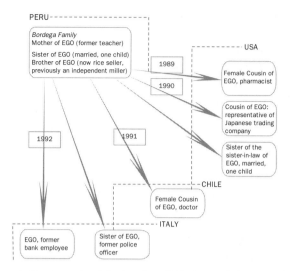

Figure 1. The transnational Bordega household. *Source*: Felicitas Hillmann, *Jenseits der Kontinente. Migrationstraditionen von Frauen nach Europa* (Opladen, 1996), 213.

and professional training to pursue gainful employment. However, little has changed in Italy with respect to social roles and the gender-specific division of work. As a result, both the care of children and household work remained largely allocated to women. Hiring domestic help to care for children and do the household chores is one way for working women to escape this dilemma.

Second, demographic change has created a large (and growing) demand for household-related services. The elderly are increasingly in need of personal care. Local care facilities usually have long waiting lists and are expensive; individual care provided by regularly employed workers is affordable to few. Italian households by now see this kind of help more as a necessity than a luxury. Especially the informal – and thus cheaper and less bureaucratic – employment of irregular household help went hand in hand with a supply of labor from countries of the southern regions of the world. Peruvian women work in Italian households on an hourly basis. Some are live-ins, which has the advantage for the migrant women that they can save a fair amount of money fairly quickly, since their living expenses are low. Migrant women who expected to return to their home countries one day preferred informal work arrangements and linked their intent to return to what was going on politically and with their families back in Peru.

The situation of the Peruvian women in Milan, for example, deteriorated with the increased immigration from Peru. The willingness to help newcomers declined in relation to the degree of one's own integration into Italian society, which in some cases became possible also for initially illegal migrants through legalization programs. Others used their good contacts within the informal sector and charged a fee for placing the newcomers in their jobs. Because most women have no residence permit, it has been clearly difficult to organize this group also over a longer period of time to press for its interests – especially since working and earning money is the top priority for nearly all migrant women.

Transnational households made the migration of Peruvian women easier and were the precondition for the consolidation of gender-specific geographies of migration. At the same time, the migrant women encountered an Italian labor market which, because of a change in gender relations and in the demographic structures, had a demand for precisely the qualifications they often already possessed as care workers or in social vocations. Their stay in Italy often became permanent because the future in their native country was uncertain, though for the majority of these women that has not led to an advanced integration into Italian society.

Cittadini stranieri. Popolazione residente per sesso e cittadinanza al 31. Dicembre 2000. Published by Istat. Rome, 2001.

Hillmann, Felicitas. *Jenseits der Kontinente. Migrationsstrategien von Frauen nach Europa*. Opladen, 1996.

Husa, Karl, and Christof Parnreiter, eds. *Internationale Migration. Die globale Herausforderung des 21. Jahrhunderts?* Vienna, 2000.

Ricerca Eurispes sul lavoro domestico in Italia. La colf del 2002 è straniera, giovane, istruita. Published by Eurispes. Rome, 2002.

Young, Brigitte. "Die 'Herrin' und die 'Magd.' Globalisierung und die neue internationale Arbeitsteilung im Haushalt." *Frauen-Dok.* 9 (1999): 39–48.

Cross-references: Italy; Latin American Migrants in Spain since the End of the 1980s; Latin American Prostitutes in the Netherlands since the 1970s

POLISH AGRICULTURAL WORKERS IN PRUSSIA-GERMANY FROM THE LATE 19TH CENTURY TO WORLD WAR II

Klaus J. Bade and Jochen Oltmer

At various times from the late 18th and early 19th centuries, Poland was part of the empire of the czar, the Habsburg monarchy, and Prussia-Germany. Short- and long-distance migrations within rural districts, migrations from the country to the city, and continental and overseas labor migration and emigration were a part of everyday working life in the decades before the First World War for probably more than a third of a population of just under 30 million. In all, around 2 million Poles left Europe between 1870 and 1914. Still, the overseas migration of Poles, 85% to 90% of which was directed to the USA, amounted annually to no more than one-third of Polish continental migration in the last 15 years before World War I, 85% to 90% of which was in turn headed for Germany: in the last decade before World War I, between 300,000 and 600,000 Poles of both genders went to northern, western, and central Europe as migrant workers – primarily as seasonal laborers.

In German economic history, the Empire (1871–1918) witnessed the structural transformation of Germany from an agrarian state with a dynamic industrial sector into an industrial state with a strong agrarian base. During a two-decade-long industrial boom – only briefly interrupted by short crises – and a long agrarian upswing before World War I, the growing need for industrial labor could not be met by domestic workers, in spite of the migration of laborers from the primary into the secondary sector. At the same time, there was a growing need to replace agricultural workers. As a result, the continental migration of foreign workers to Germany, and primarily Prussia, showed a steady rise beginning in the 1890s.

In the agricultural labor market in eastern Prussia, it was especially large-scale grain producers who complained about the scarcity of people. The most cost-effective solution from a business perspective was the recruitment of workers in the eastern regions who were "eager and cheap" because of the dramatically poor prospects of earning a living in the labor markets there: "eager" because of their material situation in the primarily Polish areas of origin; "cheap" in absolute terms because of low wages, and after the alignment of foreign wages with those of domestic workers, still relatively cheap from a business perspective through the use of seasonal contracts, which incurred no unproductive wage costs outside of the season.

The seasonalization of the labor migrations from those parts of Poland that belonged to Russia and Austria-Hungary was a result of Prussia's restrictive policy toward Poland. In Prussia, the "migrant worker question" had been from the beginning caught up in the collision between economic and political interests. On the one side, economic interests concentrated on the desire to meet the demand in the labor market for replacement workers and additional workers by drawing on foreign laborers. Diametrically opposed were the political interests that wished to contain the predominantly Polish immigration into Prussia's eastern provinces. The anti-Polish "Prussian defense policy" was dominated by a skeptical attitude toward the ineradicable dream of Prussian, Russian, and Austro-Hungarian Poles to resurrect a Polish national state. The solution to the dilemma of satisfying economic interests without endangering the strategy of the anti-Polish security policy was to prevent the necessary flow of workers from the east from turning into permanent immigration, but maintaining it as a mobile and available reserve within the paths of transnational seasonal migration.

The result was a system of restrictive control over foreigners that was developed in Prussia beginning in the 1890s and perfected in 1907. It has entered the history of labor market policy and the law pertaining to foreigners in Prussia-Germany under the keywords of *Legitimationszwang* (compulsory presentation of identity papers) and *Rückkehrzwang* (compulsory return) during the *Karenzzeit* (waiting period) in the winter: the first referred to tighter supervision of foreigners through work and residence permits that were temporary and had to be renewed every year, the second to the obligation – on pain of expulsion – that migrant workers from the east return to their region of origin during the wintertime exclusion period, with exemptions generally not granted to Poles, and only with great difficulty to other nationalities. Moreover, Polish migrant workers were admitted only as single laborers, not as family units. Children had to remain on the other side

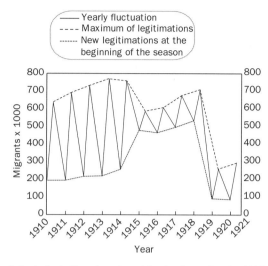

Figure 1. Yearly fluctuation of continental immigration to Prussia, 1910–1920. *Source:* "Denkschrift über die Ein- und Auswanderung nach bzw. aus Deutschland in den Jahren 1910 bis 1920," in *Verhandlungen des Reichstags. I. Wahlperiode 1920, Bd. 372. Anlagen,* 4382–404, here 4401–4.

"Workers legitimation cards" issued by the German Agricultural Workers Central Office (*Feldarbeiter-Zentralstelle*), 1910: top for the Poles, bottom for Ruthenians (*Landesarchiv Baden-Württemberg, Hauptstaatsarchiv Stuttgart*).

of the Prussian border, men and women were separated in the work gangs, and pregnancy was grounds for expulsion.

For migrant workers from Poland the combination of compulsory legitimation and compulsory return amounted

to both mobilization and immobilization: maintained in a permanent state of extreme mobility through the compulsory return every year, they were at the same immobilized in Prussia's labor market by the *Legitimationszwang*: the legitimation card, the only valid domestic identification for foreign workers, contained two names, that of the worker and that of the domestic employer, to whom foreigners were bound for the duration of their residence and work permit, on pain of expulsion. A change of job was possible only in exceptional circumstances and with the express permission of the employer. The result of this combination of compulsory legitimation and compulsory return was the characteristic structural picture of an annually fluctuating labor migration from the east to Prussia-Germany (see Figure 1), which resembles a fever curve: a rapid rise in the spring, a climax during the high season in the summer, and a rapid drop during the exclusion period in the winter.

As Prussia had the highest employment of foreign workers and other German states adopted this model, the Prussian regulations were important for the Reich as a whole: it was largely due to these acts of direct state intervention that the Reich did not change from a country of emigration to one of immigration in the decade leading up to World War I; instead, among the "worker-importing states" it became, after the USA, merely the "second-largest labor-importing country in the world" (Imre Ferenczi).

Shortly before World War I, the total number of foreign workers in Germany was estimated at 1.2 million, more than 900,000 of whom were employed in Prussia. About one-third were Poles from the Russian or Austro-Hungarian partition of Poland. Agriculture accounted for around 40% of all foreign workers in Prussia. Poles were dominant in this sector: totaling around 270,000, three-quarters of the 365,000 foreigners in the Prussian agricultural sector thus hailed from Polish areas beyond the eastern and southeastern borders of

Potato harvest at a Prussian estate around 1930 (*Deutsches Historisches Museum, Berlin*).

Prussia. Women made up just over half of all Polish workers in Prussian agriculture. Main destinations were the four Prussian provinces of Saxony, Silesia, Pomerania, and Brandenburg where agriculture employed nearly two-thirds of all Polish workers.

Polish migrant workers mainly came from the Russian partition in central Poland close to the border, and from western Galicia, which was part of the Habsburg monarchy. These were both predominantly agrarian regions with, by European standards, an extremely high population growth and very large proportions of landless people and land-poor who were dependent on a secondary income. Although the large estates that dominated both regions offered some opportunities to earn an outside income, compared to the eastern part of Prussia the wage level for agricultural laborers was very low.

In East Elbian provinces, the primary area of the agricultural economy in which Poles were active was the cultivation of potatoes and sugar beets with its strong seasonal labor spikes. The growing of potatoes required foreign laborers especially during planting and harvesting (potato diggers). The cultivation of sugar beets involved more than planting and the harvest, since the beets required constant care. Women were the dominant laborers for both crops. They generally worked in gangs under the supervision of a male, usually bilingual gang leader, who often also disbursed the wages and not infrequently diverted some portion of them into his own pocket. The situation of Polish workers was very similar in southern Sweden and Denmark.

Alongside the cultivation of root crops, the harvesting of grain was, until the introduction of labor-saving machines (mower and thresher), an area for Polish laborers in eastern Prussia before World War I, though in this case the work was done entirely by men in "reaper gangs." A special group among Polish migrant workers in Prussia were the largely male brickyard workers in enterprises that were registered as secondary agricultural enterprises because the employment of foreigners was outlawed in Prussia in brickworks that were operated outside of agriculture and were thus classified as belonging to "industry," a situation that led to serious clashes of interest.

Prussia's anti-Polish "defense policy" achieved its chief goal before World War I: migrant workers from countries to the east were available to satisfy the replacement and expansion demands in the agricultural labor markets and to act as an economic buffer during the transition from crisis to upswing. At the same time, Prussia was able to prevent the permanent settlement and integration of foreign workers with the help of a combination of compulsory legitimation and compulsory return.

This changed with the beginning of World War I: while the number of Poles from Galicia declined dramatically after the outbreak of the war as a result of the mobilization in Austria-Hungary, men from the Russian partition of central Poland who were of draft age were classified as "hostile foreigners," forbidden from returning or changing location and thus tied to a single employer. These Poles had thus de facto become forced laborers, unable to decide freely on either their place of residence or their employer.

Their regions of origin, Russian central Poland, was conquered in 1915–16 by German and Austro-Hungarian troops and developed – alongside occupied Belgium – into the most important recruitment area for the German war economy suffering from an acute labor shortage. As the number of "voluntary" signups overall fell far short of the level that was deemed necessary by the military authorities, compulsory means were used with growing frequency. An indirect effect came from the deterioration of the economic situation in the occupied Polish region: deliberately instigated by the German occupying power, it was intended to coerce broad segments of the population into working for the occupiers directly or back in the Reich. A direct measure was added at the end of 1916 in the form of a policy of deportation for work in the Reich; however, it failed within a few short months, because the German authorities were unable to either procure a larger number of sufficiently qualified workers or to coerce those forcefully recruited into working permanently in agricultural enterprises. According to estimates, more than half of the foreign civilian workers, who numbered around 1 million at the end of the war in 1918, were supposedly Poles, most of whom – now as forced laborers – worked in agriculture in eastern Prussia.

The end of the war in 1918 led to a noticeable decline in the number of foreign workers in agriculture and industry, down to perhaps a third to two-fifths of the level in the last year of the war. Because of the border conflicts between Germany and the new Polish state, which also involved the closing of the border by Poland, hardly any new Polish workers were recruited in the immediate postwar period. As a result of the returning ban between 1914 and 1918 and the fact that compulsory return was not revived after the end of the war, foreign Poles had settled down in Germany. In the mid-1920s, the German labor administration assumed that up to 100,000 Poles of both genders had become permanent workers in German agriculture. Estimates put the number of those who had been in Germany since 1914 at 70,000 to 90,000. As a result of the unclear border situation after the end of the war, many Polish workers had been able to bring over their families. German agencies estimated that the number of children brought from Poland or born in Germany was nearly as high as the number of Polish migrant workers. In addition, there were reports of numerous marriages between German and Polish citizens.

We have only sporadic information from the German administration about such visible signs of permanent settlement and integration. However, they impelled German migration policy in the mid-1920s to push for measures to reintroduce the compulsory return for Polish workers that had been suspended since 1914. The justification had not changed substantially since the prewar period: the permanent settlement of Polish laborers would lead to the "displacement" of German agricultural workers of both genders from East Elbia and threaten the national and territorial integrity of the Prussian border provinces in the east. Thus, in spite of the substantial decline in the Polish minority within the Reich after World War I as a result of the cessions under the Treaty of Versailles, the ethnonationalist image of Polish infiltration and the consequent "Polonization" of what was left of eastern Prussia continued to form the basis of an anti-Polish migration policy. This policy regarded the immigration of Poles into the Reich as a threat to Germany's internal security, its economy and labor market, and its society and culture – most especially in the East Elbian regions. And since many Polish laborers were unemployed during the winter months, their presence would also place an additional burden on poor relief; another fear was a rise in crime during the winter.

The year 1925 therefore saw the first German measures aimed at prompting as many Poles as possible to return to their homeland. At the same time, the Berlin government entered into talks with Poland about a German-Polish Recruitment Treaty. It was intended to guarantee the supply of Polish workers to German agriculture and industry, and at the same time secure Poland's agreement about the reintroduction of compulsory return. Of importance to the German government was above all Polish agreement with the extension of this measure also to those Poles who had settled in Germany since the beginning of World War I, many of whom lacked proper passports and proof of citizenship because they had crossed the border to the west before the Polish state came into being at the end of the war.

The signing of the German-Polish Migration Treaty in November 1927 allowed for the recruitment of Polish laborers in accordance with German wishes: the German Workers Agency was no longer dependent on choosing from among those workers who arrived at its border offices. Instead, in coordination with the Polish labor administration it was now able to recruit directly in the regions of origin and consistently meet the demands of German employers concerning the composition of the work gangs. Above all, this new procedure substantially boosted the percentage of female agricultural workers – highly desired because of their lower wages – from just over 50% to more than 80%.

In addition, the German-Polish Migration Treaty also revived the compulsory return for Polish agricultural laborers after an interruption of 14 years. The hopes of the German government that this would prevent a permanent settlement of Poles in the Reich, given what was seen as the continued necessity for the employment of Polish workers in the Reich, were fulfilled: the vast majority of Polish migrant workers who had been living in Germany for many years were deported to Poland by the winter of 1930–1. Exemptions applied only to Poles who were married to German citizens and had many children. Added to this group were those receiving accident or disability pensions.

The decline in the number of permanently settled Poles in the Weimar Republic accelerated with the global economic crisis, which had a severe impact also on agricultural labor markets. In 1932, the German labor administration counted fewer than 15,000 Polish agricultural laborers who were classified as permanently settled. It is likely that this number declined further as the economic crisis unfolded. With the help of restrictive instruments of migration policy, Germany had thus been able, across nearly half a century, to prevent the immigration and integration of Polish migrants or interrupt integration processes. The number of seasonal agricultural laborers from Poland rose again only in the wake of the rearmament-driven full employment in National Socialist Germany in the second half of the 1930s. After the outbreak of hostilities in 1939, it led to the employment of millions of forced laborers during World War II.

Bade, Klaus J. "Land oder Arbeit? Transnationale und interne Migration im deutschen Nordosten vor dem Ersten Weltkrieg." Manuscript, Habilitation thesis, Erlangen 1979; Internet edition 2005: www.imis.uni-osnabrueck.de/BadeHabil.pdf.

Bade, Klaus J. "'Preußengänger' und 'Abwehrpolitik.' Ausländerbeschäftigung, Ausländerpolitik und Ausländerkontrolle auf dem Arbeitsmarkt in Preußen vor dem Ersten Weltkrieg." *Archiv für Sozialgeschichte* 24 (1984): 91–162.

Ferenczi, Imre. *Kontinentale Wanderungen und die Annäherung der Völker. Ein geschichtlicher Überblick*. Jena, 1930.

Morawska, Ewa. "Labor Migrations of Poles in the Atlantic World Economy, 1880–1914." *Comparative Studies in Society and History* 31 (1989): 237–72.

Oltmer, Jochen. *Migration und Politik in der Weimarer Republik*. Göttingen, 2005.

Oltmer, Jochen. "Migration und deutsche Außenpolitik. Der deutsch-polnische Wanderungsvertrag von 1927 und die mitteleuropäischen Migrationsbeziehungen nach dem Ersten Weltkrieg." *Zeitschrift für Ostmitteleuropa-Forschung* 54/3 (2005): 399–424.

Cross references: Germany; Poland; Forced Laborers in Germany and German-occupied Europe during World War II; Polish Industrial Workers in the Ruhr (Ruhrpolen) since the End of the 19th Century; Polish Labor Migrants in Central and Western Europe after 1989

POLISH AND BELGIAN FORCED LABORERS IN GERMANY DURING WORLD WAR I

Jens Thiel

The term "forced laborers" for Polish and Belgian workers in World War I refers to a segment of workers employed in the German war economy who came from the occupied territories of Belgium and from the Kingdom of Poland that was part of Russia (Congress Poland). The backdrop to this use of forced laborers in Germany was the acute labor shortage in war-related industries and the army's need for replacements.

At the outbreak of war in August 1914, 200,000 to 300,000 Russian-Polish workers of both genders were in Germany, mostly seasonal workers in agriculture. Just under half of the Russian-Polish agricultural workers were women. Now classified as "enemy foreigners," the Poles were not allowed to return to their homeland; men of draft age were declared to be "civilian prisoners," though they were not interned. The compulsory return that was previously in force for this group of workers was replaced in the early spring of 1914 with a prohibition against returning for the duration of the war, a prohibition that was soon extended to include also the approximately 22,000 Russian-Polish industrial workers. The compulsory presentation of legitimating documents and the prohibition against changing one's residence, which made it nearly impossible to change jobs, remained in force.

The category of forced laborers also includes the workers who were recruited from the beginning of 1915 in the Russian-Polish territories occupied by Germany, with a small number also deported. Up to the end of the war, Germany recruited, from the General Government of Warsaw that was set up in August 1915, about 140,000 Polish agricultural and 100,000 Polish industrial workers, as well as about 30,000 Polish-Jewish workers. Added to this were about 35,000 workers from the occupied Russian territories in the Baltic region. The line between voluntary and forced recruitment was fluid in the occupied eastern territories; economic pressure and noneconomic coercive means complemented each other. In spite of the formally voluntary recruitment, the legal status and legal treatment of the recruited workers corresponded to the restrictive regulations that applied to the Russian-Polish forced laborers who had been working in Germany since the beginning of the war. They found employment chiefly in the Rhenish-Westphalian and Upper Silesian mining industry and in the agricultural sector east of the Elbe.

The approximately 4,200 Belgian workers who were in Germany in August 1914 also fell under the restrictive special regulations for "enemy foreigners" and were thus forced laborers. The Belgians, employed in the Rhenish-Westphalian mining industry but chiefly in the glass and mirror industry in and around Düsseldorf, lived and worked under better conditions than the Russian-Polish forced laborers. Legally classified as "civilian prisoners," they and their families initially lived as internees in the small workers' colonies that had been set up for them before the war. Because they were

few in number and posed a minor risk of causing trouble, but mostly because they were skilled, the Prussian Ministry of War relaxed the registration and residence requirements for them as of June 1915. The coercive nature of their employment was gradually lifted: first the prohibition against returning home, in January 1916 the internment, and eventually, from the middle of 1917, also the prohibition against changing location. As "free enemy foreigners," they were now subject to moderate registration and residence regulations. While the Belgian glassworkers lived relatively isolated from the surrounding society, they were appreciated by their employers and colleagues as indispensable and highly skilled workers.

A larger number of Belgian forced laborers came to Germany in the fall and winter of 1916–17 as part of the deportations from the General Government of Belgium: between the end of October 1916 and the middle of February 1917, about 60,000 Belgian jobless and workers were deported to Germany for forced labor. At the same time, the military High Command had another 60,000 civilians deported from the Belgian and northern French areas under its direct control; they were coerced into working in the Civilian Worker Battalions that were set up there. The Belgians who were taken to Germany were placed into "distribution centers" that were connected to the existing prisoner of war camps. Such camps for Belgian "deportees" or "forced Belgians" (*Zwangsbelgier*) existed in Holzminden, Guben, Wittenberg, Altengrabow, Münster, Kassel, Meschede, Soltau, and in their subsidiary and auxiliary camps. The conditions of housing and food were disastrous; inadequate hygienic and sanitary conditions led to numerous diseases: 1,316 Belgians died in the camps (other reports put the figure at 1,250). Under these conditions, only a quarter of the deported were willing to enter into a "voluntary" four-month work contract with a company. Deportees who refused to work in the German war industry were put to work as forced labor in the camps themselves or in labor gangs in agriculture, on soil improvement projects, on road construction, or in mining. Deportations from the General Government ceased in February of 1917; the last deported forced laborers returned to Belgium in June 1917. The deportees who were already working in industrial enterprises were given the status of free enemy foreigners and thus received the same status as voluntary workers recruited from Belgium.

Thanks to a system of promotion, social misery, threats, coercive measures, the dismantlement of industrial installations, and the provision of material benefits (signing-on fees, family support, vacation), the German Industrial Bureau in charge of recruitment in the General Government of Belgium was able to recruit about 160,000 workers by the end of the war. The majority of the recruited workers found employment in the large, war-related enterprises along the Rhine and the Ruhr. In contrast to the Russian-Polish workers who had been recruited and were subject to far tougher residency regulations, the term "forced laborers" does not apply to these Belgian workers. There was no general prohibition

Deported Belgian workers in the canteen of a barrack in Oberhausen, Germany, around 1916 (*Stiftung Rheinisch-Westfälisches Wirtschaftsarchiv, Cologne*).

against changing locations or returning home, and vacation regulations were also more generous. Although some of them lived in "barracks of Belgians" or fenced "camps of Belgians" under guard in direct proximity to the enterprises, their living and working conditions were often better than those for the Poles. Under certain conditions, the recruited Belgians could have their families join them. The recruitment of women was less desirable and was made more difficult by withholding benefits from them. As a result, the number of Belgian female workers did not rise above a few thousand in agriculture and industry.

The life and everyday working conditions of the Polish forced laborers were strictly regulated. Drastic punishments even for minor transgressions, disobedience, violations of the contract, or flight were used to discipline the workers. Beginning in December 1916, the Prussian Ministry of War gradually made some concessions with respect to a change of residence and workplace, as well as with respect to vacation regulations and the possibility of lodging complaints against employers. Still, these concessions did not alter the fundamentally coercive nature of this employment.

In spite of the restricted freedom of movement, the Polish-Russian industrial workers did not live completely isolated. Since the original plan of placing them in barracks could be implemented only to a limited extent, the forced laborers lived primarily in mass quarters (dormitories, workers' homes, dormitories in guest houses, homeless shelters), though some lived also in private lodgings or in separate workers' colonies and fenced-in barracks which large enterprises set up in direct proximity to their factories. Controlling the workers in the densely populated large cities was difficult. Because some spoke German, the Russian-Polish forced laborers, at least those employed in industry, were hardly visible on the outside as a separate group. Still, the special law that applied to them and their status as civilian prisoners and enemy foreigners placed them in the position of outsiders. Relations with the German population were generally limited to contact in the workplace or chance encounters in everyday life. By contrast, the forced laborers who worked in agriculture east of the Elbe, most of whom came from the

poorest strata of the Polish rural population, lived far more isolated lives. Here, contact with the native population was effectively prevented by the living and working conditions, the language barriers, and the low population density. Unlike the coerced Polish industrial workers, they remained visible as a separate group.

It was especially in agriculture that the working and living conditions of the forced Russian-Polish workers deteriorated compared to the prewar situation. Nominal and real wages declined. Forced laborers often complained about bad conditions – for example, physical abuse by employers and supervisors and policemen deployed to guard them, housing unfit for human habitation, poor food, and improper deductions from their wages. The traditionally harsh work regimen was enforced even more harshly than before the war, and the curtailment of their rights in response to the war was exploited above all by agricultural employers. As before the war, agricultural workers were housed in *Schnitterkasernen* (harvester barracks) but sometimes also in barns or accommodations with even more inadequate sanitary and hygienic conditions.

The attitude of German officials and the population toward the Russian-Polish as well as the Belgian workers was mostly one of indifference or rejection, rarely one of pity. The perception and treatment of these groups was characterized by an east-west gradient: in the hierarchy of foreign workers, Jewish and Polish workers stood at the very bottom, even though the Belgians also had to suffer defamations and poor treatment. The image of the Polish and Jewish migrant workers was founded on traditional national, racist, and anti-Semitic resentments from the prewar period. Employers and officials frequently complained about "uppity behavior" and hygienic or ethical-moral shortcomings of the Polish and Belgian workers. They were also collectively accused of slacking off at work, laziness, and unwillingness to work. Fellow workers usually looked upon them as unwanted social competition and wage depressors; in a few cases the conflicts erupted into abuse and physical assaults.

On the whole, the possibilities for Polish and Belgian forced laborers to integrate and the population's willingness to have them do so were minimal. It would also appear that there was no creation of distinct group structures, except for the "communities of need" born out of the working and living conditions, joint attendance at religious services, leisure activities, and relations among friends and family. Such beginnings of an autonomous group organization were most likely to be found in the distribution centers of the Belgian deportees or in the barracks camps and workers' colonies. The workers' homes set up for Flemish workers by the German-Flemish Society in the Rhenish-Westphalian industrial region offered integration services, but since they combined care and leisure time activities with social control and political indoctrination, workers were hesitant to use them. A few smaller clubs and institutions of Walloon workers were established in the Ruhr region. The informal *Schnittergemeinschaften* (harvesting communities) in agriculture east of the Elbe became much more active than before the war, since the workers worked and lived together not only for the harvest season – as they had before 1914 – but usually for the entire duration of the war. External efforts to promote integration hardly existed, except for the charitable work of the Catholic Church, worker welfare institutions, and the timid attempts by the unions to integrate the Poles. Most Polish-Russian and Belgian workers returned to their homeland immediately after the war without leaving any larger traces in the German society. The Jewish workers for the most part remained in Germany. The forced labor deployment of Polish and Belgian workers in World War I constituted a turning point in the labor migration with its transition to open bureaucratic coercion. Moreover, its importance as a precedent for the practice of forced labor in World War II should not be underestimated.

Heid, Ludger. *Maloche – nicht Mildtätigkeit. Ostjüdische Arbeiter in Deutschland 1914–1923*. Hildesheim, 1995.

Herbert, Ulrich. "Zwangsarbeit als Lernprozeß. Zur Beschäftigung ausländischer Arbeiter in der westdeutschen Industrie im Ersten Weltkrieg." *Archiv für Sozialgeschichte* 24 (1984): 285–304.

Oltmer, Jochen. "Zwangsmigration und Zwangsarbeit – Ausländische Arbeitskräfte und bäuerliche Ökonomie im Ersten Weltkrieg." *Tel Aviver Jahrbuch für deutsche Geschichte* 27 (1998): 135–68.

Pyta, Wolfram. "Polnische und belgische Arbeiter in Preußen während des 1. Weltkrieges." *Geschichte in Köln* 14 (1983): 62–120.

Thiel, Jens. *"Menschenbassin Belgien." Anwerbung, Deportation und Zwangsarbeit im Ersten Weltkrieg*. Essen, 2007.

Westerhoff, Christian. "Von der Friedens- zur Kriegswirtschaft. Anwerbung und Beschäftigung von Arbeitskräften aus Rußland in Deutschland 1914–1916." In *Migration und Arbeitsmarkt vom 17. bis zum 20. Jahrhundert*, edited by Dittmar Dahlmann and Margit Schulte-Beerbühl. Essen, 2009.

Zunkel, Friedrich. "Die ausländischen Arbeiter in der deutschen Kriegswirtschaftspolitik des 1. Weltkrieges." In *Entstehung und Wandel der modernen Gesellschaft. Festschrift für Hans Rosenberg zum 65. Geburtstag*, edited by Gerhard A. Ritter, 280–311. Berlin, 1970.

Cross-references: Belgium and Luxembourg; Germany; Poland; Forced Laborers in Germany and German-occupied Europe during World War II; Polish Agricultural Workers in Prussia-Germany from the Late 19th Century to World War II

POLISH INDUSTRIAL WORKERS IN THE RUHR (*RUHRPOLEN*) SINCE THE END OF THE 19TH CENTURY

Brian McCook

The German term *Ruhrpolen* refers to those ethnic Poles who migrated from the eastern Prussian provinces of West and East Prussia, Silesia, and Posen to work in the growing industries of the Ruhr region in the Prussian provinces of Westphalia and the Rhineland during the late 19th and early 20th centuries. The pattern of east-west industrial migration stimulated by German industry's demand for labor was first established in 1871 when the Prosper coal mine in Bottrop recruited a few hundred Polish miners from Upper Silesia. Soon thereafter, the number of ethnic Poles living in the Ruhr grew dramatically. By 1914, well over 400,000 Polish-speaking migrants lived in the Ruhr, where they formed a vibrant ethnic community supported by over 1,000 ethnic associations, a lively ethnic press, and the third largest coal miners' union in the Ruhr. Overall, the Polish minority in the Ruhr attained a level of influence in local affairs before the First World War that no minority group in Germany has since matched.

After the First World War, however, the Polish community in the Ruhr went into decline. Many workers returned to Poland; others moved on to the prospering industrial areas of northwestern and northern France. The inadequate integration of the group before the war combined with postwar developments, in particular the reestablishment of the Polish state and growing political and economic hardship within Weimar Germany, encouraged the majority of Poles to leave. Nevertheless, a sizable minority chose to remain and gradually assimilated into the host society. Today the historical remnants of Polish migration to the Ruhr can still be seen in aspects of the local dialect, in the many Polish sounding names, and in local cuisine.

The formation of the Polish minority in the Ruhr, 1871–1914

The causes for Polish migration from the eastern Prussian provinces to the Ruhr are varied. First were classic economic push and pull factors that affected both Poles and Germans living in eastern Germany. These economic factors included (1) excess population growth in the eastern provinces during the 19th century; (2) insufficient industrialization in eastern Germany outside of Upper Silesia; (3) the crisis in German agriculture from the 1870s onward, which constrained the ability of peasants to earn sustainable wages from the land; and (4) labor shortages and the significantly higher wages that could be earned in the industrialized Ruhr region. To these economic factors were added political factors related to the *Germanisierung*, or Germanization, campaign waged by the government in eastern Prussia. Particularly of note were elements of the campaign that lent state support to the acquisition and parcelization of Polish gentry property in eastern Prussia to German "colonists" and various regulations that impeded land sales to Poles.

Polish migration was also aided because the migration process itself was becoming easier. In the 19th century, literacy rates in the German partition of Poland grew significantly, print media became more widespread, and transportation networks were better developed, allowing the average Polish peasant to acquire increased knowledge about the outside world. Most important, after early Polish migrants settled in the Ruhr, they remained in constant contact with relatives back home. With each successive year, the putative dangers associated with migration, including dislocation and isolation, diminished while the apparent rewards increased. With the establishment of such informal networks, the phenomenon of chain migration grew and increasingly proved responsible for sustaining the high level of Polish migration to the Ruhr in the two decades before the First World War.

Early Polish migrants to the Ruhr initially tended to come from Upper Silesia. By the 1890s, however, the majority of eastern workers increasingly migrated from either East Prussia or Posen, followed distantly by workers from West Prussia and Upper Silesia. Of the 133,033 eastern workers employed in the Ruhr in 1914, 7.4% came from Upper Silesia, 41.9% from Posen, 12.9% from West Prussia, and 37.8% from East Prussia. Poles arriving in the Ruhr from the 1870s to mid-1890s settled predominantly in rural districts of the north-central Ruhr region within the present-day areas of Gelsenkirchen, Bottrop, Recklinghausen, Herne, and Bochum. The primary causes of this initial settlement pattern were the location of work, geographic origin, and religious affiliation. Most of the coal mines that employed Polish labor were new, large-scale operations located in these, for the time, rural regions of the Ruhr. Mine companies sent agents to recruit laborers from specific villages or regions in eastern Prussia and many mine owners often hired only those workers who shared their Protestant or Catholic faith.

With the subsequent influx of Polish labor after 1895, Polish settlement grew more diffuse. Increasing numbers of Poles settled in areas around Dortmund to the east and Oberhausen and Duisburg to the west. By 1914, Poles were present in every sizable community between Düsseldorf and Hamm and, though still traceable, Polish settlement areas grew less defined by specific regional or confessional origins. The process of expanded Polish settlement across the Ruhr was driven by the continued expansion of Ruhr industry, the relatively high level of fluctuation in employment, and the growing urbanization of the Ruhr. An important by-product of this expanded settlement was that Poles came into greater contact with their German host society.

Single, young men or married men who left their wives behind in their homeland dominated the first wave of Polish migration to the Ruhr from the 1870s until the early 1890s. While Polish men continued to outnumber women until after the First World War, the gender gap did gradually ease as many of those who originally intended to remain in the Ruhr for only a few years decided to settle permanently and subsequently sent for their wives or returned to their homeland, married, and brought their new wives back with them. Polish men were generally in their early to mid-20s when they married while women were in their late teens or early 20s. Over the course of a marriage, Polish couples would have on average three to four children. The rate of interethnic marriage between Germans and Poles was negligible. In 1912, only 3.2% of Polish men and 2.2% of Polish women were married to Germans.

Families lived in close quarters by present-day standards. A typical Polish family residing in a mining colony lived in an apartment with three or four rooms and a small garden plot. Within each household, the division of labor was strict. Men worked in the mines or in other industries such as steel or ironworks while women managed the household, often including the family budget, and raised the children. Women also added to the family income by selling extra produce grown in the garden and assuming odd jobs such as washing clothes or caring for boarders. Children went to German language schools until around the age of 14, when boys left for work in the mines and girls attempted to find employment as domestic servants, seamstresses, or workers in light industries. It was exceedingly rare for Polish children to obtain secondary or university education as education costs were high and most parents expected their children to enter the workforce and contribute to the family income.

To make ends meet, most Polish households also took in boarders and, despite overcrowding, the boardinghouse system remained popular well into the 20th century. Boarders preferred living with a family to the even more crowded and authoritarian environment of company dormitories. Further, the elaborate boarder system eased initial migrant dislocation and contributed significantly to establishing a stable, close-knit ethnic community. By facilitating contact with other Poles, the boardinghouse system enabled countless boarders to learn about job opportunities and ethnic organizations, hear news from the homeland, and generally become more mobile in their adopted societies.

Poles performed the most dangerous, backbreaking, and dirty work. In the early years of Polish migration, almost all Poles, nearly 90%, were employed in the mining industry. Over time, this percentage declined as Polish employment increased in other industries such as steel and chemicals. On the eve of the First World War, it is estimated that approximately 60% of Poles in the Ruhr were employed in mining while 40% worked in other industries. In addition, as Poles became more settled, a small but growing number also began opening small businesses. By 1912, over 2,000 Poles in the Ruhr were self-employed tradesmen or shopkeepers.

The initial proportion of Poles working in the mining industry was large because barriers to employment in the industry were low, occupational mobility was good, and wages relative to other forms of employment were high. At least initially, Poles generally worked in the larger mine operations of the northern and eastern Ruhr region, where workforces of over 1,000 men were commonplace. By the turn of the century, 19 of these mines became known as *Polenzechen*, or Polish mines, as over one-half of their workforce was comprised of eastern migrants. Overall, Polish-speaking migrants represented approximately 25% of the entire coal-mining workforce in the Ruhr by 1914.

Upon entering the industry, Poles found themselves employed in secondary, unskilled positions within the mine complex, as haulers, for example. However, within a few years, barring any stains on their employment record, Poles could generally expect to attain positions as miners' apprentices and finally as full miners. The ability to move up the occupational ladder was significant since wages and benefits for miners were generally double those of unskilled workers.

Within the workplace, the development of interethnic solidarity with German workers was slow. The initial isolation and regional concentration of Poles hindered cross-cultural contact and native workers initially viewed Poles as a threat to their wages and job security. Poles were castigated as wage suppressors, employers' lackeys, and strikebreakers. The word "Polack" became a term of derision widely used throughout the Ruhr.

During the 1890s the massive influx of Poles increased ethnic tensions at work. German union leaders, including members of the socialist Alter Verband and the Christian Gewerkverein, utilized nationalist-tinged rhetoric in appeals demanding that employers limit the further recruitment of Poles. When unions did attempt to reach out to Poles, they often did so in a heavy-handed, condescending manner, arguing that Poles needed to be raised to the cultural level of the enlightened, class-conscious German worker. The tensions between Germans and Poles exploded in 1899. At the beginning of the year, German unions supported the introduction of an ordinance that required Polish miners to demonstrate a proficiency in German before being employed. Later in June, German working-class organizations refused to support a wildcat strike by predominantly young Polish workers in the town of Herne. In response to the strike, one socialist newspaper remarked that Poles needed to learn that "only by organizing [in the socialist union] could they expect to better their condition."

Polish workers gathered valuable lessons from the events of 1899. However, instead of turning to join German unions, the majority of Poles mobilized their ethnic strength and formed the independent Zjednoczenie Zawodwe Polskie (ZZP), or Polish Trade Union, in 1902. The ideology of the ZZP was initially dominated by ethno-confessional principles that forbade political activity and religious conflict as well as any form of socialist activity. The goal of the union was to organize Polish industrial workers in all trades throughout Germany. However, owing to their large numbers, Polish workers from the Ruhr, particularly coal miners, dominated the union's membership until the early 1920s.

In the Ruhr, the union achieved significant success within a few short years. By 1905, the ZZP was the third largest miners' union with approximately 28,000 members. By the end of the First World War, this figure had increased to approximately 45,000. Although membership in the union did fluctuate due to economic conditions, the ZZP's achievement in organizing workers was impressive. By 1910, organization rates among Poles in the Ruhr actually exceeded those of German workers, approximately 54% to 37%, respectively. The higher rate is significant because it disproves stereotypes

popular among German trade unionists that eastern workers were less willing to organize.

Drawing from the strength of their own union, Polish workers were often at the forefront of challenging employers in the hope of achieving better working conditions. During the January 1905 coal strike, the ZZP acted as an equal partner with the larger German unions. After this strike, the ZZP became more involved in political affairs and, while remaining nationally conscious, also increasingly began to embrace socialist rhetoric in defending workers' interests. This ideological drift reflected the growing class awareness and radicalization of Polish workers, who, having chosen to permanently settle, absorbed and contributed to the working-class ethos that predominated in the Ruhr. Although tensions between Poles and Germans continued to exist, the growth of an ethnically informed class consciousness greatly aided in stabilizing the position of the Polish community by providing Poles increased representational clout in the workplace and in society.

Community stability was also gained through Polish involvement in religious life and in ethnic associations. In the first phase of Polish migration to the Ruhr in the 1870s and into the 1880s, the Catholic Church provided a symbol of continuity and became the most visible unifying element for thousands of disparate Poles. In this early period of migration, the Church actively aided the preservation of an independent Polish identity by facilitating the development of Polish ethnic associations under its roof, including *Rosenkranzvereine* (rosary societies), *Gesangvereine* (choral clubs), various *Frauen-* and *Jugendvereine* (Women's and Youth Associations) and, most significantly, *Polnisch-Katholische Arbeitervereine* (Polish-Catholic Worker Associations). Such organizations, led initially by local German priests, emphasized the need of members to concentrate on maintaining a religiously meaningful life and strictly forbade involvement in politics by members.

The Church also enabled the preservation of ethnic identity by providing Poles access to spiritual care in their native language. German priests able to speak Polish occasionally gave masses, heard confession, and attended to other Catholic rites in Polish. More striking, the Church hierarchy also initially permitted a full-time Polish priest from eastern Germany to minister in the Ruhr. The most influential of these Polish clerics was Francis Liss, who from 1890 to 1894 was a driving force in expanding Polish ethnic institutions in the Ruhr. Through his activities, the number of Polish-Catholic worker associations increased dramatically and the first and most influential Polish newspaper in the Ruhr, the *Wiarus Polski* (Old Polish Soldier) was founded in 1891.

From the mid-1890s onward, however, the relationship between Poles and the Church in the Ruhr deteriorated and interethnic confessional bonds weakened. The most important factor influencing this trend was the Prussian state, which pressured the hierarchy to curtail Polish activities within the Church deemed national in character. The changing relationship of the Church to its Polish flock was punctuated by two key events. In 1894, the Bishop of Paderborn removed the popular Polish priest Liss from his position at the behest of the Minister-President of Westphalia. Later in 1904, the Church hierarchy placed further limits on Polish spiritual care. While allowing Poles to continue to make confession and attend occasional services in Polish, the hierarchy banned the use of Polish songs without permission; prohibited baptismal, marriage, and funeral services conducted in Polish; and perhaps most inflammatory, ordered that Polish children be instructed for the sacrament of communion only in German.

The anti-Polish stance taken by Church officials provoked outrage within the Polish community. Nevertheless, most Poles remained loyal to the Church because their confessional identity was so intricately bound to their ethnicity. Consequently, Poles adopted a pragmatic approach in which they attempted to reform the Church from within. To accomplish this, Poles engaged in grassroots campaigns through the Polish Catholic associations, drafting petitions to German bishops demanding ethnically Polish priests, an increase in the number of Polish language masses, and the lifting of the 1904 restrictions. The hierarchy, however, generally ignored these official Polish entreaties for improved spiritual care until after the First World War.

Poles achieved significantly more success in influencing the Church on the local level, particularly through their efforts to capture seats on local parish executive committees and councils. These two bodies aided the local priest in the administration of a given parish and provided the parishioners with a means of voicing their concerns and influencing local church policy. At the turn of the century, despite their growing population, Polish representation on church councils and executive committees was insignificant. By 1912, however, this picture shifted dramatically and, in some areas of the Ruhr, Poles were able to attain representation commensurate with their numbers in the Catholic population.

Clearly, discontentment with the limited progress toward changing the hierarchy's anti-Polish policies motivated Poles to effect change locally. More significant, however, was the growing cooperation of Poles with German Catholics. Recognizing their growing political strength, Germans often chose to reach preelection compromises with Poles over the allotment of church office seats rather than risk losing seats in elections. Such agreements highlight that interethnic cooperation was growing and that ethnic relations, despite increasing tensions at the national level, were stabilizing at the local level in the Ruhr. Further, the Polish effort to win seats on local church councils indicates that by the eve of the First World War, Polish ties to their local communities were strengthening and Poles were gradually becoming stakeholders in the local Ruhr society.

The determination of the Poles to protect their ethnic autonomy was also directly responsible for the growing secularization of the Polish associational movement. At the turn of the century, only a handful of secular organizations existed. By 1912, however, over half the total 1,038 Polish associations was secular and the rapid growth of these associations led German officials to observe that Polish organizational activity was more intense in the Ruhr than in eastern Germany. The various secular associations were diverse and ranged from politically active *Sokoły* (gymnastic societies) and voting associations to nonpolitical singing and independent women's societies.

Polish associations were subjected throughout the prewar period to constant police supervision and their meetings were often disbanded by the police when they were considered too nationalistic in character. By 1909, Polish associations were deemed enough of a threat to the state that a centralized office under the police president in Bochum was created to coordinate surveillance across the Ruhr. The reporting activities of this office lasted well into the late 1920s. In addition to surveillance, other laws and police orders prohibited the open display of symbols, such as club flags and uniforms, deemed national in character and banned certain Polish songs, pictures, books, and newspapers. Perhaps the best example of the government's attempts to limit the growth of Polish organizations was the Reichsvereinsgesetz (Law on Associations) of 1908. The law required the use of the German language in all publicly held Polish meetings in the Ruhr except for those related to elections. Despite the various restrictions, Polish organizations persevered and thrived.

The growth of ethnic associations, participation in strikes at work, and protests against the Church highlight the growing willingness of Poles to defend their interests. Poles were increasingly active in the political arena as well. As citizens of the Kingdom of Prussia, the Poles who migrated from eastern Germany enjoyed the same right to vote in local, regional, and national elections as Germans. By the turn of the century, the Polish community formed an important political constituency in the Ruhr. While Poles had difficulty in electing their own candidates to office because in most Ruhr communities they remained numerically in the minority, Polish electoral support often determined whether a German political party won or lost an election. As a consequence, Polish influence on local and regional politics in the Ruhr was significant.

In the first phase of Polish migration to the Ruhr, Poles allied themselves politically almost exclusively with the Catholic-dominated Center Party. With the increasing tensions between the Church and Poles beginning in the 1890s, however, this support began to waver. In the elections of 1893 the leading Polish newspaper in the Ruhr, the *Wiarus Polski*, questioned whether Poles should provide such blind support to the Center Party. Four years later, Poles initially planned to withhold support for the Center before ultimately relenting and endorsing the party two days before the election in exchange for Church promises of improved spiritual care.

After the turn of the century, the ongoing tension with the Church as well as the increasingly anti-Polish line of the Center prompted Poles to run their own candidates in the national parliamentary election of 1903. Although Poles were well aware that their candidates could not be elected, their action did cause Center candidates in three Ruhr voting districts to lose. In the later parliamentary elections of 1907 and 1912, Poles similarly fielded their own candidates in the first round of elections while generally withholding their support for the Center in the second round of elections.

The political orientation of Poles, however, was also increasingly more difficult to direct from above or from afar. In the years leading up to the war, the unity of the Polish ethnic voting bloc was declining as many working-class Poles projected an independent political identity that often did not conform to the will of local Ruhr-Polish leaders or to the desires of Polish political circles in Posen. The 1912 parliamentary elections provide a telling example. In this election, Poles went against the recommendations of Polish leaders and gave critical electoral support to socialist candidates in three electoral districts in the Ruhr.

In addition to the role of Polish voters in being a deciding factor in many national elections, Polish political power was also growing on the local level after the turn of the century. In national elections, there was universal male suffrage; local elections for town councils, however, were run according to the Prussian three-class franchise system (which divided the voters by their direct tax revenue into three classes) that placed working-class Poles at a severe disadvantage. Nevertheless, by 1912, Poles were able to attain a degree of electoral success, holding 32 seats on local town councils throughout the Ruhr. In addition, the Polish community could often act as a swing vote in local politics, throwing their support behind the German party that best addressed their needs.

War, peace, and the decline of the Polish community in the Ruhr, 1914–1924

On the eve of the First World War, the Polish community had firmly established itself in the Ruhr. Although Poles continued to suffer discrimination at the hands of the state, their community was stable, vibrant, and increasingly accepted as an integral part of working-class society. The war challenged and transformed this state of affairs. Although most Poles would not have sought the outbreak of war, they were loyal to the German war effort. Polish organizations such as the ZZP declared their support and joined other German unions in the *Burgfrieden*, or civil peace. Thousands of military-age Polish men served in the German army. By the end of 1916, Germany's declared support for the establishment of a Polish state after the war was accompanied by the relaxation of most of the government's anti-Polish measures in the Ruhr. This increased freedom of action, however, brought little relief for ordinary Poles suffering under the hardships of war. Food shortages, the limited availability of consumer goods, and declining real wages were all part of daily life in the Ruhr in the last two years of the war. As a result, Poles, like their German counterparts, were growing increasingly militant. By 1917, sporadic wildcat strikes occurred at mines where Poles worked throughout the Ruhr.

The demise of Imperial Germany in 1918 was generally welcomed by a majority of Poles in the Ruhr. After 123 years, the Polish state was reestablished and the Treaty of Versailles provided Poles living in Germany with wide-ranging minority protections, including the right to Polish language education for children. The weakness of the early Weimar social order, however, also adversely affected Poles. Economically, the growing rate of inflation, which exploded with the French occupation of the Ruhr in 1923, caused a decline in real wages. Even more worrisome was the growing radicalization of politics on the left and the right, highlighted by strikes of revolutionary pro-communist groups and the right wing Kapp Putsch in 1920. Although Poles generally remained aloof from these events since they considered them "German matters," the disorder caused widespread insecurity within the community. Further, the German government suspected that Poles were behind some of the turmoil and surreptitiously began closely monitoring Polish activity again.

Poles also faced significant resentment in German society generally. Many Germans could not understand how Germany lost the war and felt that the nation had been betrayed. The enlargement of the Polish state at the expense of Germany, as called for in the Treaty of Versailles, produced widespread bitterness toward Poles among all German social classes. This antipathy grew as tensions increased between the German and Polish governments over final borders and the status of ethnic minorities in each country. Further, the fact that the new Polish state was closely allied with France made many in Germany view Poles as a potential fifth column.

Most ominous was the growing hostility of the German working class toward Poles. Although all of the German trade unions in the Ruhr spoke out against interethnic animosity, many in the rank and file ignored these appeals. Radical elements blamed Poles for thwarting the success of the revolutionary movement in the Ruhr, particularly after the Soviet defeat in the Polish-Soviet war of 1920. Newly arrived German refugees from Poland demanded that employers fire Poles in retribution for their own dislocation. Resentment against Poles was particularly bitter during the period leading up to and after the plebiscites in Upper Silesia and East Prussia and during the Ruhr occupation, when Poles, even though the majority supported the policy of passive resistance, were accused of aiding the French. Against the backdrop of growing tensions in the early 1920s, many Poles increasingly felt compelled to leave the Ruhr.

Leaders of the Polish community in the Ruhr had been preparing for an eventual return to their homeland as early as 1916. When Polish statehood was reestablished, a sizable number of Poles immediately emigrated. It is estimated that by August 1919 approximately 40,000 Ruhr-Poles had returned to Posen while figures for the other eastern provinces are not available. Many of the early return migrants, however, were disappointed by the dismal economic prospects in Poland. As news of the unstable conditions there filtered back to the Ruhr, most Poles adopted a "wait and see" attitude toward returning. By the end of 1920, however, ethnic tensions in the Ruhr and provisions in the Treaty of Versailles that required Poles who wished to acquire Polish citizenship to declare their intention to do so by January 1922 caused the Polish exodus from the Ruhr to resume. While no exact statistics are available on the number of Poles who returned to Poland, rough estimates place the total between 1919 and 1924 at approximately 100,000 to 130,000.

In addition to Poland, increasing numbers of Poles also looked to migrate to France. French mine companies were desperate for workers, and for Poles, the economic and social conditions both in the Ruhr and in their homeland made migration to France an attractive alternative. Beginning in 1920, French mine agents, with the support of the Polish government, surreptitiously began recruiting Polish workers from the Ruhr. By the end of the year, close to 3,000 Poles had migrated to France. Recruitment slowed to a near halt in 1921 after Poles who returned from France circulated reports in the Ruhr that conditions in French mines were poor. However, migration increased significantly the following year as close to 10,000 Poles left the Ruhr for France. With the occupation of the Ruhr in 1923 and labor unrest during 1924, Polish migration intensified. Polish government sources estimate that between 100,000 and 130,000 Poles from the Ruhr moved to France by the end of 1925.

Transformation and assimilation since 1925

By 1925, the Polish community in the Ruhr was a shadow of its former self. While over 100,000 Poles continued to live in the region, the vitality of the ethnic community had declined. Membership in Polish organizations throughout the Ruhr dropped significantly. For example, whereas 45,000 Poles were organized in the ZZP's miners' union in 1920, only 3,000 members remained by 1925. More important, the ability of the ethnic community to survive and reproduce itself into the second and third generation was in jeopardy. Enrollment in Polish language schools, which Poles organized with much fanfare beginning in 1919, fell dramatically. In 1921 there were approximately 10,700 students enrolled in Polish language classes. By 1932, fewer than 3,000 students participated in such courses.

The danger to the survival of the ethnic community posed by the massive emigration was of great concern to Poles who remained. As a consequence, Polish leaders in the Ruhr, together with representatives of Polish minorities in Berlin and eastern Germany, established in 1922 the Związek Polaków w Niemczech (Union of Poles in Germany, or ZPwN) in Berlin. The primary goal of the new ZPwN was to ensure the protection of Polish minority rights in Germany, an objective of increasing importance in the Weimar and Nazi periods due to the continued discrimination and derision faced by Poles in German society. The ZPwN made frequent appeals against such inequity directly to the highest levels of government. While unable to end all abuses, the ZPwN was successful in ensuring that the most egregious

examples of discrimination were corrected. The outspokenness of the ZPwN, however, came with a tragic price. After the outbreak of the Second World War, many of the leaders of the organization were imprisoned and murdered by the Nazi regime. Despite this loss, the ZPwN survived and after the war it reestablished itself in Bochum, where it remains active to this day.

The continued existence of an organization such as the ZPwN highlights the determination of Poles to preserve ethnic awareness across generations. Nevertheless, during the interwar period, Poles were unable to maintain the high level of ethnic cohesion that marked the community before the First World War. While full integration of the Polish community into German society did not occur until after the Second World War, when new immigrants from southern and later southeastern Europe displaced Poles as the leading subaltern group, the trend toward assimilation was evident in the interwar period.

In particular, the lack of significant numbers of new migrants to the Ruhr after the early 1920s limited the extent to which the ethnic community could replenish its losses and remain dynamic. Even more important, the Poles of the first generation who remained were the ones most amenable to assimilating. For them, bonds to their local communities outweighed distant ties to their homeland. This was particularly true for their children, the majority of whom were born and raised in the Ruhr, spoke fluent German, and did not need the same degree of protection that a strong ethnic community afforded. While the second generation continued to value elements of their ethnic heritage, ethnicity was increasingly becoming more of a sensibility rather than an active need-oriented system of ethnic mobilization. With this transformation, the history of the Polish community in the Ruhr gradually drew to a close.

Kleßmann, Christoph. *Polnische Bergarbeiter im Ruhrgebiet. Soziale Integration und nationale Subkultur einer Minderheit in der deutschen Industriegesellschaft.* Göttingen, 1978.

Kulczycki, John L. *The Foreign Worker and the German Labor Movement: Xenophobia and Solidarity in the Coal Fields of the Ruhr, 1871–1914.* Providence, 1994.

Murphy, Richard Charles. *Guestworkers in the German Reich: A Polish Community in Wilhelmine Germany.* Boulder, 1983.

Murzynowska, Krystyna. *Die polnischen Erwerbsauswanderer im Ruhrgebiet während der Jahre 1880–1914.* Dortmund, 1979.

Oenning, Ralf K. *"Du da mitti polnischen Farben." Sozialisationserfahrungen von Polen im Ruhrgebiet 1918–1939.* Münster, 1991.

Peters-Schildgen, Susanne. *"Schmelztiegel" Ruhrgebiet. Die Geschichte der Zuwanderung am Beispiel Herne bis 1945.* Essen, 1997.

Stefanski, Valentina-Maria. *Zum Prozeß der Emanzipation und Integration von Außenseitern: Polnische Arbeitsmigranten im Ruhrgebiet.* Dortmund, 1984.

Cross-references: Germany; Poland; French, Belgian, British, and U.S. American Occupation Troops in Western and Southwestern Germany, 1918–1930; German Immigrants in Germany from Territories Ceded after World War I; Greek Labor Migrants in Western, Central, and Northern Europe after 1950: The Examples of Germany and the Netherlands; Italian Labor Migrants in Northern, Central, and Western Europe since the End of World War II; Portuguese Labor Migrants in Northwestern Europe since the 1950s: The Examples of France and Germany; Spanish Labor Migrants in Western, Central, and Northern Europe since the End of World War II; Yugoslav Labor Migrants in Western, Central, and Northern Europe since the End of World War II

POLISH LABOR MIGRANTS IN CENTRAL AND WESTERN EUROPE AFTER 1989

Ewa Morawska

Polish seasonal workers harvesting cabbage in 2004 on a field of the "Agrar GmbH Wittow Süd" near Altenkirchen on the German island of Rügen (*ullstein bild*).

Although the collapse of the Soviet regime in eastern Europe opened the door for the accelerated incorporation of the region into the global economy, the long-term process of capitalist perestroika, including the modernization of inefficient, state-socialist economies, has thus far not diminished the long-standing gap in economic development between the eastern and western parts of the European continent. Measured in terms of per capita gross national product (GNP), the economic performance of east-central Europe in 2000 was only 36% of that of western Europe (a minimal improvement since 1910, when it was 28%) while the ratio of average wages between these two parts of the Continent in 2000 was between 1:3 and 1:4 and between 1:4 and 1:6 in 1910). The respective values for Poland reflect the same discrepancies. This enduring east-west disequilibrium in economic performance has sustained or, more precisely, revived the early 20th-century geographic pattern of income-seeking migrations from the region migrating westward, which fits into the worldwide pattern of population flows from the south and east to north and west.

The resumption of the mass westward migration of Poles has been facilitated by three factors. First, rapid advances in transportation and communication technologies have greatly increased the convenience of international movement and the cross-border lifestyle of (im)migrants. Second, changes in entry and exit policies of sending and receiving states have opened the door, literally and symbolically, between the former antagonists of the east-west conflict. Of particular consequence has been the "domestication" of passports in Poland (under the communist regime, passports were granted upon application only for specific reasons and had to be surrendered to the state authorities upon return) and the elimination of entry visas, as well as work permits, in most west European countries for east-central Europeans. Thus, in May 2004 Ireland, Sweden, and the UK opened their labor markets, followed by Greece, Italy, Spain, and Portugal in May 2006, and the Netherlands in May 2007. Countries

such as Norway, Denmark, France, and Belgium require migrants from east-central Europe to obtain (easily available) permission to work before undertaking employment. Third, the steady demand for cheap and dispensable labor on the one hand and for a highly skilled workforce in the informal and primary sectors of the postindustrial economies of west European countries on the other has created a labor market for Poles and other east Europeans seeking better wages and careers.

Two features differentiate post-1989 Polish migration from earlier waves: their temporary rather than permanent character and their primary orientation toward west European destinations in place of the USA, which earlier served as the traditional recipient of Polish immigrants. The three most common types of international migration of Poles since the last decade of the 20th century have been (1) temporary visits to the West as *Arbeitstouristen* or labor tourists who remain abroad and engage in work without the appropriate immigration documents, usually for a period of three to six months; (2) contracted seasonal and other work-related sojourns; and (3) the migration of highly educated and highly skilled members of Poland's postcommunist economy, including so-called brain-drain (e)migration.

The figures provided by agencies that track labor and population movement as well as local surveys in the sending and receiving countries suggest that the total number of temporary absentees in the prerecession era or until the spring of 2008 was 1.5 million to 2 million people; most were income-seeking migrants in the three categories discussed earlier. Of this figure, between 1 million and 1.3 million were low- and high-skilled Poles legally employed in western EU countries in jobs they found themselves: the largest numbers, 700,000–750,000 in the UK and Ireland; 200,000–250,000 in southern Europe (Italy, Spain, and Greece combined), and about the same number in the Scandinavian countries and the Netherlands. *Arbeitstouristen* primarily in Germany, Austria, and the USA numbered between 150,000 and 200,000; and the remainder – about 350,000 – were seasonal contract workers. With the onset of the economic recession in the West, an estimated 200,000–250,000 Polish labor migrants have returned to Poland since the summer of 2008; it is expected, however, that they will migrate again as soon as the labor markets recover.

The available data suggest that the typical Polish income-seeking migrants to the West have this sociodemographic profile: most (65%–70%) were of urban origin and, within this category, primarily from small- to mid-sized cities; there were slightly more (55%–65%) men than women; the typical age range was 25 to 40 years; 55%–60% had a mid-level education; and 20%–35% were unemployed at the time of migration. The majority of these male labor migrants find employment in construction, agriculture, or a wide variety of service trades. Women are most commonly employed in domestic services (as maids and housekeepers, baby-sitters, caregivers to the elderly), in bars and restaurants, and as cleaners and pieceworkers. The average monthly wages of these contract workers ranged between 800 and 1,000 euros in 2004, or two to three times more than they would have earned in Poland during the same time. Because of their legal status, the reception of seasonal and contract workers by their host employers has been friendlier than that encountered by their undocumented fellow nationals. However, the short-term sojourns of these migrant laborers and their concentration in low-pay, low-status jobs have not been conducive to their integration into west European receiver societies.

Sociological studies regarding the post-1989, low-skilled Polish migrants in the West indicate that both documented employees and "tourist-workers" tend to remain within their own social circles, largely isolated from everyday contact with the host-country institutions and their representatives. The principal reason for this isolation is the unfamiliarity of the migrants with the language of their host countries and their absorbing "*trans*national" lives. Ethnographic studies, however, suggest that during their sojourns in western Europe Polish migrants take on some habits of their host countries, such as discipline on the job and self-reliance, which are seen as evidence of their acculturation to the new, capitalist system. (The structurally induced lack of commitment to hard work and "expectant" attitudes toward the provider state among citizens of state-socialist countries – integral elements of the so-called *homo sovieticus* syndrome – have been central critiques of the communist system among social scientists and political opponents.)

Polish professionals, currently no more than 2,000–2,500 annually, make up a minority among seasonal workers. Since the 1990s they have been employed on 12- to 36-month contracts in western Europe as doctors and nurses (their primary occupations, particularly in Scandinavia as well as Germany, mainly in provincial hospitals and retirement homes) and by engineering and computer companies. These migrants, usually professional couples between 25 and 34 years old, take contract jobs in the West not only because of the much higher remuneration (4–6 times more than in Poland), but also to gain occupational experience and improve their skills in the language of their host country. They adapt well to conditions in their host countries and feel their identity as Europeans is bolstered by sojourns in the West.

The third and last group of international migrants considered here, highly skilled members of the workforce in Poland's new capitalist economy, consists of managers of successful private businesses in service and production, including those owned by east-west joint ventures and multinational companies that employ increasing numbers of native workers. They venture to the West in search of more remunerative jobs and better career opportunities either on their own or after being transferred abroad by their firms. Members of this group are mostly young (under 35), have a graduate or postgraduate education, and reside in large urban centers. They are fluent in foreign languages. In 2005, men still constituted the majority of this group, but the share of women has been on a steady increase since the 1990s. The occupational activities of the highly skilled migrants and their inclusion in corporate structures, typically on the basis of a junior partnership, facilitate their integration into European (rather than country-specific) professional and organizational culture.

Although all three categories of post-1989 migrants prefer to go abroad temporarily, some decide to remain in the West permanently. Except for sporadic data on particular professional specializations or individual towns, however, no reliable information on the number of migrants who have remained in their host country is available. The "brain drain" emigration of Poles to western Europe (and North America) most likely constitutes the largest group among the nonreturnees. While the trend has abated since the early 1990s, the exodus of highly skilled Polish professionals nevertheless continues. Currently, this group includes in particular younger employees from the occupations named above as well as contract workers, especially specialists in the medical and high-tech engineering fields and scientists and researchers, who initially leave for short-term jobs and then when these jobs end search for, and often find, jobs in the West that offer greater professional opportunities and much higher salaries than those available at home. Marriage to native citizens of the western host countries has been another reason that temporary sojourners have become permanent immigrants. Anecdotal evidence points to the concentration of such marriages in Holland, Sweden, and Italy, but the phenomenon has not yet been systematically investigated.

Fassmann, Heinz, and Rainer Münz, eds. *Ost-West-Wanderung in Europa*. Vienna and Cologne, 2000.

Favell, Adrian. "The New Face of East West Migration in Europe." *Journal of Ethnic and Migration Studies* 34 (2008), no. 5: 701–16.

Górny, Agata, and Paolo Ruspini, eds. *Migration in the New Europe: East-West Revisited*. Basingstoke, 2004.

Iglicka, Krystyna. *Kosntrasty Migracyjne Polski. Wymiar Transatlantycki*. Warsaw, 2008.

Kaczmarczyk, Paweł. "Współczesne Procesy Migracyjne z Polski." *Przegląd Polonijny* 124 (2007), no. 2: 41–74.

Pallaske, Christoph. *Migrationen aus Polen in die Bundesrepublik Deutschland in den 1980er und 1990er Jahren.* Munich and Berlin, 2002.

Cross-references: Austria; France; Germany; Italy; The Netherlands; Northern Europe; Poland; Spain and Portugal; Southeastern Europe; *Aussiedler/Spätaussiedler* in Germany since 1950; Polish Undocumented Immigrants in Berlin since the 1980s

POLISH POLITICAL REFUGEES IN CENTRAL AND WESTERN EUROPE IN THE 19TH CENTURY

Jerzy W. Borejsza

The Polish national insurrections (1830–1, 1846, 1848–9, 1863–4) against foreign domination of Poland, partitioned among Russia, Prussia, and Austria, led to the emigration of 20,000–30,000 Polish political refugees to other European countries. Most went to France, which was home to between 4,000 and 6,000 émigrés. The most important centers of exile were Paris, London, Brussels, Istanbul, and various cities in Switzerland. The emigrants were geographically highly mobile, moving from country to country, depending on living conditions and the possibilities of working for Poland's liberation. Thousands migrated between the German states and France or Switzerland, or between the Ottoman Empire and western Europe. From England, some of the émigrés went to the USA and Canada; many settled permanently in those countries and severed ties to their former comrades-in-arms in Europe. The largest geographic movement of refugees, however, occurred between the three partitioned sections of Poland.

These events are enshrined in Poland's cultural memory as the "Great Emigration," and they led in the "long" 19th century to the formation of a European network of nationalistically minded Poles. The terms "Polish emigrants" and "Polish emigration" have an unmistakably positive connotation in the Polish language. The Great Emigration created institutions that still exist in the 21st century – for example, the Polish Library in Paris, founded in 1842, and the Polish Museum in Rapperswil, Switzerland, established in 1870.

Poles were the clear majority among the refugees alongside groups from the Lithuanian-Belarus regions or Polish Jews who had participated in the uprisings. They were overwhelmingly men, especially in the initial period after 1830, which saw the flight of rebels of the nationalist movement who had refused an amnesty from the Russian czar and Polish king, Nikolas I, or had been excluded from it. Although most of the emigrants were young, they suffered an unusually high rate of mortality. Between 1831 and 1842, for example, more than 10% of all refugees died in the Polish emigration. The backdrop to this was physical and psychological stress: misery, malnourishment, poor sanitary conditions, unfamiliar climates, a foreign environment, and separation from the family.

The partition of Poland among Russia, Prussia, and Austria (1772, 1793, and 1795) had already led to the flight especially of leading Polish politicians. The first wave of emigration followed the defeat of the Confederation of Bar (a league of Polish nobles and gentry aimed against Russia) and the first partition of Poland. The refugees went to the Ottoman Empire, Switzerland, and France. A wave of refugees came to Saxony after the defeat of Poland in the war against Russia (1792) and the second partition of the country. After the collapse of the Kosciuszko Uprising in 1794 and the third partition of Poland, the destination countries of the émigrés were France and Italy.

A mass movement occurred only after 1797, when, as a result of a treaty between Polish opposition politicians and the French-controlled Lombard Republic in Italy, Polish legions were raised. They served Napoleon's political goals and were made up of Polish prisoners of war, Poles who had deserted the Austrian army, and emigrants. In five years, around 1,000 officers and about 25,000 noncommissioned officers and soldiers passed through these legions, where French pay created trained personnel who subsequently formed the basis for the army of the short-lived Duchy of Warsaw (1807–15). The Dabrowski Mazurka "Poland Is Not Yet Lost," named after Jan Henryk Dabrowski, the Polish commander of the Italian legions, is still the Polish national anthem. The idea of preserving the memory of the Polish nation within the organizational framework of the Polish legions was also carried on, down to the legions of Józef Piłsudski, which helped Poland regain its independence in 1918.

The Great Emigration

Following the failed Polish uprising against czarist rule in November of 1830, 48,000 soldiers from the Polish army who had come from the Russian partition zone were interned in Prussia and Austria. A time of mass migrations between the partition regions now began. At Russia's insistence, Prussian and Austrian officials forced the rebellious troops and noncommissioned officers whom they had disarmed to accept an amnesty from the czar. Most of amnestied troops were subsequently impressed into the Russian army. Officers predominated among those who did not accept the amnesty and left the partition zones. The flight into countries outside of the three partition states encompassed about 7,000–10,000 persons after 1830, among them members of the rebellious national government and delegates of the Polish parliament (*Sejm*). Three-quarters of the members of the political and military leadership were of noble background, with a high level of education and in part excellent foreign language skills. Hundreds of scholars, scientists, and artists left the country, among them the poet Adam Mickiewicz, the historian Joachim Lelewel (1786–1861), and the composer Fryderyk/Frédéric Chopin. Exile was also the choice of the president of the national government during the November uprising, Prince Adam Jerzy Czartoryski. They all died outside of Poland.

Until his death 30 years later, Prince Adam Jerzy Czartoryski was the "uncrowned king of Poland" who always had possibilities of intervening on behalf of Polish independence at courts and with governments. His political faction, named the "Hôtel Lambert" after his place of residence in Paris, maintained constant contact with several European states through Polish diplomatic representatives and had great influence in the Balkans. Dozens of journals and periodicals were published by the Polish émigrés in Polish, French, German, and English. Also published in emigration were important works of Polish poetry and fiction and all of the Polish literature on independence. In 1848–9, the Polish generals Józef Bem, Wojciech Chrzanowski, Henryk Dembiński, Franciszek Sznayde, Ludwik Mierosławski, and Jan Skrzynecki played the role of "albatrosses of revolution," as the Germans called it, and led revolutions in Austria, Hungary, Italy, and in the German states. Poles worked as military advisors in nearly all European countries and especially in the Ottoman Empire.

The Great Emigration was continuously replenished by new waves of refugees: after the Polish uprisings of 1846 and 1848, hundreds of new emigrants ensured that it would continue, while large numbers of the Polish participants in the Hungarian revolution of 1849 found refuge in the Ottoman Empire. Later came the Polish refugees from the Russian army, who fled during the Crimean War (1853–6). Another 10,000 refugees joined the exodus after the January uprising of 1863–4, though their social background was more diverse than that of the "people of the November uprising." They were mostly partisans and not professional soldiers, and the numbers of the nobility among them were also noticeably lower.

The integration of the refugees

In the 1830s, nationalists and democrats in the German states, in France, Belgium, and in part also in Great Britain enthusiastically welcomed the Polish immigrants as fighters for Polish liberty against the Russian army. The German national movement celebrated Polish national resistance with "Polish songs" in a veritable "mania for Poles." The governments of the July monarchy in France (1830–48) and pro-Polish committees in many European countries created a system of support and aid for Polish emigrants. The refugees from the November uprising internalized the way outsiders saw them and said of themselves: "In the face of emigration, of the eternal wanders and exiles, the kings are seized by fear, but in the people we arouse enthusiasm and determination. Consequently we hold an important position."

But that would not last. Antipathy toward the Polish emigrants grew especially after 1864. This was caused by a lack of political understanding, in part even hostile attitudes in the German states and Italy; indifference in Great Britain and many other countries; difficulties for the emigrants in finding work; language problems; political persecution; and pressure from Russian diplomats, especially in Saxony, Bavaria, and

Belgium. Only France and Switzerland were the exception. As romantics of liberty and imitators of the "springtime of nations," many Polish émigrés from the January uprising of 1863–4 felt alienated in an increasingly industrialized Europe. Thousands of Poles – emigrants from the January uprising and participants in other streams of refugees – went to the Austrian partition territory of Galicia after 1867. After the war against Prussia, the severely weakened Austria had withdrawn politically from this area and had granted this part of the empire de facto autonomous status (free development of learning and culture).

The social integration of the Polish refugees in the destination countries depended on a variety of factors. While France offered support and aid after 1830, the July monarchy was simultaneously afraid of the revolutionary extremism of the Poles, most of whom had military training. As a result, they were initially prevented from settling freely in Paris. Only around 700 Poles were living in Paris and its environs (Département Seine) in 1841, but their number was steadily growing. In the provinces, the government set up enclosed dépôts in which Polish soldiers, but also civilians, could be closely watched. Among other places, these settlements were found in Avignon (maximum occupancy about 1,200, of which nearly 900 were officers) and in Bourges (maximum occupancy 1,600, of which 200 were soldiers); smaller dépôts existed in Lons-le-Saunier, Salins, and Dijon. Most of these installations were under the authority of the Ministry of War; by contrast, the camp in Châteauroux, which was reserved for civilians, was run by the Ministry of the Interior (maximum occupancy 620, including a few military personnel). The dépôts were disbanded after 1833 and the Poles were dispersed to various locations; 70 remained in Châteauroux. The government of the "bourgeois monarch" Louis-Philippe (1830–48) granted the Poles a small subsidy in the form of military pay. The subsequent French governments continued this pay until the establishment of the Third Republic, when it was drastically cut as punishment for the participation of 600 Polish emigrants in the uprising of the Paris Commune in 1871.

According to an incomplete statistic from the end of September 1835, 4,713 Polish emigrants were living in France, 4,657 of whom received pay. By 1839, the subsidy was being paid to 5,472 Poles. Later, the number of those entitled to receive it gradually declined. If one considers that many Poles received no support, the number of Polish political émigrés in France is likely to have exceeded 6,000, especially if one takes into account the emigration following the Polish uprisings. In 1845, there were at least 4,739 Poles among the total of 12,203 émigrés of various nationalities in France. It can be estimated that between 1831 and 1847, about 11,000 Poles, mostly men, found temporary or permanent refuge in France.

A fairly large number of Polish refugees married French women. The Polish emigrants who had a profession learned in their homeland or abroad (doctors, engineers, teachers, civil servants) adjusted quickly to the host society; the same was often true of children of mixed marriages. Members of noble families, who were often financially supported from Poland, had an easier time – not only in France – in establishing contacts with families of the same social class and entering into marriages befitting their status. As a result, the Poniatowski, Palewski, Lipkowski, or Wolowski families, well known in French politics and finance to this day, have been assimilated for generations while remaining aware of their Polish roots and cultivating their family history. At the same time, Polish families, especially in and around Paris, preserved the Polish language and Polish customs across three or four generations into the 20th century, as revealed by the histories of the Gałęzowski, Mickiewicz, or Gierszyński families. Most political refugees preserved their Polish identity. Generation after generation they strived to return to an independent Poland.

In service to the Turkish sultan, Poles gained entry more quickly into the local elites than was the case in western and central Europe. Provided they converted to Islam, educated Polish military men or civilians found nearly all doors open to them. That is how Józef Bem and Michał Czajkowski became generals of the army of the Ottoman Empire, as did Konstanty Borzęcki, who also emerged as one of the fathers of pan-Turkism. In western and central Europe, the keys to integration differed from one country to the next: for example, a Catholic confession, membership in a Freemason lodge, or membership in political organizations or in professional associations could facilitate the entry of Poles into their host society.

In Belgium, following the founding of the state in 1830, a lack of personnel led to many Polish officers being taken into the army. In France, Polish émigrés were allowed to serve only in three newly established foreign legions after 1830. In Great Britain, Poles were supported much less and also much later than in France, Belgium, or some of the German states. It was only in 1834, in response to a request from the Literary Association of the Friends of Poland, that annual support for about 500 Polish emigrants was enacted.

Based on the experiences during the Great Emigration, a variety of images about the Poles endured in Europe. Because often the best-educated segments of the Polish elite emigrated after 1830–1, 1846, 1848–9, and 1863–4, the stereotype arose in central and western Europe of the "educated Poles," "chivalrous and brave soldiers" who were always ready for battle and sometimes possessed astounding language skill. For example, a number of Poles were on the editorial teams of the French encyclopedias, worked in the French banking system, or served as British agents in Asia. In all destination countries they were found as journalists, engineers, administrators, and lawyers. The Poles of the Great Migration were thus seen as educated Europeans with only slightly divergent customs and habits. The positive notions that the natives associated with the Polish emigrants were fundamentally different from the images that were generated in the late 19th and early 20th centuries by the rural labor migration that flowed from villages in Galicia or Russian-Poland to the destination areas in northern and central Europe.

The Poles brought with them to western and central Europe new knowledge about east-central and eastern Europe, in part also about Asia. Conversely, the Polish emigrants who returned to Galicia after 1867 were regarded as bearers of western European civilization. After his return to Galicia, Karol Świdziński – the cousin of Jarosław Dąbrowski, commander in chief of the troops of the Paris Commune, and like him a refugee from the uprising of 1863–4 and an officer in the Paris Commune – built railroad lines and penned one of the manifestos of Polish Positivism. Konstanty Bobczyński, a nobleman from the region of Sanok in the foothills of the Carpathians, who had participated in the Hungarian Revolution in 1849, became during his emigration a textile merchant and then secretary of the Polish Section of the First International, where he collaborated with Karl Marx. Back in Galicia, and drawing on his experiences in England, he fought for universal suffrage and became a delegate in the Galician Sejm. These are only two examples of the roles that dozens of returned emigrants played in modernizing their country.

The Great Emigration was the breeding ground for the modern political parties in Poland. Apart from the conservative group of the Hôtel Lambert and many smaller organizations, 1832 saw the emergence of the prototype of the modern political party with a freely elected leadership: the Democratic Polish Society (Towarzystwo Demokratyczne Polskie, TDP), which developed into the largest political organization of exiled Poles. In 1835, the TDP, which was also active outside of France, had 1,193 members; in 1848 there were 2,105. In the 30 years of its existence, the TDP had about 4,000 members. It published a weekly (*Demokrata Polski*, with editorial offices in Poitiers, Paris, Brussels, and London) as well as other journals and brochures. Zygmunt Miłkowski, an important member of the society, better known under his nom de plume, Teodor Tomasz Jeż, founded the Liga Polska in 1887, the germ cell of one of the great Polish political parties of the 20th century, the National Democracy (Narodowa Demokracja, ND). Another emigrant, the general of the Paris Commune and last secretary of the Polish Section of the First International, Walery Wróblewski, became the figurehead of the Polish Socialist Party (Polska Partia Socjalistyczna, PPS).

In their modern history, the Poles were never again as famous in Europe as they were after the uprisings, when "the Polish nobility was the general staff of sansculottes everywhere in the world," as one Polish writer put it. Thanks to Polish political refugees, Poles appeared in the works of Victor Hugo, Gottfried Keller, Théophile Gautier, Gustave Flaubert, Jules Michelet, Giuseppe Mazzini, Félicité Robert de Lamennais, James Fenimore Cooper, and Heinrich Heine. In general, both the great literature and the forgotten penny literature was dominated by the heroic tone of veneration for the members of one of the great refugee movements of the 19th century.

Borejsza, Jerzy W. *Emigracja polska po powstaniu styczniowym.* Warsaw, 1966.

Gadon, Lubomir. *Wielka Emigracja w pierwszych latach po powstaniu listopadowym.* Paris, 1960.

Hahn, Hans Henning. *Außenpolitik in der Emigration. Die Exildiplomatie Adam Jerzy Czartoryskis 1830–1840.* Munich, 1978.

Kalembka, Sławomir. *Wielka Emigracja 1831–1863.* Thorn, 2003.

Karpus, Zbigniew, et al., eds. *W kraju i na wychodźstwie. Księga pamiątkowa ofiarowana Profesorowi Sławomirowi Kalembce.* Thorn, 2001.

Kuśmidrowicz-Król, Anna, et al., eds. *Polenbegeisterung. Deutsche und Polen nach dem Novemberaufstand 1830.* Warsaw, 2005.

Marchlewicz, Krzysztof. *Wielka Emigracja na Wyspach Brytyjskich (1831–1863).* Poznań, 2008.

Willaume, Małgorzata, ed. *Ku Niepodległej. Ścieżki polskie i francuskie 1795–1918.* Lublin, 2005.

Cross-references: Belgium and Luxembourg; France; Germany; Great Britain; Poland; Russia and Belarus; Southeastern Europe; Switzerland; Polish Agricultural Workers in Prussia-Germany from the Late 19th Century to World War II

POLISH SETTLERS IN BOSNIA AND HERZEGOVINA SINCE THE END OF THE 19TH CENTURY

Husnija Kamberović

After the Berlin Congress of 1878, Austria-Hungary took over the administration of Bosnia, which had been formerly under the control of the Ottoman Empire. As a consequence, a small number of Poles started to immigrate to Bosnia after 1878 as civilian and military officials of the Habsburg monarchy. Between 1895 and 1905 a further colonization took place, this time by rural Poles, mainly to the areas of Bosnian Krajina, Posavina, and central Bosnia. The government gave free land to a few of these immigrants. But owing to constant opposition from the local Orthodox population, others were forced to purchase land, primarily from Muslims who were immigrating to the Ottoman Empire in those same years. Since the immigrants came mainly from Galicia, the local population called them Galicians, a term with a pejorative connotation that referred both to the Poles, who were Roman Catholics, and to the Ukrainians, who were Greek Catholic Uniates.

The Poles moved to Bosnia through a process called "external colonization." With the support of the Habsburg authorities, the agricultural population of Austria-Hungary migrated to uninhabited and uncultivated areas of the new administrative territories of Bosnia and Herzegovina. Numerous agricultural colonies of Germans, Austrians, Hungarians, Italians, Slovenians, Czechs, Poles, and Ukrainians were created in those days. According to the official data 830 Polish rural families moved to Bosnia between 1895 and 1905. In 1910 there were some 11,000 Poles, located in 12 compact rural colonies (Čelinovac, Donji Bakinci, Miljevačka Kozara, Gornji Bakinci, Dubrava, Novi Martinac, Rakovac,

Gumjera, Kotorski Lug, Smrtići-Plačkovci, Kunova, and Grabašnica) and in about 30 mixed settlements. According to the 1921 census, there were still 11,000 Poles in Bosnia and Herzegovina, while on the eve of the Second World War their number had increased to about 20,000, primarily as the consequence of natural population growth.

In the period between the two world wars, there was a minor process of emigration of the Poles from Bosnia to the USA, where they usually joined their relatives who had moved there before the end of the 19th century. Apart from two failed attempts in 1911 to persuade the Poles to return home from areas near Bosanska Gradiška and Banja Luka, there were no cases of organized repatriation of Poles from Bosnia before the end of the Second World War. After the Second World War, however, Poles were systematically moved out of the Yugoslavian constituent republics of Bosnia and Herzegovina.

Little is known about the experiences or integration of the small number of Polish civil and military government employees, who numbered only some 600 in 1910. For Polish farmers, their residence in compact rural settlements, where their way of life was favorable for preserving their ethnic characteristics, mainly determined their experiences. Polish agricultural migrants enjoyed benefits as colonists, which caused the local population to develop a negative attitude toward them, leading to their social isolation. Although these state-sponsored benefits came to an end after the First World War, the locals still viewed the colonists as privileged foreigners.

Bosnia's Poles remained outside the mainstream of Bosnian society rather than becoming a part of it. By the end of the 19th century, they operated their own schools, received their priests from Polish sections of the double monarchy, and appealed for a separate Polish church organization. After the First World War, with the establishment of a Consulate of the Republic of Poland in Banja Luka, the Polish minority in Bosnia and Herzegovina received institutional support to resist assimilation into the Kingdom of Serbia, Croatia, and Slovenia (from 1929 the Kingdom of Yugoslavia). In some primary schools, special classes were initiated in Polish, and branches of the Polish cultural society Ognisko Polskie (Polish Home) promoted cultural life, folk music, sports, and lending libraries featuring books in Polish. On the eve of the Second World War, Poles formed the Savez Poljaka (Polish Alliance), with the goal of maintaining links with the Polish homeland.

Although Catholic by religion, Polish settlers successfully resisted assimilation to the local population, part of which was also Catholic. They often mixed and married with Ukrainians, who belonged to the Uniate denomination and also came from Galicia. The close links between the Poles and Ukrainians resulted from their linguistic kinship and the affinity of Ukrainian and Polish traditional rural culture, which differed from the popular culture of the local Bosnians. Although the Poles became bilingual shortly after their arrival, they preserved their own language with only minimal influence from the Bosnian idiom. The Ukrainian language, often spread through intermarriage, had more influence on the language of Polish immigrants. Bosnia's Poles maintained, together with the Ukrainians, the status of an immigrant minority until the end of the Second World War.

After the Second World War, the political situation became unfavorable for the Poles. They were subject to attacks from other peasants. These conditions resulted in a collective request to leave for Poland and within a short period of time some 14,000 Poles were systematically moved out of Bosnia-Herzegovina. The request to leave was permitted under the terms of a protocol signed by Yugoslavia and Poland on 2 January 1946. According to the protocol, each migrant who wanted to leave had to sign a statement that he was emigrating voluntarily and renouncing any claim to real estate in Yugoslavia. After the remigration, the lands and possessions of the Poles were distributed to newly immigrated internal Yugoslavian colonists.

After the large-scale remigration in 1946, the Poles who remained in Bosnia were subjected to renewed forces of assimilation, which led to further departures. Even before 1940, some Poles, driven by agrarian overpopulation, left Bosnia and Herzegovina for Croatia. Only at the end of the 1950s and in the early 1960s did this emigration to Croatia, and to a lesser extent to Vojvodina, become significant. For some Poles, their departure for Croatia or Vojvodina was only a first step on the longer journey to the USA or Australia. Ultimately, very few Poles remained: in 1991 only 526 Poles were recorded as living in Bosnia and Herzegovina.

Drljača, Dušan. *Kolonizacija i život Poljaka u jugoslovenskim zemljama od kraja XIX do polovine XX veka.* Belgrade, 1985.

Kamberović, Husnija. "Iseljavanje Poljaka iz Bosne i Hercegovine 1946. godine." *Časopis za suvremenu povijest* 30 (1988): 95–104.

Sobolevski, Mihael. "Poljska nacionalna manjina u Jugoslaviji tijekom Drugoga svjetskog rata." *Dijalog povjesničara-istoričara* 3 (2001): 371–88.

Cross-references: Southeastern Europe; Poland

POLISH UNDOCUMENTED IMMIGRANTS IN BERLIN SINCE THE 1980S

Norbert Cyrus

"Polish illegals" in Germany are illegal immigrants of Polish citizenship who are in the country without a residence or work permit. Others, after entering the country legally as tourists, have taken a job in contravention of the law, i.e., without a work permit, and/or continued their stay illegally, i.e., without a residence and work permit, after the expiration of their tourist visa. Many maintain the center of their life in Poland and come to Germany regularly or sporadically to engage in illegal work (as "work tourists").

It is, of course, impossible to make any precise statements about the number of Polish citizens who are in Berlin illegally. Polish sources estimate that about 200,000 Poles are among the work tourists in Germany. For Berlin, uncertain information suggests that there are about as many illegal as legal Polish citizens in the city. That would put the number of illegal Polish migrants in Berlin at around 30,000. The largest group belongs to the commuters whose lives are based in Poland and who are only temporarily in Berlin, with some also traveling home on the weekends.

Within the German public the presence of illegal Polish migrants in Berlin has attracted growing attention since the beginning of the 1980s. In the process, a remarkable change in perception has become evident: during the cold war, when the east-west migration was widely seen as people voting with their feet for the competing system, immigrants from Poland who settled in Berlin after the imposition of martial law in their country in 1981 were seen uniformly as "freedom fighters" and welcomed. From the middle of the 1980s, however, even before the end of the east-west conflict, when a growing number of immigrants came to Berlin after liberalization of Polish departure regulations and applied for asylum or admission as ethnic immigrants, they were increasingly given the pejorative label of "economic refugees." The possibilities for Polish citizens to enter as ethnic immigrants or asylum seekers were strongly curtailed by the German authorities at the beginning of the 1990s, especially through the Act Dealing with the Consequences of the War (1993), and have declined considerably. What came to the fore was the stereotype of the "illegal" Pole who was abusing the visa-free entry introduced in 1991 to work without a work permit on construction sites, clean private homes, or commit crimes, especially car theft. The largely negative perception of Poland and its citizens during this time culminated in the discriminatory saying: "*Kaum gestohlen, schon in Polen*" – "Barely stolen, already in Poland."

Patterns of movement

In the decades of the east-west conflict, Polish citizens had consistently been granted a right of residence in the Federal Republic for political reasons. Against this backdrop, the presence of Poles was seen – until the change in admission requirements in 1986 – not as a problem of illegality but at most as a problem of integration.

In many cases, the numerous Polish citizens and ethnic immigrants from Poland who had been living legally in Berlin since the 1970s supported the illegal movement and the illegal presence of their fellow countrymen and women, who were often relatives, friends, or former neighbors. At the end of the 1950s and after 1975, Berlin accepted a total of about 100,000 ethnic immigrants from Poland. Beginning in the mid-1970s, Polish citizens used the relatively liberal departure regulations to visit relatives in western countries, especially Germany, and to work in agriculture or construction while they were there. Because of the existing disparity in purchasing power, this kind of "work tourism" was exceedingly lucrative: at the beginning of the 1980s, the wages for one month of off-the-books employment in Germany was the equivalent of two years' income in Poland.

In general, the Polish "work tourists" of the 1970s and early 1980s returned to Poland. However, after the imposition of martial law in their country in December of 1981, Polish citizens who were in the West at that time decided to stay. The "new migration" from Poland began with the admission of the "Solidarność refugees." The resident Polish population in Berlin began to grow. After the lifting of martial law and the renewed relaxation of departure regulations in the middle of the 1980s, the number of tourist departures from Poland rose sharply once again: from just under 6.4 million cases in 1985 to 19.3 million in 1989. In 1989, alone, 250,000 ethnic immigrants and 26,000 asylum seekers from Poland were admitted throughout the country. The size of the registered Polish residential population in Germany grew from 104,800 in 1985 to 220,000 in 1989, to about 300,000 at the end of the 1990s; 10% of those lived in Berlin. Polish tourists used visa-free entry to boost their income through illegal work, or by selling everyday household items or smuggled cigarettes and vodka on the "Polish markets." In the second half of the 1980s, up to 100,000 Polish citizens came to the "Polish markets" in Berlin on the weekends. The Berlin authorities tried to stop the illegal trading activities with police measures. But it was only with the introduction of free market structures in Poland and the growing equalization of price levels between Poland and Germany that the markets began to disappear from the cityscape at the beginning of the 1990s.

It is not possible to identify a concentration of illegal Polish migrants from specific regions of origin. In principle, the illegal migration followed the routes of the legal or at least tolerated immigration of the Solidarność refugees, ethnic immigrants, and asylum seekers. In looking for housing and work, the illegal Polish migrants depended on the help of others, often relatives, neighbors, or friends who had emigrated to Germany legally. Over time, the social structure of the illegal commuters changed: initially they were individuals from cities with good or advanced qualifications, but since the 1990s there has been a rise in the numbers of less-qualified workers from rural regions.

Patterns of (non-)integration

The (non-)integration of illegal Polish migrants is connected to the change in West Germany's immigration policy. At the beginning of the 1980s, Polish citizens in the Federal Republic did not face any obstacles in terms of legal residence. Berlin authorities recommended that the immigrants apply not for asylum, but for a Duldung (exceptional leave to remain), which was easier to obtain but gave no access

to the labor market. The initially small but growing number of Polish citizens in Berlin with a Duldung status was therefore forced to engage in illegal work. Polish commuters also entered the shadow economy. The "shock therapy" pursued by the Polish government in the period of transformation after 1989 led to a massive devaluation of the zloty and rising unemployment, which sent many Poles to Berlin in search of alternative sources of income. Subsequently, the group of Poles in Berlin became further differentiated.

Some of the Poles who had been living in Berlin for a longer period had been able to establish themselves as self-employed professionals: doctors, lawyers, insurance brokers, merchants, or translators. In addition, in response to the denial of work permits by the German authorities, Poles with temporary residence permits set up their own illegal businesses, largely in construction and sometimes even without adequate skills. From the end of the 1980s there thus existed an infrastructure of established, precariously integrated, and increasingly illegal businesses which, for commercial reasons, found new migrants jobs and housing, offered employment, or sold medical care or other services for payment in cash. Interested parties could find relevant information in Polish-language magazines published in Berlin, such as Kontakty or Kurier Polski. At religious services held in the Polish language, which were attended by some of the illegal Poles in Berlin, one could also find bulletin boards with offers of work: it was here, for example, that one could find a house cleaning job with a family in Berlin, information that was sold for one month's salary.

However, Poles who were commuters or who lacked residence permits relied not only on commercial agents but also – especially in the initial period – on help from supportive networks of relatives or friends. Free housing and help in finding work at no fee offered the opportunity to become acquainted with a life in illegality in Berlin. The situation is especially precarious for illegal commuters, who often have to do without these supportive networks. Because of their legal exclusion, they are easy targets of fraud and exploitation. In the shadow economy, workers are often cheated out of part or even all of their wages. Especially in the initial phase, illegal migrants can get caught up not only in exploitive but also criminal networks.

A particularly extreme example are the human traffickers who lure young women to Berlin with false promises of jobs, take away their passports once they have arrived, charge them with fictitious expenses, and force them into prostitution. These women do not go to the police because they are afraid of these criminals or fear deportation. This kind of trafficking affected young Polish women especially in the second half of the 1980s; now the victims tend more to be women from the Baltic countries and the Commonwealth of Independent States (CIS) countries. Since the middle of the 1980s, Polish women have been successful mostly in the informal labor market for household help.

The "Polish cleaning lady" ensures cleanliness and order in many private homes in Berlin. A few of these women have been employed 12 years or longer; some have shifted the center of their lives to Berlin and are living with school-age children under illegal circumstances. Work in private homes provides them with some protection against monitoring. For similar reasons, men who live or work illegally in Berlin for extended periods prefer employment on small construction sites or in private homes, where the risk of control is lower and employers are considered less likely to report their illegal status.

While illegal residence in Berlin is motivated largely by economic considerations, some also seek it out to realize subculture lifestyles. Poles living in Berlin illegally display a whole panoply of different life situations and life plans that exist side-by-side and barely intersect. Some illegal migrants remain in the city because they have joined an eastern religious community or the colorful subcultures of punks, squatters, jazz, the techno scene, or homeless groups. The only common characteristics are the lack of the necessary residence and work permits and the legal marginalization this entails.

Nevertheless, the weak bonds that exist between the many illegal worlds and their Berlin surroundings are important, since they open up opportunities to expand and stabilize the sphere of daily life in illegality. Illegal commuting migration and illegal residence are embedded in a border-spanning, transnational social realm that is created by the mutual interactions of a multitude of heterogeneous actors of various nationalities and different legal situations of residence. Illegal migration is made possible only by the participation of Berlin residents of diverse nationalities who shelter illegal Poles and use their services as cleaning ladies, baby-sitters, old-age care providers, construction workers, gardeners, or car mechanics. Illegal Polish migrants are perfectly integrated into the informal economy, of which they form an integral part. Legally, however, they are completely marginalized. That is the reason that some return to Poland after years of illegal commuting migration or long-term illegal residence. Many remain in the vague hope of legalizing their residence somehow for themselves and their families. Some have in fact been able to legalize their residence through an arranged or genuine love marriage to a German or a foreigner with a residence permit. Socially, illegal Polish migrants are partly embedded in subcultural milieus, limited to Polish networks, or integrated into self-created transcultural circles of friends.

Poland's accession to the European Union in 2004 changed the background conditions. Barriers to immigration have fallen. After the end of the transition regulations, which restrict the freedom of Polish citizens to work in other EU countries until 2011, there will be free access to the labor market without the need for work permits and the right to settle in Germany. However, even then it is expected that Poles will continue to be informally employed in the shadow economy. Many of the Berliners who employ and hire illegal Polish migrants will have no interest in officially registered and therefore more expensive workers.

Cyrus, Norbert. "'…als alleinstehende Mutter habe ich viel geschafft.' Lebensführung und Selbstverortung einer illegalen polnischen Arbeitsmigrantin." In *Vom Wandergesellen zum "Green Card"-Spezialisten. Interkulturelle Aspekte der Arbeitsmigration im östlichen Mitteleuropa*, edited by Klaus Roth, 227–63. Münster, 2003.

Cyrus, Norbert, and Dita Vogel. "Managing Access to the German Labour Market – How Polish (Im)Migrants Relate to German Opportunities and Restrictions." In *Illegal Immigration in Europe: Beyond Control?*, edited by Franck Düvell, 71–105. Houndmills, 2002.

Miera, Frauke. *Polski Berlin. Migration aus Polen nach Berlin.* Münster, 2006.

Morawska, Ewa. "Structuring Migration: The Case of Polish Income-seeking Travellers to the West." *Theory and Society* 31 (2001): 47–80.

Morokvasic, Mirjana. "Settled in Mobility: Engendering Post-Wall Migration in Europe." *Feminist Review* 77, 1 (2004): 7–25.

Triandafyllidou, Anna. *Contemporary Polish Migration in Europe: Complex Patterns of Movement and Settlement.* Ceredigon and Washington, DC, 2007.

Cross-references: Germany; Poland; *Aussiedler/Spätaussiedler* in Germany since 1950; Polish Labor Migrants in Central and Western Europe after 1989

POLITICAL AND INTELLECTUAL REFUGEES FROM NAZI GERMANY AND FROM GERMAN-OCCUPIED EUROPE, 1933–1945

Peter Widmann

The majority of the approximately 500,000 individuals who fled the German Reich during the Nazi dictatorship were persecuted by the regime as "non-Aryans." A smaller number were representatives of the political opposition and intellectual dissidents from the country's literary, artistic, and scientific life. They formed that majority of the political and intellectual representatives of the Weimar Republic who sought refuge abroad following Hitler's takeover of power in 1933. They were characterized as much by a diversity of political convictions and self-understanding as they were by differences in social background, worldview, or artistic focus.

The distinction between political and intellectual or artistic exiles lacks the same kind of clarity as that between those persecuted for racial reasons and those persecuted for other reasons, especially since in many cases several criteria applied simultaneously. Some of the artists and scientists also exposed themselves politically, and many political opponents and dissidents from scholarship, science, and the world of culture were also persecuted as Jews. Thus, only a biographical study of each individual case would allow us to make a judgment about the weight of various motives and factors behind an individual's flight.

Waves of flight

In the 1930s, five waves of flight from Germany and Austria can be distinguished. The first refugees sought safety through a quick exit after Hitler's assumption of power in January 1933. That was especially true for members of the political opposition. A second wave came from Austria in 1934, where an authoritarian government quashed the workers' movement and had thousands of its representatives arrested. Social democrats and communists left along with unionists, members of the Republican Protection League (Republikanischer Schutzbund), and leftist youth organizations. These refugees, like those of the first wave, found safety especially in Czechoslovakia, but also in the Soviet Union.

Every territorial addition by Nazi Germany triggered further waves of flight. The re-annexation of the Saar region to the German Reich on 1 March 1935 forced many of those who had found refuge there after Hitler's takeover of power and the freedom to engage in political work to continue their migration. The former Reich Interior Minister Wilhelm Sollmann (SPD) and the communist Herbert Wehner were among the presumably more than 5,000 individuals to whom the Saar region, under administration by the League of Nations since 1920, had become a refuge. Most of those newly displaced went from there to France.

After this third wave, the annexation of Austria and the arrival of the Wehrmacht in that country in March 1938 triggered a fourth exodus. Social democrats and communists who were still in Austria had to flee, as did supporters of the Habsburg monarchy, conservatives, and representatives of the corporate state. Finally, a fifth wave followed the annexation of the Sudeten regions in the fall of 1938. Between 4,000 and 5,000 social democrats, around 1,500 communists, and about 150 members of the German Democratic Freedom Party (Deutsch-Demokratische Freiheitspartei), established in exile in 1937, settled in other countries.

Most political opponents and cultural dissidents initially sought refuge in neighboring states. Especially France and Czechoslovakia became the most important destinations between the Nazi takeover of power and the outbreak of the war. However, they offered only temporary safety: the refugees who had settled in Czechoslovakia had to leave the country again in 1938, after the government of Edvard Beneš gave up its liberal course in refugee policy under pressure from Berlin and the London strategy of appeasement. That same year, France also tightened its policy toward exiles. After the outbreak of the war, the advancing German troops triggered another exodus in many countries of Europe. Now it was above all the USA, but also South America, Palestine, and other countries overseas, that became the destinations of the refugees; among them, the USA remained the most important final destination. Thus many refugees reached a final place of residence only after several way stations.

The constant need to continue migrating was only one factor that drove members of the political, literary, artistic, and scientific exile community into difficult living conditions after their flight. Only a few prominent individuals, like Thomas Mann or Albert Einstein, were able to continue their careers without interruption. Most other exiles had to keep afloat with occasional jobs, suffering from humiliation, fears about surviving financially, and a loss of occupational-social status; no small number ended up psychologically shattered and committed suicide.

Another reason for the precarious situation of the refugees was the Nazi Law on the Revocation of Naturalization and the Loss of German Nationality of 14 July 1933. Among the 39,000 individuals who lost their citizenship through this law were many refugees from politics, science, and culture. The first denaturalization lists of the years 1933 to 1936 read like a Who's Who of public life in Germany before the Nazi takeover of power. Later, more and more nonprominent "little people" were added, who suffered the most from being stateless.

By stripping a person of citizenship as punishment for a lack of "loyalty to the Reich and nation," as stated in §2 of the law, the German authorities could also confiscate the assets of the person in question and transfer them to the Reich. Denaturalization could also affect spouses and children, since the law permitted *Sippenhaft* (kinship liability). The law also made it possible to revoke diplomas and doctoral degrees.

Political exile

An estimated 30,000 individuals left the German Reich as politically persecuted. Many of the political opponents left the country in the first months after the Nazis came to power. The prominent political figures of the Weimar Republic were among the first refugees, as were the local functionaries of the SPD, the KPD, and the unions, who had to fear becoming victims of Nazi acts of revenge where they lived. By fleeing the country they escaped abuse by the NSDAP-Sturmabteilung (SA) and internment in the hastily established concentration camps.

After the Nazi regime had repealed basic democratic rights, oppositional work was possible only outside the country. The new rulers used the fire in the Reichstag on the night of 28 February 1933 to justify the mass arrests of communists and to expose members of the SPD and of the social democratic militia Reich Banner Black-Red-Gold (Reichsbanner Schwarz-Rot-Gold). The day after the fire, the Decree of the Reich President for the Protection of the People and the State suspended basic rights of the Weimar Constitution. It intensified the persecution, as did the Enabling Law of 24 March, the outlawing of the SPD on 22 June, and a law of 14 July, which declared the NSDAP the only legal party.

By 1935, according to the League of Nations, 6,000–8,000 communists, 5,000–6,000 social democrats, and 5,000 other opponents had left the country. They included the former minister president of Prussia, Otto Braun (SPD), who fled to Switzerland as early as the beginning of March 1933, as well as the former Reich chancellors Joseph Wirth and Heinrich Brüning (both of the Zentrum party). All told, the political refugees included 27 members of previous governments at the Reich and state levels, as well as 267 deputies of the Reichstag and state parliaments. The majority of party-affiliated political refugees were single young men.

Between 1933 and 1938, the focal point of the political exile was chiefly in France, but also in Czechoslovakia. Both countries had comparatively liberal asylum laws and allowed the refugees to engage in political activity. In May 1933, the KPD set up a foreign office in Paris; beginning in the fall of 1933, it was also home to the Politburo, the party's leadership body. Party functionaries tried to maintain contact with communist groups in Germany via border bases in the Reich's neighbor countries. In 1935, the Soviet leadership summoned the leaders of the KPD to Moscow and placed it under supervision there. A foreign secretariat remained behind in Paris. The communists formed the largest group among the political exiles: 8,000–10,000 are likely to have fled from the Reich, the Saar region, and the Sudetenland.

In Prague, the second center of political exile, the SPD, which now called itself Sopade (Social Democratic Party of Germany), set up an exile board under Otto Wels and Hans Vogel. From the Czech capital, social democrats smuggled political literature to Germany. The logistical basis for this effort was provided by 16 border secretariats encircling the Reich and run by full-time functionaries. At the same time, the "Germany reports" issued by Sopade were intended to inform the world public about conditions in the Nazi state. Sudeten German democrats supported the work of the refugees from the Reich.

In May 1938, Sopade moved its headquarters to Paris, where a social democratic group had already existed since August 1933. A little over a year later, shortly before German troops occupied Paris on 14 July 1940, the members of the Sopade board had to flee again. In 1940, the party leadership reconstituted itself in London.

Most pacifists also escaped into neighboring countries, especially to France, Czechoslovakia, and Great Britain. In Paris, a legal advisory service for refugees from Germany was set up in the spring of 1933 at the headquarters of the French League of Human Rights. Groups of the German League of Human Rights (Deutsche Liga für Menschenrechte), outlawed in the Nazi state, were set up in Paris, Strasbourg, Lyon, and London.

Political refugees from the liberal, conservative, and national milieu could count on far less support from their parties than the social democrats and communists. Left to their own devices, they participated as individuals in political initiatives – for example in the German Democratic Freedom Party, which the Center (Zentrum) politician Carl Spiecker had founded in Paris in 1937. Little political activity came from right-wing political refugees, among whom were also disappointed National Socialists. The most prominent among them was Otto Strasser, who had set up the voelkish-

social revolutionary Black Front in the summer of 1931. He tried, with little success, to run the organization from Prague after Hitler's takeover of power.

While many of those persecuted as Jews wished to leave Germany and Austria for good with their escape, most political refugees wanted to return home as soon as possible. They were hoping for the downfall of the Nazi regime, not for their integration into a country of refuge. Many saw themselves as representatives of a different Germany that was to survive in temporary exile.

Communist activists expected a workers' uprising in Germany that would overthrow Hitler. Only when they realized that their hope for proletarian self-liberation was futile did they proclaim the idea of a popular front. The executive board of the SPD in exile in Prague also placed its hopes on a revolution in its Prague Manifesto in January 1934. Communists and social democrats cultivated contacts with resistance groups in Germany, but those links broke off in the middle of the 1930s when it became clear that the dictatorship had consolidated itself and that the Gestapo was leading a successful fight against the political work in the underground.

Like the Left worldwide, many political refugees saw the Spanish Civil War as a battle against National Socialism. Refugees from all the countries of exile went to Spain in 1936 to fight against the forces of General Franco on the side of the Republicans. Two-thirds of the approximately 5,000 German fighters in Spain came from the communist ranks; about 15% were social democrats and members of smaller political groups. Between 1,500 and 2,000 of the German exiles were killed in the civil war. The defeat of the Republican troops in early 1939 led, along with the collapse of the popular front and disappointment over the Stalin-focused KPD, to a crisis of the resistance in exile.

Political refugees became involved in the resistance to German occupation in various countries. In the Second World War, refugees in uniform performed various tasks for the Allied troops. In demand for their language skills, they supported psychological warfare, interrogated prisoners of war, and served as interpreters. In 1945, the USA brought exiles to Germany as "guides" through the secret service Office of Strategic Services.

While few of those persecuted as Jews returned to the defeated Germany, the return rate after the war was higher particularly among the political refugees and stood at around 60%. Especially the social democratic returnees took over important positions in the political life of West Germany. Until the 1950s, half of the party executive of the SPD was made up of former refugees. Exile shaped many well-known social democrats, men like the mayor of Berlin, Ernst Reuter; the chairman of the SPD, Erich Ollenhauer; chancellor Willy Brandt; or the head of the SPD party group in the Bundestag, Herbert Wehner.

Returning émigrés of the KPD played a central role in the establishment of the East German state. The Soviet leadership dispatched into its occupation zone three "initiative groups" around Walter Ulbricht, Anton Ackermann, and Gustav Sobottka to take over key political and economic posts. Cadres of the KPD from exile in western countries were also deployed to advance the buildup of East Germany in line with Moscow's ideas.

The exiled opposition failed to find a common identity. As a result, no internationally recognized German government in exile was ever set up. The political orientations were simply too different, even among the groups that came out of the workers' movement. And so the attempt to unite social democratic, communists, and other opponents of the Hitler regime into a "popular front" in Paris in 1935 also came to nothing. The conflicts dating to the time after the First World War and the absence of shared parliamentary-democratic ideals were joined by a new mistrust toward the Moscow-directed KPD as a result of the purges carried out by the Soviet leadership and then the pact between Hitler and Stalin on 23 August 1939. The chasm between the two most important émigré groups, the communists and the socialists, was a crucial factor in why the political exile community lacked potency.

Only smaller initiatives had some success. In London, the Sopade and three other noncommunist leftist groups set up the Union of German Socialist Organizations in Great Britain in 1941. The Union, headed by Hans Vogel, the chairman of the Sopade, provided a forum to discuss possible postwar orders in Germany. Not until 1944 were the participants able to agree on guidelines. They had no influence on Allied policy after Germany's collapse, but they did influence the program of the newly created West German SPD.

The communist side created the National Committee of a Free Germany (Nationalkomitee Freies Deutschland, NKFG) in July 1943. It included 13 KPD politicians from the exile in Moscow, among them Walter Ulbricht and Wilhelm Pieck. Under Soviet oversight, the committee organized propaganda on the Soviet front lines to convince soldiers and officers of the Wehrmacht to stop fighting and take up the struggle against Hitler. At the end of the war, nearly 2,000 individuals were working for front-line organizations that the committee had set up for this purpose. Representatives of the committee recruited new members in the prisoners of war camps. In the Reich itself, various NKFG groups were working in the underground, in no small number of cases without contact with Moscow. The attempt to accelerate the German defeat with such means failed.

The Council for a Democratic Germany in the USA saw itself as a counter model to the National Committee. In May 1944, the Council's Initiative Committee under the leadership of the theologian Paul Tillich went public with a declaration in New York. The document, signed by 60 prominent refugees, appealed to the future victors of the war to entrust the Germans themselves with constructing a new democracy. After the invasion of Normandy in June 1944, the council called upon the Germans to fight against National Socialism.

The literary, artistic, and scientific exile

The total number of refugees from the worlds of science, literature, the press, and art should be estimated at more than 10,000. One-quarter of the group was made up of writers, publishers, and journalists. In addition, the academic-cultural exile community included actors, directors, painters, sculptors, architects, and musicians.

Most of the notable representatives of the intellectual and cultural life in the Weimar Republic fled. These included the winner of the Nobel Prize for Literature in 1929, Thomas Mann, later Nobel Prize winners like Nelly Sachs (1966) and Elias Canetti (1981), and nearly all other prominent authors of the time who stood for German and Austrian literature, such as Bertolt Brecht, Alfred Döblin, Lion Feuchtwanger, Else Lasker-Schüler, Heinrich Mann, Anna Seghers, Franz Werfel, Carl Zuckmayer, and Stefan Zweig.

Painters like Max Beckmann, Lyonel Feininger, and Paul Klee fled, as did many sculptors and architects (e.g., Walter Gropius, Ludwig Mies van der Rohe, and Bruno Taut), and those "forgotten" after they left, like the group of painters known as expressive realists, who were discovered only much later and whose artistic biographies were virtually cut off by their flight.

A first group, especially writers and journalists, went abroad shortly after the Nazi takeover of power, in the weeks between the Reichstag fire on 27 February and the book burnings on 10 May 1933. Like the representatives of political parties and organizations, they also escaped the persecution of the opposition and the punishment of every divergent, publicly voiced opinion. Other artists and scientists had to leave the country because of their Jewish origins, without having been active for the opposition. Most fled later than the dissidents. The cultural refugees, too, can be divided into two groups: while many committed enemies of National Socialism saw their future in a Germany after Hitler, the majority of those persecuted as Jews sought lasting prospects in another country.

The refugees from the world of culture also sought refuge initially in Germany's neighbor countries. Paris and Prague developed into the cultural centers of the exiled Germans. Many exile journals were published in Paris, like the *Pariser Tageblatt*, later renamed *Pariser Tageszeitung*, or *Das Neue Tage-Buch*. Theater performances were organized along with readings and exhibits.

The Czech capital offered the refugees a German-speaking public. Writers like Oskar Maria Graf, Wieland Herzfelde, or Stefan Heym found temporary refuge there. The number of German-language newspapers and journals in Czechoslovakia – already at 173 before Hitler's takeover of power – increased by 60 publications. The literature of the refugees appeared in the exile publishing houses Graphia and Malik, but also in native publishing houses. Apart from Prague and Paris, other European cities also became centers of the exile – for example, Amsterdam, where the publishing houses Querido and Allert de Lange published the exile literature, as well as Stockholm and Zurich.

As German troops invaded Germany's neighbors, the USA became the most important destination country of the refugees, where the cultural exiles gathered especially in large cities like New York and Los Angeles. A number of the most prominent German writers at the time found refuge in the USA – Thomas Mann, Franz Werfel, Lion Feuchtwanger, and Bertolt Brecht.

In addition to political refugees and cultural dissidents, many scientists also left the country after the Nazis came to power. Among them were 24 Nobel Prize winners, including Albert Einstein, Erwin Schrödinger, and Fritz Haber. About 3,000 scientists at universities and research institutions – about a third of the scientific personnel – lost their jobs during the Nazi dictatorship; of those, 2,000, mostly the younger ones, left Germany – an academic exodus without parallel in the more recent history of western Europe.

The Law for the Restoration of the Professional Civil Service of 7 April 1933 accelerated the expulsions. It allowed the dismissal of civil servants who were not of "Aryan descent," along with those who, the regime suspected, would not "support the National Socialist state at all times without reservations." The law affected an especially large number of academics from modern disciplines, for example, the social sciences, nuclear physics, and biochemistry. These were more likely than the fields dominated by national-conservative professors, such as history or German, to have Jewish scientists and supporters of democracy.

Most of the scientific refugees, about 1,300, eventually also found refuge in the USA. A larger segment of this group managed to get a professional foothold there than was the case for other groups among the refugees from German-occupied Europe. This process was helped by organizations and foundations whose goal it was to integrate the refugees into the country's scholarly life. They were also active in Great Britain, which became, second to the USA, the most important host country for scientists.

The American Emergency Committee in Aid of Displaced German/Foreign Scholars, for example, paid the salaries of immigrant scientists during a transition period, if a university agreed to continue financing the position created in this way. In Great Britain, the supporters of the Academic Assistance Council taxed themselves and used the funds to make it possible for scientists to find work with universities and research institutions. The Rockefeller Foundation financed aid programs for displaced scientists around the world.

Especially in the USA, many of the academic refugees exerted a significant influence on the development of their disciplines. The successful integration of these refugees compared to others is reflected in the low return rates after the war: only one out of 10 scientific refugees returned permanently to Germany.

Whereas integration into the job market was quick and positive for such groups, for most refugees the new beginning in their destination country meant a decline in social status. Not least the restrictions in the labor markets of the destination countries forced many to scrape by in occupations that were below their level of education and training, were poorly paid, and had little status. Material need, psychological stress, and the loss of social relationships and language were therefore as much part of the overall picture of flight as successful lives in the face of difficult circumstances.

Ash, Mitchell G., and Alfons Söllner, eds. *Forced Migration and Scientific Change: Emigré German-Speaking Scientists and Scholars after 1933*. Cambridge, 1996.

Becher, Peter, and Peter Heumos, eds. *Drehscheibe Prag. Zur deutschen Emigration in der Tschechoslowakei*. Munich, 1992.

Benz, Wolfgang. *Flucht aus Deutschland. Zum Exil im 20. Jahrhundert*. Munich, 2001.

Biographisches Handbuch der deutschsprachigen Emigration nach 1933. Published by the Institut für Zeitgeschichte. 3 vols. Munich, 1980–3.

Crohn, Klaus-Dieter, et al., eds. *Handbuch der deutschsprachigen Emigration 1933–1945*. Darmstadt, 1988.

Hepp, Michael, ed. *Die Ausbürgerung deutscher Staatsangehöriger 1933–1945 nach den im Reichsanzeiger veröffentlichten Listen*. 3 vols. Munich, 1985–8.

Lacina, Evelyn. *Emigration 1933–1945. Sozialhistorische Darstellung der deutschsprachigen Emigration und einiger ihrer Asylländer aufgrund ausgewählter zeitgenössischer Selbstzeugnisse*. Stuttgart, 1982.

Maas, Lieselotte. *Handbuch der deutschen Exilpresse 1933–1945*. 4 vols. Munich, 1976–90.

Saint Sauveur-Henn, Anne, ed. *Fluchtziel Paris. Die deutschsprachige Emigration 1933–1940*. Berlin, 2002.

Walter, Hans Albert. *Deutsche Exilliteratur 1933–1950*. Vols. 2–4. Stuttgart, 1978–88.

Cross-references: Austria; Czechia and Slovakia; France; Germany; Great Britain; The Netherlands; Northern Europe; Russia and Belarus; Jewish Refugees from Nazi Germany and from German-Occupied Europe since 1933; Spanish Political Refugees in Europe since the Beginning of the Civil War in 1936: The Example of France

PORTUGUESE LABOR MIGRANTS IN WESTERN AND CENTRAL EUROPE SINCE THE 1950S: THE EXAMPLES OF FRANCE AND GERMANY

Marcelo J. Borges

In the 1950s, Portuguese migration began to shift from traditional transatlantic destinations to northern, western, and central Europe. Intra-European migration was not an entirely new phenomenon. For centuries, temporary and seasonal migrants had left Portugal to work in fishing, agriculture, and other trades in neighboring Spain, Gibraltar, and the circum-Mediterranean world. After World War I, Portuguese workers migrated in significant numbers to France, where they worked mainly in agriculture. By 1921, there were over 10,000 Portuguese in France and by 1931, their number reached 49,000. But it was during the second half of the 20th century that this movement acquired an intensity never seen before. Like in other southern European countries, in Portugal, migrant workers responded to the labor opportunities available in the industrial countries of western Europe during the post-war years. By the 1960s, intra-European movements became the dominant system of migration in continental Portugal.

Two phases are clear in the post–World War II flows of Portuguese migrants within Europe. The first wave of migration started in the 1950s and began to decline in the 1970s. France was the dominant destination in this cycle, followed by Germany. The second wave began in the mid-1980s, with new departures to France and Germany and the development of large flows of labor migration to less traditional destinations like Switzerland, Luxembourg, and Great Britain. Interestingly, during the latter phase, Portugal also became a significant destination for permanent and temporary migrants from Africa, Latin America, and eastern Europe. According to official estimates, by the late 1990s the largest Portuguese communities in northwestern and central Europe were in France (799,000), Germany (170,000), Switzerland (155,000), the UK (60,000), Luxembourg (52,000), and Belgium (38,000).

The existence of official recruitment, the legal status of Portuguese workers in certain countries, and the initial temporary nature of their stay generalized the use of the name "guest workers." The term, however, was more popular in Germany – and later Switzerland and the Benelux countries – than in France. From the point of view of the receiving countries, the image of labor migrants depended not only on the changing situation of the economy and labor market but also on the ideas of nation and citizenship. The two main European destinations for Portuguese migrants during the second half of the 20th century, France and Germany, developed different patterns of immigrant adjustment and assimilation.

Intra-European migration went from representing 12% of the total Portuguese flow in the period 1955–9 to 83% in the period 1970–4. The absolute numbers also grew dramatically: from 165,500 migrants in the first period to 668,000 in the second. As a result of immigration restrictions and changes in the labor markets of the receiving countries following the oil crisis of 1973, the number of migrants declined steadily: 183,000 in 1975–9; 107,000 in 1980–4; and 46,500 in 1985–8. From 1965 to 1974, at the peak of emigration to northwestern Europe, France received 63% of the total Portuguese flow, followed by Germany with 14%.

The Portuguese population of France grew dramatically in the 1960s and 1970s. They numbered 759,000 in 1975, 765,000 in 1982, and then declined to 650,000 in 1990. By 1975 the Portuguese represented 22% of the foreign population in France, becoming the largest immigrant group; in 1982, with 21% of the foreign population, they occupied the

Portuguese workers in their Osnabrück hostel, 1970 (*Custoias, Antonio, Osnabrück, Germany*).

second place after the Algerians. The Portuguese population in Germany went from a peak of 122,000 in 1974 to about 69,000 in 1987. Their proportion of the immigrant population was smaller than their countrymen in France: 3% of the foreign workers in 1973 and 2% in 1987. The Portuguese population in Germany rose again after Portugal joined the European Union, especially after 1992, when Portuguese workers could move freely within the EU space.

A distinctive feature of Portuguese migration within Europe in the 1960s and 1970s was the significance of illegal or clandestine flows (62%). According to Portuguese statistics, 482,000 migrants left for France and Germany between 1950 and 1988. However, when this number is corrected with the statistics of the countries of immigration, the total of Portuguese migrants rises to 1,259,000. In other words, legal departures represented only 38% of the total number of migrants to these countries. To be sure, illegal departures were also common during the heyday of transatlantic migrations, but they were more dominant in the intra-European flows. The relative proximity and accessibility of the European destinations, when compared to the more traditional destinations across the Atlantic, and the existence of networks of informal contacts and assistance made the journey possible. For clandestine migration, this assistance included the services of a *passador* who escorted migrants across Spain and beyond the Pyrenees in what became known among Portuguese migrants as the *salto* or "the leap." Networks of information and contacts also helped the newly arrived migrants find a place to stay and secure initial work. Clandestine migration was prevalent in the Portuguese flow to France during the 1960s and 1970s. It was less common in emigration to Germany, where the authorities tightly monitored the entrance of foreign workers and their movements, and the distance and risks for illegal migration were considerably greater. There were, however, other ways of circumventing legal requirements, such as overstaying tourist visas. The proportion of emigration to France unaccounted for by Portuguese statistics was 48% in the 1960s and 81% in the 1970s; for Germany, the proportion of unregistered emigration was 27% in the 1960s and 42% in the 1970s.

The large movement of illegal migration was incited by a combination of restrictions in the countries of origin and destination. During much of the 20th century, Portuguese migratory policies were characterized by partial restrictions and selection in order to keep the flow of remittances, while protecting the internal labor market and encouraging migration to the colonies. Transatlantic flows in the 1940s were controlled through the requirement of work contracts or sponsorship by family members established abroad. In the 1960s Portugal signed migration treaties with several European countries, including France and Germany, but limited the total number of migrants and banned the emigration of workers with certain occupations. Bureaucratic limitations and expenses stimulated the growth of illegal departures. The beginning of the colonial wars in Portuguese Africa added other compelling reasons for men of military age to leave the country clandestinely.

The immigration countries restricted the arrival of foreign workers. These legal barriers contributed to the insecurity of undocumented migrant workers in the countries of arrival, but they did not stop the clandestine flows. The French case showed a peculiar combination of limitation and openness in their immigration policies that contributed to fuel the illegal flow of Portuguese and other migrants: even though legal migration was restricted, legalization after arrival was common. Broad legalizations occurred repeatedly during the 1960s and early 1970s. The economic stagnation caused by the oil crisis of 1973, however, put an end to the previous policy of "regulated open doors." Labor migration was seriously restricted or banned, as was the possibility of regularization of illegal residents. France officially ended this practice in 1977, although it implemented an exceptional regularization in 1981.

Family reunification became predominant after the restrictive French policies of the mid-1970s. This was not, however, an entirely new phenomenon. Since the mid-1960s, there was an increasing number of women and children in the Portuguese flow to France. The existence of opportunities for female migrants and the possibility of maximizing economic returns was a determining factor in the decision of thousands of Portuguese women to migrate to France. Initially, this strategy involved the migration of only husbands and wives, while their children were left in Portugal under the care of relatives. This family migration strategy was reinforced in the late 1960s by changes in government policy. Beginning in 1968, the French government sought to settle and integrate immigrants through family reunification. This policy was not replicated in other immigration countries in Europe at that time. This shift in policy and the restrictions of the early 1970s gave way to a pattern of family migration and reunification. Whereas women and children represented a third of Portuguese arrivals in France from 1960 to 1971, their share rose to almost two-thirds from 1972 to 1988.

Similarly in Germany, the end of direct recruitment in 1973 was followed by family reunification. Even though family members and friends were able to join guest workers in Germany by way of what scholars have called the "gray market" – mainly with tourist visas – legal reunification was regulated. Family reunification was available only to members of the immediate family (spouses and children) and with several limitations (for example, only children younger than 21 years old were eligible). As a result of this state intervention and due to the nature of labor recruitment, nuclear families tended to be the norm among Portuguese workers, and it was common for siblings to be scattered around Germany. Restrictions notwithstanding, family reunification occurred, as illustrated by the sharp decline of workers as a total of the Portuguese population in Germany: from 77% in 1974 to 57% in 1989.

In Portugal, the areas of emigration were not limited to the traditional migratory districts in the north and center but covered the entire country, and increasingly included urban and industrial centers. From 1950 to 1984 the district of Lisbon was the main area of origin of the Portuguese migrants to Germany and ranked among the eight largest areas of departure to France, in both cases with more than 20,000 emigrants. The vast majority of the migrants, however, were from rural areas and small towns. Chain migration and the emergence of ethnic communities or occupational specialization based on family and village networks were less prevalent in the European flows than in the transatlantic movements. There are, however, some examples of village and occupational chains in France, such as the immigrants from the rural village of Queiriga, in northern Portugal, who settled mainly in Pau, in the Lower Pyrenees, and in Orsay and Limours, in the outskirts of Paris; and the workers from the industrial town of Portimão, in southern Portugal, who migrated to the western Parisian suburb of Billancourt. The nature of labor recruitment in the German guest worker system, and the controlled access to residence and working permits, did not foster the formation of migratory chains linked to particular destinations. Evidence from Hamburg, with a population of about 6,000 Portuguese in the mid-1980s (8% of the Portuguese living in Germany), shows every region in Portugal represented among the immigrants with no clear local or regional concentration.

In France, Portuguese migrants were attracted by the labor opportunities in construction and public works; later, they also began working in the industrial sector, especially in automobile factories. With its large and diversified labor market, higher salaries, and need for both male and female unskilled workers, the Paris region attracted the majority of the immigrants. In the mid-1970s, about 40% lived in and around the French capital; the same was true in the mid-1990s. Important concentrations also emerged in Lyon, Clermont-Ferrand, Toulouse, and the Lower Pyrenees. Urban centers provided an abundance of employment opportunities for both male and female migrants. During the 1960s and 1970s, Paris had several public projects under way that provided employment opportunities for Portuguese immigrants, such as the construction of the new universities of Orsay and Jussie, the regional train network *Réseau Express Régional*, and the ring road, or "peripheral boulevard." Factory work also provided employment opportunities in Paris and other regions, like the Renault complex in Billancourt, west of Paris, and the Michelin plant in Clermont-Ferrand.

Urban centers were also attractive for female immigrants. Employment opportunities for women were important during the phase of family migration and reunification. Portuguese women in France had a high level of employment. This was an important aspect of the Portuguese migratory strategy: the employment of both the husband and the wife allowed them to earn more money and increase savings to invest back in Portugal, where they planned to return. The majority of immigrant women worked in the domestic service, as maids, cleaning ladies, and concierges. In the late 1960s, they represented a third of all women employed in this sector in Paris. In the 1970s, Portuguese women were also working in the secondary sector, but their entrance into factory work was slow.

The majority of the Portuguese immigrants in Germany worked in the industrial sector, a concentration that is reflected in their geographical distribution. In 1980 large urban-industrial centers, especially Rhineland-Westphalia, Baden-Württemberg, Hesse, north Bavaria, and Lower Saxony-Bremen were home to 81% of the Portuguese in Germany, of whom half lived in Rhineland-Westphalia. The vast majority worked in unskilled blue-collar jobs, some three-quarters in 1975. In the 1970s and 1980s, mechanical engineering, textiles, iron, and chemistry were the sectors with the largest numbers of Portuguese workers. They generally had low levels of education and no industrial training. In the mid-1970s 77% had only basic schooling without vocational training. The proportion of workers in the service sectors grew over the years, from 11% in 1975 to 22% in 1990. Immigrants' spouses in Germany had to wait several years to obtain work permits. Like other female immigrants, Portuguese women who joined their husbands in Germany routinely circumvented this legal limitation by working illegally as domestics or in the hospitality industry.

In France some social mobility has occurred among male immigrants, particularly across generations. In the early 1980s, 45% of the Portuguese men were nonqualified workers, but there was a higher proportion of technicians and supervisors among those who migrated as children, and a higher percentage of professionals among the children of Portuguese born in France. This is also visible in their patterns of education. Whereas until the 1980s, Portuguese children showed a preference for a shorter cycle of vocational education, data from the mid-1990s show that they were shifting to academic and technological education. It is important to take into account, however, that social mobility of migrants was also related to their expectations. For first-generation immigrants, it was more likely linked to the possibilities of economic progress at home – once they returned

with enough savings to invest in plots of land, a house, a store, or a restaurant – and not necessarily to their situation in the country of immigration.

Portuguese immigrants in Europe did not form ethnic enclaves. Certain areas had larger concentrations of Portuguese families, but there were no recognizable "Little Portugals." The existence of services common in classic ethnic neighborhoods, such as ethnic stores or travel agencies, was at times limited by the host countries. In the 1970s, it was impossible for Portuguese and other foreigners to own such businesses in France; the same was true in Germany until 1992, when Portuguese became full European Union citizens. More important, immigrants' work experiences and employment opportunities had a clear influence on their residential patterns and hindered the creation of ethnic clusters. In Paris, home of the largest Portuguese community in Europe, immigrants lived scattered throughout the city.

However, the two phases of migration (male and familial) were characterized by different living experiences and residential patterns. The large numbers of Portuguese migrant workers that arrived during the early phase of labor migration lived in temporary housing provided by the construction companies or in the periphery of the city. The surge in the arrival of migrant workers from Portugal and North Africa in the 1960s contributed to the growth of emergency settlements known as *bidonvilles*. The name refers to the oilcans (*bidons*) that, once flattened, served as construction material in these emergency settlements that appeared in marginal land throughout the city. In the early 1960s, more than 10,000 Portuguese lived in one of these communities in Champigny, in the outskirts of Paris. With the arrival of more women and their entrance in the labor force, the settlement patterns and living arrangements among the Portuguese of Paris changed. Employment as maids and concierges often gave women and their families access to housing (ground floor apartments or sixth floor "maid rooms"). Whereas women tended to live and work in the same geographical space, men commuted to work in construction sites or automobile factories in and around the city.

Portuguese immigrant communities created opportunities for social interaction and celebration of national heritage and culture. Following early initiatives sponsored by some Catholic churches as an extension of their Portuguese-language religious services, hundreds of Portuguese associations and clubs emerged in the 1970s and 1980s. These organizations offered opportunities for social interaction, leisure, education, and communal celebrations. France developed the largest associative network; by the mid-1980s there were over 800 Portuguese organizations, including clubs, cultural associations, religious groups, and folk dance troupes. According to official estimates, by the late 1990s the largest concentrations of Portuguese associations were in France (600), Germany (250), Switzerland (100), and Luxembourg (60).

For Portuguese migrants and their families, working in northern, western, and central European countries was another phase in their country's long history of labor migration. The traditional strategy of temporary migration with return was beneficial for the countries of origin and immigration as well as for the migrants involved. While migrants could save money and improve their socioeconomic position, Portugal took advantage of a regular influx of remittances. Money sent by migrants not only had a significant impact on family and local economies but on the country's economy as a whole: they represented 8% of the gross domestic product between 1973 and 1979, and 10% in the 1980s. For some regional economies, the contribution of migrants' transfers was even higher. For example, in the district of Guarda, in northern Portugal, they accounted for 39% of the gross regional product in 1984.

Unlike previous transatlantic migrants, Portuguese workers in France, Germany, and other European countries could visit their home country regularly. Each summer, villages throughout Portugal welcomed thousands of migrants, who participated in local festivities and family events, worked on the construction of a new house and on the land, and had the opportunity to show their accomplishments (and compare them with those of others). These visits kept the links to the home villages strong and contributed to what scholars call the identity of "being here and there," both important elements of the idea of return.

From 1960 to 1980 the annual average of Portuguese migrants who returned from France was between 25,000 and 30,000. The majority returned during the early 1980s, with an average of 42,000 a year. In the mid-1980s, the German government offered economic incentives for permanent return. About a quarter of the Portuguese took advantage of this program, resulting in a considerable decline of the Portuguese population in Germany: from 99,500 in 1983 to 77,000 in 1985. Evidence from France, however, clearly shows that a sizable number of the migrants stayed. This apparent modification of the initial strategy by a significant proportion of Portuguese migrants was not necessarily perceived as permanent settlement. Although migrant families of two or three generations were common at the turn of the 21st century, for many their initial project of return had not been completely abandoned, only postponed.

There are, however, significant variations in expectations and behavior by country of residence and across generations. Qualitative evidence suggests that Portuguese of second and third generations living in Germany have not abandoned their parents' and grandparents' idea of return. In contrast, the descendants of Portuguese immigrants in France show a stronger integration into French society. These different experiences in integration are also visible in the rates of naturalization among Portuguese immigrants in both countries. Even after the changes in citizenship legislation in Germany in the 1990s, the rate of naturalization among the Portuguese was less than 0.1%. In France, with an overall rate of 17.5%, the Portuguese were among the groups with the highest naturalization rates. The possibility of dual citizenship granted in the 1990s and access to an enlarged European space as full European Union citizens have given Portuguese immigrants and their descendants in France, Germany, and other European countries greater flexibility to negotiate their transnational lives.

Baganha, Maria, and Pedro Góis. "Migrações internacionais de e para Portugal: O que sabemos e para onde vamos?" *Revista Crítica de Ciências Sociais* 52/53 (1998/99): 229–80.

Bauer, Thomas, Pedro Pereira, Michael Vogler, and Klaus Zimmermann. *Portuguese Migrants in the German Labour Market: Performance and Self-Selection.* London, 1998.

Branco, Jorge Portugal. *A estrutura da comunidade portuguesa em França.* Porto, 1986.

Brettell, Caroline. *We Have Already Cried Many Tears: The Stories of Three Portuguese Migrant Women.* Prospect Heights, IL, 1995.

Klimt, Andrea. "Do National Narratives Matter? Identity Formation among Portuguese Migrants in France and Germany." In *European Encounters: Migrants, Migration and European Societies since 1945*, edited by Rainer Ohliger, Karen Schönwälder, and Triadafilos Triadafilopoulos, 257–80. Aldershot, 2003.

Rocha-Trindade, Maria Beatriz. *Immigrés portugais: Observation psycho-sociologique d'un groupe de portugais dans la banlieue parisienne (Orsay).* Lisbon, 1973.

Cross-references: Belgium and Luxembourg; France; Germany; Great Britain; The Netherlands; Portugal; Switzerland; Angolan and Mozambican Labor Migrants in Portugal since the 1970s; Maghrebis in France after Decolonization during the 1950s and 1960s; Portuguese *Retornados* from the Colonies in Portugal since the 1970s

PORTUGUESE *RETORNADOS* FROM THE COLONIES IN PORTUGAL SINCE THE 1970S

Cármen Maciel

The Portuguese term *retornado* literally means "those who return home" and refers to migrants who returned from Portugal's former African colonies (Mozambique, Angola, Cape Verde, Guinea-Bissau, São Tomé, and Príncipe) during and immediately after the decolonization period (1974–8). Many of the *retornados* were of European, African, Asian, or mixed ancestry who had never lived in Portugal but who fled Africa following independence because they, for example, had collaborated with the colonizers or, as white settlers, were no longer welcome. The term became a commonplace in the contemporary press, official documents, and everyday discussions and is still in wide use today. It is used to define and characterize what is a heterogeneous group of people from the colonies as "foreign" to Portuguese society.

The regime of the Portuguese dictator António de Oliveira Salazar (1932–68, succeeded by Marcello Caetano, who ruled until 1974) granted new land to foster settlement in the colonies in the 1950s and 1960s, which significantly increased the number of Portuguese settlers. This was largely a reaction to growing resistance among the native population as well as an attempt to strengthen the colonial economy. In official rhetoric, Portugal was one "indivisible nation" and the residents of the territories under Portuguese sovereignty were part of a "great pluricontinental and multiracial nation."

The Carnation Revolution of 1974 put an end to the dictatorship in Portugal as well as to the Portuguese colonial rule in Africa. After the civil wars in the former colonies and the transfer of sovereignty to the African liberation movements, many were faced with the decision of staying under the protection of the new authorities or emigrating to Portugal: within one year, approximately 500,000 persons left the former Portuguese colonies.

The first significant outflows started in 1973, before the change of regime. In early 1974, the number of *retornados* increased dramatically and seats on flights to Lisbon were in short supply. Given the urgency and the intensity of the exodus, the Portuguese authorities organized the so-called Air Bridge linking Angola with Portugal. The massive concentration of people in the Lisbon airport and the daily pictures of people arriving in total destitution seriously undermined the image of exemplary and well-organized decolonization propagated by the authorities.

The 1981 census registered 471,427 migrants from the former colonies: 62% from Angola, 34% from Mozambique, and only 5% from other African countries. This represented an increase of some 6% of the population of Portugal proper. An estimated 20,000 Portuguese chose to stay in Angola (including the Angolan-Portuguese *mestiços*). There is inadequate information on them and other Portuguese who remained in Africa. They resided chiefly in the cities in a society divided by racial discrimination and facing serious economic and social problems: inflation and costs skyrocketed, exports slumped, development plans from the colonial era were shelved for lack of funds and management, housing and construction projects were halted, and many near-complete facilities were abandoned.

In accordance with a decree from 1975, the only migrants able to receive Portuguese citizenship were either born in Portugal or naturalized, which included those born abroad with Portuguese parents and those born in the former colonies with Portuguese parents or grandparents. Those born in the former colonies without Portuguese ancestry could claim Portuguese citizenship only after living in Portugal for more than five years. This meant that the overwhelming majority of black Africans could apply for Portuguese citizenship only in exceptional cases (e.g., veterans of the Portuguese colonial army or administration). From an embracing, imperial *jus soli*–based notion of nation, the law now shifted to a *jus sanguinis* understanding of citizenship.

Although 63% of adult and 40% of younger *retornados* were born in Portugal, they have often been viewed as Africans. There were more male than female *retornados* and persons of working age were predominant. The *retornados* tended to settle in metropolitan areas like Lisbon (32%),

Porto, and Setúbal, likely due to the better opportunities in employment and housing. The arrival of a large number of young migrants diminished (at least temporarily) some asymmetries in Portugal's demographic structure. Available statistical data, however, do not allow more specific details on marriage patterns and the extent of endogamy.

The educational and occupational skills of the returnee population were above the national average: only 17% had not completed primary education in 1981 versus 51% of the total Portuguese population. They represented 16% of all Portuguese with vocational training and 11% of those with tertiary education. Some *retornados* entered professional and management occupations or political leadership positions, even if only at the local level. In 1981 the *retornados* made up over 15% of all professionals in manufacturing; 12% in the banking, financial, and public administration sectors (due to their background in agriculture, the number of *retornados* employed in the Office of Agriculture was disproportionately high); 6% in the security services; and another 6% in small trades, particularly restaurants. Although unemployment was generally low in 1981, the percentage of unemployed among *retornados* was higher, among both sexes, than within the general population, thus demonstrating that some suffered from economic and social marginalization.

The occupational integration of *retornados*, however, should not conceal the strains between locals and migrants. Most of the *retornados* possessed Portuguese citizenship, but for many locals this did not mean they had a legitimate claim to residence in the country. Their arrival and settlement was experienced as a form of invasion, and this was made clear in everyday life and the media. The returnees arrived in Portugal in a period of great turmoil as Portuguese society was rebuilding itself after the regime change. The *retornados* were seen as responsible for housing shortages, unemployment, and strains on the social service system. Various government bodies and programs were created to organize the repatriation of the *retornados* and to facilitate their integration, such as the IARN (Board for Aiding the Return of Nationals), the State Secretary for *Retornados* and the CIFRE (Interministerial Council for Financing the *Retornados*). Some banks provided credit for the acquisition or building of houses for permanent residence and the CIFRE guaranteed credits for entrepreneurial initiatives.

The *retornados* brought with them new cultural elements, such as new words, African meals, different clothes and music. They also contributed to the linguistic, ethnic, religious, and cultural pluralization of Portuguese society. Some independent organizations emerged, such as the Association of Ex-Ultramarine Combatants and the Alliance of Portuguese Returnees from Overseas. They were created in the 1980s as advocates for the returnees' rights (e.g., damage indemnities) or to organize annual meetings of specific groups of *retornados*, from Angola, for example.

Opinions vary on the outcome of the integration process of the *retornados* in Portuguese society. While some argue that it has been an unparalleled success story, others believe that integration has proceeded on only a superficial level. Optimistic critics claim that all indications point to successful integration, such as the lack of a policy of positive discrimination (e.g., quotas), the territorial dispersion of *retornados*, the network of interpersonal relations among the returnees, the support of families, the small number of returnees that organized to make claims, and occupational integration.

The more negative view, rather widespread among *retornados* themselves, points to the image of the returnees often found among native Portuguese. Although the *retornados* were full citizens, they signified a "foreign" element, personified a past age of colonial exploitation, and were blamed for social problems within the country. According to those with a negative view and to numerous *retornados* themselves, this type of stereotyping and exclusion indicates a superficial or even failed integration. This view, in turn, strengthened the argument that *retornados* were not "truly" Portuguese or belonged to a "different," undesirable Portugal.

Barreto, António, ed. *A Situação Social em Portugal, 1960–1995*. Lisbon, 1996.

Ferreira, José. "A Descolonização: Seu processo e consequências." In *História de Portugal*, vol. 8, edited by José Mattoso, 53–101. Lisbon, 1994.

Pires, Rui. "O Regresso das Colónias." In *História da Expansão Portuguesa*, vol. 5, edited by Francisco Bethencourt and Kirti Chaudhuri, 182–96. Navarra, 1999.

Smith, Andrea, ed. *Europe's Invisible Migrants*. Amsterdam, 2003.

Cross-references: Spain and Portugal; Angolan and Mozambican Labor Migrants in Portugal since the 1970s

PRISONERS OF WAR IN EUROPE, 1914–1922

Jochen Oltmer

War captivity of the First World War in Europe was a mass phenomenon of previously unknown dimensions. Prisoners of war (POWs) were very often forced to work in the European war economy; in the process, there was at times also an overlap with the employment of coerced civilian laborers. At least 7 million, and probably more like 8–9 million (soldiers, men), fell into enemy hands between 1914 and 1918. This was nearly one-seventh of all mobilized soldiers. And the internment of prisoners of war was not limited to the four years of war from August 1914 to November 1918. It remained a European mass phenomenon also in the first postwar years and a political problem until the end of the repatriation schemes and thus until the return of the last German, Austrian, and Russian POWs willing to be repatriated in July 1922. However, even after the end of the repatriations, tens of thousands of former prisoners of war did not leave the countries in which they had been interned for months or years.

Among the states whose military suffered the heaviest losses through war captivity in the First World War was czarist Russia: it is possible that more than 3.4 million Russian soldiers fell into captivity. Although the Russian army had the highest troop strength in the European theaters of war, this loss from war captivity was serious. After all, it affected well over one-fifth of all conscripted men; for the Russian army, war captivity accounted for about three-quarters of all personnel losses at the fronts. Nearly three-fifths of Russian POWs were taken by Austrian-Hungarian troops, about two-fifths by German forces. However, Austria-Hungary interned not only a particularly large number of Russian military personnel; on a more or less comparable scale, the phenomenon affected also the soldiers of the Austro-Hungarian armies: with a mobilization of 9 million men during the war, more than 2.8 million subjects of the Habsburg monarchy fell into primarily Russian war captivity – that was nearly one-third of all recruited soldiers.

By contrast, for the other warring powers, the internment of their military personnel was less significant to the conduct of the war. France's army lost around 600,000 soldiers through war captivity, Italy about the same number, Great Britain around 200,000, Germany about 1 million. This comparatively large number for Germany must be qualified, however, in terms of its importance in weakening the manpower of the German military, for the majority of the prisoners of war fell into French, British, and American hands only in the final months of the war with the failure of the German spring offensive in 1918 and the armistice in November 1918. Moreover, when it comes to the quantitative figures about POWs in the First World War, one must bear in mind that tens of thousands of escaped POWs and deserters were interned in neutral states during the war, chief among them the Netherlands and Switzerland.

War captivity as a problem of security, labor, and nationalities policy, 1914–1918

During the first weeks of war in 1914, all warring states faced the need to securely intern and house a surprisingly large number of POWs. It is consistently evident throughout Europe in the first phase of the war that there were no well-developed plans on how to accommodate larger numbers of prisoners. The military authorities in charge let themselves be guided by the simple goal – motivated by security policy – of housing the prisoners in isolation from the domestic population. For that purpose they usually had in mind military training areas and artillery ranges or barracks installations and often fortresses for officers.

The illusion entertained across Europe that the war would be over quickly led everywhere to a pronounced underestimation of the problem of interning and housing POWs. In Germany, the number of prisoners had risen to more than 100,000 by the end of the first month of the war. After three months, nearly 400,000 POWs – chiefly Russian and French – had to be taken care of in Germany. No one had any idea how it would be possible to adequately house, clothe, and feed the prisoners during the approaching winter. Much the same can be observed in Austria-Hungary: in December 1914, the Austro-Hungarian military authorities had to house and care for 200,000 POWs, a number no one within the military establishment had anticipated.

In Germany, Austria-Hungary, Russia, as well as in France and Great Britain, the available quarters were quickly filled beyond capacity. At first, primitive makeshift accommodations were used everywhere, including tent camps, mud huts, empty, sometimes near-derelict factory buildings, monasteries, barracks for harvest workers, circus tents, and horse racing tracks. A short time later began the construction of expansive barracks camps, whose facilities were oriented toward the provisioning of large numbers of prisoners only from the spring of 1915, that is, more than half a year after the outbreak of the war. Especially in Russia, Austria-Hungary, and Germany, however, the camps, because of the difficult supply situation with foods and articles of daily need, remained inadequate to the demands – in those countries, hunger therefore became one of the central everyday experiences of hundreds of thousands of POWs. For those groups for whom permanent internment in camps became the rule and whose employment in the war economy was not possible under international law, especially officers and the higher ranks of the noncommissioned officers, it was chiefly the length of camp internment that became a problem: to escape years of inactivity and isolation, whose psychological effects were already summarized at the time as "barbed wire disease," prisoners, especially in officers camps, set up cultural institutions, some with ambitious programs. They ranged from camp theaters and camp orchestras, to camp papers, arts and crafts workshops, all the way to virtual camp universities.

The transition phase in late 1914 and early 1915, which ended in the construction of a regular, extensive universe of camps, was characterized, however, by inadequate housing and provisioning: makeshift barracks that were de facto unheatable, of the kind that were used in France soon after the beginning of the war, could still be placed under the heading of "difficult housing conditions." The same could be true of the damp horse boxes in the British camp of Newbury that was set up on a horse track. In Germany, Austria-Hungary, and Russia, on the other hand, there were much more serious signs of deficient mass accommodations in completely overcrowded camps, with highly inadequate food supplies and a miserable hygienic and sanitary situation: in Germany, spotted fever spread like an epidemic. Then there were other infectious diseases such as dysentery and typhus, which likewise could not be brought under control in several camps over many months. Russia, too, experienced a typhus epidemic in the camps in the winter of 1914–15. In one camp in the east Russian government of Samara, 17,000 of 25,000 POWs are said to have died of typhus. Similar epidemic centers are also found in Austria-Hungary: in the camp of Mauthausen,

Prisoners of war in Soltau (northwestern Germany), where a large camp was situated (*Stadtarchiv Soltau*).

which housed mostly Serbs, the Ministry of War reported in the winter of 1914–15 around 12,000 victims of a typhus epidemic. The spread of these epidemics, even if limited to individual camps in Austria-Hungary, Russia, and Germany, indicates a lack of adequate medical care for the prisoners.

In terms of accommodations and medical care, the housing situation did improve everywhere through the construction of large prisoner camps with relatively solid barracks, permanent hospitals, and canteen kitchens. But this led only in a very limited way to a more favorable food situation in the camps in Germany, Austria-Hungary, and Russia, which deteriorated noticeably especially toward the end of the war – reflecting the general desperate supply situation in these countries. As a rule, the only internees who were better supplied with food were those who had been assigned work in agriculture, assignments that occurred when employment of prisoners of war in the European war economy became commonplace after the spring of 1915.

The recruitment of POWs as workers became a major issue only with the increasing needs of agricultural and industrial production to meet the demands of a war economy. By contrast, during the first six months of the war, the employment of POWs was regarded as unwelcome competition in the face of the mass unemployment caused by mobilization. As a result, during the first few months of the war, the prisoners performed work, if at all, only within the makeshift camps – in erecting or expanding their own accommodations, and in caring for, maintaining, or expanding the infrastructure of the military training grounds often used as sites for camps. The goal here was chiefly to discipline the prisoners and to reduce the costs of accommodation.

With the beginning of the second development phase of the war economy, after the beginning of 1915, using prisoners of war to replace the millions of male workers conscripted from all economic areas became one of the most important goals of the administrative labor policy: in Russia, only around 100,000 POWs had been employed outside the camps at the beginning of March 1915. That number surged to 400,000 by July 1915 and to 600,000 by September 1915, after which time it continued to rise steadily and reached 1.1 million at the beginning of 1917. Of the inmates of camp Krasnoyarsk in central Siberia, for example, around 65% were employed outside the camp in the middle of June 1916; in September 1916 it was 84%. More than two-fifths of the prisoners employed in early 1917 worked in agriculture, 27% in mines and industrial enterprises, 16% on canal and railroad construction sites. Because of the increasing employment of the POWs, many prisoners who were initially interned in the Siberian part of the Russian Empire were transported back to the European part of Russia.

Although Germany had more than 800,000 POWs in April/May 1915, they were being used very little in the war economy – for example, Prussian agriculture employed only 27,000 at that time. In the following months, the rapid rise in the number of POWs was surpassed by the even more rapid increase in the number of prisoners employed in the war economy: by September 1915, their number in Prussian agriculture alone had risen 12-fold to 330,000. The numbers had surged especially in the early summer of 1915: in Prussia, for example, from 190,000 in July to 307,000 in August. Another doubling took place over the next 12 months: in September 1916, Prussian agriculture was using 670,000 prisoners of war.

In Austria-Hungary, as well, as early as the second half of 1915 only 30% to 40% of the prisoners of war were on average still interned in the camps. In February 1915, the government had decided to employ POWs in the economy. In the dual monarchy, as in Germany, one can detect strong initial reservations on the part of the military and civilian authorities toward the employment of prisoners. In the beginning, only a few scattered attempts were made with prisoners who seemed particularly trustworthy, especially in the private economy, and here primarily in agriculture.

In the middle of the war, in July/August 1916, the French economy employed about three-quarters of all POWs; in Germany it was also around three-quarters of the 1.6 million captives (1.1 million), with agriculture accounting for more than 750,000 and far outpacing industry with 330,000. And the share of prisoners of war directly put to work in the war economy continued to rise: about a year later, in September 1917, the number of POWs in German agriculture had risen sharply to 860,000, three-quarters of whom came from czarist Russia; in industry it had grown to 400,000. Mining was clearly the single largest industrial sector with 170,000 employed prisoners. At this point, POWs likely made up more than 15% of all dependent workers in the war economy in Germany. Shortly before the end of the war, about 1.9 million prisoners were employed. A few hundreds of thousands worked directly for the military authorities, a not insignificant number in the war zone; about 1.5 million were deployed directly in the war economy, among them 940,000 in agriculture, where the supply situation for the POWs was on the whole satisfactory, and in any case much better than in the housing camps. Eventually, during the second half of the

war, so many POWs were employed in the war economy in Germany, Austria-Hungary, and Russia, that the occupancy numbers in the expansive camps built up especially in 1915 became smaller and smaller, to the point that some camps were no longer able to maintain their operations.

A seeming exception to the employment of prisoners of war was Great Britain. Here, employment in the private economy began late, at the end of 1916, and remained at a very low level compared to the rest of Europe: in December 1917, only around 27,000 POWs were employed, largely in agriculture; shortly before the end of the war that number had grown only slightly to 34,000. In terms of the housing and employment of POWs, however, the British military and civilian authorities were pursuing a different strategy from that of the warring continental powers: in the beginning, the prisoners moved to the British Isles were almost exclusively officers; only during the second half of the war did the number of prisoners from junior ranks rise somewhat. By contrast, German soldiers of the lower ranks who were captured by British troops remained in France. The British military administration deployed them directly in the military zone, though their numbers were by no means adequate for this purpose. As a result, beginning in 1916 the British military authorities recruited around 100,000 civilian Chinese laborers, who were put to work on freight handling and construction projects but toward the end of the war with growing frequency also in the zone of fire.

In their employment of POWs in the war zones or in the zones close to the front, the British military authorities were by no means the exception. On the contrary, among all the powers involved in the war, when it came to the use of prisoners the boundaries blurred between work that was permitted by international law and work that was prohibited, that is, work that was part of the war effort. The construction of trenches or artillery emplacements by prisoners could certainly be counted among the prohibited works for very good reason.

However, these boundaries had long been crossed also on the "home front," where so many POWs were employed all across Europe, as the example of Austria-Hungary shows: in Trofaiach in Styria, for example, 5,000 POWs worked on the production of gunpowder, and they were also used in considerable numbers by the largest Austro-Hungarian armament enterprise, Skoda. As in the hinterland of the British trenches in northern France, at the Austro-Hungarian home front one can see the close intertwining of the work of POWs and that of civilians who were not infrequently recruited as forced laborers: the Austro-Hungarian POW camp Auschwitz was at the same time a transit camp for agricultural laborers – many recruited (by force) among refugees from the Galician East – who worked in the war zone for the military authorities. Because of this overlap of employing forcibly recruited or deported civilian workers and POWs in the First World War, the topic of war captivity also belongs to the broad field of the interaction of forced migration and forced labor in the 20th century.

War captivity did not remain a marginal phenomenon of the war economy. This much can be said, most especially for Germany and Austria-Hungary: without the considerable potential of millions of POWs, the war economy would have been considerably less efficient. At the end of the war, for example, the 1.5 million POWs employed in the German war economy and industry were distributed, according to an official estimate, in 750,000 workplaces. Thus the employment of POWs, in particular, contributed substantially to their contact with millions of natives as part of daily life after 1915. The war of nations thus also led in Europe to an unprecedented encounter among people of different nationalities.

In all of this, nationality turned out to be a category that could have profound importance for the living situation of the POWs. National minorities made up substantial portions of the various mass armies of the First World War – that was the case much more for the troops of the three empires facing one another in the eastern theater of war than for those of the Western powers. War captivity was thus also a problem of nationality policy: POWs were instrumentalized for purposes of nationality policies – in the east more frequently than in the west. In the Russian Empire, there even developed a veritable system of privileges for prisoners of Slavic nationalities. Into this context belong also the Russian efforts – affecting probably 120,000–130,000 POWs – to raise military units out of the reservoir of Slavic and Romanian prisoners, and to separate soldiers of Italian background among the Austro-Hungarian troops and transport them to allied Italy. Similar measures were taken with respect to Alsatian soldiers of the German army, whom French officers prepared in special Russian camps for transport to the western front. The scope of these measures remained limited, however: this strategy of privileging and separating selected nationalities can be considered a political and military success only insofar as they succeeded in raising militarily effective Czech units (the Czech legion) in Russian services. They would go on to play an important military role in the Russian civil war.

In other warring states, as well, similar concepts were developed and partially implemented, though for the most part with limited success: in Austro-Hungarian camps that was especially true of efforts to separate and politically influence Ukrainians and Poles from Czarist Russia. In Germany, too, there were similar efforts at privileging. Here the policy targeted once again Ukrainians, as well as the Muslims among the Russian, French, and British POWs, Flemish, and German subjects of the czar: around 18,000 Russian Germans were privileged during the war through improved provisions and easier working conditions. Considerations about privileging ethnic German POWs culminated in Germany in a decree of 1918, which offered the possibility of a grant of German citizenship under certain conditions.

In view of the large number of POWs in the various warring European states, their very diverse regional and social background, and the contacts – differing in intensity – with the native population, it is hardly possible to make general statements about autonymous and exonymous images of the POWs. The situation of being captured during direct military confrontations, generally in connection with offensives, was usually highly risky. Offensive troops usually had no interest in taking prisoners, because their military mission required unrestricted mobility, and captured soldiers constituted a burden and a potential danger. As a result, the life of soldiers was not safe either at their surrender or during their transport to the rear. There are countless examples in all theaters of war that soldiers who had already surrendered were nevertheless killed. At the same time, there are diverse examples, again involving all warring parties, of more or less clearly articulated criminal orders not to take any prisoners or to kill already captured soldiers.

Especially in the first months of the war, the POWs, as the personification of the tamed, hostile Other, met with substantial interest from the native population – some prisoner of war camps developed into veritable tourist attractions. With the increasing employment of POWs, they had more and more contacts with the native civilians. Especially in agriculture, where a large number of prisoners were increasingly employed as permanent laborers without being under guard and lived in the households of their employers, the close personal contact meant the captured soldiers were no longer viewed as hostile foreigners but rather as fully accepted members of the family farms.

The return of the prisoners of war after the First World War and the "internationalization" of the question of repatriation

The return and repatriation of the POWs following the armistice in November 1918 were processes that could extend over many months and years in the west and the east. The armistice treaty of November 1918 forced Germany to immediately transport back the captured soldiers of the Western Allies. Within a month after the armistice, around 350,000 POWs had already been transported out of Germany back into their home countries. At the beginning of January 1919 the last 175,000 British prisoners followed; the nearly 450,000 French soldiers still interned at this time were able to return home within two weeks (by the middle of January), chiefly by train. By January 15, 1919, about two months after the signing of the armistice, nearly all French, British, American, Greek, Serbian, and Romanian POWs had been repatriated from Germany.

By contrast, the return of POWs from Great Britain and France took longer. In November 1918, around 90,000 enemy soldiers were interned on the British Isles, most of them Germans. As late as July 1919, the number of prisoners who remained interned was still at 87,000. That number dropped rapidly only with the repatriation action between the end of September and the end of November 1919. The last German POWs left the British Isles in April 1920. Until then, the majority of the German and Austro-Hungarian prisoners had been deployed in the most diverse range of jobs, with the agrarian sector dominating.

The repatriation of the majority of German POWs in France began later than in Britain. After the armistice, the approximately 300,000 POWs were given a new status as *prisonniers de guerre en régions libérées* and were placed under the Ministry for the Liberated Regions. That ministry was responsible for the nine *départements* in northern and northeastern France (from Calais in the west to Vosges in the east) especially hard hit by the war. The task of German POWs between January 1919 and January 1920 was chiefly the removal of rubble, the dismantling of war material, and reconstruction. The French government legitimized the internment and employment of POWs far beyond the de facto end of the war as reparations. Only in January 1920, after the Treaty of Versailles had come into force, did the repatriation of German POWs begin, and it was concluded within two months.

By contrast, for many reasons, the exchange of prisoners of war between the former enemies in eastern Europe proved to be a far more complex problem. The number of POWs was substantially higher, and larger distances had to be covered in regions with an inadequate transportation infrastructure. Added to this, as a crucial aspect, was the political situation in east-central and eastern Europe. The Russian revolution and the subsequent civil war destabilized any form of state authority in the former Czarist Empire. Hundreds of thousands of soldiers of the former German and Austro-Hungarian armies were caught between the front lines of the civil war. State institutions that would have been able to enforce uniform policies dealing with the POWs or carry out repatriations did not exist or possessed only very limited regulatory authority and capacities to act. Another consequence of this situation was that for many months, it was difficult for German officials or the relevant agencies in the successor states to the Austro-Hungarian monarchy to initiate contact with organizations in the former Czarist Empire to coordinate the repatriation of POWs from Russian lands.

The lack of interest on the part of the Western Allies in a regulation of the POW question in the successor states of the three empires also played a role: a repatriation of former soldiers of the czarist army seemed to entail the danger of strengthening the Bolshevist Red Army also against the Western Allies' intervention forces in the civil war. That was a central reason that the Western Allies, in January 1919, prohibited German authorities from transporting back any more Russian POWs. By that point, the number of Russian POWs in Germany had already declined substantially, from 1.2 million to around 300,000. No further orderly returns of Russian POWs took place for one year.

Most of the Russian POWs left in Germany in 1919–20 were deployed in German agriculture. They were seen as an important reservoir of labor especially because the German postwar conflicts with the newly established Polish state also meant that far fewer seasonal workers from Poland were available than in the prewar period. Even though the war had ended, the POWs continued to be restricted in their freedom of mobility: while the Russian internees were to have equal standing with native workers in respect to housing, provisions, and wages, employers had to hold back part of the earnings of the POWs and hand them over to the camp administration, which used it to pay for clothes. The personal information was passed to the local officials and the police; the POWs' place of employment was noted on the identity card of the camp administration. Leaving a place of employment was considered a breach of a labor contract and the offending POW was tracked down by the police and returned to the camp. This was intended to prevent prisoners from taking employment on their own volition. Still after 1918, the POWs remained for employers available workers with strongly restricted rights: if a prisoner was no longer needed, he could be immediately handed back to the camp. Refusal to work was also punishable by return to the camp.

Following an interruption of nearly a year and a half, the number of Russian POWs in Germany began to decline again. Negotiations with the Soviet Russian government led to a repatriation agreement. What made the implementation of the agreement technically possible, given the absence of direct borders between Germany and Soviet Russia, was the support from the International Red Cross, which entered into talks with Estonia and Lithuania and arranged for the repatriation transports to be channeled through the ports of Narva and Riga. In addition, Finland agreed to provide a transit camp. The International Committee of the Red Cross created the preconditions for the transports also in other ways: with the vast majority of the German merchant fleet having been turned over to the Allies, very few ships were available. Only in response to the intervention by the League of Nations' High Commissioner for the Repatriation of Prisoners of War, the polar explorer and Norwegian diplomat Fridtjof Nansen, was it possible to use British ships for the repatriation. The entire technical implementation of repatriation stood under the supervision of the International Red Cross in cooperation with High Commissioner Nansen.

On 1 October 1920, there were still around 130,000 Russian POWs in Germany, who continued to be employed chiefly in agriculture. A year later, the number of remaining Russian POWs had dropped to about 70,000–80,000. In November 1921, the Russian POWs who were still present, around 20,000, who did not wish to return to their homeland, were released from captivity and many were registered as foreign agricultural workers. They remained in Germany and disappeared for the observer either in the broad stream of Russian emigration or in the mass of foreign workers numbering into the tens of thousands. In spite of demands by conservative-national circles, the responsible German authorities refrained from forced repatriations in 1921–2.

In comparison, return and repatriations from the former Czarist Empire extended over a longer period of time – they began sooner and ended later. They began sooner chiefly because Russia exited the war soon after the successful October Revolution of the Bolsheviks in 1917. Of the approximately 1.9 million POWs at the end of 1917, about three-quarters were interned in the European part of Russia, one-quarter in Siberia and Central Asia. The return of POWs began immediately after the October Revolution of 1917; in the first months, up to the summer of 1918, it was usually a "wild" return movement of POWs to Austria-Hungary and Germany not organized by the state. Between July and October 1918, this was followed by repatriations organized by German and Austro-Hungarian military authorities; after the Peace of Brest-Litowsk in March 1918 and the subsequent advance of troops of the Central Powers into large parts of Ukraine, about 700,000 Austro-Hungarian as well as German POWs were liberated, and many were gradually transported back into their homelands. All told, about 1 million POWs had returned between the end of 1917 and the end of 1918.

Over the subsequent months, to the end of 1919, the withdrawal of the forces of the Central Powers following the armistice in the west and the civil war in the former Czarist Empire made the further repatriation of the still remaining 700,000–900,000 POWs (500,000 of whom were interned in Siberia) more difficult. Neither side in the civil war was interested in repatriating the POWs; rather, they saw them primarily as a potential pool from which to recruit experienced fighters for their own side. Around 100,000 former POWs probably fought – voluntarily or not – in the ranks of the Red Army, alone. The victories of the Red Army against the counter-revolutionary forces and the withdrawal of the Western Allies' intervention troops in 1919 brought greater possibilities of a state-regulated exchange of POWs. Repatriations began at the end of 1919 under the responsibility of the International Red Cross, especially from the Siberian part of Russia. They were completed in July 1922. In cooperation with the League of Nations' High Commissioner for the Repatriation of POWs, a total of 425,000 Russian, German, and Austro-Hungarian POWs had been repatriated between 10 May 1920 and 12 July 1922. In 1922, High Commissioner Nansen was awarded the Nobel Prize for Peace for his long commitment to the repatriation of POWs.

How many former POWs remained in the territory of the former Czarist Empire beyond the end of the repatriations in the middle of 1922 is unclear. Cautious estimates assume that the number exceeded 100,000. At any rate, dominant among them were former Austro-Hungarian soldiers, mostly Hungarians or Slavs. However, individual former POWs returned into the successor states of the Habsburg monarchy still into the 1930s.

The fate of the POWs, which assumed a central place during the war and the immediate postwar period in the public media and political discussion across Europe, had not only lost its political explosiveness a few years after the end of war but also its journalistic attraction and public interest. The Second World War led to significantly higher numbers of POWs (estimates put the figure at 35 million) and

the repatriations took much longer than after the First World War – the last German POWs were able to leave the USSR only in 1956. These are the crucial reasons that the phenomenon of war captivity between 1914 and 1922 and the experiences of the millions of POWs of the First World War were largely forgotten after 1945.

Becker, Annette. *Oubliés de la Grande Guerre. Humanitaire et culture de guerre 1914–1918: Populations occupées, déportés civils, prisonniers de guerre*. Paris, 1998.

Delpal, Bernard. "Prisonniers de guerre en France, 1914–1920." In *Les Exclus en Europe, 1830–1930*, edited by André Gueslin and Dominique Kalifa, 145–59. Paris, 1999.

Hinz, Uta. *Gefangen im Großen Krieg. Kriegsgefangene in Deutschland 1914–1921*. Essen, 2006.

Leidinger, Hannes, and Verena Moritz. *Gefangenschaft, Revolution, Heimkehr. Die Bedeutung der Kriegsgefangenenproblematik für die Geschichte des Kommunismus in Mittel- und Osteuropa 1917–1920*. Vienna, 2003.

Nachtigal, Reinhard. *Kriegsgefangenschaft an der Ostfront 1914 bis 1918. Literaturbericht zu einem neuen Forschungsfeld*. Frankfurt am Main, 2004.

Nachtigal, Reinhard. *Rußland und seine österreichisch-ungarischen Kriegsgefangenen (1914–1918)*. Grunbach, 2003.

Oltmer, Jochen. "Zwangsmigration und Zwangsarbeit: Ausländische Arbeitskräfte und bäuerliche Ökonomie im Deutschland des Ersten Weltkriegs." *Tel Aviver Jahrbuch für deutsche Geschichte* 27 (1998): 135–68.

Oltmer, Jochen, ed. *Kriegsgefangene im Europa des Ersten Weltkriegs*. Paderborn, 2006.

Rachamimov, Alon. *POWs and the Great War. Captivity on the Eastern Front*. Oxford and New York, 2002.

Wurzer, Georg. *Die Kriegsgefangenen der Mittelmächte in Rußland im Ersten Weltkrieg*. Göttingen, 2005.

Cross-references: Czechia and Slovakia; France; Germany; Great Britain; Russia and Belarus; Southeastern Europe; Chinese Contract Workers in France during World War I; Ethnic German "Remigrants" from Russia in Germany, 1890s to 1930s; Polish Agricultural Workers in Prussia-Germany from the Late 19th Century to World War II; Russian Emigrants in Europe since 1917

REFUGEES FROM FORMER YUGOSLAVIA IN EUROPE SINCE 1991

Pascal Goeke

All the signs had been pointing to the breakup of Yugoslavia since the 1980s. In 1989, at the latest, it was clear that the old socialist-authoritarian order would not be able to hold on much longer. While the revolutions in the other countries in eastern, east-central, and southeastern Europe were directed primarily against the political system, in Yugoslavia the process of dissolution coincided with national independence movements. The complex process of dismantling the old order and creating a new one involved the most serious military conflicts, the greatest number of casualties, and the most extensive refugee movements Europe had seen since the end of World War II and its aftermath.

Although the wars in Croatia and Bosnia-Herzegovina, and more recently in Kosovo and Serbia, had diverse causes and led to different kinds of refugee movements, they were closely interconnected. An examination of these events must take into account the starting conditions in Yugoslavia, the background to the collapse of the state, but also the reactions and signals from the West – not least because European refugee policy changed significantly in the 1990s, and with it the conditions of admission for refugees and their chances of inclusion in their host societies. A comprehensive assessment of the integration of the refugee groups is not possible at this time, because the number of refugees who are returning or leaving for other destinations is high and because the different groups are not captured in the statistics of the target countries in a way that would allow us to differentiate them clearly.

Yugoslavia on the eve of its breakup and the road to war

A thicket of political, economic, legal, religious, and social developments formed the backdrop to the breakup of Yugoslavia. The success of the "Second Yugoslavia," the Federal Republic of Yugoslavia, between 1945 and 1991 was the product of the charismatic politics of its leader, Tito, but also a heroic founding myth, a nonaligned status, economic prosperity, and social modernization. The Communist Party unified the state in an authoritarian-dictatorial fashion. There was no space to address, let alone process, the traumatic events that had happened during and after World War II. As a result, the fighting between and atrocities committed by communist partisans, Serbian-nationalist Cetniks, and the Croatian-fascist Ustasha engraved themselves in raw form upon the cultural memory of the various population groups. Lines of demarcation between population groups that were once at war always became visible when it came to making sense of and assessing economic and social crises and conflicts. The vision of an integrated Yugoslavism remained the idea of a minority.

When Tito was succeeded, after his death in 1980, not by an equally charismatic statesman but by nationalistically minded politicians intent on holding power, when the economy weakened, unemployment rose, and hyperinflation got out of control, the country broke apart. The great regional gap in development between the northwest and the southeast and the power of the Serbs within the state became obvious. At the same time, with the end of the east-west conflict, Yugoslavia simultaneously lost its special, identity-creating status as a nonaligned state. It became apparent now that the population of Yugoslavia was hardly united by citizenship in the Socialistička Federativna Republika Jugoslavija. Competing

collective identities came to the fore. Added to this, further national, linguistic, and religious dividing lines existed in the republics of Slovenia, Croatia, Bosnia-Herzegovina, Serbia, Montenegro, and Macedonia, as well as – with historical variations – in the two autonomous provinces of Kosovo and Vojvodina. The last census in 1991 conveys a sense of the relative sizes and distribution of the various groups in the republic. Table 1 reproduces the salient results.

The free elections saw victories by nationalist parties, some of whom advocated claims to independence. Slovenia and Croatia declared their independence on 25 June 1991. Slobodan Milošević, the president of the constituent Republic of Serbia, ordered his generals to occupy the Slovene capital of Ljubljana to put an end to Slovene independence. This attempt failed: Slovenia was able to break away from Yugoslavia and to develop into an economically and politically stable country, not least because the minorities had less weight than in Croatia, and because Croatia acted as a buffer to Serbia. Croatia saw the outbreak of war between Croatian government troops and paramilitary Serbian groups, a war that would eventually claim 10,000 lives.

War, expulsion, and flight from Croatia

Slovenia and Croatia were recognized by the EU member states on 15 January 1992. After Croatia's independence in June 1991, the large Serbian minority feared for its safety and the Serbian nationalist movement denounced Croatia's "foreign rule." Subsequently, the Serbs living in Krajina in Croatia declared their independence (Republic of Serbian Krajina, 1991–5). In the first phase of the war up to January 1992, the border region between this republic and Bosnia-Herzegovina as well as eastern Slavonia, at the border to Serbia, witnessed large-scale expulsions of 300,000 Croats, while 200,000 Serbs fled from the other parts of Croatia.

The majority of both groups of refugees remained within the borders of the former Yugoslavia; only about 80,000 left Yugoslav territory. Most of those were taken in by relatives and acquaintances who had gone to western, central, and northern Europe as part of the Yugoslav labor migration since the 1960s. Since Yugoslav immigrants in the various European destination countries had come from various republics, a national selection and sorting took place during the flight and in the choice of a destination country. Although a large part of these refugees returned to Croatia, the influx of refugees can also be seen as the beginning of an accelerated reunification of previously transnational families in the destination countries of the Yugoslav labor migration. This situation, which was even more important for refugees from Bosnia-Herzegovina and Kosovo, substantially eased the process of integration in the destination countries. For arriving children and spouses that was true in both legal and social terms.

Although the political situation in the Serbian Republic of Krajina had calmed down in 1992 in spite of a devastating

Table 1. The population of Yugoslavia according to "nations" and "nationalities" in the various republics and provinces, 1991 (all absolute figures in thousands)

	Population		Bosnia-Herzegovina	Monte-negro	Croatia	Mace-donia	Slo-venia	Serbia	Kosovo	Vojvo-dina
Total	23,528		4,365	615	4,784	2,034	1,963	5,809	1,965	2,014
Nations		%	%	%	%	%	%	%	%	%
Serbs	8,527	36.2	31.4	9.3	12.2	2.2	2.4	87.3	10.0	57.3
Croats	4,637	19.7	17.3	1.0	77.9		2.7			3.7
Muslims	2,353	10.0	43.7	14.6	1.0	2.1	1.4	3.0	2.9	
Slovenes	1,760	7.5					87.6			
Macedonians	1,372	5.8				64.6				
Montenegrins	539	2.3		61.8				1.3	1.0	2.1
Nationalities										
Albanians	2,178	9.3		6.6		21.1		1.3	82.2	
Hungarians	379	1.6								16.9
Roma	210	0.9				2.7		1.2	2.2	1.2
Turks	110	0.5				4.8				
Slovaks	730	0.3								3.2
Romanians	430	0.2								1.9
Yugoslavs	710	3.0	5.5	4.2	2.2			2.5		8.4

Source: Roux, *La population de la Yougoslavie en 1991,* 36, 40. The slight differences in the totals arise from the preliminary nature of the results. The peculiar division into "nations" and "nationalities" corresponds to the structure of the census. Each citizen could assign himself or herself to a group.

economic crisis, Croatia was able to retake the territory in 1995. This time between 150,000 and 200,000 Serbs took flight, most of them to Serbia. By 2003, fewer than 100,000 of the 350,000 Serbs who fled Croatia had returned. Implementing the right of return was still difficult at the beginning of the 21st century because large obstacles had been erected in Croatia on the local and national levels, and because anti-Serb feelings remained strong. In addition, Serbia and Montenegro were using international aid money for projects to integrate these refugees into their own countries and paid little attention to those who returned to Croatia. The number of Serbs in Croatia declined from 12.2% of the population in 1991 to 4.5% in 2001. Because those who remained and those who returned were mostly older individuals and more rarely families with children, the Serbian share of Croatia's population is expected to decline further in the first two decades of the 21st century. One can foresee a time when hardly any Serbs will be living in Croatia.

War, expulsion, and flight in Bosnia-Herzegovina

The situation in Bosnia-Herzegovina had deteriorated since the beginning of 1992. Encouraged by western signals, a referendum on independence was held on 1 March 1992. The majority of Muslims and Croats voted in favor, while the Serbs boycotted the referendum. On 6 April 1992, the Republic of Bosnia-Herzegovina was recognized by the USA and the member states of the EU. Subsequently, Bosnian Serbs and, a year later, Bosnian Croats, as well, tried to gain control of large sections of the country in an effort to annex them to either Serbia or Croatia. The respective minorities in the Croat- and Serb-dominated territories were expelled.

According to figures from the International Helsinki Federation for Human Rights (IHF), more than 160,000 died in the war between 1991 and 1995. About 2.5 million were forced to flee. Of those, 600,000 refugees remained in Bosnia-Herzegovina, another 600,000 in the territories of the former Yugoslavia; 1.3 million fled across the borders of the former state.

For the first time, the number of refugees from the Balkans rose appreciably also in western, central, northern, and southeastern Europe. Leaving aside the duration of the war, the reasons for this were chiefly that the entire Republic of Bosnia-Herzegovina was affected and that the Bosnian Muslims, especially, unlike the Serbs or the Croats, had no state of their own and thus no secure fallback area. There is no unanimity about the precise number of refugees in Europe because their stay in the destination countries fell under various legal categories. Moreover, it was often impossible to distinguish flight from family reunification and to clarify the ethnic and regional origins of the refugees. The existing numbers diverge so strongly as to make any reasonable comparison impossible. Few refugees were given refugee status in the sense of the 1951 Geneva Refugee Convention. The overwhelming majority was given temporary protection with very divergent possibilities of employment. Table 2 conveys an approximate and incomplete overview of the distribution of refugees two years after the Dayton Peace Accords of 1995. It also tries to offer some indication of how the refugee burden was distributed among the European destination countries.

During the peace negotiations and on the political agenda in the destination countries, the return of the refugees had priority. But in September 2004, the United Nations High

Table 2. Refugees from Bosnia in select EU countries, 1997

Country	Refugees from Bosnia-Herzegovina in select countries		Indicators of the capacity and the contribution of the destination countries to refugee protection overall	
	Estimated number of Bosnians, beginning of 1997	Returnees to Bosnia-Herzegovina, end of 1997	Number of refugees per $1 of per capita GDP, 1996	Number of refugees per 1,000 inhabitants, 1996
Austria	88,609	1,601	3.6	11.0
Belgium	6,000	104	1.5	3.5
Denmark	21,458	886	2.0	12.4
Finland	1,350	9	0.5	2.2
France	15,000	180	6.4	2.5
Germany	342,500	70,000	52.8	15.4
Greece	4,000	3	0.5	0.5
Ireland	886	87	0.0	0.0
Italy	8,827	494	3.1	1.1
Luxembourg	1,816	0	0.0	1.6
Netherlands	25,000	118	4.0	6.4
Portugal	n.a.	7	0.0	0.0
Spain	1,900	16	0.4	0.1
Sweden	60,671	285	7.4	21.6
Great Britain	6,000	460	3.8	1.7
Total	584,017	74,250		

Source: Selm, ed. *Kosovo's Refugees in the European Union*, 229; Statistical Yearbook 2002, published by the UNHCR.

Commissioner for Refugees (UNHCR) was able to announce the return of only 1 million, while 1.5 million refugees remained in their host countries.

Germany, in particular, pursued a rigorous policy of return that came in for strong criticism domestically and from the USA, for example. While the country had initially taken in the largest number of refugees, beginning in 1997 they were pressured to leave and also deported to regions in which they were part of a threatened minority. According to figures from the UNHCR, 39,688 refugees from Bosnia-Herzegovina were still living in Germany in 2003. Because the number of returnees was significantly lower in other countries, Germany's initially large contribution to the admission of refugees eventually approached the European average. As early as 1997, the USA declared its willingness to accept 18,000 refugees from the European destination countries, of which 7,000 would be from Germany.

Individual studies about the integration of the refugees point out that the refugees on average had a higher status than those who remained behind in the former Yugoslavia. Even years after their arrival in the first host country, a high mobility could be observed among the refugees. For example, at least 20,000 refugees from Germany went to the USA, which had a total of 61,834 Bosnian refugees in 2003. Australia, Canada, and New Zealand also took in refugees who had originally been given refuge in western, central, northern, and southern Europe.

Integration progressed steadily right up to the beginning of the 21st century, in spite of numerous problems. Among these, many members of the refugee groups had been traumatized and this continued to pose a serious problem; as another, often professional diplomas were not recognized in the destination countries. In Germany, the discussion about refugees remaining in the country revolved around integration in the labor market and the educational system. The integration of the refugees was promoted above all by the progressive improvement in their legal status, which led to rights of permanent residency and opened up access to the labor market. A similar effect came because the Muslims of Bosnia-Herzegovina had always been drawn more to Europe than to the Islamic world. That this group was relatively inconspicuous in the European destination countries was the result of this self-conception. At the turn of the 21st century, Kosovar refugees were increasingly displacing Bosnian refugees from the lowest rungs of the labor market in the destination countries. Public attention, too, was now directed more at the refugees from the war in Kosovo.

War, expulsion, and flight in Kosovo

As early as 28 March 1989, Serbia repealed the autonomous status of the provinces of Kosovo and Vojvodina. Thereafter, the social conditions of the Kosovo Albanians deteriorated and reports about human rights violations multiplied. Still, the international community was decidedly passive until 1998. Diplomatic pressure on Serbia was not intensified, and the peaceful protest movements in Kosovo received no meaningful international support. A major reason the crisis

Albanian refugees from Prizren in Kosovo reach the Albanian border in Morina, 28 April 1999 (*ullstein bild*).

came to a head was that the Kosovo Albanians were increasingly shut out from access to central institutions of the education system and the administration in Serbia. The Serbian government created a system of apartheid that excluded the Kosovo Albanians from any modernization processes, which subsequently also had repercussions for the integration of the refugees from Kosovo in Europe.

Even though the Kosovo Albanians responded to Serbian pressure by setting up extensive political and social parallel structures, they were not able to compensate for their exclusion. For example, the number of Kosovo Albanians in schools and universities dropped by 50% within a few years. At the same time there was a rise in applications for asylum by Kosovo Albanians; the EU member states, alone, registered 114,430 such applications from individuals from the former Yugoslavia between 1995 and 1997, and according to estimates, 90% were probably from Kosovo Albanians.

The conflict in Kosovo was militarized and the Albanian liberation army Ushtria Çlirimtare e Kosovës (UÇK) stepped up its activities. Financial support, and in some cases also new members, came from groups of Kosovo Albanians in Germany, Switzerland, Great Britain, Belgium, the USA, and other countries. While the UÇK was trying to provoke international intervention with its guerrilla warfare, the Yugoslav army and troops of the special police responded with intense repression. According to information from the Independent International Commission on Kosovo, between February and September 1998, about 1,000 civilians were murdered and 400,000 of Kosovo's population of just under 2 million were driven from their homes. Half of those remained in Kosovo and were able to return following the Holbrooke-Milošević agreement in October 1998, even though Serbia and the UÇK continued to talk openly about further offensives. As the conflict did not ease, NATO decided to intervene militarily and flew air attacks between 24 March and 19 June 1999. During that time about 10,000 people died,

most of them Kosovo Albanians killed by the Yugoslav army. About 900,000 civilians were expelled or fled from Kosovo, another 600,000 refugees remained in Kosovo. Flight and expulsions went hand in hand with rapes, torture, plundering, and blackmail.

The European governments and nongovernmental organizations (NGOs) were unprepared for the magnitude of the refugee movements. Immediately after the start of NATO's intervention it was unclear whether it or the UNHCR was in charge of providing for the refugees. The beginning of the evacuation of the refugees from the war regions as well as aid for the refugees on the ground were delayed because of a disagreement over what status the refugees should be accorded. The countries of western, central, northern, and southern Europe maintained that the refugees should in principle remain in the politically unstable region (Albania, Macedonia, and Montenegro). Given their experiences with the Bosnian refugees, the governments of potential host countries were afraid that the Kosovo refugees would not return home any time soon.

Germany, the Netherlands, and Austria proposed granting the refugees temporary protection on the basis of an EU formula that would distribute internationally the burden of taking in the refugees. Opposition to the admission of the refugees came from France, Great Britain, and Italy, who saw in the transport of refugees outside of the territory of the former Yugoslavia a measure that solidified and legitimized the Serbian policy of "ethnic cleansing." The UNHCR's response was also not favorable: it saw a threat to the principle of unconditional asylum because the receiving countries wanted to grant only temporary protection. The political quarrel, which revolved chiefly around the issue of what leeway nations would have for taking action, stood in striking contrast to the engagement of civil society. In France alone, 400,000 households declared their willingness to take in refugees, even though they would have to bear the expenses for lodging and food themselves. Only a fraction of these offers were taken up.

The evacuation program began in 1999, with the participation of 29 countries. In the end, about 92,000 refugees were able to leave the zone of conflict; 52,853 went to EU states. The admission of contingents of refugees was accompanied – as had already been the case during the Bosnian war – by illegal border crossings and entry of individuals into the host countries. Between April and June 1999, 22 different countries counted 42,290 applications for asylum: half of these applications were filed in Switzerland alone, and one-fourth in Germany.

Depending on national laws and political decisions, the status given to refugees varied. As had already been the case with Bosnian refugees, access to regular asylum proceedings was often closed to the evacuees. Generally we are talking about collective, temporary protection for refugees. In Norway, for example, this meant a status that came very close to the regulations of the Geneva Refugee Convention: a residency permit for four years, unlimited access to the labor market, and the right to family reunification. Shortly after the end of the military conflict, Norway, like many other countries, put in place programs for returning the refugees. In part the return was voluntary, and sometimes there was the possibility of returning immediately to the host country if the conditions of settlement back home were unsatisfactory. Germany provided support for orientation trips back to the regions of origin. In some cases such measures had also existed for the refugees from Bosnia-Herzegovina.

The majority of those who had fled into Serbia's neighbor states returned quickly to their original country. That is also true for a large segment of refugees who had gained admission into the EU countries. A few countries were adamant in deporting them, but in part the returns also occurred because of restrictive admission conditions in the destination countries and because staying there offered few prospects. In Germany, for example, Kosovo Albanians classified as "Refugees from war and civil war" in accordance with the Foreigners' Law, just like asylum seekers, did not receive welfare payments but material support (vouchers, packages of food and toiletries) and no work permit.

Statements about the number of refugees remain speculative because only citizenship was registered, and no ethnical affiliation. In the political discussion in Europe over the admitted contingents, the various destination countries regularly made their admission quotas look better than they were. It is noticeable that the group of Kosovo Albanians, which cannot be statistically established with absolute clarity, seemed to possess a pronounced group identity. Although a few Kosovo Albanians were also among the migrant workers from Yugoslavia after World War II, even in the favorite target countries of the Yugoslav labor migration, Switzerland and West Germany, they were perceived as a separate group only since the 1990s. Negative external descriptions were regularly found in the most important admission countries for Kosovo Albanian refugees – Germany, Austria, Switzerland, France, Great Britain, the Netherlands, Sweden, Norway, Denmark, and Italy. In Switzerland, for example, as the most recent immigrant group they replaced the Tamils as the publicly pilloried "problem group."

Kosovo Albanian refugees who had obtained permanent residency as the result of a successful application for asylum or as part of family reunification had a hard time gaining access to the labor markets in their host countries because of their generally poor education and training in their homeland. At the beginning of the 21st century, the refugees are still obliged to transfer part of their often small income to Kosovo to support relatives and acquaintances struggling with the poor economic conditions there.

Al-Ali, Nadje, Richard Black, and Khalid Koser. "Refugees and Transnationalism: The Experience of Bosnians and Eritreans in Europe." *Journal of Ethnic and Migration Studies* 27 (2001): 615–34.

Barutciski, Michael, and Astri Suhrke. "Lessons from the Kosovo Refugee Crisis: Innovations in Protection and Burden-sharing." *Journal of Refugee Studies* 14 (2001): 95–134.

Buckley, William Joseph, ed. *Kosovo: Contending Voices on Balkan Interventions*. Cambridge, 2000.

Jambrešić Kirin, Renata, and Maja Povrzanović, eds. *War, Exile, Everyday Life: Cultural Perspectives*. Zagreb, 1996.

The Kosovo Report: Conflict, International Response, Lessons Learned. Published by the Independent International Commission on Kosovo. Oxford, 2000.

Lukic, Vesna, and Vladimir Nikitovic "Refugees from Bosnia and Herzegovina in Serbia: A Study of Refugee Selectivity." *International Migration* 42 (2004): 85–110.

Roux, Michel. "La population de la Yougoslavie en 1991. Inventaire avant le chaos." *Méditerranée* (1995): 35–46.

Selm, Joanne van, ed. *Kosovo's Refugees in the European Union*. London and New York, 2000.

Cross-references: Austria; Belgium and Luxembourg; France; Germany; Great Britain; Ireland and Northern Ireland; Italy; The Netherlands; Northern Europe; Southeastern Europe; Spain and Portugal; Switzerland; Sri-Lankan Tamils in Western and Central Europe since the 1980s: The Example of Switzerland; Yugoslav Labor Migrants in Western, Central, and Northern Europe since the End of World War II

REFUGEES IN RUSSIA DURING AND AFTER WORLD WAR I

Eric Lohr

World War I brought many refugees from foreign lands into the Russian Empire. Over 100,000 Ukrainians from Galicia and the Carpathians fled to the interior after the Russian retreat from these Habsburg-occupied foreign lands in 1915. A comparable number of civilians from East Prussia were deported to Russia or went of their own accord during the occupation of the region in 1914. More than a half million Armenian refugees poured into the Caucasus and Russia in the period 1914–20, many from parts of Anatolia occupied by Russia early in the war then lost to the Ottoman army in 1918.

Hundreds of thousands of the over 2 million prisoners of war in Russian camps became refugees after 1917, during the chaos of revolution and civil war. Groups of Polish officers and soldiers trekked through Mongolia, China, and then traveled by ship from the Far East to France, in order to ultimately return to Poland. Most famous was the saga of Czech POWs, who formed an army unit within the czar's army, were embroiled in the cause of the White Russians during the civil war, and briefly seized the entire Trans-Siberian Railway, before finally managing their originally planned journey to the newly founded Czechoslovakia (1918) via Vladivostok and France.

More commonly, whether they had escaped or were among the 1 million POWs formally released according to the terms of the Brest-Litovsk treaties in 1918, refugees often had to manage the long land journey on their own. Until the middle of 1918, the new revolutionary regime was unable to control its borders, and hundreds of thousands of POWs and other refugees slipped across the western frontier. However, in 1918, the Bolsheviks created the Central Committee for Prisoners of War and Refugees (Tsentroplenbezh) and gradually began to assert more control over movements across the border. Diplomacy also became an important factor as the authorities engaged in protracted bilateral POW and civilian exchange negotiations with former enemies that stretched into the early 1920s.

In addition to captured soldiers, the Russian Army interned roughly 300,000 civilian subjects of enemy states who were living in Russia. This category of prisoner was interned under less stringent forms of oversight than POWs, and most were able to simply leave the country or even return to their homes in Russia during the chaos of 1917–18. By all accounts, the vast majority chose to leave the country, not least because many of their properties, businesses, and homes had been confiscated or destroyed during the war and revolution.

Thus, by the narrow UN definition of refugees – persons who have fled or been displaced from their homeland – the war and revolution created roughly a million refugees. A much broader definition that includes displaced Russian subjects estimates at least 7 million refugees in the Russian Empire by July 1917. Individuals and groups who fled or were forced to leave their homes in the front zones comprise the bulk of this category. Millions of Russian subjects fled the front zone as the Russian army conducted the "Great Retreat" out of the Polish kingdom, Galicia, and parts of Russian Ukraine, Belarus, and Lithuania.

The Russian army exacerbated what was already a serious refugee crisis by conducting a brutal policy of "scorched earth" for a few weeks in the summer of 1915, in some areas driving the entire population to the Russian interior. The army further added to the number of refugees by launching a sweeping program of mass deportations of Russian-subject ethnic Germans and Jews that forced over a half million people to the Russian interior. These measures were closely associated with laws passed by the civilian government to formally expropriate the properties of Germans in the western and southern parts of the empire, effectively turning them into permanent refugees with no home or farm to which they could return.

The collapse of the Russian Empire in revolution and civil war turned huge numbers of people into refugees. Poland, Lithuania, Latvia, Estonia, and Finland all gained independence early in the civil war, leaving millions outside what they or their new host states considered to be their proper homeland. Because many of these new states had been in areas of heavy military activity during the war, hundreds of thousands ended up as refugees, deportees, and evacuees in the Russian interior. Others returned through official channels. Polish authorities and the national committees of other eastern-central European states granted passports to many

of the displaced and negotiated with the Soviet regime for their return or immigration to the new states. These official repatriations were regulated by a series of bilateral treaties that gave refugees a deadline by which they could "opt" for citizenship in their new homeland state. If they did not exercise this option, they would become Soviet citizens. The new states often went to great lengths to promote the return or new arrival of citizens of their titular nationalities. They also tried to prevent the mass return of Jews and other minorities to their homes in the new states. The scale of these population movements was impressive. More than 2 million people returned from the Soviet Union to Poland, for example, between 1918 and 1924.

One could expand the definition of refugee even further to include the millions of people displaced during the civil war and revolution as a result of military operations, economic collapse, and famine. Countless numbers of people temporarily or permanently fled advancing White and Red armies on both sides of the front. At war's end, more than 2 million Russians left and became refugees in Europe and the Far East. The collapse of the urban economy after the revolution forced millions of urban workers to seek refuge and survival in the countryside, bringing about a massive decline in Russia's urban workforce to less than a third of its 1917 level by 1921. Famine, epidemic disease, and war killed over 9 million people; millions more fled famine and connected outbreaks of epidemic disease to other regions of Russia in the hope of survival. Among other things, this left 1.5 million or more orphans. Due to a severe lack of funds and institutions to house them, many took up an itinerant existence, wandering like nomads from place to place in large groups.

What happened to the refugees in their new places of residence? While there were tensions right from the start, during the first years of World War I, they were mitigated somewhat by the intense labor shortage that prevailed throughout much of the empire. Many refugees were able to quickly find work, which eased their integration into the labor market. Many refugees were able to use extended community networks to settle in regions where people of their own religious or ethnic communities could help provide for their needs. For example, many of the German refugees and forced migrants ended up settling among the German communities of the Volga region, where local churches and communities provided support. Assistance to the refugees became a popular cause in Russian society, and each national group formed aid committees that were quite effective in providing assistance.

However, many locals feared the incoming refugees because of the frequency of typhus and other epidemics among them. As the war dragged on, inflation became an increasingly serious problem and at times refugees were blamed for increasing the demand for scarce consumer goods. Many areas that had been previously uniformly Russian quite suddenly had to deal with a major influx of minorities. Tensions ran high, turning most violent against the Jews.

Jews in the Russian Empire had long been banned from settling in the Russian interior and were allowed to reside only within the Pale of Settlement, a swath of territory limited to the western parts of the empire conquered in the late 18th century. During World War I, the army command expelled a half million or more Jews from the front zones, especially when the Russian army retreated to the interior of the country during 1915. To facilitate resettlement of the Jewish refugees, officials reluctantly abolished the Pale and opened up other Russian areas to Jewish settlement. Local reactions to the migration of Jews that followed were extremely hostile. In 1919, with substantial popular support, the Ukrainian Insurgent Army, anarchist units, White armies, and Bolshevik troops massacred as many as 100,000 Jews. The pogroms affected areas of long-term Jewish settlement, but the wartime refugees and deportees were hit with particular violence.

One of the most striking general features of the refugee phenomenon in the period was its nationalizing impact – and among local communities as well as among immigrants. This was a result of tensions and violent conflict between groups of different regional and national origin. The mobilization of the displaced communities around national aid committees caused a growth in national orientations and led to new conflicts with locals; the leaders of national aid committees often ended up taking on leadership roles in national independence movements. These movements gave states the ability to pursue their state- and nation-building goals by enabling them to sort through refugees applying to return or migrate, encouraging some to return and denying permission to others. The rise of national sentiment and identity among refugees in the Russian interior helps explain why such a relatively small proportion of non-Russian refugees decided to stay in Russia.

In sum, the number of refugees in Russia between 1914 and 1920 depends on how one defines "refugee" and "Russia." War, imperial collapse, famine, epidemics, and revolution combined to cause massive and widespread population movements involving varying degrees of coercion. Rather than integrate in the host Russian society, many became more integrated in their own national communities as a result of their refugee experience. War, epidemic, and famine left refugees with few incentives to remain, and many who had alternative homelands made their way out of the country. But millions of others had little choice but to begin their lives under the revolutionary regime as refugees.

Baron, Nick, and Peter Gatrell. "Population Displacement, State-Building, and Social Identity in the Lands of the Former Russian Empire, 1917–1923." *Kritika: Explorations in Russian and Eurasian History* 4 (2003): 51–100.

Baron, Nick, and Peter Gatrell, eds. *Homelands: War, Population and Statehood in Eastern Europe and Russia, 1918–1924*. London, 2004.

Gatrell, Peter. *A Whole Empire Walking: Refugees in Russia during World War I*. Bloomington, IN, 1999.

Lohr, Eric. *Nationalizing the Russian Empire: The Campaign against Enemy Aliens during World War I*. Cambridge, 2003.

Sanborn, Joshua A. "Unsettling the Empire: Violent Migrations and Social Disaster in Russia during World War I." *Journal of Modern History* 77, 2 (2005): 290–324.

Cross-references: The Baltic Region; Czechia and Slovakia; Germany; Poland; Russia and Belarus; Southeastern Europe; Ukraine; Prisoners of War in Europe, 1914–1922; Russian Emigrants in Europe since 1917

RUSSIAN ELITES IN THE BALTIC STATES SINCE THE EARLY MODERN PERIOD

Ralph Tuchtenhagen

The modern-day Baltic states of Estonia, Latvia, and Lithuania were created between 1918 and 1920. Until then, their territories were provinces or parts of the provinces of the Czarist Empire. The phrase "Russian elites" can refer to a range of very different phenomena. In particular, a distinction must be drawn between self-description and external description. Thus, while "Russians" could think of themselves as an elite in the Czarist Empire or the Soviet Union, in the Baltic countries or states themselves they had an inferior legal status. Moreover, to this day there is a lack of clear criteria for who should be considered "Russian." For the Czarist Empire, factors such as language, religion, or a sense of nationality have only qualified usefulness as defining criteria, and that is even more true of the Soviet context, leaving aside entries into the passport. Then there is the problem that in the Baltic lands or states, different criteria of what is "Russian" could be applied from what the "Russians" in questions themselves used. Within the context of the "Russification" of the Baltic lands or states in various historical phases, a distinction between "Russians" and "Non-Russians" is nearly impossible. Consequently, for the present purpose the label "Russian elites" refers to those groups of people who hailed from Russia and held high-level political, administrative, economic, religious, or cultural positions.

For the 16th and 17th centuries, individual merchants of the Russian Orthodox faith were found in the large cities of the Swedish Baltic provinces of Estonia and Livonia. They probably came largely from the nearby Russian cities, for example, Novgorod, Pskov, and Polock. In addition, Russian religious refugees (Old Believers) had settled since the 1660s at Lake Peipus, where their descendants have been living to this day. However, the majority of neither the Old Believers nor the Russian merchants in the cities can be regarded as elites. As a rule, they enjoyed guest status and were merely tolerated.

After the conquest and annexation of the Swedish provinces of Estonia and Livonia by the Grand Duchy of Moscow at the beginning of the 18th century, it was initially only the occasional high civilian and military official, noble landowner, merchant, or high dignitary of the Russian-Orthodox

Church who made his way into the provinces. This immigration began to accelerate during the reign of Empress Catherine II (1762–96). In 1782, Russians made up about 2% of the population in the territory of modern-day Estonia, and slightly more in that of modern-day Latvia. They came from all parts of the Czarist Empire and thought of themselves as an administrative, military, and economic elite within the provinces, though they were constrained in what they could do by the estate laws of the two provinces. In fact, in their relationship to the crown they enjoyed fewer rights than did the nobility of Estonia and Livonia and the burgher class of the Baltic states, unless they were registered in the local nobility through donations of land by the crown. In that case, however, they were no longer considered "Russians" from a legal point of view, but Livonians or Estonians. Catherine II therefore tried to push through equal religious rights for the Russian Orthodox population and to align the Baltic estate rights with their Russian counterparts by introducing the Russian nobility and city code in 1786. The introduction of "normal schools" in the Baltic provinces, also in 1786, guaranteed the Russian population an elementary education that exceeded the demands of the traditional elementary education in the Baltic provinces and underscored its claim to elite status.

The integration policy initiated by Catherine II intensified considerably after the partitions of Poland-Lithuania (1772, 1793, 1795) and the Crimean War (1853–6), but especially between 1867 and 1917. In this process, a distinction was made between the "Baltic provinces" of Estonia, Livonia, and Courland, and the "northwest territory" settled by, among others, Lithuanians. The Baltic Sea provinces were subjected to a linguistic, administrative, religious, and cultural "Russification." The conversion campaigns of the 1840s – which made a part of the Estonian and Latvian population into members of the Russian Orthodox Church, with no possibility of a legal re-conversion – made it difficult to distinguish "Russians" and "Estonians" or "Latvians" after the 1840s, for at that time "Russian" and "Orthodox" were considered synonymous, and an Estonian and Latvian national consciousness was just beginning to develop.

If one applies the criteria for membership in the "Russian people" that were used back then, we can identify a "Russian" minority that was produced especially by conversion, spoke Russian only as an exception, and was hardly part of the elite. A systematic "Russification" above and beyond this through the immigration of Russian speakers would have been possible with the 1863 law about freedom of movement and settlement through the empire and with the introduction of commercial freedom in the provinces of Estonia and Livonia in 1866, though very little of that occurred until 1917. At most, there were labor migrations from the interior of the empire to the Baltic provinces in the wake of the industrialization that began there in the 1860s.

In the larger cities, a Russian educated elite organized itself into charitable, artistic, musical, literary, and journalistic circles, and in the university city of Dorpat also into Russian student fraternities. The representatives of this Russian educated elite were, on the one hand, from the families and merchants who had been settled in the Baltic cities since the 18th century, and, on the other hand, immigrant civil and military officials, who in the 19th century lived in the Baltic provinces for a short period, though sometimes also over several generations. Between the censuses of 1881 (Baltic provinces) and 1897 (all of Russia), the size of the Russian-speaking population in the Baltic provinces rose from about 3.5% to around 4.5%. The elite is likely to have made up a shrinking part of this population compared to the immigrant workers. It is not possible to say anything about "Russians" (members of the Russian Orthodox Church) of Estonian or Latvian descent, since language was the central criterion in both censuses.

In the wake of the three partitions of Poland, the better part of the former Grand Duchy of Lithuania had been divided up, under Russian rule, among various *guberniya* (provinces) of the "northwest territory," and unlike the Baltic provinces, it did not possess privileged standing within the empire. Still, the Russification measures and the conversion policy of the Russian Orthodox Church remained largely unsuccessful. As in the Russian Baltic provinces, the Russian elite in the Lithuanian territories did not form a homogeneous minority in the 19th century. High state officials and members of the military for the most part remained in the northwest territory only for the duration of their service. Merchants and clergy sometimes stayed until the end of their lives, and the subsequent generations assimilated, whereby mixed marriages often led to assimilation to German or Russian ways of life. The religious laws pertaining to mixed marriages had the decisive influence here: as a rule, children had to be raised in the religious-cultural traditions of the confession of the head of the family. Of course, mixed marriages were ruled out for members of the families of Orthodox clergy.

The points around which "Russian" identity crystallized in the provinces were the Orthodox Church and Russian schools in the larger cities (Reval, Narva, Dorpat, Riga, Libau, Windau, Vilna). So far we lack numbers and studies about the size and structure of the "Russian elites" in the Baltic provinces. The subsequent fate of the elite groups in the 20th century, to the extent that it has been studied, was quite varied. After the establishment of the Baltic states around 1920, many old-established Russian families fled into the Soviet Union, others formed a Russian minority that was initially protected by minority and autonomy laws, while still others assimilated, especially through marriage. However, these last two groups came under growing pressure in Lithuania from the middle of the 1920s, in Estonia and Latvia from the middle of the 1930s, when the authoritarian regimes of the Baltic states began to ignore the guaranteed autonomy rights of the Russian minority. This led to further emigrations in the late 1920s and 1930s, though their extent and quality have so far not been examined in detail.

Büttner, Ruth, Vera Lubina, and Michail Leonov. *Russia and the Baltic States: Political Relations, National Identity and Social Thought in XVII–XX Centuries*. Samara, 2001.

Issakov, Sergej G. *Russkie obščestvennye i kuľturnye dejateli v Èstonii. Materialy k biografičeskomu slovarju*, vol. 1. Tallinn, 1996.

Loeber, Dietrich A. "Russifizierung in den baltischen Ländern – einst und jetzt." *Baltisches Jahrbuch* 5 (1988): 144–63.

Pistohlkors, Gert von, Andrejs Plakans, and Paul Kaegbein. *Bevölkerungsverschiebungen und sozialer Wandel in den baltischen Provinzen Russlands 1850–1914*. Lüneburg, 1995.

Stranga, Aivars, ed. *Historical Minorities in Latvia*. Riga, 1994.

Viikberg, Jüri. *Eesti rahvaste raamat. Rahvusvähemused, -rühmad ja -killud*. Tallinn, 1999.

Cross-references: The Baltic Region; Poland; Russia and Belarus

A former colonel of the czarist army and his family in the refugee camp Wünsdorf near Berlin painting crockery, 1924 (*ullstein bild*).

RUSSIAN EMIGRANTS IN EUROPE SINCE 1917

Karl Schlögel

In the 20th century, Russia was the point of origin for an important emigration movement, which would prove consequential for Russia itself as well as for the host countries. This emigration, which occurred in repeated waves and thrusts, was triggered by the social and political upheavals that forced thousands to leave their homeland and settle in foreign lands. Unlike the exodus from the Czarist Empire in the late 19th and early 20th centuries, which was caused by economic misery and the pressure of persecution above all in the Jewish Pale of Settlement, and whose destination was mostly North America, the emigration after 1917 was above all a political movement: the establishment of Soviet power posed a threat to life and limb for certain groups, and leaving the country proved for many the only escape.

"Emigration from Russian lands" (rossijskaja emigracija*) and "Russian emigration"* (russkaja emigracija*): an important semantic distinction*

This emigration can be described as from "Russian lands" in that it involved by no means only (ethnic) Russians. *Rossijkij* describes the territoriality and statehood of the Russian Empire, which broke apart in revolution and civil war, and all the groups living in it – Ukrainians, Germans, Jews, Latvians, Estonians, Georgians, Armenians, Fins, Tartars, Lithuanians, or Poles. Emigration from Russian lands after 1917 thus refers to the flight of members of the Russian Empire, regardless of their nationality. Talk of "Russian emigrants" who settled in the capital cities of Europe after 1917 therefore refers nearly always to refugees from the former Russian Empire and by no means only to ethnic Russians. It was only when the Russian Empire ceased to exist and numerous new nation-states arose from its ashes (Finland, the Baltic republics, Poland, for a while also the transcaucasian republics) that the "emigration from Russian lands" also disintegrated and split into national groups (Armenian, Georgian, Ukrainian diaspora). In addition to the somewhat unaccustomed but correct designation as "emigration from Russian lands" or "diaspora from Russian lands," there are a number of other terms for the same phenomenon: "Russia beyond the borders" (*rossijskoe zarubež̌e, russkoe zarubež̌e*), "Russian diaspora," or "Russia II."

However, emigration from Russian lands in the 20th century has another meaning. It describes various, successive waves of emigration. The first wave is usually the one that was triggered by the October Revolution of 1917 and the seizure of power by the Bolsheviks. The second wave is the one that the USSR experienced during and after the end of the Second World War: Soviet citizens who were deported by the German occupiers from the USSR to forced labor in Germany and who did not return to their homeland, or who, as "voluntary assistants," members of Vlasov's army or other collaborationist organizations, had to fear punishment or revenge and therefore remained in the West after 1945. This group was numerically significant but above all socially and culturally different from the first wave: former Soviet citizens who had grown up and been socialized in the USSR and had nothing to do with the old emigrants.

The third wave refers to the surge of emigration that drew from the counter-society and civil rights movement that was emerging within the Soviet Union. These were mostly members of civil rights and dissident movements from the 1960s to the 1980s, members of networks of civil society: Helsinki committees, national independence groups in the Soviet republics, and writers and artists striving for freedom and civil liberties. These groups suffered increasing repression in the 1970s, but they could also count on political support in the West. This gave rise to a new emigration that usually took on individual – though in a few cases also collective – forms,

639

which were often dealt with in intrastate agreements. That applies, for example, to the Jewish "refuzniks," the Volga Germans, or the Pontic Greeks.

"Emigration from Russian lands," as a largely political emigration due to the pressures of oppression and persecution, came to an end with the dissolution of the USSR. Conversely, the end of the USSR triggered quantitatively important migrations, which can be traced back to the resettlement or flight of Russian minorities from the now independent former Soviet republics, especially in Central Asia, the Caucasus, and the Baltic region. The new Russian diaspora that began to take shape beginning with the 1990s can be attributed more to the newly acquired mobility, freedom of movement, and new possibilities of work – in short, to the globalization process in which Russia is now also participating. What is remarkable for the entire "short 20th century," however, is not only that Russia or the Soviet Union was the constant starting point of political emigration but also that "Russia beyond the borders," the Russian diaspora, was more or less autonomous and distinct and did not dissolve and disappear into processes of assimilation and acculturation. This also sheds light on a very specific characteristic of emigration from Russian lands: it was an emigration with a strong cultural dimension, if not a cultural mission.

Emigration from Russian lands: its driving forces and its pathways

Although we are thus dealing with three waves, the label "emigration from Russian lands" usually refers to the one that was triggered by the October Revolution and the civil war. This was probably the most massive and, in its social and cultural import, the most significant political refugee movement in the 20th century. Scholarship, which developed at a new level after the dissolution of the Soviet Union, generally estimates that 1.5 to 2 million people left Soviet Russia as a reaction to revolution, civil war, and the establishment of Soviet power and settled abroad temporarily, in the hope that after the collapse or overthrow of the revolutionary regime, they would be able to return to Russia.

To be sure, even during the period of the bourgeois provisional government there were exoduses to calmer areas (Crimea, Finland), where the émigrés intended to wait out the upheavals in the capital cities. However, a real movement of flight and exodus occurred only after the definitive victory of Soviet power, when the Bolsheviks controlled the cities and the armies of the Whites and the intervention forces of the Entente had been defeated. That was the case in most regions of the old Empire in the spring of 1920, at the latest. The visible events – which have become symbolic – were the precipitous evacuation of soldiers and civilians in the ports of Odessa, on the Crimea, and in Novorossiysk, and the movements of flight across the new Russian-Finnish border. At this time, however, the exodus tended to be seen more as an evasive maneuver or an escape in a still undecided struggle that had to be carried on – now from the headquarters of the

White Movement and from exile organizations and institutions in the centers of the diaspora.

Those who left were above all members of the propertied and governing class, who were directly and physically threatened, members of the old apparatus of power, the officer corps, and the volunteer armies and their hangers-on, as well as members of all non-Bolshevik parties – from the monarchist right to the socialist left made up of social revolutionaries, Mensheviks, and anarchists – and finally, representatives of the aristocracy, the bourgeois middle class, and the intelligentsia. The Russian emigration after 1917 had the traits of a flight of the elites, which took large segments of the cultural, intellectual, and political elite of prerevolutionary Russia abroad – in this compactness probably comparable only to the exile of the French aristocracy after 1789. Or in other words, in a massive bloodletting, Russia lost a large part of its educated and propertied elite with experience in ruling and competence at organizing, the sociocultural product of a process of accumulation and selection over generations. The flip side of this mass exodus was the vacating of posts into which thousands moved in a grand process of social upward mobility.

In its first stage, the emigration was a movement of removal and wait-and-see, and it therefore established itself in proximity to the borders and under the protection of the allies of France and Russia, who advocated a return into a "unified and indivisible Russian Empire." It is no coincidence that the temporary centers of Russian emigration were identical with stations on the path of evacuation and flight. The White Armies, which had been pushed back to the shores of the Black Sea, found their first bases in exile in Constantinople and in the evacuated barracks of the camps in the surrounding area (Gallipoli). They moved on into states of the Balkans that had always been allied to Russia and especially the Russian military – into Bulgaria (from Wrangel) and the Kingdom of Serbia, Croatia, and Slovenia. Both states had been exhausted by the war and had an urgent need for scientifically and technically qualified personnel, but above all engineers. Another part of the evacuated armies and civilians followed the Entente powers to Paris, Marseille, or other centers of the Mediterranean – port cities or marine bases such as Beirut, Alexandria, and Bizerta. But we also know of larger groups of Russian refugees in Cairo and Damascus.

A second route of flight was in northwestern Europe. Parts of the White Armies had remained in Finland, which had become independent, and had become engaged there on the side of the new government against the "Reds." Relatively large groups of emigrants were thus found again in the capital cities of the newly independent states: in Helsinki, Tallinn, Kaunas, Riga, Warsaw. Flight carried some further, to Scandinavia, to Stockholm, and Copenhagen, where traditionally good relationships to the elites of prerevolutionary Russia existed. A third route led to central Europe – into newly formed Czechoslovakia and to Germany. In President Tomas G. Masaryk and Prime Minister Karel Kramar,

Russian refugees in camp Wünsdorf near Berlin waiting for their food, 1924 (*ullstein bild*).

Czechoslovakia was led by two men who were intimately familiar with Russia; moreover, as a new nation-state it had an enormous need for highly qualified personnel. In the "Russian Action," emigrants from Russia were deliberately brought into the country, and Prague, with its numerous scientific establishments and scholarly institutions, became the "Russian Oxford."

However, the unquestioned center where the Russian diaspora initially gathered was Berlin – the capital of the former war enemy, who in the "sealed train" had brought the revolutionaries from Swiss exile to Russia and thus to power, but also one with centuries of cultural and political proximity, where Russian writers, artists, aristocrats, and members of the entrepreneurial class came and went. Around half a million refugees were found in the German Reich in the early years of the Weimar Republic (1921–4), mostly in "Russian Berlin," before, prompted by inflation and stabilization, they continued their migration to the second capital of the Russian diaspora in Europe: Paris. During the next 20 years, until the Wehrmacht occupied the city in 1940, this capital of Russia's erstwhile ally had everything a capital of the exile needed: money, intellectual brilliance, spiritual inspiration, literary glamour, an intact infrastructure, and organizational stability. After the occupation of Paris by the Germans, the center of the Russian diaspora migrated onward to the New World, to New York and San Francisco.

Another robust branch of the Russian emigration extended into the Far East, into the international concession areas of Shanghai, but above all to Harbin, the Russian metropolis on the East China railroad. Until the conquest of Manchuria by the Japanese at the beginning of the 1930s, and then by the communists after the end of the Second World War, Harbin and Shanghai were a unique exclave and a reservation of prerevolutionary Russia with everything that was part of it: schools, papers, businesses, banks, clubs. In Harbin and in Shanghai, the Russian diaspora survived until the end of

the Second World War in 1945 or the victory of Mao's communists in 1948. Some of its remnants reappeared in North America and in Australasia, or – deported there by Stalin's secret police – in Central Asia.

With this the history of the diaspora from Russian lands would have come to an end if the Second World War had not set in motion a new, robust wave. These were Soviet citizens who were deported from the German-occupied territories for forced labor into the "Greater German Reich." They were guilty of collaborating with the Nazis and had to fear retribution and punishment after the liberation. Or they were Soviet citizens – civilians or members of the military – who, after their experiences with the Stalinist dictatorship, with forced collectivization, arbitrary terror in the prewar years, and all other manifestations of communist coercion, felt no inclination to return to their homeland. Instead, they preferred to wait, as displaced persons (DPs) in former prisoner of war camps and barracks in occupied Germany (e.g., in Münsingen or Regensburg), for better times, but especially for a chance to continue on to the USA or Canada, where they reinforced the already existing Russian diaspora or became simply Americans. The second wave of emigration from Russia coincides with the incubation of the cold war, with the instrumentalization of the emigration in the emerging division of the world and Europe.

Between the first and the second wave of the emigration from Russia there was no continuity in terms of personnel or the world of ideas; often there was even animosity and enmity. The followers of the Ancien Régime had little or nothing in common with ex-Soviet citizens, who often owed their advancement to the revolutionary regime. Much the same is true of the third wave, that of dissidents and members of the civil rights movement, who wanted nothing to do with the antisoviet and anti-communist refugees from the early years of the cold war. The destination countries of the third wave were the same as for the second: chiefly the USA (A. Solzhenitsyn, P. Grigorenko), but also Paris (L. Pljushch, N. Gorbanevsaia, V. Maksimov, and others), and London (V. Bukovskii). With the radio stations (Voice of America, BBC, Radio Free Europe, Radio Liberty), entirely new media had come into play for the emigrants in the way they presented themselves: the airwaves as a forum and a public. For the third wave one can say that it found a connection much more frequently with the "old," "prerevolutionary" emigration and intelligentsia.

Summarizing, one can say that the three waves of emigration from Russian lands formed a peculiar continuity, which reflected the continuity of the Soviet regime. It was entirely logical that the end of the Soviet Union also brought to an end the exodus that had been triggered and provoked by Soviet power. With few exceptions (e.g., A. Zinoviev, V. Maksimov), however, this end did not lead to a return to the homeland. The Russian emigration remained abroad, though without being absorbed into its new home, or more precisely, without ever wanting to be absorbed into the new home.

Emigration from Russian lands – no integration, but a declaration of the permanency of exile

Characteristic of the literature about the Russian emigration is the emphasis on its cultural mission and cultural achievements. The Russian diaspora was rich in intellectual giants – artists, writers, and scientists who acquired world fame later. They include the names of the Nobel laureate in literature, Ivan Bunin; the writer and novelist Vladimir Nabokov; the philosophers Nikolay Berdiaev, Fedor Stepun, Lev Shestov, Semen Frank; the builders and engineers Igor Sikorskii, Dimitrii Riabushinskii; the economist Wassilii Leontiev; the painters Marc Chagall and Wassilii Kandinskii; the composers Igor Stravinski and Sergei Prokofiev; the choreographers and ballet dancers Sergei Diaghilev, Leonid Massine, and Tamara Karsavina; and actors like Mikhail Chekhov. Needless to say, all the prominent political figures of prerevolutionary Russia were found in exile: Pavel Miliukov and Alexandr Kerenskii, as well as the entire leadership of the Mensheviks.

The emphasis on prominent cultural figures or the prominence of culture points to a sociologically significant fact: emigration from Russia, as Vladimir Nabokov put it, displayed a "specifically high cultural coefficient." It was not characterized as an "exile government" or the "military or political arm" of this "Russia beyond the borders"; instead, it was marked by a self-understanding of the diaspora as the place where the true, the spiritual, the authentic Russia survived, and by the notion that the meaning of exile lay in preserving, indeed, saving, Russian culture. In this self-affirmation as the place of a cultural mission lay its distinction from Russia, which had supposedly fallen, temporarily, into the wrong hands, but also from the host countries, in which the diaspora always found itself only as a temporary guest, never as having arrived and ready to acculturate and integrate – as though integration were tantamount to a renunciation, indeed a betrayal of the "cultural mission" of exile.

It therefore comes as no surprise that the Russian exile communities existed everywhere as more or less self-contained microcosms with an exceedingly rich interior life. The meaning was to preserve "Russianness," not to overcome it. They formed structures that imparted continuity and coherence to life in strange lands, structures which – at least in those places where immigrants from Russia had settled permanently (as in Paris) – remained intact and viable also beyond the first generation, and to which the arrivals of the second and third waves could also connect.

Which were the most important elements and structures of the inner life of emigration? In many respects the Russian Orthodox Church abroad overarched the fragmentation of the emigrant communities; in many places the Church functioned as *the* meeting place and point of contact, even for emigrants with no confessional affiliation or religious bonds. The goings-on around the embassy church Unter den Linden and at the Hohenzollerdamm in Berlin, or at the Alexander Nevskii Cathedral in the Rue Darue in Paris is a fixed topos in all remembrances by emigrants. Even after the split of the Orthodox Church abroad in 1924 by Bishop Archimandrite Evlogii in Paris, the churches, in spite of their pro-czarist and reactionary orientation, remained the nonpartisan and charity-focused institutions par excellence. This also survived the political ruptures of the 20th century.

In proximity to the church institutions were probably the charitable ones, mostly in connection with foreign aid organizations (e.g., the YMCA, Papal Aid Organization, Nansen Committee of the League of Nations, Russian Action in Czechoslovakia). Elements of the defeated state apparatus reassembled in emigration, often as a state in reserve, as a government in waiting. Numerous members of the ministries, often with good connections to the political elites of the host countries, populated the restaurants of the diaspora. Guidebooks to Russian Berlin or Russian Paris mirrored this "state in waiting" with all its subdivisions: organizations of members of the foreign office, the general staff, the guard regiments, the national associations of bankers, merchants, and industrialists. Until the Second World War, at least, the leadership of the armies of the White Movement maintained its apparatus, its command structure, its open and secret divisions, in spite of the growing infiltration by Soviet secret agents (first in Belgrade, then in Paris and Brussels).

In the early phase of exile, the personnel of the central representation and aid organizations were recruited from members of the old state apparatus (especially former Russian ambassadors in the host countries): in Germany, for example, the "Russian Delegation" or the "Russian Commission," which functioned as a link between the emigrant community and the German officials, especially the foreign office. Of course, the position of these aid organizations was considerably weakened after diplomatic ties had been established between the Weimar Republic and the USSR. However, more important than these institutions were probably the representatives of the political parties, who now worked frequently as writers or publishers of the émigré press.

In fact, the press was probably the most important medium, which permitted self-communication, orientation, and engagement with the homeland and the new environment. To this day, the developed press system in the metropolises of the diaspora is among the most remarkable accomplishments of the Russian emigration – with respect to both the extent, diffusion, and quality of the published work. Papers like *Rul* (Berlin), *Segodnja* (Riga), *Časy* (Brussels), *Sovremennye Zapiski* and *Russkaja mysl* (Paris) were headed by the leading pressmen from old Russia and had a first-rate staff of co-workers, among them world-class writers. What must be emphasized about the press of the diaspora is that it acted across borders and had an exceptional network of correspondents – one of the few early examples for the emergence of a transnational public in 20th-century Europe.

The effectiveness of the press was reinforced by a vibrant publishing system, which at times published more titles than its counterpart in the crisis-ridden USSR. A flourishing, if not feverish, publishing scene existed above all in Berlin in the first half of the 1920s, when well over 100 Russian publishers made Berlin the capital of the Russian book. Newspapers and publishing houses created the space in which the emigrants could develop their own life. It included cafés, restaurants, theaters, cabarets, nightclubs, and specialty shops of the Russian luxury and delicatessen industry. After all, the issue for the mass of emigrants was to find or develop ways of making a living, a process that was very different in the various host countries: France, for example, had a strong need for labor (the "Cossacks" at Renault-Billancourt, the Russian taxi drivers of Paris); Yugoslavia and Czechoslovakia as new states were looking for highly qualified scientists and technical personnel, which meant that experts from the Russian Empire could find jobs fairly easily, including leading professorships at colleges and universities.

However, the misery of the refugees is a continuously recurring theme of the émigré press and émigré literature. For simple soldiers, the footmen of the White Armies, a lack of prospects was one reason behind an early return home and the decision to accept the amnesty offer of the Soviet government; for the members of the old propertied class, exile, with its loss of status and precipitous social decline, became an existential crisis. Robert C. Williams has called the exile communities of the late 1920s "communities of despair." Resignation and despair intensified when a temporary situation became permanent: one had to make decisions now – return or stay? One had to make arrangements to educate the children and young people; if one decided to stay, viable scientific and social institutions had to be created. Here, too, the emigration from Russian lands brought forth significant institutions. Examples are the Russian Scientific Institute in Berlin, the Russian Foreign Archive as the central depot of documentation in Prague, the academic organizations of Russian scholars in Belgrade, Berlin, Prague, Paris, and later in North America.

Finally, the emigration, as one from Russian lands, brought forth numerous confessional, ethnic, and nationally defined or colored groups which attest to the richness but also the disparateness of the diaspora. A particularly pronounced, special sense of self within the diaspora was displayed by the Russian Jews, who played a leading role in the press and publishing system and had their own organizations and own journals – e.g., the Association of Russian Jews, Evreyskiy mir, and Evreyskaya tribuna. But the Ukrainian, Armenian, Georgian, or Tartar branches of the Russian emigration each brought forth its own academies, organizations, and press products; of course, the multinational Russian emigration was kept together only very superficially by an anti-Bolshevik negative consensus.

The aim of the Russian emigration – at first with a certain realistic expectation, but from the middle of the 1920s with virtually no justification – was a return during the lifetime of the émigrés. The contacts with the emigrants to the environment of the host country were thus usually formal, instrumental, temporary. Still, the diaspora communities were often involved in the conflict-ridden domestic political life of their host countries; it was not rare for the domestic political front lines to run parallel to the position that the state in question assumed toward the Soviet Union. As a result, the emigrants from Russia were often drawn into the internal clashes between communists and right-wing radicals, between the power of the state and the opposition in their host countries. As a general tendency, the emigration from Russian lands kept its distance, led its own life as best it could, and awaited the day when something would happen back at home. We can speak of a definitive and probably also successful integration wherever representatives of Russian literature, language, art, and scholarship became part of an international, cosmopolitan culture. This is true, for example, of Chagall, Kandinskii, Nabokov, Stravinski, or Diaghilev. Here, integration seems almost like the continuation of a line that had already begun before the First World War and which one can associate with the globalization of culture.

The fates of the Russian emigration depended on the central developments of the political situation in Europe, especially on the relationships of the respective states with Russia. In the first half of the 20th century this meant that it got caught in the deadly conflict between communism and National Socialism, between the "hammer and the anvil," when in the period of the Second World War a marginal and nonrepresentative part had made common cause with the Germans (as *Hilfswillige*, members of the Russian Volunteer Army). In the second half of the 20th century the emigration became a dependent variable in the conflicts of the cold war and was fighting an all but hopeless battle if it tried to formulate an independent position that sought to avoid political instrumentalization.

Only for the third wave of emigration, with the end of the east-west clash and of communism, could it work toward the fulfillment of its mission, which meant also the end of the exile. The dissident emigrants lived to see the end of communism and the possibility of returning home. Before its eyes there occurred the transformation of the 1980s and 1990s, which turned the politically motivated emigration into the normality of border-crossing migrating movements that now also included Russia. However, new authoritarian tendencies indicate that this need not be the last word. The revival of an emigration from Russian lands would be one of the surest signs that the process of Russia's opening and normalization has failed once again. The ethnic communities from Russian lands in the metropolises of Europe and North America, which today are still counting hundreds of thousands, the presence of numerous Russian radio and television stations as well as newspapers, are evidence not of the existence of an emigration from Russia, but of its end and transformation into the normality of transnational migration.

While the great exodus meant for Russia an enormous loss of talent, skill, intelligence, and know-how, the reception countries on balance benefited from the arrival of the emigrants, costs and conflicts notwithstanding. The flight of artists, writers, designers, and musicians from Russian lands imparted decisive impulses to the cultural life of many host countries – beginning with the founding of opera houses and ballet companies (Constantinople), proceeding to the import of dancers, choreographers, and world-class stage designers (Paris, Milan, Monte Carlo), impulses from designers and fashion designers, and to the establishment of scientific institutions and scholarly societies (Berlin, Prague, Belgrade). The USA benefited in concentrated form – much as it did from the intellectual and cultural emigration from Germany and German-occupied central Europe in the 1930s and early 1940s – from the emigration from Russian lands (Kussevitzkii with the Boston Symphony Orchestra, the Russian Research Center at Harvard, Nabokov's "American years"). Many of the artists, writers, and scholars established schools in the New World and enriched it with the rich cultural heritage of Russia and the Old Continent. That was true, incidentally, of all three waves of emigration, in which political exile and "brain drain" seem to have gone hand in hand.

Korliakov, Andrei. *L'émigration russe en photos, France, 1917–1947*. Paris, 1999.

Literaturnaja enciklopedija Russkogo Zarubež'ja 1918–1940. Pisateli russkogo zarubež'ja. Moscow, 1997.

Raeff, Marc. *Russia Abroad: A Cultural History of the Russian Emigration 1919–1939*. New York and Oxford, 1990.

Russkoe Zarubeže. Zolotaja Kniga emigracii. Pervaja tret' XX veka. Enciklopedičeskij biografičeskijslovar'. Moscow, 1997.

Schlögel, Karl, ed. *Der große Exodus. Die russische Emigration und ihre Zentren 1917 bis 1941*. Munich, 1994.

Schlögel, Karl. *Berlin Ostbahnhof Europas. Russen und Deutsche in ihrem Jahrhundert*. Berlin, 1998.

Severjuchin, D. Ja, and O. L. Lejkind. *Chudožniki russkoj émigracii (1917–1941). Biografičeskij slovar'*. St. Petersburg, 1995.

Williams, Robert C. *Culture in Exile: Russian Emigrés in Germany, 1881–1941*. Ithaca and London, 1972.

Cross-references: Czechia and Slovakia; The Baltic Region; France; Germany; Great Britain; Northern Europe; Poland; Russia and Belarus; Southeastern Europe; *Aussiedler/Spätaussiedler* in Germany since 1950; Deportees in the Soviet Union during and after World War II; Displaced Persons (DPs) in Europe since the End of World War II; Eastern European Jews in Germany since 1990; Eastern European Jews in Berlin from the Late 19th Century to the 1930s; Eastern European Jews in London since the Late 19th Century; Eastern European Jews in Paris since the Late 19th Century; Forced Laborers in Germany and German-Occupied Europe during World War II; French Revolutionary Refugees in Europe after 1789: The Example of Germany; Greek Settlers from the Black Sea Region in New Russia since the Early Modern Period and Pontic Greeks in Greece since the End of World War II; Jewish Refugees from Nazi Germany and from German-Occupied Europe since 1933; Political and Intellectual Refugees from Nazi Germany and from German-Occupied Europe, 1933–1945; Russian Students at German Colleges and Universities in the Late 19th and Early 20th Centuries

RUSSIAN FEMALE STUDENTS IN SWITZERLAND IN THE LATE 19TH AND EARLY 20TH CENTURIES

Béatrice Ziegler and Silvia Bolliger

Beginning in the last third of the 19th century, foreign female students poured into Switzerland. From the middle of the 1860s, Switzerland – along with France – offered women for the first time ever the possibility of matriculating as regular students at a university. It was above all women from the Russian Empire who benefited from this, but also women from Germany, France, Bulgaria, Austria, England, and the USA, all of whom came to Switzerland to be educated and trained, while relatively few Swiss women entered university.

The label "foreign women students" encompasses a highly heterogeneous group, subdivided by geographic, ethnic, cultural, and social background, and by confession and age (see Figure 1). One can hardly speak of a group identity. The commonality lay in their temporary presence in Switzerland with the goal of pursuing studies or obtaining degrees that were reserved for men in other countries. Although the possibility of a higher education for women did exist in a few countries, earning a university degree or doctorate was not possible, or the diplomas were not considered equal to those obtained by men. In Russia, for instance, there were Higher Women's Courses, though they were at times closed for political reasons, and Jewish women, for example, had only limited access to them. Likewise, special women's colleges and women's universities existed in the Anglo-Saxon realm.

Between 1882 and 1913, the number of all students in Switzerland rose sixfold, from 1,245 to 7,088; the number of women students in the same period increased 20-fold, from 63 to 1,241. The quotient of Russian nationals among the foreign women was always highest and averaged 75%. After rising for years, the number of foreign women at Swiss universities declined around 1910. The backdrop to this was that universities in their countries of origin began to accept women as equal to men, or to offer them satisfactory alternatives to study abroad. Russia, for example, set up additional Higher Women's Courses beginning in 1905 – at the same time improving their quality. Moreover, beginning in 1911, women could take exams at the universities. Then, with the outbreak of World War I, the opportunities of migrating across borders for the purpose of education dropped precipitously.

The crucial factor in the choice of a field of study was the job prospects in the country of origin. The majority of women students from czarist Russia, referred to as Russians regardless of their varying nationalities, chose medicine, which comes as no surprise given the inadequate medical care of the population in their homeland. In second place were the sciences, and in third place the philosophical subjects. Many of the other foreign women also came to Switzerland primarily for medical training; in general, the medical profession was probably easiest to reconcile with the prevailing image

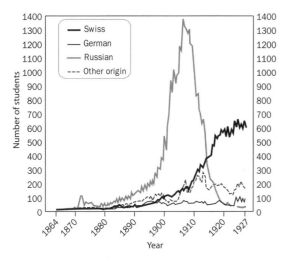

Figure 1. Female students in Switzerland by nationality, 1864–1927. *Source: De l'Académie à l'Université de Lausanne 1537–1987. 450 ans d'histoire* (Lausanne, 1987), 319.

Women dominating the anatomy classroom at the University of Bern. In 1907, more Russian women than Swiss men studied medicine in Bern (*Anatomisches Institut, Bern, Switzerland*).

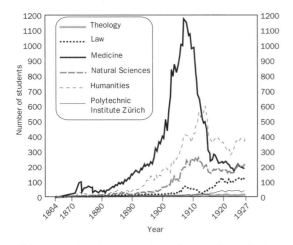

Figure 2. Female students in Switzerland by subjects, 1864–1927. *Source: De l'Académie à l'Université de Lausanne 1537–1987*, 319.

of women as caregivers. Among the other foreign women, philosophical fields were more popular than the natural sciences (see Figure 2).

With the exception of the University of Basel, which had existed since the late Middle Ages, the Swiss universities were founded between 1833 and 1910 or converted into universities from precursor institutions. The density of universities was tremendously high: there were seven universities for a population of 3.3 million (including the Polytechnical Institute in Zurich, there were eight). As a result, there was plenty of capacity to accept foreign students in large numbers. Because of this, the requirements for matriculation were initially relatively low: foreign students were urgently needed to secure the continued existence of the universities. As a result, Switzerland, compared to other European countries, had by far the most students relative to its population and also the most foreign and female students. Observers like to attribute this situation to Switzerland's humanitarian

and liberal asylum tradition, but for the reasons described above, that was not a major factor.

Between 1881 and 1913, the percentage of foreigners among students in Switzerland averaged 45%. Students from czarist Russia, alone, accounted for a third (maximum): in 1906, 2,322 of the 6,444 students were Russian nationals, 1507 women and 815 men. The highest quotient of Russians among all female students was reached in 1902–3 and 1906–7 with 79%.

In 1867, the Russian Nadeshda Suslova graduated from the University of Zurich; she was the first foreign woman – and first woman, period – to receive the degree of medical doctor at a Swiss university. Her graduation created a precedent, following which it would become possible for women to matriculate as regular students (initially only in Zurich). The number of matriculated female students rose in Zurich to 114 by 1873 (26% of the student body); of those, 109 came from the Russian Empire. From 1872 on, the universities in Bern and Geneva were also open to women, followed by Lausanne and Basel in 1890, Fribourg in 1905, and, last, the University of Neuchâtel that was newly founded in 1910. However, tradition-steeped Basel and Catholic Fribourg consciously limited access for foreign students by making the cantonal high school diploma (*Maturität*) a precondition for matriculation. Neuchâtel, meanwhile, was not all that attractive because it did not have a medical school. These background conditions explain why most foreign women chose the universities in Zurich, Bern, Geneva, or later also Lausanne.

The female students came from all regions of the Czarist Empire, from Siberia as well as Armenia and Crimea. However, the majority hailed from the western periphery (Ukraine, Poland, Latvia, Lithuania, Georgia) and belonged to ethnic and confessional minorities (Jews, Catholics, and German Balts) that experienced difficulties in entering the institutions of higher learning in Russia because of a *numerus clausus* (closed number) for non-Orthodox students. Because Jews, who made up around 5% of the Russian population, were subject to further restrictions in terms of their geographic mobility and economic activity, their socioeconomic situation deteriorated noticeably. Only a few groups within the Jewish population, including persons with university degrees, could be exempted from the regulations on settlement in certain settlement zones and enjoyed chiefly professional privileges, though the latter were not heritable. A doctoral degree thus assumed an existential significance for Jewish men and especially Jewish women and constituted an important motive behind their migration. It therefore occasions little surprise that approximately 75% of all female students from the Czarist Empire in Switzerland are said to have been Jewish.

Female students from Russia, in particular, but also American women, put up with onerous journeys lasting days or even weeks to get to Switzerland in the first place. Most were accompanied by women friends or family members who were also eager to study. Their first destination was generally a university where they already had contacts with students or could at least count on support from resident countrymen. Guest semesters at other universities were popular, whenever possible also in other countries at universities with higher prestige than those in Switzerland. Mobility was impressively high.

At least in Zurich and Bern, students from the Czarist Empire, also called "Slavs" or "Orientals" by contemporaries, lived spatially separated from the city population in separate quarters. In part they sought this segregation themselves, but in part it was also due to landlords who were in principle not interested in renting rooms to female students and/or foreigners. So-called Russian colonies grew up, and they were well organized. For example, Poles and Russian Jews set up support funds for the needy and maintained their own eating halls and libraries, where events were also staged. These places were a piece of home and offered a certain replacement for the family. The living circumstances were often precarious, with the money sometimes not sufficient. Especially Jewish female and male students from the Czarist Empire did not by any means come from the wealthier classes. Among fellow female students, the women from the Czarist Empire aroused special pity because of their poverty, but also elicited admiration on account of their persistence and willingness to make sacrifices.

Close contacts between Russian women and fellow female students were the exception. To be sure, at the University of Bern, at least, popularly referred to as "Slavic Girls' School," a female students' association that advocated the interests of women students appeared around the turn of the century. However, given its small membership, it is not likely to have acquired any major significance for intercultural understanding. Yet sometimes friendships with Swiss students led to marriages, a crucial step toward integration. Leaving aside such exceptions and cases in which Russian women were able to have a university career, the female students from the Czarist Empire along with the majority of the other foreign women left Switzerland after completing their studies and for the most part returned to their homeland, where they practiced medicine or realized their occupational goals in other professions, often as pioneers.

The first generation of overwhelmingly Russian women students in Zurich attracted considerable attention, at the university itself as well as in the city. For decades to come, their outward appearance and emancipated behavior shaped the negatively charged stereotype of the Russian woman and of the female student in Switzerland: Russian women, also called "Little Cossack horses," were caricatured as unkempt, immoral, cigarette-smoking women with short hair and blue glasses, who sacrificed themselves for revolutionary ideals and used their studies as a cover for political agitation. This reflected above all Swiss fears of emancipated and politically active women. Even if students from Russian lands, among them many women, did in fact engage in political activities especially in the early period, those remained limited to matters concerning czarist Russia; there was no interference in Swiss politics. Their chief goal was and remained a university education. Conflict with the Swiss authorities was very rare.

Time and again, however, we hear of the negative attitude of Swiss students toward female students, which could express itself in rude jokes and harassment or lead to protest rallies against the admission of women. To what extent such reactions were directed specifically against foreign women or against Russian women as the largest group among female students remains unclear. And there were also opposing voices who highlighted the willingness of fellow students to help. Likewise, there were professors who ignored female students as much as possible, and others who helped them along. In general, the university administration and especially the professors, who derived a direct financial benefit from every additional student and were themselves often of foreign background, took a benevolent attitude toward foreign female students.

All in all, it can be said that the foreign students did not generally pursue integration into Swiss society, which was in any case denied them. Free access to university study for foreigners, and especially women, was not tantamount with access to the (academic) job market. As long as foreign female students – the same was true for foreign male students – behaved discreetly during their studies and left Switzerland once they were completed, it seemed economically sensible to the university towns to tolerate their temporary presence. Foreign women students, in particular, accepted this arrangement without complaints, given the lack of alternatives.

Das Frauenstudium an den Schweizer Hochschulen. Published by the Schweizerischer Verband der Akademikerinnen. Zurich, 1928.

Neumann, Daniela. *Studentinnen aus dem Russischen Reich in der Schweiz (1867–1914).* Zurich, 1987.

Tikhonov, Natalia. "Les étudiantes russes dans les universités suisses à la fin du XIXᵉ siècle et au début du XXᵉ siècle: Les raisons d'un choix." In *Les femmes dans la société européenne – Die Frauen in der europäischen Gesellschaft*, edited by Anne-Lise Head-König and Liliane Mottu-Weber, 91–103. Geneva, 2000.

Tikhonov, Natalia. "Zwischen Öffnung und Rückzug. Die Universitäten der Schweiz und Deutschlands angesichts des Studentinnenstroms aus dem Russischen Reich." In *Universitäten als Brücken in Europa. Studien zur Geschichte der studentischen Migration – Les universités: Des ponts à travers l'Europe. Etudes sur l'histoire des migrations étudiantes*, edited by Hartmut Rüdiger Peter and Natalia Tikhonov, 157–74. Frankfurt am Main, 2003.

Cross-references: The Baltic Region; Poland; Russia and Belarus; Switzerland; Ukraine; Russian Revolutionaries in Western and Central Europe in the 19th and Early 20th Centuries; Russian Students at German Colleges and Universities in the Late 19th and Early 20th Centuries

RUSSIAN ITINERANT MERCHANTS IN THE 19TH CENTURY

Klaus Gestwa

Fixed and permanent retail trade in urban stores was not established in Russia as the dominant form of trade until well into the 19th century. The reasons for the persistent dominance of (partly seasonal) itinerant trade are to be found in the climatic and geographic parameters of the Czarist Empire. They made it extremely difficult to build up a functional infrastructure that would have ensured a rapid flow of merchandise to provide the scattered and widely separated settlements with goods on a continuous basis. Merchants resident in Russian cities were rarely able to supply a larger surrounding area with goods. The weakness of the urban economy provided most itinerant merchants of peasant stock with an opportunity to occupy important market positions and, in the process of exchanging goods, act as a conduit of information between commercial centers and peripheral economic areas. The itinerant trade was little constrained by state restrictions.

Some form of itinerant trade had always existed in Russia. As the Russian domestic market slowly grew in size and density, the number of peasants who took goods on the road increased markedly from the second half of the 18th century. Away from the large markets and important trade routes, the itinerant trade filled the growing supply vacuum. Depending on the region and their activities, the itinerant traders were called *ofeni* or *korobejniki*, as well as *prasoli*, *samovozy*, *chodebščiki*, *šabonniki*, *krasnotovarniki*, *raznoščiki*, and *sloboždani*. The heyday of the itinerant trade was in the first half of the 19th century. Its centers lay in the government of Vladimir; especially the districts of Šuja, Kovrov, and Vjazniki were widely known for their itinerant traders. In the district of Kovrov alone, 5,000 *ofeni* were counted in the

1840s, and 4,000 in the district Šuja. A large number of peasant itinerant merchants were also found in the governments of Chernihiv, Nizhny Novgorod, Yaroslavl, and Kostroma.

The unwieldy nature of the circulation of goods in Russia was overcome only with the emergence of a railroad and telegraph network and with the growing use of steamships. The resulting, massive expansion of the area in which urban trading houses could be active put considerable pressure on the itinerant trade at the beginning of the 20th century. Small itinerant traders were for the most part able to hold their own only in remote regions hardly penetrated by commerce, where they adjusted to the changed customer needs. Even after the October Revolution of 1917 they continued to traverse the land with their carts and large backpacks, until the Stalinist regime once and for all deprived them of a livelihood after 1928 with a prohibition against free trade.

The preferred wares of the itinerant merchants included, among textiles and other smaller mass market items, books and above all the *lubki*, printed, colorful pictorial broadsheets. These sheets initially contained biblical motifs and tales of heroic historical figures, and later also works of Russian literature; the works were made accessible to the peasant public in easy-to-understand illustrations and short texts.

The itinerant merchants obtained their goods either directly from producers in cities and commercial villages or at important fairs, especially at Russia's largest annual fair in Nizhny Novgorod, where in 1846 they purchased more than half of all the cotton goods on offer. Contemporary observers reported that the countless itinerant merchants were one of the most striking features of Russian trade fairs.

On their extensive commercial travels, which sometimes lasted three to five years, the itinerant merchants supplied especially small weekly bazaars in the western governments, in Ukraine, as well as in Siberia, which had many settlements with no regular contact with a market. With extraordinary skill, the itinerant traders ferreted out pockets of demand in the most remote regions and found customers for their goods even in times of crisis. They integrated the destinations of their travels into the supraregional exchange of goods and acquainted the rural folk in peripheral economic areas with developments outside of their own world. The itinerant traders thus remained for a long time indispensable to the expansion of the Russian domestic market. That is also why factory owners and wholesalers time and again advanced them larger quantities of goods, even if the traders had no capital of their own and could offer hardly any assurances or collateral. They took this risk in the hope that by prefinancing a distributor of goods they would soon acquire a permanent customer and profit from his commercial success.

The itinerant trade developed not only into an important artery for the circulation of goods but also into an indispensable part of rural cultural and social life. As a storyteller and reporter, the itinerant trader satisfied his customers' curiosity along with their consumer demands. His arrival was therefore always an event and often a cause for celebration. The peasants generously offered him lodging and food, bought his goods, and demanded in return news and answers to their questions. It was from this embeddedness within the fabric of rural life that the itinerant trade derived a large part of its strength.

The itinerant traders, most of whom saw themselves as part of traditional peasant society, developed a vibrant subculture. It was characterized, for example, by communication in a secret language, which the peddlers had devised specifically to conceal their calculations and plans from outsiders. In this way they sought to maximize their chances at turning a profit and to preserve their social exclusivity.

Part of the explanation for the long and successful history of the *ofeni*, *korobejniki*, and other groups of itinerant traders is that many of them were Old Believers. The reforms that were implemented after the middle of the 17th century had led to a schism in the Russian Orthodox Church, and the area between the upper reaches of the Oka and the Volga became a reservoir of religious dissidents. Old Believers sought refuge in the large trading and commercial villages in the governments of Vladimir, Kostroma, Yaroslavl, and Nizhny Novgorod, where they developed an active community life and engaged in successful missionary activity. Old Belief and economic success were closely connected, since membership in the dissident religious community brought with it important advantages in the marketplace. For example, Old Believers were characterized by intellectual flexibility and a higher level of education: because they refused to recognize the official doctrine of the Orthodox Church, they were compelled to articulate their own beliefs and therefore acquired early on the ability to read and write.

As a religious diaspora group, the Old Believers developed a strong sense of community. They joined forces on their trading ventures; they shared profits and losses and hoped in this way to reduce the high business risks they assumed on their travels. And unlike his Orthodox competitor, the Old Believer merchant did not have to fear going bankrupt if he ran into misfortune, miscalculated, or suffered a slump in sales, since he could hope to receive interest-free or favorable loans through the community. The dissident religious community was simultaneously one of economic solidarity. The tight cohesiveness of the Old Believers created a functioning network of communication between individual communities and important trading centers. The numerous Old Believers who were tavern keepers, postmasters, and traders formed an army of reliable and cheap agents who exchanged information about the market situation and sales trends.

The itinerant trade was hierarchically organized. For example, the *ofeni* of the government of Vladimir were divided into three groups: "lords" (*chozjainy*), "administrators" (*prikazčiki*), and "helpers" (*rebjata, rabočie, molodcy*). The lords were wealthy peasants or urban merchants who for the most part did not travel about as itinerant traders, but as the "commercial head" provided goods and capital and procured loans. The actual peddling was organized by the administrators, who with several carts and helpers traversed the land in a small trading caravan. Upon arriving at their destination area, the various helpers set out on their own as previously arranged in order to systematically scour the region and look up as many settlements as possible without competing against one another. The administrators rarely saw their lords. At the end of the trade circuit, the men would meet at fairs or important weekly bazaars to settle the accounts. The profit was often so ample that many itinerant traders were able to move up socially after a few successful years. Some lords purchased their way into the highest guilds of the urban merchant class in the central Russian commercial region and occasionally even in Moscow. Numerous administrators acquired trading patents in Siberian or Ukrainian cities, which means that new social elements were continuously flowing into the city from this group.

In spite of the itinerant merchants' important function as intermediaries, and in spite of their cooperation with entrepreneurs and trading houses, urban merchants were constantly complaining about the tenacious competition from these rural itinerant traders. The complaints culminated in the 1820s in the charge that the peasant trade was destroying the Russian merchant class. The fact is that many urban merchant families were not able to sustain their economic and social status permanently. And the old-established notables and ministerial officials in St. Petersburg saw in the simultaneous rise of peasant traders into the urban guilds proof that the merchant estate was being "debased." At the end of the 19th century, the majority of merchants and entrepreneurs in Moscow were in fact former peasants engaged in trade. In czarist Russia it was therefore not urban merchants who penetrated the countryside with their capital. Instead, the peasants, by organizing important areas of commercial life, were increasingly pushing into the urban social and economic spheres.

It was initially difficult for itinerant traders who had advanced through economic success to gain social prestige and recognition in the city. The native merchant families treated them with disdain. However, if they were able to continue their commercial careers over time, peasant families who had risen up the social ladder were integrated as accepted members into the social life of the urban middle and upper classes in the second or, at the latest, the third generation and largely left their village origins behind.

Fitzpatrick, Anne L. *The Great Russian Fair: Nizhnii Novgorod 1840–90*. Basingstoke and London, 1990.

Gestwa, Klaus. "Der Marktkontext russischer Proto-Industrialisierung." *Jahrbuch für Wirtschaftsgeschichte* 2 (1998): 97–128.

Gestwa, Klaus. *Proto-Industrialisierung in Rußland. Wirtschaft, Herrschaft und Kultur in Ivanovo und Pavlovo, 1741–1932*. Göttingen, 1999.

Hildermeier, Manfred. *Bürgertum und Stadt in Rußland 1760–1870. Rechtliche Lage und soziale Struktur*. Cologne and Vienna, 1986.

Hildermeier, Manfred. "Alter Glaube und Mobilität. Bemerkungen zur Verbreitung und sozialen Struktur des Raskol im frühindustriellen Rußland (1760–1860)." *Jahrbücher für Geschichte Osteuropas* 39 (1991): 321–38.

Mironov, Boris N. *Vnutrennij rynok Rossii vo vtoroj polovine XVIII – pervoj polovine XIX vv.* Leningrad, 1981.

Cross-references: Russia and Belarus; Ukraine

RUSSIAN LABOR MIGRANTS ON LARGE CONSTRUCTION SITES IN THE USSR SINCE THE 1920S

Klaus Gestwa

The foundations of Soviet power were by no means only in Moscow but were also where Soviet engineers and functionaries sought to conquer peripheral landscapes through large-scale construction projects. With the first Five-Year Plan (1928–32), the USSR became a technological, industrialized, and urbanized country. Impressive as well as costly giant projects, like the new steel metropolis of Magnitogorsk in the Urals, the Moscow Metro, the gigantic hydroelectric plant on the Dniepr near Zaporože (Dneproges), and the railroad from Turkmenistan to Siberia (Turksib), were inextricably tied to the rise and consolidation of the Stalinist system. The large-scale Stalinist construction sites, where migrant laborers encountered native workers and groups of diverse social and ethnic background interacted, were places of joyful community experiences and tragic clashes. Through these impressive building sites of Soviet modernity ran the front lines not only between bright future and gloomy past, civilization and barbarism, but also between reality and utopia. Even after Stalin's death in 1953, industrialization in the USSR was characterized by the existence of large-scale construction sites: the campaign for new land in Kazakhstan and Siberia, the building of the world's largest hydroelectric plant in Bratsk in eastern Siberia (1954–67), and the Baikal-Amur Mainline (1973–86).

After 1928, fascination with new and modern technology seized young people, who sought to leave behind at the large construction sites their parents' traditional life of poverty and backwardness. However, the youthful zeal in these propagandistically inflated "spheres of enthusiastic will" must not be exaggerated. For example, these construction sites for the most part resembled nomadic camps where the flotsam from the coercive "socialist restructuring" congregated. It included kulaks of refugees that appeared after the collectivization of their holdings, families driven from villages and small towns by oppressive hunger, Central Asian nomads whose way of work and life had been destroyed, and criminals seeking to escape the reach of the law. All were in desperate search of a new beginning.

The goal of the nationalities policy (*korenizacija*), in force since 1928, was to make the specialized cadres in the various Soviet Republics more aware of their ethnic origins; this policy stipulated that native peasants and nomads would be given preferential hiring on all large-scale projects in the non-Russian peripheries. For example, in Magnitogorsk, on the construction sites of the Turksib, and in the Caucasus, there were numerous Muslim workers who were attracted by this modernization and were hoping for material advantages. Still, running these construction sites depended on the influx of many European Russians, who made up the largest group of construction workers. At the large building sites a system of ethnic exclusions and hierarchies soon emerged, which made the natives into strangers in their own land and gave the immigrant European workers the putative justification for acting even far from home as though they were the real residents of the modernization zones that sprang up. There were often violent clashes between the ethnically closed workers' groups (*arteli*), which occasionally even erupted into pogroms.

In the 1930s, the state used its apparatus of repression to break up the *arteli* and thus forcefully calm relations between the immigrant and the native workers. Though this action was successful on the surface, the ethnic conflicts continued in everyday oppositional behavior. The notion of the peaceful multiethnic working class of the Soviet Union remained a political myth. The great migration movements triggered by the ambitious industrial plans and infrastructure projects did not by any means automatically bring about ethnic integration and internationalization of the Soviet population.

Moreover, in many places the urbanization of the workers was a lengthy process, as peasant society survived for a long time in the industrial centers. For example, long after 1945, Karaganda, the mining and industrial city built from scratch in the northern Caucasus, still had large open spaces in the center of the city for yurts and animal husbandry. The official statistics failed to reveal that many of the Kazaks it listed as city dwellers and industrial workers continued to live a dual existence as semi-nomads. In Magnitogorsk, the Bashkir, Tartars, and Kyrgyz set up their own suburb, living in a slum called "Little Shanghai." Physically separated from the city zone, it lacked an urban infrastructure until the 1950s.

A special meeting place of the Soviet nationalities was the enormous forced labor camps at the large construction sites. Under the aegis of the Chief Administration of the Camps (Russian acronym: GULAG), the grandiose projects of Stalinism created a mighty economic empire. Between 1930 and 1953, a total of 18 million persons were forced to pass through this shadow world of Stalinist industrial civilization. The history of the industrial Archipel GULAG began with the building of the White Sea–Baltic Sea Canal (1931–3). Roughly 126,000 forced laborers were brought to Russia's far north to move enormous amounts of earth with the simplest tools and to build complex locks. Later, entire industrial cities such as Magadan, Vorkuta, and Noril'sk were created in the mushrooming Stalinist "camp-industrial complex."

The fusion of the system of camps with large construction sites became obsolete when the use of modern machines began demanding a higher quality of work. This was already apparent before 1953 and even more so after Stalin's death. Although "improvement camps" existed also in the post-Stalinist period in spite of all the amnesties, many economic agencies were unwilling to continue using this reservoir of labor. With Stalin's death, the large-scale projects were freed from the choke hold of the GULAG system. The campaign for new land in Kazakhstan and Siberia, the construction of the hydroelectric plant in Bratsk, and the Baikal-Amur Mainline were declared to be projects near and dear to Komsomol, the party youth organization; they attracted young people eager to escape the bleakness of Soviet rural life. Along with these youthful enthusiasts, the construction overseers wooed skilled workers and specialists to the post-Stalinist large construction site with high wages and privileges. In addition, many women were drawn to the remote sites because few places in the Soviet Union had more single men. The migrant laborers also met many former camp inmates, who had no prospects of a life anywhere else and therefore did not leave their internment cities like Magadan, Vorkuta, and Noril'sk.

These groups of the most varied social and ethnic backgrounds populated the industrial centers that were conjured out of nothing in inhospitable peripheral regions, and which slowly became reasonably livable places with the development of urban infrastructures beginning in the 1960s. However, the high turnover of workers, the growing environmental pollution, and alcoholism proved to be serious problems, which could be scientifically documented, but not resolved. The pathos of being part of a "building process" was soon lost in everyday life. What made numerous migrant laborers permanent residents of the new cities in Siberia, Central Asia, and the Far East was not an attachment to the construction projects but a lack of alternatives.

At the same time, specific communities emerged in these cities. In retrospect, construction foremen, engineers, and privileged workers transfigured the large construction sites into "places to prove oneself." They were full of pride at having achieved something magnificent with their dedication. As a result, one can observe in Magnitogorsk, Noril'sk, and Vorkuta a growing local patriotism at the beginning of the 21st century, which allows many residents to overlook their city's past as a former GULAG colony and the enormous ecological damage the projects caused.

Applebaum, Anne. *GULAG: A History*. New York, 2003.

Filtzer, Donald. *Soviet Workers and De-Stalinization: The Consolidation of the Modern System of Soviet Production Relations, 1953–1964*. Cambridge, 1992.

Filtzer, Donald. *Soviet Workers and Late Stalinism: Labour and the Restoration of the Stalinist System after World War II*. Cambridge, 2002.

Gestwa, Klaus. "Technik als Kultur der Zukunft. Der Kult um die 'Stalinschen Großbauten des Kommunismus.'" *Geschichte und Gesellschaft* 30 (2004): 37–73.

Gestwa, Klaus. "Technologische Kolonisation und die Konstruktion des Sowjetvolkes. Die Schau- und Bauplätze der stalinistischen Moderne als Zukunftsräume, Erinnerungsorte und Handlungsfelder." In *Mental Maps – Raum – Erinnerung. Kulturwissenschaftliche Zugänge zum Verhältnis von Raum und Erinnerung*, edited by Sabine Damir-Geilsdorf, Angelika Hartmann, and Béatrice Hendrich, 73–115. Münster, 2005.

Gregory, Paul R., and Valery Lazarev, eds. *The Economics of Forced Labor: The Soviet Gulag*. Stanford, 2003.

Khlevniuk, Oleg V. *The History of the Gulag: From Collectivization to the Great Terror*. New Haven, 2004.

Neutatz, Dietmar. *Die Moskauer Metro. Von den ersten Plänen bis zur Großbaustelle des Stalinismus*. Cologne, 2001.

Cross-references: Russia and Belarus

RUSSIAN PEASANT LABOR MIGRANTS IN RUSSIAN FACTORIES FROM THE END OF THE 19TH CENTURY TO THE END OF THE 1920S

Klaus Gestwa

Because of a short growing season, the Russian peasant was never a pure farmer. A commercial side income was crucial in allowing the peasant family to make ends meet. In addition to various trades and proto-industries in the village, labor migration (*otchod*) always played a central role. And with the rise of modern machine manufacturing after the 1880s, factory work became increasingly important. The industrial enterprises were concentrated either in the few large cities or in numerous quasi-urban industrial villages.

In contemporary usage, the term "worker," like the term "peasant," was merely an administrative category referring to a person's estate, which usually did not coincide with social reality. Given this lack of clear criteria of classification, we therefore have no precise statistical data on the rural labor migrants (*otchodniki*) who worked in the factories. Scholars have calculated 2.5 million and 3 million factory workers in 1913. Since only 15% of the total population of the Russian Empire lived in cities at that time, only a small portion of the factory workforce was recruited from the urban lower classes. More than two-thirds of all those employed in the factories were rural migrant laborers, which means that at the end of the Czarist Empire, their number in the industrial enterprises approached 2 million. Numerous female peasant migrant laborers were also found, especially in the textile industry.

Unlike the small group of skilled urban workers, the peasant migrant laborers of both genders did not call themselves "workers" (*rabočie*) or "master" (*masterovye*). Instead, they retained the traditional peasant term *otchodniki*, which is best translated literally as "those who leave." In spite of their work in factories, they did not see themselves as part of urban society but of traditional peasant society. The urban middle and upper classes, like the urban "worker aristocracy," looked down on the *otchodniki* and referred to them disparagingly as "aliens" (*prišlye*), "gray suckers" (*serye mužiki*), or "assistant workers" (*rabotniki* and *černorabočie*).

Contemporaries themselves were at odds over the extent to which the Russian factory worker was still a peasant or already a proletarian. Lenin defined the *otchodniki* as "workers with allotment land" (*rabočie s nadelom*) as a way of underscoring that while they had by no means relinquished their claim to the land redistributed by the village community, in general they were already leading the life of a factory worker. Later Soviet historians adopted Lenin's definition. In Anglo-American scholarship, the term "peasant workers" is most common. German historians of Russia generally speak of *Arbeiterbauern* (lit.: worker peasants). Regardless of the terms used, Western researchers point to the strong peasant imprint on industrial labor migration. In the last few years, most Russian historians have followed their approach and interpretation.

In the final years of czarist Russia, St. Petersburg, with its newly established enterprises in the modern sectors of ship- and machine building, electrical engineering, and chemistry, had emerged as Russia's leading industrial metropolis. The city's factories employed around 250,000 workers, nearly 10% of all factory workers in Russia. Only a portion came from the immediate environs. Many factory workers journeyed to St. Petersburg from distant provinces. In the commercial region of central Russia, traditionally characterized by textile manufacturing, Ivanovo, the "Russian Manchester," made a name for itself as an industrial center alongside Moscow. In addition, the governments of Moscow and Vladimir had numerous industrial villages in whose cotton factories many peasant workers found employment. It was above all residents of nearby villages or neighboring districts who took advantage of this opportunity after tens of thousands of domestic weavers had become unemployed with the introduction of mechanical looms in the 1870s.

In southern Russia, the so-called Donbas region, a rapidly expanding industrial area had grown up since the 1870s with the rise of mining and heavy industry. Located in a traditionally agrarian region, the mines and factories that sprouted like mushrooms offered the surrounding peasants plenty of opportunity to earn a living as industrial workers. Here the movement from field to factory was above all an interregional process of migration. In the oldest Russian industrial region of the Ural there had been "allotted peasants" (*pripisennye krest'jane*) since the 18th century. They had been given land to use as they wished and were in return obligated to make some of the familial workers available to the mines and iron factories. This form of "working off" was retained also after the liberation of the peasants in 1861. As a result, the peasants living in the mining and industrial districts of the Urals were continuously commuting between their fields and the industrial enterprises. At times the distances were so great that a daily return to the village was impossible, and they had to seek accommodations in the mining and industrial villages for the duration of their industrial work. Contingents of Russian migrant laborers were also found in the factories of the Baltic region, in Helsinki, in Odessa, and in Baku in the Caucasus, where the accelerated production of oil since the 1870s had triggered an economic boom. Russian peasants who were attracted to these industrial sites located at the periphery of the Russian Empire often covered considerable distances during their migration from the country to the city.

Between field and factory: labor migration as part of the peasant life cycle

By the eve of the October Revolution, the differentiation process between peasants and workers had not yet progressed very far. Russian workers stood between factory and field – numerous peasants were in a state between city and country with respect to their social situation and their mentality. Peasant migrant laborers changed their jobs and place of residence depending on the economy and the circumstances of their lives. The cyclical country-city migration was by no means simply the beginning stage of permanent urban immigration. Rather, the dual existence between field and factory shaped the life experience of many generations of Russian peasants. As late as 1914, the age structure of the peasant workers pointed to an urban settlement that may have lasted many years in some cases, but in the end was only temporary. These workers began in the factories at the best working age, mostly around 20, and left them at the age of 40 or 50, at the latest. Back in the villages they replaced the father as the head of the family and ran the farm while younger family members took their place in the city.

The succession of village and factory life remained the normal situation. For one, the survival of the peasant family economy could be secured better with a mixed agrarian-commercial income. For another, only the village offered factory workers the necessary degree of social safety. Provisions for illness, disability, unemployment, and old age offered by the state and businesses were still in their infancy and were far from adequate to prevent a social decline in such cases.

Peasants could not simply leave their villages. Familial and communal impediments prevented them from migrating from the country to the city at will. For example, peasant migrant laborers were required to procure the permission of the head of the family, that is, mostly the father, at regular intervals and then have the village community issue them the requisite pass. There were also many cases of factories that entered into collective labor agreements with individual village communities. These agreements stipulated that the village would provide the enterprise with a specific number of workers, and the village assembly would then decide who would go. That is why the personal desire of the migrant laborers is simply inadequate to explain the peasant labor migration. This migration remained an economic necessity and was subject to the rigid social control of the village community.

During the migration processes at the end of czarist Russia, one can observe a bond to the village that varied in strength by region and industrial sector. Where peasant farm workers came from the immediate environs – namely, in the commercial area of central Russia, in the Donbas and the

Urals – they regularly returned to the village to help with sowing and harvesting and to spend important feast days within the circle of the family. That is why industrial production regularly slumped during the agricultural season. In these situations the *otchodniki* could be described as seasonal workers. Entrepreneurs tried to counteract the regular return to the villages with special work contracts and high wages in the summer months, though their success was limited. Only in St. Petersburg, with its electronic, chemical, and heavy industries, were the peasant workers in the factories for the most part "permanent workers" (*postojanye rabočie*) who did not return to their villages for several years. The primary reason was the large distances: traveling at periodic intervals would have entailed a substantial expense of money and time.

The commuting between field and factory that was adapted to the agricultural season and the ups and downs in the economy by no means came to an end with the October Revolution in 1917. The developments during the Russian civil war reveal once again just how strongly the peasant migrant laborers were tied to the land: when the supply situation in the cities deteriorated dramatically as a result of the "war communism," more than a million factory workers returned for good to their native villages. In times of crisis the villages offered them a place of refuge where the chances of survival were better. Because of this massive return migration, the population of Moscow, St. Petersburg, and other Russian industrial cities dropped by more than half within a short period of time.

In the phase of the "New Economic Policy" that began in 1922, the traditional pattern of the county-city migration continued under the aegis of the "class alliance" between peasants and workers (*smyčka*). Peasant migrant laborers played a dominant role in the gradual rebuilding of the destroyed industries. It was only the Stalinist collectivization and the brute industrialization after 1928 that created fundamentally new conditions by reconfiguring the existing society. The peasant family economy in the villages was destroyed, and at the same time there were attempts, with various means, to gain control of the high degree of mobility between city and countryside. The leadership of the state and the party sought to create a factory workforce that was tied to its workplace, in order to secure a minimum of stability in what Moshe Lewin has called the Soviet "quicksand society" and to ensure the survival of the Soviet system. However, the tenaciously defended remnants of village culture were lost in everyday factory life and in urban social life only in the years after World War II, when the social profile of the factory workforce had changed fundamentally through the employment of younger workers who had not grown up in the traditional Russian village.

Integration in the urban environment

Once peasant migrant laborers had arrived at their destination, they were by no means left to their own devices.

Hometown associations (*zemljačestva*) had formed everywhere. The heads of these organizations, whose members were either migrant laborers from one village or from friendly neighbor communities, procured information about the situation of the labor market and entered into agreements with entrepreneurs. If open jobs had to be filled or older workers had to be replaced, they requested new workers from their native village. Together with "countrymen" (*zemljaki*) already experienced in factory life, these newcomers formed smaller communal units, the so-called *arteli*. An *artel'* was mostly made up of 15–20 individuals who not only shared a specific workplace in a factory but also living quarters in factory barracks or private lodgings. These communal units made sure that newcomers were trained so they could hold their own in the factory and the urban labor market. Without a fixed set of regulations, the legitimacy of the *arteli* was derived entirely from customary law. They elected the eldest (*starosti*) who were responsible for distributing the wages that were handed as a lump sum to the *arteli*; these wages were then given to the workers depending on qualifications, age, productivity, and area of work. The eldest workers also made sure that the factory workers sent a portion of their wages back to their villages. In most cases the members of an *artel'* also paid for a cook. They ate together and subscribed to tabloids, the articles of which were read out loud and then heatedly discussed.

The peasant migrant laborers were very rarely on their own even outside of work and living quarters. On paydays they visited taverns together to get drunk. One popular form of entertainment was mass fistfights, where regional organizations, the residents of various apartment blocks, or the workers of a factory squared off against one another. These popular boxing spectacles served to develop a lively sense of group belonging and a publicly demonstrated social cohesion. Thus the various corporative work groups developed a specific social life of their own and a special group spirit. Even if the migrant workers in the city came into contact with urban culture and were drawn into wider contexts of communication through newspapers and social interactions, they lived largely within a closed community with traditional customs of daily life and traditional organizational structures. They succeeded in integrating structures of village life into everyday urban factory life. With the strong peasant imprint on the factory workforce and the large numbers of peasants within the urban population, one can speak in the last stages of czarist Russia of a "peasantification" of Russian cities.

The factories also had many female workers from the villages, who filled various jobs especially in the textile industry. Those who were engaged in factory work with their husbands were tied into village networks and thus socially secure. They participated in strikes and sometimes appeared in public with a self-confident demeanor. The situation was different for women who lived in their villages as outsiders, for example, as single women, widows, or mothers out of wedlock. They, too, set out for the cities, but most of them turned their back on their village community for good. With paltry wages for women and a high risk of unemployment, it was extraordinarily difficult for them to get by in city and factory life. They were often victims of insults and sexual advances. In times of crisis many had no choice but to sell their bodies. There was often a close connection between the rise of factory work and the development of prostitution, because there was an increase in both supply and demand.

The peasant workers in the factories differed from the urban, skilled workers in their hairstyles, clothes, behavior, and village language. On the eve of the 20th century, the self-proclaimed native "worker aristocracy" increasingly adopted the pretensions and needs of the property-owning urban social groups and made a greater effort to set themselves apart from the peasant migrant laborers. Skilled workers such as printers and metalworkers developed an artisanal particularism (*cechovščina*). In the factories they only trained their own and thus preserved the social segregation of their profession. Education, expensive clothes, and a disciplined lifestyle became for them important indicators of social recognition. Above all it was the undiminished fear of competition that drove skilled urban workers to show such lack of solidarity and cling to their own social exclusivity. Immigrant migrant laborers were not only verbally vilified by them. In many places the urban "worker aristocracy" formed gangs of thugs: they greeted the *otchodniki* arriving at the train stations with blows and thus made it very clear to them that the locals in the city perceived them not as brothers in affliction, but as competitors.

Contemporary observers spoke of "hatred and envy" in the Russian factories, of "differences and even opposition between the social elements." The migrant laborers accused the urban factory workers of arrogance, xenophobia, and a lack of solidarity. For example, during strikes and during the revolution, the skilled workers were intent on compromise with entrepreneurs and the authorities. By contrast, the less-qualified *otchodniki* had far less to lose and therefore often sought confrontation. The unions and social democratic party groups also had very few instruments to control the peasant migrant workers. The latter cared little about the discipline prescribed by these organizations and rarely had anything in common with the leaders of parties and unions. With their continued, traditional protest behavior they were a major reason that strikes often resembled an unruly peasant uprising (*bunt*) rather than a controlled, modern labor struggle. A large number of migrant workers also participated in the anti-Semitic pogroms that convulsed the cities in the south of the Russian Empire at the beginning of the 20th century. It often made no difference to them whom they were assaulting: every possible opportunity was used to blow off the aggression that had been building up.

A uniform working class had emerged neither in the last years of czarist Russia nor in the decade following the October Revolution. Russian cities and industrial villages were characterized by a highly fragmented proletarian milieu. The real elements of identification were not a shared class consciousness, but origin and profession. The various work groups were marked internally by strong solidarity and externally by rigid segregation. Only in individual cases can one speak of the successful integration of peasant migrant workers into urban society. The cultural gap between city and countryside remained too large to be bridged by labor migration to the factories. Although the constant migration between field and factory was creating new channels of communication through which certain elements of urban culture made their way into the countryside, this did not lead to the dissolution of the traditional order of the Russian village. For the time being, the peasant way of life was still flexible enough to hold its own against the "insults" of emerging industrial modernity.

Burds, Jeffrey. *Peasant Dreams and Market Politics: Labor Migration and the Russian Village, 1861–1905*. Pittsburgh, 1998.

Edelman, Robert. *Proletarian Peasants: The Revolution of 1905 in Russia's Southwest*. Ithaca and London, 1987.

Engel, Barbara Alpern. *Between the Fields and the City: Women, Work, and Family in Russia, 1861–1914*. Cambridge, 1994.

Gestwa, Klaus. *Proto-Industrialisierung in Rußland. Wirtschaft, Herrschaft und Kultur in Ivanovo und Pavlovo, 1741–1932*, Göttingen, 1999.

Gestwa, Klaus. "Konfrontation und Kooperation, Adaption und Tradition. Arbeiterkultur zwischen bürgerlicher und bäuerlicher Welt, Ivanovo 1800–1905." In *Gesellschaft als lokale Veranstaltung. Selbstverwaltung, Assoziierung und Geselligkeit in den Städten des ausgehenden Zarenreiches*, edited by Guido Hausmann, 445–78. Göttingen, 2002.

Hoffmann, David L. *Peasant Metropolis: Social Identities in Moscow, 1929–1941*. Ithaca, 1994.

Johnson, Robert Eugene. *Peasant and Proletarian: The Working Class of Moscow in the Late 19th Century*. New Brunswick and New York, 1979.

Cross-references: Russia and Belarus; Russian and Ukrainian Seasonal Laborers in the Grain Belt of New Russia and the North Caucasus in the Late 19th and Early 20th Centuries

RUSSIAN REVOLUTIONARIES IN WESTERN AND CENTRAL EUROPE IN THE 19TH AND EARLY 20TH CENTURIES

Michael G. Esch

Politically motivated migrations from czarist Russia to western and central Europe existed throughout the 19th century and up to World War II. In the wake of the October Revolution of 1917 came the mass exodus of political refugees and those fleeing the civil war. Several phases and forms can be differentiated. The first Russian political opponents and revolutionaries already fled after the failed constitutional-democratic Decembrist uprising of 1825–6.

However, Russian "colonies" (to use contemporary terminology) as centers of emigration emerging into larger ethnic communities are known only from the 1840s, and especially after the European revolutions of 1848–9.

It is hardly possible to clearly distinguish political reasons from economic and social motives for leaving Russia: the first departing revolutionaries, like Alexander Herzen, for example, maintained intensive contacts with participants of the Polish national-republican "Great Emigration" after the failed November uprising in 1830. Toward the end of the 19th century, in the wake of the mass migration of east European Jews into the capital cities of western Europe, revolutionaries who had departed as such could hardly be distinguished from those who became revolutionaries only in their destination country. A clear demarcation of the group is rendered more difficult by its strong social and religious-confessional heterogeneity. Along with the Orthodox-Russian majority, Russian- and sometimes Polish-assimilated Jews also arrived in the destination countries. In the early phase the migrants were above all noblemen, mostly those who had interrupted a military or administrative career to devote themselves to their political activities. They were joined by students and educational travelers, some of whom were also politicized only in their destination country. Beginning in the 1870s, the exodus was enlarged by workers, artisans, and (a very small number of) peasants who joined the revolutionary movement. Finally, after 1881 the political flight was mixed in with a largely Jewish labor migration, which was often simultaneously an escape from religious discrimination.

The migrations and their circumstances display a considerable variety in form. One must distinguish between illegal and legal migrations: in principle, everyone who left the Russian Empire needed permission, and the relevant permit could be revoked at any time. However, from the time of Peter the Great the czars promoted travel abroad for the purpose of education. After the participation of Russian migrants – e.g., Michael Bakunin – in the western and central European revolutions of 1848–9 and the growing politicization of Russian journalists and students, Nicholas I prohibited all foreign study in 1849, which meant that any departure for that purpose was necessarily illegal. However, an illegal departure meant that permission for an eventual return could be obtained only as an act of grace. It was not until after the great reforms of Alexander II in the 1860s that study abroad was permitted again. Subsequently the number of women among the (mostly revolutionary) students also increased: although a woman could journey abroad only with the express permission of her father or husband, many revolutionary young women legalized their emigration by contracting sham marriage with comrades who then provided the permission or accompanied their "spouses" abroad.

Those who refused to return to Russia after an authorized departure also became illegal migrants. Illegal border crossings led to Prussia-Germany and the Habsburg Empire. Many political refugees who wished to escape arrest and deportation chose the Ottoman Empire as their transit country. A few revolutionaries who had already been deported to Siberia fled from there via Japan and the USA to western and central Europe, as Bakunin did in 1861.

In spite of their religious-confessional and national heterogeneity (the Jews, too, were considered a separate "nationality" in czarist Russia), the revolutionaries from the Russian Empire formed an ethnic community with contacts to their homeland. Migration was based on networks and the (often merely putative) knowledge of the situation in the destination countries. The group settled in colonies in most western and central European university towns and capitals, especially in Paris, London, and Brussels, as well as in Geneva, Bern, Heidelberg, and Halle. In spite of the strong political fragmentation of the individual colonies, group members, especially the politically more active among them, moved between the various cities and even traveled to Russia to illegally smuggle brochures and books into their home country.

Until the second half of the 1880s, the overwhelming majority of the revolutionaries (Bakunin was an early exception) stayed clear of the political conflicts in their host countries. For one, this had ideological reasons: the political migrants found in the destination countries the kind of liberal conditions for freedom of opinion and political work that was almost entirely absent in Russia and for which they were fighting. For another, refugee status itself played a role not to be underestimated. To be sure, the political refugees got a fairly friendly reception in some destination countries: in Paris, for example (and similarly in London), Russian political refugees had a special status, even if they never attained the guaranteed refugee status – including the right to state support – that the Polish political refugees enjoyed after 1831 and 1863. However, meddling in domestic affairs – for example, a discussion of the social question in western and central Europe – was in no way welcome.

The Russian colonies remained largely self-contained, with their own restaurants, libraries, and aid funds. Beyond that, cultural and political events as well as public appearances on important anniversaries – e.g., March 1, the day of the successful attempt on the life of Czar Alexander I in 1881 – kept the group together. Balls, for example, were used to finance political activities, and at times also the livelihood of professional revolutionaries. The immigrants saw themselves culturally and nationally as Russian and constituted themselves – much like the group of "White" Russian refugees in the interwar period – as Russia abroad (*zarubeže*).

Especially during extended stays abroad, some revolutionaries were able to integrate into the political, and sometimes the social, milieu of their host societies: Bakunin, for example, was a known and indispensable figure in the European revolutionary movement and the First International; Alexander Herzen, Pyotr Lavrov, and Charles Rappoport were known in Paris and for a long time also quite respected personalities, though without giving up their self-conception as Russian revolutionaries, as which they were also often perceived within their environments. Much the same is true of Pyotr Kropotkin in London or later Lenin and Trotsky, who each cultivated intensive contacts with the Russian colonies as well as with the European socialist movement.

Sometimes in spite of the way they would have identified themselves, some revolutionaries became citizens of their host country. On the one hand, this could be the expression of a cultural decision or one related to perceived prospects for their lives; on the other hand, it could also be a sign of pragmatism, since naturalization brought secure residency status. The assimilation of the children of revolutionaries was, however, hardly avoidable: since the living quarters of the immigrants were usually extremely tight, their children played in the streets. After some time during their stay in Vienna, Trotsky's sons, for example, spoke Austrian German better than they did Russian, until the family was forced to leave Austria. Trotsky's son Sergei/Serge played an important role in the 1930s in the founding of Trotskyist organizations in France.

The political and social integration of Russian revolutionary immigrants did not experience a significant change even when Russian revolutionaries carried out attempted assassinations abroad from the end of 1880s. When the Polish-Russian socialist Stanislav Padlewski attempted to kill General Mikhail Seliverstov, French anarchists delighted over Padlewski's successful escape. However, then and until shortly before World War I, both Russian revolutionaries and the czar's secret police, which had a branch in Paris, regarded attempts by Russian subjects on the lives of Russian officials as internal Russian matters even if they took place abroad. These actions were aimed at revolutionizing their homeland, not their host countries. Contacts between Russian (especially Jewish) and domestic revolutionaries – and thus a focus on changing living conditions in the host countries – increased mostly on the level of proletarian-syndicalist organization, less so within the circles of the classic revolutionary emigration.

From the 1890s, Russian revolutionaries, now especially the Marxist-oriented exiles, together with a growing number of other, mostly Jewish, immigrants joined the native workers' organizations. Vladimir Burcev, a social revolutionary who worked hard at unmasking czarist agents, published his Paris magazine in Russian and French. Moreover, in many places the Russian revolutionaries of the 19th century were part of a city's folklore: their existence was widely known, and in some periods (especially after the "spring of nations" in 1848 and during the transition from educational to terrorist populism in the mid-1870s), their reputation and esteem among the interested public grew high. At certain times, the aura of Russian nihilists, anarchists, terrorists, or (during World War I) maximalists radiated also onto young Russians who were not politically organized at all.

Actions directed against the political and social conditions in their host countries also affected the conditions under which Russian revolutionaries were staying there: beginning in the 1890s, bans on residence, confiscation of journals, and

expulsions became more numerous. However, direct extradition occurred only in the German Empire. Already the Revolution of 1905, and even more so the February Revolution in 1917, led to a certain return migration, though its exact extent is impossible to accurately determine. However, after the October Revolution, some remigrants returned to their previous domiciles with the group of the "Whites."

Esch, Michael G. "Parallele Gesellschaften und soziale Räume. Osteuropäische Einwanderer in Paris 1880–1940." Habilitation thesis, Düsseldorf, 2007.

Haupt, George. "Rôle de l'exil dans la diffusion de l'image de l'intelligentsia révolutionnaire." *Cahiers du monde russe et soviétique* 19, 3 (1978): 235–49.

Kutos, Paul. *Russische Revolutionäre in Wien 1900–1917. Eine Fallstudie zur Geschichte der politischen Emigration.* Vienna, 1993.

Miller, Martin A. *The Russian Revolutionary Emigres 1825–1870.* Baltimore and London, 1986.

Neumann, Daniela. *Studentinnen aus dem Russischen Reich in der Schweiz (1867–1914).* Zurich, 1987.

Peter, Hartmut Rüdiger, ed. *Schnorrer, Verschwörer, Bombenwerfer? Studenten aus dem Russischen Reich an deutschen Hochschulen vor dem 1. Weltkrieg.* Frankfurt am Main, 2001.

Cross-references: Austria; France; Germany; Great Britain; Russia and Belarus; Switzerland; Polish Political Refugees in Central and Western Europe in the 19th Century; Russian Emigrants in Europe since 1917; Russian Female Students in Switzerland in the Late 19th and Early 20th Centuries; Russian Students at German Colleges and Universities in the Late 19th and Early 20th Centuries

RUSSIAN STUDENTS AT GERMAN COLLEGES AND UNIVERSITIES IN THE LATE 19TH AND EARLY 20TH CENTURIES

Hartmut Rüdiger Peter

Border-crossing mobility by students and teachers is as old as universities and colleges themselves and is one of the basic elements of academic life. Compared to other migratory phenomena, it involved only social minority groups, though they played an important role in the formation of social elites and in international cultural transfers. Border-crossing movements by students were closely connected with the development of the European network of universities and colleges and generally flowed from less developed regions into those with highly evolved educational systems. At the turn of the 19th to the 20th century, the primary direction of migration was from east to west.

Russia was one of the most important countries of origin for foreign students at universities and colleges in western and central Europe. By the end of the 19th century, the educational trips of young noblemen had evolved, through various forms of state-supported or privately funded education of skilled workers, into a barely regulated stream of students to the academic centers in Belgium, Germany, France, and Switzerland. Between 1698 and 1814, around 630 Russian subjects can be identified in the enrollment records of German universities. In 1895–6, Prussian statistics already recorded an annual average of 466 students from czarist Russia at German universities. By 1899–1900 that number had risen to 572, by 1905–6 it had doubled to 1,140, and by 1912–13 it had surged again to 1,891. Although Russian citizens accounted for no more than about 3.6% of all students, they made up 45% of foreigners at German universities and represented the same percentage of foreign students at Technical Colleges in 1912 (1,998 of 4,409). However, with just over 13,000 students and auditors at these institutions, their presence loomed much larger here, a situation that earned the Technical College in Darmstadt, for example, the name "Russian College" in student circles. The presence of Russians was also strong at agricultural and trade colleges, mining academies, engineering schools, and other higher technical institutions.

Along with the growth in numbers described above, there was also a change in the composition of the Russian students in Germany. Until the last third of the 19th century, most students were the sons of privileged families of the nobility, of wealthy merchants and entrepreneurs, and to a lesser extent of the independent professions. They came predominantly from the two metropolises of St. Petersburg and Moscow as well as the Baltic and Polish regions of the empire. A large percentage were members of national minorities, such as Poles and Germans. The student body at higher technical institutions, where the numbers had been on the rise since the 1870s, was from the very beginning less exclusive.

The strong influx since the turn of the century was recruited primarily from the Jewish Pale of Settlement (čerta) in the western part of the empire. The Russian public health physician L. B. Granovskij, using data from 52 German universities and colleges, calculated that Jews accounted for 66.3% of Russian students in the summer semester 1913. Statistical surveys by Russian-Jewish student organizations at the 11 largest German universities estimated a percentage of 85.4. The social composition of the migration became more heterogeneous. The number of young people from simple backgrounds increased. Although the vague term "merchant" dominates the data on the parents' background in the enrollment records, it now represented more rarely larger entrepreneurs in the large cities, but instead mostly small-scale and very small merchants in the towns and settlements of the Jewish Pale.

The background to and motives behind this educational migration from the Russian Empire were complex. Academic interests and social and political reasons often overlapped and could change during the course of study. A central trigger was the persistent structural weakness of the Russian university and college system, which was unable to satisfy the demand for classic universities and modern technical training and was forced to regulate access through entrance exams and other restrictions. The unstable political situation within Russia also played a central role. Universities and colleges were among the centers of political and social protest. The regime reacted to periodic student unrest with arrests, restrictions on academic rights, mass expulsions, and even the temporary closing of entire departments as well as universities and colleges. This often made an orderly course of studies impossible even for students who were not politically active.

In addition, the reactionary policy on higher education, in combination with social, national, or religious discrimination, hit various groups within Russian society especially hard. For example, women were – with few exceptions – excluded from full-fledged state educational institutions. Female students or auditors remained a marginal phenomenon also in the German Reich as a result of the late opening of higher education to women and a restrictive enrollment policy toward foreign women, while women students were found in larger numbers in Switzerland. In response to national discrimination within the Russian education system, which manifested itself, among other things, in the Russification of the universities in Dorpat and Warsaw, of the Polytechnical Institute in Riga, and of other institutions, members of minorities, such as Poles, Germans, and – in smaller numbers – Armenians, enrolled in foreign universities.

The czarist policy on nationalities was especially hard on the Jews. After 1887, a quota system limited their access to *Gymnasien* (upper secondary schools), universities, and most other institutions of higher learning to 3% in St. Petersburg and Moscow, 5% in the educational districts outside, and 10% in those within the Pale of Settlement. At first the regulations were rarely enforced to the fullest. But after the dissolution of the second Duma (Russian parliament) on 3 June 1907, which triggered a reactionary turnaround in the country, the government of Stolypin pushed through the strict implementation of the quota system. For Jewish graduates of the higher secondary schools, large numbers of whom were pushing to get to university, this exclusion was problematic in two ways. The social rank that came with an academic degree meant the right to settle freely within Russia, and this opened possibilities of assimilation and further social advancement. To circumvent the restrictions, an especially large number headed for foreign institutions. A segment of these students, difficult to circumscribe, also saw university study as a chance for permanent emigration, and they should therefore be seen within the context of the general Jewish emigration from east-central and eastern Europe. According to Salomon Adler Rudel, Germany, because of its favorable geographical location, moderate enrollment regulations and tuition costs, easy linguistic access, and the high renown of its academic culture, became the "promised land of the intellectually interested Jewish youth of Russia."

The above described changes in the composition and motives of the educational migrants from Russia were also reflected in their academic focus and study behavior. In 1895–6, about two-thirds of the students from czarist Russia (320 of 466) at the universities enrolled in the philosophical faculties, where, alongside the liberal arts, they entered institutes of agriculture and the natural sciences. About a quarter (112) studied medicine. Law (25) and theology (8) played a minor role. These choices corresponded to general patterns of professionalization and were aimed at the acquisition of knowledge that could be used in Russia for a socially appropriate job in government service or on an agricultural estate. In the academic year 1905–6, the philosophical faculties of the universities attracted only half of the students from Russia (577 of 1,140), and in 1911–12 only a little more than a quarter (513 of 1,891). By contrast, the number of medical students quadrupled by 1905–6 to 452, and in 1911–12 they made up more than two-thirds (1,316). At most universities, more than 90% of these students were Jewish. If one adds in technical colleges, where students flocked in large numbers to fields such as construction and machine building or electrical engineering, the dominant professional profiles were those for which there was an acute demand in Russia with a view toward the country's modernization, and which therefore provided favorable prospects for professional and social advancement.

Until the turn of the century, their background, prior education, and language skills had allowed most students from Russia to live in keeping with their social status, and their presence was hardly noticed as disruptive in the academic milieu. This changed when, as a result of the growing social differentiation of the student body, the picture was increasingly shaped by students who had to struggle to raise the necessary funds for tuition and living costs. Their primary interest was to finish their studies as quickly as possible. Their zeal and ascetic way of life were often seen by fellow German students as out of keeping with their social status and as offensive, though most university teachers took a positive view of this.

In Germany, the students from Russia developed a social life of their own, which became more diverse and differentiated as their numbers grew. In the process, they carried on forms of self-organization that had been tried in their home country and adjusted them to the conditions and legal environment abroad. The traditions and customs of German students, however, they mostly rejected as alien. All larger student colonies had academic clubs and reading halls, shared dining facilities, and relief funds; in large university and college towns there were also academic information and job-placement offices, choirs, or sports clubs. Social life centered around benefit events and balls or lecture evenings on scientific, literary, and political topics. Outside of these networks, few students from Russia could be found in professional associations. There were also contacts with the German Freistudentenschaft (Free Student Body, organizations of students who did not belong to regular fraternities and were influenced by the Youth Movement). However, social, cultural, and language barriers on the whole led to a self-isolation of Russian students that offended German students and was criticized also from within their own ranks.

Under the umbrella of the community of students from Russia, but increasingly also separately, members of the various groups went their own ways. Where German authorities allowed it, Polish students from Russia joined with Poles from Prussia and Austria-Hungary to set up independent organizations. Armenian and Finnish students likewise set up their own academic organizations. Ethnic German students from Russia joined German student fraternities, though they also had their own clubs or joined Russian ones. The "national"-confessional differentiation intensified after the turn of the century with the separation of Jewish or Zionist as well as pan-Russian organizations. Attempts to establish organizations for all of Germany or all of Europe did not succeed until 1912–13, when the Russian and especially the Russian-Jewish students were increasingly stigmatized in the public as foreigners and their possibilities of pursuing a university education were curtailed through stricter matriculation and testing requirements. This period also saw the emergence of a Russian and a Russian-Jewish student press in Germany.

Among the stereotypes of the contemporary perception was the image of students from Russia as inclined to revolution. The authorities kept a close eye on them especially in Prussia and Bavaria, and also cooperated with the Russian secret police. In fact, an interest in politics was expected among students, but such an interest was by no means an indication of practical involvement. It would appear that the number of activists tended to be low. They were concentrated in large university and college centers like Berlin, Leipzig, or Munich, cities that were also home to a political exile community. At smaller colleges and universities with a small number of Russian students, activists had only limited possibilities to do anything. Political refugees took advantage of the legal student organizations and reading halls as the basis for their work, with the various parties and factions competing against each other. The political groups outside of large cities that were made up almost exclusively of students organized lectures, distributed illegal literature, collected donations, and also cooperated with the German Social Democrats.

Both the growing number and the changes in the picture of the educational migrants from Russia were reflected in public in various contexts and in various ways. In the 1890s, their strong presence at the already overcrowded technical colleges prompted the discussion of the "issue of academic foreigners," which was later often reduced to a "Russian" or "Jewish question." The student unrest in Russia fed political distrust. Nationalistic circles within the German student body, especially the so-called Burschenschaften, called for drastic restrictions on the admission of foreign, but especially Russian, students; as arguments they invoked their "poor preparation" and "cultural backwardness," a "threat to morals," possible negative repercussions for German exports, and a "waste of tax revenue." Various professional organizations, for example, those of engineers or chemists, invoked the social anxieties of their members and put forth similar demands.

National-conservative politicians and segments of the press instrumentalized such sentiments, resorting in the process to anti-Semitic and anti-Russian stereotypes. A substantial number of professors spoke out against restrictions on Russians – or foreigners as such – studying at German universities. The Ministries of Culture tended to pursue a restrained course, and moderate voices were also heard from the economic sector and circles of the Freistudenten. It was only in the last few years before World War I that the stream of students from czarist Russia to German universities and colleges was consistently curtailed through admission regulations, fees, and a general quota system (as in Bavaria in 1911 and Prussia in 1913). After the outbreak of the war in 1914, a decree about the nonmatriculation of members of countries in a state of war with Germany excluded them from higher education in Germany. With few exceptions, students from Russia were expelled, if they were not already out of the country on account of the semester break.

Ivanov, Anatolij Evgen´evič. *Studenčestvo Rossii konca XIX – načala XX veka. Social'no-istoričeskaja sud'ba.* Moscow, 1999.

Peter, Hartmut Rüdiger, ed. *Schnorrer, Verschwörer, Bombenwerfer? Studenten aus dem Russischen Reich an deutschen Hochschulen vor dem 1. Weltkrieg.* Frankfurt am Main, 2001.

Peter, Hartmut Rüdiger, and Natalia Tikhonov, eds. *Universitäten als Brücken in Europa. Studien zur Geschichte der studentischen Migration – Les universités: Des ponts à travers l'Europe. Etudes sur l'histoire des migrations étudiantes.* Frankfurt am Main, 2003.

Weill, Claudie. *Étudiantes russes en Allemagne 1900–1914. Quand la Russie frappait aux portes de l'Europe.* Paris, 1996.

Wertheimer, Jack. *Unwelcome Strangers: East European Jews in Imperial Germany.* New York and Oxford, 1991.

Cross-references: Germany; Poland; Russia and Belarus; Ukraine; Ashkenazim in Europe since the Early Modern Period; Eastern European Jews in Berlin from the Late 19th Century to the 1930s; Eastern European Jews in London since the Late 19th Century; Eastern European Jews in Paris since the Late 19th Century; European Elites on the Grand Tour in Early Modern Europe; Russian Female Students in Switzerland in the Late 19th and Early 20th Centuries; Russian Revolutionaries in Western and Central Europe in the 19th and Early 20th Centuries

RUSSIAN AND UKRAINIAN SEASONAL LABORERS IN THE GRAIN BELT OF NEW RUSSIA AND THE NORTH CAUCASUS IN THE LATE 19TH AND EARLY 20TH CENTURIES

Gijs Kessler

One of the most spectacular forms of peasant seasonal labor migration (*otkhod*) in the late 19th-century Russian Empire was the annual migration of peasants from the Russian Central Black Earth agricultural provinces to work as hired laborers on the large grain-growing estates of the northern steppe rim of the Black Sea, known as New Russia, and of the North Caucasus. New Russia and parts of the North Caucasus, in particular the Don and Kuban provinces, produced grain for internal and external markets, profiting from fertile steppe soils, a favorable climate, and the nearness of the sea and several major ports. Having become part of the Russian Empire only at the end of the 18th century, these regions were relatively sparsely populated, and during harvest time the demand for labor could not be met locally. This attracted seasonal laborers from areas to the north and northeast, from Podolia and Volhynia in the west to the provinces of Penza and Simbirsk in the east. These areas were the old agricultural heartland of European Russia, dominated by fertile Black Earth soils, but very densely populated and home to peasant smallholding agriculture.

In the heyday of this "steppe-system," during the last two decades of the 19th century, well over a million peasants from these central provinces, almost exclusively men, worked annually as agricultural laborers in the south. Their earnings supplemented core agricultural incomes, which were under pressure from a combination of rapid population growth, a shortage of land, and primitive production techniques. During the first decades of the 20th century seasonal migration between the two regions declined in importance due to population growth in the steppe areas and a concomitant increase in the local supply of labor, as well as to the effects of mechanization in the harvesting process. The elimination of large landholdings during the agricultural revolution of 1918 finally brought an end to the extensive grain cultivation in the area and therewith to the large-scale demand for seasonal agricultural laborers.

The annual migration to the south rested on an intricate interplay of factors. The need for supplementary income drove peasants from central Russia to the south because of low demand for labor at home, where most of the larger estates had long been transferred to peasant smallholding through purchase and rental agreements as the population sought to increase the area under cultivation to offset population growth. Nonagricultural demand for labor was weakly developed in this predominantly rural region. In this situation, the nearest employment opportunities were down in the south, because the industrial centers of Moscow, St. Petersburg, and other cities farther to the north were already provided with labor from their own hinterlands. At the same time, permanent resettlement in the south was complicated by two further circumstances. Until 1906 peasants were legally bound to the land commune (*obshchina*) and therefore could not, at least legally, permanently resettle in other regions. Second, grain monoculture in the steppe areas meant that employment opportunities outside the harvest season were scarce.

Wage labor in the south was integrated in the peasant economy of the areas of departure in different ways, depending on the proximity to the pull area. The distances that had to be covered could be up to 700–800 kilometers and were traveled by train, steamship, or raft, but most often by foot, and the journey could vary from a couple of days to three weeks. Peasants from the closer areas could combine harvest work in the south with the work on their own lands, because in the steppe the harvest tended to fall somewhat earlier than up north, and as a rule they would manage to be home in time. For peasants from the most northern regions of the push area this was impossible. In these regions only those who could be missed in local agriculture went to the south, mostly young men or peasants with landholdings small enough to be cultivated by the women, the young, and the elderly.

In the steppe areas supply and demand of labor met in the most literal sense of the word at large-scale open-air hiring markets at important road junctions, riverboat terminals, and railroad stations. Set in direct negotiations, wages fluctuated with the day, ranking among the highest in European Russia. Trying to get the best possible price, workers risked remaining without a job, and employers risked remaining without workers. The foundation on which this system rested was the disequilibrium between demand for labor and labor reserves in the region. In many ways this was a transitory stage. Over the years, New Russia and the North Caucasus were colonized by peasants from the densely populated areas of the Central Black Earth districts – particularly when the peasants of these districts were no longer bound to the land commune after 1906 – but also by peasants from other regions. This process gradually increased the local supply of labor, which pushed wages downward and thus reduced the attraction of harvest work in the area for peasant migrants from the north. To this were added the effects of mechanization in steppe agriculture, which both reduced the length of the season and increased the demand for female and adolescent labor at the expense of male workers. The combined result of these developments was a gradual reduction in the size of the annual migration flow from north to south and back. Whether this caused seasonal migration to disappear entirely is unclear – in any case the abolition of large landholdings in the revolutions of 1917 and 1918 effectively eliminated the demand for labor to which the steppe system had owed its existence.

The changes in the peasant economy of the Central Black Earth Region related to the disappearance of the steppe system have been insufficiently studied. Permanent settlement of former migrant laborers in the pull area after 1906 somewhat reduced underemployment in the peasant economy of the former push area, but the magnitude of this outflow appears to have been limited. More important, the migratory current was diverted in two other directions. In the first place resettlement (*pereselenie*) to Siberia and Central Asia gathered momentum during the first decades of the 20th century as the state started to actively stimulate it. Second, the economic expansion of Moscow, St. Petersburg, and other towns of the Central Industrial Region drew in labor from farther

and farther afield, including some of the areas from which people had migrated to the south only a couple of decades earlier.

Grube, Robert. *Das Wandergewerbe in Rußland*. Berlin, 1905.

Mixter, Timothy R. "Perceptions of Agricultural Labor and Hiring-Market Disturbances in Saratov, 1872–1905." *Russian History* 7 (1980): 139–68.

Mixter, Timothy R. "The Hiring-Market as Workers' Turf: Migrant Agricultural Laborers and the Mobilization of Collective Action in the Steppe Grainbelt of European Russia, 1853–1913." In *Peasant Economy, Culture and Politics of European Russia, 1800–1921*, edited by Esther Kingston-Mann and Timothy R. Mixter, 294–340. Princeton, 1991.

Sagorsky, Simon. *Die Arbeiterfrage in der südrussischen Landwirtschaft*. Munich, 1907.

Strumilin, Stanislav G., ed. *Naemnyi trud v sel'skom khoziaistve*. Moscow, 1926.

Cross-references: Russia and Belarus; Ukraine

SALZBURG PROTESTANTS IN EAST PRUSSIA SINCE THE 18TH CENTURY

Charlotte E. Haver

The term "Salzburg emigrants" encompasses in the broader sense all residents of the Prince-Bishopric of Salzburg who left their homeland voluntarily or involuntarily after the 16th century because of their adherence to the Lutheran confession. In the narrower sense it refers to those Protestants who were exiled from the Prince-Bishopric in connection with the "Great Emigration" in 1731–3 and were subsequently able to settle in the German Empire, the Netherlands, the British colony of Georgia, and above all in Prussian Lithuania. In 1944–5, the Salzburgers, who still existed as a community of memory at the beginning of the 21st century, were expelled from East Prussia.

In the early 16th century, reformationist doctrines had been persecuted in the Prince-Bishopric of Salzburg from the very beginning – as in Bavaria but initially in contrast to neighboring Austria. Since no Protestant congregations were therefore able to establish themselves at any time, Lutheranism survived only in secret Protestantism (crypto-Protestantism), that is, with adherents outwardly participating in Catholic religious life. Especially as a result of the Counter-Reformation that also began in Austria at the end of the 16th century, the transmission of Luther's teachings remained possible only in the private sphere through conversations and writings. The migrations of the "Salzburgers" and the attendant patterns of integration can be compared to the history of other religious refugees in the early modern period.

The migrations of the Protestants from Salzburg can be divided into three phases: (1) The partly voluntary departure of individuals (preachers, schoolmasters, professors, and migrants with only qualified religious motives) prior to 1588; (2) the forced emigration of larger groups from 1588 onward (citizens of the city of Salzburg; after that peasants, miners, day laborers from, among other places, the mountain valleys); (3) the expulsion of nearly all (crypto-)Protestants who were still living in the Prince-Bishopric until 1731 (almost exclusively peasants, miners, and day laborers from the mountain regions). In the first half of the 17th century, about 2,000 Protestants fled from Salzburg. In the 16th century, the Salzburgers had still been able to emigrate to the Austrian patrimonial lands, but in the 17th century they had to search for new destinations (except for Ortenburg, Old Bavaria was Catholic, and Bohemia and Moravia were re-Catholicized in the Thirty Years' War). The only possible destinations now were the Protestant territories and cities in the German Empire, such as Franconia with Nuremberg, Ansbach-Bayreuth, Neustadt/Aisch, Erlangen, as well as Regensburg, the Swabian imperial cities, and Württemberg. At the end of the century (1684–91), about 1,000 peasants and day laborers were expelled from the Defereggental south of Gastein, and they migrated to Augsburg, Regensburg, and Ulm. Another 60–70 miners from the salt mine Dürrnberg near Hallein settled in the southern German imperial cities and in Nuremberg.

The year 1731 spelled the end of crypto-Protestantism. Prince-Bishop Leopold Firmian and his chancellor Christani de Rallo decided to set a warning example and to now "eradicate" Protestantism "completely and from the roots up" (Emigration Patent of 31 October 1731). One-fifth of the population (20,678 individuals) was exiled from the land as "heretics" and "rebels" with no regard for the agreements of the Peace of Westphalia (1648). The approximately 5,000 landless persons (*Unangesessene*) among them (for example, day laborers) had to leave the Principality of Salzburg within a few days in the middle of the winter of 1731–2. The date 24 April 1732 was fixed for the departure of the land-owning peasants (*Angesessene*). The landless moved from the mountain valleys to the Swabian imperial cities; the landed emigrants were offered an opportunity to settle in East Prussia (Prussian Lithuania: the Memelland, parts of the districts of Königsberg and Gumbinnen) through a patent of invitation from the Prussian king Frederick William I that was issued on 2 February 1732.

The invitation from Prussia was followed by a group exodus that would henceforth shape the self-image and the self-confidence of the Salzburgers: about 16,000 refugees, dressed in their traditional clothes, migrated in tightly organized treks from the Alps to the Baltic Sea on horseback, in carts, or on foot. Their routes led from the mountains (Gastein, Rauris, Kleinarl, Wagrain, St. Johann) to Salzburg, and from there, via Protestant imperial cities and territories, if at all possible (e.g., Kempten, Memmingen, Augsburg, Ulm, Nördlingen, Nuremburg [hinterland]), in the direction of Gotha, Halle, and Leipzig to Potsdam and Berlin. From there, a part moved to Stettin and onward by sea to Königsberg; the other part

The Prussian king Frederick William I greets the Salzburg emigrants (*Germanisches Nationalmuseum, Nuremberg*).

went via Danzig or Kulm. The chief areas of settlement lay east and west of Gumbinnen (around Insterburg, Lappönen, Ragnit, Tilsit, along the Pregel, and partly in Memel) as well as south of the city. For the duration of the journey Frederick William I had declared all Salzburgers Prussian subjects and had provided money and organization for the migration. And so the aimless and haphazard expulsion of the "rebels" from Salzburg turned into a "triumphal procession" of Lutheran Protestantism that was followed with interest by Europe's entire Protestant public. Engravers and writers of every kind immediately and extensively documented the fate of the Salzburgers, who were styled as "martyrs of the faith," and even "saints."

For the individual refugees themselves the flight was strenuous, marked in part by illness, death, and anxiety about the future. At a traveling speed of 20–26 kilometers per day, it lasted three months. But after a long period of crypto-Protestantism, it was for many Salzburgers also the first (and only) time that they were the widely admired focus of attention as symbols of religious faithfulness and love of freedom, even if they were in need of support. Countless illustrations show the Salzburgers as "God's wandering people." On church windows, in paintings, drawing, and historical postcards, individuals, families, or groups of expellees are depicted as being always en route. That is still true for the self-descriptions at the beginning of the 21st century.

However, the banishment of the Salzburgers did not come to an end with the "Great Emigration." During the winter of 1732–3, the miners of the Dürrnberger salt mine were expelled along with their families (a total of 780 persons). The attempt to settle this group in Cadzand in the lower Dutch province of Zealand was successful for only a few of the Salzburgers. The vast majority wandered back into the

German Empire. More important and consequential were probably the migrations of about 300 landless emigrants who settled in Swabia for a time. Between 1734 and 1741 they journeyed in four so-called transports to Georgia, the British North American colony founded in 1732.

Most – though by no means all – Salzburgers remained in the settlement places assigned or offered to them by the authorities. Some sought to make their own way to other Protestant areas. A return to Salzburg, something that many yearned for, would have been possible only through conversion to Catholicism, and Austria, too, continued to be closed to them.

Prussian Lithuania, the destination of the vast majority of the Salzburgers, had been largely depopulated, mainly due to the plague of 1708–10. Estimates put the number of deaths from the epidemic at three-quarters of the population (around 150,000 people). Immediately after assuming the throne in 1713, Frederick William I tried hard to populate the region. Within the framework of a recovery program, he sought to make Prussian Lithuania once again a productive territory through financial subsidies, new legal regulations, and the recruitment of settlers. But the project turned into a failure in every regard, in spite of the immigration of Swiss Calvinists, northwest Germans, Hessians, and Palatines after 1713 and especially between 1723 and 1727: some of the immigrants had no basic agricultural skills and moved on when their expectations (about industrial job opportunities) were disappointed. The Salzburgers seemed to offer new prospects for developing the region; in the king's eyes they promised to become pious subjects who possessed the requisite qualifications and motivation for rebuilding Prussian Lithuania.

After some resistance, the Salzburgers came to terms with what they found in Prussian Lithuania, even if not everything was in accordance with the terms of their invitation. For example, because of the earlier settlements in 1713, they were not able to be settled all together. As they saw it, they were now in a foreign cultural sphere. Moreover, the mountain peasants from the Alps had to adjust to unaccustomed agricultural conditions (for example, different soils, different seasonal rhythms, a different climate, and therefore also different crops). In addition, they discovered that while they no longer had to practice their religion in secret, they had moved from one absolutist state to another, which meant that central aspects of their lives continued to be determined by the ruling authorities.

Because of their agricultural success and their faith, which played a role in shaping their everyday lives, the vast majority of Salzburgers integrated after a number of years. They evolved into Gumbinners, Stallupöners, and so forth and were accepted as such by the locals and the other immigrants. They respected the king and the authorities and gave up any desire to return to Salzburg. That they shared the same German language, even if it was still colored by dialect, formed an important integrative factor. Still, they did not forget their common history, tended to marry within their own circle, and handed down the pride of not having submitted to the Prince-Bishops' claim of religious and political suzerainty. But it was precisely their identity, which expressed itself in its opposition to Catholicism and a sense of unity in the struggle for religious liberty, that led in the end to social integration in a Protestant environment, with a simultaneous, permanent emphasis on a shared history as a minority. In this context, the Stiftung Salzburger Anstalt, a foundation that was set up as early as 1740 and was financed with the profits from the sale of landholdings in Salzburg, was influential in preserving this identity. This charitable foundation, which cared for the poor, old, and sick Salzburgers, developed into a location of remembrance of the history of the Salzburgers. The foundation still exists at the beginning of the 21st century, having found a new center – after the expulsions of 1944–5 – in Bielefeld, Gumbinnen's sister city. It now houses, in addition to a residential home (also for non-Salzburgers) for the old, a library and an archive – institutions that ensure the cohesiveness of the Salzburgers and allow them to cultivate their traditions. Moreover, churches of the Salzburgers, for example, in Cadzand and in Gumbinnen, remain locations of remembrance even where no Salzburgers have been living for a long time.

When the search for national or group-specific characteristics was made popular during the period of historicism, the Salzburger Verein (Association of Salzburgers) was founded in Gumbinnen in 1911. Since then, its publication, *Der Salzburger*, has appeared four times a year, interrupted only by the wars. At the beginning of the 21st century, the association (membership in 2009: about 720) with its regional groups – since 1989 also in the new states of the Federal German Republic – and its magazine (circulation in 2009: 1,200) play a crucial role in creating and preserving the identity of the Salzburgers who have been living widely dispersed since 1945. That is also true of the younger generation. Contacts among the descendants of these religious refugees have remained strong. As they have married among themselves over long periods of time they are often still recognizable by their names today. There are regular conferences, annual conventions, meetings (in the regional groups), and joint outings. There are ties to the Georgia Salzburger Society founded in 1925 in Savannah, Georgia (USA) and to the Stichting tot Bestudering van Salzburger emigranten in Cadzand, the Netherlands.

What all Salzburgers share to this day is a historical group consciousness – even if it is often vague – and a pronounced pride in being the descendants of the Salzburg emigrants of 1731–2. Still today, one can describe the Salzburgers as a very lively community. The 20th century saw the first reconciliation with the old homeland of Salzburg. The first Group Tour to the Homeland of Our Ancestors took place in 1914. Because of the war, the reports about the trip ("How beautiful is Salzburg!") did not appear in the bulletin until 1921. Other tours followed. To this day, association meetings are held in the Salzburg region and, conversely, members of the Salzburg state government regularly participate in larger meetings and conventions in Germany. After 220 years in East Prussia and complete social integration, after renewed expulsion and life in the Federal Republic of Germany and in the German Democratic Republic, the Salzburg Protestants continue to refer to the state of Salzburg as their "old, unforgotten homeland."

Beheim-Schwarzbach, Max. *Friedrich Wilhelms I. Colonisationswerk in Lithauen, vornehmlich die Salzburger Kolonie.* Königsberg, 1879.

Göcking, Gerhard Gottlieb Günther. *Vollkommene Emigrations-Geschichte Von denen Aus dem Ertz-Bißthum Saltzburg vertriebenen und größtentheils nach Preussen gegangenen Lutheranern…*, 2 parts. Frankfurt am Main and Leipzig, 1733/1737.

Haver, Charlotte E. "Das Experiment des Königs. Europäische Migration und die Peuplierung Preußens am Beispiel der Salzburger Emigranten." In *Über die trockene Grenze und über das offene Meer*, edited by Mathias Beer and Dittmar Dahlmann, 67–90. Essen, 2004.

Haver, Charlotte E. *Von Salzburg nach Amerika. Mobilität und Kultur einer Gruppe religiöser Emigranten.* Paderborn, 2011.

Marsch, Angelika. *Die Salzburger Emigration in Bildern.* Weißenborn, 1977.

Reformation, Emigration. Protestanten in Salzburg. Katalog zur Ausstellung im Schloß Goldegg/Pongau, edited by the Salzburger Landesregierung. Salzburg, 1981.

Cross-references: Austria; Germany; The Netherlands; Russia and Belarus; Austrian Protestants (*Landler*) in Transylvania since the 18th Century; Huguenots in Europe since the 16th Century

SAVOYARD ITINERANT TRADERS AND MERCHANTS IN CENTRAL EUROPE IN THE EARLY MODERN PERIOD

Martin Zürn

Savoy (Lat. Sabaudia, Land of the Firs), developed in the Middle Ages into a duchy that was formally part of the Imperial Circle of Burgundy. After unification with Sardinia, Savoy became a kingdom in 1720 and remained such until 1860. It was divided into the northern regions or provinces of Chablais on the southern shore of Lake Geneva, Genevois, Faucigny along the Arbe as far as Montblanc, and Savoie Propre around Chambéry. In the center and south lay Tarentaise and Meurienne with important Alpine passes into the Savoyard territories of Val d'Aoste and Piedmont. Added to these was the County of Nizza. French dialects were prevalent. Here and there one could find islands of Alamannic language, especially in the settlements Issime and Gressoney on the Lyss south of the Monte Rosa. Migrants from these lands were often referred to disparagingly as "Savoyards." In Germany, moreover, they were often lumped together with representatives of other Romance languages under the derogatory collective name "Welsch."

Beginning in the late Middle Ages, one can find clear traces especially for the commercial migration of Savoyards in northern Switzerland, southern Germany, and the Alsace. Michal Saphoy is recorded as a foreman on church constructions in St. Gallen and Salem between 1418 and 1435. In 1442, Duke Louis of Savoy negotiated with the city of Strasbourg over the property of his subjects resident there. "Welsch spice dealers" were increasingly seen as competitors by the local merchant guilds. As a result, seasonal migration as well as definitive immigration were made more and more difficult through restrictive market regulations and the denial of petitions for naturalization. Ordinances in this regard are known from Salzburg (1525), Zurich (1539), and Basel (1546); after 1551 in Freiburg im Breisgau, a woman who married a "Welsch" man would be punished by losing her citizenship. Still, established Savoyard families in southern Germany were able to build up inter-regional trading companies. From the emigration of qualified and often wealthy Savoyards to Germany, the "German type" of Savoyard emigration, one must distinguish the "French type." To escape subsistence crises in the alpine regions, wars, and military service, day laborers and craftsmen took every job they could find in French cities, especially Lyon and Paris.

In the 18th century, 90% of the migrants from Savoy in Germany were presumably merchants and peddlers. They hailed mostly from Faucigny but also from Gressoney and the neighboring valleys in the Aosta region. Around 1750, 300 itinerant merchants supposedly remitted a total of 60,000 Savoyard livres (18,000 Reichsgulden) to their home community of Arâches in Faucigny, which was equivalent to 90% of all annual income of the individual residents. Such sums made it possible to import an adequate amount of grain. The constantly rising value of dowries in the 18th century, also among the lower classes, attests to a growing prosperity. The circulation of debt and rent notes solidified the social hierarchies at home.

There is not a uniform picture of how trade was organized and practiced. According to the literature, itinerant hucksters were subject to a strict honor code. They were to eschew all vices and sell their wares only for a specific patron. In the 18th and early 19th centuries, the company of Perrollaz-Cartier, whose partners had probably come directly from Savoy to Laufenburg on the upper Rhine, supplied the southern Black Forest with textiles and notions through their peddlers. For the early modern community, "Welsch" peddlers brought different kinds of stores on the road and reached the most remote farm. The Laufenburg company was probably among a group of independent enterprises that differed in their offerings and sales regions. To be sure, criminal files also reveal other practices. While on the road, the itinerant hucksters bought and sold at every opportunity and no doubt often on their own account. The estate inventories of some suddenly deceased traders show wares of every kind, balanced on the other side of the ledger by large debts to countrymen and German partners.

Migrants from certain communities or valleys (*Talschaften*) specialized as kettle makers, pewterers, harness makers, stone masons, bricklayers, and wood carvers – occupations, that is, for which one had to carry along relatively few tools and where the material was furnished at the place of work. In the second half of the 18th century, the rise of the Savoyard watch industry was combined with the distribution system of long-distance and peddling trade. The itinerant routes corresponded to the traditional transalpine trading routes of the early modern period. They led from the Val d'Aosta via central Switzerland or the Bünden passes to Zurich or Lake Constance and onward into the Allgäu, or via Geneva and Francophone Switzerland as well as via Basel down the Rhine, through the Black Forest, and down the Danube into the Habsburg monarchy.

The transition from seasonal migration to permanent emigration was fluid. Merchants, mostly from the circle of wealthy Savoy notables and farmers, recruited countrymen who found no employment in agriculture during the winter months for temporary work as peddlers in Germany. If they were successful, the peddlers extended their stay abroad, sometimes for several years. A former farmer could also pursue his business as a merchant or patron far from home in hostels and at markets for years, while his wife kept the farm back home running with the help of farmhands. This marital division of labor made possible a de facto independence – indeed, emancipation – of the Savoyard woman and paid for long periods of separation. Those who invested their profits in the civic rights of a German citizen were mostly younger, single men or widowers who wished to marry into the native population. By contrast, it was very rare for a Savoyard to apply for civic rights also for his Savoyard wife.

The possibility of permanent settlement depended also on confessional developments. Savoyard merchants in Augsburg and Konstanz had considerable influence in Protestant groups until the early 17th century. "Welsch" merchants are also recorded in Würrtemberg territories and in the interspersed Protestant cities – for example, Stuttgart and Esslingen. By contrast, the immigrants after 1648 were Catholic, with the exception of the Waldensians. They did not marry into the immigrant families of the prewar period. Rejected by Protestant city governments, they settled in Old Faith communities, such as Electoral Main or in lordships of the abbeys of Kempten and St. Gallen. On the whole, the territorial and confessional checkerboard in the southwest of the Empire and in northeastern Switzerland thus offered, in spite of considerable opposition from the local population, good prospects for local integration, especially after 1648. This is also shown by the enrollment lists of the Catholic universities of Freiburg im Breisgau, Dillingen, and Ingolstadt. They show Savoyard names in many small cities and market towns of Upper Swabia and Bavaria.

While the acquisition of civic rights and marriage into the local community were frequently hampered in German territories before 1648, after the Thirty Years' War, the marquisate of Baden, for example, sought to attract Savoyard shopkeepers and craftsmen by offering favorable conditions. In addition, the expansion of fortifications along the upper Rhine by France – e.g., Breisach and Freiburg – in the late 17th century attracted a good many shopkeepers, canteen proprietors, construction entrepreneurs, and construction craftsmen. However, most shied away from becoming citizens because of the costs involved and left the city again after its handover to Habsburg or the Empire. The mercantilist attitude of the territorial rulers favored the settlement of Savoyard and Genevan merchants, entrepreneurs, and workers in the second half of the 18th century, with no regard to their confession.

Once civic rights had been acquired, many families experienced a remarkable social advancement, which was even accelerated in times of crisis. Johan Georg Farket, the son of an immigrant, is recorded as Augsburg's mayor in 1639. In Freiburg im Breisgau, the merchant Karl Franz Montfort from Sallanches first became *Obristmeister* (1747) in the wake of unrest in the city, then *Schultheiß* (1756), and finally mayor (1766). Varied success was achieved by the Sarway families, who are recorded prior to the Thirty Year's War in the Catholic cities of Freiburg im Breisgau, Konstanz, Sigmaringen, Meßkirch, and Saulgau, as well as in Augsburg and in Protestant Tübingen. The descendants of the Savoyard merchant Nicolaus Sarwy (died 1614 in Tübingen) held communal, territorial, and church offices like their Catholic countrymen. These traditions reach into the educated burgher class of the 19th century, as exemplified by the lawyer Gottfried Gottlob August von Sarwey and his nephew, the minister of culture of Württemberg, Ernst Otto Claudius von Sarwey (1825–1900).

The marriage circles of immigrants who acquired citizen rights were accordingly shaped by the boundaries and opportunities offered by the urban society. On the High Rhine and the Upper Rhine, as well as along the Danube, those circles encompassed the local merchant elite, the respectable Germans (urban upper class) of neighboring territorial and residential cities, and, finally, the stratum of notables in the distant homeland. Statistically, marriage to a German woman citizen was dominant above all among immigrants of the first generation. The marriage of two spouses of Savoyard background for the most part presupposed that at least one family was integrated into the estate structure of Germany. For that reason, no regions of dense Savoyard settlement emerged within the territories. Savoyard settlement continuity in the city was tied to the intrafamilial transmission of properties. Those were often located at market squares and main roadways, had cellars and attics suitable for trading purposes, and were furnished with relatively comfortable furnishings. They confirmed the estate-identity of their owners.

It is difficult to track the cohesiveness of the Savoyards as an allochthonous group. Trade books, business correspondence, and bankruptcy files demonstrate the importance of economic geography and the fairs in Zurzach, Strasbourg, Frankfurt am Main, and Munich. They carried greater weight as against trading intertwinements with countrymen.

To be sure, there are clues to credit relationships between the homeland and the foreign lands, but their proportion of the total sales of the Savoyard merchant houses was usually not significant. The cooperation among countrymen may have been indirect, for example, in the form of agreements on how to divide up territories for itinerant trade. Relationships to customers in a city and its environs were dominated by small-scale credit.

The lion's share of the often rich inheritances was passed down locally within the core families. Although Savoyard rectories often owed their furnishings to the largess of the emigrants, many inventories of estates no longer list endowments for the old homeland. Thus, whether the trading activity promoted or loosened the cohesion among countrymen or relatives has not yet been clarified. On the whole, however, the success of Savoyard migrants was probably based on the dual integration into German urban society, on the one hand, and into the society notables of the home parish, on the other.

The strong Viennese *Landsmannschaft*, which formed under Prince Eugene of Savoy, the victor against the Turks, should be seen as a special case of Savoyard integration. Merchants imported luxury goods and semi-luxury foods for the court and therefore also became involved in important credit deals. On a smaller scale, Savoyards in the Breisgau organized military supplies, canal building, and mining. They were often related by marriage to Austrian officials in Freiburg im Breisgau, and the second or third generation of these immigrants entered into Austrian state service themselves.

While the self-perception of Savoyards as a mobile minority was fragile and multifaceted, the outside perception often remained negative. Official decrees as an element of the collective memory stereotypically denounced the less well-off peddlers as cheats and smugglers, in the wars of the 16th century even as marauders and arsonists. In the supplications of the merchants' guilds, one can identify a communalistic rhetoric that was based on the topoi of "sufficient livelihood" (for the locally resident shopkeepers) and the endangered common weal. Even well-established genuine Savoyard merchants like the Sautiers in Freiburg im Breisgau joined in these arguments. They thus placed familial, estate-based, and communal interests above possible allegiances to countrymen, and did so also – and especially – if the economic policy of the territorial ruler favored the immigration and naturalization of qualified and wealthy interested parties. Thus, the question about the communicative context in which Savoyards were present – positively or negatively – within the collective memory can be answered only by differentiating according to estate, family, and communal context. Some families responded to the assimilationist pressure that was unquestionably present by Germanizing their names. With the end of the Savoyard migration in Germany in the 19th century, the knowledge about its origins disappeared from the public into the private cultivation of tradition and into private genealogical research.

Fontaine, Laurence. *History of Pedlars in Europe*. Cambridge and Oxford, 1996.

Häberlein, Mark. "Savoyische Kaufleute und die Distribution von Konsumgütern im Oberrheingebiet, ca. 1720–1840." In *Geschichte des Konsums*, edited by Rolf Walter, 81–114. Stuttgart, 2004.

Häberlein, Mark, and Martin Zürn, eds. *Minderheiten, Obrigkeit und Gesellschaft in der Frühen Neuzeit. Integrations- und Abgrenzungsprozesse im süddeutschen Raum*. St. Katharinen, 2001.

Maistre, Chantal, Gilbert Maistre, and Georges Heitz. *Colporteurs et marchands savoyards dans l'Europe des XVIIe et XVIIIe siècles*. Annecy, 1992.

Raynaud, Franziska. *Savoyische Einwanderungen in Deutschland (15. bis 19. Jahrhundert)*. Neustadt an der Aisch, 2001.

Siddle, David J. "Migration as a Strategy of Accumulation: Social and Economic Change in 18th-Century Savoy." *Economic History Review* 50 (1997): 1–20.

Cross-references: France; Germany; Italy; Switzerland

SAXON JOURNEYMEN PURSE MAKERS IN VIENNA IN THE 18TH AND 19TH CENTURIES

Annemarie Steidl

In the old craft trades in central Europe, a period of tramping was a fixed element in the life of journeymen in nearly all crafts. Even after the official abolition of compulsory tramping, it was virtually constant as a phase in the lives of journeymen in many craft trades. This journeymen migration can be described as a multiyear phase in a circular mobility, during which times of wandering alternated with shorter and longer periods of employment in a city. While it can be assumed that for most journeymen the search for work was paramount in their wanderings, it alone does not adequately describe the various migration routes.

Vienna, until about the middle of the 19th century the largest commercial center in the German-speaking lands, was an important migration destination for workers in the most diverse trades. It does not seem far-fetched to assume that at least three-quarters of all journeymen working in Vienna in the 18th and 19th century were migrants. The area from which Viennese craftsmen were drawn extended over the entire German-speaking region, as well as into northern Italy and modern-day Slovenia and Croatia; France, too, was tied into the widely cast network. So far, scholarship has paid little attention to the larger Hungarian realm as well as Ukraine and Russia, which were also among the regions of origin.

The labor market for craft trades was regionally segmented – strictly speaking, every craft had its own area from which it drew its workers. In the 18th and 19th centuries, the region of origin of journeymen in the Viennese purse-making trade, which hardly exists today, was especially the

Kingdom of Saxony. In such specialized trades, which usually had a small number of masters and journeymen who often covered long distances, there were intensive contacts among the journeymen but also with individual masters. These migration networks contributed to the development of occupation-specific migration routes in various craft industries – in this case, those of the Saxon purse makers to Vienna – and they often lasted for centuries.

Purse making was one of those small, specialized craft trades that existed only in cities and which have had a lasting impact in shaping the perception of the world of old crafts. Only in a large city such as Vienna was there sufficient demand for its products, while villages and small towns usually had too few customers for such a specialized craft. In addition to the production of purses, trunks, backpacks, and similar containers, indicated by the name of the trade, covering chairs with leather was part of the product palette of the purse-making trade. In their workshops, purse makers worked with many materials other than leather, such as wood, metals for fittings, and cloth for lining purses.

The Viennese purse-making trade can be traced back to the 14th century; the first master, Heinrich Jans, is mentioned as early as 1367. As late as the 17th century, only four workshops in Vienna were engaged in the craft of purse making. While the number of workshops rose substantially until the 18th century, thereafter it remained fairly stable, compared to other trades, until the middle of the 19th century. A Viennese trade survey in 1736 named 15 purse-making workshops; a hundred years later, their number had risen to merely 18. Beginning in the middle of the 19th century, the growing industrialization, with the introduction of new production techniques, invigorated the purse-making trade. The number of Viennese purse-making enterprises more than doubled between 1847 and 1870, and we can also note a change in the product palette, which was now shaped above all by travel articles for a supralocal market.

Because of the broad dispersion of trade locations, the purse-making trade required a supraregional labor market for journeymen. In contrast to other trades, for example, the butcher's trade – in the 19th century more than 35% of journeymen butchers had been born in Vienna – the employment of journeymen purse makers tied to a locality was rarely found. Immigration from the immediate surroundings (*Umland*) was usually also insignificant – in the 18th and 19th centuries, more than 80% of journeymen purse makers had immigrated from further afield.

The surviving *Gesellenprotokolle* (journeymen records) for the period 1724–1859 provide information about the origin region of 435 journeymen purse makers. According to these data, more than half of all journeymen who migrated to Vienna came from regions of modern-day Germany, especially from the Kingdom of Saxony: 113 journeymen (26%) indicated that they had been born there or had completed their apprenticeship there. Immigrants from Saxony were found in all Viennese workshops that employed journeymen

between 1801 and 1830. The master purse maker Johann Stephan, for example, employed an above-average number of Saxon journeymen: between 1811 and 1830, 21 of the 37 journeymen in his workshop were from Saxony. In the shop of Johann Lerch, as well, which was later run by his widow Theresia, 8 of 19 journeymen between 1808 and 1829 had immigrated from Saxony.

The migration patterns of the journeymen purse makers, which remained fairly stable over centuries, can be traced back to the end of the 16th century. Between 1591 and 1724, 65% of the journeymen purse makers employed in Vienna originated from what is today Germany, and a mere 9% were natives of Vienna. In the last decade of the 16th century, journeymen were still migrating from the entire territory of the Reich, including the far north; only the Thirty Years' War led to a change in the directions of migration. At the beginning of the 17th century, the area from which they were drawn shifted toward Saxony, and the kingdom became the most important region of origin for journeymen purse makers alongside Silesia, Franconia, and Bavaria. The traditional migratory system of journeymen that still existed in the 18th century, supraterritorial and encompassing the guild system of the entire Old Reich, was replaced in the wake of industrialization by the emergence of labor markets within state borders. But those, too, retained an institutional and guild imprint. However, while in most Viennese trades the region of origin for journeymen shifted increasingly to Bohemia and Moravia, the share of Saxon journeymen among all those employed in the Viennese purse makers' workshops rose to 32%.

As with many other commercial products, the demand for the goods produced by purse makers was seasonal. For journeymen this meant alternating between phases of low work intensity or complete idleness and times of heavy exertion in the workshops. Journeymen were well informed about seasonal fluctuations in their particular trade and adjusted their times of migration to the demand. March, June, and October developed into peak months for the influx of journeymen purse makers into Vienna. Nearly half of the Saxon journeymen entered the city gates during these months. New journeymen arrived in April, August, and November. Since purse makers represented a trade that was fairly contained in terms of numbers even in the 19th century, the city's labor market was strongly regulated by the guild. Upon their arrival in the city, journeymen were expected to report to the guild-owned lodgings, which were in the house of the chosen guild master, and to remain there until they began their employment.

According to the Register of Arriving and Departing Journeymen, which had to be kept by the lodging-house father, the guild master, between 1 and 17 journeymen passed through Vienna's city gates in search for work each year between 1801 and 1830. Because this number was so small compared to the mass trades, it was not necessary in the purse-making trade to rent one's own lodging-house, where laborers were also recruited. Work sites were assigned to the journeymen in the house of the guild master. The names of the masters who needed an additional worker appeared on a posted list. Journeymen purse makers who came to Vienna on their wanderings had no difficulties finding a job in the city. Most spent only a day or two in the lodging-house and then moved on to the house of their employer. The guild statutes prohibited journeymen from circumventing this regulated allocation of work to search out a workshop on their own.

Most journeymen purse makers worked in the shops only for short periods, for the most part measured in days or weeks rather than months. At the same time, however, the range remained exceedingly broad, so that multiyear work relationships were not impossible. Leaving a job did not invariably mean leaving the city. Journeymen repeatedly changed workshops also within Vienna. On 13 June 1811, Karl Friedrich Brieser, who had completed his apprenticeship in Leipzig, put his name down in the register as someone in search of a job. Only a day later he found employment in the workshop of Leopold Stephan, located in the district of Leopoldstadt. That work relationship lasted nearly five years, until 20 May 1816. That September he was already working in the shop of the widow Theresia Nebe, which was also located in Leopoldstadt. The sources provide no information about where journeyman Brieser spent his time between May and September 1816. The job with widow Nebe was not of long duration, however, as he left Vienna on 11 October. After two years for which we have no information, Karl Friedrich Brieser worked another month in the purse-making workshop of Stephan Leopold.

One journeyman who changed employers especially frequently was Friedrich Adolph Möglich from Leipzig. He first arrived in Vienna in May 1808 and began working on 1 June in the shop of Johann Nebe in Braunhirschengrund, a suburb of Vienna. That same year he switched to the workshop of Master Johan Schäffler in the inner city. After a longer period, about which the sources provide no information, journeyman Möglich was entered again in the Viennese lodging book in September 1815 as looking for work, and he found employment once more with master purse maker Schäffer until January 1816. Subsequently, he moved to the shop of Franz Pschürrer at the Neustift, though he stayed there only for two weeks. He then took another job with master Leopold Stephan, in whose services he remained for four months, until 16 June 1816. Möglich left Vienna at the beginning of August 1816, and we have no further information about his subsequent career.

Looking for work in Vienna thus by no means led to a permanent stay for the journeymen from Saxony. Only one of the immigrant Saxons entered in the Viennese journeymen book is later found in the civic book of masters (*Meisterbuch*): the purse maker Johann Gottliebe Nebe from Leipzig, registered in 1788 as a journeyman, ran a workshop as *Landmeister* (master, located in the suburb) in the Viennese suburb of Braunhirschengrund beginning in 1800. On 25 October 1812, he took over the shop of Franz Wiesner and became a civic master in the district of Leopoldstadt. However, he headed this shop for only three years, since he died in 1815. His widow, Theresia, continued to run the business successfully for 20 years, until 1835. At various times and for various periods, 18 different journeymen worked in this shop. Only one other Saxon can be documented in the civic book of masters: the name of Christian Gottliebe Hoffmann was entered in 1762; in 1769 he was *Obervorsteher* (chief warden) of the guild.

Merely a tenth of the journeymen purse makers who immigrated in the 18th and 19th centuries later rose to become independent masters in Vienna. Although studies have shown that the bequest from father to son tended to have little significance in the continuation of a workshop, in the purse-making trade the sons of masters were clearly preferred over the migrants. This strongly reduced the chances for immigrant Saxons to set themselves up as independent masters. However, studies of German small-scale trades have also shown that in many trades in the 19th century, the social situation of the unmarried, flexible, and uncommitted journeymen was far more favorable than that of independent producers.

Even though Saxon journeymen purse makers accounted for only a tiny fraction of the many immigrants to Vienna in the 18th and 19th centuries, their example can be used to trace an occupation-specific migration pattern shaped by large fluctuation and few opportunities to open a workshop. While Vienna's master chimney sweeps, for example, came for centuries mostly from the Italian-speaking part of Switzerland, and these immigrants had a firm grip on the trade, Saxon immigrants left behind no permanent traces in the modern city.

Bräuer, Helmut. "Zur Wanderungsmotivation sächsischer Handwerksgesellen im 15. und 16. Jahrhundert. Quellenbefund – theoretische Erörterung – Hypothesen." In *Migration in der Feudalgesellschaft*, edited by Gerhard Jaritz and Albert Müller, 217–32. Frankfurt am Main and New York, 1988.

Ehmer, Josef. "Tramping Artisans in 19th-Century Vienna." In *Migration, Mobility, and Modernisation*, edited by David Siddle, 164–85. Liverpool, 2000.

Reith, Reinhold. "Arbeitsmigration und Gruppenkultur deutscher Handwerksgesellen im 18. und frühen 19. Jahrhundert." *Scripta Mercaturae* 23, 1/2 (1989): 1–35.

Steidl, Annemarie. *Auf nach Wien! Die Mobilität des mitteleuropäischen Handwerks im 18. und 19. Jahrhundert am Beispiel der Haupt- und Residenzstadt*. Vienna and Munich, 2003.

Wadauer, Sigrid. "Journeymen's Mobility and the Guild System: A Space of Possibilities Based on Central European Cases." In *Guilds and Associations in Europe, 900–1900*, edited by Ian A. Gadd and Patrick Wallis, 169–85. London, 2007.

Cross-references: Austria; Germany; Alpine Chimney Sweeps in Western, Central, and Southern Europe from the 16th to the Early 20th Century

SCOTTISH SOLDIERS IN EUROPE IN THE EARLY MODERN PERIOD

Steve Murdoch

In the early modern period large areas of Scotland remained largely martial in nature. The Highlands, the northeast, and the Border areas of Scotland all contained traditional kin-based armed societies. About half the population lived within these areas and, to some degree or another, were bound by a series of military alliances with or against their neighbors. The large number of Scots with military experience within the country worried the central government, but also provided the country with a depth of experienced military manpower out of proportion to its population. Many of these engaged in mercenary service, particularly in Ireland. Others were self-confessed mercenaries-for-hire on the international labor market. Large-scale military migrations to the European continent, however, most often reflected the political aspirations of the monarchy or Scottish parliament.

Scottish soldiers could be found fighting in the armies of most European powers either as individuals, in small groups, or in larger formations, including entire armies. These military migrations of the early modern period occurred in the post-1560 years as Scotland sought to ensure that her new Reformed religion became firmly established in the nation. Indeed, it is not coincidental that in the post-Reformation era the location of Scottish troops frequently mirrored a desire to strike up an alliance with a similarly Reformed state, such as the Dutch Republic, or at least nations likely to resist any attempt at a Counter-Reformation within Europe like Denmark-Norway and Sweden. Although traditional Catholic allies such as France continued to receive token military support from Scotland, larger migrations, as occurred during the 1635–42 French war against the Holy Roman Empire, required the motivation of mutual benefit to mainstream Scottish political objectives – the prevention of Habsburg hegemony in Europe. While the period of the Thirty Years' War (1618–48) undoubtedly saw the largest movement of Scottish military migrants to Europe, it by no means encompassed the phenomenon in its entirety.

Patterns of migration to the continent

Between 1573 and 1579 some 3,100 Scots were levied for service in the Low Countries to assist in the fight against Catholic Spain. Shortly after, a permanent Scotch-Dutch brigade was formed, which remained in service until the end of the 18th century. This brigade of three regiments not only ensured improved relations between the two states but also provided for a Scottish element in resisting the Counter-Reformation without actually having to commit Scotland directly to war against Spain. These regiments, like those that followed into continental service thereafter, brought with them chaplains to preach the Scottish interpretation of Calvinism in their own languages, particularly Scots, but also Gaelic. Thus the religious rationale for service and links with home were maintained throughout the life of the regiment.

Contemporaneously with the origins of the Scotch-Dutch, Scots also became a regular component of Scandinavian armies. The presence of some 1,600 Scots soldiers in Sweden was complicated by the reestablishment of the Scottish-Danish alliance of 1589, which included a mutual commitment to support their ally in all her wars. This created the likelihood of Scots facing each other in opposing armies – privately enlisted soldiers standing against an official allied force sent by their own sovereign. During the intra-Scandinavian Kalmar War (1611–13), additional clauses were added to those warrants for private contractors allowing them to recruit and serve only in armies that were not hostile to the Stuarts or their allies. With Scots soldiers now regularly engaged in France, the Dutch Republic, and the Scandinavian kingdoms, patterns of service and loyalty emerged that lasted throughout the early modern period. These countries all participated in the Thirty Years' War to various degrees and in doing so brought Scotsmen into the heart of the areas of conflict in central Europe.

When Elector Frederick of the Palatinate accepted the throne of Bohemia in defiance of the soon-to-be Habsburg emperor, Ferdinand II, war ensued. With the defeat at the hands of the Catholic League at the Battle of White Mountain in 1620, Frederick lost the Bohemian crown as well as his territory and position as *Kurfürst*, or prince-elector of the Holy Roman Empire. Frederick's marriage to Elizabeth Stuart, daughter of James VI, led some 50,000 Scots to volunteer for the protracted war to reinstate Elizabeth and her family to their electoral and regal titles. However, the army of Count Mansfeld, which included many Scottish mercenaries, disintegrated before reaching the theater of war in 1625. Having observed the decimation of Mansfeld's force by inept leadership and disease, the Scottish nobility decided that they no longer wished to participate in private ventures and even balked at future joint initiatives with the English.

As a result, they opted to levy and supply their own forces that were to serve under the leadership of Christian IV of Denmark-Norway. By March 1627, patents were issued to raise 9,000 Scots for Danish-Norwegian service. They joined 2,000 Scots already in Danish service. Perhaps more important than the numerical contribution was their role in the military command. Between 1625 and 1629, over 300 Scottish officers joined the army of Christian IV, outnumbering indigenous officers by three to one. Twenty-five of them held the rank of major or above while two became generals: Robert Scott and the Earl of Nithsdale. The efforts of the Danish army against Ferdinand came to naught and Christian IV retired from the war in 1629 through the Treaty of Lübeck. This treaty paved the way for Swedish intervention and many of the remaining Scots in Denmark transferred to the Swedish army.

By late 1630 some 12,000 Scots could be found in Swedish service and recruiting continued throughout the period.

Between 1624 and 1660 the Scots produced eight field marshals and generals, over 70 colonels and 50 lieutenant colonels, providing a military pedigree the Swedes themselves found hard to match. By the war's end in 1648, some 30,000 had fought in Germany on behalf of Sweden.

It was not only Protestant states that attempted to fend off Habsburg hegemony in Europe; any Catholic state that joined in could expect support from Scottish military units. Venice became one recipient of several thousand Scottish soldiers in the 1630s and 1640s. When Franco-Habsburg relations deteriorated and France entered the war on the same side as Sweden, Scots arrived in France. All three Scottish regiments that entered French service between 1632 and 1654 were led by Catholics. However, as Cardinal Richelieu noted, the majority of the troops were Presbyterian and the anti-Habsburg motive highlighted in earlier Scottish participation remained relevant in French service. The Scottish troops in France also served as a sweetener to ensure that France remained out of the conflict developing in Scotland between the Stuart monarchy and the Presbyterian Covenanters, who opposed a centralized religious order. When the Scottish and English King Charles I attempted to implement the Anglican church order in Scotland, Scottish troops invaded England, which culminated in the civil conflict known as the Bishops' Wars (1639–41).

By 1648, warrants for 10,320 Scottish soldiers for French service had been issued. Soon after the Treaty of Westphalia, all remaining Scottish units were merged and continued to serve as the Régiment de Douglas. They were, however, effectively barred from returning home as Scotland had been occupied by England in 1651, effectively making refugees of significant numbers of Scottish soldiers abroad. While most returned to traditional countries of service in Scandinavia and the Low Countries, some put themselves up for hire to whoever would pay them. Thus, high-profile individuals like General Patrick Gordon in Russia or colonels John Mollison and Andrew Melville in Germany became famous internationally for their military service.

Since the fortunes of the Royalist Party were in decline in Scotland in the mid-1640s, individual officers traveled across Europe with commissions from Charles I. They sought enlistment in countries friendly to the Stuart monarchy and wanted work abroad, where they could wait for a turn in the fortunes of their king at home. This led to some regiments such as the Bergenhus in Norway being commanded by a Scottish Royalist officer cadre overseeing indigenous Norwegian troops. By the 1650s, it was not just Royalists who found themselves in this position. Scots of all persuasions looked to escape the "Cromwellian Usurpation" and, indeed, the option of foreign service over imprisonment was offered by the English authorities to those Scots still in open arms as an enticement to end their uprising. Some 4,000 Scotsmen went to Sweden while other smaller groups went to France and Poland-Lithuania.

From the Stuart Restoration of 1660 until the period following the defeat of the Jacobites in 1746, various political groups held power in Scotland, resulting in streams of military refugees to the Continent. As the Stuarts returned to power in 1660, their erstwhile enemies left the country. This pattern repeated itself after William of Orange gained the "vacant" Scottish throne in 1689, leading to an exodus of Stuart supporters (more famously known as the Jacobites) to the Continent. These enlisted in various numbers in armies as far apart as Russia, Sweden, France, and Spain. However, despite the presence in Europe of several hundred Jacobite officers, the age of mass Scottish overseas enlistment had come to an end. After the establishment of the UK in 1707, the majority of Scottish servicemen fought around the world within the British armed forces. The last regular Scottish military force in continental Europe not under British control was one of the first established, the Scots-Dutch brigade, "nationalized" as a Dutch regiment in 1782.

Return migration

It is very hard to ascertain whether those who left Scotland ever intended to return or whether they saw their military migration as temporary. In any case, most never saw their homeland again. Through a combination of disease, combat, and shipwreck, rates of attrition were extremely high. William Lithgow, the widely traveled author, noted in 1633 that 12,000 out of 13,500 Scots in Danish service were killed between 1626 and 1629 alone. Nonetheless, it was not unexceptional for a Scottish mercenary to return to Scotland after lengthy periods of military service abroad. Field Marshal Alexander Leslie served in Sweden for some 30 years before he led several hundred other Scots back to Scotland to form the Army of the Covenant in 1638 to fight against Charles I. This case serves to highlight that lengthy foreign employment, even when rewarded by land and title, did not remove or displace an interest in their homeland for many of the Scottish professional soldiers. Indeed, they were prepared to risk all they had gained in demonstration of that fact.

Military chaplains in Sweden like Robert Douglas were in constant contact with the Kirk (church) in Scotland and delivered sermons aimed at persuading the soldiers of the just cause of the Covenanters. Indeed, Douglas went on to act as Moderator of the Kirk of Scotland after his return with Leslie. A similar, though less successful, return migration was orchestrated from abroad by Scottish veterans in 1649 under James Graham, the Marquis of Montrose, who was keen to dislodge the government put in place by Leslie's efforts a decade earlier. Thus, they proved that not all Scots in foreign service sang from the same hymn sheet. Indeed, Montrose's chaplain, George Wishart, fled Scotland to join the Dutch Brigade as chaplain and to preach to the Scottish congregation at Schiedam.

Two further attempts were launched on Scotland from abroad. One in 1685 by a Calvinist refugee army led by the Duke of Argyll spectacularly failed. However, the arrival in

Britain of the Scots-Dutch Brigade with William of Orange in 1688–90 ultimately saw the original idea of the brigade – the protection of Protestantism in Europe – achieve its goal in Scotland (and England) as it swept aside the forces of the last Catholic Stuart monarch, James VII and II. In doing so, it completed the Presbyterian settlement of Scotland which Leslie's army sought to achieve in 1639 and paved the way for the Treaty of Union of 1707.

Patterns of integration

Aside from Scottish veterans who returned with some political purpose, other soldiers simply retired to their homeland during times of relative peace within Scotland. For some, the allure of the Continent prevented their return, particularly those holding land grants as rewards for service. For many, there were more advantages to be gained by remaining abroad and exploiting the opportunities afforded them by their new estates than there would have been in returning to Scotland. This is highlighted by the numbers of Scots ennobled in foreign service compared to those who were ennobled for their service in Scotland. Several hundred Scots were promoted to the continental peerage throughout the 17th century with some 140 Scots and their children in Sweden alone. This is a number well in excess of those raised into the Scottish or English peerage in the same time period and this did not go unnoticed among the soldiering class. It may help to explain the preference for Swedish service over Danish-Norwegian, where only six Scottish families made it into the peerage.

Where these men can be traced, we find them integrating into their host societies, though often retaining a sense of community with fellow Scots, whether merchants or fellow soldiers. In Russia, for most of the 17th century, this meant a conversion to Orthodoxy, as in the case of Michael Monteith. However, most individuals preferred to maintain their own brand of faith and continued to attend Scottish churches, like those in Rotterdam or Kedainiai in Lithuania. Where no Scottish congregation existed, Reformed "English" churches were sought, such as those at Elbing near Danzig and Amsterdam where Scottish chaplains frequently preached. German or Dutch Reformed churches also provided good substitutes, such as Christina Kyrka in Gothenburg. However, the first Roman Catholic church in Russia was established by two Scottish soldiers, Patrick Gordon and Paul Menzies, who were determined not to convert to Orthodoxy.

Examination of existing church records, Scottish Kirk or otherwise, is revealing as to other indicators of integration, such as marriage patterns. For those countries where research on the subject has been done (Sweden and the Dutch Republic), it appears that Scots initially preferred to marry among their own nation, although no single pattern can be discerned. Some married within Scottish military families, others into the wider Scottish mercantile community. The greatest number, however, married outside their own community. For instance, Dutch marriage statistics show only a third of Scots marrying fellow Scots, the rest marrying foreigners. Swedish patterns, in contrast, show that nearly 60% of Scots married women from their own country. The discrepancy may reflect the focus of the Swedish survey on officers while the Dutch statistic takes into account marriage patterns of the entire regiment. Further, the Swedish statistic shows that specific families selected partners from other specific families with several brothers and sisters in order to cement the bond between the families.

Considering marriage patterns and trends of return migration, it is possible to conclude that the majority of soldiers retained a very distinct identity in foreign service. Not only did they gain a reputation as reliable and skilled soldiers during their overseas employment but they also demonstrated a tangible loyalty to their home country through their repeated efforts to influence the political destiny of their native land. Drawn from the few early modern texts relating to the subject, it seems that a sense of "Scottishness" could survive for several generations within the host community. However, the processes of naturalization and intermarriage meant that one's surname often remained the only marker of Scottish heritage. At the beginning of the 21st century, there are no surviving communities that can be traced back to the great migration of Scottish soldiers in the early modern period. This group of migrants, however, remains present in the cultural memory of the host countries, as is evident in the number of Scottish street and place names in Russia, Scandinavia, and Germany. However, given the large Scottish mercantile community, it remains uncertain whether such place names can be traced back specifically to the presence of Scottish soldiers.

Ameer-Ali, Torick, ed. *Memoirs of Sir Andrew Melvill and the Wars of the 17th Century*. London, 1918.

Dow, Alexander C. *Ministers to the Soldiers of Scotland*. Edinburgh, 1962.

Fischer, Thomas A. *The Scots in Germany*. Edinburgh, 1903.

Fischer, Thomas A. *The Scots in Sweden*. Edinburgh, 1907.

Grosjean, Alexia. *An Unofficial Alliance: Scotland and Sweden 1596–1654*. Leiden, 2003.

Monro, Robert. Monro. *His Expedition with the Worthy Scots Regiment Called Mac-keys*. Westport and London, 1999.

Murdoch, Steve, ed. *Scotland and the Thirty Years' War 1618–1648*. Leiden, 2001.

Murdoch, Steve. *Britain, Denmark-Norway and the House of Stuart 1603–1660: A Diplomatic and Military Analysis*. East Linton, 2003.

Murdoch, Steve, and Andrew Mackillop, eds. *Fighting for Identity: Scottish Military Experiences c. 1550–1900*. Leiden, 2002.

Cross-references: Belgium and Luxembourg; France; Great Britain; The Netherlands; Northern Europe; Jacobites in Europe, 1688–1788; Scottish Traders and Merchants in East-Central Europe in the Early Modern Period

SCOTTISH TRADERS AND MERCHANTS IN EAST-CENTRAL EUROPE IN THE EARLY MODERN PERIOD

Andreas Kossert

In the 16th and 17th centuries, the word "Scot" (German: *Schotte*) stood in the southern region of the Baltic Sea for a peddler crisscrossing the land (*institor circumforaneus*). The word had a negative connotation, which was lost only gradually with the integration of the Scots in the German and Polish linguistic and cultural sphere. In many areas of east-central Europe, the terms *Schotte* and *Kellerschotte* were synonyms for foreign small-scale merchants and shopkeepers. In the Prussian port cities of Danzig (Gdánsk), Elbing (Elblag), Königsberg (Kaliningrad), and Memel (Klaipeda), in the Duchy of Prussia, and in the Kingdom of Prussia as a whole, but also in the other territories of the Polish crown, Scots dominated this sector of the economy in some areas. As late as 1741, Frisch gave this definition in his German-Latin dictionary: *Schott, ein landfahrender Krämer* (Scot, a traveling hawker), and in Grimm's German Dictionary we read: *Schotte, herumziehender Krämer, Hausierer, Landfahrer* (Scot, migrant hawker, peddler, vagrant). Apart from these "traveling Scots," there were also Scottish mercenaries and Scottish merchants and tradesmen in the Baltic region who lived in the cities.

The Scottish traders stood outside the guild system. They were the target of envy of guild-traders and guild-merchants who sought to make their social integration difficult. Scottish hawkers enjoyed an excellent reputation in the peddling business especially among the rural population. Their activity in this economic sector survived in the Cashubian dialect to this day, where "*Szot*" means simply "trader"; if people spoke of "Scottish wares," they meant knives, scissors, boxes, and pots.

Lively trading connections between the Baltic region shaped by the Hanseatic League and the British Isles already existed from the High Middle Ages on. Especially the ports along Scotland's eastern coast – Aberdeen, Dundee, St. Andrews, Leith, and Berwick – maintained close contacts with their Hanseatic counterparts. For Scotland, east-central Europe's hinterland was of particular interest as a supplier of wood and grain. The large Baltic seaports thus had a wide presence in the Scottish trading community in the 16th century, which meant that many migrants were familiar with their destinations at least from stories.

Migration, however, did not reach its climax until the 16th and then especially the 17th century. It was primarily economic and social factors, and not religious reasons as previously believed, that drove the Scots to seek their fortune abroad. The chronicler of the Scottish migration to the east, Theodor Fischer, wrote that Poland was "the America of those days." Interest in east-central Europe dried up with the beginning of Scottish overseas emigration. Still, the magnitude of the European migration was considerable. Around 1600, Scotland had a population of just under a million.

Estimates about the number of Scots who emigrated to ducal and royal Prussia as well as to Poland-Lithuania since the 16th century range from about 15,000 to 40,000. The real number was probably much higher still, since many traveling hawkers were never registered. The immigrants hailed especially from the class of small landowners (*Lairds*), though they also came from the cities of Scotland's eastern coast.

Unlike the hawkers who crisscrossed the land with their wares, many of the Scottish merchants who settled in the cities of east-central Europe came from wealthy families. Although they were seeking their fortune in foreign lands, they continued to cultivate close contacts to their Scottish homeland. Their assimilation occurred in the second or third generation. Family names like Taylor, Wallace, Motherby, Crawford, Ross, or Morris often appeared in Prussia in a Germanicized and in Poland in a Polacized form: to this day one can find in Poland Makaliński (Macauly), Górski (Gore), or Tailorowicz (Taylor). Place and field names point to former Scottish inhabitants: Alt-Schottland as a suburb of Gdansk, the villages of Schottland near Lauenburg (Lębork) and Bromberg (Bydgoszcz) are reminders, as are the townships of Nowa Szkocja, Skotna Góra, Szkockie Wzgórza, Scotówka, Szotniki, and Szoty, and in Gdansk Szkocka Gróbla, Pasaż Szkocki, and Brama Douglasa. Until 1628, Elbing alone was home to about 170 Scottish and English families. Between 1577 and 1709, no fewer than 135 Scots were given citizenship rights in Gdansk. That is why one Englishman remarked about Gdansk in 1734 that one got the impression that "indeed a better half of the Families or Inhabitants are of Scotch Extraction."

From the perspective of the native population, the Scots held a monopoly in the peddler trade. And in fact many Scotsmen did travel as traders to fairs and traversed the land to sell their hawkers' wares. The presence of Scottish traders aroused the envy of the local competition early on. As peddlers, hawkers, and hucksters, the Scots were initially prohibited from acquiring houses and lived in cellars, which is why they were also called *Kellerschotten* (cellar Scots). Those who worked as peddlers and sold their wares from chests that were called *Paudel* in the East Prussian dialect were referred to as *Paudelschotten* in the Duchy of Prussia. That many Scotsmen were absorbed into the lower classes of the urban population is revealed by the term *Kellerschotte*, which was later used in Prussia to designate no longer a nationality but a certain economic and social status.

Envy and suspicion from the outside strengthened the internal cohesiveness of the Scots. However, the bond within the ethnic community resulted not only from their outsider status in east-central Europe but represented also a normal part of their native tradition and formed an element of the clan system. Linked to this was the development and cultivation of a group identity, whereby their self-image, as surviving correspondence shows, was closely shaped by references to their various regions of origin. After the Union of Parliaments and the creation of Great Britain in 1707, the notion of forming a community of origin manifested itself in the founding of the Brotherhood of the Esteemed Nation of Great Britain (Brüderschaft Hochlöblicher Groß-Brittannischer Nation). In its new environment, the Scottish community, which was characterized by the rapid increase in the number of Scottish merchants in the Prussian port cities, developed a social dynamic that accelerated its acculturation. They soon held honorary offices in city organizations, churches, and guilds, and distinguished themselves by their generous donations in the social and educational realms. Tilsit (Sovietsk) had a British Brotherhood with poor relief as early as 1667. One person who was socially active in his new homeland was Alexander Chalmers (Polish: Czamer), who had converted to Catholicism and served three terms as the mayor of the Polish capital of Warsaw. George Tepper-Ferguson, a delegate to the Polish parliament, laid the foundation for a banking empire. His son Bernard, honorary citizen of Edinburgh, donated the Protestant Church of the Holy Trinity in Warsaw.

On the outside the visible sign of their foreignness was above all the Reformed creed. The Reformed faith was equally opposed in Catholic Poland and in strictly Lutheran Prussia. It was not until 20 October 1616 that the adherents of this faith were given permission in Prussia to deliver the first Reformed sermon. The Reformed congregations in the Duchy of Prussia owed their existence largely to the Scots and the Dutch. The fight against the Anabaptists, Sacramentarians, and other denominations arose chiefly from the pious zeal of the Orthodox Lutherans. The city council of Königsberg denied citizenship to all adherents of the Reformed faith. In 1667, the city of Posen granted the right of citizenship to three Scotsmen – Jacobus Joachimus Watson, George Edislay from Newbattle, and Wilhelmus Aberkrambi (Abercrombie) from Aberdeen – on the condition that they attend the sermon in the Catholic church of St. Magdalen on Sundays and feast days and join the Roman church within a year. Eventually, many Reformed Scots converted to Lutheranism or Catholicism in the course of the 18th century, another central step in the integration process after the adoption of the local language.

A register of names from 1615 lists no fewer than 410 Scotsmen in the Duchy of Prussia who "are engaged with hawker's wares." The list *Sämbtlicher Crähmer auß Churfstl. Stadt Mümmell* (All hawkers from the electoral city of Memel) from 1668 contains only three non-Scotsmen among the 13 names. Countless decrees by city councils and edicts threatened the Scots with confiscation of their wares, jail, and expulsion from the land. In the Prussian territorial law of 1640, Scots were allowed to offer their wares in cities only at fairs. In the Kingdom of Prussia, an edict from 1552 that was renewed in 1636 decreed that "the itinerant Scots and other *Paudelkrämer* should not be tolerated or condoned" anywhere, neither in the countryside nor in the cities. The law of Rastenburg (Kętrzyn) prohibited the influx of Scotsmen and also stipulated that "no Scotsman shall be given here in Rastenburg the right of citizenship in the old manner." In Prussian Christburg (Dzierzgoń) a case of ethnic

discrimination is on record: a Scottish new citizen by name of Donaldson was told that he could enter into a marriage only with a German woman; otherwise he would lose his privileges.

Negative stereotypes were not infrequently aimed at Scots and Jews alike: itinerant traders who made life difficult for the honorable, Christian (Lutheran or Roman Catholic) merchants who were members of guilds. Stereotypes of the "Jewish peddler" or the "itinerant gypsy," of the kind that existed in many parts of Europe until the beginning of the 20th century, applied in early modern east-central Europe above all to the Scots. Jews and Scots were jointly mentioned in many edicts. On 12 September 1594, King Sigismund III confirmed the city of Kcyna the exclusion of Scots and Jews as foreign bodies from the urban community (*a Judaeis, Scotis et aliis ceteris vagis hominibus*). In 1699, King August II renewed for the city of Kosten (Kościan) in Greater Poland the old anti-Scottish laws that prohibited them from acquiring land in the city, because they were *a religione Romana Catholica dissidentes*.

Official British agencies evidently felt the need to counteract the negative perception of their countrymen in Prussia. To that end, the British envoy in Danzig and Prussia, Patrick Gordon, penned 80 *Articuli pro Scotis in Ducatis Prussia* in 1616. In these he enjoined the Scots to adhere strictly to codes of honor and to join together into religious brotherhoods. It was especially the suspicion of fraud and dishonest dealings that Gordon sought to dispel in several articles titled *De falsis aut corruptis mercibus et injusta mensura*. At the same time, the Scots self-confidently used the new corporate network through brotherhoods or religious communities to defend themselves against discrimination.

The documents that have been studied to date point solely to an economic migration from Scotland. This concurs with a statement by the bishop of Glasgow, who was at the court of the Polish king on an official mission in 1574 and after his return assured Queen Mary of the urgency of his mandate by noting that "outside France there was no country under the sun where the Queen's subjects traded more by sea than Poland, especially Danzig." As numerous wills attest, many Scots in east-central Europe maintained close ties with their country of origin until the end of the 17th century.

For a long time, the pioneering migrants of the Scots remained a minority to which largely negative characteristics were attributed. It was only in subsequent generations that their reputation improved. This also went hand in hand – in the third generation, at the latest – with their assimilation into the German- or Polish-speaking cultural sphere, which often also entailed a change in religious confession. The Scottish Brotherhoods and religious communities finally disbanded in the 18th century, so that family and place names were the only reminders of the Scottish migration to east-central Europe in the early modern period.

Cornwall, Mark, and Murray Frame, eds. *Scotland and the Slavs: Cultures in Contact, 1500–2000*. Newtonville, 2001.

Fischer, Theodor A. *The Scots in Eastern and Western Prussia.* Edinburgh, 1903.

Sembrzycki, Johannes. "Die Schotten und Engländer in Ostpreußen und die 'Brüderschaft Gross-Brittanischer Nation' zu Königsberg." *Altpreußische Monatsschrift* 29 (1892): 228–47, and 30 (1893): 351–6.

Smout, Thomas C., ed. *Scotland and Europe 1200–1850.* Edinburgh, 1986.

Steuart, Francis A., ed. *Papers Relating to the Scots in Poland 1576–1793.* Edinburgh, 1915.

Cross-references: Great Britain; Germany; Poland

SEPHARDIM IN EUROPE IN THE EARLY MODERN PERIOD

Jessica V. Roitman

The term *Sefardi* (pl. *Sephardim*) refers to Jews, and their descendants, living in Spain or Portugal before 1492. When King Ferdinand and Queen Isabella expelled the Jews from Spain in 1492, between 70,000 and 120,000 Jews left within three months rather than convert to Christianity, while an uncertain number of Jews converted in order to remain in Spain, joining the separate legal and ethnic class known as *conversos* (converts). Thus was set in motion what became two separate Sephardic diasporas – an Oriental and an Occidental one – that were distinct in impetus, chronology, geography, and patterns of integration and assimilation.

The majority of the exiles from Spain and Portugal initially migrated along the Mediterranean, toward North Africa, Italy, and the Ottoman Empire, at the end of the 15th and beginning of the 16th century. The Jews of this Oriental diaspora retained their distinct ethnic and religious identity, including their language and culture, until the destruction of their communities in the 20th century.

In contrast to the Oriental diaspora, the Occidental diaspora only began to form at the end of the 16th century, a process that lasted throughout the 17th and early 18th centuries. The emigration from the Iberian Peninsula was to northern Europe and was comprised of *conversos* and the so-called New Christians, the Jews and their descendants forcibly converted to Christianity in Portugal in 1497. These Sephardim fled due to a combination of inquisitorial pressure, a search for greater religious freedom, and economic opportunities. The Sephardim of the Occidental diaspora blended into the cultural milieu of Enlightenment Europe and largely disappeared as a visible ethnic and religious minority in western Europe by the 19th century.

The Ottoman Empire – the Oriental diaspora

The immigration of Sephardim to the Ottoman Empire began before 1492, though most of this immigration took place between 1492 and 1512, when Portugal, Navarre, and several Italian states expelled or became increasingly oppressive toward their Jewish populations. During the beginning phase of immigration, most of the Sephardim settled in Istanbul, Edirne, and Thessaloniki, concentrating in the port cities of the southern Balkans and western Anatolia. By the 1520s and 1530s, Sephardic communities had been founded in towns and cities that had previously had a minor Jewish presence or none at all. The Ottoman rulers supported the settlement of the Sephardim. Although non-Muslims paid higher taxes, were required to wear distinctive clothing, and were obliged to outwardly accept the superiority of Islam and Muslims, Ottoman Jewry became the hub of the Sephardic diaspora because the Ottoman Empire was relatively tolerant of religious minorities. The Ottomans recognized their right to their own religious beliefs, to autonomy in their internal affairs, and to the free choice of a place of residence. Jews were also permitted to work in almost every profession and were not subject to any travel restrictions, which allowed for the emergence of Jewish commercial networks, both within the empire itself, as well as with Europe, Iran, and India.

Although the various religious and ethnic groups in the Ottoman Empire existed peacefully side-by-side, there were tensions between the different communities and sporadic outbreaks of violence. And despite economic ties, there was little social and cultural interaction among the various communities. It was difficult to move from membership in one group to affiliation with another and there is little evidence of intermarriage between Jews and non-Jews or of religious conversion.

The Sephardim not only outnumbered local Jews in the Ottoman Empire but they also enjoyed greater economic importance and social position. Most of the well-respected rabbis and scholars in the 16th and 17th centuries were Sephardim. The Sephardic population was bolstered throughout the 16th and 17th centuries by a constant flow of immigration. This steady stream of new immigrants helped the Sephardim to attain an influential economic position within the Jewish community. The non-Sephardic Jews adopted Sephardic religious and judicial practices.

The Occidental diaspora

Portugal. The majority of the Sephardim who remained on the Iberian Peninsula after the Spanish expulsion made the journey on foot to Portugal, while a small percentage sailed on small riverboats to the Kingdom of Navarre and later left the peninsula entirely. In Portugal, the Sephardim joined anywhere from 50,000 to 100,000 of their fellow Jews. The Jews already living in Portugal prior to the Spanish expulsion were almost indistinguishable from the Spanish Sephardim in background, language, and religious practice. The two groups merged into a single large Jewish community.

In 1497, King Manoel declared that all Jews in his kingdom were now Christians, creating another group of *conversos*, or New Christians (*cristãos novos*). After this forced conversion, the Sephardim who distrusted the king's assurances of their safety or who wanted to live openly as Jews left the country, mainly for the Ottoman Empire. Although the king refused to allow New Christians to leave the country between 1499 and 1507, those who wished to escape the country mostly did so. Nevertheless, the majority of the Portuguese New Christians remained in Portugal.

The percentage of New Christians that remained loyal to Judaism is disputed. Crypto-Judaism existed in various sectors of the community of New Christians. However, not all *conversos* and their descendants were practicing crypto-Jews. There were some *conversos* who were sincere Christians; others opted for Judeo-Christian syncretism. Moreover, those who remained after 1492, even if crypto-Jews, had made a decision to acculturate and assimilate into Iberian society as they had not fled into other areas where they would have been able to practice Judaism freely.

The Portuguese Inquisition, established in 1536, resulted in the renewed persecution of the New Christians. Although inquisitorial prosecution did not mean expulsion, its consequences, such as confiscation of property, social stigmatization, imprisonment, and the threat of the death penalty, made life in Portugal difficult and thus led to large-scale emigration.

With the emigration of New Christians from Portugal begins the history of the "New Christian diaspora" in the economically prosperous areas of western Europe that were experiencing an economic boom in the late 15th and early 16th century. The number of these emigrants varied from decade to decade, but the exodus never entirely ceased until the 18th century.

The Sephardim of this diaspora referred to themselves as a nation (*Nação*) or "members of the Spanish-Portuguese Nation." The term *Nación* or *Nação* referred not only to the Sephardic diaspora but also to the "New Christians" who remained in lands where they were not allowed to practice Judaism openly – whether or not they were affiliated with Judaism. Though the boundaries defining the "Hebrew Nation" were vague, there was a genuine sense of affiliation centered mostly on shared Jewish ancestry. This sense of identity and belonging was often bolstered, or even caused, by the hostility they encountered in the surrounding society.

The Portuguese Jewish "nation" was, therefore, somewhat different from other early modern "nations": groups of foreign residents in a city usually engaged in trade or other economic activities, that were identified according to their place of origin. The Sephardic communities were in many respects merchant colonies much like others in northern Europe, but their collective sense of identity transcending religious and geographical boundaries differentiates them somewhat from the other alien trading nations.

What further distinguishes these *conversos* who went north was that they knew little about their Jewish heritage since they and their families had lived as Christians for, in some cases, five or more generations. Therefore, they were accustomed to mixing with, and living as, non-Jews. In fact, aside from their identity as members of the "Hebrew nation,"

the Sephardim of early-modern western Europe were not particularly different from their Christian neighbors. In the end, this ability to assimilate with the majority society, when combined with their numerical inferiority vis-à-vis the Ashkenazi, spelled the end of most major Sephardic communities in western Europe by the 19th century.

The Low Countries – Antwerp and Amsterdam. Starting in the mid-16th century, the Sephardim were attracted to the Habsburg Netherlands, particularly to Antwerp, due to its central role in the handling and distribution of Portuguese and Spanish colonial products. Though the community flourished, their identities as Jews remained concealed.

By 1570, there were 400 New Christians living in Antwerp. However, the rebellion of the seven northern provinces of the Netherlands against the Spanish made possible open Jewish settlement in the northern Netherlands, which had been closed to Jews up to that point. When Antwerp fell to the Spanish in 1585, many residents, including New Christians, fled to the northern provinces; this marked the start of the immigration of Sephardim into the Dutch Republic, which reached its high point in the mid-17th century. By 1672, the formative period was over and the Dutch Sephardic community was close to its height.

There were several Sephardic merchants who settled in Amsterdam with their families during the mid-1590s, before the arrival of the first group of immigrants who came directly from Portugal in 1597. There is also evidence that a substantial number came from Sephardic communities in Germany, Italy, France, Brazil, and as far afield as Angola. In 1612 nearly 500 Jews were in Amsterdam as well as smaller groups in cities such as Rotterdam and Middelburg. A great migration to Amsterdam occurred during the armistice between Spain and Holland from 1609 to 1620. And, by 1630, approximately 900 Sephardim lived in Amsterdam. The waves of New Christian immigration grew stronger from the end of the 1640s and throughout the 1650s. In 1672, there were over 2,000 Jews in Amsterdam.

In general, the members of the *Nação* were greeted with relative tolerance in Amsterdam and in the other cities in the western part of the Netherlands. Despite this tolerance, some male members of the *Nação* refused to be circumcised because they feared capture by the Inquisition if they returned to Iberia. Moreover, most Jewish merchants used two names: their Iberian alias used for business and their Hebrew name used within the synagogue or for personal use. And although Jews could buy citizenship, it gave them no right to join the guilds and it could not be passed on to their children. Marriage with non-Jews was also forbidden.

The Sephardim considered themselves more cultured, better educated, and wealthier than the Ashkenazi. When there were only a few isolated Ashkenazi refugees or immigrants, the Sephardim admitted them to their community, though not with the same rights that the Sephardim had. However, when there was a flood of Ashkenazi refugees following the Thirty Years' War (1618–48), the Sephardic community became concerned about the number of beggars. Not all the beggars were Ashkenazi – there were poor Sephardim as well. These poor Sephardim were often sent away to other countries where they could practice Judaism openly while not placing a financial burden on the Amsterdam community.

By sending away so many poor Sephardim, however, the community of the *Nação* contributed to its own decline in the 18th century. Ultimately, this form of emigration contributed to the Sephardic community being completely overwhelmed numerically and culturally by the Ashkenazi in the 19th century. Whereas most Jews in Amsterdam in the 17th century were Sephardim, by the early 18th century, Ashkenazim were the majority. Intermarriage between these two ethnic groups was rare. In fact, if a Sephardic man married an Ashkenazi woman he could lose his community rights.

This numerical decline was coupled with shifting patterns of European trade that spelled the end of Dutch commercial supremacy. The Sephardim of Amsterdam declined along with their commercial empires. The Sephardim were thus consigned to a marginal role both within the Jewish community of the Netherlands specifically and inside the overarching Dutch society generally.

France. France served as a first place of refuge for those Sephardim who fled the Spanish and Portuguese Inquisitions, even though no Jews were legally allowed there after their expulsion in 1394. Jews began drifting into the country almost immediately after the Spanish expulsion, but they were forced to live as Catholics and to settle primarily in a few places near the Spanish border, most commonly in the border town of St.-Jean-de-Luz as well as Bayonne and Bordeaux. From the middle of the 16th century and throughout the 17th century, settlements by Portuguese merchants who continued to live as New Christians were expanded in Bordeaux and Bayonne and established in Bidache, Peyrehorade, Labastide-Clairence, and other locations.

Soon after the establishment of the Inquisition in Portugal, the New Christians sought legal recognition of their settlement and protection from persecution by petitioning the French government for letters of naturalization. These were granted in 1550 and authorized the New Christians to enter France to trade there. They were given the same rights as other subjects of the king, though only as long as they did not openly practice Judaism.

For many Sephardim, settling in France was only intended to be temporary. It was viewed as a safe haven from the Inquisition, but most Sephardim intended to move on to a place where they could openly practice Judaism once their resources allowed it. Nevertheless, France became a permanent place of settlement for many Sephardim. Therefore, France was far from being only a way station on the road to Amsterdam, London, or Hamburg.

In the early 18th century, the authorities began to acknowledge these New Christians as Jews and permitted them to practice Judaism openly, leading to designation of the 18th

century as the "Golden Age" of France's Sephardim. Bayonne and Bordeaux were especially important cities with large Jewish communities, most of which were engaged in trade with France's colonial possessions. In Bordeaux, for example, the community numbered about 1,000 in the 18th century, while in Bayonne, the approximately 2,500 Sephardim comprised around one-fifth of the total population. The French communities were in active correspondence – personal, business, and religious – with members of the *Nação* in other lands, especially in Amsterdam.

The Sephardim of France were numerically overwhelmed by the Ashkenazi in the 18th century although the Ashkenazi tended to settle in the main cities and on France's border with Germany, while the Sephardim were largely in the southwestern corner of the country. Only a tiny Sephardic community remained in France by the 19th century.

Germany. The history of the Sephardim of Germany is really the history of Hamburg at the end of the 16th century. After Antwerp was recaptured by Spanish troops in 1585, a substantial proportion of the city's Portuguese New Christian community migrated to northwestern Germany. By the late 1580s about a dozen Sephardic families had settled in the city and in 1612 there were 125 Sephardic adults.

The Sephardim who settled in Hamburg at the end of the 16th century were wealthy merchants with trading connections overseas. At that time, Hamburg was the major center in northern Europe for the trade in sugar, spices, and other colonial commodities. The Sephardim were the first to open up trade with Spain and Portugal. They imported sugar, tobacco, spices, cotton, and other products from the colonies. Moreover, they played a prominent part in the foundation of the Bank of Hamburg in 1619. A charter granted in 1612 gave the first official approval for Jewish life in Hamburg but forbade public worship within the borders of the city. Permission for residence was expensive: 1,000 marks for five years.

By the end of the 17th century the Sephardic community was in decline. A number of well-respected and influential Sephardim had died. When, in 1697, the Senate and the Bürgerschaft demanded sizable annual payments from the Portuguese Jews to stay in Hamburg and rescinded their right to religious practice, some of the wealthy families emigrated to Altona, Ottensen, and Amsterdam. This emigration, when added to the internal strife within the Sephardic community, led in the 18th century to a reduction in the number and influence of the Sephardim in Hamburg.

In the meantime, the Ashkenazi were increasing in importance and number. By the second quarter of the 17th century, several Ashkenazi merchants settled in Hamburg but were again expelled in 1649. Other Ashkenazi were admitted after 1654 and they founded the Hamburg Ashkenazi congregation. In 1710 an imperial commission issued an edict that formed the legal basis for the treatment of all Jews in Hamburg, whether Sephardim or Ashkenazi, for the next century. The Ashkenazi were legally allowed to settle in Hamburg and were given the same rights as the Portuguese. As a result of Sephardic exclusiveness and due to the lack of new immigration, the Sephardic community declined in the 18th century.

The Italian City States. The Jewish population of Italy in the 16th century was small and scattered. During the second quarter of the 16th century, however, New Christian merchants began to settle in Ancona, Ferrara, Livorno, and Venice. Some of the *conversos* continued to live as Christians; others reverted to Judaism. They were joined in their settlement by Jews from the Near East, who were subjects of the Ottoman Empire and who began to migrate into Italy in order to intensify their links in Mediterranean trade.

Ferdinand de Medici as Grand Duke of Tuscany (1587–1609) invited the New Christians to settle in Pisa-Livorno and allowed them to live openly as Jews. The Sephardic settlement there thrived. After 1589 Venice allowed New Christian immigration. There they joined other Jewish communities, though throughout most of the 17th century the Sephardim were the most numerous and wealthiest Jewish group in the city.

In Italy, therefore, two major centers of Sephardim emerged during the second half of the 16th century and flourished during the 17th century: Venice and Livorno. In Venice, there were approximately 1,700 Jews in the 1580s, 2,650 in the 1640s, and 4,000 in the 1660s. The city's Jewish community consisted of three separate congregations of Levantine, Iberian, and Ashkenazi Jews. The Sephardim were not the majority. However, the Sephardic community of Venice was one of the largest populations – along with Antwerp – of the emerging Portuguese diaspora at the beginning of the 17th century.

Venice was a mixture of tolerance and intolerance for its Jewish residents. Jews could live in the city, but were confined to the Ghetto Nuova, which was locked at night, from 1516 onward. Jews were only permitted to work in pawnshops, act as moneylenders, work in the Hebrew printing press, trade in textiles, or practice medicine. Once they left the ghetto they were required to wear distinctive clothing such as a yellow circle or scarf. Jews were also faced with high taxes.

The 17th century was the ghetto's golden age; Jewish commerce and scholarship flourished. The Sephardim controlled much of Venice's foreign trade by the mid-1600s and they gained influence and wealth in the Venetian economy. The economic conditions for the Sephardim, however, deteriorated at the end of the 17th century. Anti-Jewish feelings were prevalent in the 18th century and limitations were placed on Jewish economic activity. The Jewish population decreased from 4,800 in 1655 to 1,700 in 1766 because many prominent families left for Livorno or other port cities. Taxes were high and Sephardi merchants lost their shops between 1714 and 1718. Finally in 1737, the Jewish community declared bankruptcy.

In contrast to Venice, there was no ghetto in Livorno, nor was distinctive Jewish clothing required. Moreover, Livorno was the only place in Italy where the Catholic Counter-Reformation had little effect on the Jews. This was largely because in the 16th century Grand Duke Cosimo I invited foreigners, including New Christians, to come to the young port city.

The Jewish population grew from 114 in 1601 to 3,000 by 1689, becoming the most important group of foreigners living in Livorno. Spanish and Portuguese became the official language of Jewish merchants in Livorno and remained so until the late 18th century. By the end of the 18th century, nearly 5,000 Jews lived in Livorno but, at the end of the 19th century, the Sephardim had virtually disappeared and the entire Jewish population had decreased to 2,500. This is most likely the result of the deteriorating economic situation brought about by the Napoleonic wars, which forced the Sephardim to flee to other places.

Spain. Some Portuguese New Christians fleeing the Inquisition returned to Spain during the union of Spain and Portugal (1580–1640) since New Christians could not be tried there for any crimes of "Judaizing" committed in Portugal. The Inquisitions in the two countries did exchange information on suspected crypto-Jews, but Spain did not extradite them. The Portuguese immigrants in Spain were suspected of crypto-Judaism by definition and were regarded as a separate group of Christians – *Portugueses de la nación hebrea* or simply *Portugueses de la nación*. While some of these immigrants to Spain were fleeing the Inquisition in Portugal, other Sephardic immigrants to Spain came to the country after they had returned to Judaism and lived openly in a Jewish community. They mostly came to Spain for economic reasons. However, since Jews were officially not allowed to live in the country, it is difficult to ascertain their exact numbers or the development of their community.

England. Impetus to admit Jews to England began with the overthrow of the monarchy in the middle of the 17th century. In 1655 about 100 Sephardim were living in London. Jews in England had not received official approval to live there, but there was a tacit sanctioning of their presence in the country by 1656. England's military conflict with Spain, as well as strong anti-Catholic feelings, created a climate of tolerance for Jews, mostly Sephardim, to enter the country. In 1656, the first Jewish congregation was formed. In the early 1680s, the community numbered 414 people. Around 1692, the Ashkenazi established a separate community with its own synagogue since relations between the two Jewish groups had become strained as their numbers increased.

The London Sephardic community grew in importance in the 18th century and replaced Hamburg as the second community – after Amsterdam – within the western Sephardic diaspora. However, from the beginning, the community was threatened by the ease with which the Sephardim could enter mainstream English society: mixed marriages were widespread, only one-third of the Sephardim resident in London before 1659 were buried in the Sephardi cemetery, and a noticeable number of congregants converted to Christianity.

By the second or third generation in England, many Sephardim were integrated so completely into the surrounding society that they had converted to the Church of England. Between 1740 and 1800, the number of marriages at the Sephardic synagogue fell by 43%, as assimilation undercut the size and strength of the organized community.

There was a great division between the western diaspora – Sephardim who went to the lands of western Europe and the Americas – and the eastern diaspora of Sephardim who went to North Africa and the Ottoman Empire. In the Sephardic diaspora in the Ottoman Empire, the exiles from Spain and their descendants established communities soon after the expulsions from Spain and Portugal. Due to their cultural strength as well as the segregated nature of Ottoman society, they preserved their ancestral traditions. Although economic and political stagnation affected their fortunes, they attained cultural ascendancy over the other Jewish groups in the empire and maintained their language and culture until their communities' destruction in the 20th century.

In contrast, former New Christians who had lived in isolation from Judaism for four generations or more established the western Sephardic diaspora. The Sephardim of early modern western Europe were hardly discernible from their neighbors, in dress, language, and lifestyle. Therefore, when they settled in countries in which they were granted the right to their own religious beliefs, they did not have problems adjusting. On the contrary, they often had more problems accommodating Jewish practice and ritual. Ultimately, this caused many Sephardim to give up their Judaism altogether and fully assimilate into the larger Christian society. This ability to assimilate into the greater society, when combined with their numerical decline vis-à-vis the Ashkenazi, spelled the end of most major Sephardic communities in western Europe by the 19th century.

Barnett, Richard. *The Sephardi Heritage: Essays on the Historical and Cultural Contribution of the Jews of Spain and Portugal*, vol. 2: *The Western Sephardim. The History of Some of the Communities Formed in Europe, the Mediterranean and the New World after the Expulsion of 1492*. Grendon, 1989.

Beinart, Haim. *The Expulsion of the Jews from Spain*. Oxford, 2002.

Bodian, Miriam. *Hebrews of the Portuguese Nation: Conversos and Community in Early Modern Amsterdam*. Bloomington, IN, 1997.

Endelman, Todd. *Radical Assimilation in English Jewish History, 1656–1945*. Bloomington, IN, 1990.

Gampel, Benjamin. *Crisis and Creativity in the Sephardic World: 1391–1648*. New York, 1997.

Israel, Jonathan. *Diasporas within a Diaspora: Jews, Crypto-Jews, and the World Maritime Empires (1540–1740)*. Leiden, 2002.

Kaplan, Yosef. "The Formation of the Western Sephardi Diaspora." In *The Sephardic Journey 1492–1992*, edited by Yeshiva University Museum, 136–55. New York, 1992.

Kaplan, Yosef. *An Alternative Path to Modernity: The Sephardi Diaspora in Western Europe*. Leiden, 2000.

Levy, Avigador. *The Sephardim in the Ottoman Empire*. Princeton, NJ, 1992.

Swetschinski, Daniel. *Reluctant Cosmopolitans: The Portuguese Jews of 17th-century Amsterdam*. London, 2000.

Cross-references: France; Germany; Great Britain; The Netherlands; Spain and Portugal; Southeastern Europe; Ashkenazim in Europe since the Early Modern Period; Flemish Merchants in the Iberian Peninsula in the Early Modern Period; French Maritime Merchants in Hamburg since 1680; Spanish Merchants in the Netherlands in the Early Modern Period

SERBIAN AND MONTENEGRAN COLONISTS IN VOJVODINA (SERBIA) AND IN SLAVONIA (CROATIA) SINCE THE END OF WORLD WAR I

Carl Bethke

After the First and Second World Wars, the Kingdom of the Serbs, Croats, and Slovenians (1918–29), that is, Yugoslavia, carried out agrarian reforms that had social, economic, and political goals: preferably, members of minorities in Croatia and Serbia were dispossessed, while the land was to be distributed exclusively to members of the peoples making up the national state – among them, overwhelmingly, Serbs. The agrarian reforms involved resettlements, primarily from the poorer, economically less developed Yugoslavian regions in the south to the fertile and economically stronger regions in the northeast. Settlements were to take place largely in Vojvodina (Serbia) and in Slavonia (Croatia), also with the effect of homogenizing these regions ethnically.

The newly settled colonists received certain privileges. They were at times very distinct from the natives (Serbs, Croats, some minority groups) culturally and economically, but in part also in the perception of their history and in their national-political orientation. For that reason, the newcomers were seen as a special group for decades. The agrarian reforms and the colonization in northeastern Yugoslavia they entailed are striking examples of the politically planned and legitimized migrations that shaped eastern, east-central, and southeastern Europe in the 20th century. This policy was inspired by ideas from the fields of demography and agronomy in western and central Europe since the 19th century.

Moreover, expropriations of big Muslim landowners had already occurred in the Kingdom of Serbia after its independence from the Ottoman Empire was recognized at the Congress of Berlin in 1878. Following in their wake, the demand for agrarian reforms was already part of the political program of some of the southern Slav nationalists in the Habsburg monarchy, to which Slavonia and Vojvodina belonged until 1918. In Bosnia-Herzegovina, as well as in Kosovo and Macedonia (Serbian since 1913), the big landowners were Muslim. By contrast, in Vojvodina and Slavonia the big landowners and agrarian entrepreneurs were largely Magyars and Germans. When social unrest erupted after the end of World War I especially in these regions characterized by feudal capitalism, the prince regent of the newly created Kingdom of the Serbs, Croats, and Slovenians, Alexander I. Karađorđević, proclaimed the agrarian reform that was being called for.

With an eye on the developments in revolutionary Russia and in view of the national structure of large-scale landownership, the majority of the expropriated land (about 25,000 hectares) was distributed between 1914 and 1941 to small farmers and agricultural laborers who lived there or came from the region. Many of the former big landowners emigrated to Hungary. Members of the strong Magyar and German minorities (together about 50% of the population) were excluded from the distribution of land, even though they made up the largest share of the landless agricultural workers and day laborers in the region after World War I. They were therefore all the more embittered when 21,000 families were settled in the region, chiefly Serbs from Bosnia, Krajina, and central Serbia. Moreover, war veterans had been given special preference in the land distribution.

Within the framework of the agrarian reform, some separated settlements were founded and named after the home villages of the colonists or after Serbian war heroes. Many of the colonists were unable to cope with the unaccustomed work techniques and the ecological conditions of the plain, which was part of the reason the agrarian reform was often discussed as an economic failure, even by its supporters. Between 1941 and 1944, the occupiers expelled the colonists from the now Hungarian and Croatian areas of Vojvodina. Their renamed settlements became home to Hungarians from Bukovina and Moldavia as well as Croats from the region of Zagorje (near Zagreb) and Bosnia.

The second Yugoslavian agrarian reform between 1945 and 1948 was to be socially more favorable to its beneficiaries: for example, the new farmers did not have to pay rent for the land assigned to them. This reform thus realized the results of the discussion in the later 1930s about the necessity of a "second agrarian reform." It was legitimized as part of the communist ideology of the new rulers and with reference to the experiences of World War II: apart from the churches, expropriation also targeted "hostile" minorities (especially persons of German extraction), unless they lived in mixed marriages with members of the nationalities making up the Yugoslav state or had actively supported the communist partisans. This time, expropriation encompassed not only land, but also other personal property (including even jewelry or authorship rights).

The focal point of the second agrarian reform was in Vojvodina and Slavonia as the former settlement centers of the ethnic-German "Danube Swabians." The origin regions of the approximately 250,000 colonists largely resembled those in the first agrarian reform, with a stronger participation by Montenegrans, who as a group often set themselves apart among the colonists and still referred to themselves this way in the census at the beginning of the 21st century. Victims of fascism and National Socialism and deserving veterans,

among them even some from World War I, were given preference during the land distribution.

Yugoslav agrarian geographers, historians, and ethnologists accompanied and analyzed the settlement of colonists in several large-scale research projects. The agrarian reform and the resettlements it entailed were processed in novels (e.g., those by Branko Ćopić), anecdotes, and sagas.

The colonists often attracted relatives and neighbors in their wake. Many colonists contributed to the collectivization of Yugoslav agriculture by selling their land to the agricultural production cooperatives that were strongly represented in the region. Politically, the colonists in Vojvodina – where there had been few partisans – were considered especially loyal to the regime: in an allusion to the seven offensives of the partisan war, the colonization was referred to in common parlance as Tito's "eighth offensive." Often, even in elections in the 1990s, the colonists in Vojvodina still preferred the Socialist Party of Serbia. After the wars following the breakup of Yugoslavia in the 1990s, more Serbs from Krajina and Bosnians came to Vojvodina. Family connections to the colonists of the 1940s are said to have played some role in this.

Gačeša, Nikola. *Agrarna reforma i kolonizacija u Jugoslavji. 1945–1948*. Novi Sad, 1984.

Lekić, Bogdan. *Agrarna reforma i kolonizacija u Jugoslaviji. 1945–1948*. Belgrade, 1997.

Lekić, Bogdan. *Agrarna reforma i kolonizacija u Jugoslaviji. 1918–1941*. Belgrade, 2002.

Petrović, Edit, and Andrei Simić. "Montenegrin Colonists in Vojvodina. Objective and Subjective Measures of Ethnicity." *Serbian Studies* 5, 4 (1993): 5–20.

Šimončić-Bobetko, Zdenka. *Agrarna reforma i kolonizacija u Hrvatskoj*. Zagreb, 1997.

Cross-references: Southeastern Europe; German Settlers (*Donauschwaben*) in Southeastern Europe since the Early Modern Period; Refugees from Former Yugoslavia in Europe since 1991

SERBS IN KRAJINA SINCE THE LATE 19TH CENTURY

Carolin Leutloff-Grandits

In contemporary Croatia, "Krajina" is by now a rarely used, negatively connotated term for the formerly Serb-occupied, war-torn region of Croatia that was home, between 1991 and 1995, to the self-proclaimed Republika Srpska Krajina (Republic of Serbian Krajina). The never internationally recognized Republika Srpska Krajina extended on the Croatian state territory along the border with Bosnia or rump Yugoslavia and was more or less coterminous with the historical Vojna Krajina.

During the war, the Serbian population in the Republika Srpska Krajina numbered about 300,000. After the Croatian military offensives, which led to the flight of nearly the entire Serbian element of the population from Krajina (with the exception of eastern Slavonia) and the reintegration of the region into the Croatian state, by 2005 about 117,500 Serbs who had been living there in 1991 had returned. Nevertheless, many of these returnees merely formally registered but did not, in fact, live permanently in Croatia. Most of the real returnees are older people.

The name Vojna Krajina (military frontier) describes more or less large parts of the regions of Lika, Kordun, and Banija (also referred to as Krajina proper), as well as western and eastern Slavonia and the Baranja, which, between the 16th and the second half of the 19th century, constituted a separate military frontier region of the Habsburg Empire vis-à-vis the Ottomans. In the 18th century, regions of Dalmatia (with Knin) as part of the Venetian Republic also formed a military frontier area to the Ottoman Empire. The term Krajina-Serbs or "Serbs from the Krajina" goes back to the nationalization process of the local Orthodox element of the population, a process that progressed in the 19th century and did not conclude until the 20th. During the early settlement of Krajina, the Serbs were generally referred to as Orthodox Vlachs. Alongside the Catholic element and a small group of Catholic Vlachs (Bunjevci), they constituted the largest population group in Vojna Krajina. The settlers were recruited by the Habsburgs to repopulate the regions laid waste by war and to fortify the border with the Ottoman Empire.

Over the centuries, the Orthodox Vlachs as well as the other settlers of Vojna Krajina developed a common social identity as "military farmers." In this way they set themselves apart from the population of the Habsburg realm living under feudal conditions outside the military frontier. At the same time, the language and customs of the Orthodox and Catholic population were regionally very similar, even though membership in different churches did separate them in daily life.

The process of nationalization within the two regional religious groups took off only with the dissolution of the military frontier in 1881 and the subsequent, far-reaching social transformations. It was directed by Serbian-national and Croatian-national centers outside of Krajina. For the Serbian population, those centers were especially Vojvodina (part of the Habsburg monarchy) but also Belgrade; for the Catholic population it was Zagreb. Ecclesiastical unions, a "national" system of banking and cooperatives, and the newly founded or emerging political parties became the carriers of clashing national ideologies. The abolition of military service and the simultaneous increase in the tax burden cast many residents of the former military frontier into dire social circumstances, which made them especially susceptible to the politicization and nationalization of everyday life: the Orthodox population became "Serbs," the Catholic population became "Croats."

The first half of the 20th century saw the first conflicts between Serbs and Croats over territorial claims to the region of Krajina. The split between the two population groups deepened considerably in World War II. Krajina was part of the Independent State of Croatia created by National Socialist Germany in 1941, and its existence was based on the fascist ideology of "ethnic purity." Mass executions of Serbs were carried out under the regime of Ante Pavelic, the leader of the Croatian Ustasha movement, especially in the largest concentration camp, Jasenovac. The territory of the former Krajina itself witnessed massacres, deportations, and the first mass flight of Serbs from the region to Serbia. On the Krajina-Serb side, most of the resistance against the Ustasha regime formed early on within the framework of the communist partisan movement, but in part also within the framework of the Serbian-royalist Chetnik movement (especially in the region around Knin). After the end of the war, the partisans carried out massive reprisals against the supporters of the Independent State of Croatia.

Under the socialist regime there were hardly any open conflicts between Serbs and Croats in Krajina, despite the grim wartime experience. That also had to do with the post-war order in socialist Yugoslavia, in which the population was supposed to focus less on national aspects and more on the communist ideology of the "brotherhood and unity" of the various nations.

As the consequences of the political and economic crisis in Yugoslavia deepened at the end of the 1980s, the old antagonistic national constructs reemerged in Croatia, as well as in other parts of Yugoslavia. The demands for an independent Croatia reinforced among the Serbs in Croatia the fear of losing their economic and political rights.

The situation in economically underdeveloped Krajina became more tense beginning in the summer of 1990 and eventually escalated into Croatia's declaration of independence in 1991: Serbian troops that were massed in Krajina, with help from the Yugoslav People's Army and the political leadership in Belgrade, drove out hundreds of thousands of native Croats and destroyed much of their property. In 1991, the political leaders of the Serbs proclaimed the Republic of Serbian Krajina in Krajina.

The situation reversed when Croatia launched a surprise military offensive in 1995 and recaptured the Serbian-occupied territory (with the exception of eastern Slavonia). At that point the remaining Serbian population fled into rump-Yugoslavia, the Bosnian Serb republic, and eastern Slavonia. After the end of military operations, up to 70% of Serbian houses had been destroyed in the various regions of Krajina. The return of the Serbian part of the population has proved difficult also at the beginning of the 21st century. Although the Croatian state has created the legal conditions for a return, the situation in the labor and housing markets is very tense. Clashes are still occurring, for the most part along the national borders established in the late 19th century.

Grandits, Hannes, and Christian Promitzer. "'Former Comrades' at War: Historical Perspectives on 'Ethnic Cleansing' in Croatia." In *Neighbors at War: Anthropological Perspectives on Yugoslav Ethnicity, Culture, and History*, edited by Joel M. Halpern and David A. Kideckel, 125–42. University Park, PA, 2000.

Kaser, Karl. *Freier Bauer und Soldat. Die Militarisierung der agrarischen Gesellschaft an der kroatisch-slawonischen Militärgrenze (1535–1881)*. Vienna, 1997.

Leutloff-Grandits, Carolin. *Claiming Ownership in Post-War Croatia: The Dynamics of Ethnic Conflict and Property Relations in the Knin Region*. Münster, 2006.

Roksandić, Drago. *Srbi u Hrvatskoj od 15. stoljeća do naših dana*. Zagreb, 1991.

Cross-references: Southeastern Europe; Refugees from Former Yugoslavia in Europe since 1991; Settlers on the Habsburg Military Border since the Early Modern Period

SETTLERS ON THE HABSBURG MILITARY BORDER SINCE THE EARLY MODERN PERIOD

Karl Kaser

The expansion of the Ottomans toward central Europe faltered in the middle of the 16th century in the face of defensive efforts by the Croatians and the Habsburgs. The border between the Habsburg and the Ottoman empires stabilized on Croatian territory, a substantial portion of which (the southern Croatian territories) had fallen to the Ottoman Empire. The decades-long military conflict largely destroyed the infrastructure in the contested areas. A part of the agricultural population was transferred into the safe hinterland (as far as modern-day Burgenland and Slovakia), a part lost their lives. The Croatian and Hungarian feudal lords were forced to suspend their administrative and economic activities in the border region.

As a result of the enormous material losses, the Hungarian (a large part of Hungary proper had also fallen to the Ottomans) and Croatian estates were no longer capable of mounting effective defensive measures. In this precarious situation, the estates of Inner Austria (Styria, Carynthia, Carniola, and Gorizia) became more active in border security in the second half of the 16th century, also for reasons of self-interest. The *Landtag* of Inner Austria in Bruck/Mur in 1578 decided on an extensive package of financial and military measures to protect the border in Croatia. The task of coordinating them fell to the Inner Austrian Court Council of War in Graz, which set up two so-called *Generalate* (in Varaždin and Karlovac), appointed their commanders, and moved troop contingents to Croatia.

Over the next century or two, these measures gave rise to an enclosed military border territory, a process that was complete by the middle of the 18th century. The defensive zone was completely removed from the authority of the Croatian *Landtag* (*Sabor*) and placed under the command, first of the Inner Austrian Court Council of War, and from the middle of the 18th century the Austrian Court Council of War in Vienna. What remained of Croatia was therefore divided into two parts, a military and a civilian Croatia. Because of the military successes of the Habsburgs against the Ottomans, this military border territory was substantially expanded at the beginning of the 18th century: it now ran in a wide arc from the coastal regions of Croatia right up to the gates of Belgrade.

One of the central problems from the perspective of the military administration was that the border regions were nearly completely unpopulated. The challenge therefore was how to make settlements in the Habsburg border territory, which was under constant military threat and some of which had soil that was difficult to cultivate, attractive to farming families. The solution that was found could be encapsulated in the formula "free farmer and soldier." Beginning in the second half of the 16th century, thousands of people came to the border territory as *Grenzer* (frontiersmen) from the Croatian hinterland and from Ottoman-controlled regions. The settlers enjoyed a privileged status that was noticeably different from that of the agricultural population of feudal Europe.

The settlement program of the military authorities

The emerging military frontier was settled by families of the most diverse backgrounds, although the existing sources hardly allow for a precise analysis of the motivations of the settlers. It would appear that the prospect of land free of taxes and dues in return for military service, with the men initially called upon only to defend their own property, was very attractive to the various immigrant groups.

The sources refer to the most important immigrant group in the beginning as *Uskoks*, and since the end of the 16th century with growing frequency as *Vlachs*. It is likely that there were hardly any social and ethnic differences between them; at any rate, they were families of Orthodox faith from the Ottoman-dominated section of southeastern Europe. While the term *Uskok* (renegade, refugee) allows no further inferences about the origin and social status of the families, the term *Vlach* (Aromanian) is more significant. This was evidently an originally Latin-speaking group that settled in the coastal region of Dalmatia and was displaced in the seventh century by Slavic-Avar immigrants. They found new settlement areas on the Dalmatian islands, as well as in the Dinarian and Pindos mountains. In the mountains they organized themselves as nomadic and semi-nomadic herder communities and were able to preserve their Romanic language and identity for a period that is impossible to determine with precision, though in some cases – as in the northern Greek region around the city of Metsovo – until today. Such communities of Vlachs – called *Katune* (mountain dairy farming communities) – are noted in the Middle Ages in broad swaths of the Balkan Peninsula. In many cases the medieval Balkan states and later also the Ottoman Empire granted them certain privileges. In return they guarded mountain passes and roads, carried out transports, or participated in military campaigns. They also enjoyed a certain degree of self-government under the leadership of military leaders frequently referred to as *voivods*. However, it appears that they were gradually stripped of this privileged status by the end of the 16th and the beginning of the 17th century, which might have been an additional reason for their migration to the Habsburg military frontier. By this time, however, the Vlach families had already lost their Romanic language. Their names were already Slavic, and in the wake of the later process of national integration, they would feel that they were part of the Serbian nation.

The first group of these Vlachs (*Uskoks*) obtained permission to cross the border from the Habsburg military authorities as early as September 1530. It comprised about 50 families and was led by a *voivod*. Like many of the families who arrived later, their previous living area had been in Bosnia-Herzegovina. These and subsequent families were eventually settled relatively far in the hinterland, in the Sichelburg District (in the modern-day border region between Croatia and Slovenia). By 1610, a total of 1,218 Vlach families had settled in the Varaždin *Generalat*, which is equivalent to a settlement size of about 10,000. The first 325 Vlach families were settled in the Karlovac *Generalat* in 1600, not counting the Sichelburg District, which was assigned to this *Generalat*. They founded the villages of Gomirje, Moravice, and Vrbovsko in northwestern Croatia. The following century and a half was characterized by massive immigration. A census in 1746 counted 6,789 families or 54,511 residents in the 96 free frontier villages.

Next to the Vlachs, the Croatians were the most important immigrant group in the early period of the military frontier. Our grasp of their numbers in this early period is not as good as in the case of the Vlachs. Still, various subgroups can be identified: one group was probably a remnant of the original population and many subject peasant families (referred to in the sources as *Predavzen*) who had fled from the feudal estates of the hinterland. Evidently, the feudal lords were unable to prevent the departure of their subject families. The Croatian *Sabor* regularly passed laws that made emigration to the military frontier a punishable offense, but they remained fairly ineffective. Another group was the so-called *Bunjevzen*. They were also referred to as *Valachi Catholici*, because they were similar to the Vlachs in their social organization. They came from the Dalmatian region and the Croatian coastal area to the north, and they settled primarily in the southwestern part of the military frontier.

The already mentioned population groups were joined by the German-speaking population that was living in the military frontier temporarily or permanently. It was recruited primarily from salaried garrison soldiers (the "German troops"), who were deployed to protect the important fortresses. Their number fluctuated over time. Some of these soldiers remained in the border region and their descendants merged with the local population. Then there were the higher military ranks, which were recruited chiefly from the noble families of Inner Austria and reinforced the German population. In sum, the population of the military frontier around 1775 was approximately 550,000, and in 1869, shortly before its dissolution, 753,500.

We are not well informed about the immediate settlement process. It would appear that in the early years of the military frontier, the military government had little organizational involvement in the allocation of land. While early villages had usually been unstructured, clustered settlements, beginning in the 18th century the intent was to set up planned villages, specifically in the flat terrain along the Sava in Slavonia. The occupation and settlement of the land probably followed the same pattern. In some cases the settlers seem to have simply taken as much land as they needed. The land registers indicate as much with comments like "has taken land with the sword." In the Varaždin *Generalat*, the landed property of a frontier household was called *bastine* (Croatian: *baština*: hereditary property). Calculations have shown that the term did not refer to a specific plot size, and this points to a chaotic process of settlement. Many Vlach settlers brought their animals with them. Usually they had to be immediately provisioned with grain by the military government so they could support themselves until the first harvest. In any case, speed was essential in allocating land, since fields had to be cleared or cultivated and houses built before the arrival of winter.

In the southwestern military frontier, in the region Lika-Krbava, which passed into Habsburg hands only at the end of the 17th century, the resettlement process was already an orderly one. Here the village fields were divided into *squadras* and *petinas*; one *squadra* consisted of any number of *petinas*. One *petine* could be owned by one or more households. Unmarried men also came to the military frontier alongside families; they were not given any land.

The Vlach families who migrated to the military frontier were granted certain privileges upon crossing the border; owning land exempt from dues was the most important. However, these special rights were threatened when the former noble and ecclesiastical landlords tried to assert their ownership rights, something they succeeded in doing to some extent in the hinterland. Vlachs who settled there were called "private Vlachs" in the sources. The majority had their privileges confirmed by the Habsburg rulers. The most important document was the Statuta Valachorum of 1630. Initially limited to the Vlach villages of the Varazdin *Generalat*, it confirmed the dues-exempt landholdings in return for military service when these villages were threatened. The other villages were given a kind of autonomous, civil self-government, which included the administration of justice. Its most important institution was the *knesen* (village leaders, judges). However, in the middle of the 18th century these rights of self-government were substantially curtailed.

Though these liberties were intended for the Vlach families, over time they were expanded also to Croatian villages and the rest of the frontier region. This was the basis for the territorialization of the frontier territory. The years between 1745 and 1770 witnessed a serious reorganization of the social and military structures, as the society was militarized. The military frontier was divided into regimental areas and company districts. Each regimental area had to muster a regiment that was integrated into the general military organization of the Habsburg Empire. Eventually the men called up for service had to provide their own equipment. Landed property was now also taxed, with exemption only for the structurally weak regimental areas in the western, mountainous frontier sections. This deterioration of the legal and social situation put in question the very existence of the military frontier when the liberation of the peasants was proclaimed in civilian areas in 1848 and the farmers in the military frontier had more disadvantages than advantages compared to the "civilian Croats."

The process of ethnonational differentiation among Serbs and Croats

To understand whether this ethnically nonhomogenous frontier society could be integrated into a homogenous one, several factors must be taken into account. The territorialization of the military frontier had both an integrative and disintegrative effect: tendencies toward homogenization resulted largely because the frontier families had been subject to a uniform law since the middle of the 18th century. In addition, from the middle of the 18th century, the military units were principally *not* composed along ethnic lines. Moreover, with the settlers living under military command, processes of socioeconomic stratification could hardly develop. Urbanization processes, too, were all but impossible because military service was tied to landownership. Rather, the military frontier formed a militarized enclave of free peasants within the feudally structured society of the Habsburg Empire. While this unique status had an integrative effect internally, it was also the cause of significant problems when the military frontier was dissolved for good in 1881 and the territory was reintegrated into civilian Croatia. The frontier dwellers were also conscious of their unique position and fought to preserve it. When the Varazdin *Generalat* was scheduled to be dissolved in the middle of the 18th century, because it no longer constituted an immediate frontier region in the wake of Habsburg conquests, the frontiersmen took up arms and thus prevented the loss of their privileges. Of importance for their identity-construction as frontiersmen was the general notion that they were characterized by special bravery in battle, as well as their self-conception as "the emperor's frontiersmen," since they correctly traced their special status back to the Habsburg rulers.

However, these trends toward homogenization within the emerging frontier society were opposed by growing national demarcations. Beneath the shared surface of living on the frontier, a process of national differentiation began to emerge on the basis of ethnic differences (in terms of religious confessions, language, and writing) between Serbs and Croats. Although that process was not yet very pronounced by the time the military frontier was dissolved, it was irreversible, since by then a landscape of political parties on a national basis had taken shape in civilian Croatia, and this trend would subsequently accelerate. The question arises as to why the identity as "frontiersmen" eventually receded in the face of other elements. To what extent did Catholic and Orthodox – that is, Croatian and Serbian – frontier-dwellers differ, and how evident was that on the outside? The following three elements help to explain how this distinction was maintained:

1. The immigrant Vlach families of the Orthodox confession were a problem for the administration, since a decision in favor of the integration of populations of other faiths had not yet been made in the Catholic Habsburg Empire. The potential settlers resisted a change in confession. Different solutions were found for the two old *Generalate*: the Varazdin *Generalat* was able, by applying considerable pressure on the Vlachs, to establish a united Catholic-Orthodox church organization with its center in the Marcha Monastery. This strategy had no success in the Karlovac *Generalat*, and the Vlach families there forced the preservation of their own religion. In 1600, permission was granted for the founding of the first Orthodox monastery on Habsburg soil, Gomirje. It would become the spiritual center of the Orthodox Vlachs of the military frontier. The monastery was allowed to house 20 monks. However, setting up an ecclesiastical organization was not permitted, and the establishment of churches required the approval of the Court Council of War. The situation for Orthodoxy improved only with the so-called Great Serbian Migration of 1690 and the resultant settlement of thousands of additional Orthodox Serbian families in the Habsburg Empire. The support for and training of the Orthodox clergy was much worse than it was for its Catholic counterpart. For example, parishioners had to supply the Orthodox clergy with portions from the harvest. Only from the second half of the 18th century were they paid by the frontier administration.

2. The difference between the two population groups was openly demonstrated not only by separate ecclesiastical organizations but also by language and writing. Vlach families generally spoke a dialect that was different from the Serbo-Croatian of the Croats. However, because there was significant overlap, language did not demarcate clear boundaries between the two populations. That tended to be more true for names: family and given names allowed someone to determine membership in the respective group with some certainty. In fact, family names can be used to draw well-founded inferences about the origins of a given family. For centuries, however, there were no clear linguistic differentiations, because a general school system was established only very slowly and a uniform system could not be set up in the military frontier. In 1764 it was decreed that a school with German as the language of instruction was to be set up in every larger place. In addition, there were schools run by Catholic orders. Initially there was no public support for the establishment of an Orthodox school organization. The Orthodox population largely rejected attending German schools, an option

that was open to them. On this matter there were long debates with the frontier administration; this administration pushed for the introduction of the Latin script, something the Orthodox ecclesiastical leadership rejected. That is why school instruction was organized exclusively by the parishes until 1829, when a functioning Orthodox school system could be set up with public support. The establishment of an educational system on a confessional basis – and, what it is more, with unequal support by the administration – deepened the contrast between the two population groups. It became the leaven for the national integration on a confessional basis.

3. The Croatian and Valachian-Serbian populations also differed with regard to family organization. A census in 1712, the detailed records of which have survived, conveys central information about the composition of the population for the frontier region of Lika. In the Croatian villages, the families were almost entirely structured as simple – that is, nuclear – families. In the villages of the Vlachs, but also in the those of the Catholic Bunjevci, families had a more complex structure: a household could be composed of two or several conjugal family units, resulting in larger family entities. The largest household in 1712 counted 54 members from the group of the Bunjevci.

We can infer from this that these two population groups of the military frontier also represented two distinct cultures: Vlachs and Bunjevci corresponded to the widespread pattern of the Balkan patriarchate, for which manliness and heroism, a nomadic economy in the mountains, patrilineal thinking, kinship solidarity, and Christianized ancestor-worship represented central elements. By contrast, the majority of Croatian immigrants came from an agricultural milieu of the plain, which led to other forms of economic life and social adaptation.

It is interesting to note that the military administration ordered all families in 1754 to form family conglomerates following the model among the Vlachs and Bunjevci. The reason for this was that it was hardly possible to remove a conscript from small families with one or two adult men, something that was much easier in the case of larger familial conglomerates. However, this measure only appeared to lead to a cultural harmonization of the two population groups. While Croatian households now grew substantially in terms of number, many of them split clandestinely. When free household divisions were permitted once again following the dissolution of the military frontier, the households with complex structures among the Croatian population rapidly dissolved again, more rapidly, at any rate, than those among the Serbian population.

This last example is symptomatic for the problem of integration in the military frontier: the population that immigrated from various regions was ethnically nonhomogeneous. The integration offer "free farmer and soldier" proved attractive for the immigrant families of any background. In the end, however, this frontiersman identity was not solid enough to resist alternative offers of identity. Indications suggest that while there were no significant conflicts between the Orthodox and the Catholic populations, there was also hardly any social intermixing of the two groups. The above-mentioned census of 1712 encompassed 2,000 families; among them there were merely a dozen inter-confessional marriages at the time the census was taken. The prevention of any social stratification by the military administration is likely to have contributed – much like the poor infrastructure and communication – to a situation in which "the emperor's frontiersmen" tended to live side-by-side rather than with each other. Military camaraderie could do nothing to change that.

Bracewell, Wendy. *The Uskoks of Senj: Piracy, Banditry, and Holy War in the 16th Century Adriatic*. Ithaca, NY, 1992.

Ivić, Aleksa. *Migracija Srba u Hrvatsku tokom 16., 17. i 18. stoleća*. Subotica, 1923.

Kaser, Karl. *Freier Bauer und Soldat. Die Militarisierung der agrarischen Gesellschaft an der kroatisch-slawonischen Militärgrenze (1535–1881)*. Vienna, 1997.

Moačanin, Fedor. "Vojna krajina do kantonskog uredjenja 1787." In *Vojna krajina: povijesni pregled, historiografija, rasprave*, edited by Dragutin Pavličević, 23–56. Zagreb, 1984.

Roksandić, Drago. *Srbi u Hrvatskoj*. Zagreb, 1991.

Rothenberg, Gunther E. *Die österreichische Militärgrenze in Kroatien 1522 bis 1881*. Vienna, 1970.

Valentić, Mirko. *Vojna krajina i pitanje njezina sjedinjena s Hrvatskom 1849–1881*. Zagreb, 1981.

Cross-references: Austria; Southeastern Europe; Serbs in the Krajina since the Late 19th Century

SLOVENIAN AND CROATIAN EMIGRANTS IN YUGOSLAVIA FROM TERRITORIES CEDED TO ITALY AFTER 1918

Rolf Wörsdörfer

When prince regent Aleksandar Karađorđević, in the summer of 1920, paid his first visit to his new Slovenian and Croatian subjects, united for almost two years with the Serbs into a kingdom, he was greeted in Ljubljana by a group of men dressed in black as a sign of mourning. They were the first representatives of exile and refugee movements of Slovenes and Croats from Adriatic territories that had been Austrian until 1918 and had then devolved to Italy. These movements took on endemic forms in the course of the 1920s and 1930s.

In recent times, the exile of the Slovenes and Croats has been at times also referred to as an "exodus," in reference to the departure of the Italians from the same territories after 1945. That term was not usual in the interwar period, which is the focus of this essay. The approximately 70,000 members of the Slovenian-Croatian exile in the southern

Slavic state called themselves "refugees" or "emigrants." A literary enhancement was the term *Uskoks* that is occasionally found, a reminder of the Christian southern Slavs who had fled from the Ottoman Empire in the early modern period into the neighboring spheres of Habsburg or Venetian power. The word "emigrants" appeared also in the names of those organizations who succeeded in the 1920s and 1930s in organizing about a tenth of the Slovenes and Croats who had moved from Italy to Yugoslavia.

It is striking that the exiles, especially in the period of the royal dictatorship (1929–34), did not refer to themselves as Slovenes and Croats, but as *primorci* (coastal dwellers) and *istrani* (Istrians). Those labels indicated their regions of origin: coastal Slovenia (Primorska) and the Croatian southern half of the Istrian peninsula. Official southern Slavic documents at the time always spoke of a "Yugoslav minority" in Italy, not of a Slovenian or Croatian one. Only after the Serbian-Croatian Compromise of 1939 were the refugees from Italy allowed to call themselves Slovenes and Croats again.

The boundaries between political exile and labor migration from the minority regions in northwestern Italy, which was at times deliberately promoted by the Mussolini regime through dismissals from public service and the destruction of the cooperatives, were fluid. The first Slovenes and Croats to leave former Habsburg territory that was occupied by Italy in the waning weeks of the First World War were state employees who did not believe there was any chance the new Italian authorities would keep them in their jobs. That included no small number of teachers speaking the native language, whose schools were soon closed or Italianized by the Italian military administration. Members of other minorities left territories close to the front lines that had been destroyed in the war (Karst, Isonzo Valley) or did not return after having been evacuated after 1915 and in many cases spent several years in camps.

With the definitive settling of the border issue in the Treaty of Rapallo and the Fiume Agreement (1920 and 1924), but especially with the fascist "March on Rome" in October 1922, there were now many more reasons that prompted a part of the Slavic border population to leave the territories that had come under Italian rule. Those initially affected were once again public employees and to a growing degree also the self-employed, priests, workers, or cooperatively organized farmers who followed their functionaries, the targets of disciplinary action by the dictatorship, into exile. There was an accelerated exodus after the political trials that the fascist special court pursued after the end of the 1920s against activists of the southern Slav nationalist movement in the Julian Veneto, or in connection with Italy's military intervention in Ethiopia and in the Spanish Civil War.

A clear distinction between various waves of refugees is problematic, because the fascist policy of forced assimilation extended over the entire interwar period. As a result, members of the minority (minorities) always had reasons to flee, even independent of political events. For example,

in response to the Italianization of all public and private schools, Slavic teachers who were not willing to teach in Italian lost their jobs. Self-employed professionals had to leave Italy when they lost their license or work permit. Slovenian and Croatian journalists followed suit after the regime had outlawed their papers. Slavic artists and musicians who worked at the Narodni dom (House of the People) also lost their livelihood when it was burned down by the fascists. Pupils and students from Julian Veneto who attended educational institutions in Yugoslavia were not really part of the political exile. Boarding schools existed in Zagreb and Karlovac for the children of emigrants and other members of the minorities. The young people grew up in the spirit of an integral Yugoslavism (*Jugolovenstvo*), which saw its enemy not only in fascism but also in the Italian nation as a whole; this shaped the attitude of future political activists and partisan leaders.

The rapprochement between Italy and Yugoslavia that was initiated under Minister President Milan Stojadinović in the second half of the 1930s brought only minor improvements to the minority in the country. It made the situation of the emigrants worse, as their organizations could suddenly no longer count on the funds that had been generously flowing until then from the royal house and from the government. In 1935, even the Central Congress of Emigrants was outlawed. The difficulties that the emigrants encountered in exile prompted some of them to return to Italy.

Until the middle of the 1930s, the centralized Yugoslav state was interested – for both internal and external political reasons – in keeping the exile organizations alive. Internally, the emigrants organized by the liberal Trieste establishment (Edinost Group, *narodnjaci*) constituted a reliable pillar of the government in Belgrade and of the royal house, because they adopted the Yugoslav state ideology and aggressively disseminated it in the various places of exile, above all in Slovenia and Croatia (Old Current). Exiled writers interwove the Serbian-Yugoslav founding myth, the legend of King Lazar and his *voivods*, with the experiences of the refugees from the Julian Veneto and Carinthia, with the Italian defeat at Caporetto (Kobarid) in October 1917, and with the "land robbery" by liberal and fascist Italy.

In spite – or precisely because – of this function as the mouthpiece of the centralized state, the exiles were not well liked in certain parts of Yugoslavia. Some people in this desperately poor country were envious of the support they received from the state. In some places they were even denounced as "fascists," even though they had fled precisely from the effects of fascist policies. Most problematic was the situation in Croatia, where the autonomy efforts – which sometimes became a threat of separation – on the part of the Farmers' Party under Stjepan Radić stood in striking opposition to the focus of the refugees on the centralized state. According to Italian sources, the refugees in Croatia, who were already in a precarious situation in the wake of the global economic crisis, often lost their jobs as supporters of the centralized government. Attempts by the Farmers' Party to set up its own lobby among the exiles came only after the Serbo-Croatian Agreement of 1939. By contrast, since the mid-1930s communist influence had been on the rise among the migrants (Young Current), who were joined during the Abyssinian War by hundreds of deserters from the Italian military.

Those refugees who counted themselves as part of the *inteligencija* were in demand in the labor market, and they had good opportunities for advancement in the Kingdom of Yugoslavia. Thus representatives of the Julian exile community were found in the civil service (all the way to the top echelons of the regional administration, where the Istrian Matko Laginja rose as high as administrator of a banate) and among the industrialists. Entrepreneurs from the Julian Veneto ran a kind of closed-shop system for unskilled migrant workers, who were given a job only if they joined the state-supported emigrant organizations. In some cases, the membership dues for these organizations was deducted directly from the workers' wages. Thus it became more and more difficult to distinguish between political exile and work migration. Remigrants interrogated by the Italian organs of repression (police, militia, *carabinieri*) often stated that they joined the exile organizations out of economic pressure. Whether this was true or said out of self-protection cannot be clearly determined on the basis of the sources.

Most migrants retained Italian citizenship in southern Slavia, as the acquisition of Yugoslav citizenship required a high fee that was more than the small budgets of the immigrants could afford. In fact, the spokesmen of the *istrani* and *primorci* advocated the establishment of a kind of dual citizenship that would have granted its holders all the rights of Yugoslav nationals without forcing them to give up Italian citizenship and thus also the hope of returning to Italy.

The exiles from the coastal region and from Istria were often compelled to perform "national pioneer work" in the sense of the *Jugoslovenstvo* or Slovenian national ideology: the exile organizations and patriotic clubs (*Sokol, Jugoslovenska matica*) directed the Slovenes from the coastal regions into the German minority regions of the Drava-Banat, where they were supposed to influence the "national struggle" and decide it in favor of the Slovenian side. In fact, with help from the *primorci* it was possible to gradually Slovenize a city like Maribor (Lower Styria), which still had a strong German imprint right after 1918. The emigrant organizations came up with a separate settlement policy for the rural minority regions in southern Yugoslavia, where Albanians or Macedo-Slavs were to be influenced in the sense of *Jugoslovenstvo*. This concerned above all the farmers, who had lost their rural credit funds in the province of Görz or in Istria. Their functionaries, some of whom had already emigrated, recruited them with the possibility of colonizing border areas, peripheral regions, and minority territories in the southern Slavic state.

On the ground, the emigrants were in part installed in farmsteads whose native owners had been expelled by the police. Some settlers from Italy were also overwhelmed by a wave of Serbianization and in Macedonia converted from Catholicism to Orthodoxy. Christian-Social agrarian funds that were common in the province of Görz, along with the social infrastructure connected with it (from the choir to the reading hall), were copied in Banja Luka (Bosnia).

When the Axis powers occupied Yugoslavia in 1941, the emigrants were among the most harshly persecuted segments of the Yugoslav population. That was true of the parts of the country occupied by the Wehrmacht as well as of the Hungarian occupation zone. During the war or in the postwar years, a large part of the emigrants returned to their home regions, most of which had by now been assigned once again to the Yugoslav state.

Kalc, Aleksej. "L'emigrazione slovena e croata dalla Venezia Giulia tra le due guerre ed il suo ruolo politico." *Annales (Koper)* (1996), no. 8: 23–60.

Marušič, Branko. *Domovina kje si? Zbornik ob stoletnici rojstva Alberta Rejca 1899–1976.* Gorica, 1998.

Purini, Piero. "Raznarodovanje slovenske manjšine v Trstu (Problematika ugotajljanja števila neitaljanskih izseljencev iz Julijske krajine po prvi svetovni vojni)." *Prispevki za novejšo zgodovino* (1988), no 38: 23–41.

Vovko, Andrej. "Organizacije jugoslovanskih emigrantov iz Julijske krajine do leta 1933." *Zgodovinski časopis* 32, 4 (1978): 449–73.

Vovko, Andrej. "Delovanje 'Zveze jugoslovanskih emigrantov iz Julijske krajine' v letih 1933–1940." *Zgodovinski časopis* 33, 1 (1979): 67–102.

Cross-references: Italy; Southeastern Europe; Italian Refugees in Italy from Adriatic Territories that Fell to Yugoslavia after 1945

SOUTHERN ITALIAN WORKERS IN NORTHERN ITALY, 1945–1975

John Foot

South-north migration in Italy offers an example of internal migration, but also must be considered from the same perspective as broader trends in international migration. The distances involved were often very great (over 1,000 kilometers from Sicily to Milan, for example, usually covered by fairly slow trains or ships) and Italy itself had been unified only since 1860. There were also great regional economic and social inequalities in Italy. A good argument can be made for seeing the south-north migration in Italy as occurring between two very separate territories with distinct histories, cultures, economies, and peoples, making vast migration from one area to another – despite being technically within one country.

Migration to the north

Southern Italians migrated in large numbers to the north of Italy from the end of the 19th century onward. For "southerners" we mean people from the regions of Italy below Rome, and in particular the Abruzzo, Apulia, Calabria, Campania, Basilicata, and the islands of Sicily and Sardinia. The earliest southern migrants were generally employed in public administration sectors or set up commercial enterprises – in particular, bars, wine enterprises, and street trading stalls. Nonetheless, in this period and right through the 1930s, the main bulk of southern Italian migration was directed outside of Italy, to Argentina, Brazil, the USA, and other European countries. The main bulk of mass southern migration to the north of Italy took place in the period roughly from the late 1940s until the early 1970s. During these years, with a peak in the "economic miracle" (1958–63), hundreds of thousands of southerners moved to cities all over Italy (including Rome and Naples). The highest concentrations of movement were to the industrial cities of Milan, Turin, and Genoa. Throughout this period, in addition, transnational emigration did not cease but continued apace. However, this was the first moment in Italian history when the mass southern Italians were presented with the alternative of migration internally to purely external migration, in order to earn a decent wage for themselves and their families.

Mass movement thus began in the late 1940s and early 1950s, with the revival of industrial production in the north and the demand for building workers in the big northern conurbations. The agrarian reforms of the 1950s came too late to offer most southerners any kind of realistic economic alternative to the grinding poverty of the rural south, but the reasons for migration were not purely to do with jobs. Many southerners were certainly attracted by the cultural image of the north – the glittering cities of Milan and Turin depicted in the popular press and film and, from the mid-1950s onward, on state television. This was Italy's own, homespun, "American Dream." So migrants were not purely southern peasants but also sections of the upwardly mobile lower-middle classes. The latter often ended up in public administration posts (the postal service, police, and *carabiniere*) rather than in the construction sites of the "economic miracle." In addition, a number of intellectuals also finally abandoned the south in this period and they had an important impact on the cultural milieu of the north.

In most cases, young men were the first and most numerically dominant migrants, although there were also many older men, disillusioned by the defeats of the great peasant movements for land distribution in the south (1944–5; 1949–50), and whole families. The first port of call was usually linked to the formation of immigrant "chains," through "pioneers" who had managed to establish a base in the north and could help with work contacts, housing, and wide-ranging cultural networks. The vast majority of movement was by train, particularly on the main coastal routes running up from Bari,

Naples, and Sicily on either side of Italy. Thus, many immigrants arrived in the same place (the central stations of Milan and Turin) and this moment of arrival was captured by documentaries and films, and most famously re-created in the opening scene of Luchino Visconti's *Rocco and His Brothers* (1960), which deals with the migration of a southern family to Milan during the years of the "economic miracle."

Southerners were not the only immigrants to the north and to the northern cities in those years, and, for a long time, they were not the most numerous group. For much of the early 1950s, most immigrants to Milan were from the Veneto and from the Lombard countryside, and to Turin the great bulk of early immigration was from the Piedmontese hills. It was only with the early 1960s that a mass "southernization" of immigration took place, and the equation between "southerners" and "immigrants" was cemented in the public mind, in particular in Milan and Turin. At its peak, southern immigrants made up 30% of all new arrivals in Milan between 1958 and 1963. Although all statistics from this period should be looked at critically, at least 300,000 immigrants moved from within Italy to Milan between 1951 and 1961, and Turin's population rose from 719,300 in 1951 to 1,124,714 in 1967. Internal migration was not confined to these two cities alone. At least 9.1 million Italians migrated within their own country between 1955 and 1971.

A series of immigrant chains from the south led to concentrations of regional immigration in various areas in and around the big cities. Whole villages from the rural south were more or less transported to the outskirts of the big northern cities. For example, between the 1950s and 1960s, there were concentrations of immigrants from Fuscaldo in Calabria in the small town of Pero, on the outskirts of Milan, of Sicilians in Garbagnate, also outside Milan, and of Sardinians in Turin. These geographical micro-concentrations can be traced all over these cities (over time) and right across the provinces of Milan, Turin, and Genoa in the 1950s, 1960s, and 1970s. Many of these settlement concentrations remain today, along with cultural associations, patterns of exchange, and cultural links between hometowns and the towns to which the migrants moved.

Patterns of integration

In the early period of southern migration, most migrants found work in the building industry, in street trading, or in casual industrial work. These sectors were cheap, less unionized, and less state-controlled than other industrial sectors. In the early 1960s, with the general and massive growth that accompanied the economic miracle, southerners began to find work en masse in the big factories of the north – Alfa Romeo, Pirelli, Breda, Falck in Milan; Fiat (above all) in Turin. At first, these workers were treated with some diffidence and even in racist terms by the local workers but, with time, the southern workers began to link to the struggles of the 1960s that were conducted both by the unions and by the new left organizations that concentrated on the big factories of the north. A series of theorists began to identify the southern proletariat as a new kind of worker – the "mass worker" – unintegrated and liable to rebel. This type of analysis took off after the 1962 street riots in Turin (known as the events of Piazza Statuto) where southern workers and immigrants were at the forefront of long and violent clashes with the police.

The events of 1969 in particular deserve much attention. Southern workers, in particular at Fiat but not only there, played a key role in the extraordinary strike movements of those years, which threatened the very bases of Italian capitalism and won a series of gains – above all the 1970 Worker's Statute – which remain in place to this day. The unions, and the political parties (the Communists and the Socialists, but including the Christian Democrats [DC]), played a key role in the integration of southern migrant workers both inside and outside these big factories. Many southerners became leaders of the post-1968 leftist political and union movements in the north and tried to build links with similar movements in the south itself.

Other factors and organizations contributed to the integration of southerners in the northern cities. Local administrations, especially after the abrogation of fascist anti-urbanization laws in 1961, built houses for the new arrivals (a whole belt around both Milan and Turin was constructed for the immigrants, including huge and often well-built estates). Councils also set up offices for the migrants and made sure that temporary accommodation was available. They also helped migrants find work, and great efforts were made within the schools to deal with overcrowding. In both Milan and Turin, school shifts were introduced to cope with the extraordinarily high numbers of immigrant children.

Church and Catholic organizations of all kinds also worked hard to aid immigrant integration. Priests and Catholic bodies could provide introductions to work opportunities, child care and free schooling, pastoral care, and financial help. In addition, specific organizations were set up by the Church (often through the Christian Democrats) to assist immigrants; these sometimes came with explicit political motives, as many commentators believed that the southerners would "naturally" gravitate toward the left and looked to stop this shift. One example of this was the Center for Immigrant Aid in Milan, set up in 1963. Other mediators included so-called cooperatives of various kinds, many of which were organized by immigrants themselves to either help new arrivals or to afford them access to a range of services. Immigrant organizations of various types were instituted in the cultural sphere, many of which were linked to particular places of origin, and religious and other festivals were organized to coincide with those in the immigrants' hometowns; these organizations also fostered cultural and political exchanges with the south. Additionally, intermarriage contributed to social integration. Within a short period of time, intermarriage became commonplace although no proper study has been carried out regarding this important social and cultural phenomenon.

The vast majority of immigrants did not break their links entirely with the south and returned home at some time or another in a complicated series of movements within the diaspora. Some "failed" and returned home for good. Others "succeeded," returning for holidays (summer, Christmas), family events (funerals, weddings), or to build houses in their hometowns to retire to. In August, towns all over the Italian south would fill with the Fiats and Alfa Romeos now owned by those who had migrated to the north some time before. Many returned completely to the *mezzogiorno* on retirement.

However, these inclusionary features of life in Milan and Turin were not the whole story. Many immigrants were met by racism and hostility among the local population and at a political level. In Turin, in particular, immigration was understood as a burden. A series of traditional stereotypes were applied to the migrants – especially those linking southern immigrants to criminal behavior and prostitution. Racism ranged from lurid reporting in the popular press to signs saying "we do not rent to southerners." Southerners were marginalized in particular parts of these cities – in Turin either on the extreme periphery or in very low-quality housing in the city center, or in hotel rooms rented by the hour or the day. Public housing dominated the periphery of Turin – where huge estates were built to accommodate these new migrants. In the town center, on the other hand, most migrants ended up in something close to slum dwellings.

In Milan, unlike Turin, many immigrants were able to buy land around the city and build their own houses. These zones became known as *coree* because of their supposed similarity to images being seen in Italy from the Korean War. Whole zones of this type, with small self-constructed housing, sprang up like mushrooms between the early 1950s and mid-1960s. For a long time, these zones were lacking in basic urban services, such as drains and streets, but they are, at the beginning of the 21st century, now an integral part of the city. Those able to buy land and build their own houses were the immigrant elite. They then turned to expanding their own buildings. Those who rented rooms here were often the poorest newly arrived immigrants. These immigrant spaces around Milan were and are unique, and it is estimated that something like 100,000 immigrants (mainly from the south and the Veneto) lived in these places by the mid-1960s. Integration in Milan was easier than in Turin, thanks to the multifaceted nature of the Milanese economy and the spread of the city to accommodate new arrivals. Those who ended up in public housing were often ghettoized within the city and accused of not integrating into the local population. In Milan, as in Turin, public housing was also constructed around the city for the migrants. However, unlike Turin, very few southerners in Milan were able to find housing – of whatever quality – near the city center. Speculation had already made this very difficult and thus workers in Milan (of all types) were faced with long journeys to and from work on the grimy trains of the Ferrovie Nord.

Over time, as the economic boom slowed down, so too did the migration of potential industrial workers to the north. Most migrants who moved did so in order to take up jobs in public administration such as the postal services or the education sector. The "biblical" nature of the immigration had ended by the early 1970s (the early period was often referred to as an "exodus"). By the mid-1970s, Milan and Turin were already beginning to attract foreign migrants. The divisions between northerners and southerners have softened over time. However, the few studies on the contemporary conditions of southern immigrants in these conurbations show (especially for Turin) that strong ethnic and spatial divisions remain part of everyday life and everyday discourse. The rise of the regional northern leagues in the 1980s and 1990s, which assembled into the Lega Nord in 1991, was in part based on racist propaganda directed against the south and against southerners in general. Southerners were connected to a series of ills, including the corruption of the public administrative system. However, the shift toward anti-foreign immigrant policies and propaganda has had the interesting effect of mobilizing support among ex-southern immigrants (for example, in certain central zones of Turin) and uniting Italians against a supposed foreign menace (needed to fill huge gaps at the "dirty" end of the job market). This occurred in a broader context where many southern workers were forced to reinvent themselves on the job market with the crisis of Fiat and other big industries in the 1980s and 1990s.

Historical work on this question has not been of the quality or depth deserved by the extent of the migration movement or its effects. Certain key works of the 1960s remain in use today; no extended research has been carried out since the 1970s. However, with the shift in scholarly attention to foreign immigration, comparisons have begun to be made, historically and politically, with other periods of southern Italian migration. Cinema has been the most interesting arena of research and debate: Gianni Amelio's *Cosi Ridevano* (1997) was a fascinating attempt to revisit the southern immigration to Turin in the 1960s from the point of view of contemporary Italy and its treatment of foreign immigrants. Nonetheless, the full story (at cultural, political, and economic levels, as well as on the makeup of these cities) of this mass immigration still has to be told. The contradictory and untapped memories of those who migrated, and those who did not, also have yet to be analyzed. In many ways, the impact of these migrations is still being felt at an everyday level in today's postindustrial economy as well as through the continuing and complicated links that exist and continue to develop between second- and third-generation southern migrants, the south itself, and northern cities.

Fofi, Goffredo. *L'immigrazione meridionale a Torino*. Milan, 1964.

Foot, John. "Migration and the 'Miracle' at Milan: The Neighbourhoods of Baggio, Barona, Bovisa and Comasina

in the 1950s and 1960s." *Journal of Historical Sociology* 10 (1997): 184–211.

Foot, John. *Milan since the Miracle: City, Culture and Identity*. Oxford, 2001.

Gabaccia, Donna. *Italy's Many Diasporas*. London, 2000.

Ginsborg, Paul. *A History of Contemporary Italy: Society and Politics, 1943–1980*. London, 2002.

Petrillo, Gianfranco. "Immigrati a Milano, 1951–1963." *Annali dell'Istituto milanese per la storia della resistenza e del movimento operaio*, 631–61. Milan, 1992.

Treves, Anna. *Le migrazioni interne nell'Italia fascista*. Torino, 1976.

Cross-references: Italy; Italian Labor Migrants in Northern, Central, and Western Europe since the End of World War II

SOVIET MIGRANT CONSTRUCTION WORKERS (*SHABASHNIKI*) SINCE THE 1950S

Hans Oversloot

The term *shabashnik* derives from the Russian word for Sabbath (*shabash*). When the second syllable is stressed, the word *shabash* means "enough" or "I call it quits." The verb *shabashit'* can mean "to take off after work done"; the noun *shabashka* can mean "free time," but it can also mean "work outside the confines of one's regular job" or "moonlighting." In many instances *shabashnik* is the near equivalent of *otkhodnik* or *sezonnik* (migrant worker and seasonal worker, respectively). *Shabashka* and *shabashnik* can be used neutrally but also and most often disparagingly. In some (Russian-speaking) regions of the Soviet Union, *kalymshik* was used more often than *shabashnik*; *kalym* originally meant dowry, but with an additional second meaning of "income received for an activity detrimental to society" (colloquial, derogatory), as the 1978 edition of the authoritative Ozhegov's dictionary has it. *Kalymshik* came to stand for a man who leaves home to make money – in a way that is not completely reputable– and then returns home once he has made his fortune.

The phenomenon of *shabashnichestvo* was never studied properly by Soviet academics, although it grew to enormous proportions: it involved semilegal and illegal seasonal construction work by entire brigades of migrant workers as well as agricultural work performed by seasonal migrant labor, partially in return for a portion of the crops harvested. Soviet scholarship's neglect of *shabashnichestvo* can be accounted for by two separate but related reasons. First, gaining insight into semilegal and illegal work is difficult regardless of the context. Second, "wild brigades" were not a proper subject for academic research as they did not fit the ideal of a planned socioeconomic order. *Shabashnichestvo* was, however, a phenomenon of interest to, among others, the USSR Ministry of Internal Affairs and to State Committees of Labor in the USSR's union republics.

Not much is known about the *shabashniki*-sharecroppers, often referred to as *gektarniki*. *Gektarniki* were nearly always from a rural background and specialized in the early planting of easily marketable crops that benefit from proper care and extra nonmechanized labor (e.g., melons and onions, but not wheat). Family ties and local ties were important. Old Believers – Orthodox Christians who rejected Patriarch Nikon's modernization of faith and church in 1666 and who have been persecuted on and off ever since – were active as *gektarniki*. Ethnic minorities such as the Koreans, who had been transported to Central Asia under Stalin, were also active as *gektarniki*. As renowned onion growers, Koreans not only worked in Kazakhstan and Tadzhikistan but also migrated as far as the Don River delta, southern Ukraine, and the Crimea. *Getarniki* also worked in other places like Lithuania, Belarus, Ukraine, south-central Russia, and Tadzhikistan and other Central Asian republics. In some regions as much as 5% of arable land was cultivated by *gektarniki*, yielding four times as much per hectare than the average. The number of *gektarniki* in the 1970s and early 1980s is unknown, yet there were likely many tens of thousands of them.

Much more is known about illegal seasonal construction work by brigades of migrant workers. From the late 1960s until the mid 1980s – and the estimate can only be very rough – between 500,000 and up to 2.3 million people were involved in the work of construction brigades each year, working for a couple weeks or even up to six or eight months (a full construction season). *Shabashniki* were almost exclusively men; some worked for a few seasons, others for their full working life, starting in their early 20s and continuing until their mid-40s. Most work was physically very demanding; "organizers" could continue well into their 50s. In the early 1980s brigades of *shabashniki* were responsible for some 6% to 8% of *all* construction work in the Soviet Union, and for some 25% to 30% to potentially 35% or even 40% of all construction work done in agricultural regions of the Soviet Union. In the Union Republic of Kazakhstan *shabashniki* were responsible for over 40% of all construction work in agricultural regions; in the province (*oblast'*) of Kurgan (in the Russian Soviet Federative Socialist Republic, or RSFSR) *shabashniki* completed 60% of construction work in agricultural areas. *Shabashniki* came from major cities as well as from rural areas: in the rural areas of Ivano-Frankovsk in the western part of the Union Republic of Ukraine, in Chechnya-Ingushetia (part of the RSFSR, close to the Caucasian mountains), and Armenia, *shabashnichestvo* was by far the most important source of income in some areas.

The phenomenon of seasonal and migrant labor such as it existed in the 1960s to 1980s in the Soviet Union can be traced back to forms and organization of migrant seasonal labor in the pre-Soviet era (*artel'* and *otkhodnichestvo*), but was (re)shaped by the conditions that were specific to the economic system of the Soviet Union in general and to its industrial development in particular. The state organization *orgnabor* oversaw the large-scale permanent as well as seasonal relocation of labor to build the new industrial

centers. In 1940, for example, almost 2.4 million people were put to work via *orgnabor* for a period of eight to nine months. After the Second World War the numbers were far smaller: between 1946 and 1956 from 0.7 to 0.8 million workers per year, in 1958 0.5 million. From 1953 onward the majority of laborers recruited by *orgnabor* no longer came from the countryside but from cities. In fact, in the course of the 1950s, but especially in the 1960s – in a tendency that has never been reversed – large-scale emigration from agricultural areas of the Soviet Union set in. Young men more so than young women sought to get away from country life. In many instances young men did not return to their villages (or rather kolkhoz or collective farm) of origin after completing the obligatory military service and instead sought employment in cities. Labor shortages became endemic in large parts of the Soviet Union's agricultural areas, which not only posed a problem at harvest time (each year millions of high school and college students and hundreds of thousands of soldiers were sent in to help), but also for seasonal work in the construction industry, which could take place only during the five to eight frost-free months of the year.

It was especially difficult for the kolkhozes to organize at least the formal allocation of adequate provisions (permits, material, and/or credit) for construction work. Even when these preconditions had been met, the "realization" (*realizatsiya*) of planned construction work often remained a problem. In such cases, *shabashniki*, among others, stepped in. A leader (*brigadir*) of a "wild brigade" could provide the manpower and various specialists required for the job. Older, more experienced construction brigade leaders, some of whom had worked in the same or in surrounding regions for over a decade and were therefore well acquainted with key figures in the region, could sometimes help the president (*predsedatel'*) of the kolkhoz or the director of a state organization who wanted or needed to hire a wild brigade to get hold of (*dostat'*) the required materials as well. Leaders of wild brigades either did business directly with the kolkhoz or state organization requiring construction work or with an inter-kolkhoz-construction organization (*mezhkolkhozstroi*). Brigades consisted of between 5 and 35 members. Some brigade leaders were in fact leaders of several brigades working sometimes, but not always, in the same area. Some kolkhozes and state organizations hired several brigades at the same time for different projects.

The leader(s) of a brigade of *shabashniki* independently organized the brigade's work regime. Depending on the kind of work, the kind of brigade, the duration of the project, and the location of the work, the work regime varied: six or nine days of work with very long hours followed by one day off or three or six weeks at a remote location with little time off followed by a few days of vacation in a nearby town before returning to work. The *brigadir* or the wild brigade's "leading collective" also decided on payment of its members and of other hired hands.

Officially hiring *shabashniki* was of course impossible in the Soviet Union's planned economic system. Wild brigades as such could not be contracted, registered, or paid. The "formal hiring" of *shabashniki* therefore proceeded along other lines: if possible, which was often the case, *shabashniki* were listed as regular employees of the organization that required their services. Very often a far greater number of employees were registered in the organization's account than were actually present and longer periods of time were registered than the *shabashniki* required for the work. The reason for this was the necessity of distributing the actual earnings in such a way that the activities of the *shabashniki* would correspond to the targets of the economic plan. The actual monthly earnings of approximately 800–1200 rubles per *shabashnik* in the late 1970s and early 1980s had to be registered as the monthly salary of three, four, or more officially registered employees since the latter earned 200 rubles per month. Financial departments could not justify payment of salaries of much more than 200 rubles for construction work without coming into conflict with financial supervisors or the economic police.

Brigades of *shabashniki* from major towns were usually ethnically mixed. The informal character of the work and the inevitability of working and living together for an extended period of time, sometimes under considerable stress and quite often in rather primitive conditions, made *brigadirs* look for healthy men who were not only qualified professionally but who would fit the specific labor regime. They sought men whom they could trust and who could get along together. Kinship and friendship ties as well as ethnic and/or religious background typically did not play a role in the composition of wild brigades from major cities, but there were some exceptions. From the late 1970s to the mid-1980s, for example, some brigades from Moscow were exclusively Jewish, providing a livelihood for a number of *refuzniki*, or Jewish Soviet citizens whose applications for exit visas had been rejected and who as a result had been relegated to marginal positions in the official economy.

Family ties in general played a far more prominent role in the makeup and organization of brigades of *shabashniki* from rural areas, villages, and small towns, as well as for brigades consisting mostly of Chechens, Armenians, Greeks, or Ukrainians (many from the region of Ivano-Frankovsk) or for brigades from Dagestan. As a rule, there was less ethnic diversity among wild brigades originating in rural areas. Marriages of visiting *shabashniki* with local women were infrequent and members of visiting brigades rarely took up permanent residence in the region. *Shabashnichestvo* in its many varieties remained a form of seasonal migration.

After the late 1950s there was an absolute decline in population in the agricultural areas of the former Soviet Union, including Belarus, the Baltic Republics, Ukraine, and the RSFSR. This decline was particularly pronounced among the male population. Most wild brigades were employed in the RSFSR, by far the most important union republic. In other union republics, but also in some parts of the RSFSR (notably Chechnya-Ingushetia), the rural population actually increased. In these regions the lack of earning opportunities

(combined with sometimes substantial local unemployment) provided incentive for the seasonal trek of *shabasniki* to places hundreds or even thousands of miles away from home.

However, the limited opportunities for employment for a growing rural populace provide neither the sole nor the most important explanatory factor. The absolute growth of the rural populace in the period 1959–81 was highest in the union republics of Uzbekistan (75%), Turkmenistan (83%), and Tajikistan (97%), but young men from the rural areas of these republics did not venture out to, for example, the south-central Siberian regions of the RSFSR, where labor shortages were endemic and where *shabashniki* from places farther away like Armenia and the Ivano-Frankovsk province in western Ukraine found work.

The breakup of the Soviet Union in the early 1990s and the economic decline in most parts of the (former) USSR since the late 1980s put an end to the phenomenon of *shabashnichestvo*, at least in its specific Soviet variety. Regions of the former Soviet Union that had been especially dependent upon the earnings of *shabashniki* were hit very hard, such as parts of Chechnya, Ingushetia, Armenia, and Ivano-Frankovsk; only in some regions could compensation be found in seasonal construction work outside the former Soviet Union. Western Ukrainians and some Russians, for example, found illegal work in Poland, Germany, and elsewhere.

Aleksandrov, L. "Kak ostanovit' shabshnika." *Sovety narodnykh deputatov* 9 (1986): 101–5.

Alekseenko, N. "Shabashniki: stereotipy i real'nost." *Sotsiologicheskie issledovaniya* 6 (1987): 89–94.

Gal'chenko, Viktor. "Zhitie odnogo shabashnika." *Ėkonomika i organizatsia promyshlennogo proizvodstva (ĖKO)* 153, 3 (1987): 101–36.

Murphy, Patrick. "Soviet *Shabashniki*: Material Incentives at Work." *Problems of Communism* 34, 6 (1985): 48–57.

Oversloot, Johannes. *Sabbatswerkers in de Sovjetunie*. Leiden, 1990.

Cross-references: The Baltic Region; Russia and Belarus; Ukraine; Russian Peasant Labor Migrants in Russian Factories from the End of the 19th Century to the End of the 1920s

SPANISH LABOR MIGRANTS IN WESTERN, CENTRAL, AND NORTHERN EUROPE SINCE THE END OF WORLD WAR II

Dietrich Thränhardt

The Spanish migration to western, central, and northern Europe was part of the labor migrations from the Mediterranean countries into the European industrialized states between 1945 and the oil price shock of 1973. The first labor migrations across the Pyrenees to France after the Second World War were informal, because the Franco regime sought to curtail emigration as part of its policy of autarchy.

Break of Spanish labor migrants at the Karmann company in Osnabrück in the 1970s (*Molina Rodriguez, Julio, Osnabrück, Germany*).

It was only after the economic opening of Spain in 1959 that France was able to establish a recruitment office for Spanish workers in Irún. Subsequently, Spain signed recruitment treaties with Germany (1960), Switzerland (1961), and the Netherlands (1964). Within the context of the European economic upswing that lasted until 1973, extensive, organized labor migrations took place into those countries as well as to Great Britain, Belgium, and Sweden. Parallel to this, the largely informal migration to France continued. Following the recruitment stop in Sweden (1972), Germany (1973), France and the Benelux states (1974), only Switzerland continued organized recruitment, though within the framework of the *Saisonnier* Programs, which permitted only a seasonal migration of workers.

Much more than comparable immigrant groups, the Spaniards responded to the end of the recruitment phase by returning home, driven by the hope of a better future in Spain in the wake of that country's democratization in 1974. Those who remained abroad integrated quickly into the host countries. Especially their rates of exogamy rose more rapidly than those of other migrant workers. Even though many Spaniards had immigrated as illiterates and came from the poorest provinces of Spain, especially Andalusia and Galicia, the second generation showed good integration success with respect to education, work, and income. An effective organization and pragmatic orientation toward the system of education and training in the destination countries, as well as support from the homeland, formed the basis of this success. It was all made easier because the Spanish immigrants did not become the central target of xenophobic campaigns in any of the destination countries.

Migratory movements and destination countries

After the Second World War, migrations into European industrialized countries replaced emigration to Latin America, which had dominated Spain for centuries. In contrast to emigration to America, this migration occurred with the expectation of a return home. According to the official figures of the Spanish Instituto Espanõl de Emigración (IEE), 1961 was the first year of more migrations to other European countries than overseas, even if the official statistics did not include the ongoing informal migration to France. Since 1945, France, for demographic and economic reasons, favored the immigration of people from neighboring Romance countries, who were considered especially assimilable. By virtue of the treaties of 1862 and 1932, Spaniards were free to settle in France. The new immigration after 1945 thus picked up on older migratory traditions, which reached from the Spanish agricultural laborers in France since the late 19th century to the Republican refugees fleeing the Franco regime. This continuity facilitated the social and political organization and adaptation of the new migrants of both genders.

Given its geographic proximity, France was always the most important European destination country for migrations from Spain. When the Italian migration to France began to dry up because of higher wages in Switzerland and Germany and the dynamic economic development in Italy, the Spaniards became the largest immigrant group in France in 1959. As early as 1966, when France counted 367,000 Spaniards, the Portuguese replaced them as the largest group because of the slower economic growth in Portugal and its colonial war in Africa. In 1974 there were 587,400 Spaniards in France, of whom 250,000 were employable.

After signing its recruitment treaty, which from the outset made possible also the immigration of families, Germany quickly developed into the second-most important European destination country for Spaniards. The migration to Germany was comprehensively organized by the state and overseen by the Federal Labor Office (Bundesanstalt für Arbeit). At the height of the labor migration in 1973, the 287,000 Spaniards in Germany were the fifth-largest group of foreigners from recruitment countries, after the Turks, Italians, Yugoslavs, and Greeks. They were more evenly spread across Germany than these other groups and like the Greeks, they immigrated in large numbers as family units. Smaller groups came under similar conditions to the Netherlands, Belgium, Great Britain, and Sweden. Beginning in 1971, most of those placed officially went to Switzerland. After Italy had won greater rights for its citizens in Switzerland in 1964, Spaniards were recruited in larger numbers. They had to allow themselves to be recruited as seasonal workers five years in a row before they acquired the status of a "resident," which allowed them to remain in the country continuously and to have their families join them.

All in all, the IEE speaks of 1,472,000 individuals who left Spain between 1955 and 1972 (see Table 1). Half of those were nonemployable family members. The return remittances from migrant workers were a substantial asset to the Spanish foreign currency balance in the crucial years of transition to a dynamic economic development and a greater intertwining with the global economy. Remittances rose from $50 million in 1959 to $200 million in 1963, $627 million in 1970, to as high as $1.185 billion in 1973, before declining again in the wake of the oil crisis. Remittances from Germany rose

Table 1. Workers officially placed by the Spanish authorities, 1961–1975

Year	Germany	Belgium	France	Great Britain	The Netherlands	Switzerland	Other countries	Total
1961	29,991	111	23,075	1,206	744	4,070	46	59,243
1962	35,936	1,936	13,416	736	2,584	10,190	542	65,336
1963	35,364	1,570	21,222	1,509	4,172	19,052	839	83,728
1964	45,899	904	20,772	1,194	4,048	28,965	364	102,146
1965	41,114	316	8,446	1,601	2,660	20,145	257	74,539
1966	26,927	131	8,357	1,698	1,602	17,991	89	56,795
1967	3,422	34	6,543	847	551	14,383	131	25,911
1968	23,565	9	25,136	950	1,374	15,609	56	66,699
1969	42,778	49	32,008	941	4,308	20,664	92	100,840
1970	40,658	26	22,727	885	6,373	26,777	211	97,657
1971	30,317	42	24,266	1,087	5,922	51,751	317	113,702
1972	23,271	6	22,114	758	2,089	53,711	185	104,134
1973	27,919	22	11,631	464	2,591	53,284	177	96,088
1974	245	4	5,601	319	2,338	42,029	159	50,695
1975	85	3	1,751	286	394	17,992	97	20,618

Source: Instituto Español de Emigracion; Mision Catolica 1986: 14.

Table 2. Children born to German-foreign and to foreign marriages in West Germany, 1980–1997

	Children born to foreign marriages				Children born to German-foreign marriages				Ratio %
	1980	1990	1995	1997	1980	1990	1995	1997	1997
Turks	39,658	43,921	41,733	44,956	1,336	2,572	4,275	6,880	13.5
Former Yugoslavs	9,287	4,870	7,121	7,492	2,454	2,505	1,789	2,333	23.7
Italians	9,871	6,096	4,776	5,215	3,819	4,258	3,728	3,814	42.2
Greeks	3,904	3,124	3,578	3,698	834	1,022	1,071	1,101	22.9
Spaniards	1,723	495	305	282	1,068	1,238	1,201	1,272	81.2

Source: Statistische Jahrbücher der Bundesrepublik Deutschland; author's calculations.

from $50 million in 1960 to $700 million in 1974 and then declined to $250 million by 1984.

Because of return migrations, high rates of exogamy, and in France also high rates of naturalization in the period before Spain entered the European Community (EC) in 1986, the number of Spaniards in the foreigner statistics of the European states dropped sharply: in France from 607,200 in 1968 to 161,800 in 1999; in Germany from 287,000 in 1973 to 129,000 in 2000; in Belgium from 67,534 in 1971 to 45,917 in 2000. Only in Switzerland did the number of Spaniards continue to increase – from 108,400 in 1985 to 116,100 in 1990 – and dropped sharply only at the end of the 1990s, when the *Saisonnier* recruitment system was abolished for EU Europeans. Today, most Spanish citizens are found in France, Germany, Switzerland, Great Britain, the Netherlands, and Belgium.

Assimilation and return migration

When it comes to the integration of the Spanish immigrants into the economy and the educational system, we can make fairly transparent statements for France and Germany. For France, they are based on a survey in 1992, which is representative of all immigrants resident in France, both naturalized and nonnaturalized. This survey is especially important because the differentiation according to groups of origin or ethnic categories is not made in France. For Germany, the figures are based on the foreigners' statistics, which are fairly precise in this regard, since Spaniards – like other EU citizens in Germany – rarely became naturalized.

The most far-reaching indicator for integration is intermarriage with locals, especially since the children of such unions generally receive both citizenships and are at home in the culture of the country of residence. This is especially true if the immigrant group has a weaker status than the native population. In Germany, Spanish immigrants had higher rates of exogamy than comparable groups from other recruitment countries, and these rates rose steadily. At the turn of the 20th century, this meant that 80% of the children of Spaniards in Germany were from mixed marriages – an extraordinarily high rate of exogamy (see Table 2) – and thus possessed the citizenship of both parents.

A similar development was evident in France: 70% of the immigrant Spanish women and 65% of the men had married

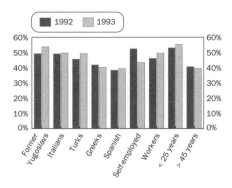

Figure 1. Future in Germany, 1992-3: among selected immigrants groups, those who intend to remain in Germany as long as possible (in %). *Source: Marplan,* 1992-3.

natives (*Français de souche*) in 1992 – far more than comparable groups. The question of where the next generation met their partners or friends showed results that underscore the successful process of integration: the children of Spaniards met them in the public sphere and less through their parents. Moreover, the rates of naturalization of Spaniards in France were also the highest compared to other nationality groups.

Both the German and the French data show that the Spaniards arrived with fairly poor occupational and social qualifications. Largely, they came from the poorest provinces and a rural milieu. French data point to a high documented rate of illiterates among the immigrants, and the data of the Federal Labor Office show a very low percentage of skilled workers among the Spaniards recruited: only 7.7%, compared to an average of 21.2% for all recruited workers. Nevertheless, the children of Spaniards achieved higher academic success rates than the children from all other recruitment groups in Germany. For France, data about the good command of French by the Spaniards also points to an advanced process of integration. The strongly developed self-organization of the immigrants in Spanish organizations and a strong affirmation of full integration in the school system – in Germany at times in opposition to the authorities, which wanted to set up special classes – led to good school diplomas, rapid placement into training positions, and integration careers with corresponding professional success. In Switzerland this development was less pronounced, because the *Saisonnier* system made self-organization more difficult. With support from Spanish agencies, there were also Europewide meetings of Spanish migrants and thus an exchange of experiences about migration and integration could take place.

In spite of the fast integration process that after only one generation made the Spanish immigrants barely visible as a separate group in official statistics and in public opinion, a strong orientation toward a return home exists within this group (see Figure 1). The financial per capita transfers to Spain were accordingly high still in the 1990s. Return seems not to happen because of social or economic pressures. It parallels the old-age migration of northern Europeans to Spain. A breakdown by age of Spanish immigrants in France

today suggests that the older generation returned in large numbers to Spain upon reaching retirement age, while the younger generations have integrated well in France. This is also in line with the trend in Germany. All in all, the Spanish migration to EU countries is a story of success, parallel to Spain's entry in the EU.

Anuario de migraciones 2000. Published by the Ministerio de Trabajo y Asuntos Sociales. Madrid, 2000.

Breitenbach, Barbara von. *Italiener und Spanier als Arbeitnehmer in der Bundesrepublik Deutschland.* Munich and Mainz, 1982.

Jamin, Mathilde. "Die deutsch-türkische Anwerbevereinbarung von 1961 und 1964." In *Fremde Heimat. Eine Geschichte der Einwanderung aus der Türkei,* edited by Aytaç Erlyımaz and Mathilde Jamin, 69–83. Essen, 1998.

Lopéz-Blasco, Andrés. *Sozialisationsprozesse und Identitätskrisen spanischer Jugendlicher in der Bundesrepublik Deutschland.* Munich, 1983.

Massenet, Michel. "Action sociale et politique d'immigration." *Hommes et Migrations Documents* 761 (15.2.1969).

Thränhardt, Dietrich. "Einwandererkulturen und soziales Kapital." In *Einwanderernetzwerke und ihre Integrationsqualität in Deutschland und Israel,* edited by Dietrich Thränhardt and Uwe Hunger, 15–51. Münster and London, 2000.

Trends in International Migration. Published by the OECD. Paris, various years.

Tribalat, Michèle. *25 años son mucho.* Published by the Mision Catolica española en Alemania. Bonn, 1986.

Tribalat, Michèle. *De l'immigration à l'assimilation. Enquête sur les populations d'origine étrangère en France.* Paris, 1996.

Viet, Vincent. *La France Immigrée. Construction d'une politique 1914–1997.* Paris, 1998.

Cross-references: Belgium and Luxembourg; France; Germany; Great Britain; The Netherlands; Northern Europe; Spain and Portugal; German Affluence Migrants in Spain since the Late 20th Century; Greek Labor Migrants in Western, Central, and Northern Europe after 1950: The Examples of Germany and the Netherlands; Italian Labor Migrants in Northern, Central, and Western Europe since the End of World War II; Latin American Migrants in Spain since the End of the 1980s; Portuguese Labor Migrants in Western and Central Europe since the 1950s: The Examples of France and Germany; Spanish Political Refugees in Europe since the Beginning of the Civil War in 1936: The Example of France; Turkish Labor Migrants in Western, Central, and Northern Europe since the Mid-1950s; Yugoslav Labor Migrants in Western, Central, and Northern Europe since the End of World War II

SPANISH MERCHANTS IN THE NETHERLANDS IN THE EARLY MODERN PERIOD

Raymond P. Fagel

Between 1450 and 1570, Spanish merchants played an important role in the trade centers of the Netherlands. Their main activity was the import of Spanish wool for the textile industry. Other important products were wine, iron, olive oil, and fruits. From the Low Countries they mostly sent textile products back to Spain. The fact that both the Low Countries and the Spanish Kingdoms became a part of the Habsburg monarchy at the beginning of the 16th century strengthened the economic relations between the two countries. After 1550, economic changes caused the downfall of this trade and the outbreak of a long and violent civil war, known historically as the Eighty-Year War, in the Low Countries after 1568 speeded up this development. The bad reputation of Spanish soldiers from the 1550s onward, and outrage about the politics of the Spanish governor, the Duke of Alba, and his Council of Troubles after 1567, limited the commercial prospects of merchants from Spain even further. Until then, they were able to reside in the Low Countries without arousing too much enmity or jealousy in the local population.

The Spanish merchants in the Low Countries possessed their own organizations, called "nations," which brought together merchants originating from the same region. These mercantile "nations" were based on a contract between the sovereign of the merchants' homeland, the host city, and the foreign community, in which all the special privileges and prohibitions were stated. The Spanish merchants thus did not have to pay all of the cities' taxes but on the other hand were not allowed to engage in retail trade. These contracts gave the merchants of a Spanish nation a different legal position compared to the citizens of the city.

In 1428, the merchants from the territories of the crown of Castile received the status of nation in the Flemish city of Bruges. This nation, often called the "Spanish nation," would remain an important feature in the commercial landscape of the city for a long time. Besides two episodes, around 1490 and during the 1580s, this nation resided in Bruges up to 1705. The Spanish nation of Bruges can be regarded as the focal point of Spanish life in the Netherlands.

Yet there were other Spanish nations as well. The first nation in Bruges had been that of the lands of Aragon, Valencia, and Catalonia, dating from 1330. They left Bruges in 1527 and moved to Antwerp, but it remains unclear whether their nation kept functioning after 1540. The merchants and seamen from the Spanish north coast, separated from the Castilian nation after a commercial struggle in 1455, joined together and founded their own nation. This nation, often called the "Vizcayan nation," stayed in Bruges until its dissolution in 1585. Besides these, merchants from Navarre and Andalusia founded some smaller nations.

Antwerp, the city that would become the main commercial center of the Netherlands in the 16th century, came too late to be granted many official organizations of Spanish merchants. The Spanish nation resided in this city between 1488 and 1494 and the Aragonese settled there only after 1527. The city did try to organize an official Spanish nation in 1551, meant to include merchants from the entire Spanish region, but the central government, the city of Bruges, and the

Castilian nation in Bruges succeeded in blocking these plans. Although the Spanish merchants in Antwerp expanded to become the largest group of international merchants in the city, new attempts to organize a Spanish nation in Antwerp all failed.

The presence of the Spanish merchants is difficult to quantify. Surviving records of the official notary of the Castilian nation in Bruges from 1549 mention 184 Spaniards, of whom 130 were described as residing in Bruges, 54 as present, and a further 11 as servants. Although some Vizcayans and Aragonese appear in these sources, they almost certainly are not all the merchants of these nations. In 1549, the heyday of Spanish trade, at least a few hundred Spanish merchants resided in the city or passed through. For the city of Antwerp, estimates are based on the registers of (only) two notaries dating from 1540. In that year, some 210 Spaniards appeared in their documents, but more Spaniards were likely active in the city. In 1560, a list of Spaniards from all parts of the Iberian Peninsula living in Antwerp mentioned 60 married merchants and 38 unmarried ones. This can be considered the more permanent group of resident merchants in Antwerp.

The information about resident merchants is richer than that about temporarily resident traders, but the group of merchants who stayed only temporarily was probably more numerous. The Aragonese merchant Pedro de Casanova possessed a large house in Antwerp and it is said that 20 merchants at a time often used his house. Some of them stayed for more than one year; others came and went repeatedly. The overall picture is that the traveling merchants could benefit from the presence of the Spanish resident merchants, who were often members of a nation in the city. With their commercial networks, houses, and warehouses, the large majority of traveling merchants, some staying for a seasonal visit, others for their apprentice years, could easily function within the foreign city.

In Middelburg and Antwerp, the nations were less important than in Bruges. The evidence suggests that this more or less forced the Spaniards to integrate into the host society. They often bought the citizenship of the city or married into a local family. In Middelburg, a new citizen could enter directly into the magistrate, while the Spaniards entering into the Antwerp magistrate were generally from the next generation of already mixed origin. Another marked difference is that integration in Middelburg did not lead to abandonment of commerce, while in Antwerp the mixed families disappeared from Iberian trade.

In Bruges the situation was different. The existence of foreign nations enabled the merchants to acquire a fixed position in the host society without the necessity to integrate. The Castilian nation had its own laws, its notary, its buildings, and its own chapel. The street where the nation was located, together with some of the private houses of the merchants, was already in the 16th century called "the Street of the Spaniards." Resident merchants brought their wives from

Spain, or were married in Bruges to women from other resident Spanish families. This was possible because, compared to the immigrants from other countries, there were quite a lot of Spanish families in the Netherlands. Although they were less numerous, the Aragonese, the Vizcayans, and the Navarrese in Bruges fit into this pattern. At the same time, there was conflict between Spanish of different regional origins, and their mutual relations were no stronger than with Italians, Germans, Portuguese, or with merchants from the Low Countries.

A merchant of the Castilian nation was not allowed to marry a local woman or obtain the citizenship of Bruges without first returning to Spain to settle his business affairs. If he failed to do so, the city authorities had to imprison him and send him to Spain by force. Only after that could his legal status be changed. The citizenship of Bruges and the membership of the Castilian nation conferred clearly different and incompatible sets of privileges. This can be illustrated with the example of Fernando de Matute, who was married to a local woman and citizen of Bruges. Although he was often present in the reunions of the nation, he never occupied the position of consul of the nation. A former mayor of Bruges of Spanish descent, Jean Pardo, had to give up his citizenship of Bruges to gain the privileges of the Castilian nation. The last consuls of the nation, who in 1705 closed down the nation and handed over its possessions to the city, became citizens of Bruges only in that same year.

The outbreak of the Dutch Revolt and the religious division within the Low Countries had its effect on the Spanish merchants. In a secret report on heresy in Antwerp dating from 1566, we find the names of some Spanish Calvinist merchants. It is interesting to note that these were mostly Antwerp-born Spaniards from mixed marriages and of Jewish origin. Especially among the merchants from Burgos, there were converts to be found – Calvinists of Jewish origin. The great majority of the Spanish merchants, however, remained faithful to the Catholic Church and loyal to their king. The example of Ursula López de Villanueva illustrates that a conversion could put a whole family into an awkward position. As a Calvinist and convert, she sought refuge from the Duke of Alba in Basel and left her children behind in Antwerp, while her half-sister Eleonora was married to a treasurer of Alba's Council of Troubles, who as a "Blood councilor" stood as a symbol of Spanish foreign dominance par excellence.

Some Spanish families who had resided for generations in Middelburg remained in the rebellious northern provinces. Salvador de la Palma, for example, had to flee to England, but after his return in 1574 he became a mayor of the city in 1591. His son occupied the same office in 1606. Another Spanish family from Middelburg, called De Valladolid, moved to Utrecht and married into the local nobility, and one member obtained a canonry in that city. Some members of the Ayala family also chose to live in the rebellious provinces, while the greater part of this family would serve Philip II.

Many other descendants of the Spanish merchants were also in Philip's government in Brussels. The fact that they were loyal to Spain but knew the Low Countries and spoke several languages made them very useful in the royal service.

This process of integration continued during the 17th century. During the early modern period, a relatively large group of Spanish merchant families mixed with local families of both noble and bourgeois origin. The fact that some of the rich Spaniards bought estates with the right to bear a noble title and had connections with the Spanish military stationed in the Netherlands made their entrance into the local and national elites even more fluid.

At the close of the 16th century, merchants from the Low Countries secured the trade between Spain and the Netherlands, using their own agents in the Spanish ports and trade centers. Merchants of Spanish origin born in the Netherlands were often well prepared for this kind of work in Spain. An interesting example is the son of Willem van der Beecke, who traded with Spain from Antwerp before ultimately moving to Spain. There, he always used his mother's name and was known as Baltasar de Compostela. Another example is the Antwerp merchant Gaspar de Añastro, the main figure behind the 1582 attempt on the life of William of Orange, who left for Spain in that same year.

The war in the Netherlands also changed the trade routes of the Spanish wool, which was taken more and more to cities such as Rouen, Lille, and St. Omer. Following the flow of their main merchandise, part of the Spanish merchants also changed their residence to these cities. Rouen especially received a large group of Spanish merchants. While this city did not have a "Spanish nation," many Spaniards became citizens of Rouen to gain a stable legal position in the city.

The presence of Spanish merchants in Bruges rapidly diminished. In 1605, Diego de Aranda complained that people who were not merchants anymore governed the Spanish nation, which was against the regulations of the nation. In 1617, two members of that same Aranda family were the last real merchants present in the nation. The rest, probably some 20 others, were no longer involved in international trade. The Aranda family would eventually hand over possessions of the nation to the city of Bruges in 1705.

In Antwerp the same process of abandonment of international trade took place, but the city also kept attracting new merchants. Their relatively small numbers seem to have fluctuated during the 17th century. Around 1610 there were probably some 40 Spanish merchants in Antwerp, but 20 years later only half that number remained.

Fagel, Raymond. "Spanish Merchants in the Low Countries: Stabilitas Loci or Peregrinatio?" In *International Trade in the Low Countries (14th–16th Centuries): Merchants, Organisation, Infrastructure*, edited by Peter Stabel, Bruno Blondé, and Anke Greve, 87–104. Louvain and Apeldoorn, 2000.

Phillips, William D. "Merchants of the Fleece: Castilians in Bruges and the Wool Trade." In *International Trade in the Low Countries (14th-16th Centuries): Merchants, Organisation, Infrastructure*, edited by Peter Stabel, Bruno Blondé, and Anke Greve, 75–85. Louvain and Apeldoorn, 2000.

Vandewalle, André. "Bruges and the Iberian Peninsula." In *Bruges and Europe*, edited by Valentin Vermeersch, 159–81. Antwerp, 1992.

Cross-references: Belgium and Luxembourg; The Netherlands; Spain and Portugal; Spanish Troops in the Netherlands in the 16th and 17th Centuries: The Example of Geldern

SPANISH POLITICAL REFUGEES IN EUROPE SINCE THE BEGINNING OF THE CIVIL WAR IN 1936: THE EXAMPLE OF FRANCE

Jean-François Berdah

Even today, the Spanish Civil War (1936–9) looms in the collective memory of the Spaniards as an event full of symbolism. The war seems like a prototype of or prelude to World War II and as an ideological battle between democracy and dictatorship. After the Spanish conflict, air raids – like those on Guernica and the large republican cities – and the Blitzkrieg were part of military strategy. The tragedy of the Spanish people triggered a lively echo throughout the world. Writers, artists, politicians, but also the broader public in many countries recognized the enormous and also international dimension of this war.

The defeats of the republican army in the fight against the putschists led to the mass flight of civilians and soldiers into neighboring France. Estimates put the number of refugees who crossed the border between 1936 and 1939 at 500,000. In the narrower sense, only the members of political parties (Social Democrats, Socialists, Communists, and Anarchists) and union organizations can be regarded as political refugees. In the end, however, those who stood up for the Republic as party members, soldiers, or committed citizens were labeled by the putschists as "political enemies," "Republicans," and "Red Spaniards." In accordance with these labels, the following discussion will regard the refugees from the Spanish Civil War as political refugees. Their political exile was marked by camp life and labor service in the French "Third Republic," by forced labor and deportation following France's defeat in the war and during the Vichy regime, and by a resistance struggle against Nazi rule; for some, this exile would turn into permanent settlement in France.

Spaniards had been settling throughout Europe since the 19th century, chiefly in France. According to the census of March 1936, 253,599 Spaniards were living in the territory of Spain's northern neighbor, where they made up the third-largest group of foreigners. They were mostly poorly skilled migrant laborers who worked in construction and

Refugees from the Spanish civil war crossing the Spanish-French border at Perthus in the foothills of the Pyrenees, February 1939 (*ullstein bild*).

agriculture; the majority were illiterate. As a result of the revision of France's citizenship law in 1927, many Spaniards acquired French citizenship. By the middle of the 1930s, more than 200,000 Frenchman were Spanish by birth.

After the first battles of the civil war and since the front lines cut across the Basque provinces in the summer of 1936, that region saw the first movement of refugees across the French border. A second wave was formed after the collapse of the northern front and the occupation of the last remnants of the Republican territory in western Spain in June/July 1937. About 125,000 people were able to flee on foot or in fishing boats toward France. Only a part of them, about 35,000, decided to remain in the neighboring country: the majority of the soldiers and civilians were unwilling to accept the defeat of the Republic and returned to Spain across the Pyrenees to fight the Nationalists in Aragon and Catalonia. Following the occupation of Aragon in the spring of 1938, a third wave of refugees brought 23,000 to 24,000 Republicans to France. At the end of 1938, a total of 40,000 to 45,000 Spanish refugees were in France, among them more than 10,000 children.

The fourth and final wave was also the largest. When the troops commanded by Francisco Franco, at that time the Generalísimo of the putschist forces, launched their campaign to take Catalonia in December 1938, the military situation of the Republican army was all but hopeless: the border between France and Spain had been officially closed for several months, and Soviet aid was no longer able to reach the Republican camp but by sea and erratically. The French government, which had already spent more than 88 million francs on aid to the refugees since the beginning of the war, feared an influx of hundreds of thousands of refugees. And in fact, at the end of January and the beginning of February 1939, about 170,000 civilians and 295,000 soldiers arrived in the "Sister Republic." French authorities were able to organize the reception of these masses of refugees only by mobilizing all their resources, even if the Red Spaniards also encountered political opposition and xenophobia.

Other countries took in smaller contingents of refugees. At the beginning of 1939, thousands of Republicans escaped falling into the enemy's hands by crossing on boats from Alicante to Algeria and Tunisia. The onward migration of about 15,000 refugees from France to South and Central America (Mexico, Chile, and the Dominican Republic) was organized – until the German occupation of France in June 1940 – by SERE (Servicio de Evacuación de Refugiados Españoles) and JARE (Junta de Auxilio a los Republicanos Españoles). After the first defeats in the Basque region, several groups of children were sent off to France, as well as to Belgium, Great Britain, the USSR, and Switzerland. In England alone, around 4,000 Basque children were welcomed by the Basque Children's Committee in 1937, and that same year the Soviet Union took in 3,000 children. All told, more than 70,000 children were evacuated between 1936 and 1939 according to the most recent figures.

Most Republicans were forced to remain in France. Other European countries showed no willingness to admit refugees in larger numbers. Return to Spain was impossible for those who were politically active, around 125,000–135,000 individuals, given the immediate danger of execution. Some took that risk and went back to Spain before the end of the year, among them also soldiers who, upon crossing the border, were immediately disarmed and brought into internment camps – that is, concentration camps according to their official designation by military and civilian authorities.

The occupation of northern France by the German Wehrmacht and the signing of the armistice between France and Germany on 22 June 1940 put a swift end to the relative freedom of opinion and action that the Spanish Republican government agencies and organizations had enjoyed in French exile. The vast majority of the Republican political and military elite was forced to leave the country as quickly as possible. Some, however, could not or would not flee. Lluis Companys, the leader of the Republican Left of Catalonia (Esquerra Republicana de Catalunya) was arrested by the Germans, handed over to Franco's Spain, sentenced to death, and executed on 15 October 1940. Manuel Azaña, president of the Republic, escaped the same fate only through his death on 3 November in Montauban shortly before he was to be arrested. The Republicans who were now fleeing Nazi Germany sought refuge in Central and South America and in European countries that were not occupied by or allied with Germany: about 3,000 went to the Soviet Union, several hundred to Great Britain, Switzerland, and the Baltic region. These were mainly officers (e.g., Antonio Cordón, Juan Modesto), intellectuals (e.g., Cernuda, Salvador de Madariaga, José Carner), artists (e.g., Ángel Gutiérrez, Alberto Sánchez), and politicians (e.g., José Díaz, Juan Negrín, Pablo de Azcárate, Marcelino Pascua).

Refugees who arrived in France after 1936 were initially aggregated in improvised camps erected on the Mediterranean seashore, which lacked barracks, toilets, and shower units. The first two camps, Argelès-sur-Mer and Saint-Cyprien, hosted nearly 275,000 persons. After a few months, the situation of the exiles began to improve as additional internment camps were set up (Barcarès, Le Vernet, Gurs, Bram, Septfonds), but also because the total number of internees dropped to about 95,000 from the end of July in response to the integration policy of the French bureaucracy; Prime Minister Édouard Daladier had already emphasized at the end of March 1939 that the only solution to the refugee question was to integrate the Republican soldiers into the Foreign Legion or into the economy as workers.

On 12 April 1939, compulsory labor service was announced for all Spanish men between the ages of 20 and 48 who were living in France. However, the civilian authorities pushed the recruitment of Spaniards more vigorously only after the declaration of war against Germany and the mobilization of the French army in September 1939. Within a few months, the interment camps emptied out as men flowed into the Compagnies de Travailleurs Étrangers (Labor Service Units for Foreigners). In May 1940, shortly before the defeat and collapse of the Third Republic, they comprised about 56,500 Spanish refugees. Of those men who had not moved on to America with the help of SERE or JARE, or had returned home in accordance with the French-Spanish Bérard-Jordana Treaty signed in March 1939, most were put to work in agriculture, the construction industry or projects (especially the consolidation of the Maginot Line), and even, but rather belatedly, in the armament industry. In addition to the Compagnies de Travailleurs Étrangers, 5,000 Spanish internees worked in industry under the direct oversight of the Ministry of Defense or the Ministry of Labor.

With the French defeat in May 1940, a fairly large number of Spanish Republicans ended up in German captivity, while others withdrew to the south with the remnants of the French army. More than 7,000 Red Spaniards were deported to the Mauthausen concentration camp in August 1940. For the Spanish Republicans it was therefore clear, from the summer of 1940, at the latest, that National Socialists and the Vichy government would regard them as enemies and treat them as such. That was true even though the French authorities made possible their flight into the "Free French Zone" that was not yet occupied by German troops and where there was still at that time no internment or deportation. However, the new Law on National Defense and the Restoration of Public Security promulgated on 3 September 1940 was to change the situation radically. Internment camps (internement administratif) were to be set up. The administration and especially the prefects who had considerable legal powers at a departmental level were instructed to intern in these camps individuals who posed a threat to "public order." At the end of 1940, 10,000 Spaniards were back in Argelès, 3,000 in Le Vernet, 4,500 in Bram, and 2,500 each in Gurs and Septfonds.

The Persecution Law passed on 27 September 1940 also shaped the life of all Spanish Republicans in France right up to the end of the war: henceforth, individuals assigned to the units of the labor service (now Groupements de Travailleurs Étrangers, GTE) could no longer receive any wages, but were given only arbitrarily assigned performance bonuses. In the fall of 1940, the GTE consisted almost entirely of Red Spaniards between the ages of 18 and 55, alongside smaller groups of Jews who did not hold French citizenship. In the Free Zone, one GTE camp was generally established for each *département*, though some had three or four, for example, Lozère, Haute-Garonne, and Bouches-du-Rhône. Contrary to what happened a few months earlier German military authorities, too, recognized that the interned Red Spaniards could be put to use as forced laborers or auxiliary personnel for the German army and navy.

The new military strategy developed by the Wehrmacht during the fall of 1940 after the failure of the battle of Britain, which included submarine warfare against the British fleet in the Atlantic and the Mediterranean, prompted the German occupiers to resort increasingly to Spanish Republicans as laborers. These included also the so-called *Transportspanier*, i.e., Spanish forced workers who were deployed in building and maintaining German U-boat bases on the French Atlantic coast and on the western English Channel. As early as the beginning of 1941, the German occupation authorities were pulling thousands of Red Spaniards out of the GTE camps, in spite of the vigorous protests of the Vichy government. Sealed railway cars took them to their destinations, usually a forced labor camp or a barracks of the German navy. The *Transportspanier* were forced to work a minimum of 10 hours a day for the German occupiers. Abuse was a daily occurrence. The most important camps, under the direct authority of the Organization Todt, were in the restricted coastal region in Brest, Lorient, Saint-Nazaire, La Pallice (La Rochelle), Bordeaux, Royan, Arcachon, and Cherbourg.

The Red Spaniards in the GTE camps and the forced labor camps played an important role in the organization of the *résistance* and the liberation of France in 1944–5. The first Spanish resistance groups were set up in the fall of 1940 in Haute-Savoie, Haute-Vienne, Brittany, and the Pyrenees. They worked with the French resistance movements and had close contacts with British and American agents. The first attacks against industrial and technical installations in southern France came as early as 1941. In addition, there was fighting between Spanish workers and German troops in the restricted region of the Atlantic zone. The Spanish resistance groups increased their capacity for action in 1942 by establishing a new organizational structure. They set up, for example, the 14th Spanish Partisan corps (Cuerpo de Guerrilleros Españoles) and the Main d'Œuvre Immigrée (MOI), which was attached to the French FTP (Franc-Tireurs et Partisans); both participated in a decisive way in the liberation of many *départements*, with other French resistance groups or alone, in Aude, Ariège, Haute-Garonne, Gard, Pyrénées orientales, Puy-de-Dôme, Corrèze, and Haute-Loire. All told, more than

21,000 Spaniards took part effectively in the liberation of France in various resistance groups. Another 15,000 fought in the Forces Françaises Libres, especially with the Second Tank Division under General Leclerc.

After the liberation of France, the Spanish partisans directed their attention to their own country. The hope that the victorious democracies, especially France under the provisional republican government of General De Gaulle, would support them proved unrealistic. To the Allies, and especially the British, the Iberian Peninsula was seen as too important strategically to carry out a military action against Franco. The failure of an invasion by Red Spaniards in the Val d'Aran in 1944–5 led for many of those who had fled Spain between 1936 and 1939 to permanent banishment from their homeland. Exile organizations developed after World War II in Great Britain under the former head of the government, Juan Negrín, and especially in France, where a Basque, a Catalan, and eventually a Spanish exile government was formed, the latter in Paris in 1946 under President Martínez Barrio. The exile government dissolved voluntarily only in 1977, following the first democratic elections in Spain.

Although the reception of the Spanish refugees in France may also have been marked by political and xenophobic exclusion in the beginning, the remembrance was dominated by the common republican struggle against fascism and National Socialism. With the labor migrations from Franco's Spain in the 1960s and 1970s, the former political refugees became a minority among the Spaniards in France. Nevertheless, the memory of their presence is still very pronounced. This is especially true of southern France, where numerous Spanish Republicans found a permanent home and, together with their families, have kept the remembrance of the Spanish Civil War and of exile alive to this day.

Abellán, José Luis, ed. *El exilio español de 1939*. 6 vols. Madrid, 1976.

Alted-Vigil, Alicia. *La voz de los vencidos. El exilio republicano de 1939*. Madrid, 2005.

Cuesta, Josefina, and Benito Bermejo, eds. *Emigración y exilio. Españoles en Francia, 1936–1946*. Madrid, 1996.

Dreyfus-Armand, Geneviève. *L'exil des républicains espagnols en France. De la guerre civile à la mort de Franco*. Paris, 1999.

Rubio, Javier. *La emigración de la guerra civil de 1936–1939. Historia del éxodo que se produce con el fin de la II República española*. 3 vols. Madrid, 1977.

Soriano, Antonio. *Éxodos. Historia oral del exilio republicano en Francia*. Barcelona, 1989.

Stein, Louis. *Beyond Death and Exile: The Spanish Republicans in France, 1939–1955*. Cambridge and London, 1979.

Vargas, Bruno, ed. *La Seconde République espagnole en exil en France*. Albi, 2008.

Cross-references: France; Spain and Portugal; Spanish Labor Migrants in Western, Central, and Northern Europe since the End of World War II

SPANISH TROOPS IN THE NETHERLANDS IN THE 16TH AND 17TH CENTURIES: THE EXAMPLE OF GELDERN

Martin Papenheim

In 1567, Duke Alba, the new governor for King Philip II of Spain, came to the Netherlands with an army to break the resistance of the Dutch nobility and cities against the repressive political, religious, and financial measures by the House of Habsburg. His arrival began a period of constant, intense military conflicts in northwestern Europe, which came to an end – and a temporary one at that – with the Peace of Utrecht in 1713. During that time, the lower Rhine was a constant scene of warfare and always connected with the events in the Netherlands. The war against Alba's tyranny that broke out in 1568, and ended only 80 years later with the independence of the Republic of the United Provinces in 1648, also spilled over into the neutral lower Rhenish territories of the United Duchies of Cleves-Jülich-Berg, where Spanish troops constructed fortifications. Schenkenschanz (part of Cleves) between the Rhine and the Waal housed the strongest Dutch fortress anywhere, while the Spanish presence in the southern lower Rhine region had pushed forward as far as Neuss and Grevenbroich. Geldern was part of this fortified landscape on the lower Rhine.

Emperor Charles V had already wrested the Duchy of Geldern from William of Jülich-Cleves. The northern section, the three northern quarters, became part of the United Netherlands. The southern section, the southern quarter with the city of Geldern, remained Spanish from 1555–6 to 1703. Only between 1578 and 1587 was it under the suzerainty of the Dutch Estates-General. Geldern was the largest Spanish fortress north of the Alps. The Spaniards modified the older structure after Italian models and constructed bastions. The final fortifications were built in the 1660s. The fortified position was captured for the first time in 1703, following a bombardment by Prussian troops. King Frederick II had the fortress razed in 1764.

The Spanish king's army of Flanders was a multicultural force of foot soldiers recruited predominantly from the lower social strata. The cavalry played only a secondary role. Most soldiers came from territories belonging to the Spanish crown or from Habsburg lands. Soldiers who were also subjects were considered especially reliable. At the same time, the military leadership was paying attention to confessional homogeneity. In the well-studied period between 1567 and 1665, German and Dutch (Walloon) infantry constituted the largest contingents. The German mercenaries hailed chiefly from Austria, Tyrol, and the Alsace. In numerical terms, they were followed by soldiers from Spain (chiefly from Old Castile and Cantabria), Italy (mostly from the Kingdom of Naples), Burgundy (Franche Comté), and finally, the remaining troops, among them above all British mercenaries (mostly Catholics) or Dutch defectors. The total size of the army of Flanders ranged from around 10,000 soldiers in 1567 to nearly 90,000 in the 1570s and 1640s.

In terms of their military quality, the assessment of these different contingents varied a great deal. Without a doubt, the Spaniards were considered the best soldiers, followed by the Italians, the British, the Burgundians, and well below them the Walloons and the Germans. While the Germans were always suspected of being sympathetic to the Protestants and were therefore used primarily for auxiliary services, the Walloons were suspect because of their close ties to the land and its people. It was a basic military belief of the Spaniards that soldiers fought well only in foreign lands, because they were then free of ties and inhibitions. That is why the Spaniards liked to deploy units of soldiers who had no connections of any kind with the embattled land. This "military expatriation" (a term coined by the military historian Geoffrey Parker) and not some supposed national character formed the basis for the military assessment of the troops. Even the Spaniards, the most feared soldiers in Europe at this time, were considered unenthusiastic warriors in their own country. However, when the transport of troops from southern German and Austrian regions and from southern Europe became increasingly difficult after 1600, the Spaniards found themselves compelled to recruit more and more soldiers from regions near the areas of conflict, especially the Rhineland.

In 1603, Geldern had a garrison of as many as 6,000 soldiers, a number that far exceeded the local population (about 1,500). Soldiers of the most diverse backgrounds rotated in and out: Burgundians arrived in 1605, English in 1608, Italians in 1618–20, and Portuguese and Neapolitans in 1620. In the last quarter of the 16th century, the first casemates were constructed in the city, which served as defensive positions and possible quarters. Generally, however, the soldiers lived in the houses of the burghers, who were obligated to provide food and lodging. Barracks were constructed in the course of the 17th century, and the Spaniards switched over to demanding monetary contributions instead of payments in kind. However, alongside these burdens on the native population, the garrison also constituted a positive economic factor: for example, building barracks for the soldiers was a profitable business in Geldern.

The soldiers lived according to their own laws and customs. The Spaniards, in particular, cultivated a close cohesiveness and special culture in the *camerada*. However, the close cohabitation of mercenaries and natives in the town was by no means characterized only by separation and the resulting tensions and dislikes. In the 17th century, soldiers are listed in Geldern as house owners, and the town's church registers document marriages between soldiers and natives, with the names suggesting that the soldiers in question were Flemings or Germans. The worlds of the soldiers and townspeople was thus not sharply separated.

Of all the foreigners they encountered – and this included also the Germans if they spoke a diverging dialect – the Netherlanders and northern Germans had a particularly negative perception of the Spaniards. Savage acts of destruction (for example, of Aalst in 1576 by Spanish mutineers),

More than once Antwerp fell victim to the "Spanish Fury." Contemporary impression of the pillage in November 1575 (*Deutsches Historisches Museum, Berlin*).

acts of extreme violence, and the military strength of the Spanish units spread fear. But the image of the "cruel and cunning Spaniards," the so-called Black Legend, was also a stereotype that was cultivated within German Protestantism. And even in Spain itself it was used to criticize the cruel conquest of America. In the Dutch War of Independence, the Black Legend was deliberately used as war propaganda. By contrast, the image that the Spanish soldiers had of the Netherlands and its people was characterized by a positive exoticism. The foreigners marveled at the unfamiliar vegetation and food (for example, butter), at the relaxed manner in which the genders interacted, and at how much the Flemings could drink.

Because of the high turnover in troop contingents, the presence in Geldern of large numbers of soldiers in service to Spain did not lead to the formation of minorities. The military presence was important above all for the adoption of Spanish loan words from the military sphere. However, being part of Spain also promoted a special consciousness vis-à-vis the Dutch Estates-General and the German lordships of the lower Rhine, and traces of that identity can be found to this day. The native population experienced the culture of the ruling power especially within the framework of symbolic actions (e.g., memorial ceremonies for a deceased regent, the bestowal of a Spanish title on a local noble), but also through imported art oriented toward Brussels and Madrid, and not least by an active religious policy, which also included the Maria pilgrimage to Kevelaer.

The memory of the Spanish period is still present among the population of Geldern. For example, a street named Kroatenstraße (Croat Street) in Kevelaer is a reminder of mercenaries from that time. A Spanish colonel is said to be buried in a crypt in one of that town's churches, and the priest of Walbeck was supposedly able to identify precisely who was a descendant of the Spaniards from their darker complexion. It is not so important whether these last two claims

have proven false or unverifiable. Rather, what matters is that the Spanish period has left traces in the memory of the population through the centuries.

Brouwer, Johannes, ed. *Kronieken van spaansche soldaten uit het begin van den tachtigjarigen oorlog.* Zutphen, 1933.

Kaiser, Michael. "Die Söldner und die Bevölkerung. Überlegungen zu Konstituierung und Überwindung eines lebensweltlichen Antagonismus." In *Militär und ländliche Gesellschaft in der frühen Neuzeit,* edited by Stefan Kroll and Kersten Krüger, 79–120. Münster, 2000.

Parker, Geoffrey. *The Army of Flanders and the Spanish Road 1567–1659. The Logistics of Spanish Victory and Defeat in the Low Countries' Wars.* Cambridge, 1972.

Pollmann, Judith. "Eine natürliche Feindschaft: Ursprung und Funktion der schwarzen Legende über Spanien in den Niederlanden, 1560–1581." In *Feindbilder. Die Darstellung des Gegners in der politischen Publizistik des Mittelalters und der Neuzeit,* edited by Franz Bosbach, 73–93. Cologne, 1992.

Schepper, Hugo de. "Flandres y su Leyenda negra." In *España: ¿Ruptura 1492?* edited by Maxi P. A. M. Kerkhof, Hugo de Schepper, and Otto Ywartjes, 115–25. Amsterdam and Atlanta, 1993.

Cross-references: The Netherlands; Spain and Portugal

SRI LANKAN TAMILS IN WESTERN AND CENTRAL EUROPE SINCE THE 1980S: THE EXAMPLE OF SWITZERLAND

Damaris Lüthi

From the early 1980s to the present, Sri Lanka has been torn by a bloody conflict between a Tamil minority and the Sinhalese majority, a conflict that had claimed more than 60,000 lives by the beginning of the 21st century. The political efforts of the Sinhalese since the 1950s to establish a Sinhalese-Buddhist nationalism (Sinhalese as the sole national language, restrictive admission of Tamils to universities, Buddhism as the declared state religion) radicalized the Tamils who were thereby disadvantaged. Eventually, that led to the formation of armed underground organizations. In the 1970s these took up the struggle for an independent Tamil state in the north and east of the island. At the turn of the 21st century, the strongest of these groups was the LTTE (Liberation Tigers of Tamil Eelam).

Ever since the escalation of the conflict in 1983, Tamil refugees have been fleeing into neighboring countries (India, Malaysia), but also to Europe, North America, and Australia. At the beginning of the 21st century, the largest refugee communities were living in Canada (around 200,000), India (110,000), Great Britain (90,000), Germany (65,000), France (60,000), the USA (50,000), Australia (20,000), and Norway (20,000); another 442,000 Tamils emigrated to other countries. Between 1982 and 2003, a total of 43,662 persons of Sri Lankan origin applied for political asylum in Switzerland; a

Tamil Hindus pray in the temple in Adliswil, canton Zurich (*ullstein bild*).

mere 803 were recognized as refugees. During roughly the same period (1986–June 2005), the largest number of asylum applications – with varying rates of success – were submitted by refugees from Serbia-Montenegro (123,855), Turkey (59,365), Bosnia-Herzegovina (27,679), Albania (14,542), Somalia (12,561), and Lebanon (11,896).

The vast majority of Tamils were granted residence permits because a return to their crisis-ridden homeland was unacceptable on humanitarian grounds – deportation was not an option. At the end of 2003, Switzerland, with around 40,000 persons of Sri Lankan origin, had the highest concentration of Tamil refugees in Europe in proportion to the native population: 4,575 nationalized individuals, 31,390 with permanent residence in Switzerland (2% of the approximately 1.5 million foreign nationals), and 3,867 asylum seekers. To this number must be added thousands of Tamils who went underground after rejection of their application for regular residence status and who remained in Switzerland as illegals or moved to another country.

The integration process of the Tamils during the 1980s and 1990s was marked by Switzerland's restrictive asylum policy, which downplayed the political causes of the flight of the Tamils. Labeled "economic refugees," the immigrants were unpopular with the native population. The government made numerous revisions to the asylum law primarily because of the growing influx of Tamil asylum seekers. Whereas only six persons from Sri Lanka had applied for asylum in the 1970s, the number of applications rose in the early 1980s. Since the beginning of the 21st century, the number of Sri Lankan nationals seeking asylum has been declining again. At the end of January 2005, 2,965 Tamils (5.6% of the 55,103 applicants of various nationalities) were registered as asylum seekers. They currently still face deportation to Sri Lanka, with potentially coercive measures such as custody pending deportation. At the same time, nationalizations have increased since 1997 among refugees with secure residence status. In 2003, alone, 1,138 Tamils acquired Swiss citizenship; one-third of these were born in Switzerland.

The first Tamil refugees were young, well-educated men, most of them (62% between 1983 and 1991) from the high-status Vellalar landowning caste – next to the Brahmins the highest caste in northern Sri Lanka. They hailed from the city and region of Jaffna or were native to Pungudutivu, an island off the western coast of the Jaffna peninsula: 12% were middle-caste craftsmen with less education; 13% were lower-caste Karaiyar from the northwestern coast of the peninsula and engaged in local government service, deep-sea fishing, or coastal trade; and 11% were from various lower castes. Only 2% were high-caste Brahmins. The immigrant men were either married or later wed a Tamil asylum seeker. Of the small number of women who arrived in the beginning, half were married; the others came to marry a husband chosen for them in a transnational arranged marriage. The first immigrants were the pioneers of a later chain migration.

Circumstances permitting, the wealthy and well-educated Tamils did not remain in Switzerland but moved on to anglophone countries. The Tamils remaining in Switzerland found employment relatively quickly and almost exclusively in the catering, nursing, and cleaning sectors, that is, in service industries that demanded no specific vocational qualifications. The trend toward the social de-differentiation of the group was reinforced by chain migration: the proportion of refugees with a rural background, little education, and low-caste status increased. The majority developed into members of a Swiss underclass. Nearly 90% of Tamils living in Switzerland are Hindus; the remainder are Christians, primarily Roman Catholics. The several hundred Tamil-speaking Muslims from Sri Lanka do not consider themselves Tamils.

Among the Swiss Tamils are tensions that derive in part from their diverse sociogeographic backgrounds, but in part also from the length of their stay in Switzerland. For example, the Jaffna-Tamils regard the inhabitants of the island of Pungudutivu as conservative and uneducated; the Pungudutivans, in return, complain that the inhabitants of Jaffna had kept the "English education" for themselves and left them no option but to focus on other lines of work, such as trade. Moreover, the first immigrants, who already enjoy certain securities (family reunion, legal status, employment, savings), feel superior to the later arrivals. In addition, there are political-ideological differences. While the LTTE, which dominates the conflict in Sri Lanka and recruits in large part from Karaiyar and other residents of the Jaffna peninsula, propagates a "victim diaspora," the Pungudutivans take a less negative view of exile, are more focused on economic success in the host country, and emphasize self-help.

The perception of the Tamils by the native Swiss has changed from one of pronounced xenophobia to a rather marked acceptance. In the beginning, the refugee group had a bad reputation because of internal conflicts and drug trafficking. In 1984 the first Tamil jokes started circulating, and until 1988 there was at least one documented assault on a Tamil every year. The years from 1989 and 1991 saw a growing number of attacks on refugee camps. Since the mid-1990s, however, the Tamils have generally been regarded as "likable" and "integrated." They are in fact quite popular, especially among their primary employers, the restaurant owners, who describe them as "hardworking" and "frugal." Presumably, the Tamils are accepted primarily because they try to avoid attracting attention within the public sphere in Switzerland.

Economically, the Tamils adapted quite well to Swiss society, and in their external appearance they also adjusted to the customs of the natives. However, a sociocultural integration of the refugee generation did not take place. In private life they kept mostly to themselves. The primary focus was on cultivating relationships with relatives inside and outside Switzerland. This tendency showed already when the immigration began and was able to stabilize itself as a result of chain migration. Also important were relations with countrymen from the same village, former fellow students, companions in flight, work colleagues, and members of the LTTE or Tamil cultural organizations. The preference for these social ties goes hand in hand with the widespread wish to return to a state – Tamil Eelam – of their own, though it does not exclude onward migration to other countries with a Tamil population. On weekends and during vacations, Tamils go to see relatives domestically and abroad, visit Hindu temples or churches, and participate in Tamil weddings, birthdays, puberty rites, soccer tournaments, and cultural events that draw fellow Tamils from all over Europe.

The conventional pattern of relationships allows them to maintain "cultural" autonomy, which is regarded as central for the return to a Tamil Eelam. Leisure time is filled with activities for Tamil schools or associations, which exist in impressive numbers: there are temple, church, soccer, theater, dance (Bharata Natyam), choral, poetry, and cultural societies. Many women, for example, are active in the Melmaruvattur Atiparacakti Cultural, Prayer, and Social Association of Tamil Women in Switzerland. Moreover, there are several Tamil radio and TV stations, screenings of south-Indian-Tamil films, and grocery stores with goods from Southeast Asia. Every Tamil living room has a video or DVD player that will play Tamil movies. Classes in "Tamil culture" (language, history, Bharata Natyam), but also in computer science, English, and soccer are offered primarily by the LTTE's cultural association Tamil Illam. The goal is to make especially the second generation sensitive to political issues and cultural values relating to the homeland. However, in spite of the commitment to native traditions, the skills of the children – for example, in the Tamil language – often lag behind their parents' expectations.

Traditional caste habits are to some extent still alive among the refugee generation. Although these are branded as immoral in official discourse, their continuing importance shows, for example, in the persistent relevance of the concepts of purity – central to the hierarchical structuring of society – in connection with diet, occupation, marriage, menstruation, birth, and death. One area in which these values manifest themselves is the central importance of traditional

marriage alliances within the caste or even the caste sub-group. Individuals whose behavior does not conform face the threat of social isolation also in Switzerland. Diet, too, is oriented toward one's own caste's degree of purity. Moreover, pride in one's own caste, combined with condescending statements about the lower-caste membership of other compatriots, exemplifies traditional status thinking. The relevance of conventional notions of purity has tended to weaken in the areas of commensality and occupation, where the fear of contamination seems to be gradually waning. Education, income, and wealth reinforce the importance of caste membership also in Switzerland – as they do in "semi-traditional" Sri Lanka, where the primary effect of class aspects was to prop up the traditional caste hierarchy.

Many forms of behavior and values in Swiss society are rejected outright and are seen as incompatible with Tamil "culture." Those include, for example, the tolerant attitude toward the consumption of alcohol and tobacco, rather egalitarian gender relations, the lack of respect for the elderly (principle of seniority), and the options of divorce and pre-marital sex. The fear is that Tamil society, and especially its female members, could be negatively influenced. Many Tamil parents also regard the Swiss school system with suspicion, believing that it discriminates against their children. The often very ambitious parents feel that many young Tamils have far greater difficulties obtaining higher school and university degrees in Switzerland than in anglophone countries. One obstacle is the lack of language skills among the parents, who are unable to offer adequate help with homework. At the same time they lament a loss of authority, the result of what they presume to be the stronger social integration of their children compared to other countries of immigration. Some parents therefore try to shield their children – especially daughters – from contact with Swiss children. This attitude often encounters strong resistance among children during puberty, and in the end it has a negative effect on their language competency and thus on their ability to obtain higher educational degrees. In addition, many Tamils are afraid that as they grow old in Switzerland they will be abandoned by their children or put in a nursing home, which many are familiar with from their work in caring for old people.

The expectation of the Tamil community that their economically integrated women should act as the guardians of Tamil culture in the spheres of religion, the family, and marriage, and should shield themselves from "amoral" Swiss influences, leads to burdensome conflicts over roles, power struggles, and jealousy in marriage. On the whole, the relations to Swiss society, in keeping with the pronounced sociocultural priorities, are rather restrained. As it is, social contacts are often more likely to exist with other foreigners than with natives, also because of the work and housing situation. Many members of the first generation would welcome the opportunity to live even more closely among each other – for example, in the sort of separate neighborhoods that are found in Great Britain or Canada. At the same time, however, Switzerland is appreciated as a host country because of its quiet political situation and the job opportunities.

The lack of sociocultural integration thus results less from exclusion by the host society than from a withdrawal into one's own group. The idea of diaspora, the belief that a nation-state of their own will eventually emerge in Sri Lanka, reinforces the group's backward orientation and cultural conservatism. This attitude is promoted by the ethnonationalist stance of the LTTE.

This "cultural segregation," however, is less pronounced among the second generation. While contacts within the group remain important for the second generation, young people have a positive attitude toward both the Tamil and the Swiss value systems. Still, in certain areas – for example, marriage – the Tamil norms hold sway. Boys are in principle more strongly integrated into the Swiss value system than the very protected girls. However, to avoid conflict, the second generation engages in behavior that deviates from Tamil rules only clandestinely. On the whole, this generation, socialized in Switzerland, prefers to remain in exile, which is at the same time home.

Fankhauser, Marie-Anne. "Tamilische Jugendliche in der Schweiz." *Tsantsa* 8 (2003): 173–6.

Lüthi, Damaris. *Soziale Beziehungen und Werte im Exil bewahren. Tamilische Flüchtlinge aus Sri Lanka im Raum Bern.* Bern, 2005.

McDowell, Christopher. *A Tamil Asylum Diaspora. Sri Lankan Migration, Settlement and Politics in Switzerland.* Oxford, 1996.

Moret, Joëlle, Denise Efionayi, and Fabienne Stants. *Die srilankische Diaspora in der Schweiz.* Bern, 2007.

Stürzinger, Martin. *Mapping der srilankischen Diaspora in der Schweiz. Kurzstudie für das Berghof Forschungszentrum für konstruktive Konfliktbearbeitung.* Berlin and Zurich, 2002.

Vögeli, Johanna. *Ohne Shakti ist Shiva nichts. Tamilische Geschlechterbeziehungen in der Schweiz.* Bern, 2005.

Cross-references: Switzerland; Great Britain

SWEDISH LABOR MIGRANTS IN DENMARK AND NORWAY IN THE 19TH AND EARLY 20TH CENTURIES

Jan Eivind Myhre

Swedish migration to neighboring Norway and Denmark began around 1850, continuing into the first decade of the 20th century, when it decreased during the great exodus to the USA. Although Swedish migrants did not have a distinct social or occupational profile, it was primarily labor migration and included both men and women.

Swedish registration authorities recorded 66,400 migrants to Norway between 1850 and 1910 and 82,800 to Denmark. An additional 25,600 to Germany were registered after 1866.

The actual figures were certainly higher, with probably more than 100,000 to both Denmark and Norway each. At the turn of the century some 50,000 Swedish-born persons were registered as living in Norway and 35,000 in Denmark. As these censuses were taken in winter, the considerable number of Swedish seasonal laborers was not included. In comparison with the small populations of the Scandinavian countries, this was indeed a mass migration. Denmark had a population of 2 million in the early 1880s, Norway reached that number in 1890, when the population of Sweden surpassed 5 million.

For several reasons this sizable migration did not attract very much attention in Norway and Denmark. In the first place, the cultural barriers were quite low because the languages were related and the religions were quite similar. Second, public attention in this period was directed toward overseas emigration, not immigration. The Swedes were quite preoccupied with emigration to Denmark and Norway and conducted a large public investigation after 1900 to analyze and remedy the situation (The Emigration Inquiry, 21 volumes). Third, much of the emigration to Denmark and Norway was a regional phenomenon. Parts of southern Sweden and eastern Denmark functioned as one labor market, as did parts of western Sweden and southeastern Norway. In these regions, the Copenhagen area and the Oslofjord area stood out as the industrial and urban centers. Thus, Swedish-Norwegian and Swedish-Danish migration formed part of the related processes of industrialization and urbanization, whereby internal migration in these regions was numerically more important than immigration from Sweden.

Most Swedish migrants were, as everywhere in Europe, young and unmarried. More men than women went from Sweden to Norway, but the difference was not large. There were fewer married couples than in the overseas migration, but more than in internal Norwegian country-to-town migration.

Patterns of movement

The centuries-long rivalry between Denmark, Norway, and Sweden influenced local attitudes toward the migrants. This was particularly the case in the 19th century, when nationalist tendencies were increasing and Norway was struggling to dissolve the personal union with Sweden. Nevertheless, no deep, irreconcilable national antagonism developed among the three nations. Danes, Norwegians, and Swedes could settle freely in neighboring countries and passports were abolished in the 1860s.

For Swedes, neighboring Denmark and Norway were sometimes characterized as the "poor man's America" or "Little America." Most Swedish migrants to Denmark and Norway were common people from the countryside with little or no property. The exodus of Swedes to the two little Americas may be regarded as two distinct, yet parallel, phenomena. The migrants to Norway and Denmark originated from different places in Sweden. Some 80% of the Swedes who migrated to Norway between 1850 and 1910 came from the three counties (out of a total of 25) closest to the Oslofjord area: Värmland, Gothenburg och Bohus, and Älfsborg. From the two latter counties, the surrounding areas of Bohuslän and Dalsland, respectively, provided almost all the migrants. Only very few people from these areas went to Denmark. Swedes in Denmark originated mainly (75%) from the four southernmost counties: Malmöhus (42%), Kristianstad, Halland, and Blekinge, areas that hardly saw any migration to Norway.

Within the two clearly delineated target regions, people migrated from less developed areas to areas with a higher rate of urbanization, growing manufacturing industries, and higher wages, which were to be found in both rural and urban areas. In Norway, the major destination for Swedish migrants was the Oslofjord region with its many towns and the city of Oslo, then called Kristiania. This was not only the most industrialized part of Norway but also the region where agriculture was most advanced. In 1900 more than 70% of Swedish-born persons lived in four small counties surrounding the Oslofjord. To a lesser extent, Swedes also settled in the Norwegian border counties and along the coast southeast of the Oslofjord, where shipping flourished in the decades after 1850. Numerous Swedes also moved to northern Norway, which offered jobs in mining and fishing and provided a certain amount of virgin land for agricultural development. Most of the coastal areas and the inland areas were thinly settled with Swedes, with the exception of construction sites.

In Denmark, Copenhagen attracted migrating Swedes as did the neighboring areas in northern Zealand. In 1901 some 68% of Swedish-born persons lived in Zealand, two-thirds of whom had settled in the city of Copenhagen. Eastern Jutland, particularly the Århus and Randers districts, the island of Bornholm (south of Sweden), and the sugar beet–growing southern islands of Lolland and Falster also attracted many Swedes.

Both long-term economic developments and short-term economic trends have always had an influence on mass migration. The push factors in Swedish society between the middle of the 19th century and the beginning of the 20th were rural economic hardship and increasing proletarianization. Famine in some districts aggravated the situation in the late 1860s. In Norway the boost in shipping on the south coast attracted many Swedes until about 1880, thereafter relatively few. Migration currents sharply increased due to a great demand for workers for the construction of railways, harbors, roads, telegraph lines, and urban housing. The peak of the immigration waves seems to have coincided with periods of prosperity, in Denmark above all in the 1880s, in Norway in the mid-1870s and the late 1890s. The thriving economies in the Danish and Norwegian core regions provide the major explanation for Swedish immigration. This also undermines the theory, occasionally advanced, that Swedish migrants replaced the Danish and Norwegian emigrants who left for America.

Annual variations in the number of migrants were strikingly small. In the peak year of Swedish immigration, Norway took in less than twice as many immigrants as in the year with the least immigration, Denmark between two and three times as many. There was, therefore, a rather steady stream of Swedish immigration to Norway and Denmark.

The costs of migration were relatively low, which meant that the costs of return migration were low as well. Although there is a lack of concrete information, return migration seems to have been significant considering that Swedish labor migration to Denmark and Norway was frequently seasonal. Migrants sometimes did not return voluntarily but rather were deported. According to an agreement between Norway and Sweden reached in 1855, both countries could expel each other's citizens when they lacked the means of existence. The Norwegian Aliens Act (1901) facilitated the expulsion of "idle" and "criminal" immigrants. Local authorities sometimes financed the return ticket when there was a shortage of work, as in Kristiania after the business crash of 1899. The Danish Aliens Act of 1875 enabled the police to expel criminal or unemployed foreigners. Between 1875 and 1920 a total of around 30,000 persons were expelled, almost half of whom were Swedes.

Immigrants at work

There were striking similarities in the daily work of Swedish immigrants in Denmark and Norway. Most immigrants hailed from the Swedish countryside and many, although a minority, got a rural job. Both Denmark and Norway were dominated by family farms and ownership was hard to achieve for outsiders. Many immigrants worked as farmhands or domestic servants, some ended up as smallholders or tenant farmers. When, due to increasing commercialization, more farms were offered for sale, some Swedes in Norway succeeded in acquiring property and became independent farmers.

Swedes in Norway were also known as specialists in building fences, draining bogs, and opening up new land. Well-to-do farmers or suburban house owners often employed a Swedish gardener. Swedish men were also known to be skilled stonemasons. In both Denmark and Norway, Swedish immigrants were highly represented in tile works situated in rural areas or just outside towns and cities. Tile working was a seasonal activity, just like much of the agricultural work, like harvesting sugar beets (Denmark) and threshing hay, wheat, barley, or oats. This tradition of Swedish seasonal migrant workers in agriculture dates back to the period before 1840 but continued alongside more permanent migration long after the mid-19th century.

Swedish migrants in urban areas or in industrialized rural districts were mainly employed as domestic servants, industrial workers, artisans, or casual laborers. Most worked unskilled or semiskilled jobs, typically as glassworkers, stonecutters, metalworkers, miners, or textile workers, including many women, who were actively recruited by Norwegian companies in Swedish textile centers like Borås. A small minority of Swedish immigrants was recruited as experts, comparable to specialists from Germany or England. Glassworkers may serve as an example. These qualified Swedish migrants, just like clerks, engineers, shopkeepers, entrepreneurs, and other businessmen, commonly hailed from other parts of Sweden than the great majority of unskilled workers.

A special group of these skilled workers were the so-called *rallare*, navvies roaming the Norwegian and Danish countryside from one construction site to another. With their distinctive appearance (large black hats), physical strength, occupational pride, staunch independence, coarse language, and oppositional spirit, they were sometimes seen as the typical Swedish immigrant. This was far from the truth, since they represented only a small minority of all Swedish immigrants, although there were several thousands of them. Their fame or notoriety also rested on their radical political views: the *rallare* spread socialist ideas to distant parts of Denmark and Norway and contributed to the formation of trade unions. Their employers certainly viewed them ambivalently: they disliked their utter lack of subordination and humility but were in constant need of their professional skills.

Aspects of integration

Several municipalities in Norway witnessed the chain migration of Swedes. Although they clustered in certain counties and towns, the creation of ghettoes in either Norway or Denmark was rather rare. Higher concentrations of Swedes in certain blocks or neighborhoods were particularly noticeable in some Danish towns, especially near large employers (wharfs, tile works, or construction sites). These concentrations, however, consisted mainly of adult men, which meant that few children grew up in an ethnically one-sided milieu. Accordingly, one cannot quite compare them to the Chinatowns or Little Italys known from American migration history, although in the late 19th and early 20th century some areas in Norwegian and Danish towns were known as "Little Sweden."

A minority of the Swedish immigrants between 1860 and 1910 was married. Of all Swedish migrants to Denmark aged 15 and over, only 12% were married; of those who went to Norway, the number was close to 30%. Intermarriage with Norwegians and Danes was quite common. The Swedes tended to marry among themselves when an abundance of Swedish partners was available, but more than half of the migrants married a native. Even in the Norwegian town of Arendal, with a great surplus of Swedish men, half of the Swedish women who married chose a Norwegian husband. Toward the end of the 19th century only one-quarter of Swedish marriages in the town of Kragerø involved two Swedish partners.

Swedish migrants usually participated in the social life of their host countries together with the natives, either in musical societies, sporting clubs, temperance societies, or trade unions.

Both in Denmark and Norway, Swedes were among the pioneers in the labor movement. In the 1890s Swedish social democrats in Kristiania (Oslo) formed their own organization, Manhem, that was affiliated with the Norwegian labor party. Although the three Scandinavian countries were all Lutheran, they had separate churches. In the larger towns and cities, in particular Copenhagen (from the 1860s) and Kristiania (from the 1880s), Swedish migrants formed their own social clubs, mainly reading societies, organizations for mutual support, or religious congregations. Such organizations were typically headed by members of the middle class, but there were working-class members as well. In both Copenhagen and Kristiania (especially after the breakup of the union in 1905), Swedish middle-class groups formed mutual aid societies for the relief of needy countrymen. These Swedish organizations should not be seen as an obstacle to the integration of Swedish migrants into Danish or Norwegian society. On the contrary, they were probably conducive to that process.

The integration of the Swedes was further simplified by the affinity of the Scandinavian languages. Dialects within one country sometimes differed more than the three languages themselves, which, however, also displayed some noticeable differences, often prompting immigrants to adapt their dialect or name to the new language. Thus, for many immigrants the Swedish patronymic "son" soon changed into the Norwegian or Danish "–sen," either voluntarily or simply because a minister changed their names while registering them in church records.

Although many Swedes adapted rather quickly and easily to their new surroundings, they were still sometimes seen as different from the local population, particularly when national sentiments came to the fore. The labor market was a main arena for national rivalries, and lack of employment could lead to conflicts and protests against foreign workers. Apart from an ordinance for the preferential treatment of native workers in public works in both Norway and Denmark (1894), no measures were taken against the employment of foreigners. However, local resentment against foreign workers could be rather strong and Norwegian municipalities often preferred local workers to foreigners.

In both Denmark and Norway, Swedes could often, but not always, be identified by their surnames, which might be one of the reasons that some altered their patronymic to correspond to local usage. Whereas locals were seen as thrifty, industrious, sober, and honest, Swedes often had the reputation of being spendthrifts (the *rallare* in particular), lazy, drunkards, or criminal. On the job, they were sometimes accused of undercutting wages, ingratiating themselves to employers, serving as strikebreakers, and resistant to becoming union members. Some derogatory names have survived to the present day, like *svenskeradd*, where *radd* is an old word for scoundrel. Although the continued existence of such concepts is interesting, studies have illustrated that there was little substance behind these names.

Swedish culture was rarely considered a threat and Norwegians displayed few resentments against the Swedes.

The Swedes, accordingly, had little reason to organize politically to protect their interests against the Danish or Norwegian governments. Their nationalism was similar to neither irredenta nor *risorgimento* nationalism and they did not view themselves as part of a diaspora.

Although Swedish migrants were in most respects not very different from the native population, they were more or less a recognizable minority in Danish and Norwegian society during the second half of the 19th and the first decades of the 20th century. In some cases and under some circumstances they were treated as foreigners: when unemployment increased, when expenditures for poor relief sharply increased, and when nationalistic issues gained importance. However, since Swedes are ethnically, religiously, and linguistically close to Danes and Norwegians, second-generation immigrants were hardly recognizable as such and were usually fully integrated into the majority society.

Bråstad, Kjell J. "Svensk innvandring til Arendalsområdet på 1800-tallet." In *Aust-Agder-Arv*, 27–66. Arendal, 2000.

Brochmann, Grete, and Knut Kjeldstadli. *A History of Immigration: The Case of Norway 900–2000*. Oslo, 2008.

Emigrationsutredningen, vol. 20. *Svenskarna i utlandet*. Stockholm, 1911.

Myhre, Jan Eivind. "Vicini e lontani: Svedesi nelle città norvegesi (1814–1914)." *Quaderni storici* 107 (2001): 517–40.

Myhre, Jan Eivind. "Kajsa, Sven og hundre tusen svensker – innvandring fra Sverige til Norge på 1800-tallet." *Norsk-svenske relasjoner i 200 år*, edited by Øystein Sørensen and Thorbjörn Nilsson, 89–104. Oslo, 2005.

Niemi, Einar, Jan Eivind Myhre, and Knut Kjeldstadli. *Norsk innvandringshistorie*, vol. 2. *I nasjonalstatens tid 1814–1940*. Oslo, 2003.

Østergaard, Bent. *Indvandrerne i Danmarks historie: kultur og religionsmøter*. Odense, 2007.

Wirén, Agnes. "Den glömda utvandringen i nytt perspektiv. Om svenska invandrare i Danmark och Tyskland." In *Över gränser. Festskrift til Birgitta Odén*, 459–72. Lund, 1987.

Zip Sane, Henrik. "Kriminalitet og fremmedangst – politiets forhold til svenske indvandrere I København 1868–1898." *Scandia* 2 (1998): 225–43.

Zip Sane, Henrik. *Billige og villige? Af indvandringens historie i Danmark*. Farum, 2000.

Cross-references: Northern Europe; Swedish Labor Migrants in Germany in the Late 19th and Early 20th Centuries

SWEDISH LABOR MIGRANTS IN GERMANY IN THE LATE 19TH AND EARLY 20TH CENTURIES

Claudius H. Riegler

The year 1868 saw the beginning of an extensive migration by Swedes to Germany in search of work. It was the high point of a famine that was affecting nearly all of Sweden due to catastrophic weather and subsequent poor harvests and became the direct trigger of border-crossing mass movements. The migration into northern Germany, which took place largely in groups, followed in the footsteps of older migratory traditions in the triangle Sweden-Denmark-Germany.

During the high phase of the exodus 1868–72 and 1879–85, the Swedes who migrated to Germany were a socially homogeneous group, made up of (mostly younger) members of the rural lower classes who were placed in the German labor market as domestics. Among them were those who came directly from the class of the village poor, as well as those who were unsuccessful in the first country-city migrations in the early stages of Sweden's partial industrialization. The proportion of women was higher than that of men. They hailed from the southern provinces of the kingdom – the regions of Scania, Blekinge, Halland, Småland (including the island of Öland), and parts of Östergötland and Bohuslän. Women found employment chiefly as milkmaids on the estates in northern Germany; men were farmhands and day laborers in agriculture and in various sectors of the construction industry (canals, ports, urban excavation, railroads). Those who went to Germany between 1890 and 1920 were primarily single men from the cities who were trained tradesmen. The total number for the period 1868 to 1920 was 60,000 to 80,000 persons.

The influx was a temporary labor migration with a high seasonal component. It was dictated by the necessity "of exporting our people because we do not know how to employ them," as one Swedish diplomat put it in 1896 while criticizing the weaknesses in his country's path of development: a lopsided export of raw materials from agriculture, mining, and iron smelting without investments in additional processing because of a lack of technical know-how.

In the Kingdom of Sweden and in the German Empire, the political establishment and the public perceived this migratory movement as a group phenomenon until the 1890s. In Sweden, labor migration was seen as a functioning outlet for "overpopulation," though it was at the same time referred to derogatorily as the "German disease" and its magnitude was noted with regret. In Germany, estate owners welcomed it as a remedy against a "shortage of people." Employers and their organizations in the emerging industry of goods for mass consumption appreciated them as a reservoir of workers.

The geographical population movements that were characteristic of Sweden were shaped by the parallel existence of internal migrations, an overseas emigration and remigration that took hold of the entire country, and labor migrations into the neighboring states. Overseas emigration, which was a rural settlement migration until the 1880s, was different from the labor migration into a small number of European neighboring countries (Denmark, Norway, and Russia). The migration patterns of people who went to European countries in search of jobs were initially characterized by organized group migrations.

The Swedish labor migration to northern Germany was headed for Schleswig-Holstein and Mecklenburg and the northern areas of Lower Saxony. The mostly young immigrants of both genders came to Germany as farmhands as part of an extensive recruitment system run by estate owners. In 1879 their number was about 3,700 in Schleswig-Holstein and around 6,000 in Mecklenburg. At the same time, though, industrial workers were also recruited in large numbers. In 1871, 250 shipyard workers arrived in Kiel as strikebreakers. In 1872 their number had risen to 800. The year 1879 saw extensive dismissals. The unemployed found work in canal building on the Trave (1879–83) and – provided they remained on German soil and were not deported or voluntarily returned to Sweden where they would wait for new employment opportunities in Germany – in the shipyards of Stettin in 1886–7 and from 1887 on in the construction of the Kaiser Wilhelm Canal, which was later renamed the North Sea–Baltic Sea Canal.

Beginning in the 1890s, the social composition of the immigration changed noticeably. Tradesmen, skilled workers, and technicians now pushed into the labor markets of the German Reich, often with a clear intent of acquiring further training. The large cities (Berlin, Hamburg) and industrially developed regions now became attractive, and many began to arrive with support from the Swedish government (travel grants). Swedes were also hired by shipyards in Bremen (1911) and factories in the rubber and cigarette industry in the greater Hamburg region. During World War I, the German Central Office for Workers, which was in charge of bringing in foreign workers, recruited several hundred skilled metalworkers for the German armament industry.

The Swedish migrant workers were clearly perceived as an immigrant minority. That was true of the countryside, where, even though they integrated into the lower class, they stood out because of their language and divergent social behavior (group solidarity, resistance to the despotic power of estate owners). The Swedes scattered over a wide area tried to maintain contact beyond the boundaries of the estate districts and supported countrymen and –women who had fallen on hard times. They attracted the attention of the police for petty criminal behavior, which they often engaged in while inebriated. Over time they showed increasing signs of mental disturbances, phenomena that one must describe – because of their frequency – as the self-destructive consequences of social deracination.

The flight of Swedish farmhands from the unexpectedly harsh working conditions especially on the estates in Mecklenburg soon turned into a nightmare for landowners. In December 1871, the police office in Bützow reported behavior that was typical for this form of collective resistance: the migrants, who had been brought into the country and had been hamstrung through work contracts and additional material obligations toward the middlemen who rented out the domestics, "used to escape in groups, probably under suitable leaders, often right after entering into their service and receiving an advance payment." To

be on the safe side, the Prussian authorities often expelled them before the end of the 10-year period during which they could retain their Swedish citizenship, for if they were expelled after their citizenship had been revoked, they expected problems with their readmission into Sweden. In the cities they merged with the native proletariat in the 1880s. They participated early in organizations representing their interests (aid funds and organizations, unions) and were often singled out and punished as instigators during actions by the organized workers' movement. As early as 1872, native and Swedish shipyard workers in Kiel joined forces to strike for wage hikes. The Swedes learned to be more class conscious. Over a period of 10 years, the Swedish shipyard workers in Kiel formed a settlement colony with its own way of life. Including family members, it encompassed about 2,000 persons in 1876–7.

The traces of the labor migrants who settled in the countryside disappeared with the beginning of the 20th century, in Mecklenburg sooner than in Schleswig-Holstein. There the officials used various forms of harassment in an effort to prevent an integration desired by many Swedes: although they didn't bother those who had begun the process of integration (e.g., through marriage with natives, applications for citizenship), they expelled all migrants who had become useless to the labor market, thereby imposing all the social costs for this migratory group on the country of origin. Thus, pregnant maids were taken to Sweden under demeaning circumstances, and disobedient workers were deported after serving draconian sentences in the infamous workhouses, like the one in Güstrow.

At the end of the 19th century, a brief Slavophobia seemed to alter the attitude of agricultural employers toward the Swedish workers: between 1897 and 1900, Chambers of Agriculture in East Prussia and Pomerania, acting as the spokesmen for estate owners, declared that in the face of a supposedly imminent avalanche of settlement by "foreign workers of Slavic extraction," the salvation of agriculture lay in the recruitment of Swedish agricultural workers. This strategy – conceived of as a bulwark against the immigration of Russian-Polish and Galician agricultural workers – of once again "importing" tens of thousands of rural workers "of Germanic origin" from Sweden was not realized.

Of the members of Sweden's rural underclasses and of the subsequent tradesmen, skilled workers, and engineers who came to Germany, only a fraction remained. For a while they benefited from their reputation – not universally shared – of being "more obedient, modest, and hardworking than the native domestics," as a contemporary observer put it in 1877. Integration succeeded above all in the cities. Around 1885 there were about 2,400 Swedes in Hamburg; around 1910 there were only 1,650. However, since nationalized individuals born in Sweden were not captured by the statistics, we must posit the existence of a small, ethnic Swedish population minority in all coastal towns along the North and Baltic Seas, something that is also indicated by the spelling – in part assimilated – of certain family names.

Haack, Hanna, and Silke Rossow. "Die Integration schwedischer Arbeitsimmigranten im Großherzogtum Mecklenburg-Schwerin." *Migration: A European Journal of International Migration and Ethnic Relations. Special Issue on Migration in the Southern Baltic Region* 20 (1993/1994): 63–84.

Hoerder, Dirk, ed. *Labor Migration in the Atlantic Economies in the Period of Industrialization.* Westport, CT, 1985.

Riegler, Claudius H. *Emigration und Arbeitswanderung aus Schweden nach Norddeutschland 1868–1914.* Neumünster, 1985.

Cross-references: Germany; Northern Europe; Central and Western European Miners and Smelters in Sweden and Denmark-Norway from the 16th to the 18th Century; Polish Agricultural Workers in Prussia-Germany from the Late 19th Century to World War II; Swedish Return Migrants from the United States, 1875–1930

SWEDISH RETURN MIGRANTS FROM THE UNITED STATES, 1875–1930

Per-Olof Grönberg

Swedish mass emigration to the USA started in 1845. Between 1845 and 1930, some 1,150,000 Swedish immigrants were officially registered; the unregistered number may have been around 100,000. About three-fourths of these emigrants left the country between 1868 and 1913. The proportion of emigration was high in relation to the Swedish population and exceeded only by Ireland, Norway, and Iceland within Europe.

There are no statistics available on return migration before 1875, but it was probably almost nonexistent. Between 1875 and 1890 the return frequency was low, but a shift occurred in the 1890s, when almost a fourth of all migrants returned. The average Swedish return frequency between 1875 and 1930 was 18%, which means that the share was high compared to Ireland (10% in 1815–1914), but low compared to Italy and other countries whose emigration culminated in a later period than Sweden (see Table 1).

Farming families who left with the intention to stay permanently in the USA initially dominated Swedish emigration. There was a successive shift toward single labor migrants, of whom many wanted to take temporary jobs and return to Sweden. The predominant family migration in the first period helps to explain the low return rates. When the individual labor migration increased, return migration to Sweden increased as well, although the return rate was never over 50% at any point in time.

Of all the Swedes who migrated to the USA between 1851 and 1930, roughly 57% were men and 43% women. Only in the late 1890s and late 1910s were female migrants dominant. Return migrants were predominantly male. In the 1880s, almost three-fourths of return migrants were male, which decreased to two-thirds in the 1890s and only slightly less in the 1920s. Gender differences in return migration related to social and economic circumstances. Men were

Table 1. Return migration from the United States to Sweden, 1875–1930		
Years	**Return Migration**	**in % of emigration**
1875–1880	3,691	5.8
1881–1890	18,766	5.8
1891–1900	47,138	23.5
1901–1910	44,029	20.1
1911–1920	37,153	45.6
1921–1930	27,474	29.9
TOTAL	178,251	18.2

Source: Bidrag till Sveriges officiella statistik, Serie A; Sveriges officiella statistik. Ut- och invandring.

mostly employed as laborers, while women often had jobs in domestic service that brought with it greater interaction with Americans. Women more often married in America. Besides, they had fewer opportunities to take over a farm or to start a business should they return to Sweden. More women than men chose to stay in the USA, a country where female emancipation was more advanced and where they had more independence and greater opportunities for employment.

The period of stay in the USA was generally short: almost three-quarters remained four years or less. Migrants who returned to Sweden between 1880 and 1930 were mostly in their 20s or 30s (65%), the largest group being aged 25 to 34. Almost 30% of the male and 40% of the female returnees were married. A comparison of these figures with those of the Swedish emigrants in this period illustrates that an average of 10% of the male and 15% of the female returnees had married during their stay in the USA.

Emigration drew primarily from nonurban areas, which, however, does not imply that all the emigrants worked in the agricultural sector. Between 1851 and 1930 some 28% worked in agricultural occupations while 23% were domestic servants, 19% were wage earners, and 18% worked in manufacturing and handicrafts. Return migration was, according to official statistics, strongest in agrarian counties with little industrialization. Between 1875 and 1913, return migration amounted to 15% for Sweden as a whole, whereas the percentage in four southern agrarian counties was between 17% and 26%. This rural pattern possibly correlated with a high degree of laborers among the emigrants, who preferred a temporary stay in North America to internal migration and proletarization in an urban settlement.

Urban return migration was significant only in an early phase of migration overall. In 1881–5 the share of return emigration to urban areas was 14%, while 22% of the return migrants went to towns. Between 1926 and 1930 those shares were equal (31%). Thus, despite the higher degree of urbanization, which doubled between 1881 and 1930, there was no rise in the share of return migration to urban areas. Return migrants generally went back to their home parishes. There are even indications of migrants who had lived in industrial or urban areas prior to their emigration, but who moved to agrarian parishes after their return.

Although return migration generally did not enhance urbanization or industrialization, a small group of migrant engineers were important in the exchange of ideas between the countries. The USA was the major destination for engineers; almost 20% of all engineers educated in Sweden between 1880 and 1919 went there, whereas 11% went to Germany. They did not go to Minnesota and other major Swedish destinations, but choose places like Pittsburgh in Pennsylvania and Schenectady in upstate New York. Their primary goal was employment with large corporations such as General Electric, Westinghouse, or Carnegie Steel, where they could acquire experience of mass production and American technology. Around 1900 Swedish industrialists and politicians viewed America as a model for industrial development. Experience in the USA was advantageous in the Swedish job market and for further professional mobility. Almost a third of the returned engineers reached positions as managing directors or chief engineers, compared with less than 20% of nonemigrants. Although many laborers also intended to stay for a limited period in the USA, this pattern was especially significant for the engineers, of whom almost 60% returned.

Less than half of the returnees stayed in the area where they first settled upon return. Others moved to another parish in Sweden or again to America, some even making several journeys across the Atlantic. In particular, migrants from urban areas, of whom many did not return to their original hometown, tended to move again. Rural returnees either remained where they came from or returned to the USA. Many must have been disappointed by their homecoming – such repeated migrations commonly led to permanent settlement in America.

Roughly 10% of all the returnees died within a year or two of their return to their former homes; many of them were older, but some were still young. Others returned to marry in Sweden. In rural areas, having a fiancée waiting at home was more common than in urban areas. Within three years well over a third of the unmarried rural returnees had married, in comparison to less than a fourth of the urban ones. Rural returnees often used their American savings for farm and land purchases. An inquiry into 23 returnees in one village has shown that 16 of them used their money for this purpose; a fourth of all real estate purchases between 1897 and 1941 in this village were paid for in dollars. The migration experience rarely resulted in upward social mobility, except for some returnees who started their own businesses. Roughly 10% of the returnees did so and sometimes the stay in America was crucially influential. In Hälsingland, returnees established three of the four furniture factories. Returnee shopkeeper Alfred Geijer in the southern Swedish village of Långasjö is described as always being "one step ahead," which made him successful. Erik Öhman, who returned from Minnesota in 1920, started a forge in Hälsingland as well as one of the area's first car repair shops. He became known for manufacturing joints for chains and truck cabins on American models.

Returned engineers influenced Swedish technology. J. Sigfrid Edström spent four years with Westinghouse and General Electric in the 1890s and became director of Sweden's largest electro-technical company ASEA in 1903. Under his leadership this company was organized according to American principles. Naval architect Hugo Hammar returned from Boston and later developed the Götaverken shipyard, with his American knowledge of warships and the use of templates, into one of the world's largest shipyards. Paul Palèn and Oscar Falkman became familiar with copper smelting in America and used several ideas in the Boliden mining company. Labor-management relations and a kind of social welfare policy, inspired by American companies, influenced many of these engineers as well.

Returnees were also important in spreading religious nonconformity. A Baptist returnee started the first Sunday school in 1855; two years later Sweden had eight Baptist congregations and the number steadily increased in the 1860s. The first Methodist congregation was founded in 1868 on the initiative of two returnees, and Methodism had an early growth despite official opposition. Mormonism also gained a foothold. Returnees were critical of the Swedish State Lutheran Church. The priests no longer received the same kind of respect they had known earlier, and one returnee became known for refusing to raise his hat in greeting for the old pastor. Free churches were connected with the temperance movement, which spread from America through letters, publications, temporary visits, and return migration. A national temperance society was founded in 1837 and a Swedish branch of the international temperance movement appeared in 1879. Later, Minnesota returnees started a local temperance movement.

Sweden did receive return migrants who had been members of the International Workers of the World (IWW), but they never became a major impulse toward a radical union movement. Some labor activists pursued ideas and dreams inspired by the ideals discussed in American mining towns and meeting halls. Returnee Edward Mattsson became a leader of the ironworkers' union. There are indications that returnees were active within local as well as national politics, but unlike Norway and Finland, Sweden never had a return migrant who became prime minister.

Carlsson, Sten. "Chronology and Composition of Swedish Emigration to America." In *From Sweden to America: A History of the Migration*, edited by Harald Runblom and Hans Norman, 114–48. Uppsala and Minneapolis, 1976.

Grönberg, Per-Olof. *Learning and Returning: Return Migration of Swedish Engineers from the United States, 1880–1940.* Umeå, 2003.

Lindblad, Hans. "Impulser som förändrade Sverige." In *Tur och retur Amerika. Utvandrare som förändrade Sverige*, edited by Ingvar Henricsson and Hans Lindblad, 99–272. Stockholm, 1995.

Tedebrand, Lars-Göran. "Remigration from America to Sweden." In *From Sweden to America: A History of the Migration*, edited by Harald Runblom and Hans Norman, 201–27. Uppsala and Minneapolis, 1976.

Wyman, Mark. *Round-Trip to America: The Immigrants Return to Europe, 1880–1930*. Ithaca and London, 1993.

Cross-references: Northern Europe; Irish Return Migrants from the United States in the 19th and Early 20th Centuries

SWEDISH TROOPS ON THE COASTS OF THE NORTH SEA AND THE BALTIC SEA IN THE EARLY MODERN PERIOD

Stefan Kroll

In Swedish history, the period from the early 17th century to the end of the Great Nordic War of 1721 is generally referred to as the "Great Power Period." During this stretch of about a century, the Scandinavian Kingdom not only participated successfully in the struggle for hegemony in the region of the Baltic Sea but it also possessed considerable weight as a major power in central, east-central, and eastern Europe. Although its foreign policy was at times defensive in orientation, the Swedish kings needed a powerful army. In the course of the 17th century, Sweden developed a model of raising armies that was based – unlike the model in nearly all other European countries – essentially on the conscripting of native farmers and was referred to as *indelningsverk*. After the reform of 1682, every Swedish province was required to maintain a regiment. Losses that were incurred had to be defrayed first of all by the farmers who were not drafted for service into an active unit (usually 10 men between the ages of 15 and 60). The soldiers were given a cottager's allotment to provide a livelihood, and through it they remained closely tied to their surrounding world of relatives and neighbors.

These Swedish and Finnish regiments, composed entirely of native subjects, formed the core of the Swedish army far beyond the end of Sweden's "Great Power Period." However, especially in the Thirty Years' War and in the Great Nordic War, but also in the intervening military conflicts, this army was not adequate for pursuing offensive goals of power politics beyond the Baltic Sea. Alongside a smaller number of regiments recruited in Sweden itself, the Swedish kings deployed in the theaters of war in central, east-central, and eastern Europe numerous units that were made up of foreign mercenaries who had not been born in Sweden or Finland. The regional makeup of these recruited regiments depended essentially on where they were levied and stationed. For example, scholars put the strength of the Swedish army in 1632 at 108,000 men, 95,000 of whom were not from Sweden but had been recruited in the European theaters of war.

From the turn of the 16th century, the power-political ambitions of their king Gustav II Adolf led the Swedish troops to the southern shores of the North and Baltic Seas. After Estonia had passed into Swedish hands as early as 1582, Karelia, Ingermanland, and Livonia followed also between 1617 and 1629. Gustav II Adolf's successors won Hither Pomerania, Wismar, and Bremen-Verden for the Swedish crown in the Peace of Westphalia in 1648. Subsequently, Sweden was also involved in the three Nordic Wars (1655–60, 1674–9, and 1700–12). Troops were repeatedly moved across the Baltic Sea during those wars. However, the largest troop movements had occurred in the years 1630–48, when Sweden became active in Germany during the Thirty Years' War.

The leadership of the Swedish army separated the so-called National Regiments in the important port cities and fortresses along the German North Sea and Baltic Sea coast – regiments regarded as reliable, made up exclusively of Swedes and Finns, and levied by conscription – from the field army that operated deep into southern Germany. To the end of the war and several years beyond, the National Regiments formed the garrisons in cities like Stettin, Stralsund, Wismar (at times also Stade), which served the Swedish army as important military bridgeheads. The number of soldiers stationed in the garrison cities (in many cases they were joined by their wives and children) fluctuated strongly. For example, in the fall of 1630, 4,230 soldiers were stationed in Stettin and 3,130 in Stralsund, but by 1640 there were only 1,106 and 905, respectively. At times the percentage of soldiers among the total population of these cities probably reached as high as 40%, but especially after the end of the war it is likely to have dropped in most cases below 10%. It was only in garrison cities and towns that a sustained process of integration could take place in the end, since the field armies rarely remained in one place for any length of time.

After the end of the war, two-thirds of the Swedish and Finnish soldiers moved back home across the Baltic Sea as early as 1649. Only a small part – mostly deserters – joined other European armies. In the following decades, down to the end of the Great Nordic War in 1721 (and beyond that to the end of the presence of Swedish troops on the southern coast of the Baltic Sea at the beginning of the 19th century), the troops serving in northern German territories were largely recruited locally and had a high percentage of natives. They took the place of the National Regiments. Exceptions were made only during a number of different wars, but in no case was there any long-term stationing of troops.

For the population along the shores of the North and Baltic Seas, the regular appearance of foreign armies during the Thirty Years' War was nothing unusual in itself, for they were familiar with this from previous wars. What was new was that the soldiers remained even after the fighting had shifted to other regions. The Swedes were the first to establish permanent garrisons there and to fortify the most important cities into defensive fortresses as an external sign of a new era. Henceforth, the native urban population had to adjust to the presence of an entirely new social group within its walls, especially since the soldiers were at times accompanied by their wives and children. They were all quartered in the houses of the burghers – a drastic experience that would shape the daily life of many city dwellers from then on. The age of the standing armies had begun.

Various processes of demarcation but also accommodation began, the latter especially after the 1650s, when the National Regiments were increasingly replaced by troops recruited locally. While the military population was clearly separated from the burghers and other residents of the city legally, a multitude of connections developed in nearly all other spheres. This is evident among other things from the many marriages between soldiers and the daughters of civilians, from the frequency with which they acted as godparents for one another, and from business relationships. For example, many soldiers worked as laborers, handymen, or journeymen in the employment of burghers or they produced and sold affordable goods to the less well-off city residents, especially shoes, clothing, and food.

Soldiers were also welcome as consumers of tobacco products and as paying guests in taverns. However, the trade guilds, in particular, regularly saw the soldiers, who depended on sources of income in addition to their pay, as unwelcome competition and persecuted them accordingly. Moreover, the close encounters in the taverns regularly led to conflicts that were not infrequently settled violently. It was no doubt in the longer periods of peace – which also brought more stability and less fluctuation among the garrison troops – that the world of the soldiers and that of the burghers drew closest. Time and again, members of one group switched to the other, as former soldiers became burghers and vice versa. The fact that the Swedish troops nevertheless always preserved a certain autonomy as a group in the garrison cities had two main reasons: the discontinuity in personnel in response to military necessities, and the special legal status of the soldiers.

So far we have very few insights into integration processes and possible remigrations in the rural areas. However, there are some indications, especially for Swedish-Pomerania, which was heavily depopulated by the Thirty Years' War, that point to a partly nondirected, but partly also intentional settlement of Swedish families after 1650, often concentrated in specific locations. Entries in church registers show that there were many former Swedish soldiers among the new farmers, shepherds, weavers, and day laborers.

Many legends about the Swedish troops have persisted to this day in the Swedish garrison cities along the German coast of the North and Baltic Seas. The popular tradition does not distinguish between the members of the National Regiments and the soldiers of non-Swedish background. Anyone who wore the requisite uniform was considered a Swedish soldier. For the period of the Thirty Years' War, heavily negative images prevailed here as elsewhere in the Empire. The Swedish soldiers were described primarily as "arsonists," "plunderers," and "murderers." These characterizations dissipated with the end of the war. In the subsequent course of the 17th and into the 18th century they gave way to a more differentiated view, because the marauding field armies became in times of peace rather tolerable occupiers with whom one could get along quite well.

Ericson, Lars. *Svenska knektar. Indelta soldater, ryttare och båtsmän i krig och fred.* 2nd ed. Lund, 2002.

Kroll, Stefan. *Stadtgesellschaft und Krieg. Sozialstruktur, Bevölkerung und Wirtschaft in Stralsund und Stade 1700–1715.* Göttingen, 1997.

Krusenstjern, Benigna von, and Hans Medick, eds. *Zwischen Alltag und Katastrophe. Der Dreißigjährige Krieg aus der Nähe.* Göttingen, 1999.

Langer, Herbert. "Die Anfänge des Garnisonswesens in Pommern." In *Gemeinsame Bekannte. Schweden und Deutschland in der Frühen Neuzeit*, edited by Ivo Asmus, Heiko Droste, and Jens E. Olesen, 397–417. Münster, 2003.

Tessin, Georg. *Die deutschen Regimenter der Krone Schweden.* 2 parts. Cologne and Graz, 1965/67.

Cross-references: The Baltic Region; Germany; Northern Europe; Poland; Scottish Soldiers in Europe in the Early Modern Period; Spanish Troops in the Netherlands in the 16th and 17th Centuries: The Example of Geldern

SWISS MERCENARIES IN EUROPE FROM THE 17TH TO THE 19TH CENTURY: THE EXAMPLE OF FRANCE

Alain-Jacques Czouz-Tornare

From the 14th century on, nearly 2 million Swiss, mostly from the rural Catholic cantons, were engaged in "foreign service" as mercenaries in other European states. Nearly half went to France. The lack of opportunities for a secure livelihood and strong population growth in the region of origin led to the massive emigration of mercenaries into the 19th century. In 1701, 54,350 Swiss were in military service abroad: 24,700 in France, 11,200 in the Netherlands, 6,400 in Spain, 4,925 in Savoy-Piedmont, 4,800 in Austria, and 2,000 in Poland. In 1789, more than 14,000 Swiss soldiers were in France, 9,800 in the Netherlands, 5,834 in the Kingdom of Naples, and 4,868 in Spain. In the 16th century the outflow was equal to excess births, in the 17th century it amounted to two-thirds, and in the 18th century to nearly half of excess births. In the first half of the 18th century, the peak period of foreign service, 50,000–60,000 Swiss were continuously employed by foreign armies. All told, 300,000–350,000 Swiss mercenaries were abroad during the 18th century. The number of Swiss who volunteered for foreign military service in the 17th and 18th centuries has been estimated at between one-sixth and one-third of a generation of men between the ages of 16 and 45. Although ever larger segments of the population were benefiting from the upswing in the textile industry since the 18th century, foreign military service remained an important factor for the Swiss economy.

Two phases can be identified: the period until the second half of the 17th century was dominated by a mercenary service (*Reisläuferei*) characterized by the temporally limited recruitment of bands of mercenaries and later also of entire companies. Private military contractors, whose activities peaked in the 17th century, offered military commanders troops in return for payment. Beginning in the late 17th century, the Swiss increasingly served in the standing armies of their destination countries on a permanent basis. Foreign service gradually became an essential component of the administration of the Patrician oligarchies that had emerged in various parts of the Swiss Confederacy. The authorities took over the organization of the military migration and transformed the system of mercenaries that was unproductive for them into a useful economic and political instrument. The exodus was directed into allied states and regulated through contracts. The nonlegalized migration of mercenaries developed into a system for marketing mercenaries overseen by the authorities.

To prevent illegal recruitment on the old model, every Swiss state, following the example of Bern from 1684, established a recruitment board that processed all matters relating to foreign military service and registered all mercenaries recruited by the recruitment officers. The mercenary set out with the approval of his territorial lordship, which was represented by the rural or urban administrative and judicial lord (*Schultheiß*). Both for the state and for the mercenary, foreign military service could be a lucrative alternative to emigration as a civilian. Often, however, the authorities also used forced recruitments to rid themselves of vagrants, beggars, and "immoral," "rebellious," and "troublesome" individuals.

Leaving aside the economic advantages, military service abroad also supported the political relationships between the cantons and the destination states, among them especially France, which had developed into the protector of the balance between the cantons within Switzerland. By making Swiss troops available, the elites in the cantons close to France in a sense purchased their dominant position, especially after the time of Louis XIV. The troops reinforced the French army but also represented the political strength of the cantons, who until 1792 could summon their soldiers back at any time. In the process, political reasons for providing the troops could make economic considerations recede into the background: for example, in 1752, the canton of Zurich sent a regiment to France, even though its manufactures had acquired considerable economic importance and needed workers.

Freiburg im Üechtland, for example, a Catholic and largely Francophone enclave within the state of Bern, became, on the basis of military contracts, a crucial partner and outpost for France in the 18th century. Its elites had an unusually strong influence over foreign military service in France. The city-state on the banks of the Sarine exported human beings, cattle, and cheese, and received in return, under royal protection, French military pensions and salt. Shortly before the French Revolution, at least half of Freiburg's 2,000 men fit for military service were in foreign service in France. Preferred by the court, they had a monopolistic hold on the highest ranks within the Swiss troops of the French kings, especially within the Swiss guard.

The Swiss soldiers in France formed an army within the army and, in a broader sense, a state within the state. The French kings had heaped so many privileges on the soldiers from the neighboring country to the east that they had a better status than French soldiers. For example, tax exemptions, lower court fees, and religious liberty eventually applied to the entire community of Swiss origin in France. The French Revolution put an end to this special status.

The Swiss generally enlisted for four years, but the receiving states for the most part tried to keep them longer in their regiments. The sending states were hardly interested in the return of the soldiers and did not keep any statistic on returnees. Relatively few mercenaries came back to their regions of origin, not because they had been killed in war but mostly because they recognized the advantages of settling in the countries of their service. Longtime former members of the Swiss guard who had been stationed for many years in the Paris region usually settled in suburbs (e.g., Rueil, Courbevoie, Suresnes) and married local women, who were attracted by the Swiss men's privileges.

The more time the Swiss could invest in agricultural activities during their military service, the more frequently they became farmers in France after the end of their service. They were regarded as especially reliable and were not infrequently given jobs as porters, caretakers, or sextons, who were commonly referred to in France as "Suisse" as late as the 20th century. A frequent alternation between military and civilian activities occurred in the 18th century. In many cases, soldiers engaged after their military service in tasks they had also performed within their regiments: sutlers became tavern keepers, and tailors and cobblers also continued their professions.

Even after the crushing defeat of the Swiss guard in Paris during the revolutionary assault on the Tuileries on 10 August 1792, followed by their dismissal back to their home country, more than one-quarter of their soldiers remained in France. As late as 1794, in the midst of the Terror, about 200 Swiss were counted in Rueil among a total population of 2,484. A reintegration of the returnees into the rural world of Switzerland was unlikely, since they had adopted a way of life that ran counter to its social norms. The majority of the remigrants remained poor and in debt. Few returnees were able to move into the service of Swiss law enforcement forces.

Foreign military service declined after the middle of the 18th century. Commanders and warlords went deeper and deeper into debt, while the simple soldier saw his purchasing power erode. The attractiveness of this service also waned because the opportunities for a livelihood in the rising Swiss manufacturing sector surpassed the earnings prospects as a soldier abroad. The system of recruiting mercenaries exerted its influence in the field of overseas emigration from Switzerland: the practice at the beginning and the middle of the 19th century of sending socially marginal groups to Brazil as settlers and plantation workers imitated the military model.

Foreign service in Great Britain disappeared in 1816; the Swiss were recruited only one more time, for the Crimean War. No Swiss troops existed any longer in Spain after 1823, or in the Netherlands after 1829. The state-organized foreign service in France collapsed in the July Revolution of 1830. Thereafter, Swiss mercenaries were still found in service to the pope and in Naples, and in large numbers also in the French Foreign Legion (created 1831). In Algeria, for example, the Swiss foreign legionnaires protected those settlers from Switzerland who had emigrated in 1853, with the help of an organization in Geneva and on the basis of French land concessions and subsidies, to Sétif (province of Constantine). After the conclusion of their service as legionnaires, some of the soldiers likewise became settlers in Algeria.

The signing of new military agreements was outlawed in 1848 and 1859. Only private contracts still existed in the 20th century. The only Swiss military formation in foreign service that still exists in the 21st century is the Swiss Guard at the Vatican, which celebrated its two-hundredth anniversary in 2006.

Czouz-Tornare, Alain-Jacques. *Les troupes suisses capitulées et les relations franco-helvétiques à la fin du XVIIIe siècle*. Paris, 1996.

Hausmann, Germain. "Suisses au service de France. Étude économique et sociologique (1763–1792)." 2 vols., PhD diss, Paris, 1980.

Head, Anne-Lise. "Démographie et société en pays glaronnais (XVIIe–XVIIIe siècles)." PhD diss, Geneva, 1986.

Henry, Philippe. "Fremde Dienste." In *Historisches Lexikon der Schweiz*, vol. 4, 789–96. Basel, 2005.

Cross-references: France; Italy; Switzerland; German Soldiers in the French Foreign Legion in the 19th and 20th Centuries

SWISS PROTESTANT PEASANTS IN ALSACE, SOUTHWESTERN GERMANY, AND BRANDENBURG-PRUSSIA SINCE THE MID-17TH CENTURY

Matthias Asche

The sometimes far-flung migrations of Swiss population groups in the 17th and 18th centuries to the "Niderland," that is, the northward migration into the territories of the Holy Roman Empire, were prominently characterized by a high number of migrants from the strata of small farmers and below, as well as from nonguild agricultural and construction workers. They were mostly driven by economic reasons and were dependent on the fluctuating opportunities to make a living in an agrarian world that was susceptible to crisis and poor in natural resources. Seasonal migrations and permanent emigration occurred equally among German-, French-, and Italian-speaking population groups of all religious denominations. At the center here are the German Swiss and the French-speaking Swiss (*Welschschweizer*) of the Reformed denomination, whose migration paths can at least be reconstructed in rough outline, even if the total size of the group remains unknown.

Potential target lands for the rural Swiss migrants were the neighboring territories in Alsace and along the upper Rhine that had been devastated and depopulated in the Thirty Years' War. The Swiss Reformed authorities generally acceded to the desire of their subjects to emigrate, given the existing socio-economic tensions that could often not be resolved any other way; at times they even actively promoted their departure, if the countries of destination belonged to a related denomination. Between 1649 and 1662, more than 4,300 largely impoverished persons from the territory of Zurich, about 5% of the rural subjects of the canton, moved to Electoral Palatinate, Württemberg, Baden-Durlach, and the imperial knights' territories of Lower Alsace. At the beginning of the Swiss mass exodus in the second half of the 17th century was also the last phase of the expulsion of the Anabaptists from the Protestant cantons, which took them above all to the territories of the tolerant counts of Rappoltsweiler (Ribeauvillé) and the Imperial Knightage in Alsace (around Colmar), as well as to the Electoral Palatinate and the territories of the imperial knights in the Kraichgau.

In view of the expansionary policy of France's King Louis XIV along the border of the Rhine, the Swiss migrants increasingly preferred target regions east of the Rhine instead of west of the Rhine, which had initially been part of their destinations, too. In the process, the Electoral Palatinate rapidly became the favored immigration region, especially since the reformed prince-elector was actively recruiting fellow Protestants to rebuild his lands. By contrast, the Reformed French-speaking Swiss, chiefly from the Bern Waadtland, the territories of Basle's prince-bishop in the Bern Jura, or the Principality of Neuchâtel, migrated largely to the francophone county of Mömpelgard (Montbéliard) which belonged to the Duke of Württemberg.

The migration of Reformed Swiss into the territories along the upper Rhine declined markedly as early as the 1680s. The transfer of the Electoral Palatinate to the Catholic Neuburg line of the House of Wittelsbach (1685) and the War of the Palatine Succession (1689–97) virtually brought an end to immigration (a trickle of new arrivals into the 1720s, notwithstanding), especially since there no longer were any Reformed territories in the south of the Empire, apart from smaller territories like the Counties of Hanau-Lichtenberg (1650–1700, receiving around 1,350 immigrants, mostly from Bern and Zurich) and Nassau-Saarwerden (Bliesgau), the Duchy of Zweibrücken (Westrich), and a few territories of imperial knights in the Kraichgau and the Odenwald. Moreover, the economic situation had improved markedly in the departure areas at the turn of the 18th century, as a result of which emigration from Switzerland as a whole waned and the authorities also took a much more restrictive stance on the wishes of their subjects to leave.

The only exceptions from this generally restrictive policy were two treks of settlers to Brandenburg-Prussia, which were arranged by treaties between the magistrates of Bern and Zurich, on the one side, and the prince-electors of Brandenburg, on the other. Much like the emigration to the

Upper Rhine after 1648, the settlement of Swiss colonists in the Margraviate of Brandenburg in the early 1690s and in northern East Prussia (Prussian Lithuania) was intended to offset the demographic imbalances after the devastating plague of 1709–10, a consequence of the Great Nordic War.

The prelude was the reception of 14 families from the Berner Oberland into the riparian lowland near Potsdam in 1685. Following the success of this settlement in the Schweizerbruch, seven villages in the environs of Neuruppin were newly established in the early 1690s by about 1,500 Swiss colonists from the canton of Bern. The approximately 1,000 settlers who left Zurich at the same time – previously most of them had worked in their rural homes producing textiles – proved little suited for agriculture in the settlement villages in Brandenburg and soon moved to larger cities.

King Frederick I sought to make up for the loss of around 60% of the population in Prussian Lithuania from the plague by using the model of the successful Swiss settlements in Brandenburg. Even before the letter of invitation for the "Building of Lithuania" (1711) was proclaimed, the first Reformed Swiss colonists were settled in the environs of Gumbinnen and Insterburg. The peak of Swiss immigration occurred in 1721, when more than 350 families of Swiss colonists – about two-thirds French-speaking and one-third German-Swiss – were settled. They were not only distributed among the new settlements according to linguistic criteria but also on the basis of regional affiliation. The king's invitation had also been taken up by unprovided descendants of German-speaking Swiss colonists from the Ruppin area and of the *réfugiés* (Huguenots) who had settled in the Uckermark after 1685; as a result, there were already 23 francophone villages in Prussian Lithuania by 1713. The legal sphere of the "Swiss colonists" in Prussian Lithuania included other groups of settlers alongside colonists from all parts of Brandenburg-Prussia, Hessians, Nassauans, and Franconians. Given the total number of colonists in East Prussia – in 1727 around 17,000; another 11,000 exiles from Salzburg arrived in 1732–3 – the Swiss as the original pioneer settlers made up only a small portion.

Paths and forms of integration of the Swiss in Alsace and southwestern Germany

Given the strikingly high number of children among the colonists, the importance of immigrants from Switzerland into Alsace and the Upper Rhine after the Thirty Years' War to the population growth should not be underestimated. Nevertheless, historians in the past have set the total volume of the immigration too high because of counting many temporary labor migrants as permanent immigrants. However, we are most likely to deal with fluid transitions between seasonal or permanent labor migration, permanent settlement migration, and – after a few years and even decades of settlement – even remigrations back home.

The social composition of the emigrants – chiefly single men – already points to forms of labor migration. For a while they settled as *Hintersassen* (without land of their own) in thinly settled places suffering from labor shortages to perform all manner of casual work. Acquiring a farmstead was either impossible for financial reasons or undesirable because they wanted to keep the option of returning home. Instead, after some time most of them moved on, following favorable work opportunities. Only a few immigrants – often specialized craftsmen – were able to marry into established families, which would have turned the original labor migrants into new real settlers who were then given the usual subject status. The rule, however, was a frequent change of residence, endogamous marriages and godparenthood within the migrant group, as well as remigration home. To date, though, there are no studies about these aspects.

The migration of pastors from Reformed congregations who had been unable to find a position in Switzerland was intimately linked to this migratory movement. This institution – pastors suggested and paid for by the Protestant cantons – existed in most destination territories, but especially in the Electoral Palatine and after 1666 in Markirch in Alsace (Sainte Marie-aux-Mines). These "Swiss preachers" were not only supposed to strengthen the Reformed creed of the countrymen abroad, but they also formed the most important points of contact and crystallization for Swiss immigrant groups, and therefore the central connecting element between the old and the new homeland through which the influence of the old authorities over their subjects was also preserved abroad.

By contrast, the Reformed authorities in Switzerland looked rather askance at the extensive migration of Swiss into the Lutheran territories of Württemberg and Baden-Durlach. They demanded that the migrants stay away from religious services of other denominations and attend the Reformed Eucharist at least once a year, if possible in their home parishes back in Switzerland. Absolutely forbidden, however, was the settlement of subjects in Catholic territories, with the exception of temporary work stays. If such settlement occurred and was discovered, subjects were punished by having their citizenship (*Mannrecht*) revoked, which automatically entailed the confiscation of their remaining property in their homeland. Only the voluntary relinquishing of the heritable *Mannrecht* – which did not often happen until the second or even third generation of migrants – and thus the renunciation of the status of a cantonal subject and the complete liquidation of the remaining property in the home community can be seen as an indicator of the complete integration of a Swiss immigrant into the new homeland. But even in those cases, contacts with the old community could often continue for some time through Swiss preachers or visits to relatives. Swiss migrants and their descendants were readily absorbed into the local host community, not least because their Alamannic dialect was understood in Alsace, Baden, and the adjoining regions.

Paths and forms of integration of Swiss migrants in Brandenburg and Prussian Lithuania

In the Hohenzoller territories far from the Swiss homeland, on the other hand, language barriers stood in the way of a rapid integration of the German-Swiss and the French-speaking Swiss colonists from the beginning. Prince-Elector Frederick William and his son Frederick III/I had deliberately recruited Swiss immigrants – usually young families – and had agreed beforehand to settle them in places that were separated from the native population. The Swiss colonies formed separate legal corporations protected by the territorial ruler. For example, they had even possessed a certain degree of political autonomy in the office of the Swiss Inspector since 1690 or 1711 or the institution of the "Swiss Day" as the central meeting of all Swiss village mayors (*Dorfschulzen*) in Prussian Lithuania. These institutions, the exemption from compulsory labor and serfdom, as well as the favorable status under property law as *Erbzinsbauern* (hereditary tenant farmers) set the outsiders apart from the natives and often engendered envy.

In terms of religious denomination, as well, the Swiss colonists, with their French Reformed or German Reformed creed, formed a foreign body in the otherwise almost purely Lutheran state of Brandenburg-Prussia. As in some southwest German and Alsatian territories, we can find the central institution of the Swiss pastors – alternately dispatched and paid for by the authorities in Bern and Zurich (in Prussian Lithuania only by Bern) – in the form of the "Swiss colony benefice." This special institution allowed the two cities to repeatedly intervene in the internal affairs of the Swiss colonies. Moreover, if the migration enterprise failed, Swiss colonists – who remained on the whole very mobile, at least in the first generation – always had the option of returning to their homeland although few colonist families might have actually returned to Switzerland. Still, contacts with the homeland remained vigorous for a long time, as numerous inheritance matters or renewals of citizenship (*Mannrecht*) reveal.

Seven German Reformed parishes were set up in Brandenburg, as well as two French Reformed and two German Reformed parishes in Prussian Lithuania. Their church buildings were paid for by funds collected during services in Switzerland. In the initial years at least, the congregations and political communities were homogeneous because their members came from the same region in Switzerland. Endogamy, still widely practiced among colonist families of the second and third generations, was an expression of this group coherence. At first the gradual opening of the exclusive marriage circles led among the Swiss colonists in Brandenburg to marriages with members of the other Reformed demoninations, for example, with the *réfugiés* in the Uckermarck, and only in a second step – mostly not until the third generation – to family bonds with native Lutherans. Individuals who married into old colonist families followed the denomination of the spouse, if the family continued to live in the community. The children from such mixed marriages were oriented toward the local parishes. The mutual tolerance was generally very high between French Reformed and German Reformed, provided that a French Reformed church also offered religious services in German. While the willingness to accept native Lutherans into German-Reformed parishes was very high, the reverse was rarely the case.

The Swiss colony in Prussian Lithuania has not yet been studied in this regard, but the situation was probably similar. The reciprocal attendance of German Reformed and French Reformed services was undoubtedly higher than in Brandenburg, as separate parishes for German-Swiss or French-speaking Swiss were not always within easy reach, given the large distances. As a result, knowledge of French declined rapidly among the descendants of French-speaking colonists in the second half of the 18th century. For example, many French family names became linguistically corrupted and were changed in order to sound German or Lithuanian, or were directly translated into those languages.

Already under King Frederick William I, who had very concrete absolutist ideas about centralized administration and personal control over the Church, the special status of all Swiss colonists in Brandenburg-Prussia had gradually been dismantled. Although the Swiss colonists were able, with some effort, to preserve their privileges relating to personal or property law (exemption from *corvée* labor and hereditary possession of their farmsteads), the institution of the Swiss preachers disappeared for good in the 1730s in favor of native German Reformed pastors; as a result, the contacts of the Swiss colonists to the old homeland were gradually lost. The merger of French Reformed and German Reformed congregations and the "Old Prussian Church Union" put an end to the ecclesiastical autonomy of the colonist communities. Today, both Swiss colonies have almost completely vanished from historical memory.

Asche, Matthias. *Neusiedler im verheerten Land – Kriegsfolgenbewältigung, Migrationssteuerung und Konfessions politik im Zeichen des Landeswiederaufbaus. Die Mark Brandenburg nach den Kriegen des 17. Jahrhunderts.* Münster, 2006.

Bastian, Margarete. *Schweizer Einwanderer im Westrich 1650–1750.* Zweibrücken, 1995.

Bodmer, Walter. *L'immigration suisse dans le comté de Hanau-Lichtenberg au dix-septième siècle.* Strasbourg, 1930.

Bonnaud-Delamare, Roger. *L'immigration helvétique dans les Principautés de Murbach et de Lure après la guerre de Trente Ans (1649–1715).* Paris, 1966.

Debor, Herbert Wilhelm. "Schweizer in Südhessen." *Hessische Familienkunde* 17 (1985): 353–68, 417–36.

Diefenbacher, Karl, et al. *Schweizer Einwanderer in den Kraichgau nach dem Dreißigjährigen Krieg.* Sinsheim, 1983.

Greib, Robert. *L'immigration suisse dans les paroisses du Comté de Nassau-Sarrewerden après la guerre de Trente Ans.* Saverne, 1972.

Heinzmann, Kurt. "Zur Einwanderung der Schweizer nach dem Dreißigjährigen Krieg. Ihr Beitrag zur Wiederbesiedlung des Breisgaus und des Markgräflerlandes und ihre Integration, dargestellt am Beispiel der Gemeinde Eichstetten am Kaiserstuhl." In *Minderheiten, Obrigkeit und Gesellschaft in der Frühen Neuzeit*, edited by Mark Häberlein and Martin Zürn, 109–39. St. Katharinen, 2001.

Kenkel, Horst. *Französische Schweizer und Réfugiés als Siedler im nördlichen Ostpreußen (Litauen) 1710–1750.* Hamburg, 1970.

Stintzi, Paul. *L'immigration suisse dans le Sundgau après la Guerre de Trente Ans.* Strasbourg and Paris, 1952.

Wunder, Gerd. "Die Schweizer Kolonisten in Ostpreußen 1710–1730 als Beispiel für Koloniebauern." In *Bauernschaft und Bauernstand 1500–1970*, edited by Günther Franz, 183–94. Limburg, 1975.

Zbinden, Karl. "Die Pfalz als Ziel und Etappe schweizerischer Auswanderung." In *Pfälzer – Palatines*, edited by Karl Scherer, 177–206. Kaiserslautern, 1981.

Cross-references: France; Germany; Poland; Switzerland; Dutch Calvinist Refugees in Europe since the Early Modern Period; Huguenots in Europe since the Early Modern Period; Palatines in Europe since the 17th Century; Salzburg Protestants in East Prussia since the 18th Century; Waldensians in Central Europe since the Early Modern Period

TRAVELLERS IN IRELAND SINCE THE 19TH CENTURY

Jane Helleiner

In 2002, the Irish census included the question "are you a member of the Traveller community?" for the first time. The result was a figure of 23,681 Travelling People in the Southern Republic. Irish Travellers have attracted scholarly attention since the late 19th century and have been referred to by a variety of terms including "gypsies," "tinkers," and "itinerants." Since the 1980s the term "Travellers" or "Travelling People" is most frequently used with other terms having derogatory connotations. Unlike many Gypsy, Roma, and other Travellers in Europe whose origins are outside of their respective "host" nations, Travellers in Ireland were an indigenous minority. Attributions of origin have emphasized the essential "Irishness" of Travellers. The origin stories told about and by Travellers in Ireland have focused not on where they are from, so much as when and why they emerged as a socially and culturally distinct group within Ireland.

The history of wandering people both before and during the period when Ireland was a part of the UK is controversial. It is difficult to come to any conclusion regarding the relationship between these wanderers and the "tinkers" that attracted scholarly attention at the end of the 19th century. The term "tynker" was known as a trade name in England by 1175 and as a surname by 1265. This fact is frequently cited in support of claims that the presence of Irish Travellers can be dated from this period. The extent to which the term referred

to a distinct category of people is, however, unclear and although the term "tinker" has been used in recent decades to refer (usually in a derogatory way) to Irish Travellers living in England, it is not clear that the term had a specifically Irish referent in the past.

One account of Irish Traveller origins that was widely accepted among non-Travellers from the 1960s onward suggested that Irish Travellers were the descendants of peasants forced into landlessness and mobility by the evictions and famines suffered by the Irish during the centuries of British domination. This particular account of Traveller origins was effectively used as part of the justification of a state settlement program for Travellers. According to this understanding of Traveller origins, for example, the settlement program could be promoted as the action of a benevolent state motivated by a national duty to resettle victims of colonialism. The ascription of "dispossessed peasant" and his colonial origins have, however, been challenged by Travellers and their advocates. Traveller activists and non-Traveller supporters involved in resisting aspects of the state settlement program have pointed to earlier theories (some of which can be found in the late 19th-century literature on "Gypsies") that traced Traveller origins to a much older precolonial Ireland. Claims to a much deeper Traveller history in Ireland have been evoked in the context of contemporary struggles over the legitimacy of Traveller identity and culture at the beginning of the 21st century.

The limited archival research available suggests that "tinkers" were not particularly visible (as least to the elite), within the larger itinerant population prior to the 19th century. By the 1830s, however, the Commission on the Condition of the Poorer Classes (1835) included passages that appeared to identify the "tinkers" as forming a "class" distinguished by particular economic activities (e.g., tinkering or begging) as well as distinctive social relations – notably, mobile family-based units, linked by ties of kinship and affinity to one another. Evidence for an already distinctive population is also suggested by the presence of Irish Travellers in the southern USA who claim that their ancestors emigrated from Ireland during the famine period of the 1840s.

The development of the group in the 20th century is easier to uncover. The Traveller economy in the past and present has been marked by a flexible multioccupationality that includes both paid and unpaid forms of work performed by men, women, and children largely in the informal sector. Outsider accounts, however, have often focused on particular Traveller men's trades (e.g., tinsmithing, horse dealing). Perceptions of their alleged obsolescence were used as evidence for pessimistic assessments of the economic base of the Traveller way of life. Claims that the economic basis for a Traveller way of life is disappearing can be documented back to the late 19th century and continue into the present. The assumption that the Traveller economy is linked to particular male trades neglects the range and flexibility of Travellers' work activities and downplays the significance of the work of women and children.

Published autobiographical accounts describing the first half of the 20th century reveal that Travellers were involved in such activities as the production, sale, and repair of tinware, dealing in horses, and the collection and resale of feathers, rags, bottles and jars, scrap, and other recyclable items from the non-Traveller population. Travellers also provided musical entertainment, had casual employment as farmworkers, and engaged in subsistence activities such as hunting and fishing. Traveller family units relied on a strategy of flexible multioccupationality that involved all members and their activities. This strategy facilitated and/or mediated links between less commodified rural Irish households and wider commodified urban markets through the first half of the 20th century.

While Traveller mobility was economically driven, it was also often violently produced by anti-Traveller racism. From the beginning of the foundation of the Irish state in the 1920s there is evidence of local authorities targeting Traveller camps for harassment and eviction. It also appears that Travellers were at least in some regions actively excluded from local authority housing. Anti-Traveller rhetoric and action is also apparent at the level of the national government. By the 1950s, politicians from several urban areas called for state action to be taken against Traveller camps. By 1960, the national government responded by creating a Commission on Itinerancy. The 1963 report of this commission outlined a wide-ranging program aimed at Traveller settlement in permanent accommodation and assimilation through wage labor and schooling. The commissions' recommendations were adopted as official government policy in 1964. The new goal was to facilitate the assimilation of the "itinerant" population into the wider "settled community" within a generation. The settlement policy for Travelling people dovetailed with a larger government policy of economic and social "modernization" in Ireland.

Since the introduction of this policy, many Travellers have taken up housing accommodation and some official camping sites (hardstands) have been provided for those living in trailer-caravans. The provision of housing and official sites, however, has never been sufficient for the growing number of Traveller families in Ireland. Many therefore live in unofficial camps, often without basic services and under constant threat of eviction. Despite the premise of the settlement program – that housing Travellers would result in their settlement and "absorption" into the "settled community" – many Travellers living in houses retain their identity as Travellers. They pursue the same economic activities as those living in trailers in camps and maintain close ties with relatives in both houses and camps. There is also considerable mobility in and out of housing, often linked to different points of the life cycle. Research in Galway City in the 1980s revealed that some younger married couples who had spent part of their childhood in a house were camping in trailers, often hoping to reenter houses when their families were larger.

While some Travellers stay sedentary for long periods (whether in houses or camps), others are more mobile. Movement may be localized between two towns in the same county or more long distance, e.g., between Dublin and the West. In some cases, it may involve travell between Ireland and the British Isles (Northern Ireland, England, Wales, and/or Scotland). Economic resources and opportunities as well as kinship networks shape their movement. Camping and housing patterns reveal a preference for living alongside close kin.

Despite policies and programs aimed at bringing adult (especially male) Travellers into conventional wage labor, wage labor remains for the most part either linked to particular training programs and/or casual and short term in nature. Some Travellers find that they must hide their Traveller identity in the context of a mainstream labor force that continues to actively discriminate against them. While anti-Traveller racism mitigates against opportunities for Travellers in the formal sector, there is an identifiable Traveller economy characterized by a combination of short-term employment and a more economically significant range of income-generating activities in the informal sector. In the beginning of the 21st century, the most significant sources of income would include recycling, trading in small markets, gardening and treetopping, and horse breeding and dealing.

The introduction of the Traveller settlement policy in the 1960s included targeting Traveller children for compulsory schooling. There have been experiments with separate Traveller schools, special Traveller classrooms within regular schools, and integration into regular classrooms. Traveller advocates point to the limitations of an Irish school system that does not easily accommodate mobility and is insufficiently intercultural in its pedagogy and curriculum. There continue to be instances where Traveller children are actively excluded from schools, and those who are successfully enrolled may find themselves subject to racist harassment.

Advocacy organizations such as the Irish Traveller Movement and Pavee Point have spearheaded mobilization around legal protection from anti-Traveller racism, lobbied for Traveller representation in policy making and implementation, and worked to improve provision of basic services for Travellers, e.g., official public camping sites. There are important links between the Traveller organizations in Ireland and Gypsy/Traveller organizations in the wider European Union. Traveller advocacy organizations have also been part of a broader Irish antiracist movement. After years of lobbying, "membership in the travelling community" was included as one of the grounds of protection in Ireland's Equal Status legislation of 2000. Despite formal legal recognition and protection, however, there is continued debate over the legitimacy of Traveller culture, especially mobility and living in trailers. Most Travellers continue to experience extreme marginalization and intense struggles over access to camping land in Ireland.

Fanning, Bryan. *Racism and Social Change in the Republic of Ireland.* Manchester, 2002.

Gmelch, George. *The Irish Tinkers: The Urbanization of an Itinerant People.* Menlo Park, CA, 1977.

Helleiner, Jane. *Irish Travellers: Racism and the Politics of Culture.* Toronto, 2000.

Lentin, Ronit, and Robbie McVeigh, eds. *Racism and Anti-Racism in Ireland.* Belfast, 2002.

McCann, May, Séamas O Síocháin, and Joseph Ruane, eds. *Irish Travellers: Culture and Ethnicity.* Belfast, 1994.

Cross-references: Ireland and Northern Ireland; Bosnian Bear Leaders in Western and Central Europe, 1868–1940; Dutch Caravan Dwellers in the Netherlands since 1870; Hungarian Coppersmiths in Western Europe from the 1860s to World War I

TURKISH LABOR MIGRANTS IN WESTERN, CENTRAL, AND NORTHERN EUROPE SINCE THE MID-1950S

Yasemin Karakaşoğlu

Turkish mass emigration to western, central, and northern Europe commenced in the mid-1950s. It is continuing also at the beginning of the 21st century and is leading to the formation of a considerable Turkish minority in the European destination countries. In 1970, the number of Turkish citizens in western, central, and northern Europe stood at 430,000. By 2002, it had grown to around 3.2 million. A large majority of Turks live in Germany (1.9 million). They also have a relatively strong presence in the Netherlands and France (about 300,000 each), in Austria (140,000), Switzerland (80,000), Great Britain (73,000), Belgium (70,000), Denmark (37,000), and Sweden (36,000). These figures do not include those natives of Turkish origin who have by now adopted the citizenship of their host country or have received it automatically at birth. In Germany, alone, that number was 97,000 in 2002. As ethnic-religious minorities, Turks have by now become integral elements of the societies in their immigration countries.

However, it is necessary to draw distinctions within this group based on ethnic and religious background, regions of origin, and motivations for the migration. The group identifier "Turks" refers to the nationality of the immigrants, whose ethnic background reflects the entire spectrum of the more than 40 different population groups living in Turkey. The most important internal differentiation is that between Turks and Kurds. An estimated 30% of the total Turkish population in Europe is of Kurdish background. Another differentiation concerns religion. The majority of Turks belong to the Sunni-Hanefite branch of Islamic jurisprudence, Kurds largely to the Sunni-Shafite branch. Both population groups contain about 20% to 30% Alevites, an Anatolian variant of Shi'ite Islam.

The vast majority of Turks living in the European destination countries came to western, central, and northern Europe since the end of the 1950s for economic reasons as part of the selective labor recruitment that was directed by the government and was originally intended to be temporary, or they are descended from these labor migrants. The German word *Gastarbeiter* (guest workers) goes back to this context. Another segment arrived and is arriving in the destination countries of this labor migration by way of family reunification – at the beginning of the 21st century especially as part of marriage migration. Another influx from Turkey occurs when visitors overstay their tourist visas to seek work illegally. In addition, there were always some political refugees among the immigrants (especially after the military coups of 1972 and 1980). Among those, the Christian Assyrians and the Kurds from southeastern Turkey are especially prominent because of their large numbers.

The Turks in Germany are a topic of the social debate over migration and integration in a way they are not in any other European country. They form not only the largest Islamic population group in that country but also the majority of all foreigners living there. In Germany they have also preserved, in a very pronounced form, their specific characteristics as an ethnocultural minority. That is exemplified by the many ethnic clubs, the existence of a vigorous Turkish press, and the development of an ethnic economy and ethnically dominated neighborhoods in the large cities.

Migration and remigration from the 1950s to the 1980s

Turkish migration to western, central, and northern Europe began – initially as an unorganized influx to Germany – already before the official recruitment treaties between the governments of the European states and Turkey. This phase is referred to as the initial experimental phase, since it laid the groundwork for the "guest worker migration" that followed. At the end of the 1950s and the beginning of the 1960s, individual, qualified Turkish workers had already made their way to northern Germany, in particular, through the deliberate recruitment of a few companies. The primary goal here was further training for these workers by way of internships: "developmental aid" was to be rendered for the emerging industry in the Turkish republic.

Turkish immigration to West Germany experienced a noticeable quantitative and qualitative leap with the signing of the official recruitment treaty in 1961. Another boost came from the new constitution enacted in Turkey that same year, which for the first time granted Turkish citizens the right of freedom of movement. Until 1973, only the economic crisis in 1966–7 interrupted the rise in the number of Turks in West Germany. The majority of those Turks who lost their jobs during this recessionary period did not return home but sought employment in neighboring European countries, which had likewise entered into bilateral recruitment treaties with Turkey: Austria, the Netherlands, and Belgium in 1964, France in 1965, and Switzerland in 1967.

The economic upswing in postwar Europe and the demand this created in industry for workers who were available on short notice and could be used in a flexible way in industry formed the backdrop of the transfer of "guest workers" from Mediterranean countries to western, central, and northern Europe. Responding to the needs of the economy, the workers who were recruited in the beginning were mostly young Turkish men. In 1965, a mere 13% of guest workers from Turkey were female.

The motives driving the migration and the social background of the migrants were always diverse. Among the Turks one could find jobless agricultural laborers as well as elementary school teachers or small merchants. No fewer than 30% of the Turkish guest workers between 1966 and 1973 were qualified workers because of their education or work background. Still, in the host societies they were employed mostly as unskilled or semiskilled workers. In addition to state intervention in immigration, the recruitment phase was also characterized by specific requests for workers from employers. Conversely, workers themselves sought to obtain a work contract in companies in which relatives and acquaintances were already employed. The result was chain migrations from certain regions. They led to the reconstruction of regional and kinship ties in the host society and eventually also to the formation of migrant networks.

In the beginning, Turkish workers intended to return home – after a temporary stay – with savings and specialized skills they expected to acquire in order to create an independent livelihood for themselves at home or take on higher positions in industrial enterprises. The Turkish government supported the outflow of workers: in the face of rapid population growth (2.7% in 1965) and a high rate of unemployment, it was hoping primarily to take pressure off the domestic labor market and to benefit from the remittance of hard currencies. Between 1963 and 1973, half of all recruited workers came from the eight economically most highly developed provinces in western and northern Turkey, which included also the country's three largest cities, Ankara, Izmir, and Istanbul; 20% of the recruited workers migrated from Istanbul, alone. Only 1% were from the underdeveloped provinces in southeastern Turkey. However, many of the workers recruited from the large cities came from the urban subproletariat that had developed only recently. The backdrop to the strong growth of the subproletariat was the internal migration – triggered by a rapid mechanization of agriculture – from the rural regions especially of central and southern Anatolia in the mid-1950s.

The recruitment phase lasted until the mid-1970s: 1973 in Germany, 1974 in Austria and Belgium, 1976 in the Netherlands. During this phase the guest workers initially lived in gender-separated dormitories set up by employers. Their living conditions were marked by great thriftiness, large remittances back home, and on the whole meager circumstances. The continuously extended stays of the Turkish workers and the subsequent arrival of family members consolidated this group. The migration policy of the European countries, which was characterized by a stop to recruitment, unintentionally intensified this pattern of consolidation, since legal immigration from Turkey was now possible only through family reunification or asylum. One exception was Sweden, which responded to the oil price crisis by expanding

the range of available jobs and recruited immigrants until the 1990s.

During the consolidation phase, the center of life for the former guest workers shifted increasingly to the host country. Family reunification proved a basic precondition for the development of heterogeneous population structures and the formation of specific Turkish migrant cultures. The arrival especially of wives not only caused gender ratios to approximate those in the host countries but it also led to a stronger integration of women into the workplace, with all the changes to social relations within the family this entailed. In addition, there was the problem of how to integrate the children of the immigrants into the European educational and vocational systems.

As early as the late 1960s, the Turkish guest workers created their own infrastructure with political and religious organizations and media of their own. At the same time an ethnic economy emerged, which largely had a niche character. Until the mid-1980s, the goals of the political and religious organizations were still strongly focused on the home country, and political conflicts between various groups abroad essentially mirrored the political conditions in Turkey. This changed in the late 1980s. The growing orientation of the Turkish migrants toward a permanent life abroad was closely connected with the rather negative experience of many remigrants with social and cultural reintegration into Turkish society. That is especially true of the approximately 200,000 Turks who took advantage of the German government's 1983–4 law encouraging the return of immigrants.

As the presence of the immigrants became increasingly a permanent prospect, their problems adjusting to majority society attracted the growing attention of the public. These difficulties were largely interpreted as the lack of a willingness to integrate. For example, the debate over questions of policy dealing with foreigners revolved especially in West Germany in the 1980s increasingly around the problems of Turkish children in schools, ethnically dominated neighborhoods, the above-average family size compared to majority culture, and the high unemployment among Turkish immigrants. The federal government responded by tightening the policy and laws dealing with foreigners, a stance that was reflected, among other things, in the introduction of a visa requirement for Turks. A growing xenophobia manifested itself as early as the beginning of the 1990s, and in Germany it expressed itself especially as hostility toward Turks.

Turkish migrant society between integration and disintegration.

As European host countries realized that the presence of immigrants was irreversible and that additional immigration was economically necessary, the question about how to promote integration became more and more important in the 1990s. In this regard, the Netherlands with its open integration policy (municipal voting rights, secure residency, facilitated naturalization, integration courses, official designation as an "immigrant country") was long considered exemplary. And in fact, unlike in Germany, the majority of the Turks in the Netherlands are naturalized and thus also politically equal. However, that has not protected them from a higher rate of unemployment than that found among Turks in Germany and from even worse achievements in school. At the beginning of the 21st century, the Dutch model of integration has lost its exemplary function also against the backdrop of an increase in xenophobia in the Netherlands, as well as tendencies among segments of the immigrants ranging from self-segregation to radicalization.

With respect to a participatory voice in politics and the situation pertaining to residency law and work permits, the Turkish immigrants encountered very different conditions in the various host countries. While participation in local elections is possible for them in the Netherlands and Sweden, they are excluded in Germany, France, and Great Britain. In Austria, in contrast to Germany, they are also blocked from participating in representative bodies in the workplace.

A profound transformation has taken place within the population of Turkish origin: from guest workers to members of a permanent immigrant minority. Germany has witnessed an extensive demographic assimilation to the majority society: in 2003, the gender ratios were 46% females to 54% males. Women had accounted for only 17.5% of the immigrants in 1961 and 36% in 1974. The younger age cohorts remain particularly strong. One-third of the Turks in Germany are under the age of 18, and more than 80% of those were born in the host country. Those recruited in the mid-1960s at the age of 20 to 30 are now of retirement age and are collecting social security. Since older immigrants are affected by poverty at above-average rates because of lower wages, shorter periods of social security eligibility, and more frequent health problems as they age, the system of social and medical care in the European host countries is an important factor – alongside the desire to remain with their children and grandchildren – behind their strong orientation to remain where they are.

The occupational structure of the working population of Turkish origin has become differentiated. Although the status of the unskilled or semiskilled workers continues to shape the image of Turkish workers in northern, central, and western Europe, a gradual shift toward white-collar work, especially in the service sector, is apparent. In the face of the frequent lack of formal qualifications and unemployment rates that are nearly double those among the native population in all European countries, self-employment represents one option for many of the former guest workers. In 2002, there were about 74,000 self-employed Turks in the European Union. However, the majority of the Turkish population is made up of nonworking family members such as children, housewives/househusbands, pensioners, and the jobless. In 2005, about 28% of the Turks in northern, central, and western

Turkish workers of the Salzgitter company in their hostel (*Stadtarchiv Peine, Germany, Dep PSAG*).

Europe were engaged in work that was subject to social security contributions.

The population of Turkish origin in most northern, central, and western European countries has thus long since moved beyond the stage where it can be defined solely through its participation in the labor market. A growing interest in acquiring apartments and houses illustrates that the center of life of the Turks is shifting to the respective immigration country. In Germany alone, 96,200 residents of Turkish origin owned apartments and homes at the beginning of the 21st century. This means that 15.9% of Turkish households own their real estate, though its acquisition must also be seen against the backdrop of their often poor living conditions. For example, an above-average number of Turkish households live in relatively small, overpriced, and poorly furnished apartments. Often several generations will purchase a low-priced property – mostly in the same residential neighborhood – which they then renovate themselves. However, those of the second generation with a good education and training tend to move away from living in neighborhoods that are largely inhabited by migrants.

Immigrants from Turkey have developed a dense network of organizations in all European countries. In most instances the headquarters of the European organizations are found in Germany, and these are concentrated in Berlin and Cologne. The organizations, too, are displaying a growing diversity of target groups and goals. Alongside the classic workers' culture clubs there have arisen a growing number of organizations of Turkish entrepreneurs, Turkish academics, and a multitude of religiously motivated ones that cover the entire spectrum of Islamic religiosity, from secular orientations to religious fundamentalism. Within these organizations, in turn, a growing diversity and specialization point to the very divergent interests of the respective target groups. For example, there are branches especially for young people, women, and seniors. Next to the nonpolitical organizations there are also political interest groups that follow the model of the

German party system, with the spectrum in Germany ranging from the Turkish Greens to Turkish Social Democrats all the way to Turkish conservatives. Moreover, a number of German politicians of Turkish descent have been elected to state assemblies as well as the Bundestag and the European parliament.

The establishment of ethnic organizations and clubs, like the creation of companies and the purchase of housing, certainly has an ambivalent character when it comes to the integration process. For one, the creation of organizations points to an adaptation to the pluralistic group formation within the majority society. On the other hand, these organizations support the persistence of ethnic enclaves and allow a segment of their members to remain active without learning the language of the majority society and integrating themselves into its social structures. And while the self-employed in the ethnic niche economy demonstrate an entrepreneurial spirit focused on the immigration country, along with the requisite willingness to take risks, they are at the same time also supporting the formation of ethnic enclaves. The same is true for the purchase of real estate in existing ethnic neighborhoods. The sense of "we" that is created and preserved in these neighborhoods on the one hand stabilizes the individuals and gives them a sense of belonging, and on the other hand reinforces the perception of difference between natives and immigrants on both sides.

The educational realm, in particular, is characterized by great discrepancies among the European immigration countries. In Germany, Turks make up 44% of all foreign students. They are underrepresented at higher secondary schools compared to the majority society and other foreign groups of students (with the exception of the Italians), and overrepresented at schools of lower status (*Hauptschulen* or special schools for the learning disabled). Another problem area is the transition from school to job. Estimates suggest that up to 40% of the young Turks of a school cohort in Germany leave school without the ability to begin vocational training. In France and Belgium twice as many young Turks attend middle and higher schools than is the case in Germany, Austria, or the Netherlands. On the other hand, the proportion of Turkish dropouts is especially high in France and the Netherlands compared to Germany, Austria, and Belgium. While Germany and Austria are more successful than Belgium, France, and the Netherlands in placing Turkish graduates in jobs, the differences in educational status between children without and those with a migration background are especially glaring.

The data illustrates less the (in)capacity of young Turks to integrate than the integration-specific performance by various segments of the different educational systems. Only a very small – though rising – percentage of graduates meet the requirements for admission to university. About 25,000 Turkish men and women were studying at German universities at the beginning of the 21st century. Three-quarters of them had obtained their *Abitur* (highest secondary school degree) in Germany; one-third were female students.

A large part of the Turkish residential population can look back on a lengthy stay in the various European countries. In Germany alone, 64% of the Turks have been in the country for more than 10 years; 40% have been there for more than 20 years. In representative polls among Turks in Germany since the early 1990s, two-thirds of those surveyed indicated that they were not planning to return to Turkey. The long duration of their stay and strong focus on remaining runs counter to the legal residency situation of the Turks in Germany. Only 24% hold the most secure residency permit, the *Aufenthaltsberechtigung*, the permanent right of residence. Thirty-three percent hold an unlimited and 34% a limited resident permit. The others hold residence permits for certain purposes, permits for humanitarian reasons, and temporary toleration (*befristete Duldung*).

The Aliens Act of 1991, in particular, led to a growing nationalization of Turks in Germany. Analogous trends occurred in the neighboring European countries. Since the revision of the German Citizenship Law on 1 January 2000, many children of Turkish nationals in Germany are given German citizenship from birth in addition to their Turkish one. However, contrary to the hopes of many Turks, the majority of which had favored the right of dual citizenship, the new law requires that children must choose one citizenship by the time they turn 23.

Artists of Turkish background are achieving growing recognition and popularity and are becoming a normal element of the pluralistic cultural scene in Germany. The actors, directors, writers, and cabaretists of Turkish origin are representatives of a new self-image of the Turks in Germany. While they embrace their roots, which they also use as a device of artistic alienation, they emphasize their ties to Germany and the autonomy of a Turkish migrant culture vis-à-vis the culture of the Turkish society of origin. The fact that Turks have evolved into a self-evident theme and protagonists in literature and movies points to their acceptance as an element of German popular culture.

The changes within the Turkish minority are evident especially in the younger generation. Turks represent the youngest population group in Germany: 80% of foreigners under the age of 18 are Turks. By now, three-quarters of underage Turks were born in Germany. Their parents and grandparents, who were born and raised in Turkey and initially came to Germany only temporarily, often developed a guest worker "mentality." It was characterized by an effort to be as inconspicuous as possible in public, by keeping quiet in the face of xenophobic comments or behavior, having as little contact as possible with natives, clinging to traditional values, being content with low-level jobs, and focusing politically on Turkey. The mentality of the second and third generation is considerably different. They see themselves as a natural part of the immigration societies. Even those who do not identify with Germany define themselves as Turks from Hamburg or Berlin, or even more specifically as residents of their neighborhood. Their self-descriptions combined elements of their parents' culture of origin and of the immigration society into something new. The result, for example, is the emergence, especially in the large cities, of expressions of youth culture in both music and language in which Turkish elements enter into new combinations with German or English ones. In the religious realm, too, the members of the second and third generations are developing their own ideas: they continue to feel a strong bond to Islam but interpret their religious obligations more liberally than their parents' generation and seek to find their own access to their faith through reading. In this context, the headscarf that is worn by some women of the second and third generations also takes on a different, modern meaning as the expression of a self-chosen, specifically Islamic way of life, while their mothers still wore their head covering for traditional reasons that were barely ever questioned.

Xenophobia attacks, however, can be noticeably unsettling to this sense of belonging. Especially the xenophobic and sometimes fatal attacks by right-wing radicals on Turkish families in Mölln (1992) and Solingen (1993) have revealed the potential of the young generation to emphasize, in response to what they experience as exclusion, their own patterns of identification in the sense of a stronger public embrace of religion or nation. At the same time, though, the connections to modern forms of expression and ways of life are not relinquished.

The growing number of university students, politicians, the self-employed, and artists of Turkish background clearly point to a successful integration. In all immigration countries, however, education and training for children and young people and the housing and job market situations pose a particular problem. In all reception countries, Turks are among the population groups most affected by poverty. Here it is evident that the low social status created by the "guest worker recruitment" has a negative effect on the opportunities of the next generation for social advancement. One cannot simply posit the automatic and self-evident integration of Turkish immigrants as one generation gives rise to the next. The marriage behavior of the Turks, which is especially endogamous compared to other immigrant groups, favors the formation of an ethnic community. In addition, the continuing migration as part of family reunification, especially in the form of marriage migration, is diluting the division of immigrant society into a first, second, and third generation and ensures that there is always a "first generation." These new immigrants have no knowledge of the German language upon their arrival. Their language of daily life, and thus also the language in which they raise their children, is Turkish. The broad offering of Turkish-language media in Europe reinforces this tendency. Other educational institutions therefore face the task of providing the children with the language skills necessary for integration into their respective host societies.

In no way is it possible to speak of completed integration processes. In all European host countries, immigrants of Turkish background belong largely to the urban subproletariat. As a result, they face disadvantages in the labor, housing, and education markets not only vis-à-vis majority society, but also vis-à-vis many other minority groups. However, compared to many other labor migrants of the postwar era, they remain in their host countries at especially high rates and show a pronounced orientation toward staying. Elements of the identification with the culture of origin are preserved in the process, even though the interest in the culture and politics of Turkey declines noticeably from one generation to the next. In the integration process, ethnoreligious demarcations from the host society take on a special, identity-creating importance, even as they are newly interpreted by the subsequent generations and are thus developed into an autonomous (Turkish) migrant culture. This dualism is no doubt the most striking characteristic of the life orientation of a great many Turkish immigrants. Especially in Germany, the Turks have established themselves as a visible minority. Material evidence of their presence is part of the landscape of the large cities – from Turkish fast-food restaurants and specialty shops to mosques in the Ottoman style.

Abadan-Unat, Nermin. *Turkish Workers in Europe 1960–1975: A Socio-Economic Reappraisal.* Leiden, 1976.

Abadan-Unat, Nermin, and Bitmeyen Göç. *Konuk işçilikten ulus-ötesi yurttaşliğa.* Istanbul, 2002.

Akgündüz, Ahmet. *Labour Migration from Turkey to Western Europe, 1960–1974: A Multidisciplinary Analysis.* Aldershot, 2008.

Bericht der Beauftragten der Bundesregierung für Ausländerfragen über die Lage der Ausländer in der Bundesrepublik Deutschland, edited by the Beauftragte der Bundesregierung für Ausländerfragen. Berlin, 2005.

Böcker, Anita, and Dietrich Thränhardt. "Erfolge und Mißerfolge der Integration – Deutschland und die Niederlande im Vergleich." *Aus Politik und Zeitgeschichte* 26 (2003): 3–11.

Crul, Maurice, and Hans Vermeulen. "The Second Generation in Europe: Introduction." *International Migration Review* 27 (2003): 965–87.

Eryilmaz, Aytaç, and Mathilde Jamin, eds. *Fremde Heimat – Eine Geschichte der Einwanderung aus der Türkei. Yaban Silan oldu – Türkiye´den Almanya´ya Göçün tarihi.* Essen, 1998.

Gestring, Norbert, Andrea Janßen, and Ayca Polat. *Prozesse der Integration und Ausgrenzung: Türkische Migranten der zweiten Generation.* Wiesbaden, 2006.

Karakaşoğlu, Yasemin. "Vom Gastarbeiter zum Einwanderer. Zur Lebenssituation der türkischen Bevölkerung." In *Von der Ausländer- zur Einwanderungspolitik*, edited by the Forschungsinstitut der Friedrich-Ebert-Stiftung, Abt. Arbeits- und Sozialforschung, 87–96. Düsseldorf, 1994.

Manço, Ural. "Des organisations socio-politiques comme solidarités islamiques dans l'immigration turque en Europe." *Les Annales de l'Autre Islam* 4 (1997): 97–133.

Özüdiken, Şule, and Ronald van Kempen, eds. *Turks in European Cities: Housing and Urban Segregation.* Utrecht, 1997.

Straßburger, Gaby. "Türkische Migrantenkolonien in Deutschland und Frankreich." *Archiv für Sozialgeschichte* 42 (2002): 173–89.

TYROLEAN CONSTRUCTION WORKERS IN CENTRAL EUROPE FROM THE 17TH TO THE 19TH CENTURY

Reinhold Reith

Beginning in the 16th century, but especially after the end of the Thirty Years' War in 1648, Tyrolean construction workers migrated north and sought work on building projects in German-speaking central Europe. At first it was individual workers, and then – in the wake of the rebuilding after the Thirty Year's War – also large groups who set out from West Tyrol, especially from the Außerfern, to take jobs during the building season. While the Tyroleans were probably the best known among the seasonal migrant laborers in the building trade, until the 20th century workers came to the cities and to larger construction sites during the building season also from the Oberallgäu, Graubünden, Vorarlberg, as from the central uplands in general (e.g., Vogtland, Bohemia). Within the framework of the Tyrolean migration, the construction workers (bricklayers, stonemasons, plasterers, stonecarvers, and carpenters, but also pond diggers and pond cleaners) formed the strongest group, alongside which one should also mention the traders from the Lechtal and the glove merchants from the Zillertal, whereby the trade migration cannot be clearly distinguished from the seasonal migration of craftsmen.

After the end of the Thirty Years' War, building workers came from the areas of West Tyrol that were poorer and – measured against resources – the most densely populated, the areas of the upper Lech and the upper Inn rivers. Hundreds of construction workers now migrated north annually from the Lech Valley, the Stanzer Valley, and the Paznaun Valley. They set out in March in large groups and returned in the fall. Participants in the seasonal migration ranged from 14-year-old apprentices to 70-year-old craftsmen, with the result that in the poorer regions and communities of Tyrol,

nearly every male inhabitant who was fit to work was gone during the season.

The destinations for the Tyrolean building trade workers were above all the Catholic lands of the Habsburg Empire, first of all the nearby bishoprics. In the 18th century more distant places were also reached (Westphalia, Lower Saxony), and individual journeymen migrated all the way to Vienna, Prague, and Hungary; Switzerland, Luxembourg, and the Netherlands also attracted Tyrolean construction workers. Although return home after the end of the season was the norm, a significant percentage left for good. In defiance of the religious mandates, construction workers settled also in Protestant regions (the Palatinate, Zweibrücken); Upper Hesse is said to have experienced a "genuine invasion" in the second half of the 17th century, and the Reformed settlement of Contwig in the Palatinate developed into a Catholic bricklayers' village as early as the end of the 17th century.

As for the Tryoleans themselves, their migration was probably triggered by the reduced employment opportunities in their home region: real division had led to a strong fragmentation of landed property, and the Thirty Years' War had dried up the transit traffic in goods from Venice to the north, which had offered numerous employment opportunities. The personal freedom of the Tyroleans made the migration easier. At the same time, many territories had a demand for workers, also because of the construction projects of the spiritual and secular princes. Since most Tyroleans had only a small farm, they generally had a second job, and many were skilled in the technique of building walls and vaults. This was the case even though initially most of them did not have any formal training; it was only in the late 17th century that the seasonal labor led to the formation of so-called *Nebenladen* (secondary guild organizations) that split off from the *Vororte*, for example, the Innsbruck *Hauptlade* (main guild organization). At the location of a so-called *Lade* there was an annual meeting of craftsmen (usually on January 20th), during which disagreements were aired and apprentices and masters were entered into or taken off the rolls. As a result, formal training structures were established also for apprentices hired by the mobile Tyrolean masters, and this reinforced the process of professionalization.

In the Lech Valley, where seasonal migration was most pronounced, the building trade workers came together in 1693 to establish the Brotherhood and *Hauptlade* of St. Joseph in Bichelbach, where they also built a guild church. Those enrolled as masters in the guild migrated and took their journeymen and apprentices with them; from the 18th century there are also several references to Westphalian apprentices who were enrolled in the *Laden* in Außerfern as apprentices. Scattered documentation – for example, the *Verfachbücher* (which recorded, among other things, real estate holdings, and which were replaced in the 19th century by the land register) of the parish of Aschau – shows that girls and women, possibly as helpers, participated in the seasonal migration. The joint seasonal migration of spouses is repeatedly recorded for the building trade in the 19th century; in the 1860s, Bohemian laborers and their wives, who worked as helpers, were often found in Leipzig, and after the turn of the century there are still reports of this from cities and towns in Upper Silesia.

The demand for workers from Tyrol was high: for example, a large number of well-known Tyrolean stonemasons were hired for the construction of the castle in Zweibrücken in 1720–30. Beginning in 1740, many bricklayers from the Tannheim Valley worked as plasterers and found employment all over Europe until World War I. In Augsburg, too, the Tyroleans were valued workers and hired in large numbers; in the 1790s, the city had nearly a hundred Tyrolean journeymen bricklayers during the season. The local journeymen saw the Tyroleans as unwelcome competition, especially since the masters favored them (some Tyroleans had managed to become master bricklayers for the court, the cathedral, or the city). It was made clear to the Augsburg journeymen that one could not regard the outside journeymen who had been coming to Augsburg for 30–40 years, including the "Tyrollers," as foreigners; rather, the Augsburgers should "be equally hardworking, equally unflagging, equally orderly." The Tyroleans were frequently perceived as a group: in Augsburg, the journeymen bricklayers maintained a separate hostel, which was run by a Tyrolean hostel keeper, and in Zurich, where the Tyrolean journeymen bricklayers still had a strong presence in the early 19th century, they shared lodgings.

The sources frequently remark on the Tyroleans' willingness to take any jobs that came their way, their diligence, and their special qualifications: when the bricklayers of the Principality of Hersfeld complained in 1667 that "foreign Tyroleans" had been given a large bridge-building job in Fulda, the mayor and town council replied that "it is widely known that the local masters are not good at this kind of work." They should work together with the foreigners so that they might "absorb the Tyrolean way." In Hesse, bricklaying and construction work (probably vaulting or plastering) was soon referred to as "Tyrolean work," which is also how it appears in the accounts. In Western Palatinate, Tyrolean master bricklayers were often charged with inspecting and approving new construction.

In the wake of the seasonal migration, the monetary economy in the home regions improved because of the returning craftsmen, but workers also settled abroad, although we have no comprehensive information about their number and centers of settlement and nothing concrete can be said about their integration. Although settlements in cities are known, the Tyroleans preferred to settle in villages near residences and administrative towns in order to be able to cultivate their small farming plots on the side. Seasonal migration, and with it the exodus of Tyrolean building trade workers, waned in the 19th century, especially in the second half of the century, and stopped altogether after World War I. Rarely can one still find traces of this migratory tradition, which for many Tyrolean communities across centuries had considerable economic and social importance. One example comes from the Western Palatinate, where the inhabitants of the village of Fehrbach, which had developed through settlement into a real village of bricklayers, were still referred to as "Tyroleans" in the 1960s.

Drumm, Ernst. *Die Einwanderung Tiroler Bauhandwerker in das linke Rheingebiet 1660–1730.* Zweibrücken, 1950.

Höck, Alfred. "Tiroler Bauhandwerker in Hessen nach dem Dreißigjährigen Krieg." *Hessische Blätter für Volks- und Kulturraumforschung* 23 (1988): 12–28.

Pieper-Lippe, Maria, and Othmar Aschauer. "Oberdeutsche Bauhandwerker in Westfalen. Untersuchungen zur gewerblichen Wanderbewegung, besonders vom 17. bis zum 19. Jahrhundert, unter Einbeziehung des Wanderhandels." *Westfälische Forschungen* 20 (1967): 119–93.

Reith, Reinhold. "Arbeitsmigration und Gruppenkultur deutscher Handwerksgesellen im 18. und frühen 19. Jahrhundert." *Scripta Mercaturae. Zeitschrift für Wirtschafts- und Sozialgeschichte* 23 (1989): 1–35.

Reith, Reinhold. "Kommunikation und Migration: Der Arbeitsmarkt des Augsburger Handwerks im 17./18. Jahrhundert in räumlicher Dimension." In *Kommunikation und Region*, edited by Carl A. Hoffmann and Rolf Kießling, 327–56. Konstanz, 2001.

Cross-references: Austria; Belgium and Luxembourg; Germany; The Netherlands; Southeastern Europe; Switzerland

TYROLESE AND VORARLBERGER CHILDREN IN WÜRTTEMBERG, BADEN, AND BAVARIA FROM THE EARLY MODERN PERIOD TO WORLD WAR I

Roman Spiss

The Austrian children employed in agriculture in Württemberg Upper Swabia, in Bavarian Swabia, and in Baden were given different labels in the sources: the phrase "Swabian children" is misleading and points to the destination area of the movement, not its region of origin. These were not children of Swabians or from Swabia, but children in Swabia between the ages of 8 and 14 who hailed from Vorarlberg, Tyrol, or the Swiss Grisons. The alternative term "herding children" (*Hütekinder*) in turn encompasses only one aspect of their activities (watching animals, watching children). Children especially from the age of 12 had to perform tasks that were also given to grown farmhands and maids. Those included, in addition to stable work, milk processing, the removal of rocks from pastures in the spring, or peat cutting in the fall; for girls – who for the most part made up one-fifth to one-third of the migrations – it was largely kitchen work. "Drive boys," working in the correct rhythm, had to drive the horses yoked before the plow and not under the control of the farmer behind the plow. This placed demands on physical strength that went clearly beyond what was needed for animal herding. Moreover, the workday began between four and six in the morning, during harvest times as early as three, and lasted into the evening hours.

The labor of children far from home should be seen as a survival strategy and a safety valve for the most abject economic misery. The farmsteads in western Tyrol and in Vorarlberg, utterly fragmented because of the prevailing practice of real division, could not feed a family of even the most modest needs. The plots were often so small that only two or three cows could be kept on them. As a result, itinerant trading spread in the Lech Valley as a supplemental income alternative as early as the early modern period, with Bavaria and Swabia as the favored destination areas of the traders. Beginning in the 17th century, thousands of small farmers also headed for areas north of the Alps year after year, mostly as seasonal laborers in the building trade. Like those who had taken employment as domestics, they brought back the news that the well-off farmers of the Lake Constance region could also offer children room and board and even wages. In Upper Swabia, a large number of laborers were indeed needed to work the farms. Alongside the farmhands and maids employed year-round and the short-term harvest workers, there was a demand for many other cheap workers. A shortage of domestics also existed in the Allgäu, where the change to grassland farming and a dairy economy had taken place in the first half of the 19th century. For the Catholic farmers from Upper Swabia, aside from economic considerations, confessional differences also argued against taking in young workers from the surrounding Protestant Württemberg lands. And in the Catholic homeland of the Swabian migrants, as well, zealous care was taken that no Protestant farmers in Upper Swabia took in a child.

The first report about the "little subjects" from Montafon in Vorarlberg from the year 1625 was still an exceptional case. The migrations of children grew noticeably in the 18th century and peaked in the first half of the 19th. Around 1800 there were up to 3,000 Swabian migrants from Tyrol and Vorarlberg; estimates for the 1830s, which may be a little high, speak of 1,800 to 2,000 children from Vorarlberg and 2,500 from Tyrol. Around the middle of the century there were probably also 700 children from the Swiss Grisons along with 1,500 from Austria, and 600 to 800 Swabian migrants from western Austria were still found around 1900. Brought to a halt by the First World War, the migrations revived on a modest scale after 1918, but then came to an end with the outbreak of the Second World War. The late end to the migrations, which many already regarded as an anachronism around 1900, suggests that something like a tradition-shaped "occupational consciousness" of the Swabian migrants had developed with the consistent economic need, and that we can speak of "migrations from tradition" by this time.

The "herding children" from Vorarlberg and Außerfern in Tyrol (district of Reutte) reached the Swabian land before the others, but even they traveled at least a day or two. The longest distance had to be covered by the children from the Vinschgau in southern Tyrol, who had to cross not one but two passes, the Reschen Pass and then either the Arlberg

"The slave market in Ravensburg" (*Otto Uhlig. Die Schwabenkinder aus Tirol und Vorarlberg [Innsbruck, 1983], figure 59*).

Pass (1,793 m) or the Fern Pass (1,210 m.). Distances of up to two hundred kilometers had to be traversed on poor roads during a time of year when cold, snow, and storms made the migration even more difficult. Employment began between St. Joseph (19 March) and the end of March, while the traditional days of return were Saints Simon and Jude (28 October), but also St. Martin (11 November). Only the opening of the Arlberg Railway line (1884) brought some relief.

Separate children's markets developed as a special form of markets for domestics, which had likewise arisen at the periphery of general markets. In Württemberg they were found in Friedrichshafen, Ravensburg, Wangen, and Waldsee; in Baden in Überlingen and Pfullendorf; in the Bavarian Allgäu, Kempten remained the most important one, though Füssen, Kaufbeuren, Immenstadt, and Oberstdorf should also be mentioned.

The pay for the children depended on gender, age, and region, and it increased slowly over the decades. In addition to free room and board, it consisted of material benefits in the form of a full set of clothes – in Upper Swabia eventually even two sets of clothes (for work and for leisure) – and a small nominal wage, which was lower in Bavaria than in the other destination areas. But it was especially this wage that the parents awaited eagerly, since their small plots, as subsistence farms, produced hardly any cash. The children therefore made a significant contribution to paying debts and taxes and buying food for the winter. Even the Austrian administrative authorities emphasized the great economic importance of the remittances from abroad, while the regret over the fate of the children was for a long time only half-hearted.

The Association for the Welfare of the Swabian Children and Youthful Workers, founded in 1891, was able to get some kind of handle on the worst excesses of the system of herding children, at least in the Tyrolean Oberland. The association registered and collected the children, organized their journey to and from their destination, and also looked after their earnings. Under leadership of the priest Alois Gaim, who undertook his inspection tours of the children's work sites by bicycle, humanitarian as well as material requirements could be imposed upon employers. The conditions agreed upon between the "herding child" and the farmer were recorded on a form. Gaim even brought lawsuits against farmers who violated the terms of the agreement.

The stay of the foreign children in the destination regions led to rules of exception for obligatory school attendance. Back at home the Austrian children did attend the "winter school," of which they missed about eight weeks. The "summer school," however, which was scheduled to last three to four months, increasingly turned into a farce because of the almost general absence of the Swabian children, especially since numerous exemption petitions were filed by all the communities. In Württemberg, the influence of the agricultural lobby made sure that the Austrian exemption from summer school was recognized by the Württemberg school authorities without any problems. Even after the First World War, the Swabian children did not attend school in Württemberg.

In 1892, Baden extended obligatory school attendance by law also to foreign children. However, this created a host of separate problems that served for the most part merely as a pretext: the children, it was said, could "not possibly keep up with the natives" because of the "foreign accent, the difference in methods, teaching materials, and so on," as a result of which "they sit apathetically on the benches and are usually entirely neglected by the teachers." The local school councils therefore tolerated the constant absence of the Austrians. The situation was similar in Bavaria, where the existing obligatory school attendance was for the most part not enforced by local inspectors and town councils (*Ortsvorstände*).

This illustrates, therefore, not only the economic but also the educational gap between the native children and those who arrived for temporary stays. The children from Vorarlberg and Tyrol were excluded from the entire educational culture in which the natives grew up. Demeaning outside descriptions of the societies from which the children came found a breeding ground here. A perfect example was an interjection by the deputy Franz Speth during a debate about obligatory school attendance for foreign herding children in the Second Chamber of the Württemberg *Landtag* in 1913: "That does not concern us!" It is equally revealing that the children's market was ridiculed during the carnival in Friedrichshafen in 1909 with the depiction of the "paradisiacal life" of the herding children – this shortly after the press in the USA had already declared the town the "place of the German slave trade" and there was growing talk in Austria of an "evil."

The children could be described as well liked but not as integrated. They remained foreign workers who were supposed to show patient obedience, even if this was rarely stated openly. A genuine appreciation for their work would have shown itself by the unreserved reception of the Swabian children into the circles of their native cohorts. That,

however, almost never happened. The children of Upper Swabia saw them as outsiders, mocked them for their dialect and poor education, and also got into fights with them. To the farmhands and maids they remained intruders and inferior humans. Quite apart from the confessional questions, young Württembergers would have hardly worked voluntarily in Upper Swabia under these poor conditions. Even Unterlanders living in direst poverty were not interested in taking over the jobs of the foreigners.

The herding children therefore joined together and met their compatriots in their sparse free time on Sundays in church for mass and religious instruction. They also congregated on feast days to gather strength for the remaining time of their employment. Despised and exploited, they certainly did develop a group consciousness and, connected with it, the feeling of constant foreignness. This also prevented a larger number of those from Vorarlberg and Tyrol from deciding to stay and settle down. Apart from the personal ties to family, farm, and homeland, another important factor was that the combination of commercial work abroad during the summer and farming work at home in the winter made possible an adequate livelihood. The children's migration thus made a substantial contribution to preserving over long periods the traditional economic and social structures in the origin regions.

In their homeland, the Swabian children in turn stood out not only through their better clothes; many had also adopted expressions of the foreign dialect – they were "speaking Swabian." They were laughed at especially in school, where it was sometimes even said: "Here come the Swabians (*Schwabenländer*) again!" It took a few weeks for the Swabian or Bavarian expressions to gradually disappear. Still, they had become children of two worlds: of their homeland in Tyrol or Vorarlberg, and of the destination regions of their labor migration. In the latter they could be children even less than was possible at home.

Laferton, Siegfried. "Schwabengänger. Kinderarbeit in der Fremde." In *Fremde auf dem Land*, edited by Hermann Heidrich et al., 157–79. Bad Windsheim. 2000.

Spiss, Roman. *Saisonwanderer, Schwabenkinder und Landfahrer. Die 'gute alte Zeit' im Stanzertal*. Innsbruck, 1993.

Uhlig, Otto. *Die Schwabenkinder aus Tirol und Vorarlberg*. 3rd ed. Innsbruck, 1998.

Ulmer, Ferdinand. *Die Schwabenkinder*. Prague, 1943.

Cross-references: Austria; Germany

UKRAINIAN LABOR MIGRANTS FROM GALICIA IN THE CZARIST EMPIRE IN THE 19TH AND EARLY 20TH CENTURIES

Kerstin S. Jobst

The Kingdom of Galicia and Lodomeria, the official name of the crown lands that belonged to the Habsburg monarchy after the partitioning of Poland, was the most important Austro-Hungarian region of outmigration in both relative and absolute terms. Out of a population exceeding 8 million, more than 1 million individuals left the land – considered by contemporaries "Europe's poor house" – at least temporarily between 1850 and 1914. Overseas destinations were above all the USA, Brazil, Canada, and Argentina. The continental migration, which was mostly seasonal in nature, took Galician migrant laborers from the 1860s mainly to other parts of the monarchy, to Prussia-Germany, Scandinavia, or France.

By contrast, Galician migrants rarely went to the Czarist Empire in the last decades of the 19th century. While various movements can be identified, they have so far not been systematically studied. In those cases, where the migrants did move to destinations within the czarist realm – driven mostly by economic but also by ethnic, religious, and political motivations – these places were generally the Kingdom of Poland, Bessarabia, and the Ukrainian lands east of the Zbruč.

In the years before World War I, Galicia had become a focal point of national conflicts between Poles and Ukrainians. According to the results of the census of 1910 (whose criteria were controversial, however), the ethnically diverse crown land was dominated by the Polish population, compactly settled mostly in western Galicia, with about 47% as against the Ukrainian population with 42%. Although the Ukrainians were the absolute majority in the eastern portions of the land, in the urban centers they were underrepresented vis-à-vis the Polish and Jewish population (the latter group averaged around 10%). Added were numerous other nationalities such as Armenians, Germans, or Tartars, who made up about 1% of the population of Galicia. This entry focuses on the migration to Russia by Galicians, usually referred to as "Ruthenians" in the official usage of the monarchy, as they are the only group for which statements of any reliability can be made about their integration process.

In the 1860s and 1870s, Ukrainian teachers and Greek Orthodox priests, in response to official Russian recruitment, took over teaching jobs and parishes in the Kingdom of Poland, and here especially in the area of Chelm, which was not unlike eastern Galicia in terms of its social and national structure. The recruitment of Ukrainians was part of the reform of higher education in the Czarist Empire under the aegis of Minister of Education D. A. Tolstoi; the teachers in highest demand were graduates from the university departments of ancient languages in Cisleithania, who were regarded as well educated and from disciplines that had been long neglected in the Czarist Empire. It was therefore not only Ruthenians but also the Slavic-speaking Habsburg subjects with the requisite training who were recruited. From the perspective of the Russian administrators, pragmatic considerations argued in favor of the recruitment, since speakers of Slavic as their mother tongue were believed to have greater facility in learning Russian. But political reasons

also played a role: according to widely held pan-Slavic ideas, these groups were seen as being part of Greater Russia.

Because of the close kinship of the Ukrainian vernacular (not yet codified at this time) with Russian, Galician immigrants generally had an easier time with the language than did the Czechs, for example, and this facilitated their integration. Although we have no precise figures, some Galician secondary school teachers rose to higher positions within the Russian education system, for example, as school principals. This rise was made possible because the immigrants, unlike the majority of the members of the Polish educational elite, accepted Russian rule in the kingdom and acted as pillars of the system.

Something similar seems to have been true of the 136 Greek Catholic clergymen from Galicia who began their service in the Czarist Empire in the years 1866–70. They profited from the anti-Polish backlash within the Russian bureaucracy following the January uprising in 1863, in the wake of which priests suspected of pro-Polish sympathies had lost their jobs. A larger number of remigrants from this group is not recorded, especially since Polish as well as Ukrainian nationalist circles in Galicia would have regarded entry into Russian service as treason, which would have made reintegration into their homeland difficult.

Of relevance in terms of both domestic and foreign politics was also the illegal crossing, in 1892–3, of mostly Ukrainian peasant families from the eastern Galician districts of Borshchiv, Husiatyn, Sokal, Zalischyky, and Zbarazh, which were close to the border; between 5,000 and 10,000 individuals entered Russian territory without valid passports but were left unmolested. This migration was triggered by rumors that the Russian czar intended to distribute free land to destitute Ukrainian-Galician peasants. Such stories about a "better life" beyond the border circulated in many different forms. They were, among other things, linked with the person of the Habsburg crown prince Rudolph, who had already died in 1889 and was considered a benefactor of the Ruthenian peasantry. The great receptiveness to such rumors is an indication of the poverty of information among the peasants and their low level of education.

The Cisleithanian/Galician public was long dominated by a mercantilist ideology which said that the loss of population was harmful to the national economy and that emigration therefore had to be prevented. Only slowly did the realization take hold that emigration could be useful in raising the economic level, especially in backward and – measured by its economic productivity – overpopulated Galicia. In response, the efforts were aimed primarily at protecting those willing to leave, for example, against unscrupulous emigration agents. In the special case of the exodus of 1892–3, the Habsburg administration reacted on the one hand with threats of punishment (e.g., for illegal crossing of the border), and on the other, in cooperation with Russian officials, with an information campaign; the rumors about a distribution of land were officially denied and work creation measures were agreed upon, though these could be implemented only in rudimentary form. Especially the Polish-nationalist camp in Galicia welcomed the exodus of the Ukrainian population as a presumptive solution to the Polish-Ukrainian conflict, since every departing Ukrainian increased the size of the Polish segment of the population.

Emigration resulted primarily from the outdated semi-feudal agrarian structures, landlessness, and a high birth surplus. The central government in Vienna largely neglected the area, dispensing, for example, with efforts to improve the infrastructure out of consideration for the Polish-Galician upper class that was hostile to innovations. The migration of the Ukrainian teachers and priests was also influenced by their realization that social advancement was impossible or at least very difficult for them in Polish-dominated Galicia. The activities of the so-called Ukrainian Russophiles, who were culturally or politically oriented toward Russia, did not fail to have an effect on some segments of the Galician Ukrainians. No small number of migrants considered themselves part of the Russian nation. The Ruthenian-Galician emigrants for the most part approved of the at times harsh measures of the Russian bureaucracy against the Polish population, which was, after all, seen as the oppressor of the Russian ethnic group in Galicia.

The Czarist Empire, and here especially the regions of the Kingdom of Poland close to the border, offered an alternative to the migrants heading for Russia; although these migrants were small in number compared to the overall emigration from Galicia, their homeland was near, the resettlement costs were low, the geography and climate were familiar, and the language was the same or very similar. These were also the reasons that no minority created by immigration is discernible in these regions, although there are no concrete studies about this. Moreover, the number of remigrants was very high: more than half of the Ukrainians who left in 1892–3 are likely to have returned to Galicia. One reason was that, contrary to expectations, no land was distributed. The denial of civic rights also argued against permanent settlement; it would appear that until the beginning of World War I, the desire for Russian citizenship expressed by many immigrant Ruthenians was not fulfilled or citizenship was gained only with the greatest of difficulties.

Himka, John-Paul. "Hope in the Tsar: Displaced Naïve Monarchism among the Ukrainian Peasants of the Habsburg Empire." *Russian History/Histoire Russe* 7 (1980): 125–38.

Mark, Rudolf A. *Galizien unter Österreichischer Herrschaft. Verwaltung – Kirche – Bevölkerung*. Marburg, 1994.

Pilch, Andrzej. "Emigracja z ziem zaboru austriackiego (od połowy XIX w. do 1919 r.)." In *Emigracja z ziem polskich w czasach nowożytnych i najnowszych (XVIII–XX w.)*, edited by Andrzej Pilch, 252–325. Warsaw, 1984.

Wendland, Anna Veronika. *Die Russophilen in Galizien. Ukrainische Konservative zwischen Österreich und Rußland 1848–1915*, 444–66. Vienna, 2001.

Cross-references: Poland; Russia and Belarus; Ukraine

UKRAINIAN AND RUSSIAN SETTLERS IN NEW RUSSIA SINCE THE 18TH CENTURY

Detlef Brandes

In czarist times, southern Ukraine with the regions (*oblasti*) Odessa, Cherson, Nikolayev, Kirovograd, Dnepropetrovsk, Lugansk, and Zaporizhia, as well as the Autonomous Republic of Crimea were called New Russia (Novorossia). Between 1802 and 1922, it consisted of the *gubernia* of Cherson with the large city of Odessa, the *gubernia* of Yekaterinoslav (Dnepropetrovsk), and the *gubernia* of Tauria, i.e., Crimea and a region lying in front of this peninsula. Since the middle of the 18th century this was the destination of Ukrainian and Russian peasants who were fleeing serfdom, but it was also the place where the czarist government directed especially immigrants from abroad, "state farmers" from densely settled governments, and members of various Orthodox sects.

Russia conquered New Russia in several stages. In the Peace Treaty of Belgrade (1739), a border to the Ottoman Empire was drawn in the southern Russian steppe, a border that followed natural obstacles only in a few areas. That is why demilitarized zones at the Sea of Azov and the "free land" of the Zaporozhian Cossacks were supposed to separate the hostile states. Into the narrow strip of land that was later given to New Russia and into the land of the Zaporozhian Cossacks wandered peasants who had fled serfdom, mostly from the neighboring *gubernii* of "Little Russia" and "Greater Russia." Because their settlements, however, were repeatedly ravaged by the Tatars, only 22,400 taxpaying persons ("souls") of the male gender were living there in 1745.

Russia solidified its position along the border east of the Dnieper under Empress Elizabeth (1741–62). Serbian officers of the Habsburg monarchy who had protested against the transfer of the self-governed military border to the Hungarian civilian administration were given permission to settle their own regiments – which were to consist entirely of Balkan Christians – on two strips of border land, a "New Serbia" and a "Slavic Serbia." By 1762, the population of New Russia had risen to 64,500 "souls of the male gender." In 1764, Empress Catherine II combined the two "Serbian" colonies and another border strip into the *gubernia* of New Russia. In her settlement plan, certain parcels of land were reserved for military settlers, others for civilian settlers, and others still for foreigners, Old Believers, and "returnees from abroad." Anyone who decided on military service would receive a plot of land as heritable property. Civilian settlers were promised that they would not be impressed into military service. New settlers would be given a land allocation of 26–30 *desjatins* (1 *desjatin* = 1.09 hectares). Depending on their origins and the settlement area, they would be exempted from dues for 6 to 16 years. "Members of every estates," but not peasants, were to receive 48 such parcels free of charge and be able to work them with farmers.

Through Catherine's First Turkish War (1768–74), Russia gained territory up to the estuary of the Dnieper and turned the Khanate of Crimea into a satellite state; as a result, the Zaporozhian Cossacks lost their value as a buffer and were subjected in 1775. Following the annexation of the Khanate of Crimea (1783), the governor general of New Russia appointed by Catherine, Grigory Potemkin, was concerned above all with settling – and thus securing – the conquered territories as quickly as possible. Noblemen, officials, and merchants were given large estates, with the obligation of settling them with peasants. The proportion of these "noble peasants," who, in contrast to the interior of the land, retained their personal freedom, rose from 1% in 1762 to 28% in 1782. By 1782, 193,500 men were already registered on the territory of the expanded New Russia.

When the Ukraine west of the Dnieper, the so-called Hetmanate that was dissolved in 1782–3, was assimilated into the administrative structures of the other *gubernii*, the peasants there were tied to the land and had to pay the poll tax. Thereafter, a large number of Ukrainians fled to Poland, and many of them returned to Russia soon after under false names. In New Russia, such "returnees" were given the now increased land grant of 60 *desjatins* per farm. Others settled in military settlements or on the holdings of landlords, where the labor shortage allowed them to negotiate more favorable *corvée* conditions than existed in the regions where they had come from.

After the Second Turkish War (1787–92), Catherine had several cities founded in the newly acquired region between the southern Bug and the Dniester, of which Odessa would become the most important. Through the annexation of densely settled areas in the north, but above all through migration gains, New Russia already had a population of 489,000 men in 1801. About half of the settlers had come with permission from the authorities or their former masters, the other half without. Fifty-seven percent of the population lived on state land, 43% on noble land. At 4,200, the number of merchants was just as small as that of the 21,800 so-called state citizens (*meshchane*), the majority of whom were active in agriculture on urban soil or as tenants. In 1796, the peasants of New Russia were also prohibited from changing their place of residence; however, they continued to be set apart from serfs by their personal freedom and the right to their movable property. For some peasants, however, the implementation of this binding to the land was sufficient warning to veer off into the neighboring "Land of the Don Army."

In 1802, Czar Alexander I (1801–25) subdivided New Russia into the *gubernii* of Yekaterinoslav, Tauria, and Nikolayev (later Cherson). To promote foreign trade, the port cities of Taganrog and Odessa were separated off as administrative subdistricts. At the head of Odessa, the czar placed Count Richelieu. In the first third of the 19th century, the government promoted the resettlement of Ukrainian and Russian state peasants to New Russia. Farmers who had settled in New Russia between 1805 and 1812 were given, on Richelieu's instigation, exemption from dues for five years and loans for furnishings which they had to repay after 10 years. Still, the subsidies they received from the authorities

and the privileges given to them remained far behind those granted to foreign colonists.

Immigration began to falter during these years because of the new Turkish War (1806–12) and a new plague epidemic. In the 1820s, the government reduced its subsidies not only for the settlement of foreigners but also for settlers from the interior. A decree from 1824 promoted the resettlement of peasants only within the respective *gubernii*. They were allowed to leave villages in which they owned fewer than 5 *desjatins* and move to areas in which they could be allocated 8 to 15 *desjatins*. There they were now exempted from taxation for only three years; their tax obligations had to be assumed by their fellow villagers who remained behind and who could expect larger land allocations after the departure of the settlers. A deterrent to potential immigrants was the arbitrary conversion of 80 villages into military settlements in 1817: the commander of the settled regiments subjected their soldiers to strict control, leased them out to estate holders, or deployed them for all kinds of heavy labor – for example, the transportation of wood. Above all, however, willing settlers from the Ukrainian and central Russian governments were drawn from the 1820s on to the lower Volga, the southern Urals, and the northern Caucasus, where, in contrast to New Russia, free state land was being handed out.

In 1827, the peasantry comprised 797,000 men. The number of merchants (3,100) and urban dwellers (69,700) was still low, especially since these categories continued to include a high proportion of sharecroppers. The chief source of income for the peasants and estate holders in the early phase was sheep and cattle raising. Slowly, however, the importance of grain cultivation increased; the grain was not only sold within the Russian Empire but also shipped abroad through ports on the northern coast of the Black Sea. From the 1820s on, the population of New Russia grew far more rapidly through natural increase than through immigration – by 1858 there were 1,332,000 men, about three-quarters of whom spoke Ukrainian or Russian.

The majority of Orthodox Ukrainians and Russians had immigrated at the same time with groups of different ethnicities and confessions – Jews, Germans, Bulgarians, and Greeks, and in the *gubernia* of Tauria also the autochthonous Tatars and Nogayans. A multiethnic society arose. Conflicts dominated the relationship between the new settlers and the government, on the one hand, and the Muslim Tatars and Nogayans, on the other. The latter emigrated into the Ottoman Empire in several waves, especially after the annexation of the Khanate (1783) and the Crimean War (1853–6). What contributed to the rapid economic development of New Russia and southern Ukraine was the symbiosis between the Ukrainian-Russian peasant majority, the important merchants of Greek origin, and the mostly Jewish and German tradesmen and manufacturers in the port cities. Most groups were large enough so as not to have to rely on intermarriage with partners speaking a different language. Well into the Soviet period, the differing confessions were an obstacle to marriages between certain ethnic groups.

Družinina, Elena I. *Severnoe Pričernomor'e v 1775–1800 gg.* Moscow, 1959.

Družinina, Elena I. *Južnaja Ukraina 1800–1825.* Moscow, 1970.

Družinina, Elena I. *Južnaja Ukraina v period krizisa feodalizma 1825–1860 gg.* Moscow, 1981.

Kabuzan, Vladimir M. *Zaselenie Novorossii (Ekaterinoslavskoj i Chersonskoj gubernii) v XVIII – pervoj polovine XIX v. (1719–1858).* Moscow, 1976.

Cross-references: Russia and Belarus; Southeastern Europe; Ukraine; Bulgarian and Gagauzian Settlers in New Russia and Bessarabia since the 18th Century; German Merchants and Industrial Entrepreneurs in Russia since the 18th Century; German Settlers in Russia since the 18th Century; Greek Settlers from the Black Sea Region in New Russia since the Early Modern Period and Pontic Greeks in Greece since the End of World War II

VIETNAMESE COLONIAL AND POSTCOLONIAL IMMIGRANTS IN FRANCE SINCE WORLD WAR I

Ida Simon-Barouh

Since the First World War, Vietnamese have been immigrating into the motherland of the Union Indochinoise, which formally existed from 1887 to 1954. Four waves of immigration can be distinguished. Migrations in the colonial period were followed by postcolonial repatriations and movements of Vietnamese refugees coming to France to escape war, civil war, and political persecution. Although the immigrants came from the same country and shared the same cultural foundations, the circumstances of their departure from Vietnam and the ways in which they were received in France led to the formation of heterogeneous groups. Moreover, social background and knowledge of the French language also varied quite considerably among the immigrants. It is therefore not possible to speak of a homogeneous Vietnamese community in France. What the Vietnamese immigrants share is an often inconspicuous presence in their host society and their ties to their country of origin, independent of the political situation there.

In scholarly discourse and in official parlance, the immigrants are described either as Vietnamese or as French nationals of Vietnamese extraction, depending on whether the focus is on their culture of origin or their legal status. During the colonial period, they were referred to colloquially as Annamites (French Indochina was made up of the three protectorates of Annam, Tonking, and Cochinchina), Indochinese, or disparagingly as "Yellows." Postcolonially they were often given the derisive names "Chinese" or "Chinetok," before the generalizing term "Asians" came to prevail. The immigrants described themselves in public, depending on the situation, as "Asians," "Vietnamese," or "Frenchmen." Within their own group and in their country of origin they called themselves Viêt Kiêu (Vietnamese outside the country), or Viêt for short. They referred to their children who were born and raised in France as Francophones. They accepted their

visibility with more or less equanimity, depending on the phase of life (childhood, youth, adulthood). The French census of 1990 counted about 72,000 Vietnamese, just slightly more than half of whom held French citizenship.

The first wave of immigration from Vietnam to France was the result of the wars in Europe in the first half of the 20th century; during the First and Second World Wars, a total of 50,000 "Indochinese" worked in the French war economy. There were also 20,000 infantry soldiers among the colonial forces. Only a small number of Vietnamese remained in France after the end of the Second World War. They settled primarily in Paris and in a few of the large cities in southern France, where they formed the first Vietnamese ethnic community as soldiers, seamen, craftsmen, merchants, restaurateurs, and above all as factory workers.

Within the French unions they worked actively on behalf of equality with the natives. Their political engagement was aimed emphatically at a change in the situation in Vietnam, where national, socialist, and anticolonial movements had emerged during the interwar period. The French police suspected that their intent was to contribute to the destabilization of colonial rule from France.

The majority of Vietnamese in France were men. Many married French women. In keeping with the prevailing attitude within French society that immigrants should integrate thoroughly, their children became largely assimilated. The census of 1954 counted 8,000 Vietnamese workers, intellectuals, and students.

A second wave of immigration brought the "repatriates from Indochina" to France. After 1945, the open anticolonial resistance led to the First Indochina War. It was ended through the Geneva Agreement on Indochina of 21 July 1954, which granted the French colonies independence. Between 30,000 and 35,000 "repatriates" from Indochina were taken in by France in 1955–65: for the most part these were families of two or three generations, Eurasians, and Catholic or Buddhist Vietnamese with French citizenship who had taken the side of France against the independence movement. Especially the women and children were deeply rooted in Vietnamese culture.

Some of the "repatriates," often of elevated social status, joined their families already living in France and dispersed themselves throughout the country. Others, the poorest among them, received welfare and housing in smaller towns – for example, in Noyant d'Allier and Sainte-Livrade-sur-Lot – where some of them were still living in 2000 at a very advanced age. In these two communities there were pagodas and temples (*temples aux Génies*). Mothers who had to leave Vietnam during the dramatic events of the war and experienced a cultural uprooting in France tried to raise their children in the traditional Vietnamese way. Today, the second generation, more than 40 years after the end of the First Indochina War, does not see itself as fully French, in spite of French citizenship, but also no longer as Vietnamese. Although among the public they continue to be seen as Vietnamese, professionally and socially they are, unlike their parents, by no means outsiders. Emotionally they remained strongly tied to Vietnam: for many, the villages from which their families came are special places of memory in which they root their identity.

The third wave of Vietnamese immigration to France was the result of the Second Indochina War, which ended on 30 April 1975 when the communist troops of North Vietnam entered Saigon, the capital of South Vietnam. The war had tremendous significance for the Vietnamese in France. They organized themselves, often under the cloak of culture or religion, into political organizations that sometimes advocated diametrically opposed positions. Some were hoping for a Vietnam liberated from capitalism, where, after their return with the skills and experience gained in France, they could contribute to the development of the country. Others condemned communism and sought to reestablish their privileges in the country. However, running through all the political activity was the situation in Vietnam and the hope of a return after the end of the war. And all, independent of their political orientation, were eager to preserve the Vietnamese culture and language in France as well as possible, also in the second generation.

The fourth wave of immigration was Vietnamese refugees seeking to escape communist rule in Vietnam and who made their way to France, legally or illegally, between the end of the Second Indochina War in 1975 and the mid-1980s. According to the censuses, the number of Vietnamese in France rose from 8,000 (1954), to 22,300 (1975), to 57,000 (1982), and eventually reached more than 72,000 in 1990. Since the 1970s, the gender ratios have been balanced. In 1975, nearly 50% of all Vietnamese held French citizenship. By 1982, that share had declined to 40%, but by 1990 it was up again over 50%.

Despite the varied backgrounds and social positions of the immigrants, they shared many qualities and attitudes. They adopted the formal and informal rules of the majority society (good neighborly relations, discretion, politeness). They also achieved integration in socioeconomic terms, even if some of them, especially in the closing years of the 20th century, were affected by unemployment. Privately, however, Vietnamese ways of life dominated: the Vietnamese cultivate their often far-flung family relationships and strive to pass central elements of their culture of origin on to subsequent generations. Although the Vietnamese have, over the decades, for the most part given up the notion of returning to or settling permanently in their country of origin, a strong bond to Vietnam persists. In their value system and norms of social behavior, most take their guidance from the Confucian tradition. That applies especially to the place of the individual within the group held together by the cult of the ancestors and respect for the generational hierarchy. But it also holds for their relationship to work and the value they put on it, for their striving for academic success, for their desire to accomplish their tasks successfully, and for the positive effect that professional and social success has on the life of the entire family. Daily

life is shaped by the Vietnamese cuisine, the religion they brought with them, and the rhythm of the Vietnamese year (New Year's, Mid-Autumn Festival). The group is characterized by various religious currents: Catholics, Buddhists, or Caodaists maintain separate religious sites and a multitude of different religious organizations and institutions.

Although the Vietnamese live dispersed all over France, there are presently settlement concentrations in a few cities (the city of Paris and the greater Paris region, and in southwestern France). Over the long term, this could lead to a change in the current perception of the Vietnamese by the majority society, which is committed to the idea of assimilation and fears enclaves that dissociate themselves. However, initial accounts of tendencies toward segregation overlook the many mixed marriages and the capacity, especially of the second generation, to integrate itself into French culture.

Hémery, Daniel. "Du patriotisme au marxisme: L'immigration viêtnamienne en France de 1926 à 1930." *Le Mouvement Social* (1975), no. 90: 3–54.

Khoa, Lê Huu. *Les Viêtnamiens en France. Insertion et identité*. Paris, 1985.

Lhorme, Véronique, and Marc Nardino. "Enfants de Noyant et d'Indochine." Documentary (film). Lyon, 2006.

Linh, Nguyên Xuân. "Le riz est plus parfumé: Alimentation des Viêtnamiens en France." In *Autour du riz. Le repas chez quelques populations d'Asie du Sud-Est*, edited by Nelly Krowolski, 165–96. Paris, 1993.

Simon, Pierre-Jean. *Rapatriés d'Indochine. Un village franco-indochinois en Bourbonnais. Aspects de la colonisation et de la décolonisation de l'Indochine*. Paris, 1981.

Simon-Barouh, Ida. *Rapatriés d'Indochine, deuxième génération. Les enfants d'origine indochinoise à Noyant d'Allier*. Paris, 1981.

Simon-Barouh, Ida. "Les Viêtnamiens, des 'rapatriés' aux boat people." In *Immigration et intégration, l'état des savoirs*, edited by Philippe Dewitte, 134–42. Paris, 1999.

Cross-references: France; Vietnamese Refugees in Western, Central, and Northern Europe since the 1970s: The Examples of France, Great Britain, and Germany

VIETNAMESE REFUGEES IN WESTERN, CENTRAL, AND NORTHERN EUROPE SINCE THE 1970S: THE EXAMPLES OF FRANCE, GREAT BRITAIN, AND GERMANY

Olaf Beuchling

Beginning in the mid-1970s, hundreds of thousands of Vietnamese made their way to northern, central, and western Europe as well as other parts of the world. Until the 1980s, they could expect to be recognized in their resettlement countries as refugees on humanitarian and political grounds. Many of these refugees, most of whom came from

South Vietnam, were referred to as "Boat people" who had managed to flee in vessels that were often unsuited for the high seas. In the South China Seas they were picked up by merchant or rescue ships or made it to the coast of a neighboring country. Although the Boat People attracted special attention from the world public because of the often dramatic circumstances of their flight, they were only a part of the Vietnamese refugees. Others came to Europe as part of family reunification or through asylum procedures.

Nearly all western and central European states took in Vietnamese refugees. France, the Federal Republic of Germany, and the UK accepted the largest contingents. Currently about 300,000 exile Vietnamese live in France, around 50,000 in Germany, and about 40,000 in the UK. However, because of statistical problems, high rates of naturalization, and the presence of additional migrants who are not refugees, these figures are only reference points. The countries of northern Europe also participated in the international initiatives to alleviate the refugee crisis in Southeast Asia. Norway, in particular, accepted a larger number of Vietnamese refugees. After the immigrants of Pakistani origin, the more than 16,000 Vietnamese constitute the second largest immigrant group in that country. The majority of the Vietnamese diaspora is found in the classic immigrant countries of the USA (well over 1.2 million), Canada (around 300,000), and Australia (160,000). In addition, small Vietnamese communities are found in many other countries, including Japan, New Zealand, and the Ivory Coast.

The exodus of Vietnamese refugees was triggered by the capture of the pro-Western Republic of Vietnam (South Vietnam) by the army of the Communist Democratic Republic of Vietnam (North Vietnam) in the spring of 1975. A first wave occurred during the advance of the North Vietnamese Revolutionary Army and the capitulation of Saigon in April 1975. About 13,000 individuals who had been close to the former South Vietnamese government were evacuated by the US military and settled mostly in the USA. In subsequent years, political repression (such as reeducation campaigns, internment in labor camps, and expropriations), economic misery as a result of mistakes in the planned economy and failed harvests, and military conflicts with Cambodia and the People's Republic of China led to growing discontent among wide segments of the population.

The exodus reached its high point between 1979 and 1982. While around 200,000 members of the Chinese minority made their way into the People's Republic of China overland, hundreds of thousands tried to leave South Vietnam by sea. By July 1979, more than 200,000 Vietnamese boat refugees had already reached the coasts of neighboring states in Southeast and east Asia. Housed initially in temporary camps, they were hoping to be recognized as refugees by third-party states. Tens of thousands of boat refugees perished: they were drowned during storms, died of thirst on the open sea, or were killed by pirates who were lying in wait for the refugees in the Gulf of Thailand.

"Boat people" are taken aboard the rescue ship *Cap Anamur* in the South China Sea, 1980 (*ullstein bild*).

The announcement by the Association of Southeast Asian Nations (ASEAN) that member states would not accept any more refugees and the practice by some governments of pushing boats filled with refugees back out to sea prompted a response from the United Nations High Commission for Refugees (UNHCR), which declared that temporarily the Vietnamese boat refugees would be under its jurisdiction. The UN's first Indochina Refugee Conference in Geneva in July 1979, attended by 65 nations, agreed, among other things, to establish new transit camps in the region and to accelerate and expand the admission of refugees from the camps into third-party states. Moreover, the uncontrolled exodus of refuges from Vietnam was to be stopped in favor of the Orderly Departure Program (ODP), which made possible the orderly reunification of family members in the destination countries.

The exodus from Vietnam mirrors in a revealing way the changes in how refugee movements have been perceived by international organizations like the UNHRC and national governments in Europe since the 1970s. In the beginning, the UNHCR primarily wanted to ensure humane living conditions for the boat refugees in the transit camps in Southeast Asia, coordinate their onward journey to third countries, and arrange for the possibility of an orderly departure from Vietnam. Following the collapse of the Eastern Bloc in 1989–90, the efforts of the international community were aimed chiefly at gradually shutting down the camps and supporting the voluntary return of refugees and their reintegration into Vietnamese society. Accordingly, the European states who were strongly supportive of the admission and settlement of Vietnamese refugees in the 1970s and 1980s increasingly pulled back from this policy and have severely restricted the admission of any more refugees.

The attention that the media gave to the events in Southeast Asia promoted the willingness, at the end of the 1970s and the beginning of the 1980s, to admit Vietnamese refugees into Europe. The governments pursued a fairly engaged refugee policy and the public displayed a pronounced sense of solidarity, with integration programs developed everywhere. As a result, the reception of Vietnamese refugees was substantially similar in the various European countries (allowing for differences in the size and origins of the refugee groups).

In France, the private organization France Terre d'Asile was responsible for overseeing the immigration and integration of Vietnamese refugees. It arranged for the initial support for refugees in reception centers and coordinated the work of other charitable organizations as well as of the state-run Comité National d'Entraide, which took over coordination tasks in the admission of refugees. The chief focus was on allocating housing and running language and integration courses as well as vocational training. After the initial settlement in *départements* throughout the country, Paris developed into a special center of immigration. By the time of the first Indochina Refugee Conference in 1979, France had already admitted 50,000 refugees. These refugees, as well as subsequent immigrants from Vietnam, were generally accorded refugee status and given the chance to acquire French citizenship. By 1985, the number of refugees had risen to over 110,000 – Vietnamese but also Laotians and Khmer. As in other European countries that were offering asylum to Vietnamese refugees, reservations grew in France in the 1980s: there were growing doubts as to whether the Vietnamese had in fact left their country for political reasons. As a result, the generous practice of asylum and integration that was practiced in the 1970s and early 1980s gradually became much more restrictive.

The Federal Republic of Germany had already declared its willingness, in principle, to admit refugees from Vietnam right after the fall of Saigon. The government guaranteed a contingent that was increased several times and eventually resulted in the admission of 38,000 refugees. It included refugees from the transit camps in Southeast Asia as well as boat refugees and their families rescued at sea. Over and above this contingent, Germany admitted further refugees, including through special actions (like the reception of 277 refugees in 1979 initiated by the weekly *Die Zeit* and the Hamburg state government) or as part of the regular asylum process. In the wake of the refugee conference in Geneva, the federal government drew up a catalog of measures and combined them into the Program of the Federal Government for Foreign Refugees. On the one hand, the catalog included participation in international aid efforts – for example, the Indochina programs of the UNHCR and the International Red Cross – which the Federal Republic supported financially and logistically. On the other hand, it clarified, on the

federal and state levels, the legal basis for granting residency and work permits, for language instruction, and for social services for the refugees.

The modalities of admission differed only slightly from one federal state to the next: for example, in Hamburg the refugees were given sponsors on a voluntary basis, while Hesse deliberately did not do that. After about 23,000 refugees had been admitted by the middle of 1982, the federal authorities limited immigration to family reunification. All other refugees who after this point where picked up by German merchant or rescue vessels (like the *Cap Anamur*) or arrived in the Federal Republic in some other way had to go through an asylum process. As a result, the immigration of Vietnamese refugees declined markedly in the following years. At the beginning of the 21st century, the number of Vietnamese refugees and their descendants in Germany is estimated to be at least 50,000. In general, Vietnamese refugees are found in all old federal states as well as outside of the urban conurbations. Larger communities established themselves in Berlin and Hamburg, among other places. Well over half of the Vietnamese refugees have adopted German citizenship.

In the UK, the Vietnamese refugee migrations occurred during a period of fairly restrictive immigration policies. By 1979, only a few hundred Vietnamese refugees and orphaned children had been admitted, and these were looked after by a private organization. At the refugee conference in Geneva, the Thatcher government agreed to take in an initial contingent of 10,000 refugees, largely to provide relief for the first asylum camps in Hong Kong. The initial care for refugees had clear parallels to the practice in France and West Germany: housing was provided for several months in transit domiciles where the refugees were given medical care and introduced to the language and society of their host country. Their subsequent dispersal to subsidized housing was – as in Germany – guided by the idea that this would avoid the creation of segregated neighborhoods, prevent unequal financial burdens on the communities, and offer the refugees opportunities for integration through contacts with the majority population. The integration of the refugees into the labor market confronted problems that were also similar to the situation in West Germany: economic integration was made more difficult by a recession, on the one hand, and by problems of communication and the absence of skills that were useful in the British labor market, on the other hand. Unlike in West Germany, however, the subsequent migration within the country played a major role in the UK. By 1989, more than half of the refugees had already left their first domicile and had moved to the large urban centers, where Vietnamese communities began to take shape.

The integration of the Vietnamese refugees in the various host countries deepened with the establishment of Vietnamese organizations and associations on the regional, national, and international levels. They fostered and passed on cultural traditions, provided mutual support in the integration process, and offered a forum for political work in exile. The political activities of the opposition groups, exile parties, and refugee organizations were initially marked by a (sometimes militant) anticommunism that in the beginning could still harbor ideas about bringing about violent change in Vietnam. The experiences in Vietnam and while trying to get out had bred a deep political mistrust of leftist movements: for example, in the 1980s a small band of Vietnamese refugees from Italy arrived in Hamburg to request asylum there after the leftist parties in Italy had made substantial gains in the elections. With the gradual opening of Vietnam, the position of the exile organizations moderated and the work for democracy and human rights moved to the fore. However, even at the beginning of the 21st century, many political activities continue to be focused on the homeland. Criticism of the political developments in the homeland is continually voiced within the framework of cultural events or on the occasion of rallies to mark the anniversary of the fall of Saigon. At times this leads to conflicts with Vietnamese who had originally come to the former GDR and other areas of east-central and eastern Europe as temporary labor migrants, with some eventually staying on.

The reception and integration of Vietnamese refugees led to the establishment of Vietnamese Buddhism in Europe. Two currents can be identified; one is the Congregation of the United Vietnamese-Buddhist Church Abroad, which was set up as the exile organization of the United Vietnamese-Buddhist Church that was outlawed in Vietnam. At the beginning of the 21st century, it had pagodas and lay groups in various European cities. In France alone there are 35 pagodas; England has 10 and Germany 12. The largest monastery of the organization was built in the 1990s in Hanover (Lower Saxony) on a property of 4,000 square meters, and shortly after its inauguration it hosted the first World Congress of the Vietnamese-Buddhist Order in Exile. For another, Vietnamese Buddhism has become known to a broad public in Europe through the work of the monk Thich Nhat Hanh. His international seminars, focused on daily life, annually draw thousands of people of diverse backgrounds to the "plum village" in Thénac near Bordeaux; his books have been translated into many languages and are popular beyond the group of believers of Vietnamese background. Vietnamese Catholicism has also gained a foothold in Europe in close cooperation with local congregations. In some parishes, priests of Vietnamese background are already ministering to both Vietnamese and non-Vietnamese faithful.

The social and economic development of the group in northern, central, and western Europe depends on very diverse individual factors, which include the socioeconomic status before the exodus, attendance at educational institutions in the reception countries, and the age of the migrants at the time of their settlement in Europe. Sweeping statements about the integration of the first or second generation are impossible given the heterogeneity of the immigrant group: on the one hand, among the boat refugees were many young people whose parents or grandparents could follow only much later and who therefore had much less chance to make their way in the majority society. On the other hand, individuals who had been studying in Europe before 1975 and were then granted refugee status had academic qualifications that led to prestigious and high-earning professions. This applies especially to the former students in France but also to the approximately 2,000 Vietnamese who had come to Germany to study before the Vietnamese refugee crisis began.

An "ethnic economy" developed in the form of restaurants and Asian markets, a striking example of which can be found in the 13th *arrondissement* in Paris. Among the Vietnamese refugees in France – perhaps a reflection that some of them came from comparatively privileged backgrounds – there are numerous artists who have also won international acclaim with their work as writers, filmmakers, or painters. Filmmakers like Lam Le or Tran Anh Hung, women writers like Linda Le, or painters like Tran Trong Vu process their intercultural experiences in characteristic Franco-Vietnamese works of a kind that are only beginning to emerge in other parts of the Vietnamese diaspora in Europe.

For refugees who came to Europe as children or adolescents, educational and vocational institutions were the passageway to economic integration. Even if secondary school qualifications or even a university degree were no guarantees for a well-paying profession, they were the requirement for access to a multitude of prestigious jobs and the privileges that came with them. In Germany, the younger generation succeeded fairly quickly in making its way in the educational system. In the 1990s, girls and boys of Vietnamese background attended higher secondary schools at higher rates than their German counterparts. Another reason the educational opportunities – which were regarded as better than in the country of origin – were often taken advantage of is that education holds a special place within the Vietnamese culture of origin. Serious economic problems are documented for only a part of the Vietnamese who live in the UK. These are especially evident among individuals who were admitted only at the end of the 1980s from camps in Hong Kong; this group shows clear disadvantages of educational and economic integration compared to their countrymen who immigrated earlier. Whether that is due largely to the late arrival or differences in the motivation behind the migration must remain an open question.

In summary, one can say that the Vietnamese refugees in various European countries succeeded in establishing themselves in the societies that received them, primarily through success in school and university. The integration process was far more successful in families who already possessed secondary education diplomas in Vietnam than in families from rural, poorer regions. Moreover, as a rule the younger generation oriented itself more strongly toward the social and cultural customs of the host society than did older family members who arrived only later as part of the program of family reunification.

Beuchling, Olaf. *Vom Bootsflüchtling zum Bundesbürger. Migration, Integration und schulischer Erfolg in einer vietnamesischen Exilgemeinschaft.* Münster and New York, 2003.

Bun Chan, Kwok, and Kenneth Christie. "Past, Present and Future: The Indochinese Refugee Experience Twenty Years Later." *Journal of Refugee Studies* 8, 1 (1995): 75–94.

Duke, Karen, and Tony Marshall. *Vietnamese Refugees since 1982.* London, 1995.

Mignot, Michel. "Refugees from Cambodia, Laos and Vietnam, 1975–1993." In *The Cambridge Survey of Migration*, edited by Robin Cohen, 452–6. Cambridge, 1995.

Robinson, W. Courtland. *Terms of Refuge: The Indochinese Exodus and the International Response.* London, 1998.

Cross-references: France; Germany; Great Britain; Vietnamese Colonial and Postcolonial Immigrants in France since World War I; Vietnamese, Mozambican, and Cuban Labor Migrants in East Germany since the 1970s

VIETNAMESE, MOZAMBICAN, AND CUBAN LABOR MIGRANTS IN EAST GERMANY SINCE THE 1970S

Sandra Gruner-Domić

A large number of migrant workers from European and non-European countries came to East German enterprises as "contract workers." Beginning in the 1970s, the GDR signed bilateral treaties with non-European socialist countries to recruit workers, including Cuba (1978), Mozambique (1979), and Vietnam (1980). The workers of both genders, most of whom were young, remained in East Germany for four to five years and were then replaced by new workers. A mere 15% were women. The goal of the GDR in signing these treaties was to remedy the country's serious labor shortage in certain manufacturing areas. According to the official propaganda, the purpose behind this arrangement was to train workers from less developed, fellow socialist countries. By using this premise of vocational training, the East German government was hoping to avoid the accusation that it was recruiting and exploiting foreign workers.

Even before these treaties were signed, Vietnamese and Cuban trainees and students, in particular, but also Mozambican students, made their way to the GDR. They studied at technical colleges and universties, especially in the natural sciences and engineering, or were trained as skilled workers, for example, in the textile and chemical industries. The number of these young immigrants from all three countries did not exceed 2,000. The number of contract workers who arrived was on an entirely different order of magnitude. They came to East Germany in groups of 100. At the beginning of the 1980s, on average 6,000 Cubans and 5,000 Mozambicans were working in East German enterprises. In the second half of the 1980s, an average of 11,000 Cubans, 12,000 Mozambicans, and 34,000 Vietnamese were working in the GDR, where especially the number of Vietnamese was continually rising.

The recruitment treaties had stipulated that the contract workers were to receive German language instruction and specialized training in addition to their daily work. In the 1970s, the GDR abided by this training program. However, in the 1980s the recruitment increasingly brought in individuals who already had vocational training or even a university education. Some workers were so disappointed by their situation in East Germany that they returned to their home countries before the end of their work contract. Termination of a contract could be justified with health or personal problems. Freedom of movement was in principle restricted for foreign workers, who were seen by the GDR and the respective treaty states as "delegates."

The contracts under which the workers arrived regulated the organization and manner of their stay down to the smallest detail. The workers were recruited through state offices, which arranged everything – from the flight, to the necessary documents, to the organization of daily life. The collective accommodation of the migrant workers in dormitories had direct consequences for their life and nonintegration in East Germany. They lived as close as possible to the enterprises in which they worked, and in keeping with the contract several workers shared one fully furnished room. This concentrated housing was officially justified with reference to the housing shortage in East Germany and the temporary, short-term stay of the migrants. As a result, the contract workers for the most part lived isolated from the native population, which wanted to know as little as possible about the reasons behind their presence. Even though some dormitories were located in the middle of residential areas, contact with neighbors was very restricted. Locals who encountered groups of "foreign" men at a bus stop or while shopping often reacted with racist prejudices and xenophobia, which further limited relations with the migrants especially in smaller towns. Some German women also felt harassed by the Cuban or Mozambican men. German men feared competition in the local discotheques where the workers went for entertainment. To avoid conflicts, the East German authorities set up clubs in the dormitories that were closed to the public. That created even more distance, as even friends were not allowed entry into the dormitories, which were supervised by porters, after 10 P.M. As a result of this isolation, many women migrant workers found a partner among their fellow contract workers, especially since there was a considerable excess of men. The East German government threatened to deport pregnant migrant workers since they were no longer regarded as fit to work and were not to be given any maternity benefits.

Intensive contact between natives and foreigners occurred in the workplace. Nevertheless, here, too, there were many prejudices. One large disadvantage for the immigrants was their poor language skills, for which their work colleagues mocked them on the job or treated them as inferior. Dark-skinned Mozambicans and Cubans had an especially difficult time. For the most part they ignored the provocations so as to avoid conflicts, since that would generally have led to a negative evaluation of the entire work group's discipline.

Contract workers in East Berlin in the 1980s (*ullstein bild*).

Friendships with colleagues were rare. Relationships between young East German women and immigrants, especially dark-skinned Mozambicans and Cubans, got a negative public reception. But there were also positive descriptions of "hardworking and soft-spoken" Vietnamese and "happy and sociable" Cubans, some of whom consciously adopted these stereotypes. For example, Vietnamese were eager not to draw undue attention and tried to articulate the language very well. Cuban and Mozambican workers invoked their "exotic background" and became active musically, formed bands, and even gave some performances. They had a better chance this way of getting German friends and girlfriends.

The fact that East German citizens had few experiences with immigrants or minorities promoted the guiding notion of a homogeneous GDR society. That in turn generally prompted foreigners to adapt as much as possible. Still, Vietnamese, Mozambicans, and Cubans stood out because of the way they looked. The situation for migrant workers changed profoundly with the fall of the Berlin Wall. They now experienced "Western" patterns of behavior and for the first time met larger groups of immigrants who had been living in Germany for a long time and had become integrated. A few Cubans and Mozambicans who remained in Germany after losing their jobs took advantage of opportunities in the music and entertainment industry. Vietnamese sought a path to independence as street vendors or small entrepreneurs, including work in the ethnic commercial sector – for example, in Asian fast food.

All in all, few of the former contract workers remained in Germany after the German unification in 1990. In 1989 there were 8,300 Cubans, 15,400 Mozambicans, and 59,600 Vietnamese in East Germany. The last East German government under Prime Minister Lothar de Maizière had negotiated an immediate stop to recruitment with the treaty states. Those workers who had just arrived in East Germany were allowed to remain until the end of their contractual term. However, Cuba immediately recalled its citizens. After unification, the German government paid bonuses to those Mozambican workers who had arrived shortly before 1989

and agreed to return voluntarily. Some workers who had already completed the better part of their work contract in East Germany accepted this offer, seeing the wave of dismissals in their companies and the growing outbreaks of xenophobia.

However, contrary to the expectations of the government, the immigration of Vietnamese, Mozambicans, and Cubans to Germany continued. Many of the workers who had arrived only shortly before the end of the GDR adjusted to the upheaval. A few even sought to make a living as street vendors in West Germany, where, in the country's effort to restrict further immigration, they were prohibited from looking for work. Many of those in binational marriages remained in Germany. Vietnamese, in particular, brought their families to join them. In this way, friends, acquaintances, relatives, and even migrant workers who had in the meantime returned made their way to Germany, even after the East German recruitment treaties had been terminated.

Bui, Pipo. *Envisioning Vietnamese Migrants in Germany: Ethnic Stigma, Immigrant Origin Narratives and Partial Masking.* Münster, 2003.

Cala Fuentes, Leonel. *Kubaner im Realen Paradies. Ausländer-Alltag in der DDR. Eine Erinnerung.* Berlin, 2007

"*…da sind wir keine Ausländer mehr.*" *Eingewanderte ArbeiterInnen in Berlin 1961–1993*, edited by the Berliner Geschichtswerkstatt. Berlin, 1993.

Gruner-Domić, Sandra. "Zur Geschichte der Arbeitskräftemigration in der DDR. Die bilateralen Verträge zur Beschäftigung ausländischer Arbeiter (1961–1989)." *Internationale Wissenschaftliche Korrespondenz zur Geschichte der deutschen Arbeiterbewegung* 32 (1996), no 2: 204–30.

Gruner-Domić, Sandra. *Kubanische Arbeitskräftemigration in die DDR 1978–1989. Das Arbeitskräfteabkommen Kuba-DDR und dessen Realisierung.* Berlin, 1997.

Scherzer, Landolf. *Die Fremden. Unerwünschte Begegnungen und verbotene Protokolle.* Berlin, 2002.

Trong, Phan Duc. "Vietnamesische Vertragsarbeitnehmer in der BRD. Probleme der Integration in Deutschland. Wege und Programme der Reintegration in der SRV." PhD diss, Berlin, 1998.

Zwengel, Almut, ed. *Die 'Gastarbeiter' der DDR.* Münster, 2009.

Cross-references: Germany; Chinese Restaurant Owners in the Netherlands and Germany in the Second Half of the 20th Century; Vietnamese Refugees in Western, Central, and Northern Europe since the 1970s: The Examples of France, Great Britain, and Germany

WALDENSIANS IN CENTRAL EUROPE SINCE THE EARLY MODERN PERIOD

Matthias Asche

The word "Waldensians" (Lat. *waldenses*, Fr. *vaudois*, Ital. *valdesi*) goes back to the founder of the sect, (Petrus) Waldes, who traveled through southern France around 1174–5 as a charismatic itinerant preacher. By the 15th century, the Waldensians had not only spread in their original territories in France and Savoy but throughout the entire European continent, from Spain and Italy to the Baltic region. The Waldensians were for the first time excommunicated as heretics at the Council of Verona (1184) and suffered numerous waves of persecution throughout the Middle Ages. As a result, they could practice their religion only in secrecy. Their lay churches were led by preachers (*barbes*) who lived lives of personal poverty and chastity, but otherwise they had no official ecclesiastical hierarchy. Waldensian theology centered on the Bible as the only source of faith. Because of that they found common ground in their diaspora with other late medieval reform movements of the medieval church (Lollards, Bohemian Brothers), into which they were sometimes absorbed.

The concentration on the Gospels as the sole guide allowed Waldensian communities a certain openness to contact with the francophone Reformation in its Swiss incarnation. The majority of these communities joined that movement out of political grounds at a synod in Chanforan in 1532. After the destruction of their last larger settlements in the Provence (1545) as well as in Apulia and Calabria (1560), the Waldensians only survived as mountain farmers in the remote valleys of the Cottian Alps west of Turin, and especially in the Chisone Valley (Val Clusone) that was politically divided between France and Savoy (outsiders referred to them as the "valley people").

Since the middle of the 16th century, the Chisone Valley had seen the establishment of permanent French Reformed parishes with a synodal-presbyterian organization, modeled after Calvin's Geneva. Although the idiosyncratic character of the old Waldensian church had been lost with the adoption of the Calvinist church constitution, the Waldensian parishes did assume a special place within the French Reformed church, because – with the exception of their pastors who often came from western Switzerland – they largely consisted of peasants. The identity-creating term "Waldensians" experienced a revival only in exile, as a legal-social demarcation vis-à-vis other groups of French Reformed refugees.

Because of their religious denomination, the Waldensians in many ways shared the experiences of the French Huguenots with persecution and migration. However, a precise differentiation of the Huguenots of France from the Waldensians from the French-Savoyan border region is problematic, especially since the Waldensians on the French side of the Chisone Valley (Val Pragela) were rightly seen by the French king as Huguenots because of their creed. The constant state of mobility on the part of the French and Savoyan Waldensians because of the persecutions of the 16th and 17th centuries (1562–1629 10 "Huguenot wars" in France; 1560–1 and 1655 "Waldensian wars" in Savoy) led to a lasting intermingling of the two groups in the border region. To complicate the situation further, the Val Pérouse, originally part of Savoy, was for

a time occupied by the French. Here, as in the rest of France, the 1685 Edict of Fontainebleu, the "Edict of Revocation" that triggered the great Huguenot exodus, was in force. By contrast, the Val Pragela was conquered after 1708 by the Duke of Savoy, later king of Sardinia-Piedmont, which made all remaining Waldensians in the valleys his subjects.

The pressure of re-Catholicization exerted by the Duke of Savoy, which did not relent even after the Patent of Mercy of Pinerolo (1655), led to a first wave of emigration by Savoyan Waldensians. In addition to smaller groups of refugees who went to areas in Limburg and Brabant that were directly ruled by the Dutch States General and to the French-speaking part of Switzerland, the first real Waldensian colony arose in Mörlheim in the Electoral Palatinate (1665), where other groups of Calvinist refugees also settled until the outbreak of the War of the Palatine Succession. After 1688, most of the *réfugiés* settled in the Palatinate fled to Brandenburg-Prussia, where all of the refugees were indiscriminately called "people from the Palatinate (*Pfälzer*)."

More important in quantitative terms was the exodus of French Waldensians after the Edict of Fontainebleau (1685): the Val Pragal lost about 2,500 individuals, one-quarter of its population. The following year, Duke Victor Amadeus II issued a similar edict for the Savoyan Waldensians. A co-coordinated French-Savoyan military operation against the valleys of the Waldensians led to death, captivity, flight, and mass conversions among those who were left. The Waldensian refugees of 1685–7 initially moved to the Swiss Confederation, where special "chambers of exiles" had been set up in Bern (since 1683) and Zurich (since 1685) to look after all west European refugees. Until their final destination outside the overcrowded Confederation had been clarified, they were distributed among the various Reformed cantons with francophone populations.

With the exception of the admission into a few cities in Brandenburg-Prussia (ca. 900 Waldensians) as well as smaller contingents in the landgraviates of Hesse-Darmstadt (ca. 350) and Hesse-Kassel (ca. 200), and the in the Duchy of Holzappel (later the Principality of Nassau-Schaumburg), nearly all attempted settlements in the Holy Roman Empire in the late 1680s failed. The reasons were either the high expectations placed by the princes on the farming Waldensians, who were not suited for settlement in cities, opposition by the territorial Lutheran churches, or, not least, advances by French troops into southwestern Germany in the War of the Palatine Succession. Large numbers of the Waldensians were forced to return to the Swiss Confederation after 1688. Only the Savoyan Waldensians were able to return to their original valleys in 1690, after the duke joined the anti-French war party (Glorieuse Rentrée). Then the area also took in French Waldensians and Huguenots.

However, the greatest exodus of Waldensians was triggered by the separate peace between France and Savoy (1696), in which the duke agreed to no longer tolerate Protestants. The relevant edict of 1698 led to the renewed flight of about 3,000 Waldensians, who, after a lengthy interlude in the Swiss Confederation, found a permanent home in territories of the Holy Roman Empire. Between 1699 and 1701, Waldensians – with occasional participation by other groups of refugees – founded more than a dozen villages: in the Duchy of Württemberg (ca. 1,650 Waldensians in new settlements with francophone names like Lucerne, Villars, Pinache, Serres, Perouse), in the Principalities of Ysenburg-Wächtersbach (ca. 350) and Nassau-Schaumburg (ca. 50), in the Landgraviates of Hesse-Darmstadt (ca. 300) and Hesse-Homburg (ca. 160), as well as in the Margraviate of Baden-Durlach (ca. 130). A few villages inhabited largely by Waldensians, who had come from Württemberg and Baden-Durlach, also arose in the Landgraviate of Hesse-Kassel in the 1720s.

Finally, the Savoyan Waldensians experienced a last, religiously motivated wave of emigration in 1730, after Savoy outlawed the practice of the Protestant religion for good. More than 500 Waldensians were evacuated via the Swiss Confederation to those areas in Brabant and Limburg that were directly governed by the Dutch States General. All that remained in the valleys until the declaration of freedom of religion by the Kingdom of Piedmont-Sardinia (1848) was a small minority of secret Protestants without any clergy.

As they did with other groups of refugees, German territorial rulers granted the Waldensians separate privileges, which allowed them a special status in political, ecclesiastical, and economic-social terms. Before their great exodus around 1700, the Waldensians were usually admitted on the conditions found in the general privileges for refugees. A small group of delegates negotiated separate Waldensian privileges in 1698–1701; the policy of privileges took the place of integration – desired by neither the Waldensians nor the territorial rulers – into an environment with a foreign language, a foreign confession, and a foreign culture. The isolation of the Waldensians, settled for the most part in separated village communities, was intended to ensure the homogeneity and autonomy of the colony and to prevent the abuse of the privileges. By contrast, given the rural and agricultural background of the Waldensians, settling them in cities always proved problematic. The identity of the few Waldensians in German, Swiss, and Dutch cities were absorbed into the "French" identity of the refugee groups dominant there.

What prevented the rapid integration of the Waldensians into their new homelands – apart from the physical remoteness of their villages (combined with a prohibition against natives moving there) and their French Reformed confession – were the problems of everyday life – for example, the transition from mountain farming to small and large animal husbandry, ignorance of three-field farming, and the lack of German language skills. Moreover, the Waldensians were not only set apart from other refugee groups in the host country by their consistently lower social origins and low level of education, but also, and especially, by the use of

their own language, which was part of Occitan; of course, the German authorities did not notice the peculiarities of that language, which for a long time proved remarkably resistant in the destination lands to the reception of German loan words.

While neighboring Waldensian villages were closely linked by numerous ties of kinship, there was hardly any coordination in terms of church politics. Although the Waldensian communities in Baden-Durlach, Württemberg, and Hesse initially formed a common synodal union in each area, the assemblies were held very irregularly and the individual parishes sent representatives independently of one another. The "South Hesse Waldensian Synod" (three meetings or colloquies) ended in 1704, the "Württemberg Waldensian Synod" (13 colloquies) in 1769, the communities of Baden-Durlach having already ceased to send representatives to that synod in 1714. The Reformed landgrave of Hesse-Kassel did not permit any synod, but integrated the French Reformed congregations into the highest church office under the supervision of an inspector.

The general prohibition for natives to move into Waldensian settlements, mentioned in nearly all Waldensian privileges, was already circumvented in the first half of the 18th century, especially because the homogenous settlements of colonists had virtually no qualified artisans. In the long run, the gradual arrival of natives, initially admitted to the Waldensian villages as less-privileged immigrant villagers or *Beisassen*, broke open the originally strong isolation of the separate farming communities in nearly all spheres of life. That opening up occurred fully with the appearance of mixed confessional marriages, which, of course, entailed the problem of baptism and the religious upbringing of the children from such unions.

Growing signs of assimilation in the Waldensian villages appeared from the middle of the 18th century, which led, for example, to a mixed language, initially among pastors and schoolteachers. From around 1800, at the latest, Waldensian villages conducted their entire correspondence with the authorities in German. This circumstance, combined with the disappearing knowledge of the correct use of their original language, led to a growing problem with the comprehensibility of religious services. That problem also existed because the language of ritual and the church was high French, which deviated strongly from the Waldensian dialect.

The final integration of the Waldensians was initiated by the various authorities at the beginning of the 19th century, especially through church unions (1821 Hesse-Darmstadt and Baden, 1830s Hesse-Kassel). Because the self-confident French Reformed Church in Württemberg resisted plans of a union, King Wilhelm I outlawed the French language in church and school (1820–3), although in many French Reformed churches the preaching had already been done in German since the end of the 18th century. Shortly before that, the special administration for the Waldensians had been abolished (French Chancellery in Kassel, Waldensian

Deputation in Stuttgart). In some villages in Württemberg and northern Hesse, remnants of the Waldensian language persisted – revealingly enough in the sacral sphere – in some old-established families into the 1930s.

During the anniversary celebrations in 1885, held by the large French Reformed urban parishes to commemorate the admission of the Huguenots into German territories in 1685, especially in Prussia and Hesse-Kassel, the memory of the peasant Waldensians did not play a part. Of central importance to the rediscovery of the Waldensian legacy were the village anniversaries celebrated in Württemberg in 1899. The German Waldensian Association was founded in 1936, nearly half a century later than the German Huguenot Association (1890); today it is headquartered in Schönenberg-Ötisheim near Pforzheim and maintains there a Waldensian Museum in the Henri Arnaud House.

In spite of all the waves of persecution, small and for a long time clergy-less French Reformed congregations were able to survive underground in the old Waldensian valleys. Encouraged by Swiss and English revivalist preachers at the beginning of the 19th century, and for the first time recognized as a church in the constitution of the Kingdom of Piedmont-Sardinia (1848), these communities were eventually able to consolidate. However, poor economic opportunities in the remote Alpine valleys led to constant emigration. One result was the appearance of Reformed Waldensian communities; first in Turin (1849), then in all large Italian cities as well as in France and Switzerland, and in the second half of the 19th century even in Uruguay (Colonia Valdese near Montevideo) and the USA (Valdese in North Carolina). The synodal-presbyterian *Chiesa valdese*, headquartered in Torre Pelice near Turin – with about 45,000 members – points to the unbroken tradition of what is, next to the Hussite-Utraquist church and its offshoots, the only pre-Reformation movement that has survived until today.

Armand-Hugon, Augusto, and Valdo Vinay. *Storia dei Valdesi*. 3 vols. Turin, 1974–80.

Audisio, Gabriel. *Les "Vaudois." Naissance, vie et mort d'une dissidence (XXIIme–XVIme siècles)*. Turin, 1989.

Bischoff, Johannes E. *Lexikon deutscher Hugenotten-Orte*. Bad Karlshafen, 1994.

Jalla, Jean. *Histoire des Vaudois des Alpes et leurs colonies.* 4th ed. Torre Pelice, 1934.

Kiefner, Theo, ed. *Die Privilegien der nach Deutschland gekommenen Waldenser.* Stuttgart, 1990.

Kiefner, Theo. *Die Waldenser auf ihrem Weg aus dem Val Cluson durch die Schweiz nach Deutschland 1532–1755.* 5 vols. to date. Göttingen, 1980–2005.

Molnár, Amedeo. *Die Waldenser. Geschichte und europäisches Ausmaß einer Ketzerbewegung.* Freiburg im Breisgau, 1993.

Tourn, Giorgio. *I valdesi. La singolare vicenda di un popolo-chiesa (1170–1999).* 3rd ed. Turin, 1999.

Cross-references: France; Germany; Italy; The Netherlands; Switzerland; Dutch Calvinist Refugees in Europe since the Early Modern Period; Huguenots in Europe since the Early Modern Period; Moravian Brethren in Europe since the Early Modern Period

WALLOON STRAW HAT MAKERS IN THE NETHERLANDS IN THE 19TH CENTURY

Annemarie Cottaar

The river Jeker (French: Geer) originates in the region Hesbaye west of Liège and joins the river Meuse not far from Maastricht. In the villages along this river, like Heure-le-Romain, Rocklenge, Glons, and Bassenge, the production of straw hats began to flourish at the end of the 18th century. In a surprisingly short period, a growing number of people from this region specialized in the making and selling of straw hats. Apart from exporting the hats, to Scandinavia, Russia, and the USA, a number of producers established businesses in the big cities in western Europe making use of male migrant labor from their home villages. They opened shops and more or less monopolized this line of trade. Around the middle of the 19th century a few hundred Jeker men owned shops and workshops in almost every big and middle-sized town in the Netherlands, whereas at that time Dutch competitors were virtually absent. From the 1890s onward, the number of shops dwindled and the industry came to a halt. The competition from Italy and China became too heavy and the Netherlands and other neighboring countries introduced an import tax on straw plait, which still could not halt the decline of the industry. In the Jeker Valley, the industry continued, albeit on a more modest scale.

Until 1800 straw hat manufacturers mostly migrated within Belgium or to northern France; after 1800, they also went to the Netherlands and to French towns farther away, especially Paris. The migration from the villages in the department Meuse Inférieure – like Roclenge, Bassenge, and Wonck – was entirely directed to the Netherlands. Arnoldus Gielson, who owned a straw hat shop in Utrecht in 1749, is the earliest example of this type of migration. From the beginning of the 19th century straw hat manufacturers visited towns all over the country, but Amsterdam was the most important destination, with 53 Jeker shops between 1850 and 1920. These shops sometimes passed from father to son.

In the main cities the stores and workshops were located in the center of the town on the most important shopping streets, underlining the fact that straw hats were considered a luxury good, sold to the middle and upper classes. Advertisements and signs indicate that the shopkeepers not only produced new hats but also washed and dyed used hats. To decorate the hats they engaged in the trade in hatbands, feathers, flowers, and all kinds of embroidery, which they sometimes obtained from their fellow villagers who had established their own shops in Paris.

The manufacturers relied exclusively on migrant workers from their home area, particularly male seasonal workers of various ages, who traveled in groups and stayed in Dutch cities for four or five months. Women from the Jeker region were not employed in the Netherlands either as workers or as saleswomen, as the latter occupation was dominated by Dutch women. Between autumn and January men and women in the Jeker Valley prepared and plaited the straw. In the beginning of the year the semimanufactured plaiting, mostly in bundles of long small strings, was brought to the workshops in the Dutch cities. The seasonal migrants' main task was stitching (by hand, until the 1880s) the semimanufactured plaiting into many different kinds of hats, following the latest fashion. In the Hague and Rotterdam the workers stayed in the houses of their employers; in Amsterdam they were accommodated in boardinghouses. This yearly pattern involved hundreds of people and lasted almost a century.

The manufacturers themselves mostly settled for good in the Netherlands, while a minority commuted between their homeland and the location of their business. Marriage partners seem to have been decisive in this respect. Those who married a woman from their home region remained oriented toward the Jeker Valley. Despite their successful business in the Netherlands they invested their capital in their home region and returned when they retired. The manufacturers who married Dutch women, however, displayed a more integrative orientation and did not return to their home region. Thirteen of the 18 first-generation Jeker migrant manufacturers who settled in the Hague were also buried there. Eleven of them were married to Dutch women and two to Belgian women from outside the Jeker area.

Although there are strong indications that first- or second-generation migrants from the Jeker Valley dominated the Dutch straw hat market for a century, it would be inaccurate to label them "ethnic entrepreneurs." Even the first generation of migrants who set up business in Dutch cities often married Dutch women and, more important, they were far from enclave businessmen. They aimed at a wide market and did not advertise their hats as "typical Belgian" or "product of the Jeker Valley." After the decline of the straw hat industry they vanished in Dutch society. Although common names like Fraikin or Mathot still exist, no one connects them with the Walloon straw hat makers.

Ansiaux, Maurice. *L'industrie du tressage de la paille de la vallée du Geer*. Bruxelles, 1900.

Cottaar, Annemarie, and Leo Lucassen. "Naar de laatste Parijse mode. Strohoedenmakers uit het Jekerdal in Nederland 1750–1900." In *Jaarboek van het Sociaal Historisch centrum Limburg*, edited by Ad Knotter and Willibrord Rutten, 45–52. Maastricht, 2001. ["A la dernière mode parisienne, les fabricants de chapeaux de paille wallons aux Pays-Bas, 1750–1900." *Actes de l'histoire de l'immigration. Revue électronique* 3 (2003).]

Cross-references: Belgium and Luxembourg; The Netherlands

WEST INDIANS IN GREAT BRITAIN, FRANCE, AND THE NETHERLANDS SINCE THE END OF WORLD WAR II

Pieter C. Emmer

West Indians in Europe originate from former British, French, and Dutch colonies in the Caribbean. Until the end of the colonial period, after World War II, residents of Caribbean colonies could settle unhindered in their respective European motherlands. After independence, residents of the former British colonies and the former Dutch colony of Suriname lost this right. West Indians from the former Spanish islands, which had gained independence in the 19th century, migrated primarily to the American mainland.

The vast majority of West Indians are of African or Indian origin. The indigenous Carib population of the Caribbean region died out – and mainland populations were likewise decimated – in the decades following Spanish conquest from diseases introduced by the Spanish. Europeans imported African slaves and, after the abolition of slavery, brought Indian contract laborers to work on plantations on the West Indian islands. Between 1600 and 1850, around 4 million African slaves of both sexes were brought to the West Indies. After 1850, around 500,000 Indian contract workers immigrated.

After the plantation economy in the Caribbean had taken root, black West Indians migrated to Europe, accompanying expatriate European planters and merchants who returned home from time to time. Slaves from the Caribbean doubtless came to settle permanently in Spain, England, France, and the Netherlands in this way. In London, they numbered between 5,000 and 10,000 in 1780. With the decline of the plantation economy in the 19th century, this migration movement came to an end.

Toward the end of the 19th century, a small trickle of students from the West Indies came to Europe. Most West Indians migrated to other parts of the Caribbean and to the American mainland in search of work, and not to Europe, as the trip was too expensive. During World War I, Caribbean migrant laborers started to arrive in Britain and France. A free passage was provided by the recruiting organizations as part of their temporary labor contracts, and most of these migrants returned to the Caribbean afterward.

During the interwar period, the number of West Indians in Europe remained small and mainly consisted of students, trainees, and artists. During the Second World War, Great Britain and France recruited West Indian soldiers, who returned to their homelands after the end of the war. In the decades after the Second World War, the volume of Caribbean immigrants in Europe increased dramatically. In 2000, the ex-Caribbean populations in the UK, France, and the Netherlands alike were estimated at 350,000 to 500,000 each, half of whom had been born in the Caribbean. Today, migration from the Caribbean to Europe has been largely prevented by immigration restrictions in the countries of destination. However, unrestricted migration still continues from the French Antilles and French Guyana as well as from the Dutch Antilles, as the inhabitants of these ex-colonies have either a French or Dutch passport, allowing them to travel freely between their place of birth and Europe and also to settle in Europe.

Migration motives

The main reasons for Caribbean migrants to move to Europe or North America were work and education. The island economies are not able to offer similar opportunities to those available in a metropolis. Before independence, ethnic and political refugees also left the Caribbean for Europe and North America. These refugee movements were due to racial tensions between the ex-Africans and ex-Indians in former British Guyana as well as in colonial Suriname. In other cases, migrants left in fear of the repressive dictatorships and amid threats to their lives and safety in Cuba, Haiti, Guyana, and Suriname. Migration to Europe also offered social security: because the standard of living in destination countries was so much better than at home, unemployment rates in Europe hardly affected the number of Caribbean migrants to Europe.

Migration

Until 1945, the number of Caribbean migrants in the UK had been small. The war years had been an exception, when both France and the UK had recruited black soldiers from the Caribbean and tropical Africa. Between 1950 and 1960, the number of colored immigrants from Africa, Asia, and the Caribbean in Britain increased 10 times, from 20,000 to more than 200,000. The majority of these migrants came from Jamaica. As a consequence, xenophobic riots occurred and right-wing racist parties gained some popularity. In order to limit the immigration from the former colonies, the government introduced the Commonwealth Immigrants Act (CIA) in 1962. The act gave only people with a British passport and a work permit the right to settle in Britain. Immediately after the law's passage, West Indian migration increased still further. In 1968, Enoch Powell, a Conservative Member of Parliament, predicted that race conflicts in British society would end in "rivers of blood," becoming as violent as those in the USA. Only after 1970 did immigration from former colonies decline as a consequence of the CIA.

Most migrants settled in the large urban areas and in the vicinity of relatives and neighbors who had migrated before, founding urban ethnic communities. Many found employment in the lower ranks of the public sector, such as hospitals, public transport, the postal service, and education. These jobs offered a steady income, allowing the Caribbean

West Indian church in the London neighborhood Brixton, around 1960 (*ullstein bild*).

migrants to send home a regular flow of remittances. These transfers had a very significant impact on the economy of the smaller islands; in 1960 they made up a quarter of the national income of Montserrat.

Migration rates from the West Indies are quite diverse. While rates for the small island of Montserrat were nearly 50% of the total population of that island, those of the four largest countries of the British Caribbean were much lower in 1962 – when the free migration from former colonies to Great Britain was limited – Jamaica, 9.2%; Barbados, 8.1%; Trinidad, 1.2%; and Guyana, 1.3%. The migration from the Caribbean to France and the Netherlands was much larger and long-lasting: in 1990, the immigrant population from the Caribbean living in France and the Netherlands had risen to numbers that equaled about half the the population of the French and Dutch Caribbean. The migration from Suriname to the Netherlands declined sharply after 1980, when restrictions were put in place.

In contrast to Britain, government policies in France toward Caribbean migrants after the First World War did not undergo a restrictive change. During the late 1940s, West Indian labor migration to France was welcomed and seen as beneficial to both the countries of origin and France itself: this migration would defuse the demographic pressure in the primarily agricultural Caribbean, reducing social tension, and at the same time diminish the shortages on the labor market in France. When the French Antilles became an overseas department in 1946, all young men from Guadeloupe and Martinique were drafted into the army and brought to France or to Algeria, where the French were involved in suppressing the independence movement. Many Caribbean soldiers stayed in France after demobilization. Around 1955, there were about 15,000 West Indians in France, mainly students, civil servants, and former soldiers. In 2000, the number of West Indians in France reached 350,000, and the size of the group continues to increase. One of the reasons for the continuing migration to France is the comparatively high unemployment rate in the Antilles.

In 1963, the French government attempted to channel the migration from the West Indies to France via the Bureau pour le développement des Migrations intéressant les Départements d'Outre-Mer (BUMIDOM). This institution tried to regulate migration by offering courses to prospective migrants before their departure as well as after their arrival in France; it provided information for migrants about personal hygiene, how to dress, the right table manners, and the use of a washing machine, telephone, and refrigerator. Over time, BUMIDOM was criticized for the low level of its introductory courses, which frequently lasted only two weeks. They were also faulted for offering only low-paid jobs, and for the fact that most Caribbean migrants came to France without using its services. Judging from the data collected by BUMIDOM, between 1962 and 1982 about two-fifths of the migrants were male, one-fifth was female, and the remainder consisted of children and elderly men. The BUMIDOM schemes brought twice as many children to France (14% of all Caribbean immigrants) as did British migration policies. In France and the UK, half of Caribbean immigrant women found hospital jobs in urban areas and most immigrant men worked on building sites.

The experience of West Indians migrating to the Netherlands falls between the French and British experiences. As in the UK, migration from Suriname was halted in 1980 as the country had obtained independence in 1975, while immigration from the Dutch Antilles continues. The Dutch Antilles were given wide-ranging autonomy in 1954 but remained part of the Dutch Kingdom. Residents of the six islands of the Dutch Antilles (Curaçao, Aruba, Bonaire, St. Eustatius, St. Maarten, and Saba) all have Dutch passports and can still settle in the Netherlands without further formalities. In 2005, the total number of immigrants from the Dutch Antilles living in the Netherlands was estimated at 90,000, while the population of all the islands totaled around 200,000. There is no special organization with the aim of regulating or organizing the migration from the Dutch West Indies to the Netherlands.

Because of the potential for higher income, better social services, and better medical care in the Netherlands, migration from Suriname to the Netherlands reached a high point in the 1970s. The rapidly growing number of migrants, the development of self-contained ethnic communities, and the high crime rate among them spurred the Dutch government to give Suriname its independence and to severely limit migration after 1980. More than 50,000 migrants moved from Suriname to the Netherlands in 1974 and 1975 alone, taking advantage of their right of free migration, and a similar wave of about 30,000 migrants arrived in 1979 and 1980. After 1980 each year on average 5,000 Surinamese migrated legally to the Netherlands, except in 1993 when more than 9,000 were admitted. In 2005, the total number of people of Surinamese origin living in the Netherlands was estimated to be more than 300,000, of whom 182,000 were born in Suriname. There are about as many Surinamese in the Netherlands as in Suriname itself, whose remaining population is estimated at 400,000.

In light of the negative political and economic developments in postcolonial Suriname, the last remnants of the Dutch colonial empire, the Dutch Antilles, now resist decolonization. They avoid talking about independence because they would also lose the right of unlimited migration to the Netherlands. In the past 10 years, a disproportionate number of young male minors without any family ties but with a criminal record, as well as single teenage mothers with their children, have migrated to the Netherlands. That has resulted in extremely high unemployment and crime rates among these young migrants. To limit the consequences of this migration, understood as "negative selection," the Dutch government has attempted to compel people who want to migrate to the Netherlands to take a Dutch language test and to inform themselves about the requirements of the Dutch labor market. However, the Dutch Antillean government has refused to cooperate, pointing out that everyone with a Dutch passport has the right to reside in the Netherlands.

The end of unlimited post-independence migration from the West Indies to Britain, and from Suriname to the Netherlands, on the one hand, and the continuing migration from the Antilles to the Netherlands and to France, on the other hand, have led to two different demographic profiles. Among West Indian migrants in Britain and the Surinamese in the Netherlands, people between the ages of 40 and 60 predominate, while among Caribbean immigrants in France and Antillean immigrants in the Netherlands, the age cohort between 15 and 40 is the largest.

Integration

The integration of the West Indians into the British society progressed, albeit with several setbacks. During the 1990s, the negative prejudice toward blacks (whether of African or of West Indian origin) in Britain was dwarfed by the negative public sentiments toward Muslim fundamentalism among the large South Asian community. That does not mean, however, that black West Indians are fully integrated into British society. Unemployment among this group in 2001 was 11.6%, against 4.7% among Britons. In this respect West Indians took second place, after the Indians (7.3%) and before Africans (14.1%), Pakistanis (16.1%), and Bangladeshis (21.3%). However, Caribbean immigrants, especially women, are moving out of lower skilled jobs toward professional and nonmanual labor jobs at a higher rate than Britons, thus reducing the wage gap between them. The percentage of unemployed West Indian men in the lower segment of the labor market is higher than that among white nonimmigrants. This can be attributed to discrimination as well as to the widespread tendency among the black poor in Britain toward separation and avoidance of integration.

As far as education, intermarriage, and housing are concerned, the situation of Caribbean blacks in Britain is improving, but the statistics do not indicate that the first- and second-generation migrants are completely integrated.

The percentage of black (mainly Caribbean) boys and girls obtaining university entrance is smaller than that of Indian (first place) and British (second place) students. The number of dropouts among Caribbean pupils is also much higher than among other groups: 38 per 10,000 against 13 for whites and only 3 for Indians, with black girls showing much better results than black boys. As far as intermarriage is concerned, both male and female Caribbean immigrants of the first and second generation marry more partners of other ethnic groups than other immigrant groups in the UK and the Netherlands, while for France no statistics are available. The average intermarriage rate of Caribbean men of the first generation is 26% and of the second generation 60%. For women these percentages are 26% and 46%, respectively. These percentages are much higher than among the Caribbean immigrants in the USA. Similarly, the housing sector has shown improvement. Around 1970 more than half of the Caribbean immigrants lived in segregated areas in the poorer sections of London, Birmingham, Manchester, Leeds, and Bradford, but that proportion has declined during the past decades. In fact, during the 19th century more immigrants from Russia, Poland, and Italy lived in segregated housing areas in the USA than Caribbean communities do in Britain at the beginning of the 21st century.

In France, the official optimism toward immigrants changed during the 1970s, as French society was faced with the same problems as Britain a decade earlier: failing integration and its corollary, xenophobic riots. Around 1970, estimates of the number of Caribbean immigrants ranged from 70,000 to 150,000 and only 30,000 had come to France under the auspices of BUMIDOM. Official estimates also indicate that about half the migrants were women with little education. Between the 1960s and the early 1980s, the French government, some large private firms such as the Post Office and the State Railways, and certain car manufacturers tried to regulate migration by recruiting migrants in the Caribbean with specific job qualifications, offering clothing, pocket money, and housing after arrival in France. During those years, it seems that immigrants from the Caribbean were better integrated in French society than West Indians in the UK and the Netherlands. However, the situation changed later, and immigration during the years of the socialist president Mitterrand (1981–95) was not more successful than the nonintervention politics in Britain under conservative Prime Minister Margaret Thatcher.

The BUMIDOM was replaced by the Agence Nationale pour l'insertion de la promotion des Travailleurs d'outre-mer (ANT), an organization that would not only provide training and jobs for immigrants but also stimulate return migration. It is extremely difficult to establish how many migrants returned definitely, as both France and the Netherlands consider moving back and forth to their territories in the West Indies as internal migration and do not monitor it. A similar lack of statistics makes it impossible to estimate the number of interethnic marriages. About one-third to one-fourth of all Caribbean immigrants in France have married a partner born in France. These percentages, however, are no indication of a reduction in ethnic homogeneity as, no doubt, many of these marriage partners are of Caribbean descent.

As far as the labor market, housing, and education are concerned, Caribbean immigrants and their children in France attract little public attention, as most discriminatory acts are directed toward the immigrants from North Africa. In France, cultural variations from mainstream society, and not color, are seen as the real impediment to integration. Yet, as in Britain, most Caribbean immigrants live in poorer sections of the big cities and two-thirds live in the greater Paris suburbs, but their numbers are never higher than 2% of the resident population, too small to speak of as closed ethnic communities. The housing accommodations of Caribbean immigrants resemble those of the lower income French laborers and is usually of a better quality than that of the immigrants from North Africa. In the educational system, immigrants from the French Caribbean and their children also perform better on average than those from North Africa, but not as well as students from metropolitan France. Culturally, French Caribbean authors and musicians are seen as part of the French culture and not of an international black culture as is commonly the case in the UK and USA.

In the Netherlands, the West Indian immigrants split into at least four entities as soon as they arrived. In most cases, migrants from Suriname are seen as separate from those coming from the Antilles, and the many welfare and social organizations catering to these immigrants are based on that distinction. Another distinction is made between the ex-Africans (Creoles), the ex-Indians (Hindustani), ex-Javanese from Suriname, and the migrants from the Dutch Antilles. In the West Indies, racial stereotyping is strong. Blacks are considered to be disorganized, hedonistic, jolly, with weak family ties resulting in a high percentage of one-parent families with an absent father. The ex-Indians have a reputation as misers, with strong family ties, marrying at an extremely young age and with a strong drive to climb the social ladder. In the Netherlands such stereotypes are defied by the social reality of economic and social integration of the ex-African immigrants from Suriname into Dutch society. A recent study shows that the position of the black Surinamese in the Netherlands is little different from that of the ex-Indians. This result, unexpected by many, is based on the fact that in Suriname, Creoles were overrepresented in the civil service and better prepared for the Dutch labor market, while the Hindustanis in Suriname had worked largely in small agriculture and trade before their migration to the Netherlands.

More than three-quarters of the West Indian immigrants settled in urban areas in the western part of Holland, with a concentration of Creoles in Amsterdam and of Hindustanis in the Hague. There is no specific economic niche where any of the West Indian groups are dominant, nor did any of these groups create special economic organizations or institutions, with the exception of some Surinamese restaurants and shops in the large cities. Special mention should be made of the prominent role of second-generation Surinamese Creole

Table 1. Social and demographic characteristics of West Indian immigrants in France, the UK, and the Netherlands around 1990, in percentages

Inhabitants coming from	Unemployment	Labor market participation	Civil servants	Working in industry	Home owners	In social housing	Living in large urban areas
Martinique	10.8	78	55	11	27	47	72
Guadeloupe	12.2	77	53	12	26	48	75
France	11.1	55	34	23	54	21	19
British Caribbean	19	73		17	53	34	58
UK	9.2	61		18	66	21	12
Suriname	19	62		43	14	70	59
Dutch Antilles	16	57		27	16	65	34
The Netherlands	7	60		20	43	40	13

Source: Ramón Grossfogel, "Les Migrations Caraïbes vers la France, les Pays-Bas, la Grande Bretagne et les États-Unis," *Des Amériques noires* 1213 (May/June 1998): 30–46.

immigrants on many of the Dutch soccer teams, and they make up about 25% of the players of the Dutch national team. Similarly, first- and second-generation Antillean immigrants feature prominently in Dutch baseball teams (see Table 1 for information on West Indian immigrants to France, the UK, and the Netherlands).

Brock, Colin, ed. *The Caribbean in Europe: Aspects of the West Indian Experience in Britain, France and the Netherlands*. London, 1968.

Brown, Laurence. "Afro-Caribbean Migrants in France and the United Kingdom." In *Paths of Integration: Migrants in Western Europe (1880–2004)*, edited by Leo Lucassen, David Feldman, and Jochen Oltmer, 177–97. Amsterdam, 2006.

Levine, Barry B., ed. *The Caribbean Exodus*. New York, 1987.

Lucassen, Leo. *The Immigrant Threat: The Integration of Old and New Migrants in Western Europe since 1850*. Urbana, 2005.

Lucassen, Leo, and Charlotte Laarman. "Immigration, Intermarriage and the Changing Face of Europe in the Post War Period." *History of the Family* 14 (2009), no. 1: 52–68.

Niekerk, Mies van. "*De krekel en de mier.*" *Fabels en feiten over maatschappelijke stijging van creoolse en hindoestaanse Surinamers in Nederland*. Amsterdam, 2000.

Cross-references: France; Great Britain; The Netherlands; Africans from the Former Colonies in France since the 1960s; Indian, Pakistani, and Bangladeshi Migrants in Great Britain since 1947; Maghrebis in France after Decolonization during the 1950s and 1960s; Pakistanis in Great Britain since the 1950s

WESTERN AND CENTRAL EUROPEAN SOLDIERS IN THE DUTCH COLONIAL ARMY, 1815–1909

Martin P. Bossenbroek

The expansion of the Dutch colonial empire in the Indonesian archipelago during the 19th century was realized partly by foreign military manpower. Of the 175,000 European non-commissioned officers and soldiers recruited for the Dutch Colonial Army from 1815 to 1909, 105,000 (60%) were born in the Netherlands. The other 70,000 (40%) came from other European countries. The largest groups among the foreign volunteers were Belgians and Germans, each represented by some 24,000 men (14%). They were followed by the Swiss, the French, and others, each represented by some 7,500 men (4%).

Unlike the time of the VOC (Verenigde Oost-Indische Compagnie, the Dutch East India Company, 1602–1799), in the 19th century the Netherlands was no longer a natural destination for foreign job seekers. Apart from the fairly stable but limited number of foreigners who spontaneously enrolled in the colonial service, potential candidates had to be recruited chiefly from ports and industrial centers such as Hamburg, Bremen, Frankfurt am Main, Brussels, and Lille. There, Dutch colonial recruiters were limited to recruiting individuals; the increasing scale and the "nationalization" of war from the end of the early modern period had made the practice of hiring an entire corps of foreign mercenaries obsolete.

The recruitment of individual volunteers in foreign parts met with a number of problems. In all surrounding countries, laws were made in connection with compulsory military service, regulating the recruitment of subjects by other states. Several treaties were also signed for the extradition of deserters. Officially, the Dutch government kept to these treaties. Volunteers for the Dutch colonial army, for instance, had to be able to produce legally valid documents. In this it was different from the French Foreign Legion, founded in 1831, which selected recruits only on the basis of their physical ability.

In practice, however, the Dutch colonial recruiters often bent the rules, especially during periods of colonial crisis (1815–30, 1856–60, 1873–9). Dutch recruiting methods, combined with the dubious past of the VOC and the low chance of survival for volunteers in the first decades of the 19th century, gave colonial service a bad reputation. From the beginning, service in the Dutch colonial troops carried the stigma of social reprobation. Stricter recruiting criteria were gradually introduced during the second half of the 19th century, but nevertheless the colonial recruitment depot in the Zuyderzee town of Harderwijk remained known as the "gutter of Europe."

In the 19th century, two clear tendencies can be distinguished in the social-economic background and the geographical origin of the foreign volunteers: a shift from a military to a civilian background among the recruits and an expansion of the recruitment area. Up to 1860 the proportion of former military men and civilian volunteers was roughly equal. Professional soldiers consisted of large groups of Germans from diverse military units dismantled after the Napoleonic wars (after 1815), French deserters (around 1820), Belgian deserters (after the Belgian separation in 1839), and Swiss dismissed from the British and Napoleonic service (after the second half of the 1850s). Most civilian volunteers in this period were Belgians from the provinces of Brabant, West and East Flanders, Germans from the states to the north and southwest of Prussia (fewer from Prussia, where the authorities were very sensitive to violations of conscription regulations), Swiss from the predominantly German-speaking northwestern cantons, and French from the northern departments.

From the 1860s onward, the portion of former soldiers from foreign armies strongly decreased. The number of foreign civilian volunteers – the large majority of whom could be categorized as workmen – remained constant, at least until the end of the 19th century. In the first years of the Achin War (1873–9) civilian volunteers reached an unprecedented level, with an average of 1,650 men per year. The countries of origin of the civilian volunteers were the same as those of the military men of the earlier period, but within those countries remarkable changes took place: the Belgians now came from Flanders as well as the Walloon provinces, the Germans mainly from Rhineland-Westphalia and from the central Prussian area in the northeast (most of them, however, after completing their military service), and the French also from regions to the south of the imaginary line connecting Le Havre, Paris, and Mulhouse. Only the Swiss contingent showed an unchanged picture, the northwestern cantons still being overrepresented.

This twofold shift can be partly explained by changes in the recruitment of volunteers. The Dutch government tried to make the colonial service more attractive by improving its public image and through financial incentives. Bounties were increased – from 10 guilders in the beginning to a maximum of 300 guilders in the 1870s for a six-year contract – as were reappointment bonuses and pensions. The introduction of stricter criteria for admission, improvements in the working conditions in the Dutch East Indies, and medical and social care for retired soldiers enhanced the colonial service's reputation. Moreover, the structural involvement of Dutch diplomatic and consular representatives now ensured that the terms of recruitment were widely known throughout Europe.

This shift was also due to changes in the supply of potential volunteers. Especially in the second half of the 19th century, Dutch recruits were drawn not only from the hundreds of thousands of unemployed who crossed the border from Belgium but also from the millions of willing migrants drifting in from the German hinterland. For the unencumbered and adventurous, entry into the colonial service was an alternative to migration overseas. The specific geographical origins of the colonial volunteers suggest that the Dutch colonial recruiters succeeded in draining some of the flows of the successive *Auswanderungswellen* (waves of emigration). The volunteers for the Dutch Colonial Army – at least the civilian volunteers among them – can therefore be considered *Auswanderer* (emigrants), namely, the more free and adventurous among them.

For most volunteers, entry into the colonial army meant a radical break with the past. Before their departure to the colonies they were a transient part of the Harderwijk society for a couple of months – a time too short to settle but long enough to generate income and inconvenience for the locals. The colonial soldiers were forbidden to leave the town except for military exercises. Their freedom of movement was limited to the quarter-square kilometer within the town walls. Most of the original population of fishermen and farmers kept away from the soldiers; contact tended to be superficial and professional. The only point of contact between the permanent and temporary residents was the free spending pattern of the latter. The uncertain fate awaiting them under the tropical sun made the new colonial soldiers careless spenders of their bounties and pay. The local middle class was eager to take advantage of this. As long as they spent their money, soldiers were welcomed in the local establishments; once stripped of their cash, and therefore of their economic value, only their invariably inferior social status remained.

Upon arrival in the Indonesian archipelago, the foreign colonial soldiers found no relatives, friends, or an existing German community, but rather an international military community with its own laws. Apart from expeditions, they spent the time of their service in their barracks or the immediate vicinity, where they were allowed to live with a native woman (*njai* or housekeeper). For the large majority of foreign colonials, their departure from Europe was definitive: either they did not survive the first term or they renewed their contract once or a few times before leaving the service and remaining in the Indies. Of those who did return to the Netherlands, a number chose to sign a further contract with the colonial troops.

As a rule, foreign colonials who after their return did not opt for a new contract were not allowed to stay in the Netherlands. Since the passage of the Aliens Act in 1849, unwanted foreigners were deported – and both unaccepted volunteers and foreign colonial soldiers with a passport were classified as such. The state constables, stationed at Harderwijk, deported some 100 to 400 foreigners per year, depending on the influx.

Only foreigners who had built up pension claims during their service (originally after 20 years, at the end of the

19th century also after 12 years) were allowed to stay in the Netherlands. Often they chose a place of residence near Harderwijk. At the beginning of the 20th century some 400 pensioners lived in the Veluwe region, the large majority of whom were foreigners. It was not always a purely positive choice: there were quite a few who had pawned their pension contracts, and therefore their freedom of movement, to local landlords and shopkeepers.

Ultimately, only a few hundred of the 70,000 foreign volunteers recruited for the Dutch Colonial Army from 1815 to 1909 remained recognizable as a group. Their group identity, however, was no longer based on their original Belgian or German provenance but on their common service in the Indonesian archipelago. They were not so much identified as Belgians or Germans but piled on one heap with their Dutch brothers-in-arms as "colonials," "pensioners," or, if they had become addicted to alcohol, as "binge drinkers." It was with reference to these distinctions that they composed a very small but recognizable minority on the margin of Dutch society.

Bossenbroek, Martin. *Volk voor Indië. De werving van Europese militairen voor de Nederlandse koloniale dienst 1814–1909.* Amsterdam, 1992.

Bossenbroek, Martin. "De stad van de kolonialen." In *Harderwijk als militaire stad en de geschiedenis van 4 Divisie*, edited by M. Elands, 24–53. The Hague, 1994.

Bossenbroek, Martin. "The 'Living' Tools of Empire: The Recruitment of European Soldiers for the Dutch Colonial Army, 1814–1909." *Journal of Imperial and Commonwealth History* 23 (1995): 26–53.

Horresco. Gepensioneerden. *Een kijkje in hun leven op de Veluwe.* Harderwijk, 1907.

Cross-references: Belgium and Luxembourg; Germany; The Netherlands; German Soldiers in the French Foreign Legion in the 19th and 20th Centuries

YUGOSLAV LABOR MIGRANTS IN WESTERN, CENTRAL, AND NORTHERN EUROPE SINCE THE END OF WORLD WAR II

Pascal Goeke

The Socijalistička Federativna Republika Jugoslavija existed until 1992. This multiethnic state consisted of Slovenia, Croatia, Bosnia-Herzegovina, Serbia, Montenegro, Macedonia, and, at various times, the two autonomous provinces of Kosovo and Vojvodina. The primary languages were Slovenian, Serbo-Croatian, Macedonian, and Albanian; the majority of Yugoslavs were Catholic, Orthodox, or Muslim. But it was not only these political, social, and cultural dividing lines that made the group of Yugoslav migrant workers in northern, western, and central Europe so diverse. Additional factors were the demarcations between various

Yugoslav labor migrants arriving at Munich central station, 1963 (*SV Bilderdienst*).

groups within the immigrant population on the basis of different historical and cultural origins as well as divergent economic and social developments in the various regions of origin. All this had consequences for their integration in the destination countries. The diversity of the immigrant group stood in opposition to the way it was received in the host countries. Even though "Yugoslavia" was barely recognizable as a political framework after the 1990s, at the latest, the immigrants continued to be referred to with the collective term "Yugoslavs."

Slovenia and Croatia had been origin regions of overseas migration before World War I. Beginning in the 1920s, France, Belgium, the Netherlands, and later Germany emerged as the most important destination countries for Yugoslav migrant workers. The founding of the "Second Yugoslavia" after 1945 initially led to the flight of members of national minorities and of political opponents of the communists. These emigrants were quickly able to get a footing in the labor markets in their destination countries. The Tito regime in Yugoslavia tried to prevent extensive emigration, and in fact it remained moderate in the 1950s. As late as 1962, the Yugoslav government turned down Austria's request to officially permit the employment of Yugoslav workers. Yugoslavia's restrictive migration policy came under pressure only when large age-cohorts pushed onto the Yugoslav labor market in the 1960s and economic reforms were freeing up many workers.

In 1964, Yugoslav authorities began a tentative cooperation with foreign employers. Yugoslavia developed into the only socialist country that concluded recruitment treaties with states in the West. The first such treaty with Austria went into effect in 1965. Following were treaties with France (1966), Sweden (1967), West Germany and Luxembourg (1969), as well as Belgium and the Netherlands (1970). Although Switzerland did not sign a special treaty with Yugoslavia, it did become an important destination country.

Table 1. Number of Yugoslav labor migrants abroad at the end of 1973		
Destination country	**Number**	**% of all Yugoslav migrants**
Germany	469,000	50.1
Austria	197,000	19.9
France	54,000	5.5
Switzerland	28,000	2.8
Sweden	25,000	2.5
Benelux states	14,000	1.4
Other European countries	16,000	1.6
Overseas countries	160,000	16.2

Source: Ivo Baučić, "Yugoslavia as a Country of Emigration," *Options Méditerranéennes* 22 (1973): 55–66, here 62. The numbers are based on Yugoslav statistics. In the destination countries, the figures are on average 15% higher, but they are not comparable because rates of nationalization differed and the numbers were collected at various times.

In the beginning, Yugoslav authorities organized the emigration directly. Because the federal Yugoslav offices primarily placed workers with lesser qualifications, the skill level of the emigrants remained lower than that of the Yugoslav population as a whole. This negative selection clashed with the expectations of the foreign employers, who soon switched to recruiting and selecting their workers individually and increasingly dispensed with official help. As a result, better qualified workers began to emigrate in increasing numbers. Switzerland had left the recruitment entirely in the hands of the associations of employers.

Among the origin regions of the Yugoslav emigrants, Croatia was dominant. This can be attributed not only to networks, chain migrations, or traditions of migration. Rather, one must bear in mind that many "Croatian" migrants came from families that had previously migrated within Yugoslavia, and it was only the border-crossing migration that identified them and others as emigrants from Croatia. What the statistics conceal is that during the strong internal migration, which resulted from the difference in economic development within Yugoslavia, the migrants may have crossed linguistic, national, or religious boundaries and accomplished feats of assimilation comparable to the border-crossing migrations.

Recruitment came to an end at the beginning of the 1970s. The destination countries ceased their recruitment, and Yugoslavia itself passed the Law for the Protection of Workers Employed Abroad in 1973, which was intended to limit the placement of workers to the unemployed and members of select occupational groups. As a result, the sending regions shifted southward. Now it was especially Kosovars who left, their preferred destination being Switzerland. As Table 1 illustrates, the number of Yugoslav migrant workers and their families in the destination countries in Europe had risen to 803,000 by 1973; more than half of them lived in West Germany.

The migratory behavior of some of the migrant workers was determined by their unhappiness over the political situation in Yugoslavia. They saw in the recruitment agreements a chance to leave the country and make a new life for themselves elsewhere. In this way, many Yugoslavs escaped the restrictions imposed in their home country on their choice of job and job training. However, the state restricted the freedoms of its citizens not only domestically but also abroad. Under the premise that the stay abroad would be only temporary and given the fact that obtaining citizenship was difficult or impossible in many destination countries, the Yugoslav government disposed of an effective threat: workers who attracted negative political attention abroad had to be afraid that their visas would not be extended. Individuals to whom a visa was denied had the choice of returning to Yugoslavia, where they could expect harassment, or applying for asylum in the destination country.

As a result, Yugoslav migrant workers were highly accommodating toward state authorities. Although the indicators of social inequality were not clearly better or worse than among comparable groups, because of this attitude, the Yugoslav workers were often praised as exemplary pupils of the integration process in the host countries.

Beginning in the late 1970s, the composition of the group changed through remigration and family reunification. However, transnational family forms could be found among the Yugoslavs as late as the 1980s. In the case of Germany this meant that in 1985, a total of 42.9% of children under the age of 16 in Yugoslav households did not live in Germany but in Yugoslavia (Turks 31.3%, Greeks 29%, Italians 28.7%). With a majority of Yugoslavs preparing themselves for longer stays and the customary lifestyle of large families that had previously prevailed in Yugoslavia dissolving, which meant that child care at home was no longer guaranteed, that number plunged to 3.4% in 2001 (Turks 0.9%, Greeks 3%, Italians 1.1%).

The total number of Yugoslav immigrants in Europe declined up until around 1987, largely because of the strong remigration. Subsequently the composition of the group changed again with the arrival of refugees from war and civil war in the former Yugoslavia. In Germany alone, the number of individuals from the territory of the former Yugoslavia rose from 551,600 in 1987 to 975,800 in 2004. The line between work migration and flight was often fluid, since migrant workers especially from Bosnia-Herzegovina brought their children to the host countries during the war years, while other Yugoslavs who migrated only because of the war used the networks of labor migration to do so.

In the 1990s, immigrants of all generations had to deal with changes taking place in the regions from which they came. Most immigrants showed a heightened engagement for the future of their (now independent) homeland: their participation ranged from honorary offices in political parties to the extreme case of direct participation in military conflicts. In many cases, the death of close relatives in the war or the loss of savings and real estate necessitated painful adjustments to plans for the future. Many had to put off plans to return.

Even after the end of the wars, the situation of the migrant workers from the former Yugoslavia continued to be shaped by the regions from which they came. For example, the differences in the political, economic, and social situation could hardly be greater between Slovenia, a new EU member since 2004, and economically underdeveloped Bosnia-Herzegovina. This affected the situation of the migrant workers and their willingness to integrate, since remigration to Slovenia, for example, increasingly took on the characteristics of an old-age migration, while immigrants from Bosnia-Herzegovina continued to place great importance upon financial support for family members living back home.

Migrant workers from the former Yugoslavia formed numerous organizations in the destination countries. The first migrant workers encountered organizations that had been founded by political refugees. For example, in Munich the first Serbian Orthodox congregation in Germany had been founded in 1946, and two years later the first Croatian Catholic mission. The religious congregations grew in size with the rise in immigration, but so did the many Yugoslav clubs, which often cooperated closely with the consulates and competed with the churches in the influence they exerted on the migrants. The collapse of Yugoslavia led to a decline in the number of clubs – at times they dissolved entirely – while the religious communities once again experienced a strong influx.

At the beginning of the 21st century, the Yugoslav immigrants were far more attached to their faith than was the native population in the destination countries, but the surge in membership brought about by the war had ebbed again. Presently one can observe a progressive secularization as well as processes of shrinkage and fragmentation within the congregations. Macedonian as well as Montenegran Orthodox are seeking autocephaly (autonomy under their own leader), and the Croatian missions are finding it increasingly difficult in Catholic regions to make clear what separates them from the local Catholic church. Muslims from Bosnia-Herzegovina or Kosovo are participating in the religious life of Muslims from other geographic regions as least as frequently as they do in the activities of their own mosques.

Like other migrant workers, Yugoslavs encountered resentment, became victims of discriminatory practices, and occupied primarily the low-status segments of the labor market. Still, they never became the distinct target of xenophobic attacks. In part this was because Austrians and Germans, in particular, had vacationed in some of the regions from which the Yugoslav immigrants came and they were familiar with these areas, though areas like Kosovo remained foreign to them. Moreover, its status as a nonaligned state earned Yugoslavia a lot of good feelings in western Europe, which had a positive effect on the image of the immigrants. Yugoslavia even participated in the Grand Prix Eurovision de la Chanson and was able to win the contest in 1989.

However, during the wars of the 1990s that led to the breakup of Yugoslavia, it also became clear that the closeness to the West was in some ways fragile. The immigrants from the various and, at the beginning of the 21st century, independent former Yugoslav regions of origin for the most part ran into incomprehension when it came to legitimizing their particular group interests. The pejorative term "Balkanization" as the symbol of "irrational behavior" and "senseless fragmentation" was repeatedly used in media and public commentaries on the events and affected the perception of the migrant workers from the former Yugoslavia in the European destination countries. Henceforth, the "Balkans" and "Europe" (or more precisely, the EU) were seen as opposites. The events of the war, the end of the Yugoslav state, and the desire to be part of "Europe" and not the "Balkans" led the migrant workers from the various regions of origin in the former Yugoslavia to distance themselves from one another. The once visible culture and economy of the emigrants from the former Yugoslavia has largely disappeared from the landscape of the large cities.

Božić, Saša. *Kroaten in Wien. Immigranten und Integration im Zusammenhang mehrschichtiger ethnischer Beziehungen.* Zagreb, 2000.

Ellis, Mark, and Richard Wright. "The Balkanization Metaphor in the Analysis of U.S. Immigration." *Annals of the Association of American Geographers* 88 (1998): 686–98.

Kalter, Frank, and Nadia Granato. "Sozialer Wandel und strukturelle Assimilation in der Bundesrepublik. Empirische Befunde mit Mikrodaten der amtlichen Statistik." *IMIS-Beiträge* (2004), no 23: 61–81.

Klarić, Josip P., ed. *Hrvatska obitelj u pokretu/Die kroatische Migrantenfamilie. Pastorale Jahrestagung.* Frankfurt am Main, 2001.

Lichtenberger, Elisabeth. *Gastarbeiter. Leben in zwei Gesellschaften.* Vienna, 1984.

Morokvašić, Mirjana. *Jugoslawische Frauen. Die Emigration – und danach.* Stroemfeld, 1987.

Schierup, Carl-Ulrik. *Migration, Socialism and the International Division of Labour.* Aldershot, 1990.

Torche, Denis. "Structuration d'un espace migratoire. Le cas des émigrés albanais des Yougoslavie vers la Suisse," *Geographica Helvetica* 48 (1993): 159–64.

Venema, Mathias, and Claus Grimm. *Situation der ausländischen Arbeitnehmer und ihrer Familienangehörigen in der Bundesrepublik Deutschland. Repräsentativuntersuchung 2001, Tabellenband.* Berlin, 2002.

Cross-references: Austria; Germany; Southeastern Europe; Switzerland; Greek Labor Migrants in Western, Central, and Northern Europe after 1950: The Examples of Germany and the Netherlands; Italian Labor Migrants in Northern, Central, and Western Europe since the End of World War II; Moroccan Labor Migrants in Western, Central, and Northern Europe since the 1960s: The Example of Great Britain; Portuguese Labor Migrants in Western and Central Europe since the 1950s: The Examples of France and Germany; Refugees from Former Yugoslavia in Europe since 1991; Turkish Labor Migrants in Western, Central, and Northern Europe since the Mid-1950s

APPENDIX

Numbers are opening page numbers of articles.

[†] Deceased.

Thiel, Jens (Berlin, Germany), 599

Thränhardt, Dietrich (Berlin, Germany), 689

Thunø, Mette (Copenhagen, Denmark), 283

Tilmatine, Mohand (Cádiz, Spain), 579

Tuchtenhagen, Ralph (Hamburg, Germany), 637

Vaculík, Jaroslav (Brno, Czechia), 304

Vasili, Phil (London, United Kingdom), 216

Vermeulen, Hans (Milies-Volou, Greece), 457

Vuilleumier, Marc (Geneva, Switzerland), 94, 519

Walker, Melvin (Liverpool, United Kingdom), 545

Walz, Markus (Leipzig, Germany), 229, 515

Wang, Nora (Paris, France), 281, 291

Weber, Klaus (Hamburg, Germany), 258, 393, 421

Widmann, Peter (Berlin, Germany), 615

Wiedemann, Andreas (Prague, Czechia), 306

Willems, Wim (The Hague, The Netherlands), 327

Wörsdörfer, Rolf (Darmstadt, Germany), 517, 682

Xiujing, Liang (Aalborg, Denmark), 289

Zappi, Elda Gentili (New York, NY, USA), 521

Zedinger, Renate (Vienna, Austria), 473

Zeitlhofer, Hermann (Vienna, Austria), 152

Zelepos, Ioannis (Vienna, Austria), 468, 472

Ziegler, Béatrice (Hinterkappelen, Switzerland), 644

Zucchi, John (Montreal, Canada), 522

Zhuravlev, Sergej (Moscow, Russia), 448

Zürcher, Erik-Jan (Amsterdam, The Netherlands), 460

Zürn, Martin (Meersburg, Germany), 662

SCIENTIFIC ADVISORY COUNCIL AND COUNTRY COORDINATORS

Arlettaz, Gérald (Avry-sur-Matran, Switzerland)

Brandes, Detlef (Berlin, Germany)

Bustos Rodríguez, Manuel (Cádiz, Spain)

Canny, Nicholas (Galway, Ireland)

Conzen, Kathleen (Chicago, IL, USA)

Entzinger, Han (Rotterdam, The Netherlands)

François, Etienne (Berlin, Germany, and Paris, France)

Gabaccia, Donna R. (Minneapolis, MN, USA)

Glettler, Monika (Munich, Germany)

Golczewski, Frank (Hamburg, Germany)

Green, Nancy L. (Paris, France)

Harzig, Christiane[†]

Hassauer, Friederike (Vienna, Austria)

Haumann, Heiko (Basel, Switzerland)

Hoerder, Dirk (Tempe, AZ, USA)

Jersch-Wenzel, Stefi (Berlin, Germany)

Kjeldstadli, Knut (Oslo, Norway)

Linden, Marcel van der (Amsterdam, The Netherlands)

Lindner, Rolf (Berlin, Germany)

Lucassen, Jan (Amsterdam, The Netherlands)

Münz, Rainer (Vienna, Austria)

Obdeijn, Herman (Oegstgeest, The Netherlands)

Oksaar, Els (Hamburg, Germany)

Page Moch, Leslie (East Lansing, MI, USA)

Pietschmann, Horst (Cologne, Germany)

Reif, Heinz (Berlin, Germany)

Rosental, Paul-André (Paris, France)

Schilling, Heinz (Berlin, Germany)

Schindling, Anton (Tübingen, Germany)

Schubert, Ernst[†]

Sundhaussen, Holm (Berlin, Germany)

Wimmer, Andreas (Los Angeles, CA, USA)

EDITORS

Klaus J. Bade, born 1944, Dr. phil. habil., Professor Emeritus for Modern History, Chair, Expert Council of German Foundations on Integration and Migration, Founder of the Institute for Migration Research and Intercultural Studies (IMIS) at Osnabrück University, Germany, as well as of the German Rat für Migration (RfM). Fellow, Center for European Studies, Harvard University 1976–7; St. Antony's College, Oxford University 1985; Wissenschaftskolleg zu Berlin 2000–1; Netherlands Institute for Advanced Study (NIAS) 1996–7 and 2002–3; author and editor of more than 40 books on colonial history, economic, social, and cultural history, and especially on the development of population and migration past and present, e.g.:

(ed.) *Auswanderer – Wanderarbeiter – Gastarbeiter*, 2 vols. Ostfildern, 1984 (2nd ed. 1986)

(ed.) *Deutsche im Ausland – Fremde in Deutschland: Migration in Geschichte und Gegenwart*. Munich, 1992 (3rd ed. Munich, 1993; other ed. Frankfurt a.M., 1992, and Gütersloh, 1992)

(ed.) *Das Manifest der 60: Deutschland und die Einwanderung*. Munich, 1994; *Ausländer – Aussiedler – Asyl: Eine Bestandsaufnahme*. Munich, 1994

(ed.) *Migration – Ethnizität – Konflikt: Systemfragen und Fallstudien* (IMIS-Schriften, vol. 1). Osnabrück, 1996

(ed. with Rainer Münz) *Migrationsreport 2000: Fakten – Analysen – Perspektiven*. Frankfurt a.M. and New York, 2000

(ed. with Rainer Münz) *Migrationsreport 2002: Fakten – Analysen – Perspektiven*. Frankfurt a.M. and New York, 2002

Europe on the Move. Oxford, 2003 (German ed. Munich, 2000; Italian ed. Rome, 2001; French ed. Paris, 2002; Spanish ed. Barcelona, 2003)

Sozialhistorische Migrationsforschung. Gesammelte Beiträge, ed. by Michael Bommes and Jochen Oltmer (Studien zur Historischen Migrationsforschung, vol. 13). Göttingen, 2004

(with Jochen Oltmer) *Normalfall Migration: Deutschland im 20. und frühen 21. Jahrhundert* (Bundeszentrale für politische Bildung, Zeitbilder, vol. 15). Bonn, 2004

(ed. with Michael Bommes and Rainer Münz) *Migrationsreport 2004. Fakten – Analysen – Perspektiven*. Frankfurt a.M. and New York, 2004 (ed. with Michael Bommes) *Migration – Integration – Bildung: Grundfragen und Problembereiche* (IMIS-Beiträge, H. 23). Osnabrück, 2004

(ed. with Hans-Georg Hiesserich) *Nachholende Integrationspolitik und Gestaltungsperspektiven der Integrationspraxis* (Beiträge der Akademie für Migration und Integration, H. 11). Göttingen, 2007.

Pieter C. Emmer, born 1944, Ph.D., Professor of the History of European Expansion and Migrations, University of Leiden, the Netherlands. Fellow, Churchill College, Cambridge (1978–9), Wissenschaftskolleg zu Berlin (2000–1), Netherlands Institute of Advanced Study (NIAS) (2002–3), Visiting Professor University of Texas (Austin, USA), University of Hamburg, Germany, Université de Bretagne-Sud (Lorient, France), member of the Academia Europaea (London), advisory council of the journals *Itinerario, European Journal of Overseas History* (Leiden), *Journal of Imperial and Commonwealth History* (London), *Journal of Caribbean History* (Kingston, Jamaica), *Jahrbuch für Geschichte Lateinamerikas* (Cologne), *Revue d'histoire maritime* (Paris), and of the series *Studien zur Historischen Migrationsforschung* (SHM). Author and editor of books on the history of European expansion and transatlantic migration, e.g.:

(ed.) *Colonialism and Migration: Indentured Labour before and after Slavery.* Dordrecht and Boston, 1986

(ed. with Magnus Mörner) *European Expansion and Migration.* Oxford, 1992

(ed. with Femme Gaastra) *The Organisation of Interoceanic Trade in European Expansion, 1450–1800.* Aldershot, 1996

(ed.) *General History of the Caribbean,* vol. 2: *The New Societies in the Long Sixteenth Century.* London and Basingstoke, 1999

The Dutch in the Atlantic Economy, 1500–1850: Trade, Slavery and Emancipation. Aldershot, 1998

The Dutch Slave Trade, 1500–1850. Oxford and New York, 2006.

Leo Lucassen, born 1959, Ph.D., Professor of Social History, University of Leiden, the Netherlands. Author and editor of books on the history of Gypsies and of migration and integration, mainly in the 19th and 20th centuries, e.g.:

En men noemde hen zigeuners'. De geschiedenis van Kaldarasch, Ursari, Lowara en Sinti in Nederland 1750–1944. Amsterdam and the Hague, 1990

(with Annemarie Cottaar and Wim Willems) *Mensen van de reis: woonwagenbewoners en zigeuners in Nederland (1868–1995).* Zwolle, 1995

Zigeuner. Die Geschichte eines polizeilichen Ordnungsbegriffes. Cologne and Vienna, 1996

(with Wim Willems und Annemarie Cottaar) *Gypsies and Other Itinerant Groups: A Socio-historical Approach.* Basingstoke and New York, 1998

(ed. with Jan Lucassen) *Migration, Migration History, History: Old Paradigms and New Perspectives.* Bern, 1997 (2nd ed. 1999, 3rd ed. 2006)

(ed.) *Amsterdammer worden. Migranten, hun organisaties en inburgering, 1600–2000.* Amsterdam, 2004

The Immigrant Threat: Old and New Migrants in Western Europe since 1850. Urbana and Chicago, 2005

(ed. with David Feldman and Jochen Oltmer) *Paths of Integration: Migrants in Western Europe (1880–2004).* Amsterdam, 2006

(with Wim Willems) *Gelijkheid en onbehagen. Over steden, nieuwkomers en nationaal geheugenverlies.* Amsterdam, 2006

(ed. with Wim Willems) *De Krachtige Stad. Een eeuw omgang en ontwijking.* Amsterdam, 2007

(ed. with Jan Lucassen and Patrick Manning) *Migration History in World History: Multidisciplinary Approaches.* Leiden and Boston, 2010.

Jochen Oltmer, born 1965, Dr. phil. habil., Associate Professor of Modern History at the Institute for Migration Research and Intercultural Studies (IMIS), University of Osnabrück. Author and editor of several books on the history of the labor market, migration and migration politics, mainly in the 19th and 20th centuries, e.g., 2003–10:

(ed. with Klaus J. Bade) *Aussiedler: deutsche Einwanderer aus Osteuropa* (IMIS-Schriften, vol. 8). 2nd ed. Göttingen, 2003

(ed.) *Migration steuern und verwalten. Deutschland vom späten 19. Jahrhundert bis zur Gegenwart* (IMIS-Schriften, vol. 12). Göttingen, 2003

(with Klaus J. Bade) *Normalfall Migration: Deutschland im 20. und frühen 21. Jahrhundert* (Bundeszentrale für politische Bildung, Zeitbilder, vol. 15). Bonn, 2004

(with Michael Schubert) *Migration und Integration in Europa seit der Frühen Neuzeit. Eine Bibliographie zur Historischen Migrationsforschung.* Osnabrück, 2005

Migration und Politik in der Weimarer Republik. Göttingen, 2005

(ed.) *Kriegsgefangene im Europa des Ersten Weltkriegs* (Krieg in der Geschichte, vol. 24). Paderborn, 2006

(with David Feldman and Leo Lucassen) *Paths of Integration: Migrants in Europe (1880–2004)* (IMISCOE-Research, vol. 1). Amsterdam, 2006

(ed. with Ute Frevert) "Europäische Migrationsregime." *Geschichte und Gesellschaft* 35 (2009)

"Migration im 19. und 20. Jahrhundert" (*Enzyklopädie deutscher Geschichte*, vol. 86). Munich 2010.

INDEX OF MIGRATION TYPES

Most page numbers indicate the first pages of articles that deal predominantly with this specific migration form. In cases where a specific migration form is mentioned in a larger article with a different topic, the exact page numbers are indicated.

INDEX OF COUNTRIES, REGIONS, AND PLACES